Census of the Co

of Massachusetts, 1895

(Volume I)

Population and Social Statistics.

Horace G. Wadlin

Alpha Editions

This edition published in 2020

ISBN : 9789354017988

Design and Setting By
Alpha Editions
email - alphaedis@gmail.com

CENSUS

OF THE COMMONWEALTH OF

MASSACHUSETTS:

1895.

PREPARED UNDER THE DIRECTION OF

HORACE G. WADLIN,

CHIEF OF THE BUREAU OF STATISTICS OF LABOR.

VOLUME I.

POPULATION AND SOCIAL STATISTICS.

BOSTON:
WRIGHT & POTTER PRINTING CO., STATE PRINTERS,
18 POST OFFICE SQUARE.
1896.

TABLE OF CONTENTS.

TABLE OF CONTENTS.   V

THE

DECENNIAL CENSUS OF THE COMMONWEALTH.

1895.

VOLUME I.

INTRODUCTION.

The Decennial Census taken in 1895 was the fifth regular decennial enumeration of the people, conducted in accordance with the Constitution and laws made in conformity thereto. The enumeration of the population and the collection of social statistics began May 1. By the provisions of the Census law, however, the collection of information relating to other branches of the work, chiefly Manufactures, Agriculture, Commerce, and the Fisheries, was not undertaken until a later date, or until the industrial operations of the entire year 1895 had been completed; so that in the main, the industrial and commercial returns of the Census will cover the year ending December 31, 1895.

Although the first decennial enumeration was made in 1855, there were several previous enumerations, by order of the Legislature, the first occurring in 1837, and others following in 1840 and 1850. In connection with the Censuses taken decennially by the United States beginning with 1790, and the earlier provincial Censuses taken in 1765 and 1776, we are able to trace the growth of the Commonwealth during 130 years. Industrial statistics, including statistics of Agriculture, were collected in the Census of 1837, also in 1845, and regularly in connection with the decennial enumerations begun in 1855.

The results of the Census of 1885 were nominally published in three volumes, but, as one of these consisted of two Parts, four books were actually issued, aggregating 4,493 pages of tabular matter, accompanied by analytical text. The results of the present Census, while requiring in their presentation approximately the same number of pages, will be published in smaller volumes, probably eight in number, which will be more conveniently consulted by the reader.

Each separate section of the work, as fast as completed, is issued in preliminary pamphlet form, intended mainly for the press, in order that the information may reach the public at the earliest possible moment. In accordance with this plan, the matter contained in the five Parts comprising the present volume, has been published seriatim, at dates much earlier than would have been possible under the plan formerly followed of issuing practically nothing until the bound volumes were ready. A full statement of the organization and methods of the Census will be given in the final volume, and for that reason will not be otherwise referred to here.

The present volume, the first of the series, contains the following:

Part 1.
Population and Legal Voters.
Population: By Towns, Alphabetically.
Population for 1885 and 1895: Increase and Decrease. By Towns.
Population and Sex.
Population for 1885 and 1895: Increase and Decrease. By Sex.

Part 2.
Villages: By Towns.
Villages, Sections, Etc.: Alphabetically.
Censuses of Population: 1765–1895. Dates of Incorporation, Changes in Name, Area, Boundaries, Population, Etc., for Counties, Cities, Towns, and The State.

Part 3.
Polls and Voters.
Political Condition: By Sex.
Political Condition: By Age Periods.

Part 4.
Families: Number and Average Size.
Size of Families and Composition by Sex.
Rooms: Occupied Dwelling Houses.
Rooms: Occupied and Unoccupied Dwelling Houses.
Tenements: Occupied Dwelling Houses.
Dwelling Houses: Number of Stories and Materials.
Averages and Comparative Totals: Rooms, Tenements, and Dwelling Houses.

Part 5.
    Native and Foreign Born.
    Color and Race.
    Conjugal Condition.
    Soldiers, Sailors, and Marines.

Each tabular presentation is accompanied with full analytical text, to which the attention of the reader is especially called.

HORACE G. WADLIN,

Chief.

BUREAU OF STATISTICS OF LABOR,
  20 BEACON STREET, BOSTON,
    December, 1896.

Population and Legal Voters.

POPULATION AND LEGAL VOTERS.

COUNTIES, CITIES, AND TOWNS.	Popula-tion	Legal Voters	COUNTIES, CITIES, AND TOWNS.	Popula-tion	Legal Voters
BARNSTABLE.	27,654	7,620	**BERKSHIRE — Con.**		
Barnstable,	4,065	1,220	Tyringham,	363	102
Bourne,	1,580	434	Washington,	423	105
Brewster,	901	266	West Stockbridge,	1,257	327
Chatham,	1,809	603	Williamstown,	4,887	1,234
Dennis,	2,545	738	Windsor,	556	155
Eastham,	476	152			
Falmouth,	2,655	721	**BRISTOL.**	219,019	42,495
Harwich,	2,532	693			
Mashpee,	330	90	Acushnet,	1,115	315
Orleans,	1,198	342	Attleborough,	8,288	1,814
Provincetown,	4,555	920	Berkley,	955	276
Sandwich,	1,580	437	Dartmouth,	3,107	811
Truro,	815	188	Dighton,	1,797	470
Wellfleet,	968	284	Easton,	4,452	1,124
Yarmouth,	1,655	532	Fairhaven,	3,338	893
			FALL RIVER,	89,203	14,566
BERKSHIRE.	86,292	20,186	Ward 1,	11,146	1,929
Adams,	7,837	1,470	Ward 2,	8,724	1,274
Alford,	280	90	Ward 3,	11,451	1,826
Becket,	888	211	Ward 4,	10,468	1,941
Cheshire,	1,176	319	Ward 5,	10,609	1,635
Clarksburg,	1,009	214	Ward 6,	12,264	1,236
Dalton,	3,210	769	Ward 7,	6,397	1,532
Egremont,	836	235	Ward 8,	7,382	1,663
Florida,	425	99	Ward 9,	10,812	1,530
Great Barrington,	4,794	1,226	Freetown,	1,405	390
Hancock,	511	121	Mansfield,	3,722	933
Hinsdale,	1,650	364	NEW BEDFORD,	55,251	10,096
Lanesborough,	848	243	Ward 1,	13,192	1,731
Lee,	4,066	958	Ward 2,	7,791	1,602
Lenox,	2,872	678	Ward 3,	5,636	1,546
Monterey,	464	120	Ward 4,	6,388	1,636
Mount Washington,	136	33	Ward 5,	9,104	1,797
New Ashford,	116	37	Ward 6,	13,140	1,784
New Marlborough,	1,288	378	North Attleborough,	6,576	1,541
NORTH ADAMS,*	19,135	4,065	Norton,	1,614	443
Otis,	518	162	Raynham,	1,518	402
Peru,	305	79	Rehoboth,	1,810	510
PITTSFIELD,	20,461	4,801	Seekonk,	1,465	346
Ward 1,	2,836	614	Somerset,	1,983	481
Ward 2,	3,526	858	Swansea,	1,627	385
Ward 3,	2,625	683	TAUNTON,	27,115	5,993
Ward 4,	2,780	664	Ward 1,	2,802	760
Ward 5,	2,687	552	Ward 2,	2,872	774
Ward 6,	3,474	751	Ward 3,	3,039	707
Ward 7,	2,533	679	Ward 4,	2,989	769
Richmond,	701	170	Ward 5,	3,841	774
Sandisfield,	802	240	Ward 6,	3,102	731
Savoy,	504	154	Ward 7,	3,033	728
Sheffield,	1,897	494	Ward 8,	5,437	750
Stockbridge,	2,077	538	Westport,	2,678	697

* Incorporated as a city, March 22, 1895; Act accepted, April 8, 1895. Population not distributed by wards.

POPULATION AND LEGAL VOTERS — Continued.

Counties, Cities, and Towns.	Population	Legal Voters
DUKES.	4,238	1,236
Chilmark,	304	107
Cottage City,	1,038	252
Edgartown,	1,125	340
Gay Head,	169	41
Gosnold,	140	46
Tisbury,	1,002	301
West Tisbury,	460	149
ESSEX.	330,393	77,282
Amesbury,	9,986	2,310
Andover,	6,145	1,505
BEVERLY,	11,806	3,034
Ward 1,	2,676	686
Ward 2,	2,443	636
Ward 3,	2,442	576
Ward 4,	2,011	537
Ward 5,	1,203	336
Ward 6,	1,031	263
Boxford,	727	191
Bradford,	4,756	1,159
Danvers,	8,181	1,756
Essex,	1,587	492
Georgetown,	2,050	691
GLOUCESTER,	28,211	6,444
Ward 1,	3,198	838
Ward 2,	5,028	999
Ward 3,	5,190	1,196
Ward 4,	3,461	864
Ward 5,	4,344	1,039
Ward 6,	2,943	738
Ward 7,	2,838	432
Ward 8,	1,209	356
Groveland,	2,333	592
Hamilton,	1,356	262
HAVERHILL,	30,299	7,456
Ward 1,	2,648	877
Ward 2,	2,513	681
Ward 3,	3,543	972
Ward 4,	3,985	1,013
Ward 5,	11,268	2,383
Ward 6,	6,252	1,530
Ipswich,	4,720	1,070
LAWRENCE,	52,164	10,178
Ward 1,	8,568	1,811
Ward 2,	6,984	1,483
Ward 3,	8,978	1,593
Ward 4,	9,969	1,645
Ward 5,	9,933	1,956
Ward 6,	7,732	1,690
LYNN,	62,354	15,437
Ward 1,	1,579	424
Ward 2,	3,936	997
Ward 3,	14,859	3,654
Ward 4,	11,512	3,243
Ward 5,	12,860	3,197
Ward 6,	14,932	3,324
Ward 7,	2,676	598

Counties, Cities, and Towns.	Population	Legal Voters
ESSEX — Con.		
Lynnfield,	818	228
Manchester,	1,876	450
Marblehead,	7,671	2,295
Merrimac,	2,301	613
Methuen,	5,690	1,168
Middleton,	838	228
Nahant,	865	209
Newbury,	1,489	428
NEWBURYPORT,	14,552	3,507
Ward 1,	2,372	593
Ward 2,	2,331	457
Ward 3,	2,666	696
Ward 4,	2,321	593
Ward 5,	2,236	494
Ward 6,	2,626	674
North Andover,	3,569	912
Peabody,	10,507	2,647
Rockport,	5,289	1,055
Rowley,	1,272	381
SALEM,	34,473	7,411
Ward 1,	5,006	1,107
Ward 2,	5,647	1,435
Ward 3,	4,385	1,062
Ward 4,	5,235	1,206
Ward 5,	9,911	1,478
Ward 6,	4,289	1,123
Salisbury,	1,300	394
Saugus,	4,497	1,152
Swampscott,	3,259	874
Topsfield,	1,033	305
Wenham,	886	274
West Newbury,	1,643	464
FRANKLIN.	40,145	10,332
Ashfield,	1,013	300
Bernardston,	778	222
Buckland,	1,548	416
Charlemont,	1,041	294
Colrain,	1,619	409
Conway,	1,304	336
Deerfield,	3,007	722
Erving,	964	241
Gill,	1,082	280
Greenfield,	6,229	1,657
Hawley,	468	143
Heath,	476	124
Leverett,	744	235
Leyden,	363	106
Monroe,	298	72
Montague,	6,058	1,287
New Salem,	869	240
Northfield,	1,851	456
Orange,	5,361	1,444
Rowe,	498	111
Shelburne,	1,560	416
Shutesbury,	444	137
Sunderland,	696	192

POPULATION AND LEGAL VOTERS — Continued.

COUNTIES, CITIES, AND TOWNS.	Population	Legal Voters	COUNTIES, CITIES, AND TOWNS.	Population	Legal Voters
FRANKLIN — Con.			**HAMPSHIRE — Con.**		
Warwick,	599	136	Easthampton,	4,790	965
Wendell,	529	135	Enfield,	990	234
Whately,	755	221	Goshen,	304	73
			Granby,	748	182
HAMPDEN.	152,938	31,568	Greenwich,	481	146
Agawam,	2,408	530	Hadley,	1,704	398
Blandford,	849	256	Hatfield,	1,262	320
Brimfield,	962	290	Huntington,	1,450	319
Chester,	1,429	379	Middlefield,	386	86
CHICOPEE,	16,420	2,749	NORTHAMPTON,	16,746	3,290
Ward 1,	3,269	470	Ward 1,	2,170	525
Ward 2,	1,752	398	Ward 2,	3,244	464
Ward 3,	2,817	344	Ward 3,	2,872	599
Ward 4,	2,258	392	Ward 4,	2,488	432
Ward 5,	2,650	542	Ward 5,	2,136	456
Ward 6,	1,698	308	Ward 6,	1,903	436
Ward 7,	1,976	295	Ward 7,	1,933	378
East Longmeadow,	1,591	239	Pelham,	486	137
Granville,	1,005	255	Plainfield,	450	135
Hampden,	743	180	Prescott,	401	126
Holland,	199	54	Southampton,	1,054	282
HOLYOKE,	40,322	6,597	South Hadley,	4,443	839
Ward 1,	6,014	966	Ware,	7,651	1,271
Ward 2,	8,858	916	Westhampton,	476	120
Ward 3,	5,923	846	Williamsburg,	1,955	468
Ward 4,	6,781	855	Worthington,	648	184
Ward 5,	3,579	818			
Ward 6,	5,698	1,103	**MIDDLESEX.**	499,217	109,577
Ward 7,	4,369	1,093	Acton,	1,978	545
Longmeadow,	620	143	Arlington,	6,515	1,545
Ludlow,	2,562	372	Ashby,	804	259
Monson,	3,746	851	Ashland,	2,090	482
Montgomery,	275	79	Ayer,	2,191	515
Palmer,	6,858	1,196	Bedford,	1,169	264
Russell,	846	181	Belmont,	2,843	550
Southwick,	961	261	Billerica,	2,577	640
SPRINGFIELD,	51,522	12,240	Boxborough,	307	89
Ward 1,	6,899	1,717	Burlington,	574	140
Ward 2,	7,898	1,617	CAMBRIDGE,	81,643	17,018
Ward 3,	6,197	1,747	Ward 1,	15,881	3,747
Ward 4,	6,209	1,586	Ward 2,	22,932	4,707
Ward 5,	6,426	1,625	Ward 3,	13,996	2,462
Ward 6,	6,153	1,333	Ward 4,	18,681	3,999
Ward 7,	4,650	1,189	Ward 5,	10,453	2,103
Ward 8,	7,090	1,426	Carlisle,	492	125
Tolland,	309	84	Chelmsford,	3,162	771
Wales,	783	177	Concord,	5,175	943
Westfield,	10,668	2,752	Dracut,	2,443	534
West Springfield,	6,125	1,374	Dunstable,	400	134
Wilbraham,	1,740	359	EVERETT,	18,573	4,090
			Ward 1,	3,138	617
HAMPSHIRE.	54,710	11,888	Ward 2,	2,627	610
Amherst,	4,785	1,339	Ward 3,	3,090	609
Belchertown,	2,161	557	Ward 4,	2,876	702
Chesterfield,	559	192	Ward 5,	3,153	651
Cummington,	750	225	Ward 6,	3,689	901

POPULATION AND LEGAL VOTERS — Continued.

COUNTIES, CITIES, AND TOWNS.	Population	Legal Voters	COUNTIES, CITIES, AND TOWNS.	Population	Legal Voters
MIDDLESEX — Con.			**MIDDLESEX — Con.**		
Framingham,	9,512	2,308	SOMERVILLE,	52,200	11,839
Groton,	2,192	494	Ward 1,	10,127	2,272
Holliston,	2,718	734	Ward 2,	17,196	3,573
Hopkinton,	2,984	902	Ward 3,	13,056	3,239
Hudson,	5,308	1,296	Ward 4,	11,821	2,755
Lexington,	3,498	848	Stoneham,	6,284	1,757
Lincoln,	1,111	229	Stow,	920	240
Littleton,	1,136	274	Sudbury,	1,141	319
LOWELL,	84,367	16,408	Tewksbury,	3,379	423
Ward 1,	9,508	2,128	Townsend,	1,780	535
Ward 2,	10,493	1,742	Tyngsborough,	635	157
Ward 3,	9,243	1,901	Wakefield,	8,304	1,885
Ward 4,	9,241	1,995	WALTHAM,	20,876	4,574
Ward 5,	8,452	1,717	Ward 1,	2,920	624
Ward 6,	9,332	1,750	Ward 2,	2,936	574
Ward 7,	13,118	1,678	Ward 3,	3,376	594
Ward 8,	7,940	1,911	Ward 4,	3,071	632
Ward 9,	7,088	1,586	Ward 5,	2,887	763
MALDEN,	29,708	6,522	Ward 6,	2,918	765
Ward 1,	4,105	939	Ward 7,	2,768	622
Ward 2,	5,330	914	Watertown,	7,788	1,751
Ward 3,	3,579	854	Wayland,	2,026	535
Ward 4,	4,860	1,065	Westford,	2,418	506
Ward 5,	3,931	971	Weston,	1,710	394
Ward 6,	4,212	941	Wilmington,	1,420	333
Ward 7,	3,751	838	Winchester,	6,150	1,390
MARLBOROUGH,	14,977	3,445	WOBURN,	14,178	3,327
Ward 1,	1,335	368	Ward 1,	2,625	619
Ward 2,	2,295	515	Ward 2,	2,881	684
Ward 3,	2,969	573	Ward 3,	2,509	605
Ward 4,	3,302	635	Ward 4,	2,622	601
Ward 5,	1,934	492	Ward 5,	1,161	259
Ward 6,	1,689	468	Ward 6,	1,413	338
Ward 7,	1,543	394	Ward 7,	967	221
Maynard,	3,090	598			
MEDFORD,	14,474	3,321	**NANTUCKET.**	3,016	886
Ward 1,	3,012	589	Nantucket,	3,016	886
Ward 2,	2,305	557			
Ward 3,	1,924	485			
Ward 4,	1,956	485	**NORFOLK.**	134,819	31,565
Ward 5,	2,955	634	Avon,	1,626	469
Ward 6,	2,322	571	Bellingham,	1,481	323
Melrose,	11,965	2,851	Braintree,	5,311	1,381
Natick,	8,814	2,334	Brookline,	16,164	3,243
NEWTON,	27,590	5,617	Canton,	4,636	1,096
Ward 1,	4,287	668	Cohasset,	2,474	665
Ward 2,	5,412	1,072	Dedham,	7,211	1,702
Ward 3,	3,433	761	Dover,	668	169
Ward 4,	3,574	691	Foxborough,	3,219	858
Ward 5,	4,114	964	Franklin,	5,136	1,184
Ward 6,	4,240	846	Holbrook,	2,298	645
Ward 7,	2,530	615	Hyde Park,	11,826	2,772
North Reading,	835	228	Medfield,	1,872	447
Pepperell,	3,321	800	Medway,	2,913	818
Reading,	4,717	1,184	Millis,	1,006	231
Sherborn,	1,446	269	Milton,	5,518	1,171
Shirley,	1,399	315	Needham,	3,511	763

POPULATION AND LEGAL VOTERS — Continued.

Counties, Cities, and Towns.	Population	Legal Voters	Counties, Cities, and Towns.	Population	Legal Voters
NORFOLK — Con.			**SUFFOLK — Con.**		
Norfolk, ...	882	193	BOSTON — Con.		
Norwood, ...	4,574	1,133	Ward 2, ...	21,588	4,357
QUINCY, ...	20,712	4,325	Ward 3, ...	13,943	3,538
Ward 1, ...	3,562	803	Ward 4, ...	13,375	3,311
Ward 2, ...	2,741	658	Ward 5, ...	12,986	3,266
Ward 3, ...	4,696	834	Ward 6, ...	27,860	4,190
Ward 4, ...	4,964	874	Ward 7, ...	16,975	4,237
Ward 5, ...	2,669	646	Ward 8, ...	23,130	5,173
Ward 6, ...	2,080	510	Ward 9, ...	23,174	5,504
Raudolph, ...	3,694	1,123	Ward 10, ...	22,554	6,007
Sharon, ...	1,717	423	Ward 11, ...	19,930	4,886
Stoughton, ...	5,272	1,333	Ward 12, ...	21,591	5,731
Walpole, ...	2,994	715	Ward 13, ...	24,900	4,795
Wellesley, ...	4,229	694	Ward 14, ...	19,186	4,381
Weymouth, ...	11,291	3,039	Ward 15, ...	18,628	4,324
Wrentham, ...	2,584	700	Ward 16, ...	16,320	3,933
			Ward 17, ...	21,114	4,501
PLYMOUTH.	101,498	26,956	Ward 18, ...	21,679	4,830
			Ward 19, ...	22,372	4,467
Abington, ...	4,207	1,258	Ward 20, ...	21,528	5,225
Bridgewater, ...	4,686	992	Ward 21, ...	19,274	4,793
BROCKTON, ...	33,165	8,531	Ward 22, ...	22,289	4,879
Ward 1, ...	4,169	1,253	Ward 23, ...	18,283	4,032
Ward 2, ...	4,327	1,310	Ward 24, ...	18,240	4,371
Ward 3, ...	5,045	1,273	Ward 25, ...	15,001	3,577
Ward 4, ...	4,792	1,042	CHELSEA, ...	31,264	7,066
Ward 5, ...	5,046	1,164	Ward 1, ...	7,479	1,561
Ward 6, ...	4,940	1,202	Ward 2, ...	7,585	1,631
Ward 7, ...	4,846	1,287	Ward 3, ...	7,122	1,493
Carver, ...	1,016	269	Ward 4, ...	5,387	1,265
Duxbury, ...	1,966	555	Ward 5, ...	3,691	1,116
East Bridgewater, . .	2,894	780	Revere, ...	7,423	1,818
Halifax, ...	497	146	Winthrop, ...	4,192	825
Hanover, ...	2,051	584			
Hanson, ...	1,380	286	**WORCESTER.**	306,445	66,109
Hingham, ...	4,819	1,256			
Hull, ...	1,044	192	Ashburnham, ...	2,148	548
Kingston, ...	1,746	473	Athol, ...	7,364	1,846
Lakeville, ...	870	254	Auburn, ...	1,598	270
Marion, ...	759	207	Barre, ...	2,278	543
Marshfield, ...	1,760	536	Berlin, ...	897	238
Mattapoisett, ...	1,032	296	Blackstone, ...	6,939	1,393
Middleborough, . . .	6,689	1,843	Bolton, ...	797	210
Norwell, ...	1,540	473	Boylston, ...	729	197
Pembroke, ...	1,223	369	Brookfield, ...	3,279	760
Plymouth, ...	7,957	1,966	Charlton, ...	1,877	487
Plympton, ...	549	158	Clinton, ...	11,497	2,418
Rochester, ...	1,021	283	Dana, ...	717	180
Rockland, ...	5,523	1,571	Douglas, ...	2,026	493
Scituate, ...	2,246	673	Dudley, ...	3,203	528
Wareham, ...	3,367	828	FITCHBURG, ...	26,409	5,231
West Bridgewater, . .	1,747	461	Ward 1, ...	4,376	828
Whitman, ...	5,744	1,616	Ward 2, ...	6,510	884
			Ward 3, ...	4,299	821
SUFFOLK.	539,799	123,102	Ward 4, ...	3,214	817
			Ward 5, ...	3,350	932
Boston, ...	496,920	113,393	Ward 6, ...	4,660	949
Ward 1, ...	21,007	4,785	Gardner, ...	9,182	1,980

POPULATION AND LEGAL VOTERS — Concluded.

COUNTIES, CITIES, AND TOWNS.	Population	Legal Voters	COUNTIES, CITIES, AND TOWNS.	Population	Legal Voters
WORCESTER — Con.			**WORCESTER — Con.**		
Grafton,	5,101	990	Southborough,	2,223	448
Hardwick,	2,655	479	Southbridge,	8,250	1,414
Harvard,	1,162	306	Spencer,	7,614	1,570
Holden,	2,602	522	Sterling,	1,218	337
Hopedale,	1,377	351	Sturbridge,	1,910	423
Hubbardston,	1,274	338	Sutton,	3,420	555
Lancaster,	2,180	413	Templeton,	2,915	770
Leicester,	3,239	744	Upton,	2,150	519
Leominster,	9,211	2,260	Uxbridge,	3,546	743
Lunenburg,	1,237	357	Warren,	4,430	859
Mendon,	889	263	Webster,	7,799	1,248
Milford,	8,950	2,323	Westborough,	5,235	1,128
Millbury,	5,222	963	West Boylston,	2,968	517
New Braintree,	542	112	West Brookfield,	1,467	407
Northborough,	1,940	407	Westminster,	1,315	354
Northbridge,	5,286	974	Winchendon,	4,490	1,049
North Brookfield,	4,635	1,070	WORCESTER,	98,767	21,128
Oakham,	605	175	Ward 1,	11,100	2,788
Oxford,	2,390	559	Ward 2,	13,089	2,686
Paxton,	426	131	Ward 3,	14,637	2,695
Petersham,	952	258	Ward 4,	13,491	2,577
Phillipston,	460	133	Ward 5,	15,285	2,646
Princeton,	962	254	Ward 6,	11,835	2,656
Royalston,	890	255	Ward 7,	10,352	2,554
Rutland,	978	257	Ward 8,	8,978	2,526
Shrewsbury,	1,524	444			

RECAPITULATION.

THE STATE, AND COUNTIES.	Population	Legal Voters
THE STATE.	2,500,183	560,802
Barnstable,	27,654	7,620
Berkshire,	86,292	20,186
Bristol,	219,019	42,495
Dukes,	4,238	1,236
Essex,	330,393	77,282
Franklin,	40,145	10,332
Hampden,	152,938	31,568
Hampshire,	54,710	11,888
Middlesex,	499,217	109,577
Nantucket,	3,016	886
Norfolk,	134,819	31,565
Plymouth,	101,498	26,956
Suffolk,	539,799	123,102
Worcester,	306,445	66,109

POPULATION:
BY TOWNS, ALPHABETICALLY.

POPULATION: BY TOWNS, ALPHABETICALLY.

CITY OR TOWN.	County	Population	CITY OR TOWN.	County	Population
Abington,	Plymouth,	4,207	CAMBRIDGE,	Middlesex,	81,643
Acton,	Middlesex,	1,978	Canton,	Norfolk,	4,836
Acushnet,	Bristol,	1,115	Carlisle,	Middlesex,	492
Adams,	Berkshire,	7,837	Carver,	Plymouth,	1,016
Agawam,	Hampden,	2,408	Charlemont,	Franklin,	1,041
Alford,	Berkshire,	280	Charlton,	Worcester,	1,877
Amesbury,	Essex,	9,986	Chatham,	Barnstable,	1,809
Amherst,	Hampshire,	4,785	Chelmsford,	Middlesex,	3,162
Andover,	Essex,	6,145	CHELSEA,	Suffolk,	31,264
Arlington,	Middlesex,	6,515	Cheshire,	Berkshire,	1,176
Ashburnham,	Worcester,	2,148	Chester,	Hampden,	1,429
Ashby,	Middlesex,	804	Chesterfield,	Hampshire,	589
Ashfield,	Franklin,	1,013	CHICOPEE,	Hampden,	16,420
Ashland,	Middlesex,	2,606	Chilmark,	Dukes,	304
Athol,	Worcester,	7,364	Clarksburg,	Berkshire,	1,069
Attleborough,	Bristol,	8,288	Clinton,	Worcester,	11,497
Auburn,	Worcester,	1,598	Cohasset,	Norfolk,	2,474
Avon,	Norfolk,	1,926	Colrain,	Franklin,	1,610
Ayer,	Middlesex,	2,101	Concord,	Middlesex,	5,175
			Conway,	Franklin,	1,304
Barnstable,	Barnstable,	4,055	Cottage City,	Dukes,	1,038
Barre,	Worcester,	2,278	Cummington,	Hampshire.	750
Becket,	Berkshire,	888			
Bedford,	Middlesex,	1,169			
Belchertown,	Hampshire,	2,161	Dalton,	Berkshire,	3,210
Bellingham,	Norfolk,	1,481	Dana,	Worcester,	717
Belmont,	Middlesex,	2,843	Danvers,	Essex,	8,181
Berkley,	Bristol,	955	Dartmouth,	Bristol,	3,107
Berlin,	Worcester,	897	Dedham,	Norfolk,	7,211
Bernardston,	Franklin,	778	Deerfield,	Franklin,	3,007
BEVERLY,	Essex,	11,806	Dennis,	Barnstable,	2,545
Billerica,	Middlesex,	2,577	Dighton,	Bristol,	1,797
Blackstone,	Worcester,	6,030	Douglas,	Worcester,	2,026
Blandford,	Hampden,	840	Dover,	Norfolk,	668
Bolton,	Worcester,	797	Dracut,	Middlesex,	2,443
BOSTON,	Suffolk,	496,920	Dudley,	Worcester,	3,203
Bourne,	Barnstable,	1,580	Dunstable,	Middlesex,	400
Boxborough,	Middlesex,	307	Duxbury,	Plymouth,	1,966
Boxford,	Essex,	727			
Boylston,	Worcester,	729	East Bridgewater,	Plymouth,	2,894
Bradford,	Essex,	4,736	Eastham,	Barnstable,	476
Braintree,	Norfolk,	5,311	Easthampton,	Hampshire,	4,790
Brewster,	Barnstable,	901	East Longmeadow,	Hampden,	1,591
Bridgewater,	Plymouth,	4,686	Easton,	Bristol,	4,452
Brimfield,	Hampden,	962	Edgartown,	Dukes,	1,125
BROCKTON,	Plymouth,	33,165	Egremont,	Berkshire,	836
Brookfield,	Worcester,	3,279	Enfield,	Hampshire,	990
Brookline,	Norfolk,	16,164	Erving,	Franklin,	964
Buckland,	Franklin,	1,548	Essex,	Essex,	1,587
Burlington,	Middlesex,	574	EVERETT,	Middlesex,	18,573

POPULATION: BY TOWNS — Continued.

City or Town.	County	Population	City or Town.	County	Population
Fairhaven, . . .	Bristol, . .	3,338	Lakeville, ...	Plymouth, .	870
FALL RIVER, . . .	Bristol, . .	89,203	Lancaster, . . .	Worcester, .	2,180
Falmouth, . . .	Barnstable, .	2,655	Lanesborough, . .	Berkshire, .	848
FITCHBURG, . . .	Worcester, .	26,409	LAWRENCE, . . .	Essex, . .	52,164
Florida, ...	Berkshire, .	425	Lee, ...	Berkshire, . .	4,066
Foxborough, . . .	Norfolk, .	3,219	Leicester, ...	Worcester, . .	3,239
Framingham, . . .	Middlesex, .	9,512	Lenox, ...	Berkshire, .	2,872
Franklin, ...	Norfolk, .	5,136	Leominster, . . .	Worcester, .	9,211
Freetown, . . .	Bristol, . .	1,405	Leverett, ...	Franklin, .	744
			Lexington, . . .	Middlesex, .	3,498
Gardner, ...	Worcester, .	9,182	Leyden, ...	Franklin, .	363
Gay Head, . . .	Dukes, . .	169	Lincoln, ...	Middlesex, .	1,111
Georgetown, . . .	Essex, . .	2,050	Littleton, ...	Middlesex, . .	1,136
Gill, ...	Franklin, .	1,082	Longmeadow, . . .	Hampden, .	620
GLOUCESTER, . . .	Essex, . .	28,211	LOWELL, . . .	Middlesex, .	84,367
Goshen, ...	Hampshire, .	304	Ludlow, ...	Hampden, .	2,562
Gosnold, ...	Dukes, . .	140	Lunenburg, . . .	Worcester, .	1,237
Grafton, ...	Worcester, .	5,101	LYNN, ...	Essex, . .	62,354
Granby, ...	Hampshire, .	748	Lynnfield, . . .	Essex, . .	818
Granville, ...	Hampden, .	1,095			
Great Barrington, .	Berkshire, .	4,794	MALDEN, ...	Middlesex, .	29,708
Greenfield, . . .	Franklin, .	6,229	Manchester, . . .	Essex, . .	1,876
Greenwich, . . .	Hampshire, .	481	Mansfield, . . .	Bristol, . .	3,722
Groton, ...	Middlesex, .	2,192	Marblehead, . . .	Essex, . .	7,671
Groveland, . . .	Essex, . .	2,333	Marion, ...	Plymouth, .	759
			MARLBOROUGH, . .	Middlesex, .	14,977
Hadley, ...	Hampshire, .	1,704	Marshfield, . . .	Plymouth, .	1,760
Halifax, ...	Plymouth, .	497	Mashpee, . . .	Barnstable, .	330
Hamilton, . . .	Essex, . .	1,356	Mattapoisett, . . .	Plymouth, .	1,032
Hampden, . . .	Hampden, .	743	Maynard, ...	Middlesex, .	3,090
Hancock, ...	Berkshire, .	511	Medfield, ...	Norfolk, .	1,872
Hanover, ...	Plymouth, .	2,051	MEDFORD, . . .	Middlesex, .	14,474
Hanson, ...	Plymouth, .	1,380	Medway, ...	Norfolk, .	2,913
Hardwick, . . .	Worcester, .	2,655	Melrose, ...	Middlesex, .	11,965
Harvard, ...	Worcester, .	1,162	Mendon, ...	Worcester, .	889
Harwich, ...	Barnstable, .	2,532	Merrimac, . . .	Essex, . .	2,301
Hatfield, ...	Hampshire, .	1,262	Methuen, ...	Essex, . .	5,090
HAVERHILL, . . .	Essex, . .	30,209	Middleborough, . .	Plymouth, .	6,689
Hawley, ...	Franklin, .	468	Middlefield, . . .	Hampshire, .	386
Heath, ...	Franklin, .	476	Middleton, . . .	Essex, . .	838
Hingham, ...	Plymouth, .	4,819	Milford, ...	Worcester, .	8,959
Hinsdale, ...	Berkshire, .	1,650	Millbury, ...	Worcester, .	5,222
Holbrook, ...	Norfolk, .	2,298	Mills, ...	Norfolk, .	1,006
Holden, ...	Worcester, .	2,602	Milton, ...	Norfolk, .	5,518
Holland, ...	Hampden, .	199	Monroe, ...	Franklin, .	298
Holliston, ...	Middlesex, .	2,718	Monson, ...	Hampden, .	3,746
HOLYOKE, . . .	Hampden, .	40,322	Montague, . . .	Franklin, .	6,058
Hopedale, ...	Worcester, .	1,377	Monterey, . . .	Berkshire, .	464
Hopkinton, . . .	Middlesex, .	2,984	Montgomery, . . .	Hampden, .	275
Hubbardston, . . .	Worcester, .	1,274	Mount Washington,	Berkshire, .	136
Hudson, ...	Middlesex, .	5,398			
Hull, ...	Plymouth, .	1,044	Nahant, ...	Essex, . .	865
Huntington, . . .	Hampshire, .	1,450	Nantucket, . . .	Nantucket, .	3,016
Hyde Park, . . .	Norfolk, .	11,826	Natick, ...	Middlesex, .	8,814
			Needham, . . .	Norfolk, .	3,511
Ipswich, ...	Essex, . .	4,720	New Ashford, . .	Berkshire, .	116
			NEW BEDFORD, . .	Bristol, . .	55,251
Kingston, ...	Plymouth, .	1,746	New Braintree, . .	Worcester, .	542

POPULATION: BY TOWNS — Continued.

CITY OR TOWN.	County	Population	CITY OR TOWN.	County	Population
Newbury,	Essex,	1,489	SALEM,	Essex,	34,473
NEWBURYPORT,	Essex,	14,552	Salisbury,	Essex,	1,300
New Marlborough,	Berkshire,	1,288	Sandisfield,	Berkshire,	862
New Salem,	Franklin,	869	Sandwich,	Barnstable,	1,580
NEWTON,	Middlesex,	27,590	Saugus,	Essex,	4,497
Norfolk,	Norfolk,	882	Savoy,	Berkshire,	504
NORTH ADAMS,	Berkshire,	19,135	Scituate,	Plymouth,	2,246
NORTHAMPTON,	Hampshire,	16,746	Seekonk,	Bristol,	1,465
North Andover,	Essex,	3,969	Sharon,	Norfolk,	1,717
North Attleborough,	Bristol,	6,576	Sheffield,	Berkshire,	1,887
Northborough,	Worcester,	1,940	Shelburne,	Franklin,	1,590
Northbridge,	Worcester,	5,286	Sherborn,	Middlesex,	1,446
North Brookfield,	Worcester,	4,635	Shirley,	Middlesex,	1,389
Northfield,	Franklin,	1,851	Shrewsbury,	Worcester,	1,524
North Reading,	Middlesex,	835	Shutesbury,	Franklin,	444
Norton,	Bristol,	1,614	Somerset,	Bristol,	1,583
Norwell,	Plymouth,	1,540	SOMERVILLE,	Middlesex,	52,200
Norwood,	Norfolk,	4,574	Southampton,	Hampshire,	1,054
			Southborough,	Worcester,	2,223
Oakham,	Worcester,	665	Southbridge,	Worcester,	8,250
Orange,	Franklin,	5,961	South Hadley,	Hampshire,	4,443
Orleans,	Barnstable,	1,198	Southwick,	Hampden,	983
Otis,	Berkshire,	518	Spencer,	Worcester,	7,614
Oxford,	Worcester,	2,390	SPRINGFIELD,	Hampden,	51,522
			Sterling,	Worcester,	1,218
Palmer,	Hampden,	6,858	Stockbridge,	Berkshire,	2,077
Paxton,	Worcester,	423	Stoneham,	Middlesex,	6,284
Peabody,	Essex,	10,507	Stoughton,	Norfolk,	5,272
Pelham,	Hampshire,	486	Stow,	Middlesex,	920
Pembroke,	Plymouth,	1,223	Sturbridge,	Worcester,	1,910
Pepperell,	Middlesex,	3,321	Sudbury,	Middlesex,	1,141
Peru,	Berkshire,	305	Sunderland,	Franklin,	696
Petersham,	Worcester,	952	Sutton,	Worcester,	3,420
Phillipston,	Worcester,	460	Swampscott,	Essex,	3,259
PITTSFIELD,	Berkshire,	20,461	Swansea,	Bristol,	1,627
Plainfield,	Hampshire,	450			
Plymouth,	Plymouth,	7,367	TAUNTON,	Bristol,	27,115
Plympton,	Plymouth,	549	Templeton,	Worcester,	2,915
Prescott,	Hampshire,	401	Tewksbury,	Middlesex,	3,379
Princeton,	Worcester,	952	Tisbury,	Dukes,	1,062
Provincetown,	Barnstable,	4,555	Tolland,	Hampden,	309
			Topsfield,	Essex,	1,033
QUINCY,	Norfolk,	20,712	Townsend,	Middlesex,	1,780
			Truro,	Barnstable,	815
Randolph,	Norfolk,	3,694	Tyngsborough,	Middlesex,	635
Raynham,	Bristol,	1,518	Tyringham,	Berkshire,	363
Reading,	Middlesex,	4,717			
Rehoboth,	Bristol,	1,810	Upton,	Worcester,	2,150
Revere,	Suffolk,	7,423	Uxbridge,	Worcester,	3,546
Richmond,	Berkshire,	701			
Rochester,	Plymouth,	1,021	Wakefield,	Middlesex,	8,304
Rockland,	Plymouth,	5,523	Wales,	Hampden,	783
Rockport,	Essex,	5,289	Walpole,	Norfolk,	2,994
Rowe,	Franklin,	498	WALTHAM,	Middlesex,	20,876
Rowley,	Essex,	1,272	Ware,	Hampshire,	7,651
Royalston,	Worcester,	800	Wareham,	Plymouth,	3,367
Russell,	Hampden,	846	Warren,	Worcester,	4,430
Rutland,	Worcester,	978	Warwick,	Franklin,	599

POPULATION: BY TOWNS — Concluded.

CITY OR TOWN.	County	Population	CITY OR TOWN.	County	Population
Washington, . . .	Berkshire, .	423	West Stockbridge, . .	Berkshire, .	1,257
Watertown, . . .	Middlesex, .	7,788	West Tisbury, . . .	Dukes, . .	460
Wayland, ...	Middlesex, .	2,026	Weymouth, . . .	Norfolk, .	11,291
Webster, ...	Worcester, .	7,799	Whately, ...	Franklin, .	755
Wellesley, . . .	Norfolk, .	4,229	Whitman, ...	Plymouth, .	5,744
Wellfleet, . . .	Barnstable, .	968	Wilbraham, . . .	Hampden, .	1,740
Wendell, ...	Franklin, .	529	Williamsburg, . .	Hampshire, .	1,955
Wenham, ...	Essex, . .	886	Williamstown, . .	Berkshire, .	4,887
Westborough, . . .	Worcester, .	5,235	Wilmington, . . .	Middlesex, .	1,420
West Boylston, . .	Worcester, .	2,968	Winchendon, . . .	Worcester, .	4,490
West Bridgewater, . .	Plymouth, .	1,747	Winchester, . . .	Middlesex, .	6,150
West Brookfield, . .	Worcester, .	1,467	Windsor, ...	Berkshire, .	556
Westfield, ...	Hampden, .	10,663	Winthrop, . . .	Suffolk, . .	4,192
Westford, ...	Middlesex, .	2,418	WOBURN, ...	Middlesex, .	14,178
Westhampton, . . .	Hampshire, .	476	WORCESTER, . . .	Worcester, .	98,767
Westminster, . . .	Worcester, .	1,315	Worthington, . . .	Hampshire, .	648
West Newbury, . .	Essex, . .	1,643	Wrentham, . . .	Norfolk, .	2,584
Weston, ...	Middlesex, .	1,710			
Westport, ...	Bristol, . .	2,678	Yarmouth, . . .	Barnstable, .	1,655
West Springfield, . .	Hampden, .	6,125			

POPULATION FOR 1885 AND 1895:

INCREASE AND DECREASE.

BY TOWNS.

POPULATION — 1885 AND 1895.

TOWNS SHOWING INCREASE.

[The asterisk indicates new towns, changes in area, boundaries, etc., since 1885. See CENSUSES OF POPULATION : 1765-1895.]

COUNTIES, CITIES, AND TOWNS.	1885	1895	INCREASE Number	Percentage	COUNTIES, CITIES, AND TOWNS.	1885	1895	INCREASE Number	Percentage
BARNSTABLE.	13,980	14,373	473	3.40	ESSEX — Con.				
Barnstable,*	4,050	4,055	5	0.12	BEVERLY,	9,186	11,806	2,620	28.52
Bourne,	1,363	1,580	217	15.92	Bradford,	3,106	4,796	1,690	52.48
Falmouth,*	2,520	2,655	135	5.36	Danvers,	7,061	8,181	1,120	15.86
Mashpee,*	311	330	19	6.11	GLOUCESTER,*	21,703	28,211	6,508	29.99
Orleans,	1,176	1,198	22	1.87	Groveland,	2,272	2,333	61	2.68
Provincetown,	4,480	4,555	75	1.67	Hamilton,	851	1,356	505	59.34
					HAVERHILL,	21,795	30,209	8,414	38.61
BERKSHIRE.	41,007	57,204	16,197	39.50	Ipswich,*	4,207	4,720	513	12.19
Clarksburg,	708	1,009	301	42.51	LAWRENCE,	38,862	52,164	13,302	34.23
Dalton,	2,113	3,210	1,097	51.92	LYNN,	45,867	62,354	16,487	35.95
Egremont,	826	836	10	1.21	Lynnfield,	766	818	52	6.79
Great Barrington,	4,471	4,794	323	7.22	Manchester,	1,639	1,876	237	14.46
Lenox,	2,154	2,872	718	33.33	Marblehead,	7,517	7,671	154	2.05
NORTH ADAMS,	12,540	19,135	6,595	52.59	Methuen,	4,507	5,690	1,183	26.25
PITTSFIELD,	14,466	20,461	5,995	41.44	Nahant,	637	865	228	35.79
Williamstown,	3,729	4,887	1,158	31.05	NEWBURYPORT,	13,716	14,552	836	6.10
					North Andover,	3,425	3,569	144	4.20
BRISTOL.	131,984	198,426	66,442	50.34	Peabody,	9,530	10,507	977	10.25
Acushnet,	1,071	1,115	44	4.11	Rockport,	3,888	5,289	1,401	36.03
Berkley,	941	955	14	1.49	Rowley,	1,183	1,272	89	7.52
Dighton,	1,782	1,797	15	0.84	SALEM,	28,090	34,473	6,383	22.72
Easton,	3,948	4,452	504	12.77	Saugus,	2,855	4,497	1,642	57.51
Fairhaven,	2,880	3,338	458	15.90	Swampscott,	2,471	3,259	788	31.89
FALL RIVER,*	56,870	89,203	32,333	56.85	Wenham,	871	886	15	1.72
Mansfield,	2,939	3,722	783	26.64					
NEW BEDFORD,*	33,393	55,251	21,858	65.46	FRANKLIN.	21,666	25,892	4,226	19.51
N. Attleborough,*	-	6,576	6,576	-	Charlemont,	958	1,041	83	8.66
Rehoboth,	1,788	1,810	22	1.23	Colrain,	1,605	1,610	5	0.31
Seekonk,	1,295	1,465	170	13.13	Erving,	873	964	91	10.42
Swansea,	1,403	1,627	224	15.97	Gill,	860	1,082	222	25.81
TAUNTON,	23,674	27,115	3,441	14.53	Greenfield,	4,869	6,229	1,360	27.93
					Monroe,	176	298	122	69.32
DUKES.	831	1,638	807	97.11	Montague,	5,629	6,058	429	7.62
Cottage City,	709	1,038	329	46.40	New Salem,	832	869	37	4.45
Gosnold,	122	140	18	14.75	Northfield,	1,705	1,851	146	8.56
West Tisbury,*	-	460	460	-	Orange,	3,650	5,361	1,711	46.88
					Wendell,	509	529	20	3.93
ESSEX.	246,119	317,425	71,306	28.97	HAMPDEN.	103,396	141,640	38,274	37.03
Amesbury,*	4,403	9,986	5,583	126.80	Agawam,	2,357	2,408	51	2.16
Andover,	5,711	6,145	434	7.60	Chester,	1,318	1,429	111	8.42

18   CENSUS OF MASSACHUSETTS — 1895.

TOWNS SHOWING INCREASE — Continued.

COUNTIES, CITIES, AND TOWNS.	1885	1895	Increase Number	Increase Percentage
HAMPDEN—Con.				
CHICOPEE, . .	11,516	16,420	4,904	42.58
E. Longmeadow,*	-	1,591	1,591	-
HOLYOKE, . .	27,895	40,322	12,427	44.55
Ludlow, . .	1,649	2,562	913	55.37
Palmer, . . .	5,923	6,858	935	15.79
SPRINGFIELD,* .	37,575	51,522	13,947	37.12
Westfield, . .	8,961	10,663	1,702	18.99
West Springfield,	4,448	6,125	1,677	37.70
Wilbraham, . .	1,724	1,740	16	0.93
HAMPSHIRE.	34,359	41,667	7,308	21.27
Amherst, . .	4,199	4,785	586	13.96
Easthampton, .	4,291	4,790	499	11.63
Granby,. . .	729	748	19	2.61
Huntington,. .	1,267	1,450	183	14.44
NORTHAMPTON, .	12,896	16,746	3,850	29.85
Southampton, .	1,025	1,054	29	2.83
South Hadley, .	3,949	4,443	494	12.51
Ware, . . .	6,003	7,651	1,648	27.45
MIDDLESEX.	337,995	482,071	144,076	42.63
Acton, . . .	1,785	1,978	193	10.81
Arlington, . .	4,673	6,515	1,842	39.42
Bedford, . .	930	1,169	239	25.70
Belmont,* . .	1,639	2,843	1,204	73.46
Billerica, . .	2,161	2,577	416	19.25
CAMBRIDGE,* .	59,658	81,643	21,985	36.85
Chelmsford, . .	2,304	3,162	858	37.24
Concord, . .	3,727	5,175	1,448	38.85
Dracut, . . .	1,927	2,443	516	26.78
EVERETT, . .	5,825	18,573	12,748	218.85
Framingham, .	8,275	9,512	1,237	14.95
Groton, . . .	1,987	2,192	205	10.32
Hudson, . .	3,968	5,308	1,340	33.77
Lexington,* . .	2,718	3,498	780	28.70
Lincoln, . .	901	1,111	210	23.31
Littleton,* . .	1,067	1,136	69	6.47
LOWELL,* . .	64,107	84,367	20,260	31.60
MALDEN, . .	16,407	29,708	13,301	81.07
MARLBOROUGH,.	10,941	14,977	4,036	36.89
Maynard, . .	2,703	3,090	387	14.32
MEDFORD, . .	9,042	14,474	5,432	60.08
Melrose,* . .	6,101	11,965	5,864	96.12
Natick, . . .	8,460	8,814	354	4.18
NEWTON, . .	19,759	27,590	7,831	39.63
Pepperell . .	2,587	3,321	734	28.37
Reading, . .	3,539	4,717	1,178	33.29
Sherborn, . .	1,391	1,446	55	3.95
Shirley, . . .	1,242	1,399	157	12.64
SOMERVILLE,* .	29,971	52,260	22,229	74.17
Stoneham,* . .	5,659	6,284	625	11.04
Tewksbury,* .	2,333	3,379	1,046	44.83
Tyngsborough, .	604	635	31	5.13
Wakefield,* . .	6,060	8,304	2,244	37.03
WALTHAM,*. .	14,609	20,876	6,267	42.90
Watertown, . .	6,238	7,788	1,550	24.85
Wayland, . .	1,946	2,026	80	4.11
MIDDLESEX—Con.				
Westford, . .	2,193	2,418	225	10.26
Weston, . . .	1,427	1,710	283	19.83
Wilmington,. .	991	1,420	429	43.29
Winchester, . .	4,390	6,150	1,760	40.09
WOBURN,* . .	11,750	14,178	2,428	20.66
NORFOLK.	93,291	126,243	32,952	35.32
Avon,* . . .	-	1,626	1,626	-
Bellingham, . .	1,198	1,481	283	23.62
Braintree, . .	4,040	5,311	1,271	31.46
Brookline,* . .	9,196	16,164	6,968	75.77
Canton, . . .	4,380	4,636	256	5.84
Cohasset, . .	2,216	2,474	258	11.64
Dedham, . .	6,641	7,211	570	8.58
Dover, . . .	664	668	4	0.60
Foxborough, .	2,814	3,219	405	14.39
Franklin, . .	3,983	5,136	1,153	28.95
Hyde Park, . .	8,276	11,826	3,450	41.19
Medfield, . .	1,594	1,872	278	17.44
Medway, . .	2,777	2,913	136	4.90
Millis, . . .	683	1,006	323	47.29
Milton, . . .	3,555	5,518	1,963	55.22
Needham, . .	2,586	3,511	925	35.77
Norfolk, . .	825	882	57	6.91
Norwood, . .	2,921	4,574	1,653	56.59
QUINCY, . .	12,145	20,712	8,567	70.54
Sharon, . . .	1,328	1,717	389	29.29
Stoughton,* . .	5,173	5,272	99	1.91
Walpole, . .	2,443	2,994	551	22.55
Wellesley, . .	3,013	4,229	1,216	40.36
Weymouth, . .	10,740	11,291	551	5.13
PLYMOUTH.	71,047	91,766	20,719	29.16
Abington, . .	3,699	4,207	508	13.73
Bridgewater, .	3,827	4,686	859	22.45
BROCKTON,* .	20,783	33,165	12,382	59.58
Duxbury, . .	1,924	1,966	42	2.18
East Bridgewater,	2,812	2,894	82	2.92
Hanover, . .	1,966	2,051	85	4.32
Hanson,. . .	1,227	1,380	153	12.47
Hingham, . .	4,375	4,819	444	10.15
Hull, . . .	451	1,044	593	131.49
Kingston, . .	1,570	1,746	176	11.21
Marshfield,* . .	1,649	1,760	111	6.73
Middleborough, .	5,163	6,689	1,526	29.56
Plymouth, . .	7,239	7,957	718	9.92
Rochester,* . .	1,021	1,021	†	-
Rockland, . .	4,785	5,523	738	15.42
Wareham,* . .	3,254	3,367	113	3.47
W. Bridgewater,*	1,707	1,747	40	2.34
Whitman, . .	3,595	5,744	2,149	59.78
SUFFOLK.	421,109	539,799	118,690	28.19
BOSTON,* . .	390,393	496,920	106,527	27.29
CHELSEA, . .	25,709	31,264	5,555	21.61
Revere, . . .	3,637	7,423	3,786	104.10
Winthrop, . .	1,370	4,192	2,822	205.99

† No change since 1885.

TOWNS SHOWING INCREASE — Concluded.

COUNTIES, CITIES, AND TOWNS.	1885	1895	INCREASE Number	Percentage	COUNTIES, CITIES, AND TOWNS.	1885	1895	INCREASE Number	Percentage
WORCESTER.	200,558	266,556	65,998	32.91	WORCESTER — Con.				
Ashburnham,	2,058	2,148	90	4.37	Millbury,	4,555	5,222	667	14.64
Athol,	4,758	7,364	2,606	54.77	Northborough,	1,853	1,940	87	4.70
Auburn,	1,268	1,598	330	26.03	Northbridge,	3,786	5,286	1,500	39.62
Barre,	2,093	2,278	185	8.84	North Brookfield,	4,201	4,635	434	10.33
Blackstone,	5,436	6,039	603	11.09	Oxford,	2,355	2,390	35	1.49
Brookfield,	3,013	3,279	266	8.83	Rutland,	963	978	15	1.56
Charlton,	1,823	1,877	54	2.96	Shrewsbury,	1,450	1,524	74	5.10
Clinton,	8,945	11,497	2,552	28.53	Southborough,	2,100	2,223	123	5.86
Dana,	695	717	22	3.17	Southbridge,	6,500	8,250	1,750	26.92
Dudley,	2,742	3,203	461	16.81	Sutton,	3,101	3,420	319	10.29
FITCHBURG,	15,375	26,409	11,034	71.77	Templeton,*	2,627	2,915	288	10.96
Gardner,	7,283	9,182	1,899	26.07	Uxbridge,	2,948	3,546	598	20.28
Grafton,	4,498	5,101	603	13.41	Warren,	4,032	4,430	398	9.87
Holden,	2,471	2,602	131	5.30	Webster,	6,220	7,799	1,579	25.39
Hopedale,*	-	1,377	1,377	-	Westborough,	4,880	5,235	355	7.27
Lancaster,	2,050	2,180	130	6.34	West Boylston,	2,927	2,968	41	1.40
Leicester,	2,923	3,239	316	10.81	Winchendon,	3,872	4,490	618	15.96
Leominster,	5,297	9,211	3,914	73.89	WORCESTER,	68,389	98,767	30,378	44.42
Lunenburg,	1,071	1,237	166	15.50					

TOWNS SHOWING DECREASE.

Counties, Cities, and Towns.	1885	1895	Decrease Number	Decrease Percentage
BARNSTABLE.	15,945	13,281	2,664	16.71
Brewster,	964	901	33	3.53
Chatham,	2,028	1,809	219	10.80
Dennis,	2,923	2,545	378	12.93
Eastham,*	638	476	162	25.39
Harwich,	2,783	2,532	251	9.02
Sandwich,*	2,124	1,580	544	25.61
Truro,	972	815	157	16.15
Wellfleet,*	1,687	968	719	42.62
Yarmouth,	1,856	1,655	201	10.83
BERKSHIRE.	32,821	29,088	3,733	11.37
Adams,	8,283	7,837	446	5.38
Alford,	341	280	61	17.89
Becket,	938	888	50	5.33
Cheshire,	1,448	1,176	272	18.78
Florida,	487	425	62	12.73
Hancock,	613	511	102	16.64
Hinsdale,	1,656	1,650	6	0.36
Lanesborough,	1,212	848	364	30.03
Lee,	4,274	4,066	208	4.87
Monterey,	571	464	107	18.74
Mt. Washington,	160	136	24	15.00
New Ashford,	163	116	47	28.83
New Marlborough,	1,661	1,288	373	22.46
Otis,	703	518	185	26.32
Peru,	368	305	63	17.12
Richmond,	854	701	153	17.92
Sandisfield,	1,019	802	217	21.30
Savoy,	691	504	187	27.06
Sheffield,	2,033	1,897	136	6.69
Stockbridge,	2,114	2,077	37	1.75
Tyringham,	457	363	94	20.57
Washington,	470	423	47	10.00
West Stockbridge,	1,648	1,257	391	23.73
Windsor,	657	556	101	15.37
BRISTOL.	26,514	20,593	5,921	22.33
Attleborough,*	13,175	8,288	4,887	37.09
Dartmouth,*	3,448	3,107	341	9.80
Freetown,	1,457	1,405	52	3.57
Norton,	1,718	1,614	104	6.05
Raynham,	1,535	1,518	17	1.11
Somerset,	2,475	1,983	492	19.88
Westport,*	2,706	2,678	28	1.03
DUKES.	3,304	2,600	704	21.31
Chilmark,	412	304	108	26.21
Edgartown,	1,165	1,125	40	3.43
Gay Head,	186	169	17	9.14
Tisbury,*	1,541	1,002	539	34.98

Counties, Cities, and Towns.	1885	1895	Decrease Number	Decrease Percentage
ESSEX.	17,608	12,968	4,640	26.35
Boxford,	840	727	113	13.45
Essex,*	1,722	1,587	135	7.84
Georgetown,	2,299	2,050	249	10.83
Merrimac,	2,378	2,301	77	3.24
Middleton,	899	838	61	6.79
Newbury,	1,590	1,489	101	6.35
Salisbury,*	4,840	1,300	3,540	73.14
Topsfield,	1,141	1,033	108	9.47
West Newbury,	1,899	1,643	256	13.48
FRANKLIN.	15,783	14,253	1,530	9.69
Ashfield,	1,097	1,013	84	7.66
Bernardston,*	930	778	152	16.34
Buckland,	1,760	1,548	212	12.05
Conway,	1,573	1,304	269	17.10
Deerfield,	3,042	3,007	35	1.15
Hawley,	545	468	77	14.13
Heath,	568	476	92	16.20
Leverett,	779	744	35	4.49
Leyden,*	447	363	84	18.79
Rowe,	582	498	84	14.43
Shelburne,	1,614	1,560	54	3.35
Shutesbury,	485	444	41	8.45
Sunderland,	700	696	4	0.57
Warwick,	662	599	63	9.52
Whately,	999	755	244	24.42
HAMPDEN.	13,398	11,298	2,100	15.67
Blandford,	954	849	105	11.01
Brimfield,	1,137	962	175	15.39
Granville,	1,193	1,005	188	15.76
Hampden,	868	743	125	14.40
Holland,	229	199	30	13.10
Longmeadow,*	1,677	620	1,057	63.03
Monson,	3,958	3,746	212	5.36
Montgomery,	278	275	3	1.08
Russell,	847	846	1	0.12
Southwick,	982	961	21	2.14
Tolland,	422	309	113	26.78
Wales,	853	783	70	8.21
HAMPSHIRE.	14,113	13,043	1,070	7.58
Belchertown,	2,307	2,161	146	6.33
Chesterfield,	698	589	109	15.62
Cummington,	805	750	55	6.83
Enfield,	1,010	980	20	1.98
Goshen,	336	304	32	9.52
Greenwich,	532	481	51	9.59
Hadley,	1,747	1,704	43	2.46
Hatfield,	1,367	1,262	105	7.68

TOWNS SHOWING DECREASE — Concluded.

COUNTIES, CITIES, AND TOWNS.	1885	1895	DECREASE		COUNTIES, CITIES, AND TOWNS.	1885	1895	DECREASE	
			Number	Percentage				Number	Percentage
HAMPSHIRE — Con.					PLYMOUTH.	10,633	9,732	901	8.47
Middlefield, . .	513	386	127	24.76	Carver, . . .	1,091	1,016	75	6.87
Pelham, . .	549	486	63	11.48	Halifax, . .	530	497	33	6.23
Plainfield, .	453	450	3	0.66	Lakeville, . .	980	870	110	11.22
Prescott, .	448	401	47	10.49	Marion, . . .	965	759	206	21.35
Westhampton,	541	476	65	12.01	Mattapoisett, .	1,215	1,032	183	15.06
Williamsburg, .	2,044	1,955	89	4.35	Norwell, . .	1,589	1,540	49	3.08
Worthington,	763	648	115	15.07	Pembroke, . .	1,313	1,223	90	6.85
					Plympton, . .	600	549	51	8.50
MIDDLESEX.	19,316	17,146	2,170	11.23	Scituate,* . .	2,350	2,246	104	4.43
Ashby, . . .	871	804	67	7.69	WORCESTER.	43,481	39,889	3,592	8.26
Ashland, .	2,633	2,090	543	20.62	Berlin, . . .	899	897	2	0.22
Ayer, . . .	2,190	2,101	89	4.06	Bolton, . . .	876	797	79	9.02
Boxborough,* .	348	307	41	11.78	Boylston, . .	834	729	105	12.59
Burlington, .	604	574	30	4.97	Douglas, . .	2,205	2,026	179	8.12
Carlisle, . .	526	492	34	6.46	Hardwick, . .	3,145	2,655	490	15.58
Dunstable, .	431	400	31	7.19	Harvard, . .	1,184	1,162	22	1.86
Holliston, . .	2,926	2,718	208	7.11	Hubbardston, .	1,303	1,274	29	2.23
Hopkinton, . .	3,922	2,984	968	23.92	Mendon, . .	945	889	56	5.93
North Reading, .	878	835	43	4.90	Milford,* . .	9,343	8,959	384	4.11
Stow, . . .	976	920	56	5.74	New Braintree, .	558	542	16	2.87
Sudbury, . .	1,165	1,141	24	2.06	Oakham, . .	749	605	144	19.23
Townsend, . .	1,846	1,780	66	3.58	Paxton, . . .	561	426	135	24.06
					Petersham, . .	1,032	952	80	7.75
NANTUCKET.	3,142	3,016	126	4.01	Phillipston,* .	560	490	70	13.21
					Princeton, . .	1,038	952	86	8.29
Nantucket, . .	3,142	3,016	126	4.01	Royalston, . .	1,153	890	263	22.81
					Spencer, . .	8,247	7,614	633	7.68
NORFOLK.	8,851	8,576	275	3.11	Sterling, . .	1,331	1,218	113	8.49
					Sturbridge, . .	1,980	1,910	70	3.54
Holbrook,* .	2,334	2,298	36	1.54	Upton, . . .	2,265	2,150	115	5.08
Randolph,* .	3,807	3,694	113	2.97	West Brookfield,.	1,747	1,467	280	16.06
Wrentham, . .	2,710	2,584	126	4.65	Westminster, .	1,556	1,315	241	15.49

RECAPITULATION — INCREASE.

THE STATE, AND COUNTIES.	Towns	Number Show-ing Gain	1885	1895	INCREASE	
					Number	Percentage
THE STATE.	353	210	1,717,232	2,304,700	587,468	34.21
Barnstable, ...	15	6	13,900	14,373	473	3.40
Berkshire, ...	32	8	41,007	57,204	16,197	39.50
Bristol, ...	20	13	131,984	198,426	66,442	50.34
Dukes, ...	7	3	831	1,638	807	97.11
Essex, ...	35	26	246,119	317,425	71,306	28.97
Franklin, ...	26	11	21,666	25,892	4,226	19.51
Hampden, ...	23	11	103,366	141,640	38,274	37.03
Hampshire, ...	23	8	34,359	41,667	7,308	21.27
Middlesex, ...	54	41	337,995	482,071	144,076	42.63
Nantucket, ...	1	–	–	–	–	–
Norfolk, ...	27	24	93,291	126,243	32,952	35.32
Plymouth, ...	27	18	71,047	91,766	20,719	29.16
Suffolk, ...	4	4	421,109	539,799	118,690	28.19
Worcester, ...	59	37	200,558	266,556	65,998	32.91

RECAPITULATION — DECREASE.

THE STATE, AND COUNTIES.	Towns	Number Show-ing Loss	1885	1895	DECREASE	
					Number	Percentage
THE STATE.	353	†143	224,909	195,483	29,426	13.08
Barnstable, ...	15	9	15,945	13,281	2,664	16.71
Berkshire, ...	32	24	32,821	29,088	3,733	11.37
Bristol, ...	20	7	26,514	20,593	5,921	22.33
Dukes, ...	7	4	3,304	2,600	704	21.31
Essex, ...	35	9	17,608	12,968	4,640	26.35
Franklin, ...	26	15	15,783	14,253	1,530	9.69
Hampden, ...	23	12	13,398	11,298	2,100	15.67
Hampshire, ...	23	15	14,113	13,043	1,070	7.58
Middlesex, ...	54	13	19,316	17,146	2,170	11.23
Nantucket, ...	1	1	3,142	3,016	126	4.01
Norfolk, ...	27	3	8,851	8,576	275	3.11
Plymouth, ...	27	9	10,633	9,732	901	8.47
Suffolk, ...	4	–	–	–	–	–
Worcester, ...	59	22	43,481	39,889	3,592	8.26

† [Of the total decrease in population since 1885, or 29,426 for 143 towns, 6,867, or 23.34 per cent, is directly due to loss of territory caused by the division of existing towns and the incorporation of new towns, as follows: — Attleborough loses 4,887 to North Attleborough; Tisbury, 539 to West Tisbury; Longmeadow, 1,657 to East Longmeadow; Milford, 384 to Hopedale. If the towns named had remained intact all but Tisbury would have shown an increase in population, representing in the aggregate 3,216, or 13.29 per cent, over their population in 1885, while Tisbury would have shown a decrease in population of 79, or 5.13 per cent. Assuming then, that, with the exception of Tisbury, the entire loss in these towns is apparent only, the actual decrease in population for 140 towns is found to be 22,559, or 11.33 per cent, of their population in 1885. Although Avon was set off from the town of Stoughton, the latter town not only regained the population lost by the division, but gained 99 more in total population.]

COMBINED RECAPITULATION — INCREASE AND DECREASE.

THE STATE, AND COUNTIES.	Towns in State and County	Number of Towns showing Gain	Number of Towns showing Loss	POPULATION		Net Gain Since 1885	Net Loss Since 1885	Net Percentage of Increase	Net Percentage of Decrease
				1885	1895	1885	1885		
THE STATE.†	353	210	143	1,942,141	2,500,183	560,359	2,317	28.85	0.12
Barnstable, . .	15	6	9	29,845	27,654	-	2,191	-	7.34
Berkshire, . . .	32	8	24	73,828	86,292	12,464	-	16.88	-
Bristol, . . .	20	13	7	158,498	219,019	60,521	-	38.18	-
Dukes, ...	7	3	4	4,135	4,238	103	-	2.49	-
Essex, ...	35	26	9	263,727	330,393	66,666	-	25.28	-
Franklin, . . .	26	11	15	37,449	40,145	2,696	-	7.20	-
Hampden, . . .	23	11	12	116,764	152,938	36,174	-	30.98	-
Hampshire, . .	23	8	15	48,472	54,710	6,238	-	12.87	-
Middlesex, . .	54	41	13	357,311	499,217	141,906	-	39.71	-
Nantucket, . . .	1	-	1	3,142	3,016	-	126	-	4.01
Norfolk, . . .	27	24	3	102,142	134,819	32,677	-	31.99	-
Plymouth, . . .	27	18	9	81,680	101,498	19,818	-	24.26	-
Suffolk, . . .	4	4	-	421,160	539,799	118,630	-	28.19	-
Worcester, . . .	59	37	22	244,930	306,445	62,406	-	25.57	-

† The actual net gain since 1885, for the whole state, is 558,042; the actual net percentage of increase, 28.73.

POPULATION AND SEX.

POPULATION AND SEX.

COUNTIES, CITIES, AND TOWNS.	Males	Females	Population	Percentages M	Percentages F
BARNSTABLE.	13,294	14,360	27,654	48.07	51.93
Barnstable,	1,944	2,111	4,055	47.94	52.06
Bourne,	772	808	1,580	48.86	51.14
Brewster,	437	464	901	48.50	51.50
Chatham,	898	911	1,809	49.64	50.36
Dennis,	1,164	1,381	2,545	45.74	54.26
Eastham,	234	242	476	49.16	50.84
Falmouth,	1,283	1,372	2,655	48.32	51.68
Harwich,	1,253	1,279	2,532	49.49	50.51
Mashpee,	178	152	330	53.94	46.06
Orleans,	559	639	1,198	46.66	53.34
Provincetown,	2,215	2,340	4,555	48.63	51.37
Sandwich,	734	846	1,580	46.46	53.54
Truro,	402	413	815	49.33	50.67
Wellfleet,	449	519	968	46.38	53.62
Yarmouth,	772	883	1,655	46.65	53.35
BERKSHIRE.	42,525	43,767	86,292	49.28	50.72
Adams,	3,712	4,125	7,837	47.37	52.63
Alford,	152	128	280	54.29	45.71
Becket,	483	405	888	54.39	45.61
Cheshire,	599	577	1,176	50.94	49.06
Clarksburg,	502	507	1,009	49.75	50.25
Dalton,	1,506	1,704	3,210	46.92	53.08
Egremont,	406	430	836	48.56	51.44
Florida,	223	202	425	52.47	47.53
Great Barrington,	2,332	2,462	4,794	48.64	51.36
Hancock,	266	245	511	52.05	47.95
Hinsdale,	821	829	1,650	49.76	50.24
Lanesborough,	434	414	848	51.18	48.82
Lee,	1,973	2,093	4,066	48.52	51.48
Lenox,	1,529	1,343	2,872	53.24	46.76
Monterey,	241	223	464	51.94	48.06
Mt. Washington,	76	60	136	55.88	44.12
New Ashford,	68	48	116	58.62	41.38
New Marlborough,	682	606	1,288	52.95	47.05
NORTH ADAMS,	9,350	9,785	19,135	48.86	51.14
Otis,	289	229	518	55.79	44.21
Peru,	146	159	305	47.87	52.13
PITTSFIELD,	9,838	10,623	20,461	48.08	51.92
Ward 1,	1,428	1,408	2,836	50.35	49.65
Ward 2,	1,658	1,868	3,526	47.02	52.98
Ward 3,	1,285	1,340	2,625	48.95	51.05
Ward 4,	1,198	1,582	2,780	43.09	56.91
Ward 5,	1,328	1,359	2,687	49.42	50.58
Ward 6,	1,684	1,790	3,474	48.47	51.53
Ward 7,	1,257	1,276	2,533	49.62	50.38
Richmond,	354	347	701	50.50	49.50
Sandisfield,	401	401	802	50.00	50.00
Savoy,	256	248	504	50.79	49.21
Sheffield,	944	953	1,897	49.76	50.24
Stockbridge,	996	1,081	2,077	47.95	52.05

COUNTIES, CITIES, AND TOWNS.	Males	Females	Population	Percentages M	Percentages F
BERKSHIRE —Con.					
Tyringham,	186	177	363	51.24	48.76
Washington,	236	187	423	55.79	44.21
West Stockbridge,	608	649	1,257	48.37	51.63
Williamstown,	2,615	2,272	4,887	53.51	46.49
Windsor,	301	255	556	54.14	45.86
BRISTOL.	105,582	113,437	219,019	48.21	51.79
Acushnet,	568	547	1,115	50.94	49.06
Attleborough,	4,029	4,259	8,288	48.61	51.39
Berkley,	482	473	955	50.47	49.53
Dartmouth,	1,599	1,598	3,197	51.46	48.54
Dighton,	916	881	1,797	50.97	49.03
Easton,	2,286	2,166	4,452	51.35	48.65
Fairhaven,	1,554	1,784	3,338	46.55	53.45
FALL RIVER,	42,704	46,499	89,203	47.87	52.13
Ward 1,	5,410	5,736	11,146	48.54	51.46
Ward 2,	4,192	4,532	8,724	48.05	51.95
Ward 3,	5,624	5,827	11,451	49.11	50.89
Ward 4,	4,824	5,644	10,468	46.08	53.92
Ward 5,	5,135	5,474	10,609	48.40	51.60
Ward 6,	6,004	6,260	12,264	48.96	51.04
Ward 7,	2,970	3,427	6,397	46.43	53.57
Ward 8,	3,278	4,054	7,332	44.71	55.29
Ward 9,	5,267	5,545	10,812	48.71	51.29
Freetown,	725	680	1,405	51.60	48.40
Mansfield,	1,793	1,929	3,722	48.17	51.83
NEW BEDFORD,	26,158	29,093	55,251	47.34	52.66
Ward 1,	6,456	6,736	13,192	48.94	51.06
Ward 2,	3,730	4,061	7,791	47.88	52.12
Ward 3,	2,451	3,185	5,636	43.49	56.51
Ward 4,	2,943	3,445	6,388	46.07	53.93
Ward 5,	4,144	4,960	9,104	45.52	54.48
Ward 6,	6,434	6,706	13,140	48.96	51.04
No. Attleborough,	3,145	3,431	6,576	47.83	52.17
Norton,	760	854	1,614	47.09	52.91
Raynham,	751	767	1,518	49.47	50.53
Rehoboth,	958	852	1,810	52.93	47.07
Seekonk,	793	672	1,465	54.13	45.87
Somerset,	1,040	943	1,983	52.45	47.55
Swansea,	830	797	1,627	51.01	48.99
TAUNTON,	13,147	13,968	27,115	48.49	51.51
Ward 1,	1,389	1,413	2,802	49.57	50.43
Ward 2,	1,365	1,507	2,872	47.53	52.47
Ward 3,	1,460	1,579	3,039	48.04	51.96
Ward 4,	1,394	1,595	2,989	46.64	53.36
Ward 5,	1,850	1,991	3,841	48.16	51.84
Ward 6,	1,539	1,563	3,102	49.61	50.39
Ward 7,	1,509	1,524	3,033	49.75	50.25
Ward 8,	2,641	2,796	5,437	48.57	51.43
Westport,	1,344	1,334	2,678	50.19	49.81

POPULATION AND SEX — Continued.

COUNTIES, CITIES, AND TOWNS.	Males	Females	Population	Percentages M	F
DUKES.	2,057	2,181	4,238	48.54	51.46
Chilmark,	151	153	304	49.67	50.33
Cottage City,	508	530	1,038	48.94	51.06
Edgartown,	527	598	1,125	46.84	53.16
Gay Head,	90	79	169	53.25	46.75
Gosnold,	88	52	140	62.86	37.14
Tisbury,	477	525	1,002	47.60	52.40
West Tisbury,	216	244	460	46.96	53.04
ESSEX.	161,913	168,480	330,393	49.01	50.99
Amesbury,	4,780	5,206	9,986	47.87	52.13
Andover,	2,913	3,232	6,145	47.40	52.60
BEVERLY,	5,728	6,078	11,806	48.52	51.48
Ward 1,	1,328	1,348	2,676	49.63	50.37
Ward 2,	1,124	1,319	2,443	46.01	53.99
Ward 3,	1,176	1,266	2,442	48.16	51.84
Ward 4,	952	1,059	2,011	47.34	52.66
Ward 5,	601	602	1,203	49.96	50.04
Ward 6,	547	484	1,031	53.06	46.94
Boxford,	359	368	727	49.38	50.62
Bradford,	2,222	2,514	4,736	46.92	53.08
Danvers,	3,958	4,223	8,181	48.38	51.62
Essex,	809	778	1,587	50.98	49.02
Georgetown,	999	1,051	2,050	48.73	51.27
GLOUCESTER,	16,257	11,954	28,211	57.63	42.37
Ward 1,	1,682	1,516	3,198	52.60	47.40
Ward 2,	2,763	2,305	5,028	54.95	45.05
Ward 3,	3,467	1,723	5,190	66.80	33.20
Ward 4,	2,276	1,185	3,461	65.76	34.24
Ward 5,	2,296	2,048	4,344	52.85	47.15
Ward 6,	1,464	1,479	2,943	49.75	50.25
Ward 7,	1,697	1,141	2,838	59.80	40.20
Ward 8,	612	597	1,209	50.62	49.38
Groveland,	1,118	1,215	2,333	47.92	52.08
Hamilton,	685	671	1,356	50.52	49.48
HAVERHILL,	14,535	15,674	30,209	48.11	51.89
Ward 1,	1,271	1,377	2,648	48.00	52.00
Ward 2,	1,105	1,408	2,513	43.97	56.03
Ward 3,	1,696	1,847	3,543	47.87	52.13
Ward 4,	1,890	2,095	3,985	47.43	52.57
Ward 5,	5,632	5,636	11,268	49.98	50.02
Ward 6,	2,941	3,311	6,252	47.04	52.96
Ipswich,	2,178	2,542	4,720	46.14	53.86
LAWRENCE,	25,107	27,057	52,164	48.13	51.87
Ward 1,	4,199	4,368	8,568	49.01	50.99
Ward 2,	3,374	3,610	6,984	48.31	51.69
Ward 3,	4,161	4,817	8,978	46.35	53.65
Ward 4,	4,892	5,167	9,969	48.17	51.83
Ward 5,	4,764	5,169	9,933	47.96	52.04
Ward 6,	3,897	3,925	7,732	49.24	50.76
LYNN,	30,173	32,181	62,354	48.39	51.61
Ward 1,	765	814	1,579	48.45	51.55
Ward 2,	1,933	2,003	3,936	49.11	50.89
Ward 3,	7,046	7,813	14,859	47.42	52.58
Ward 4,	5,669	5,843	11,512	49.24	50.76
Ward 5,	6,076	6,784	12,860	47.25	52.75
Ward 6,	7,316	7,616	14,932	49.00	51.00
Ward 7,	1,368	1,308	2,676	51.12	48.88
ESSEX — Con.					
Lynnfield,	408	410	818	49.88	50.12
Manchester,	893	983	1,876	47.60	52.40
Marblehead,	3,649	4,022	7,671	47.57	52.43
Merrimac,	1,111	1,190	2,301	48.28	51.72
Methuen,	2,760	2,930	5,690	48.51	51.49
Middleton,	428	410	838	51.07	48.93
Nahant,	425	440	865	49.13	50.87
Newbury,	760	729	1,489	51.04	48.96
NEWBURYPORT,	6,616	7,936	14,552	45.46	54.54
Ward 1,	1,097	1,275	2,372	46.25	53.75
Ward 2,	1,046	1,285	2,331	44.87	55.13
Ward 3,	1,196	1,470	2,666	44.86	55.14
Ward 4,	1,029	1,292	2,321	44.33	55.67
Ward 5,	1,016	1,220	2,236	45.44	54.56
Ward 6,	1,232	1,384	2,626	46.92	53.08
North Andover,	1,765	1,804	3,569	49.45	50.55
Peabody,	5,262	5,245	10,507	50.08	49.92
Rockport,	2,966	2,323	5,289	56.08	43.92
Rowley,	656	616	1,272	51.57	48.43
SALEM,	16,270	18,203	34,473	47.20	52.80
Ward 1,	2,369	2,637	5,006	47.32	52.68
Ward 2,	2,692	2,955	5,647	47.67	52.33
Ward 3,	1,925	2,460	4,385	43.90	56.10
Ward 4,	2,429	2,806	5,235	46.40	53.60
Ward 5,	4,816	5,095	9,911	48.59	51.41
Ward 6,	2,039	2,250	4,289	47.54	52.46
Salisbury,	642	658	1,300	49.38	50.62
Saugus,	2,189	2,308	4,497	48.68	51.32
Swampscott,	1,534	1,725	3,259	47.07	52.93
Topsfield,	516	517	1,033	49.95	50.05
Wenham,	431	455	886	48.65	51.35
West Newbury,	811	832	1,643	49.36	50.64
FRANKLIN,	20,293	19,852	40,145	50.55	49.45
Ashfield,	523	490	1,013	51.63	48.37
Bernardston,	389	389	778	50.00	50.00
Buckland,	785	763	1,548	50.71	49.29
Charlemont,	526	515	1,041	50.53	49.47
Colrain,	851	759	1,610	52.86	47.14
Conway,	657	647	1,304	50.38	49.62
Deerfield,	1,550	1,457	3,007	51.55	48.45
Erving,	490	474	964	50.83	49.17
Gill,	699	383	1,082	64.60	35.40
Greenfield,	2,987	3,242	6,229	47.95	52.05
Hawley,	250	218	468	53.42	46.58
Heath,	250	226	476	52.52	47.48
Leverett,	379	365	744	50.94	49.06
Leyden,	185	178	363	50.96	49.04
Monroe,	176	122	298	59.06	40.94
Montague,	3,076	2,982	6,058	50.78	49.22
New Salem,	438	431	869	50.40	49.60
Northfield,	754	1,097	1,851	40.73	59.27
Orange,	2,690	2,671	5,361	50.18	49.82
Rowe,	283	215	498	56.83	43.17
Shelburne,	750	810	1,560	48.08	51.92
Shutesbury,	218	226	444	49.10	50.90
Sunderland,	381	315	696	54.74	45.26

POPULATION AND SEX — Continued.

Counties, Cities, and Towns.	Males	Females	Population	M	F
FRANKLIN — Con.					
Warwick,	321	278	599	53.59	46.41
Wendell,	293	236	529	55.39	44.61
Whately,	392	363	755	51.92	48.08
HAMPDEN.	74,133	78,805	152,938	48.47	51.53
Agawam,	1,237	1,171	2,408	51.37	48.63
Blandford,	437	412	849	51.47	48.53
Brimfield,	498	464	962	51.77	48.23
Chester,	700	729	1,429	48.99	51.01
CHICOPEE,	8,095	8,325	16,420	49.30	50.70
Ward 1,	1,608	1,661	3,269	49.19	50.81
Ward 2,	802	950	1,752	45.78	54.22
Ward 3,	1,440	1,377	2,817	51.12	48.88
Ward 4,	1,050	1,208	2,258	46.50	53.50
Ward 5,	1,360	1,290	2,650	51.32	48.68
Ward 6,	822	876	1,638	48.41	51.59
Ward 7,	1,013	963	1,976	51.27	48.73
East Longmeadow	833	728	1,561	54.24	45.76
Granville,	522	483	1,005	51.94	48.06
Hampden,	374	369	743	50.34	49.66
Holland,	107	92	199	53.77	46.23
HOLYOKE,	19,198	21,124	40,322	47.61	52.39
Ward 1,	2,849	3,165	6,014	47.37	52.63
Ward 2,	4,373	4,485	8,858	49.37	50.63
Ward 3,	2,461	2,562	5,023	48.99	51.01
Ward 4,	3,233	3,548	6,781	47.68	52.32
Ward 5,	1,574	2,005	3,579	43.98	56.02
Ward 6,	2,717	2,981	5,698	47.68	52.32
Ward 7,	1,991	2,378	4,369	45.57	54.43
Longmeadow,	290	330	620	46.77	53.23
Ludlow,	1,314	1,248	2,562	51.29	48.71
Monson,	1,862	1,884	3,746	49.71	50.29
Montgomery,	151	124	275	54.91	45.09
Palmer,	3,345	3,513	6,858	48.78	51.22
Russell,	440	406	846	52.01	47.99
Southwick,	510	451	961	53.07	46.93
SPRINGFIELD,	24,651	26,871	51,522	47.85	52.15
Ward 1,	3,405	3,494	6,899	49.35	50.65
Ward 2,	3,886	4,012	7,898	49.20	50.80
Ward 3,	3,152	3,045	6,197	50.86	49.14
Ward 4,	2,652	3,557	6,209	42.71	57.29
Ward 5,	2,886	3,540	6,426	44.91	55.09
Ward 6,	2,983	3,170	6,153	48.48	51.52
Ward 7,	2,202	2,448	4,650	47.35	52.65
Ward 8,	3,485	3,605	7,090	49.15	50.85
Tolland,	171	138	309	55.34	44.66
Wales,	405	378	783	51.72	48.28
Westfield,	5,175	5,488	10,663	48.53	51.47
West Springfield,	2,951	3,174	6,125	48.18	51.82
Wilbraham,	837	903	1,740	48.10	51.90
HAMPSHIRE.	26,061	28,649	54,710	47.63	52.37
Amherst,	2,427	2,358	4,785	50.72	49.28
Belchertown,	1,115	1,046	2,161	51.60	48.40
Chesterfield,	301	288	589	51.10	48.90
Cummington,	367	383	750	48.93	51.07

Counties, Cities, and Towns.	Males	Females	Population	M	F
HAMPSHIRE — Con.					
Easthampton,	2,242	2,548	4,790	46.81	53.19
Enfield,	512	478	990	51.72	48.28
Goshen,	160	144	304	52.63	47.37
Granby,	394	354	748	52.67	47.33
Greenwich,	243	238	481	50.52	49.48
Hadley,	894	810	1,704	52.46	47.54
Hatfield,	669	593	1,262	53.01	46.99
Huntington,	722	728	1,450	49.79	50.21
Middlefield,	197	189	386	51.04	48.96
NORTHAMPTON,	7,434	9,342	16,776	44.39	55.61
Ward 1,	1,013	1,157	2,170	46.68	53.32
Ward 2,	967	2,277	3,244	29.81	70.19
Ward 3,	1,370	1,502	2,872	47.70	52.30
Ward 4,	1,239	1,249	2,488	49.80	50.20
Ward 5,	1,046	1,090	2,136	48.97	51.03
Ward 6,	871	1,032	1,903	45.77	54.23
Ward 7,	928	1,005	1,933	48.01	51.99
Pelham,	246	240	486	50.62	49.38
Plainfield,	231	219	450	51.33	48.67
Prescott,	208	193	401	51.87	48.13
Southampton,	537	517	1,054	50.95	49.05
South Hadley,	2,054	2,389	4,443	46.23	53.77
Ware,	3,576	4,075	7,651	46.74	53.26
Westhampton,	241	235	476	50.63	49.37
Williamsburg,	950	1,005	1,955	48.59	51.41
Worthington,	341	307	648	52.62	47.38
MIDDLESEX.	239,323	259,894	499,217	47.94	52.06
Acton,	980	998	1,978	49.54	50.46
Arlington,	3,067	3,448	6,515	47.08	52.92
Ashby,	413	391	804	51.37	48.63
Ashland,	1,015	1,075	2,090	48.56	51.44
Ayer,	1,018	1,083	2,101	48.45	51.55
Bedford,	623	546	1,169	53.29	46.71
Belmont,	1,519	1,324	2,843	53.43	46.57
Billerica,	1,301	1,276	2,577	50.49	49.51
Boxborough,	172	135	307	56.03	43.97
Burlington,	316	258	574	55.05	44.95
CAMBRIDGE,	39,831	41,812	81,643	48.79	51.21
Ward 1,	7,814	8,067	15,881	49.20	50.80
Ward 2,	10,894	11,738	22,632	48.14	51.86
Ward 3,	7,303	6,693	13,996	52.18	47.82
Ward 4,	8,914	9,767	18,681	47.72	52.28
Ward 5,	4,906	5,547	10,453	46.93	53.07
Carlisle,	268	224	492	54.47	45.53
Chelmsford,	1,611	1,551	3,162	50.95	49.05
Concord,	3,157	2,018	5,175	61.00	39.00
Dracut,	1,325	1,118	2,443	54.24	45.76
Dunstable,	207	193	400	51.75	48.25
EVERETT,	9,057	9,516	18,573	48.76	51.24
Ward 1,	1,586	1,548	3,138	50.67	49.33
Ward 2,	1,289	1,338	2,627	49.07	50.93
Ward 3,	1,515	1,575	3,090	49.03	50.97
Ward 4,	1,380	1,496	2,876	47.98	52.02
Ward 5,	1,539	1,614	3,153	48.81	51.19
Ward 6,	1,744	1,945	3,689	47.28	52.72

POPULATION AND SEX — Continued.

COUNTIES, CITIES, AND TOWNS.	Males	Females	Population	M	F	COUNTIES, CITIES, AND TOWNS.	Males	Females	Population	M	F
MIDDLESEX — Con.						**MIDDLESEX — Con.**					
Framingham,	4,570	4,942	9,512	48.01	51.96	SOMERVILLE,	24,917	27,283	52,200	47.73	52.27
Groton,	1,078	1,114	2,192	49.18	50.82	Ward 1,	4,834	5,293	10,127	47.73	52.27
Holliston,	1,309	1,409	2,718	48.16	51.84	Ward 2,	8,338	8,858	17,196	48.49	51.51
Hopkinton,	1,469	1,515	2,984	49.23	50.77	Ward 3,	6,158	6,808	13,056	47.17	52.83
Hudson,	2,533	2,775	5,308	47.72	52.28	Ward 4,	5,587	6,234	11,821	47.26	52.74
Lexington,	1,692	1,806	3,498	48.37	51.63	Stoneham,	3,070	3,214	6,284	48.85	51.15
Lincoln,	626	485	1,111	56.35	43.65	Stow,	473	447	920	51.41	48.59
Littleton,	569	567	1,136	50.09	49.91	Sudbury,	603	538	1,141	52.85	47.15
LOWELL,	38,931	45,436	84,367	46.14	53.86	Tewksbury,	1,653	1,726	3,379	48.92	51.08
Ward 1,	4,085	5,423	9,508	42.96	57.04	Townsend,	880	900	1,780	49.44	50.56
Ward 2,	5,034	5,459	10,493	47.97	52.03	Tyngsborough,	324	311	635	51.02	48.98
Ward 3,	4,301	4,944	9,245	46.52	53.48	Wakefield,	3,962	4,342	8,304	47.71	52.29
Ward 4,	4,385	4,856	9,241	47.45	52.55	WALTHAM,	9,638	11,238	20,876	46.17	53.83
Ward 5,	4,003	4,449	8,452	47.36	52.64	Ward 1,	1,426	1,494	2,920	48.84	51.16
Ward 6,	4,236	4,966	9,332	46.46	53.54	Ward 2,	1,390	1,546	2,936	47.34	52.66
Ward 7,	6,018	7,100	13,118	45.88	54.12	Ward 3,	1,590	1,786	3,376	47.10	52.90
Ward 8,	3,653	4,287	7,940	46.01	53.99	Ward 4,	1,414	1,657	3,071	46.04	53.96
Ward 9,	3,116	3,922	7,038	44.27	55.73	Ward 5,	1,222	1,665	2,887	42.33	57.67
MALDEN,	13,923	15,785	29,708	46.87	53.13	Ward 6,	1,274	1,644	2,918	43.66	56.34
Ward 1,	1,795	2,310	4,105	43.73	56.27	Ward 7,	1,322	1,446	2,768	47.76	52.24
Ward 2,	2,633	2,697	5,330	49.40	50.60	Watertown,	3,740	4,048	7,788	48.02	51.98
Ward 3,	1,524	2,055	3,579	42.58	57.42	Wayland,	1,026	1,000	2,026	50.64	49.36
Ward 4,	2,325	2,475	4,800	48.44	51.56	Westford,	1,223	1,195	2,418	50.58	49.42
Ward 5,	1,822	2,109	3,961	46.35	53.65	Weston,	877	833	1,710	51.29	48.71
Ward 6,	2,017	2,195	4,212	47.89	52.11	Wilmington,	715	705	1,420	50.35	49.65
Ward 7,	1,807	1,944	3,751	48.17	51.83	Winchester,	2,928	3,222	6,150	47.61	52.39
MARLBOROUGH,	7,469	7,508	14,977	49.87	50.13	WOBURN,	7,000	7,178	14,178	49.37	50.63
Ward 1,	679	656	1,335	50.86	49.14	Ward 1,	1,314	1,311	2,625	50.06	49.94
Ward 2,	1,072	1,133	2,205	48.62	51.38	Ward 2,	1,478	1,403	2,881	51.30	48.70
Ward 3,	1,522	1,447	2,969	51.26	48.74	Ward 3,	1,165	1,344	2,509	46.43	53.57
Ward 4,	1,613	1,689	3,302	48.85	51.15	Ward 4,	1,248	1,374	2,622	47.60	52.40
Ward 5,	969	965	1,934	50.10	49.90	Ward 5,	602	559	1,161	51.85	48.15
Ward 6,	841	848	1,689	49.79	50.21	Ward 6,	689	724	1,413	48.76	51.24
Ward 7,	773	770	1,543	50.10	49.90	Ward 7,	504	463	967	52.12	47.88
Maynard,	1,520	1,570	3,090	49.19	50.81						
MEDFORD,	7,043	7,431	14,474	48.66	51.34	**NANTUCKET.**	1,315	1,701	3,016	43.60	56.40
Ward 1,	1,521	1,491	3,012	50.50	49.50	Nantucket,	1,315	1,701	3,016	43.60	56.40
Ward 2,	1,054	1,251	2,305	45.73	54.27						
Ward 3,	829	1,095	1,924	43.09	56.91	**NORFOLK.**	64,780	70,039	134,819	48.05	51.95
Ward 4,	1,010	946	1,956	51.64	48.36	Avon,	818	808	1,626	50.31	49.69
Ward 5,	1,518	1,437	2,955	51.37	48.63	Bellingham,	721	760	1,481	48.68	51.32
Ward 6,	1,111	1,211	2,322	47.85	52.15	Braintree,	2,660	2,651	5,311	50.08	49.92
Melrose,	5,546	6,417	11,963	46.37	53.63	Brookline,	6,826	9,338	16,164	42.23	57.77
Natick,	4,234	4,580	8,814	48.04	51.96	Canton,	2,207	2,429	4,636	47.61	52.39
NEWTON,	12,355	15,235	27,590	44.78	55.22	Cohasset,	1,148	1,326	2,474	46.40	53.60
Ward 1,	1,993	2,294	4,287	46.49	53.51	Dedham,	3,476	3,735	7,211	48.20	51.80
Ward 2,	2,488	2,924	5,412	45.97	54.03	Dover,	345	323	668	51.65	48.35
Ward 3,	1,484	1,949	3,433	43.23	56.77	Foxborough,	1,542	1,677	3,219	47.90	52.10
Ward 4,	1,509	2,065	3,574	42.22	57.78	Franklin,	2,459	2,677	5,136	47.88	52.12
Ward 5,	1,939	2,175	4,114	47.13	52.87	Holbrook,	1,127	1,171	2,298	49.04	50.96
Ward 6,	1,931	2,309	4,240	45.54	54.46	Hyde Park,	5,790	6,009	11,826	48.71	51.29
Ward 7,	1,011	1,519	2,530	39.96	60.04	Medfield,	883	989	1,872	47.17	52.83
North Reading,	422	413	835	50.54	49.46	Medway,	1,438	1,475	2,913	49.36	50.64
Pepperell,	1,650	1,671	3,321	49.68	50.32	Millis,	484	522	1,006	48.11	51.89
Reading,	2,235	2,482	4,717	47.38	52.62	Milton,	2,562	2,956	5,518	46.43	53.57
Sherborn,	584	862	1,446	40.39	59.61	Needham,	1,749	1,762	3,511	49.81	50.19
Shirley,	654	745	1,399	46.75	53.25						

POPULATION AND SEX — Continued.

COUNTIES, CITIES, AND TOWNS.	Males	Females	Population	M	F	COUNTIES, CITIES, AND TOWNS.	Males	Females	Population	M	F
NORFOLK—Con.						SUFFOLK—Con.					
Norfolk, . .	471	411	882	53.40	46.60	BOSTON—Con.					
Norwood,	2,437	2,137	4,574	53.28	46.72	Ward 2, .	11,505	10,083	21,588	53.29	46.71
QUINCY,	10,608	10,104	20,712	51.22	48.78	Ward 3, .	6,841	7,102	13,943	49.06	50.94
Ward 1,	1,742	1,850	3,592	48.06	51.94	Ward 4, .	6,654	6,721	13,375	49.75	50.25
Ward 2,	1,408	1,333	2,741	51.37	48.63	Ward 5, .	6,994	5,992	12,986	53.86	46.14
Ward 3,	2,502	2,194	4,696	53.28	46.72	Ward 6, .	14,805	13,055	27,860	53.14	46.86
Ward 4,	2,658	2,306	4,964	53.55	46.45	Ward 7, .	9,049	7,924	16,973	53.31	46.69
Ward 5,	1,297	1,372	2,669	48.59	51.41	Ward 8, .	12,143	10,987	23,130	52.50	47.50
Ward 6,	1,031	1,049	2,080	49.57	50.43	Ward 9, .	11,398	11,776	23,174	49.18	50.82
Randolph,	1,825	1,869	3,694	49.40	50.60	Ward 10, .	10,070	12,484	22,554	44.65	55.35
Sharon, .	839	878	1,717	48.86	51.14	Ward 11, .	7,375	12,555	19,930	37.00	63.00
Stoughton,	2,570	2,702	5,272	48.75	51.25	Ward 12, .	9,188	12,403	21,591	42.55	57.45
Walpole,	1,500	1,494	2,994	50.10	49.90	Ward 13, .	12,695	12,205	24,900	50.98	49.02
Wellesley,	1,470	2,759	4,229	34.76	65.24	Ward 14, .	9,635	9,551	19,186	50.22	49.78
Weymouth,	5,592	5,699	11,291	49.53	50.47	Ward 15, .	8,975	9,648	18,623	48.19	51.81
Wrentham, .	1,263	1,321	2,584	48.88	51.12	Ward 16, .	7,664	8,656	16,320	46.96	53.04
						Ward 17, .	10,128	10,986	21,114	47.97	52.03
						Ward 18, .	10,641	11,068	21,679	49.08	50.92
PLYMOUTH.	50,694	50,804	101,498	49.95	50.05	Ward 19, .	10,508	11,864	22,372	46.97	53.03
Abington,	2,040	2,167	4,207	48.49	51.51	Ward 20, .	9,893	11,635	21,528	45.95	54.05
Bridgewater,	2,722	1,964	4,686	58.09	41.91	Ward 21, .	8,079	11,195	19,274	41.92	58.08
BROCKTON, .	16,559	16,606	33,165	49.93	50.07	Ward 22, .	10,445	11,844	22,289	46.86	53.14
Ward 1,	2,059	2,110	4,169	49.39	50.61	Ward 23, .	8,736	9,547	18,283	47.78	52.22
Ward 2,	2,067	2,260	4,327	47.77	52.23	Ward 24, .	8,589	9,651	18,240	47.09	52.91
Ward 3,	2,567	2,478	5,045	50.88	49.12	Ward 25, .	7,293	7,708	15,001	48.62	51.38
Ward 4,	2,369	2,423	4,792	49.44	50.56	CHELSEA, .	15,273	15,991	31,264	48.85	51.15
Ward 5,	2,566	2,480	5,046	50.85	49.15	Ward 1, .	3,666	3,813	7,479	49.02	50.98
Ward 6,	2,596	2,344	4,940	52.55	47.45	Ward 2, .	3,723	3,862	7,585	49.08	50.92
Ward 7,	2,335	2,511	4,846	48.18	51.82	Ward 3, .	3,521	3,601	7,122	49.44	50.56
Carver, .	546	470	1,016	53.74	46.26	Ward 4, .	2,530	2,857	5,387	46.96	53.04
Duxbury, .	945	1,021	1,966	48.07	51.93	Ward 5, .	1,833	1,858	3,691	49.66	50.34
East Bridgewater,	1,441	1,453	2,894	49.79	50.21	Revere, .	3,721	3,702	7,423	50.13	49.87
Halifax, .	266	231	497	53.52	46.48	Winthrop,	2,015	2,177	4,192	48.07	51.93
Hanover,	1,009	1,042	2,051	49.20	50.80						
Hanson,	708	672	1,380	51.30	48.70						
Hingham,	2,299	2,520	4,819	47.71	52.29	WORCESTER.	152,056	154,389	306,445	49.62	50.38
Hull, .	536	508	1,044	51.34	48.66	Ashburnham,	1,070	1,078	2,148	49.81	50.19
Kingston,	847	899	1,746	48.51	51.49	Athol, . .	3,735	3,629	7,364	50.72	49.28
Lakeville,	439	431	870	50.46	49.54	Auburn,	821	777	1,598	51.38	48.62
Marion, .	328	431	759	43.21	56.79	Barre, .	1,150	1,128	2,278	50.48	49.52
Marshfield, .	850	910	1,760	48.30	51.70	Berlin, .	451	446	897	50.28	49.72
Mattapoisett,	490	542	1,032	47.48	52.52	Blackstone, .	3,116	2,923	6,039	51.60	48.40
Middleborough, .	3,205	3,484	6,689	47.91	52.09	Bolton, .	398	399	797	49.94	50.06
Norwell,	771	769	1,540	50.06	49.94	Boylston,	389	340	729	53.36	46.64
Pembroke,	634	589	1,223	51.84	48.16	Brookfield,	1,689	1,590	3,279	51.51	48.49
Plymouth,	3,863	4,094	7,957	48.55	51.45	Charlton, .	975	902	1,877	51.94	48.06
Plympton,	268	281	549	48.82	51.18	Clinton, .	5,291	6,206	11,497	46.02	53.98
Rochester,	535	486	1,021	52.46	47.60	Dana, .	353	364	717	49.23	50.77
Rockland,	2,757	2,766	5,523	49.92	50.08	Douglas, .	1,033	993	2,026	50.99	49.01
Scituate,	1,115	1,131	2,246	49.64	50.36	Dudley, .	1,611	1,592	3,203	50.30	49.70
Wareham, .	1,765	1,602	3,367	52.42	47.58	FITCHBURG, .	13,037	13,372	26,409	49.37	50.63
West Bridgewater,	877	870	1,747	50.20	49.80	Ward 1, .	2,197	2,179	4,376	50.21	49.79
Whitman, .	2,879	2,865	5,744	50.12	49.88	Ward 2, .	3,289	3,221	6,510	50.52	49.48
						Ward 3, .	2,108	2,191	4,299	49.03	50.97
SUFFOLK.	260,675	279,124	539,799	48.29	51.71	Ward 4, .	1,497	1,717	3,214	46.58	53.42
BOSTON, .	239,675	257,254	496,920	48.23	51.77	Ward 5, .	1,646	1,704	3,350	49.13	50.87
Ward 1, .	10,363	10,644	21,007	49.33	50.67	Ward 6, .	2,300	2,360	4,660	49.36	50.64

POPULATION AND SEX — Concluded.

COUNTIES, CITIES, AND TOWNS.	Males	Females	Population	Percentages M	F	COUNTIES, CITIES, AND TOWNS.	Males	Females	Population	Percentages M	F
WORCESTER —Con.						WORCESTER —Con.					
Gardner,	4,735	4,447	9,182	51.57	48.43	Shrewsbury,	784	740	1,524	51.44	48.56
Grafton,	2,455	2,646	5,101	48.13	51.87	Southborough,	1,274	949	2,223	57.31	42.69
Hardwick,	1,376	1,279	2,655	51.83	48.17	Southbridge,	4,043	4,207	8,250	49.01	50.99
Harvard,	574	588	1,162	49.40	50.60	Spencer,	3,784	3,830	7,614	49.70	50.30
Holden,	1,302	1,300	2,602	50.04	49.96	Sterling,	604	614	1,218	49.59	50.41
Hopedale,	698	679	1,377	50.69	49.31	Sturbridge,	948	962	1,910	49.63	50.37
Hubbardston,	659	615	1,274	51.73	48.27	Sutton,	1,770	1,650	3,420	51.75	48.25
Lancaster,	978	1,202	2,180	44.86	55.14	Templeton,	1,488	1,427	2,915	51.05	48.95
Leicester,	1,541	1,698	3,239	47.58	52.42	Upton,	908	1,242	2,150	42.23	57.77
Leominster,	4,504	4,707	9,211	48.90	51.10	Uxbridge,	1,780	1,766	3,546	50.20	49.80
Lunenburg,	626	611	1,237	50.61	49.39	Warren,	2,197	2,233	4,430	49.59	50.41
Mendon,	462	427	889	51.97	48.03	Webster,	3,766	4,000	7,766	48.71	51.29
Milford,	4,354	4,605	8,959	48.60	51.40	Westborough,	2,611	2,624	5,235	49.88	50.12
Millbury,	2,619	2,603	5,222	50.15	49.85	West Boylston,	1,447	1,521	2,968	48.75	51.25
New Braintree,	292	250	542	53.87	46.13	West Brookfield,	717	750	1,467	48.88	51.12
Northborough,	975	965	1,940	50.26	49.74	Westminster,	632	683	1,315	48.06	51.94
Northbridge,	2,732	2,554	5,286	51.68	48.32	Winchendon,	2,257	2,233	4,490	50.27	49.73
North Brookfield,	2,248	2,387	4,635	48.50	51.50	WORCESTER,	48,863	49,904	98,767	49.47	50.53
Oakham,	308	297	605	50.91	49.09	Ward 1,	5,611	5,489	11,100	50.55	49.45
Oxford,	1,147	1,243	2,390	47.99	52.01	Ward 2,	6,424	6,095	13,089	49.08	50.92
Paxton,	234	192	426	54.93	45.07	Ward 3,	7,636	7,001	14,637	52.17	47.83
Petersham,	493	459	952	51.79	48.21	Ward 4,	6,729	6,762	13,491	49.88	50.12
Phillipston,	248	212	460	53.91	46.09	Ward 5,	8,053	7,232	15,285	52.69	47.81
Princeton,	491	461	952	51.58	48.42	Ward 6,	5,677	6,158	11,835	47.97	52.03
Royalston,	454	436	890	51.01	48.99	Ward 7,	4,756	5,596	10,352	45.94	54.06
Rutland,	526	452	978	53.78	46.22	Ward 8,	3,977	5,001	8,978	44.30	55.70

RECAPITULATION.

THE STATE, AND COUNTIES.	Males	Females	Population	Percentages Males	Females
THE STATE.	1,214,701	1,285,482	2,500,183	48.58	51.42
Barnstable,	13,294	14,360	27,654	48.07	51.93
Berkshire,	42,525	43,767	86,292	49.28	50.72
Bristol,	105,582	113,437	219,019	48.21	51.79
Dukes,	2,057	2,181	4,238	48.54	51.46
Essex,	161,913	168,480	330,393	49.01	50.99
Franklin,	20,293	19,852	40,145	50.55	49.45
Hampden,	74,133	78,805	152,938	48.47	51.53
Hampshire,	26,061	28,649	54,710	47.63	52.37
Middlesex,	239,323	259,894	499,217	47.94	52.06
Nantucket,	1,315	1,701	3,016	43.60	56.40
Norfolk,	64,780	70,039	134,819	48.05	51.95
Plymouth,	50,694	50,804	101,498	49.95	50.05
Suffolk,	260,675	279,124	539,799	48.29	51.71
Worcester,	152,056	154,389	306,445	49.62	50.38

POPULATION FOR 1885 AND 1895:

INCREASE AND DECREASE.

BY SEX.

POPULATION — 1885 AND 1895.

INCREASE OR DECREASE BY SEX.

COUNTIES, CITIES, AND TOWNS.	MALES				FEMALES			
	1885	1895	Increase or Decrease Number	Percentage	1885	1895	Increase or Decrease Number	Percentage
BARNSTABLE.	14,466	13,294	−1,172	−8.10	15,379	14,360	−1,019	−6.63
Barnstable,	1,904	1,944	+ 40	+ 2.10	2,146	2,111	− 35	− 1.63
Bourne,	677	772	+ 95	+14.03	686	808	+ 122	+17.78
Brewster,	423	437	+ 14	+ 3.31	511	464	− 47	− 9.20
Chatham,	902	808	− 94	− 9.48	1,036	911	− 125	−12.07
Dennis,	1,397	1,164	− 233	−16.68	1,526	1,381	− 145	− 9.50
Eastham,	317	234	− 83	−26.18	321	242	− 79	−24.61
Falmouth,	1,244	1,283	+ 39	+ 3.14	1,276	1,372	+ 96	+ 7.52
Harwich,	1,384	1,253	− 131	− 9.47	1,399	1,279	− 120	− 8.58
Mashpee,	170	178	+ 8	+ 4.71	141	152	+ 11	+ 7.80
Orleans,	539	559	+ 20	+ 3.71	637	639	+ 2	+ 0.31
Provincetown,	2,212	2,215	+ 3	+ 0.14	2,268	2,340	+ 72	+ 3.17
Sandwich,	1,029	734	− 295	−28.67	1,095	846	− 249	−22.74
Truro,	467	402	− 65	−13.92	505	413	− 92	−18.22
Wellfleet,	832	449	− 383	−46.03	855	519	− 336	−39.30
Yarmouth,	879	772	− 107	−12.17	977	883	− 94	− 9.62
BERKSHIRE.	36,144	42,525	+6,381	+17.65	37,684	43,767	+6,083	+16.14
Adams,	4,032	3,712	− 320	− 7.94	4,251	4,125	− 126	− 2.96
Alford,	176	152	− 24	−13.64	165	128	− 37	−22.42
Becket,	485	483	− 2	− 0.41	453	405	− 48	−10.60
Cheshire,	742	599	− 143	−19.27	706	577	− 129	−18.27
Clarksburg,	373	502	+ 129	+34.58	335	507	+ 172	+51.34
Dalton,	949	1,506	+ 557	+58.69	1,164	1,704	+ 540	+46.39
Egremont,	389	406	+ 17	+ 4.37	437	430	− 7	− 1.60
Florida,	266	223	− 43	−16.17	221	202	− 19	− 8.60
Great Barrington,	2,126	2,332	+ 206	+ 9.69	2,345	2,462	+ 117	+ 4.99
Hancock,	296	266	− 30	−10.14	317	245	− 72	−22.71
Hinsdale,	804	821	+ 17	+ 2.11	852	829	− 23	− 2.70
Lanesborough,	618	434	− 184	−29.77	594	414	− 180	−30.30
Lee,	2,053	1,973	− 80	− 3.90	2,221	2,093	− 128	− 5.76
Lenox,	1,106	1,529	+ 423	+38.25	1,048	1,343	+ 295	+28.15
Monterey,	283	241	− 42	−14.84	288	223	− 65	−22.57
Mount Washington,	81	76	− 5	− 6.17	79	60	− 19	−24.05
New Ashford,	80	68	− 12	−15.00	83	48	− 35	−42.17
New Marlborough,	841	682	− 159	−18.91	820	606	− 214	−26.10
NORTH ADAMS,	6,059	9,350	+3,291	+54.32	6,481	9,785	+3,304	+50.98
Otis,	364	289	− 75	−20.60	339	229	− 110	−32.45
Peru,	198	146	− 52	−26.26	170	159	− 11	− 6.47
PITTSFIELD,	6,870	9,838	+2,968	+43.20	7,596	10,623	+3,027	+39.85
Richmond,	414	354	− 60	−14.49	440	347	− 93	−21.14
Sandisfield,	517	401	− 116	−22.44	502	401	− 101	−20.12
Savoy,	356	256	− 100	−28.09	335	248	− 87	−25.97
Sheffield,	1,021	944	− 77	− 7.54	1,012	953	− 59	− 5.83

INCREASE OR DECREASE BY SEX — Continued.

COUNTIES, CITIES, AND TOWNS.	MALES		INCREASE OR DECREASE		FEMALES		INCREASE OR DECREASE	
	1885	1895	Number	Percentage	1885	1895	Number	Percentage
BERKSHIRE — Con.								
Stockbridge, ...	1,030	996	— 34	— 3.30	1,084	1,081	— 3	— 0.28
Tyringham, ...	226	186	— 40	— 17.70	231	177	— 54	— 23.38
Washington, ...	251	236	— 15	— 5.98	219	187	— 32	— 14.61
West Stockbridge, . . .	830	608	— 222	— 26.75	818	649	— 169	— 20.66
Williamstown, ...	1,959	2,615	+ 656	+ 33.49	1,770	2,272	+ 502	+ 28.36
Windsor, ...	349	301	— 48	— 13.75	308	255	— 53	— 17.21
BRISTOL.	75,856	105,582	+29,726	+ 39.19	82,642	113,437	+30,795	+ 37.26
Acushnet, ...	533	568	+ 35	+ 6.57	538	547	+ 9	+ 1.67
Attleborough, ...	6,472	4,029	— 2,443	— 37.75	6,703	4,259	— 2,444	— 36.46
Berkley, ...	488	482	— 6	— 1.23	453	473	+ 20	+ 4.42
Dartmouth, ...	1,709	1,599	— 110	— 6.44	1,739	1,508	— 231	— 13.28
Dighton, ...	909	916	+ 7	+ 0.77	873	881	+ 8	+ 0.92
Easton, ...	2,011	2,286	+ 275	+ 13.67	1,937	2,166	+ 229	+ 11.82
Fairhaven, ...	1,318	1,554	+ 236	+ 17.91	1,562	1,784	+ 222	+ 14.21
FALL RIVER, ...	26,807	42,704	+15,897	+ 59.30	30,063	46,499	+16,436	+ 54.67
Freetown, ...	720	725	+ 5	+ 0.69	737	680	— 57	— 7.73
Mansfield, ...	1,410	1,793	+ 383	+ 27.16	1,529	1,929	+ 400	+ 26.16
NEW BEDFORD, ...	15,413	26,158	+10,745	+ 69.71	17,980	29,093	+11,113	+ 61.81
North Attleborough, . . .	-	3,145	+ 3,145	-	-	3,431	+ 3,431	-
Norton, ...	815	760	— 55	— 6.75	903	854	— 49	— 5.43
Raynham, ...	763	751	— 12	— 1.57	772	767	— 5	— 0.65
Rehoboth, ...	941	958	+ 17	+ 1.81	847	852	+ 5	+ 0.59
Seekonk, ...	671	793	+ 122	+ 18.18	624	672	+ 48	+ 7.69
Somerset, ...	1,321	1,040	— 281	— 21.27	1,154	943	— 211	— 18.28
Swansea, ...	710	830	+ 120	+ 16.90	693	797	+ 104	+ 15.01
TAUNTON, ...	11,528	13,147	+ 1,619	+ 14.04	12,146	13,968	+ 1,822	+ 15.00
Westport, ...	1,317	1,344	+ 27	+ 2.05	1,389	1,334	— 55	— 3.96
DUKES.	2,006	2,057	+ 51	+ 2.54	2,129	2,181	+ 52	+ 2.44
Chilmark, ...	206	151	— 55	— 26.70	206	153	— 53	— 25.73
Cottage City, ...	357	508	+ 151	+ 42.30	352	530	+ 178	+ 50.57
Edgartown, ...	557	527	— 30	— 5.39	608	598	— 10	— 1.64
Gay Head, ...	94	90	— 4	— 4.26	92	79	— 13	— 14.13
Gosnold, ...	71	88	+ 17	+ 23.94	51	52	+ 1	+ 1.96
Tisbury, ...	721	477	— 244	— 33.84	820	525	— 295	— 35.98
West Tisbury, ...	-	216	+ 216	-	-	244	+ 244	-
ESSEX.	126,011	161,913	+35,902	+ 28.49	137,716	168,480	+30,764	+ 22.34
Amesbury, ...	2,100	4,780	+ 2,680	+127.62	2,303	5,206	+ 2,903	+126.05
Andover, ...	2,714	2,913	+ 199	+ 7.33	2,997	3,232	+ 235	+ 7.84
BEVERLY, ...	4,349	5,728	+ 1,379	+ 31.71	4,837	6,078	+ 1,241	+ 25.66
Boxford, ...	407	359	— 48	— 11.79	433	368	— 65	— 15.01
Bradford, ...	1,412	2,222	+ 810	+ 57.37	1,694	2,514	+ 820	+ 48.41
Danvers, ...	3,358	3,958	+ 600	+ 17.87	3,703	4,223	+ 520	+ 14.04
Essex, ...	872	809	— 63	— 7.22	850	778	— 72	— 8.47
Georgetown, ...	1,123	999	— 124	— 11.04	1,176	1,051	— 125	— 10.63
GLOUCESTER, ...	11,723	16,257	+ 4,534	+ 38.68	9,980	11,954	+ 1,974	+ 19.78
Groveland, ...	1,070	1,118	+ 48	+ 4.49	1,202	1,215	+ 13	+ 1.08
Hamilton, ...	420	685	+ 265	+ 63.10	431	671	+ 240	+ 55.68
HAVERHILL, ...	10,455	14,535	+ 4,080	+ 39.02	11,340	15,674	+ 4,334	+ 38.22
Ipswich, ...	1,950	2,178	+ 208	+ 10.56	2,237	2,542	+ 305	+ 13.63
LAWRENCE, ...	17,706	25,107	+ 7,401	+ 41.80	21,156	27,057	+ 5,901	+ 27.89
LYNN, ...	21,752	30,173	+ 8,421	+ 38.71	24,115	32,181	+ 8,066	+ 33.45
Lynnfield, ...	373	408	+ 35	+ 9.38	393	410	+ 17	+ 4.33
Manchester, ...	824	893	+ 69	+ 8.37	815	983	+ 168	+ 20.61

INCREASE OR DECREASE BY SEX — Continued.

COUNTIES, CITIES, AND TOWNS.	MALES				FEMALES			
	1885	1895	INCREASE OR DECREASE Number	Percentage	1885	1895	INCREASE OR DECREASE Number	Percentage
ESSEX — Con.								
Marblehead, ...	3,605	3,649	+ 44	+ 1.22	3,912	4,022	+ 110	+ 2.81
Merrimac, ...	1,187	1,111	— 76	— 6.40	1,191	1,190	— 1	— 0.08
Methuen, ...	2,101	2,760	+ 659	+31.37	2,406	2,930	+ 524	+21.78
Middleton, ...	457	428	— 29	— 6.35	442	410	— 32	— 7.24
Nahant, ...	318	425	+ 107	+33.65	319	440	+ 121	+37.93
Newbury, ...	829	760	— 69	— 8.32	761	729	— 32	— 4.20
NEWBURYPORT, . . .	6,162	6,616	+ 454	+ 7.37	7,554	7,936	+ 382	+ 5.06
North Andover, . . .	1,710	1,765	+ 55	+ 3.22	1,715	1,804	+ 89	+ 5.19
Peabody, ...	4,737	5,262	+ 525	+11.08	4,793	5,245	+ 452	+ 9.43
Rockport, ...	1,999	2,906	+ 907	+48.37	1,889	2,323	+ 434	+22.98
Rowley, ...	609	656	+ 47	+ 7.72	574	616	+ 42	+ 7.32
SALEM, ...	12,775	16,270	+ 3,495	+27.36	15,315	18,203	+ 2,888	+18.86
Salisbury, ...	2,380	642	— 1,738	—73.03	2,460	658	— 1,802	—73.25
Saugus, ...	1,394	2,189	+ 795	+57.06	1,461	2,308	+ 847	+57.97
Swampscott, ...	1,158	1,534	+ 376	+32.47	1,313	1,725	+ 412	+31.38
Topsfield, ...	575	516	— 59	—10.26	566	517	— 49	— 8.66
Wenham, ...	425	431	+ 6	+ 1.41	446	455	+ 9	+ 2.02
West Newbury, . . .	962	811	— 151	—15.70	937	832	— 105	—11.21
FRANKLIN.	18,761	20,293	+ 1,532	+ 8.17	18,688	19,852	+ 1,164	+ 6.23
Ashfield, ...	547	523	— 24	— 4.39	550	490	— 60	—10.91
Bernardston, ...	465	389	— 76	—16.34	465	389	— 76	—16.34
Buckland, ...	895	785	— 110	—12.29	865	763	— 102	—11.79
Charlemont, ...	477	526	+ 49	+10.27	481	515	+ 34	+ 7.07
Colrain, ...	812	851	+ 39	+ 4.80	793	759	— 34	— 4.29
Conway, ...	786	657	— 129	—16.41	787	647	— 140	—17.79
Deerfield, ...	1,553	1,550	— 3	— 0.19	1,489	1,457	— 32	— 2.15
Erving, ...	452	490	+ 38	+ 8.41	421	474	+ 53	+12.59
Gill, ...	482	699	+ 217	+45.02	378	383	+ 5	+ 1.32
Greenfield, ...	2,311	2,987	+ 676	+29.25	2,558	3,242	+ 684	+26.74
Hawley, ...	292	250	— 42	—14.38	253	218	— 35	—13.83
Heath, ...	287	250	— 37	—12.89	281	226	— 55	—19.57
Leverett, ...	398	379	— 19	— 4.77	381	365	— 16	— 4.20
Leyden, ...	217	185	— 32	—14.75	230	178	— 52	—22.61
Monroe, ...	96	176	+ 80	+83.33	80	122	+ 42	+52.56
Montague, ...	2,809	3,076	+ 267	+ 9.51	2,820	2,982	+ 162	+ 5.74
New Salem, ...	412	438	+ 26	+ 6.31	420	431	+ 11	+ 2.62
Northfield, ...	783	754	— 29	— 3.70	922	1,097	+ 175	+18.98
Orange, ...	1,836	2,690	+ 854	+46.51	1,814	2,671	+ 857	+47.24
Rowe, ...	336	283	— 53	—15.77	246	215	— 31	—12.60
Shelburne, ...	757	750	— 7	— 0.92	857	810	— 47	— 5.48
Shutesbury, ...	244	218	— 26	—10.66	241	226	— 15	— 6.22
Sunderland, ...	372	381	+ 9	+ 2.42	328	315	— 13	— 3.96
Warwick, ...	330	321	— 9	— 2.73	332	278	— 54	—16.27
Wendell, ...	271	293	+ 22	+ 8.12	238	236	— 2	— 0.84
Whately, ...	541	392	— 149	—27.54	458	363	— 95	—20.74
HAMPDEN.	55,922	74,133	+18,211	+32.57	60,842	78,805	+17,963	+29.52
Agawam, ...	1,155	1,237	+ 82	+ 7.10	1,202	1,171	— 31	— 2.58
Blandford, ...	493	437	— 56	—11.36	461	412	— 49	—10.63
Brimfield, ...	564	438	— 66	—11.70	573	464	— 109	—19.02
Chester, ...	679	700	+ 21	+ 3.09	639	729	+ 90	+14.08
CHICOPEE, ...	5,357	8,095	+ 2,738	+51.11	6,159	8,325	+ 2,166	+35.17
East Longmeadow, . .	-	863	+ 863	-	-	728	+ 728	-
Granville, ...	634	522	— 112	—17.67	559	483	— 76	—13.60
Hampden, ...	442	374	— 68	—15.38	426	369	— 57	—13.38

INCREASE OR DECREASE BY SEX — Continued.

COUNTIES, CITIES, AND TOWNS.	MALES				FEMALES			
	1885	1895	Increase or Decrease		1885	1895	Increase or Decrease	
			Number	Percentage			Number	Percentage
HAMPDEN — Con.								
Holland,	119	107	− 12	−10.08	110	92	− 18	−16.36
HOLYOKE, .	13,218	19,198	+ 5,980	+45.24	14,677	21,124	+ 6,447	+43.93
Longmeadow,	881	290	− 591	−67.08	796	330	− 466	−58.54
Ludlow,	828	1,314	+ 486	+58.70	821	1,248	+ 427	+52.01
Monson,	1,924	1,862	− 62	− 3.22	2,034	1,884	− 150	− 7.37
Montgomery,	146	151	+ 5	+ 3.42	132	124	− 8	− 6.06
Palmer,	2,820	3,345	+ 525	+18.62	3,103	3,513	+ 410	+13.21
Russell,	399	440	+ 41	+10.28	448	406	− 42	− 9.38
Southwick, .	494	510	+ 16	+ 3.24	488	451	− 37	− 7.58
SPRINGFIELD,	17,877	24,651	+ 6,774	+37.89	19,698	26,871	+ 7,173	+36.41
Tolland,	231	171	− 60	−25.97	191	138	− 53	−27.75
Wales, .	421	405	− 16	− 3.80	432	378	− 54	−12.50
Westfield, .	4,296	5,175	+ 879	+20.46	4,665	5,488	+ 823	+17.64
West Springfield,	2,100	2,951	+ 851	+40.52	2,348	3,174	+ 826	+35.18
Wilbraham,	844	837	− 7	− 0.83	880	903	+ 23	+ 2.61
HAMPSHIRE.	22,921	26,061	+ 3,140	+13.70	25,551	28,649	+ 3,098	+12.12
Amherst, .	2,076	2,427	+ 351	+16.91	2,123	2,358	+ 235	+11.07
Belchertown,	1,160	1,115	− 45	− 3.88	1,147	1,046	− 101	− 8.81
Chesterfield,	361	301	− 60	−16.62	337	288	− 49	−14.54
Cummington,	397	367	− 30	− 7.56	408	383	− 25	− 6.13
Easthampton,	1,902	2,242	+ 340	+17.88	2,389	2,548	+ 159	+ 6.66
Enfield,	507	512	+ 5	+ 0.99	503	478	− 25	− 4.97
Goshen,	177	160	− 17	− 9.60	159	144	− 15	− 9.43
Granby,	360	394	+ 34	+ 9.44	369	354	− 15	− 4.07
Greenwich, .	266	243	− 23	− 8.65	266	238	− 28	−10.53
Hadley,	906	894	− 12	− 1.32	841	810	− 31	− 3.69
Hatfield,	704	669	− 35	− 4.97	663	593	− 70	−10.56
Huntington,	623	722	+ 99	+15.89	644	728	+ 84	+13.04
Middlefield,	250	197	− 53	−21.20	263	189	− 74	−28.14
NORTHAMPTON,	5,852	7,434	+ 1,582	+27.06	7,044	9,312	+ 2,268	+32.20
Pelham,	262	246	− 16	− 6.11	287	240	− 47	−16.38
Plainfield,	225	231	+ 6	+ 2.67	228	219	− 9	− 3.95
Prescott,	220	208	− 12	− 5.45	228	193	− 35	−15.35
Southampton,	499	537	+ 38	+ 7.62	526	517	− 9	− 1.71
South Hadley,	1,790	2,054	+ 264	+14.75	2,159	2,389	+ 230	+10.65
Ware, .	2,721	3,576	+ 855	+31.42	3,282	4,075	+ 793	+24.16
Westhampton,	280	241	− 39	−13.93	261	235	− 26	− 9.96
Williamsburg,	998	950	− 48	− 4.81	1,046	1,005	− 41	− 3.92
Worthington,	385	341	− 44	−11.43	378	307	− 71	−18.78
MIDDLESEX.	169,491	239,323	+69,832	+41.20	187,820	259,894	+72,074	+38.37
Acton,	898	980	+ 82	+ 9.13	887	998	+ 111	+12.51
Arlington, .	2,205	3,067	+ 862	+39.09	2,468	3,448	+ 980	+39.71
Ashby,	436	413	− 23	− 5.28	435	391	− 44	−10.11
Ashland,	1,392	1,045	− 347	−25.48	1,271	1,075	− 196	−15.42
Ayer, .	1,106	1,018	− 88	− 7.96	1,084	1,083	− 1	− 0.09
Bedford,	459	623	+ 164	+35.73	471	546	+ 75	+15.92
Belmont,	767	1,519	+ 752	+98.04	872	1,324	+ 452	+51.83
Billerica,	1,051	1,301	+ 250	+23.79	1,110	1,276	+ 166	+14.95
Boxborough,	173	172	− 1	− 0.58	175	135	− 40	−22.86
Burlington,	310	316	+ 6	+ 1.94	294	258	− 36	−12.24
CAMBRIDGE,	28,609	39,831	+11,222	+39.23	31,049	41,812	+10,763	+34.66
Carlisle,	278	268	− 10	− 3.60	248	224	− 24	− 9.68
Chelmsford,	1,142	1,611	+ 469	+41.07	1,162	1,551	+ 389	+33.48
Concord,	2,013	3,157	+ 1,144	+56.83	1,714	2,018	+ 304	+17.74

INCREASE OR DECREASE BY SEX — Continued.

COUNTIES, CITIES, AND TOWNS.	MALES				FEMALES			
	1885	1895	Number	Percentage	1885	1895	Number	Percentage
MIDDLESEX — Con.								
Dracut,	1,058	1,325	+ 267	+ 25.24	869	1,118	+ 249	+ 28.65
Dunstable,	217	207	− 10	− 4.61	214	193	− 21	− 9.81
EVERETT,	2,881	9,057	+ 6,176	+214.37	2,944	9,516	+ 6,572	+223.23
Framingham,	4,010	4,570	+ 560	+ 13.97	4,265	4,942	+ 677	+ 15.87
Groton,	976	1,078	+ 102	+ 10.45	1,011	1,114	+ 103	+ 10.19
Holliston,	1,384	1,309	− 75	− 5.42	1,542	1,469	− 133	− 8.63
Hopkinton,	1,972	1,469	− 503	− 25.51	1,950	1,515	− 435	− 22.31
Hudson,	1,938	2,533	+ 595	+ 30.70	2,030	2,775	+ 745	+ 36.70
Lexington,	1,357	1,692	+ 335	+ 24.69	1,361	1,806	+ 445	+ 32.70
Lincoln,	472	626	+ 154	+ 32.63	429	485	+ 56	+ 13.05
Littleton,	537	569	+ 32	+ 5.96	530	567	+ 37	+ 6.98
LOWELL,	28,517	38,931	+10,414	+ 36.52	35,590	45,436	+ 9,846	+ 27.66
MALDEN,	7,690	13,923	+ 6,233	+ 81.05	8,717	15,785	+ 7,068	+ 81.08
MARLBOROUGH,	5,567	7,469	+ 1,902	+ 34.17	5,374	7,508	+ 2,134	+ 39.71
Maynard,	1,342	1,520	+ 178	+ 13.26	1,361	1,570	+ 209	+ 15.36
MEDFORD,	4,418	7,043	+ 2,625	+ 59.42	4,624	7,431	+ 2,807	+ 60.71
Melrose,	2,834	5,548	+ 2,714	+ 95.77	3,267	6,417	+ 3,150	+ 96.42
Natick,	4,185	4,234	+ 49	+ 1.17	4,275	4,580	+ 305	+ 7.13
NEWTON,	8,741	12,355	+ 3,614	+ 41.35	11,018	15,235	+ 4,217	+ 38.27
North Reading,	451	422	− 29	− 6.43	427	413	− 14	− 3.28
Pepperell,	1,270	1,650	+ 380	+ 29.92	1,317	1,671	+ 354	+ 26.88
Reading,	1,582	2,235	+ 653	+ 41.28	1,957	2,482	+ 525	+ 26.83
Sherborn,	561	584	+ 23	+ 4.10	830	862	+ 32	+ 3.86
Shirley,	585	654	+ 69	+ 11.79	657	745	+ 88	+ 13.39
SOMERVILLE,	14,190	24,917	+10,727	+ 75.60	15,781	27,283	+11,502	+ 72.89
Stoneham,	2,726	3,070	+ 344	+ 12.62	2,963	3,214	+ 281	+ 9.58
Stow,	484	473	− 11	− 2.27	492	447	− 45	− 9.15
Sudbury,	583	603	+ 20	+ 3.43	582	538	− 44	− 7.56
Tewksbury,	1,037	1,653	+ 616	+ 59.40	1,296	1,726	+ 430	+ 33.18
Townsend,	894	880	− 14	− 1.57	952	900	− 52	− 5.46
Tyngsborough,	299	324	+ 25	+ 8.36	305	311	+ 6	+ 1.97
Wakefield,	2,882	3,962	+ 1,080	+ 37.47	3,178	4,342	+ 1,164	+ 36.63
WALTHAM,	6,708	9,638	+ 2,930	+ 43.68	7,901	11,238	+ 3,337	+ 42.24
Watertown,	3,004	3,740	+ 736	+ 24.50	3,234	4,048	+ 814	+ 25.17
Wayland,	987	1,026	+ 39	+ 3.95	959	1,000	+ 41	+ 4.28
Westford,	1,059	1,223	+ 164	+ 15.49	1,134	1,195	+ 61	+ 5.38
Weston,	744	877	+ 133	+ 17.88	683	833	+ 150	+ 21.96
Wilmington,	486	715	+ 229	+ 47.12	505	705	+ 200	+ 39.60
Winchester,	2,152	2,928	+ 776	+ 36.06	2,238	3,222	+ 984	+ 43.97
WOBURN,	5,902	7,000	+ 1,098	+ 18.60	5,848	7,178	+ 1,330	+ 22.74
NANTUCKET.	1,340	1,315	− 25	− 1.87	1,802	1,701	− 101	− 5.60
Nantucket,	1,340	1,315	− 25	− 1.87	1,802	1,701	− 101	− 5.60
NORFOLK.	49,000	64,780	+15,780	+ 32.20	53,142	70,039	+16,897	+ 31.80
Avon,	-	818	+ 818	-	-	808	+ 808	-
Bellingham,	594	721	+ 127	+ 21.38	604	760	+ 156	+ 25.83
Braintree,	1,943	2,660	+ 717	+ 36.90	2,097	2,651	+ 554	+ 26.42
Brookline,	3,939	6,826	+ 2,887	+ 73.29	5,257	9,338	+ 4,081	+ 77.63
Canton,	2,093	2,207	+ 114	+ 5.45	2,287	2,429	+ 142	+ 6.21
Cohasset,	1,058	1,148	+ 90	+ 8.51	1,158	1,326	+ 168	+ 14.51
Dedham,	3,149	3,476	+ 327	+ 10.38	3,492	3,735	+ 243	+ 6.96
Dover,	351	345	− 6	− 1.71	313	323	+ 10	+ 3.19
Foxborough,	1,243	1,542	+ 299	+ 24.05	1,571	1,677	+ 106	+ 6.75
Franklin,	1,911	2,459	+ 548	+ 28.68	2,072	2,677	+ 605	+ 29.20
Holbrook,	1,155	1,127	− 28	− 2.42	1,179	1,171	− 8	− 0.68

INCREASE OR DECREASE BY SEX — Continued.

COUNTIES, CITIES, AND TOWNS.	MALES		INCREASE OR DECREASE		FEMALES		INCREASE OR DECREASE	
	1885	1895	Number	Percentage	1885	1895	Number	Percentage
NORFOLK — Con.								
Hyde Park, ...	4,047	5,760	+ 1,713	+ 42.33	4,329	6,066	+ 1,737	+ 40.12
Medfield, ...	674	883	+ 209	+ 31.01	920	989	+ 69	+ 7.50
Medway, ...	1,382	1,438	+ 56	+ 4.05	1,395	1,475	+ 80	+ 5.73
Millis, ...	332	484	+ 152	+ 45.78	351	522	+ 171	+ 48.72
Milton, ...	1,661	2,562	+ 901	+ 54.24	1,894	2,956	+ 1,062	+ 56.07
Needham, ...	1,284	1,749	+ 465	+ 36.21	1,302	1,762	+ 460	+ 35.33
Norfolk, ...	410	471	+ 61	+ 14.88	415	411	— 4	— 0.96
Norwood, ...	1,514	2,437	+ 923	+ 60.96	1,407	2,137	+ 730	+ 51.88
QUINCY, ...	6,192	10,608	+ 4,416	+ 71.32	5,953	10,104	+ 4,151	+ 69.73
Randolph, ...	1,871	1,825	— 46	— 2.46	1,936	1,869	— 67	— 3.46
Sharon, ...	660	839	+ 179	+ 27.12	668	878	+ 210	+ 31.44
Stoughton, ...	2,543	2,570	+ 27	+ 1.06	2,630	2,702	+ 72	+ 2.74
Walpole, ...	1,291	1,500	+ 209	+ 24.90	1,242	1,494	+ 252	+ 20.29
Wellesley, ...	1,114	1,470	+ 356	+ 31.96	1,899	2,759	+ 860	+ 45.29
Weymouth, ...	5,349	5,592	+ 243	+ 4.54	5,391	5,699	+ 308	+ 5.71
Wrentham, ...	1,330	1,263	— 67	— 5.04	1,380	1,321	— 59	— 4.28
PLYMOUTH.	40,553	50,694	+10,141	+ 25.01	41,127	50,804	+ 9,677	+ 23.53
Abington, ...	1,816	2,040	+ 224	+ 12.33	1,883	2,167	+ 284	+ 15.08
Bridgewater, ...	1,995	2,722	+ 727	+ 36.44	1,832	1,964	+ 132	+ 7.21
BROCKTON, ...	10,398	16,559	+ 6,161	+ 59.25	10,385	16,606	+ 6,221	+ 59.90
Carver, ...	572	546	— 26	— 4.55	519	470	— 49	— 9.44
Duxbury, ...	887	945	+ 58	+ 6.54	1,037	1,021	— 16	— 1.54
East Bridgewater, . .	1,411	1,441	+ 30	+ 2.13	1,401	1,453	+ 52	+ 3.71
Halifax, ...	257	266	+ 9	+ 3.50	273	231	— 42	— 15.38
Hanover, ...	950	1,009	+ 59	+ 6.21	1,016	1,042	+ 26	+ 2.56
Hanson, ...	633	708	+ 75	+ 11.85	594	672	+ 78	+ 13.13
Hingham, ...	2,040	2,299	+ 259	+ 12.70	2,335	2,520	+ 185	+ 7.92
Hull, ...	240	536	+ 296	+123.33	211	508	+ 297	+140.76
Kingston, ...	753	847	+ 94	+ 12.48	817	899	+ 82	+ 10.04
Lakeville, ...	485	439	— 46	— 9.48	495	431	— 64	— 12.93
Marion, ...	449	328	— 121	— 26.95	516	431	— 85	— 16.47
Marshfield, ...	825	850	+ 25	+ 3.03	824	910	+ 86	+ 10.44
Mattapoisett, ...	554	490	— 64	— 11.55	661	542	— 119	— 18.00
Middleborough, . . .	2,452	3,205	+ 753	+ 30.71	2,711	3,484	+ 773	+ 28.51
Norwell, ...	800	771	— 29	— 3.63	789	769	— 20	— 2.53
Pembroke, ...	663	634	— 29	— 4.37	650	589	— 61	— 9.38
Plymouth, ...	3,556	3,863	+ 307	+ 8.63	3,683	4,094	+ 411	+ 11.16
Plympton, ...	290	268	— 22	— 7.59	310	281	— 29	— 9.35
Rochester, ...	509	535	+ 26	+ 5.11	512	486	— 26	— 5.08
Rockland, ...	2,418	2,757	+ 339	+ 14.02	2,367	2,766	+ 399	+ 16.86
Scituate, ...	1,176	1,115	— 61	— 5.19	1,174	1,131	— 43	— 3.66
Wareham, ...	1,732	1,765	+ 33	+ 1.91	1,522	1,602	+ 80	+ 5.26
West Bridgewater, . .	868	877	+ 9	+ 1.04	839	870	+ 31	+ 3.69
Whitman, ...	1,824	2,879	+ 1,055	+ 57.84	1,771	2,865	+ 1,094	+ 61.77
SUFFOLK.	200,808	260,675	+59,867	+ 29.81	220,301	279,124	+58,823	+ 26.70
BOSTON, ...	186,182	239,666	+53,484	+ 28.73	204,211	257,254	+53,043	+ 25.97
CHELSEA, ...	12,139	15,273	+ 3,134	+ 25.82	13,570	15,991	+ 2,421	+ 17.84
Revere, ...	1,833	3,721	+ 1,888	+103.00	1,804	3,702	+ 1,898	+105.21
Winthrop, ...	654	2,015	+ 1,361	+208.10	716	2,177	+ 1,461	+204.05
WORCESTER.	119,605	152,056	+32,451	+ 27.13	124,434	154,389	+29,955	+ 24.07
Ashburnham, ...	1,001	1,070	+ 69	+ 6.89	1,057	1,078	+ 21	+ 1.99
Athol, ...	2,271	3,735	+ 1,464	+ 64.46	2,487	3,629	+ 1,142	+ 45.92
Auburn, ...	621	821	+ 200	+ 32.21	647	777	+ 130	+ 20.09

INCREASE OR DECREASE BY SEX — Continued.

COUNTIES, CITIES, AND TOWNS.	MALES				FEMALES			
	1885	1895	Increase or Decrease Number	Percentage	1885	1895	Increase or Decrease Number	Percentage
WORCESTER—Con.								
Barre,	1,002	1,150	+ 148	+14.77	1,091	1,128	+ 37	+ 3.39
Berlin,	439	451	+ 12	+ 2.73	460	446	— 14	— 3.04
Blackstone,	2,743	3,116	+ 373	+13.60	2,693	2,923	+ 230	+ 8.54
Bolton,	423	398	— 25	— 5.91	453	399	— 54	—11.92
Boylston,	413	389	— 24	— 5.81	421	340	— 81	—19.24
Brookfield,	1,481	1,689	+ 208	+14.04	1,532	1,590	+ 58	+ 3.79
Charlton,	937	975	+ 38	+ 4.06	886	902	+ 16	+ 1.81
Clinton,	4,022	5,291	+ 1,269	+31.55	4,923	6,206	+ 1,283	+26.06
Dana,	341	353	+ 12	+ 3.52	354	364	+ 10	+ 2.82
Douglas,	1,119	1,033	— 86	— 7.69	1,086	993	— 93	— 8.56
Dudley,	1,341	1,611	+ 270	+20.13	1,401	1,592	+ 191	+13.63
FITCHBURG,	7,502	13,037	+ 5,535	+73.78	7,873	13,372	+ 5,499	+69.85
Gardner,	3,752	4,735	+ 983	+26.20	3,531	4,447	+ 916	+25.94
Grafton,	2,194	2,455	+ 261	+11.90	2,304	2,646	+ 342	+14.84
Hardwick,	1,652	1,376	— 276	—16.71	1,493	1,279	— 214	—14.33
Harvard,	564	574	+ 10	+ 1.77	620	588	— 32	— 5.16
Holden,	1,232	1,302	+ 70	+ 5.68	1,239	1,300	+ 61	+ 4.92
Hopedale,	–	698	+ 698	–	–	679	+ 679	–
Hubbardston,	662	659	— 3	— 0.45	641	615	— 26	— 4.06
Lancaster,	928	978	+ 50	+ 5.39	1,122	1,202	+ 80	+ 7.13
Leicester,	1,378	1,541	+ 163	+11.83	1,545	1,698	+ 153	+ 9.90
Leominster,	2,568	4,504	+ 1,935	+75.32	2,728	4,707	+ 1,979	+72.54
Lunenburg	553	626	+ 73	+13.20	518	611	+ 93	+17.95
Mendon,	466	462	— 4	— 0.86	479	427	— 52	—10.86
Milford,	4,556	4,354	— 202	— 4.43	4,787	4,605	— 182	— 3.80
Millbury,	2,170	2,619	+ 449	+20.69	2,385	2,606	+ 218	+ 9.14
New Braintree,	296	292	— 4	— 1.35	262	250	— 12	— 4.58
Northborough,	942	975	+ 33	+ 3.50	911	965	+ 54	+ 5.93
Northbridge,	1,890	2,732	+ 842	+44.55	1,896	2,554	+ 658	+34.70
North Brookfield,	2,098	2,248	+ 150	+ 7.15	2,103	2,387	+ 284	+13.50
Oakham,	384	308	— 76	—19.79	365	297	— 68	—18.63
Oxford,	1,130	1,147	+ 17	+ 1.50	1,225	1,243	+ 18	+ 1.47
Paxton,	304	234	— 70	—23.03	257	192	— 65	—25.29
Petersham,	515	493	— 22	— 4.27	517	459	— 58	—11.22
Phillipston,	270	248	— 22	— 8.15	260	212	— 48	—18.46
Princeton,	523	491	— 32	— 6.12	515	461	— 54	—10.49
Royalston,	568	454	— 114	—20.07	585	436	— 149	—25.47
Rutland,	516	526	+ 10	+ 1.94	447	452	+ 5	+ 1.12
Shrewsbury,	728	784	+ 56	+ 7.69	722	740	+ 18	+ 2.49
Southborough,	1,061	1,274	+ 213	+20.08	1,039	949	— 90	— 8.66
Southbridge,	3,129	4,043	+ 914	+29.21	3,371	4,207	+ 836	+24.80
Spencer,	4,190	3,784	— 406	— 9.69	4,057	3,830	— 227	— 5.60
Sterling,	641	604	— 37	— 5.77	690	614	— 76	—11.01
Sturbridge,	957	948	— 9	— 0.94	1,023	962	— 61	— 5.96
Sutton,	1,552	1,770	+ 218	+14.05	1,549	1,650	+ 101	+ 6.52
Templeton,	1,302	1,488	+ 186	+14.29	1,325	1,427	+ 102	+ 7.70
Upton,	923	908	— 15	— 1.63	1,342	1,242	— 100	— 7.45
Uxbridge,	1,409	1,780	+ 371	+26.33	1,539	1,766	+ 227	+14.75
Warren,	1,992	2,197	+ 205	+10.29	2,040	2,233	+ 196	+ 9.46
Webster,	3,031	3,799	+ 768	+25.34	3,189	4,000	+ 811	+25.43
Westborough,	2,299	2,611	+ 312	+13.57	2,581	2,624	+ 43	+ 1.67
West Boylston,	1,419	1,447	+ 28	+ 1.97	1,508	1,521	+ 13	+ 0.86
West Brookfield,	825	717	— 108	—13.09	922	750	— 172	—18.66
Westminster,	757	632	— 125	—16.51	799	683	— 116	—14.52
Winchendon,	1,940	2,257	+ 317	+16.34	1,932	2,233	+ 301	+15.58
WORCESTER,	33,682	48,863	+15,181	+45.07	34,707	49,904	+15,197	+43.79

INCREASE OR DECREASE BY SEX — Concluded.
RECAPITULATION.

THE STATE, AND COUNTIES.	MALES		INCREASE OR DECREASE		FEMALES		INCREASE OR DECREASE	
	1885	1895	Number	Percentage	1885	1895	Number	Percentage
THE STATE.	932,884	1,214,701	+281,817	+30.21	1,009,257	1,285,482	+276,225	+27.37
Barnstable, . . .	14,466	13,294	− 1,172	− 8.10	15,379	14,360	− 1,019	− 6.63
Berkshire, . . .	36,144	42,525	+ 6,381	+17.65	37,684	43,767	+ 6,083	+16.14
Bristol, ...	75,856	105,582	+ 29,726	+39.19	82,642	113,437	+ 30,795	+37.26
Dukes, ...	2,006	2,057	+ 51	+ 2.54	2,129	2,181	+ 52	+ 2.44
Essex, ...	126,011	161,913	+ 35,902	+28.49	137,716	168,480	+ 30,764	+22.34
Franklin, . . .	18,761	20,293	+ 1,532	+ 8.17	18,688	19,852	+ 1,164	+ 6.23
Hampden, . . .	55,922	74,133	+ 18,211	+32.57	60,842	78,805	+ 17,963	+29.52
Hampshire, . . .	22,921	26,061	+ 3,140	+13.70	25,551	28,649	+ 3,098	+12.12
Middlesex, . . .	169,491	239,323	+ 69,832	+41.20	187,820	259,894	+ 72,074	+38.37
Nantucket, . . .	1,340	1,315	− 25	− 1.87	1,802	1,701	− 101	− 5.60
Norfolk, . . .	49,000	64,780	+ 15,780	+32.20	53,142	70,039	+ 16,897	+31.80
Plymouth, . . .	40,553	50,694	+ 10,141	+25.01	41,127	50,804	+ 9,677	+23.53
Suffolk, ...	200,808	260,675	+ 59,867	+29.81	220,301	279,124	+ 58,823	+26.70
Worcester, . . .	119,605	152,056	+ 32,451	+27.13	124,434	154,389	+ 29,955	+24.07

Tabular Analyses

For the Following Presentations:

The presentation, pages 1 to 8, shows the population of the cities and towns, together with the number of legal voters, with a recapitulation by counties and for the State. The total population of the State is 2,500,183, and the total number of legal voters, 560,-802. It should be said that in the enumeration taken by the Census the term "legal voters" means persons who have the constitutional requisites for voting, and such persons are to be distinguished from registered voters or persons who have not only the constitutional requisites, but have complied with certain regulations under which the constitutional right is to be exercised, such as, for instance, registration. In other words, legal voters, as enumerated in the Census, are potential voters, or those who might vote if all merely temporary disabilities which it is in the power of the voter himself to overcome were removed. The number of such voters enumerated in the Census of 1885 was 442,616, or 22.79 per cent of the entire population: the legal voters enumerated in 1895 constituted 22.43 per cent of the population. There were 118,186 more voters in 1895 than in 1885, or an increase of 26.70 per cent.

The presentation, pages 9 to 14, shows the population by towns, arranged alphabetically. The presentation, pages 15 to 19, exhibits the towns showing an increase in population from 1885 to 1895, while this is followed upon pages 20 to 22 by a presentation of the towns showing a decrease. The recapitulation, page 23, will enable the reader to see at a glance the number of towns showing a gain and the number showing a loss, with the net gain or loss since 1885, with net percentages of increase or decrease. The actual numerical net gain since 1885 for the whole State is 558,042, the actual net percentage of increase being 28.73. There are 210 towns which show an increase in population, while 143 towns show a loss. The largest number of towns showing increase in any single county is found in the county of Middlesex, namely, 41: while on the other hand, 13 towns in this county show a loss. The net percentage of increase for the county is, however, 39.71, a larger percentage of gain than is found in any other county. The county of Nantucket shows a net loss of 126 persons, or a percentage of decrease of 4.01. The county of Barnstable contains nine towns which show a net loss numerically of 2,191, or a net percentage of decrease of 7.34. Every county except Barnstable and Nantucket shows a net percentage of increase, the highest percentage being found in Middlesex, as just cited, and the lowest in the county of Dukes, namely, 2.49. The county having the largest number of towns showing a loss is Berkshire, which contains 24 such towns; but this county, nevertheless, makes a net gain of 12,464 persons, and a net percentage of increase of 16.88. Worcester County contains 22 towns which show a loss, against 37 towns which show a gain, the numerical net gain for the county being 62,406, and the net percentage of increase, 25.57. In 1885, there were 153

[43]

towns which exhibited a loss, as compared with the year 1875, the actual loss in these towns between 1875 and 1885 being 34,675. The present Census, therefore, shows a less number of towns which have suffered a loss in population during the preceding decade than was found in 1885, and the actual numerical decrease in these towns is but 29,426, a percentage of decrease of 13.08, as against 34,675, the loss in actual population between 1875 and 1885, which was a percentage of decrease for the decade of 13.10 While, therefore, the number of towns showing a loss is less in the present Census than in that of 1885, and the numerical loss is also less, the percentage of loss in the towns which have declined is substantially the same as the percentage of loss in such towns shown in the Census taken ten years ago.

In 1885, the counties of Barnstable and Nantucket showed a net loss, the actual numerical decline, between 1875 and 1885, in these counties taken together being 2,358. The same counties show, as will be seen from the figures just cited, a further decline between 1885 and 1895 of 2,317. Barnstable County lost 7.15 per cent of its population between 1875 and 1885 ; it has also lost 7.34 per cent of its population between 1885 and 1895. Nantucket County lost 1.84 per cent of its population between 1875 and 1885, and now exhibits a further decline of 4.01 per cent. Notwithstanding the losses exhibited in the tables in certain portions of the State, the actual net percentage of increase is, as we have said, 28.73 per cent, while the actual net percentage of increase between 1875 and 1885 was only 17.57 per cent   The towns which show a decline are mainly the small and remote agricultural towns, such, for instance, as are found in some parts of Berkshire, Franklin, and Worcester counties, or the shore towns, whose main reliance is the fishing industry. Towns of this class have suffered a loss for many years, the general tendency of the population being toward the larger cities and towns.

Towns Showing Continuous Loss for 20 Years.

The following table shows the towns which have suffered a continuous loss in population during twenty years :

Adams,*	Eastham,*	Middlefield,
Alford,	Edgartown,*	Middleton,
Ashby,	Enfield,	Milford,*
Ashfield,	Florida,	Monterey,
Becket,	Gay Head,	Montgomery.
Belchertown,	Goshen,	Mount Washington,
Berlin,	Granville,	Nantucket,
Bernardston,*	Greenwich,	New Braintree.
Blandford,	Hadley,	New Marlborough,
Bolton.	Halifax,	North Reading.
Boylston,	Hancock,	Norwell,*
Brewster,	Harvard,	Oakham,
Brimfield,	Harwich,	Otis,
Buckland,	Hatfield,	Paxton,
Burlington,	Hawley,	Pelham,
Carlisle,	Holland,	Pembroke,*
Carver,	Holliston,	Peru,
Chatham,	Hopkinton,	Petersham,*
Cheshire,	Hubbardston,	Phillipston,*
Chesterfield,	Lakeville,	Plainfield,
Chilmark,*	Lanesborough,	Plympton,
Cummington,	Leverett,	Prescott,
Deerfield,	Leyden,*	Princeton,
Dennis,	Mattapoisett,	Randolph,*
Dunstable,	Mendon,	Raynham,

* Loss either wholly or partly due to change in territory by the incorporation of new towns, changes in area, boundaries, etc., as will be more fully shown in a presentation hereinafter given. See " Censuses of Population, 1765-1895 " with accompanying notes.

Richmond,
Rowe,
Royalston,
Sandisfield,*
Sandwich,*
Savoy,
Scituate,*
Sheffield,
Shutesbury,
Southwick,
Sterling.

Stow,
Sturbridge,
Sudbury,
Sunderland,
Tolland,
Topsfield,
Townsend,
Truro,
Tyringham,
Wales,
Warwick.

Washington,
Wellfleet.*
West Brookfield,
Westhampton,
Westminster,
West Newbury,
Westport,*
West Stockbridge,
Worthington,
Yarmouth.

The following towns, which showed a loss in 1885 as compared with 1875, show a gain in 1895, as compared with 1885:

Ashburnham,
Barnstable,
Barre,
Bellingham,
Belmont,†
Braintree,
Bridgewater,
Charlemont,
Charlton,
Chelmsford,
Chester,
Colrain,
Dana,†
Duxbury,
Egremont,
Foxborough,

Granby,
Hanson,
Hingham,
Lunenburg,
Lynnfield,
Marblehead,
Marshfield,
Medway.†
Monroe,
Nahant,
Needham,†
New Salem,
Norfolk,
Northbridge,
Orleans,

Oxford,
Rehoboth,
Rockport,
Rutland,
Sharon,
Shirley,
Shrewsbury,
Southampton,
Templeton,
Tyngsborough,
Uxbridge,
Wenham,
Westborough,
West Bridgewater,
Wilbraham.†

The following towns, which showed a gain in 1885 as compared with 1875, show a loss during the decade closing in 1895:

Ashland,
Attleborough,*
Ayer,
Boxborough,*
Boxford,
Conway,
Dartmouth,*
Douglas,
Essex,*
Freetown,
Georgetown,
Hardwick,

Heath,
Hinsdale,
Holbrook,*
Lee,
Longmeadow,*
Marion,
Merrimac,
Monson,
New Ashford,
Newbury,
Norton,
Russell,

Salisbury,*
Shelburne,
Somerset,
Spencer,
Stockbridge,
Tisbury,*
Upton,
Whately,
Williamsburg,
Windsor,
Wrentham.

Concentration of Population.

The tendency exhibited in previous censuses toward concentration of the population in the vicinity of the city of Boston still continues. The following table shows the

* See note on page 44.
† The loss in 1885 was either wholly or partly due to a change in territory during the previous decade.

population in municipalities located within a circle including eight miles in every direction from the State House, so presented as to show the gain for each city and town between 1885 and 1895:

CITIES AND TOWNS.	POPULATION		Gain
	1885	1895	
Boston, ...	390,393	496,920	100,527
Cambridge, ...	59,658	81,643	21,985
Chelsea, ...	25,709	31,264	5,555
Everett, ...	5,825	18,573	12,748
Malden, ...	16,407	29,708	13,301
Medford, ...	9,042	14,471	5,432
Somerville, ...	29,971	52,200	22,229
Arlington, ...	4,673	6,515	1,812
Belmont, ...	1,639	2,843	1,204
Brookline, ...	9,196	16,164	6,968
Melrose, ...	6,101	11,965	5,864
Revere, ...	3,637	7,423	3,786
Watertown, ...	6,238	7,788	1,550
Winchester, ...	4,390	6,150	1,760
Winthrop, ...	1,370	4,192	2,822
Totals, ...	574,249	787,822	213,573

The above table shows that 787,822 persons, or 31.51 per cent of the entire population of the State, resided in the immediate vicinity of the city of Boston, in 1895. The same towns and cities contained in 1885, 574,249, or 29.57 per cent of the population of the State; the gain upon this territory since 1885 has been 213,573, or 37.19 per cent

If the population is desired of the cities and towns within ten miles of the State House the following should be included in addition to those shown in the preceding table:

CITIES AND TOWNS.	POPULATION		Gain
	1885	1895	
Dedham, ...	6,641	7,211	570
Hyde Park, ...	8,376	11,826	3,450
Lexington, ...	2,718	3,498	780
Lynn, ...	45,867	62,354	16,487
Milton, ...	3,555	5,518	1,963
Nahant, ...	637	865	228
Needham, ...	2,586	3,511	925
Newton, ...	19,759	27,590	7,831
Quincy, ...	12,145	20,712	8,567
Saugus, ...	2,855	4,497	1,642
Stoneham, ...	5,659	6,284	625
Swampscott, ...	2,471	3,259	788
Wakefield, ...	6,060	8,304	2,244
Waltham, ...	14,609	20,876	6,267
Woburn, ...	11,750	14,178	2,428
Totals, ...	115,688	200,483	54,795

The cities and towns shown in these two tables are included in the so-called Metropolitan district, or "Greater Boston," as that term is usually employed, or has been fixed by various commissions which have considered subjects relating to the city of Boston and its immediate suburbs The total population for 1895 of the cities and towns within this area is 988,395, and the municipalities thus united include all whose nearest boundary is within ten miles of the State House, except the town of Wellesley which at one point extends over the ten-mile line, and including also the town of Swampscott which lies just outside the ten-mile line. The Metropolitan District Commission which reported to the Legislature of 1896 respecting the subject of a general municipal administration for the city of Boston and adjoining municipalities, included all of these cities and towns, except Needham, in its plan for the creation of a new Metropolitan county.

If the circle be enlarged to comprise the cities and towns within 12 miles of the State House, the following table results :

CITIES AND TOWNS.	POPULATION		Gain
	1885	1895	
Boston, ...	390,393	496,920	106,527
Cambridge, ...	59,658	81,643	21,985
Chelsea, ...	25,709	31,264	5,555
Everett, ...	5,825	18,573	12,748
Lynn, ...	45,867	62,354	16,487
Malden, ...	16,407	29,708	13,301
Medford, ...	9,042	11,474	5,432
Newton, ...	19,759	27,590	7,831
Quincy, ...	12,145	20,712	8,567
Somerville, ...	29,971	52,200	22,229
Waltham, ...	14,609	20,876	6,267
Woburn, ...	11,750	14,178	2,428
Arlington, ...	4,673	6,515	1,842
Belmont, ...	1,639	2,843	1,204
Braintree, ...	4,040	5,311	1,271
Brookline, ...	9,196	16,164	6,968
Dedham, ...	6,641	7,211	570
Hull, ...	451	1,044	593
Hyde Park, ...	8,376	11,826	3,450
Lexington, ...	2,718	3,498	780
Lynnfield, ...	766	818	52
Melrose, ...	6,101	11,965	5,864
Milton, ...	3,555	5,518	1,963
Nahant, ...	637	865	228
Needham, ...	2,586	3,511	925
Reading, ...	3,539	4,717	1,178
Revere.	3,637	7,423	3,786
Saugus, ...	2,855	4,497	1,642
Stoneham, ...	5,659	6,284	625
Swampscott, ...	2,471	3,259	788
Wakefield, ...	6,060	8,304	2,244
Watertown, ...	6,238	7,788	1,550
Wellesley, ...	3,013	4,229	1,216
Winchester, ...	4,390	6,150	1,760
Winthrop, ...	1,370	4,192	2,822
Totals, ...	731,746	1,004,424	272,678

The cities and towns within the twelve-mile circle had, in 1885, a population of 731,746, or 37.68 per cent of the entire population of the State. The population upon this territory is now 1,004,424, or 40.17 per cent of the population of the State, the gain being 272,678, or 37.26 per cent.

City and Town Population Contrasted.

Since 1885, nine towns have been incorporated as cities, including the town of North Adams, which has been under city government since January, 1896, the act authorizing the change having been passed before the taking of the Census, although the town had not at that time actually become a city. It is, however, included in the following table, which shows the population of the cities incorporated since 1885, with comparisons for the years 1885 and 1895:

CITIES.	1885	1895
Beverly, ...	9,186	11,806
Chicopee, ...	11,516	16,420
Everett, ...	5,825	18,573
Marlborough, ...	10,941	14,977
Medford, ...	9,042	14,474
North Adams, ...	12,540	19,135
Pittsfield, ...	14,466	20,461
Quincy, ...	12,145	20,712
Woburn, ...	11,750	14,178
Totals, ...	97,411	150,736

It will be seen from the foregoing table that these places had a population of 97,411 in 1885, and 150,736 in 1895, the rate of increase being 54.74 per cent. The Commonwealth now has 32 cities, including North Adams. The population of these cities, with the numerical gain and percentage of increase since 1885, is shown in the following table, the names of cities which have been incorporated since 1885 being printed in italics:

CITIES.	POPULATION		INCREASE	
	1885	1895	Number	Percentages
Beverly, ...	9,186	11,806	2,620	28.52
Boston, ...	390,393	496,920	106,527	27.29
Brockton, ...	26,783	33,165	12,382	59.58
Cambridge, ...	59,658	81,643	21,985	36.85
Chelsea, ...	25,709	31,264	5,555	21.61
Chicopee, ...	11,516	16,420	4,904	42.58
Everett, ...	5,825	18,573	12,748	218.85
Fall River, ...	56,870	89,203	32,333	56.85
Fitchburg, ...	15,375	26,409	11,034	71.77
Gloucester, ...	21,703	28,211	6,508	29.99
Haverhill, ...	21,795	30,209	8,414	38.61
Holyoke, ...	27,895	40,322	12,427	44.55
Lawrence, ...	38,862	52,164	13,302	34.23
Lowell, ...	64,107	84,367	20,260	31.60
Lynn, ...	45,867	62,354	16,487	35.95

CITIES.	POPULATION		INCREASE	
	1885	1895	Number	Percentages
Malden, ...	16,407	29,708	13,301	81.07
Marlborough, ...	10,941	14,977	4,036	36.89
Medford, ...	9,042	14,474	5,432	60.08
New Bedford, ...	33,393	55,251	21,858	65.46
Newburyport, ...	13,716	14,552	836	6.10
Newton, ...	19,759	27,590	7,831	39.63
North Adams, ...	12,540	19,135	6,595	52.59
Northampton, ...	12,896	16,746	3,850	29.85
Pittsfield, ...	14,466	20,461	5,995	41.44
Quincy, ...	12,145	20,712	8,567	70.54
Salem, ...	28,090	34,473	6,383	22.72
Somerville, ...	29,971	52,200	22,229	74.17
Springfield, ...	37,575	51,522	13,947	37.12
Taunton, ...	23,674	27,115	3,441	14.53
Waltham, ...	14,609	20,876	6,267	42.90
Woburn, ...	11,750	14,178	2,428	20.66
Worcester, ...	68,389	98,767	30,378	44.42
TOTALS, ...	1,184,907	1,635,767	450,860	38.05

From this table we note that the population under city government is now 1,635,767, or 65.43 per cent of the total population. Upon the same territory in 1885 there was a population of 1,184,907, or 61.01 per cent of the total population, the numerical increase being 450,860, or 38.05 per cent. The towns outside the territorial limits of these cities contained in 1885 a population of 757,234, or 38.99 per cent of the total population, which has risen to 864,416, or 34.57 per cent of the total population, a gain of but 14.15 per cent. That is to say, upon the territory now under city government there has been a gain of 38.05 per cent in ten years, while the gain in the towns outside these municipal limits has been but 14.15 per cent in the same time. Marked differences in the rate of growth during the decade appear in the different municipalities. The city which has made the largest percentage of growth is Everett, incorporated as a city in 1892, and showing an increase of 218.85 per cent. This rate is, of course, entirely unusual, and due to the rapid development of a residence section within easy distance of the city of Boston. The rate of increase in Boston itself is 27.29 per cent, but this has been secured without annexation. The cities of Malden, Medford, Somerville, and Quincy also show great gains, due to the development of suburban residential sections, the percentages of increase being respectively, 81.07, 60.08, 74.17, and 70.54. The city which, remote from the vicinity of Boston, shows the largest percentage of growth during the decade is Fitchburg, in Worcester County, this percentage being 71.77. Other cities which show an increase greater than 50 per cent are Brockton, 59.58; Fall River, 56.85; New Bedford, 65.46; and North Adams, 52.59. It will be noted that the percentage rate of increase in the municipalities now under city government since 1885 is 38.05, while the percentage rate of increase in the State at large has been but 28.73.

Population Rank of Cities and Towns.

The following table exhibits the ranking, upon the basis of population, of all the cities and towns in the Commonwealth, the names of cities being printed in small capitals:

Cities and Towns.	Counties	Population	Rank in 1885	Rank in 1895
Boston,	Suffolk,	496,920	1	1
Worcester,	Worcester,	98,767	2	2
Fall River,	Bristol,	89,203	5	3
Lowell,	Middlesex,	84,367	3	4
Cambridge,	Middlesex,	81,643	4	5
Lynn,	Essex,	62,354	6	6
New Bedford,	Bristol,	55,251	9	7
Somerville,	Middlesex,	52,200	10	8
Lawrence,	Essex,	52,164	7	9
Springfield,	Hampden,	51,522	8	10
Holyoke,	Hampden,	40,322	12	11
Salem,	Essex,	34,473	11	12
Brockton,	Plymouth,	33,165	17	13
Chelsea,	Suffolk,	31,264	13	14
Haverhill,	Essex,	30,209	15	15
Malden,	Middlesex,	29,708	19	16
Gloucester,	Essex,	28,211	16	17
Newton,	Middlesex,	27,590	18	18
Taunton,	Bristol,	27,115	14	19
Fitchburg,	Worcester,	26,409	20	20
Waltham,	Middlesex,	20,876	21	21
Quincy,	Norfolk,	20,712	27	22
Pittsfield,	Berkshire,	20,461	22	23
North Adams,	Berkshire,	19,135	26	24
Everett,	Middlesex,	18,573	56	25
Northampton,	Hampshire,	16,746	25	26
Chicopee,	Hampden,	16,420	29	27
Brookline,	Norfolk,	16,164	34	28
Marlborough,	Middlesex,	14,977	30	29
Newburyport,	Essex,	14,552	23	30
Medford,	Middlesex,	14,474	36	31
Woburn,	Middlesex,	14,178	28	32
Melrose,	Middlesex,	11,965	52	33
Hyde Park,	Norfolk,	11,826	40	34
Beverly,	Essex,	11,806	35	35
Clinton,	Worcester,	11,397	38	36
Weymouth,	Norfolk,	11,291	31	37
Westfield,	Hampden,	10,663	37	38
Peabody,	Essex,	10,507	32	39
Amesbury,	Essex,	9,986	76	40
Framingham,	Middlesex,	9,512	42	41
Leominster,	Worcester,	9,211	61	42
Gardner,	Worcester,	9,182	45	43
Milford,	Worcester,	8,959	33	44
Natick,	Middlesex,	8,814	39	45
Wakefield,	Middlesex,	8,304	53	46
Attleborough,	Bristol,	8,288	24	47
Southbridge,	Worcester,	8,250	49	48
Danvers,	Essex,	8,181	47	49
Plymouth,	Plymouth,	7,957	46	50
Adams,	Berkshire,	7,837	41	51

Cities and Towns.	Counties	Population	Rank in 1885	Rank in 1895
Webster,	Worcester,	7,799	51	52
Watertown,	Middlesex,	7,788	50	53
Marblehead,	Essex,	7,671	44	54
Ware,	Hampshire,	7,651	54	55
Spencer,	Worcester,	7,614	43	56
Revere,	Suffolk,	7,423	103	57
Athol,	Worcester,	7,364	68	58
Dedham,	Norfolk,	7,211	48	59
Palmer,	Hampden,	6,858	55	60
Middleborough,	Plymouth,	6,689	63	61
North Attleborough,	Bristol,	6,576	–	62
Arlington,	Middlesex,	6,515	69	63
Stoneham,	Middlesex,	6,284	58	64
Greenfield,	Franklin,	6,229	65	65
Winchester,	Middlesex,	6,150	77	66
Andover,	Essex,	6,145	57	67
West Springfield,	Hampden,	6,125	75	68
Montague,	Franklin,	6,058	59	69
Blackstone,	Worcester,	6,029	60	70
Whitman,	Plymouth,	5,744	104	71
Methuen,	Essex,	5,690	71	72
Rockland,	Plymouth,	5,523	67	73
Milton,	Norfolk,	5,518	105	74
Orange,	Franklin,	5,361	102	75
Braintree,	Norfolk,	5,311	86	76
Hudson,	Middlesex,	5,308	89	77
Rockport,	Essex,	5,289	94	78
Northbridge,	Worcester,	5,284	98	79
Stoughton,	Norfolk,	5,272	62	80
Westborough,	Worcester,	5,255	64	81
Millbury,	Worcester,	5,222	70	82
Concord,	Middlesex,	5,175	100	83
Franklin,	Norfolk,	5,136	88	84
Grafton,	Worcester,	5,101	72	85
Williamstown,	Berkshire,	4,887	99	86
Hingham,	Plymouth,	4,819	79	87
Great Barrington,	Berkshire,	4,794	74	88
Easthampton,	Hampshire,	4,790	80	89
Amherst,	Hampshire,	4,785	84	90
Bradford,	Essex,	4,736	112	91
Ipswich,	Essex,	4,720	82	92
Reading,	Middlesex,	4,717	106	93
Bridgewater,	Plymouth,	4,686	96	94
Canton,	Norfolk,	4,636	78	95
North Brookfield,	Worcester,	4,635	83	96
Norwood,	Norfolk,	4,574	123	97
Provincetown,	Barnstable,	4,555	73	98
Saugus,	Essex,	4,497	125	99
Winchendon,	Worcester,	4,490	95	100
Easton,	Bristol,	4,452	92	101
South Hadley,	Hampshire,	4,443	91	102

CITIES AND TOWNS.	Counties	Population	Rank in 1885	Rank in 1895
Warren, ...	Worcester, . . .	4,430	87	103
Wellesley, ...	Norfolk, ...	4,229	116	104
Abington, ...	Plymouth, . . .	4,207	101	105
Winthrop, ...	Suffolk, ...	4,192	218	106
Lee, ...	Berkshire, . . .	4,066	81	107
Barnstable, ...	Barnstable, . . .	4,055	85	108
Monson, ...	Hampden, . . .	3,746	90	109
Mansfield, ...	Bristol, . . .	3,722	118	110
Randolph, ...	Norfolk, ...	3,694	97	111
North Andover, ...	Essex, ...	3,569	108	112
Uxbridge, ...	Worcester, . . .	3,546	117	113
Needham, ...	Norfolk, ...	3,511	138	114
Lexington, ...	Middlesex, . . .	3,498	131	115
Sutton, ...	Worcester, . . .	3,420	113	116
Tewksbury, ...	Middlesex, . . .	3,379	149	117
Wareham, ...	Plymouth, . . .	3,367	109	118
Fairhaven, ...	Bristol, . . .	3,338	124	119
Pepperell, ...	Middlesex, . . .	3,321	137	120
Brookfield, ...	Worcester, . . .	3,279	115	121
Swampscott, ...	Essex, ...	3,259	142	122
Leicester, ...	Worcester, . . .	3,239	122	123
Foxborough, ...	Norfolk, ...	3,219	126	124
Dalton, ...	Berkshire, . . .	3,210	163	125
Dudley, ...	Worcester, . . .	3,203	130	126
Chelmsford, ...	Middlesex, . . .	3,162	151	127
Dartmouth, ...	Bristol, . . .	3,107	107	128
Maynard, ...	Middlesex, . . .	3,090	134	129
Nantucket, ...	Nantucket, . . .	3,016	111	130
Deerfield, ...	Franklin, . . .	3,007	114	131
Walpole, ...	Norfolk, ...	2,994	143	132
Hopkinton, ...	Middlesex, . . .	2,984	93	133
West Boylston, ...	Worcester, . . .	2,968	119	134
Templeton, ...	Worcester, . . .	2,915	136	135
Medway, ...	Norfolk, ...	2,913	129	136
East Bridgewater, . . .	Plymouth, . . .	2,894	127	137
Lenox, ...	Berkshire, . . .	2,872	160	138
Belmont, ...	Middlesex, . . .	2,843	200	139
Holliston, ...	Middlesex, . . .	2,718	120	140
Westport, ...	Bristol, . . .	2,678	133	141
Falmouth, ...	Barnstable, . . .	2,655	139	142
Hardwick, ...	Worcester, . . .	2,655	110	143
Holden, ...	Worcester, . . .	2,602	141	144
Wrentham, ...	Norfolk, ...	2,584	132	145
Billerica, ...	Middlesex, . . .	2,577	159	146
Ludlow, ...	Hampden, . . .	2,562	197	147
Dennis, ...	Barnstable, . . .	2,545	121	148
Harwich, ...	Barnstable, . . .	2,532	128	149
Cohasset, ...	Norfolk, ...	2,474	155	150
Dracut, ...	Middlesex, . . .	2,443	175	151
Westford, ...	Middlesex, . . .	2,418	157	152
Agawam, ...	Hampden, . . .	2,408	145	153

Cities and Towns.	Counties	Population	Rank in 1885	Rank in 1895
Oxford,	Worcester,	2,390	146	154
Groveland,	Essex,	2,333	153	155
Merrimac,	Essex,	2,301	144	156
Holbrook,	Norfolk,	2,298	148	157
Barre,	Worcester,	2,278	165	158
Scituate,	Plymouth,	2,246	147	159
Southborough,	Worcester,	2,223	164	160
Groton,	Middlesex,	2,192	171	161
Lancaster,	Worcester,	2,180	167	162
Belchertown,	Hampshire,	2,161	150	163
Upton,	Worcester,	2,150	154	164
Ashburnham,	Worcester,	2,148	166	165
Ayer,	Middlesex,	2,101	158	166
Ashland,	Middlesex,	2,090	135	167
Stockbridge,	Berkshire,	2,077	162	168
Hanover,	Plymouth,	2,051	173	169
Georgetown,	Essex,	2,050	152	170
Douglas,	Worcester,	2,026	156	171
Wayland,	Middlesex,	2,026	174	172
Somerset,	Bristol,	1,983	140	173
Acton,	Middlesex,	1,978	183	174
Duxbury,	Plymouth,	1,966	176	175
Williamsburg,	Hampshire,	1,955	168	176
Northborough,	Worcester,	1,940	179	177
Sturbridge,	Worcester,	1,910	172	178
Sheffield,	Berkshire,	1,897	169	179
Charlton,	Worcester,	1,877	181	180
Manchester,	Essex,	1,876	201	181
Medfield,	Norfolk,	1,872	204	182
Northfield,	Franklin,	1,851	192	183
Rehoboth,	Bristol,	1,810	182	184
Chatham,	Barnstable,	1,809	170	185
Dighton,	Bristol,	1,797	184	186
Townsend,	Middlesex,	1,780	180	187
Marshfield,	Plymouth,	1,760	198	188
West Bridgewater,	Plymouth,	1,747	191	189
Kingston,	Plymouth,	1,746	208	190
Wilbraham,	Hampden,	1,740	188	191
Sharon,	Norfolk,	1,717	222	192
Weston,	Middlesex,	1,710	215	193
Hadley,	Hampshire,	1,704	186	194
Yarmouth,	Barnstable,	1,655	178	195
Hinsdale,	Berkshire,	1,650	196	196
West Newbury,	Essex,	1,643	177	197
Swansea,	Bristol,	1,627	216	198
Avon,	Norfolk,	1,626	–	199
Norton,	Bristol,	1,614	190	200
Colrain,	Franklin,	1,610	203	201
Auburn,	Worcester,	1,598	227	202
East Longmeadow,	Hampden,	1,591	–	203
Essex,	Essex,	1,587	189	204

Cities and Towns.	Counties	Population	Rank in 1885	Rank in 1895
Bourne,	Barnstable,	1,580	220	205
Sandwich,	Barnstable,	1,580	161	206
Shelburne,	Franklin,	1,560	202	207
Buckland,	Franklin,	1,548	185	208
Norwell,	Plymouth,	1,540	206	209
Shrewsbury,	Worcester,	1,524	213	210
Raynham,	Bristol,	1,518	211	211
Newbury,	Essex,	1,489	205	212
Bellingham,	Norfolk,	1,481	233	213
West Brookfield,	Worcester,	1,467	187	214
Seekonk,	Bristol,	1,465	226	215
Huntington,	Hampshire,	1,450	228	216
Sherborn,	Middlesex,	1,446	217	217
Chester,	Hampden,	1,429	223	218
Wilmington,	Middlesex,	1,420	255	219
Freetown,	Bristol,	1,405	212	220
Shirley,	Middlesex,	1,399	229	221
Hanson,	Plymouth,	1,380	230	222
Hopedale,	Worcester,	1,377	-	223
Hamilton,	Essex,	1,356	282	224
Westminster,	Worcester,	1,315	209	225
Conway,	Franklin,	1,304	207	226
Salisbury,	Essex,	1,300	66	227
New Marlborough,	Berkshire,	1,288	195	228
Hubbardston,	Worcester,	1,274	225	229
Rowley,	Essex,	1,272	236	230
Hatfield,	Hampshire,	1,262	219	231
West Stockbridge,	Berkshire,	1,257	199	232
Lunenburg,	Worcester,	1,237	246	233
Pembroke,	Plymouth,	1,223	224	234
Sterling,	Worcester,	1,218	221	235
Orleans,	Barnstable,	1,198	237	236
Cheshire,	Berkshire,	1,176	214	237
Bedford,	Middlesex,	1,169	268	238
Harvard,	Worcester,	1,162	235	239
Sudbury,	Middlesex,	1,141	239	240
Littleton,	Middlesex,	1,136	247	241
Edgartown,	Dukes,	1,125	238	242
Acushnet,	Bristol,	1,115	245	243
Lincoln,	Middlesex,	1,111	270	244
Gill,	Franklin,	1,082	279	245
Southampton,	Hampshire,	1,054	250	246
Hull,	Plymouth,	1,044	331	247
Charlemont,	Franklin,	1,041	262	248
Cottage City,	Dukes,	1,038	295	249
Topsfield,	Essex,	1,033	241	250
Mattapoisett,	Plymouth,	1,032	231	251
Rochester,	Plymouth,	1,021	251	252
Carver,	Plymouth,	1,016	244	253
Ashfield,	Franklin,	1,013	243	254
Clarksburg,	Berkshire,	1,009	206	255

Cities and Towns.	Counties	Population	Rank in 1885	Rank in 1895
Millis,	Norfolk,	1,006	302	256
Granville,	Hampden,	1,005	234	257
Tisbury,	Dukes,	1,002	210	258
Enfield,	Hampshire,	990	253	259
Rutland,	Worcester,	978	261	260
Wellfleet,	Barnstable,	968	193	261
Erving,	Franklin,	964	275	262
Brimfield,	Hampden,	962	242	263
Southwick,	Hampden,	961	256	264
Berkley,	Bristol,	955	265	265
Petersham,	Worcester,	952	249	266
Princeton,	Worcester,	952	248	267
Stow,	Middlesex,	920	258	268
Brewster,	Barnstable,	901	267	269
Berlin,	Worcester,	897	271	270
Royalston,	Worcester,	890	240	271
Mendon,	Worcester,	889	264	272
Becket,	Berkshire,	888	266	273
Wenham,	Essex,	886	277	274
Norfolk,	Norfolk,	882	288	275
Lakeville,	Plymouth,	870	257	276
New Salem,	Franklin,	869	286	277
Nahant,	Essex,	865	307	278
Blandford,	Hampden,	849	263	279
Lanesborough,	Berkshire,	848	232	280
Russell,	Hampden,	846	283	281
Middleton,	Essex,	838	272	282
Egremont,	Berkshire,	836	287	283
North Reading,	Middlesex,	835	273	284
Lynnfield,	Essex,	818	291	285
Truro,	Barnstable,	815	259	286
Ashby,	Middlesex,	804	276	287
Sandisfield,	Berkshire,	802	252	288
Bolton,	Worcester,	797	274	289
Wales,	Hampden,	783	281	290
Bernardston,	Franklin,	778	269	291
Marion,	Plymouth,	759	260	292
Whately,	Franklin,	755	254	293
Cummington,	Hampshire,	750	289	294
Granby,	Hampshire,	748	294	295
Leverett,	Franklin,	744	290	296
Hampden,	Hampden,	743	278	297
Boylston,	Worcester,	729	285	298
Boxford,	Essex,	727	284	299
Dana,	Worcester,	717	300	300
Richmond,	Berkshire,	701	280	301
Sunderland,	Franklin,	696	298	302
Dover,	Norfolk,	668	303	303
Worthington,	Hampshire,	648	292	304
Tyngsborough,	Middlesex,	635	310	305
Longmeadow,	Hampden,	620	194	306

Cities and Towns.	Counties	Population	Rank in 1885	Rank in 1895
Oakham,	Worcester,	605	293	307
Warwick,	Franklin,	599	304	308
Chesterfield,	Hampshire,	589	299	309
Burlington,	Middlesex,	574	309	310
Windsor,	Berkshire,	556	305	311
Plympton,	Plymouth,	549	311	312
New Braintree,	Worcester,	542	316	313
Wendell,	Franklin,	529	325	314
Otis,	Berkshire,	518	297	315
Hancock,	Berkshire,	511	308	316
Savoy,	Berkshire,	504	301	317
Rowe,	Franklin,	498	312	318
Halifax,	Plymouth,	497	321	319
Carlisle,	Middlesex,	492	323	320
Pelham,	Hampshire,	486	317	321
Greenwich,	Hampshire,	481	320	322
Eastham,	Barnstable,	476	306	323
Heath,	Franklin,	476	314	324
Westhampton,	Hampshire,	476	319	325
Hawley,	Franklin,	468	318	326
Monterey,	Berkshire,	464	313	327
Phillipston,	Worcester,	460	322	328
West Tisbury,	Dukes,	460	–	329
Plainfield,	Hampshire,	450	330	330
Shutesbury,	Franklin,	444	327	331
Paxton,	Worcester,	426	315	332
Florida,	Berkshire,	425	326	333
Washington,	Berkshire,	423	328	334
Prescott,	Hampshire,	401	332	335
Dunstable,	Middlesex,	400	334	336
Middlefield,	Hampshire,	386	324	337
Leyden,	Franklin,	363	333	338
Tyringham,	Berkshire,	363	329	339
Mashpee,	Barnstable,	330	341	340
Tolland,	Hampden,	309	335	341
Boxborough,	Middlesex,	307	338	342
Peru,	Berkshire,	305	337	343
Chilmark,	Dukes,	304	336	344
Goshen,	Hampshire,	304	340	345
Monroe,	Franklin,	298	345	346
Alford,	Berkshire,	280	339	347
Montgomery,	Hampden,	275	342	348
Holland,	Hampden,	199	343	349
Gay Head,	Dukes,	169	344	350
Gosnold,	Dukes,	140	348	351
Mount Washington,	Berkshire,	136	347	352
New Ashford,	Berkshire,	116	346	353

An inspection of the foregoing table shows that 27 of the cities rank in numerical order, the city of Boston standing first, and the city of Chicopee ranking 27. The town of Brookline, containing a population of 16,164, ranks next to the city of Chicopee, and stands 28 in the table. After Brookline, rank in regular order the cities of Marlborough, Newburyport, Medford, and Woburn. Woburn is followed by the towns of Melrose and Hyde Park, ranking respectively 33 and 34, and the city of Beverly ranking 35. The population of Beverly, as determined by the Census, was 11,806, just within the limit required for incorporation as a city. It should be said, however, that Beverly, being a shore town, has an increase of population during the summer months, and, prior to its incorporation as a city, the results of a special census, taken during the summer, showed that it had a sufficient population. The Decennial Census was taken earlier in the year however, and at a time when a depression in the boot and shoe industry undoubtedly affected results.

The smallest town in the State is New Ashford, in Berkshire County, its population being but 116, and its rank among the cities and towns, 353. Gosnold, in Dukes County, ranked as the smallest town in 1885, its population at that time being 122; the town has made a gain of 18 persons in 10 years and thereby changed its rank.

The following table is a summary showing the number of cities and towns within certain ranges of population, the total population and average population for each range, and percentages for each range of the whole number of towns, and of the total population :

RANGE OF POPULATION.	Number of Cities and Towns	Total Population	Average Population	PERCENTAGES —	
				Of Towns	Of Population
Boston, ...	1	496,920	496,920	0.28	19.88
90,000 to 100,000, ...	1	98,767	98,767	0.28	3.95
80,000 to 90,000, ...	3	255,213	85,071	0.85	10.21
60,000 to 70,000, ...	1	62,354	62,354	0.28	2.49
50,000 to 60,000, ...	4	211,137	52,784	1.13	8.45
40,000 to 50,000, ...	1	40,322	40,322	0.28	1.61
30,000 to 40,000, ...	4	129,111	32,278	1.13	5.17
20,000 to 30,000, ...	8	201,082	25,135	2.27	8.04
15,000 to 20,000, ...	5	87,068	17,408	1.42	3.48
10,000 to 15,000, ...	11	137,736	12,521	3.12	5.51
5,000 to 10,000, ...	46	314,841	6,844	13.03	12.59
3,000 to 5,000, ...	46	181,297	3,941	13.03	7.25
2,500 to 3,000, ...	18	49,491	2,750	5.10	1.98
2,000 to 2,500, ...	23	51,064	2,220	6.52	2.04
1,500 to 2,000, ...	39	67,476	1,730	11.05	2.70
1,000 to 1,500, ...	47	57,243	1,218	13.32	2.29
500 to 1,000, ...	59	45,804	776	16.71	1.83
Under 500.	36	13,287	369	10.20	0.53
TOTALS, ...	353	2,500,183	7,083	100.00	100.00

The city of Boston, containing a population of 496,920, stands alone in its class, and contains 19.88 per cent of the total population of the State. Outside of the city of Boston there is no city containing more than 100,000 persons. In the class ranging from 90,000 to 100,000 is found the city of Worcester, containing 3.95 per cent of the total population of the State. In the class ranging from 80,000 to 90,000 are found three cities, the total population therein contained being 10.21 per cent of the total population of the State. There are no cities in which the population ranges from 70,000 to 80,000. In the class ranging from 60,000 to 70,000 there is one city, its population being 2.49 per cent of the entire population of the State. There are four cities in which the population ranges from 50,000 to 60,000 ; one in the class ranging from 40,000 to 50,000 ; four, ranging from 30,000 to 40,000 ; eight, ranging from 20,000 to 30,000 ; and five cities and towns in which the population ranges from 15,000 to 20,000. In the class ranging from 10,000 to 15,000 are found 11 cities and towns. The classes to which we have so far referred, namely, those ranging from 10,000 to 100,000, together with the city of Boston, represent 11.04 per cent of the total number of cities and towns in the Commonwealth, and contain 68.79 per cent of the entire population At the other end of the scale, there are found 36 towns having a population under 500; 59 ranging from 500 to 1,000; 47, from 1,000 to 1,500; 39, from 1,500 to 2,000; 23, from 2,000 to 2,500; 18, from 2,500 to 3,000; 46, from 3,000 to 5,000; and 46, from 5,000 to 10,000. These towns taken together constitute 88.96 per cent of the total number of the cities and towns, while they contain 31.21 per cent of the entire population of the State.

The total number of cities and towns January 1, 1896, was 353, of which, as we have said, 32 were cities and 321 were towns. In 1885 there were 23 cities and 325 towns, making a total of 348 cities and towns. The newly incorporated cities have been mentioned. The new towns since 1885 are North Attleborough, in Bristol County, set off from Attleborough, June 14, 1887; West Tisbury, in Dukes County, set off from the town of Tisbury, April 28, 1892; East Longmeadow, in Hampden County, set off from the town of Longmeadow, July 1, 1894; Avon, in Norfolk County, which was set off from the town of Stoughton, February 21, 1888, and afterwards received additional territory from the towns of Holbrook and Randolph; and Hopedale, in Worcester County, which was set off from the town of Milford, April 7, 1886. In a subsequent presentation we shall give full information as to the dates of incorporation, changes in name and boundaries, population, etc., of the counties, cities, and towns.

Estimated Population to 1905.

To enable calculations of population to be readily made for years between the census periods, the following table is inserted, containing an estimate for all years between 1895 and 1905. The figures contained in this table are estimated upon a purely mathematical basis, except for the year 1895, which is, of course, the census year.

Years.	Population	Years.	Population
1895,	2,500,183	1901,	2,962,812
1896,	2,571,938	1902,	3,047,845
1897,	2,645,753	1903,	3,135,318
1898,	2,721,686	1904,	3,225,302
1899,	2,799,798	1905,	3,317,868
1900,	2,880,152		

Comparisons of Population in Classified Industrial Districts.

Chief among the causes which have led to the increase in population of the State is the growth and prosperity of our manufacturing industries.

In the Decennial Census of 1885 it was found that, exclusive of the city of Boston, there were 100 cities and towns leading in manufacturing, each showing a product exceeding one million dollars in value for the Census year. These 100 cities and towns contained 59.24 per cent of the population of the State, and for the last decade they exhibit an increase of 34.60 per cent, a rate of increase relatively greater than that shown in other municipalities, inasmuch as the growth shown in all other cities and towns taken together, including the city of Boston, is at the rate of 20.20 per cent. As these 100 cities and towns include the suburban cities near Boston it is, of course, true that part of their growth is due to causes other than their prominence in manufacturing, as in fact they share in the prosperity of the metropolis. Broadly considered, however, it remains true that to manufacturing the growth of these 100 municipalities is largely due.

The leading industries of the State include Textiles, Boots and Shoes, Metals and Metallic Goods, Leather, and Paper and Paper Goods. Under these designations about 50 per cent of the total product of the State is found. If, under these industry heads, we classify the cities and towns, placing each in the class representing the principal industry of the city or town, on the basis of persons employed in 1885, and include no municipality in which the product in the specified industry for that year did not reach $300,000 in value, we arrive at certain results which are interesting as showing the growth of the leading industrial cities and towns.

Under the classification "Textiles" we group the following, comparing their population for 1885 and 1895:

CITIES AND TOWNS.	POPULATION		INCREASE (+), OR DECREASE (—), IN 1895 AS COMPARED WITH 1885	
	1885	1895	Number	Percentages
Adams, ...	8,283	7,837	—446	—5.38
Amesbury, ...	4,403	9,986	+5,583	+126.80
Andover, ...	5,711	6,145	+434	+7.60
Billerica, ...	2,161	2,577	+416	+19.25
Chicopee, ...	11,516	16,420	+4,904	+42.58
Clinton, ...	8,945	11,497	+2,552	+28.53
Dracut, ...	1,927	2,443	+516	+26.78
Dedham, ...	6,641	7,211	+570	+8.58
Dudley, ...	2,742	3,203	+461	+16.81
Fall River, ...	56,870	89,203	+32,333	+56.85
Fitchburg, ...	15,375	26,409	+11,034	+71.77
Grafton, ...	4,498	5,101	+603	+13.41
Great Barrington, ...	4,471	4,794	+323	+7.22
Groveland, ...	2,272	2,333	+61	+2.68
Hinsdale, ...	1,656	1,650	—6	—0.36
Holden, ...	2,471	2,602	+131	+5.30
Hyde Park, ...	8,376	11,826	+3,450	+41.19
Ipswich, ...	4,207	4,720	+513	+12.19
Lawrence, ...	38,862	52,164	+13,302	+34.23
Leicester, ...	2,923	3,239	+316	+10.81
Lowell, ...	64,107	84,367	+20,260	+31.60
Ludlow, ...	1,649	2,562	+913	+55.37
Maynard, ...	2,703	3,090	+387	+14.32
Methuen, ...	4,507	5,690	+1,183	+26.25
Millbury, ...	4,555	5,222	+667	+14.64
New Bedford, ...	33,393	55,251	+21,858	+65.46
North Adams, ...	12,540	19,135	+6,595	+52.59
Northbridge, ...	3,786	5,280	+1,494	+39.46
Palmer, ...	5,923	6,858	+935	+15.79
Pittsfield, ...	14,466	20,461	+5,995	+41.44
Saugus, ...	2,855	4,497	+1,642	+57.51
Southbridge, ...	6,500	8,250	+1,750	+26.92
Sutton, ...	3,101	3,420	+319	+10.29
Taunton, ...	23,674	27,115	+3,441	+14.53
Uxbridge, ...	2,948	3,546	+598	+20.28
Walpole, ...	2,443	2,994	+551	+22.55
Ware, ...	6,003	7,651	+1,648	+27.45
Warren, ...	4,032	4,430	+398	+9.87
Watertown, ...	6,238	7,788	+1,550	+24.85
Webster, ...	6,220	7,799	+1,579	+25.39
West Boylston, ...	2,927	2,968	+41	+1.40
Westford, ...	2,193	2,418	+225	+10.26
Totals, ...	411,073	562,152	+151,079	+36.75

The population of these textile cities and towns in 1885 was 411,073. It has now become 562,152, a gain of 36.75 per cent.

The Boot and Shoe cities and towns appear in the following table:

CITIES AND TOWNS.	POPULATION		INCREASE (+) OR DECREASE (—), IN 1895 AS COMPARED WITH 1885	
	1885	1895	Number	Percentages
Abington, ...	3,699	4,207	+508	+13.73
Ashland, ...	2,633	2,090	—543	—20.62
Athol, ...	4,758	7,364	+2,606	+54.77
Beverly, ...	9,186	11,806	+2,620	+28.52
Braintree, ...	4,040	5,311	+1,271	+31.46
Brockton, ...	20,783	33,165	+12,382	+59.58
Brookfield, ...	3,013	3,279	+266	+8.83
Danvers, ...	7,061	8,181	+1,120	+15.86
Essex, ...	1,722	1,587	—135	—7.84
Georgetown, ...	2,299	2,050	—249	—10.83
Haverhill, ...	21,795	30,209	+8,414	+38.61
Holbrook, ...	2,334	2,298	—36	—1.54
Holliston, ...	2,926	2,718	—208	—7.11
Hopkinton, ...	3,922	2,984	—938	—23.92
Hudson, ...	3,968	5,308	+1,340	+33.77
Lynn, ...	45,867	62,354	+16,487	+35.95
Marblehead, ...	7,517	7,671	+154	+2.05
Marlborough, ...	10,941	14,977	+4,036	+36.89
Medway, ...	2,777	2,913	+136	+4.90
Milford, ...	9,343	8,959	—384	—4.11
Natick, ...	8,460	8,814	+354	+4.18
Newburyport, ...	13,716	14,552	+836	+6.10
North Brookfield, ...	4,201	4,635	+434	+10.33
Pepperell, ...	2,587	3,321	+734	+28.37
Randolph, ...	3,807	3,694	—113	—2.97
Rockland, ...	4,785	5,523	+738	+15.42
Rowley, ...	1,183	1,272	+89	+7.52
Salem, ...	28,090	34,473	+6,383	+22.72
Spencer, ...	8,247	7,614	—633	—7.68
Stoneham, ...	5,659	6,284	+625	+11.04
Stoughton, ...	5,173	5,272	+99	+1.91
Westborough, ...	4,880	5,235	+355	+7.27
Weymouth, ...	10,740	11,291	+551	+5.13
Whitman, ...	3,595	5,744	+2,149	+59.78
Totals, ...	275,707	337,155	+61,448	+22.29

The cities and towns grouped in the preceding table contained a population of 275,707 in 1885. This has risen to 337,155, a gain of 22.29 per cent. It will be noticed that while the towns as a whole exhibit growth, nevertheless a decrease appears in certain places. In a subsequent presentation the changes in population due to changes in area or other exceptional causes will be especially pointed out. It is sufficient to note here that some of the decreases appearing in this table may be thus legitimately accounted for, as, for instance, in the town of Milford which lost territory by the incorporation of the town of Hopedale. In other cases a slight depression of the boot and shoe industry at the time the Census of 1895 was taken accounts for the failure to show an increase over the figures for 1885.

The next table presents the cities and towns which lead in the manufacture of metals and metallic goods.

CITIES AND TOWNS.	POPULATION		INCREASE (+), OR DECREASE (—), IN 1895 AS COMPARED WITH 1885	
	1885	1895	Number	Percentages
Attleborough,*	13,175	14,864	+1,689	+12.82
Bridgewater, ...	3,827	4,686	+859	+22.45
Canton, ...	4,380	4,636	+256	+5.84
Mansfield, ...	2,939	3,722	+783	+26.64
Montague, ...	5,629	6,058	+429	+7.62
Somerset, ...	2,475	1,983	—492	—19.88
Wareham, ...	3,254	3,367	+113	+3.47
WORCESTER, ...	68,389	98,767	+30,378	+44.42
TOTALS.	104,068	138,083	+34,015	+32.69

* Including also North Attleborough in 1895.

These towns had a population of 104,068 in 1885 which has risen to 138,083, a gain of 32.69 per cent. Every municipality in the group shows an increase except the town of Somerset which has suffered industrial reverses.

The cities and towns in which the manufacture of leather is the leading industry appear below.

CITIES AND TOWNS.	POPULATION		INCREASE (+), OR DECREASE (—), IN 1895 AS COMPARED WITH 1885	
	1885	1895	Number	Percentages
Peabody, ...	9,530	10,507	+977	+10.25
Winchester, ...	4,390	6,150	+1,760	+40.09
WOBURN, ...	11,750	14,178	+2,428	+20.66
TOTALS, ...	25,670	30,835	+5,165	+20.12

In these cities and towns the population has risen from 25,670 in 1885 to 30,835, a gain of 20.12 per cent. Growth in each municipality has contributed to this result, although the large percentage shown in Winchester is mainly due to the development of the town as a place of residence, the Leather industry at present being an incidental rather than a prominent factor in the prosperity of the town, which is residential rather than industrial.

The concluding table presents the cities and towns devoted largely to the Paper and Paper Goods industry.

CITIES AND TOWNS.	POPULATION		INCREASE (+), OR DECREASE (—), IN 1895 AS COMPARED WITH 1885	
	1885	1895	Number	Percentages
Dalton, ...	2,113	3,210	+1,097	+51.92
HOLYOKE, ...	27,895	40,322	+12,427	+44.55
Lee, ...	4,274	4,066	—208	—4.87
Russell, ...	847	846	—1	—0.12
South Hadley, ...	3,949	4,443	+494	+12.51
West Springfield, ...	4,448	6,125	+1,677	+37.70
TOTALS.	43,526	59,012	+15,486	+35.58

The population of the cities and towns in this group was 43,526 in 1885 The percentage of increase is 35.58, the population now being 59,012, although the growth is seen to be quite unequal when the municipalities are compared with one another.

The several groups are brought together in the following recapitulation:

CLASSIFICATION BY INDUSTRIES.	INCREASE IN **1895** AS COMPARED WITH **1885**		CLASSIFICATION BY INDUSTRIES.	INCREASE IN **1895** AS COMPARED WITH **1885**	
	Number	Percentages		Number	Percentages
Textiles, ...	+151,079	+36.75	Leather, ...	+5,165	+20.12
Boots and shoes, . .	+61,448	+22.29	Paper and paper goods,	+15,489	+35.58
Metals and metallic goods,	+34,015	+32.69			

If we rank the cities and towns by industries according to the percentage of growth in each class, shown in 1895 as compared with 1885, the groups take the following order: Textiles, Paper and Paper Goods, Metals and Metallic Goods, Boots and Shoes, and Leather. It must be remembered that in forming the groups of cities and towns under the foregoing heads, the classification is somewhat arbitrary, and is made, as before stated, upon the basis of the industry which leads for the city and town in the number of persons employed in 1885, the industrial returns for 1895 not being available as yet. Some of the places have diversified industries which of course have contributed to their growth. For example, Holyoke, classed as a paper town, has large textile interests; Taunton, classed under textiles, is largely engaged in metals and metallic goods; Lowell, besides textiles, has extensive manufactories of metals and metallic goods and machinery; Lynn, besides boots and shoes, is connected with the leather industry, and Worcester, classed under metals and metallic goods, has also various other extensive industries. Within the limitations stated, however, the classification is indicative.

Special Presentations for the City of Boston.

Before closing the analytical consideration of the growth in population, we present, for the city of Boston, a table showing the population according to the old ward lines, that is to say, according to the ward lines which had existed since 1875, being superseded by a new division taking effect, so far as the Census was concerned, in May of the census year.

CITY OF BOSTON.	POPULATION		INCREASE (+), OR DECREASE (—), IN **1895** AS COMPARED WITH **1885**	
	1885	1895	Number	Percentages
Boston, ...	390,393	496,920	+106,527	+27.29
Ward 1, ...	15,659	23,821	+8,162	+52.12
Ward 2, ...	15,760	18,774	+3,014	+19.12
Ward 3, ...	12,328	13,943	+1,615	+13.10
Ward 4, ...	12,518	13,375	+857	+6.85
Ward 5, ...	12,827	12,986	+159	+1.24
Ward 6, ...	17,256	18,194	+938	+5.44
Ward 7, ...	12,038	12,965	+927	+7.70
Ward 8, ...	11,986	13,990	+2,004	+16.72
Ward 9, ...	11,239	11,857	+618	+5.50
Ward 10, ...	9,746	5,883	—3,863	—39.64
Ward 11, ...	17,863	25,729	+7,866	+44.04

CITY OF BOSTON.	POPULATION		INCREASE (+), OR DECREASE (—), IN 1895 AS COMPARED WITH 1885	
	1885	1895	Number	Percentages
Boston — Con.				
Ward 12,	13,845	10,748	—3,097	—22.37
Ward 13,	22,547	20,506	—2,041	—9.05
Ward 14,	22,741	27,906	+5,165	+22.71
Ward 15,	16,237	19,501	+3,264	+20.10
Ward 16,	16,459	16,343	—116	—0.70
Ward 17,	14,747	16,715	+1,968	+13.35
Ward 18,	14,140	17,725	+3,585	+25.35
Ward 19,	20,557	22,622	+2,065	—10.05
Ward 20,	20,994	30,261	+9,267	+44.14
Ward 21,	15,627	28,364	+12,737	+81.51
Ward 22,	15,838	26,012	+10,174	—64.24
Ward 23,	17,425	32,761	+15,336	+88.01
Ward 24,	21,500	40,938	+19,438	+90.41
Ward 25,	8,516	15,001	+6,485	+76.15

An inspection of the percentages in the preceding table will enable the reader to trace the growth of different sections of the city since 1885. In a subsequent presentation the growth of the city proper, and the growth of the annexed and outlying sections will be shown, with comparisons from the earliest years.

In order to comply with requests received from persons desiring the figures, the population of Boston has been distributed according to police and missionary districts, the first being arbitrary divisions of the city made for police purposes by the Board of Police Commissioners, and the second administrative districts for missionary work in charge of the City Missionary. As these tabulations may possibly be of wider interest they are inserted below, it being understood, however, that the distribution in each case, although fairly accurate, is approximate, for the reason that boundaries of the wards are seldom coterminous, either wholly or in part, with those of the districts named, and, therefore, in making up the district population, in some instances, arbitrary divisions of the ward figures were necessary. The first presentation exhibits the population by Police Divisions.

POLICE DIVISIONS.	Estimated Population in 1895	POLICE DIVISIONS.	Estimated Population in 1895
Boston,	496,920	Boston — Con.	
Number 1,	22,288	Number 9,	51,798
Number 2,	10,970	Number 10,	44,171
Number 3,	25,070	Number 11,	42,004
Number 4,	12,241	Number 12,	35,828
Number 5,	52,809	Number 13,	36,116
Number 6,	20,555	Number 14,	15,001
Number 7,	39,995	Number 15,	40,304
Number 8,	2,600	Number 16,	36,167

The next presentation shows the population by Missionary Districts, and in this case it is possible to give the population within the same territorial divisions in 1885.

MISSIONARY DISTRICTS.	Estimated Population in 1885	Estimated Population in 1895
Boston,	390,393	496,920
Number 1,	15,659	23,821
Number 2,	15,760	18,774
Number 3,	23,275	24,676
Number 4,	34,117	36,252
Number 5,	26,947	20,880
Number 6,	9,931	17,609
Number 7,	11,391	15,079
Number 8,	15,603	16,530
Number 9,	8,788	10,132
Number 10,	11,660	15,540
Number 11,	13,215	13,630
Number 12,	30,665	29,800
Number 13,	30,860	37,657
Number 14,	12,379	19,509
Number 15,	25,426	38,240
Number 16,	19,603	29,787
Number 17,	17,425	32,761
Number 18,	21,500	40,938
Number 19,	37,673	40,304
Number 20,	8,516	15,001

Comparisons of the Male and Female Population.

The presentation, pages 25 to 32, shows the number of males and females, together with the total population, and the percentages of males and females of the whole population, for each county, city, ward, and town, and for the State. This is followed by the presentation, pages 33 to 42, which shows the increase and decrease of the population by sex, for each municipality, by counties, and for the State. By these presentations we find that in 1895 the males in the State numbered 1,214,701, and the females 1,285,482, these tables indicating that the males represented 48.58 per cent of the entire population, and the females, 51.42, the excess of females representing 2.84 per cent of the entire population.

Analyzing the final presentation, we find that the males in 1885 numbered 932,884, or 48.03 per cent of the whole population, while the females numbered 1,009,257, or 51.97 per cent of the total population, the excess of females representing 3.94 of the whole population. Thus it will be seen that while the females still remain in excess, the proportion which this excess of females represents of the whole population has declined during the decade. The results may be more readily compared by means of the following table, which recapitulates the figures for 1885 and 1895, with percentages:

CENSUS YEARS.	Males	Females	Population	PERCENTAGES Males	PERCENTAGES Females
1895,	1,214,701	1,285,482	2,500,183	48.58	51.42
1885,	932,884	1,009,257	1,942,141	48.03	51.97
INCREASE,	281,817	276,225	558,042	+0.55	—0.55

The final line of the foregoing table shows at once that the numerical increase in males during the decade has been 281,817, the numerical increase in females being 276,225;

and while the percentage which the males constitute of the total population has increased 0.55 per cent, the percentage which the females constitute of the total population exhibits a corresponding decline.

The following table presents a similar comparison for the years 1885 and 1875:

CENSUS YEARS.	Males	Females	Population	PERCENTAGES	
				Males	Females
1885, ...	932,884	1,009,257	1,942,141	48.03	51.97
1875, ...	794,383	857,529	1,651,912	48.09	51.91
INCREASE, ...	138,501	151,728	290,229	—0.06	+0.06

The males in 1875 numbered 794,383, and represented 48.09 per cent of the whole population, the females numbering 857,529, constituting 51.91 per cent of the whole population. Comparing these figures with those for 1885 it will be seen that the excess of females was slightly greater, when considered as a percentage of the total population, in 1885 than in 1875. In 1875, there were 107.95 females to 100 males; in 1885, 108.19 females to 100 males; while in 1895 there are 105.83 females to 100 males. In 1840, the excess of females over males was but 7.672, or 102.13 females to every 100 males; in 1855 there was an excess of females over males of 32.301, or 105.87 females to every 100 males; in 1865 the excess of females was 63.011, or 110.46 females to every 100 males. During the last 55 years, the percentage of females of the whole population was highest in 1865, being 52.48 per cent, and lowest in 1840, or 50.53 per cent.

The following table exhibits the percentages of males and females respectively of the total population in 1885 and 1895, with the increase or decrease in percentages in 1895 as compared with 1885:

THE STATE, AND COUNTIES.	PERCENTAGES OF MALES IN —		Increase (+), or Decrease (—), in Percentages in 1895 as compared with 1885	PERCENTAGES OF FEMALES IN —		Increase (+), or Decrease (—), in Percentages in 1895 as compared with 1885
	1885	1895		1885	1895	
THE STATE.	48.03	48.58	+0.55	51.97	51.42	—0.55
Barnstable, . . .	48.47	48.07	—0.40	51.53	51.93	+0.40
Berkshire, . . .	48.96	49.28	+0.32	51.04	50.72	—0.32
Bristol, ...	47.86	48.21	+0.35	52.14	51.79	—0.35
Dukes, ...	48.51	48.54	+0.03	51.49	51.46	—0.03
Essex, ...	47.78	49.01	+1.23	52.22	50.99	—1.23
Franklin, . . .	50.10	50.55	+0.45	49.90	49.45	—0.45
Hampden, . . .	47.89	48.47	+0.58	52.11	51.53	—0.58
Hampshire, . . .	47.29	47.63	+0.34	52.71	52.37	—0.34
Middlesex, . . .	47.44	47.94	+0.50	52.56	52.06	—0.50
Nantucket, . . .	42.65	43.60	+0.95	57.35	56.40	—0.95
Norfolk, . . .	47.97	48.05	+0.08	52.03	51.95	—0.08
Plymouth, . . .	49.65	49.95	+0.30	50.35	50.05	—0.30
Suffolk, . . .	47.69	48.29	+0.60	52.31	51.71	—0.60
Worcester, . . .	49.01	49.62	+0.61	50.99	50.38	—0.61

In the counties of Barnstable, Bristol, Dukes, Hampden, Hampshire, Middlesex, Nantucket, Norfolk, and Suffolk, the percentages of females of the total population are slightly greater than for the State at large. All of the counties show a decrease in the percentages of females of the total population in 1895 as compared with 1885, except the county of Barnstable, which shows an increase. The increases and decreases are, of course, comparatively slight. Similar comparisons for each of the cities are brought forward in the following table:

CITIES.	PERCENTAGES OF MALES IN —		Increase (+), or Decrease (—), in Percentages in 1895 as compared with 1885	PERCENTAGES OF FEMALES IN —		Increase (+), or Decrease (—), in Percentages in 1895 as compared with 1885
	1885	1895		1885	1895	
Beverly,	47.34	48.52	+1.18	52.66	51.48	—1.18
Boston,	47.69	48.23	+0.54	52.31	51.77	—0.54
Brockton,	50.03	49.93	—0.10	49.97	50.07	+0.10
Cambridge,	47.96	48.79	+0.83	52.04	51.21	—0.83
Chelsea,	47.22	48.85	+1.63	52.78	51.15	—1.63
Chicopee,	46.52	49.30	+2.78	53.48	50.70	—2.78
Everett,	49.46	48.76	—0.70	50.54	51.24	+0.70
Fall River,	47.14	47.87	+0.73	52.86	52.13	—0.73
Fitchburg,	48.79	49.37	+0.58	51.21	50.63	—0.58
Gloucester,	54.02	57.63	+3.61	45.98	42.37	—3.61
Haverhill,	47.97	48.11	+0.14	52.03	51.89	—0.14
Holyoke,	47.38	47.61	+0.23	52.62	52.39	—0.23
Lawrence,	45.56	48.13	+2.57	54.44	51.87	—2.57
Lowell,	44.48	46.14	+1.66	55.52	53.86	—1.66
Lynn,	47.42	48.39	+0.97	52.58	51.61	—0.97
Malden,	46.87	46.87	*—	53.13	53.13	*—
Marlborough,	50.88	49.87	—1.01	49.12	50.13	+1.01
Medford,	48.86	48.66	—0.20	51.14	51.34	+0.20
New Bedford,	46.16	47.34	+1.18	53.84	52.66	—1.18
Newburyport,	44.93	45.46	+0.53	55.07	54.54	—0.53
Newton,	44.24	44.78	+0.54	55.76	55.22	—0.54
North Adams,	48.32	48.86	+0.54	51.68	51.14	—0.54
Northampton,	45.38	44.39	—0.99	54.62	55.61	+0.99
Pittsfield,	47.49	48.08	+0.59	52.51	51.92	—0.59
Quincy,	50.98	51.22	+0.24	49.02	48.78	—0.24
Salem,	45.48	47.20	+1.72	54.52	52.80	—1.72
Somerville,	47.35	47.73	+0.38	52.65	52.27	—0.38
Springfield,	47.58	47.85	+0.27	52.42	52.15	—0.27
Taunton,	48.69	48.49	—0.20	51.31	51.51	+0.20
Waltham,	45.92	46.17	+0.25	54.08	53.83	—0.25
Woburn,	50.23	49.37	—0.86	49.77	50.63	+0.86
Worcester,	49.25	49.47	+0.22	50.75	50.53	—0.22

* The same for both years.

The females constitute more than 50 per cent of the population in each of the cities except Gloucester and Quincy, the highest percentage, 55.61, being found in the city of Northampton, and the lowest in the city of Gloucester, 42.37. In other words, in each of the cities there is an excess of females except in Gloucester, where the males are considerably in excess, this excess being due to the peculiar character of the city as the centre of the fishing industry. In 1885, there were five cities in which males were in excess of females, namely, Brockton, Gloucester, Marlborough, Quincy, and Woburn. The percentage which the females constitute of the whole population has declined in every city except Brockton, Everett, Marlborough, Medford, Northampton, Taunton, and Woburn. The greatest decline is found in the city of Gloucester. In the city of Malden, the percentage of females in 1885 and 1895 is identical. The distribution of the excess of males and the excess of females as regards the relative location in cities and towns is shown in the following table:

THE STATE, AND COUNTIES.	EXCESS OF MALES				EXCESS OF FEMALES				Net Excess of Females
	Number of Cities or Towns	Males	Females	Excess of Males	Number of Cities or Towns	Males	Females	Excess of Females	
THE STATE, . .	165	176,211	160,528	15,683	186	1,037,700	1,124,164	86,464	70,781
(cities), .	2	26,865	22,058	4,807	30	762,566	824,278	61,712	56,905
(towns), .	163	149,346	138,470	10,876	156	275,134	299,886	24,752	13,876
Barnstable (towns),	1	178	152	26	14	13,116	14,208	1,092	1,066
Berkshire (cities), .	-	-	-	-	2	19,188	20,408	1,220	1,220
(towns),*	18	8,990	7,966	1,024	11	13,946	14,992	1,046	22
Bristol (cities), .	-	-	-	-	3	82,009	89,560	7,551	7,551
(towns), .	11	11,541	10,853	688	6	12,032	13,024	992	304
Dukes (towns), .	2	178	131	47	5	1,879	2,050	171	124
Essex (cities), .	1	16,257	11,954	4,303	6	98,429	107,129	8,700	4,397
(towns), .	7	11,566	10,772	794	21	35,661	38,625	2,964	2,170
Franklin (towns),*	21	15,195	14,088	1,107	4	4,709	5,375	666	-441
Hampden (cities), .	-	-	-	-	3	51,914	56,320	4,376	4,376
(towns), .	13	7,029	6,464	565	7	15,160	16,021	861	296
Hampshire (cities),	-	-	-	-	1	7,434	9,312	1,878	1,878
(towns),	16	8,716	8,209	507	6	9,911	11,128	1,217	710
Middlesex (cities),.	-	-	-	-	10	170,364	188,422	18,258	18,258
(towns),	21	17,770	15,528	2,242	23	51,389	55,944	4,555	2,313
Nantucket (towns),	-	-	-	-	1	1,315	1,701	386	386
Norfolk (cities), .	1	10,608	10,104	504	-	-	-	-	-504
(towns), .	6	8,231	7,824	407	20	45,941	52,111	6,170	5,763
Plymouth (cities),.	-	-	-	-	1	16,559	16,606	47	47
(towns),	12	12,678	11,457	1,221	14	21,457	22,741	1,284	63
Suffolk (cities), .	-	-	-	-	2	254,939	273,245	18,306	18,306
(towns), .	1	3,721	3,702	19	1	2,015	2,177	162	143
Worcester (cities),..	-	-	-	-	2	61,900	63,276	1,376	1,376
(towns),	34	43,558	41,324	2,229	23	46,603	49,789	3,186	957

* Two towns (Sandisfield in Berkshire, and Bernardston in Franklin) show no excess, there being an equal number of males and females.

From this table it is seen that for the State, two cities, representing a population of 48,923, or 1.96 per cent of the whole population, show an excess of 4,807 males, while 30 cities, with a population of 1,586,844, or 63.47 per cent of the total population, show an excess of 61,712 females, the net excess of females in the cities as a whole being 56,905. It may be mentioned in passing that the net excess of females in the cities as a whole in 1885 was 56,244. Thus, notwithstanding changes in the cities when considered individually, the net excess of females within municipalities under city government is, numerically, substantially the same as in 1885. On the other hand, 163 towns, having a population of 287,816, or 11.51 per cent of the whole population, show an excess of 10,876 males, while 156 towns, having a total population of 575,020, or 23 per cent of the total population of the State, show an excess of 24,752 females, the net excess of females in the towns taken as a whole being 13,876, as against 20,129, the numerical net excess of females in towns in 1885. In 1895, the cities show 30.65 per cent of the total excess of males, 71.37 per cent of the total excess of females, and 80.40 per cent of the net excess of females; while the towns show 69.35 per cent of the total excess of males, 28.63 per cent of the total excess of females, and 19.60 per cent of the net excess of females. The cities in each of the counties when taken together show an excess of females, except in the county of Norfolk, which contains but one city, namely, Quincy, wherein the males are in excess. When the towns of each of the counties are grouped together, each group exhibits an excess of females, except in Franklin County, wherein the 21 towns when taken together show an excess of males. In the town of Sandisfield, in Berkshire County, and Bernardston, in Franklin County, there is an equal number of males and females.

VILLAGES: BY TOWNS.

VILLAGES: BY TOWNS.

[This presentation shows the number of families, the number of males and females, and the total population of each city and town, and the same facts for the several villages or sections of which each city or town is composed. The population which lies outside of the well defined limits of the villages or sections is included under the name of the city or town itself which is, of necessity, repeated under its own name in order to present the total population for the town. In those cases where the name of the city or town is simply repeated, it means that no villages or sections were reported separately owing to lack of definite boundaries, although such undefined villages or sections are actually located in some cities and towns.]

COUNTIES, CITIES, TOWNS, AND VILLAGES.	Number of Families	Males	Females	Population	COUNTIES, CITIES, TOWNS, AND VILLAGES.	Number of Families	Males	Females	Population
BARNSTABLE.					**BARNSTABLE – Con.**				
Barnstable, . . .	1,173	1,544	2,111	4,055	Falmouth, . . .	722	1,283	1,372	2,655
Barnstable, . .	169	279	321	600	Davisville, . .	22	34	36	70
Centreville, . .	118	168	211	379	East Falmouth, .	59	109	100	209
Cotuit, . . .	137	221	243	464	Falmouth, . . .	211	360	412	772
Hyannis, . .	361	599	638	1,237	Falmouth Heights,	12	26	20	46
Hyannisport, . .	46	91	82	173	Hatchville, . .	30	53	60	113
Marston's Mills, .	68	132	129	261	North Falmouth, .	54	81	102	183
Osterville, . .	125	208	220	428	Quissett, . . .	21	41	42	83
Santuit, . . .	28	55	57	112	Teaticket, . .	43	77	76	153
South Hyannis, .	20	26	30	56	Waquoit, . . .	62	105	108	213
West Barnstable, .	101	165	180	345	West Falmouth, .	94	163	166	329
Bourne, . . .	429	772	808	1,580	Wood's Holl, . .	114	234	250	484
Bourne, . . .	124	232	222	454	Harwich, . . .	783	1,253	1,279	2,532
Bournedale, . .	29	46	50	96	East Harwich, .	73	134	126	260
Buzzard's Bay, .	61	123	128	251	Harwich, . . .	189	323	325	648
Cataumet, . .	49	85	82	167	Harwichport, . .	189	236	266	502
Monument Beach, .	40	71	77	148	North Harwich, .	65	99	96	195
Pocasset, . . .	61	93	104	197	Pleasant Lake, .	75	151	144	295
Sagamore, . .	65	122	145	267	South Harwich, .	72	97	107	204
Brewster, . . .	255	437	464	901	West Harwich, .	132	213	215	428
Brewster, . . .	113	156	207	363	Mashpee, . . .	81	178	152	330
East Brewster, .	47	98	81	179	Mashpee, . . .	68	151	132	283
South Brewster, .	34	51	55	106	South Mashpee, .	13	27	20	47
West Brewster, .	61	132	121	253	Orleans, . . .	375	559	639	1,198
Chatham, . . .	543	898	911	1,809	East Orleans, .	102	137	175	312
Chatham, . . .	332	556	544	1,100	Orleans, . . .	219	350	382	732
Chathamport, .	38	57	67	124	South Orleans, .	54	72	82	154
North Chatham, .	43	63	74	137	Provincetown, .	1,216	2,215	2,340	4,555
South Chatham, .	86	145	152	297	Provincetown, .	1,216	2,215	2,340	4,555
West Chatham, .	44	77	74	151	Sandwich, . . .	442	734	846	1,580
Dennis, . . .	817	1,164	1,381	2,545	East Sandwich, .	42	66	73	139
Dennis, . . .	113	171	188	359	Forestdale, . .	19	27	29	56
Dennisport, . .	257	353	425	778	Sandwich, . .	301	518	571	1,089
East Dennis, .	103	147	191	338	South Sandwich, .	26	42	52	94
South Dennis, .	132	203	234	437	Spring Hill, . .	54	81	121	202
West Dennis, .	210	290	343	633	Truro, ...	229	402	413	815
Eastham, . . .	137	234	242	476	North Truro, .	70	101	116	217
Eastham, . . .	107	181	189	370	South Truro, .	35	57	56	113
North Eastham, .	30	53	53	106	Truro, ...	124	244	241	485

CENSUS OF MASSACHUSETTS — 1895.

VILLAGES: BY TOWNS — Continued.

Counties, Cities, Towns, and Villages.	Number of Families.	Males.	Females.	Population.
BARNSTABLE - Con.				
Wellfleet,	332	449	519	968
South Wellfleet,	47	59	62	121
Wellfleet,	285	390	457	847
Yarmouth,	535	772	883	1,655
South Yarmouth,	223	306	329	635
West Yarmouth,	80	133	131	264
Yarmouth,	107	151	194	345
Yarmouthport,	125	182	229	411
BERKSHIRE.				
Adams,	1,604	3,712	4,125	7,837
Adams,	1,431	2,589	2,881	5,470
Maple Grove,	107	235	264	499
Renfrew,	277	682	779	1,461
Zylonite,	89	206	201	407
Alford,	76	152	128	280
Alford,	76	152	128	280
Becket,	219	483	405	888
Becket,	184	389	347	736
Becket Centre,	13	33	21	54
West Becket,	22	61	37	98
Cheshire,	297	599	577	1,176
Cheshire,	297	599	577	1,176
Clarksburg,	214	502	507	1,009
Briggsville,	40	111	119	230
Clarksburg,	174	391	388	779
Dalton,	688	1,506	1,704	3,210
Dalton,	688	1,506	1,704	3,210
Egremont,	211	406	430	836
Egremont,	120	252	238	490
North Egremont,	29	40	49	89
South Egremont,	62	114	143	257
Florida,	93	223	202	425
Florida,	68	159	147	306
Hoosac Tunnel,	25	64	55	119
Great Barrington,	1,136	2,332	2,462	4,794
Great Barrington,	857	1,791	1,843	3,634
Housatonic,	247	487	556	1,043
Van Deusenville,	32	54	63	117
Hancock,	117	296	245	541
Hancock,	112	244	215	459
Shaker Settlement,	5	22	30	52
Hinsdale,	346	821	829	1,650
Hinsdale,	346	821	829	1,650
Lanesborough,	210	434	414	848
Berkshire,	66	147	145	292
Lanesborough,	144	287	269	556
Lee,	922	1,963	2,093	4,066
East Lee,	108	187	220	407
Lee,	699	1,551	1,585	3,136
South Lee,	115	235	288	523
Lenox,	581	1,529	1,343	2,872
Lenox,	405	1,039	973	2,012
Lenox Dale,	110	329	236	565
New Lenox,	66	161	134	295
Monterey,	115	241	223	464
Monterey,	115	241	223	464
BERKSHIRE — Con.				
Mount Washington,	31	76	60	136
Mt. Washington,	31	76	60	136
New Ashford,	30	68	48	116
New Ashford,	30	68	48	116
New Marlborough,	325	682	606	1,288
Clayton,	41	98	76	174
Hartsville,	39	75	69	144
Mill River,	120	241	233	474
New Marlborough,	75	164	135	299
Southfield,	50	104	93	197
NORTH ADAMS,	3,361	9,350	9,785	19,135
Blackinton,	81	187	182	369
Greylock,	109	335	317	652
NORTH ADAMS,	3,741	8,828	9,286	18,114
Otis,	136	289	229	518
East Otis,	42	93	71	164
North Otis,	22	43	35	78
Otis,	62	128	107	235
West Otis,	10	25	16	41
Peru,	71	116	159	305
Peru,	71	116	159	305
PITTSFIELD,	4,342	9,838	10,623	20,461
Barkerville,	71	177	155	332
Bel Air,	86	213	220	433
Coltsville,	80	191	202	393
PITTSFIELD,	3,506	8,717	9,560	18,277
Pontoosuc,	159	427	389	816
West Pitt-field,	40	113	97	210
Richmond,	164	354	347	701
Richmond,	121	260	252	512
Richmond Furnace,	43	94	95	189
Sandisfield,	213	401	401	802
Montville,	34	46	65	111
New Boston,	32	56	51	107
Sandisfield,	97	184	185	369
So. Sandisfield,	24	58	46	104
West New Boston,	26	57	54	111
Savoy,	133	256	248	504
Brier,	31	60	58	118
Savoy,	73	132	136	268
Savoy Centre,	29	64	54	118
Sheffield,	481	944	953	1,897
Ashley Falls,	88	135	149	284
Sheffield,	393	809	804	1,613
Stockbridge,	471	996	1,081	2,077
Curtisville,	79	181	164	345
Glendale,	118	261	274	535
Stockbridge,	274	554	643	1,197
Tyringham,	90	186	177	363
Tyringham,	90	186	177	363
Washington,	87	236	187	423
Washington,	87	236	187	423
West Stockbridge,	324	608	649	1,257
State Line,	21	46	45	91
West Stockbridge,	230	415	457	872
West Stockbridge Centre,	34	73	57	130
Williamsville,	39	74	90	164

VILLAGES: BY TOWNS — Continued.

COUNTIES, CITIES, TOWNS, AND VILLAGES.	Number of Families	Males	Females	Population
BERKSHIRE — Con.				
Williamstown, . .	1,017	2,615	2,272	4,887
Blackinton, . .	126	291	280	571
So. Williamstown, .	88	192	179	371
Williamstown, .	569	1,516	1,238	2,754
Williamstown Station, . . .	234	616	575	1,191
Windsor, . . .	135	301	255	556
Windsor, . . .	135	301	255	556
BRISTOL.				
Acushnet, . .	294	568	547	1,115
Acushnet, . .	227	457	415	872
Long Plain, . .	67	111	132	243
Attleborough, . .	1,830	4,029	4,259	8,288
Attleborough, . .	1,433	2,936	3,147	6,083
Dodgeville, . .	131	342	358	700
Hebronville, . .	131	342	323	665
South Attleborough,	189	429	431	860
Berkley, . . .	256	482	473	955
Berkley, . . .	165	313	306	619
Berkley Bridge, .	34	67	58	125
Myrickville, . .	57	102	109	211
Dartmouth, . .	814	1,559	1,508	3,107
Apponegansett, .	29	54	53	107
Dartmouth, . .	587	1,214	1,091	2,305
North Dartmouth, .	77	131	154	285
South Dartmouth, .	121	200	210	410
Dighton, . . .	461	916	881	1,797
Dighton, . . .	461	916	881	1,797
Easton, . . .	1,061	2,286	2,166	4,452
Easton, . . .	15	31	31	62
Eastondale, . .	92	175	153	328
Furnace Village, .	157	318	291	609
North Easton, . .	674	1,492	1,445	2,937
South Easton, . .	123	270	246	516
Fairhaven, . . .	898	1,554	1,784	3,338
Fairhaven, . . .	898	1,554	1,784	3,338
FALL RIVER, . .	17,948	42,794	46,469	89,203
Bowenville, . .	336	977	1,008	1,985
FALL RIVER, . .	16,758	39,782	43,414	83,196
Flint Village, . .	135	323	343	666
Globe Village, . .	402	1,118	1,176	2,294
New Boston, . .	59	128	131	259
Oak Grove Village,	27	64	67	131
Steep Brook, . .	171	312	360	672
Freetown, . . .	342	725	680	1,405
Assonet, . . .	101	210	204	414
East Freetown, .	134	276	253	529
Freetown, . . .	107	239	223	462
Mansfield, . . .	946	1,793	1,929	3,722
Mansfield, . . .	834	1,558	1,707	3,265
West Mansfield, .	112	235	222	457
NEW BEDFORD, .	12,221	26,158	29,093	55,251
NEW BEDFORD, .	12,192	26,101	29,039	55,140
Shawmut, . . .	29	57	54	111
North Attleborough, .	1,499	3,145	3,431	6,576
Adamsdale, . .	38	91	75	166

COUNTIES, CITIES, TOWNS, AND VILLAGES.	Number of Families	Males	Females	Population
BRISTOL — Con.				
No. Attleboro' — Con.				
Attleborough Falls,	250	516	580	1,096
North Attleborough,	1,179	2,453	2,700	5,153
Old Town, . .	32	85	76	161
Norton, ...	401	760	854	1,614
Barrowsville, . .	63	117	127	244
Chartley, . . .	83	181	172	353
East Norton, . .	132	248	251	499
Norton, . . .	105	179	267	446
Norton Furnace, .	18	35	37	72
Raynham, . . .	397	751	767	1,518
Judson, . . .	44	81	79	160
North Raynham, .	143	267	261	528
Raynham, . . .	46	75	84	159
Raynham Centre, .	106	187	206	393
South Raynham, .	58	141	137	278
Rehoboth, . . .	451	958	852	1,810
Rehoboth, . . .	451	958	852	1,810
Seekonk, . . .	334	793	672	1,465
Seekonk, . . .	334	793	672	1,465
Somerset, . . .	497	1,040	943	1,983
Somerset, . . .	497	1,040	943	1,983
Swansea, . . .	411	830	797	1,627
Hortonville, . .	69	151	138	289
North Swansea, .	69	139	134	273
South Swansea, .	41	79	83	162
Swansea Centre, .	86	156	157	313
Swansea Village, .	146	305	285	590
TAUNTON, . . .	5,885	13,147	13,968	27,115
TAUNTON, . . .	5,885	13,147	13,968	27,115
Westport, . . .	702	1,344	1,334	2,678
Central Village, .	26	47	44	91
North Westport, .	91	188	204	392
South Westport, .	21	41	37	78
Westport, . . .	502	973	949	1,922
Westport Harbor, .	5	15	8	23
Westport Point, .	57	80	92	172
DUKES.				
Chilmark, . . .	95	151	153	304
Chilmark, . . .	52	85	85	170
Noman's Land, .	3	10	8	18
Squibnocket, . .	40	56	60	116
Cottage City, . .	313	508	530	1,038
Cottage City, . .	313	508	530	1,038
Edgartown, . . .	377	527	598	1,125
Chappaquiddic, .	22	37	34	71
Edgartown, . . .	355	490	564	1,054
Gay Head, . . .	40	90	79	169
Gay Head, . . .	40	90	79	169
Gosnold, . . .	38	88	52	140
Cuttyhunk, . .	29	60	40	100
Nashawena Island,	1	3	1	4
Naushon Island, .	6	20	10	30
Pasque Island, .	1	4	1	5
Penikese Island, .	1	1	-	1

VILLAGES: BY TOWNS — Continued.

COUNTIES, CITIES, TOWNS, AND VILLAGES.	Number of Families	Males	Females	Population	COUNTIES, CITIES, TOWNS, AND VILLAGES.	Number of Families	Males	Females	Population
DUKES — Con.					**ESSEX — Con.**				
Tisbury, . . .	289	477	525	1,002	Groveland, . . .	560	1,118	1,215	2,333
Tisbury, . .	3	14	8	22	Groveland, . .	363	611	653	1,264
Vineyard Haven, .	272	446	496	942	South Groveland, .	197	507	562	1,069
West Chop, . .	14	17	21	38	Hamilton, . . .	315	685	671	1,356
West Tisbury, . .	154	216	244	460	Asbury Grove, . .	56	58	89	147
North Tisbury, .	73	111	118	229	Hamilton, . .	157	398	352	750
West Tisbury, .	81	105	126	231	South District, .	102	229	230	459
					HAVERHILL, . .	6,902	14,535	15,674	30,209
					Ayer's Village, .	58	107	103	210
ESSEX.					East Haverhill, .	39	79	82	161
Amesbury, . . .	2,281	4,780	5,206	9,986	HAVERHILL, . .	6,939	14,089	15,219	29,308
Amesbury, . .	2,160	4,553	4,951	9,504	North Parish, .	56	96	104	200
Salisbury Point, .	121	227	255	482	Rock's Village, .	67	113	121	234
Andover, . . .	1,296	2,913	3,232	6,145	Rosemont, . .	23	51	45	96
Andover, . . .	810	1,850	2,099	3,949	Ipswich, . . .	1,104	2,178	2,542	4,720
Ballardvale, . .	200	397	468	865	Ipswich, . . .	1,070	2,108	2,476	4,584
Frye Village, . .	93	201	257	458	Linebrook Parish, .	34	70	66	136
West Andover, .	184	465	408	873	LAWRENCE, . .	10,783	25,107	27,057	52,164
BEVERLY, . . .	2,914	5,728	6,078	11,806	LAWRENCE, . .	9,206	21,522	23,336	44,858
BEVERLY, . .	2,221	4,330	4,696	9,026	South Lawrence, .	1,577	3,585	3,721	7,306
Beverly Cove, . .	185	348	391	739	LYNN, . . .	14,144	30,173	32,181	62,354
Beverly Farms, .	205	425	408	833	East Lynn, . .	1,239	2,588	2,732	5,320
Montserrat, . .	86	193	142	335	Glenmere, . .	908	1,830	1,879	3,709
North Beverly, .	217	432	441	873	Highlands, . .	814	1,743	1,847	3,590
Boxford, . . .	186	359	368	727	Lakeside, . .	60	103	124	227
Boxford, . . .	115	196	202	398	LYNN, . . .	8,365	17,966	19,367	37,333
West Boxford, .	71	163	166	329	West Lynn, . .	2,698	5,943	6,232	12,175
Bradford, . . .	1,121	2,222	2,514	4,736	Lynnfield, . .	211	408	410	818
Bradford, . .	1,024	2,023	2,321	4,344	Lynnfield, . .	117	224	209	433
Ward Hill, . .	97	199	193	392	South Lynnfield, .	94	184	201	385
Danvers, . . .	1,653	3,958	4,223	8,181	Manchester, . .	488	893	983	1,876
Danvers, . . .	786	2,050	2,266	4,316	Manchester, . .	488	893	983	1,876
Danvers Centre, .	155	325	365	690	Marblehead, . .	2,603	3,649	4,022	7,671
Danversport, . .	350	833	802	1,635	Devereaux, . .	39	89	85	174
Putnamville, . .	57	110	108	218	Marblehead, . .	1,954	3,543	3,905	7,448
Tapleyville, . .	286	640	682	1,322	Marblehead Neck, .	10	17	32	49
Essex, ...	445	809	778	1,587	Merrimac, . . .	605	1,111	1,190	2,301
Essex, . . .	250	469	441	910	Merrimac, . .	112	206	204	410
Essex Falls, . .	72	137	128	265	Merrimac Centre, .	401	745	821	1,566
South Essex, . .	123	203	209	412	Merrimacport, .	92	160	165	325
Georgetown, . .	541	999	1,051	2,050	Methuen, . . .	1,317	2,760	2,930	5,690
Byfield, . . .	53	104	88	192	Ayer's Village, .	9	19	15	34
Georgetown, . .	414	745	816	1,561	Methuen, . . .	1,308	2,741	2,915	5,656
Marlborough, . .	24	54	52	106	Middleton, . .	219	428	410	838
South Georgetown, .	50	96	95	191	Middleton, . .	211	392	390	782
GLOUCESTER, . .	5,416	16,257	11,954	28,211	South Middleton, .	8	36	20	56
Annisquam, . .	98	160	174	334	Nahant, ...	204	425	440	865
Bay View, . .	228	583	482	1,065	Nahant, . . .	204	425	440	865
East Gloucester, .	696	1,682	1,516	3,198	Newbury, . . .	360	760	729	1,489
Fresh Water Cove					Byfield, . . .	199	396	390	786
Village, . .	24	39	52	91	Newbury, . . .	161	364	339	703
GLOUCESTER, . .	3,692	11,983	8,548	20,531	NEWBURYPORT, . .	3,479	6,616	7,936	14,552
Lanesville, . .	359	1,114	659	1,773	NEWBURYPORT, . .	3,479	6,616	7,936	14,552
Magnolia, . .	57	134	113	247	North Andover, . .	796	1,765	1,804	3,569
Riverdale, . .	155	294	321	615	North Andover, .	222	507	499	1,006
West Gloucester, .	137	268	289	557	N. Andover Depot, .	574	1,258	1,305	2,563

VILLAGES: BY TOWNS—Continued.

COUNTIES, CITIES, TOWNS, AND VILLAGES	Number of Families	Males	Females	Population
ESSEX—Con.				
Peabody, . . .	2,373	5,262	5,245	10,507
Peabody, . .	2,049	4,560	4,594	9,154
South Peabody, .	201	440	407	847
West Peabody, .	123	262	244	506
Rockport, . . .	1,236	2,906	2,323	5,289
Pigeon Cove, .	406	1,247	793	2,040
Rockport, . .	830	1,719	1,530	3,243
Rowley, . . .	340	656	616	1,272
Millwood, .	39	74	64	138
Rowley, . .	301	582	552	1,134
SALEM, . . .	7,623	16,270	18,203	34,473
Baker's Island,	3	5	6	11
Lowell Island,	1	1	4	5
Misery Island,	2	5	7	12
North Salem, .	472	923	1,049	1,972
SALEM, . .	5,985	11,876	13,689	25,565
South Salem, .	1,158	3,433	3,443	6,876
Winter Island,	2	27	5	32
Salisbury, . .	351	642	658	1,300
Salisbury, . .	344	629	645	1,274
Salisbury Beach, .	7	13	13	26
Saugus, . . .	1,065	2,189	2,308	4,497
Cliftondale, .	383	783	864	1,647
East Saugus, .	221	421	470	891
North Saugus, .	42	95	88	183
Saugus, . .	142	302	308	610
Saugus Centre, .	277	588	578	1,166
Swampscott, . .	823	1,534	1,725	3,259
Beach Bluff, .	4	15	19	34
Swampscott, .	819	1,519	1,706	3,225
Topsfield, . .	264	516	517	1,033
Topsfield, . .	264	516	517	1,033
Wenham, . .	234	431	455	886
Wenham, . .	234	431	455	886
West Newbury, .	440	811	832	1,643
West Newbury,	440	811	832	1,643
FRANKLIN.				
Ashfield, . .	252	523	490	1,013
Ashfield, . .	169	414	344	758
Ashfield Plain, .	61	80	111	191
South Ashfield, .	22	29	35	64
Bernardston, .	269	389	389	778
Bernardston, .	269	389	389	778
Buckland, . .	387	785	763	1,548
Buckland, .	149	259	283	542
Shelburne Falls, .	238	526	480	1,006
Charlemont, . .	275	526	515	1,041
Charlemont, . .	192	366	366	732
East Charlemont, .	49	90	89	179
Zoar, . . .	34	70	60	130
Colrain, . . .	366	851	759	1,610
Adamsville, .	52	128	108	236
Colrain, . .	156	318	309	627
Elm Grove, . .	30	76	63	139

COUNTIES, CITIES, TOWNS, AND VILLAGES	Number of Families	Males	Females	Population
FRANKLIN—Con.				
Colrain—Con.				
Griswoldville, . .	69	178	138	316
Shattuckville, . .	35	76	68	144
Willis Place, . .	24	75	73	148
Conway, . . .	309	657	647	1,304
Conway, . . .	309	657	647	1,304
Deerfield, . . .	674	1,550	1,457	3,007
Cheapside, .	44	133	90	223
Deerfield, . .	110	232	255	487
East Deerfield, .	39	87	61	148
Green River, . .	143	326	317	643
Pettis Plain, . .	31	69	69	138
South Deerfield, .	241	543	528	1,071
Wapping, . . .	21	50	47	97
West Deerfield, .	45	110	90	200
Erving, . . .	256	490	474	964
Erving, . . .	148	274	263	537
Farley, . . .	32	66	60	126
Miller's Falls, . .	76	150	151	301
Gill, . . .	197	689	383	1,082
Gill, . . .	97	190	174	364
Mount Hermon, .	25	338	34	572
Riverside, . .	75	171	175	346
Greenfield, . .	1,450	2,987	3,242	6,229
Greenfield, . .	1,450	2,987	3,242	6,229
Hawley, . . .	110	250	218	468
Bozrah, . . .	14	35	31	66
Hawley, . . .	42	96	79	175
West Hawley, .	54	119	108	227
Heath, . . .	120	250	226	476
Dell, . . .	15	35	26	61
Heath, . . .	60	127	116	243
North Heath, . .	45	88	84	172
Leverett, . . .	200	379	365	744
East Leverett, .	44	77	82	159
Leverett, . .	57	107	98	205
Long Plain, .	23	52	46	98
Moore's Corner, .	26	52	47	99
North Leverett, .	50	91	92	183
Leyden, . . .	88	185	178	363
Leyden, . . .	68	149	114	263
West Leyden, . .	20	36	34	70
Monroe, . . .	65	176	122	298
Monroe, . . .	65	176	122	298
Montague, . .	1,349	3,076	2,982	6,058
Lake Pleasant, .	29	22	36	58
Miller's Falls, . .	128	282	246	528
Montague, . .	241	459	444	903
Montague City, .	81	196	171	367
Turner's Falls, .	870	2,117	2,085	4,202
New Salem, . .	253	438	431	869
Cooleyville, .	19	36	33	69
Millington, . .	13	33	26	59
New Salem, . .	184	345	350	695
North New Salem, .	17	24	22	46
Northfield, . . .	419	754	1,097	1,851

VILLAGES: BY TOWNS — Continued.

Counties, Cities, Towns, and Villages.	Number of Families	Males	Females	Population
FRANKLIN — Con.				
Northfield — Con.				
East Northfield,	84	127	496	623
Northfield,	224	397	425	822
Northfield Farms,	55	107	75	182
West Northfield,	56	123	101	224
Orange,	1,390	2,690	2,671	5,361
North Orange,	26	62	65	127
Orange,	1,263	2,450	2,445	4,895
Tully,	37	61	69	130
West Orange,	37	63	61	124
Wheeler,	17	54	31	85
Rowe,	123	283	215	498
Rowe,	123	283	215	498
Shelburne,	392	750	810	1,560
Shelburne,	119	298	263	561
Shelburne Falls,	273	452	547	999
Shutesbury,	125	218	226	444
Shutesbury,	125	218	226	444
Sunderland,	166	381	315	696
Sunderland,	166	381	315	696
Warwick,	158	321	278	599
Warwick,	158	321	278	599
Wendell,	129	293	236	529
Wendell,	70	166	134	300
Wendell Centre,	37	68	58	126
Wendell Depot,	22	59	44	103
Whately,	195	392	363	755
East Whately,	71	150	135	285
West Whately,	43	83	77	160
Whately,	81	159	151	310
HAMPDEN.				
Agawam,	553	1,237	1,171	2,408
Agawam,	201	450	399	849
Feeding Hills,	168	351	311	662
Mittineague,	184	436	461	897
Blandford,	206	437	412	849
Blandford,	173	385	356	741
North Blandford,	33	52	56	108
Brimfield,	228	498	464	962
Brimfield,	119	263	240	503
Brimfield Centre,	65	100	117	217
East Brimfield,	39	82	74	156
West Brimfield,	15	53	33	86
Chester,	354	700	729	1,429
Chester,	290	555	609	1,164
Chester Centre,	25	67	54	121
Littleville,	20	37	27	64
North Chester,	19	41	39	80
CHICOPEE,	3,942	8,095	8,325	16,420
Aldenville,	22	65	55	120
CHICOPEE,	1,624	4,364	4,562	8,926
Chicopee Falls,	1,086	2,887	2,964	5,851
Fairview,	95	237	232	469
Willimansett,	215	542	512	1,054

Counties, Cities, Towns, and Villages.	Number of Families	Males	Females	Population
HAMPDEN — Con.				
East Longmeadow,	330	863	728	1,591
East Longmeadow,	330	863	728	1,591
Granville,	252	522	483	1,005
Granville,	157	301	283	584
Granville Centre,	32	78	72	150
West Granville,	63	143	128	271
Hampden,	194	374	369	743
Hampden,	115	234	231	465
Hampden Centre,	79	140	138	278
Holland,	55	107	92	199
Holland,	55	107	92	199
HOLYOKE,	7,894	19,198	21,124	40,322
HOLYOKE,	7,839	19,040	20,980	40,020
Rock Valley,	24	73	68	141
West Holyoke,	31	85	76	161
Longmeadow,	146	290	330	620
Longmeadow,	146	290	330	620
Ludlow,	473	1,314	1,248	2,562
Ludlow,	444	1,259	1,190	2,449
Ludlow Centre,	29	55	58	113
Monson,	872	1,862	1,884	3,746
Monson,	743	1,616	1,600	3,216
North Monson,	19	36	36	72
South Monson,	110	210	248	458
Montgomery,	63	151	124	275
Montgomery,	63	151	124	275
Palmer,	1,382	3,345	3,513	6,858
Bondsville,	209	573	606	1,179
Palmer,	553	1,127	1,161	2,288
Thorndike,	280	715	788	1,503
Three Rivers,	340	930	958	1,888
Russell,	185	440	406	846
Crescent Mills,	18	55	38	93
Fairfield,	65	153	165	318
Russell,	73	162	140	302
Russell Mountain,	29	70	63	133
Southwick,	239	510	451	961
Southwick,	239	510	451	961
SPRINGFIELD,	11,741	24,651	26,871	51,522
Brightwood,	188	438	412	850
Indian Orchard,	461	1,108	1,081	2,189
Sixteen Acres,	51	115	116	231
SPRINGFIELD,	11,041	22,990	25,262	48,252
*Tolland,	67	171	138	309
Tolland,	67	171	138	309
Wales,	191	405	378	783
Wales,	191	405	378	783
Westfield,	2,596	5,175	5,488	10,663
East Farms,	18	35	29	64
Middle Farms,	31	106	58	164
Mundale,	40	81	77	158
Pochassic,	30	61	58	119
West Farms,	35	66	60	126
Westfield,	2,439	4,826	5,206	10,032
West Springfield,	1,360	2,951	3,174	6,125
Merrick,	749	1,649	1,730	3,379

VILLAGES : BY TOWNS -- Continued.

COUNTIES, CITIES, TOWNS, AND VILLAGES.	Number of Families	Males	Females	Population	COUNTIES, CITIES, TOWNS, AND VILLAGES.	Number of Families	Males	Females	Population
HAMPDEN — Con.					**HAMPSHIRE — Con.**				
West Springfield-Con.					NORTHAMPTON, . .	3,270	7,434	9,312	16,746
Mittineague, . .	287	607	730	1,337	Bay State Village, .	222	574	558	1,132
West Springfield, .	324	695	714	1,409	Florence, . . .	610	1,285	1,512	2,797
Wilbraham, . . .	363	837	903	1,740	Leeds, . . .	180	467	513	980
North Wilbraham, .	106	227	249	476	Loudville, . .	7	21	16	37
Wilbraham, . .	257	610	654	1,264	Mount Tom, . .	22	113	45	158
HAMPSHIRE.					NORTHAMPTON, . .	2,142	4,770	6,498	11,268
Amherst, . . .	1,064	2,427	2,358	4,785	North Farms, . .	12	30	21	51
Amherst, . . .	770	1,873	1,782	3,655	Park Hill, . .	5	14	8	22
North Amherst, .	186	327	361	688	Pine Grove, . .	11	36	23	59
South Amherst, .	108	227	215	442	Roberts' Meadow, .	9	18	14	32
Belchertown, .	524	1,115	1,046	2,161	Smith's Ferry, .	19	47	52	99
Belchertown, . .	502	1,064	1,008	2,072	West Farms, . .	51	59	52	111
Dwight, . . .	22	51	38	89	Pelham, . . .	126	246	240	486
Chesterfield, . .	162	301	288	589	Packardsville, . .	19	37	37	74
Chesterfield, . .	114	210	205	415	Pelham, . .	62	114	107	221
West Chesterfield, .	48	91	83	174	West Pelham, . .	45	95	96	191
Cummington, .	204	367	383	750	Plainfield, . . .	169	231	219	450
Cummington, . .	141	263	277	540	Plainfield, . .	169	231	219	450
Swift River, . .	15	28	27	55	Prescott, . . .	106	208	193	401
West Cummington,	45	76	79	155	North Prescott, .	59	109	101	210
Easthampton, .	1,019	2,242	2,548	4,790	Prescott, . . .	47	99	92	191
Easthampton, .	875	1,817	2,157	3,974	Southampton, . .	252	537	517	1,054
Glendale, . .	10	32	31	63	Russellville, . .	16	38	28	66
Loudville, . .	3	7	10	17	Southampton, . .	236	499	489	988
Mount Tom, . .	30	98	71	169	South Hadley, . .	894	2,054	2,389	4,443
Park Hill, . .	7	17	27	44	South Hadley, . .	233	486	816	1,302
Williston Mills, .	94	271	252	523	So. Hadley Falls, .	661	1,568	1,573	3,141
Enfield, . . .	264	512	478	990	Ware, ...	1,523	3,576	4,075	7,651
Enfield, . . .	188	351	322	673	Ware, . . .	1,508	3,549	4,047	7,596
Smith's, . .	73	161	156	317	West Ware, . .	15	27	28	55
Goshen, . . .	66	160	144	304	Westhampton, . .	124	241	235	476
Goshen, . . .	66	160	144	304	Loudville, . .	22	45	36	81
Granby, . . .	171	394	354	748	Westhampton, .	102	196	199	395
Granby, . . .	156	366	319	685	Williamsburg, . .	473	950	1,005	1,955
Granby Centre, .	15	28	35	63	Haydenville, . .	235	514	550	1,064
Greenwich, . . .	142	243	238	481	Williamsburg, .	238	436	455	891
Greenwich, . .	104	188	176	364	Worthington, . .	155	341	307	648
Greenwich Village, .	38	55	62	117	Ringville, . .	7	12	9	21
Hadley, ...	390	894	810	1,704	So. Worthington, .	20	43	36	79
Hadley, . . .	245	575	517	1,092	West Worthington, .	19	35	33	68
North Hadley, .	145	319	293	612	Worthington, . .	96	226	206	432
Hatfield, . . .	291	669	593	1,262	Worthington Centre, ...	13	25	23	48
Hatfield, . . .	188	417	379	796	**MIDDLESEX.**				
North Hatfield, .	65	166	126	292	Acton, ...	529	980	998	1,978
West Hatfield, .	38	86	88	174	Acton, . . .	189	406	356	762
Huntington, . .	329	722	728	1,450	Acton Centre, .	63	94	102	196
Huntington, . .	232	517	537	1,054	South Acton, . .	143	255	273	528
Indian Hollow, .	10	24	18	42	West Acton, . .	134	225	267	492
Knightville, . .	24	47	46	93	Arlington, . . .	1,362	3,067	3,448	6,515
Norwich, . . .	41	83	86	169	Arlington, . .	1,204	2,696	3,027	5,723
Norwich Bridge, .	22	51	41	92	Arlington Heights,	158	371	421	792
Middlefield, . .	92	197	189	386	Ashby, ...	233	413	391	804
Bancroft, . . .	16	36	39	75	Ashby, . . .	184	352	305	657
Factory Village, .	23	53	48	101	Ashby Centre, .	49	61	86	147
Middlefield, . .	53	108	102	210					

VILLAGES: BY TOWNS — Continued.

COUNTIES, CITIES, TOWNS, AND VILLAGES.	Number of Families	Males	Females	Population	COUNTIES, CITIES, TOWNS, AND VILLAGES.	Number of Families	Males	Females	Population
MIDDLESEX — Con.					**MIDDLESEX — Con.**				
Ashland, . . .	486	1,015	1,075	2,090	Framingham — Con.				
Ashland, . .	486	1,015	1,075	2,090	Nobscot, . . .	37	89	87	176
Ayer, ...	528	1,018	1,083	2,101	Saxonville, . .	409	757	932	1,689
Ayer, . . .	528	1,018	1,083	2,101	South Framingham,	1,270	2,887	2,883	5,770
Bedford, . . .	251	623	546	1,169	Groton, ...	508	1,078	1,114	2,192
Bedford, . .	251	623	546	1,169	Groton, . . .	439	952	975	1,927
Belmont, . . .	565	1,519	1,324	2,843	West Groton, . .	69	126	139	265
Belmont, . .	357	1,174	943	2,117	Holliston, . . .	701	1,309	1,409	2,718
Waverley, . .	148	345	381	726	Braggville, . .	21	47	51	98
Billerica, . . .	582	1,301	1,276	2,577	East Holliston, .	81	132	155	287
Billerica, . .	163	337	335	672	Holliston, . . .	150	304	280	594
East Billerica, .	53	116	104	220	Holliston Centre, .	430	786	877	1,663
North Billerica,	254	577	614	1,191	Metcalf, . . .	19	40	36	76
South Billerica, .	36	89	79	168	Hopkinton, . . .	752	1,469	1,515	2,984
South East, .	41	102	82	184	Hayden Row, . .	54	106	109	215
West Billerica, .	35	80	62	142	Hopkinton, . .	624	1,217	1,280	2,497
Boxborough, . .	78	172	135	307	Woodville, . .	74	146	126	272
Boxborough, . .	78	172	135	307	Hudson, ...	1,245	2,533	2,775	5,308
Burlington, . . .	129	316	258	574	Hudson, . . .	1,245	2,533	2,775	5,308
Burlington, . .	129	316	258	574	Lexington, . . .	775	1,692	1,806	3,498
CAMBRIDGE, . .	17,193	39,831	41,812	81,643	East Lexington, .	150	291	336	627
CAMBRIDGE, . .	3,040	8,020	8,323	16,343	Lexington, . .	625	1,401	1,470	2,871
Cambridgeport, .	9,234	19,808	21,505	41,313	Lincoln, ...	209	626	485	1,111
East Cambridge, .	2,812	7,303	6,683	13,986	Lincoln, . .	209	626	485	1,111
North Cambridge, .	2,107	4,700	5,291	9,991	Littleton, . . .	256	569	567	1,136
Carlisle, . .	126	268	224	492	Littleton, . .	173	394	372	766
Carlisle, . . .	126	268	224	492	Littleton Centre, .	75	159	174	333
Chelmsford, . .	747	1,611	1,551	3,162	Littleton Common, .	8	16	21	37
Chelmsford, . .	300	603	602	1,205	**LOWELL,** . . .	16,885	38,931	45,436	84,367
East Chelmsford, .	56	139	117	256	Ayer City, . .	135	331	332	663
North Chelmsford,	244	574	538	1,112	Centralville, . .	2,567	5,442	6,387	11,829
South Chelmsford,	67	128	124	252	LOWELL, . . .	13,760	32,228	37,685	69,913
West Chelmsford, .	80	167	170	337	Middlesex Village, .	48	103	133	236
Concord, . . .	874	3,157	2,018	5,175	Pawtucketville, .	375	827	899	1,726
Concord, . .	625	1,513	1,492	3,005	**MALDEN,** . . .	6,638	13,923	15,785	29,708
West Concord, .	187	1,486	377	1,863	Bell Rock, . .	112	236	266	502
Westvale, . .	62	158	149	307	Edgeworth, . .	980	2,422	2,488	4,910
Dracut, ...	475	1,325	1,118	2,443	Faulkner, . . .	515	994	1,073	2,067
Collinsville, . .	138	444	374	818	Linden, . .	255	512	558	1,070
Dracut, . . .	89	214	162	376	MALDEN, . . .	3,989	8,138	9,640	17,778
Dracut Centre, .	79	211	167	378	Maplewood, . .	777	1,621	1,760	3,381
Navy, . . .	169	456	415	871	**MARLBOROUGH,** .	3,159	7,369	7,508	14,977
Dunstable, . . .	106	207	193	400	MARLBOROUGH, .	3,159	7,369	7,508	14,977
Dunstable, . .	106	207	193	400	Maynard, . . .	642	1,520	1,570	3,090
EVERETT, . . .	4,504	9,057	9,516	18,573	Maynard, . . .	642	1,520	1,570	3,090
East Everett, . .	317	691	743	1,434	**MEDFORD,** . . .	3,172	7,043	7,431	14,474
EVERETT, . .	1,986	4,126	4,381	8,507	Glenwood, . .	298	767	667	1,434
Glendale, . .	724	1,502	1,563	3,065	MEDFORD, . .	2,023	4,478	4,710	9,188
Mt. Washington, .	108	247	262	509	Park Street, . .	161	353	410	763
South Everett, .	430	1,026	983	2,009	Wellington, . .	95	183	224	407
Washington Park, .	35	84	87	171	West Medford, .	595	1,262	1,420	2,682
West Everett, . .	704	1,381	1,497	2,878	Melrose, . . .	2,685	5,548	6,417	11,965
Framingham, . .	2,115	4,570	4,942	9,512	Fells, . . .	54	157	190	347
Framingham, . .	29	65	67	132	Melrose, . . .	1,071	2,103	2,514	4,617
Framingham Centre, .	370	772	973	1,745	Melrose Highlands,	478	868	1,039	1,907
					Wyoming, . .	1,082	2,420	2,614	5,034

VILLAGES : BY TOWNS — Continued.

Counties, Cities, Towns, and Villages.	Number of Families.	Males	Females	Population	Counties, Cities, Towns, and Villages.	Number of Families.	Males	Females	Population
MIDDLESEX — Con.					MIDDLESEX — Con.				
Natick,	2,080	4,234	4,580	8,814	Wakefield,	1,958	3,962	4,342	8,304
Felchville,	153	334	323	657	Greenwood,	192	400	402	802
Natick,	1,593	3,138	3,486	6,624	Montrose,	104	224	241	465
North Natick,	60	113	124	237	Wakefield,	1,662	3,338	3,699	7,037
South Natick,	283	649	647	1,296	WALTHAM,	4,276	9,638	11,238	20,876
NEWTON,	5,528	12,355	15,235	27,590	WALTHAM,	4,276	9,638	11,238	20,876
Auburndale,	534	1,142	1,674	2,846	Watertown,	1,650	3,740	4,048	7,788
NEWTON,	1,808	3,899	5,102	9,001	Watertown,	1,650	3,740	4,048	7,788
Newton Centre,	364	831	981	1,812	Wayland,	446	1,026	1,000	2,026
Newton Highlands,	404	835	1,078	1,943	Cochituate,	280	654	620	1,274
Newton Lower Falls,	145	353	339	692	Wayland,	166	372	380	752
Newton Upper Falls,	340	790	782	1,572	Westford,	526	1,223	1,195	2,418
Newtonville,	720	1,645	1,941	3,586	Brookside,	18	37	47	84
Nonantum,	412	1,130	1,118	2,248	Cold Spring,	9	21	17	38
Riverside,	35	80	104	184	Forge Village,	83	202	244	446
Thompsonville,	14	45	32	77	Graniteville,	133	347	326	673
Waban,	42	100	132	232	Westford,	283	616	561	1,177
West Newton,	720	1,595	1,852	3,457	Weston,	367	877	833	1,710
North Reading,	228	422	413	835	Kendal Green,	83	208	181	389
North Reading,	228	422	413	835	Weston,	284	669	652	1,321
Pepperell,	787	1,650	1,671	3,321	Wilmington,	338	715	705	1,420
East Pepperell,	276	676	639	1,315	North Wilmington,	67	120	123	243
Pepperell,	511	974	1,032	2,006	Wilmington,	165	350	334	684
Reading,	1,150	2,235	2,482	4,717	Wilmington Centre,	106	245	248	493
Reading,	1,150	2,235	2,482	4,717	Winchester,	1,301	2,928	3,222	6,150
Sherborn,	286	554	862	1,446	Winchester,	1,301	2,928	3,222	6,150
North Sherborn,	73	176	486	662	WOBURN,	3,012	7,000	7,178	14,178
Sherborn,	122	210	212	422	Cummingsville,	65	151	157	308
South Sherborn,	51	118	93	211	East Woburn,	248	607	571	1,178
West Sherborn,	40	80	71	151	North Woburn,	248	510	537	1,047
Shirley,	324	654	745	1,399	WOBURN,	2,390	5,586	5,757	11,343
Shirley,	91	166	166	332	Woburn Highlands,	61	146	156	302
Shirley Village,	233	488	579	1,067					
SOMERVILLE,	11,903	24,917	27,283	52,200	NANTUCKET.				
SOMERVILLE,	11,903	24,917	27,283	52,200	Nantucket,	981	1,315	1,701	3,016
Stoneham,	1,581	3,070	3,214	6,284	Muskegat,	1	1	–	1
Stoneham,	1,581	3,070	3,214	6,284	Nantucket,	928	1,222	1,611	2,833
Stow,	234	473	447	920	Polpis,	12	25	24	49
Rock Bottom,	80	156	150	306	Siasconset,	28	43	46	89
Stow,	154	317	297	614	Tuckernuck,	12	24	20	44
Sudbury,	272	603	538	1,141					
North Sudbury,	34	98	64	162	NORFOLK.				
South Sudbury,	127	273	252	525	Avon,	385	818	808	1,626
Sudbury,	111	232	222	454	Avon,	385	818	808	1,626
Tewksbury,	473	1,653	1,726	3,379	Bellingham,	358	721	760	1,481
South Lowell,	47	106	107	213	Bellingham,	98	178	195	373
Tewksbury,	240	573	543	1,116	Caryville,	51	108	122	230
Tewksbury Centre,	62	682	759	1,441	North Bellingham,	195	210	213	423
Wamesit,	27	56	72	128	South Bellingham,	104	225	230	455
Wigginville,	97	236	245	481	Braintree,	1,254	2,660	2,651	5,311
Townsend,	512	880	900	1,780	Braintree,	403	821	901	1,722
Townsend,	293	496	514	1,010	East Braintree,	318	637	685	1,322
Townsend Harbor,	70	128	133	261	South Braintree,	533	1,202	1,065	2,267
West Townsend,	149	256	253	509	Brookline,	3,148	6,826	9,338	16,164
Tyngsborough,	163	324	311	635	Brookline,	3,148	6,826	9,338	16,164
Tyngsborough,	163	324	311	635					

VILLAGES: BY TOWNS — Continued.

Counties, Cities, Towns, and Villages.	Number of Families	Males	Females	Population
NORFOLK — Con.				
Canton, . . .	968	2,207	2,429	4,636
Canton, . . .	854	1,956	2,176	4,132
Canton Junction, . .	22	42	54	96
Ponkapoag, . .	92	209	199	408
Cohasset, . .	586	1,148	1,326	2,474
Beechwood, . .	87	172	170	342
Cohasset, . .	403	788	925	1,713
North Cohasset,	96	188	231	419
Dedham, . . .	1,613	3,476	3,735	7,211
Ashcroft, . .	16	34	40	74
Dedham, . .	718	1,508	1,730	3,238
East Dedham, . .	388	898	889	1,787
Endicott, . . .	31	71	82	153
Islington, . . .	29	53	65	118
Oakdale, . . .	112	217	232	449
Riverdale, . . .	30	86	74	160
Walnut Hill, . .	121	227	260	487
West Dedham, . .	198	382	363	745
Dover, ...	148	345	323	668
Dover, . . .	148	345	323	668
Foxborough, . . .	828	1,542	1,677	3,219
East Foxborough, .	100	194	163	357
Foxborough, . .	512	874	1,062	1,936
Foxvale, . . .	48	105	101	206
Lakeview, . . .	14	30	31	61
North Foxborough,	46	99	99	198
South Foxborough,	88	204	187	391
West Foxborough,	29	36	34	70
Franklin, . . .	1,176	2,459	2,677	5,136
Franklin, . . .	1,057	2,225	2,415	4,640
North Franklin,	34	67	82	149
South Franklin,	28	58	56	114
Unionville, . .	57	109	124	233
Holbrook, . . .	571	1,127	1,171	2,298
Brookville, . .	100	188	202	390
Holbrook, . .	250	548	520	1,068
Holbrook Centre, .	221	391	449	840
Hyde Park, . . .	2,561	5,790	6,066	11,826
Clarendon Hills, .	492	1,061	1,144	2,205
Fairmount, . .	556	1,161	1,282	2,443
Hyde Park, . .	777	1,739	1,878	3,617
Readville, . .	274	679	659	1,338
Sunnyside, . .	462	1,120	1,103	2,223
Medfield, . . .	415	883	989	1,872
Medfield, . . .	415	883	989	1,872
Medway, . . .	732	1,438	1,475	2,913
Medway, . .	296	586	666	1,252
West Medway, . .	436	852	809	1,661
Millis, . . .	226	484	522	1,006
Millis, . . .	175	373	409	782
Rockville, . . .	51	111	113	224
Milton, . . .	1,106	2,562	2,956	5,518
East Milton, . .	257	560	601	1,161
Mattapan, . .	183	425	453	878
Milton, . . .	666	1,577	1,902	3,479
Needham, . . .	802	1,749	1,762	3,511

Counties, Cities, Towns, and Villages.	Number of Families	Males	Females	Population
NORFOLK — Con.				
Needham — Con.				
Charles River Village, . .	40	94	85	179
Greendale, . .	35	95	70	165
Highlandville, . .	265	569	581	1,150
Needham, . .	385	808	825	1,633
The Falls, . .	77	183	201	384
Norfolk, . .	210	471	411	882
City Mills, . .	46	115	108	223
Norfolk, . . .	140	299	261	560
Stony Brook, . .	24	57	42	99
Norwood, . .	983	2,437	2,137	4,574
Norwood, . .	983	2,437	2,137	4,574
QUINCY, . . .	4,373	10,608	10,104	20,712
Atlantic, . . .	461	1,035	1,056	2,091
Hough's Neck, . .	79	159	146	305
QUINCY, . . .	1,137	2,589	2,679	5,268
Quincy Point, . .	153	366	340	706
South Quincy, . .	388	2,508	2,212	4,720
West Quincy, . .	390	2,658	2,306	4,964
Wollaston, . .	565	1,293	1,365	2,658
Randolph, . . .	905	1,825	1,869	3,694
Randolph, . .	905	1,825	1,869	3,694
Sharon, . . .	326	839	878	1,717
East Sharon, . .	14	26	32	58
Sharon, . . .	357	765	793	1,558
Sharon Heights, . .	22	48	53	101
Stoughton, . . .	1,241	2,570	2,702	5,272
North Stoughton, . .	38	72	74	146
Stoughton, . . .	1,121	2,317	2,445	4,762
West Stoughton, . .	82	181	183	364
Walpole, . . .	688	1,500	1,494	2,994
East Walpole, . .	122	291	236	527
South Walpole, . .	87	141	177	318
Walpole, . . .	479	1,068	1,081	2,149
Wellesley, . . .	738	1,470	2,759	4,229
Newton Lower Falls,	120	317	283	600
Wellesley, . .	336	589	1,749	2,338
Wellesley Hills, . .	273	564	727	1,291
Weymouth, . . .	2,696	5,592	5,699	11,291
East Weymouth, . .	862	1,860	1,868	3,728
North Weymouth, . .	326	824	679	1,503
South Weymouth, . .	787	1,573	1,626	3,199
Weymouth, . .	605	1,173	1,349	2,522
Weymouth Heights,	86	162	177	339
Wrentham, . . .	631	1,263	1,321	2,584
Plainville, . .	209	433	451	884
Sheldonville, . .	86	152	168	320
Shepardville, . .	23	42	50	92
West Wrentham, . .	29	59	58	117
Wrentham, . .	284	577	594	1,171
PLYMOUTH.				
Abington, . . .	1,076	2,040	2,167	4,207
Abington, . .	526	976	1,060	2,036

VILLAGES : BY TOWNS — Continued.

PLYMOUTH — Con.

Counties, Cities, Towns, and Villages	Number of Families	Males	Females	Population
Abington — Con.				
North Abington,	550	1,064	1,107	2,171
Bridgewater,	854	2,722	1,964	4,686
Bridgewater,	792	2,595	1,848	4,443
Scotland,	62	127	116	243
BROCKTON,	7,700	16,559	16,606	33,165
BROCKTON,	5,666	12,076	12,327	24,403
Brockton Heights,	39	91	84	175
Campello,	1,305	2,779	2,715	5,494
Montello,	690	1,613	1,480	3,093
Carver,	262	546	470	1,016
Carver,	72	134	129	263
East Carver,	35	60	63	123
North Carver,	70	143	117	260
South Carver,	85	209	161	370
Duxbury,	552	945	1,021	1,966
Ashdod,	16	32	23	55
Duxbury,	242	416	488	904
Island Creek,	47	89	93	182
Millbrook,	68	128	135	263
North Duxbury,	31	50	48	98
South Duxbury,	94	169	173	342
West Duxbury,	34	61	61	122
East Bridgewater,	726	1,441	1,453	2,894
Beaver,	58	129	113	242
Curtisville,	34	65	67	132
East Bridgewater,	324	615	654	1,269
Eastville,	44	95	81	176
Elmwood,	110	200	212	412
Matfield,	27	65	70	135
Northville,	57	107	98	205
Satucket,	39	72	89	161
Westdale,	33	93	69	162
Halifax,	148	266	231	497
Halifax,	148	266	231	497
Hanover,	544	1,009	1,042	2,051
Assinippi,	39	66	66	132
Hanover,	150	309	313	622
North Hanover,	120	208	213	421
South Hanover,	83	135	154	289
West Hanover,	152	291	296	587
Hanson,	380	708	672	1,380
Hanson,	296	542	518	1,060
North Hanson,	18	31	37	68
South Hanson,	66	135	117	252
Hingham,	1,164	2,299	2,520	4,819
Downer Landing,	11	21	37	58
Hingham,	318	651	755	1,406
Hingham Centre,	291	620	613	1,233
South Hingham,	251	450	504	954
West Hingham,	236	557	611	1,168
Hull,	229	536	508	1,044
Calf Island,	2	4	2	6
Great Brewster,	2	2	1	3
Hull,	34	93	69	162
Hull Village,	65	133	157	290

PLYMOUTH — Con.

Counties, Cities, Towns, and Villages	Number of Families	Males	Females	Population
Hull — Con.				
Kenberma,	7	17	24	41
Little Brewster,	3	4	2	6
Middle Brewster,	3	5	5	10
Nantasket,	88	194	183	377
Point Allerton,	12	30	28	58
Stony Beach,	10	41	30	71
Waveland,	3	13	7	20
Kingston,	477	847	899	1,746
Kingston,	433	769	834	1,603
Silver Lake,	44	78	65	143
Lakeville,	233	439	431	870
Lakeville,	233	439	431	870
Marion,	213	328	431	759
Marion,	213	328	431	759
Marshfield,	511	850	910	1,760
Brant Rock,	41	66	65	131
Green Harbor,	47	64	70	134
Marshfield,	181	325	392	687
Marshfield Centre,	26	42	48	90
Marshfield Hills,	165	173	164	337
North Marshfield,	72	113	127	240
Sea View,	39	67	74	141
Mattapoisett,	301	490	542	1,032
East Mattapoisett,	51	101	102	203
Mattapoisett,	250	389	440	829
Middleborough,	1,673	3,205	3,484	6,689
Fire District,	1,020	1,925	2,216	4,141
Middleborough,	463	949	911	1,860
N. Middleborough,	129	223	255	478
Rock,	61	108	102	210
Norwell,	422	771	769	1,540
Assinippi,	73	116	132	248
Church Hill,	74	137	140	277
Mount Blue,	42	89	75	164
Norwell,	166	306	305	611
Ridge Hill,	67	123	117	240
Pembroke,	367	634	589	1,223
Bryantville,	65	107	103	210
East Pembroke,	41	61	63	124
North Pembroke,	66	109	112	221
Pembroke,	132	252	212	464
Pembroke Centre,	63	105	99	204
Plymouth,	1,869	3,863	4,094	7,957
Cedarville,	23	46	34	80
Chiltonville,	151	333	335	668
Ellisville,	8	23	12	35
Manomet,	93	187	183	370
North Plymouth,	112	281	269	550
Plymouth,	1,582	2,993	3,261	6,254
Plympton,	162	268	281	549
Plympton,	162	268	281	549
Rochester,	280	535	486	1,021
Rochester,	260	535	486	1,021
Rockland,	1,331	2,757	2,766	5,523
Hatherly,	113	256	236	492

VILLAGES: BY TOWNS — Continued.

COUNTIES, CITIES, TOWNS, AND VILLAGES.	Number of Families	Males	Females	Population	COUNTIES, CITIES, TOWNS, AND VILLAGES.	Number of Families	Males	Females	Population
PLYMOUTH — Con.					**WORCESTER — Con.**				
Rockland — Con.					Barre — Con.				
Rockland, .	1,218	2,501	2,530	5,031	Barre Plains, .	26	71	49	120
Scituate, . . .	607	1,115	1,131	2,246	Smithville, . .	30	61	79	140
Egypt, . . .	48	78	96	174	Berlin, ...	225	451	446	897
Greenbush, . .	61	120	110	230	Berlin, . . .	123	219	242	461
North Scituate, .	227	393	403	796	Carterville, . .	13	33	34	67
Scituate, . . .	60	95	94	189	South Berlin, . .	39	102	85	187
Scituate Harbor, .	211	429	428	857	West Berlin, . .	44	97	85	182
Wareham, . .	891	1,765	1,602	3,367	Blackstone, . . .	1,266	3,116	2,923	6,039
East Wareham, .	178	335	279	614	Blackstone, . .	688	1,548	1,671	3,219
Onset, . . .	165	218	234	452	East Blackstone, .	71	151	153	304
South Wareham, .	98	247	189	436	Millville, . . .	507	1,417	1,099	2,516
Wareham, . .	334	683	669	1,352	Bolton, . . .	206	398	399	797
West Wareham, .	116	272	231	503	Bolton, . . .	206	398	399	797
West Bridgewater, .	409	877	870	1,747	Boylston, . . .	177	389	340	729
Cochesett, . .	104	215	195	410	Boylston, . . .	137	321	271	592
Jerusalem, . .	39	86	76	162	Boylston Centre, .	40	68	69	137
Mattield, . . .	42	88	82	170	Brookfield, . . .	756	1,689	1,590	3,279
West Bridgewater, .	180	389	432	821	Brookfield, . .	518	1,118	1,079	2,197
Westdale, . .	44	99	85	184	East Brookfield, .	238	571	511	1,082
Whitman, . .	1,389	2,879	2,865	5,744	Charlton, . . .	470	975	902	1,877
Auburnville, . .	74	132	143	275	Charlton, . . .	291	590	518	1,108
East Whitman, .	237	481	480	961	Charlton City, .	106	231	249	480
Whitman, . .	1,078	2,266	2,242	4,508	Charlton Depot, .	73	154	135	289
SUFFOLK.					Clinton, ...	2,278	5,291	6,206	11,497
Boston, . . .	103,396	239,666	257,254	496,920	Clinton, . . .	2,278	5,291	6,206	11,497
Boston (city proper),	30,824	76,393	83,950	160,349	Dana, ...	196	353	364	717
Brighton, . . .	3,172	7,293	7,708	15,001	Dana, ...	74	129	121	250
Charlestown, . .	8,762	20,489	19,815	40,304	North Dana, . .	122	224	243	467
Dorchester, . .	10,004	21,332	24,577	45,909	Douglas, . . .	483	1,033	993	2,026
East Boston, . .	8,815	21,868	20,727	42,595	Douglas, . . .	111	218	218	436
Roxbury, . . .	19,072	43,103	48,985	92,088	East Douglas, . .	372	815	775	1,590
South Boston, . .	14,062	33,853	34,060	67,913	Dudley, ...	628	1,611	1,592	3,203
West Roxbury, .	7,025	15,335	17,426	32,761	Chaseville, . .	42	112	109	221
Chelsea, . . .	6,934	15,273	15,991	31,264	Dudley, . . .	140	318	306	624
Chelsea, . . .	6,934	15,273	15,991	31,264	Jericho, . . .	148	375	360	735
Revere, ...	1,652	3,721	3,702	7,423	Merino Village, .	197	488	511	999
Revere, . . .	1,652	3,721	3,702	7,423	Perryville, . .	40	121	123	244
Winthrop, . . .	910	2,015	2,177	4,192	Stevens' Village, .	44	150	139	289
Winthrop, . .	910	2,015	2,177	4,192	West Dudley, . .	17	47	44	91
WORCESTER.					Fitchburg, . . .	5,686	13,037	13,372	26,409
Ashburnham, . .	530	1,070	1,078	2,148	East Fitchburg, .	32	80	64	144
Ashburnham, . .	311	618	643	1,261	Fitchburg, . .	5,014	11,265	11,699	22,964
No. Ashburnham, .	38	76	65	141	South Fitchburg, .	205	701	562	1,263
So. Ashburnham, .	181	376	370	746	West Fitchburg, .	435	991	1,047	2,038
Athol, ...	1,750	3,735	3,629	7,364	Gardner, . . .	2,062	4,735	4,447	9,182
Athol, . . .	1,189	2,744	2,550	5,294	Gardner, . . .	624	1,323	1,313	2,636
Athol Centre, . .	538	944	1,044	1,988	South Gardner, .	444	853	831	1,684
South Athol, . .	23	47	35	82	West Gardner, .	994	2,559	2,303	4,862
Auburn, . . .	345	821	777	1,598	Grafton, . . .	1,106	2,455	2,646	5,101
Auburn, . . .	230	520	468	988	Farnumsville, . .	119	294	276	570
Stoneville, . .	81	214	230	444	Fisherville, . .	132	378	403	781
West Auburn, . .	34	87	79	166	Grafton, . . .	382	716	771	1,487
Barre, ...	558	1,150	1,128	2,278	North Grafton, .	366	839	944	1,783
Barre, . . .	502	1,018	1,000	2,018	Saundersville, .	81	180	200	380
					Wilkinsonville, .	26	48	52	100

VILLAGES: BY TOWNS — Continued.

Counties, Cities, Towns, and Villages.	Number of Families	Males	Females	Population
WORCESTER — Con.				
Hardwick, . . .	533	1,376	1,279	2,655
Furnace, . . .	18	41	41	82
Gilbertville, . .	291	765	779	1,544
Hardwick, . .	204	512	405	917
Wheelwright, . .	20	58	54	112
Harvard, . . .	279	574	588	1,162
Harvard, . .	240	506	520	1,026
Still River, . .	39	68	68	136
Holden, . . .	555	1,392	1,300	2,692
Chaffinville, . .	43	120	106	226
Dawsonville, . .	38	102	101	203
Holden, . . .	174	274	326	600
Jeffersonville, .	153	411	415	826
North Woods, . .	21	72	48	120
Quinapoxet, . .	66	185	176	361
Springdale, . .	30	75	68	143
Unionville, . .	30	63	60	123
Hopedale, . . .	307	698	679	1,377
Hopedale, . .	307	698	679	1,377
Hubbardston, . .	348	659	615	1,274
East Hubbardston,	9	23	20	43
Hubbardston,. .	318	597	555	1,152
Williamsville,. .	21	39	40	79
Lancaster, . . .	452	978	1,202	2,180
Lancaster, . .	248	519	679	1,198
South Lancaster, .	204	459	523	982
Leicester, . .	731	1,541	1,688	3,239
Cherry Valley, .	211	468	532	1,001
Leicester,. . .	372	768	839	1,607
Rochdale,. . .	148	304	327	631
Leominster, . . .	2,181	4,504	4,707	9,211
Leominster, . .	1,945	4,020	4,233	8,253
North Leominster,.	236	484	474	958
Lunenburg,. .	302	626	611	1,237
Lunenburg, . .	302	626	611	1,237
Mendon, . . .	234	462	427	889
Mendon, . . .	234	462	427	889
Milford,. . .	2,116	4,354	4,605	8,959
Milford, . . .	2,116	4,354	4,605	8,959
Millbury, . .	1,300	2,619	2,603	5,222
Aldrichville, . .	40	92	106	198
Armory Village, .	558	1,309	1,274	2,583
Bramanville, . .	255	663	680	1,343
Buck's Village, .	17	38	46	84
Burling Mills,. .	26	53	48	101
Millbury,. . .	116	241	245	486
West Millbury, .	64	151	148	299
Wheelersville, .	24	72	56	128
New Braintree, .	114	292	250	542
New Braintree, .	114	292	250	542
Northborough, .	451	975	965	1,940
Chapinville, .	57	165	142	307
Northborough, .	345	690	709	1,399
Woodside Mills, .	49	120	114	234
Northbridge, . .	1,070	2,732	2,554	5,286
Linwood, . .	84	227	269	496

Counties, Cities, Towns, and Villages.	Number of Families	Males	Females	Population
WORCESTER — Con.				
Northbridge — Con.				
Northbridge, . .	154	468	454	922
Northbridge Centre,	95	187	156	343
Riverdale, . .	39	111	103	214
Whitinsville, . .	698	1,739	1,572	3,311
North Brookfield, .	1,630	2,248	2,387	4,635
North Brookfield, .	1,630	2,248	2,387	4,635
Oakham, . . .	161	308	297	605
Coldbrook, . .	28	59	57	116
Oakham, . . .	133	249	240	489
Oxford, ...	618	1,147	1,243	2,390
Bartlett's Village, .	30	53	74	127
Buffum's Village, .	3	6	6	12
Chase's Village, .	13	37	19	56
Combs' Village, .	13	27	27	54
Howarth's Village,	23	48	57	105
North Oxford, .	50	112	108	220
Oxford, . . .	439	753	808	1,561
Texas Village, .	47	111	144	255
Paxton, ...	114	234	192	426
Paxton, . . .	114	234	192	426
Petersham, . .	254	493	459	952
Nichewaug, . .	13	28	22	50
Peter-ham, . .	241	465	437	902
Phillipston, . .	114	248	212	460
East Phillipston, .	7	9	15	24
Phillipston, . .	107	239	197	436
Princeton, . . .	236	491	461	952
East Hubbardston,	6	14	14	28
East Princeton, .	34	61	55	116
Princeton, . . .	196	416	392	808
Royalston, . . .	254	454	436	890
Royalston, . .	163	305	294	599
South Royalston, .	91	149	142	291
Rutland, . . .	225	526	452	978
North Rutland, .	8	14	17	31
Rutland, . . .	196	458	388	846
West Rutland,. .	21	54	47	101
Shrewsbury.. .	381	784	740	1,524
Shrewsbury, . .	381	784	740	1,524
Southborough, .	442	1,274	949	2,223
Cordaville, . .	57	131	112	243
Fayville, . . .	106	249	197	446
Southborough, .	207	751	456	1,244
Southville, . .	72	143	147	290
Southbridge, . .	1,688	4,043	4,207	8,250
Globe Village, .	753	1,813	1,878	3,691
Southbridge. . .	935	2,230	2,329	4,559
Spencer, . . .	1,625	3,784	3,830	7,614
Hillsville, . . .	47	125	102	227
North Spencer, .	26	83	66	149
South Spencer, .	32	79	71	150
Spencer, . . .	1,454	3,307	3,434	6,741
Wire Village, . .	66	190	157	347
Sterling, ...	342	604	614	1,218
Pratt's Junction, .	24	52	45	97

VILLAGES: BY TOWNS — Concluded.

Counties, Cities, Towns, and Villages.	Number of Families	Males	Females	Population	Counties, Cities, Towns, and Villages.	Number of Families	Males	Females	Population
WORCESTER — Con.					**WORCESTER — Con.**				
Sterling — Con.					Westborough, . .	1,031	2,611	2,624	5,235
Sterling, . . .	279	476	496	972	Westborough, .	1,031	2,611	2,624	5,235
Sterling Junction, .	22	44	38	82	West Boylston, . .	648	1,447	1,521	2,968
West Sterling, .	17	32	35	67	Harrisville, . .	46	127	106	233
Sturbridge, . . .	434	948	962	1,910	Oakdale, . . .	248	644	651	1,295
Fiskdale, . . .	228	553	595	1,148	South Boylston, .	164	290	343	633
Sturbridge, . .	206	395	367	762	West Boylston, .	190	386	421	807
Sutton, ...	714	1,770	1,650	3,420	West Brookfield, .	469	717	750	1,467
Aldrichville, . .	25	67	54	121	West Brookfield, .	469	717	750	1,467
Manchaug, . .	267	798	768	1,566	Westminster, . .	370	632	683	1,315
Marbleville, . .	15	27	28	55	North Common, .	9	14	9	23
Smithville, . .	11	28	24	52	South Westminster,	42	80	78	158
South Sutton, . .	54	104	111	215	Wachusett Park, .	4	8	11	19
Sutton, . . .	175	344	328	672	Wachusettville, .	19	32	29	61
West Sutton, . .	47	81	74	155	Westminster, . .	115	229	224	453
Wilkinsonville, .	120	321	263	584	Westminster Cen-				
Templeton, . . .	718	1,488	1,427	2,915	tre, . . .	147	206	272	478
Baldwinville, . .	284	638	602	1,240	Westminster Depot,	24	49	46	95
East Templeton, .	116	184	196	380	Whitman's Village,	10	14	14	28
Otter River, . .	96	228	206	434	Winchendon, . .	1,078	2,257	2,233	4,490
Templeton, . .	222	438	423	861	Bullardville, . .	38	68	50	118
Upton, . . .	524	908	1,242	2,150	Glenallen, . .	23	90	87	177
Upton, . . .	371	616	662	1,278	Harrisville, . .	5	15	7	22
West Upton, . .	153	292	580	872	Hydeville, . .	18	42	37	79
Uxbridge, . . .	812	1,780	1,766	3,546	New Boston, . .	28	58	43	101
Calumet, . . .	41	94	88	182	Waterville, . .	139	289	243	532
Elmdale, . . .	26	67	57	124	Winchendon, . .	726	1,434	1,469	2,903
Hecla, . . .	56	157	140	297	Winchendon Centre,	24	47	46	93
North Uxbridge, .	166	387	387	774	Winchendon Springs,	77	214	251	465
South Uxbridge, .	19	44	33	77	**WORCESTER, . .**	20,861	48,863	49,904	98,767
Uxbridge, . .	173	356	344	700	Barnardville, . .	22	73	54	127
Uxbridge Centre, .	289	579	626	1,205	Bloomingdale, . .	126	825	844	1,669
Wheelocksville, .	42	96	91	187	Greendale, . .	126	263	279	542
Warren, . . .	980	2,197	2,233	4,430	Jamesville, . .	46	119	107	226
Warren, . . .	656	1,443	1,467	2,910	Lake View, . .	181	352	376	728
West Warren, . .	324	754	766	1,520	New Worcester, .	327	709	692	1,401
Webster, . . .	1,716	3,709	4,090	7,799	North Worcester, .	14	27	33	60
East Village, . .	101	258	234	492	Quinsigamond, .	522	1,375	1,194	2,569
North Village, .	135	382	358	740	South Worcester, .	1,002	2,802	2,633	5,435
South Village, .	237	527	592	1,119	Trowbridgeville, .	22	53	64	117
Webster, . . .	1,133	2,357	2,510	4,867	Valley Falls, . .	88	215	235	450
Webster Depot, .	110	275	306	581	WORCESTER, . .	18,325	42,050	43,363	85,443

VILLAGES, SECTIONS, ETC.:

ALPHABETICALLY.

VILLAGES, SECTIONS, ETC.: ALPHABETICALLY.

In this presentation the villages, sections, etc., in each town and city of the State are arranged alphabetically. Following the name of the village, section, etc., is given the name of the city or town, the county, and, in the case of villages, the number of families and the number of males, females, and total population.

In this presentation the aggregate population of the cities and towns is not given. This may, of course, be found by referring to the preceding table, "VILLAGES: BY TOWNS." The population which, in any city or town, exists outside the limits of the villages or sections for which population figures are given in this table, may also be found in the preceding table, but, to avoid confusion, is omitted here.

It has been found impossible to give the population of each locality, as many of the popular names given indicate sections to which there are no definite boundaries, but for the larger sections or villages the number of families and the population by sex are presented.

The asterisk (*) indicates post offices, the parallel (‖) railroad stations, and the section sign (§) steamboat landings.]

CITIES, TOWNS, VILLAGES, SECTIONS, ETC.	Cities and Towns	Counties	Number of Families	Males	Females	Population
Abbott Village,	Andover,	Essex, .	–	–	–	–
Aberdeen,	BOSTON,	Suffolk,	–	–	–	–
Abington,* ‖ .	Abington,	Plymouth, .	–	–	–	–
Academy Hill,	BOSTON,	Suffolk,	–	–	–	–
Acre,	Clinton, .	Worcester, .	–	–	–	–
Acton,* ‖	Acton, .	Middlesex, .	–	–	–	–
Acton Centre,	Acton, .	Middlesex,	63	94	102	196
Acushnet,* ‖ ¹	Acushnet,	Bristol, .	–	–	–	–
Adams,* ‖	Adams, .	Berkshire, .	–	–	–	–
Adams' Corners, .	Northbridge,	Worcester, .	–	–	–	–
Adamsdale,* ‖	North Attleborough, .	Bristol, .	38	91	75	166
Adamsville,* .	Colrain, .	Franklin, .	52	128	108	236
Agawam,*	Agawam,	Hampden, .	–	–	–	–
Alander,*	Mount Washington, .	Berkshire, .	–	–	–	–
Albeeville,	Mendon,	Worcester, .	–	–	–	–
Aldenville, .	CHICOPEE, .	Hampden, .	22	65	55	120
Aldrichville, .	Granby, .	Hampshire,	–	–	–	–
Aldrichville, .	Millbury,	Worcester, .	40	92	106	198
Aldrichville, .	Sutton, .	Worcester, .	25	67	54	121
Alford,* .	Alford, .	Berkshire, .	–	–	–	–
Algeria, .	Otis, .	Berkshire, .	–	–	–	–
Algerine,	Berkley,	Bristol, .	–	–	-	–
Allen's Corner, .	Amesbury, .	Essex, .	–	–	-	–
Allenville,	Walpole,	Norfolk, .	–	–	–	–
Allenville,	WOBURN,	Middlesex, .	–	–	–	–
Allston,* ‖	BOSTON,	Suffolk, .	–	–	–	–
Allston Heights, .	BOSTON,	Suffolk, .	–	–	–	–
Almont, ‖	Tewksbury, .	Middlesex, .	–	–	–	–
Amesbury,* ‖	Amesbury, .	Essex, .	–	–	–	–
Amherst,* ‖ .	Amherst, .	Hampshire, .	–	–	–	–
Amherst City,	Amherst, .	Hampshire,	–	–	–	–
Amostown, .	West Springfield, .	Hampden, .	–	–	–	–
Anawam, .	BOSTON,	Suffolk, .	–	–	–	–
Andover,* ‖ .	Andover, .	Essex, .	–	–	–	–
Annisquam,*.	GLOUCESTER,	Essex, .	98	160	174	334

¹ R. R. station in the city of New Bedford.

[87]

VILLAGES, SECTIONS, ETC.: ALPHABETICALLY — Continued.

Cities, Towns, Villages, Sections, Etc.	Cities and Towns	Counties	Number of Families	Males	Females	Population
Apponegansett,* . . .	Dartmouth, . . .	Bristol, . .	29	54	53	107
Aquashenet, ...	Mashpee, . . .	Barnstable, .	–	–	–	–
Argilla, ...	Ipswich, . . .	Essex, . . .	–	–	–	–
Arlington,* ‖	Arlington, . . .	Middlesex, . .	–	–	–	–
Arlington District, . .	LAWRENCE, . . .	Essex, . . .	–	–	–	–
Arlington Heights,* ‖ . .	Arlington, . . .	Middlesex, . .	158	371	421	792
Armory, ‖	SPRINGFIELD, . .	Hampden, . .	–	–	–	–
Armory Hill, . . .	SPRINGFIELD, . .	Hampden, . .	–	–	–	–
Armory Village, . . .	Millbury, . . .	Worcester, . .	558	1,309	1,274	2,583
Arnoldsville, ...	Adams, ...	Berkshire, . .	–	–	–	–
Arsenal, ...	Watertown, . . .	Middlesex, . .	–	–	–	–
Artichoke, ...	NEWBURYPORT, . .	Essex, . . .	–	–	–	–
Asbury Grove,* . . .	Hamilton, . . .	Essex, . . .	56	58	89	147
Ashburnham,* ‖ . . .	Ashburnham, . .	Worcester, . .	–	–	–	–
Ashby,*	Ashby, ...	Middlesex, . .	–	–	–	–
Ashby Centre, . . .	Ashby, ...	Middlesex, . .	49	61	86	147
Ashcroft,* ‖	Dedham, . . .	Norfolk, . .	16	34	40	74
Ashdale, ...	BROCKTON, . . .	Plymouth, . .	–	–	–	–
Ashdod, ...	Duxbury, . . .	Plymouth, . .	16	32	23	55
Ashfield,*	Ashfield, . . .	Franklin, . .	–	–	–	–
Ashfield Plain, . . .	Ashfield, . . .	Franklin, . .	61	80	111	191
Ashland,* ‖	Ashland, . . .	Middlesex, . .	–	–	–	–
Ashley Falls,* ‖ . . .	Sheffield, . . .	Berkshire, . .	88	135	149	284
Ashleyville, ...	West Springfield, .	Hampden, . .	–	–	–	–
Ashmont, ‖	BOSTON, . . .	Suffolk, . .	–	–	–	–
Assinippi,*	Hanover, . . .	Plymouth, . .	39	66	66	132
Assinippi, ...	Norwell, . . .	Plymouth, . .	73	116	132	248
Assonet, ‖	Freetown, . . .	Bristol, . .	101	210	204	414
Assonet Neck, . . .	Berkley, . . .	Bristol, . .	–	–	–	–
Asylum Station,* ‖ . .	Danvers, . . .	Essex, . . .	–	–	–	–
Athol,* ‖	Athol, ...	Worcester, . .	–	–	–	–
Athol Centre,* . . .	Athol, ...	Worcester, . .	538	944	1,044	1,988
Atlantic,* ‖	QUINCY, . . .	Norfolk, . .	461	1,035	1,056	2,091
Atlantic, ‖	SALEM, ...	Essex, . . .	–	–	–	–
Atlantic Hill, . . .	Hull, ...	Plymouth, . .	–	–	–	–
Attleborough,* ‖ . . .	Attleborough, . .	Bristol, . .	–	–	–	–
Attleborough Falls,* ‖ [1]	North Attleborough, .	Bristol, . .	250	516	580	1,096
Auburn,* ‖	Auburn, . . .	Worcester, . .	–	–	–	–
Auburndale,* ‖ . . .	NEWTON, . . .	Middlesex, . .	534	1,142	1,674	2,816
Auburnville, ...	Whitman, . . .	Plymouth, . .	74	132	143	275
Avon,* ‖	Avon, ...	Norfolk, . .	–	–	–	–
Ayer,* ‖	Ayer, ...	Middlesex, . .	–	–	–	–
Ayer City, ...	LOWELL, . . .	Middlesex, . .	135	331	332	663
Ayer's Village,* . . .	HAVERHILL, . .	Essex, . . .	58	107	103	210
Ayer's Village, . . .	Methuen, . . .	Essex, . . .	9	19	15	34
Babb. tassett, . . .	Pepperell, . . .	Middlesex, . .	–	–	–	–
Back Bay,*	BOSTON, . . .	Suffolk, . .	–	–	–	–
Back Row, ...	North Reading, . .	Middlesex, . .	–	–	–	–
Baker's Island, . . .	SALEM, ...	Essex, . . .	3	5	6	11
Bakerville, ...	Dartmouth, . . .	Bristol, . .	–	–	–	–
Baldwinville,* ‖ . . .	Templeton, . . .	Worcester, . .	284	638	602	1,240
Ballardvale,* ‖ . . .	Andover, . . .	Essex, . . .	209	397	468	865
Ballville, ...	Bolton, ...	Worcester, . .	–	–	–	–
Bancroft,* ‖	Middlefield, . . .	Hampshire, . .	16	36	39	75
Baptist Village, . . .	East Longmeadow, .	Hampden, . .	–	–	–	–
Barber's, ‖	WORCESTER, . .	Worcester, . .	–	–	–	–
Bardwell's Ferry,* ‖ . .	Shelburne, . . .	Franklin, . .	–	–	–	–

[1] R. R. name Falls Village.

VILLAGES, SECTIONS, ETC.: ALPHABETICALLY — Continued.

Cities, Towns, Villages, Sections, Etc.	Cities and Towns	Counties	Number of Families	Males	Fe-males	Population
Bare Hill, ...	Harvard, . . .	Worcester, . .	–	–	–	–
Barkersville,. . . .	PITTSFIELD,. . .	Berkshire, . .	71	177	155	342
Barleyneck, ...	Orleans,. . . .	Barnstable, . .	–	–	–	–
Barnardville, . . .	WORCESTER, . .	Worcester, . .	22	73	54	127
Barneyville, ...	Swansea, . . .	Bristol, . . .	–	–	–	–
Barnstable,* ‖ . . .	Barnstable, . . .	Barnstable, . .	–	–	–	–
Barrack Hill, . . .	Rutland, . . .	Worcester, . .	–	–	–	–
Barre,* ‖	Barre, ...	Worcester, . .	–	–	–	–
Barre Falls, ...	Barre, ...	Worcester, . .	–	–	–	–
Barre Four Corners, . .	Barre, ...	Worcester, . .	–	–	–	–
Barre Plains,* ‖ . . .	Barre, ...	Worcester, . .	26	71	49	120
Barrett's Junction, ‖ .	Belchertown, . .	Hampshire, . .	–	–	–	–
Barrowsville,* ‖ . .	Norton, ...	Bristol, . .	63	117	127	244
Barry's Corner, . . .	BOSTON, . . .	Suffolk, . .	–	–	–	–
Bartlett Park, . . .	Winthrop, . . .	Suffolk, . .	–	–	–	–
Bartlett's Village, . .	Oxford, ...	Worcester, . .	30	53	74	127
Bartonville, ...	Dalton, . . .	Berkshire, . .	–	–	–	–
Bass Point, . . .	Nahant, . . .	Essex, . . .	–	–	–	–
Bass Rocks, ...	GLOUCESTER, . .	Essex, . . .	–	–	–	–
Bayside, ...	Hull, ...	Plymouth, . .	–	–	–	–
Bay State Village,* 1 .	NORTHAMPTON, .	Hampshire, . .	222	574	558	1,132
Bay View, ...	BOSTON, . . .	Suffolk, . .	–	–	–	–
Bay View,*	GLOUCESTER, .	Essex, . . .	228	583	482	1,065
Beach Bluff,* ‖ . . .	Swampscott,. . .	Essex, . . .	4	15	19	34
Beachmont, ‖ . . .	Revere, ...	Suffolk, . .	–	–	–	–
Beacon Park, . . .	BOSTON, . . .	Suffolk, . .	–	–	–	–
Bearcroft, ‖	Attleborough, . .	Bristol, . .	–	–	–	–
Bear Hill, ...	Merrimac, . . .	Essex, . . .	–	–	–	–
Bear Town, ...	Great Barrington, .	Berkshire, . .	–	–	–	–
Beaver, ...	East Bridgewater, .	Plymouth, . .	58	129	113	242
Beaver, ...	NORTH ADAMS, .	Berkshire, . .	–	–	–	–
Beaver Brook, ‖ . .	WALTHAM, . . .	Middlesex, . .	–	–	–	–
Becket,* ‖	Becket, . . .	Berkshire, . .	–	–	–	–
Becket Centre,* . . .	Becket, ...	Berkshire, . .	13	33	21	54
Bedford,* ‖	Bedford, . . .	Middlesex, . .	–	–	–	–
Bedford Springs,* ‖ .	Bedford, . . .	Middlesex, . .	–	–	–	–
Beech Plain, . . .	Sandisfield, . . .	Berkshire, . .	–	–	–	–
Beechwood,* ‖ . . .	Cohasset, . . .	Norfolk, . .	87	172	170	342
Beechwoods,. . . .	Lakeville, . . .	Plymouth, . .	–	–	–	–
Bel Air, ...	PITTSFIELD, . .	Berkshire, . .	86	213	220	433
Belcher's Corner, . .	Stoughton, . . .	Norfolk, . .	–	–	–	–
Belchertown,* ‖ . .	Belchertown, . .	Hampshire, . .	–	–	–	–
Belleville, ...	NEW BEDFORD, .	Bristol, . .	–	–	–	–
Belleville, ...	NEWBURYPORT, .	Essex, . . .	–	–	–	–
Bellingham,* ‖ 2 . .	Bellingham, . . .	Norfolk, . .	–	–	–	–
Bell Rock, ‖	MALDEN, . . .	Middlesex, . .	112	236	266	502
Belmont,* ‖	Belmont, . . .	Middlesex, . .	–	–	–	–
Belvidere, ...	LOWELL, . . .	Middlesex, . .	–	–	–	–
Belvidere Plain, . . .	Falmouth, . . .	Barnstable, . .	–	–	–	–
Bemis,* ‖	Watertown, . .	Middlesex, . .	–	–	–	–
Berkley Bridge, . . .	Berkley, . . .	Bristol, . .	34	67	58	125
Berkshire,* ‖. . . .	Lanesborough, .	Berkshire, . .	66	147	145	292
Berlin,* ‖	Berlin, ...	Worcester, . .	–	–	–	–
Bernardston,* ‖ . . .	Bernardston, . .	Franklin, . .	–	–	–	–
BEVERLY,* ‖ . . .	BEVERLY, . . .	Essex, . . .	–	–	–	–
Beverly Cove, . . .	BEVERLY, . . .	Essex, . . .	185	348	391	739
Beverly Farms,* ‖ . .	BEVERLY, . . .	Essex, . . .	205	425	408	833
Bigelow Hill, . . .	BOSTON, . . .	Suffolk, . .	–	–	–	–

1 P. O. name Bay State.   2 R. R. name Bellingham Junction.

VILLAGES, SECTIONS, ETC.: ALPHABETICALLY — Continued.

Cities, Towns, Villages, Sections, Etc.	Cities and Towns	Counties	Number of Families	Males	Fe-males	Popula-tion
Billerica,* ‖	Billerica,	Middlesex,	–	–	–	–
Billingsgate,	Wellfleet,	Barnstable,	–	–	–	–
Billings' Mill,	Montague,	Franklin,	–	–	–	–
Birch Meadow,	Merrimac,	Essex,	–	–	–	–
Bird Street, ‖	Boston,	Suffolk,	–	–	–	–
Blackinton,* ‖	NORTH ADAMS,	Berkshire,	81	187	182	369
Blackinton,	Williamstown,	Berkshire,	126	291	280	571
Blackstone,* ‖	Blackstone,	Worcester,	–	–	–	–
Blackwater,	Kingston,	Plymouth,	–	–	–	–
Blanchardville,	Palmer,	Hampden,	–	–	–	–
Blandford,*	Blandford,	Hampden,	–	–	–	–
Bleachery, ‖	LOWELL,	Middlesex,	–	–	–	–
Bleachery, ‖	WALTHAM,	Middlesex,	–	–	–	–
Blissville,	Orange,	Franklin,	–	–	–	–
Bloomingdale,	WORCESTER,	Worcester,	126	825	844	1,669
Blue Hill,*	Milton,	Norfolk,	–	–	–	–
Blue Hill Terrace,	Milton,	Norfolk,	–	–	–	–
Bolton,* ‖	Bolton,	Worcester,	–	–	–	–
Bolton Centre,	Bolton,	Worcester,	–	–	–	–
Bondsville,* ‖	Palmer,	Hampden,	209	573	606	1,179
Border City Village,	FALL RIVER,	Bristol,	–	–	–	–
Boston,* ‖	BOSTON,	Suffolk,	–	–	–	–
Boston Highlands,	BOSTON,	Suffolk,	–	–	–	–
Bostonville,	Wellesley,	Norfolk,	–	–	–	–
Bourne,* ‖	Bourne,	Barnstable,	–	–	–	–
Bournedale,* ‖	Bourne,	Barnstable,	29	46	50	96
Bowenville,	FALL RIVER,	Bristol,	336	977	1,008	1,985
Boxborough, ‖	Boxborough,	Middlesex,	–	–	–	–
Boxford,* ‖	Boxford,	Essex,	–	–	–	–
Boylston, ‖	BOSTON,	Suffolk,	–	–	–	–
Boylston,* ‖	Boylston,	Worcester,	–	–	–	–
Boylston Centre,*	Boylston,	Worcester,	40	68	69	137
Boyntonville,	Wakefield,	Middlesex,	–	–	–	–
Bozrah,	Hawley,	Franklin,	14	35	31	66
Bradford,* ‖	Bradford,	Essex,	–	–	–	–
Braggville,* ‖	Holliston,	Middlesex,	21	47	51	98
Braggville,	Milford,	Worcester,	–	–	–	–
Braintree,* ‖	Braintree,	Norfolk,	–	–	–	–
Braley's, ‖	Freetown,	Bristol,	–	–	–	–
Bramanville,	Millbury,	Worcester,	275	663	680	1,343
Brant Rock,*.	Marshfield,	Plymouth,	41	66	65	131
Brattles, ‖	Arlington,	Middlesex,	–	–	–	–
Brayton, ‖	Somerset,	Bristol,	–	–	–	–
Brayton Point, ‖	Somerset,	Bristol,	–	–	–	–
Braytonville, ‖	NORTH ADAMS,	Berkshire,	–	–	–	–
Breed's Island,	BOSTON,	Suffolk,	–	–	–	–
Brewster,* ‖	Brewster,	Barnstable,	–	–	–	–
Bridgewater,* ‖	Bridgewater,	Plymouth,	–	–	–	–
Bridgewater Iron Works, ‖	Bridgewater,	Plymouth,	–	–	–	–
Brier,*	Savoy,	Berkshire,	31	60	58	118
Briggs' Corner,*	Attleborough,	Bristol,	–	–	–	–
Briggsville,*	Clarksburg,	Berkshire,	40	111	119	230
Brighton,* ‖	BOSTON,	Suffolk,	3,172	7,293	7,708	15,001
Brighton Hill,	BOSTON,	Suffolk,	–	–	–	–
Brightside,	HOLYOKE,	Hampden,	–	–	–	–
Brightwood,* ‖	SPRINGFIELD,	Hampden,	188	438	412	850
Brimfield,*	Brimfield,	Hampden,	–	–	–	–
Brimfield Centre,	Brimfield,	Hampden,	65	100	117	217

VILLAGES, SECTIONS, ETC.: ALPHABETICALLY — Continued.

CITIES, TOWNS, VILLAGES, SECTIONS, ETC.	Cities and Towns	Counties	Number of Families	Males	Females	Population
Brittaniaville, . . .	TAUNTON, . . .	Bristol, . .	-	-	-	-
Broad Cove, ...	Hingham, . . .	Plymouth, . .	-	-	-	-
Broadway, ‖ . . .	MALDEN, . . .	Middlesex, . .	-	-	-	-
BROCKTON,* ‖ . .	BROCKTON, . . .	Plymouth, . .	-	-	-	-
Brockton Heights, . .	BROCKTON, . . .	Plymouth, . .	39	91	84	175
Brookdale, ...	Peabody, . . .	Essex, . . .	-	-	-	-
Brookfield,* ‖ . . .	Brookfield, . . .	Worcester, . .	-	-	-	-
Brookline,* ‖ . . .	Brookline, . . .	Norfolk, . . .	-	-	-	-
Brookline Hills, ‖ . .	Brookline, . . .	Norfolk, . .	-	-	-	-
Brooks' Hollow, . .	New Marlborough, .	Berkshire, . .	-	-	-	-
Brookside, ‖	Westford, . . .	Middlesex, . .	18	37	47	84
Brooks' Station,* ‖ . .	Princeton, . . .	Worcester, . .	-	-	-	-
Brooks' Village, . .	Templeton, . . .	Worcester, . .	-	-	-	-
Brookville,*	Holbrook, . . .	Norfolk, . .	100	188	202	390
Broomshire, ...	Conway, . . .	Franklin, . .	-	-	-	-
Brown's Crossing, ‖ . .	East Bridgewater, .	Plymouth, . .	-	-	-	-
Brown's Crossing, ‖ . .	Wilmington, . .	Middlesex, . .	-	-	-	-
Brush Hill, ...	Milton, ...	Norfolk, . .	-	-	-	-
Bryantville,*. . . .	Pembroke, . . .	Plymouth, . .	65	107	103	210
Buckland,* ‖ . . .	Buckland, . . .	Franklin, . .	-	-	-	-
Buck's Village, . . .	Millbury, . . .	Worcester, . .	17	38	46	84
Buffum's Village, . .	Oxford, ...	Worcester, . .	3	6	6	12
Bullardville, ...	Winchendon, . .	Worcester, . .	38	68	50	118
Bumpus Corner, . . .	BROCKTON, . .	Plymouth, . .	-	-	-	-
Bunker Hill, ...	BOSTON, . . .	Suffolk, . .	-	-	-	-
Bardin Hill, ...	Clinton, . . .	Worcester, . .	-	-	-	-
Burkinshaw, ...	Pepperell, . . .	Middlesex, . .	-	-	-	-
Burling Mills, . . .	Millbury, . . .	Worcester, . .	26	53	48	101
Burlington,*	Burlington, . . .	Middlesex, . .	-	-	-	-
Burt's Corners, . . .	Berkley, . . .	Bristol, . .	-	-	-	-
Burtt's, ‖	Tewksbury, . . .	Middlesex, . .	-	-	-	-
Bush, ...	BROCKTON, . .	Plymouth, . .	-	-	-	-
Bush Corner, . . .	Middleton, . . .	Essex, . . .	-	-	-	-
Butlerville, ...	Wilbraham, . . .	Hampden, . .	-	-	-	-
Buzzard's Bay,* ‖ . .	Bourne, . . .	Barnstable, . .	61	123	128	251
Byfield, ...	Georgetown, . .	Essex, . . .	53	104	88	192
Byfield,* ‖	Newbury, . . .	Essex, . . .	130	396	390	786
Calf Island, ...	Hull, ...	Plymouth, . .	2	4	2	6
California, ...	Clinton, . . .	Worcester, . .	-	-	-	-
Calumet, ...	Uxbridge, . . .	Worcester, . .	41	94	88	182
CAMBRIDGE,* ‖ . .	CAMBRIDGE, . .	Middlesex, . .	-	-	-	-
Cambridgeport,* . . .	CAMBRIDGE, . .	Middlesex, . .	9,234	19,808	21,505	41,313
Campello,* ‖	BROCKTON, . .	Plymouth, . .	1,705	2,779	2,715	5,494
Canada, ...	Sunderland, . .	Franklin, . .	-	-	-	-
Candlewood, ...	Ipswich, . . .	Essex, . . .	-	-	-	-
Cannonville, ...	Mattapoisett, . .	Plymouth, . .	-	-	-	-
Cannonville, ...	NEW BEDFORD, .	Bristol, . .	-	-	-	-
Canterbury, ...	BOSTON, . . .	Suffolk, . .	-	-	-	-
Canton,* ‖	Canton, . . .	Norfolk, . .	-	-	-	-
Canton Corner, . . .	Canton, . . .	Norfolk, . .	-	-	-	-
Canton Junction,* ‖ . .	Canton, . . .	Norfolk, . .	22	42	54	96
Cape Poge, ...	Edgartown, . . .	Dukes, . . .	-	-	-	-
Captain's Hill, . . .	Duxbury, . . .	Plymouth, . .	-	-	-	-
Careyville, ...	CHELSEA, . . .	Suffolk, . .	-	-	-	-
Carlisle,*	Carlisle, . . .	Middlesex, . .	-	-	-	-
Carltonville, ‖ . . .	SALEM, ...	Essex, . . .	-	-	-	-
Carsonville, ...	Dalton, ...	Berkshire, . .	-	-	-	-

VILLAGES, SECTIONS, ETC.: ALPHABETICALLY — Continued.

Cities, Towns, Villages, Sections, Etc.	Cities and Towns	Counties	Number of Families	Males	Females	Population
Carterville, ‖ [1]	Berlin,	Worcester,	19	33	34	67
Carterville,	CHELSEA,	Suffolk,	–	–	–	–
Carver,*	Carver,	Plymouth,	–	–	–	–
Cary Hill,	BROCKTON,	Plymouth,	–	–	–	–
Caryville,* ‖	Bellingham,	Norfolk,	51	108	122	230
Castle Hill,	SALEM,	Essex,	–	–	–	–
Castle Village,	Truro,	Barnstable,	–	–	–	–
Cataumet,* ‖	Bourne,	Barnstable,	49	85	82	167
Cedar Grove, ‖	BOSTON,	Suffolk,	–	–	–	–
Cedar Hill,	Clinton,	Worcester,	–	–	–	–
Cedarville,	Plymouth,	Plymouth,	23	46	34	80
Central, ‖	BOSTON,	Suffolk,	–	–	–	–
Central Avenue, ‖	Milton,	Norfolk,	–	–	–	–
Central Hill,	SOMERVILLE,	Middlesex,	–	–	–	–
Central Village,	Seekonk,	Bristol,	–	–	–	–
Central Village,*	Westport,	Bristol,	26	47	44	91
Centralville,	LOWELL,	Middlesex,	2,567	5,442	6,387	11,829
Centre Hill,	Hull,	Plymouth,	–	–	–	–
Centreville,*	Barnstable,	Barnstable,	118	168	211	379
Centreville,	BROCKTON,	Plymouth,	–	–	–	–
Centreville,	Winchendon,	Worcester,	–	–	–	–
Chace's,	Freetown,	Bristol,	–	–	–	–
Chace's, ‖	TAUNTON,	Bristol,	–	–	–	–
Chaffinville, ‖ [2]	Holden,	Worcester,	43	120	106	226
Chapel Station,	Brookline,	Norfolk,	–	–	–	–
Chapinsville,	LAWRENCE,	Essex,	–	–	–	–
Chapinville,*	Northborough,	Worcester,	57	165	142	307
Chappaquiddic,	Edgartown,	Dukes,	22	37	34	71
Charityville,	Williamstown,	Berkshire,	–	–	–	–
Charlemont,* ‖	Charlemont,	Franklin,	–	–	–	–
Charles River Village,* ‖	Needham,	Norfolk,	40	94	85	179
Charlestown,* ‖	BOSTON,	Suffolk,	8,762	20,489	19,815	40,304
Charlton,*	Charlton,	Worcester,	–	–	–	–
Charlton City,*	Charlton,	Worcester,	106	231	249	480
Charlton Depot,* ‖	Charlton,	Worcester,	73	154	135	289
Chartley,* ‖	Norton,	Bristol,	83	181	172	353
Chase's Village,	Oxford,	Worcester,	13	37	19	56
Chaseville,	Dudley,	Worcester,	42	112	109	221
Chatham,* ‖	Chatham,	Barnstable,	–	–	–	–
Chathamport,*	Chatham,	Barnstable,	38	57	67	124
Chattanooga,	Ashland,	Middlesex,	–	–	–	–
Cheapside,	Deerfield,	Franklin,	44	133	90	223
Chelmsford,* ‖	Chelmsford,	Middlesex,	–	–	–	–
CHELSEA,* ‖	CHELSEA,	Suffolk,	–	–	–	–
Cherry Brook, ‖	Weston,	Middlesex,	–	–	–	–
Cherry Valley,*	Leicester,	Worcester,	211	469	532	1,001
Cherry Valley,	Ludlow,	Hampden,	–	–	–	–
Cheshire,* ‖	Cheshire,	Berkshire,	–	–	–	–
Cheshire Corner,	Cheshire,	Berkshire,	–	–	–	–
Cheshire Harbor, ‖	Cheshire,	Berkshire,	–	–	–	–
Chester,* ‖	Chester,	Hampden,	–	–	–	–
Chester Centre,	Chester,	Hampden,	25	67	54	121
Chesterfield,*	Chesterfield,	Hampshire,	–	–	–	–
Chestnut Hill,	Brookline,	Norfolk,	–	–	–	–
Chestnut Hill, ‖	NEWTON,	Middlesex,	–	–	–	–
Chickering, ‖	BOSTON,	Suffolk,	–	–	–	–
CHICOPEE,* ‖	CHICOPEE,	Hampden,	–	–	–	–
Chicopee Falls,* ‖	CHICOPEE,	Hampden,	1,086	2,887	2,964	5,851

[1] R. R. name Berlin. [2] R. R. name Chaffins.

VILLAGES, SECTIONS, ETC.: ALPHABETICALLY — Continued.

Cities, Towns, Villages, Sections, Etc.	Cities and Towns	Counties	Number of Families	Males	Females	Population
Chiltonville,*	Plymouth,	Plymouth,	151	333	335	668
Chimquist,	Mashpee,	Barnstable,	–	–	–	–
Church Hill,	Norwell,.	Plymouth,	74	137	140	277
Cinder Hill,	East Bridgewater,	Plymouth,	–	–	–	–
City Mills,* ‖	Norfolk,	Norfolk,	46	115	108	223
City Point,	BOSTON,	Suffolk,	–	–	–	–
Clarendon Hills,‖	Hyde Park,	Norfolk,	492	1,061	1,144	2,205
Clarendon Hills,	SOMERVILLE,	Middlesex,	–	–	–	–
Clark's Point,	NEW BEDFORD,	Bristol,	–	–	–	–
Claverack,	Whately,	Franklin,	–	–	–	–
Clayton,*	New Marlborough,	Berkshire,	41	98	76	174
Cleghorn,	FITCHBURG,	Worcester,	–	–	–	–
Clematis Brook,‖	WALTHAM,	Middlesex,	–	–	–	–
Clifford,*	NEW BEDFORD,	Bristol,	–	–	–	–
Clifton,* ‖	Marblehead,.	Essex,	–	–	–	–
Cliftondale,* ‖	Saugus,	Essex,	383	783	864	1,647
Clifton Heights,	BROCKTON,	Plymouth,	–	–	–	–
Clinton,* ‖	Clinton,	Worcester,	–	–	–	–
Coatue,	Nantucket,	Nantucket,	–	–	–	–
Cochesett,* ‖	West Bridgewater,	Plymouth,	104	215	195	410
Cochituate,*	Wayland,	Middlesex,	280	654	620	1,274
Cohasset,* ‖	Cohasset,	Norfolk,	–	–	–	–
Coldbrook,* ‖ [1]	Oakham,	Worcester,	28	59	57	116
Cold Spring,	Otis,	Berkshire,	–	–	–	–
Cold Spring,*	Westford,	Middlesex,	9	21	17	38
Cole's Station,‖	Swansea,	Bristol,	–	–	–	–
Coleville,	Williamstown,	Berkshire,	–	–	–	–
College Hill,‖	MEDFORD,	Middlesex,	–	–	–	–
College Hill,	WORCESTER,	Worcester,	–	–	–	–
Collins,‖	Ludlow,	Hampden,	–	–	–	–
Collins Street,‖	Danvers,	Essex,	–	–	–	–
Collinsville,*.	Dracut,	Middlesex,	138	444	374	818
Colrain,*.	Colrain,	Franklin,	–	–	–	–
Coltsville,‖	PITTSFIELD,.	Berkshire,	80	191	202	393
Columbus Park,	WORCESTER,	Worcester,	–	–	–	–
Comins' Village,	Oxford,	Worcester,	13	27	27	54
Commercial Point,	BOSTON,	Suffolk,	–	–	–	–
Concord,* ‖	Concord,	Middlesex,	–	–	–	–
Concord Junction,* ‖	Concord,	Middlesex,	–	–	–	–
Congamuck,‖	Southwick,	Hampden,	–	–	–	–
Conway,* ‖	Conway.	Franklin,	–	–	–	–
Cook Street,‖	NEWTON,	Middlesex,	–	–	–	–
Cooleyville,*.	New Salem,	Franklin,	19	36	33	69
Coolidge Corner,	Brookline,	Norfolk,	–	–	–	–
Coolidgeville,	Hudson,	Middlesex,	–	–	–	–
Copecut,	FALL RIVER,	Bristol,	–	–	–	–
Cordaville,* ‖	Southborough,	Worcester,	57	131	112	243
Cordis Mills,	Millbury,	Worcester,	–	–	–	–
Corey Hill,	Brookline,	Norfolk,	–	–	–	–
Corriganville,	Hyde Park,	Norfolk,	–	–	–	–
Cottage City,* §	Cottage City,	Dukes,.	–	–	–	–
Cottage Farm,‖	BOSTON,	Suffolk,	–	–	–	–
Cottage Farm,	Brookline,	Norfolk,	–	–	–	–
Cottage Hill,	Winthrop,	Suffolk,	–	–	–	–
Cottage Park,	Winthrop,	Suffolk,	–	–	–	–
Cotuit,*	Barnstable,	Barnstable,.	137	221	243	464
Craigville,*	Barnstable,	Barnstable,.	–	–	–	–
Crane's,‖	Norton,	Bristol,	–	–	–	–

[1] P. O, name Coldbrook Springs.

VILLAGES, SECTIONS, ETC.: ALPHABETICALLY — Continued.

CITIES, TOWNS, VILLAGES, SECTIONS, ETC.	Cities and Towns	Counties	Number of Families	Males	Females	Population
Craneville, ...	Dalton, ...	Berkshire, . .	–	–	–	–
Crescent Avenue, ‖ .	BOSTON, . . .	Suffolk, . .	–	–	–	–
Crescent Beach, ‖ . .	Revere, ...	Suffolk, . .	–	–	–	–
Crescent Hill, . .	SPRINGFIELD, . .	Hampden, . .	–	–	–	–
Crescent Mills, . .	Russell, . . .	Hampden, . .	18	55	38	93
Crescent Park, . .	WALTHAM, . . .	Middlesex, . .	–	–	–	–
Cricket Hill, . . .	Conway, . . .	Franklin, . .	–	–	–	–
Crookertown, . .	Pembroke, . .	Plymouth, . .	–	–	–	–
Cross Street, ‖ . .	Winchester, . .	Middlesex, . .	–	–	–	–
Crystal Spring, ‖ . .	Freetown, . . .	Bristol, . .	–	–	–	–
Cummings' Corner, .	Phillipston, . .	Worcester, . .	–	–	–	–
Cummingsville,* . .	WOBURN, . . .	Middlesex, . .	65	151	157	308
Cummington,* . .	Cummington, . .	Hampshire, . .	–	–	–	–
Cummington Hill, .	Cummington, . .	Hampshire, . .	–	–	–	–
Cumston Village, .	Burlington, . .	Middlesex, . .	–	–	–	–
Curson's Mills, . .	NEWBURYPORT, .	Essex, . . .	–	–	–	–
Curtisville, . . .	East Bridgewater, .	Plymouth, . .	34	65	67	132
Curtisville,* . . .	Stockbridge, . .	Berkshire, . .	79	181	164	345
Cutter Village, . .	Winchester, . .	Middlesex, . .	–	–	–	–
Cuttyhunk,* § . . .	Gosnold, . . .	Dukes, . . .	29	60	40	100
Dalton,* ‖	Dalton, ...	Berkshire, . .	–	–	–	–
Dalton Centre, . .	Dalton, . . .	Berkshire, . .	–	–	–	–
Daltonville, . . .	NEWBURYPORT, .	Essex, . .	–	–	–	–
Dana,*	Dana, . . .	Worcester, . .	–	–	–	–
Danvers,* ‖ . . .	Danvers, . .	Essex, . . .	–	–	–	–
Danvers Centre,* . .	Danvers, . .	Essex, . .	155	325	305	630
Danvers Junction ‖ .	Danvers, . .	Essex, . .	–	–	–	–
Danversport,* ‖ . .	Danvers, . .	Essex, . .	330	833	802	1,635
Darby, ‖	Plymouth, . .	Plymouth, . .	–	–	–	–
Dartmouth,* . . .	Dartmouth, . .	Bristol, . .	–	–	–	–
Davis,*	Rowe, . . .	Franklin, . .	–	–	–	–
Davisville, . . .	Falmouth, . .	Barnstable, . .	22	34	36	70
Dawsonville, ‖ [1] .	Holden, . . .	Worcester, . .	38	102	101	203
Dayville, ...	Chester, . . .	Hampden, . .	–	–	–	–
Deantown, . . .	Attleborough, . .	Bristol, . .	–	–	–	–
Dedham,* ‖ . . .	Dedham, . . .	Norfolk, . .	–	–	–	–
Deerfield,* ‖ . . .	Deerfield, . .	Franklin, . .	–	–	–	–
Dell,*	Heath, . . .	Franklin, . .	15	35	26	61
Dennis,*	Dennis, . . .	Barnstable, . .	–	–	–	–
Dennison District, .	Southbridge, . .	Worcester, . .	–	–	–	–
Dennisport,* ‖ . .	Dennis, . . .	Barnstable, . .	257	353	425	778
Depot Hill, . . .	HOLYOKE, . .	Hampden, . .	–	–	–	–
Devereaux, ‖ . . .	Marblehead, . .	Essex, . .	39	89	85	174
Dighton,* ‖ . . .	Dighton, . .	Bristol, . .	–	–	–	–
Dodgeville,* ‖ . .	Attleborough, . .	Bristol, . .	131	342	358	700
Dog Town, . . .	Wellfleet, . .	Barnstable, . .	–	–	–	–
Dorchester,* ‖ . .	BOSTON, . . .	Suffolk, . .	10,004	21,332	24,577	45,909
Dorchester Heights, .	BOSTON, . . .	Suffolk, . .	–	–	–	–
Dorchester Lower Mills, .	BOSTON, . . .	Suffolk, . .	–	–	–	–
Douglas,* ‖ . . .	Douglas, . . .	Worcester, . .	–	–	–	–
Douglas Park, . .	BROCKTON, . .	Plymouth, . .	–	–	–	–
Dover,* ‖	Dover, . . .	Norfolk, . .	–	–	–	–
Downer Landing, § .	Hingham, . . .	Plymouth, . .	11	21	37	58
Dracut,*	Dracut, . . .	Middlesex, . .	–	–	–	–
Dracut Centre, . .	Dracut, . . .	Middlesex, . .	79	211	167	378
Dragon Corner, . .	Reading, . . .	Middlesex, . .	–	–	–	–
Dresser Hill, . . .	Charlton, . .	Worcester, . .	–	–	–	–

[1] R. R. name Dawsons.

VILLAGES, SECTIONS, ETC.: ALPHABETICALLY — Continued.

Cities, Towns, Villages, Sections, Etc.	Cities and Towns	Counties	Number of Families	Males	Females	Population
Dry Pond,	Stoughton,	Norfolk,	–	–	–	–
Duck Harbor,	Clinton,	Worcester,	–	–	–	–
Duckville,	Palmer,	Hampden,	–	–	–	–
Dudley,*	Dudley,	Worcester,	–	–	–	–
Dudley Street, ‖	BOSTON,	Suffolk,	–	–	–	–
Dudleyville,	Leverett,	Franklin,	–	–	–	–
Dunstable,* ‖	Dunstable,	Middlesex,	–	–	–	–
Durensville,	WOBURN,	Middlesex,	–	–	–	–
Duxbury,* ‖	Duxbury,	Plymouth,	–	–	–	–
Dwight,* ‖	Belchertown,	Hampshire,	22	51	38	89
Eagleville,	Orange,	Franklin,	–	–	–	–
East Acton,*	Acton,	Middlesex,	–	–	–	–
East Barnstable,	Barnstable,	Barnstable,	–	–	–	–
East Billerica,* ‖	Billerica,	Middlesex,	55	116	104	220
East Blackstone,* ‖	Blackstone,	Worcester,	71	151	153	304
East Bolton,	Bolton,	Worcester,	–	–	–	–
East Boston,* ‖	BOSTON,	Suffolk,	8,815	21,868	20,727	42,595
East Boxford,* ‖	Boxford,	Essex,	–	–	–	–
East Braintree,* ‖	Braintree,	Norfolk,	318	637	685	1,322
East Brewster,* ‖	Brewster,	Barnstable,	47	98	81	179
East Bridgewater,* ‖	East Bridgewater,	Plymouth,	–	–	–	–
East Brimfield,*	Brimfield,	Hampden,	39	82	74	156
East Brookfield,* ‖	Brookfield,	Worcester,	248	571	511	1,082
East Cambridge,* ‖	CAMBRIDGE,	Middlesex,	2,812	7,363	6,686	13,996
East Carver,*	Carver,	Plymouth,	35	60	63	123
East Charlemont,*	Charlemont,	Franklin,	49	90	80	179
East Chelmsford,	Chelmsford,	Middlesex,	56	139	117	256
East Danvers,	Danvers,	Essex,	–	–	–	–
East Dedham,	Dedham,	Norfolk,	388	898	889	1,787
East Deerfield,* ‖	Deerfield,	Franklin,	39	87	61	118
East Dennis,*	Dennis,	Barnstable,	108	147	191	338
East Douglas,* ‖	Douglas,	Worcester,	372	845	775	1,590
East End,	Wenham,	Essex,	–	–	–	–
East Everett, ‖	EVERETT,	Middlesex,	317	691	743	1,434
East Falmouth,*	Falmouth,	Barnstable,	59	109	100	209
East Farms,	Westfield,	Hampden,	18	35	29	64
East Fitchburg,	FITCHBURG,	Worcester,	32	80	64	144
East Foxborough,* ‖	Foxborough,	Norfolk,	190	194	163	357
East Freetown,* ‖	Freetown,	Bristol,	134	276	253	529
East Gloucester,	GLOUCESTER,	Essex,	696	1,682	1,516	3,198
East Groton, ‖	Groton,	Middlesex,	–	–	–	–
East Hadley,	Hadley,	Hampshire,	–	–	–	–
Eastham,*	Eastham,	Barnstable,	–	–	–	–
Easthampton,*	Easthampton,	Hampshire,	–	–	–	–
East Harwich,*	Harwich,	Barnstable,	73	134	126	260
East Haverhill,*	HAVERHILL,	Essex,	39	79	82	161
East Hawley,	Hawley,	Franklin,	–	–	–	–
East Holliston,* ‖	Holliston,	Middlesex,	81	132	155	287
East Hubbardston,	Hubbardston,	Worcester,	9	23	20	43
East Hubbardston,*	Princeton,	Worcester,	6	14	14	28
East Junction, ‖	Attleborough,	Bristol,	–	–	–	–
East Lee,*	Lee,	Berkshire,	108	187	220	407
East Leverett,*	Leverett,	Franklin,	44	77	82	159
East Lexington,* ‖	Lexington,	Middlesex,	150	291	336	627
East Littleton, ‖ [1]	Littleton,	Middlesex,	–	–	–	–
East Longmeadow,* ‖	East Longmeadow,	Hampden,	–	–	–	–
East Lynn, ‖	LYNN,	Essex,	1,260	2,588	2,732	5,320

[1] R. R. station in town of Westford.

VILLAGES, SECTIONS, ETC.: ALPHABETICALLY — Continued.

CITIES, TOWNS, VILLAGES, SECTIONS, ETC.	Cities and Towns	Counties	Number of Families	Males	Females	Population
East Mansfield,*	Mansfield,	Bristol,	–	–	–	–
East Mashpee,	Mashpee,	Barnstable,	–	–	–	–
East Mattapoisett,*	Mattapoisett,	Plymouth,	51	101	102	203
East Middleton,	Middleton,	Essex,	–	–	–	–
East Millis, ‖	Millis,	Norfolk,	–	–	–	–
East Milton,* ‖	Milton,	Norfolk,	257	560	601	1,161
East Northfield,*	Northfield,	Franklin,	84	127	496	623
East Norton,*	Norton,	Bristol,	132	248	251	499
Easton,* ‖	Easton,	Bristol,	–	–	–	–
Eastondale,* ‖	Easton,	Bristol,	92	175	153	328
East Orleans,*	Orleans,	Barnstable,	102	137	175	312
East Otis,	Otis,	Berkshire,	42	93	71	164
East Parish,	HAVERHILL,	Essex,	–	–	–	–
East Pembroke,*	Pembroke,	Plymouth,	41	61	63	124
East Pepperell,*	Pepperell,	Middlesex,	276	676	639	1,315
East Phillipston,	Phillipston,	Worcester,	7	9	15	24
East Princeton,*	Princeton,	Worcester,	34	61	55	116
East Quarter,	Concord,	Middlesex,	–	–	–	–
East Rochester,	Rochester,	Plymouth,	–	–	–	–
East Sandwich,* ‖	Sandwich,	Barnstable,	42	66	73	139
East Saugus,* ‖	Saugus,	Essex,	221	421	470	891
East Sharon,	Sharon,	Norfolk,	14	26	32	58
East Shelburne,*	Shelburne,	Franklin,	–	–	–	–
East Shirley,	Shirley,	Middlesex,	–	–	–	–
East Somerville,* ‖	SOMERVILLE,	Middlesex,	–	–	–	–
East Sudbury, ‖	Sudbury,	Middlesex,	–	–	–	–
East Swansea,	Swansea,	Bristol,	–	–	–	–
East Taunton,* ‖	TAUNTON,	Bristol,	–	–	–	–
East Templeton,*.	Templeton,	Worcester,	116	184	196	380
East Village,	Amherst,	Hampshire,	–	–	–	–
East Village,	Clinton,	Worcester,	–	–	–	–
East Village, ‖ [1]	Webster,	Worcester,	101	258	234	492
Eastville,	Cottage City,	Dukes,	–	–	–	–
Eastville,	East Bridgewater,	Plymouth,	44	95	81	176
East Walpole,* ‖	Walpole,	Norfolk,	122	291	236	527
East Wareham,*	Wareham,	Plymouth,	178	335	279	614
East Watertown, ‖	Watertown,	Middlesex,	–	–	–	–
East Weymouth,* ‖	Weymouth,	Norfolk,	862	1,860	1,868	3,728
East Whately,*	Whately,	Franklin,	71	150	135	285
East Whitman,	Whitman,	Plymouth,	237	481	480	961
East Wilmington,	Wilmington,	Middlesex,	–	–	–	–
East Windsor,*	Windsor,	Berkshire,	–	–	–	–
East Woburn,	WOBURN,	Middlesex,	248	607	571	1,178
East Worcester,	WORCESTER,	Worcester,	–	–	–	–
Eddyville,*	Middleborough,	Plymouth,	–	–	–	–
Edgartown,* §	Edgartown,	Dukes,	–	–	–	–
Edgeworth, ‖	MALDEN,	Middlesex,	990	2,422	2,488	4,910
Egleston Square,	BOSTON,	Suffolk,	–	–	–	–
Egremont Plain,*	Egremont,	Berkshire,	–	–	–	–
Egypt,*	Scituate,	Plymouth,	48	78	96	174
Eliot. ‖	NEWTON,	Middlesex,	–	–	–	–
Ellis,* ‖ [2]	Dedham,	Norfolk,	–	–	–	–
Ellisville,	Plymouth,	Plymouth,	8	23	12	35
Elmdale,	Uxbridge,	Worcester,	26	67	57	124
Elm Grove,*	Colrain,	Franklin,	30	76	63	139
Elm Hill,	BOSTON,	Suffolk,	–	–	–	–
Elmwood,* ‖	East Bridgewater,	Plymouth,	116	200	212	412
Elmwood,	HOLYOKE,	Hampden,	–	–	–	–

[1] R. R. name East Webster.   [2] R. R. station in town of Norwood.

VILLAGES, SECTIONS, ETC. : ALPHABETICALLY — Continued.

Cities, Towns, Villages, Sections, Etc.	Cities and Towns	Counties	Number of Families	Males	Females	Population Total
Endicott,* ‖	Dedham, . . .	Norfolk, . .	31	71	82	153
Enfield,* ‖	Enfield, ...	Hampshire, .	–	–	–	–
Englewood, ...	BOSTON, . . .	Suffolk, . .	–	–	–	–
Erving,* ‖	Erving, . . .	Franklin, . .	–	–	–	–
Essex,* ‖	Essex, ...	Essex, . . .	–	–	–	–
Essex Falls, ‖ . . .	Essex, ...	Essex, . . .	72	137	128	265
Evening Side, . . .	PITTSFIELD, .	Berkshire, . .	–	–	–	–
EVERETT,* ‖ . . .	EVERETT, . .	Middlesex, . .	–	–	–	–
Everettville, ...	Princeton, . .	Worcester, .	–	–	–	–
Factory Village, . . .	Ashburnham, .	Worcester, . .	–	–	–	–
Factory Village, . . .	Greenfield, . .	Franklin, . .	–	–	–	–
Factory Village, . . .	Middlefield, . .	Hampshire, .	23	53	48	101
Fairfield,* ‖ . . .	Russell, . . .	Hampden, . .	65	153	165	318
Fairhaven,* ‖ . . .	Fairhaven, . .	Bristol, . .	–	–	–	–
Fairmount, ...	Brookline, . .	Norfolk, . .	–	–	–	–
Fairmount, ...	HOLYOKE, . .	Hampden, . .	–	–	–	–
Fairmount, ...	Hyde Park, . .	Norfolk, . .	556	1,161	1,282	2,443
Fairmount, ...	WORCESTER, .	Worcester, . .	–	–	–	–
Fairview,*	CHICOPEE, . .	Hampden, . .	95	237	232	469
FALL RIVER,* ‖ . .	FALL RIVER, .	Bristol, . .	–	–	–	–
Falmouth,* ‖ . . .	Falmouth, . .	Barnstable, .	–	–	–	–
Falmouth Heights,* . .	Falmouth, . .	Barnstable, .	12	26	20	46
Falulah Park, . . .	FITCHBURG, .	Worcester, . .	–	–	–	–
Faneuil, ‖	BOSTON, . .	Suffolk, . .	–	–	–	–
Farley,*	Erving, . . .	Franklin, . .	32	66	60	126
Farley, ‖	Wendell, . .	Franklin, . .	–	–	–	–
Farmersville,* 1 . .	Attleborough, .	Bristol, . .	–	–	–	–
Farmer-ville, . . .	Sandwich, . .	Barnstable, .	–	–	–	–
Farm Hill, ‖ . . .	Stoneham, . .	Middlesex, . .	–	–	–	–
Farm Neck, ...	Cottage City, .	Dukes, . .	–	–	–	–
Farm Street, ‖ . .	Medfield, . .	Norfolk, . .	–	–	–	–
Farnams, ‖ . . .	Cheshire, . .	Berkshire, . .	–	–	–	–
Farnumsville,* ‖ . .	Grafton, . .	Worcester, . .	119	294	276	570
Faulkner, ‖ . . .	MALDEN, . .	Middlesex, . .	515	994	1,073	2,067
Fayville,* ‖ . . .	Southborough, .	Worcester, . .	106	249	197	446
Feeding Hills,* . . .	Agawam, . .	Hampden, . .	168	351	311	662
Felchville, ...	Natick, . . .	Middlesex, . .	153	334	323	657
Felix Neck, ...	Edgartown, . .	Dukes, . .	–	–	–	–
Fells,* ‖	Melrose, . .	Middlesex, . .	54	157	190	347
Felting Mills, . . .	Norfolk, . .	Norfolk, . .	–	–	–	–
Fenno's Corner, . . .	Revere, . . .	Suffolk, . .	–	–	–	–
Fern Croft, ‖ . . .	Danvers, . .	Essex, . .	–	–	–	–
Fernside, ...	Tyringham, . .	Berkshire, . .	–	–	–	–
Fernwood, ...	GLOUCESTER, .	Essex, . .	–	–	–	–
Field's Corner, ‖ . .	BOSTON, . .	Suffolk, . .	–	–	–	–
Fire District, ‖ . .	Middleborough, .	Plymouth, . .	1,020	1,925	2,216	4,141
First Parish, ...	Boxford, . .	Essex, . .	–	–	–	–
First Parish, ...	West Newbury, .	Essex, . .	–	–	–	–
Fisherville, ...	Attleborough, .	Bristol, . .	–	–	–	–
Fisherville,*	Grafton, . .	Worcester, . .	132	378	403	781
Fiskdale,*	Sturbridge, . .	Worcester, . .	228	553	595	1,148
FITCHBURG,* ‖ . .	FITCHBURG, .	Worcester, . .	–	–	–	–
Five Corners, . . .	BOSTON, . .	Suffolk, . .	–	–	–	–
Five Corners, . . .	Granby, . . .	Hampshire, . .	–	–	–	–
Five Roads, ...	NORTH ADAMS, .	Berkshire, . .	–	–	–	–
Flint Village, ‖ . .	FALL RIVER, .	Bristol, . .	135	323	343	666
Florence,* ‖ . . .	NORTHAMPTON, .	Hampshire, .	610	1,285	1,512	2,797

1 R. R. name Farmers.

VILLAGES, SECTIONS, ETC.: ALPHABETICALLY — Continued.

Cities, Towns, Villages, Sections, Etc.	Cities and Towns	Counties	Number of Families	Males	Females	Population
Florida,*	Florida, ...	Berkshire, . .	–	–	–	–
Folly Cove Village, . .	GLOUCESTER, . .	Essex, ...	–	–	–	–
Fordville, ...	Duxbury, . . .	Plymouth, . .	–	–	–	–
Forest Avenue, ‖ . .	BOSTON, . . .	Suffolk, . .	–	–	–	–
Forestdale,*	Sandwich, . . .	Barnstable,. .	19	27	29	56
Forest Hills, ‖ . . .	BOSTON, . . .	Suffolk, . .	–	–	–	–
Forest River, ‖ . . .	SALEM, ...	Essex, . . .	–	–	–	–
Forge Village,* ‖ . .	Westford, . . .	Middlesex, . .	83	202	244	446
Foskett's Mills, . . .	Brimfield, . . .	Hampden, . .	–	–	–	–
Four Corners, . . .	BOSTON, . . .	Suffolk, . .	–	–	–	–
Four Corners, . . .	Middleborough, . .	Plymouth, . .	–	–	–	–
Four Corners, . . .	West Stockbridge, .	Berkshire, . .	–	–	–	–
Foxborough,* ‖ . . .	Foxborough, . .	Norfolk, . .	–	–	–	–
Foxvale,* 1	Foxborough, . .	Norfolk, . .	48	105	101	206
Framingham,* ‖ . . .	Framingham, . .	Middlesex, . .	–	–	–	–
Framingham Centre, . .	Framingham, . .	Middlesex, . .	370	772	973	1,745
Franconia, ...	Longmeadow, . .	Hampden, . .	–	–	–	–
Franklin,* ‖	Franklin, . . .	Norfolk, . .	–	–	–	–
Franklin Park,* ‖. . .	Revere, ...	Suffolk, . .	–	–	–	–
Free Quarter, . . .	Sandisfield, . . .	Berkshire, . .	–	–	–	–
Freetown,*	Freetown, . . .	Bristol, . .	–	–	–	–
Fresh Brook Village, . .	Wellfleet, . . .	Barnstable,. .	–	–	–	–
Fresh Pond, ‖ . . .	CAMBRIDGE, . .	Middlesex, . .	–	–	–	–
Fresh Water Cove Village,	GLOUCESTER, . .	Essex, . . .	24	39	52	91
Frye Village, . . .	Andover, . . .	Essex, . . .	93	201	257	458
Fryeville, ...	Athol, ...	Worcester, . .	–	–	–	–
Fryeville, ...	Orange, ...	Franklin, . .	–	–	–	–
Fullerton, ...	Halifax, . . .	Plymouth, . .	–	–	–	–
Fullerville, ...	Clinton, . . .	Worcester, . .	–	–	–	–
Furnace, ...	Freetown, . . .	Bristol, . .	–	–	–	–
Furnace,* ‖	Hardwick, . . .	Worcester, . .	18	41	41	82
Furnace Village, . . .	Easton, ...	Bristol, . .	157	318	291	609
Gallows Hill, . . .	SALEM, ...	Essex, . . .	–	–	–	–
Gannett's Corner, . .	Scituate, . . .	Plymouth, . .	–	–	–	–
Garden City, ...	Dudley, ...	Worcester, . .	–	–	–	–
Gardner,* ‖	Gardner, . . .	Worcester, . .	–	–	–	–
Gardnerville, . . .	Duxbury, . . .	Plymouth, . .	–	–	–	–
Gates' Crossing, ‖ . .	Leominster, . . .	Worcester, . .	–	–	–	–
Gay Head,*	Gay Head, . . .	Dukes, . . .	–	–	–	–
Georgetown,* ‖ . . .	Georgetown, . .	Essex, . . .	–	–	–	–
Germantown, . . .	BOSTON, . . .	Suffolk, . .	–	–	–	–
Germantown, . . .	Clinton, . . .	Worcester, . .	–	–	–	–
Germantown, . . .	NEW BEDFORD, . .	Bristol, . .	–	–	–	–
Germantown, . . .	QUINCY, . . .	Norfolk, . .	–	–	–	–
Gilbertville,* ‖ 2 . .	Hardwick, . . .	Worcester, . .	294	765	779	1,544
Gill,*	Gill, ...	Franklin, . .	–	–	–	–
Gilmanville, ...	Tewksbury, . . .	Middlesex, . .	–	–	–	–
Glenallen, ...	Winchendon, . .	Worcester, . .	23	90	87	177
Glendale, ...	Easthampton, . .	Hampshire, . .	10	32	31	63
Glendale, ...	EVERETT, . . .	Middlesex, . .	724	1,502	1,563	3,065
Glendale, ...	Middlefield, . . .	Hampshire, . .	–	–	–	–
Glendale, ...	Southampton, . .	Hampshire, . .	–	–	–	–
Glendale,* ‖	Stockbridge, . . .	Berkshire, . .	118	261	274	535
Glendale, ...	Wilbraham, . . .	Hampden, . .	–	–	–	–
Glenmere, ...	LYNN, ...	Essex, . . .	968	1,830	1,879	3,709
Glenn Mills, ...	Rowley, ...	Essex, . . .	–	–	–	–
Glennonville, . . .	Dalton, ...	Berkshire, . .	–	–	–	–

1 R. R. name Rockdale.　　　　　2 R. R. station in town of Ware.

VILLAGES, SECTIONS, ETC.: ALPHABETICALLY — Continued.

Cities, Towns, Villages, Sections, Etc.	Cities and Towns	Counties	Number of Families	Males	Females	Population
Glenwood,* ||	Medford,	Middlesex,	208	767	667	1,434
Glenwood,	Springfield,	Hampden,	-	-	-	-
Glenwood,	Wrentham,	Norfolk,	-	-	-	-
Glenwood Avenue,||	Hyde Park,	Norfolk,	-	-	-	-
Globe Village,	Fall River,	Bristol,	462	1,118	1,176	2,294
Globe Village,* ||	Southbridge,	Worcester,	753	1,813	1,878	3,691
GLOUCESTER,* ||	GLOUCESTER,	Essex,	-	-	-	-
Glover's Corner,	Boston,	Suffolk,	-	-	-	-
Goodrich Hollow,	Hancock,	Berkshire,	-	-	-	-
Goshen,*	Goshen,	Hampshire,	-	-	-	-
Grafton,*	Grafton,	Worcester,	-	-	-	-
Grafton Centre,||	Grafton,	Worcester,	-	-	-	-
Granby,*	Granby,	Hampshire,	-	-	-	-
Granby Centre,	Granby,	Hampshire,	15	28	35	63
Granite Bridge,||	Boston,	Suffolk,	-	-	-	-
Graniteville,* ||	Westford,	Middlesex,	133	347	326	673
Grantville,	Seekonk,	Bristol,	-	-	-	-
Granville,*	Granville,	Hampden,	-	-	-	-
Granville Centre,*	Granville,	Hampden,	32	78	72	150
Grasshopper Plains,	Newburyport,	Essex,	-	-	-	-
Gravesville,	Hudson,	Middlesex,	-	-	-	-
Great Barrington,* ||	Great Barrington,	Berkshire,	-	-	-	-
Great Brewster,	Hull,	Plymouth,	2	2	1	3
Great Head,	Winthrop,	Suffolk,	-	-	-	-
Great Neck,	Marion,	Plymouth,	-	-	-	-
Great River,	Deerfield,	Franklin,	-	-	-	-
Greenbush,* ||	Scituate,	Plymouth,	61	120	110	230
Greendale,	Needham,	Norfolk,	35	95	70	165
Greendale,* ||	Worcester,	Worcester,	126	263	279	542
Green District,	Bolton,	Worcester,	-	-	-	-
Greenfield,* ||	Greenfield,	Franklin,	-	-	-	-
Green Harbor,*	Marshfield,	Plymouth,	47	64	70	134
Green Hill,	Hull,	Plymouth,	-	-	-	-
Green River,	Deerfield,	Franklin,	143	326	317	643
Greenville,	Leicester,	Worcester,	-	-	-	-
Greenwich,* ||	Greenwich,	Hampshire,	-	-	-	-
Greenwich Village,* ||	Greenwich,	Hampshire,	38	55	62	117
Greenwood,* ||	Wakefield,	Middlesex,	192	400	402	802
Greylock,	North Adams,	Berkshire,	109	335	317	652
Griswoldville,*	Colrain,	Franklin,	69	178	138	316
Groton,* ||	Groton,	Middlesex,	-	-	-	-
Grove Hall,	Boston,	Suffolk,	-	-	-	-
Groveland,* ||	Groveland,	Essex,	-	-	-	-
Guinea,	Newburyport,	Essex,	-	-	-	-
Gurney's Corners,	Hanson,	Plymouth,	-	-	-	-
Hadley,* ||	Hadley,	Hampshire,	-	-	-	-
Hadley,	Merrimac,	Essex,	-	-	-	-
Haggett's,||	Andover,	Essex,	-	-	-	-
Halifax,* ||	Halifax,	Plymouth,	-	-	-	-
Hallsville,	Lawrence,	Essex,	-	-	-	-
Hamilton,* ||	Hamilton,	Essex,	-	-	-	-
Hammondtown,	Mattapoisett,	Plymouth,	-	-	-	-
Hampden,*	Hampden,	Hampden,	-	-	-	-
Hampden Centre,	Hampden,	Hampden,	79	140	138	278
Hancock,*	Hancock,	Berkshire,	-	-	-	-
Hanover,* ||	Hanover,	Plymouth,	-	-	-	-
Hanson,*	Hanson,	Plymouth,	-	-	-	-

VILLAGES, SECTIONS, ETC.: ALPHABETICALLY — Continued.

Cities, Towns, Villages, Sections, Etc.	Cities and Towns	Counties	Number of Families	Males	Females	Population
Happy Alley, . . .	Marion, ...	Plymouth, . .	–	–	–	–
Happy Hollow, . . .	BROCKTON, . .	Plymouth, . .	–	–	–	–
Harbor View, ‖ . . .	BOSTON, . . .	Suffolk, . .	–	–	–	–
Hardwick,* ‖	Hardwick, . . .	Worcester, . .	–	–	–	–
Harmony, ...	East Bridgewater, .	Plymouth, . .	–	–	–	–
Harris,*	Rehoboth, . . .	Bristol, . .	–	–	–	–
Harrison Square, ‖ . .	BOSTON, . . .	Suffolk, . .	–	–	–	–
Harrisville, ...	Clinton, ...	Worcester, . .	–	–	–	–
Harrisville, ...	West Boylston, . .	Worcester, . .	46	127	106	233
Harrisville, ...	Winchendon, . .	Worcester, . .	5	15	7	22
Hart's Brook, . . .	Hadley, ...	Hampshire, . .	–	–	–	–
Hartsville,*	New Marlborough, .	Berkshire, . .	39	75	69	144
Harvard,* ‖	Harvard, . . .	Worcester, . .	–	–	–	–
Harvard Street, ‖ .	BOSTON, . . .	Suffolk, . .	–	–	–	–
Harwich,* ‖	Harwich, . . .	Barnstable, . .	–	–	–	–
Harwich Centre, ‖ . .	Harwich, . . .	Barnstable, . .	–	–	–	–
Harwichport,* . . .	Harwich, . . .	Barnstable, . .	180	236	266	502
Hastings, ‖	Weston, . . .	Middlesex, . .	–	–	–	–
Hastingsville, . . .	Framingham, . .	Middlesex, . .	–	–	–	–
Hatchville, ...	Duxbury, . . .	Plymouth, . .	–	–	–	–
Hatchville,*	Falmouth, . . .	Barnstable, . .	30	53	60	113
Hatfield,* ‖ . . .	Hatfield, . . .	Hampshire, . .	–	–	–	–
Hatherly,*	Rockland, . . .	Plymouth, . .	113	256	236	492
Havenville, ...	Burlington, . . .	Middlesex, . .	–	–	–	–
HAVERHILL,* ‖ . . .	HAVERHILL, . . .	Essex, . . .	–	–	–	–
Haverhill Bridge, ‖ .	Bradford, . . .	Essex, . . .	–	–	–	–
Hawley,*	Hawley, . . .	Franklin, . .	–	–	–	–
Hayden Row,* ‖ [1] .	Hopkinton, . . .	Middlesex, . .	54	106	109	215
Haydenville,* ‖ . .	Williamsburg, . .	Hampshire, . .	235	514	550	1,064
Hazelwood, ‖ . . .	Hyde Park, . . .	Norfolk, . .	–	–	–	–
Head Pamet, . . .	Truro, ...	Barnstable, . .	–	–	–	–
Heald Village, . . .	Barre, ...	Worcester, . .	–	–	–	–
Heath, ‖	BOSTON, . . .	Suffolk, . .	–	–	–	–
Heath,*	Heath, ...	Franklin, . .	–	–	–	–
Hebronville,* ‖ . .	Attleborough, . .	Bristol, . .	131	342	323	665
Hecla, ...	Uxbridge, . . .	Worcester, . .	56	157	140	297
Hemlock, ‖	Westport, . . .	Bristol, . .	–	–	–	–
Hendersonville, . .	Arlington, . . .	Middlesex, . .	–	–	–	–
Hendersonville, ‖ . .	EVERETT, . . .	Middlesex, . .	–	–	–	–
Heywood's, ‖ . . .	Gardner, . . .	Worcester, . .	–	–	–	–
Heywood's, ‖ . . .	Rowe, ...	Franklin, . .	–	–	–	–
Hicksville, ‖ . . .	Dartmouth, . . .	Bristol, . .	–	–	–	–
Highfield, ...	Falmouth, . . .	Barnstable, . .	–	–	–	–
High Head, ...	Truro, . . .	Barnstable, . .	–	–	–	–
Highland, ‖	BOSTON, . . .	Suffolk, . .	–	–	–	–
Highland, ...	Truro, . . .	Barnstable, . .	–	–	–	–
Highland, ...	WORCESTER, . .	Worcester, . .	–	–	–	–
Highland Lake, ‖ . .	Norfolk, . . .	Norfolk, . .	–	–	–	–
Highlands, ...	HAVERHILL, . . .	Essex, . . .	–	–	–	–
Highlands, ...	HOLYOKE, . . .	Hampden, . .	–	–	–	–
Highlands, ...	LOWELL, . . .	Middlesex, . .	–	–	–	–
Highlands, ...	LYNN, ...	Essex, . . .	844	1,743	1,847	3,590
Highlands, ...	Merrimac, . . .	Essex, . . .	–	–	–	–
Highland Terrace, . .	BROCKTON, . . .	Plymouth, . .	–	–	–	–
Highlandville,* ‖ . .	Needham, . . .	Norfolk, . .	265	569	581	1,150
Hill's Crossing, ‖ . .	Belmont, . . .	Middlesex, . .	–	–	–	–
Hillside, ...	Deerfield, . . .	Franklin, . .	–	–	–	–

[1] R. R. name Hayden.

VILLAGES, SECTIONS, ETC.: ALPHABETICALLY — Continued.

CITIES, TOWNS, VILLAGES, SECTIONS, ETC.	Cities and Towns	Counties	Number of Families	Males	Females	Population
Hillside Park, . . .	Southbridge,. . .	Worcester, . .	–	–	–	–
Hillsville, ...	Spencer,. . . .	Worcester, . .	47	125	102	227
Hingham,* ‖	Hingham, . . .	Plymouth, . .	–	–	–	–
Hingham Centre,* . .	Hingham, . . .	Plymouth, . .	291	620	613	1,233
Hinsdale,* ‖	Hinsdale, . . .	Berkshire, . .	–	–	–	–
Hockanum, ...	Hadley, ...	Hampshire, . .	–	–	–	–
Hoggs Bridge, . . .	BOSTON, . . .	Suffolk, . .	–	–	–	–
Holbrook,* ‖	Holbrook, . . .	Norfolk, . .	–	–	–	–
Holbrook Centre,. . .	Holbrook, . . .	Norfolk, . .	221	391	449	840
Holden,* ‖	Holden, . . .	Worcester, . .	–	–	–	–
Holland,*	Holland, . . .	Hampden, . .	–	–	–	–
Hollingsworth, ‖ . .	Groton, ...	Middlesex, . .	–	–	–	–
Holliston,* ‖ . . .	Holliston, . . .	Middlesex, . .	–	–	–	–
Holliston Centre, . .	Holliston, . . .	Middlesex, . .	430	786	877	1,663
Holtshire, ...	Orange, ...	Franklin, . .	–	–	–	–
HOLYOKE,* ‖ . . .	HOLYOKE, . . .	Hampden, . .	–	–	–	–
Hometield, ...	Hyde Park, . . .	Norfolk, . .	–	–	–	–
Hoosac, ...	Conway, ...	Franklin, . .	–	–	–	–
Hoosac, ...	Deerfield, . . .	Franklin, . .	–	–	–	–
Hoosac Tunnel,* ‖ [1] .	Florida, ...	Berkshire, . .	25	64	55	119
Hopedale,* ‖ . . .	Hopedale, . . .	Worcester, . .	–	–	–	–
Hopeville, ...	WORCESTER, . .	Worcester, . .	–	–	–	–
Hopewell, ...	TAUNTON, . . .	Bristol, . .	–	–	–	–
Hopkinton,* ‖ . . .	Hopkinton, . . .	Middlesex, . .	–	–	–	–
Horseneck, ...	Westport, . . .	Bristol, . .	–	–	–	–
Hortonville,*. . . .	Swansea, . . .	Bristol, . .	69	151	138	289
Hospital Hill, . . .	NORTHAMPTON, . .	Hampshire, . .	–	–	–	–
Hospital Station, ‖ .	Northborough, . .	Worcester, . .	–	–	–	–
Hough's Neck,* . . .	QUINCY,. . . .	Norfolk, . .	79	159	146	305
Houghtonville, . . .	NORTH ADAMS, .	Berkshire, . .	–	–	–	–
Housatonic,* ‖ . . .	Great Barrington, .	Berkshire, . .	247	487	556	1,043
Hovendon Park, . . .	BROCKTON, . . .	Plymouth, . .	–	–	–	–
Howarth's Village, . .	Oxford, ...	Worcester, . .	23	48	57	105
Howe's Station, ‖ . .	Middleton, . . .	Essex, . .	–	–	–	–
Howe Village, . . .	Boxford, . . .	Essex, . .	–	–	–	–
Howland's, ‖	Lakeville, . . .	Plymouth, . .	–	–	–	–
Howland Village, . .	NEW BEDFORD, . .	Bristol, . .	–	–	–	–
Hubbardston,* ‖ . . .	Hubbardston, . .	Worcester, . .	–	–	–	–
Hudson,* ‖	Hudson, . . .	Middlesex, . .	–	–	–	–
Hull,* §	Hull, ...	Plymouth, . .	–	–	–	–
Hull Village,. . . .	Hull, ...	Plymouth, . .	65	133	157	290
Huntington,* ‖ . . .	Huntington, . . .	Hampshire, . .	–	–	–	–
Hyannis,* ‖	Barnstable, . . .	Barnstable,. .	361	599	638	1,237
Hyannisport,* . . .	Barnstable, . . .	Barnstable,. .	46	91	82	173
Hyde Park,* ‖ . . .	Hyde Park, . . .	Norfolk, . .	–	–	–	–
Hydeville, ...	Winchendon, . .	Worcester, . .	18	42	37	79
Iceville, ...	SPRINGFIELD, . .	Hampden, . .	–	–	–	–
Indian Hollow, . . .	Huntington, . . .	Hampshire, . .	10	24	18	42
Indian Orchard,* ‖ .	SPRINGFIELD, . .	Hampden, . .	461	1,108	1,081	2,189
Indian Pond, . . .	Kingston, . . .	Plymouth, . .	–	–	–	–
Indiantown, ...	FALL RIVER, . .	Bristol, . .	–	–	–	–
Ingall's, ‖	North Andover, . .	Essex, . .	–	–	–	–
Ingleside, ‖	HOLYOKE, . . .	Hampden, . .	–	–	–	–
Intervale Park, . . .	BROCKTON, . . .	Plymouth, . .	–	–	–	–
Ipswich,* ‖	Ipswich, . . .	Essex, . .	–	–	–	–
Island, ...	WORCESTER, . .	Worcester, . .	–	–	–	–

[1] R. R. station in town of Rowe.

VILLAGES, SECTIONS, ETC.: ALPHABETICALLY — Continued.

CITIES, TOWNS, VILLAGES, SECTIONS, ETC.	Cities and Towns	Counties	Number of Families	Males	Females	Population
Island Creek,* ‖	Duxbury,	Plymouth,	47	89	93	182
Island Park, ‖	Bradford,	Essex,	-	-	-	-
Islington,* ‖	Dedham,	Norfolk,	29	53	65	118
Jacksonville,	FITCHBURG,	Worcester,	-	-	-	-
Jamaica Plain,* ‖	BOSTON,	Suffolk,	-	-	-	-
Jamesville, ‖	WORCESTER,	Worcester,	46	119	107	226
Jeffersonville,* ‖ 1	Holden,	Worcester,	153	411	415	826
Jeffries Point,	BOSTON,	Suffolk,	-	-	-	-
Jenksville,	SPRINGFIELD,	Hampden,	-	-	-	-
Jericho,	Dudley,	Worcester,	148	375	360	735
Jericho,	Scituate,	Plymouth,	-	-	-	-
Jerusalem,	Tyringham,	Berkshire,	-	-	-	-
Jerusalem,	West Bridgewater,	Plymouth,	39	86	76	162
Jesseville,	NEW BEDFORD,	Bristol,	-	-	-	-
Johnson's Ground,	NORTH ADAMS,	Berkshire,	-	-	-	-
Joppa,	GLOUCESTER,	Essex,	-	-	-	-
Joppa,	NEWBURYPORT,	Essex,	-	-	-	-
Judson,*.	Raynham,	Bristol,	44	81	79	160
Juniper Point,	SALEM,	Essex,	-	-	-	-
Katama,	Edgartown,	Dukes,	-	-	-	-
Keephickon,	Chilmark,	Dukes,	-	-	-	-
Kempville,	NORTH ADAMS,	Berkshire,	-	-	-	-
Kenberma, ‖	Hull,	Plymouth,	7	17	24	41
Kendal Green,* ‖	Weston,	Middlesex,	83	208	181	389
Kenersonville,	NEW BEDFORD,	Bristol,	-	-	-	-
Kingston,* ‖	Kingston,	Plymouth,	-	-	-	-
King Street, ‖	Cohasset,	Norfolk,	-	-	-	-
Kittle Cove Village,	Manchester,	Essex,	-	-	-	-
Kittredgeville,	Dalton,	Berkshire,	-	-	-	-
Knife Works,	Sharon,	Norfolk,	-	-	-	-
Knightville,	Huntington,	Hampshire,	24	47	46	93
Lagoon Heights,	Cottage City,	Dukes,	-	-	-	-
Lake Crossing, ‖	Natick,	Middlesex,	-	-	-	-
Lake Pleasant,* ‖	Montague,	Franklin,	29	22	36	58
Lake Shore Park,	LYNN,	Essex,	-	-	-	-
Lakeside,	Leicester,	Worcester,	-	-	-	-
Lakeside,	LYNN,	Essex,	60	103	124	227
Laketown,	Essex,	Essex,	-	-	-	-
Lakeview,	Foxborough,	Norfolk,	14	30	31	61
Lake View,*	WORCESTER,	Worcester,	181	352	376	728
Lake Village,	Topsfield,	Essex,	-	-	-	-
Lakeville,* ‖	Lakeville,	Plymouth,	-	-	-	-
Lakeville,	Shirley,	Middlesex,	-	-	-	-
Lamb City,	Phillipston,	Worcester,	-	-	-	-
Lambert's Cove,	West Tisbury,	Dukes,	-	-	-	-
Lancaster,* ‖	Lancaster,	Worcester,	-	-	-	-
Lanesborough,*	Lanesborough,	Berkshire,	-	-	-	-
Lanesville,*	GLOUCESTER,	Essex,	359	1,114	659	1,773
Lane Village,	Ashburnham,	Worcester,	-	-	-	-
LAWRENCE,* ‖	LAWRENCE,	Essex,	-	-	-	-
Lebanon,	Seekonk,	Bristol,	-	-	-	-
Ledgeville,	Petersham,	Worcester,	-	-	-	-
Lee,* ‖	Lee,	Berkshire,	-	-	-	-
Leeds,* ‖	NORTHAMPTON,	Hampshire,	180	467	513	980
Leet Ore Beds,	West Stockbridge,	Berkshire,	-	-	-	-
Leicester,*	Leicester,	Worcester,	-	-	-	-

1 R. R. and P. O. name Jefferson.

VILLAGES, SECTIONS, ETC. : ALPHABETICALLY — Continued.

Cities, Towns, Villages, Sections, Etc.	Cities and Towns	Counties	Number of Families	Males	Females	Population
Lelandville, ...	Charlton, . . .	Worcester, .	–	–	–	–
Lenox,* ‖	Lenox, ...	Berkshire, . .	–	–	–	–
Lenox Dale,* ‖ . . .	Lenox, ...	Berkshire, . .	110	329	236	565
Lensdale, ...	Southbridge,. . .	Worcester, . .	–	–	–	–
Leominster,* ‖ ¹ . .	Leominster, . . .	Worcester, . .	–	–	–	–
Leverett,* ‖ . . .	Leverett, . . .	Franklin, . .	–	–	–	–
Lexington,* ‖ . . .	Lexington, . . .	Middlesex, . .	–	–	–	–
Leyden,*	Leyden,. . . .	Franklin, . .	–	–	–	–
Leyden Park, . . .	BROCKTON, . . .	Plymouth, . .	–	–	–	–
Liberty Hill, ...	SALEM, ...	Essex, . . .	–	–	–	–
Lincoln,* ‖ . . .	Lincoln,. . . .	Middlesex, . .	–	–	–	–
Lincoln Square,* . .	WORCESTER, . .	Worcester, . .	–	–	–	–
Linden, ‖	MALDEN, . . .	Middlesex, . .	255	512	558	1,070
Lindenwood,‖ . . .	Stoneham, . . .	Middlesex, . .	–	–	–	–
Line,*	Colrain, ...	Franklin, . .	–	–	–	–
Linebrook Parish, . .	Ipswich,. . . .	Essex, . . .	34	70	66	136
Linwood, ‖ ²	Northbridge, . .	Worcester, . .	84	227	269	496
Linwood Park, . . .	LYNN, ...	Essex, . . .	–	–	–	–
Lion's Mouth, . . .	Amesbury, . . .	Essex, . . .	–	–	–	–
Little Brewster, . . .	Hull, ...	Plymouth, . .	3	4	2	6
Little Canada, . . .	LOWELL, . . .	Middlesex, . .	–	–	–	–
Little Nahant, . . .	Nahant, . . .	Essex, . . .	–	–	–	–
Little River, ...	Westfield, . . .	Hampden, . .	–	–	–	–
Little South, ...	Natick, ...	Middlesex, . .	–	–	–	–
Littleton,* ‖	Littleton, . . .	Middlesex, . .	–	–	–	–
Littleton Centre, . . .	Littleton, . . .	Middlesex, . .	75	159	174	333
Littleton Common,* . .	Littleton, . . .	Middlesex, . .	8	16	21	37
Littleville,*	Chester, ...	Hampden, . .	20	37	27	64
Lock's Village, . . .	Shutesbury, . .	Franklin, . .	–	–	–	–
Lock's Village,* . . .	Wendell, . . .	Franklin, . .	–	–	–	–
Logan's, ‖	Rowe, ...	Franklin, . .	–	–	–	–
Lokerville, ...	Wayland, . . .	Middlesex, . .	–	–	–	–
Long Hill, ...	Rehoboth, . . .	Bristol, . .	–	–	–	–
Longmeadow,* ‖ . . .	Longmeadow, . .	Hampden, . .	–	–	–	–
Lougnook, ...	Truro, ...	Barnstable, .	–	–	–	–
Long Plain,*. . . .	Acushnet, . . .	Bristol, . .	67	111	132	243
Long Plain, ...	Leverett, . . .	Franklin, . .	23	52	46	98
Longwood, ‖	Brookline, . . .	Norfolk, . .	–	–	–	–
Look's Mills, ...	Rochester, . . .	Plymouth, . .	–	–	–	–
Loudville, ...	Easthampton, . .	Hampshire, . .	3	7	10	17
Loudville, ...	NORTHAMPTON, .	Hampshire, . .	7	21	16	37
Loudville,*	Westhampton, . .	Hampshire, . .	22	45	36	81
Lovell's Corners, . . .	Weymouth, . . .	Norfolk, . .	–	–	–	–
Lovell's Grove, ‖ . . .	Weymouth, . . .	Norfolk, . .	–	–	–	–
LOWELL,* ‖	LOWELL, . . .	Middlesex, . .	–	–	–	–
Lowell Island, . . .	SALEM, ...	Essex, . . .	1	1	4	5
Lowell Junction, ‖ ³ . .	LOWELL, . . .	Middlesex, . .	–	–	–	–
Lowell Street, ‖ . . .	Wakefield, . . .	Middlesex, . .	–	–	–	–
Lower Corner, . . .	Merrimac, . . .	Essex, . . .	–	–	–	–
Lower End, ...	North Reading, . .	Middlesex, . .	–	–	–	–
Lower Village, . . .	Warren,. . . .	Worcester, . .	–	–	–	–
Ludlow,* ‖	Ludlow,. . . .	Hampden, . .	–	–	–	–
Ludlow Centre,* . . .	Ludlow,. . . .	Hampden, . .	29	55	58	113
Ludlow City, ...	Granby,. . . .	Hampshire, . .	–	–	–	–
Ludlow City, ...	Ludlow,. . . .	Hampden, . .	–	–	–	–
Lund's Corner, . . .	NEW BEDFORD, . .	Bristol, . .	–	–	–	–
Lunenburg,* ‖ . . .	Lunenburg, . . .	Worcester, . .	–	–	–	–
Lyndhurst, ...	Saugus, ...	Essex, . . .	–	–	–	–

¹ R. R. name Leominster Centre.   ² R. R. name Whitins.   ³ R. R. station in town of Tewksbury.

VILLAGES, SECTIONS, ETC.: ALPHABETICALLY — Continued.

Cities, Towns, Villages, Sections, Etc.	Cities and Towns	Counties	Number of Families	Males	Females	Population
Lynn,*‖	Lynn, ...	Essex, ...	-	-	-	-
Lynn Common,‖ . .	Lynn, ...	Essex, ...	-	-	-	-
Lynnfield,*‖ . . .	Lynnfield, . .	Essex, ...	-	-	-	-
Lynnfield Centre,*‖ .	Lynnfield, . .	Essex, ...	-	-	-	-
Lynnhurst, . . .	Lynn, ...	Essex, ...	-	-	-	-
Lyonsville,* . . .	Colrain, . . .	Franklin, . .	-	-	-	-
Lyonville, . . .	Halifax,. . . .	Plymouth, . .	-	-	-	-
Machine Shop, ‖ . .	North Andover, .	Essex, ...	-	-	-	-
Madaket, . . .	Nantucket, . .	Nantucket, . .	-	-	-	-
Magnolia,*‖ ¹ . .	GLOUCESTER, .	Essex, . . .	57	134	113	247
Makonikey, . . .	Tisbury, . . .	Dukes,. . .	-	-	-	-
MALDEN,*‖ . .	MALDEN, . .	Middlesex, . .	-	-	-	-
Manchaug.* . . .	Sutton, . . .	Worcester, . .	267	798	768	1,566
Manchester,*‖ . .	Manchester, . .	Essex, . . .	-	-	-	-
Mann's Hill, . . .	Sharon, . . .	Norfolk, . .	-	-	-	-
Manomet,* . . .	Plymouth, . .	Plymouth, . .	93	187	183	370
Mansfield,*‖ . . .	Mansfield, . .	Bristol, . .	-	-	-	-
Manville, . . .	Leicester, . .	Worcester, . .	-	-	-	-
Maple Grove,‖ . .	Adams, . . .	Berkshire, . .	107	235	264	499
Mapleville, . . .	Wenham, . .	Essex, . . .	-	-	-	-
Maplewood, . . .	FALL RIVER, .	Bristol, . .	-	-	-	-
Maplewood,‖ . . .	MALDEN, . .	Middlesex, . .	777	1,621	1,760	3,381
Marblehead,*‖ . .	Marblehead, . .	Essex, . . .	-	-	-	-
Marblehead Neck,* ² .	Marblehead,. .	Essex, . . .	10	17	32	49
Marble Ridge,‖ . .	North Andover, .	Essex, . . .	-	-	-	-
Marbleville, . . .	Sutton, . . .	Worcester, . .	13	27	28	55
Marion,*‖ . . .	Marion, . . .	Plymouth, . .	-	-	-	-
Market Street,‖ . .	Lynn, . . .	Essex, . . .	-	-	-	-
Marland Village, . .	Andover, . . .	Essex, . . .	-	-	-	-
Marlborough, . .	Georgetown,. .	Essex, . . .	24	54	52	106
MARLBOROUGH,*‖ .	MARLBOROUGH, .	Middlesex, . .	-	-	-	-
Marlborough Junction,‖	MARLBOROUGH, .	Middlesex, . .	-	-	-	-
Marshall's Corner, .	BROCKTON, .	Plymouth, . .	-	-	-	-
Marshfield,*‖ . .	Marshfield, . .	Plymouth, . .	-	-	-	-
Marshfield Centre,*‖ .	Marshfield, . .	Plymouth, . .	26	42	48	90
Marshfield Hills,*‖ .	Marshfield, . .	Plymouth, . .	165	173	164	337
Marston's Mills,* . .	Barnstable, . .	Barnstable, . .	68	132	129	261
Mashpee,* . . .	Mashpee, . .	Barnstable, . .	-	-	-	-
Matfield, . . .	East Bridgewater, .	Plymouth, . .	27	65	70	135
Matfield,*‖ . . .	West Bridgewater, .	Plymouth, . .	42	88	82	170
Mattapan,*‖ . .	BOSTON, . .	Suffolk, . .	-	-	-	-
Mattapan, . . .	Milton, . . .	Norfolk, . .	183	425	453	878
Mattapoisett,*‖ . .	Mattapoisett, .	Plymouth, . .	-	-	-	-
Maynard,*‖ . . .	Maynard, . .	Middlesex, . .	-	-	-	-
Meadows, . . .	Sunderland, . .	Franklin, . .	-	-	-	-
Mechanicsville, . .	Attleborough, .	Bristol, . .	-	-	-	-
Mechanicsville, . .	FALL RIVER, .	Bristol, . .	-	-	-	-
Medfield,*‖ . . .	Medfield, . .	Norfolk, . .	-	-	-	-
Medfield Junction,‖ .	Medfield, . .	Norfolk, . .	-	-	-	-
MEDFORD,*‖ . .	MEDFORD, . .	Middlesex, . .	-	-	-	-
Medway,*‖ . . .	Medway, . .	Norfolk, . .	-	-	-	-
Meeting House Hill, .	BOSTON, . .	Suffolk, . .	-	-	-	-
Melrose,*‖ . . .	Melrose, . .	Middlesex, . .	-	-	-	-
Melrose Highlands,*‖	Melrose, . .	Middlesex, . .	478	808	1,069	1,877
Menamsha, . . .	Chilmark, . .	Dukes,. . .	-	-	-	-
Menauhant,*. . .	Falmouth, . .	Barnstable, . .	-	-	-	-
Mendon,* . . .	Mendon, . .	Worcester, . .	-	-	-	-

¹ R. R. station in town of Manchester.   ² P. O. name Nanepashemet.

VILLAGES, SECTIONS, ETC.: ALPHABETICALLY — Continued.

Cities, Towns, Villages, Sections, Etc.	Cities and Towns	Counties	Number of Families	Males	Females	Population
Menlo Park, ...	Brockton, . . .	Plymouth, .	–	–	–	–
Merino Village, . . .	Dudley, ...	Worcester, . .	197	488	511	999
Merrick,*	West Springfield,	Hampden, . .	749	1,649	1,730	3,379
Merrimac,* ‖	Merrimac, . . .	Essex, ...	–	–	–	–
Merrimac Centre, . .	Merrimac, . . .	Essex, . . .	401	745	821	1,566
Merrimacport,* . . .	Merrimac, . . .	Essex, . .	92	160	165	325
Metcalf,* ‖	Holliston, . . .	Middlesex, . .	19	40	36	76
Methuen,* ‖	Methuen, . . .	Essex, ...	–	–	–	–
Mica Mill, ...	Chester, . . .	Hampden, . .	–	–	–	–
Michawum, ‖	Woburn, . . .	Middlesex, . .	–	–	–	–
Middleborough.* ‖ . .	Middleborough, .	Plymouth, . .	–	–	–	–
Middle Brewster, . .	Hull, ...	Plymouth, . .	3	5	5	10
Middle Farms, . . .	Westfield, . . .	Hampden, . .	31	106	58	164
Middlefield,* ‖ . . .	Middlefield, . . .	Hampshire, . .	–	–	–	–
Middlesex Junction,‖ .	Lowell, . . .	Middlesex, . .	–	–	–	–
Middlesex Village,* ‖ [1]	Lowell, ...	Middlesex, . .	48	103	133	236
Middleton,* ‖ . . .	Middleton, . . .	Essex, . . .	–	–	–	–
Middletown, ...	West Tisbury, . .	Dukes, . . .	–	–	–	–
Middletown, ...	Yarmouth, . . .	Barnstable, . .	–	–	–	–
Miles' River, ‖ . . .	Hamilton, . . .	Essex, . . .	–	–	–	–
Milford,* ‖	Milford, . . .	Worcester, . .	–	–	–	–
Milk Hill, ...	Chelsea, . . .	Suffolk, . . .	–	–	–	–
Milk Row, ...	Somerville, . .	Middlesex, . .	–	–	–	–
Millbrook,*	Duxbury, . . .	Plymouth, . .	68	128	135	263
Millbury,* ‖	Millbury, . . .	Worcester, . .	–	–	–	–
Millbury Junction, ‖ . .	Millbury, . . .	Worcester, . .	–	–	–	–
Miller's Falls, . . .	Erving, ...	Franklin, . .	76	150	151	301
Miller's Falls,* ‖ . . .	Montague, . . .	Franklin, . .	128	282	246	528
Millington,*	New Salem, . . .	Franklin, . .	13	33	26	59
Millis,* ‖	Millis, ...	Norfolk, . .	–	–	–	–
Mill River, ...	Deerfield, . . .	Franklin, . .	–	–	–	–
Mill River,*	New Marlborough,	Berkshire, . .	120	241	233	474
Millvale, ...	Haverhill, . . .	Essex, . . .	–	–	–	–
Mill Valley, ...	Amherst, . . .	Hampshire, . .	–	–	–	–
Mill Village, ...	Ashby, ...	Middlesex, . .	–	–	–	–
Millville,* ‖	Blackstone, . .	Worcester, . .	507	1,417	1,099	2,516
Millward, ...	Charlton, . . .	Worcester, . .	–	–	–	–
Millwood, ...	Framingham, . .	Middlesex, . .	–	–	–	–
Millwood,*	Rowley, ...	Essex, . . .	39	74	64	138
Milton,* ‖	Milton, ...	Norfolk, . .	–	–	–	–
Milton Hill, ...	Milton, ...	Norfolk, . .	–	–	–	–
Misery Island, . . .	Salem, ...	Essex, . . .	2	5	7	12
Mittineague, ...	Agawam, . . .	Hampden, . .	184	436	461	897
Mittineague,* ‖ . . .	West Springfield, .	Hampden, . .	287	607	730	1,337
Monroe,*	Monroe, . . .	Franklin, . .	–	–	–	–
Monroe Bridge,* ‖ . .	Monroe, . . .	Franklin, . .	–	–	–	–
Monson,* ‖	Monson, . . .	Hampden, . .	–	–	–	–
Montague,* ‖ . . .	Montague, . . .	Franklin, . .	–	–	–	–
Montague City,* . .	Montague, . . .	Franklin, . .	81	196	171	367
Montclair, ...	Milton, ...	Norfolk, . .	–	–	–	–
Montclair, ‖	Quincy, . . .	Norfolk, . .	–	–	–	–
Montello, ‖	Brockton, . . .	Plymouth, . .	680	1,613	1,480	3,093
Monterey,* ‖ . . .	Monterey, . . .	Berkshire, . .	–	–	–	–
Montgomery,* . . .	Montgomery, . .	Hampden, . .	–	–	–	–
Montrose,* ‖ . . .	Wakefield, . . .	Middlesex, . .	104	224	241	465
Montserrat, ‖ . . .	Beverly, . . .	Essex, . . .	86	193	142	335
Montvale, ‖	Woburn, . . .	Middlesex, . .	–	–	–	–
Montville,*	Sandisfield, . . .	Berkshire, . .	34	46	65	111

[1] R. R. name Middlesex.

VILLAGES, SECTIONS, ETC.: ALPHABETICALLY — Continued.

CITIES, TOWNS, VILLAGES, SECTIONS, ETC.	Cities and Towns	Counties	Number of Families	Males	Females	Population
Monument Beach,* ‖ . . .	Bourne, ...	Barnstable,	40	71	77	148
Monument Valley, . .	Great Barrington, .	Berkshire, . .	–	–	–	–
Moore's Corner,* . . .	Leverett, . . .	Franklin, . .	26	52	47	99
Moose Hill, . . .	Sharon, . . .	Norfolk, . .	–	–	–	–
Morning Side, . . .	PITTSFIELD, . .	Berkshire, . .	–	–	–	–
Morse Hollow, . . .	Leominster, . . .	Worcester, . .	–	–	–	–
Morse Village, . . .	New Salem, . .	Franklin, . .	–	–	–	–
Mosquito Valley, . .	Hamilton, . . .	Essex, . .	–	–	–	–
Moultonville, . . .	NEWBURYPORT, . .	Essex, . . .	–	–	–	–
Mountain Park, . . .	Swampscott, . .	Essex, . .	–	–	–	–
Mount Auburn, . .	CAMBRIDGE, . .	Middlesex, .	–	–	–	–
Mount Auburn,* ‖ . .	Watertown, . .	Middlesex, . .	–	–	–	–
Mount Bellingham, . .	CHELSEA, . . .	Suffolk, . .	–	–	–	–
Mount Blue, . . .	Hingham, . . .	Plymouth, . .	–	–	–	–
Mount Blue,* . . .	Norwell, . . .	Plymouth, . .	42	89	75	164
Mount Bowdoin, ‖ . .	BOSTON, . .	Suffolk, . .	–	–	–	–
Mount Carmel, ‖ . .	Middleborough, . .	Plymouth, . .	–	–	–	–
Mount Hermon,* . .	Gill, ...	Franklin, . .	25	338	34	372
Mount Hermon, ‖ . .	Northfield, . .	Franklin, . .	–	–	–	–
Mount Hope, ‖ . .	BOSTON, . .	Suffolk, . .	–	–	–	–
Mount Pleasant, . .	BOSTON, . .	Suffolk, . .	–	–	–	–
Mount Pleasant, ‖ . .	NEW BEDFORD, . .	Bristol, . .	–	–	–	–
Mount Tom,* ‖ . .	Easthampton, . .	Hampshire, . .	30	98	71	169
Mount Tom, . . .	NORTHAMPTON, . .	Hampshire, . .	22	113	45	158
Mount Wachusett,* . .	Princeton, . . .	Worcester, . .	–	–	–	–
Mount Washington, . .	BOSTON, . .	Suffolk, . .	–	–	–	–
Mount Washington, . .	CHELSEA, . .	Suffolk, . .	–	–	–	–
Mount Washington, . .	EVERETT, . . .	Middlesex, . .	108	247	262	509
Mount Washington, . .	HAVERHILL, . .	Essex, . .	–	–	–	–
Mount Washington,* . .	Mount Washington, . .	Berkshire, . .	–	–	–	–
Mundale,*	Westfield, . . .	Hampden, . .	40	81	77	158
Munroe, ‖	Lexington, . . .	Middlesex, . .	–	–	–	–
Muschopauge, ‖ . .	Rutland, . . .	Worcester, . .	–	–	–	–
Mus-kegat, ...	Nantucket, . . .	Nantucket, . .	1	1	–	1
Myricksville,* ‖ [1] . .	Berkley, . . .	Bristol, . .	57	102	109	211
Mystic, ‖	Winchester, . .	Middlesex, . .	–	–	–	–
Nahant,* §	Nahant, ...	Essex, . . .	–	–	–	–
Namasket, ...	Middleborough, . .	Plymouth, . .	–	–	–	–
Namequoit, ...	Orleans, . . .	Barnstable, .	–	–	–	–
Namskaket, ...	Orleans, ...	Barnstable, .	–	–	–	–
Nantasket,'	Cohasset, . . .	Norfolk, . .	–	–	–	–
Nantasket, ‖ § . . .	Hull, ...	Plymouth, . .	88	194	183	377
Nantasket Junction, ‖ . .	Hingham, . . .	Plymouth, . .	–	–	–	–
Nantucket,* §	Nantucket, . . .	Nantucket, . .	–	–	–	–
Nash,*	Weymouth, . .	Norfolk, . .	–	–	–	–
Nashaquitsa, . . .	Chilmark, . . .	Dukes, . .	–	–	–	–
Nashawannuck, . . .	Easthampton, . .	Hampshire, . .	–	–	–	–
Nashawena Island, . .	Gosnold, . . .	Dukes, . .	1	3	1	4
Nashoba,*	Westford, . . .	Middlesex, . .	–	–	–	–
Nash's Mills, ...	Greenfield, . . .	Franklin, . .	–	–	–	–
Nasketucket, ...	Fairhaven, . . .	Bristol, . .	–	–	–	–
Natick,* ‖	Natick, ...	Middlesex, . .	–	–	–	–
Nauset, ...	Eastham, . . .	Barnstable, . .	–	–	–	–
Nanshon Island, . . .	Gosnold, . . .	Dukes, . .	6	20	10	30
Navy, ...	Dracut, . . .	Middlesex, . .	169	456	415	871
Nebroska Plain, . . .	Natick, . . .	Middlesex, . .	–	–	–	–
Neck, ...	Lakeville, . . .	Plymouth, . .	–	–	–	–

[1] R. R. and P. O. name Myricks.

VILLAGES, SECTIONS, ETC.: ALPHABETICALLY — Continued.

Cities. Towns, Villages, Sections, Etc.	Cities and Towns	Counties	Number of Families	Males	Females	Population
Neck, ...	North Reading, . .	Middlesex, . .	–	–	–	–
Neck, ...	Truro, ...	Barnstable, .	–	–	–	–
Needham,* . . .	Needham, . . .	Norfolk, . .	–	–	–	–
Neponset, ...	BOSTON, . . .	Suffolk, . .	–	–	–	–
New Ashford,* . . .	New Ashford, . .	Berkshire, . .	–	–	–	–
NEW BEDFORD,* .	NEW BEDFORD, . .	Bristol, . .	–	–	–	–
New Boston, . . .	Dracut	Middlesex, . .	–	–	–	–
New Boston, ...	Fairhaven, . . .	Bristol, . .	–	–	–	–
New Boston, ...	FALL RIVER, . .	Bristol, . .	59	128	131	259
New Boston, . . .	Rutland, . . .	Worcester, . .	–	–	–	–
New Boston,* . . .	Sandisfield, . .	Berkshire, . .	32	56	51	107
New Boston, ...	Winchendon, . .	Worcester, . .	28	58	43	101
New Braintree,* .	New Braintree, . .	Worcester, . .	–	–	–	–
Newbury,* . . .	Newbury, . . .	Essex, . . .	–	–	–	–
Newbury Lower Green, .	Newbury, . . .	Essex, . . .	–	–	–	–
NEWBURYPORT,* .	NEWBURYPORT, . .	Essex, . . .	–	–	–	–
Newbury Upper Green,	Newbury, . . .	Essex, . . .	–	–	–	–
Newhall Heights, .	LYNN, . . .	Essex, . . .	–	–	–	–
Newhall's, . . .	Peabody, . . .	Essex, . . .	–	–	–	–
New Jerusalem, . .	Clinton, . . .	Worcester, . .	–	–	–	–
New Lenox,* .	Lenox, ...	Berkshire, . .	66	161	134	295
New Maine, . . .	Foxborough, . .	Norfolk, . .	–	–	–	–
New Marlborough,* .	New Marlborough, .	Berkshire, . .	–	–	–	–
New Salem,* .	New Salem, . .	Franklin, . .	–	–	–	–
New State, ...	Foxborough, . .	Norfolk, . .	–	–	–	–
NEWTON,* . .	NEWTON, . .	Middlesex. .	–	–	–	–
Newton Centre,* .	NEWTON, . .	Middlesex, . .	564	831	981	1,812
Newton Highlands,* .	NEWTON, . .	Middlesex, . .	404	835	1,078	1,913
Newton Lower Falls,*	NEWTON, . .	Middlesex, . .	135	353	339	692
Newton Lower Falls, .	Wellesley, . .	Norfolk, . .	129	317	283	600
Newton Street, .	WALTHAM, . .	Middlesex. .	–	–	–	–
Newton Upper Falls,*	NEWTON, . .	Middlesex, . .	340	790	782	1,572
Newtonville,* .	NEWTON, . .	Middlesex, . .	720	1,045	1,541	2,586
New Town, . . .	Barnstable, . .	Barnstable, .	–	–	–	–
New Worcester,* . .	WORCESTER, .	Worcester, . .	327	709	692	1,401
Nichewaug,* . .	Petersham, . .	Worcester, . .	13	28	22	50
Nine Acre Corner, .	Concord, . .	Middlesex, . .	–	–	–	–
Nissitissett, ...	Pepperell, . .	Middlesex, . .	–	–	–	–
Nobscot,* .	Framingham, . .	Middlesex, . .	37	89	87	176
Noman's Land, . .	Chilmark, . .	Dukes, . . .	3	10	8	18
Nonantum, . . .	NEWTON, . .	Middlesex, . .	412	1,130	1,118	2,248
Nonantum Hill, . .	BOSTON, . .	Suffolk, . .	–	–	–	–
Nonquitt,* . . .	Dartmouth, . .	Bristol, . .	–	–	–	–
Norfolk,*	Norfolk, . .	Norfolk, . .	–	–	–	–
Norfolk Downs, .	QUINCY, . .	Norfolk, . .	–	–	–	–
North Abington,* .	Abington, . .	Plymouth, . .	550	1,064	1,107	2,171
North Acton,* . .	Acton, . . .	Middlesex, . .	–	–	–	–
NORTH ADAMS,* .	NORTH ADAMS, .	Berkshire, . .	–	–	–	–
North Amherst, .	Amherst, . . .	Hampshire, . .	189	327	361	688
NORTHAMPTON,* .	NORTHAMPTON, .	Hampshire, . .	–	–	–	–
North Andover,* .	North Andover, . .	Essex, . . .	–	–	–	–
North Andover Depot,* .	North Andover, . .	Essex, . .	574	1,258	1,305	2,563
North Ashburnham,* .	Ashburnham, . .	Worcester, . .	38	76	65	141
North Attleborough,* .	North Attleborough, .	Bristol, . .	–	–	–	–
North Bellingham,* .	Bellingham, . .	Norfolk, . .	105	210	213	423
North Beverly, .	BEVERLY, . .	Essex, . .	217	432	441	873
North Billerica,* .	Billerica, . .	Middlesex, . .	254	577	614	1,191
North Blandford,* . .	Blandford, . .	Hampden, . .	33	52	56	108

VILLAGES, SECTIONS, ETC.: ALPHABETICALLY — Continued.

CITIES, TOWNS, VILLAGES, SECTIONS, ETC.	Cities and Towns	Counties	Number of Families	Males	Females	Population
Northborough,* ‖ . . .	Northborough, . .	Worcester, . .	–	–	–	–
Northbridge,* ‖ . . .	Northbridge, . .	Worcester, . .	–	–	–	–
Northbridge Centre,* . .	Northbridge, . .	Worcester, . .	95	187	156	343
North Brookfield,* ‖ . .	North Brookfield, .	Worcester, . .	–	–	–	–
North Cambridge,* ‖ . .	CAMBRIDGE, . .	Middlesex, . .	2,107	4,700	5,291	9,991
North Carver,* ‖ . . .	Carver, ...	Plymouth, . .	70	143	117	260
North Chatham,* . . .	Chatham, . . .	Barnstable, . .	43	63	74	137
North Chelmsford,* ‖ . .	Chelmsford, . .	Middlesex, . .	244	574	538	1,112
North Chester,* . . .	Chester, ...	Hampden, . .	19	41	39	80
North Cohasset, ‖ ¹ . .	Cohasset, . . .	Norfolk, . .	96	188	231	419
North Common, . . .	Westminster, . .	Worcester, . .	9	14	9	23
North Dana,* ‖ . . .	Dana, ...	Worcester, . .	122	224	243	467
North Dartmouth,* ‖ . .	Dartmouth, . .	Bristol, . .	77	131	154	285
North Dennis, . . .	Dennis, ...	Barnstable, . .	–	–	–	–
North Dighton,* ‖ ² . .	Dighton, . . .	Bristol, . .	–	–	–	–
North Duxbury,* . . .	Duxbury, . . .	Plymouth, . .	31	50	48	98
North Eastham,* ‖ . .	Eastham, . . .	Barnstable, . .	30	53	53	106
North Easton,* ‖ . .	Easton, ...	Bristol, . .	674	1,492	1,445	2,937
North Egremont,* . .	Egremont, . . .	Berkshire, . .	29	40	49	89
North End, ...	BOSTON, . . .	Suffolk, . .	–	–	–	–
North End, ...	NEW BEDFORD, . .	Bristol, . .	–	–	–	–
North Falmouth,* ‖ . .	Falmouth, . . .	Barnstable, . .	54	81	102	183
North Farms, . . .	NORTHAMPTON, . .	Hampshire, . .	12	30	21	51
Northfield,* ‖ . . .	Northfield, . . .	Franklin, . .	–	–	–	–
Northfield Farms,* ‖ . .	Northfield, . . .	Franklin, . .	55	107	75	182
North Foxborough,* ‖. .	Foxborough, . .	Norfolk, . .	46	99	99	198
North Franklin, . . .	Franklin, . . .	Norfolk, . .	34	67	82	149
North Grafton,* ‖. . .	Grafton, . . .	Worcester, . .	366	839	944	1,783
North Groveland, . .	Groveland, . . .	Essex, . .	–	–	–	–
North Hadley,* . . .	Hadley, ...	Hampshire, . .	145	319	293	612
North Hanover,* . . .	Hanover, . . .	Plymouth, . .	120	208	213	421
North Hanson,* ‖. . .	Hanson, ...	Plymouth, . .	18	31	37	68
North Harwich,* ‖ . .	Harwich, . . .	Barnstable, . .	65	99	96	195
North Hatfield,* ‖ . .	Hatfield, . . .	Hampshire, . .	65	166	126	292
North Heath,* . . .	Heath, ...	Franklin, . .	45	88	84	172
North Lancaster, . . .	Lancaster, . . .	Worcester, . .	–	–	–	–
North Lawrence, . . .	LAWRENCE, . . .	Essex, . .	–	–	–	–
North Leominster,* ‖ . .	Leominster, . . .	Worcester, . .	236	484	474	958
North Leverett,* . . .	Leverett, . . .	Franklin, . .	50	91	92	183
North Lexington, ‖ . .	Lexington, . . .	Middlesex, . .	–	–	–	–
North Littleton,* ‖. .	Littleton, . . .	Middlesex, . .	–	–	–	–
North Marshfield,* . .	Marshfield, . . .	Plymouth, . .	72	113	127	240
North Mashpee, . . .	Mashpee, . . .	Barnstable, . .	–	–	–	–
North Middleborough,* .	Middleborough, . .	Plymouth, . .	129	223	255	478
North Middleton, . . .	Middleton, . . .	Essex, . .	–	–	–	–
North Milford, . . .	Milford, . . .	Worcester, . .	–	–	–	–
North Monson, . . .	Monson, . . .	Hampden, . .	19	36	36	72
North Natick,* . . .	Natick, ...	Middlesex, . .	60	113	124	237
North New Salem,* . .	New Salem, . . .	Franklin, . .	17	24	22	46
North Orange,* . . .	Orange, ...	Franklin, . .	36	62	65	127
North Otis, ...	Otis, ...	Berkshire, . .	22	43	35	78
North Oxford,* ‖ . .	Oxford, ...	Worcester, . .	50	112	108	220
North Oxford Mills, ‖ . .	Oxford, ...	Worcester, . .	–	–	–	–
North Parish, . . .	HAVERHILL, . .	Essex, . .	56	96	104	200
North Pembroke,* . .	Pembroke, . . .	Plymouth, . .	66	109	112	221
North Pepperell,* ‖ ³ . .	Pepperell, . . .	Middlesex, . .	–	–	–	–
North Plymouth,* ‖ ⁴ . .	Plymouth, . . .	Plymouth, . .	112	281	269	550

VILLAGES, SECTIONS, ETC.: ALPHABETICALLY — Continued.

Cities, Towns, Villages, Sections, Etc.	Cities and Towns	Counties	Number of Families	Males	Females	Population
North Plympton, . . .	Plympton, . . .	Plymouth, . .	–	–	–	–
North Prescott,* . . .	Prescott, . . .	Hampshire, .	59	109	101	210
North Quarter, . . .	Concord, . . .	Middlesex, . .	–	–	–	–
North Raynham,* . .	Raynham, . . .	Bristol, . .	143	267	261	528
North Reading,* ‖ . .	North Reading, . .	Middlesex, . .	–	–	–	–
North Rehoboth,*. . .	Rehoboth, . . .	Bristol, . .	–	–	–	–
North Rochester,* . .	Rochester, . . .	Plymouth, . .	–	–	–	–
North Rutland,* . . .	Rutland, . . .	Worcester, . .	8	14	17	31
North Salem, ...	SALEM, ...	Essex, . . .	472	923	1,049	1,972
North Saugus, . . .	Saugus, ...	Essex, . . .	42	95	88	183
North Scituate,* ‖ . .	Scituate, . . .	Plymouth, . .	227	393	403	796
North Sherborn, . . .	Sherborn, . . .	Middlesex, . .	73	176	486	662
North Shirley, . . .	Shirley, ...	Middlesex, . .	–	–	–	–
North Side, ...	Charlton, . . .	Worcester, . .	–	–	–	–
North Somerville, ‖ . .	SOMERVILLE, . .	Middlesex, . .	–	–	–	–
North Spencer, . . .	Spencer, . . .	Worcester, . .	26	83	66	149
North Stoughton,* ‖ . .	Stoughton, . . .	Norfolk, . .	38	72	74	146
North Sudbury,* ‖ . .	Sudbury, . . .	Middlesex, . .	34	98	64	162
North Sunderland, . .	Sunderland, . . .	Franklin, . .	–	–	–	–
North Swansea,* . . .	Swansea, . . .	Bristol, . .	69	139	134	273
North Taunton, . . .	TAUNTON, . . .	Bristol, . .	–	–	–	–
North Tisbury,* . . .	West Tisbury, . .	Dukes, . . .	73	111	118	229
North Truro,* ‖ . . .	Truro, ...	Barnstable, . .	70	101	116	217
North Uxbridge,*. . .	Uxbridge, . . .	Worcester, . .	166	387	387	774
North Village, . . .	Lancaster, . . .	Worcester, . .	–	–	–	–
North Village, . . .	Truro, ...	Barnstable, . .	–	–	–	–
North Village, ‖ [1] . . .	Webster, . . .	Worcester, . .	135	382	358	740
Northville, ...	East Bridgewater, .	Plymouth, . .	57	107	98	205
North Westport,* ‖ . .	Westport, . . .	Bristol, . .	91	188	204	392
North Weymouth,* ‖ .	Weymouth, . . .	Norfolk, . .	326	824	679	1,503
North Wilbraham,* ‖ .	Wilbraham, . . .	Hampden, . .	106	227	249	476
North Wilmington,* ‖ .	Wilmington, . . .	Middlesex, . .	67	120	123	243
North Woburn, ‖ . . .	WOBURN, . . .	Middlesex, . .	248	510	537	1,047
North Woods, ‖ . . .	Holden, ...	Worcester, . .	21	72	48	120
North Worcester, ‖ . .	WORCESTER, . .	Worcester, . .	14	27	33	60
Norton,* ‖	Norton, ...	Bristol, . .	–	–	–	–
Norton Furnace,* ‖ . .	Norton, ...	Bristol, . .	18	35	37	72
Norwell,*	Norwell, . . .	Plymouth, . .	–	–	–	–
Norwich,*	Huntington, . . .	Hampshire, . .	41	83	86	169
Norwich Bridge, . . .	Huntington, . . .	Hampshire, . .	22	51	41	92
Norwood,* ‖	Norwood, . . .	Norfolk, . .	–	–	–	–
Norwood Central, ‖ . .	Norwood, . . .	Norfolk, . .	–	–	–	–
Notch, ...	NORTH ADAMS, . .	Berkshire, . .	–	–	–	–
Oakdale, ...	Dedham, . . .	Norfolk, . .	112	217	232	449
Oakdale, ...	HOLYOKE, . . .	Hampden, . .	–	–	–	–
Oakdale,* ‖	West Boylston, . .	Worcester, . .	248	644	651	1,295
Oak Grove, ‖	MALDEN, . . .	Middlesex, . .	–	–	–	–
Oak Grove Village, . .	FALL RIVER, . .	Bristol, . .	27	64	67	131
Oakham,*	Oakham, . . .	Worcester, . .	–	–	–	–
Oak Hill, ...	BROCKTON, . . .	Plymouth, . .	–	–	–	–
Oak Hill, ...	Harvard, . . .	Worcester, . .	–	–	–	–
Oak Hill, ...	NEWTON, . . .	Middlesex, . .	–	–	–	–
Oak Hill, ...	Pepperell, . . .	Middlesex, . .	–	–	–	–
Oak Island, ‖	Revere, ...	Suffolk, . .	–	–	–	–
Oak Knoll, ...	SPRINGFIELD, . .	Hampden, . .	–	–	–	–
Oakland, ...	TAUNTON, . . .	Bristol, . .	–	–	–	–

[1] R. R. names North Webster and Webster Mills.

VILLAGES, SECTIONS, ETC.: ALPHABETICALLY — Continued.

Cities, Towns, Villages, Sections, Etc.	Cities and Towns	Counties	Number of Families	Males	Females	Population
Oaklands,	Lowell,	Middlesex,	–	–	–	–
Oaklands,	Springfield,	Hampden,	–	–	–	–
Oaklandvale,	Saugus,	Essex,	–	–	–	–
Oakwood Park,	Hyde Park,	Norfolk,	–	–	–	–
Ocean Bluff,	Marshfield,	Plymouth,	–	–	–	–
Ocean Pier,	Revere,	Suffolk,	–	–	–	–
Ocean Spray,	Winthrop,	Suffolk,	–	–	–	–
Oklahoma,	Tisbury,	Dukes,	–	–	–	–
Old City,	Townsend,	Middlesex,	–	–	–	–
Old Colony Hill,	Hingham,	Plymouth,	–	–	–	–
Old Common,	Millbury,	Worcester,	–	–	–	–
Old Landing,	Marion,	Plymouth,	–	–	–	–
Old Mill,	Harvard,	Worcester,	–	–	–	–
Old Town,*	North Attleborough,	Bristol,	32	85	76	161
Onset,*	Wareham,	Plymouth,	165	218	234	452
Orange,*	Orange,	Franklin,	–	–	–	–
Orchard Park,	Lynn,	Essex,	–	–	–	–
Oregon,	Ashland,	Middlesex,	–	–	–	–
Orient Heights,	Boston,	Suffolk,	–	–	–	–
Orleans,*	Orleans,	Barnstable,	–	–	–	–
Osgood Heights,	Medford,	Middlesex,	–	–	–	–
Osterville,*	Barnstable,	Barnstable,	125	208	220	428
Otis,*	Otis,	Berkshire,	–	–	–	–
Otter River,*	Templeton,	Worcester,	96	228	206	434
Oxford,	Fairhaven,	Bristol,	–	–	–	–
Oxford,*	Oxford,	Worcester,	–	–	–	–
Packachoag Hill,	Auburn,	Worcester,	–	–	–	–
Packardsville,	Pelham,	Hampshire,	19	37	37	74
Painsville,	Wellfleet,	Barnstable,	–	–	–	–
Palmer,*	Palmer,	Hampden,	–	–	–	–
Pansy Park,	Belchertown,	Hampshire,	–	–	–	–
Parker Hill,	Boston,	Suffolk,	–	–	–	–
Parker Mills,	Wareham,	Plymouth,	–	–	–	–
Parkerville,	Westford,	Middlesex,	–	–	–	–
Park Hill,	Easthampton,	Hampshire,	7	17	27	44
Park Hill,	Millbury,	Worcester,	–	–	–	–
Park Hill,	Northampton,	Hampshire,	5	14	8	22
Parks' Corner,	Framingham,	Middlesex,	–	–	–	–
Park Street,	Medford,	Middlesex,	161	353	410	763
Parley Vale,	Boston,	Suffolk,	–	–	–	–
Partridgeville,	Athol,	Worcester,	–	–	–	–
Partridgeville,	Templeton,	Worcester,	–	–	–	–
Pasque Island,	Gosnold,	Dukes,	1	4	1	5
Patch,	Auburn,	Worcester,	–	–	–	–
Pattenville,	Tewksbury,	Middlesex,	–	–	–	–
Pawtucketville,	Lowell,	Middlesex,	375	827	899	1,726
Paxton,*	Paxton,	Worcester,	–	–	–	–
Peabody,*	Peabody,	Essex,	–	–	–	–
Pearl Hill,	Fitchburg,	Worcester,	–	–	–	–
Peck's,	Pittsfield,	Berkshire,	–	–	–	–
Pecowsic,	Springfield,	Hampden,	–	–	–	–
Pelham,*	Pelham,	Hampshire,	–	–	–	–
Pemberton, §	Hull,	Plymouth,	–	–	–	–
Pembroke,*	Pembroke,	Plymouth,	–	–	–	–
Pembroke Centre,	Pembroke,	Plymouth,	63	105	99	204
Penikese Island,	Gosnold,	Dukes,	1	1	–	1
Pepperell,*	Pepperell,	Middlesex,	–	–	–	–

VILLAGES, SECTIONS, ETC.: ALPHABETICALLY — Continued.

CITIES, TOWNS, VILLAGES, SECTIONS, ETC.	Cities and Towns	Counties	Number of Families	Males	Females	Population
Perrin's Bridge,	Seekonk,	Bristol,	–	–	–	–
Perrin's Crossing,	Seekonk,	Bristol,	–	–	–	–
Perryville,	Dudley,	Worcester,	40	121	123	244
Peru,*	Peru,	Berkshire,	–	–	–	–
Petersham,*	Petersham,	Worcester,	–	–	–	–
Pettis Plain,	Deerfield,	Franklin,	31	69	69	138
Phelps' Mills,	Peabody,	Essex,	–	–	–	–
Phillips Beach,	Swampscott,	Essex,	–	–	–	–
Phillipston,*	Phillipston,	Worcester,	–	–	–	–
Phoenix,[1]	Tewksbury,	Middlesex,	–	–	–	–
Piety Corner,	WALTHAM,	Middlesex,	–	–	–	–
Pigeon Cove,*	Rockport,	Essex,	406	1,247	793	2,040
Pine Bank,	BOSTON,	Suffolk,	–	–	–	–
Pinedale,	Athol,	Worcester,	–	–	–	–
Pine Grove,	NORTHAMPTON,	Hampshire,	11	36	23	59
Pine Hill,	LYNN,	Essex,	–	–	–	–
Pine Island,	BOSTON,	Suffolk,	–	–	–	–
Pine Ridge,	Westford,	Middlesex,	–	–	–	–
Pingreyville,	Littleton,	Middlesex,	–	–	–	–
PITTSFIELD,*	PITTSFIELD,	Berkshire,	–	–	–	–
Pittsfield Junction,	PITTSFIELD,	Berkshire,	–	–	–	–
Plainfield,*	Plainfield,	Hampshire,	–	–	–	–
Plains,	Edgartown,	Dukes,	–	–	–	–
Plainville,	Hadley,	Hampshire,	–	–	–	–
Plainville,	Marshfield,	Plymouth,	–	–	–	–
Plainville,	NEW BEDFORD,	Bristol,	–	–	–	–
Plainville,*	Wrentham,	Norfolk,	209	433	451	884
Pleasant Hills,	Saugus,	Essex,	–	–	–	–
Pleasant Lake,*	Harwich,	Barnstable,	75	151	144	295
Pleasant Park,	BROCKTON,	Plymouth,	–	–	–	–
Pleasant Valley,	Amesbury,	Essex,	–	–	–	–
Pleasantville,	BROCKTON,	Plymouth,	–	–	–	–
Plimptonville,	Walpole,	Norfolk,	–	–	–	–
Plum Island,	NEWBURYPORT,	Essex,	–	–	–	–
Plummer's,	Northbridge,	Worcester,	–	–	–	–
Plumtrees,	Sunderland,	Franklin,	–	–	–	–
Plymouth,*	Plymouth,	Plymouth,	–	–	–	–
Plympton,*	Plympton,	Plymouth,	–	–	–	–
Pocasset,*	Bourne,	Barnstable,	61	36	104	197
Pochassic,	Westfield,	Hampden,	30	61	58	119
Pochet,	Orleans,	Barnstable,	–	–	–	–
Pohoganut,	Edgartown,	Dukes,	–	–	–	–
Point,	North Reading,	Middlesex,	–	–	–	–
Point Allerton,*[2]	Hull,	Plymouth,	12	30	28	58
Point Holes,	QUINCY,	Norfolk,	–	–	–	–
Point of Pines,	Revere,	Suffolk,	–	–	–	–
Point Shirley,[3]	Winthrop,	Suffolk,	–	–	–	–
Poland,	Conway,	Franklin,	–	–	–	–
Polpis,	Nantucket,	Nantucket,	12	25	24	49
Pomeroy,	PITTSFIELD,	Berkshire,	–	–	–	–
Pond Hills,	Amesbury,	Essex,	–	–	–	–
Pond Village,	Barnstable,	Barnstable,	–	–	–	–
Pond Village,	Yarmouth,	Barnstable,	–	–	–	–
Pondville,	Auburn,	Worcester,	–	–	–	–
Pondville,*	Norfolk,	Norfolk,	–	–	–	–
Poniken,	Lancaster,	Worcester,	–	–	–	–
Ponkapoag,*	Canton,	Norfolk,	92	209	199	408
Pontoosuc,*	PITTSFIELD,	Berkshire,	159	427	389	816

[1] R. R. name Atherton.   [2] P. O. and R. R. name Allerton.   [3] R. R. name Shirley.

VILLAGES, SECTIONS, ETC.: ALPHABETICALLY — Continued.

CITIES, TOWNS, VILLAGES, SECTIONS, ETC.	Cities and Towns	Counties	Number of Families	Males	Fe- males	Popula- tion
Pope's Hill, ‖ .	BOSTON,	Suffolk,	–	–	–	–
Poquanticut, .	Easton,	Bristol,	–	–	–	–
Porter's Station, .	CAMBRIDGE,	Middlesex, .	–	–	–	–
Portnomequot, .	Orleans,.	Barnstable,	–	–	–	–
Port Norfolk.	BOSTON,	Suffolk,	–	–	–	–
Pottersville,*	Somerset,	Bristol,	–	–	–	–
Pound Hill, .	FITCHBURG, .	Worcester, .	–	–	–	–
Pound Hill, .	Rutland,	Worcester, .	–	–	–	–
Powder Horn Hill,	CHELSEA,	Suffolk,	–	–	–	–
Power Station, ‖ .	Hingham,	Plymouth, .	–	–	–	–
Pratt's Junction,* ‖	Sterling,.	Worcester, .	24	52	45	97
Pratt Town, .	Bridgewater.	Plymouth, .	–	–	–	–
Prattville,	CHELSEA,	Suffolk,	–	–	–	–
Prattville,	Raynham,	Bristol,	–	–	–	–
Precinct,	Lakeville,	Plymouth, .	–	–	–	–
Prescott,*	Prescott,	Hampshire,	–	–	–	–
Pride's,* ‖ [1]	BEVERLY,	Essex, .	–	–	–	–
Princeton,*	Princeton,	Worcester, .	–	–	–	–
Princeton Depot,* ‖	Princeton,	Worcester, .	–	–	–	–
Prison Point,	BOSTON,	Suffolk,	–	–	–	–
Proctor's, ‖	Peabody,	Essex, .	–	–	–	–
Prospect Hill,	BROCKTON,	Plymouth, .	–	–	–	–
Prospect Hill,	Easthampton,	Hampshire,	–	–	–	–
Prospect Hill,	Hingham,	Plymouth, .	–	–	–	–
Prospect Hill, ‖	SOMERVILLE,	Middlesex, .	–	–	–	–
Prospect Hill,	West Springfield,	Hampden, .	–	–	–	–
Prospect Park,	BROCKTON,	Plymouth, .	–	–	–	–
Provincetown,* ‖ .	Provincetown,	Barnstable,	–	–	–	–
Pumpkin Hollow,	Conway,	Franklin, .	–	–	–	–
Putnam's, ‖ .	Middleborough, .	Plymouth, .	–	–	–	–
Putnamville, ‖	Danvers.	Essex, .	57	110	108	218
Quaise, .	Nantucket,	Nantucket, .	–	–	–	–
Quaker District, .	Northbridge,.	Worcester, .	–	–	–	–
Quakerville, .	Bolton,	Worcester, .	–	–	–	–
Quality Hill, .	BROCKTON,	Plymouth, .	–	–	–	–
Quampache, .	Edgartown,	Dukes,.	–	–	–	–
Quansue,	Chilmark,	Dukes, .	–	–	–	–
Queen Anne's Corner,	Norwell,	Plymouth, .	–	–	–	–
Quidnet,.	Nantucket,	Nantucket, .	–	–	–	–
Quinapoxet,* ‖	Holden,	Worcester, .	66	185	176	361
QUINCY,* ‖	QUINCY,	Norfolk,	–	–	–	–
Quincy Adams, ‖ .	QUINCY,	Norfolk,	–	–	–	–
Quincy Neck,	QUINCY,	Norfolk,	–	–	–	–
Quincy Point, ‖	QUINCY,	Norfolk,	153	366	340	706
Quinsigamond,* .	WORCESTER,	Worcester, .	522	1,375	1,194	2,569
Quissett,*	Falmouth,	Barnstable,	21	41	42	83
Rabbit Hill, .	Wrentham,	Norfolk,	–	–	–	–
Raddins, ‖	LYNN,	Essex, .	–	–	–	–
Randall Town,	Mattapoisett,	Plymouth, .	–	–	–	–
Randolph,* ‖,	Randolph,	Norfolk,	–	–	–	–
Rangeley Park,	BROCKTON, .	Plymouth, .	–	–	–	–
Raynham,* ‖ .	Raynham,	Bristol,	–	–	–	–
Raynham Centre,.	Raynham,	Bristol,	106	187	206	393
Reading,* ‖	Reading,	Middlesex, .	–	–	–	–
Reading Highlands, ‖ .	Reading,	Middlesex, .	–	–	–	–
Readville,* ‖ .	Hyde Park,	Norfolk,	274	679	659	1,338

[1] P. O. name Pride's Crossing.

VILLAGES, SECTIONS, ETC. : ALPHABETICALLY — Continued.

Cities, Towns, Villages, Sections, Etc.	Cities and Towns	Counties	Number of Families	Males	Females	Population
Bed Bridge, ‖	Ludlow,	Hampden,	–	–	–	–
Reed's Hill,	Marblehead,	Essex,	–	–	–	–
Reformatory, ‖	Concord,	Middlesex,	–	–	–	–
Rehoboth,*	Rehoboth,	Bristol,	–	–	–	–
Rehoboth Village,	Rehoboth,	Bristol,	–	–	–	–
Renfrew, ‖	Adams,	Berkshire,	277	682	779	1,461
Renfrew,	Dalton,	Berkshire,	–	–	–	–
Reservoir, ‖	Brookline,	Norfolk,	–	–	–	–
Reservoir Hill,	CAMBRIDGE,	Middlesex,	–	–	–	–
Revere,* ‖	Revere,	Suffolk,	–	–	–	–
Revere Beach,	Revere,	Suffolk,	–	–	–	–
Revere Highlands,	Revere,	Suffolk,	–	–	–	–
Rice Village,	Barre,	Worcester,	–	–	–	–
Riceville,	Athol,	Worcester,	–	–	–	–
Richmond,*	Richmond,	Berkshire,	–	–	–	–
Richmond Furnace,* ‖	Richmond,	Berkshire,	43	94	95	189
Ridge Hill,*	Norwell,	Plymouth,	67	123	117	240
King's Island,	Salisbury,	Essex,	–	–	–	–
Ringville,*	Worthington,	Hampshire,	7	12	9	21
Riverdale,	Dedham,	Norfolk,	36	86	74	160
Riverdale,	GLOUCESTER,	Essex,	155	294	321	615
Riverdale,	Northbridge,	Worcester,	39	111	103	214
Riverdale,	West Springfield,	Hampden,	–	–	–	–
Riverside,*	Gill,	Franklin,	75	171	175	346
Riverside,	HAVERHILL,	Essex,	–	–	–	–
Riverside, ‖	NEWTON,	Middlesex,	35	80	104	184
Riverside,	Williamstown,	Berkshire,	–	–	–	–
River Street, ‖	Hyde Park,	Norfolk,	–	–	–	–
River View, ‖	WALTHAM,	Middlesex,	–	–	–	–
Roberts' Crossing, ‖ [1]	WALTHAM,	Middlesex,	–	–	–	–
Roberts' Meadow,	NORTHAMPTON,	Hampshire,	9	18	14	32
Robinsville,	Walpole,	Norfolk,	–	–	–	–
Rochdale,* ‖	Leicester,	Worcester,	148	304	327	631
Rochdale,	Spencer,	Worcester,	–	–	–	–
Rochester,*	Rochester,	Plymouth,	–	–	–	–
Rochester Centre,	Rochester,	Plymouth,	–	–	–	–
Rock,* ‖	Middleborough,	Plymouth,	61	108	102	210
Rock Bottom,* ‖	Stow,	Middlesex,	80	156	150	306
Rock Dale,	NEW BEDFORD,	Bristol,	–	–	–	–
Rock Dale Mills,*.	West Stockbridge,	Berkshire,	–	–	–	–
Rock Harbor,	Orleans,	Barnstable,	–	–	–	–
Rockland,* ‖	Rockland,	Plymouth,	–	–	–	–
Rockport,* ‖	Rockport,	Essex,	–	–	–	–
Rock's Village,	HAVERHILL,	Essex,	67	113	121	234
Rock Valley,	HOLYOKE,	Hampden,	24	73	68	141
Rockville,	FITCHBURG,	Worcester,	–	–	–	–
Rockville,*	Millis,	Norfolk,	51	111	113	224
Rocky Hill,	Amesbury,	Essex,	–	–	–	–
Rocky Nook,	Hingham,	Plymouth,	–	–	–	–
Rocky Nook,	Kingston,	Plymouth,	–	–	–	–
Rosemont,	HAVERHILL,	Essex,	23	51	45	96
Roslindale,* ‖	BOSTON,	Suffolk,	–	–	–	–
Round Hill,	SPRINGFIELD,	Hampden,	–	–	–	–
Rounseville Mills,	Rochester,	Plymouth,	–	–	–	–
Rowe,*	Rowe,	Franklin,	–	–	–	–
Rowley,* ‖	Rowley,	Essex,	–	–	–	–
Roxbury,* ‖	BOSTON,	Suffolk,	19,972	43,103	48,985	92,088
Roxbury Crossing,*	BOSTON,	Suffolk,	–	–	–	–

[1] R. R. name Roberts.

VILLAGES, SECTIONS, ETC.: ALPHABETICALLY — Continued.

CITIES, TOWNS, VILLAGES, SECTIONS, ETC.	Cities and Towns	Counties	Number of Families	Males	Females	Population
Royalston,* ‖	Royalston,	Worcester,	-	-	-	-
Rubber District,	CHELSEA,	Suffolk,	-	-	-	-
Rugby, ‖	BOSTON,	Suffolk,	-	-	-	-
Rugby,	Hyde Park,	Norfolk,	-	-	-	-
Russell,* ‖	Russell,	Hampden,	-	-	-	-
Russell Mountain,	Russell,	Hampden,	29	70	63	133
Russell's,	PITTSFIELD,	Berkshire,	-	-	-	-
Russellville,	Hadley,	Hampshire,	-	-	-	-
Russellville,	Southampton,	Hampshire,	16	38	28	66
Rutland,* ‖	Rutland,	Worcester,	-	-	-	-
Ryall's Side,	BEVERLY,	Essex,	-	-	-	-
Ryder Village,	Barre,	Worcester,	-	-	-	-
Sagamore,* ‖	Bourne,	Barnstable,	65	122	145	267
Sagamore Hill,	Hull,	Plymouth,	-	-	-	-
Sagamore Village,	FALL RIVER,	Bristol,	-	-	-	-
SALEM,* ‖	SALEM,	Essex,	-	-	-	-
Salem Neck,	SALEM,	Essex,	-	-	-	-
Salisbury,* ‖	Salisbury,	Essex,	-	-	-	-
Salisbury Beach,	Salisbury,	Essex,	7	13	13	26
Salisbury Heights,	BROCKTON,	Plymouth,	-	-	-	-
Salisbury Plains,	Salisbury,	Essex,	-	-	-	-
Salisbury Point,* ‖	Amesbury,	Essex,	121	227	255	482
Salisbury Square,	BROCKTON,	Plymouth,	-	-	-	-
Sandersdale, ‖	Southbridge,	Worcester,	-	-	-	-
Sand Hills,	Scituate,	Plymouth,	-	-	-	-
Sandisfield,*	Sandisfield,	Berkshire,	-	-	-	-
Sandwich,* ‖	Sandwich,	Barnstable,	-	-	-	-
Santuit,*.	Barnstable,	Barnstable,	28	55	57	112
Satucket,	East Bridgewater,	Plymouth,	39	72	89	161
Saugus,* ‖	Saugus,	Essex,	-	-	-	-
Saugus Centre,	Saugus,	Essex,	277	588	578	1,166
Saundersville,* ‖	Grafton,	Worcester,	81	180	200	380
Savin Hill, ‖	BOSTON,	Suffolk,	-	-	-	-
Savoy,*	Savoy,	Berkshire,	-	-	-	-
Savoy Centre,*	Savoy,	Berkshire,	29	64	54	118
Sawtelleville,	BROCKTON,	Plymouth,	-	-	-	-
Saxonville,* ‖	Framingham,	Middlesex,	469	757	932	1,689
Scantic,	Hampden,	Hampden,	-	-	-	-
Scituate,* ‖	Scituate,	Plymouth,	-	-	-	-
Scituate Centre,*	Scituate,	Plymouth,	-	-	-	-
Scituate Harbor,	Scituate,	Plymouth,	211	429	428	857
Scotient Neck,	Fairhaven,	Bristol,	-	-	-	-
Scorton,	Sandwich,	Barnstable,	-	-	-	-
Scotland,*	Bridgewater,	Plymouth,	62	127	116	243
Scotland,	Newbury,	Essex,	-	-	-	-
Scrabbletown,	Cheshire,	Berkshire,	-	-	-	-
Searsville,	Dennis,	Barnstable,	-	-	-	-
Searsville,	Williamsburg,	Hampshire,	-	-	-	-
Sea View,* ‖	Marshfield,	Plymouth,	39	67	74	141
Second Parish,	West Newbury,	Essex,	-	-	-	-
Seekonk,	Great Barrington,	Berkshire,	-	-	-	-
Seekonk,*	Seekonk,	Bristol,	-	-	-	-
Segreganset,*	Dighton,	Bristol,	-	-	-	-
Shaboken,	Harvard,	Worcester,	-	-	-	-
Shaker Settlement,	Hancock,	Berkshire,	5	22	30	52
Shaker Village,	Harvard,	Worcester,	-	-	-	-
Shaker Village,	PITTSFIELD,	Berkshire,	-	-	-	-

VILLAGES, SECTIONS, ETC.: ALPHABETICALLY — Continued.

Cities, Towns, Villages, Sections, Etc.	Cities and Towns	Counties	Number of Families	Males	Females	Population
Shaker Village,	Shirley,	Middlesex,	–	–	–	–
Sharon,* ‖	Sharon,	Norfolk,	–	–	–	–
Sharon Corner,	Walpole,	Norfolk,	–	–	–	–
Sharon Heights, ‖	Sharon,	Norfolk,	22	48	53	101
Shattuckville,*	Colrain,	Franklin,	35	76	68	144
Shawmut, ‖	Boston,	Suffolk,	–	–	–	–
Shawmut,*	New Bedford,	Bristol,	29	57	54	111
Shaw's Corner,	Brockton,	Plymouth,	–	–	–	–
Shawville,	Wales,	Hampden,	–	–	–	–
Sheffield,* ‖	Sheffield,	Berkshire,	–	–	–	–
Shelburne,*	Shelburne,	Franklin,	–	–	–	–
Shelburne Falls, ‖	Buckland,	Franklin,	238	526	480	1,006
Shelburne Falls,*.	Shelburne,	Franklin,	273	452	547	999
Sheldonville,*	Wrentham,	Norfolk,	86	152	168	320
Shepardville,	Wrentham,	Norfolk,	23	42	50	92
Sherborn,* ‖	Sherborn,	Middlesex,	–	–	–	–
Shirkshire,	Conway,	Franklin,	–	–	–	–
Shirley,* ‖	Shirley,	Middlesex,	–	–	–	–
Shirley Centre,*¹.	Shirley,	Middlesex,	–	–	–	–
Shirley Village,	Shirley,	Middlesex,	233	488	579	1,067
Shoosett,	Pembroke,	Plymouth,	–	–	–	–
Shrewsbury,*	Shrewsbury,	Worcester,	–	–	–	–
Shutesbury,*.	Shutesbury,	Franklin,	–	–	–	–
Siasconset,* ‖	Nantucket,	Nantucket,	28	43	46	89
Silver Hill, ‖.	Weston,	Middlesex,	–	–	–	–
Silver Lake,*	Kingston,	Plymouth,	44	78	65	143
Silver Lake, .	Plympton,	Plymouth,	–	–	–	–
Silver Lake, ‖	Wilmington,	Middlesex,	–	–	–	–
Sippican,	Marion,	Plymouth,	–	–	–	–
Sixteen Acres,* ‖.	Springfield,	Hampden,	51	115	116	231
Skinnerville, .	Williamsburg,	Hampshire,	–	–	–	–
Slab City,	Leverett,	Franklin,	–	–	–	–
Smith Hollow,	Middlefield,	Hampshire,	–	–	–	–
Smith's,* ‖	Enfield,	Hampshire,	73	161	156	317
Smith's Ferry,* ‖.	Northampton,	Hampshire,	19	47	52	99
Smithville,* ‖	Barre,	Worcester,	30	61	79	140
Smithville,	Sutton,	Worcester,	11	28	24	52
Snellville,	Sturbridge,	Worcester,	–	–	–	–
Sodom,	Scituate,	Plymouth,	–	–	–	–
Sodom,	Tyringham,	Berkshire,	–	–	–	–
Somerset,* ‖.	Somerset,	Bristol,	–	–	–	–
Somerset Hill,*	Cambridge,	Middlesex,	–	–	–	–
Somerset Junction, ‖.	Fall River,	Bristol,	–	–	–	–
Somerville,* ‖	Somerville,	Middlesex,	–	–	–	–
Somerville Highlands, ‖	Somerville,	Middlesex,	–	–	–	–
Somerville Junction, ‖	Somerville,	Middlesex,	–	–	–	–
South Abington Station,* .	Whitman,	Plymouth,	–	–	–	–
South Acton,* ‖	Acton,	Middlesex,	143	255	273	528
South Amherst,* ‖	Amherst,	Hampshire,	108	227	215	442
Southampton,* ‖ ·	Southampton,	Hampshire,	–	–	–	–
Southardville,	Athol,	Worcester,	–	–	–	–
South Ashburnham,* ‖	Ashburnham,	Worcester,	181	376	370	746
South Ashfield,* .	Ashfield,	Franklin,	22	29	35	64
South Athol,* ‖	Athol,	Worcester,	23	47	35	82
South Attleborough,* .	Attleborough,	Bristol,	189	429	431	860
South Barre, .	Barre,	Worcester,	–	–	–	–
South Bellingham,*	Bellingham,	Norfolk,	194	225	230	455
South Berlin,*	Berlin,	Worcester,	39	102	85	187

¹ P. O. name Shirleyville.

VILLAGES, SECTIONS, ETC.: ALPHABETICALLY — Continued.

CITIES, TOWNS, VILLAGES, SECTIONS, ETC.	Cities and Towns	Counties	Number of Families	Males	Females	Population
South Billerica,* ‖	Billerica,	Middlesex, .	36	89	79	168
South Bolton, ‖	Bolton, .	Worcester, .	–	–	–	–
Southborough,* ‖	Southborough,	Worcester, .	–	–	–	–
South Boston,* ‖	BOSTON,	Suffolk,	14,602	33,853	34,060	67,913
South Boylston, ‖	West Boylston,	Worcester, .	164	290	343	633
South Braintree,* ‖	Braintree,	Norfolk,	533	1,202	1,065	2,267
South Brewster,* .	Brewster,	Barnstable,	34	51	55	106
Southbridge,* ‖	Southbridge,.	Worcester, .	–	–	–	–
South Byfield,*	Newbury,	Essex, .	–	–	–	–
South Canton,	Canton, .	Norfolk,	–	–	–	–
South Carver,*	Carver, .	Plymouth, .	85	209	161	370
South Chatham,* ‖	Chatham,	Barnstable,	86	145	152	297
South Chelmsford,* ‖	Chelmsford, .	Middlesex, .	67	128	124	252
South Clinton, ‖ [1]	Clinton, .	Worcester, .	–	–	–	–
South Dartmouth,*	Dartmouth, .	Bristol,	121	200	210	410
South Deerfield,* ‖	Deerfield,	Franklin,	241	543	528	1,071
South Dennis,* ‖	Dennis,	Barnstable,	132	203	234	437
South District,	Hamilton,	Essex, .	102	229	230	459
South Douglas,	Douglas,	Worcester, .	–	–	–	–
South Duxbury,* ‖	Duxbury,	Plymouth, .	94	169	173	342
South East, .	Billerica,	Middlesex, .	41	102	82	184
South Eastham, .	Eastham,	Barnstable,	–	–	–	–
South Easton,* ‖	Easton, .	Bristol,	123	270	246	516
South Egremont,*	Egremont,	Berkshire, .	62	114	143	257
South End,* .	BOSTON,	Suffolk,	–	–	–	–
South End,	Leominster, .	Worcester, .	–	–	–	–
South End,	NEW BEDFORD, .	Bristol,	–	–	–	–
South Essex,* ‖ [2]	Essex, .	Essex, .	123	203	209	412
South Everett,	EVERETT,	Middlesex, .	430	1,026	983	2,009
Southfield,*	New Marlborough,	Berkshire, .	50	104	93	197
South Fitchburg,* ‖	FITCHBURG, .	Worcester, .	205	701	562	1,263
South Foxborough,	Foxborough,	Norfolk,	88	204	187	391
South Framingham,* ‖	Framingham,	Middlesex, .	1,270	2,887	2,883	5,770
South Franklin,* ‖ [3]	Franklin,	Norfolk,	28	58	56	114
South Gardner,* .	Gardner,	Worcester, .	444	853	831	1,684
South Georgetown, ‖	Georgetown,	Essex, .	50	96	95	191
South Groveland,*	Groveland, .	Essex, .	197	507	562	1,069
South Hadley,*	South Hadley,	Hampshire,	–	–	–	–
South Hadley Falls,* .	South Hadley,	Hampshire,	663	1,568	1,573	3,141
South Hanover,* ‖	Hanover,	Plymouth, .	85	135	154	289
South Hanson,* ‖ .	Hanson, .	Plymouth, .	66	135	117	252
South Harwich,* ‖	Harwich,	Barnstable,	72	97	107	204
South Hingham,* .	Hingham,	Plymouth, .	254	450	504	954
South Holyoke,	HOLYOKE,	Hampden,	–	–	–	–
South Hyannis,* .	Barnstable,	Barnstable,	20	26	30	56
South Lancaster,* ‖	Lancaster,	Worcester, .	204	459	523	982
South Lawrence, ‖	LAWRENCE, .	Essex, .	1,577	3,585	3,721	7,306
South Lee,* ‖	Lee, .	Berkshire, .	115	235	288	523
South Lincoln,*	Lincoln,	Middlesex, .	–	–	–	–
South Lowell,	Tewksbury, .	Middlesex, .	47	106	107	213
South Lynnfield, .	Lynnfield,	Essex, .	94	184	201	385
South Mashpee,	Mashpee,	Barnstable,	13	27	20	47
South Medford, .	MEDFORD,	Middlesex, .	–	–	–	–
South Middleborough,* ‖	Middleborough,	Plymouth, .	–	–	–	–
South Middleton,* ‖	Middleton,	Essex, .	8	36	20	56
South Milford,* ‖ .	Hopedale,	Worcester, .	–	–	–	–
South Monson,	Monson,.	Hampden, .	110	210	248	458
South Natick,*	Natick, .	Middlesex, .	283	649	647	1,296

---

[1] R. R. station in town of Boylston.   [2] R. R. name Conomo.   [3] R. R. name Wadsworth.

VILLAGES, SECTIONS, ETC.: ALPHABETICALLY — Continued.

CITIES, TOWNS, VILLAGES, SECTIONS, ETC.	Cities and Towns	Counties	Number of Families	Males	Females	Population
South New Salem,	New Salem,	Franklin,	–	–	–	–
South Orleans,*	Orleans,	Barnstable,	54	72	82	154
South Peabody,	Peabody,	Essex,	201	440	407	847
South Quincy,	QUINCY,	Norfolk,	988	2,508	2,212	4,720
South Raynham,	Raynham,	Bristol,	58	141	137	278
South Rehoboth,*	Rehoboth,	Bristol,	–	–	–	–
South Royalston,*	Royalston,	Worcester,	91	149	142	291
South Salem,	SALEM,	Essex,	1,158	3,433	3,443	6,876
South Sandisfield,*	Sandisfield,	Berkshire,	24	58	46	104
South Sandwich,*	Sandwich,	Barnstable,	26	42	52	94
South Seekonk,	Seekonk,	Bristol,	–	–	–	–
South Sherborn,* ‖	Sherborn,	Middlesex,	51	118	93	211
South Shrewsbury,	Shrewsbury,	Worcester,	–	–	–	–
South Side,	WALTHAM,	Middlesex,	–	–	–	–
South Somerset,	Somerset,	Bristol,	–	–	–	–
South Spencer, ‖	Spencer,	Worcester,	32	79	71	150
South Sudbury,* ‖	Sudbury,	Middlesex,	127	273	252	525
South Sutton,	Sutton,	Worcester,	54	104	111	215
South Swansea,* ‖	Swansea,	Bristol,	41	79	83	162
South Truro,* ‖	Truro,	Barnstable,	35	57	56	113
South Uxbridge, ‖	Uxbridge,	Worcester,	19	44	33	77
South Village,	Dennis,	Barnstable,	–	–	–	–
South Village, ‖¹	Webster,	Worcester,	237	527	592	1,119
Southville,* ‖	Southborough,	Worcester,	72	143	147	290
South Walpole,* ‖	Walpole,	Norfolk,	87	141	177	318
South Wareham,* ‖	Wareham,	Plymouth,	98	247	189	436
South Wellfleet,* ‖	Wellfleet,	Barnstable,	47	59	62	121
South Westminster,*	Westminster,	Worcester,	42	80	78	158
South Westport,*	Westport,	Bristol,	21	41	37	78
South Weymouth,* ‖	Weymouth,	Norfolk,	757	1,573	1,626	3,199
Southwick,* ‖	Southwick,	Hampden,	–	–	–	–
South Williamstown,*	Williamstown,	Berkshire,	88	192	179	371
South Wilmington, ‖	Wilmington,	Middlesex,	–	–	–	–
South Worcester,* ‖	WORCESTER,	Worcester,	1,062	2,802	2,633	5,435
South Worthington,*	Worthington,	Hampshire,	20	43	36	79
South Yarmouth,* ‖	Yarmouth,	Barnstable,	223	306	329	635
Spencer,* ‖	Spencer,	Worcester,	–	–	–	–
Sprague's Hill,	Bridgewater,	Plymouth,	–	–	–	–
Springdale, ‖	Canton,	Norfolk,	–	–	–	–
Springdale,	Holden,	Worcester,	30	75	68	143
Springdale,	HOLYOKE,	Hampden,	–	–	–	–
Springdale,	Westfield,	Hampden,	–	–	–	–
SPRINGFIELD,* ‖	SPRINGFIELD,	Hampden,	–	–	–	–
Spring Hill,*	Sandwich,	Barnstable,	54	81	121	202
Spring Hill,	SOMERVILLE,	Middlesex,	–	–	–	–
Springside,	PITTSFIELD,	Berkshire,	–	–	–	–
Spring Street, ‖	BOSTON,	Suffolk,	–	–	–	–
Springville,	Topsfield,	Essex,	–	–	–	–
Spruce Corner,*	Ashfield,	Franklin,	–	–	–	–
Squantum,	QUINCY,	Norfolk,	–	–	–	–
Square-hire,	Sterling,	Worcester,	–	–	–	–
Squibnocket,*	Chilmark,	Dukes,	40	56	60	116
Stafford's Hill,	Cheshire,	Berkshire,	–	–	–	–
State Farm,*	Bridgewater,	Plymouth,	–	–	–	–
State Line,* ‖	West Stockbridge,	Berkshire,	21	46	45	91
Stearnsville,	PITTSFIELD,	Berkshire,	–	–	–	–
Steelville,	FALL RIVER,	Bristol,	–	–	–	–
Steep Brook,* ‖	FALL RIVER,	Bristol,	171	312	360	672

¹ R. R. name South Webster.

VILLAGES, SECTIONS, ETC.: ALPHABETICALLY — Continued.

Cities, Towns, Villages, Sections, Etc.	Cities and Towns	Counties	Number of Families	Males	Females	Population
Sterling,* ‖	Sterling, . . .	Worcester, . .	–	–	–	–
Sterling Junction,* ‖ .	Sterling, . . .	Worcester, . .	22	44	38	82
Stetsonville, ...	LYNN, ...	Essex, ...	–	–	–	–
Stevens' Village, . .	Dudley, ...	Worcester, . .	44	150	139	289
Stevens' Village, ‖ 1 .	North Andover, . .	Essex, ...	–	–	–	–
Still River,* ‖ . . .	Harvard, . . .	Worcester, . .	39	68	68	136
Stockbridge,* ‖ . . .	Stockbridge, . . .	Berkshire, . .	–	–	–	–
Stoneham,* ‖	Stoneham, . . .	Middlesex, . .	–	–	–	–
Stone Haven, ‖ . . .	Dedham, . . .	Norfolk, . . .	–	–	–	–
Stoneville, ...	Auburn. . . .	Worcester, . .	81	214	230	444
Stoneville, ...	Erving, ...	Franklin, . .	–	–	–	–
Stony Beach, ‖ . . .	Hull, ...	Plymouth, . .	10	41	30	71
Stony Brook, . . .	Norfolk, ...	Norfolk, . .	24	57	42	99
Stony Brook, ‖ . . .	Weston, ...	Middlesex, . .	–	–	–	–
Stoughton,* ‖ . . .	Stoughton, . . .	Norfolk, . .	–	–	–	–
Stow.* ‖	Stow, ...	Middlesex, . .	–	–	–	–
Strawberry Hill, . .	CAMBRIDGE, . . .	Middlesex, . .	–	–	–	–
Straw Hollow, . . .	Boylston, . . .	Worcester, . .	–	–	–	–
Sturbridge,*	Sturbridge, . . .	Worcester, . .	–	–	–	–
Succanesett, . . .	Falmouth, . . .	Barnstable, . .	–	–	–	–
Sudbury,* ‖	Sudbury, . . .	Middlesex, . .	–	–	–	–
Summit, ...	WORCESTER, . .	Worcester, . .	–	–	–	–
Sunderland,* . . .	Sunderland, . . .	Franklin, . .	–	–	–	–
Sunnyside, ...	BROCKTON, . . .	Plymouth, . .	–	–	–	–
Sunnyside, ...	Hyde Park, . .	Norfolk, . .	462	1,120	1,103	2,223
Surfside, ‖	Hull, ...	Plymouth, . .	–	–	–	–
Surfside, ...	Nantucket, . . .	Nantucket, . .	–	–	–	–
Sutton,*	Sutton, ...	Worcester, . .	–	–	–	–
Swampscott,* ‖ . . .	Swampscott, . .	Essex, ...	–	–	–	–
Swansea Centre,* . .	Swansea, . . .	Bristol, . .	86	156	157	313
Swansea Village,* . .	Swansea, . . .	Bristol, . .	146	305	285	590
Sweeneyville, . . .	Topsfield, . . .	Essex, ...	–	–	–	–
Sweet's Corner, . .	Williamstown, . .	Berkshire, . .	–	–	–	–
Swift River,* . . .	Cummington, . .	Hampshire, . .	15	28	27	55
Sylvester Corner, . .	BROCKTON, . . .	Plymouth, . .	–	–	–	–
Symmes' Corner, . .	Winchester, . . .	Middlesex, . .	–	–	–	–
Taconic, ...	PITTSFIELD, . .	Berkshire, . .	–	–	–	–
Tainter Hill, . . .	Millbury, . . .	Worcester, . .	–	–	–	–
Tapleyville,* ‖ . . .	Danvers, . . .	Essex, ...	296	640	682	1,322
Tarpaulin Cove,* . .	Gosnold, . . .	Dukes, ...	–	–	–	–
Tar Hill, ...	FITCHBURG, . . .	Worcester, . .	–	–	–	–
Tatham, ‖	West Springfield, .	Hampden, . .	–	–	–	–
Tatnuck, ...	WORCESTER, . .	Worcester, . .	–	–	–	–
TAUNTON,* ‖ . .	TAUNTON, . . .	Bristol, . .	–	–	–	–
Teatickett,*	Falmouth, . . .	Barnstable, . .	43	77	76	153
Templeton,* ‖ . . .	Templeton, . . .	Worcester, . .	–	–	–	–
Tenneyville, . . .	Palmer, . . .	Hampden, . .	–	–	–	–
Tewksbury,* ‖ . . .	Tewksbury, . . .	Middlesex, . .	–	–	–	–
Tewksbury Centre, ‖ .	Tewksbury, . . .	Middlesex, . .	62	682	759	1,441
Tewksbury Junction, ‖	Tewksbury, . . .	Middlesex, . .	–	–	–	–
Texas Village, . . .	Oxford, ...	Worcester, . .	47	111	144	255
The Bars, ...	Deerfield, . . .	Franklin, . .	–	–	–	–
The Falls, ...	Needham, . . .	Norfolk, . .	77	183	201	384
The Island, . . .	Wayland, . . .	Middlesex, . .	–	–	–	–
The Laurels, . . .	NEWBURYPORT, . .	Essex, ...	–	–	–	–
The Mill, ...	Deerfield, . . .	Franklin, . .	–	–	–	–
The Neck, ...	Mattapoisett, . .	Plymouth, . .	–	–	–	–

1 R. R. name Stevens.

VILLAGES, SECTIONS, ETC.: ALPHABETICALLY — Continued.

CITIES, TOWNS, VILLAGES, SECTIONS, ETC.	Cities and Towns	Counties	Number of Families	Males	Females	Population
The Pines, ...	NEWBURYPORT, . .	Essex, ...	–	–	–	–
The Plains, ...	Leominster, . . .	Worcester, . .	–	–	–	–
Thomaston Park, . .	BROCKTON, . . .	Plymouth, . .	–	–	–	–
Thompsonville, . .	NEWTON, . . .	Middlesex, . .	14	45	32	77
Thorndike,* ‖ . . .	Palmer, ...	Hampden, . .	280	715	788	1,503
Three-Mile Hill, . .	Great Barrington, .	Berkshire, . .	–	–	–	–
Three Rivers,* ‖ . .	Palmer, ...	Hampden, . .	340	960	958	1,888
Tihonet, ...	Wareham, . . .	Plymouth, . .	–	–	–	–
Tillotson's, ...	PITTSFIELD, . .	Berkshire, . .	–	–	–	–
Tilton's Corner, . .	HAVERHILL, . .	Essex, ...	–	–	–	–
Tinkhamtown, . .	Mattapoisett, .	Plymouth, . .	–	–	–	–
Tipperary, ...	BROCKTON, . . .	Plymouth, . .	–	–	–	–
Tisbury, ...	Tisbury, . . .	Dukes, . . .	–	–	–	–
Titicut, ‖	Bridgewater, . .	Plymouth, . .	–	–	–	–
Titicut, ...	Middleborough, .	Plymouth, . .	–	–	–	–
Tolland,*	Tolland, . . .	Hampden, . .	–	–	–	–
Tonset, ...	Orleans, . . .	Barnstable, .	–	–	–	–
Topsfield,* ‖ . . .	Topsfield, . . .	Essex, ...	–	–	–	–
Tower Hill, . . .	BROCKTON, . . .	Plymouth, . .	–	–	–	–
Tower Hill, . . .	Randolph, . . .	Norfolk, . .	–	–	–	–
Tower Hill, ‖ . . .	Wayland, . . .	Middlesex, . .	–	–	–	–
Townsend,* ‖ . . .	Townsend, . . .	Middlesex, . .	–	–	–	–
Townsend Harbor,* ‖ .	Townsend, . . .	Middlesex, . .	70	128	133	261
Traskville, ...	FITCHBURG, . .	Worcester, . .	–	–	–	–
Trowbridgeville, . .	WORCESTER, . .	Worcester, . .	22	53	64	117
Trowel Works, . .	Sharon, . . .	Norfolk, . .	–	–	–	–
Truro,* ‖	Truro, ...	Barnstable, .	–	–	–	–
Tuckernuck, . . .	Nantucket, . . .	Nantucket, . .	12	24	20	44
Tufts College,* ‖ [1]. .	MEDFORD, . . .	Middlesex, . .	–	–	–	–
Tugmanug, . . .	Hingham, . . .	Plymouth, . .	–	–	–	–
Tully,*	Orange, . . .	Franklin, . .	37	61	69	130
Turkey Hill, . . .	NEWBURYPORT, . .	Essex, . . .	–	–	–	–
Turner's Falls,* ‖ .	Montague, . . .	Franklin, . .	870	2,117	2,085	4,202
Turnerville, . . .	NEW BEDFORD, . .	Bristol, . .	–	–	–	–
Tylerville, . . .	Belchertown, . .	Hampshire, . .	–	–	–	–
Tyngsborough,* ‖ .	Tyngsborough, . .	Middlesex, . .	–	–	–	–
Tyringham,* . .	Tyringham, . .	Berkshire, . .	–	–	–	–
Union Heights, . .	North Andover, . .	Essex, ...	–	–	–	–
Union Hill, . . .	WORCESTER, . .	Worcester, . .	–	–	–	–
Union Market, . .	Watertown, . . .	Middlesex, . .	–	–	–	–
Union Square, . .	BOSTON, . . .	Suffolk, . .	–	–	–	–
Union Square, ‖ . .	SOMERVILLE, . .	Middlesex, . .	–	–	–	–
Unionville,* ‖ . .	Franklin, . . .	Norfolk, . .	57	109	124	233
Unionville, . . .	Holden, . . .	Worcester, . .	30	63	60	123
Unionville, . . .	Wellesley, . .	Norfolk, . .	–	–	–	–
Upham's Corner,* .	BOSTON, . . .	Suffolk, . .	–	–	–	–
Upper Four Corners, .	Lakeville, . . .	Plymouth, . .	–	–	–	–
Upper Houghtonville,	Clarksburg, . .	Berkshire, . .	–	–	–	–
Upper Marsh, . .	CAMBRIDGE, . .	Middlesex, . .	–	–	–	–
Upton,* ‖	Upton, ...	Worcester, . .	–	–	–	–
Uxbridge,* ‖ . . .	Uxbridge, . . .	Worcester, . .	–	–	–	–
Uxbridge Centre, .	Uxbridge, . . .	Worcester, . .	289	579	626	1,205
Valley Falls, . . .	WORCESTER, . .	Worcester, . .	88	215	235	450
Van Deusenville,* ‖ .	Great Barrington, .	Berkshire, . .	32	54	63	117
Vernon Square,* . .	WORCESTER, . .	Worcester, . .	–	–	–	–

VILLAGES, SECTIONS, ETC.: ALPHABETICALLY — Continued.

Cities, Towns, Villages, Sections. Etc.	Cities and Towns	Counties	Number of Families	Males	Females	Population
Vineyard Haven,* § . .	Tisbury, . . .	Dukes,. . .	272	446	496	942
Vineyard Highlands, . .	Cottage City, . .	Dukes,. . .	–	–	–	–
Waban,* ‖	NEWTON, . . .	Middlesex, . .	42	100	132	232
Wachogue, ...	SPRINGFIELD, . .	Hampden, . .	–	–	–	–
Wachusett, ‖	FITCHBURG, . .	Worcester, . .	–	–	–	–
Wachusett Park, . .	Westminster, . .	Worcester, . .	4	8	11	19
Wachusettville, . . .	Westminster, . .	Worcester, . .	19	32	29	61
Wakeby, ...	Mashpee, . . .	Barnstable, . .	–	–	–	–
Wakeby, ...	Sandwich, . . .	Barnstable, . .	–	–	–	–
Wakefield,* ‖ . . .	Wakefield, . . .	Middlesex, . .	–	–	–	–
Wakefield Junction, ‖ .	Wakefield, . . .	Middlesex, . .	–	–	–	–
Wakefield Park, . .	Wakefield, . . .	Middlesex, . .	–	–	–	–
Wales,*	Wales, ...	Hampden, . .	–	–	–	–
Walker, ...	TAUNTON, . . .	Bristol, . .	–	–	–	–
Walnut Bottom, . .	BROCKTON, . .	Plymouth, . .	–	–	–	–
Walnut Hill,* ‖ . .	Dedham, . . .	Norfolk, . .	121	227	260	487
Walnut Hill, . . .	Orange, ...	Franklin, . .	–	–	–	–
Walnut Hill, ‖ . .	WOBURN, . . .	Middlesex, . .	–	–	–	–
Walpole,* ‖ . . .	Walpole, . . .	Norfolk, . .	–	–	–	–
Walpole Centre, ‖ .	Walpole, . . .	Norfolk, . .	–	–	–	–
Walpole Junction, ‖ .	Walpole, . . .	Norfolk, . .	–	–	–	–
WALTHAM,* ‖ . .	WALTHAM, . .	Middlesex, . .	–	–	–	–
Waltham Highlands, ‖ .	WALTHAM, . .	Middlesex, . .	–	–	–	–
Wamesit,* ‖ . . .	Tewksbury, . .	Middlesex, . .	27	56	72	128
Wampum, ‖ . . .	Wrentham, . .	Norfolk, . .	–	–	–	–
Wapping, ...	Deerfield, . . .	Franklin, . .	21	50	47	97
Wapping, ...	Kingston, . . .	Plymouth, . .	–	–	–	–
Waquoit,*	Falmouth, . . .	Barnstable, . .	62	105	108	213
Ward Hill,* ‖ . .	Bradford, . . .	Essex, ...	97	199	193	392
Ware,* ‖.	Ware, ...	Hampshire, . .	–	–	–	–
Wareham,* ‖ . . .	Wareham, . . .	Plymouth, . .	–	–	–	–
Warfield's Village, . .	West Boylston, .	Worcester, . .	–	–	–	–
Warren,* ‖	Warren, ...	Worcester, . .	–	–	–	–
Warwick,*	Warwick, . . .	Franklin, . .	–	–	–	–
Washington,* ‖ . .	Washington,. .	Berkshire, . .	–	–	–	–
Washington City, . .	Washington,. .	Berkshire, . .	–	–	–	–
Washington Park, . .	EVERETT, . . .	Middlesex, . .	35	84	87	171
Washington Village, . .	BOSTON, . . .	Suffolk, . .	–	–	–	–
Water Hill, ...	LYNN, ...	Essex, ...	–	–	–	–
Watertown,* ‖ . .	Watertown, . .	Middlesex, . .	–	–	–	–
Waterville,* ‖ . . .	Winchendon, . .	Worcester, . .	139	289	243	532
Watuppa, ‖ . . .	FALL RIVER, .	Bristol, . .	–	–	–	–
Wauwinet, ...	Nantucket, . .	Nantucket, . .	–	–	–	–
Waveland, ‖ . . .	Hull, ...	Plymouth, . .	3	13	7	20
Waverley,* ‖ . . .	Belmont, . . .	Middlesex, . .	148	345	381	726
Wayland,* ‖ . . .	Wayland, . . .	Middlesex, . .	–	–	–	–
Wayside Inn, ‖ . .	Sudbury, . . .	Middlesex, . .	–	–	–	–
Webster,* ‖ . . .	Webster, . . .	Worcester, . .	–	–	–	–
Webster Depot, . .	Webster, . . .	Worcester, . .	110	275	306	581
Webster Gore, . .	Webster, . . .	Worcester, . .	–	–	–	–
Weir Junction, ‖ . .	TAUNTON, . .	Bristol, . .	–	–	–	–
Weir River, ‖ . . .	Hingham, . . .	Plymouth, . .	–	–	–	–
Weir Village, ‖ . .	TAUNTON, . .	Bristol, . .	–	–	–	–
Weir Village, . . .	Yarmouth, . .	Barnstable, . .	–	–	–	–
Wellesley,* ‖ . . .	Wellesley, . . .	Norfolk, . .	–	–	–	–
Wellesley Farms, ‖ .	Wellesley, . . .	Norfolk, . .	–	–	–	–
Wellesley Hills,* ‖ .	Wellesley, . . .	Norfolk, . .	273	564	727	1,291

VILLAGES, SECTIONS, ETC. : ALPHABETICALLY — Continued.

Cities, Towns, Villages, Sections, Etc.	Cities and Towns	Counties	Number of Families	Males	Females	Population
Wellfleet,* ‖	Wellfleet, . . .	Barnstable, .	–	–	–	–
Wellington,* ‖ . . .	MEDFORD, . . .	Middlesex, . .	95	183	224	407
Wenaumet, ‖	Bourne, ...	Barnstable, .	–	–	–	–
Wendell, *	Wendell, . . .	Franklin, . .	–	–	–	–
Wendell Centre, . . .	Wendell, . . .	Franklin, . .	37	68	58	126
Wendell Depot,* ‖ . .	Wendell, . . .	Franklin, . .	22	59	44	103
Wenham,* ‖	Wenham, . . .	Essex, . . .	–	–	–	–
Wenham Depot,* . . .	Wenham, . . .	Essex, . . .	–	–	–	–
Wenham Neck, . . .	Wenham, . . .	Essex, . . .	–	–	–	–
West Abington, . . .	Abington, . . .	Plymouth, . .	–	–	–	–
West Acton,* ‖ . . .	Acton, ...	Middlesex, . .	134	225	267	492
West Andover, ‖ . .	Andover, . . .	Essex, . . .	184	465	408	873
West Auburn,* . . .	Auburn, . . .	Worcester, . .	34	87	79	166
West Barnstable,* ‖ .	Barnstable, . . .	Barnstable, .	101	165	180	345
West Becket,* . . .	Becket, ...	Berkshire, . .	22	61	37	98
West Bedford, ‖ . .	Bedford, . . .	Middlesex, . .	–	–	–	–
West Berlin,* ‖ . . .	Berlin, ...	Worcester, . .	44	97	85	182
West Billerica, . . .	Billerica, . . .	Middlesex, . .	35	80	62	142
Westborough,* ‖ . .	Westborough, . .	Worcester, . .	–	–	–	–
West Boxford,* . . .	Boxford, . . .	Essex, . . .	71	163	166	329
West Boylston,* ‖ . .	West Boylston, . .	Worcester, . .	–	–	–	–
West Brewster,* . . .	Brewster, . . .	Barnstable, .	61	132	121	253
West Bridgewater,* ‖ .	West Bridgewater, .	Plymouth, . .	–	–	–	–
West Brimfield, ‖ . .	Brimfield, . . .	Hampden, . .	15	53	33	86
West Brookfield,* ‖ .	West Brookfield, .	Worcester, . .	–	–	–	–
West Cambridge, ‖ . .	CAMBRIDGE, . .	Middlesex, . .	–	–	–	–
West Chatham,* . . .	Chatham, . . .	Barnstable, .	44	77	74	151
West Chelmsford,* ‖ .	Chelmsford, . . .	Middlesex, . .	80	167	170	337
West Chesterfield,* . .	Chesterfield, . .	Hampshire, . .	48	91	83	174
West Chop,* § . . .	Tisbury, ...	Dukes, . . .	14	17	21	38
West Concord,* . . .	Concord, . . .	Middlesex . .	187	1,486	377	1,863
West Corners, . . .	Randolph, . . .	Norfolk, . .	–	–	–	–
West Cummington,* . .	Cummington, . .	Hampshire, . .	45	76	79	155
Westdale,* ‖ . . .	East Bridgewater, .	Plymouth, . .	33	93	69	162
Westdale, ...	West Bridgewater, .	Plymouth, . .	44	99	85	184
West Dedham,* . . .	Dedham, . . .	Norfolk, . .	168	382	363	745
West Deerfield,* ‖	Deerfield, . . .	Franklin, . .	45	110	90	200
West Dennis,* . . .	Dennis, ...	Barnstable, .	210	290	343	633
West Dighton,* . . .	Dighton, . . .	Bristol, . .	–	–	–	–
West Douglas, . . .	Douglas, . . .	Worcester, . .	–	–	–	–
West Dudley,* ‖ . .	Dudley, ...	Worcester, . .	17	47	44	91
West Duxbury,* . . .	Duxbury, . . .	Plymouth, . .	34	61	61	122
West End, ...	BOSTON, . . .	Suffolk, . .	–	–	–	–
West End, ...	MALDEN, . . .	Middlesex, . .	–	–	–	–
West Everett, ‖ . . .	EVERETT, . . .	Middlesex, . .	704	1,384	1,497	2,878
West Falmouth,* ‖ . .	Falmouth, . . .	Barnstable, .	94	163	166	329
West Farms,* . . .	NORTHAMPTON, . .	Hampshire, . .	34	59	52	111
West Farms, ...	Westfield, . . .	Hampden, . .	35	66	60	126
Westfield,* ‖ . . .	Westfield, . . .	Hampden, . .	–	–	–	–
West Fitchburg,* ‖ .	FITCHBURG, . . .	Worcester, . .	435	991	1,047	2,038
Westford,* ‖ . . .	Westford, . . .	Middlesex, . .	–	–	–	–
Westford Corner, . .	Westford, . . .	Middlesex, . .	–	–	–	–
West Foxborough, . .	Foxborough, . . .	Norfolk, . .	20	36	34	70
West Gardner,* . . .	Gardner, . . .	Worcester, . .	994	2,559	2,303	4,862
West Gloucester,* ‖ .	GLOUCESTER, . .	Essex, . . .	137	268	289	557
West Graniteville, ‖ .	Westford, . . .	Middlesex, . .	–	–	–	–
West Granville,* . .	Granville, . . .	Hampden, . .	63	143	128	271
West Groton,* ‖ . .	Groton, ...	Middlesex, . .	69	126	139	265

VILLAGES, SECTIONS, ETC.: ALPHABETICALLY — Continued.

Cities, Towns, Villages, Sections, Etc.	Cities and Towns	Counties	Number of Families	Males	Females	Population
Westhampton,*	Westhampton,	Hampshire,	–	–	–	–
West Hanover,* ‖	Hanover,	Plymouth,	152	291	296	587
West Harwich,*	Harwich,	Barnstable,	132	213	215	428
West Hatfield,*	Hatfield,	Hampshire,	38	86	88	174
West Hawley,*	Hawley,	Franklin,	54	119	108	227
Westhill,	Middlefield,	Hampshire,	–	–	–	–
West Hingham,* ‖	Hingham,	Plymouth,	263	557	611	1,168
West Holyoke,	HOLYOKE,	Hampden,	31	85	76	161
West Leominster,‖	Leominster,	Worcester,	–	–	–	–
West Leyden,*	Leyden,	Franklin,	20	36	34	70
West Lynn,‖	LYNN,	Essex,	2,898	5,943	6,232	12,175
West Manchester,‖	Manchester,	Essex,	–	–	–	–
West Mansfield,* ‖	Mansfield,	Bristol,	112	235	222	457
West Medford,* ‖	MEDFORD,	Middlesex,	595	1,262	1,420	2,682
West Medway,* ‖	Medway,	Norfolk,	436	852	809	1,661
West Millbury,*	Millbury,	Worcester,	64	151	148	299
Westminster,* ‖	Westminster,	Worcester,	–	–	–	–
Westminster Centre,	Westminster,	Worcester,	147	206	272	478
Westminster Depot,* ‖	Westminster,	Worcester,	24	49	46	95
West Natick,	Natick,	Middlesex,	–	–	–	–
West New Boston,	Sandisfield,	Berkshire,	26	57	54	111
West Newbury,* ‖	West Newbury,	Essex,	–	–	–	–
West Newton,* ‖	NEWTON,	Middlesex,	720	1,505	1,952	3,457
West Northfield,*	Northfield,	Franklin,	56	123	101	224
Weston,* ‖	Weston,	Middlesex,	–	–	–	–
West Orange,	Orange,	Franklin,	37	63	61	124
West Otis,*	Otis,	Berkshire,	10	25	16	41
West Parish,	Granby,	Hampshire,	–	–	–	–
West Parish,	HAVERHILL,	Essex,	–	–	–	–
West Peabody,* ‖	Peabody,	Essex,	123	262	244	506
West Pelham,	Pelham,	Hampshire,	45	95	96	191
West Pittsfield,* ‖	PITTSFIELD,	Berkshire,	40	113	97	210
Westport,*	Westport,	Bristol,	–	–	–	–
Westport Factory Village,	Dartmouth,	Bristol,	–	–	–	–
Westport Factory Village, ‖	Westport,	Bristol,	–	–	–	–
Westport Harbor,	Westport,	Bristol,	5	15	8	23
Westport Point,*	Westport,	Bristol,	57	80	92	172
West Quincy, ‖	QUINCY,	Norfolk,	990	2,658	2,306	4,964
West Roxbury,* ‖	BOSTON,	Suffolk,	7,095	15,335	17,426	32,761
West Rutland,* ‖	Rutland,	Worcester,	21	54	47	141
West Sherborn,	Sherborn,	Middlesex,	40	80	71	151
West Shrewsbury,	Shrewsbury,	Worcester,	–	–	–	–
Westside,	Hampden,	Hampden,	–	–	–	–
West Side,	WORCESTER,	Worcester,	–	–	–	–
West Somerville,* ‖	SOMERVILLE,	Middlesex,	–	–	–	–
West Springfield,*	West Springfield,	Hampden,	–	–	–	–
West Sterling,*	Sterling,	Worcester,	17	32	35	67
West Stockbridge,* ‖	West Stockbridge,	Berkshire,	–	–	–	–
West Stockbridge Centre,*.	West Stockbridge,	Berkshire,	34	73	57	130
West Stoughton,* ‖	Stoughton,	Norfolk,	82	181	183	364
West Sutton,*	Sutton,	Worcester,	47	81	74	155
West Tisbury,*	West Tisbury,	Dukes,	–	–	–	–
West Townsend,* ‖	Townsend,	Middlesex,	149	256	253	509
West Upton,* ‖	Upton,	Worcester,	153	292	580	872
Westvale,*	Concord,	Middlesex,	62	158	149	307
Westville,	Southbridge,	Worcester,	–	–	–	–
Westville,	Spencer,	Worcester,	–	–	–	–
Westville,	Sturbridge,	Worcester,	–	–	–	–

VILLAGES, SECTIONS, ETC.: ALPHABETICALLY — Continued.

Cities, Towns, Villages, Sections, Etc.	Cities and Towns	Counties	Number of Families	Males	Females	Population
Westville, ...	TAUNTON, . . .	Bristol, . . .	–	–	–	–
West Ware, ‖ . .	Ware, ...	Hampshire, . .	15	27	28	55
West Wareham,* ‖ ¹ .	Wareham, . . .	Plymouth, . .	116	272	231	503
West Warren,* ‖ . .	Warren, . . .	Worcester, . .	324	754	766	1,520
West Whately, . . .	Whately, . . .	Franklin, . .	43	83	77	160
West Worthington,* .	Worthington, . .	Hampshire, . .	19	35	33	68
West Wrentham, ‖ . .	Wrentham, . .	Norfolk, . . .	29	59	58	117
West Yarmouth,*. . .	Yarmouth, . . .	Barnstable, . .	80	133	131	264
Weymouth,* ‖ . . .	Weymouth, . .	Norfolk, . . .	–	–	–	–
Weymouth Centre,* . .	Weymouth, . . .	Norfolk, . . .	–	–	–	–
Weymouth Heights,* .	Weymouth, . . .	Norfolk, . . .	86	162	177	339
Whately,* ‖	Whately, . . .	Franklin, . .	–	–	–	–
Wheeler, ...	Orange, ...	Franklin, . .	17	54	31	85
Wheeler Park, . . .	BROCKTON, . . .	Plymouth, . .	–	–	–	–
Wheelersville, . . .	Millbury, . . .	Worcester, . .	24	72	56	128
Wheelocksville, . . .	Uxbridge, . . .	Worcester, . .	42	96	91	187
Wheelwright,* ‖ . . .	Hardwick, . . .	Worcester, . .	29	58	54	112
Wheldon Factory, . .	Acushnet, . . .	Bristol, . . .	–	–	–	–
Whitehall, ...	Rutland, . . .	Worcester, . .	–	–	–	–
Whitehead, ...	Hull, ...	Plymouth, . .	–	–	–	–
White Oaks, ...	Williamstown, .	Berkshire, . .	–	–	–	–
White's Factory, . .	Acushnet, . . .	Bristol, . . .	–	–	–	–
Whiteville, ...	Mansfield, . . .	Bristol, . . .	–	–	–	–
Whitingsville, . . .	West Boylston, .	Worcester, . .	–	–	–	–
Whitinsville,* . . .	Northbridge, . .	Worcester, . .	608	1,739	1,572	3,311
Whitman,* ‖	Whitman, . . .	Plymouth, . .	–	–	–	–
Whitman's Crossing, ‖ .	Littleton, . . .	Middlesex, . .	–	–	–	–
Whitman's Village, . .	Westminster, . .	Worcester, . .	10	14	14	28
Whittenton, ‖ . . .	TAUNTON, . . .	Bristol, . . .	–	–	–	–
Whittenton Junction, ‖	TAUNTON, . . .	Bristol, . . .	–	–	–	–
Wianno,*	Barnstable, . .	Barnstable, . .	–	–	–	–
Wigginville, ...	Tewksbury, . . .	Middlesex, . .	97	236	245	481
Wilbraham,*	Wilbraham, . . .	Hampden, . .	–	–	–	–
Wilkinsonville, . . .	Grafton, . . .	Worcester, . .	26	48	52	100
Wilkinsonville,* ‖ . .	Sutton, ...	Worcester, . .	120	321	263	584
Wilkinsville, ...	Hudson, ...	Middlesex, . .	–	–	–	–
Williamsburg,* ‖ . .	Williamsburg, . .	Hampshire, . .	–	–	–	–
Williamstown,* . . .	Williamstown, .	Berkshire, . .	–	–	–	–
Williamstown Station,* ‖ .	Williamstown, .	Berkshire, . .	234	616	575	1,191
Williamsville,* ‖ . .	Hubbardston, . .	Worcester, . .	21	39	40	79
Williamsville, . . .	West Stockbridge, .	Berkshire, . .	39	74	90	164
Willimansett,* ‖ . . .	CHICOPEE, . . .	Hampden, . .	215	542	512	1,054
Wills Place, ...	Colrain, ...	Franklin, . .	24	75	73	148
Willston Mills, . . .	Easthampton, . .	Hampshire, . .	94	271	252	523
Willowdale, ...	Ipswich, ...	Essex, . . .	–	–	–	–
Willows, ‖	Ayer, ...	Middlesex, . .	–	–	–	–
Wilmington,* ‖ . . .	Wilmington, . .	Middlesex, . .	–	–	–	–
Wilmington Centre, . .	Wilmington, . .	Middlesex, . .	106	245	248	493
Wilmington Junction, ‖	Wilmington, . .	Middlesex, . .	–	–	–	–
Wilsonville, ...	WOBURN, . . .	Middlesex, . .	–	–	–	–
Winchendon,* ‖ . . .	Winchendon, . .	Worcester, . .	–	–	–	–
Winchendon Centre, . .	Winchendon, . .	Worcester, . .	24	47	46	93
Winchendon Springs,* .	Winchendon, . .	Worcester, . .	77	214	251	465
Winchester,* ‖ . . .	Winchester, . .	Middlesex, . .	–	–	–	–
Winchester Highlands, ‖ .	Winchester, . .	Middlesex, . .	–	–	–	–
Winchester Park, . .	BROCKTON, . . .	Plymouth, . .	–	–	–	–
Windemere, ...	Cottage City, . .	Dukes, . . .	–	–	–	–
Windermere, ‖ . . .	Hull, ...	Plymouth, . .	–	–	–	–

¹ R. R. name Tremont.

VILLAGES, SECTIONS, ETC.: ALPHABETICALLY — Concluded.

Cities, Towns, Villages, Sections, Etc.	Cities and Towns	Counties	Number of Families	Males	Females	Population
Windsor,*	Windsor,	Berkshire,	–	–	–	–
Windsor Hill,	Windsor,	Berkshire,	–	–	–	–
Winctuxet,	Plympton,	Plymouth,	–	–	–	–
Winneconnet,	Norton,	Bristol,	–	–	–	–
Winslow's, ‖	Norwood,	Norfolk,	–	–	–	–
Winter Hill,* ‖	SOMERVILLE,	Middlesex,	–	–	–	–
Winter Island,	SALEM,	Essex,	2	27	5	32
Winter's Corner,	BROCKTON,	Plymouth,	–	–	–	–
Winterville,	NEW BEDFORD,	Bristol,	–	–	–	–
Winthrop,* ‖	Winthrop,	Suffolk,	–	–	–	–
Winthrop Beach, ‖	Winthrop,	Suffolk,	–	–	–	–
Winthrop Centre, ‖	Winthrop,	Suffolk,	–	–	–	–
Winthrop Highlands, ‖	Winthrop,	Suffolk,	–	–	–	–
Winthrop Square,	BROCKTON,	Plymouth,	–	–	–	–
Wire Village,	Spencer,	Worcester,	66	190	157	347
WOBURN,* ‖	WOBURN,	Middlesex,	–	–	–	–
Woburn Highlands, ‖	WOBURN,	Middlesex,	61	146	156	302
Wollaston,* ‖	QUINCY,	Norfolk,	565	1,293	1,365	2,658
Woodbury's, ‖	Hamilton,	Essex,	–	–	–	–
Wood Island,	BOSTON,	Suffolk,	–	–	–	–
Woodruff Heights,	Clinton,	Worcester,	–	–	–	–
Wood's Holl,* ‖	Falmouth,	Barnstable,	114	234	250	484
Woodside Mills,	Northborough,	Worcester,	49	120	114	234
Woodville,*	Hopkinton,	Middlesex,	74	146	126	272
Woodville,	Wakefield,	Middlesex,	–	–	–	–
Woonsocket Junction, ‖	Blackstone,	Worcester,	–	–	–	–
WORCESTER,* ‖	WORCESTER,	Worcester,	–	–	–	–
Worthington,*	Worthington,	Hampshire,	–	–	–	–
Worthington Centre,	Worthington,	Hampshire,	13	25	23	48
Wrentham,* ‖	Wrentham,	Norfolk,	–	–	–	–
Wyoma,	LYNN,	Essex,	–	–	–	–
Wyoming, ‖	Melrose,	Middlesex,	1,082	2,420	2,614	5,034
Yarmouth,* ‖	Yarmouth,	Barnstable,	–	–	–	–
Yarmouth Farms,*	Yarmouth,	Barnstable,	–	–	–	–
Yarmouthport,*	Yarmouth,	Barnstable,	125	182	229	411
Yellow Town,	Wareham,	Plymouth,	–	–	–	–
York,	Canton,	Norfolk,	–	–	–	–
Zoar,* ‖	Charlemont,	Franklin,	34	70	60	130
Zylonite,* ‖	Adams,	Berkshire,	89	206	201	407

TABULAR ANALYSES

FOR THE FOLLOWING PRESENTATIONS:

The presentations of the population by villages require no special analysis, but a brief explanation is needed in order to prevent misconception as to their significance.

The villages or sections within town or city limits, as presented in the tables, have neither exact geographical boundaries nor legal autonomy. They are aggregations of population, sometimes separated by considerable territory, and sometimes divided by imaginary lines, concerning which no exact information can be obtained, and as to the location of which no general agreement exists. In some cases the village has grown up around a factory, in others it is the development of a distinct settlement made in early years, that has never reached the importance of a separate municipal organization. Frequently the village is also a railway station, and sometimes it possesses a post office.

The rapid growth of certain parts of the Commonwealth, and the settlement of problems relating to water supply and sewerage and other important questions which have arisen in consequence of this growth, make it essential to determine the population of these villages. This has been attempted in previous censuses, but until now without success, owing principally to the lack of agreement as to the village boundaries. Unusual care has, however, been devoted to the determination of the village and section population in the present census, and it is believed that the results as given in the presentations, although for obvious reasons approximate, are nevertheless fairly accurate. The returns, as originally made by the enumerator, have been carefully scanned, and so far as the village names are concerned, compared with the census of 1885. All discrepancies have been noted, and the lists submitted to the town and city clerks, accompanied by the following letter:

Upon the other side of this letter sheet you will find a statement in regard to the names of villages in your town, as reported by the Census Enumerators for 1885, and also those reported for 1895. Will you kindly inform us upon the back of this sheet in the blank space at the right why certain villages that were named in 1885 do not appear in the 1895 returns; also please give the dates between 1885 and 1895 when the new villages returned in 1895 were first designated by their present names.

In the tabular statement on the back part of this sheet we give the number of families and the population for each of the villages returned by the Census Enumerators in your town for the year 1895. Please examine this list and inform us whether the list of villages so reported is complete, whether the names are properly spelled, and whether each village mentioned is really a village and known as such in your town.

If there are any so-called village designations which are simply "popular" designations or "nicknames" for sections of your town, but which should be properly combined with some other village, will you kindly mark out these popular designations and indicate at the right of the tabular presentation to which line they should be added?

It is obviously difficult for this office to obtain a proper knowledge of the villages in each city and town without the experienced co-operation of town officers who are thoroughly familiar with the town or city in which they reside. Any information that you can supply in relation to this matter which we have not asked for specifically above will be greatly appreciated by this office and will contribute to making the village presentation for your town of more value to your citizens and to the Commonwealth.

[125]

The results, after making such changes and corrections as were suggested by the city and town clerks, were submitted to the postmasters of the various towns, to whom the following letter was sent:

Upon the other side of this sheet you will find a statement of the villages and localities in your town, with certain designations, namely, — "V" for village, "P D" for popular or local name, "P O" for post office, and "R R" for railway station. Will you kindly state whether the names so given are correct and whether they include all the villages, localities, etc., in your town; and if not, will you please give us the additional names and make such correction in the spelling as will make the names conform to local usage?

It may be that one place is given two names; if so, will you indicate such and suggest which of the two names is the more popular and to be retained in print?

It is obviously difficult for this office to obtain a proper knowledge of the villages in each town without the experienced co-operation of town officials who are thoroughly familiar with the town in which they reside. Any information that you can supply in relation to this matter which we have not asked for specifically above will be greatly appreciated by this office and will contribute to making the village presentation for your town of more value to your citizens and to the Commonwealth.

In the presentation "VILLAGES: BY TOWNS," the population as finally determined is presented for every section which was found to possess an individuality sufficient to justify its separate presentation. In the subsequent presentation the villages are presented alphabetically, and with these are included the names of localities or districts which have a local significance or are found in local usage, but which are not sufficiently distinct as to boundaries, or are not of sufficient importance to warrant the presentation of separate population figures. In this table, also, the railway stations and post offices throughout the Commonwealth are designated.

The following table shows the number of cities and towns, villages, and localities with popular designations. It should be borne in mind that only the cities and towns have fixed boundaries and legal status.

THE STATE, AND COUNTIES.	Number of Cities and Towns	Number of Villages	Number of Localities with Popular Designations	Totals
THE STATE.	353	759	1,031	2,143
Barnstable,	15	56	46	117
Berkshire,	32	47	58	137
Bristol,	20	44	91	155
Dukes,	7	11	20	38
Essex,	35	67	121	223
Franklin,	26	49	44	119
Hampden,	23	38	45	106
Hampshire,	23	46	25	94
Middlesex,	54	101	153	308
Nantucket,	1	4	6	11
Norfolk,	27	64	71	162
Plymouth,	27	81	117	225
Suffolk,	4	7	105	116
Worcester,	59	144	129	332

In some cases, particularly in the cities and larger towns, villages which were formerly quite distinct have now grown together so as to present a practically homogeneous population. In such cases no attempt has been made to give the village or section population, although the names, which are still used, may be found in the alphabetical table. An example in point is found in the city of Somerville.

In order to complete the information as to post offices it should be stated that the following stations are comprised in the Boston postal district:

A	. . .	South End.	N	. . .	Jamaica Plain.

A . . . South End.   N . . . Jamaica Plain.
B . . . Back Bay.   O . . . Mattapan.
C . . . Brighton.   P . . . North Cambridge.
D . . . Brookline.   R . . . Revere.
E . . . Cambridge.   S . . . Roslindale.
F . . . Cambridgeport.   T . . . Roxbury.
G . . . Charlestown.   U . . . Somerville.
H . . . Chelsea.   V . . . South Boston.
K . . . Dorchester.   W . . . West Roxbury.
L . . . East Boston.   X . . . Winthrop.
M . . . East Cambridge.

Sub-stations within the Boston district for receiving registered matter, and for domestic money orders, are established as follows:

No. 1 Allston, in Brighton.   No. 5 Tremont, in South End.
No. 2 East Somerville.   No. 6 Upham's Corner, in Dorchester.
No. 3 Roxbury Crossing, in Roxbury.   No. 7 West Somerville.
No. 4 Somerset Hill, in Cambridge.   No. 8 Winter Hill, in Somerville.

CENSUSES OF POPULATION — 1765-1895 — Continued.

TOWN OF HARWICH — concluded.

YEARS AND CENSUS.	Population	Increase (+), or Decrease (−), as Compared with Previous Census
1870 (U. S.)	3,080	−460
1875 (State)	3,355	+275
1880 (U. S.)	3,265	− 90
1885 (State)	2,783	−482
1890 (U. S.)	2,734	− 49
1895 (State)	2,532	−202

TOWN OF MASHPEE.

Established June 14, 1763, as the District of Mashpee, to remain in force three years. Above Act revived March 20, 1767 to remain in force until July 1, 1770. On November 15, 1770, Act again revived, and to remain in force until the end of the session of the General Court next after November 1, 1775. On February 9, 1776, the Act was again continued in force until the end of the session next after November 1, 1779. On November 25, 1779, the Act again continued until November 1, 1785. On June 13, 1788, the above Act was repealed and three "Guardians to the Proprietors" appointed, Act to remain in force for 10 years. March 7, 1797, the last named Act made perpetual until repealed by the Legislature. Part of the plantation of Marshpee annexed to Sandwich, February 26, 1811. On March 31, 1834, the "Plantation of Marshpee" established as the "District of Marshpee," to be under the guardianship of a commissioner appointed by the Governor. A part of the land formerly in the plantation of Marshpee annexed to Falmouth March 17, 1841, and part to Sandwich April 1, 1859, and another part to Sandwich March 13, 1860. May 28, 1870, the District of Marshpee abolished and the town of Mashpee established. Part of Sandwich reannexed to Mashpee March 19, 1872. Boundary lines established as follows: between Mashpee and Falmouth June 18, 1885; between Mashpee and Sandwich May 27, 1887, and a part of Sandwich annexed; and between Mashpee and Barnstable March 28, 1894.

1765 (Prov.)	108	−
1776 (Prov.)	82	− 26
1790 (U. S.)	308	+226
1800 (U. S.)	155	−153
1810 (U. S.)	139	− 16
1820 (U. S.)	150	+ 11
1840 (U. S.)	309	+159
1860 (U. S.)	322	+ 13
1870 (U. S.)	348	+ 26
1875 (State)	278	− 70
1880 (U. S.)	346	+ 68
1885 (State)	311	− 35
1890 (U. S.)	298	− 13
1895 (State)	330	+ 32

TOWN OF ORLEANS.

Established March 3, 1797, from the southerly part of Eastham. Part of Eastham annexed to Orleans March 9, 1839. Boundary lines established as follows: between Orleans and Brewster February 20, 1861; between Orleans and Harwich April 4, 1862; between Orleans and Chatham April 14, 1862; between Orleans and Eastham March 23, 1867, and part of each town annexed to the other town.

1800 (U. S.)	1,095	−
1810 (U. S.)	1,248	+153

TOWN OF ORLEANS — concluded.

YEARS AND CENSUS.	Population	Increase (+), or Decrease (−), as Compared with Previous Census
1820 (U. S.)	1,343	+ 95
1830 (U. S.)	1,789	+446
1840 (U. S.)	1,974	+185
1850 (U. S.)	1,848	−126
1855 (State)	1,754	− 94
1860 (U. S.)	1,678	− 76
1865 (State)	1,585	− 93
1870 (U. S.)	1,323	−262
1875 (State)	1,373	+ 50
1880 (U. S.)	1,294	− 79
1885 (State)	1,176	−118
1890 (U. S.)	1,219	+ 43
1895 (State)	1,198	− 21

TOWN OF PROVINCETOWN.

Precinct of Cape Cod established as Provincetown June 14, 1727. Parts of Truro annexed and boundary lines established June 12, 1813, March 2, 1829, and March 30, 1836.

1765 (Prov.)	[205]	−
1776 (Prov.)	205	=
1790 (U. S.)	454	+ 249
1800 (U. S.)	812	+ 358
1810 (U. S.)	936	+ 124
1820 (U. S.)	1,252	+ 316
1830 (U. S.)	1,710	+ 458
1840 (U. S.)	2,122	+ 412
1850 (U. S.)	3,157	+1,035
1855 (State)	3,096	− 61
1860 (U. S.)	3,206	+ 110
1865 (State)	3,472	+ 266
1870 (U. S.)	3,865	+ 393
1875 (State)	4,357	+ 492
1880 (U. S.)	4,346	− 11
1885 (State)	4,480	+ 134
1890 (U. S.)	4,642	+ 162
1895 (State)	4,555	− 87

TOWN OF SANDWICH.

On March 6, 1638, certain persons were ordered to go to "Sanditch" to set forth the bounds (Plymouth Colony Records, Volume I, p. 80). Boundary line between Sandwich and Barnstable established March 2, 1652, and June 10, 1662. The boundary lines established January 19, 1663, ordered to be entered on the records of the court, June 7, 1670. October 28, 1684, boundaries established. Part of the plantation of Marshpee annexed February 26, 1811. Parts of the District of Marshpee annexed April 1, 1859, and March 13, 1860. Part of Sandwich reannexed to Mashpee March 19, 1872. Boundary between Sandwich and Falmouth established March 19, 1880. Part of Sandwich set off as a new town, Bourne, April 2, 1884. Boundary between Sandwich and Mashpee established May 27, 1887, and a part annexed to Mashpee.

1765 (Prov.)	1,376	−
1776 (Prov.)	1,912	+536

CENSUSES OF POPULATION — 1765-1895 — Continued.

TOWN OF SANDWICH — concluded.

YEARS AND CENSUS.	Population	Increase (+), or Decrease (−), as Compared with Previous Census
1790 (U. S.)	1,991	+ 79
1800 (U. S.)	2,024	+ 33
1810 (U. S.)	2,382	+ 358
1820 (U. S.)	2,484	+ 102
1830 (U. S.)	3,361	+ 877
1840 (U. S.)	3,719	+ 358
1850 (U. S.)	4,368	+ 649
1855 (State)	4,496	+ 128
1860 (U. S.)	4,479	− 17
1865 (State)	4,158	− 321
1870 (U. S.)	3,694	− 464
1875 (State)	3,417	− 277
1880 (U. S.)	3,543	+ 126
1885 (State)	2,124	−1,419
1890 (U. S.)	1,819	− 305
1895 (State)	1,580	− 239

TOWN OF TRURO.

Established July 16, 1709, from common land called Pawmett as the township of "Truroe." (Prov. Laws, Vol. 1, p. 642.) Part of Truro annexed to Provincetown June 12, 1813, and boundary between the towns established. Another part annexed to Provincetown March 2, 1829, and the boundaries again established. Another part annexed to Provincetown March 30, 1836, and on February 22, 1837, the boundaries between Truro and Wellfleet established.

YEARS AND CENSUS.	Population	Increase / Decrease
1765 (Prov.)	924	-
1776 (Prov.)	1,227	+303
1790 (U. S.)	1,193	− 34
1800 (U. S.)	1,152	− 41
1810 (U. S.)	1,209	+ 57
1820 (U. S.)	1,241	+ 32
1830 (U. S.)	1,547	+306
1840 (U. S.)	1,920	+373
1850 (U. S.)	2,051	+131
1855 (State)	1,917	−134
1860 (U. S.)	1,583	−334
1865 (State)	1,447	−136
1870 (U. S.)	1,269	−178
1875 (State)	1,098	−171
1880 (U. S.)	1,017	− 81
1885 (State)	972	− 45
1890 (U. S.)	919	− 53
1895 (State)	815	−104

TOWN OF WELLFLEET.

Established as a district June 16, 1763, from the North Precinct of Eastham. Made a town by Act of August 23, 1775. Boundary between Wellfleet and Truro established February 22, 1837. Part of Eastham annexed April 26, 1847. Boundary between the tidewaters of Wellfleet and Eastham established May 6, 1887.

YEARS AND CENSUS.	Population	Increase / Decrease
1765 (Prov.)	917	-
1776 (Prov.)	1,235	+318
1790 (U. S.)	1,117	−118

TOWN OF WELLFLEET — concluded.

YEARS AND CENSUS.	Population	Increase (+), or Decrease (−), as Compared with Previous Census
1800 (U. S.)	1,207	+ 90
1810 (U. S.)	1,402	+195
1820 (U. S.)	1,472	+ 70
1830 (U. S.)	2,046	+574
1840 (U. S.)	2,377	+331
1850 (U. S.)	2,411	+ 34
1855 (State)	2,325	− 86
1860 (U. S.)	2,322	− 3
1865 (State)	2,296	− 26
1870 (U. S.)	2,135	−161
1875 (State)	1,988	−147
1880 (U. S.)	1,875	−113
1885 (State)	1,687	−188
1890 (U. S.)	1,291	−396
1895 (State)	968	−323

TOWN OF YARMOUTH.

The first mention of this town occurs in Plymouth Colony Laws, Volume 1, p. 108, on January 7, 1639, "the land at Mattacheeset, now called Yarmouth." Boundary line between Yarmouth and Barnstable established June 17, 1641. Yarmouth and Barnstable agreed upon boundary line March 11, 1658. Part of Yarmouth set off and established as the town of Dennis June 19, 1793.

YEARS AND CENSUS.	Population	Increase / Decrease
1765 (Prov.)	1,740	-
1776 (Prov.)	2,227	+487
1790 (U. S.)	2,678	+451
1800 (U. S.)	1,727	−951
1810 (U. S.)	2,134	+407
1820 (U. S.)	2,232	+ 98
1830 (U. S.)	2,251	+ 19
1840 (U. S.)	2,554	+303
1850 (U. S.)	2,595	+ 41
1855 (State)	2,592	− 3
1860 (U. S.)	2,752	+160
1865 (State)	2,472	−280
1870 (U. S.)	2,423	− 49
1875 (State)	2,264	−159
1880 (U. S.)	2,173	− 91
1885 (State)	1,856	−317
1890 (U. S.)	1,760	− 96
1895 (State)	1,655	−105

COUNTY OF BERKSHIRE.

Incorporated April 21, 1761, from the westerly part of Hampshire County; Act took effect June 30, 1761. (Province Laws, Vol. IV, p. 432.)

YEARS AND CENSUS.	Population	Increase / Decrease
1765 (Prov.)	8,640	-
1776 (Prov.)	17,952	+ 9,312
1790 (U. S.) .* . . .	30,213	+12,261
1800 (U. S.)	33,670	+ 3,457
1810 (U. S.)	35,787	+ 2,117

* Includes population of 67 for Boston Corner (ceded to New York); 425 for the gore adjoining Adams and Windsor; and 51 for the gore adjoining Williamstown.

CENSUSES OF POPULATION — 1765-1895 — Continued.

COUNTY OF BERKSHIRE — concluded.

YEARS AND CENSUS.	Population	Increase (+), or Decrease (−), as Compared with Previous Census
1820 (U. S.)*. . . .	35,570	− 217
1830 (U. S.)*. . . .	37,706	+2,136
1840 (U. S.)*. . . .	41,745	+4,039
1850 (U. S.)*. . . .	49,591	+7,846
1855 (State)	52,791	+3,200
1860 (U. S.)	55,120	+2,329
1865 (State)	56,944	+1,824
1870 (U. S.)	64,827	+7,883
1875 (State)	68,270	+3,443
1880 (U. S.)	69,032	+ 762
1885 (State)	73,828	+4,796
1890 (U. S.)	81,108	+7,280
1895 (State)	86,292	+5,184

TOWN OF ADAMS.

Established October 15, 1778, from the plantation called East Hoosuck. The plantation called New Providence annexed April 10, 1780. Part of Adams included in the new town of Cheshire March 14, 1793, and on April 16, 1878, a part was set off and established as North Adams. The date of establishment of this town is subsequent to the date of the earliest census in which population appears. This is due, probably, to the fact that the territory in question was well defined and recognized in census enumerations prior to the date of its formal incorporation as a district or town.

1776 (Prov.)	932	-
1790 (U. S.)	2,040	+ 1,108
1800 (U. S.)	1,688	− 352
1810 (U. S.)	1,763	+ 75
1820 (U. S.)	1,836	+ 73
1830 (U. S.)	2,649	+ 813
1840 (U. S.)	3,703	+ 1,054
1850 (U. S.)	6,172	+ 2,469
1855 (State)	6,980	+ 808
1860 (U. S.)	6,924	− 56
1865 (State)	8,298	+ 1,374
1870 (U. S.)	12,090	+ 3,792
1875 (State)	15,760	+ 3,670
1880 (U. S.)	5,591	−10,169
1885 (State)	8,283	+ 2,692
1890 (U. S.)	9,213	+ 930
1895 (State)	7,837	− 1,376

TOWN OF ALFORD.

Established as a district February 16, 1773, from the westerly part of Great Barrington and certain common lands. Made a town by Act of August 23, 1775. Part of Great Barrington annexed February 11, 1779. Boundary lines between Alford and Egremont established February 6, 1790. Another part of Great Barrington annexed February 18, 1819. Part of West Stockbridge annexed March 17, 1847.

1776 (Prov.)	298	-
1790 (U. S.)	577	+279
1800 (U. S.)	518	− 59
1810 (U. S.)	522	+ 4

TOWN OF ALFORD — concluded.

YEARS AND CENSUS.	Population	Increase (+), or Decrease (−), as Compared with Previous Census
1820 (U. S.)	570	+48
1830 (U. S.)	512	−58
1840 (U. S.)	481	−31
1850 (U. S.)	502	+21
1855 (State)	526	+24
1860 (U. S.)	542	+16
1865 (State)	461	−81
1870 (U. S.)	430	−31
1875 (State)	389	−41
1880 (U. S.)	348	−41
1885 (State)	341	− 7
1890 (U. S.)	297	−44
1895 (State)	280	−17

TOWN OF BECKET.

Established June 21, 1765, from the plantation called "Number Four." On March 12, 1783, a part included in the new town of Middlefield (Hampshire County). On February 3, 1798, certain common lands lying between Becket, Blandford, Chester, and Loudon annexed. Part of Loudon (Bethlehem District) annexed March 1, 1810.

1765 (Prov.)	[414]	-
1776 (Prov.)	414	=
1790 (U. S.)	751	+337
1800 (U. S.)	930	+179
1810 (U. S.)	1,028	+ 98
1820 (U. S.)	984	− 44
1830 (U. S.)	1,063	+ 79
1840 (U. S.)	1,342	+279
1850 (U. S.)	1,223	−119
1855 (State)	1,472	+249
1860 (U. S.)	1,578	+106
1865 (State)	1,393	−185
1870 (U. S.)	1,346	− 47
1875 (State)	1,329	− 17
1880 (U. S.)	1,123	−206
1885 (State)	938	−185
1890 (U. S.)	946	+ 8
1895 (State)	888	− 58

TOWN OF CHESHIRE.

Established March 14, 1793, from parts of Adams, Lanesborough, Windsor, and the district of New Ashford. Part of Cheshire reannexed to Windsor February 26, 1794. Part of the district of New Ashford annexed February 6, 1798.

1800 (U. S.)	1,325	-
1810 (U. S.)	1,315	− 10
1820 (U. S.)	1,202	−113
1830 (U. S.)	1,050	−152
1840 (U. S.)	985	− 65
1850 (U. S.)	1,298	+313
1855 (State)	1,532	+234
1860 (U. S.)	1,533	+ 1
1865 (State)	1,650	+117

* Includes population of Boston Corner as follows : 1820, 92; 1830, 64; 1840, 65; 1850, 73.

CENSUSES OF POPULATION — 1765-1895 — Continued.

TOWN OF CHESHIRE — concluded.

YEARS AND CENSUS.	Popula-tion	Increase (+), or Decrease (—), as Compared with Previous Census
1870 (U. S.)	1,758	+ 108
1875 (State)	1,693	— 65
1880 (U. S.)	1,537	—156
1885 (State)	1,448	— 89
1890 (U. S.)	1,308	—140
1895 (State)	1,176	—132

TOWN OF CLARKSBURG.

Established March 2, 1798, from a gore of unincorporated land lying north of Adams. Part of Clarksburg annexed to Florida May 2, 1848, and on May 20, 1852, a part of Florida annexed to Clarksburg.

1800 (U. S.)	253	-
1810 (U. S.)	231	— 22
1820 (U. S.)	274	+ 43
1830 (U. S.)	315	+ 41
1840 (U. S.)	370	+ 55
1850 (U. S.)	384	+ 14
1855 (State)	424	+ 40
1860 (U. S.)	420	— 4
1865 (State)	530	+110
1870 (U. S.)	686	+156
1875 (State)	670	— 16
1880 (U. S.)	724	+ 54
1885 (State)	708	— 16
1890 (U. S.)	884	+176
1895 (State)	1,009	+125

TOWN OF DALTON.

Established March 20, 1784, from the new plantation of Ashuelot Equivalent. Part of Windsor annexed February 28, 1795.

1790 (U. S.)	554	-
1800 (U. S.)	859	+305
1810 (U. S.)	779	— 80
1820 (U. S.)	817	+ 38
1830 (U. S.)	827	+ 10
1840 (U. S.)	1,255	+428
1850 (U. S.)	1,020	—235
1855 (State)	1,064	+ 44
1860 (U. S.)	1,243	+179
1865 (State)	1,137	—106
1870 (U. S.)	1,252	+115
1875 (State)	1,759	+507
1880 (U. S.)	2,052	+293
1885 (State)	2,113	+ 61
1890 (U. S.)	2,885	+772
1895 (State)	3,210	+325

TOWN OF EGREMONT.

Established February 13, 1760, as a district from certain common lands lying west of Sheffield. Made a town by Act of August 23, 1775. Boundary line between Egremont and Alford established February

TOWN OF EGREMONT — concluded

6, 1790. Part of Sheffield annexed February 22, 1790. Boundary line established June 17, 1817, between Egremont and Mount Washington and a part of each town annexed to the other town. Part of Sheffield annexed February 16, 1824. Boundary line between Egremont and Sheffield established June 4, 1869.

YEARS AND CENSUS.	Popula-tion	Increase (+), or Decrease (—), as Compared with Previous Census
1765 (Prov.)	[671]	-
1776 (Prov.)	671	=
1790 (U. S.)	759	+ 88
1800 (U. S.)	835	+ 76
1810 (U. S.)	790	— 45
1820 (U. S.)	865	+ 75
1830 (U. S.)	890	+ 25
1840 (U. S.)	1,038	+148
1850 (U. S.)	1,013	— 25
1855 (State)	992	— 21
1860 (U. S.)	1,079	+ 87
1865 (State)	928	—151
1870 (U. S.)	931	+ 3
1875 (State)	890	— 41
1880 (U. S.)	875	— 15
1885 (State)	826	— 49
1890 (U. S.)	845	+ 19
1895 (State)	836	— 9

TOWN OF FLORIDA.

Established June 15, 1805, from Barnardstone's Grant and part of Bullock's Grant, unincorporated lands. Part of Clarksburg annexed to Florida May 2, 1848. Part of Florida annexed to Clarksburg May 20, 1852.

1810 (U. S.)	392	-
1820 (U. S.)	431	+ 39
1830 (U. S.)	454	+ 23
1840 (U. S.)	441	— 13
1850 (U. S.)	561	+120
1855 (State)	612	+ 51
1860 (U. S.)	645	+ 33
1865 (State)	1,173	+528
1870 (U. S.)	1,322	+149
1875 (State)	572	—750
1880 (U. S.)	459	—113
1885 (State)	487	+ 28
1890 (U. S.)	436	— 51
1895 (State)	425	— 11

TOWN OF GREAT BARRINGTON.

Established June 30, 1761, from a part of Sheffield, called the "North Parish." Part of Great Barrington included in the new district of Alford February 16, 1773. Adjoining lands annexed to Great Barrington February 16, 1773. Part of Great Barrington included in the new town of Lee October 21, 1777. Parts of Great Barrington annexed to Alford February 11, 1779, and February 18, 1819.

1765 (Prov.)	550	-
1776 (Prov.)	961	+411
1790 (U. S.)	1,373	+412

CENSUSES OF POPULATION — 1765-1895 — Continued.

TOWN OF GREAT BARRINGTON — concluded.

Years and Census.	Population	Increase (+), or Decrease (—), as Compared with Previous Census
1800 (U. S.)	1,754	+381
1810 (U. S.)	1,784	+ 30
1820 (U. S.)	1,908	+124
1830 (U. S.)	2,264	+356
1840 (U. S.)	2,704	+440
1850 (U. S.)	3,264	+560
1855 (State)	3,449	+185
1860 (U. S.)	3,871	+422
1865 (State)	3,920	+ 49
1870 (U. S.)	4,320	+400
1875 (State)	4,385	+ 65
1880 (U. S.)	4,653	+268
1885 (State)	4,471	—182
1890 (U. S.)	4,612	+141
1895 (State)	4,794	+182

TOWN OF HANCOCK.

Established July 2, 1776, from the plantation called "Jerico." Part of Hancock annexed to district of New Ashford June 26, 1798. Boundary line between Hancock and New Ashford established May 20, 1851.

1776 (Prov.)	977	-
1790 (U. S.)	1,211	+284
1800 (U. S.)	1,157	— 24
1810 (U. S.)	1,049	—138
1820 (U. S.)	1,165	+116
1830 (U. S.)	1,052	—113
1840 (U. S.)	922	—130
1850 (U. S.)	789	—133
1855 (State)	848	+ 59
1860 (U. S.)	816	— 32
1865 (State)	937	+121
1870 (U. S.)	882	— 55
1875 (State)	730	—152
1880 (U. S.)	642	— 88
1885 (State)	613	— 29
1890 (U. S.)	506	—107
1895 (State)	511	+ 5

TOWN OF HINSDALE.

Established June 21, 1804, from the Westerly Parish of Partridgefield (now Peru).

1810 (U. S.)	822	-
1820 (U. S.)	822	=
1830 (U. S.)	780	— 42
1840 (U. S.)	955	+175
1850 (U. S.)	1,253	+298
1855 (State)	1,361	+108
1860 (U. S.)	1,511	+150
1865 (State)	1,517	+ 6
1870 (U. S.)	1,695	+178
1875 (State)	1,571	—124
1880 (U. S.)	1,595	+ 24

TOWN OF HINSDALE — concluded.

Years and Census.	Population	Increase (+), or Decrease (—), as Compared with Previous Census
1885 (State)	1,656	+ 61
1890 (U. S.)	1,739	+ 83
1895 (State)	1,650	— 89

TOWN OF LANESBOROUGH.

Established June 21, 1765, from the plantation of New Framingham. Part of Lanesborough included in the new town of Cheshire March 14, 1793.

1765 (Prov.)	[1,434]	-
1776 (Prov.)	1,434	=
1790 (U. S.)	2,142	+708
1800 (U. S.)	1,443	—699
1810 (U. S.)	1,303	—140
1820 (U. S.)	1,319	+ 16
1830 (U. S.)	1,192	—127
1840 (U. S.)	1,140	— 52
1850 (U. S.)	1,229	+ 89
1855 (State)	1,235	+ 6
1860 (U. S.)	1,308	+ 73
1865 (State)	1,294	— 14
1870 (U. S.)	1,393	+ 99
1875 (State)	1,357	— 36
1880 (U. S.)	1,286	— 71
1885 (State)	1,212	— 74
1890 (U. S.)	1,018	—194
1895 (State)	848	—170

TOWN OF LEE.

Established October 21, 1777, from parts of Great Barrington and Washington, the Glass Works Grant, and part of Williams' Grant. Boundary lines between Lee and Lenox established March 7, 1806, and February 7, 1820.

1790 (U. S.)	1,170	-
1800 (U. S.)	1,267	+ 97
1810 (U. S.)	1,305	+ 38
1820 (U. S.)	1,584	+ 79
1830 (U. S.)	1,825	+ 441
1840 (U. S.)	2,428	+ 605
1850 (U. S.)	3,220	+ 792
1855 (State)	4,226	+1,006
1860 (U. S.)	4,420	+ 194
1865 (State)	4,035	— 385
1870 (U. S.)	3,866	— 169
1875 (State)	3,900	+ 34
1880 (U. S.)	3,939	+ 39
1885 (State)	4,274	+ 335
1890 (U. S.)	3,785	— 489
1895 (State)	4,066	+ 281

TOWN OF LENOX.

Established as a district February 26, 1767, from the easterly part of "Richmont," now Richmond. Lands adjoining annexed to Lenox November 20, 1770. Made

CENSUSES OF POPULATION — 1765-1895 — Continued.

TOWN OF LENOX — concluded.

a town by Act of August 23, 1775. Parts of Washington annexed January 31, 1795, and February 18, 1802. Boundary lines between Lenox and Lee established March 7, 1806, and February 7, 1820.

YEARS AND CENSUS.	Population	Increase (+), or Decrease (—), as Compared with Previous Census
1776 (Prov.)	931	-
1790 (U. S.)	1,169	+238
1800 (U. S.)	1,041	—128
1810 (U. S.)	1,310	+269
1820 (U. S.)	1,315	+ 5
1830 (U. S.)	1,359	+ 44
1840 (U. S.)	1,313	— 46
1850 (U. S.)	1,599	+286
1855 (State)	1,921	+322
1860 (U. S.)	1,711	—210
1865 (State)	1,660	— 51
1870 (U. S.)	1,965	+305
1875 (State)	1,845	—120
1880 (U. S.)	2,043	+198
1885 (State)	2,154	+111
1890 (U. S.)	2,889	+735
1895 (State)	2,872	— 17

TOWN OF MONTEREY.

Established April 12, 1847, from a part of Tyringham. Part of New Marlborough annexed May 24, 1854. Part of Sandisfield annexed by Act of April 24, 1875, accepted by the town May 19, 1875, to take effect June 1, 1875.

1850 (U. S.)	791	-
1855 (State)	823	+62
1860 (U. S.)	758	—65
1865 (State)	737	—21
1870 (U. S.)	653	—84
1875 (State)	703	+50
1880 (U. S.)	635	—68
1885 (State)	571	—64
1890 (U. S.)	495	—76
1895 (State)	464	—31

TOWN OF MOUNT WASHINGTON.

Established June 21, 1779, from the plantation called Tauconnuck Mountain. Boundary line between Mount Washington and Egremont established June 17, 1817, and part of each town annexed to the other town. Boundary line between Mount Washington and the District of Boston Corner established March 12, 1847. The District of Boston Corner was established April 14, 1838, from common land, but owing to its inconvenient location was a constant source of annoyance, being the resort of prize fighters and other law breakers, who were there secure from the jurisdiction of the State, and for this reason the district was ceded to the State of New York May 14, 1853. The population of Boston Corner was 67 in 1790; 92 in 1820; 64 in 1830; 65 in 1840; and 73 in 1850. The date of establishment of Mount Washington is subsequent to the date of the earliest census in which population appears. This is due, probably, to the fact that the territory in question was well defined and recognized in census enumerations prior to the date of its formal incorporation as a district or town.

1776 (Prov.)	259	-
1790 (U. S.)	261	+2

TOWN OF MOUNT WASHINGTON — concluded.

YEARS AND CENSUS.	Population	Increase (+), or Decrease (—), as Compared with Previous Census
1800 (U. S.)	291	+ 30
1810 (U. S.)	474	+183
1820 (U. S.)	467	— 7
1830 (U. S.)	345	—122
1840 (U. S.)	438	+ 93
1850 (U. S.)	351	— 87
1855 (State)	344	— 7
1860 (U. S.)	321	— 23
1865 (State)	237	— 84
1870 (U. S.)	256	+ 19
1875 (State)	182	— 74
1880 (U. S.)	205	+ 23
1885 (State)	160	— 45
1890 (U. S.)	148	— 12
1895 (State)	136	— 12

TOWN OF NEW ASHFORD.

Established as a district February 26, 1781, from land called New Ashford, lying between Adams, Hancock, Lanesborough, and Williamstown. Part of the district of New Ashford included in the new town of Cheshire March 14, 1793, and on February 6, 1798, another part was annexed to Cheshire. Part of Hancock annexed to the district of New Ashford June 26, 1798. On May 1, 1836, the district was made a town by Chapter 15 of the Revised Statutes. Boundary line between New Ashford and Hancock established May 20, 1851. The date of establishment of this town is subsequent to the date of the earliest census in which population appears. This is due, probably, to the fact that the territory in question was well defined and recognized in census enumerations prior to the date of its formal incorporation as a district or town.

1776 (Prov.)	215	-
1790 (U. S.)	460	+245
1800 (U. S.)	390	— 70
1810 (U. S.)	411	+ 21
1820 (U. S.)	358	— 53
1830 (U. S.)	285	— 73
1840 (U. S.)	227	— 58
1850 (U. S.)	186	— 41
1855 (State)	195	+ 9
1860 (U. S.)	239	+ 44
1865 (State)	178	— 61
1870 (U. S.)	208	+ 30
1875 (State)	160	— 48
1880 (U. S.)	203	+ 43
1885 (State)	163	— 40
1890 (U. S.)	125	— 38
1895 (State)	116	— 9

TOWN OF NEW MARLBOROUGH.

Established as a district June 15, 1759, from the plantation of the same name. Made a town by Act of August 23, 1775. Parts of Sheffield annexed June 19, 1795, and February 7, 1798. Part of Tyringham annexed February 27, 1811. Part of New Marlborough annexed to Tyringham February 11, 1812. Part of New Marlborough annexed to Monterey May 24, 1851. Part of Sheffield annexed April 19, 1871, and boundary line established.

1765 (Prov.)	[1,087]	-
1776 (Prov.)	1,087	=

CENSUSES OF POPULATION — 1765-1895 — Continued.

TOWN OF NEW MARLBOROUGH — concluded.

YEARS AND CENSUS.	Population	Increase (+), or Decrease (—), as Compared with Previous Census
1790 (U. S.)	1,550	+463
1800 (U. S.)	1,848	+298
1810 (U. S.)	1,832	— 16
1820 (U. S.)	1,668	—164
1830 (U. S.)	1,656	— 12
1840 (U. S.)	1,682	+ 26
1850 (U. S.)	1,847	+165
1855 (State)	1,647	—200
1860 (U. S.)	1,782	+135
1865 (State)	1,649	—133
1870 (U. S.)	1,855	+206
1875 (State)	2,037	+182
1880 (U. S.)	1,876	—161
1885 (State)	1,661	—215
1890 (U. S.)	1,305	—356
1895 (State)	1,288	— 17

CITY OF NORTH ADAMS.

Established as a town April 16, 1878, from a part of Adams. Incorporated as a city March 22, 1895. Act of incorporation accepted by the town April 8, 1895.

1880 (U. S.)	10,191	-
1885 (State)	12,540	+2,349
1890 (U. S.)	16,074	+3,534
1895 (State)	19,135	+3,061

TOWN OF OTIS.

Established February 27, 1773, as "London" from a tract of common land called "Tyringham Equivalent." London and the District of Bethlehem united as the town of London June 19, 1809. (The District of Bethlehem established June 24, 1789, from the North Eleven Thousand Acres.) Act of June 19, 1809, took effect March 1, 1810, and part of London (Bethlehem District) was annexed to Becket. The name of London changed to Otis June 13, 1810. Part of the common lands called East Eleven Thousand Acres annexed to Otis April 9, 1838.

1776 (Prov.)	200	-
1790 (U. S.)	695	+495
1800 (U. S.)	1,102	+407
1810 (U. S.)	1,111	+ 9
1820 (U. S.)	981	—130
1830 (U. S.)	1,012	+ 31
1840 (U. S.)	1,177	+165
1850 (U. S.)	1,224	+ 47
1855 (State)	1,018	—206
1860 (U. S.)	998	— 20
1865 (State)	956	— 42
1870 (U. S.)	960	+ 4
1875 (State)	855	—105
1880 (U. S.)	785	— 70
1885 (State)	703	— 82
1890 (U. S.)	583	—120
1895 (State)	518	— 65

TOWN OF PERU.

Established July 4, 1771, from the new plantation called "Number Two," as Partridgefield. Part of Partridgefield included in the new town of Middlefield March 12, 1783. Part of Partridgefield established as the new town of Hinsdale June 21, 1804. Name changed to Peru June 19, 1806.

YEARS AND CENSUS.	Population	Increase (+), or Decrease (—), as Compared with Previous Census
1776 (Prov.)	376	-
1790 (U. S.)	1,041	+665
1800 (U. S.)	1,361	+320
1810 (U. S.)	912	—449
1820 (U. S.)	748	—164
1830 (U. S.)	729	— 19
1840 (U. S.)	576	—153
1850 (U. S.)	519	— 57
1855 (State)	487	— 32
1860 (U. S.)	499	+ 12
1865 (State)	494	— 5
1870 (U. S.)	455	— 39
1875 (State)	443	— 12
1880 (U. S.)	403	— 40
1885 (State)	368	— 35
1890 (U. S.)	305	— 63
1895 (State)	305	=

CITY OF PITTSFIELD.

Established as a town April 21, 1761, from the plantation called Pontoosuck. Incorporated as a city June 5, 1889. Act of incorporation accepted by the town February 11, 1890.

1765 (Prov.)	428	-
1776 (Prov.)	1,132	+ 704
1790 (U. S.)	1,992	+ 860
1800 (U. S.)	2,261	+ 269
1810 (U. S.)	2,665	+ 404
1820 (U. S.)	2,768	+ 103
1830 (U. S.)	3,559	+ 791
1840 (U. S.)	3,747	+ 188
1850 (U. S.)	5,872	+2,125
1855 (State)	6,501	+ 629
1860 (U. S.)	8,045	+1,544
1865 (State)	9,676	+1,631
1870 (U. S.)	11,112	+1,436
1875 (State)	12,267	+1,155
1880 (U. S.)	13,364	+1,097
1885 (State)	14,466	+1,102
1890 (U. S.)	17,281	+2,815
1895 (State)	20,461	+3,180

TOWN OF RICHMOND.

Established as "Richmont" June 21, 1765, from the new plantation called "Yokum Town" and "Mount Ephraim." Part of Richmont established as the District of Lenox February 26, 1767. Name changed to Richmond March 3, 1785. Boundary line established March 27, 1834, between Richmond and West Stockbridge.

1765 (Prov.)	[921]	-
1776 (Prov.)	921	=

142   CENSUS OF MASSACHUSETTS — 1895.

CENSUSES OF POPULATION — 1765-1895 — Continued.

TOWN OF RICHMOND — concluded.

YEARS AND CENSUS.	Population.	Increase (+), or Decrease (—), as Compared with Previous Census
1790 (U. S.)	1,255	+334
1800 (U. S.)	1,044	—211
1810 (U. S.)	1,041	— 3
1820 (U. S.)	923	—118
1830 (U. S.)	844	— 79
1840 (U. S.)	1,097	+253
1850 (U. S.)	907	—190
1855 (State)	970	+ 63
1860 (U. S.)	914	— 56
1865 (State)	944	+ 30
1870 (U. S.)	1,091	+147
1875 (State)	1,141	+ 50
1880 (U. S.)	1,124	— 17
1885 (State)	854	—270
1890 (U. S.)	796	— 58
1895 (State)	701	— 95

TOWN OF SANDISFIELD.

Established March 6, 1762, from the new plantation called "Number Three." The district of Southfield (established June 19, 1797, from the South Eleven Thousand Acres) and the town of Sandisfield united as the town of Sandisfield February 10, 1819. Part of the common lands called East Eleven Thousand Acres annexed April 9, 1838. Boundary lines between Sandisfield and Tolland (Hampden County) established May 4, 1853, and May 15, 1855. Part of Sandisfield annexed to Monterey by Act of April 24, 1875, accepted by Monterey May 19, 1875, to take effect June 1, 1875.

1765 (Prov.)	409	-
1776 (Prov.)	1,044	+635
1790 (U. S.)	1,742	+698
1800 (U. S.)	1,857	+115
1810 (U. S.)	1,795	— 62
1820 (U. S.)	1,646	—149
1830 (U. S.)	1,655	+ 9
1840 (U. S.)	1,464	—191
1850 (U. S.)	1,649	+185
1855 (State)	1,615	— 34
1860 (U. S.)	1,585	— 30
1865 (State)	1,411	—174
1870 (U. S.)	1,482	+ 71
1875 (State)	1,172	—310
1880 (U. S.)	1,107	— 65
1885 (State)	1,019	— 88
1890 (U. S.)	807	—212
1895 (State)	802	— 5

TOWN OF SAVOY.

Established February 20, 1797, from certain common land.

1800 (U. S.)	430	-
1810 (U. S.)	711	+281
1820 (U. S.)	852	+141
1830 (U. S.)	927	+ 75
1840 (U. S.)	915	— 12

TOWN OF SAVOY — concluded.

YEARS AND CENSUS.	Population.	Increase (+), or Decrease (—), as Compared with Previous Census
1850 (U. S.)	955	+ 40
1855 (State)	919	— 36
1860 (U. S.)	904	— 15
1865 (State)	866	— 38
1870 (U. S.)	861	— 5
1875 (State)	730	—131
1880 (U. S.)	715	— 15
1885 (State)	691	— 24
1890 (U. S.)	569	—122
1895 (State)	504	— 65

TOWN OF SHEFFIELD.

Established June 22, 1733, from part of the lower plantation called "Housatannick." Part of Sheffield established as Great Barrington June 30, 1761. Part of Sheffield annexed to Egremont February 22, 1790. Parts of Sheffield annexed to New Marlborough June 19, 1795, and February 7, 1798. Part of Sheffield annexed to Egremont February 16, 1824. Boundary line established between Sheffield and Egremont June 4, 1869. Part of Sheffield annexed to New Marlborough April 19, 1871, and boundary line established.

1765 (Prov.)	1,073	-
1776 (Prov.)	1,722	+649
1790 (U. S.)	1,899	+177
1800 (U. S.)	2,050	+151
1810 (U. S.)	2,439	+389
1820 (U. S.)	2,476	+ 37
1830 (U. S.)	2,382	— 94
1840 (U. S.)	2,322	— 60
1850 (U. S.)	2,769	+447
1855 (State)	2,624	—145
1860 (U. S.)	2,621	— 3
1865 (State)	2,459	—162
1870 (U. S.)	2,535	+ 76
1875 (State)	2,233	—302
1880 (U. S.)	2,204	— 29
1885 (State)	2,033	—171
1890 (U. S.)	1,954	— 79
1895 (State)	1,897	— 57

TOWN OF STOCKBRIDGE.

Established June 22, 1739, from the plantation called the "Indian Town." Part of Stockbridge established as the district of West Stockbridge March 9, 1774. Part of Stockbridge annexed to West Stockbridge March 2, 1829. Act of March 2, 1829, perfected February 6, 1830.

1765 (Prov.)	244	-
1776 (Prov.)	907	+663
1790 (U. S.)	1,336	+429
1800 (U. S.)	1,261	— 75
1810 (U. S.)	1,372	+111
1820 (U. S.)	1,377	+ 5
1830 (U. S.)	1,580	+203
1840 (U. S.)	1,992	+412
1850 (U. S.)	1,941	— 51

CENSUSES OF POPULATION — 1765-1895 — Continued.

TOWN OF STOCKBRIDGE — concluded.

YEARS AND CENSUS.	Population	Increase (+), or Decrease (—), as Compared with Previous Census
1855 (State)	2,058	+117
1860 (U. S.)	2,136	+ 78
1865 (State)	1,967	—169
1870 (U. S.)	2,003	+ 36
1875 (State)	2,089	+ 86
1880 (U. S.)	2,357	+268
1885 (State)	2,114	—243
1890 (U. S.)	2,132	+ 18
1895 (State)	2,077	— 55

TOWN OF TYRINGHAM.

Established March 6, 1762, from the new plantation called "Number One." Part of Tyringham annexed to New Marlborough February 27, 1811, and a part of New Marlborough annexed to Tyringham February 11, 1812. Part of Tyringham set off and established as Monterey April 12, 1847.

1765 (Prov.)	326	-
1776 (Prov.)	809	+483
1790 (U. S.)	1,397	+588
1800 (U. S.)	1,712	+315
1810 (U. S.)	1,689	— 23
1820 (U. S.)	1,443	—246
1830 (U. S.)	1,350	— 93
1840 (U. S.)	1,477	+127
1850 (U. S.)	821	—656
1855 (State)	710	—111
1860 (U. S.)	730	+ 20
1865 (State)	650	— 80
1870 (U. S.)	557	— 93
1875 (State)	517	— 40
1880 (U. S.)	542	+ 25
1885 (State)	457	— 85
1890 (U. S.)	412	— 45
1895 (State)	363	— 49

TOWN OF WASHINGTON.

Established April 12, 1777, from the plantation called "Hartwood" and several contiguous grants. Part of Washington included in Lee October 21, 1777. Part of Washington included in Middlefield (Hampshire County) March 12, 1783. Parts of Washington annexed to Lenox January 31, 1795, and February 18, 1802. The date of establishment of this town is subsequent to the date of the earliest census in which population appears. This is due, probably, to the fact that the territory in question was well defined and recognized in census enumerations prior to the date of its formal incorporation as a district or town.

1776 (Prov.)	750	-
1790 (U. S.)	588	—162
1800 (U. S.)	914	+326
1810 (U. S.)	942	+ 28
1820 (U. S.)	750	—192
1830 (U. S.)	701	— 49
1840 (U. S.)	991	+290
1850 (U. S.)	953	— 38
1855 (State)	1,068	+115

TOWN OF WASHINGTON — concluded.

YEARS AND CENSUS.	Population	Increase (+), or Decrease (—), as Compared with Previous Census
1860 (U. S.)	948	—120
1865 (State)	859	— 89
1870 (U. S.)	694	—165
1875 (State)	603	— 91
1880 (U. S.)	493	—110
1885 (State)	470	— 23
1890 (U. S.)	434	— 36
1895 (State)	423	— 11

TOWN OF WEST STOCKBRIDGE.

Established March 9, 1774, as the District of West Stockbridge, from the west part of Stockbridge. Made a town by Act of August 23, 1775. A gore of common land annexed March 2, 1793. Part of Stockbridge annexed March 2, 1829. Act of March 2, 1829, perfected February 6, 1830. Boundary line between West Stockbridge and Richmond established March 27, 1834. Part of West Stockbridge annexed to Alford March 17, 1847.

1776 (Prov.)	370	-
1790 (U. S.)	1,113	+743
1800 (U. S.)	1,002	—111
1810 (U. S.)	1,049	+ 47
1820 (U. S.)	1,034	— 15
1830 (U. S.)	1,209	+175
1840 (U. S.)	1,448	+239
1850 (U. S.)	1,713	+265
1855 (State)	1,736	+ 23
1860 (U. S.)	1,589	—147
1865 (State)	1,620	+ 31
1870 (U. S.)	1,924	+304
1875 (State)	1,981	+ 57
1880 (U. S.)	1,923	— 58
1885 (State)	1,648	—275
1890 (U. S.)	1,492	—156
1895 (State)	1,257	—235

TOWN OF WILLIAMSTOWN.

Established June 21, 1765, from the plantation called "West Hoosuck." Certain unincorporated lands bounded west by the State of New York annexed April 9, 1838.

1765 (Prov.)	[1,083]	-
1776 (Prov.)	1,083	=
1790 (U. S.)	1,769	+ 686
1800 (U. S.)	2,086	+ 317
1810 (U. S.)	1,843	— 243
1820 (U. S.)	2,010	+ 167
1830 (U. S.)	2,134	+ 124
1840 (U. S.)	2,153	+ 19
1850 (U. S.)	2,626	+ 473
1855 (State)	2,529	— 97
1860 (U. S.)	2,611	+ 82
1865 (State)	2,555	— 56
1870 (U. S.)	3,559	+1,004
1875 (State)	3,683	+ 124
1880 (U. S.)	3,394	— 289

CENSUSES OF POPULATION — 1765-1895 — Continued.

TOWN OF WILLIAMSTOWN — concluded.

YEARS AND CENSUS.	Popula-tion	Increase (+), or Decrease (—), as Compared with Previous Census
1885 (State)	3,729	+335
1890 (U. S.)	4,221	+492
1895 (State)	4,887	+666

TOWN OF WINDSOR.

Established as the town of "Gageborough" July 4, 1771, from the new plantation called "Number Four." Part of the plantation called "Number Five" annexed October 16, 1778, and the town of Gageborough, together with this annexed tract of land, established as the new town of Windsor. Part of Windsor included in the new town of Cheshire March 14, 1793. Part of Cheshire reannexed February 26, 1794. Part of Windsor annexed to Dalton February 28, 1795.

1776 (Prov.)	459	-
1790 (U. S.)	916	+457
1800 (U. S.)	961	+ 45
1810 (U. S.)	1,108	+147
1820 (U. S.)	1,085	— 23
1830 (U. S.)	1,042	— 43
1840 (U. S.)	897	—145
1850 (U. S.)	897	=
1855 (State)	905	+ 8
1860 (U. S.)	839	— 66
1865 (State)	753	— 86
1870 (U. S.)	686	— 67
1875 (State)	624	— 62
1880 (U. S.)	644	+ 20
1885 (State)	657	+ 13
1890 (U. S.)	612	— 45
1895 (State)	556	— 56

COUNTY OF BRISTOL.

Incorporated June 2, 1685. (Plymouth Colony Laws, edition 1836, p. 295.)

1765 (Prov.)	21,301	-
1776 (Prov.)	26,700	+ 5,399
1790 (U. S.)	31,709	+ 5,009
1800 (U. S.)	33,880	+ 2,171
1810 (U. S.)	37,168	+ 3,288
1820 (U. S.)	40,908	+ 3,740
1830 (U. S.)*	49,592	+ 8,684
1840 (U. S.)*	60,165	+10,573
1850 (U. S.)*	76,192	+16,027
1855 (State)*	87,425	+11,233
1860 (U. S.)*	93,794	+ 6,369
1865 (State)	89,395	— 4,399
1870 (U. S.)	102,886	+13,491
1875 (State)	131,087	+28,201
1880 (U. S.)	139,040	+ 7,953
1885 (State)	158,498	+19,458
1890 (U. S.)	186,465	+27,967
1895 (State)	219,019	+32,554

TOWN OF ACUSHNET.

Established February 13, 1860, from the northerly part of Fairhaven. Part of Acushnet annexed to New Bedford April 9, 1875.

YEARS AND CENSUS.	Popula-tion	Increase (+), or Decrease (—), as Compared with Previous Census
1860 (U. S.)	1,387	-
1865 (State)	1,251	—136
1870 (U. S.)	1,132	—119
1875 (State)	1,059	— 73
1880 (U. S.)	1,105	+ 46
1885 (State)	1,071	— 34
1890 (U. S.)	1,027	— 44
1895 (State)	1,115	+ 88

TOWN OF ATTLEBOROUGH.

Established October 19, 1694, from that part of Rehoboth called the "North Purchase," and which was granted to Rehoboth July 5, 1671. Boundary line between Attleborough and Rehoboth established September 10, 1697. Boundary line between Attleborough and Wrentham established February 18, 1830, and part of Attleborough annexed to Wrentham. Part of Attleborough set off as the new town of North Attleborough by Act of June 14, 1887; accepted by the town July 30, 1887, and said acceptance confirmed March 6, 1888.

1765 (Prov.)	1,739	-
1776 (Prov.)	2,200	+. 461
1790 (U. S.)	2,166	— 34
1800 (U. S.)	2,480	+ 314
1810 (U. S.)	2,716	+ 236
1820 (U. S.)	3,055	+ 339
1830 (U. S.)	3,215	+ 160
1840 (U. S.)	3,585	+ 370
1850 (U. S.)	4,200	+ 615
1855 (State)	5,451	+1,251
1860 (U. S.)	6,066	+ 615
1865 (State)	6,200	+ 134
1870 (U. S.)	6,769	+ 569
1875 (State)	9,224	+2,455
1880 (U. S.)	11,111	+1,887
1885 (State)	13,175	+2,064
1890 (U. S.)	7,577	—5,598
1895 (State)	8,288	+ 711

TOWN OF BERKLEY.

Established April 18, 1735, from parts of Dighton and Taunton. Part of Dighton annexed February 26, 1799. Certain lands in Berkley belonging to Taunton annexed February 6, 1810, and March 3, 1842. Centre of main ship channel in Taunton Great River established as boundary line of Berkley, Dighton, Freetown, Fall River, and Somerset March 17, 1847. Part of Taunton, known as Myricks District, annexed by Act of April 1, 1879; Act accepted by the town April 12, 1879.

1765 (Prov.)	659	-
1776 (Prov.)	787	+128
1790 (U. S.)	850	+ 63
1800 (U. S.)	1,013	+163

* Includes population of Pawtucket (ceded to Rhode Island) as follows: 1830, 1,459; 1840, 2,184; 1850, 3,753; 1855, 4,132; 1860, 4,200.

CENSUSES OF POPULATION — 1765-1895 — Continued.

TOWN OF BERKLEY — concluded.

Years and Census.	Population	Increase (+), or Decrease (—), as Compared with Previous Census
1810 (U. S.)	1,014	+ 1
1820 (U. S.)	1,060	+ 46
1830 (U. S.)	907	—153
1840 (U. S.)	886	— 21
1850 (U. S.)	908	+ 22
1855 (State)	924	+ 16
1860 (U. S.)	825	— 99
1865 (State)	847	+ 22
1870 (U. S.)	744	—103
1875 (State)	781	+ 37
1880 (U. S.)	927	+146
1885 (State)	941	+ 14
1890 (U. S.)	894	— 47
1895 (State)	955	+ 61

TOWN OF DARTMOUTH.

The first mention of this town occurs on page 19, Volume III, Plymouth Colony Records, October 5, 1652, as follows: "Dartmouth is to pay £2." The tract of land called Acushena, Ponnagansett, and Coaksett established as Dartmouth June 8, 1664. Boundaries established June 3, 1668. Part of Dartmouth established as New Bedford February 23, 1787. Part of Dartmouth established as Westport July 2, 1787. Parts of Dartmouth annexed to Westport February 25, 1793, February 28, 1795, and March 4, 1805. Boundary line between Dartmouth and Westport established February 20, 1828. Boundary line between Dartmouth and New Bedford established February 19, 1841. Part of Dartmouth annexed to New Bedford March 20, 1845. Boundary line between Dartmouth and New Bedford changed and a part of Dartmouth annexed to New Bedford May 3, 1888.

Year and Census	Population	Increase/Decrease
1765 (Prov.)	4,506	-
1776 (Prov.)	6,773	+2,267
1790 (U. S.)	2,499	—4,274
1800 (U. S.)	2,660	+ 161
1810 (U. S.)	3,219	+ 559
1820 (U. S.)	3,636	+ 417
1830 (U. S.)	3,866	+ 230
1840 (U. S.)	4,135	+ 269
1850 (U. S.)	3,868	— 267
1855 (State)	3,658	— 210
1860 (U. S.)	3,883	+ 225
1865 (State)	3,435	— 448
1870 (U. S.)	3,367	— 68
1875 (State)	3,434	+ 67
1880 (U. S.)	3,430	— 4
1885 (State)	3,448	+ 18
1890 (U. S.)	3,122	— 326
1895 (State)	3,107	— 15

TOWN OF DIGHTON.

Established May 30, 1712, from the South Precinct of Taunton. Part of Dighton included in the new town of Berkley April 18, 1735. Boundary lines reported by a committee March 2, 1743, and established January 8, 1745. Part of Dighton annexed to Berkley February 26, 1799. Part of Dighton established as Wellington June 9, 1814. Boundary line

TOWN OF DIGHTON — concluded.

established between Dighton and Wellington and part of Dighton annexed to Wellington February 12, 1824. Dighton and Wellington united as one town February 22, 1826, if the Act is accepted previous to March 1, 1826. Act accepted by Dighton February 25, 1826. Wellington revived as a separate town June 16, 1827, to exist one year. Centre of main ship channel of Taunton Great River established as boundary line of Berkley, Dighton, Freetown, Fall River, and Somerset March 17, 1847. Part of Dighton annexed to Somerset April 4, 1854.

Years and Census.	Population	Increase (+), or Decrease (—), as Compared with Previous Census
1765 (Prov.)	1,174	-
1776 (Prov.)	1,420	+246
1790 (U. S.)	1,793	+373
1800 (U. S.)	1,666	—127
1810 (U. S.)	1,659	— 7
1820 (U. S.)	1,607	— 52
1830 (U. S.)	1,723	+116
1840 (U. S.)	1,378	—345
1850 (U. S.)	1,641	+263
1855 (State)	1,729	+ 88
1860 (U. S.)	1,733	+ 4
1865 (State)	1,813	— 80
1870 (U. S.)	1,817	+ 4
1875 (State)	1,755	— 62
1880 (U. S.)	1,791	+ 36
1885 (State)	1,782	— 9
1890 (U. S.)	1,889	+107
1895 (State)	1,797	— 92

TOWN OF EASTON.

Established December 21, 1725, from part of the land in Norton called the "Taunton North Purchase."

Year and Census	Population	Increase/Decrease
1765 (Prov.)	837	-
1776 (Prov.)	1,172	+335
1790 (U. S.)	1,466	+294
1800 (U. S.)	1,550	+ 84
1810 (U. S.)	1,557	+ 7
1820 (U. S.)	1,803	+246
1830 (U. S.)	1,756	— 47
1840 (U. S.)	2,074	+318
1850 (U. S.)	2,337	+263
1855 (State)	2,748	+411
1860 (U. S.)	3,067	+319
1865 (State)	3,076	+ 9
1870 (U. S.)	3,668	+592
1875 (State)	3,898	+230
1880 (U. S.)	3,902	+ 4
1885 (State)	3,948	+ 46
1890 (U. S.)	4,493	+545
1895 (State)	4,452	— 41

TOWN OF FAIRHAVEN.

Established February 22, 1812, from the easterly part of New Bedford. Part of Freetown annexed June 15, 1815. Part of Rochester (Plymouth County)

CENSUSES OF POPULATION — 1765-1895 — Continued.

TOWN OF FAIRHAVEN — concluded.

annexed and boundary line established April 9, 1836. Part of Fairhaven set off as the town of Acushnet February 13, 1860.

YEARS AND CENSUS.	Popula- tion	Increase (+), or Decrease (—), as Com- pared with Pre- vious Census
1820 (U. S.)	2,733	-
1830 (U. S.)	3,034	+ 301
1840 (U. S.)	3,951	+ 917
1850 (U. S.)	4,304	+ 353
1855 (State)	4,693	+ 389
1860 (U. S.)	3,118	—1,575
1865 (State)	2,547	— 571
1870 (U. S.)	2,626	+ 79
1875 (State)	2,768	+ 142
1880 (U. S.)	2,875	+ 107
1885 (State)	2,880	+ 5
1890 (U. S.)	2,919	+ 39
1895 (State)	3,338	+ 419

CITY OF FALL RIVER.

Established February 26, 1803, from the southerly part of Freetown. Name of Fall River changed to Troy June 18, 1804. Name changed from Troy to Fall River February 12, 1834. Centre of main ship channel in Taunton Great River established as boundary line of Berkley, Dighton, Fall River, Freetown, and Somerset March 17, 1847. Fall River incorporated as a city by Act of April 12, 1854. Act of incorporation accepted by the town April 22, 1854. Certain lands on the east side of Mount Hope Bay annexed by the change of the boundary lines of Massachusetts and Rhode Island April 10, 1861. Boundary line between Fall River and Westport located and defined June 14, 1894.

1810 (U. S.)	1,296	-
1820 (U. S.)	1,594	+ 298
1830 (U. S.)	4,158	+ 2,564
1840 (U. S.)	6,738	+ 2,580
1850 (U. S.)	11,524	+ 4,786
1855 (State)	12,680	+ 1,156
1860 (U. S.)	14,026	+ 1,346
1865 (State)	17,481	+ 3,455
1870 (U. S.)	26,766	+ 9,285
1875 (State)	45,340	+18,574
1880 (U. S.)	48,961	+ 3,621
1885 (State)	56,870	+ 7,909
1890 (U. S.)	74,398	+17,528
1895 (State)	89,203	+14,805

TOWN OF FREETOWN.

No exact date of establishment is given to this town other than that recorded in July, 1683, on page 113, Volume VI, Plymouth Colony Records: "The inhabitants of the freemen's land at the Fall River shall be a township and be henceforth called by the name of Freetowne." Boundary line between Freetown and Tiverton, R. I., established June 17, 1790. Part of Freetown established as Fall River February 26, 1803. Part of Freetown annexed to Fairhaven June 15, 1815. Centre of main ship channel in Taunton Great River established as boundary line of Berkley, Dighton, Freetown, Fall River, and Somerset March 17, 1847.

TOWN OF FREETOWN — concluded.

YEARS AND CENSUS.	Popula- tion	Increase (+), or Decrease (—), as Com- pared with Pre- vious Census
1765 (Prov.)	1,492	-
1776 (Prov.)	1,901	+409
1790 (U. S.)	2,202	+301
1800 (U. S.)	2,535	+333
1810 (U. S.)	1,878	—657
1820 (U. S.)	1,863	— 15
1830 (U. S.)	1,909	+ 46
1840 (U. S.)	1,772	—137
1850 (U. S.)	1,615	—157
1855 (State)	1,585	— 30
1860 (U. S.)	1,521	— 64
1865 (State)	1,485	— 36
1870 (U. S.)	1,372	—113
1875 (State)	1,396	+ 24
1880 (U. S.)	1,329	— 67
1885 (State)	1,457	+128
1890 (U. S.)	1,417	— 40
1895 (State)	1,405	— 12

TOWN OF MANSFIELD.

Established as a district April 26, 1770, from the North Precinct of Norton. Made a town by the general Act of August 23, 1775.

1776 (Prov.)	944	-
1790 (U. S.)	983	+ 39
1800 (U. S.)	1,016	+ 33
1810 (U. S.)	1,030	+ 14
1820 (U. S.)	1,222	+192
1830 (U. S.)	1,172	— 50
1840 (U. S.)	1,382	+210
1850 (U. S.)	1,789	+407
1855 (State)	2,119	+330
1860 (U. S.)	2,114	— 5
1865 (State)	2,130	+ 16
1870 (U. S.)	2,432	+302
1875 (State)	2,656	+224
1880 (U. S.)	2,765	+109
1885 (State)	2,939	+174
1890 (U. S.)	3,432	+493
1895 (State)	3,722	+290

CITY OF NEW BEDFORD.

Established as a town February 23, 1787, from the easterly part of Dartmouth. Part of New Bedford set off as the new town of Fairhaven February 22, 1812. Boundary line between Dartmouth and New Bedford established February 19, 1831. Part of Dartmouth annexed to New Bedford March 20, 1845. Incorporated as a city by Act of March 9, 1847; Act of incorporation accepted by the town March 18, 1847. Part of Acushnet annexed April 9, 1875. Boundary line between New Bedford and Dartmouth changed and a part of Dartmouth annexed to New Bedford May 3, 1888.

1790 (U. S.)	3,313	-
1800 (U. S.)	4,361	+1,048
1810 (U. S.)	5,651	+1,290

CENSUSES OF POPULATION — 1765-1895 — Continued.

CITY OF NEW BEDFORD — concluded.

Years and Census.	Popula-tion	Increase (+), or Decrease (—), as Compared with Previous Census
1820 (U. S.)	3,947	— 1,704
1830 (U. S.)	7,592	+ 3,645
1840 (U. S.)	12,087	+ 4,495
1850 (U. S.)	16,443	+ 4,356
1855 (State)	20,389	+ 3,946
1860 (U. S.)	22,300	+ 1,911
1865 (State)	20,853	— 1,447
1870 (U. S.)	21,320	+ 467
1875 (State)	25,895	+ 4,575
1880 (U. S.)	26,845	+ 950
1885 (State)	33,393	+ 6,548
1890 (U. S.)	40,733	+ 7,340
1895 (State)	55,251	+14,518

TOWN OF NORTH ATTLEBOROUGH.

Established June 14, 1887, from a part of Attleborough. Act of incorporation accepted by the town of Attleborough July 30, 1887, and acceptance of said Act confirmed March 6, 1888.

1890 (U. S.)	6,727	-
1895 (State)	6,576	—151

TOWN OF NORTON.

The North Precinct of Taunton granted to be the town of Norton March 17, 1710. Bill to perfect the grant passed June 12, 1711. Part of Norton set off as the new town of Easton December 21, 1725. Part of Norton set off as the District of Mansfield April 26, 1770.

1765 (Prov.)	1,942	-
1776 (Prov.)	1,929	—613
1790 (U. S.)	1,428	+ 99
1800 (U. S.)	1,481	+ 53
1810 (U. S.)	1,598	+117
1820 (U. S.)	1,600	+ 2
1830 (U. S.)	1,479	—121
1840 (U. S.)	1,545	+ 66
1850 (U. S.)	1,966	+421
1855 (State)	1,894	— 72
1860 (U. S.)	1,848	— 46
1865 (State)	1,709	—139
1870 (U. S.)	1,821	+112
1875 (State)	1,595	—226
1880 (U. S.)	1,732	+137
1885 (State)	1,718	— 14
1890 (U. S.)	1,785	+ 67
1895 (State)	1,614	—171

TOWN OF RAYNHAM.

Established April 2, 1731, from a part of Taunton. Boundary line between Raynham and Taunton established February 27, 1866.

1765 (Prov.)	687	-
1776 (Prov.)	940	+253
1790 (U. S.)	1,094	+154

TOWN OF RAYNHAM — concluded.

Years and Census.	Popula-tion	Increase (+), or Decrease (—), as Compared with Previous Census
1800 (U. S.)	1,181	+ 87
1810 (U. S.)	1,154	— 27
1820 (U. S.)	1,071	— 83
1830 (U. S.)	1,208	+137
1840 (U. S.)	1,329	+121
1850 (U. S.)	1,541	+212
1855 (State)	1,634	+ 93
1860 (U. S.)	1,746	+112
1865 (State)	1,868	+122
1870 (U. S.)	1,713	—155
1875 (State)	1,687	— 26
1880 (U. S.)	1,681	— 6
1885 (State)	1,535	—146
1890 (U. S.)	1,340	—195
1895 (State)	1,518	+178

TOWN OF REHOBOTH.

Established June 4, 1645, from common land called "Seacunck." Boundary lines "to be" established June 6, 1649. Part of Rehoboth included in the new town of Swansea March 5, 1668. Certain common lands annexed to Rehoboth June 3, 1668. Boundary line between Rehoboth and Swansea established August 11, 1670. The land called the North Purchase granted to Rehoboth July 5, 1671. Boundary lines established July 7, 1682. The part called the North Purchase established as the new town of Attleborough October 19, 1694. Boundary line between Rehoboth and Attleborough established September 10, 1697. Part of Rehoboth established as the new town of Seekonk February 26, 1812.

1765 (Prov.)	3,090	-
1776 (Prov.)	4,191	+ 501
1790 (U. S.)	4,710	+ 519
1800 (U. S.)	4,743	+ 33
1810 (U. S.)	4,866	+ 123
1820 (U. S.)	2,740	—2,126
1830 (U. S.)	2,459	— 281
1840 (U. S.)	2,169	— 290
1850 (U. S.)	2,104	— 65
1855 (State)	2,107	+ 3
1860 (U. S.)	1,932	— 175
1865 (State)	1,843	— 89
1870 (U. S.)	1,895	+ 52
1875 (State)	1,827	— 68
1880 (U. S.)	1,891	+ 64
1885 (State)	1,788	— 103
1890 (U. S.)	1,786	— 2
1895 (State)	1,810	+ 24

TOWN OF SEEKONK.

Established February 26, 1812, from a part of Rehoboth. A portion of the territory was called Pawtucket (established March 1, 1828), and by Act of April 10, 1861, all of Pawtucket, except that part lying easterly of Seven Mile River, was annexed to Rhode Island and new boundary lines established. The excepted part of the above territory was annexed to Seekonk. On January 29, 1862, a municipal district by name of East Seekonk established to consist of the excepted territory named in the Act of April 10, 1861. Said

CENSUSES OF POPULATION — 1765-1895 — Continued.

TOWN OF SEEKONK — concluded.

district to cease "so soon as the proper officers of the future town of Seekonk shall have been elected and qualified." Population of Pawtucket was, for 1830, 1,459; 1840, 2,184; 1850, 3,753; 1855, 4,132; and 1860, 4,200.

YEARS AND CENSUS.	Popula- tion	Increase (+), or Decrease (—), as Com- pared with Pre- vious Census
1820 (U. S.)	2,775	-
1830 (U. S.)	2,133	— 642
1840 (U. S.)	1,996	— 137
1850 (U. S.)	2,243	+ 247
1855 (State)	2,304	+ 61
1860 (U. S.)	2,662	+ 358
1865 (State)	928	—1,734
1870 (U. S.)	1,021	+ 93
1875 (State)	1,167	+ 146
1880 (U. S.)	1,227	+ 60
1885 (State)	1,295	+ 68
1890 (U. S.)	1,317	+ 22
1895 (State)	1,445	+ 148

TOWN OF SOMERSET.

Established February 20, 1790, from that part of Swansea called the "Shewamet Purchase." Centre of main ship channel in Taunton Great River estab- lished as boundary line of Berkley, Dighton, Free- town, Fall River, and Somerset March 17, 1847. Part of Dighton annexed April 4, 1854.

YEARS AND CENSUS.	Popula- tion	Increase (+), or Decrease (—)
1790 (U. S.)	1,151	-
1800 (U. S.)	1,232	+ 81
1810 (U. S.)	1,199	— 33
1820 (U. S.)	1,116	— 83
1830 (U. S.)	1,023	— 93
1840 (U. S.)	1,005	— 18
1850 (U. S.)	1,166	+161
1855 (State)	1,339	+173
1860 (U. S.)	1,793	+454
1865 (State)	1,789	— 4
1870 (U. S.)	1,776	— 13
1875 (State)	1,940	+164
1880 (U. S.)	2,006	+ 66
1885 (State)	2,475	+469
1890 (U. S.)	2,106	—369
1895 (State)	1,983	—123

TOWN OF SWANSEA.

Established as "Swansey" March 5, 1668, from a part of Rehoboth called the "Township of Wanna- moisett," and places adjacent. A neck of land called "Papasquash Neck," excepting 100 acres, annexed July 5, 1669. Boundary line between Swansea and Rehoboth established August 11, 1670. Boundary lines established July 5, 1679. Boundary line between Swansea and Mount Hope "to be" established Novem- ber 4, 1679. Part of Swansea established as Somerset February 20, 1790. The name of this town is variously spelled. It is derived from Swansea in Wales, Rev. John Miles, who came here from Wales with a part of his church in 1663, being the first minister. The termination of the Welch name is "sea." Notwith- standing this, the spelling that appears in the earliest records of the town is Swansey, and this was retained in the records until 1718, after which it was changed to Swanzey, this continuing consecutively, or nearly

TOWN OF SWANSEA — concluded.

so, until 1865, when the form Swansey was again adopted, and from that date to the present the name has been so spelled in the town records. The State Department of the Commonwealth, however, follow- ing ancient departmental and legislative usage, still retains the form Swanzey. On the other hand, the U. S. Departmental usage, including the name of the Post Office, is Swansea. The name of the Railroad Station of the town is similarly spelled by the Rail- road Corporation, and this form is used in the legis- lative manual. It would seem to be historically accurate if the Welch derivation is taken into account, and the others seem to be corrupt spellings, that of Swansey being the more ancient. The form Swansea is also taught in the public schools of the town, is in use by a large proportion of the people, and so far as usage is concerned, any other spelling is rapidly be- coming obsolete. This manner of spelling the name has been used in the State Censuses since 1875, and is therefore retained in the present Census.

YEARS AND CENSUS.	Popula- tion	Increase (+), or Decrease (—), as Com- pared with Pre- vious Census.
1765 (Prov.)	1,840	-
1776 (Prov.)	[1,784]	— 56
1790 (U. S.)	1,784	=
1800 (U. S.)	1,741	— 43
1810 (U. S.)	1,839	+ 98
1820 (U. S.)	1,933	+ 94
1830 (U. S.)	1,678	—255
1840 (U. S.)	1,484	—194
1850 (U. S.)	1,554	+ 70
1855 (State)	1,467	— 87
1860 (U. S.)	1,430	— 37
1865 (State)	1,336	— 94
1870 (U. S.)	1,294	— 42
1875 (State)	1,308	+ 14
1880 (U. S.)	1,355	+ 47
1885 (State)	1,403	+ 48
1890 (U. S.)	1,456	+ 53
1895 (State)	1,627	+171

CITY OF TAUNTON.

Established March 3, 1639, from common land called Cohannett. Land at Assonet granted to Taunton March 3, 1640. Boundary lines established June 19, 1640. Certain lands granted to Taunton October 26, 1672. The land called Assonet Neck annexed to Taunton July -, 1682. The North Precinct of Taun- ton granted to be a town by name of Norton March 17, 1710. Bill to perfect said grant passed June 12, 1711. South Precinct of Taunton established as Dighton May 30, 1712. Part of Taunton estab- lished as Raynham April 2, 1731. Part of Taunton included in the new town of Berkley April 18, 1735. Certain lands in Berkley belonging to Taunton an- nexed to Berkley February 6, 1810, and March 3, 1842. Taunton incorporated as a city by Act of May 11, 1864. Act accepted by the town June 6, 1864. Boundary line between Taunton and Raynham established Feb- ruary 27, 1866. Boundary line between Taunton and Lakeville (Plymouth County) established June 1, 1867. Part of Taunton, known as Myricks District, annexed to Berkley by Act of April 1, 1879, said Act accepted by town of Berkley April 12, 1879.

YEARS AND CENSUS.	Popula- tion	Increase (+), or Decrease (—), as Com- pared with Pre- vious Census.
1765 (Prov.)	2,735	-
1776 (Prov.)	3,259	+524
1790 (U. S.)	3,804	+545
1800 (U. S.)	3,860	+ 56
1810 (U. S.)	3,907	+ 47

CENSUSES OF POPULATION — 1765-1895 — Continued.

CITY OF TAUNTON — concluded.

YEARS AND CENSUS.	Population	Increase (+), or Decrease (—), as Compared with Previous Census
1820 (U. S.)	4,520	+ 613
1830 (U. S.)	6,042	+1,522
1840 (U. S.)	7,645	+1,603
1850 (U. S.)	10,441	+2,796
1855 (State)	13,750	+3,309
1860 (U. S.)	15,376	+1,626
1865 (State)	16,005	+ 629
1870 (U. S.)	18,629	+2,624
1875 (State)	20,445	+1,816
1880 (U. S.)	21,213	+ 768
1885 (State)	23,674	+2,461
1890 (U. S.)	25,448	+1,774
1895 (State)	27,115	+1,667

TOWN OF WESTPORT.

Established July 2, 1787, from a part of Dartmouth. Parts of Dartmouth annexed to Westport February 25, 1793, February 28, 1795, and March 4, 1805. Boundary line between Westport and Dartmouth established February 20, 1828. Certain lands lying east and south of a line described, after the entry of the decree of the United States Supreme Court concerning the Rhode Island boundary, to be a part of Westport April 10, 1861. Boundary line between Westport and Fall River located and defined June 14, 1894.

YEARS AND CENSUS.	Population	Increase/Decrease
1790 (U. S.)	2,466	-
1800 (U. S.)	2,361	— 105
1810 (U. S.)	2,585	+224
1820 (U. S.)	2,633	+ 48
1830 (U. S.)	2,779	+ 146
1840 (U. S.)	2,820	+ 41
1850 (U. S.)	2,795	— 25
1855 (State)	2,822	+ 27
1860 (U. S.)	2,767	— 55
1865 (State)	2,799	+ 32
1870 (U. S.)	2,724	— 75
1875 (State)	2,912	+188
1880 (U. S.)	2,894	— 18
1885 (State)	2,706	—188
1890 (U. S.)	2,599	—107
1895 (State)	2,678	+ 79

COUNTY OF DUKES COUNTY.

This county was incorporated November 1, 1683, by the State of New York, to which it belonged, and contained the Island of Nantucket, "Martins" Vineyard, Elizabeth Island, and No-Man's Land. By the Province Charter of 1692 the "Isles of Cappawock and Nantuckett near Cape Cod" were granted to the Province of Massachusetts Bay. On June 13, 1693 (Province Laws, Volume I, page 117), the "Islands of Capawock, alias Martha's Vineyard," are referred to, and on June 22, 1695 (Province Laws, Volume I, page 216), it was ordered that the "Islands of Martha's Vineyard, Elsabeth Islands, the islands called Noman's land and all the dependencies formerly belonging to Dukes County (the island of Nantucket only excepted) shall be and remain, and continue to be one county to all intents and purposes, by the name of Dukes County."

YEARS AND CENSUS.	Population	Increase/Decrease
1765 (Prov.)	2,346	-
1776 (Prov.)	2,822	+476

COUNTY OF DUKES COUNTY — concluded.

YEARS AND CENSUS.	Population	Increase (+), or Decrease (—), as Compared with Previous Census
1790 (U. S.)	3,265	+443
1800 (U. S.)	3,118	—147
1810 (U. S.)	3,290	+172
1820 (U. S.)	3,292	+ 2
1830 (U. S.)	3,517	+225
1840 (U. S.)	3,958	+441
1850 (U. S.)	4,540	+582
1855 (State)	4,401	—139
1860 (U. S.)	4,403	+ 2
1865 (State)	4,200	—203
1870 (U. S.)	3,787	—413
1875 (State)	4,071	+284
1880 (U. S.)	4,300	+229
1885 (State)	4,135	—165
1890 (U. S.)	4,369	+234
1895 (State)	4,238	—131

TOWN OF CHILMARK.

There is considerable ambiguity concerning the date of establishment of this town and of Tisbury. In the New York State Book of Patents, Volume IV, page 73, under date of July 8, 1671, appears a grant headed "Tisbury Mannor." By it Governor Lovelace granted to Thomas Mayhew, Senior, and Thomas Mayhew, Junior, a certain island containing lands bought of the Indians called Chickemote, Keep-hickon, Quia-naines, Nashowa-Kemmuck, together with two of the Elizabeth Islands called Kataymuck and Nanname-sitt, and several other small and inconsiderable islands in Monument Bay to be called and known by the name of "Tysbury Mannor." September 14, 1694, Chilmark is mentioned in the Tax Act (also Tisbury). On June 17, 1696, it was Resolved, the constable of Chilmark empowered to collect the tax levied in 1694, while on October 30, 1714, it was Resolved, "the Mannour of Tisbury, commonly called Chilmark" to have all the powers of a town; whether under the name of Chilmark or Tisbury is not stated. Boundary lines between Chilmark and Gay Head, as established May 9, 1855, confirmed May 28, 1856. Part of Chilmark known as Elizabeth Islands established as Gosnold March 17, 1864. Boundary line between Chilmark and Tisbury established February 27, 1882.

YEARS AND CENSUS.	Population	Increase/Decrease
1765 (Prov.)	663	-
1776 (Prov.)	769	+106
1790 (U. S.)	771	+ 2
1800 (U. S.)	800	— 29
1810 (U. S.)	723	— 77
1820 (U. S.)	695	— 28
1830 (U. S.)	691	— 4
1840 (U. S.)	702	+ 11
1850 (U. S.)	747	+ 45
1855 (State)	676	— 71
1860 (U. S.)	654	— 22
1865 (State)	548	—106
1870 (U. S.)	476	— 72
1875 (State)	508	+ 32
1880 (U. S.)	494	— 14
1885 (State)	412	— 82
1890 (U. S.)	353	— 59
1895 (State)	304	— 49

CENSUSES OF POPULATION — 1765-1895 — Continued.

TOWN OF COTTAGE CITY.

Established February 17, 1880, from a part of Edgartown.

YEARS AND CENSUS.	Population	Increase (+), or Decrease (—), as Compared with Previous Census
1880 (U. S.)	672	-
1885 (State)	709	+ 37
1890 (U. S.)	1,080	+371
1895 (State)	1,038	— 42

TOWN OF EDGARTOWN.

Established July 8, 1671 (N. Y. Book of Patents, Vol. IV, p. 75). "The said Towne being formerly known by the name of Great Harbour . . . And the said Towne which for the future shall bee called by the name of Edgar Towne." Boundary line between Edgartown and Tisbury established February 5, 1830, and April 23, 1862. Part of the town set off as the new town Cottage City February 17, 1880.

1765 (Prov.)	944	-
1776 (Prov.)	1,020	+ 76
1790 (U. S.)	1,352	+332
1800 (U. S.)	1,226	—126
1810 (U. S.)	1,365	+139
1820 (U. S.)	1,374	+ 9
1830 (U. S.)	1,509	+135
1840 (U. S.)	1,736	+227
1850 (U. S.)	1,990	+254
1855 (State)	1,898	— 92
1860 (U. S.)	2,118	+220
1865 (State)	1,846	—272
1870 (U. S.)	1,516	—330
1875 (State)	1,707	+191
1880 (U. S.)	1,303	—404
1885 (State)	1,195	—138
1890 (U. S.)	1,156	— 9
1895 (State)	1,125	— 31

TOWN OF GAY HEAD.

The first mention of this town is on May 28, 1856, when the boundary lines between the land of the Indians of Gay Head and the town of Chilmark, as established May 9, 1855, were confirmed May 28, 1856. April 30, 1870, the District of Gay Head made the town of Gay Head.

1870 (U. S.)	160	-
1875 (State)	216	+56
1880 (U. S.)	161	—55
1885 (State)	186	+25
1890 (U. S.)	139	—47
1895 (State)	160	+30

TOWN OF GOSNOLD.

Established March 17, 1864, from that part of Chilmark known as the Elizabeth Islands.

1865 (State)	108	-
1870 (U. S.)	99	— 9
1875 (State)	115	+16

TOWN OF GOSNOLD — concluded.

YEARS AND CENSUS.	Population	Increase (+), or Decrease (—), as Compared with Previous Census
1880 (U. S.)	152	+37
1885 (State)	122	—30
1890 (U. S.)	135	+13
1895 (State)	140	+ 5

TOWN OF TISBURY.

As noted under Chilmark, the establishment of this town is indefinite though a grant given in New York July 8, 1671, states "Whereas there is a certain Island . . . granted to Thomas Mayhew Senr & Thomas Mayhew Junr who granted a proportion near the middle of the said Island for a township formerly known as Middletowne, said Towne to be called Tisbury-Towne." Boundary line between Tisbury and Edgartown established February 5, 1830, and April 23, 1862. Boundary line between Tisbury and Chilmark established February 27, 1882. Part of Tisbury established as West Tisbury April 28, 1892.

1765 (Prov.)	739	-
1776 (Prov.)	1,033	+294
1790 (U. S.)	1,142	+109
1800 (U. S.)	1,092	— 50
1810 (U. S.)	1,202	+110
1820 (U. S.)	1,223	+ 21
1830 (U. S.)	1,317	+ 94
1840 (U. S.)	1,520	+203
1850 (U. S.)	1,803	+283
1855 (State)	1,827	+ 24
1860 (U. S.)	1,631	—196
1865 (State)	1,698	+ 67
1870 (U. S.)	1,536	—162
1875 (State)	1,525	— 11
1880 (U. S.)	1,518	— 7
1885 (State)	1,541	+ 23
1890 (U. S.)	1,506	— 35
1895 (State)	1,002	—504

TOWN OF WEST TISBURY.

Established April 28, 1892, from a part of Tisbury.

1895 (State)	460	-

COUNTY OF ESSEX.

Incorporated May 10, 1643, from a part of Norfolk County. (Mass. Rec., Vol. II, p. 38.)

1765 (Prov.)	43,524	-
1776 (Prov.)	50,923	+ 7,399
1790 (U. S.)	57,913	+ 6,990
1800 (U. S.)	61,196	+ 3,283
1810 (U. S.)	71,888	+10,692
1820 (U. S.)	74,655	+ 2,767
1830 (U. S.)	82,859	+ 8,204
1840 (U. S.)	94,987	+12,128
1850 (U. S.)	131,300	+36,313
1855 (State)	151,018	+19,718
1860 (U. S.)	165,611	+14,593

CENSUSES OF POPULATION — 1765-1895 — Continued.

COUNTY OF ESSEX — concluded.

YEARS AND CENSUS.	Popula-tion	Increase (+), or Decrease (—), as Compared with Previous Census
1865 (State)	171,034	+ 5,423
1870 (U. S.)	200,843	+29,809
1875 (State)	223,342	+22,499
1880 (U. S.)	244,535	+21,193
1885 (State)	263,727	+19,192
1890 (U. S.)	299,995	+36,268
1895 (State)	330,392	+30,398

TOWN OF AMESBURY.

Established May 27, 1668, from a part of Salisbury. On May 12, 1675, boundary lines were allowed to Amesbury. Part of Salisbury called "Little Salisbury" annexed March 15, 1844. Part of Amesbury established as Merrimac April 11, 1876. Another part of Salisbury was annexed by Act of June 16, 1886, taking effect July 1, 1886.

1765 (Prov.)	1,567	-
1776 (Prov.)	1,795	+ 228
1790 (U. S.)	1,801	+ 6
1800 (U. S.)	1,757	— 44
1810 (U. S.)	1,890	+ 133
1820 (U. S.)	1,956	+ 66
1830 (U. S.)	2,445	+ 489
1840 (U. S.)	2,471	+ 26
1850 (U. S.)	3,143	+ 672
1855 (State)	3,585	+ 442
1860 (U. S.)	3,877	+ 292
1865 (State)	4,181	+ 304
1870 (U. S.)	5,581	+1,400
1875 (State)	3,816	—1,765
1880 (U. S.)	3,355	— 461
1885 (State)	4,403	+1,048
1890 (U. S.)	9,798	+5,395
1895 (State)	9,986	+ 188

TOWN OF ANDOVER.

First mentioned May 22, 1646, in Massachusetts Records, Volume II, page 139, "Cochicawick now called Andiver." Boundary line between Andover and Billerica (Middlesex County) established May 26, 1658. Boundary line between Andover and "Wills Hill" established May 9, 1678. Part of Andover included in the new town of Middleton June 20, 1728. Part of Andover included in the new town of Lawrence April 17, 1847. Part of Andover established as North Andover April 7, 1855. Part of Andover annexed to Lawrence February 4, 1879.

1765 (Prov.)	2,442	-
1776 (Prov.)	2,953	+ 511
1790 (U. S.)	2,863	— 90
1800 (U. S.)	2,941	+ 78
1810 (U. S.)	3,164	+ 223
1820 (U. S.)	3,889	+ 725
1830 (U. S.)	4,530	+ 641
1840 (U. S.)	5,207	+ 677
1850 (U. S.)	6,945	+1,738
1855 (State)	4,810	—2,135

TOWN OF ANDOVER — concluded.

YEARS AND CENSUS.	Popula-tion	Increase (+), or Decrease (—), as Compared with Previous Census
1860 (U. S.)	4,765	— 45
1865 (State)	5,314	+549
1870 (U. S.)	4,873	—441
1875 (State)	5,097	+224
1880 (U. S.)	5,169	+ 72
1885 (State)	5,711	+542
1890 (U. S.)	6,142	+431
1895 (State)	6,145	+ 3

CITY OF BEVERLY.

Established October 14, 1668, from that part of Salem called "Bass River." Part of Salem annexed to Beverly September 11, 1753. Part of Beverly annexed to Danvers April 27, 1857. Beverly incorporated as a city March 23, 1894. Act of incorporation accepted by the town May 1, 1894.

1765 (Prov.)	2,164	-
1776 (Prov.)	2,754	+ 590
1790 (U. S.)	3,290	+ 536
1800 (U. S.)	3,881	+ 591
1810 (U. S.)	4,608	+ 727
1820 (U. S.)	4,283	— 325
1830 (U. S.)	4,073	— 210
1840 (U. S.)	4,689	+ 616
1850 (U. S.)	5,376	+ 687
1855 (State)	5,944	+ 568
1860 (U. S.)	6,154	+ 210
1865 (State)	5,942	— 212
1870 (U. S.)	6,507	+ 565
1875 (State)	7,271	+ 764
1880 (U. S.)	8,456	+1,185
1885 (State)	9,186	+ 730
1890 (U. S.)	10,821	+1,635
1895 (State)	11,806	+ 985

TOWN OF BOXFORD.

On September 14, 1694, Boxford is named in the Tax Act. Boundary line between Boxford and Topsfield fixed February 25, 1701. Part of Boxford included in the new town of Middleton June 20, 1728. Part of Rowley annexed to Boxford June 10, 1808. Boundary line between Boxford and Rowley established June 18, 1825. Part of Ipswich annexed March 7, 1846. Part of Boxford annexed to Groveland March 21, 1850.

1765 (Prov.)	851	-
1776 (Prov.)	989	+138
1790 (U. S.)	925	— 64
1800 (U. S.)	852	— 73
1810 (U. S.)	880	+ 28
1820 (U. S.)	906	+ 26
1830 (U. S.)	935	+ 29
1840 (U. S.)	942	+ 7
1850 (U. S.)	982	+ 40
1855 (State)	1,034	+ 52
1860 (U. S.)	1,020	— 14
1865 (State)	868	—152

CENSUSES OF POPULATION — 1765–1895 — Continued.

TOWN OF BOXFORD — concluded.

YEARS AND CENSUS.	Population	Increase (+), or Decrease (—), as Compared with Previous Census
1870 (U. S.)	847	— 21
1875 (State)	834	— 13
1880 (U. S.)	824	— 10
1885 (State)	840	+ 16
1890 (U. S.)	865	+ 25
1895 (State)	727	—138

TOWN OF BRADFORD.

On October 13, 1675, Bradford is mentioned in the Tax Act and was established from a part of Rowley called "Merrimak" or "Rowley Village." Boundary line between Bradford and Rowley confirmed February 24, 1701. Part of Bradford established as Groveland March 8, 1850.

YEARS AND CENSUS.	Population	Increase/Decrease
1765 (Prov.)	1,125	-
1776 (Prov.)	1,240	+ 115
1790 (U. S.)	1,371	+ 131
1800 (U. S.)	1,420	+ 49
1810 (U. S.)	1,369	— 51
1820 (U. S.)	1,600	+ 231
1830 (U. S.)	1,856	+ 256
1840 (U. S.)	2,222	+ 366
1850 (U. S.)	1,328	— 894
1855 (State)	1,372	+ 44
1860 (U. S.)	1,688	+ 316
1865 (State)	1,566	— 122
1870 (U. S.)	2,014	+ 448
1875 (State)	2,347	+ 333
1880 (U. S.)	2,643	+ 296
1885 (State)	3,106	+ 463
1890 (U. S.)	3,720	+ 614
1895 (State)	4,736	+1,016

TOWN OF DANVERS.

Established as a district January 28, 1752, from the village and Middle Parishes in Salem. Made a town June 16, 1757, but the Act was disallowed by the Privy Council August 10, 1759; however, by general Act of August 23, 1775, the district was made a town. Boundary line between Danvers and Salem established March 17, 1840. Part of Danvers set off as the new town of South Danvers May 18, 1855, the name of the latter town being changed April 13, 1868, to Peabody. Boundary line between Danvers and South Danvers established May 31, 1856. Part of Beverly annexed April 27, 1857.

YEARS AND CENSUS.	Population	Increase/Decrease
1765 (Prov.)	2,133	-
1776 (Prov.)	2,284	+ 151
1790 (U. S.)	2,425	+ 141
1800 (U. S.)	2,643	+ 218
1810 (U. S.)	3,127	+ 484
1820 (U. S.)	3,646	+ 519
1830 (U. S.)	4,228	+ 582
1840 (U. S.)	5,020	+ 792
1850 (U. S.)	8,109	+3,089
1855 (State)	4,000	—4,109
1860 (U. S.)	5,110	+1,110

TOWN OF DANVERS — concluded.

YEARS AND CENSUS.	Population	Increase (+), or Decrease (—), as Compared with Previous Census
1865 (State)	5,144	+ 34
1870 (U. S.)	5,600	+456
1875 (State)	6,024	+424
1880 (U. S.)	6,598	+574
1885 (State)	7,061	+463
1890 (U. S.)	7,454	+393
1895 (State)	8,181	+727

TOWN OF ESSEX.

Established February 15, 1819, from a part of Ipswich. Boundary lines in tide-water between Essex and Gloucester, and Essex and Ipswich established April 19, 1892.

YEARS AND CENSUS.	Population	Increase/Decrease
1820 (U. S.)	1,107	-
1830 (U. S.)	1,333	+226
1840 (U. S.)	1,450	+117
1850 (U. S.)	1,585	+135
1855 (State)	1,668	+ 83
1860 (U. S.)	1,701	+ 33
1865 (State)	1,630	— 71
1870 (U. S.)	1,614	— 16
1875 (State)	1,713	+ 99
1880 (U. S.)	1,670	— 43
1885 (State)	1,722	+ 52
1890 (U. S.)	1,713	— 9
1895 (State)	1,587	—126

TOWN OF GEORGETOWN.

Established April 21, 1838, from a part of Rowley.

YEARS AND CENSUS.	Population	Increase/Decrease
1840 (U. S.)	1,540	-
1850 (U. S.)	2,052	+512
1855 (State)	2,042	— 10
1860 (U. S.)	2,075	+ 33
1865 (State)	1,926	—149
1870 (U. S.)	2,088	+162
1875 (State)	2,214	+126
1880 (U. S.)	2,231	+ 17
1885 (State)	2,299	+ 68
1890 (U. S.)	2,117	—182
1895 (State)	2,050	— 67

CITY OF GLOUCESTER.

Established May 18, 1642, from common lands called "Cape Anne." Boundary line between Gloucester and Manchester established May 15, 1672. Part of Gloucester set off as the new town of Rockport February 27, 1840. Incorporated as a city April 28, 1873. Act of incorporation accepted by the town May 15, 1873. Boundary lines in tide-water between Gloucester, and Essex and Ipswich established April 19, 1892.

YEARS AND CENSUS.	Population	Increase/Decrease
1765 (Prov.)	3,763	-
1776 (Prov.)	4,512	+749
1790 (U. S.)	5,317	+805
1800 (U. S.)	5,313	— 4

CENSUSES OF POPULATION — 1765-1895 — Continued.

CITY OF GLOUCESTER — concluded.

YEARS AND CENSUS.	Population	Increase (+), or Decrease (−), as Compared with Previous Census
1810 (U. S.)	5,943	+ 630
1820 (U. S.)	6,384	+ 441
1830 (U. S.)	7,510	+1,126
1840 (U. S.)	6,350	−1,160
1850 (U. S.)	7,786	+1,436
1855 (State)	8,935	+1,149
1860 (U. S.)	10,904	+1,969
1865 (State)	11,937	+1,033
1870 (U. S.)	15,389	+3,452
1875 (State)	16,754	+1,365
1880 (U. S.)	19,329	+2,575
1885 (State)	21,703	+2,374
1890 (U. S.)	24,651	+2,948
1895 (State)	28,211	+3,560

TOWN OF GROVELAND.

Established March 8, 1850, from a part of Bradford. Part of Boxford annexed March 21, 1856.

1850 (U. S.)	1,286	-
1855 (State)	1,367	+ 81
1860 (U. S.)	1,448	+ 81
1865 (State)	1,619	+171
1870 (U. S.)	1,776	+157
1875 (State)	2,084	+308
1880 (U. S.)	2,227	+143
1885 (State)	2,272	+ 45
1890 (U. S.)	2,191	− 81
1895 (State)	2,333	+142

TOWN OF HAMILTON.

Established June 21, 1793, from that part of Ipswich called the "Parish of Ipswich Hamlet."

1800 (U. S.)	749	-
1810 (U. S.)	780	+ 31
1820 (U. S.)	802	+ 22
1830 (U. S.)	748	− 54
1840 (U. S.)	818	+ 70
1850 (U. S.)	889	+ 71
1855 (State)	896	+ 7
1860 (U. S.)	789	−107
1865 (State)	799	+ 10
1870 (U. S.)	790	− 9
1875 (State)	797	+ 7
1880 (U. S.)	935	+138
1885 (State)	851	− 84
1890 (U. S.)	961	+110
1895 (State)	1,356	+395

CITY OF HAVERHILL.

First mention, June 2, 1641, boundary lines to be set out "between Salsberry and Pantucket, all : Haverell." On May 10, 1643, Haverhill is named as in one of the

CITY OF HAVERHILL. — concluded.

four shires established. An island in the Merrimack River was granted to Haverhill on May 23, 1659, unless some person prove a clear title to it within three years. Boundary lines established October 30, 1651. Boundary line between Haverhill and Salisbury established November 1, 1654. Boundary line between Haverhill and "lands of Maj. Gen'l Dennison established," May 18, 1664. Boundary lines established May 15, 1667, and May 12, 1675. Part of Haverhill included in the new town of Methuen December 8, 1725. Haverhill incorporated as a city March 10, 1869. Act of incorporation accepted by the town May 15, 1869.

YEARS AND CENSUS.	Population	Increase (+), or Decrease (−), as Compared with Previous Census
1765 (Prov.)	1,980	-
1776 (Prov.)	2,810	+ 830
1790 (U. S.)	2,408	− 402
1800 (U. S.)	2,730	+ 322
1810 (U. S.)	2,682	− 48
1820 (U. S.)	3,070	+ 388
1830 (U. S.)	3,896	+ 826
1840 (U. S.)	4,336	+ 440
1850 (U. S.)	5,877	+1,541
1855 (State)	7,932	+2,055
1860 (U. S.)	9,995	+2,063
1865 (State)	10,740	+ 745
1870 (U. S.)	13,092	+2,352
1875 (State)	14,628	+1,536
1880 (U. S.)	18,472	+3,844
1885 (State)	21,795	+3,323
1890 (U. S.)	27,412	+5,617
1895 (State)	30,209	+2,797

TOWN OF IPSWICH.

Established August 5, 1634, from common land called "Aggawam." Part of Ipswich called the "Village" at the New Meadows was named "Toppesfield" October 18, 1648. Boundary line between Ipswich and Topsfield established February 28, 1694. Part of Ipswich annexed to Rowley November 29, 1785. Part of Ipswich set off as the new town of Hamilton June 21, 1793. Part of Ipswich set off as the new town of Essex February 15, 1819. Part of Ipswich annexed to Boxford March 9, 1846. Boundary lines in tide-water between Ipswich and Essex and Ipswich and Gloucester established April 19, 1892.

1765 (Prov.)	3,745	-
1776 (Prov.)	4,508	+ 765
1790 (U. S.)	4,562	+ 54
1800 (U. S.)	3,305	−1,257
1810 (U. S.)	3,569	+ 264
1820 (U. S.)	2,553	−1,016
1830 (U. S.)	2,949	+ 396
1840 (U. S.)	3,000	+ 51
1850 (U. S.)	3,349	+ 349
1855 (State)	3,421	+ 72
1860 (U. S.)	3,300	− 121
1865 (State)	3,311	+ 11
1870 (U. S.)	3,720	+ 409
1875 (State)	3,674	− 46
1880 (U. S.)	3,699	+ 25
1885 (State)	4,207	+ 508
1890 (U. S.)	4,439	+ 232
1895 (State)	4,720	+ 281

CENSUSES OF POPULATION — 1765-1895 — Continued.

CITY OF LAWRENCE.

Established as a town April 17, 1847, from parts of Andover and Methuen. Incorporated as a city March 21, 1853. Act of incorporation accepted by the town March 29, 1853. Part of Methuen annexed April 4, 1854. Parts of Andover and North Andover annexed February 4, 1879.

Years and Census.	Population	Increase (+), or Decrease (—), as Compared with Previous Census
1850 (U. S.)	8,282	-
1855 (State)	16,114	+7,832
1860 (U. S.)	17,639	+1,525
1865 (State)	21,698	+4,059
1870 (U. S.)	28,921	+7,223
1875 (State)	34,916	+5,995
1880 (U. S.)	39,151	+4,235
1885 (State)	38,862	— 289
1890 (U. S.)	44,654	+5,792
1895 (State)	52,164	+7,510

CITY OF LYNN.

Originally called "Saugus," a plantation, the first mention being made in the Tax Act, July 5, 1631. Boundary lines between Saugus and Salem, and Saugus and Marble Harbor "to be" established March 4, 1635. On November 20, 1637, "Saugus is called Lin." (Mass. Records, Vol. I, p. 211.) Part of Lynn set off as the new town of Reading (Middlesex County) May 29, 1644. Part of Lynn established as the District of Lynnfield July 3, 1782. Part of Lynn set off as the new town of Saugus February 17, 1815. Incorporated as a city April 10, 1850. Act of incorporation accepted by the town April 10, 1850. Part of Lynn set off as the new town of Swampscott May 21, 1852. Part of Lynn set off as the new town of Nahant March 29, 1853.

1765 (Prov.)	2,198	-
1776 (Prov.)	2,755	+ 557
1790 (U. S.)	2,291	— 464
1800 (U. S.)	2,837	+ 546
1810 (U. S.)	4,087	+1,250
1820 (U. S.)	4,515	+ 428
1830 (U. S.)	6,138	+1,623
1840 (U. S.)	9,367	+3,229
1850 (U. S.)	14,257	+4,890
1855 (State)	15,713	+1,456
1860 (U. S.)	19,083	+3,370
1865 (State)	20,747	+1,664
1870 (U. S.)	28,233	+7,486
1875 (State)	32,600	+4,367
1880 (U. S.)	38,274	+5,674
1885 (State)	45,867	+7,593
1890 (U. S.)	55,727	+9,860
1895 (State)	62,354	+6,627

TOWN OF LYNNFIELD.

Established as a district July 3, 1782, from a part of Lynn. Made a town February 28, 1814. Boundary line between Lynnfield and Reading (Middlesex County) established April 19, 1854. Boundary line between Lynnfield and North Reading (Middlesex County) established and part of each town annexed to the other town May 27, 1857. The provisions of this Act were accepted by Lynnfield November 3, 1857, and by North Reading January 7, 1858.

TOWN OF LYNNFIELD — concluded.

Years and Census.	Population	Increase (+), or Decrease (—), as Compared with Previous Census
1790 (U. S.)	491	-
1800 (U. S.)	468	— 23
1810 (U. S.)	509	+ 41
1820 (U. S.)	596	+ 87
1830 (U. S.)	617	+ 21
1840 (U. S.)	707	+ 90
1850 (U. S.)	1,723	+1,016
1855 (State)	883	— 840
1860 (U. S.)	866	— 17
1865 (State)	725	— 141
1870 (U. S.)	818	+ 93
1875 (State)	769	— 49
1880 (U. S.)	686	— 83
1885 (State)	766	+ 80
1890 (U. S.)	787	+ 21
1895 (State)	818	+ 31

TOWN OF MANCHESTER.

Established May 14, 1645, from that part of Salem called "Jeffreyes Creeke." Boundary line between Manchester and Gloucester established May 15, 1672.

1765 (Prov.)	732	-
1776 (Prov.)	949	+217
1790 (U. S.)	965	+ 16
1800 (U. S.)	1,082	+117
1810 (U. S.)	1,137	+ 55
1820 (U. S.)	1,201	+ 64
1830 (U. S.)	1,236	+ 35
1840 (U. S.)	1,355	+119
1850 (U. S.)	1,638	+283
1855 (State)	1,864	+226
1860 (U. S.)	1,698	—166
1865 (State)	1,643	— 55
1870 (U. S.)	1,665	+ 22
1875 (State)	1,560	—105
1880 (U. S.)	1,640	+ 80
1885 (State)	1,639	— 1
1890 (U. S.)	1,789	+150
1895 (State)	1,876	+ 87

TOWN OF MARBLEHEAD.

Marblehead mentioned July 2, 1633, on page 106 of Mass. Records, Vol. I. A plantation established at Marblehead May 6, 1635. Established as a town May 2, 1649, from a part of Salem.

1765 (Prov.)	4,954	-
1776 (Prov.)	4,386	— 568
1790 (U. S.)	5,661	+1,275
1800 (U. S.)	5,211	— 450
1810 (U. S.)	5,900	+ 689
1820 (U. S.)	5,630	— 270
1830 (U. S.)	5,149	— 481
1840 (U. S.)	5,575	+ 426
1850 (U. S.)	6,167	+ 592
1855 (State)	6,928	+ 761

CENSUSES OF POPULATION — 1765-1895 — Continued.

TOWN OF MARBLEHEAD — concluded.

YEARS AND CENSUS.	Population	Increase (+), or Decrease (—), as Compared with Previous Census
1860 (U. S.)	7,646	+ 718
1865 (State)	7,308	— 338
1870 (U. S.)	7,703	+ 395
1875 (State)	7,677	— 26
1880 (U. S.)	7,467	— 210
1885 (State)	7,517	+ 50
1890 (U. S.)	8,202	+ 685
1895 (State)	7,671	— 531

TOWN OF MERRIMAC.

Established April 11, 1876, from a part of Amesbury. The date of establishment of this town is subsequent to the date of the earliest census in which population appears. The returns for the town of Amesbury, of which Merrimac constituted a part at the time of the taking of the State Census in 1875, were divided after the enumeration was completed and the results for Merrimac were presented separately.

1875 (State)	2,171	-
1880 (U. S.)	2,287	+ 66
1885 (State)	2,278	+141
1890 (U. S.)	2,633	+355
1895 (State)	2,301	—332

TOWN OF METHUEN.

Established December 8, 1725, from a part of Haverhill and certain common lands. Part of Methuen included in the new town of Lawrence April 17, 1847, and another part annexed to Lawrence April 4, 1854.

1765 (Prov.)	932	-
1776 (Prov.)	1,326	+ 393
1790 (U. S.)	1,297	— 29
1800 (U. S.)	1,253	— 44
1810 (U. S.)	1,181	— 72
1820 (U. S.)	1,371	+ 190
1830 (U. S.)	2,006	+ 635
1840 (U. S.)	2,251	+ 245
1850 (U. S.)	2,538	+ 287
1855 (State)	2,582	+ 44
1860 (U. S.)	2,566	— 16
1865 (State)	2,576	+ 10
1870 (U. S.)	2,959	+ 383
1875 (State)	4,205	+1,246
1880 (U. S.)	4,392	+ 187
1885 (State)	4,507	+ 115
1890 (U. S.)	4,814	+ 307
1895 (State)	5,690	+ 876

TOWN OF MIDDLETON.

Established June 20, 1728, from parts of Andover, Boxford, Salem, and Topsfield.

1765 (Prov.)	581	-
1776 (Prov.)	650	+ 69
1790 (U. S.)	682	+ 32

TOWN OF MIDDLETON — concluded.

YEARS AND CENSUS.	Population	Increase (+), or Decrease (—), as Compared with Previous Census
1800 (U. S.)	598	— 84
1810 (U. S.)	541	— 57
1820 (U. S.)	596	+ 55
1830 (U. S.)	607	+ 11
1840 (U. S.)	657	+ 50
1850 (U. S.)	832	+175
1855 (State)	880	+ 48
1860 (U. S.)	940	+ 60
1865 (State)	922	— 18
1870 (U. S.)	1,010	+ 88
1875 (State)	1,092	+ 82
1880 (U. S.)	1,000	— 92
1885 (State)	899	—101
1890 (U. S.)	924	+ 25
1895 (State)	838	— 86

TOWN OF NAHANT.

Established March 29, 1853, from a part of Lynn.

1855 (State)	270	-
1860 (U. S.)	380	+110
1865 (State)	313	— 67
1870 (U. S.)	475	+162
1875 (State)	766	+291
1880 (U. S.)	808	+ 42
1885 (State)	637	—171
1890 (U. S.)	880	+243
1895 (State)	865	— 15

TOWN OF NEWBURY.

Established May 6, 1635, from the plantation called "Wessacucon." Part of Newbury established as Newburyport January 28, 1764. Part of Newbury established as Parsons February 18, 1819; the name of the latter was afterward (June 14, 1820,) changed to West Newbury. Part of Newbury annexed to Newburyport April 17, 1851.

1765 (Prov.)	2,960	-
1776 (Prov.)	3,239	+ 279
1790 (U. S.)	3,972	+ 733
1800 (U. S.)	4,076	+ 104
1810 (U. S.)	5,176	+ 1,100
1820 (U. S.)	3,671	—1,505
1830 (U. S.)	3,603	— 68
1840 (U. S.)	3,789	+ 186
1850 (U. S.)	4,426	+ 637
1855 (State)	1,484	—2,942
1860 (U. S.)	1,444	— 40
1865 (State)	1,362	— 82
1870 (U. S.)	1,430	+ 68
1875 (State)	1,423	— 4
1880 (U. S.)	1,566	+ 140
1885 (State)	1,590	+ 24
1890 (U. S.)	1,427	— 163
1895 (State)	1,489	+ 62

CENSUSES OF POPULATION — 1765–1895 — Continued.

CITY OF NEWBURYPORT.

Established as a town January 28, 1764, from a part of Newbury. Part of Newbury annexed April 17, 1851. Incorporated as a city May 24, 1851. Act of incorporation accepted by the town June 3, 1851.

YEARS AND CENSUS.	Popula- tion	Increase (+), or Decrease (—), as Com- pared with Pre- vious Census
1765 (Prov.)	2,882	–
1776 (Prov.)	3,681	+ 799
1790 (U. S.)	4,837	+1,156
1800 (U. S.)	5,946	+1,109
1810 (U. S.)	7,634	+1,688
1820 (U. S.)	6,852	— 782
1830 (U. S.)	6,375	— 477
1840 (U. S.)	7,161	+ 786
1850 (U. S.)	9,572	+2,411
1855 (State)	13,357	+3,785
1860 (U. S.)	13,401	+ 44
1865 (State)	12,976	— 425
1870 (U. S.)	12,595	— 381
1875 (State)	13,323	+ 728
1880 (U. S.)	13,538	+ 215
1885 (State)	13,716	+ 178
1890 (U. S.)	13,947	+ 231
1895 (State)	14,552	+ 605

TOWN OF NORTH ANDOVER.

Established April 7, 1855, from a part of Andover. Part annexed to Lawrence February 4, 1879.

1855 (State)	2,218	–
1860 (U. S.)	2,343	+125
1865 (State)	2,622	+279
1870 (U. S.)	2,549	— 73
1875 (State)	2,981	+432
1880 (U. S.)	3,217	+236
1885 (State)	3,425	+208
1890 (U. S.)	3,742	+317
1895 (State)	3,569	—173

TOWN OF PEABODY.

Established May 18, 1855, as South Danvers from a part of Danvers. Boundary line between South Danvers and Salem established and part of each place annexed to the other place April 30, 1856. Boundary line between South Danvers and Danvers established May 31, 1856. Name changed to Peabody April 13, 1868. Change of name accepted by the town April 30, 1868. Part of Peabody annexed to Salem March 27, 1882.

1855 (State)	5,348	–
1860 (U. S.)	6,549	+1,201
1865 (State)	6,051	— 498
1870 (U. S.)	7,343	+1,292
1875 (State)	8,066	+ 723
1880 (U. S.)	9,028	+ 962
1885 (State)	9,530	+ 502
1890 (U. S.)	10,158	+ 628
1895 (State)	10,507	+ 349

TOWN OF ROCKPORT.

Established February 27, 1840, from a part of Gloucester.

YEARS AND CENSUS.	Popula- tion	Increase (+), or Decrease (—), as Com- pared with Pre- vious Census
1840 (U. S.)	2,650	–
1850 (U. S.)	3,274	+ 624
1855 (State)	3,498	+ 224
1860 (U. S.)	3,237	— 261
1865 (State)	3,367	+ 130
1870 (U. S.)	3,904	+ 537
1875 (State)	4,480	+ 576
1880 (U. S.)	3,912	— 568
1885 (State)	3,888	— 24
1890 (U. S.)	4,087	+ 199
1895 (State)	5,289	+1,202

TOWN OF ROWLEY.

Established September 4, 1639, from "Mr. Ezechi Rogers plantation." Part established as Bradford in 1675, and another part as Boxford in 1694. Boundary line between Rowley and Bradford established February 24, 1701. Part of Ipswich annexed November 29, 1785. Part of Rowley annexed to Boxford June 10, 1808. Boundary line between Rowley and Boxford established June 18, 1825. Part of Rowley set off as the new town of Georgetown April 21, 1838.

1765 (Prov.)	1,477	–
1776 (Prov.)	1,678	+201
1790 (U. S.)	1,772	+ 94
1800 (U. S.)	1,557	—215
1810 (U. S.)	1,682	+125
1820 (U. S.)	1,825	+143
1830 (U. S.)	2,044	+219
1840 (U. S.)	1,203	—841
1850 (U. S.)	1,075	—128
1855 (State)	1,214	+139
1860 (U. S.)	1,278	+ 64
1865 (State)	1,191	— 87
1870 (U. S.)	1,157	— 34
1875 (State)	1,162	+ 5
1880 (U. S.)	1,201	+ 39
1885 (State)	1,183	— 18
1890 (U. S.)	1,248	+ 65
1895 (State)	1,272	+ 24

CITY OF SALEM.[*]

Common land, Nahumkeke. Nahumkeke men- tioned, 1628. Present name appears Aug. 23, 1639. Boundary lines between Salem and Saugus (now Lynn) and Salem and Marble Harbor "to be" established March 4, 1635. That part of Salem called "Enon" set off as Wenham September 7, 1643. That part known as "Jeffreyes Creeke" set off as Manchester May 14, 1645. Part established as Marblehead May 2, 1649. Boundary lines between Salem and Topsfield estab- lished October 19, 1658, and May 29, 1664. That part called "Bass River" set off as Beverly October 14, 1668. Part of Salem included in the new town of Middleton June 20, 1728. Part of Salem established as the District of Danvers January 28, 1752. Part of Salem annexed to Beverly, September 11, 1753. Incorporated as a city March 23, 1836. Act of incor- poration accepted by the town April 4, 1836. Boun-

CENSUSES OF POPULATION — 1765-1895 — Continued.

CITY OF SALEM — concluded.

dary line between Salem and Danvers established March 17, 1840. Boundary line between Salem and South Danvers established and part of each place annexed to the other place April 30, 1856. Part of Salem annexed to Swampscott April 3, 1867. Part of Peabody annexed to Salem March 27, 1882.

YEARS AND CENSUS.	Population	Increase (+), or Decrease (—), as Compared with Previous Census.
1765 (Prov.)	4,427	-
1776 (Prov.)	5,337	+ 910
1790 (U. S.)	7,921	+2,584
1800 (U. S.)	9,457	+1,536
1810 (U. S.)	12,613	+3,156
1820 (U. S.)	12,731	+ 118
1830 (U. S.)	13,895	+1,164
1840 (U. S.)	15,082	+1,187
1850 (U. S.)	20,264	+5,182
1855 (State)	20,934	+ 670
1860 (U. S.)	22,252	+1,318
1865 (State)	21,189	—1,063
1870 (U. S.)	24,117	+2,928
1875 (State)	25,958	+1,841
1880 (U. S.)	27,563	+1,605
1885 (State)	28,090	+ 527
1890 (U. S.)	30,801	+2,711
1895 (State)	34,473	+3,672

TOWN OF SALISBURY.

Established October 7, 1640, from common lands called "Colechester." Boundary line between Salisbury and "Pantucket, ali: Haverell" established June 2, 1641. Boundary line between Salisbury and Haverhill established November 1, 1654. Part of Salisbury set off as Amesbury May 27, 1668. Parts of Salisbury annexed to Amesbury March 15, 1844, and June 16, 1886. The latter Act took effect July 1, 1886.

1765 (Prov.)	1,329	-
1776 (Prov.)	1,666	+ 337
1790 (U. S.)	1,780	+ 114
1800 (U. S.)	1,855	+ 75
1810 (U. S.)	2,047	+ 192
1820 (U. S.)	2,006	— 41
1830 (U. S.)	2,519	+ 513
1840 (U. S.)	2,739	+ 220
1850 (U. S.)	3,100	+ 361
1855 (State)	3,185	+ 85
1860 (U. S.)	3,310	+ 125
1865 (State)	3,609	+ 299
1870 (U. S.)	3,776	+ 167
1875 (State)	4,078	+ 302
1880 (U. S.)	4,079	+ 1
1885 (State)	4,840	+ 761
1890 (U. S.)	1,316	—3,524
1895 (State)	1,300	— 16

TOWN OF SAUGUS.

Established February 17, 1815, from a part of Lynn. Part of Chelsea (Suffolk County) annexed February 22, 1841.

TOWN OF SAUGUS — concluded.

YEARS AND CENSUS.	Population	Increase (+), or Decrease (—), as Compared with Previous Census.
1820 (U. S.)	748	-
1830 (U. S.)	960	+212
1840 (U. S.)	1,098	+138
1850 (U. S.)	1,552	+454
1855 (State)	1,788	+236
1860 (U. S.)	2,024	+236
1865 (State)	2,006	— 18
1870 (U. S.)	2,247	+241
1875 (State)	2,578	+331
1880 (U. S.)	2,625	+ 47
1885 (State)	2,855	+230
1890 (U. S.)	3,673	+818
1895 (State)	4,497	+824

TOWN OF SWAMPSCOTT.

Established May 21, 1852, from a part of Lynn. Part of Salem annexed April 3, 1867.

1855 (State)	1,335	-
1860 (U. S.)	1,530	+195
1865 (State)	1,535	+ 5
1870 (U. S.)	1,846	+311
1875 (State)	2,128	+282
1880 (U. S.)	2,500	+372
1885 (State)	2,471	— 29
1890 (U. S.)	3,198	+727
1895 (State)	3,250	— 61

TOWN OF TOPSFIELD.

On October 18, 1648, that part of Ipswich called the "Village" at the New Meadows was named "Toppesfield." Established as a town October 18, 1650. Boundary lines between Topsfield and Salem established October 19, 1658, and May 29, 1664. Boundary line between Topsfield and Ipswich established February 28, 1694. Boundary line between Ipswich and Boxford established February 25, 1701. Part of Topsfield included in the new town of Middleton June 20, 1728.

1765 (Prov.)	719	-
1776 (Prov.)	773	+ 54
1790 (U. S.)	780	+ 7
1800 (U. S.)	789	+ 9
1810 (U. S.)	815	+ 26
1820 (U. S.)	866	+ 51
1830 (U. S.)	1,010	+144
1840 (U. S.)	1,059	+ 49
1850 (U. S.)	1,170	+111
1855 (State)	1,250	+ 80
1860 (U. S.)	1,292	+ 42
1865 (State)	1,212	— 80
1870 (U. S.)	1,213	+ 1
1875 (State)	1,221	+ 8
1880 (U. S.)	1,165	— 56
1885 (State)	1,141	— 24
1890 (U. S.)	1,022	—119
1895 (State)	1,033	+ 11

CENSUSES OF POPULATION — 1765-1895 — Continued.

TOWN OF WENHAM.

Established September 7, 1643, from that part of Salem called "Enon."

YEARS AND CENSUS.	Population	Increase (+), or Decrease (—), as Compared with Previous Census
1765 (Prov.)	564	-
1776 (Prov.)	638	+ 74
1790 (U. S.)	502	—136
1800 (U. S.)	476	— 26
1810 (U. S.)	554	+ 78
1820 (U. S.)	572	+ 18
1830 (U. S.)	611	+ 39
1840 (U. S.)	689	+ 78
1850 (U. S.)	977	+288
1855 (State)	1,073	+ 96
1860 (U. S.)	1,105	+ 32
1865 (State)	918	—187
1870 (U. S.)	985	+ 67
1875 (State)	911	— 74
1880 (U. S.)	889	— 22
1885 (State)	871	— 18
1890 (U. S.)	886	+ 15
1895 (State)	886	=

TOWN OF WEST NEWBURY.

Established February 18, 1819, as "Parsons" from a part of Newbury. Name changed to West Newbury June 14, 1820.

1820 (U. S.)	1,279	-
1830 (U. S.)	1,586	+307
1840 (U. S.)	1,560	— 26
1850 (U. S.)	1,746	+186
1855 (State)	2,094	+348
1860 (U. S.)	2,202	+108
1865 (State)	2,087	—115
1870 (U. S.)	2,006	— 81
1875 (State)	2,021	+ 15
1880 (U. S.)	1,989	— 32
1885 (State)	1,899	— 90
1890 (U. S.)	1,796	—103
1895 (State)	1,643	—153

COUNTY OF FRANKLIN.

Incorporated June 24, 1811, from a part of Hampshire County; Act took effect December 2, 1811. The date of incorporation of this county is subsequent to the date of the earliest census in which population appears. This is due, probably, to the fact that the territory in question was well defined and recognized in census enumerations prior to the date of its formal incorporation as a county.

1765 (Prov.)	5,057	-
1776 (Prov.)	10,294	+ 5,237
1790 (U. S.)*	21,743	+11,449
1800 (U. S.)*	26,300	+ 4,557
1810 (U. S.)*	27,421	+ 1,121

COUNTY OF FRANKLIN — concluded.

YEARS AND CENSUS.	Population	Increase (+), or Decrease (—), as Compared with Previous Census
1820 (U. S.)*	29,418	+ 1,997
1830 (U. S.)*	29,630	+ 212
1840 (U. S.)	28,812	— 818
1850 (U. S.)	30,870	+ 2,058
1855 (State)	31,652	+ 782
1860 (U. S.)	31,434	— 218
1865 (State)	31,340	— 94
1870 (U. S.)	32,635	+ 1,295
1875 (State)	33,696	+ 1,061
1880 (U. S.)	36,001	+ 2,305
1885 (State)	37,449	+ 1,448
1890 (U. S.)	38,610	+ 1,161
1895 (State)	40,145	+ 1,535

TOWN OF ASHFIELD.

Established June 21, 1765, from the new plantation called "Huntstown."

1765 (Prov.)	[628]	-
1776 (Prov.)	628	=
1790 (U. S.)	1,459	+831
1800 (U. S.)	1,741	+282
1810 (U. S.)	1,809	+ 68
1820 (U. S.)	1,748	— 61
1830 (U. S.)	1,732	— 16
1840 (U. S.)	1,610	—122
1850 (U. S.)	1,394	—216
1855 (State)	1,342	— 52
1860 (U. S.)	1,302	— 40
1865 (State)	1,221	— 81
1870 (U. S.)	1,180	— 41
1875 (State)	1,190	+ 10
1880 (U. S.)	1,066	—124
1885 (State)	1,097	+ 31
1890 (U. S.)	1,025	— 72
1895 (State)	1,013	— 12

TOWN OF BERNARDSTON.

Established March 6, 1762, from the new plantation called "Falltown." Part annexed to Colrain December 2, 1779. Part established as the District of Leyden March 12, 1784. Part of Greenfield annexed April 14, 1888. Part of Leyden annexed by Act of May 7, 1886; Act accepted by the town June 7, 1886.

1765 (Prov.)	230	-
1776 (Prov.)	607	+377
1790 (U. S.)	691	+ 84
1800 (U. S.)	780	+ 89
1810 (U. S.)	811	+ 31
1820 (U. S.)	912	+101
1830 (U. S.)	918	+ 6
1840 (U. S.)	992	+ 74

* Includes population of plantation of Zoar (annexed to Charlemont and Rowe) as follows: 1790, 78; 1800, 215; 1810, 120; 1820, 150; 1830, 120.

CENSUSES OF POPULATION — 1765-1895 — Continued.

TOWN OF BERNARDSTON — concluded.

YEARS AND CENSUS.	Population	Increase (+), or Decrease (—), as Compared with Previous Census
1850 (U. S.)	937	— 55
1855 (State)	908	— 29
1860 (U. S.)	968	+ 60
1865 (State)	902	— 66
1870 (U. S.)	961	+ 59
1875 (State)	991	+ 30
1880 (U. S.)	934	— 57
1885 (State)	930	— 4
1890 (U. S.)	770	—160
1895 (State)	778	+ 8

TOWN OF BUCKLAND.

Established April 14, 1779, from the plantation called "No-town" and a part of Charlemont. Part of Conway annexed April 14, 1838.

YEARS AND CENSUS.	Population	Increase/Decrease
1790 (U. S.)	718	-
1800 (U. S.)	1,041	+323
1810 (U. S.)	1,097	+ 56
1820 (U. S.)	1,037	— 60
1830 (U. S.)	1,039	+ 2
1840 (U. S.)	1,084	+ 45
1850 (U. S.)	1,056	— 28
1855 (State)	1,614	+558
1860 (U. S.)	1,702	+ 88
1865 (State)	1,922	+220
1870 (U. S.)	1,946	+ 24
1875 (State)	1,921	— 25
1880 (U. S.)	1,739	—182
1885 (State)	1,760	+ 21
1890 (U. S.)	1,570	—190
1895 (State)	1,548	— 22

TOWN OF CHARLEMONT.

Established June 21, 1765, from the new plantation called "Charlemont." Part included in the new town of Buckland April 14, 1779. Part included in the new town of Heath February 14, 1785. Certain common lands lying between Charlemont and North River annexed March 19, 1793. Part of the common lands called "Zoar" annexed April 2, 1838, and the balance annexed to Rowe. The population of the plantation of Zoar was in 1790, 78; 1800, 215; 1810, 120; 1820, 150; and 1830, 129.

YEARS AND CENSUS.	Population	Increase/Decrease
1765 (Prov.)	[665]	-
1776 (Prov.)	[665]	=
1790 (U. S.)	665	=
1800 (U. S.)	875	+210
1810 (U. S.)	987	+112
1820 (U. S.)	1,081	+ 94
1830 (U. S.)	1,065	— 16
1840 (U. S.)	1,127	+ 62
1850 (U. S.)	1,173	+ 46
1855 (State)	1,113	— 60
1860 (U. S.)	1,075	— 38
1865 (State)	994	— 81

TOWN OF CHARLEMONT — concluded.

YEARS AND CENSUS.	Population	Increase (+), or Decrease (—), as Compared with Previous Census
1870 (U. S.)	1,005	+ 11
1875 (State)	1,029	+ 24
1880 (U. S.)	932	— 97
1885 (State)	958	+ 26
1890 (U. S.)	972	+ 14
1895 (State)	1,041	+ 69

TOWN OF COLRAIN.

Established June 30, 1761, from the new plantation called "Colrain." Part of Bernardston annexed December 2, 1779.

YEARS AND CENSUS.	Population	Increase/Decrease
1765 (Prov.)	297	-
1776 (Prov.)	566	+269
1790 (U. S.)	1,417	+851
1800 (U. S.)	2,014	+597
1810 (U. S.)	2,016	+ 2
1820 (U. S.)	1,961	— 55
1830 (U. S.)	1,877	— 84
1840 (U. S.)	1,971	+ 94
1850 (U. S.)	1,785	—186
1855 (State)	1,604	—181
1860 (U. S.)	1,798	+194
1865 (State)	1,726	— 72
1870 (U. S.)	1,742	+ 16
1875 (State)	1,699	— 43
1880 (U. S.)	1,777	+ 78
1885 (State)	1,605	—172
1890 (U. S.)	1,671	+ 66
1895 (State)	1,610	— 61

TOWN OF CONWAY.

Established as a district June 17, 1767, from a part of Deerfield. Made a town by Act of August 23, 1775. Part of Shelburne annexed February 19, 1781. Part of Conway annexed to Goshen (Hampshire County) February 9, 1785. Parts of Deerfield annexed to Conway June 17, 1791, and June 21, 1811. Boundary line between Conway and Whately and Conway and Deerfield established June 21, 1811. Part of Conway annexed to Buckland April 14, 1838.

YEARS AND CENSUS.	Population	Increase/Decrease
1776 (Prov.)	897	-
1790 (U. S.)	2,092	+1,195
1800 (U. S.)	2,013	— 79
1810 (U. S.)	1,784	— 229
1820 (U. S.)	1,705	— 79
1830 (U. S.)	1,563	— 142
1840 (U. S.)	1,409	— 154
1850 (U. S.)	1,831	+ 422
1855 (State)	1,784	— 47
1860 (U. S.)	1,689	— 95
1865 (State)	1,538	— 151
1870 (U. S.)	1,460	— 78
1875 (State)	1,452	— 8
1880 (U. S.)	1,760	+ 308
1885 (State)	1,573	— 187
1890 (U. S.)	1,451	— 122
1895 (State)	1,304	— 147

CENSUSES OF POPULATION — 1765-1895 — Continued.

TOWN OF DEERFIELD.

"Deerefeild" is mentioned October 22, 1677 (Mass. Records, Vol. V, p. 167). The encouraging of the rebuilding of the plantation of Deerfield provided for October -, 1678. Part of Deerfield established as the District of Greenfield June 9, 1753. Part established as the District of Conway June 17, 1767. Part established as the District of Shelburne June 21, 1768. Part of Deerfield annexed to Conway June 17, 1791. Part annexed to Whately March 5, 1810. Part annexed to Conway and boundary line established June 21, 1811.

YEARS AND CENSUS.	Population	Increase (+), or Decrease (—), as Compared with Previous Census
1765 (Prov.)	737	-
1776 (Prov.)	836	+ 99
1790 (U. S.)	1,330	+494
1800 (U. S.)	1,531	+201
1810 (U. S.)	1,570	+ 39
1820 (U. S.)	1,868	+298
1830 (U. S.)	2,003	+135
1840 (U. S.)	1,912	— 91
1850 (U. S.)	2,421	+509
1855 (State)	2,766	+345
1860 (U. S.)	3,073	+307
1865 (State)	3,038	— 35
1870 (U. S.)	3,632	+594
1875 (State)	3,414	—218
1880 (U. S.)	3,543	+129
1885 (State)	3,042	—501
1890 (U. S.)	2,910	—132
1895 (State)	3,007	+ 97

TOWN OF ERVING.

Established April 17, 1838, from the common lands called "Erving's Grant." Boundary line between Erving and Orange established February 27, 1841. Part of Northfield called "Hack's Grant," annexed February 10, 1869. The date of establishment of this town is subsequent to the date of the earliest census in which population appears. This is due, probably, to the fact that the territory in question was well defined and recognized in census enumerations prior to the date of its formal incorporation as a district or town.

1810 (U. S.)	160	-
1820 (U. S.)	331	+171
1830 (U. S.)	488	+157
1840 (U. S.)	309	—179
1850 (U. S.)	449	+140
1855 (State)	471	+ 22
1860 (U. S.)	527	+ 56
1865 (State)	576	+ 49
1870 (U. S.)	579	+ 3
1875 (State)	794	+215
1880 (U. S.)	872	+ 78
1885 (State)	873	+ 1
1890 (U. S.)	972	+ 99
1895 (State)	964	— 8

TOWN OF GILL.

Established September 28, 1793, from a part of Greenfield. Part of Northfield annexed February 28, 1795. The island called "Great Island" annexed after April 1, 1805, by Act of March 14, 1805.

TOWN OF GILL — concluded.

YEARS AND CENSUS.	Population	Increase (+), or Decrease (—), as Compared with Previous Census
1800 (U. S.)	700	-
1810 (U. S.)	762	+ 62
1820 (U. S.)	800	+ 38
1830 (U. S.)	864	+ 64
1840 (U. S.)	798	— 66
1850 (U. S.)	754	— 44
1855 (State)	732	— 22
1860 (U. S.)	683	— 49
1865 (State)	635	— 48
1870 (U. S.)	653	+ 18
1875 (State)	673	+ 20
1880 (U. S.)	733	+ 60
1885 (State)	860	+127
1890 (U. S.)	960	+100
1895 (State)	1,082	+122

TOWN OF GREENFIELD.

Established as a district June 9, 1753, from a part of Deerfield. Made a town by Act of August 23, 1775. Part set off as Gill September 28, 1793. Part annexed to Bernardston April 14, 1838.

1765 (Prov.)	368	-
1776 (Prov.)	735	+367
1790 (U. S.)	1,498	+763
1800 (U. S.)	1,254	—244
1810 (U. S.)	1,165	— 89
1820 (U. S.)	1,361	+196
1830 (U. S.)	1,540	+179
1840 (U. S.)	1,756	+216
1850 (U. S.)	2,580	+824
1855 (State)	2,945	+365
1860 (U. S.)	3,198	+253
1865 (State)	3,211	+ 13
1870 (U. S.)	3,589	+378
1875 (State)	3,540	— 49
1880 (U. S.)	3,903	+363
1885 (State)	4,869	+966
1890 (U. S.)	5,252	+383
1895 (State)	6,229	+977

TOWN OF HAWLEY.

Established February 6, 1792, from the plantation called "Number Seven." A certain part of the plantation Number Seven, accidentally omitted in the boundary description, annexed to Hawley March 9, 1795. Part of Hawley annexed to the District of Plainfield (Hampshire County) June 21, 1803. The date of establishment of this town is subsequent to the date of the earliest census in which population appears. This is due, probably, to the fact that the territory in question was well defined and recognized in census enumerations prior to the date of its formal incorporation as a district or town.

1776 (Prov.)	244	-
1790 (U. S.)	539	+295
1800 (U. S.)	878	+339
1810 (U. S.)	1,031	+153
1820 (U. S.)	1,089	+ 58

CENSUSES OF POPULATION — 1765-1895 — Continued.

TOWN OF HAWLEY — concluded.

YEARS AND CENSUS.	Popula-tion	Increase (+), or Decrease (—), as Compared with Previous Census
1830 (U. S.)	1,037	— 52
1840 (U. S.)	977	— 60
1850 (U. S.)	881	— 96
1855 (State)	774	—107
1860 (U. S.)	671	—103
1865 (State)	687	+ 16
1870 (U. S.)	672	— 15
1875 (State)	588	— 84
1880 (U. S.)	592	+ 4
1885 (State)	545	— 47
1890 (U. S.)	515	— 30
1895 (State)	468	— 47

TOWN OF HEATH.

Established February 14, 1785, from a part of Charlemont and common lands called "Green and Walker's Land."

1790 (U. S.)	379	-
1800 (U.S.)	604	+225
1810 (U. S.)	917	+313
1820 (U. S.)	1,122	+205
1830 (U. S.)	1,199	+ 77
1840 (U. S.)	895	—304
1850 (U. S.)	803	— 92
1855 (State)	741	— 62
1860 (U. S.)	661	— 80
1865 (State)	642	— 19
1870 (U. S.)	613	— 29
1875 (State)	545	— 68
1880 (U. S.)	560	+ 15
1885 (State)	568	+ 8
1890 (U. S.)	503	— 65
1895 (State)	476	— 27

TOWN OF LEVERETT.

Established March 5, 1774, from a part of Sunderland.

1776 (Prov.)	293	-
1790 (U. S.)	524	+231
1800 (U. S.)	711	+187
1810 (U. S.)	769	+ 58
1820 (U. S.)	857	+ 88
1830 (U. S.)	939	+ 82
1840 (U. S.)	875	— 64
1850 (U. S.)	948	+ 73
1855 (State)	982	+ 34
1860 (U. S.)	964	— 18
1865 (State)	914	— 50
1870 (U. S.)	877	— 37
1875 (State)	831	— 46
1880 (U. S.)	742	— 89
1885 (State)	779	+ 37
1890 (U. S.)	702	— 77
1895 (State)	744	+ 42

TOWN OF LEYDEN.

Established as a district March 12, 1784, from a part of Bernardston. Made a town February 22, 1809. Part annexed to Bernardston May 7, 1886; Act accepted by Bernardston June 7, 1886.

YEARS AND CENSUS.	Popula-tion	Increase (+), or Decrease (—), as Compared with Previous Census
1790 (U. S.)	989	-
1800 (U. S.)	1,095	+106
1810 (U. S.)	1,009	— 86
1820 (U. S.)	974	— 35
1830 (U. S.)	796	—178
1840 (U. S.)	632	—164
1850 (U. S.)	716	+ 84
1855 (State)	653	— 63
1860 (U. S.)	606	— 47
1865 (State)	592	— 14
1870 (U. S.)	518	— 74
1875 (State)	524	+ 6
1880 (U. S.)	507	— 17
1885 (State)	447	— 69
1890 (U. S.)	407	— 40
1895 (State)	363	— 44

TOWN OF MONROE.

Established February 21, 1822, from a part of Rowe and a gore of common lands lying north of Florida.

1830 (U. S.)	265	-
1840 (U. S.)	282	+ 17
1850 (U. S.)	254	— 28
1855 (State)	217	— 37
1860 (U. S.)	236	+ 19
1865 (State)	191	— 45
1870 (U. S.)	201	+ 10
1875 (State)	190	— 11
1880 (U. S.)	166	— 24
1885 (State)	176	+ 10
1890 (U. S.)	282	+106
1895 (State)	298	+ 16

TOWN OF MONTAGUE.

Established as a district January 25, 1754, from a part of Sunderland. Made a town by Act of August 23, 1775. Part annexed to Wendell February 28, 1803.

1765 (Prov.)	392	-
1776 (Prov.)	575	+ 183
1790 (U. S.)	906	+ 331
1800 (U. S.)	1,222	+ 316
1810 (U. S.)	934	— 288
1820 (U. S.)	1,074	+ 140
1830 (U. S.)	1,152	+ 78
1840 (U. S.)	1,255	+ 103
1850 (U. S.)	1,518	+ 263
1855 (State)	1,509	— 9
1860 (U. S.)	1,593	+ 84
1865 (State)	1,574	— 19
1870 (U. S.)	2,224	+ 650

CENSUSES OF POPULATION — 1765–1895 — Continued.

TOWN OF MONTAGUE — concluded.

YEARS AND CENSUS.	Population	Increase (+), or Decrease (—), as Compared with Previous Census
1875 (State)	3,380	+1,156
1880 (U. S.)	4,875	+1,495
1885 (State)	5,629	+ 754
1890 (U. S.)	6,296	+ 667
1895 (State)	6,058	— 238

TOWN OF NEW SALEM.

Established as a district June 15, 1753, from the township of New Salem and an additional grant of land made to said township. Made a town by Act of August 23, 1775. Part included in the new town of Prescott, (Hampshire County) January 28, 1822. Part of Shutesbury annexed February 20, 1824. Part annexed to Athol (Worcester County) February 5, 1830. Part called "Little Grant" annexed to Orange and a part to Athol March 16, 1837.

YEARS AND CENSUS.	Population	Increase/Decrease
1765 (Prov.)	375	–
1776 (Prov.)	940	+535
1790 (U. S.)	1,543	+633
1800 (U. S.)	1,949	+406
1810 (U. S.)	2,107	+158
1820 (U. S.)	2,146	+ 39
1830 (U. S.)	1,889	—257
1840 (U. S.)	1,305	—584
1850 (U. S.)	1,253	— 52
1855 (State)	1,221	— 32
1860 (U. S.)	957	—264
1865 (State)	1,116	+159
1870 (U. S.)	987	—129
1875 (State)	923	— 64
1880 (U. S.)	869	— 54
1885 (State)	832	— 37
1890 (U. S.)	856	+ 24
1895 (State)	869	+ 13

TOWN OF NORTHFIELD.

Established February 22, 1713, from the plantation called "Squakead." Two tracts of land lying south of Northfield annexed June 29, 1773. Part annexed to Gill February 28, 1795. Part called "Hack's Grant" annexed to Erving February 10, 1860.

YEARS AND CENSUS.	Population	Increase/Decrease
1765 (Prov.)	415	–
1776 (Prov.)	580	+165
1790 (U. S.)	868	+288
1800 (U. S.)	1,047	+179
1810 (U. S.)	1,218	+171
1820 (U. S.)	1,584	+366
1830 (U. S.)	1,757	+173
1840 (U. S.)	1,673	— 84
1850 (U. S.)	1,772	+ 99
1855 (State)	1,951	+179
1860 (U. S.)	1,712	—239
1865 (State)	1,660	— 52
1870 (U. S.)	1,720	+ 60
1875 (State)	1,641	— 79

TOWN OF NORTHFIELD — concluded.

YEARS AND CENSUS.	Population	Increase (+), or Decrease (—), as Compared with Previous Census
1880 (U. S.)	1,663	— 28
1885 (State)	1,705	+102
1890 (U. S.)	1,869	+164
1895 (State)	1,851	— 18

TOWN OF ORANGE.

Established as a district October 15, 1783, from parts of Warwick and certain common lands called "Erving-shire" (Franklin County), and parts of Athol and Royalston (Worcester County). Made a town February 24, 1810. Part annexed to Athol February 7, 1816. Part of the common lands called "Erving's Grant" annexed March 16, 1837. Part of New Salem called "Little Grant" annexed March 16, 1837. Boundary line between Orange and Erving established February 27, 1841.

YEARS AND CENSUS.	Population	Increase/Decrease
1790 (U. S.)	784	–
1800 (U. S.)	766	— 18
1810 (U. S.)	764	— 2
1820 (U. S.)	829	+ 65
1830 (U. S.)	880	+ 51
1840 (U. S.)	1,501	+621
1850 (U. S.)	1,701	+200
1855 (State)	1,753	+ 52
1860 (U. S.)	1,622	—131
1865 (State)	1,909	+287
1870 (U. S.)	2,091	+182
1875 (State)	2,497	+406
1880 (U. S.)	3,169	+672
1885 (State)	3,650	+481
1890 (U. S.)	4,568	+918
1895 (State)	5,361	+793

TOWN OF ROWE.

Established February 9, 1785, from the common lands called "Myrifield" and lands adjoining. Part of Rowe and certain common lands established as Monroe February 21, 1822. Part of the common lands called "Zoar" annexed April 2, 1878.

YEARS AND CENSUS.	Population	Increase/Decrease
1790 (U. S.)	443	–
1800 (U. S.)	575	+132
1810 (U. S.)	839	+264
1820 (U. S.)	851	+ 12
1830 (U. S.)	716	—135
1840 (U. S.)	703	— 13
1850 (U. S.)	659	— 44
1855 (State)	601	— 58
1860 (U. S.)	619	+ 18
1865 (State)	563	— 56
1870 (U. S.)	581	+ 18
1875 (State)	661	+ 80
1880 (U. S.)	502	—159
1885 (State)	582	+ 80
1890 (U. S.)	541	— 41
1895 (State)	498	— 43

CENSUSES OF POPULATION — 1765-1895 — Continued.

TOWN OF SHELBURNE.

Established as a district June 21, 1768, from a part of Deerfield Made a town by Act of August 23, 1775. Part annexed to Conway February 19, 1781. Certain common lands lying between Shelburne and North River annexed March 19, 1793.

YEARS AND CENSUS.	Popula-tion	Increase (+), or Decrease (—), as Compared with Previous Census
1776 (Prov.)	575	—
1790 (U. S.)	1,183	+608
1800 (U. S.)	1,079	—104
1810 (U. S.)	961	—118
1820 (U. S.)	1,022	+ 61
1830 (U. S.)	995	— 27
1840 (U. S.)	1,022	+ 27
1850 (U. S.)	1,239	+217
1855 (State)	1,401	+162
1860 (U. S.)	1,448	+ 47
1865 (State)	1,564	+116
1870 (U. S.)	1,582	+ 18
1875 (State)	1,590	+ 8
1880 (U. S.)	1,621	+ 31
1885 (State)	1,614	— 7
1890 (U. S.)	1,553	— 61
1895 (State)	1,560	+ 7

TOWN OF SHUTESBURY.

Established June 30, 1761, from the plantation called "Roadtown." Part included in the new town of Wendell May 8, 1781. Part annexed to New Salem February 20, 1824.

1765 (Prov.)	330	—
1776 (Prov.)	508	+208
1790 (U. S.)	674	+ 76
1800 (U. S.)	930	+256
1810 (U. S.)	939	+ 9
1820 (U. S.)	1,029	+ 90
1830 (U. S.)	986	— 43
1840 (U. S.)	987	+ 1
1850 (U. S.)	912	— 75
1855 (State)	939	+ 27
1860 (U. S.)	798	—141
1865 (State)	788	— 10
1870 (U. S.)	614	—174
1875 (State)	558	— 56
1880 (U. S.)	529	— 29
1885 (State)	485	— 44
1890 (U. S.)	453	— 32
1895 (State)	444	— 9

TOWN OF SUNDERLAND.

Established November 12, 1718, from common lands. Boundary line between Sunderland and Hadley (Hampshire County) established January 2, 1749. Part established as the District of Montague January 25, 1754. Part established as Leverett March 5, 1774.

1765 (Prov.)	[409]	—
1776 (Prov.)	409	=

TOWN OF SUNDERLAND — concluded.

YEARS AND CENSUS.	Popula-tion	Increase (+), or Decrease (—), as Compared with Previous Census
1790 (U. S.)	462	+ 53
1800 (U. S.)	537	+ 75
1810 (U. S.)	551	+ 14
1820 (U. S.)	597	+ 46
1830 (U. S.)	666	+ 69
1840 (U. S.)	719	+ 53
1850 (U. S.)	792	+ 73
1855 (State)	839	+ 47
1860 (U. S.)	839	=
1865 (State)	861	+22
1870 (U. S.)	832	— 29
1875 (State)	860	+ 28
1880 (U. S.)	755	—105
1885 (State)	700	— 55
1890 (U. S.)	663	— 37
1895 (State)	696	+ 33

TOWN OF WARWICK.

Established February 17, 1763, from the plantation called "Roxbury Canada" with sundry farms lying therein, and certain common lands. Part included in the new town of Orange October 15, 1783.

1765 (Prov.)	191	—
1776 (Prov.)	766	+575
1790 (U. S.)	1,246	+480
1800 (U. S.)	1,233	— 13
1810 (U. S.)	1,227	— 6
1820 (U. S.)	1,256	+ 29
1830 (U. S.)	1,150	—106
1840 (U. S.)	1,071	— 79
1850 (U. S.)	1,021	— 50
1855 (State)	1,002	— 19
1860 (U. S.)	932	— 70
1865 (State)	901	— 31
1870 (U. S.)	769	—132
1875 (State)	744	— 25
1880 (U. S.)	713	— 31
1885 (State)	662	— 51
1890 (U. S.)	565	— 97
1895 (State)	599	+ 34

TOWN OF WENDELL.

Established May 8, 1781, from a part of Shutesbury and a part of the common lands called "Ervingshire." Part of Montague and a gore of common lands annexed February 28, 1803.

1790 (U. S.)	519	—
1800 (U. S.)	737	+218
1810 (U. S.)	983	+246
1820 (U. S.)	958	— 25
1830 (U. S.)	874	— 84
1840 (U. S.)	875	+ 1
1850 (U. S.)	920	+ 45

CENSUSES OF POPULATION — 1765–1895 — Continued.

TOWN OF WENDELL — concluded.

YEARS AND CENSUS.	Population	Increase (+), or Decrease (−), as Compared with Previous Census
1855 (State)	738	−182
1860 (U. S.)	704	− 34
1865 (State)	603	−101
1870 (U. S.)	539	− 64
1875 (State)	503	− 36
1880 (U. S.)	465	− 38
1885 (State)	509	+ 44
1890 (U. S.)	505	− 4
1895 (State)	529	+ 24

TOWN OF WHATELY.

Established April 24, 1771, from a part of Hatfield (Hampshire County). Part of Deerfield annexed March 5, 1810. Boundary line between Whately and Conway established June 21, 1811. Boundary line between Whately and Williamsburg (Hampshire County) established February 2, 1849.

1776 (Prov.)	410	–
1790 (U. S.)	736	+326
1800 (U. S.)	773	+ 37
1810 (U. S.)	891	+118
1820 (U. S.)	1,076	+185
1830 (U. S.)	1,111	+ 35
1840 (U. S.)	1,072	− 39
1850 (U. S.)	1,101	+ 29
1855 (State)	1,052	− 49
1860 (U. S.)	1,057	+ 5
1865 (State)	1,012	− 45
1870 (U. S.)	1,068	+ 56
1875 (State)	958	−110
1880 (U. S.)	1,074	+116
1885 (State)	999	− 75
1890 (U. S.)	779	−220
1895 (State)	755	− 24

COUNTY OF HAMPDEN.

Incorporated February 25, 1812, from a part of Hampshire County; Act took effect August 1, 1812. The date of incorporation of this county is subsequent to the date of the earliest census in which population appears. This is due, probably, to the fact that the territory in question was well defined and recognized in census enumerations prior to the date of its formal incorporation as a county.

1765 (Prov.)	8,307	–
1776 (Prov.)	13,274	+ 4,967
1790 (U. S.)	19,193	+ 5,919
1800 (U. S.)	23,462	+ 4,269
1810 (U. S.)	24,421	+ 959
1820 (U. S.)	28,021	+ 3,600
1830 (U. S.)	31,639	+ 3,618
1840 (U. S.)	37,366	+ 5,727
1850 (U. S.)	51,283	+13,917
1855 (State)	54,849	+ 3,566
1860 (U. S.)	57,366	+ 2,517

COUNTY OF HAMPDEN — concluded.

YEARS AND CENSUS.	Population	Increase (+), or Decrease (−), as Compared with Previous Census
1865 (State)	64,570	+ 7,204
1870 (U. S.)	78,409	+13,839
1875 (State)	94,304	+15,895
1880 (U. S.)	104,142	+ 9,838
1885 (State)	116,764	+12,622
1890 (U. S.)	135,713	+18,949
1895 (State)	152,938	+17,225

TOWN OF AGAWAM.

Established May 17, 1855, from a part of West Springfield.

1855 (State)	1,543	–
1860 (U. S.)	1,698	+155
1865 (State)	1,664	− 34
1870 (U. S.)	2,001	+337
1875 (State)	2,248	+247
1880 (U. S.)	2,216	− 32
1885 (State)	2,357	+141
1890 (U. S.)	2,352	− 5
1895 (State)	2,408	+ 56

TOWN OF BLANDFORD.

Established April 10, 1741, from Suffield Equivalent lands, commonly called "Glasgow." Boundary line between Blandford and Russell and Blandford and Chester established February 22, 1803. Boundary line between Blandford and Chester established June 13, 1810. Part annexed to Norwich (now Huntington, Hampshire County) May 25, 1853.

1765 (Prov.)	406	–
1776 (Prov.)	772	+366
1790 (U. S.)	1,416	+644
1800 (U. S.)	1,778	+362
1810 (U. S.)	1,613	−165
1820 (U. S.)	1,515	− 98
1830 (U. S.)	1,590	+ 75
1840 (U. S.)	1,427	−163
1850 (U. S.)	1,418	− 9
1855 (State)	1,271	−147
1860 (U. S.)	1,256	− 15
1865 (State)	1,087	−169
1870 (U. S.)	1,026	− 61
1875 (State)	964	− 62
1880 (U. S.)	979	+ 15
1885 (State)	954	− 25
1890 (U. S.)	871	− 83
1895 (State)	849	− 22

TOWN OF BRIMFIELD.

First mentioned August 16, 1722, in a list of frontier towns. The town incorporated December 24, 1731; the Act of incorporation, which is lost, passed both Houses to be enacted on this date, and was signed by the Governor before February 2, 1732, when the Legislature was prorogued. Part included in the new town of Western (now Warren, Worcester County) January

CENSUSES OF POPULATION — 1765-1895 — Continued.

TOWN OF BRIMFIELD — concluded.

16, 1742. Part established as the District of Monson April 28, 1760. Part established as the District of South Brimfield September 18, 1762. Boundary lines definitely established February 7, 1763.

YEARS AND CENSUS.	Popula-tion	Increase (+), or Decrease (—), as Com-pared with Pre-vious Census
1765 (Prov.)	773	-
1776 (Prov.)	1,064	+291
1790 (U. S.)	1,211	+147
1800 (U. S.)	1,384	+173
1810 (U. S.)	1,325	— 59
1820 (U. S.)	1,612	+287
1830 (U. S.)	1,599	— 13
1840 (U. S.)	1,419	—180
1850 (U. S.)	1,420	+ 1
1855 (State)	1,343	— 77
1860 (U. S.)	1,363	+ 20
1865 (State)	1,316	— 47
1870 (U. S.)	1,288	— 28
1875 (State)	1,201	— 87
1880 (U. S.)	1,203	+ 2
1885 (State)	1,137	— 66
1890 (U. S.)	1,096	— 41
1895 (State)	962	—134

TOWN OF CHESTER.

Formerly called "Murrayfield," which, as a planta-tion, was established as a town October 31, 1765. On June 29, 1773, part of Murrayfield established as the Dis-trict of Norwich and on May 8, 1781, another part was annexed to Norwich. The name was changed from Murrayfield to Chester February 21, 1783. Part in-cluded in the new town of Middlefield (Hampshire County) March 12, 1783. Part annexed to Worthington (Hampshire County) June 21, 1799. Boundary lines be-tween Chester and Blandford established February 22, 1809, and June 13, 1810. Part annexed to Norwich May 25, 1853.

YEARS AND CENSUS.	Popula-tion	Increase
1765 (Prov.)	(495)	-
1776 (Prov.)	495	=
1790 (U. S.)	1,119	+714
1800 (U. S.)	1,542	+423
1810 (U. S.)	1,534	— 8
1820 (U. S.)	1,526	— 8
1830 (U. S.)	1,407	—119
1840 (U. S.)	1,632	+225
1850 (U. S.)	1,521	—111
1855 (State)	1,255	—266
1860 (U. S.)	1,314	+ 59
1865 (State)	1,266	— 48
1870 (U. S.)	1,253	— 13
1875 (State)	1,296	+43
1880 (U. S.)	1,473	+ 77
1885 (State)	1,318	—155
1890 (U. S.)	1,295	— 23
1895 (State)	1,429	+134

CITY OF CHICOPEE.

Established April 29, 1848, from part of Springfield. Incorporated as a city April 18, 1890. Act of incor-poration accepted by the town May 6, 1890.

CITY OF CHICOPEE — concluded.

YEARS AND CENSUS.	Popula-tion	Increase (+), or Decrease (—), as Com-pared with Pre-vious Census
1850 (U. S.)	8,291	-
1855 (State)	7,576	— 715
1860 (U. S.)	7,261	— 315
1865 (State)	7,577	+ 316
1870 (U. S.)	9,607	+2,030
1875 (State)	10,335	+ 728
1880 (U. S.)	11,286	+ 951
1885 (State)	11,516	+ 230
1890 (U. S.)	14,050	+2,534
1895 (State)	16,420	+2,370

TOWN OF EAST LONGMEADOW.

Established May 19, 1894, from part of Long-meadow; Act to take effect July 1, 1894.

YEARS AND CENSUS.	Popula-tion	Increase
1895 (State)	1,591	-

TOWN OF GRANVILLE.

Established as a district January 25, 1754, from the plantation of "Bedford." Made a town by Act of Au-gust 23, 1775. Part established as Tolland June 14, 1810.

YEARS AND CENSUS.	Popula-tion	Increase
1765 (Prov.)	682	-
1776 (Prov.)	1,126	+444
1790 (U. S.)	1,979	+853
1800 (U. S.)	2,309	+330
1810 (U. S.)	1,504	—805
1820 (U. S.)	1,643	+139
1830 (U. S.)	1,649	+ 6
1840 (U. S.)	1,414	—235
1850 (U. S.)	1,305	—109
1855 (State)	1,316	+ 11
1860 (U. S.)	1,385	+ 60
1865 (State)	1,367	— 18
1870 (U. S.)	1,293	— 74
1875 (State)	1,240	— 53
1880 (U. S.)	1,205	— 35
1885 (State)	1,193	— 12
1890 (U. S.)	1,061	—132
1895 (State)	1,005	— 56

TOWN OF HAMPDEN.

Established March 28, 1878, from part of Wilbra-ham.

YEARS AND CENSUS.	Popula-tion	Increase
1880 (U. S.)	958	-
1885 (State)	868	— 90
1890 (U. S.)	831	— 37
1895 (State)	743	— 88

TOWN OF HOLLAND.

Established as a district July 5, 1783, from the east parish of South Brimfield. Boundary line between the

CENSUSES OF POPULATION — 1765-1895 — Continued.

TOWN OF HOLLAND — concluded.

District of Holland and South Brimfield established February 8, 1796. Made a town by Chapter 15 of the Revised Statutes May 1, 1836.

YEARS AND CENSUS.	Popula-tion	Increase (+), or Decrease (—), as Com-pared with Pre-vious Census
1790 (U. S.)	428	-
1800 (U. S.)	445	+17
1810 (U. S.)	420	—25
1820 (U. S.)	453	+33
1830 (U. S.)	453	=
1840 (U. S.)	423	—30
1850 (U. S.)	449	+26
1855 (State)	392	—57
1860 (U. S.)	419	+27
1865 (State)	368	—51
1870 (U. S.)	344	—24
1875 (State)	334	—10
1880 (U. S.)	302	—32
1885 (State)	229	—73
1890 (U. S.)	201	—28
1895 (State)	199	— 2

CITY OF HOLYOKE.

Established March 14, 1850, from part of West Springfield. Incorporated as a city April 7, 1873. Act of incorporation accepted by the town May 29, 1873.

1850 (U. S.)	3,245	-
1855 (State)	4,639	+1,394
1860 (U. S.)	4,997	+ 358
1865 (State)	5,648	+ 651
1870 (U. S.)	10,733	+5,085
1875 (State)	16,260	+5,527
1880 (U. S.)	21,915	+5,655
1885 (State)	27,895	+5,980
1890 (U. S.)	35,637	+7,742
1895 (State)	40,322	+4,685

TOWN OF LONGMEADOW.

Established October 13, 1783, from that part of Springfield called "Longmeadow." Certain common lands called "The Gore" annexed November 16, 1787. Part annexed to Springfield June 2, 1890. Part of Longmeadow established as East Longmeadow by Act of May 19, 1894, to take effect July 1, 1894.

1790 (U. S.)	744	-
1800 (U. S.)	973	+ 229
1810 (U. S.)	1,036	+ 63
1820 (U. S.)	1,171	+ 135
1830 (U. S.)	1,257	+ 86
1840 (U. S.)	1,270	+ 13
1850 (U. S.)	1,252	— 18
1855 (State)	1,348	+ 96
1860 (U. S.)	1,376	+ 28
1865 (State)	1,480	+ 104
1870 (U. S.)	1,342	— 138

TOWN OF LONGMEADOW — concluded.

YEARS AND CENSUS.	Popula-tion	Increase (+), or Decrease (—), as Com-pared with Pre-vious Census
1875 (State)	1,467	+ 125
1880 (U. S.)	1,401	— 66
1885 (State)	1,677	+ 276
1890 (U. S.)	2,183	+ 506
1895 (State)	620	—1,563

TOWN OF LUDLOW.

Established February 28, 1774, from that part of Springfield called "Stony Hill." Made a town by Act of August 23, 1775. Boundary line between Ludlow and Springfield established June 5, 1830.

1776 (Prov.)	413	-
1790 (U. S.)	560	+147
1800 (U. S.)	650	+ 90
1810 (U. S.)	730	+ 80
1820 (U. S.)	1,246	+516
1830 (U. S.)	1,327	+ 81
1840 (U. S.)	1,268	— 59
1850 (U. S.)	1,186	— 82
1855 (State)	1,191	+ 5
1860 (U. S.)	1,174	— 17
1865 (State)	1,232	+ 58
1870 (U. S.)	1,136	— 96
1875 (State)	1,222	+ 86
1880 (U. S.)	1,526	+304
1885 (State)	1,649	+123
1890 (U. S.)	1,939	+290
1895 (State)	2,562	+623

TOWN OF MONSON.

Established April 25, 1760, from part of Brimfield as the District of Monson. Boundary lines definitely established February 7, 1765. Made a town by Act of August 23, 1775. Boundary line between Monson and Palmer established February 8, 1828.

1765 (Prov.)	389	-
1776 (Prov.)	813	+424
1790 (U. S.)	1,351	+518
1800 (U. S.)	1,655	+304
1810 (U. S.)	1,674	+ 39
1820 (U. S.)	2,126	+452
1830 (U. S.)	2,263	+137
1840 (U. S.)	2,151	—112
1850 (U. S.)	2,831	+680
1855 (State)	2,942	+111
1860 (U. S.)	3,164	+222
1865 (State)	3,272	+108
1870 (U. S.)	3,204	— 68
1875 (State)	3,733	+529
1880 (U. S.)	3,758	+ 25
1885 (State)	3,958	+200
1890 (U. S.)	3,650	—308
1895 (State)	3,746	+ 96

CENSUSES OF POPULATION — 1765-1895 — Continued.

TOWN OF MONTGOMERY.

Established November 28, 1780, from parts of Westfield (Hampden County) and Norwich and Southampton (Hampshire County). Part included in the new town of Russell February 25, 1792. Parts of Norwich and Southampton annexed March 6, 1792.

YEARS AND CENSUS.	Population	Increase (+), or Decrease (—), as Compared with Previous Census
1790 (U. S.)	449	-
1800 (U. S.)	560	+111
1810 (U. S.)	595	+ 35
1820 (U. S.)	604	+ 9
1830 (U. S.)	579	— 25
1840 (U. S.)	740	+161
1850 (U. S.)	393	—347
1855 (State)	413	+ 20
1860 (U. S.)	371	— 42
1865 (State)	353	— 18
1870 (U. S.)	318	— 35
1875 (State)	304	— 14
1880 (U. S.)	303	— 1
1885 (State)	278	— 25
1890 (U. S.)	266	— 12
1895 (State)	275	+ 9

TOWN OF PALMER.

Established as a district January 30, 1752, from the plantation called "The Elbows." Boundary lines definitely established February 7, 1763. Made a town by Act of August 23, 1775. Boundary line between Palmer and Monson established February 8, 1828. Part of Western (now Warren, Worcester County) annexed February 7, 1831.

1765 (Prov.)	508	-
1776 (Prov.)	727	+ 219
1790 (U. S.)	809	+ 82
1800 (U. S.)	1,039	+ 230
1810 (U. S.)	1,114	+ 75
1820 (U. S.)	1,197	+ 83
1830 (U. S.)	1,237	+ 40
1840 (U. S.)	2,139	+ 902
1850 (U. S.)	3,974	+1,835
1855 (State)	4,012	+ 38
1860 (U. S.)	4,082	+ 70
1865 (State)	3,080	—1,002
1870 (U. S.)	3,631	+ 551
1875 (State)	4,572	+ 941
1880 (U. S.)	5,504	+ 932
1885 (State)	5,923	+ 419
1890 (U. S.)	6,520	+ 597
1895 (State)	6,858	+ 338

TOWN OF RUSSELL.

Established February 25, 1792, from parts of Westfield and Montgomery. Boundary line between Blandford and Russell established February 22, 1809.

1800 (U. S.)	431	-
1810 (U. S.)	422	— 9

TOWN OF RUSSELL — concluded.

YEARS AND CENSUS.	Population	Increase (+), or Decrease (—), as Compared with Previous Census
1820 (U. S.)	491	+ 69
1830 (U. S.)	507	+ 16
1840 (U. S.)	955	+448
1850 (U. S.)	521	—434
1855 (State)	677	+156
1860 (U. S.)	605	— 72
1865 (State)	618	+ 13
1870 (U. S.)	635	+ 17
1875 (state)	643	+ 8
1880 (U. S.)	823	+180
1885 (State)	847	+ 24
1890 (U. S.)	870	+ 22
1895 (State)	846	— 23

TOWN OF SOUTHWICK.

Established as a district November 7, 1770, from part of Westfield. Made a town by Act of August 23, 1775. Part of Westfield annexed October 6, 1779. Boundary line between Southwick and Westfield established March 20, 1837.

1776 (Prov.)	[841]	-
1790 (U. S.)	841	=
1800 (U. S.)	867	+ 26
1810 (U. S.)	1,229	+362
1820 (U. S.)	1,255	+ 26
1830 (U. S.)	1,355	+100
1840 (U. S.)	1,214	—141
1850 (U. S.)	1,120	— 94
1855 (State)	1,130	+ 10
1860 (U. S.)	1,188	+ 58
1865 (State)	1,155	— 33
1870 (U. S.)	1,100	— 55
1875 (State)	1,114	+ 14
1880 (U. S.)	1,104	— 10
1885 (State)	982	—122
1890 (U. S.)	914	— 68
1895 (State)	961	+ 47

CITY OF SPRINGFIELD.

First mention June 2, 1641, in Mass. Records, Vol. I, p. 320, of a letter from the General Court to Mr. Pinchen and others of "Agawam now Springfeild." "Woronoko" to be a part of Springfield Nov. 11, 1647 (Mass. Records, Vol. II, p. 224). Certain common lands annexed March, - 1648. Part called "Woronoake" established as Westfield May 19, 1669. Boundary line between Springfield and Westfield established May 31, 1670. Boundary line established May 17, 1684. Boundary line between Springfield and Northampton (Hampshire County) established June 4, 1685. Part established as Wilbraham June 15, 1763. Part called "Stony Hill" established as the District of Ludlow February 28, 1774. Part established as Longmeadow October 13, 1783. Part annexed to Wilbraham June 11, 1799. Boundary line between Springfield and Ludlow established June 5, 1830. Part established as Chicopee April 29, 1848. Springfield incorporated as a city April 12, 1852. Act accepted by the town April 21, 1852. Part of Longmeadow annexed June 2, 1890.

CENSUSES OF POPULATION — 1765-1895 — Continued.

CITY OF SPRINGFIELD — concluded.

YEARS AND CENSUS.	Popula-tion	Increase (+), or Decrease (—), as Compared with Previous Census
1765 (Prov.)	2,755	-
1776 (Prov.)	1,974	— 781
1790 (U. S.)	1,574	— 400
1800 (U. S.)	2,312	+ 738
1810 (U. S.)	2,767	+ 455
1820 (U. S.)	3,914	+1,147
1830 (U. S.)	6,784	+2,870
1840 (U. S.)	10,985	+4,201
1850 (U. S.)	11,766	+ 781
1855 (State)	13,788	+2,022
1860 (U. S.)	15,199	+1,411
1865 (State)	22,035	+6,836
1870 (U. S.)	26,703	+4,668
1875 (State)	31,053	+4,350
1880 (U. S.)	33,340	+2,287
1885 (State)	37,575	+4,235
1890 (U. S.)	44,179	+6,604
1895 (State)	51,522	+7,343

TOWN OF TOLLAND.

Established June 14, 1810, from part of Granville. Boundary lines between Tolland and Sandisfield (Berkshire County) established May 4, 1853, and May 15, 1855.

YEARS AND CENSUS	Population	Increase/Decrease
1810 (U. S.)	798	-
1820 (U. S.)	692	—106
1830 (U. S.)	723	+ 31
1840 (U. S.)	627	— 96
1850 (U. S.)	594	— 33
1855 (State)	603	+ 9
1860 (U. S.)	596	— 7
1865 (State)	511	— 85
1870 (U. S.)	509	— 2
1875 (State)	452	— 57
1880 (U. S.)	452	=
1885 (State)	422	— 30
1890 (U. S.)	393	— 29
1895 (State)	309	— 84

TOWN OF WALES.

Formerly called "South Brimfield" having been established as a district September 18, 1762. On February 21, 1766, the district was divided into two parishes, the east and west, and by Act of August 23, 1775, was made a town. The east parish was established as the District of Holland July 5, 1783. Boundary line between South Brimfield and Holland established February 8, 1796. Name changed to Wales February 20, 1828.

YEARS AND CENSUS	Population	Increase/Decrease
1765 (Prov.)	574	-
1776 (Prov.)	850	+276
1790 (U. S.)	606	—244
1800 (U. S.)	774	+168
1810 (U. S.)	645	—129
1820 (U. S.)	683	+ 38
1830 (U. S.)	665	— 18

TOWN OF WALES — concluded.

YEARS AND CENSUS.	Population	Increase (+), or Decrease (—), as Compared with Previous Census
1840 (U. S.)	686	+ 21
1850 (U. S.)	711	+ 25
1855 (State)	713	+ 2
1860 (U. S.)	677	— 36
1865 (State)	696	+ 19
1870 (U. S.)	831	+135
1875 (State)	1,020	+189
1880 (U. S.)	1,030	+ 10
1885 (State)	853	—177
1890 (U. S.)	700	—153
1895 (State)	783	+ 83

TOWN OF WESTFIELD.

Established May 19, 1669, from part of Springfield called "Woronoake." Boundary line between Westfield and Springfield established May 31, 1670. A strip of common land divided between Westfield and Northampton (Hampshire County) June 4, 1701. Part established as the District of Southwick November 7, 1770. Part annexed to Southwick October 6, 1779. Part included in the new town of Montgomery November 28, 1780. Part included in the new town of Russell February 25, 1792. Part annexed to West Springfield March 3, 1802. Boundary line between Westfield and Southwick established March 20, 1837.

YEARS AND CENSUS	Population	Increase/Decrease
1765 (Prov.)	1,324	-
1776 (Prov.)	1,488	+ 164
1790 (U. S.)	2,204	+ 716
1800 (U. S.)	2,185	— 19
1810 (U. S.)	2,130	— 55
1820 (U. S.)	2,668	+ 538
1830 (U. S.)	2,940	+ 272
1840 (U. S.)	3,526	+ 586
1850 (U. S.)	4,180	+ 654
1855 (State)	4,575	+ 395
1860 (U. S.)	5,055	+ 480
1865 (State)	5,634	+ 579
1870 (U. S.)	6,519	+ 885
1875 (State)	8,431	+1,912
1880 (U. S.)	7,587	— 844
1885 (State)	8,961	+1,374
1890 (U. S.)	9,805	+ 844
1895 (State)	10,663	+ 858

TOWN OF WEST SPRINGFIELD.

Established February 23, 1774, from a part of Springfield. Part of Westfield annexed March 3, 1802. Part established as Holyoke March 14, 1850. Part established as Agawam May 17, 1855.

YEARS AND CENSUS	Population	Increase/Decrease
1776 (Prov.)	1,744	-
1790 (U. S.)	2,367	+ 623
1800 (U. S.)	2,835	+ 468
1810 (U. S.)	3,109	+ 274
1820 (U. S.)	3,246	+ 137
1830 (U. S.)	3,270	+ 24
1840 (U. S.)	3,626	+ 356

TOWN OF WEST SPRINGFIELD — concluded.

YEARS AND CENSUS.	Population.	Increase (+), or Decrease (—), as Compared with Previous Census.
1850 (U. S.)	2,979	— 647
1855 (State)	2,090	— 889
1860 (U. S.)	2,105	+ 15
1865 (State)	2,100	— 5
1870 (U. S.)	2,606	+ 506
1875 (State)	3,739	+1,133
1880 (U. S.)	4,149	+ 419
1885 (State)	4,448	+ 299
1890 (U. S.)	5,077	+ 629
1895 (State)	6,125	+1,048

TOWN OF WILBRAHAM.

Established June 15, 1763, from part of Springfield. Part of Springfield called "The Elbows" annexed June 11, 1799. Part of Wilbraham established as Hampden March 28, 1878.

1765 (Prov.)	494	-
1776 (Prov.)	1,057	+566
1790 (U. S.)	1,555	+498
1800 (U. S.)	1,743	+188
1810 (U. S.)	1,776	+ 33
1820 (U. S.)	1,979	+203
1830 (U. S.)	2,034	+ 55
1840 (U. S.)	1,864	—170
1850 (U. S.)	2,127	+263
1855 (State)	2,032	— 95
1860 (U. S.)	2,081	+ 49
1865 (State)	2,111	+ 30
1870 (U. S.)	2,350	+219
1875 (State)	2,576	+226
1880 (U. S.)	1,928	—948
1885 (State)	1,724	+ 96
1890 (U. S.)	1,814	+ 90
1895 (State)	1,740	— 74

COUNTY OF HAMPSHIRE.

Incorporated May 7, 1662. On April 21, 1761, the westerly part was set off and established as Berkshire County; June 24, 1811, the northerly part was erected into a new county by the name of Franklin; and February 25, 1812, the southerly portion of the remaining part was incorporated as the county of Hampden.

1765 (Prov.)	6,429	-
1776 (Prov.)	12,154	+5,725
1790 (U. S.)	18,823	+6,669
1800 (U. S.)	22,885	+4,062
1810 (U. S.)	24,553	+1,668
1820 (U. S.)	26,487	+1,934
1830 (U. S.)	30,254	+3,767
1840 (U. S.)	30,897	+ 643
1850 (U. S.)	35,732	+4,835
1855 (State)	35,485	— 247
1860 (U. S.)	37,823	+2,338
1865 (State)	39,269	+1,446
1870 (U. S.)	44,388	+5,119
1875 (State)	44,821	+ 433

COUNTY OF HAMPSHIRE — concluded.

YEARS AND CENSUS.	Population.	Increase (+), or Decrease (—), as compared with Previous Census.
1880 (U. S.)	47,232	+2,411
1885 (State)	48,472	+1,240
1890 (U. S.)	51,859	+3,387
1895 (State)	54,710	+2,851

TOWN OF AMHERST.

Established as a district February 13, 1759, from part of Hadley. Made a town by Act of August 23, 1775. Parts of Hadley annexed January 15, 1789, February 28, 1811, February 18, 1812, and February 17, 1814. Boundary line between Amherst and Hadley established and part of each town annexed to the other town March 1, 1815.

1765 (Prov.)	645	-
1776 (Prov.)	915	+270
1790 (U. S.)	1,233	+318
1800 (U. S.)	1,358	+125
1810 (U. S.)	1,469	—111
1820 (U. S.)	1,917	+448
1830 (U. S.)	2,631	+714
1840 (U. S.)	2,550	— 81
1850 (U. S.)	3,057	+507
1855 (State)	2,937	—120
1860 (U. S.)	3,206	+269
1865 (State)	3,415	+209
1870 (U. S.)	4,035	+620
1875 (State)	3,937	— 98
1880 (U. S.)	4,298	+361
1885 (State)	4,199	— 99
1890 (U. S.)	4,512	+313
1895 (State)	4,785	+273

TOWN OF BELCHERTOWN.

Established as "Belcher's Town" June 30, 1761, from the plantation called "Cold Spring." Part annexed to Greenwich June 22, 1771. Part annexed to Pelham June 16, 1788. Part included in the new town of Enfield February 15, 1817.

1765 (Prov.)	418	-
1776 (Prov.)	972	+554
1790 (U. S.)	1,485	+513
1800 (U. S.)	1,878	+393
1810 (U. S.)	2,270	+392
1820 (U. S.)	2,426	+156
1830 (U. S.)	2,491	+ 65
1840 (U. S.)	2,554	+ 63
1850 (U. S.)	2,080	—126
1855 (State)	2,098	+ 18
1860 (U. S.)	2,709	— 11
1865 (State)	2,636	— 73
1870 (U. S.)	2,428	—208
1875 (State)	2,315	—113
1880 (U. S.)	2,346	+ 31
1885 (State)	2,307	— 39
1890 (U. S.)	2,120	—187
1895 (State)	2,161	+ 41

CENSUSES OF POPULATION — 1765-1895 — Continued.

TOWN OF CHESTERFIELD.

Established June 11, 1762, from the new plantation called "New Hingham." Certain common lands annexed January 31, 1763. Part of Chesterfield and the plantation called Chesterfield Gore established as Goshen May 14, 1781. Part of Goshen annexed June 8, 1789. Part of Norwich annexed February 22, 1794. Boundary lines between Chesterfield and Williamsburg established June 24, 1795, and February 7, 1797. Boundary lines between Chesterfield, Goshen, and Williamsburg established February 16, 1810.

YEARS AND CENSUS.	Population.	Increase (+), or Decrease (—), as compared with Previous Census.
1765 (Prov.)	161	-
1776 (Prov.)	1,092	+931
1790 (U. S.)	1,183	+ 91
1800 (U. S.)	1,323	+140
1810 (U. S.)	1,408	+ 85
1820 (U. S.)	1,447	+ 39
1830 (U. S.)	1,416	- 31
1840 (U. S.)	1,132	-284
1850 (U. S.)	1,014	-118
1855 (State)	950	- 64
1860 (U. S.)	897	- 53
1865 (State)	801	- 96
1870 (U. S.)	811	+ 10
1875 (State)	746	- 65
1880 (U. S.)	769	+ 23
1885 (State)	698	- 71
1890 (U. S.)	608	- 90
1895 (State)	589	- 19

TOWN OF CUMMINGTON.

Established June 23, 1779, from part of the plantation called "Number Five." Part established as the District of Plainfield March 16, 1785. Certain common lands called "Murrayfield Grant" and "Minot's Grant," and a gore of 2,200 acres annexed March 21, 1788. Part annexed to Plainfield February 4, 1794.

1790 (U. S.)	873	-
1800 (U. S.)	985	+112
1810 (U. S.)	1,009	+ 24
1820 (U. S.)	1,060	+ 51
1830 (U. S.)	1,261	+201
1840 (U. S.)	1,237	- 24
1850 (U. S.)	1,172	- 65
1855 (State)	1,004	-168
1860 (U. S.)	1,085	+ 81
1865 (State)	980	-105
1870 (U. S.)	1,037	+ 57
1875 (State)	916	-121
1880 (U. S.)	881	- 35
1885 (State)	805	- 76
1890 (U. S.)	787	- 18
1895 (State)	750	- 37

TOWN OF EASTHAMPTON.

Established as a district June 17, 1785, from parts of Northampton and Southampton. Made a town June 16, 1809. Boundary line between Easthampton and Southampton established February 1, 1828. Parts of Southampton annexed March 13, 1841, and April 4, 1850. Boundary line between Easthampton and South-

TOWN OF EASTHAMPTON — concluded.

ampton established February 21, 1862. Boundary line between Easthampton and Westhampton established March 12, 1872.

YEARS AND CENSUS.	Population.	Increase (+), or Decrease (—), as compared with Previous Census.
1790 (U. S.)	457	-
1800 (U. S.)	586	+129
1810 (U. S.)	660	+ 74
1820 (U. S.)	712	+ 52
1830 (U. S.)	745	+ 33
1840 (U. S.)	717	- 28
1850 (U. S.)	1,342	+625
1855 (State)	1,386	+ 44
1860 (U. S.)	1,916	+530
1865 (State)	2,869	+953
1870 (U. S.)	3,620	+751
1875 (State) . . . /.	3,972	+352
1880 (U. S.)	4,206	+234
1885 (State)	4,291	+ 85
1890 (U. S.)	4,395	+104
1895 (State)	4,790	+395

TOWN OF ENFIELD.

Established February 15, 1816, from all the lands in Belchertown and Greenwich which are comprised within the South Parish of Greenwich, together with the farm of Robert Hathaway in said Greenwich. Boundary line between Enfield and Greenfield established and part of each town annexed to the other town June 12, 1818.

1820 (U. S.)	873	-
1830 (U. S.)	1,056	+183
1840 (U. S.)	976	- 80
1850 (U. S.)	1,036	+ 60
1855 (State)	1,056	=
1860 (U. S.)	1,025	- 11
1865 (State)	997	- 28
1870 (U. S.)	1,023	+ 26
1875 (State)	1,065	+ 42
1880 (U. S.)	1,043	- 22
1885 (State)	1,010	- 33
1890 (U. S.)	952	- 58
1895 (State)	990	+ 38

TOWN OF GOSHEN.

Established May 14, 1781, from part of Chesterfield and the plantation called "Chesterfield Gore." Part of Conway (Franklin County) annexed February 9, 1785. Part annexed to Chesterfield June 8, 1789. Boundary lines between Goshen and Williamsburg established June 24, 1795, and February 7, 1797. Boundary lines between Goshen, Chesterfield, and Williamsburg established February 16, 1810.

1790 (U. S.)	681	-
1800 (U. S.)	724	+43
1810 (U. S.)	652	-72
1820 (U. S.)	632	-20
1830 (U. S.)	617	-15
1840 (U. S.)	556	-61
1850 (U. S.)	512	-44

CENSUSES OF POPULATION — 1765–1895 — Continued.

TOWN OF GOSHEN — concluded.

YEARS AND CENSUS.	Population	Increase (+), or Decrease (—), as Compared with Previous Census
1855 (State)	471	—41
1860 (U. S.)	439	—32
1865 (State)	411	—28
1870 (U. S.)	368	—43
1875 (State)	349	—19
1880 (U. S.)	327	—22
1885 (State)	336	+ 9
1890 (U. S.)	297	—39
1895 (State)	304	+ 7

TOWN OF GRANBY.

Established June 11, 1768, from part of South Hadley. Boundary line between Granby and South Hadley established June 28, 1781. Part of South Hadley annexed March 9, 1792. Boundary lines between Granby and South Hadley established June 12, 1824, June 20, 1826, and June 16, 1827.

1776 (Prov.)	491	-
1790 (U. S.)	596	+105
1800 (U. S.)	786	+190
1810 (U. S.)	850	+ 64
1820 (U. S.)	1,066	+216
1830 (U. S.)	1,064	— 2
1840 (U. S.)	971	— 93
1850 (U. S.)	1,104	+133
1855 (State)	1,001	—103
1860 (U. S.)	907	— 94
1865 (State)	908	+ 1
1870 (U. S.)	863	— 45
1875 (State)	812	— 51
1880 (U. S.)	753	— 59
1885 (State)	729	— 24
1890 (U. S.)	765	+ 36
1895 (State)	748	— 17

TOWN OF GREENWICH.

Established April 20, 1754, from the plantation called "Quabin." Part of Belchertown annexed June 22, 1771. Part included in the new town of Dana (Worcester County) February 18, 1801. Boundary line between Greenwich and Dana established June 19, 1811. Part included in the new town of Enfield February 15, 1816. Boundary line between Greenwich and Enfield established and part of each town annexed to the other town June 12, 1818.

1765 (Prov.)	434	
1776 (Prov.)	890	+456
1790 (U. S.)	1,045	+155
1800 (U. S.)	1,460	+415
1810 (U. S.)	1,225	—235
1820 (U. S.)	778	—447
1830 (U. S.)	813	+ 35
1840 (U. S.)	824	+ 11
1850 (U. S.)	838	+ 14
1855 (State)	803	— 35
1860 (U. S.)	699	—104
1865 (State)	648	— 51

TOWN OF GREENWICH — concluded.

YEARS AND CENSUS.	Population	Increase (+), or Decrease (—), as Compared with Previous Census
1870 (U. S.)	665	+ 17
1875 (State)	606	— 59
1880 (U. S.)	633	+ 27
1885 (State)	532	—101
1890 (U. S.)	526	— 6
1895 (State)	481	— 45

TOWN OF HADLEY.

Established May 22, 1661, from the new plantation near Northampton. Boundary lines established October 21, 1663. Certain common lands granted to Hadley May 15, 1664. Part established as Hatfield May 31, 1670. Certain common lands granted to Hadley May 7, 1673, and May 16, 1683. Boundary line between Hadley and Sunderland (Franklin County) established January 2, 1740. Part made the District of South Hadley April 12, 1753. Part made the District of Amherst February 13, 1759. Parts annexed to Amherst January 15, 1789, February 28, 1811, February 18, 1812, and February 17, 1814. Boundary line between Hadley and Amherst established and part of each town annexed to the other town March 1, 1815. Part annexed to Northampton April 15, 1850.

1765 (Prov.)	575	-
1776 (Prov.)	681	+106
1790 (U. S.)	882	+201
1800 (U. S.)	1,073	+191
1810 (U. S.)	1,247	+174
1820 (U. S.)	1,461	+214
1830 (U. S.)	1,686	+225
1840 (U. S.)	1,814	+128
1850 (U. S.)	1,986	+172
1855 (State)	1,928	— 58
1860 (U. S.)	2,105	+177
1865 (State)	2,246	+141
1870 (U. S.)	2,301	+ 55
1875 (State)	2,125	—176
1880 (U. S.)	1,938	—187
1885 (State)	1,747	—191
1890 (U. S.)	1,669	— 78
1895 (State)	1,704	+ 35

TOWN OF HATFIELD.

Established as "Hatfields" May 31, 1670, from part of Hadley. Boundary lines established October 9, 1672. Certain common lands annexed November 26, 1695. Part established as Whately (Franklin County) April 24, 1771. Part included in the District of Williamsburg April 24, 1771. Boundary line between Hatfield and Williamsburg established and part of each town annexed to the other town March 14, 1845, and March 19, 1846.

1765 (Prov.)	803	-
1776 (Prov.)	582	—221
1790 (U. S.)	703	+121
1800 (U. S.)	809	+106
1810 (U. S.)	805	— 4
1820 (U. S.)	823	+ 18
1830 (U. S.)	893	+ 70
1840 (U. S.)	933	+ 40
1850 (U. S.)	1,073	+140

CENSUSES OF POPULATION — 1765-1895 — Continued.

TOWN OF HATFIELD — concluded.

YEARS AND CENSUS.	Population.	Increase (+), or Decrease (—), as Compared with Previous Census.
1855 (State)	1,162	+ 89
1860 (U. S.)	1,337	+175
1865 (State)	1,405	+ 68
1870 (U. S.)	1,594	+189
1875 (State)	1,600	+ 6
1880 (U. S.)	1,495	—105
1885 (State)	1,367	—128
1890 (U. S.)	1,246	—121
1895 (State)	1,262	+ 16

TOWN OF HUNTINGTON.

Formerly called the "District of Norwich," being established June 29, 1773, from part of Murrayfield (now Chester, Hampden County). Made a town by Act of August 23, 1775. Part included in the new town of Montgomery (Hampden County) November 28, 1780. Part of Murrayfield annexed May 8, 1781. Part annexed to Montgomery March 6, 1792, and a part to Chesterfield February 22, 1794. Parts of Blandford and Chester (Hampden County) annexed May 25, 1853. Name changed to Huntington March 9, 1855.

YEARS AND CENSUS.	Population.	Increase / Decrease
1776 (Prov.)	[742]	-
1790 (U. S.)	742	=
1800 U. S.	959	+217
1810 U. S.	968	+ 9
1820 (U. S.)	849	—119
1830 (U. S.)	795	— 54
1840 U. S.	750	— 45
1850 (U. S.)	756	+ 6
1855 (State)	1,172	+416
1860 (U. S.)	1,216	+ 44
1865 (State)	1,163	— 53
1870 U. S.	1,156	— 7
1875 (State)	1,095	— 61
1880 (U. S.)	1,236	+141
1885 (State)	1,267	+ 31
1890 U. S.	1,385	+118
1895 (State)	1,450	+ 65

TOWN OF MIDDLEFIELD.

Established March 12, 1783, from parts of Becket, Partridgefield, and Washington, Berkshire County; Chester, Hampden County; and Worthington and the common lands called "Prescott's Grant."

YEARS AND CENSUS.	Population.	Increase / Decrease
1790 U. S.	608	-
1800 (U. S.)	877	+269
1810 (U. S.)	822	— 55
1820 (U. S.)	755	— 67
1830 (U. S.)	720	— 35
1840 U. S.	1,717	+997
1850 U. S.	797	—920
1855 (State)	677	— 60
1860 U. S.	748	+ 71
1865 (State)	727	— 21
1870 U. S.	728	+ 1
1875 (State)	603	—125

TOWN OF MIDDLEFIELD — concluded.

YEARS AND CENSUS.	Population.	Increase (+), or Decrease (—), as Compared with Previous Census.
1880 (U. S.)	648	— 45
1885 (State)	513	—135
1890 (U. S.)	455	— 58
1895 (State)	386	— 69

CITY OF NORTHAMPTON.

First mentioned May 14, 1656, on page 250, Vol. IV, Part 1, Mass. Records, "Forasmuch as the towns of Springfield and North Hampton are so remote," and the second mention is on page 271, same volume, "Northwottock, alias North Hampton." Boundary line between Northampton and Springfield (Hampden County) established June 4, 1685. A strip of common land divided between Northampton and Westfield (Hampden County) June 4, 1701. Part established as Southampton January 5, 1753. Part established as Westhampton September 29, 1778. Part annexed to Southampton September 29, 1778. Part included in the District of Easthampton June 17, 1785. Part of Hadley annexed April 15, 1850. Boundary line between Northampton and Westhampton established March 12, 1872. Northampton incorporated as a city June 23, 1883. Act of incorporation accepted by the town September 5, 1883.

YEARS AND CENSUS.	Population.	Increase / Decrease
1765 (Prov.)	1,285	-
1776 (Prov.)	1,790	— 505
1790 (U. S.)	1,628	— 162
1800 (U. S.)	2,190	+ 562
1810 (U. S.)	2,631	+ 441
1820 U. S.	2,854	+ 223
1830 U. S.	3,613	+ 759
1840 (U. S.)	3,750	+ 137
1850 U. S.	5,278	+1,528
1855 (State)	5,819	— 541
1860 (U. S.)	6,788	— 969
1865 (State)	7,925	+1,137
1870 (U. S.)	10,160	+2,235
1875 (State)	11,108	+ 948
1880 (U. S.)	12,172	+1,064
1885 (State)	12,896	+ 724
1890 (U. S.)	14,990	—2,694
1895 (State)	16,746	+1,756

TOWN OF PELHAM.

Established January 15, 1743, from common land called "New Lisburne." Part of Belchertown annexed June 16, 1788. Part included in the new town of Prescott January 28, 1822.

YEARS AND CENSUS.	Population.	Increase / Decrease
1765 (Prov.)	571	-
1776 (Prov.)	729	+558
1790 (U. S.)	1,040	—311
1800 U. S.	1,144	—104
1810 U. S.	1,185	+ 41
1820 U. S.	1,278	— 93
1830 U. S.	904	—374
1840 U. S.	956	+ 52
1850 U. S.	983	— 27
1855 (State)	789	—194
1860 U. S.	748	— 41

CENSUSES OF POPULATION — 1765-1895 — Continued.

TOWN OF PELHAM — concluded.

YEARS AND CENSUS.	Popula- tion	Increase (+), or Decrease (—), as Com- pared with Pre- vious Census
1865 (State)	737	— 11
1870 (U. S.)	673	— 64
1875 (State)	633	— 40
1880 (U. S.)	614	— 19
1885 (State)	549	— 65
1890 (U. S.)	486	— 63
1895 (State)	486	=

TOWN OF PLAINFIELD.

Established as a district March 16, 1785, from part of Cummington. Part of Cummington annexed to the District of Plainfield February 4, 1794. Part of Hawley (Franklin County) annexed June 21, 1803. Made a town June 15, 1807.

1790 (U. S.)	458	-
1800 (U. S.)	797	+339
1810 (U. S.)	977	+180
1820 (U. S.)	936	— 41
1830 (U. S.)	984	+ 48
1840 (U. S.)	910	— 74
1850 (U. S.)	814	— 96
1855 (State)	652	—162
1860 (U. S.)	639	— 13
1865 (State)	579	— 60
1870 (U. S.)	521	— 58
1875 (State)	481	— 40
1880 (U. S.)	457	— 24
1885 (State)	453	— 4
1890 (U. S.)	435	— 18
1895 (State)	450	+ 15

TOWN OF PRESCOTT.

There is considerable ambiguity about the early establishment of this town. In the Mass. Records, Vol. III, p. 392, on May 18, 1653, it is stated: "Consid- ering that there is already at Nashaway about 9 fami- lies . . . this Court doth hereby give and grant them liberties of a township and at the request of the in- habitants do order it to be called 'Prescott.'" This record is confusing in regard to Nashaway, which ap- pears to have been made Prescott, West Towne, and Lancaster by one Act (See Lancaster, Worcester County). Parts of New Salem (Franklin County) and Pelham established as Prescott January 28, 1822.

1820 (U. S.)	758	-
1840 (U. S.)	780	+22
1850 (U. S.)	737	—43
1855 (State)	643	—94
1860 (U. S.)	611	—32
1865 (State)	596	—15
1870 (U. S.)	541	—55
1875 (State)	493	—48
1880 (U. S.)	460	—33
1885 (State)	448	—12
1890 (U. S.)	376	—72
1895 (State)	401	+25

TOWN OF SOUTHAMPTON.

Established as a district January 5, 1753, from part of Northampton. Made a town by Act of August 23, 1775. Part of Northampton annexed September 29, 1778. Part included in the new town of Montgomery (Hampden County) November 28, 1780. Part included in the District of Easthampton June 17, 1785. Part an- nexed to Montgomery March 6, 1792. Boundary line between Southampton and Easthampton established February 1, 1828. Parts annexed to Easthampton March 13, 1841, and April 4, 1850. Boundary line between Southampton and Easthampton established February 21, 1862. Boundary line between South- ampton and Westhampton established March 12, 1872.

YEARS AND CENSUS.	Popula- tion	Increase (+), or Decrease (—), as Com- pared with Pre- vious Census
1765 (Prov.)	437	-
1776 (Prov.)	740	+303
1790 (U. S.)	829	+ 89
1800 (U. S.)	983	+154
1810 (U. S.)	1,171	+188
1820 (U. S.)	1,160	— 11
1830 (U. S.)	1,244	+ 84
1840 (U. S.)	1,157	— 87
1850 (U. S.)	1,060	— 97
1855 (State)	1,195	+135
1860 (U. S.)	1,130	— 65
1865 (State)	1,216	+ 86
1870 (U. S.)	1,159	— 57
1875 (State)	1,050	—109
1880 (U. S.)	1,046	— 4
1885 (State)	1,025	— 21
1890 (U. S.)	1,017	— 8
1895 (State)	1,054	+ 37

TOWN OF SOUTH HADLEY.

Established as a district April 12, 1753, from part of Hadley. Part established as Granby June 11, 1768. Made a town by Act of August 23, 1775. Boundary line between South Hadley and Granby established June 28, 1781. Part annexed to Granby March 9, 1792. Boundary lines between South Hadley and Granby established June 12, 1824, June 20, 1826, and June 16, 1827.

1765 (Prov.)	817	
1776 (Prov.)	584	— 233
1790 (U. S.)	759	+ 175
1800 (U. S.)	801	+ 42
1810 (U. S.)	902	+ 101
1820 (U. S.)	1,047	+ 145
1830 (U. S.)	1,185	+ 138
1840 (U. S.)	1,458	+ 273
1850 (U. S.)	2,495	+1,037
1855 (State)	2,051	— 444
1860 (U. S.)	2,277	+ 226
1865 (State)	2,099	— 178
1870 (U. S.)	2,840	+ 741
1875 (State)	3,370	+ 530
1880 (U. S.)	3,538	+ 168
1885 (State)	3,949	+ 411
1890 (U. S.)	4,261	+ 312
1895 (State)	4,443	+ 182

CENSUSES OF POPULATION — 1765–1895 — Continued.

TOWN OF WARE.

Established as a district November 25, 1761, from parts of Palmer (Hampden County), Brookfield and Western (Worcester County), and certain common lands all forming the so-called "Ware-River Parish." Made a town by Act of August 23, 1775. Parts of Brookfield and Western (now Warren) annexed February 8, 1823.

YEARS AND CENSUS.	Population	Increase (+), or Decrease (—), as Compared with Previous Census
1765 (Prov.)	485	–
1776 (Prov.)	[773]	+ 288
1790 (U. S.)	773	=
1800 (U. S.)	997	+ 224
1810 (U. S.)	996	— 1
1820 (U. S.)	1,154	+ 158
1830 (U. S.)	2,045	+ 891
1840 (U. S.)	1,890	— 155
1850 (U. S.)	3,785	+1,895
1855 (State)	3,498	— 287
1860 (U. S.)	3,597	+ 99
1865 (State)	3,374	— 223
1870 (U. S.)	4,259	+ 885
1875 (State)	4,142	— 117
1880 (U. S.)	4,817	+ 675
1885 (State)	6,003	+1,186
1890 (U. S.)	7,329	+1,326
1895 (State)	7,651	+ 322

TOWN OF WESTHAMPTON.

Established September 29, 1778, from part of Northampton. Boundary lines between Westhampton and Easthampton, Northampton, and Southampton established March 12, 1872.

YEARS AND CENSUS.	Population	Increase/Decrease
1790 (U. S.)	683	–
1800 (U. S.)	756	+ 73
1810 (U. S.)	793	+ 37
1820 (U. S.)	896	+103
1830 (U. S.)	918	+ 22
1840 (U. S.)	759	—159
1850 (U. S.)	602	—157
1855 (State)	670	+ 68
1860 (U. S.)	608	— 62
1865 (State)	636	+ 28
1870 (U. S.)	587	— 49
1875 (State)	556	— 31
1880 (U. S.)	563	+ 7
1885 (State)	541	— 22
1890 (U. S.)	477	— 64
1895 (State)	476	— 1

TOWN OF WILLIAMSBURG.

Established as a district April 24, 1771, from part of Hatfield and certain common lands adjoining. Made a town by Act of August 23, 1775. Boundary lines between Williamsburg and Chesterfield and Goshen established June 24, 1795, February 7, 1797, and February 16, 1819. Boundary line between Williamsburg and Hatfield established and part of each town annexed

TOWN OF WILLIAMSBURG — concluded.

to the other town March 14, 1845, and March 19, 1846. Boundary line between Williamsburg and Whately (Franklin County) established February 2, 1849.

YEARS AND CENSUS.	Population	Increase (+), or Decrease (—), as Compared with Previous Census
1776 (Prov.)	554	–
1790 (U. S.)	1,049	—515
1800 (U. S.)	1,176	+127
1810 (U. S.)	1,122	— 54
1820 (U. S.)	1,087	— 35
1830 (U. S.)	1,236	+149
1840 (U. S.)	1,509	+ 73
1850 (U. S.)	1,537	+228
1855 (State)	1,831	+294
1860 (U. S.)	2,095	+264
1865 (State)	1,976	—119
1870 (U. S.)	2,159	+183
1875 (State)	2,029	—130
1880 (U. S.)	2,234	+205
1885 (State)	2,044	—190
1890 (U. S.)	2,057	+ 13
1895 (State)	1,955	—102

TOWN OF WORTHINGTON.

Established June 30, 1768, from the new plantation called "Number Three." Part included in the new town of Middlefield March 12, 1783. Part of Chester (Hampden County) annexed June 21, 1799.

YEARS AND CENSUS.	Population	Increase/Decrease
1776 (Prov.)	639	–
1790 (U. S.)	1,116	+477
1800 (U. S.)	1,223	+107
1810 (U. S.)	1,391	+168
1820 (U. S.)	1,276	—115
1830 (U. S.)	1,179	— 97
1840 (U. S.)	1,197	+ 18
1850 (U. S.)	1,134	— 63
1855 (State)	1,112	— 22
1860 (U. S.)	1,041	— 71
1865 (State)	925	—116
1870 (U. S.)	860	— 65
1875 (State)	818	— 42
1880 (U. S.)	758	— 60
1885 (State)	763	+ 5
1890 (U. S.)	714	— 49
1895 (State)	648	— 66

COUNTY OF MIDDLESEX.

Incorporated May 10, 1643, from a part of Norfolk County (Mass. Records, Vol. II, p. 38).

1765 (Prov.)*	34,859	–
1776 (Prov.)*	40,321	+ 5,225
1790 (U. S.)*	42,737	+ 2,016
1800 (U. S.)*	46,928	+ 4,191
1810 (U. S.)*	52,789	+ 5,861
1820 (U. S.)*	61,472	+ 8,683

* Includes the population of Brighton and Charlestown (annexed to Boston) as follows: 1765, 2,061; 1776, 309; 1790, 1,583; 1800, 2,751; 1810, 5,567; 1820, 7,293; 1830, 9,755; 1840, 12,909; 1850, 19,572; 1855, 24,595; 1860, 28,440; 1865, 30,233; 1870, 33,290.

CENSUSES OF POPULATION — 1765-1895 — Continued.

COUNTY OF MIDDLESEX — concluded.

Years and Censuses	Population	Increase (+), or Decrease (—), as compared with Previous Census
1830 (U. S.)*	77,961	+16,489
1840 (U. S.)*	106,611	+28,650
1850 (U. S.)*	161,383	+54,772
1855 (State)*	194,023	—32,640
1860 (U. S.)*	216,354	+22,331
1865 (State)*	220,384	+ 4,030
1870 (U. S.)*	274,353	+53,969
1875 (State)	284,112	+ 9,759
1880 (U. S.)	317,830	+33,718
1885 (State)	357,311	+39,481
1890 (U. S.)	431,167	+73,856
1895 (State)	499,217	+68,050

TOWN OF ACTON.

Established July 3, 1735, from part of Concord called "The Village" or "New Grant," together with "Willard's Farms." Part included in the second District of Carlisle April 28, 1780.

Years and Censuses	Population	Increase/Decrease
1765 (Prov.)	611	-
1776 (Prov.)	769	+158
1790 (U. S.)	853	+ 84
1800 (U. S.)	901	+ 48
1810 (U. S.)	885	— 16
1820 (U. S.)	1,047	+162
1830 (U. S.)	1,128	+ 81
1840 (U. S.)	1,121	— 7
1850 (U. S.)	1,605	+484
1855 (State)	1,678	+ 73
1860 (U. S.)	1,726	+ 48
1865 (State)	1,660	— 66
1870 (U. S.)	1,593	— 67
1875 (State)	1,708	+115
1880 (U. S.)	1,797	+ 89
1885 (State)	1,785	— 12
1890 (U. S.)	1,897	+112
1895 (State)	1,978	+ 81

TOWN OF ARLINGTON.

Formerly called "West Cambridge" being established as such February 27, 1807, from a part of Cambridge. Part of Charlestown annexed February 25, 1842. Part included in the new town of Winchester April 30, 1850, and another part included in the new town of Belmont March 18, 1859. Boundary line between West Cambridge and Belmont established January 31, 1861. Boundary line between West Cambridge and Cambridge established and a part of each place annexed to the other place February 25, 1862. Name of West Cambridge changed to Arlington April 13, 1867; Act took effect April 30, 1867. By the Province Laws, Volume II, page 990, the plantation of Arlington in the county of Hampshire was established June 16, 1739, as the township of Winchester, but no Act has been found abolishing the town of Winchester.

Years and Censuses	Population	Increase/Decrease
1810 (U. S.)	971	-
1820 (U. S.)	1,064	+ 93
1830 (U. S.)	1,230	+166
1840 (U. S.)	1,363	+133
1850 (U. S.)	2,202	+839

TOWN OF ARLINGTON — concluded.

Years and Censuses	Population	Increase (+), or Decrease (—), as compared with Previous Census
1855 (State)	2,670	+468
1860 (U. S.)	2,681	+ 11
1865 (State)	2,760	+ 79
1870 (U. S.)	3,261	+501
1875 (State)	3,906	+645
1880 (U. S.)	4,100	+194
1885 (State)	4,673	+573
1890 (U. S.)	5,620	+956
1895 (State)	6,515	+886

TOWN OF ASHBY.

Established March 6, 1767, from parts of Townsend and Ashburnham and Fitchburg (Worcester County). Part of Ashburnham annexed November 16, 1792. Part of Fitchburg annexed March 3, 1829.

Years and Censuses	Population	Increase/Decrease
1776 (Prov.)	422	-
1790 (U. S.)	751	+329
1800 (U. S.)	941	+190
1810 (U. S.)	1,103	+162
1820 (U. S.)	1,188	+ 85
1830 (U. S.)	1,240	+ 52
1840 (U. S.)	1,246	+ 6
1850 (U. S.)	1,208	— 38
1855 (State)	1,176	— 32
1860 (U. S.)	1,091	— 85
1865 (State)	1,080	— 11
1870 (U. S.)	994	— 86
1875 (State)	962	— 32
1880 (U. S.)	914	— 48
1885 (State)	871	— 43
1890 (U. S.)	825	— 46
1895 (State)	804	— 21

TOWN OF ASHLAND.

Established March 16, 1846, from parts of Framingham, Holliston, and Hopkinton. Part to be annexed to Hopkinton when a certain sum is paid by Hopkinton April 28, 1853; three hundred dollars paid by Hopkinton and the Act took effect May 2, 1853.

Years and Censuses	Population	Increase/Decrease
1850 (U. S.)	1,304	-
1855 (State)	1,308	+ 4
1860 (U. S.)	1,554	+246
1865 (State)	1,702	+148
1870 (U. S.)	2,186	+484
1875 (State)	2,211	+ 25
1880 (U. S.)	2,394	+183
1885 (State)	2,693	+299
1890 (U. S.)	2,592	—101
1895 (State)	2,090	—442

TOWN OF AYER.

Established February 14, 1871, from parts of Groton and Shirley.

Years and Censuses	Population	Increase/Decrease
1875 (State)	1,872	-
1880 (U. S.)	1,881	+ 9
1885 (State)	2,190	+309

* See foot-note on page 174.

CENSUSES OF POPULATION — 1765-1895 — Continued.

TOWN OF AYER — concluded.

YEARS AND CENSUS.	Population	Increase (+), or Decrease (—), as Compared with Previous Census
1890 (U. S.)	2,148	— 42
1895 (State)	2,101	— 47

TOWN OF BEDFORD.

Established September 23, 1729, from parts of Billerica and Concord. Part of Billerica annexed February 26, 1767.

YEARS AND CENSUS.	Population	Increase (+), or Decrease (—)
1765 (Prov.)	457	-
1776 (Prov.)	482	+ 25
1790 (U. S.)	523	+ 41
1800 (U. S.)	538	+ 15
1810 (U. S.)	592	+ 54
1820 (U. S.)	648	+ 56
1830 (U. S.)	685	+ 37
1840 (U. S.)	929	+244
1850 (U. S.)	975	+ 46
1855 (State)	986	+ 11
1860 (U. S.)	843	—143
1865 (State)	820	— 23
1870 (U. S.)	849	+ 29
1875 (State)	900	+ 51
1880 (U. S.)	931	+ 31
1885 (State)	930	— 1
1890 (U. S.)	1,092	+162
1895 (State)	1,169	+ 77

TOWN OF BELMONT.

Established March 18, 1859, from parts of Waltham, Watertown, and West Cambridge. Boundary line between Belmont and West Cambridge established January 31, 1861. Boundary line between Belmont and Cambridge established and a part of each place annexed to the other place February 25, 1862. Part annexed to Cambridge April 19, 1880. Boundary line between Belmont and Cambridge readjusted and part of each place annexed to the other place April 28, 1891.

YEARS AND CENSUS.	Population	Increase/Decrease
1860 (U. S.)	1,198	-
1865 (State)	1,279	+ 81
1870 (U. S.)	1,513	+234
1875 (State)	1,937	+424
1880 (U. S.)	1,615	—322
1885 (State)	1,639	+ 24
1890 (U. S.)	2,098	+459
1895 (State)	2,843	+745

TOWN OF BILLERICA.

On May 29, 1655, by Mass. Records, Vol. IV, Part 1, p. 237, certain proprietors and inhabitants of Shawshine were granted a tract of land on Concord River, the name of the plantation to be "Billirikeyea." Eight thousand acres of common land granted to Billerica May 14, 1656. Certain lands granted to Billerica May 15, 1657. Boundary line between Billerica and Andover (Essex County) established May 26, 1658. Four thousand acres of land granted to Billerica June 7, 1661. Boundary line between Billerica and Woburn established October 10, 1666. Boundary lines between Billerica and Chelmsford and Concord established June 27, 1701. Part included in the new town of Bedford September 23, 1729. Part established as Tewks-

TOWN OF BILLERICA — concluded.

bury December 17, 1734. Part annexed to Bedford February 26, 1767. Part included in the second District of Carlisle April 28, 1780.

YEARS AND CENSUS.	Population	Increase (+), or Decrease (—), as Compared with Previous Census
1765 (Prov.)	1,334	-
1776 (Prov.)	1,500	+166
1790 (U. S.)	1,191	—309
1800 (U. S.)	1,383	+192
1810 (U. S.)	1,289	— 94
1820 (U. S.)	1,380	+ 91
1830 (U. S.)	1,374	— 6
1840 (U. S.)	1,632	+258
1850 (U. S.)	1,646	+ 14
1855 (State)	1,772	+126
1860 (U. S.)	1,776	+ 4
1865 (State)	1,808	+ 32
1870 (U. S.)	1,833	+ 25
1875 (State)	1,881	+ 48
1880 (U. S.)	2,000	+119
1885 (State)	2,161	+161
1890 (U. S.)	2,380	+219
1895 (State)	2,577	+197

TOWN OF BOXBOROUGH.

Established as a district February 25, 1783, from parts of Harvard (Worcester County), Littleton, and Stow. Boundary line between Boxborough and Littleton established February 29, 1794. Made a town by chapter 15 of the Revised Statutes May 1, 1836. Boundary line between Boxborough and Littleton established April 30, 1890.

YEARS AND CENSUS.	Population	Increase/Decrease
1790 (U. S.)	412	-
1800 (U. S.)	387	— 25
1810 (U. S.)	388	+ 1
1820 (U. S.)	424	+ 36
1830 (U. S.)	474	+ 50
1840 (U. S.)	426	— 48
1850 (U. S.)	395	— 31
1855 (State)	413	+ 18
1860 (U. S.)	403	— 10
1865 (State)	454	+ 51
1870 (U. S.)	338	—116
1875 (State)	318	— 20
1880 (U. S.)	319	+ 1
1885 (State)	348	+ 29
1890 (U. S.)	325	— 23
1895 (State)	307	— 18

TOWN OF BURLINGTON.

Established February 28, 1799, from part of Woburn. Part annexed to Lexington January 29, 1800.

YEARS AND CENSUS.	Population	Increase/Decrease
1800 (U. S.)	534	-
1810 (U. S.)	471	— 63
1820 (U. S.)	508	+ 27
1830 (U. S.)	446	— 62
1840 (U. S.)	510	+ 64
1850 (U. S.)	545	+ 35

CENSUSES OF POPULATION — 1765-1895 — Continued.

TOWN OF BURLINGTON — concluded.

YEARS AND CENSUS.	Population	Increase (+), or Decrease (−), as Compared with Previous Census
1855 (State)	564	+ 19
1860 (U. S.)	606	+ 42
1865 (State)	594	− 12
1870 (U. S.)	626	+ 32
1875 (State)	650	+ 24
1880 (U. S.)	711	+ 61
1885 (State)	604	−107
1890 (U. S.)	617	+ 13
1895 (State)	574	− 43

CITY OF CAMBRIDGE.

Originally called "Newtowne." First mentioned in Mass. Records, Vol. I, p. 90, "Charlton, Misticke and the newe town," July 26, 1631. The same volume on page 94, states that the "Bounds between Charles-Towne and Newe Towne" were established March 6, 1632. On page 129 under date of September 25, 1634, a part of New Towne to revert to Watertown "if Mr. Hooker and his congregation shall remove hence." Boundary line between Watertown and New Towne established April 7, 1635 (page 144). On September 8, 1636, on page 180, same volume, "Newe Town now called Cambridge," while in the same volume, page 228, "it is ordered that Newtowne shall henceforward be called Cambridge," this, on May 2, 1638. Boundary line between Cambridge and Watertown established March 13, 1639. Boundary line between Cambridge and Boston established October 7, 1641. One thousand acres of land granted to Cambridge November 12, 1659. The grant renewed October 19, 1664. The North Precinct in Cambridge established as Lexington March 20, 1713. Parts of Charlestown annexed April 18, 1761, and March 6, 1802. Part established as Brighton February 24, 1807. Part established as West Cambridge February 27, 1807. Parts of Charlestown annexed February 12, 1818, and June 17, 1820. Cambridge incorporated as a city March 17, 1846. Act of incorporation accepted by the town March 30, 1846. Part of Watertown annexed April 27, 1855. Boundary line between Cambridge and Somerville established and part of each place annexed to the other place April 30, 1856. Boundary lines established February 25, 1862, between Cambridge and Belmont and West Cambridge and parts of each town annexed to Cambridge and part of Cambridge annexed to Belmont and West Cambridge. Boundary line between Cambridge and Somerville established and part of each place annexed to the other place April 29, 1882. Part of Belmont annexed April 19, 1880. Part of Watertown annexed March 10, 1885. Boundary line between Cambridge and Belmont readjusted and part of each place annexed to the other place April 28, 1891.

1765 (Prov.)	1,571	-
1776 (Prov.)	1,586	+ 15
1790 (U. S.)	2,115	+ 529
1800 (U. S.)	2,453	+ 338
1810 (U. S.)	2,323	− 130
1820 (U. S.)	3,295	+ 972
1830 (U. S.)	6,072	+ 2,777
1840 (U. S.)	8,409	+ 2,337
1850 (U. S.)	15,215	+ 6,806
1855 (State)	20,473	+ 5,258
1860 (U. S.)	26,060	+ 5,587
1865 (State)	29,112	+ 3,052
1870 (U. S.)	39,634	+10,522
1875 (State)	47,838	+ 8,204
1880 (U. S.)	52,669	+ 4,831

CITY OF CAMBRIDGE — concluded.

YEARS AND CENSUS.	Population	Increase (+), or Decrease (−), as Compared with Previous Census
1885 (State)	59,658	+ 6,989
1890 (U. S.)	70,028	+10,370
1895 (State)	81,643	+11,615

TOWN OF CARLISLE.

The original, or first, District of Carlisle was established April 19, 1754, from a part of Concord, and on October 6, 1756, the district was annexed to Concord. The second District of Carlisle was formed from parts of Acton, Billerica, Chelmsford, and Concord, and incorporated April 28, 1780. Part of the District of Carlisle annexed to Concord September 12, 1780. Part of the District of Carlisle annexed to Chelmsford March 1, 1783. Made a town February 18, 1805. Part of Chelmsford annexed to Carlisle and boundary line established February 17, 1865.

1790 (U. S.)	555	
1800 (U. S.)	634	+ 79
1810 (U. S.)	672	+ 38
1820 (U. S.)	681	+ 9
1830 (U. S.)	566	−115
1840 (U. S.)	556	− 10
1850 (U. S.)	632	+ 76
1855 (State)	630	− 2
1860 (U. S.)	621	− 9
1865 (State)	642	+ 21
1870 (U. S.)	569	− 73
1875 (State)	548	− 21
1880 (U. S.)	478	− 70
1885 (State)	526	+ 48
1890 (U. S.)	481	− 45
1895 (State)	492	+ 11

TOWN OF CHELMSFORD.

A new plantation "the name thereof to be called Chelmsford" is mentioned May 29, 1655, in the Mass. Records, Vol. IV, Part 1, p. 237. Boundary line between Chelmsford and the Indian plantation at Patucket established May 31, 1660. Boundary line between Chelmsford and Billerica established June 27, 1701. "Wameset" annexed June 13, 1726. Part included in the second District of Carlisle April 28, 1780. Part of the second District of Carlisle annexed March 1, 1783. Part established as Lowell March 1, 1826. Part annexed to Carlisle and boundary line established February 17, 1865. Part annexed to Lowell May 18, 1874. Act accepted by Lowell June 23, 1874, taking effect August 1, 1874.

1765 (Prov.)	1,012	-
1776 (Prov.)	1,341	+329
1790 (U. S.)	1,144	−197
1800 (U. S.)	1,290	+146
1810 (U. S.)	1,396	+106
1820 (U. S.)	1,535	+139
1830 (U. S.)	1,387	−148
1840 (U. S.)	1,697	+310
1850 (U. S.)	2,097	+400
1855 (State)	2,140	+ 43
1860 (U. S.)	2,291	+151
1865 (State)	2,291	=

TOWN OF CHELMSFORD — concluded.

YEARS AND CENSUS.	Population	Increase (+), or Decrease (—), as Compared with Previous Census
1870 (U. S.)	2,374	+ 83
1875 (State)	2,372	— 2
1880 (U. S.)	2,553	+181
1885 (State)	2,304	—249
1890 (U. S.)	2,695	+391
1895 (State)	3,162	+467

TOWN OF CONCORD.

Established September 3, 1635, from a plantation at "Musketequid." Boundary lines between Concord, Dedham (Norfolk County), and Watertown established August 29, 1638. Boundary line between Concord and Billerica established June 27, 1701. Part included in the new town of Bedford September 23, 1729. Part included in the new town of Acton July 3, 1735. Part included in the new town of Lincoln April 19, 1754. Part made the first District of Carlisle April 19, 1754. The first District of Carlisle annexed October 6, 1756. Part included in the second District of Carlisle April 28, 1780. Part of the District of Carlisle annexed September 12, 1780.

1765 (Prov.)	1,564	-
1776 (Prov.)	1,927	+ 363
1790 (U. S.)	1,590	— 337
1800 (U. S.)	1,679	+ 89
1810 (U. S.)	1,633	— 46
1820 (U. S.)	1,788	+ 155
1830 (U. S.)	2,017	+ 229
1840 (U. S.)	1,784	— 233
1850 (U. S.)	2,249	+ 465
1855 (State)	2,244	— 5
1860 (U. S.)	2,246	+ 2
1865 (State)	2,232	— 14
1870 (U. S.)	2,412	+ 180
1875 (State)	2,676	+ 264
1880 (U. S.)	3,922	+1,246
1885 (State)	3,727	— 195
1890 (U. S.)	4,427	+ 700
1895 (State)	5,175	+ 748

TOWN OF DRACUT.

Established February 26, 1701, from common land. Parts annexed to Lowell February 28, 1851, and May 18, 1874, the latter annexation accepted by Lowell June 23, 1874, taking effect August 1, 1874. Part annexed to Lowell April 1, 1879.

1765 (Prov.)	[1,173]	-
1776 (Prov.)	1,173	=
1790 (U. S.)	1,217	+ 44
1800 (U. S.)	1,274	+ 57
1810 (U. S.)	1,301	+ 27
1820 (U. S.)	1,407	+ 106
1830 (U. S.)	1,615	+ 208
1840 (U. S.)	2,188	+ 573
1850 (U. S.)	3,503	+1,315
1855 (State)	1,966	—1,537
1860 (U. S.)	1,881	— 85
1865 (State)	1,905	+ 24

TOWN OF DRACUT — concluded.

YEARS AND CENSUS.	Population	Increase (+), or Decrease (—), as Compared with Previous Census
1870 (U. S.)	2,078	+ 173
1875 (State)	1,116	— 962
1880 (U. S.)	1,595	+ 479
1885 (State)	1,927	+ 332
1890 (U. S.)	1,996	+ 69
1895 (State)	2,443	+ 447

TOWN OF DUNSTABLE.

Certain men were empowered October 17, 1673, to begin a plantation beyond Chelmsford and Groton but no name was given to it. A marginal note in the Mass. Records, Vol. IV, Part 2, p. 570, says, "a plantation about Groaton, called Dunstable." On October 13, 1680, Dunstable is mentioned in a military list (Mass. Records, Vol. V, p. 295). Part established as Nottingham (N. H.) January 4, 1733. Part included in the new town of Litchfield (N. H.) July 4, 1735. Part established as the District of Tyngsborough June 22, 1789. Part annexed to the District of Tyngsborough March 3, 1792. Parts of Groton annexed February 25, 1793, January 26, 1796, and June 18, 1803. Boundary lines between Dunstable and Tyngsborough established January 29, 1798, and a part of Dunstable annexed to Tyngsborough. Boundary line between Dunstable and Tyngsborough established June 10, 1814. Boundary line between Dunstable and Groton established February 15, 1820.

1765 (Prov.)	559	-
1776 (Prov.)	679	+120
1790 (U. S.)	380	—299
1800 (U. S.)	485	+105
1810 (U. S.)	475	— 10
1820 (U. S.)	584	+109
1830 (U. S.)	593	+ 9
1840 (U. S.)	603	+ 10
1850 (U. S.)	590	— 13
1855 (State)	533	— 57
1860 (U. S.)	487	— 46
1865 (State)	533	+ 46
1870 (U. S.)	471	— 62
1875 (State)	452	— 19
1880 (U. S.)	453	+ 1
1885 (State)	431	— 22
1890 (U. S.)	416	— 15
1895 (State)	400	— 16

CITY OF EVERETT.

Established March 9, 1870, from part of Malden. Part annexed to Medford April 20, 1875. Incorporated as a city June 11, 1892. Act of incorporation accepted by the town July 19, 1892.

1870 (U. S.)	2,220	-
1875 (State)	3,651	+1,431
1880 (U. S.)	4,159	+ 508
1885 (State)	5,825	+1,666
1890 (U. S.)	11,068	+5,243
1895 (State)	18,573	+7,505

TOWN OF FRAMINGHAM.

Mentioned in the Tax Act October 13, 1675 (Mass. Records, Vol. V, p. 56). The plantation of Framing-

CENSUSES OF POPULATION — 1765-1895 — Continued.

TOWN OF FRAMINGHAM — concluded.

ham established as Framingham June 25, 1700. Certain common lands annexed July 5, 1700. Part of Sherborn annexed July 11, 1700. Boundary line between Framingham and Sudbury established June 13, 1701. Part annexed to Southborough (Worcester County) March 7, 1786. Part annexed to Marlborough February 23, 1791. Part of Holliston annexed February 11, 1833. Part included in the new town of Ashland March 16, 1846. Part of Natick annexed April 22, 1871.

Years and Census.	Population	Increase (+), or Decrease (—), as Compared with Previous Census.
1765 (Prov.)	1,305	—
1776 (Prov.)	1,574	+ 269
1790 (U. S.)	1,598	+ 24
1800 (U. S.)	1,625	+ 27
1810 (U. S.)	1,670	+ 45
1820 (U. S.)	2,037	+ 367
1830 (U. S.)	2,313	+ 276
1840 (U. S.)	3,030	+ 717
1850 (U. S.)	4,252	+1,222
1855 (State)	4,676	+ 424
1860 (U. S.)	4,227	— 449
1865 (State)	4,665	+ 438
1870 (U. S.)	4,968	+ 303
1875 (State)	5,167	+ 199
1880 (U. S.)	6,235	+1,068
1885 (State)	8,275	+2,040
1890 (U. S.)	9,239	+ 964
1895 (State)	9,512	+ 273

TOWN OF GROTON.

Established as "Groaten" May 29, 1655, from the plantation of "Petapawag." Part included in the new town of Harvard (Worcester County) June 29, 1732. Part established as the District of Shirley January 5, 1753. Part established as the District of Pepperell April 12, 1753. Parts annexed to Dunstable February 24, 1793, January 26, 1796, and June 18, 1803. Part annexed to Shirley February 6, 1798. Part of Pepperell annexed February 3, 1803. Boundary line between Groton and Dunstable established February 15, 1820. Part annexed to Pepperell May 18, 1857. Part included in the new town of Ayer February 14, 1871.

1765 (Prov.)	1,423	—
1776 (Prov.)	1,639	+ 216
1790 (U. S.)	1,840	+ 201
1800 (U. S.)	1,802	— 38
1810 (U. S.)	1,886	+ 84
1820 (U. S.)	1,897	+ 11
1830 (U. S.)	1,925	+ 28
1840 (U. S.)	2,139	+ 214
1850 (U. S.)	2,515	+ 376
1855 (State)	2,745	+ 230
1860 (U. S.)	3,193	+ 448
1865 (State)	3,176	— 17
1870 (U. S.)	3,584	+ 408
1875 (State)	1,908	—1,676
1880 (U. S.)	1,862	— 46
1885 (State)	1,987	+ 125
1890 (U. S.)	2,057	+ 70
1895 (State)	2,192	+ 135

TOWN OF HOLLISTON.

Established December 3, 1724, from part of Sherborn. Part of Hopkinton annexed April 28, 1781. Boundary line between Holliston and Medway (Norfolk County) established March 3, 1829, and a part of each town annexed to the other town. Part annexed to Framingham February 11, 1833. Part annexed to Milford (Worcester County) March 27, 1835, and boundary lines between Holliston, Hopkinton, and Milford established. Part included in the new town of Ashland March 16, 1846. Boundary line between Holliston and Milford established April 1, 1859.

Years and Census.	Population	Increase (+), or Decrease (—) as Compared with Previous Census.
1765 (Prov.)	705	—
1776 (Prov.)	909	+204
1790 (U. S.)	875	— 34
1800 (U. S.)	783	— 92
1810 (U. S.)	989	+206
1820 (U. S.)	1,042	+ 53
1830 (U. S.)	1,304	+262
1840 (U. S.)	1,782	+478
1850 (U. S.)	2,428	+646
1855 (State)	2,894	+466
1860 (U. S.)	3,339	+445
1865 (State)	3,125	—214
1870 (U. S.)	3,073	— 52
1875 (State)	3,399	+326
1880 (U. S.)	3,098	—301
1885 (State)	2,926	—172
1890 (U. S.)	2,619	—307
1895 (State)	2,718	+ 99

TOWN OF HOPKINTON.

Established December 13, 1715, from certain common lands and the plantation called "Moguncoy." Part included in the new town of Upton (Worcester County) June 14, 1735. Part annexed to Holliston April 28, 1781. Part annexed to Upton March 8, 1808. Part of Milford (Worcester County) annexed to Hopkinton, part of Hopkinton annexed to Milford, and boundary lines between Hopkinton, Holliston, and Milford established March 27, 1835. Part included in the new town of Ashland March 16, 1846. Part of Ashland annexed upon the payment of $300 by Hopkinton, May 2, 1853, in conformity with Act passed April 28, 1855.

1765 (Prov.)	1,027	—
1776 (Prov.)	1,134	+ 107
1790 (U. S.)	1,317	+ 183
1800 (U. S.)	1,372	+ 55
1810 (U. S.)	1,345	— 27
1820 (U. S.)	1,655	+ 310
1830 (U. S.)	1,809	+ 154
1840 (U. S.)	2,245	+ 436
1850 (U. S.)	2,801	+ 556
1855 (State)	3,934	+1,133
1860 (U. S.)	4,340	+ 406
1865 (State)	4,132	— 208
1870 (U. S.)	4,419	+ 287
1875 (State)	4,503	+ 84
1880 (U. S.)	4,601	+ 98
1885 (State)	3,922	— 679
1890 (U. S.)	4,088	+ 166
1895 (State)	2,984	—1,104

CENSUSES OF POPULATION — 1765-1895 — Continued.

TOWN OF HUDSON.

Established March 19, 1866, from parts of Marlborough and Stow. Part of Bolton (Worcester County) annexed March 20, 1868.

YEARS AND CENSUS.	Population	Increase (+), or Decrease (—), as Compared with Previous Census
1870 (U. S.)	3,389	-
1875 (State)	3,493	+104
1880 (U. S.)	3,739	+246
1885 (State)	3,968	+229
1890 (U. S.)	4,670	+702
1895 (State)	5,308	+638

TOWN OF LEXINGTON.

Established March 20, 1713, from the North Precinct in Cambridge. Part included in the new town of Lincoln April 19, 1754. Part of Burlington annexed January 29, 1800. Boundary line between Lexington and Lincoln established February 28, 1855. Boundary line between Lexington and Waltham located and defined April 4, 1895.

1765 (Prov.)	912	-
1776 (Prov.)	1,088	+176
1790 (U. S.)	941	—147
1800 (U. S.)	1,006	+ 65
1810 (U. S.)	1,052	+ 46
1820 (U. S.)	1,200	+148
1830 (U. S.)	1,543	+343
1840 (U. S.)	1,642	+ 99
1850 (U. S.)	1,893	+251
1855 (State)	2,549	+656
1860 (U. S.)	2,329	—220
1865 (State)	2,220	—109
1870 (U. S.)	2,277	+ 57
1875 (State)	2,505	+228
1880 (U. S.)	2,460	— 45
1885 (State)	2,718	+258
1890 (U. S.)	3,197	+479
1895 (State)	3,498	+301

TOWN OF LINCOLN.

Established April 19, 1754, from parts of Concord, Lexington, and Weston. Boundary line between Lincoln and Lexington established February 28, 1855.

1765 (Prov.)	649	-
1776 (Prov.)	775	+126
1790 (U. S.)	740	— 35
1800 (U. S.)	756	+ 16
1810 (U. S.)	713	— 43
1820 (U. S.)	706	— 7
1830 (U. S.)	709	+ 3
1840 (U. S.)	686	— 23
1850 (U. S.)	719	+ 33
1855 (State)	721	+ 2
1860 (U. S.)	718	— 3
1865 (State)	711	— 7
1870 (U. S.)	791	+ 80
1875 (State)	834	+ 43

TOWN OF LINCOLN — concluded.

YEARS AND CENSUS.	Population	Increase (+), or Decrease (—), as Compared with Previous Census
1880 (U. S.)	907	+ 73
1885 (State)	901	— 6
1890 (U. S.)	987	+ 86
1895 (State)	1,111	+124

TOWN OF LITTLETON.

By a Resolve dated December 3, 1715, the ownership of a grant made November 2, 1714, is corrected and it is "ordered that the name of the township be henceforth called Littleton." Part included in the District of Boxborough February 23, 1783. Boundary lines between Littleton and Boxborough established February 29, 1794, and April 30, 1890.

1765 (Prov.)	773	-
1776 (Prov.)	1,047	+274
1790 (U. S.)	854	—193
1800 (U. S.)	904	+ 50
1810 (U. S.)	773	—131
1820 (U. S.)	955	+182
1830 (U. S.)	947	— 8
1840 (U. S.)	927	— 20
1850 (U. S.)	987	+ 60
1855 (State)	985	— 2
1860 (U. S.)	1,063	+ 78
1865 (State)	967	— 96
1870 (U. S.)	983	+ 16
1875 (State)	950	— 33
1880 (U. S.)	994	+ 44
1885 (State)	1,067	+ 73
1890 (U. S.)	1,025	— 42
1895 (State)	1,136	+111

CITY OF LOWELL.

Established March 1, 1826, from part of Chelmsford. Part of Tewksbury annexed March 29, 1834. Incorporated as a city April 1, 1836. Act of incorporation accepted by the town April 11, 1836. Part of Dracut annexed February 28, 1851. Parts of Chelmsford and Dracut annexed May 18, 1874; Act accepted by Lowell June 23, 1874, taking effect August 1, 1874. Part of Tewksbury annexed June 5, 1874. Part of Dracut annexed April 1, 1879. Part of Tewksbury annexed May 17, 1888.

1830 (U. S.)	6,474	-
1840 (U. S.)	20,796	+14,322
1850 (U. S.)	33,383	+12,587
1855 (State)	37,554	+ 4,171
1860 (U. S.)	36,827	— 727
1865 (State)	30,990	— 5,837
1870 (U. S.)	40,928	+ 9,938
1875 (State)	49,688	+ 8,760
1880 (U. S.)	59,475	+ 9,787
1885 (State)	64,107	+ 4,632
1890 (U. S.)	77,696	+13,589
1895 (State)	84,367	+ 6,671

CENSUSES OF POPULATION — 1765-1895 — Continued.

CITY OF MALDEN.

On May 2, 1649, "Mistieke side men" granted to be a town to be called "Mauldon" (Mass. Records, Vol. II, p. 274). Part annexed to Medford June 10, 1817. Part established as Melrose May 3, 1850. Part established as Everett March 9, 1870. Part of Medford annexed April 20, 1877. Boundary line between Malden and Medford established February 20, 1878. Malden incorporated as a city March 31, 1881. Act of incorporation accepted by the town June 9, 1881.

YEARS AND CENSUS.	Popula-tion	Increase (+), or Decrease (−), as Compared with Previous Census
1765 (Prov.)	983	–
1776 (Prov.)	1,030	+ 47
1790 (U. S.)	1,033	+ 3
1800 (U. S.)	1,059	+ 26
1810 (U. S.)	1,384	+ 325
1820 (U. S.)	1,731	+ 347
1830 (U. S.)	2,010	+ 279
1840 (U. S.)	2,514	+ 504
1850 (U. S.)	3,520	+1,006
1855 (State)	4,592	+1,072
1860 (U. S.)	5,865	+1,273
1865 (State)	6,840	+ 975
1870 (U. S.)	7,367	+ 527
1875 (State)	10,843	+3,476
1880 (U. S.)	12,017	+1,174
1885 (State)	16,407	+4,390
1890 (U. S.)	23,031	+6,624
1895 (State)	29,708	+6,677

CITY OF MARLBOROUGH.

On May 31, 1660, the grant to the Whip sufferage planters confirmed, the name of the plantation to be "Marlborow" (Mass. Records, Vol. IV, Part 1, p. 424). Certain lands granted to Marlborough July 2, 1700. On November 16, 1716, the title of a tract of land called "Agaganquamasset" confirmed to Marlborough (Resolve). Part called "Chauncy" established as Westborough (Worcester County) November 18, 1717. Part established as Southborough (Worcester County) July 6, 1727. Part included in the District of Berlin (Worcester County) March 16, 1784. Part of Framingham annexed February 23, 1791. Part annexed to Northborough (Worcester County) and boundary line established June 20, 1807. Part annexed to Bolton (Worcester County) February 11, 1829. Boundary line between Marlborough and Bolton established March 16, 1858. Part of Southborough annexed March 24, 1843. Part included in the new town of Hudson March 19, 1866. Marlborough incorporated as a city May 23, 1890. Act of incorporation accepted by the town July 14, 1890.

1765 (Prov.)	1,287	–
1776 (Prov.)	1,554	+ 267
1790 (U. S.)	1,554	=
1800 (U. S.)	1,735	+ 181
1810 (U. S.)	1,674	− 61
1820 (U. S.)	1,952	+ 278
1830 (U. S.)	2,077	+ 125
1840 (U. S.)	2,101	+ 24
1850 (U. S.)	2,941	+ 840
1855 (State)	4,288	+1,347
1860 (U. S)	5,911	+1,623
1865 (State)	7,164	+1,253
1870 (U. S.)	8,474	+1,310

CITY OF MARLBOROUGH — concluded.

YEARS AND CENSUS.	Popula-tion	Increase (+), or Decrease (−), as Compared with Previous Census
1875 (State)	8,424	− 50
1880 (U. S.)	10,127	+1,703
1885 (State)	10,941	+ 814
1890 (U. S.)	13,805	+2,864
1895 (State)	14,977	+1,172

TOWN OF MAYNARD.

Established April 19, 1871, from parts of Sudbury and Stow.

1875 (State)	1,965	–
1880 (U. S.)	2,291	+326
1885 (State)	2,703	+412
1890 (U. S.)	2,700	− 3
1895 (State)	3,090	+390

CITY OF MEDFORD.

On September 28, 1630, "Meadford" is mentioned in a Tax Act (Mass. Records, Vol. I, p. 77). Part annexed to Charlestown June 21, 1811. Part of Malden annexed June 10, 1817. Part included in the new town of Winchester April 30, 1850. Part of Everett annexed April 20, 1875. Part annexed to Malden April 20, 1877. Boundary line between Medford and Malden established February 20, 1878. Medford incorporated as a city May 31, 1892. Act of incorporation accepted by the town October 6, 1892.

1765 (Prov.)	790	–
1776 (Prov.)	967	+ 177
1790 (U. S.)	1,029	+ 62
1800 (U. S.)	1,114	+ 85
1810 (U. S.)	1,443	+ 329
1820 (U. S.)	1,474	+ 31
1830 (U. S.)	1,755	+ 281
1840 (U. S.)	2,478	+ 723
1850 (U. S.)	3,749	+1,271
1855 (State)	4,603	+ 854
1860 (U. S.)	4,842	+ 239
1865 (State)	4,839	− 3
1870 (U. S.)	5,717	+ 878
1875 (State)	6,627	+ 910
1880 (U. S.)	7,573	+ 946
1885 (State)	9,042	+1,469
1890 (U. S.)	11,079	+2,037
1895 (State)	14,474	+3,395

TOWN OF MELROSE.

Established May 3, 1850, from part of Malden. Part of Stoneham annexed March 15, 1853. Boundary line between Melrose and Stoneham located and defined March 27, 1895.

1850 (U. S.)	1,260	–
1855 (State)	1,976	+ 716
1860 (U. S.)	2,532	+ 556
1865 (State)	2,865	+ 333
1870 (U. S.)	3,414	+ 549

CENSUSES OF POPULATION — 1765-1895 — Continued.

TOWN OF MELROSE — concluded.

YEARS AND CENSUS.	Population	Increase (+), or Decrease (—), as Compared with Previous Census
1875 (State)	3,990	+ 576
1880 (U. S.)	4,560	+ 570
1885 (State)	6,101	+1,541
1890 (U. S.)	8,519	+2,418
1895 (State)	11,965	+3,446

TOWN OF NATICK.

First mentioned in Mass. Records, Vol. V, p. 227, on April 16, 1679, relative to an exchange of land made between the plantation of Natick and Sherborn, said exchange being ratified by the General Court May 30, 1679. Boundary line between Natick and Dedham (Norfolk County) established October 18, 1701. In the Province Laws, Vol. III, p. 234, "the plantation of Natick, belonging to no particular town" is mentioned June 28, 1745. On February 28, 1762, the Parish of Natick is established as the District of Natick. On February 19, 1781, the District of Natick made the town of Natick, being an Act confirmatory of the general Act of August 23, 1775. Boundary line between Natick and Needham (Norfolk County) established and part of each town annexed to the other town June 22, 1797. Part of Sherborn annexed February 7, 1820. Boundary line between Natick and Wayland established April 26, 1850. Part annexed to Framingham April 22, 1871.

1765 (Prov.)	474	-
1776 (Prov.)	535	+ 61
1790 (U. S.)	615	+ 80
1800 (U. S.)	694	+ 79
1810 (U. S.)	766	+ 72
1820 (U. S.)	849	+ 83
1830 (U. S.)	890	+ 41
1840 (U. S.)	1,285	+ 395
1850 (U. S.)	2,744	+1,459
1855 (State)	4,138	+1,394
1860 (U. S.)	5,515	+1,377
1865 (State)	5,208	— 307
1870 (U. S.)	6,404	+1,196
1875 (State)	7,419	+1,015
1880 (U. S.)	8,479	+1,060
1885 (State)	8,460	— 19
1890 (U. S.)	9,118	+ 658
1895 (State)	8,814	— 304

CITY OF NEWTON.

As recorded in Mass. Archives, Vol. CXII, p. 421, December 15, 1691, the petition of the inhabitants of "Cambridge Village sometimes called Little Cambridge" for a name for their town was granted, the name to be Newton and the town's brandmark to be N. An island in Charles River annexed June 21, 1803. Part annexed to Roxbury April 23, 1838. Part annexed to Waltham April 16, 1849. Newton incorporated as a city June 2, 1873. Act of incorporation accepted by the town October 13, 1873. Boundary line between Newton and Boston established May 29, 1874. Part of Boston annexed May 5, 1875; Act accepted by Newton June 23, 1875, taking effect July 1, 1875.

1765 (Prov.)	1,308	-
1776 (Prov.)	1,625	+ 317

CITY OF NEWTON — concluded.

YEARS AND CENSUS.	Population	Increase (+), or Decrease (—), as Compared with Previous Census
1790 (U. S.)	1,360	— 265
1800 (U. S.)	1,491	+ 131
1810 (U. S.)	1,709	+ 218
1820 (U. S.)	1,850	+ 141
1830 (U. S.)	2,376	+ 526
1840 (U. S.)	3,351	+ 975
1850 (U. S.)	5,258	+1,907
1855 (State)	6,768	+1,510
1860 (U. S.)	8,382	+1,614
1865 (State)	8,975	+ 593
1870 (U. S.)	12,825	+3,850
1875 (State)	16,105	+3,280
1880 (U. S.)	16,995	+ 890
1885 (State)	19,759	+2,764
1890 (U. S.)	24,379	+4,620
1895 (State)	27,590	+3,211

TOWN OF NORTH READING.

Established March 22, 1853, from part of Reading. Boundary line between North Reading and Lynnfield (Essex County) established and part of each town annexed to the other town May 27, 1857, provided the Act is accepted by both towns; Act accepted by North Reading January 7, 1858, and by Lynnfield November 3, 1857.

1855 (State)	1,050	-
1860 (U. S.)	1,203	+153
1865 (State)	987	—216
1870 (U. S.)	942	— 45
1875 (State)	979	+ 37
1880 (U. S.)	900	— 79
1885 (State)	878	— 22
1890 (U. S.)	874	— 4
1895 (State)	835	— 39

TOWN OF PEPPERELL.

Established April 12, 1753, from the second precinct of Groton as the district of "Pepperell." Made a town by Act of August 23, 1775. Part annexed to Groton February 3, 1803. Part of Groton annexed May 18, 1857.

1765 (Prov.)	758	-
1776 (Prov.)	1,034	+276
1790 (U. S.)	1,132	+ 98
1800 (U. S.)	1,198	+ 66
1810 (U. S.)	1,333	+135
1820 (U. S.)	1,439	+106
1830 (U. S.)	1,440	+ 1
1840 (U. S.)	1,571	+131
1850 (U. S.)	1,754	+183
1855 (State)	1,765	+ 11
1860 (U. S.)	1,895	+130
1865 (State)	1,709	—186
1870 (U. S.)	1,842	+133
1875 (State)	1,927	+ 85
1880 (U. S.)	2,348	+421

CENSUSES OF POPULATION — 1765-1895 — Continued.

TOWN OF PEPPERELL — concluded.

YEARS AND CENSUS.	Population	Increase (+), or Decrease (—), as Compared with Previous Census
1885 (State)	2,587	+239
1890 (U. S.)	3,127	+540
1895 (State)	3,321	+194

TOWN OF READING.

Established May 29, 1644, "Linn Village shall be called Redding" (Mass. Records, Vol. II, p. 75). Boundary line between Reading and Woburn established May 29, 1644. Part included in the new town of Wilmington September 25, 1730. First or South Parish of Reading established as South Reading (now Wakefield) February 25, 1812. Part of South Reading annexed June 16, 1813. Part established as North Reading March 22, 1853. Boundary line between Reading and Lynnfield (Essex County) established April 16, 1854.

1765 (Prov.)	1,530	-
1776 (Prov.)	1,984	+454
1790 (U. S.)	1,802	—182
1800 (U. S.)	2,025	+223
1810 (U. S.)	2,228	+203
1820 (U. S.)	2,797	+569
1830 (U. S.)	1,806	—991
1840 (U. S.)	2,193	+387
1850 (U. S.)	3,108	+915
1855 (State)	2,522	—586
1860 (U. S.)	2,662	+140
1865 (State)	2,436	—226
1870 (U. S.)	2,664	+228
1875 (State)	3,186	+522
1880 (U. S.)	3,181	— 5
1885 (State)	3,539	+358
1890 (U. S.)	4,088	+549
1895 (State)	4,717	+629

TOWN OF SHERBORN.*

On October 7, 1674, more land was granted to the inhabitants and proprietors of the land at or near Boggestow, the place to be called "Sherborne" (Mass. Records, Vol. V, p. 23). Exchange of land made with the plantation of Natick April 16, 1679, said exchange being ratified by the General Court May 30, 1679. Grant of October 7, 1674, and the name Sherborne, then given, confirmed May 17, 1684. Part of "Sherburn" annexed to Framingham July 11, 1700. Part of "Sherburn" established as Holliston December 3, 1724. Boundary line between "Sherburne" and Medway (Norfolk County) established March 3, 1792. Part of "Sherburne" annexed to Natick February 7, 1820. The name of the town of "Sherburne" changed to Sherborn May 3, 1852.

1765 (Prov.)	670	-
1776 (Prov.)	699	+ 29
1790 (U. S.)	801	+102
1800 (U. S.)	775	— 26
1810 (U. S.)	770	— 5
1820 (U. S.)	811	+ 41
1830 (U. S.)	899	+ 88
1840 (U. S.)	995	+ 96
1850 (U. S.)	1,043	+ 48

TOWN OF SHERBORN — concluded.

YEARS AND CENSUS.	Population	Increase (+), or Decrease (—), as Compared with Previous Census
1855 (State)	1,071	+ 28
1860 (U. S.)	1,129	+ 58
1865 (State)	1,049	— 80
1870 (U. S.)	1,062	+ 13
1875 (State)	999	— 63
1880 (U. S.)	1,401	+402
1885 (State)	1,391	— 10
1890 (U. S.)	1,381	— 10
1895 (State)	1,446	+ 65

TOWN OF SHIRLEY.

Established as a district January 5, 1753, from part of Groton. Made a town by Act of August 23, 1775. Part of Groton annexed February 6, 1798. Boundary lines between Shirley and Lunenburg (Worcester County) established March 3, 1846, and April 25, 1848. Part included in the new town of Ayer February 14, 1871.

1765 (Prov.)	430	-
1776 (Prov.)	704	+274
1790 (U. S.)	677	— 27
1800 (U. S.)	713	+ 36
1810 (U. S.)	814	+101
1820 (U. S.)	922	+108
1830 (U. S.)	991	+ 69
1840 (U. S.)	957	— 34
1850 (U. S.)	1,158	+201
1855 (State)	1,479	+321
1860 (U. S.)	1,468	— 11
1865 (State)	1,217	—251
1870 (U. S.)	1,451	+234
1875 (State)	1,352	— 99
1880 (U. S.)	1,365	+ 13
1885 (State)	1,242	—123
1890 (U. S.)	1,191	— 51
1895 (State)	1,399	+208

CITY OF SOMERVILLE.

Established March 3, 1842, from part of Charlestown. Boundary lines between Somerville and Cambridge established and parts of each place annexed to the other place April 30, 1856, and April 29, 1862. Somerville incorporated as a city April 14, 1871. Act of incorporation accepted by the town April 27, 1871. Boundary line between Somerville and Boston established May 4, 1891.

1850 (U. S.)	3,540	-
1855 (State)	5,806	+ 2,266
1860 (U. S.)	8,025	+ 2,219
1865 (State)	9,353	+ 1,328
1870 (U. S.)	14,685	+ 5,332
1875 (State)	21,868	+ 7,183
1880 (U. S.)	24,933	+ 3,065
1885 (State)	29,971	+ 5,038
1890 (U. S.)	40,152	+10,181
1895 (State)	52,200	+12,048

* The spelling of the town name is given, in each instance, as found in the records.

CENSUSES OF POPULATION — 1765-1895 — Continued.

TOWN OF STONEHAM.

Established December 17, 1725, from part of Charlestown. Part annexed to Melrose March 15, 1853. Part annexed to South Reading (Wakefield) April 5, 1856. Part annexed to Wakefield March 13, 1889. Boundary line between Stoneham and Melrose located and defined March 27, 1895. Part of Woburn annexed April 20, 1895.

YEARS AND CENSUS.	Population	Increase (+), or Decrease (−), as Compared with Previous Census
1765 (Prov.)	340	-
1776 (Prov.)	319	− 21
1790 (U. S.)	381	+ 62
1800 (U. S.)	380	− 1
1810 (U. S.)	467	+ 87
1820 (U. S.)	615	+ 148
1830 (U. S.)	732	+ 117
1840 (U. S.)	1,017	+ 285
1850 (U. S.)	2,085	+1,068
1855 (State)	2,518	+ 433
1860 (U. S.)	3,206	+ 688
1865 (State)	3,298	+ 92
1870 (U. S.)	4,513	+1,215
1875 (State)	4,984	+ 471
1880 (U. S.)	4,890	− 94
1885 (State)	5,659	+ 769
1890 (U. S.)	6,155	+ 496
1895 (State)	6,284	+ 129

TOWN OF STOW.

Established May 16, 1683, from the plantation between Concord and Lancaster called "Pompositticut." Part included in the new town of Harvard (Worcester County) June 29, 1732. Part included in the new town of Boxborough February 25, 1783. Part included in the new town of Hudson March 19, 1866. Part included in the new town of Maynard April 19, 1871.

1765 (Prov.)	794	-
1776 (Prov.)	915	+121
1790 (U. S.)	891	−114
1800 (U. S.)	890	+ 89
1810 (U. S.)	885	− 5
1820 (U. S.)	1,071	+186
1830 (U. S.)	1,220	+149
1840 (U. S.)	1,230	+ 10
1850 (U. S.)	1,455	+225
1855 (State)	1,485	+ 30
1860 (U. S.)	1,641	+156
1865 (State)	1,537	−104
1870 (U. S.)	1,813	+276
1875 (State)	1,022	−791
1880 (U. S.)	1,945	+ 23
1885 (State)	976	− 69
1890 (U. S.)	903	− 73
1895 (State)	920	+ 17

TOWN OF SUDBURY.

Established September 4, 1639, from the new plantation by Concord. Boundary line between Sudbury and Watertown established April 10, 1651. Boundary line between Sudbury and Framingham established

TOWN OF SUDBURY — concluded.

June 13, 1701. Part established as East Sudbury (now Wayland) April 10, 1780. Part included in the new town of Maynard April 19, 1871.

YEARS AND CENSUS.	Population	Increase (+), or Decrease (−), as Compared with Previous Census
1765 (Prov.)	1,773	-
1776 (Prov.)	2,160	+387
1790 (U. S.)	1,290	−870
1800 (U. S.)	1,303	+ 13
1810 (U. S.)	1,287	− 16
1820 (U. S.)	1,417	+130
1830 (U. S.)	1,423	+ 6
1840 (U. S.)	1,422	− 1
1850 (U. S.)	1,578	+156
1855 (State)	1,673	+ 95
1860 (U. S.)	1,691	+ 18
1865 (State)	1,703	+ 12
1870 (U. S.)	2,091	+388
1875 (State)	1,177	−914
1880 (U. S.)	1,178	+ 1
1885 (State)	1,165	− 13
1890 (U. S.)	1,197	+ 32
1895 (State)	1,141	− 56

TOWN OF TEWKSBURY.

Established December 17, 1734, from a part of Billerica. Parts annexed to Lowell March 29, 1834, June 5, 1874, and May 17, 1888.

1765 (Prov.)	781	-
1776 (Prov.)	821	+ 40
1790 (U. S.)	958	+137
1800 (U. S.)	944	− 14
1810 (U. S.)	943	− 1
1820 (U. S.)	1,008	+ 65
1830 (U. S.)	1,527	+519
1840 (U. S.)	906	−621
1850 (U. S.)	1,044	+138
1855 (State)	1,716	+672
1860 (U. S.)	1,744	+ 28
1865 (State)	1,801	+ 57
1870 (U. S.)	1,944	+143
1875 (State)	1,997	+ 53
1880 (U. S.)	2,179	+182
1885 (State)	2,333	+154
1890 (U. S.)	2,515	+182
1895 (State)	3,379	+864

TOWN OF TOWNSEND.

Established June 29, 1732, from the north part of Turkey Hills. Part included in the new town of Ashby March 6, 1767.

1765 (Prov.)	598	-
1776 (Prov.)	794	+196
1790 (U. S.)	993	+199
1800 (U. S.)	1,149	+156
1810 (U. S.)	1,246	+ 97

CENSUSES OF POPULATION — 1765-1895 — Continued.

TOWN OF TOWNSEND — concluded.

YEARS AND CENSUS.	Population	Increase (+), or Decrease (—), as Compared with Previous Census
1820 (U. S.)	1,482	+236
1830 (U. S.)	1,506	+ 24
1840 (U. S.)	1,882	+386
1850 (U. S.)	1,947	+ 55
1855 (State)	2,092	+145
1860 (U. S.)	2,005	— 87
1865 (State)	2,042	+ 37
1870 (U. S.)	1,962	— 80
1875 (State)	2,196	+234
1880 (U. S.)	1,967	—229
1885 (State)	1,846	—121
1890 (U. S.)	1,750	— 96
1895 (State)	1,780	+ 30

TOWN OF TYNGSBOROUGH.

Established as a district June 22, 1789, from a part of Dunstable. Parts of Dunstable annexed March 3, 1792, and January 29, 1798, and boundary lines established. Made a town February 23, 1809. Boundary line between Tyngsborough and Dunstable established June 19, 1814.

YEARS AND CENSUS.	Population	Increase (+), etc.
1790 (U. S.)	582	-
1800 (U. S.)	696	+314
1810 (U. S.)	704	+ 8
1820 (U. S.)	808	+104
1830 (U. S.)	822	+ 14
1840 (U. S.)	870	+ 48
1850 (U. S.)	799	— 71
1855 (State)	714	— 85
1860 (U. S.)	626	— 88
1865 (State)	578	— 48
1870 (U. S.)	629	+ 51
1875 (State)	665	+ 36
1880 (U. S.)	631	— 34
1885 (State)	604	— 27
1890 (U. S.)	632	+ 58
1895 (State)	635	— 27

TOWN OF WAKEFIELD.

Formerly called South Reading, being established February 25, 1812, from a part of Reading. Part of South Reading annexed to Reading June 16, 1813. Part of Stoneham annexed to South Reading April 5, 1856. Name changed to Wakefield February 25, 1868, taking effect June 30, 1868. Part of Stoneham annexed March 13, 1889.

YEARS AND CENSUS.	Population	Increase (+), etc.
1830 (U. S.)	1,311	-
1840 (U. S.)	1,517	+ 206
1850 (U. S.)	2,407	+ 890
1855 (State)	2,758	+ 351
1860 (U. S)	3,207	+ 449
1865 (State)	3,244	+ 37
1870 (U. S.)	4,135	+ 891
1875 (State)	5,349	+1,214
1880 (U. S.)	5,547	+ 198
1885 (State)	6,060	+ 513
1890 (U. S.)	6,982	+ 922
1895 (State)	8,304	+1,322

CITY OF WALTHAM.

Established January 4, 1738, from part of Watertown. Part of Newton annexed April 16, 1849. Part included in the new town of Belmont March 18, 1859. Waltham incorporated as a city June 2, 1884. Act of incorporation accepted by the town July 16, 1884. Boundary line between Waltham and Lexington located and defined April 4, 1895.

YEARS AND CENSUS.	Population	Increase (+), or Decrease (—), as Compared with Previous Census
1765 (Prov.)	663	-
1776 (Prov.)	870	+ 207
1790 (U. S.)	882	+ 12
1800 (U. S.)	903	+ 21
1810 (U. S.)	1,014	+ 111
1820 (U. S.)	1,677	+ 663
1830 (U. S.)	1,857	+ 180
1840 (U. S.)	2,504	+ 647
1850 (U. S.)	4,464	+1,960
1855 (State)	6,049	+1,585
1860 (U. S.)	6,397	+ 348
1865 (State)	6,896	+ 499
1870 (U. S.)	9,065	+2,169
1875 (State)	9,967	+ 902
1880 (U. S.)	11,712	+1,745
1885 (State)	14,609	+2,897
1890 (U. S.)	18,707	+4,098
1895 (State)	20,876	+2,169

TOWN OF WATERTOWN.

Established September 7, 1630, "The town upon Charles River to be called Waterton." Part of New Towne to revert to Watertown "if Mr. Hooker and his congregation shall remove hence," September 25, 1634. Boundary line between Watertown and New Towne established April 7, 1635. Boundary lines between Watertown, Concord, and Dedham (Norfolk County) established August 20, 1638. Boundary line between Watertown and Cambridge established March 13, 1639. Boundary line between Watertown and Dedham established May 22, 1629. Boundary line between Watertown and Sudbury established April 10, 1651. Part established as Weston January 1, 1712. Part established as Waltham January 4, 1738. Part annexed to Cambridge April 27, 1855. Part included in the new town of Belmont March 18, 1859. Part annexed to Cambridge March 19, 1885.

YEARS AND CENSUS.	Population	Increase (+), etc.
1765 (Prov.)	693	-
1776 (Prov.)	1,057	+ 364
1790 (U. S.)	1,091	+ 34
1800 (U. S.)	1,207	+ 116
1810 (U. S.)	1,531	+ 324
1820 (U. S.)	1,518	— 13
1830 (U. S.)	1,641	+ 123
1840 (U. S.)	1,810	+ 169
1850 (U. S.)	2,837	+1,027
1855 (State)	3,578	+ 741
1860 (U. S.)	3,270	— 308
1865 (State)	3,779	+ 509
1870 (U. S.)	4,326	+ 547
1875 (State)	5,099	+ 773
1880 (U. S.)	5,426	+ 327
1885 (State)	6,238	+ 812
1890 (U. S.)	7,073	+ 835
1895 (State)	7,788	+ 715

CENSUSES OF POPULATION — 1765–1895 — Continued.

TOWN OF WAYLAND.

Originally established as East Sudbury April 10, 1780, from a part of Sudbury. Name changed to Wayland March 11, 1835. Boundary line between Wayland and Natick established April 26, 1850.

YEARS AND CENSUS.	Population	Increase (+), or Decrease (−), as Compared with Previous Census
1790 (U. S.)	801	–
1800 (U. S.)	835	+ 34
1810 (U. S.)	824	− 11
1820 (U. S.)	962	+138
1830 (U. S.)	944	− 18
1840 (U. S.)	998	+ 54
1850 (U. S.)	1,115	+117
1855 (State)	1,178	+ 63
1860 (U. S.)	1,188	+ 10
1865 (State)	1,137	− 51
1870 (U. S.)	1,240	+103
1875 (State)	1,766	+526
1880 (U. S.)	1,962	+196
1885 (State)	1,946	− 16
1890 (U. S.)	2,060	+114
1895 (State)	2,026	− 34

TOWN OF WESTFORD.

Established September 23, 1729, from part of Chelmsford, as "Wesford."

YEARS AND CENSUS.	Population	Increase (+), or Decrease (−)
1765 (Prov.)	962	–
1776 (Prov.)	1,193	+231
1790 (U. S.)	1,229	+ 36
1800 (U. S.)	1,267	+ 38
1810 (U. S.)	1,330	+ 63
1820 (U. S.)	1,409	+ 79
1830 (U. S.)	1,329	− 80
1840 (U. S.)	1,436	+107
1850 (U. S.)	1,473	+ 37
1855 (State)	1,586	+113
1860 (U. S.)	1,624	+ 38
1865 (State)	1,568	− 56
1870 (U. S.)	1,803	+235
1875 (State)	1,933	+130
1880 (U. S.)	2,147	+214
1885 (State)	2,193	+ 46
1890 (U. S.)	2,250	+ 57
1895 (State)	2,418	+168

TOWN OF WESTON.

Established January 1, 1712, from the West Precinct of Watertown. Part included in the new town of Lincoln April 19, 1754.

YEARS AND CENSUS.	Population	Increase (+), or Decrease (−)
1765 (Prov.)	768	–
1776 (Prov.)	1,027	+259
1790 (U. S.)	1,010	− 17
1800 (U. S.)	1,027	+ 17
1810 (U. S.)	1,008	− 19
1820 (U. S.)	1,041	+ 33

TOWN OF WESTON — concluded.

YEARS AND CENSUS.	Population	Increase (+), or Decrease (−), as Compared with Previous Census
1830 (U. S.)	1,091	+ 50
1840 (U. S.)	1,092	+ 1
1850 (U. S.)	1,205	+113
1855 (State)	1,205	=
1860 (U. S.)	1,243	+ 38
1865 (State)	1,231	− 12
1870 (U. S.)	1,261	+ 30
1875 (State)	1,282	+ 21
1880 (U. S.)	1,448	+166
1885 (State)	1,427	− 21
1890 (U. S.)	1,664	+237
1895 (State)	1,710	+ 46

TOWN OF WILMINGTON.

Established September 25, 1730, from parts of Reading and Woburn.

YEARS AND CENSUS.	Population	Increase (+), or Decrease (−)
1765 (Prov.)	673	–
1776 (Prov.)	737	+ 64
1790 (U. S.)	710	− 27
1800 (U. S.)	797	+ 87
1810 (U. S.)	716	− 81
1820 (U. S.)	786	+ 70
1830 (U. S.)	731	− 55
1840 (U. S.)	859	+128
1850 (U. S.)	874	+ 15
1855 (State)	958	+ 84
1860 (U. S.)	919	− 39
1865 (State)	850	− 69
1870 (U. S.)	866	+ 16
1875 (State)	879	+ 13
1880 (U. S.)	933	+ 54
1885 (State)	991	+ 58
1890 (U. S.)	1,213	+222
1895 (State)	1,420	+207

TOWN OF WINCHESTER.

Established April 30, 1850, from parts of Medford, West Cambridge, and Woburn. Part annexed to Woburn May 12, 1873. By the Province Laws, Vol. II, p. 990, the plantation of Arlington in the county of Hampshire was established as the township of Winchester (June 16, 1739), but no Act has been found abolishing the town of Winchester.

YEARS AND CENSUS.	Population	Increase (+), or Decrease (−)
1850 (U. S.)	1,353	–
1855 (State)	1,801	+448
1860 (U. S.)	1,937	+136
1865 (State)	1,968	+ 31
1870 (U. S.)	2,645	+677
1875 (State)	3,099	+454
1880 (U. S.)	3,802	+703
1885 (State)	4,390	+588
1890 (U. S.)	4,861	+471
1895 (State)	6,150	+1,289

CENSUSES OF POPULATION — 1765-1895 — Continued.

CITY OF WOBURN.

On September 27, 1642, "Charlestowne Village is called Wooborne" (Mass. Records, Vol. II, p. 28). Boundary line between Woburn and Reading established May 29, 1644. Two thousand acres of land granted to Woburn October 19, 1661. Boundary line between Woburn and Billerica established October 10, 1666. Part included in the new town of Wilmington September 25, 1730. Part established as Burlington February 28, 1799. Part included in the new town of Winchester April 30, 1850. Part of Winchester annexed May 12, 1873. Woburn incorporated as a city May 1, 1888. Act of incorporation accepted by the town May 29, 1888. Part annexed to Stoneham April 20, 1895.

YEARS AND CENSUS.	Population	Increase (+), or Decrease (—), as compared with Previous Census
1765 (Prov.)	1,515	-
1776 (Prov.)	1,691	+ 176
1790 (U. S.)	1,727	+ 36
1800 (U. S.)	1,228	— 499
1810 (U. S.)	1,219	— 9
1820 (U. S.)	1,519	+ 300
1830 (U. S.)	1,977	+ 458
1840 (U. S.)	2,993	+1,016
1850 (U. S.)	3,956	+ 963
1855 (State)	5,448	+1,492
1860 (U. S.)	6,287	+ 839
1865 (State)	6,999	+ 712
1870 (U. S.)	8,560	+1,561
1875 (State)	9,568	+1,008
1880 (U. S.)	10,931	+1,363
1885 (State)	11,750	+ 819
1890 (U. S.)	13,499	+1,749
1895 (State)	14,178	+ 679

COUNTY OF NANTUCKET.

Incorporated June 22, 1695. (Province Laws, Vol. I, p. 216.)

	Population	
1765 (Prov.)	3,320	-
1776 (Prov.)	4,412	+1,092
1790 (U. S.)	4,620	+ 208
1800 (U. S.)	5,617	+ 997
1810 (U. S.)	6,807	+1,190
1820 (U. S.)	7,266	+ 459
1830 (U. S.)	7,202	— 64
1840 (U. S.)	9,012	+1,810
1850 (U. S.)	8,452	— 560
1855 (State)	8,064	— 388
1860 (U. S.)	6,094	—1,970
1865 (State)	4,748	—1,346
1870 (U. S.)	4,123	— 625
1875 (State)	3,201	— 922
1880 (U. S.)	3,727	+ 526
1885 (State)	3,142	— 585
1890 (U. S.)	3,268	+ 126
1895 (State)	3,016	— 252

TOWN OF NANTUCKET.

The original name was "Nantuckett" but was changed by the State of New York, to which it

TOWN OF NANTUCKET — concluded.

belonged, June 27, 1687, "to be called by the Name of the Trustees of the ffreeholders & Comonalty of the Towne of Sharborn." The island was granted to the Province of Massachusetts Bay in 1692, and the name was changed from "Sherburn" to Nantucket June 8, 1795.

YEARS AND CENSUS.	Population	Increase (+), or Decrease (—), as compared with Previous Census
1765 (Prov.)	3,320	
1776 (Prov.)	4,412	+1,092
1790 (U. S.)	4,620	+ 208
1800 (U. S.)	5,617	+ 997
1810 (U. S.)	6,807	+1,190
1820 (U. S.)	7,266	+ 459
1830 (U. S.)	7,202	— 64
1840 (U. S.)	9,012	+1,810
1850 (U. S.)	8,452	— 560
1855 (State)	8,064	— 388
1860 (U. S.)	6,094	—1,970
1865 (State)	4,748	—1,346
1870 (U. S.)	4,123	— 625
1875 (State)	3,201	— 922
1880 (U. S.)	3,727	+ 526
1885 (State)	3,142	— 585
1890 (U. S.)	3,268	+ 126
1895 (State)	3,016	— 252

COUNTY OF NORFOLK.

On May 10, 1643, the Colony was divided into four counties: Essex, Middlesex, Suffolk, and Norfolk. The latter was composed of the towns of Haverhill, Salisbury, Hampton, Exeter, Dover, and Strawberry Bank (Portsmouth). The four last named towns having been "taken off," upon the separation of New Hampshire from Massachusetts, January 1, 1680, the others were set back to Essex February 4, 1680, and the original county of Norfolk ceased to exist. The present Norfolk County was incorporated March 26, 1793. The date of incorporation of this county is subsequent to the date of the earliest census in which population appears. It is evident that the territory was well defined and recognized for census purposes prior to the date of its formal incorporation as a county.

	Population	
1765 (Prov.)* . . .	17,682	-
1776 (Prov.)* . . .	22,124	+ 4,442
1790 (U. S.)* . . .	23,878	+ 1,754
1800 (U. S.)* . . .	27,216	+ 3,338
1810 (U. S.)* . . .	31,245	+ 4,029
1820 (U. S.)* . . .	36,471	+ 5,226
1830 (U. S.)* . . .	41,972	+ 5,501
1840 (U. S.)* . . .	53,140	+11,168
1850 (U. S.)* . . .	78,892	+25,752
1855 (State)* . . .	94,367	+15,475
1860 (U. S.)* . . .	109,950	+15,583
1865 (State)* . . .	116,306	+ 6,356
1870 (U. S.)* . . .	89,443	—26,863
1875 (State)	88,321	— 1,122
1880 (U. S.)	96,507	+ 8,186
1885 (State)	102,142	+ 5,635
1890 (U. S.)	118,950	+16,808
1895 (State)	134,819	+15,869

* Includes the population of Dorchester, Roxbury, and West Roxbury (annexed to Boston), as follows: 1765, 2,847; 1776, 2,946; 1790, 3,948; 1800, 5,112; 1810, 6,599; 1820, 7,819; 1830, 9,321; 1840, 13,964; 1850, 26,333; 1855, 31,621; 1860, 41,216; 1865, 46,055; 1870, 8,683.

CENSUSES OF POPULATION — 1765–1895 — Continued.

TOWN OF AVON.

Established February 21, 1888, from part of Stoughton. Parts of Holbrook and Randolph annexed April 16, 1889.

YEARS AND CENSUS.	Population	Increase (+), or Decrease (−), as Compared with Previous Census
1890 (U. S.)	1,384	-
1895 (State)	1,626	+242

TOWN OF BELLINGHAM.

Established November 27, 1719, from parts of Dedham and Wrentham and Mendon (Worcester County). Boundary line between Bellingham and Franklin established February 23, 1832. Boundary line between Bellingham and Mendon established March 7, 1872.

YEARS AND CENSUS.	Population	Increase/Decrease
1765 (Prov.)	468	-
1776 (Prov.)	627	+159
1790 (U. S.)	735	+108
1800 (U. S.)	704	− 31
1810 (U. S.)	766	+ 62
1820 (U. S.)	1,034	+268
1830 (U. S.)	1,102	+ 68
1840 (U. S.)	1,055	− 47
1850 (U. S.)	1,281	+226
1855 (State)	1,413	+132
1860 (U. S.)	1,313	−100
1865 (State)	1,240	− 73
1870 (U. S.)	1,282	+ 42
1875 (State)	1,247	− 35
1880 (U. S.)	1,223	− 24
1885 (State)	1,198	− 25
1890 (U. S.)	1,334	+136
1895 (State)	1,481	+147

TOWN OF BRAINTREE.

Established May 13, 1640, from land belonging to Boston called "Mount Woollaston." Part included in the new town of Quincy February 22, 1792. Part established as Randolph March 9, 1793. Certain estates in Braintree re-annexed to Randolph June 22, 1811. Part annexed to Quincy April 24, 1856.

YEARS AND CENSUS.	Population	Increase/Decrease
1765 (Prov.)	2,433	-
1776 (Prov.)	2,871	+ 438
1790 (U. S.)	2,771	− 100
1800 (U. S.)	1,285	−1,486
1810 (U. S.)	1,351	+ 66
1820 (U. S.)	1,466	+ 115
1830 (U. S.)	1,758	+ 292
1840 (U. S.)	2,168	+ 410
1850 (U. S.)	2,969	+ 801
1855 (State)	3,472	+ 503
1860 (U. S.)	3,468	− 4
1865 (State)	3,725	+ 257
1870 (U. S.)	3,948	+ 223
1875 (State)	4,156	+ 208
1880 (U. S.)	3,855	− 301
1885 (State)	4,040	+ 185
1890 (U. S.)	4,848	+ 808
1895 (State)	5,311	+ 463

TOWN OF BROOKLINE.

Established as "Brookline" November 13, 1705, from part of Boston called "Muddy River." Boundary line between Brookline and Boston established February 22, 1825. Part of Roxbury annexed February 24, 1844. Part annexed to Boston June 18, 1870. The Act accepted by Boston November 4, 1870. Boundary line between Brookline and Boston established April 27, 1872. Part annexed to Boston May 8, 1874. Boundary lines between Brookline and Boston established May 27, 1890 and April 13, 1894.

YEARS AND CENSUS.	Population	Increase/Decrease
1765 (Prov.)	338	-
1776 (Prov.)	502	+ 164
1790 (U. S.)	484	− 18
1800 (U. S.)	605	+ 121
1810 (U. S.)	784	+ 179
1820 (U. S.)	900	+ 116
1830 (U. S.)	1,043	+ 143
1840 (U. S.)	1,365	+ 322
1850 (U. S.)	2,516	+1,151
1855 (State)	3,737	+1,221
1860 (U. S.)	5,164	+1,427
1865 (State)	5,262	+ 98
1870 (U. S.)	6,650	+1,388
1875 (State)	6,675	+ 25
1880 (U. S.)	8,057	+1,382
1885 (State)	9,196	+1,139
1890 (U. S.)	12,103	+2,907
1895 (State)	16,164	+4,061

TOWN OF CANTON.

Established February 23, 1797, from part of Stoughton. Part annexed to Stoughton March 31, 1847.

YEARS AND CENSUS.	Population	Increase/Decrease
1800 (U. S.)	1,110	-
1810 (U. S.)	1,353	+243
1820 (U. S.)	1,268	− 85
1830 (U. S.)	1,515	+247
1840 (U. S.)	1,995	+480
1850 (U. S.)	2,598	+603
1855 (State)	3,115	+517
1860 (U. S.)	3,242	+127
1865 (State)	3,318	+ 76
1870 (U. S.)	3,879	+561
1875 (State)	4,192	+313
1880 (U. S.)	4,516	+324
1885 (State)	4,380	−136
1890 (U. S.)	4,538	+158
1895 (State)	4,636	+ 98

TOWN OF COHASSET.

Established as a district April 26, 1770, from a part of Hingham (Plymouth County). Made a town by Act of August 23, 1775. Part of Scituate (Plymouth County) annexed June 14, 1823. Boundary line between Cohasset and Scituate established March 20, 1840, and part of each town annexed to the other town.

YEARS AND CENSUS.	Population	Increase/Decrease
1776 (Prov.)	754	-
1790 (U. S.)	817	+63
1800 (U. S.)	849	+32

CENSUSES OF POPULATION — 1765-1895 — Continued.

TOWN OF COHASSET — concluded.

YEARS AND CENSUS.	Population	Increase (+), or Decrease (—), as Compared with Previous Census.
1810 (U. S.)	994	+145
1820 (U. S.)	1,099	+105
1830 (U. S.)	1,233	+134
1840 (U. S.)	1,471	+238
1850 (U. S.)	1,775	+304
1855 (State)	1,879	+104
1860 (U. S.)	1,953	+ 74
1865 (State)	2,048	+ 95
1870 (U. S.)	2,130	+ 82
1875 (State)	2,197	+ 67
1880 (U. S.)	2,182	— 15
1885 (State)	2,216	+ 34
1890 (U. S.)	2,448	+232
1895 (State)	2,474	+ 26

TOWN OF DEDHAM.

On September 8, 1636, the plantation to be settled above the falls of the Charles River established as "Deddam" (Mass. Records, Vol. I, p. 179). Boundary line between Dedham and Roxbury established May 16, 1638. Boundary line between Dedham and Dorchester established May 17, 1638. Boundary line between Dedham, and Concord and Watertown (Middlesex County) established August 20, 1638. Boundary line between Dedham and Watertown established May 22, 1639. Part established as Medfield May 22, 1650. Boundary line between Dedham and Natick (Middlesex County) established October 18, 1701. Part established as Needham November 5, 1711. Part included in the new town of Bellingham November 27, 1719. Part established as Walpole December 10, 1724. Parts of Stoughton annexed April 25, 1733, and December 10, 1737. Boundary line between Dedham and Stoughton established December 11, 1738. Part annexed to Dorchester June 7, 1739. Part of Stoughton annexed June 17, 1780. Part established as the District of Dover July 7, 1784. Boundary line between Dedham and Dover established March 7, 1791. Part reannexed to Walpole June 21, 1811. Part annexed to Dorchester June 17, 1831. Part of Dedham annexed by Act of April 21, 1852 to West Roxbury upon payment of $400 by West Roxbury; the Act accepted by West Roxbury April 30, 1852; amount paid by West Roxbury July 4, 1855. Part annexed to Walpole April 30, 1852. Part included in the new town of Hyde Park April 22, 1868. Boundary line, fixed by the Act of April 22, 1868, changed May 1, 1868. Part included in the new town of Norwood February 23, 1872.

YEARS AND CENSUS.	Population	Increase (+), or Decrease (—), as Compared with Previous Census.
1765 (Prov.)	1,909	-
1776 (Prov.)	1,937	+ 28
1790 (U. S.)	1,659	— 278
1800 (U. S.)	1,973	+ 314
1810 (U. S.)	2,172	+ 199
1820 (U. S.)	2,493	+ 321
1830 (U. S.)	3,117	+ 624
1840 (U. S.)	3,290	+ 173
1850 (U. S.)	4,447	+1,157
1855 (State)	5,633	+1,186
1860 (U. S.)	6,330	+ 697
1865 (State)	7,195	+ 865
1870 (U. S.)	7,342	+ 147
1875 (State)	5,756	—1,586
1880 (U. S.)	6,233	+ 477

TOWN OF DEDHAM — concluded.

YEARS AND CENSUS.	Population	Increase (+), or Decrease (—), as Compared with Previous Census.
1885 (State)	6,641	+408
1890 (U. S.)	7,123	+482
1895 (State)	7,211	+ 88

TOWN OF DOVER.

Established as a district July 7, 1784, from part of Dedham. Boundary line between the District of Dover and Dedham established March 7, 1791. Made a town March 31, 1836. Act accepted by the district May 2, 1836. Boundary line between Dover and Walpole established February 27, 1872.

YEARS AND CENSUS.	Population	Increase (+), or Decrease (—), as Compared with Previous Census.
1790 (U. S.)	485	-
1800 (U. S.)	511	+ 26
1810 (U. S.)	548	+ 37
1820 (U. S.)	548	=
1830 (U. S.)	497	— 51
1840 (U. S.)	520	+ 23
1850 (U. S.)	631	+111
1855 (State)	745	+114
1860 (U. S.)	679	— 66
1865 (State)	616	— 63
1870 (U. S.)	645	+ 29
1875 (State)	650	+ 5
1880 (U. S.)	653	+ 3
1885 (State)	664	+ 11
1890 (U. S.)	727	+ 63
1895 (State)	668	— 59

TOWN OF FOXBOROUGH.

Established June 10, 1778, from parts of Stoughton, Stoughtonham (now Sharon), Walpole, and Wrentham. Parts of Sharon and Stoughton annexed and boundary lines established March 12, 1793. Boundary line between Foxborough and Wrentham established February 3, 1819. Part of Wrentham annexed February 7, 1831. Boundary line between Foxborough and Sharon established March 29, and part of each town annexed to the other town January 30, 1833. Parts annexed to Walpole March 27, 1833, and March 28, 1834. Part of Sharon annexed February 28, 1850.

YEARS AND CENSUS.	Population	Increase (+), or Decrease (—), as Compared with Previous Census.
1790 (U. S.)	674	-
1800 (U. S.)	779	+105
1810 (U. S.)	870	+ 91
1820 (U. S.)	1,004	+134
1830 (U. S.)	1,165	+161
1840 (U. S.)	1,298	+133
1850 (U. S.)	1,880	+582
1855 (State)	2,570	+690
1860 (U. S.)	2,879	+309
1865 (State)	2,778	—101
1870 (U. S.)	3,057	+279
1875 (State)	3,168	+111
1880 (U. S.)	2,950	—218
1885 (State)	2,814	—136
1890 (U. S.)	2,933	+119
1895 (State)	3,219	+286

CENSUSES OF POPULATION — 1765-1895 — Continued.

TOWN OF FRANKLIN.

Established March 2, 1778, from part of Wrentham. Part of Medway annexed June 25, 1792. Boundary line between Franklin and Medway established November 13, 1792. Boundary lines between Franklin and Bellingham and Medway established February 23, 1832. Boundary line between Franklin and Medway established March 13, 1839, and a part of Franklin annexed to Medway. Part included in the new town of Norfolk February 23, 1870.

YEARS AND CENSUS.	Population.	Increase (+), or Decrease (—), as compared with Previous Census.
1790 (U. S.)	1,101	–
1800 (U. S.)	1,285	+ 184
1810 (U. S.)	1,398	+ 113
1820 (U. S.)	1,630	+ 232
1830 (U. S.)	1,662	+ 32
1840 (U. S.)	1,717	+ 55
1850 (U. S.)	1,818	+ 101
1855 (State)	2,044	+ 226
1860 (U. S.)	2,172	+ 128
1865 (State)	2,510	+ 338
1870 (U. S.)	2,512	+ 2
1875 (State)	2,983	+ 471
1880 (U. S.)	4,051	+1,068
1885 (State)	3,983	— 68
1890 (U. S.)	4,831	+ 848
1895 (State)	5,136	+ 305

TOWN OF HOLBROOK.

Established February 29, 1872, from part of Randolph. Part annexed to Avon April 16, 1889.

1875 (State)	1,726	–
1880 (U. S.)	2,150	+424
1885 (State)	2,354	+204
1890 (U. S.)	2,474	+140
1895 (State)	2,298	—176

TOWN OF HYDE PARK.

Established April 22, 1868, from parts of Dedham, Dorchester, and Milton. Act amended and boundary line changed May 1, 1868.

1870 (U. S.)	4,136	–
1875 (State)	6,316	+2,180
1880 (U. S.)	7,088	+ 772
1885 (State)	8,376	+1,288
1890 (U. S.)	10,193	+1,817
1895 (State)	11,826	+1,633

TOWN OF MEDFIELD.

Established May 22, 1650. "At the request of the inhabitants of Dedham, the village there is by this Court named Meadfeild" (Mass. Records, Vol. IV, Part 1, p. 7). Land granted to Medfield May 28, 1659. Part established as Medway October 24, 1713.

1765 (Prov.)	628	–
1776 (Prov.)	775	+147
1790 (U. S.)	731	— 44
1800 (U. S.)	745	+ 14

TOWN OF MEDFIELD — concluded.

YEARS AND CENSUS.	Population.	Increase (+), or Decrease (—), as compared with Previous Census.
1810 (U. S.)	786	+ 41
1820 (U. S.)	892	+106
1830 (U. S.)	817	— 75
1840 (U. S.)	883	+ 66
1850 (U. S.)	966	+ 83
1855 (State)	984	+ 18
1860 (U. S.)	1,082	+ 98
1865 (State)	1,012	— 70
1870 (U. S.)	1,142	+130
1875 (State)	1,163	+ 21
1880 (U. S.)	1,371	+208
1885 (State)	1,594	+223
1890 (U. S.)	1,493	—101
1895 (State)	1,872	+379

TOWN OF MEDWAY.

Established October 24, 1713, from part of Medfield. Boundary line between Medway and Sherborn (Middlesex County) established March 3, 1792. Part annexed to Franklin June 25, 1792. Boundary line between Medway and Franklin established November 13, 1792. Boundary line between Medway and Holliston (Middlesex County) established and part of each town annexed to the other town March 3, 1829. Boundary line between Medway and Franklin established February 23, 1832. Part of Franklin annexed and boundary line established March 13, 1839. Part included in the new town of Norfolk February 23, 1870. Part established as Millis February 24, 1885.

1765 (Prov.)	785	–
1776 (Prov.)	912	+ 127
1790 (U. S.)	1,035	+ 123
1800 (U. S.)	1,050	+ 15
1810 (U. S.)	1,213	+ 163
1820 (U. S.)	1,523	+ 310
1830 (U. S.)	1,756	+ 233
1840 (U. S.)	2,043	+ 287
1850 (U. S.)	2,778	+ 735
1855 (State)	3,230	+ 452
1860 (U. S.)	3,195	— 35
1865 (State)	3,219	+ 24
1870 (U. S.)	3,721	+ 502
1875 (State)	4,242	+ 521
1880 (U. S.)	3,956	— 286
1885 (State)	2,777	—1,179
1890 (U. S.)	2,985	+ 208
1895 (State)	2,913	— 72

TOWN OF MILLIS.

Established February 24, 1885, from part of Medway.

1885 (State)	683	–
1890 (U. S.)	786	+103
1895 (State)	1,006	+220

TOWN OF MILTON.

Established May 7, 1662, from part of Dorchester called "Uncataquissett." Part included in the new

CENSUSES OF POPULATION — 1765-1895 — Continued.

TOWN OF MILTON — concluded.

town of Hyde Park April 22, 1868. The Act amended and boundary lines changed May 1, 1868. Boundary line between Milton and Quincy established and part of each town annexed to the other town April 16, 1885.

YEARS AND CENSUS.	Population	Increase (+), or Decrease (—), as Compared with Previous Census
1765 (Prov.)	943	
1776 (Prov.)	1,213	+ 270
1790 (U. S.)	1,039	— 174
1800 (U. S.)	1,143	+ 104
1810 (U. S.)	1,264	+ 121
1820 (U. S.)	1,502	+ 238
1830 (U. S.)	1,576	+ 74
1840 (U. S.)	1,822	+ 246
1850 (U. S.)	2,241	+ 419
1855 (State)	2,656	+ 415
1860 (U. S.)	2,669	+ 13
1865 (State)	2,770	+ 101
1870 (U. S.)	2,683	— 87
1875 (State)	2,738	+ 55
1880 (U. S.)	3,206	+ 468
1885 (State)	3,555	+ 349
1890 (U. S.)	4,278	+ 723
1895 (State)	5,518	+1,240

TOWN OF NEEDHAM.

Established November 5, 1711, from part of Dedham. Boundary line between Needham and Natick (Middlesex County) established and part of each town annexed to the other town June 22, 1797. Part established as Wellesley April 6, 1881.

1765 (Prov.)	945	
1776 (Prov.)	912	— 33
1790 (U. S.)	1,130	+ 218
1800 (U. S.)	1,072	— 58
1810 (U. S.)	1,097	+ 25
1820 (U. S.)	1,227	+ 130
1830 (U. S.)	1,418	+ 191
1840 (U. S.)	1,488	+ 70
1850 (U. S.)	1,944	+ 456
1855 (State)	2,401	+ 457
1860 (U. S.)	2,658	+ 257
1865 (State)	2,793	+ 135
1870 (U. S.)	3,607	+ 814
1875 (State)	4,548	+ 941
1880 (U. S.)	5,252	+ 704
1885 (State)	2,586	—2,666
1890 (U. S.)	3,035	+ 449
1895 (State)	3,511	+ 476

TOWN OF NORFOLK.

Established February 23, 1870, from parts of Franklin, Medway, Walpole, and Wrentham. Boundary line between Norfolk and Wrentham established April 19, 1871.

1870 (U. S.)	1,081	
1875 (State)	920	—161
1880 (U. S.)	930	+ 10

TOWN OF NORFOLK — concluded.

YEARS AND CENSUS.	Population	Increase (+), or Decrease (—), as Compared with Previous Census
1885 (State)	825	—105
1890 (U. S.)	913	+ 88
1895 (State)	882	— 31

TOWN OF NORWOOD.

Established February 23, 1872, from parts of Dedham and Walpole.

1875 (State)	1,749	
1880 (U. S.)	2,345	+596
1885 (State)	2,921	+576
1890 (U. S.)	3,733	+812
1895 (State)	4,574	+841

CITY OF QUINCY.

Established February 22, 1792, from part of Braintree as Quincy, and part of that part of Dorchester called "Squantum and the Farms" annexed. Another part of "Squantum and the Farms" annexed February 10,1814. Part of Dorchester annexed February 12,1819. Boundary line between Quincy and Dorchester established, and part of Dorchester annexed February 21, 1820. Part of Dorchester annexed May 2, 1855. Part of Braintree annexed April 24, 1856. Boundary line between Quincy and Milton established and part of each town annexed to the other town April 16, 1885. Quincy incorporated as a city May 17, 1888. Act of incorporation accepted by the town June 11, 1888.

1800 (U. S.)	1,081	
1810 (U. S.)	1,281	+ 200
1820 (U. S.)	1,623	+ 342
1830 (U. S.)	2,201	+ 578
1840 (U. S.)	3,486	+1,285
1850 (U. S.)	5,017	+1,531
1855 (State)	5,921	+ 904
1860 (U. S.)	6,778	+ 857
1865 (State)	6,718	— 60
1870 (U. S.)	7,442	+ 724
1875 (State)	9,155	+1,713
1880 (U. S.)	10,570	+1,415
1885 (State)	12,145	+1,575
1890 (U. S.)	16,723	+4,578
1895 (State)	20,712	+3,989

TOWN OF RANDOLPH.

Established March 9, 1793, from part of Braintree. Certain estates in Braintree re-annexed June 22, 1811. Boundary line between Randolph and Abington (Plymouth County) established March 21, 1861. Part established as Holbrook February 29, 1872. Part annexed to Avon April 16, 1889.

1800 (U. S.)	1,021	
1810 (U. S.)	1,170	+ 149
1820 (U. S.)	1,546	+ 376
1830 (U. S.)	2,200	+ 654
1840 (U. S.)	3,213	+1,013
1850 (U. S.)	4,741	+1,528
1855 (State)	5,538	+ 797

CENSUSES OF POPULATION — 1765-1895 — Continued.

TOWN OF RANDOLPH — concluded.

YEARS AND CENSUS.	Population.	Increase (+), or Decrease (—), as Compared with Previous Census.
1860 (U. S.)	5,760	+ 222
1865 (State)	5,734	— 26
1870 (U. S.)	5,642	— 92
1875 (State)	4,064	—1,578
1880 (U. S.)	4,027	— 37
1885 (State)	3,807	— 220
1890 (U. S.)	3,946	+ 139
1895 (State)	3,694	— 252

TOWN OF SHARON.

Originally established as the District of Stoughtonham June 21, 1765, from part of Stoughton. Made a town by Act of August 23, 1775. Part included in the new town of Foxborough June 10, 1778. Name changed to Sharon February 25, 1783. Parts of Stoughton annexed February 16, 1789, and February 22, 1792. Boundary line between Sharon and Foxborough established and parts of Sharon and Stoughton annexed to Foxborough March 12, 1793. Parts annexed to Walpole February 28, 1804, and June 21, 1811. Boundary line between Sharon and Foxborough established and part of each town annexed to the other town January 30, 1833. Part annexed to Foxborough February 28, 1850. Part of Stoughton annexed March 26, 1864. Part annexed to Walpole May 1, 1874.

1776 (Prov.)	1,261	-
1790 (U. S.)	1,034	—227
1800 (U. S.)	1,018	— 16
1810 (U. S.)	1,000	— 18
1820 (U. S.)	1,010	+ 10
1830 (U. S.)	1,023	+ 13
1840 (U. S.)	1,076	+ 53
1850 (U. S.)	1,128	+ 52
1855 (State)	1,331	+203
1860 (U. S.)	1,377	+ 46
1865 (State)	1,393	+ 16
1870 (U. S.)	1,508	+115
1875 (State)	1,330	—178
1880 (U. S.)	1,492	+162
1885 (State)	1,328	—164
1890 (U. S.)	1,634	+306
1895 (State)	1,717	+ 83

TOWN OF STOUGHTON.

Established December 22, 1726, from part of Dorchester. Parts annexed to Dedham April 25, 1735, and December 10, 1737. Boundary line between Stoughton and Dedham established December 11, 1738. Part established as the District of Stoughtonham June 21, 1765. Part annexed to Bridgewater (Plymouth County) November 20, 1776. Part included in the new town of Foxborough June 10, 1778. Part annexed to Dedham June 17, 1780. Parts annexed to Sharon February 16, 1789, and February 22, 1792. Part annexed to Foxborough March 12, 1793. Part established as Canton February 23, 1797. Part annexed to Bridgewater February 8, 1798. Part of Canton annexed March 31, 1847. Part annexed to Sharon March 26, 1864. Part established as Avon February 21, 1888.

| 1765 (Prov.) . . . . | 2,321 | - |
| 1776 (Prov.) . . . . | 2,097 | —224 |

TOWN OF STOUGHTON — concluded.

YEARS AND CENSUS.	Population.	Increase (+), or Decrease (—), as Compared with Previous Census.
1790 (U. S.)	1,994	— 103
1800 (U. S.)	1,020	— 974
1810 (U. S.)	1,134	+ 114
1820 (U. S.)	1,313	+ 179
1830 (U. S.)	1,591	+ 278
1840 (U. S.)	2,142	+ 551
1850 (U. S.)	3,494	+1,352
1855 (State)	4,370	+ 876
1860 (U. S.)	4,830	+ 460
1865 (State)	4,855	+ 25
1870 (U. S.)	4,914	+ 59
1875 (State)	4,842	— 72
1880 (U. S.)	4,875	+ 33
1885 (State)	5,173	+ 298
1890 (U. S.)	4,852	— 321
1895 (State)	5,272	+ 420

TOWN OF WALPOLE.

Established December 10, 1724, from part of Dedham. Part included in the new town of Foxborough June 10, 1778. Part of Sharon annexed February 28, 1804. Part of Sharon annexed and part of Dedham re-annexed June 21, 1811. Parts of Foxborough annexed March 27, 1833, and March 28, 1834. Part of Dedham annexed April 30, 1852. Part included in the new town of Norfolk February 23, 1870. Part included in the new town of Norwood February 23, 1872. Boundary line between Walpole and Dover established February 27, 1872. Part of Sharon annexed May 1, 1874.

1765 (Prov.)	785	-
1776 (Prov.)	967	+182
1790 (U. S.)	1,005	+ 38
1800 (U. S.)	989	— 16
1810 (U. S.)	1,098	+109
1820 (U. S.)	1,366	+268
1830 (U. S.)	1,442	+ 76
1840 (U. S.)	1,491	+ 49
1850 (U. S.)	1,929	+438
1855 (State)	1,935	+ 6
1860 (U. S.)	2,037	+102
1865 (State)	2,018	— 19
1870 (U. S.)	2,137	+119
1875 (State)	2,290	+153
1880 (U. S.)	2,494	+204
1885 (State)	2,443	— 51
1890 (U. S.)	2,604	+161
1895 (State)	2,994	+390

TOWN OF WELLESLEY.

Established April 6, 1881, from part of Needham.

1885 (State)	3,013	-
1890 (U. S.)	3,600	+587
1895 (State)	4,229	+629

CENSUSES OF POPULATION — 1765-1895 — Continued.

TOWN OF WEYMOUTH.

On September 2, 1635, the name of the plantation of "Wessaguscus" changed to "Waymothe" (Mass. Records, Vol 1, p. 156). Boundary line between Weymouth and Abington (Plymouth County) established March 31, 1847.

YEARS AND CENSUS.	Popula-tion	Increase (+), or Decrease (—), as Compared with Previous Census
1765 (Prov.)	1,258	-
1776 (Prov.)	1,471	+ 213
1790 (U. S.)	1,469	— 2
1800 (U. S.)	1,803	+ 334
1810 (U. S.)	1,889	+ 86
1820 (U. S.)	2,407	+ 518
1830 (U. S.)	2,837	+ 430
1840 (U. S.)	3,738	+ 901
1850 (U. S.)	5,369	+1,631
1855 (State)	6,530	+1,161
1860 (U. S.)	7,742	+1,212
1865 (State)	7,975	+ 233
1870 (U. S.)	9,010	+1,035
1875 (State)	9,819	+ 809
1880 (U. S.)	10,570	+ 751
1885 (State)	10,740	+ 170
1890 (U. S.)	10,866	+ 126
1895 (State)	11,291	+ 425

TOWN OF WRENTHAM.

On October 15, 1673, lands granted to the inhabitants of Wollonopang, and name changed to Wrentham. Part included in the new town of Bellingham November 27, 1719. Part established as Franklin March 2, 1778. Part included in the new town of Foxborough June 10, 1778. Boundary line between Wrentham and Foxborough established February 3, 1819. Boundary line between Wrentham and Attleborough (Bristol County) established and part of Attleborough annexed February 18, 1830. Part annexed to Foxborough February 7, 1831. Part included in the new town of Norfolk February 23, 1870. Boundary line between Wrentham and Norfolk established April 19, 1871.

1765 (Prov.)	2,022	-
1776 (Prov.)	2,879	+ 857
1790 (U. S.)	1,767	—1,112
1800 (U. S.)	2,061	+ 294
1810 (U. S.)	2,478	+ 417
1820 (U. S.)	2,801	+ 323
1830 (U. S.)	2,698	— 103
1840 (U. S.)	2,915	+ 217
1850 (U. S.)	3,037	+ 122
1855 (State)	3,242	+ 205
1860 (U. S.)	3,406	+ 164
1865 (State)	3,072	— 334
1870 (U. S.)	2,292	— 780
1875 (State)	2,395	+ 103
1880 (U. S.)	2,481	+ 86
1885 (State)	2,710	+ 229
1890 (U. S.)	2,566	— 144
1895 (State)	2,584	+ 18

COUNTY OF PLYMOUTH.

Incorporated June 2, 1685 (Plymouth Colony Laws, edition 1836, p. 295).

COUNTY OF PLYMOUTH — concluded.

YEARS AND CENSUS.	Popula-tion	Increase (+), or Decrease (—), as Compared with Previous Census
1765 (Prov.)	29,777	-
1776 (Prov.)	29,113	+ 3,336
1790 (U. S.)	31,740	+ 2,627
1800 (U. S.)	32,302	+ 562
1810 (U. S.)	35,169	+ 2,867
1820 (U. S.)	38,136	+ 2,967
1830 (U. S.)	43,044	+ 4,908
1840 (U. S.)	47,373	+ 4,329
1850 (U. S.)	55,697	+ 8,324
1855 (State)	61,495	+ 5,798
1860 (U. S.)	64,768	+ 3,273
1865 (State)	63,107	— 1,661
1870 (U. S.)	65,365	+ 2,258
1875 (State)	69,362	+ 3,997
1880 (U. S.)	74,018	+ 4,656
1885 (State)	81,680	+ 7,662
1890 (U. S.)	92,700	+11,020
1895 (State)	101,498	+ 8,798

TOWN OF ABINGTON.

Established June 10, 1712, from part of Bridgewater and certain lands adjoining, as "Abington." Part included in the new town of Hanover June 14, 1727. Boundary line between Abington and Weymouth (Norfolk County) established March 31, 1847. Boundary line between Abington and Randolph (Norfolk County) established March 21, 1861. Boundary line between Abington and Hingham established March 21, 1861. Part established as Rockland March 9, 1874. Part included in the new town of South Abington (now Whitman) March 4, 1875.

1765 (Prov.)	1,253	-
1776 (Prov.)	1,295	+ 30
1790 (U. S.)	1,453	+ 160
1800 (U. S.)	1,623	+ 170
1810 (U. S.)	1,704	+ 81
1820 (U. S.)	1,920	+ 216
1830 (U. S.)	2,423	+ 503
1840 (U. S.)	3,214	+ 791
1850 (U. S.)	5,269	+2,055
1855 (State)	6,937	+1,668
1860 (U. S.)	8,527	+1,590
1865 (State)	8,576	+ 49
1870 (U. S.)	9,308	+ 732
1875 (State)	3,241	—6,067
1880 (U. S.)	3,697	+ 456
1885 (State)	3,699	+ 2
1890 (U. S.)	4,260	+ 561
1895 (State)	4,207	— 53

TOWN OF BRIDGEWATER.

"Ordered (June 3, 1656) that henceforth Duxburrow New Plantation bee allowed to bee a townshipe of yt selfe, destinct from Duxburrow, and to bee called by the name of Bridgewater" (Ply. Col. Rec., Vol. I, p. 101). Certain lands granted to Bridgewater June 3, 1662. Lands between Bridgewater and Weymouth (Norfolk County), called Foord's Farms, and lands adjoining annexed February 11, 1691. Part included in the new town of Abington June 10, 1712. Parts of

CENSUSES OF POPULATION — 1765-1895 — Continued.

TOWN OF BRIDGEWATER — concluded.

Stoughton (Norfolk County) annexed November 20, 1770, and February 8, 1798. Part established as North Bridgewater (now Brockton) June 15, 1821. Part established as West Bridgewater February 16, 1822. Part established as East Bridgewater June 14, 1823. Part annexed to Halifax February 20, 1824. Boundary line between Bridgewater and East Bridgewater established February 23, 1838. Boundary line between Bridgewater and East Bridgewater established and part of each town annexed to the other town March 20, 1846.

YEARS AND CENSUS.	Popula-tion	Increase (+), or Decrease (—), as Compared with Previous Census
1765 (Prov.)	3,942	-
1776 (Prov.)	4,364	+ 422
1790 (U. S.)	4,975	+ 611
1800 (U. S.)	5,200	+ 225
1810 (U. S.)	5,157	— 43
1820 (U. S.)	1,700	—3,457
1830 (U. S.)	1,855	+ 155
1840 U. S.)	2,131	+ 276
1850 (U. S.)	2,790	+ 659
1855 (State)	3,363	+ 573
1860 (U. S.)	3,761	+ 398
1865 (State)	4,196	+ 435
1870 (U. S.)	3,660	— 536
1875 (State)	3,969	+ 309
1880 (U. S.)	3,620	— 349
1885 (State)	3,827	+ 207
1890 (U. S.)	4,249	+ 422
1895 (State)	4,686	+ 437

CITY OF BROCKTON.

Originally established as North Bridgewater June 15, 1821, from part of Bridgewater. Boundary line between North Bridgewater and West Bridgewater established January 26, 1825. Name authorized to be changed March 28, 1874. Brockton adopted as the name May 5, 1874. Part annexed to South Abington (now Whitman) and parts of East Bridgewater and South Abington annexed April 24, 1875. Brockton incorporated as a city April 9, 1881. Act of Incorporation accepted by the town May 23, 1881. Part of West Bridgewater annexed to Brockton, if the Act is accepted February, May 8, 1893. Act accepted by Brockton November 7, 1893, taking effect March 1, 1894. Act of May 8, 1893, amended March 12, 1894. The date of establishment of North Bridgewater is subsequent to the date of the earliest census in which population appears. This is due, probably, to the fact that the territory was well defined and recognized in census enumerations prior to the date of its formal incorporation as a town.

1820 (U. S.)	1,480	-
1830 (U. S.)	1,953	+ 473
1840 (U. S.)	2,616	+ 663
1850 (U. S.)	3,939	+1,323
1855 (State)	5,205	+1,266
1860 (U. S.)	6,584	+1,379
1865 (State)	6,332	— 252
1870 (U. S.)	8,007	+1,675
1875 (State)	10,578	+2,571
1880 (U. S.)	13,608	+3,030
1885 (State)	20,783	+7,175
1890 (U. S.)	27,294	+6,511
1895 (State)	33,165	+5,871

TOWN OF CARVER.

Established June 9, 1790, from part of Plympton. Boundary line between Carver and Plympton established February 8, 1793. Part annexed to Wareham January 20, 1827. Boundary line between Carver and Middleborough established March 24, 1849.

YEARS AND CENSUS.	Popula-tion	Increase (+), or Decrease (—), as Compared with Previous Census
1790 (U. S.)	847	-
1800 (U. S.)	863	+ 16
1810 (U. S.)	858	— 5
1820 (U. S.)	839	— 19
1830 (U. S.)	970	+131
1840 (U. S.)	995	+ 25
1850 (U. S.)	1,186	+191
1855 (State)	1,205	+ 19
1860 (U. S.)	1,186	— 19
1865 (State)	1,059	—127
1870 (U. S.)	1,092	+ 33
1875 (State)	1,127	+ 35
1880 (U. S.)	1,039	— 88
1885 (State)	1,091	+ 52
1890 (U. S.)	994	— 97
1895 (State)	1,016	+ 22

TOWN OF DUXBURY.

"Ducksburrow" made "a township and to have the priviledges of a towne" June 7, 1637 (Ply. Col. Rec., Vol. I, p. 62). Boundary lines established March 2, 1641. Part called the "Duxborrow New Plantation" established as Bridgewater June 3, 1656. Namassakeesett annexed March 2, 1658. Certain lands granted to Duxbury and Marshfield March 5, 1661. Boundary line between Duxbury and "the Major's Purchase" established July 5, 1670. Boundary lines established June 5, 1678. Boundary line between Duxbury and Marshfield established February 23, 1683. Part called "Mattakeeset" included in the new town of Pembroke March 21, 1712. Boundary line between Duxbury and Marshfield established June 14, 1813. Part annexed to Kingston April 14, 1857.

1765 (Prov.)	1,050	-
1776 (Prov.)	1,254	+204
1790 (U. S.)	1,454	+200
1800 (U. S)	1,664	+210
1810 (U. S.)	2,201	+537
1820 (U. S.)	2,403	+202
1830 (U. S.)	2,716	+313
1840 (U. S.)	2,798	+ 82
1850 (U. S.)	2,679	—119
1855 (State)	2,620	— 59
1860 (U. S.)	2,597	— 23
1865 (State)	2,384	—213
1870 (U. S.)	2,341	— 43
1875 (State)	2,245	— 96
1880 (U. S.)	2,196	— 49
1885 (State)	1,924	—272
1890 (U. S.)	1,908	— 16
1895 (State)	1,966	+ 58

TOWN OF EAST BRIDGEWATER.

Established June 14, 1823, from part of Bridgewater. Boundary line between East Bridgewater and Bridge-

CENSUSES OF POPULATION — 1765-1895 — Continued.

TOWN OF EAST BRIDGEWATER — concluded.

water established February 23, 1858. Boundary line between East Bridgewater and Bridgewater established and part of each town annexed to the other town March 20, 1846. Part of Halifax annexed and boundary line established April 11, 1857. Part included in the new town of South Abington (Whitman) March 4, 1875. Part annexed to Brockton April 24, 1875. The date of establishment of this town is subsequent to the date of the earliest census in which population appears. This is due, probably, to the fact that the territory in question was well defined and recognized in census enumerations prior to the date of its formal incorporation as a district or town.

YEARS AND CENSUS.	Population	Increase (+), or Decrease (—), as Compared with Previous Census.
1820 (U. S.)	1,435	–
1830 (U. S.)	1,653	+218
1840 (U. S.)	1,950	+297
1850 (U. S.)	2,545	+595
1855 (State)	2,930	+385
1860 (U. S.)	3,207	+277
1865 (State)	2,976	—231
1870 (U. S.)	3,017	+ 41
1875 (State)	2,808	—209
1880 (U. S.)	2,710	— 98
1885 (State)	2,812	+102
1890 (U. S.)	2,911	+ 99
1895 (State)	2,894	— 17

TOWN OF HALIFAX.

Established July 4, 1734, from parts of Middleborough, Pembroke, and Plympton, as "Hallifax." Part of Bridgewater annexed February 20, 1824. Part of Plympton annexed March 16, 1831. Part annexed to East Bridgewater and boundary line established April 11, 1857. Boundary line between Halifax and Plympton established and part of each town annexed to the other town February 6, 1863.

1765 (Prov.)	556	–
1776 (Prov.)	672	+116
1790 (U. S.)	664	— 8
1800 (U. S.)	642	— 22
1810 (U. S.)	703	+ 61
1820 (U. S.)	749	+ 46
1830 (U. S.)	708	— 41
1840 (U. S.)	734	+ 26
1850 (U. S.)	784	+ 50
1855 (State)	786	+ 2
1860 (U. S.)	766	— 20
1865 (State)	722	— 44
1870 (U. S.)	619	—103
1875 (State)	568	— 51
1880 (U. S.)	542	— 26
1885 (State)	530	— 12
1890 (U. S.)	562	+ 32
1895 (State)	497	— 65

TOWN OF HANOVER.

Established June 14, 1727, from parts of Abington and Scituate. Boundary line between Hanover and Pembroke established March 6, 1835. Boundary line between Hanover and South Scituate (Norwell) established May 15, 1857. Boundary line between Hanover

TOWN OF HANOVER — concluded.

and South Scituate established and part of each town annexed to the other town February 11, 1878. Boundary line between Hanover and Rockland established and part of each town annexed to the other town March 23, 1878. Boundary line between Hanover and Pembroke established April 23, 1885.

YEARS AND CENSUS.	Population	Increase (+), or Decrease (—), as Compared with Previous Census.
1765 (Prov.)	[1,105]	–
1776 (Prov.)	1,105	=
1790 (U. S.)	1,084	— 21
1800 (U. S.)	958	—126
1810 (U. S.)	1,171	+213
1820 (U. S.)	1,211	+ 40
1830 (U. S.)	1,303	+ 92
1840 (U. S.)	1,488	+185
1850 (U. S.)	1,592	+104
1855 (State)	1,674	+ 82
1860 (U. S.)	1,565	—109
1865 (State)	1,545	— 20
1870 (U. S.)	1,628	+ 83
1875 (State)	1,801	+173
1880 (U. S.)	1,897	+ 96
1885 (State)	1,966	+ 69
1890 (U. S.)	2,093	+127
1895 (State)	2,051	— 42

TOWN OF HANSON.

Established February 22, 1820, from part of Pembroke.

1820 (U. S.)	917	–
1830 (U. S.)	1,030	+113
1840 (U. S.)	1,040	+ 10
1850 (U. S.)	1,217	+177
1855 (State)	1,231	+ 14
1860 (U. S.)	1,245	+ 14
1865 (State)	1,196	— 49
1870 (U. S.)	1,219	+ 23
1875 (State)	1,265	+ 46
1880 (U. S.)	1,309	+ 44
1885 (State)	1,227	— 82
1890 (U. S.)	1,267	+ 40
1895 (State)	1,380	+113

TOWN OF HINGHAM.

Established September 2, 1635, from common land called "Barecove." Land at Conihasset granted to Hingham May 15, 1640. Part established as the District of Cohasset (Norfolk County) April 26, 1770. Boundary line between Hingham and Abington established March 21, 1861.

1765 (Prov.)	2,467	–
1776 (Prov.)	2,087	—380
1790 (U. S.)	2,085	— 2
1800 (U. S.)	2,112	+ 27
1810 (U. S.)	2,382	+270
1820 (U. S.)	2,857	+475
1830 (U. S.)	3,387	+530
1840 (U. S.)	3,564	+177

CENSUSES OF POPULATION — 1765-1895 — Continued.

TOWN OF HINGHAM — concluded.

Years and Census.	Population.	Increase (+), or Decrease (—), as Compared with Previous Census.
1850 (U. S.)	3,980	+416
1855 (State)	4,257	+277
1860 (U. S.)	4,351	+ 94
1865 (State)	4,176	—175
1870 (U. S.)	4,422	+246
1875 (State)	4,654	+232
1880 (U. S.)	4,485	—169
1885 (State)	4,375	—110
1890 (U. S.)	4,564	+189
1895 (State)	4,819	+255

TOWN OF HULL.

The date of establishment of Hull is not positively known. On May 20, 1642, according to Mass. Records, Vol. I, p. 5, a report of a committee was made to the General Court concerning the allotment of lands at Nantasket, said report being dated "9th of the 2d mouth," 1642. "Nantasket" is again mentioned May 10, 1643, as being within the shire of Suffolk. On Sept. 7, 1643, a former grant to "Nantascot" was confirmed. On May 29, 1644, it was ordered "that Nantascot shall be called Hull" and on May 26, 1647, Hull is mentioned as a town.

1765 (Prov.)	370	-
1776 (Prov.)	[120]	— 50
1790 (U. S.)	120	—
1800 (U. S.)	117	— 3
1810 (U. S.)	139	+ 22
1820 (U. S.)	172	+ 33
1830 (U. S.)	198	+ 26
1840 (U. S.)	231	+ 33
1850 (U. S.)	253	+ 22
1855 (State)	292	+ 39
1860 (U. S.)	285	— 7
1865 (State)	260	— 25
1870 (U. S.)	261	+ 1
1875 (State)	316	+ 55
1880 (U. S.)	383	+ 67
1885 (State)	451	+ 68
1890 (U. S.)	989	+538
1895 (State)	1,044	+ 55

TOWN OF KINGSTON.

Established June 16, 1726, from part of Plymouth. Part of Duxbury annexed April 14, 1857.

1765 (Prov.)	759	-
1776 (Prov.)	980	+221
1790 (U. S.)	1,004	+ 24
1800 (U. S.)	1,037	+ 33
1810 (U. S.)	1,137	+100
1820 (U. S.)	1,313	+176
1830 (U. S.)	1,321	+ 8
1840 (U. S.)	1,440	+119
1850 (U. S.)	1,591	+151
1855 (State)	1,571	— 20
1860 (U. S.)	1,655	+ 84
1865 (State)	1,626	— 29

TOWN OF KINGSTON — concluded.

Years and Census.	Population.	Increase (+), or Decrease (—), as Compared with Previous Census.
1870 (U. S.)	1,694	— 22
1875 (State)	1,569	— 35
1880 (U. S.)	1,524	— 45
1885 (State)	1,570	+46
1890 (U. S.)	1,659	+89
1895 (State)	1,746	+87

TOWN OF LAKEVILLE.

Established May 13, 1853, from part of Middleborough. Boundary line between Lakeville and Taunton (Bristol County) established June 1, 1867.

1855 (State)	1,188	-
1860 (U. S.)	1,160	—28
1865 (State)	1,110	—50
1870 (U. S.)	1,159	+49
1875 (State)	1,061	—98
1880 (U. S.)	1,008	—53
1885 (State)	980	—28
1890 (U. S.)	935	—45
1895 (State)	870	—65

TOWN OF MARION.

Established May 14, 1852, from part of Rochester. Boundary line between Marion and Rochester established April 8, 1853. Boundary lines between Marion and Wareham established February 18, 1859 and February 13, 1866.

1855 (State)	969	-
1860 (U. S.)	918	— 51
1865 (State)	960	+ 42
1870 (U. S.)	896	— 64
1875 (State)	862	— 34
1880 (U. S.)	958	+ 96
1885 (State)	965	+ 7
1890 (U. S.)	871	— 94
1895 (State)	759	—112

TOWN OF MARSHFIELD.

On March 2, 1641, it was "enacted by the Court that Green's Harbour shall be a township . . . and that it shall be called by the name Rexhame" (Plymouth Colony Records, Vol. XI, p. 37). On the same date, but in Vol. II, p. 9, of Plymouth Colony Records, "Rexame" is in the list of places for which constables were chosen. On June 1, 1641, Rexhame is mentioned in a list of towns and the name then disappears from the records. Name of Rexhame was changed to Marshfield about this time though the transaction was not recorded. On March 1, 1642, Marshfield is mentioned as one of the towns for which officers were chosen (Plymouth Colony Records, Vol. II, p. 34). Boundary lines established March 7, 1643. Certain lands granted to Marshfield and Duxbury March 5, 1661. Boundary line between Marshfield and Duxbury established February 23, 1685. Part included in the new town of Pembroke March 21, 1712. Part of Scituate annexed March 10, 1788. Boundary line between Marshfield and Duxbury established June 14, 1813. Boundary line between Marshfield and Scituate established May 11, 1887.

1765 (Prov.)	1,147	-
1776 (Prov.)	1,157	+10

CENSUSES OF POPULATION — 1765-1895 — Continued.

TOWN OF MARSHFIELD — concluded.

YEARS AND CENSUS.	Population.	Increase (+), or Decrease (—), as Compared with Previous Census.
1790 (U. S.)	1,269	+ 112
1800 (U. S.)	1,256	— 13
1810 (U. S.)	1,364	+108
1820 (U. S.)	1,532	+168
1830 (U. S.)	1,565	+ 33
1840 (U. S.)	1,761	+196
1850 (U. S.)	1,837	+ 76
1855 (State)	1,876	+ 39
1860 (U. S.)	1,870	— 6
1865 (State)	1,809	— 61
1870 (U. S.)	1,659	—150
1875 (State)	1,817	+158
1880 (U. S.)	1,781	— 36
1885 (State)	1,649	—132
1890 (U. S.)	1,713	+ 64
1895 (State)	1,760	+ 47

TOWN OF MATTAPOISETT.

Established May 20, 1857, from part of Rochester.

1860 (U. S.)	1,483	-
1865 (State)	1,451	— 32
1870 (U. S.)	1,361	— 90
1875 (State)	1,261	=
1880 (U. S.)	1,365	+ 4
1885 (State)	1,215	—150
1890 (U. S.)	1,148	— 67
1895 (State)	1,032	—116

TOWN OF MIDDLEBOROUGH.

Established as "Middleberry" June 1, 1669, from common land called "Namasakett." Certain lands at Assowamsett Neck and places adjacent granted to Middleborough September 28, 1680. Part included in the new town of Halifax July 4, 1734. Boundary line between Middleborough and Carver established March 24, 1849. Part established as Lakeville May 13, 1853.

1765 (Prov.)	3,412	-
1776 (Prov.)	4,119	+ 707
1790 (U. S.)	4,526	+ 407
1800 (U. S.)	4,458	— 68
1810 (U. S.)	4,400	— 58
1820 (U. S.)	4,687	+ 287
1830 (U. S.)	5,008	+ 321
1840 (U. S.)	5,085	+ 77
1850 (U. S.)	5,236	+ 251
1855 (State)	4,324	—1,012
1860 (U. S.)	4,553	+ 229
1865 (State)	4,565	+ 12
1870 (U. S.)	4,687	+ 122
1875 (State)	5,023	+ 336
1880 (U. S.)	5,237	+ 214
1885 (State)	5,163	— 74
1890 (U. S.)	6,065	+ 902
1895 (State)	6,689	+ 624

TOWN OF NORWELL.

Originally established as South Scituate February 14, 1849, from part of Scituate. Boundary line between South Scituate and Hanover established May 15, 1857. Boundary line between South Scituate and Hanover established and part of each town annexed to the other town February 11, 1878. South Scituate authorized to change its name February 27, 1888. The name of Norwell adopted March 5, 1888.

YEARS AND CENSUS.	Population.	Increase (+), or Decrease (—), as Compared with Previous Census.
1850 (U. S.)	1,770	-
1855 (State)	1,786	+ 16
1860 (U. S.)	1,774	— 12
1865 (State)	1,635	—139
1870 (U. S.)	1,661	+ 26
1875 (State)	1,818	+157
1880 (U. S.)	1,820	+ 2
1885 (State)	1,589	—231
1890 (U. S.)	1,635	+ 46
1895 (State)	1,540	— 95

TOWN OF PEMBROKE.

Established March 21, 1712, from part of Duxbury called "Mattakeesett," a tract of land known as "the Major's Purchase," and the land called Marshfield Upper Lands at Mattakeesett. Part included in the new town of Halifax July 4, 1734. Part established as Hanson February 22, 1820. Boundary line between Pembroke and Hanover established March 6, 1835, and April 23, 1885.

1765 (Prov.)	1,409	-
1776 (Prov.)	1,768	+359
1790 (U. S.)	1,954	+186
1800 (U. S.)	1,943	— 11
1810 (U. S.)	2,051	+108
1820 (U. S.)	1,297	—754
1830 (U. S.)	1,325	+ 28
1840 (U. S.)	1,258	— 67
1850 (U. S.)	1,388	+130
1855 (State)	1,500	+112
1860 (U. S.)	1,524	+ 24
1865 (State)	1,489	— 35
1870 (U. S.)	1,447	— 42
1875 (State)	1,399	— 48
1880 (U. S.)	1,405	+ 6
1885 (State)	1,313	— 92
1890 (U. S.)	1,320	+ 7
1895 (State)	1,223	— 97

TOWN OF PLYMOUTH.

The first mention of Plymouth in the records is in "Plimouth's great Book of Deeds of Lands Enrolled," under the date of 1620. The boundary line between Plymouth and Sandwich established January 19, 1665, not being recorded, was ordered to be entered on the Records of the Court June 7, 1670. Part established as Plympton June 4, 1707. Part established as Kingston June 16, 1726. A plantation in Plymouth called "Agawam" included in the new town of Wareham July 10, 1739. Part annexed to Wareham January 29, 1827.

| 1765 (Prov.) . . . . | 2,177 | - |
| 1776 (Prov.) . . . . | 2,655 | +478 |

CENSUSES OF POPULATION — 1765-1895 — Continued.

TOWN OF PLYMOUTH — concluded.

YEARS AND CENSUS.	Popula-tion	Increase (+), or Decrease (—), as Compared with Previous Census
1790 (U. S.)	2,995	+340
1800 (U. S.)	3,524	+529
1810 (U. S.)	4,228	+704
1820 (U. S.)	4,348	+120
1830 (U. S.)	4,758	+410
1840 (U. S.)	5,281	+523
1850 (U. S.)	6,024	+743
1855 (State)	6,484	+460
1860 (U. S.)	6,272	—212
1865 (State)	6,068	—204
1870 (U. S.)	6,238	+170
1875 (State)	6,370	+132
1880 (U. S.)	7,093	+723
1885 (State)	7,239	+146
1890 (U. S.)	7,314	+ 75
1895 (State)	7,957	+643

TOWN OF PLYMPTON.

Established June 4, 1707, from part of Plymouth. Part included in the new town of Halifax July 4, 1734. Part established as Carver June 9, 1790. Boundary line between Plympton and Carver established February 8, 1793. Part annexed to Halifax March 16, 1831. Boundary line between Plympton and Halifax established and part of each town annexed to the other town February 6, 1865.

1765 (Prov.)	1,390	-
1776 (Prov.)	1,707	+317
1790 (U. S.)	956	—751
1800 (U. S.)	861	— 95
1810 (U. S.)	900	+ 39
1820 (U. S.)	930	+ 30
1830 (U. S.)	920	— 10
1840 (U. S.)	834	— 86
1850 (U. S.)	927	+ 93
1855 (State)	1,000	+ 73
1860 (U. S.)	994	— 6
1865 (State)	924	— 70
1870 (U. S.)	804	—120
1875 (State)	755	— 49
1880 (U. S.)	604	— 61
1885 (State)	600	— 94
1890 (U. S.)	597	— 3
1895 (State)	549	— 48

TOWN OF ROCHESTER.

Established June 4, 1686, from common land called "Sippican." Part included in the new town of Wareham July 10, 1739. Part annexed to Fairhaven (Bristol County) and boundary line established April 9, 1836. Part established as Marion May 14, 1852. Boundary line between Rochester and Marion established April 8, 1853. Part established as Mattapoisett May 20, 1857. Boundary lines between Rochester and Wareham established April 29, 1864, February 15, 1866, and June 3, 1887.

1765 (Prov.)	1,959	-
1776 (Prov.)	2,449	+510

TOWN OF ROCHESTER — concluded.

YEARS AND CENSUS.	Popula-tion	Increase (+), or Decrease (—), as Compared with Previous Census
1790 (U. S.)	2,644	+ 195
1800 (U. S.)	2,546	— 98
1810 (U. S.)	2,954	+ 408
1820 (U. S.)	3,034	+ 80
1830 (U. S.)	3,556	+ 522
1840 (U. S.)	3,864	+ 308
1850 (U. S.)	3,808	— 56
1855 (State)	3,048	— 760
1860 (U. S.)	1,232	—1,816
1865 (State)	1,156	— 76
1870 (U. S.)	1,024	— 132
1875 (State)	1,001	— 23
1880 (U. S.)	1,043	+ 42
1885 (State)	1,021	— 22
1890 (U. S.)	1,012	— 9
1895 (State)	1,021	+ 9

TOWN OF ROCKLAND.

Established March 9, 1874, from part of Abington. Boundary line between Rockland and Hanover established and part of each town annexed to the other town March 23, 1878.

1875 (State)	4,203	-
1880 (U. S.)	4,553	+350
1885 (State)	4,785	+232
1890 (U. S.)	5,213	+428
1895 (State)	5,523	+310

TOWN OF SCITUATE.

On July 1, 1633, the "brooke at Scituate" is mentioned in Plymouth Colony Records, Vol. I, p. 13. On October 4, 1636, "the towne of Scituate (viz't the purchasers and freemen)" was authorized to dispose of lands. Land granted to Scituate November 30, 1640. Boundary line established March 7, 1643. Part included in the new town of Hanover June 14, 1727. Part annexed to Marshfield March 10, 1788. Part annexed to Cohasset (Norfolk County) June 14, 1823. Boundary line between Scituate and Cohasset established and part of each town annexed to the other town March 20, 1840. Part established as South Scituate (Norwell) February 14, 1849. Boundary line between Scituate and Marshfield established May 11, 1887.

1765 (Prov.)	2,488	-
1776 (Prov.)	2,672	+ 184
1790 (U. S.)	2,856	+ 184
1800 (U. S.)	2,728	— 128
1810 (U. S.)	2,969	+ 241
1820 (U. S.)	3,305	+ 336
1830 (U. S.)	3,468	+ 163
1840 (U. S.)	3,886	+ 418
1850 (U. S.)	2,149	—1,737
1855 (State)	2,269	+ 120
1860 (U. S.)	2,227	— 42
1865 (State)	2,269	+ 42
1870 (U. S.)	2,350	+ 81
1875 (State)	2,463	+ 113
1880 (U. S.)	2,466	+ 3

CENSUSES OF POPULATION — 1765-1895 — Continued.

TOWN OF SCITUATE — concluded.

YEARS AND CENSUS.	Popula-tion	Increase (+), or Decrease (−), as Compared with Previous Census
1885 (State)	2,350	−116
1890 (U. S.)	2,318	− 32
1895 (State)	2,246	− 72

TOWN OF WAREHAM.

Established July 10, 1739, from part of Rochester and a plantation in Plymouth called "Agawam." Parts of Carver and Plymouth annexed January 20, 1827. Boundary line between Wareham and Marion established February 18, 1859. Boundary line between Wareham and Rochester established April 20, 1864. Boundary line between Wareham and Marion established February 13, 1866. Boundary line between Wareham and Rochester established February 15, 1866, and June 3, 1887.

1765 (Prov.)	503	−
1776 (Prov.)	711	+ 208
1790 (U. S.)	854	+ 143
1800 (U. S.)	770	− 84
1810 (U. S.)	851	+ 81
1820 (U. S.)	952	+ 101
1830 (U. S.)	1,885	+ 933
1840 (U. S.)	2,002	+ 117
1850 (U. S.)	3,186	+1,184
1855 (State)	3,246	+ 60
1860 (U. S.)	3,186	− 60
1865 (State)	2,798	− 388
1870 (U. S.)	3,098	+ 300
1875 (State)	2,874	− 224
1880 (U. S.)	2,896	+ 22
1885 (State)	3,254	+ 358
1890 (U. S.)	3,451	+ 197
1895 (State)	3,367	− 84

TOWN OF WEST BRIDGEWATER.

Established February 16, 1822, from part of Bridgewater. Boundary line between West Bridgewater and North Bridgewater established January 26, 1825. Part of West Bridgewater annexed to Brockton if the Act is accepted by Brockton May 8, 1893; Act accepted by Brockton November 7, 1893, taking effect March 1, 1894. Act of May 8, 1893 amended March 12, 1894. The date of establishment of this town is subsequent to the date of the earliest census in which population appears. This is due, probably, to the fact that the territory in question was well defined and recognized in census enumerations prior to the date of its formal incorporation as a town.

1820 (U. S.)	1,055	−
1830 (U. S.)	1,042	− 13
1840 (U. S.)	1,201	+159
1850 (U. S.)	1,447	+246
1855 (State)	1,734	+287
1860 (U. S.)	1,846	+112
1865 (State)	1,825	− 21
1870 (U. S.)	1,803	− 22
1875 (State)	1,758	− 45
1880 (U. S.)	1,665	− 93
1885 (State)	1,707	+ 42
1890 (U. S.)	1,917	+210
1895 (State)	1,747	−170

TOWN OF WHITMAN.

Originally established as South Abington March 4, 1875, from parts of Abington and East Bridgewater. Part annexed to Brockton and part of Brockton annexed April 24, 1875. South Abington authorized to change its name March 5, 1886. The name of Whitman adopted May 3, 1886.

YEARS AND CENSUS.	Popula-tion	Increase (+), or Decrease (−), as Compared with Previous Census
1875 (State)	2,456	−
1880 (U. S.)	3,024	+ 568
1885 (State)	3,595	+ 571
1890 (U. S.)	4,441	+ 846
1895 (State)	5,744	+1,303

COUNTY OF SUFFOLK.

Incorporated May 10, 1643. (Mass. Records, Vol. II, p. 58.)

1765 (Prov.)	15,982	−
1776 (Prov.)	3,208	−12,774
1790 (U. S.)	18,792	+15,584
1800 (U. S.)	25,786	+ 6,994
1810 (U. S.)	34,381	+ 8,595
1820 (U. S.)	43,940	+ 9,559
1830 (U. S.)	62,163	+18,223
1840 (U. S.)	95,773	+33,610
1850 (U. S.)	144,517	+48,744
1855 (State)	171,841	+27,324
1860 (U. S.)	192,700	+20,859
1865 (State)	208,212	+15,512
1870 (U. S.)	270,802	+62,590
1875 (State)	364,886	+94,084
1880 (U. S.)	387,927	+23,041
1885 (State)	421,109	+33,182
1890 (U. S.)	484,780	+63,671
1895 (State)	539,799	+55,019

CITY OF BOSTON.

On September 7, 1630, "Ordered that Tri-mountain shall be called Boston" (Mass. Records, Vol. I, p. 75). On November 7, 1632, "Ordered that the neck of land betwixt Powder Horne Hill and Pullen Poynte shall belong to Boston" (Mass. Records, Vol. I, p. 101). Boundary line between Boston and Roxbury established March 4, 1633. On May 14, 1634, "Boston shall have convenient enlargement at Mount Woolliston," to be reported to the next General Court (Mass. Records, Vol. I, p. 119). On September 3, 1634, "Ordered that Wynetsemit shall belong to Boston" (Mass Records, Vol. I, p. 125). On September 25, 1634, "Boston shall have inlargement at Mount Woolliston and Rumney Marshe" (Mass. Records, Vol. I, p. 130). Deer, Hog, Long, and Spectacle Islands granted to Boston March 4, 1635. Boundary line between Boston and Charlestown established March 8, 1635. Boundary lines between Boston and Charlestown and Boston and Dorchester established March 28, 1636. Noddle's Island annexed March 9, 1637. "Mount Woollaston" established as Braintree May 13, 1640. Boundary line between Boston and Roxbury, at Muddy River, established October 7, 1641. Boundary line between Boston and Cambridge established October 7, 1641. Part called "Muddy River" established as Brookline (Norfolk County) November 13, 1705. Part called "Winnisimet, Rumney Marsh, and Pullin Point, or otherwise called Number Thirteen (excepting Noddle's Island and Hog Island)," established as Chelsea January 10, 1739. Part of Dorchester annexed March 6, 1804. Boston incorporated as a city February 23, 1822. Act of incorporation accepted by the town March 4, 1822.

CENSUSES OF POPULATION — 1765–1895 — Continued.

CITY OF BOSTON — continued.

Boundary line between Boston and Brookline established February 22, 1825. Thompson's Island set off from Dorchester and annexed to Boston, while it shall be used for charitable purposes, March 25, 1834. Boundary line between Boston and Roxbury established March 16, 1836, and April 19, 1837. Part of Roxbury annexed and boundary line established May 3, 1850. Part of Dorchester annexed May 21, 1855. Part of Roxbury annexed and boundary line established if the Act is accepted by both cities April 3, 1860; accepted by Roxbury April 16, 1860; accepted by Boston May 8, 1860. Roxbury annexed if the Act is accepted by both cities June 1, 1867; accepted by both September 9, 1867, taking effect January 5, 1868. Dorchester annexed if the Act is accepted by both places June 4, 1869; accepted by both June 22, 1869; taking effect January 3, 1870. Boundary line between Boston and West Roxbury established April 2, 1870. Part of Brookline annexed June 18, 1870; Act accepted by Boston November 4, 1870. Part of West Roxbury (Mount Hope Cemetery) annexed April 12, 1872. Boundary line between Boston and Brookline established April 27, 1872. Charlestown annexed if the Act is accepted by both cities May 14, 1873. Brighton annexed if the Act is accepted by both places May 21, 1873. West Roxbury annexed if the Act is accepted by both places May 29, 1873. Acts of annexation accepted by Boston, Charlestown, Brighton, and West Roxbury October 7, 1873, taking effect January 5, 1874. Part of Brookline annexed May 8, 1874. Boundary line between Boston and Newton (Middlesex County) established May 29, 1874. Part annexed to Newton May 5, 1875; Act accepted by Newton June 23, 1875, taking effect July 1, 1875. Boundary line between Boston and Brookline established May 27, 1890. Boundary line between Boston and Somerville (Middlesex County) established May 4, 1891. Boundary line between Boston and Brookline established April 13, 1894.

YEARS AND CENSUS.	Population	Increase (+), or Decrease (−), as Compared with Previous Census
1765 (Prov.)	15,520	−
1776 (Prov.)	2,719	−12,801
1790 (U. S.)	18,320	+15,601
1800 (U. S.)	24,937	+ 6,617
1810 (U. S.)	33,787	+ 8,850
1820 (U. S.)	43,298	+ 9,511
1830 (U. S.)	61,392	+18,094
1840 (U. S.)	93,383	+31,991
1850 (U. S.)	136,881	+43,498
1855 (State)	160,490	+23,609
1860 (U. S.)	177,840	+17,350
1865 (State)	192,318	+14,478
1870 (U. S.)	250,526	+58,208
1875 (State)	341,919	+91,393
1880 (U. S.)	362,839	+20,920
1885 (State)	390,393	+27,554
1890 (U. S.)	448,477	+58,084
1895 (State)	496,920	+48,443

BRIGHTON.

Established February 24, 1807, from a part of Cambridge (Middlesex County). Part of Cambridge annexed to Brighton January 27, 1816. By Act of May 21, 1873, Brighton was annexed to Boston, the Act being accepted by both places October 7, 1873, taking effect January 5, 1874.

1810 (U. S.)	608	
1820 (U. S.)	702	+ 94
1830 (U. S.)	972	+270
1840 (U. S.)	1,425	+453

CITY OF BOSTON (BRIGHTON) — continued.

YEARS AND CENSUS.	Population	Increase (+), or Decrease (−), as Compared with Previous Census
1850 (U. S.)	2,356	+ 931
1855 (State)	2,895	+ 539
1860 (U. S.)	3,375	+ 480
1865 (State)	3,854	+ 479
1870 (U. S.)	4,967	−1,113

CHARLESTOWN.

First mention of Charlestown occurs in Mass. Records, Vol. I, p. 73, August 23, 1630, where it is stated that the first Court of Assistants was held at "Charlton." Boundary lines between Charlestown and Newe Towne (now Cambridge, Middlesex County) established March 6, 1632. Boundary lines between Charlestown and Boston established July 8, 1635. Boundary lines established "eight miles into the country from their meeting-house" March 3, 1636. Boundary lines between Charlestown and Boston established March 28, 1636. "Lovels Iland is granted to Charlestowne, provided they imploy it for fishing by their own townesmen or hinder not others," October 28, 1636. Certain common lands granted to Charlestown May 13 and October 7, 1640. "The Iland called Lovels Iland" granted to Charlestown, "provided half the timber and fire-wood shall belong to the garrison at the castle," October 27, 1648. One thousand acres of land granted to Charlestown November 12, 1639. Certain common lands granted to Charlestown October 21, 1663. The grant made November 12, 1659, renewed October 19, 1664. Part of Charlestown established as Stoneham (Middlesex County) December 17, 1725. Parts of Charlestown annexed to Cambridge April 18, 1761, March 6, 1802, February 12, 1818, and June 17, 1820. Part of Medford (Middlesex County) annexed to Charlestown June 21, 1811. Part of Charlestown annexed to West Cambridge (Middlesex County) February 25, 1842. Part of Charlestown established as Somerville (Middlesex County) March 3, 1842. Charlestown incorporated as a city February 22, 1847. Act of incorporation accepted by the town March 10, 1847. By Act of May 14, 1873, Charlestown was annexed to the city of Boston, the Act being accepted by both cities October 7, 1873, taking effect January 5, 1874.

1765 (Prov.)	2,031	−
1776 (Prov.)	360	−1,671
1790 (U. S.)	1,583	+1,223
1800 (U. S.)	2,751	−1,168
1810 (U. S.)	4,959	+2,208
1820 (U. S.)	6,591	+1,632
1830 (U. S.)	8,783	+2,192
1840 (U. S.)	11,484	+2,701
1850 (U. S.)	17,216	+5,732
1855 (State)	21,700	+4,484
1860 (U. S.)	25,065	+3,365
1865 (State)	26,399	+1,334
1870 (U. S.)	28,323	+1,924

DORCHESTER.

In Mass. Records, Vol. I, p. 75, it was ordered that Mattapan be called Dorchester September 7, 1630. Boundary lines established between Boston and Dorchester March 28, 1636. "Squantums Neck and Mennens Moone are layd to Dorchester" June 2, 1641. One thousand acres of common lands granted to Dorchester November 12, 1639. Part of Dorchester established as Milton (Norfolk County) May 7, 1662. Part of Dorchester established as Stoughton (Norfolk County) December 22, 1726. Part of Dedham annexed to Dorchester June 2, 1739. Part of Dor-

CENSUSES OF POPULATION — 1765-1895 — Continued.

CITY OF BOSTON (DORCHESTER) — continued.

chester called "Squantum and the Farms" annexed to the new town of Quincy (Norfolk County) February 22, 1792. Another part of the same territory annexed to Quincy February 10, 1814, and other parts of Dorchester annexed to Quincy February 12, 1819, and May 2, 1855. Part of Dorchester annexed to Boston March 6, 1804. Boundary lines between Dorchester and Quincy established and part of Dorchester annexed to Quincy February 21, 1820. Part of Dedham (Norfolk County) annexed to Dorchester June 17, 1831. Thompson's Island set off from Dorchester and annexed to Boston, while it shall be used for charitable purposes, March 25, 1834. Part of Dorchester annexed to Boston May 21, 1855. Part of Dorchester included in the new town of Hyde Park (Norfolk County) April 22, 1868. Act of April 22, 1868, amended and boundary lines changed May 1, 1868. By Act of June 4, 1869, Dorchester was annexed to Boston, the Act being accepted by both places June 22, 1869, taking effect January 3, 1870.

YEARS AND CENSUS.	Population	Increase (+), or Decrease (—) as Compared with Previous Census.
1765 (Prov.)	1,330	-
1776 (Prov.)	1,513	+ 153
1790 (U. S.)	1,722	+ 209
1800 (U. S.)	2,347	+ 625
1810 (U. S.)	2,930	+ 583
1820 (U. S.)	3,684	+ 754
1830 (U. S.)	4,074	+ 390
1840 (U. S.)	4,875	+ 801
1850 (U. S.)	7,969	+3,094
1855 (State)	8,340	+ 371
1860 (U. S.)	9,769	+1,429
1865 (State)	10,717	+ 948

ROXBURY.

"Roxbury" is mentioned in the list of plantations September 28, 1630, on page 77, Vol. I of Mass. Records. Boundary lines between Roxbury and Boston established March 4, 1633. Boundary lines between Roxbury and Newe Towne (now Cambridge, Middlesex County) established April 7, 1635. Certain lands granted to Roxbury May 25, 1636, May 2, 1638, and October 16, 1690. Boundary lines between Roxbury and Dedham (Norfolk County) established May 16, 1638. Boundary lines between Roxbury and Boston at Muddy River established October 7, 1641. Boundary lines between Roxbury and Dedham established May 12, 1675. Boundary lines between Roxbury and Boston established March 16, 1836, and April 19, 1837. Part of Newton (Middlesex County) annexed to Roxbury April 23, 1838. Part of Roxbury annexed to Brookline (Norfolk County) February 24, 1844. Roxbury incorporated as a city March 12, 1846. Act of incorporation accepted by the town March 25, 1846. Boundary line between Roxbury and Boston established May 3, 1850, and part of Roxbury annexed to Boston. Part of Roxbury established as West Roxbury May 24, 1851. By Act of April 3, 1860, a part of Roxbury to be annexed to Boston, and boundary lines established if accepted by both cities; accepted by Roxbury April 16, 1860, by Boston May 8, 1860. By Act of June 1, 1867, Roxbury annexed to Boston the Act being accepted by both cities September 9, 1867, taking effect January 5, 1868.

1765 (Prov.)	1,487	-
1776 (Prov.)	1,433	— 54
1790 (U. S.)	2,226	+ 793
1800 (U. S.)	2,765	+ 539
1810 (U. S.)	3,669	+ 904
1820 (U. S.)	4,135	+ 466
1830 (U. S.)	5,247	+1,112

CITY OF BOSTON (ROXBURY) — concluded.

YEARS AND CENSUS.	Population	Increase (+), or Decrease (—) as Compared with Previous Census.
1840 (U. S.)	9,089	+3,842
1850 (U. S.)	18,364	+9,275
1855 (State)	18,469	+ 105
1860 (U. S.)	25,137	+6,668
1865 (State)	28,426	+3,289

WEST ROXBURY.

Established from a part of Roxbury May 24, 1851. Part of Dedham (Norfolk County) by Act of April 21, 1852, annexed to West Roxbury upon payment of $400; Act accepted by West Roxbury April 30, 1852, and amount paid by West Roxbury July 4, 1853. Boundary lines between West Roxbury and Boston established April 2, 1870. Part of West Roxbury (Mount Hope Cemetery) annexed to Boston April 12, 1872. By Act of May 29, 1873, West Roxbury was annexed to Boston the Act being accepted by both places October 7, 1873, taking effect January 5, 1874.

1855 (State)	4,812	-
1860 (U. S.)	6,310	+1,498
1865 (State)	6,912	+ 602
1870 (U. S.)	8,683	+1,771

CITY OF CHELSEA.

Established January 10, 1739, from part of Boston called "Winnissimet, Rumney Marsh, and Pulin Point, or otherwise called Number Thirteen (excepting Noddle's Island and Hog Island)." Part annexed to Saugus (Essex County) February 22, 1841. Part established as North Chelsea (now Revere) March 19, 1846. Chelsea incorporated as a city March 13, 1857. Act of incorporation accepted by the town March 23, 1857.

1765 (Prov.)	462	-
1776 (Prov.)	489	— 27
1790 (U. S.)	472	— 17
1800 (U. S.)	849	— 577
1810 (U. S.)	594	— 255
1820 (U. S.)	642	+ 48
1830 (U. S.)	771	— 129
1840 (U. S.)	2,390	+1,619
1850 (U. S.)	6,701	+4,311
1855 (State)	10,151	+3,450
1860 (U. S.)	13,395	+3,244
1865 (State)	14,403	+1,008
1870 (U. S.)	18,547	+4,144
1875 (State)	20,737	+2,190
1880 (U. S.)	21,782	+1,045
1885 (State)	25,709	+3,927
1890 (U. S.)	27,909	+2,200
1895 (State)	31,264	+3,355

TOWN OF REVERE.

Originally established as North Chelsea March 19, 1846, from part of Chelsea. Part established as Winthrop March 27, 1852. Name changed to Revere if accepted within ninety days March 24, 1871. Act accepted April 6, 1871.

CENSUSES OF POPULATION — 1765-1895 — Continued.

TOWN OF REVERE — concluded.

YEARS AND CENSUS.	Population	Increase (+), or Decrease (—), as Compared with Previous Census
1850 (U. S.)	935	-
1855 (State)	793	— 142
1860 (U. S.)	921	+ 128
1865 (State)	858	— 63
1870 (U. S.)	1,197	+ 339
1875 (State)	1,603	+ 406
1880 (U. S.)	2,263	+ 660
1885 (State)	3,637	+1,374
1890 (U. S.)	5,668	+2,031
1895 (State)	7,423	+1,755

TOWN OF WINTHROP.

Established March 27, 1852, from part of North Chelsea (Revere).

YEARS AND CENSUS.	Population	Increase (+), or Decrease (—)
1855 (State)	407	-
1860 (U. S.)	544	+ 137
1865 (State)	633	+ 89
1870 (U. S.)	532	— 101
1875 (State)	627	+ 95
1880 (U. S.)	1,043	+ 416
1885 (State)	1,370	+ 327
1890 (U. S.)	2,726	+1,356
1895 (State)	4,192	+1,466

COUNTY OF WORCESTER.

Incorporated April 2, 1731; Act took effect July 10, 1731. (Province Laws, Vol. II, p. 584.)

YEARS AND CENSUS.	Population	Increase (+), or Decrease (—)
1765 (Prov.)	32,827	-
1776 (Prov.)	46,437	+13,610
1790 (U. S.)*. . . .	56,807	+10,370
1800 (U. S.)	61,192	+ 4,385
1810 (U. S.)	64,910	+ 3,718
1820 (U. S.)	73,625	+ 8,715
1830 (U. S.)*. . . .	84,355	+10,730
1840 (U. S.)	95,313	+10,958
1850 (U. S.)	130,789	+35,476
1855 (State)	149,516	+18,727
1860 (U. S.)	159,659	+10,143
1865 (State)	162,912	+ 3,253
1870 (U. S.)	192,716	+29,804
1875 (State)	210,295	+17,579
1880 (U. S.)	226,897	+16,602
1885 (State)	244,039	+17,142
1890 (U. S.)	280,787	+36,748
1895 (State)	306,445	+25,658

TOWN OF ASHBURNHAM.

Established February 22, 1765, from the plantation of "Dorchester Canada." Part included in the new town of Ashby (Middlesex County) March 6, 1767. Part included in the new town of Gardner June 27, 1785. Part annexed to Ashby November 14, 1792. Part of Gardner annexed February 16, 1815. Part of Westminster annexed January 28, 1824.

TOWN OF ASHBURNHAM — concluded.

YEARS AND CENSUS.	Population	Increase (+), or Decrease (—), as Compared with Previous Census
1765 (Prov.)	[551]	-
1776 (Prov.)	551	=
1790 (U. S.)	951	+400
1800 (U. S.)	994	+ 43
1810 (U. S.)	1,036	+ 42
1820 (U. S.)	1,230	+194
1830 (U. S.)	1,402	+172
1840 (U. S.)	1,652	+250
1850 (U. S.)	1,875	+223
1855 (State)	2,211	+336
1860 (U. S.)	2,108	—103
1865 (State)	2,153	+ 45
1870 (U. S.)	2,172	+ 19
1875 (State)	2,141	— 31
1880 (U. S.)	1,666	—475
1885 (State)	2,058	+392
1890 (U. S.)	2,074	+ 16
1895 (State)	2,148	+ 74

TOWN OF ATHOL.

Established March 6, 1762, from the plantation called "Payquage." Part included in the District of Orange (Franklin County) October 15, 1783. Part included in the new town of Gerry (now Phillipston) October 20, 1786. Parts annexed to Royalston February 26, 1799, and March 7, 1803. Part of Gerry annexed February 28, 1806. Part of Orange annexed February 7, 1816. Certain common lands annexed June 11, 1829. Part of New Salem (Franklin County) annexed February 5, 1830. Part of New Salem called "Little Grant" annexed March 16, 1837.

YEARS AND CENSUS.	Population	Increase (+), or Decrease (—)
1765 (Prov.)	359	-
1776 (Prov.)	[848]	+ 489
1790 (U. S.)	848	=
1800 (U. S.)	993	+ 145
1810 (U. S.)	1,041	+ 48
1820 (U. S.)	1,211	+ 170
1830 (U. S.)	1,325	+ 114
1840 (U. S.)	1,591	+ 266
1850 (U. S.)	2,034	+ 443
1855 (State)	2,395	+ 361
1860 (U. S.)	2,604	+ 209
1865 (State)	2,814	+ 210
1870 (U. S.)	3,517	+ 703
1875 (State)	4,134	+ 617
1880 (U. S.)	4,307	+ 173
1885 (State)	4,758	+ 451
1890 (U. S.)	6,319	+1,561
1895 (State)	7,364	+1,045

TOWN OF AUBURN.

Originally established as "Ward" April 10, 1778, from the parish set off from Leicester, Oxford, Sutton, and Worcester. Name changed to Auburn February 17, 1837. Part of Auburn annexed to Millbury May 24, 1851.

* Includes population in 1790 of the following gores: adjoining Oxford, 237; adjoining Sturbridge, 64; adjoining Leominster, 27; adjoining Fitchburg, 14; adjoining Princeton, 26; total, 368; and for 1830, a tract of land called No-town, 69.

CENSUSES OF POPULATION — 1765-1895 — Continued.

TOWN OF AUBURN — concluded.

YEARS AND CENSUS.	Population	Increase (+), or Decrease (−), as Compared with Previous Census
1790 (U. S.)	473	–
1800 (U. S.)	532	+ 59
1810 (U. S.)	540	+ 8
1820 (U. S.)	608	+ 68
1830 (U. S.)	690	+ 82
1840 (U. S.)	649	− 41
1850 (U. S.)	879	+230
1855 (State)	885	+ 6
1860 (U. S.)	914	+ 29
1865 (State)	959	+ 45
1870 (U. S.)	1,178	+219
1875 (State)	1,233	+ 55
1880 (U. S.)	1,317	+ 84
1885 (State)	1,268	− 49
1890 (U. S.)	1,532	+264
1895 (State)	1,598	+ 66

TOWN OF BARRE.

Originally established as the "Rutland District" April 12, 1753, from a part of the town of Rutland. Rutland District established as Hutchinson June 17, 1774. The name of the town of Hutchinson changed to Barre November 7, 1776.

YEARS AND CENSUS.	Population	Increase (+), or Decrease (−)
1765 (Prov.)	734	–
1776 (Prov.)	1,329	+595
1790 (U. S.)	1,613	+284
1800 (U. S.)	1,937	+324
1810 (U. S.)	1,971	+ 34
1820 (U. S.)	2,077	+106
1830 (U. S.)	2,503	+426
1840 (U. S.)	2,751	+248
1850 (U. S.)	2,976	+225
1855 (State)	2,787	−189
1860 (U. S.)	2,973	+186
1865 (State)	2,856	−117
1870 (U. S.)	2,572	−284
1875 (State)	2,460	−112
1880 (U. S.)	2,419	− 41
1885 (State)	2,093	−326
1890 (U. S.)	2,239	+146
1895 (State)	2,278	+ 39

TOWN OF BERLIN.

Established March 16, 1784, from parts of Bolton and Marlborough (Middlesex County) as the District of Berlin. Part of Lancaster annexed February 8, 1791. Boundary line between Berlin and Northborough established and part of each town annexed to the other town February 15, 1806. Made a town February 6, 1812.

YEARS AND CENSUS.	Population	Increase (+), or Decrease (−)
1790 (U. S.)	512	–
1800 (U. S.)	590	+78
1810 (U. S.)	591	+ 1
1820 (U. S.)	625	+34
1830 (U. S.)	692	+67

TOWN OF BERLIN — concluded.

YEARS AND CENSUS.	Population	Increase (+), or Decrease (−), as Compared with Previous Census
1840 (U. S.)	763	+ 71
1850 (U. S.)	866	+103
1855 (State)	976	+110
1860 (U. S.)	1,106	+130
1865 (State)	1,061	− 45
1870 (U. S.)	1,016	− 45
1875 (State)	987	− 29
1880 (U. S.)	977	− 10
1885 (State)	899	− 78
1890 (U. S.)	884	− 15
1895 (State)	897	+ 13

TOWN OF BLACKSTONE.

Established March 25, 1845, from part of Mendon.

YEARS AND CENSUS.	Population	Increase (+), or Decrease (−)
1850 (U. S.)	4,391	–
1855 (State)	5,346	+955
1860 (U. S.)	5,453	+107
1865 (State)	4,857	−596
1870 (U. S.)	5,421	+564
1875 (State)	4,640	−781
1880 (U. S.)	4,907	+267
1885 (State)	5,436	+529
1890 (U. S.)	6,138	+702
1895 (State)	6,039	− 99

TOWN OF BOLTON.

Established June 24, 1738, from part of Lancaster. Part included in the District of Berlin March 16, 1784. Part of Marlborough (Middlesex County) annexed February 11, 1829. Boundary line between Bolton and Marlborough established March 16, 1838. Part annexed to Hudson (Middlesex County) March 20, 1868.

YEARS AND CENSUS.	Population	Increase (+), or Decrease (−)
1765 (Prov.)	925	–
1776 (Prov.)	1,210	+285
1790 (U. S.)	861	−349
1800 (U. S.)	945	+ 84
1810 (U. S.)	1,037	+ 92
1820 (U. S.)	1,229	+192
1830 (U. S.)	1,253	+ 24
1840 (U. S.)	1,186	− 67
1850 (U. S.)	1,263	+ 77
1855 (State)	1,255	− 8
1860 (U. S.)	1,348	+ 93
1865 (State)	1,502	+154
1870 (U. S.)	1,014	−488
1875 (State)	987	− 27
1880 (U. S.)	903	− 84
1885 (State)	876	− 27
1890 (U. S.)	827	− 49
1895 (State)	797	− 30

TOWN OF BOYLSTON.

Established March 1, 1786, from part of Shrewsbury. Part included in the new town of West Boylston Jan-

CENSUSES OF POPULATION — 1765-1895 — Continued.

TOWN OF BOYLSTON — concluded.

uary 30, 1808. Parts annexed to West Boylston February 10, 1820, and June 17, 1820.

YEARS AND CENSUS.	Population	Increase (+), or Decrease (—), as Compared with Previous Census
1790 (U. S.)	839	-
1800 (U. S.)	1,058	+219
1810 (U. S.)	800	−258
1820 (U. S.)	902	+102
1830 (U. S.)	820	− 82
1840 (U. S.)	797	− 23
1850 (U. S.)	918	+121
1855 (State)	835	− 83
1860 (U. S.)	929	+ 94
1865 (State)	792	−137
1870 (U. S.)	800	+ 8
1875 (State)	895	+ 95
1880 (U. S.)	854	− 41
1885 (State)	834	− 20
1890 (U. S.)	770	− 64
1895 (State)	729	− 41

TOWN OF BROOKFIELD.

On October 15, 1673, Quobauge to be the town of "Brookefeild," when forty or fifty families shall have settled there (Mass. Records, Vol. IV, Part 2, p. 568). Brookfield invested with the privileges of a town November 12, 1718. Part included in the new town of Western (now Warren) January 16, 1742. Boundary line between Brookfield and New Braintree established and part of each town annexed to the other town June 10, 1791, and March 8, 1792. Part established as North Brookfield February 28, 1812. Part annexed to Ware (Hampshire County) February 8, 1823. Part established as West Brookfield March 3, 1848. Part of North Brookfield annexed April 15, 1854.

1765 (Prov.)	1,811	-
1776 (Prov.)	2,649	+838
1790 (U. S.)	3,100	+451
1800 (U. S.)	3,284	+184
1810 (U. S.)	3,170	−114
1820 (U. S.)	2,292	−878
1830 (U. S.)	2,342	+ 50
1840 (U. S.)	2,472	+130
1850 (U. S.)	1,674	−798
1855 (State)	2,007	+333
1860 (U. S.)	2,276	+269
1865 (State)	2,101	−175
1870 (U. S.)	2,527	+426
1875 (State)	2,660	+133
1880 (U. S.)	2,820	+160
1885 (State)	3,013	+193
1890 (U. S.)	3,352	+339
1895 (State)	3,279	− 73

TOWN OF CHARLTON.

Established November 21, 1754, from part of Oxford as the District of Charlton. The district made a town by Act of August 23, 1775. Part annexed to Oxford January 5, 1789. Part annexed to Sturbridge June 26, 1792. Part annexed to Oxford February 23, 1809. Part included in the new town of Southbridge February 15, 1816.

TOWN OF CHARLTON — concluded.

YEARS AND CENSUS.	Population	Increase (+), or Decrease (—), as Compared with Previous Census
1765 (Prov.)	739	-
1776 (Prov.)	1,310	+571
1790 (U. S.)	1,905	+595
1800 (U. S.)	2,120	+215
1810 (U. S.)	2,180	+ 60
1820 (U. S.)	2,134	− 46
1830 (U. S.)	2,173	+ 39
1840 (U. S.)	2,117	− 56
1850 (U. S.)	2,015	−102
1855 (State)	2,059	+ 44
1860 (U. S.)	2,047	− 12
1865 (State)	1,925	−122
1870 (U. S.)	1,878	− 47
1875 (State)	1,852	− 26
1880 (U. S.)	1,900	+ 48
1885 (State)	1,823	− 77
1890 (U. S.)	1,847	+ 24
1895 (State)	1,877	+ 30

TOWN OF CLINTON.

Established March 14, 1850, from part of Lancaster.

1850 (U. S.)	3,115	-
1855 (State)	3,636	+ 523
1860 (U. S.)	3,859	+ 223
1865 (State)	4,021	+ 162
1870 (U. S.)	5,429	−1,408
1875 (State)	6,781	−1,352
1880 (U. S.)	8,029	−1,248
1885 (State)	8,945	+ 916
1890 (U. S.)	10,424	−1,479
1895 (State)	11,497	−1,073

TOWN OF DANA.

Established February 18, 1801, from parts of Greenwich (Hampshire County), Hardwick, and Petersham. Boundary line between Dana and Petersham established February 12, 1802. Boundary line between Dana and Greenwich established June 19, 1811. Parts of Hardwick and Petersham annexed February 4, 1842. Boundary line between Dana and Petersham established April 10, 1882.

1810 (U. S.)	625	-
1820 (U. S.)	664	+ 39
1830 (U. S.)	623	− 41
1840 (U. S.)	691	+ 68
1850 (U. S.)	842	+151
1855 (State)	824	− 18
1860 (U. S.)	876	+ 52
1865 (State)	789	− 87
1870 (U. S.)	758	− 31
1875 (State)	760	+ 2
1880 (U. S.)	736	− 24
1885 (State)	695	− 41
1890 (U. S.)	700	+ 5
1895 (State)	717	+ 17

CENSUSES OF POPULATION — 1765-1895 — Continued.

TOWN OF DOUGLAS.

Established as a district June 5, 1746, from the district of "New Sherburn." Made a town by Act of August 23, 1775. Boundary line between Douglas and Webster established February 27, 1841. Boundary line between Douglas and Uxbridge established April 25, 1864.

YEARS AND CENSUS.	Population	Increase (+), or Decrease (—), as Compared with Previous Census
1765 (Prov.)	521	–
1776 (Prov.)	800	+279
1790 (U. S.)	1,079	+279
1800 (U. S.)	1,083	+ 4
1810 (U. S.)	1,142	+ 59
1820 (U. S.)	1,375	+233
1830 (U. S.)	1,742	+367
1840 (U. S.)	1,617	—125
1850 (U. S.)	1,878	+261
1855 (State)	2,320	+442
1860 (U. S.)	2,442	+122
1865 (State)	2,155	—287
1870 (U. S.)	2,182	+ 27
1875 (State)	2,202	+ 20
1880 (U. S.)	2,241	+ 39
1885 (State)	2,205	— 36
1890 (U. S.)	1,908	—297
1895 (State)	2,026	+118

TOWN OF DUDLEY.

Established February 2, 1732, from part of Oxford and certain common lands. Part of a gore of common land known as "Middlesex Gore" annexed June 25, 1794. Part included in the new town of Southbridge February 15, 1816. Part annexed to Southbridge February 23, 1822. Part included in the new town of Webster March 6, 1832.

	Population	Increase/Decrease
1765 (Prov.)	748	–
1776 (Prov.)	875	+127
1790 (U. S.)	1,114	+239
1800 (U. S.)	1,140	+ 26
1810 (U. S.)	1,226	+ 86
1820 (U. S.)	1,615	+389
1830 (U. S.)	2,155	+540
1840 (U. S.)	1,352	—803
1850 (U. S.)	1,443	+ 91
1855 (State)	1,523	+ 80
1860 (U. S.)	1,736	+213
1865 (State)	2,076	+340
1870 (U. S.)	2,388	+312
1875 (State)	2,653	+265
1880 (U. S.)	2,803	+150
1885 (State)	2,742	— 61
1890 (U. S.)	2,944	+202
1895 (State)	3,203	+259

CITY OF FITCHBURG.

Established February 3, 1764, from part of Lunenburg. Part included in the new town of Ashby (Middlesex County) March 6, 1767. Certain common lands annexed February 26, 1783. Parts annexed to Westminster February 27, 1796, and February 16, 1815. Part annexed to Ashby March 3, 1829. Fitchburg incorporated as a city March 8, 1872. Act of Incorporation accepted by the town April 8, 1872.

YEARS AND CENSUS.	Population	Increase (+), or Decrease (—), as Compared with Previous Census
1765 (Prov.)	259	–
1776 (Prov.)	643	+ 384
1790 (U. S.)	1,151	+ 508
1800 (U. S.)	1,390	+ 239
1810 (U. S.)	1,566	+ 176
1820 (U. S.)	1,736	+ 170
1830 (U. S.)	2,169	+ 433
1840 (U. S.)	2,604	+ 435
1850 (U. S.)	5,120	+2,516
1855 (State)	6,442	+1,322
1860 (U. S.)	7,805	+1,363
1865 (State)	8,118	+ 313
1870 (U. S.)	11,260	+3,142
1875 (State)	12,289	+1,029
1880 (U. S.)	12,429	+ 140
1885 (State)	15,375	+2,946
1890 (U. S.)	22,037	+6,662
1895 (State)	26,409	+4,372

TOWN OF GARDNER.

Established June 27, 1785, from parts of Ashburnham, Templeton, Westminster, and Winchendon. Part annexed to Winchendon March 2, 1787. Part of Winchendon annexed February 22, 1794. Part annexed to Ashburnham February 16, 1815. Part of Winchendon annexed May 24, 1851.

	Population	Increase/Decrease
1790 (U. S.)	531	–
1800 (U. S.)	667	+ 136
1810 (U. S.)	815	+ 148
1820 (U. S.)	911	+ 96
1830 (U. S.)	1,023	+ 112
1840 (U. S.)	1,260	+ 237
1850 (U. S.)	1,533	+ 273
1855 (State)	2,183	+ 650
1860 (U. S.)	2,646	+ 463
1865 (State)	2,553	— 93
1870 (U. S.)	3,333	+ 780
1875 (State)	3,730	+ 397
1880 (U. S.)	4,988	+1,258
1885 (State)	7,283	+2,295
1890 (U. S.)	8,424	+1,141
1895 (State)	9,182	+ 758

TOWN OF GRAFTON.

Established April 18, 1735, from the plantation of "Hassanamisco." Certain common lands annexed June 14, 1825. Part of Shrewsbury annexed March 3, 1826. Part of Sutton annexed March 3, 1842.

	Population	Increase/Decrease
1765 (Prov.)	763	–
1776 (Prov.)	861	+ 98
1790 (U. S.)	872	+ 11
1800 (U. S.)	985	+ 113
1810 (U. S.)	946	— 39
1820 (U. S.)	1,154	+ 208
1830 (U. S.)	1,889	+ 735

CENSUSES OF POPULATION — 1765-1895 — Continued.

TOWN OF GRAFTON — concluded.

YEARS AND CENSUS.	Population	Increase (+), or Decrease (—), as compared with Previous Census
1840 (U. S.)	2,943	+1,054
1850 (U. S.)	3,904	+ 961
1855 (State)	4,409	+ 505
1860 (U. S.)	4,317	— 92
1865 (State)	3,961	— 356
1870 (U. S.)	4,594	+ 633
1875 (State)	4,442	— 152
1880 (U. S.)	4,030	— 412
1885 (State)	4,498	+ 468
1890 (U. S.)	5,002	+ 504
1895 (State)	5,101	+ 99

TOWN OF HARDWICK.

Established January 10, 1739, from the plantation called "Lambstown." Part of Hardwick included in the District of New Braintree January 31, 1751. Part included in the new town of Dana February 18, 1801. Part of New Braintree annexed June 10, 1814. Certain common lands annexed February 7, 1831. Certain common lands called "Hardwick Gore" annexed February 6, 1835. Part annexed to Dana February 4, 1842.

YEARS AND CENSUS.	Population	Increase/Decrease
1765 (Prov.)	1,010	-
1776 (Prov.)	1,393	+383
1790 (U. S.)	1,725	+332
1800 (U. S.)	1,727	+ 2
1810 (U. S.)	1,657	— 70
1820 (U. S.)	1,836	+179
1830 (U. S.)	1,885	+ 49
1840 (U. S.)	1,789	— 96
1850 (U. S.)	1,631	—158
1855 (State)	1,523	—168
1860 (U. S.)	1,521	— 2
1865 (State)	1,967	+446
1870 (U. S.)	2,219	+252
1875 (State)	1,992	—227
1880 (U. S.)	2,233	+241
1885 (State)	3,145	+912
1890 (U. S.)	2,922	—223
1895 (State)	2,655	—267

TOWN OF HARVARD.

Established June 29, 1732, from parts of Groton and Stow (Middlesex County) and Lancaster. Part included in the District of Boxborough (Middlesex County) February 25, 1783.

YEARS AND CENSUS.	Population	Increase/Decrease
1765 (Prov.)	1,126	-
1776 (Prov.)	1,315	+189
1790 (U. S.)	1,387	+ 72
1800 (U. S.)	1,319	— 68
1810 (U. S.)	1,431	+112
1820 (U. S.)	1,597	+166
1830 (U. S.)	1,600	+ 3
1840 (U. S.)	1,571	— 29
1850 (U. S.)	1,630	+ 59
1855 (State)	1,533	— 97

TOWN OF HARVARD — concluded.

YEARS AND CENSUS.	Population	Increase (+), or Decrease (—), as compared with Previous Census
1860 (U. S.)	1,507	— 26
1865 (State)	1,355	—152
1870 (U. S.)	1,341	— 14
1875 (State)	1,304	— 37
1880 (U. S.)	1,253	— 51
1885 (State)	1,184	— 69
1890 (U. S.)	1,095	— 89
1895 (State)	1,162	+ 67

TOWN OF HOLDEN.

Established January 9, 1741, from part of Worcester called North Worcester. Boundary line between Holden and Paxton established March 27, 1793. Part annexed to Paxton February 13, 1804. Part included in the new town of West Boylston January 30, 1808. Part of Paxton annexed March 19, 1831. Part annexed to Paxton April 9, 1838.

YEARS AND CENSUS.	Population	Increase/Decrease
1765 (Prov.)	495	-
1776 (Prov.)	749	+254
1790 (U. S.)	1,077	+328
1800 (U. S.)	1,142	+ 65
1810 (U. S.)	1,072	— 70
1820 (U. S.)	1,402	+330
1830 (U. S.)	1,719	+317
1840 (U. S.)	1,874	+155
1850 (U. S.)	1,933	+ 59
1855 (State)	2,114	+181
1860 (U. S.)	1,945	—169
1865 (State)	1,846	— 99
1870 (U. S.)	2,062	+216
1875 (State)	2,180	+118
1880 (U. S.)	2,499	+319
1885 (State)	2,471	— 28
1890 (U. S.)	2,623	+152
1895 (State)	2,602	— 21

TOWN OF HOPEDALE.

Established April 7, 1886, from part of Milford.

YEARS AND CENSUS.	Population	Increase/Decrease
1890 (U. S.)	1,176	
1895 (State)	1,377	+201

TOWN OF HUBBARDSTON.

Established as a district June 13, 1767, from part of Rutland. Made a town by Act of August 23, 1775. Part annexed to Princeton February 16, 1810.

YEARS AND CENSUS.	Population	Increase/Decrease
1776 (Prov.)	488	-
1790 (U. S.)	933	+445
1800 (U. S.)	1,113	+180
1810 (U. S.)	1,127	+ 14
1820 (U. S.)	1,367	+240
1830 (U. S.)	1,674	+307
1840 (U. S.)	1,784	+110
1850 (U. S.)	1,825	+ 41

CENSUSES OF POPULATION — 1765–1895 — Continued.

TOWN OF HUBBARDSTON — concluded.

YEARS AND CENSUS.	Population	Increase (+), or Decrease (—), as Compared with Previous Census
1855 (State)	1,744	— 81
1860 (U. S.)	1,621	—123
1865 (State)	1,546	— 75
1870 (U. S.)	1,654	+108
1875 (State)	1,440	—214
1880 (U. S.)	1,386	— 54
1885 (State)	1,303	— 83
1890 (U. S.)	1,346	+ 43
1895 (State)	1,274	— 72

TOWN OF LANCASTER.

On May 18, 1653, "The court taking the condition of Nashaway into further consideration do order, that it shall be called henceforth West Towne" (Mass. Records, Vol. III, p. 303). Under the same date Nashaway is made a township and is ordered to be called Prescott, and then Prescott is ordered to be called Lancaster, but no Act has been found which abolishes the township of West Towne. (See Prescott, Hampshire County.) Boundary lines established October 11, 1672. Part included in the new town of Harvard June 29, 1732. Part established as Bolton June 24, 1738. Part established as Leominster June 23, 1740. Part of Shrewsbury annexed February 27, 1768. Part annexed to Shrewsbury February 26, 1781. Part established as Sterling April 25, 1781. Part annexed to Berlin February 8, 1791. Boundary line between Lancaster and Sterling established March 12, 1793. Part annexed to Sterling and boundary line established March 7, 1857. Part established as Clinton March 14, 1850.

1765 (Prov.)	1,999	-
1776 (Prov.)	2,746	+ 747
1790 (U. S.)	1,460	—1,286
1800 (U. S.)	1,584	+ 124
1810 (U. S.)	1,694	+ 110
1820 (U. S.)	1,862	+ 168
1830 (U. S.)	2,014	+ 152
1840 (U. S.)	2,019	+ 5
1850 (U. S.)	1,688	— 331
1855 (State)	1,728	+ 40
1860 (U. S.)	1,932	+ 204
1865 (State)	1,752	— 180
1870 (U. S.)	1,845	+ 93
1875 (State)	1,957	+ 112
1880 (U. S.)	2,008	+ 51
1885 (State)	2,050	+ 42
1890 (U. S.)	2,201	+ 151
1895 (State)	2,180	— 21

TOWN OF LEICESTER.

Established February 15, 1713, from common lands called "Towtaid." Part made the District of Spencer April 12, 1753. Part included in the District of Paxton February 12, 1765. A parish lately set off from Leicester and other towns established as Ward (now Auburn) April 10, 1778.

1765 (Prov.)	770	-
1776 (Prov.)	1,005	+235
1790 (U. S.)	1,076	+ 71

TOWN OF LEICESTER — concluded.

YEARS AND CENSUS.	Population	Increase (+), or Decrease (—), as Compared with Previous Census
1800 (U. S.)	1,103	+ 27
1810 (U. S.)	1,181	+ 78
1820 (U. S.)	1,252	+ 71
1830 (U. S.)	1,782	+530
1840 (U. S.)	1,707	— 75
1850 (U. S.)	2,269	+562
1855 (State)	2,589	+320
1860 (U. S.)	2,748	+159
1865 (State)	2,527	—221
1870 (U. S.)	2,768	+241
1875 (State)	2,770	+ 2
1880 (U. S.)	2,779	+ 9
1885 (State)	2,923	+144
1890 (U. S.)	3,120	+197
1895 (State)	3,239	+119

TOWN OF LEOMINSTER.

Established June 23, 1740, from part of Lancaster. Part of certain common lands called "No Town" annexed April 13, 1829.

1765 (Prov.)	743	-
1776 (Prov.)	978	+ 235
1790 (U. S.)	1,189	+ 211
1800 (U. S.)	1,486	+ 297
1810 (U. S.)	1,584	+ 98
1820 (U. S.)	1,790	+ 206
1830 (U. S.)	1,861	+ 71
1840 (U. S.)	2,069	+ 208
1850 (U. S.)	3,121	+1,052
1855 (State)	3,200	+ 79
1860 (U. S.)	3,522	+ 322
1865 (State)	3,313	— 209
1870 (U. S.)	3,894	+ 581
1875 (State)	5,201	+1,307
1880 (U. S.)	5,772	+ 571
1885 (State)	5,297	— 475
1890 (U. S.)	7,269	+1,972
1895 (State)	9,211	+1,942

TOWN OF LUNENBURG.

Established August 1, 1728, from the south part of Turkey Hills. Part established as Fitchburg February 3, 1764. Boundary line between Lunenburg and Shirley (Middlesex County) established March 3, 1846, and April 25, 1848.

1765 (Prov.)	821	-
1776 (Prov.)	1,265	+444
1790 (U. S.)	1,277	+ 12
1800 (U. S.)	1,243	— 34
1810 (U. S.)	1,371	+128
1820 (U. S.)	1,209	—162
1830 (U. S.)	1,317	+108
1840 (U. S.)	1,272	— 45
1850 (U. S.)	1,249	— 23
1855 (State)	1,224	— 25

CENSUSES OF POPULATION — 1765-1895 — Continued.

TOWN OF LUNENBURG — concluded.

YEARS AND CENSUS.	Population.	Increase (+), or Decrease (—), as Compared with Previous Census.
1860 (U. S.)	1,212	— 12
1865 (State)	1,167	—45
1870 (U. S.)	1,121	—46
1875 (State)	1,153	+32
1880 (U. S.)	1,101	—52
1885 (State)	1,071	—30
1890 (U. S.)	1,146	+75
1895 (State)	1,237	+91

TOWN OF MENDON.

On May 15, 1667, it was ordered that the name of Mendon be given to " the Court's grant at Quntipauge, being the township of Qunshapage as it was laid out according to the grant of the General Court," and that Mendon be settled as a town (Mass. Records, Vol. IV, Part 2, p. 341). Certain lands granted to Mendon May 20, 1669. Certain lands annexed June 29, 1719. Part included in the new town of Bellingham (Norfolk County) November 27, 1719. Part established as Uxbridge June 27, 1727. Part included in the new town of Upton June 14, 1735. Part of Uxbridge annexed April 24, 1770. Part established as Milford April 11, 1780. Part established as Blackstone March 25, 1845. Boundary line between Mendon and Bellingham established March 7, 1872.

1765 (Prov.)	1,808	-
1776 (Prov.)	2,392	+ 484
1790 (U. S.)	1,555	— 767
1800 (U. S.)	1,628	+ 73
1810 (U. S.)	1,819	+ 191
1820 (U. S.)	2,254	+ 435
1830 (U. S.)	3,152	+ 898
1840 (U. S.)	3,524	+ 372
1850 (U. S.)	1,300	—2,224
1855 (State)	1,382	+ 82
1860 (U. S.)	1,351	— 31
1865 (State)	1,207	— 144
1870 (U. S.)	1,175	— 32
1875 (State)	1,176	+ 1
1880 (U. S.)	1,094	— 82
1885 (State)	945	— 149
1890 (U. S.)	919	— 26
1895 (State)	889	— 30

TOWN OF MILFORD.

Established April 11, 1780, from part of Mendon. Boundary line between Milford and Holliston and Hopkinton (Middlesex County) established and parts of Holliston and Hopkinton annexed to Milford, and part of Milford annexed to Hopkinton March 27, 1835. Boundary line between Milford and Holliston established April 1, 1859. Part established as Hopedale April 7, 1886.

1790 (U. S.)	829	-
1800 (U. S.)	907	+ 68
1810 (U. S.)	973	+ 66
1820 (U. S.)	1,160	+187
1830 (U. S.)	1,360	+200
1840 (U. S.)	1,773	+413

TOWN OF MILFORD — concluded.

YEARS AND CENSUS.	Population.	Increase (+), or Decrease (—), as Compared with Previous Census.
1850 (U. S.)	4,819	+3,046
1855 (State)	7,489	+2,670
1860 (U. S.)	9,132	+1,643
1865 (State)	9,108	— 24
1870 (U. S.)	9,890	+ 782
1875 (State)	9,818	— 72
1880 (U. S.)	9,310	— 508
1885 (State)	9,343	+ 33
1890 (U. S.)	8,780	— 563
1895 (State)	8,959	+ 179

TOWN OF MILLBURY.

Established June 11, 1813, from part of Sutton. Part of Auburn annexed May 24, 1851.

1820 (U. S.)	926	-
1830 (U. S.)	1,611	+685
1840 (U. S.)	2,171	+560
1850 (U. S.)	3,081	+910
1855 (State)	3,286	+205
1860 (U. S.)	3,296	+ 10
1865 (State)	3,780	+484
1870 (U. S.)	4,397	+617
1875 (State)	4,529	+132
1880 (U. S.)	4,741	+212
1885 (State)	4,555	—186
1890 (U. S.)	4,428	—127
1895 (State)	5,222	+794

TOWN OF NEW BRAINTREE.

On January 31, 1751, " The precinct consisting of the lands called New Braintree, and part of the town of Hardwick is erected into a district" (Resolve). Made a town by Act of August 23, 1775. Boundary line between New Braintree and Brookfield established and parts of each town annexed to the other town June 10, 1791, and March 8, 1792. Part annexed to Hardwick June 10, 1814.

1765 (Prov.)	594	-
1776 (Prov.)	798	+204
1790 (U. S.)	939	+141
1800 (U. S.)	875	— 64
1810 (U. S.)	912	+ 37
1820 (U. S.)	888	— 24
1830 (U. S.)	825	— 63
1840 (U. S.)	752	— 73
1850 (U. S.)	852	+100
1855 (State)	775	— 77
1860 (U. S.)	805	+ 30
1865 (State)	752	— 53
1870 (U. S.)	640	—112
1875 (State)	606	— 34
1880 (U. S.)	610	+ 4
1885 (State)	558	— 52
1890 (U. S.)	573	+ 15
1895 (State)	542	— 31

CENSUSES OF POPULATION — 1765-1895 — Continued.

TOWN OF NORTHBOROUGH.

Established January 24, 1766, from part of West-borough as the District of Northborough. Made a town by Act of August 23, 1775. Boundary line be-tween Northborough and Berlin established and part of each town annexed to the other town February 15, 1806. Part of Marlborough (Middlesex County) an-nexed and boundary line established June 20, 1807.

YEARS AND CENSUS.	Popula-tion	Increase (+), or Decrease (—), as Com-pared with Pre-vious Census
1776 (Prov.)	562	-
1790 (U. S.)	619	+ 57
1800 (U. S.)	698	+ 79
1810 (U. S.)	794	+ 96
1820 (U. S.)	1,018	+224
1830 (U. S.)	992	— 26
1840 (U. S.)	1,248	+256
1850 (U. S.)	1,535	+287
1855 (State)	1,602	+ 67
1860 (U. S.)	1,565	— 37
1865 (State)	1,623	+ 58
1870 (U. S.)	1,504	—119
1875 (State)	1,398	—106
1880 (U. S.)	1,676	+278
1885 (State)	1,853	+177
1890 (U. S.)	1,952	+ 99
1895 (State)	1,940	— 12

TOWN OF NORTHBRIDGE.

Established July 14, 1772, from part of Uxbridge as the District of Northbridge. Made a town by Act of August 23, 1775. Part of Sutton annexed April 29, 1780, and February 17, 1801. Part annexed to Sutton June 15, 1831. Boundary line between Northbridge and Sutton established March 7, 1837. Part of Sut-ton annexed March 16, 1844. Boundary line between Northbridge and Uxbridge established and part of each town annexed to the other town April 29, 1856.

1776 (Prov.)	481	-
1790 (U. S.)	569	+ 88
1800 (U. S.)	544	— 25
1810 (U. S.)	713	+ 169
1820 (U. S.)	905	+ 192
1830 (U. S.)	1,053	+ 148
1840 (U. S.)	1,449	+ 396
1850 (U. S.)	2,230	+ 781
1855 (State)	2,104	— 126
1860 (U. S.)	2,633	+ 529
1865 (State)	2,642	+ 9
1870 (U. S.)	3,774	+1,132
1875 (State)	4,030	+ 256
1880 (U. S.)	4,053	+ 23
1885 (State)	3,786	— 267
1890 (U. S.)	4,603	+ 817
1895 (State)	5,286	+ 683

TOWN OF NORTH BROOKFIELD.

Established February 28, 1812, from part of Brook-field. Part annexed to Brookfield April 15, 1854.

TOWN OF NORTH BROOKFIELD — concluded.

YEARS AND CENSUS.	Popula-tion	Increase (+), or Decrease (—), as Com-pared with Pre-vious Census
1820 (U. S.)	1,095	-
1830 (U. S.)	1,241	+146
1840 (U. S.)	1,485	+244
1850 (U. S.)	1,939	+454
1855 (State)	2,349	+410
1860 (U. S.)	2,760	+411
1865 (State)	2,514	—246
1870 (U. S.)	3,343	+829
1875 (State)	3,749	+406
1880 (U. S.)	4,459	+710
1885 (State)	4,201	—258
1890 (U. S.)	3,871	—330
1895 (State)	4,635	+764

TOWN OF OAKHAM.

Established June 7, 1762, from part of Rutland. Made a town by Act of August 23, 1775.

1765 (Prov.)	270	-
1776 (Prov.)	598	+328
1790 (U. S.)	772	+174
1800 (U. S.)	801	+ 29
1810 (U. S.)	848	+ 47
1820 (U. S.)	986	+138
1830 (U. S.)	1,010	+ 24
1840 (U. S.)	1,038	+ 28
1850 (U. S.)	1,137	+ 99
1855 (State)	1,062	— 75
1860 (U. S.)	959	—103
1865 (State)	925	— 34
1870 (U. S.)	860	— 65
1875 (State)	873	+ 13
1880 (U. S.)	869	— 4
1885 (State)	749	—120
1890 (U. S.)	738	— 11
1895 (State)	605	—133

TOWN OF OXFORD.

The records are very deficient in regard to the suc-cessive settlements of this town, the first mention being May 31, 1693, in Mass. Archives, Vol. VI, p. 278, where Daniel Allen is recorded as Represent-ative from Oxford. The name of the town is also mentioned in the Tax Act September 14, 1694. Part included in the new town of Dudley February 2, 1732. Part established as the District of Charlton November 21, 1754. A parish lately set off from Oxford and other towns established as Ward (now Auburn) April 10, 1778. Part of Charlton annexed January 5, 1789. Part of Sutton annexed February 18, 1795. The Ox-ford South Gore annexed February 6, 1807. Part of Charlton annexed February 23, 1809. Part included in the new town of Webster March 6, 1832. The Oxford North Gore annexed March 22, 1838.

1765 (Prov.)	890	-
1776 (Prov.)	1,112	+222
1790 (U. S.)	1,000	—112
1800 (U. S.)	1,237	+237
1810 (U. S.)	1,277	+ 40

CENSUSES OF POPULATION — 1765-1895 — Continued.

TOWN OF OXFORD — concluded.

YEARS AND CENSUS.	Population	Increase (+), or Decrease (−), as Compared with Previous Census
1820 (U. S.)	1,562	+285
1830 (U. S.)	2,034	+472
1840 (U. S.)	1,742	−292
1850 (U. S.)	2,380	+638
1855 (State)	2,808	+428
1860 (U. S.)	3,034	+226
1865 (State)	2,713	−321
1870 (U. S.)	2,669	− 44
1875 (State)	2,938	+269
1880 (U. S.)	2,604	−334
1885 (State)	2,355	−249
1890 (U. S.)	2,616	+261
1895 (State)	2,390	−226

TOWN OF PAXTON.

Established as a district February 12, 1765, from parts of Leicester and Rutland. Part of Rutland adjudged to belong to the District of Paxton July 14, 1772. Made a town by Act of August 23, 1775. Boundary line between Paxton and Holden established March 27, 1793. Part of Holden annexed February 13, 1804. Boundary line between Paxton and Rutland established February 20, 1829. Part annexed to Holden March 19, 1831. Part of Holden annexed April 9, 1838. Part of Rutland annexed May 24, 1851.

YEARS AND CENSUS.	Population	Increase / Decrease
1776 (Prov.)	[558]	-
1790 (U. S.)	558	=
1800 (U. S.)	582	+ 24
1810 (U. S.)	619	+ 37
1820 (U. S.)	613	− 6
1830 (U. S.)	597	− 16
1840 (U. S.)	670	+ 73
1850 (U. S.)	820	+150
1855 (State)	792	− 28
1860 (U. S.)	725	− 67
1865 (State)	626	− 99
1870 (U. S.)	646	+ 20
1875 (State)	600	− 46
1880 (U. S.)	592	− 8
1885 (State)	561	− 31
1890 (U. S.)	445	−116
1895 (State)	426	− 19

TOWN OF PETERSHAM.

Established April 20, 1754, from the plantation called "Nichewoag." Part included in the new town of Dana February 18, 1801. Boundary line between Petersham and Dana established February 12, 1803. Part annexed to Dana February 4, 1842. Boundary line between Petersham and Dana established April 10, 1882.

YEARS AND CENSUS.	Population	Increase / Decrease
1765 (Prov.)	707	-
1776 (Prov.)	1,235	+528
1790 (U. S.)	1,560	+325
1800 (U. S.)	1,794	+234
1810 (U. S.)	1,490	−304
1820 (U. S.)	1,623	+133
1830 (U. S.)	1,696	+ 73

TOWN OF PETERSHAM — concluded.

YEARS AND CENSUS.	Population	Increase (+), or Decrease (−), as Compared with Previous Census
1840 (U. S.)	1,775	+ 79
1850 (U. S.)	1,527	−248
1855 (State)	1,553	+ 26
1860 (U. S.)	1,465	− 88
1865 (State)	1,428	− 37
1870 (U. S.)	1,335	− 93
1875 (State)	1,203	−132
1880 (U. S.)	1,109	− 94
1885 (State)	1,032	− 77
1890 (U. S.)	1,050	+ 18
1895 (State)	952	− 98

TOWN OF PHILLIPSTON.

Originally established as "Gerry" October 20, 1786, from parts of Athol and Templeton. Part annexed to Royalston February 26, 1799. Part annexed to Athol February 28, 1806. Name changed to Phillipston February 5, 1814. Boundary line between Phillipston and Royalston established March 29, 1837. Part of Phillipston annexed to Templeton April 5, 1892.

YEARS AND CENSUS.	Population	Increase / Decrease
1790 (U. S.)	740	-
1800 (U. S.)	802	+ 62
1810 (U. S.)	839	+ 37
1820 (U. S.)	916	+ 77
1830 (U. S.)	932	+ 16
1840 (U. S.)	919	− 13
1850 (U. S.)	809	−110
1855 (State)	799	− 10
1860 (U. S.)	764	− 35
1865 (State)	725	− 39
1870 (U. S.)	693	− 32
1875 (State)	666	− 27
1880 (U. S.)	621	− 45
1885 (State)	530	− 91
1890 (U. S.)	502	− 28
1895 (State)	460	− 42

TOWN OF PRINCETON.

Established as the District of "Prince-town" October 20, 1759, from part of Rutla d and certain common lands adjacent. The district and all lands adjacent not belonging to any town or district established as Princeton April 24, 1771. All lands which did not belong to Princeton wh n it was a district set off as they were before the passage of the Act of April 24, 1771, on March 6, 1775. Part of Hubbardston annexed February 16, 1810. Part of the common lands of No Town annexed April 4, 1838. Part of Westminster annexed April 22, 1870.

YEARS AND CENSUS.	Population	Increase / Decrease
1765 (Prov.)	284	-
1776 (Prov.)	701	+417
1790 (U. S.)	1,016	+315
1800 (U. S.)	1,021	+ 5
1810 (U. S.)	1,062	+ 41
1820 (U. S.)	1,261	+199
1830 (U. S.)	1,346	+ 85
1840 (U. S.)	1,347	+ 1
1850 (U. S.)	1,318	− 29

CENSUSES OF POPULATION — 1765-1895 — Continued.

TOWN OF PRINCETON — concluded.

YEARS AND CENSUS.	Population	Increase (+), or Decrease (—), as Compared with Previous Census
1855 (State)	1,317	— 1
1860 (U. S.)	1,201	—116
1865 (State)	1,239	+ 38
1870 (U. S.)	1,279	+ 40
1875 (State)	1,063	—216
1880 (U. S.)	1,100	+ 37
1885 (State)	1,038	— 62
1890 (U. S.)	982	— 56
1895 (State)	952	— 30

TOWN OF ROYALSTON.

Established February 19, 1765, from a tract of land called "Royalshire." Part annexed to Winchendon June 17, 1780. Part included in the District of Orange (Franklin County) October 15, 1783. Parts of Athol and Gerry (Phillipston) annexed February 26, 1799. Part of Athol annexed March 7, 1803. Boundary line between Royalston and Phillipston established March 29, 1837.

	Population	Increase (+), or Decrease (—)
1765 (Prov.)	[617]	-
1776 (Prov.)	617	=
1790 (U. S.)	1,130	+513
1800 (U. S.)	1,243	+113
1810 (U. S.)	1,415	+172
1820 (U. S.)	1,424	+ 9
1830 (U. S.)	1,493	+ 69
1840 (U. S.)	1,667	+174
1850 (U. S.)	1,546	—121
1855 (State)	1,469	— 77
1860 (U. S.)	1,486	+ 17
1865 (State)	1,441	— 45
1870 (U. S.)	1,354	— 87
1875 (State)	1,260	— 94
1880 (U. S.)	1,192	— 68
1885 (State)	1,153	— 39
1890 (U. S.)	1,030	—123
1895 (State)	890	—140

TOWN OF RUTLAND.

Established February 23, 1713, from common lands called "Naquag." Rutland granted the privileges that other towns enjoy June 18, 1722. Part established as the Rutland District April 12, 1753. Part established as Princeton October 20, 1759. Part established as the District of Oakham June 7, 1762. Part included in the new town of Paxton February 12, 1765. Part established as Hubbardston June 13, 1767. Part adjudged to belong to Paxton July 14, 1772. Boundary line between Rutland and Paxton established February 20, 1829. Part annexed to Paxton May 24, 1851.

	Population	Increase (+), or Decrease (—)
1765 (Prov.)	1,090	
1776 (Prov.)	1,006	— 84
1790 (U. S.)	1,072	+ 66
1800 (U. S.)	1,202	+130
1810 (U. S.)	1,231	+ 29
1820 (U. S.)	1,262	+ 31
1830 (U. S.)	1,276	+ 14
1840 (U. S.)	1,260	— 16
1850 (U. S.)	1,223	— 37

TOWN OF RUTLAND — concluded.

YEARS AND CENSUS.	Population	Increase (+), or Decrease (—), as Compared with Previous Census
1855 (State)	1,102	—121
1860 (U. S.)	1,076	— 26
1865 (State)	1,011	— 65
1870 (U. S.)	1,024	+ 13
1875 (State)	1,030	+ 6
1880 (U. S.)	1,059	+ 29
1885 (State)	963	— 96
1890 (U. S.)	980	+ 17
1895 (State)	978	— 2

TOWN OF SHREWSBURY.

On December 6, 1720, a committee was paid for "running the lines of Whitehall Farm and Shrewsbury . . . which service they performed in July, 1717." Shrewsbury is mentioned in a list of frontier towns August 16, 1722. Shrewsbury endowed with equal powers with any other town in the province December 19, 1727. Part annexed to Westborough June 3, 1762. Part annexed to Lancaster February 27, 1768. Part of Lancaster annexed February 26, 1781. Part established as Boylston March 1, 1786. Part annexed to Westborough March 2, 1793. Part annexed to Grafton March 3, 1826.

	Population	Increase (+), or Decrease (—)
1765 (Prov.)	1,401	-
1776 (Prov.)	1,475	+ 74
1790 (U. S.)	963	—512
1800 (U. S.)	1,048	+ 85
1810 (U. S.)	1,210	+162
1820 (U. S.)	1,458	+248
1830 (U. S.)	1,386	— 72
1840 (U. S.)	1,481	+ 95
1850 (U. S.)	1,596	+115
1855 (State)	1,636	+ 40
1860 (U. S.)	1,558	— 78
1865 (State)	1,570	+ 12
1870 (U. S.)	1,610	+ 40
1875 (State)	1,524	— 86
1880 (U. S.)	1,500	— 24
1885 (State)	1,450	— 50
1890 (U. S.)	1,449	— 1
1895 (State)	1,524	+ 75

TOWN OF SOUTHBOROUGH.

Established July 6, 1727, from part of Marlborough (Middlesex County). Part of Framingham (Middlesex County) annexed March 7, 1786. Boundary line between Southborough and Westborough established March 5, 1835. Part annexed to Marlborough March 24, 1843.

	Population	Increase (+), or Decrease (—)
1765 (Prov.)	731	-
1776 (Prov.)	753	+ 22
1790 (U. S.)	837	+ 84
1800 (U. S.)	871	+ 34
1810 (U. S.)	926	+ 55
1820 (U. S.)	1,030	+104
1830 (U. S.)	1,080	+ 50
1840 (U. S.)	1,145	+ 65

CENSUSES OF POPULATION — 1765-1895 — Continued.

TOWN OF SOUTHBOROUGH — concluded.

YEARS AND CENSUS.	Population	Increase (+), or Decrease (—), as compared with Previous Census
1850 (U. S.)	1,347	+202
1855 (State)	1,602	+255
1860 (U. S.)	1,854	+252
1865 (State)	1,750	—104
1870 (U. S.)	2,135	+385
1875 (State)	1,986	—149
1880 (U. S.)	2,142	+156
1885 (State)	2,100	— 42
1890 (U. S.)	2,114	+ 14
1895 (State)	2,223	+109

TOWN OF SOUTHBRIDGE.

Established February 15, 1816, from parts of Charlton, Dudley, and Sturbridge. Part of Dudley annexed February 23, 1822. Part of Sturbridge annexed April 6, 1839. Boundary line between Southbridge and Sturbridge established May 4, 1871.

1820 (U. S.)	1,066	-
1830 (U. S.)	1,444	+ 378
1840 (U. S.)	2,031	+ 587
1850 (U. S.)	2,824	+ 703
1855 (State)	3,429	+ 605
1860 (U. S.)	3,575	+ 146
1865 (State)	4,131	+ 556
1870 (U. S.)	5,208	+1,077
1875 (State)	5,740	+ 532
1880 (U. S.)	6,464	+ 724
1885 (State)	6,500	+ 36
1890 (U. S.)	7,655	+1,155
1895 (State)	8,250	+ 595

TOWN OF SPENCER.

Established as a district April 12, 1753, from part of Leicester. Made a town by Act of August 23, 1775.

1765 (Prov.)	664	-
1776 (Prov.)	1,042	+ 378
1790 (U. S.)	1,322	+ 280
1800 (U. S.)	1,432	+ 110
1810 (U. S.)	1,453	+ 21
1820 (U. S.)	1,548	+ 95
1830 (U. S.)	1,618	+ 70
1840 (U. S.)	1,604	— 14
1850 (U. S.)	2,244	+ 640
1855 (State)	2,527	+ 283
1860 (U. S.)	2,777	+ 250
1865 (State)	3,024	+ 247
1870 (U. S.)	3,952	+ 928
1875 (State)	5,451	+1,499
1880 (U. S.)	7,466	+2,015
1885 (State)	8,247	+ 781
1890 (U. S.)	8,747	+ 500
1895 (State)	7,614	—1,133

TOWN OF STERLING.

Established April 25, 1781, from part of Lancaster. Boundary line between Sterling and Lancaster established March 12, 1793. Part included in the new town of West Boylston January 30, 1808. Boundary line between Sterling and Lancaster established and a part of Lancaster annexed to Sterling March 7, 1837.

YEARS AND CENSUS.	Population	Increase (+), or Decrease (—), as compared with Previous Census
1790 (U. S.)	1,428	-
1800 (U. S.)	1,614	+186
1810 (U. S.)	1,472	—142
1820 (U. S.)	1,710	+238
1830 (U. S.)	1,794	+ 84
1840 (U. S.)	1,647	—147
1850 (U. S.)	1,805	+158
1855 (State)	1,838	+ 33
1860 (U. S.)	1,881	+ 43
1865 (State)	1,668	—213
1870 (U. S.)	1,670	+ 2
1875 (State)	1,569	—101
1880 (U. S.)	1,414	—155
1885 (State)	1,331	— 83
1890 (U. S.)	1,244	— 87
1895 (State)	1,218	— 26

TOWN OF STURBRIDGE.

Established June 24, 1738, from a tract of land called "New Medfield." Part of Charlton annexed June 26, 1792. Part of Middlesex Gore annexed June 25, 1794. Part included in the new town of Southbridge February 15, 1816. Part annexed to Southbridge April 6, 1839. Boundary line between Sturbridge and Southbridge established May 4, 1871.

1765 (Prov.)	896	-
1776 (Prov.)	1,374	+478
1790 (U. S.)	1,704	+330
1800 (U. S.)	1,846	+142
1810 (U. S.)	1,927	+ 81
1820 (U. S.)	1,633	—294
1830 (U. S.)	1,688	+ 55
1840 (U. S.)	2,005	+317
1850 (U. S.)	2,119	+114
1855 (State)	2,188	+ 69
1860 (U. S.)	2,291	+103
1865 (State)	1,993	—298
1870 (U. S.)	2,101	+108
1875 (State)	2,213	+112
1880 (U. S.)	2,062	—151
1885 (State)	1,980	— 82
1890 (U. S.)	2,074	+ 94
1895 (State)	1,910	—164

TOWN OF SUTTON.

On October 28, 1714, "voted in concurrence with the Representatives approving and confirming a survey and plat of the laying out of the township of Sutton" (Resolves). Certain common lands allowed to the proprietors of Sutton June 21, 1715. Part annexed to Westborough June 5, 1728. Part included in the new town of Upton June 14, 1735. A parish lately set off from Sutton and other towns established as Ward (now

CENSUSES OF POPULATION — 1765-1895 — Continued.

TOWN OF SUTTON — concluded.

Auburn) April 10, 1778. Part annexed to Northbridge April 20, 1780. A certain gore of land annexed June 5, 1789. Part annexed to Oxford February 18, 1793. Part annexed to Northbridge February 17, 1801. Part established as Millbury June 11, 1813. Part of Northbridge annexed June 15, 1831. Boundary line between Sutton and Northbridge established March 7, 1837. Part annexed to Grafton March 3, 1842. Part annexed to Northbridge March 16, 1844.

Years and Census.	Population	Increase (+), or Decrease (—), as Compared with Previous Census
1765 (Prov.)	2,138	–
1776 (Prov.)	2,644	+506
1790 (U. S.)	2,642	– 2
1800 (U. S.)	2,513	—129
1810 (U. S.)	2,660	+147
1820 (U. S.)	2,056	—604
1830 (U. S.)	2,186	+130
1840 (U. S.)	2,370	+184
1850 (U. S.)	2,595	+225
1855 (State)	2,718	+123
1860 (U. S.)	2,676	– 42
1865 (State)	2,363	—313
1870 (U. S.)	2,699	+336
1875 (State)	3,051	+352
1880 (U. S.)	3,105	+ 54
1885 (State)	3,101	– 4
1890 (U. S.)	3,180	+ 79
1895 (State)	3,420	+240

TOWN OF TEMPLETON.

Established as "Templetown" March 6, 1762, from the plantation called "Narragansett Number Six." Part included in the new town of Gardner June 27, 1785. Part included in the new town of Gerry (Phillipston) October 20, 1786. Part of Phillipston annexed April 5, 1892.

1765 (Prov.)	348	-
1776 (Prov.)	1,016	+668
1790 (U. S.)	950	– 66
1800 (U. S.)	1,068	+118
1810 (U. S.)	1,205	+137
1820 (U. S.)	1,331	+126
1830 (U. S.)	1,552	+221
1840 (U. S.)	1,776	+224
1850 (U. S.)	2,173	+397
1855 (State)	2,618	+445
1860 (U. S.)	2,816	+198
1865 (State)	2,390	—426
1870 (U. S.)	2,802	+412
1875 (State)	2,764	– 38
1880 (U. S.)	2,789	+ 25
1885 (State)	2,627	—162
1890 (U. S.)	2,999	+372
1895 (State)	2,915	– 84

TOWN OF UPTON.

Established June 14, 1735, from parts of Hopkinton (Middlesex County), Mendon, Sutton, and Uxbridge. Part annexed to Westborough January 24, 1763. Part of Hopkinton annexed March 8, 1808.

TOWN OF UPTON — concluded.

Years and Census.	Population	Increase (+), or Decrease (—), as Compared with Previous Census
1765 (Prov.)	614	–
1776 (Prov.)	702	+ 88
1790 (U. S.)	833	+131
1800 (U. S.)	854	+ 21
1810 (U. S.)	995	+141
1820 (U. S.)	1,088	+ 93
1830 (U. S.)	1,167	+ 79
1840 (U. S.)	1,466	+299
1850 (U. S.)	2,023	+557
1855 (State)	2,035	+ 12
1860 (U. S.)	1,986	– 49
1865 (State)	2,018	+ 32
1870 (U. S.)	1,989	– 29
1875 (State)	2,125	+136
1880 (U. S.)	2,023	—102
1885 (State)	2,265	+242
1890 (U. S.)	1,878	—387
1895 (State)	2,150	+272

TOWN OF UXBRIDGE.

Established June 27, 1727, from part of Mendon. Part included in the new town of Upton June 14, 1735. Part annexed to Mendon April 24, 1770. Part established as the District of Northbridge July 14, 1772. Boundary line between Uxbridge and Northbridge established and part of each town annexed to the other town April 30, 1856. Boundary line between Uxbridge and Douglas established April 25, 1864.

1765 (Prov.)	1,213	-
1776 (Prov.)	1,110	—103
1790 (U. S.)	1,308	+198
1800 (U. S.)	1,404	+ 96
1810 (U. S.)	1,404	=
1820 (U. S.)	1,551	+147
1830 (U. S.)	2,086	+535
1840 (U. S.)	2,004	– 82
1850 (U. S.)	2,457	+453
1855 (State)	3,068	+611
1860 (U. S.)	3,133	+ 65
1865 (State)	2,838	—295
1870 (U. S.)	3,058	+220
1875 (State)	3,029	– 29
1880 (U. S.)	3,111	+ 82
1885 (State)	2,948	—163
1890 (U. S.)	3,408	+460
1895 (State)	3,546	+138

TOWN OF WARREN.

Originally established as "Western" January 16, 1742, from parts of Brimfield (Hampden County), Brookfield, and Kingsfield.* Part annexed to Ware (Hampshire County) February 8, 1823. Part annexed to Palmer (Hampden County) February 7, 1831. Name changed to Warren March 13, 1834.

1765 (Prov.)	583	-
1776 (Prov.)	827	+244
1790 (U. S.)	899	+ 72

* Variously designated as Kingsfield, New Marlborough, and The Elbows.

CENSUSES OF POPULATION — 1765–1895 — Continued.

TOWN OF WARREN — concluded.

YEARS AND CENSUS.	Population	Increase (+), or Decrease (—), as Compared with Previous Census
1800 (U. S.)	979	+ 80
1810 (U. S.)	1,014	+ 35
1820 (U. S.)	1,112	+ 98
1830 (U. S.)	1,189	+ 77
1840 (U. S.)	1,290	+101
1850 (U. S.)	1,777	+487
1855 (State)	1,793	+ 16
1860 (U. S.)	2,107	+314
1865 (State)	2,180	+ 73
1870 (U. S.)	2,625	+445
1875 (State)	3,260	+635
1880 (U. S.)	3,889	+629
1885 (State)	4,032	+143
1890 (U. S.)	4,681	+649
1895 (State)	4,430	—251

TOWN OF WEBSTER.

Established March 6, 1832, from common lands, and parts of Dudley and Oxford. Boundary line between Webster and Douglas established February 27, 1841.

1840 (U. S.)	1,403	-
1850 (U. S.)	2,371	+ 968
1855 (State)	2,727	+ 356
1860 (U. S.)	2,912	+ 185
1865 (State)	3,608	+ 696
1870 (U. S.)	4,763	+1,155
1875 (State)	5,064	+ 301
1880 (U. S.)	5,696	+ 632
1885 (State)	6,220	+ 524
1890 (U. S.)	7,031	+ 811
1895 (State)	7,799	+ 768

TOWN OF WESTBOROUGH.

Established November 18, 1717, from part of Marlborough (Middlesex County) called "Chauncy," and other lands. Part of Sutton annexed June 5, 1728. Part of Shrewsbury annexed June 3, 1762. Part of Upton annexed January 24, 1763. Part established as the District of Northborough January 24, 1766. Part of Shrewsbury annexed March 2, 1793. Boundary line between Westborough and Southborough established March 5, 1835.

1765 (Prov.)	1,110	-
1776 (Prov.)	900	—210
1790 (U. S.)	934	+ 34
1800 (U. S.)	922	— 12
1810 (U. S.)	1,048	+126
1820 (U. S.)	1,326	+278
1830 (U. S.)	1,438	+112
1840 (U. S.)	1,658	+220
1850 (U. S.)	2,371	+713
1855 (State)	3,014	+643
1860 (U. S.)	2,913	—101
1865 (State)	3,141	+228
1870 (U. S.)	3,601	+460

TOWN OF WESTBOROUGH — concluded.

YEARS AND CENSUS.	Population	Increase (+), or Decrease (—), as Compared with Previous Census
1875 (State)	5,141	+1,540
1880 (U. S.)	5,214	+ 73
1885 (State)	4,880	— 334
1890 (U. S.)	5,195	+ 315
1895 (State)	5,235	+ 40

TOWN OF WEST BOYLSTON.

Established January 30, 1808, from parts of Boylston, Holden, and Sterling. Parts of Boylston annexed February 10, 1820, and June 17, 1820.

1810 (U. S.)	632	-
1820 (U. S.)	886	+254
1830 (U. S.)	1,055	+169
1840 (U. S.)	1,187	+132
1850 (U. S.)	1,749	+562
1855 (State)	2,310	+561
1860 (U. S.)	2,509	+199
1865 (State)	2,294	—215
1870 (U. S.)	2,862	+568
1875 (State)	2,902	+ 40
1880 (U. S.)	2,994	+ 92
1885 (State)	2,927	— 67
1890 (U. S.)	3,019	+ 92
1895 (State)	2,968	— 51

TOWN OF WEST BROOKFIELD.

Established March 3, 1848, from part of Brookfield.

1850 (U. S.)	1,344	
1855 (State)	1,364	+ 20
1860 (U. S.)	1,548	+184
1865 (State)	1,549	+ 1
1870 (U. S.)	1,842	+293
1875 (State)	1,903	+ 61
1880 (U. S.)	1,917	+ 14
1885 (State)	1,747	—170
1890 (U. S.)	1,592	—155
1895 (State)	1,467	—125

TOWN OF WESTMINSTER.

Established as a district October 20, 1759, from the plantation called "Narragansett Number Two." Made a town April 26, 1770. Part included in the new town of Gardner June 27, 1785. Parts of Fitchburg annexed February 27, 1796, and February 16, 1813. Part annexed to Ashburnham January 28, 1824. Part of the common lands called No Town annexed April 10, 1838. Part annexed to Princeton April 22, 1870.

1765 (Prov.)	468	-
1776 (Prov.)	1,145	+677
1790 (U. S.)	1,176	+ 31
1800 (U. S.)	1,369	+193
1810 (U. S.)	1,419	+ 50
1820 (U. S.)	1,634	+215

CENSUSES OF POPULATION — 1765-1895 — Continued.

TOWN OF WESTMINSTER — concluded.

YEARS AND CENSUS.	Popula-tion	Increase (+), or Decrease (—), as Compared with Previous Census
1829 (U. S.)	1,696	+ 62
1840 (U. S.)	1,645	— 51
1850 (U. S.)	1,914	+269
1855 (State)	1,979	+ 65
1860 (U. S.)	1,840	—139
1865 (State)	1,639	—201
1870 (U. S.)	1,770	+131
1875 (State)	1,712	— 58
1880 (U. S.)	1,652	— 60
1885 (State)	1,556	— 96
1890 (U. S.)	1,688	+132
1895 (State)	1,315	—373

TOWN OF WINCHENDON.

Established June 14, 1764, from the plantation called "Ipswich-Canada." Part of Royalston annexed and the bounds of Winchendon extended to embrace all the lands on the north as far as the New Hampshire State line June 17, 1780. Part included in the new town of Gardner June 27, 1785. Part of Gardner annexed March 2, 1787. Parts annexed to Gardner February 22, 1794, and May 24, 1851.

YEARS AND CENSUS.	Popula-tion	Increase (+), or Decrease (—), as Compared with Previous Census
1765 (Prov.)	(519)	-
1776 (Prov.)	519	=
1790 (U. S.)	946	+427
1800 (U. S.)	1,092	+146
1810 (U. S.)	1,173	+ 81
1820 (U. S.)	1,263	+ 90
1830 (U. S.)	1,463	+200
1840 (U. S.)	1,754	+291
1850 (U. S.)	2,445	+691
1855 (State)	2,747	+302
1860 (U. S.)	2,624	—123
1865 (State)	2,801	+177

TOWN OF WINCHENDON — concluded.

YEARS AND CENSUS.	Popula-tion	Increase (+), or Decrease (—), as Compared with Previous Census
1870 (U. S.)	3,398	+597
1875 (State)	3,762	+364
1880 (U. S.)	3,722	— 40
1885 (State)	3,872	+150
1890 (U. S.)	4,390	+518
1895 (State)	4,490	+100

CITY OF WORCESTER.

Established October 15, 1684, from the plantation called "Quansigamond." Part called North Worcester established as Holden January 9, 1741. The parish lately set off from Worcester and other towns established as Ward (now Auburn) April 10, 1778. Certain common lands annexed June 14, 1785. Grafton Gore annexed March 22, 1838. Worcester incorporated as a city February 29, 1848. Act of incorporation accepted by the town March 18, 1848.

YEARS AND CENSUS.	Popula-tion	Increase (+), or Decrease (—), as Compared with Previous Census
1765 (Prov.)	1,478	-
1776 (Prov.)	1,925	+ 447
1790 (U. S.)	2,095	+ 170
1800 (U. S.)	2,411	+ 316
1810 (U. S.)	2,577	+ 166
1820 (U. S.)	2,962	+ 385
1830 (U. S.)	4,173	+ 1,211
1840 (U. S.)	7,497	+ 3,324
1850 (U. S.)	17,049	+ 9,552
1855 (State)	22,286	+ 5,237
1860 (U. S.)	24,960	+ 2,674
1865 (State)	30,055	+ 5,095
1870 (U. S.)	41,105	+11,050
1875 (State)	49,317	+ 8,212
1880 (U. S.)	58,291	+ 8,974
1885 (State)	68,389	+10,098
1890 (U. S.)	84,655	+16,266
1895 (State)	98,767	+14,112

CENSUSES OF POPULATION — 1765-1895 — Concluded.

THE STATE.

The Commonwealth of Massachusetts covers part of the territory originally granted to the Plymouth Company of England. It grew out of the consolidation of the colonies of Plymouth and Massachusetts Bay. The settlement at Plymouth began with the landing of the Pilgrims, December 22, 1620. The colony of Massachusetts Bay originated with the settlement under John Endecott at Salem, in 1628. In 1643, a confederacy was formed consisting of the colonies of Massachusetts Bay, Plymouth, Connecticut, and New Haven. In 1692, under a new charter given by William III, the colonies of Massachusetts Bay and Plymouth were consolidated as a royal province, including also Maine. In 1780, after the Revolution, the present State Constitution was adopted. In January, 1788, the Constitution of the United States was ratified by Massachusetts. The colonists in New Hampshire, in 1641, as a measure of protection and defence against the Indians, allied themselves with the colony of Massachusetts Bay and remained part of said colony until 1679, when New Hampshire was made a separate royal province, Massachusetts thereby losing part of its territory, January 1, 1680 (see Norfolk County). The territory now comprising the State of Maine was set off from Massachusetts by an Act passed March 3, 1820, taking effect March 15, 1820. By the Province Charter of 1692, certain islands now comprising the county of Dukes County and Nantucket County were ceded to Massachusetts from New York (see county of Dukes County). Certain common lands in Berkshire County, known as the District of Boston Corner, were ceded to the State of New York May 14, 1853 (see town of Mount Washington, Berkshire County). By a settlement of a boundary controversy between Massachusetts and Rhode Island, certain exchanges of territory were made between these States April 10, 1861 (see Fall River, Seekonk, and Westport).

YEARS AND CENSUS.														Population	Increase (+), or Decrease(—), as compared with Previous Census
1765 (Prov.)*	.	.	.	.	.	.	.	.	.	.	.	.	.	239,764	–
1776 (Prov.)†	.	.	.	.	.	.	.	.	.	.	.	.	.	299,841	+ 60,077
1790 (U. S.)	.	.	.	.	.	.	.	.	.	.	.	.	.	378,787	+ 78,946
1800 (U. S.)	.	.	.	.	.	.	.	.	.	.	.	.	.	422,845	+ 44,058
1810 (U. S.)	.	.	.	.	.	.	.	.	.	.	.	.	.	472,040	+ 49,195
1820 (U. S.)	.	.	.	.	.	.	.	.	.	.	.	.	.	523,287	+ 51,247
1830 (U. S.)	.	.	.	.	.	.	.	.	.	.	.	.	.	610,408	+ 87,121
1840 (U. S.)	.	.	.	.	.	.	.	.	.	.	.	.	.	737,700	+127,292
1850 (U. S.)	.	.	.	.	.	.	.	.	.	.	.	.	.	994,514	+256,814
1855 (State)	.	.	.	.	.	.	.	.	.	.	.	.	.	1,132,369	+137,855
1860 (U. S.)	.	.	.	.	.	.	.	.	.	.	.	.	.	1,231,066	+ 98,697
1865 (State)	.	.	.	.	.	.	.	.	.	.	.	.	.	1,267,031	+ 35,965
1870 (U. S.)	.	.	.	.	.	.	.	.	.	.	.	.	.	1,457,351	+190,320
1875 (State)	.	.	.	.	.	.	.	.	.	.	.	.	.	1,651,912	+194,561
1880 (U. S.)	.	.	.	.	.	.	.	.	.	.	.	.	.	1,783,085	+131,173
1885 (State)	.	.	.	.	.	.	.	.	.	.	.	.	.	1,942,141	+159,056
1890 (U. S.)	.	.	.	.	.	.	.	.	.	.	.	.	.	2,238,943	+296,802
1895 (State)	.	.	.	.	.	.	.	.	.	.	.	.	.	2,500,183	+261,240

* Includes 1,569 Indians distributed by counties as follows: Barnstable, 515 (of which 230 were in Mashpee); Berkshire, 221 (in Stockbridge); Bristol, 167 (principally in Dartmouth and Freetown), Dukes, 313 (of which 188 were in Chilmark); Middlesex, 37 (in Natick); Nantucket, 93; Plymouth, 223.

† Includes 4,761 colored population distributed by counties as follows: Barnstable, 171; Berkshire, 216; Bristol, 585; Dukes, 59; Essex, 1,049; Franklin, Hampden, and Hampshire (one county), 245; Middlesex, 702; Nantucket, 133; Plymouth, 487; Norfolk and Suffolk (one county), 682; Worcester, 432.

TABULAR ANALYSIS.

This presentation requires no extended analytical treatment. The information, while requiring much research on the part of the Bureau to ensure accuracy, has been so presented that the reader may easily follow the growth of the towns and cities from the earliest years. The student of the Census returns of the Commonwealth will note that a consolidation of two distinct presentations, as shown in Part 1, Volume I, of the Census of 1885, has been made for the Census of 1895, combining the historical features of the settlement and acquisition of additional territory with the purely statistical information as to the numerical gain or loss in population of the counties, cities, and towns. This arrangement, it is thought, will make the presentation easy of reference, as the notes relating to the establishment or incorporation of cities and towns, changes in boundary lines, annexation of one city or town to another, etc., appear in connection with the Census figures for each city and town, while the increases or decreases for each Census, as compared with the one preceding, being computed, will save the reader much time.

The dates relative to the establishment or incorporation of the cities and towns, as given in the Census of 1885, have been carefully compared with those contained in the first and subsequent reports of the Commissioner of Public Records and with other official sources of information. Each date has been subjected to careful scrutiny by the Bureau and it is believed that, as far as the archives of the Commonwealth show, those printed in this volume are correct. The authorities consulted have been

Reports of the Commissioner of Public Records,	Massachusetts Archives,
	Resolves and Orders (unprinted),
Manual of the General Court,	Province Laws,
Massachusetts Records,	Acts and Resolves,
Plymouth Colony Laws,	Boston Town Records.
Plymouth Colony Records,	

As will be noted, there are a number of instances where the actual date of establishment of certain towns cannot be given, as up to the present time no authentic knowledge exists. In cases of this kind the method adopted has been to give the date when the first mention of the town appears in some of the volumes of record. For instance, while it is not certainly known in what year Rev. William Blackstone settled at the place called Shawmut (one of the olden time names for Boston), it is supposed to have been between 1623 and 1626. In April, 1630, Charlestown was settled by colonists, and it is a matter of record that many of these colonists, acting upon the suggestion of Mr. Blackstone, settled at Trimountain (apparently the original name for Boston) in August 1630, yet it was not until September 7 (17, new style) that any mention is found in the Massachusetts Records, and on this date the Great and General Court ordered that Trimountain should be called Boston. No prior mention can be found of the establishment of the city of Boston or its boundaries.

In 1626, Roger Conant, who had previously removed from Nantasket to Cape Ann in charge of a party of settlers, built the first house at Naumkeag on the site of the present city of Salem. Capt. John Endecott and his followers landed there in 1628, yet the name Salem first appears in the Massachusetts Records in August, 1630; although Naumkeag (Nahumkeke) is mentioned in 1628.

The town records of Sutton show that by an order dated May 15, 1704, a township was granted, but the first mention of Sutton in the State records is October 28, 1714. Many other instances may be found of the lack of actual dates in the history of many of the older towns.

There is no record in the State archives of the incorporation of the following cities and towns:

Andover,	Eastham,	Plymouth,
Barnstable,	Falmouth,	SALEM,
BOSTON,	Gay Head,	Sandwich,
Boxford,	HAVERHILL,	Scituate,
Bradford,	Hull,	Shrewsbury,
Brimfield,	LYNN,	SPRINGFIELD,
CAMBRIDGE,	Marblehead,	Sutton,
Chilmark,	MEDFORD,	Tisbury,
Dartmouth,	Natick,	Weymouth,
Deerfield,	NORTHAMPTON,	Wrentham,
Dunstable,	Oxford,	Yarmouth.

We have retained, wherever practicable, the language used by the authors of the various original acts, together with the old form of spelling town names whenever it has been deemed advisable to do so, the authority for dates and quotations being given for purposes of reference. Undoubtedly many dates which are now lacking or obscure will be brought out when the forthcoming volume of the Province Laws, containing resolves, orders, etc., relating to the establishment of towns, is published.

We call particular attention to the notes on page 131, which should be read carefully in connection with the historical and statistical data contained in the presentation itself.

For the purpose of showing the percentages of increase or decrease in population in the different counties, and for the State, the following table is introduced:

	PERCENTAGES OF INCREASE OR DECREASE IN POPULATION							
CENSUS PERIODS.	COUNTIES							
	Barnstable	Berkshire	Bristol	Dukes	Essex	Franklin	Hampden	Hampshire
1765-1776* (Provincial)	28.19	107.78	25.35	20.29	17.00	104.37	59.79	89.05
1776-1790† (U. S.)	11.63	68.30	18.76	15.70	13.73	111.22	44.59	54.87
1790-1800 (U. S.)	11.17	11.44	6.84	—4.19	5.66	20.95	22.24	21.58
1800-1810 (U. S.)	15.12	6.28	9.70	5.51	17.47	4.26	4.08	7.28
1810-1820 (U. S.)	8.17	—0.60	10.06	–	3.84	7.28	14.74	7.87
1820-1830 (U. S.)	18.67	6.31	21.22	6.83	10.98	0.72	12.91	14.29
1830-1840 (U. S.)	14.14	10.71	21.31	12.53	14.63	—2.76	18.10	2.12
1840-1850 (U. S.)	8.38	18.79	26.64	14.70	38.22	7.32	37.24	15.65
1850-1860 (U. S.)	2.02	11.15	25.10	—3.02	26.13	1.83	11.86	5.85
1855-1865 (State)	—2.34	7.87	2.25	—4.52	13.25	—0.99	17.72	10.06
1860-1870 (U. S.)	—8.94	17.61	9.69	—13.90	21.27	3.82	36.68	17.36
1865-1875 (State)	—7.13	19.89	46.64	—3.07	30.58	7.32	46.05	14.11
1870-1880 (U. S.)	—2.68	6.49	35.14	13.55	21.75	10.31	32.82	6.41
1875-1885 (State)	—7.15	8.14	20.91	1.57	18.08	11.14	23.82	8.15
1880-1890 (U. S.)	—8.54	17.49	34.11	1.60	22.68	7.25	30.32	9.80
1885-1895 (State)	—7.34	16.88	38.18	2.49	25.28	7.20	30.98	12.87
1765-1895‡	128.04	808.75	928.21	80.65	659.11	697.00	1,741.07	750.99

* 11 years.   † 14 years.   ‡ 130 years.

CENSUS PERIODS.	PERCENTAGES OF INCREASE OR DECREASE IN POPULATION						THE STATE
	COUNTIES						
	Middlesex	Nantucket	Norfolk	Plymouth	Suffolk	Worcester	
1765–1776* (Provincial)	14.97	32.89	25.12	12.94	−79.93	41.46	*23.88
1776–1790† (U. S.)	6.52	4.71	7.93	9.62	485.79	22.33	†28.37
1790–1800 (U. S.)	9.80	21.58	13.97	1.77	37.21	7.72	11.63
1800–1810 (U. S.)	12.48	21.18	14.89	9.18	33.33	6.07	11.63
1810–1820 (U. S.)	16.44	6.74	16.72	8.43	27.80	13.42	16.85
1820–1830 (U. S.)	26.89	−0.85	15.08	12.86	41.47	14.57	16.64
1830–1840 (U. S.)	36.74	25.15	26.60	10.05	54.06	12.99	20.85
1840–1850 (U. S.)	51.37	−6.21	48.46	17.57	50.89	37.22	34.81
1850–1860 (U. S.)	34.06	27.89	39.37	16.29	33.34	22.67	23.79
1855–1865 (State)	13.58	−11.12	23.25	2.62	21.17	8.96	11.89
1860–1870 (U. S.)	26.81	−32.34	−18.65	0.92	40.53	20.70	18.38
1865–1875 (State)	28.92	−32.58	−24.06	9.01	75.25	29.08	30.38
1870–1880 (U. S.)	15.85	−9.61	7.90	13.24	43.25	17.74	22.85
1875–1885 (State)	25.76	−1.84	15.65	17.76	15.41	16.05	17.57
1880–1890 (U. S.)	35.66	−12.32	23.26	25.21	24.97	23.75	25.57
1885–1895 (State)	39.71	−4.01	31.99	24.26	28.19	25.57	28.73
1765–1895‡	1,330.59	−9.16	662.46	293.75	3,277.54	833.52	‡949.64

* 11 years. † 14 years. ‡ 130 years.

The final line indicates the percentages of increase or decrease during 130 years. It shows, for example, that the State has increased its population since 1765, the date of the first provincial census, to the extent of 949.64 per cent. The percentage of gain in the different counties varies from 89.65, in Dukes County, to 3,277.54, in Suffolk County. The county of Nantucket, however, shows a loss of 9.16 per cent in the 130 years. While the total percentages of increase are thus shown, the table also exhibits the percentages of increase during each census period, respectively. For example, in the first census period, 1765–1776, the State gained 23.88 per cent. This was a period of 11 years. The next census was taken in 1790, 14 years later, and in this period, 1776–1790, the gain was 28.37 per cent. After 1790, censuses were taken at regular intervals of ten years, until 1850 and since 1850 at intervals of five years; and the percentages for each period, for each of the counties, and for the State, may be readily found in the table.

It will be noted that Barnstable County shows a decline since 1855, and Nantucket County a decline since 1820, with the exception of the periods 1830–1840 and 1850–1860, in which increases appear. Between the years 1790 and 1800 and between 1850 and 1875, declines are noticed in Dukes County ; in the period 1810–1820, a slight decline is found in the county of Berkshire ; also, in Norfolk County, a considerable decrease in the periods 1860–1870 and 1865–1875 ; and in the periods 1830–1840 and 1855–1865, Franklin County shows a decline of 2.76 per cent and 0.99 per cent, respectively. In the first period, 1765–1776, the county of Suffolk shows a decline of 79.93 per cent. With these exceptions, every county in the State shows an increase during each census period. The increases are, however, not uniform. The gain in Suffolk, which is entirely out of proportion to that which is elsewhere exhibited, is of course due to the growth of the city of Boston, and the increase in Boston as estimated and taken at different periods since and including 1638, representing the growth of the metropolis on its original territory, and by annexation, is presented in the following table, which was first prepared and published by this Department in 1882, and is now brought forward to include the census figures of 1895 :

	Census Years.	Census taken by —	Boston, including Annexations	a Boston proper: Settled, 1630; Made a City, 1822	Annexed Territory	Annexations East Boston (1637)	The Islands (See Notes)
1	1638,	-	-	b 150	-	-	-
2	1675,	-	-	b 4,000	-	-	-
3	1698,	-	-	b 7,000	-	-	-
4	1704,	-	-	b 6,750	-	-	-
5	1720,	-	-	b 11,000	-	-	-
6	1722,	Town,	-	10,567	-	-	-
7	1742,	Town,	-	16,382	-	-	-
8	1752,	Town,	-	15,731	-	-	-
9	1765,	Province,	-	15,520	-	-	-
10	1775,	Gen. Gage,	-	6,573	-	-	-
11	1776,	Province,	-	2,719	-	-	-
12	1781,	Province,	-	c 10,000	-	-	-
13	1784,	Province,	-	c 15,870	-	-	-
14	1789,	Town,	-	d 17,880	-	-	-
15	1790,	U. S.,	18,320	18,038	282	-	282
16	1800,	U. S.,	24,937	24,655	282	-	f 282
17	1810,	U. S.,	33,787	32,896	891	18	519
18	1820,	U. S.,	43,298	-	-	-	-
19	1825,	City,	58,277	56,003	2,274	24	264
20	1830,	U. S.,	61,392	-	-	-	-
21	1835,	City,	78,603	72,057	6,546	607	344
22	1840,	U. S.,	e 93,383	85,475	7,908	1,455	277
23	1845,	City,	114,366	99,036	15,330	5,018	292
24	1850,	U. S.,	136,881	113,721	23,160	9,526	325
25	1855,	State,	160,490	126,296	34,194	15,433	f 530
26	1860,	U. S.,	177,840	133,563	44,277	18,356	f 1,000
27	1865,	State,	192,318	141,083	51,235	20,572	f 1,300
28	1870,	U. S.,	250,526	138,781	111,745	23,816	f 1,700
29	1875,	State,	341,919	140,669	201,250	27,420	1,927
30	1880,	U. S.,	362,839	147,075	215,764	k 28,381	m 1,545
31	1885,	State,	390,393	147.138	243,255	k 29,280	m 2,139
32	1890,	U. S.,	418,477	161,330	287,147	36,930	n —
33	1895,	State,	496,920	160,349	336,571	39,889	m 2,706

a By Boston proper is meant the territory of Boston, independent of all annexations.

b Estimates made in the years named. Those for 1675 and 1698 were probably too large.

c Estimates based on censuses of polls.

d Estimate based on actual number of houses in 1789, and the average persons to a house, as shown by the U. S. census of 1790.

e By the census of May, 1840, the population of Boston was 84,401. Mr. Shattuck, in his report on the census of Boston for 1845, shows clearly that the U. S. census of 1840 was incorrect.

f Estimated.

g Included also in the population of Dorchester in this year. After 1855, Washington Village is included in south Boston.

h The population of South Boston could not be stated definitely for 1875, because the wards including South Boston also included a part of Boston proper. The figures given are very close, however.

If we trace the growth of Boston as presented in the preceding table, we begin with the population shown on the original territory, settled in 1630, and estimated and presented for the year 1638, namely, 150. Upon substantially the same territory, the population in 1895 is 160,349. The first gain from annexed territory appears in the enumeration for 1790, the gain being very slight. In recent years, however, the gain by

ANNEXATIONS

South Boston (1804)	Washington Village (1855)	Roxbury (1867)	Dorchester (1869)	West Roxbury (1873)	Brighton (1873)	Charlestown (1873)	
-	-	-	-	-	-	-	1
-	-	-	-	-	-	-	2
-	-	-	-	-	-	-	3
-	-	-	-	-	-	-	4
-	-	-	-	-	-	-	5
-	-	-	-	-	-	-	6
-	-	-	-	-	-	-	7
-	-	-	-	-	-	-	8
-	-	1,487	1,360	-	-	2,031	9
-	-	-	-	-	-	-	10
-	-	1,433	1,513	-	-	360	11
-	-	c 1,650	c 1,840	-	-	c 725	12
-	-	c 2,150	c 2,060	-	-	c 1,310	13
-	-	-	-	-	-	-	14
-	-	2,226	1,722	-	-	1,583	15
-	-	2,705	2,347	-	-	2,751	16
354	-	3,669	2,930	-	608	4,959	17
-	-	4,135	3,984	-	702	6,591	18
1,986	-	-	-	-	-	-	19
-	-	5,247	4,074	-	972	8,783	20
5,595	-	-	-	-	-	-	21
6,176	-	9,089	4,875	-	1,425	11,484	22
10,020	-	-	-	-	-	-	23
13,309	-	18,364	7,969	-	2,356	17,216	24
16,912	g 1,319	18,469	8,340	4,812	2,895	21,700	25
24,921	-	25,137	9,769	6,310	3,375	25,065	26
29,363	-	28,426	10,717	6,912	3,854	26,399	27
39,215	-	34,753	12,264	8,686	4,967	28,323	28
h 54,147	-	50,129	15,788	11,783	6,200	33,556	29
56,369	-	i 57,123	i 17,890	14,032	6,693	33,731	30
61,534	-	65,965	20,717	17,424	8,523	37,673	31
66,791	-	78,411	29,688	24,997	12,032	38,348	32
67,913	-	92,088	45,909	32,761	15,001	40,304	33

i The territory of Roxbury and Dorchester was not kept intact by ward boundaries in the ward division of 1875; it is difficult, therefore, to give the exact population of each district by the census of 1880. The figures given are the result of very careful study of the population by census enumeration districts, of which there were 208 in Boston for the U. S. census of 1880.

k The population, as usually given in census tables, includes that of the islands in the harbor.

m For the separate islands as follows: 1880 — Breed's, 152; Deer, 451; Galloupe, 5; Rainsford, 187; Long, 49; Lovell, 5; Spectacle, 55; Thompson's, 106; Fort Independence, 13; Fort Warren, 112; Fort Winthrop, 12. 1885 — Breed's, 348; Deer, 1,145; Galloupe, 6; Rainsford, 204; Long, 81; Lovell, 7; Spectacle, 61; Thompson's, 112; Fort Independence, 11; Fort Warren, 129; Fort Winthrop, 25. 1895 — Breed's, included in East Boston; Deer, 1,620; Galloupe, 6; Rainsford, 83; Long, 612; Lovell, 3; Spectacle, 94; Thompson's, 119; Fort Independence, 2; Fort Warren, 164; Fort Winthrop, 3.

n Included in East Boston.

annexation has been quite important, beginning with Roxbury, annexed in 1867, followed by Dorchester, annexed in 1869, and by West Roxbury, Brighton, and Charlestown, which were annexed in 1873. The population upon territory which has been annexed since the original settlement of the city is 336,571, out of 496,920, the total population of the city in 1895. The population on the territory acquired by the annexation of East Boston is now 39,889; South Boston, 67,913; Roxbury, 92,088; Dorchester, 45,909; West Roxbury, 32,761; Brighton, 15,001; and Charlestown, 40,304. The population upon the islands in the harbor is 2,706.

The population of the original territory shows a decline as compared with the last preceding enumeration, the United States census of 1890, from 161,330 to 160,349. A decline between two census periods has never before been found since the Revolution, except between the years 1865 and 1870. The present decline is due to the encroachment of business upon the residential section.

During the ten years, 1885 to 1895, however, there has been a gain upon the original territory from 147,138 to 160,349. The gain upon the annexed territory since 1885 is from 243,255 to 336,571, the largest numerical gain being shown in the Roxbury district, and the next largest in Dorchester. In percentages of gain during this period, the Dorchester section leads all others, as will appear from the following table, showing the percentages for 1895 as compared with 1885, in the city proper, and in each of the annexed districts :

Divisions of Boston.	Increase in 1895 as compared with 1885	Percentages of Increase
The City proper,	13,211	+ 8.98
East Boston (including the islands),	11,176	+ 35.57
South Boston,	6,379	+ 10.37
Dorchester,	25,192	+121.60
West Roxbury,	15,337	+ 88.02
Brighton,	6,478	+ 76.01
Charlestown,	2,631	+ 6.98
Roxbury,	26,123	+ 39.60
THE CITY,	106,527	+ 27.29

The following table shows the percentages of population of the entire city, found in the different territorial divisions :

Divisions of Boston.	Population	Percentages
The City proper,	160,349	32.27
East Boston (including the islands),	42,595	8.57
South Boston,	67,913	13.67
Dorchester,	45,909	9.24
West Roxbury,	32,761	6.59
Brighton,	15,001	3.02
Charlestown,	40,304	8.11
Roxbury,	92,088	18.53
THE CITY,	496,920	100.00

It will be seen from this table that while the population on the annexed territory is much larger, when considered in its entirety, than the population on the original territory, or city proper, nevertheless, the city proper contains the largest fraction of the total population which is found in any single subdivision, namely, 32.27 per cent. It may be pointed out in passing that in 1890 the city proper contained 35.97 per cent of the entire population of the city. Roxbury contains 18.53 per cent of the total population, as against 17.49 per cent in 1890; South Boston, 13.67 per cent, as against 14.89 per cent in 1890; Dorchester, 9.24 per cent, as against 6.61 per cent in 1890; West Roxbury, 6.59 per cent, as against 5.57 per cent in 1890; Brighton, 3.02 per cent, as against 2.68 per cent in 1890. The population in East Boston, including the islands, constitutes 8.57 per cent of the total population of the city, and the population of Charlestown, 8.11 per cent of the total population, these proportions being about the same as obtained in 1890. That is to say, the city proper to-day, while containing nearly one-third of the total population of the city, has a smaller proportion of the population than it held five years ago, and while the districts of Roxbury, Dorchester, West Roxbury, and Brighton have each of them gained a larger proportion of the population than they held in 1890, South Boston has a smaller proportion, and East Boston and Charlestown retain about the same proportion as they held five years ago.

POLLS AND VOTERS.

POLLS AND VOTERS.

COUNTIES, CITIES, AND TOWNS.	RATABLE POLLS				LEGAL VOTERS		
	Total Polls	PERCENTAGES OF TOTAL RATABLE POLLS			Total Voters	PERCENTAGES OF TOTAL LEGAL VOTERS	
		Voters	Not Voters	Aliens		Native Born Voters	Foreign Born Naturalized Voters
BARNSTABLE.	8,874	85.87	5.13	9.00	7,620	94.24	5.76
Barnstable, ...	1,311	93.06	3.81	3.13	1,220	96.31	3.69
Bourne, ...	515	84.27	10.49	5.24	434	98.39	1.61
Brewster, ...	285	93.33	1.41	5.26	266	94.36	5.64
Chatham, ...	616	97.89	1.79	0.32	603	97.35	2.65
Dennis, ...	786	93.89	3.31	2.80	738	97.29	2.71
Eastham, ...	168	90.48	8.93	0.59	152	98.68	1.32
Falmouth, ...	865	83.35	5.32	11.33	721	93.90	6.10
Harwich, ...	841	82.40	12.37	5.23	686	98.12	1.88
Mashpee, ...	98	91.84	5.10	3.06	90	98.89	1.11
Orleans, ...	390	87.69	7.69	4.62	342	98.54	1.46
Provincetown, ...	1,395	65.95	3.73	30.32	920	79.67	20.33
Sandwich, ...	496	88.11	5.24	6.65	437	87.41	12.59
Truro, ...	236	79.66	0.85	19.49	188	95.74	4.26
Wellfleet, ...	309	91.91	4.21	3.88	284	96.48	3.52
Yarmouth, ...	563	94.49	3.02	2.49	532	97.93	2.07
BERKSHIRE.	25,897	77.95	7.06	14.99	20,186	79.30	20.70
Adams, ...	2,057	71.46	5.59	22.95	1,470	64.76	35.24
Alford, ...	99	90.91	5.05	4.04	90	92.22	7.78
Becket, ...	295	71.53	9.83	18.64	211	86.73	13.27
Cheshire, ...	394	80.96	5.08	13.96	319	86.21	13.79
Clarksburg, ...	311	68.81	14.15	17.04	214	86.92	13.08
Dalton, ...	878	87.59	6.72	5.69	769	81.27	18.73
Egremont, ...	272	86.40	11.03	2.57	255	96.60	3.40
Florida, ...	141	70.21	7.09	22.70	99	86.87	13.13
Great Barrington, . . .	1,517	80.82	7.45	11.73	1,226	85.15	14.85
Hancock, ...	155	78.07	16.77	5.16	121	96.69	3.51
Hinsdale, ...	487	74.74	6.57	18.69	364	79.40	20.60
Lanesborough, ...	277	87.72	6.14	6.14	243	84.36	15.64
Lee, ...	1,208	75.55	10.10	14.35	958	78.39	21.61
Lenox, ...	938	71.75	2.88	25.37	673	77.56	22.44
Monterey, ...	142	84.50	7.75	7.75	120	90.83	9.17
Mount Washington, . . .	41	80.49	2.44	17.07	33	96.97	3.03
New Ashford, ...	42	88.10	9.52	2.38	37	91.89	8.11
New Marlborough, . . .	423	89.36	2.36	8.28	378	88.89	11.11
NORTH ADAMS, ...	5,537	73.42	6.28	20.30	4,065	73.60	26.40
Otis, ...	182	89.01	8.24	2.75	162	99.38	0.62
Peru, ...	98	80.61	11.23	8.16	79	89.87	10.13
PITTSFIELD, ...	6,031	79.61	7.03	13.36	4,801	76.67	23.33
Ward 1, ...	812	75.62	3.69	20.69	614	64.01	35.99
Ward 2, ...	1,025	83.71	8.88	7.41	858	79.37	20.63
Ward 3, ...	808	84.53	4.95	10.52	683	81.84	18.16
Ward 4, ...	777	85.46	5.53	9.01	664	85.54	14.46
Ward 5, ...	782	79.59	11.12	18.29	552	73.37	26.63
Ward 6, ...	955	78.64	3.56	17.80	751	68.58	31.42
Ward 7, ...	872	77.87	11.35	10.78	679	82.47	17.53

POLLS AND VOTERS — Continued.

COUNTIES, CITIES, AND TOWNS.	Total Polls	RATABLE POLLS			LEGAL VOTERS		
		PERCENTAGES OF TOTAL RATABLE POLLS			Total Voters	PERCENTAGES OF TOTAL LEGAL VOTERS	
		Voters	Not Voters	Aliens		Native Born Voters	Foreign Born Naturalized Voters
BERKSHIRE — Con.							
Richmond, ...	214	79.44	7.94	12.62	170	72.94	27.06
Sandisfield, ...	270	88.89	8.15	2.96	240	93.75	6.25
Savoy, ...	177	87.01	8.47	4.52	154	93.51	6.49
Sheffield, ...	586	84.30	8.87	6.83	494	90.08	9.92
Stockbridge, ...	630	85.40	3.65	10.95	538	83.09	16.91
Tyringham, ...	121	84.30	9.92	5.78	102	97.06	2.94
Washington, ...	133	78.95	6.77	14.28	105	83.81	16.19
West Stockbridge, . . .	385	84.93	3.90	11.17	327	80.43	19.57
Williamstown, ...	1,612	76.55	10.24	13 21	1,234	86.47	13.53
Windsor, ...	184	84.24	10.33	5.43	155	92.90	7.10
BRISTOL.	62,352	68.16	4.93	26.91	42,495	69.67	30.33
Acushnet, ...	375	84.00	7.20	8.80	315	95.87	4.13
Attleborough, ...	2,457	73.83	6.31	19.86	1,814	83.13	16.87
Berkley, ...	323	85.45	3.41	11.14	276	93.84	6.16
Dartmouth, ...	1,020	79.51	5.98	14.51	811	92.48	7.52
Dighton, ...	591	79.53	6.43	14.04	470	94.04	5.96
Easton, ...	1,407	79.89	4.90	15.21	1,124	74.91	25.09
Fairhaven, ...	1,053	84.80	3.23	11.97	893	94.06	5.94
FALL RIVER, ...	23,767	61.29	4.35	34.36	14,566	50.95	49.05
Ward 1, ...	2,951	65.37	3.35	31.28	1,929	47.38	52.62
Ward 2, ...	2,238	56.93	3.75	39.32	1,274	42.78	57.22
Ward 3, ...	3,150	57.80	4.75	37.45	1,826	44.85	55.15
Ward 4, ...	2,800	69.32	4.25	26.43	1,941	53.53	46.47
Ward 5, ...	2,877	56.83	4.21	38.96	1,635	42.26	57.74
Ward 6, ...	2,921	42.31	5.07	52.62	1,236	31.63	68.37
Ward 7, ...	2,035	75.28	4.67	20.05	1,532	72.72	27.28
Ward 8, ...	2,002	83.07	3.05	13.88	1,663	69.69	30.31
Ward 9, ...	2,784	54.96	5.67	39.37	1,530	48.95	51.05
Freetown, ...	479	81.42	4.18	14.40	390	93.33	6.67
Mansfield, ...	1,146	81.41	6.11	12.48	933	91.00	9.00
NEW BEDFORD, ...	15,798	63.91	4.83	31.26	10,096	71.43	28.57
Ward 1, ...	3,571	48.47	4.15	47.38	1,731	52.74	47.26
Ward 2, ...	2,231	71.81	3.72	24.47	1,602	72.03	27.97
Ward 3, ...	1,691	91.43	3.19	5.38	1,546	89.78	10.22
Ward 4, ...	2,081	78.62	9.37	12.01	1,636	84.84	15.16
Ward 5, ...	2,652	67.76	3.92	28.32	1,797	82.97	17.03
Ward 6, ...	3,572	49.94	5.04	45.02	1,784	49.22	50.78
North Attleborough, . . .	1,916	80.43	5.74	13.83	1,541	77.09	22.91
Norton, ...	520	85.19	5.00	9.81	443	92.10	7.90
Raynham, ...	496	81.05	6.05	12.90	402	95.02	4.98
Rehoboth, ...	653	79.48	8.12	12.40	519	94.61	5.39
Seekonk, ...	514	67.32	12.06	20.62	346	91.91	8.09
Somerset, ...	674	71.36	5.79	22.85	481	88.57	11.43
Swansea, ...	560	68.75	16.43	14.82	385	87.01	12.99
TAUNTON, ...	7,746	77.37	4.56	18.07	5,993	76.96	23.04
Ward 1, ...	853	89.10	2.34	8.56	760	85.00	15.00
Ward 2, ...	891	86.87	5.39	7.74	774	84.63	15.37
Ward 3, ...	908	77.86	5.07	17.07	707	68.60	31.40
Ward 4, ...	901	85.35	4.22	10.43	769	87.26	12.74
Ward 5, ...	1,058	73.16	4.44	22.40	774	63.05	36.95
Ward 6, ...	944	77.44	2.65	19.91	731	81.12	18.88
Ward 7, ...	877	83.01	3.19	13.80	728	79.95	20.05
Ward 8, ...	1,314	57.08	7.69	35.23	750	65.60	34.40
Westport, ...	857	81.33	3.15	15.52	697	94.26	5.74

POLLS AND VOTERS — Continued.

COUNTIES, CITIES, AND TOWNS.	RATABLE POLLS				LEGAL VOTERS		
	Total Polls	PERCENTAGES OF TOTAL RATABLE POLLS			Total Voters	PERCENTAGES OF TOTAL LEGAL VOTERS	
		Voters	Not Voters	Aliens		Native Born Voters	Foreign Born Naturalized Voters
DUKES.	1,473	83.91	5.97	10.12	1,236	94.50	5.50
Chilmark,	121	88.43	10.74	0.83	107	100.00	–
Cottage City,	336	75.00	7.14	17.86	252	89.29	10.71
Edgartown,	392	86.74	4.08	9.18	340	95.59	4.41
Gay Head,	44	93.18	2.27	4.55	41	97.56	2.44
Gosnold,	72	63.89	20.83	15.28	46	89.13	10.87
Tisbury,	341	88.27	4.69	7.04	301	95.02	4.98
West Tisbury,	167	89.22	1.80	8.98	149	96.64	3.36
ESSEX.	105,920	73.58	5.11	21.31	77,282	77.70	22.30
Amesbury,	3,066	75.34	5.48	19.18	2,316	81.17	18.83
Andover,	1,701	76.72	6.82	16.46	1,305	76.86	23.14
BEVERLY,	3,782	80.22	6.56	13.22	3,034	88.69	11.31
Ward 1,	873	78.58	8.13	13.29	686	84.26	15.74
Ward 2,	768	82.81	4.43	12.76	636	88.84	11.16
Ward 3,	774	74.42	9.69	15.89	576	91.67	8.33
Ward 4,	601	89.35	2.16	8.49	537	89.94	10.06
Ward 5,	394	85.28	5.84	8.88	336	94.35	5.65
Ward 6,	372	70.70	8.60	20.70	263	83.65	16.35
Boxford,	231	82.68	7.36	9.96	191	94.76	5.24
Bradford,	1,428	81.16	6.65	12.19	1,159	88.87	11.13
Danvers,	2,263	77.60	8.13	14.27	1,756	82.18	17.82
Essex,	573	85.86	3.84	10.30	492	94.31	5.69
Georgetown,	668	89.97	3.89	6.14	601	91.85	8.15
GLOUCESTER,	11,829	54.48	3.25	42.27	6,444	69.10	30.90
Ward 1,	1,136	73.77	3.61	22.62	838	70.41	29.59
Ward 2,	1,904	52.00	2.99	45.01	990	67.27	32.73
Ward 3,	2,827	42.31	2.44	55.25	1,196	56.19	43.81
Ward 4,	1,900	45.47	3.79	50.74	864	62.27	37.73
Ward 5,	1,581	65.15	2.97	31.88	1,030	73.30	26.70
Ward 6,	886	83.30	4.06	12.64	738	81.30	18.70
Ward 7,	1,177	36.71	3.65	59.64	432	72.45	27.55
Ward 8,	418	85.17	4.78	10.05	356	89.61	10.39
Groveland,	700	84.57	3.43	12.00	592	86.49	13.51
Hamilton,	481	54.47	20.17	25.36	262	95.80	4.20
HAVERHILL,	9,432	79.05	4.95	16.00	7,456	82.39	17.61
Ward 1,	1,002	87.52	6.59	5.89	877	90.42	9.58
Ward 2,	780	87.31	4.10	8.59	681	92.07	7.93
Ward 3,	1,249	77.82	5.13	17.05	972	71.30	28.70
Ward 4,	1,168	86.73	4.62	8.65	1,013	88.75	11.25
Ward 5,	3,413	69.82	4.45	25.73	2,383	77.84	22.16
Ward 6,	1,820	84.07	5.44	10.49	1,530	83.40	16.60
Ipswich,	1,441	74.25	6.18	19.57	1,070	88.88	11.12
LAWRENCE,	15,340	66.35	5.25	28.40	10,178	52.99	47.01
Ward 1,	2,564	70.63	3.98	25.39	1,811	45.67	54.33
Ward 2,	2,270	65.33	5.33	29.34	1,483	56.10	43.90
Ward 3,	2,508	63.52	4.98	31.50	1,593	49.09	50.91
Ward 4,	2,990	55.02	9.76	35.22	1,645	53.01	46.99
Ward 5,	2,856	68.49	3.25	28.26	1,956	53.58	46.42
Ward 6,	2,152	78.53	3.35	18.12	1,690	61.07	38.93
LYNN,	19,820	77.85	4.89	17.26	15,437	81.38	18.62
Ward 1,	482	87.97	2.49	9.54	424	93.16	6.84
Ward 2,	1,232	80.92	5.44	13.64	997	89.07	10.93
Ward 3,	4,462	81.89	3.70	14.41	3,654	86.97	13.03
Ward 4,	4,136	78.41	6.24	15.35	3,243	81.99	18.01
Ward 5,	4,177	76.54	5.34	18.12	3,197	80.17	19.83

POLLS AND VOTERS — Continued.

COUNTIES, CITIES, AND TOWNS.	RATABLE POLLS				LEGAL VOTERS		
	Total Polls	PERCENTAGES OF TOTAL RATABLE POLLS			Total Voters	PERCENTAGES OF TOTAL LEGAL VOTERS	
		Voters	Not Voters	Aliens		Native Born Voters	Foreign Born Naturalized Voters
ESSEX — Con.							
LYNN — Con.							
Ward 6, ...	4,541	73.20	4.73	22.07	3,324	72.47	27.53
Ward 7, ...	799	74.84	3.63	21.53	598	78.76	21.24
Lynnfield, ...	290	78.62	8.97	12.41	228	96.49	3.51
Manchester, ...	631	71.32	6.02	22.66	450	89.56	10.44
Marblehead, ...	2,482	92.47	2.82	4.71	2,295	91.50	8.50
Merrimac, ...	731	83.86	3.15	12.99	613	89.89	10.11
Methuen, ...	1,665	70.15	6.31	23.54	1,168	72.69	27.31
Middleton, ...	281	81.14	7.12	11.74	228	90.79	9.21
Nahant, ...	299	69.90	14.72	15.38	209	74.64	25.36
Newbury, ...	531	80.60	6.40	13.00	428	93.93	6.07
NEWBURYPORT, . . .	4,201	83.48	3.98	12.54	3,507	85.54	14.46
Ward 1, ...	686	86.44	3.79	9.77	593	92.75	7.25
Ward 2, ...	634	72.08	3.16	24.76	457	87.09	12.91
Ward 3, ...	789	88.21	3.04	8.75	696	85.34	14.66
Ward 4, ...	690	85.94	5.80	8.26	593	82.46	17.54
Ward 5, ...	639	77.31	5.01	17.68	494	75.91	24.09
Ward 6, ...	763	88.33	3.28	8.39	674	88.13	11.87
North Andover, . . .	1,112	82.01	6.75	11.24	912	66.45	33.55
Peabody, ...	3,293	80.38	4.16	15.46	2,647	74.23	25.77
Rockport, ...	2,027	52.05	3.21	44.74	1,055	83.22	16.78
Rowley, ...	436	87.39	6.19	6.42	381	96.06	3.94
SALEM, ...	10,193	72.71	5.80	21.49	7,411	77.80	22.20
Ward 1, ...	1,504	73.61	4.85	21.54	1,107	73.80	26.20
Ward 2, ...	1,893	75.81	13.10	11.09	1,435	88.36	11.64
Ward 3, ...	1,263	84.09	2.69	13.22	1,062	78.44	21.56
Ward 4, ...	1,537	78.46	3.97	17.57	1,206	69.15	30.85
Ward 5, ...	2,705	54.64	4.29	41.07	1,478	73.88	26.12
Ward 6, ...	1,291	86.99	4.57	8.44	1,123	82.10	17.90
Salisbury, ...	434	90.78	5.30	3.92	394	94.16	5.84
Saugus, ...	1,378	83.60	5.73	10.67	1,152	83.07	16.93
Swampscott, . . .	1,056	82.77	4.92	12.31	874	90.96	9.04
Topsfield, ...	353	86.40	8.78	4.82	305	93.11	6.89
Wenham, ...	316	86.71	3.80	9.49	274	97.45	2.55
West Newbury, . . .	556	83.45	6.30	10.25	464	85.56	14.44
FRANKLIN.	12,832	80.52	6.11	13.37	10,332	87.13	12.87
Ashfield, ...	355	84.51	9.01	6.48	300	96.67	3.33
Bernardston, . . .	261	85.06	8.43	6.51	222	97.30	2.70
Buckland, ...	486	85.60	3.91	10.49	416	73.56	26.44
Charlemont, ...	340	86.47	7.35	6.18	294	97.62	2.38
Colrain, ...	513	79.73	2.53	17.74	409	95.11	4.89
Conway, ...	415	80.96	9.40	9.64	336	90.77	9.23
Deerfield, ...	979	73.75	7.05	19.20	722	83.93	16.07
Erving, ...	309	77.99	6.47	15.54	241	89.63	10.37
Gill, ...	408	68.63	14.21	17.16	280	93.21	6.79
Greenfield, ...	1,945	85.19	5.66	9.15	1,657	84.25	15.75
Hawley, ...	160	89.38	8.12	2.50	143	98.60	1.40
Heath, ...	142	87.32	4.23	8.45	124	97.58	2.42
Leverett, ...	256	91.80	5.08	3.12	235	98.72	1.28
Leyden, ...	122	86.88	8.20	4.92	106	93.40	6.60
Monroe, ...	123	58.54	6.50	34.96	72	94.44	5.56
Montague, ...	1,735	74.18	4.96	20.86	1,287	64.65	35.35
New Salem, ...	293	81.91	9.90	8.19	240	95.00	5.00
Northfield, ...	511	89.24	2.74	8.02	456	93.86	6.14

POLLS AND VOTERS — Continued.

COUNTIES, CITIES, AND TOWNS.	RATABLE POLLS				LEGAL VOTERS		
	Total Polls	PERCENTAGES OF TOTAL RATABLE POLLS			Total Voters	PERCENTAGES OF TOTAL LEGAL VOTERS	
		Voters	Not Voters	Aliens		Native Born Voters	Foreign Born Naturalized Voters
FRANKLIN — Con.							
Orange,	1,740	82.99	3.22	13.79	1,444	91.76	8.24
Rowe,	184	60.32	11.96	27.72	111	98.20	1.80
Shelburne,	501	83.04	8.38	8.58	416	94.23	5.77
Shutesbury,	146	93.84	2.74	3.42	137	96.35	3.65
Sunderland,	254	75.59	4.72	19.69	192	92.71	7.29
Warwick,	211	64.45	15.17	20.38	136	95.59	4.41
Wendell,	179	75.42	7.26	17.32	135	91.85	8.15
Whately,	264	83.71	6.44	9.85	221	86.43	13.57
HAMPDEN.	45,582	69.56	6.52	23.92	31,568	76.06	23.94
Agawam,	745	71.14	10.74	18.12	530	82.45	17.55
Blandford,	283	90.46	6.71	2.83	256	98.83	1.17
Brimfield,	325	80.00	8.00	12.00	260	94.23	5.77
Chester,	459	82.57	5.88	11.55	379	95.51	4.49
CHICOPEE,	5,013	54.84	5.86	39.30	2,749	69.99	30.01
Ward 1,	967	48.61	4.96	46.43	470	61.49	38.51
Ward 2,	514	77.43	4.48	18.09	398	74.12	25.88
Ward 3,	948	36.29	7.59	56.12	344	67.15	32.85
Ward 4,	651	60.21	4.92	34.87	392	76.79	23.21
Ward 5,	883	61.38	7.25	31.37	542	77.68	22.32
Ward 6,	518	59.46	3.67	36.87	308	69.16	30.84
Ward 7,	532	55.45	6.77	37.78	295	58.98	41.02
East Longmeadow,	517	46.23	2.51	51.26	239	79.92	20.08
Granville,	313	81.47	8.95	9.58	255	93.33	6.67
Hampden,	242	74.38	11.16	14.46	180	86.67	13.33
Holland,	64	84.38	6.25	9.37	54	94.44	5.56
HOLYOKE,	10,742	61.41	4.98	33.61	6,597	56.74	43.26
Ward 1,	1,543	62.61	5.18	32.21	966	53.11	46.89
Ward 2,	2,307	39.71	6.11	54.18	916	46.07	53.93
Ward 3,	1,315	64.34	4.64	31.02	846	50.83	49.17
Ward 4,	1,784	47.92	5.16	46.92	855	38.95	61.05
Ward 5,	960	85.21	3.96	10.83	818	65.16	34.84
Ward 6,	1,596	69.11	4.14	26.75	1,103	59.75	40.25
Ward 7,	1,237	88.36	4.61	7.03	1,093	78.04	21.96
Longmeadow,	193	74.09	10.36	15.55	143	88.81	11.19
Ludlow,	739	50.34	9.34	40.32	372	82.80	17.20
Monson,	1,150	74.00	6.96	19.04	851	87.07	12.93
Montgomery,	87	90.80	3.45	5.75	79	96.20	3.80
Palmer,	2,063	57.97	7.76	34.27	1,196	81.61	18.39
Russell,	267	67.79	14.23	17.98	181	85.64	14.36
Southwick,	330	79.09	12.12	8.79	261	90.04	9.96
SPRINGFIELD,	15,911	76.93	6.96	16.11	12,240	80.01	19.99
Ward 1,	2,122	80.92	6.36	12.72	1,717	82.88	17.12
Ward 2,	2,393	67.57	5.77	26.66	1,617	71.43	28.57
Ward 3,	2,333	74.88	7.42	17.70	1,747	78.76	21.24
Ward 4,	1,866	84.99	4.93	10.08	1,586	83.42	16.58
Ward 5,	1,881	86.39	5.05	8.56	1,625	86.40	13.60
Ward 6,	1,935	68.89	13.90	17.21	1,333	74.57	25.43
Ward 7,	1,363	87.23	3.08	9.69	1,189	82.93	17.07
Ward 8,	2,018	70.66	8.08	21.26	1,426	79.38	20.62
Tolland,	108	77.78	9.26	12.96	84	92.86	7.14
Wales,	251	79.52	12.35	17.13	177	90.40	9.60
Westfield,	3,352	82.10	6.18	11.72	2,752	84.70	15.30
West Springfield,	1,757	78.20	6.15	15.65	1,374	81.30	18.70
Wilbraham,	471	76.22	7.22	16.56	359	87.74	12.26

POLLS AND VOTERS — Continued.

COUNTIES, CITIES, AND TOWNS.	RATABLE POLLS				LEGAL VOTERS		
	Total Polls	PERCENTAGES OF TOTAL RATABLE POLLS			Total Voters	PERCENTAGES OF TOTAL LEGAL VOTERS	
		Voters	Not Voters	Aliens		Native Born Voters	Foreign Born Naturalized Voters
HAMPSHIRE.	15,754	75.46	6.27	18.27	11,888	82.87	17.13
Amherst,	1,591	84.16	9.81	6.03	1,339	93.35	6.65
Belchertown,	689	80.84	6.82	12.34	557	91.38	8.62
Chesterfield,	212	90.57	5.19	4.24	192	98.44	1.56
Cummington,	258	87.21	8.53	4.26	225	98.22	1.78
Easthampton,	1,360	70.96	8.45	20.59	965	72.75	27.25
Enfield,	314	74.52	6.05	19.43	234	89.32	10.68
Goshen,	90	81.11	12.22	6.67	73	97.26	2.74
Granby,	251	72.51	7.97	19.52	182	92.31	7.69
Greenwich,	159	91.83	3.77	4.40	146	97.26	2.74
Hadley,	573	69.46	5.06	25.48	398	90.95	9.05
Hatfield,	434	73.73	3.00	23.27	320	85.00	15.00
Huntington,	422	75.59	9.95	14.46	319	87.77	12.23
Middlefield,	118	72.88	11.02	16.10	86	96.51	3.49
NORTHAMPTON,	4,341	75.79	5.14	19.07	3,290	76.63	23.37
Ward 1,	669	78.48	4.33	17.19	525	79.05	20.95
Ward 2,	564	82.27	4.96	12.77	464	80.17	19.83
Ward 3,	852	70.31	6.57	23.12	599	76.13	23.87
Ward 4,	622	69.45	5.79	24.76	432	83.80	16.20
Ward 5,	594	76.77	3.70	19.53	456	62.28	37.72
Ward 6,	527	82.73	3.99	13.28	436	78.21	21.79
Ward 7,	513	73.09	6.04	20.27	378	76.98	23.02
Pelham,	154	88.96	9.09	1.95	137	94.89	5.11
Plainfield,	153	88.23	8.50	3.27	135	100.00	–
Prescott,	146	86.30	10.27	3.43	126	100.00	–
Southampton,	351	80.34	3.99	15.67	282	94.68	5.32
South Hadley,	1,213	69.17	4.86	25.97	839	77.12	22.88
Ware,	2,008	63.30	5.03	31.67	1,271	69.32	30.68
Westhampton,	146	82.19	2.06	15.75	120	95.83	4.17
Williamsburg,	564	82.98	4.79	12.23	468	83.97	16.03
Worthington,	207	88.89	7.25	3.86	184	97.28	2.72
MIDDLESEX.	150,610	72.76	6.18	21.06	109,577	74.61	25.39
Acton,	697	78.19	7.89	13.92	545	89.17	10.83
Arlington,	1,970	78.43	3.65	17.92	1,545	69.97	30.03
Ashby,	294	88.10	7.48	4.42	259	96.91	3.09
Ashland,	636	75.79	9.59	14.62	482	82.16	17.84
Ayer,	650	79.23	10.15	10.62	515	83.50	16.50
Bedford,	437	60.41	13.96	25.63	264	87.50	12.50
Belmont,	1,043	52.73	6.81	40.46	550	78.55	21.45
Billerica,	813	78.72	4.67	16.61	640	74.06	25.94
Boxborough,	108	74.07	12.04	13.89	80	88.75	11.25
Burlington,	219	63.93	16.89	19.18	140	92.14	7.86
CAMBRIDGE,	25,105	67.79	7.55	24.66	17,018	71.20	28.80
Ward 1,	5,291	70.82	13.38	15.80	3,747	79.80	20.20
Ward 2,	6,728	69.96	4.65	25.39	4,707	67.94	32.06
Ward 3,	4,581	53.74	9.07	36.59	2,462	58.98	41.02
Ward 4,	5,565	71.86	5.43	22.71	3,999	72.07	27.93
Ward 5,	2,940	71.55	4.42	24.05	2,103	75.84	24.16
Carlisle,	177	70.62	7.91	21.47	125	96.00	4.00
Chelmsford,	1,019	75.66	7.66	16.68	771	79.90	20.10
Concord,	1,934	48.76	29.73	21.51	943	83.03	16.97
Dracut,	839	63.65	12.87	23.48	534	69.66	30.34
Dunstable,	152	88.16	4.60	7.24	134	91.04	8.96
EVERETT,	5,530	73.96	5.37	20.67	4,090	77.97	22.03
Ward 1,	921	66.99	7.82	25.19	617	74.88	25.12

POLLS AND VOTERS — Continued.

Counties, Cities, and Towns.	Total Polls	Voters	Not Voters	Aliens	Total Voters	Native Born Voters	Foreign Born Naturalized Voters
MIDDLESEX — Con.							
Everett — Con.							
Ward 2,	770	79.22	2.60	18.18	610	75.74	24.26
Ward 3,	914	66.63	9.30	24.07	669	73.40	26.60
Ward 4,	884	79.41	3.17	17.42	702	80.34	19.66
Ward 5,	945	68.89	6.56	24.55	651	76.65	23.35
Ward 6,	1,096	82.21	2.74	15.05	901	83.80	16.20
Framingham,	2,831	81.53	5.93	12.54	2,308	78.99	21.01
Groton,	614	80.46	7.49	12.05	494	91.30	8.70
Holliston,	872	84.17	5.39	10.44	734	83.65	16.35
Hopkinton,	983	91.76	3.36	4.88	902	77.16	22.84
Hudson,	1,639	79.07	3.78	17.15	1,296	82.72	17.28
Lexington,	1,189	71.32	6.48	22.20	848	82.55	17.45
Lincoln,	446	51.35	17.04	31.61	229	80.79	19.21
Littleton,	370	74.05	6.76	19.19	274	87.23	12.77
Lowell,	23,792	68.96	4.85	26.19	16,408	60.48	39.52
Ward 1,	2,910	73.13	4.50	22.37	2,128	62.69	37.31
Ward 2,	3,102	56.16	5.29	38.55	1,742	43.92	56.08
Ward 3,	2,683	70.85	4.36	24.79	1,901	75.22	24.78
Ward 4,	2,569	77.66	6.15	16.19	1,995	45.51	54.49
Ward 5,	2,542	67.55	4.52	27.93	1,717	53.41	46.59
Ward 6,	2,502	69.94	4.64	25.42	1,750	62.17	37.83
Ward 7,	3,298	50.88	5.15	43.97	1,678	63.77	36.23
Ward 8,	2,249	84.97	4.98	10.05	1,911	75.35	24.65
Ward 9,	1,937	81.88	3.67	14.45	1,586	61.29	38.71
Malden,	8,856	73.64	5.30	21.06	6,522	77.25	22.75
Ward 1,	1,173	80.05	4.09	15.86	939	81.36	18.64
Ward 2,	1,504	60.77	5.52	33.71	914	44.64	55.36
Ward 3,	1,026	83.24	4.97	11.79	854	87.59	12.41
Ward 4,	1,629	65.38	5.16	29.46	1,065	82.72	17.28
Ward 5,	1,185	81.94	4.98	13.08	971	87.13	12.87
Ward 6,	1,232	76.38	5.93	17.69	941	76.83	23.17
Ward 7,	1,107	75.70	6.41	17.89	838	79.71	20.29
Marlborough,	4,470	77.07	5.46	17.47	3,445	74.02	25.98
Ward 1,	439	83.83	3.87	12.30	368	84.78	15.22
Ward 2,	673	76.52	6.39	17.09	515	74.95	25.05
Ward 3,	798	71.80	4.64	23.56	573	66.67	33.33
Ward 4,	885	71.11	5.26	23.63	635	66.30	33.70
Ward 5,	622	79.10	6.91	13.99	492	83.54	16.46
Ward 6,	536	87.31	2.61	10.08	468	73.93	26.07
Ward 7,	509	77.41	8.45	14.14	394	74.11	25.89
Maynard,	948	63.08	5.38	31.54	598	62.71	37.29
Medford,	4,489	73.98	7.17	18.85	3,321	81.42	18.58
Ward 1,	986	59.74	11.26	29.00	589	78.61	21.39
Ward 2,	643	86.63	2.64	10.73	557	82.76	17.24
Ward 3,	553	87.70	4.70	7.60	485	85.77	14.23
Ward 4,	701	69.19	4.56	26.25	485	68.04	31.96
Ward 5,	920	68.91	10.76	20.33	634	83.75	16.25
Ward 6,	686	83.24	5.39	11.37	571	88.09	11.91
Melrose,	3,566	79.95	4.01	16.04	2,851	81.27	18.73
Natick,	2,714	86.00	4.94	9.06	2,334	78.41	21.59
Newton,	7,874	71.34	4.91	23.75	5,617	80.08	19.92
Ward 1,	1,176	56.80	3.91	39.29	668	71.11	28.89
Ward 2,	1,564	68.54	5.18	26.28	1,072	77.33	22.67
Ward 3,	933	81.56	3.86	14.58	761	84.49	15.51
Ward 4,	966	71.53	7.66	20.81	691	78.44	21.56

POLLS AND VOTERS — Continued.

		RATABLE POLLS				LEGAL VOTERS		
COUNTIES, CITIES, AND TOWNS.	Total Polls	PERCENTAGES OF TOTAL RATABLE POLLS			Total Voters	PERCENTAGES OF TOTAL LEGAL VOTERS		
		Voters	Not Voters	Aliens		Native Born Voters	Foreign Born Naturalized Voters	

COUNTIES, CITIES, AND TOWNS.	Total Polls	Voters	Not Voters	Aliens	Total Voters	Native Born Voters	Foreign Born Naturalized Voters
MIDDLESEX — Con.							
NEWTON — Con.							
Ward 5, ...	1,247	77.30	3.53	19.17	964	77.70	22.30
Ward 6, ...	1,273	66.46	5.89	27.65	846	81.68	18.32
Ward 7, ...	715	86.01	4.34	9.65	615	92.52	7.48
North Reading, . . .	284	80.28	7.75	11.97	228	92.98	7.02
Pepperell, ...	1,035	77.29	5.22	17.49	800	90.63	9.37
Reading, ...	1,485	79.73	7.00	13.27	1,184	86.40	13.60
Sherborn, ...	375	71.73	7.20	21.07	269	86.99	13.01
Shirley, ...	410	76.83	6.34	16.83	315	86.67	13.33
SOMERVILLE, ...	15,960	74.18	5.57	20.25	11,839	77.80	22.20
Ward 1, ...	3,133	72.52	7.82	19.66	2,272	82.35	17.65
Ward 2, ...	5,253	68.02	5.46	26.52	3,573	71.54	28.46
Ward 3, ...	4,038	80.21	4.83	14.96	3,239	79.84	20.16
Ward 4, ...	3,536	77.91	4.58	17.51	2,755	79.78	20.22
Stoneham, ...	2,062	85.21	3.25	11.54	1,757	82.24	17.76
Stow, ...	325	73.85	7.69	18.46	240	87.50	12.50
Sudbury, ...	418	76.31	3.83	19.86	319	90.91	9.09
Tewksbury, ...	698	60.60	12.47	26.93	423	70.69	29.31
Townsend, ...	619	86.43	5.82	7.75	535	92.90	7.10
Tyngsborough, . . .	218	72.02	9.17	18.81	157	94.90	5.10
Wakefield, ...	2,491	75.67	5.22	19.11	1,885	78.25	21.75
WALTHAM, ...	6,057	75.52	4.85	19.63	4,574	74.75	25.25
Ward 1, ...	895	69.72	4.36	25.92	624	75.48	24.52
Ward 2, ...	837	68.58	11.83	19.59	574	79.09	20.91
Ward 3, ...	956	63.46	4.59	31.95	594	60.61	39.39
Ward 4, ...	852	74.18	3.76	22.06	632	77.22	22.78
Ward 5, ...	899	84.87	4.12	11.01	763	87.81	12.19
Ward 6, ...	866	88.34	2.65	9.01	765	84.31	15.69
Ward 7, ...	772	80.57	2.72	16.71	622	53.22	46.78
Watertown, ...	2,438	71.82	7.01	21.17	1,751	74.19	25.81
Wayland, ...	658	81.31	3.65	15.04	535	85.79	14.21
Westford, ...	746	67.83	8.98	23.19	506	78.26	21.74
Weston, ...	585	67.35	5.98	26.67	394	90.36	9.64
Wilmington, . . .	436	76.38	2.52	21.10	333	85.89	14.11
Winchester, ...	1,866	74.49	6.70	18.81	1,390	74.60	25.40
WOBURN, ...	4,368	79.82	4.10	16.08	3,527	64.56	35.44
Ward 1, ...	768	80.60	4.56	14.84	619	58.16	41.84
Ward 2, ...	893	76.60	4.14	19.26	684	54.68	45.32
Ward 3, ...	699	86.55	2.86	10.59	605	68.93	31.07
Ward 4, ...	747	80.46	4.15	15.39	601	71.05	28.95
Ward 5, ...	338	76.63	5.32	18.05	259	57.53	42.47
Ward 6, ...	420	80.48	3.57	15.95	338	80.77	19.23
Ward 7, ...	396	72.94	4.95	22.11	221	66.97	33.03
NANTUCKET.	948	93.46	3.06	3.48	886	94.02	5.98
Nantucket, ...	948	93.46	3.06	3.48	886	94.02	5.98
NORFOLK.	41,120	76.76	5.32	17.92	31,565	77.88	22.12
Avon, ...	540	86.85	7.59	5.56	469	85.50	14.50
Bellingham, ...	453	71.30	9.05	19.65	323	87.00	13.00
Braintree, ...	1,779	74.82	3.82	21.36	1,331	85.20	14.80
Brookline, ...	4,371	74.19	5.06	20.75	3,243	72.77	27.23
Canton, ...	1,547	81.37	3.93	14.70	1,096	73.81	26.19
Cohasset, ...	784	84.82	2.42	12.76	665	86.17	13.88

POLLS AND VOTERS — Continued.

COUNTIES, CITIES, AND TOWNS.	Total Polls	RATABLE POLLS			LEGAL VOTERS		
		PERCENTAGES OF TOTAL RATABLE POLLS			Total Voters	PERCENTAGES OF TOTAL LEGAL VOTERS	
		Voters	Not Voters	Aliens		Native Born Voters	Foreign Born Naturalized Voters
NORFOLK — Con.							
Dedham,	2,223	76.56	9.45	13.99	1,702	74.15	25.85
Dover,	217	77.88	10.60	11.52	169	75.15	24.85
Foxborough,	1,054	81.41	9.20	9.39	858	87.76	12.24
Franklin,	1,552	76.29	5.15	18.56	1,184	82.60	17.40
Holbrook,	713	90.46	4.77	4.77	645	86.20	13.80
Hyde Park,	3,539	78.33	5.90	15.77	2,772	72.87	27.13
Medfield,	639	69.95	10.33	19.72	447	87.70	12.30
Medway,	918	89.11	3.27	7.62	818	83.25	16.75
Millis,	307	75.25	7.49	17.26	231	83.98	16.02
Milton,	1,586	73.83	4.67	21.50	1,171	77.03	22.97
Needham,	1,118	68.25	8.05	23.70	763	71.82	28.18
Norfolk,	293	65.87	8.53	25.60	193	86.01	13.99
Norwood,	1,551	73.05	5.09	21.86	1,133	71.14	28.86
QUINCY,	6,394	67.96	5.31	26.73	4,325	66.38	33.62
Ward 1,	1,130	71.06	8.59	20.35	803	76.71	23.29
Ward 2,	819	80.34	5.01	14.65	658	75.84	24.16
Ward 3,	1,450	57.16	4.39	38.45	834	49.88	50.12
Ward 4,	1,487	58.78	3.83	37.39	874	48.05	51.95
Ward 5,	824	78.40	5.10	16.50	646	83.90	16.10
Ward 6,	645	79.07	5.74	15.19	510	74.12	25.88
Randolph,	1,222	91.90	2.13	5.97	1,123	80.77	19.23
Sharon,	570	74.21	6.14	19.65	423	85.58	14.42
Stoughton,	1,601	83.26	3.31	13.43	1,333	82.82	17.18
Walpole,	951	75.18	2.42	22.40	715	83.64	16.36
Wellesley,	924	75.11	2.92	21.97	694	76.66	23.34
Weymouth,	3,704	82.05	4.40	13.55	3,039	87.56	12.44
Wrentham,	800	87.50	4.75	7.75	700	86.57	13.43
PLYMOUTH.	33,325	80.89	6.65	12.46	26,956	87.41	12.59
Abington,	1,384	90.90	4.48	4.62	1,258	86.80	13.20
Bridgewater,	1,697	58.46	33.53	8.01	992	87.60	12.40
BROCKTON,	10,701	79.72	4.64	15.64	8,531	80.80	19.20
Ward 1,	1,472	85.12	4.69	10.19	1,253	91.62	8.38
Ward 2,	1,468	89.24	3.95	6.81	1,310	87.25	12.75
Ward 3,	1,599	79.61	3.07	17.32	1,273	76.67	23.33
Ward 4,	1,497	69.61	5.34	25.05	1,042	67.08	32.92
Ward 5,	1,554	74.90	4.83	20.27	1,164	80.67	19.33
Ward 6,	1,641	73.25	7.25	19.50	1,202	80.20	19.80
Ward 7,	1,470	87.55	3.13	9.32	1,287	79.56	20.44
Carver,	355	75.77	8.17	16.06	269	96.28	3.72
Duxbury,	640	86.72	2.81	10.47	555	96.94	3.06
East Bridgewater,	996	80.75	6.21	13.04	780	91.67	8.33
Halifax,	174	83.91	3.45	12.64	146	94.52	5.48
Hanover,	705	82.84	8.65	8.51	584	94.86	5.14
Hanson,	472	81.78	6.14	12.08	386	97.15	2.85
Hingham,	1,568	80.10	4.59	15.31	1,256	87.42	12.58
Hull,	393	48.85	36.90	14.25	192	82.81	17.19
Kingston,	562	84.16	5.70	10.14	473	90.91	9.09
Lakeville,	304	83.55	6.58	9.87	254	96.46	3.54
Marion,	220	94.09	4.09	1.82	207	98.07	1.93
Marshfield,	604	88.74	2.15	9.11	536	97.39	2.61
Mattapoisett,	343	86.30	6.70	7.00	296	98.31	1.69
Middleborough,	2,182	84.47	5.45	10.08	1,843	92.57	7.43
Norwell,	522	90.61	4.41	4.98	473	96.19	3.81

POLLS AND VOTERS — Continued.

COUNTIES, CITIES, AND TOWNS	RATABLE POLLS				LEGAL VOTERS		
	Total Polls	PERCENTAGES OF TOTAL RATABLE POLLS			Total Voters	PERCENTAGES OF TOTAL LEGAL VOTERS	
		Voters	Not Voters	Aliens		Native Born Voters	Foreign Born Naturalized Voters
PLYMOUTH — Con.							
Pembroke,	428	86.22	3.97	9.81	369	94.04	5.96
Plymouth,	2,441	80.54	3.97	15.49	1,966	89.37	10.63
Plympton,	192	82.29	8.33	9.38	158	96.20	3.80
Rochester,	332	85.24	6.33	8.43	283	96.82	3.18
Rockland,	1,765	89.01	3.34	7.65	1,571	81.73	18.27
Scituate,	757	88.90	2.64	8.46	673	90.64	9.36
Wareham,	1,155	71.69	8.40	19.91	828	91.91	8.09
West Bridgewater,	582	79.21	4.47	16.32	461	87.20	12.80
Whitman,	1,881	85.91	4.15	9.94	1,616	88.68	11.32
SUFFOLK.	169,496	72.63	5.48	21.89	123,102	68.03	31.97
Boston,	156,084	72.65	5.46	21.89	113,393	67.43	32.57
Ward 1,	6,281	76.18	2.82	21.00	4,785	66.50	33.50
Ward 2,	7,166	60.80	13.44	25.76	4,357	55.52	44.48
Ward 3,	4,355	81.61	2.91	15.48	3,538	68.03	31.97
Ward 4,	4,207	78.70	3.40	17.90	3,311	72.61	27.39
Ward 5,	4,962	65.82	15.50	18.68	3,266	67.51	32.49
Ward 6,	9,371	44.71	6.29	49.00	4,190	52.03	47.97
Ward 7,	6,888	61.51	8.65	29.84	4,237	66.75	33.25
Ward 8,	8,232	62.84	4.24	32.92	5,173	67.41	32.59
Ward 9,	8,044	68.42	6.50	25.08	5,504	68.53	31.47
Ward 10,	7,604	79.00	5.14	15.86	6,007	80.36	19.64
Ward 11,	5,767	84.72	4.49	10.79	4,886	82.23	17.77
Ward 12,	6,963	82.31	4.42	13.27	5,731	80.07	19.93
Ward 13,	7,543	63.57	4.12	32.31	4,795	50.78	49.22
Ward 14,	6,071	72.16	10.08	17.76	4,381	66.15	33.85
Ward 15,	5,447	79.58	3.80	16.82	4,324	65.06	34.94
Ward 16,	4,904	80.20	3.55	16.25	3,933	72.31	27.69
Ward 17,	6,175	77.75	3.50	18.95	4,801	62.01	37.99
Ward 18,	6,779	71.25	3.27	25.48	4,830	61.78	38.22
Ward 19,	6,084	73.42	3.22	23.36	4,467	49.90	50.10
Ward 20,	6,372	82.00	4.52	13.48	5,225	74.20	25.80
Ward 21,	5,550	86.36	3.91	9.73	4,793	78.09	21.91
Ward 22,	6,214	78.52	3.86	17.62	4,879	61.98	38.02
Ward 23,	5,087	79.26	4.91	15.83	4,032	62.85	37.15
Ward 24,	5,358	81.58	3.85	14.59	4,371	74.63	25.37
Ward 25,	4,680	76.43	4.30	19.27	3,577	70.59	29.41
Chelsea,	9,732	72.61	4.68	22.83	7,066	74.57	25.43
Ward 1,	2,289	68.19	4.24	27.57	1,561	72.39	27.61
Ward 2,	2,260	72.17	4.03	23.80	1,631	70.45	29.55
Ward 3,	2,219	67.28	3.70	29.02	1,493	70.26	29.74
Ward 4,	1,648	76.76	5.16	18.08	1,265	81.34	18.66
Ward 5,	1,316	84.80	6.76	8.44	1,116	81.72	18.28
Revere,	2,301	79.01	2.74	18.25	1,818	73.32	26.68
Winthrop,	1,379	59.83	19.65	20.52	825	83.03	16.97
WORCESTER.	95,141	70.98	6.69	22.33	66,109	77.59	22.41
Ashburnham,	657	83.41	3.50	13.09	548	91.06	8.94
Athol,	2,572	71.77	9.25	18.98	1,846	93.50	6.50
Auburn,	471	57.32	10.83	31.85	270	82.22	17.78
Barre,	742	73.18	8.63	18.19	543	93.74	6.26
Berlin,	308	77.27	8.77	13.96	238	94.54	5.46
Blackstone,	1,921	72.51	2.55	24.94	1,393	60.16	39.84
Bolton,	268	78.36	9.33	12.31	210	91.43	8.57

POLLS AND VOTERS — Continued.

COUNTIES, CITIES, AND TOWNS.	RATABLE POLLS				LEGAL VOTERS		
	Total Polls	PERCENTAGES OF TOTAL RATABLE POLLS			Total Voters	PERCENTAGES OF TOTAL LEGAL VOTERS	
		Voters	Not Voters	Aliens		Native Born Voters	Foreign Born Naturalized Voters
WORCESTER — Con.							
Boylston,	251	78.48	5.58	15.94	197	90.36	9.64
Brookfield,	1,077	70.57	8.08	21.35	760	87.63	12.37
Charlton,	612	79.58	9.15	11.27	487	93.02	6.98
Clinton,	3,079	78.53	5.13	16.34	2,418	53.52	46.48
Dana,	248	72.58	10.89	16.53	180	98.33	1.67
Douglas,	675	73.04	7.70	19.26	493	88.03	11.97
Dudley,	864	61.11	4.75	34.14	528	71.02	28.98
FITCHBURG,	7,950	65.80	7.58	26.62	5,231	74.57	25.43
Ward 1,	1,312	63.11	13.26	23.63	828	66.55	33.45
Ward 2,	1,894	46.67	5.65	47.68	884	59.16	40.84
Ward 3,	1,311	62.62	6.64	30.74	821	67.72	32.28
Ward 4,	1,057	77.29	11.26	11.45	817	89.72	10.28
Ward 5,	1,084	85.98	6.73	7.29	932	86.91	13.09
Ward 6,	1,292	73.45	3.33	23.22	949	76.71	23.29
Gardner,	2,987	66.29	4.55	29.16	1,980	81.92	18.08
Grafton,	1,456	68.00	4.60	27.40	990	84.55	15.45
Hardwick,	808	59.28	7.55	33.17	479	77.24	22.76
Harvard,	416	73.56	10.09	16.35	396	89.87	10.13
Holden,	768	67.97	3.78	28.25	522	84.87	15.13
Hopedale,	464	75.65	12.93	11.42	351	86.32	13.68
Hubbardston,	436	77.52	11.70	10.78	338	91.72	8.28
Lancaster,	591	69.88	9.14	20.98	413	82.57	17.43
Leicester,	960	77.50	6.15	16.35	744	78.09	21.91
Leominster,	2,928	76.92	7.59	15.49	2,290	86.50	13.50
Lunenburg,	396	90.15	1.52	8.33	357	94.12	5.88
Mendon,	306	85.95	7.84	6.21	263	92.78	7.22
Milford,	2,873	80.86	4.35	14.79	2,323	76.67	23.33
Millbury,	1,621	59.41	6.11	34.48	963	80.17	19.83
New Braintree,	189	59.26	12.17	28.57	112	97.32	2.68
Northborough,	597	68.17	4.86	26.97	407	88.70	11.30
Northbridge,	1,651	59.00	7.81	33.19	974	66.22	33.78
North Brookfield,	1,399	76.48	5.86	17.66	1,070	82.80	17.20
Oakham,	208	84.13	5.77	10.10	175	95.43	4.57
Oxford,	706	79.18	4.39	16.43	559	89.80	10.20
Paxton,	158	82.91	2.53	14.56	131	94.66	5.34
Petersham,	341	75.66	12.90	11.44	258	90.70	9.30
Phillipston,	160	83.13	9.37	7.50	132	97.74	2.26
Princeton,	328	77.44	7.01	15.55	254	91.34	8.66
Royalston,	296	86.15	5.40	8.45	255	93.33	6.67
Rutland,	316	75.00	6.96	18.04	237	89.87	10.13
Shrewsbury,	516	86.05	4.46	9.49	444	93.24	6.76
Southborough,	821	54.57	6.94	38.49	448	83.26	16.74
Southbridge,	2,189	64.60	5.66	29.74	1,414	71.00	29.00
Spencer,	2,141	73.33	5.79	20.88	1,570	77.96	22.04
Sterling,	419	80.43	10.26	9.31	337	94.36	5.64
Sturbridge,	557	75.94	6.11	17.95	423	84.63	15.37
Sutton,	973	57.04	7.61	35.35	555	88.65	11.35
Templeton,	930	82.80	5.27	11.93	770	89.61	10.39
Upton,	614	84.53	7.00	8.47	519	92.10	7.90
Uxbridge,	1,127	65.93	7.01	27.06	743	86.41	13.59
Warren,	1,332	64.49	10.66	24.85	859	83.82	16.18
Webster,	2,198	56.78	6.73	36.49	1,248	67.63	32.37
Westborough,	1,488	75.81	12.97	11.22	1,128	85.37	14.63
West Boylston,	812	63.67	5.17	31.16	517	83.95	16.05
West Brookfield,	468	86.97	6.41	6.62	407	86.00	14.00

POLLS AND VOTERS — Concluded.

COUNTIES, CITIES, AND TOWNS.	Total Polls	RATABLE POLLS			LEGAL VOTERS		
		PERCENTAGES OF TOTAL RATABLE POLLS			Total Voters	PERCENTAGES OF TOTAL LEGAL VOTERS	
		Voters	Not Voters	Aliens		Native Born Voters	Foreign Born Naturalized Voters
WORCESTER — Con.							
Westminster, ...	423	83.69	8.04	8.27	354	92.94	7.06
Winchendon, ...	1,403	74.77	7.70	17.53	1,049	87.13	12.87
WORCESTER, . . .	29,666	71.22	6.43	22.35	21,128	71.21	28.79
Ward 1, ...	3,763	74.09	5.77	20.14	2,788	75.11	24.89
Ward 2, ...	3,805	70.59	3.76	25.65	2,686	72.60	27.40
Ward 3, ...	4,438	60.73	12.32	26.95	2,695	64.23	35.77
Ward 4, ...	3,700	69.65	4.70	25.65	2,577	55.06	44.94
Ward 5, ...	4,580	57.77	7.10	35.13	2,646	51.25	48.75
Ward 6, ...	3,418	77.71	5.12	17.17	2,656	78.09	21.91
Ward 7, ...	3,103	82.31	5.86	11.83	2,554	83.44	16.56
Ward 8, ...	2,859	88.35	5.07	6.58	2,526	90.70	9.30

RECAPITULATION.

THE STATE, AND COUNTIES.	Total Polls	RATABLE POLLS			LEGAL VOTERS		
		PERCENTAGES OF TOTAL RATABLE POLLS			Total Voters	PERCENTAGES OF TOTAL LEGAL VOTERS	
		Voters	Not Voters	Aliens		Native Born Voters	Foreign Born Naturalized Voters
THE STATE.	766,233	73.19	5.85	20.96	560,802	75.37	24.63
Barnstable, ...	8,874	85.87	5.13	9.00	7,620	94.24	5.76
Berkshire, ...	25,897	77.95	7.06	14.99	20,186	79.30	20.70
Bristol, ...	62,352	68.16	4.93	26.91	42,495	69.67	30.33
Dukes, ...	1,473	83.91	5.97	10.12	1,236	94.50	5.50
Essex, ...	105,029	73.58	5.11	21.31	77,282	77.70	22.30
Franklin, ...	12,832	80.52	6.11	13.37	10,332	87.13	12.87
Hampden, ...	45,382	69.56	6.52	23.92	31,568	76.06	23.94
Hampshire, ...	15,754	75.46	6.27	18.27	11,888	82.87	17.13
Middlesex, ...	150,610	72.76	6.18	21.06	109,577	74.61	25.39
Nantucket, ...	948	93.46	3.06	3.48	886	94.02	5.98
Norfolk, ...	41,120	76.76	5.32	17.92	31,565	77.88	22.12
Plymouth, ...	33,325	80.89	6.65	12.46	26,956	87.41	12.59
Suffolk, ...	169,496	72.63	5.48	21.89	123,102	68.03	31.97
Worcester, ...	93,141	70.98	6.69	22.33	66,109	77.59	22.41

POLITICAL CONDITION: BY SEX.

POLITICAL CONDITION: BY SEX.

The object of the presentation which follows is to show a classification of the political condition of the male population of the Commonwealth 20 years of age and over, and a similarly classified showing for the total population, including both sexes and all ages.

Although this presentation contains the more important facts in relation to the political condition of the male population 20 years of age and over, and also of the total population, yet reference may advantageously be had, in a full consideration of the question of political condition, to the following presentations, which appear in this and the second volume of the Census:

Population and Legal Voters,   Ages: By Five Year Periods,
Polls and Voters,   Ages: By Ten Year Periods,
Political Condition: By Age Periods,   Ages: By Selected Age Periods.

It is evidently impossible to combine in one table all the information relating to political condition; but by the use of the presentations mentioned above all desired information relating to the subject can undoubtedly be secured.

If we take a town and consider the figures in detail we shall learn the proper method of reading one line of the table. The method of reading calculated to bring out the facts for one town is equally applicable to the lines devoted to the remaining towns and cities of the Commonwealth.

In the town of Barnstable there are 1,311 ratable polls and four male persons with no political condition. The total, 1,315, is the total male population 20 years of age and over. There are 1,220 voters, 50 males above 20 years of age, who are all ratable polls, some of whom have not yet become voters on account of age limitation, while the balance have not complied with certain constitutional requirements, 41 aliens (that is, male persons born in foreign countries who have not yet become naturalized), and four persons having no political condition. If these four numbers are added together, the total is 1,315, which is the male population 20 years of age and over in the town.

Of the total male population 20 years of age and over, 99.70 per cent are ratable polls, while 0.30 per cent have no political condition; the total is 100 per cent, or the total male population 20 years of age and over. The total voters represent 92.78 per cent of the total male population 20 years of age and over. Of this 92.78 per cent, 89.36 per cent are native born voters and 3.42 per cent are foreign born naturalized voters. Of the total male population 20 years of age and over, as we have seen, 92.78 per cent are voters; the remaining 7.22 per cent is composed of 3.12 per cent aliens, 3.80 per cent of not voters, and 0.30 per cent of persons having no political condition; the total is 100 per cent, which means the total male population 20 years of age and over.

There are in the town of Barnstable 1,311 ratable polls and 2,744 persons having no political condition, the latter being males under 20 and females of all ages. The sum of these two numbers (1,311 and 2,744), or 4,055, is the total population of the town. If we add together the 1,220 voters, 50 not voters, 41 aliens, and the 2,744 persons of both sexes having no political condition, the total is 4,055, or the total population of the town.

Of the 4,055 persons in the town, the ratable polls, which are always males 20 years of age and over, represent 32.33 per cent, and the total voters comprise 30.09 per cent of the total population of the town. This percentage is composed of 28.98 per cent of native born voters and 1.11 per cent of foreign born naturalized voters. If we subtract 30.09 per cent from 32.33 per cent we secure 2.24 per cent, which represents 1.23 per cent of ratable polls, some of whom cannot become voters until they reach the age of 21, while the balance have not complied with certain constitutional requirements, and 1.01 per cent who have not yet taken proper steps to become citizens.

If we consider 4,055, the total population of the town, as being 100 per cent, 30.09 per cent are voters, 1.01 per cent aliens, 1.23 per cent not voters, while 67.67 per cent have no political condition; in other words, the actual political governing force in the town of Barnstable is 30.09 out of a total of 100 per cent.

The number of females 20 years of age and over may be found in the presentation entitled "AGES: BY SELECTED AGE PERIODS," in the second volume of the Census. This figure will allow of a direct comparison with the column in the first section of this presentation, which shows the total male population 20 years of age and over.

Assuming that women are endowed with the franchise on identically the same terms as men, the relative percentages of ratable polls for native born voters, foreign born naturalized voters, aliens, not voters, and women with no political condition, would approximate very closely to those shown in this presentation for men. If these percentages are applied to the female population 20 years of age and over it will be possible to construct a table for each city and town showing the political condition of women on the bases assumed. One of the principal objects in the preparation of this presentation has been to supply authoritative bases for such a computation.

POLITICAL CONDITION: BY SEX.

COUNTIES, CITIES, AND TOWNS.	MALE POPULATION 20 YEARS OF AGE AND OVER						PERCENTAGES OF MALE POPULATION 20 YEARS OF AGE AND OVER						
	Voters	Not Voters	Aliens	Total Ratable Polls	No. Political Condition	Total Male Population 20 Years of Age and Over	Ratable Polls	Native Born Voters	Foreign Born Naturalized Voters	Total Voters	Aliens	Not Voters	No Political Condition
1 BARNSTABLE.	7,020	455	799	8,874	63	8,937	99.30	80.35	4.92	85.27	8.94	5.09	0.70
2 Barnstable, .	1,220	50	41	1,311	4	1,315	99.70	89.36	3.42	92.78	3.12	3.80	0.30
3 Bourne, . .	434	54	27	515	–	515	100.00	82.91	1.36	84.27	5.24	10.49	–
4 Brewster, .	266	4	15	285	5	290	98.28	86.55	5.17	91.72	5.18	1.38	1.72
5 Chatham, .	603	11	2	616	2	618	99.67	94.98	2.59	97.57	0.33	1.77	0.33
6 Dennis, .	738	26	22	786	7	793	99.12	90.54	2.52	93.06	2.78	3.28	0.88
7 Eastham, .	152	15	1	168	1	169	99.41	88.76	1.18	89.94	0.59	8.88	0.59
8 Falmouth, .	721	46	98	865	4	869	99.54	77.91	5.06	82.97	11.28	5.29	0.46
9 Harwich, .	693	104	44	841	8	849	99.06	80.10	1.53	81.63	5.18	12.25	0.94
10 Mashpee, .	90	5	3	98	–	98	100.00	90.82	1.02	91.84	3.06	5.10	–
11 Orleans, .	342	30	18	390	–	390	100.00	86.41	1.28	87.69	4.62	7.69	–
12 Provincetown, .	920	52	423	1,395	12	1,407	99.15	52.10	13.29	65.39	30.06	3.70	0.85
13 Sandwich, .	437	26	33	496	10	506	98.02	75.49	10.87	86.36	6.52	5.14	1.98
14 Truro, . .	188	2	46	236	4	240	98.33	75.00	3.33	78.33	19.17	0.83	1.67
15 Wellfleet, .	284	13	12	309	2	311	99.36	88.10	3.22	91.32	3.86	4.18	0.64
16 Yarmouth, .	532	17	14	563	4	567	99.29	91.89	1.94	93.83	2.47	2.99	0.71
17 BERKSHIRE.	20,186	1,828	3,883	25,897	109	26,006	99.58	61.55	16.07	77.62	14.93	7.03	0.42
18 Adams, . .	1,470	115	472	2,057	3	2,060	99.85	46.21	25.15	71.36	22.91	5.58	0.15
19 Alford, . .	90	5	4	99	–	99	100.00	83.84	7.07	90.91	4.04	5.05	–
20 Becket, . .	211	29	55	295	4	299	98.66	61.20	9.37	70.57	18.39	9.70	1.34
21 Cheshire, .	319	20	55	394	7	401	98.25	68.58	10.97	79.55	13.71	4.99	1.75
22 Clarksburg, .	214	44	53	311	–	311	100.00	59.81	9.00	68.81	17.04	14.15	–
23 Dalton, . .	769	59	50	878	2	880	99.77	71.02	16.37	87.39	5.68	6.70	0.23
24 Egremont, .	235	30	7	272	1	273	99.63	83.15	2.93	86.08	2.56	10.98	0.37
25 Florida, . .	99	10	32	141	–	141	100.00	60.99	9.22	70.21	22.70	7.09	–
26 Gt. Barrington, .	1,226	113	178	1,517	–	1,517	100.00	68.82	12.00	80.82	11.73	7.45	–
27 Hancock, .	121	26	8	155	–	155	100.00	75.49	2.58	78.07	5.16	16.77	–
28 Hinsdale, . .	364	32	91	487	4	491	99.19	58.86	15.27	74.13	18.54	6.52	0.81
29 Lanesborough, .	243	17	17	277	3	280	98.96	73.22	13.57	86.79	6.07	6.07	1.07
30 Lee, . . .	958	128	182	1,268	8	1,276	99.37	58.86	16.22	75.08	14.26	10.03	0.63
31 Lenox, . .	673	27	238	938	1	939	99.89	55.59	16.08	71.67	25.35	2.87	0.11
32 Monterey, .	120	11	11	142	–	142	100.00	76.75	7.75	84.50	7.75	7.75	–
33 Mt. Washington,	38	1	2	41	1	42	97.62	76.19	2.38	78.57	16.67	2.38	2.38
34 New Ashford, .	37	4	1	42	–	42	100.00	80.95	7.15	88.10	2.38	9.52	–
35 N. Marlborough,	378	10	35	423	2	425	99.53	79.06	9.88	88.94	8.24	2.35	0.47
36 NORTH ADAMS,	4,065	348	1,124	5,537	22	5,559	99.60	53.82	19.30	73.12	20.22	6.26	0.40
37 Otis, . . .	162	15	5	182	1	183	99.45	87.97	0.55	88.52	2.73	8.20	0.55
38 Peru, . . .	79	11	8	98	1	99	98.99	71.72	8.08	79.80	8.08	11.11	1.01
39 PITTSFIELD,	4,801	424	806	6,031	28	6,059	99.54	61.75	18.49	79.24	13.30	7.00	0.46
40 Ward 1, .	614	30	168	812	25	837	97.01	46.95	26.41	73.36	20.07	3.58	2.99
41 Ward 2, .	858	91	76	1,025	–	1,025	100.00	66.44	17.27	83.71	7.41	8.88	–
42 Ward 3, .	683	40	85	808	1	809	99.88	69.10	15.33	84.43	10.51	4.94	0.12
43 Ward 4, .	664	43	70	777	1	778	99.87	73.01	12.34	85.35	9.00	5.52	0.13
44 Ward 5, .	552	87	143	782	1	783	99.87	51.72	18.77	70.49	18.27	11.11	0.13
45 Ward 6, .	751	34	170	955	–	955	100.00	53.93	24.71	78.64	17.80	3.56	–
46 Ward 7, .	679	99	94	872	–	872	100.00	64.22	13.65	77.87	10.78	11.35	–
47 Richmond, .	170	17	27	214	–	214	100.00	57.94	21.50	79.44	12.62	7.94	–

POLITICAL CONDITION: BY SEX.

	Total Population. Both Sexes. All Ages					Percentages of Total Population							
Voters	Not Voters	Aliens	Total Ratable Polls	No Political Condition	Total Population Both Sexes All Ages	Ratable Polls	Native Born Voters	Foreign Born Naturalized Voters	Total Voters	Aliens	Not Voters	No Political Condition	
7,620	455	799	8,874	18,780	27,654	32.09	25.97	1.59	27.56	2.88	1.95	67.91	1
1,220	50	41	1,311	2,744	4,055	32.33	28.98	1.11	30.09	1.01	1.23	67.67	2
434	54	27	515	1,065	1,580	32.59	27.03	0.44	27.47	1.70	3.42	67.41	3
266	4	15	285	616	901	31.63	27.86	1.66	29.52	1.66	0.45	68.37	4
603	11	2	616	1,193	1,809	34.05	32.45	0.88	33.33	0.11	0.61	65.95	5
738	26	22	786	1,759	2,545	30.88	28.21	0.79	29.00	0.86	1.02	69.12	6
152	15	1	168	308	476	35.29	31.51	0.42	31.93	0.21	3.15	64.71	7
721	46	98	865	1,790	2,655	32.58	25.50	1.66	27.16	3.69	1.73	67.42	8
686	104	44	841	1,691	2,532	33.21	26.86	0.51	27.37	1.73	4.11	66.79	9
90	5	3	98	232	330	29.70	26.97	0.30	27.27	0.91	1.52	70.30	10
342	30	18	390	808	1,198	32.55	28.13	0.42	28.55	1.50	2.50	67.45	11
920	52	423	1,395	3,160	4,555	30.63	16.09	4.11	20.20	9.29	1.14	69.37	12
437	26	33	496	1,084	1,580	31.39	24.18	3.48	27.66	2.09	1.64	68.61	13
188	2	46	236	579	815	28.96	22.09	0.98	23.07	5.64	0.25	71.04	14
284	13	12	309	659	968	31.92	28.31	1.03	29.34	1.24	1.34	68.08	15
532	17	14	563	1,092	1,655	34.02	31.48	0.67	32.15	0.84	1.03	65.98	16
20,186	1,828	3,883	25,897	60,395	86,292	30.01	18.55	4.84	23.39	4.50	2.12	69.99	17
1,470	115	472	2,057	5,780	7,837	26.25	12.15	6.61	18.76	6.02	1.47	73.75	18
90	5	4	99	181	280	35.36	29.64	2.50	32.14	1.43	1.79	64.64	19
211	29	55	295	593	888	33.22	20.61	3.15	23.76	6.19	3.27	66.78	20
319	20	55	394	782	1,176	33.50	23.39	3.74	27.13	4.67	1.70	66.50	21
214	44	53	311	698	1,009	30.82	18.43	2.79	21.21	5.25	4.36	69.18	22
769	59	50	878	2,332	3,210	27.35	19.47	4.48	23.95	1.56	1.84	72.65	23
235	30	7	272	564	836	32.54	27.15	0.96	28.11	0.84	3.59	67.46	24
99	10	32	141	284	425	33.18	20.24	3.06	23.30	7.53	2.35	66.82	25
1,226	113	178	1,517	3,277	4,794	31.64	21.78	3.79	25.57	3.71	2.36	68.36	26
121	26	8	155	356	511	30.33	22.90	0.78	23.68	1.56	5.09	69.67	27
364	32	91	487	1,163	1,650	29.52	17.51	4.55	22.06	5.52	1.94	70.48	28
243	17	17	277	571	848	32.66	24.18	4.48	28.66	2.00	2.00	67.34	29
958	128	182	1,268	2,798	4,066	31.19	18.47	5.09	23.56	4.48	3.15	68.81	30
673	27	238	938	1,934	2,872	32.66	18.17	5.26	23.43	8.29	0.94	67.34	31
120	11	11	142	322	464	30.60	23.49	2.37	25.86	2.37	2.37	69.40	32
33	1	7	41	95	136	30.15	23.52	0.74	24.26	5.15	0.74	69.85	33
37	4	1	42	74	116	36.21	29.31	2.59	31.90	0.86	3.45	63.79	34
378	10	35	423	865	1,288	32.84	26.09	3.26	29.35	2.72	0.77	67.16	35
4,065	348	1,124	5,537	13,598	19,135	28.94	15.64	5.61	21.25	5.87	1.82	71.06	36
162	15	5	182	336	518	35.14	31.08	0.19	31.27	0.97	2.90	64.86	37
79	11	8	98	207	305	32.13	23.28	2.62	25.90	2.62	3.61	67.87	38
4,801	424	806	6,031	14,430	20,461	29.48	17.99	5.47	23.46	3.94	2.08	70.52	39
614	30	168	812	2,024	2,836	28.63	13.86	7.79	21.65	5.92	1.06	71.37	40
858	91	76	1,025	2,501	3,526	29.07	19.31	5.02	24.33	2.16	2.58	70.93	41
683	40	85	808	1,817	2,625	30.78	21.30	4.72	26.02	3.24	1.52	69.22	42
664	43	70	777	2,003	2,780	27.95	20.43	3.45	23.88	2.52	1.55	72.05	43
552	87	143	782	1,905	2,687	29.10	15.07	5.47	20.54	5.32	3.24	70.90	44
751	34	170	955	2,519	3,474	27.49	14.83	6.79	21.62	4.89	0.98	72.51	45
679	99	94	872	1,661	2,533	34.43	22.11	4.70	26.81	3.71	3.91	65.57	46
170	17	27	214	487	701	30.53	17.69	6.56	24.25	3.85	2.43	69.47	47

POLITICAL CONDITION: BY SEX — Continued.

COUNTIES, CITIES, AND TOWNS.	MALE POPULATION 20 YEARS OF AGE AND OVER						PERCENTAGES OF MALE POPULATION 20 YEARS OF AGE AND OVER						
	Voters	Not Voters	Aliens	Total Ratable Polls	No. Political Condition	Total Male Population 20 Years of Age and Over	Ratable Polls	Native Born Voters	Foreign Born Naturalized Voters	Total Voters	Aliens	Not Voters	No Political Condition
BERKSHIRE — Con.													
1 Sandisfield,	240	22	8	270	1	271	99.63	83.03	5.53	88.56	2.95	8.12	0.37
2 Savoy,	154	15	8	177	1	178	99.44	80.90	5.62	86.52	4.49	8.43	0.56
3 Sheffield,	494	52	40	586	4	590	99.32	75.42	8.31	83.73	6.78	8.81	0.68
4 Stockbridge,	538	23	69	630	7	637	98.90	70.17	14.29	84.46	10.83	3.61	1.10
5 Tyringham,	102	12	7	121	3	124	97.58	79.84	2.42	82.26	5.64	9.68	2.42
6 Washington,	105	9	19	133	–	133	100.00	66.17	12.78	78.95	14.28	6.77	–
7 W. Stockbridge,	327	15	43	385	1	386	99.74	68.13	16.58	84.71	11.14	3.89	0.26
8 Williamstown,	1,234	165	213	1,612	4	1,616	99.75	66.03	10.33	76.36	13.18	10.21	0.25
9 Windsor,	155	19	10	184	–	184	100.00	78.26	5.98	84.24	5.43	10.33	–
10 **BRISTOL.**	42,495	3,076	16,781	62,352	565	62,917	99.10	47.05	20.49	67.54	26.67	4.89	0.90
11 Acushnet,	315	27	33	375	6	381	98.43	79.27	3.41	82.68	8.66	7.09	1.57
12 Attleborough,	1,814	155	488	2,457	5	2,462	99.80	61.25	12.43	73.68	19.82	6.30	0.20
13 Berkley,	276	11	36	323	2	325	99.38	79.69	5.23	84.92	11.08	3.38	0.62
14 Dartmouth,	811	61	148	1,020	8	1,028	99.22	72.96	5.36	78.89	14.40	5.93	0.78
15 Dighton,	470	38	83	591	1	592	99.83	74.66	4.73	79.39	14.02	6.42	0.17
16 Easton,	1,124	69	214	1,407	8	1,415	99.43	50.50	19.93	79.43	15.12	4.88	0.57
17 Fairhaven,	883	34	126	1,053	6	1,059	99.43	79.32	5.00	84.32	11.90	3.21	0.57
18 **FALL RIVER,**	14,566	1,635	8,166	23,767	60	23,827	99.75	31.14	29.99	61.13	34.27	4.35	0.25
19 Ward 1,	1,929	99	923	2,951	–	2,951	100.00	30.97	34.40	65.37	31.28	3.35	–
20 Ward 2,	1,274	84	880	2,238	–	2,238	100.00	24.35	32.58	56.93	39.32	3.75	–
21 Ward 3,	1,826	150	1,183	3,159	–	3,159	100.00	25.92	31.88	57.80	37.45	4.75	–
22 Ward 4,	1,941	119	740	2,800	7	2,807	99.75	37.02	32.13	69.15	26.36	4.24	0.25
23 Ward 5,	1,635	121	1,121	2,877	–	2,877	100.00	24.02	32.81	56.83	38.96	4.21	–
24 Ward 6,	1,236	148	1,537	2,921	1	2,922	99.97	13.38	28.92	42.30	52.60	5.07	0.03
25 Ward 7,	1,532	95	408	2,035	–	2,035	100.00	54.74	20.54	75.28	20.05	4.67	–
26 Ward 8,	1,663	61	278	2,002	48	2,050	97.66	56.54	24.58	81.12	13.56	2.98	2.34
27 Ward 9,	1,530	158	1,066	2,784	4	2,788	99.86	26.87	28.01	54.88	39.31	5.67	0.14
28 Freetown,	380	20	69	479	3	482	99.38	75.52	5.39	80.91	14.32	4.15	0.62
29 Mansfield,	933	70	143	1,146	4	1,150	99.65	73.87	7.20	81.13	12.43	6.09	0.35
30 **NEW BEDFORD,**	10,096	764	4,938	15,798	38	15,836	99.76	45.54	18.21	63.75	31.18	4.83	0.24
31 Ward 1,	1,731	148	1,692	3,571	–	3,571	100.00	25.57	22.90	48.47	47.38	4.15	–
32 Ward 2,	1,692	83	546	2,231	–	2,231	100.00	51.73	20.08	71.81	24.47	3.72	–
33 Ward 3,	1,546	54	91	1,691	6	1,697	99.65	81.79	9.31	91.10	5.37	3.18	0.35
34 Ward 4,	1,636	195	250	2,081	–	2,081	100.00	66.70	11.92	78.62	12.01	9.37	–
35 Ward 5,	1,797	104	751	2,652	–	2,652	100.00	56.22	11.54	67.76	28.32	3.92	–
36 Ward 6,	1,784	180	1,608	3,572	32	3,604	99.11	24.36	25.14	49.50	44.62	4.99	0.89
37 N. Attleborough,	1,541	110	265	1,916	9	1,925	99.53	61.71	18.34	80.05	13.77	5.71	0.47
38 Norton,	443	26	51	520	3	523	99.43	78.01	6.70	84.71	9.75	4.97	0.57
39 Raynham,	402	30	64	496	2	498	99.60	76.71	4.01	80.72	12.85	6.03	0.40
40 Rehoboth,	519	53	81	653	3	656	99.54	74.84	4.27	79.11	12.35	8.08	0.46
41 Seekonk,	346	62	106	514	4	518	99.23	61.39	5.41	66.80	20.46	11.97	0.77
42 Somerset,	481	39	154	674	4	678	99.41	62.83	8.12	70.95	22.71	5.75	0.59
43 Swansea,	385	92	83	560	1	561	99.82	59.72	8.91	68.63	14.79	16.40	0.18
44 **TAUNTON,**	5,986	355	1,400	7,746	395	8,141	95.15	56.65	16.96	73.61	17.20	4.34	4.85
45 Ward 1,	760	20	73	853	–	853	100.00	75.73	13.37	89.10	8.56	2.34	–
46 Ward 2,	774	48	69	891	2	893	99.78	73.35	13.32	86.67	7.73	5.38	0.22
47 Ward 3,	707	46	155	908	–	908	100.00	53.41	24.45	77.86	17.07	5.07	–
48 Ward 4,	769	38	94	901	–	901	100.00	74.47	10.88	85.35	10.43	4.22	–
49 Ward 5,	774	47	237	1,058	–	1,058	100.00	46.12	27.03	73.15	22.40	4.45	–
50 Ward 6,	731	25	188	944	–	944	100.00	62.82	14.62	77.44	19.91	2.65	–
51 Ward 7,	728	28	121	877	25	902	97.23	64.52	16.19	80.71	13.42	3.10	2.77
52 Ward 8,	750	101	463	1,314	368	1,682	78.12	29.25	15.34	44.59	27.53	6.00	21.88
53 Westport,	697	27	133	857	3	860	99.65	76.40	4.65	81.05	15.46	3.14	0.35

POLITICAL CONDITION: BY SEX — Continued.

TOTAL POPULATION. BOTH SEXES. ALL AGES						PERCENTAGES OF TOTAL POPULATION							
Voters	Not Voters	Aliens	Total Ratable Polls	No Political Condition	Total Population. Both Sexes. All Ages	Ratable Polls	Native Born Voters	Foreign Born Naturalized Voters	Total Voters	Aliens	Not Voters	No Political Condition	
240	22	8	270	532	802	33.67	28.06	1.87	29.93	1.00	2.74	66.33	1
154	15	8	177	327	504	35.12	28.57	1.98	30.55	1.59	2.98	64.88	2
494	52	40	586	1,311	1,897	30.89	23.46	2.58	26.04	2.11	2.74	69.11	3
538	23	69	630	1,447	2,077	30.33	21.52	4.38	25.90	3.32	1.11	69.67	4
102	12	7	121	242	363	33.33	27.27	0.83	28.10	1.93	3.30	66.67	5
105	9	19	133	290	423	31.44	20.80	4.02	24.82	4.49	2.13	68.56	6
327	15	43	385	872	1,257	30.63	20.92	5.09	26.01	3.42	1.20	69.37	7
1,234	165	213	1,612	3,275	4,887	32.99	21.83	3.42	25.25	4.36	3.38	67.01	8
155	19	10	184	372	556	33.09	25.90	1.98	27.88	1.80	3.41	66.91	9
42,495	3,076	16,781	62,352	156,667	219,019	28.47	13.52	5.88	19.40	7.66	1.41	71.53	10
315	27	33	375	740	1,115	33.63	27.08	1.17	28.25	2.96	2.42	66.37	11
1,814	155	488	2,457	5,831	8,288	29.65	18.20	3.69	21.89	5.89	1.87	70.35	12
276	11	36	323	632	955	33.82	27.12	1.78	28.90	3.77	1.15	66.18	13
811	61	148	1,020	2,087	3,107	32.83	24.14	1.96	26.10	4.77	1.96	67.17	14
470	38	83	591	1,206	1,797	32.89	24.60	1.56	26.16	4.62	2.11	67.11	15
1,124	69	214	1,407	3,045	4,452	31.60	18.91	6.34	25.25	4.80	1.55	68.40	16
886	34	126	1,053	2,285	3,338	31.55	25.16	1.59	26.75	3.78	1.02	68.45	17
14,566	1,035	8,166	23,767	65,436	89,203	26.64	8.32	8.01	16.33	9.15	1.16	73.36	18
1,929	99	923	2,951	8,195	11,146	26.48	8.20	9.11	17.31	8.28	0.89	73.52	19
1,274	84	880	2,238	6,486	8,724	25.65	6.25	8.35	14.60	10.09	0.96	74.35	20
1,826	150	1,183	3,159	8,292	11,451	27.59	7.15	8.80	15.95	10.33	1.31	72.41	21
1,941	119	740	2,800	7,668	10,468	26.75	9.92	8.62	18.54	7.07	1.14	73.25	22
1,935	121	1,121	2,877	7,732	10,609	27.12	6.51	8.90	15.41	10.57	1.14	72.88	23
1,236	148	1,537	2,921	9,343	12,264	23.82	3.19	6.89	10.08	12.53	1.21	76.18	24
1,532	95	408	2,035	4,362	6,397	31.81	17.42	6.53	23.95	6.38	1.48	68.19	25
1,663	61	278	2,002	5,330	7,332	27.30	15.81	6.87	22.68	3.79	0.83	72.70	26
1,590	158	1,096	2,784	8,028	10,812	25.75	6.93	7.22	14.15	10.14	1.46	74.25	27
390	20	69	479	926	1,405	34.09	25.91	1.85	27.76	4.91	1.42	65.91	28
163	70	143	1,146	2,576	3,722	30.79	22.81	2.26	25.07	3.84	1.88	69.21	29
10,086	764	4,368	15,798	39,453	55,251	28.59	13.05	5.22	18.27	8.94	1.38	71.41	30
1,731	148	1,692	3,571	9,621	13,192	27.07	6.92	6.20	13.12	12.83	1.12	72.93	31
1,602	83	546	2,231	5,560	7,791	28.64	14.81	5.75	20.56	7.01	1.07	71.36	32
1,546	54	91	1,691	3,945	5,636	30.00	24.63	2.80	27.43	1.61	0.96	70.00	33
1,636	195	250	2,081	4,307	6,388	32.58	21.73	3.88	25.61	3.92	3.05	67.42	34
1,797	104	751	2,652	6,452	9,104	29.13	16.38	3.36	19.74	8.25	1.14	70.87	35
1,784	180	1,608	3,572	9,568	13,140	27.18	6.68	6.89	13.57	12.24	1.37	72.82	36
1,541	110	265	1,916	4,660	6,576	29.14	18.07	5.37	23.44	4.03	1.67	70.86	37
443	26	51	520	1,094	1,614	32.22	25.28	2.17	27.45	3.16	1.61	67.78	38
402	30	64	496	1,022	1,518	32.67	25.16	1.32	26.48	4.21	1.98	67.33	39
519	53	81	653	1,157	1,810	36.08	27.13	1.54	28.67	4.48	2.93	63.92	40
346	62	106	514	951	1,465	35.09	21.71	1.91	23.62	7.24	4.23	64.91	41
481	39	154	674	1,309	1,983	33.99	21.48	2.78	24.26	7.76	1.97	66.01	42
385	92	83	560	1,067	1,627	34.42	20.59	3.07	23.66	5.10	5.66	65.58	43
5,986	353	1,400	7,746	19,369	27,115	28.57	17.01	5.09	22.10	5.17	1.30	71.43	44
760	20	73	853	1,949	2,802	30.44	23.05	4.07	27.12	2.61	0.71	69.56	45
774	48	69	891	1,981	2,872	31.02	22.81	4.14	26.95	2.40	1.67	68.98	46
707	46	155	908	2,131	3,039	29.88	15.96	7.31	23.27	5.10	1.51	70.12	47
769	38	94	901	2,088	2,989	30.14	22.45	3.28	25.73	3.14	1.27	69.86	48
774	47	237	1,058	2,783	3,841	27.54	12.70	7.45	20.15	6.17	1.22	72.46	49
731	25	188	944	2,158	3,102	30.43	19.11	4.45	23.56	6.06	0.81	69.57	50
728	28	121	877	2,156	3,033	28.92	19.19	4.81	24.00	3.99	0.93	71.08	51
750	101	463	1,314	4,123	5,437	24.17	9.05	4.74	13.79	8.52	1.86	75.83	52
697	27	133	857	1,821	2,678	32.00	24.53	1.49	26.02	4.97	1.01	68.00	53

POLITICAL CONDITION: BY SEX — Continued.

	COUNTIES, CITIES, AND TOWNS.	MALE POPULATION 20 YEARS OF AGE AND OVER						PERCENTAGES OF MALE POPULATION 20 YEARS OF AGE AND OVER						
		Voters	Not Voters	Aliens	Total Ratable Polls	No Political Condition	Total Male Population 20 Years of Age and Over	Ratable Polls	Native Born Voters	Foreign Born Naturalized Voters	Total Voters	Aliens	Not Voters	No Political Condition
1	DUKES.	1,236	88	149	1,473	6	1,479	99.59	78.97	4.60	83.57	10.07	5.95	0.41
2	Chilmark, .	107	13	1	121	2	123	98.37	86.99	–	86.99	0.81	10.57	1.63
3	Cottage City, .	252	24	60	336	–	336	100.00	66.96	8.04	75.00	17.86	7.14	–
4	Edgartown, .	340	16	36	392	2	394	99.49	82.49	3.80	86.29	9.14	4.06	0.51
5	Gay Head, .	41	1	2	44	–	44	100.00	90.91	2.27	93.18	4.55	2.27	–
6	Gosnold, .	46	15	11	72	–	72	100.00	56.95	6.94	63.89	15.28	20.83	–
7	Tisbury, .	301	16	24	341	1	342	99.71	83.62	4.39	88.01	7.02	4.68	0.29
8	West Tisbury, .	149	3	15	167	1	168	99.40	85.71	2.98	88.69	8.93	1.78	0.60
9	ESSEX.	77,282	5,396	22,381	105,029	775	105,804	99.27	56.75	16.29	73.04	21.16	5.07	0.73
10	Amesbury, .	2,310	168	588	3,066	5	3,071	99.84	61.06	14.16	75.22	19.15	5.47	0.16
11	Andover, .	1,305	116	280	1,701	8	1,709	99.53	58.69	17.67	76.36	16.38	6.79	0.47
12	BEVERLY, .	3,034	248	500	3,782	15	3,797	99.60	70.87	9.03	79.90	13.17	6.53	0.40
13	Ward 1, .	686	71	116	873	–	873	100.00	66.21	12.37	78.58	13.29	8.13	–
14	Ward 2, .	636	34	98	768	–	768	100.00	73.57	9.24	82.81	12.76	4.43	–
15	Ward 3, .	576	75	123	774	3	777	99.61	67.95	6.18	74.13	15.83	9.65	0.39
16	Ward 4, .	537	13	51	601	12	613	98.04	78.79	8.81	87.60	8.32	2.12	1.96
17	Ward 5, .	336	23	35	394	–	394	100.00	80.46	4.82	85.28	8.88	5.84	–
18	Ward 6, .	263	32	77	372	–	372	100.00	59.14	11.56	70.70	20.70	8.60	–
19	Boxford, .	191	17	23	231	3	234	98.72	77.35	4.27	81.62	9.83	7.27	1.28
20	Bradford, .	1,159	95	174	1,428	–	1,428	100.00	72.13	9.03	81.16	12.19	6.65	–
21	Danvers, .	1,756	184	323	2,263	426	2,689	84.16	53.67	11.64	65.31	12.01	6.84	15.84
22	Essex, .	492	22	59	573	3	576	99.48	80.56	4.86	85.42	10.24	3.82	0.52
23	Georgetown, .	601	26	41	668	8	676	98.82	81.66	7.25	88.91	6.06	3.85	1.18
24	GLOUCESTER, .	6,444	385	5,000	11,829	18	11,847	99.85	37.59	16.80	54.39	42.21	3.25	0.15
25	Ward 1, .	838	41	257	1,136	1	1,137	99.91	51.89	21.81	73.70	22.60	3.61	0.09
26	Ward 2, .	930	57	857	1,904	1	1,905	99.95	34.96	17.01	51.97	44.99	2.99	0.05
27	Ward 3, .	1,196	69	1,562	2,827	–	2,827	100.00	23.77	18.54	42.31	55.25	2.44	–
28	Ward 4, .	864	72	964	1,900	–	1,900	100.00	28.31	17.16	45.47	50.74	3.79	–
29	Ward 5, .	1,030	47	504	1,581	16	1,597	99.00	47.28	17.22	64.50	31.56	2.94	1.00
30	Ward 6, .	738	36	112	886	–	886	100.00	67.72	15.58	83.30	12.64	4.06	–
31	Ward 7, .	432	43	702	1,177	–	1,177	100.00	26.59	10.11	36.70	59.64	3.66	–
32	Ward 8, .	356	20	42	418	–	418	100.00	76.32	8.85	85.17	10.05	4.78	–
33	Groveland,	592	24	84	700	1	701	99.86	73.04	11.41	84.45	11.98	3.43	0.14
34	Hamilton, .	262	97	122	481	2	483	99.59	51.97	2.28	54.25	25.26	20.08	0.41
35	HAVERHILL, .	7,456	467	1,509	9,432	39	9,471	99.59	64.86	13.86	78.72	15.94	4.93	0.41
36	Ward 1, .	877	66	59	1,002	–	1,002	100.00	79.14	8.38	87.52	5.89	6.59	–
37	Ward 2, .	681	32	67	780	–	780	100.00	80.39	6.92	87.31	8.59	4.10	–
38	Ward 3, .	972	64	213	1,249	–	1,249	100.00	55.48	22.34	77.82	17.05	5.13	–
39	Ward 4, .	1,013	54	101	1,168	38	1,206	96.85	74.54	9.45	83.99	8.38	4.48	3.15
40	Ward 5, .	2,383	152	878	3,413	1	3,414	99.97	54.33	15.47	69.80	25.72	4.45	0.03
41	Ward 6, .	1,530	99	191	1,820	–	1,820	100.00	70.11	13.96	84.07	10.49	5.44	–
42	Ipswich, .	1,070	89	282	1,441	13	1,454	99.11	65.41	8.18	73.59	19.40	6.12	0.89
43	LAWRENCE,	10,178	805	4,357	15,340	42	15,382	99.73	35.06	31.11	66.17	28.33	5.23	0.27
44	Ward 1, .	1,811	102	651	2,564	40	2,604	98.46	31.76	37.79	69.55	25.00	3.91	1.54
45	Ward 2, .	1,483	121	666	2,270	–	2,270	100.00	36.65	28.68	65.33	29.34	5.33	–
46	Ward 3, .	1,593	125	790	2,508	1	2,509	99.96	31.17	32.32	63.49	31.49	4.98	0.04
47	Ward 4, .	1,645	292	1,053	2,990	1	2,991	99.97	29.15	25.85	55.00	35.21	9.76	0.03
48	Ward 5, .	1,956	93	807	2,856	–	2,856	100.00	36.70	31.79	68.49	28.25	3.26	–
49	Ward 6, .	1,690	72	390	2,152	–	2,152	100.00	47.95	30.58	78.53	18.12	3.35	–
50	LYNN, .	15,437	969	3,423	19,829	51	19,880	99.74	63.19	14.46	77.65	17.22	4.87	0.26
51	Ward 1, .	424	12	46	482	–	482	100.00	81.95	6.02	87.97	9.54	2.49	–
52	Ward 2, .	997	67	168	1,232	–	1,232	100.00	72.08	8.85	80.93	13.63	5.44	–
53	Ward 3, .	3,654	165	643	4,462	–	4,462	100.00	71.22	10.67	81.89	14.41	3.70	–
54	Ward 4, .	3,245	258	635	4,136	2	4,138	99.95	64.26	14.11	78.37	15.35	6.23	0.05

POLITICAL CONDITION: BY SEX — Continued.

Total Population. Both Sexes. All Ages						Percentages of Total Population					
Voters	Not Voters	Aliens	Total Ratable Polls	No Political Condition	Total Population. Both Sexes. All Ages	Ratable Polls	Native Born Voters	Foreign Born Naturalized Voters	Total Voters	Aliens	Not Voters	No Political Condition	
1,236	88	149	1,473	2,765	4,238	34.76	27.56	1.60	29.16	3.52	2.08	65.24	1
107	13	1	121	183	304	39.80	35.20	–	35.20	0.33	4.27	60.20	2
252	24	60	336	702	1,038	32.37	21.68	2.60	24.28	5.78	2.31	67.63	3
340	16	36	392	733	1,125	34.84	28.89	1.33	30.22	3.20	1.42	65.16	4
41	1	2	44	125	169	26.04	23.67	0.59	24.26	1.19	0.59	73.96	5
46	15	11	72	68	140	51.43	29.29	3.57	32.86	7.86	10.71	48.57	6
301	16	24	341	661	1,002	34.03	28.54	1.50	30.04	2.39	1.60	65.97	7
149	3	15	167	293	460	36.30	31.30	1.09	32.39	3.26	0.65	63.70	8
77,282	5,396	22,381	105,029	225,364	330,386	31.79	18.17	5.22	23.39	6.77	1.63	68.21	9
2,310	168	588	3,066	6,920	9,386	30.70	18.78	4.35	23.13	5.89	1.68	69.30	10
1,305	116	280	1,701	4,444	6,145	27.68	16.32	4.92	21.24	4.56	1.88	72.32	11
3,034	248	500	3,782	8,024	11,806	32.03	22.79	2.91	25.70	4.23	2.10	67.97	12
686	71	116	873	1,803	2,676	32.62	21.60	4.04	25.64	4.33	2.65	67.38	13
636	54	98	768	1,675	2,443	31.44	23.13	2.91	26.04	4.01	1.39	68.56	14
576	75	123	774	1,668	2,442	31.70	21.62	1.97	23.59	5.04	3.07	68.30	15
537	13	51	601	1,410	2,011	29.89	24.02	2.68	26.70	2.54	0.65	70.11	16
336	23	35	394	869	1,203	32.75	26.35	1.58	27.93	2.91	1.91	67.25	17
283	32	77	372	659	1,031	36.08	21.34	4.17	25.51	7.47	3.10	63.92	18
191	17	23	231	496	727	31.77	24.90	1.37	26.27	3.16	2.34	68.23	19
1,159	95	174	1,428	3,308	4,736	30.15	21.75	2.72	24.47	3.67	2.01	69.85	20
1,756	184	323	2,263	5,918	8,181	27.66	17.64	3.82	21.46	3.95	2.25	72.34	21
492	22	59	573	1,014	1,587	36.11	29.24	1.76	31.00	3.72	1.39	63.89	22
601	26	41	668	1,382	2,050	32.59	26.93	2.39	29.32	2.00	1.27	67.41	23
6,444	385	5,000	11,829	16,382	28,211	41.93	15.78	7.06	22.84	17.72	1.37	58.07	24
838	41	257	1,136	2,062	3,198	35.52	18.45	7.75	26.20	8.04	1.28	64.48	25
990	57	857	1,904	3,124	5,028	37.87	13.25	6.44	19.69	17.05	1.13	62.13	26
1,196	69	1,562	2,827	2,363	5,190	54.47	12.95	10.10	23.05	30.09	1.33	45.53	27
864	72	964	1,900	1,561	3,461	54.90	15.54	9.42	24.96	27.86	2.08	45.10	28
1,030	47	504	1,581	2,763	4,344	36.40	17.38	6.33	23.71	11.61	1.08	63.60	29
738	36	112	886	2,057	2,943	30.11	20.39	4.69	25.08	3.81	1.22	69.89	30
432	43	702	1,177	1,661	2,838	41.47	11.03	4.19	15.22	24.74	1.51	58.53	31
356	20	42	418	791	1,209	34.57	26.39	3.06	29.45	3.47	1.65	65.43	32
562	24	84	700	1,633	2,333	30.00	21.94	3.43	25.37	3.60	1.03	70.00	33
262	97	122	481	875	1,356	35.47	18.51	0.81	19.32	9.00	7.15	64.53	34
7,456	467	1,509	9,432	20,777	30,209	31.22	20.33	4.35	24.68	5.00	1.54	68.78	35
877	66	59	1,002	1,646	2,648	37.84	29.95	3.17	33.12	2.23	2.49	62.16	36
681	32	67	780	1,733	2,543	31.04	24.95	2.15	27.10	2.67	1.27	68.96	37
972	64	213	1,249	2,294	3,543	35.25	19.56	7.87	27.43	6.01	1.81	64.75	38
1,013	54	101	1,168	2,817	3,985	29.31	22.56	2.86	25.42	2.53	1.36	70.69	39
2,383	152	878	3,413	7,855	11,268	30.29	16.46	4.69	21.15	7.79	1.35	69.71	40
1,530	99	191	1,820	4,432	6,252	29.11	20.41	4.06	24.47	3.06	1.58	70.89	41
1,070	80	282	1,441	3,279	4,720	30.53	20.15	2.52	22.67	5.97	1.89	69.47	42
10,178	805	4,357	15,340	36,824	52,164	29.41	10.34	9.17	19.51	8.35	1.55	70.59	43
1,811	102	651	2,564	6,004	8,568	29.93	9.66	11.48	21.14	7.60	1.19	70.07	44
1,483	121	666	2,270	4,714	6,984	32.50	11.92	9.32	21.24	9.53	1.73	67.50	45
1,583	125	790	2,508	6,470	8,978	27.93	8.71	9.03	17.74	8.80	1.39	72.07	46
1,645	292	1,053	2,990	6,979	9,969	29.99	8.75	7.75	16.50	10.56	2.93	70.01	47
1,956	93	807	2,856	7,077	9,933	28.75	10.55	9.14	19.69	8.12	0.94	71.25	48
1,630	72	390	2,152	5,580	7,732	27.83	13.35	8.51	21.89	5.04	0.93	72.17	49
15,437	969	3,423	19,829	42,525	62,354	31.80	20.15	4.61	24.76	5.49	1.55	68.20	50
424	12	46	482	1,097	1,579	30.53	23.02	1.84	26.86	2.91	0.76	69.47	51
997	67	168	1,232	2,704	3,936	31.30	22.56	2.77	25.33	4.27	1.70	68.70	52
3,654	165	643	4,462	10,397	14,859	30.03	21.39	3.20	24.59	4.33	1.11	69.97	53
3,243	258	635	4,136	7,376	11,512	35.93	23.10	5.07	28.17	5.52	2.24	64.07	54

POLITICAL CONDITION: BY SEX — Continued.

COUNTIES, CITIES, AND TOWNS.	MALE POPULATION 20 YEARS OF AGE AND OVER						PERCENTAGES OF MALE POPULATION 20 YEARS OF AGE AND OVER						
	Voters	Not Voters	Aliens	Total Ratable Polls	No Political Condition	Total Male Population 20 Years of Age and Over	Ratable Polls	Native Born Voters	Foreign Born Naturalized Voters	Total Voters	Aliens	Not Voters	No Political Condition
ESSEX — Con.													
LYNN — Con.													
1 Ward 5, . .	3,197	223	757	4,177	–	4,177	100.00	61.36	15.18	76.54	18.12	5.34	–
2 Ward 6, .	3,324	215	1,002	4,541	2	4,543	99.96	53.03	20.14	73.17	22.06	4.73	0.04
3 Ward 7, .	598	29	172	799	47	846	94.44	55.67	15.01	70.68	20.33	3.43	5.56
4 Lynnfield, . .	228	26	36	290	–	290	100.00	75.86	2.76	78.62	12.41	8.97	–
5 Manchester, .	450	38	143	631	3	634	99.53	63.57	7.41	70.98	22.56	5.99	0.47
6 Marblehead, .	2,295	70	117	2,482	9	2,491	99.64	84.30	7.83	92.13	4.70	2.81	0.36
7 Merrimac, . .	613	23	95	731	–	731	100.00	75.58	8.48	83.86	12.99	3.15	–
8 Methuen, . .	1,168	105	392	1,665	3	1,668	99.82	50.90	19.12	70.02	23.50	6.30	0.18
9 Middleton, .	228	20	33	281	1	282	99.65	73.40	7.45	80.85	11.70	7.10	0.35
10 Nahant, . .	209	44	46	299	–	299	100.00	52.17	17.73	69.90	15.38	14.72	–
11 Newbury, . .	428	34	69	531	1	532	99.81	75.56	4.89	80.45	12.97	6.39	0.19
12 NEWBURYPORT,	3,507	167	527	4,201	31	4,232	99.27	70.89	11.38	82.87	12.45	3.95	0.73
13 Ward 1, .	593	26	67	686	–	686	100.00	80.17	6.27	86.44	9.77	3.79	–
14 Ward 2, .	457	20	157	634	–	634	100.00	62.78	9.30	72.08	24.76	3.16	–
15 Ward 3, .	696	24	69	789	–	789	100.00	75.28	12.93	88.21	8.75	3.04	–
16 Ward 4, .	593	40	57	690	1	691	99.86	70.77	15.05	85.82	8.25	5.79	0.14
17 Ward 5, .	494	32	113	639	–	639	100.00	58.69	18.62	77.31	17.68	5.01	–
18 Ward 6, .	674	25	64	763	30	793	96.22	74.90	10.09	84.99	8.07	3.16	3.78
19 North Andover,	912	75	125	1,112	3	1,115	99.73	54.35	27.44	81.79	11.21	6.73	0.27
20 Peabody, . .	2,647	137	509	3,293	22	3,315	99.34	59.28	20.57	79.85	15.36	4.13	0.66
21 Rockport, . .	1,055	65	907	2,027	4	2,031	99.80	43.23	8.71	51.94	44.66	3.20	0.20
22 Rowley, . .	381	27	28	436	5	441	98.87	83.00	3.40	86.40	6.35	6.12	1.13
23 SALEM, . .	7,411	591	2,191	10,193	50	10,243	99.51	56.29	16.06	72.35	21.39	5.77	0.49
24 Ward 1, . .	1,107	73	324	1,504	49	1,553	96.84	52.61	18.67	71.28	20.86	4.70	3.16
25 Ward 2, .	1,435	248	210	1,893	–	1,893	100.00	66.99	8.82	75.81	11.09	13.10	–
26 Ward 3, .	1,062	34	167	1,263	1	1,264	99.92	65.90	18.12	84.02	13.21	2.69	0.08
27 Ward 4, .	1,206	61	270	1,537	–	1,537	100.00	54.26	24.20	78.46	17.57	3.97	–
28 Ward 5, .	1,478	116	1,111	2,705	–	2,705	100.00	40.37	14.27	54.64	41.07	4.29	–
29 Ward 6, .	1,123	59	109	1,291	–	1,291	100.00	71.42	15.57	86.99	8.44	4.57	–
30 Salisbury, . .	394	23	17	434	1	435	99.77	85.28	5.29	90.57	3.91	5.29	0.23
31 Saugus, . .	1,152	79	147	1,378	5	1,383	99.64	69.20	14.10	83.30	10.63	5.71	0.36
32 Swampscott, .	874	52	130	1,056	–	1,056	100.00	75.29	7.48	82.77	12.31	4.92	–
33 Topsfield, . .	305	31	17	353	2	355	99.44	80.00	5.92	85.92	4.79	8.73	0.56
34 Wenham, . .	274	12	30	316	–	316	100.00	84.49	2.22	86.71	9.49	3.80	–
35 West Newbury,	464	35	57	556	1	557	99.82	71.27	12.63	83.30	10.23	6.29	0.18
36 **FRANKLIN.**	10,732	784	1,716	12,832	50	12,882	99.61	69.88	10.32	80.20	13.32	6.09	0.39
37 Ashfield, . .	300	32	23	355	3	358	99.16	81.01	2.79	83.80	6.42	8.94	0.84
38 Bernardston, .	222	22	17	261	2	263	99.24	82.13	2.28	84.41	6.46	8.37	0.76
39 Buckland, . .	416	19	51	486	3	489	99.39	62.58	22.49	85.07	10.43	3.89	0.61
40 Charlemont, .	294	25	21	340	1	341	99.71	84.17	2.05	86.22	6.16	7.33	0.29
41 Colrain, . .	409	13	91	513	–	513	100.00	75.83	3.90	79.73	17.74	2.53	–
42 Conway, . .	336	39	40	415	4	419	99.05	72.79	7.40	80.19	9.55	9.31	0.95
43 Deerfield, . .	722	69	188	979	5	984	99.49	61.58	11.79	73.37	19.11	7.01	0.51
44 Erving, . .	241	20	48	309	2	311	99.36	69.45	8.04	77.49	15.44	6.43	0.64
45 Gill, . . .	280	58	70	408	–	408	100.00	63.97	4.66	68.63	17.16	14.21	–
46 Greenfield, . .	1,657	116	175	1,945	3	1,948	99.85	71.66	13.40	85.06	9.44	5.95	0.15
47 Hawley, . .	143	13	4	160	2	162	98.77	87.04	1.23	88.27	2.47	8.03	1.23
48 Heath, . .	124	6	12	142	–	142	100.00	85.21	2.11	87.32	8.45	4.23	–
49 Leverett, . .	235	13	8	256	2	258	99.22	89.92	1.46	91.68	3.10	5.04	0.78
50 Leyden, . .	106	10	6	122	–	122	100.00	81.14	5.74	86.88	4.92	8.20	–
51 Monroe, . .	72	8	43	123	–	123	100.00	55.29	3.25	58.54	34.96	6.50	–
52 Montague, . .	1,287	86	362	1,735	9	1,744	99.48	47.70	26.09	73.79	20.76	4.93	0.52

POLITICAL CONDITION: BY SEX — Continued.

Voters	Not Voters	Aliens	Total Ratable Polls	No Political Condition	Total Population. Both Sexes. All Ages	Ratable Polls	Native Born Voters	Foreign Born Naturalized Voters	Total Voters	Aliens	Not Voters	No Political Condition	
3,197	223	757	4,177	8,683	12,860	32.48	19.93	4.93	24.86	5.89	1.73	67.52	1
3,324	215	1,002	4,541	10,391	14,932	30.41	16.13	6.13	22.26	6.71	1.44	69.59	2
398	29	172	799	1,877	2,676	29.86	17.60	4.75	22.35	6.43	1.08	70.14	3
228	26	36	290	528	818	35.45	26.89	0.98	27.87	4.40	3.18	64.55	4
450	38	143	631	1,245	1,876	33.64	21.48	2.51	23.99	7.62	2.03	66.36	5
2,295	70	117	2,482	5,189	7,671	32.36	27.38	2.54	29.92	1.53	0.91	67.64	6
613	23	95	731	1,570	2,301	31.77	23.35	2.89	26.64	4.13	1.00	68.23	7
1,168	105	392	1,665	4,025	5,690	29.26	14.92	5.81	20.73	6.89	1.84	70.71	8
228	20	33	281	557	838	33.53	24.70	2.51	27.21	3.94	2.38	66.47	9
209	44	46	299	566	865	34.57	18.03	6.13	24.16	5.32	5.09	65.43	10
428	34	69	531	858	1,489	35.66	27.00	1.75	28.75	4.63	2.28	64.34	11
3,507	167	527	4,201	10,351	14,552	28.87	20.62	3.48	24.10	3.62	1.15	71.13	12
593	26	67	686	1,686	2,372	28.92	23.19	1.81	25.00	2.82	1.10	71.08	13
457	20	157	634	2,331	2,831	27.20	17.08	2.53	19.61	6.73	0.86	72.80	14
686	24	69	789	1,877	2,666	29.59	22.28	3.82	26.10	2.59	0.90	70.41	15
563	40	57	680	1,631	2,321	29.73	21.07	4.48	25.55	2.46	1.72	70.27	16
494	32	113	639	1,597	2,236	28.58	16.77	5.32	22.09	5.06	1.43	71.42	17
674	25	64	763	1,863	2,626	29.06	22.62	3.05	25.67	2.44	0.95	70.34	18
912	75	125	1,112	2,457	3,569	31.16	16.98	8.57	25.55	3.51	2.10	68.84	19
2,647	137	509	3,293	7,214	10,507	31.34	18.70	6.49	25.19	4.85	1.30	68.66	20
1,055	65	907	2,027	3,262	5,289	38.32	16.60	3.34	19.94	17.15	1.23	61.68	21
381	27	28	436	836	1,272	34.28	28.78	1.18	29.96	2.20	2.12	65.72	22
7,411	591	2,194	10,196	24,280	34,473	29.57	16.73	4.77	21.50	6.36	1.71	70.43	23
1,107	73	324	1,504	3,502	5,006	30.04	16.32	5.79	22.11	6.47	1.46	69.96	24
1,435	248	210	1,893	3,754	5,647	33.52	22.45	2.96	25.41	3.72	4.39	66.48	25
1,602	34	167	1,263	3,122	4,385	28.80	19.00	5.22	24.22	3.81	0.77	71.20	26
1,206	61	270	1,537	3,698	5,235	29.36	13.16	7.41	23.04	5.16	1.16	70.64	27
1,478	116	1,111	2,705	7,206	9,911	27.29	11.92	3.89	14.91	11.21	1.17	72.71	28
1,123	59	109	1,291	2,998	4,289	30.10	21.50	4.68	26.18	2.54	1.38	69.90	29
394	23	17	434	866	1,300	33.38	28.54	1.77	30.31	1.30	1.77	66.62	30
1,152	79	147	1,378	3,119	4,497	30.64	21.28	4.34	25.62	3.27	1.75	69.36	31
874	52	130	1,056	2,203	3,259	32.40	24.39	2.43	26.82	3.99	1.59	67.60	32
305	31	17	353	680	1,033	34.17	27.49	2.03	29.52	1.65	3.00	65.83	33
274	12	30	316	570	886	35.67	30.14	0.79	30.93	3.39	1.35	64.33	34
494	35	57	556	1,087	1,643	33.84	24.16	4.08	28.24	3.47	2.13	66.16	35
10,832	784	1,716	12,882	27,313	40,145	31.96	22.43	3.31	25.74	4.27	1.95	68.04	36
300	32	23	355	658	1,013	35.04	28.63	0.98	29.61	2.27	3.16	64.96	37
222	22	17	261	517	778	33.55	27.76	0.77	28.53	2.19	2.83	66.45	38
416	19	51	486	1,062	1,548	31.40	19.77	7.10	26.87	3.30	1.23	68.60	39
294	25	21	340	701	1,041	32.66	27.57	0.67	28.24	2.02	2.40	67.34	40
409	13	91	513	1,097	1,610	31.86	24.16	1.24	25.40	5.65	0.81	68.14	41
336	39	40	415	889	1,304	31.83	23.39	2.38	25.77	3.07	2.99	68.17	42
722	69	188	979	2,028	3,007	32.56	20.15	3.86	24.01	6.25	2.30	67.44	43
241	20	48	309	655	964	32.05	22.41	2.59	25.00	4.98	2.07	67.95	44
280	58	70	408	674	1,082	37.71	24.12	1.76	25.88	6.47	5.36	62.29	45
1,657	110	178	1,945	4,284	6,229	31.22	22.41	4.19	26.60	2.86	1.76	68.78	46
143	13	4	160	308	468	34.19	30.13	0.43	30.56	0.85	2.78	65.81	47
124	6	12	142	334	476	29.83	25.42	0.63	26.05	2.52	1.26	70.17	48
235	13	8	256	488	744	34.41	31.18	0.41	31.59	1.07	1.75	65.59	49
106	10	6	122	241	363	33.61	27.27	1.93	29.20	1.65	2.76	66.39	50
72	8	43	123	175	298	41.28	22.82	1.34	24.16	14.43	2.69	58.72	51
1,287	86	362	1,735	4,323	6,058	28.64	13.73	7.51	21.24	5.98	1.42	71.36	52

POLITICAL CONDITION: BY SEX — Continued.

COUNTIES, CITIES, AND TOWNS.	MALE POPULATION 20 YEARS OF AGE AND OVER						PERCENTAGES OF MALE POPULATION 20 YEARS OF AGE AND OVER						
	Voters	Not Voters	Aliens	Total Ratable Polls	No Political Condition	Total Male Population 20 Years of Age and Over	Ratable Polls	Native Born Voters	Foreign Born Naturalized Voters	Total Voters	Aliens	Not Voters	No Political Condition
FRANKLIN — Con.													
1 New Salem, .	240	29	24	293	1	294	99.66	77.55	4.08	81.63	8.16	9.87	0.34
2 Northfield, .	456	14	41	511	1	512	99.80	83.79	5.47	89.06	8.01	2.73	0.20
3 Orange, .	1,444	56	240	1,740	1	1,741	99.94	76.11	6.83	82.94	13.78	3.22	0.06
4 Rowe, .	111	22	51	184	1	185	99.46	58.92	1.08	60.00	27.57	11.89	0.54
5 Shelburne, .	416	42	43	501	2	503	99.60	77.03	4.77	82.70	8.55	8.35	0.40
6 Shutesbury, .	137	4	5	146	1	147	99.32	89.80	3.40	93.20	3.40	2.72	0.68
7 Sunderland, .	192	12	50	254	1	255	99.61	69.80	5.49	75.29	19.61	4.71	0.39
8 Warwick, .	136	32	43	211	3	214	98.90	60.75	2.80	63.55	20.10	14.95	1.40
9 Wendell, .	135	13	31	179	1	180	99.44	68.89	6.11	75.00	17.22	7.22	0.56
10 Whately, .	221	17	26	264	2	266	99.25	71.80	11.28	83.08	9.78	6.39	0.75
11 **HAMPDEN.**	31,568	2,960	10,854	45,382	199	45,581	99.56	52.68	16.58	69.26	23.81	6.49	0.44
12 Agawam, .	550	80	135	745	3	748	99.60	58.42	12.44	70.86	18.05	10.69	0.40
13 Blandford, .	256	19	8	283	1	284	99.65	89.08	1.06	90.14	2.82	6.69	0.35
14 Brimfield, .	260	26	39	325	7	332	97.89	73.79	4.52	78.31	11.75	7.83	2.11
15 Chester, .	379	27	53	459	4	463	99.14	78.19	3.67	81.86	11.45	5.83	0.86
16 **CHICOPEE,**	2,749	294	1,970	5,013	18	5,031	99.64	38.24	16.40	54.64	39.16	5.84	0.36
17 Ward 1, .	470	48	449	967	3	970	99.69	29.79	18.66	48.45	46.29	4.95	0.31
18 Ward 2, .	398	23	93	514	-	514	100.00	57.39	20.04	77.43	18.09	4.48	-
19 Ward 3, .	344	72	532	948	-	948	100.00	24.36	11.93	36.29	56.12	7.59	-
20 Ward 4, .	392	32	227	651	15	666	97.75	45.20	13.66	58.86	34.08	4.81	2.25
21 Ward 5, .	542	64	277	883	-	883	100.00	47.68	13.70	61.38	31.37	7.25	-
22 Ward 6, .	308	19	191	518	-	518	100.00	41.12	18.34	59.46	36.87	3.67	-
23 Ward 7, .	295	36	201	532	-	532	100.00	32.71	22.74	55.45	37.78	6.77	-
24 E. Longmeadow, .	239	13	265	517	-	517	100.00	36.94	9.29	46.23	51.26	2.51	-
25 Granville, .	255	28	30	313	9	322	97.20	73.91	5.28	79.19	9.32	8.69	2.80
26 Hampden, .	180	27	35	242	1	243	99.59	64.20	9.87	74.07	14.41	11.11	0.41
27 Holland, .	54	4	6	64	1	65	98.46	78.46	4.62	83.08	9.23	6.15	1.54
28 **HOLYOKE,** .	6,597	535	3,610	10,742	28	10,770	99.74	34.75	26.50	61.25	33.52	4.97	0.26
29 Ward 1, .	966	80	497	1,543	-	1,543	100.00	33.25	29.36	62.61	32.21	5.18	-
30 Ward 2, .	916	141	1,250	2,307	1	2,308	99.96	18.29	21.40	39.69	54.16	6.11	0.04
31 Ward 3, .	846	61	408	1,315	25	1,340	98.13	32.09	31.04	63.13	30.45	4.55	1.87
32 Ward 4, .	855	92	837	1,784	1	1,785	99.94	18.66	29.24	47.90	46.89	5.15	0.06
33 Ward 5, .	818	38	104	960	-	960	100.00	55.52	29.69	85.21	10.83	3.96	-
34 Ward 6, .	1,103	66	427	1,596	-	1,596	100.00	41.29	27.82	69.11	26.75	4.14	-
35 Ward 7, .	1,093	57	87	1,237	1	1,238	99.92	68.90	19.39	88.29	7.03	4.60	0.08
36 Longmeadow, .	143	20	30	193	1	194	99.48	65.46	8.25	73.71	15.46	10.31	0.52
37 Ludlow, .	372	69	298	739	3	742	99.60	41.51	8.63	50.14	40.16	9.30	0.40
38 Monson, .	851	80	219	1,150	14	1,164	98.80	63.66	9.45	73.11	18.82	6.87	1.20
39 Montgomery, .	79	3	5	87	5	92	94.56	82.60	3.26	85.86	5.44	3.26	5.44
40 Palmer, .	1,196	100	767	2,063	10	2,073	99.52	47.66	10.61	57.69	34.11	7.72	0.48
41 Russell, .	181	38	48	267	4	271	98.52	57.20	9.59	66.79	17.71	14.02	1.48
42 Southwick, .	261	40	29	330	3	333	99.10	70.57	7.81	78.38	8.71	12.01	0.90
43 **SPRINGFIELD,** .	12,240	1,107	2,564	15,911	70	15,981	99.56	61.28	15.31	76.59	16.04	6.93	0.44
44 Ward 1, .	1,717	135	270	2,122	1	2,123	99.95	67.03	13.85	80.88	12.71	6.36	0.05
45 Ward 2, .	1,617	138	638	2,393	-	2,393	100.00	48.26	19.31	67.57	26.66	5.77	-
46 Ward 3, .	1,747	173	413	2,333	-	2,333	100.00	58.98	15.90	74.88	17.70	7.42	-
47 Ward 4, .	1,586	92	188	1,866	-	1,866	100.00	70.90	14.09	84.99	10.08	4.93	-
48 Ward 5, .	1,625	95	161	1,881	-	1,881	100.00	74.64	11.75	86.39	8.56	5.05	-
49 Ward 6, .	1,333	269	333	1,935	-	1,935	100.00	51.37	17.52	68.89	17.21	13.90	-
50 Ward 7, .	1,189	42	132	1,363	-	1,363	100.00	72.31	14.89	87.23	9.69	3.08	-
51 Ward 8, .	1,426	163	429	2,018	69	2,087	96.69	54.24	14.09	68.33	20.55	7.81	3.31
52 Tolland, .	84	10	14	108	-	108	100.00	72.22	5.56	77.78	12.96	9.26	-

POLITICAL CONDITION: BY SEX — Continued.

			TOTAL POPULATION. BOTH SEXES. ALL AGES						PERCENTAGES OF TOTAL POPULATION				
Voters	Not Voters	Aliens	Total Ratable Polls	No Political Condition	Total Population. Both Sexes. All Ages	Ratable Polls	Native Born Voters	Foreign Born Naturalized Voters	Total Voters	Aliens	Not Voters	No Political Condition	
240	29	24	296	576	889	33.72	26.24	1.38	27.62	2.76	3.34	66.28	1
456	14	41	511	1,340	1,851	27.61	23.12	1.52	24.64	2.21	0.76	72.39	2
1,444	56	240	1,740	3,621	5,361	32.46	24.72	2.22	26.94	4.48	1.04	67.54	3
111	22	51	184	314	498	36.95	21.89	0.40	22.29	10.24	4.42	63.05	4
416	42	43	501	1,059	1,560	32.12	25.13	1.54	26.67	2.76	2.69	67.88	5
157	4	5	146	298	444	32.88	29.72	1.13	30.85	1.13	0.90	67.12	6
192	12	50	254	442	696	36.49	25.58	2.01	27.59	7.18	1.72	63.51	7
136	32	43	211	388	599	35.23	21.71	1.00	22.71	7.18	5.34	64.77	8
135	13	31	179	350	529	33.84	23.44	2.08	25.52	5.86	2.46	66.16	9
221	17	26	264	491	755	34.97	25.30	3.97	29.27	3.45	2.25	65.03	10
31,568	2,960	10,854	45,382	107,556	152,968	29.67	15.70	4.94	20.64	7.10	1.93	70.33	11
530	80	135	745	1,663	2,408	30.94	18.15	3.86	22.01	5.61	3.32	69.06	12
256	19	8	283	566	849	33.33	29.80	0.35	30.15	0.94	2.24	66.67	13
260	26	39	325	617	982	33.78	25.47	1.56	27.03	4.05	2.70	66.22	14
379	27	53	459	970	1,429	32.12	25.33	1.19	26.52	3.71	1.89	67.88	15
2,749	294	1,970	5,013	11,407	16,420	30.53	11.72	5.02	16.74	12.00	1.79	69.47	16
470	48	449	967	2,302	3,269	29.58	8.84	5.54	14.38	13.73	1.47	70.42	17
398	23	93	514	1,238	1,752	29.34	16.84	5.88	22.72	5.31	1.31	70.66	18
344	72	532	948	1,869	2,817	33.65	8.20	4.01	12.21	18.89	2.55	66.35	19
392	32	227	651	1,607	2,258	28.83	13.33	4.03	17.36	10.05	1.42	71.17	20
542	64	277	883	1,767	2,650	33.32	15.89	4.56	20.45	10.45	2.42	66.68	21
308	19	191	518	1,180	1,698	30.51	12.55	5.59	18.14	11.25	1.12	69.49	22
295	36	201	532	1,444	1,976	26.92	8.81	6.12	14.93	10.17	1.82	73.08	23
239	13	265	517	1,074	1,591	32.50	12.00	3.42	15.92	16.66	0.82	67.50	24
255	28	30	313	692	1,005	31.14	23.68	1.69	25.37	2.98	2.79	68.86	25
180	27	35	242	501	743	32.57	21.00	3.23	24.23	4.71	3.63	67.43	26
54	4	6	64	135	199	32.16	25.63	1.51	27.14	3.01	2.01	67.84	27
6,597	535	3,610	10,742	29,580	40,322	26.64	9.28	7.08	16.36	8.95	1.33	73.36	28
996	80	497	1,543	4,471	6,014	25.66	8.53	7.53	16.06	8.27	1.33	74.34	29
906	141	1,250	2,307	5,858	8,165	28.04	4.76	5.58	10.34	14.11	1.59	73.96	30
846	61	408	1,315	3,708	5,023	26.18	8.56	8.28	16.84	8.12	1.22	73.82	31
855	92	857	1,784	4,997	6,781	26.31	4.91	7.70	12.61	12.34	1.36	73.69	32
818	38	104	960	2,619	3,579	26.82	14.89	7.96	22.85	2.91	1.06	73.18	33
1,103	66	427	1,596	4,102	5,698	28.01	11.57	7.79	19.36	7.49	1.16	71.99	34
1,066	57	87	1,237	3,132	4,369	28.31	19.53	5.49	25.02	1.99	1.30	71.69	35
143	20	30	193	427	620	31.13	20.48	2.58	23.06	4.84	3.23	68.87	36
372	69	208	739	1,823	2,562	28.84	12.02	2.50	14.52	11.63	2.69	71.16	37
851	80	219	1,150	2,596	3,746	30.70	19.78	2.94	22.72	5.85	2.13	69.30	38
79	3	5	87	188	275	31.64	27.64	1.09	28.73	1.82	1.09	68.36	39
1,196	160	707	2,063	4,795	6,858	30.08	14.23	3.21	17.44	10.31	2.33	69.92	40
181	38	48	267	579	846	31.36	18.32	3.07	21.39	5.68	4.49	68.44	41
261	40	29	330	631	961	34.34	24.45	2.71	27.16	3.02	4.16	65.66	42
12,240	1,107	2,564	15,911	35,611	51,522	30.88	19.01	4.75	23.76	4.97	2.15	69.12	43
1,717	135	270	2,122	4,777	6,899	30.76	20.63	4.26	24.89	3.91	1.96	69.24	44
1,617	138	638	2,393	5,505	7,898	30.30	14.62	5.85	20.47	8.08	1.75	69.70	45
1,747	173	413	2,333	3,864	6,197	37.65	22.20	5.59	28.19	6.67	2.79	62.35	46
1,586	92	188	1,896	4,343	6,209	30.05	21.31	4.23	25.54	3.03	1.48	69.95	47
1,625	95	161	1,881	4,545	6,426	29.27	21.85	3.44	25.29	2.50	1.48	70.73	48
1,333	269	333	1,935	4,218	6,153	31.45	16.15	5.51	21.66	5.42	4.37	68.55	49
1,189	42	132	1,363	3,287	4,650	29.31	21.20	4.37	25.57	2.84	0.90	70.69	50
1,426	163	429	2,018	5,072	7,090	28.46	15.96	4.15	20.11	6.05	2.30	71.54	51
84	10	14	108	201	309	34.95	25.24	1.94	27.18	4.53	3.24	65.05	52

POLITICAL CONDITION: BY SEX — Continued.

	COUNTIES, CITIES, AND TOWNS.	MALE POPULATION 20 YEARS OF AGE AND OVER						PERCENTAGES OF MALE POPULATION 20 YEARS OF AGE AND OVER						
		Voters	Not Voters	Aliens	Total Ratable Polls	No Political Condition	Total Male Population 20 Years of Age and Over	Ratable Polls	Native Born Voters	Foreign Born Naturalized Voters	Total Voters	Aliens	Not Voters	No Political Condition
	HAMPDEN — Con.													
1	Wales, . .	177	31	43	251	–	251	100.00	63.75	6.77	70.52	17.13	12.35	–
2	Westfield, . .	2,752	207	393	3,352	16	3,368	99.52	69.21	12.50	81.71	11.67	6.14	0.48
3	W. Springfield, .	1,374	108	275	1,757	–	1,757	100.00	63.57	14.63	78.20	15.65	6.15	–
4	Wilbraham, .	359	34	78	471	1	472	99.79	66.74	9.32	76.06	16.53	7.20	0.21
5	**HAMPSHIRE.**	11,888	988	2,878	15,754	319	16,073	98.02	61.29	12.07	73.96	17.91	6.15	1.98
6	Amherst, . .	1,339	156	96	1,591	4	1,595	99.75	78.37	5.58	83.95	6.02	9.78	0.25
7	Belchertown, .	557	47	85	689	2	691	99.71	73.66	6.95	80.61	12.30	6.80	0.29
8	Chesterfield, .	192	11	9	212	3	215	98.60	87.91	1.39	89.30	4.19	5.11	1.40
9	Cummington, .	225	22	11	258	5	263	98.10	84.03	1.52	85.55	4.18	8.37	1.90
10	Easthampton, .	965	115	280	1,360	6	1,366	99.56	51.39	19.25	70.64	20.50	8.42	0.44
11	Enfield, . .	234	19	61	314	1	315	99.68	66.35	7.93	74.28	19.37	6.03	0.32
12	Goshen, . .	73	11	6	90	7	97	92.78	73.20	2.06	75.26	6.18	11.34	7.22
13	Granby, . .	182	20	49	251	2	253	99.21	66.40	5.53	71.93	19.37	7.91	0.79
14	Greenwich, .	146	6	7	159	4	163	97.55	87.12	2.45	89.57	4.30	3.68	2.45
15	Hadley, . .	398	29	146	573	4	577	99.31	62.74	6.24	68.98	25.30	5.03	0.69
16	Hatfield, . .	320	13	101	434	1	435	99.77	62.53	11.03	73.56	23.22	2.99	0.23
17	Huntington, .	319	42	61	422	3	425	99.29	65.88	9.18	75.06	14.35	9.88	0.71
18	Middlefield, .	86	13	19	118	1	119	99.16	69.75	2.52	72.27	15.97	10.92	0.84
19	NORTHAMPTON,	3,290	223	828	4,341	253	4,594	94.49	54.88	16.74	71.62	18.02	4.85	5.51
20	Ward 1, .	525	29	115	669	–	669	100.00	62.04	16.44	78.48	17.19	4.33	–
21	Ward 2, .	464	28	72	564	9	573	98.43	64.92	16.06	80.98	12.56	4.89	1.57
22	Ward 3, .	599	56	197	852	–	852	100.00	53.52	16.79	70.31	23.12	6.57	–
23	Ward 4, .	432	36	154	622	244	866	71.82	41.80	8.08	49.88	17.78	4.16	28.18
24	Ward 5, .	456	22	116	594	–	594	100.00	47.81	28.95	76.76	19.53	3.71	–
25	Ward 6, .	436	21	70	527	–	527	100.00	64.71	18.02	82.73	13.28	3.99	–
26	Ward 7, .	378	31	104	513	–	513	100.00	56.73	16.96	73.69	20.27	6.04	–
27	Pelham, . .	137	14	3	154	–	154	100.00	84.42	4.54	88.96	1.95	9.09	–
28	Plainfield, . .	135	13	5	153	–	153	100.00	88.24	–	88.24	3.27	8.49	–
29	Prescott, . .	126	15	5	146	1	147	99.32	85.71	–	85.71	3.40	10.21	0.68
30	Southampton, .	282	14	55	351	–	351	100.00	76.07	4.27	80.34	15.67	3.99	–
31	South Hadley, .	839	59	315	1,213	3	1,216	99.75	53.23	15.79	69.60	25.90	4.85	0.25
32	Ware, . . .	1,271	101	636	2,008	12	2,020	99.41	44.61	19.31	62.92	31.49	5.00	0.59
33	Westhampton, .	120	3	23	146	–	146	100.00	78.77	3.42	82.19	15.75	2.06	–
34	Williamsburg, .	468	27	69	564	7	571	98.77	68.83	13.13	81.96	12.08	4.73	1.23
35	Worthington, .	184	15	8	207	–	207	100.00	86.47	2.42	88.89	3.86	7.25	–
36	**MIDDLESEX.**	109,577	9,310	31,723	150,610	836	151,446	99.45	53.98	18.37	72.35	20.95	6.15	0.55
37	Acton, . .	545	55	97	697	–	697	100.00	69.73	8.46	78.19	13.92	7.89	–
38	Arlington, . .	1,545	72	353	1,970	4	1,974	99.80	54.76	23.51	78.27	17.88	3.65	0.20
39	Ashby, . .	259	22	13	294	1	295	99.66	85.08	2.71	87.79	4.41	7.46	0.34
40	Ashland, . .	482	61	93	636	9	645	98.60	61.40	13.33	74.73	14.42	9.45	1.40
41	Ayer, . .	515	66	69	650	3	653	99.54	65.85	13.02	78.87	10.56	10.11	0.46
42	Bedford, . .	264	61	112	437	3	440	99.32	52.50	7.50	60.00	25.46	13.86	0.68
43	Belmont, . .	550	71	422	1,043	10	1,053	99.05	41.02	11.21	52.23	40.08	6.74	0.95
44	Billerica, . .	640	38	135	813	3	816	99.63	58.80	20.34	78.43	16.54	4.66	0.37
45	Boxborough, .	80	13	15	108	–	108	100.00	65.74	8.33	74.07	13.89	12.04	–
46	Burlington, .	140	57	42	219	4	223	98.21	57.85	4.93	62.78	18.84	16.59	1.79
47	CAMBRIDGE, .	17,018	1,896	6,191	25,105	51	25,156	99.80	48.17	19.48	67.65	24.61	7.54	0.20
48	Ward 1, .	3,747	708	836	5,291	–	5,291	100.00	56.51	14.31	70.82	15.80	13.38	–
49	Ward 2, .	4,707	313	1,708	6,728	–	6,728	100.00	47.53	22.43	69.96	25.39	4.65	–
50	Ward 3, .	2,462	443	1,676	4,581	1	4,582	99.98	31.69	22.04	53.73	36.58	9.67	0.02

POLITICAL CONDITION: BY SEX — Continued.

Voters	Not Voters	Aliens	Total Ratable Polls	No Political Condition	Total Population. Both Sexes. All Ages	Ratable Polls	Native Born Voters	Foreign Born Naturalized Voters	Total Voters	Aliens	Not Voters	No Political Condition	
177	31	43	251	532	783	32.06	20.44	2.17	22.61	5.49	3.96	67.94	1
2,752	207	393	3,352	7,311	10,663	31.44	21.86	3.35	25.81	3.69	1.94	68.56	2
1,574	168	275	1,757	4,368	6,125	28.69	18.24	4.49	22.43	4.49	1.77	71.31	3
359	34	78	471	1,269	1,740	27.07	18.10	2.53	20.63	4.48	1.96	72.93	4
11,888	988	2,878	15,754	38,956	54,710	28.80	18.01	3.72	21.73	5.26	1.81	71.20	5
1,339	156	96	1,591	3,194	4,785	33.25	26.12	1.86	27.98	2.01	3.26	66.75	6
557	47	85	689	1,472	2,161	31.88	23.56	2.22	25.78	3.93	2.17	68.12	7
192	11	9	212	377	589	35.99	32.09	0.51	32.60	1.53	1.86	64.01	8
225	22	11	258	492	750	34.40	29.47	0.53	30.00	1.47	2.93	65.60	9
965	115	280	1,360	3,430	4,790	28.39	14.65	5.49	20.14	5.85	2.40	71.61	10
234	19	61	314	676	990	31.72	21.11	2.53	23.64	6.16	1.92	68.28	11
73	11	6	90	214	304	29.61	23.35	0.66	24.01	1.98	3.62	70.39	12
182	20	49	251	497	748	33.56	22.46	1.87	24.33	6.55	2.68	66.44	13
146	6	7	159	322	481	33.06	29.52	0.83	30.35	1.46	1.25	66.94	14
398	29	146	573	1,131	1,704	33.63	21.25	2.11	23.36	8.57	1.70	66.37	15
320	13	101	434	828	1,262	34.33	21.56	3.80	25.36	8.00	1.03	65.61	16
319	42	61	422	1,028	1,450	29.10	19.31	2.69	22.00	4.21	2.89	70.90	17
86	13	19	118	268	386	30.57	21.50	0.78	22.28	4.92	3.37	69.43	18
3,290	223	828	4,341	12,405	16,746	25.92	15.06	4.59	19.65	4.94	1.33	74.08	19
525	29	115	669	1,501	2,170	30.83	19.12	5.07	24.19	5.30	1.34	69.17	20
464	28	72	564	2,680	3,244	17.39	11.47	2.83	14.30	2.22	0.87	82.61	21
599	56	197	852	2,020	2,872	29.07	15.88	4.98	20.86	6.86	1.95	70.33	22
432	36	154	622	1,866	2,488	25.00	14.55	2.81	17.36	6.19	1.45	75.00	23
456	22	116	594	1,542	2,136	27.81	13.30	8.05	21.35	5.43	1.03	72.19	24
436	21	70	527	1,376	1,903	27.69	17.92	4.90	22.91	3.68	1.10	72.31	25
378	31	104	513	1,420	1,933	29.54	15.06	4.50	19.56	5.38	1.60	73.46	26
137	14	3	154	332	486	31.69	26.75	1.44	28.19	0.62	2.88	68.31	27
135	13	5	153	297	450	34.00	30.00	-	30.00	1.11	2.89	66.00	28
126	15	5	146	255	401	36.41	31.42	-	31.42	1.25	3.74	63.59	29
282	14	55	351	703	1,054	33.30	25.33	1.42	26.75	5.22	1.33	66.70	30
839	59	315	1,213	3,230	4,443	27.30	14.56	4.32	18.88	7.09	1.33	72.70	31
1,271	101	636	2,008	5,643	7,651	26.24	11.54	5.10	16.64	8.31	1.32	73.76	32
120	3	23	146	330	476	30.67	24.16	1.05	25.21	4.83	0.63	69.33	33
468	27	69	564	1,391	1,955	28.85	20.10	3.84	23.94	3.53	1.38	71.15	34
184	15	8	207	441	648	31.95	27.62	0.77	28.39	1.24	2.32	68.05	35
109,577	9,310	31,723	150,610	348,607	499,217	30.17	16.38	5.57	21.95	6.35	1.87	69.83	36
545	55	97	697	1,281	1,978	35.24	24.57	2.98	27.55	4.91	2.78	64.76	37
1,545	72	333	1,950	4,565	6,515	30.24	16.59	7.12	23.71	5.42	1.11	69.76	38
259	22	13	294	510	804	36.57	31.22	0.99	32.21	1.62	2.74	63.43	39
482	61	93	636	1,454	2,080	30.43	18.95	4.11	23.06	4.45	2.92	69.57	40
515	66	69	650	1,451	2,101	30.94	20.47	4.04	24.51	3.29	3.14	69.06	41
264	61	112	437	732	1,169	37.38	19.76	2.82	22.58	9.58	5.22	62.62	42
550	71	422	1,043	1,800	2,843	36.69	15.20	4.15	19.35	14.84	2.50	63.31	43
640	38	135	813	1,764	2,577	31.55	18.40	6.44	24.84	5.24	1.47	68.45	44
80	13	15	108	199	307	35.18	23.13	2.93	26.06	4.89	4.23	64.82	45
140	37	42	219	355	574	38.15	22.47	1.92	24.39	7.32	6.44	61.85	46
17,618	1,896	6,191	25,705	56,538	81,643	30.75	14.84	6.01	20.85	7.58	2.32	69.25	47
3,747	708	836	5,291	10,580	15,881	33.32	18.83	4.77	23.60	5.26	4.46	66.68	48
4,707	313	1,708	6,728	15,904	22,632	29.73	14.13	6.67	20.80	7.55	1.38	70.27	49
2,462	443	1,676	4,581	9,415	13,996	32.73	10.37	7.22	17.59	11.97	3.17	67.27	50

POLITICAL CONDITION: BY SEX — Continued.

	COUNTIES, CITIES, AND TOWNS.	MALE POPULATION 20 YEARS OF AGE AND OVER						PERCENTAGES OF MALE POPULATION 20 YEARS OF AGE AND OVER						
		Voters	Not Voters	Aliens	Total Ratable Polls	No Political Condition	Total Male Population 20 Years of Age and Over	Ratable Polls	Native Born Voters	Foreign Born Naturalized Voters	Total Voters	Aliens	Not Voters	No Political Condition
	MIDDLESEX — Con. CAMBRIDGE — Con.													
1	Ward 4, .	3,969	302	1,294	5,565	1	5,566	99.98	51.78	20.07	71.85	22.71	5.42	0.02
2	Ward 5, .	2,106	136	707	2,940	49	2,989	98.36	53.36	17.00	70.36	23.65	4.35	1.64
3	Carlisle, .	125	14	38	177	2	179	98.88	67.04	2.79	69.83	21.23	7.82	1.12
4	Chelmsford,	771	78	170	1,019	3	1,022	99.71	60.27	15.17	75.44	16.64	7.63	0.29
5	Concord, .	943	575	416	1,934	6	1,940	99.69	40.26	8.25	48.61	21.44	29.64	0.31
6	Dracut, .	539	108	196	839	4	843	99.53	44.13	19.22	63.35	23.37	12.81	0.47
7	Dunstable,	134	7	11	152	-	152	100.00	80.26	7.90	88.16	7.24	4.60	-
8	EVERETT, .	4,090	297	1,143	5,530	-	5,530	100.00	57.67	16.29	73.96	20.67	5.37	-
9	Ward 1, .	617	72	232	921	-	921	100.00	50.16	16.83	66.99	25.19	7.82	-
10	Ward 2, .	610	20	140	770	-	770	100.00	60.00	19.22	79.22	18.18	2.60	-
11	Ward 3, .	609	85	220	914	-	914	100.00	48.91	17.72	66.63	24.07	9.30	-
12	Ward 4, .	702	28	154	884	-	884	100.00	63.80	15.61	79.41	17.42	3.17	-
13	Ward 5, .	651	62	232	945	-	945	100.00	52.80	16.09	68.89	24.55	6.56	-
14	Ward 6, .	901	30	165	1,096	-	1,096	100.00	68.89	13.32	82.21	15.05	2.74	-
15	Framingham,	2,308	168	355	2,831	7	2,838	99.75	64.23	17.09	81.32	12.51	5.92	0.25
16	Groton, .	494	46	74	614	3	617	99.51	73.09	6.97	80.06	11.99	7.46	0.49
17	Holliston, .	734	47	91	872	9	881	98.98	69.69	13.62	83.31	10.33	5.34	1.02
18	Hopkinton, .	902	33	48	983	11	994	98.89	70.02	20.72	90.74	4.83	3.32	1.11
19	Hudson, .	1,298	62	281	1,639	1	1,640	99.94	65.36	13.66	79.02	17.14	3.78	0.06
20	Lexington, .	848	77	264	1,189	5	1,194	99.58	58.65	12.39	71.02	22.11	6.45	0.42
21	Lincoln, .	229	76	141	446	1	447	99.78	41.39	9.84	51.23	31.55	17.00	0.22
22	Littleton, .	274	25	71	370	-	370	100.00	64.50	9.46	74.05	19.19	6.76	-
23	LOWELL, .	16,408	1,154	6,230	23,792	83	23,875	99.65	41.57	27.16	68.73	26.09	4.83	0.35
24	Ward 1, .	2,128	131	651	2,910	1	2,911	99.97	45.83	27.27	73.10	22.37	4.50	0.03
25	Ward 2, .	1,742	164	1,198	3,102	3	3,105	99.90	24.64	31.46	56.10	38.52	5.28	0.10
26	Ward 3, .	1,901	117	665	2,683	-	2,683	100.00	53.30	17.55	70.85	24.79	4.36	-
27	Ward 4, .	1,995	158	416	2,569	-	2,569	100.00	35.35	42.31	77.66	16.19	6.15	-
28	Ward 5, .	1,717	115	710	2,542	1	2,543	99.96	36.06	31.46	67.52	27.92	4.52	0.04
29	Ward 6, .	1,750	116	636	2,502	-	2,502	100.00	43.48	26.46	69.94	25.42	4.64	-
30	Ward 7, .	1,678	170	1,456	3,298	-	3,298	100.00	32.44	18.44	50.88	43.97	5.15	-
31	Ward 8, .	1,911	112	226	2,249	78	2,327	96.65	61.88	20.24	82.12	9.71	4.82	3.35
32	Ward 9, .	1,586	71	280	1,937	-	1,937	100.00	50.18	31.70	81.88	14.45	3.67	-
33	MALDEN, .	6,522	469	1,865	8,856	9	8,865	99.90	56.83	16.74	73.57	21.04	5.29	0.10
34	Ward 1, .	939	48	186	1,173	-	1,173	100.00	65.13	14.92	80.05	15.86	4.09	-
35	Ward 2, .	914	83	507	1,504	-	1,504	100.00	27.13	33.64	60.77	33.71	5.52	-
36	Ward 3, .	854	51	121	1,026	1	1,027	99.90	72.83	10.32	83.15	11.78	4.97	0.10
37	Ward 4, .	1,065	84	480	1,629	-	1,629	100.00	54.08	11.30	65.38	29.46	5.16	-
38	Ward 5, .	971	59	155	1,185	8	1,193	99.33	70.91	10.48	81.39	12.99	4.95	0.67
39	Ward 6, .	941	73	218	1,232	-	1,232	100.00	58.02	17.69	76.38	17.69	5.36	-
40	Ward 7, .	838	71	198	1,107	-	1,107	100.00	60.34	15.36	75.70	17.89	6.41	-
41	MARLBOROUGH,	3,445	244	781	4,470	19	4,489	99.58	56.80	19.94	76.74	17.40	5.44	0.42
42	Ward 1, .	368	17	54	439	18	457	96.06	68.27	12.25	80.52	11.82	3.72	3.94
43	Ward 2, .	545	43	115	673	-	673	100.00	57.35	19.17	76.52	17.09	6.39	-
44	Ward 3, .	573	37	188	798	1	799	99.87	47.81	23.90	71.71	23.53	4.63	0.13
45	Ward 4, .	635	47	211	893	-	893	100.00	47.14	23.97	71.11	23.63	5.26	-
46	Ward 5, .	492	43	87	622	-	622	100.00	66.08	13.02	79.10	13.99	6.91	-
47	Ward 6, .	468	14	54	536	-	536	100.00	64.55	22.76	87.31	10.08	2.61	-
48	Ward 7, .	394	43	72	509	-	509	100.00	57.37	20.04	77.41	14.14	8.45	-
49	Maynard, .	598	51	299	948	8	956	99.16	39.22	23.33	62.55	31.28	5.33	0.84
50	MEDFORD, .	3,821	322	846	4,489	15	4,504	99.67	60.04	13.70	73.74	18.78	7.15	0.33
51	Ward 1, .	586	111	286	986	-	986	100.00	46.96	12.78	59.74	29.00	11.26	-
52	Ward 2, .	557	17	69	643	1	644	99.84	71.58	14.91	86.49	10.71	2.64	0.16
53	Ward 3, .	485	26	42	553	13	566	97.70	73.50	12.19	85.69	7.42	4.59	2.30
54	Ward 4, .	485	32	184	701	-	701	100.00	47.08	22.11	69.19	26.25	4.56	-

POLITICAL CONDITION: BY SEX — Continued.

	TOTAL POPULATION. BOTH SEXES. ALL AGES						PERCENTAGES OF TOTAL POPULATION						
Voters	Not Voters	Aliens	Total Ratable Polls	No Political Condition	Total Population. Both Sexes. All Ages	Ratable Polls	Native Born Voters	Foreign Born Naturalized Voters	Total Voters	Aliens	Not Voters	No Political Condition	
3,969	392	1,264	5,565	13,116	18,681	29.79	15.43	5.98	21.41	6.76	1.62	70.21	1
2,103	130	707	2,940	7,513	10,453	28.43	15.26	4.86	20.12	6.76	1.25	71.87	2
125	14	38	177	315	492	35.98	24.39	1.02	25.41	7.72	2.85	64.02	3
771	78	170	1,019	2,143	3,162	32.23	19.48	4.90	24.38	5.38	2.47	67.77	4
943	575	416	1,364	3,241	5,175	37.37	15.13	3.09	18.22	8.04	11.11	62.63	5
534	108	197	839	1,604	2,443	34.34	15.23	6.63	21.86	8.06	4.42	65.66	6
134	7	11	152	248	400	38.00	30.50	3.00	33.50	2.75	1.75	62.00	7
4,080	297	1,143	5,530	13,043	18,573	29.77	17.17	4.85	22.02	6.15	1.60	70.23	8
617	72	232	921	2,217	3,138	29.55	14.72	4.94	19.66	7.39	2.30	70.65	9
610	20	140	770	1,857	2,627	29.31	17.59	5.63	23.22	5.33	0.76	70.69	10
609	85	220	914	2,176	3,090	29.58	14.47	5.24	19.71	7.12	2.75	70.42	11
702	28	154	884	1,992	2,876	30.74	19.61	4.80	24.41	5.36	0.97	69.26	12
651	62	232	945	2,208	3,153	29.07	15.83	4.82	20.65	7.36	1.96	70.03	13
901	30	165	1,096	2,593	3,689	29.71	20.47	3.96	24.43	4.47	0.81	70.29	14
2,308	168	355	2,831	6,681	9,512	29.76	19.16	5.10	24.26	3.73	1.77	70.24	15
494	46	74	614	1,578	2,192	28.01	20.58	1.96	22.54	3.37	2.10	71.99	16
734	47	91	872	1,846	2,718	32.08	22.59	4.41	27.00	3.35	1.73	67.92	17
902	33	48	983	2,001	2,984	32.34	23.32	6.90	30.22	1.61	1.11	67.06	18
1,206	62	281	1,659	3,649	5,308	30.88	20.20	4.22	24.42	5.29	1.17	69.12	19
848	77	264	1,189	2,309	3,498	33.99	20.01	4.23	24.24	7.55	2.20	66.01	20
229	76	141	446	665	1,111	40.34	16.65	3.36	20.01	12.69	6.84	59.86	21
274	25	71	370	766	1,136	32.57	21.04	3.08	24.12	6.25	2.20	67.43	22
16,408	1,154	6,230	23,792	60,575	84,367	28.20	11.76	7.69	19.45	7.38	1.37	71.80	23
2,128	131	651	2,910	6,598	9,508	30.61	14.03	8.35	22.38	6.85	1.38	69.39	24
1,742	164	1,196	3,102	7,394	10,496	29.56	7.20	9.31	16.60	11.40	1.56	70.44	25
1,901	117	665	2,683	6,562	9,245	29.02	15.47	5.09	20.56	7.19	1.27	70.98	26
1,995	158	416	2,569	6,672	9,241	27.80	9.83	11.76	21.59	4.50	1.71	72.20	27
1,717	115	710	2,542	5,910	8,452	30.08	16.85	9.47	20.32	8.40	1.36	69.92	28
1,750	116	636	2,502	6,830	9,332	26.84	11.66	7.09	18.75	6.82	1.24	73.19	29
1,678	170	1,450	3,298	9,820	13,118	25.14	8.16	4.63	12.79	11.05	1.30	74.86	30
1,911	112	226	2,249	5,691	7,940	28.32	18.14	5.36	24.07	2.84	1.41	71.68	31
1,586	71	280	1,937	5,101	7,038	27.52	13.81	8.72	22.53	3.98	1.01	72.48	32
6,522	464	1,865	8,856	20,852	29,708	29.84	16.96	4.99	21.95	6.28	1.58	70.19	33
939	48	186	1,173	2,932	4,105	28.57	18.61	4.26	22.87	4.53	1.17	71.43	34
914	83	507	1,504	3,826	5,330	28.22	7.66	9.49	17.15	9.51	1.56	71.78	35
854	51	121	1,026	2,553	3,579	28.07	20.30	2.96	23.86	3.38	1.43	71.33	36
1,065	84	480	1,929	3,171	4,800	33.94	18.36	3.83	22.19	10.00	1.75	66.06	37
971	59	155	1,185	2,746	3,931	30.15	21.52	3.18	24.70	3.95	1.50	69.85	38
941	73	218	1,232	2,980	4,212	29.25	17.16	5.18	22.34	5.18	1.73	70.75	39
838	71	198	1,107	2,644	3,751	29.51	17.81	4.53	22.34	5.28	1.89	70.49	40
3,445	244	781	4,470	10,507	14,977	29.85	17.03	5.97	23.00	5.22	1.63	70.15	41
368	17	54	439	896	1,335	32.88	23.37	4.19	27.56	4.05	1.27	67.12	42
515	43	115	673	1,532	2,205	30.52	17.51	5.85	23.36	5.21	1.95	69.48	43
573	37	188	798	2,171	2,969	26.88	12.87	6.43	19.30	6.33	1.25	73.12	44
635	47	211	893	2,409	3,302	27.04	12.75	6.48	19.23	6.39	1.42	72.96	45
492	43	87	622	1,312	1,934	32.16	21.25	4.19	25.44	4.50	2.22	67.84	46
468	14	54	536	1,153	1,689	31.73	20.49	7.22	27.71	3.19	0.83	68.27	47
394	43	72	509	1,034	1,543	32.99	18.92	6.61	25.53	4.67	2.79	67.01	48
598	51	299	948	2,142	3,090	30.68	12.13	7.22	19.35	9.68	1.65	69.32	49
3,321	322	846	4,489	9,985	14,474	31.61	18.68	4.26	22.94	5.85	2.22	68.99	50
589	111	286	986	2,026	3,012	32.74	15.37	4.18	19.55	9.50	3.69	67.26	51
557	17	69	643	1,662	2,305	27.90	20.00	4.16	24.16	3.00	0.74	72.10	52
485	26	42	553	1,371	1,924	28.74	21.62	3.59	25.21	2.18	1.35	71.26	53
485	32	184	701	1,255	1,956	35.84	16.87	7.92	24.79	9.41	1.64	64.16	54

POLITICAL CONDITION: BY SEX — Continued.

	COUNTIES, CITIES, AND TOWNS.	Voters	Not Voters	Aliens	Total Ratable Polls	No Political Condition	Total Male Population 20 Years of Age and Over	Ratable Polls	Native Born Voters	Foreign Born Naturalized Voters	Total Voters	Aliens	Not Voters	No Political Condition
	MIDDLESEX — Con.													
	MEDFORD—Con.													
1	Ward 5, . .	634	99	187	920	1	921	99.89	57.66	11.18	68.84	20.30	10.75	0.11
2	Ward 6, . .	571	37	78	686	-	686	100.00	73.33	9.91	83.24	11.37	5.39	-
3	Melrose, . .	2,851	143	572	3,566	2	3,568	99.94	64.94	14.96	79.90	16.03	4.01	0.06
4	Natick, . .	2,334	134	246	2,714	12	2,726	99.56	67.13	18.49	85.62	9.02	4.92	0.44
5	NEWTON, . .	5,617	387	1,870	7,874	8	7,882	99.90	57.06	14.20	71.26	23.73	4.91	0.10
6	Ward 1, . .	668	46	462	1,176	-	1,176	100.00	40.39	16.41	56.80	39.29	3.91	-
7	Ward 2, . .	1,072	81	411	1,564	-	1,564	100.00	53.00	15.54	68.54	26.28	5.18	-
8	Ward 3, . .	761	36	136	933	-	933	100.00	68.92	12.64	81.56	14.58	3.80	-
9	Ward 4, . .	691	74	201	966	-	966	100.00	56.11	15.42	71.53	20.81	7.66	-
10	Ward 5, . .	964	44	239	1,247	8	1,255	99.36	59.68	17.13	76.81	19.04	3.51	0.64
11	Ward 6, . .	846	75	352	1,273	-	1,273	100.00	54.25	12.18	66.46	27.65	5.89	-
12	Ward 7, . .	615	31	69	715	-	715	100.00	79.58	6.43	86.01	9.65	4.34	-
13	North Reading, .	228	22	34	284	-	284	100.00	74.65	5.63	80.28	11.97	7.75	-
14	Pepperell, . .	800	54	181	1,035	5	1,040	99.52	69.71	7.21	76.92	17.41	5.19	0.48
15	Reading, . .	1,184	104	197	1,485	5	1,490	99.66	68.66	10.80	79.46	13.22	6.98	0.34
16	Sherborn, . .	269	27	79	375	1	376	99.73	62.23	9.31	71.54	21.01	7.18	0.27
17	Shirley, . .	315	26	69	410	-	410	100.00	66.59	10.24	76.83	16.83	6.34	-
18	SOMERVILLE, .	11,889	889	3,232	15,960	-	15,960	100.00	57.71	16.47	74.18	20.25	5.57	-
19	Ward 1, . .	2,272	245	616	3,133	-	3,133	100.00	59.72	12.80	72.52	19.66	7.82	-
20	Ward 2, . .	3,573	287	1,393	5,253	-	5,253	100.00	48.06	19.96	68.02	26.52	5.46	-
21	Ward 3, . .	3,239	195	604	4,038	-	4,038	100.00	64.04	16.17	80.21	14.96	4.83	-
22	Ward 4, . .	2,755	162	619	3,536	-	3,536	100.00	62.16	15.75	77.91	17.51	4.58	-
23	Stoneham, . .	1,757	67	238	2,062	11	2,073	99.47	69.71	15.05	84.76	11.48	3.23	0.53
24	Stow, . . .	240	25	60	325	1	326	99.69	64.42	9.20	73.62	18.40	7.67	0.31
25	Sudbury, . .	319	16	83	418	4	422	99.05	68.72	6.87	75.59	19.67	3.79	0.95
26	Tewksbury, .	423	87	188	698	444	1,142	61.12	26.18	10.86	37.04	16.46	7.62	38.88
27	Townsend, .	535	36	48	619	5	624	99.29	79.65	6.09	85.74	7.69	5.77	0.80
28	Tyngsborough, .	157	20	41	218	1	219	99.54	68.04	3.65	71.69	18.72	9.13	0.46
29	Wakefield, . .	1,885	130	476	2,491	5	2,496	99.80	59.09	16.43	75.52	19.07	5.21	0.20
30	WALTHAM, .	4,574	294	1,189	6,057	17	6,074	99.72	56.29	19.01	75.30	19.58	4.84	0.28
31	Ward 1, . .	624	39	232	895	-	895	100.00	52.63	17.09	69.72	25.92	4.36	-
32	Ward 2, . .	574	99	164	837	-	837	100.00	54.24	14.34	68.58	19.59	11.83	-
33	Ward 3, . .	594	43	299	936	-	936	100.00	38.46	25.00	63.46	31.95	4.59	-
34	Ward 4, . .	632	32	188	852	17	869	98.04	56.16	16.57	72.73	21.63	3.68	1.96
35	Ward 5, . .	763	37	99	899	-	899	100.00	74.53	10.34	84.87	11.01	4.12	-
36	Ward 6, . .	765	23	78	866	-	866	100.00	74.48	13.86	88.34	9.01	2.65	-
37	Ward 7, . .	622	21	129	772	-	772	100.00	42.88	37.69	80.57	16.71	2.72	-
38	Watertown, .	1,751	171	516	2,438	7	2,445	99.71	53.13	18.49	71.62	21.10	6.99	0.29
39	Wayland, . .	535	24	99	658	2	660	99.70	69.55	11.51	81.06	15.00	3.64	0.30
40	Westford, . .	596	67	173	746	4	750	99.47	52.80	14.67	67.47	23.07	8.26	0.53
41	Weston, . .	394	35	156	585	2	587	99.66	60.65	6.47	67.12	26.58	5.96	0.34
42	Wilmington, .	333	11	92	436	2	438	99.54	65.30	10.73	76.03	21.00	2.51	0.46
43	Winchester, .	1,390	125	351	1,866	2	1,868	99.89	55.51	18.90	74.41	18.79	6.69	0.11
44	WOBURN, . .	3,327	171	670	4,168	22	4,190	99.47	51.26	28.14	79.40	15.99	4.08	0.53
45	Ward 1, . .	619	35	114	768	-	768	100.00	46.88	33.72	80.60	14.84	4.56	-
46	Ward 2, . .	684	37	172	893	-	893	100.00	41.88	34.72	76.60	19.26	4.14	-
47	Ward 3, . .	605	20	74	699	-	699	100.00	59.66	26.89	86.55	10.59	2.86	-
48	Ward 4, . .	601	31	115	747	21	768	97.27	55.60	22.66	78.26	14.97	4.04	2.73
49	Ward 5, . .	259	18	61	338	-	338	100.00	44.09	32.54	76.63	18.05	5.32	-
50	Ward 6, . .	338	15	67	420	1	421	99.76	64.85	15.44	80.29	15.91	3.56	0.24
51	Ward 7, . .	221	15	67	303	-	303	100.00	48.85	24.09	72.94	22.11	4.95	-
52	NANTUCKET .	886	29	33	948	11	959	98.85	86.86	5.53	92.39	3.44	3.02	1.15
53	Nantucket, .	886	29	33	948	11	959	98.85	86.86	5.53	92.39	3.44	3.02	1.15

POLITICAL CONDITION: BY SEX — Continued.

POLITICAL CONDITION: BY SEX -- Continued.

	COUNTIES, CITIES, AND TOWNS.	MALE POPULATION 20 YEARS OF AGE AND OVER						PERCENTAGES OF MALE POPULATION 20 YEARS OF AGE AND OVER						
		Voters	Not Voters	Aliens	Total Ratable Polls	No Political Condition	Total Male Population 20 Years of Age and over	Ratable Polls	Native Born Voters	Foreign Born Naturalized Voters	Total Voters	Aliens	No Voters	No Political Condition
1	NORFOLK.	31,565	2,186	7,369	41,120	137	41,257	99.67	59.53	16.92	76.51	17.86	5.30	0.33
2	Avon, . . .	499	41	50	540	1	541	99.82	74.12	12.57	86.69	5.55	7.58	0.18
3	Bellingham, .	323	41	89	453	3	456	99.34	61.62	9.21	70.83	19.52	8.90	0.66
4	Braintree, . .	1,331	68	380	1,779	7	1,786	99.61	63.49	11.05	74.52	21.28	3.81	0.39
5	Brookline, . .	3,243	221	907	4,371	-	4,371	100.00	53.99	20.20	74.19	20.75	5.06	-
6	Canton, . .	1,096	53	198	1,347	11	1,358	99.19	59.57	21.14	80.71	14.58	3.90	0.81
7	Cohasset, . .	695	19	100	784	6	790	99.24	72.53	11.65	84.18	12.66	2.46	0.76
8	Dedham, . .	1,702	210	311	2,223	6	2,229	99.73	56.62	19.74	76.36	13.95	9.42	0.27
9	Dover, . . .	169	23	25	217	-	217	100.00	58.53	19.35	77.88	11.52	10.59	-
10	Foxborough, .	858	97	99	1,054	7	1,061	99.34	70.97	9.90	80.87	9.33	9.14	0.66
11	Franklin, . .	1,184	80	288	1,552	2	1,554	99.87	62.93	13.29	76.19	18.53	5.15	0.13
12	Holbrook, . .	645	34	34	713	11	724	98.48	76.79	12.29	89.08	4.70	4.70	1.52
13	Hyde Park, .	2,772	209	558	3,539	2	3,541	99.94	57.04	21.24	78.28	15.76	5.90	0.06
14	Medfield, . .	447	66	126	639	3	642	99.53	61.06	8.57	69.63	19.62	10.28	0.47
15	Medway, . .	818	30	70	918	11	929	98.82	73.30	14.75	88.05	7.54	3.23	1.18
16	Millis, . .	231	23	53	307	-	307	100.00	63.19	12.05	75.24	17.27	7.49	-
17	Milton, . .	1,171	74	341	1,586	7	1,593	99.56	56.62	16.89	73.51	21.41	4.64	0.44
18	Needham, . .	763	90	265	1,118	2	1,120	99.82	48.93	19.20	68.13	23.66	8.04	0.18
19	Norfolk, . .	193	25	75	293	2	295	99.32	56.27	9.15	65.42	25.42	8.28	0.68
20	Norwood, . .	1,133	79	339	1,551	1	1,552	99.94	51.93	21.07	73.00	21.85	5.09	0.06
21	QUINCY, . .	4,325	338	1,701	6,364	8	6,372	99.87	45.06	22.82	67.88	26.69	5.30	0.13
22	Ward 1, .	803	97	230	1,130	7	1,137	99.38	54.18	16.44	70.62	20.23	8.53	0.62
23	Ward 2, .	658	41	120	819	-	819	100.00	60.93	19.41	80.34	14.65	5.01	-
24	Ward 3, .	834	64	561	1,459	-	1,459	100.00	28.51	28.65	57.16	38.45	4.35	-
25	Ward 4, .	874	57	556	1,487	1	1,488	99.93	28.23	30.51	58.74	37.36	3.83	0.07
26	Ward 5, .	646	42	136	824	-	824	100.00	65.78	12.62	78.40	16.50	5.10	-
27	Ward 6, .	510	37	98	645	-	645	100.00	58.60	20.47	79.07	15.19	5.73	-
28	Randolph, .	1,123	26	73	1,222	8	1,230	99.35	73.74	17.56	91.30	5.94	2.11	0.65
29	Sharon, . .	423	35	112	570	-	570	100.00	63.51	10.70	74.21	19.65	6.14	-
30	Stoughton, .	1,333	53	215	1,601	10	1,611	99.38	68.53	14.21	82.74	13.35	3.29	0.62
31	Walpole, . .	715	23	213	951	2	953	99.79	62.75	12.28	75.03	22.35	2.41	0.21
32	Wellesley, . .	694	27	203	924	1	925	99.89	57.52	17.51	75.03	21.94	2.92	0.11
33	Weymouth, .	3,639	163	502	3,704	25	3,729	99.33	71.36	10.14	81.50	13.46	4.37	0.67
34	Wrentham, .	700	38	62	800	1	801	99.88	75.66	11.73	87.39	7.74	4.75	0.12
35	PLYMOUTH.	26,956	2,217	4,152	33,325	608	33,933	98.21	69.44	10.00	79.44	12.24	6.53	1.79
36	Abington, . .	1,258	62	64	1,384	7	1,391	99.50	78.54	11.93	90.44	4.60	4.46	0.50
37	Bridgewater, .	992	90	139	1,221	433	2,150	78.93	40.42	5.72	46.14	6.33	26.46	21.07
38	BROCKTON, .	8,531	496	1,674	10,701	17	10,718	99.84	64.31	15.28	79.59	15.62	4.63	0.16
39	Ward 1, .	1,253	69	150	1,472	-	1,472	100.00	77.99	7.13	85.12	10.19	4.69	-
40	Ward 2, .	1,310	58	100	1,468	-	1,468	100.00	77.86	11.38	89.24	6.81	3.95	-
41	Ward 3, .	1,273	49	277	1,599	-	1,599	100.00	61.04	18.57	79.61	17.32	3.07	-
42	Ward 4, .	1,042	80	375	1,497	-	1,497	100.00	46.69	22.31	69.00	25.05	5.35	-
43	Ward 5, .	1,164	75	315	1,554	15	1,569	99.04	59.85	14.34	74.19	20.07	4.78	0.96
44	Ward 6, .	1,202	139	320	1,641	1	1,642	99.94	58.71	14.49	73.20	19.49	7.25	0.06
45	Ward 7, .	1,287	46	137	1,470	1	1,471	99.93	69.61	17.88	87.49	9.31	3.13	0.07
46	Carver, . .	269	29	57	355	3	358	99.16	72.35	2.79	75.14	15.92	8.10	0.84
47	Duxbury, . .	555	18	67	640	8	648	98.77	83.03	2.62	85.65	10.34	2.78	1.23
48	E. Bridgewater,	780	60	126	966	5	971	99.49	73.64	6.69	80.33	12.98	6.18	0.51
49	Halifax, . .	146	6	22	174	-	174	100.00	79.31	4.60	83.91	12.64	3.45	-
50	Hanover, . .	584	61	60	705	11	716	98.46	77.37	4.19	81.56	8.38	8.52	1.54
51	Hanson, . .	386	29	57	472	6	478	98.74	78.45	2.30	80.75	11.92	6.07	1.26
52	Hingham, . .	1,256	72	240	1,568	4	1,572	99.75	68.85	10.05	78.90	15.27	4.58	0.25
53	Hull, . . .	192	145	56	393	-	393	100.00	40.46	8.39	48.85	14.25	36.90	-

POLITICAL CONDITION : BY SEX — Continued.

	TOTAL POPULATION. BOTH SEXES. ALL AGES						PERCENTAGES OF TOTAL POPULATION							
Voters	Not Voters	Aliens	Total Ratable Polls	No Political Condition	Total Population, Both Sexes, All Ages	Ratable Polls	Native Born Voters	Foreign Born Naturalized Voters	Total Voters	Aliens	Not Voters	No Political Condition	
31,565	2,186	7,369	41,120	95,669	134,849	30.50	18.23	5.18	23.41	5.47	1.62	69.50	1
169	30	340	540	1,086	1,626	33.21	24.00	4.18	28.84	1.85	2.52	66.79	2
523	41	89	453	1,028	1,481	30.59	18.97	2.84	21.81	6.01	2.77	69.41	3
1,531	68	380	1,779	3,532	5,311	33.50	21.35	3.71	25.06	7.16	1.28	66.50	4
3,243	221	907	4,371	11,793	16,164	27.04	14.60	5.46	20.06	5.61	1.37	72.96	5
1,096	53	198	1,347	3,289	4,636	29.06	17.45	6.49	23.94	4.27	1.15	70.94	6
665	19	100	784	1,680	2,474	31.69	23.16	3.72	26.88	4.04	0.77	68.31	7
1,702	210	311	2,223	4,988	7,211	30.83	17.50	6.10	23.60	4.32	2.91	69.17	8
169	23	25	217	451	668	32.49	19.01	6.29	25.30	3.74	3.45	67.51	9
868	97	99	1,054	2,165	3,219	32.74	23.39	5.26	26.65	3.08	3.01	67.26	10
1,184	80	288	1,552	3,584	5,136	30.22	19.04	4.61	23.65	5.61	1.56	69.78	11
645	34	34	713	1,585	2,298	31.03	24.20	3.87	28.07	1.48	1.48	68.97	12
2,772	290	558	3,539	8,287	11,826	29.93	17.08	6.36	23.44	4.72	1.77	70.07	13
447	66	126	639	1,233	1,872	34.13	20.94	2.94	23.88	6.73	3.52	65.87	14
818	30	70	918	1,995	2,913	31.51	23.58	4.70	28.08	2.40	1.03	68.49	15
234	23	53	307	699	1,006	30.52	19.28	3.68	22.96	5.27	2.29	69.48	16
1,171	74	341	1,586	3,932	5,518	28.74	16.35	4.87	21.22	6.18	1.34	71.26	17
703	80	265	1,118	2,396	3,514	31.84	15.61	6.12	21.73	7.55	2.96	68.16	18
136	23	75	236	589	882	33.22	18.82	3.06	21.88	8.50	2.84	66.78	19
1,133	79	339	1,551	3,023	4,574	33.94	17.62	7.15	24.77	7.41	1.73	66.49	20
4,325	338	1,701	6,364	14,348	20,712	30.73	13.86	7.02	20.88	8.22	1.63	69.27	21
803	97	230	1,130	2,432	3,562	31.72	17.29	5.25	22.54	6.46	2.72	68.28	22
658	44	120	819	1,922	2,741	29.88	18.21	5.80	24.01	4.38	1.49	70.12	23
834	64	561	1,459	3,237	4,696	31.07	8.86	8.90	17.76	11.95	1.36	68.93	24
874	57	556	1,487	4,064	5,551	26.96	8.46	9.15	17.61	11.20	1.15	70.04	25
646	42	136	824	1,845	2,669	30.87	20.31	3.89	24.20	5.10	1.57	69.13	26
510	37	98	645	1,435	2,080	31.01	18.17	6.35	24.52	4.71	1.78	68.99	27
1,423	26	73	1,222	2,472	3,694	33.08	24.55	5.85	30.40	1.98	0.70	66.92	28
423	35	112	570	1,147	1,717	33.20	21.08	3.55	24.63	6.53	2.04	66.80	29
1,333	53	215	1,601	3,671	5,272	30.37	20.94	4.34	25.28	4.08	1.01	69.63	30
715	25	213	951	2,043	2,994	31.76	19.07	5.91	25.88	7.11	0.77	68.24	31
694	27	203	924	3,305	4,229	21.85	12.58	3.83	16.41	4.80	0.64	78.15	32
3,029	163	502	3,704	7,587	11,291	32.80	23.57	3.35	26.92	4.44	1.44	67.20	33
700	38	62	800	1,784	2,584	30.96	23.45	3.64	27.09	2.40	1.47	69.04	34
26,966	2,217	4,152	33,325	68,173	101,498	32.83	23.22	3.34	26.56	4.09	2.18	67.17	35
1,258	62	64	1,384	2,823	4,207	32.90	25.96	3.94	29.90	1.52	1.48	67.10	36
992	560	136	1,697	2,989	4,686	36.21	18.55	2.62	21.17	2.90	12.44	63.79	37
8,531	496	1,674	10,701	22,464	33,165	32.27	20.78	4.94	25.72	5.05	1.50	67.73	38
1,253	69	150	1,472	2,697	4,169	35.31	27.54	2.52	30.06	3.60	1.65	64.69	39
1,310	58	100	1,468	2,859	4,327	33.93	26.42	3.86	30.28	2.31	1.34	66.07	40
1,273	49	277	1,360	3,446	5,045	31.69	19.34	5.89	25.23	5.49	0.97	68.31	41
1,042	80	375	1,497	3,295	4,792	31.24	14.58	7.16	21.74	7.84	1.07	68.76	42
1,164	75	315	1,554	3,492	5,046	30.80	18.61	4.46	23.07	6.24	1.49	69.20	43
1,202	119	320	1,641	3,299	4,940	33.22	19.51	4.82	24.33	6.48	2.41	66.78	44
1,287	46	137	1,470	3,376	4,846	30.33	21.13	5.43	26.56	2.82	0.95	69.67	45
269	29	57	355	661	1,016	34.94	25.49	0.98	26.47	5.61	2.86	65.06	46
555	18	67	640	1,326	1,966	32.55	27.37	0.86	28.23	3.41	0.91	67.45	47
780	60	126	966	1,928	2,894	33.38	24.71	2.21	26.95	4.36	2.07	66.62	48
146	6	22	174	323	497	35.01	27.77	1.61	29.38	4.42	1.21	64.99	49
584	61	60	705	1,346	2,051	34.37	27.04	1.46	28.47	2.93	2.97	65.63	50
386	29	57	472	908	1,380	34.20	27.47	0.80	27.97	4.13	2.10	65.80	51
1,256	72	240	1,568	3,251	4,819	32.54	22.78	3.28	26.06	4.98	1.50	67.46	52
192	145	56	393	651	1,044	37.64	15.23	3.16	18.39	5.36	13.89	62.36	53

POLITICAL CONDITION: BY SEX — Continued.

COUNTIES, CITIES, AND TOWNS.	MALE POPULATION 20 YEARS OF AGE AND OVER						PERCENTAGES OF MALE POPULATION 20 YEARS OF AGE AND OVER					
	Voters	Not Voters	Aliens	Total Ratable Polls	No Political Condition	Total Male Population 20 Years of Age and Over	Ratable Polls	Native Born Voters	Foreign Born Naturalized Voters	Total Voters	Aliens	Not Voters	No Political Condition
PLYMOUTH — Con.													
1 Kingston,	473	32	57	562	–	562	100.00	76.51	7.65	84.16	10.14	5.70	–
2 Lakeville,	254	20	30	304	1	305	99.67	80.33	2.95	83.28	9.83	6.56	0.33
3 Marion,	207	9	4	220	1	221	99.55	91.86	1.81	93.67	1.81	4.07	0.45
4 Marshfield,	596	13	55	604	4	608	99.34	83.86	2.30	88.16	9.04	2.14	0.66
5 Mattapoisett,	296	23	24	343	3	346	99.13	84.16	1.45	85.55	6.93	6.95	0.87
6 Middleborough,	1,843	119	220	2,182	12	2,194	99.45	77.76	6.24	84.00	10.03	5.42	0.55
7 Norwell,	473	23	26	522	1	523	99.81	87.00	3.14	90.44	4.97	4.40	0.19
8 Pembroke,	389	17	42	428	5	433	98.85	80.14	5.08	85.22	9.70	3.93	1.15
9 Plymouth,	1,999	97	378	2,441	12	2,453	99.51	71.63	8.52	80.15	15.41	3.95	0.49
10 Plympton,	158	16	18	192	–	192	100.00	79.17	3.12	82.29	9.38	8.33	–
11 Rochester,	283	21	28	332	4	336	98.81	81.55	2.68	84.23	8.33	6.25	1.19
12 Rockland,	1,571	59	135	1,765	31	1,796	98.27	71.49	15.98	87.47	7.52	3.28	1.73
13 Scituate,	673	20	64	757	–	757	100.00	80.58	8.32	88.90	8.16	2.64	–
14 Wareham,	828	97	230	1,155	6	1,161	99.48	65.55	5.77	71.32	19.81	8.35	0.52
15 W. Bridgewater,	461	26	95	582	6	588	98.98	68.37	10.03	78.40	16.16	4.42	1.02
16 Whitman,	1,646	78	187	1,881	8	1,889	99.58	75.86	9.68	85.55	9.90	4.13	0.42
17 **SUFFOLK.**	123,102	9,298	37,096	169,496	527	170,023	99.69	49.26	23.14	72.40	21.82	5.47	0.31
18 BOSTON,	113,393	8,520	34,171	156,084	524	156,608	99.67	48.83	23.58	72.41	21.82	5.41	0.33
19 , Ward 1,	4,785	177	1,319	6,281	–	6,281	100.00	50.66	25.52	76.18	21.00	2.82	–
20 Ward 2,	4,357	903	1,846	7,166	252	7,418	96.60	32.61	26.13	58.74	24.88	12.38	3.40
21 Ward 3,	3,528	126	671	4,335	1	4,336	99.98	55.51	26.08	81.59	15.48	2.91	0.02
22 Ward 4,	3,311	143	733	4,207	45	4,252	98.94	56.54	21.33	77.87	17.71	3.36	1.06
23 Ward 5,	3,295	789	927	4,962	1	4,963	99.98	44.43	21.38	65.81	18.68	15.40	0.02
24 Ward 6,	4,180	589	4,592	9,371	–	9,371	100.00	23.26	21.45	44.71	49.00	6.29	–
25 Ward 7,	4,237	306	2,055	6,888	1	6,889	99.99	41.05	20.45	61.50	29.83	8.66	0.01
26 Ward 8,	5,173	349	2,710	8,232	4	8,236	99.95	42.34	29.47	62.84	32.90	4.24	0.05
27 Ward 9,	5,504	523	2,017	8,044	–	8,044	100.00	46.89	21.53	68.42	25.08	6.50	–
28 Ward 10,	6,067	304	1,206	7,604	–	7,604	100.00	63.48	15.52	79.00	15.86	5.14	–
29 Ward 11,	4,886	259	622	5,767	–	5,767	100.00	69.07	15.05	84.72	10.79	4.49	–
30 Ward 12,	5,731	308	924	6,963	48	7,011	99.32	65.45	16.29	81.74	13.18	4.40	0.68
31 Ward 13,	4,705	311	2,437	7,543	11	7,554	99.85	32.21	31.24	63.48	32.26	4.11	0.15
32 Ward 14,	4,381	642	1,075	6,074	–	6,074	100.00	47.73	24.43	72.16	17.76	10.08	–
33 Ward 15,	4,324	207	946	5,447	4	5,451	99.93	51.61	27.72	79.33	16.80	3.80	0.07
34 Ward 16,	3,363	174	797	4,304	–	4,304	100.00	57.60	22.21	80.20	16.25	3.55	–
35 Ward 17,	4,801	204	1,470	6,475	2	6,477	99.97	48.19	29.53	77.72	18.91	3.31	0.03
36 Ward 18,	4,830	222	1,727	6,779	1	6,780	99.98	44.01	27.25	71.24	25.47	3.25	0.01
37 Ward 19,	4,467	196	1,421	6,084	–	6,084	100.00	36.61	36.78	73.42	23.36	3.22	–
38 Ward 20,	5,225	288	858	6,372	1	6,373	99.98	60.84	21.15	81.99	13.47	4.52	0.02
39 Ward 21,	4,716	217	510	5,556	2	5,552	99.96	67.42	18.91	86.33	9.72	3.91	0.04
40 Ward 22,	4,829	240	1,065	6,211	–	6,211	100.00	48.67	29.85	78.52	17.62	3.86	–
41 Ward 23,	4,032	250	805	5,087	148	5,235	97.17	48.40	28.62	77.02	15.38	4.77	2.83
42 Ward 24,	4,371	205	782	5,558	1	5,559	99.98	60.87	20.09	81.56	14.50	3.83	0.02
43 Ward 25,	3,577	204	902	4,680	2	4,682	99.96	53.95	22.47	76.40	19.27	4.29	0.04
44 CHELSEA,	7,069	411	2,222	9,732	2	9,734	99.98	54.53	18.46	72.59	22.83	4.56	0.02
45 Ward 1,	1,561	97	631	2,289	1	2,290	99.96	49.55	18.82	68.47	27.55	4.24	0.04
46 Ward 2,	1,931	91	368	2,390	–	2,390	100.00	50.84	21.33	72.17	23.80	4.03	–
47 Ward 3,	1,433	82	644	2,219	1	2,220	99.95	47.25	20.00	67.25	29.01	3.69	0.05
48 Ward 4,	1,265	85	298	1,648	–	1,648	100.00	62.14	14.32	76.76	18.08	5.16	–
49 Ward 5,	1,116	89	111	1,316	–	1,316	100.00	69.30	15.50	84.80	8.44	6.76	–
50 Revere,	1,818	63	420	2,301	1	2,302	99.96	57.30	21.07	78.97	18.25	2.74	0.04
51 Winthrop,	825	271	283	1,379	–	1,379	100.00	49.68	10.15	59.83	20.52	19.65	–

POLITICAL CONDITION: BY SEX — Continued.

					TOTAL POPULATION. BOTH SEXES. ALL AGES				PERCENTAGES OF TOTAL POPULATION				
Voters	Not Voters	Aliens	Total Ratable Polls	No Political Condition	Total Population. Both sexes. All Ages	Ratable Polls	Native Born Voters	Foreign Born Naturalized Voters	Total Voters	Aliens	Not Voters	No Political Condition	
473	32	57	562	1,184	1,706	32.49	24.63	2.46	27.09	3.27	1.83	67.81	1
254	20	50	304	566	870	31.94	28.16	1.03	29.19	3.45	2.30	65.06	2
207	9	4	220	539	759	28.99	26.74	0.53	27.27	0.53	1.19	71.01	3
536	13	55	604	1,156	1,760	34.32	29.06	0.79	30.45	3.13	0.74	65.68	4
296	23	24	343	689	1,032	33.24	28.20	0.48	28.68	2.33	2.23	66.76	5
1,843	119	220	2,182	4,507	6,689	32.62	25.50	2.05	27.55	3.29	1.78	67.38	6
473	23	26	522	1,018	1,540	33.90	29.55	1.17	30.72	1.69	1.49	66.10	7
369	17	42	428	795	1,223	35.00	28.37	1.80	30.17	3.44	1.39	65.00	8
1,909	97	378	2,441	5,516	7,957	30.68	22.08	2.63	24.71	4.75	1.22	69.32	9
158	16	18	192	357	549	34.97	27.69	1.09	28.78	3.28	2.91	65.03	10
283	21	28	332	689	1,021	32.52	26.84	0.88	27.72	2.74	2.06	67.18	11
1,571	30	135	1,705	3,758	5,528	31.06	23.25	3.20	28.15	2.44	1.07	68.91	12
673	29	64	757	1,489	2,246	33.70	27.16	2.80	29.96	2.85	0.89	69.30	13
828	97	230	1,155	2,212	3,367	34.30	22.60	1.60	24.20	6.83	2.88	65.70	14
461	26	95	582	1,165	1,747	33.31	23.01	2.28	26.29	5.43	1.49	66.68	15
1,616	78	187	1,881	3,863	5,744	32.75	24.95	3.18	28.13	3.26	1.36	67.25	16
123,102	9,298	37,096	169,496	370,363	539,799	31.40	15.52	7.29	22.81	6.87	1.72	68.60	17
113,383	8,520	34,171	156,084	340,836	496,920	31.41	15.39	7.43	22.82	6.88	1.71	68.30	18
4,785	177	1,319	6,281	14,726	21,007	29.90	15.15	7.63	22.78	6.28	0.84	70.10	19
4,357	983	1,846	7,196	14,422	21,588	33.19	11.20	8.98	20.18	8.55	4.46	66.81	20
3,548	126	671	4,335	9,608	13,943	31.09	17.26	8.11	25.37	4.81	0.94	68.91	21
3,311	143	753	4,207	9,168	13,375	31.45	17.97	6.78	24.75	5.63	1.07	68.55	22
3,265	769	927	4,962	8,024	12,986	38.21	16.98	8.47	25.15	7.14	5.92	61.79	23
4,190	589	4,592	9,571	18,489	27,890	33.64	7.83	7.21	15.04	16.48	2.12	66.36	24
4,237	596	2,055	6,888	10,085	16,973	40.58	16.66	8.30	24.96	12.11	3.51	59.42	25
5,173	349	2,710	8,232	14,898	23,130	35.59	15.07	7.29	22.36	11.72	1.51	64.41	26
5,504	523	2,017	8,044	15,130	23,174	34.71	16.28	7.47	23.75	8.70	2.26	65.29	27
6,007	394	1,206	7,904	14,950	22,554	33.71	21.40	5.23	26.63	5.35	1.73	69.29	28
4,886	259	622	5,767	14,163	19,930	28.94	20.16	4.36	24.52	3.12	1.30	71.06	29
5,731	308	924	6,963	14,628	21,791	32.25	21.25	5.29	26.54	4.28	1.43	67.75	30
4,795	311	2,437	7,543	17,357	24,900	30.29	9.78	9.48	19.26	9.78	1.25	69.71	31
4,381	612	1,078	6,071	13,115	19,186	31.64	15.10	7.73	22.83	5.62	3.19	68.36	32
4,324	207	916	5,447	13,176	18,623	29.25	15.11	8.11	23.22	4.92	1.11	70.75	33
3,833	174	797	4,804	11,416	16,320	30.65	17.43	6.67	24.10	4.88	1.07	69.95	34
4,801	204	1,170	6,175	14,939	21,114	29.25	14.10	8.64	22.74	5.54	0.97	70.75	35
4,830	222	1,727	6,779	14,900	21,679	31.27	13.76	8.52	22.28	7.97	1.02	68.73	36
4,467	196	1,421	6,084	16,288	22,372	27.19	9.96	10.01	19.97	6.35	0.87	72.81	37
5,225	288	859	6,372	15,156	21,528	29.60	18.01	6.26	24.27	3.99	1.34	70.40	38
4,793	217	540	5,550	13,724	19,274	28.80	19.42	5.45	24.87	2.80	1.13	71.20	39
4,879	240	1,095	6,214	16,075	22,289	27.88	13.57	8.32	21.89	4.91	1.08	72.12	40
4,032	209	805	5,087	14,196	19,283	27.82	13.86	8.19	22.05	4.40	1.37	72.18	41
4,371	205	782	5,358	12,882	18,240	29.37	17.88	6.08	23.96	4.29	1.12	70.63	42
3,577	201	902	4,680	10,321	15,001	31.20	16.84	7.01	23.85	6.01	1.34	68.80	43
7,066	444	2,222	9,732	21,532	31,264	31.13	16.85	5.75	22.60	7.11	1.42	68.87	44
1,561	97	631	2,289	5,190	7,479	30.61	15.11	5.76	20.87	8.44	1.30	69.39	45
1,633	91	548	2,260	5,325	7,585	29.80	15.15	6.35	21.50	7.10	1.20	70.20	46
1,493	82	644	2,219	4,903	7,122	31.16	14.73	6.23	20.96	9.05	1.15	68.84	47
1,265	85	298	1,648	3,739	5,387	30.59	19.10	4.38	23.48	5.53	1.58	69.41	48
1,116	89	111	1,316	2,375	3,691	35.65	24.71	5.53	30.24	3.00	2.41	64.35	49
1,818	63	420	2,301	5,122	7,423	31.00	17.96	6.53	24.49	5.66	0.85	69.00	50
825	271	283	1,379	2,813	4,192	32.90	16.34	3.34	19.68	6.75	6.47	67.10	51

POLITICAL CONDITION: BY SEX — Continued.

	MALE POPULATION 20 YEARS OF AGE AND OVER						PERCENTAGES OF MALE POPULATION 20 YEARS OF AGE AND OVER						
COUNTIES, CITIES, AND TOWNS.	Voters	Not Voters	Aliens	Total Ratable Polls	No Political Condition	Total Male Population 20 Years of Age and Over	Ratable Polls	Native Born Voters	Foreign Born Naturalized Voters	Total Voters	Aliens	Not Voters	No Political Condition
1 WORCESTER,	66,169	6,236	20,796	93,141	1,268	94,409	98.66	54.33	15.69	70.02	22.03	6.61	1.34
2 Ashburnham, .	548	23	86	657	4	661	99.39	75.49	7.41	82.90	13.01	3.48	0.61
3 Athol, . . .	1,846	238	488	2,572	9	2,581	99.65	66.87	4.65	71.52	18.91	9.22	0.35
4 Auburn, . .	270	51	150	471	–	471	100.00	47.13	10.19	57.32	31.85	10.83	–
5 Barre, . .	543	64	135	742	53	795	93.33	64.02	4.28	68.30	16.98	8.05	6.67
6 Berlin, . .	238	27	43	308	3	311	99.04	72.35	4.18	76.53	13.83	8.68	0.96
7 Blackstone, .	1,303	40	479	1,921	17	1,938	99.12	43.24	28.64	71.88	24.71	2.53	0.88
8 Bolton, . .	210	25	33	268	5	273	98.17	70.33	6.59	76.92	12.09	9.16	1.83
9 Boylston, . .	197	14	40	251	4	255	98.43	69.80	7.45	77.25	15.69	5.49	1.57
10 Brookfield, .	760	87	230	1,077	1	1,078	99.91	61.78	8.72	70.50	21.34	8.07	0.09
11 Charlton, . .	487	56	69	612	4	616	99.35	73.54	5.52	79.06	11.20	9.09	0.65
12 Clinton, . .	2,418	158	503	3,079	7	3,086	99.77	41.36	36.42	78.35	16.30	5.12	0.23
13 Dana, . . .	180	27	41	248	–	248	100.00	71.37	1.21	72.58	16.53	10.89	–
14 Douglas, . .	493	52	130	675	3	678	99.56	64.01	8.70	72.71	19.18	7.67	0.44
15 Dudley, . .	528	41	295	864	3	867	99.65	43.25	17.65	60.90	34.02	4.73	0.35
16 FITCHBURG,	5,231	603	2,116	7,950	39	7,989	99.51	48.83	16.65	65.48	26.48	7.55	0.49
17 Ward 1, .	828	174	310	1,312	38	1,350	97.19	40.82	20.52	61.34	22.96	12.89	2.81
18 Ward 2, .	884	107	903	1,894	1	1,895	99.95	27.60	19.05	46.65	47.65	5.65	0.05
19 Ward 3, .	821	87	403	1,311	–	1,311	100.00	42.41	20.21	62.62	30.74	6.64	–
20 Ward 4, .	817	119	121	1,057	–	1,057	100.00	69.35	7.94	77.29	11.45	11.26	–
21 Ward 5, .	932	73	79	1,084	–	1,084	100.00	74.72	11.26	85.98	7.29	6.73	–
22 Ward 6, .	949	43	300	1,292	–	1,292	100.00	56.35	17.10	73.45	23.22	3.33	–
23 Gardner, . .	1,380	136	871	2,387	14	3,001	99.53	54.05	11.93	65.98	29.02	4.53	0.47
24 Grafton, . .	990	67	399	1,456	10	1,466	99.32	57.09	10.44	67.53	27.22	4.57	0.68
25 Hardwick, . .	479	61	268	808	8	816	99.02	45.34	13.36	58.70	32.84	7.48	0.98
26 Harvard, . .	306	42	68	416	4	420	99.05	65.48	7.38	72.86	16.19	10.00	0.95
27 Holden, . .	522	29	217	768	5	773	99.35	57.31	10.22	67.53	28.07	3.75	0.65
28 Hopedale, . .	351	60	53	464	1	465	99.78	65.16	10.32	75.48	11.40	12.90	0.22
29 Hubbardston, .	338	51	47	436	1	437	99.77	70.94	6.41	77.35	10.75	11.67	0.23
30 Lancaster, . .	413	54	124	591	6	597	98.99	57.12	12.06	69.18	20.77	9.04	1.01
31 Leicester, . .	744	50	157	960	6	966	99.38	48.15	16.87	77.02	16.25	6.11	0.62
32 Leominster, .	2,260	223	455	2,938	6	2,944	99.80	66.41	10.36	76.77	15.46	7.57	0.20
33 Lunenburg, .	357	6	33	396	8	404	98.02	83.17	5.20	88.37	8.17	1.48	1.98
34 Mendon, . .	263	24	19	306	2	308	98.35	79.22	6.17	85.39	6.17	7.79	0.65
35 Milford, . .	2,323	125	425	2,873	30	2,903	98.97	63.35	18.67	80.02	14.64	4.31	1.03
36 Millbury, . .	983	88	550	1,621	4	1,625	99.75	47.51	11.75	59.26	34.40	6.06	0.25
37 New Braintree, .	112	23	54	189	1	190	99.47	57.37	1.58	58.95	28.42	12.10	0.53
38 Northborough, .	407	29	161	597	1	598	99.83	60.37	7.69	68.06	26.92	4.85	0.17
39 Northbridge, .	974	129	548	1,651	5	1,656	99.70	38.95	19.87	58.82	33.09	7.79	0.30
40 N. Brookfield, .	1,070	82	247	1,399	5	1,404	99.64	63.11	13.10	76.21	17.59	5.84	0.36
41 Oakham, . .	175	12	21	208	–	208	100.00	80.29	3.84	84.13	10.10	5.77	–
42 Oxford, . .	550	31	116	706	6	712	99.16	70.51	8.00	78.51	16.29	4.36	0.84
43 Paxton, . .	131	4	23	158	2	160	98.75	79.31	4.38	81.88	14.37	2.50	1.25
44 Petersham, .	258	44	39	341	6	347	98.27	67.43	6.92	74.35	11.24	12.68	1.73
45 Phillipston, .	133	15	12	160	3	163	98.16	79.76	1.84	81.60	7.36	9.20	1.84
46 Princeton, . .	254	23	51	328	2	330	99.39	75.00	4.48	79.48	15.45	6.97	0.61
47 Royalston, . .	255	16	25	296	1	297	99.66	80.14	5.72	85.86	8.42	5.38	0.34
48 Rutland, . .	237	22	57	316	1	317	99.68	67.19	7.57	74.76	17.98	6.94	0.32
49 Shrewsbury, .	444	23	49	516	6	522	98.85	79.31	5.75	85.06	9.39	4.40	1.15
50 Southborough, .	448	57	316	821	3	824	99.64	45.27	9.10	54.37	38.35	6.92	0.36
51 Southbridge, .	1,414	124	651	2,189	9	2,198	99.59	45.68	18.65	64.33	29.62	5.64	0.41
52 Spencer, . .	1,570	124	447	2,141	9	2,150	99.58	56.33	16.69	73.02	20.79	5.77	0.42
53 Sterling, . .	357	43	19	419	5	424	98.82	75.00	4.48	79.48	9.20	10.14	1.18
54 Sturbridge, .	423	34	100	557	4	561	99.29	63.81	11.59	75.40	17.83	6.06	0.71
55 Sutton, . .	555	74	344	973	11	984	98.88	50.00	6.40	56.40	34.96	7.52	1.12

POLITICAL CONDITION: BY SEX — Continued.

	TOTAL POPULATION. BOTH SEXES. ALL AGES					PERCENTAGES OF TOTAL POPULATION							
Voters	Not Voters	Aliens	Total Ratable Polls	No Political Condition	Total Population. Both Sexes. All Ages	Ratable Polls	Native Born Voters	Foreign Born Naturalized Voters	Total Voters	Aliens	Not Voters	No Political Condition	
66,109	6,236	20,796	93,141	213,394	306,445	30.39	16.74	4.83	21.57	6.79	2.03	69.61	1
548	23	86	657	1,491	2,148	30.59	23.28	2.28	25.51	4.01	1.07	69.41	2
1,846	238	488	2,572	4,792	7,364	34.93	23.44	1.63	25.07	6.63	3.23	65.07	3
270	51	150	471	1,127	1,598	29.47	13.89	3.00	16.89	9.39	3.19	70.53	4
543	64	135	742	1,536	2,278	32.57	22.35	1.49	23.84	5.92	2.81	67.43	5
238	27	43	308	589	897	34.34	25.08	1.45	26.53	4.80	3.01	65.66	6
1,363	49	479	1,921	4,118	6,039	31.81	13.88	9.19	23.07	7.93	0.81	68.19	7
210	25	33	268	529	797	33.63	24.09	2.26	26.35	4.14	3.14	66.37	8
197	14	40	251	478	729	34.43	24.42	2.60	27.02	5.49	1.92	65.57	9
790	57	230	1,077	2,202	3,279	32.85	20.31	2.87	23.18	7.02	2.05	67.15	10
487	56	69	612	1,265	1,877	32.61	24.14	1.81	25.95	3.68	2.98	67.39	11
2,448	158	503	3,079	8,418	11,497	26.78	11.25	9.78	21.03	4.38	1.37	73.22	12
180	27	41	248	469	717	34.59	24.68	0.42	25.10	5.72	3.77	65.41	13
493	52	130	675	1,351	2,026	33.32	21.42	2.91	24.33	6.42	2.57	66.68	14
528	41	295	864	2,339	3,203	26.97	11.71	4.77	16.48	9.21	1.28	73.06	15
5,231	603	2,116	7,950	18,450	26,400	30.10	14.77	5.04	19.81	8.01	2.28	69.90	16
828	174	310	1,312	3,064	4,376	29.98	12.59	6.33	18.92	7.08	3.98	70.02	17
884	107	903	1,894	4,616	6,510	29.09	8.03	5.55	13.58	13.87	1.64	70.91	18
821	87	403	1,311	2,988	4,299	30.50	12.93	6.17	19.10	9.38	2.02	69.50	19
817	119	121	1,057	2,157	3,214	32.89	22.81	2.61	25.42	3.77	3.70	67.11	20
932	73	79	1,084	2,266	3,350	32.36	24.18	3.64	27.82	2.36	2.18	67.64	21
949	43	300	1,292	3,368	4,660	27.73	15.62	4.75	20.37	6.44	0.92	72.27	22
1,060	156	871	2,987	6,195	9,182	32.53	17.66	3.90	21.56	9.49	1.48	67.47	23
900	67	389	1,456	3,645	5,101	28.54	16.44	3.00	19.44	7.92	1.31	71.46	24
479	61	268	808	1,847	2,655	30.43	13.94	4.10	18.04	10.09	2.30	69.57	25
596	42	68	416	746	1,162	35.80	25.96	2.67	26.63	5.85	3.62	64.20	26
522	29	217	768	1,834	2,602	29.52	17.02	3.04	20.06	8.34	1.12	70.48	27
351	60	53	464	913	1,377	33.70	22.06	3.40	25.49	3.85	4.36	66.30	28
338	51	47	436	838	1,274	34.22	24.33	2.20	26.53	3.69	4.00	65.78	29
415	54	124	593	1,589	2,180	27.11	15.94	3.30	18.94	5.69	2.48	72.89	30
744	59	157	960	2,279	3,239	29.64	17.94	5.03	22.97	4.85	1.82	70.36	31
2,299	223	455	2,958	6,273	9,211	31.00	21.23	3.31	24.54	4.94	2.42	68.10	32
357	6	33	396	841	1,237	32.04	27.16	1.70	28.86	2.67	0.48	67.50	33
263	24	19	306	583	889	34.42	27.44	2.14	29.58	2.14	2.70	65.58	34
2,323	125	425	2,873	6,086	8,959	32.07	19.88	6.05	25.93	4.74	1.40	67.93	35
963	99	559	1,621	3,601	5,222	31.04	14.78	3.66	18.44	10.70	1.90	68.96	36
112	23	54	189	353	542	34.87	20.11	0.55	20.66	9.96	4.25	65.13	37
407	29	161	597	1,343	1,940	30.77	18.61	2.37	20.98	8.30	1.49	69.23	38
954	129	548	1,651	3,635	5,286	31.23	12.20	6.22	18.42	10.37	2.44	68.77	39
1,070	82	247	1,399	3,236	4,635	30.18	19.12	3.97	23.09	5.32	1.77	69.82	40
175	12	21	208	397	605	34.38	27.61	1.32	28.93	3.47	1.98	65.62	41
550	31	116	706	1,684	2,390	29.54	21.00	2.39	23.39	4.85	1.30	70.46	42
131	4	23	158	268	426	37.09	29.11	1.64	30.75	5.40	0.94	62.91	43
258	44	39	341	611	952	35.82	24.58	2.52	27.10	4.10	4.62	64.18	44
133	15	12	160	300	460	34.78	28.26	0.65	28.91	2.61	3.26	65.22	45
254	23	51	328	624	952	34.45	24.37	2.31	26.68	5.36	2.41	65.55	46
255	16	25	296	594	890	33.26	26.74	1.91	28.65	2.81	1.80	66.74	47
237	22	57	316	662	978	32.31	21.78	2.45	24.23	5.83	2.25	67.69	48
444	25	49	546	1,008	1,524	33.86	27.16	1.97	29.13	3.22	1.51	66.14	49
448	57	346	821	1,402	2,223	36.96	20.15	14.22	20.15	14.22	2.56	63.07	50
1,411	124	651	2,189	6,061	8,250	26.53	12.17	4.97	17.14	7.89	1.50	73.47	51
1,570	124	447	2,141	5,473	7,614	28.12	16.08	4.54	20.62	5.87	1.63	71.88	52
557	43	39	419	799	1,218	34.40	26.11	1.56	27.67	3.20	3.53	65.60	53
423	34	100	557	1,353	1,910	29.16	18.74	3.40	22.14	5.24	1.78	70.84	54
555	74	344	973	2,447	3,420	28.45	14.39	1.84	16.23	10.06	2.16	71.55	55

POLITICAL CONDITION: BY SEX — Concluded.

COUNTIES, CITIES, AND TOWNS.	MALE POPULATION 20 YEARS OF AGE AND OVER						PERCENTAGES OF MALE POPULATION 20 YEARS OF AGE AND OVER					
	Voters	Not Voters	Aliens	Total Ratable Polls	No Political Condition	Total Male Population 20 Years of Age and over	Ratable Polls	Native Born Voters	Foreign Born Naturalized Voters	Total Voters	Aliens	Not Political Condition
WORCESTER — Con.												
1 Templeton,	770	49	111	830	4	934	89.57	73.88	8.56	82.44	11.88	0.43
2 Upton,	519	43	52	614	4	618	99.35	77.35	6.63	83.98	8.41	0.65
3 Uxbridge,	743	79	395	1,127	5	1,132	99.56	56.72	8.92	65.64	26.94	0.44
4 Warren,	850	142	331	1,332	6	1,338	99.55	53.81	10.59	64.20	24.74	0.45
5 Webster,	1,248	148	802	2,198	13	2,211	99.41	38.47	18.27	56.44	36.27	0.59
6 Westborough,	1,128	193	167	1,488	194	1,682	88.47	57.25	9.81	67.06	9.93	11.53
7 West Boylston,	517	42	253	812	–	812	100.00	52.45	10.22	63.67	31.16	–
8 W. Brookfield,	407	30	31	468	4	472	99.15	74.15	12.08	86.23	6.57	0.85
9 Westminster,	354	34	35	423	2	425	99.53	77.41	5.88	83.26	8.23	0.47
10 Winchendon,	1,049	108	246	1,403	9	1,412	99.36	64.73	9.56	74.26	17.42	0.64
11 WORCESTER,	21,428	1,308	6,659	29,695	680	30,356	97.73	49.50	20.04	69.60	21.84	2.27
12 Ward 1,	2,788	217	758	3,763	1	3,764	99.97	55.95	18.44	74.07	20.14	0.03
13 Ward 2,	2,686	143	976	3,805	457	4,262	89.28	45.75	17.27	63.02	22.90	10.72
14 Ward 3,	2,635	547	1,496	4,438	230	4,668	95.07	37.08	20.45	57.53	32.02	4.93
15 Ward 4,	2,577	174	949	3,700	–	3,700	100.00	38.35	31.30	69.65	25.65	–
16 Ward 5,	2,646	325	1,606	4,580	1	4,584	99.98	29.60	28.16	57.76	35.12	0.02
17 Ward 6,	2,656	175	587	3,418	1	3,419	99.97	60.96	17.02	77.68	17.37	0.03
18 Ward 7,	2,554	182	367	3,163	–	3,163	100.00	68.68	13.63	82.31	11.83	–
19 Ward 8,	2,526	145	188	2,859	–	2,859	100.00	80.13	8.22	88.35	6.58	–

RECAPITULATION.

THE STATE, AND COUNTIES.	MALE POPULATION 20 YEARS OF AGE AND OVER						PERCENTAGES OF MALE POPULATION 20 YEARS OF AGE AND OVER					
	Voters	Not Voters	Aliens	Total Ratable Polls	No Political Condition	Total Male Population 20 Years of Age and Over	Ratable Polls	Native Born Voters	Foreign Born Naturalized Voters	Total Voters	Aliens	No Political Condition
1 THE STATE.	569,802	44,821	160,610	766,233	5,473	771,706	99.29	54.77	17.90	72.67	20.81	0.71
2 Barnstable,	7,620	455	790	8,874	63	8,937	99.30	80.35	4.92	85.27	8.94	0.70
3 Berkshire,	20,486	1,828	3,883	25,807	109	26,006	99.58	61.55	16.07	77.62	14.96	0.42
4 Bristol,	42,495	3,076	16,781	62,352	565	62,917	99.10	47.05	20.49	67.54	26.67	0.90
5 Dukes,	1,236	88	149	1,473	6	1,479	99.59	78.47	4.60	83.57	10.07	0.41
6 Essex,	77,282	5,396	22,384	105,026	775	105,804	99.27	56.75	16.29	73.04	21.16	0.73
7 Franklin,	10,332	784	1,716	12,832	50	12,882	99.61	69.88	10.32	80.20	13.32	0.39
8 Hampden,	31,568	2,960	10,854	45,382	199	45,584	99.56	52.68	16.58	69.26	23.81	0.44
9 Hampshire,	11,888	988	2,878	15,754	319	16,073	98.02	61.29	12.67	73.96	17.90	1.98
10 Middlesex,	109,577	9,310	31,723	150,610	836	151,446	99.45	53.98	18.37	72.35	20.95	0.55
11 Nantucket,	880	29	33	948	11	959	98.85	86.86	5.53	92.39	3.44	1.15
12 Norfolk,	31,565	2,186	7,369	41,120	137	41,257	99.67	59.59	16.92	76.51	17.86	0.33
13 Plymouth,	26,956	2,217	4,152	33,325	608	33,933	98.21	69.44	10.00	79.44	12.24	1.79
14 Suffolk,	123,102	9,268	37,006	169,496	527	170,023	99.69	49.26	23.14	72.40	21.82	0.31
15 Worcester,	65,169	6,236	20,796	93,141	1,268	94,409	98.66	54.33	15.69	70.02	22.03	1.34

POLITICAL CONDITION: BY SEX — Concluded.

TOTAL POPULATION. BOTH SEXES. ALL AGES						**PERCENTAGES OF TOTAL POPULATION**						
Voters	Not Voters	Aliens	Total Ratable Polls	No Political Condition	Total Population. Both Sexes. All Ages	Rata-ble Polls	Native Born Voters	Foreign Born Natural-ized Voters	Total Voters	Aliens	Not Voters	No Political Condition	
770	49	111	830	1,985	2,915	31.90	23.67	2.74	26.41	3.81	1.68	68.10	1
519	43	52	614	1,536	2,150	28.56	22.23	1.91	24.14	2.42	2.00	71.44	2
743	79	305	1,127	2,419	3,546	31.78	18.10	2.85	20.95	8.60	2.23	68.22	3
859	142	331	1,332	3,068	4,430	30.07	16.25	3.14	19.30	7.47	3.21	69.26	4
1,248	148	802	2,198	5,601	7,799	28.18	10.82	5.18	16.00	10.28	1.90	71.82	5
1,128	193	167	1,488	3,747	5,235	28.42	18.40	3.15	21.55	3.19	3.68	71.78	6
517	42	253	812	2,156	2,968	27.36	14.92	2.80	17.42	8.52	1.42	72.64	7
407	30	31	468	969	1,467	31.90	23.86	3.88	27.74	2.11	2.05	68.10	8
354	34	35	423	892	1,315	32.17	25.02	1.90	26.92	2.66	2.59	67.83	9
1,049	108	246	1,403	3,087	4,490	31.25	20.35	3.01	23.36	5.48	2.41	68.75	10
21,128	1,908	6,630	29,666	68,101	18,767	30.04	15.23	6.16	21.39	6.72	1.95	69.90	11
2,758	217	758	3,768	7,337	11,105	33.90	18.87	6.25	25.12	6.83	1.95	66.10	12
2,686	143	976	3,805	9,284	13,089	29.07	14.90	5.62	20.52	7.46	1.09	70.46	13
2,895	347	1,196	4,468	10,169	14,637	30.52	11.83	6.58	18.41	8.17	3.74	69.08	14
2,577	174	949	3,700	9,791	13,491	27.43	10.52	8.58	19.10	7.04	1.29	72.57	15
2,646	325	1,609	4,580	10,705	15,285	29.96	8.87	8.44	17.31	10.53	2.12	70.04	16
2,656	175	587	3,418	8,417	11,835	28.88	17.52	4.92	22.44	4.96	1.48	71.12	17
2,654	182	307	3,103	7,249	10,352	29.97	20.38	4.09	24.97	3.54	1.70	70.03	18
2,526	145	188	2,859	6,119	8,978	31.84	25.52	2.62	28.14	2.09	1.61	68.16	19

RECAPITULATION.

TOTAL POPULATION. BOTH SEXES. ALL AGES						**PERCENTAGES OF TOTAL POPULATION**						
Voters	Not Voters	Aliens	Total Ratable Polls	No Political Condition	Total Population. Both Sexes. All Ages	Rata-ble Polls	Native Born Voters	Foreign Born Natural-ized Voters	Total Voters	Aliens	Not Voters	No Political Condition	
500,802	44,821	160,610	766,233	1,733,950	2,500,183	30.65	16.90	5.53	22.43	6.43	1.79	69.55	1
7,620	455	799	8,874	18,780	27,654	32.09	25.97	1.59	27.56	2.88	1.65	67.91	2
20,186	1,828	3,883	25,897	60,395	86,292	30.01	18.55	4.84	23.39	4.50	2.12	69.99	3
42,495	3,076	16,781	62,352	156,667	219,019	28.47	13.52	5.88	19.40	7.66	1.41	71.53	4
1,236	88	149	1,473	2,765	4,238	34.76	27.56	1.69	29.16	3.52	2.08	65.24	5
77,282	5,366	22,281	105,029	225,364	330,393	31.79	18.17	5.22	23.39	6.77	1.65	68.21	6
10,832	784	1,716	12,832	27,313	40,145	31.96	22.43	3.31	25.74	4.27	1.95	68.04	7
31,568	2,980	10,854	45,382	107,556	152,868	29.67	15.70	4.94	20.64	7.10	1.96	70.33	8
11,888	988	2,878	15,754	38,956	54,710	28.80	18.01	3.72	21.73	5.26	1.81	71.20	9
109,577	9,310	31,723	150,610	348,607	486,217	30.47	16.38	5.57	21.95	6.35	1.87	69.83	10
886	29	33	948	2,068	3,016	31.43	27.62	1.76	29.38	1.09	0.96	68.57	11
31,565	2,186	7,369	41,120	93,699	134,819	30.50	18.23	5.18	23.41	5.47	1.62	69.50	12
26,956	2,217	4,152	33,325	68,173	101,498	32.83	23.22	3.34	26.56	4.09	2.18	67.17	13
123,102	9,208	37,096	169,406	370,303	539,709	31.40	15.52	7.29	22.81	6.87	1.72	68.00	14
96,109	6,236	20,796	93,141	213,304	306,445	30.39	16.74	4.83	21.57	6.79	2.03	69.61	15

POLITICAL CONDITION: BY AGE PERIODS.

POLITICAL CONDITION: BY AGE PERIODS.

Counties, Cities, Towns, and Voting Precincts.	Ratable Polls (Not Voters)	Ratable Polls and Native-Born Voters	Ratable Polls and Foreign-Born Naturalized Voters	Ratable Polls and Aliens	No Political Condition	Total Male Population 20 Years of Age and Over
BARNSTABLE.						
Barnstable, . . .	50	1,175	45	41	4	1,347
20 to 29 years, . .	38	216	1	17	-	272
30 to 39 years, . .	4	254	6	13	-	277
40 to 49 years, . .	3	216	9	6	-	234
50 to 59 years, . .	4	198	6	4	-	212
60 to 79 years, . .	1	250	23	1	4	288
80 years and over, .	-	32	-	-	-	32
Bourne, ...	54	427	7	7	-	17
20 to 29 years, . .	25	78	1	10	-	114
30 to 39 years, . .	13	95	2	8	-	117
40 to 49 years, . .	12	81	1	6	-	100
50 to 59 years, . .	2	69	2	2	-	75
60 to 79 years, . .	2	97	2	1	-	102
80 years and over, .	-	6	-	-	-	6
Age unknown, . .	-	1	-	-	-	1
Brewster, ...	4	24	15	15	5	230
20 to 29 years, . .	2	37	-	3	1	43
30 to 39 years, . .	1	40	1	7	2	60
40 to 49 years, . .	1	48	2	2	-	53
50 to 59 years, . .	-	48	3	1	-	52
60 to 79 years, . .	-	61	9	2	1	73
80 years and over, .	-	7	-	-	1	8
Age unknown, . .	-	1	-	-	-	1
Chatham, ...	11	587	15	2	2	618
20 to 29 years, . .	10	118	-	-	-	128
30 to 39 years, . .	1	141	2	1	-	145
40 to 49 years, . .	-	118	5	-	-	123
50 to 59 years, . .	-	96	4	1	1	102
60 to 79 years, . .	-	114	6	-	1	121
80 years and over, .	-	10	1	-	-	11
Dennis, ...	26	718	24	22	7	796
20 to 29 years, . .	17	94	1	1	1	114
30 to 39 years, . .	7	134	2	5	-	148
40 to 49 years, . .	-	140	3	7	2	152
50 to 59 years, . .	1	143	5	-	-	154
60 to 79 years, . .	1	162	8	7	2	180
80 years and over, .	-	25	1	-	2	28
Eastham, ...	15	130	2	1	1	139
20 to 29 years, . .	8	25	-	1	-	34
30 to 39 years, . .	4	34	-	-	-	38
40 to 49 years, . .	1	20	-	-	-	21
50 to 59 years, . .	2	34	1	-	-	37
60 to 79 years, . .	-	36	1	-	1	38
80 years and over, .	-	1	-	-	-	1
Falmouth, ...	46	677	44	98	4	829
20 to 29 years, . .	35	122	4	33	1	195
30 to 39 years, . .	5	135	17	28	1	186
40 to 49 years, . .	3	134	14	26	-	177
50 to 59 years, . .	2	120	6	8	-	136

POLITICAL CONDITION: BY AGE PERIODS — Continued.

COUNTIES, CITIES, TOWNS, AND AGE PERIODS.	Ratable Polls (Not Voters.)	Ratable Polls and Native Born Voters.	Ratable Polls and Foreign Born Naturalized Voters.	Ratable Polls and Aliens.	No Political Condition.	Total Male Population 20 Years of Age and over.
BARNSTABLE — Con.						
Falmouth — Con.						
60 to 79 years,	1	149	3	2	2	157
80 years and over,	-	17	-	1	-	18
Harwich,	104	680	13	44	8	849
20 to 29 years,	44	98	-	11	1	154
30 to 39 years,	12	128	1	13	-	154
40 to 49 years,	20	122	4	9	1	156
50 to 59 years,	13	139	2	8	1	163
60 to 79 years,	15	176	4	2	4	201
80 years and over,	-	17	2	1	1	21
Mashpee,	5	89	1	3	-	98
20 to 29 years,	4	29	-	1	-	34
30 to 39 years,	1	22	-	2	-	25
40 to 49 years,	-	11	-	-	-	11
50 to 59 years,	-	19	-	-	-	19
60 to 79 years,	-	8	1	-	-	9
Orleans,	30	207	5	18	-	260
20 to 29 years,	13	42	-	2	-	57
30 to 39 years,	6	72	1	4	-	83
40 to 49 years,	4	51	2	4	-	61
50 to 59 years,	5	60	1	3	-	69
60 to 79 years,	2	97	1	3	-	103
80 years and over,	-	15	-	2	-	17
Provincetown,	52	733	187	423	12	1,407
20 to 29 years,	48	177	16	134	2	377
30 to 39 years,	1	148	39	125	2	315
40 to 49 years,	1	133	60	78	3	275
50 to 59 years,	1	113	34	53	3	204
60 to 79 years,	1	149	34	31	2	217
80 years and over,	-	13	4	1	-	18
Age unknown,	-	-	-	1	-	1
Sandwich,	26	382	55	83	10	506
20 to 29 years,	16	76	3	4	-	99
30 to 39 years,	2	73	6	6	-	87
40 to 49 years,	5	60	11	5	1	80
50 to 59 years,	4	69	10	8	5	96
60 to 79 years,	1	95	21	7	4	128
80 years and over,	-	9	4	1	-	14
Age unknown,	-	-	-	2	-	2
Truro,	2	180	8	46	4	240
20 to 29 years,	1	40	-	11	1	53
30 to 39 years,	1	26	1	8	-	36
40 to 49 years,	-	35	1	12	-	48
50 to 59 years,	-	30	2	7	2	41
60 to 79 years,	-	46	4	8	-	58
80 years and over,	-	3	-	-	1	4
Wellfleet,	13	274	10	12	2	311
20 to 29 years,	7	23	1	-	-	31
30 to 39 years,	3	47	1	3	-	54
40 to 49 years,	1	63	3	4	-	71
50 to 59 years,	-	44	1	1	-	46
60 to 79 years,	2	87	4	4	2	99
80 years and over,	-	9	-	-	-	9
Age unknown,	-	1	-	-	-	1
Yarmouth,	17	521	11	14	4	567
20 to 29 years,	15	97	-	3	-	115

POLITICAL CONDITION: BY AGE PERIODS — Continued.

COUNTIES, CITIES, TOWNS, AND AGE PERIODS.	Ratable Polls (Not Voters)	Ratable Polls and Native Born Voters	Ratable Polls and Foreign Born Naturalized Voters	Ratable Polls and Aliens	No Political Condition	Total Male Population 20 Years of Age and Over
BARNSTABLE — Con.						
Yarmouth — Con.						
30 to 39 years,	1	97	1	6	–	105
40 to 49 years,	–	98	1	1	1	101
50 to 59 years,	1	87	1	3	–	92
60 to 79 years,	–	120	8	2	2	151
80 years and over,	–	21	–	–	1	22
Age unknown,	–	1	–	–	–	1
BERKSHIRE.						
Adams, .	115	952	518	472	5	2,060
20 to 29 years,	97	335	93	127	1	653
30 to 39 years,	7	266	128	126	–	527
40 to 49 years,	7	174	124	96	–	401
50 to 59 years,	4	89	100	59	–	252
60 to 79 years,	–	80	73	63	2	218
80 years and over,	–	8	–	1	–	9
Alford, .	5	83	7	4	–	99
20 to 29 years,	2	17	1	1	–	21
30 to 39 years,	2	9	–	1	–	12
40 to 49 years,	1	15	2	–	–	18
50 to 59 years,	–	17	3	2	–	22
60 to 79 years,	–	24	1	–	–	25
80 years and over,	–	1	–	–	–	1
Becket, .	29	183	28	55	4	299
20 to 29 years,	15	45	–	8	1	69
30 to 39 years,	7	36	4	17	–	64
40 to 49 years,	4	25	4	14	–	47
50 to 59 years,	1	37	5	3	–	46
60 to 79 years,	2	36	14	10	1	63
80 years and over,	–	4	1	3	2	10
Cheshire, .	20	275	44	55	7	401
20 to 29 years,	14	67	3	15	–	99
30 to 39 years,	5	54	2	13	–	75
40 to 49 years,	–	55	11	6	–	72
50 to 59 years,	1	38	8	7	–	54
60 to 79 years,	–	58	18	10	6	92
80 years and over,	–	3	2	3	1	9
Clarksburg, .	44	186	28	63	–	311
20 to 29 years,	18	52	2	16	–	88
30 to 39 years,	11	45	4	20	–	81
40 to 49 years,	8	25	10	7	–	51
50 to 59 years,	3	30	7	4	–	44
60 to 79 years,	4	31	4	6	–	45
80 years and over,	–	1	1	–	–	2
Dalton, .	59	625	144	50	2	880
20 to 29 years,	37	217	12	9	–	275
30 to 39 years,	8	183	27	8	1	227
40 to 49 years,	8	105	42	8	–	163
50 to 59 years,	5	62	31	17	–	115
60 to 79 years,	–	35	50	7	1	91
80 years and over,	1	5	2	1	–	9
Egremont, .	30	227	8	7	1	273
20 to 29 years,	11	43	–	1	–	55
30 to 39 years,	7	54	1	5	–	65
40 to 49 years,	7	49	2	–	–	58
50 to 59 years,	2	38	1	2	–	43

POLITICAL CONDITION: BY AGE PERIODS — Continued.

Counties, Cities, Towns, and Age Periods.	Ratable Polls (Not Voters)	Ratable Polls and Native Born Voters	Ratable Polls and Foreign Born Naturalized Voters	Ratable Polls and Aliens	No Political Condition	Total Male Population 20 Years of Age and Over
BERKSHIRE — Con.						
Egremont — Con.						
60 to 79 years,	3	40	4	-	-	47
80 years and over,	-	3	-	1	1	5
Florida,	10	86	13	32	-	141
20 to 29 years,	6	21	2	7	-	36
30 to 39 years,	2	22	3	11	-	38
40 to 49 years,	1	10	2	8	-	21
50 to 59 years,	-	22	3	4	-	29
60 to 79 years,	1	10	5	1	-	15
80 years and over,	-	1	-	1	-	2
Great Barrington,	113	1,044	182	178	-	1,517
20 to 29 years,	74	316	16	48	-	454
30 to 39 years,	17	242	29	44	-	332
40 to 49 years,	9	182	38	38	-	267
50 to 59 years,	3	125	34	28	-	190
60 to 79 years,	10	155	62	19	-	246
80 years and over,	-	24	3	1	-	28
Hancock,	26	117	4	8	-	155
20 to 29 years,	12	16	-	4	-	32
30 to 39 years,	6	22	-	2	-	30
40 to 49 years,	5	28	2	1	-	36
50 to 59 years,	-	20	1	1	-	22
60 to 79 years,	3	24	1	-	-	28
80 years and over,	-	7	-	-	-	7
Hinsdale,	32	289	75	91	4	491
20 to 29 years,	24	121	9	23	1	178
30 to 39 years,	6	53	15	21	1	96
40 to 49 years,	-	43	12	14	1	70
50 to 59 years,	2	34	21	16	-	73
60 to 79 years,	-	35	17	16	1	69
80 years and over,	-	3	1	1	-	5
Lanesborough,	17	205	38	17	3	280
20 to 29 years,	9	62	2	4	-	77
30 to 39 years,	3	37	5	6	1	50
40 to 49 years,	1	24	7	3	-	35
50 to 59 years,	2	36	8	1	1	48
60 to 79 years,	2	38	18	2	1	61
80 years and over,	-	8	-	1	-	9
Lee,	128	751	207	182	8	1,276
20 to 29 years,	70	227	8	39	-	344
30 to 39 years,	28	180	51	54	1	294
40 to 49 years,	16	132	55	32	1	236
50 to 59 years,	7	95	42	23	1	169
60 to 79 years,	7	102	65	13	3	190
80 years and over,	-	14	6	1	2	23
Lenox,	27	522	151	238	1	939
20 to 29 years,	21	188	13	94	-	316
30 to 39 years,	3	142	40	69	-	254
40 to 49 years,	2	91	35	41	-	169
50 to 59 years,	-	57	33	18	-	108
60 to 79 years,	1	43	30	15	1	90
80 years and over,	-	1	-	1	-	2
Monterey,	11	109	11	11	-	142
20 to 29 years,	6	21	-	2	-	29
30 to 39 years,	1	25	1	4	-	31
40 to 49 years,	3	15	3	2	-	23

POLITICAL CONDITION: BY AGE PERIODS — Continued.

COUNTIES, CITIES, TOWNS, AND AGE PERIODS.	Ratable Polls (Not Voters)	Ratable Polls and Native-Born Voters	Ratable Polls and Foreign Born Naturalized Voters	Ratable Polls and Aliens	No Political Condition	Total Male Population 20 Years of Age and Over
BERKSHIRE — Con.						
Monterey — Con.						
50 to 59 years, ...	-	20	2	1	-	23
60 to 79 years, ...	1	22	4	2	-	29
80 years and over, . . .	-	6	1	-	-	7
Mount Washington, ...	1	32	1	7	1	42
20 to 29 years, ...	-	5	-	1	-	6
30 to 39 years, ...	-	8	1	2	-	11
40 to 49 years, ...	-	4	-	4	-	8
50 to 59 years, ...	-	6	-	-	1	7
60 to 79 years, ...	1	6	-	-	-	7
80 years and over, . . .	-	3	-	-	-	3
New Ashford, ...	4	34	3	1	-	42
20 to 29 years, ...	1	4	1	-	-	6
30 to 39 years, ...	2	9	-	-	-	11
40 to 49 years, ...	1	4	-	1	-	6
50 to 59 years, ...	-	4	2	-	-	6
60 to 79 years, ...	-	13	-	-	-	13
New Marlborough, ...	10	336	42	35	2	425
20 to 29 years, ...	10	80	1	9	-	100
30 to 39 years, ...	-	74	2	13	-	89
40 to 49 years, ...	-	63	10	6	-	79
50 to 59 years, ...	-	45	9	3	-	57
60 to 79 years, ...	-	65	19	4	1	89
80 years and over, . . .	-	9	1	-	1	11
NORTH ADAMS, ...	348	2,992	1,073	1,124	22	5,559
20 to 29 years, ...	277	1,113	196	402	1	1,989
30 to 39 years, ...	34	776	297	306	2	1,415
40 to 49 years, ...	22	512	235	194	3	966
50 to 59 years, ...	10	314	216	136	4	680
60 to 79 years, ...	4	253	123	83	11	474
80 years and over, . . .	1	24	5	3	1	34
Age unknown, ...	-	-	1	-	-	1
Otis, ...	15	161	1	5	1	183
20 to 29 years, ...	8	28	-	1	-	37
30 to 39 years, ...	3	29	-	2	-	34
40 to 49 years, ...	3	24	-	-	-	27
50 to 59 years, ...	-	28	1	-	-	29
60 to 79 years, ...	-	49	-	2	-	51
80 years and over, . . .	1	3	-	-	1	5
Peru, ...	11	71	8	8	1	99
20 to 29 years, ...	6	14	1	1	-	22
30 to 39 years, ...	3	16	-	-	-	19
40 to 49 years, ...	1	12	2	2	-	17
50 to 59 years, ...	1	12	3	3	-	19
60 to 79 years, ...	-	13	2	2	-	17
80 years and over, . . .	-	4	-	-	1	5
PITTSFIELD, ...	424	3,681	1,120	806	28	6,059
20 to 29 years, ...	301	1,312	149	280	4	2,046
30 to 39 years, ...	68	1,030	218	212	6	1,534
40 to 49 years, ...	35	642	262	157	3	1,099
50 to 59 years, ...	11	359	219	86	2	677
60 to 79 years, ...	9	311	254	67	11	652
80 years and over, . . .	-	27	18	2	2	49
Age unknown, ...	-	-	-	2	-	2
Richmond, ...	17	124	46	27	-	214
20 to 29 years, ...	9	23	3	2	-	37

POLITICAL CONDITION: BY AGE PERIODS — Continued.

COUNTIES, CITIES, TOWNS, AND AGE PERIODS.	Ratable Polls (Not Voters)	Ratable Polls and Native Born Voters	Ratable Polls and Foreign Born Naturalized Voters	Ratable Polls and Aliens	No Political Condition	Total Male Population 20 Years of Age and Over
BERKSHIRE — Con.						
Richmond — Con.						
30 to 39 years,	6	30	9	11	-	56
40 to 49 years,	-	21	7	6	-	34
50 to 59 years,	1	15	10	2	-	28
60 to 79 years,	1	32	15	6	-	54
80 years and over,	-	3	2	-	-	5
Sandisfield,	22	225	15	8	1	271
20 to 29 years,	11	49	2	2	-	64
30 to 39 years,	6	45	-	3	-	54
40 to 49 years,	3	39	3	-	-	45
50 to 59 years,	1	34	7	3	-	45
60 to 79 years,	1	54	3	-	1	59
80 years and over,	-	4	-	-	-	4
Savoy,	15	144	10	8	1	178
20 to 29 years,	9	31	-	2	-	42
30 to 39 years,	2	26	3	4	-	35
40 to 49 years,	2	22	-	1	-	25
50 to 59 years,	-	20	3	1	-	24
60 to 79 years,	2	39	4	-	-	45
80 years and over,	-	6	-	-	1	7
Sheffield,	52	445	49	40	4	590
20 to 29 years,	26	109	1	12	1	149
30 to 39 years,	10	83	3	5	2	103
40 to 49 years,	8	82	12	8	-	110
50 to 59 years,	2	63	17	5	-	87
60 to 79 years,	5	99	13	8	-	125
80 years and over,	-	9	3	-	1	13
Age unknown,	1	-	-	2	-	3
Stockbridge,	23	447	91	69	7	637
20 to 29 years,	19	124	5	21	-	169
30 to 39 years,	-	110	15	21	1	147
40 to 49 years,	3	85	9	14	-	111
50 to 59 years,	1	55	21	8	-	85
60 to 79 years,	-	67	41	5	5	118
80 years and over,	-	6	-	-	1	7
Tyringham,	12	99	3	7	3	124
20 to 29 years,	5	21	-	2	-	28
30 to 39 years,	1	21	1	1	-	24
40 to 49 years,	3	20	-	-	-	23
50 to 59 years,	2	15	1	1	-	19
60 to 79 years,	1	22	1	3	2	29
80 years and over,	-	-	-	-	1	1
Washington,	9	88	17	19	-	133
20 to 29 years,	3	23	-	4	-	30
30 to 39 years,	2	18	4	2	-	26
40 to 49 years,	2	19	1	5	-	27
50 to 59 years,	-	8	4	3	-	15
60 to 79 years,	2	19	6	4	-	31
80 years and over,	-	1	2	1	-	4
West Stockbridge,	15	263	64	43	1	386
20 to 29 years,	11	54	4	6	-	75
30 to 39 years,	1	59	7	3	-	70
40 to 49 years,	2	54	13	3	-	72
50 to 59 years,	1	42	13	13	-	69
60 to 79 years,	-	47	26	15	1	89
80 years and over,	-	7	1	2	-	10
Age unknown,	-	-	-	1	-	1

POLITICAL CONDITION: BY AGE PERIODS — Continued.

COUNTIES, CITIES, TOWNS, AND AGE PERIODS.	Ratable Polls (Not Voters)	Ratable Polls and Native Born Voters	Ratable Polls and Foreign Born Naturalized Voters	Ratable Polls and Aliens	No Political Condition	Total Male Population 20 Years of Age and Over
BERKSHIRE — Con.						
Williamstown, ...	165	1,067	167	213	4	1,616
20 to 29 years, ...	146	426	33	77	1	683
30 to 39 years, ...	9	240	36	59	-	344
40 to 49 years, ...	6	167	31	33	1	238
50 to 59 years, ...	1	118	32	20	1	172
60 to 79 years, ...	3	103	34	20	1	161
80 years and over, . . .	-	13	1	4	-	18
Windsor, ...	19	144	11	10	-	184
20 to 29 years, ...	9	32	-	3	-	44
30 to 39 years, ...	4	36	1	4	-	45
40 to 49 years, ...	2	24	-	1	-	27
50 to 59 years, ...	1	16	5	2	-	24
60 to 79 years, ...	3	32	5	-	-	40
80 years and over, . . .	-	4	-	-	-	4
BRISTOL.						
Acushnet, ...	27	302	13	33	6	381
20 to 29 years, ...	25	54	-	11	2	92
30 to 39 years, ...	1	66	1	10	2	80
40 to 49 years, ...	-	45	5	7	-	57
50 to 59 years, ...	1	56	3	2	1	63
60 to 79 years, ...	-	68	3	2	1	74
80 years and over, . . .	-	13	1	1	-	15
Attleborough, ...	155	1,508	306	488	5	2,462
20 to 29 years, ...	96	425	69	146	-	736
30 to 39 years, ...	19	417	82	142	-	660
40 to 49 years, ...	13	282	62	104	1	462
50 to 59 years, ...	7	187	54	51	1	300
60 to 79 years, ...	4	174	38	44	3	263
80 years and over, . . .	-	22	1	1	-	24
Age unknown, ...	16	1	-	-	-	17
Berkley, ...	11	259	17	36	2	325
20 to 29 years, ...	10	39	1	20	-	70
30 to 39 years, ...	-	48	4	15	-	67
40 to 49 years, ...	-	52	7	-	-	59
50 to 59 years, ...	-	43	2	1	-	46
60 to 79 years, ...	1	70	2	-	2	75
80 years and over, . . .	-	7	1	-	-	8
Dartmouth, ...	61	750	61	148	8	1,028
20 to 29 years, ...	39	143	8	70	2	262
30 to 39 years, ...	9	155	15	37	-	196
40 to 49 years, ...	4	147	8	21	-	180
50 to 59 years, ...	5	121	10	14	-	150
60 to 79 years, ...	4	188	18	6	5	221
80 years and over, . . .	-	15	2	-	1	18
Age unknown, ...	-	1	-	-	-	1
Dighton, ...	38	442	28	83	1	592
20 to 29 years, ...	37	89	5	42	1	174
30 to 39 years, ...	-	94	2	21	-	117
40 to 49 years, ...	1	77	6	10	-	94
50 to 59 years, ...	-	83	9	3	-	95
60 to 79 years, ...	-	83	6	7	-	96
80 years and over, . . .	-	16	-	-	-	16
Easton, ...	69	842	282	214	8	1,415
20 to 29 years, ...	48	237	32	81	-	398
30 to 39 years, ...	6	197	61	60	2	326

POLITICAL CONDITION: BY AGE PERIODS — Continued.

Counties, Cities, Towns, and Age Periods.	Ratable Polls (Not Voters)	Ratable Polls and Native Born Voters	Ratable Polls and Foreign Born Naturalized Voters	Ratable Polls and Aliens	No Political Condition	Total Male Population 20 Years of Age and Over
BRISTOL. — Con.						
Easton — Con.						
40 to 49 years,	4	136	83	35	-	258
50 to 59 years,	4	111	56	21	1	193
60 to 79 years,	7	149	50	16	4	226
80 years and over,	-	12	-	1	1	14
Fairhaven,	34	840	53	126	6	1,059
20 to 29 years,	32	179	4	67	-	282
30 to 39 years,	-	170	16	23	-	209
40 to 49 years,	-	159	14	23	2	198
50 to 59 years,	-	119	9	7	1	136
60 to 79 years,	2	195	9	4	2	212
80 years and over,	-	18	1	2	1	22
Fall River,	1,035	7,421	7,145	8,166	60	23,827
20 to 29 years,	945	3,085	1,443	3,157	6	8,636
30 to 39 years,	42	1,977	1,930	2,099	9	6,057
40 to 49 years,	26	1,293	1,655	1,452	6	4,342
50 to 59 years,	15	633	1,297	892	8	2,845
60 to 79 years,	3	477	795	541	20	1,836
80 years and over,	1	45	24	17	11	98
Age unknown,	3	1	1	8	-	13
Freetown,	20	364	26	69	3	482
20 to 29 years,	14	81	1	25	-	121
30 to 39 years,	1	76	2	16	-	95
40 to 49 years,	3	70	7	16	1	97
50 to 59 years,	2	56	8	5	-	71
60 to 79 years,	-	69	6	7	1	83
80 years and over,	-	12	2	-	1	15
Mansfield,	70	849	84	143	4	1,150
20 to 29 years,	42	190	6	41	-	279
30 to 39 years,	11	232	17	39	-	299
40 to 49 years,	8	179	15	32	1	235
50 to 59 years,	4	95	22	15	-	136
60 to 79 years,	5	139	23	15	1	183
80 years and over,	-	14	1	1	2	18
New Bedford,	764	7,232	2,884	4,938	38	15,836
20 to 29 years,	617	2,145	549	1,988	2	5,301
30 to 39 years,	69	1,843	838	1,356	5	4,111
40 to 49 years,	46	1,273	624	845	5	2,793
50 to 59 years,	20	930	512	459	8	1,929
60 to 79 years,	11	903	344	280	17	1,555
80 years and over,	-	116	17	8	1	142
Age unknown,	1	2	-	2	-	5
North Attleborough,	110	1,188	553	265	9	1,925
20 to 29 years,	92	297	48	82	-	519
30 to 39 years,	9	368	76	70	2	525
40 to 49 years,	4	220	76	59	1	360
50 to 59 years,	4	140	86	30	2	262
60 to 79 years,	1	153	65	22	3	244
80 years and over,	-	10	2	1	1	14
Age unknown,	-	-	-	1	-	1
Norton,	26	408	35	51	3	523
20 to 29 years,	12	90	2	16	1	121
30 to 39 years,	10	85	5	20	-	120
40 to 49 years,	3	82	3	4	-	92
50 to 59 years,	-	66	11	7	-	84

POLITICAL CONDITION: BY AGE PERIODS — Continued.

Counties, Cities, Towns, and Age Periods.	Ratable Polls (Not Voters)	Ratable Polls and Native Born Voters	Ratable Polls and Foreign Born Naturalized Voters	Ratable Polls and Aliens	No Political Condition	Total Male Population Years of Age and Over
BRISTOL — Con.						
Norton — Con.						
60 to 79 years,	-	74	14	4	2	94
80 years and over,	1	11	-	-	-	12
Raynham,	30	382	20	64	2	498
20 to 29 years,	14	76	-	21	1	112
30 to 39 years,	7	70	5	16	-	98
40 to 49 years,	3	72	5	17	-	97
50 to 59 years,	5	65	6	6	-	82
60 to 79 years,	1	84	3	4	1	93
80 years and over,	-	15	1	-	-	16
Rehoboth,	53	491	28	81	3	656
20 to 29 years,	34	105	-	39	-	178
30 to 39 years,	7	107	4	16	1	135
40 to 49 years,	4	78	1	15	-	98
50 to 59 years,	2	73	9	6	-	90
60 to 79 years,	4	112	12	5	2	135
80 years and over,	-	15	2	-	-	17
Age unknown,	2	1	-	-	-	3
Seekonk,	62	318	28	106	4	518
20 to 29 years,	46	66	4	55	-	171
30 to 39 years,	7	66	9	27	-	109
40 to 49 years,	4	61	3	11	-	79
50 to 59 years,	2	47	7	4	1	61
60 to 79 years,	3	72	5	8	1	89
80 years and over,	-	6	-	-	2	8
Age unknown,	-	-	-	1	-	1
Somerset,	29	426	55	154	4	678
20 to 29 years,	22	103	-	55	-	180
30 to 39 years,	8	102	4	31	-	145
40 to 49 years,	4	71	6	18	-	99
50 to 59 years,	2	64	15	5	-	86
60 to 79 years,	1	81	13	10	4	109
80 years and over,	-	4	2	-	-	6
Age unknown,	2	1	15	35	-	53
Swansea,	92	335	50	83	1	561
20 to 29 years,	22	76	6	54	-	158
30 to 39 years,	64	36	17	14	-	131
40 to 49 years,	3	72	7	6	-	88
50 to 59 years,	3	54	6	5	-	68
60 to 79 years,	-	86	12	3	1	102
80 years and over,	-	11	2	1	-	14
TAUNTON,	353	4,612	1,381	1,400	395	8,141
20 to 29 years,	273	1,387	171	534	58	2,423
30 to 39 years,	29	1,156	325	390	91	1,991
40 to 49 years,	19	908	316	215	91	1,549
50 to 59 years,	12	581	303	143	70	1,109
60 to 79 years,	17	523	250	106	76	972
80 years and over,	1	57	14	6	9	87
Age unknown,	2	-	2	6	-	10
Westport,	27	657	40	133	3	860
20 to 29 years,	20	110	5	59	1	195
30 to 39 years,	6	120	13	23	-	162
40 to 49 years,	-	131	6	25	-	162
50 to 59 years,	1	108	7	12	1	129
60 to 79 years,	-	172	6	10	-	188
80 years and over,	-	16	2	1	1	20
Age unknown,	-	-	1	3	-	4

POLITICAL CONDITION: BY AGE PERIODS — Continued.

COUNTIES, CITIES, TOWNS, AND AGE PERIODS.	Ratable Polls (Not Voters)	Ratable Polls and Native Born Voters	Ratable Polls and Foreign Born Naturalized Voters	Ratable Polls and Aliens	No Political Condition	Total Male Population 20 Years of Age and Over
DUKES.						
Chilmark,	13	107	-	1	2	123
20 to 29 years,	6	14	-	1	-	21
30 to 39 years,	3	25	-	-	-	28
40 to 49 years,	-	24	-	-	-	24
50 to 59 years,	1	15	-	-	-	16
60 to 79 years,	2	24	-	-	-	26
80 years and over,	-	5	-	-	2	7
Age unknown,	1	-	-	-	-	1
Cottage City,	24	225	27	60	-	336
20 to 29 years,	18	42	1	27	-	88
30 to 39 years,	2	44	6	16	-	68
40 to 49 years,	2	41	7	13	-	63
50 to 59 years,	1	48	7	2	-	58
60 to 79 years,	1	47	6	2	-	56
80 years and over,	-	3	-	-	-	3
Edgartown,	16	325	15	36	2	394
20 to 29 years,	6	47	5	16	-	74
30 to 39 years,	3	68	1	7	-	79
40 to 49 years,	1	63	2	5	1	72
50 to 59 years,	3	52	5	3	-	63
60 to 79 years,	3	84	2	5	-	94
80 years and over,	-	11	-	-	1	12
Gay Head,	1	40	1	2	-	44
20 to 29 years,	1	10	1	-	-	12
30 to 39 years,	-	9	-	-	-	9
40 to 49 years,	-	11	-	-	-	11
50 to 59 years,	-	5	-	2	-	7
60 to 79 years,	-	4	-	-	-	4
80 years and over,	-	1	-	-	-	1
Gosnold,	15	41	5	11	-	72
20 to 29 years,	7	8	3	6	-	24
30 to 39 years,	4	7	1	2	-	14
40 to 49 years,	2	11	-	3	-	16
50 to 59 years,	1	10	1	-	-	12
60 to 79 years,	1	5	-	-	-	6
Tisbury,	16	286	15	24	1	342
20 to 29 years,	9	52	1	13	1	76
30 to 39 years,	3	59	5	4	-	71
40 to 49 years,	-	55	3	3	-	61
50 to 59 years,	1	55	2	4	-	62
60 to 79 years,	3	58	3	-	-	64
80 years and over,	-	7	1	-	-	8
West Tisbury,	3	144	5	15	1	168
20 to 29 years,	2	22	-	11	-	35
30 to 39 years,	-	22	3	-	-	25
40 to 49 years,	1	30	2	3	-	36
50 to 59 years,	-	24	-	-	-	24
60 to 79 years,	-	42	-	1	1	44
80 years and over,	-	4	-	-	-	4
ESSEX.						
Amesbury,	168	1,875	435	588	5	3,071
20 to 29 years,	101	555	62	221	-	949
30 to 39 years,	18	454	120	177	1	770
40 to 49 years,	12	358	89	89	1	549
50 to 59 years,	6	237	93	62	1	399

POLITICAL CONDITION: BY AGE PERIODS — Continued.

COUNTIES, CITIES, TOWNS, AND AGE PERIODS.	Ratable Polls (Not Voters)	Ratable Polls and Native Born Voters	Ratable Polls and Foreign Born Naturalized Voters	Ratable Polls and Aliens	No Political Condition	Total Male Population 20 Years of Age and Over
ESSEX — Con.						
Amesbury — Con.						
60 to 79 years,	3	227	65	26	–	341
80 years and over,	–	24	6	3	2	35
Age unknown,	28	–	–	–	–	28
Andover,	116	1,003	302	280	8	1,709
20 to 29 years,	95	296	35	103	–	529
30 to 39 years,	14	234	57	68	3	376
40 to 49 years,	3	178	72	37	2	292
50 to 59 years,	2	130	64	41	–	237
60 to 79 years,	2	139	71	30	3	245
80 years and over,	–	26	3	1	–	30
BEVERLY,	248	2,691	343	500	15	3,797
20 to 29 years,	155	727	43	202	2	1,129
30 to 39 years,	30	716	82	136	1	965
40 to 49 years,	14	479	73	72	4	642
50 to 59 years,	6	394	79	39	2	520
60 to 79 years,	43	336	62	20	5	466
80 years and over,	–	39	4	4	1	48
Age unknown,	–	–	–	27	–	27
Boxford,	17	181	10	23	3	234
20 to 29 years,	9	29	–	7	–	45
30 to 39 years,	1	30	1	4	1	37
40 to 49 years,	4	36	6	3	–	49
50 to 59 years,	3	25	1	5	1	35
60 to 79 years,	–	53	2	4	–	59
80 years and over,	–	8	–	–	1	9
Bradford,	95	1,030	129	174	–	1,428
20 to 29 years,	52	276	21	70	–	419
30 to 39 years,	23	291	36	50	–	400
40 to 49 years,	16	200	27	24	–	267
50 to 59 years,	2	123	29	13	–	167
60 to 79 years,	2	132	15	14	–	163
80 years and over,	–	8	1	1	–	10
Age unknown,	–	–	–	2	–	2
Danvers,	184	1,443	313	323	426	2,689
20 to 29 years,	103	392	40	151	65	751
30 to 39 years,	27	345	65	69	116	622
40 to 49 years,	21	278	73	53	90	515
50 to 59 years,	14	204	73	29	79	399
60 to 79 years,	16	198	58	18	70	360
80 years and over,	3	26	4	3	6	42
Essex,	22	464	28	59	3	576
20 to 29 years,	17	92	1	27	–	137
30 to 39 years,	4	101	4	13	–	122
40 to 49 years,	1	83	2	9	–	95
50 to 59 years,	–	68	6	4	1	79
60 to 79 years,	–	108	15	6	2	131
80 years and over,	–	12	–	–	–	12
Georgetown,	26	552	49	41	8	676
20 to 29 years,	17	106	4	8	–	135
30 to 39 years,	7	107	6	10	1	131
40 to 49 years,	1	99	11	8	1	120
50 to 59 years,	–	98	13	7	1	119
60 to 79 years,	1	116	15	8	3	143
80 years and over,	–	26	–	–	2	28
GLOUCESTER,	385	4,453	1,991	5,000	18	11,847
20 to 29 years,	310	1,406	275	2,515	–	4,506

POLITICAL CONDITION: BY AGE PERIODS — Continued.

Counties, Cities, Towns, and Age Periods	Ratable Polls (Not Voters)	Ratable Polls and Native Born Voters	Ratable Polls and Foreign Born Naturalized Voters	Ratable Polls and Aliens	No Political Condition	Total Male Population 20 Years of Age and Over
ESSEX — Con.						
GLOUCESTER — Con.						
30 to 39 years,	33	1,144	651	1,578	2	3,408
40 to 49 years,	22	779	489	612	2	1,904
50 to 59 years,	6	572	318	196	3	1,095
60 to 79 years,	1	496	248	87	9	841
80 years and over,	-	50	6	1	2	59
Age unknown,	13	6	4	11	-	34
Groveland,	24	512	80	84	1	701
20 to 29 years,	17	143	7	27	-	194
30 to 39 years,	4	111	17	27	-	159
40 to 49 years,	-	93	19	11	-	123
50 to 59 years,	1	73	17	7	-	98
60 to 79 years,	1	81	20	12	1	115
80 years and over,	1	11	-	-	-	12
Hamilton,	97	251	11	122	2	483
20 to 29 years,	32	49	1	60	-	142
30 to 39 years,	19	56	6	31	-	112
40 to 49 years,	13	43	-	22	1	79
50 to 59 years,	18	40	1	4	1	64
60 to 79 years,	15	54	3	4	-	76
80 years and over,	-	9	-	1	-	10
HAVERHILL,	467	6,143	1,313	1,509	39	9,471
20 to 29 years,	344	1,832	284	633	2	3,095
30 to 39 years,	54	1,648	372	410	7	2,491
40 to 49 years,	32	1,172	280	227	4	1,715
50 to 59 years,	16	806	219	154	6	1,201
60 to 79 years,	10	633	156	83	16	898
80 years and over,	2	52	2	2	4	62
Age unknown,	9	-	-	-	-	9
Ipswich,	89	951	119	282	13	1,454
20 to 29 years,	57	221	17	151	4	450
30 to 39 years,	20	214	21	56	1	312
40 to 49 years,	5	109	25	39	1	230
50 to 59 years,	4	161	22	27	5	219
60 to 79 years,	3	173	32	8	1	217
80 years and over,	-	22	2	1	1	26
LAWRENCE,	805	5,383	4,785	4,357	42	15,382
20 to 29 years,	627	2,156	869	1,833	2	5,487
30 to 39 years,	90	1,519	1,211	1,147	3	3,970
40 to 49 years,	58	882	1,181	715	5	2,841
50 to 59 years,	19	450	948	375	12	1,804
60 to 79 years,	7	369	558	279	14	1,218
80 years and over,	-	25	18	8	6	57
Age unknown,	4	1	-	-	-	5
LYNN,	969	12,563	2,874	3,423	51	19,880
20 to 29 years,	726	3,983	461	1,448	3	6,621
30 to 39 years,	123	3,453	798	1,089	6	5,469
40 to 49 years,	48	2,468	704	459	7	3,686
50 to 59 years,	37	1,610	547	264	9	2,467
60 to 79 years,	14	1,249	350	156	22	1,791
80 years and over,	-	99	14	6	4	123
Age unknown,	21	1	-	1	-	23
Lynnfield,	26	220	8	36	-	290
20 to 29 years,	11	33	-	17	-	61
30 to 39 years,	5	45	1	6	-	57
40 to 49 years,	4	52	3	3	-	62
50 to 59 years,	3	38	3	5	-	49

POLITICAL CONDITION: BY AGE PERIODS — Continued.

COUNTIES, CITIES, TOWNS, AND AGE PERIODS.	Ratable Polls (Not Voters)	Ratable Polls and Native Born Voters	Ratable Polls and Foreign Born Naturalized Voters	Ratable Polls and Aliens	No Political Condition	Total Male Population 20 Years of Age and Over
ESSEX — Con.						
Lynnfield — Con.						
60 to 79 years,	3	46	-	5	-	54
80 years and over,	-	6	1	-	-	7
Manchester,	38	403	47	143	3	634
20 to 29 years,	27	95	5	51	-	178
30 to 39 years,	6	89	15	43	-	153
40 to 49 years,	2	85	9	19	-	115
50 to 59 years,	-	55	9	20	1	85
60 to 79 years,	3	72	8	9	1	93
80 years and over,	-	6	1	1	1	9
Age unknown,	-	1	-	-	-	1
Marblehead,	70	2,160	195	117	9	2,491
20 to 29 years,	55	509	19	37	1	621
30 to 39 years,	7	490	32	29	1	559
40 to 49 years,	5	384	33	19	3	446
50 to 59 years,	3	351	63	15	-	432
60 to 79 years,	-	332	45	15	3	395
80 years and over,	-	32	3	2	1	38
Merrimac,	23	551	62	95	-	731
20 to 29 years,	14	124	6	25	-	169
30 to 39 years,	3	119	13	32	-	167
40 to 49 years,	3	132	21	9	-	165
50 to 59 years,	2	81	11	15	-	109
60 to 79 years,	1	89	10	13	-	113
80 years and over,	-	6	1	1	-	8
Methuen,	105	849	319	392	3	1,668
20 to 29 years,	70	220	55	138	1	484
30 to 39 years,	14	191	92	122	-	419
40 to 49 years,	10	145	62	63	1	281
50 to 59 years,	2	135	69	47	-	253
60 to 79 years,	9	147	37	22	-	215
80 years and over,	-	11	4	-	1	16
Middleton,	20	207	21	33	1	282
20 to 29 years,	13	43	3	13	-	72
30 to 39 years,	4	36	4	3	-	47
40 to 49 years,	1	47	5	5	1	59
50 to 59 years,	1	35	4	6	-	46
60 to 79 years,	1	42	5	6	-	54
80 years and over,	-	4	-	-	-	4
Nahant,	44	156	53	46	-	299
20 to 29 years,	19	49	8	18	-	94
30 to 39 years,	12	38	12	12	-	74
40 to 49 years,	7	24	10	6	-	47
50 to 59 years,	4	24	15	4	-	47
60 to 79 years,	2	19	7	5	-	33
80 years and over,	-	2	-	-	-	2
Age unknown,	-	-	1	1	-	2
Newbury,	34	402	26	69	1	532
20 to 29 years,	27	82	4	46	-	159
30 to 39 years,	3	73	5	12	-	93
40 to 49 years,	3	89	5	6	-	103
50 to 59 years,	-	65	5	3	-	73
60 to 79 years,	1	81	7	2	-	91
80 years and over,	-	12	-	-	1	13
NEWBURYPORT,	167	3,000	507	527	31	4,232
20 to 29 years,	137	768	69	208	4	1,186

POLITICAL CONDITION: BY AGE PERIODS — Continued.

Counties, Cities, Towns, and Age Periods.	Ratable Polls (Not Voters)	Ratable Polls and Native Born Voters	Ratable Polls and Foreign Born Naturalized Voters	Ratable Polls and Aliens	No Political Condition	Total Male Population 20 Years of Age and Over
ESSEX — Con.						
NEWBURYPORT — Con.						
30 to 39 years, ...	14	737	80	144	4	979
40 to 49 years, ...	5	566	107	84	5	767
50 to 59 years, ...	7	358	126	56	5	552
60 to 79 years, ...	4	522	121	31	9	687
80 years and over, ...	-	49	4	4	4	61
North Andover, ...	75	606	306	125	3	1,115
20 to 29 years, ...	59	169	32	58	-	318
30 to 39 years, ...	8	159	66	37	-	270
40 to 49 years, ...	5	126	85	12	-	228
50 to 59 years, ...	2	67	72	13	-	154
60 to 79 years, ...	1	78	50	5	1	135
80 years and over, ...	-	7	1	-	2	10
Peabody, ...	137	1,965	682	509	22	3,315
20 to 29 years, ...	103	626	67	205	1	1,002
30 to 39 years, ...	22	479	203	140	1	845
40 to 49 years, ...	4	339	182	83	4	612
50 to 59 years, ...	5	255	140	50	1	431
60 to 79 years, ...	2	261	88	30	14	395
80 years and over, ...	-	25	2	1	1	29
Age unknown, ...	1	-	-	-	-	1
Rockport, ...	65	878	177	907	4	2,031
20 to 29 years, ...	62	183	16	388	1	650
30 to 39 years, ...	2	187	43	300	-	532
40 to 49 years, ...	-	152	46	170	1	369
50 to 59 years, ...	-	150	46	37	1	234
60 to 79 years, ...	1	187	25	12	1	226
80 years and over, ...	-	19	1	-	-	20
Rowley, ...	27	366	15	28	5	441
20 to 29 years, ...	15	69	2	12	-	98
30 to 39 years, ...	5	78	4	5	1	93
40 to 49 years, ...	-	77	1	2	1	81
50 to 59 years, ...	2	40	5	3	1	51
60 to 79 years, ...	5	92	3	6	1	107
80 years and over, ...	-	10	-	-	1	11
SALEM, ...	591	5,766	1,645	2,191	50	10,243
20 to 29 years, ...	394	1,775	257	883	2	3,311
30 to 39 years, ...	106	1,406	394	605	9	2,520
40 to 49 years, ...	51	1,064	398	322	16	1,851
50 to 59 years, ...	23	690	319	228	7	1,267
60 to 79 years, ...	8	738	267	126	13	1,152
80 years and over, ...	-	88	10	9	3	110
Age unknown, ...	9	5	-	18	-	32
Salisbury, ...	23	371	23	17	1	435
20 to 29 years, ...	15	77	1	5	-	98
30 to 39 years, ...	5	87	5	4	-	101
40 to 49 years, ...	2	75	4	6	-	87
50 to 59 years, ...	1	51	6	-	-	58
60 to 79 years, ...	-	74	5	2	1	82
80 years and over, ...	-	7	1	-	-	8
Age unknown, ...	-	-	1	-	-	1
Saugus, ...	79	957	195	147	5	1,383
20 to 29 years, ...	48	233	22	50	-	353
30 to 39 years, ...	17	238	55	35	3	348
40 to 49 years, ...	7	198	46	28	1	280
50 to 59 years, ...	3	150	35	18	1	187

POLITICAL CONDITION: BY AGE PERIODS — Continued.

COUNTIES, CITIES, TOWNS, AND AGE PERIODS.	Ratable Polls (Not Voters)	Ratable Polls and Native Born Voters	Ratable Polls and Foreign Born Naturalized Voters	Ratable Polls and Aliens	No Political Condition	Total Male Population 20 Years of Age and Over
ESSEX — Con.						
Saugus — Con.						
60 to 79 years, ...	4	145	33	15	-	197
80 years and over, ...	-	13	4	1	-	18
Swampscott, ...	52	795	79	130	-	1,056
20 to 29 years, ...	34	186	11	45	-	276
30 to 39 years, ...	6	210	13	44	-	273
40 to 49 years, ...	6	161	15	20	-	202
50 to 59 years, ...	5	110	21	10	-	146
60 to 79 years, ...	1	119	19	10	-	149
80 years and over, ...	-	9	-	1	-	10
Topsfield, ...	31	284	21	17	2	355
20 to 29 years, ...	13	58	3	8	-	82
30 to 39 years, ...	7	52	2	3	-	64
40 to 49 years, ...	4	51	4	1	-	60
50 to 59 years, ...	5	57	5	2	1	70
60 to 79 years, ...	1	61	6	3	1	72
80 years and over, ...	1	5	1	-	-	7
Wenham, ...	12	267	7	30	-	316
20 to 29 years, ...	7	52	3	19	-	81
30 to 39 years, ...	3	49	-	4	-	56
40 to 49 years, ...	1	45	-	1	-	47
50 to 59 years, ...	-	48	2	2	-	52
60 to 79 years, ...	1	57	2	4	-	64
80 years and over, ...	-	16	-	-	-	16
West Newbury, ...	35	397	67	57	1	557
20 to 29 years, ...	24	86	3	18	-	131
30 to 39 years, ...	5	96	3	12	-	116
40 to 49 years, ...	2	67	13	8	-	90
50 to 59 years, ...	3	64	9	6	-	82
60 to 79 years, ...	1	72	36	13	-	122
80 years and over, ...	-	12	3	-	1	16
FRANKLIN.						
Ashfield, ...	32	290	10	23	3	358
20 to 29 years, ...	24	62	-	11	-	97
30 to 39 years, ...	3	51	1	7	-	62
40 to 49 years, ...	4	50	3	1	-	58
50 to 59 years, ...	-	52	1	1	-	54
60 to 79 years, ...	1	64	5	2	2	74
80 years and over, ...	-	11	-	-	1	12
Age unknown, ...	-	-	-	1	-	1
Bernardston, ...	22	216	6	17	2	263
20 to 29 years, ...	12	31	-	6	1	50
30 to 39 years, ...	-	40	1	6	-	47
40 to 49 years, ...	1	41	1	2	-	45
50 to 59 years, ...	3	36	1	2	1	43
60 to 79 years, ...	4	60	3	1	-	68
80 years and over, ...	-	7	-	-	-	7
Age unknown, ...	2	1	-	-	-	3
Buckland, ...	19	306	110	51	3	489
20 to 29 years, ...	15	92	11	17	-	135
30 to 39 years, ...	2	67	19	16	-	104
40 to 49 years, ...	2	49	31	5	1	88
50 to 59 years, ...	-	45	24	5	1	75
60 to 79 years, ...	-	44	25	8	-	77
80 years and over, ...	-	9	-	-	1	10

POLITICAL CONDITION: BY AGE PERIODS — Continued.

Counties, Cities, Towns, and Age Periods.	Ratable Polls (Not Voters)	Ratable Polls and Native Born Voters	Ratable Polls and Foreign Born Naturalized Voters	Ratable Polls and Aliens	No Political Condition	Total Male Population 20 Years of Age and Over
FRANKLIN — Con.						
Charlemont, ...	25	287	7	21	1	341
20 to 29 years, ...	15	44	1	6	-	66
30 to 39 years, ...	3	63	-	7	1	74
40 to 49 years, ...	3	63	1	3	-	70
50 to 59 years, ...	2	41	2	4	-	49
60 to 79 years, ...	2	69	3	1	-	75
80 years and over, . . .	-	7	-	-	-	7
Colrain, ...	13	389	20	91	-	513
20 to 29 years, ...	9	88	2	37	-	136
30 to 39 years, ...	3	72	5	21	-	101
40 to 49 years, ...	-	80	6	14	-	100
50 to 59 years, ...	1	70	1	11	-	83
60 to 79 years, ...	-	72	4	8	-	84
80 years and over, . . .	-	7	2	-	-	9
Conway, ...	39	305	31	40	4	419
20 to 29 years, ...	26	73	3	14	-	116
30 to 39 years, ...	8	64	4	9	1	86
40 to 49 years, ...	1	62	6	5	1	75
50 to 59 years, ...	-	40	6	5	1	52
60 to 79 years, ...	4	56	11	7	1	79
80 years and over, . . .	-	10	-	-	-	10
Age unknown, ...	-	-	1	-	-	1
Deerfield, ...	69	606	116	188	5	984
20 to 29 years, ...	41	150	15	89	2	297
30 to 39 years, ...	10	147	18	34	1	210
40 to 49 years, ...	9	107	27	25	-	168
50 to 59 years, ...	4	72	27	20	-	123
60 to 79 years, ...	4	114	27	17	2	164
80 years and over, . . .	1	16	2	3	-	22
Erving, ...	20	216	25	48	2	311
20 to 29 years, ...	8	36	2	14	-	60
30 to 39 years, ...	3	55	7	13	-	78
40 to 49 years, ...	6	52	7	11	-	76
50 to 59 years, ...	2	40	4	4	-	50
60 to 79 years, ...	-	28	5	3	2	38
80 years and over, . . .	1	5	-	-	-	6
Age unknown, ...	-	-	-	3	-	3
Gill, ...	58	261	19	70	-	408
20 to 29 years, ...	53	105	5	49	-	212
30 to 39 years, ...	3	40	4	11	-	58
40 to 49 years, ...	-	34	4	4	-	42
50 to 59 years, ...	1	34	5	4	-	44
60 to 79 years, ...	1	42	1	2	-	46
80 years and over, . . .	-	6	-	-	-	6
Greenfield, ...	110	1,396	261	178	3	1,948
20 to 29 years, ...	77	427	27	73	1	605
30 to 39 years, ...	25	336	60	33	1	455
40 to 49 years, ...	4	255	56	24	-	339
50 to 59 years, ...	4	180	78	23	-	285
60 to 79 years, ...	-	183	35	17	1	236
80 years and over, . . .	-	14	5	2	-	21
Age unknown, ...	2	1	-	6	-	9
Hawley, ...	13	141	2	4	2	162
20 to 29 years, ...	8	28	1	2	-	39
30 to 39 years, ...	3	23	1	-	-	27
40 to 49 years, ...	2	23	-	2	-	27

POLITICAL CONDITION: BY AGE PERIODS — Continued.

Counties, Cities, Towns, and Age Periods.	Ratable Polls (Not Voters)	Ratable Polls and Native Born Voters	Ratable Polls and Foreign Born Naturalized Voters	Ratable Polls and Aliens	No Political Condition	Total Male Population 20 Years of Age and over
FRANKLIN — Con.						
Hawley — Con.						
50 to 59 years,	-	24	-	-	1	25
60 to 79 years,	-	39	-	-	1	40
80 years and over,	-	4	-	-	-	4
Heath,	6	121	3	12	-	142
20 to 29 years,	2	16	1	8	-	27
30 to 39 years,	-	28	-	1	-	29
40 to 49 years,	3	26	-	1	-	30
50 to 59 years,	-	23	-	1	-	24
60 to 79 years,	1	27	1	-	-	29
80 years and over,	-	1	1	1	-	3
Leverett,	13	232	3	8	2	258
20 to 29 years,	10	42	-	3	-	55
30 to 39 years,	1	53	-	3	-	57
40 to 49 years,	1	41	-	2	-	44
50 to 59 years,	1	39	1	-	-	41
60 to 79 years,	-	48	2	-	-	50
80 years and over,	-	9	-	-	2	11
Leyden,	10	99	7	6	-	122
20 to 29 years,	7	19	-	2	-	28
30 to 39 years,	2	13	-	-	-	15
40 to 49 years,	-	16	2	2	-	20
50 to 59 years,	1	23	1	2	-	27
60 to 79 years,	-	20	3	-	-	23
80 years and over,	-	8	1	-	-	9
Monroe,	8	68	4	43	-	123
20 to 29 years,	7	26	-	18	-	51
30 to 39 years,	1	16	3	16	-	36
40 to 49 years,	-	10	-	8	-	18
50 to 59 years,	-	6	1	1	-	8
60 to 79 years,	-	10	-	-	-	10
Montague,	86	832	455	362	9	1,744
20 to 29 years,	60	261	79	135	-	535
30 to 39 years,	9	197	129	106	3	444
40 to 49 years,	7	151	117	61	1	337
50 to 59 years,	1	120	78	40	1	240
60 to 79 years,	6	90	49	18	4	167
80 years and over,	-	12	3	2	-	17
Age unknown,	3	1	-	-	-	4
New Salem,	29	228	12	24	1	294
20 to 29 years,	15	40	-	10	-	65
30 to 39 years,	4	36	7	6	-	53
40 to 49 years,	8	39	1	5	-	53
50 to 59 years,	-	42	3	3	-	48
60 to 79 years,	2	63	1	-	-	66
80 years and over,	-	8	-	-	1	9
Northfield,	14	428	28	41	1	512
20 to 29 years,	11	87	2	18	-	118
30 to 39 years,	2	86	4	12	-	104
40 to 49 years,	1	74	6	5	1	87
50 to 59 years,	-	59	5	4	-	68
60 to 79 years,	-	107	10	2	-	119
80 years and over,	-	15	1	-	-	16
Orange,	56	1,325	119	240	1	1,741
20 to 29 years,	43	270	31	98	-	442
30 to 39 years,	8	411	35	87	-	541

POLITICAL CONDITION: BY AGE PERIODS — Continued.

COUNTIES, CITIES, TOWNS, AND AGE PERIODS.	Ratable Polls (Not Voters)	Ratable Polls and Native Born Voters	Ratable Polls and Foreign Born Naturalized Voters	Ratable Polls and Aliens	No Political Condition	Total Male Population 20 Years of Age and Over
FRANKLIN — Con.						
Orange — Con,						
40 to 49 years,	4	277	25	29	-	335
50 to 59 years,	-	189	19	13	1	222
60 to 79 years,	1	163	9	12	-	185
80 years and over,	-	15	-	1	-	16
Rowe,	22	109	2	51	1	185
20 to 29 years,	15	26	1	16	-	58
30 to 39 years,	4	24	-	14	-	42
40 to 49 years,	1	17	1	15	-	34
50 to 59 years,	-	18	-	3	-	21
60 to 79 years,	1	19	-	3	1	24
80 years and over,	1	5	-	-	-	6
Shelburne,	42	392	24	43	2	503
20 to 29 years,	23	72	1	17	-	113
30 to 39 years,	7	85	2	13	-	107
40 to 49 years,	9	75	5	5	-	94
50 to 59 years,	2	55	9	3	1	70
60 to 79 years,	1	91	7	5	1	105
80 years and over,	-	14	-	-	-	14
Shutesbury,	4	132	5	5	1	147
20 to 29 years,	2	21	-	-	1	24
30 to 39 years,	-	17	2	2	-	21
40 to 49 years,	2	27	1	2	-	32
50 to 59 years,	-	26	1	-	-	27
60 to 79 years,	-	37	1	1	-	39
80 years and over,	-	4	-	-	-	4
Sunderland,	12	178	14	50	1	255
20 to 29 years,	8	38	-	37	-	83
30 to 39 years,	-	35	3	7	-	45
40 to 49 years,	1	32	2	4	-	39
50 to 59 years,	-	25	2	-	-	27
60 to 79 years,	2	43	6	2	1	54
80 years and over,	1	5	1	-	-	7
Warwick,	32	130	6	43	3	214
20 to 29 years,	12	20	-	20	-	52
30 to 39 years,	8	20	2	9	1	40
40 to 49 years,	4	23	2	8	-	37
50 to 59 years,	7	22	1	4	1	35
60 to 79 years,	1	39	1	2	1	44
80 years and over,	-	6	-	-	-	6
Wendell,	13	124	11	31	1	180
20 to 29 years,	7	26	-	12	-	45
30 to 39 years,	2	20	4	13	-	39
40 to 49 years,	3	26	2	4	-	35
50 to 59 years,	-	22	2	2	1	27
60 to 79 years,	1	26	3	-	-	30
80 years and over,	-	4	-	-	-	4
Whately,	17	191	30	26	2	266
20 to 29 years,	12	34	1	17	-	64
30 to 39 years,	1	37	2	3	-	43
40 to 49 years,	1	33	7	2	-	43
50 to 59 years,	3	32	8	3	-	46
60 to 79 years,	-	48	12	1	2	63
80 years and over,	-	6	-	-	-	6
Age unknown,	-	1	-	-	-	1

POLITICAL CONDITION: BY AGE PERIODS — Continued.

COUNTIES, CITIES, TOWNS, AND AGE PERIODS.	Ratable Polls (Not Voters)	Ratable Polls and Native Born Voters	Ratable Polls and Foreign Born Naturalized Voters	Ratable Polls and Aliens	No Political Condition	Total Male Population 20 Years of Age and Over
HAMPDEN.						
Agawam,	80	437	93	135	3	748
20 to 29 years,	45	111	6	35	-	197
30 to 39 years,	15	107	28	31	-	181
40 to 49 years,	10	72	23	24	1	130
50 to 59 years,	5	69	19	21	-	114
60 to 79 years,	5	70	17	22	1	115
80 years and over,	-	8	-	2	1	11
Blandford,	19	253	3	8	1	284
20 to 29 years,	13	62	1	3	-	79
30 to 39 years,	3	53	-	1	-	57
40 to 49 years,	1	34	1	1	-	37
50 to 59 years,	1	41	-	3	-	45
60 to 79 years,	1	60	1	-	1	63
80 years and over,	-	3	-	-	-	3
Brimfield,	26	245	15	39	7	332
20 to 29 years,	17	44	-	13	2	76
30 to 39 years,	1	36	3	13	1	54
40 to 49 years,	1	47	1	5	1	55
50 to 59 years,	4	34	6	4	1	49
60 to 79 years,	3	76	4	3	1	87
80 years and over,	-	8	1	-	1	10
Age unknown,	-	-	-	1	-	1
Chester,	27	362	17	53	4	463
20 to 29 years,	15	77	2	14	1	109
30 to 39 years,	4	84	2	15	-	105
40 to 49 years,	5	75	7	5	-	92
50 to 59 years,	1	50	3	7	-	61
60 to 79 years,	2	67	3	11	3	86
80 years and over,	-	9	-	1	-	10
Chicopee,	294	1,924	825	1,970	18	5,031
20 to 29 years,	257	767	153	907	-	2,084
30 to 39 years,	11	518	233	510	-	1,272
40 to 49 years,	14	295	150	252	4	715
50 to 59 years,	6	176	173	178	2	535
60 to 79 years,	1	156	109	116	11	393
80 years and over,	-	12	7	6	1	26
Age unknown,	5	-	-	1	-	6
East Longmeadow,	13	191	48	265	-	517
20 to 29 years,	9	37	7	96	-	149
30 to 39 years,	1	45	18	109	-	173
40 to 49 years,	1	35	13	43	-	92
50 to 59 years,	2	25	6	13	-	46
60 to 79 years,	-	45	4	3	-	52
80 years and over,	-	4	-	-	-	4
Age unknown,	-	-	-	1	-	1
Granville,	28	238	17	30	9	322
20 to 29 years,	17	48	-	7	2	74
30 to 39 years,	8	55	5	7	2	77
40 to 49 years,	2	39	4	4	-	49
50 to 59 years,	-	37	2	7	-	46
60 to 79 years,	1	52	6	5	4	68
80 years and over,	-	7	-	-	1	8
Hampden,	27	156	24	35	1	243
20 to 29 years,	15	28	-	12	-	55
30 to 39 years,	5	33	1	8	-	47

POLITICAL CONDITION: BY AGE PERIODS — Continued.

COUNTIES, CITIES, TOWNS, AND AGE PERIODS.	Ratable Polls (Not Voters)	Ratable Polls and Native-Born Voters	Ratable Polls and Foreign-Born Naturalized Voters	Ratable Polls and Aliens	No Political Condition	Total Male Population 20 Years of Age and Over
HAMPDEN — Con.						
Hampden — Con.						
40 to 49 years,	3	24	7	4	1	39
50 to 59 years,	4	32	9	5	-	50
60 to 79 years,	-	34	7	6	-	47
80 years and over,	-	5	-	-	-	5
Holland,	4	51	3	6	1	65
20 to 29 years,	2	7	-	2	-	11
30 to 39 years,	2	13	1	2	-	18
40 to 49 years,	-	8	1	1	-	10
50 to 59 years,	-	6	-	-	1	7
60 to 79 years,	-	16	1	1	-	18
80 years and over,	-	1	-	-	-	1
HOLYOKE,	535	3,743	2,854	3,610	28	10,770
20 to 29 years,	462	1,577	640	1,434	6	4,119
30 to 39 years,	41	1,087	891	961	7	2,987
40 to 49 years,	16	575	628	578	3	1,800
50 to 59 years,	8	290	456	367	4	1,125
60 to 79 years,	4	204	232	251	5	696
80 years and over,	1	10	7	15	3	36
Age unknown,	3	-	-	4	-	7
Longmeadow,	20	127	16	30	1	194
20 to 29 years,	9	32	1	10	-	52
30 to 39 years,	4	27	4	5	-	40
40 to 49 years,	3	20	2	5	-	30
50 to 59 years,	3	13	4	5	-	25
60 to 79 years,	-	32	5	5	1	43
80 years and over,	1	3	-	-	-	4
Ludlow,	69	308	64	298	3	742
20 to 29 years,	48	89	9	115	1	262
30 to 39 years,	6	67	15	76	-	164
40 to 49 years,	8	48	16	60	-	132
50 to 59 years,	6	39	14	29	-	88
60 to 79 years,	1	63	9	17	2	92
80 years and over,	-	2	1	1	-	4
Monson,	80	741	110	219	14	1,164
20 to 29 years,	37	180	18	58	-	293
30 to 39 years,	14	196	14	57	1	282
40 to 49 years,	13	121	22	46	2	204
50 to 59 years,	8	118	28	32	1	187
60 to 79 years,	8	112	25	21	9	175
80 years and over,	-	14	3	5	1	23
Montgomery,	3	76	3	5	5	92
20 to 29 years,	1	13	-	2	2	18
30 to 39 years,	1	13	-	2	-	16
40 to 49 years,	-	14	2	-	2	18
50 to 59 years,	1	11	1	1	1	15
60 to 79 years,	-	24	-	-	-	24
80 years and over,	-	1	-	-	-	1
Palmer,	160	976	220	707	10	2,073
20 to 29 years,	104	305	26	304	1	740
30 to 39 years,	25	251	53	175	2	506
40 to 49 years,	14	165	46	121	1	347
50 to 59 years,	5	108	48	43	1	205
60 to 79 years,	5	132	42	57	5	241
80 years and over,	-	15	5	4	-	24
Age unknown,	7	-	-	3	-	10

POLITICAL CONDITION: BY AGE PERIODS — Continued.

COUNTIES, CITIES, TOWNS, AND AGE PERIODS.	Ratable Polls (Not Voters)	Ratable Polls and Native Born Voters	Ratable Polls and Foreign Born Naturalized Voters	Ratable Polls and Aliens	No Political Condition	Total Male Population 20 Years of Age and Over
HAMPDEN — Con.						
Russell, ...	38	155	26	48	4	271
20 to 29 years, ...	20	41	4	21	-	86
30 to 39 years, ...	9	41	4	8	-	62
40 to 49 years, ...	5	30	2	11	-	48
50 to 59 years, ...	2	20	5	3	-	30
60 to 79 years, ...	2	23	10	5	2	42
80 years and over, ...	-	-	1		2	3
Southwick, ...	40	235	26	29	3	333
20 to 29 years, ...	20	49	3	12	1	85
30 to 39 years, ...	5	39	4	5	-	53
40 to 49 years, ...	4	41	8	2	2	57
50 to 59 years, ...	3	35	3	5	-	46
60 to 79 years, ...	7	66	8	2	-	83
80 years and over, ...	1	5	-	3	-	9
SPRINGFIELD, ...	1,107	9,793	2,447	2,564	70	15,981
20 to 29 years, ...	757	2,934	374	1,039	6	5,110
30 to 39 years, ...	184	2,596	675	811	15	4,281
40 to 49 years, ...	99	1,825	562	365	14	2,865
50 to 59 years, ...	30	1,198	402	297	2	1,929
60 to 79 years, ...	9	1,161	327	127	30	1,654
80 years and over, ...	1	79	15	10	1	106
Age unknown, ...	27	-	2	5	2	36
Tolland, ...	10	78	6	14	-	108
20 to 29 years, ...	5	14	-	4	-	23
30 to 39 years, ...	1	17	1	3	-	22
40 to 49 years, ...	2	15	-	4	-	21
50 to 59 years, ...	1	12	3	2	-	18
60 to 79 years, ...	1	17	2	-	-	20
80 years and over, ...	-	3	-	1	-	4
Wales, ...	31	160	17	43	-	251
20 to 29 years, ...	21	30	2	10	-	63
30 to 39 years, ...	5	40	5	13	-	63
40 to 49 years, ...	2	23	4	7	-	36
50 to 59 years, ...	3	27	2	7	-	39
60 to 79 years, ...	-	28	4	5	-	47
80 years and over, ...	-	2	-	1	-	3
Westfield, ...	207	2,331	421	393	16	3,368
20 to 29 years, ...	147	644	67	154	1	983
30 to 39 years, ...	34	563	97	112	-	806
40 to 49 years, ...	9	459	136	54	3	661
50 to 59 years, ...	9	323	97	37	-	466
60 to 79 years, ...	6	355	60	33	10	464
80 years and over, ...	-	37	4	3	2	46
Age unknown, ...	2	-	-	-	-	2
West Springfield, ...	108	1,117	257	275	-	1,757
20 to 29 years, ...	70	392	45	67	-	574
30 to 39 years, ...	17	282	49	83	-	431
40 to 49 years, ...	12	196	77	46	-	331
50 to 59 years, ...	3	123	49	37	-	212
60 to 79 years, ...	2	110	36	39	-	187
80 years and over, ...	-	14	1	3	-	18
Age unknown, ...	4	-	-	-	-	4
Wilbraham, ...	34	315	44	78	1	472
20 to 29 years, ...	33	85	10	35	-	163
30 to 39 years, ...	-	66	7	13	-	86
40 to 49 years, ...	-	54	7	15	-	76

POLITICAL CONDITION: BY AGE PERIODS — Continued.

COUNTIES, CITIES, TOWNS, AND AGE PERIODS.	Ratable Polls (Not Voters)	Ratable Polls and Native Born Voters	Ratable Polls and Foreign Born Naturalized Voters	Ratable Polls and Aliens	No Political Condition	Total Male Population 20 Years of Age and Over
HAMPDEN — Con.						
Wilbraham — Con.						
50 to 59 years,	-	46	16	3	-	65
60 to 79 years,	1	53	4	11	-	69
80 years and over,	-	11	-	1	1	13
HAMPSHIRE.						
Amherst,	156	1,250	89	96	4	1,595
20 to 29 years,	149	455	10	47	4	665
30 to 39 years,	1	219	15	18	-	253
40 to 49 years,	2	185	18	13	-	218
50 to 59 years,	-	166	21	7	-	194
60 to 79 years,	4	209	24	9	-	246
80 years and over,	-	16	1	2	-	19
Belchertown,	47	509	48	85	2	691
20 to 29 years,	25	110	1	20	-	156
30 to 39 years,	5	98	4	27	-	134
40 to 49 years,	6	85	6	9	-	106
50 to 59 years,	4	71	15	7	-	97
60 to 79 years,	2	132	22	18	2	176
80 years and over,	1	12	-	3	-	16
Age unknown,	4	1	-	1	-	6
Chesterfield,	11	189	3	9	3	215
20 to 29 years,	9	39	-	3	-	51
30 to 39 years,	1	34	1	5	-	41
40 to 49 years,	-	38	-	1	1	40
50 to 59 years,	-	22	1	-	-	23
60 to 79 years,	1	50	1	-	2	54
80 years and over,	-	6	-	-	-	6
Cummington,	22	221	4	11	5	263
20 to 29 years,	10	50	-	4	-	64
30 to 39 years,	3	34	1	2	1	41
40 to 49 years,	1	37	2	1	-	41
50 to 59 years,	4	38	-	2	-	44
60 to 79 years,	4	55	1	2	2	64
80 years and over,	-	7	-	-	2	9
Easthampton,	115	702	263	280	6	1,366
20 to 29 years,	77	252	43	84	-	456
30 to 39 years,	21	169	50	80	1	321
40 to 49 years,	12	101	57	40	2	212
50 to 59 years,	1	75	57	35	2	170
60 to 79 years,	4	101	53	40	1	199
80 years and over,	-	4	3	1	-	8
Enfield,	19	209	25	61	1	315
20 to 29 years,	9	35	5	23	-	72
30 to 39 years,	2	39	8	16	1	66
40 to 49 years,	4	37	2	11	-	54
50 to 59 years,	3	37	4	7	-	51
60 to 79 years,	1	55	6	4	-	66
80 years and over,	-	6	-	-	-	6
Goshen,	11	71	2	6	7	97
20 to 29 years,	6	11	-	2	-	19
30 to 39 years,	3	19	1	4	-	27
40 to 49 years,	2	7	-	-	1	10
50 to 59 years,	-	12	1	-	2	15
60 to 79 years,	-	22	-	-	1	23
80 years and over,	-	-	-	-	1	1
Age unknown,	-	-	-	-	2	2

POLITICAL CONDITION: BY AGE PERIODS — Continued.

Counties, Cities, Towns, and Age Periods.	Ratable Polls (Not Voters)	Ratable Polls and Native Born Voters	Ratable Polls and Foreign Born Naturalized Voters	Ratable Polls and Aliens	No Political Condition	Total Male Population 20 Years of Age and Over
HAMPSHIRE — Con.						
Granby, ...	20	168	14	49	2	253
20 to 29 years, ...	14	48	1	18	-	76
30 to 39 years, ...	4	29	1	11	1	46
40 to 49 years, ...	-	30	1	7	-	38
50 to 59 years, ...	1	31	3	7	-	42
60 to 79 years, ...	1	32	8	6	-	47
80 years and over,. . . .	-	3	-	-	1	4
Greenwich, ...	6	142	4	7	4	163
20 to 29 years, ...	3	19	-	2	-	24
30 to 39 years, ...	-	20	-	1	-	21
40 to 49 years, ...	1	39	-	2	-	42
50 to 59 years, ...	1	19	3	1	-	24
60 to 79 years, ...	1	43	1	1	4	50
80 years and over,. . . .	-	2	-	-	-	2
Hadley, ...	29	362	36	146	4	577
20 to 29 years, ...	18	85	-	56	-	159
30 to 39 years, ...	6	79	4	30	-	119
40 to 49 years, ...	5	64	3	19	3	92
50 to 59 years, ...	1	45	11	23	-	80
60 to 79 years, ...	1	83	18	16	1	119
80 years and over,. . . .	-	6	-	2	-	8
Hatfield, ...	13	272	48	101	1	435
20 to 29 years, ...	13	87	5	34	-	139
30 to 39 years, ...	-	55	5	21	-	81
40 to 49 years, ...	-	48	12	22	-	82
50 to 59 years, ...	-	34	16	10	-	60
60 to 79 years, ...	-	43	10	14	1	68
80 years and over,. . . .	-	5	-	-	-	5
Huntington, ...	42	280	39	61	3	425
20 to 29 years, ...	22	55	3	15	1	94
30 to 39 years, ...	9	82	7	9	-	107
40 to 49 years, ...	5	58	11	19	-	93
50 to 59 years, ...	2	33	7	7	-	49
60 to 79 years, ...	4	51	11	11	-	77
80 years and over,. . . .	-	3	-	-	2	5
Middlefield, ...	13	83	3	19	1	119
20 to 29 years, ...	9	19	-	6	-	34
30 to 39 years, ...	1	18	-	4	-	23
40 to 49 years, ...	1	12	2	2	-	17
50 to 59 years, ...	1	11	-	3	-	15
60 to 79 years, ...	1	22	1	4	-	28
80 years and over,. . . .	-	1	-	-	1	2
NORTHAMPTON, ...	223	2,321	769	828	253	4,594
20 to 29 years, ...	171	845	113	299	37	1,465
30 to 39 years, ...	23	610	157	218	53	1,061
40 to 49 years, ...	8	408	190	137	63	806
50 to 59 years, ...	14	300	173	79	39	605
60 to 79 years, ...	6	331	132	85	56	610
80 years and over,. . . .	1	27	4	10	5	47
Pelham, ...	14	130	7	3	-	154
20 to 29 years, ...	9	13	1	-	-	23
30 to 39 years, ...	-	29	-	1	-	30
40 to 49 years, ...	3	28	1	1	-	33
50 to 59 years, ...	1	22	-	-	-	23
60 to 79 years, ...	-	34	5	1	-	40
80 years and over,. . . .	1	4	-	-	-	5

POLITICAL CONDITION: BY AGE PERIODS — Continued.

Counties, Cities, Towns, and Age Periods.	Ratable Polls (Not Voters)	Ratable Polls and Native Born Voters	Ratable Polls and Foreign Born Naturalized Voters	Ratable Polls and Aliens	No Political Condition	Total Male Population 20 Years of Age and Over
HAMPSHIRE — Con.						
Plainfield,	13	135	-	5	-	153
20 to 29 years,	4	26	-	2	-	32
30 to 39 years,	6	27	-	3	-	36
40 to 49 years,	-	20	-	-	-	20
50 to 59 years,	-	25	-	-	-	25
60 to 79 years,	2	32	-	-	-	34
80 years and over,	1	5	-	-	-	6
Prescott,	15	126	-	5	1	147
20 to 29 years,	8	26	-	2	-	36
30 to 39 years,	2	24	-	-	-	26
40 to 49 years,	-	22	-	2	-	24
50 to 59 years,	2	19	-	1	-	22
60 to 79 years,	2	33	-	-	1	36
80 years and over,	1	2	-	-	-	3
Southampton,	14	267	15	55	-	351
20 to 29 years,	11	53	2	19	-	85
30 to 39 years,	2	62	2	10	-	76
40 to 49 years,	-	54	4	11	-	69
50 to 59 years,	1	30	3	5	-	39
60 to 79 years,	-	61	4	9	-	74
80 years and over,	-	7	-	1	-	8
South Hadley,	59	647	192	315	3	1,216
20 to 29 years,	45	190	26	136	-	397
30 to 39 years,	5	182	42	80	-	309
40 to 49 years,	5	105	34	50	-	194
50 to 59 years,	4	61	55	32	1	153
60 to 79 years,	-	102	34	17	1	154
80 years and over,	-	7	1	-	1	9
Ware,	101	881	390	636	12	2,020
20 to 29 years,	82	313	78	208	-	681
30 to 39 years,	13	292	87	141	2	445
40 to 49 years,	6	159	85	121	2	373
50 to 59 years,	-	84	79	77	1	241
60 to 79 years,	-	116	59	82	7	264
80 years and over,	-	7	2	7	-	16
Westhampton,	3	115	5	23	-	146
20 to 29 years,	1	20	-	7	-	28
30 to 39 years,	-	26	-	8	-	34
40 to 49 years,	1	16	1	2	-	20
50 to 59 years,	-	19	2	2	-	23
60 to 79 years,	1	33	2	4	-	40
80 years and over,	-	1	-	-	-	1
Williamsburg,	27	393	75	69	7	571
20 to 29 years,	14	104	5	19	1	143
30 to 39 years,	7	96	18	20	-	141
40 to 49 years,	4	58	24	14	1	101
50 to 59 years,	-	66	12	7	3	88
60 to 79 years,	1	63	15	8	2	89
80 years and over,	1	6	1	1	-	9
Worthington,	15	179	5	8	-	207
20 to 29 years,	10	28	-	4	-	42
30 to 39 years,	3	35	1	2	-	41
40 to 49 years,	2	34	1	2	-	39
50 to 59 years,	-	35	-	-	-	35
60 to 79 years,	-	43	3	-	-	46
80 years and over,	-	4	-	-	-	4

POLITICAL CONDITION: BY AGE PERIODS — Continued.

Counties, Cities, Towns, and Age Periods.	Ratable Polls (Not Voters)	Ratable Polls and Native Born Voters	Ratable Polls and Foreign Born Naturalized Voters	Ratable Polls and Aliens	No Political Condition	Total Male Population 20 Years of Age and Over
MIDDLESEX.						
Acton, ...	55	486	59	97	-	697
20 to 29 years, . . .	31	100	8	49	-	188
30 to 39 years, . . .	11	108	16	25	-	160
40 to 49 years, . . .	8	81	12	14	-	115
50 to 59 years, . . .	2	85	8	7	-	102
60 to 79 years, . . .	3	101	13	2	-	119
80 years and over, . .	-	11	2	-	-	13
Arlington, ...	72	1,081	464	353	4	1,974
20 to 29 years, . . .	67	308	80	184	-	639
30 to 39 years, . . .	1	295	121	92	-	509
40 to 49 years, . . .	3	186	110	47	-	346
50 to 59 years, . . .	-	129	72	24	-	225
60 to 79 years, . . .	1	144	78	6	3	232
80 years and over, . .	-	19	3	-	1	23
Ashby, ...	22	251	8	13	1	295
20 to 29 years, . . .	12	40	2	5	-	59
30 to 39 years, . . .	5	50	-	4	-	59
40 to 49 years, . . .	3	45	1	2	-	51
50 to 59 years, . . .	-	40	2	-	-	42
60 to 79 years, . . .	-	66	3	1	1	71
80 years and over, . .	-	10	-	-	-	10
Age unknown, ...	2	-	-	1	-	3
Ashland, ...	61	396	86	93	9	645
20 to 29 years, . . .	29	96	10	35	-	170
30 to 39 years, . . .	14	104	17	24	-	159
40 to 49 years, . . .	7	60	25	11	4	107
50 to 59 years, . . .	6	61	19	9	3	98
60 to 79 years, . . .	5	69	15	13	1	103
80 years and over, . .	-	6	-	1	1	8
Ayer, ...	66	430	85	69	3	653
20 to 29 years, . . .	37	112	4	18	-	171
30 to 39 years, . . .	8	102	14	17	-	141
40 to 49 years, . . .	12	78	31	15	1	137
50 to 59 years, . . .	4	59	18	8	1	90
60 to 79 years, . . .	4	73	18	8	1	104
80 years and over, . .	1	6	-	3	-	10
Bedford, ...	61	231	33	112	3	440
20 to 29 years, . . .	42	64	6	62	-	174
30 to 39 years, . . .	11	47	3	30	-	91
40 to 49 years, . . .	6	43	4	11	-	64
50 to 59 years, . . .	-	34	7	5	-	46
60 to 79 years, . . .	2	36	12	4	2	56
80 years and over, . .	-	7	1	-	1	9
Belmont, ...	71	432	118	422	10	1,053
20 to 29 years, . . .	57	120	13	202	6	398
30 to 39 years, . . .	7	105	27	135	2	276
40 to 49 years, . . .	6	83	35	57	1	182
50 to 59 years, . . .	-	63	26	22	-	111
60 to 79 years, . . .	1	53	17	6	1	78
80 years and over, . .	-	8	-	-	-	8
Billerica, ...	38	474	166	135	3	816
20 to 29 years, . . .	37	128	24	55	-	244
30 to 39 years, . . .	1	118	43	39	-	201
40 to 49 years, . . .	-	80	32	19	2	133
50 to 59 years, . . .	-	74	34	11	-	119
60 to 79 years, . . .	-	67	30	11	1	109
80 years and over, . .	-	7	3	-	-	10

POLITICAL CONDITION: BY AGE PERIODS — Continued.

COUNTIES, CITIES, TOWNS, AND AGE PERIODS.	Ratable Polls (Not Voters)	Ratable Polls and Native Born Voters	Ratable Polls and Foreign Born Naturalized Voters	Ratable Polls and Aliens	No Political Condition	Total Male Population 20 Years of Age and Over
MIDDLESEX — Con.						
Boxborough,	13	71	9	15	-	108
20 to 29 years,	7	4	3	7	-	21
30 to 39 years,	4	15	1	4	-	24
40 to 49 years,	1	17	1	-	-	19
50 to 59 years,	-	9	3	1	-	13
60 to 79 years,	1	24	1	3	-	29
80 years and over,	-	2	-	-	-	2
Burlington,	37	129	11	42	4	223
20 to 29 years,	20	35	1	23	-	79
30 to 39 years,	2	25	1	5	-	33
40 to 49 years,	8	22	3	7	-	40
50 to 59 years,	2	13	4	-	-	19
60 to 79 years,	5	28	2	5	3	43
80 years and over,	-	6	-	1	-	7
Age unknown,	-	-	-	1	1	2
CAMBRIDGE,	1,896	12,117	4,901	6,191	51	25,156
20 to 29 years,	1,498	4,802	775	2,575	-	9,650
30 to 39 years,	183	3,023	1,313	1,851	3	6,373
40 to 49 years,	111	2,014	1,202	901	9	4,237
50 to 59 years,	42	1,202	923	507	11	2,685
60 to 79 years,	40	968	659	326	27	2,020
80 years and over,	3	107	28	26	1	165
Age unknown,	19	1	1	5	-	26
Carlisle,	14	120	5	38	2	179
20 to 29 years,	3	20	-	14	-	37
30 to 39 years,	5	31	-	10	1	47
40 to 49 years,	4	24	-	5	-	33
50 to 59 years,	2	19	2	6	1	30
60 to 79 years,	-	22	3	3	-	28
80 years and over,	-	4	-	-	-	4
Chelmsford,	78	616	155	170	3	1,022
20 to 29 years,	50	137	18	67	-	272
30 to 39 years,	10	128	44	38	-	220
40 to 49 years,	8	114	21	22	1	166
50 to 59 years,	5	103	35	28	1	172
60 to 79 years,	4	121	36	13	1	175
80 years and over,	1	13	-	2	-	16
Age unknown,	-	-	1	-	-	1
Concord,	575	783	160	416	6	1,940
20 to 29 years,	496	242	25	241	-	1,004
30 to 39 years,	64	166	35	100	1	366
40 to 49 years,	9	142	44	33	-	228
50 to 59 years,	4	101	26	20	2	153
60 to 79 years,	2	122	29	20	2	175
80 years and over,	-	10	1	2	1	14
Dracut,	108	372	162	197	4	843
20 to 29 years,	62	99	33	91	-	285
30 to 39 years,	15	95	30	32	-	172
40 to 49 years,	9	67	38	30	-	144
50 to 59 years,	7	52	33	19	-	111
60 to 79 years,	6	53	26	18	3	106
80 years and over,	-	5	2	-	1	8
Age unknown,	9	1	-	7	-	17
Dunstable,	7	122	12	11	-	152
20 to 29 years,	5	23	2	4	-	34
30 to 39 years,	1	21	3	3	-	28

POLITICAL CONDITION: BY AGE PERIODS — Continued.

Counties, Cities, Towns, and Age Periods.	Ratable Polls (Not Voters)	Ratable Polls and Native Born Voters	Ratable Polls and Foreign Born Naturalized Voters	Ratable Polls and Aliens	No Political Condition	Total Male Population 20 Years of Age and over
MIDDLESEX — Con.						
Dunstable — Con.						
40 to 49 years,	1	12	5	1	–	19
50 to 59 years,	–	20	2	1	–	23
60 to 79 years,	–	39	–	2	–	41
80 years and over,	–	7	–	–	–	7
EVERETT,	207	3,189	901	1,143	–	5,530
20 to 29 years,	200	929	136	434	–	1,699
30 to 39 years,	49	870	279	366	–	1,564
40 to 49 years,	23	630	236	188	–	1,077
50 to 59 years,	19	420	147	99	–	685
60 to 79 years,	5	318	100	55	–	476
80 years and over,	–	22	2	3	–	27
Age unknown,	1	–	1	–	–	2
Framingham,	168	1,823	485	355	7	2,838
20 to 29 years,	104	505	56	141	–	806
30 to 39 years,	17	517	127	96	1	758
40 to 49 years,	19	339	121	61	–	540
50 to 59 years,	6	212	94	33	1	346
60 to 79 years,	8	224	79	21	2	334
80 years and over,	–	26	7	2	3	38
Age unknown,	14	–	1	1	–	16
Groton,	46	451	43	74	3	617
20 to 29 years,	25	88	–	24	–	137
30 to 39 years,	7	117	8	16	1	149
40 to 49 years,	9	87	12	12	2	122
50 to 59 years,	1	60	11	6	–	78
60 to 79 years,	4	85	10	16	–	115
80 years and over,	–	14	2	–	–	16
Holliston,	47	614	120	91	9	881
20 to 29 years,	24	151	1	25	–	201
30 to 39 years,	11	138	18	29	–	196
40 to 49 years,	10	109	19	11	2	151
50 to 59 years,	1	89	38	11	4	143
60 to 79 years,	1	107	40	12	2	162
80 years and over,	–	20	4	3	1	28
Hopkinton,	33	696	206	48	11	994
20 to 29 years,	28	214	4	8	–	254
30 to 39 years,	2	177	8	9	1	197
40 to 49 years,	3	120	34	9	–	166
50 to 59 years,	–	70	76	10	2	158
60 to 79 years,	–	105	79	10	8	202
80 years and over,	–	10	5	2	–	17
Hudson,	62	1,072	224	281	1	1,640
20 to 29 years,	53	328	16	97	–	494
30 to 39 years,	3	270	55	80	–	408
40 to 49 years,	3	187	51	47	–	288
50 to 59 years,	3	131	60	26	–	220
60 to 79 years,	–	145	41	28	1	215
80 years and over,	–	11	1	3	–	15
Lexington,	77	700	148	264	5	1,194
20 to 29 years,	58	163	13	112	–	346
30 to 39 years,	11	170	43	81	1	306
40 to 49 years,	2	138	33	27	–	200
50 to 59 years,	3	99	26	28	–	156
60 to 79 years,	3	114	27	14	3	161
80 years and over,	–	16	6	2	1	25

POLITICAL CONDITION : BY AGE PERIODS — Continued.

COUNTIES, CITIES, TOWNS, AND AGE PERIODS.	Ratable Polls (Not Voters)	Ratable Polls and Native Born Voters	Ratable Polls and Foreign Born Naturalized Voters	Ratable Polls and Aliens	No Political Condition	Total Male Population 20 Years of Age and Over
MIDDLESEX — Con.						
Lincoln, ...	76	185	44	141	1	447
20 to 29 years, ...	43	53	13	68	-	177
30 to 39 years, ...	14	55	6	28	- ·	103
40 to 49 years, ...	15	32	9	15	-	71
50 to 59 years, ...	3	9	10	19	-	41
60 to 79 years, ...	1	33	5	11	-	50
80 years and over,. . . .	-	3	1	-	1	5
Littleton, ...	25	239	35	71	-	370
20 to 29 years, ...	15	58	3	32	-	108
30 to 39 years, ...	2	59	3	22	-	86
40 to 49 years, ...	4	40	11	6	-	61
50 to 59 years, ...	2	23	7	6	-	38
60 to 79 years, ...	2	52	8	5	-	67
80 years and over,. . . .	-	7	3	-	-	10
LOWELL, ...	1,154	9,924	6,484	6,230	83	23,875
20 to 29 years, ...	929	3,334	1,481	2,711	4	8,459
30 to 39 years, ...	123	2,765	1,846	1,509	10	6,253
40 to 49 years, ...	54	1,839	1,469	968	13	4,343
50 to 59 years, ...	20	1,006	968	614	19	2,627
60 to 79 years, ...	15	907	690	394	34	2,040
80 years and over,. . . .	-	72	26	29	3	130
Age unknown, ...	13	1	4	5	-	23
MALDEN, ...	469	5,038	1,484	1,865	9	8,865
20 to 29 years, ...	341	1,405	260	786	1	2,793
30 to 39 years, ...	61	1,451	422	556	1	2,491
40 to 49 years, ...	30	965	352	275	1	1,623
50 to 59 years, ...	14	638	247	140	3	1,042
60 to 79 years, ...	11	537	192	98	3	841
80 years and over,. . . .	-	42	10	7	-	59
Age unknown, ...	12	-	1	3	-	16
MARLBOROUGH, ...	244	2,550	895	781	19	4,489
20 to 29 years, ...	190	972	104	236	2	1,504
30 to 39 years, ...	36	741	186	238	2	1,203
40 to 49 years, ...	8	405	212	133	2	760
50 to 59 years, ...	3	227	204	93	5	532
60 to 79 years, ...	5	194	181	74	6	460
80 years and over,. . . .	-	11	8	5	1	25
Age unknown, ...	2	-	-	2	1	5
Maynard, ...	51	375	223	299	8	956
20 to 29 years, ...	35	124	30	117	-	306
30 to 39 years, ...	10	128	53	87	-	278
40 to 49 years, ...	3	58	54	46	2	163
50 to 59 years, ...	2	35	52	24	-	113
60 to 79 years, ...	1	28	34	23	5	91
80 years and over,. . . .	-	2	-	2	1	5
MEDFORD, ...	322	2,704	617	846	15	4,504
20 to 29 years, ...	213	800	89	380	-	1,482
30 to 39 years, ...	41	710	158	219	1	1,129
40 to 49 years, ...	19	510	146	135	2	812
50 to 59 years, ...	40	336	125	72	-	573
60 to 79 years, ...	9	318	92	39	9	467
80 years and over,. . . .	-	30	7	1	3	41
Melrose, ...	143	2,317	534	572	2	3,568
20 to 29 years, ...	106	568	90	269	-	1,033
30 to 39 years, ...	18	646	175	174	-	1,013
40 to 49 years, ...	10	508	95	73	-	686

POLITICAL CONDITION: BY AGE PERIODS — Continued.

COUNTIES, CITIES, TOWNS, AND AGE PERIODS.	Ratable Polls (Not Voters)	Ratable Polls and Native Born Voters	Ratable Polls and Foreign Born Naturalized Voters	Ratable Polls and Aliens	No Political Condition	Total Male Population 20 Years of Age and over
MIDDLESEX — Con.						
Melrose — Con.						
50 to 59 years,	6	305	84	33	2	431
60 to 79 years,	2	261	87	20	-	370
80 years and over,	-	28	3	2	-	33
Age unknown,	1	-	-	1	-	2
Natick,	134	1,830	504	246	12	2,726
20 to 29 years,	83	532	56	96	-	767
30 to 39 years,	30	452	83	72	-	637
40 to 49 years,	10	367	113	34	2	526
50 to 59 years,	5	241	132	27	2	407
60 to 79 years,	5	227	118	17	8	375
80 years and over,	1	11	2	-	-	14
NEWTON,	387	4,498	1,119	1,870	8	7,882
20 to 29 years,	274	1,294	181	820	-	2,479
30 to 39 years,	52	1,115	267	538	2	1,972
40 to 49 years,	24	951	258	281	1	1,515
50 to 59 years,	20	606	221	143	3	993
60 to 79 years,	7	561	175	81	2	826
80 years and over,	-	59	12	2	-	73
Age unknown,	10	4	5	5	-	24
North Reading,	22	212	16	34	-	284
20 to 29 years,	13	39	1	17	-	70
30 to 39 years,	5	34	5	8	-	52
40 to 49 years,	1	45	5	5	-	56
50 to 59 years,	2	38	2	1	-	45
60 to 79 years,	1	51	3	3	-	58
80 years and over,	-	5	-	-	-	5
Pepperell,	54	725	75	181	5	1,040
20 to 29 years,	36	166	9	46	1	258
30 to 39 years,	7	171	20	69	1	279
40 to 49 years,	7	135	24	37	1	204
50 to 59 years,	1	99	10	26	-	136
60 to 79 years,	3	131	12	10	2	158
80 years and over,	-	23	-	2	-	25
Reading,	104	1,023	161	197	5	1,490
20 to 29 years,	51	244	47	75	-	417
30 to 39 years,	34	238	32	62	-	366
40 to 49 years,	11	227	34	32	1	305
50 to 59 years,	6	134	18	19	2	179
60 to 79 years,	2	155	27	9	1	194
80 years and over,	-	25	3	-	1	29
Sherborn,	27	234	35	79	1	376
20 to 29 years,	15	31	3	31	-	80
30 to 39 years,	6	48	12	33	-	99
40 to 49 years,	1	56	3	6	-	66
50 to 59 years,	3	30	8	4	-	45
60 to 79 years,	2	62	8	4	-	76
80 years and over,	-	7	1	-	1	9
Age unknown,	-	-	-	1	-	1
Shirley,	26	273	42	69	-	410
20 to 29 years,	18	64	4	20	-	106
30 to 39 years,	3	49	11	12	-	75
40 to 49 years,	4	48	3	13	-	68
50 to 59 years,	1	46	13	11	-	71
60 to 79 years,	-	60	11	10	-	81
80 years and over,	-	6	-	1	-	7
Age unknown,	-	-	-	2	-	2

POLITICAL CONDITION: BY AGE PERIODS — Continued.

Counties, Cities, Towns, and Age Periods.	Ratable Polls (Not Voters)	Ratable Polls and Native Born Voters	Ratable Polls and Foreign Born Naturalized Voters	Ratable Polls and Aliens	No Political Condition	Total Male Population 20 Years of Age and Over
MIDDLESEX — Con.						
SOMERVILLE, ...	889	9,211	2,628	3,262	-	15,960
20 to 29 years, ...	605	2,874	373	1,284	-	5,136
30 to 39 years, ...	136	2,458	753	994	-	4,321
40 to 49 years, ...	66	1,827	628	475	-	2,996
50 to 59 years, ...	39	1,113	462	261	-	1,875
60 to 79 years, ...	39	892	381	194	-	1,506
80 years and over,. . . .	-	65	23	16	-	104
Age unknown, ...	4	2	8	8	-	22
Stoneham, ...	67	1,445	312	238	11	2,073
20 to 29 years, ...	55	419	40	121	4	639
30 to 39 years, ...	5	319	61	69	-	454
40 to 49 years, ...	5	257	56	26	-	344
50 to 59 years, ...	1	198	91	15	2	307
60 to 79 years, ...	1	228	60	6	4	299
80 years and over,. . . .	-	24	4	1	1	30
Stow, ...	25	210	30	60	1	326
20 to 29 years, ...	18	44	1	27	-	90
30 to 39 years, ...	3	37	6	18	-	64
40 to 49 years, ...	3	40	7	6	-	56
50 to 59 years, ...	1	27	7	7	-	42
60 to 79 years, ...	-	58	9	2	-	69
80 years and over,. . . .	-	4	-	-	1	5
Sudbury, ...	16	290	29	83	4	422
20 to 29 years, ...	7	59	1	38	-	105
30 to 39 years, ...	3	62	2	18	1	86
40 to 49 years, ...	4	63	10	12	1	90
50 to 59 years, ...	1	42	5	4	-	52
60 to 79 years, ...	1	55	11	11	2	80
80 years and over,. . . .	-	9	-	-	-	9
Tewksbury, ...	87	299	124	188	444	1,142
20 to 29 years, ...	51	70	14	77	48	260
30 to 39 years, ...	17	69	34	52	75	247
40 to 49 years, ...	6	69	30	31	88	224
50 to 59 years, ...	5	29	27	16	89	166
60 to 79 years, ...	7	56	16	11	124	214
80 years and over,. . . .	-	5	2	-	13	20
Age unknown, ...	1	1	1	1	7	11
Townsend, ...	36	497	38	48	5	624
20 to 29 years, ...	20	94	1	16	-	131
30 to 39 years, ...	7	82	7	13	-	109
40 to 49 years, ...	6	93	12	8	-	119
50 to 59 years, ...	1	89	8	5	-	103
60 to 79 years, ...	1	119	8	6	3	137
80 years and over,. . . .	-	20	2	-	2	24
Age unknown, ...	1	-	-	-	-	1
Tyngsborough, ...	20	149	8	41	1	219
20 to 29 years, ...	13	22	2	17	-	54
30 to 39 years, ...	3	36	1	12	1	53
40 to 49 years, ...	1	29	1	5	-	36
50 to 59 years, ...	2	30	3	1	-	36
60 to 79 years, ...	1	26	1	5	-	33
80 years and over,. . . .	-	6	-	-	-	6
Age unknown, ...	-	-	-	1	-	1
Wakefield, ...	150	1,475	410	476	5	2,496
20 to 29 years, ...	85	361	57	218	-	721
30 to 39 years, ...	27	362	98	126	-	613

POLITICAL CONDITION: BY AGE PERIODS — Continued.

Counties, Cities, Towns, and Age Periods.	Ratable Polls (Not Voters)	Ratable Polls and Native Born Voters	Ratable Polls and Foreign Born Naturalized Voters	Ratable Polls and Aliens	No Political Condition	Total Male Population 20 Years of Age and Over
MIDDLESEX — Con.						
Wakefield — Con.						
40 to 49 years,	7	284	110	69	-	470
50 to 59 years,	7	198	86	38	2	331
60 to 79 years,	2	249	59	21	2	333
80 years and over,	-	20	-	1	1	22
Age unknown,	2	1	-	3	-	6
WALTHAM,	294	3,419	1,155	1,189	17	6,074
20 to 29 years,	244	1,050	201	448	1	1,944
30 to 39 years,	25	996	335	390	-	1,746
40 to 49 years,	13	619	246	169	4	1,051
50 to 59 years,	4	373	211	104	1	693
60 to 79 years,	3	344	153	70	10	580
80 years and over,	-	35	9	6	1	51
Age unknown,	5	2	-	2	-	9
Watertown,	171	1,299	452	516	7	2,445
20 to 29 years,	112	418	60	242	-	832
30 to 39 years,	27	337	110	129	-	603
40 to 49 years,	16	238	111	80	-	445
50 to 59 years,	6	154	90	38	2	290
60 to 79 years,	8	128	80	24	4	234
80 years and over,	-	14	1	3	1	19
Age unknown,	2	-	-	-	-	2
Wayland,	24	459	76	99	2	660
20 to 29 years,	21	144	6	37	-	208
30 to 39 years,	1	111	18	18	-	148
40 to 49 years,	1	85	25	23	-	134
50 to 59 years,	-	60	18	9	1	88
60 to 79 years,	1	50	9	12	1	73
80 years and over,	-	9	-	-	-	9
Westford,	67	396	110	173	4	790
20 to 29 years,	41	80	22	63	-	206
30 to 39 years,	9	88	17	47	-	161
40 to 49 years,	8	66	13	33	-	120
50 to 59 years,	5	74	28	19	-	126
60 to 79 years,	4	83	29	11	1	128
80 years and over,	-	5	1	-	3	9
Weston,	35	356	38	156	2	587
20 to 29 years,	15	76	5	84	-	180
30 to 39 years,	5	69	15	34	-	123
40 to 49 years,	10	77	6	16	-	109
50 to 59 years,	2	53	5	13	1	74
60 to 79 years,	3	74	6	7	1	91
80 years and over,	-	7	1	2	-	10
Wilmington,	11	286	47	92	2	438
20 to 29 years,	11	48	6	32	-	97
30 to 39 years,	-	68	12	28	-	108
40 to 49 years,	-	55	15	21	-	91
50 to 59 years,	-	46	8	6	-	60
60 to 79 years,	-	64	6	5	2	77
80 years and over,	-	5	-	-	-	5
Winchester,	125	1,037	353	351	2	1,868
20 to 29 years,	84	292	61	163	-	600
30 to 39 years,	21	268	92	88	-	469
40 to 49 years,	11	217	90	63	-	581
50 to 59 years,	5	118	63	25	2	213
60 to 79 years,	4	130	46	11	-	191
80 years and over,	-	12	1	1	-	14

POLITICAL CONDITION: BY AGE PERIODS — Continued.

COUNTIES, CITIES, TOWNS, AND AGE PERIODS.	Ratable Polls (Not Voters)	Ratable Polls and Native Born Voters	Ratable Polls and Foreign Born Naturalized Voters	Ratable Polls and Aliens	No Political Condition	Total Male Population 20 Years of Age and Over
MIDDLESEX — Con.						
WOBURN,	171	2,148	1,179	670	22	4,190
20 to 29 years,	142	724	150	291	1	1,308
30 to 39 years,	17	561	315	186	2	1,081
40 to 49 years,	5	388	317	95	1	806
50 to 59 years,	6	194	221	63	4	488
60 to 79 years,	1	250	172	32	13	468
80 years and over,	-	31	4	3	1	39
NANTUCKET.						
Nantucket,	29	883	53	33	11	959
20 to 29 years,	17	132	5	15	1	170
30 to 39 years,	3	179	7	8	-	197
40 to 49 years,	5	154	5	5	2	171
50 to 59 years,	2	123	10	3	4	142
60 to 79 years,	2	210	24	2	3	241
80 years and over,	-	35	2	-	1	38
NORFOLK.						
Avon,	41	401	68	30	1	541
20 to 29 years,	20	120	3	11	-	154
30 to 39 years,	8	99	6	9	-	122
40 to 49 years,	7	76	10	7	-	100
50 to 59 years,	2	49	17	1	-	69
60 to 79 years,	4	53	32	1	1	91
80 years and over,	-	4	-	1	-	5
Bellingham,	41	281	42	89	3	456
20 to 29 years,	15	64	6	35	-	120
30 to 39 years,	13	62	10	26	-	111
40 to 49 years,	4	46	9	12	-	71
50 to 59 years,	3	41	11	7	-	62
60 to 79 years,	5	63	6	9	1	84
80 years and over,	1	5	-	-	2	8
Braintree,	68	1,134	197	380	7	1,786
20 to 29 years,	59	287	31	178	-	555
30 to 39 years,	6	315	45	126	-	492
40 to 49 years,	-	199	46	41	-	286
50 to 59 years,	-	153	40	14	1	208
60 to 79 years,	2	167	35	17	4	225
80 years and over,	-	13	-	3	2	18
Age unknown,	1	-	-	1	-	2
Brookline,	221	2,360	883	907	-	4,371
20 to 29 years,	165	654	133	416	-	1,368
30 to 39 years,	25	698	225	272	-	1,220
40 to 49 years,	13	439	231	114	-	797
50 to 59 years,	10	302	156	68	-	536
60 to 79 years,	8	233	132	34	-	407
80 years and over,	-	34	6	2	-	42
Age unknown,	-	-	-	1	-	1
Canton,	53	809	287	198	11	1,358
20 to 29 years,	49	268	32	59	1	409
30 to 39 years,	3	227	70	50	-	350
40 to 49 years,	-	126	57	29	3	215
50 to 59 years,	1	78	64	20	-	163
60 to 79 years,	-	98	60	40	5	203
80 years and over,	-	12	4	-	2	18

POLITICAL CONDITION: BY AGE PERIODS — Continued.

COUNTIES, CITIES, TOWNS, AND AGE PERIODS.	Ratable Polls (Not Voters)	Ratable Polls and Native Born Voters	Ratable Polls and Foreign Born Naturalized Voters	Ratable Polls and Aliens	No Political Condition	Total Male Population 20 Years of Age and Over
NORFOLK — Con.						
Cohasset, ...	19	573	92	100	6	790
20 to 29 years, ...	19	134	11	40	–	204
30 to 39 years, ...	–	142	15	26	–	183
40 to 49 years, ...	–	93	28	13	1	135
50 to 59 years, ...	–	82	21	8	2	113
60 to 79 years, ...	–	108	16	10	3	137
80 years and over, ...	–	14	1	3	–	18
Dedham, ...	210	1,262	440	311	6	2,229
20 to 29 years, ...	130	379	42	113	2	666
30 to 39 years, ...	35	346	86	78	–	545
40 to 49 years, ...	25	216	98	43	–	382
50 to 59 years, ...	8	140	83	37	1	269
60 to 79 years, ...	8	162	123	29	3	325
80 years and over, ...	–	19	3	4	–	26
Age unknown, ...	4	–	5	7	–	16
Dover, ...	23	127	42	25	–	217
20 to 29 years, ...	7	38	13	1	–	59
30 to 39 years, ...	6	22	4	8	–	40
40 to 49 years, ...	6	18	4	4	–	32
50 to 59 years, ...	2	19	4	7	–	32
60 to 79 years, ...	2	28	17	5	–	52
80 years and over, ...	–	2	–	–	–	2
Foxborough, ...	97	732	105	99	7	1,061
20 to 29 years, ...	45	144	7	25	–	221
30 to 39 years, ...	16	186	13	25	4	244
40 to 49 years, ...	14	135	27	18	1	195
50 to 59 years, ...	15	99	20	17	–	151
60 to 79 years, ...	7	172	34	13	1	227
80 years and over, ...	–	17	4	1	1	23
Franklin, ...	80	978	204	288	2	1,554
20 to 29 years, ...	58	284	16	109	2	469
30 to 39 years, ...	11	247	27	88	–	373
40 to 49 years, ...	6	171	64	45	–	286
50 to 59 years, ...	2	121	49	32	–	204
60 to 79 years, ...	3	144	48	13	–	208
80 years and over, ...	–	11	2	1	–	14
Holbrook, ...	34	556	89	34	11	724
20 to 29 years, ...	27	144	8	11	–	190
30 to 39 years, ...	3	118	18	7	2	148
40 to 49 years, ...	3	127	20	10	3	163
50 to 59 years, ...	–	70	24	2	3	99
60 to 79 years, ...	1	84	18	4	2	109
80 years and over, ...	–	12	1	–	1	14
Age unknown, ...	–	1	–	–	–	1
Hyde Park, ...	209	2,920	752	558	2	3,541
20 to 29 years, ...	156	642	113	217	2	1,130
30 to 39 years, ...	28	500	189	149	–	866
40 to 49 years, ...	16	405	172	92	–	685
50 to 59 years, ...	3	240	169	63	–	475
60 to 79 years, ...	4	215	105	33	–	357
80 years and over, ...	–	18	4	2	–	24
Age unknown, ...	2	–	–	2	–	4
Medfield, ...	66	392	55	126	3	642
20 to 29 years, ...	39	83	7	68	1	198
30 to 39 years, ...	16	99	10	37	–	162
40 to 49 years, ...	5	74	17	14	2	112

POLITICAL CONDITION: BY AGE PERIODS — Continued.

COUNTIES, CITIES, TOWNS, AND AGE PERIODS.	Ratable Polls (Not Voters)	Ratable Polls and Native Born Voters	Ratable Polls and Foreign Born Naturalized Voters	Ratable Polls and Aliens	No Political Condition	Total Male Population 20 Years of Age and over
NORFOLK — Con.						
Medfield — Con.						
50 to 59 years,	3	58	12	5	-	78
60 to 79 years,	1	64	8	2	-	75
80 years and over,	1	14	1	-	-	16
Age unknown,	1	-	-	-	-	1
Medway,	30	681	137	70	11	929
20 to 29 years,	21	174	9	18	-	222
30 to 39 years,	5	168	17	15	1	206
40 to 49 years,	4	123	24	15	2	168
50 to 59 years,	-	90	45	13	2	150
60 to 79 years,	-	107	40	8	5	160
80 years and over,	-	18	2	1	1	22
Age unknown,	-	1	-	-	-	1
Millis,	23	194	37	53	-	307
20 to 29 years,	13	33	3	21	-	70
30 to 39 years,	6	55	7	15	-	83
40 to 49 years,	1	32	10	8	-	51
50 to 59 years,	1	31	5	5	-	42
60 to 79 years,	2	40	11	4	-	57
80 years and over,	-	3	1	-	-	4
Milton,	74	902	269	341	7	1,593
20 to 29 years,	59	267	40	160	-	526
30 to 39 years,	9	243	72	85	-	409
40 to 49 years,	3	176	64	46	-	289
50 to 59 years,	1	97	53	23	-	174
60 to 79 years,	1	102	38	25	5	171
80 years and over,	1	17	2	2	2	24
Needham,	90	548	215	265	2	1,120
20 to 29 years,	57	184	14	107	-	362
30 to 39 years,	16	120	51	85	-	272
40 to 49 years,	7	88	55	31	-	181
50 to 59 years,	8	75	43	18	-	144
60 to 79 years,	2	73	50	22	2	149
80 years and over,	-	8	2	2	-	12
Norfolk,	25	166	27	75	2	295
20 to 29 years,	17	46	1	31	-	95
30 to 39 years,	4	25	4	18	-	51
40 to 49 years,	2	32	9	11	1	55
50 to 59 years,	1	26	9	8	-	44
60 to 79 years,	1	33	4	6	-	44
80 years and over,	-	4	-	1	1	6
Norwood,	79	806	327	339	1	1,552
20 to 29 years,	59	268	43	182	1	553
30 to 39 years,	9	221	95	99	-	424
40 to 49 years,	6	137	90	31	-	264
50 to 59 years,	1	83	46	16	-	146
60 to 79 years,	2	84	51	10	-	147
80 years and over,	-	13	2	1	-	16
Age unknown,	2	-	-	-	-	2
QUINCY,	338	2,871	1,454	1,701	8	6,372
20 to 29 years,	241	875	240	740	1	2,097
30 to 39 years,	46	796	448	545	1	1,836
40 to 49 years,	24	528	371	235	1	1,159
50 to 59 years,	12	335	220	105	2	674
60 to 79 years,	14	305	161	65	1	546
80 years and over,	1	32	14	9	2	58
Age unknown,	-	-	-	2	-	2

POLITICAL CONDITION: BY AGE PERIODS — Continued.

Counties, Cities, Towns, and Age Periods.	Ratable Polls (Not Voters)	Ratable Polls and Native Born Voters	Ratable Polls and Foreign Born Naturalized Voters	Ratable Polls and Aliens	No Political Condition	Total Male Population 20 Years of Age and Over
NORFOLK — Con.						
Randolph, ...	26	907	216	73	8	1,230
20 to 29 years, . . .	20	236	18	24	-	298
30 to 39 years, . . .	5	233	21	15	-	274
40 to 49 years, . . .	-	177	42	8	4	231
50 to 59 years, . . .	1	126	51	12	-	190
60 to 79 years, . . .	-	122	79	14	4	219
80 years and over, . . .	-	13	5	-	-	18
Sharon, ...	35	362	61	112	-	570
20 to 29 years, . . .	25	66	6	55	-	152
30 to 39 years, . . .	5	73	14	32	-	124
40 to 49 years, . . .	3	63	14	14	-	94
50 to 59 years, . . .	2	77	16	6	-	101
60 to 79 years, . . .	-	73	11	4	-	88
80 years and over, . . .	-	10	-	1	-	11
Stoughton, ...	53	1,104	229	215	10	1,611
20 to 29 years, . . .	45	306	27	66	-	444
30 to 39 years, . . .	4	272	44	73	-	393
40 to 49 years, . . .	3	222	44	28	1	298
50 to 59 years, . . .	-	126	54	34	-	214
60 to 79 years, . . .	1	153	59	14	7	234
80 years and over, . . .	-	24	1	-	2	27
Age unknown, . . .	-	1	-	-	-	1
Walpole, ...	23	598	117	213	2	953
20 to 29 years, . . .	23	154	23	82	2	284
30 to 39 years, . . .	-	145	31	52	-	228
40 to 49 years, . . .	-	123	25	28	-	176
50 to 59 years, . . .	-	77	21	25	-	123
60 to 79 years, . . .	-	89	16	22	-	127
80 years and over, . . .	-	10	1	3	-	14
Age unknown, . . .	-	-	-	1	-	1
Wellesley, ...	27	592	162	203	1	925
20 to 29 years, . . .	21	156	24	84	-	265
30 to 39 years, . . .	2	126	38	66	-	232
40 to 49 years, . . .	1	115	45	28	-	189
50 to 59 years, . . .	-	69	28	14	-	111
60 to 79 years, . . .	-	82	25	10	1	118
80 years and over, . . .	-	4	2	1	-	7
Age unknown, . . .	3	-	-	-	-	3
Weymouth, ...	163	2,061	378	592	25	3,729
20 to 29 years, . . .	125	752	14	167	-	1,058
30 to 39 years, . . .	15	603	52	166	3	839
40 to 49 years, . . .	14	498	86	105	4	707
50 to 59 years, . . .	3	345	111	33	7	499
60 to 79 years, . . .	5	424	119	31	6	576
80 years and over, . . .	1	38	4	-	5	48
Age unknown, . . .	-	1	1	-	-	2
Wrentham, ...	38	606	94	62	1	801
20 to 29 years, . . .	27	118	13	15	-	173
30 to 39 years, . . .	4	133	17	22	1	177
40 to 49 years, . . .	1	131	23	12	-	167
50 to 59 years, . . .	2	89	17	7	-	115
60 to 79 years, . . .	4	118	23	6	-	151
80 years and over, . . .	-	17	1	-	-	18
PLYMOUTH.						
Abington, ...	62	1,262	166	64	7	1,561
20 to 29 years, . . .	41	271	12	25	2	351

POLITICAL CONDITION: BY AGE PERIODS — Continued.

Counties, Cities, Towns, and Age Periods.	Ratable Polls (Not Voters)	Ratable Polls and Native Born Voters	Ratable Polls and Foreign Born Naturalized Voters	Ratable Polls and Aliens	No Political Condition	Total Male Population 20 Years of Age and Over
PLYMOUTH — Con.						
Abington — Con.						
30 to 39 years,	8	305	24	16	1	354
40 to 49 years,	7	206	28	6	1	248
50 to 59 years,	3	141	34	4	1	183
60 to 79 years,	2	151	66	13	2	234
80 years and over,	-	17	2	-	-	19
Age unknown,	1	1	-	-	-	2
Bridgewater,	569	869	123	136	453	2,150
20 to 29 years,	183	212	12	42	41	490
30 to 39 years,	173	228	21	29	111	562
40 to 49 years,	122	158	16	24	82	402
50 to 59 years,	72	193	27	22	89	313
60 to 79 years,	19	148	46	18	114	345
80 years and over,	-	19	1	1	4	25
Age unknown,	-	1	-	-	12	13
BROCKTON,	496	6,893	1,638	1,674	17	10,718
20 to 29 years,	355	2,105	320	736	4	3,520
30 to 39 years,	49	2,052	567	525	-	3,193
40 to 49 years,	24	1,391	357	235	4	2,011
50 to 59 years,	17	712	241	107	1	1,078
60 to 79 years,	7	596	147	64	5	819
80 years and over,	-	37	5	6	3	51
Age unknown,	44	-	1	1	-	46
Carver,	29	259	10	57	3	358
20 to 29 years,	20	56	-	23	-	99
30 to 39 years,	4	58	3	17	-	82
40 to 49 years,	2	42	3	11	-	58
50 to 59 years,	3	48	2	3	1	57
60 to 79 years,	-	46	2	3	2	53
80 years and over,	-	9	-	-	-	9
Duxbury,	18	538	17	67	8	648
20 to 29 years,	15	84	1	21	1	122
30 to 39 years,	1	91	4	20	1	117
40 to 49 years,	1	100	6	16	1	124
50 to 59 years,	-	87	2	8	-	97
60 to 79 years,	1	147	4	2	2	156
80 years and over,	-	29	-	-	3	32
East Bridgewater,	60	715	65	126	5	971
20 to 29 years,	39	164	5	44	-	252
30 to 39 years,	7	131	10	58	1	187
40 to 49 years,	5	143	16	20	1	185
50 to 59 years,	6	107	17	12	-	142
60 to 79 years,	1	152	15	12	3	183
80 years and over,	2	18	2	-	-	22
Halifax,	6	138	8	22	-	174
20 to 29 years,	5	29	3	7	-	44
30 to 39 years,	1	19	-	4	-	24
40 to 49 years,	-	20	5	8	-	33
50 to 59 years,	-	28	-	1	-	29
60 to 79 years,	-	37	-	1	-	38
80 years and over,	-	5	-	1	-	6
Hanover,	61	554	50	60	11	716
20 to 29 years,	44	108	1	24	-	177
30 to 39 years,	7	112	6	18	-	143
40 to 49 years,	4	111	4	10	-	129
50 to 59 years,	1	79	14	4	1	99
60 to 79 years,	5	133	4	3	9	154

POLITICAL CONDITION: BY AGE PERIODS — Continued.

COUNTIES, CITIES, TOWNS, AND AGE PERIODS.	Ratable Polls (Not Voters)	Ratable Polls and Native Born Voters	Ratable Polls and Foreign Born Naturalized Voters	Ratable Polls and Aliens	No Political Condition	Total Male Population 20 Years of Age and Over
PLYMOUTH — Con.						
Hanover — Con.						
80 years and over,	-	11	-	-	1	12
Age unknown,	-	-	1	1	-	2
Hanson,	29	375	11	57	6	478
20 to 29 years,	22	64	2	22	-	110
30 to 39 years,	2	79	-	15	-	96
40 to 49 years,	3	71	3	8	2	87
50 to 59 years,	1	57	3	7	2	70
60 to 79 years,	1	85	2	4	2	94
80 years and over,	-	19	1	1	-	21
Hingham,	72	1,098	158	240	4	1,572
20 to 29 years,	47	245	22	101	-	415
30 to 39 years,	9	232	24	73	-	338
40 to 49 years,	8	195	33	31	-	267
50 to 59 years,	3	169	30	22	1	225
60 to 79 years,	5	220	48	11	2	286
80 years and over,	-	37	1	2	1	41
Hull,	145	159	33	56	-	393
20 to 29 years,	48	32	4	26	-	110
30 to 39 years,	27	33	15	18	-	93
40 to 49 years,	30	44	8	5	-	87
50 to 59 years,	29	33	1	5	-	68
60 to 79 years,	10	15	5	2	-	32
80 years and over,	1	2	-	-	-	3
Kingston,	32	430	43	57	-	562
20 to 29 years,	16	88	5	16	-	128
30 to 39 years,	7	97	4	17	-	125
40 to 49 years,	4	81	9	9	-	103
50 to 59 years,	1	69	6	10	-	86
60 to 79 years,	1	82	16	4	-	103
80 years and over,	-	13	3	1	-	17
Lakeville,	20	245	9	30	1	305
20 to 29 years,	12	36	2	13	-	63
30 to 39 years,	3	47	1	9	-	60
40 to 49 years,	2	32	2	2	-	38
50 to 59 years,	1	44	1	4	-	50
60 to 79 years,	2	77	3	2	1	85
80 years and over,	-	9	-	-	-	9
Marion,	9	203	4	4	1	221
20 to 29 years,	6	26	-	3	-	35
30 to 39 years,	1	46	-	1	-	48
40 to 49 years,	1	39	2	-	-	42
50 to 59 years,	1	38	-	-	-	39
60 to 79 years,	-	50	2	-	1	53
80 years and over,	-	4	-	-	-	4
Mar-hfield,	13	522	14	55	4	608
20 to 29 years,	11	79	1	16	-	107
30 to 39 years,	1	77	5	17	-	100
40 to 49 years,	1	100	2	7	1	111
50 to 59 years,	-	94	1	5	1	101
60 to 79 years,	-	150	5	8	1	164
80 years and over,	-	22	-	1	1	24
Age unknown,	-	-	-	1	-	1
Mattapoisett,	23	294	5	24	3	346
20 to 29 years,	20	43	-	15	-	78
30 to 39 years,	1	47	-	6	1	55
40 to 49 years,	1	47	1	2	-	51

POLITICAL CONDITION: BY AGE PERIODS — Continued.

Counties, Cities, Towns, and Age Periods.	Ratable Polls (Not Voters)	Ratable Polls and Native Born Voters	Ratable Polls and Foreign Born Naturalized Voters	Ratable Polls and Aliens	No Political Condition	Total Male Population 20 Years of Age and Over
PLYMOUTH — Con.						
Mattapoi-ett — Con.						
50 to 59 years,	1	61	1	-	-	63
60 to 79 years,	-	82	1	1	2	86
80 years and over,	-	11	1	-	-	12
Age unknown,	-	-	1	-	-	1
Middleborough,	119	1,706	137	220	12	2,194
20 to 29 years,	72	399	16	92	2	581
30 to 39 years,	15	403	27	66	1	512
40 to 49 years,	10	299	33	33	2	377
50 to 59 years,	7	256	33	15	2	313
60 to 79 years,	10	306	25	14	3	358
80 years and over,	3	42	3	-	2	50
Age unknown,	2	1	-	-	-	3
Norwell,	23	455	18	26	1	523
20 to 29 years,	17	96	2	14	-	129
30 to 39 years,	2	93	4	6	-	105
40 to 49 years,	3	71	3	3	-	80
50 to 59 years,	1	91	4	-	1	97
60 to 79 years,	-	95	5	3	-	103
80 years and over,	-	9	-	-	-	9
Pembroke,	17	347	22	42	5	433
20 to 29 years,	11	61	1	6	-	79
30 to 39 years,	2	61	2	14	1	80
40 to 49 years,	-	59	5	7	1	72
50 to 59 years,	2	53	6	10	-	71
60 to 79 years,	2	104	8	3	1	118
80 years and over,	-	9	-	2	2	13
Plymouth,	97	1,757	209	378	12	2,453
20 to 29 years,	71	409	25	134	-	639
30 to 39 years,	14	408	31	120	1	574
40 to 49 years,	11	341	49	62	3	466
50 to 59 years,	1	278	46	37	1	363
60 to 79 years,	-	289	53	23	5	370
80 years and over,	-	32	5	2	2	41
Plympton,	16	152	6	18	-	192
20 to 29 years,	8	32	-	4	-	44
30 to 39 years,	3	21	-	5	-	29
40 to 49 years,	-	23	-	4	-	27
50 to 59 years,	1	26	2	2	-	31
60 to 79 years,	4	43	3	3	-	53
80 years and over,	-	7	1	-	-	8
Rochester,	21	274	9	28	4	336
20 to 29 years,	13	52	-	14	-	79
30 to 39 years,	1	58	5	7	-	71
40 to 49 years,	5	53	2	4	-	64
50 to 59 years,	-	55	1	3	-	59
60 to 79 years,	1	50	1	-	3	55
80 years and over,	-	6	-	-	1	7
Age unknown,	1	-	-	-	-	1
Rockland,	59	1,284	287	135	31	1,796
20 to 29 years,	52	368	34	45	6	505
30 to 39 years,	3	365	54	37	9	468
40 to 49 years,	2	232	51	22	-	397
50 to 59 years,	-	167	66	14	6	253
60 to 79 years,	2	138	81	15	8	244
80 years and over,	-	14	1	1	2	18
Age unknown,	-	-	-	1	-	1

POLITICAL CONDITION: BY AGE PERIODS — Continued.

Counties, Cities, Towns, and Age Periods.	Ratable Polls (Not Voters)	Ratable Polls and Native Born Voters	Ratable Polls and Foreign Born Naturalized Voters	Ratable Polls and Aliens	No Political Condition	Total Male Population 20 Years of Age and Over
PLYMOUTH — Con.						
Scituate,	20	610	63	64	–	757
20 to 29 years,	15	128	5	32	–	180
30 to 39 years,	3	131	8	15	–	157
40 to 49 years,	2	105	11	6	–	124
50 to 59 years,	–	82	11	6	–	99
60 to 79 years,	–	143	28	4	–	175
80 years and over,	–	21	–	1	–	22
Wareham,	97	761	67	230	6	1,161
20 to 29 years,	49	178	4	109	–	340
30 to 39 years,	14	176	11	69	–	270
40 to 49 years,	10	148	16	20	–	194
50 to 59 years,	10	92	11	13	1	127
60 to 79 years,	8	158	24	15	4	209
80 years and over,	1	7	1	–	1	10
Age unknown,	5	2	–	4	–	11
West Bridgewater,	26	402	59	95	6	588
20 to 29 years,	19	92	7	51	–	169
30 to 39 years,	–	88	13	17	–	118
40 to 49 years,	5	81	10	13	2	111
50 to 59 years,	2	50	14	8	1	75
60 to 79 years,	–	76	15	6	2	99
80 years and over,	–	15	–	–	1	16
Whitman,	78	1,433	183	187	8	1,889
20 to 29 years,	57	402	30	67	–	556
30 to 39 years,	8	380	45	54	1	488
40 to 49 years,	7	276	45	35	–	363
50 to 59 years,	5	198	35	15	2	255
60 to 79 years,	1	160	26	15	2	204
80 years and over,	–	17	2	1	3	23
SUFFOLK.						
Boston,	8,520	76,483	36,800	34,171	524	156,608
20 to 29 years,	5,673	27,253	6,185	13,782	68	52,959
30 to 39 years,	1,257	21,730	10,416	10,906	95	44,413
40 to 49 years,	702	13,445	8,873	5,085	90	28,195
50 to 59 years,	321	7,819	6,548	2,627	65	17,380
60 to 79 years,	157	5,728	4,672	1,617	165	12,339
80 years and over,	7	428	217	105	41	798
Age unknown,	403	51	21	49	–	524
Chelsea,	444	5,209	1,797	2,222	2	9,734
20 to 29 years,	315	1,570	332	948	–	3,165
30 to 39 years,	27	1,310	459	692	2	2,490
40 to 49 years,	30	991	414	284	–	1,719
50 to 59 years,	43	737	340	168	–	1,288
60 to 79 years,	27	622	243	122	–	1,014
80 years and over,	–	39	9	7	–	55
Age unknown,	2	–	–	1	–	3
Revere,	63	1,333	485	420	1	2,302
20 to 29 years,	53	381	103	152	1	690
30 to 39 years,	–	397	142	112	–	651
40 to 49 years,	3	272	123	86	–	484
50 to 59 years,	–	161	76	41	–	278
60 to 79 years,	7	115	38	25	–	185
80 years and over,	–	6	3	1	–	10
Age unknown,	–	1	–	3	–	4

POLITICAL CONDITION: BY AGE PERIODS — Continued.

COUNTIES, CITIES, TOWNS, AND AGE PERIODS.	Ratable Polls (Not Voters)	Ratable Polls and Native Born Voters	Ratable Polls and Foreign Born Naturalized Voters	Ratable Polls and Aliens	No Political Condition	Total Male Population 20 Years of Age and Over
SUFFOLK — Con.						
Winthrop, ...	271	685	140	283	-	1,379
20 to 29 years, ...	116	167	24	120	-	427
30 to 39 years, ...	71	189	37	75	-	372
40 to 49 years, ...	45	153	39	48	-	285
50 to 59 years, ...	27	85	22	27	-	161
60 to 79 years, ...	12	85	17	12	-	126
80 years and over,. . . .	-	6	1	1	-	8
WORCESTER.						
Ashburnham, ...	23	499	49	86	4	661
20 to 29 years, ...	23	112	7	25	-	167
30 to 39 years, ...	-	112	15	22	1	150
40 to 49 years, ...	-	77	11	17	1	106
50 to 59 years, ...	-	81	10	14	1	106
60 to 79 years, ...	-	104	6	7	-	117
80 years and over,. . . .	-	13	-	1	1	15
Athol, ...	238	1,726	120	488	9	2,581
20 to 29 years, ...	146	481	16	175	-	818
30 to 39 years, ...	50	371	25	172	1	619
40 to 49 years, ...	27	332	19	86	1	465
50 to 59 years, ...	6	254	27	33	· 1	321
60 to 79 years, ...	8	262	32	20	3	325
80 years and over,. . . .	-	26	1	2	3	32
Age unknown, ...	1	-	-	-	-	1
Auburn, ...	51	222	48	150	-	471
20 to 29 years, ...	33	55	9	36	-	133
30 to 39 years, ...	9	57	12	40	-	118
40 to 49 years, ...	3	39	13	31	-	86
50 to 59 years, ...	4	27	9	23	-	63
60 to 79 years, ...	2	37	4	18	-	61
80 years and over,. . . .	-	7	1	2	-	10
Barre, ...	64	509	34	135	53	795
20 to 29 years, ...	34	104	4	69	16	227
30 to 39 years, ...	14	103	3	34	16	170
40 to 49 years, ...	8	82	8	17	7	122
50 to 59 years, ...	6	91	7	9	7	120
60 to 79 years, ...	2	114	11	5	7	139
80 years and over,. . . .	-	15	1	-	-	16
Age unknown, ...	-	-	-	1	-	1
Berlin, ...	27	225	13	43	3	311
20 to 29 years, ...	17	49	1	20	-	87
30 to 39 years, ...	6	37	-	8	-	51
40 to 49 years, ...	3	42	1	5	-	51
50 to 59 years, ...	-	38	3	7	1	49
60 to 79 years, ...	1	53	8	2	1	65
80 years and over,. . . .	-	6	-	1	1	8
Blackstone, ...	49	838	555	479	17	1,938
20 to 29 years, ...	44	375	127	213	-	759
30 to 39 years, ...	2	208	148	132	1	491
40 to 49 years, ...	1	99	86	47	-	233
50 to 59 years, ...	1	63	90	48	3	205
60 to 79 years, ...	-	85	98	37	10	230
80 years and over,. . . .	1	8	6	2	3	20
Bolton, ...	25	192	18	33	5	273
20 to 29 years, ...	12	36	-	18	1	67
30 to 39 years, ...	4	32	2	6	2	46

POLITICAL CONDITION: BY AGE PERIODS — Continued.

COUNTIES, CITIES, TOWNS, AND AGE PERIODS.	Ratable Polls (Not Voters)	Ratable Polls and Native Born Voters	Ratable Polls and Foreign Born Naturalized Voters	Ratable Polls and Aliens	No Political Condition	Total Male Population 20 Years of Age and Over
WORCESTER — Con.						
Bolton — Con.						
40 to 49 years,	2	30	1	6	-	39
50 to 59 years,	2	36	6	2	-	46
60 to 79 years,	5	43	9	1	-	58
80 years and over,	-	15	-	-	2	17
Boylston,	14	178	19	40	4	255
20 to 29 years,	9	40	3	15	1	68
30 to 39 years,	2	37	3	9	-	51
40 to 49 years,	1	29	2	9	-	41
50 to 59 years,	1	33	7	5	-	46
60 to 79 years,	1	35	4	2	3	45
80 years and over,	-	4	-	-	-	4
Brookfield,	87	666	94	230	1	1,078
20 to 29 years,	51	176	6	79	-	312
30 to 39 years,	18	150	26	62	-	256
40 to 49 years,	10	121	24	46	-	201
50 to 59 years,	6	86	16	23	-	131
60 to 79 years,	2	123	20	20	1	166
80 years and over,	-	10	2	-	-	12
Charlton,	56	453	34	69	4	616
20 to 29 years,	31	99	-	24	1	155
30 to 39 years,	11	93	4	16	-	124
40 to 49 years,	8	77	7	14	-	106
50 to 59 years,	2	64	9	10	-	85
60 to 79 years,	3	108	11	5	2	129
80 years and over,	1	12	3	-	1	17
Clinton,	158	1,294	1,124	503	7	3,086
20 to 29 years,	128	496	268	234	2	1,128
30 to 39 years,	18	354	277	120	2	771
40 to 49 years,	9	206	233	61	-	509
50 to 59 years,	2	122	183	47	1	355
60 to 79 years,	1	110	153	37	2	303
80 years and over,	-	6	8	4	-	18
Age unknown,	-	-	2	-	-	2
Dana,	27	177	3	41	-	248
20 to 29 years,	10	25	1	13	-	49
30 to 39 years,	6	30	1	11	-	48
40 to 49 years,	3	41	-	7	-	51
50 to 59 years,	1	31	-	3	-	35
60 to 79 years,	7	44	1	7	-	59
80 years and over,	-	6	-	-	-	6
Douglas,	52	434	59	130	3	678
20 to 29 years,	28	97	6	44	-	175
30 to 39 years,	8	88	8	46	3	153
40 to 49 years,	6	74	13	19	-	112
50 to 59 years,	8	56	20	13	-	97
60 to 79 years,	1	110	11	6	-	128
80 years and over,	1	9	1	1	-	12
Age unknown,	-	-	-	1	-	1
Dudley,	41	375	153	295	3	867
20 to 29 years,	40	165	20	88	1	314
30 to 39 years,	1	76	35	69	1	182
40 to 49 years,	-	60	27	69	-	156
50 to 59 years,	-	30	46	49	-	125
60 to 79 years,	-	40	24	17	1	82
80 years and over,	-	4	1	3	-	8

POLITICAL CONDITION: BY AGE PERIODS — Continued.

COUNTIES, CITIES, TOWNS, AND AGE PERIODS.	Ratable Polls (Not Voters)	Ratable Polls and Native Born Voters	Ratable Polls and Foreign Born Naturalized Voters	Ratable Polls and Aliens	No Political Condition	Total Male Population 20 Years of Age and Over
WORCESTER — Con.						
FITCHBURG, ...	603	3,901	1,330	2,116	39	7,989
20 to 29 years, ...	418	1,164	263	875	2	2,722
30 to 39 years, ...	109	1,077	382	602	8	2,178
40 to 49 years, ...	42	733	289	308	5	1,377
50 to 59 years, ...	24	447	227	217	7	922
60 to 79 years, ...	5	445	161	103	17	731
80 years and over, . . .	1	34	8	11	-	54
Age unknown, ...	4	1	-	-	-	5
Gardner, ...	136	1,622	358	871	14	3,001
20 to 29 years, ...	112	426	78	354	-	970
30 to 39 years, ...	12	424	105	256	1	798
40 to 49 years, ...	7	328	84	123	4	546
50 to 59 years, ...	4	234	45	79	2	364
60 to 79 years, ...	1	187	44	52	5	289
80 years and over, . . .	-	23	2	7	2	34
Grafton, ...	67	837	153	399	10	1,466
20 to 29 years, ...	54	232	24	121	-	431
30 to 39 years, ...	5	208	31	83	-	327
40 to 49 years, ...	6	141	29 .	74	2	252
50 to 59 years, ...	2	96	37	61	3	199
60 to 79 years, ...	-	147	31	58	2	238
80 years and over, . . .	-	13	1	2	3	19
Hardwick, ...	61	370	109	268	8	816
20 to 29 years, ...	45	113	19	118	-	295
30 to 39 years, ...	9	94	30	61	-	194
40 to 49 years, ...	3	47	21	39	1	111
50 to 59 years, ...	4	38	19	20	2	83
60 to 79 years, ...	-	68	19	27	5	119
80 years and over, . . .	-	10	1	2	-	13
Age unknown, ...	-	-	-	1	-	
Harvard, ...	42	275	31	68	4	420
20 to 29 years, ...	25	50	2	30	-	107
30 to 39 years, ...	9	56	2	13	1	81
40 to 49 years, ...	5	41	7	6	-	59
50 to 59 years, ...	1	38	7	5	-	51
60 to 79 years, ...	1	78	12	14	2	107
80 years and over, . . .	1	12	1	-	1	15
Holden, ...	29	443	79	217	5	773
20 to 29 years, ...	27	117	4	60	-	208
30 to 39 years, ...	1	103	18	58	-	180
40 to 49 years, ...	-	71	19	43	-	133
50 to 59 years, ...	-	70	14	25	1	110
60 to 79 years, ...	1	71	21	28	3	124
80 years and over, . . .	-	11	3	3	1	18
Hopedale, ...	60	303	48	53	1	465
20 to 29 years, ...	42	99	9	25	-	175
30 to 39 years, ...	8	74	15	13	-	110
40 to 49 years, ...	3	61	9	6	1	80
50 to 59 years, ...	2	33	8	5	-	48
60 to 79 years, ...	3	34	7	4	-	48
80 years and over, . . .	-	2	-	-	-	2
Age unknown, ...	2	-	-	-	-	2
Hubbardston, ...	51	310	28	47	1	437
20 to 29 years, ...	22	53	5	14	-	94
30 to 39 years, ...	11	61	2	6	-	80
40 to 49 years, ...	9	52	4	13	-	78

POLITICAL CONDITION: BY AGE PERIODS — Continued.

COUNTIES, CITIES, TOWNS, AND AGE PERIODS.	Ratable Polls (Not Voters)	Ratable Polls and Native Born Voters	Ratable Polls and Foreign Born Naturalized Voters	Ratable Polls and Aliens	No Political Condition	Total Male Population 20 Years of Age and Over
WORCESTER — Con.						
Hubbardston — Con.						
50 to 59 years, ...	6	44	5	5	-	60
60 to 79 years, ...	3	91	11	9	1	115
80 years and over, ...	-	9	1	-	-	10
Lancaster, ...	54	341	72	124	6	597
20 to 29 years, ...	30	79	6	57	1	173
30 to 39 years, ...	15	91	15	28	-	149
40 to 49 years, ...	6	54	7	19	3	89
50 to 59 years, ...	1	45	18	9	2	75
60 to 79 years, ...	2	63	24	11	-	100
80 years and over, ...	-	9	2	-	-	11
Leicester, ...	59	581	163	157	6	966
20 to 29 years, ...	42	200	13	42	1	298
30 to 39 years, ...	10	131	23	33	-	197
40 to 49 years, ...	4	101	41	43	-	189
50 to 59 years, ...	3	66	41	22	1	133
60 to 79 years, ...	-	76	40	16	4	136
80 years and over, ...	-	7	5	1	-	13
Leominster, ...	223	1,955	305	455	6	2,944
20 to 29 years, ...	146	525	45	175	-	891
30 to 39 years, ...	38	502	78	129	2	749
40 to 49 years, ...	21	391	73	82	1	568
50 to 59 years, ...	6	264	65	37	-	372
60 to 79 years, ...	11	242	40	29	2	324
80 years and over, ...	-	31	4	3	1	39
Age unknown, ...	1	-	-	-	-	1
Lunenburg, ...	6	336	21	33	8	404
20 to 29 years, ...	6	63	2	14	1	86
30 to 39 years, ...	-	77	6	10	1	94
40 to 49 years, ...	-	53	6	5	-	64
50 to 59 years, ...	-	55	2	3	2	62
60 to 79 years, ...	-	83	5	1	3	92
80 years and over, ...	-	5	-	-	1	6
Mendon, ...	24	244	19	19	2	308
20 to 29 years, ...	11	51	-	4	-	66
30 to 39 years, ...	4	39	4	4	-	51
40 to 49 years, ...	4	43	2	3	-	52
50 to 59 years, ...	4	43	5	4	-	56
60 to 79 years, ...	1	56	7	4	2	70
80 years and over, ...	-	12	1	-	-	13
Milford, ...	125	1,781	542	425	30	2,903
20 to 29 years, ...	96	607	42	142	2	889
30 to 39 years, ...	12	485	80	141	2	720
40 to 49 years, ...	11	306	106	59	5	487
50 to 59 years, ...	2	165	137	46	4	354
60 to 79 years, ...	4	203	169	33	16	425
80 years and over, ...	-	15	8	3	1	27
Age unknown, ...	-	-	-	-	1	1
Millbury, ...	99	772	191	559	4	1,625
20 to 29 years, ...	67	270	13	143	-	493
30 to 39 years, ...	17	197	33	116	-	363
40 to 49 years, ...	9	114	39	96	1	259
50 to 59 years, ...	4	93	54	55	-	206
60 to 79 years, ...	2	89	45	42	2	180
80 years and over, ...	-	9	7	4	1	21
Age unknown, ...	-	-	-	103	-	103

POLITICAL CONDITION : BY AGE PERIODS — Continued.

COUNTIES, CITIES, TOWNS, AND AGE PERIODS.	Ratable Polls (Not Voters)	Ratable Polls and Native Born Voters	Ratable Polls and Foreign Born Naturalized Voters	Ratable Polls and Aliens	No Political Condition	Total Male Population 20 Years of Age and Over
WORCESTER — Con.						
New Braintree,	23	109	3	54	1	190
20 to 29 years,	11	24	-	20	-	55
30 to 39 years,	4	18	-	12	-	34
40 to 49 years,	6	17	1	11	-	35
50 to 59 years,	-	23	2	2	1	28
60 to 79 years,	2	24	-	9	-	35
80 years and over,.	-	3	-	-	-	3
Northborough,	29	361	46	161	1	598
20 to 29 years,	20	81	7	47	-	155
30 to 39 years,	1	81	10	39	-	131
40 to 49 years,	3	64	10	31	-	108
50 to 59 years,	3	54	4	17	-	78
60 to 79 years,	2	71	12	26	1	112
80 years and over,.	-	10	3	1	-	14
Northbridge,	129	645	329	548	5	1,656
20 to 29 years,	102	218	83	209	-	612
30 to 39 years,	13	172	80	143	-	408
40 to 49 years,	5	111	71	100	3	290
50 to 59 years,	7	64	56	54	1	182
60 to 79 years,	2	71	37	38	-	148
80 years and over,.	-	9	2	4	1	16
North Brookfield,	82	886	184	247	5	1,404
20 to 29 years,	63	294	13	72	-	442
30 to 39 years,	8	230	36	54	-	328
40 to 49 years,	6	139	48	56	3	252
50 to 59 years,	1	106	46	30	-	183
60 to 79 years,	3	102	37	34	1	177
80 years and over,.	1	15	4	1	1	22
Oakham,	12	167	8	21	-	208
20 to 29 years,	6	32	-	3	-	41
30 to 39 years,	3	30	-	8	-	41
40 to 49 years,	2	37	3	4	-	46
50 to 59 years,	1	24	2	3	-	30
60 to 79 years,	-	41	3	3	-	47
80 years and over,.	-	3	-	-	-	3
Oxford, .	31	502	57	116	6	712
20 to 29 years,	22	89	1	18	1	131
30 to 39 years,	6	121	10	32	1	170
40 to 49 years,	1	96	15	36	2	147
50 to 59 years,	1	81	13	15	-	110
60 to 79 years,	1	105	16	15	2	139
80 years and over,.	-	13	2	-	-	15
Paxton, .	4	124	7	23	2	160
20 to 29 years,	4	20	1	6	-	31
30 to 39 years,	-	22	-	2	-	24
40 to 49 years,	-	16	2	3	-	21
50 to 59 years,	-	17	-	3	1	21
60 to 79 years,	-	41	3	7	1	52
80 years and over,.	-	8	1	2	-	11
Petersham, .	44	234	24	39	6	347
20 to 29 years,	23	34	2	19	2	80
30 to 39 years,	11	49	3	10	1	74
40 to 49 years,	5	37	4	7	1	54
50 to 59 years,	4	44	4	1	1	54
60 to 79 years,	1	62	10	2	1	76
80 years and over,.	-	8	1	-	-	9

POLITICAL CONDITION: BY AGE PERIODS — Continued.

COUNTIES, CITIES, TOWNS, AND AGE PERIODS.	Ratable Polls (Not Voters)	Ratable Polls and Native Born Voters	Ratable Polls and Foreign Born Naturalized Voters	Ratable Polls and Aliens	No Political Condition	Total Male Population 20 Years of Age and Over
WORCESTER — Con.						
Phillipston,	15	130	3	12	3	163
20 to 29 years,	7	30	-	4	-	41
30 to 39 years,	3	20	-	3	-	26
40 to 49 years,	-	21	2	1	-	24
50 to 59 years,	4	23	-	1	-	28
60 to 79 years,	1	27	1	3	1	33
80 years and over,	-	9	-	-	2	11
Princeton,	23	232	22	51	2	330
20 to 29 years,	19	36	3	13	1	72
30 to 39 years,	1	48	4	16	-	69
40 to 49 years,	1	52	2	9	1	65
50 to 59 years,	-	35	8	3	-	46
60 to 79 years,	2	52	5	8	-	67
80 years and over,	-	9	-	2	-	11
Royalston,	16	238	17	25	1	297
20 to 29 years,	9	33	1	14	-	57
30 to 39 years,	6	47	2	7	-	62
40 to 49 years,	1	42	3	1	-	47
50 to 59 years,	-	43	4	3	-	50
60 to 79 years,	-	65	7	-	1	73
80 years and over,	-	7	-	-	-	7
Age unknown,	-	1	-	-	-	1
Rutland,	22	213	24	57	1	317
20 to 29 years,	16	45	3	20	1	85
30 to 39 years,	3	37	-	13	-	53
40 to 49 years,	2	33	5	8	-	48
50 to 59 years,	1	38	4	11	-	54
60 to 79 years,	-	54	12	5	-	71
80 years and over,	-	6	-	-	-	6
Shrewsbury,	23	414	30	49	6	522
20 to 29 years,	17	92	3	14	1	127
30 to 39 years,	3	80	6	10	-	99
40 to 49 years,	1	72	8	12	2	95
50 to 59 years,	1	59	2	3	2	67
60 to 79 years,	1	95	11	9	-	116
80 years and over,	-	16	-	1	1	18
Southborough,	57	373	75	316	3	824
20 to 29 years,	24	87	8	136	-	255
30 to 39 years,	18	100	18	88	-	224
40 to 49 years,	10	59	17	63	1	150
50 to 59 years,	5	45	13	18	-	81
60 to 79 years,	-	72	19	11	-	102
80 years and over,	-	10	-	-	2	12
Southbridge,	124	1,004	410	651	9	2,198
20 to 29 years,	103	382	59	173	-	717
30 to 39 years,	10	241	127	149	-	527
40 to 49 years,	8	152	107	129	2	398
50 to 59 years,	2	100	58	111	1	272
60 to 79 years,	1	116	55	85	4	261
80 years and over,	-	13	4	4	2	23
Spencer,	124	1,224	346	447	9	2,150
20 to 29 years,	86	366	28	75	2	557
30 to 39 years,	18	323	67	95	-	503
40 to 49 years,	13	206	106	109	1	435
50 to 59 years,	5	148	69	92	1	315
60 to 79 years,	1	155	76	69	5	306

POLITICAL CONDITION: BY AGE PERIODS — Continued.

COUNTIES, CITIES, TOWNS, AND AGE PERIODS.	Ratable Polls (Not Voters)	Ratable Polls and Native Born Voters	Ratable Polls and Foreign Born Naturalized Voters	Ratable Polls and Aliens	No Political Condition	Total Male Population 20 Years of Age and Over
WORCESTER — Con.						
Spencer — Con.						
80 years and over,	-	26	-	7	-	33
Age unknown,	1	-	-	-	-	1
Sterling,	43	318	19	59	5	424
20 to 29 years,	22	55	1	16	-	94
30 to 39 years,	10	57	1	13	-	81
40 to 49 years,	7	68	3	4	1	83
50 to 59 years,	1	47	7	3	1	59
60 to 79 years,	3	78	7	3	2	93
80 years and over,	-	13	-	-	1	14
Sturbridge,	34	358	65	100	4	561
20 to 29 years,	27	74	11	25	-	137
30 to 39 years,	2	78	12	25	-	117
40 to 49 years,	1	82	11	24	-	118
50 to 59 years,	3	46	8	13	-	70
60 to 79 years,	1	67	23	12	3	106
80 years and over,	-	11	-	1	1	13
Sutton,	74	492	63	344	11	984
20 to 29 years,	52	136	8	98	4	298
30 to 39 years,	12	88	12	95	3	210
40 to 49 years,	6	82	17	79	-	184
50 to 59 years,	2	67	12	37	2	120
60 to 79 years,	1	104	14	34	1	154
80 years and over,	1	15	-	1	1	18
Templeton,	49	690	80	111	4	934
20 to 29 years,	32	168	6	40	-	246
30 to 39 years,	8	146	13	33	2	202
40 to 49 years,	5	137	19	11	-	172
50 to 59 years,	3	106	16	17	-	142
60 to 79 years,	1	119	26	9	1	156
80 years and over,	-	14	-	1	1	16
Upton,	43	478	41	52	4	618
20 to 29 years,	15	116	3	12	-	146
30 to 39 years,	2	87	5	14	-	108
40 to 49 years,	-	106	3	7	1	117
50 to 59 years,	1	71	15	9	-	96
60 to 79 years,	-	81	13	8	3	105
80 years and over,	-	14	1	1	-	16
Age unknown,	25	3	1	1	-	30
Uxbridge,	79	642	161	305	5	1,192
20 to 29 years,	52	181	8	110	-	351
30 to 39 years,	12	182	13	77	-	284
40 to 49 years,	6	111	22	39	2	180
50 to 59 years,	3	64	24	36	1	128
60 to 79 years,	3	98	33	43	2	179
80 years and over,	-	6	1	-	-	7
Age unknown,	3	-	-	-	-	3
Warren,	142	720	139	331	6	1,338
20 to 29 years,	82	203	20	99	-	404
30 to 39 years,	32	191	30	92	1	346
40 to 49 years,	14	145	34	60	2	255
50 to 59 years,	6	80	33	42	-	161
60 to 79 years,	8	96	22	37	2	165
80 years and over,	-	5	-	1	1	7
Webster,	148	844	404	802	13	2,211
20 to 29 years,	88	280	48	288	-	704

POLITICAL CONDITION: BY AGE PERIODS — Continued.

COUNTIES, CITIES, TOWNS, AND AGE PERIODS.	Ratable Polls (Not Voters)	Ratable Polls and Native Born Voters	Ratable Polls and Foreign Born Naturalized Voters	Ratable Polls and Aliens	No Political Condition	Total Male Population 20 Years of Age and Over
WORCESTER — Con.						
Webster — Con.						
30 to 39 years,	17	296	98	227	1	549
40 to 49 years,	11	151	103	132	3	400
50 to 59 years,	6	98	95	88	1	288
60 to 79 years,	1	98	56	61	7	223
80 years and over,	-	11	4	6	1	22
Age unknown,	25	-	-	-	-	25
Westborough,	193	963	165	167	194	1,682
20 to 29 years,	110	236	12	67	41	466
30 to 39 years,	38	230	29	46	52	395
40 to 49 years,	24	194	26	27	32	303
50 to 59 years,	10	120	47	10	32	219
60 to 79 years,	10	161	49	15	32	267
80 years and over,	1	22	2	2	3	30
Age unknown,	-	-	-	-	2	2
West Boylston,	42	434	83	253	-	812
20 to 29 years,	27	128	13	72	-	240
30 to 39 years,	7	91	24	66	-	188
40 to 49 years,	2	71	13	54	-	140
50 to 59 years,	2	63	16	29	-	110
60 to 79 years,	4	72	16	31	-	123
80 years and over,	-	8	1	1	-	10
Age unknown,	-	1	-	-	-	1
West Brookfield,	30	350	57	31	4	472
20 to 29 years,	14	68	4	6	-	92
30 to 39 years,	7	65	5	9	-	86
40 to 49 years,	4	72	8	6	-	90
50 to 59 years,	3	58	19	5	1	86
60 to 79 years,	2	77	19	4	3	105
80 years and over,	-	9	2	-	-	11
Age unknown,	-	1	-	1	-	2
Westminster,	34	329	25	35	2	425
20 to 29 years,	21	49	1	8	-	79
30 to 39 years,	4	61	2	7	1	75
40 to 49 years,	3	63	5	9	-	80
50 to 59 years,	2	56	5	3	-	66
60 to 79 years,	4	84	12	5	-	105
80 years and over,	-	16	-	3	1	20
Winchendon,	108	914	135	246	9	1,412
20 to 29 years,	75	215	18	96	-	404
30 to 39 years,	21	208	30	54	1	314
40 to 49 years,	7	187	27	41	-	262
50 to 59 years,	3	115	32	29	-	179
60 to 79 years,	2	172	26	24	5	229
80 years and over,	-	17	2	2	3	24
WORCESTER,	1,908	15,046	6,082	6,630	690	30,356
20 to 29 years,	1,356	5,074	946	2,771	103	10,250
30 to 39 years,	266	4,013	1,725	1,971	174	8,149
40 to 49 years,	142	2,709	1,527	971	195	5,544
50 to 59 years,	87	1,646	1,158	514	135	3,540
60 to 79 years,	47	1,473	702	359	80	2,661
80 years and over,	5	119	21	26	3	174
Age unknown,	5	12	3	18	-	38

POLITICAL CONDITION : BY AGE PERIODS — Continued.

RECAPITULATION : BY COUNTIES.

COUNTIES, AND AGE PERIODS.	Ratable Polls (Not Voters)	Ratable Polls and Native Born Voters	Ratable Polls and Foreign Born Naturalized Voters	Ratable Polls and Aliens	No Political Condition	Total Male Population 20 Years of Age and Over
BARNSTABLE COUNTY, . . .	455	7,181	439	799	63	8,437
20 to 29 years, ...	283	1,272	27	231	7	1,820
30 to 39 years, ...	62	1,465	79	229	5	1,840
40 to 49 years, ...	49	1,330	114	157	8	1,658
50 to 59 years, ...	35	1,269	78	104	12	1,498
60 to 79 years, ...	26	1,656	129	69	25	1,905
80 years and over, . . .	-	185	12	6	6	209
Age unknown, ...	-	4	-	3	-	7
BERKSHIRE COUNTY, . . .	1,828	16,007	4,179	3,883	109	26,006
20 to 29 years, ...	1,267	5,196	557	1,243	10	8,273
30 to 39 years, ...	264	3,981	885	1,048	15	6,193
40 to 49 years, ...	165	2,768	934	705	9	4,581
50 to 59 years, ...	62	1,875	862	472	10	3,281
60 to 79 years, ...	66	1,975	890	383	49	3,363
80 years and over, . . .	3	212	50	27	16	308
Age unknown, ...	1	-	1	5	-	7
BRISTOL COUNTY, . . .	3,076	29,606	12,889	16,781	565	62,917
20 to 29 years, ...	2,440	8,977	2,354	6,563	74	20,408
30 to 39 years, ...	305	7,365	3,426	4,425	112	15,633
40 to 49 years, ...	149	5,318	2,909	2,915	108	11,399
50 to 59 years, ...	89	3,632	2,432	1,688	94	7,935
60 to 79 years, ...	64	3,872	1,674	1,094	146	6,850
80 years and over, . . .	3	435	75	40	31	584
Age unknown, ...	26	7	19	56	-	108
DUKES COUNTY, ...	88	1,168	68	149	6	1,479
20 to 29 years, ...	49	195	11	74	1	330
30 to 39 years, ...	15	234	16	29	-	294
40 to 49 years, ...	6	235	14	27	1	283
50 to 59 years, ...	7	209	15	11	-	242
60 to 79 years, ...	10	264	11	8	1	294
80 years and over, . . .	-	31	1	-	3	35
Age unknown, ...	1	-	-	-	-	1
ESSEX COUNTY, ...	5,366	60,045	17,237	22,381	775	105,804
20 to 29 years, ...	3,809	17,410	2,706	9,700	88	33,713
30 to 39 years, ...	721	15,282	4,489	6,457	161	27,110
40 to 49 years, ...	372	11,189	4,100	3,247	151	19,059
50 to 59 years, ...	205	7,775	3,395	1,767	139	13,281
60 to 79 years, ...	167	7,599	2,444	1,099	191	11,500
80 years and over, . . .	7	776	97	51	45	976
Age unknown, ...	85	14	6	60	-	165
FRANKLIN COUNTY, . . .	784	9,002	1,330	1,716	50	12,882
20 to 29 years, ...	522	2,134	183	729	5	3,573
30 to 39 years, ...	110	2,036	313	449	8	2,916
40 to 49 years, ...	77	1,683	313	249	4	2,326
50 to 59 years, ...	32	1,335	280	158	9	1,814
60 to 79 years, ...	32	1,602	224	112	19	1,989
80 years and over, . . .	4	208	16	9	5	242
Age unknown, ...	7	4	1	10	-	22
HAMPDEN COUNTY, . . .	2,960	24,012	7,556	10,854	199	45,581
20 to 29 years, ...	2,124	7,536	1,368	4,354	23	15,405
30 to 39 years, ...	396	6,220	2,110	3,020	28	11,783
40 to 49 years, ...	224	4,195	1,679	1,653	34	7,785
50 to 59 years, ...	105	2,833	1,436	1,016	13	5,403
60 to 79 years, ...	59	2,966	916	740	85	4,766
80 years and over, . . .	4	253	45	56	14	372
Age unknown, ...	48	-	2	15	2	67

POLITICAL CONDITION: BY AGE PERIODS — Continued.
RECAPITULATION: BY COUNTIES — Concluded.

COUNTIES, AND AGE PERIODS.	Ratable Polls (Not Voters)	Ratable Polls and Native Born Voters	Ratable Polls and Foreign Born Naturalized Voters	Ratable Polls and Aliens	No Political Condition	Total Male Population 20 Years of Age and Over
HAMPSHIRE COUNTY,	988	9,852	2,036	2,878	319	16,073
20 to 29 years,	719	2,876	293	1,010	43	4,941
30 to 39 years,	117	2,188	404	711	59	3,479
40 to 49 years,	66	1,645	454	486	73	2,724
50 to 59 years,	40	1,255	403	312	48	2,118
60 to 79 years,	36	1,746	410	331	81	2,604
80 years and over,	6	141	12	27	13	199
Age unknown,	4	1	-	1	2	8
MIDDLESEX COUNTY,	9,510	81,759	27,818	31,723	836	151,446
20 to 29 years,	6,831	25,077	4,601	13,335	68	49,912
30 to 39 years,	1,190	21,255	7,361	8,926	107	38,839
40 to 49 years,	628	15,271	6,535	4,721	141	27,296
50 to 59 years,	320	9,717	5,190	2,737	166	18,040
60 to 79 years,	237	9,477	4,007	1,821	299	15,841
80 years and over,	6	949	191	134	46	1,326
Age unknown,	98	13	23	49	9	192
NANTUCKET COUNTY,	29	833	53	33	11	959
20 to 29 years,	17	132	5	15	1	170
30 to 39 years,	3	179	7	8	-	197
40 to 49 years,	5	154	5	5	2	171
50 to 59 years,	2	123	10	3	4	142
60 to 79 years,	2	210	24	2	3	241
80 years and over,	-	35	2	-	1	38
NORFOLK COUNTY,	2,186	24,584	6,981	7,969	137	41,257
20 to 29 years,	1,542	6,856	807	3,035	12	12,342
30 to 39 years,	300	6,274	1,029	2,180	12	10,404
40 to 49 years,	168	4,770	1,685	1,042	23	7,488
50 to 59 years,	81	3,068	1,589	600	18	5,186
60 to 79 years,	77	3,396	1,312	451	51	5,287
80 years and over,	5	386	63	38	21	513
Age unknown,	13	4	6	14	-	37
PLYMOUTH COUNTY,	2,217	23,562	3,394	4,152	608	33,933
20 to 29 years,	1,271	5,859	514	1,702	56	9,402
30 to 39 years,	396	5,858	884	1,223	128	8,449
40 to 49 years,	270	4,468	720	603	100	6,161
50 to 59 years,	168	3,218	609	337	111	4,443
60 to 79 years,	82	3,733	635	249	174	4,873
80 years and over,	7	441	29	20	27	524
Age unknown,	53	5	3	8	12	81
SUFFOLK COUNTY,	9,298	83,750	39,352	37,066	527	170,923
20 to 29 years,	6,157	29,371	6,642	15,092	69	57,241
30 to 39 years,	1,355	23,635	11,054	11,785	97	47,926
40 to 49 years,	780	14,861	9,449	5,503	90	30,683
50 to 59 years,	391	8,802	6,986	2,863	65	19,107
60 to 79 years,	263	6,550	4,970	1,776	165	13,664
80 years and over,	7	479	230	114	41	871
Age unknown,	405	52	21	53	-	531
WORCESTER COUNTY,	6,236	51,263	14,816	20,796	1,298	94,409
20 to 29 years,	4,254	15,205	2,304	7,778	185	29,726
30 to 39 years,	955	12,689	3,745	5,710	279	23,378
40 to 49 years,	507	9,174	3,403	3,397	284	16,765
50 to 59 years,	269	6,284	2,889	2,081	219	11,742
60 to 79 years,	171	7,134	2,350	1,554	252	11,491
80 years and over,	13	788	119	119	47	1,086
Age unknown,	67	19	6	127	2	221

POLITICAL CONDITION: BY AGE PERIODS — Concluded.

RECAPITULATION. FOR THE STATE.

THE STATE, AND AGE PERIODS.	Ratable Polls (Not Voters)	Ratable Polls and Native-Born Voters	Ratable Polls and Foreign Born Naturalized Voters	Ratable Polls and Aliens	No Political Condition	Total Male Population 20 Years of Age and Over
THE STATE, ...	44,821	422,654	138,148	160,610	5,473	771,706
20 to 29 years, ...	31,285	128,096	22,462	64,771	642	247,256
30 to 39 years, ...	6,159	108,650	36,402	46,219	1,011	198,441
40 to 49 years, ...	3,466	76,861	32,314	24,710	1,028	138,379
50 to 59 years, ...	1,806	51,425	25,944	14,149	908	94,232
60 to 79 years, ...	1,232	52,180	19,996	9,719	1,541	84,668
80 years and over, . .	65	5,319	942	641	316	7,283
Age unknown, ...	808	123	88	401	27	1,447

Tabular Analyses

For the Following Presentations:

The presentations, pages 225 to 318, relate to the political condition of the people. The first table, pages 225 to 238, shows for each city and town, with a recapitulation for the State and counties, the number of polls and the number of legal voters, each class being subdivided so as to show first, with respect to the total polls, the percentage of voters, the percentage not voters, and the percentage of aliens; and, second, with respect to the total voters, the percentage native born and the percentage which, being of foreign birth, has acquired the franchise by naturalization.

Referring to the recapitulation on page 238, it will be seen that the total number of polls in the State is 766,233. It should be borne in mind that by law every male twenty years of age residing in the State on the first of May, in any year, and not a pauper or exempt by law, is a poll, and subject to a poll tax. The polls thus defined are made up of three classes: first, those who are aliens and who are not voters by reason of that fact; second, those who are not voters by reason of disability other than the incident of foreign birth, included under the head of "not voters" in the table; and, third, those who are legal voters. The total voters number 560,802, or 73.19 per cent of the total polls. We repeat that the term "voters," as used in the Census, means potential voters; in other words, a legal voter under the Census enumeration is a person who possesses the constitutional requisites for voting, or who could vote under the Constitution should he see fit to do so; that is, who has no disabilities other than those of a temporary character, for example, those relating to registration. The constitutional requisites for voting are thus set forth: "Every male citizen of twenty-one years of age and upwards, excepting paupers and persons under guardianship, who shall have resided within the commonwealth one year, and within the town or district in which he may claim a right to vote, six calendar months next preceding any election of governor, lieutenant-governor, senators, or representatives, shall have a right to vote in such election." This is further limited by a provision that "No person shall have a right to vote * * * * who shall not be able to read the Constitution in the English language, and write his name." It is provided, however, that this limitation shall not apply to any person prevented by physical disability from complying with its requisitions, or to any person who had a right to vote at the time of the adoption of the amendment under which the limitation was made, namely, May 1, 1857, nor to any person who was 60 years of age at that time.

In a previous report treating of this subject we have said that "Registered voters constitute the voting force fully equipped and in the field for action at any particular time. This force varies in numbers according to the varying conditions of different political campaigns. Besides these active voters there is always a reserve corps made up of those who for various reasons are not registered, but who constitute, nevertheless, part of the voting strength of the State." The legal voters, as included in the tables we are now considering, comprise both the active and reserve voters. They represent, in fact, the ultimate voting strength of the State.

In the Census taken in 1885, the legal voters constituted 77.93 per cent of the polls. It will be seen, therefore, that the proportion in the present Census is somewhat less than at that date. In 1895, the persons who are polls, and not aliens, but who nevertheless are not voters, constitute 5.85 per cent of total polls. This class includes persons who had passed their twentieth birthday at the date of the Census, and also paupers, persons under guardianship, and others who, although polls, are debarred by the constitutional provisions just cited. The aliens, or persons of foreign birth without the right of franchise on account of insufficient length of residence in the country, or who although resident here sufficiently long, have neglected to acquire citizenship, constitute 20.96 per cent of the total polls. In 1885, 4.62 per cent of the polls were not voters, and 17.15 per cent were aliens. It will be seen, therefore, that the alien and non-voter classes each constitute larger percentages of the total polls than was the case in 1885. In the present Census the total voters number 560,802. Of these, 75.37 per cent are native born and 24.63 per cent foreign born. By way of comparison it may be stated that the native born voters in 1875 constituted 80.27 per cent of the total voters, and in 1885, 77.69 per cent. These percentages, taken in connection with that shown in the present Census, exhibit a constant decline during the 20 years. The foreign born naturalized voters constituted 19.73 per cent of the total voters in 1875, the percentage rising to 22.31 per cent in 1885, and now forming, as above stated, 24.63 per cent. The percentage of voters of total polls is largest in the county of Nantucket, being 93.46. On the other hand, it is smallest in Bristol County, being but 68.16. The percentage of aliens of total voters is smallest in Nantucket County, being only 3.48, and largest in Bristol County, being 26.91 per cent. The percentage of voters of total polls is larger than the percentage for the State in the counties of Barnstable, Berkshire, Dukes, Essex, Franklin, Hampshire, Nantucket, Norfolk, and Plymouth. The percentage of aliens is larger than the percentage for the State in the counties of Bristol, Essex, Hampden, Middlesex, Suffolk, and Worcester. The largest percentage of native born voters of total voters is found in the county of Dukes, this percentage being 94.50, closely matched by the percentage 94.24 in Barnstable County, and 94.02 in Nantucket County These counties, of course, respectively, contain the smallest percentages of foreign born naturalized voters of total voters. The county which shows the largest percentage of foreign born naturalized voters of total voters is Suffolk, the percentage being 31.97. Next to this is found Bristol County, the percentage being 30.33. In Middlesex County the foreign born naturalized voters constitute 25.39 per cent of the total voters. In every other county except Suffolk, Bristol, and Middlesex the percentage of foreign born naturalized voters of total voters is less than the percentage for the State.

The following table brings forward a recapitulation for the cities:

| CITIES. | RATABLE POLLS | | | | LEGAL VOTERS | | |
| | Total Polls | PERCENTAGES OF TOTAL RATABLE POLLS | | | Total Voters | PERCENTAGES OF TOTAL LEGAL VOTERS | |
		Voters	Not Voters	Aliens		Native Born Voters	Foreign Born Naturalized Voters
Beverly, ...	3,782	80.22	6.56	13.22	3,034	88.69	11.31
Boston, ...	156,084	72.65	5.46	21.89	113,393	67.43	32.57
Brockton, ...	10,701	79.72	4.64	15.64	8,531	80.80	19.20
Cambridge, ...	25,105	67.79	7.55	24.66	17,018	71.20	28.80
Chelsea, ...	9,732	72.61	4.56	22.83	7,066	74.57	25.43
Chicopee, ...	5,013	54.84	5.86	39.30	2,749	69.99	30.01
Everett, ...	5,530	73.96	5.37	20.67	4,090	77.97	22.03
Fall River, ...	23,767	61.29	4.35	34.36	14,566	50.95	49.05
Fitchburg, ...	7,950	65.80	7.58	26.62	5,231	74.57	25.43
Gloucester, ...	11,829	54.48	3.25	42.27	6,444	69.10	30.90
Haverhill, ...	9,432	79.05	4.95	16.00	7,456	82.39	17.61

CITIES.	RATABLE POLLS				LEGAL VOTERS		
	Total Polls	PERCENTAGES OF TOTAL RATABLE POLLS			Total Voters	PERCENTAGES OF TOTAL LEGAL VOTERS	
		Voters	Not Voters	Aliens		Native Born Voters	Foreign Born Naturalized Voters
Holyoke, ...	10,742	61.41	4.98	33.61	6,597	56.74	43.26
Lawrence, ...	15,340	66.35	5.25	28.40	10,178	52.99	47.01
Lowell, ...	23,792	68.96	4.85	26.19	16,408	60.48	39.52
Lynn.	19,829	77.85	4.89	17.26	15,437	81.38	18.62
Malden, ...	8,856	73.64	5.30	21.06	6,522	77.25	22.75
Marlborough, . . .	4,470	77.07	5.46	17.47	3,445	74.02	25.98
Medford, ...	4,489	73.98	7.17	18.85	3,321	81.42	18.58
New Bedford, . . .	15,798	63.91	4.83	31.26	10,096	71.43	28.57
Newburyport, . . .	4,201	83.48	3.98	12.54	3,507	85.54	14.46
Newton, ...	7,874	71.34	4.91	23.75	5,617	80.08	19.92
North Adams, . . .	5,537	73.42	6.28	20.30	4,065	73.60	26.40
Northampton, . . .	4,341	75.79	5.14	19.07	3,290	76.63	23.37
Pittsfield, ...	6,031	79.61	7.03	13.36	4,801	76.67	23.33
Quincy, ...	6,364	67.96	5.31	26.73	4,325	66.38	33.62
Salem, ...	10,193	72.71	5.80	21.49	7,411	77.80	22.20
Somerville, . . .	15,960	74.18	5.57	20.25	11,839	77.80	22.20
Springfield, . . .	15,911	76.93	6.96	16.11	12,240	80.01	19.99
Taunton, ...	7,746	77.37	4.56	18.07	5,993	76.96	23.04
Waltham, ...	6,057	75.52	4.85	19.63	4,574	74.75	25.25
Woburn, ...	4,168	79.82	4.10	16.08	3,327	64.56	35.44
Worcester, . . .	29,666	71.22	6.43	22.35	21,128	71.21	28.79

The presentation, pages 239 to 266, shows very completely the political condition of the population by sex for each city and town, with a recapitulation for the State and counties. No table similar to this has ever been presented before in the Census reports, and the facts contained in it are of very great interest and importance. Referring to the recapitulation on pages 264, 265 we note a subdivision of the male population twenty years of age and over so as to exhibit its political condition. The total male population twenty years of age and over numbers 771,706. Of this population, the ratable polls number 766,233, or 99.29 per cent; the aliens, 160,610, or 20.81 per cent; the persons not voters for reasons other than birth, 44,821, or 5.81 per cent; the voters, 560,802, or 72.67 per cent. The native born voters constitute 54.77 per cent of the male population 20 years of age and over, while the foreign born naturalized voters constitute 17.90 per cent of this population. These percentages may be compared with those shown in the table previously analyzed. To express the facts in another way in connection with those of the preceding table, it may be said that of the total male population 20 years of age and over, nearly 55 persons in every 100 (54.77) are native born voters, while nearly 18 persons in every 100 (17.90) are foreign born naturalized voters. In other words, while of the total legal voters nearly 25 persons in every 100 are foreign born naturalized voters, such voters constitute only about 18 persons in every 100 of the total male population 20 years of age and over. Nearly six (5.81) persons in every 100 of the male population 20 years of age and over while not aliens are still not voters, while nearly 21 persons in every 100 (20.81) are aliens. Only 5,473 persons included in the male population 20 years of age and over are without political status, such persons constituting less than one in every one hundred. For the purpose of comparison the political condition of the population is shown in the table in terms of percentages of the total population as well as the male population 20 years of age and over. For example, referring again to the recapitulation for the State, the total population of both sexes is 2,500,183; and while of the male population 20 years of age and over only 0.71 per cent

322 CENSUS OF MASSACHUSETTS — 1895.

is without political status, nevertheless, of the total population, 1,733,950 persons, constituting 69.35 per cent, are without political status, such persons comprising minors, paupers, and persons otherwise debarred, including those who are debarred on account of sex. The total voters constitute 22.43 per cent of the total population, the aliens only 6.43 per cent, the persons not voters, although males of voting age and not aliens, 1.79 per cent. The native born voters constitute 16.90 per cent of the total population, and the foreign born naturalized voters 5.53 per cent.

Comparing these percentages with the facts as they existed in 1875, or 20 years ago, we find that at that date the voters constituted 78.08 per cent of polls and 21.25 per cent of the population; while the aliens were 17.60 per cent of polls and 4.79 per cent of the total population. It appears, therefore, that during the 20 years the aggregate number

	CITIES.		MALE POPULATION 20 YEARS OF AGE AND OVER					PERCENTAGES OF MALE POPULATION 20 YEARS OF AGE AND OVER						
		Voters	Not Voters	Aliens	Total Ratable Polls	No Political Condition	Total Male Population 20 Years of Age and Over	Ratable Polls	Native Born Voters	Foreign Born Naturalized Voters	Total Voters	Aliens	Not Voters	No Political Condition
1	Beverly,	3,034	248	500	3,782	15	3,797	99.60	70.87	9.03	79.90	13.17	6.53	0.40
2	Boston,	113,386	8,520	34,171	156,084	524	156,608	99.67	48.83	23.58	72.41	21.82	5.44	0.33
3	Brockton,	8,531	496	1,674	10,701	17	10,718	99.84	64.31	15.28	79.59	15.62	4.63	0.16
4	Cambridge,	17,018	1,896	6,191	25,105	51	25,156	99.80	48.17	19.48	67.65	24.61	7.54	0.20
5	Chelsea,	7,066	444	2,222	9,732	2	9,734	99.98	54.13	18.46	72.59	22.83	4.56	0.02
6	Chicopee,	2,749	294	1,970	5,013	18	5,031	99.64	38.24	16.40	54.64	39.16	5.84	0.36
7	Everett,	4,060	297	1,143	5,530	–	5,530	100.00	37.67	16.20	73.96	20.67	5.37	–
8	Fall River,	14,566	1,635	8,166	23,767	60	23,827	99.75	31.14	29.99	61.13	34.27	4.35	0.25
9	Fitchburg,	5,231	603	2,116	7,950	39	7,989	99.51	48.83	16.65	65.48	26.48	7.55	0.49
10	Gloucester,	6,444	385	5,000	11,829	18	11,847	99.85	37.59	16.80	54.39	42.21	3.25	0.15
11	Haverhill,	7,456	467	1,509	9,432	39	9,471	99.59	64.86	13.86	78.72	15.94	4.95	0.41
12	Holyoke,	6,597	535	3,610	10,742	28	10,770	99.74	34.75	26.50	61.25	33.52	4.97	0.26
13	Lawrence,	10,478	805	4,257	15,540	42	15,582	99.73	35.06	31.11	66.17	28.33	5.23	0.27
14	Lowell,	16,408	1,154	6,230	23,792	83	23,875	99.65	41.57	27.16	68.73	26.09	4.83	0.35
15	Lynn,	15,457	969	3,423	19,829	51	19,880	99.74	63.19	14.46	77.65	17.22	4.87	0.26
16	Malden,	6,522	469	1,865	8,856	9	8,865	99.90	56.83	16.74	73.57	21.04	5.29	0.10
17	Marlborough,	3,445	244	781	4,470	19	4,489	99.58	56.80	19.94	76.74	17.40	5.44	0.42
18	Medford,	3,321	322	846	4,489	15	4,504	99.67	60.04	13.70	73.74	18.78	7.15	0.33
19	New Bedford,	10,996	764	4,038	15,798	38	15,836	99.76	45.54	18.21	63.75	31.18	4.83	0.24
20	Newburyport,	3,507	167	527	4,201	31	4,232	99.27	70.89	11.98	82.87	12.45	3.95	0.73
21	Newton,	5,617	387	1,870	7,874	8	7,882	99.90	57.06	14.20	71.26	23.73	4.91	0.10
22	North Adams,	4,065	348	1,124	5,537	22	5,559	99.60	53.82	19.30	73.12	20.22	6.26	0.40
23	Northampton,	3,290	223	828	4,341	253	4,594	94.49	54.88	16.74	71.62	18.02	4.85	5.51
24	Pittsfield,	4,801	424	806	6,031	28	6,059	99.54	60.75	18.49	79.24	13.30	7.00	0.46
25	Quincy,	4,325	338	1,701	6,364	8	6,372	99.87	45.06	22.82	67.88	26.69	5.30	0.13
26	Salem,	7,411	591	2,191	10,193	50	10,243	99.51	56.29	16.06	72.35	21.39	5.77	0.49
27	Somerville,	11,830	889	3,232	15,960	–	15,960	100.00	57.71	16.47	74.18	20.25	5.57	–
28	Springfield,	12,240	1,107	2,564	15,911	70	15,981	99.56	61.28	15.31	76.59	16.04	6.93	0.44
29	Taunton,	5,993	353	1,400	7,746	395	8,141	95.15	56.65	16.96	73.61	17.20	4.34	4.85
30	Waltham,	4,574	294	1,189	6,057	17	6,074	99.72	56.29	19.01	75.30	19.58	4.84	0.28
31	Woburn,	3,527	171	670	4,368	22	4,390	99.47	51.26	28.14	79.40	15.99	4.08	0.53
32	Worcester,	21,128	1,308	6,530	29,966	690	30,656	97.73	49.56	20.04	69.60	21.84	6.29	2.27

The final presentation, pages 267 to 318, exhibits the political condition of the total male population 20 years of age and over, by age periods. As before, we continue our analysis to the recapitulation, presented on page 318. The total male population 20 years of age and over being 771,706, we find 247,256 in the period 20 to 29; 198,411 in the period 30 to 39; 138,379 in the period 40 to 49; 94,232 in the period 50 to 59; 84,668 in the period 60 to 79; 7,283 in the period 80 years of age and over; while for 1,447 persons the facts as to age are unknown. Of the ratable polls who are not voters for reasons other than foreign birth, the total number being 44,821, the largest number is found in the period 20 to 29, it being understood that a person 20 years of age becomes of voters and of aliens has not only increased, but the relative proportion of voters of population and the proportion of aliens of polls and of total population has also increased. In other words, while the relative voting strength of the population has increased, naturalization has not, apparently, quite kept pace with the growth of population. In 1885 as compared with 1875, the proportion of aliens to the total population of which they formed a part had not materially changed. It follows, therefore, that as to the aliens who have come into the State since 1885, naturalization has not proceeded quite so far as among those who came into the State between 1875 and 1885. In a subsequent tabulation, relating to the foreign born, we shall be able to show the extent to which naturalization has taken place among foreign born males of different nationalities.

The following table presents a recapitulation for the cities:

	TOTAL POPULATION, BOTH SEXES, ALL AGES					PERCENTAGES OF TOTAL POPULATION							
Voters	Not Voters	Aliens	Total Ratable Polls	No Political Condition	Total Population. Both Sexes, All Ages	Ratable Polls	Native Born Voters	Foreign Born Naturalized Voters	Total Voters	Aliens	Not Voters	No Political Condition	
3,034	248	500	3,782	8,024	11,806	32.03	22.79	2.91	25.70	4.23	2.10	67.97	1
113,396	8,520	34,171	156,084	340,836	496,920	31.41	15.79	7.43	22.82	6.88	1.71	68.59	2
8,531	496	1,674	10,701	22,464	33,165	32.27	20.78	4.94	25.72	5.05	1.50	67.73	3
17,018	1,896	6,191	25,105	56,538	81,643	30.75	14.84	6.01	30.85	7.58	2.32	69.25	4
7,066	444	2,222	9,732	21,532	31,264	31.13	16.85	5.75	22.60	7.11	1.42	68.87	5
2,749	294	1,970	5,013	11,407	16,420	30.53	11.72	5.02	16.74	12.00	1.79	69.47	6
4,060	297	1,143	5,500	13,043	18,573	29.77	17.17	4.85	22.02	6.15	1.60	70.23	7
14,566	1,035	8,166	23,767	65,496	89,263	26.64	8.32	8.01	16.33	9.15	1.16	73.36	8
5,231	603	2,116	7,950	18,459	26,409	30.10	14.77	5.04	19.81	8.01	2.28	69.90	9
6,444	385	5,000	11,829	16,382	28,211	41.93	15.78	7.06	22.84	17.72	1.37	58.07	10
7,456	467	1,509	9,432	20,777	30,209	31.22	20.33	4.35	24.68	5.00	1.54	68.78	11
6,597	535	3,610	10,742	29,580	40,322	26.64	9.28	7.08	16.36	8.95	1.33	73.33	12
10,178	805	4,357	15,340	36,824	52,164	29.41	10.34	9.17	19.51	8.35	1.55	70.59	13
16,408	1,154	6,230	23,792	60,575	84,367	28.20	11.76	7.69	19.45	7.38	1.37	71.80	14
15,437	963	3,423	19,829	42,525	62,354	31.80	20.15	4.61	24.76	5.49	1.55	68.20	15
6,522	469	1,865	8,856	20,852	29,708	29.81	16.96	4.99	21.95	6.28	1.58	70.19	16
3,445	241	784	4,470	10,507	14,977	29.85	17.03	5.97	23.00	5.22	1.63	70.15	17
3,321	322	846	4,489	9,985	14,474	31.01	18.68	4.26	22.94	5.85	2.22	68.99	18
10,696	764	4,968	15,798	39,453	55,251	28.59	13.05	5.22	18.27	8.94	1.38	71.41	19
3,507	167	527	4,201	10,351	14,552	28.87	20.62	3.48	24.10	3.62	1.15	71.13	20
5,617	387	1,870	7,874	19,716	27,590	28.54	16.30	4.06	20.36	6.78	1.40	71.46	21
4,065	348	1,124	5,537	13,598	19,135	28.94	15.64	5.61	21.25	5.87	1.82	71.06	22
3,280	223	828	4,331	12,405	16,746	25.92	15.06	4.59	19.65	4.94	1.33	74.08	23
4,801	424	806	6,031	14,430	20,461	29.48	17.99	5.47	23.46	3.94	2.08	70.52	24
4,325	338	1,701	6,364	14,348	20,712	30.75	13.56	7.02	20.88	8.22	1.63	69.27	25
7,411	591	2,191	10,193	24,280	34,473	29.57	16.73	4.77	21.50	6.36	1.71	70.43	26
11,839	889	3,232	15,960	36,240	52,200	30.57	17.65	5.05	22.68	6.19	1.70	69.43	27
12,240	1,107	2,564	15,911	35,611	51,522	30.88	19.01	4.75	23.76	4.97	2.15	69.12	28
5,966	355	1,400	7,746	19,369	27,115	28.57	17.01	5.09	22.10	5.17	1.50	71.43	29
4,374	294	1,189	6,057	14,819	20,876	29.01	16.38	5.53	21.91	5.69	1.41	70.99	30
3,327	171	670	4,168	10,010	14,178	29.40	15.15	8.32	23.47	4.72	1.21	70.60	31
21,128	1,908	6,630	29,666	69,101	98,767	30.04	15.23	6.16	21.39	6.72	1.95	69.96	32

a ratable poll, but is not a legal voter until his twenty-first birthday has been passed. Of persons having no political status, including paupers and others legally debarred, the total number being 5,473, 642 are found in the period 20 to 29; 1,011 in the period 30 to 39; 1,028 in the period 40 to 49; 908 in the period 50 to 59; 1,541 in the period 60 to 79; 316 are 80 years of age and over; while for 27 the age is unknown.

The table also exhibits the number of native born voters, foreign born naturalized voters, and aliens for each of the age periods, but it is not necessary to point out the facts in detail. We conclude the analysis with a table showing these facts for the cities, with percentages for the city of Boston and for the State.

CITIES.	Ratable Polls (Not Voters)	Ratable Polls and Native Born Voters	Ratable Polls and Foreign Born Naturalized Voters	Ratable Polls and Aliens	No Political Condition	Total Male Population 20 Years of Age and Over
Beverly, ...	248	2,691	343	500	15	3,797
20 to 29 years, ...	155	727	43	202	2	1,129
30 to 39 years, ...	30	716	82	136	1	965
40 to 49 years, ...	14	479	73	72	4	642
50 to 59 years, ...	6	394	79	39	2	520
60 to 79 years, ...	43	336	62	20	5	466
80 years and over, . . .	-	39	4	4	1	48
Age unknown, ...	-	-	-	27	-	27
Boston, ...	8,520	76,463	36,930	34,171	524	156,608
20 to 29 years, ...	5,673	27,253	6,183	13,782	68	52,959
30 to 39 years, ...	1,257	21,739	10,416	10,906	95	44,413
40 to 49 years, ...	702	13,445	8,873	5,085	90	28,195
50 to 59 years, ...	321	7,819	6,548	2,627	65	17,380
60 to 79 years, ...	157	5,728	4,672	1,617	165	12,339
80 years and over, . . .	7	428	217	105	41	798
Age unknown, ...	403	51	21	49	-	524
Brockton, ...	496	6,893	1,638	1,674	17	10,718
20 to 29 years, ...	355	2,105	320	736	4	3,520
30 to 39 years, ...	49	2,052	567	525	-	3,193
40 to 49 years, ...	24	1,391	357	235	4	2,011
50 to 59 years, ...	17	712	241	107	1	1,078
60 to 79 years, ...	7	596	147	64	5	819
80 years and over, . . .	-	37	5	6	3	51
Age unknown, ...	44	-	1	1	-	46
Cambridge, ...	1,896	12,117	4,901	6,191	51	25,156
20 to 29 years, ...	1,498	4,802	775	2,575	-	9,650
30 to 39 years, ...	183	3,023	1,313	1,851	3	6,373
40 to 49 years, ...	111	2,014	1,202	901	9	4,237
50 to 59 years, ...	42	1,202	923	507	11	2,685
60 to 79 years, ...	40	968	659	326	27	2,020
80 years and over, . . .	3	107	28	26	1	165
Age unknown, ...	19	1	1	5	-	26
Chelsea, ...	444	5,269	1,797	2,222	2	9,734
20 to 29 years, ...	315	1,570	332	948	-	3,165
30 to 39 years, ...	27	1,310	459	692	2	2,490
40 to 49 years, ...	30	991	414	284	-	1,719
50 to 59 years, ...	43	737	340	168	-	1,288
60 to 79 years, ...	27	622	243	122	-	1,014
80 years and over, . . .	-	39	9	7	-	55
Age unknown, ...	2	-	-	1	-	3
Chicopee, ...	294	1,924	825	1,970	18	5,031
20 to 29 years, ...	257	767	153	907	-	2,084
30 to 39 years, ...	11	518	233	510	-	1,272
40 to 49 years, ...	14	295	150	252	4	715
50 to 59 years, ...	6	176	173	178	2	535
60 to 79 years, ...	1	156	109	116	11	393
80 years and over, . . .	-	12	7	6	1	26
Age unknown, ...	5	-	-	1	-	6
Everett, ...	297	3,189	901	1,143	-	5,530
20 to 29 years, ...	200	929	136	434	-	1,699

CITIES.	Ratable Polls (Not Voters)	Ratable Polls and Native Born Voters	Ratable Polls and Foreign Born Naturalized Voters	Ratable Polls and Aliens	No Political Condition	Total Male Population 20 Years of Age and Over
Everett — Con.						
30 to 39 years, ...	19	870	279	366	–	1,564
40 to 49 years, ...	23	630	236	188	–	1,077
50 to 59 years, ...	19	420	147	99	–	685
60 to 79 years, ...	5	318	100	53	–	476
80 years and over, . . .	–	22	2	3	–	27
Age unknown, ...	1	–	1	–	–	2
Fall River, ...	1,035	7,421	7,145	8,166	60	23,827
20 to 29 years, ...	945	3,085	1,443	3,157	6	8,636
30 to 39 years, ...	42	1,977	1,930	2,099	9	6,057
40 to 49 years, ...	26	1,203	1,655	1,452	6	4,342
50 to 59 years, ...	15	633	1,297	892	8	2,845
60 to 79 years, ...	3	477	795	541	20	1,836
80 years and over, . . .	1	45	24	17	11	98
Age unknown, ...	3	1	1	8	–	13
Fitchburg, ...	603	3,991	1,330	2,116	39	7,980
20 to 29 years, ...	418	1,164	263	875	2	2,722
30 to 39 years, ...	109	1,077	382	602	8	2,178
40 to 49 years, ...	42	733	289	308	5	1,377
50 to 59 years, ...	24	447	227	217	7	922
60 to 79 years, ...	5	445	161	103	17	731
80 years and over, . . .	1	34	8	11	–	54
Age unknown, ...	4	1	–	–	–	5
Gloucester, ...	385	4,453	1,991	5,000	18	11,847
20 to 29 years, ...	310	1,406	275	2,515	–	4,506
30 to 39 years, ...	33	1,144	651	1,578	2	3,408
40 to 49 years, ...	22	779	489	612	2	1,904
50 to 59 years, ...	6	572	318	196	3	1,095
60 to 79 years, ...	1	496	248	87	9	841
80 years and over, . . .	–	50	6	1	2	59
Age unknown, ...	13	6	4	11	–	34
Haverhill, ...	467	6,143	1,313	1,509	39	9,471
20 to 29 years, ...	344	1,832	284	633	2	3,095
30 to 39 years, ...	54	1,648	372	410	7	2,491
40 to 49 years, ...	32	1,172	280	227	4	1,715
50 to 59 years, ...	16	806	219	154	6	1,201
60 to 79 years, ...	10	633	156	83	16	898
80 years and over, . . .	2	52	2	2	4	62
Age unknown, ...	9	–	–	–	–	9
Holyoke, ...	535	3,743	2,854	3,610	28	10,770
20 to 29 years, ...	462	1,577	640	1,434	6	4,119
30 to 39 years, ...	41	1,087	891	961	7	2,987
40 to 49 years, ...	16	575	628	578	3	1,800
50 to 59 years, ...	8	290	456	367	4	1,125
60 to 79 years, ...	4	204	232	251	5	696
80 years and over, . . .	1	10	7	15	3	36
Age unknown, ...	3	–	–	4	–	7
Lawrence, ...	805	5,393	4,785	4,357	42	15,382
20 to 29 years, ...	627	2,156	869	1,833	2	5,487
30 to 39 years, ...	90	1,519	1,211	1,147	3	3,970

CITIES.	Ratable Polls (Not Voters)	Ratable Polls and Native Born Voters	Ratable Polls and Foreign Born Naturalized Voters	Ratable Polls and Aliens	No Political Condition	Total Male Population 20 Years of Age and Over
Lawrence — Con.						
40 to 49 years, ...	58	882	1,181	715	5	2,841
50 to 59 years, ...	19	450	948	375	12	1,804
60 to 79 years, ...	7	360	558	279	14	1,218
80 years and over, . . .	-	25	18	8	6	57
Age unknown, ...	4	1	-	-	-	5
Lowell, ...	1,154	9,924	6,484	6,230	83	23,875
20 to 29 years, ...	929	3,334	1,481	2,711	4	8,459
30 to 39 years, ...	123	2,765	1,846	1,509	10	6,253
40 to 49 years, ...	54	1,839	1,469	968	13	4,343
50 to 59 years, ...	20	1,006	968	614	19	2,627
60 to 79 years, ...	15	907	690	394	34	2,040
80 years and over, . . .	-	72	26	29	3	130
Age unknown, ...	13	1	4	5	-	23
Lynn, ...	969	12,563	2,874	3,423	51	19,880
20 to 29 years, ...	726	3,683	461	1,448	3	6,321
30 to 39 years, ...	123	3,453	798	1,089	6	5,469
40 to 49 years, ...	48	2,468	704	459	7	3,686
50 to 59 years, ...	37	1,610	547	264	9	2,467
60 to 79 years, ...	14	1,249	350	156	22	1,791
80 years and over, . . .	-	99	14	6	4	123
Age unknown, ...	21	1	-	1	-	23
Malden, ...	469	5,038	1,484	1,865	9	8,865
20 to 29 years, ...	341	1,405	260	786	1	2,793
30 to 39 years, ...	61	1,451	422	556	1	2,491
40 to 49 years, ...	30	965	352	275	1	1,623
50 to 59 years, ...	14	638	247	140	3	1,042
60 to 79 years, ...	11	537	192	98	3	841
80 years and over, . . .	-	42	10	7	-	59
Age unknown, ...	12	-	1	3	-	16
Marlborough, ...	244	2,550	895	781	19	4,489
20 to 29 years, ...	190	972	104	236	2	1,504
30 to 39 years, ...	36	741	186	238	2	1,203
40 to 49 years, ...	8	405	212	133	2	760
50 to 59 years, ...	3	227	204	93	5	532
60 to 79 years, ...	5	194	181	74	6	460
80 years and over, . . .	-	11	8	5	1	25
Age unknown, ...	2	-	-	2	1	5
Medford, ...	322	2,704	617	846	15	4,504
20 to 29 years, ...	213	800	89	380	-	1,482
30 to 39 years, ...	41	710	158	219	1	1,129
40 to 49 years, ...	19	510	146	135	2	812
50 to 59 years, ...	40	336	125	72	-	573
60 to 79 years, ...	9	318	92	39	9	467
80 years and over, . . .	-	30	7	1	3	41
New Bedford, ...	764	7,212	2,884	4,938	38	15,836
20 to 29 years, ...	617	2,145	549	1,988	2	5,301
30 to 39 years, ...	69	1,843	838	1,356	5	4,111
40 to 49 years, ...	46	1,273	624	845	5	2,793
50 to 59 years, ...	20	930	512	459	8	1,929

Cities.	Ratable Polls (Not Voters)	Ratable Polls and Native Born Voters	Ratable Polls and Foreign Born Naturalized Voters	Ratable Polls and Aliens	No Political Condition	Total Male Population 20 Years of Age and Over
New Bedford — Con.						
60 to 79 years,	11	903	344	280	17	1,555
80 years and over,	-	116	17	8	1	142
Age unknown,	1	2	-	2	-	5
Newburyport,	167	3,000	507	527	31	4,232
20 to 29 years,	137	768	69	208	4	1,186
30 to 39 years,	14	737	80	144	4	979
40 to 49 years,	5	566	107	84	5	767
50 to 59 years,	7	358	126	56	5	552
60 to 79 years,	4	522	121	31	9	687
80 years and over,	-	49	4	4	4	61
Newton,	387	4,498	1,119	1,870	8	7,882
20 to 29 years,	274	1,204	181	820	-	2,479
30 to 39 years,	52	1,113	267	538	2	1,972
40 to 49 years,	24	951	258	281	1	1,515
50 to 59 years,	20	606	221	143	3	993
60 to 79 years,	7	561	175	81	2	826
80 years and over,	-	59	12	2	-	73
Age unknown,	10	4	5	5	-	24
North Adams,	348	2,992	1,073	1,124	22	5,559
20 to 29 years,	277	1,113	196	402	1	1,989
30 to 39 years,	34	776	297	306	2	1,415
40 to 49 years,	22	512	235	194	3	966
50 to 59 years,	10	314	216	136	4	680
60 to 79 years,	4	253	123	83	11	474
80 years and over,	1	24	5	3	1	34
Age unknown,	-	-	1	-	-	1
Northampton,	223	2,521	769	828	253	4,594
20 to 29 years,	171	845	113	299	37	1,465
30 to 39 years,	23	610	157	218	53	1,061
40 to 49 years,	8	408	190	137	63	806
50 to 59 years,	14	300	173	79	39	605
60 to 79 years,	6	331	132	85	56	610
80 years and over,	1	27	4	10	5	47
Pittsfield,	424	3,681	1,120	806	28	6,059
20 to 29 years,	301	1,312	149	280	4	2,046
30 to 39 years,	68	1,030	218	212	6	1,534
40 to 49 years,	35	642	262	157	3	1,099
50 to 59 years,	11	359	219	86	2	677
60 to 79 years,	9	311	254	67	11	652
80 years and over,	-	27	18	2	2	49
Age unknown,	-	-	-	2	-	2
Quincy,	338	2,871	1,454	1,701	8	6,372
20 to 29 years,	211	875	240	740	1	2,097
30 to 39 years,	46	796	448	545	1	1,836
40 to 49 years,	24	528	371	235	1	1,159
50 to 59 years,	12	335	220	105	2	674
60 to 79 years,	14	305	161	65	1	546
80 years and over,	1	32	14	9	2	58
Age unknown,	-	-	-	2	-	2

CITIES.	Ratable Polls (Not Voters)	Ratable Polls and Native Born Voters	Ratable Polls and Foreign Born Naturalized Voters	Ratable Polls and Aliens	No Political Condition	Total Male Population 20 Years of Age and Over
Salem, ...	591	5,766	1,645	2,191	50	10,243
20 to 29 years, ...	394	1,775	257	883	2	3,311
30 to 39 years, ...	106	1,406	394	605	9	2,520
40 to 49 years, ...	51	1,064	398	322	16	1,851
50 to 59 years, ...	23	690	319	228	7	1,267
60 to 79 years, ...	8	738	267	126	13	1,152
80 years and over, . . .	–	88	10	9	3	110
Age unknown, ...	9	5	–	18	–	32
Somerville, ...	889	9,211	2,628	3,232	–	15,960
20 to 29 years, ...	605	2,874	373	1,284	–	5,136
30 to 39 years, ...	136	2,438	753	994	–	4,321
40 to 49 years, ...	66	1,827	628	475	–	2,996
50 to 59 years, ...	39	1,113	462	261	–	1,875
60 to 79 years, ...	39	892	381	194	–	1,506
80 years and over, . . .	–	65	23	16	–	104
Age unknown, ...	4	2	8	8	–	22
Springfield, . . .	1,107	9,793	2,447	2,564	70	15 981
20 to 29 years, ...	757	2,934	374	1,039	6	5,110
30 to 39 years, ...	184	2,596	675	811	15	4,281
40 to 49 years, ...	99	1,825	562	365	14	2,865
50 to 59 years, ...	30	1,198	492	207	2	1,929
60 to 79 years, ...	9	1,161	327	127	30	1,654
80 years and over, . . .	1	79	15	10	1	106
Age unknown, ...	27	–	2	5	2	36
Taunton, ...	353	4,612	1,381	1,400	395	8,141
20 to 29 years, ...	273	1,387	171	534	58	2,423
30 to 39 years, ...	29	1,156	325	390	91	1,991
40 to 49 years, ...	19	908	316	215	91	1,549
50 to 59 years, ...	12	581	303	143	70	1,109
60 to 79 years, ...	17	523	250	106	76	972
80 years and over, . . .	1	57	14	6	9	87
Age unknown, ...	2	–	2	6	–	10
Waltham, ...	294	3,419	1,155	1,189	17	6,074
20 to 29 years, ...	244	1,050	201	448	1	1,944
30 to 39 years, ...	25	996	335	390	–	1,746
40 to 49 years, ...	13	619	246	169	4	1,051
50 to 59 years, ...	4	373	211	104	1	693
60 to 79 years, ...	3	344	153	70	10	580
80 years and over, . . .	–	35	9	6	1	51
Age unknown, ...	5	2	–	2	–	9
Woburn, ...	171	2,448	1,179	670	22	4,490
20 to 29 years, ...	142	724	150	291	1	1,308
30 to 39 years, ...	17	561	315	186	2	1,081
40 to 49 years, ...	5	388	317	95	1	806
50 to 59 years, ...	6	194	221	63	4	488
60 to 79 years, ...	1	250	172	32	13	468
80 years and over, . . .	–	31	4	3	1	39

CITIES.	Ratable Polls (Not Voters)	Ratable Polls and Native Born Voters	Ratable Polls and Foreign Born Naturalized Voters	Ratable Polls and Aliens	No Political Condition	Total Male Population 20 Years of Age and Over
Worcester, ...	1,908	15,046	6,082	6,630	690	30,356
20 to 29 years, ...	1,356	5,074	946	2,771	103	10,250
30 to 39 years, ...	266	4,013	1,725	1,971	174	8,149
40 to 49 years, ...	142	2,709	1,527	971	195	5,544
50 to 59 years, ...	87	1,646	1,158	514	135	3,540
60 to 79 years, ...	47	1,473	702	359	80	2,661
80 years and over, . . .	5	119	21	26	3	174
Age unknown, ...	5	12	3	18	–	38

The following table presents the figures for the city of Boston, as shown on page 324, reduced to percentages :

CITY OF BOSTON, AND AGE PERIODS.	Ratable Polls (Not Voters)	Ratable Polls and Native Born Voters	Ratable Polls and Foreign Born Naturalized Voters	Ratable Polls and Aliens	No Political Condition	Total Male Population 20 Years of Age and Over
CITY OF BOSTON, ...	100.00	100.00	100.00	100.00	100.00	100.00
20 to 29 years, . . .	66.59	35.64	16.74	40.33	12.98	33.82
30 to 39 years, . . .	14.77	28.43	28.20	31.92	18.13	28.36
40 to 49 years, . . .	8.24	17.58	24.06	14.88	17.18	18.00
50 to 59 years, . . .	3.77	10.23	17.73	7.69	12.40	11.10
60 to 79 years, . . .	1.84	7.49	12.65	4.73	31.49	7.88
80 years and over, . . .	0.08	0.56	0.59	0.31	7.82	0.51
Age unknown, . . .	1.73	0.07	0.06	0.14	–	0.33

From the above table, we find that 33.82 per cent of the total male population 20 years of age and over is classified in the age period 20 to 29 years; 28.36 per cent in the 30 to 39 year period; 18 per cent in the 40 to 49 year period; 11.10 per cent in the 50 to 59 year period; 7.88 per cent in the 60 to 79 year period; 0.51 per cent in the period 80 years and over, while for 0.33 per cent the age is unknown.

A similar analysis table follows for the State :

THE STATE, AND AGE PERIODS.	Ratable Polls (Not Voters)	Ratable Polls and Native Born Voters	Ratable Polls and Foreign Born Naturalized Voters	Ratable Polls and Aliens	No Political Condition	Total Male Population 20 Years of Age and Over
THE STATE, ...	100.00	100.00	100.00	100.00	100.00	100.00
20 to 29 years, ...	69.80	30.31	16.26	40.33	11.73	32.04
30 to 39 years, ...	13.74	25.71	26.35	28.78	18.47	25.72
40 to 49 years, ...	7.73	18.18	23.39	15.38	18.78	17.93
50 to 59 years, ...	4.03	12.17	18.78	8.81	16.59	12.21
60 to 79 years, ...	2.75	12.34	14.48	6.05	28.16	10.97
80 years and over, . . .	0.15	1.26	0.68	0.40	5.78	0.94
Age unknown, ...	1.80	0.03	0.06	0.25	0.49	0.19

FAMILIES:

NUMBER AND AVERAGE SIZE.

FAMILIES : NUMBER AND AVERAGE SIZE.

Counties, Cities, and Towns.	Number	Average Size	Counties, Cities, and Towns.	Number	Average Size	Counties, Cities, and Towns.	Number	Average Size
BARNSTABLE.	8,069	3.43	BERKSHIRE — Con.			DUKES.	1,306	3.25
Barnstable, . .	1,175	3.46	Tyringham, . .	90	4.66	Chilmark, . .	95	3.20
Bourne,. . .	429	3.68	Washington, .	87	4.86	Cottage City, .	313	3.32
Brewster, . .	255	3.53	West Stockbridge,	324	3.88	Edgartown, . .	377	2.98
Chatham, . .	543	3.33	Williamstown, .	1,017	4.81	Gay Head, . .	40	4.23
Dennis,. . .	817	3.42	Windsor, . .	135	4.12	Gosnold, . .	38	3.68
Eastham, . .	137	3.47				Tisbury, . . .	289	3.47
Falmouth, . .	722	3.68	BRISTOL.	17,708	4.39	West Tisbury, .	154	2.99
Harwich, . .	783	3.23				ESSEX.	74,092	4.46
Mashpee, . .	81	4.07	Acushnet, . .	294	3.79			
Orleans, . .	375	3.49	Attleborough, .	1,890	4.39	Amesbury, . .	2,281	4.38
Provincetown, .	1,216	3.75	Berkley, . .	256	3.73	Andover, . .	1,296	4.74
Sandwich, . .	442	3.57	Dartmouth, . .	814	3.82	BEVERLY, . .	2,914	4.05
Truro, . . .	229	3.56	Dighton, . .	461	3.90	Ward 1, . .	598	4.47
Wellfleet, . .	332	2.92	Easton, . . .	1,061	4.20	Ward 2, . .	618	3.95
Yarmouth, . .	535	3.09	Fairhaven, . .	898	3.72	Ward 3, . .	610	4.00
			FALL RIVER, .	17,348	4.97	Ward 4, . .	528	3.81
BERKSHIRE.	18,810	4.59	Ward 1, . .	2,342	4.76	Ward 5, . .	306	3.93
Adams,. . .	1,904	4.89	Ward 2, . .	1,977	5.20	Ward 6, . .	254	4.06
Alford, . . .	76	3.68	Ward 3, . .	2,247	5.10	Boxford, . .	186	3.91
Becket, . . .	219	4.05	Ward 4, . .	2,241	4.07	Bradford, . .	1,121	4.22
Cheshire, . .	297	3.96	Ward 5, . .	2,129	4.98	Danvers, . .	1,053	4.95
Clarksburg, . .	214	4.71	Ward 6, . .	2,179	5.63	Essex, . . .	445	3.57
Dalton, . . .	688	4.07	Ward 7, . .	1,396	4.58	Georgetown, .	541	3.79
Egremont, . .	211	3.96	Ward 8, . .	1,607	4.56	GLOUCESTER, .	5,416	5.21
Florida,. . .	93	4.57	Ward 9, . .	2,130	5.08	Ward 1, . .	690	4.59
Great Barrington,	1,136	4.22	Freetown, . .	342	4.11	Ward 2, . .	982	5.12
Hancock, . .	117	4.37	Mansfield, . .	946	3.93	Ward 3, . .	743	6.99
Hinsdale, . .	346	4.77	NEW BEDFORD, .	12,221	4.52	Ward 4, . .	520	6.66
Lanesborough, .	210	4.04	Ward 1, . .	2,500	5.28	Ward 5, . .	893	4.86
Lee, . . .	922	4.41	Ward 2, . .	1,792	4.35	Ward 6, . .	704	4.18
Lenox, . . .	581	4.34	Ward 3, . .	1,553	3.63	Ward 7, . .	587	4.83
Monterey, . .	145	4.02	Ward 4, . .	1,615	3.96	Ward 8, . .	291	4.15
Mt. Washington,.	51	3.87	Ward 5, . .	2,172	4.19	Groveland, . .	560	4.17
New Ashford, .	34	3.87	Ward 6, . .	2,589	5.08	Hamilton, . .	315	4.30
New Marlborough,	325	3.96	No. Attleborough,	1,499	4.39	HAVERHILL, .	6,902	4.58
NORTH ADAMS, .	3,981	4.87	Norton, . . .	491	4.02	Ward 1, . .	573	4.92
Otis, . . .	136	3.81	Raynham, . .	397	3.82	Ward 2, . .	631	3.98
Peru, . . .	71	4.30	Rehoboth, . .	451	4.01	Ward 3, . .	781	4.54
PITTSFIELD, .	4,342	4.71	Seekonk, . .	334	4.39	Ward 4, . .	957	4.16
Ward 1, . .	552	5.14	Somerset, . .	497	3.99	Ward 5, . .	2,452	4.60
Ward 2, . .	722	4.88	Swansea, . .	411	3.96	Ward 6, . .	1,508	4.95
Ward 3, . .	599	4.38	TAUNTON, . .	5,885	4.61	Ipswich, . .	1,104	4.28
Ward 4, . .	604	4.60	Ward 1, . .	669	4.19	LAWRENCE,. .	10,783	4.84
Ward 5, . .	546	4.92	Ward 2, . .	687	4.18	Ward 1, . .	1,805	4.75
Ward 6, . .	742	4.68	Ward 3, . .	691	4.40	Ward 2, . .	1,331	5.25
Ward 7, . .	577	4.39	Ward 4, . .	737	4.06	Ward 3, . .	1,879	4.78
Richmond, . .	164	4.27	Ward 5, . .	815	4.71	Ward 4, . .	1,888	5.28
Sandisfield, . .	213	3.76	Ward 6, . .	715	4.34	Ward 5, . .	2,215	4.48
Savoy, . . .	133	3.79	Ward 7, . .	673	4.51	Ward 6, . .	1,665	4.64
Sheffield, . .	481	3.94	Ward 8, . .	808	6.05	LYNN, . . .	14,144	4.41
Stockbridge, .	471	4.41	Westport, . .	702	3.81	Ward 1, . .	387	4.08

FAMILIES: NUMBER AND AVERAGE SIZE — Continued.

COUNTIES, CITIES, AND TOWNS.	Number	Average Size
ESSEX — Con.		
LYNN — Con.		
Ward 2, . .	968	4.67
Ward 3, . .	3,602	4.13
Ward 4, . .	2,384	4.83
Ward 5, . .	2,875	4.47
Ward 6, . .	3,324	4.49
Ward 7, . .	604	4.43
Lynnfield, . .	211	3.88
Manchester, .	488	3.84
Marblehead, .	2,063	3.83
Merrimac, .	605	3.80
Methuen, . .	1,317	4.32
Middleton, . .	219	3.83
Nahant, . .	204	4.24
Newbury, . .	360	4.14
NEWBURYPORT, .	3,479	4.18
Ward 1, . .	601	3.95
Ward 2, . .	510	4.57
Ward 3, . .	615	4.33
Ward 4, . .	559	4.15
Ward 5, . .	538	4.16
Ward 6, . .	656	4.00
North Andover, .	796	4.48
Peabody, . .	2,373	4.43
Rockport, . .	1,296	4.28
Rowley, . .	340	3.74
SALEM, . .	7,623	4.52
Ward 1, . .	1,109	4.51
Ward 2, . .	1,369	4.12
Ward 3, . .	1,028	4.27
Ward 4, . .	1,181	4.43
Ward 5, . .	1,881	5.27
Ward 6, . .	1,055	4.07
Salisbury, . .	351	3.70
Saugus, . .	1,065	4.22
Swampscott, .	823	3.96
Topsfield, . .	264	3.94
Wenham, . .	234	3.79
West Newbury, .	440	3.73
FRANKLIN.	9,637	4.17
Ashfield, .	252	4.02
Bernardston, .	209	3.72
Buckland, .	387	4.00
Charlemont, .	275	3.79
Colrain, . .	366	4.40
Conway, . .	369	4.22
Deerfield, .	674	4.46
Erving, . .	256	3.77
Gill, . .	197	5.49
Greenfield, .	1,450	4.30
Hawley, . .	110	4.25
Heath, . .	120	3.97
Leverett, . .	200	3.72
Leyden, . .	88	4.13
Monroe, . .	65	4.58

COUNTIES, CITIES, AND TOWNS.	Number	Average Size
FRANKLIN — Con.		
Montague, . .	1,349	4.49
New Salem, . .	233	3.73
Northfield, . .	419	4.42
Orange, . .	1,330	3.86
Rowe, . .	123	4.05
Shelburne, . .	392	3.98
Shutesbury, . .	125	3.55
Sunderland, . .	166	4.19
Warwick, . .	158	3.79
Wendell, . .	129	4.10
Whately, . .	195	3.87
HAMPDEN.	32,793	4.66
Agawam, . .	553	4.35
Blandford, . .	206	4.12
Brimfield, . .	238	4.04
Chester, . .	354	4.04
CHICOPEE, . .	3,042	5.40
Ward 1, . .	570	5.74
Ward 2, . .	394	4.45
Ward 3, . .	417	6.76
Ward 4, . .	421	5.36
Ward 5, . .	505	5.25
Ward 6, . .	333	5.10
Ward 7, . .	402	4.92
E. Longmeadow, .	330	4.82
Granville, . .	252	3.90
Hampden, . .	194	3.83
Holland, . .	55	3.62
HOLYOKE, . .	7,894	5.41
Ward 1, . .	1,145	5.25
Ward 2, . .	1,690	5.24
Ward 3, . .	968	5.24
Ward 4, . .	1,256	5.40
Ward 5, . .	768	4.66
Ward 6, . .	1,152	4.95
Ward 7, . .	925	4.72
Longmeadow, . .	146	4.25
Ludlow, . .	473	5.42
Monson, . .	872	4.30
Montgomery, .	63	4.37
Palmer, . .	1,382	4.36
Russell, . .	185	4.57
Southwick, . .	239	4.02
SPRINGFIELD, .	11,741	4.39
Ward 1, . .	1,604	4.30
Ward 2, . .	1,758	4.49
Ward 3, . .	1,390	4.56
Ward 4, . .	1,435	4.33
Ward 5, . .	1,534	4.19
Ward 6, . .	1,390	4.43
Ward 7, . .	1,135	4.49
Ward 8, . .	1,524	4.65
Tolland, . .	67	4.63
Wales, . .	191	4.10
Westfield, . .	2,563	4.11

COUNTIES, CITIES, AND TOWNS.	Number	Average Size
HAMPDEN — Con.		
West Springfield,	1,360	4.50
Wilbraham, . .	363	4.79
HAMPSHIRE.	11,744	4.06
Amherst, . .	1,094	4.50
Belchertown, .	521	4.12
Chesterfield, .	192	3.64
Cummington, .	201	3.73
Easthampton, .	1,019	4.70
Enfield, . .	261	3.79
Goshen, . .	65	4.61
Granby, . .	173	4.37
Greenwich, . .	142	3.29
Hadley, . .	380	4.37
Hatfield, . .	291	4.34
Huntington, .	329	4.41
Middlefield, . .	92	4.20
NORTHAMPTON, .	3,270	5.12
Ward 1, . .	480	4.52
Ward 2, . .	507	6.40
Ward 3, . .	697	4.73
Ward 4, . .	423	5.88
Ward 5, . .	445	4.80
Ward 6, . .	412	4.62
Ward 7, . .	396	4.88
Pelham, . .	129	3.86
Plainfield, . .	109	4.13
Prescott, . .	106	3.78
Southampton, .	252	4.18
South Hadley, .	894	4.97
Ware, . .	1,523	5.02
Westhampton, .	124	3.84
Williamsburg, .	473	4.43
Worthington, .	155	4.18
MIDDLESEX.	167,654	4.64
Acton, . .	529	3.74
Arlington, . .	1,362	4.78
Ashby, . .	233	3.45
Ashland, . .	486	4.30
Ayer, . .	528	3.98
Bedford, . .	251	4.06
Belmont, . .	505	5.63
Billerica, . .	552	4.43
Boxborough, .	78	3.94
Burlington, . .	129	4.45
CAMBRIDGE, .	17,136	4.75
Ward 1, . .	2,945	5.40
Ward 2, . .	4,369	4.55
Ward 3, . .	2,812	4.38
Ward 4, . .	4,225	4.41
Ward 5, . .	2,204	4.74
Carlisle, . .	126	3.80
Chelmsford, . .	747	4.28
Concord, . .	874	5.92
Dracut, . .	475	5.14

FAMILIES: NUMBER AND AVERAGE SIZE — Continued.

COUNTIES, CITIES, AND TOWNS	Number	Average Size
MIDDLESEX — Con.		
Dunstable, . .	106	3.77
EVERETT, . .	4,304	4.32
Ward 1, . .	673	4.66
Ward 2, . .	583	4.51
Ward 3, . .	729	4.24
Ward 4, . .	703	4.09
Ward 5, . .	779	4.05
Ward 6, . .	837	4.41
Framingham, .	2,115	4.50
Groton, . . .	508	4.31
Holliston, . .	701	3.88
Hopkinton, . .	752	3.97
Hudson, . .	1,245	4.26
Lexington, . .	775	4.51
Lincoln, . .	209	5.32
Littleton, . .	256	4.44
LOWELL, . .	16,885	5.00
Ward 1, . .	1,633	5.82
Ward 2, . .	1,879	5.58
Ward 3, . .	2,608	4.54
Ward 4, . .	1,881	4.91
Ward 5, . .	1,765	4.79
Ward 6, . .	1,369	4.67
Ward 7, . .	2,383	5.50
Ward 8, . .	1,785	4.45
Ward 9, . .	1,522	4.62
MALDEN, . .	6,638	4.48
Ward 1, . .	953	4.31
Ward 2, . .	1,091	4.89
Ward 3, . .	763	4.69
Ward 4, . .	1,024	4.69
Ward 5, . .	943	4.17
Ward 6, . .	977	4.31
Ward 7, . .	887	4.23
MARLBOROUGH, .	3,159	4.74
Ward 1, . .	317	4.21
Ward 2, . .	455	4.85
Ward 3, . .	564	5.26
Ward 4, . .	636	5.19
Ward 5, . .	460	4.20
Ward 6, . .	395	4.28
Ward 7, . .	332	4.65
Maynard, . .	642	4.81
MEDFORD, . .	3,172	4.56
Ward 1, . .	642	4.69
Ward 2, . .	544	4.24
Ward 3, . .	411	4.08
Ward 4, . .	426	4.59
Ward 5, . .	627	4.71
Ward 6, . .	522	4.45
Melrose, . .	2,685	4.46
Natick, . . .	2,689	4.22
NEWTON, . .	5,528	4.80
Ward 1, . .	830	5.17
Ward 2, . .	1,107	4.89
Ward 3, . .	719	4.77
Ward 4, . .	685	5.22

COUNTIES, CITIES, AND TOWNS	Number	Average Size
MIDDLESEX — Con.		
NEWTON — Con.		
Ward 5, . .	856	4.81
Ward 6, . .	836	5.07
Ward 7, . .	495	5.11
North Reading, .	228	3.66
Pepperell, . .	787	4.22
Reading, . .	1,150	4.10
Sherborn, . .	286	5.06
Shirley, . .	324	4.32
SOMERVILLE, .	11,903	4.39
Ward 1, . .	2,302	4.40
Ward 2, . .	3,875	4.44
Ward 3, . .	3,056	4.27
Ward 4, . .	2,670	4.43
Stoneham, . .	1,581	3.97
Stow, . . .	234	3.46
Sudbury, . .	272	4.19
Tewksbury, . .	473	7.14
Townsend, . .	512	3.48
Tyngsborough, .	163	3.90
Wakefield, . .	1,958	4.24
WALTHAM, . .	4,276	4.88
Ward 1, . .	615	4.75
Ward 2, . .	500	5.87
Ward 3, . .	651	5.19
Ward 4, . .	646	4.75
Ward 5, . .	639	4.52
Ward 6, . .	647	4.51
Ward 7, . .	578	4.79
Watertown, . .	1,950	4.72
Wayland, . .	446	4.54
Westford, . .	526	4.60
Weston, . .	367	4.66
Wilmington, . .	338	4.20
Winchester, . .	1,301	4.73
WOBURN, . .	3,012	4.71
Ward 1, . .	509	5.16
Ward 2, . .	580	4.88
Ward 3, . .	561	4.47
Ward 4, . .	574	4.57
Ward 5, . .	242	4.50
Ward 6, . .	343	4.12
Ward 7, . .	193	5.01
NANTUCKET.		
Nantucket, . .	981	3.07
NORFOLK.	29,685	4.54
Avon, . . .	385	4.22
Bellingham, . .	358	4.14
Braintree, . .	1,254	4.24
Brookline, . .	3,148	5.13
Canton, . .	968	4.79
Cohasset, . .	586	4.22
Dedham, . .	1,615	4.47
Dover, . . .	148	4.51

COUNTIES, CITIES, AND TOWNS	Number	Average Size
NORFOLK — Con.		
Foxborough, . .	828	3.89
Franklin, . .	1,176	4.37
Holbrook, . .	571	4.02
Hyde Park, . .	2,561	4.62
Medfield, . .	415	4.51
Medway, . .	732	3.98
Mills, . . .	226	4.45
Milton, . .	1,106	4.29
Needham, . .	802	4.38
Norfolk, . .	210	4.20
Norwood, . .	983	4.75
QUINCY, . .	4,373	4.74
Ward 1, . .	790	4.51
Ward 2, . .	584	4.69
Ward 3, . .	983	4.78
Ward 4, . .	960	5.01
Ward 5, . .	568	4.70
Ward 6, . .	458	4.54
Randolph, . .	905	4.08
Sharon, . .	386	4.37
Stoughton, . .	1,241	4.25
Walpole, . .	688	4.35
Wellesley, . .	738	5.73
Weymouth, . .	2,666	4.24
Wrentham, . .	631	4.10
PLYMOUTH.	24,830	4.09
Abington, . .	1,076	3.91
Bridgewater, . .	854	5.49
BROCKTON, . .	7,700	4.31
Ward 1, . .	935	4.46
Ward 2, . .	1,070	4.04
Ward 3, . .	1,188	4.21
Ward 4, . .	1,089	4.40
Ward 5, . .	1,126	4.48
Ward 6, . .	1,086	4.55
Ward 7, . .	1,196	4.05
Carver, . .	262	3.88
Duxbury, . .	532	3.70
East Bridgewater, .	726	3.99
Halifax, . .	148	3.96
Hanover, . .	544	3.77
Hanson, . .	380	3.63
Hingham, . .	1,164	4.14
Hull, . . .	229	4.56
Kingston, . .	477	3.66
Lakeville, . .	233	3.73
Marion, . .	213	3.56
Marshfield, . .	511	3.44
Mattapoisett, . .	301	3.43
Middleborough, .	1,673	4.00
Norwell, . .	422	3.65
Pembroke, . .	367	3.33
Plymouth, . .	1,989	4.04
Plympton, . .	162	3.39
Rochester, . .	260	3.93

FAMILIES: NUMBER AND AVERAGE SIZE — Continued.

COUNTIES, CITIES, AND TOWNS.	Number	Average Size	COUNTIES, CITIES, AND TOWNS.	Number	Average Size	COUNTIES, CITIES, AND TOWNS.	Number	Average Size
PLYMOUTH — Con.			**SUFFOLK — Con.**			**WORCESTER — Con.**		
Rockland,	1,331	4.15	Revere,	1,652	4.49	Millbury,	1,100	4.75
Scituate,	607	3.70	Winthrop,	910	4.61	New Braintree,	114	4.75
Wareham,	894	3.78				Northborough,	451	4.30
West Bridgewater,	469	4.27	**WORCESTER.**	67,274	4.56	Northbridge,	1,070	4.94
Whitman,	1,389	4.14				North Brookfield,	1,030	4.50
			Ashburnham,	530	4.05	Oakham,	161	3.76
SUFFOLK.	112,802	4.79	Athol,	1,750	4.21	Oxford,	618	3.87
Boston,	103,306	4.81	Auburn,	945	4.63	Paxton,	114	3.74
Ward 1,	4,671	4.50	Barre,	558	4.08	Petersham,	254	3.75
Ward 2,	4,144	5.21	Berlin,	225	3.99	Phillipston,	114	4.04
Ward 3,	3,164	4.41	Black-stone,	1,296	4.77	Princeton,	236	4.03
Ward 4,	3,010	4.44	Bolton,	206	3.87	Royalston,	254	3.50
Ward 5,	2,588	5.02	Boylston,	177	4.12	Rutland,	225	4.35
Ward 6,	5,559	5.01	Brookfield,	756	4.34	Shrewsbury,	381	4.00
Ward 7,	3,137	5.41	Charlton,	470	3.99	Southborough,	442	5.03
Ward 8,	4,370	5.29	Clinton,	2,278	5.05	Southbridge,	1,688	4.89
Ward 9,	4,682	4.95	Dana,	196	3.66	Spencer,	1,625	4.89
Ward 10,	4,471	5.04	Douglas,	483	4.19	Sterling,	342	3.56
Ward 11,	3,770	5.29	Dudley,	628	5.10	Sturbridge,	434	4.40
Ward 12,	3,518	6.14	**FITCHBURG,**	5,686	4.64	Sutton,	714	4.79
Ward 13,	5,453	4.57	Ward 1,	897	4.88	Templeton,	718	4.06
Ward 14,	4,074	4.71	Ward 2,	1,241	5.25	Upton,	524	4.10
Ward 15,	3,992	4.67	Ward 3,	911	4.72	Uxbridge,	812	4.37
Ward 16,	3,735	4.37	Ward 4,	793	4.05	Warren,	980	4.52
Ward 17,	4,656	4.53	Ward 5,	843	3.97	Webster,	1,716	4.54
Ward 18,	4,960	4.37	Ward 6,	1,001	4.66	Westborough,	1,631	5.08
Ward 19,	4,620	4.84	Gardner,	2,062	4.45	West Boylston,	648	4.58
Ward 20,	4,674	4.61	Grafton,	1,106	4.61	West Brookfield,	409	3.59
Ward 21,	4,306	4.48	Hardwick,	533	4.98	Westminster,	370	3.55
Ward 22,	4,770	4.67	Harvard,	279	4.16	Winchendon,	1,078	4.17
Ward 23,	3,866	4.73	Holden,	555	4.69	**WORCESTER,**	20,861	4.73
Ward 24,	3,944	4.62	Hopedale,	307	4.49	Ward 1,	2,417	4.59
Ward 25,	3,172	4.73	Hubbardston,	348	3.66	Ward 2,	2,653	4.93
CHELSEA,	6,934	4.51	Lancaster,	452	4.82	Ward 3,	2,825	5.18
Ward 1,	1,655	4.52	Leicester,	731	4.43	Ward 4,	2,742	4.92
Ward 2,	1,712	4.43	Leominster,	2,181	4.22	Ward 5,	3,028	5.05
Ward 3,	1,561	4.56	Lunenburg,	302	4.10	Ward 6,	2,591	4.57
Ward 4,	1,241	4.34	Mendon,	234	3.80	Ward 7,	2,452	4.22
Ward 5,	765	4.82	Milford,	2,116	4.23	Ward 8,	2,153	4.17

FAMILIES: NUMBER AND AVERAGE SIZE — Concluded.

RECAPITULATION.

THE STATE, AND COUNTIES.	Number	Average Size
THE STATE.	547,385	4.57
Barnstable, ...	8,069	3.43
Berkshire, ...	18,810	4.59
Bristol, ...	47,708	4.50
Dukes, ...	1,306	3.25
Essex, ...	74,092	4.46
Franklin, ...	9,637	4.17
Hampden, ...	32,783	4.66
Hampshire, ...	11,744	4.66
Middlesex, ...	107,054	4.64
Nantucket, ...	981	3.07
Norfolk, ...	29,085	4.54
Plymouth, ...	24,830	4.09
Suffolk, ...	112,802	4.79
Worcester, ...	67,274	4.56

SIZE OF FAMILIES

AND

COMPOSITION BY SEX.

SIZE OF FAMILIES AND COMPOSITION BY SEX.

The distribution of the total number of families, by exact size, for each city, town, and for the State, is shown in this presentation. In addition, the composition by sex is shown for each city and for the State. By "composition by sex" is meant the number of males and number of females, respectively, in families of each specified size.

A description of the various columns in that portion of the presentation which relates to towns is herewith given. In the first column, to the right of the name, the full face figures (1, 2, etc.) indicate the number of persons to a family, that is, show the size of the family. The second column shows the number of families of the specified size.

In the third and fourth columns are given percentages which show the proportions as regards total families and total population for families of each size; in other words, if the whole number of families in the town is considered as representing 100 per cent, and the total population is also considered as being represented by 100 per cent, the percentages given opposite each size of family show what proportion of the total families and of the total population is represented by the number of families and population comprehended by families of that size.

The proper method of reading this presentation is as follows: In the town of Barnstable there are 1,173 families. Of these 1,173 families, 124 are composed of one person each, this number of families being 10.57 per cent of the total number of families and containing 3.96 per cent of the total population of the town. There are 272 families composed of two persons each, this number of families being 23.19 per cent of the total number of families and containing 13.41 per cent of the total population. The other lines may be read in a similar manner.

In that portion of the presentation devoted to the cities and the State, the composition by sex is shown, which requires a different arrangement of the table and additional description. We supply a description of the second form of presentation.

In the first column the full face figures (1, 2, etc.) indicate the number of persons to a family, or the size of the family; the figures in parentheses show the number of families of the specified size.

In the second column M indicates males and F females. Thus 1 M 1 F means a family of two persons, composed of one male and one female.

The third column gives the number of families of the specified size and sex composition.

In the fourth and fifth columns are given percentages which show the proportions, as regards total families and total population, of families of each size. A description of these percentages is given above.

We present a particular description of the manner of reading the presentation for cities which also applies to the presentation for the State.

If we look at the figures for the city of North Adams we find that there are 93 families containing one person each. By reference to the second and third columns we find that of these 93 families, 40 are composed of one male person each and 53 of one female person each. There are 722 families of four persons each. Of these, 229 families contain one male and three females each, 331 contain two males and two females each, 144 contain three males and one female each, one contains four males, and 17 contain four females each. The percentages given in the fourth and fifth columns relate to the whole number of families of the sizes designated, and the total population of those families, and not to the detail lines which are required to show the composition of family. In other words, the percentages 18.36 and 15.09 show, respectively, the proportion that 722 families of four persons each bear to the total number of families, while the population of those families, or 2,888, is 15.09 per cent of the total population of the city. The percentages contained in the fourth and fifth columns are to be read in the same manner as previously described in connection with the presentation for towns.

In many cases it happens that the percentages are less than one one-hundredth of one per cent, in which cases an asterisk (*) has been placed in the percentage column to indicate that fact.

In the presentation FAMILIES: NUMBER AND AVERAGE SIZE, which precedes SIZE OF FAMILIES AND COMPOSITION BY SEX, some families of very large average size appear in certain cities and towns. These cities and towns contain large aggregations of people in hotels, boarding and lodging houses, hospitals, asylums, jails, prisons, charitable institutions, etc., these being counted, for Census purposes, as families; and to this fact are due the high averages. The influence of these large families on city or town averages can be accurately determined, and, if desired, the large families may be eliminated, and the average size of family for the city or town as a whole obtained without taking them into account.

The space at the disposal of the Bureau would not permit of the printing in detail of the composition by sex of families of each size in each of the towns in the State, as such a presentation would have taken three times the space which is devoted to it in this volume; but the composition by sex of each of these large families, where they are located in cities, is shown in detail, and also in the recapitulation for the State. If for any purpose the composition of the families by sex is desired for any town in the Commonwealth, it can be supplied by the Bureau.

[341]

SIZE OF FAMILIES : FOR TOWNS.

COUNTIES, TOWNS, AND SIZE OF FAMILIES.	Number of Families	PERCENTAGES — Total Families	PERCENTAGES — Total Population
BARNSTABLE.			
Barnstable, . . .	1,173	100.00	100.00
1	124	10.57	3.06
2	272	23.19	13.41
3	296	25.23	21.90
4	215	18.33	21.21
5	127	10.83	15.66
6	61	5.20	9.03
7	41	3.50	7.08
8	20	1.71	3.94
9	4	0.34	0.89
10	3	0.26	0.74
11	5	0.43	1.36
12	2	0.17	0.59
13	1	0.08	0.32
14	1	0.08	0.34
19	1	0.08	0.47
Bourne, . . .	429	100.00	100.00
1	45	10.49	2.85
2	84	19.58	10.63
3	86	20.05	16.33
4	87	20.28	22.03
5	57	13.29	18.04
6	32	7.46	12.15
7	24	5.59	10.63
8	11	2.56	5.57
9	2	0.47	1.14
10	1	0.23	0.63
Brewster, . . .	255	100.00	100.00
1	20	7.84	2.22
2	71	27.84	15.76
3	56	21.96	18.65
4	51	20.00	22.64
5	20	7.84	11.10
6	14	5.49	9.32
7	11	4.31	8.55
8	8	3.14	7.10
10	2	0.79	2.22
11	2	0.79	2.44
Chatham, . . .	543	100.00	100.00
1	56	10.31	3.10
2	142	26.15	15.70
3	140	25.78	23.22
4	88	16.21	19.46
5	60	11.05	16.58
6	28	5.16	9.29
7	15	2.76	5.80
8	6	1.10	2.65
9	4	0.74	1.99
10	4	0.74	2.21
BARNSTABLE - Con.			
Dennis, . . .	817	100.00	100.00
1	103	12.61	4.05
2	235	28.76	18.47
3	203	24.85	23.93
4	134	16.40	21.06
5	74	9.06	14.54
6	37	4.53	8.72
7	18	2.20	4.95
8	9	1.10	2.83
9	3	0.37	1.06
10	1	0.12	0.39
Eastham, . . .	137	100.00	100.00
1	15	10.95	3.15
2	24	17.52	10.08
3	42	30.65	26.47
4	25	18.25	21.02
5	14	10.22	14.71
6	8	5.84	10.09
7	4	2.92	5.88
8	4	2.92	6.72
9	1	0.73	1.89
Falmouth, . . .	722	100.00	100.00
1	79	10.94	2.98
2	157	21.75	11.83
3	148	20.50	16.72
4	135	18.70	20.34
5	92	12.74	17.33
6	44	6.09	9.94
7	32	4.43	8.44
8	18	2.49	5.42
9	6	0.83	2.03
10	4	0.55	1.51
11	2	0.28	0.83
13	3	0.42	1.47
15	1	0.14	0.56
16	1	0.14	0.60
Harwich, . . .	783	100.00	100.00
1	87	11.11	3.44
2	225	28.74	17.77
3	184	23.50	21.80
4	121	15.45	19.12
5	90	11.49	17.77
6	49	6.26	11.61
7	15	1.91	4.15
8	6	0.77	1.90
9	4	0.51	1.42
10	1	0.13	0.39
16	1	0.13	0.63
Mashpee, . . .	81	100.00	100.00

SIZE OF FAMILIES: FOR TOWNS — Continued.

COUNTIES, TOWNS, AND SIZE OF FAMILIES.	Number of Families	PERCENTAGES Total Families	PERCENTAGES Total Population
BARNSTABLE—Con.			
Mashpee—Con.			
1	7	8.64	2.42
2	14	17.28	8.48
3	12	14.82	10.91
4	21	25.93	25.46
5	11	13.58	16.67
6	6	7.41	10.91
7	3	3.70	6.36
8	4	4.94	9.70
10	2	2.47	6.06
11	1	1.23	3.33
Orleans, . . .	375	100.00	100.00
1	36	9.60	3.00
2	126	33.60	21.04
3	90	24.00	22.54
4	53	14.13	17.70
5	31	8.27	12.94
6	16	4.27	8.01
7	11	2.93	6.43
8	9	2.40	6.01
9	2	0.53	1.50
10	1	0.27	0.83
Provincetown, . .	1,216	100.00	100.00
1	84	6.91	1.84
2	303	24.92	13.30
3	285	23.44	18.77
4	185	15.21	16.25
5	140	11.51	15.37
6	93	7.65	12.25
7	50	4.11	7.68
8	41	3.37	7.29
9	26	2.14	5.14
10	3	0.25	0.66
11	4	0.33	0.97
12	1	0.08	0.26
14	1	0.08	0.31
Sandwich, . . .	442	100.00	100.00
1	55	12.44	3.48
2	94	21.27	11.90
3	107	24.21	20.32
4	74	16.74	18.74
5	44	9.95	13.92
6	28	6.33	10.63
7	21	4.75	9.50
8	7	1.58	3.54
9	4	0.91	2.28
10	5	1.13	3.16
11	1	0.23	0.70
12	1	0.23	0.76
20	1	0.23	1.27
Truro, ...	229	100.00	100.00
1	34	14.85	4.17
2	57	24.89	13.99
3	44	19.21	16.20
4	35	15.28	17.18
5	19	8.30	11.66
6	17	7.42	12.51

COUNTIES, TOWNS, AND SIZE OF FAMILIES.	Number of Families	PERCENTAGES Total Families	PERCENTAGES Total Population
BARNSTABLE—Con.			
Truro—Con.			
7	7	3.06	6.01
8	4	1.74	3.95
9	7	3.06	7.75
10	3	1.31	3.68
11	1	0.44	1.35
13	1	0.44	1.59
Wellfleet, . . .	332	100.00	100.00
1	62	18.67	6.41
2	94	28.31	19.42
3	82	24.70	25.41
4	50	15.06	20.66
5	17	5.12	8.78
6	14	4.22	8.68
7	5	1.51	3.92
8	5	1.51	4.15
9	2	0.60	1.86
10	1	0.30	1.05
Yarmouth, . . .	535	100.00	100.00
1	60	11.21	3.35
2	177	33.08	21.39
3	123	22.99	22.39
4	79	14.77	19.00
5	52	9.72	15.71
6	24	4.49	8.70
7	13	2.43	5.50
8	5	0.93	2.42
9	1	0.19	0.54
12	1	0.19	0.72
BERKSHIRE.			
Adams, ...	1,604	100.00	100.00
1	31	1.93	0.39
2	222	13.84	5.67
3	276	17.21	10.57
4	262	16.33	13.37
5	254	15.84	16.27
6	214	13.34	16.38
7	126	7.84	11.25
8	89	5.55	9.09
9	55	3.43	6.32
10	35	2.18	4.47
11	18	1.12	2.53
12	10	0.62	1.53
13	4	0.25	0.66
14	3	0.19	0.55
15	3	0.19	0.57
16	1	0.06	0.20
20	1	0.06	0.25
Alford, ...	76	100.00	100.00
1	6	7.89	2.14
2	15	19.74	10.71
3	19	25.00	20.36
4	15	19.74	21.43
5	8	10.52	14.29
6	7	9.21	15.00

SIZE OF FAMILIES: FOR TOWNS — Continued.

COUNTIES, TOWNS, AND SIZE OF FAMILIES.	Number of Families	PERCENTAGES Total Families	PERCENTAGES Total Population
BERKSHIRE — Con.			
Alford — Con.			
7	3	3.95	7.50
8	3	3.95	8.57
Becket,	219	100.00	100.00
1	14	6.39	1.58
2	49	22.37	11.04
3	53	24.20	17.91
4	31	14.15	13.96
5	20	9.13	11.26
6	16	7.31	10.81
7	17	7.76	13.40
8	4	1.83	3.60
9	7	3.20	7.10
10	7	3.20	7.88
13	1	0.46	1.46
Cheshire,	297	100.00	100.00
1	22	7.41	1.87
2	60	20.20	10.20
3	70	23.57	17.86
4	44	14.82	14.97
5	38	12.79	16.16
6	24	8.08	12.24
7	19	6.40	11.31
8	10	3.37	6.80
9	5	1.68	3.83
10	2	0.67	1.70
11	2	0.67	1.87
14	1	0.34	1.19
Clarksburg,	214	100.00	100.00
1	9	4.21	0.89
2	35	16.36	6.94
3	44	20.56	13.08
4	25	11.68	9.91
5	31	14.49	15.36
6	20	9.34	11.89
7	22	10.28	15.26
8	13	6.07	10.31
9	6	2.80	5.35
10	5	2.34	4.96
12	2	0.93	2.38
13	1	0.47	1.29
24	1	0.47	2.38
Dalton,	688	100.00	100.00
1	31	4.51	0.97
2	94	13.66	5.86
3	122	17.73	11.40
4	112	16.28	13.96
5	103	14.97	16.04
6	94	13.66	17.57
7	51	7.41	11.12
8	35	5.09	8.72
9	20	2.91	5.61
10	16	2.32	4.98
11	6	0.87	2.06
12	2	0.29	0.75
13	1	0.15	0.40
18	1	0.15	0.56

COUNTIES, TOWNS, AND SIZE OF FAMILIES.	Number of Families	PERCENTAGES Total Families	PERCENTAGES Total Population
BERKSHIRE — Con.			
Egremont,	211	100.00	100.00
1	12	5.68	1.44
2	43	20.38	10.29
3	41	19.43	14.71
4	41	19.43	19.62
5	30	14.22	17.94
6	22	10.43	15.79
7	13	6.16	10.88
8	5	2.37	4.78
9	3	1.42	3.23
11	1	0.48	1.32
Florida,	93	100.00	100.00
1	5	5.38	1.18
2	4	4.30	1.88
3	24	25.81	16.94
4	18	19.35	16.94
5	14	15.05	16.47
6	11	11.83	15.53
7	8	8.60	13.18
8	6	6.45	11.29
9	2	2.15	4.24
10	1	1.08	2.35
Great Barrington,	1,136	100.00	100.00
1	70	6.16	1.46
2	196	17.25	8.18
3	235	20.69	14.70
4	208	18.31	17.55
5	146	12.85	15.23
6	114	10.03	14.27
7	78	6.87	11.39
8	47	4.14	7.84
9	22	1.94	4.13
10	9	0.79	1.88
11	4	0.35	0.92
12	3	0.26	0.75
13	1	0.09	0.27
14	1	0.09	0.29
31	1	0.09	0.65
33	1	0.09	0.69
Hancock,	117	100.00	100.00
1	9	7.69	1.73
2	20	17.09	7.83
3	19	16.24	11.15
4	26	22.22	20.35
5	12	10.25	11.74
6	15	12.82	17.61
7	4	3.42	5.48
8	5	4.27	7.83
9	4	3.42	7.05
10	1	0.86	1.96
13	1	0.86	2.54
24	1	0.86	4.70
Hinsdale,	346	100.00	100.00
1	16	4.62	0.97
2	56	16.18	5.79
3	58	16.76	10.54
4	52	15.03	12.61

SIZE OF FAMILIES: FOR TOWNS — Continued.

COUNTIES, TOWNS, AND SIZE OF FAMILIES.	Number of Families	PERCENTAGES		COUNTIES, TOWNS, AND SIZE OF FAMILIES.	Number of Families	PERCENTAGES	
		Total Families	Total Population			Total Families	Total Population
BERKSHIRE — Con.				BERKSHIRE — Con.			
Hinsdale — Con.				Monterey, . .	115	100.00	100.00
5	44	12.71	13.63	1	8	6.96	1.72
6	35	10.17	12.73	2	21	18.26	9.05
7	33	9.53	14.00	3	25	21.74	19.16
8	24	6.93	11.64	4	17	14.78	14.66
9	12	3.47	6.54	5	22	19.13	23.71
10	6	1.73	3.64	6	12	10.43	15.52
11	4	1.15	2.67	7	4	3.48	6.03
12	3	0.86	2.18	8	1	0.87	1.72
13	3	0.86	2.36	9	2	1.74	3.88
Lanesborough, . .	210	100.00	100.00	10	1	0.87	2.16
1	14	6.67	1.65	12	1	0.87	2.59
2	46	21.90	10.85	13	1	0.87	2.80
3	34	16.19	12.03	Mount Washington, .	31	100.00	100.00
4	40	19.05	18.87	1	1	3.22	0.74
5	29	13.81	17.10	2	2	6.45	2.94
6	20	9.52	14.15	3	8	25.81	17.65
7	12	5.71	9.91	4	8	25.81.	23.53
8	9	4.29	8.49	5	5	16.13	18.38
9	3	,1.43	3.18	6	2	6.45	8.82
10	1	0.48	1.18	7	2	6.45	11.29
11	2	0.95	2.59	8	3	9.68	17.65
Lee, ...	922	100.00	100.00	New Ashford, . .	30	100.00	100.00
1	60	6.51	1.48	1	1	3.33	0.86
2	144	15.62	7.08	2	9	30.00	15.52
3	203	22.02	14.98	3	4	13.34	10.35
4	152	16.49	14.95	4	6	20.00	20.69
5	112	12.15	13.77	5	6	20.00	25.86
6	80	9.65	15.13	6	1	3.33	5.17
7	58	6.29	9.99	8	2	6.67	13.79
8	30	3.25	5.90	9	1	3.33	7.76
9	32	3.47	7.08	New Marlborough, .	325	100.00	100.00
10	18	1.95	4.43	1	28	8.62	2.17
11	10	1.08	2.71	2	67	20.62	10.40
12	6	0.65	1.77	3	67	20.62	15.61
13	4	0.43	1.28	4	46	14.15	11.29
14	2	0.22	0.69	5	40	12.30	13.73
15	1	0.11	0.37	6	29	8.92	12.31
16	1	0.11	0.39	7	28	8.62	15.22
Lenox, ...	581	100.00	100.00	8	12	3.69	7.45
1	37	6.37	1.29	9	5	1.54	3.49
2	71	12.22	4.94	10	3	0.92	2.33
3	94	16.18	9.82	Otis, ...	136	100.00	100.00
4	80	13.82	12.40	1	13	9.56	2.31
5	89	15.32	15.49	2	23	16.91	8.88
6	52	8.95	10.86	3	36	26.47	23.85
7	59	10.16	14.38	4	20	14.71	15.44
8	33	5.68	9.19	5	19	13.97	18.34
9	19	3.27	5.95	6	9	6.62	10.43
10	14	2.41	4.88	7	10	7.35	13.51
11	10	1.72	3.83	8	3	2.21	4.63
12	6	1.03	2.51	9	2	1.47	3.48
13	5	0.86	2.26	10	1	0.73	1.93
14	1	0.17	0.49	Peru, ...	71	100.00	100.00
16	1	0.17	0.56	1	3	4.23	0.98
33	1	0.17	1.15	2	11	15.49	7.21

SIZE OF FAMILIES: FOR TOWNS — Continued.

COUNTIES, TOWNS, AND SIZE OF FAMILIES	Number of Families	Total Families	Total Population
BERKSHIRE — Con.			
Peru — Con.			
3	16	22.53	15.74
4	12	16.90	15.74
5	7	9.86	11.48
6	10	14.08	19.67
7	9	12.68	20.66
8	1	1.41	2.62
9	2	2.82	5.90
Richmond, . . .	164	100.00	100.00
1	8	4.88	1.14
2	27	16.46	7.70
3	36	21.95	15.41
4	32	19.51	18.26
5	23	14.02	16.41
6	9	5.49	7.70
7	11	6.71	10.98
8	8	4.88	9.13
9	8	4.88	10.27
10	1	0.61	1.43
11	1	0.61	1.57
Sandisfield, . . .	213	100.00	100.00
1	21	9.86	2.62
2	43	20.19	10.72
3	44	20.66	16.46
4	38	17.84	18.95
5	34	15.96	21.20
6	14	6.57	10.48
7	8	3.75	6.98
8	4	1.88	3.99
9	3	1.41	3.37
10	2	0.94	2.49
11	2	0.94	2.74
Savoy, ...	133	100.00	100.00
1	5	3.76	0.99
2	31	23.31	12.30
3	30	22.56	17.86
4	27	20.30	21.43
5	16	12.03	15.87
6	14	10.52	16.67
7	5	3.76	6.94
8	5	3.76	7.94
Sheffield, ...	481	100.00	100.00
1	33	6.86	1.74
2	112	23.28	11.81
3	95	19.75	15.03
4	73	15.18	15.39
5	62	12.89	16.34
6	46	9.56	14.55
7	28	5.82	10.33
8	19	3.95	8.01
9	5	1.04	2.37
10	5	1.04	2.64
11	2	0.42	1.16
12	1	0.21	0.63
Stockbridge, . .	471	100.00	100.00
1	20	4.25	0.96

COUNTIES, TOWNS, AND SIZE OF FAMILIES	Number of Families	Total Families	Total Population
BERKSHIRE — Con.			
Stockbridge — Con.			
2	97	20.59	9.34
3	80	16.99	11.55
4	82	17.41	15.70
5	57	12.10	13.72
6	57	12.10	16.47
7	28	5.95	9.44
8	22	4.67	8.47
9	14	2.97	6.07
10	7	1.49	3.67
11	4	0.85	2.42
12	1	0.21	0.58
13	1	0.21	0.63
34	1	0.21	1.49
Tyringham, . . .	90	100.00	100.00
1	5	5.55	1.38
2	14	15.56	7.71
3	20	22.22	13.55
4	21	23.33	25.14
5	14	15.56	15.28
6	6	6.67	9.92
7	2	2.22	3.86
8	6	6.67	13.22
9	2	2.22	4.93
Washington, . . .	87	100.00	100.00
1	4	4.60	0.95
2	14	16.09	6.92
3	7	8.04	4.96
4	20	22.99	18.94
5	11	12.64	7.09
6	8	9.20	11.35
7	8	9.20	15.24
8	11	12.64	20.80
9	1	1.15	2.13
11	2	2.30	5.20
12	1	1.15	2.84
West Stockbridge, .	324	100.00	100.00
1	21	6.48	1.07
2	77	23.76	12.25
3	67	20.68	15.39
4	55	16.35	14.87
5	44	13.58	17.50
6	26	8.02	12.41
7	16	4.94	8.91
8	11	3.39	7.60
9	3	0.93	2.15
10	3	0.93	2.39
11	1	0.31	0.88
12	1	0.31	0.95
13	1	0.31	1.03
Williamstown, . .	1,017	100.00	100.00
1	50	4.92	1.02
2	145	14.26	5.94
3	197	19.37	12.09
4	172	16.91	14.05
5	148	14.55	15.14

SIZE OF FAMILIES: FOR TOWNS — Continued.

COUNTIES, TOWNS, AND SIZE OF FAMILIES.	Number of Families	PERCENTAGES Total Families	PERCENTAGES Total Population	COUNTIES, TOWNS, AND SIZE OF FAMILIES.	Number of Families	PERCENTAGES Total Families	PERCENTAGES Total Population
BERKSHIRE — Con.				BRISTOL — Con.			
Williamstown — Con.				Attleborough — Con.			
6	107	10.52	13.14	15	2	0.11	0.36
7	75	7.37	10.74	16	2	0.11	0.39
8	51	5.01	8.35	18	1	0.05	0.22
9	32	3.15	5.89	20	1	0.05	0.24
10	16	1.57	3.27	22	1	0.05	0.26
11	10	0.98	2.25	25	1	0.05	0.29
12	6	0.59	1.47	26	1	0.05	0.31
13	2	0.20	0.53	Berkley, . . .	256	100.00	100.00
14	1	0.10	0.29	1	24	9.38	2.51
15	1	0.10	0.31	2	56	21.88	11.73
17	2	0.20	0.70	3	50	19.53	15.71
18	1	0.10	0.37	4	52	20.31	21.78
216	1	0.10	4.42	5	30	11.72	15.71
Windsor, . . .	135	100.00	100.00	6	16	6.25	10.05
1	9	6.67	1.62	7	17	6.64	12.46
2	28	20.74	10.07	8	8	3.12	6.70
3	26	19.26	14.03	9	1	0.39	0.94
4	21	15.56	15.11	10	1	0.39	1.05
5	19	14.07	17.08	13	1	0.39	1.36
6	15	11.11	16.19	Dartmouth, . . .	814	100.00	100.00
7	7	5.19	8.81	1	65	7.98	2.09
8	4	2.96	5.75	2	206	25.31	13.26
9	2	1.48	3.24	3	153	18.80	14.77
10	1	0.74	1.80	4	141	17.32	18.15
11	1	0.74	1.98	5	94	11.55	15.13
12	2	1.48	4.32	6	69	8.48	13.32
BRISTOL.				7	37	4.55	8.34
Acushnet, . . .	294	100.00	100.00	8	19	2.33	4.80
1	31	10.54	2.78	9	13	1.60	3.77
2	57	19.39	10.22	10	8	0.98	2.57
3	62	21.09	16.68	11	4	0.49	1.42
4	58	19.73	20.81	12	1	0.12	0.39
5	33	11.23	14.80	13	1	0.12	0.42
6	16	5.44	8.61	14	1	0.12	0.45
7	18	6.12	11.39	16	2	0.25	1.03
8	11	3.74	7.89	Dighton, . . .	461	100.00	100.00
9	5	1.70	4.04	1	36	7.81	2.00
10	2	0.68	1.70	2	99	21.47	11.02
12	1	0.34	1.08	3	93	20.17	15.52
Attleborough, . .	1,890	100.00	100.00	4	77	16.70	17.14
1	63	3.33	0.76	5	62	13.45	17.25
2	331	17.51	7.99	6	42	9.11	14.02
3	385	20.37	13.96	7	28	6.07	10.91
4	353	18.68	17.04	8	10	2.17	4.45
5	275	14.55	16.59	9	8	1.74	4.01
6	198	10.48	14.33	10	1	0.22	0.56
7	123	6.51	10.39	11	4	0.87	2.45
8	67	3.55	6.47	12	1	0.22	0.67
9	38	2.01	4.13	Easton, . . .	1,061	100.00	100.00
10	25	1.32	3.02	1	60	5.66	1.35
11	10	0.53	1.33	2	179	16.87	8.04
12	9	0.48	1.30	3	217	20.45	14.62
13	3	0.16	0.47	4	204	19.23	18.33
14	1	0.05	0.17	5	155	14.61	17.41
				6	99	9.33	13.34

SIZE OF FAMILIES: FOR TOWNS — Continued.

COUNTIES, TOWNS, AND SIZE OF FAMILIES.	Number of Families	PERCENTAGES		COUNTIES, TOWNS, AND SIZE OF FAMILIES.	Number of Families	PERCENTAGES	
		Total Families	Total Population			Total Families	Total Population
BRISTOL — Con.				BRISTOL — Con.			
Easton — Con.				No. Attleborough — Con.			
7	58	5.47	3.12	5	206	13.74	15.96
8	51	4.81	3.16	6	148	9.88	13.50
9	20	1.89	4.04	7	98	6.54	10.45
10	8	0.75	1.80	8	67	4.47	8.15
11	6	0.57	1.48	9	39	2.60	5.34
12	1	0.09	0.27	10	19	1.27	2.89
14	1	0.09	0.32	11	7	0.47	1.17
15	1	0.09	0.34	12	4	0.27	0.73
17	1	0.09	0.38	13	1	0.06	0.20
Fairhaven, . . .	898	100.00	100.00	14	2	0.13	0.45
1	61	6.79	1.83	15	1	0.06	0.22
2	217	24.16	13.00	22	1	0.06	0.54
3	197	21.94	17.70	27	1	0.06	0.81
4	159	17.71	19.05	Norton, ...	404	100.00	100.00
5	118	13.14	17.68	1	35	8.23	2.05
6	65	7.24	11.68	2	77	19.20	9.54
7	43	4.79	9.02	3	88	21.94	16.96
8	19	2.12	4.55	4	68	16.96	13.87
9	11	1.22	2.97	5	62	15.46	19.21
10	5	0.76	1.50	6	33	8.23	12.27
11	2	0.22	0.65	7	20	4.99	8.67
12	1	0.11	0.36	8	7	1.74	3.47
Freetown, . . .	342	100.00	100.00	9	4	1.00	2.23
1	32	9.35	2.28	10	5	1.25	3.10
2	63	18.42	8.97	11	2	0.50	1.36
3	52	15.20	11.10	12	1	0.25	0.74
4	83	24.27	25.63	67	1	0.25	4.15
5	42	12.28	14.95	Raynham, ...	397	100.00	100.00
6	20	5.85	8.54	1	22	5.54	1.45
7	20	5.85	9.96	2	88	22.17	11.59
8	12	3.51	6.83	3	101	25.44	19.96
9	7	2.05	4.48	4	67	16.88	17.60
10	3	0.88	2.71	5	47	11.84	15.48
11	3	0.88	2.35	6	33	8.31	13.04
12	3	0.88	2.56	7	21	5.29	9.58
15	1	0.29	1.07	8	5	1.26	2.64
16	1	0.29	1.14	9	7	1.76	4.15
Mansfield, . . .	946	100.00	100.00	10	1	0.25	0.65
1	60	6.34	1.64	11	4	1.01	2.60
2	201	21.25	10.80	12	1	0.25	0.75
3	194	20.51	15.64	Rehoboth, ...	443	100.00	100.00
4	179	18.92	19.24	1	37	8.21	2.04
5	128	13.53	17.19	2	96	21.29	10.63
6	79	8.35	12.73	3	89	19.73	14.75
7	47	4.97	8.84	4	74	16.41	16.35
8	25	2.64	5.37	5	56	12.42	15.47
9	20	2.11	4.84	6	38	8.43	12.60
10	8	0.85	2.15	7	24	5.32	9.28
11	3	0.32	0.89	8	18	3.99	7.96
13	2	0.21	0.70	9	9	2.00	4.47
North Attleborough, .	1,499	100.00	100.00	10	3	0.66	1.65
1	50	3.34	0.76	11	1	0.22	0.61
2	250	16.68	7.60	12	3	0.66	1.90
3	305	20.35	13.91	13	2	0.44	1.44
4	300	20.02	18.25	14	1	0.22	0.77

SIZE OF FAMILIES: FOR TOWNS — Continued.

COUNTIES, TOWNS, AND SIZE OF FAMILIES.	Number of Families	PERCENTAGES		COUNTIES, TOWNS, AND SIZE OF FAMILIES.	Number of Families	PERCENTAGES	
		Total Families	Total Population			Total Families	Total Population
BRISTOL — Con.				DUKES.			
Seekonk,	354	100.00	100.00	Chilmark,	95	100.00	100.00
1	22	6.58	1.50	1	14	14.74	4.69
2	54	16.17	7.37	2	19	20.00	12.50
3	69	20.66	14.13	3	29	30.53	28.62
4	66	19.76	18.02	4	16	16.84	21.05
5	35	10.48	11.95	5	6	6.31	9.87
6	28	8.38	11.47	6	7	7.37	13.82
7	19	5.69	9.08	7	5	3.16	6.91
8	12	3.59	6.55	8	1	1.05	2.63
9	17	5.09	10.44	Cottage City,	313	100.00	100.00
10	5	1.50	3.41	1	46	14.70	4.45
11	1	0.30	0.75	2	83	26.52	15.99
12	2	0.60	1.64	3	65	20.77	18.79
13	3	0.90	2.66	4	48	15.33	18.50
15	1	0.30	1.03	5	33	10.54	15.90
Somerset,	497	100.00	100.00	6	12	3.83	6.94
1	47	9.46	2.37	7	15	4.79	10.11
2	97	19.52	9.78	8	6	1.92	4.62
3	102	20.52	15.43	9	2	0.64	1.73
4	76	15.29	15.32	10	2	0.64	1.93
5	61	12.27	15.38	11	1	0.32	1.06
6	45	9.06	13.62	Edgartown,	377	100.00	100.00
7	32	6.44	11.30	1	63	16.71	5.60
8	16	3.22	6.46	2	124	32.89	22.04
9	14	2.82	6.35	3	71	18.83	18.93
10	3	0.60	1.51	4	56	14.86	19.91
11	1	0.20	0.55	5	29	7.69	12.89
12	1	0.20	0.61	6	15	3.98	8.00
13	2	0.40	1.31	7	12	3.18	7.47
Swansea,	411	100.00	100.00	8	5	1.33	3.56
1	27	6.57	1.66	9	2	0.53	1.60
2	83	20.19	10.20	Gay Head,	40	100.00	100.00
3	77	18.74	14.20	1	5	12.50	2.96
4	95	23.11	23.36	2	8	20.00	9.47
5	50	12.17	15.36	3	8	20.00	14.20
6	31	7.54	11.43	4	2	5.00	4.73
7	24	5.84	10.32	5	4	10.00	11.83
8	10	2.43	4.92	6	4	10.00	14.20
9	5	1.22	2.77	7	4	10.00	16.57
10	6	1.46	3.69	8	3	7.50	14.20
11	2	0.49	1.35	9	1	2.50	5.33
12	1	0.24	0.74	11	1	2.50	6.51
Westport,	702	100.00	100.00	Gosnold,	38	100.00	100.00
1	59	8.41	2.20	1	3	7.90	2.14
2	145	20.66	10.83	2	5	13.16	7.14
3	160	22.79	17.92	3	14	36.84	30.00
4	126	17.95	18.82	4	11	28.95	31.43
5	87	12.39	16.24	5	2	5.26	7.14
6	54	7.69	12.10	7	1	2.63	5.90
7	29	4.13	7.58	8	1	2.63	5.72
8	16	2.28	4.78	16	1	2.63	11.43
9	13	1.85	4.37	Tisbury,	289	100.00	100.00
10	7	1.00	2.62	1	42	14.53	4.19
11	5	0.71	2.05	2	72	24.91	14.37
13	1	0.14	0.49	3	55	19.03	16.47

SIZE OF FAMILIES: FOR TOWNS — Continued.

COUNTIES, TOWNS, AND SIZE OF FAMILIES.	Number of Families	Percentages — Total Families	Percentages — Total Population
DUKES — Con.			
Tisbury — Con.			
4	50	17.30	19.96
5	29	10.03	14.47
6	18	6.23	10.78
7	8	2.77	5.59
8	3	1.04	2.39
9	9	3.11	8.08
11	1	0.35	1.10
12	1	0.35	1.20
14	1	0.35	1.40
West Tisbury,	154	100.00	100.00
1	17	11.04	3.70
2	47	30.52	20.43
3	46	29.87	30.00
4	25	16.23	21.74
5	10	6.49	10.87
6	4	2.60	5.22
7	3	1.95	4.56
8	2	1.30	3.48
ESSEX.			
Amesbury,	2,281	100.00	100.00
1	88	3.86	0.88
2	365	16.00	7.31
3	481	21.09	14.45
4	433	18.98	17.35
5	327	14.34	16.37
6	265	11.62	15.92
7	137	6.01	9.60
8	68	2.98	5.45
9	54	2.37	4.87
10	29	1.27	2.91
11	14	0.62	1.54
12	8	0.35	0.96
13	6	0.26	0.78
16	3	0.13	0.48
19	1	0.04	0.19
26	1	0.04	0.26
68	1	0.04	0.68
Andover,	1,296	100.00	100.00
1	58	4.47	0.94
2	208	16.05	6.77
3	203	15.66	9.91
4	252	19.44	16.40
5	188	14.51	15.30
6	150	11.57	14.65
7	96	7.41	10.94
8	53	4.09	6.90
9	30	2.31	4.39
10	21	1.62	3.42
11	13	1.00	2.33
12	8	0.62	1.56
13	2	0.15	0.42
14	5	0.38	1.14
15	1	0.08	0.24

COUNTIES, TOWNS, AND SIZE OF FAMILIES.	Number of Families	Percentages — Total Families	Percentages — Total Population
ESSEX — Con.			
Andover — Con.			
16	1	0.08	0.26
22	1	0.08	0.36
23	1	0.08	0.37
24	1	0.08	0.39
30	1	0.08	0.49
32	1	0.08	0.52
59	1	0.08	0.96
82	1	0.08	1.34
Boxford,	186	100.00	100.00
1	19	10.22	2.61
2	41	22.04	11.28
3	35	18.82	14.44
4	41	22.04	22.56
5	14	7.53	9.63
6	10	5.38	8.25
7	8	4.30	7.70
8	6	3.23	6.60
9	2	1.07	2.48
10	7	3.76	9.63
11	2	1.07	3.03
13	1	0.54	1.79
Bradford,	1,121	100.00	100.00
1	24	2.14	0.51
2	204	18.20	8.61
3	275	24.53	17.42
4	222	19.80	18.75
5	170	15.16	17.95
6	103	9.19	13.05
7	59	5.26	8.72
8	25	2.23	4.22
9	18	1.61	3.42
10	11	0.98	2.32
11	2	0.18	0.46
12	2	0.18	0.51
13	2	0.18	0.55
14	1	0.09	0.39
16	1	0.09	0.34
20	1	0.09	0.42
116	1	0.09	2.45
Danvers,	1,653	100.00	100.00
1	72	4.36	0.88
2	294	17.79	7.19
3	359	21.72	13.17
4	296	17.91	14.47
5	227	13.73	15.87
6	157	9.50	11.51
7	110	6.65	9.41
8	59	3.57	5.77
9	34	2.06	3.74
10	18	1.09	2.20
11	5	0.30	0.67
12	4	0.24	0.59
13	7	0.42	1.11
14	3	0.18	0.51

SIZE OF FAMILIES: FOR TOWNS — Continued.

COUNTIES, TOWNS, AND SIZE OF FAMILIES.	Number of Families	PERCENTAGES		COUNTIES, TOWNS, AND SIZE OF FAMILIES.	Number of Families	PERCENTAGES	
		Total Families	Total Population			Total Families	Total Population
ESSEX — Con.				ESSEX — Con.			
Danvers — Con.				Hamilton — Con.			
15	2	0.12	0.37	5	42	13.33	15.49
16	1	0.06	0.20	6	28	8.89	12.39
17	1	0.06	0.21	7	15	4.76	7.74
18	1	0.06	0.22	8	12	3.81	7.08
19	1	0.06	0.23	9	7	2.22	4.65
32	1	0.06	0.39	10	3	0.95	2.21
1,087	1	0.06	13.29	11	4	1.27	3.24
Essex, ...	445	100.00	100.00	12	1	0.32	0.89
1	27	6.07	1.70	13	1	0.32	0.96
2	114	25.62	14.37	15	1	0.32	1.11
3	114	25.62	21.55	16	1	0.32	1.18
4	84	18.88	21.17	19	1	0.32	1.40
5	47	10.56	14.81	28	1	0.32	2.07
6	28	6.29	10.59	Ipswich, ...	1,104	100.00	100.00
7	17	3.82	7.50	1	80	7.25	1.70
8	6	1.35	3.02	2	202	18.30	8.56
9	3	0.67	1.70	3	240	21.74	15.25
10	3	0.67	1.89	4	200	18.12	16.95
12	1	0.22	0.76	5	133	12.05	14.09
15	1	0.22	0.94	6	88	7.97	11.19
Georgetown, . .	541	100.00	100.00	7	47	4.26	6.97
1	41	7.58	2.00	8	36	3.26	6.10
2	121	22.37	11.81	9	36	3.26	6.83
3	120	22.18	17.56	10	14	1.27	2.97
4	85	15.71	16.59	11	9	0.81	2.10
5	76	14.05	18.54	12	5	0.45	1.27
6	46	8.50	13.46	13	6	0.54	1.65
7	27	4.99	9.22	14	2	0.18	0.59
8	10	1.85	3.99	15	1	0.09	0.32
9	10	1.85	4.38	16	1	0.09	0.34
10	3	0.55	1.46	17	1	0.09	0.36
11	2	0.37	1.07	21	1	0.09	0.44
Groveland, . . .	560	100.00	100.00	34	1	0.09	0.72
1	33	5.89	1.41	74	1	0.09	1.57
2	109	19.46	9.34	Lynnfield, . . .	211	100.00	100.00
3	123	21.96	15.82	1	12	5.69	1.47
4	92	16.43	15.77	2	54	25.59	13.29
5	78	13.96	16.72	3	43	20.38	15.77
6	51	9.11	13.12	4	29	13.74	14.18
7	35	6.25	10.50	5	30	14.22	18.34
8	10	1.78	3.43	6	19	9.01	13.94
9	12	2.14	4.63	7	12	5.69	10.27
10	4	0.71	1.72	8	7	3.32	6.84
11	3	0.54	1.41	9	3	1.42	3.30
12	2	0.36	1.03	10	1	0.47	1.22
13	2	0.36	1.11	12	1	0.47	1.47
14	3	0.54	1.80	Manchester, . . .	488	100.00	100.00
15	1	0.18	0.64	1	50	10.25	2.07
16	1	0.18	0.69	2	93	19.06	9.91
20	1	0.18	0.86	3	106	21.72	16.95
Hamilton, . . .	315	100.00	100.00	4	79	16.19	16.84
1	21	6.66	1.55	5	68	13.94	18.12
2	66	20.95	9.73	6	46	9.43	14.71
3	60	19.05	13.27	7	23	4.71	8.58
4	51	16.19	15.04	8	8	1.64	3.41

SIZE OF FAMILIES: FOR TOWNS — Continued.

COUNTIES, TOWNS, AND SIZE OF FAMILIES.	Number of Families	Percentages Total Families	Percentages Total Population
ESSEX — Con.			
Manchester — Con.			
9	4	0.82	1.92
10	6	1.23	3.20
11	1	0.20	0.50
12	1	0.20	0.64
13	2	0.41	1.39
20	1	0.20	1.07
Marblehead, . . .	2,003	100.00	100.00
1	141	7.04	1.84
2	418	20.87	10.90
3	460	22.96	17.99
4	378	18.87	19.71
5	265	13.23	17.27
6	150	7.49	11.73
7	83	4.14	7.57
8	46	2.30	4.80
9	27	1.35	3.17
10	24	1.20	3.13
11	6	0.39	0.86
12	2	0.10	0.31
13	2	0.10	0.34
29	1	0.05	0.38
Merrimac, . . .	605	100.00	100.00
1	30	4.96	1.30
2	136	22.48	11.82
3	152	25.12	19.82
4	114	18.84	19.82
5	80	13.22	17.38
6	44	7.27	11.47
7	21	3.47	6.39
8	13	2.15	4.52
9	6	0.99	2.55
10	4	0.66	1.74
11	1	0.17	0.48
14	2	0.33	1.22
15	1	0.17	0.65
24	1	0.17	1.04
Methuen, . . .	1,317	100.00	100.00
1	43	3.26	0.75
2	244	18.53	8.58
3	275	20.88	14.50
4	225	17.08	15.82
5	185	14.05	16.26
6	149	11.31	15.71
7	85	6.45	10.46
8	58	4.40	8.15
9	25	1.90	3.95
10	15	1.14	2.64
11	8	0.61	1.55
12	2	0.15	0.42
14	1	0.08	0.25
19	1	0.08	0.33
36	1	0.08	0.63
Middleton, . . .	219	100.00	100.00
1	27	12.33	3.22
2	35	15.98	8.35

COUNTIES, TOWNS, AND SIZE OF FAMILIES.	Number of Families	Percentages Total Families	Percentages Total Population
ESSEX — Con.			
Middleton — Con.			
3	47	21.46	16.83
4	46	21.00	21.96
5	27	12.33	16.11
6	16	7.30	11.46
7	10	4.57	8.35
8	4	1.83	3.82
9	1	0.46	1.07
10	2	0.91	2.39
11	2	0.91	2.62
12	1	0.46	1.43
20	1	0.46	2.39
Nahant, . . .	204	100.00	100.00
1	19	9.31	2.20
2	45	22.06	10.40
3	35	17.16	12.14
4	31	15.20	14.34
5	27	13.24	15.61
6	13	6.37	9.02
7	10	4.90	8.09
8	9	4.41	8.52
9	5	2.45	5.20
10	3	1.47	3.47
11	2	0.98	2.54
12	1	0.49	1.39
13	1	0.49	1.50
14	1	0.49	1.62
15	1	0.49	1.73
21	1	0.49	2.43
Newbury, . . .	360	100.00	100.00
1	21	5.83	1.41
2	70	19.45	9.40
3	75	20.83	15.11
4	72	20.00	19.34
5	49	13.61	16.45
6	21	5.83	8.46
7	22	6.11	10.34
8	6	1.67	3.22
9	9	2.50	5.44
10	10	2.78	6.72
11	3	0.83	2.22
12	1	0.28	0.81
16	1	0.28	1.08
North Andover, . . .	796	100.00	100.00
1	26	3.27	0.73
2	130	16.33	7.29
3	156	19.60	13.11
4	145	18.22	16.25
5	131	16.46	18.35
6	73	9.17	12.27
7	48	6.03	9.42
8	46	5.78	10.31
9	17	2.14	4.29
10	9	1.13	2.52
11	4	0.51	1.23
12	7	0.88	2.35

SIZE OF FAMILIES: FOR TOWNS — Continued.

COUNTIES, TOWNS, AND SIZE OF FAMILIES.	Number of Families	PERCENTAGES		COUNTIES, TOWNS, AND SIZE OF FAMILIES.	Number of Families	PERCENTAGES	
		Total Families	Total Population			Total Families	Total Population
ESSEX — Con.				ESSEX — Con.			
North Andover — Con.				Salisbury — Con.			
13	1	0.12	0.36	3	86	24.50	19.85
16	1	0.12	0.45	4	69	19.66	21.23
17	1	0.12	0.48	5	46	13.11	17.69
21	1	0.12	0.59	6	32	9.12	14.77
Peabody, . . .	2,373	100.00	100.00	7	13	3.70	7.00
1	82	3.46	0.78	8	7	2.00	4.31
2	403	16.98	7.67	9	1	0.28	0.69
3	465	19.60	13.28	10	1	0.28	0.77
4	450	18.96	17.13	12	1	0.28	0.92
5	332	13.99	15.80	Saugus, . . .	1,065	100.00	100.00
6	246	10.37	14.05	1	36	3.38	0.80
7	160	6.74	10.66	2	168	15.77	7.47
8	100	4.21	7.61	3	262	24.60	17.48
9	72	3.04	6.17	4	205	19.25	18.23
10	33	1.39	3.14	5	161	15.12	17.90
11	12	0.51	1.26	6	101	9.48	13.48
12	9	0.38	1.03	7	61	5.73	9.49
13	5	0.21	0.62	8	25	2.35	4.45
14	1	0.04	0.13	9	17	1.60	3.40
17	1	0.04	0.16	10	12	1.13	2.67
19	1	0.04	0.18	11	8	0.75	1.96
35	1	0.04	0.33	12	3	0.28	0.80
Rockport, . . .	1,236	100.00	100.00	13	4	0.38	1.16
1	96	7.77	1.82	14	1	0.09	0.31
2	238	19.26	9.00	18	1	0.09	0.40
3	255	20.63	14.46	Swampscott, . .	823	100.00	100.00
4	201	16.26	15.20	1	37	4.50	1.13
5	121	9.79	11.44	2	169	20.53	10.37
6	120	9.71	13.61	3	199	24.18	18.32
7	69	5.58	9.13	4	160	19.44	19.64
8	51	4.13	7.71	5	101	12.27	15.50
9	36	2.91	6.13	6	60	7.29	11.05
10	23	1.86	4.35	7	46	5.59	9.88
11	9	0.73	1.87	8	28	3.40	6.87
12	4	0.32	0.91	9	10	1.22	2.76
13	5	0.41	1.23	10	5	0.61	1.53
14	2	0.16	0.53	11	5	0.61	1.69
15	3	0.24	0.85	13	2	0.24	0.80
19	1	0.08	0.36	15	1	0.12	0.46
21	1	0.08	0.40	Topsfield, . . .	264	100.00	100.00
53	1	0.08	1.00	1	42	15.91	4.07
Rowley, . . .	340	100.00	100.00	2	38	14.39	7.36
1	13	3.82	1.02	3	41	15.53	11.91
2	72	21.18	11.32	4	50	18.94	19.56
3	83	24.41	19.58	5	37	14.01	17.91
4	79	23.24	24.84	6	27	10.23	15.68
5	50	14.71	19.65	7	12	4.55	8.13
6	17	5.00	8.02	8	8	3.03	6.20
7	17	5.00	9.36	9	4	1.51	3.48
8	6	1.76	3.77	10	2	0.76	1.94
10	2	0.59	1.57	11	1	0.38	1.06
11	1	0.29	0.87	12	1	0.38	1.16
Salisbury, . . .	351	100.00	100.00	18	1	0.38	1.74
1	24	6.84	1.85	Wenham, . . .	234	100.00	100.00
2	71	20.23	10.92	1	20	8.55	2.26

SIZE OF FAMILIES: FOR TOWNS — Continued.

COUNTIES, TOWNS, AND SIZE OF FAMILIES.	Number of Families	PERCENTAGES Total Families	PERCENTAGES Total Population	COUNTIES, TOWNS, AND SIZE OF FAMILIES.	Number of Families	PERCENTAGES Total Families	PERCENTAGES Total Population
ESSEX — Con.				FRANKLIN — Con.			
Wenham — Con.				Buckland — Con.			
2	56	25.93	12.64	6	41	10.59	15.89
3	44	18.80	14.50	7	14	3.62	6.65
4	44	18.80	19.87	8	13	3.36	9.72
5	28	11.97	15.80	9	5	1.29	2.91
6	20	8.55	13.54	10	3	0.77	1.94
7	8	3.42	6.32	11	2	0.52	1.42
8	6	2.57	5.42	12	2	0.52	1.55
9	2	0.85	2.03	13	2	0.52	1.68
10	3	1.28	3.39	Charlemont, . . .	275	100.00	100.00
11	2	0.85	2.48	1	12	4.36	1.15
12	1	0.43	1.25	2	68	24.73	13.06
West Newbury, . .	440	100.00	100.00	3	62	22.55	17.87
1	39	8.86	2.37	4	51	18.55	19.00
2	85	19.32	10.55	5	39	14.18	18.73
3	98	22.27	17.89	6	18	6.54	10.38
4	89	20.23	21.67	7	10	3.64	6.72
5	61	13.86	18.56	8	10	3.64	7.99
6	33	7.50	12.05	9	1	0.36	0.86
7	18	4.09	7.67	10	3	1.09	2.88
8	4	0.91	1.95	11	1	0.36	1.06
9	8	1.82	4.58	Colrain, . . .	366	100.00	100.00
10	4	0.91	2.44	1	18	4.92	1.12
11	1	0.23	0.67	2	67	18.31	8.32
FRANKLIN.				3	65	17.76	12.11
Ashfield, . . .	252	100.00	100.00	4	61	16.67	15.16
1	22	8.73	2.17	5	49	13.39	15.22
2	48	19.05	9.48	6	44	12.02	16.40
3	44	17.46	13.03	7	26	7.10	11.30
4	46	18.25	18.16	8	15	4.10	7.45
5	34	13.49	16.78	9	9	2.46	5.03
6	29	11.51	17.18	10	7	1.91	4.35
7	13	5.16	8.98	11	4	1.09	2.73
8	9	3.57	7.11	13	1	0.27	0.81
9	3	1.19	2.66	Conway, . . .	309	100.00	100.00
10	1	0.40	0.99	1	15	4.85	1.15
11	1	0.40	1.09	2	55	17.80	8.44
12	2	0.79	2.37	3	56	18.12	12.88
Bernardston, . .	289	100.00	100.00	4	66	21.36	20.24
1	16	7.05	2.06	5	43	13.92	16.49
2	53	25.36	13.92	6	34	11.09	15.64
3	40	19.14	15.42	7	16	5.18	8.59
4	35	16.75	17.99	8	14	4.53	8.59
5	31	14.83	19.92	9	2	0.65	1.38
6	15	7.18	11.57	10	4	1.29	3.07
7	7	3.33	6.20	11	2	0.65	1.99
8	7	3.35	7.20	12	2	0.65	1.84
9	4	1.91	4.63	Deerfield, . . .	674	100.00	100.00
10	1	0.48	1.29	1	30	4.45	1.00
Buckland, . . .	387	100.00	100.00	2	119	17.66	7.91
1	22	5.68	1.42	3	140	20.77	13.97
2	77	19.90	9.95	4	111	16.47	14.77
3	98	25.32	18.99	5	86	12.76	14.30
4	57	14.73	14.73	6	74	10.98	14.77
5	51	13.18	16.47	7	31	4.60	7.22
				8	35	5.19	9.31

SIZE OF FAMILIES: FOR TOWNS — Continued.

COUNTIES, TOWNS, AND SIZE OF FAMILIES	Number of Families	Total Families	Total Population
FRANKLIN — Con.			
Deerfield — Con.			
9	17	2.52	5.09
10	17	2.52	5.65
11	7	1.04	2.56
12	3	0.44	1.20
13	1	0.15	0.43
14	1	0.15	0.46
17	1	0.15	0.56
24	1	0.15	0.80
Erving, ...	256	100.00	100.00
1	20	7.81	2.08
2	44	17.19	9.13
3	62	24.22	19.29
4	53	20.70	21.99
5	35	13.67	18.15
6	22	8.60	13.69
7	13	5.08	9.44
8	4	1.56	3.32
9	2	0.78	1.87
10	1	0.39	1.04
Gill, ...	197	100.00	100.00
1	11	5.58	1.02
2	35	17.77	6.47
3	37	18.78	10.26
4	39	19.80	14.42
5	18	9.14	8.32
6	19	9.64	10.53
7	16	8.12	10.35
8	3	1.52	2.22
9	6	3.04	4.99
10	6	3.04	5.54
11	1	0.51	1.02
18	2	1.02	3.33
20	1	0.51	1.85
21	1	0.51	1.94
24	1	0.51	2.22
168	1	0.51	15.52
Greenfield, . . .	1,450	100.00	100.00
1	64	4.41	1.03
2	265	18.27	8.51
3	308	21.24	14.83
4	256	17.66	16.44
5	219	15.10	17.58
6	144	9.93	13.87
7	96	6.62	10.79
8	39	2.69	5.01
9	24	1.66	3.47
10	11	0.76	1.77
11	8	0.55	1.41
12	5	0.34	0.96
13	1	0.07	0.21
14	1	0.07	0.22
17	1	0.07	0.27
18	2	0.14	0.58
24	2	0.14	0.77
33	1	0.07	0.53

COUNTIES, TOWNS, AND SIZE OF FAMILIES	Number of Families	Total Families	Total Population
FRANKLIN — Con.			
Greenfield — Con.			
34	1	0.07	0.54
36	1	0.07	0.58
39	1	0.07	0.63
Hawley, . . .	110	100.00	100.00
1	1	0.91	0.21
2	16	14.54	6.84
3	25	22.73	16.06
4	22	20.00	18.80
5	22	20.00	23.50
6	15	13.64	19.23
7	6	5.45	8.98
9	2	1.82	3.85
12	1	0.91	2.56
Heath, ...	120	100.00	100.00
1	9	7.50	1.89
2	18	15.00	7.56
3	27	22.50	17.02
4	27	22.50	22.69
5	16	13.34	16.81
6	10	8.33	12.61
7	7	5.83	10.29
8	2	1.67	3.36
9	3	2.50	5.67
10	1	0.83	2.10
Leverett, . . .	200	100.00	100.00
1	17	8.50	2.28
2	42	21.00	11.29
3	42	21.00	16.93
4	39	19.50	23.97
5	29	14.50	19.49
6	16	8.00	12.90
7	7	3.50	6.59
8	3	1.50	3.23
9	3	1.50	3.63
10	2	1.00	2.69
Leyden, . . .	88	100.00	100.00
1	5	5.67	1.38
2	15	17.04	8.26
3	17	19.32	14.05
4	19	21.59	20.94
5	12	13.64	16.53
6	9	10.23	14.88
7	7	7.95	13.50
8	1	1.14	2.20
9	1	1.14	2.48
10	1	1.14	2.75
11	1	1.14	3.03
Monroe, . . .	65	100.00	100.00
1	2	3.08	0.67
2	14	21.54	9.40
3	9	13.85	9.06
4	11	16.92	14.77
5	14	21.54	23.49
6	4	6.15	8.05
7	5	7.69	11.74

SIZE OF FAMILIES: FOR TOWNS — Continued.

COUNTIES, TOWNS, AND SIZE OF FAMILIES.	Number of Families	Percentages Total Families	Percentages Total Population
FRANKLIN — Con.			
Monroe — Con.			
8	1	1.54	2.68
9	1	1.54	3.02
10	3	4.61	10.07
21	1	1.54	7.05
Montague, . . .	1,349	100.00	100.00
1	63	4.67	1.04
2	211	15.64	6.97
3	250	18.53	12.38
4	243	18.01	16.05
5	206	15.27	17.00
6	145	10.75	14.36
7	87	6.45	10.05
8	59	4.37	7.79
9	44	3.26	6.54
10	23	1.70	3.80
11	9	0.66	1.63
12	3	0.22	0.60
14	2	0.15	0.46
16	1	0.08	0.26
17	1	0.08	0.28
23	1	0.08	0.38
25	1	0.08	0.41
New Salem, . .	233	100.00	100.00
1	23	9.87	2.65
2	55	23.60	12.66
3	49	21.03	16.92
4	40	17.17	18.41
5	24	10.30	13.81
6	17	7.30	11.74
7	9	3.86	7.25
8	7	3.00	6.44
9	3	1.29	3.11
10	5	2.15	5.75
11	1	0.43	1.26
Northfield, . .	419	100.00	100.00
1	20	4.77	1.08
2	94	22.43	10.16
3	101	24.10	16.37
4	69	16.47	14.91
5	60	14.32	16.21
6	34	8.11	11.02
7	13	3.10	4.91
8	9	2.15	3.89
9	5	1.19	2.43
10	3	0.72	1.62
11	3	0.72	1.78
20	2	0.48	2.16
22	1	0.24	1.19
23	1	0.24	1.24
24	1	0.24	1.50
44	1	0.24	2.38
57	1	0.24	3.08
79	1	0.24	4.27
Orange, . . .	1,390	100.00	100.00
1	70	5.04	1.31

COUNTIES, TOWNS, AND SIZE OF FAMILIES.	Number of Families	Percentages Total Families	Percentages Total Population
FRANKLIN — Con.			
Orange — Con.			
2	284	20.43	10.59
3	343	24.68	19.19
4	259	18.63	19.32
5	210	15.11	19.59
6	99	7.12	11.08
7	62	4.46	8.10
8	30	2.16	4.48
9	17	1.22	2.85
10	5	0.36	0.93
11	3	0.22	0.62
12	5	0.36	1.12
13	1	0.07	0.24
15	1	0.07	0.28
16	1	0.07	0.30
Rowe, . . .	123	100.00	100.00
1	6	4.88	1.21
2	21	17.07	8.43
3	28	22.76	16.87
4	29	23.58	23.29
5	15	12.19	15.06
6	9	7.32	10.84
7	6	4.88	8.43
8	4	3.25	6.43
9	3	2.44	5.42
10	2	1.63	4.02
Shelburne, . .	392	100.00	100.00
1	18	4.59	1.15
2	88	22.45	11.28
3	76	19.39	14.62
4	78	19.90	20.00
5	54	13.78	17.31
6	36	9.18	13.85
7	22	5.61	9.87
8	7	1.79	3.50
9	9	2.30	5.19
10	2	0.51	1.28
11	1	0.25	0.71
18	1	0.25	1.15
Shutesbury, . .	125	100.00	100.00
1	12	9.60	2.70
2	31	24.80	13.97
3	24	19.20	16.22
4	26	20.80	23.42
5	15	12.00	16.89
6	9	7.20	12.16
7	2	1.60	3.15
8	5	4.00	9.01
11	1	0.80	2.48
Sunderland, . .	166	100.00	100.00
1	8	4.82	1.15
2	30	18.07	8.62
3	35	21.08	15.09
4	26	15.66	14.94
5	24	14.46	17.24
6	21	12.65	18.10

SIZE OF FAMILIES: FOR TOWNS — Continued.

COUNTIES, TOWNS, AND SIZE OF FAMILIES.	Number of Families	Total Families	Total Population	COUNTIES, TOWNS, AND SIZE OF FAMILIES.	Number of Families	Total Families	Total Population
FRANKLIN — Con.				HAMPDEN — Con.			
Sunderland — Con.				Blandford, . . .	206	100.00	100.00
7	12	7.23	12.07	1	18	8.74	2.12
8	4	2.41	4.60	2	33	16.02	7.77
9	3	1.81	3.88	3	39	18.93	13.78
10	3	1.81	4.31	4	42	20.39	19.79
Warwick, . . .	158	100.00	100.00	5	30	14.56	17.67
1	11	6.95	1.84	6	20	9.71	14.13
2	36	22.78	12.02	7	8	3.88	6.60
3	42	26.58	21.04	8	7	3.40	6.60
4	30	18.99	20.03	9	3	1.46	3.18
5	9	5.70	7.51	10	1	0.48	1.18
6	9	5.70	9.01	11	2	0.97	2.59
7	6	3.80	7.01	13	3	1.46	4.59
8	10	6.33	13.96	Brimfield, . . .	238	100.00	100.00
9	2	1.27	3.00	1	15	6.31	1.56
10	2	1.27	3.84	2	58	24.37	12.06
11	1	0.63	1.84	3	57	23.95	17.78
Wendell, . . .	129	100.00	100.00	4	35	14.71	14.55
1	15	11.63	2.84	5	20	8.40	10.39
2	24	18.60	9.07	6	20	8.40	12.47
3	17	13.18	9.64	7	14	5.88	10.19
4	21	16.28	15.88	8	4	1.68	3.33
5	22	17.05	20.79	9	5	2.10	4.68
6	13	10.08	14.75	10	5	2.10	5.20
7	3	2.33	3.97	11	1	0.42	1.14
8	8	6.20	12.10	12	1	0.42	1.25
9	2	1.55	3.40	13	1	0.42	1.35
10	4	3.10	7.56	19	1	0.42	1.97
Whately, . . .	195	100.00	100.00	20	1	0.42	2.08
1	16	8.20	2.12	Chester, . . .	354	100.00	100.00
2	46	23.59	12.19	1	11	3.11	0.77
3	37	18.97	14.70	2	69	19.49	9.66
4	31	15.90	16.42	3	89	25.14	18.68
5	26	13.33	17.22	4	70	19.78	19.59
6	13	6.67	10.33	5	38	10.73	13.30
7	12	6.15	11.13	6	32	9.04	13.43
8	9	4.62	9.54	7	22	6.21	10.78
9	2	1.03	2.38	8	15	4.24	8.40
10	3	1.54	3.97	9	4	1.13	2.52
HAMPDEN.				10	3	0.85	2.10
				11	1	0.28	0.77
Agawam, . . .	583	100.00	100.00	East Longmeadow, .	330	100.00	100.00
1	32	5.79	1.33	1	8	2.42	0.50
2	94	17.00	7.81	2	51	15.46	6.41
3	96	17.36	11.98	3	63	19.09	11.88
4	92	16.64	15.28	4	50	15.15	12.57
5	86	15.55	17.80	5	49	14.85	15.40
6	58	10.49	14.45	6	55	16.61	15.20
7	49	8.86	14.24	7	29	8.79	12.76
8	21	5.80	6.98	8	17	5.15	8.55
9	16	2.89	3.98	9	11	3.33	6.22
10	4	0.72	1.66	10	7	2.12	4.40
11	2	0.56	0.91	11	2	0.61	1.38
12	2	0.56	1.00	12	3	0.91	2.26
13	1	0.18	0.54	13	2	0.61	1.64
				14	1	0.30	0.88

SIZE OF FAMILIES: FOR TOWNS — Continued.

COUNTIES, TOWNS, AND SIZE OF FAMILIES.	Number of Families	Percentages Total Families	Percentages Total Population
HAMPDEN — Con.			
E. Longmeadow — Con.			
15	1	0.30	0.94
16	1	0.30	1.01
Granville, . . .	252	100.00	100.00
1	25	9.92	2.49
2	37	14.68	7.36
3	68	26.99	20.30
4	37	14.68	14.73
5	25	9.92	12.44
6	28	11.11	16.72
7	13	5.16	9.05
8	9	3.57	7.16
9	5	1.99	4.48
10	2	0.79	1.99
11	3	1.19	3.28
Hampden, . . .	194	100.00	100.00
1	12	6.19	1.62
2	44	22.68	11.84
3	41	21.14	16.55
4	39	20.10	21.00
5	22	11.34	14.80
6	17	8.76	13.75
7	10	5.15	9.42
8	4	2.06	4.37
9	2	1.03	2.42
10	1	0.52	1.35
11	2	1.03	2.96
Holland, . . .	55	100.00	100.00
1	8	14.54	4.02
2	14	25.46	14.07
3	12	21.82	18.09
4	8	14.54	16.08
5	3	5.45	7.54
6	5	9.09	15.08
7	1	1.82	3.52
8	1	1.82	4.02
9	1	1.82	4.52
12	1	1.82	6.03
14	1	1.82	7.03
Longmeadow, . .	146	100.00	100.00
1	10	6.85	1.61
2	26	17.81	8.39
3	25	17.12	12.10
4	34	23.29	21.94
5	14	9.59	11.29
6	12	8.22	11.61
7	10	6.85	11.29
8	6	4.11	7.74
9	7	4.79	10.16
12	2	1.37	3.87
Ludlow, . . .	473	100.00	100.00
1	23	4.86	0.90
2	48	10.15	3.75
3	79	16.70	9.25
4	67	14.17	10.46
5	62	13.11	12.10

COUNTIES, TOWNS, AND SIZE OF FAMILIES.	Number of Families	Percentages Total Families	Percentages Total Population
HAMPDEN — Con.			
Ludlow — Con.			
6	55	11.63	12.88
7	43	9.09	11.75
8	34	7.19	10.62
9	23	4.86	8.08
10	11	2.33	4.29
11	10	2.12	4.29
12	2	0.42	0.94
13	5	1.06	2.54
14	2	0.42	1.09
15	1	0.21	0.58
17	2	0.42	1.33
18	1	0.21	0.70
21	2	0.42	1.64
22	1	0.21	0.86
25	2	0.42	1.95
Monson, . . .	872	100.00	100.00
1	53	6.08	1.42
2	200	22.94	10.68
3	164	18.81	13.14
4	130	14.91	13.88
5	116	13.30	15.48
6	92	10.55	14.74
7	51	5.85	9.53
8	29	3.33	6.19
9	12	1.38	2.88
10	8	0.92	2.14
11	4	0.46	1.18
12	2	0.23	0.64
13	2	0.23	0.69
14	1	0.11	0.37
15	2	0.23	0.80
17	2	0.23	0.91
20	1	0.11	0.53
31	1	0.11	0.83
35	1	0.11	0.93
114	1	0.11	3.04
Montgomery, . .	63	100.00	100.00
1	2	3.17	0.73
2	9	14.28	6.54
3	15	23.81	16.36
4	13	20.63	18.91
5	8	12.70	14.55
6	4	6.35	8.73
7	8	12.70	20.36
8	1	1.59	2.91
9	1	1.59	3.27
10	1	1.59	3.64
11	1	1.59	4.00
Palmer, . . .	1,382	100.00	100.00
1	54	3.91	0.79
2	190	13.75	5.54
3	290	18.81	11.37
4	237	17.15	13.82
5	196	13.97	14.07
6	117	8.47	10.24

SIZE OF FAMILIES: FOR TOWNS — Continued.

COUNTIES, TOWNS, AND SIZE OF FAMILIES.	Number of Families	PERCENTAGES Total Families	PERCENTAGES Total Population	COUNTIES, TOWNS, AND SIZE OF FAMILIES.	Number of Families	PERCENTAGES Total Families	PERCENTAGES Total Population
HAMPDEN — Con.				HAMPDEN — Con.			
Palmer — Con.				Wales — Con.			
7	107	7.74	10.92	2	45	23.56	11.49
8	74	5.36	8.63	3	34	17.80	13.06
9	47	3.40	6.17	4	22	11.52	11.24
10	41	2.97	5.98	5	35	18.33	22.35
11	16	1.16	2.57	6	15	7.85	11.49
12	15	1.09	2.62	7	13	6.81	11.62
13	9	0.65	1.71	8	4	2.09	4.09
14	5	0.36	1.02	9	3	1.57	3.45
15	3	0.22	0.66	10	3	1.57	3.83
16	6	0.43	1.40	11	3	1.57	4.22
17	2	0.14	0.50	12	1	0.52	1.53
18	2	0.14	0.52	Westfield, . . .	2,593	100.00	100.00
20	1	0.07	0.29	1	125	4.82	1.17
22	1	0.07	0.32	2	474	18.28	8.89
27	1	0.07	0.39	3	593	22.87	16.68
32	1	0.07	0.47	4	499	19.24	18.72
Russell, . . .	185	100.00	100.00	5	578	14.58	17.72
1	10	5.41	1.18	6	218	8.41	12.27
2	21	11.35	4.96	7	137	5.28	8.99
3	46	24.87	16.31	8	74	2.85	5.55
4	39	21.08	18.44	9	47	1.81	3.97
5	18	9.73	10.64	10	24	0.93	2.25
6	18	9.73	12.77	11	12	0.46	1.24
7	6	3.24	4.96	12	2	0.08	0.22
8	6	3.24	5.67	13	3	0.11	0.37
9	9	4.86	9.58	15	1	0.04	0.14
10	10	5.41	11.82	17	1	0.04	0.16
12	1	0.54	1.42	18	1	0.04	0.17
19	1	0.54	2.23	22	1	0.04	0.21
Southwick, . . .	239	100.00	100.00	30	1	0.04	0.28
1	16	6.69	1.66	34	1	0.04	0.32
2	45	18.83	9.37	72	1	0.04	0.68
3	52	21.76	16.23	West Springfield, . . .	1,360	100.00	100.00
4	33	13.81	13.74	1	26	1.91	0.42
5	44	18.41	22.89	2	229	16.84	7.48
6	23	9.62	14.36	3	264	19.41	12.93
7	13	5.44	9.47	4	265	19.49	17.31
8	6	2.51	4.99	5	198	14.56	16.16
9	4	1.67	3.75	6	146	10.73	14.30
10	1	0.42	1.04	7	108	7.94	12.34
12	2	0.84	2.50	8	51	3.75	6.66
Tolland, . . .	67	100.00	100.00	9	29	2.13	4.26
1	4	5.97	1.29	10	25	1.84	4.08
2	12	17.91	7.77	11	10	0.73	1.80
3	13	19.40	12.62	12	1	0.07	0.20
4	9	13.43	11.65	13	2	0.15	0.42
5	8	11.94	12.94	14	2	0.15	0.46
6	7	10.45	13.59	15	2	0.15	0.49
7	3	4.48	6.80	24	2	0.15	0.69
8	3	4.48	7.77	Wilbraham, . . .	563	100.00	100.00
9	3	4.48	8.74	1	24	6.61	1.38
10	3	4.48	9.71	2	66	18.18	7.59
11	2	2.98	7.12	3	77	21.21	13.28
Wales, . . .	191	100.00	100.00	4	64	17.63	14.71
1	13	6.81	1.66	5	49	13.50	14.08

SIZE OF FAMILIES: FOR TOWNS — Continued.

COUNTIES, TOWNS, AND SIZE OF FAMILIES.	Number of Families	PERCENTAGES Total Families	PERCENTAGES Total Population
HAMPDEN — Con.			
Wilbraham — Con.			
6	23	6.33	7.93
7	20	5.51	8.04
8	12	3.30	5.52
9	10	2.75	5.17
10	8	2.20	4.60
11	3	0.83	1.90
12	3	0.83	2.07
13	1	0.28	0.75
14	1	0.28	0.80
19	1	0.28	1.09
193	1	0.28	11.09
HAMPSHIRE.			
Amherst, . . .	1,064	100.00	100.00
1	46	4.32	0.96
2	208	19.55	8.69
3	244	22.93	15.30
4	168	15.79	14.04
5	129	12.13	13.48
6	99	9.31	12.41
7	66	6.20	9.66
8	31	2.91	5.18
9	28	2.63	5.27
10	17	1.60	3.55
11	4	0.58	0.92
12	3	0.28	0.75
13	2	0.19	0.54
14	2	0.19	0.59
15	2	0.19	0.63
16	2	0.19	0.67
17	1	0.09	0.36
18	2	0.19	0.75
19	2	0.19	0.80
22	1	0.09	0.46
29	2	0.19	1.21
30	2	0.19	1.25
35	1	0.09	0.73
42	1	0.09	0.88
44	1	0.09	0.92
Belchertown, . .	524	100.00	100.00
1	43	8.21	1.99
2	105	20.04	9.72
3	110	20.99	15.27
4	74	14.12	13.70
5	61	11.64	14.11
6	40	7.63	11.11
7	42	8.02	13.60
8	21	4.01	7.77
9	18	3.44	7.50
10	2	0.38	0.92
11	4	0.76	2.04
12	3	0.57	1.67
13	1	0.19	0.60
Chesterfield, . .	162	100.00	100.00
1	14	8.64	2.38

COUNTIES, TOWNS, AND SIZE OF FAMILIES.	Number of Families	PERCENTAGES Total Families	PERCENTAGES Total Population
HAMPSHIRE — Con.			
Chesterfield — Con.			
2	40	24.69	13.58
3	32	19.75	16.30
4	25	15.43	16.98
5	24	14.82	20.37
6	16	9.88	16.30
7	7	4.32	8.32
8	3	1.85	4.07
10	1	0.62	1.70
Cummington, . .	201	100.00	100.00
1	14	6.96	1.86
2	35	17.41	9.33
3	52	25.87	20.80
4	41	20.40	21.87
5	33	16.42	22.00
6	11	5.47	8.80
7	9	4.48	8.40
8	4	1.99	4.27
9	1	0.50	1.20
11	1	0.50	1.47
Easthampton, . .	1,019	100.00	100.00
1	53	5.20	1.11
2	149	14.62	6.22
3	179	17.57	11.21
4	185	18.15	15.45
5	145	14.23	15.14
6	110	10.79	13.78
7	80	7.85	11.69
8	46	4.51	7.68
9	28	2.75	5.26
10	18	1.77	3.76
11	9	0.88	2.07
12	8	0.78	2.00
13	2	0.20	0.54
15	2	0.20	0.63
22	1	0.10	0.46
24	1	0.10	0.50
28	1	0.10	0.58
33	1	0.10	0.69
59	1	0.10	1.23
Enfield, . . .	261	100.00	100.00
1	18	6.89	1.82
2	62	23.75	12.53
3	62	23.75	18.79
4	34	13.03	13.74
5	34	13.03	17.17
6	27	10.34	16.36
7	12	4.60	8.48
8	6	2.30	4.85
9	2	0.77	1.82
10	2	0.77	2.02
12	2	0.77	2.42
Goshen, . . .	66	100.00	100.00
1	2	3.03	0.66
2	12	18.18	7.90
3	8	12.12	7.90

SIZE OF FAMILIES: FOR TOWNS — Continued.

COUNTIES, TOWNS, AND SIZE OF FAMILIES.	Number of Families	PERCENTAGES		COUNTIES, TOWNS, AND SIZE OF FAMILIES.	Number of Families	PERCENTAGES	
		Total Families	Total Population			Total Families	Total Population
HAMPSHIRE — Con.				HAMPSHIRE — Con.			
Goshen — Con.				Huntington,	329	100.00	100.00
4	9	13.63	11.84	1	12	3.65	0.83
5	13	19.70	21.38	2	51	15.50	7.03
6	10	15.15	19.73	3	59	17.93	12.21
7	8	12.12	18.42	4	73	22.19	20.14
8	1	1.52	2.63	5	38	11.55	13.10
9	1	1.52	2.96	6	49	14.90	20.27
10	2	3.03	6.58	7	24	7.30	11.59
Granby,	171	100.00	100.00	8	8	2.43	4.41
1	9	5.26	1.20	9	5	1.52	3.10
2	26	15.21	6.95	10	7	2.13	4.83
3	29	16.96	11.63	11	1	0.30	0.76
4	31	18.13	16.55	12	1	0.30	0.83
5	30	17.54	20.05	13	1	0.30	0.90
6	22	12.87	17.65	Middlefield,	92	100.00	100.00
7	13	7.60	12.17	1	6	6.52	1.55
8	4	2.34	4.28	2	20	21.74	10.36
10	6	3.51	8.02	3	20	21.74	15.55
11	1	0.58	1.47	4	8	8.70	8.29
Greenwich,	142	100.00	100.00	5	12	13.04	15.55
1	19	13.38	5.95	6	11	11.96	17.10
2	41	28.87	17.05	7	6	6.52	10.88
3	32	22.54	19.96	8	5	5.43	10.36
4	17	11.97	14.14	9	2	2.17	4.66
5	12	8.45	12.47	10	1	1.09	2.59
6	8	5.63	9.98	12	1	1.09	3.11
7	4	2.82	5.82	Pelham,	126	100.00	100.00
8	3	2.11	4.99	1	7	5.56	1.44
9	4	2.82	7.48	2	33	26.19	13.58
10	2	1.41	4.16	3	26	20.64	16.05
Hadley,	390	100.00	100.00	4	23	18.25	18.93
1	20	5.13	1.17	5	12	9.52	12.34
2	58	14.87	6.81	6	8	6.35	9.88
3	77	19.74	13.56	7	9	7.14	12.96
4	66	16.92	15.49	8	5	3.97	8.23
5	65	16.67	19.07	10	1	0.79	2.06
6	46	11.79	16.20	11	2	1.59	4.53
7	22	5.64	9.04	Plainfield,	109	100.00	100.00
8	20	5.13	9.39	1	4	3.67	0.89
9	8	2.05	4.23	2	25	22.94	11.11
10	5	1.28	2.93	3	18	16.51	12.00
11	1	0.26	0.65	4	14	12.84	12.45
12	1	0.26	0.70	5	25	22.94	27.78
13	1	0.26	0.76	6	10	9.17	13.23
Hatfield,	291	100.00	100.00	7	6	5.50	9.33
1	16	5.50	1.27	8	5	4.59	8.89
2	50	17.18	7.93	9	1	0.92	2.00
3	51	17.53	12.12	10	1	0.92	2.22
4	55	18.90	17.45	Prescott,	106	100.00	100.00
5	42	14.43	15.64	1	5	4.72	1.25
6	26	8.94	12.36	2	29	27.36	14.47
7	24	8.25	13.31	3	26	24.53	19.45
8	14	4.81	8.88	4	13	12.27	12.97
9	9	3.09	6.42	5	15	14.15	18.70
10	1	0.34	0.79	6	7	6.60	19.47
11	2	0.69	1.74	7	4	3.77	6.98
14	1	0.34	1.11				

SIZE OF FAMILIES: FOR TOWNS -- Continued.

COUNTIES, TOWNS, AND SIZE OF FAMILIES.	Number of Families	PERCENTAGES Total Families	Total Population	COUNTIES, TOWNS, AND SIZE OF FAMILIES.	Number of Families	PERCENTAGES Total Families	Total Population
HAMPSHIRE—Con.				HAMPSHIRE—Con.			
Prescott—Con.				Westhampton—Con.			
8	3	2.83	5.99	2	21	16.93	8.82
9	2	1.89	4.49	3	23	18.55	14.50
10	1	0.94	2.49	4	22	17.74	18.49
11	1	0.94	2.74	5	26	16.13	21.01
Southampton,	252	100.00	100.00	6	11	8.87	13.87
1	23	9.13	2.18	7	5	4.03	7.35
2	44	17.46	8.65	8	4	3.23	6.72
3	45	17.86	12.81	9	2	1.61	3.78
4	43	17.06	16.32	11	1	0.81	2.31
5	32	12.70	15.18	Williamsburg,	473	100.00	100.00
6	23	9.13	13.09	1	26	5.50	1.33
7	20	7.94	13.28	2	101	21.35	10.33
8	12	4.76	9.11	3	96	20.30	14.73
9	3	1.19	2.56	4	92	19.45	18.82
10	3	1.19	2.85	5	59	12.47	15.09
11	3	1.19	3.13	6	30	6.34	9.21
12	1	0.39	1.14	7	27	5.71	9.67
South Hadley,	834	100.00	100.00	8	11	2.33	4.50
1	31	3.47	0.70	9	14	2.96	6.45
2	131	14.65	5.90	10	5	1.06	2.56
3	161	18.01	10.87	11	7	1.48	3.94
4	162	18.12	14.56	12	3	0.63	1.84
5	144	16.11	16.27	13	1	0.21	0.66
6	98	10.96	13.24	17	1	0.21	0.87
7	61	6.85	9.67	Worthington,	155	100.00	100.00
8	48	5.37	8.94	1	11	7.10	1.70
9	22	2.46	4.46	2	27	17.42	8.33
10	16	1.79	3.60	3	29	18.71	13.43
11	17	1.68	3.72	4	28	18.06	17.28
12	1	0.11	0.27	5	21	13.55	16.20
14	1	0.11	0.32	6	16	10.32	14.82
15	1	0.11	0.34	7	10	6.45	10.80
28	1	0.11	0.63	8	6	3.87	7.41
308	1	0.11	0.63	9	5	3.23	6.94
Ware,	1,523	100.00	100.00	10	2	1.29	3.09
1	55	3.61	0.72	MIDDLESEX.			
2	201	13.20	5.27	Acton,	529	100.00	100.00
3	249	13.35	9.76	1	28	5.29	1.41
4	254	16.68	13.28	2	128	23.25	12.44
5	195	12.80	12.74	3	124	23.44	18.81
6	200	13.13	15.68	4	112	21.17	22.65
7	113	7.42	10.34	5	59	11.15	14.91
8	100	6.56	10.46	6	58	7.19	11.53
9	59	3.87	6.94	7	24	4.54	8.49
10	40	2.63	5.23	8	7	1.32	2.83
11	21	1.38	3.02	9	8	1.51	3.64
12	15	0.98	2.35	10	3	0.57	1.52
13	6	0.39	1.02	11	2	0.38	1.11
14	6	0.39	1.10	13	1	0.19	0.66
15	3	0.20	0.59	Arlington,	1,392	100.00	100.00
16	1	0.07	0.21	1	24	1.91	0.40
18	3	0.20	0.71	2	172	12.03	5.28
22	1	0.07	0.23	3	277	19.90	12.48
24	1	0.07	0.31	4	225	16.52	13.81
Westhampton,	124	100.00	100.00	5	200	15.35	16.04
1	15	12.10	3.15				

SIZE OF FAMILIES: FOR TOWNS — Continued.

COUNTIES, TOWNS, AND SIZE OF FAMILIES.	Number of Families	PERCENTAGES Total Families	PERCENTAGES Total Population	COUNTIES, TOWNS, AND SIZE OF FAMILIES.	Number of Families	PERCENTAGES Total Families	PERCENTAGES Total Population
MIDDLESEX — Con.				MIDDLESEX — Con.			
Arlington — Con.				Bedford — Con.			
6	190	13.95	17.50	6	25	9.96	12.83
7	115	8.90	12.14	7	12	4.78	7.19
8	71	5.21	8.72	8	8	3.19	5.48
9	34	2.50	4.70	9	9	3.58	6.93
10	21	1.54	3.22	10	5	1.99	4.28
11	10	0.73	1.69	11	4	1.59	3.76
12	9	0.66	1.66	12	1	0.40	1.03
13	8	0.59	1.60	13	1	0.40	1.11
14	1	0.07	0.21	15	1	0.40	1.28
15	1	0.07	0.23	16	1	0.40	1.37
21	1	0.07	0.32	17	1	0.40	1.45
Ashby, ...	233	100.00	100.00	18	1	0.40	1.54
1	18	7.72	2.24	36	1	0.40	3.08
2	54	23.17	13.43	Belmont, . . .	505	100.00	100.00
3	64	27.47	23.88	1	12	2.38	0.42
4	49	21.03	24.38	2	64	12.67	4.50
5	23	9.87	14.30	3	80	15.84	8.44
6	12	5.15	8.96	4	87	17.23	12.24
7	5	2.15	4.35	5	79	15.64	13.89
8	5	2.15	4.98	6	58	11.49	12.24
9	2	0.86	2.24	7	30	5.94	7.39
10	1	0.43	1.24	8	38	7.53	10.69
Ashland, ...	486	100.00	100.00	9	18	3.56	5.70
1	34	6.99	1.63	10	15	2.97	5.28
2	88	18.11	8.42	11	4	0.79	1.55
3	97	19.96	13.92	12	9	1.78	3.80
4	81	16.67	15.50	13	3	0.59	1.37
5	56	11.52	13.40	14	3	0.59	1.48
6	40	8.23	11.48	38	1	0.20	1.94
7	39	8.02	13.06	39	1	0.20	1.37
8	19	3.91	7.27	53	1	0.20	1.87
9	14	2.88	6.03	80	1	0.20	2.81
10	8	1.65	3.83	103	1	0.20	3.62
11	8	1.65	4.21	Billerica, . . .	582	100.00	100.00
13	2	0.41	1.25	1	36	6.19	1.40
Ayer, ...	528	100.00	100.00	2	87	14.95	6.75
1	39	7.38	1.86	3	105	18.04	12.22
2	114	21.59	10.85	4	111	19.07	17.23
3	107	20.26	15.28	5	85	14.60	16.49
4	86	16.29	16.37	6	61	10.48	14.20
5	70	13.26	16.66	7	47	8.08	12.77
6	38	7.29	10.85	8	25	4.30	7.76
7	41	7.76	13.66	9	8	1.37	2.79
8	15	2.84	5.71	10	10	1.72	3.88
9	11	2.08	4.71	11	3	0.52	1.28
10	2	0.38	0.95	12	1	0.17	0.47
11	2	0.38	1.05	13	1	0.17	0.51
13	2	0.38	1.24	16	1	0.17	0.62
17	1	0.19	0.81	42	1	0.17	1.63
Bedford, . . .	251	100.00	100.00	Boxborough, . .	78	100.00	100.00
1	14	5.58	1.20	1	6	7.69	1.95
2	47	18.72	8.04	2	14	17.95	9.12
3	44	17.53	11.29	3	20	25.64	19.55
4	51	20.32	17.45	4	15	19.23	19.55
5	25	9.96	10.69	5	7	8.98	11.40

SIZE OF FAMILIES: FOR TOWNS — Continued.

COUNTIES, TOWNS, AND SIZE OF FAMILIES.	Number of Families	Total Families	Total Population
MIDDLESEX — Con.			
Boxborough — Con.			
6	6	7.69	11.73
7	3	3.85	6.84
8	4	5.13	10.42
9	2	2.56	5.86
11	1	1.28	3.58
Burlington, . . .	128	100.00	100.00
1	11	8.53	1.92
2	24	18.60	8.36
3	23	17.83	12.02
4	20	15.50	13.94
5	7	5.43	6.10
6	12	9.30	12.54
7	16	12.40	19.51
8	8	6.20	11.15
9	3	2.32	4.70
10	2	1.55	3.48
11	1	0.78	1.92
12	1	0.78	2.09
13	1	0.78	2.27
Carlisle, . . .	126	100.00	100.00
1	10	7.94	2.05
2	30	23.81	12.20
3	21	16.67	12.80
4	20	15.87	16.26
5	17	13.49	17.28
6	16	12.70	19.51
7	5	3.97	7.11
8	3	2.38	4.88
9	2	1.59	3.66
10	1	0.79	2.05
11	1	0.79	2.24
Chelmsford, . . .	747	100.00	100.00
1	30	4.02	0.95
2	139	18.61	8.79
3	167	22.36	15.84
4	144	19.28	18.22
5	112	14.99	17.71
6	57	7.63	10.82
7	46	6.16	10.18
8	27	3.62	6.83
9	8	1.07	2.28
10	7	0.94	2.21
11	4	0.54	1.39
12	1	0.13	0.38
14	1	0.13	0.44
16	1	0.13	0.51
17	1	0.13	0.54
23	1	0.13	0.73
69	1	0.13	2.18
Concord, . . .	874	100.00	100.00
1	32	3.66	0.62
2	131	14.99	5.06
3	146	16.71	8.46
4	167	19.11	12.91
5	123	14.08	11.89
MIDDLESEX — Con.			
Concord — Con.			
6	91	10.41	10.55
7	61	6.98	8.25
8	53	6.07	8.19
9	29	3.32	5.04
10	18	2.06	3.48
11	7	0.80	1.49
12	5	0.57	1.16
13	2	0.23	0.50
14	4	0.46	1.08
15	1	0.11	0.29
16	1	0.11	0.31
18	1	0.11	0.35
22	1	0.11	0.43
1.032	1	0.11	19.94
Dracut, . . .	475	100.00	100.00
1	12	2.53	0.49
2	65	13.69	5.32
3	88	18.53	10.81
4	64	13.47	10.48
5	78	16.42	15.96
6	47	9.90	11.54
7	41	8.63	11.75
8	33	6.95	19.81
9	23	4.84	8.47
10	5	1.05	2.05
11	7	1.47	3.15
12	3	0.63	1.47
13	2	0.42	1.06
16	1	0.21	0.66
17	2	0.42	1.39
18	1	0.21	0.74
23	1	0.21	0.94
29	1	0.21	1.19
42	1	0.21	1.72
Dunstable, . . .	106	100.00	100.00
1	11	10.38	2.75
2	23	21.70	11.50
3	22	20.76	16.50
4	13	12.26	13.00
5	17	16.04	21.25
6	9	8.49	13.50
7	5	4.72	8.75
8	4	3.77	8.00
9	1	0.94	2.25
10	1	0.94	2.50
Framingham, . .	2,115	100.00	100.00
1	84	3.97	0.88
2	361	17.07	7.59
3	413	19.53	13.02
4	374	17.68	15.73
5	332	15.70	17.45
6	201	9.50	12.68
7	125	5.91	9.20
8	98	4.63	8.24
9	57	2.70	5.39

SIZE OF FAMILIES: FOR TOWNS — Continued.

COUNTIES, TOWNS, AND SIZE OF FAMILIES.	Number of Families	Total Families	Total Population	COUNTIES, TOWNS, AND SIZE OF FAMILIES.	Number of Families	Total Families	Total Population
MIDDLESEX — Con.				MIDDLESEX — Con.			
Framingham — Con.				Hopkinton — Con.			
10	30	1.42	3.15	9	13	1.73	3.92
11	10	0.47	1.16	10	4	0.53	1.34
12	11	0.52	1.39	11	6	0.80	2.21
13	5	0.24	0.68	12	1	0.13	0.40
15	2	0.09	0.52	13	1	0.13	0.44
16	2	0.09	0.54	14	1	0.13	0.47
17	2	0.09	0.56	15	1	0.13	0.50
19	1	0.05	0.20	18	1	0.13	0.60
21	1	0.05	0.22	Hudson,	1,245	100.00	100.00
23	2	0.09	0.48	1	49	3.94	0.92
28	1	0.05	0.29	2	234	18.80	8.82
30	1	0.05	0.32	3	277	22.25	15.66
32	1	0.05	0.34	4	229	18.39	17.26
51	1	0.05	0.57	5	153	12.29	14.41
Groton,	508	100.00	100.00	6	128	10.28	14.47
1	42	8.27	1.92	7	64	5.14	8.44
2	92	18.11	8.39	8	47	3.77	7.08
3	109	21.46	14.92	9	24	1.93	4.07
4	95	18.70	17.33	10	18	1.45	3.39
5	59	11.61	13.46	11	10	0.80	2.07
6	43	8.46	11.77	12	4	0.32	0.90
7	30	5.91	9.58	13	2	0.16	0.49
8	15	2.95	5.47	14	2	0.16	0.53
9	8	1.57	3.28	15	1	0.08	0.28
10	5	0.98	2.28	19	2	0.16	0.72
11	4	0.79	2.01	26	1	0.08	0.49
12	1	0.20	0.55	Lexington,	775	100.00	100.00
13	3	0.59	1.78	1	36	4.65	1.03
19	1	0.20	0.87	2	109	14.06	6.23
110	1	0.20	6.59	3	147	18.97	12.61
Holliston,	701	100.00	100.00	4	153	19.74	17.50
1	54	7.70	1.99	5	106	13.68	15.15
2	144	20.54	10.60	6	90	11.61	15.44
3	156	22.26	17.22	7	48	6.19	9.61
4	138	19.69	20.31	8	42	5.42	9.61
5	75	10.70	13.80	9	20	2.58	5.15
6	55	7.85	12.14	10	9	1.16	2.57
7	35	4.99	9.01	11	8	1.03	2.51
8	16	2.28	4.71	12	4	0.52	1.37
9	17	2.43	5.63	13	2	0.26	0.74
10	6	0.86	2.21	17	1	0.13	0.48
11	1	0.14	0.40	Lincoln,	209	100.00	100.00
12	1	0.14	0.44	1	12	5.74	1.08
13	1	0.14	0.48	2	21	10.05	3.78
14	1	0.14	0.51	3	32	15.31	8.64
15	1	0.14	0.55	4	36	17.22	12.96
Hopkinton,	752	100.00	100.00	5	24	11.48	10.80
1	59	7.85	1.98	6	22	10.53	11.88
2	147	19.55	9.85	7	24	11.48	15.13
3	170	22.61	17.09	8	11	5.26	7.92
4	127	16.89	17.02	9	8	3.83	6.48
5	87	11.57	14.58	10	7	3.35	6.30
6	73	9.71	14.68	11	2	0.96	1.98
7	43	5.72	10.09	12	1	0.48	1.08
8	18	2.39	4.83	13	4	1.91	4.68

SIZE OF FAMILIES: FOR TOWNS — Continued.

COUNTIES, TOWNS, AND SIZE OF FAMILIES.	Number of Families	Percentages Total Families	Percentages Total Population
MIDDLESEX — Con.			
Lincoln — Con.			
11	1	0.48	1.26
15	1	0.48	1.35
16	1	0.48	1.44
17	1	0.48	1.53
19	1	0.48	1.71
Littleton, . . .	256	100.00	100.00
1	11	4.30	0.97
2	44	17.19	7.75
3	43	16.80	11.36
4	43	16.80	15.14
5	42	16.40	18.49
6	27	10.55	14.26
7	23	8.98	14.17
8	15	5.86	10.56
9	5	1.95	3.96
10	1	0.39	0.88
13	1	0.39	1.14
15	1	0.39	1.32
Maynard, . . .	642	100.00	100.00
1	15	2.34	0.49
2	77	11.99	4.98
3	119	18.54	11.55
4	128	19.94	16.57
5	100	15.58	16.18
6	61	9.50	11.85
7	53	8.25	12.01
8	39	6.07	10.10
9	24	3.74	6.99
10	12	1.87	3.88
11	7	1.09	2.49
12	4	0.62	1.55
13	2	0.31	0.84
16	1	0.16	0.52
Melrose, . . .	2,685	100.00	100.00
1	50	1.86	0.42
2	392	14.60	6.55
3	518	19.29	12.99
4	581	21.63	19.42
5	463	17.25	19.35
6	312	11.62	15.65
7	174	6.48	10.18
8	95	3.53	6.35
9	35	1.31	2.63
10	32	1.19	2.67
11	16	0.59	1.47
12	5	0.19	0.50
13	1	0.04	0.11
14	3	0.11	0.35
15	3	0.11	0.38
16	1	0.04	0.13
18	1	0.04	0.15
19	1	0.04	0.16
20	1	0.04	0.17
44	1	0.04	0.37
Natick, . . .	2,089	100.00	100.00
1	106	5.07	1.20
MIDDLESEX — Con.			
Natick — Con.			
2	367	17.57	8.33
3	436	20.87	14.84
4	400	19.15	18.15
5	312	14.93	17.70
6	176	8.42	11.98
7	139	6.65	11.04
8	63	3.02	5.72
9	35	1.68	3.57
10	25	1.20	2.84
11	12	0.57	1.50
12	8	0.38	1.09
13	3	0.14	0.44
14	2	0.10	0.32
15	1	0.05	0.17
18	2	0.10	0.41
24	1	0.05	0.27
38	1	0.05	0.43
North Reading, . .	228	100.00	100.00
1	21	9.21	2.51
2	46	20.18	11.02
3	59	25.88	21.20
4	48	21.05	22.99
5	22	9.65	13.17
6	9	3.95	6.47
7	12	5.26	10.06
8	4	1.75	3.83
9	3	1.31	3.23
10	2	0.88	2.40
11	1	0.44	1.32
15	1	0.44	1.80
Pepperell, . . .	787	100.00	100.00
1	52	6.61	1.57
2	150	19.06	9.03
3	151	19.19	13.64
4	135	17.15	16.26
5	108	13.72	16.26
6	78	9.91	14.09
7	39	4.95	8.22
8	28	3.56	6.75
9	21	2.67	5.69
10	14	1.78	4.22
11	6	0.76	1.99
12	2	0.25	0.72
15	1	0.13	0.45
17	1	0.13	0.51
20	1	0.13	0.60
Reading, . . .	1,150	100.00	100.00
1	45	3.91	0.95
2	237	20.61	10.05
3	244	21.22	15.52
4	226	19.65	19.16
5	142	12.34	15.05
6	102	8.87	12.97
7	82	7.13	12.17
8	36	3.13	6.11
9	14	1.22	2.67

SIZE OF FAMILIES: FOR TOWNS — Continued.

COUNTIES, TOWNS, AND SIZE OF FAMILIES.	Number of Families	PERCENTAGES	
		Total Families	Total Population
MIDDLESEX — Con.			
Reading — Con.			
10	10	0.87	2.12
11	6	0.52	1.40
12	1	0.09	0.25
13	3	0.26	0.83
14	1	0.09	0.30
21	1	0.09	0.45
Sherborn, . . .	286	100.00	100.00
1	18	6.29	1.24
2	61	21.33	8.44
3	60	20.98	12.45
4	50	17.48	13.83
5	46	16.08	15.91
6	18	6.29	7.47
7	14	4.90	6.78
8	6	2.10	3.32
9	7	2.45	4.36
10	3	1.05	2.07
11	1	0.35	0.76
12	1	0.35	0.83
326	1	0.35	22.54
Shirley, . . .	324	100.00	100.00
1	21	6.48	1.50
2	62	19.13	8.86
3	59	18.21	12.65
4	64	19.75	18.30
5	38	11.73	13.58
6	25	7.72	10.72
7	25	7.72	12.51
8	8	2.47	4.58
9	10	3.08	6.43
10	7	2.16	5.00
11	2	0.62	1.57
17	1	0.31	1.22
18	1	0.31	1.29
25	1	0.31	1.79
Stoneham, . . .	1,581	100.00	100.00
1	84	5.31	1.84
2	370	23.40	11.78
3	345	21.82	16.47
4	285	18.03	18.14
5	197	12.46	15.67
6	111	7.02	10.60
7	85	5.38	9.47
8	45	2.85	5.73
9	21	1.33	3.01
10	14	0.89	2.23
11	8	0.51	1.40
12	6	0.38	1.14
13	3	0.19	0.62
15	1	0.06	0.24
16	1	0.06	0.25
20	2	0.13	0.64
22	1	0.06	0.35
24	1	0.06	0.38
34	1	0.06	0.54
MIDDLESEX — Con.			
Stow, ...	234	100.00	100.00
1	12	5.13	1.30
2	51	21.80	11.09
3	49	20.94	15.98
4	40	17.09	17.39
5	42	17.95	22.83
6	17	7.27	11.09
7	12	5.13	9.13
8	6	2.56	5.22
10	2	0.85	2.17
11	2	0.85	2.39
13	1	0.43	1.41
Sudbury, . . .	272	100.00	100.00
1	20	7.35	1.75
2	53	19.48	9.29
3	50	18.38	13.15
4	47	17.28	16.48
5	35	12.87	15.34
6	30	11.03	15.77
7	16	5.88	9.82
8	5	1.84	3.51
9	9	3.31	7.10
10	3	1.10	2.63
11	2	0.74	2.45
15	1	0.37	1.31
16	1	0.37	1.40
Tewksbury, . . .	473	100.00	100.00
1	14	2.96	0.41
2	79	16.70	4.68
3	75	15.86	6.66
4	89	18.82	10.54
5	65	13.74	9.62
6	56	11.84	9.94
7	39	8.25	8.08
8	21	4.44	4.97
9	16	3.38	4.26
10	6	1.27	1.78
11	4	0.85	1.30
12	2	0.42	0.71
13	1	0.21	0.39
14	3	0.63	1.24
15	1	0.21	0.44
16	1	0.21	0.47
1.166	1	0.21	34.51
Townsend, . . .	512	100.00	100.00
1	50	9.76	2.81
2	149	29.10	16.74
3	109	21.29	18.37
4	81	15.82	18.29
5	56	10.94	15.73
6	30	5.86	10.11
7	12	2.34	4.72
8	12	2.34	5.39
9	7	1.37	3.54
10	3	0.58	1.69
12	1	0.20	0.68

SIZE OF FAMILIES: FOR TOWNS — Continued.

COUNTIES, TOWNS, AND SIZE OF FAMILIES.	Number of Families	PERCENTAGES Total Families	PERCENTAGES Total Population
MIDDLESEX — Con.			
Townsend — Con.			
16	1	0.20	0.90
20	1	0.20	1.12
Tyngsborough, . .	163	100.00	100.00
1	16	9.82	2.52
2	37	22.70	11.65
3	32	19.63	15.12
4	25	15.34	15.75
5	19	11.66	14.96
6	12	7.36	11.34
7	10	6.13	11.02
8	3	1.84	3.78
9	6	3.68	8.50
10	1	0.61	1.58
12	2	1.23	3.78
Wakefield, . . .	1,958	100.00	100.00
1	68	3.47	0.82
2	355	18.13	8.55
3	414	21.15	14.96
4	378	19.31	18.21
5	279	14.25	16.80
6	212	10.83	15.32
7	104	5.31	8.77
8	70	3.58	6.74
9	37	1.89	4.01
10	20	1.02	2.41
11	12	0.61	1.59
12	2	0.10	0.29
13	1	0.05	0.15
14	2	0.10	0.34
15	1	0.05	0.18
20	1	0.05	0.24
25	1	0.05	0.30
27	1	0.05	0.32
Watertown, . . .	1,650	100.00	100.00
1	30	1.82	0.39
2	242	14.67	6.21
3	305	18.49	11.75
4	297	18.00	15.25
5	259	15.70	16.65
6	204	12.37	15.72
7	119	7.21	10.70
8	84	5.09	8.63
9	56	3.39	6.47
10	18	1.09	2.31
11	23	1.39	3.25
12	5	0.30	0.77
13	3	0.18	0.50
15	1	0.06	0.19
17	1	0.06	0.22
19	1	0.06	0.24
28	1	0.06	0.36
32	1	0.06	0.41
Wayland, . . .	446	100.00	100.00
1	20	4.48	0.99
2	69	15.47	6.81

COUNTIES, TOWNS, AND SIZE OF FAMILIES.	Number of Families	PERCENTAGES Total Families	PERCENTAGES Total Population
MIDDLESEX — Con.			
Wayland — Con.			
3	80	17.94	11.85
4	86	19.28	16.98
5	63	14.13	15.55
6	51	11.44	15.10
7	32	7.18	11.06
8	14	3.14	5.53
9	12	2.69	5.33
10	9	2.02	4.44
11	5	1.12	2.71
12	1	0.22	0.59
13	2	0.45	1.28
16	1	0.22	0.79
20	1	0.22	0.99
Westford, . . .	526	100.00	100.00
1	25	4.75	1.05
2	95	18.06	7.86
3	99	18.82	12.28
4	86	16.35	14.23
5	62	11.79	12.82
6	62	11.79	15.59
7	26	4.94	7.53
8	28	5.33	9.26
9	14	2.66	5.21
10	9	1.71	3.72
11	4	0.76	1.82
12	8	1.52	3.97
13	3	0.57	1.61
14	2	0.38	1.16
16	1	0.19	0.66
17	1	0.19	0.70
18	1	0.19	0.75
Weston, . . .	367	100.00	100.00
1	10	2.72	0.59
2	52	14.17	6.08
3	70	19.07	12.28
4	75	20.44	17.55
5	55	14.99	16.08
6	36	9.81	12.63
7	27	7.36	11.05
8	13	3.54	6.08
9	14	3.81	7.37
10	7	1.91	4.09
11	3	0.82	1.93
12	1	0.27	0.70
13	1	0.27	0.76
14	2	0.55	1.64
20	1	0.27	1.17
Wilmington, . . .	338	100.00	100.00
1	20	5.92	1.41
2	63	18.64	8.87
3	68	20.12	14.37
4	59	17.46	16.62
5	46	13.61	16.20
6	32	9.46	13.52
7	19	5.62	9.37

SIZE OF FAMILIES: FOR TOWNS — Continued.

Counties, Towns, and Size of Families.	Number of Families	Percentages Total Families	Total Population
MIDDLESEX — Con.			
Wilmington — Con.			
8	17	5.03	9.58
9	5	1.48	3.17
10	5	1.48	3.52
11	1	0.29	0.77
12	2	0.60	1.69
13	1	0.29	0.91
Winchester, . . .	1,301	100.00	100.00
1	33	2.54	0.54
2	182	13.99	5.92
3	201	15.45	9.81
4	253	19.45	16.45
5	221	16.99	17.97
6	168	12.91	16.39
7	98	7.53	11.15
8	71	5.46	9.24
9	43	3.30	6.29
10	13	1.00	2.11
11	5	0.38	0.89
12	2	0.15	0.39
13	4	0.31	0.85
15	2	0.15	0.49
16	3	0.23	0.78
18	1	0.08	0.29
27	1	0.08	0.44
NANTUCKET.			
Nantucket, . . .	981	100.00	100.00
1	149	15.19	4.94
2	295	30.07	19.56
3	218	22.22	21.68
4	159	16.21	21.09
5	80	8.16	13.26
6	38	3.88	7.56
7	22	2.24	5.11
8	9	0.92	2.39
9	5	0.51	1.49
10	1	0.10	0.33
11	2	0.20	0 73
12	1	0.10	0.40
16	1	0 10	0.53
28	1	0.10	0.93
NORFOLK.			
Avon, ...	385	100.00	100.00
1	13	3.38	0.80
2	74	19.22	9.10
3	86	22.34	15.87
4	68	17.66	16.73
5	56	14.54	17.22
6	34	8.83	12.55
7	24	6.23	10.33
8	16	4.16	7.87
9	7	1.82	3.87
10	3	0.78	1.85
11	2	0.52	1.35

Counties, Towns, and Size of Families.	Number of Families	Percentages Total Families	Total Population
NORFOLK — Con.			
Avon — Con.			
14	1	0.26	0.86
26	1	0.26	1.60
Bellingham, . . .	558	100.00	100.00
1	23	6.42	1.55
2	80	22.85	10.80
3	71	19.83	14.38
4	54	15.08	14.59
5	34	9.50	11.48
6	46	12.85	18.64
7	16	4.47	7.56
8	14	3.91	7.56
9	9	2.51	5.47
10	6	1.68	4.05
11	4	1.12	2.97
14	1	0.28	0.95
Braintree, . . .	1,254	100.00	100.00
1	51	4.07	0.96
2	245	19.54	9.23
3	277	22.09	15.65
4	243	19.38	18.30
5	179	14.27	16.85
6	103	8.21	11.64
7	58	4.62	7.64
8	49	3.91	7.38
9	25	1.99	4.24
10	10	0.80	1.88
11	6	0.48	1.24
12	3	0.24	0.68
13	1	0.08	0.24
15	1	0 08	0.28
19	1	0.08	0.36
20	1	0.08	0.38
162	1	0.08	3.05
Brookline, . . .	3,148	100.00	100.00
1	113	3.59	0.70
2	319	10.14	3.95
3	459	14.58	8.52
4	510	16.20	12.62
5	527	16.74	16.30
6	450	14.30	16.70
7	311	9.88	13.47
8	186	5.91	9.21
9	120	3.81	6.68
10	57	1.81	3.53
11	40	1.27	2.72
12	16	0.51	1.19
13	13	0.41	1.05
14	7	0.22	0.61
15	5	0.16	0.46
16	3	0.10	0.30
17	1	0.03	0.10
18	2	0.07	0.22
19	1	0.03	0.12
20	1	0.03	0.12
22	1	0.03	0.14

SIZE OF FAMILIES: FOR TOWNS — Continued.

COUNTIES, TOWNS, AND SIZE OF FAMILIES.	Number of Families	Total Families	Total Population
NORFOLK — Con.			
Brookline — Con.			
25	1	0.03	0.15
26	1	0.03	0.16
27	1	0.03	0.17
29	1	0.03	0.18
31	1	0.03	0.19
72	1	0.03	0.44
Canton, . . .	968	100.00	100.00
1	35	3.62	0.76
2	151	15.60	6.51
3	158	16.32	10.22
4	155	16.01	13.37
5	138	14.26	14.88
6	110	11.36	14.24
7	86	8.88	12.99
8	51	5.27	8.80
9	48	4.96	9.32
10	12	1.24	2.59
11	15	1.55	3.56
12	5	0.52	1.29
13	1	0.10	0.28
17	1	0.10	0.37
19	2	0.21	0.82
Cohasset, . . .	586	100.00	100.00
1	43	7.34	1.74
2	123	20.99	9.94
3	110	18.77	13.51
4	96	16.38	15.52
5	68	11.61	13.74
6	51	8.70	12.37
7	27	4.62	10.47
8	23	3.58	6.79
9	14	2.39	5.09
10	7	1.20	2.83
11	6	1.02	2.67
12	5	0.53	1.45
13	4	0.68	2.10
14	1	0.17	0.57
15	1	0.17	0.61
19	1	0.17	0.77
Dedham, . . .	1,613	100.00	100.00
1	82	5.08	1.14
2	260	16.12	7.21
3	311	19.28	12.94
4	294	18.23	16.31
5	216	13.39	14.98
6	183	11.35	15.23
7	126	7.81	12.23
8	59	3.66	6.54
9	35	2.17	4.37
10	23	1.43	3.19
11	7	0.43	1.07
12	4	0.25	0.66
13	5	0.31	0.90
14	4	0.25	0.78
19	1	0.06	0.26
38	1	0.06	0.53

COUNTIES, TOWNS, AND SIZE OF FAMILIES.	Number of Families	Total Families	Total Population
NORFOLK — Con.			
Dedham — Con.			
40	1	0.06	0.55
80	1	0.06	1.11
Dover, ...	148	100.00	100.00
1	9	6.08	1.35
2	22	14.86	6.59
3	31	20.93	13.92
4	23	15.54	13.77
5	20	13.51	14.97
6	14	9.46	12.57
7	12	8.11	12.57
8	6	4.05	7.19
9	6	4.05	8.08
10	1	0.68	1.50
11	1	0.68	1.65
12	1	0.68	1.80
13	1	0.68	1.95
14	1	0.68	2.09
Foxborough, . .	828	100.00	100.00
1	69	8.33	2.14
2	195	23.55	12.12
3	175	21.14	16.31
4	154	18.60	19.14
5	82	9.90	12.74
6	74	8.94	13.80
7	34	4.11	7.39
8	25	3.02	6.21
9	8	0.97	2.24
10	5	0.60	1.55
11	2	0.24	0.68
12	1	0.12	0.37
13	1	0.12	0.40
18	1	0.12	0.56
22	1	0.12	0.68
118	1	0.12	3.67
Franklin, . . .	1,176	100.00	100.00
1	58	4.93	1.13
2	217	18.45	8.45
3	242	20.58	14.14
4	229	19.47	17.83
5	164	13.94	15.97
6	108	9.18	12.62
7	51	4.34	6.95
8	37	3.14	5.76
9	33	2.80	5.78
10	15	1.27	2.92
11	4	0.34	0.86
12	8	0.68	1.87
13	1	0.09	0.25
14	2	0.17	0.55
18	2	0.17	0.70
19	1	0.09	0.57
33	1	0.09	0.64
34	1	0.09	0.66
35	1	0.09	0.68
96	1	0.09	1.87

SIZE OF FAMILIES: FOR TOWNS — Continued.

COUNTIES, TOWNS, AND SIZE OF FAMILIES.	Number of Families	Total Families	Total Population
NORFOLK — Con.			
Holbrook, . . .	571	100.00	100.00
1	34	5.95	1.48
2	113	19.79	9.84
3	125	21.89	16.32
4	100	17.51	17.41
5	77	13.49	16.75
6	49	8.58	12.79
7	36	6.30	10.97
8	19	3.33	6.61
9	8	1.40	3.13
10	3	0.53	1.31
11	6	1.05	2.87
12	1	0.18	0.52
Hyde Park, . . .	2,561	100.00	100.00
1	82	3.20	0.69
2	365	14.25	6.17
3	461	18.00	11.69
4	498	19.45	16.84
5	393	15.35	16.62
6	297	11.60	15.07
7	197	7.69	11.66
8	121	4.72	8.19
9	54	2.11	4.11
10	45	1.76	3.81
11	17	0.66	1.58
12	13	0.51	1.32
13	6	0.23	0.66
14	5	0.19	0.59
15	1	0.04	0.13
16	3	0.12	0.41
17	1	0.04	0.14
18	1	0.04	0.15
20	1	0.04	0.17
Medfield, . . .	415	100.00	100.00
1	25	6.03	1.34
2	81	19.52	8.65
3	83	20.00	13.30
4	66	15.91	14.10
5	55	13.25	14.69
6	41	9.88	13.14
7	20	4.82	7.48
8	13	3.13	5.56
9	14	3.37	6.73
10	5	1.21	2.67
11	3	0.72	1.76
13	1	0.24	0.69
14	1	0.24	0.75
15	1	0.24	0.80
16	1	0.24	0.86
18	1	0.24	0.96
19	1	0.24	1.02
21	1	0.24	1.28
34	1	0.24	1.82
45	1	0.24	2.40
Medway, . . .	732	100.00	100.00
1	55	7.51	1.89
NORFOLK — Con.			
Medway — Con.			
2	163	22.27	11.19
3	142	19.40	14.63
4	133	18.17	18.26
5	84	11.47	14.42
6	66	9.02	13.59
7	40	5.46	9.61
8	18	2.46	4.94
9	13	1.77	4.02
10	10	1.37	3.43
11	4	0.54	1.51
12	1	0.14	0.41
13	1	0.14	0.45
21	1	0.14	0.72
27	1	0.14	0.93
Millis, . . .	226	100.00	100.00
1	11	4.87	1.00
2	33	14.60	6.56
3	51	22.57	15.21
4	36	15.93	14.32
5	34	15.05	16.90
6	22	9.74	13.12
7	14	6.19	9.74
8	8	3.54	6.36
9	9	3.98	8.05
10	5	2.21	4.97
11	2	0.88	2.19
15	1	0.44	1.49
Milton, . . .	1,106	100.00	100.00
1	38	3.44	0.69
2	157	14.20	5.69
3	191	17.27	10.58
4	170	15.37	12.32
5	156	14.10	14.14
6	141	12.75	15.33
7	87	7.87	11.04
8	68	6.15	9.86
9	39	3.53	6.36
10	19	1.72	3.44
11	12	1.08	2.39
12	13	1.17	2.83
13	4	0.36	0.94
14	3	0.27	0.76
15	4	0.36	1.09
18	1	0.09	0.33
26	1	0.09	0.47
30	1	0.09	0.91
57	1	0.09	1.03
Needham, . . .	802	100.00	100.00
1	39	4.86	1.11
2	134	16.71	7.63
3	162	20.20	13.84
4	147	18.33	16.75
5	101	12.59	14.39
6	82	10.22	14.01
7	58	7.23	11.56

SIZE OF FAMILIES: FOR TOWNS — Continued.

COUNTIES, TOWNS, AND SIZE OF FAMILIES.	Number of Families	Total Families	Total Population	COUNTIES, TOWNS, AND SIZE OF FAMILIES.	Number of Families	Total Families	Total Population
NORFOLK — Con.				NORFOLK — Con.			
Needham — Con.				Sharon — Con.			
8	41	5.11	9.34	6	41	10.43	11.33
9	17	2.12	4.36	7	28	7.12	11.42
10	10	1.25	2.85	8	13	3.31	6.06
11	3	0.38	0.94	9	5	1.27	2.62
12	3	0.38	1.03	10	4	1.02	2.33
13	3	0.38	1.11	11	2	0.51	1.28
14	1	0.12	0.40	12	2	0.51	1.40
24	1	0.12	0.68	13	2	0.51	1.51
Norfolk, . . .	210	100.00	100.00	14	1	0.25	0.81
1	11	5.24	1.25	18	1	0.25	1.05
2	36	17.14	8.16	24	1	0.25	1.40
3	44	20.95	14.96	Stoughton, . . .	1,241	100.00	100.00
4	36	17.14	16.33	1	77	6.20	1.46
5	30	14.29	17.01	2	233	18.78	8.84
6	25	11.90	17.01	3	235	18.94	13.37
7	13	6.19	10.32	4	213	17.16	16.16
8	5	2.38	4.33	5	175	14.10	16.60
9	9	4.29	9.18	6	129	10.39	14.68
11	1	0.48	1.25	7	68	5.48	9.03
Norwood, . . .	963	100.00	100.00	8	45	3.63	6.83
1	23	2.39	0.50	9	35	2.82	5.97
2	134	13.91	5.84	10	12	0.97	2.28
3	171	17.76	11.22	11	3	0.24	0.63
4	179	18.59	15.65	12	11	0.89	2.50
5	148	15.37	16.18	14	1	0.08	0.26
6	121	12.56	15.87	16	2	0.16	0.61
7	74	7.68	11.32	19	1	0.08	0.56
8	42	4.36	7.35	22	1	0.08	0.42
9	33	3.43	6.49	Walpole, . . .	688	100.00	100.00
10	15	1.56	3.28	1	33	4.80	1.10
11	12	1.25	2.88	2	125	18.17	8.35
12	7	0.73	1.84	3	143	20.79	14.33
13	2	0.21	0.57	4	124	18.02	16.57
20	1	0.10	0.44	5	82	11.92	13.69
25	1	0.10	0.55	6	73	10.61	14.63
Randolph, . . .	905	100.00	100.00	7	45	6.54	10.52
1	61	6.74	1.65	8	26	3.78	6.95
2	170	18.79	9.20	9	20	2.91	6.01
3	178	19.67	14.46	10	7	1.02	2.34
4	181	20.00	19.60	11	3	0.44	1.10
5	112	12.38	15.16	12	4	0.58	1.60
6	82	9.06	13.32	18	1	0.14	0.60
7	50	5.52	9.47	23	1	0.14	0.77
8	38	4.20	8.23	43	1	0.14	1.44
9	19	2.10	4.63	Wellesley, . . .	758	100.00	100.00
10	9	0.99	2.44	1	28	3.80	0.66
11	2	0.22	0.60	2	116	15.72	5.49
12	1	0.11	0.32	3	130	17.62	9.22
17	2	0.22	0.92	4	142	19.25	13.43
Sharon, . . .	393	100.00	100.00	5	96	13.01	11.35
1	35	8.91	2.04	6	72	9.76	10.22
2	53	13.49	6.17	7	55	7.46	9.10
3	65	16.54	11.36	8	24	3.26	4.54
4	78	19.85	18.17	9	22	2.99	4.68
5	62	15.78	18.05	10	13	1.77	3.07

SIZE OF FAMILIES: FOR TOWNS — Continued.

COUNTIES, TOWNS, AND SIZE OF FAMILIES.	Number of Families	Total Families (Percentages)	Total Population (Percentages)	COUNTIES, TOWNS, AND SIZE OF FAMILIES.	Number of Families	Total Families (Percentages)	Total Population (Percentages)
NORFOLK — Con.				PLYMOUTH — Con.			
Wellesley — Con.				Abington — Con.			
11	12	1.63	3.12	2	221	20.54	10.51
12	4	0.55	1.14	3	243	22.58	17.33
13	4	0.55	1.23	4	205	19.05	19.49
14	3	0.41	0.99	5	154	14.31	18.30
15	2	0.27	0.71	6	101	9.39	14.41
16	1	0.13	0.38	7	51	4.74	8.49
17	1	0.13	0.40	8	25	2.32	4.75
20	1	0.13	0.47	9	11	1.02	2.35
21	1	0.13	0.50	10	7	0.65	1.06
24	1	0.13	0.57	11	3	0.28	0.78
25	1	0.13	0.59	14	2	0.19	0.67
29	1	0.13	0.68	Bridgewater, . .	854	100.00	100.00
32	1	0.13	0.76	1	39	4.57	0.83
33	1	0.13	0.78	2	188	22.01	8.02
40	1	0.13	0.95	3	167	19.55	10.69
55	1	0.13	1.30	4	154	18.03	13.15
59	1	0.13	1.40	5	114	13.35	12.16
71	1	0.13	1.68	6	84	9.84	10.76
124	1	0.13	2.93	7	42	4.92	6.27
324	1	0.13	7.66	8	32	3.75	5.46
Weymouth, . . .	2,666	100.00	100.00	9	16	1.87	3.07
1	102	3.82	0.90	10	2	0.23	0.43
2	503	18.87	8.91	11	4	0.47	0.94
3	599	22.47	15.92	12	2	0.23	0.51
4	501	18.79	17.75	13	3	0.35	0.83
5	367	13.77	16.25	14	3	0.35	0.90
6	230	8.63	12.22	15	1	0.12	0.32
7	156	5.85	9.67	18	1	0.12	0.39
8	111	4.16	7.87	169	1	0.12	3.61
9	42	1.57	3.35	1,015	1	0.12	21.66
10	27	1.01	2.39	Carver, ...	262	100.00	100.00
11	15	0.56	1.46	1	30	11.45	2.95
12	5	0.19	0.53	2	50	19.09	9.84
13	4	0.15	0.46	3	55	20.99	16.24
15	1	0.04	0.13	4	41	15.65	16.14
26	1	0.04	0.23	5	34	12.98	16.73
38	1	0.04	0.34	6	24	9.16	14.18
183	1	0.04	1.62	7	11	4.20	7.58
Wrentham, . . .	631	100.00	100.00	8	7	2.67	5.51
1	41	6.50	1.59	9	2	0.76	1.77
2	125	19.81	9.68	10	3	1.15	2.95
3	120	19.02	13.93	11	2	0.76	2.17
4	125	19.81	19.35	12	2	0.76	2.36
5	83	13.15	16.06	16	1	0.38	1.58
6	57	9.03	13.24	Duxbury, ...	532	100.00	100.00
7	27	4.28	7.31	1	48	9.02	2.44
8	24	3.80	7.43	2	140	26.31	14.24
9	15	2.38	5.22	3	115	21.62	17.55
10	6	0.95	2.32	4	94	17.67	19.13
11	4	0.63	1.70	5	51	9.59	12.97
13	2	0.32	1.01	6	33	6.20	10.07
15	2	0.32	1.16	7	22	4.13	7.83
PLYMOUTH.				8	10	1.88	4.07
Abington, . . .	1,076	100.00	100.00	9	11	2.07	5.04
1	53	4.93	1.26	10	5	0.94	2.54
				12	1	0.19	0.61

SIZE OF FAMILIES: FOR TOWNS — Continued.

COUNTIES, TOWNS, AND SIZE OF FAMILIES.	Number of Families	Percentages Total Families	Total Population	COUNTIES, TOWNS, AND SIZE OF FAMILIES.	Number of Families	Percentages Total Families	Total Population
PLYMOUTH — Con.				PLYMOUTH — Con.			
Duxbury — Con.				Hingham — Con.			
49	1	0.49	0.97	2	227	19.50	9.42
50	1	0.49	2.54	3	239	20.53	14.88
East Bridgewater, .	726	100.00	100.00	4	209	17.96	17.35
1	43	5.92	1.49	5	147	12.63	15.25
2	140	19.28	9.67	6	109	9.36	13.57
3	155	21.35	16.07	7	58	4.98	8.42
4	158	21.76	21.84	8	38	3.26	6.31
5	90	12.40	15.55	9	21	1.80	3.92
6	65	8.95	13.48	10	17	1.46	3.53
7	33	4.55	7.98	11	4	0.34	0.91
8	18	2.48	4.97	12	4	0.34	1.00
9	10	1.38	3.11	13	2	0.17	0.54
10	5	0.69	1.73	15	1	0.09	0.81
11	4	0.55	1.52	17	2	0.17	0.71
12	3	0.41	1.24	20	1	0.09	0.41
15	1	0.14	0.52	22	1	0.09	0.46
24	1	0.14	0.85	26	1	0.09	0.54
Halifax, . . .	148	100.00	100.00	37	1	0.09	0.77
1	24	16.22	4.83	Hull, ...	229	100.00	100.00
2	35	23.65	14.08	1	10	4.37	0.96
3	29	19.59	17.50	2	35	15.28	6.70
4	26	17.57	20.93	3	43	18.78	12.96
5	11	7.43	11.07	4	44	19.21	16.86
6	12	8.11	14.49	5	30	13.10	14.37
7	7	4.73	9.86	6	27	11.79	15.52
8	2	1.35	3.22	7	19	8.30	12.74
10	2	1.35	4.02	8	9	3.93	6.90
Hanover, . . .	534	100.00	100.00	9	4	1.74	3.45
1	40	7.56	1.95	10	4	1.74	3.83
2	120	22.06	11.70	11	1	0.44	1.05
3	135	24.82	19.75	13	1	0.44	1.24
4	101	18.57	19.70	14	1	0.44	1.34
5	52	9.56	12.68	28	1	0.44	2.68
6	42	7.72	12.29	Kingston, . . .	477	100.00	100.00
7	29	5.33	9.99	1	29	6.08	1.66
8	11	2.02	4.29	2	117	24.53	13.40
9	5	0.92	2.19	3	105	22.01	18.04
10	3	0.55	1.46	4	106	22.22	24.29
12	1	0.18	0.58	5	44	9.22	12.60
13	2	0.37	1.27	6	39	8.18	15.40
14	1	0.18	0.68	7	20	4.19	8.92
15	1	0.18	0.73	8	9	1.89	4.12
17	1	0.18	0.83	9	5	1.05	2.58
Hanson, . . .	380	100.00	100.00	11	3	0.63	1.89
1	24	6.32	1.74	Lakeville, . . .	233	100.00	100.00
2	84	22.10	12.17	1	24	10.30	2.76
3	104	27.37	22.61	2	48	20.60	11.03
4	66	17.37	19.13	3	49	21.03	16.99
5	49	12.89	17.75	4	45	18.45	19.77
6	28	7.37	12.17	5	28	12.02	16.09
7	12	3.16	6.09	6	16	6.87	11.03
8	6	1.58	3.48	7	15	6.44	12.07
9	3	0.79	1.96	8	5	2.14	4.60
10	4	1.05	2.90	9	1	0.43	1.04
Hingham, . . .	1,164	100.00	100.00	10	3	1.29	3.45
1	82	7.05	1.70	11	1	0.43	1.26

SIZE OF FAMILIES: FOR TOWNS — Continued.

COUNTIES, TOWNS, AND SIZE OF FAMILIES.	Number of Families	PERCENTAGES Total Families	PERCENTAGES Total Population	COUNTIES, TOWNS, AND SIZE OF FAMILIES.	Number of Families	PERCENTAGES Total Families	PERCENTAGES Total Population
PLYMOUTH — Con.				PLYMOUTH — Con.			
Marion, . . .	213	100.00	100.00	Norwell — Con.			
1	12	5.63	1.58	5	49	11.61	15.91
2	49	23.00	12.91	6	22	5.21	8.57
3	58	27.23	22.93	7	16	3.79	7.27
4	42	19.72	22.13	8	10	2.37	5.20
5	26	12.21	17.13	9	9	2.13	5.26
6	15	7.04	11.86	11	4	0.95	2.86
7	3	1.41	2.77	13	1	0.24	0.84
8	6	2.82	6.32	Pembroke, . . .	367	100.00	100.00
9	2	0.94	2.37	1	50	13.62	4.09
Marshfield, . . .	511	100.00	100.00	2	93	25.34	15.21
1	47	9.20	2.67	3	80	21.80	19.62
2	136	26.61	15.45	4	68	18.53	22.24
3	127	24.85	21.65	5	30	8.17	12.27
4	85	16.63	19.32	6	22	5.99	10.79
5	48	9.39	13.64	7	10	2.73	5.72
6	33	6.46	11.25	8	7	1.91	4.58
7	19	3.72	7.56	9	4	1.09	2.94
8	5	0.98	2.27	10	2	0.55	1.64
9	4	0.78	2.05	11	1	0.27	0.90
10	5	0.98	2.84	Plymouth, . . .	1,969	100.00	100.00
11	1	0.20	0.62	1	119	6.05	1.49
12	1	0.20	0.68	2	372	18.89	9.35
Mattapoisett, . .	301	100.00	100.00	3	454	23.06	17.12
1	32	10.63	3.10	4	358	18.18	18.00
2	82	27.24	15.89	5	263	13.36	16.53
3	69	22.92	20.06	6	169	8.58	12.74
4	42	13.95	16.28	7	111	5.64	9.76
5	42	13.95	20.35	8	55	2.79	5.53
6	11	3.66	6.39	9	31	1.58	3.51
7	11	3.66	7.46	10	17	0.86	2.14
8	3	1.00	2.33	11	6	0.31	0.83
9	6	1.99	5.23	12	4	0.20	0.60
10	3	1.00	2.91	13	2	0.10	0.33
Middleborough, .	1,675	100.00	100.00	14	2	0.10	0.35
1	85	5.08	1.27	15	1	0.05	0.19
2	333	19.90	9.96	16	1	0.05	0.20
3	394	23.55	17.67	17	1	0.05	0.21
4	310	18.53	18.54	18	1	0.05	0.23
5	221	13.21	16.52	21	1	0.05	0.26
6	144	8.61	12.92	50	1	0.05	0.63
7	92	5.50	9.63	Plympton, . . .	162	100.00	100.00
8	40	2.39	4.78	1	18	11.11	3.28
9	22	1.31	2.96	2	42	25.92	15.30
10	15	0.90	2.24	3	38	23.46	20.76
11	8	0.48	1.31	4	27	16.67	19.67
12	4	0.24	0.72	5	16	9.88	14.57
13	2	0.12	0.39	6	10	6.17	10.93
18	1	0.06	0.27	7	7	4.32	8.93
20	1	0.06	0.30	8	1	0.62	1.46
35	1	0.06	0.52	9	2	1.23	3.28
Norwell, . . .	422	100.00	100.00	10	1	0.62	1.82
1	38	9.01	2.47	Rochester, . . .	260	100.00	100.00
2	96	22.75	12.47	1	13	5.00	1.27
3	105	24.88	20.45	2	56	21.54	10.97
4	72	17.06	18.70	3	56	21.54	16.45

SIZE OF FAMILIES: FOR TOWNS — Continued.

COUNTIES, TOWNS, AND SIZE OF FAMILIES.	Number of Families	PERCENTAGES Total Families	PERCENTAGES Total Population
PLYMOUTH — Con.			
Rochester — Con.			
4	44	16.92	17.24
5	36	13.85	17.63
6	32	12.31	18.81
7	14	5.38	9.60
8	5	1.92	5.92
9	2	0.77	1.76
12	2	0.77	2.35
Rockland, . . .	1,331	100.00	100.00
1	64	4.81	1.16
2	254	19.09	9.20
3	276	20.74	14.99
4	259	19.46	18.76
5	189	14.20	17.11
6	119	8.94	12.93
7	62	4.66	7.86
8	51	3.83	7.39
9	25	1.88	4.07
10	16	1.20	2.90
11	7	0.53	1.39
12	4	0.30	0.87
13	2	0.15	0.47
14	1	0.07	0.25
17	1	0.07	0.31
19	1	0.07	0.84
Scituate, . . .	607	100.00	100.00
1	65	10.71	2.89
2	129	21.25	11.49
3	133	21.91	17.76
4	114	18.78	20.30
5	60	9.89	13.36
6	47	7.74	12.56
7	26	4.28	8.10
8	16	2.64	5.70
9	4	0.66	1.60
10	7	1.15	3.12
11	3	0.49	1.47
12	2	0.33	1.07
13	1	0.17	0.58
Wareham, . . .	891	100.00	100.00
1	90	10.10	2.67
2	197	22.11	11.70
3	194	21.77	17.29
4	139	15.60	16.51
5	103	11.56	15.30
6	68	7.63	12.12
7	47	5.28	9.77
8	20	2.24	4.75
9	15	1.68	4.01
10	10	1.12	2.97
11	2	0.23	0.65
12	3	0.34	1.07
13	2	0.23	0.77
14	1	0.11	0.42
West Bridgewater, .	409	100.00	100.00
1	25	6.11	1.43

COUNTIES, TOWNS, AND SIZE OF FAMILIES.	Number of Families	PERCENTAGES Total Families	PERCENTAGES Total Population
PLYMOUTH — Con.			
W. Bridgewater — Con.			
2	85	20.78	9.73
3	84	20.54	14.42
4	71	17.36	16.28
5	47	11.49	13.45
6	45	11.00	15.46
7	19	4.65	7.61
8	10	2.45	4.58
9	9	2.20	4.64
10	5	1.22	2.86
11	4	0.98	2.52
12	2	0.49	1.37
15	2	0.49	1.72
69	1	0.24	3.95
Whitman, . . .	1,389	100.00	100.00
1	49	3.53	0.85
2	269	19.87	9.37
3	302	21.74	15.77
4	287	20.66	19.99
5	194	13.97	16.89
6	125	9.00	13.06
7	62	4.46	7.55
8	51	3.67	7.10
9	21	1.51	3.29
10	16	1.15	2.78
11	4	0.29	0.77
12	3	0.22	0.63
13	1	0.07	0.23
16	2	0.15	0.56
21	1	0.07	0.36
22	1	0.07	0.38
21	1	0.07	0.42
SUFFOLK.			
Revere, ...	1,652	100.00	100.00
1	31	1.88	0.42
2	273	16.65	7.41
3	342	20.70	13.82
4	289	17.49	15.57
5	243	16.10	17.92
6	193	11.68	15.60
7	93	5.63	8.77
8	69	4.18	7.44
9	46	2.79	5.58
10	16	0.97	2.15
11	17	1.03	2.52
12	7	0.42	1.13
13	3	0.18	0.52
14	3	0.18	0.57
17	1	0.06	0.23
26	1	0.06	0.35
Winthrop, . . .	916	100.00	100.00
1	17	1.87	0.41
2	122	13.41	5.82
3	188	20.66	13.46
4	187	20.55	17.84

SIZE OF FAMILIES: FOR TOWNS — Continued.

COUNTIES, TOWNS, AND SIZE OF FAMILIES.	Number of Families	PERCENTAGES		COUNTIES, TOWNS, AND SIZE OF FAMILIES.	Number of Families	PERCENTAGES	
		Total Families	Total Population			Total Families	Total Population
SUFFOLK — Con.				WORCESTER — Con.			
Winthrop — Con.				Athol — Con.			
5	143	15.71	17.06	58	1	0.06	0.79
6	105	11.54	15.03	160	1	0.06	2.17
7	62	6.81	10.35	Auburn, . . .	345	100.00	100.00
8	40	4.39	7.63	1	15	4.35	0.94
9	16	1.76	3.44	2	49	14.20	6.13
10	11	1.21	2.62	3	65	18.84	12.20
11	10	1.10	2.62	4	60	17.39	15.02
12	1	0.11	0.29	5	51	14.78	15.96
13	3	0.33	0.93	6	34	9.86	12.77
14	1	0.11	0.33	7	32	9.27	14.02
15	1	0.11	0.36	8	16	4.64	8.01
16	1	0.11	0.38	9	9	2.61	5.07
18	1	0.11	0.43	10	6	1.74	3.75
42	1	0.11	1.00	11	4	1.16	2.75
WORCESTER.				12	1	0.29	0.75
Ashburnham, . .	530	100.00	100.00	13	2	0.58	1.63
1	29	5.47	1.35	16	1	0.29	1.00
2	118	22.26	10.99	Barre, ...	558	100.00	100.00
3	119	22.45	16.62	1	55	9.86	2.41
4	99	18.68	18.44	2	136	24.37	11.94
5	54	10.19	12.57	3	117	20.97	15.41
6	45	8.49	12.57	4	88	15.77	15.45
7	31	5.85	10.10	5	66	11.83	14.49
8	11	2.08	4.10	6	39	6.99	10.27
9	12	2.26	5.03	7	22	3.94	6.76
10	4	0.75	1.86	8	12	2.15	4.22
11	2	0.38	1.02	9	6	1.07	2.37
12	1	0.19	0.56	10	6	1.07	2.63
13	1	0.19	0.61	11	2	0.36	0.97
14	1	0.19	0.65	12	3	0.54	1.58
19	1	0.19	0.88	13	2	0.36	1.32
26	1	0.19	1.21	18	1	0.18	0.79
31	1	0.19	1.44	20	1	0.18	0.88
Athol, ...	1,750	100.00	100.00	60	1	0.18	2.63
1	108	6.17	1.47	134	1	0.18	5.88
2	340	19.43	9.23	Berlin, ...	225	100.00	100.00
3	391	22.34	15.93	1	18	8.00	2.01
4	337	19.26	18.31	2	57	25.33	12.71
5	218	12.46	14.80	3	35	15.55	11.70
6	143	8.17	11.65	4	38	16.89	16.95
7	77	4.40	7.32	5	29	12.89	16.16
8	55	3.14	5.98	6	18	8.00	12.04
9	31	1.77	3.79	7	10	4.44	7.80
10	20	1.14	2.72	8	9	4.00	8.03
11	7	0.40	1.05	9	5	2.22	5.02
12	8	0.45	1.30	10	3	1.33	3.34
13	5	0.28	0.88	11	1	0.45	1.23
15	1	0.06	0.20	13	1	0.45	1.45
17	2	0.11	0.36	14	1	0.45	1.56
21	1	0.06	0.28	Blackstone, . . .	1,266	100.00	100.00
22	1	0.06	0.30	1	43	3.39	0.71
29	1	0.06	0.39	2	199	15.72	6.59
31	1	0.06	0.42	3	228	18.01	11.33
44	1	0.06	0.56	4	233	18.40	15.43
				5	152	12.01	12.59

SIZE OF FAMILIES: FOR TOWNS — Continued.

COUNTIES, TOWNS, AND SIZE OF FAMILIES.	Number of Families	Total Families	Total Population
WORCESTER — Con.			
Blackstone — Con.			
6	135	10.03	13.41
7	109	8.61	12.64
8	72	5.69	9.54
9	32	2.53	4.77
10	29	2.29	4.80
11	14	1.10	2.55
12	5	0.39	0.99
13	6	0.47	1.29
14	2	0.16	0.46
15	2	0.16	0.50
20	1	0.08	0.33
25	1	0.08	0.41
26	1	0.08	0.43
33	1	0.08	0.55
41	1	0.08	0.78
Bolton, . .	206	100.00	100.00
1	13	6.31	1.63
2	46	22.33	11.54
3	42	20.39	15.81
4	46	22.33	23.09
5	22	10.68	13.80
6	14	6.79	10.54
7	11	5.34	9.66
8	4	1.34	4.02
9	4	1.34	4.52
10	2	0.97	2.51
11	1	0.49	1.58
12	1	0.49	1.50
Boylston, . . .	177	100.00	100.00
1	17	9.61	2.36
2	34	19.21	9.33
3	28	15.82	11.52
4	27	15.25	14.82
5	26	14.69	17.83
6	20	11.30	16.46
7	11	6.21	10.56
8	7	3.95	7.08
9	2	1.13	2.47
10	4	2.26	5.49
11	1	0.56	1.51
Brookfield, . . .	756	100.00	100.00
1	40	5.29	1.22
2	158	18.25	8.42
3	153	20.24	14.09
4	143	18.92	17.44
5	85	11.24	12.96
6	78	10.32	14.27
7	42	5.56	8.97
8	34	4.50	8.50
9	18	2.38	4.94
10	7	0.93	2.13
11	8	1.06	2.68
12	2	0.26	0.73
13	1	0.13	0.40
14	3	0.40	1.25

COUNTIES, TOWNS, AND SIZE OF FAMILIES.	Number of Families	Total Families	Total Population
WORCESTER — Con.			
Brookfield — Con.			
15	1	0.13	0.46
18	1	0.13	0.55
20	1	0.13	0.61
21	1	0.13	0.64
Charlton, . . .	470	100.00	100.00
1	25	5.32	1.53
2	105	22.34	11.19
3	105	22.34	16.78
4	86	18.30	18.53
5	56	11.91	14.92
6	38	8.09	12.15
7	22	4.68	8.20
8	9	1.91	2.84
9	12	2.55	5.75
10	4	0.85	2.13
11	2	0.43	1.17
12	3	0.64	1.92
13	2	0.43	1.58
17	1	0.21	0.91
Clinton, ...	2,278	100.00	100.00
1	55	2.42	0.48
2	321	14.10	5.58
3	372	16.33	9.71
4	423	18.57	14.72
5	331	14.53	14.39
6	260	11.42	15.57
7	173	7.60	10.53
8	127	5.58	8.84
9	82	3.60	6.42
10	66	2.90	5.74
11	28	1.23	2.68
12	11	0.49	1.15
13	8	0.35	0.90
14	5	0.22	0.97
16	1	0.04	0.14
19	1	0.04	0.17
22	1	0.04	0.19
24	1	0.04	0.21
26	1	0.04	0.23
28	1	0.04	0.24
36	1	0.04	0.31
38	2	0.09	0.66
42	1	0.04	0.37
53	1	0.04	0.46
66	1	0.04	0.57
88	1	0.04	0.77
Dana, ...	196	100.00	100.00
1	24	12.24	3.35
2	48	24.49	13.39
3	40	20.41	16.74
4	26	13.27	14.50
5	28	14.29	19.52
6	7	3.57	5.86
7	9	4.59	8.79
8	4	2.04	4.46

SIZE OF FAMILIES: FOR TOWNS — Continued.

COUNTIES, TOWNS, AND SIZE OF FAMILIES.	Number of Families	PERCENTAGES		COUNTIES, TOWNS, AND SIZE OF FAMILIES.	Number of Families	PERCENTAGES	
		Total Families	Total Population			Total Families	Total Population
WORCESTER — Con.				WORCESTER — Con.			
Dana — Con.				Grafton — Con.			
9	6	3.06	7.53	2	190	17.18	7.45
10	2	1.02	2.79	3	188	17.00	11.06
11	2	1.02	3.07	4	176	15.91	13.80
Douglas, . . .	483	100.00	100.00	5	156	14.11	15.29
1	38	7.87	1.88	6	109	9.86	12.82
2	90	18.63	8.88	7	101	9.13	13.86
3	98	20.29	14.51	8	45	4.07	7.06
4	76	15.73	15.00	9	38	3.44	6.70
5	70	14.49	17.28	10	20	1.81	3.92
6	33	6.83	9.77	11	10	0.90	2.16
7	29	6.01	10.02	12	6	0.54	1.41
8	28	5.80	11.06	13	2	0.18	0.51
9	6	1.24	2.67	14	2	0.18	0.55
10	6	1.24	2.96	15	4	0.36	1.18
11	6	1.24	3.26	18	2	0.18	0.70
13	1	0.21	0.64	22	1	0.09	0.43
15	1	0.21	0.74	Hardwick, . . .	533	100.00	100.00
27	1	0.21	1.33	1	18	3.38	0.68
Dudley, . . .	628	100.00	100.00	2	69	12.94	5.20
1	19	3.03	0.59	3	93	17.45	10.51
2	75	11.94	4.68	4	87	16.32	13.11
3	100	15.92	9.37	5	74	13.88	13.94
4	107	17.04	13.36	6	59	11.07	13.33
5	88	14.01	13.74	7	55	10.32	14.50
6	71	11.30	13.39	8	24	4.50	7.23
7	50	7.96	10.93	9	22	4.12	7.46
8	43	6.85	10.74	10	16	3.00	6.03
9	40	6.37	11.24	11	7	1.31	2.90
10	19	3.03	5.93	12	2	0.38	0.90
11	9	1.43	3.09	13	2	0.38	0.98
12	1	0.16	0.38	14	2	0.38	1.05
13	2	0.32	0.84	15	1	0.19	0.56
14	3	0.48	1.31	17	1	0.19	0.64
17	1	0.16	0.53	26	1	0.19	0.98
Gardner, . . .	2,062	100.00	100.00	Harvard, . . .	279	100.00	100.00
1	61	2.96	0.67	1	16	5.73	1.38
2	338	16.39	7.36	2	56	20.07	9.64
3	427	20.71	13.95	3	62	22.22	16.01
4	388	18.82	16.90	4	53	19.00	18.25
5	321	15.57	17.48	5	34	12.19	14.63
6	182	8.82	11.89	6	17	6.09	8.78
7	141	6.84	10.76	7	18	6.45	10.84
8	86	4.17	7.49	8	12	4.30	8.26
9	52	2.52	5.10	9	4	1.43	3.10
10	32	1.55	3.43	10	1	0.36	0.86
11	15	0.73	1.80	11	2	0.72	1.89
12	6	0.29	0.78	12	1	0.36	1.03
13	5	0.24	0.71	14	1	0.36	1.29
15	3	0.14	0.49	24	2	0.72	4.13
16	1	0.05	0.17	Holden, . . .	555	100.00	100.00
21	1	0.05	0.23	1	36	6.49	1.38
22	2	0.10	0.48	2	90	16.22	6.92
24	1	0.05	0.26	3	88	15.85	10.15
Grafton, . . .	1,106	100.00	100.00	4	90	16.22	13.84
1	56	5.06	1.10	5	74	13.33	14.22

SIZE OF FAMILIES: FOR TOWNS — Continued.

COUNTIES, TOWNS, AND SIZE OF FAMILIES.	Number of Families	PERCENTAGES		COUNTIES, TOWNS, AND SIZE OF FAMILIES.	Number of Families	PERCENTAGES	
		Total Families	Total Population			Total Families	Total Population
WORCESTER — Con.				WORCESTER — Con.			
Holden — Con.				Leicester, . . .	731	100.00	100.00
6	46	8.29	10.61	1	34	4.65	1.05
7	48	8.65	12.91	2	115	15.73	7.10
8	36	6.49	11.07	3	140	19.15	12.97
9	21	3.78	7.26	4	141	19.29	17.41
10	11	1.98	4.23	5	110	15.05	16.98
11	7	1.26	2.96	6	75	10.26	15.80
12	3	0.54	1.38	7	38	5.20	8.21
13	1	0.18	0.50	8	31	4.24	7.66
14	3	0.54	1.61	9	18	2.46	5.00
25	1	0.18	0.96	10	17	2.33	5.25
Hopedale, . . .	307	100.00	100.00	11	6	0.82	2.04
1	12	3.91	0.87	12	3	0.41	1.11
2	59	19.22	8.57	13	1	0.14	0.40
3	50	16.29	10.90	15	2	0.27	0.93
4	63	20.52	18.39	Leominster, . . .	2,181	100.00	100.00
5	38	12.38	13.80	1	92	4.22	1.00
6	36	11.73	15.09	2	417	19.12	9.06
7	23	7.49	11.69	3	477	21.87	15.54
8	14	4.56	8.33	4	396	18.16	17.20
9	3	0.98	1.98	5	288	13.20	15.63
10	5	1.63	3.63	6	207	9.49	13.48
11	2	0.65	1.60	7	121	5.55	9.20
21	1	0.32	1.74	8	89	4.08	7.73
43	1	0.32	3.12	9	36	1.65	3.52
Hubbardston, . .	348	100.00	100.00	10	20	0.92	2.17
1	35	10.06	2.75	11	16	0.73	1.91
2	78	22.41	12.24	12	7	0.32	0.91
3	80	22.99	18.84	13	4	0.18	0.57
4	55	15.80	17.27	14	2	0.09	0.50
5	46	13.22	18.05	15	1	0.05	0.16
6	22	6.32	10.36	16	1	0.05	0.17
7	18	5.17	9.89	17	2	0.09	0.37
8	5	1.44	3.14	19	2	0.09	0.41
9	4	1.15	2.83	20	2	0.09	0.43
10	2	0.57	1.57	22	1	0.05	0.24
12	1	0.29	0.94	Lunenburg, . . .	302	100.00	100.00
13	1	0.29	1.02	1	17	5.63	1.37
14	1	0.29	1.10	2	65	21.52	10.51
Lancaster, . . .	452	100.00	100.00	3	65	21.52	15.76
1	22	4.87	1.01	4	51	16.89	16.49
2	87	19.25	7.98	5	37	12.25	14.96
3	83	18.36	11.42	6	26	8.61	12.61
4	83	18.36	15.23	7	14	4.64	7.92
5	59	13.06	13.53	8	13	4.31	8.41
6	48	10.62	13.21	9	5	1.66	3.64
7	29	6.42	9.31	10	3	0.99	2.43
8	18	3.98	6.61	11	3	0.99	2.67
9	9	1.99	3.72	12	2	0.66	1.94
10	5	1.11	2.30	16	1	0.33	1.29
11	3	0.66	1.51	Mendon, . . .	234	100.00	100.00
15	1	0.22	0.69	1	21	8.97	2.36
16	1	0.22	0.73	2	51	21.79	11.48
19	1	0.22	0.87	3	50	21.37	16.87
48	1	0.22	2.20	4	35	14.96	15.75
71	1	0.22	3.26	5	35	14.96	19.69
140	1	0.22	6.42				

SIZE OF FAMILIES: FOR TOWNS — Continued.

COUNTIES, TOWNS, AND SIZE OF FAMILIES.	Number of Families	Total Families	Total Population
WORCESTER — Con.			
Mendon — Con.			
6	15	6.41	10.12
7	15	6.41	11.81
8	6	2.56	5.40
9	5	2.14	5.06
13	1	0.43	1.46
Milford, . . .	2,116	100.00	100.00
1	114	5.39	1.27
2	395	18.67	8.82
3	453	21.41	15.17
4	390	18.43	17.41
5	265	12.52	14.79
6	202	9.55	13.53
7	119	5.62	9.30
8	84	3.97	7.50
9	37	1.75	3.72
10	22	1.04	2.45
11	14	0.66	1.72
12	4	0.19	0.54
13	1	0.05	0.14
14	3	0.14	0.47
15	3	0.14	0.50
16	2	0.09	0.36
17	3	0.14	0.57
19	2	0.09	0.42
26	1	0.05	0.29
41	1	0.05	0.46
51	1	0.05	0.57
Millbury, . . .	1,100	100.00	100.00
1	40	3.64	0.76
2	178	16.18	6.82
3	290	18.18	11.49
4	211	19.18	16.16
5	153	13.91	14.65
6	140	9.09	11.49
7	71	6.36	9.52
8	45	4.09	6.89
9	45	4.09	7.75
10	32	2.91	6.13
11	12	1.09	2.53
12	5	0.46	1.15
13	3	0.27	0.75
14	2	0.18	0.54
18	1	0.09	0.34
62	1	0.09	1.19
96	1	0.09	1.84
New Braintree, . .	114	100.00	100.00
1	4	3.51	0.74
2	16	14.03	5.90
3	14	12.28	7.75
4	27	23.68	19.92
5	19	16.67	17.53
6	13	11.40	14.39
7	6	5.26	7.75
8	4	3.51	5.90
9	8	7.02	15.28
WORCESTER — Con.			
New Braintree — Con.			
10	1	0.88	1.85
11	1	0.88	2.03
16	1	0.88	2.95
Northborough, . .	451	100.00	100.00
1	26	5.77	1.34
2	72	15.96	7.42
3	99	21.95	15.31
4	78	17.30	16.08
5	63	13.97	16.24
6	39	8.65	12.06
7	32	7.10	11.55
8	19	4.21	7.84
9	13	2.88	6.03
10	3	0.67	1.55
11	2	0.44	1.13
12	1	0.22	0.62
13	2	0.44	1.34
14	1	0.22	0.72
15	1	0.22	0.77
Northbridge, . .	1,070	100.00	100.00
1	39	3.65	0.74
2	145	13.55	5.49
3	198	18.51	11.24
4	159	14.86	12.03
5	152	14.21	14.38
6	125	11.68	14.19
7	91	8.51	12.05
8	68	6.36	10.29
9	41	3.83	6.98
10	15	1.40	2.84
11	20	1.87	4.16
12	5	0.47	1.13
13	3	0.28	0.74
14	1	0.09	0.26
16	3	0.28	0.91
17	1	0.09	0.32
20	1	0.09	0.38
22	1	0.09	0.42
33	1	0.09	0.62
44	1	0.09	0.83
North Brookfield, .	1,050	100.00	100.00
1	44	4.27	0.95
2	197	19.13	8.50
3	184	17.86	11.91
4	154	14.95	13.29
5	147	14.27	15.86
6	100	9.71	12.94
7	98	9.51	14.80
8	46	4.46	7.94
9	26	2.52	5.05
10	15	1.46	3.24
11	8	0.78	1.90
12	3	0.29	0.78
13	3	0.29	0.84
14	1	0.10	0.30

SIZE OF FAMILIES: FOR TOWNS — Continued.

COUNTIES, TOWNS, AND SIZE OF FAMILIES.	Number of Families	PERCENTAGES Total Families	PERCENTAGES Total Population
WORCESTER — Con.			
No. Brookfield — Con.			
15	1	0.10	0.32
16	1	0.10	0.34
23	1	0.10	0.50
25	1	0.10	0.54
Oakham, . . .	161	100.00	100.00
1	18	11.18	2.98
2	28	17.39	9.26
3	35	21.74	17.35
4	25	15.53	16.53
5	27	16.77	22.31
6	17	10.56	16.86
7	4	2.48	4.63
8	6	3.73	7.93
13	1	0.62	2.15
Oxford, . . .	618	100.00	100.00
1	53	8.58	2.22
2	157	25.40	13.14
3	117	18.93	14.69
4	103	16.67	17.24
5	67	10.84	14.02
6	44	7.12	11.04
7	28	4.53	8.20
8	16	2.59	5.35
9	14	2.27	5.27
10	8	1.29	3.35
11	6	0.97	2.76
12	3	0.49	1.51
14	1	0.16	0.58
15	1	0.16	0.63
Paxton, . . .	114	100.00	100.00
1	5	4.38	1.17
2	25	21.93	11.74
3	28	24.56	19.72
4	29	25.44	27.23
5	10	8.77	11.74
6	7	6.14	9.86
7	5	4.39	8.22
8	3	2.63	5.63
9	1	0.88	2.11
11	1	0.88	2.58
Petersham, . . .	254	100.00	100.00
1	25	9.84	2.63
2	56	22.05	11.76
3	64	25.20	20.17
4	36	14.17	15.13
5	30	11.81	15.76
6	16	6.30	10.08
7	12	4.73	8.82
8	6	2.36	5.04
9	5	1.97	4.73
12	3	1.18	3.78
20	1	0.39	2.10
Phillipston, . . .	114	100.00	100.00
1	2	1.75	0.44
2	35	30.70	15.22

COUNTIES, TOWNS, AND SIZE OF FAMILIES.	Number of Families	PERCENTAGES Total Families	PERCENTAGES Total Population
WORCESTER — Con.			
Phillipston — Con.			
3	25	21.93	16.30
4	17	14.92	14.78
5	7	6.14	7.61
6	9	7.90	11.74
7	8	7.02	12.17
8	5	4.39	8.70
9	2	1.75	3.91
10	2	1.75	4.35
11	2	1.75	4.78
Princeton, . . .	236	100.00	100.00
1	16	6.78	1.68
2	50	21.19	10.50
3	54	22.88	17.02
4	39	16.53	16.39
5	20	8.47	10.50
6	23	9.75	14.50
7	16	6.78	11.76
8	6	2.54	5.04
9	3	1.27	2.84
10	6	2.54	6.30
11	3	1.27	3.47
Royalston, . . .	254	100.00	100.00
1	19	7.48	2.15
2	62	24.41	13.93
3	66	25.98	22.25
4	45	17.72	20.22
5	26	10.23	14.61
6	21	8.27	14.16
7	10	3.94	7.87
8	2	0.79	1.80
9	3	1.18	3.03
Rutland, . . .	225	100.00	100.00
1	15	6.67	1.53
2	44	19.56	9.00
3	30	13.33	9.20
4	40	17.78	16.36
5	38	16.89	19.43
6	19	8.45	11.66
7	18	8.00	12.88
8	10	4.44	8.18
9	4	1.78	3.68
10	3	1.33	3.07
11	1	0.44	1.13
12	2	0.89	2.45
14	1	0.44	1.43
Shrewsbury, . . .	381	100.00	100.00
1	29	7.61	1.90
2	81	21.26	10.63
3	73	19.16	14.37
4	67	17.59	17.59
5	49	12.86	16.08
6	30	7.87	11.81
7	26	6.83	11.94
8	10	2.63	5.25
9	10	2.63	5.91

SIZE OF FAMILIES: FOR TOWNS — Continued.

COUNTIES, TOWNS, AND SIZE OF FAMILIES.	Number of Families	PERCENTAGES Total Families	PERCENTAGES Total Population
WORCESTER — Con.			
Shrewsbury — Con.			
10	2	0.52	1.31
11	2	0.52	1.44
13	1	0.26	0.85
14	1	0.26	0.92
Southborough,	442	100.00	100.00
1	22	4.97	0.99
2	85	19.23	7.65
3	89	20.13	12.01
4	74	16.74	13.82
5	47	10.63	10.57
6	52	11.76	14.04
7	27	6.11	8.50
8	11	2.49	3.96
9	12	2.71	4.86
10	5	1.13	2.25
11	1	0.23	0.49
12	1	0.23	0.54
13	3	0.68	1.75
14	1	0.23	0.63
15	1	0.23	0.67
17	2	0.45	1.53
18	3	0.68	2.43
20	1	0.23	0.90
21	2	0.45	1.89
55	1	0.23	2.47
62	1	0.23	2.79
128	1	0.23	5.76
Southbridge,	1,688	100.00	100.00
1	63	3.73	0.76
2	240	14.22	5.82
3	308	18.25	11.20
4	267	15.82	12.95
5	202	11.97	12.24
6	196	11.61	14.26
7	155	9.18	13.15
8	93	5.51	9.02
9	61	3.61	6.66
10	51	3.02	6.18
11	28	1.66	3.73
12	13	0.77	1.89
13	3	0.18	0.47
14	4	0.23	0.68
16	1	0.06	0.19
24	2	0.12	0.51
24	1	0.06	0.29
Spencer,	1,625	100.00	100.00
1	55	3.39	0.72
2	246	15.14	6.46
3	328	20.18	12.92
4	271	16.68	14.24
5	217	13.35	14.25
6	164	10.09	12.92
7	126	7.75	11.59
8	86	5.29	9.04
9	61	3.75	7.21

COUNTIES, TOWNS, AND SIZE OF FAMILIES.	Number of Families	PERCENTAGES Total Families	PERCENTAGES Total Population
WORCESTER — Con.			
Spencer — Con.			
10	37	2.28	4.86
11	11	0.68	1.59
12	13	0.80	2.05
13	3	0.19	0.51
14	3	0.19	0.55
15	1	0.06	0.20
19	1	0.06	0.25
20	1	0.06	0.26
29	1	0.06	0.38
Sterling,	342	100.00	100.00
1	39	11.41	3.20
2	80	23.39	13.14
3	80	23.39	19.71
4	62	18.13	20.36
5	26	7.60	19.67
6	22	6.43	10.84
7	13	3.80	7.47
8	9	2.63	5.91
9	7	2.05	5.17
10	3	0.88	2.46
13	1	0.29	1.07
Sturbridge,	434	100.00	100.00
1	26	5.99	1.36
2	86	19.82	9.01
3	81	18.67	12.72
4	69	15.90	14.45
5	56	12.90	14.66
6	27	6.22	8.48
7	30	6.91	10.99
8	21	4.84	8.80
9	21	4.84	9.90
10	8	1.84	4.19
11	6	1.38	3.45
12	2	0.46	1.26
14	1	0.23	0.73
Sutton,	714	100.00	100.00
1	33	4.62	0.96
2	130	18.21	7.60
3	118	16.53	10.35
4	107	14.99	12.51
5	92	12.89	13.45
6	80	11.20	14.04
7	57	7.98	11.67
8	27	3.78	6.32
9	22	3.08	5.79
10	17	2.38	4.97
11	13	1.82	4.18
12	8	1.12	2.81
13	6	0.84	2.28
14	2	0.28	0.82
31	1	0.14	0.91
46	1	0.14	1.34
Templeton,	718	100.00	100.00
1	39	5.43	1.34
2	172	23.96	11.80

SIZE OF FAMILIES: FOR TOWNS — Continued.

COUNTIES, TOWNS, AND SIZE OF FAMILIES.	Number of Families	PERCENTAGES Total Families	PERCENTAGES Total Population
WORCESTER — Con.			
Templeton — Con.			
3	169	23.54	17.30
4	126	17.55	17.29
5	87	12.12	14.92
6	48	6.68	9.88
7	26	3.62	6.24
8	20	2.78	5.49
9	13	1.81	4.01
10	7	0.97	2.40
11	3	0.42	1.13
12	1	0.14	0.41
13	1	0.14	0.45
14	1	0.14	0.48
15	2	0.28	1.03
18	1	0.14	0.62
20	1	0.14	0.69
129	1	0.14	4.45
Upton, . . .	524	100.00	100.00
1	46	8.78	2.14
2	120	22.90	11.16
3	124	23.66	17.30
4	90	17.18	16.74
5	62	11.83	14.42
6	37	7.06	10.33
7	18	3.44	5.86
8	9	1.72	3.35
9	9	1.72	3.77
10	1	0.19	0.47
11	1	0.19	0.51
14	1	0.19	0.65
18	1	0.19	0.84
20	1	0.19	0.93
25	1	0.19	1.16
28	1	0.19	1.30
31	1	0.19	1.44
161	1	0.19	7.65
Uxbridge, . . .	812	100.00	100.00
1	37	4.56	1.04
2	162	19.95	9.14
3	138	17.00	11.68
4	154	18.97	17.37
5	108	13.30	15.23
6	79	9.73	13.37
7	44	5.42	8.68
8	46	5.66	10.38
9	20	2.46	5.08
10	11	1.35	3.10
11	4	0.49	1.24
12	4	0.49	1.35
13	1	0.12	0.37
14	2	0.25	0.79
21	2	0.25	1.18
Warren, . . .	980	100.00	100.00
1	30	3.06	0.68
2	152	15.51	6.86
3	213	21.74	14.43

COUNTIES, TOWNS, AND SIZE OF FAMILIES.	Number of Families	PERCENTAGES Total Families	PERCENTAGES Total Population
WORCESTER — Con.			
Warren — Con.			
4	180	18.37	16.25
5	132	13.47	14.90
6	102	10.41	13.81
7	66	6.74	10.43
8	41	4.18	7.40
9	37	3.78	7.52
10	10	1.02	2.26
11	5	0.51	1.24
12	6	0.61	1.63
13	1	0.10	0.29
14	1	0.10	0.32
16	1	0.10	0.36
21	1	0.10	0.47
22	1	0.10	0.50
29	1	0.10	0.65
Webster, . . .	1,716	100.00	100.00
1	90	5.24	1.15
2	256	14.92	6.56
3	345	20.10	13.27
4	307	17.89	15.75
5	210	12.24	13.46
6	194	11.30	14.93
7	116	6.76	10.41
8	83	4.84	8.51
9	62	3.61	7.16
10	24	1.40	3.08
11	15	0.87	2.12
12	7	0.41	1.08
17	1	0.06	0.22
19	1	0.06	0.24
22	1	0.06	0.28
23	1	0.06	0.29
32	1	0.06	0.41
34	1	0.06	0.44
50	1	0.06	0.64
Westborough, . . .	1,031	100.00	100.00
1	63	6.11	1.20
2	198	19.21	7.56
3	230	22.31	13.18
4	185	17.94	14.14
5	145	14.06	13.85
6	78	7.57	8.94
7	65	6.30	8.69
8	25	2.42	3.82
9	20	1.94	3.44
10	10	0.97	1.91
11	2	0.19	0.42
12	1	0.10	0.23
13	1	0.10	0.25
14	2	0.19	0.53
19	2	0.19	0.73
25	1	0.10	0.48
27	1	0.10	0.52
301	1	0.10	5.75
752	1	0.10	14.36

SIZE OF FAMILIES: FOR TOWNS — Concluded.

COUNTIES, TOWNS, AND SIZE OF FAMILIES.	Number of Families	PERCENTAGES		COUNTIES, TOWNS, AND SIZE OF FAMILIES.	Number of Families	PERCENTAGES	
		Total Families	Total Population			Total Families	Total Population
WORCESTER — Con.				WORCESTER — Con.			
West Boylston, . .	648	100.00	100.00	Westminster — Con.			
1	37	5.71	1.25	2	107	28.92	16.27
2	107	16.51	7.21	3	73	19.73	16.65
3	119	18.36	12.03	4	69	18.65	20.99
4	106	16.36	14.29	5	38	10.27	14.45
5	84	12.96	14.15	6	21	5.68	9.58
6	71	10.96	14.35	7	15	4.05	7.99
7	51	7.87	12.03	8	8	2.16	4.87
8	31	4.78	8.36	9	4	1 08	2.74
9	17	2.62	5.15	10	2	0.54	1.52
10	7	1.08	2.36	11	2	0.54	1.67
11	7	1.08	2.59	13	1	0.27	0.99
12	6	0.92	2.42	Winchendon, . .	1,078	100.00	100.00
13	2	0.31	0.88	1	60	5.57	1.34
14	1	0.16	0.47	2	215	19.94	9.58
18	1	0.16	0.61	3	242	22.45	16.17
55	1	0.16	1.85	4	185	17.16	16.48
West Brookfield, . .	409	100.00	100.00	5	129	11.97	14.36
1	41	10.02	2.80	6	99	9.18	13.23
2	108	26.41	14.72	7	57	5.29	8.89
3	76	18.58	15.54	8	45	4.18	8.02
4	64	15.65	17.45	9	15	1.39	3.01
5	55	13.45	18.75	10	12	1.11	2.67
6	31	7.58	12.08	11	5	0.46	1.23
7	18	4.40	8.59	12	2	0.19	0.53
8	8	1.96	4.36	13	5	0.46	1.45
9	6	1.47	3.68	14	2	0.19	0.62
10	1	0.24	0.68	17	1	0.09	0.38
11	1	0.24	0.75	19	1	0.09	0.42
Westminster, . .	370	100.00	100.00	23	2	0.19	1.02
1	30	8.11	2.28	27	1	0.09	0.60

SIZE OF FAMILIES AND COMPOSITION BY SEX: FOR CITIES.

COUNTIES, CITIES, SIZE OF FAMILIES, AND NUMBER OF EACH SIZE.	Composition of Families	Number of Families	Total Families	Total Population
BERKSHIRE.				
NORTH ADAMS, .	-	3,961	100.00	100.00
(93) 1	1 M	40	2.36	0.49
	1 F	53		
(550) 2	1 M 1 F	492	13.99	5.75
	2 M	6		
	2 F	52		
(646) 3	1 M 2 F	333	16.43	10.13
	2 M 1 F	268		
	3 M	6		
	3 F	39		
(722) 4	1 M 3 F	229	18.36	15.09
	2 M 2 F	351		
	3 M 1 F	144		
	4 M	1		
	4 F	17		
(616) 5	1 M 4 F	91	15.67	16.10
	2 M 3 F	220		
	3 M 2 F	213		
	4 M 1 F	67		
	5 M	3		
	5 F	3		
(432) 6	1 M 5 F	28	10.99	13.54
	2 M 4 F	121		
	3 M 3 F	141		
	4 M 2 F	104		
	5 M 1 F	34		
	6 F	4		
(348) 7	1 M 6 F	12	8.85	12.73
	2 M 5 F	64		
	3 M 4 F	105		
	4 M 3 F	90		
	5 M 2 F	55		
	6 M 1 F	15		
(224) 8	1 M 7 F	7	5.70	9.36
	2 M 6 F	14		
	3 M 5 F	50		
	4 M 4 F	56		
	5 M 3 F	58		
	6 M 2 F	32		
	7 M 1 F	7		
(126) 9	2 M 7 F	12	3.20	5.93
	3 M 6 F	15		
	4 M 5 F	25		
	5 M 4 F	37		
	6 M 3 F	22		
	7 M 2 F	12		
	8 M 1 F	3		

COUNTIES, CITIES, SIZE OF FAMILIES, AND NUMBER OF EACH SIZE.	Composition of Families	Number of Families	Total Families	Total Population
BERKSHIRE —Con.				
NO. ADAMS —Con.				
(73) 10	2 M 8 F	2	1.86	3.81
	3 M 7 F	11		
	4 M 6 F	14		
	5 M 5 F	15		
	6 M 4 F	16		
	7 M 3 F	11		
	8 M 2 F	4		
(53) 11	2 M 9 F	1	1.55	3.05
	3 M 8 F	3		
	4 M 7 F	8		
	5 M 6 F	12		
	6 M 5 F	11		
	7 M 4 F	13		
	8 M 3 F	1		
	9 M 2 F	3		
	11 F	1		
(17) 12	4 M 8 F	2	0.43	1.07
	5 M 7 F	2		
	6 M 6 F	3		
	7 M 5 F	3		
	8 M 4 F	3		
	9 M 3 F	3		
	11 M 1 F	1		
(14) 13	5 M 8 F	5	0.35	0.95
	6 M 7 F	2		
	7 M 6 F	2		
	8 M 5 F	3		
	11 M 2 F	1		
	13 F	1		
(3) 14	6 M 8 F	1	0.08	0.22
	7 M 7 F	1		
	11 M 3 F	1		
(2) 15	4 M 11 F	1	0.05	0.16
	11 M 4 F	1		
(3) 16	5 M 11 F	1	0.08	0.25
	7 M 9 F	1		
	10 M 6 F	1		
(1) 21	18 M 3 F	1	0.03	0.11
(3) 22	12 M 10 F	1	0.08	0.34
	16 M 6 F	1		
	17 M 5 F	1		
(1) 25	2 M 23 F	1	0.03	0.13
(2) 37	21 M 16 F	1	0.05	0.39
	26 M 11 F	1		
(1) 38	16 M 22 F	1	0.03	0.20
(1) 39	20 M 19 F	1	0.03	0.20

SIZE OF FAMILIES AND COMPOSITION BY SEX: FOR CITIES — Continued.

COUNTIES, CITIES, SIZE OF FAMILIES, AND NUMBER OF EACH SIZE.	Composition of Families	Number of Families	PERCENTAGES: EACH SIZE OF — Total Families	Total Population
BERKSHIRE — Con.				
PITTSFIELD, . .	-	4,342	100.00	100.00
(114) 1	1 M	60	3.32	0.70
	1 F	84		
(640) 2	1 M 1 F	533	14.74	6.26
	2 M	22		
	2 F	85		
(852) 3	1 M 2 F	438	19.62	12.49
	2 M 1 F	357		
	3 M	7		
	3 F	50		
(754) 4	1 M 3 F	229	17.37	14.74
	2 M 2 F	358		
	3 M 1 F	146		
	4 M	3		
	4 F	18		
(641) 5	1 M 4 F	108	14.76	15.66
	2 M 3 F	255		
	3 M 2 F	209		
	4 M 1 F	62		
	5 M	1		
	5 F	6		
(489) 6	1 M 5 F	57	11.26	14.34
	2 M 4 F	103		
	3 M 3 F	179		
	4 M 2 F	123		
	5 M 1 F	26		
	6 F	1		
(297) 7	1 M 6 F	8	6.84	10.16
	2 M 5 F	40		
	3 M 4 F	106		
	4 M 3 F	90		
	5 M 2 F	39		
	6 M 1 F	14		
(199) 8	1 M 7 F	6	4.59	7.78
	2 M 6 F	18		
	3 M 5 F	47		
	4 M 4 F	72		
	5 M 3 F	40		
	6 M 2 F	11		
	7 M 1 F	4		
	8 F	1		
(140) 9	1 M 8 F	1	3.23	6.16
	2 M 7 F	15		
	3 M 6 F	19		
	4 M 5 F	57		
	5 M 4 F	36		
	6 M 3 F	19		
	7 M 2 F	11		
	8 M 1 F	2		
(95) 10	2 M 8 F	2	2.19	4.64
	3 M 7 F	12		
	4 M 6 F	15		
	5 M 5 F	22		
	6 M 4 F	19		
	7 M 3 F	19		

COUNTIES, CITIES, SIZE OF FAMILIES, AND NUMBER OF EACH SIZE.	Composition of Families	Number of Families	PERCENTAGES: EACH SIZE OF — Total Families	Total Population
BERKSHIRE — Con.				
PITTSFIELD - Con.				
	8 M 2 F	4		
	9 M 1 F	1		
	10 M	1		
(34) 11	2 M 9 F	1	0.78	1.83
	3 M 8 F	8		
	4 M 7 F	4		
	5 M 6 F	9		
	6 M 5 F	5		
	7 M 4 F	2		
	8 M 3 F	4		
	9 M 2 F	1		
(15) 12	2 M 10 F	2	0.35	0.88
	3 M 9 F	1		
	4 M 8 F	1		
	5 M 7 F	1		
	6 M 6 F	5		
	7 M 5 F	3		
	8 M 4 F	2		
(11) 13	5 M 8 F	2	0.26	0.70
	6 M 7 F	3		
	7 M 6 F	1		
	9 M 4 F	1		
	10 M 3 F	3		
	13 M	1		
(6) 14	4 M 10 F	1	0.14	0.41
	5 M 9 F	1		
	8 M 6 F	1		
	9 M 5 F	1		
	10 M 4 F	1		
	12 M 2 F	1		
(4) 15	6 M 9 F	1	0.09	0.29
	7 M 8 F	1		
	9 M 6 F	1		
	11 M 4 F	1		
(3) 16	7 M 9 F	2	0.07	0.23
	12 M 4 F	1		
(1) 17	9 M 8 F	1	0.02	0.08
(1) 18	6 M 12 F	1	0.02	0.09
(4) 19	14 M 5 F	2	0.09	0.37
	15 M 4 F	1		
	19 F	1		
(1) 20	17 M 3 F	1	0.02	0.10
(2) 21	17 M 4 F	1	0.05	0.21
	18 M 3 F	1		
(1) 22	17 M 5 F	1	0.02	0.11
(1) 24	24 F	1	0.02	0.12
(2) 34	22 M 12 F	1	0.05	0.33
	25 M 9 F	1		
(1) 36	21 M 15 F	1	0.02	0.18
(1) 37	18 M 19 F	1	0.02	0.18
(1) 51	30 M 21 F	1	0.02	0.25
(1) 70	12 M 58 F	1	0.02	0.34
(1) 75	68 M 7 F	1	0.02	0.37

SIZE OF FAMILIES AND COMPOSITION BY SEX: FOR CITIES — Continued.

COUNTIES, CITIES, SIZE OF FAMILIES, AND NUMBER OF EACH SIZE.	Composition of Families	Number of Families	PERCENTAGES: EACH SIZE OF —	
			Total Families	Total Population
BRISTOL.				
FALL RIVER, . .		- 17,948	100.00	100.00
(511) 1	1 M	162	2.85	0.57
	1 F	349		
(2,539) 2	1 M 1 F	2,100	14.15	5.69
	2 M	56		
	2 F	383		
(3,029) 3	1 M 2 F	1,506	16.88	10.19
	2 M 1 F	1,292		
	3 M	25		
	3 F	206		
(2,927) 4	1 M 3 F	837	16.31	13.13
	2 M 2 F	1,412		
	3 M 1 F	572		
	4 M	12		
	4 F	94		
(2,582) 5	1 M 4 F	429	14.39	14.47
	2 M 3 F	952		
	3 M 2 F	880		
	4 M 1 F	278		
	5 M	5		
	5 F	38		
(2,086) 6	1 M 5 F	191	11.63	14.05
	2 M 4 F	515		
	3 M 3 F	761		
	4 M 2 F	471		
	5 M 1 F	125		
	6 M	5		
	6 F	18		
(1,490) 7	1 M 6 F	70	8.30	11.69
	2 M 5 F	272		
	3 M 4 F	446		
	4 M 3 F	448		
	5 M 2 F	207		
	6 M 1 F	42		
	7 M	2		
	7 F	3		
(1,091) 8	1 M 7 F	28	6.08	9.79
	2 M 6 F	115		
	3 M 5 F	254		
	4 M 4 F	357		
	5 M 3 F	227		
	6 M 2 F	95		
	7 M 1 F	33		
	8 M	2		
(715) 9	1 M 8 F	8	3.99	7.21
	2 M 7 F	35		
	3 M 6 F	136		
	4 M 5 F	177		
	5 M 4 F	187		
	6 M 3 F	121		
	7 M 2 F	37		
	8 M 1 F	12		
	9 M	1		
	9 F	1		
(419) 10	1 M 9 F	3	2.34	4.70
	2 M 8 F	18		

COUNTIES, CITIES, SIZE OF FAMILIES, AND NUMBER OF EACH SIZE.	Composition of Families	Number of Families	PERCENTAGES: EACH SIZE OF —	
			Total Families	Total Population
BRISTOL — Con.				
FALL RIVER - Con.				
	3 M 7 F	43		
	4 M 6 F	89		
	5 M 5 F	123		
	6 M 4 F	77		
	7 M 3 F	42		
	8 M 2 F	18		
	9 M 1 F	5		
	10 F	1		
(267) 11	1 M 10 F	2	1.49	3.29
	2 M 9 F	8		
	3 M 8 F	16		
	4 M 7 F	45		
	5 M 6 F	51		
	6 M 5 F	65		
	7 M 4 F	49		
	8 M 3 F	21		
	9 M 2 F	6		
	10 M 1 F	2		
	11 M	1		
	11 F	1		
(124) 12	2 M 10 F	3	0.69	1.67
	3 M 9 F	5		
	4 M 8 F	19		
	5 M 7 F	19		
	6 M 6 F	22		
	7 M 5 F	31		
	8 M 4 F	17		
	9 M 3 F	4		
	10 M 2 F	1		
	11 M 1 F	2		
	12 F	1		
(75) 13	3 M 10 F	1	0.42	1.09
	4 M 9 F	7		
	5 M 8 F	15		
	6 M 7 F	11		
	7 M 6 F	14		
	8 M 5 F	11		
	9 M 4 F	12		
	10 M 3 F	3		
	12 M 1 F	1		
(31) 14	3 M 11 F	1	0.18	0.49
	4 M 10 F	1		
	5 M 9 F	4		
	6 M 8 F	3		
	7 M 7 F	7		
	8 M 6 F	8		
	9 M 5 F	4		
	10 M 4 F	1		
	11 M 3 F	1		
	13 M 1 F	1		
(19) 15	4 M 11 F	1	0.11	0.32
	5 M 10 F	2		
	6 M 9 F	3		
	7 M 8 F	4		
	8 M 7 F	3		

SIZE OF FAMILIES AND COMPOSITION BY SEX: FOR CITIES — Continued.

COUNTIES, CITIES, SIZE OF FAMILIES, AND NUMBER OF EACH SIZE.	Composition of Families	Number of Families	PERCENTAGES: EACH SIZE OF — Total Families	Total Population
BRISTOL — Con.				
FALL RIVER - Con.				
	9 M 6 F	1		
	10 M 5 F	3		
	11 M 4 F	1		
	15 F	1		
(5) 16	7 M 9 F	1	0.03	0.09
	11 M 5 F	2		
	13 M 3 F	1		
	15 M 1 F	1		
(6) 17	9 M 8 F	1	0.04	0.12
	11 M 6 F	2		
	12 M 5 F	1		
	13 M 4 F	1		
	17 F	1		
(2) 18	9 M 9 F	1	0.01	0.04
	17 M 1 F	1		
(3) 19	12 M 7 F	1	0.02	0.06
	13 M 6 F	1		
	17 M 2 F	1		
(4) 20	11 M 9 F	1	0.02	0.09
	15 M 5 F	2		
	16 M 4 F	1		
(1) 21	17 M 4 F	1	*-	0.02
(3) 22	13 M 9 F	1	0.02	0.07
	14 M 8 F	1		
	15 M 7 F	1		
(3) 24	13 M 11 F	1	0.02	0.08
	15 M 9 F	1		
	16 M 8 F	1		
(1) 26	8 M 18 F	1	*-	0.03
(1) 27	27 M	1	*-	0.03
1) 28	26 M 2 F	1	*-	0.03
(2) 29	23 M 6 F	1	0.01	0.07
	25 M 4 F	1		
2) 33	24 M 9 F	1	0.01	0.07
	33 F	1		
2) 36	15 M 21 F	1	0.01	0.08
	33 M 3 F	1		
1) 44	31 M 10 F	1	*-	0.05
(1) 45	19 M 26 F	1	*-	0.05
(1) 53	27 M 26 F	1	*-	0.06
(1) 82	34 M 48 F	1	*-	0.09
(1) 86	1 M 85 F	1	*-	0.10
1) 119	42 M 77 F	1	*-	0.13
1) 271	141 M 133 F	1	*-	0.31
NEW BEDFORD, .	—	12,221	100.00	100.00
(855) 1	1 M	127	4.38	0.97
	1 F	408		
2,263) 2	1 M 1 F	1,819	18.02	7.97
	2 M	36		
	2 F	348		
(2,343) 3	1 M 2 F	1,221	19.17	12.72
	2 M 1 F	941		
	3 M	16		
	3 F	165		
BRISTOL — Con.				
NEW BEDFORD — Con.				
(2,041) 4	1 M 3 F	611	16.70	14.78
	2 M 2 F	979		
	3 M 1 F	389		
	4 M	5		
	4 F	57		
(1,639) 5	1 M 4 F	273	13.41	14.83
	2 M 3 F	623		
	3 M 2 F	551		
	4 M 1 F	167		
	5 F	25		
(1,199) 6	1 M 5 F	108	9.81	13.02
	2 M 4 F	304		
	3 M 3 F	447		
	4 M 2 F	265		
	5 M 1 F	68		
	6 M	1		
	6 F	6		
(841) 7	1 M 6 F	55	6.88	10.65
	2 M 5 F	152		
	3 M 4 F	234		
	4 M 3 F	267		
	5 M 2 F	109		
	6 M 1 F	21		
	7 F	3		
(553) 8	1 M 7 F	11	4.52	8.01
	2 M 6 F	51		
	3 M 5 F	126		
	4 M 4 F	181		
	5 M 3 F	132		
	6 M 2 F	43		
	7 M 1 F	8		
	8 F	1		
(354) 9	1 M 8 F	1	2.89	5.77
	2 M 7 F	30		
	3 M 6 F	48		
	4 M 5 F	91		
	5 M 4 F	92		
	6 M 3 F	58		
	7 M 2 F	26		
	8 M 1 F	8		
(212) 10	1 M 9 F	1	1.73	3.84
	2 M 8 F	4		
	3 M 7 F	21		
	4 M 6 F	45		
	5 M 5 F	69		
	6 M 4 F	47		
	7 M 3 F	24		
	8 M 2 F	9		
	9 M 1 F	1		
(149) 11	2 M 9 F	2	1.22	2.97
	3 M 8 F	17		
	4 M 7 F	25		
	5 M 6 F	40		
	6 M 5 F	28		

SIZE OF FAMILIES AND COMPOSITION BY SEX: FOR CITIES — Continued.

COUNTIES, CITIES, SIZE OF FAMILIES, AND NUMBER OF EACH SIZE.	Composition of Families	Number of Families	PERCENTAGES: EACH SIZE OF — Total Families	Total Population
BRISTOL — Con.				
NEW BEDFORD — Con.				
	7 M 4 F	22		
	8 M 3 F	7		
	9 M 2 F	6		
	10 M 1 F	2		
(67) 12	2 M 10 F	1	0.55	1.45
	3 M 9 F	2		
	4 M 8 F	7		
	5 M 7 F	13		
	6 M 6 F	7		
	7 M 5 F	16		
	8 M 4 F	11		
	9 M 3 F	8		
	10 M 2 F	1		
	11 M 1 F	1		
(33) 13	4 M 9 F	2	0.27	0.78
	5 M 8 F	4		
	6 M 7 F	6		
	7 M 6 F	8		
	8 M 5 F	4		
	9 M 4 F	4		
	10 M 3 F	3		
	11 M 2 F	2		
(16) 14	2 M 12 F	1	0.13	0.40
	4 M 10 F	1		
	6 M 8 F	2		
	7 M 7 F	5		
	8 M 6 F	2		
	10 M 4 F	2		
	11 M 3 F	1		
	12 M 2 F	2		
(13) 15	6 M 9 F	1	0.10	0.35
	7 M 8 F	2		
	8 M 7 F	2		
	9 M 6 F	2		
	10 M 5 F	1		
	11 M 4 F	5		
(4) 16	4 M 12 F	1	0.03	0.12
	8 M 8 F	1		
	10 M 6 F	1		
	13 M 3 F	1		
(2) 17	10 M 7 F	2	0.02	0.06
(3) 18	10 M 8 F	1	0.03	0.10
	11 M 7 F	1		
	12 M 6 F	1		
(2) 19	12 M 7 F	1	0.02	0.07
	19 F	1		
(2) 21	6 M 15 F	1	0.02	0.08
	11 M 10 F	1		
(1) 22	9 M 13 F	1	0.01	0.04
(1) 26	1 M 25 F	1	0.01	0.05
(1) 27	19 M 8 F	1	0.01	0.05
(2) 29	18 M 11 F	1	0.02	0.10
	21 M 8 F	1		
(1) 35	35 M	1	0.01	0.06

COUNTIES, CITIES, SIZE OF FAMILIES, AND NUMBER OF EACH SIZE.	Composition of Families	Number of Families	PERCENTAGES: EACH SIZE OF — Total Families	Total Population
BRISTOL — Con.				
NEW BEDFORD — Con.				
(1) 37	21 M 16 F	1	0.01	0.07
(1) 78	42 M 36 F	1	0.01	0.14
(1) 84	39 M 45 F	1	0.01	0.15
(1) 221	187 M 34 F	1	0.01	0.40
TAUNTON, . .	-	5,885	100.00	100.00
(220) 1	1 M	64	3.74	0.81
	1 F	156		
(973) 2	1 M 1 F	838	16.53	7.18
	2 M	20		
	2 F	115		
(1,169) 3	1 M 2 F	619	19.86	12.93
	2 M 1 F	477		
	3 M	7		
	3 F	66		
(1,090) 4	1 M 3 F	275	18.01	15.64
	2 M 2 F	540		
	3 M 1 F	223		
	4 M	3		
	4 F	19		
(878) 5	1 M 4 F	139	14.92	16.19
	2 M 3 F	518		
	3 M 2 F	397		
	4 M 1 F	104		
	5 M	1		
	5 F	9		
(636) 6	1 M 5 F	45	10.80	14.07
	2 M 4 F	159		
	3 M 3 F	220		
	4 M 2 F	179		
	5 M 1 F	30		
	6 M	2		
	6 F	1		
(373) 7	1 M 6 F	13	6.34	9.63
	2 M 5 F	55		
	3 M 4 F	112		
	4 M 3 F	110		
	5 M 2 F	66		
	6 M 1 F	9		
	7 M	1		
(209) 8	1 M 7 F	5	4.23	7.35
	2 M 6 F	21		
	3 M 5 F	64		
	4 M 4 F	58		
	5 M 3 F	71		
	6 M 2 F	23		
	7 M 1 F	7		
(152) 9	1 M 8 F	2	2.58	5.04
	2 M 7 F	7		
	3 M 6 F	25		
	4 M 5 F	44		
	5 M 4 F	34		
	6 M 3 F	26		
	7 M 2 F	12		
	8 M 1 F	1		

SIZE OF FAMILIES AND COMPOSITION BY SEX: FOR CITIES — Continued.

COUNTIES, CITIES, SIZE OF FAMILIES, AND NUMBER OF EACH SIZE.	Composition of Families	Number of Families	PERCENTAGES: EACH SIZE OF —		COUNTIES, CITIES, SIZE OF FAMILIES, AND NUMBER OF EACH SIZE.	Composition of Families	Number of Families	PERCENTAGES: EACH SIZE OF —	
			Total Families	Total Population				Total Families	Total Population
BRISTOL — Con.					ESSEX — Con.				
TAUNTON — Con.					BEVERLY — Con.				
	9 F	1				2 M	15		
(78) 10	2 M 8 F	3	1.32	2.88		2 F	85		
	3 M 7 F	14			(642) 3	1 M 2 F	327	22.03	16.31
	4 M 6 F	12				2 M 1 F	274		
	5 M 5 F	16				3 M	5		
	6 M 4 F	22				3 F	36		
	7 M 3 F	8			(521) 4	1 M 3 F	156	17.88	17.65
	8 M 2 F	2				2 M 2 F	242		
	9 M 1 F	1				3 M 1 F	109		
(54) 11	2 M 9 F	1	0.92	2.19		4 M	2		
	3 M 8 F	5				4 F	12		
	4 M 7 F	15			(390) 5	1 M 4 F	57	13.39	16.52
	5 M 6 F	9				2 M 3 F	142		
	6 M 5 F	12				3 M 2 F	127		
	7 M 4 F	8				4 M 1 F	56		
	8 M 3 F	4				5 M	1		
	10 M 1 F	1				5 F	7		
	11 F	1			(256) 6	1 M 5 F	15	8.79	13.01
(16) 12	3 M 9 F	1	0.27	0.71		2 M 4 F	60		
	5 M 7 F	1				3 M 3 F	110		
	6 M 6 F	2				4 M 2 F	55		
	7 M 5 F	4				5 M 1 F	14		
	8 M 4 F	4				6 M	1		
	9 M 3 F	2				6 F	1		
	10 M 2 F	2			(156) 7	1 M 6 F	5	5.36	9.25
(7) 13	6 M 7 F	2	0.12	0.34		2 M 5 F	27		
	7 M 6 F	3				3 M 4 F	43		
	9 M 4 F	2				4 M 3 F	46		
(5) 14	6 M 8 F	1	0.08	0.25		5 M 2 F	28		
	7 M 7 F	2				6 M 1 F	5		
	8 M 6 F	1				7 M	1		
	9 M 5 F	1				7 F	1		
(1) 15	6 M 9 F	1	0.02	0.05	(94) 8	1 M 7 F	1	3.23	6.37
(2) 16	1 M 15 F	1	0.03	0.12		2 M 6 F	10		
	9 M 7 F	1				3 M 5 F	16		
(1) 17	12 M 5 F	1	0.02	0.06		4 M 4 F	35		
(1) 18	15 M 3 F	1	0.02	0.07		5 M 3 F	21		
(3) 19	15 M 4 F	1	0.05	0.21		6 M 2 F	8		
	17 M 2 F	1				7 M 1 F	2		
	19 F	1				8 M	1		
(1) 20	15 M 5 F	1	0.02	0.07	(41) 9	3 M 6 F	8	1.41	3.12
(1) 21	16 M 5 F	1	0.02	0.08		4 M 5 F	6		
(1) 22	3 M 19 F	1	0.02	0.08		5 M 4 F	10		
(1) 28	19 M 9 F	1	0.02	0.10		6 M 3 F	14		
(1) 46	36 M 10 F	1	0.02	0.17		7 M 2 F	2		
(1) 65	31 M 34 F	1	0.02	0.24		8 M 1 F	1		
(1) 957	474 M 483 F	1	0.02	3.55	(24) 10	2 M 8 F	1	0.83	2.03
						3 M 7 F	4		
ESSEX.						4 M 6 F	4		
						5 M 5 F	4		
BEVERLY, . .	—	2,914	100.00	100.00		6 M 4 F	6		
(194) 1	1 M	48	6.66	1.64		7 M 3 F	2		
	1 F	146				8 M 2 F	3		
(559) 2	1 M 1 F	459	19.19	9.57	(12) 11	3 M 8 F	2	0.41	1.12

SIZE OF FAMILIES AND COMPOSITION BY SEX: FOR CITIES — Continued.

COUNTIES, CITIES, SIZE OF FAMILIES, AND NUMBER OF EACH SIZE.	Composition of Families	Number of Families	PERCENTAGES: EACH SIZE OF — Total Families	PERCENTAGES: EACH SIZE OF — Total Population
ESSEX — Con.				
BEVERLY — Con.				
	4 M 7 F	1		
	5 M 6 F	3		
	6 M 5 F	2		
	7 M 4 F	4		
(5) 12	5 M 7 F	1	0.17	0.51
	6 M 6 F	1		
	7 M 5 F	2		
	8 M 4 F	1		
(4) 13	6 M 7 F	1	0.14	0.44
	8 M 5 F	1		
	11 M 2 F	1		
	13 M	1		
(3) 14	5 M 9 F	1	0.10	0.56
	9 M 5 F	1		
	14 M	1		
(3) 15	8 M 7 F	1	0.10	0.58
	11 M 4 F	1		
	12 M 3 F	1		
(3) 16	9 M 7 F	2	0.10	0.41
	12 M 4 F	1		
(1) 17	14 M 3 F	1	0.03	0.14
(1) 19	16 M 3 F	1	0.03	0.16
(1) 22	16 M 6 F	1	0.03	0.19
(1) 24	21 M	1	0.03	0.20
(1) 27	13 M 14 F	1	0.03	0.23
(1) 28	16 M 12 F	1	0.03	0.24
(1) 29	29 M	1	0.03	0.25
GLOUCESTER, .	—	5,416	100.00	100.00
(216) 1	1 M	106	3.99	0.77
	1 F	113		
(821) 2	1 M 1 F	714	15.16	5.82
	2 M	20		
	2 F	87		
(1,057) 3	1 M 2 F	557	19.51	11.24
	2 M 1 F	477		
	3 M	5		
	3 F	38		
(963) 4	1 M 3 F	237	17.22	13.23
	2 M 2 F	472		
	3 M 1 F	206		
	4 M	4		
	4 F	14		
(738) 5	1 M 4 F	99	13.62	13.08
	2 M 3 F	256		
	3 M 2 F	285		
	4 M 1 F	97		
	5 F	1		
(584) 6	1 M 5 F	40	10.78	12.42
	2 M 4 F	137		
	3 M 3 F	213		
	4 M 2 F	143		
	5 M 1 F	48		
	6 M	2		
	6 F	1		

COUNTIES, CITIES, SIZE OF FAMILIES, AND NUMBER OF EACH SIZE.	Composition of Families	Number of Families	PERCENTAGES: EACH SIZE OF — Total Families	PERCENTAGES: EACH SIZE OF — Total Population
ESSEX — Con.				
GLOUCESTER-Con.				
(383) 7	1 M 6 F	11	7.07	9.50
	2 M 5 F	50		
	3 M 4 F	93		
	4 M 3 F	120		
	5 M 2 F	84		
	6 M 1 F	25		
(242) 8	1 M 7 F	2	4.47	6.86
	2 M 6 F	12		
	3 M 5 F	44		
	4 M 4 F	65		
	5 M 3 F	68		
	6 M 2 F	35		
	7 M 1 F	15		
	8 F	1		
(124) 9	1 M 8 F	2	2.29	3.96
	2 M 7 F	5		
	3 M 6 F	13		
	4 M 5 F	37		
	5 M 4 F	22		
	6 M 3 F	22		
	7 M 2 F	17		
	8 M 1 F	5		
	9 M	1		
(62) 10	1 M 9 F	1	1.14	2.20
	4 M 6 F	12		
	5 M 5 F	15		
	6 M 4 F	11		
	7 M 3 F	13		
	8 M 2 F	5		
	9 M 1 F	5		
(57) 11	3 M 8 F	4	1.05	2.22
	4 M 7 F	5		
	5 M 6 F	7		
	6 M 5 F	10		
	7 M 4 F	6		
	8 M 3 F	11		
	9 M 2 F	7		
	10 M 1 F	7		
(30) 12	3 M 9 F	1	0.55	1.28
	5 M 7 F	1		
	6 M 6 F	5		
	7 M 5 F	5		
	8 M 4 F	4		
	9 M 3 F	8		
	10 M 2 F	2		
	11 M 1 F	4		
(19) 13	6 M 7 F	1	0.35	0.88
	7 M 6 F	3		
	8 M 5 F	2		
	9 M 4 F	4		
	10 M 3 F	5		
	11 M 2 F	2		
	12 M 1 F	2		
(23) 14	6 M 8 F	2	0.42	1.14

SIZE OF FAMILIES AND COMPOSITION BY SEX: FOR CITIES — Continued.

Counties, Cities, Size of Families, and Number of Each Size.	Composition of Families	Number of Families	Percentages: Each Size of — Total Families	Percentages: Each Size of — Total Population
ESSEX — Con.				
GLOUCESTER-Con.				
	7 M 7 F	2		
	8 M 6 F	2		
	9 M 5 F	1		
	10 M 4 F	1		
	11 M 3 F	2		
	12 M 2 F	10		
	13 M 1 F	3		
(10) 15	9 M 6 F	2	0.18	0.53
	11 M 4 F	1		
	12 M 3 F	3		
	13 M 2 F	3		
	14 M 1 F	1		
(11) 16	11 M 5 F	1	0.20	0.62
	13 M 3 F	6		
	14 M 2 F	3		
	15 M 1 F	1		
(14) 17	13 M 4 F	3	0.26	0.84
	14 M 3 F	7		
	15 M 2 F	3		
	16 M 1 F	1		
(9) 18	13 M 5 F	1	0.16	0.57
	14 M 4 F	2		
	15 M 3 F	1		
	16 M 2 F	5		
(5) 19	14 M 5 F	1	0.09	0.34
	16 M 3 F	3		
	17 M 2 F	1		
(6) 20	16 M 4 F	2	0.11	0.43
	17 M 3 F	2		
	18 M 2 F	2		
(2) 21	17 M 4 F	2	0.04	0.15
(4) 22	15 M 7 F	2	0.07	0.31
	17 M 5 F	1		
	18 M 4 F	1		
(2) 23	16 M 7 F	1	0.04	0.16
	17 M 6 F	1		
(4) 24	17 M 7 F	1	0.07	0.34
	19 M 5 F	1		
	20 M 4 F	1		
	21 M 3 F	1		
(3) 25	21 M 4 F	1	0.05	0.27
	22 M 3 F	1		
	23 M 2 F	1		
(3) 27	22 M 5 F	1	0.05	0.29
	23 M 4 F	2		
(3) 28	20 M 8 F	1	0.04	0.20
	25 M 3 F	1		
(3) 29	25 M 4 F	1	0.04	0.21
	28 M 1 F	1		
(1) 30	28 M 2 F	1	0.02	0.11
(1) 31	26 M 5 F	1	0.02	0.11
(1) 32	29 M 3 F	1	0.02	0.11
(2) 33	31 M 2 F	2	0.04	0.23
(2) 35	31 M 4 F	1	0.04	0.25
	33 M 2 F	1		
ESSEX — Con.				
GLOUCESTER-Con.				
(2) 36	33 M 3 F	2	0.04	0.26
(1) 37	18 M 19 F	1	0.02	0.13
(3) 39	35 M 4 F	2	0.05	0.42
	36 M 3 F	1		
(1) 40	36 M 4 F	1	0.02	0.14
(2) 41	38 M 3 F	2	0.04	0.29
(1) 42	40 M 2 F	1	0.02	0.15
(1) 43	40 M 3 F	1	0.02	0.15
(2) 46	43 M 3 F	1	0.04	0.33
	44 M 2 F	1		
(2) 47	45 M 2 F	2	0.04	0.33
(2) 49	42 M 7 F	1	0.04	0.35
	45 M 4 F	1		
(2) 50	49 M 1 F	2	0.04	0.35
(2) 51	47 M 4 F	1	0.04	0.36
	49 M 2 F	1		
(1) 54	49 M 5 F	1	0.02	0.19
(2) 56	35 M 21 F	1	0.04	0.40
	54 M 2 F	1		
(3) 57	54 M 3 F	1	0.05	0.61
	55 M 2 F	2		
(1) 66	63 M 3 F	1	0.02	0.23
(1) 71	66 M 5 F	1	0.02	0.25
(2) 75	75 M	2	0.04	0.55
(1) 77	73 M 4 F	1	0.02	0.27
(1) 78	78 M	1	0.02	0.28
(1) 80	80 M	1	0.02	0.28
(2) 82	77 M 5 F	1	0.04	0.58
	79 M 3 F	1		
(1) 85	84 M 1 F	1	0.02	0.30
(1) 91	87 M 4 F	1	0.02	0.32
(1) 93	89 M 4 F	1	0.02	0.33
(1) 99	97 M 2 F	1	0.02	0.35
(1) 105	101 M 4 F	1	0.02	0.37
(1) 109	106 M 3 F	1	0.02	0.39
(1) 111	111 M	1	0.02	0.39
HAVERHILL. . .	-	6,962	100.00	100.00
(222) 1	1 M	66	3.22	0.73
	1 F	156		
(1,245) 2	1 M 1 F	1,062	18.04	8.24
	2 M	19		
	2 F	174		
(1,398) 3	1 M 2 F	797	20.26	13.88
	2 M 1 F	618		
	3 M	7		
	3 F	66		
(1,582) 4	1 M 3 F	582	19.30	17.64
	2 M 2 F	632		
	3 M 1 F	273		
	4 M	1		
	4 F	24		
(1,009) 5	1 M 4 F	154	14.62	16.70
	2 M 3 F	393		
	3 M 2 F	355		
	4 M 1 F	92		

SIZE OF FAMILIES AND COMPOSITION BY SEX: FOR CITIES — Continued.

COUNTIES, CITIES, SIZE OF FAMILIES, AND NUMBER OF EACH SIZE.	Composition of Families	Number of Families	PERCENTAGES: EACH SIZE OF — Total Families	Total Population
ESSEX — Con.				
HAVERHILL — Con.				
	5 M	4		
	5 F	11		
(683) 6	1 M 5 F	51	9.90	13.57
	2 M 4 F	162		
	3 M 3 F	256		
	4 M 2 F	159		
	5 M 1 F	48		
	6 M	4		
	6 F	3		
(423) 7	1 M 6 F	19	6.13	9.80
	2 M 5 F	77		
	3 M 4 F	126		
	4 M 3 F	133		
	5 M 2 F	56		
	6 M 1 F	12		
(243) 8	1 M 7 F	4	3.52	6.44
	2 M 6 F	30		
	3 M 5 F	47		
	4 M 4 F	73		
	5 M 3 F	64		
	6 M 2 F	23		
	7 M 1 F	2		
(144) 9	1 M 8 F	3	2.05	4.20
	2 M 7 F	6		
	3 M 6 F	21		
	4 M 5 F	40		
	5 M 4 F	28		
	6 M 3 F	26		
	7 M 2 F	11		
	8 M 1 F	5		
	9 F	1		
(78) 10	1 M 9 F	1	1.13	2.58
	2 M 8 F	1		
	3 M 7 F	8		
	4 M 6 F	12		
	5 M 5 F	24		
	6 M 4 F	23		
	7 M 3 F	4		
	8 M 2 F	5		
(40) 11	2 M 9 F	1	0.58	1.46
	3 M 8 F	3		
	4 M 7 F	2		
	5 M 6 F	10		
	6 M 5 F	9		
	7 M 4 F	4		
	8 M 3 F	8		
	9 M 2 F	1		
	10 M 1 F	1		
	11 F	1		
(22) 12	3 M 9 F	2	0.32	0.87
	4 M 8 F	1		
	5 M 7 F	6		
	6 M 6 F	5		
	7 M 5 F	5		
	8 M 4 F	3		
ESSEX — Con.				
HAVERHILL — Con.				
(20) 13	5 M 10 F	1	0.29	0.86
	4 M 9 F	3		
	5 M 8 F	1		
	6 M 7 F	1		
	7 M 6 F	5		
	8 M 5 F	3		
	9 M 4 F	3		
	10 M 3 F	2		
	11 M 2 F	1		
(15) 14	2 M 12 F	1	0.22	0.70
	5 M 9 F	2		
	6 M 8 F	2		
	7 M 7 F	4		
	8 M 6 F	2		
	9 M 5 F	3		
	10 M 4 F	1		
(5) 15	6 M 9 F	1	0.07	0.25
	8 M 7 F	1		
	9 M 6 F	1		
	10 M 5 F	1		
	12 M 3 F	1		
(4) 16	5 M 11 F	1	0.06	0.21
	9 M 7 F	1		
	12 M 4 F	1		
	13 M 3 F	1		
(5) 18	9 M 9 F	1	0.07	0.30
	13 M 5 F	2		
	14 M 4 F	1		
	18 F	1		
(1) 19	14 M 5 F	1	0.01	0.06
(4) 20	5 M 15 F	1	0.06	0.26
	9 M 11 F	1		
	11 M 9 F	1		
	12 M 8 F	1		
(4) 21	6 M 15 F	1	0.06	0.28
	13 M 8 F	1		
	14 M 7 F	1		
	21 F	1		
(2) 22	13 M 9 F	1	0.03	0.15
	15 M 7 F	1		
(1) 23	21 M 2 F	1	0.01	0.08
(1) 27	19 M 8 F	1	0.01	0.09
(1) 28	16 M 12 F	1	0.01	0.09
(1) 31	19 M 12 F	1	0.01	0.11
(1) 47	25 M 22 F	1	0.01	0.16
(1) 89	58 M 31 F	1	0.01	0.29
LAWRENCE, . . .	—	10,783	100.00	100.00
(344) 1	1 M	105	3.19	0.66
	1 F	239		
(1,617) 2	1 M 1 F	1,324	14.99	6.20
	2 M	38		
	2 F	255		
(2,057) 3	1 M 2 F	1,160	19.07	11.83
	2 M 1 F	789		
	3 M	8		

SIZE OF FAMILIES AND COMPOSITION BY SEX: FOR CITIES — Continued.

Counties, Cities, Size of Families, and Number of Each Size	Composition of Families	Number of Families	Percentages: Each Size of — Total Families	Percentages: Each Size of — Total Population
ESSEX — Con.				
LAWRENCE—Con.				
	3 F	159		
(1,966) 4	1 M 3 F	554	18.23	15.08
	2 M 2 F	933		
	3 M 1 F	400		
	4 M	6		
	4 F	73		
(1,573) 5	1 M 4 F	239	14.59	15.08
	2 M 3 F	596		
	3 M 2 F	540		
	4 M 1 F	169		
	5 M	8		
	5 F	21		
(1,182) 6	1 M 5 F	107	10.96	13.60
	2 M 4 F	366		
	3 M 3 F	427		
	4 M 2 F	250		
	5 M 1 F	75		
	6 M	5		
	6 F	9		
(775) 7	1 M 6 F	36	7.19	10.40
	2 M 5 F	139		
	3 M 4 F	248		
	4 M 3 F	212		
	5 M 2 F	110		
	6 M 1 F	25		
	7 F	5		
(495) 8	1 M 7 F	10	4.57	7.56
	2 M 6 F	44		
	3 M 5 F	123		
	4 M 4 F	150		
	5 M 3 F	99		
	6 M 2 F	55		
	7 M 1 F	4		
	8 M	7		
	8 F			
(294) 9	1 M 8 F	6	2.73	5.07
	2 M 7 F	20		
	3 M 6 F	39		
	4 M 5 F	73		
	5 M 4 F	89		
	6 M 3 F	41		
	7 M 2 F	20		
	8 M 1 F	4		
	9 M	1		
	9 F	1		
(165) 10	1 M 9 F	1	1.53	3.16
	2 M 8 F	4		
	3 M 7 F	15		
	4 M 6 F	54		
	5 M 5 F	56		
	6 M 4 F	32		
	7 M 3 F	13		
	8 M 2 F	5		
	9 M 1 F	2		

Counties, Cities, Size of Families, and Number of Each Size	Composition of Families	Number of Families	Percentages: Each Size of — Total Families	Percentages: Each Size of — Total Population
ESSEX — Con.				
LAWRENCE—Con.				
(111) 11	2 M 9 F	4	1.03	2.34
	3 M 8 F	7		
	4 M 7 F	13		
	5 M 6 F	23		
	6 M 5 F	28		
	7 M 4 F	18		
	8 M 3 F	7		
	9 M 2 F	5		
	10 M 1 F	3		
	11 M	2		
	11 F	1		
(47) 12	2 M 10 F	1	0.43	1.08
	3 M 9 F	2		
	4 M 8 F	8		
	5 M 7 F	10		
	6 M 6 F	6		
	7 M 5 F	11		
	8 M 4 F	3		
	9 M 3 F	2		
	10 M 2 F	1		
	11 M 1 F	2		
	12 M	1		
(31) 13	3 M 10 F	1	0.29	0.77
	4 M 9 F	1		
	5 M 8 F	3		
	6 M 7 F	2		
	7 M 6 F	3		
	8 M 5 F	8		
	9 M 4 F	6		
	10 M 3 F	1		
	11 M 2 F	3		
	12 M 1 F	1		
	13 M	2		
(19) 14	3 M 11 F	1	0.17	0.51
	4 M 10 F	1		
	5 M 9 F	1		
	6 M 8 F	2		
	7 M 7 F	4		
	8 M 6 F	2		
	9 M 5 F	3		
	11 M 3 F	2		
	12 M 2 F	2		
	13 M 1 F	1		
(10) 15	4 M 11 F	1	0.09	0.29
	5 M 10 F	2		
	9 M 6 F	1		
	10 M 5 F	2		
	11 M 4 F	1		
	12 M 3 F	2		
	13 M 2 F	1		
(7) 16	7 M 9 F	1	0.06	0.21
	8 M 8 F	3		
	9 M 7 F	1		
	12 M 4 F	1		

SIZE OF FAMILIES AND COMPOSITION BY SEX: FOR CITIES — Continued.

ESSEX — Con.
LAWRENCE — Con.

Size of Families, and Number of Each Size	Composition of Families	Number of Families	Percentages: Each Size of — Total Families	Percentages: Each Size of — Total Population
	16 M	1		
(6) 17	4 M 13 F	1	0.05	0.19
	7 M 10 F	2		
	10 M 7 F	1		
	11 M 6 F	1		
	12 M 5 F	1		
(7) 18	3 M 15 F	1	0.06	0.24
	8 M 10 F	1		
	9 M 9 F	2		
	11 M 7 F	1		
	13 M 5 F	1		
	14 M 4 F	1		
(4) 19	1 M 18 F	1	0.04	0.15
	5 M 14 F	1		
	10 M 9 F	1		
	15 M 4 F	1		
(8) 20	6 M 14 F	1	0.07	0.31
	7 M 13 F	1		
	11 M 9 F	1		
	12 M 8 F	1		
	13 M 7 F	2		
	16 M 4 F	1		
	18 M 2 F	1		
(2) 21	7 M 14 F	1	0.02	0.08
	15 M 6 F	1		
(3) 22	11 M 11 F	1	0.03	0.13
	13 M 9 F	1		
	14 M 8 F	1		
(4) 23	9 M 14 F	1	0.04	0.18
	12 M 11 F	1		
	13 M 10 F	1		
	14 M 9 F	1		
(3) 24	10 M 14 F	1	0.03	0.14
	12 M 12 F	1		
	14 M 10 F	1		
(7) 25	5 M 20 F	1	0.06	0.33
	14 M 11 F	1		
	16 M 9 F	2		
	17 M 8 F	1		
	18 M 7 F	1		
	19 M 6 F	1		
(1) 26	14 M 12 F	1	0.01	0.05
(2) 27	2 M 25 F	1	0.02	0.10
	17 M 10 F	1		
(3) 28	15 M 13 F	1	0.03	0.16
	25 M 3 F	1		
	28 F	1		
(1) 29	16 M 13 F	1	0.01	0.06
(1) 30	10 M 20 F	1	0.01	0.06
(2) 32	1 M 31 F	1	0.02	0.12
	17 M 15 F	1		
(2) 33	5 M 28 F	1	0.02	0.13
	19 M 14 F	1		
(3) 34	15 M 19 F	1	0.03	0.19

ESSEX — Con.
LAWRENCE — Con.

Size of Families, and Number of Each Size	Composition of Families	Number of Families	Percentages: Each Size of — Total Families	Percentages: Each Size of — Total Population
	24 M 10 F	1		
	28 M 6 F	1		
(2) 35	25 M 10 F	1	0.02	0.13
	35 M	1		
(1) 36	29 M 7 F	1	0.01	0.07
(2) 37	20 M 17 F	1	0.02	0.14
	28 M 9 F	1		
(2) 38	19 M 19 F	1	0.02	0.15
	31 M 4 F	1		
(1) 39	17 M 22 F	1	0.01	0.07
(4) 40	11 M 29 F	1	0.04	0.31
	21 M 19 F	1		
(2) 41	21 M 20 F	1	0.02	0.16
	22 M 19 F	1		
(2) 42	28 M 14 F	1	0.02	0.16
	36 M 6 F	1		
(3) 43	19 M 24 F	1	0.03	0.25
	25 M 18 F	1		
	29 M 14 F	1		
(1) 44	33 M 11 F	1	0.01	0.08
(3) 45	24 M 21 F	1	0.03	0.26
	27 M 18 F	1		
	28 M 17 F	1		
(2) 47	19 M 28 F	1	0.02	0.18
	28 M 19 F	1		
(1) 50	33 M 17 F	1	0.01	0.10
(1) 52	38 M 14 F	1	0.01	0.10
(1) 57	51 M 6 F	1	0.01	0.11
(1) 59	27 M 32 F	1	0.01	0.11
(1) 60	10 M 50 F	1	0.01	0.11
1 141	60 M 81 F	1	0.01	0.27
1 144	52 M 92 F	1	0.01	0.28
1) 261	227 M 34 F	1	0.01	0.50
LYNN, ...	–	14,144	100.00	100.00
(456) 1	1 M	123	3.08	0.70
	1 F	315		
(2,428) 2	1 M 1 F	2,947	17.15	7.79
	2 M	30		
	2 F	351		
(2,956) 3	1 M 2 F	1,508	20.90	14.22
	2 M 1 F	1,273		
	3 M	17		
	3 F	158		
(2,847) 4	1 M 3 F	799	20.13	18.26
	2 M 2 F	1,406		
	3 M 1 F	574		
	4 M	5		
	4 F	63		
(2,094) 5	1 M 4 F	294	14.80	16.79
	2 M 3 F	832		
	3 M 2 F	746		
	4 M 1 F	206		

SIZE OF FAMILIES AND COMPOSITION BY SEX: FOR CITIES — Continued.

Counties, Cities, Size of Families, and Number of Each Size.	Composition of Families	Number of Families	Percentages: Each size of — Total Families	Percentages: Each size of — Total Population
ESSEX — Con.				
LYNN — Con.				
	5 M	1		
	5 F	15		
(1,305) 6	1 M 5 F	92	9.23	12.56
	2 M 4 F	336		
	3 M 3 F	487		
	4 M 2 F	319		
	5 M 1 F	67		
	6 M	1		
	6 F	3		
(871) 7	1 M 6 F	35	6.16	9.78
	2 M 5 F	134		
	3 M 4 F	278		
	4 M 3 F	271		
	5 M 2 F	123		
	6 M 1 F	27		
	7 M	1		
	7 F	2		
(506) 8	1 M 7 F	7	3.58	6.49
	2 M 6 F	49		
	3 M 5 F	130		
	4 M 4 F	152		
	5 M 3 F	111		
	6 M 2 F	48		
	7 M 1 F	9		
(271) 9	1 M 8 F	4	1.91	3.91
	2 M 7 F	9		
	3 M 6 F	41		
	4 M 5 F	71		
	5 M 4 F	79		
	6 M 3 F	48		
	7 M 2 F	16		
	8 M 1 F	2		
	9 M	1		
(153) 10	2 M 8 F	8	1.08	2.45
	3 M 7 F	18		
	4 M 6 F	26		
	5 M 5 F	49		
	6 M 4 F	21		
	7 M 3 F	23		
	8 M 2 F	4		
	9 M 1 F	3		
	10 M	1		
(72) 11	2 M 9 F	1	0.51	1.27
	3 M 8 F	5		
	4 M 7 F	12		
	5 M 6 F	12		
	6 M 5 F	15		
	7 M 4 F	18		
	8 M 3 F	5		
	9 M 2 F	3		
	11 M	1		
(53) 12	2 M 10 F	1	0.37	1.02
	3 M 9 F	1		
	4 M 8 F	2		

Counties, Cities, Size of Families, and Number of Each Size.	Composition of Families	Number of Families	Percentages: Each size of — Total Families	Percentages: Each size of — Total Population
ESSEX — Con.				
LYNN — Con.				
	5 M 7 F	11		
	6 M 6 F	11		
	7 M 5 F	14		
	8 M 4 F	6		
	9 M 3 F	5		
	10 M 2 F	1		
	12 M	1		
(35) 13	1 M 12 F	1	0.25	0.73
	3 M 10 F	3		
	4 M 9 F	1		
	5 M 8 F	2		
	6 M 7 F	5		
	7 M 6 F	5		
	8 M 5 F	9		
	9 M 4 F	4		
	10 M 3 F	3		
	11 M 2 F	1		
	12 M 1 F	1		
(22) 14	5 M 9 F	3	0.15	0.49
	6 M 8 F	1		
	7 M 7 F	4		
	8 M 6 F	5		
	9 M 5 F	4		
	10 M 4 F	3		
	11 M 3 F	2		
(19) 15	4 M 11 F	1	0.13	0.46
	5 M 10 F	1		
	6 M 9 F	1		
	7 M 8 F	1		
	8 M 7 F	3		
	9 M 6 F	2		
	10 M 5 F	4		
	11 M 4 F	1		
	12 M 3 F	1		
	13 M 2 F	1		
	15 M	2		
	15 F	1		
(13) 16	5 M 11 F	1	0.09	0.33
	6 M 10 F	1		
	7 M 9 F	2		
	8 M 8 F	2		
	9 M 7 F	3		
	10 M 6 F	1		
	11 M 5 F	2		
	12 M 4 F	1		
(6) 17	6 M 11 F	1	0.04	0.16
	9 M 8 F	3		
	12 M 5 F	2		
(7) 18	7 M 11 F	1	0.05	0.20
	8 M 10 F	1		
	10 M 8 F	1		
	12 M 6 F	1		
	13 M 5 F	1		
	14 M 4 F	1		

SIZE OF FAMILIES AND COMPOSITION BY SEX: FOR CITIES — Continued.

Counties, Cities, Size of Families, and Number of Each Size.	Composition of Families	Number of Families	Total Families	Total Population
ESSEX — Con.				
LYNN — Con.				
(5) 19	15 M 3 F	1		
	19 M 9 F	2	0.03	0.15
	13 M 6 F	1		
	16 M 3 F	1		
	18 M 1 F	1		
(5) 20	10 M 10 F	1	0.03	0.16
	11 M 9 F	1		
	12 M 8 F	2		
	16 M 4 F	1		
(5) 21	10 M 11 F	2	0.03	0.17
	11 M 10 F	1		
	12 M 9 F	2		
(1) 22	14 M 8 F	1	0.01	0.04
(7) 23	12 M 11 F	1	0.05	0.26
	15 M 8 F	2		
	17 M 6 F	1		
	18 M 5 F	1		
	19 M 4 F	1		
	23 M	1		
(4) 24	5 M 19 F	1	0.03	0.15
	13 M 11 F	1		
	14 M 10 F	1		
	18 M 6 F	1		
(7) 25	1 M 24 F	1	0.05	0.28
	10 M 15 F	1		
	13 M 12 F	1		
	17 M 8 F	1		
	19 M 6 F	1		
	20 M 5 F	1		
	25 M	1		
(2) 26	20 M 6 F	2	0.01	0.08
(1) 28	18 M 10 F	1	0.01	0.05
(1) 30	20 M 10 F	1	0.01	0.05
(1) 31	22 M 9 F	1	0.01	0.05
(1) 34	20 M 14 F	1	0.01	0.06
(1) 35	27 M 8 F	1	0.01	0.06
(1) 40	22 M 18 F	1	0.01	0.07
(1) 43	27 M 16 F	1	0.01	0.07
(1) 44	28 M 15 F	1	0.01	0.07
(1) 51	33 M 18 F	1	0.01	0.08
(1) 57	47 M 10 F	1	0.01	0.09
(1) 61	38 M 23 F	1	0.01	0.10
(1) 70	57 M 13 F	1	0.01	0.11
(1) 72	59 M 13 F	1	0.01	0.12
(1) 75	42 M 33 F	1	0.01	0.12
NEWBURYPORT, .	-	3,470	100.00	100.00
(233) 1	1 M	54	6.70	1.60
	1 F	179		
(648) 2	1 M 1 F	484	18.63	8.91
	2 M	16		
	2 F	148		
(672) 3	1 M 2 F	399	19.31	13.85
	2 M 1 F	237		
	3 M	5		
	3 F	61		

Counties, Cities, Size of Families, and Number of Each Size.	Composition of Families	Number of Families	Total Families	Total Population
ESSEX — Con.				
NEWBURYPORT — Con.				
(939) 4	1 M 3 F	192	18.37	17.57
	2 M 2 F	310		
	3 M 1 F	111		
	4 F	26		
(509) 5	1 M 4 F	87	14.63	17.49
	2 M 3 F	203		
	3 M 2 F	163		
	4 M 1 F	45		
	5 M	2		
	5 F	9		
(301) 6	1 M 5 F	22	8.65	12.41
	2 M 4 F	77		
	3 M 3 F	114		
	4 M 2 F	66		
	5 M 1 F	20		
	6 F	2		
(205) 7	1 M 6 F	3	5.89	9.86
	2 M 5 F	38		
	3 M 4 F	69		
	4 M 3 F	62		
	5 M 2 F	20		
	6 M 1 F	4		
(103) 8	1 M 7 F	5	2.96	5.66
	2 M 6 F	16		
	3 M 5 F	13		
	4 M 4 F	33		
	5 M 3 F	24		
	6 M 2 F	11		
	7 M 1 F	1		
(73) 9	1 M 8 F	2	2.10	4.52
	2 M 7 F	7		
	3 M 6 F	15		
	4 M 5 F	19		
	5 M 4 F	16		
	6 M 3 F	9		
	7 M 2 F	4		
	8 M 1 F	1		
(45) 10	2 M 8 F	1	1.29	3.09
	3 M 7 F	5		
	4 M 6 F	8		
	5 M 5 F	18		
	6 M 4 F	7		
	7 M 3 F	5		
	8 M 2 F	1		
(23) 11	1 M 10 F	1	0.66	1.74
	2 M 9 F	2		
	3 M 8 F	1		
	4 M 7 F	7		
	5 M 6 F	4		
	6 M 5 F	2		
	7 M 4 F	2		
	8 M 3 F	4		
(8) 12	3 M 9 F	1	0.23	0.66
	4 M 8 F	1		

SIZE OF FAMILIES AND COMPOSITION BY SEX: FOR CITIES — Continued.

COUNTIES, CITIES, SIZE OF FAMILIES, AND NUMBER OF EACH SIZE.	Composition of Families	Number of Families	Percentages: Each Size of — Total Families	Percentages: Each Size of — Total Population
ESSEX — Con.				
NEWBURYPORT — Con.				
	6 M 6 F	3		
	7 M 5 F	2		
	10 M 2 F	1		
(3) 13	6 M 7 F	1	0.08	0.27
	7 M 6 F	1		
	8 M 5 F	1		
(3) 14	4 M 10 F	1	0.08	0.29
	6 M 8 F	1		
	7 M 7 F	1		
(2) 15	7 M 8 F	1	0.06	0.21
	15 F	1		
(2) 16	10 M 6 F	1	0.06	0.22
	16 M	1		
(1) 17	11 M 6 F	1	0.03	0.12
(1) 18	18 F	1	0.03	0.12
(2) 19	13 M 6 F	1	0.06	0.26
	14 M 5 F	1		
(1) 20	9 M 11 F	1	0.03	0.14
(1) 21	21 F	1	0.03	0.14
(2) 25	9 M 16 F	1	0.06	0.34
	15 M 10 F	1		
(1) 31	19 M 12 F	1	0.03	0.21
(1) 47	30 M 17 F	1	0.03	0.32
SALEM, . . .	-	7,623	100.00	100.00
(353) 1	1 M	61	4.63	1.02
	1 F	292		
(1,320) 2	1 M 1 F	1,046	17.32	7.66
	2 M	26		
	2 F	248		
(1,465) 3	1 M 2 F	758	19.22	12.75
	2 M 1 F	580		
	3 M	14		
	3 F	113		
(1,326) 4	1 M 3 F	410	17.40	15.39
	2 M 2 F	613		
	3 M 1 F	248		
	4 M	4		
	4 F	51		
(1,099) 5	1 M 4 F	171	14.42	15.94
	2 M 3 F	399		
	3 M 2 F	398		
	4 M 1 F	113		
	5 F	18		
(769) 6	1 M 5 F	68	10.09	13.58
	2 M 4 F	216		
	3 M 3 F	274		
	4 M 2 F	163		
	5 M 1 F	42		
	6 F	6		
(509) 7	1 M 6 F	23	6.68	10.34
	2 M 5 F	100		
	3 M 4 F	158		
	4 M 3 F	139		
	5 M 2 F	72		
ESSEX — Con.				
SALEM — Con.				
	6 M 1 F	14		
	7 M	1		
	7 F	2		
(327) 8	1 M 7 F	7	4.29	7.59
	2 M 6 F	31		
	3 M 5 F	69		
	4 M 4 F	104		
	5 M 3 F	80		
	6 M 2 F	28		
	7 M 1 F	7		
	8 M	1		
(179) 9	1 M 8 F	4	2.35	4.67
	2 M 7 F	12		
	3 M 6 F	29		
	4 M 5 F	42		
	5 M 4 F	49		
	6 M 3 F	28		
	7 M 2 F	11		
	8 M 1 F	4		
(119) 10	1 M 9 F	1	1.56	3.45
	2 M 8 F	3		
	3 M 7 F	11		
	4 M 6 F	22		
	5 M 5 F	33		
	6 M 4 F	28		
	7 M 3 F	15		
	8 M 2 F	6		
(62) 11	2 M 9 F	1	0.81	1.98
	3 M 8 F	3		
	4 M 7 F	11		
	5 M 6 F	13		
	6 M 5 F	9		
	7 M 4 F	17		
	8 M 3 F	7		
	10 M 1 F	1		
(62) 12	3 M 9 F	1	0.42	1.11
	4 M 8 F	2		
	5 M 7 F	5		
	6 M 6 F	9		
	7 M 5 F	7		
	8 M 4 F	5		
	9 M 3 F	2		
	10 M 2 F	1		
(19) 13	5 M 8 F	1	0.25	0.72
	6 M 7 F	5		
	7 M 6 F	5		
	8 M 5 F	3		
	10 M 3 F	4		
	11 M 2 F	1		
(9) 14	4 M 10 F	1	0.12	0.37
	6 M 8 F	1		
	7 M 7 F	1		
	8 M 6 F	2		
	9 M 5 F	2		

SIZE OF FAMILIES AND COMPOSITION BY SEX: FOR CITIES — Continued.

COUNTIES, CITIES, SIZE OF FAMILIES, AND NUMBER OF EACH SIZE.	Composition of Families	Number of Families	PERCENTAGES: EACH SIZE OF — Total Families	PERCENTAGES: EACH SIZE OF — Total Population
ESSEX — Con.				
SALEM — Con.				
	14 M	1		
	14 F	1		
(7) 15	5 M 10 F	1	0.09	0.30
	8 M 7 F	2		
	10 M 5 F	1		
	11 M 4 F	1		
	15 M	2		
(6) 16	6 M 10 F	1	0.08	0.28
	7 M 9 F	1		
	9 M 7 F	1		
	11 M 5 F	1		
	16 F	2		
(5) 17	8 M 9 F	1	0.07	0.25
	9 M 8 F	2		
	12 M 5 F	1		
	17 M	1		
(2) 18	7 M 11 F	1	0.03	0.10
	12 M 6 F	1		
(1) 19	15 M 4 F	1	0.01	0.06
(1) 20	15 M 5 F	1	0.01	0.06
(1) 21	17 M 4 F	1	0.01	0.06
(1) 22	15 M 7 F	1	0.01	0.06
(2) 28	6 M 22 F	1	0.03	0.16
	28 F	1		
(2) 29	25 M 4 F	2	0.03	0.17
(1) 38	38 F	1	0.01	0.11
(1) 42	16 M 26 F	1	0.01	0.12
(1) 49	26 M 23 F	1	0.01	0.14
(1) 58	9 M 49 F	1	0.01	0.17
(1) 113	55 M 58 F	1	0.01	0.33
(1) 136	63 M 73 F	1	0.01	0.39
(1) 299	274 M 25 F	1	0.01	0.87
HAMPDEN.				
CHICOPEE, . .	—	5,042	100.00	100.00
(97) 1	1 M	46	2.20	0.41
	1 F	51		
(389) 2	1 M 1 F	300	12.13	4.49
	2 M	4		
	2 F	65		
(584) 3	1 M 2 F	284	17.56	9.76
	2 M 1 F	229		
	3 M	3		
	3 F	27		
(501) 4	1 M 3 F	128	16.47	12.20
	2 M 2 F	240		
	3 M 1 F	127		
	4 M	3		
	4 F	3		
(441) 5	1 M 4 F	67	14.50	13.43
	2 M 3 F	176		
	3 M 2 F	144		
	4 M 1 F	49		
	5 M	2		

COUNTIES, CITIES, SIZE OF FAMILIES, AND NUMBER OF EACH SIZE.	Composition of Families	Number of Families	PERCENTAGES: EACH SIZE OF — Total Families	PERCENTAGES: EACH SIZE OF — Total Population
HAMPDEN — Con.				
CHICOPEE — Con.				
	5 F	3		
(355) 6	1 M 5 F	28	11.67	12.97
	2 M 4 F	90		
	3 M 3 F	129		
	4 M 2 F	90		
	5 M 1 F	16		
	6 M	1		
	6 F	1		
(237) 7	1 M 6 F	6	7.79	10.10
	2 M 5 F	58		
	3 M 4 F	85		
	4 M 3 F	60		
	5 M 2 F	40		
	6 M 1 F	8		
(167) 8	1 M 7 F	5	5.49	8.14
	2 M 6 F	14		
	3 M 5 F	41		
	4 M 4 F	52		
	5 M 3 F	41		
	6 M 2 F	12		
	7 M 1 F	2		
(101) 9	2 M 7 F	6	3.32	5.54
	3 M 6 F	23		
	4 M 5 F	30		
	5 M 4 F	24		
	6 M 3 F	8		
	7 M 2 F	9		
	8 M 1 F	1		
(77) 10	2 M 8 F	3	2.53	4.60
	3 M 7 F	8		
	4 M 6 F	15		
	5 M 5 F	22		
	6 M 4 F	14		
	7 M 3 F	12		
	8 M 2 F	3		
(46) 11	3 M 8 F	6	1.51	3.05
	4 M 7 F	3		
	5 M 6 F	8		
	6 M 5 F	13		
	7 M 4 F	10		
	8 M 3 F	3		
	10 M 1 F	2		
	11 M	1		
(28) 12	3 M 9 F	3	0.92	2.05
	4 M 8 F	2		
	5 M 7 F	7		
	6 M 6 F	3		
	7 M 5 F	7		
	8 M 4 F	3		
	9 M 3 F	2		
	10 M 2 F	1		
(28) 13	4 M 9 F	2	0.92	2.22
	5 M 8 F	3		
	6 M 7 F	6		

SIZE OF FAMILIES AND COMPOSITION BY SEX: FOR CITIES — Continued.

HAMPDEN - Con.

CHICOPEE — Con.

Counties, Cities, Size of Families, and Number of Each Size.	Composition of Families	Number of Families	Percentages: Each Size of — Total Families	Percentages: Each Size of — Total Population
	7 M 6 F	6		
	8 M 5 F	4		
	9 M 4 F	3		
	10 M 3 F	1		
	11 M 2 F	1		
	12 M 1 F	1		
	13 F	1		
(24) 14	2 M 12 F	1	0.79	2.05
	4 M 10 F	2		
	5 M 9 F	1		
	6 M 8 F	2		
	7 M 7 F	6		
	8 M 6 F	5		
	9 M 5 F	5		
	10 M 4 F	1		
	11 M 3 F	1		
(12) 15	7 M 8 F	4	0.39	1.10
	8 M 7 F	2		
	9 M 6 F	3		
	10 M 5 F	1		
	11 M 4 F	2		
(7) 16	7 M 9 F	1	0.23	0.68
	9 M 7 F	3		
	10 M 6 F	3		
(10) 17	6 M 11 F	1	0.33	1.04
	8 M 9 F	1		
	9 M 8 F	2		
	10 M 7 F	3		
	11 M 6 F	1		
	13 M 4 F	2		
(6) 18	8 M 10 F	1	0.20	0.66
	10 M 8 F	2		
	11 M 7 F	1		
	12 M 6 F	1		
	14 M 4 F	1		
(5) 19	6 M 13 F	1	0.17	0.58
	9 M 10 F	2		
	11 M 8 F	1		
	13 M 6 F	1		
(5) 20	5 M 15 F	1	0.17	0.61
	10 M 10 F	2		
	13 M 7 F	2		
(3) 21	6 M 15 F	1	0.10	0.38
	10 M 11 F	1		
	12 M 9 F	1		
(1) 22	12 M 10 F	1	0.03	0.13
(1) 23	9 M 14 F	1	0.06	0.14
(3) 24	14 M 10 F	1	0.10	0.44
	15 M 9 F	2		
(1) 25	17 M 8 F	1	0.03	0.15
(3) 26	12 M 14 F	1	0.10	0.47
	15 M 11 F	1		
	19 M 7 F	1		
(2) 27	17 M 10 F	1	0.07	0.33

HAMPDEN - Con.

CHICOPEE — Con.

Counties, Cities, Size of Families, and Number of Each Size.	Composition of Families	Number of Families	Percentages: Each Size of — Total Families	Percentages: Each Size of — Total Population
	19 M 8 F	1		
(1) 28	15 M 13 F	1	0.03	0.17
(1) 33	30 M 3 F	1	0.03	0.20
(1) 34	15 M 19 F	1	0.03	0.21
(1) 37	17 M 20 F	1	0.03	0.22
(2) 50	30 M 20 F	1	0.07	0.61
	31 M 19 F	1		
(1) 55	28 M 27 F	1	0.03	0.33
(1) 69	27 M 42 F	1	0.03	0.42
HOLYOKE, . .	-	7,894	100.00	100.00
(153) 1	1 M	59	1.94	0.58
	1 F	94		
(931) 2	1 M 1 F	753	11.80	4.62
	2 M	21		
	2 F	157		
(1,289) 3	1 M 2 F	648	16.33	9.50
	2 M 1 F	539		
	3 M	19		
	3 F	83		
(1,362) 4	1 M 3 F	379	17.26	13.51
	2 M 2 F	650		
	3 M 1 F	290		
	4 M	6		
	4 F	37		
(1,221) 5	1 M 4 F	201	15.47	15.14
	2 M 3 F	463		
	3 M 2 F	465		
	4 M 1 F	129		
	5 M	2		
	5 F	21		
(1,021) 6	1 M 5 F	86	12.94	15.19
	2 M 4 F	290		
	3 M 3 F	362		
	4 M 2 F	234		
	5 M 1 F	38		
	6 M	2		
	6 F	9		
(731) 7	1 M 6 F	38	9.26	12.69
	2 M 5 F	116		
	3 M 4 F	253		
	4 M 3 F	196		
	5 M 2 F	108		
	6 M 1 F	18		
	7 F	2		
(404) 8	1 M 7 F	13	6.26	9.80
	2 M 6 F	59		
	3 M 5 F	108		
	4 M 4 F	158		
	5 M 3 F	113		
	6 M 2 F	30		
	7 M 1 F	11		
	8 F	2		
(289) 9	1 M 8 F	3	3.66	6.45
	2 M 7 F	19		

SIZE OF FAMILIES AND COMPOSITION BY SEX: FOR CITIES — Continued.

COUNTIES, CITIES, SIZE OF FAMILIES, AND NUMBER OF EACH SIZE.	Composition of Families	Number of Families	PERCENTAGES: EACH SIZE OF — Total Families	PERCENTAGES: EACH SIZE OF — Total Population
HAMPDEN - Con.				
HOLYOKE — Con.				
	3 M 6 F	55		
	4 M 5 F	68		
	5 M 4 F	77		
	6 M 3 F	46		
	7 M 2 F	20		
	8 M 1 F	1		
(182) 10	1 M 9 F	2	2.31	4.51
	2 M 8 F	6		
	3 M 7 F	20		
	4 M 6 F	44		
	5 M 5 F	47		
	6 M 4 F	36		
	7 M 3 F	16		
	8 M 2 F	9		
	9 M 1 F	1		
	10 M	1		
(89) 11	2 M 9 F	3	1.13	2.43
	3 M 8 F	5		
	4 M 7 F	13		
	5 M 6 F	18		
	6 M 5 F	24		
	7 M 4 F	18		
	8 M 3 F	4		
	9 M 2 F	3		
	10 M 1 F	1		
(48) 12	3 M 9 F	1	0.61	1.48
	4 M 8 F	6		
	5 M 7 F	8		
	6 M 6 F	11		
	7 M 5 F	10		
	8 M 4 F	4		
	9 M 3 F	5		
	10 M 2 F	1		
	12 F	2		
(31) 13	4 M 9 F	3	0.39	1.00
	5 M 8 F	6		
	6 M 7 F	4		
	7 M 6 F	9		
	8 M 5 F	7		
	10 M 3 F	2		
(19) 14	6 M 8 F	3	0.24	0.66
	7 M 7 F	8		
	8 M 6 F	4		
	9 M 5 F	2		
	10 M 4 F	1		
	14 M	1		
(4) 15	9 M 6 F	1	0.05	0.15
	10 M 5 F	2		
	11 M 4 F	1		
(4) 16	5 M 11 F	1	0.05	0.16
	8 M 8 F	1		
	9 M 7 F	1		
	11 M 5 F	1		
(4) 17	10 M 7 F	1	0.05	0.17
HAMPDEN - Con.				
HOLYOKE — Con.				
	12 M 5 F	1		
	14 M 3 F	1		
	17 F	1		
(1) 18	11 M 7 F	1	0.01	0.04
(4) 19	10 M 9 F	1	0.05	0.19
	15 M 4 F	3		
(4) 20	13 M 7 F	1	0.05	0.20
	17 M 3 F	2		
	20 F	1		
(1) 21	8 M 13 F	1	0.01	0.05
(1) 26	26 F	1	0.01	0.06
(2) 28	11 M 17 F	1	0.03	0.14
	20 M 8 F	1		
(1) 29	14 M 15 F	1	0.01	0.07
(1) 35	12 M 23 F	1	0.01	0.09
(1) 36	17 M 19 F	1	0.01	0.09
(1) 46	11 M 35 F	1	0.01	0.12
(1) 57	3 M 54 F	1	0.01	0.14
(1) 63	59 M 4 F	1	0.01	0.16
(1) 66	32 M 34 F	1	0.01	0.16
(1) 112	7 M 105 F	1	0.01	0.28
(1) 134	108 M 26 F	1	0.01	0.33
SPRINGFIELD, .	-	11,741	100.00	100.00
(403) 1	1 M	94	3.43	0.78
	1 F	309		
(2,043) 2	1 M 1 F	1,734	17.40	7.93
	2 M	35		
	2 F	274		
(2,531) 3	1 M 2 F	1,351	21.55	14.74
	2 M 1 F	1,019		
	3 M	14		
	3 F	147		
(2,221) 4	1 M 3 F	678	18.91	17.24
	2 M 2 F	1,077		
	3 M 1 F	418		
	4 M	6		
	4 F	42		
(1,724) 5	1 M 4 F	250	14.68	16.73
	2 M 3 F	674		
	3 M 2 F	584		
	4 M 1 F	188		
	5 M	5		
	5 F	14		
(1,171) 6	1 M 5 F	102	9.97	13.64
	2 M 4 F	317		
	3 M 3 F	414		
	4 M 2 F	257		
	5 M 1 F	71		
	6 M	3		
	6 F	7		
(690) 7	1 M 6 F	35	5.87	9.38
	2 M 5 F	117		
	3 M 4 F	202		
	4 M 3 F	207		

SIZE OF FAMILIES AND COMPOSITION BY SEX: FOR CITIES — Continued.

HAMPDEN - Con.
SPRINGFIELD — Con.

Counties, Cities, Size and Number of Each Size	Composition of Families	Number of Families	% Total Families	% Total Population
	5 M 2 F	98		
	6 M 1 F	25		
	7 M	4		
	7 F	2		
(411) 8	1 M 7 F	12	3.50	6.38
	2 M 6 F	48		
	3 M 5 F	94		
	4 M 4 F	117		
	5 M 3 F	92		
	6 M 2 F	31		
	7 M 1 F	13		
	8 M	1		
	8 F	3		
(211) 9	1 M 8 F	6	1.80	3.69
	2 M 7 F	10		
	3 M 6 F	25		
	4 M 5 F	65		
	5 M 4 F	48		
	6 M 3 F	34		
	7 M 2 F	17		
	8 M 1 F	5		
	9 M	1		
(135) 10	2 M 8 F	7	1.15	2.62
	3 M 7 F	16		
	4 M 6 F	22		
	5 M 5 F	35		
	6 M 4 F	27		
	7 M 3 F	19		
	8 M 2 F	7		
	9 M 1 F	2		
(72) 11	2 M 9 F	2	0.61	1.54
	3 M 8 F	1		
	4 M 7 F	11		
	5 M 6 F	12		
	6 M 5 F	14		
	7 M 4 F	15		
	8 M 3 F	10		
	9 M 2 F	4		
	10 M 1 F	2		
	11 M	1		
(35) 12	3 M 9 F	2	0.30	0.82
	4 M 8 F	2		
	5 M 7 F	6		
	6 M 6 F	6		
	7 M 5 F	7		
	8 M 4 F	7		
	9 M 3 F	3		
	10 M 2 F	2		
(20) 13	2 M 11 F	1	0.17	0.50
	3 M 10 F	1		
	5 M 8 F	3		
	6 M 7 F	2		
	7 M 6 F	3		
	8 M 5 F	3		
	9 M 4 F	2		
	10 M 3 F	2		
	11 M 2 F	2		
	13 M	1		
(15) 14	4 M 10 F	1	0.12	0.41
	5 M 9 F	1		
	6 M 8 F	1		
	7 M 7 F	5		
	8 M 6 F	3		
	9 M 5 F	2		
	10 M 4 F	1		
	14 F	1		
(12) 15	6 M 9 F	1	0.10	0.35
	7 M 8 F	1		
	8 M 7 F	1		
	9 M 6 F	1		
	10 M 5 F	2		
	11 M 4 F	2		
	12 M 3 F	2		
	13 M 2 F	1		
	15 F	1		
(4) 16	1 M 15 F	1	0.03	0.12
	8 M 8 F	1		
	13 M 3 F	1		
	14 M 2 F	1		
(6) 17	5 M 12 F	1	0.05	0.20
	6 M 11 F	1		
	8 M 9 F	2		
	10 M 7 F	1		
	13 M 4 F	1		
(3) 18	13 M 5 F	1	0.02	0.10
	14 M 4 F	2		
(2) 20	9 M 11 F	1	0.02	0.04
	17 M 3 F	1		
(2) 21	18 M 3 F	1	0.02	0.08
	19 M 2 F	1		
(2) 22	12 M 10 F	1	0.02	0.09
	14 M 8 F	1		
(2) 23	17 M 6 F	1	0.02	0.09
	23 F	1		
(2) 24	19 M 5 F	1	0.02	0.09
	22 M 2 F	1		
(2) 27	15 M 12 F	1	0.02	0.10
	25 M 2 F	1		
(2) 28	23 M 5 F	1	0.02	0.11
	24 M 4 F	1		
(2) 30	1 M 29 F	1	0.02	0.12
	30 M	1		
(2) 31	10 M 21 F	1	0.02	0.12
	19 M 12 F	1		
(1) 32	32 F	1	0.01	0.06
(1) 33	23 M 10 F	1	0.01	0.06
(2) 34	20 M 14 F	1	0.02	0.13
	34 F	1		

SIZE OF FAMILIES AND COMPOSITION BY SEX: FOR CITIES — Continued.

COUNTIES, CITIES, SIZE OF FAMILIES, AND NUMBER OF EACH SIZE.	Composition of Families	Number of Families	Total Families	Total Population	COUNTIES, CITIES, SIZE OF FAMILIES, AND NUMBER OF EACH SIZE.	Composition of Families	Number of Families	Total Families	Total Population
HAMPDEN - Con.					HAMPSHIRE — Con.				
SPRINGFIELD — Con.					NORTHAMPTON — Con.				
(1) 35	17 M 18 F	1	0.01	0.07	(101) 9	2 M 7 F	10	3.09	5.45
(1) 37	35 M 2 F	1	0.01	0.07		3 M 6 F	17		
(2) 38	18 M 20 F	1	0.02	0.15		4 M 5 F	22		
	31 M 7 F	1				5 M 4 F	19		
(2) 39	18 M 21 F	1	0.02	0.15		6 M 3 F	18		
	19 M 20 F	1				7 M 2 F	9		
(1) 47	26 M 21 F	1	0.01	0.09		8 M 1 F	4		
(1) 49	32 M 17 F	1	0.01	0.10		9 F	2		
(1) 50	16 M 34 F	1	0.01	0.10	(54) 10	1 M 9 F	1	1.65	3.22
(1) 74	34 M 40 F	1	0.01	0.14		2 M 8 F	6		
(1) 171	78 M 93 F	1	0.01	0.33		3 M 7 F	5		
(1) 259	228 M 31 F	1	0.01	0.50		4 M 6 F	9		
HAMPSHIRE.						5 M 5 F	15		
NORTHAMPTON, .	-	3,270	100.00	100.00		6 M 4 F	11		
(124) 1	1 M	43	3.79	0.74		7 M 3 F	3		
	1 F	81				8 M 2 F	3		
(507) 2	1 M 1 F	407	15.51	6.05		10 F	1		
	2 M	5			(31) 11	1 M 10 F	1	0.95	2.04
	2 F	95				3 M 8 F	5		
(614) 3	1 M 2 F	348	18.78	11.00		4 M 7 F	4		
	2 M 1 F	217				5 M 6 F	6		
	3 M	5				6 M 5 F	8		
	3 F	44				7 M 4 F	4		
(574) 4	1 M 3 F	196	17.55	13.71		8 M 3 F	1		
	2 M 2 F	277				10 M 1 F	1		
	3 M 1 F	103				11 F	1		
	4 M	2			(12) 12	2 M 10 F	1	0.37	0.86
	4 F	26				3 M 9 F	1		
(450) 5	1 M 4 F	63	13.76	13.44		4 M 8 F	1		
	2 M 3 F	181				5 M 7 F	3		
	3 M 2 F	141				6 M 6 F	2		
	4 M 1 F	58				8 M 4 F	2		
	5 F	7				10 M 2 F	1		
(333) 6	1 M 5 F	28	10.19	11.93		12 F	1		
	2 M 4 F	82			(18) 13	1 M 12 F	1	0.55	1.40
	3 M 3 F	121				4 M 9 F	3		
	4 M 2 F	85				5 M 8 F	4		
	5 M 1 F	15				6 M 7 F	1		
	6 F	2				7 M 6 F	3		
(243) 7	1 M 6 F	16	7.43	10.16		9 M 4 F	2		
	2 M 5 F	36				11 M 2 F	1		
	3 M 4 F	84				13 F	2		
	4 M 3 F	64			(4) 14	1 M 13 F	4	0.12	0.33
	5 M 2 F	36			(6) 15	1 M 14 F	2	0.19	0.54
	6 M 1 F	7				5 M 10 F	1		
(165) 8	1 M 7 F	8	5.05	7.88		8 M 7 F	2		
	2 M 6 F	18				9 M 6 F	1		
	3 M 5 F	34			(2) 16	11 M 5 F	1	0.06	0.19
	4 M 4 F	48				16 F	1		
	5 M 3 F	21			(1) 17	9 M 8 F	1	0.03	0.10
	6 M 2 F	18			(2) 18	8 M 10 F	1	0.06	0.21
	7 M 1 F	6				18 F	1		
	8 F	2			(2) 22	14 M 8 F	1	0.06	0.26
						22 F	1		

SIZE OF FAMILIES AND COMPOSITION BY SEX: FOR CITIES — Continued.

COUNTIES, CITIES, SIZE OF FAMILIES, AND NUMBER OF EACH SIZE.	Composition of Families	Number of Families	Percentages: Each Size of — Total Families	Percentages: Each Size of — Total Population	COUNTIES, CITIES, SIZE OF FAMILIES, AND NUMBER OF EACH SIZE.	Composition of Families	Number of Families	Percentages: Each Size of — Total Families	Percentages: Each Size of — Total Population
HAMPSHIRE — Con.					**MIDDLESEX** — Con.				
NORTHAMPTON — Con.					CAMBRIDGE — Con.				
(1) 23	17 M 6 F	1	0.03	0.14		6 F	26		
(2) 24	12 M 12 F	1	0.06	0.29	(1,359) 7	1 M 6 F	62	7.90	11.65
	20 M 4 F	1				2 M 5 F	248		
(3) 25	1 M 24 F	2	0.09	0.45		3 M 4 F	405		
	25 F	1				4 M 3 F	403		
(1) 28	28 F	1	0.03	0.17		5 M 2 F	190		
(1) 29	29 F	1	0.03	0.17		6 M 1 F	41		
(2) 34	13 M 21 F	1	0.06	0.41		7 M	4		
	34 F	1				7 F	6		
(1) 35	35 F	1	0.03	0.21	(845) 8	1 M 7 F	23	4.91	8.28
(1) 40	2 M 38 F	1	0.03	0.24		2 M 6 F	103		
(1) 43	39 M 4 F	1	0.03	0.26		3 M 5 F	174		
(1) 45	39 M 6 F	1	0.03	0.27		4 M 4 F	245		
(1) 49	4 M 45 F	1	0.03	0.29		5 M 3 F	192		
(1) 50	50 F	1	0.03	0.30		6 M 2 F	84		
(2) 54	1 M 53 F	1	0.06	0.64		7 M 1 F	21		
	54 F	1				8 F	3		
(1) 57	21 M 36 F	1	0.03	0.34	(482) 9	1 M 8 F	10	2.80	5.51
(1) 59	1 M 58 F	1	0.03	0.35		2 M 7 F	40		
(1) 60	60 F	1	0.03	0.36		3 M 6 F	70		
(1) 63	63 F	1	0.03	0.38		4 M 5 F	122		
(1) 64	31 M 33 F	1	0.03	0.38		5 M 4 F	111		
(1) 66	66 F	1	0.03	0.39		6 M 3 F	86		
(1) 68	68 F	1	0.03	0.41		7 M 2 F	34		
(1) 72	30 M 42 F	1	0.03	0.43		8 M 1 F	7		
(1) 608	298 M 310 F	1	0.03	3.63		9 M	1		
MIDDLESEX.						9 F	1		
CAMBRIDGE, . .	—	17,193	100.00	100.00	(231) 10	1 M 9 F	1	1.34	2.86
(447) 1	1 M	130	2.60	0.55		2 M 8 F	9		
	1 F	317				3 M 7 F	26		
(2,580) 2	1 M 1 F	2,130	15.00	6.32		4 M 6 F	51		
	2 M	56				5 M 5 F	44		
	2 F	394				6 M 4 F	37		
(3,143) 3	1 M 2 F	1,668	18.28	11.55		7 M 3 F	34		
	2 M 1 F	1,267				8 M 2 F	22		
	3 M	12				9 M 1 F	5		
	3 F	196				10 F	2		
(3,150) 4	1 M 3 F	936	18.32	15.43	(145) 11	1 M 10 F	4	0.84	1.95
	2 M 2 F	1,403				2 M 9 F	7		
	3 M 1 F	654				3 M 8 F	11		
	4 M	10				4 M 7 F	19		
	4 F	87				5 M 6 F	23		
(2,637) 5	1 M 4 F	416	15.33	16.15		6 M 5 F	28		
	2 M 5 F	990				7 M 4 F	25		
	3 M 2 F	905				8 M 3 F	17		
	4 M 1 F	291				9 M 2 F	8		
	5 M	2				10 M 1 F	1		
	5 F	33				11 M	2		
(1,975) 6	1 M 5 F	163	11.48	14.51	(61) 12	2 M 10 F	1	0.35	0.90
	2 M 4 F	503				3 M 9 F	4		
	3 M 3 F	688				4 M 8 F	4		
	4 M 2 F	462				5 M 7 F	11		
	5 M 1 F	153				6 M 6 F	9		
						7 M 5 F	9		

SIZE OF FAMILIES AND COMPOSITION BY SEX: FOR CITIES — Continued.

COUNTIES, CITIES, SIZE OF FAMILIES, AND NUMBER OF EACH SIZE.	Composition of Families	Number of Families	Percentages: Each Size of — Total Families	Percentages: Each Size of — Total Population
MIDDLESEX —Con.				
CAMBRIDGE—Con.				
	8 M 4 F	14		
	9 M 3 F	7		
	12 M	1		
	12 F	1		
(47) 13	2 M 11 F	1	0.27	0.75
	3 M 10 F	1		
	4 M 9 F	3		
	5 M 8 F	5		
	6 M 7 F	4		
	7 M 6 F	4		
	8 M 5 F	13		
	9 M 4 F	7		
	10 M 3 F	3		
	11 M 2 F	3		
	12 M 1 F	2		
	13 F	1		
(17) 14	1 M 13 F	2	0.10	0.29
	5 M 9 F	1		
	6 M 8 F	1		
	7 M 7 F	4		
	8 M 6 F	3		
	10 M 4 F	3		
	11 M 3 F	1		
	12 M 2 F	1		
	14 F	1		
(17) 15	1 M 14 F	1	0.10	0.31
	3 M 12 F	2		
	5 M 10 F	1		
	6 M 9 F	1		
	7 M 8 F	1		
	8 M 7 F	1		
	11 M 4 F	4		
	12 M 3 F	2		
	13 M 2 F	2		
	14 M 1 F	1		
	15 F	1		
(10) 16	3 M 13 F	1	0.05	0.20
	6 M 10 F	1		
	8 M 8 F	3		
	11 M 5 F	2		
	12 M 4 F	1		
	13 M 3 F	1		
	16 F	1		
(5) 17	8 M 9 F	1	0.03	0.10
	10 M 7 F	1		
	11 M 6 F	1		
	13 M 4 F	1		
	15 M 2 F	1		
(4) 18	8 M 10 F	1	0.02	0.09
	14 M 4 F	1		
	15 M 3 F	1		
	18 M	1		
(1) 19	3 M 16 F	1	0.01	0.02
(4) 20	1 M 19 F	1	0.02	0.10

COUNTIES, CITIES, SIZE OF FAMILIES, AND NUMBER OF EACH SIZE.	Composition of Families	Number of Families	Percentages: Each Size of — Total Families	Percentages: Each Size of — Total Population
MIDDLESEX —Con.				
CAMBRIDGE—Con.				
	3 M 17 F	1		
	17 M 3 F	1		
	18 M 2 F	1		
(3) 21	16 M 5 F	1	0.01	0.08
	17 M 4 F	1		
	21 M	1		
(3) 22	20 M 2 F	1	0.01	0.08
	22 M	1		
	22 F	1		
(1) 23	23 M	1	0.01	0.06
(1) 24	17 M 7 F	1	0.01	0.03
(1) 26	21 M 5 F	1	0.01	0.03
(1) 27	27 M	1	0.01	0.03
(2) 32	23 M 9 F	1	0.01	0.08
	32 M	1		
(1) 38	38 M	1	0.01	0.05
(1) 39	14 M 25 F	1	0.01	0.05
(1) 41	41 M	1	0.01	0.05
(2) 43	41 M 2 F	1	0.01	0.10
	43 M	1		
(1) 44	18 M 26 F	1	0.01	0.05
(1) 47	47 M	1	0.01	0.06
(1) 48	44 M 4 F	1	0.01	0.06
(1) 49	49 M	1	0.01	0.06
(2) 53	53 M	2	0.01	0.13
(1) 57	57 M	1	0.01	0.07
(1) 78	78 M	1	0.01	0.10
(1) 80	80 M	1	0.01	0.10
(1) 96	96 M	1	0.01	0.12
(1) 98	98 M	1	0.01	0.12
(2) 99	98 M 1 F	1	0.01	0.24
	99 M	1		
(1) 120	120 M	1	0.01	0.15
(1) 122	62 M 60 F	1	0.01	0.15
(1) 564	488 M 76 F	1	0.01	0.69
EVERETT, . . .	-	4,304	100.00	100.00
(96) 1	1 M	34	2.23	0.52
	1 F	62		
(715) 2	1 M 1 F	648	16.61	7.70
	2 M	12		
	2 F	55		
(941) 3	1 M 2 F	497	21.87	15.20
	2 M 1 F	420		
	3 M	3		
	3 F	21		
(837) 4	1 M 3 F	230	19.45	18.03
	2 M 2 F	424		
	3 M 1 F	171		
	4 M	7		
	4 F	11		
(671) 5	1 M 4 F	90	15.59	18.06
	2 M 3 F	244		
	3 M 2 F	273		
	4 M 1 F	60		

SIZE OF FAMILIES AND COMPOSITION BY SEX: FOR CITIES — Continued.

MIDDLESEX — Con.

EVERETT — Con.

COUNTIES, CITIES, SIZE OF FAMILIES, AND NUMBER OF EACH SIZE.	Composition of Families	Number of Families	PERCENTAGES: EACH SIZE OF — Total Families	PERCENTAGES: EACH SIZE OF — Total Population
	5 M	1		
	5 F	3		
(475) 6	1 M 5 F	34	11.04	15.34
	2 M 4 F	120		
	3 M 3 F	172		
	4 M 2 F	112		
	5 M 1 F	28		
(254) 7	1 M 6 F	7	5.90	9.57
	2 M 5 F	37		
	3 M 4 F	80		
	4 M 3 F	72		
	5 M 2 F	40		
	6 M 1 F	9		
(148) 8	1 M 7 F	5	3.44	6.57
	2 M 6 F	17		
	3 M 5 F	28		
	4 M 4 F	40		
	5 M 5 F	40		
	6 M 2 F	14		
	7 M 1 F	4		
(87) 9	2 M 7 F	8	2.02	4.22
	3 M 6 F	8		
	4 M 5 F	26		
	5 M 4 F	19		
	6 M 3 F	17		
	7 M 2 F	7		
	8 M 1 F	2		
(41) 10	2 M 8 F	1	0.95	2.21
	3 M 7 F	3		
	4 M 6 F	7		
	5 M 5 F	10		
	6 M 4 F	12		
	7 M 3 F	6		
	8 M 2 F	2		
(20) 11	2 M 9 F	2	0.47	1.18
	4 M 7 F	3		
	5 M 6 F	5		
	6 M 5 F	5		
	7 M 4 F	4		
	8 M 3 F	1		
(8) 12	3 M 9 F	1	0.19	0.52
	6 M 6 F	4		
	8 M 4 F	2		
	11 M 1 F	1		
(3) 13	5 M 8 F	1	0.07	0.21
	6 M 7 F	1		
	9 M 4 F	1		
(3) 14	3 M 11 F	1	0.07	0.23
	6 M 8 F	1		
	7 M 7 F	1		
(1) 18	5 M 13 F	1	0.02	0.10
(1) 22	12 M 10 F	1	0.02	0.12
(1) 23	1 M 22 F	1	0.02	0.12

MIDDLESEX — Con.

EVERETT — Con.

COUNTIES, CITIES, SIZE OF FAMILIES, AND NUMBER OF EACH SIZE.	Composition of Families	Number of Families	PERCENTAGES: EACH SIZE OF — Total Families	PERCENTAGES: EACH SIZE OF — Total Population
(1) 27	21 M 6 F	1	0.02	0.14
(1) 29	26 M 3 F	1	0.02	0.16
LOWELL, . .	—	16,885	100.00	100.00
(465) 1	1 M	117	2.75	0.55
	1 F	348		
(2,451) 2	1 M 1 F	1,652	14.51	5.81
	2 M	49		
	2 F	450		
(3,005) 3	1 M 2 F	1,645	17.80	10.69
	2 M 1 F	1,076		
	3 M	26		
	3 F	258		
(2,913) 4	1 M 3 F	914	17.25	13.81
	2 M 2 F	1,352		
	3 M 1 F	526		
	4 M	14		
	4 F	110		
(2,472) 5	1 M 4 F	385	14.64	14.65
	2 M 3 F	983		
	3 M 2 F	801		
	4 M 1 F	226		
	5 M	16		
	5 F	61		
(1,935) 6	1 M 5 F	196	11.46	13.76
	2 M 4 F	526		
	3 M 3 F	706		
	4 M 2 F	404		
	5 M 1 F	79		
	6 M	13		
	6 F	11		
(1,297) 7	1 M 6 F	88	7.68	10.76
	2 M 5 F	242		
	3 M 4 F	394		
	4 M 3 F	370		
	5 M 2 F	155		
	6 M 1 F	35		
	7 M	4		
	7 F	9		
(871) 8	1 M 7 F	23	5.16	8.26
	2 M 6 F	103		
	3 M 5 F	207		
	4 M 4 F	207		
	5 M 3 F	180		
	6 M 2 F	75		
	7 M 1 F	10		
	8 M	4		
	8 F	2		
(542) 9	1 M 8 F	12	3.21	5.78
	2 M 7 F	41		
	3 M 6 F	92		
	4 M 5 F	146		
	5 M 4 F	147		
	6 M 3 F	70		

SIZE OF FAMILIES AND COMPOSITION BY SEX: FOR CITIES — Continued.

COUNTIES, CITIES, SIZE OF FAMILIES, AND NUMBER OF EACH SIZE.	Composition of Families	Number of Families	Total Families	Total Population
MIDDLESEX — Con.				
LOWELL — Con.				
	7 M 2 F	25		
	8 M 1 F	8		
	9 F	3		
(392) 10	1 M 9 F	1	1.96	3.93
	2 M 8 F	16		
	3 M 7 F	42		
	4 M 6 F	62		
	5 M 5 F	85		
	6 M 4 F	64		
	7 M 3 F	44		
	8 M 2 F	14		
	9 M 1 F	1		
	10 M	1		
	10 F	2		
(186) 11	1 M 10 F	2	1.10	2.42
	2 M 9 F	4		
	3 M 8 F	12		
	4 M 7 F	35		
	5 M 6 F	42		
	6 M 5 F	49		
	7 M 4 F	28		
	8 M 3 F	14		
	9 M 2 F	1		
	11 M	1		
(99) 12	1 M 11 F	2	0.58	1.41
	2 M 10 F	1		
	3 M 9 F	5		
	4 M 8 F	7		
	5 M 7 F	18		
	6 M 6 F	25		
	7 M 5 F	21		
	8 M 4 F	12		
	9 M 3 F	5		
	10 M 2 F	2		
	12 M	1		
(61) 13	1 M 12 F	1	0.36	0.94
	3 M 10 F	2		
	4 M 9 F	4		
	5 M 8 F	8		
	6 M 7 F	16		
	7 M 6 F	13		
	8 M 5 F	10		
	9 M 4 F	4		
	10 M 3 F	2		
	11 M 2 F	1		
(57) 14	2 M 12 F	1	0.34	0.95
	3 M 11 F	2		
	4 M 10 F	5		
	5 M 9 F	4		
	6 M 8 F	8		
	7 M 7 F	7		
	8 M 6 F	9		
	9 M 5 F	11		
	10 M 4 F	5		
MIDDLESEX — Con.				
LOWELL — Con.				
	11 M 3 F	5		
	12 M 2 F	2		
(29) 15	5 M 12 F	1	0.17	0.52
	5 M 10 F	4		
	6 M 9 F	5		
	7 M 8 F	4		
	8 M 7 F	5		
	9 M 6 F	3		
	10 M 5 F	4		
	11 M 4 F	2		
	12 M 3 F	3		
(15) 16	5 M 13 F	1	0.09	0.28
	6 M 10 F	3		
	7 M 9 F	1		
	8 M 8 F	3		
	9 M 7 F	1		
	10 M 6 F	3		
	11 M 5 F	1		
	13 M 3 F	1		
	16 M	1		
(17) 17	5 M 12 F	2	0.10	0.34
	7 M 10 F	2		
	8 M 9 F	1		
	9 M 8 F	2		
	10 M 7 F	3		
	11 M 6 F	2		
	12 M 5 F	2		
	13 M 4 F	2		
	14 M 3 F	1		
(15) 18	1 M 17 F	1	0.09	0.32
	5 M 13 F	1		
	4 M 14 F	1		
	7 M 11 F	1		
	8 M 10 F	1		
	9 M 9 F	5		
	10 M 8 F	1		
	12 M 6 F	4		
	18 F	2		
(9) 19	8 M 11 F	2	0.05	0.20
	9 M 10 F	1		
	11 M 8 F	1		
	12 M 7 F	4		
	13 M 6 F	1		
(14) 20	1 M 19 F	2	0.08	0.33
	2 M 18 F	1		
	4 M 16 F	1		
	8 M 12 F	2		
	9 M 11 F	2		
	11 M 9 F	1		
	14 M 6 F	2		
	16 M 4 F	2		
	20 M	1		
(6) 21	1 M 20 F	1	0.03	0.15
	5 M 18 F	1		

SIZE OF FAMILIES AND COMPOSITION BY SEX: FOR CITIES — Continued.

COUNTIES, CITIES, SIZE OF FAMILIES, AND NUMBER OF EACH SIZE.	Composition of Families	Number of Families	Total Families	Total Population	COUNTIES, CITIES, SIZE OF FAMILIES, AND NUMBER OF EACH SIZE.	Composition of Families	Number of Families	Total Families	Total Population
MIDDLESEX — Con.					**MIDDLESEX — Con.**				
LOWELL — Con.					**LOWELL — Con.**				
8 M 13 F	1				(2) 33	4 M 29 F	1	0.01	0.08
9 M 12 F	1					16 M 17 F	1		
11 M 10 F	1				(1) 34	19 M 15 F	1	0.01	0.04
21 F	1				(5) 35	1 M 34 F	1	0.03	0.21
(6) 22	2 M 20 F	1	0.03	0.16		16 M 19 F	2		
	10 M 12 F	1				20 M 9 F	1		
	11 M 11 F	1				27 M 8 F	1		
	13 M 9 F	1			(4) 36	6 M 30 F	1	0.02	0.17
	14 M 8 F	1				12 M 24 F	1		
	22 F	1				14 M 22 F	1		
(6) 23	7 M 16 F	2	0.03	0.16		25 M 11 F	1		
	12 M 11 F	2			(4) 37	1 M 36 F	1	0.02	0.18
	16 M 7 F	1				22 M 15 F	2		
	17 M 6 F	1				37 F	- 1		
(5) 24	13 M 11 F	1	0.03	0.14	(3) 38	4 M 34 F	1	0.02	0.13
	14 M 10 F	3				6 M 32 F	1		
	16 M 8 F	1				38 F	1		
(10) 25	1 M 24 F	1	0.06	0.30	(3) 39	20 M 19 F	1	0.02	0.14
	3 M 22 F	1				31 M 8 F	1		
	8 M 17 F	1				32 M 7 F	1		
	12 M 13 F	1			(1) 40	7 M 33 F	1	0.01	0.05
	13 M 12 F	1			(1) 43	35 M 8 F	1	0.01	0.05
	14 M 11 F	1			(2) 44	5 M 39 F	1	0.01	0.10
	15 M 10 F	1				13 M 31 F	1		
	17 M 8 F	2			(1) 46	35 M 11 F	1	0.01	0.05
	25 F	1			(1) 47	17 M 30 F	1	0.01	0.06
(4) 26	1 M 25 F	1	0.02	0.12	(1) 48	30 M 18 F	1	0.01	0.06
	5 M 21 F	1			(1) 49	10 M 39 F	1	0.01	0.06
	6 M 20 F	1			(1) 50	29 M 21 F	1	0.01	0.06
	25 M 1 F	1			(1) 52	13 M 39 F	1	0.01	0.06
(5) 27	3 M 24 F	1	0.03	0.16	(1) 53	6 M 47 F	1	0.01	0.06
	7 M 20 F	1			(1) 64	64 F	1	0.01	0.08
	10 M 17 F	1			(1) 70	70 F	1	0.01	0.08
	13 M 14 F	1			(1) 107	84 M 23 F	1	0.01	0.13
	18 M 9 F	1			(1) 113	87 M 26 F	1	0.01	0.13
(4) 28	11 M 17 F	1	0.02	0.15	(1) 342	144 M 198 F	1	0.01	0.41
	14 M 14 F	1			**MALDEN, . .**		-	6,638	100.00	100.00
	19 M 9 F	1			(178) 1	1 M	57	2.68	0.60
	20 M 8 F	1				1 F	121		
(6) 29	9 M 20 F	1	0.03	0.21	(1,007) 2	1 M 1 F	860	15.17	6.78
	11 M 18 F	1				2 M	13		
	16 M 13 F	1				2 F	134		
	18 M 11 F	1			(1,205) 3	1 M 2 F	716	19.51	13.08
	19 M 10 F	1				2 M 1 F	510		
	21 M 8 F	1				3 M	7		
(5) 30	2 M 28 F	1	0.03	0.18		3 F	62		
	3 M 27 F	1			(1,345) 4	1 M 3 F	440	20.26	18.11
	13 M 17 F	2				2 M 2 F	635		
	23 M 7 F	1				3 M 1 F	243		
(3) 31	4 M 27 F	1	0.02	0.11		4 M	5		
	13 M 18 F	1				4 F	24		
	19 M 12 F	1			(1,072) 5	1 M 4 F	186	16.15	18.04
(2) 32	19 M 13 F	1	0.01	0.08		2 M 3 F	414		
	25 M 7 F	1				3 M 2 F	343		

SIZE OF FAMILIES AND COMPOSITION BY SEX: FOR CITIES — Continued.

Counties, Cities, Size of Families, and Number of Each Size	Composition of Families	Number of Families	% Total Families	% Total Population
MIDDLESEX — Con.				
MALDEN — Con.				
	4 M 1 F	107		
	5 M	4		
	5 F	18		
(752) 6	1 M 5 F	59	11.52	15.19
	2 M 4 F	214		
	3 M 3 F	305		
	4 M 2 F	144		
	5 M 1 F	26		
	6 F	4		
(487) 7	1 M 6 F	21	6.58	10.59
	2 M 5 F	81		
	3 M 4 F	143		
	4 M 3 F	123		
	5 M 2 F	57		
	6 M 1 F	9		
	7 M	2		
	7 F	1		
(230) 8	1 M 7 F	5	3.46	6.19
	2 M 6 F	24		
	3 M 5 F	79		
	4 M 4 F	60		
	5 M 3 F	52		
	6 M 2 F	17		
	7 M 1 F	2		
(140) 9	1 M 8 F	3	2.11	4.24
	2 M 7 F	11		
	3 M 6 F	22		
	4 M 5 F	40		
	5 M 4 F	31		
	6 M 3 F	26		
	7 M 2 F	7		
(84) 10	2 M 8 F	2	1.26	2.83
	3 M 7 F	10		
	4 M 6 F	22		
	5 M 5 F	22		
	6 M 4 F	11		
	7 M 3 F	12		
	8 M 2 F	5		
(34) 11	2 M 9 F	1	0.51	1.26
	3 M 8 F	4		
	4 M 7 F	2		
	5 M 6 F	4		
	6 M 5 F	6		
	7 M 4 F	10		
	8 M 3 F	4		
	9 M 2 F	3		
(22) 12	4 M 8 F	3	0.33	0.89
	5 M 7 F	4		
	6 M 6 F	7		
	7 M 5 F	3		
	8 M 4 F	3		
	9 M 3 F	1		
	10 M 2 F	1		
(11) 13	6 M 7 F	2	0.16	0.48
MIDDLESEX — Con.				
MALDEN — Con.				
	7 M 6 F	3		
	8 M 5 F	1		
	9 M 4 F	2		
	10 M 3 F	2		
	11 M 2 F	1		
(9) 14	5 M 9 F	1	0.13	0.42
	6 M 8 F	1		
	8 M 6 F	4		
	9 M 5 F	2		
	11 M 3 F	1		
(2) 15	9 M 6 F	1	0.03	0.10
	10 M 5 F	1		
(6) 16	8 M 8 F	2	0.09	0.32
	9 M 7 F	1		
	11 M 5 F	1		
	12 M 4 F	1		
	13 M 3 F	1		
(3) 17	6 M 11 F	1	0.05	0.17
	12 M 5 F	1		
	13 M 4 F	1		
(5) 18	6 M 12 F	1	0.05	0.18
	7 M 11 F	1		
	10 M 8 F	1		
(5) 20	8 M 12 F	1	0.05	0.20
	10 M 10 F	1		
	20 F	1		
(1) 23	20 M 3 F	1	0.02	0.08
(1) 24	12 M 12 F	1	0.02	0.08
(1) 31	5 M 26 F	1	0.02	0.10
(1) 43	43 M	1	0.02	0.15
(1) 61	61 M	1	0.02	0.21
MARLBOROUGH, .	-	3,150	100.00	100.00
(73) 1	1 M	26	2.31	0.49
	1 F	47		
(489) 2	1 M 1 F	439	15.48	6.55
	2 M	10		
	2 F	40		
(595) 3	1 M 2 F	390	18.77	11.88
	2 M 1 F	259		
	3 M	10		
	3 F	24		
(565) 4	1 M 3 F	148	17.89	15.09
	2 M 2 F	284		
	3 M 1 F	117		
	4 M	2		
	4 F	14		
(469) 5	1 M 4 F	65	14.56	15.36
	2 M 3 F	181		
	3 M 2 F	156		
	4 M 1 F	51		
	5 M	1		
	5 F	6		
(347) 6	1 M 5 F	24	10.98	13.90
	2 M 4 F	81		

SIZE OF FAMILIES AND COMPOSITION BY SEX: FOR CITIES — Continued.

COUNTIES, CITIES, SIZE OF FAMILIES, AND NUMBER OF EACH SIZE.	Composition of Families	Number of Families	Total Families	Total Population
MIDDLESEX — Con.				
MARLBOROUGH — Con.				
	3 M 3 F	125		
	4 M 2 F	101		
	5 M 1 F	14		
	6 F	2		
(244) 7	1 M 6 F	9	7.72	11.40
	2 M 5 F	37		
	3 M 4 F	75		
	4 M 3 F	81		
	5 M 2 F	35		
	6 M 1 F	7		
(162) 8	1 M 7 F	5	5.13	8.65
	2 M 6 F	6		
	3 M 5 F	43		
	4 M 4 F	33		
	5 M 3 F	33		
	6 M 2 F	16		
	7 M 1 F	6		
(102) 9	2 M 7 F	8	3.23	6.15
	3 M 6 F	13		
	4 M 5 F	27		
	5 M 4 F	26		
	6 M 3 F	19		
	7 M 2 F	8		
	8 M 1 F	1		
(47) 10	3 M 7 F	3	1.49	3.14
	4 M 6 F	15		
	5 M 5 F	13		
	6 M 4 F	7		
	7 M 3 F	8		
	8 M 2 F	2		
(33) 11	3 M 8 F	1	1.04	2.42
	4 M 7 F	5		
	5 M 6 F	8		
	6 M 5 F	8		
	7 M 4 F	7		
	8 M 3 F	2		
	9 M 2 F	2		
(17) 12	4 M 8 F	4	0.54	1.36
	5 M 7 F	1		
	6 M 6 F	5		
	7 M 5 F	3		
	8 M 4 F	3		
	9 M 3 F	1		
(9) 13	5 M 8 F	1	0.29	0.78
	6 M 7 F	2		
	7 M 6 F	1		
	8 M 5 F	5		
	9 M 4 F	2		
(5) 14	8 M 6 F	2	0.16	0.47
	10 M 4 F	1		
	11 M 3 F	1		
	12 M 2 F	1		
(3) 15	5 M 10 F	1	0.10	0.30
MIDDLESEX — Con.				
MARLBOROUGH — Con.				
	7 M 8 F	1		
	11 M 4 F	1		
(1) 16	12 M 4 F	1	0.03	0.11
(3) 19	13 M 6 F	1	0.10	0.38
	14 M 5 F	2		
(1) 21	12 M 9 F	1	0.03	0.14
(1) 26	26 M	1	0.03	0.17
(2) 29	22 M 7 F	2	0.06	0.39
(1) 37	25 M 12 F	1	0.03	0.25
(1) 99	99 M	1	0.03	0.66
MEDFORD, . .	-	3,172	100.00	100.00
(86) 1	1 M	23	2.71	0.59
	1 F	63		
(510) 2	1 M 1 F	447	16.08	7.05
	2 M	6		
	2 F	57		
(615) 3	1 M 2 F	345	19.35	12.71
	2 M 1 F	228		
	3 M	1		
	3 F	39		
(993) 4	1 M 3 F	162	19.04	16.66
	2 M 2 F	323		
	3 M 1 F	108		
	4 F	12		
(477) 5	1 M 4 F	80	15.04	16.48
	2 M 3 F	186		
	3 M 2 F	163		
	4 M 1 F	35		
	5 F	4		
(365) 6	1 M 5 F	31	11.51	15.13
	2 M 4 F	98		
	3 M 3 F	137		
	4 M 2 F	69		
	5 M 1 F	27		
	6 M	2		
	6 F	1		
(204) 7	1 M 6 F	11	6.43	9.87
	2 M 5 F	26		
	3 M 4 F	59		
	4 M 3 F	64		
	5 M 2 F	23		
	6 M 1 F	11		
(148) 8	1 M 7 F	2	4.67	8.18
	2 M 6 F	14		
	3 M 5 F	45		
	4 M 4 F	37		
	5 M 3 F	27		
	6 M 2 F	17		
	7 M 1 F	5		
	8 M	1		
(82) 9	1 M 8 F	1	2.59	5.10
	2 M 7 F	4		
	3 M 6 F	10		

SIZE OF FAMILIES AND COMPOSITION BY SEX: FOR CITIES — Continued.

Counties, Cities, Size of Families, and Number of Each Size.	Composition of Families	Number of Families	Percentages: Each Size of — Total Families	Total Population	Counties, Cities, Size of Families, and Number of Each Size.	Composition of Families	Number of Families	Percentages: Each Size of — Total Families	Total Population
MIDDLESEX — Con.					MIDDLESEX — Con.				
MEDFORD — Con.					NEWTON — Con.				
	4 M 5 F	18			(920) 3	1 M 2 F	532	16.64	10.00
	5 M 4 F	25				2 M 1 F	314		
	6 M 3 F	16				3 M	6		
	7 M 2 F	7				3 F	68		
	8 M 1 F	1			(1,069) 4	1 M 3 F	361	18.25	14.63
(30) 10	3 M 7 F	4	0.95	2.07		2 M 2 F	455		
	4 M 6 F	2				3 M 1 F	165		
	5 M 5 F	11				4 M	3		
	6 M 4 F	7				4 F	27		
	7 M 3 F	4			(931) 5	1 M 4 F	199	16.84	16.87
	8 M 2 F	1				2 M 3 F	390		
	9 M 1 F	1				3 M 2 F	265		
(19) 11	3 M 8 F	1	0.60	1.44		4 M 1 F	63		
	4 M 7 F	3				5 M	3		
	5 M 6 F	1				5 F	11		
	6 M 5 F	4			(689) 6	1 M 5 F	85	12.46	14.98
	7 M 4 F	4				2 M 4 F	222		
	8 M 3 F	4				3 M 3 F	236		
	9 M 2 F	1				4 M 2 F	118		
	11 F	1				5 M 1 F	23		
(13) 12	4 M 8 F	1	0.41	1.08		6 M	1		
	5 M 7 F	2				6 F	4		
	6 M 6 F	2			(495) 7	1 M 6 F	33	8.95	12.36
	7 M 5 F	4				2 M 5 F	111		
	8 M 4 F	1				3 M 4 F	151		
	9 M 3 F	2				4 M 3 F	119		
	10 M 2 F	1				5 M 2 F	64		
(3) 13	7 M 6 F	1	0.09	0.27		6 M 1 F	15		
	8 M 5 F	1				7 F	2		
	13 M	1			(315) 8	1 M 7 F	12	5.70	9.13
(1) 14	11 M 3 F	1	0.03	0.10		2 M 6 F	41		
(5) 15	6 M 9 F	1	0.16	0.52		3 M 5 F	84		
	7 M 8 F	1				4 M 4 F	97		
	10 M 5 F	1				5 M 3 F	60		
	12 M 3 F	2				6 M 2 F	16		
(2) 16	8 M 8 F	1	0.06	0.22		7 M 1 F	5		
	14 M 3 F	1			(170) 9	1 M 8 F	2	3.08	5.55
(1) 17	11 M 6 F	1	0.03	0.12		2 M 7 F	22		
(1) 19	17 M 2 F	1	0.03	0.13		3 M 6 F	34		
(2) 20	6 M 14 F	1	0.06	0.28		4 M 5 F	36		
	20 M	1				5 M 4 F	32		
(2) 21	20 M 1 F	1	0.06	0.29		6 M 3 F	29		
	21 M	1				7 M 2 F	13		
(1) 29	17 M 12 F	1	0.03	0.20		9 M	2		
(1) 35	35 M	1	0.03	0.24	(102) 10	2 M 8 F	6	1.84	3.70
(1) 38	33 M 5 F	1	0.03	0.26		3 M 7 F	14		
(1) 47	47 M	1	0.03	0.32		4 M 6 F	31		
(1) 100	100 M	1	0.03	0.69		5 M 5 F	23		
NEWTON,	-	5,528	100.00	100.00		6 M 4 F	13		
(117) 1	1 M	38	2.12	0.42		7 M 3 F	8		
	1 F	79				8 M 2 F	3		
(653) 2	1 M 1 F	533	11.81	4.73		9 M 1 F	2		
	2 M	19				10 M	2		
	2 F	101			(40) 11	2 M 9 F	2	0.72	1.59

SIZE OF FAMILIES AND COMPOSITION BY SEX: FOR CITIES — Continued.

COUNTIES, CITIES, SIZE OF FAMILIES, AND NUMBER OF EACH SIZE.	Composition of Families	Number of Families	PERCENTAGES: EACH SIZE OF — Total Families	Total Population
MIDDLESEX — Con.				
NEWTON — Con.				
	3 M 8 F	6		
	4 M 7 F	8		
	5 M 6 F	10		
	6 M 5 F	7		
	7 M 4 F	3		
	8 M 3 F	1		
	9 M 2 F	1		
	10 M 1 F	1		
	11 M	1		
(50) 12	3 M 9 F	5	0.54	1.30
	4 M 8 F	3		
	5 M 7 F	2		
	6 M 6 F	7		
	7 M 5 F	5		
	8 M 4 F	3		
	10 M 2 F	2		
	11 M 1 F	2		
	12 F	1		
(19) 13	2 M 11 F	1	0.54	0.90
	3 M 10 F	3		
	4 M 9 F	1		
	5 M 8 F	1		
	6 M 7 F	2		
	7 M 6 F	3		
	8 M 5 F	3		
	9 M 4 F	2		
	13 M	1		
	13 F	2		
(8) 14	4 M 10 F	1	0.14	0.41
	5 M 9 F	3		
	7 M 7 F	1		
	8 M 6 F	1		
	9 M 5 F	2		
(4) 15	5 M 10 F	1	0.07	0.22
	6 M 9 F	1		
	9 M 6 F	1		
	15 M	1		
(2) 16	6 M 10 F	1	0.04	0.12
	8 M 8 F	1		
(3) 17	9 M 8 F	1	0.05	0.19
	10 M 7 F	1		
	12 M 5 F	1		
(4) 18	5 M 13 F	1	0.07	0.26
	13 M 5 F	1		
	16 M 2 F	1		
	18 M	1		
(2) 19	1 M 18 F	1	0.04	0.14
	9 M 10 F	1		
(1) 20	20 M	1	0.02	0.07
(2) 22	11 M 11 F	1	0.04	0.16
	17 M 5 F	1		
(2) 23	20 M 3 F	1	0.04	0.17
	23 F	1		
(1) 25	9 M 16 F	1	0.02	0.09

COUNTIES, CITIES, SIZE OF FAMILIES, AND NUMBER OF EACH SIZE.	Composition of Families	Number of Families	PERCENTAGES: EACH SIZE OF — Total Families	Total Population
MIDDLESEX — Con.				
NEWTON — Con.				
(1) 26	26 M	1	0.02	0.09
1) 27	3 M 24 F	1	0.02	0.10
1) 29	14 M 15 F	1	0.02	0.11
1) 30	28 M 2 F	1	0.02	0.11
(2) 36	9 M 27 F	1	0.04	0.26
	30 M 6 F	1		
(1) 84	24 M 60 F	1	0.02	0.50
(1) 85	39 M 46 F	1	0.02	0.51
(1) 147	3 M 144 F	1	0.02	0.53
SOMERVILLE, .	-	11,963	100.00	100.00
(188) 1	1 M	43	1.58	0.36
	1 F	145		
(2,001) 2	1 M 1 F	1,770	16.81	7.67
	2 M	27		
	2 F	204		
(2,479) 3	1 M 2 F	1,334	20.83	14.25
	2 M 1 F	1,037		
	3 M	11		
	3 F	97		
(2,500) 4	1 M 3 F	727	21.00	19.16
	2 M 2 F	1,227		
	3 M 1 F	504		
	4 M	5		
	4 F	37		
(1,849) 5	1 M 4 F	268	15.53	17.71
	2 M 3 F	735		
	3 M 2 F	644		
	4 M 1 F	183		
	5 F	19		
(1,233) 6	1 M 5 F	116	10.35	14.17
	2 M 4 F	336		
	3 M 3 F	408		
	4 M 2 F	295		
	5 M 1 F	74		
	6 M	2		
	6 F	2		
(758) 7	1 M 6 F	26	6.37	10.16
	2 M 5 F	133		
	3 M 4 F	253		
	4 M 3 F	210		
	5 M 2 F	101		
	6 M 1 F	23		
	7 M	2		
(432) 8	1 M 7 F	10	3.63	6.92
	2 M 6 F	44		
	3 M 5 F	91		
	4 M 4 F	122		
	5 M 3 F	113		
	6 M 2 F	43		
	7 M 1 F	8		
	8 M	1		
(226) 9	1 M 8 F	1	1.90	3.90
	2 M 7 F	16		
	3 M 6 F	38		

SIZE OF FAMILIES AND COMPOSITION BY SEX: FOR CITIES — Continued.

MIDDLESEX —Con.
SOMERVILLE—Con.

COUNTIES, CITIES, SIZE OF FAMILIES, AND NUMBER OF EACH SIZE.	Composition of Families	Number of Families	Total Families	Total Population
	4 M 5 F	55		
	5 M 4 F	67		
	6 M 3 F	34		
	7 M 2 F	11		
	8 M 1 F	4		
(121) 10	1 M 9 F	3	1.01	2.52
	2 M 8 F	4		
	3 M 7 F	11		
	4 M 6 F	24		
	5 M 5 F	31		
	6 M 4 F	20		
	7 M 3 F	12		
	8 M 2 F	5		
	9 M 1 F	1		
(58) 11	3 M 8 F	3	0.49	1.22
	4 M 7 F	14		
	5 M 6 F	9		
	6 M 5 F	17		
	7 M 4 F	7		
	8 M 3 F	2		
	9 M 2 F	3		
	10 M 1 F	3		
(24) 12	3 M 9 F	1	0.20	0.55
	4 M 8 F	2		
	5 M 7 F	2		
	6 M 6 F	3		
	7 M 5 F	7		
	8 M 4 F	3		
	9 M 3 F	4		
	11 M 1 F	2		
(12) 13	4 M 9 F	1	0.10	0.30
	5 M 8 F	2		
	6 M 7 F	2		
	7 M 6 F	1		
	8 M 5 F	2		
	10 M 3 F	2		
	11 M 2 F	2		
(6) 14	5 M 9 F	2	0.05	0.16
	7 M 7 F	2		
	9 M 5 F	1		
	11 M 3 F	1		
(3) 15	7 M 8 F	1	0.02	0.09
	10 M 5 F	1		
	12 M 3 F	1		
(4) 16	5 M 11 F	1	0.03	0.12
	12 M 4 F	2		
	16 F	1		
(1) 18	12 M 6 F	1	0.01	0.03
(1) 19	10 M 9 F	1	0.01	0.04
(1) 24	18 M 3 F	1	0.01	0.04
(1) 22	18 M 4 F	1	0.01	0.04
(1) 23	23 F	1	0.01	0.04
(1) 37	8 M 29 F	1	0.01	0.07
(1) 41	25 M 16 F	1	0.01	0.08

MIDDLESEX —Con.
SOMERVILLE—Con.

COUNTIES, CITIES, SIZE OF FAMILIES, AND NUMBER OF EACH SIZE.	Composition of Families	Number of Families	Total Families	Total Population
(1) 145	61 M 84 F	1	0.01	0.28
(1) 323	144 M 179 F	1	0.01	0.62
WALTHAM, . .	-	4,276	100.00	100.00
(125) 1	1 M	36	2.93	0.60
	1 F	89		
(582) 2	1 M 1 F	455	13.31	5.58
	2 M	16		
	2 F	111		
(778) 3	1 M 2 F	448	18.20	11.18
	2 M 1 F	274		
	3 M	3		
	3 F	53		
(819) 4	1 M 3 F	235	19.16	15.69
	2 M 2 F	377		
	3 M 1 F	175		
	4 M	1		
	4 F	33		
(685) 5	1 M 4 F	98	16.02	16.41
	2 M 3 F	281		
	3 M 2 F	239		
	4 M 1 F	58		
	5 M	1		
	5 F	8		
(480) 6	1 M 5 F	37	11.23	13.80
	2 M 4 F	150		
	3 M 3 F	167		
	4 M 2 F	97		
	5 M 1 F	19		
	6 F	1		
(304) 7	1 M 6 F	15	7.11	10.19
	2 M 5 F	66		
	3 M 4 F	110		
	4 M 3 F	73		
	5 M 2 F	32		
	6 M 1 F	5		
	7 M	1		
	7 F	2		
(210) 8	1 M 7 F	2	4.92	8.95
	2 M 6 F	30		
	3 M 5 F	45		
	4 M 4 F	66		
	5 M 3 F	33		
	6 M 2 F	18		
	7 M 1 F	2		
	8 M	1		
	8 F	1		
(129) 9	1 M 8 F	1	3.02	5.56
	2 M 7 F	12		
	3 M 6 F	26		
	4 M 5 F	33		
	5 M 4 F	22		
	6 M 3 F	26		
	7 M 2 F	8		
	8 M 1 F	1		

SIZE OF FAMILIES AND COMPOSITION BY SEX: FOR CITIES — Continued.

COUNTIES, CITIES, SIZE OF FAMILIES, AND NUMBER OF EACH SIZE.	Composition of Families	Number of Families	PERCENTAGES: EACH SIZE OF — Total Families	Total Population
MIDDLESEX — Con.				
WALTHAM — Con.				
(77) 10	1 M 9 F	1	1.80	3.69
	2 M 8 F	3		
	3 M 7 F	13		
	4 M 6 F	16		
	5 M 5 F	18		
	6 M 4 F	16		
	7 M 3 F	8		
	8 M 2 F	2		
(24) 11	3 M 8 F	4	0.57	1.27
	4 M 7 F	4		
	5 M 6 F	6		
	6 M 5 F	4		
	7 M 4 F	2		
	8 M 3 F	2		
	9 M 2 F	2		
(15) 12	3 M 9 F	2	0.35	0.86
	4 M 8 F	2		
	5 M 7 F	1		
	6 M 6 F	3		
	7 M 5 F	3		
	8 M 4 F	1		
	9 M 3 F	2		
	10 M 2 F	1		
(17) 13	3 M 10 F	2	0.40	1.06
	4 M 9 F	3		
	5 M 8 F	3		
	6 M 7 F	1		
	7 M 6 F	3		
	8 M 5 F	4		
	9 M 4 F	1		
(6) 14	8 M 6 F	2	0.14	0.40
	11 M 3 F	2		
	12 M 2 F	2		
(4) 15	7 M 8 F	1	0.10	0.29
	9 M 6 F	1		
	15 F	2		
(2) 17	6 M 11 F	1	0.05	0.16
	10 M 7 F	1		
(2) 18	13 M 5 F	1	0.05	0.17
	14 M 4 F	1		
(1) 19	19 F	1	0.02	0.09
(1) 20	14 M 6 F	1	0.02	0.10
(1) 21	13 M 8 F	1	0.02	0.10
(1) 26	26 F	1	0.02	0.12
(1) 27	20 M 7 F	1	0.02	0.13
(1) 30	6 M 24 F	1	0.02	0.14
(1) 31	9 M 22 F	1	0.02	0.15
(1) 33	30 M 3 F	1	0.02	0.16
(1) 41	34 M 7 F	1	0.02	0.20
(1) 43	22 M 21 F	1	0.02	0.21
(1) 53	25 M 28 F	1	0.02	0.25
(1) 78	78 F	1	0.02	0.37
(1) 80	80 F	1	0.02	0.38
(1) 85	7 M 78 F	1	0.02	0.41

COUNTIES, CITIES, SIZE OF FAMILIES, AND NUMBER OF EACH SIZE.	Composition of Families	Number of Families	PERCENTAGES: EACH SIZE OF — Total Families	Total Population
MIDDLESEX — Con.				
WALTHAM — Con.				
(1) 99	99 M	1	0.02	0.47
(1) 170	160 M 10 F	1	0.02	0.81
(1) 198	71 M 127 F	1	0.02	0.95
WOBURN,	. . —	3,012	100.00	100.00
(80) 1	1 M	22	2.96	0.63
	1 F	67		
(447) 2	1 M 1 F	359	14.84	6.31
	2 M	9		
	2 F	79		
(535) 3	1 M 2 F	279	17.76	11.32
	2 M 1 F	228		
	3 M	2		
	3 F	26		
(524) 4	1 M 3 F	134	17.40	14.78
	2 M 2 F	249		
	3 M 1 F	128		
	4 M	2		
	4 F	11		
(458) 5	1 M 4 F	54	15.21	16.15
	2 M 3 F	177		
	3 M 2 F	173		
	4 M 1 F	51		
	5 M	1		
	5 F	2		
(357) 6	1 M 5 F	22	11.85	15.11
	2 M 4 F	91		
	3 M 3 F	125		
	4 M 2 F	89		
	5 M 1 F	29		
	6 F	1		
(232) 7	1 M 6 F	6	7.70	11.45
	2 M 5 F	44		
	3 M 4 F	70		
	4 M 3 F	59		
	5 M 2 F	38		
	6 M 1 F	14		
	7 F	1		
(167) 8	1 M 7 F	2	5.54	9.42
	2 M 6 F	15		
	3 M 5 F	43		
	4 M 4 F	47		
	5 M 3 F	35		
	6 M 2 F	24		
	7 M 1 F	1		
(96) 9	2 M 7 F	3	3.19	6.09
	3 M 6 F	12		
	4 M 5 F	25		
	5 M 4 F	22		
	6 M 3 F	24		
	7 M 2 F	10		
(53) 10	1 M 9 F	1	1.76	3.74
	3 M 7 F	7		
	4 M 6 F	12		
	5 M 5 F	12		

SIZE OF FAMILIES AND COMPOSITION BY SEX: FOR CITIES — Continued.

COUNTIES, CITIES, SIZE OF FAMILIES, AND NUMBER OF EACH SIZE.	Composition of Families	Number of Families	Total Families	Total Population	COUNTIES, CITIES, SIZE OF FAMILIES, AND NUMBER OF EACH SIZE.	Composition of Families	Number of Families	Total Families	Total Population
MIDDLESEX — Con.					NORFOLK — Con.				
WOBURN — Con.					QUINCY — Con.				
	6 M 4 F	12				3 M 2 F	274		
	7 M 3 F	7				4 M 1 F	101		
	8 M 2 F	1				5 M	1		
	9 M 1 F	1				5 F	7		
(24) 11	2 M 9 F	1	0.80	1.86	(569) 6	1 M 5 F	32	11.64	14.75
	3 M 8 F	2				2 M 4 F	125		
	4 M 7 F	4				3 M 3 F	170		
	5 M 6 F	6				4 M 2 F	132		
	6 M 5 F	3				5 M 1 F	47		
	7 M 4 F	4				6 F	3		
	8 M 3 F	1			(343) 7	1 M 6 F	9	7.84	11.59
	9 M 2 F	2				2 M 5 F	38		
	10 M 1 F	1				3 M 4 F	107		
(11) 12	4 M 8 F	2	0.37	0.93		4 M 3 F	111		
	5 M 7 F	1				5 M 2 F	54		
	6 M 6 F	1				6 M 1 F	24		
	7 M 5 F	4			(212) 8	1 M 7 F	4	4.85	8.19
	8 M 4 F	2				2 M 6 F	22		
	9 M 3 F	1				3 M 5 F	39		
(10) 13	3 M 10 F	1	0.33	0.92		4 M 4 F	60		
	5 M 8 F	1				5 M 3 F	59		
	6 M 7 F	2				6 M 2 F	25		
	7 M 6 F	1				7 M 1 F	12		
	9 M 4 F	3			(135) 9	1 M 8 F	1	3.09	5.87
	13 F	2				2 M 7 F	3		
(2) 14	8 M 6 F	1	0.07	0.20		3 M 6 F	13		
	10 M 4 F	1				4 M 5 F	37		
(3) 16	9 M 7 F	1	0.10	0.34		5 M 4 F	35		
	11 M 5 F	1				6 M 3 F	30		
	16 M	1				7 M 2 F	13		
(1) 17	14 M 3 F	1	0.03	0.12		8 M 1 F	2		
(1) 20	20 M	1	0.03	0.14		9 M	1		
(1) 34	22 M 12 F	1	0.03	0.24	(80) 10	2 M 8 F	1	1.83	3.86
(1) 35	25 M 10 F	1	0.03	0.25		3 M 7 F	5		
						4 M 6 F	15		
NORFOLK.						5 M 5 F	16		
QUINCY,	-	4,373	100.00	100.00		6 M 4 F	22		
(134) 1	1 M	64	3.07	0.65		7 M 3 F	12		
	1 F	70				8 M 2 F	7		
(615) 2	1 M 1 F	525	14.06	5.94		9 M 1 F	2		
	2 M	20			(37) 11	4 M 7 F	4	0.85	1.96
	2 F	70				5 M 6 F	10		
(756) 3	1 M 2 F	371	17.29	10.95		6 M 5 F	9		
	2 M 1 F	350				7 M 4 F	5		
	3 M	6				8 M 3 F	5		
	3 F	29				9 M 2 F	4		
(785) 4	1 M 3 F	202	17.95	15.16	(21) 12	5 M 7 F	3	0.48	1.22
	2 M 2 F	405				6 M 6 F	2		
	3 M 1 F	169				7 M 5 F	7		
	4 M	2				8 M 4 F	5		
	4 F	7				9 M 3 F	4		
(717) 5	1 M 4 F	78	16.40	17.31	(8) 13	5 M 8 F	2	0.18	0.50
	2 M 3 F	256				6 M 7 F	2		
						8 M 5 F	3		

SIZE OF FAMILIES AND COMPOSITION BY SEX: FOR CITIES — Continued.

Counties, Cities, Size of Families, and Number of Each Size.	Composition of Families	Number of Families	Total Families	Total Population
NORFOLK — Con.				
QUINCY — Con.				
(7) 14	9 M 4 F	1		
	5 M 9 F	1	0.16	0.47
	6 M 8 F	1		
	7 M 7 F	1		
	8 M 6 F	2		
	10 M 4 F	1		
	13 M 1 F	1		
(4) 15	5 M 10 F	1	0.09	0.29
	10 M 5 F	1		
	12 M 3 F	1		
	13 M 2 F	1		
(1) 16	10 M 6 F	1	0.02	0.08
(2) 17	8 M 9 F	1	0.05	0.16
	14 M 3 F	1		
(1) 19	14 M 5 F	1	0.02	0.09
(1) 23	11 M 12 F	1	0.02	0.11
(2) 25	7 M 18 F	1	0.05	0.24
	19 M 6 F	1		
(1) 32	22 M 10 F	1	0.02	0.15
(1) 45	40 M 5 F	1	0.02	0.22
(1) 49	42 M 7 F	1	0.02	0.24
PLYMOUTH.				
BROCKTON, . .	-	7,700	100.00	100.00
(217) 1	1 M	78	2.82	0.65
	1 F	139		
(1,320) 2	1 M 1 F	1,164	17.14	7.96
	2 M	32		
	2 F	124		
(1,692) 3	1 M 2 F	860	21.97	15.31
	2 M 1 F	752		
	3 M	10		
	3 F	70		
(1,517) 4	1 M 3 F	400	19.70	18.30
	2 M 2 F	738		
	3 M 1 F	347		
	4 M	6		
	4 F	26		
(1,168) 5	1 M 4 F	163	15.17	17.61
	2 M 3 F	413		
	3 M 2 F	431		
	4 M 1 F	150		
	5 M	1		
	5 F	10		
(760) 6	1 M 5 F	44	9.87	13.75
	2 M 4 F	180		
	3 M 3 F	277		
	4 M 2 F	196		
	5 M 1 F	62		
	6 M	1		
	6 F	2		
(440) 7	1 M 6 F	15	5.72	9.29
	2 M 5 F	76		

Counties, Cities, Size of Families, and Number of Each Size.	Composition of Families	Number of Families	Total Families	Total Population
PLYMOUTH — Con.				
BROCKTON — Con.				
	3 M 4 F	117		
	4 M 3 F	146		
	5 M 2 F	70		
	6 M 1 F	15		
	7 F	1		
(263) 8	1 M 7 F	3	3.42	6.54
	2 M 6 F	22		
	3 M 5 F	55		
	4 M 4 F	89		
	5 M 3 F	66		
	6 M 2 F	25		
	7 M 1 F	11		
	8 F	1		
(154) 9	1 M 8 F	2	2.00	4.18
	2 M 7 F	7		
	3 M 6 F	23		
	4 M 5 F	42		
	5 M 4 F	36		
	6 M 3 F	22		
	7 M 2 F	20		
	8 M 1 F	2		
(60) 10	1 M 9 F	2	0.78	1.81
	3 M 7 F	6		
	4 M 6 F	7		
	5 M 5 F	15		
	6 M 4 F	14		
	7 M 3 F	8		
	8 M 2 F	7		
	9 M 1 F	1		
(38) 11	3 M 8 F	1	0.49	1.26
	4 M 7 F	2		
	5 M 6 F	9		
	6 M 5 F	6		
	7 M 4 F	7		
	8 M 3 F	9		
	9 M 2 F	4		
(18) 12	4 M 8 F	1	0.23	0.65
	5 M 7 F	2		
	6 M 6 F	3		
	7 M 5 F	3		
	8 M 4 F	3		
	9 M 3 F	2		
	10 M 2 F	3		
	11 M 1 F	1		
(16) 13	5 M 8 F	1	0.21	0.63
	6 M 7 F	2		
	7 M 6 F	3		
	8 M 5 F	3		
	9 M 4 F	4		
	10 M 3 F	2		
	11 M 2 F	1		
(5) 14	7 M 7 F	2	0.07	0.21
	9 M 5 F	2		
	14 F	1		

SIZE OF FAMILIES AND COMPOSITION BY SEX: FOR CITIES — Continued.

COUNTIES, CITIES, SIZE OF FAMILIES, AND NUMBER OF EACH SIZE.	Composition of Families	Number of Families	PERCENTAGES: EACH SIZE OF — Total Families	PERCENTAGES: EACH SIZE OF — Total Population
PLYMOUTH — Con.				
BROCKTON — Con.				
(5) 15	10 M 5 F	1	0.07	0.23
	12 M 3 F	2		
	13 M 2 F	1		
	15 M	1		
(9) 16	7 M 9 F	1	0.12	0.43
	8 M 8 F	1		
	9 M 7 F	1		
	10 M 6 F	1		
	11 M 5 F	1		
	13 M 3 F	2		
	16 M	2		
(4) 17	7 M 10 F	1	0.05	0.20
	11 M 6 F	1		
	12 M 5 F	1		
	14 M 3 F	1		
(2) 19	7 M 12 F	1	0.03	0.11
	15 M 4 F	1		
(2) 21	11 M 10 F	1	0.03	0.13
	15 M 6 F	1		
(2) 22	12 M 10 F	1	0.03	0.13
	15 M 7 F	1		
(1) 25	25 M	1	0.01	0.08
(1) 29	29 M	1	0.01	0.09
(1) 30	19 M 11 F	1	0.01	0.09
(1) 31	17 M 14 F	1	0.01	0.09
(1) 33	26 M 7 F	1	0.01	0.10
(1) 37	18 M 19 F	1	0.01	0.11
(1) 42	42 M	1	0.01	0.13
(1) 44	20 M 24 F	1	0.01	0.13
SUFFOLK.				
BOSTON, . . .	-	103,206	100.00	100.00
(3,421) 1	1 M	1,042	3.31	0.69
	1 F	2,379		
(16,399) 2	1 M 1 F	13,564	15.88	6.60
	2 M	429		
	2 F	2,406		
(18,952) 3	1 M 2 F	9,556	18.35	11.44
	2 M 1 F	7,929		
	3 M	184		
	3 F	1,283		
(18,530) 4	1 M 3 F	5,278	17.94	14.92
	2 M 2 F	8,656		
	3 M 1 F	3,940		
	4 M	82		
	4 F	574		
(15,077) 5	1 M 4 F	2,347	14.60	15.17
	2 M 3 F	5,550		
	3 M 2 F	5,215		
	4 M 1 F	1,712		
	5 M	33		
	5 F	220		
(11,063) 6	1 M 5 F	931	10.71	13.36

COUNTIES, CITIES, SIZE OF FAMILIES, AND NUMBER OF EACH SIZE.	Composition of Families	Number of Families	PERCENTAGES: EACH SIZE OF — Total Families	PERCENTAGES: EACH SIZE OF — Total Population
SUFFOLK — Con.				
BOSTON — Con.				
	2 M 4 F	2,884		
	3 M 3 F	3,964		
	4 M 2 F	2,544		
	5 M 1 F	660		
	6 M	20		
	6 F	90		
(7,616) 7	1 M 6 F	358	7.37	10.73
	2 M 5 F	1,197		
	3 M 4 F	2,318		
	4 M 3 F	2,226		
	5 M 2 F	1,107		
	6 M 1 F	395		
	7 M	11		
	7 F	34		
(4,734) 8	1 M 7 F	134	4.58	7.62
	2 M 6 F	488		
	3 M 5 F	1,095		
	4 M 4 F	1,308		
	5 M 3 F	1,049		
	6 M 2 F	528		
	7 M 1 F	116		
	8 M	7		
	8 F	12		
(2,769) 9	1 M 8 F	34	2.68	5.02
	2 M 7 F	197		
	3 M 6 F	407		
	4 M 5 F	740		
	5 M 4 F	682		
	6 M 3 F	453		
	7 M 2 F	191		
	8 M 1 F	47		
	9 M	7		
	9 F	11		
(1,664) 10	1 M 9 F	17	1.61	3.35
	2 M 8 F	75		
	3 M 7 F	203		
	4 M 6 F	318		
	5 M 5 F	395		
	6 M 4 F	342		
	7 M 3 F	191		
	8 M 2 F	87		
	9 M 1 F	21		
	10 M	9		
	10 F	6		
(945) 11	1 M 10 F	4	0.92	2.09
	2 M 9 F	29		
	3 M 8 F	70		
	4 M 7 F	133		
	5 M 6 F	179		
	6 M 5 F	212		
	7 M 4 F	155		
	8 M 3 F	97		
	9 M 2 F	39		
	10 M 1 F	16		

SIZE OF FAMILIES AND COMPOSITION BY SEX: FOR CITIES — Continued.

Counties, Cities, Size of Families, and Number of Each Size	Composition of Families	Number of Families	Percentages: Each Size of — Total Families	Percentages: Each Size of — Total Population
SUFFOLK — Con.				
Boston — Con.				
	11 M	5		
	11 F	6		
(571) 12	1 M 11 F	2	0.55	1.38
	2 M 10 F	9		
	3 M 9 F	45		
	4 M 8 F	53		
	5 M 7 F	95		
	6 M 6 F	109		
	7 M 5 F	97		
	8 M 4 F	82		
	9 M 3 F	42		
	10 M 2 F	22		
	11 M 1 F	6		
	12 M	5		
	12 F	4		
(366) 13	1 M 12 F	3	0.36	0.96
	2 M 11 F	8		
	3 M 10 F	16		
	4 M 9 F	26		
	5 M 8 F	35		
	6 M 7 F	57		
	7 M 6 F	75		
	8 M 5 F	56		
	9 M 4 F	45		
	10 M 3 F	20		
	11 M 2 F	16		
	12 M 1 F	5		
	13 M	2		
	13 F	2		
(295) 14	1 M 13 F	1	0.29	0.85
	2 M 12 F	3		
	3 M 11 F	8		
	4 M 10 F	18		
	5 M 9 F	27		
	6 M 8 F	28		
	7 M 7 F	53		
	8 M 6 F	33		
	9 M 5 F	44		
	10 M 4 F	35		
	11 M 3 F	22		
	12 M 2 F	12		
	13 M 1 F	2		
	14 M	2		
	14 F	7		
(188) 15	1 M 14 F	3	0.18	0.57
	2 M 13 F	1		
	3 M 12 F	9		
	4 M 11 F	8		
	5 M 10 F	18		
	6 M 9 F	19		
	7 M 8 F	19		
	8 M 7 F	26		
	9 M 6 F	21		
	10 M 5 F	19		

Counties, Cities, Size of Families, and Number of Each Size	Composition of Families	Number of Families	Percentages: Each Size of — Total Families	Percentages: Each Size of — Total Population
SUFFOLK — Con.				
Boston — Con.				
	11 M 4 F	16		
	12 M 3 F	13		
	13 M 2 F	11		
	14 M 1 F	2		
	15 M	2		
	15 F	1		
(151) 16	1 M 15 F	3	0.15	0.49
	2 M 14 F	1		
	3 M 13 F	2		
	4 M 12 F	4		
	5 M 11 F	9		
	6 M 10 F	10		
	7 M 9 F	15		
	8 M 8 F	20		
	9 M 7 F	14		
	10 M 6 F	21		
	11 M 5 F	17		
	12 M 4 F	18		
	13 M 3 F	11		
	14 M 2 F	5		
	16 F	1		
(109) 17	1 M 16 F	1	0.11	0.37
	3 M 14 F	3		
	4 M 13 F	4		
	5 M 12 F	5		
	6 M 11 F	7		
	7 M 10 F	8		
	8 M 9 F	13		
	9 M 8 F	17		
	10 M 7 F	9		
	11 M 6 F	12		
	12 M 5 F	12		
	13 M 4 F	7		
	14 M 3 F	5		
	15 M 2 F	4		
	17 M	1		
	17 F	1		
(81) 18	1 M 17 F	1	0.08	0.29
	4 M 14 F	2		
	5 M 13 F	2		
	6 M 12 F	4		
	7 M 11 F	2		
	8 M 10 F	9		
	9 M 9 F	12		
	10 M 8 F	10		
	11 M 7 F	10		
	12 M 6 F	9		
	13 M 5 F	5		
	14 M 4 F	5		
	15 M 3 F	5		
	16 M 2 F	1		
	18 M	1		
	18 F	3		
(55) 19	5 M 14 F	2	0.05	0.21

SIZE OF FAMILIES AND COMPOSITION BY SEX: FOR CITIES — Continued.

Counties, Cities, Size of Families, and Number of Each Size.	Composition of Families	Number of Families	Percentages: Each Size of — Total Families	Percentages: Each Size of — Total Population	Counties, Cities, Size of Families, and Number of Each Size.	Composition of Families	Number of Families	Percentages: Each Size of — Total Families	Percentages: Each Size of — Total Population
SUFFOLK — Con.					SUFFOLK — Con.				
BOSTON — Con.					BOSTON — Con.				
	6 M 13 F	3				16 M 6 F	2		
	7 M 12 F	3				17 M 5 F	1		
	9 M 10 F	7				18 M 4 F	2		
	10 M 9 F	6			(12) 23	2 M 21 F	1	0.01	0.06
	11 M 8 F	7				3 M 20 F	1		
	12 M 7 F	5				6 M 17 F	1		
	13 M 6 F	6				9 M 14 F	1		
	14 M 5 F	7				10 M 13 F	2		
	15 M 4 F	4				12 M 11 F	1		
	16 M 3 F	2				14 M 9 F	1		
	17 M 2 F	2				15 M 8 F	1		
	19 F	1				16 M 7 F	1		
(45) 20	5 M 15 F	1	0.05	0.18		21 M 2 F	1		
	6 M 14 F	1				23 F	1		
	7 M 13 F	3			(11) 24	5 M 19 F	1	0.01	0.05
	8 M 12 F	1				8 M 16 F	1		
	9 M 11 F	5				12 M 12 F	3		
	10 M 10 F	8				14 M 10 F	1		
	11 M 9 F	3				15 M 9 F	1		
	12 M 8 F	5				17 M 7 F	1		
	13 M 7 F	4				18 M 6 F	1		
	14 M 6 F	3				20 M 4 F	1		
	15 M 5 F	2				24 F	1		
	16 M 4 F	3			(9) 25	8 M 17 F	1	0.01	0.05
	17 M 3 F	1				9 M 16 F	1		
	18 M 2 F	1				13 M 12 F	1		
	20 M	2				15 M 10 F	1		
	20 F	2				16 M 9 F	1		
(42) 21	4 M 17 F	1	0.04	0.18		17 M 8 F	1		
	5 M 16 F	1				19 M 6 F	1		
	6 M 15 F	1				20 M 5 F	1		
	7 M 14 F	1				25 F	1		
	8 M 13 F	2			(8) 26	6 M 20 F	1	0.01	0.04
	9 M 12 F	4				11 M 15 F	1		
	10 M 11 F	5				13 M 13 F	1		
	11 M 10 F	6				17 M 9 F	1		
	12 M 9 F	2				20 M 6 F	1		
	13 M 8 F	3				21 M 5 F	2		
	14 M 7 F	6				26 F	1		
	15 M 6 F	3			(11) 27	1 M 26 F	1	0.01	0.06
	17 M 4 F	2				7 M 20 F	1		
	18 M 3 F	2				11 M 16 F	1		
	20 M 1 F	1				14 M 13 F	1		
	21 M	1				17 M 10 F	1		
	21 F	1				18 M 9 F	1		
(28) 22	4 M 18 F	1	0.03	0.12		20 M 7 F	2		
	8 M 14 F	1				22 M 5 F	1		
	9 M 13 F	4				23 M 4 F	1		
	10 M 12 F	2				25 M 2 F	1		
	11 M 11 F	2			(5) 28	10 M 18 F	2	0.01	0.03
	12 M 10 F	2				14 M 14 F	1		
	13 M 9 F	1				16 M 12 F	1		
	14 M 8 F	5				28 M	1		
	15 M 7 F	5			(9) 29	3 M 26 F	2	0.01	0.05

SIZE OF FAMILIES AND COMPOSITION BY SEX: FOR CITIES — Continued.

COUNTIES, CITIES, SIZE OF FAMILIES, AND NUMBER OF EACH SIZE.	Composition of Families	Number of Families	PERCENTAGES: EACH SIZE OF — Total Families	PERCENTAGES: EACH SIZE OF — Total Population	COUNTIES, CITIES, SIZE OF FAMILIES, AND NUMBER OF EACH SIZE.	Composition of Families	Number of Families	PERCENTAGES: EACH SIZE OF — Total Families	PERCENTAGES: EACH SIZE OF — Total Population
SUFFOLK — Con.					SUFFOLK — Con.				
BOSTON — Con.					BOSTON — Con.				
	15 M 14 F	1				25 M 17 F	1		
	17 M 12 F	2				27 M 16 F	1		
	19 M 10 F	1				41 M 2 F	1		
	25 M 4 F	1			(1) 44	2 M 42 F	1	*-	0.01
	28 M 1 F	1			(3) 45	16 M 29 F	1	*-	0.03
	29 F	1				22 M 23 F	1		
(9) 30	11 M 19 F	1	0.01	0.05		40 M 5 F	1		
	13 M 17 F	1			(3) 46	1 M 45 F	1	*-	0.03
	15 M 15 F	1				46 M	2		
	18 M 12 F	1			(2) 47	16 M 31 F	1	*-	0.02
	20 M 10 F	1				23 M 24 F	1		
	22 M 8 F	1			(5) 48	7 M 41 F	1	0.01	0.05
	24 M 6 F	1				17 M 31 F	1		
	25 M 5 F	1				30 M 18 F	1		
	30 M	1				35 M 13 F	1		
(5) 31	3 M 28 F	1	0.01	0.05		48 F	1		
	6 M 25 F	1			(1) 50	43 M 7 F	1	*-	0.01
	13 M 18 F	1			(1) 51	51 F	1	*-	0.01
	23 M 8 F	1			(2) 52	30 M 22 F	1	*-	0.02
	31 F	1				37 M 15 F	1		
(4) 32	16 M 16 F	1	0.01	0.05	(1) 56	39 M 17 F	1	*-	0.01
	17 M 15 F	1			(2) 59	34 M 25 F	1	*-	0.02
	19 M 13 F	1				41 M 18 F	1		
	20 M 12 F	1			(2) 62	55 M 7 F	1	*-	0.02
(3) 33	12 M 21 F	1	*-	0.02		62 M	1		
	17 M 16 F	1			(1) 66	13 M 53 F	1	*-	0.01
	33 F	1			(1) 68	27 M 41 F	1	*-	0.01
(4) 34	13 M 21 F	1	0.01	0.05	(1) 69	69 M	1	*-	0.01
	22 M 12 F	1			(1) 70	7 M 63 F	1	*-	0.01
	25 M 9 F	1			(1) 71	71 F	1	*-	0.01
	26 M 8 F	1			(2) 72	14 M 58 F	1	*-	0.03
(5) 35	1 M 34 F	1	0.01	0.04		22 M 50 F	1		
	8 M 27 F	1			(1) 73	29 M 44 F	1	*-	0.02
	14 M 21 F	1			(1) 76	33 M 43 F	1	*-	0.02
	24 M 11 F	1			(2) 77	5 M 72 F	1	*-	0.03
	26 M 9 F	1				77 F	1		
	29 M 6 F	1			(2) 78	16 M 62 F	1	*-	0.03
(2) 36	1 M 35 F	1	*-	0.01		75 M 3 F	1		
	3 M 33 F	1			(1) 79	58 M 21 F	1	*-	0.02
(5) 37	1 M 36 F	1	0.01	0.04	(1) 81	38 M 43 F	1	*-	0.02
	2 M 35 F	1			(1) 82	30 M 52 F	1	*-	0.02
	18 M 19 F	1			(1) 86	42 M 44 F	1	*-	0.02
	24 M 13 F	1			(2) 87	34 M 53 F	1	*-	0.03
	37 M	1				37 M 50 F	1		
(1) 38	38 M	1	*-	0.01	(1) 88	1 M 87 F	1	*-	0.02
(3) 39	2 M 37 F	1	*-	0.02	(1) 89	34 M 55 F	1	*-	0.02
	3 M 36 F	1			(2) 91	90 M 1 F	1	*-	0.04
	24 M 15 F	1				91 F	1		
(4) 40	3 M 37 F	1	0.01	0.05	(1) 93	34 M 59 F	1	*-	0.02
	18 M 22 F	1			(1) 94	23 M 71 F	1	*-	0.02
	40 M	2			(1) 96	5 M 91 F	1	*-	0.02
(1) 41	29 M 12 F	1	*-	0.01	(1) 97	3 M 94 F	1	*-	0.02
(1) 42	24 M 18 F	1	*-	0.01	(1) 101	3 M 98 F	1	*-	0.02
(4) 43	20 M 23 F	1	0.01	0.05	(1) 107	50 M 57 F	1	*-	0.02

SIZE OF FAMILIES AND COMPOSITION BY SEX: FOR CITIES — Continued.

COUNTIES, CITIES, SIZE OF FAMILIES, AND NUMBER OF EACH SIZE.	Composition of Families	Number of Families	Total Families	Total Population
SUFFOLK — Con.				
BOSTON — Con.				
(2) 109	98 M 11 F	1	*-	0.04
	109 F	1		
(1) 112	25 M 87 F	1	*-	0.02
(1) 114	52 M 62 F	1	*-	0.02
(1) 116	42 M 74 F	1	*-	0.02
(2) 118	1 M 117 F	1	*-	0.05
	30 M 88 F	1		
(1) 119	108 M 11 F	1	*-	0.02
(1) 121	17 M 104 F	1	*-	0.02
(2) 124	24 M 100 F	1	*-	0.05
	101 M 23 F	1		
(1) 129	53 M 76 F	1	*-	0.03
(1) 132	42 M 90 F	1	*-	0.03
(1) 134	81 M 53 F	1	*-	0.03
(1) 135	58 M 77 F	1	*-	0.03
(1) 137	46 M 91 F	1	*-	0.03
(1) 145	145 M	1	*-	0.03
(1) 156	133 M 23 F	1	*-	0.03
(1) 158	1 M 157 F	1	*-	0.03
(1) 183	152 M 31 F	1	*-	0.04
(1) 194	1 M 193 F	1	*-	0.04
(1) 200	83 M 117 F	1	*-	0.04
(1) 212	94 M 118 F	1	*-	0.04
(1) 214	103 M 111 F	1	*-	0.04
(1) 220	71 M 149 F	1	*-	0.04
(1) 268	92 M 176 F	1	*-	0.05
(1) 276	276 M	1	*-	0.06
(1) 352	4 M 348 F	1	*-	0.07
(1) 397	252 M 145 F	1	*-	0.08
(1) 399	4 M 395 F	1	*-	0.08
(1) 412	176 M 236 F	1	*-	0.08
(1) 599	273 M 326 F	1	*-	0.12
(1) 680	600 M 80 F	1	*-	0.14
(1) 691	334 M 357 F	1	*-	0.14
(1) 741	736 M 5 F	1	*-	0.15
(1) 1,596	1,251 M 345 F	1	*-	0.32
CHELSEA.	-	6,954	100.00	100.00
(165) 1	1 M	32	2.38	0.53
	1 F	133		
(1,194) 2	1 M 1 F	1,017	17.22	7.64
	2 M	25		
	2 F	152		
(1,413) 3	1 M 2 F	770	20.38	13.56
	2 M 1 F	565		
	3 M	7		
	3 F	71		
(1,266) 4	1 M 3 F	364	18.26	16.20
	2 M 2 F	606		
	3 M 1 F	270		
	4 M	7		
	4 F	25		
(1,011) 5	1 M 4 F	145	14.58	16.17
	2 M 3 F	386		
	3 M 2 F	365		

COUNTIES, CITIES, SIZE OF FAMILIES, AND NUMBER OF EACH SIZE.	Composition of Families	Number of Families	Total Families	Total Population
SUFFOLK — Con.				
CHELSEA — Con.				
	4 M 1 F	107		
	5 M	3		
	5 F	5		
(725) 6	1 M 5 F	33	10.50	13.97
	2 M 4 F	171		
	3 M 3 F	293		
	4 M 2 F	155		
	5 M 1 F	51		
	6 M	3		
	6 F	4		
(483) 7	1 M 6 F	16	6.97	10.81
	2 M 5 F	70		
	3 M 4 F	144		
	4 M 3 F	154		
	5 M 2 F	77		
	6 M 1 F	20		
	7 F	2		
(292) 8	1 M 7 F	8	4.21	7.47
	2 M 6 F	17		
	3 M 5 F	69		
	4 M 4 F	92		
	5 M 3 F	64		
	6 M 2 F	30		
	7 M 1 F	12		
(169) 9	2 M 7 F	7	2.44	4.87
	3 M 6 F	32		
	4 M 5 F	36		
	5 M 4 F	50		
	6 M 3 F	27		
	7 M 2 F	6		
	8 M 1 F	2		
(99) 10	3 M 7 F	12	1.43	3.17
	4 M 6 F	19		
	5 M 5 F	32		
	6 M 4 F	26		
	7 M 3 F	8		
	8 M 2 F	2		
(56) 11	3 M 8 F	7	0.81	1.97
	4 M 7 F	7		
	5 M 6 F	12		
	6 M 5 F	11		
	7 M 4 F	9		
	8 M 3 F	6		
	9 M 2 F	2		
	10 M 1 F	1		
	11 F	1		
(22) 12	4 M 8 F	3	0.32	0.84
	5 M 7 F	1		
	6 M 6 F	9		
	7 M 5 F	3		
	8 M 4 F	3		
	9 M 3 F	3		
(14) 13	4 M 9 F	2	0.20	0.58
	5 M 8 F	2		

SIZE OF FAMILIES AND COMPOSITION BY SEX: FOR CITIES — Continued.

Counties, Cities, Size of Families, and Number of Each Size.	Composition of Families	Number of Families	Percentages: Each Size of — Total Families	Percentages: Each Size of — Total Population
SUFFOLK — Con.				
CHELSEA — Con.				
	6 M 7 F	1		
	8 M 5 F	4		
	9 M 4 F	2		
	10 M 3 F	3		
(5) 14	7 M 7 F	1	0.08	0.22
	8 M 6 F	2		
	9 M 5 F	1		
	11 M 3 F	1		
(2) 15	4 M 11 F	1	0.05	0.10
	11 M 4 F	1		
(3) 16	8 M 8 F	1	0.05	0.15
	13 M 3 F	2		
(2) 17	8 M 9 F	1	0.05	0.11
	13 M 4 F	1		
(1) 20	11 M 9 F	1	0.01	0.06
(2) 22	16 M 6 F	1	0.05	0.14
	22 F	1		
(1) 23	5 M 18 F	1	0.01	0.07
(1) 29	13 M 16 F	1	0.01	0.09
(1) 30	20 M 10 F	1	0.01	0.10
(1) 31	16 M 15 F	1	0.01	0.10
(1) 34	25 M 9 F	1	0.01	0.11
(1) 47	27 M 20 F	1	0.01	0.15
(1) 255	251 M 4 F	1	0.01	0.82
WORCESTER.				
FITCHBURG, . .	-	5,686	100.00	100.00
(149) 1	1 M	44	2.62	0.56
	1 F	105		
(919) 2	1 M 1 F	785	16.16	6.96
	2 M	28		
	2 F	106		
(1,136) 3	1 M 2 F	621	19.98	12.91
	2 M 1 F	466		
	3 M	11		
	3 F	38		
(1,035) 4	1 M 3 F	274	18.20	15.68
	2 M 2 F	523		
	3 M 1 F	209		
	4 M	7		
	4 F	22		
(781) 5	1 M 4 F	123	13.74	14.79
	2 M 3 F	269		
	3 M 2 F	287		
	4 M 1 F	92		
	5 M	5		
	5 F	5		
(579) 6	1 M 5 F	36	10.18	13.15
	2 M 4 F	151		
	3 M 3 F	218		
	4 M 2 F	121		
	5 M 1 F	51		
	6 F	2		
(421) 7	1 M 6 F	16	7.40	11.16

Counties, Cities, Size of Families, and Number of Each Size.	Composition of Families	Number of Families	Percentages: Each Size of — Total Families	Percentages: Each Size of — Total Population
WORCESTER — Con.				
FITCHBURG — Con.				
	2 M 5 F	77		
	3 M 4 F	107		
	4 M 3 F	133		
	5 M 2 F	76		
	6 M 1 F	11		
	7 M	1		
(264) 8	1 M 7 F	6	4.64	8.00
	2 M 6 F	36		
	3 M 5 F	59		
	4 M 4 F	64		
	5 M 3 F	66		
	6 M 2 F	30		
	7 M 1 F	2		
	8 M	1		
(173) 9	2 M 7 F	8	3.04	5.90
	3 M 6 F	23		
	4 M 5 F	54		
	5 M 4 F	46		
	6 M 3 F	27		
	7 M 2 F	10		
	8 M 1 F	4		
	9 M	1		
(83) 10	2 M 8 F	5	1.46	3.14
	3 M 7 F	9		
	4 M 6 F	10		
	5 M 5 F	20		
	6 M 4 F	23		
	7 M 3 F	12		
	8 M 2 F	3		
	10 M	1		
(68) 11	1 M 10 F	1	1.20	2.83
	2 M 9 F	1		
	3 M 8 F	6		
	4 M 7 F	9		
	5 M 6 F	11		
	6 M 5 F	15		
	7 M 4 F	14		
	8 M 3 F	5		
	9 M 2 F	5		
	10 M 1 F	1		
(35) 12	4 M 8 F	2	0.62	1.59
	5 M 7 F	2		
	6 M 6 F	17		
	7 M 5 F	9		
	8 M 4 F	1		
	9 M 3 F	2		
	10 M 2 F	2		
(16) 13	4 M 9 F	1	0.28	0.79
	5 M 8 F	3		
	6 M 7 F	2		
	7 M 6 F	5		
	8 M 5 F	1		
	9 M 4 F	3		
	10 M 3 F	1		

SIZE OF FAMILIES AND COMPOSITION BY·SEX: FOR CITIES — Continued.

COUNTIES, CITIES, SIZE OF FAMILIES, AND NUMBER OF EACH SIZE.	Composition of Families	Number of Families	PERCENTAGES: EACH SIZE OF — Total Families	PERCENTAGES: EACH SIZE OF — Total Population
WORCESTER — Con.				
FITCHBURG — Con.				
(4) 14	8 M 6 F	2	0.07	0.21
	9 M 5 F	1		
	10 M 4 F	1		
(7) 15	6 M 9 F	1	0.12	0.40
	7 M 8 F	1		
	9 M 6 F	1		
	10 M 5 F	2		
	11 M 4 F	1		
	13 M 2 F	1		
(4) 17	9 M 8 F	1	0.07	0.26
	11 M 6 F	1		
	14 M 3 F	1		
	15 M 2 F	1		
(1) 18	13 M 5 F	1	0.02	0.07
(1) 22	16 M 6 F	1	0.02	0.08
(3) 23	14 M 9 F	1	0.05	0.26
	21 M 2 F	1		
	23 F	1		
(2) 24	8 M 16 F	1	0.03	0.18
	18 M 6 F	1		
(1) 27	13 M 14 F	1	0.02	0.10
(1) 32	28 M 4 F	1	0.02	0.12
(1) 37	19 M 18 F	1	0.02	0.14
(1) 80	47 M 33 F	1	0.02	0.30
(1) 111	107 M 4 F	1	0.02	0.42
WORCESTER, .	—	20,861	100.00	100.00
(585) 1	1 M	175	2.81	0.59
	1 F	410		
(3,255) 2	1 M 1 F	2,759	15.61	6.59
	2 M	79		
	2 F	417		
(3,945) 3	1 M 2 F	2,075	18.91	11.98
	2 M 1 F	1,692		
	3 M	21		
	3 F	157		
(3,906) 4	1 M 3 F	1,084	19.02	16.06
	2 M 2 F	1,955		
	3 M 1 F	841		
	4 M	19		
	4 F	76		
(3,164) 5	1 M 4 F	450	15.17	16.02
	2 M 3 F	1,175		
	3 M 2 F	1,135		
	4 M 1 F	373		
	5 M	8		
	5 F	23		
(2,170) 6	1 M 5 F	153	10.41	13.18
	2 M 4 F	533		
	3 M 3 F	798		
	4 M 2 F	506		
	5 M 1 F	166		
	6 M	8		
	6 F	6		
(1,570) 7	1 M 6 F	56	7.53	11.13

COUNTIES, CITIES, SIZE OF FAMILIES, AND NUMBER OF EACH SIZE.	Composition of Families	Number of Families	PERCENTAGES: EACH SIZE OF — Total Families	PERCENTAGES: EACH SIZE OF — Total Population
WORCESTER — Con.				
WORCESTER - Con.				
	2 M 5 F	258		
	3 M 4 F	444		
	4 M 3 F	493		
	5 M 2 F	242		
	6 M 1 F	69		
	7 M	5		
	7 F	3		
(955) 8	1 M 7 F	17	4.58	7.74
	2 M 6 F	88		
	3 M 5 F	212		
	4 M 4 F	275		
	5 M 3 F	213		
	6 M 2 F	121		
	7 M 1 F	21		
	8 M	6		
	8 F	2		
(573) 9	1 M 8 F	4	2.75	5.22
	2 M 7 F	31		
	3 M 6 F	85		
	4 M 5 F	143		
	5 M 4 F	152		
	6 M 3 F	105		
	7 M 2 F	39		
	8 M 1 F	12		
	9 M	2		
(259) 10	1 M 9 F	3	1.25	2.62
	2 M 8 F	11		
	3 M 7 F	24		
	4 M 6 F	50		
	5 M 5 F	69		
	6 M 4 F	52		
	7 M 3 F	32		
	8 M 2 F	11		
	9 M 1 F	4		
	10 M	3		
(160) 11	1 M 10 F	1	0.77	1.78
	2 M 9 F	2		
	3 M 8 F	8		
	4 M 7 F	23		
	5 M 6 F	33		
	6 M 5 F	32		
	7 M 4 F	30		
	8 M 3 F	16		
	9 M 2 F	12		
	11 M	2		
	11 F	1		
(92) 12	1 M 11 F	1	0.44	1.12
	2 M 10 F	2		
	3 M 9 F	5		
	4 M 8 F	7		
	5 M 7 F	10		
	6 M 6 F	16		
	7 M 5 F	18		
	8 M 4 F	13		

SIZE OF FAMILIES AND COMPOSITION BY SEX: FOR CITIES — Concluded.

WORCESTER — Con.

WORCESTER — Con.

Counties, Cities, Size of Families, and Number of Each Size	Composition of Families	Number of Families	Total Families %	Total Population %
	9 M 3 F	9		
	10 M 2 F	7		
	11 M 1 F	3		
	12 M	1		
(54) 13	2 M 11 F	1	0.17	0.45
	4 M 9 F	1		
	5 M 8 F	3		
	6 M 7 F	7		
	7 M 6 F	6		
	8 M 5 F	7		
	9 M 4 F	4		
	10 M 3 F	3		
	11 M 2 F	1		
	13 F	1		
(24) 14	3 M 11 F	1	0.12	0.34
	5 M 9 F	2		
	6 M 8 F	3		
	7 M 7 F	3		
	8 M 6 F	3		
	9 M 5 F	3		
	10 M 4 F	3		
	11 M 3 F	3		
	12 M 2 F	2		
	14 M	1		
(22) 15	6 M 9 F	2	0.11	0.33
	8 M 7 F	1		
	9 M 6 F	3		
	10 M 5 F	6		
	11 M 4 F	5		
	12 M 3 F	2		
	14 M 1 F	1		
(10) 16	5 M 11 F	1	0.05	0.16
	6 M 10 F	1		
	8 M 8 F	2		
	10 M 6 F	1		
	11 M 5 F	1		
	12 M 4 F	1		
	13 M 3 F	1		
	14 M 2 F	1		
	15 M 1 F	1		
(9) 17	7 M 10 F	2	0.05	0.16
	8 M 9 F	2		
	9 M 8 F	2		
	11 M 6 F	1		
	12 M 5 F	2		
(7) 18	8 M 10 F	1	0.04	0.13
	11 M 7 F	1		
	12 M 6 F	1		
	13 M 5 F	1		
	15 M 3 F	1		
	18 M	2		
(5) 19	11 M 8 F	2	0.03	0.10
	15 M 4 F	1		
	16 M 3 F	1		

WORCESTER — Con.

WORCESTER — Con.

Counties, Cities, Size of Families, and Number of Each Size	Composition of Families	Number of Families	Total Families %	Total Population %
	19 M	1		
(3) 20	5 M 15 F	1	0.02	0.06
	12 M 8 F	1		
	13 M 7 F	1		
(2) 21	15 M 6 F	1	0.01	0.04
	17 M 4 F	1		
(3) 22	14 M 8 F	1	0.02	0.07
	15 M 7 F	1		
	22 M	1		
(4) 23	4 M 19 F	1	0.02	0.06
	11 M 12 F	2		
	15 M 8 F	1		
(8) 24	12 M 12 F	2	0.04	0.10
	17 M 7 F	3		
	18 M 6 F	1		
	19 M 5 F	1		
	24 F	1		
(4) 25	15 M 10 F	1	0.02	0.10
	16 M 9 F	1		
	17 M 8 F	1		
	18 M 7 F	1		
(1) 27	19 M 8 F	1	*-	0.03
(2) 28	20 M 8 F	1	0.01	0.06
	24 M 4 F	1		
(1) 29	29 F	1	*-	0.03
(2) 31	17 M 14 F	1	0.01	0.06
	31 F	1		
(2) 32	15 M 17 F	1	0.01	0.06
	24 M 8 F	1		
(1) 35	28 M 7 F	1	*-	0.04
(2) 37	23 M 14 F	1	0.01	0.08
	24 M 13 F	1		
(1) 38	30 M 8 F	1	*-	0.04
(2) 40	19 M 21 F	1	0.01	0.08
	20 M 20 F	1		
(1) 41	31 M 10 F	1	*-	0.04
(1) 44	42 M 2 F	1	*-	0.04
(1) 46	26 M 20 F	1	*-	0.05
(1) 49	20 M 29 F	1	*-	0.05
(1) 53	39 M 14 F	1	*-	0.05
(1) 63	1 M 62 F	1	*-	0.06
(1) 64	14 M 50 F	1	*-	0.06
(1) 66	38 M 28 F	1	*-	0.07
(1) 69	61 M 8 F	1	*-	0.07
(1) 99	33 M 66 F	1	*-	0.10
(1) 113	48 M 65 F	1	*-	0.12
(1) 150	131 M 19 F	1	*-	0.15
(1) 172	73 M 99 F	1	*-	0.17
(1) 188	177 M 11 F	1	*-	0.19
(1) 205	205 M	1	*-	0.21
(1) 227	120 M 107 F	1	*-	0.23
(1) 529	263 M 266 F	1	*-	0.54
(1) 1,055	495 M 560 F	1	*-	1.07

SIZE OF FAMILIES AND COMPOSITION BY SEX: FOR THE STATE.

THE STATE, SIZE OF FAMILIES, AND NUMBER OF EACH SIZE.	Composition of Families	Number of Families	PERCENTAGES: EACH SIZE OF — Total Families	Total Population	THE STATE, SIZE OF FAMILIES, AND NUMBER OF EACH SIZE.	Composition of Families	Number of Families	PERCENTAGES: EACH SIZE OF — Total Families	Total Population
THE STATE,		547,385	100.00	100.00	THE STATE — Con.				
(21,836) 1	1 M	7,456	5.99	0.87		3 M 6 F	2,077		
	1 F	14,380				4 M 5 F	3,531		
(91,786) 2	1 M 1 F	76,722	16.77	7.34		5 M 4 F	3,525		
	2 M	2,355				6 M 3 F	2,360		
	2 F	12,709				7 M 2 F	971		
(106,436) 3	1 M 2 F	54,801	19.45	12.77		8 M 1 F	215		
	2 M 1 F	45,090				9 M	32		
	3 M	773				9 F	23		
	3 F	5,772			(7,892) 10	1 M 9 F	55	1.43	3.13
(99,152) 4	1 M 3 F	27,583	18.12	15.86		2 M 8 F	286		
	2 M 2 F	48,017				3 M 7 F	855		
	3 M 1 F	20,910				4 M 6 F	1,525		
	4 M	342				5 M 5 F	1,973		
	4 F	2,300				6 M 4 F	1,634		
(78,150) 5	1 M 4 F	11,535	14.28	15.63		7 M 3 F	966		
	2 M 3 F	29,354				8 M 2 F	412		
	3 M 2 F	27,576				9 M 1 F	89		
	4 M 1 F	8,030				10 M	25		
	5 M	164				10 F	16		
	5 F	857			(4,652) 11	1 M 10 F	23	0.80	1.91
(56,160) 6	1 M 5 F	4,367	10.26	13.48		2 M 9 F	104		
	2 M 4 F	14,263				3 M 8 F	311		
	3 M 3 F	20,128				4 M 7 F	621		
	4 M 2 F	13,243				5 M 6 F	859		
	5 M 1 F	3,410				6 M 5 F	984		
	6 M	109				7 M 4 F	732		
	6 F	310				8 M 3 F	412		
(37,173) 7	1 M 6 F	1,506	6.79	10.41		9 M 2 F	194		
	2 M 5 F	6,061				10 M 1 F	62		
	3 M 4 F	11,384				11 M	26		
	4 M 3 F	11,695				11 F	24		
	5 M 2 F	5,596			(2,281) 12	1 M 11 F	11	0.42	1.09
	6 M 1 F	1,519				2 M 10 F	35		
	7 M	58				3 M 9 F	117		
	7 F	114				4 M 8 F	197		
(23,202) 8	1 M 7 F	544	4.24	7.42		5 M 7 F	356		
	2 M 6 F	2,321				6 M 6 F	469		
	3 M 5 F	5,185				7 M 5 F	429		
	4 M 4 F	6,707				8 M 4 F	331		
	5 M 3 F	5,360				9 M 3 F	188		
	6 M 2 F	2,415				10 M 2 F	89		
	7 M 1 F	549				11 M 1 F	33		
	8 M	49				12 M	15		
	8 F	42				12 F	13		
(13,771) 9	1 M 8 F	161	2.52	4.96	(1,289) 13	1 M 12 F	9	0.26	0.73
	2 M 7 F	876				2 M 11 F	19		

SIZE OF FAMILIES AND COMPOSITION BY SEX: FOR THE STATE — Continued.

THE STATE, SIZE OF FAMILIES, AND NUMBER OF EACH SIZE.	Composition of Families	Number of Families	PERCENTAGES: EACH SIZE OF — Total Families	Total Population
THE STATE — Con.				
	3 M 10 F	41		
	4 M 9 F	90		
	5 M 8 F	144		
	6 M 7 F	223		
	7 M 6 F	272		
	8 M 5 F	236		
	9 M 4 F	168		
	10 M 3 F	95		
	11 M 2 F	57		
	12 M 1 F	18		
	13 M	11		
	13 F	16		
(877) 14	1 M 13 F	8	0.16	0.49
	2 M 12 F	8		
	3 M 11 F	18		
	4 M 10 F	44		
	5 M 9 F	75		
	6 M 8 F	87		
	7 M 7 F	152		
	8 M 6 F	134		
	9 M 5 F	125		
	10 M 4 F	86		
	11 M 3 F	62		
	12 M 2 F	47		
	13 M 1 F	10		
	14 M	10		
	14 F	11		
(547) 15	1 M 14 F	7	0.10	0.33
	2 M 13 F	7		
	3 M 12 F	14		
	4 M 11 F	18		
	5 M 10 F	38		
	6 M 9 F	48		
	7 M 8 F	57		
	8 M 7 F	61		
	9 M 6 F	60		
	10 M 5 F	72		
	11 M 4 F	63		
	12 M 3 F	48		
	13 M 2 F	28		
	14 M 1 F	7		
	15 M	10		
	15 F	9		
(381) 16	1 M 15 F	6	0.07	0.24
	2 M 14 F	3		
	3 M 13 F	7		
	4 M 12 F	6		
	5 M 11 F	16		
	6 M 10 F	23		
	7 M 9 F	32		
	8 M 8 F	49		
	9 M 7 F	43		
	10 M 6 F	46		
	11 M 5 F	39		
	12 M 4 F	35		
THE STATE — Con.				
	13 M 3 F	41		
	14 M 2 F	13		
	15 M 1 F	5		
	16 M	10		
	16 F	7		
(285) 17	1 M 16 F	1	0.05	0.19
	2 M 15 F	2		
	3 M 14 F	3		
	4 M 13 F	6		
	5 M 12 F	8		
	6 M 11 F	12		
	7 M 10 F	19		
	8 M 9 F	26		
	9 M 8 F	38		
	10 M 7 F	29		
	11 M 6 F	29		
	12 M 5 F	36		
	13 M 4 F	27		
	14 M 3 F	26		
	15 M 2 F	13		
	16 M 1 F	2		
	17 M	5		
	17 F	3		
(224) 18	1 M 17 F	3	0.04	0.16
	3 M 15 F	2		
	4 M 14 F	3		
	5 M 13 F	4		
	6 M 12 F	8		
	7 M 11 F	10		
	8 M 10 F	16		
	9 M 9 F	24		
	10 M 8 F	19		
	11 M 7 F	18		
	12 M 6 F	23		
	13 M 5 F	25		
	14 M 4 F	24		
	15 M 3 F	13		
	16 M 2 F	13		
	17 M 1 F	3		
	18 M	8		
	18 F	8		
(165) 19	1 M 18 F	2	0.03	0.12
	2 M 17 F	2		
	3 M 16 F	1		
	5 M 14 F	5		
	6 M 13 F	4		
	7 M 12 F	6		
	8 M 11 F	4		
	9 M 10 F	12		
	10 M 9 F	17		
	11 M 8 F	14		
	12 M 7 F	16		
	13 M 6 F	15		
	14 M 5 F	19		
	15 M 4 F	15		

SIZE OF FAMILIES AND COMPOSITION BY SEX: FOR THE STATE—Continued.

THE STATE, SIZE OF FAMILIES, AND NUMBER OF EACH SIZE.	Composition of Families	Number of Families	PERCENTAGES: EACH SIZE OF— Total Families	Total Population
THE STATE —Con.				
	16 M 3 F	12		
	17 M 2 F	7		
	18 M 1 F	1		
	19 M	6		
	19 F	5		
(156) 20	1 M 19 F	4	0.03	0.12
	2 M 18 F	1		
	3 M 17 F	3		
	4 M 16 F	1		
	5 M 15 F	4		
	6 M 14 F	3		
	7 M 13 F	4		
	8 M 12 F	7		
	9 M 11 F	11		
	10 M 10 F	12		
	11 M 9 F	14		
	12 M 8 F	15		
	13 M 7 F	10		
	14 M 6 F	13		
	15 M 5 F	9		
	16 M 4 F	13		
	17 M 3 F	12		
	18 M 2 F	5		
	20 M	7		
	20 F	8		
(115) 21	1 M 20 F	1	0.02	0.10
	3 M 18 F	1		
	4 M 17 F	2		
	5 M 16 F	1		
	6 M 15 F	4		
	7 M 14 F	3		
	8 M 13 F	4		
	9 M 12 F	7		
	10 M 11 F	9		
	11 M 10 F	10		
	12 M 9 F	9		
	13 M 8 F	5		
	14 M 7 F	10		
	15 M 6 F	9		
	16 M 5 F	7		
	17 M 4 F	12		
	18 M 3 F	10		
	19 M 2 F	1		
	20 M 1 F	2		
	21 M	4		
	21 F	4		
(191) 22	1 M 21 F	1	0.02	0.09
	2 M 20 F	1		
	3 M 19 F	1		
	4 M 18 F	1		
	7 M 15 F	1		
	8 M 14 F	1		
	9 M 13 F	6		
	10 M 12 F	4		
	11 M 11 F	5		

THE STATE, SIZE OF FAMILIES, AND NUMBER OF EACH SIZE.	Composition of Families	Number of Families	PERCENTAGES: EACH SIZE OF— Total Families	Total Population
THE STATE —Con.				
	12 M 10 F	11		
	13 M 9 F	6		
	14 M 8 F	13		
	15 M 7 F	14		
	16 M 6 F	9		
	17 M 5 F	11		
	18 M 4 F	7		
	20 M 2 F	3		
	22 M	2		
	22 F	4		
(63) 23	1 M 22 F	1	0.01	0.06
	2 M 21 F	1		
	3 M 20 F	1		
	4 M 19 F	1		
	5 M 18 F	1		
	6 M 17 F	1		
	7 M 16 F	2		
	8 M 15 F	1		
	9 M 14 F	3		
	10 M 13 F	2		
	11 M 12 F	3		
	12 M 11 F	5		
	13 M 10 F	1		
	14 M 9 F	5		
	15 M 8 F	5		
	16 M 7 F	5		
	17 M 6 F	6		
	18 M 5 F	2		
	19 M 4 F	1		
	20 M 3 F	5		
	21 M 2 F	3		
	23 M	2		
	23 F	6		
(76) 24	1 M 23 F	2	0.02	0.07
	4 M 20 F	1		
	5 M 19 F	3		
	8 M 16 F	2		
	10 M 14 F	2		
	12 M 12 F	8		
	13 M 11 F	5		
	14 M 10 F	7		
	15 M 9 F	7		
	16 M 8 F	3		
	17 M 7 F	7		
	18 M 6 F	8		
	19 M 5 F	3		
	20 M 4 F	4		
	21 M 3 F	4		
	22 M 2 F	1		
	23 M 1 F	1		
	24 M	3		
	24 F	5		
(65) 25	1 M 24 F	4	0.01	0.06
	2 M 23 F	2		
	3 M 22 F	1		

SIZE OF FAMILIES AND COMPOSITION BY SEX: FOR THE STATE — Continued.

THE STATE, SIZE OF FAMILIES, AND NUMBER OF EACH SIZE.	Composition of Families	Number of Families	PERCENTAGES: EACH SIZE OF — Total Families	Total Population	THE STATE, SIZE OF FAMILIES, AND NUMBER OF EACH SIZE.	Composition of Families	Number of Families	PERCENTAGES: EACH SIZE OF — Total Families	Total Population
THE STATE —Con.					THE STATE —Con.				
	5 M 20 F	1				25 M 2 F	2		
	7 M 18 F	1				27 M	2		
	8 M 17 F	2			(28) 28	1 M 27 F	1	0.01	0.04
	9 M 16 F	3				6 M 22 F	1		
	10 M 15 F	2				10 M 18 F	2		
	11 M 14 F	1				11 M 17 F	2		
	12 M 13 F	3				12 M 16 F	2		
	13 M 12 F	5				14 M 14 F	3		
	14 M 11 F	3				15 M 13 F	2		
	15 M 10 F	5				16 M 12 F	3		
	16 M 9 F	4				17 M 11 F	1		
	17 M 8 F	7				18 M 10 F	1		
	18 M 7 F	3				19 M 9 F	3		
	19 M 6 F	5				20 M 8 F	5		
	20 M 5 F	2				23 M 5 F	1		
	21 M 4 F	2				24 M 4 F	2		
	22 M 3 F	2				25 M 3 F	2		
	23 M 2 F	1				26 M 2 F	1		
	25 M	2				28 M	3		
	25 F	4				28 F	3		
(39) 26	1 M 25 F	2	0.01	0.04	(44) 29	3 M 26 F	2	0.01	0.05
	5 M 21 F	1				9 M 20 F	1		
	6 M 20 F	2				11 M 18 F	1		
	7 M 19 F	1				12 M 17 F	1		
	8 M 18 F	1				13 M 16 F	2		
	10 M 16 F	1				14 M 15 F	2		
	11 M 15 F	1				15 M 14 F	1		
	12 M 14 F	1				16 M 13 F	2		
	13 M 13 F	1				17 M 12 F	5		
	14 M 12 F	1				18 M 11 F	3		
	15 M 11 F	1				19 M 10 F	3		
	16 M 10 F	2				21 M 8 F	2		
	17 M 9 F	2				22 M 7 F	3		
	19 M 7 F	3				23 M 6 F	1		
	20 M 6 F	6				24 M 5 F	1		
	21 M 5 F	5				25 M 4 F	5		
	25 M 1 F	2				26 M 3 F	1		
	26 M	3				28 M 1 F	2		
	26 F	3				29 M	3		
(44) 27	1 M 26 F	1	0.01	0.05		29 F	3		
	2 M 25 F	2			(28) 30	1 M 29 F	1	0.01	0.03
	3 M 24 F	2				2 M 28 F	1		
	7 M 20 F	2				3 M 27 F	1		
	10 M 17 F	2				6 M 24 F	1		
	11 M 16 F	1				10 M 20 F	1		
	13 M 14 F	3				11 M 19 F	1		
	14 M 13 F	1				13 M 17 F	3		
	15 M 12 F	2				15 M 15 F	1		
	17 M 10 F	3				17 M 13 F	1		
	18 M 9 F	3				18 M 12 F	1		
	19 M 8 F	5				19 M 11 F	1		
	20 M 7 F	4				20 M 10 F	4		
	21 M 6 F	1				22 M 8 F	1		
	22 M 5 F	4				23 M 7 F	1		
	23 M 4 F	4				24 M 6 F	1		

SIZE OF FAMILIES AND COMPOSITION BY SEX: FOR THE STATE — Continued.

THE STATE, SIZE OF FAMILIES, AND NUMBER OF EACH SIZE.	Composition of Families	Number of Families	PERCENTAGES: EACH SIZE OF — Total Families	Total Population
THE STATE — Con.				
	25 M 5 F	1		
	28 M 2 F	2		
	30 M	5		
(27) 31	2 M 29 F	1	0.01	0.03
	3 M 28 F	1		
	4 M 27 F	1		
	5 M 26 F	1		
	6 M 25 F	1		
	9 M 22 F	1		
	10 M 21 F	1		
	12 M 19 F	1		
	13 M 18 F	2		
	15 M 16 F	1		
	16 M 15 F	2		
	17 M 14 F	3		
	19 M 12 F	3		
	20 M 11 F	1		
	21 M 10 F	1		
	22 M 9 F	1		
	23 M 8 F	1		
	24 M 7 F	1		
	26 M 5 F	1		
	31 F	2		
(25) 32	1 M 31 F	1	0.01	0.03
	15 M 17 F	1		
	16 M 16 F	1		
	17 M 15 F	2		
	19 M 13 F	2		
	20 M 12 F	3		
	22 M 10 F	1		
	23 M 9 F	1		
	24 M 8 F	1		
	25 M 7 F	1		
	27 M 5 F	1		
	28 M 4 F	1		
	29 M 3 F	2		
	32 M	1		
	32 F	4		
(23) 33	1 M 32 F	1	0.01	0.03
	4 M 29 F	1		
	5 M 28 F	1		
	12 M 21 F	1		
	14 M 19 F	1		
	15 M 18 F	1		
	16 M 17 F	1		
	17 M 16 F	2		
	19 M 14 F	2		
	23 M 10 F	1		
	24 M 9 F	2		
	26 M 7 F	1		
	29 M 4 F	1		
	30 M 3 F	3		
	31 M 2 F	2		
	33 F	2		
(26) 34	13 M 21 F	2	0.01	0.03

THE STATE, SIZE OF FAMILIES, AND NUMBER OF EACH SIZE.	Composition of Families	Number of Families	PERCENTAGES: EACH SIZE OF — Total Families	Total Population
THE STATE — Con.				
	15 M 19 F	2		
	18 M 16 F	1		
	19 M 15 F	4		
	20 M 14 F	3		
	22 M 12 F	3		
	24 M 10 F	2		
	25 M 9 F	3		
	26 M 8 F	1		
	28 M 6 F	2		
	34 M	1		
	34 F	2		
(28) 35	1 M 34 F	2	0.01	0.04
	8 M 27 F	1		
	12 M 23 F	1		
	14 M 21 F	1		
	16 M 19 F	2		
	17 M 18 F	1		
	20 M 15 F	2		
	23 M 12 F	1		
	24 M 11 F	1		
	25 M 10 F	2		
	26 M 9 F	2		
	27 M 8 F	2		
	28 M 7 F	2		
	29 M 6 F	1		
	31 M 4 F	2		
	33 M 2 F	1		
	35 M	3		
	35 F	1		
(19) 36	1 M 35 F	1	*-	0.03
	3 M 33 F	1		
	6 M 30 F	1		
	9 M 27 F	1		
	12 M 24 F	1		
	14 M 22 F	1		
	15 M 21 F	1		
	17 M 19 F	1		
	18 M 18 F	1		
	21 M 15 F	1		
	23 M 13 F	1		
	25 M 11 F	1		
	29 M 7 F	1		
	30 M 6 F	1		
	33 M 3 F	4		
	34 M 2 F	1		
(25) 37	1 M 36 F	2	0.01	0.04
	2 M 35 F	1		
	8 M 29 F	1		
	17 M 20 F	1		
	18 M 19 F	4		
	19 M 18 F	1		
	20 M 17 F	1		
	21 M 16 F	2		
	22 M 15 F	2		
	23 M 14 F	1		

SIZE OF FAMILIES AND COMPOSITION BY SEX : FOR THE STATE—Continued.

THE STATE, SIZE OF FAMILIES, AND NUMBER OF EACH SIZE.	Composition of Families	Number of Families	PERCENTAGES: EACH SIZE OF — Total Families	PERCENTAGES: EACH SIZE OF — Total Population	THE STATE, SIZE OF FAMILIES, AND NUMBER OF EACH SIZE.	Composition of Families	Number of Families	PERCENTAGES: EACH SIZE OF — Total Families	PERCENTAGES: EACH SIZE OF — Total Population
THE STATE — Con.					THE STATE — Con.				
	24 M 13 F	2				31 M 10 F	2		
	25 M 12 F	1				34 M 7 F	1		
	26 M 11 F	1	*			37 M 4 F	1		
	28 M 9 F	1				38 M 3 F	2		
	35 M 2 F	1				41 M	1		
	37 M	2			(11) 42	16 M 26 F	1	*—	0.02
	37 F	1				17 M 25 F	1		
(19) 38	4 M 34 F	1	*—	0.03		21 M 18 F	1		
	6 M 32 F	1				28 M 14 F	1		
	16 M 22 F	1				34 M 8 F	1		
	18 M 20 F	1				36 M 6 F	1		
	19 M 19 F	1				39 M 3 F	1		
	23 M 15 F	1				40 M 2 F	1		
	25 M 13 F	1				42 M	3		
	26 M 12 F	1			(17) 43	19 M 24 F	1	*—	0.03
	30 M 8 F	1				20 M 23 F	1		
	31 M 7 F	1				22 M 21 F	1		
	32 M 6 F	2				25 M 18 F	1		
	33 M 5 F	1				26 M 17 F	1		
	34 M 4 F	1				27 M 16 F	2		
	38 M	3				29 M 14 F	1		
	38 F	2				30 M 13 F	1		
(16) 39	2 M 37 F	1	*—	0.02		35 M 8 F	2		
	3 M 36 F	1				39 M 4 F	1		
	14 M 25 F	1				40 M 3 F	1		
	17 M 22 F	1				41 M 2 F	2		
	18 M 21 F	1				43 M	2		
	19 M 20 F	3			(12) 44	2 M 42 F	1	*—	0.02
	20 M 19 F	2				5 M 39 F	1		
	24 M 15 F	1				13 M 31 F	1		
	31 M 8 F	1				18 M 26 F	1		
	32 M 7 F	1				19 M 25 F	1		
	35 M 4 F	2				20 M 24 F	1		
	36 M 3 F	1				28 M 16 F	1		
(16) 40	1 M 39 F	1	*—	0.03		33 M 11 F	1		
	2 M 38 F	1				38 M 6 F	1		
	3 M 37 F	1				42 M 2 F	1		
	4 M 36 F	1				44 M	1		
	7 M 33 F	1				44 F	1		
	11 M 29 F	1			(10) 45	16 M 29 F	1	*—	0.02
	18 M 22 F	1				19 M 26 F	1		
	19 M 21 F	1				22 M 23 F	2		
	20 M 20 F	1				24 M 21 F	1		
	21 M 19 F	1				27 M 18 F	1		
	22 M 18 F	1				28 M 17 F	1		
	27 M 13 F	1				39 M 6 F	1		
	31 M 9 F	1				40 M 5 F	2		
	36 M 4 F	1			(10) 46	1 M 45 F	1	*—	0.02
	40 M	2				11 M 35 F	1		
(13) 41	21 M 20 F	1	*—	0.02		26 M 20 F	1		
	22 M 19 F	1				35 M 11 F	1		
	25 M 16 F	1				36 M 10 F	1		
	26 M 15 F	1				41 M 5 F	1		
	27 M 14 F	1				43 M 3 F	1		
	29 M 12 F	1				44 M 2 F	1		

SIZE OF FAMILIES AND COMPOSITION BY SEX: FOR THE STATE — Continued.

THE STATE. SIZE OF FAMILIES. AND NUMBER OF EACH SIZE.	Composition of Families	Number of Families	PERCENTAGES: EACH SIZE OF — Total Families	Total Population	THE STATE. SIZE OF FAMILIES. AND NUMBER OF EACH SIZE.	Composition of Families	Number of Families	PERCENTAGES: EACH SIZE OF — Total Families	Total Population
THE STATE — Con.					THE STATE — Con.				
	46 M	2			(4) 54	1 M 53 F	1	*-	0.01
13) 47	16 M 31 F	1	*-	0.02		49 M 5 F	1		
	17 M 30 F	1				54 F	2		
	19 M 28 F	1			(4) 55	1 M 54 F	1	*-	0.01
	23 M 24 F	1				28 M 27 F	1		
	25 M 22 F	1				41 M 14 F	1		
	26 M 21 F	1				45 M 10 F	1		
	27 M 20 F	1			(3) 56	35 M 21 F	1	*-	0.01
	28 M 19 F	1				39 M 17 F	1		
	30 M 17 F	1				54 M 2 F	1		
	45 M 2 F	2			(10) 57	3 M 54 F	1	*-	0.02
	47 M	2				21 M 36 F	1		
(8) 48	7 M 41 F	1	*-	0.02		34 M 23 F	1		
	17 M 31 F	1				47 M 10 F	1		
	30 M 18 F	2				51 M 6 F	1		
	35 M 13 F	1				54 M 3 F	1		
	44 M 4 F	1				55 M 2 F	2		
	46 M 2 F	1				57 M	1		
	48 F	1				57 F	1		
(9) 49	4 M 45 F	1	*-	0.02	(2) 58	9 M 49 F	1	*-	*-
	10 M 39 F	1				38 M 20 F	1		
	20 M 29 F	1			(7) 59	1 M 58 F	2	*-	0.02
	26 M 23 F	1				27 M 32 F	1		
	32 M 17 F	1				34 M 25 F	1		
	42 M 7 F	2				41 M 18 F	1		
	45 M 4 F	1				59 M	2		
	49 M	1			(3) 60	10 M 50 F	1	*-	0.01
(13) 50	16 M 34 F	1	*-	0.03		60 M	1		
	29 M 21 F	1				60 F	1		
	30 M 20 F	1			(1) 61	61 M	1	*-	*-
	31 M 19 F	1			(4) 62	55 M 7 F	1	*-	0.01
	33 M 17 F	1				62 M	3		
	36 M 14 F	1			(5) 63	1 M 62 F	1	*-	0.01
	38 M 12 F	1				59 M 4 F	1		
	42 M 8 F	1				63 F	1		
	43 M 7 F	1			(4) 64	14 M 50 F	1	*-	0.01
	47 M 3 F	1				31 M 33 F	1		
	49 M 1 F	2				38 M 26 F	1		
	50 F	1				64 F	1		
(6) 51	30 M 21 F	1	*-	0.01	(1) 65	31 M 34 F	1	*-	*-
	33 M 18 F	2			(6) 66	13 M 53 F	1	*-	0.02
	47 M 4 F	1				19 M 47 F	1		
	49 M 2 F	1				32 M 34 F	1		
	51 F	1				38 M 28 F	1		
(4) 52	13 M 39 F	1	*-	0.01		63 M 3 F	1		
	30 M 22 F	1				66 F	1		
	37 M 15 F	1			(1) 67	3 M 64 F	1	*-	*-
	38 M 14 F	1			(3) 68	27 M 41 F	1	*-	0.01
(9) 53	6 M 47 F	1	*-	0.02		52 M 16 F	1		
	23 M 30 F	1				68 F	1		
	25 M 28 F	1			(5) 69	4 M 65 F	1	*-	0.01
	27 M 26 F	1				27 M 42 F	1		
	39 M 14 F	2				61 M 8 F	1		
	40 M 13 F	1				64 M 5 F	1		
	53 M	2				69 M	1		

SIZE OF FAMILIES AND COMPOSITION BY SEX: FOR THE STATE—Continued.

THE STATE, SIZE OF FAMILIES, AND NUMBER OF EACH SIZE.	Composition of Families	Number of Families	PERCENTAGES: EACH SIZE OF — Total Families	Total Population
THE STATE —Con.				
(4) 70	7 M 63 F	1	*-	0.01
	12 M 58 F	1		
	57 M 13 F	1		
	70 F	1		
(4) 71	58 M 33 F	1	*-	0.01
	66 M 5 F	1		
	71 F	2		
(6) 72	5 M 67 F	1	*-	0.02
	14 M 58 F	1		
	15 M 57 F	1		
	22 M 50 F	1		
	30 M 42 F	1		
	59 M 13 F	1		
(2) 74	34 M 40 F	1	*-	0.01
	61 M 13 F	1		
(5) 75	29 M 46 F	1	*-	0.01
	42 M 33 F	1		
	68 M 7 F	1		
	75 M	2		
(1) 76	33 M 43 F	1	*-	*-
(3) 77	5 M 72 F	1	*-	0.01
	73 M 4 F	1		
	77 F	1		
(6) 78	16 M 62 F	1	*-	0.02
	42 M 36 F	1		
	75 M 3 F	1		
	78 M	2		
	78 F	1		
(2) 79	58 M 21 F	1	*-	0.01
	79 F	1		
(6) 80	47 M 33 F	1	*-	0.02
	77 M 3 F	1		
	80 M	3		
	80 F	1		
(1) 81	38 M 43 F	1	*-	*-
(5) 82	1 M 81 F	1	*-	0.02
	30 M 52 F	1		
	34 M 48 F	1		
	77 M 5 F	1		
	79 M 3 F	1		
(2) 84	24 M 60 F	1	*-	0.01
	39 M 45 F	1		
(3) 85	7 M 78 F	1	*-	0.01
	39 M 46 F	1		
	84 M 1 F	1		
(2) 86	1 M 85 F	1	*-	0.01
	42 M 44 F	1		
(2) 87	34 M 53 F	1	*-	0.01
	37 M 50 F	1		
(2) 88	1 M 87 F	1	*-	0.01
	39 M 49 F	1		
(2) 89	34 M 55 F	1	*-	0.01
	58 M 31 F	1		
(3) 91	87 M 4 F	1	*	0.01
	90 M 1 F	1		
THE STATE —Con.				
	91 F	1		
(2) 93	34 M 59 F	1	*-	0.01
	89 M 4 F	1		
(1) 94	23 M 71 F	1	*-	*-
(4) 96	5 M 91 F	1	*-	0.02
	44 M 52 F	1		
	96 M	2		
(1) 97	3 M 94 F	1	*-	*-
(1) 98	98 M	1	*-	*-
(6) 99	33 M 66 F	1	*-	0.02
	97 M 2 F	1		
	98 M 1 F	1		
	99 M	3		
(1) 100	100 M	1	*-	*-
(1) 101	3 M 98 F	1	*-	*-
(1) 103	103 M	1	*-	*-
(1) 105	101 M 4 F	1	*-	*-
(2) 107	50 M 57 F	1	*-	0.01
	84 M 23 F	1		
(3) 109	98 M 11 F	1	*-	0.01
	106 M 3 F	1		
	109 F	1		
(2) 111	107 M 4 F	1	*-	0.01
	111 M	1		
(2) 112	7 M 105 F	1	*-	0.01
	25 M 87 F	1		
(3) 113	48 M 65 F	1	*-	0.01
	55 M 58 F	1		
	87 M 26 F	1		
(2) 114	52 M 62 F	1	*-	0.01
	95 M 19 F	1		
(2) 116	2 M 114 F	1	*-	0.01
	42 M 74 F	1		
(3) 118	1 M 117 F	1	*-	0.01
	30 M 88 F	1		
	114 M 4 F	1		
(2) 119	42 M 77 F	1	*-	0.01
	108 M 11 F	1		
(1) 120	120 M	1	*-	*-
(1) 121	17 M 104 F	1	*-	*-
(1) 122	62 M 60 F	1	*-	*-
(3) 124	3 M 121 F	1	*-	0.01
	24 M 100 F	1		
	101 M 23 F	1		
(1) 128	99 M 29 F	1	*-	0.01
(2) 129	53 M 76 F	1	*-	0.01
	73 M 56 F	1		
(1) 132	42 M 90 F	1	*-	0.01
(3) 134	78 M 56 F	1	*-	0.02
	81 M 53 F	1		
	108 M 26 F	1		
(1) 135	58 M 77 F	1	*-	0.01
(1) 136	63 M 73 F	1	*-	0.01
(1) 137	46 M 91 F	1	*-	0.01
(2) 140	2 M 138 F	1	*-	0.01

SIZE OF FAMILIES AND COMPOSITION BY SEX: FOR THE STATE--Concluded.

THE STATE, SIZE OF FAMILIES, AND NUMBER OF EACH SIZE.	Composition of Families	Number of Families	Percentages: Each size of— Total Families	Total Population
THE STATE —Con.				
	118 M 22 F	1		
(1) 141	60 M 81 F	1	*-	0.01
(1) 144	52 M 92 F	1	*-	0.01
(2) 145	61 M 84 F	1	*-	0.01
	145 M	1		
(1) 147	3 M 144 F	1	*-	0.01
(1) 150	131 M 19 F	1	*-	0.01
(1) 156	133 M 23 F	1	*-	0.01
(1) 158	1 M 157 F	1	*-	0.01
(1) 160	160 M	1	*-	0.01
(1) 162	162 M	1	*-	0.01
(1) 164	1 M 163 F	1	*-	0.01
(1) 168	168 M	1	*-	0.01
(1) 169	32 M 137 F	1	*-	0.01
(1) 170	160 M 10 F	1	*-	0.01
(1) 171	78 M 93 F	1	*-	0.01
(1) 172	73 M 99 F	1	*-	0.01
(2) 183	152 M 31 F	1	*-	0.01
	181 M 2 F	1		
(1) 188	177 M 11 F	1	*-	0.01
(1) 193	96 M 97 F	1	*-	0.01
(1) 194	1 M 193 F	1	*-	0.01
(1) 198	71 M 127 F	1	*-	0.01
(1) 200	83 M 117 F	1	*-	0.01
(1) 205	205 M	1	*-	0.01
(1) 212	94 M 118 F	1	*-	0.01
(1) 214	103 M 111 F	1	*-	0.01
(1) 216	214 M 2 F	1	*-	0.01
(1) 220	71 M 149 F	1	*-	0.01
(1) 221	187 M 34 F	1	*-	0.01
(1) 227	120 M 107 F	1	*-	0.01
(1) 255	251 M 4 F	1	*-	0.01
THE STATE —Con.				
(1) 259	228 M 31 F	1	*-	0.01
(1) 261	227 M 34 F	1	*-	0.01
(1) 268	92 M 176 F	1	*-	0.01
(1) 274	141 M 133 F	1	*-	0.01
(1) 276	276 M	1	*-	0.01
(1) 299	274 M 25 F	1	*-	0.01
(1) 301	265 M 36 F	1	*-	0.01
(1) 308	308 F	1	*-	0.01
(1) 323	144 M 179 F	1	*-	0.01
(1) 324	1 M 323 F	1	*-	0.01
(1) 326	6 M 320 F	1	*-	0.01
(1) 342	144 M 198 F	1	*-	0.01
(1) 352	4 M 348 F	1	*-	0.01
(1) 397	252 M 145 F	1	*-	0.02
(1) 399	4 M 395 F	1	*-	0.02
(1) 412	176 M 236 F	1	*-	0.02
(1) 529	263 M 266 F	1	*-	0.02
(1) 564	488 M 76 F	1	*-	0.02
(1) 599	273 M 326 F	1	*-	0.02
(1) 608	298 M 310 F	1	*-	0.02
(1) 680	660 M 80 F	1	*-	0.03
(1) 691	334 M 357 F	1	*-	0.03
(1) 741	736 M 5 F	1	*-	0.03
(1) 752	309 M 443 F	1	*-	0.03
(1) 957	474 M 483 F	1	*-	0.04
(1) 1,015	989 M 26 F	1	*-	0.04
(1) 1,032	1,032 M	1	*-	0.04
(1) 1,055	495 M 560 F	1	*-	0.04
(1) 1,087	554 M 533 F	1	*-	0.04
(1) 1,166	543 M 623 F	1	*-	0.05
(1) 1,596	1,251 M 345 F	1	*-	0.06

RECAPITULATION. SIZE OF FAMILIES.

SIZE OF FAMILIES.		Barnstable	Berkshire	Bristol	Dukes	Essex	Franklin
1	1	867	803	1,995	190	3,219	526
2	2	2,075	2,966	8,014	358	12,887	1,856
3	3	1,898	3,548	8,935	288	15,139	2,034
4	4	1,353	3,239	8,206	208	13,786	1,745
5	5	848	2,714	6,640	113	10,513	1,363
6	6	471	2,019	4,935	60	7,193	899
7	7	270	1,389	3,362	46	4,591	508
8	8	157	899	2,266	21	2,725	398
9	9	66	538	1,452	14	1,576	173
10	10	31	323	819	2	918	113
11	11	16	167	525	3	497	46
12	12	5	77	237	1	263	23
13	13	5	51	131	-	180	6
14	14	2	18	58	1	116	4
15	15	1	11	39	-	69	1
16	16	2	9	16	1	57	2
17	17	-	3	10	-	37	3
18	18	-	3	7	-	34	5
19	19	1	4	8	-	25	-
20	20	1	2	6	-	29	3
21	21	-	3	4	-	19	2
22	22	-	4	7	-	13	1
23	23	-	-	-	-	15	2
24	24	-	3	3	-	14	5
25	25	-	1	1	-	19	1
26	26	-	-	3	-	4	-
27	27	-	-	3	-	7	-
28	28	-	-	2	-	11	-
29	29	-	-	4	-	7	-
30	30	-	-	-	-	4	-
31	31	-	2	-	-	3	-
32	32	-	-	-	-	5	-
33	33	-	2	2	-	4	1
34	34	-	2	-	-	6	1
35	35	-	-	1	-	6	-
36	36	-	1	2	-	4	1
37	37	-	3	1	-	3	-
38	38	-	1	-	-	3	-
39	39	-	1	-	-	4	1
40	40	-	-	-	-	6	-
41	41	-	-	1	-	4	-
42	42	-	-	-	-	4	-
43	43	-	-	-	-	5	-
44	44	-	-	-	-	2	1
45	45	-	-	1	-	3	-
46	46	-	-	1	-	2	-
47	47	-	-	-	-	6	-
48	48	-	-	-	-	-	-
49	49	-	-	-	-	3	-
50	50	-	-	-	-	3	-
51	51	-	1	-	-	3	-
52	52	-	-	-	-	1	-
53	53	-	-	1	-	1	-
54	54	-	-	-	-	1	-
55	55	-	-	-	-	-	-
56	56	-	-	-	-	2	-

RECAPITULATION. SIZE OF FAMILIES.

		COUNTIES						THE STATE	
Hampden	Hampshire	Middlesex	Nantucket	Norfolk	Plymouth	Suffolk	Worcester		
1,112	573	3,250	149	1,325	1,370	3,634	2,813	21,836	1
5,108	1,976	16,951	295	4,842	4,918	17,990	11,550	91,786	2
6,441	2,242	20,571	218	5,576	5,501	20,895	13,150	100,436	3
5,869	2,011	20,138	159	5,340	4,682	20,272	12,144	99,152	4
4,782	1,611	16,187	80	4,256	3,206	16,497	9,256	78,156	5
3,492	1,211	11,749	38	3,210	2,202	12,089	6,502	56,160	6
2,523	815	7,601	22	2,066	1,258	8,254	4,668	37,173	7
1,450	525	4,778	9	1,292	715	5,135	2,922	23,292	8
843	315	2,769	5	794	399	3,000	1,827	13,771	9
552	187	1,512	1	409	212	1,790	967	7,836	10
281	104	796	2	225	100	1,028	562	4,352	11
149	51	406	1	127	56	601	284	2,281	12
108	52	263	-	64	35	386	138	1,399	13
71	14	145	-	39	16	304	89	877	14
38	14	90	-	23	12	191	58	547	15
22	5	62	1	11	13	155	25	381	16
27	3	45	-	8	9	112	28	285	17
14	7	40	-	19	3	82	19	224	18
12	2	25	-	10	4	55	17	163	19
14	-	34	-	5	2	46	14	159	20
10	-	17	-	2	4	42	12	115	21
6	5	15	-	3	4	30	13	101	22
3	1	16	-	2	-	13	11	63	23
5	4	9	-	4	2	11	16	79	24
3	3	13	-	5	1	9	9	65	25
4	-	9	-	4	1	9	5	39	26
5	-	11	-	2	-	11	5	44	27
5	3	6	1	-	1	5	4	38	28
1	3	12	-	2	1	10	4	44	29
3	2	8	-	-	1	10	-	28	30
3	-	5	-	1	1	6	6	27	31
2	-	6	-	2	-	4	4	23	32
2	1	3	-	2	1	3	2	23	33
4	2	3	-	2	-	5	1	26	34
3	2	7	-	1	1	6	1	28	35
1	-	7	-	-	-	2	1	19	36
2	-	6	-	-	2	5	3	25	37
2	-	7	-	2	-	1	3	19	38
2	-	5	-	-	-	3	-	16	39
-	1	1	-	2	-	4	2	16	40
-	-	3	-	-	-	1	4	13	41
-	1	2	-	-	1	2	1	11	42
-	1	5	-	1	-	4	1	17	43
-	1	4	-	-	1	1	2	12	44
-	1	-	-	2	-	3	-	10	45
1	-	1	-	-	-	3	2	10	46
1	-	3	-	-	-	3	-	13	47
-	-	2	-	-	-	5	1	8	48
1	1	2	-	1	-	-	1	9	49
3	1	1	-	1	2	1	1	13	50
-	-	-	-	-	-	1	1	6	51
-	-	1	-	-	-	2	-	4	52
-	-	5	-	-	-	-	2	9	53
-	2	1	-	-	-	-	-	4	54
1	-	-	-	1	-	-	2	4	55
-	-	-	-	-	-	1	-	3	56

RECAPITULATION. SIZE OF FAMILIES — Continued.

SIZE OF FAMILIES		Counties					
		Barnstable	Berkshire	Bristol	Dukes	Essex	Franklin
1	57	-	-	-	-	5	1
2	58	-	-	-	-	1	-
3	59	-	-	-	-	2	-
4	60	-	-	-	-	1	-
5	61	-	-	-	-	-	-
6	62	-	-	-	-	-	-
7	63	-	-	-	-	-	-
8	64	-	-	-	-	1	-
9	65	-	-	1	-	-	-
10	66	-	-	-	-	1	-
11	67	-	-	1	-	-	-
12	68	-	-	-	-	1	-
13	69	-	-	-	-	-	-
14	70	-	-	-	-	1	-
15	71	-	-	-	-	1	-
16	72	-	-	-	-	1	-
17	74	-	-	-	-	1	-
18	75	-	1	-	-	3	-
19	76	-	-	-	-	-	-
20	77	-	-	-	-	1	-
21	78	-	-	1	-	1	-
22	79	-	-	-	-	-	1
23	80	-	-	-	-	1	-
24	81	-	-	-	-	-	-
25	82	-	-	1	-	3	-
26	84	-	-	1	-	-	-
27	85	-	-	-	-	1	-
28	86	-	-	1	-	-	-
29	87	-	-	-	-	-	-
30	88	-	-	-	-	-	-
31	89	-	-	-	-	1	-
32	91	-	-	-	-	1	-
33	93	-	-	-	-	1	-
34	94	-	-	-	-	-	-
35	96	-	-	-	-	-	-
36	97	-	-	-	-	-	-
37	98	-	-	-	-	-	-
38	99	-	-	-	-	1	-
39	100	-	-	-	-	-	-
40	101	-	-	-	-	-	-
41	103	-	-	-	-	-	-
42	105	-	-	-	-	1	-
43	107	-	-	-	-	-	-
44	109	-	-	-	-	1	-
45	111	-	-	-	-	1	-
46	112	-	-	-	-	-	-
47	113	-	-	-	-	1	-
48	114	-	-	-	-	-	-
49	116	-	-	-	-	1	-
50	118	-	-	-	-	-	-
51	119	-	-	1	-	-	-
52	120	-	-	-	-	-	-
53	121	-	-	-	-	-	-
54	122	-	-	-	-	-	-
55	124	-	-	-	-	-	-
56	128	-	-	-	-	-	-
57	129	-	-	-	-	-	-

RECAPITULATION. SIZE OF FAMILIES — Continued.

		COUNTIES						THE STATE	
Hampden	Hampshire	Middlesex	Nantucket	Norfolk	Plymouth	Suffolk	Worcester		
1	1	1	-	1	-	-	-	10	1
-	-	-	-	-	-	-	1	2	2
-	2	-	-	1	-	2	-	7	3
-	1	-	-	-	-	-	1	3	4
-	-	1	-	-	-	-	-	1	5
-	-	-	-	-	-	2	2	4	6
1	1	-	-	-	-	-	1	3	7
-	1	1	-	-	-	-	1	4	8
-	-	-	-	-	-	-	-	1	9
1	1	-	-	-	-	1	2	6	10
-	-	-	-	-	-	-	-	1	11
-	1	-	-	-	-	1	-	3	12
1	-	1	-	-	1	1	1	5	13
-	-	1	-	-	-	1	-	4	14
-	-	-	-	1	-	1	1	4	15
1	1	-	-	1	-	2	-	6	16
1	-	-	-	-	-	-	-	2	17
-	-	-	-	-	-	1	-	5	18
-	-	-	-	-	-	1	-	1	19
-	-	-	-	-	-	2	-	3	20
-	-	2	-	-	-	2	-	6	21
-	-	-	-	-	-	1	-	2	22
-	-	3	-	1	-	-	1	6	23
-	-	-	-	-	-	1	-	1	24
-	-	-	-	-	-	1	-	5	25
-	-	1	-	-	-	-	-	2	26
-	-	2	-	-	-	-	-	3	27
-	-	-	-	-	-	1	-	2	28
-	-	-	-	-	-	2	-	2	29
-	-	-	-	-	-	1	1	2	30
-	-	-	-	-	-	1	-	2	31
-	-	-	-	-	-	2	-	3	32
-	-	-	-	-	-	1	-	2	33
-	-	-	-	-	-	1	-	1	34
-	-	1	-	1	-	1	1	4	35
-	-	-	-	-	-	1	-	1	36
-	-	1	-	-	-	-	-	1	37
-	-	4	-	-	-	-	1	6	38
-	-	1	-	-	-	-	-	1	39
-	-	-	-	-	-	1	-	1	40
-	-	1	-	-	-	-	-	1	41
-	-	-	-	-	-	-	-	1	42
-	-	1	-	-	-	1	-	2	43
-	-	-	-	-	-	2	-	3	44
-	-	-	-	-	-	-	1	2	45
1	-	-	-	-	-	1	-	2	46
-	-	1	-	-	-	-	1	3	47
1	-	-	-	-	-	1	-	2	48
-	-	-	-	-	-	1	-	2	49
-	-	-	-	1	-	2	-	3	50
-	-	-	-	-	-	1	-	2	51
-	-	1	-	-	-	-	-	1	52
-	-	-	-	-	-	1	-	1	53
-	-	1	-	-	-	-	-	1	54
-	-	-	-	1	-	2	-	3	55
-	-	-	-	-	-	-	1	1	56
-	-	-	-	-	-	1	1	2	57

RECAPITULATION.   SIZE OF FAMILIES — Continued.

	SIZE OF FAMILIES.	COUNTIES					
		Barnstable	Berkshire	Bristol	Dukes	Essex	Franklin
1	132	-	-	-	-	-	-
2	134	-	-	-	-	-	-
3	135	-	-	-	-	-	-
4	136	-	-	-	-	1	-
5	137	-	-	-	-	-	-
6	140	-	-	-	-	-	-
7	141	-	-	-	-	1	-
8	144	-	-	-	-	1	-
9	145	-	-	-	-	-	-
10	147	-	-	-	-	-	-
11	150	-	-	-	-	-	-
12	156	-	-	-	-	-	-
13	158	-	-	-	-	-	-
14	160	-	-	-	-	-	-
15	162	-	-	-	-	-	-
16	164	-	-	-	-	-	-
17	168	-	-	-	-	-	1
18	169	-	-	-	-	-	-
19	170	-	-	-	-	-	-
20	171	-	-	-	-	-	-
21	172	-	-	-	-	-	-
22	185	-	-	-	-	-	-
23	188	-	-	-	-	-	-
24	193	-	-	-	-	-	-
25	194	-	-	-	-	-	-
26	198	-	-	-	-	-	-
27	200	-	-	-	-	-	-
28	205	-	-	-	-	-	-
29	212	-	-	-	-	-	-
30	214	-	-	-	-	-	-
31	216	-	1	-	-	-	-
32	220	-	-	-	-	-	-
33	221	-	-	1	-	-	-
34	227	-	-	-	-	-	-
35	255	-	-	-	-	-	-
36	259	-	-	-	-	-	-
37	261	-	-	-	-	1	-
38	268	-	-	-	-	-	-
39	274	-	-	1	-	-	-
40	276	-	-	-	-	-	-
41	290	-	-	-	-	1	-
42	301	-	-	-	-	-	-
43	308	-	-	-	-	-	-
44	323	-	-	-	-	-	-
45	324	-	-	-	-	-	-
46	326	-	-	-	-	-	-
47	342	-	-	-	-	-	-
48	352	-	-	-	-	-	-
49	397	-	-	-	-	-	-
50	399	-	-	-	-	-	-
51	412	-	-	-	-	-	-
52	520	-	-	-	-	-	-
53	564	-	-	-	-	-	-
54	599	-	-	-	-	-	-
55	608	-	-	-	-	-	-
56	680	-	-	-	-	-	-
57	691	-	-	-	-	-	-

RECAPITULATION. SIZE OF FAMILIES — Continued.

			COUNTIES					THE STATE	
Hampden	Hampshire	Middlesex	Nantucket	Norfolk	Plymouth	Suffolk	Worcester		
-	-	-	-	-	-	1	-		1
1	-	-	-	-	-	1	1		2
-	-	-	-	-	-	1	-	1	3
-	-	-	-	-	-	-	-		4
-	-	-	-	-	-	1	-		5
-	-	1	-	-	-	-	1		6
-	-	-	-	-	-	-	-		7
-	-	-	-	-	-	-	-		8
-	-	1	-	-	-	1	-		9
-	-	1	-	-	-	-	-		10
-	-	-	-	-	-	-	1		11
-	-	-	-	-	-	1	-		12
-	-	-	-	-	-	1	-		13
-	-	-	-	-	-	-	1		14
-	-	-	-	1	-	-	-		15
-	-	-	-	-	-	-	1		16
-	-	-	-	-	-	-	-		17
-	-	-	-	-	1	-	-		18
-	-	1	-	-	-	-	-		19
1	-	-	-	-	-	-	-		20
-	-	-	-	-	-	-	1		21
-	-	-	-	1	-	1	-		22
-	-	-	-	-	-	-	1		23
1	-	-	-	-	-	-	-		24
-	-	-	-	-	-	1	-		25
-	-	1	-	-	-	-	-		26
-	-	-	-	-	-	1	-		27
-	-	-	-	-	-	-	1		28
-	-	-	-	-	-	1	-		29
-	-	-	-	-	-	1	-		30
-	-	-	-	-	-	-	-		31
-	-	-	-	-	-	1	-		32
-	-	-	-	-	-	-	-		33
-	-	-	-	-	-	-	1		34
-	-	-	-	-	-	1	-		35
1	-	-	-	-	-	-	-		36
-	-	-	-	-	-	-	-		37
-	-	-	-	-	-	1	-		38
-	-	-	-	-	-	-	-		39
-	-	-	-	-	-	1	-		40
-	-	-	-	-	-	-	-		41
-	-	-	-	-	-	-	1		42
-	1	-	-	-	-	-	-		43
-	-	1	-	-	-	-	-		44
-	-	-	-	1	-	-	-		45
-	-	1	-	-	-	-	-		46
-	-	1	-	-	-	-	-		47
-	-	-	-	-	-	1	-		48
-	-	-	-	-	-	1	-		49
-	-	-	-	-	-	1	-		50
-	-	-	-	-	-	1	-		51
-	-	-	-	-	-	-	1		52
-	-	1	-	-	-	-	-		53
-	-	-	-	-	-	1	-		54
-	1	-	-	-	-	-	-		55
-	-	-	-	-	-	1	-		56
-	-	-	-	-	-	1	-		57

RECAPITULATION. SIZE OF FAMILIES — Concluded.

SIZE OF FAMILIES.	COUNTIES					
	Barnstable	Berkshire	Bristol	Dukes	Essex	Franklin
1 741	-	-	-	-	-	-
2 772	-	-	-	-	-	-
3 957	-	-	1	-	-	-
4 1,015	-	-	-	-	-	-
5 1,082	-	-	-	-	-	-
6 1,055	-	-	-	-	-	-
7 1,087	-	-	-	-	1	-
8 1,196	-	-	-	-	-	-
9 1,596	-	-	-	-	-	-
10 TOTALS, ...	8,069	18,810	47,708	1,206	74,092	9,637

RECAPITULATION. SIZE OF FAMILIES — Concluded.

		COUNTIES						THE STATE	
Hampden	Hampshire	Middlesex	Nantucket	Norfolk	Plymouth	Suffolk	Worcester		
-	-	-	-	-	-	1	-	1	1
-	-	-	-	-	-	-	1	1	2
-	-	-	-	-	-	-	-	1	3
-	-	-	-	-	1	-	-	1	4
-	-	1	-	-	-	-	-	1	5
-	-	-	-	-	-	-	1	1	6
-	-	-	-	-	-	-	-	1	7
-	-	1	-	-	-	-	-	1	8
-	-	-	-	-	-	1	-	1	9
2,796	11,744	107,654	981	29,685	24,839	112,802	67,274	547,385	10

TABULAR ANALYSES

FOR THE FOLLOWING PRESENTATIONS:

The statistics relative to families are contained in two presentations. First, Families: Number and Average Size (pages 331 to 338) ; second, Size of Families and Composition by Sex (339 to 443).

From the recapitulation of the first presentation, contained on page 337, we note that the total number of families in the State is 547,385, the average size of each family being 4.57. In 1875, the average size of each family for the State was 4.60, and in 1885, 4.58. It is, therefore, plain that the average size of the family remains practically the same as it was in 1875, notwithstanding the increase in population and the changes that have taken place in the composition of the population, the most important of which are due to immigration. The average size of the family in Suffolk County is 4.79. This is the highest average reached in any county, the lowest being found in Nantucket, where the average size of the family is 3.67.

In conducting the Census enumeration, every aggregation of individuals living under one roof, or related directly to one head, either arbitrarily or otherwise, is considered a family. This interpretation of the term "family" varies somewhat from that ordinarily given to the word, and it follows, of course, that the Census family is not exactly identical with the normal family. For instance, a number of people living together in a hotel is considered a single family, the proprietor being taken as the head. In the same way, a penal or reformatory institution is considered a single family, the superintendent being the head. In 1885, however, it was shown by a careful analysis of the different families enumerated under this plan that, eliminating the families coming under an artificial designation, such as we have explained, the average size of the actual normal family in the State was 4.45, and, therefore, that the influence upon the average by including the artificial or arbitrary families, so classed for Census purposes, was immaterial, so far as the State taken as a whole was concerned, being but 0.13 ; and, as stated in that Census, " It makes but little difference, so far as great bodies of people are concerned, as, for instance, the population of the State, whether the families are considered on the basis of the actual normal family, or on the ordinary Census basis which includes all aggregations living under one roof, or having certain relations to one head."

For the purpose of showing the influence of the Census method of classification upon the average size of the families in the present Census, the following table is introduced :

CLASSIFICATION.	Number	Population	Average Size
Private families, ...	546,533	2,452,617	4.49
Hotels, ...	354	8,779	24.80
Penal and reformatory institutions, . . .	35	7,850	224.29

CLASSIFICATION.	Number	Population	Average Size
Religious institutions and associations, . .	46	1,638	35 61
Public or private charitable institutions, . .	201	11,481	57.12
Hospitals and asylums, ...	57	8,656	151.86
Boarding schools, academies, etc., . . .	58	3,624	62.48
College dormitories, ...	68	3,784	55.65
Government stations, ...	7	413	59 00
Camps, ...	26	1,341	51.58
ALL FAMILIES, ...	547,385	2,500,183	4.57

The final line of the foregoing table reproduces the total number of families under the Census classification, the total population, and the average size of the family, the latter figure being 4.57, as previously cited The total number of families, 547,385, comprises 546,533 private families, 354 hotels, 35 penal and reformatory institutions, 46 religious institutions and associations, 201 public or private charitable institutions, 57 hospitals and asylums, 58 boarding schools, academies, etc , 68 college dormitories, seven government stations, and 26 " camps; " the latter term being applied to temporary settlements of Italian or other laborers, employed on railroads or public works, and living together in a single community or camp. Excluding the private families, the other families named in the above classification are classed as families under the arbitrary method of Census classification as previously described. Excluding all such families, it will be seen, from the first line of the table, that the private families included 2,452,617 persons, the average size of each family being 4.49 If this figure is compared with the average given in the final line of the table, 4.57, it will also be seen that, as in 1885, the average size of the family for the State is not materially affected by including the arbitrary Census families.

It is found, nevertheless, repeating the experience of previous Censuses, that while the average size of the family for the State as a whole is not materially affected by the Census method of classification, which has been explained, the average for certain towns which happen to contain large institutions is somewhat affected The exact effect is seen in the following table, which shows for each of the towns in which a family of 25 persons or more was found, the total population, the population of the large families, the population excluding large families, and the average number of persons to a family, based upon the total population, and also upon the population excluding the large families :

TOWNS.	Total Population	POPULATION OF LARGE FAMILIES			Population excluding Large Families	AVERAGE NUMBER OF PERSONS TO A FAMILY	
		Schools, Colleges, etc.	Prisons, Reformatories, Hospitals, etc.	Other Large Families		Total Population	Population excluding Large Families
Amesbury, ...	9,986	–	–	94	9,892	4.38	4.34
Amherst, ...	4,785	210	–	29	4,546	4.50	4.27
Andover, ...	6,145	171	–	32	5,942	4.74	4.58
Ashburnham, ...	2,148	57	–	–	2,091	4.05	3.95
Athol, ...	7,364	–	–	319	7,045	4.21	4.03
Attleborough, ...	8,288	–	–	51	8,237	4 39	4.36
Avon, ...	1,626	–	–	26	1,600	4.22	4.16
Barre, ...	2,278	–	134	60	2,084	4.08	3.73
Bedford, ...	1,169	–	–	36	1,133	4.66	4.51

Towns.	Total Population	Population of Large Families — Schools, Colleges, etc.	Prisons, Reformatories, Hospitals, etc.	Other Large Families	Population excluding Large Families	Average Number of Persons to a Family — Total Population	Population excluding Large Families
Belmont,	2,843	–	–	313	2,530	5.63	5.01
Billerica,	2,577	42	–	–	2,535	4.43	4.36
Blackstone,	6,039	–	26	99	5,914	4.77	4.67
Bradford,	4,736	116	–	–	4,620	4.22	4.12
Braintree,	5,311	–	–	162	5,149	4.24	4.11
Bridgewater,	4,686	169	1,015	–	3,502	5.49	4.10
Brookline,	16,164	–	99	111	15,954	5.13	5.07
Chelmsford,	3,162	–	69	–	3,093	4.23	4.14
Clinton,	11,497	–	–	415	11,082	5.05	4.86
Concord,	5,175	–	1,032	–	4,143	5.92	4.74
Danvers,	8,181	–	1,087	32	7,062	4.95	4.27
Dedham,	7,211	–	80	78	7,053	4.47	4.37
Douglas,	2,026	–	–	27	1,999	4.19	4.14
Dracut,	2,443	–	–	71	2,372	5.14	4.99
Duxbury,	1,966	50	–	–	1,916	3.70	3.69
Easthampton,	4,790	59	–	61	4,670	4.70	4.58
Foxborough,	3,219	–	118	–	3,101	3.89	3.75
Framingham,	9,512	–	–	144	9,368	4.50	4.43
Franklin,	5,136	96	–	102	4,938	4.37	4.20
Gill,	1,082	168	–	–	914	5.49	4.64
Great Barrington,	4,794	31	–	33	4,730	4.22	4.16
Greenfield,	6,229	–	34	108	6,087	4.30	4.20
Groton,	2,192	140	–	–	2,052	4.31	4.04
Hamilton,	1,356	–	–	28	1,328	4.30	4.22
Hardwick,	2,655	–	–	26	2,629	4.98	4.93
Hingham,	4,819	–	–	63	4,756	4.14	4.09
Holden,	2,602	–	–	25	2,577	4.69	4.64
Hopedale,	1,377	–	–	43	1,334	4.49	4.35
Hudson,	5,308	–	–	26	5,282	4.26	4.24
Hull,	1,044	–	–	28	1,016	4.56	4.44
Ipswich,	4,720	–	74	34	4,612	4.28	4.18
Lancaster,	2,180	211	–	48	1,921	4.82	4.25
Lenox,	2,872	33	–	–	2,839	4.94	4.89
Ludlow,	2,562	–	–	50	2,512	5.42	5.31
Marblehead,	7,671	–	29	–	7,642	3.83	3.82
Medfield,	1,872	–	–	79	1,793	4.51	4.32
Medway,	2,913	–	–	27	2,886	3.98	3.94
Melrose,	11,965	–	–	44	11,921	4.46	4.44
Methuen,	5,690	–	–	36	5,654	4.32	4.29
Middleborough,	6,689	–	–	35	6,654	4.00	3.98
Milford,	8,959	–	51	67	8,841	4.23	4.18
Millbury,	5,222	–	–	158	5,064	4.75	4.60
Milton,	5,518	50	57	26	5,385	4.99	4.87
Monson,	3,746	–	114	66	3,566	4.30	4.09
Montague,	6,058	–	–	25	6,033	4.49	4.47
Nantucket,	3,016	–	28	–	2,988	3.07	3.05
Natick,	8,814	–	38	–	8,776	4.22	4.20
North Attleborough,	6,576	–	27	–	6,549	4.39	4.37
Northbridge,	5,286	–	–	77	5,209	4.94	4.87
North Brookfield,	4,635	–	–	25	4,610	4.50	4.48

Towns.	Total Population	Population of Large Families			Population excluding Large Families	Average Number of Persons to a Family	
		Schools, Colleges, etc.	Prisons, Reformatories, Hospitals, etc.	Other Large Families		Total Population	Population excluding Large Families
Northfield, ...	1,851	480	-	-	1,071	4.42	3.99
Norton, ...	1,614	67	-	-	1,547	4.02	3.86
Norwood, ...	4,574	-	-	25	4,549	4.75	4.72
Palmer, ...	6,858	-	-	59	6,799	4.96	4.92
Peabody, ...	10,507	-	35	-	10,472	4.43	4.41
Plymouth, ...	7,957	-	-	50	7,907	4.04	4.02
Revere, ...	7,423	-	-	26	7,397	4.49	4.48
Rockport, ...	5,289	-	-	53	5,236	4.28	4.24
Sherborn, ...	1,446	-	326	-	1,120	5.06	3.92
Shirley, ...	1,399	-	-	25	1,374	4.32	4.24
Southborough, ...	2,223	183	-	62	1,978	5.03	4.48
South Hadley, ...	4,443	308	-	28	4,107	4.97	4.50
Spencer, ...	7,614	-	-	29	7,585	4.69	4.67
Stockbridge, ...	2,077	-	-	31	2,046	4.41	4.34
Stoneham, ...	6,284	-	-	34	6,250	3.97	3.95
Sutton, ...	3,420	-	31	46	3,343	4.79	4.68
Templeton, ...	2,915	-	-	129	2,786	4.06	3.85
Tewksbury, ...	3,379	-	1,166	-	2,213	7.14	4.68
Upton, ...	2,150	-	-	248	1,902	4.10	3.63
Wakefield, ...	8,304	-	-	52	8,252	4.24	4.21
Walpole, ...	2,994	-	-	43	2,951	4.35	4.29
Warren, ...	4,430	-	-	29	4,401	4.52	4.49
Watertown, ...	7,788	-	-	60	7,728	4.72	4.68
Webster, ...	7,799	-	-	116	7,683	4.54	4.48
Wellesley, ...	4,229	551	29	212	3,437	5.73	4.66
Westborough, ...	5,235	-	1,053	52	4,130	5.08	4.01
West Boylston, . . .	2,968	-	55	-	2,913	4.58	4.50
West Bridgewater, . .	1,747	69	-	-	1,678	4.27	4.10
Westfield, ...	10,663	72	34	30	10,527	4.11	4.06
Weymouth, ...	11,291	183	38	26	11,044	4.24	4.14
Wilbraham, ...	1,740	193	-	-	1,547	4.79	4.26
Williamstown, ...	4,887	216	-	-	4,671	4.81	4.50
Winchendon, ...	4,490	-	-	27	4,463	4.17	4.14
Winchester, ...	6,150	-	-	27	6,123	4.73	4.71
Winthrop, ...	4,192	-	-	42	4,150	4.61	4.56

A typical town shown in the foregoing table is Concord, in Middlesex County, the seat of the Massachusetts Reformatory. By referring to the figures, it will be seen that the average size of the family for this town, based upon the Census returns, including the large families, is 5.92. This is considerably above the average size of the family for Middlesex County, in which Concord is situated, the county average being 4.64. The average in Concord is increased by including as a single large family, the Massachusetts Reformatory, containing 1,032 persons. If this is excluded, the average number of persons to a family in the town becomes 4.74. Another such town is Wellesley, in Norfolk County, containing Wellesley College. When the whole population is used as a basis to determine the average number of persons to a family, the average is 5.73, the average for Norfolk County being only 4.54. Excluding certain large families, as shown in the table, the largest single family at Wellesley being at Wellesley College, the average number of persons to a family is found to be 4.66. It is not necessary to point out other towns in the table, as the facts for any town in which a family exceeding

25 persons in size is found can be readily ascertained. The cities have been excluded from this table, as the influence of the large families is not material when the population of a city is taken into account.

The second presentation relative to families, pages 339 to 443, exhibits the size of families by towns and the composition of the families by sex, in detail, for the cities and for the State, and brings out somewhat forcibly the presence or absence of abnormally large families in certain cities and towns.

This presentation is subdivided into three sections. The reader should follow carefully the note contained on page 341, which explains fully the manner in which the table is to be read. The first subdivision of the table relates entirely to the size of families for towns, and is contained upon pages 343 to 386, a recapitulation for both cities and towns, by counties, being found on pages 436 to 443. The last column of this recapitulation exhibits the facts for the State, showing, for example, that there are 21,836 families of one person each, 91,786 families of two persons each, 106,436 families of three persons each, families of this size being the most numerous. Families of four persons each number 99,152, after which the figures show a constant decline in number of families as the family increases in size.

In the following analysis table, the number of families of one, two, three, or more persons in the cities, towns, and State is shown with the percentages which such families form of the total number of families and total population in the cities, towns, and State, respectively:

SIZE OF FAMILIES.	CITIES			TOWNS			THE STATE		
	Number of Families	Total Families	Total Population	Number of Families	Total Families	Total Population	Number of Families	Total Families	Total Population
1	10,783	3.11	0.66	11,053	5.50	1.28	21,836	3.99	0.87
2	54,530	15.74	6.67	37,256	18.54	8.62	91,786	16.77	7.34
3	65,450	18.89	12.00	40,986	20.40	14.22	106,436	19.45	12.77
4	63,090	18.21	15.43	36,062	17.95	16.69	99,152	18.12	15.86
5	51,234	14.79	15.66	26,922	13.40	15.57	78,156	14.28	15.63
6	37,219	10.74	13.65	18,941	9.43	13.15	56,160	10.26	13.48
7	25,029	7.23	10.71	12,144	6.05	9.83	37,173	6.79	10.41
8	15,809	4.56	7.73	7,393	3.68	6.84	23,202	4.24	7.42
9	9,341	2.70	5.14	4,430	2.21	4.61	13,771	2.52	4.96
10	5,334	1.54	3.26	2,502	1.25	2.89	7,836	1.43	3.13
11	3,059	0.88	2.06	1,293	0.64	1.65	4,352	0.80	1.91
12	1,618	0.47	1.19	663	0.33	0.92	2,281	0.42	1.09
13	1,014	0.29	0.81	385	0.19	0.58	1,399	0.26	0.73
14	671	0.19	0.57	206	0.10	0.33	877	0.16	0.49
15	424	0.12	0.39	123	0.06	0.21	547	0.10	0.33
16	297	0.09	0.29	84	0.04	0.16	381	0.07	0.24
17	226	0.07	0.23	59	0.03	0.12	285	0.05	0.19
18	169	0.05	0.19	55	0.03	0.11	224	0.04	0.16
19	121	0.04	0.14	42	0.02	0.09	163	0.03	0.12
20	117	0.03	0.14	39	0.02	0.09	156	0.03	0.12
21	88	0.03	0.11	27	0.01	0.07	115	0.02	0.10
22	75	0.02	0.10	26	0.01	0.07	101	0.02	0.09
23	51	0.02	0.07	12	0.01	0.03	63	0.01	0.06
24	51	0.02	0.07	25	0.01	0.07	76	0.02	0.07
25	51	0.02	0.08	14	0.01	0.04	65	0.01	0.06
26	25	0.01	0.04	14	0.01	0.04	39	0.01	0.04
27	35	0.01	0.06	9	0.01	0.03	44	0.01	0.05

SIZE OF FAMILIES.	CITIES			TOWNS			THE STATE		
	Number of Families	Total Families	Total Population	Number of Families	Total Families	Total Population	Number of Families	Total Families	Total Population
28	29	0.01	0.05	9	0.01	0.03	38	0.01	0.04
29	35	0.01	0.06	9	0.01	0.03	44	0.01	0.05
30	23	0.01	0.04	5	*	0.02	28	0.01	0.03
31	19	0.01	0.04	8	0.01	0.03	27	0.01	0.03
32	16	0.01	0.03	7	0.01	0.03	23	0.01	0.03
33	15	0.01	0.03	8	0.01	0.03	23	0.01	0.03
34	19	0.01	0.04	7	0.01	0.03	26	0.01	0.03
35	23	0.01	0.05	5	*	0.02	28	0.01	0.04
36	15	0.01	0.03	4	*	0.02	19	*	0.03
37	24	0.01	0.05	1	*	*	25	0.01	0.04
38	13	*	0.03	6	*	0.03	19	*	0.03
39	14	0.01	0.03	2	*	0.01	16	*	0.02
40	14	0.01	0.03	2	*	0.01	16	*	0.03
41	10	*	0.02	3	*	0.01	13	*	0.02
42	6	*	0.02	5	*	0.02	11	*	0.02
43	15	0.01	0.04	2	*	0.01	17	*	0.03
44	8	*	0.02	4	*	0.02	12	*	0.02
45	9	*	0.02	1	*	*	10	*	0.02
46	9	*	0.03	1	*	*	10	*	0.02
47	13	*	0.04	-	-	-	13	*	0.02
48	7	*	0.02	1	*	0.01	8	*	0.02
49	9	*	0.03	-	-	-	9	*	0.02
50	9	*	0.03	4	*	0.02	13	*	0.03
51	5	*	0.02	1	*	0.01	6	*	0.01
52	4	*	0.01	-	-	-	4	*	0.01
53	6	*	0.02	3	*	0.02	9	*	0.02
54	3	*	0.01	1	*	0.01	4	*	0.01
55	1	*	*	3	*	0.02	4	*	0.01
56	3	*	0.01	-	-	-	3	*	0.01
57	8	*	0.03	2	*	0.01	10	*	0.02
58	1	*	*	1	*	0.01	2	*	*
59	4	*	0.01	3	*	0.02	7	*	0.02
60	2	*	0.01	1	*	0.01	3	*	0.01
61	1	*	*	-	-	-	1	*	*
62	2	*	0.01	2	*	0.01	4	*	0.01
63	3	*	0.01	-	-	-	3	*	0.01
64	4	*	0.02	-	-	-	4	*	0.01
65	1	*	*	-	-	-	1	*	*
66	5	*	0.02	1	*	0.01	6	*	0.02
67	-	-	-	1	*	0.01	1	*	*
68	2	*	0.01	1	*	0.01	3	*	0.01
69	3	*	0.01	2	*	0.02	5	*	0.01
70	4	*	0.02	-	-	-	4	*	0.01
71	2	*	0.01	2	*	0.02	4	*	0.01
72	4	*	0.02	2	*	0.02	6	*	0.02
74	1	*	*	1	*	0.01	2	*	0.01
75	5	*	0.02	-	-	-	5	*	0.01
76	1	*	*	-	-	-	1	*	*
77	3	*	0.01	-	-	-	3	*	0.01

* Less than one one-hundredth of one per cent.

SIZE OF FAMILIES.	CITIES			TOWNS			THE STATE		
	Number of Families	PERCENTAGES		Number of Families	PERCENTAGES		Number of Families	PERCENTAGES	
		Total Families	Total Population		Total Families	Total Population		Total Families	Total Population
78 . . .	6	*-	0.03	-	-	-	6	*-	0.02
79 . . .	1	*-	*-	1	*-	0 01	2	*-	0.01
80 . . .	4	*-	0.02	2	*-	0.02	6	*-	0.02
81 . . .	1	*-	*-	-	-	-	1	*-	*-
82 . . .	4	*-	0.02	1	*-	0.01	5	*-	0.02
84 . . .	2	*-	0.01	-	-	-	2	*-	0.01
85 . . .	3	*-	0.02	-	-	-	3	*-	0 01
86 . . .	2	*-	0.01	-	-	-	2	*-	0.01
87 . . .	2	*-	0.01	-	-	-	2	*-	0.01
88 . . .	1	*-	0.01	1	*-	0.01	2	*-	0.01
89 . . .	2	*-	0.01	-	-	-	2	*-	0.01
91 . . .	3	*-	0.02	-	-	-	3	*-	0.01
93 . . .	2	*-	0.01	-	-	-	2	*-	0.01
94 . . .	1	*-	0.01	-	-	-	1	*-	*-
96 . . .	2	*-	0.01	2	*-	0.02	4	*-	0.02
97 . . .	1	*-	0.01	-	-	-	1	*-	*-
98 . . .	1	*-	0.01	-	-	-	1	*-	*-
99 . . .	6	*-	0.04	-	-	-	6	*-	0.02
100 . . .	1	*-	0.01	-	-	-	1	*-	*-
101 . . .	1	*-	0.01	-	-	-	1	*-	*-
103 . . .	-	-	-	1	*-	0.01	1	*-	*-
105 . . .	1	*-	0.01	-	-	-	1	*-	*-
107 . . .	2	*-	0.01	-	-	-	2	*-	0.01
109 . . .	3	*-	0.02	-	-	-	3	*-	0.01
111 . . .	2	*-	0.01	-	-	-	2	*-	0.01
112 . . .	2	*-	0.01	-	-	-	2	*-	0.01
113 . . .	3	*-	0.02	-	-	-	3	*-	0 01
114 . . .	1	*-	0.01	1	*-	0 01	2	*-	0.01
116 . . .	1	*-	0.01	1	*-	0 01	2	*-	0.01
118 . . .	2	*-	0.01	1	*-	0 01	3	*-	0.01
119 . . .	2	*-	0 01	-	-	-	2	*-	0.01
120 . . .	1	*-	0.01	-	-	-	1	*-	*-
121 . . .	1	*-	0.01	-	-	-	1	*-	*-
122 . . .	1	*-	0 01	-	-	-	1	*-	*-
124 . . .	2	*-	0.02	1	*-	0 01	3	*-	0.01
128 . . .	-	-	-	1	*-	0.01	1	*-	0.01
129 . . .	1	*-	0.01	1	*-	0.01	2	*-	0.01
132 . . .	1	*-	0.01	-	-	-	1	*-	0.01
134 . . .	2	*-	0.02	1	*-	0.02	3	*-	0.02
135 . . .	1	*-	0.01	-	-	-	1	*-	0.01
136 . . .	1	*-	0.01	-	-	-	1	*-	0.01
137 . . .	1	*-	0.01	-	-	-	1	*-	0 01
140 . . .	-	-	-	2	*-	0.03	2	*-	0.01
141 . . .	1	*-	0.01	-	-	-	1	*-	0.01
144 . . .	1	*-	0.01	-	-	-	1	*-	0 01
145 . . .	2	*-	0 02	-	-	-	2	*-	0.01
147 . . .	1	*-	0.01	-	-	-	1	*-	0.01
150 . . .	1	*-	0.01	-	-	-	1	*-	0.01
156 . . .	1	*-	0 01	-	-	-	1	*-	0.01

* Less than one one-hundredth of one per cent.

SIZE OF FAMILIES.	CITIES			TOWNS			THE STATE		
	Number of Families	Total Families	Total Population	Number of Families	Total Families	Total Population	Number of Families	Total Families	Total Population
158 . . .	1	*_	0.01	–	–	–	1	*_	0.01
160 . . .	–	–	–	1	*_	0.02	1	*_	0.01
162 . . .	–	–	–	1	*_	0.02	1	*_	0.01
164 . . .	–	–	–	1	*_	0.02	1	*_	0.01
168 . . .	–	–	–	1	*_	0.02	1	*_	0.01
169 . . .	–	–	–	1	*_	0.02	1	*_	0.01
170 . . .	1	*_	0.01	–	–	–	1	*_	0.01
171 . . .	1	*_	0.01	–	–	–	1	*_	0.01
172 . . .	1	*_	0.01	–	–	–	1	*_	0.01
183 . . .	1	*_	0.01	1	*_	0.02	2	*_	0.01
188 . . .	1	*_	0.01	–	–	–	1	*_	0.01
193 . . .	–	–	–	1	*_	0.02	1	*_	0.01
194 . . .	1	*_	0.01	–	–	–	1	*_	0.01
198 . . .	1	*_	0.01	–	–	–	1	*_	0.01
200 . . .	1	*_	0.01	–	–	–	1	*_	0.01
205 . . .	1	*_	0.01	–	–	–	1	*_	0.01
212 . . .	1	*_	0.01	–	–	–	1	*_	0.01
214 . . .	1	*_	0.01	–	–	–	1	*_	0.01
216 . . .	–	–	–	1	*_	0.02	1	*_	0.01
220 . . .	1	*_	0.01	–	–	–	1	*_	0.01
221 . . .	1	*_	0.01	–	–	–	1	*_	0.01
227 . . .	1	*_	0.01	–	–	–	1	*_	0.01
255 . . .	1	*_	0.02	–	–	–	1	*_	0.01
259 . . .	1	*_	0.02	–	–	–	1	*_	0.01
261 . . .	1	*_	0.02	–	–	–	1	*_	0.01
268 . . .	1	*_	0.02	–	–	–	1	*_	0.01
274 . . .	1	*_	0.02	–	–	–	1	*_	0.01
276 . . .	1	*_	0.02	–	–	–	1	*_	0.01
299 . . .	1	*_	0.02	–	–	–	1	*_	0.01
301 . . .	–	–	–	1	*_	0.03	1	*_	0.01
308 . . .	–	–	–	1	*_	0.04	1	*_	0.01
323 . . .	1	*_	0.02	–	–	–	1	*_	0.01
324 . . .	–	–	–	1	*_	0.04	1	*_	0.01
326 . . .	–	–	–	1	*_	0.04	1	*_	0.01
342 . . .	1	*_	0.02	–	–	–	1	*_	0.01
352 . . .	1	*_	0.02	–	–	–	1	*_	0.01
397 . . .	1	*_	0.02	–	–	–	1	*_	0.02
399 . . .	1	*_	0.02	–	–	–	1	*_	0.02
412 . . .	1	*_	0.03	–	–	–	1	*_	0.02
529 . . .	1	*_	0.03	–	–	–	1	*_	0.02
564 . . .	1	*_	0.03	–	–	–	1	*_	0.02
599 . . .	1	*_	0.04	–	–	–	1	*_	0.02
608 . . .	1	*_	0.04	–	–	–	1	*_	0.02
680 . . .	1	*_	0.04	–	–	–	1	*_	0.03
691 . . .	1	*_	0.04	–	–	–	1	*_	0.03
741 . . .	1	*_	0.05	–	–	–	1	*_	0.03
752 . . .	–	–	–	1	*_	0.09	1	*_	0.03
957 . . .	1	*_	0.06	–	–	–	1	*_	0.04
1,015 . . .	–	–	–	1	*_	0.12	1	*_	0.04

* Less than one one-hundredth of one per cent.

SIZE OF FAMILIES.	CITIES			TOWNS			THE STATE		
	Number of Families	PERCENTAGES		Number of Families	PERCENTAGES		Number of Families	PERCENTAGES	
		Total Families	Total Population		Total Families	Total Population		Total Families	Total Population
1,032 . . .	–	–	–	1	*–	0.12	1	*–	0.04
1,055 . . .	1	*–	0.06	–	–	–	1	*–	0.04
1,087 . . .	–	–	–	1	*–	0.13	1	*–	0.04
1,166 . . .	–	–	–	1	*–	0.13	1	*–	0.05
1,596 . . .	1	*–	0 10	–	–.	–	1	*–	0.06
Totals, . .	346,465	100.00	100.00	200,920	100.00	100.00	547,385	100.00	100.00

* Less than one one-hundredth of one per cent.

From the preceding table it will be seen that in the cities there are 10,783 families of one person each, and in the towns 11,053 such families. The families of one person each constitute in the cities, 3.11 per cent of the total city families, and, in the towns, 5.50 per cent of the total town families. The city families of one person each constitute 0.66 per cent of the total city population, while the town families of one person each constitute 1.28 per cent of the total town population. The relative preponderance of families of certain sizes exhibits no radical changes since 1875. The families of one person each, while naturally showing a constant numerical increase, constitute, so far as the State as a whole is concerned, a slightly smaller percentage of the total number of families than was the case in 1885. The percentage at that time was 4.04, while in the present Census, as shown in the preceding table, it is found to be 3.99. The percentage which such families constituted of total population of the State in 1885 was 0.88, while in 1895 it is 0.87. Families of from two to seven persons constituted 85.34 per cent of the total families in the State in 1885, and contained 75.24 per cent of the total population. These percentages in 1895 are, respectively, 85.67 and 75.49. For purposes of comparison we may also say that in 1885, families of from eight to 13 persons constituted 9.91 per cent of the total families, and contained 19.72 per cent of the population. In 1895 the percentages are 9.67 and 19.24, respectively. Families of from 14 to 22 persons constituted 0.52 per cent of the total families in 1885, and contained 1.86 per cent of the total population. In 1895 such families constitute 0.52 per cent of the total families, and 1 84 per cent of the total population. In 1885, families of 23 persons and over constituted 0.19 per cent of the total families, and contained 2.30 per cent of the total population. These percentages are now 0.15 and 2.56, respectively. In 1895, as in former censuses, families of three persons are the most numerous, such families constituting 18.89 per cent of the total city families, and containing 12 per cent of the total city population: they also form 20.40 per cent of the total town families, and contain 14.22 per cent of the total town population. When the town and city population is noted, and families of this size are considered with reference to the total State population, we find that they constitute 19.45 per cent of the total families in the State, and contain 12.77 per cent of the total population of the State. There are 220,058 families in the State containing from one to three persons, inclusive, and comprising in the aggregate 524,716 persons. These families represent 40.21 per cent of all the families, and contain 20.98 per cent of the total population. In the cities there are 130,763 such families, containing in the aggregate 316,193 persons, or 19.33 per cent of the total city population, while the families constitute 37.74 per cent of the total number of families in cities. In the towns there are 89,295 such families, containing in the aggregate 208,523 persons, constituting 24.12 per cent of the total town population, while the families constitute 44.44 per cent of the total families in towns. Of the 220,058 families in the State, each containing from one to three persons, inclusive, 59.42 per cent are found in the cities and 40.58 per cent in the towns. Of the 524,716 persons living in families of this class in the State, 60.26 per cent reside in the cities and 39.74 per cent in the towns.

The second and third sections of the presentation, showing the size of families and composition by sex, exhibit the composition of each family by sex for the cities and for the State. This table is entirely novel, never having been introduced in any previous Census. The second section, contained upon pages 387 to 426, relates to the cities in detail, while the facts as to the State, including both cities and towns, are shown in the third section, pages 427 to 435.

This table, at first glance, seems complicated, but if read in connection with the note on page 341, to which we have previously referred, it will be readily understood. It has already been pointed out that the families of three persons each were most numerous. Referring to such families in this table, page 427, we find, taking the figures in parenthesis, in the first column, that they number 106,436; and from the second and third columns of the table we find that this aggregate is made up of 54,801 families, each of which is composed of one male and two females, 45,090 families, each composed of two males and one female, 773 families comprising three males each, and 5,772 families comprising three females each. In the same manner the composition of all the families of various sizes in the State is shown.

The following analysis table shows the number of families which are composed of one sex only:

SIZE OF FAMILIES.	MALES		FEMALES		BOTH SEXES	
	Families	Persons	Families	Persons	Families	Persons
1	7,456	7,456	14,380	14,380	21,836	21,836
2	2,355	4,710	12,709	25,418	15,064	30,128
3	773	2,319	5,772	17,316	6,545	19,635
4	342	1,368	2,300	9,200	2,642	10,568
5	164	820	837	4,185	1,001	5,005
6	109	654	310	1,860	419	2,514
7	58	406	114	798	172	1,204
8	49	392	42	336	91	728
9	32	288	23	207	55	495
10	25	250	16	160	41	410
11	26	286	21	231	47	517
12	15	180	13	156	28	336
13	11	143	16	208	27	351
14	10	140	11	154	21	294
15	10	150	9	135	19	285
16	10	160	7	112	17	272
17	5	85	3	51	8	136
18	8	144	8	144	16	288
19	6	114	5	95	11	209
20	7	140	8	160	15	300
21	4	84	4	84	8	168
22	2	44	4	88	6	132
23	2	46	6	138	8	184
24	3	72	5	120	8	192
25	2	50	4	100	6	150
26	3	78	3	78	6	156
27	2	54	–	–	2	54
28	3	84	3	84	6	168
29	3	87	3	87	6	174
30	5	150	–	–	5	150
31	–	–	2	62	2	62
32	1	32	4	128	5	160
33	–	–	2	66	2	66

SIZE OF FAMILIES.	MALES		FEMALES		BOTH SEXES	
	Families	Persons	Families	Persons	Families	Persons
34 . . .	1	34	2	68	3	102
35 . . .	3	105	1	35	4	140
37 . . .	2	74	1	37	3	111
38 . . .	3	114	2	76	5	190
40 . . .	2	80	-	-	2	80
41 . . .	1	41	-	-	1	41
42 . . .	3	126	-	-	3	126
43 . . .	2	86	-	-	2	86
44 . . .	1	44	1	44	2	88
46 . . .	2	92	-	-	2	92
47 . . .	2	94	-	-	2	94
48 . . .	-	-	1	48	1	48
49 . . .	1	49	-	-	1	49
50 . . .	-	-	1	50	1	50
51 . . .	-	-	1	51	1	51
53 . . .	2	106	-	-	2	106
54 . . .	-	-	2	108	2	108
57 . . .	1	57	1	57	2	114
59 . . .	2	118	-	-	2	118
60 . . .	1	60	1	60	2	120
61 . . .	1	61	-	-	1	61
62 . . .	3	186	-	-	3	186
63 . . .	-	-	1	63	1	63
64 . . .	-	-	1	64	1	64
66 . . .	-	-	1	66	1	66
68 . . .	-	-	1	68	1	68
69 . . .	1	69	-	-	1	69
70 . . .	-	-	1	70	1	70
71 . . .	-	-	2	142	2	142
75 . . .	2	150	-	-	2	150
77 . . .	-	-	1	77	1	77
78 . . .	2	156	1	78	3	234
79 . . .	-	-	1	79	1	79
80 . . .	3	240	1	80	4	320
91 . . .	-	-	1	91	1	91
96 . . .	2	192	-	-	2	192
98 . . .	1	98	-	-	1	98
99 . . .	3	297	-	-	3	297
100 . . .	1	100	-	-	1	100
103 . . .	1	103	-	-	1	103
109 . . .	-	-	1	109	1	109
111 . . .	1	111	-	-	1	111
120 . . .	1	120	-	-	1	120
145 . . .	1	145	-	-	1	145
160 . . .	1	160	-	-	1	160
162 . . .	1	162	-	-	1	162
168 . . .	1	168	-	-	1	168
205 . . .	1	205	-	-	1	205
276 . . .	1	276	-	-	1	276
308 . . .	-	-	1	308	1	308
1,032 . . .	1	1,032	-	-	1	1,032
Totals, . .	11,559	26,297	36,672	78,270	48,231	104,567

The aggregate number of families of one person each has been brought out in preceding tables, but, taken in connection with the analysis table now presented, which is based upon the presentation showing size of families and composition by sex, we find that the 21.836 families of one person each in the State are made up of 14,380 families which contain only females, and 7,456 families which contain only males. The existence of so-called families of but one person each is largely due to the industrial and commercial development of the cities and larger towns of the Commonwealth in which numerous single persons are employed, who are living in lodging rooms and providing their own meals in their rooms or taking their meals at restaurants. Every such person constitutes, in the Census, an independent family, as they recognize no other family head, and the preponderance of families of this class composed of females over those composed of males is due to the larger employment of single women who live in the manner stated. Proceeding farther with the analysis table, we find that there are 15,064 families of two persons each, this aggregate being composed of 12,709 families comprising two females each, and 2,355 families comprising two males each. This peculiar composition of families of two persons, each of the same sex, also reflects the conditions which we have noted in accounting for the families of one person each, and indicates the combination in single families of males or females, who are thus living together in family relations, although families of this kind composed of females only largely preponderate over those of males only. The families of three persons each which are composed of one sex only number 6,545, including 5,772 families composed of three females each, and 773 families composed of three males each. The number of three-person families, each composed of a single sex, thus exhibits a considerable decline numerically from the number of two-person families of this class. From this point upwards, as the families increase in size, the number rapidly decreases, there being among the single-sex families only 2,642 families of four persons each, and of these, 2,300 are composed of four females each. Families of five persons each, composed of one sex only, number but 1,001; single-sex families of six persons each, but 419; and single-sex families of seven persons each, but 172. The aggregate number of each numerical class then drops below 100 as the families increase in size. The largest family of but one sex is, as shown in the table, composed of 1,032 males; this being a penal institution, and, as previously explained, classed as a single family for Census purposes only.

Rooms:

Occupied Dwelling Houses.

ROOMS: OCCUPIED DWELLING HOUSES.

[For typographical reasons certain condensations have been made in column headings. The second column, headed " Number of Families of Specified Size," means the total number of families of the size specified in the first column, this number of families occupying the total number of rooms enumerated in the third column. The fourth column shows the average number of rooms occupied by families of each specified size, and the fifth column shows the average number of persons to a room. For instance, in the town of Barnstable there are 124 families of one person each occupying in all 799 rooms; this is an average of 6.44 rooms to a family and 0.16 persons to a room. Other lines may be read in a similar manner.]

Counties, Cities, Towns, and Number of Persons to a Family.	Number of Families of Specified Size	Total Number of Rooms Occupied	Average Number of Rooms Occupied	Average Number of Persons to a Room	Counties, Cities, Towns, and Number of Persons to a Family.	Number of Families of Specified Size	Total Number of Rooms Occupied	Average Number of Rooms Occupied	Average Number of Persons to a Room
BARNSTABLE.					**BARNSTABLE —Con.**				
Barnstable,	1,173	8,557	7.29	0.47	Chatham — Con.				
1 person,	124	799	6.44	0.16	4 persons,	88	799	9.08	0.44
2 persons,	272	1,849	6.80	0.29	5 persons,	60	489	8.15	0.61
3 persons,	296	2,216	7.49	0.40	6 persons,	28	297	10.61	0.57
4 persons,	215	1,553	7.22	0.55	7 persons,	15	135	9.00	0.78
5 persons,	127	978	7.70	0.65	8 persons,	6	58	9.67	0.83
6 persons,	61	481	7.89	0.76	9 persons,	4	35	8.75	1.03
7 persons,	41	326	7.95	0.88	10 persons,	4	29	7.25	1.38
8 persons,	20	149	7.45	1.07	Dennis,	817	4,222	5.17	0.60
9 persons,	4	40	10.00	0.90	1 person,	103	482	4.68	0.21
10 persons,	3	24	8.00	1.25	2 persons,	235	1,224	5.21	0.38
11 persons,	5	44	8.80	1.25	3 persons,	203	1,050	5.17	0.58
12 persons,	2	23	11.50	1.04	4 persons,	134	726	5.42	0.74
13 persons,	1	30	30.00	0.43	5 persons,	74	382	5.16	0.97
14 persons,	1	15	15.00	0.96	6 persons,	37	183	4.95	1.21
19 persons,	1	30	30.00	0.63	7 persons,	18	102	5.67	1.24
Bourne,	429	3,094	7.21	0.51	8 persons,	9	58	6.44	1.24
1 person,	45	216	4.80	0.21	9 persons,	3	12	4.00	2.25
2 persons,	84	597	7.11	0.28	10 persons,	1	3	3.00	3.33
3 persons,	86	599	6.97	0.43	Eastham,	137	988	7.21	0.48
4 persons,	87	602	6.92	0.58	1 person,	15	91	6.07	0.16
5 persons,	57	441	7.74	0.65	2 persons,	24	171	7.13	0.28
6 persons,	32	261	8.16	0.74	3 persons,	42	306	7.29	0.41
7 persons,	24	213	8.88	0.79	4 persons,	25	182	7.28	0.55
8 persons,	11	133	12.09	0.66	5 persons,	14	107	7.64	0.65
9 persons,	2	23	11.50	0.78	6 persons,	8	68	8.50	0.71
10 persons,	1	9	9.00	1.11	7 persons,	4	24	6.00	1.17
Brewster,	255	1,827	7.16	0.49	8 persons,	4	31	7.75	1.03
1 person,	20	133	6.65	0.15	9 persons,	1	8	8.00	1.13
2 persons,	71	506	7.13	0.28	Falmouth,	722	5,576	7.72	0.48
3 persons,	56	432	7.71	0.39	1 person,	79	481	6.09	0.16
4 persons,	51	396	7.18	0.56	2 persons,	157	1,088	6.93	0.29
5 persons,	20	151	7.55	0.66	3 persons,	148	1,085	7.33	0.41
6 persons,	14	83	5.93	1.01	4 persons,	135	1,054	7.81	0.51
7 persons,	11	71	6.45	1.08	5 persons,	92	815	8.86	0.56
8 persons,	8	55	6.88	1.16	6 persons,	44	358	8.14	0.74
10 persons,	2	17	8.50	1.18	7 persons,	32	273	8.53	0.82
11 persons,	2	13	6.50	1.69	8 persons,	18	171	9.50	0.84
Chatham,	543	4,553	8.38	0.40	9 persons,	6	62	10.33	0.87
1 person,	56	390	6.96	0.14	10 persons,	4	53	13.25	0.75
2 persons,	142	1,166	8.21	0.24	11 persons,	2	24	12.00	0.92
3 persons,	140	1,155	8.25	0.36	13 persons,	3	38	12.67	1.03

ROOMS: OCCUPIED DWELLING HOUSES — Continued.

Counties, Cities, Towns, and Number of Persons to a Family.	Number of Families of Specified Size	Total Number of Rooms Occupied	Average Number of Rooms Occupied	Average Number of Persons to a Room
BARNSTABLE — Con.				
Falmouth — Con.				
15 persons,	1	24	24.00	0.63
16 persons,	1	50	50.00	0.32
Harwich,	783	4,820	6.17	0.52
1 person,	87	502	5.77	0.17
2 persons,	225	1,385	6.16	0.32
3 persons,	184	1,106	6.01	0.50
4 persons,	121	753	6.22	0.64
5 persons,	90	518	5.98	0.84
6 persons,	49	337	6.88	0.87
7 persons,	15	100	6.67	1.05
8 persons,	6	43	7.17	1.12
9 persons,	4	30	7.50	1.20
10 persons,	1	10	10.00	1.00
16 persons,	1	25	25.00	0.64
Mashpee,	81	388	4.79	0.85
1 person,	7	19	2.71	0.37
2 persons,	14	59	4.21	0.47
3 persons,	12	58	4.83	0.62
4 persons,	21	116	5.52	0.72
5 persons,	11	47	4.27	1.17
6 persons,	6	39	6.50	0.92
7 persons,	3	18	6.00	1.17
8 persons,	4	19	4.75	1.68
10 persons,	2	9	4.50	2.22
11 persons,	1	4	4.00	2.75
Orleans,	375	2,820	7.52	0.42
1 person,	36	223	6.19	0.16
2 persons,	126	910	7.22	0.28
3 persons,	90	689	7.77	0.39
4 persons,	53	424	8.00	0.50
5 persons,	31	232	7.48	0.67
6 persons,	16	137	8.56	0.70
7 persons,	11	86	7.82	0.90
8 persons,	9	67	7.44	1.07
9 persons,	2	32	16.00	0.56
10 persons,	1	10	10.00	1.00
Provincetown,	1,216	7,650	6.29	0.60
1 person,	84	418	4.98	0.20
2 persons,	303	1,912	6.31	0.32
3 persons,	285	1,824	6.40	0.47
4 persons,	185	1,174	6.35	0.63
5 persons,	140	913	6.52	0.77
6 persons,	93	546	5.87	1.02
7 persons,	50	304	6.08	1.15
8 persons,	41	295	6.46	1.24
9 persons,	26	173	6.65	1.35
10 persons,	3	35	11.67	0.86
11 persons,	4	35	8.75	1.26
12 persons,	1	41	41.00	0.29
14 persons,	1	10	10.00	1.40
Sandwich,	442	3,245	7.32	0.49
1 person,	55	318	5.78	0.17
2 persons,	94	659	7.01	0.29
3 persons,	107	768	7.18	0.42
BARNSTABLE — Con.				
Sandwich — Con.				
4 persons,	74	566	7.65	0.52
5 persons,	44	359	8.16	0.61
6 persons,	28	222	7.93	0.76
7 persons,	21	156	7.43	0.94
8 persons,	7	61	8.71	0.92
9 persons,	4	29	7.25	1.24
10 persons,	5	47	9.40	1.06
11 persons,	1	9	9.00	1.22
12 persons,	1	4	4.00	3.00
20 persons,	1	37	37.00	0.54
Truro,	229	1,714	7.48	0.48
1 person,	34	228	6.71	0.15
2 persons,	57	425	7.46	0.27
3 persons,	44	324	7.36	0.41
4 persons,	35	271	7.74	0.52
5 persons,	19	151	7.95	0.63
6 persons,	17	132	7.76	0.77
7 persons,	7	60	8.57	0.82
8 persons,	4	31	7.75	1.03
9 persons,	7	55	7.86	1.15
10 persons,	3	23	7.67	1.30
11 persons,	1	6	6.00	1.83
13 persons,	1	8	8.00	1.63
Wellfleet,	332	2,341	7.05	0.41
1 person,	62	353	5.69	0.18
2 persons,	94	640	6.81	0.29
3 persons,	82	616	7.51	0.40
4 persons,	50	383	7.66	0.52
5 persons,	17	127	7.47	0.67
6 persons,	14	115	8.21	0.73
7 persons,	5	41	8.20	0.85
8 persons,	5	48	9.60	0.83
9 persons,	2	11	5.50	1.64
10 persons,	1	7	7.00	1.43
Yarmouth,	535	4,062	7.59	0.41
1 person,	60	448	7.47	0.13
2 persons,	177	1,324	7.48	0.27
3 persons,	123	928	7.54	0.40
4 persons,	79	593	7.51	0.53
5 persons,	52	404	7.77	0.64
6 persons,	24	186	7.75	0.77
7 persons,	13	94	7.23	0.97
8 persons,	5	42	8.40	0.95
9 persons,	1	8	8.00	1.13
12 persons,	1	35	35.00	0.34
BERKSHIRE.				
Adams,	1,604	10,477	6.34	0.77
1 person,	31	137	4.42	0.23
2 persons,	222	1,238	5.58	0.36
3 persons,	276	1,621	5.87	0.51
4 persons,	262	1,614	6.16	0.65
5 persons,	254	1,689	6.65	0.75
6 persons,	214	1,451	6.78	0.88

ROOMS: OCCUPIED DWELLING HOUSES — Continued.

Counties, Cities, Towns, and Number of Persons to a Family.	Number of Families of Specified Size	Total Number of Rooms Occupied	Average Number of Rooms Occupied	Average Number of Persons to a Room
BERKSHIRE - Con.				
Adams — Con.				
7 persons,	126	835	6.63	1.06
8 persons,	89	579	6.51	1.23
9 persons,	55	389	7.07	1.27
10 persons,	35	271	7.74	1.29
11 persons,	18	127	7.06	1.56
12 persons,	10	103	10.30	1.17
13 persons,	4	34	8.50	1.53
14 persons,	3	22	7.33	1.91
15 persons,	3	39	13.00	1.15
16 persons,	1	8	8.00	2.00
20 persons,	1	20	20.00	1.00
Alford,	76	639	8.41	0.44
1 person,	6	30	5.00	0.20
2 persons,	15	116	7.73	0.26
3 persons,	19	152	8.00	0.38
4 persons,	15	134	8.93	0.45
5 persons,	8	76	9.50	0.53
6 persons,	7	76	10.86	0.55
7 persons,	3	30	10.00	0.70
8 persons,	3	25	8.33	0.96
Becket,	219	1,616	7.38	0.55
1 person,	14	86	6.14	0.16
2 persons,	49	299	6.10	0.33
3 persons,	53	378	7.13	0.42
4 persons,	31	216	6.97	0.57
5 persons,	20	200	10.00	0.50
6 persons,	16	125	7.81	0.77
7 persons,	17	155	9.12	0.77
8 persons,	4	38	9.50	0.84
9 persons,	7	56	8.00	1.13
10 persons,	7	56	8.00	1.25
13 persons,	1	7	7.00	1.86
Cheshire,	297	2,705	9.11	0.43
1 person,	22	134	6.09	0.16
2 persons,	60	484	8.07	0.25
3 persons,	70	620	8.86	0.34
4 persons,	44	454	10.32	0.39
5 persons,	38	352	9.26	0.54
6 persons,	24	250	10.42	0.58
7 persons,	19	202	10.63	0.66
8 persons,	10	105	10.50	0.76
9 persons,	5	48	9.60	0.94
10 persons,	2	14	7.00	1.43
11 persons,	2	32	16.00	0.69
14 persons,	1	10	10.00	1.40
Clarksburg,	214	1,500	7.01	0.67
1 person,	9	43	4.78	0.21
2 persons,	35	216	6.17	0.32
3 persons,	44	297	6.75	0.44
4 persons,	25	181	7.24	0.55
5 persons,	31	257	8.29	0.60
6 persons,	20	137	6.85	0.88
7 persons,	22	150	6.82	1.63
8 persons,	13	93	7.15	1.12
BERKSHIRE - Con.				
Clarksburg — Con.				
9 persons,	6	44	7.33	1.23
10 persons,	5	38	7.60	1.32
12 persons,	2	16	8.00	1.50
13 persons,	1	5	5.00	2.60
24 persons,	1	23	23.00	1.04
Dalton,	688	4,818	7.00	0.67
1 person,	31	163	5.26	0.19
2 persons,	94	581	6.18	0.32
3 persons,	122	800	6.56	0.46
4 persons,	112	776	6.93	0.58
5 persons,	103	725	7.04	0.71
6 persons,	94	692	7.36	0.82
7 persons,	51	402	7.88	0.89
8 persons,	35	270	7.71	1.04
9 persons,	20	160	8.00	1.13
10 persons,	16	117	7.31	1.37
11 persons,	6	60	10.00	1.10
12 persons,	2	20	10.00	1.20
13 persons,	1	9	9.00	1.44
18 persons,	1	43	43.00	0.42
Egremont,	211	1,631	7.73	0.51
1 person,	12	63	5.25	0.19
2 persons,	43	305	7.09	0.28
3 persons,	41	294	7.17	0.42
4 persons,	41	306	7.46	0.54
5 persons,	30	278	9.27	0.54
6 persons,	22	169	7.68	0.78
7 persons,	13	132	10.15	0.69
8 persons,	5	45	9.00	0.89
9 persons,	3	28	9.33	0.96
11 persons,	1	11	11.00	1.00
Florida,	93	650	6.99	0.65
1 person,	5	21	4.20	0.24
2 persons,	4	18	4.50	0.44
3 persons,	24	156	6.50	0.46
4 persons,	18	150	8.33	0.48
5 persons,	14	91	6.50	0.77
6 persons,	11	72	6.55	0.92
7 persons,	8	69	8.63	0.81
8 persons,	6	48	8.00	1.00
9 persons,	2	17	8.50	1.06
10 persons,	1	8	8.00	1.25
Great Barrington,	1,136	8,332	7.33	0.58
1 person,	70	354	5.06	0.20
2 persons,	196	1,229	6.27	0.32
3 persons,	235	1,595	6.79	0.44
4 persons,	208	1,516	7.29	0.53
5 persons,	146	1,092	7.48	0.67
6 persons,	114	886	7.77	0.77
7 persons,	78	709	9.09	0.77
8 persons,	47	423	9.00	0.89
9 persons,	22	186	8.45	1.06
10 persons,	9	75	8.33	1.20
11 persons,	4	44	11.00	1.00

ROOMS: OCCUPIED DWELLING HOUSES — Continued.

COUNTIES, CITIES, TOWNS, AND NUMBER OF PERSONS TO A FAMILY.	Number of Families of Specified Size	Total Number of Rooms Occupied	Average Number of Rooms Occupied	Average Number of Persons to a Room
BERKSHIRE - Con.				
Great Barrington — Con.				
12 persons,	3	53	17.67	0.68
13 persons,	1	14	14.00	0.93
14 persons,	1	29	29.00	0.48
31 persons,	1	27	27.00	1.15
33 persons,	1	100	100.00	0.33
Hancock,	117	1,013	8.66	0.50
1 person,	9	66	7.33	0.14
2 persons,	20	149	7.45	0.27
3 persons,	19	167	8.79	0.34
4 persons,	26	248	9.54	0.42
5 persons,	12	163	8.58	0.58
6 persons,	15	142	9.47	0.63
7 persons,	4	29	7.25	0.97
8 persons,	5	45	9.00	0.89
9 persons,	4	33	8.25	1.09
10 persons,	1	8	8.00	1.25
13 persons,	1	7	7.00	1.86
24 persons,	1	16	16.00	1.50
Hinsdale,	346	2,434	7.03	0.68
1 person,	16	84	5.38	0.49
2 persons,	56	353	6.30	0.32
3 persons,	58	336	6.83	0.44
4 persons,	52	371	7.13	0.56
5 persons,	44	337	7.66	0.65
6 persons,	35	255	7.29	0.82
7 persons,	33	256	7.76	0.90
8 persons,	24	180	7.50	1.07
9 persons,	12	84	7.00	1.29
10 persons,	6	40	6.67	1.50
11 persons,	4	25	6.25	1.76
12 persons,	3	25	8.33	1.44
13 persons,	3	26	8.67	1.50
Lanesborough,	210	1,630	7.76	0.52
1 person,	14	58	4.14	0.24
2 persons,	46	313	6.80	0.29
3 persons,	34	275	8.09	0.37
4 persons,	40	322	8.05	0.50
5 persons,	29	253	8.72	0.57
6 persons,	20	162	8.10	0.74
7 persons,	12	115	9.58	0.73
8 persons,	9	85	9.44	0.85
9 persons,	3	25	8.33	1.08
10 persons,	1	10	10.00	1.00
11 persons,	2	12	6.00	1.83
Lee,	922	6,732	7.30	0.60
1 person,	60	297	4.95	0.20
2 persons,	144	888	6.17	0.32
3 persons,	207	1,493	7.25	0.41
4 persons,	152	1,121	7.38	0.54
5 persons,	112	867	7.74	0.65
6 persons,	83	688	7.73	0.78
7 persons,	58	449	7.74	0.90
8 persons,	30	210	7.00	1.14
BERKSHIRE - Con.				
Lee — Con.				
9 persons,	32	286	8.94	1.01
10 persons,	18	149	8.28	1.21
11 persons,	10	105	10.50	1.05
12 persons,	6	53	8.83	1.36
13 persons,	4	35	8.75	1.49
14 persons,	2	43	21.50	0.65
15 persons,	1	12	12.00	1.25
16 persons,	1	36	36.00	0.44
Lenox,	581	4,442	7.65	0.65
1 person,	37	220	5.95	0.17
2 persons,	71	461	6.49	0.31
3 persons,	94	676	7.19	0.42
4 persons,	89	584	6.56	0.61
5 persons,	89	674	7.57	0.66
6 persons,	52	406	7.81	0.77
7 persons,	59	453	7.68	0.91
8 persons,	33	285	8.64	0.93
9 persons,	19	180	9.47	0.95
10 persons,	14	120	8.57	1.17
11 persons,	10	99	9.90	1.11
12 persons,	6	66	11.00	1.09
13 persons,	5	58	11.60	1.12
14 persons,	1	20	20.00	0.70
16 persons,	1	33	33.00	0.48
33 persons,	1	107	107.00	0.31
Monterey,	115	1,021	8.88	0.45
1 person,	8	41	5.13	0.20
2 persons,	21	167	7.95	0.25
3 persons,	25	227	9.08	0.33
4 persons,	17	166	9.41	0.43
5 persons,	22	204	9.27	0.54
6 persons,	12	115	9.58	0.63
7 persons,	4	44	11.00	0.64
8 persons,	1	11	11.00	0.73
9 persons,	2	29	14.50	0.62
10 persons,	1	6	6.00	1.67
12 persons,	1	9	9.00	1.33
13 persons,	1	8	8.00	1.63
Mount Washington,	31	355	11.45	0.38
1 person,	1	9	9.00	0.11
2 persons,	2	17	8.50	0.24
3 persons,	8	69	8.25	0.36
4 persons,	8	67	8.38	0.48
5 persons,	5	63	12.60	0.40
6 persons,	2	54	27.00	0.22
7 persons,	2	11	5.50	1.27
8 persons,	3	68	22.67	0.35
New Ashford,	30	263	8.77	0.44
1 person,	1	8	8.00	0.13
2 persons,	9	66	7.33	0.27
3 persons,	4	28	7.00	0.43
4 persons,	6	69	11.50	0.35
5 persons,	6	50	8.33	0.60
6 persons,	1	8	8.00	0.75

ROOMS: OCCUPIED DWELLING HOUSES — Continued.

COUNTIES, CITIES, TOWNS, AND NUMBER OF PERSONS TO A FAMILY.	Number of Families of Specified Size	Total Number of Rooms Occupied	Average Number of Rooms Occupied	Average Number of Persons to a Room	COUNTIES, CITIES, TOWNS, AND NUMBER OF PERSONS TO A FAMILY.	Number of Families of Specified Size	Total Number of Rooms Occupied	Average Number of Rooms Occupied	Average Number of Persons to a Room
BERKSHIRE - Con.					**BERKSHIRE - Con.**				
New Ashford — Con.					Peru — Con.				
8 persons,	2	20	10.00	0.80	7 persons,	9	89	9.89	0.71
9 persons,	1	14	14.00	0.64	8 persons,	1	9	9.00	0.89
New Marlborough,	325	2,858	8.79	0.45	9 persons,	2	21	10.50	0.86
1 person,	28	229	8.18	0.12	PITTSFIELD,	4,342	30,994	7.14	0.66
2 persons,	67	522	7.79	0.26	1 person,	144	538	3.74	0.27
3 persons,	67	607	9.06	0.33	2 persons,	646	3,659	5.72	0.35
4 persons,	46	403	8.76	0.46	3 persons,	852	5,443	6.39	0.47
5 persons,	40	390	9.75	0.51	4 persons,	754	5,166	6.85	0.58
6 persons,	29	267	9.21	0.65	5 persons,	641	4,717	7.36	0.68
7 persons,	28	262	9.36	0.75	6 persons,	489	3,748	7.66	0.78
8 persons,	12	110	9.17	0.87	7 persons,	297	2,331	7.85	0.89
9 persons,	5	43	8.60	1.05	8 persons,	199	1,875	9.42	0.85
10 persons,	3	25	8.33	1.20	9 persons,	140	1,139	8.14	1.11
NORTH ADAMS,	3,931	25,383	6.46	0.75	10 persons,	95	804	8.46	1.18
1 person,	93	326	3.51	0.29	11 persons,	34	310	9.12	1.21
2 persons,	550	2,990	5.44	0.37	12 persons,	15	139	10.60	1.13
3 persons,	646	3,962	6.13	0.49	13 persons,	11	97	8.82	1.47
4 persons,	722	4,660	6.45	0.62	14 persons,	6	71	11.83	1.18
5 persons,	616	4,122	6.69	0.75	15 persons,	4	52	13.00	1.15
6 persons,	432	2,835	6.56	0.91	16 persons,	3	38	12.67	1.26
7 persons,	348	2,316	6.66	1.05	17 persons,	1	7	7.00	2.43
8 persons,	224	1,556	6.95	1.15	18 persons,	1	23	23.00	0.78
9 persons,	126	901	7.15	1.26	19 persons,	4	67	16.75	1.13
10 persons,	73	531	7.27	1.37	20 persons,	1	16	16.00	1.25
11 persons,	53	449	8.47	1.30	21 persons,	2	42	21.00	1.00
12 persons,	17	139	8.18	1.47	22 persons,	1	40	40.00	0.55
13 persons,	14	123	8.79	1.48	24 persons,	1	33	33.00	0.73
14 persons,	3	30	10.00	1.40	34 persons,	2	88	44.00	0.77
15 persons,	2	18	9.00	1.67	36 persons,	1	115	115.00	0.31
16 persons,	3	46	15.33	1.04	37 persons,	1	110	110.00	0.34
21 persons,	1	10	10.00	2.10	51 persons,	1	90	90.00	0.57
22 persons,	3	47	15.67	1.40	70 persons,	1	68	68.00	1.03
25 persons,	1	33	33.00	0.76	75 persons,	1	148	148.00	0.51
37 persons,	2	87	43.50	0.85	*Pittsfield. Ward 1,*	552	3,574	6.47	0.79
38 persons,	1	112	112.00	0.34	1 person,	9	41	4.56	0.22
39 persons,	1	100	100.00	0.39	2 persons,	66	357	5.41	0.37
Otis,	136	1,053	7.74	0.49	3 persons,	93	522	5.61	0.53
1 person,	13	55	4.23	0.24	4 persons,	87	522	6.00	0.67
2 persons,	23	168	7.30	0.27	5 persons,	86	549	6.38	0.78
3 persons,	36	281	7.81	0.38	6 persons,	81	551	6.80	0.88
4 persons,	20	178	8.90	0.45	7 persons,	45	317	7.04	0.99
5 persons,	19	172	9.05	0.55	8 persons,	35	238	6.80	1.18
6 persons,	9	71	7.89	0.76	9 persons,	20	149	7.45	1.21
7 persons,	10	71	7.10	0.99	10 persons,	19	132	6.95	1.44
8 persons,	3	22	7.33	1.09	11 persons,	3	22	7.33	1.50
9 persons,	2	22	11.00	0.82	12 persons,	1	6	6.00	2.00
10 persons,	1	13	13.00	0.77	13 persons,	2	14	7.00	1.86
Peru,	71	569	8.01	0.54	14 persons,	2	20	10.00	1.40
1 person,	3	14	4.67	0.21	16 persons,	1	6	6.00	2.67
2 persons,	11	60	5.45	0.37	21 persons,	1	38	38.00	0.55
3 persons,	16	128	8.00	0.38	51 persons,	1	90	90.00	0.57
4 persons,	12	111	9.25	0.43	*Pittsfield. Ward 2,*	722	5,215	7.22	0.68
5 persons,	7	50	7.14	0.70	1 person,	11	56	5.09	0.20
6 persons,	10	87	8.70	0.69	2 persons,	99	575	5.81	0.34

ROOMS: OCCUPIED DWELLING HOUSES — Continued.

COUNTIES, CITIES, TOWNS, AND NUMBER OF PERSONS TO A FAMILY.	Number of Families of Specified Size	Total Number of Rooms Occupied	Average Number of Rooms Occupied	Average Number of Persons to a Room	COUNTIES, CITIES, TOWNS, AND NUMBER OF PERSONS TO A FAMILY.	Number of Families of Specified Size	Total Number of Rooms Occupied	Average Number of Rooms Occupied	Average Number of Persons to a Room
BERKSHIRE - Con.					BERKSHIRE - Con.				
Pittsfield. Ward 2 — Con.					*Pittsfield. Ward 5 — Con.*				
3 persons, . .	136	888	6.53	0.46	8 persons, . .	24	187	7.79	1.03
4 persons, . .	143	945	6.61	0.61	9 persons, . .	19	146	7.68	1.17
5 persons, . .	104	798	7.67	0.65	10 persons, . .	16	135	8.44	1.19
6 persons, . .	84	658	7.83	0.77	11 persons, . .	4	29	7.25	1.52
7 persons, . .	48	354	7.38	0.95	12 persons, . .	1	19	19 00	0.63
8 persons, . .	33	270	8.18	0.98	13 persons, . .	2	26	13 00	1.00
9 persons, . .	36	282	7.83	1.15	16 persons, . .	2	32	16.00	1.00
10 persons, . .	10	89	8.90	1.12	17 persons, . .	1	7	7.00	2.43
11 persons, . .	6	49	8.17	1.35	18 persons, . .	1	23	23.00	0.78
12 persons, . .	4	32	8.00	1.50	21 persons, . .	1	4	4.00	5.25
13 persons, . .	4	37	9.25	1.41	36 persons, . .	1	115	115.00	0.31
14 persons, . .	2	18	9.00	1.56	*Pittsfield. Ward 6, .*	742	5,057	6.82	0.69
20 persons, . .	1	16	16.00	1.25	1 person, . .	19	70	3.68	0.27
75 persons, . .	1	148	148.00	0.51	2 persons, . .	120	646	5.38	0.37
Pittsfield. Ward 3, .	599	4,072	6.80	0.64	3 persons, . .	144	866	6.01	0.50
1 person, . .	22	97	4.41	0.23	4 persons, . .	129	857	6.64	0.60
2 persons, . .	104	578	5.56	0.36	5 persons, . .	112	705	6.29	0.79
3 persons, . .	125	791	6.33	0.47	6 persons, . .	79	562	7.11	0.84
4 persons, . .	105	703	6.70	0.60	7 persons, . .	50	344	6.88	1.02
5 persons, . .	80	579	7.24	0.69	8 persons, . .	36	517	14.36	0.56
6 persons, . .	57	455	7.98	0.75	9 persons, . .	24	180	7.50	1.20
7 persons, . .	46	364	7.91	0.88	10 persons, . .	15	117	7.80	1.28
8 persons, . .	30	244	8.13	0.98	11 persons, . .	7	57	8.14	1.35
9 persons, . .	16	141	8.81	1.02	12 persons, . .	4	37	9.25	1.30
10 persons, . .	8	65	8.13	1.23	15 persons, . .	1	12	12.00	1.25
11 persons, . .	3	24	8.00	1.38	19 persons, . .	1	19	19.00	1.00
12 persons, . .	2	16	8.00	1.50	70 persons, . .	1	68	68.00	1.03
15 persons, . .	1	15	15.00	1.00	*Pittsfield. Ward 7, .*	577	4,080	7.07	0.62
Pittsfield. Ward 4, .	604	5,027	8.32	0.55	1 person, . .	50	128	2.56	0.39
1 person, . .	26	112	4.31	0.23	2 persons, . .	89	482	5.42	0.37
2 persons, . .	84	542	6.45	0.31	3 persons, . .	119	735	6.18	0.49
3 persons, . .	136	992	7.29	0.41	4 persons, . .	90	613	6.81	0.59
4 persons, . .	103	852	8.27	0.48	5 persons, . .	78	611	7.83	0.64
5 persons, . .	92	836	9.09	0.55	6 persons, . .	67	522	7.79	0.77
6 persons, . .	58	531	9.16	0.66	7 persons, . .	28	247	8.82	0.79
7 persons, . .	39	403	10.33	0.68	8 persons, . .	20	187	9.35	0.86
8 persons, . .	21	232	11.05	0 72	9 persons, . .	11	100	9.09	0.99
9 persons, . .	14	141	10.07	0.89	10 persons, . .	13	104	8.00	1.25
10 persons, . .	14	162	11.57	0.86	11 persons, . .	3	55	18.33	0.60
11 persons, . .	8	74	9.25	1.19	12 persons, . .	1	20	20.00	0.60
12 persons, . .	2	29	14.50	0.83	13 persons, . .	2	15	7.50	1.73
13 persons, . .	1	5	5.00	2.60	14 persons, . .	2	33	16.50	0.85
15 persons, . .	2	25	12.50	1.20	18 persons, . .	1	18	18.00	1.06
19 persons, . .	2	30	15.00	1.27	22 persons, . .	1	40	40.00	0.55
24 persons, . .	1	33	33.00	0.73	34 persons, . .	1	60	60.00	0.57
34 persons, . .	1	28	28.00	1.21	37 persons, . .	1	110	110.00	0.34
Pittsfield. Ward 5, .	546	3,969	7.27	0.68	Richmond, . .	164	1,377	8.40	0.51
1 person, . .	7	34	4.86	0.21	1 person, . .	8	45	5.63	0.18
2 persons, . .	78	479	6.14	0.33	2 persons, . .	27	206	7.63	0.26
3 persons, . .	99	649	6.56	0.46	3 persons, . .	36	302	8.39	0.36
4 persons, . .	97	674	6.95	0.58	4 persons, . .	32	272	8.50	0.47
5 persons, . .	89	639	7.18	0.70	5 persons, . .	23	204	8 87	0.56
6 persons, . .	63	469	7.44	0.81	6 persons, . .	9	89	9.89	0.61
7 persons, . .	41	302	7.37	0.95	7 persons, . .	11	108	9.82	0.71

ROOMS: OCCUPIED DWELLING HOUSES — Continued.

Counties, Cities, Towns, and Number of Persons to a Family.	Number of Families of Specified Size	Total Number of Rooms Occupied	Average Number of Rooms Occupied	Average Number of Persons to a Room	Counties, Cities, Towns, and Number of Persons to a Family.	Number of Families of Specified Size	Total Number of Rooms Occupied	Average Number of Rooms Occupied	Average Number of Persons to a Room
BERKSHIRE - Con.					**BERKSHIRE - Con.**				
Richmond — Con.					Tyringham — Con.				
8 persons, . .	8	85	10.63	0.75	1 person, . .	5	35	7.00	0.14
9 persons, . .	8	55	6.88	1.31	2 persons, . .	14	117	8.36	0.24
10 persons, . .	1	5	5.00	2.00	3 persons, . .	20	163	8.15	0.37
11 persons, . .	1	6	6.00	1.83	4 persons, . .	21	191	9.10	0.44
Sandisfield, . .	213	1,794	8.42	0.45	5 persons, . .	14	131	9.36	0.53
1 person, . .	21	113	5.38	0.19	6 persons, . .	6	77	12.83	0.47
2 persons, . .	43	328	7.63	0.26	7 persons, . .	2	18	9.00	0.78
3 persons, . .	44	384	8.96	0.35	8 persons, . .	6	50	8.33	0.96
4 persons, . .	38	350	9.21	0.43	9 persons, . .	2	20	10.00	0.90
5 persons, . .	34	317	9.32	0.54	Washington, . .	87	712	8.18	0.59
6 persons, . .	14	125	8.93	0.67	1 person, . .	4	19	4.75	0.21
7 persons, . .	8	79	9.88	0.71	2 persons, . .	14	92	6.57	0.30
8 persons, . .	4	37	9.25	0.86	3 persons, . .	7	58	8.29	0.36
9 persons, . .	3	23	7.67	1.17	4 persons, . .	20	163	8.15	0.49
10 persons, . .	2	23	11.50	0.87	5 persons, . .	11	98	8.91	0.56
11 persons, . .	2	18	9.00	1.22	6 persons, . .	8	73	9.13	0.66
Savoy, . .	133	977	7.35	0.52	7 persons, . .	8	83	10.38	0.67
1 person, . .	5	24	4.80	0.21	8 persons, . .	11	99	9.00	0.89
2 persons, . .	31	194	6.26	0.32	9 persons, . .	1	7	7.00	1.29
3 persons, . .	30	215	7.17	0.42	11 persons, . .	2	13	6.50	1.69
4 persons, . .	27	201	7.44	0.54	12 persons, . .	1	7	7.00	1.71
5 persons, . .	16	133	8.31	0.60	West Stockbridge, . .	324	2,319	7.16	0.54
6 persons, . .	14	128	9.14	0.66	1 person, . .	21	98	4.67	0.21
7 persons, . .	5	48	9.60	0.73	2 persons, . .	77	547	7.10	0.28
8 persons, . .	5	34	6.80	1.18	3 persons, . .	67	475	7.09	0.42
Sheffield, . .	481	3,725	7.74	0.51	4 persons, . .	53	384	7.25	0.55
1 person, . .	33	147	4.45	0.22	5 persons, . .	44	323	7.34	0.68
2 persons, . .	112	768	6.86	0.29	6 persons, . .	26	212	8.15	0.74
3 persons, . .	95	690	7.26	0.41	7 persons, . .	16	118	7.38	0.95
4 persons, . .	73	632	8.66	0.46	8 persons, . .	11	102	9.27	0.86
5 persons, . .	62	537	8.66	0.58	9 persons, . .	3	21	7.00	1.29
6 persons, . .	46	366	8.61	0.70	10 persons, . .	3	19	6.33	1.58
7 persons, . .	28	232	8.29	0.84	11 persons, . .	1	7	7.00	1.57
8 persons, . .	19	154	8.11	0.86	12 persons, . .	1	6	6.00	2.00
9 persons, . .	5	36	7.20	1.25	13 persons, . .	1	7	7.00	1.86
10 persons, . .	5	94	18.80	0.53	Williamstown, . .	1,017	7,535	7.41	0.65
11 persons, . .	2	34	17.00	0.65	1 person, . .	50	211	4.22	0.24
12 persons, . .	1	5	5.00	2.40	2 persons, . .	145	850	5.86	0.34
Stockbridge, . .	474	3,779	8.02	0.55	3 persons, . .	197	1,281	6.50	0.46
1 person, . .	20	101	5.05	0.20	4 persons, . .	172	1,233	7.17	0.56
2 persons, . .	97	625	6.44	0.31	5 persons, . .	148	1,107	7.48	0.67
3 persons, . .	80	634	7.93	0.38	6 persons, . .	107	796	7.44	0.81
4 persons, . .	82	655	7.99	0.50	7 persons, . .	75	603	8.04	0.87
5 persons, . .	57	499	8.75	0.57	8 persons, . .	51	413	8.10	0.99
6 persons, . .	57	444	7.79	0.77	9 persons, . .	32	281	8.78	1.02
7 persons, . .	28	250	8.36	0.78	10 persons, . .	16	128	8.00	1.25
8 persons, . .	22	184	8.36	0.96	11 persons, . .	10	73	7.30	1.51
9 persons, . .	14	115	8.21	1.10	12 persons, . .	6	61	10.17	1.18
10 persons, . .	7	76	10.86	0.92	13 persons, . .	2	14	7.00	1.86
11 persons, . .	4	41	10.25	1.07	14 persons, . .	1	28	28.00	0.50
12 persons, . .	1	7	7.00	1.71	15 persons, . .	1	14	14.00	1.07
13 persons, . .	1	14	14.00	0.93	17 persons, . .	2	45	22.50	0.76
31 persons, . .	1	134	134.00	0.23	18 persons, . .	1	4	4.00	4.50
Tyringham, . .	90	802	8.91	0.45	216 persons, . .	1	393	393.00	0.55

ROOMS: OCCUPIED DWELLING HOUSES — Continued.

COUNTIES, CITIES, TOWNS, AND NUMBER OF PERSONS TO A FAMILY.	Number of Families of Specified Size	Total Number of Rooms Occupied	Average Number of Rooms Occupied	Average Number of Persons to a Room	COUNTIES, CITIES, TOWNS, AND NUMBER OF PERSONS TO A FAMILY.	Number of Families of Specified Size	Total Number of Rooms Occupied	Average Number of Rooms Occupied	Average Number of Persons to a Room
BERKSHIRE - Con.					**BRISTOL — Con.**				
Windsor, . . .	135	1,019	7.55	0.55	Berkley — Con.				
1 person,	9	35	3.89	0.26	6 persons, . .	16	114	7.13	0.84
2 persons, . .	28	201	7.18	0.28	7 persons, . .	17	142	8.35	0.84
3 persons, . .	26	188	7.23	0.41	8 persons, . .	8	64	8.00	1.00
4 persons, . .	21	168	8.00	0.50	9 persons, . .	1	11	11.00	0.82
5 persons, . .	19	153	8.05	0.62	10 persons, . .	1	8	8.00	1.25
6 persons, . .	15	131	8.73	0.69	13 persons, . .	1	8	8.00	1.63
7 persons, . .	7	64	9.44	0.77	Dartmouth, . .	844	6,187	7.60	0.50
8 persons, . .	4	29	7.25	1.10	1 person, . .	65	390	6.00	0.17
9 persons, . .	2	17	8.50	1.06	2 persons, . .	206	1,454	7.06	0.28
10 persons, . .	1	8	8.00	1.25	3 persons, . .	153	1,124	7.35	0.41
11 persons, . .	1	9	9.00	1.22	4 persons, . .	141	1,158	8.21	0.49
12 persons, . .	2	16	8.00	1.50	5 persons, . .	94	722	7.68	0.65
					6 persons, . .	69	588	8.52	0.70
BRISTOL.					7 persons, . .	37	309	8.35	0.84
Acushnet, .	294	2,282	7.76	0.49	8 persons, . .	19	171	9.00	0.89
1 person,	31	186	6.00	0.17	9 persons, . .	13	107	8.23	1.09
2 persons, . .	57	379	6.65	0.30	10 persons, . .	8	60	7.50	1.33
3 persons, . .	62	485	7.82	0.38	11 persons, . .	4	30	7.50	1.47
4 persons, . .	58	484	8.34	0.48	12 persons, . .	1	14	14.00	0.86
5 persons, . .	33	265	8.03	0.62	13 persons, . .	1	13	13.00	1.00
6 persons, . .	16	143	8.94	0.67	14 persons, . .	1	16	16.00	0.88
7 persons, . .	18	169	9.39	0.75	16 persons, . .	2	31	15.50	1.03
8 persons, . .	11	90	8.18	0.98	Dighton, . .	461	3,254	7.06	0.55
9 persons, . .	5	47	9.40	0.96	1 person, . .	36	197	5.47	0.18
10 persons, . .	2	23	11.50	0.87	2 persons, . .	99	632	6.38	0.31
12 persons, . .	1	11	11.00	1.09	3 persons, . .	93	639	6.87	0.44
Attleborough, .	1,890	12,623	6.68	0.66	4 persons, . .	77	568	7.38	0.54
1 person, . .	63	291	4.62	0.22	5 persons, . .	62	468	7.55	0.63
2 persons, . .	331	1,984	5.98	0.33	6 persons, . .	42	311	7.40	0.81
3 persons, . .	385	2,448	6.36	0.47	7 persons, . .	28	220	7.86	0.89
4 persons, . .	353	2,410	6.83	0.59	8 persons, . .	10	80	8.00	1.00
5 persons, . .	275	1,931	7.02	0.71	9 persons, . .	8	83	10.38	0.87
6 persons, . .	198	1,382	6.98	0.86	10 persons, . .	1	5	5.00	2.00
7 persons, . .	123	815	6.63	1.06	11 persons, . .	4	37	9.25	1.19
8 persons, . .	67	463	6.96	1.15	12 persons, . .	1	14	14.00	0.86
9 persons, . .	38	286	7.53	1.20	Easton, . .	1,061	7,145	6.73	0.62
10 persons, . .	25	191	7.64	1.31	1 person, . .	60	246	4.10	0.24
11 persons, . .	10	69	6.90	1.59	2 persons, . .	179	1,121	6.26	0.32
12 persons, . .	9	89	9.89	1.21	3 persons, . .	217	1,481	6.82	0.44
13 persons, . .	3	36	12.00	1.08	4 persons, . .	204	1,431	7.01	0.57
14 persons, . .	1	12	12.00	1.17	5 persons, . .	155	1,098	7.08	0.71
15 persons, . .	2	32	16.00	0.94	6 persons, . .	99	672	6.79	0.88
16 persons, . .	2	35	17.50	0.91	7 persons, . .	58	426	7.34	0.95
18 persons, . .	1	31	31.00	0.58	8 persons, . .	51	377	7.39	1.08
20 persons, . .	1	25	25.00	0.80	9 persons, . .	20	139	6.95	1.29
22 persons, . .	1	18	18.00	1.22	10 persons, . .	8	68	8.50	1.18
25 persons, . .	1	45	45.00	0.56	11 persons, . .	6	37	6.17	1.78
26 persons, . .	1	30	30.00	0.87	12 persons, . .	1	6	6.00	2.00
Berkley, . .	256	1,913	7.47	0.50	14 persons, . .	1	14	14.00	1.00
1 person, . .	24	151	6.29	0.16	15 persons, . .	1	20	20.00	0.75
2 persons, . .	56	403	7.20	0.28	17 persons, . .	1	9	9.00	1.89
3 persons, . .	50	362	7.24	0.41	Fairhaven, . .	898	6,468	7.20	0.52
4 persons, . .	52	418	8.04	0.50	1 person, . .	61	340	5.57	0.18
5 persons, . .	30	232	7.73	0.65	2 persons, . .	217	1,509	6.95	0.29

ROOMS. 467

ROOMS: OCCUPIED DWELLING HOUSES — Continued.

Counties, Cities, Towns, and Number of Persons to a Family.	Number of Families Specified Size	Total Number of Rooms Occupied	Average Number of Rooms Occupied	Average Number of Persons to a Room
BRISTOL — Con.				
Fairhaven — Con.				
3 persons,	197	1,371	6.96	0.43
4 persons,	159	1,114	7.01	0.57
5 persons,	118	919	7.79	0.64
6 persons,	65	519	7.98	0.75
7 persons,	43	371	8.63	0.81
8 persons,	19	164	8.63	0.96
9 persons,	11	90	8.18	1.10
10 persons,	5	33	6.60	1.52
11 persons,	2	12	6.00	1.83
12 persons,	1	26	26.00	0.46
FALL RIVER,	17,948	100,713	5.61	0.89
1 person,	511	2,156	4.22	0.24
2 persons,	2,539	12,765	5.03	0.40
3 persons,	3,029	16,470	5.44	0.55
4 persons,	2,927	16,144	5.52	0.73
5 persons,	2,582	14,529	5.63	0.89
6 persons,	2,086	12,080	5.79	1.04
7 persons,	1,490	8,795	5.90	1.19
8 persons,	1,091	6,354	5.82	1.37
9 persons,	715	4,258	5.96	1.51
10 persons,	419	2,588	6.18	1.62
11 persons,	267	1,780	6.70	1.64
12 persons,	124	783	6.31	1.90
13 persons,	75	492	6.56	1.98
14 persons,	31	253	8.16	1.72
15 persons,	19	148	7.79	1.93
16 persons,	5	56	11.20	1.43
17 persons,	6	66	11.00	1.55
18 persons,	2	22	11.00	1.64
19 persons,	3	147	49.00	0.39
20 persons,	4	60	15.00	1.33
21 persons,	1	17	17.00	1.24
22 persons,	3	31	10.33	2.13
24 persons,	3	122	40.67	0.59
26 persons,	1	34	34.00	0.76
27 persons,	1	25	25.00	1.08
28 persons,	1	25	25.00	1.12
29 persons,	2	79	39.50	0.73
33 persons,	2	68	34.00	0.97
36 persons,	2	111	55.50	0.65
41 persons,	1	34	34.00	1.21
45 persons,	1	13	13.00	3.46
53 persons,	1	24	24.00	2.21
82 persons,	1	25	25.00	3.28
86 persons,	1	30	30.00	2.87
119 persons,	1	62	62.00	1.92
274 persons,	1	57	57.00	4.84
Fall River. Ward 1,	2,342	13,322	5.69	0.84
1 person,	61	236	4.20	0.24
2 persons,	330	1,705	5.17	0.39
3 persons,	447	2,475	5.54	0.54
4 persons,	383	2,228	5.82	0.69
5 persons,	341	1,984	5.82	0.86
6 persons,	277	1,580	5.70	1.05
BRISTOL — Con.				
Fall River. Ward 1 — Con.				
7 persons,	191	1,138	5.96	1.17
8 persons,	131	778	5.94	1.35
9 persons,	91	568	6.24	1.44
10 persons,	40	260	6.50	1.54
11 persons,	28	192	6.86	1.60
12 persons,	15	108	7.20	1.67
13 persons,	6	39	6.50	2.00
15 persons,	1	11	11.00	1.36
Fall River. Ward 2,	1,677	9,462	5.64	0.92
1 person,	40	166	4.15	0.24
2 persons,	207	1,065	5.14	0.39
3 persons,	259	1,380	5.33	0.56
4 persons,	248	1,400	5.64	0.71
5 persons,	252	1,433	5.69	0.88
6 persons,	216	1,281	5.93	1.01
7 persons,	147	864	5.88	1.19
8 persons,	122	732	6.00	1.33
9 persons,	71	412	5.80	1.55
10 persons,	45	292	5.82	1.72
11 persons,	34	217	6.38	1.72
12 persons,	18	116	6.44	1.86
13 persons,	9	61	6.78	1.92
14 persons,	3	20	6.67	2.10
15 persons,	4	24	6.00	2.50
20 persons,	1	17	17.00	1.18
22 persons,	1	12	12.00	1.83
Fall River. Ward 3,	2,247	10,249	4.56	1.12
1 person,	64	199	3.11	0.32
2 persons,	288	1,155	4.01	0.50
3 persons,	348	1,451	4.17	0.72
4 persons,	370	1,598	4.32	0.93
5 persons,	327	1,497	4.58	1.09
6 persons,	282	1,331	4.72	1.27
7 persons,	173	803	4.64	1.51
8 persons,	162	792	4.89	1.64
9 persons,	96	522	5.44	1.66
10 persons,	51	256	5.02	1.99
11 persons,	33	181	5.48	2.01
12 persons,	23	120	5.48	2.19
13 persons,	13	69	5.31	2.45
14 persons,	7	45	6.43	2.18
15 persons,	4	41	10.25	1.46
17 persons,	2	21	10.50	1.62
18 persons,	1	14	14.00	1.29
19 persons,	1	125	125.00	0.15
20 persons,	1	16	16.00	1.25
22 persons,	1	7	7.00	3.14
Fall River. Ward 4,	2,241	13,396	5.98	0.75
1 person,	76	333	4.38	0.23
2 persons,	333	1,840	5.59	0.36
3 persons,	425	2,524	5.93	0.51
4 persons,	374	2,193	5.86	0.68
5 persons,	328	2,006	6.12	0.82
6 persons,	248	1,519	6.13	0.98

ROOMS: OCCUPIED DWELLING HOUSES — Continued.

Counties, Cities, Towns, and Number of Persons to a Family	Number of Families of Specified Size	Total Number of Rooms Occupied	Average Number of Rooms Occupied	Average Number of Persons to a Room
BRISTOL — Con.				
Fall River, Ward 4 — Con.				
7 persons,	178	1,122	6.30	1.11
8 persons,	121	764	6.31	1.27
9 persons,	78	469	6.01	1.50
10 persons,	38	259	6.82	1.47
11 persons,	19	144	7.58	1.45
12 persons,	11	72	6.55	1.83
13 persons,	7	48	6.86	1.90
14 persons,	2	18	9.00	1.56
17 persons,	1	6	6.00	2.83
21 persons,	1	17	17.00	1.24
33 persons,	1	45	45.00	0.73
Fall River, Ward 5,	2,120	9,771	4.59	1.09
1 person,	72	226	3.14	0.32
2 persons,	320	1,276	3.99	0.50
3 persons,	303	1,297	4.28	0.70
4 persons,	346	1,516	4.38	0.91
5 persons,	299	1,391	4.65	1.07
6 persons,	248	1,157	4.67	1.29
7 persons,	205	1,040	5.07	1.38
8 persons,	132	674	5.11	1.57
9 persons,	81	412	5.09	1.77
10 persons,	63	354	5.62	1.78
11 persons,	30	180	6.00	1.83
12 persons,	9	58	6.44	1.86
13 persons,	11	72	6.55	1.99
14 persons,	1	6	6.00	2.33
15 persons,	4	26	6.50	2.31
16 persons,	1	12	12.00	1.33
17 persons,	1	8	8.00	2.13
20 persons,	1	12	12.00	1.67
27 persons,	1	25	25.00	1.08
36 persons,	1	29	29.00	1.24
Fall River, Ward 6,	2,179	11,432	5.25	1.07
1 person,	34	129	3.79	0.26
2 persons,	241	1,118	4.64	0.43
3 persons,	296	1,420	4.83	0.62
4 persons,	351	1,787	5.09	0.79
5 persons,	312	1,577	5.05	0.99
6 persons,	259	1,418	5.47	1.10
7 persons,	208	1,136	5.46	1.28
8 persons,	171	930	5.61	1.43
9 persons,	117	670	5.73	1.57
10 persons,	87	497	5.71	1.75
11 persons,	50	294	5.88	1.87
12 persons,	24	123	5.86	2.05
13 persons,	17	111	6.53	1.99
14 persons,	6	33	5.50	2.55
15 persons,	4	22	5.50	2.73
16 persons,	1	10	10.00	1.60
19 persons,	1	8	8.00	2.38
33 persons,	1	23	23.00	1.43
86 persons,	1	30	30.00	2.87
274 persons,	1	57	57.00	4.81
BRISTOL — Con.				
Fall River, Ward 7,	1,386	9,733	6.97	0.66
1 person,	62	344	5.55	0.18
2 persons,	267	1,527	5.72	0.35
3 persons,	261	1,728	6.62	0.45
4 persons,	234	1,547	6.61	0.61
5 persons,	188	1,282	6.82	0.73
6 persons,	136	983	7.30	0.82
7 persons,	94	714	7.60	0.92
8 persons,	53	375	7.08	1.13
9 persons,	36	241	6.69	1.24
10 persons,	17	186	10.94	0.91
11 persons,	18	196	10.89	1.01
12 persons,	5	45	9.00	1.33
13 persons,	4	39	9.75	1.33
14 persons,	6	89	14.83	0.94
15 persons,	2	24	12.00	1.25
16 persons,	2	25	12.50	1.28
17 persons,	1	9	9.00	1.89
20 persons,	1	15	15.00	1.33
22 persons,	1	12	12.00	1.83
24 persons,	3	122	40.67	0.59
28 persons,	1	25	25.00	1.12
29 persons,	2	79	39.50	0.73
36 persons,	1	82	82.00	0.44
41 persons,	1	34	34.00	1.21
Fall River, Ward 8,	1,607	11,369	7.07	0.64
1 person,	49	275	5.61	0.18
2 persons,	261	1,551	5.94	0.34
3 persons,	327	2,237	6.84	0.44
4 persons,	295	2,066	7.00	0.57
5 persons,	250	1,768	7.07	0.71
6 persons,	159	1,252	7.87	0.76
7 persons,	110	892	8.11	0.86
8 persons,	65	484	7.45	1.07
9 persons,	46	384	8.35	1.08
10 persons,	20	138	6.90	1.45
11 persons,	12	104	8.67	1.27
12 persons,	6	45	7.50	1.60
14 persons,	2	18	9.00	1.56
17 persons,	1	22	22.00	0.77
26 persons,	1	34	34.00	0.76
45 persons,	1	13	13.00	3.46
53 persons,	1	24	24.00	2.21
119 persons,	1	62	62.00	1.92
Fall River, Ward 9,	2,430	11,979	5.02	0.90
1 person,	53	228	4.30	0.23
2 persons,	292	1,508	5.16	0.39
3 persons,	363	1,952	5.38	0.56
4 persons,	326	1,809	5.55	0.72
5 persons,	285	1,594	5.58	0.90
6 persons,	261	1,549	5.93	1.01
7 persons,	184	1,086	5.90	1.19
8 persons,	154	795	5.16	1.35
9 persons,	99	580	5.86	1.54
10 persons,	58	376	6.48	1.54

ROOMS: OCCUPIED DWELLING HOUSES — Continued.

COUNTIES, CITIES, TOWNS, AND NUMBER OF PERSONS TO A FAMILY.	Number of Families Specified Size	Total Number of Rooms Occupied	Average Number of Rooms Occupied	Average Number of Persons to a Room	COUNTIES, CITIES, TOWNS, AND NUMBER OF PERSONS TO A FAMILY.	Number of Families Specified Size	Total Number of Rooms Occupied	Average Number of Rooms Occupied	Average Number of Persons to a Room
BRISTOL — Con.					**BRISTOL — Con.**				
Fall River. Ward 9 — Con.					NEW BEDFORD—Con.				
11 persons,	43	282	6.56	1.68	18 persons,	3	42	14.00	1.29
12 persons,	16	90	5.63	2.43	19 persons,	2	39	19.50	0.97
13 persons,	8	53	6.63	1.96	21 persons,	2	27	13.50	1.59
14 persons,	4	24	6.00	2.33	22 persons,	1	25	25.00	0.88
16 persons,	1	9	9.00	1.78	26 persons,	1	24	24.00	1.08
18 persons,	1	8	8.00	2.25	27 persons,	1	119	119.00	0.23
19 persons,	1	14	14.00	1.36	29 persons,	2	55	27.50	1.05
82 persons,	1	25	25.00	3.28	35 persons,	1	35	35.00	1.00
Freetown,	342	2,123	6.21	0.86	37 persons,	1	20	20.00	1.85
1 person,	32	159	4.97	0.20	78 persons,	1	28	28.00	2.79
2 persons,	63	384	6.05	0.33	84 persons,	1	60	60.00	1.40
3 persons,	52	290	5.58	0.54	221 persons,	1	235	235.00	0.94
4 persons,	83	534	6.43	0.62	*New Bedford. Wd. 1,*	2,500	14,064	5.63	0.94
5 persons,	42	290	6.90	0.72	1 person,	57	259	4.54	0.22
6 persons,	20	135	6.75	0.89	2 persons,	306	1,582	5.91	0.40
7 persons,	20	146	7.30	0.96	3 persons,	395	2,110	5.34	0.56
8 persons,	12	66	5.50	1.45	4 persons,	360	1,960	5.44	0.73
9 persons,	7	37	5.29	1.70	5 persons,	353	1,964	5.56	0.90
10 persons,	3	20	6.67	1.50	6 persons,	316	1,788	5.66	1.06
11 persons,	3	22	7.33	1.50	7 persons,	227	1,358	5.98	1.17
12 persons,	3	21	7.00	1.71	8 persons,	162	1,011	6.24	1.28
15 persons,	1	8	8.00	1.88	9 persons,	130	794	6.11	1.47
16 persons,	1	14	14.00	1.14	10 persons,	70	455	6.50	1.54
Mansfield,	946	6,790	7.18	0.55	11 persons,	70	445	6.36	1.73
1 person,	60	284	4.73	0.21	12 persons,	26	175	6.73	1.78
2 persons,	201	1,371	6.82	0.29	13 persons,	14	92	6.57	1.98
3 persons,	194	1,355	6.98	0.43	14 persons,	5	31	6.20	2.26
4 persons,	179	1,346	7.52	0.53	15 persons,	5	48	9.60	1.56
5 persons,	128	971	7.59	0.66	16 persons,	1	7	7.00	2.29
6 persons,	79	625	7.91	0.76	18 persons,	2	22	11.00	1.64
7 persons,	47	371	7.89	0.89	21 persons,	1	13	13.00	1.62
8 persons,	25	185	7.40	1.08	*New Bedford. Wd. 2,*	1,792	11,269	6.26	0.70
9 persons,	20	176	8.80	1.02	1 person,	69	311	4.51	0.22
10 persons,	8	64	8.00	1.25	2 persons,	346	2,042	5.82	0.34
11 persons,	3	18	6.00	1.83	3 persons,	365	2,257	6.18	0.49
13 persons,	2	24	12.00	1.08	4 persons,	318	1,976	6.21	0.64
NEW BEDFORD,	12,221	75,827	6.20	0.73	5 persons,	231	1,493	6.46	0.77
1 person,	535	2,347	4.39	0.23	6 persons,	159	1,055	6.64	0.90
2 persons,	2,203	12,301	5.58	0.36	7 persons,	118	792	6.71	1.04
3 persons,	2,343	14,106	6.02	0.50	8 persons,	83	569	6.86	1.17
4 persons,	2,041	12,643	6.19	0.65	9 persons,	44	284	6.45	1.39
5 persons,	1,639	10,477	6.39	0.78	10 persons,	29	202	6.97	1.44
6 persons,	1,199	7,764	6.48	0.93	11 persons,	14	94	6.71	1.64
7 persons,	841	5,584	6.64	1.05	12 persons,	8	65	8.13	1.48
8 persons,	553	3,732	6.75	1.19	13 persons,	4	42	10.50	1.24
9 persons,	354	2,323	6.56	1.37	15 persons,	1	7	7.00	2.14
10 persons,	212	1,546	7.29	1.37	16 persons,	1	11	11.00	1.45
11 persons,	149	1,070	7.18	1.53	19 persons,	1	15	15.00	1.27
12 persons,	67	495	7.39	1.62	26 persons,	1	24	24.00	1.08
13 persons,	33	354	10.73	1.21	*New Bedford. Wd. 3,*	1,553	10,431	6.72	0.54
14 persons,	16	138	8.63	1.62	1 person,	110	567	5.15	0.19
15 persons,	13	130	10.00	1.50	2 persons,	463	2,387	5.92	0.34
16 persons,	4	88	22.00	0.73	3 persons,	373	2,468	6.62	0.45
17 persons,	2	20	10.00	1.70	4 persons,	277	1,924	6.95	0.58

ROOMS: OCCUPIED DWELLING HOUSES — Continued.

COUNTIES, CITIES, TOWNS, AND NUMBER OF PERSONS TO A FAMILY.	Number of Families of Specified Size	Total Number of Rooms Occupied	Average Number of Rooms Occupied	Average Number of Persons to a Room
BRISTOL — Con.				
New Bedford. Wd. 3 — Con.				
5 persons,	180	1,340	7.44	0.67
6 persons,	89	688	7.73	0.78
7 persons,	55	444	8.07	0.87
8 persons,	28	234	8.36	0.96
9 persons,	18	154	8.56	1.05
10 persons,	7	63	9.00	1.11
11 persons,	6	65	10.83	1.02
12 persons,	5	55	11.00	1.09
14 persons,	1	14	14.00	1.00
78 persons,	1	28	28.00	2.79
New Bedford. Wd. 4,	1,615	11,745	7.27	0.54
1 person,	140	558	3.99	0.25
2 persons,	356	2,198	6.17	0.32
3 persons,	350	2,361	6.75	0.44
4 persons,	291	2,144	7.37	0.54
5 persons,	200	1,533	7.67	0.65
6 persons,	113	946	8.37	0.72
7 persons,	72	633	8.79	0.80
8 persons,	42	346	8.24	0.97
9 persons,	19	164	8.63	1.04
10 persons,	12	128	10.67	0.94
11 persons,	5	57	11.40	0.96
12 persons,	2	21	10.50	1.14
13 persons,	4	122	30.50	0.43
14 persons,	1	18	18.00	0.78
15 persons,	2	24	12.00	1.25
16 persons,	1	65	65.00	0.25
17 persons,	1	13	13.00	1.31
22 persons,	1	25	25.00	0.88
27 persons,	1	119	119.00	0.23
35 persons,	1	35	35.00	1.00
221 persons,	1	235	235.00	0.94
New Bedford. Wd. 5,	2,172	14,170	6.52	0.64
1 person,	109	462	4.24	0.24
2 persons,	438	2,425	5.54	0.36
3 persons,	440	2,729	6.20	0.48
4 persons,	376	2,438	6.48	0.62
5 persons,	291	2,045	7.03	0.71
6 persons,	199	1,423	7.15	0.84
7 persons,	139	1,044	7.51	0.93
8 persons,	83	654	7.88	1.02
9 persons,	39	336	8.62	1.04
10 persons,	31	308	9.94	1.01
11 persons,	19	193	10.16	1.08
12 persons,	1	6	6.00	2.00
13 persons,	1	14	14.00	0.93
14 persons,	1	10	10.00	1.40
15 persons,	1	16	16.00	0.94
16 persons,	1	5	5.00	3.20
19 persons,	1	24	24.00	0.79
21 persons,	1	14	14.00	1.50
29 persons,	1	24	24.00	1.21
New Bedford. Wd. 6,	2,589	14,208	5.49	0.92
1 person,	50	190	3.80	0.26

COUNTIES, CITIES, TOWNS, AND NUMBER OF PERSONS TO A FAMILY.	Number of Families of Specified Size	Total Number of Rooms Occupied	Average Number of Rooms Occupied	Average Number of Persons to a Room
BRISTOL — Con.				
New Bedford. Wd. 6 — Con.				
2 persons,	354	1,747	4.93	0.41
3 persons,	420	2,181	5.19	0.58
4 persons,	419	2,201	5.25	0.76
5 persons,	384	2,102	5.47	0.91
6 persons,	323	1,864	5.77	1.04
7 persons,	230	1,313	5.71	1.23
8 persons,	155	918	5.92	1.35
9 persons,	104	591	5.68	1.58
10 persons,	63	389	6.19	1.62
11 persons,	35	216	6.17	1.75
12 persons,	25	173	6.92	1.73
13 persons,	10	84	8.40	1.55
14 persons,	8	65	8.13	1.72
15 persons,	4	35	8.75	1.71
17 persons,	1	7	7.00	2.43
18 persons,	1	20	20.00	0.90
29 persons,	1	31	31.00	0.94
37 persons,	1	20	20.00	1.85
84 persons,	1	60	60.00	1.40
North Attleborough,	1,499	10,357	6.91	0.43
1 person,	50	206	4.12	0.24
2 persons,	250	1,517	6.07	0.33
3 persons,	305	2,101	6.89	0.44
4 persons,	300	1,996	6.65	0.60
5 persons,	206	1,502	7.29	0.68
6 persons,	148	1,078	7.28	0.82
7 persons,	98	732	7.47	0.94
8 persons,	67	552	8.24	0.97
9 persons,	39	306	7.85	1.15
10 persons,	19	160	8.42	1.19
11 persons,	7	64	9.14	1.20
12 persons,	4	46	11.50	1.04
13 persons,	1	13	13.00	1.00
14 persons,	2	16	8.00	1.75
15 persons,	1	22	22.00	0.68
22 persons,	1	16	16.00	1.38
27 persons,	1	30	30.00	0.90
Norton,	401	3,080	7.68	0.52
1 person,	33	140	4.24	0.24
2 persons,	77	524	6.81	0.29
3 persons,	88	670	7.61	0.39
4 persons,	68	528	7.76	0.52
5 persons,	62	510	8.23	0.61
6 persons,	33	259	7.85	0.76
7 persons,	20	189	9.45	0.74
8 persons,	7	63	9.00	0.89
9 persons,	4	40	10.00	0.90
10 persons,	5	52	10.40	0.96
11 persons,	2	14	7.00	15.71
12 persons,	1	6	6.00	2.00
67 persons,	1	85	85.00	0.79
Raynham,	397	3,557	8.96	0.43
1 person,	22	130	5.91	0.17
2 persons,	88	776	8.82	0.23

ROOMS: OCCUPIED DWELLING HOUSES — Continued.

COUNTIES, CITIES, TOWNS, AND NUMBER OF PERSONS TO A FAMILY.	Number of Families of Specified Size	Total Number of Rooms Occupied	Average Number of Rooms Occupied	Average Number of Persons to a Room
BRISTOL — Con.				
Raynham — Con.				
3 persons, . .	101	898	8.89	0.34
4 persons, . .	67	604	9.01	0.44
5 persons, . .	47	463	9.85	0.51
6 persons, . .	33	338	10.27	0.58
7 persons, . .	21	186	8.86	0.79
8 persons, . .	5	46	9.20	0.87
9 persons, . .	7	59	8.43	1.07
10 persons, . .	1	4	4.00	2.50
11 persons, . .	4	44	11.00	1.00
12 persons, . .	1	8	8.00	1.50
Rehoboth, . . .	451	3,352	7.43	0.54
1 person, . .	37	213	5.76	0.17
2 persons, . .	96	623	6.49	0.31
3 persons, . .	89	639	7.18	0.42
4 persons, . .	74	589	7.96	0.50
5 persons, . .	56	406	7.25	0.69
6 persons, . .	38	332	8.74	0.69
7 persons, . .	24	186	7.75	0.90
8 persons, . .	18	147	8.17	0.98
9 persons, . .	9	103	11.44	0.79
10 persons, . .	3	23	7.67	1.30
11 persons, . .	1	10	10.00	1.10
12 persons, . .	3	46	15.33	0.78
13 persons, . .	2	18	9.00	1.44
14 persons, . .	1	17	17.00	0.82
Seekonk, . . .	334	2,428	7.27	0.60
1 person, . .	22	99	4.50	0.22
2 persons, . .	54	357	6.61	0.30
3 persons, . .	69	481	6.97	0.43
4 persons, . .	66	494	7.48	0.53
5 persons, . .	35	270	7.71	0.65
6 persons, . .	28	208	7.43	0.81
7 persons, . .	19	144	7.58	0.92
8 persons, . .	12	106	8.83	0.91
9 persons, . .	17	142	8.35	1.08
10 persons, . .	5	44	8.80	1.34
11 persons, . .	1	10	10.00	1.10
12 persons, . .	2	25	12.50	0.96
13 persons, . .	3	35	11.67	1.11
15 persons, . .	1	13	13.00	1.15
Somerset, . . .	497	3,865	7.78	0.51
1 person, . .	47	249	5.30	0.19
2 persons, . .	97	752	7.75	0.26
3 persons, . .	102	758	7.43	0.40
4 persons, . .	76	637	8.38	0.48
5 persons, . .	61	510	8.36	0.60
6 persons, . .	45	376	8.36	0.72
7 persons, . .	32	271	8.47	0.83
8 persons, . .	16	124	7.75	1.03
9 persons, . .	14	121	8.64	1.04
10 persons, . .	3	21	7.00	1.43
11 persons, . .	1	14	14.00	0.79
12 persons, . .	1	7	7.00	1.71
13 persons, . .	2	25	12.50	1.04

COUNTIES, CITIES, TOWNS, AND NUMBER OF PERSONS TO A FAMILY.	Number of Families of Specified Size	Total Number of Rooms Occupied	Average Number of Rooms Occupied	Average Number of Persons to a Room
BRISTOL — Con.				
Swansea, . .	411	3,214	7.82	0.51
1 person, . .	27	170	6.30	0.16
2 persons, . .	83	588	7.08	0.28
3 persons, . .	77	590	7.66	0.39
4 persons, . .	95	754	7.94	0.50
5 persons, . .	50	422	8.44	0.59
6 persons, . .	31	255	8.23	0.73
7 persons, . .	24	215	8.96	0.78
8 persons, . .	10	76	7.60	1.05
9 persons, . .	5	41	8.20	1.10
10 persons, . .	6	65	10.83	0.92
11 persons, . .	2	23	11.50	0.96
12 persons, . .	1	15	15.00	0.80
TAUNTON, . .	5,885	41,645	7.08	0.65
1 person, . .	229	1,079	4.90	0.20
2 persons, . .	973	6,216	6.39	0.31
3 persons, . .	1,169	8,053	6.89	0.44
4 persons, . .	1,060	7,377	6.96	0.57
5 persons, . .	878	6,336	7.22	0.69
6 persons, . .	636	4,607	7.24	0.83
7 persons, . .	373	2,733	7.33	0.96
8 persons, . .	249	1,826	7.33	1.09
9 persons, . .	152	1,068	7.22	1.25
10 persons, . .	78	651	8.35	1.20
11 persons, . .	54	420	7.78	1.41
12 persons, . .	16	161	10.06	1.19
13 persons, . .	7	82	11.71	1.41
14 persons, . .	5	77	15.40	0.91
15 persons, . .	1	7	7.00	2.14
16 persons, . .	2	28	14.00	1.14
17 persons, . .	1	12	12.00	1.42
18 persons, . .	1	22	22.00	0.82
19 persons, . .	3	57	19.00	1.00
20 persons, . .	1	15	15.00	1.33
21 persons, . .	1	32	32.00	0.66
22 persons, . .	1	29	29.00	0.76
28 persons, . .	1	20	20.00	1.40
46 persons, . .	1	8	8.00	5.75
65 persons, . .	1	15	15.00	4.33
957 persons, . .	1	684	684.00	1.40
Taunton. Ward 1, .	669	4,963	7.42	0.76
1 person, . .	17	89	5.24	0.19
2 persons, . .	118	831	7.04	0.28
3 persons, . .	147	1,070	7.28	0.41
4 persons, . .	129	956	7.41	0.54
5 persons, . .	113	874	7.73	0.65
6 persons, . .	73	574	7.86	0.76
7 persons, . .	29	236	8.14	0.86
8 persons, . .	20	157	7.85	1.02
9 persons, . .	11	74	6.73	1.34
10 persons, . .	8	74	9.25	1.08
11 persons, . .	2	15	7.50	1.47
12 persons, . .	1	5	5.00	2.40
13 persons, . .	1	8	8.00	1.63

ROOMS: OCCUPIED DWELLING HOUSES — Continued.

Counties, Cities, Towns, and Number of Persons to a Family.	Number of Families of Specified Size	Total Number of Rooms Occupied	Average Number of Rooms Occupied	Average Number of Persons to a Room	Counties, Cities, Towns, and Number of Persons to a Family.	Number of Families of Specified Size	Total Number of Rooms Occupied	Average Number of Rooms Occupied	Average Number of Persons to a Room
BRISTOL — Con.					**BRISTOL — Con.**				
Taunton. Ward 2,	687	5,453	7.94	0.55	*Taunton. Ward 5 — Con.*				
1 person,	39	170	4.36	0.23	6 persons,	107	691	6.46	0.93
2 persons,	133	907	6.82	0.29	7 persons,	70	458	6.54	1.07
3 persons,	147	1,113	7.57	0.40	8 persons,	40	286	7.15	1.12
4 persons,	124	993	8.01	0.50	9 persons,	31	215	6.94	1.30
5 persons,	85	741	8.72	0.57	10 persons,	8	75	9.38	1.07
6 persons,	78	691	8.86	0.68	11 persons,	8	58	7.25	1.52
7 persons,	37	334	9.03	0.78	12 persons,	3	19	6.33	1.89
8 persons,	11	90	8.18	0.98	13 persons,	1	5	5.00	2.60
9 persons,	12	112	9.33	0.96	14 persons,	2	16	8.00	1.75
10 persons,	8	91	11.38	0.88	16 persons,	2	28	14.00	1.14
11 persons,	4	39	9.75	1.13	19 persons,	1	23	23.00	0.83
12 persons,	3	55	18.33	0.65	*Taunton. Ward 6,*	715	4,858	6.79	0.64
13 persons,	2	32	16.00	0.81	1 person,	24	118	4.92	0.20
14 persons,	1	48	48.00	0.29	2 persons,	126	816	6.48	0.31
17 persons,	1	12	12.00	1.42	3 persons,	138	923	6.69	0.45
19 persons,	1	17	17.00	1.12	4 persons,	135	942	6.98	0.57
16 persons,	1	8	8.00	5.75	5 persons,	116	797	6.87	0.73
Taunton. Ward 3,	691	4,730	6.85	0.64	6 persons,	70	476	6.80	0.88
1 person,	46	223	4.85	0.21	7 persons,	41	277	6.76	1.04
2 persons,	116	736	6.29	0.32	8 persons,	35	256	7.31	1.09
3 persons,	128	828	6.47	0.46	9 persons,	14	106	7.57	1.19
4 persons,	135	914	6.77	0.50	10 persons,	8	65	8.13	1.23
5 persons,	101	679	6.72	0.74	11 persons,	3	18	6.00	1.83
6 persons,	50	376	7.52	0.80	12 persons,	4	42	10.50	1.14
7 persons,	40	287	7.18	0.98	18 persons,	1	22	22.00	0.82
8 persons,	30	224	7.47	1.07	*Taunton. Ward 7,*	673	4,478	6.65	0.68
9 persons,	15	138	9.27	0.97	1 person,	20	112	5.60	0.18
10 persons,	7	51	7.29	1.37	2 persons,	110	677	6.15	0.32
11 persons,	15	133	8.87	1.24	3 persons,	153	1,043	6.82	0.44
12 persons,	1	10	10.00	1.20	4 persons,	111	732	6.77	0.59
13 persons,	2	30	15.00	0.87	5 persons,	96	655	6.82	0.73
14 persons,	1	8	8.00	1.75	6 persons,	68	440	6.47	0.93
19 persons,	1	17	17.00	1.12	7 persons,	44	290	6.59	1.06
21 persons,	1	32	32.00	0.66	8 persons,	32	239	7.47	1.07
22 persons,	1	29	29.00	0.76	9 persons,	20	128	6.40	1.41
28 persons,	1	20	20.00	1.40	10 persons,	9	58	6.44	1.55
Taunton. Ward 4,	737	5,782	7.85	0.52	11 persons,	7	58	8.29	1.33
1 person,	35	188	5.37	0.19	12 persons,	1	6	6.00	2.00
2 persons,	134	956	7.13	0.28	14 persons,	1	5	5.00	2.80
3 persons,	174	1,364	7.84	0.38	65 persons,	1	15	15.00	4.33
4 persons,	122	960	7.87	0.51	*Taunton. Ward 8,*	808	6,164	6.86	0.88
5 persons,	107	909	8.50	0.59	1 person,	16	74	4.63	0.22
6 persons,	78	645	8.27	0.73	2 persons,	120	640	5.33	0.38
7 persons,	46	412	8.96	0.78	3 persons,	120	711	5.93	0.51
8 persons,	25	206	8.24	0.97	4 persons,	172	1,005	5.84	0.68
9 persons,	11	86	7.82	1.15	5 persons,	151	958	6.34	0.79
10 persons,	4	47	11.75	0.85	6 persons,	112	714	6.38	0.94
12 persons,	1	9	9.00	1.33	7 persons,	66	439	6.95	1.05
Taunton. Ward 5,	815	5,217	6.40	0.74	8 persons,	56	368	6.57	1.22
1 person,	23	105	4.57	0.22	9 persons,	38	238	6.26	1.44
2 persons,	116	658	5.68	0.35	10 persons,	26	190	7.31	1.37
3 persons,	162	1,001	6.18	0.49	11 persons,	15	80	6.80	1.97
4 persons,	132	855	6.48	0.62	12 persons,	2	15	7.50	1.60
5 persons,	108	723	6.63	0.75	13 persons,	1	7	7.00	1.86

ROOMS: OCCUPIED DWELLING HOUSES — Continued.

Counties, Cities, Towns, and Number of Persons to a Family	Number of Families of Specified Size	Total Number of Rooms Occupied	Average Number of Rooms Occupied	Average Number of Persons to a Room
BRISTOL - Con.				
Taunton. Ward 8 — Con.				
15 persons,	1	7	7.00	2.14
20 persons,	1	15	15.00	1.33
357 persons,	1	684	684.00	1.40
Westport,	702	5,008	7.13	0.53
1 person,	59	327	5.54	0.18
2 persons,	145	1,011	6.97	0.29
3 persons,	160	1,132	7.08	0.42
4 persons,	126	863	6.85	0.58
5 persons,	87	695	7.99	0.63
6 persons,	54	431	7.98	0.75
7 persons,	29	237	8.17	0.86
8 persons,	16	114	7.13	1.12
9 persons,	13	96	7.38	1.22
10 persons,	7	42	6.00	1.67
11 persons,	5	52	10.40	1.06
13 persons,	1	8	8.00	1.63
DUKES.				
Chilmark,	95	754	7.91	0.40
1 person,	14	90	6.43	0.16
2 persons,	19	141	7.42	0.27
3 persons,	29	239	8.24	0.36
4 persons,	16	134	8.31	0.48
5 persons,	6	54	9.00	0.56
6 persons,	7	53	7.57	0.79
7 persons,	3	30	10.00	0.70
8 persons,	1	10	10.00	0.80
Cottage City,	313	2,279	7.28	0.46
1 person,	46	269	5.85	0.17
2 persons,	85	567	6.83	0.29
3 persons,	65	508	7.82	0.38
4 persons,	48	377	7.85	0.51
5 persons,	33	265	8.03	0.62
6 persons,	12	114	9.50	0.63
7 persons,	15	106	7.07	0.80
8 persons,	6	38	6.33	1.26
9 persons,	2	11	5.50	1.64
10 persons,	2	17	8.50	1.18
11 persons,	1	7	7.00	1.57
Edgartown,	377	2,932	7.78	0.38
1 person,	63	367	5.83	0.17
2 persons,	124	965	7.78	0.26
3 persons,	71	606	8.54	0.35
4 persons,	56	461	8.23	0.49
5 persons,	29	222	7.66	0.65
6 persons,	15	136	9.07	0.66
7 persons,	12	117	9.75	0.72
8 persons,	5	44	8.80	0.91
9 persons,	2	14	7.00	1.29
Gay Head,	40	215	5.38	0.79
1 person,	5	29	5.80	0.17
2 persons,	8	35	4.38	0.46
3 persons,	8	48	6.00	0.50

Counties, Cities, Towns, and Number of Persons to a Family	Number of Families of Specified Size	Total Number of Rooms Occupied	Average Number of Rooms Occupied	Average Number of Persons to a Room
DUKES - Con.				
Gay Head — Con.				
4 persons,	2	15	7.50	0.53
5 persons,	4	23	5.75	0.87
6 persons,	4	16	4.00	1.50
7 persons,	4	23	5.75	1.22
8 persons,	3	17	5.67	1.41
9 persons,	1	5	5.00	1.80
11 persons,	1	4	4.00	2.75
Gosnold,	38	279	7.34	0.50
1 person,	3	39	13.00	0.08
2 persons,	5	30	6.00	0.33
3 persons,	14	82	5.86	0.51
4 persons,	11	76	6.91	0.58
5 persons,	2	15	7.50	0.67
7 persons,	1	7	7.00	1.00
8 persons,	1	8	8.00	1.00
16 persons,	1	22	22.00	0.73
Tisbury,	289	2,236	7.74	0.45
1 person,	42	249	5.93	0.17
2 persons,	72	531	7.38	0.27
3 persons,	55	408	7.42	0.40
4 persons,	50	414	8.28	0.48
5 persons,	29	236	8.14	0.64
6 persons,	18	142	7.89	0.76
7 persons,	8	74	9.25	0.76
8 persons,	3	26	8.67	0.92
9 persons,	3	88	9.78	0.92
11 persons,	1	12	12.00	0.92
12 persons,	1	11	11.00	1.09
14 persons,	1	45	45.00	0.31
West Tisbury,	154	1,183	7.68	0.39
1 person,	17	110	6.47	0.15
2 persons,	47	348	7.40	0.27
3 persons,	46	370	8.04	0.37
4 persons,	25	201	8.04	0.50
5 persons,	10	70	7.00	0.71
6 persons,	4	37	9.25	0.65
7 persons,	3	29	9.67	0.72
8 persons,	2	18	9.00	0.89
ESSEX.				
Amesbury,	2,281	15,395	6.74	0.65
1 person,	88	399	4.53	0.22
2 persons,	365	2,266	6.21	0.32
3 persons,	481	3,143	6.53	0.46
4 persons,	433	2,923	6.75	0.59
5 persons,	327	2,210	6.76	0.74
6 persons,	205	1,578	7.69	0.85
7 persons,	137	964	7.04	0.99
8 persons,	68	467	6.87	1.46
9 persons,	54	437	8.09	1.11
10 persons,	29	217	7.48	1.34
11 persons,	14	167	11.36	0.92
12 persons,	8	93	11.63	1.03
13 persons,	6	55	9.17	1.42

ROOMS: OCCUPIED DWELLING HOUSES — Continued.

COUNTIES, CITIES, TOWNS, AND NUMBER OF PERSONS TO A FAMILY.	Number of Families of Specified Size	Total Number of Rooms Occupied	Average Number of Rooms Occupied	Average Number of Persons to a Room	COUNTIES, CITIES, TOWNS, AND NUMBER OF PERSONS TO A FAMILY.	Number of Families of Specified Size	Total Number of Rooms Occupied	Average Number of Rooms Occupied	Average Number of Persons to a Room
ESSEX - Con.					ESSEX — Con.				
Amesbury — Con.					Beverly. Ward 1 — Con.				
16 persons,	3	28	9.33	1.71	2 persons,	99	549	5.55	0.36
19 persons,	1	18	18.00	1.06	3 persons,	109	652	5.98	0.50
26 persons,	1	50	50.00	0.52	4 persons,	108	718	6.65	0.60
68 persons,	1	50	50.00	1.36	5 persons,	92	628	6.83	0.73
Andover,	1,296	10,039	7.75	0.61	6 persons,	69	492	7.13	0.84
1 person,	58	270	4.66	0.21	7 persons,	31	225	7.26	0.96
2 persons,	208	1,332	6.40	0.31	8 persons,	27	206	7.63	1.05
3 persons,	203	1,384	6.82	0.44	9 persons,	11	81	7.36	1.22
4 persons,	252	1,802	7.15	0.56	10 persons,	8	89	11.13	0.90
5 persons,	188	1,458	7.76	0.64	11 persons,	4	53	13.25	0.83
6 persons,	150	1,199	7.99	0.75	12 persons,	3	50	16.67	0.72
7 persons,	96	755	7.86	0.89	13 persons,	2	22	11.00	1.18
8 persons,	53	452	8.53	0.94	15 persons,	1	8	8.00	1.88
9 persons,	30	254	8.47	1.06	16 persons,	2	36	18.00	0.89
10 persons,	21	218	10.38	0.96	22 persons,	1	50	50.00	0.44
11 persons,	13	147	11.31	0.97	28 persons,	1	30	30.00	0.93
12 persons,	8	94	11.75	1.02	Beverly. Ward 2,	618	4,170	6.75	0.59
13 persons,	2	35	17.50	0.74	1 person,	51	213	4.18	0.24
14 persons,	5	91	18.20	0.77	2 persons,	116	689	5.94	0.34
15 persons,	1	24	24.00	0.63	3 persons,	139	873	6.28	0.48
16 persons,	1	22	22.00	0.73	4 persons,	104	717	6.89	0.58
22 persons,	1	50	50.00	0.44	5 persons,	80	631	7.89	0.63
23 persons,	1	18	18.00	1.28	6 persons,	52	414	7.96	0.75
24 persons,	1	70	70.00	0.34	7 persons,	41	317	7.73	0.91
30 persons,	1	120	120.00	0.25	8 persons,	17	153	9.00	0.89
32 persons,	1	25	25.00	1.28	9 persons,	7	63	9.00	1.00
59 persons,	1	59	59.00	1.00	10 persons,	3	19	6.33	1.58
82 persons,	1	160	160.00	0.51	11 persons,	4	29	7.25	1.52
BEVERLY,	2,914	18,811	6.46	0.63	13 persons,	2	25	12.50	1.04
1 person,	194	827	4.26	0.23	14 persons,	1	14	14.00	1.00
2 persons,	559	3,138	5.61	0.26	15 persons,	1	13	13.00	1.15
3 persons,	642	3,975	6.19	0.48	Beverly. Ward 3,	610	3,805	6.24	0.64
4 persons,	521	3,358	6.45	0.62	1 person,	36	147	4.08	0.24
5 persons,	390	2,685	6.88	0.73	2 persons,	132	730	5.53	0.36
6 persons,	256	1,864	7.28	0.82	3 persons,	133	807	6.07	0.49
7 persons,	156	1,131	7.25	0.97	4 persons,	117	726	6.21	0.64
8 persons,	94	734	7.81	1.02	5 persons,	70	478	6.83	0.73
9 persons,	41	321	7.83	1.15	6 persons,	47	329	7.00	0.86
10 persons,	24	231	9.63	1.04	7 persons,	27	189	7.00	1.00
11 persons,	12	108	9.00	1.22	8 persons,	28	225	8.04	1.00
12 persons,	5	64	12.80	0.94	9 persons,	9	61	6.78	1.33
13 persons,	4	47	11.75	1.11	10 persons,	5	44	8.80	1.14
14 persons,	3	33	11.00	1.27	11 persons,	1	7	7.00	1.57
15 persons,	3	35	11.67	1.29	12 persons,	1	9	9.00	1.33
16 persons,	3	54	18.00	0.89	14 persons,	1	7	7.00	2.00
17 persons,	1	25	25.00	0.68	16 persons,	1	18	18.00	0.89
19 persons,	1	24	24.00	0.79	17 persons,	1	25	25.00	0.68
22 persons,	1	50	50.00	0.44	29 persons,	1	3	3.00	9.67
24 persons,	1	24	24.00	1.00	Beverly. Ward 4,	528	3,224	6.11	0.62
27 persons,	1	50	50.00	0.54	1 person,	38	176	4.63	0.22
28 persons,	1	30	30.00	0.93	2 persons,	115	641	5.57	0.36
29 persons,	1	3	3.00	9.67	3 persons,	126	759	6.02	0.50
Beverly. Ward 1,	538	4,014	6.71	0.67	4 persons,	82	478	5.83	0.69
1 person,	30	125	4.17	0.24	5 persons,	72	459	6.38	0.78

ROOMS: OCCUPIED DWELLING HOUSES — Continued.

COUNTIES, CITIES, TOWNS, AND NUMBER OF PERSONS TO A FAMILY.	Number of Families of Specified Size	Total Number of Rooms Occupied	Average Number of Rooms Occupied	Average Number of Persons to a Room.	COUNTIES, CITIES, TOWNS, AND NUMBER OF PERSONS TO A FAMILY.	Number of Families of Specified Size	Total Number of Rooms Occupied	Average Number of Rooms Occupied	Average Number of Persons to a Room.
ESSEX — Con.					ESSEX — Con.				
Beverly. Ward 4 — Con.					Bradford — Con.				
6 persons,	49	339	6.92	0.87	6 persons,	103	714	6.93	0.87
7 persons,	25	186	7.44	0.94	7 persons,	59	445	7.54	0.93
8 persons,	8	55	6.88	1.16	8 persons,	25	198	7.92	1.01
9 persons,	6	42	7.00	1.29	9 persons,	18	145	8.06	1.12
10 persons,	4	26	6.50	1.54	10 persons,	11	100	9.09	1.10
11 persons,	1	8	8.00	1.38	11 persons,	2	19	9.50	1.16
12 persons,	1	5	5.00	2.40	12 persons,	2	16	8.00	1.50
27 persons,	1	50	50.00	0.54	13 persons,	2	16	8.00	1.62
Beverly. Ward 5.	306	2,055	6.72	0.59	14 persons,	1	14	14.00	1.00
1 person,	11	51	4.64	0.22	16 persons,	1	24	24.00	0.67
2 persons,	51	303	5.94	0.34	20 persons,	1	20	20.00	1.00
3 persons,	85	561	6.60	0.45	116 persons,	1	325	325.00	0.36
4 persons,	63	417	6.62	0.60	Danvers,	1,653	12,275	7.43	0.67
5 persons,	49	326	6.65	0.75	1 person,	72	333	4.63	0.22
6 persons,	19	159	8.37	0.72	2 persons,	294	1,815	6.17	0.32
7 persons,	13	95	7.31	0.96	3 persons,	359	2,417	6.73	0.45
8 persons,	9	68	7.56	1.06	4 persons,	296	2,174	7.34	0.54
9 persons,	3	29	9.67	0.93	5 persons,	227	1,645	7.25	0.69
10 persons,	2	34	17.00	0.59	6 persons,	157	1,229	7.83	0.77
14 persons,	1	12	12.00	1.17	7 persons,	110	818	7.44	0.94
Beverly. Ward 6,	254	1,543	6.07	0.67	8 persons,	59	511	8.66	0.92
1 person,	28	115	4.11	0.24	9 persons,	34	305	8.97	1.00
2 persons,	46	226	4.91	0.41	10 persons,	18	162	9.00	1.11
3 persons,	50	323	6.46	0.46	11 persons,	5	46	9.20	1.20
4 persons,	47	302	6.43	0.62	12 persons,	4	35	8.75	1.37
5 persons,	27	163	6.04	0.83	13 persons,	7	96	13.71	0.95
6 persons,	20	131	6.55	0.92	14 persons,	3	31	10.33	1.35
7 persons,	19	119	6.26	1.12	15 persons,	2	28	14.00	1.07
8 persons,	5	27	5.40	1.48	16 persons,	1	16	16.00	1.00
9 persons,	5	45	9.00	1.00	17 persons,	1	19	19.00	0.89
10 persons,	2	19	9.50	1.05	18 persons,	1	18	18.00	1.00
11 persons,	2	11	5.50	2.00	19 persons,	1	7	7.00	2.71
15 persons,	1	14	14.00	1.07	32 persons,	1	12	12.00	2.67
19 persons,	1	24	24.00	0.79	1,087 persons,	1	558	558.00	1.95
24 persons,	1	24	24.00	1.00	Essex,	445	2,858	6.42	0.56
Boxford,	186	1,543	8.30	0.47	1 person,	27	129	4.78	0.21
1 person,	19	133	7.00	0.14	2 persons,	114	695	6.10	0.33
2 persons,	41	334	8.15	0.25	3 persons,	114	720	6.32	0.48
3 persons,	35	272	7.77	0.39	4 persons,	84	524	6.24	0.64
4 persons,	41	341	8.32	0.48	5 persons,	47	315	6.70	0.75
5 persons,	14	133	9.50	0.53	6 persons,	28	220	7.86	0.76
6 persons,	10	80	8.00	0.75	7 persons,	17	122	7.18	0.98
7 persons,	8	80	10.00	0.70	8 persons,	6	61	10.17	0.79
8 persons,	6	53	8.83	0.91	9 persons,	3	18	6.00	1.50
9 persons,	2	21	10.50	0.86	10 persons,	3	25	8.33	1.20
10 persons,	7	62	8.86	1.13	12 persons,	1	14	14.00	0.86
11 persons,	2	24	12.00	0.92	15 persons,	1	15	15.00	1.00
13 persons,	1	10	10.00	1.30	Georgetown,	541	3,973	7.34	0.52
Bradford,	1,121	8,067	7.20	0.59	1 person,	41	204	4.80	0.20
1 person,	24	116	4.83	0.21	2 persons,	121	843	6.97	0.29
2 persons,	204	1,296	6.24	0.32	3 persons,	120	894	7.43	0.40
3 persons,	275	1,846	6.71	0.45	4 persons,	85	624	7.34	0.54
4 persons,	222	1,581	7.12	0.56	5 persons,	76	624	8.21	0.61
5 persons,	170	1,222	7.19	0.70	6 persons,	46	360	7.83	0.77

ROOMS: OCCUPIED DWELLING HOUSES — Continued.

COUNTIES, CITIES, TOWNS, AND NUMBER OF PERSONS TO A FAMILY.	Number of Families of Specified Size	Total Number of Rooms Occupied	Average Number of Rooms Occupied	Average Number of Persons to a Room	COUNTIES, CITIES, TOWNS, AND NUMBER OF PERSONS TO A FAMILY.	Number of Families of Specified Size	Total Number of Rooms Occupied	Average Number of Rooms Occupied	Average Number of Persons to a Room
ESSEX — Con.					**ESSEX — Con.**				
Georgetown — Con.					*GLOUCESTER — Con.*				
7 persons,	27	233	8.63	0.81	66 persons,	1	10	10.00	6.60
8 persons,	10	76	7.60	1.05	71 persons,	1	10	10.00	7.10
9 persons,	10	69	6.90	1.30	75 persons,	2	150	75.00	1.00
10 persons,	3	37	12.33	0.81	77 persons,	1	14	14.00	5.50
11 persons,	2	15	7.50	1.47	78 persons,	1	78	78.00	1.00
GLOUCESTER,	5,416	32,156	5.94	0.88	80 persons,	1	80	80.00	1.00
1 person,	216	899	4.16	0.24	82 persons,	2	37	18.50	4.43
2 persons,	821	4,166	5.07	0.39	85 persons,	1	7	7.00	12.14
3 persons,	1,057	5,675	5.37	0.56	91 persons,	1	20	20.00	4.55
4 persons,	933	5,220	5.59	0.71	93 persons,	1	12	12.00	7.75
5 persons,	738	4,494	6.09	0.82	98 persons,	1	17	17.00	5.82
6 persons,	584	3,711	6.35	0.94	105 persons,	1	21	21.00	5.00
7 persons,	383	2,416	6.31	1.11	109 persons,	1	18	18.00	6.06
8 persons,	242	1,632	6.66	1.20	111 persons,	1	111	111.00	1.00
9 persons,	124	784	6.32	1.42	*Gloucester, Ward 1,*	686	4,140	5.95	0.77
10 persons,	62	410	6.61	1.51	1 person,	29	162	5.59	0.18
11 persons,	57	423	7.42	1.48	2 persons,	102	474	4.65	0.43
12 persons,	30	210	7.00	1.71	3 persons,	137	700	5.11	0.59
13 persons,	19	132	6.95	1.87	4 persons,	138	770	5.58	0.72
14 persons,	23	180	7.83	1.79	5 persons,	104	665	6.39	0.78
15 persons,	10	108	10.80	1.39	6 persons,	81	528	6.52	0.92
16 persons,	11	96	8.73	1.83	7 persons,	40	281	7.03	1.00
17 persons,	14	116	8.29	2.05	8 persons,	26	172	6.62	1.21
18 persons,	9	68	7.56	2.38	9 persons,	18	129	7.17	1.26
19 persons,	5	54	10.80	1.76	10 persons,	6	42	7.00	1.43
20 persons,	6	45	7.50	2.67	11 persons,	7	51	7.29	1.51
21 persons,	2	15	7.50	2.80	12 persons,	4	28	7.00	1.71
22 persons,	4	52	13.00	1.69	13 persons,	1	8	8.00	1.63
23 persons,	2	15	7.50	3.07	17 persons,	1	9	9.00	1.89
24 persons,	4	34	8.50	2.82	20 persons,	1	10	10.00	2.00
25 persons,	3	43	14.33	1.74	111 persons,	1	111	111.00	1.00
27 persons,	3	35	11.67	2.31	*Gloucester, Ward 2,*	982	4,900	4.99	1.03
28 persons,	2	13	6.50	4.31	1 person,	35	168	3.09	0.52
29 persons,	2	21	10.50	2.76	2 persons,	131	538	4.11	0.49
30 persons,	1	18	18.00	1.67	3 persons,	179	776	4.34	0.69
31 persons,	1	18	18.00	1.72	4 persons,	173	824	4.76	0.84
32 persons,	1	12	12.00	2.67	5 persons,	137	695	5.07	0.99
33 persons,	2	23	11.50	2.87	6 persons,	116	597	5.15	1.17
35 persons,	2	42	21.00	1.67	7 persons,	74	411	5.55	1.26
36 persons,	2	20	10.00	3.60	8 persons,	51	305	5.94	1.35
37 persons,	1	50	50.00	0.74	9 persons,	33	174	5.27	1.70
39 persons,	3	42	14.00	2.79	10 persons,	17	103	6.06	1.65
40 persons,	1	9	9.00	1.44	11 persons,	13	89	6.85	1.61
41 persons,	2	15	7.50	5.47	12 persons,	2	11	5.50	2.18
42 persons,	1	6	6.00	7.00	13 persons,	1	6	6.00	2.17
43 persons,	1	14	14.00	3.07	14 persons,	4	30	7.50	1.87
46 persons,	2	26	13.00	3.54	15 persons,	2	14	7.00	2.14
47 persons,	2	29	14.50	3.24	16 persons,	1	7	7.00	2.29
49 persons,	2	33	16.50	2.97	18 persons,	3	30	10.00	1.70
50 persons,	2	25	12.50	4.00	21 persons,	1	8	8.00	2.25
51 persons,	2	18	9.00	5.67	23 persons,	1	7	7.00	3.29
54 persons,	1	22	22.00	2.45	33 persons,	1	16	16.00	2.06
56 persons,	2	65	32.50	1.72	39 persons,	1	12	12.00	3.25
57 persons,	3	37	12.33	4.62					

ROOMS: OCCUPIED DWELLING HOUSES — Continued.

COUNTIES, CITIES, TOWNS, AND NUMBER OF PERSONS TO A FAMILY.	Number of Families of Specified Size	Total Number of Rooms Occupied	Average Number of Rooms Occupied	Average Number of Persons to a Room	COUNTIES, CITIES, TOWNS, AND NUMBER OF PERSONS TO A FAMILY.	Number of Families of Specified Size	Total Number of Rooms Occupied	Average Number of Rooms Occupied	Average Number of Persons to a Room
ESSEX — Con.					ESSEX — Con.				
Gloucester, Ward 2 — Con.					*Gloucester, Ward 4,*	520	3,541	6.81	0.98
45 persons, . .	1	8	8.00	5.13	1 person, . .	31	119	3.84	0.26
46 persons, . .	1	10	10.00	4.60	2 persons, . .	67	320	4.78	0.42
47 persons, . .	1	21	21.00	2.24	3 persons, . .	90	507	5.63	0.53
49 persons, . .	1	17	17.00	2.88	4 persons, . .	72	451	6.26	0.64
78 persons, . .	1	78	78.00	1.00	5 persons, . .	66	455	6.89	0.73
Gloucester, Ward 3,	743	4,738	6.38	1.10	6 persons, . .	51	349	6.84	0.88
1 person,	24	81	3.38	0.30	7 persons, . .	45	321	7.13	0.98
2 persons, . .	90	433	4.81	0.42	8 persons, . .	27	170	6.30	1.27
3 persons, . .	141	759	5.38	0.56	9 persons, . .	11	74	6.73	1.34
4 persons, . .	118	659	5.59	0.72	10 persons, . .	3	22	7.33	1.36
5 persons, . .	107	702	6.56	0.76	11 persons, . .	10	104	10.40	1.06
6 persons, . .	82	560	6.83	0.88	12 persons, . .	4	23	5.75	2.09
7 persons, . .	59	404	6.85	1.02	13 persons, . .	3	24	8.00	1.63
8 persons, . .	35	261	7.46	1.07	14 persons, . .	4	48	12.00	1.17
9 persons, . .	11	59	5.36	1.68	15 persons, . .	3	53	17.67	0.85
10 persons, . .	8	61	7.63	1.31	16 persons, . .	3	27	9.00	1.78
11 persons, . .	5	43	8.60	1.28	17 persons, . .	3	21	7.00	2.43
12 persons, . .	7	58	8.29	1.45	18 persons, . .	2	19	9.50	1.89
13 persons, . .	5	45	9.00	1.44	19 persons, . .	4	49	12.25	1.55
14 persons, . .	4	27	6.75	2.07	20 persons, . .	3	25	8.33	2.40
15 persons, . .	1	12	12.00	1.25	21 persons, . .	1	8	8.00	2.63
16 persons, . .	3	20	6.67	2.40	24 persons, . .	1	15	15.00	1.60
17 persons, . .	3	28	9.33	1.82	25 persons, . .	2	37	18.50	1.35
18 persons, . .	3	23	7.67	2.35	27 persons, . .	2	25	12.50	2.16
20 persons, . .	1	4	4.00	5.00	35 persons, . .	1	14	14.00	2.50
22 persons, . .	4	52	13.00	1.69	42 persons, . .	1	6	6.00	7.00
23 persons, . .	1	8	8.00	2.88	43 persons, . .	1	14	14.00	3.07
24 persons, . .	1	6	6.00	4.00	46 persons, . .	1	16	16.00	2.88
27 persons, . .	1	10	10.00	2.70	49 persons, . .	1	16	16.00	3.06
28 persons, . .	2	13	6.50	4.31	50 persons, . .	1	10	10.00	5.00
29 persons, . .	1	7	7.00	4.14	56 persons, . .	2	65	32.50	1.70
30 persons, . .	1	18	18.00	1.67	75 persons, . .	1	75	75.00	1.02
32 persons, . .	1	12	12.00	2.67	82 persons, . .	1	22	22.00	3.73
36 persons, . .	1	7	7.00	4.71	91 persons, . .	1	20	20.00	4.55
38 persons, . .	1	28	28.00	1.25	99 persons, . .	1	17	17.00	5.82
30 persons, . .	2	20	10.00	3.40	*Gloucester, Ward 5,*	893	5,844	6.54	0.74
32 persons. . .	2	30	15.00	2.00	1 person,	20	66	3.30	0.30
40 persons, . .	1	9	9.00	4.44	2 persons, . .	137	796	5.81	0.34
41 persons, . .	1	7	7.00	5.86	3 persons, . .	191	1,163	6.09	0.49
47 persons, . .	1	8	8.00	5.88	4 persons, . .	171	1,028	6.01	0.67
50 persons, . .	1	15	15.00	3.33	5 persons, . .	115	767	6.67	0.75
52 persons, . .	1	8	8.00	6.38	6 persons, . .	98	735	7.50	0.80
54 persons, . .	1	22	22.00	2.45	7 persons, . .	60	424	7.07	0.99
57 persons, . .	3	37	12.33	4.62	8 persons, . .	40	277	6.93	1.16
64 persons, . .	1	10	10.00	6.60	9 persons, . .	22	154	7.00	1.29
72 persons, . .	1	10	10.00	7.10	10 persons, . .	9	74	8.22	1.22
75 persons, . .	1	75	75.00	1.00	11 persons, . .	4	29	7.25	1.52
77 persons, . .	1	14	14.00	5.50	12 persons, . .	5	54	6.80	1.76
82 persons, . .	1	15	15.00	5.47	13 persons, . .	3	20	6.67	1.95
85 persons, . .	1	7	7.00	12.14	14 persons, . .	4	38	9.50	1.47
96 persons, . .	1	12	12.00	7.75	16 persons, . .	2	18	9.00	1.78
102 persons, . .	1	21	21.00	5.00	17 persons, . .	2	18	9.00	1.89
109 persons, . .	1	18	18.00	6.06	18 persons, . .	2	12	6.00	3.00

ROOMS: OCCUPIED DWELLING HOUSES — Continued.

COUNTIES, CITIES, TOWNS, AND NUMBER OF PERSONS TO A FAMILY.	Number of Families of Specified Size	Total Number of Rooms Occupied	Average Number of Rooms Occupied	Average Number of Persons to a Room	COUNTIES, CITIES, TOWNS, AND NUMBER OF PERSONS TO A FAMILY.	Number of Families of Specified Size	Total Number of Rooms Occupied	Average Number of Rooms Occupied	Average Number of Persons to a Room
ESSEX — Con.					**ESSEX — Con.**				
Gloucester. Ward 5 — Con.					*Gloucester. Ward 8 — Con.*				
24 persons,	2	13	6.50	3.69	12 persons,	1	8	8.00	1.50
25 persons,	1	6	6.00	4.17	13 persons,	1	9	9.00	1.44
29 persons,	1	14	14.00	2.07	15 persons,	1	14	14.00	1.07
31 persons,	1	18	18.00	1.72	16 persons,	1	19	19.00	0.84
37 persons,	1	50	50.00	0.74	Groveland,	560	3,631	6.48	0.64
51 persons,	1	10	10.00	5.10	1 person,	33	166	5.03	0.20
80 persons,	1	80	80.00	1.00	2 persons,	109	681	6.25	0.32
Gloucester. Ward 6,	704	4,048	5.75	0.73	3 persons,	123	794	6.46	0.46
1 person,	31	148	4.77	0.21	4 persons,	92	617	6.71	0.60
2 persons,	128	705	5.51	0.36	5 persons,	78	503	6.45	0.78
3 persons,	156	889	5.70	0.53	6 persons,	51	338	6.63	0.91
4 persons,	133	747	5.62	0.71	7 persons,	35	240	6.86	1.02
5 persons,	89	732	5.98	0.84	8 persons,	10	60	6.00	1.33
6 persons,	69	422	6.12	0.98	9 persons,	12	79	6.58	1.37
7 persons,	46	269	5.85	1.20	10 persons,	4	33	8.25	1.21
8 persons,	25	150	6.00	1.33	11 persons,	3	19	6.33	1.74
9 persons,	10	66	6.60	1.36	12 persons,	2	21	10.50	1.14
10 persons,	8	49	6.13	1.63	13 persons,	2	13	6.50	2.00
11 persons,	5	37	7.40	1.49	14 persons,	3	26	8.67	1.62
12 persons,	3	29	9.67	1.24	15 persons,	1	10	10.00	1.50
14 persons,	1	5	5.00	2.80	16 persons,	1	17	17.00	0.94
Gloucester. Ward 7,	587	3,023	5.15	0.94	20 persons,	1	14	14.00	1.43
1 person,	21	85	4.05	0.25	Hamilton,	315	2,411	7.65	0.56
2 persons,	108	560	5.19	0.39	1 person,	21	134	6.38	0.16
3 persons,	116	589	5.08	0.59	2 persons,	66	396	6.00	0.33
4 persons,	79	406	5.14	0.78	3 persons,	60	416	6.93	0.43
5 persons,	76	367	4.83	1.04	4 persons,	51	389	7.63	0.52
6 persons,	59	329	5.58	1.08	5 persons,	42	354	8.43	0.59
7 persons,	43	207	4.81	1.45	6 persons,	28	246	8.79	0.68
8 persons,	29	199	6.86	1.17	7 persons,	15	138	9.20	0.76
9 persons,	11	55	5.00	1.80	8 persons,	12	92	7.67	1.04
10 persons,	9	47	5.22	1.91	9 persons,	7	69	8.57	1.05
11 persons,	12	61	5.08	2.16	10 persons,	3	38	12.67	0.79
12 persons,	4	19	4.75	2.53	11 persons,	4	38	9.50	1.16
13 persons,	5	20	4.00	3.25	12 persons,	1	14	14.00	0.86
14 persons,	6	32	5.33	2.63	13 persons,	1	8	8.00	1.63
15 persons,	3	15	5.00	3.00	15 persons,	1	18	18.00	0.83
16 persons,	1	5	5.00	3.20	16 persons,	1	23	23.00	0.70
17 persons,	2	10	5.00	3.40	19 persons,	1	19	19.00	1.00
18 persons,	1	6	6.00	3.00	28 persons,	1	28	28.00	1.00
19 persons,	1	5	5.00	3.80	HAVERHILL,	6,302	46,545	6.74	0.65
20 persons,	1	6	6.00	3.33	1 person,	222	1,027	4.63	0.22
Gloucester. Ward 8,	261	1,922	6.90	0.63	2 persons,	1,215	7,388	5.56	0.34
1 person,	25	130	5.20	0.19	3 persons,	1,398	8,950	6.40	0.47
2 persons,	58	340	5.86	0.34	4 persons,	1,332	8,851	6.64	0.60
3 persons,	47	292	6.21	0.49	5 persons,	1,009	6,840	6.78	0.74
4 persons,	49	335	6.84	0.59	6 persons,	683	4,757	6.96	0.86
5 persons,	44	311	7.07	0.71	7 persons,	423	3,032	7.17	0.98
6 persons,	28	191	6.82	0.88	8 persons,	243	1,877	7.72	1.04
7 persons,	16	99	6.19	1.13	9 persons,	141	1,145	8.12	1.11
8 persons,	9	80	8.89	0.90	10 persons,	78	659	8.45	1.18
9 persons,	8	73	9.13	0.99	11 persons,	40	354	8.85	1.24
10 persons,	2	12	6.00	1.67	12 persons,	22	245	11.14	1.08
11 persons,	1	9	9.00	1.22	13 persons,	20	333	17.65	0.74

ROOMS: OCCUPIED DWELLING HOUSES — Continued.

COUNTIES, CITIES, TOWNS, AND NUMBER OF PERSONS TO A FAMILY	Number of Families specified size	Total Number of Rooms Occupied	Average Number of Rooms Occupied	Average Number of Persons to a Room
ESSEX — Con.				
HAVERHILL — Con.				
14 persons,	15	175	11.67	1.20
15 persons,	5	56	11.20	1.34
16 persons,	4	64	16.00	1.00
18 persons,	5	99	19.80	0.91
19 persons,	1	16	16.00	1.19
20 persons,	4	147	36.75	0.54
21 persons,	4	117	29.25	0.72
22 persons,	2	54	27.00	0.81
23 persons,	1	27	27.00	0.85
27 persons,	1	56	56.00	0.48
28 persons,	1	76	76.00	0.37
34 persons,	1	80	80.00	0.43
47 persons,	1	20	20.00	2.35
89 persons,	1	50	50.00	1.78
Haverhill. Ward 1,	573	4,581	7.99	0.58
1 person,	27	118	4.37	0.23
2 persons,	118	728	6.17	0.32
3 persons,	118	808	6.85	0.44
4 persons,	88	660	7.50	0.53
5 persons,	73	555	7.60	0.66
6 persons,	46	363	7.89	0.76
7 persons,	25	248	9.92	0.71
8 persons,	26	255	9.81	0.82
9 persons,	10	98	9.80	0.92
10 persons,	14	151	10.79	0.94
11 persons,	7	97	13.86	0.79
12 persons,	5	63	12.60	0.95
13 persons,	4	121	30.25	0.43
14 persons,	2	26	13.00	1.08
16 persons,	2	33	16.50	0.97
18 persons,	2	35	17.50	1.03
19 persons,	1	16	16.00	1.19
21 persons,	1	30	30.00	0.70
22 persons,	1	17	17.00	1.29
23 persons,	1	27	27.00	0.85
27 persons,	1	56	56.00	0.48
28 persons,	1	76	76.00	0.37
Haverhill. Ward 2,	631	4,888	7.75	0.51
1 person,	37	184	4.97	0.20
2 persons,	131	845	6.37	0.31
3 persons,	150	1,046	6.97	0.43
4 persons,	118	902	7.64	0.52
5 persons,	83	720	8.67	0.58
6 persons,	37	309	8.35	0.72
7 persons,	39	315	8.08	0.87
8 persons,	16	158	9.88	0.81
9 persons,	8	82	10.25	0.88
10 persons,	3	40	13.33	0.75
11 persons,	1	6	6.00	1.83
12 persons,	1	15	15.00	0.80
13 persons,	3	162	54.00	0.38
15 persons,	1	9	9.00	1.67
20 persons,	1	45	45.00	0.44
21 persons,	1	40	40.00	0.53
34 persons,	1	80	80.00	0.43
ESSEX — Con.				
Haverhill. Ward 3,	784	5,151	6.60	0.89
1 person,	29	106	3.66	0.27
2 persons,	147	810	5.51	0.36
3 persons,	145	845	5.83	0.51
4 persons,	149	904	6.07	0.66
5 persons,	99	651	6.58	0.76
6 persons,	78	537	6.88	0.87
7 persons,	45	304	6.76	1.04
8 persons,	31	243	7.84	1.02
9 persons,	23	215	9.35	0.96
10 persons,	11	119	10.82	0.92
11 persons,	6	59	9.83	1.12
12 persons,	2	37	18.50	0.65
13 persons,	3	43	14.33	0.91
14 persons,	4	59	14.75	0.95
15 persons,	2	32	16.00	0.94
16 persons,	2	31	15.50	1.03
18 persons,	2	50	25.00	0.72
20 persons,	1	49	49.00	0.41
21 persons,	1	20	20.00	1.05
22 persons,	1	37	37.00	0.59
Haverhill. Ward 4,	957	6,686	6.60	0.60
1 person,	38	172	4.53	0.22
2 persons,	190	1,193	6.28	0.32
3 persons,	183	1,230	6.68	0.45
4 persons,	184	1,332	7.24	0.55
5 persons,	154	1,126	7.31	0.68
6 persons,	99	723	7.30	0.82
7 persons,	49	384	7.84	0.89
8 persons,	21	174	8.29	0.97
9 persons,	14	129	9.21	0.98
10 persons,	4	34	8.50	1.18
11 persons,	5	35	7.00	1.57
12 persons,	2	23	11.50	1.04
14 persons,	2	16	8.00	1.75
15 persons,	1	5	5.00	3.00
89 persons,	1	50	50.00	1.78
Haverhill. Ward 5,	2,452	15,685	6.15	0.75
1 person,	59	291	4.93	0.20
2 persons,	359	2,018	5.62	0.35
3 persons,	461	2,764	6.00	0.50
4 persons,	485	2,926	6.03	0.66
5 persons,	384	2,287	5.96	0.84
6 persons,	278	1,787	6.43	0.92
7 persons,	175	1,123	6.42	1.09
8 persons,	102	691	6.77	1.18
9 persons,	67	484	7.22	1.25
10 persons,	55	298	6.74	1.48
11 persons,	19	146	7.53	1.46
12 persons,	8	67	8.38	1.43
13 persons,	10	57	5.70	1.49
14 persons,	7	74	10.57	1.32
15 persons,	1	10	10.00	1.50
18 persons,	1	14	14.00	1.29
20 persons,	1	33	33.00	0.61

ROOMS: OCCUPIED DWELLING HOUSES — Continued.

Counties, Cities, Towns, and Number of Persons to a Family.	Number of Families of Specified Size	Total Number of Rooms Occupied	Average Number of Rooms Occupied	Average Number of Persons to a Room
ESSEX – Con.				
Haverhill. Ward 6,	1,508	10,174	6.75	0.61
2 person,	32	156	4.88	0.21
2 persons,	390	1,804	6.01	0.33
3 persons,	331	2,197	6.64	0.45
4 persons,	308	2,127	6.91	0.58
5 persons,	216	1,501	6.95	0.72
6 persons,	145	1,028	7.16	0.84
7 persons,	90	658	7.31	0.96
8 persons,	47	356	7.57	1.06
9 persons,	19	137	7.21	1.25
10 persons,	11	79	7.18	1.39
11 persons,	2	14	7.00	1.57
12 persons,	4	40	10.00	1.20
20 persons,	1	20	20.00	1.00
21 persons,	1	27	27.00	0.78
47 persons,	1	20	20.00	2.63
Ipswich,	1,104	7,945	7.20	0.59
1 person,	80	358	4.48	0.22
2 persons,	202	1,304	6.44	0.31
3 persons,	240	1,662	6.93	0.43
4 persons,	200	1,480	7.40	0.54
5 persons,	133	953	7.17	0.70
6 persons,	88	655	7.44	0.81
7 persons,	47	353	7.51	0.93
8 persons,	36	307	8.53	0.94
9 persons,	36	307	8.53	1.06
10 persons,	14	149	10.64	0.94
11 persons,	9	88	9.78	1.13
12 persons,	5	37	7.40	1.62
13 persons,	6	59	9.83	1.32
14 persons,	2	20	10.00	1.40
15 persons,	1	20	20.00	0.75
16 persons,	1	10	10.00	1.60
17 persons,	1	50	50.00	0.34
21 persons,	1	26	26.00	0.81
24 persons,	1	36	36.00	0.94
74 persons,	1	74	74.00	1.00
LAWRENCE,	10,783	62,591	5.80	0.83
1 person,	344	1,120	3.26	0.51
2 persons,	1,617	7,878	4.87	0.41
3 persons,	2,057	10,757	5.23	0.57
4 persons,	1,903	10,363	5.59	0.72
5 persons,	1,573	9,127	5.80	0.86
6 persons,	1,182	7,087	6.00	1.00
7 persons,	775	4,676	6.03	1.16
8 persons,	463	3,161	6.41	1.25
9 persons,	294	1,886	6.41	1.40
10 persons,	165	1,175	7.12	1.40
11 persons,	111	800	7.21	1.53
12 persons,	47	326	6.94	1.73
13 persons,	31	274	8.84	1.47
14 persons,	19	229	12.05	1.16
15 persons,	10	111	11.10	1.35
16 persons,	7	107	15.29	1.05
17 persons,	6	107	17.83	0.95

Counties, Cities, Towns, and Number of Persons to a Family.	Number of Families of Specified Size	Total Number of Rooms Occupied	Average Number of Rooms Occupied	Average Number of Persons to a Room
ESSEX – Con.				
LAWRENCE — Con.				
18 persons,	7	139	19.86	0.91
19 persons,	4	69	17.25	1.10
20 persons,	8	137	17.13	1.17
21 persons,	2	38	19.00	1.11
22 persons,	3	61	20.33	1.08
23 persons,	4	94	23.50	0.98
24 persons,	3	73	24.33	0.99
25 persons,	7	157	22.43	1.11
26 persons,	1	20	20.00	1.30
27 persons,	2	72	36.00	0.75
28 persons,	3	183	61.00	0.46
29 persons,	1	30	30.00	0.97
30 persons,	1	40	40.00	0.75
32 persons,	2	59	29.50	1.08
33 persons,	2	62	31.00	1.06
34 persons,	3	71	23.67	1.44
35 persons,	2	82	41.00	0.85
36 persons,	1	30	30.00	1.20
37 persons,	2	85	42.50	0.87
38 persons,	2	68	34.00	1.12
39 persons,	1	46	46.00	0.85
40 persons,	4	147	36.75	1.09
41 persons,	2	64	32.00	1.28
42 persons,	2	52	26.00	1.62
43 persons,	3	146	48.67	0.88
44 persons,	1	36	36.00	1.22
45 persons,	3	119	39.67	1.13
47 persons,	2	94	47.00	1.00
50 persons,	1	41	41.00	1.22
52 persons,	1	56	56.00	0.93
57 persons,	1	42	42.00	1.36
59 persons,	1	50	50.00	1.18
60 persons,	1	48	48.00	1.25
141 persons,	1	65	65.00	2.17
144 persons,	1	66	66.00	2.18
261 persons,	1	145	135.00	1.83
Lawrence. Ward 1,	1,805	10,060	5.57	0.85
1 person,	41	136	3.32	0.30
2 persons,	294	1,372	4.67	0.43
3 persons,	339	1,697	5.01	0.60
4 persons,	347	1,852	5.34	0.75
5 persons,	302	1,694	5.61	0.89
6 persons,	195	1,129	5.79	1.04
7 persons,	119	687	5.77	1.21
8 persons,	68	435	6.40	1.25
9 persons,	46	291	6.33	1.42
10 persons,	16	118	7.38	1.36
11 persons,	9	56	6.22	1.77
12 persons,	4	26	6.50	1.85
13 persons,	7	52	7.43	1.75
14 persons,	2	33	16.50	0.85
15 persons,	1	6	6.00	2.50
22 persons,	1	26	26.00	0.85
24 persons,	1	25	25.00	0.96

ROOMS: OCCUPIED DWELLING HOUSES — Continued.

COUNTIES, CITIES, TOWNS, AND NUMBER OF PERSONS TO A FAMILY.	Number of Families of Specified Size	Total Number of Rooms Occupied	Average Number of Rooms Occupied	Average Number of Persons to a Room	COUNTIES, CITIES, TOWNS, AND NUMBER OF PERSONS TO A FAMILY.	Number of Families of Specified Size	Total Number of Rooms Occupied	Average Number of Rooms Occupied	Average Number of Persons to a Room
ESSEX — Con.					ESSEX — Con.				
Lawrence. Ward 1 — Con.					*Lawrence. Ward 3* — Con.				
25 persons,	2	47	23.50	1.06	7 persons,	142	832	5.86	1.19
26 persons,	1	20	20.00	1.50	8 persons,	96	576	6.00	1.33
34 persons,	3	71	23.67	1.44	9 persons,	49	313	6.39	1.41
35 persons,	1	50	50.00	0.70	10 persons,	25	192	7.68	1.30
37 persons,	1	50	50.00	0.74	11 persons,	21	153	7.29	1.51
40 persons,	1	26	26.00	1.54	12 persons,	7	55	7.86	1.53
41 persons,	1	24	24.00	1.71	13 persons,	5	48	9.60	1.35
42 persons,	1	21	21.00	2.00	14 persons,	3	53	17.67	0.79
50 persons,	1	50	50.00	1.18	16 persons,	2	58	29.00	0.55
144 persons,	1	66	66.00	2.18	17 persons,	3	62	20.67	0.82
Lawrence. Ward 2,	1,331	8,654	6.50	0.81	18 persons,	2	45	22.50	0.80
1 person,	37	133	3.59	0.28	20 persons,	1	8	8.00	2.50
2 persons,	185	875	4.73	0.42	23 persons,	1	16	16.00	1.44
3 persons,	250	1,436	5.74	0.52	25 persons,	1	18	18.00	1.39
4 persons,	233	1,368	5.87	0.68	27 persons,	1	40	40.00	0.68
5 persons,	196	1,231	6.28	0.80	28 persons,	2	63	31.50	0.89
6 persons,	147	940	6.39	0.94	32 persons,	1	35	35.00	0.91
7 persons,	94	632	6.72	1.04	33 persons,	1	30	30.00	1.10
8 persons,	62	495	7.98	1.00	37 persons,	1	35	35.00	1.06
9 persons,	30	199	6.63	1.26	38 persons,	1	26	26.00	1.46
10 persons,	29	245	8.45	1.18	39 persons,	1	46	46.00	0.85
11 persons,	18	142	7.89	1.39	60 persons,	1	48	48.00	1.25
12 persons,	5	35	7.00	1.71	141 persons,	1	65	65.00	2.47
13 persons,	6	86	14.33	0.91	*Lawrence. Ward 4,*	1,888	11,264	5.97	0.89
14 persons,	6	83	13.83	1.01	1 person,	75	224	2.99	0.33
15 persons,	3	31	10.33	1.45	2 persons,	240	1,218	5.08	0.39
16 persons,	1	10	10.00	1.60	3 persons,	349	1,820	5.21	0.58
17 persons,	1	12	12.00	1.42	4 persons,	322	1,797	5.58	0.72
18 persons,	4	68	17.00	1.06	5 persons,	253	1,474	5.83	0.94
19 persons,	3	49	16.33	1.16	6 persons,	215	1,217	5.80	1.03
20 persons,	4	75	18.75	1.07	7 persons,	146	849	5.82	1.20
21 persons,	1	18	18.00	1.17	8 persons,	88	516	5.86	1.36
22 persons,	1	20	20.00	1.10	9 persons,	65	400	6.15	1.46
23 persons,	1	18	18.00	1.28	10 persons,	39	234	6.00	1.67
24 persons,	1	18	18.00	1.33	11 persons,	34	237	6.97	1.58
25 persons,	2	41	20.50	1.22	12 persons,	20	138	6.90	1.74
33 persons,	1	32	32.00	1.03	13 persons,	8	53	6.63	1.96
35 persons,	1	32	32.00	1.09	14 persons,	7	50	7.14	1.96
36 persons,	1	30	30.00	1.20	15 persons,	1	7	7.00	2.14
40 persons,	1	33	33.00	1.21	16 persons,	2	13	6.50	2.46
42 persons,	1	31	31.00	1.35	17 persons,	1	23	23.00	0.74
43 persons,	1	40	40.00	1.08	18 persons,	1	26	26.00	0.69
44 persons,	1	36	36.00	1.22	19 persons,	1	20	20.00	0.95
45 persons,	1	32	32.00	1.41	20 persons,	2	38	19.00	1.05
47 persons,	1	42	42.00	1.12	21 persons,	1	20	20.00	1.05
50 persons,	1	41	41.00	1.22	22 persons,	1	15	15.00	1.47
57 persons,	1	42	42.00	1.38	23 persons,	1	28	28.00	0.82
Lawrence. Ward 3,	1,879	10,069	5.36	0.89	24 persons,	1	30	30.00	0.80
1 person,	108	295	2.73	0.37	25 persons,	1	33	33.00	0.76
2 persons,	298	1,270	4.26	0.47	27 persons,	1	32	32.00	0.84
3 persons,	338	1,608	4.76	0.63	28 persons,	1	120	120.00	0.23
4 persons,	305	1,568	5.14	0.78	29 persons,	1	30	30.00	0.97
5 persons,	257	1,339	5.21	0.96	30 persons,	1	40	40.00	0.75
6 persons,	205	1,172	5.72	1.05	32 persons,	1	24	24.00	1.33

ROOMS: OCCUPIED DWELLING HOUSES — Continued.

Counties, Cities, Towns, and Number of Persons to a Family.	Number of Families Specified Size	Total Number of Rooms Occupied	Average Number of Rooms Occupied	Average Number of Persons to a Room	Counties, Cities, Towns, and Number of Persons to a Family.	Number of Families Specified Size	Total Number of Rooms Occupied	Average Number of Rooms Occupied	Average Number of Persons to a Room
ESSEX — Con.					**ESSEX — Con.**				
Lawrence. Ward 4 — Con.					LYNN — Con.				
40 persons,	2	88	44.00	0.91	10 persons,	153	1,434	9.37	1.07
41 persons,	1	40	40.00	1.03	11 persons,	72	768	10.67	1.03
43 persons,	2	106	53.00	0.81	12 persons,	53	615	11.60	1.03
45 persons,	2	87	43.50	1.03	13 persons,	35	458	13.09	0.99
47 persons,	1	52	52.00	0.90	14 persons,	22	292	13.27	1.05
261 persons,	1	135	135.00	1.93	15 persons,	19	279	14.68	1.02
Lawrence. Ward 5,	2,215	12,667	5.72	0.78	16 persons,	13	232	17.85	0.90
1 person,	51	198	3.88	0.26	17 persons,	6	113	18.83	0.90
2 persons,	368	1,911	5.19	0.39	18 persons,	7	134	19.14	0.94
3 persons,	468	2,466	5.27	0.57	19 persons,	5	114	22.80	0.83
4 persons,	432	2,476	5.73	0.70	20 persons,	5	169	33.80	0.59
5 persons,	291	1,733	5.96	0.84	21 persons,	5	118	23.60	0.89
6 persons,	237	1,417	5.98	1.00	22 persons,	1	45	45.00	0.49
7 persons,	146	907	6.21	1.13	23 persons,	7	149	21.29	1.08
8 persons,	100	616	6.16	1.30	24 persons,	4	137	34.25	0.70
9 persons,	59	379	6.42	1.40	25 persons,	7	162	23.14	1.08
10 persons,	30	191	6.37	1.57	26 persons,	2	41	20.50	1.27
11 persons,	14	95	6.79	1.62	28 persons,	1	23	23.00	1.22
12 persons,	7	49	7.00	1.71	30 persons,	1	38	38.00	0.79
13 persons,	3	19	6.33	2.05	31 persons,	1	34	34.00	0.91
14 persons,	1	10	10.00	1.40	34 persons,	1	26	26.00	1.31
15 persons,	4	54	13.50	1.11	35 persons,	1	31	31.00	1.13
20 persons,	1	16	16.00	1.25	40 persons,	1	41	41.00	0.98
23 persons,	1	32	32.00	0.72	43 persons,	1	56	56.00	0.77
38 persons,	1	42	42.00	0.90	44 persons,	1	60	60.00	0.73
52 persons,	1	56	56.00	0.93	51 persons,	1	63	63.00	0.81
Lawrence. Ward 6,	1,695	9,880	5.93	0.78	57 persons,	1	47	47.00	1.21
1 person,	32	134	4.19	0.24	64 persons,	1	125	125.00	0.51
2 persons,	232	1,232	5.31	0.38	70 persons,	1	50	50.00	1.40
3 persons,	313	1,730	5.53	0.54	72 persons,	1	72	72.00	1.00
4 persons,	327	1,932	5.91	0.68	75 persons,	1	36	36.00	2.08
5 persons,	274	1,656	6.04	0.83	*Lynn. Ward 1,*	387	2,312	5.97	0.68
6 persons,	183	1,182	6.46	0.93	1 person,	11	43	3.91	0.26
7 persons,	128	769	6.01	1.17	2 persons,	77	424	5.51	0.36
8 persons,	79	523	6.62	1.21	3 persons,	75	440	5.87	0.51
9 persons,	45	304	6.76	1.33	4 persons,	86	503	5.85	0.68
10 persons,	26	195	7.50	1.33	5 persons,	55	348	6.33	0.79
11 persons,	15	117	7.80	1.41	6 persons,	42	269	6.40	0.94
12 persons,	4	23	5.75	2.09	7 persons,	21	153	7.29	0.96
13 persons,	2	16	8.00	1.63	8 persons,	14	86	6.14	1.50
15 persons,	1	13	13.00	1.15	9 persons,	2	14	7.00	1.29
16 persons,	2	26	13.00	1.23	10 persons,	3	22	7.33	1.36
17 persons,	1	10	10.00	1.70	11 persons,	1	10	10.00	1.10
25 persons,	1	18	18.00	1.39	*Lynn. Ward 2,*	968	5,949	6.11	0.69
LYNN,	14,144	89,855	6.35	0.69	1 person,	28	103	3.68	0.27
1 person,	436	1,576	3.61	0.28	2 persons,	183	1,023	5.59	0.36
2 persons,	2,428	12,973	5.34	0.37	3 persons,	209	1,279	6.12	0.49
3 persons,	2,956	17,060	5.78	0.52	4 persons,	218	1,345	6.17	0.65
4 persons,	2,847	17,525	6.16	0.65	5 persons,	152	958	6.30	0.79
5 persons,	2,091	13,591	6.49	0.77	6 persons,	75	478	6.37	0.94
6 persons,	1,305	8,808	6.75	0.89	7 persons,	55	367	6.67	1.05
7 persons,	871	6,317	7.25	0.97	8 persons,	25	191	7.64	1.05
8 persons,	506	3,790	7.49	1.07	9 persons,	7	49	7.00	1.29
9 persons,	271	2,184	8.06	1.12	10 persons,	8	62	7.75	1.29

ROOMS: OCCUPIED DWELLING HOUSES — Continued.

Counties, Cities, Towns, and Number of Persons to a Family.	Number of Families of Specified Size	Total Number of Rooms Occupied	Average Number of Rooms Occupied	Average Number of Persons to a Room	Counties, Cities, Towns, and Number of Persons to a Family.	Number of Families of Specified Size	Total Number of Rooms Occupied	Average Number of Rooms Occupied	Average Number of Persons to a Room
ESSEX — Con.					**ESSEX — Con.**				
Lynn. Ward 2 - Con.					*Lynn. Ward 4 - Con.*				
11 persons, . .	4	32	8.00	1.38	64 persons, . .	1	125	125.00	0.51
12 persons, . .	2	12	6.00	2.00	72 persons, . .	1	72	72.00	1.00
14 persons, . .	1	7	7.00	2.00	*Lynn. Ward 5,*	2,875	19,197	6.68	0.67
23 persons, . .	1	13	13.00	1.77	1 person,	98	344	3.51	0.28
Lynn. Ward 3,	3,602	21,898	6.08	0.98	2 persons, . .	481	2,645	5.50	0.36
1 person,	126	483	3.83	0.26	3 persons, . .	612	3,626	5.92	0.51
2 persons, . .	631	3,395	5.33	0.38	4 persons, . .	573	3,621	6.32	0.63
3 persons, . .	767	4,420	5.76	0.52	5 persons, . .	396	2,717	6.86	0.73
4 persons, . .	785	4,844	6.17	0.65	6 persons, . .	263	1,863	7.08	0.85
5 persons, . .	541	3,451	6.38	0.78	7 persons, . .	183	1,406	7.68	0.91
6 persons, . .	343	2,318	6.76	0.89	8 persons, . .	99	775	7.83	1.02
7 persons, . .	197	1,389	7.05	0.99	9 persons, . .	62	506	8.16	1.10
8 persons, . .	114	802	7.04	1.14	10 persons, . .	27	317	11.74	0.85
9 persons, . .	55	414	7.53	1.20	11 persons, . .	18	187	10.39	1.06
10 persons, . .	25	195	7.80	1.28	12 persons, . .	21	285	13.57	0.88
11 persons, . .	9	88	9.78	1.13	13 persons, . .	8	121	15.13	0.86
12 persons, . .	4	48	12.00	1.00	14 persons, . .	8	111	13.88	1.01
13 persons, . .	2	42	21.00	0.62	15 persons, . .	6	89	14.83	1.01
15 persons, . .	1	8	8.00	1.88	16 persons, . .	4	67	16.75	0.96
18 persons, . .	1	13	13.00	1.38	17 persons, . .	2	38	19.00	0.89
25 persons, . .	1	18	18.00	1.39	18 persons, . .	1	35	35.00	0.51
Lynn. Ward 4,	2,384	16,743	7.02	0.92	19 persons, . .	3	70	23.33	0.81
1 person,	92	323	3.51	0.28	20 persons, . .	1	70	70.00	0.29
2 persons, . .	413	2,095	5.07	0.39	21 persons, . .	2	58	29.00	0.72
3 persons, . .	471	2,652	5.63	0.53	22 persons, . .	1	45	45.00	0.49
4 persons, . .	429	2,716	6.33	0.63	23 persons, . .	1	24	24.00	0.96
5 persons, . .	342	2,330	6.81	0.73	24 persons, . .	2	70	35.00	0.69
6 persons, . .	191	1,446	7.57	0.79	28 persons, . .	1	23	23.00	1.22
7 persons, . .	160	1,331	8.32	0.84	31 persons, . .	1	34	34.00	0.91
8 persons, . .	77	717	9.31	0.86	70 persons, . .	1	50	50.00	1.40
9 persons, . .	56	540	9.64	0.93	*Lynn. Ward 6,*	3,324	20,162	6.07	0.74
10 persons, . .	51	507	9.94	1.01	1 person,	64	226	3.53	0.28
11 persons, . .	19	281	14.79	0.74	2 persons, . .	533	2,828	5.31	0.38
12 persons, . .	12	140	11.67	1.03	3 persons, . .	688	3,957	5.67	0.53
13 persons, . .	15	209	13.93	0.93	4 persons, . .	633	3,784	5.98	0.67
14 persons, . .	8	112	14.00	1.00	5 persons, . .	524	3,250	6.22	0.80
15 persons, . .	7	111	15.86	0.95	6 persons, . .	331	2,081	6.29	0.95
16 persons, . .	7	133	19.00	0.84	7 persons, . .	220	1,490	6.64	1.05
17 persons, . .	4	75	18.75	0.91	8 persons, . .	155	1,066	6.88	1.16
18 persons, . .	1	30	30.00	0.60	9 persons, . .	79	584	7.39	1.22
19 persons, . .	2	44	22.00	0.86	10 persons, . .	28	239	8.54	1.17
20 persons, . .	3	72	24.00	0.83	11 persons, . .	19	157	8.26	1.33
21 persons, . .	3	60	20.00	1.05	12 persons, . .	12	119	9.92	1.21
23 persons, . .	5	112	22.40	1.03	13 persons, . .	9	76	8.44	1.54
24 persons, . .	1	27	27.00	0.89	14 persons, . .	5	62	12.40	1.13
25 persons, . .	4	97	24.25	1.03	15 persons, . .	4	59	14.75	1.02
26 persons, . .	1	24	24.00	1.08	16 persons, . .	2	32	16.00	1.00
30 persons, . .	1	38	38.00	0.79	18 persons, . .	4	56	14.00	1.29
34 persons, . .	1	26	26.00	1.31	20 persons, . .	1	27	27.00	0.74
35 persons, . .	1	31	31.00	1.13	24 persons, . .	1	40	40.00	0.60
40 persons, . .	1	41	41.00	0.98	25 persons, . .	1	33	33.00	0.76
43 persons, . .	1	56	56.00	0.77	26 persons, . .	1	17	17.00	1.53
44 persons, . .	1	60	60.00	0.73	*Lynn. Ward 7,*	604	3,604	5.97	0.74
51 persons, . .	1	63	63.00	0.81	1 person,	17	54	3.18	0.31
57 persons, . .	1	47	47.00	1.21	2 persons, . .	110	593	5.39	0.37

ROOMS: OCCUPIED DWELLING HOUSES — Continued.

COUNTIES, CITIES, TOWNS, AND NUMBER OF PERSONS TO A FAMILY.	Number of Families of Specified Size	Total Number of Rooms Occupied	Average Number of Rooms Occupied	Average Number of Persons to a Room	COUNTIES, CITIES, TOWNS, AND NUMBER OF PERSONS TO A FAMILY.	Number of Families of Specified Size	Total Number of Rooms Occupied	Average Number of Rooms Occupied	Average Number of Persons to a Room
ESSEX — Con.					ESSEX — Con.				
Lynn. Ward 7 - Con.					Marblehead — Con.				
3 persons, . .	124	725	5.85	0.51	13 persons, .	2	32	16.00	0.81
4 persons, . .	123	722	5.87	0.68	20 persons, . .	1	29	29.00	1.00
5 persons, . .	84	528	6.29	0.80	Merrimac, . .	605	4,282	7.08	0.54
6 persons, . .	60	353	5.88	1.02	1 person, . .	30	153	5.10	0.20
7 persons, . .	35	211	6.03	1.16	2 persons, . .	136	913	6.71	0.30
8 persons, . .	22	153	6.95	1.15	3 persons, . .	152	1,084	7.13	0.42
9 persons, . .	10	77	7.70	1.17	4 persons, . .	114	794	6.96	0.57
10 persons, . .	11	92	8.36	1.20	5 persons, . .	80	591	7.39	0.68
11 persons, . .	2	13	6.50	1.69	6 persons, . .	44	339	7.70	0.78
12 persons, . .	2	11	5.50	2.18	7 persons, . .	21	150	7.14	0.98
13 persons, . .	1	10	10.00	1.30	8 persons, . .	13	105	8.08	0.99
15 persons, . .	1	12	12.00	1.25	9 persons, . .	6	52	8.67	1.04
25 persons, . .	1	14	14.00	1.79	10 persons, . .	4	26	6.50	1.54
75 persons, . .	1	36	36.00	2.08	11 persons, . .	1	8	8.00	1.38
Lynnfield, . .	211	1,515	7.18	0.54	14 persons, . .	2	16	8.00	1.75
1 person, . .	12	75	6.25	0.46	15 persons, . .	1	16	16.00	0.94
2 persons, . .	54	380	7.04	0.28	24 persons, . .	1	35	35.00	0.69
3 persons, . .	43	294	6.84	0.44	Methuen, . .	1,317	8,933	6.78	0.64
4 persons, . .	29	211	7.28	0.55	1 person, . .	43	257	5.38	1.67
5 persons, . .	30	232	7.73	0.65	2 persons, . .	244	1,545	6.33	0.32
6 persons, . .	19	126	6.63	0.90	3 persons, . .	275	1,761	6.40	0.47
7 persons, . .	12	104	8.67	0.81	4 persons, . .	225	1,515	6.72	0.59
8 persons, . .	7	59	8.43	0.95	5 persons, . .	185	1,305	7.05	0.71
9 persons, . .	3	22	7.33	1.23	6 persons, . .	149	1,017	6.83	0.88
10 persons, . .	1	6	6.00	1.67	7 persons, . .	85	661	7.78	0.90
12 persons, . .	1	6	6.00	2.00	8 persons, . .	58	429	7.40	1.08
Manchester, . .	488	3,430	7.03	0.55	9 persons, . .	25	181	7.24	1.24
1 person, . .	50	203	4.06	0.25	10 persons, . .	15	106	7.07	1.42
2 persons, . .	93	593	6.38	0.31	11 persons, . .	8	63	7.88	1.40
3 persons, . .	106	683	6.44	0.47	12 persons, . .	2	20	10.00	1.20
4 persons, . .	79	555	7.03	0.57	14 persons, . .	1	30	30.00	0.47
5 persons, . .	68	531	7.81	0.64	19 persons, . .	1	17	17.00	1.12
6 persons, . .	46	370	8.04	0.75	36 persons, . .	1	28	28.00	1.29
7 persons, . .	23	182	7.91	0.88	Middleton, . .	219	1,471	6.72	0.57
8 persons, . .	8	88	11.00	0.73	1 person, . .	27	145	5.37	0.19
9 persons, . .	4	41	10.25	0.88	2 persons, . .	35	201	5.74	0.35
10 persons, . .	6	91	15.17	0.66	3 persons, . .	47	321	6.83	0.44
11 persons, . .	1	14	14.00	0.79	4 persons, . .	46	322	7.00	0.57
12 persons, . .	1	11	11.00	1.09	5 persons, . .	27	203	7.52	0.67
13 persons, . .	2	48	24.00	0.54	6 persons, . .	16	109	6.81	0.88
20 persons, . .	1	20	20.00	1.00	7 persons, . .	10	77	7.70	0.91
Marblehead, . .	2,003	12,015	6.00	0.64	8 persons, . .	4	30	7.50	1.07
1 person, . .	141	566	4.01	0.25	9 persons, . .	1	5	5.00	1.80
2 persons, . .	418	2,278	5.45	0.37	10 persons, . .	2	18	9.00	1.11
3 persons, . .	460	2,622	5.70	0.53	11 persons, . .	2	17	8.50	1.29
4 persons, . .	378	2,283	6.04	0.66	16 persons, . .	1	8	8.00	1.50
5 persons, . .	265	1,723	6.50	0.77	20 persons, . .	1	15	15.00	1.33
6 persons, . .	150	1,085	7.23	0.83	Nahant, . .	204	1,426	6.99	0.61
7 persons, . .	83	583	7.02	1.00	1 person, . .	19	80	4.21	0.24
8 persons, . .	46	330	7.17	1.12	2 persons, . .	45	267	5.93	0.34
9 persons, . .	27	193	7.15	1.26	3 persons, . .	35	203	5.80	0.52
10 persons, . .	24	195	8.13	1.23	4 persons, . .	31	217	7.00	0.57
11 persons, . .	6	72	12.00	0.92	5 persons, . .	27	191	7.07	0.71
12 persons, . .	2	24	12.00	1.00	6 persons, . .	13	125	9.62	0.62

ROOMS: OCCUPIED DWELLING HOUSES — Continued.

COUNTIES, CITIES, TOWNS, AND NUMBER OF PERSONS TO A FAMILY.	Number of Families of Specified Size	Total Number of Rooms Occupied	Average Number of Rooms Occupied	Average Number of Persons to a Room
ESSEX — Con.				
Nahant — Con.				
7 persons,	10	84	8.40	0.83
8 persons,	9	66	7.33	1.09
9 persons,	5	46	9.20	0.98
10 persons,	3	25	8.33	1.20
11 persons,	2	35	17.50	0.63
12 persons,	1	10	10.00	1.20
13 persons,	1	8	8.00	1.63
14 persons,	1	27	27.00	0.52
15 persons,	1	18	18.00	0.83
21 persons,	1	24	24.00	0.88
Newbury,	360	2,671	7.42	0.56
1 person,	21	94	4.48	0.22
2 persons,	70	433	6.19	0.32
3 persons,	75	522	6.96	0.43
4 persons,	72	530	7.36	0.54
5 persons,	49	405	8.27	0.60
6 persons,	21	169	8.05	0.75
7 persons,	22	197	8.95	0.78
8 persons,	6	55	9.17	0.87
9 persons,	9	90	10.00	0.90
10 persons,	10	169	10.90	0.92
11 persons,	3	44	14.67	0.75
12 persons,	1	8	8.00	1.50
16 persons,	1	15	15.00	1.07
NEWBURYPORT,	3,479	24,227	6.96	0.90
1 person,	237	1,082	4.64	0.22
2 persons,	648	4,062	6.27	0.32
3 persons,	672	4,542	6.76	0.44
4 persons,	639	4,523	7.08	0.57
5 persons,	509	3,787	7.44	0.67
6 persons,	301	2,181	7.25	0.83
7 persons,	205	1,558	7.60	0.92
8 persons,	103	768	7.46	1.07
9 persons,	73	613	8.40	1.07
10 persons,	45	396	8.80	1.14
11 persons,	23	205	8.91	1.23
12 persons,	8	70	8.75	1.37
13 persons,	3	24	8.00	1.63
14 persons,	3	42	14.00	1.00
15 persons,	2	30	15.00	1.00
16 persons,	2	22	11.00	1.45
17 persons,	1	52	52.00	0.33
18 persons,	1	17	17.00	1.06
19 persons,	2	22	11.00	1.73
20 persons,	1	30	30.00	0.67
21 persons,	1	20	20.00	1.05
25 persons,	2	32	16.00	1.56
31 persons,	1	53	53.00	0.58
47 persons,	1	96	96.00	0.49
Newburyport. Wd.1,	601	3,883	6.46	0.48
1 person,	42	214	5.10	0.20
2 persons,	113	680	6.02	0.33
3 persons,	138	889	6.44	0.47
4 persons,	113	761	6.73	0.59

COUNTIES, CITIES, TOWNS, AND NUMBER OF PERSONS TO A FAMILY.	Number of Families of Specified Size	Total Number of Rooms Occupied	Average Number of Rooms Occupied	Average Number of Persons to a Room
ESSEX — Con.				
Newburyport. Wd. 1 — Con.				
5 persons,	85	575	6.76	0.74
6 persons,	40	270	6.75	0.89
7 persons,	37	267	7.22	0.97
8 persons,	8	57	7.13	1.12
9 persons,	12	83	6.92	1.30
10 persons,	9	60	6.67	1.50
11 persons,	1	7	7.00	1.57
12 persons,	1	8	8.00	1.50
14 persons,	1	11	11.00	1.27
15 persons,	1	11	11.00	1.36
Newburyport. Wd.2,	510	3,386	6.64	0.69
1 person,	45	162	3.60	0.28
2 persons,	70	416	5.94	0.34
3 persons,	100	658	6.55	0.46
4 persons,	66	473	7.17	0.56
5 persons,	83	605	7.29	0.69
6 persons,	38	266	7.00	0.86
7 persons,	37	257	6.95	1.01
8 persons,	25	180	7.20	1.11
9 persons,	17	143	8.41	1.07
10 persons,	12	89	7.42	1.35
11 persons,	9	69	7.67	1.43
12 persons,	3	26	8.67	1.38
13 persons,	3	24	8.00	1.63
14 persons,	1	8	8.00	1.75
19 persons,	1	10	10.00	1.90
Newburyport. Wd.3,	615	4,308	7.38	0.64
1 person,	25	134	5.36	0.19
2 persons,	110	796	7.24	0.28
3 persons,	122	925	7.58	0.40
4 persons,	116	895	7.72	0.52
5 persons,	93	775	8.33	0.60
6 persons,	59	482	8.17	0.73
7 persons,	37	328	8.86	0.79
8 persons,	22	201	9.14	0.88
9 persons,	12	99	8.25	1.09
10 persons,	12	135	11.25	0.89
11 persons,	3	44	14.67	0.75
12 persons,	2	21	10.50	1.14
21 persons,	1	20	20.00	1.05
31 persons,	1	53	53.00	0.58
Newburyport. Wd.4,	530	3,862	7.09	0.59
1 person,	38	172	4.53	0.22
2 persons,	116	716	6.17	0.32
3 persons,	106	694	6.55	0.46
4 persons,	108	788	7.30	0.55
5 persons,	78	563	7.60	0.66
6 persons,	38	290	7.63	0.79
7 persons,	30	250	8.33	0.84
8 persons,	16	109	6.81	1.17
9 persons,	14	103	7.36	1.22
10 persons,	3	38	12.67	0.79
11 persons,	3	22	7.33	1.50
12 persons,	1	8	8.00	1.50

ROOMS: OCCUPIED DWELLING HOUSES — Continued.

Counties, Cities, Towns, and Number of Persons to a Family.	Number of Families of Specified Size.	Total Number of Rooms Occupied.	Average Number of Rooms Occupied.	Average Number of Persons to a Room.
ESSEX — Con.				
Newburyport. Wd. 4 — Con.				
14 persons,	1	23	23.00	0.61
15 persons,	1	19	19.00	0.79
16 persons,	1	14	14.00	1.14
17 persons,	1	52	52.00	0.33
18 persons,	1	17	17.00	1.06
19 persons,	1	12	12.00	1.58
20 persons,	1	30	30.00	0.67
25 persons,	1	12	12.00	2.08
Newburyport. Wd. 5,	538	3,576	6.65	0.63
1 person,	35	166	4.74	0.21
2 persons,	88	526	5.98	0.33
3 persons,	97	681	7.02	0.43
4 persons,	119	794	6.67	0.60
5 persons,	74	521	7.04	0.71
6 persons,	59	406	6.88	0.87
7 persons,	31	212	6.84	1.02
8 persons,	18	126	7.00	1.14
9 persons,	9	77	8.56	1.05
10 persons,	2	14	7.00	1.43
11 persons,	4	38	9.50	1.16
12 persons,	1	7	7.00	1.71
16 persons,	1	8	8.00	2.00
Newburyport. Wd. 6,	656	4,502	6.86	0.58
1 person,	48	234	4.88	0.21
2 persons,	151	928	6.15	0.33
3 persons,	109	695	6.38	0.47
4 persons,	117	812	6.94	0.58
5 persons,	96	718	7.48	0.67
6 persons,	67	467	6.97	0.86
7 persons,	33	244	7.39	0.95
8 persons,	14	95	6.79	1.18
9 persons,	9	108	12.00	0.75
10 persons,	7	60	8.57	1.17
11 persons,	3	25	8.33	1.32
25 persons,	1	20	20.00	1.25
47 persons,	1	96	96.00	0.49
North Andover.	796	5,569	6.92	0.65
1 person,	26	126	4.85	0.21
2 persons,	130	836	6.43	0.31
3 persons,	156	1,021	6.54	0.46
4 persons,	145	984	6.77	0.59
5 persons,	131	904	6.88	0.73
6 persons,	73	531	7.27	0.82
7 persons,	48	349	7.27	0.96
8 persons,	46	352	7.65	1.05
9 persons,	17	112	6.59	1.37
10 persons,	9	83	9.22	1.08
11 persons,	4	35	8.75	1.26
12 persons,	7	115	16.43	0.73
13 persons,	1	11	11.00	1.18
16 persons,	1	11	11.00	1.45
17 persons,	1	15	15.00	1.13
21 persons,	1	30	30.00	0.70
ESSEX — Con.				
Peabody,	2,373	15,466	6.52	0.68
1 person,	82	406	4.95	0.20
2 persons,	406	2,336	5.35	0.34
3 persons,	465	2,994	6.44	0.47
4 persons,	450	2,931	6.51	0.61
5 persons,	332	2,183	6.58	0.76
6 persons,	246	1,667	6.78	0.89
7 persons,	150	1,058	6.61	1.05
8 persons,	100	745	7.45	1.07
9 persons,	72	529	7.35	1.22
10 persons,	33	246	7.45	1.34
11 persons,	12	103	8.58	1.28
12 persons,	9	79	8.78	1.37
13 persons,	5	51	10.20	1.27
14 persons,	1	12	12.00	1.17
17 persons,	1	15	15.00	1.13
19 persons,	1	23	23.00	0.83
35 persons,	1	28	28.00	1.25
Rockport,	1,236	6,367	5.65	0.76
1 person,	96	430	4.48	0.22
2 persons,	238	1,273	5.35	0.37
3 persons,	255	1,470	5.76	0.52
4 persons,	201	1,161	5.78	0.69
5 persons,	121	702	5.80	0.86
6 persons,	120	741	6.18	0.97
7 persons,	69	408	5.91	1.18
8 persons,	51	304	5.96	1.34
9 persons,	36	202	5.61	1.60
10 persons,	23	125	5.43	1.84
11 persons,	9	40	4.44	2.48
12 persons,	4	20	5.00	2.40
13 persons,	5	42	8.40	1.55
14 persons,	2	15	7.50	1.87
15 persons,	3	21	7.00	2.14
19 persons,	1	26	26.00	0.73
21 persons,	1	3	3.00	7.00
53 persons,	1	14	14.00	3.79
Rowley,	340	2,373	6.98	0.54
1 person,	13	76	5.85	0.17
2 persons,	72	466	6.47	0.31
3 persons,	83	572	6.89	0.44
4 persons,	79	587	7.43	0.54
5 persons,	50	349	6.98	0.72
6 persons,	47	333	7.82	0.77
7 persons,	17	126	7.41	0.94
8 persons,	6	43	7.17	1.12
10 persons,	2	16	8.00	1.25
11 persons,	1	5	5.00	2.20
SALEM,	7,623	48,372	6.35	0.71
1 person,	353	1,507	4.27	0.23
2 persons,	1,320	7,282	5.52	0.36
3 persons,	1,465	9,168	6.26	0.48
4 persons,	1,326	8,562	6.46	0.62
5 persons,	1,089	7,196	6.55	0.76
6 persons,	769	5,057	6.58	0.91

ROOMS: OCCUPIED DWELLING HOUSES — Continued.

COUNTIES, CITIES, TOWNS, AND NUMBER OF PERSONS TO A FAMILY.	Number of Families of Specified Size	Total Number of Rooms Occupied	Average Number of Rooms Occupied	Average Number of Persons to a Room
ESSEX — Con.				
SALEM — Con.				
7 persons,	569	3,455	6.78	1.03
8 persons,	327	2,280	6.97	1.15
9 persons,	179	1,257	7.02	1.28
10 persons,	119	824	6.92	1.44
11 persons,	62	437	7.05	1.56
12 persons,	32	210	6.56	1.83
13 persons,	19	141	7.42	1.75
14 persons,	9	85	9.44	1.48
15 persons,	7	74	10.57	1.42
16 persons,	6	94	15.67	1.02
17 persons,	5	56	11.20	1.52
18 persons,	2	22	11.00	1.64
19 persons,	1	16	16.00	1.19
20 persons,	1	50	50.00	0.40
21 persons,	1	19	19.00	1.11
22 persons,	1	26	26.00	0.85
28 persons,	2	57	28.50	0.98
29 persons,	2	68	34.00	0.85
38 persons,	1	26	26.00	1.46
42 persons,	1	43	43.00	0.98
43 persons,	1	45	45.00	1.09
58 persons,	1	21	21.00	2.76
113 persons,	1	96	96.00	1.18
196 persons,	1	65	65.00	2.09
296 persons,	1	135	135.00	2.21
Salem. Ward 1,	1,109	6,197	5.59	0.81
1 person,	90	400	4.44	0.23
2 persons,	199	933	4.69	0.43
3 persons,	217	1,168	5.38	0.56
4 persons,	167	917	5.49	0.73
5 persons,	139	734	5.28	0.95
6 persons,	106	580	5.47	1.10
7 persons,	67	392	5.85	1.20
8 persons,	46	269	5.85	1.57
9 persons,	34	212	6.24	1.44
10 persons,	14	102	7.29	1.37
11 persons,	7	43	6.14	1.79
12 persons,	6	38	6.33	1.89
13 persons,	4	24	6.00	2.17
14 persons,	1	6	6.00	2.33
15 persons,	1	6	6.00	2.50
16 persons,	2	33	16.50	0.97
19 persons,	1	16	16.00	1.19
20 persons,	1	50	50.00	0.40
21 persons,	1	19	19.00	1.11
22 persons,	1	26	26.00	0.85
28 persons,	1	22	22.00	1.27
29 persons,	2	68	34.00	0.85
42 persons,	1	43	43.00	0.98
113 persons,	1	96	96.00	1.18
Salem. Ward 2,	1,369	9,356	6.83	0.60
1 person,	71	307	4.32	0.23
2 persons,	281	1,630	5.80	0.34
3 persons,	369	2,014	6.52	0.46
ESSEX — Con.				
Salem. Ward 2-Con.				
4 persons,	270	1,898	7.03	0.57
5 persons,	189	1,402	7.42	0.67
6 persons,	108	761	7.05	0.85
7 persons,	74	569	7.69	0.91
8 persons,	34	307	9.03	0.89
9 persons,	17	140	8.24	1.09
10 persons,	10	89	8.90	1.12
12 persons,	1	14	14.00	0.86
13 persons,	1	18	18.00	0.72
15 persons,	1	32	32.00	0.47
16 persons,	2	40	20.00	0.80
299 persons,	1	135	135.00	2.21
Salem. Ward 3,	1,028	6,964	6.77	0.63
1 person,	53	237	4.47	0.22
2 persons,	202	1,145	5.67	0.35
3 persons,	183	1,265	6.91	0.43
4 persons,	179	1,158	6.36	0.63
5 persons,	154	1,097	7.12	0.70
6 persons,	99	720	7.27	0.83
7 persons,	78	583	7.47	0.94
8 persons,	35	316	9.03	0.89
9 persons,	16	158	9.88	0.91
10 persons,	17	144	8.47	1.18
11 persons,	7	74	10.57	1.04
12 persons,	2	19	9.50	1.26
14 persons,	1	17	17.00	0.82
16 persons,	1	16	16.00	1.00
28 persons,	1	35	35.00	0.80
Salem. Ward 4,	1,181	7,598	6.43	0.69
1 person,	63	212	3.37	0.30
2 persons,	186	1,016	5.46	0.37
3 persons,	223	1,423	6.38	0.47
4 persons,	217	1,448	6.67	0.60
5 persons,	178	1,226	6.89	0.73
6 persons,	144	981	6.81	0.88
7 persons,	57	386	6.77	1.03
8 persons,	55	386	7.02	1.14
9 persons,	22	184	8.36	1.08
10 persons,	14	106	7.57	1.32
11 persons,	7	45	6.43	1.71
12 persons,	5	42	8.40	1.43
13 persons,	1	20	20.00	0.65
14 persons,	3	40	13.33	1.05
15 persons,	2	18	9.00	1.67
17 persons,	2	30	15.00	1.13
18 persons,	1	14	14.00	1.29
28 persons,	1	21	21.00	2.76
Salem. Ward 5,	1,881	11,399	6.06	0.87
1 person,	31	147	4.74	0.21
2 persons,	244	1,364	5.59	0.36
3 persons,	318	1,918	6.03	0.50
4 persons,	285	1,766	6.20	0.65
5 persons,	279	1,659	5.95	0.84
6 persons,	217	1,345	6.20	0.97

ROOMS: OCCUPIED DWELLING HOUSES — Continued.

COUNTIES, CITIES, TOWNS, AND NUMBER OF PERSONS TO A FAMILY.	Number of Families of Specified Size	Total Number of Rooms Occupied	Average Number of Rooms Occupied	Average Number of Persons to a Room	COUNTIES, CITIES, TOWNS, AND NUMBER OF PERSONS TO A FAMILY.	Number of Families of Specified Size	Total Number of Rooms Occupied	Average Number of Rooms Occupied	Average Number of Persons to a Room
ESSEX — Con.					**ESSEX — Con.**				
Salem. Ward 5-Con.					*Saugus — Con.*				
7 persons,	167	1,052	6.30	1.11	12 persons,	3	34	11.33	1.06
8 persons,	124	752	6.06	1.32	13 persons,	4	31	7.75	1.68
9 persons,	78	459	5.88	1.53	14 persons,	1	9	9.00	1.56
10 persons,	58	337	5.81	1.72	18 persons,	1	16	16.00	1.13
11 persons,	38	243	6.39	1.72	Swampscott,	823	5,702	6.93	0.57
12 persons,	16	85	5.31	2.26	1 person,	37	160	4.32	0.23
13 persons,	12	72	6.00	2.17	2 persons,	169	1,044	6.18	0.32
14 persons,	4	22	5.50	2.55	3 persons,	190	1,298	6.52	0.46
15 persons,	3	18	6.00	2.50	4 persons,	160	1,082	6.76	0.59
16 persons,	1	5	5.00	3.20	5 persons,	101	753	7.46	0.67
17 persons,	2	11	5.50	3.09	6 persons,	60	492	7.70	0.78
18 persons,	1	8	8.00	2.25	7 persons,	46	386	8.67	0.81
38 persons,	1	26	26.00	1.46	8 persons,	28	244	8.71	0.92
49 persons,	1	45	45.00	1.09	9 persons,	10	92	9.20	1.08
136 persons,	1	65	65.00	2.09	10 persons,	5	51	10.20	0.98
Salem. Ward 6,	1,055	6,858	6.50	0.63	11 persons,	5	77	15.40	0.71
1 person,	45	204	4.53	0.22	13 persons,	2	25	12.70	1.04
2 persons,	208	1,194	5.74	0.35	15 persons,	1	15	15.00	1.00
3 persons,	215	1,380	6.42	0.47	Topsfield,	264	1,940	7.35	0.53
4 persons,	208	1,395	6.71	0.60	1 person,	42	190	4.52	0.22
5 persons,	160	1,078	6.74	0.74	2 persons,	38	245	6.45	0.31
6 persons,	95	670	7.05	0.85	3 persons,	41	293	7.15	0.42
7 persons,	66	471	7.14	0.98	4 persons,	50	420	8.40	0.48
8 persons,	33	250	7.58	1.06	5 persons,	37	289	8.08	0.62
9 persons,	12	104	8.67	1.04	6 persons,	27	223	8.26	0.73
10 persons,	6	46	7.67	1.30	7 persons,	12	115	9.58	0.73
11 persons,	3	32	10.67	1.03	8 persons,	8	67	8.38	0.96
12 persons,	2	12	6.00	2.00	9 persons,	4	47	11.75	0.77
13 persons,	1	7	7.00	1.86	10 persons,	2	18	9.00	1.11
17 persons,	1	15	15.00	1.13	11 persons,	1	7	7.00	1.57
Salisbury,	351	2,380	6.78	0.55	12 persons,	1	4	4.00	3.00
1 person,	24	117	4.88	0.21	18 persons,	1	12	12.00	1.50
2 persons,	71	438	6.17	0.32	Wenham,	234	1,738	7.43	0.51
3 persons,	86	559	6.50	0.46	1 person,	20	126	6.30	0.16
4 persons,	69	487	7.06	0.57	2 persons,	56	355	6.30	0.32
5 persons,	46	286	6.22	0.80	3 persons,	44	320	7.27	0.41
6 persons,	32	288	9.00	0.67	4 persons,	44	352	8.00	0.50
7 persons,	13	117	9.00	0.78	5 persons,	28	207	7.39	0.68
8 persons,	7	57	8.14	0.98	6 persons,	20	162	8.10	0.74
9 persons,	1	9	9.00	1.00	7 persons,	8	80	10.00	0.70
10 persons,	1	8	8.00	1.25	8 persons,	6	56	9.33	0.86
12 persons,	1	14	14.00	0.86	9 persons,	2	13	6.50	1.38
Saugus,	1,065	7,060	6.63	0.64	10 persons,	3	26	8.67	1.15
1 person,	36	178	4.94	0.20	11 persons,	2	35	17.50	0.43
2 persons,	168	999	5.95	0.34	12 persons,	1	8	8.00	1.50
3 persons,	262	1,688	6.44	0.47	West Newbury,	440	3,282	7.46	0.50
4 persons,	205	1,359	6.63	0.60	1 person,	39	225	5.77	0.17
5 persons,	161	1,104	6.86	0.73	2 persons,	85	597	7.02	0.28
6 persons,	101	692	6.85	0.88	3 persons,	98	688	7.02	0.43
7 persons,	61	440	7.21	0.97	4 persons,	89	682	7.66	0.52
8 persons,	25	186	7.44	1.08	5 persons,	61	498	8.16	0.61
9 persons,	17	147	8.65	1.04	6 persons,	33	310	9.39	0.64
10 persons,	12	79	6.58	1.52	7 persons,	18	149	8.28	0.85
11 persons,	8	98	12.25	0.90	8 persons,	4	46	11.50	0.70

ROOMS: OCCUPIED DWELLING HOUSES — Continued.

COUNTIES, CITIES, TOWNS, AND NUMBER OF PERSONS TO A FAMILY.	Number of Families of Specified Size	Total Number of Rooms Occupied	Average Number of Rooms Occupied	Average Number of Persons to a Room	COUNTIES, CITIES, TOWNS, AND NUMBER OF PERSONS TO A FAMILY.	Number of Families of Specified Size	Total Number of Rooms Occupied	Average Number of Rooms Occupied	Average Number of Persons to a Room
ESSEX — Con.					FRANKLIN — Con.				
West Newbury-Con.					Colrain,	366	2,514	6.87	0.64
9 persons,	8	45	5.63	1.60	1 person,	18	82	4.56	0.22
10 persons,	4	28	7.00	1.43	2 persons,	67	402	6.00	0.33
11 persons,	1	14	14.00	0.79	3 persons,	65	454	6.98	0.43
FRANKLIN.					4 persons,	61	455	7.46	0.54
					5 persons,	49	353	7.20	0.69
Ashfield,	252	2,210	8.77	0.46	6 persons,	44	332	7.55	0.80
1 person,	22	128	5.82	0.17	7 persons,	26	168	6.46	1.08
2 persons,	48	342	7.13	0.28	8 persons,	15	122	8.13	0.98
3 persons,	44	375	8.52	0.35	9 persons,	9	62	6.89	1.31
4 persons,	46	412	8.96	0.45	10 persons,	7	55	7.86	1.27
5 persons,	34	315	9.26	0.54	11 persons,	4	42	10.50	1.05
6 persons,	29	275	9.48	0.63	13 persons,	1	7	7.00	1.86
7 persons,	13	136	10.46	0.67	Conway,	309	2,357	7.63	0.55
8 persons,	9	107	11.89	0.67	1 person,	15	75	5.00	0.20
9 persons,	3	33	11.00	0.82	2 persons,	55	365	6.64	0.30
10 persons,	1	9	9.00	1.11	3 persons,	56	400	7.14	0.42
11 persons,	1	14	14.00	0.79	4 persons,	66	524	7.94	0.50
12 persons,	2	64	32.00	0.38	5 persons,	43	334	7.77	0.64
Bernardston,	266	1,885	9.07	0.41	6 persons,	34	296	8.71	0.69
1 person,	16	129	8.06	0.12	7 persons,	16	147	9.19	0.76
2 persons,	53	427	8.06	0.25	8 persons,	14	117	8.36	0.81
3 persons,	40	385	9.63	0.31	9 persons,	2	21	10.50	0.89
4 persons,	35	318	9.09	0.44	10 persons,	4	41	10.25	0.98
5 persons,	31	292	9.42	0.53	11 persons,	2	14	7.00	1.57
6 persons,	15	167	11.13	0.54	12 persons,	2	23	11.50	1.04
7 persons,	7	79	11.29	0.62	Deerfield,	674	5,097	7.56	0.70
8 persons,	7	59	8.43	0.95	1 person,	30	150	5.00	0.20
9 persons,	4	33	8.25	1.09	2 persons,	119	794	6.67	0.30
10 persons,	1	6	6.00	1.67	3 persons,	140	1,024	7.31	0.41
Buckland,	387	2,585	6.68	0.60	4 persons,	111	840	7.57	0.53
1 person,	22	126	5.73	0.17	5 persons,	86	688	8.00	0.62
2 persons,	77	468	6.08	0.33	6 persons,	74	579	7.82	0.77
3 persons,	98	618	6.31	0.48	7 persons,	31	240	7.74	0.90
4 persons,	57	389	6.82	0.59	8 persons,	35	306	8.74	0.92
5 persons,	51	372	7.29	0.69	9 persons,	17	155	9.12	0.99
6 persons,	41	286	6.98	0.86	10 persons,	17	157	9.24	1.08
7 persons,	14	111	7.93	0.88	11 persons,	7	46	6.57	1.67
8 persons,	13	104	8.00	1.00	12 persons,	3	32	10.67	1.13
9 persons,	5	29	5.80	1.55	13 persons,	1	12	12.00	1.08
10 persons,	3	21	7.00	1.43	14 persons,	1	12	12.00	1.17
11 persons,	2	16	8.00	1.38	17 persons,	1	90	90.00	0.57
12 persons,	2	29	14.50	0.83	24 persons,	1	2	2.00	12.00
13 persons,	2	16	8.00	1.63	Erving,	256	1,614	6.30	0.60
Charlemont,	275	2,034	7.40	0.51	1 person,	20	81	4.05	0.25
1 person,	12	54	4.50	0.22	2 persons,	44	257	5.84	0.34
2 persons,	68	470	6.91	0.29	3 persons,	62	372	6.00	0.50
3 persons,	62	448	7.23	0.42	4 persons,	53	354	6.68	0.60
4 persons,	51	370	7.25	0.55	5 persons,	35	244	6.97	0.72
5 persons,	39	328	8.41	0.59	6 persons,	22	170	7.73	0.78
6 persons,	18	156	8.67	0.69	7 persons,	13	94	7.23	0.97
7 persons,	10	80	8.00	0.88	8 persons,	4	26	6.50	1.23
8 persons,	10	85	8.50	0.94	9 persons,	2	12	6.00	1.50
9 persons,	1	18	18.00	0.50	10 persons,	1	4	4.00	2.50
10 persons,	3	15	5.00	2.00	Gill,	197	1,633	8.29	0.65
11 persons,	1	10	10.00	1.10	1 person,	11	66	6.00	0.17

ROOMS: OCCUPIED DWELLING HOUSES — Continued.

Counties, Cities, Towns, and Number of Persons to a Family.	Number of Families of Specified Size	Total Number of Rooms Occupied	Average Number of Rooms Occupied	Average Number of Persons to a Room	Counties, Cities, Towns, and Number of Persons to a Family.	Number of Families of Specified Size	Total Number of Rooms Occupied	Average Number of Rooms Occupied	Average Number of Persons to a Room
FRANKLIN — Con.					**FRANKLIN — Con.**				
Gill — Con.					Heath — Con.				
2 persons,	35	232	6.63	0.30	7 persons,	7	52	7.43	0.94
3 persons,	37	265	7.16	0.42	8 persons,	2	17	8.50	0.94
4 persons,	39	311	7.97	0.50	9 persons,	3	26	8.67	1.04
5 persons,	18	128	7.11	0.70	10 persons,	1	5	5.00	2.00
6 persons,	19	182	9.58	0.63	Leverett,	200	1,349	6.75	0.55
7 persons,	16	127	7.94	0.88	1 person,	17	95	5.59	0.18
8 persons,	3	22	7.33	1.09	2 persons,	42	239	5.69	0.35
9 persons,	6	64	10.67	0.84	3 persons,	42	296	7.05	0.43
10 persons,	6	47	7.83	1.28	4 persons,	39	279	7.15	0.56
11 persons,	1	14	14.00	0.79	5 persons,	29	198	6.83	0.73
18 persons,	2	32	16.00	1.13	6 persons,	16	128	8.00	0.75
20 persons,	1	18	18.00	1.11	7 persons,	7	54	7.71	0.91
21 persons,	1	14	14.00	1.50	8 persons,	3	21	7.00	1.14
24 persons,	1	15	15.00	1.60	9 persons,	3	18	6.00	1.50
18 persons,	1	96	96.00	1.75	10 persons,	2	21	10.50	0.95
Greenfield,	1,450	10,509	7.25	0.50	Leyden,	88	705	8.01	0.51
1 person,	64	265	4.14	0.24	1 person,	5	25	5.00	0.20
2 persons,	265	1,592	6.01	0.33	2 persons,	15	96	6.40	0.31
3 persons,	308	2,137	6.94	0.43	3 persons,	17	127	7.47	0.40
4 persons,	256	1,876	7.33	0.55	4 persons,	19	163	8.58	0.47
5 persons,	219	1,673	7.64	0.65	5 persons,	12	104	8.67	0.58
6 persons,	144	1,099	7.63	0.79	6 persons,	9	73	8.11	0.74
7 persons,	96	727	7.57	0.92	7 persons,	7	76	10.86	0.64
8 persons,	39	351	9.00	0.89	8 persons,	1	12	12.00	0.67
9 persons,	24	185	7.71	1.17	9 persons,	1	7	7.00	1.29
10 persons,	11	116	10.55	0.95	10 persons,	1	9	9.00	1.11
11 persons,	8	73	9.13	1.21	13 persons,	1	13	13.00	0.85
12 persons,	5	65	13.00	0.92	Monroe,	65	392	6.03	0.76
13 persons,	1	8	8.00	1.63	1 person,	2	2	1.00	1.00
14 persons,	1	15	15.00	0.93	2 persons,	14	75	5.36	0.37
17 persons,	1	25	25.00	0.68	3 persons,	9	38	4.22	0.71
18 persons,	2	44	22.00	0.82	4 persons,	11	84	7.64	0.52
24 persons,	2	36	18.00	1.33	5 persons,	14	84	6.00	0.83
33 persons,	1	35	35.00	0.94	6 persons,	4	23	5.75	1.04
54 persons,	1	75	75.00	0.45	7 persons,	5	31	6.20	1.13
36 persons,	1	20	20.00	1.80	8 persons,	1	6	6.00	1.33
39 persons,	1	92	92.00	0.42	9 persons,	1	7	7.00	1.29
Hawley,	110	869	7.90	0.54	10 persons,	3	20	6.67	1.50
1 person,	1	1	1.00	1.00	21 persons,	1	22	22.00	0.95
2 persons,	16	100	6.25	0.32	Montague,	1,349	8,231	6.10	0.74
3 persons,	25	198	7.92	0.38	1 person,	63	260	4.13	0.24
4 persons,	22	163	7.41	0.54	2 persons,	211	1,124	5.33	0.38
5 persons,	22	192	8.73	0.57	3 persons,	250	1,523	6.09	0.49
6 persons,	15	129	8.60	0.70	4 persons,	243	1,515	6.23	0.64
7 persons,	6	55	9.17	0.76	5 persons,	206	1,302	6.32	0.79
9 persons,	2	23	11.50	0.78	6 persons,	145	923	6.37	0.94
12 persons,	1	8	8.00	1.50	7 persons,	87	545	6.26	1.12
Heath,	120	879	7.33	0.54	8 persons,	59	376	6.37	1.26
1 person,	9	35	3.89	0.26	9 persons,	44	301	6.84	1.32
2 persons,	18	119	6.61	0.30	10 persons,	23	167	7.26	1.38
3 persons,	27	208	7.70	0.39	11 persons,	9	54	6.00	1.83
4 persons,	27	196	7.26	0.55	12 persons,	3	14	4.67	2.57
5 persons,	16	130	8.13	0.62	14 persons,	2	34	17.00	0.82
6 persons,	10	91	9.10	0.66	16 persons,	1	24	24.00	0.67

ROOMS: OCCUPIED DWELLING HOUSES — Continued.

COUNTIES, CITIES, TOWNS, AND NUMBER OF PERSONS TO A FAMILY.	Number of Families of Specified Size	Total Number of Rooms Occupied	Average Number of Rooms Occupied	Average Number of Persons to a Room
FRANKLIN — Con.				
Montague — Con.				
17 persons,	1	10	10.00	1.70
2? persons,	1	19	19.00	1.24
2? persons,	1	40	40.00	0.67
New Salem,	253	1,929	6.73	0.55
1 person,	25	124	5.39	0.49
2 persons,	55	355	6.45	0.54
3 persons,	49	305	6.22	0.48
4 persons,	40	287	7.18	0.56
5 persons,	24	183	7.63	0.66
6 persons,	17	131	7.71	0.78
7 persons,	9	63	7.00	1.00
8 persons,	7	62	8.86	0.90
9 persons,	3	20	6.67	1.35
10 persons,	5	25	5.00	2.00
11 persons,	1	14	14.00	0.79
Northfield,	419	3,341	7.97	0.55
1 person,	20	147	7.35	0.44
2 persons,	94	627	6.67	0.30
3 persons,	101	743	7.36	0.41
4 persons,	69	532	7.71	0.52
5 persons,	60	461	7.68	0.65
6 persons,	34	288	8.47	0.71
7 persons,	13	100	7.69	0.91
8 persons,	9	78	8.67	0.92
9 persons,	5	58	11.60	0.78
10 persons,	3	33	11.00	0.91
11 persons,	3	62	20.67	0.53
20 persons,	2	30	15.00	1.33
2? persons,	1	21	21.00	1.05
2? persons,	1	19	19.00	1.24
24 persons,	1	15	15.00	1.60
4? persons,	1	29	29.00	1.52
5? persons,	1	42	42.00	1.36
7? persons,	1	56	56.00	1.41
Orange,	1,390	8,775	6.31	0.61
1 person,	70	273	3.90	0.26
2 persons,	284	1,649	5.81	0.34
3 persons,	343	2,133	6.22	0.48
4 persons,	259	1,676	6.47	0.62
5 persons,	210	1,345	6.40	0.78
6 persons,	99	654	6.61	0.94
7 persons,	62	439	7.08	0.99
8 persons,	30	222	7.40	1.08
9 persons,	17	162	9.53	0.94
10 persons,	5	50	10.00	1.06
11 persons,	3	28	9.33	1.18
12 persons,	5	38	7.60	1.58
1? persons,	1	48	48.00	0.27
1? persons,	1	20	20.00	0.75
1? persons,	1	38	38.00	0.42
Rowe,	123	785	6.38	0.63
1 person,	6	18	3.00	0.33
2 persons,	21	111	5.29	0.38
3 persons,	28	184	6.57	0.46
4 persons,	29	193	6.66	0.60

COUNTIES, CITIES, TOWNS, AND NUMBER OF PERSONS TO A FAMILY.	Number of Families of Specified Size	Total Number of Rooms Occupied	Average Number of Rooms Occupied	Average Number of Persons to a Room
FRANKLIN — Con.				
Rowe — Con.				
5 persons,	15	121	8.07	0.62
6 persons,	9	61	6.78	0.89
7 persons,	6	31	5.17	1.35
8 persons,	4	26	6.50	1.23
9 persons,	3	24	8.00	1.33
10 persons,	2	16	8.00	1.25
Shelburne,	392	3,052	7.73	0.54
1 person,	18	70	3.89	0.26
2 persons,	88	592	6.73	0.30
3 persons,	76	587	7.72	0.39
4 persons,	78	587	7.53	0.53
5 persons,	54	484	8.91	0.56
6 persons,	36	305	8.47	0.71
7 persons,	22	209	9.50	0.74
8 persons,	7	63	9.00	0.89
9 persons,	9	77	8.56	1.05
10 persons,	2	12	6.00	1.67
11 persons,	1	13	13.00	0.85
1? persons,	1	36	36.00	0.50
Shutesbury,	125	820	6.64	0.53
1 person,	12	49	4.08	0.24
2 persons,	31	135	6.29	0.52
3 persons,	24	164	6.83	0.44
4 persons,	26	167	6.42	0.62
5 persons,	15	129	8.60	0.58
6 persons,	9	57	6.33	0.95
7 persons,	2	17	8.50	0.82
8 persons,	5	42	8.40	0.95
11 persons,	1	10	10.00	1.10
Sunderland,	196	1,299	7.83	0.54
1 person,	8	36	4.50	0.22
2 persons,	30	186	6.20	0.32
3 persons,	35	284	8.11	0.37
4 persons,	26	210	8.08	0.50
5 persons,	24	192	8.00	0.63
6 persons,	21	195	9.29	0.95
7 persons,	12	99	8.25	0.85
8 persons,	4	34	8.50	0.34
9 persons,	3	29	9.67	0.36
10 persons,	3	34	11.33	0.88
Warwick,	158	1,207	8.21	0.46
1 person,	11	74	6.73	0.15
2 persons,	36	307	8.53	0.23
3 persons,	42	364	8.60	0.35
4 persons,	30	238	7.93	0.50
5 persons,	9	69	7.67	0.65
6 persons,	9	84	9.33	0.64
7 persons,	6	42	7.00	1.00
8 persons,	10	88	8.80	0.91
9 persons,	2	12	6.00	1.50
10 persons,	2	17	8.50	1.18
11 persons,	1	5	5.00	2.20
Wendell,	129	802	6.22	0.65
1 person,	15	76	5.07	0.20
2 persons,	24	153	6.38	0.31

ROOMS: OCCUPIED DWELLING HOUSES — Continued.

COUNTIES, CITIES, TOWNS, AND NUMBER OF PERSONS TO A FAMILY.	Number of Families of Specified Size	Total Number of Rooms Occupied	Average Number of Rooms Occupied	Average Number of Persons to a Room	COUNTIES, CITIES, TOWNS, AND NUMBER OF PERSONS TO A FAMILY.	Number of Families of Specified Size	Total Number of Rooms Occupied	Average Number of Rooms Occupied	Average Number of Persons to a Room
FRANKLIN — Con.					HAMPDEN — Con.				
Wendell — Con.					Brimfield — Con.				
3 persons,	17	105	6.18	0.49	6 persons,	20	187	9.35	0.64
4 persons,	21	125	5.95	0.67	7 persons,	14	124	8.86	0.79
5 persons,	22	135	6.14	0.81	8 persons,	4	29	7.25	1.10
6 persons,	13	91	7.00	0.86	9 persons,	5	34	6.80	1.32
7 persons,	3	19	6.33	1.11	10 persons,	5	54	10.80	0.93
8 persons,	8	59	7.38	1.08	11 persons,	1	9	9.00	1.22
9 persons,	2	11	5.50	1.64	12 persons,	1	12	12.00	1.00
10 persons,	4	28	7.00	1.43	13 persons,	1	8	8.00	1.63
Whately,	195	1,604	8.23	0.47	19 persons,	1	20	20.00	0.95
1 person,	16	76	4.75	0.21	20 persons,	1	7	7.00	2.86
2 persons,	46	314	6.83	0.29	Chester,	354	2,525	7.13	0.57
3 persons,	37	313	8.46	0.35	1 person,	11	59	5.36	0.19
4 persons,	31	263	8.48	0.47	2 persons,	69	424	6.14	0.33
5 persons,	26	263	10.12	0.49	3 persons,	89	612	6.88	0.44
6 persons,	13	126	9.69	0.62	4 persons,	70	503	7.19	0.56
7 persons,	12	123	10.25	0.68	5 persons,	38	310	8.16	0.61
8 persons,	9	87	9.67	0.83	6 persons,	32	266	8.31	0.72
9 persons,	2	14	7.00	1.29	7 persons,	22	155	7.05	0.99
10 persons,	3	25	8.33	1.20	8 persons,	15	129	8.60	0.93
HAMPDEN.					9 persons,	4	32	8.00	1.13
					10 persons,	3	27	9.00	1.11
Agawam,	553	3,711	6.71	0.65	11 persons,	1	8	8.00	1.38
1 person,	32	137	4.28	0.23	CHICOPEE,	3,042	18,973	6.24	0.87
2 persons,	94	601	6.39	0.31	1 person,	67	270	4.03	0.25
3 persons,	96	626	6.52	0.46	2 persons,	369	2,033	5.51	0.36
4 persons,	92	628	6.83	0.59	3 persons,	534	3,180	5.96	0.50
5 persons,	86	612	7.12	0.70	4 persons,	501	2,953	5.89	0.68
6 persons,	58	424	7.31	0.82	5 persons,	441	2,748	6.23	0.80
7 persons,	49	331	6.76	1.04	6 persons,	355	2,277	6.41	0.94
8 persons,	21	151	7.19	1.11	7 persons,	237	1,489	6.32	1.11
9 persons,	16	137	8.56	1.05	8 persons,	167	1,131	6.77	1.18
10 persons,	4	27	6.75	1.48	9 persons,	101	681	6.74	1.33
11 persons,	2	12	6.00	1.83	10 persons,	77	526	6.83	1.46
12 persons,	2	16	8.00	1.50	11 persons,	46	302	6.57	1.68
13 persons,	1	9	9.00	1.44	12 persons,	28	225	8.04	1.49
Blandford,	206	1,859	9.02	0.46	13 persons,	28	199	7.11	1.83
1 person,	18	115	6.39	0.16	14 persons,	24	175	7.29	1.92
2 persons,	33	280	8.48	0.24	15 persons,	12	74	6.17	2.43
3 persons,	39	357	9.15	0.33	16 persons,	7	44	6.29	2.55
4 persons,	42	362	8.62	0.46	17 persons,	10	65	6.50	2.62
5 persons,	30	319	10.63	0.47	18 persons,	6	39	6.50	2.77
6 persons,	20	201	10.05	0.60	19 persons,	5	73	14.60	1.30
7 persons,	8	70	8.75	0.80	20 persons,	5	51	10.20	1.96
8 persons,	7	65	9.29	0.86	21 persons,	3	29	9.67	2.17
9 persons,	3	31	10.33	0.87	22 persons,	1	9	9.00	2.44
10 persons,	1	9	9.00	1.11	23 persons,	1	7	7.00	3.29
11 persons,	2	21	10.50	1.05	24 persons,	3	85	28.33	0.85
13 persons,	3	29	9.67	1.34	25 persons,	1	7	7.00	3.57
Brimfield,	238	1,882	7.91	0.51	26 persons,	3	36	12.00	2.17
1 person,	15	76	5.07	0.20	27 persons,	2	63	31.50	0.86
2 persons,	58	414	7.14	0.28	28 persons,	1	6	6.00	4.67
3 persons,	57	415	7.28	0.41	33 persons,	1	6	6.00	5.50
4 persons,	35	315	9.00	0.44	34 persons,	1	13	13.00	2.62
5 persons,	20	178	8.90	0.56	37 persons,	1	27	27.00	1.37

ROOMS: OCCUPIED DWELLING HOUSES — Continued.

COUNTIES, CITIES, TOWNS, AND NUMBER OF PERSONS TO A FAMILY.	Number of Families of Specified Size	Total Number of Rooms Occupied	Average Number of Rooms Occupied	Average Number of Persons to a Room	COUNTIES, CITIES, TOWNS, AND NUMBER OF PERSONS TO A FAMILY.	Number of Families of Specified Size	Total Number of Rooms Occupied	Average Number of Rooms Occupied	Average Number of Persons to a Room
HAMPDEN — Con.					**HAMPDEN — Con.**				
CHICOPEE — Con.					*Chicopee, Ward 3 — Con.*				
50 persons, . .	2	73	36.50	1.37	14 persons, . .	8	72	9.00	1.56
55 persons, . .	1	32	32.00	1.72	15 persons, . .	7	41	5.86	2.56
60 persons, . .	1	35	35.00	1.97	16 persons, . .	3	19	6.33	2.53
Chicopee, Ward 1, .	570	3,085	5.41	1.06	17 persons, . .	6	43	7.17	2.37
1 person, . .	11	38	3.45	0.29	18 persons, . .	2	12	6.00	3.00
2 persons, . .	56	251	4.48	0.45	19 persons, . .	3	58	19.33	0.98
3 persons, . .	85	427	5.02	0.60	20 persons, . .	1	11	11.00	1.82
4 persons, . .	81	409	5.05	0.79	21 persons, . .	2	14	7.00	3.00
5 persons, . .	79	408	5.16	0.97	24 persons, . .	1	15	15.00	1.60
6 persons, . .	75	405	5.40	1.11	50 persons, . .	1	46	46.00	1.09
7 persons, . .	56	307	5.48	1.28	55 persons, . .	1	32	32.00	1.72
8 persons, . .	39	237	6.08	1.32	62 persons, . .	1	35	35.00	1.97
9 persons, . .	20	152	7.60	1.18	*Chicopee, Ward 4,* .	421	3,008	7.14	0.75
10 persons, . .	22	128	5.82	1.72	1 person, . .	9	40	4.44	0.23
11 persons, . .	13	91	7.00	1.57	2 persons, . .	57	391	6.86	0.29
12 persons, . .	10	73	7.30	1.64	3 persons, . .	80	577	7.21	0.42
13 persons, . .	6	33	5.50	2.36	4 persons, . .	66	476	7.21	0.55
14 persons, . .	7	39	5.57	2.51	5 persons, . .	53	392	7.40	0.68
15 persons, . .	2	12	6.00	2.50	6 persons, . .	51	370	7.25	0.83
16 persons, . .	3	18	6.00	2.67	7 persons, . .	31	223	7.19	0.97
17 persons, . .	1	7	7.00	2.43	8 persons, . .	24	177	7.38	1.08
18 persons, . .	1	10	10.00	1.80	9 persons, . .	11	74	6.73	1.34
19 persons, . .	1	10	10.00	1.90	10 persons, . .	13	94	7.23	1.38
21 persons, . .	1	15	15.00	1.40	11 persons, . .	3	19	6.33	1.74
26 persons, . .	1	15	15.00	1.73	12 persons, . .	3	27	9.00	1.33
Chicopee, Ward 2, .	384	2,757	7.00	0.64	13 persons, . .	3	25	8.33	1.56
1 person, . .	15	79	5.27	0.19	14 persons, . .	5	34	6.80	2.06
2 persons, . .	59	369	6.25	0.32	15 persons, . .	2	10	5.00	3.00
3 persons, . .	89	594	6.67	0.45	16 persons, . .	1	7	7.00	2.29
4 persons, . .	68	439	6.46	0.62	17 persons, . .	2	10	5.00	3.40
5 persons, . .	55	418	7.60	0.66	18 persons, . .	3	17	5.67	3.18
6 persons, . .	45	366	8.13	0.74	20 persons, . .	1	5	5.00	4.00
7 persons, . .	24	160	6.67	1.05	25 persons, . .	1	7	7.00	3.57
8 persons, . .	21	188	8.95	0.89	28 persons, . .	1	6	6.00	4.67
9 persons, . .	8	62	7.75	1.16	37 persons, . .	1	27	27.00	1.37
10 persons, . .	3	34	11.33	0.88	*Chicopee, Ward 5,* .	505	3,373	6.68	0.79
11 persons, . .	3	14	4.67	2.36	1 person, . .	8	33	4.13	0.24
12 persons, . .	1	6	6.00	2.00	2 persons, . .	64	348	5.44	0.37
15 persons, . .	2	21	10.50	1.24	3 persons, . .	99	591	5.97	0.50
20 persons, . .	1	7	7.00	3.71	4 persons, . .	100	628	6.28	0.64
Chicopee, Ward 3, .	417	2,541	6.09	1.11	5 persons, . .	71	465	6.55	0.76
1 person, . .	13	44	3.38	0.30	6 persons, . .	57	385	6.75	0.89
2 persons, . .	41	224	5.46	0.37	7 persons, . .	36	234	6.50	1.08
3 persons, . .	52	266	5.12	0.59	8 persons, . .	18	126	7.00	1.14
4 persons, . .	62	342	5.52	0.73	9 persons, . .	16	122	7.63	1.18
5 persons, . .	58	325	5.60	0.89	10 persons, . .	9	69	7.67	1.30
6 persons, . .	35	203	5.80	1.03	11 persons, . .	6	46	7.67	1.43
7 persons, . .	31	190	6.13	1.14	12 persons, . .	4	34	8.50	1.41
8 persons, . .	24	135	5.63	1.42	13 persons, . .	3	30	10.00	1.30
9 persons, . .	22	122	5.55	1.62	14 persons, . .	2	20	10.00	1.40
10 persons, . .	12	73	6.08	1.64	15 persons, . .	1	11	11.00	1.36
11 persons, . .	13	87	6.69	1.64	20 persons, . .	3	35	11.67	1.71
12 persons, . .	6	52	8.67	1.38	22 persons, . .	1	9	9.00	2.44
13 persons, . .	12	80	6.67	1.95	24 persons, . .	2	70	35.00	0.69

ROOMS: OCCUPIED DWELLING HOUSES — Continued.

Counties, Cities, Towns, and Number of Persons to a Family.	Number of Families of Specified Size	Total Number of Rooms Occupied	Average Number of Rooms Occupied	Average Number of Persons to a Room
HAMPDEN — Con.				
Chicopee. Ward 5 — Con.				
26 persons,	1	14	14.00	1.86
27 persons,	2	63	31.50	0.86
34 persons,	1	13	13.00	2.62
50 persons,	1	27	27.00	1.85
Chicopee. Ward 6,	333	1,918	5.76	0.89
1 person,	7	22	3.14	0.32
2 persons,	44	211	4.80	0.42
3 persons,	59	324	5.49	0.55
4 persons,	46	254	5.52	0.72
5 persons,	54	313	5.80	0.86
6 persons,	44	273	6.20	0.97
7 persons,	28	190	6.79	1.03
8 persons,	20	133	6.65	1.20
9 persons,	10	62	6.20	1.45
10 persons,	7	54	7.71	1.30
11 persons,	5	28	5.60	1.96
12 persons,	2	17	8.50	1.41
13 persons,	2	10	5.00	2.60
14 persons,	2	10	5.00	2.80
17 persons,	1	5	5.00	3.40
19 persons,	1	5	5.00	3.80
23 persons,	1	7	7.00	3.29
Chicopee. Ward 7,	402	2,291	5.70	0.86
1 person,	4	14	3.50	0.29
2 persons,	48	239	4.98	0.40
3 persons,	70	401	5.73	0.52
4 persons,	78	405	5.19	0.77
5 persons,	71	427	6.01	0.83
6 persons,	48	275	5.73	1.05
7 persons,	31	195	6.29	1.11
8 persons,	21	135	6.43	1.24
9 persons,	14	87	6.21	1.45
10 persons,	11	74	6.73	1.49
11 persons,	3	17	5.67	1.94
12 persons,	2	16	8.00	1.50
33 persons,	1	6	6.00	5.50
East Longmeadow,	330	2,082	6.31	0.76
1 person,	8	37	4.63	0.22
2 persons,	51	320	6.27	0.32
3 persons,	63	394	6.25	0.48
4 persons,	50	311	6.22	0.64
5 persons,	49	326	6.65	0.75
6 persons,	35	232	6.63	0.91
7 persons,	29	179	6.17	1.13
8 persons,	17	102	6.00	1.33
9 persons,	11	62	5.64	1.60
10 persons,	7	44	6.29	1.59
11 persons,	2	17	8.50	1.29
12 persons,	3	17	5.67	2.12
13 persons,	2	14	7.00	1.86
14 persons,	1	13	13.00	1.08
15 persons,	1	6	6.00	2.50
16 persons,	1	8	8.00	2.00
HAMPDEN — Con.				
Granville,	252	2,032	8.06	0.49
1 person,	25	147	5.88	0.17
2 persons,	37	272	7.35	0.27
3 persons,	68	553	8.13	0.37
4 persons,	37	294	7.95	0.50
5 persons,	25	234	9.36	0.53
6 persons,	28	241	8.61	0.70
7 persons,	13	134	10.31	0.68
8 persons,	9	74	8.22	0.97
9 persons,	5	43	8.60	1.05
10 persons,	2	15	7.50	1.33
11 persons,	3	25	8.33	1.32
Hampden,	194	1,438	7.41	0.52
1 person,	12	66	5.50	0.18
2 persons,	44	285	6.48	0.31
3 persons,	41	300	7.32	0.41
4 persons,	39	310	7.95	0.50
5 persons,	22	174	7.91	0.63
6 persons,	17	133	7.82	0.77
7 persons,	10	89	8.90	0.79
8 persons,	4	34	8.50	0.94
9 persons,	2	16	8.00	1.13
10 persons,	1	11	11.00	0.91
11 persons,	2	20	10.00	1.10
Holland,	55	454	8.20	0.44
1 person,	8	42	5.25	0.19
2 persons,	14	112	8.00	0.25
3 persons,	12	108	9.00	0.33
4 persons,	8	67	8.38	0.48
5 persons,	3	19	6.33	0.79
6 persons,	5	50	10.00	0.90
7 persons,	1	9	9.00	0.78
8 persons,	1	7	7.00	1.14
9 persons,	1	9	9.00	1.00
12 persons,	1	8	8.00	1.50
14 persons,	1	20	20.00	0.70
HOLYOKE,	7,894	43,167	5.47	0.35
1 person,	153	507	3.31	0.30
2 persons,	931	4,302	4.62	0.43
3 persons,	1,289	6,630	5.14	0.58
4 persons,	1,362	7,210	5.29	0.76
5 persons,	1,221	6,647	5.44	0.92
6 persons,	1,021	5,706	5.59	1.07
7 persons,	731	4,106	5.62	1.25
8 persons,	494	2,856	5.78	1.38
9 persons,	289	1,796	6.21	1.45
10 persons,	182	1,167	6.41	1.56
11 persons,	89	562	6.31	1.74
12 persons,	48	360	7.50	1.60
13 persons,	31	238	7.68	1.69
14 persons,	19	195	10.26	1.36
15 persons,	4	60	15.00	1.00
16 persons,	4	25	6.25	2.56
17 persons,	4	45	11.25	1.51
18 persons,	1	9	9.00	2.00

ROOMS: OCCUPIED DWELLING HOUSES — Continued.

COUNTIES, CITIES, TOWNS, AND NUMBER OF PERSONS TO A FAMILY.	Number of Families of Specified Size	Total Number of Rooms Occupied	Average Number of Rooms Occupied	Average Number of Persons to a Room
HAMPDEN — Con.				
HOLYOKE — Con.				
19 persons, . .	4	103	25.75	0.74
20 persons, . .	4	51	12.75	1.57
21 persons, . .	1	20	20.00	1.05
26 persons, . .	1	10	10.00	2.60
28 persons, . .	2	68	34.00	0.82
29 persons, . .	1	60	60.00	0.48
35 persons, . .	1	40	40.00	0.88
36 persons, . .	1	100	100.00	0.36
46 persons, . .	1	31	31.00	1.48
57 persons, . .	1	106	106.00	0.54
63 persons, . .	1	45	45.00	1.40
66 persons, . .	1	54	54.00	1.22
112 persons, . .	1	45	45.00	2.49
134 persons, . .	1	13	13.00	10.31
Holyoke. Ward 1, .	1,145	5,764	5.03	1.04
1 person, . .	18	53	2.94	0.34
2 persons, . .	137	603	4.40	0.45
3 persons, . .	159	760	4.78	0.63
4 persons, . .	207	973	4.70	0.85
5 persons, . .	163	808	4.96	1.01
6 persons, . .	144	745	5.17	1.16
7 persons, . .	114	590	5.18	1.35
8 persons, . .	75	399	5.32	1.50
9 persons, . .	56	301	5.38	1.67
10 persons, . .	28	149	5.32	1.88
11 persons, . .	22	128	5.82	1.89
12 persons, . .	8	46	5.75	2.09
13 persons, . .	8	43	5.38	2.42
14 persons, . .	3	48	16.00	0.88
16 persons, . .	1	6	6.00	2.67
20 persons, . .	1	12	12.00	1.67
36 persons, . .	1	100	100.00	0.36
Holyoke. Ward 2, .	1,690	7,831	4.63	1.13
1 person, . .	40	123	3.08	0.33
2 persons, . .	191	750	3.93	0.51
3 persons, . .	237	985	4.16	0.72
4 persons, . .	257	1,102	4.29	0.93
5 persons, . .	274	1,280	4.67	1.07
6 persons, . .	239	1,146	4.79	1.25
7 persons, . .	155	763	4.92	1.42
8 persons, . .	129	649	5.03	1.59
9 persons, . .	68	343	5.04	1.78
10 persons, . .	42	225	5.36	1.87
11 persons, . .	22	125	5.68	1.94
12 persons, . .	14	91	6.50	1.85
13 persons, . .	9	50	5.56	2.34
14 persons, . .	4	26	6.50	2.15
15 persons, . .	1	30	30.00	0.50
16 persons, . .	2	14	7.00	2.20
17 persons, . .	1	16	16.00	1.06
19 persons, . .	3	83	27.67	0.69
20 persons, . .	2	30	15.00	1.33
Holyoke. Ward 3, .	958	5,562	5.81	0.90
1 person, . .	20	83	4.15	0.24
HAMPDEN — Con.				
Holyoke. Ward 3 — Con.				
2 persons, . .	114	557	4.89	0.41
3 persons, . .	156	836	5.36	0.56
4 persons, . .	164	897	5.47	0.73
5 persons, . .	169	902	5.69	0.88
6 persons, . .	137	832	6.07	0.99
7 persons, . .	76	446	5.87	1.19
8 persons, . .	57	375	6.58	1.22
9 persons, . .	24	159	6.63	1.36
10 persons, . .	19	124	6.53	1.53
11 persons, . .	7	37	5.29	2.08
12 persons, . .	7	55	7.86	1.53
14 persons, . .	2	16	8.00	1.75
15 persons, . .	1	11	11.00	1.36
28 persons, . .	1	29	29.00	0.97
46 persons, . .	1	31	31.00	1.48
66 persons, . .	1	54	54.00	1.22
112 persons, . .	1	45	45.00	2.49
134 persons, . .	1	13	13.00	10.31
Holyoke. Ward 4, .	1,256	5,968	4.75	1.14
1 person, . .	33	94	2.85	0.35
2 persons, . .	160	627	3.92	0.51
3 persons, . .	171	719	4.20	0.71
4 persons, . .	169	756	4.47	0.89
5 persons, . .	177	830	4.69	1.07
6 persons, . .	173	854	4.94	1.22
7 persons, . .	140	663	4.74	1.48
8 persons, . .	90	451	5.01	1.60
9 persons, . .	55	290	5.27	1.71
10 persons, . .	39	241	6.18	1.62
11 persons, . .	15	78	5.20	2.12
12 persons, . .	9	51	5.67	2.12
13 persons, . .	6	61	10.17	1.28
14 persons, . .	7	37	5.29	2.05
15 persons, . .	2	19	9.50	1.58
16 persons, . .	1	5	5.00	3.20
17 persons, . .	2	9	4.50	3.78
18 persons, . .	1	9	9.00	2.00
19 persons, . .	1	20	20.00	0.95
20 persons, . .	1	9	9.00	2.22
21 persons, . .	1	20	20.00	1.05
26 persons, . .	1	10	10.00	2.60
35 persons, . .	1	40	40.00	0.88
63 persons, . .	1	45	45.00	1.40
Holyoke. Ward 5, .	768	4,772	6.21	0.75
1 person, . .	16	61	3.81	0.26
2 persons, . .	109	552	5.06	0.39
3 persons, . .	163	949	5.82	0.52
4 persons, . .	155	776	5.75	0.70
5 persons, . .	107	623	5.82	0.86
6 persons, . .	91	589	6.47	0.93
7 persons, . .	77	516	6.70	1.04
8 persons, . .	29	181	6.24	1.28
9 persons, . .	17	175	10.29	0.87
10 persons, . .	12	129	10.75	0.93

ROOMS: OCCUPIED DWELLING HOUSES — Continued.

Counties, Cities, Towns, and Number of Persons to a Family.	Number of Families of Specified Size	Total Number of Rooms Occupied	Average Number of Rooms Occupied	Average Number of Persons to a Room
HAMPDEN — Con.				
Holyoke. Ward 5 — Con.				
11 persons, . .	6	47	7.83	1.40
12 persons, . .	2	33	16.50	0.73
13 persons, . .	1	5	5.00	2.60
14 persons, . .	1	10	10.00	1.40
17 persons, . .	1	20	20.00	0.85
57 persons, . .	1	106	106.00	0.54
Holyoke. Ward 6, .	1,132	6,126	5.32	0.36
1 person, . .	20	66	3.30	0.30
2 persons, . .	125	540	4.32	0.46
3 persons, . .	208	1,024	4.92	0.61
4 persons, . .	223	1,141	5.12	0.78
5 persons, . .	179	949	5.30	0.94
6 persons, . .	140	757	5.41	1.11
7 persons, . .	103	562	5.46	1.28
8 persons, . .	64	370	5.78	1.38
9 persons, . .	38	227	5.97	1.51
10 persons, . .	26	151	5.81	1.72
11 persons, . .	11	84	7.64	1.44
12 persons, . .	7	67	9.57	1.25
13 persons, . .	4	31	7.75	1.68
14 persons, . .	2	58	29.00	0.48
28 persons, . .	1	39	39.00	0.72
29 persons, . .	1	60	60.00	0.48
Holyoke. Ward 7, .	925	7,174	7.76	0.61
1 person, . .	6	27	4.50	0.22
2 persons, . .	95	673	7.08	0.28
3 persons, . .	195	1,357	6.96	0.43
4 persons, . .	207	1,565	7.56	0.53
5 persons, . .	152	1,195	7.86	0.64
6 persons, . .	97	783	8.07	0.74
7 persons, . .	66	566	8.58	0.82
8 persons, . .	50	431	8.62	0.93
9 persons, . .	31	301	9.71	0.93
10 persons, . .	16	148	9.25	1.08
11 persons, . .	6	63	10.50	1.05
12 persons, . .	1	17	17.00	0.71
13 persons, . .	3	48	16.00	0.81
Longmeadow, . .	146	1,108	7.59	0.56
1 person, . .	10	55	5.50	0.18
2 persons, . .	26	169	6.50	0.31
3 persons, . .	25	174	6.96	0.43
4 persons, . .	34	275	8.09	0.49
5 persons, . .	14	99	7.07	0.71
6 persons, . .	12	101	8.42	0.71
7 persons, . .	10	97	9.70	0.72
8 persons, . .	6	49	8.17	0.98
9 persons, . .	7	61	8.71	1.03
12 persons, . .	2	28	14.00	0.86
Ludlow, . . .	473	2,911	6.15	0.88
1 person, . .	23	90	3.91	0.26
2 persons, . .	48	267	5.56	0.36
3 persons, . .	79	473	5.99	0.50
4 persons, . .	67	404	6.03	0.66
5 persons, . .	62	418	6.74	0.74

Counties, Cities, Towns, and Number of Persons to a Family.	Number of Families of Specified Size	Total Number of Rooms Occupied	Average Number of Rooms Occupied	Average Number of Persons to a Room
HAMPDEN — Con.				
Ludlow — Con.				
6 persons, . .	55	362	6.58	0.91
7 persons, . .	43	275	6.40	1.09
8 persons, . .	34	213	6.26	1.28
9 persons, . .	23	133	5.78	1.56
10 persons, . .	11	57	5.18	1.93
11 persons, . .	10	68	6.80	1.62
12 persons, . .	2	15	7.50	1.60
13 persons, . .	5	37	7.40	1.76
14 persons, . .	2	13	6.50	2.15
15 persons, . .	1	7	7.00	2.14
17 persons, . .	2	13	6.50	2.62
18 persons, . .	1	17	17.00	1.06
21 persons, . .	2	11	5.50	3.82
22 persons, . .	1	27	27.00	0.81
25 persons, . .	2	11	5.50	4.55
Monson, . . .	872	6,220	7.13	0.56
1 person, . .	53	268	5.06	0.20
2 persons, . .	200	1,270	6.35	0.31
3 persons, . .	164	1,132	6.90	0.43
4 persons, . .	130	973	7.48	0.53
5 persons, . .	116	845	7.28	0.69
6 persons, . .	92	678	7.37	0.81
7 persons, . .	51	388	7.61	0.92
8 persons, . .	29	226	7.79	1.03
9 persons, . .	12	91	7.58	1.19
10 persons, . .	8	64	8.00	1.25
11 persons, . .	4	35	8.75	1.26
12 persons, . .	2	18	9.00	1.33
13 persons, . .	2	17	8.50	1.53
14 persons, . .	1	6	6.00	2.33
15 persons, . .	2	11	5.50	2.73
17 persons, . .	2	47	23.50	0.72
20 persons, . .	1	11	11.00	1.82
31 persons, . .	1	30	30.00	1.03
35 persons, . .	1	39	39.00	0.90
114 persons, . .	1	74	74.00	1.61
Montgomery, . .	63	535	8.49	0.51
1 person, . .	2	6	3.00	0.33
2 persons, . .	9	65	7.22	0.28
3 persons, . .	15	125	8.33	0.36
4 persons, . .	13	120	9.23	0.43
5 persons, . .	8	86	10.75	0.47
6 persons, . .	4	31	7.75	0.77
7 persons, . .	8	59	7.38	0.95
8 persons, . .	1	10	10.00	0.80
9 persons, . .	1	12	12.00	0.75
10 persons, . .	1	10	10.00	1.00
11 persons, . .	1	11	11.00	1.00
Palmer, . . .	1,382	9,367	6.78	0.73
1 person, . .	54	246	4.56	0.22
2 persons, . .	190	1,126	5.93	0.34
3 persons, . .	260	1,780	6.85	0.44
4 persons, . .	237	1,628	6.87	0.58
5 persons, . .	196	1,322	6.85	0.73

ROOMS: OCCUPIED DWELLING HOUSES — Continued.

COUNTIES, CITIES, TOWNS, AND NUMBER OF PERSONS TO A FAMILY.	Number of Families of Specified Size	Total Number of Rooms Occupied	Average Number of Rooms occupied	Average Number of Persons to a Room	COUNTIES, CITIES, TOWNS, AND NUMBER OF PERSONS TO A FAMILY.	Number of Families of Specified Size	Total Number of Rooms Occupied	Average Number of Rooms occupied	Average Number of Persons to a Room
HAMPDEN — Con.					**HAMPDEN — Con.**				
Palmer — Con.					SPRINGFIELD — Con.				
6 persons,	117	828	7.08	0.85	12 persons,	35	373	10.66	1.13
7 persons,	107	706	6.60	1.06	13 persons,	20	222	11.10	1.17
8 persons,	74	520	7.03	1.14	14 persons,	15	227	15.13	0.93
9 persons,	47	312	6.64	1.36	15 persons,	12	199	16.58	0.90
10 persons,	41	281	6.85	1.46	16 persons,	4	58	14.50	1.10
11 persons,	16	101	6.31	1.74	17 persons,	6	161	26.83	0.63
12 persons,	15	110	7.33	1.64	18 persons,	3	71	23.67	0.76
13 persons,	9	67	7.44	1.75	20 persons,	2	26	13.00	1.54
14 persons,	5	47	9.40	1.49	21 persons,	2	42	21.00	1.00
15 persons,	3	18	6.00	2.50	22 persons,	2	46	23.00	0.96
16 persons,	6	32	5.33	3.00	23 persons,	2	49	24.50	0.94
17 persons,	2	34	17.00	1.00	24 persons,	2	24	12.00	2.00
18 persons,	2	78	39.00	0.46	27 persons,	2	56	28.00	0.96
20 persons,	1	30	30.00	0.67	28 per-ons,	2	34	17.00	1.65
22 persons,	1	24	24.00	0.92	30 persons,	2	37	18.50	1.62
27 persons,	1	27	27.00	1.00	31 persons,	2	159	79.50	0.39
32 persons,	1	50	50.00	0.64	32 persons,	1	24	24.00	1.33
Russell,	185	1,209	6.54	0.70	33 persons,	1	41	41.00	0.80
1 person,	10	49	4.90	0.20	34 persons,	1	62	31.00	1.10
2 persons,	21	126	6.00	0.33	35 persons,	1	51	51.00	0.69
3 persons,	46	302	6.57	0.46	37 persons,	1	44	44.00	0.84
4 persons,	39	233	5.97	0.67	38 persons,	1	67	33.50	1.13
5 persons,	18	114	6.33	0.79	39 persons,	2	235	117.50	0.33
6 persons,	18	136	7.56	0.79	47 persons,	1	100	100.00	0.47
7 persons,	6	40	6.67	1.05	49 persons,	1	35	35.00	1.40
8 persons,	6	41	6.83	1.17	50 persons,	1	16	16.00	3.13
9 persons,	9	74	8.22	1.09	74 persons,	1	235	235.00	0.31
10 persons,	10	65	6.50	1.54	171 persons,	1	86	86.00	1.99
12 persons,	1	6	6.00	2.00	259 persons,	1	287	287.00	0.90
19 persons,	1	23	23.00	0.83	*Springfield. Ward 1,*	1,604	10,855	6.75	0.64
Southwick,	239	1,754	7.34	0.55	1 person,	32	189	5.91	0.17
1 person,	16	70	4.38	0.23	2 persons,	255	1,588	6.23	0.32
2 persons,	45	307	6.82	0.29	3 persons,	398	2,549	6.40	0.47
3 persons,	52	375	7.21	0.42	4 persons,	312	2,170	6.96	0.58
4 persons,	33	265	8.03	0.50	5 persons,	262	1,749	6.68	0.75
5 persons,	44	333	7.57	0.66	6 persons,	131	924	7.05	0.85
6 persons,	23	188	8.17	0.73	7 persons,	94	700	7.45	0.94
7 persons,	13	120	9.23	0.76	8 persons,	50	365	7.30	1.10
8 persons,	6	41	6.83	1.17	9 persons,	28	210	7.50	1.20
9 persons,	4	37	9.25	0.97	10 persons,	20	148	7.40	1.35
10 persons,	1	4	4.00	2.50	11 persons,	10	88	8.80	1.25
12 persons,	2	14	7.00	1.71	12 persons,	2	13	6.50	1.85
SPRINGFIELD,	11,741	77,438	6.60	0.67	13 persons,	3	32	10.67	1.22
1 person,	403	1,627	4.04	0.25	14 persons,	1	10	10.00	1.40
2 persons,	2,043	11,295	5.51	0.36	15 persons,	2	14	7.00	2.14
3 persons,	2,531	15,686	6.20	0.48	16 persons,	1	14	14.00	1.14
4 persons,	2,221	14,487	6.52	0.61	21 persons,	1	20	20.00	1.05
5 persons,	1,724	11,586	6.72	0.74	24 persons,	1	8	8.00	3.00
6 persons,	1,171	8,147	6.96	0.86	31 persons,	1	44	44.00	0.70
7 persons,	690	4,958	7.19	0.97	*Springfield. Ward 2,*	1,758	9,876	5.62	0.80
8 persons,	411	3,144	7.65	1.05	1 person,	49	176	3.59	0.28
9 persons,	211	1,692	8.02	1.12	2 persons,	287	1,384	4.82	0.41
10 persons,	135	1,160	8.59	1.16	3 persons,	342	1,828	5.35	0.56
11 persons,	72	619	8.60	1.28	4 persons,	328	1,777	5.42	0.74

ROOMS: OCCUPIED DWELLING HOUSES — Continued.

Counties, Cities, Towns, and Number of Persons to a Family.	Number of Families of Specified Size	Total Number of Rooms Occupied	Average Number of Rooms Occupied	Average Number of Persons to a Room	Counties, Cities, Towns, and Number of Persons to a Family.	Number of Families of Specified Size	Total Number of Rooms Occupied	Average Number of Rooms Occupied	Average Number of Persons to a Room
HAMPDEN — Con.					**HAMPDEN — Con.**				
Springfield. Ward 2 — Con.					*Springfield. Ward 4 — Con.*				
5 persons,	276	1,530	5.54	0.90	8 persons,	45	423	9.40	0.85
6 persons,	205	1,109	5.41	1.11	9 persons,	25	258	10.32	0.87
7 persons,	120	672	5.60	1.25	10 persons,	21	217	10.33	0.97
8 persons,	67	404	6.03	1.33	11 persons,	12	119	9.92	1.11
9 persons,	39	259	6.64	1.36	12 persons,	4	40	10.00	1.20
10 persons,	17	129	7.59	1.32	13 persons,	4	41	10.25	1.27
11 persons,	15	113	7.53	1.46	14 persons,	1	17	17.00	0.82
12 persons,	7	64	9.14	1.31	16 persons,	1	17	17.00	0.94
14 persons,	1	16	16.00	0.88	30 persons,	2	37	18.50	1.62
17 persons,	1	27	27.00	0.63	32 persons,	1	24	24.00	1.33
21 persons,	1	22	22.00	0.95	*Springfield. Ward 5,*	1,534	11,391	7.43	0.56
24 persons,	1	16	16.00	1.50	1 person,	36	195	5.42	0.18
31 persons,	1	115	115.00	0.27	2 persons,	285	1,733	6.08	0.33
74 persons,	1	235	235.00	0.31	3 persons,	359	2,478	6.90	0.43
Springfield. Ward 3,	1,369	8,678	6.38	0.71	4 persons,	278	2,081	7.49	0.53
1 person,	133	370	2.78	0.36	5 persons,	234	1,891	8.08	0.62
2 persons,	278	1,137	4.09	0.49	6 persons,	156	1,323	8.48	0.71
3 persons,	240	1,298	5.41	0.55	7 persons,	86	730	8.49	0.82
4 persons,	205	1,144	5.58	0.72	8 persons,	51	454	8.90	0.90
5 persons,	154	964	6.26	0.80	9 persons,	27	263	9.74	0.92
6 persons,	120	815	6.79	0.88	10 persons,	15	161	10.73	0.93
7 persons,	72	527	7.32	0.96	11 persons,	4	36	9.00	1.22
8 persons,	49	442	9.02	0.89	13 persons,	1	13	13.00	1.00
9 persons,	24	221	9.21	0.98	15 persons,	1	17	17.00	0.88
10 persons,	19	199	10.47	0.95	50 persons,	1	16	16.00	3.13
11 persons,	7	73	10.43	1.05	*Springfield. Ward 6,*	1,390	8,480	6.10	0.73
12 persons,	13	177	13.62	0.88	1 person,	40	183	4.58	0.22
13 persons,	8	109	13.63	0.95	2 persons,	245	1,267	5.17	0.39
14 persons,	10	168	16.80	0.83	3 persons,	316	1,746	5.53	0.54
15 persons,	5	97	19.40	0.77	4 persons,	255	1,483	5.85	0.68
16 persons,	1	11	11.00	1.45	5 persons,	199	1,179	5.92	0.84
17 persons,	5	134	26.80	0.63	6 persons,	144	918	6.38	0.94
18 persons,	1	37	37.00	0.49	7 persons,	91	638	7.01	1.00
20 persons,	1	19	19.00	1.05	8 persons,	49	384	7.84	1.02
22 persons,	2	46	23.00	0.96	9 persons,	22	151	6.86	1.31
23 persons,	1	29	29.00	0.79	10 persons,	11	81	7.36	1.36
27 persons,	2	56	28.00	0.96	11 persons,	9	72	8.00	1.38
28 persons,	1	23	23.00	1.22	12 persons,	5	48	9.60	1.25
33 persons,	1	41	41.00	0.80	13 persons,	2	17	8.50	1.53
34 persons,	2	62	31.00	1.10	15 persons,	1	16	16.00	0.94
35 persons,	1	51	51.00	0.69	259 persons,	1	287	287.00	0.90
37 persons,	1	44	44.00	0.84	*Springfield. Ward 7,*	1,136	7,638	6.72	0.61
38 persons,	1	49	49.00	0.78	1 person,	38	170	4.47	0.22
39 persons,	2	235	117.50	0.33	2 persons,	210	1,238	5.90	0.34
47 persons,	1	100	100.00	0.47	3 persons,	258	1,759	6.78	0.44
Springfield. Ward 4,	1,435	10,636	7.41	0.58	4 persons,	246	1,756	7.14	0.56
1 person,	48	205	4.27	0.23	5 persons,	156	1,070	6.86	0.73
2 persons,	234	1,401	5.99	0.33	6 persons,	98	672	6.86	0.88
3 persons,	308	2,050	6.66	0.45	7 persons,	68	488	7.18	0.98
4 persons,	300	2,143	7.14	0.56	8 persons,	37	270	7.30	1.10
5 persons,	224	1,793	8.00	0.62	9 persons,	11	89	8.09	1.11
6 persons,	135	1,247	9.24	0.65	10 persons,	7	52	7.43	1.35
7 persons,	70	604	8.63	0.84	11 persons,	4	38	9.50	1.46

ROOMS: OCCUPIED DWELLING HOUSES — Continued.

Counties, Cities, Towns, and Number of Persons to a Family.	Number of Families of Specified Size	Total Number of Rooms Occupied	Average Number of Rooms Occupied	Average Number of Persons to a Room
HAMPDEN — Con.				
Springfield. Ward 7 — Con.				
20 persons,	1	7	7.00	2.86
23 persons,	1	20	20.00	1.15
38 persons,	1	18	18.00	2.11
Springfield. Ward 8,	1,524	9,904	6.50	0.72
1 person,	27	139	5.15	0.19
2 persons,	249	1,547	6.09	0.33
3 persons,	310	1,987	6.41	0.47
4 persons,	297	1,923	6.47	0.62
5 persons,	219	1,410	6.44	0.78
6 persons,	182	1,139	6.26	0.96
7 persons,	89	580	6.73	1.04
8 persons,	63	402	6.38	1.25
9 persons,	35	241	6.89	1.31
10 persons,	25	173	6.92	1.45
11 persons,	11	80	7.27	1.51
12 persons,	4	31	7.75	1.55
13 persons,	2	10	5.00	2.60
14 persons,	2	16	8.00	1.75
15 persons,	3	55	18.33	0.82
16 persons,	1	16	16.00	1.00
18 persons,	2	34	17.00	1.06
28 persons,	1	11	11.00	2.55
49 persons,	1	35	35.00	1.40
171 persons,	1	86	86.00	1.99
Tolland,	67	651	9.72	0.47
1 person,	4	32	8.00	0.13
2 persons,	12	103	8.58	0.23
3 persons,	13	110	8.46	0.35
4 persons,	9	95	10.56	0.38
5 persons,	8	82	10.25	0.49
6 persons,	7	78	11.14	0.54
7 persons,	3	40	13.33	0.53
8 persons,	3	29	9.67	0.82
9 persons,	3	39	13.00	0.69
10 persons,	3	25	8.33	1.20
11 persons,	2	18	9.00	1.22
Wales,	191	1,436	7.52	0.55
1 person,	13	96	7.38	0.14
2 persons,	45	321	7.13	0.28
3 persons,	34	246	7.24	0.41
4 persons,	22	184	8.36	0.48
5 persons,	35	261	7.46	0.67
6 persons,	15	114	7.60	0.79
7 persons,	13	114	8.77	0.80
8 persons,	4	25	6.25	1.28
9 persons,	3	23	7.67	1.17
10 persons,	3	13	4.33	2.31
11 persons,	3	32	10.67	1.03
12 persons,	1	7	7.00	1.71
Westfield,	2,533	17,232	6.65	0.62
1 person,	125	498	3.98	0.25
2 persons,	474	2,713	5.72	0.35
3 persons,	593	3,685	6.21	0.48
4 persons,	499	3,330	6.67	0.60
HAMPDEN — Con.				
Westfield — Con.				
5 persons,	378	2,764	7.31	0.68
6 persons,	218	1,582	7.26	0.83
7 persons,	137	1,054	7.69	0.91
8 persons,	74	540	7.30	1.10
9 persons,	47	361	7.68	1.17
10 persons,	24	204	8.50	1.18
11 persons,	12	141	11.75	0.94
12 persons,	2	38	19.00	0.63
13 persons,	3	37	12.33	1.05
15 persons,	1	40	40.00	0.38
17 persons,	1	14	14.00	1.21
18 persons,	1	40	40.00	0.45
22 persons,	1	6	6.00	3.67
30 persons,	1	70	70.00	0.43
34 persons,	1	30	30.00	1.13
72 persons,	1	85	85.00	0.85
West Springfield,	1,390	8,186	6.24	0.72
1 person,	26	103	3.96	0.25
2 persons,	229	1,323	5.80	0.34
3 persons,	264	1,614	6.11	0.49
4 persons,	265	1,579	5.96	0.67
5 persons,	198	1,279	6.46	0.77
6 persons,	146	949	6.50	0.92
7 persons,	108	703	6.51	1.08
8 persons,	51	342	6.71	1.19
9 persons,	29	179	6.17	1.46
10 persons,	25	220	8.80	1.14
11 persons,	10	83	8.30	1.33
12 persons,	1	7	7.00	1.71
13 persons,	2	15	7.50	1.73
14 persons,	2	11	5.50	2.55
15 persons,	2	25	12.50	1.20
21 persons,	2	48	24.00	0.88
Wilbraham,	363	3,021	8.32	0.58
1 person,	24	164	6.83	0.15
2 persons,	66	475	7.20	0.28
3 persons,	77	592	7.69	0.39
4 persons,	64	513	8.02	0.50
5 persons,	49	411	8.45	0.59
6 persons,	23	192	8.35	0.72
7 persons,	20	178	8.90	0.79
8 persons,	12	88	7.33	1.09
9 persons,	10	83	8.30	1.08
10 persons,	8	43	5.38	1.86
11 persons,	3	20	6.67	1.65
12 persons,	3	26	8.67	1.38
13 persons,	1	11	11.00	1.18
14 persons,	1	30	30.00	0.47
19 persons,	1	30	30.00	0.63
133 persons,	1	102	162.00	1.19
HAMPSHIRE.				
Amherst,	1,064	8,622	8.10	0.55
1 person,	46	265	5.76	0.17

ROOMS: OCCUPIED DWELLING HOUSES — Continued.

COUNTIES, CITIES, TOWNS, AND NUMBER OF PERSONS TO A FAMILY.	Number of Families of Specified Size	Total Number of Rooms Occupied	Average Number of Rooms Occupied	Average Number of Persons to a Room	COUNTIES, CITIES, TOWNS, AND NUMBER OF PERSONS TO A FAMILY.	Number of Families of Specified Size	Total Number of Rooms Occupied	Average Number of Rooms Occupied	Average Number of Persons to a Room
HAMPSHIRE — Con.					**HAMPSHIRE — Con.**				
Amherst — Con.					**Cummington — Con.**				
2 persons, . .	208	1,400	6.73	0.30	6 persons, . .	11	107	9.73	0.62
3 persons, . .	244	1,786	7.32	0.41	7 persons, . .	9	97	10.78	0.65
4 persons, . .	168	1,208	7.73	0.52	8 persons, . .	4	40	10.00	0.80
5 persons, . .	129	986	7.72	0.65	9 persons, . .	1	24	24.00	0.38
6 persons, . .	99	849	8.58	0.70	11 persons, . .	1	12	12.00	0.92
7 persons, . .	66	604	9.15	0.76	**Easthampton,** . .	1,019	6,809	6.68	0.70
8 persons, . .	31	278	8.97	0.89	1 person, . .	53	184	3.47	0.29
9 persons, . .	28	295	10.54	0.85	2 persons, . .	149	821	5.51	0.36
10 persons, . .	17	201	11.82	0.85	3 persons, . .	179	1,134	6.34	0.47
11 persons, . .	4	50	12.50	0.88	4 persons, . .	185	1,216	6.57	0.61
12 persons, . .	3	61	20.33	0.59	5 persons, . .	145	977	6.74	0.74
13 persons, . .	2	30	15.00	0.87	6 persons, . .	110	789	7.17	0.84
14 persons, . .	2	45	22.50	0.62	7 persons, . .	80	572	7.15	0.98
15 persons, . .	2	40	20.00	0.75	8 persons, . .	46	341	7.41	1.08
16 persons, . .	2	34	17.00	0.94	9 persons, . .	28	188	6.71	1.34
17 persons, . .	1	21	21.00	0.81	10 persons, . .	18	168	9.33	1.07
18 persons, . .	2	47	23.50	0.77	11 persons, . .	9	98	10.89	1.01
19 persons, . .	2	48	24.00	0.79	12 persons, . .	8	65	8.13	1.48
22 persons, . .	1	27	27.00	0.81	13 persons, . .	2	20	10.00	1.30
29 persons, . .	2	88	44.00	0.66	15 persons, . .	2	41	20.50	0.73
30 persons, . .	2	65	32.50	0.92	22 persons, . .	1	24	24.00	0.92
35 persons, . .	1	8	8.00	4.38	24 persons, . .	1	36	36.00	0.67
42 persons, . .	1	42	42.00	1.00	28 persons, . .	1	65	65.00	0.43
44 persons, . .	1	44	44.00	1.00	33 persons, . .	1	28	28.00	1.18
Belchertown, . .	524	3,952	7.54	0.55	59 persons, . .	1	42	42.00	1.40
1 person, . .	43	227	5.28	0.19	**Enfield,** . . .	261	1,921	7.36	0.52
2 persons, . .	105	757	7.21	0.28	1 person, . .	18	91	5.06	0.20
3 persons, . .	110	791	7.19	0.42	2 persons, . .	62	439	7.08	0.28
4 persons, . .	74	608	8.22	0.48	3 persons, . .	62	453	7.31	0.41
5 persons, . .	61	460	7.54	0.66	4 persons, . .	34	254	7.47	0.54
6 persons, . .	40	296	7.40	0.81	5 persons, . .	34	281	8.26	0.60
7 persons, . .	42	347	8.26	0.85	6 persons, . .	27	219	8.11	0.74
8 persons, . .	21	192	9.14	0.88	7 persons, . .	12	92	7.67	0.91
9 persons, . .	18	160	8.89	1.01	8 persons, . .	6	43	7.17	1.12
10 persons, . .	2	29	14.50	0.69	9 persons, . .	2	14	7.00	1.29
11 persons, . .	4	35	8.75	1.26	10 persons, . .	2	14	7.00	1.43
12 persons, . .	3	24	8.00	1.50	12 persons, . .	2	21	10.50	1.14
13 persons, . .	1	26	26.00	0.50	**Goshen,** . . .	66	516	7.82	0.59
Chesterfield, . .	162	1,123	6.93	0.52	1 person, . .	2	7	3.50	0.29
1 person, . .	14	63	4.50	0.22	2 persons, . .	12	83	6.92	0.29
2 persons, . .	40	252	6.30	0.32	3 persons, . .	8	57	7.13	0.42
3 persons, . .	32	218	6.81	0.44	4 persons, . .	9	74	8.22	0.49
4 persons, . .	25	173	6.92	0.58	5 persons, . .	13	96	7.38	0.68
5 persons, . .	21	192	8.00	0.63	6 persons, . .	10	89	8.90	0.67
6 persons, . .	16	138	8.63	0.70	7 persons, . .	8	67	8.38	0.84
7 persons, . .	7	52	7.43	0.94	8 persons, . .	1	6	6.00	1.33
8 persons, . .	3	23	7.67	1.04	9 persons, . .	1	9	9.00	1.00
10 persons, . .	1	12	12.00	0.83	10 persons, . .	2	28	14.00	0.71
Cummington, . .	204	1,731	8.61	0.43	**Granby,** . . .	171	1,332	7.79	0.56
1 person, . .	14	64	4.71	0.21	1 person, . .	9	63	7.00	0.14
2 persons, . .	35	271	7.74	0.26	2 persons, . .	26	163	6.27	0.32
3 persons, . .	52	453	8.71	0.34	3 persons, . .	29	227	7.83	0.38
4 persons, . .	41	370	9.02	0.44	4 persons, . .	31	232	7.48	0.53
5 persons, . .	33	291	8.82	0.57	5 persons, . .	30	244	8.13	0.61

ROOMS: OCCUPIED DWELLING HOUSES — Continued.

Counties, Cities, Towns, and Number of Persons to a Family.	Number of Families of Specified Size	Total Number of Rooms Occupied	Average Number of Rooms Occupied	Average Number of Persons to a Room
HAMPSHIRE — Con.				
Granby — Con.				
6 persons, . .	22	186	8.45	0.71
7 persons, . .	13	125	9.62	0.73
8 persons, . .	4	22	5.50	1.45
10 persons, . .	6	64	10.67	0.94
11 persons, . .	1	6	6.00	1.83
Greenwich, . .	142	1,061	7.47	0.45
1 person, . .	19	123	6.47	0.15
2 persons, . .	41	306	7.46	0.27
3 persons, . .	32	229	7.16	0.42
4 persons, . .	17	121	7.12	0.56
5 persons, . .	12	92	7.67	0.65
6 persons, . .	8	63	7.88	0.76
7 persons, . .	4	43	10.75	0.65
8 persons, . .	3	37	12.33	0.65
9 persons, . .	4	33	8.25	1.09
10 persons, . .	2	14	7.00	1.43
Hadley, . .	389	3,129	8.02	0.54
1 person, . .	20	121	6.05	0.17
2 persons, . .	58	448	7.72	0.26
3 persons, . .	77	557	7.23	0.41
4 persons, . .	66	539	8.17	0.49
5 persons, . .	65	542	8.34	0.60
6 persons, . .	46	360	7.83	0.77
7 persons, . .	22	212	9.64	0.73
8 persons, . .	20	188	9.40	0.85
9 persons, . .	8	72	9.00	1.00
10 persons, . .	5	50	10.00	1.00
11 persons, . .	1	9	9.00	1.22
12 persons, . .	1	14	14.00	0.86
13 persons, . .	1	17	17.00	0.76
Hatfield, . .	291	2,215	7.61	0.57
1 person, . .	16	81	5.06	0.20
2 persons, . .	50	319	6.38	0.31
3 persons, . .	51	369	7.24	0.41
4 persons, . .	55	441	8.02	0.50
5 persons, . .	42	314	7.48	0.67
6 persons, . .	26	226	8.69	0.69
7 persons, . .	24	217	9.04	0.77
8 persons, . .	14	114	8.14	0.98
9 persons, . .	9	88	9.78	0.92
10 persons, . .	1	10	10.00	1.00
11 persons, . .	2	18	9.00	1.22
14 persons, . .	1	18	18.00	0.78
Huntington, . .	329	2,326	7.07	0.62
1 person, . .	12	46	3.83	0.26
2 persons, . .	51	312	6.12	0.33
3 persons, . .	59	418	7.08	0.42
4 persons, . .	73	542	7.42	0.54
5 persons, . .	38	279	7.34	0.68
6 persons, . .	49	377	7.69	0.78
7 persons, . .	24	190	7.92	0.88
8 persons, . .	8	52	6.50	1.23
9 persons, . .	5	35	7.00	1.29
10 persons, . .	7	48	6.86	1.46
HAMPSHIRE — Con.				
Huntington — Con.				
11 persons, . .	1	10	10.00	1.10
12 persons, . .	1	6	6.00	2.00
13 persons, . .	1	11	11.00	1.18
Middlefield, . .	92	808	8.78	0.48
1 person, . .	6	46	7.67	0.13
2 persons, . .	20	190	9.50	0.21
3 persons, . .	20	152	7.60	0.39
4 persons, . .	8	59	7.38	0.54
5 persons, . .	12	111	9.25	0.54
6 persons, . .	11	108	9.91	0.61
7 persons, . .	6	57	9.50	0.74
8 persons, . .	5	51	10.20	0.78
9 persons, . .	2	20	10.00	0.90
10 persons, . .	1	8	8.00	1.25
12 persons, . .	1	5	5.00	2.40
NORTHAMPTON, . .	3,270	23,272	7.12	0.72
1 person, . .	124	509	4.10	0.24
2 persons, . .	507	3,007	5.93	0.34
3 persons, . .	614	3,898	6.30	0.48
4 persons, . .	574	3,885	6.68	0.60
5 persons, . .	450	3,197	7.10	0.70
6 persons, . .	333	2,311	6.94	0.86
7 persons, . .	243	1,799	7.40	0.95
8 persons, . .	165	1,227	7.44	1.08
9 persons, . .	101	764	7.56	1.19
10 persons, . .	54	400	7.41	1.35
11 persons, . .	31	296	8.58	1.28
12 persons, . .	12	96	8.00	1.50
13 persons, . .	18	212	11.78	1.10
14 persons, . .	4	59	14.75	0.95
15 persons, . .	6	60	10.00	1.50
16 persons, . .	2	18	9.00	1.78
17 persons, . .	1	60	60.00	0.28
18 persons, . .	2	62	31.00	0.58
22 persons, . .	2	120	60.00	0.37
23 persons, . .	1	13	13.00	1.77
24 persons, . .	2	66	33.00	0.73
25 persons, . .	3	83	27.67	0.90
28 persons, . .	1	22	22.00	1.27
29 persons, . .	1	23	23.00	1.26
34 persons, . .	2	73	36.50	0.93
35 persons, . .	1	32	32.00	1.09
40 persons, . .	1	55	55.00	0.73
43 persons, . .	1	32	32.00	1.34
45 persons, . .	1	56	56.00	0.80
49 persons, . .	1	45	45.00	1.09
50 persons, . .	1	33	33.00	1.52
54 persons, . .	2	96	48.00	1.13
57 persons, . .	1	55	55.00	1.04
59 persons, . .	1	62	62.00	0.95
60 persons, . .	1	50	50.00	1.20
63 persons, . .	1	65	65.00	0.97
64 persons, . .	1	55	55.00	1.16
66 persons, . .	1	63	63.00	1.05

ROOMS: OCCUPIED DWELLING HOUSES — Continued.

Counties, Cities, Towns, and Number of Persons to a Family	Number of Families of Specified Size	Total Number of Rooms Occupied	Average Number of Rooms Occupied	Average Number of Persons to a Room
HAMPSHIRE — Con.				
NORTHAMPTON — Con.				
68 persons,	1	65	65.00	1.05
72 persons,	1	65	65.00	1.11
608 persons,	1	295	295.00	2.06
Northampton. Wd. 1,	480	3,151	6.56	0.69
1 person,	37	99	2.68	0.37
2 persons,	87	492	5.66	0.35
3 persons,	89	559	6.28	0.48
4 persons,	75	459	6.12	0.65
5 persons,	62	431	6.95	0.72
6 persons,	42	260	6.19	0.97
7 persons,	32	225	7.03	1.00
8 persons,	22	150	6.82	1.17
9 persons,	11	84	7.64	1.18
10 persons,	6	42	7.00	1.43
11 persons,	5	39	7.80	1.41
12 persons,	1	5	5.00	2.40
13 persons,	4	71	17.75	0.73
15 persons,	1	10	10.00	1.50
16 persons,	1	6	6.00	2.67
18 persons,	1	41	41.00	0.44
22 persons,	1	100	100.00	0.22
23 persons,	1	13	13.00	1.77
24 persons,	1	40	40.00	0.60
34 persons,	1	25	25.00	1.36
Northampton. Wd. 2,	507	4,690	9.25	0.69
1 person,	11	58	5.27	0.19
2 persons,	79	493	6.24	0.32
3 persons,	103	719	6.98	0.43
4 persons,	80	584	7.30	0.55
5 persons,	65	524	8.06	0.62
6 persons,	48	422	8.79	0.68
7 persons,	32	315	9.84	0.71
8 persons,	25	218	8.72	0.92
9 persons,	17	175	10.29	0.87
10 persons,	8	81	10.13	0.99
11 persons,	6	72	12.00	0.92
12 persons,	2	22	11.00	1.09
13 persons,	4	49	12.25	1.06
14 persons,	4	59	14.75	0.95
15 persons,	2	25	12.50	1.20
16 persons,	1	12	12.00	1.33
18 persons,	1	21	21.00	0.86
22 persons,	1	20	20.00	1.10
25 persons,	2	42	21.00	1.19
28 persons,	1	22	22.00	1.27
29 persons,	1	23	23.00	1.26
34 persons,	1	48	48.00	0.71
35 persons,	1	32	32.00	1.09
49 persons,	1	45	45.00	1.09
50 persons,	1	33	33.00	1.52
54 persons,	2	96	48.00	1.13
57 persons,	1	55	55.00	1.04
59 persons,	1	62	62.00	0.95
HAMPSHIRE — Con.				
Northampton. Wd. 2 — Con.				
60 persons,	1	50	50.00	1.20
63 persons,	1	65	65.00	0.97
64 persons,	1	55	55.00	1.16
66 persons,	1	63	63.00	1.05
68 persons,	1	65	65.00	1.05
72 persons,	1	65	65.00	1.11
Northampton. Wd. 3,	607	4,160	6.85	0.69
1 person,	13	57	4.38	0.23
2 persons,	98	552	5.75	0.35
3 persons,	114	709	6.22	0.48
4 persons,	126	842	6.68	0.60
5 persons,	80	577	7.21	0.69
6 persons,	55	390	7.09	0.85
7 persons,	50	376	7.52	0.93
8 persons,	29	200	6.90	1.16
9 persons,	15	97	6.47	1.39
10 persons,	13	93	7.15	1.40
11 persons,	4	31	7.75	1.42
12 persons,	4	33	8.25	1.45
13 persons,	5	46	9.20	1.41
17 persons,	1	60	60.00	0.28
25 persons,	1	41	41.00	0.61
45 persons,	1	56	56.00	0.80
Northampton. Wd. 4,	423	3,116	7.37	0.80
1 person,	23	113	4.91	0.20
2 persons,	69	437	6.33	0.32
3 persons,	98	566	6.09	0.49
4 persons,	66	422	6.39	0.63
5 persons,	55	396	7.20	0.69
6 persons,	39	269	6.90	0.87
7 persons,	35	265	7.57	0.92
8 persons,	23	174	7.57	1.06
9 persons,	8	52	6.50	1.38
10 persons,	3	20	6.67	1.50
11 persons,	4	25	6.25	1.76
12 persons,	1	7	7.00	1.71
13 persons,	1	17	17.00	0.76
24 persons,	1	26	26.00	0.92
43 persons,	1	32	32.00	1.34
608 persons,	1	295	295.00	2.06
Northampton. Wd. 5,	445	2,806	6.31	0.76
1 person,	11	52	4.73	0.21
2 persons,	59	341	5.78	0.35
3 persons,	76	442	5.82	0.52
4 persons,	80	516	6.45	0.62
5 persons,	64	405	6.33	0.79
6 persons,	56	357	6.38	0.94
7 persons,	44	284	6.45	1.08
8 persons,	26	171	6.58	1.22
9 persons,	15	120	8.00	1.13
10 persons,	7	53	7.57	1.32
11 persons,	5	51	10.20	1.08
12 persons,	1	8	8.00	1.50
15 persons,	1	6	6.00	2.50

ROOMS: OCCUPIED DWELLING HOUSES — Continued.

COUNTIES, CITIES, TOWNS, AND NUMBER OF PERSONS TO A FAMILY.	Number of Families of Specified size	Total Number of Rooms Occupied	Average Number of Rooms Occupied	Average Number of Persons to a Room
HAMPSHIRE — Con.				
Northampton. Wd.6,	412	2,780	6.75	0.68
1 person,	17	81	4.76	0.21
2 persons,	67	413	6.16	0.32
3 persons,	67	410	6.12	0.49
4 persons,	73	485	6.64	0.60
5 persons,	75	530	7.07	0.71
6 persons,	39	267	6.85	0.88
7 persons,	25	162	6.48	1.08
8 persons,	22	184	8.36	0.36
9 persons,	11	84	7.64	1.18
10 persons,	11	72	6.55	1.53
11 persons,	2	14	7.00	1.57
13 persons,	1	9	9.00	1.44
15 persons,	1	14	14.00	1.07
40 persons,	1	55	55.00	0.73
Northampton. Wd.7,	396	2,569	6.49	0.75
1 person,	12	49	4.08	0.24
2 persons,	50	279	5.58	0.36
3 persons,	72	461	6.40	0.47
4 persons,	74	527	7.12	0.56
5 persons,	49	334	6.82	0.73
6 persons,	54	346	6.41	0.94
7 persons,	25	172	6.88	1.02
8 persons,	18	130	7.22	1.11
9 persons,	24	152	6.33	1.42
10 persons,	6	39	6.50	1.54
11 persons,	5	34	6.80	1.62
12 persons,	3	21	7.00	1.71
13 persons,	3	20	6.67	1.95
15 persons,	1	5	5.00	3.00
Pelham,	126	858	6.81	0.57
1 person,	7	28	4.00	0.25
2 persons,	33	190	5.76	0.35
3 persons,	26	213	8.19	0.37
4 persons,	23	169	7.35	0.54
5 persons,	12	74	6.17	0.81
6 persons,	8	54	6.75	0.89
7 persons,	9	69	7.67	0.91
8 persons,	5	36	7.20	1.11
10 persons,	1	6	6.00	1.67
11 persons,	2	19	9.50	1.16
Plainfield,	109	1,113	10.21	0.40
1 person,	4	16	4.00	0.25
2 persons,	25	223	8.92	0.22
3 persons,	18	186	10.33	0.29
4 persons,	14	137	9.79	0.41
5 persons,	25	306	12.24	0.41
6 persons,	10	109	10.90	0.55
7 persons,	6	58	9.67	0.72
8 persons,	5	55	11.00	0.73
9 persons,	1	8	8.00	1.13
10 persons,	1	15	15.00	0.67
Prescott,	106	812	7.66	0.49
1 person,	5	21	4.20	0.24
2 persons,	29	205	7.07	0.28

COUNTIES, CITIES, TOWNS, AND NUMBER OF PERSONS TO A FAMILY.	Number of Families of Specified size	Total Number of Rooms Occupied	Average Number of Rooms Occupied	Average Number of Persons to a Room
HAMPSHIRE — Con.				
Prescott — Con.				
3 persons,	26	196	7.54	0.40
4 persons,	13	102	7.85	0.51
5 persons,	15	123	8.20	0.61
6 persons,	7	69	9.86	0.61
7 persons,	4	35	8.75	0.80
8 persons,	3	24	8.00	1.00
9 persons,	2	18	9.00	1.00
10 persons,	1	7	7.00	1.43
11 persons,	1	12	12.00	0.92
Southampton,	252	1,809	7.18	0.58
1 person,	23	108	4.70	0.21
2 persons,	44	319	7.25	0.28
3 persons,	45	292	6.49	0.46
4 persons,	43	315	7.33	0.55
5 persons,	32	258	8.06	0.62
6 persons,	23	178	7.74	0.78
7 persons,	20	159	7.95	0.88
8 persons,	12	99	8.25	0.97
9 persons,	3	17	5.67	1.59
10 persons,	3	35	11.67	0.86
11 persons,	3	21	7.00	1.57
12 persons,	1	8	8.00	1.50
South Hadley,	894	6,071	6.79	0.73
1 person,	31	139	4.48	0.22
2 persons,	131	786	6.00	0.33
3 persons,	161	988	6.14	0.49
4 persons,	162	1,096	6.77	0.59
5 persons,	144	965	6.70	0.75
6 persons,	98	689	7.03	0.85
7 persons,	61	412	6.75	1.04
8 persons,	48	415	8.65	0.93
9 persons,	22	122	5.55	1.62
10 persons,	16	163	6.44	1.55
11 persons,	15	112	7.47	1.47
12 persons,	1	14	14.00	0.86
14 persons,	1	14	14.00	1.00
15 persons,	1	10	10.00	1.50
28 persons,	1	24	24.00	1.17
30 persons,	1	182	182.00	1.69
Ware,	1,523	10,223	6.71	0.75
1 person,	55	252	4.58	0.22
2 persons,	261	1,225	6.60	0.33
3 persons,	249	1,653	6.64	0.45
4 persons,	254	1,772	6.98	0.57
5 persons,	195	1,368	7.02	0.71
6 persons,	200	1,327	6.64	0.80
7 persons,	113	775	6.86	1.02
8 persons,	100	665	6.65	1.20
9 persons,	59	425	7.20	1.25
10 persons,	40	297	7.43	1.35
11 persons,	21	154	7.33	1.50
12 persons,	15	110	7.33	1.64
13 persons,	6	46	7.67	1.70
14 persons,	6	36	6.00	2.33

ROOMS: OCCUPIED DWELLING HOUSES — Continued.

COUNTIES, CITIES, TOWNS, AND NUMBER OF PERSONS TO A FAMILY.	Number of Families of Specified Size	Total Number of Rooms Occupied	Average Number of Rooms Occupied	Average Number of Persons to a Room	COUNTIES, CITIES, TOWNS, AND NUMBER OF PERSONS TO A FAMILY.	Number of Families of Specified Size	Total Number of Rooms Occupied	Average Number of Rooms Occupied	Average Number of Persons to a Room
HAMPSHIRE — Con.					**MIDDLESEX — Con.**				
Ware — Con.					Acton — Con.				
15 persons,	3	37	12.33	1.22	9 persons,	8	84	10.50	0.86
16 persons,	1	5	5.00	3.20	10 persons,	3	28	9.33	1.07
18 persons,	3	19	6.33	2.84	11 persons,	2	23	11.50	0.96
22 persons,	1	8	8.00	2.75	13 persons,	1	11	11.00	1.18
24 persons,	1	49	49.00	0.49	Arlington, .	1,362	10,228	7.51	0.64
Westhampton, .	124	861	6.94	0.55	1 person,	26	128	4.92	0.20
1 person,	15	63	4.20	0.24	2 persons,	172	1,019	5.92	0.34
2 persons,	21	153	7.29	0.27	3 persons,	271	1,821	6.72	0.45
3 persons,	23	162	7.04	0.43	4 persons,	225	1,626	7.23	0.55
4 persons,	22	154	7.00	0.57	5 persons,	209	1,657	7.93	0.63
5 persons,	20	161	8.05	0.62	6 persons,	190	1,566	8.24	0.73
6 persons,	11	80	7.27	0.83	7 persons,	113	943	8.35	0.84
7 persons,	5	37	7.40	0.95	8 persons,	71	613	8.63	0.93
8 persons,	4	34	8.50	0.94	9 persons,	34	302	8.88	1.01
9 persons,	2	7	3.50	2.57	10 persons,	21	175	8.33	1.20
11 persons,	1	10	10.00	1.10	11 persons,	10	103	10.30	1.07
Williamsburg, .	473	3,259	6.89	0.60	12 persons,	9	100	11.11	1.08
1 person,	26	145	5.58	0.18	13 persons,	8	112	14.00	0.93
2 persons,	101	648	6.42	0.31	14 persons,	1	13	13.00	1.08
3 persons,	96	656	6.83	0.44	15 persons,	1	20	20.00	0.75
4 persons,	92	651	7.08	0.57	21 persons,	1	30	30.00	0.97
5 persons,	59	408	6.92	0.72	Ashby, .	233	1,723	7.39	0.47
6 persons,	30	218	7.27	0.83	1 person,	18	110	6.11	0.16
7 persons,	27	199	7.37	0.95	2 persons,	54	379	7.02	0.28
8 persons,	11	72	6.55	1.22	3 persons,	64	485	7.58	0.40
9 persons,	14	104	7.43	1.21	4 persons,	49	381	7.78	0.51
10 persons,	5	36	7.20	1.39	5 persons,	23	179	7.78	0.64
11 persons,	7	51	7.29	1.51	6 persons,	12	97	8.08	0.74
12 persons,	3	22	7.33	1.64	7 persons,	5	31	6.20	1.13
13 persons,	1	15	15.00	0.87	8 persons,	5	36	7.20	1.11
17 persons,	1	34	34.00	0.50	9 persons,	2	18	9.00	1.00
Worthington,	155	1,239	7.99	0.52	10 persons,	1	7	7.00	1.43
1 person,	11	66	6.00	0.17	Ashland, .	486	3,560	7.33	0.59
2 persons,	27	185	6.85	0.29	1 person,	34	174	5.12	0.20
3 persons,	29	225	7.76	0.39	2 persons,	88	571	6.49	0.31
4 persons,	28	228	8.14	0.49	3 persons,	97	689	7.10	0.42
5 persons,	21	185	8.81	0.57	4 persons,	81	639	7.89	0.51
6 persons,	16	157	9.81	0.61	5 persons,	56	397	7.09	0.71
7 persons,	10	88	8.80	0.80	6 persons,	40	309	7.73	0.78
8 persons,	6	52	8.67	0.92	7 persons,	38	296	7.59	0.92
9 persons,	5	32	6.40	1.41	8 persons,	19	151	7.95	1.01
10 persons,	2	21	10.50	0.95	9 persons,	14	112	8.00	1.13
					10 persons,	8	86	10.75	0.93
					11 persons,	8	89	11.13	0.99
MIDDLESEX.					13 persons,	2	47	23.50	0.55
Acton, .	529	3,824	7.23	0.52	Ayer, .	528	3,516	6.66	0.60
1 person,	28	125	4.46	0.22	1 person,	39	174	4.46	0.22
2 persons,	123	778	6.33	0.32	2 persons,	114	686	6.02	0.33
3 persons,	124	863	6.96	0.43	3 persons,	107	700	6.54	0.46
4 persons,	112	866	7.73	0.52	4 persons,	86	566	6.58	0.61
5 persons,	59	471	7.98	0.63	5 persons,	70	518	7.40	0.68
6 persons,	38	288	7.58	0.79	6 persons,	38	269	7.08	0.85
7 persons,	24	223	9.29	0.75	7 persons,	41	312	7.61	0.92
8 persons,	7	64	9.14	0.88	8 persons,	15	99	6.60	1.21

ROOMS: OCCUPIED DWELLING HOUSES — Continued.

MIDDLESEX — Con.

Ayer — Con.

Counties, Cities, Towns, and Number of Persons to a Family	Number of Families of Specified Size	Total Number of Rooms Occupied	Average Number of Rooms Occupied	Average Number of Persons to a Room
9 persons,	11	91	8.27	1.09
10 persons,	2	19	9.50	1.05
11 persons,	2	14	6.50	1.69
13 persons,	2	43	21.50	0.90
17 persons,	1	26	26.00	0.65
Bedford,	251	1,956	7.79	0.60
1 person,	14	71	5.07	0.20
2 persons,	47	322	6.85	0.29
3 persons,	44	304	6.91	0.43
4 persons,	51	409	8.02	0.50
5 persons,	25	194	7.76	0.64
6 persons,	25	204	8.16	0.74
7 persons,	12	104	8.67	0.81
8 persons,	8	65	8.13	0.98
9 persons,	9	72	8.00	1.13
10 persons,	5	65	13.00	0.77
11 persons,	4	47	11.75	0.94
12 persons,	1	6	6.00	2.00
13 persons,	1	13	13.00	1.00
15 persons,	1	8	8.00	1.88
16 persons,	1	17	17.00	0.94
17 persons,	1	27	27.00	0.63
18 persons,	1	18	18.00	1.00
36 persons,	1	10	10.00	3.60
Belmont,	505	4,020	7.96	0.71
1 person,	12	52	4.33	0.23
2 persons,	64	394	6.16	0.32
3 persons,	80	583	7.29	0.41
4 persons,	87	678	7.79	0.51
5 persons,	79	614	7.77	0.64
6 persons,	58	457	7.88	0.76
7 persons,	30	262	8.73	0.80
8 persons,	38	338	8.89	0.90
9 persons,	18	145	8.06	1.12
10 persons,	15	134	8.93	1.12
11 persons,	4	49	12.25	0.90
12 persons,	9	115	12.78	0.94
13 persons,	3	28	9.33	1.39
14 persons,	3	63	21.00	0.67
38 persons,	1	38	38.00	1.00
39 persons,	1	25	25.00	1.56
53 persons,	1	25	25.00	2.12
80 persons,	1	10	10.00	8.00
103 persons,	1	10	10.00	10.30
Billerica,	582	4,114	7.07	0.63
1 person,	36	149	4.14	0.24
2 persons,	87	551	6.33	0.32
3 persons,	105	715	6.81	0.44
4 persons,	111	813	7.32	0.55
5 persons,	85	640	7.53	0.66
6 persons,	61	461	7.56	0.79
7 persons,	47	319	6.79	1.03
8 persons,	25	205	8.20	0.98
9 persons,	8	55	6.88	1.31

MIDDLESEX — Con.

Billerica — Con.

Counties, Cities, Towns, and Number of Persons to a Family	Number of Families of Specified Size	Total Number of Rooms Occupied	Average Number of Rooms Occupied	Average Number of Persons to a Room
10 persons,	10	85	8.50	1.18
11 persons,	3	33	11.00	1.00
12 persons,	1	9	9.00	1.33
13 persons,	1	14	14.00	0.93
16 persons,	1	21	21.00	0.76
42 persons,	1	44	44.00	0.95
Boxborough,	78	556	7.13	0.55
1 person,	6	22	3.67	0.27
2 persons,	14	83	5.93	0.34
3 persons,	20	142	7.10	0.42
4 persons,	15	112	7.47	0.54
5 persons,	7	67	9.57	0.52
6 persons,	6	46	7.67	0.78
7 persons,	3	24	8.00	0.88
8 persons,	4	33	8.25	0.97
9 persons,	2	18	9.00	1.00
11 person,	1	9	9.00	1.22
Burlington,	129	938	7.27	0.61
1 person,	11	58	5.27	0.19
2 persons,	24	132	5.50	0.36
3 persons,	23	147	6.39	0.47
4 persons,	20	143	7.15	0.56
5 persons,	7	64	9.14	0.55
6 persons,	12	106	8.83	0.68
7 persons,	16	138	8.63	0.81
8 persons,	8	69	8.63	0.93
9 persons,	3	26	8.67	1.04
10 persons,	2	12	6.00	1.67
11 persons,	1	10	10.00	1.10
12 persons,	1	13	13.00	0.92
13 persons,	1	20	20.00	0.65
CAMBRIDGE,	17,116	104,028	6.05	0.78
1 person,	447	1,638	3.66	0.27
2 persons,	2,580	12,147	4.71	0.42
3 persons,	3,143	16,849	5.36	0.56
4 persons,	3,150	18,346	5.82	0.69
5 persons,	2,637	16,245	6.16	0.81
6 persons,	1,975	12,899	6.53	0.92
7 persons,	1,359	9,210	6.78	1.03
8 persons,	845	6,152	7.28	1.10
9 persons,	482	3,606	7.48	1.20
10 persons,	231	1,940	8.40	1.19
11 persons,	145	1,345	9.28	1.19
12 persons,	61	595	9.75	1.23
13 persons,	47	519	11.04	1.18
14 persons,	17	207	12.18	1.15
15 persons,	17	245	14.41	1.04
16 persons,	10	131	13.10	1.22
17 persons,	5	73	14.60	1.16
18 persons,	4	81	20.25	0.89
19 persons,	1	20	20.00	0.95
20 persons,	4	97	24.25	0.82
21 persons,	3	65	21.67	0.97
22 persons,	3	65	21.67	1.02

ROOMS: OCCUPIED DWELLING HOUSES — Continued.

Counties, Cities, Towns, and Number of Persons to a Family	Number of Families of Specified Size	Total Number of Rooms Occupied	Average Number of Rooms Occupied	Average Number of Persons to a Room
MIDDLESEX-Con.				
CAMBRIDGE — Con.				
23 persons,	1	6	6.00	3.83
24 persons,	1	20	20.00	1.20
26 persons,	1	40	40.00	0.65
27 persons,	1	37	37.00	0.73
32 persons,	2	98	49.00	0.65
38 persons,	1	32	32.00	1.19
39 persons,	1	20	20.00	1.95
41 persons,	1	6	6.00	6.83
43 persons,	2	91	45.50	0.95
44 persons,	1	21	21.00	2.10
47 persons,	1	43	43.00	1.09
48 persons,	1	7	7.00	6.86
49 persons,	1	32	32.00	1.53
53 persons,	2	84	42.00	1.26
57 persons,	1	48	48.00	1.19
78 persons,	1	60	60.00	1.30
80 persons,	1	53	53.00	1.51
96 persons,	1	68	68.00	1.41
98 persons,	1	60	60.00	1.63
99 persons,	2	129	64.50	1.53
120 persons,	1	88	88.00	1.36
122 persons,	1	42	42.00	2.90
564 persons,	1	468	468.00	1.21
Cambridge. Ward 1,	2,943	22,615	7.68	0.70
1 person,	74	313	4.23	0.24
2 persons	366	1,843	5.04	0.40
3 persons,	451	2,769	6.14	0.49
4 persons,	534	3,697	6.92	0.57
5 persons,	460	3,458	7.47	0.67
6 persons,	356	2,934	8.24	0.73
7 persons,	267	2,166	8.11	0.86
8 persons,	155	1,406	9.07	0.88
9 persons,	100	1,053	10.53	0.85
10 persons,	61	648	10.62	0.94
11 persons,	44	515	11.70	0.94
12 persons,	17	206	12.12	0.99
13 persons,	12	185	15.42	0.84
14 persons,	5	85	17.00	0.82
15 persons,	7	120	17.14	0.88
16 persons,	3	56	18.67	0.86
17 persons,	2	32	16.00	1.66
18 persons,	3	65	21.67	0.83
20 persons,	2	53	26.50	0.75
21 persons,	1	20	20.00	1.05
22 persons,	1	31	31.00	0.71
24 persons,	1	20	20.00	1.20
26 persons,	1	40	40.00	0.65
27 persons,	1	37	37.00	0.73
32 persons,	1	47	47.00	0.68
38 persons,	1	32	32.00	1.19
39 persons,	1	20	20.00	1.95
43 persons,	2	91	45.50	0.95
44 persons,	1	21	21.00	2.10
47 persons,	1	43	43.00	1.95
MIDDLESEX-Con.				
Cambridge. Ward 1 — Con.				
48 persons,	1	7	7.00	6.86
49 persons,	1	32	32.00	1.53
53 persons,	2	84	42.00	1.26
57 persons,	1	48	48.00	1.19
78 persons,	1	60	60.00	1.30
80 persons,	1	53	53.00	1.51
96 persons,	1	68	68.00	1.41
98 persons,	1	60	60.00	1.63
99 persons,	2	129	64.50	1.53
120 persons,	1	88	88.00	1.36
Cambridge. Ward 2,	4,369	27,924	5.59	0.81
1 person,	116	392	3.38	0.30
2 persons,	818	3,684	4.50	0.44
3 persons,	905	4,923	5.40	0.59
4 persons,	912	4,956	5.43	0.74
5 persons,	756	4,361	5.81	0.86
6 persons,	554	3,404	6.14	0.98
7 persons,	388	2,509	6.47	1.08
8 persons,	220	1,498	6.81	1.17
9 persons,	137	935	6.82	1.32
10 persons,	61	513	8.41	1.19
11 persons,	26	185	7.12	1.55
12 persons,	15	146	9.73	1.23
13 persons,	15	169	11.27	1.15
14 persons,	5	59	11.80	1.19
15 persons,	5	55	11.00	1.36
16 persons,	2	22	11.00	1.45
17 persons,	1	20	20.00	0.85
18 persons,	1	16	16.00	1.13
19 persons,	1	20	20.00	0.95
22 persons,	1	30	30.00	0.73
Cambridge. Ward 3,	2,812	14,173	5.04	0.99
1 person,	83	255	3.07	0.33
2 persons,	393	1,576	4.01	0.50
3 persons,	469	2,111	4.50	0.67
4 persons,	463	2,132	4.60	0.87
5 persons,	453	2,241	4.95	1.01
6 persons,	366	1,918	5.24	1.44
7 persons,	243	1,303	5.36	1.31
8 persons,	149	905	6.07	1.32
9 persons,	101	594	5.88	1.53
10 persons,	40	247	6.18	1.62
11 persons,	23	164	7.13	1.54
12 persons,	11	77	7.00	1.71
13 persons,	7	59	8.43	1.54
14 persons,	2	14	7.00	2.00
15 persons,	2	31	15.50	0.97
16 persons,	2	21	10.50	1.52
17 persons,	2	21	10.50	1.62
20 persons,	1	11	11.00	1.82
21 persons,	1	25	25.00	0.84
564 persons,	1	468	468.00	1.21
Cambridge. Ward 4,	4,235	24,398	5.76	0.77
1 person,	122	454	3.72	0.27

ROOMS: OCCUPIED DWELLING HOUSES — Continued.

COUNTIES, CITIES, TOWNS, AND NUMBER OF PERSONS TO A FAMILY.	Number of Families of Specified Size	Total Number of Rooms Occupied	Average Number of Rooms Occupied	Average Number of Persons to a Room	COUNTIES, CITIES, TOWNS, AND NUMBER OF PERSONS TO A FAMILY.	Number of Families of Specified Size	Total Number of Rooms Occupied	Average Number of Rooms Occupied	Average Number of Persons to a Room
MIDDLESEX - Con.					**MIDDLESEX - Con.**				
Cambridge. Ward 4 — Con.					Chelmsford — Con.				
2 persons,	707	3,419	4.84	0.41	4 persons,	144	1,063	7.38	0.54
3 persons,	861	4,562	5.30	0.57	5 persons,	112	836	7.46	0.67
4 persons,	799	4,601	5.76	0.69	6 persons,	57	415	7.28	0.82
5 persons,	643	3,852	5.99	0.83	7 persons,	46	363	7.89	0.89
6 persons,	407	2,526	6.21	0.97	8 persons,	27	231	8.56	0.94
7 persons,	297	1,941	6.54	1.07	9 persons,	8	56	7.00	1.29
8 persons,	196	1,428	7.29	1.10	10 persons,	7	56	8.00	1.25
9 persons,	96	693	7.22	1.25	11 persons,	4	42	10.50	1.05
10 persons,	45	326	7.24	1.38	12 persons,	1	9	9.00	1.33
11 persons,	34	302	8.88	1.24	14 persons,	1	5	5.00	2.80
12 persons,	13	119	9.15	1.31	16 persons,	1	15	15.00	1.07
13 persons,	6	51	8.50	1.53	17 persons,	1	10	10.00	1.70
14 persons,	3	31	10.33	1.35	23 persons,	1	22	22.00	1.05
15 persons,	2	28	14.00	1.07	69 persons,	1	20	20.00	3.45
16 persons,	3	32	10.67	1.50	Concord,	874	7,575	8.67	0.68
20 persons,	1	33	33.00	0.60	1 person,	52	145	4.53	0.22
Cambridge. Ward 5,	2,204	14,918	6.77	0.70	2 persons,	131	863	6.59	0.30
1 person,	52	224	4.31	0.23	3 persons,	146	1,013	6.94	0.43
2 persons,	296	1,628	5.50	0.36	4 persons,	167	1,205	7.22	0.55
3 persons,	397	2,484	6.26	0.48	5 persons,	123	981	7.81	0.64
4 persons,	442	2,960	6.70	0.60	6 persons,	91	744	8.18	0.73
5 persons,	325	2,323	7.15	0.70	7 persons,	61	472	7.74	0.90
6 persons,	292	2,117	7.25	0.83	8 persons,	53	418	7.89	1.01
7 persons,	164	1,291	7.87	0.89	9 persons,	29	289	9.97	0.90
8 persons,	125	915	7.32	1.09	10 persons,	18	149	8.28	1.21
9 persons,	48	331	6.90	1.31	11 persons,	7	59	8.43	1.31
10 persons,	24	206	8.58	1.17	12 persons,	5	58	11.60	1.03
11 persons,	18	179	9.94	1.11	13 persons,	2	27	13.50	0.96
12 persons,	5	47	9.40	1.28	14 persons,	4	61	15.25	0.92
13 persons,	7	55	7.86	1.65	15 persons,	1	11	11.00	1.36
14 persons,	2	18	9.00	1.56	16 persons,	1	23	23.00	0.70
15 persons,	1	11	11.00	1.36	18 persons,	1	18	18.00	1.00
21 persons,	1	20	20.00	1.05	22 persons,	1	24	24.00	0.92
22 persons,	1	4	4.00	5.50	1,632 persons,	1	1,635	1635.00	1.00
23 persons,	1	6	6.00	3.83	Dracut,	475	3,380	7.13	0.72
32 persons,	1	51	51.00	0.63	1 person,	12	55	4.58	0.22
41 persons,	1	6	6.00	6.83	2 persons,	65	386	6.09	0.33
122 persons,	1	42	42.00	2.90	3 persons,	88	617	7.01	0.43
Carlisle,	126	889	7.06	0.55	4 persons,	64	425	6.64	0.60
1 person,	10	52	5.20	0.19	5 persons,	78	564	7.23	0.69
2 persons,	30	188	6.27	0.32	6 persons,	47	336	7.15	0.84
3 persons,	21	148	7.05	0.43	7 persons,	41	272	6.63	1.06
4 persons,	20	144	7.20	0.56	8 persons,	33	253	7.67	1.04
5 persons,	17	123	7.24	0.69	9 persons,	23	176	7.65	1.18
6 persons,	16	121	7.56	0.79	10 persons,	5	45	9.00	1.11
7 persons,	5	48	9.60	0.73	11 persons,	7	69	9.86	1.12
8 persons,	3	25	8.33	0.96	12 persons,	3	26	8.67	1.38
9 persons,	2	22	11.00	0.82	13 persons,	2	20	10.00	1.30
10 persons,	1	8	8.00	1.25	16 persons,	1	10	10.00	1.60
11 persons,	1	10	10.00	1.10	17 persons,	2	31	15.50	1.10
Chelmsford,	747	5,413	7.25	0.58	18 persons,	1	7	7.00	2.57
1 person,	30	147	4.90	0.20	23 persons,	1	34	34.00	0.68
2 persons,	139	919	6.61	0.30	29 persons,	1	32	32.00	0.91
3 persons,	167	1,204	7.21	0.42	42 persons,	1	21	21.00	2.00

ROOMS: OCCUPIED DWELLING HOUSES — Continued.

Counties, Cities, Towns, and Number of Persons to a Family.	Number of Families of Specified Size	Total Number of Rooms Occupied	Average Number of Rooms Occupied	Average Number of Persons to a Room
MIDDLESEX - Con.				
Dunstable, . .	106	729	6.88	0.55
1 person, . .	11	43	3.91	0.26
2 persons, . .	23	132	5.74	0.35
3 persons, . .	22	167	7.59	0.40
4 persons, . .	13	102	7.85	0.51
5 persons, . .	17	135	7.94	0.63
6 persons, . .	9	63	7.00	0.86
7 persons, . .	5	43	8.60	0.81
8 persons, . .	4	33	8.25	0.97
9 persons, . .	1	7	7.00	1.29
10 persons, . .	1	4	*4.00	2.50
EVERETT, . . .	4,304	26,948	6.26	0.69
1 person, . .	96	418	4.35	0.23
2 persons, . .	715	3,937	5.51	0.36
3 persons, . .	941	5,518	5.86	0.51
4 persons, . .	837	5,267	6.29	0.64
5 persons, . .	671	4,421	6.59	0.76
6 persons, . .	475	3,235	6.81	0.88
7 persons, . .	254	1,783	7.02	1.00
8 persons, . .	148	1,040	7.03	1.14
9 persons, . .	87	622	7.15	1.26
10 persons, . .	41	325	7.36	1.26
11 persons, . .	20	151	7.55	1.46
12 persons, . .	8	88	11.00	1.09
13 persons, . .	3	21	7.00	1.86
14 persons, . .	3	37	12.33	1.14
18 persons, . .	1	11	11.00	1.64
22 persons, . .	1	12	12.00	1.83
23 persons, . .	1	35	35.00	0.66
27 persons, . .	1	19	19.00	1.42
29 persons, . .	1	8	8.00	3.63
Everett. Ward 1, .	673	3,904	5.80	0.80
1 person, . .	17	92	5.41	0.18
2 persons, . .	36	450	4.84	0.41
3 persons, . .	130	725	5.58	0.54
4 persons, . .	128	732	5.72	0.70
5 persons, . .	100	599	5.99	0.83
6 persons, . .	84	496	5.90	1.02
7 persons, . .	39	254	6.51	1.07
8 persons, . .	40	273	6.33	1.26
9 persons, . .	25	167	6.68	1.35
10 persons, . .	8	57	7.13	1.40
11 persons, . .	3	23	7.67	1.43
12 persons, . .	2	17	8.50	1.41
13 persons, . .	1	7	7.00	1.86
14 persons, . .	1	13	13.00	1.08
18 persons, . .	1	11	11.00	1.64
29 persons, . .	1	8	8.00	3.63
Everett. Ward 2, .	583	3,674	6.30	0.72
1 person, . .	15	53	3.53	0.28
2 persons, . .	87	470	5.40	0.37
3 persons, . .	125	720	5.76	0.52
4 persons, . .	92	589	6.40	0.62
5 persons, . .	97	651	6.71	0.75
6 persons, . .	63	429	6.81	0.88
MIDDLESEX - Con.				
Everett. Ward 2 — Con.				
7 persons, . .	47	320	6.81	1.03
8 persons, . .	29	222	7.66	1.05
9 persons, . .	16	119	7.44	1.21
10 persons, . .	7	62	8.86	1.13
11 persons, . .	4	34	8.50	1.29
13 persons, . .	1	5	5.00	2.60
Everett. Ward 3, .	729	4,506	6.18	0.69
1 person, . .	14	61	4.36	0.23
2 persons, . .	137	782	5.71	0.35
3 persons, . .	142	816	5.75	0.52
4 persons, . .	157	966	6.15	0.65
5 persons, . .	116	753	6.49	0.77
6 persons, . .	77	523	6.79	0.88
7 persons, . .	39	257	6.59	1.06
8 persons, . .	21	143	6.81	1.17
9 persons, . .	13	94	7.23	1.24
10 persons, . .	8	60	7.50	1.33
11 persons, . .	2	14	7.00	1.57
12 persons, . .	2	25	12.50	0.96
22 persons, . .	1	12	12.00	1.83
Everett. Ward 4, .	703	4,525	6.44	0.64
1 person, . .	14	58	4.14	0.24
2 persons, . .	115	664	5.77	0.35
3 persons, . .	186	1,096	5.89	0.51
4 persons, . .	144	955	6.63	0.60
5 persons, . .	102	699	6.85	0.73
6 persons, . .	76	551	7.25	0.83
7 persons, . .	31	237	7.65	0.92
8 persons, . .	17	128	7.53	1.06
9 persons, . .	11	80	7.27	1.24
10 persons, . .	3	22	7.33	1.36
11 persons, . .	1	8	8.00	1.38
12 persons, . .	1	10	10.00	1.20
13 persons, . .	1	9	9.00	1.44
14 persons, . .	1	8	8.00	1.75
Everett. Ward 5, .	779	4,514	5.79	0.70
1 person, . .	19	78	4.11	0.24
2 persons, . .	162	843	5.20	0.38
3 persons, . .	181	994	5.49	0.55
4 persons, . .	135	771	5.71	0.70
5 persons, . .	129	776	6.02	0.83
6 persons, . .	72	464	6.44	0.93
7 persons, . .	41	299	7.29	0.96
8 persons, . .	19	125	6.58	1.22
9 persons, . .	9	57	6.63	1.42
10 persons, . .	6	46	7.67	1.30
11 persons, . .	4	29	7.25	1.52
12 persons, . .	1	16	16.00	0.75
14 persons, . .	1	16	16.00	0.88
Everett. Ward 6, .	837	5,925	6.96	0.65
1 person, . .	17	76	4.47	0.22
2 persons, . .	121	728	6.02	0.33
3 persons, . .	177	1,167	6.59	0.46
4 persons, . .	181	1,254	6.93	0.58

ROOMS: OCCUPIED DWELLING HOUSES — Continued.

Counties, Cities, Towns, and Number of Persons to a Family.	Number of Families of Specified Size.	Total Number of Rooms Occupied.	Average Number of Rooms Occupied.	Average Number of Persons to a Room.	Counties, Cities, Towns, and Number of Persons to a Family.	Number of Families of Specified Size.	Total Number of Rooms Occupied.	Average Number of Rooms Occupied.	Average Number of Persons to a Room.
MIDDLESEX—Con.					**MIDDLESEX—Con.**				
Everett. Ward 6—Con.					Holliston—Con.				
5 persons,	127	943	7.43	0.67	4 persons,	138	1,013	7.34	0.54
6 persons,	103	772	7.50	0.80	5 persons,	75	585	7.80	0.64
7 persons,	57	416	7.30	0.96	6 persons,	55	445	8.09	0.74
8 persons,	22	169	7.68	1.04	7 persons,	35	268	7.66	0.91
9 persons,	13	105	8.08	1.11	8 persons,	16	135	8.44	0.95
10 persons,	9	78	8.67	1.15	9 persons,	17	163	9.59	0.94
11 persons,	6	43	7.17	1.53	10 persons,	6	55	9.17	1.09
12 persons,	2	20	10.00	1.20	11 persons,	1	25	25.00	0.44
23 persons,	1	35	35.00	0.66	12 persons,	1	10	10.00	1.20
27 persons,	1	19	19.00	1.42	13 persons,	1	27	27.00	0.48
Framingham,	2,115	15,468	7.31	0.61	14 persons,	1	25	25.00	0.56
1 person,	84	424	5.05	0.20	15 persons,	1	7	7.00	2.14
2 persons,	361	2,355	6.52	0.31	Hopkinton,	752	5,504	7.32	0.54
3 persons,	413	2,838	6.87	0.44	1 person,	59	299	5.07	0.20
4 persons,	374	2,605	6.97	0.57	2 persons,	147	1,031	7.01	0.29
5 persons,	332	2,474	7.45	0.67	3 persons,	170	1,221	7.18	0.42
6 persons,	201	1,500	7.46	0.80	4 persons,	127	981	7.72	0.52
7 persons,	125	1,021	8.17	0.86	5 persons,	87	671	7.71	0.65
8 persons,	98	812	8.29	0.97	6 persons,	73	547	7.49	0.80
9 persons,	57	480	8.42	1.07	7 persons,	43	365	8.49	0.82
10 persons,	30	279	9.30	1.08	8 persons,	18	131	7.28	1.10
11 persons,	10	124	12.40	0.89	9 persons,	13	105	8.08	1.41
12 persons,	11	151	13.73	0.87	10 persons,	4	29	7.25	1.38
13 persons,	5	43	8.60	1.51	11 persons,	6	49	8.17	1.35
15 persons,	2	19	9.50	1.58	12 persons,	1	10	10.00	1.20
16 persons,	2	26	13.00	1.23	13 persons,	1	7	7.00	1.86
17 persons,	2	29	14.50	1.17	14 persons,	1	30	30.00	0.47
19 persons,	1	55	55.00	0.35	15 persons,	1	13	13.00	1.15
21 persons,	1	20	20.00	1.05	18 persons,	1	15	15.00	1.20
23 persons,	2	45	22.50	1.02	Hudson,	1,245	7,901	6.27	0.68
28 persons,	1	28	28.00	1.00	1 person,	49	169	3.45	0.29
30 persons,	1	42	42.00	0.71	2 persons,	234	1,241	5.30	0.38
32 persons,	1	43	43.00	0.74	3 persons,	277	1,634	5.30	0.51
54 persons,	1	55	55.00	0.98	4 persons,	229	1,484	6.48	0.62
Groton,	508	3,963	7.80	0.55	5 persons,	153	1,001	6.54	0.76
1 person,	42	229	5.45	0.18	6 persons,	128	868	6.78	0.88
2 persons,	92	603	6.55	0.31	7 persons,	64	444	6.94	1.01
3 persons,	109	774	7.10	0.42	8 persons,	47	358	7.62	1.05
4 persons,	95	739	7.78	0.51	9 persons,	24	168	7.00	1.29
5 persons,	59	522	8.85	0.57	10 persons,	18	161	8.94	1.12
6 persons,	43	330	7.67	0.78	11 persons,	10	90	9.00	1.22
7 persons,	30	267	8.90	0.79	12 persons,	4	28	7.00	1.71
8 persons,	15	141	9.40	0.85	13 persons,	2	36	18.00	0.72
9 persons,	8	105	13.13	0.69	14 persons,	2	19	9.50	1.47
10 persons,	5	48	9.60	1.04	15 persons,	1	21	21.00	0.71
11 persons,	4	31	7.75	1.42	19 persons,	2	34	17.00	1.12
12 persons,	1	6	6.00	2.00	26 persons,	1	45	45.00	0.58
13 persons,	3	60	20.00	0.65	Lexington,	775	6,016	7.76	0.58
19 persons,	1	28	28.00	0.68	1 person,	36	196	5.44	0.18
140 persons,	1	80	80.00	1.75	2 persons,	109	694	6.37	0.31
Holliston,	701	5,149	7.35	0.53	3 persons,	147	1,043	7.10	0.42
1 person,	54	244	4.52	0.22	4 persons,	153	1,131	7.39	0.54
2 persons,	144	989	6.87	0.29	5 persons,	106	875	8.25	0.61
3 persons,	156	1,158	7.42	0.40	6 persons,	90	784	8.71	0.69

ROOMS: OCCUPIED DWELLING HOUSES — Continued.

Counties, Cities, Towns, and Number of Persons to a Family.	Number of Families Specified Size	Total Number of Rooms Occupied	Average Number of Rooms Occupied	Average Number of Persons to a Room
MIDDLESEX - Con.				
Lexington — Con.				
7 persons,	48	420	8.75	0.80
8 persons,	42	402	9.57	0.84
9 persons,	20	183	9.15	0.98
10 persons,	9	74	8.22	1.22
11 persons,	8	76	9.50	1.16
12 persons,	4	52	13.00	0.92
13 persons,	2	70	35.00	0.37
17 persons,	1	16	16.00	1.06
Lincoln,	209	1,631	7.80	0.68
1 person,	12	37	3.08	0.32
2 persons,	21	152	7.24	0.28
3 persons,	32	221	6.91	0.43
4 persons,	36	272	7.56	0.53
5 persons,	24	186	7.75	0.65
6 persons,	22	183	8.32	0.72
7 persons,	24	229	9.54	0.73
8 persons,	11	101	9.18	0.87
9 persons,	8	58	7.25	1.24
10 persons,	7	77	11.00	0.91
11 persons,	2	11	5.50	2.00
12 persons,	1	7	7.00	1.71
13 persons,	4	48	12.00	1.08
14 persons,	1	12	12.00	1.17
15 persons,	1	11	11.00	1.36
16 persons,	1	8	8.00	2.00
17 persons,	1	11	11.00	1.55
19 persons,	1	7	7.00	2.71
Littleton,	256	2,001	7.82	0.57
1 person,	11	60	5.45	0.18
2 persons,	44	309	7.02	0.28
3 persons,	43	290	6.74	0.44
4 persons,	43	324	7.53	0.53
5 persons,	42	336	8.00	0.62
6 persons,	27	232	8.59	0.70
7 persons,	23	219	9.52	0.74
8 persons,	15	124	8.27	0.97
9 persons,	5	68	13.60	0.66
10 persons,	1	6	6.00	1.67
13 persons,	1	16	16.00	0.81
15 persons,	1	17	17.00	0.88
LOWELL,	16,885	106,124	6.28	0.80
1 person,	465	2,004	4.31	0.23
2 persons,	2,451	13,318	5.43	0.37
3 persons,	3,005	17,506	5.86	0.51
4 persons,	2,913	17,509	6.01	0.67
5 persons,	2,472	15,478	6.26	0.80
6 persons,	1,895	12,113	6.41	0.94
7 persons,	1,297	8,213	6.33	1.10
8 persons,	871	5,718	6.56	1.22
9 persons,	542	3,702	6.83	1.32
10 persons,	332	2,324	7.00	1.43
11 persons,	186	1,386	7.54	1.47
12 persons,	99	778	7.86	1.53
13 persons,	61	571	9.36	1.39
MIDDLESEX - Con.				
LOWELL — Con.				
14 persons,	57	667	11.70	1.20
15 persons,	29	291	10.03	1.49
16 persons,	15	164	10.93	1.46
17 persons,	17	238	14.00	1.21
18 persons,	15	201	13.40	1.34
19 persons,	9	136	15.11	1.26
20 persons,	14	292	20.86	0.96
21 persons,	6	120	20.00	1.05
22 persons,	6	119	19.83	1.11
23 persons,	6	168	28.00	0.82
24 persons,	5	171	34.20	0.70
25 persons,	10	233	23.30	1.07
26 persons,	4	81	20.25	1.28
27 persons,	5	150	30.00	0.90
28 persons,	4	79	19.75	1.42
29 persons,	6	148	24.67	1.18
30 persons,	5	160	32.00	0.94
31 persons,	3	96	32.00	0.97
32 persons,	2	51	25.50	1.25
33 persons,	2	50	25.00	1.32
34 persons,	1	27	27.00	1.26
35 persons,	5	171	34.20	1.02
36 persons,	4	105	26.25	1.37
37 persons,	4	111	27.75	1.33
38 persons,	3	115	38.33	0.99
39 persons,	3	81	27.00	1.44
40 persons,	1	35	35.00	1.14
43 persons,	1	27	27.00	1.59
44 persons,	2	49	24.50	1.80
46 persons,	1	26	26.00	1.77
47 persons,	1	54	54.00	0.87
48 persons,	1	67	67.00	0.72
49 persons,	1	26	26.00	1.88
50 persons,	1	38	38.00	1.32
52 persons,	1	35	35.00	1.49
53 persons,	1	37	37.00	1.43
64 persons,	1	12	12.00	5.33
70 persons,	1	15	15.00	4.67
107 persons,	1	90	90.00	1.19
113 persons,	1	117	117.00	0.97
242 persons,	1	221	221.00	1.55
Lowell, Ward 1,	1,633	11,382	6.97	0.84
1 person,	88	270	3.07	0.33
2 persons,	267	1,261	4.72	0.42
3 persons,	257	1,464	5.70	0.53
4 persons,	270	1,580	5.85	0.68
5 persons,	208	1,335	6.44	0.78
6 persons,	145	925	6.40	0.94
7 persons,	108	751	6.95	1.01
8 persons,	72	518	7.19	1.11
9 persons,	43	320	7.44	1.21
10 persons,	33	249	7.55	1.33
11 persons,	23	230	10.00	1.10
12 persons,	8	105	13.13	0.91

ROOMS: OCCUPIED DWELLING HOUSES — Continued.

Counties, Cities, Towns, and Number of Persons to a Family.	Number of Families of Specified Size.	Total Number of Rooms Occupied.	Average Number of Rooms Occupied.	Average Number of Persons to a Room.
MIDDLESEX - Con.				
Lowell. Ward 1 — Con.				
13 persons,	14	156	11.14	1.47
14 persons,	10	136	13.60	1.03
15 persons,	6	79	13.17	1.14
16 persons,	2	20	10.00	1.60
17 persons,	2	24	12.00	1.42
18 persons,	6	85	14.17	1.27
19 persons,	1	14	14.00	1.36
20 persons,	8	164	20.50	0.98
21 persons,	5	99	19.80	1.06
22 persons,	4	82	20.50	1.07
23 persons,	4	113	28.25	0.81
24 persons,	2	89	44.50	0.54
25 persons,	7	171	24.43	1.02
26 persons,	3	48	16.00	1.63
27 persons,	2	39	19.50	1.38
28 persons,	2	40	20.00	1.40
29 persons,	3	76	25.33	1.15
30 persons,	2	68	34.00	0.88
31 persons,	1	35	35.00	0.89
32 persons,	2	51	25.50	1.25
33 persons,	2	50	25.00	1.32
34 persons,	1	27	27.00	1.26
35 persons,	2	95	47.50	0.74
36 persons,	3	79	26.33	1.37
37 persons,	3	85	28.33	1.31
38 persons,	2	69	34.50	1.10
39 persons,	2	54	27.00	1.44
40 persons,	1	35	35.00	1.14
43 persons,	1	27	27.00	1.59
44 persons,	2	49	24.50	1.80
46 persons,	1	26	26.00	1.77
48 persons,	1	67	67.00	0.72
49 persons,	1	26	26.00	1.88
50 persons,	1	38	38.00	1.32
53 persons,	1	37	37.00	1.43
64 persons,	1	12	12.00	5.33
Lowell. Ward 2.	1,879	9,883	5.27	1.06
1 person,	16	119	3.24	0.31
2 persons,	236	968	4.10	0.49
3 persons,	260	1,137	4.37	0.89
4 persons,	287	1,376	4.79	0.83
5 persons,	282	1,371	4.86	1.06
6 persons,	225	1,180	5.24	1.14
7 persons,	195	1,013	5.19	1.35
8 persons,	109	570	5.23	1.53
9 persons,	81	497	6.14	1.47
10 persons,	45	292	6.49	1.54
11 persons,	28	199	7.11	1.55
12 persons,	23	161	7.00	1.71
13 persons,	9	77	8.56	1.52
14 persons,	11	126	11.45	1.22
15 persons,	6	68	11.33	1.32
16 persons,	3	39	13.00	1.23
17 persons,	10	163	16.30	1.04
MIDDLESEX - Con.				
Lowell. Ward 2 — Con.				
18 persons,	5	57	11.40	1.58
19 persons,	2	34	17.00	1.12
20 persons,	2	37	18.50	1.08
23 persons,	1	23	23.00	1.00
24 persons,	1	22	22.00	1.09
27 persons,	1	17	17.00	1.59
28 persons,	2	39	19.50	1.44
29 persons,	2	49	24.50	1.18
31 persons,	1	21	21.00	1.48
35 persons,	3	76	25.33	1.38
39 persons,	1	27	27.00	1.44
70 persons,	1	15	15.00	1.67
107 persons,	1	90	90.00	1.19
Lowell. Ward 3.	2,038	12,869	6.31	0.72
1 person,	39	174	4.46	0.22
2 persons,	353	2,032	5.76	0.35
3 persons,	415	2,519	6.07	0.43
4 persons,	365	2,228	6.10	0.66
5 persons,	300	2,014	6.71	0.74
6 persons,	224	1,544	6.88	0.87
7 persons,	135	839	6.21	1.13
8 persons,	90	560	6.22	1.29
9 persons,	43	284	6.53	1.38
10 persons,	34	228	6.71	1.49
11 persons,	16	114	7.13	1.54
12 persons,	6	57	9.50	1.26
13 persons,	1	7	7.00	1.86
14 persons,	6	89	14.83	0.94
15 persons,	4	46	11.50	1.30
16 persons,	1	7	7.00	2.29
18 persons,	1	14	14.00	1.29
19 persons,	1	22	22.00	0.86
22 persons,	1	17	17.00	1.29
24 persons,	1	15	15.00	1.60
25 persons,	1	35	35.00	0.71
30 persons,	1	30	30.00	1.00
Lowell. Ward 4.	1,881	10,691	5.68	0.86
1 person,	51	240	4.71	0.21
2 persons,	262	1,263	4.82	0.41
3 persons,	315	1,606	5.10	0.59
4 persons,	314	1,686	5.40	0.74
5 persons,	311	1,779	5.72	0.87
6 persons,	217	1,241	5.72	1.05
7 persons,	168	1,052	6.26	1.12
8 persons,	101	608	6.02	1.33
9 persons,	59	413	7.00	1.29
10 persons,	36	254	7.06	1.42
11 persons,	19	117	6.16	1.79
12 persons,	8	84	10.50	1.14
13 persons,	6	61	10.17	1.28
14 persons,	5	51	10.20	1.37
15 persons,	2	20	10.00	1.50
16 persons,	2	26	13.00	1.23
19 persons,	1	10	10.00	1.90

ROOMS: OCCUPIED DWELLING HOUSES — Continued.

Counties, Cities, Towns, and Number of Persons to a Family.	Number of Families of Specified Size	Total Number of Rooms Occupied	Average Number of Rooms Occupied	Average Number of Persons to a Room	Counties, Cities, Towns, and Number of Persons to a Family.	Number of Families of Specified Size	Total Number of Rooms Occupied	Average Number of Rooms Occupied	Average Number of Persons to a Room
MIDDLESEX - Con.					MIDDLESEX - Con.				
Lowell. Ward 4 — Con.					*Lowell. Ward 7 — Con.*				
25 persons,	2	27	13.50	1.85	7 persons,	204	1,207	6.00	1.17
35 persons,	1	26	26.00	1.38	8 persons,	187	1,186	6.34	1.26
113 persons,	1	117	117.00	0.97	9 persons,	126	728	5.78	1.56
Lowell. Ward 5,	1,765	9,836	5.57	0.86	10 persons,	85	493	5.80	1.72
1 person,	84	290	3.45	0.29	11 persons,	45	254	5.64	1.95
2 persons,	259	1,143	4.41	0.45	12 persons,	31	201	6.48	1.85
3 persons,	317	1,572	4.96	0.60	13 persons,	19	148	7.79	1.67
4 persons,	315	1,587	5.04	0.79	14 persons,	13	112	8.62	1.63
5 persons,	231	1,272	5.51	0.91	15 persons,	4	28	7.00	2.14
6 persons,	205	1,227	5.99	1.00	16 persons,	5	44	8.80	1.82
7 persons,	121	721	5.96	1.17	17 persons,	2	14	7.00	2.43
8 persons,	82	565	6.89	1.16	18 persons,	2	27	13.50	1.33
9 persons,	56	420	7.50	1.20	21 persons,	1	21	21.00	1.00
10 persons,	37	292	7.89	1.27	22 persons,	1	20	20.00	1.10
11 persons,	19	196	10.32	1.07	26 persons,	1	33	33.00	0.79
12 persons,	8	58	7.25	1.66	30 persons,	1	35	35.00	0.86
13 persons,	4	42	10.50	1.24	38 persons,	1	46	46.00	0.83
14 persons,	8	92	11.50	1.22	47 persons,	1	54	54.00	0.87
15 persons,	3	25	8.33	1.80	52 persons,	1	35	35.00	1.49
16 persons,	2	28	14.00	1.14	*Lowell. Ward 8,*	1,785	12,904	7.23	0.62
17 persons,	2	25	12.50	1.36	1 person,	44	239	5.43	0.18
19 persons,	4	56	14.00	1.36	2 persons,	319	2,115	6.63	0.30
20 persons,	1	8	8.00	2.50	3 persons,	375	2,546	6.79	0.44
23 persons,	1	32	32.00	0.72	4 persons,	362	2,570	7.10	0.56
24 persons,	1	45	45.00	0.53	5 persons,	264	1,910	7.23	0.69
27 persons,	1	24	24.00	1.13	6 persons,	191	1,478	7.74	0.78
29 persons,	1	23	23.00	1.26	7 persons,	98	733	7.48	0.94
30 persons,	1	27	27.00	1.11	8 persons,	59	472	8.00	1.00
31 persons,	1	40	40.00	0.78	9 persons,	42	324	7.71	1.17
37 persons,	1	26	26.00	1.42	10 persons,	14	126	9.00	1.11
Lowell. Ward 6,	1,969	12,797	6.40	0.73	11 persons,	10	88	8.80	1.25
1 person,	39	209	5.36	0.19	12 persons,	1	12	12.00	1.00
2 persons,	272	1,678	6.17	0.32	13 persons,	1	14	14.00	0.93
3 persons,	400	2,534	6.34	0.47	14 persons,	1	16	16.00	0.88
4 persons,	371	2,332	6.29	0.64	15 persons,	1	6	6.00	2.50
5 persons,	305	1,938	6.35	0.79	17 persons,	1	12	12.00	1.42
6 persons,	236	1,558	6.60	0.91	20 persons,	1	22	22.00	0.91
7 persons,	153	1,004	6.56	1.07	342 persons,	1	221	221.00	1.55
8 persons,	104	697	6.70	1.19	*Lowell. Ward 9,*	1,522	10,994	7.22	0.64
9 persons,	52	341	6.56	1.37	1 person,	29	194	6.69	0.15
10 persons,	27	211	7.81	1.28	2 persons,	207	1,229	5.94	0.34
11 persons,	18	136	7.56	1.46	3 persons,	298	2,003	6.72	0.45
12 persons,	12	73	6.08	1.97	4 persons,	290	2,054	7.08	0.56
13 persons,	5	32	6.40	2.06	5 persons,	235	1,710	7.28	0.69
14 persons,	2	25	12.50	1.12	6 persons,	200	1,500	7.50	0.80
15 persons,	2	11	5.50	2.73	7 persons,	118	923	7.82	0.93
18 persons,	1	18	18.00	1.00	8 persons,	67	542	8.09	0.99
Lowell. Ward 7,	2,383	14,755	6.19	0.89	9 persons,	40	378	9.45	0.95
1 person,	45	239	5.31	0.19	10 persons,	21	179	8.52	1.17
2 persons,	276	1,629	5.90	0.34	11 persons,	8	62	7.75	1.42
3 persons,	368	2,213	6.01	0.50	12 persons,	2	27	13.50	0.89
4 persons,	339	2,083	6.14	0.65	13 persons,	2	34	17.00	0.76
5 persons,	336	2,145	6.38	0.78	14 persons,	1	20	20.00	0.70
6 persons,	292	1,760	6.03	1.00	15 persons,	1	8	8.00	1.88

ROOMS: OCCUPIED DWELLING HOUSES — Continued.

COUNTIES, CITIES, TOWNS, AND NUMBER OF PERSONS TO A FAMILY.	Number of Families of Specified Size	Total Number of Rooms Occupied	Average Number of Rooms Occupied	Average Number of Persons to a Room
MIDDLESEX—Con.				
Lowell. Ward 9—Con.				
26 persons,	2	61	30.50	0.99
27 persons,	1	70	70.00	0.39
MALDEN,	6,638	45,049	6.79	0.96
1 person,	178	775	4.35	0.23
2 persons,	1,007	5,681	5.64	0.35
3 persons,	1,295	8,225	6.35	0.47
4 persons,	1,345	9,490	6.83	0.59
5 persons,	1,072	7,682	7.17	0.70
6 persons,	752	5,472	7.28	0.82
7 persons,	437	3,294	7.54	0.93
8 persons,	230	1,798	7.82	1.02
9 persons,	140	1,120	8.00	1.13
10 persons,	84	646	7.62	1.31
11 persons,	34	267	7.85	1.40
12 persons,	22	212	9.64	1.25
13 persons,	11	117	10.64	1.22
14 persons,	9	162	11.33	1.24
15 persons,	2	49	24.50	0.61
16 persons,	6	85	14.17	1.13
17 persons,	3	53	17.67	0.96
18 persons,	3	54	18.00	1.00
20 persons,	3	51	17.00	1.18
23 persons,	1	26	26.00	0.88
24 persons,	1	30	30.00	0.80
31 persons,	1	22	22.00	1.41
43 persons,	1	43	43.00	1.00
61 persons,	1	61	61.00	1.00
Malden. Ward 1,	953	6,542	6.86	0.63
1 person,	23	108	4.70	0.24
2 persons,	146	826	5.66	0.35
3 persons,	208	1,311	6.30	0.48
4 persons,	213	1,521	7.14	0.56
5 persons,	127	882	6.94	0.72
6 persons,	102	783	7.68	0.78
7 persons,	71	559	7.87	0.89
8 persons,	32	266	8.31	0.96
9 persons,	17	143	8.41	1.07
10 persons,	7	69	9.86	1.01
11 persons,	2	18	9.00	1.22
12 persons,	3	30	10.00	1.20
13 persons,	1	10	10.00	1.30
20 persons,	1	16	16.00	1.25
Malden. Ward 2,	1,091	5,714	5.24	0.93
1 person,	30	102	3.40	0.29
2 persons,	160	719	4.49	0.45
3 persons,	165	755	4.58	0.66
4 persons,	184	920	5.00	0.80
5 persons,	173	912	5.27	0.95
6 persons,	144	784	5.44	1.10
7 persons,	90	512	5.69	1.23
8 persons,	52	338	6.50	1.23
9 persons,	40	261	6.53	1.38
10 persons,	28	182	6.50	1.54
11 persons,	12	82	6.83	1.61

COUNTIES, CITIES, TOWNS, AND NUMBER OF PERSONS TO A FAMILY.	Number of Families of Specified Size	Total Number of Rooms Occupied	Average Number of Rooms Occupied	Average Number of Persons to a Room
MIDDLESEX—Con.				
Malden. Ward 2—Con.				
12 persons,	5	37	7.40	1.62
13 persons,	2	23	11.50	1.13
14 persons,	3	24	8.00	1.75
15 persons,	1	9	9.00	1.67
16 persons,	1	11	11.00	1.45
43 persons,	1	43	43.00	1.00
Malden. Ward 3,	763	6,669	8.74	0.54
1 person,	8	63	7.88	0.13
2 persons,	81	553	6.83	0.29
3 persons,	151	1,226	8.12	0.37
4 persons,	166	1,453	8.75	0.46
5 persons,	149	1,367	9.17	0.54
6 persons,	94	859	9.14	0.66
7 persons,	52	464	8.92	0.78
8 persons,	24	227	9.46	0.85
9 persons,	19	191	10.05	0.90
10 persons,	9	91	10.11	0.89
11 persons,	1	7	7.00	1.57
12 persons,	2	22	11.00	1.09
13 persons,	1	11	11.00	1.18
14 persons,	2	28	14.00	1.00
15 persons,	1	40	40.00	0.38
20 persons,	1	15	15.00	1.33
24 persons,	1	30	30.00	0.80
31 persons,	1	22	22.00	1.41
Malden. Ward 4,	1,024	7,251	7.08	0.66
1 person,	38	132	3.47	0.29
2 persons,	141	792	5.62	0.36
3 persons,	200	1,315	6.58	0.46
4 persons,	193	1,321	6.84	0.58
5 persons,	181	1,373	7.59	0.66
6 persons,	96	692	7.21	0.83
7 persons,	71	589	8.30	0.84
8 persons,	31	237	7.65	1.05
9 persons,	28	231	8.25	1.09
10 persons,	10	78	7.80	1.28
11 persons,	11	96	8.73	1.26
12 persons,	6	70	11.67	1.03
13 persons,	3	35	11.67	1.11
14 persons,	3	40	13.33	1.05
16 persons,	4	52	13.00	1.23
17 persons,	2	37	18.50	0.92
18 persons,	3	54	18.00	1.00
20 persons,	1	20	20.00	1.00
23 persons,	1	26	26.00	0.88
61 persons,	1	61	61.00	1.00
Malden. Ward 5,	943	6,723	7.13	0.58
1 person,	26	122	4.69	0.21
2 persons,	162	974	6.01	0.33
3 persons,	208	1,428	6.84	0.44
4 persons,	194	1,365	7.15	0.56
5 persons,	153	1,175	7.68	0.65
6 persons,	105	827	7.88	0.76
7 persons,	47	404	8.60	0.81

ROOMS: OCCUPIED DWELLING HOUSES — Continued.

Counties, Cities, Towns, and Number of Persons to a Family.	Number of Families of Specified Size	Total Number of Rooms Occupied	Average Number of Rooms Occupied	Average Number of Persons to a Room
MIDDLESEX - Con.				
Malden. Ward 5 — Con.				
8 persons,	28	234	8.36	0.96
9 persons,	6	56	9.33	0.96
10 persons,	8	61	7.63	1.31
11 persons,	4	32	8.00	1.38
12 persons,	3	25	8.33	1.44
14 persons,	1	10	10.00	1.40
17 persons,	1	16	16.00	1.06
Malden. Ward 6,	977	6,548	6.70	0.84
1 person,	36	166	4.61	0.22
2 persons,	160	936	5.85	0.34
3 persons,	178	1,124	6.31	0.48
4 persons,	210	1,396	6.65	0.60
5 persons,	147	1,056	7.18	0.70
6 persons,	111	820	7.39	0.81
7 persons,	60	442	7.37	0.95
8 persons,	40	316	7.90	1.01
9 persons,	21	166	7.90	1.14
10 persons,	10	79	7.90	1.27
11 persons,	1	9	9.00	1.22
12 persons,	1	8	8.00	1.50
13 persons,	1	8	8.00	1.63
16 persons,	1	22	22.00	0.73
Malden. Ward 7,	887	5,602	6.32	0.67
1 person,	17	82	4.82	0.21
2 persons,	157	881	5.61	0.36
3 persons,	185	1,072	5.79	0.52
4 persons,	188	1,214	6.46	0.62
5 persons,	142	917	6.46	0.77
6 persons,	100	707	7.07	0.85
7 persons,	46	324	7.04	0.99
8 persons,	23	180	7.83	1.02
9 persons,	9	72	8.00	1.13
10 persons,	12	80	6.67	1.50
11 persons,	3	23	7.67	1.43
12 persons,	2	20	10.00	1.20
13 persons,	3	30	10.00	1.30
MARLBOROUGH,	3,159	19,451	6.16	0.77
1 person,	73	315	4.32	0.23
2 persons,	489	2,581	5.28	0.38
3 persons,	593	3,384	5.71	0.53
4 persons,	565	3,340	5.91	0.68
5 persons,	460	2,891	6.28	0.80
6 persons,	347	2,260	6.51	0.92
7 persons,	244	1,575	6.45	1.08
8 persons,	162	1,123	6.93	1.15
9 persons,	102	731	7.17	1.26
10 persons,	47	349	7.43	1.35
11 persons,	33	268	8.12	1.35
12 persons,	17	153	9.00	1.33
13 persons,	9	88	9.78	1.33
14 persons,	5	71	14.20	0.99
15 persons,	3	33	11.00	1.36
16 persons,	1	11	11.00	1.45
MIDDLESEX - Con.				
MARLBOROUGH — Con.				
19 persons,	3	58	19.33	0.98
21 persons,	1	35	35.00	0.60
26 persons,	1	3	3.00	8.67
29 persons,	2	81	40.50	0.72
37 persons,	1	50	50.00	0.74
99 persons,	1	51	51.00	1.94
Marlborough. Wd. 1,	317	2,196	6.93	0.61
1 person,	6	26	4.33	0.23
2 persons,	68	408	6.00	0.33
3 persons,	66	413	6.26	0.48
4 persons,	63	434	6.89	0.58
5 persons,	45	341	7.58	0.69
6 persons,	27	217	8.04	0.75
7 persons,	19	125	6.58	1.06
8 persons,	12	97	8.08	0.99
9 persons,	6	55	9.17	0.98
10 persons,	2	27	13.50	0.74
11 persons,	1	8	8.00	1.38
13 persons,	1	16	16.00	0.81
29 persons,	1	29	29.00	1.00
Marlborough. Wd. 2,	455	3,002	6.60	0.73
1 person,	8	43	5.38	0.19
2 persons,	56	307	5.48	0.36
3 persons,	94	580	6.17	0.49
4 persons,	82	502	6.12	0.65
5 persons,	67	457	6.82	0.73
6 persons,	50	374	7.48	0.80
7 persons,	40	288	7.20	0.97
8 persons,	29	198	6.83	1.17
9 persons,	11	82	7.45	1.21
10 persons,	7	61	8.71	1.15
11 persons,	4	30	7.50	1.47
12 persons,	3	26	8.67	1.38
15 persons,	1	5	5.00	3.00
19 persons,	2	46	23.00	0.83
26 persons,	1	3	3.00	8.67
Marlborough. Wd. 3,	564	3,363	5.96	0.88
1 person,	20	88	4.40	0.23
2 persons,	82	414	5.05	0.40
3 persons,	80	409	5.11	0.59
4 persons,	80	446	5.58	0.72
5 persons,	72	432	6.00	0.83
6 persons,	68	435	6.40	0.94
7 persons,	64	366	5.72	1.22
8 persons,	43	296	6.81	1.17
9 persons,	26	181	6.96	1.29
10 persons,	12	83	6.92	1.45
11 persons,	5	39	7.80	1.41
12 persons,	5	42	8.40	1.43
13 persons,	3	21	7.00	1.86
14 persons,	1	7	7.00	2.00
15 persons,	1	4	4.00	3.75
29 persons,	1	52	52.00	0.56
99 persons,	1	51	51.00	1.94

ROOMS: OCCUPIED DWELLING HOUSES — Continued.

Counties, Cities, Towns, and Number of Persons to a Family.	Number of Families of Specified Size	Total Number of Rooms Occupied	Average Number of Rooms Occupied	Average Number of Persons to a Room.	Counties, Cities, Towns, and Number of Persons to a Family.	Number of Families of Specified Size	Total Number of Rooms Occupied	Average Number of Rooms Occupied	Average Number of Persons to a Room.
MIDDLESEX - Con.					MIDDLESEX - Con.				
Marlborough. Wd. 4,	636	3,655	5.75	0.90	Marlborough. Wd. 7 — Con.				
1 person,	5	22	4.40	0.23	9 persons,	9	83	9.22	0.98
2 persons,	75	372	4.96	0.40	10 persons,	4	38	9.50	1.05
3 persons,	102	572	5.61	0.53	11 persons,	3	47	15.67	0.70
4 persons,	105	571	5.44	0.74	12 persons,	4	44	11.00	1.09
5 persons,	95	521	5.48	0.91	14 persons,	1	35	35.00	0.40
6 persons,	86	478	5.56	1.08	37 persons,	1	50	50.00	0.74
7 persons,	58	375	6.47	1.08	Maynard,	642	4,287	6.68	0.72
8 persons,	42	284	6.76	1.18	1 person,	15	67	4.47	0.22
9 persons,	29	184	6.34	1.42	2 persons,	77	457	5.94	0.34
10 persons,	19	118	6.21	1.61	3 persons,	119	766	6.44	0.47
11 persons,	10	70	7.00	1.57	4 persons,	128	851	6.65	0.60
12 persons,	4	29	7.25	1.66	5 persons,	100	624	6.24	0.80
13 persons,	5	51	10.20	1.27	6 persons,	61	440	7.21	0.83
14 persons,	1	8	8.00	1.75	7 persons,	53	376	7.09	0.99
Marlborough. Wd. 5,	460	2,774	6.03	0.70	8 persons,	39	275	7.05	1.13
1 person,	11	43	3.91	0.26	9 persons,	24	170	7.08	1.27
2 persons,	87	473	5.44	0.37	10 persons,	12	97	8.08	1.24
3 persons,	107	613	5.73	0.52	11 persons,	7	52	7.43	1.48
4 persons,	96	563	5.86	0.68	12 persons,	4	67	16.75	0.72
5 persons,	62	392	6.32	0.79	13 persons,	2	15	7.50	1.73
6 persons,	45	308	6.84	0.88	16 persons,	1	30	30.00	0.53
7 persons,	17	98	5.76	1.21	MEDFORD,	3,172	22,854	7.20	0.63
8 persons,	11	71	6.45	1.24	1 person,	86	352	4.09	0.24
9 persons,	14	93	6.64	1.35	2 persons,	510	3,195	6.26	0.32
10 persons,	1	5	5.00	2.00	3 persons,	613	4,100	6.69	0.45
11 persons,	5	34	6.80	1.62	4 persons,	603	4,381	7.27	0.55
14 persons,	1	11	11.00	1.27	5 persons,	477	3,645	7.64	0.65
15 persons,	1	24	24.00	0.63	6 persons,	365	2,758	7.56	0.79
16 persons,	1	11	11.00	1.45	7 persons,	204	1,625	7.97	0.88
21 persons,	1	35	35.00	0.60	8 persons,	148	1,233	8.33	0.96
Marlborough. Wd. 6,	385	2,338	5.92	0.72	9 persons,	82	680	8.29	1.09
1 person,	13	54	4.15	0.24	10 persons,	30	250	8.43	1.16
2 persons,	73	363	4.97	0.40	11 persons,	19	172	9.05	1.22
3 persons,	82	451	5.50	0.55	12 persons,	13	123	9.46	1.27
4 persons,	75	455	6.07	0.66	13 persons,	3	32	10.67	1.22
5 persons,	60	360	6.00	0.83	14 persons,	1	7	7.00	2.00
6 persons,	35	222	6.34	0.95	15 persons,	5	63	12.60	1.19
7 persons,	29	211	7.28	0.98	16 persons,	2	28	14.00	1.14
8 persons,	11	78	7.09	1.13	17 persons,	1	12	12.00	1.42
9 persons,	7	53	7.57	1.19	19 persons,	1	13	13.00	1.46
10 persons,	2	17	8.50	1.18	20 persons,	2	27	13.50	1.48
11 persons,	5	40	8.00	1.38	21 persons,	2	38	19.00	1.11
12 persons,	1	12	12.00	1.00	29 persons,	1	22	22.00	1.32
14 persons,	1	10	10.00	1.40	35 persons,	1	36	36.00	0.97
19 persons,	1	12	12.00	1.58	38 persons,	1	4	4.00	9.50
Marlborough. Wd. 7,	332	2,123	6.39	0.73	47 persons,	1	34	34.00	1.38
1 person,	10	39	3.90	0.26	100 persons,	1	15	15.00	6.67
2 persons,	48	244	5.08	0.39	Medford. Ward 1,	642	4,514	7.03	0.67
3 persons,	62	346	5.58	0.54	1 person,	13	64	4.92	0.21
4 persons,	64	369	5.77	0.69	2 persons,	99	640	6.46	0.31
5 persons,	59	388	6.58	0.76	3 persons,	122	809	6.63	0.45
6 persons,	36	226	6.28	0.96	4 persons,	120	854	7.12	0.56
7 persons,	17	112	6.59	1.06	5 persons,	109	810	7.43	0.67
8 persons,	14	102	7.29	1.10	6 persons,	70	509	7.27	0.83

ROOMS: OCCUPIED DWELLING HOUSES — Continued.

COUNTIES, CITIES, TOWNS, AND NUMBER OF PERSONS TO A FAMILY.	Number of Families of Specified Size	Total Number of Rooms Occupied	Average Number of Rooms Occupied	Average Number of Persons to a Room
MIDDLESEX-Con.				
Medford. Ward 1—Con.				
7 persons,	49	345	7.04	0.99
8 persons,	29	221	7.62	1.05
9 persons,	14	115	8.21	1.10
10 persons,	8	69	8.63	1.16
11 persons,	2	19	9.50	1.16
12 persons,	2	21	10.50	1.14
13 persons,	1	5	5.00	2.60
14 persons,	1	7	7.00	2.00
15 persons,	1	12	12.00	1.25
21 persons,	1	2	2.00	10.50
100 persons,	1	15	15.00	6.67
Medford. Ward 2,	544	3,693	6.79	0.62
1 person,	26	109	4.19	0.24
2 persons,	94	577	6.14	0.33
3 persons,	107	689	6.44	0.47
4 persons,	102	731	7.17	0.56
5 persons,	85	605	7.12	0.70
6 persons,	60	423	7.05	0.85
7 persons,	24	176	7.33	0.95
8 persons,	23	193	8.39	0.95
9 persons,	14	114	8.14	1.11
10 persons,	4	31	7.75	1.29
11 persons,	4	33	8.25	1.33
15 persons,	1	12	12.00	1.25
Medford. Ward 3,	111	3,487	8.48	0.55
1 person,	17	60	3.53	0.28
2 persons,	63	433	6.87	0.29
3 persons,	66	516	7.82	0.38
4 persons,	77	625	8.12	0.49
5 persons,	60	545	9.08	0.55
6 persons,	45	399	8.87	0.68
7 persons,	38	394	10.37	0.68
8 persons,	22	249	11.32	0.71
9 persons,	14	131	9.36	0.96
10 persons,	2	23	11.50	0.87
11 persons,	1	14	14.00	0.79
12 persons,	1	17	17.00	0.71
13 persons,	1	13	13.00	1.00
15 persons,	1	12	12.00	1.25
17 persons,	1	12	12.00	1.42
20 persons,	1	22	22.00	0.91
29 persons,	1	22	22.00	1.32
Medford. Ward 4,	426	2,861	6.72	0.68
1 person,	11	38	3.45	0.29
2 persons,	72	384	5.33	0.38
3 persons,	90	574	6.38	0.47
4 persons,	67	453	6.76	0.59
5 persons,	55	411	7.53	0.66
6 persons,	58	432	7.45	0.81
7 persons,	23	183	7.96	0.88
8 persons,	20	144	7.20	1.11
9 persons,	13	90	6.92	1.30
10 persons,	5	37	7.40	1.35
11 persons,	6	46	7.67	1.43
MIDDLESEX-Con.				
Medford. Ward 4—Con.				
12 persons,	3	33	11.00	1.09
15 persons,	1	10	10.00	1.50
16 persons,	1	10	10.00	1.60
19 persons,	1	13	13.00	1.46
Medford. Ward 5,	627	4,311	6.88	0.69
1 person,	6	32	5.33	0.19
2 persons,	102	624	6.12	0.33
3 persons,	130	801	6.16	0.49
4 persons,	121	848	7.01	0.57
5 persons,	82	552	6.73	0.74
6 persons,	81	582	7.19	0.84
7 persons,	44	310	7.05	0.99
8 persons,	28	205	7.32	1.09
9 persons,	14	112	8.00	1.13
10 persons,	4	42	10.50	0.95
11 persons,	5	45	9.00	1.22
12 persons,	4	29	7.25	1.66
13 persons,	1	14	14.00	0.93
20 persons,	1	5	5.00	4.00
21 persons,	1	36	36.00	0.58
35 persons,	1	36	36.00	0.97
38 persons,	1	4	4.00	9.50
47 persons,	1	34	34.00	1.38
Medford. Ward 6,	522	3,988	7.64	0.58
1 person,	13	52	4.00	0.25
2 persons,	80	537	6.71	0.30
3 persons,	98	711	7.26	0.41
4 persons,	116	870	7.50	0.53
5 persons,	86	719	8.36	0.60
6 persons,	51	413	8.10	0.74
7 persons,	26	217	8.35	0.84
8 persons,	26	221	8.50	0.94
9 persons,	13	118	9.08	0.99
10 persons,	7	57	8.14	1.23
11 persons,	1	15	15.00	0.73
12 persons,	3	23	7.67	1.57
15 persons,	1	17	17.00	0.88
16 persons,	1	18	18.00	0.89
Melrose,	2,685	20,071	7.48	0.60
1 person,	50	231	4.62	0.22
2 persons,	392	2,496	6.37	0.31
3 persons,	518	3,782	7.30	0.41
4 persons,	581	4,286	7.38	0.54
5 persons,	463	3,641	7.86	0.64
6 persons,	312	2,505	8.03	0.75
7 persons,	174	1,453	8.35	0.84
8 persons,	95	771	8.12	0.99
9 persons,	35	296	8.37	1.08
10 persons,	32	250	7.81	1.28
11 persons,	16	122	7.63	1.44
12 persons,	5	51	10.20	1.18
13 persons,	1	11	11.00	1.18
14 persons,	3	32	10.67	1.31
15 persons,	3	28	9.33	1.61

ROOMS: OCCUPIED DWELLING HOUSES — Continued.

COUNTIES, CITIES, TOWNS, AND NUMBER OF PERSONS TO A FAMILY.	Number of Families of Specified Size	Total Number of Rooms Occupied	Average Number of Rooms Occupied	Average Number of Persons to a Room
MIDDLESEX - Con.				
Melrose — Con.				
16 persons,	1	5	5.00	3.20
18 persons,	1	20	20.00	0.90
19 persons,	1	23	23.00	0.83
20 persons,	1	30	30.00	0.67
44 persons,	1	41	41.00	1.07
Natick,	2,089	13,551	6.49	0.65
1 person,	106	360	3.40	0.29
2 persons,	367	2,091	5.70	0.35
3 persons,	436	2,695	6.18	0.49
4 persons,	400	2,626	6.57	0.61
5 persons,	312	2,155	6.91	0.72
6 persons,	176	1,272	7.23	0.83
7 persons,	139	1,047	7.53	0.93
8 persons,	63	489	7.76	1.03
9 persons,	35	282	8.06	1.12
10 persons,	25	190	7.60	1.32
11 persons,	12	96	8.00	1.38
12 persons,	8	98	12.25	0.98
13 persons,	3	39	13.00	1.00
14 persons,	2	29	14.50	0.97
15 persons,	1	7	7.00	2.14
18 persons,	2	44	22.00	0.82
24 persons,	1	15	15.00	1.60
38 persons,	1	16	16.00	2.38
NEWTON,	5,528	41,911	8.12	0.64
1 person,	117	489	4.18	0.24
2 persons,	653	4,037	6.18	0.32
3 persons,	920	6,695	7.28	0.41
4 persons,	1,009	8,012	7.94	0.50
5 persons,	931	7,795	8.37	0.60
6 persons,	689	6,095	8.85	0.68
7 persons,	495	4,446	8.98	0.78
8 persons,	315	2,877	9.13	0.88
9 persons,	170	1,605	9.44	0.95
10 persons,	102	997	9.77	1.02
11 persons,	40	387	9.68	1.14
12 persons,	30	311	10.37	1.16
13 persons,	19	287	15.11	0.86
14 persons,	8	93	11.63	1.20
15 persons,	4	47	11.75	1.28
16 persons,	2	37	18.50	0.86
17 persons,	3	25	8.33	2.04
18 persons,	4	40	10.00	1.80
19 persons,	2	54	27.00	0.70
20 persons,	1	6	6.00	3.33
22 persons,	2	68	34.00	0.65
23 persons,	2	27	13.50	1.70
25 persons,	1	14	14.00	1.79
26 persons,	1	13	13.00	2.00
27 persons,	1	18	18.00	1.50
29 persons,	1	40	40.00	0.73
30 persons,	1	52	52.00	0.58
36 persons,	2	43	21.50	1.67
84 persons,	1	60	60.00	1.40

COUNTIES, CITIES, TOWNS, AND NUMBER OF PERSONS TO A FAMILY.	Number of Families of Specified Size	Total Number of Rooms Occupied	Average Number of Rooms Occupied	Average Number of Persons to a Room
MIDDLESEX - Con.				
NEWTON — Con.				
85 persons,	1	120	120.00	0.71
147 persons,	1	121	121.00	1.21
Newton. Ward 1,	830	5,663	6.82	0.76
1 person,	13	34	2.62	0.38
2 persons,	98	491	5.01	0.40
3 persons,	133	836	6.29	0.48
4 persons,	135	878	6.50	0.62
5 persons,	139	961	6.91	0.72
6 persons,	106	811	7.65	0.78
7 persons,	73	558	7.64	0.92
8 persons,	49	379	7.73	1.03
9 persons,	26	190	7.31	1.23
10 persons,	33	304	9.21	1.09
11 persons,	8	59	7.38	1.49
12 persons,	5	42	8.40	1.43
13 persons,	3	22	7.33	1.77
14 persons,	2	19	9.50	1.47
15 persons,	1	6	6.00	2.50
17 persons,	3	25	8.33	2.04
18 persons,	1	9	9.00	2.00
19 persons,	1	24	24.00	0.79
23 persons,	1	15	15.00	1.53
Newton. Ward 2,	1,107	8,548	7.71	0.63
1 person,	17	62	3.65	0.27
2 persons,	110	653	5.94	0.34
3 persons,	205	1,451	7.08	0.42
4 persons,	212	1,628	7.68	0.52
5 persons,	195	1,539	7.89	0.63
6 persons,	137	1,172	8.55	0.70
7 persons,	101	814	8.06	0.87
8 persons,	65	553	8.51	0.94
9 persons,	27	249	9.22	0.98
10 persons,	16	156	9.75	1.03
11 persons,	10	105	10.50	1.05
12 persons,	6	61	10.17	1.18
13 persons,	3	62	20.67	0.63
18 persons,	1	14	14.00	1.29
20 persons,	1	6	6.00	3.33
26 persons,	1	13	13.00	2.00
Newton. Ward 3,	719	6,480	9.01	0.53
1 person,	14	72	5.14	0.19
2 persons,	121	849	7.02	0.29
3 persons,	117	929	7.94	0.38
4 persons,	112	982	8.77	0.46
5 persons,	118	1,137	9.64	0.52
6 persons,	84	853	10.15	0.59
7 persons,	74	743	10.04	0.70
8 persons,	39	416	10.67	0.75
9 persons,	17	197	11.59	0.78
10 persons,	10	116	11.60	0.86
11 persons,	5	51	10.20	1.08
12 persons,	3	38	12.67	0.95
13 persons,	1	28	28.00	0.46
14 persons,	1	9	9.00	1.56

ROOMS: OCCUPIED DWELLING HOUSES — Continued.

Counties, Cities, Towns, and Number of Persons to a Family.	Number of Families of Specified Size	Total Number of Rooms Occupied	Average Number of Rooms Occupied	Average Number of Persons to a Room
MIDDLESEX — Con.				
Newton. Ward 3 — Con.				
22 persons,	1	18	18.00	1.22
25 persons,	1	14	14.00	1.79
36 persons,	1	28	28.00	1.29
Newton, Ward 4,	685	5,530	8.07	0.65
1 person,	23	86	3.74	0.27
2 persons,	81	478	5.90	0.34
3 persons,	107	804	7.51	0.40
4 persons,	125	1,001	8.01	0.50
5 persons,	118	979	8.30	0.60
6 persons,	88	648	7.36	0.76
7 persons,	48	387	8.06	0.87
8 persons,	41	353	8.61	0.83
9 persons,	23	192	8.35	1.08
10 persons,	11	91	8.27	1.21
11 persons,	5	42	8.40	1.31
12 persons,	7	70	10.00	1.20
13 persons,	4	60	15.00	0.87
19 persons,	1	30	30.00	0.63
27 persons,	1	18	18.00	1.50
85 persons,	1	120	120.00	0.71
147 persons,	1	121	121.00	1.21
Newton. Ward 5,	886	6,709	7.84	0.61
1 person,	19	116	6.11	0.16
2 persons,	118	785	6.65	0.30
3 persons,	147	1,062	7.22	0.42
4 persons,	175	1,329	7.59	0.53
5 persons,	147	1,168	7.95	0.63
6 persons,	94	762	8.11	0.74
7 persons,	61	523	8.57	0.82
8 persons,	39	298	7.64	1.05
9 persons,	31	250	8.06	1.12
10 persons,	8	71	8.88	1.13
11 persons,	5	50	10.00	1.10
12 persons,	3	34	11.33	1.06
13 persons,	3	62	20.67	0.63
14 persons,	1	11	11.00	1.27
18 persons,	1	14	14.00	1.29
22 persons,	1	50	50.00	0.44
23 persons,	1	12	12.00	1.92
30 persons,	1	52	52.00	0.58
84 persons,	1	60	60.00	1.40
Newton. Ward 6,	836	6,861	8.33	0.61
1 person,	26	103	3.96	0.25
2 persons,	88	515	5.85	0.34
3 persons,	136	966	7.10	0.42
4 persons,	136	1,281	8.21	0.49
5 persons,	114	970	8.51	0.59
6 persons,	106	1,013	9.56	0.63
7 persons,	83	791	9.53	0.73
8 persons,	53	522	9.85	0.81
9 persons,	33	359	10.88	0.83
10 persons,	19	197	10.37	0.96
11 persons,	5	53	10.60	1.04
12 persons,	5	53	10.60	1.13
MIDDLESEX — Con.				
Newton. Ward 6 — Con.				
13 persons,	5	53	10.60	1.23
14 persons,	2	21	10.50	1.33
15 persons,	2	23	11.50	1.30
16 persons,	1	23	23.00	0.70
18 persons,	1	3	3.00	6.00
36 persons,	1	15	15.00	2.40
Newton. Ward 7,	495	5,050	10.16	0.50
1 person,	5	16	3.20	0.31
2 persons,	37	296	7.19	0.28
3 persons,	75	647	8.63	0.35
4 persons,	94	913	9.71	0.41
5 persons,	100	1,041	10.41	0.48
6 persons,	74	786	10.62	0.56
7 persons,	55	630	11.45	0.61
8 persons,	29	356	12.28	0.65
9 persons,	13	168	12.92	0.70
10 persons,	5	62	12.40	0.81
11 persons,	2	27	13.50	0.81
12 persons,	1	13	13.00	0.92
14 persons,	2	33	16.50	0.85
15 persons,	1	18	18.00	0.83
16 persons,	1	14	14.00	1.14
20 persons,	1	40	40.00	0.73
North Reading,	228	1,589	6.97	0.53
1 person,	21	94	4.48	0.22
2 persons,	46	291	6.33	0.32
3 persons,	59	418	7.08	0.42
4 persons,	48	331	6.90	0.58
5 persons,	22	188	8.55	0.59
6 persons,	9	71	7.89	0.76
7 persons,	12	97	8.08	0.87
8 persons,	4	37	9.25	0.86
9 persons,	3	19	6.33	1.42
10 persons,	2	28	14.00	0.71
11 persons,	1	4	4.00	2.75
15 persons,	1	11	11.00	1.36
Pepperell,	787	5,306	6.74	0.63
1 person,	52	234	4.50	0.22
2 persons,	150	938	6.25	0.32
3 persons,	151	963	6.38	0.47
4 persons,	135	918	6.80	0.59
5 persons,	108	740	6.85	0.73
6 persons,	78	589	7.55	0.79
7 persons,	39	289	6.90	1.01
8 persons,	28	197	7.04	1.14
9 persons,	21	183	8.71	1.03
10 persons,	14	114	8.14	1.23
11 persons,	6	44	7.33	1.50
12 persons,	2	19	9.50	1.26
15 persons,	1	21	21.00	0.71
17 persons,	1	38	38.00	0.45
20 persons,	1	39	39.00	0.51
Reading,	1,150	8,198	7.13	0.58
1 person,	45	210	4.67	0.21

ROOMS: OCCUPIED DWELLING HOUSES — Continued.

Counties, Cities, Towns, and Number of Persons to a Family.	Number of Families of Specified Size	Total Number of Rooms Occupied	Average Number of Rooms Occupied	Average Number of Persons to a Room
MIDDLESEX — Con.				
Reading — Con.				
2 persons,	237	1,469	6.20	0.52
3 persons,	244	1,694	6.82	0.44
4 persons,	226	1,659	7.34	0.54
5 persons,	142	1,073	7.56	0.66
6 persons,	102	826	8.10	0.74
7 persons,	82	606	8.12	0.86
8 persons,	36	286	7.94	1.01
9 persons,	14	120	8.57	1.05
10 persons,	10	97	9.70	1.03
11 persons,	6	58	9.67	1.14
12 persons,	1	8	8.00	1.50
13 persons,	3	38	12.67	1.03
14 persons,	1	7	7.00	2.00
21 persons,	1	17	17.00	1.24
Sherborn,	286	2,210	7.73	0.65
1 person,	18	106	5.89	0.17
2 persons,	61	478	7.84	0.26
3 persons,	60	446	7.43	0.40
4 persons,	50	390	7.80	0.51
5 persons,	46	377	8.20	0.61
6 persons,	18	144	8.00	0.75
7 persons,	14	99	7.07	0.99
8 persons,	6	49	8.17	0.98
9 persons,	7	42	6.00	1.50
10 persons,	3	22	7.33	1.36
11 persons,	1	7	7.00	1.57
12 persons,	1	7	7.00	1.71
326 persons,	1	43	43.00	7.58
Shirley,	324	2,254	6.95	0.62
1 person,	21	115	5.48	0.18
2 persons,	62	394	6.35	0.31
3 persons,	59	405	6.86	0.44
4 persons,	64	461	7.20	0.56
5 persons,	38	265	6.97	0.72
6 persons,	25	177	7.08	0.85
7 persons,	25	170	6.80	1.03
8 persons,	8	55	6.88	1.16
9 persons,	10	83	8.30	1.08
10 persons,	7	54	7.71	1.30
11 persons,	2	12	6.00	1.83
17 persons,	1	19	19.00	0.89
18 persons,	1	16	16.00	1.13
25 persons,	1	25	25.00	1.00
SOMERVILLE,	11,863	74,418	6.25	0.70
1 person,	188	712	3.79	0.26
2 persons,	2,001	10,525	5.26	0.38
3 persons,	2,479	14,394	5.77	0.52
4 persons,	2,500	15,576	6.23	0.64
5 persons,	1,849	12,170	6.59	0.76
6 persons,	1,233	8,448	6.85	0.88
7 persons,	758	5,366	7.08	0.99
8 persons,	432	3,126	7.24	1.11
9 persons,	226	1,699	7.52	1.20
10 persons,	121	996	8.23	1.21
11 persons,	58	471	8.12	1.35

Counties, Cities, Towns, and Number of Persons to a Family.	Number of Families of Specified Size	Total Number of Rooms Occupied	Average Number of Rooms Occupied	Average Number of Persons to a Room
MIDDLESEX — Con.				
SOMERVILLE — Con.				
12 persons,	24	245	10.21	1.18
13 persons,	12	117	9.75	1.33
14 persons,	6	58	9.67	1.45
15 persons,	3	36	12.00	1.25
16 persons,	4	70	17.50	0.91
18 persons,	1	13	13.00	1.38
19 persons,	1	40	40.00	0.48
21 persons,	1	2	2.00	10.50
22 persons,	1	24	24.00	0.92
23 persons,	1	20	20.00	1.15
37 persons,	1	32	32.00	1.16
41 persons,	1	45	45.00	0.91
145 persons,	1	30	30.00	4.83
323 persons,	1	284	284.00	1.14
Somerville. Ward 1,	2,302	14,018	6.09	0.72
1 person,	48	157	3.27	0.31
2 persons,	398	2,073	5.21	0.38
3 persons,	499	2,804	5.62	0.53
4 persons,	485	2,851	5.88	0.68
5 persons,	340	2,218	6.52	0.77
6 persons,	225	1,506	6.69	0.90
7 persons,	143	950	6.64	1.05
8 persons,	78	510	6.54	1.22
9 persons,	47	352	7.49	1.20
10 persons,	19	152	8.00	1.25
11 persons,	9	64	7.11	1.55
12 persons,	3	25	8.33	1.44
13 persons,	3	20	6.67	1.95
14 persons,	1	11	11.00	1.27
15 persons,	1	13	13.00	1.15
16 persons,	2	28	14.00	1.14
323 persons,	1	284	284.00	1.14
Somerville. Ward 2,	3,875	22,470	5.80	0.77
1 person,	58	207	3.57	0.28
2 persons,	658	3,237	4.92	0.41
3 persons,	756	4,055	5.36	0.56
4 persons,	798	4,589	5.76	0.69
5 persons,	605	3,580	5.92	0.84
6 persons,	409	2,593	6.34	0.95
7 persons,	261	1,712	6.56	1.07
8 persons,	150	1,000	6.67	1.20
9 persons,	81	593	7.32	1.23
10 persons,	55	423	7.69	1.30
11 persons,	22	177	8.05	1.37
12 persons,	9	96	10.67	1.13
13 persons,	5	55	11.00	1.18
14 persons,	3	29	9.67	1.45
16 persons,	1	12	12.00	1.33
18 persons,	1	13	13.00	1.38
22 persons,	1	24	24.00	0.92
23 persons,	1	20	20.00	1.15
41 persons,	1	45	45.00	0.91
Somerville. Ward 3,	3,056	20,079	6.57	0.65
1 person,	50	197	3.94	0.25
2 persons,	502	2,736	5.45	0.37

ROOMS: OCCUPIED DWELLING HOUSES — Continued.

COUNTIES, CITIES, TOWNS, AND NUMBER OF PERSONS TO A FAMILY.	Number of Families of Specified Size	Total Number of Rooms Occupied	Average Number of Rooms Occupied	Average Number of Persons to a Room	COUNTIES, CITIES, TOWNS, AND NUMBER OF PERSONS TO A FAMILY.	Number of Families of Specified Size	Total Number of Rooms Occupied	Average Number of Rooms Occupied	Average Number of Persons to a Room
MIDDLESEX - Con.					**MIDDLESEX - Con.**				
Somerville. Ward 3 — Con.					Stow, ...	234	1,787	7.64	0.51
3 persons, . .	657	4,067	6.19	0.49	1 person, . .	12	66	5.50	0.18
4 persons, . .	686	4,632	6.75	0.59	2 persons, . .	51	328	6.43	0.31
5 persons, . .	457	3,252	7.12	0.70	3 persons, . .	49	369	7.53	0.40
6 persons, . .	323	2,318	7.18	0.84	4 persons, . .	40	307	7.68	0.52
7 persons, . .	184	1,407	7.65	0.92	5 persons, . .	42	323	7.69	0.65
8 persons, . .	104	798	7.67	1.04	6 persons, . .	17	155	9.12	0.66
9 persons, . .	41	287	7.00	1.29	7 persons, . .	12	123	10.25	0.68
10 persons, . .	25	219	8.76	1.14	8 persons, . .	6	71	11.83	0.68
11 persons, . .	16	130	8.13	1.35	10 persons, . .	2	21	10.50	0.65
12 persons, . .	5	47	9.40	1.28	11 persons, . .	2	16	8.00	1.38
13 persons, . .	3	30	10.00	1.30	13 persons, . .	1	8	8.00	1.63
14 persons, . .	1	6	6.00	2.33	Sudbury, . . .	272	1,979	7.28	0.58
15 persons, . .	1	11	11.00	1.36	1 person, . .	20	99	4.95	0.20
21 persons, . .	1	2	2.00	10.50	2 persons, . .	53	329	6.21	0.32
Somerville. Ward 4,	2,670	17,851	6.69	0.66	3 persons, . .	50	341	6.82	0.44
1 person, . .	32	151	4.72	0.21	4 persons, . .	47	380	8.09	0.49
2 persons, . .	443	2,479	5.60	0.36	5 persons, . .	35	247	7.06	0.71
3 persons, . .	567	3,438	6.06	0.49	6 persons, . .	30	257	8.57	0.70
4 persons, . .	531	3,494	6.58	0.61	7 persons, . .	16	137	8.56	0.82
5 persons, . .	447	3,129	7.00	0.71	8 persons, . .	5	38	7.60	1.05
6 persons, . .	276	2,031	7.36	0.82	9 persons, . .	9	79	8.78	1.03
7 persons, . .	170	1,297	7.63	0.92	10 persons, . .	3	28	9.33	1.07
8 persons, . .	100	818	8.18	0.98	14 persons, . .	2	20	10.00	1.40
9 persons, . .	57	467	8.19	1.10	15 persons, . .	1	13	13.00	1.15
10 persons, . .	22	202	9.18	1.09	16 persons, . .	1	11	11.00	1.45
11 persons, . .	11	100	9.09	1.21	Tewksbury, . .	473	4,511	9.54	0.75
12 persons, . .	7	77	11.00	1.09	1 person, . .	14	78	5.57	0.18
13 persons, . .	1	12	12.00	1.08	2 persons, . .	79	471	5.96	0.34
14 persons, . .	1	12	12.00	1.17	3 persons, . .	75	458	6.11	0.49
15 persons, . .	1	12	12.00	1.25	4 persons, . .	89	612	6.88	0.58
16 persons, . .	1	30	30.00	0.53	5 persons, . .	65	489	7.52	0.66
19 persons, . .	1	40	40.00	0.48	6 persons, . .	56	374	6.68	0.90
37 persons, . .	1	32	32.00	1.16	7 persons-, . .	39	318	8.15	0.86
145 persons, . .	1	30	30.00	4.83	8 persons, . .	21	191	9.10	0.88
Stoneham, . .	1,581	10,567	6.65	0.69	9 persons, . .	16	150	9.38	0.96
1 person, . .	84	355	4.23	0.24	10 persons, . .	6	50	8.33	1.20
2 persons, . .	370	2,332	6.30	0.32	11 persons, . .	4	51	12.75	0.86
3 persons, . .	345	2,161	6.26	0.48	12 persons, . .	2	31	15.50	0.77
4 persons, . .	285	1,915	6.72	0.60	13 persons, . .	1	11	11.00	1.18
5 persons, . .	197	1,411	7.16	0.70	14 persons, . .	3	30	10.00	1.40
6 persons, . .	111	783	7.05	0.85	15 persons, . .	1	11	11.00	1.36
7 persons, . .	85	600	7.06	0.99	16 persons, . .	1	20	20.00	0.80
8 persons, . .	45	318	7.07	1.13	1,166 persons, . .	1	1,166	1,166.00	1.00
9 persons, . .	21	161	7.67	1.17	Townsend, . .	512	3,614	7.06	0.49
10 persons, . .	14	128	9.14	1.09	1 person, . .	50	302	6.04	0.17
11 persons, . .	8	67	8.38	1.31	2 persons, . .	149	964	6.47	0.31
12 persons, . .	6	74	12.33	0.97	3 persons, . .	108	752	6.90	0.43
13 persons, . .	3	37	12.33	1.05	4 persons, . .	81	605	7.47	0.54
15 persons, . .	1	30	30.00	0.50	5 persons, . .	56	433	7.73	0.65
16 persons, . .	1	8	8.00	2.00	6 persons, . .	30	228	7.60	0.79
20 persons, . .	2	53	26.50	0.75	7 persons, . .	12	103	8.58	0.82
22 persons, . .	1	25	25.00	0.88	8 persons, . .	12	79	6.58	1.22
24 persons, . .	1	11	11.00	2.18	9 persons, . .	7	57	8.14	1.11
34 persons, . .	1	38	38.00	0.89	10 persons, . .	3	27	9.00	1.11

ROOMS: OCCUPIED DWELLING HOUSES — Continued.

Counties, Cities, Towns, and Number of Persons to a Family.	Number of Families of Specified Size	Total Number of Rooms Occupied	Average Number of Rooms Occupied	Average Number of Persons to a Room
MIDDLESEX — Con.				
Townsend — Con.				
12 persons, . .	1	14	14.00	0.86
16 persons, . .	1	20	20.00	0.80
20 persons, . .	1	30	30.00	0.67
Tyngsborough, .	163	1,166	6.79	0.57
1 person, . .	16	64	4.00	0.25
2 persons, . .	37	218	5.89	0.34
3 persons, . .	32	202	6.31	0.48
4 persons, . .	25	194	7.76	0.52
5 persons, . .	19	149	7.84	0.64
6 persons, . .	12	93	7.75	0.77
7 persons, . .	10	82	8.20	0.85
8 persons, . .	3	22	7.33	1.09
9 persons, . .	6	45	7.50	1.20
10 persons, . .	1	14	14.00	0.71
12 persons, . .	2	23	11.50	1.04
Wakefield, . .	1,958	12,944	6.61	0.64
1 person, . .	68	287	4.22	0.24
2 persons, . .	355	2,033	5.73	0.35
3 persons, . .	414	2,614	6.31	0.48
4 persons, . .	378	2,553	6.75	0.59
5 persons, . .	279	2,011	7.21	0.69
6 persons, . .	212	1,515	7.15	0.84
7 persons, . .	104	741	7.13	0.98
8 persons, . .	70	506	7.23	1.11
9 persons, . .	37	285	7.70	1.17
10 persons, . .	20	164	8.20	1.22
11 persons, . .	12	91	7.58	1.45
12 persons, . .	2	17	8.50	1.41
13 persons, . .	1	18	18.00	0.72
14 persons, . .	2	26	13.00	1.08
15 persons, . .	1	22	22.00	0.68
20 persons, . .	1	14	14.00	1.43
25 persons, . .	1	22	22.00	1.14
27 persons, . .	1	25	25.00	1.08
WALTHAM, . .	4,276	28,985	6.78	0.72
1 person, . .	125	546	4.37	0.23
2 persons, . .	582	3,284	5.64	0.35
3 persons, . .	778	4,716	6.06	0.49
4 persons, . .	819	5,368	6.55	0.61
5 persons, . .	685	4,757	6.94	0.72
6 persons, . .	480	3,421	7.13	0.84
7 persons, . .	304	2,187	7.19	0.97
8 persons, . .	210	1,670	7.95	1.01
9 persons, . .	129	1,043	8.09	1.11
10 persons, . .	77	658	8.55	1.17
11 persons, . .	24	226	9.42	1.17
12 persons, . .	15	160	10.67	1.13
13 persons, . .	17	203	11.94	1.09
14 persons, . .	6	50	8.33	1.68
15 persons, . .	4	63	15.75	0.95
17 persons, . .	2	22	11.00	1.55
18 persons, . .	2	35	17.50	1.03
19 persons, . .	1	16	16.00	1.19
20 persons, . .	1	15	15.00	1.33
21 persons, . .	1	17	17.00	1.24

Counties, Cities, Towns, and Number of Persons to a Family.	Number of Families of Specified Size	Total Number of Rooms Occupied	Average Number of Rooms Occupied	Average Number of Persons to a Room
MIDDLESEX — Con.				
WALTHAM — Con.				
26 persons, . .	1	44	44.00	0.59
27 persons, . .	1	14	14.00	1.93
30 persons, . .	1	32	32.00	0.94
31 persons, . .	1	30	30.00	1.03
33 persons, . .	1	16	16.00	2.06
41 persons, . .	1	40	40.00	1.03
43 persons, . .	1	51	51.00	0.84
53 persons, . .	1	45	45.00	1.18
78 persons, . .	1	36	36.00	2.17
80 persons, . .	1	10	10.00	8.00
85 persons, . .	1	73	73.00	1.16
99 persons, . .	1	99	99.00	1.00
170 persons, . .	1	23	23.00	7.39
198 persons, . .	1	25	25.00	7.92
Waltham. Ward 1, .	615	4,162	6.77	0.70
1 person, . .	13	59	4.54	0.22
2 persons, . .	85	504	5.93	0.34
3 persons, . .	111	691	6.23	0.48
4 persons, . .	122	816	6.68	0.60
5 persons, . .	106	703	6.63	0.75
6 persons, . .	64	439	6.86	0.87
7 persons, . .	54	378	7.00	1.00
8 persons, . .	27	219	8.11	0.98
9 persons, . .	18	145	8.05	1.12
10 persons, . .	8	71	8.88	1.13
11 persons, . .	5	32	6.40	1.72
12 persons, . .	1	6	6.00	2.00
99 persons, . .	1	99	99.00	1.00
Waltham. Ward 2, .	500	3,359	7.92	0.74
1 person, . .	32	133	4.16	0.24
2 persons, . .	69	397	5.75	0.35
3 persons, . .	73	491	6.73	0.45
4 persons, . .	85	632	7.44	0.54
5 persons, . .	79	648	8.20	0.61
6 persons, . .	48	419	8.73	0.69
7 persons, . .	36	286	7.94	0.88
8 persons, . .	25	258	10.32	0.78
9 persons, . .	12	109	9.08	0.99
10 persons, . .	11	109	9.94	1.01
11 persons, . .	8	101	12.63	0.87
12 persons, . .	3	47	15.67	0.77
13 persons, . .	6	99	16.50	0.79
14 persons, . .	4	32	8.00	1.75
18 persons, . .	1	17	17.00	1.06
19 persons, . .	1	16	16.00	1.19
21 persons, . .	1	17	17.00	1.24
26 persons, . .	1	44	44.00	0.59
31 persons, . .	1	30	30.00	1.03
33 persons, . .	1	16	16.00	2.06
80 persons, . .	1	10	10.00	8.00
170 persons, . .	1	23	23.00	7.39
198 persons, . .	1	25	25.00	7.92
Waltham. Ward 3, .	654	4,200	6.45	0.80
1 person, . .	18	87	4.83	0.21
2 persons, . .	86	462	5.37	0.37

ROOMS: OCCUPIED DWELLING HOUSES — Continued.

COUNTIES, CITIES, TOWNS, AND NUMBER OF PERSONS TO A FAMILY.	Number of Families of Specified Size	Total Number of Rooms Occupied	Average Number of Rooms Occupied	Average Number of Persons to a Room	COUNTIES, CITIES, TOWNS, AND NUMBER OF PERSONS TO A FAMILY.	Number of Families of Specified Size	Total Number of Rooms Occupied	Average Number of Rooms Occupied	Average Number of Persons to a Room
MIDDLESEX - Con.					MIDDLESEX - Con.				
Waltham, Ward 3 — Con.					*Waltham, Ward 6* — Con.				
3 persons, .	100	605	6.05	0.50	2 persons, . .	86	511	5.94	0.34
4 persons, .	105	612	5.83	0.69	3 persons, . .	143	854	5.97	0.50
5 persons, . .	95	622	6.55	0.76	4 persons, . .	137	900	6.57	0.64
6 persons, . .	89	565	6.35	0.95	5 persons, . .	111	826	7.44	0.67
7 persons, . .	54	354	6.56	1.07	6 persons, . .	68	499	7.34	0.82
8 persons, . .	45	319	7.09	1.13	7 persons, . .	42	319	7.60	0.92
9 persons, . .	25	223	8.92	1.01	8 persons, . .	20	163	8.15	0.98
10 persons, . .	18	143	7.94	1.26	9 persons, . .	17	141	8.29	1.09
11 persons, . .	3	18	6.00	1.83	10 persons, . .	7	69	9.86	1.01
12 persons, . .	4	36	9.00	1.33	12 persons, . .	1	14	14.00	0.86
13 persons, . .	2	17	8.50	1.53	13 persons, . .	3	28	9.33	1.39
14 persons, . .	1	11	11.00	1.27	15 persons, . .	1	18	18.00	0.83
15 persons, . .	2	28	14.00	1.07	33 persons, . .	1	45	45.00	1.18
17 persons, . .	1	8	8.00	2.13	*Waltham, Ward 7,* .	578	3,388	5.86	0.82
27 persons, . .	1	14	14.00	1.93	1 person, . .	16	54	3.38	0.30
41 persons, . .	1	40	40.00	1.03	2 persons, . .	72	357	4.96	0.40
75 persons, . .	1	36	36.00	2.17	3 persons, . .	96	527	5.49	0.55
Waltham, Ward 4, .	646	4,277	6.62	0.72	4 persons, . .	108	619	5.73	0.70
1 person, . .	16	69	4.31	0.23	5 persons, . .	99	584	5.90	0.85
2 persons, . .	86	507	5.90	0.34	6 persons, . .	66	423	6.41	0.94
3 persons, . .	117	716	6.12	0.49	7 persons, . .	47	303	6.45	1.09
4 persons, . .	134	853	6.37	0.63	8 persons, . .	30	191	6.37	1.26
5 persons, . .	98	637	6.50	0.77	9 persons, . .	24	169	7.04	1.28
6 persons, . .	77	539	7.00	0.86	10 persons, . .	15	123	8.20	1.22
7 persons, . .	41	296	7.22	0.97	11 persons, . .	1	6	6.00	1.83
8 persons, . .	32	250	7.81	1.02	12 persons, . .	2	16	8.00	1.50
9 persons, . .	22	154	7.00	1.29	13 persons, . .	1	9	9.00	1.44
10 persons, . .	10	70	7.00	1.43	14 persons, . .	1	7	7.00	2.00
11 persons, . .	5	54	10.80	1.02	Watertown, . .	1,650	11,789	7.14	0.66
12 persons, . .	3	26	8.67	1.38	1 person, . .	30	119	3.97	0.25
13 persons, . .	3	23	7.67	1.70	2 persons, . .	242	1,430	5.91	0.34
30 persons, . .	1	32	32.00	0.94	3 persons, . .	305	2,075	6.80	0.44
43 persons, . .	1	51	51.00	0.84	4 persons, . .	297	2,093	7.05	0.57
Waltham, Ward 5, .	639	4,569	7.15	0.63	5 persons, . .	259	1,950	7.53	0.66
1 person, . .	20	91	4.55	0.22	6 persons, . .	204	1,545	7.57	0.79
2 persons, . .	98	546	5.57	0.36	7 persons, . .	119	845	7.10	0.99
3 persons, . .	138	832	6.03	0.50	8 persons, . .	84	679	8.08	0.99
4 persons, . .	128	936	7.31	0.55	9 persons, . .	56	443	7.91	1.14
5 persons, . .	97	737	7.60	0.66	10 persons, . .	18	154	8.56	1.17
6 persons, . .	68	537	7.90	0.76	11 persons, . .	23	226	9.83	1.12
7 persons, . .	30	251	8.37	0.84	12 persons, . .	5	45	9.00	1.33
8 persons, . .	31	270	8.71	0.92	13 persons, . .	3	31	10.33	1.26
9 persons, . .	11	102	9.27	0.97	15 persons, . .	1	11	11.00	1.36
10 persons, . .	8	73	9.13	1.10	17 persons, . .	1	21	21.00	0.81
11 persons, . .	2	15	7.50	1.47	19 persons, . .	1	10	10.00	1.90
12 persons, . .	1	15	15.00	0.80	28 persons, . .	1	42	42.00	0.67
13 persons, . .	2	27	13.50	0.96	32 persons, . .	1	70	70.00	0.46
15 persons, . .	1	17	17.00	0.88	Wayland, . .	446	3,074	6.89	0.66
17 persons, . .	1	14	14.00	1.21	1 person, . .	20	104	5.20	0.19
18 persons, . .	1	18	18.00	1.00	2 persons, . .	69	422	6.12	0.33
20 persons, . .	1	15	15.00	1.33	3 persons, . .	80	502	6.28	0.48
85 persons, . .	1	73	73.00	1.16	4 persons, . .	86	591	6.87	0.58
Waltham, Ward 6, .	647	4,440	6.86	0.66	5 persons, . .	63	466	7.40	0.68
1 person, . .	10	53	5.30	0.19	6 persons, . .	51	373	7.31	0.82

CITIES, CITIES, TOWNS, AND NUMBER OF PERSONS TO A FAMILY.	Number of Families of Specified Size	Total Number of Rooms Occupied	Average Number of Rooms Occupied	Average Number of Persons to a Room	COUNTIES, CITIES, TOWNS, AND NUMBER OF PERSONS TO A FAMILY.	Number of Families of Specified Size	Total Number of Rooms Occupied	Average Number of Rooms Occupied	Average Number of Persons to a Room
MIDDLESEX – Con.					MIDDLESEX – Con.				
Wayland — Con.					Wilmington — Con.				
7 persons,	32	237	7.41	0.95	11 persons,	1	5	5.00	2.20
8 persons,	14	109	7.79	1.03	12 persons,	2	17	8.50	1.41
9 persons,	12	94	7.83	1.15	13 persons,	1	11	11.00	1.18
10 persons,	9	75	8.33	1.20	Winchester,	1,394	9,868	7.56	0.63
11 persons,	5	38	7.60	1.45	1 person,	33	118	3.58	0.28
12 persons,	1	6	6.00	2.00	2 persons,	182	1,155	6.35	0.32
13 persons,	2	23	11.50	1.13	3 persons,	201	1,352	6.73	0.45
16 persons,	1	10	10.00	1.60	4 persons,	253	1,940	7.55	0.53
20 persons,	1	24	24.00	0.83	5 persons,	221	1,721	7.79	0.64
Westford,	526	3,655	6.91	0.67	6 persons,	198	1,427	8.49	0.71
1 person,	25	132	5.28	0.19	7 persons,	98	782	7.98	0.88
2 persons,	95	597	6.28	0.32	8 persons,	71	624	8.79	0.91
3 persons,	99	659	6.63	0.45	9 persons,	45	413	9.00	0.94
4 persons,	86	609	7.08	0.56	10 persons,	13	107	8.23	1.21
5 persons,	62	470	7.58	0.66	11 persons,	5	44	8.80	1.25
6 persons,	62	444	7.16	0.84	12 persons,	2	22	11.00	1.09
7 persons,	26	186	7.15	0.98	13 persons,	4	42	10.50	1.24
8 persons,	28	206	7.36	1.09	15 persons,	2	36	18.00	0.83
9 persons,	14	111	7.93	1.14	16 persons,	3	43	14.33	1.12
10 persons,	9	65	7.22	1.38	18 persons,	1	20	20.00	0.90
11 persons,	4	23	5.75	1.91	27 persons,	1	22	22.00	1.23
12 persons,	8	46	5.75	2.09	WOBURN,	3,012	19,029	6.52	0.72
13 persons,	3	22	7.33	1.77	1 person,	89	400	4.49	0.22
14 persons,	2	20	10.00	1.40	2 persons,	447	2,580	5.77	0.35
16 persons,	1	12	12.00	1.33	3 persons,	535	3,459	6.47	0.46
17 persons,	1	15	15.00	1.13	4 persons,	524	3,335	6.36	0.63
18 persons,	1	21	21.00	0.86	5 persons,	458	3,080	6.72	0.74
Weston,	367	3,019	8.23	0.57	6 persons,	357	2,395	6.71	0.89
1 person,	10	68	6.80	0.15	7 persons,	232	1,598	6.84	1.02
2 persons,	52	346	6.65	0.30	8 persons,	167	1,147	6.87	1.16
3 persons,	70	485	6.93	0.43	9 persons,	96	671	6.99	1.29
4 persons,	75	584	7.79	0.51	10 persons,	53	388	7.32	1.37
5 persons,	55	463	8.42	0.59	11 persons,	24	192	8.00	1.38
6 persons,	36	309	8.58	0.70	12 persons,	11	97	8.82	1.36
7 persons,	27	248	9.19	0.76	13 persons,	10	113	11.30	1.15
8 persons,	13	154	11.85	0.68	14 persons,	2	18	9.00	1.56
9 persons,	14	153	10.93	0.82	16 persons,	3	47	15.67	1.02
10 persons,	7	74	10.57	0.95	17 persons,	1	11	11.00	1.55
11 persons,	3	56	18.67	0.59	20 persons,	1	20	20.00	1.00
12 persons,	1	11	11.00	1.09	34 persons,	1	54	54.00	0.63
13 persons,	1	8	8.00	1.63	35 persons,	1	36	36.00	0.97
14 persons,	2	48	24.00	0.58	Woburn, Ward 1,	509	3,519	6.91	0.75
20 persons,	1	12	12.00	1.67	1 person,	4	25	6.25	0.16
Wilmington,	338	2,202	6.51	0.64	2 persons,	63	368	5.84	0.34
1 person,	20	75	3.75	0.27	3 persons,	73	510	6.99	0.43
2 persons,	63	417	6.62	0.30	4 persons,	78	520	6.67	0.60
3 persons,	68	453	6.66	0.45	5 persons,	92	605	6.58	0.76
4 persons,	59	419	7.10	0.56	6 persons,	73	507	6.95	0.86
5 persons,	46	289	6.28	0.80	7 persons,	46	332	7.22	0.97
6 persons,	32	205	6.41	0.94	8 persons,	35	275	7.86	1.02
7 persons,	19	128	6.74	1.04	9 persons,	21	165	7.86	1.15
8 persons,	17	118	6.94	1.15	10 persons,	10	62	6.20	1.61
9 persons,	5	33	6.60	1.36	11 persons,	5	42	8.40	1.31
10 persons,	5	32	6.40	1.56	12 persons,	3	33	11.00	1.09

ROOMS: OCCUPIED DWELLING HOUSES — Continued.

Counties, Cities, Towns, and Number of Persons to a Family.	Number of Families of Specified Size	Total Number of Rooms Occupied	Average Number of Rooms Occupied	Average Number of Persons to a Room	Counties, Cities, Towns, and Number of Persons to a Family.	Number of Families of Specified Size	Total Number of Rooms Occupied	Average Number of Rooms Occupied	Average Number of Persons to a Room
MIDDLESEX — Con.					**MIDDLESEX — Con.**				
Woburn. Ward 1 — Con.					*Woburn. Ward 5 —* Con.				
13 persons,	4	40	10.00	1.30	6 persons,	33	194	5.88	1.02
16 persons,	2	35	17.50	0.91	7 persons,	24	136	5.67	1.24
Woburn. Ward 2,	590	3,713	6.29	0.78	8 persons,	14	86	6.14	1.30
1 person,	8	32	4.00	0.25	9 persons,	9	57	6.33	1.42
2 persons,	77	417	5.42	0.37	10 persons,	2	13	6.50	1.54
3 persons,	98	609	6.21	0.48	11 persons,	2	18	9.00	1.22
4 persons,	106	659	6.22	0.64	12 persons,	2	19	9.50	1.26
5 persons,	99	664	6.71	0.75	13 persons,	1	6	6.00	2.17
6 persons,	71	424	5.97	1.00	*Woburn. Ward 6,*	343	2,269	6.92	0.92
7 persons,	53	372	7.02	1.00	1 person,	18	83	4.61	0.22
8 persons,	41	271	6.61	1.21	2 persons,	64	398	6.22	0.32
9 persons,	17	108	6.35	1.42	3 persons,	67	467	6.97	0.43
10 persons,	9	60	6.67	1.50	4 persons,	70	463	6.61	0.60
11 persons,	4	32	8.00	1.38	5 persons,	46	314	6.83	0.73
12 persons,	2	15	7.50	1.60	6 persons,	32	211	6.59	0.91
13 persons,	2	20	10.00	1.30	7 persons,	23	145	6.30	1.11
14 persons,	2	18	9.00	1.56	8 persons,	12	89	7.42	1.08
16 persons,	1	12	12.00	1.33	9 persons,	7	49	7.00	1.29
Woburn. Ward 3,	561	3,634	6.48	0.69	10 persons,	2	22	11.00	0.91
1 person,	29	133	4.59	0.22	11 persons,	1	8	8.00	1.38
2 persons,	87	490	5.63	0.36	13 persons,	1	20	20.00	0.65
3 persons,	115	699	6.08	0.49	*Woburn. Ward 7,*	193	1,247	6.46	0.78
4 persons,	98	620	6.33	0.63	1 person,	2	16	8.00	0.13
5 persons,	70	512	7.31	0.68	2 persons,	22	111	5.05	0.40
6 persons,	56	423	7.55	0.79	3 persons,	41	258	6.29	0.48
7 persons,	46	311	6.76	1.04	4 persons,	28	176	6.29	0.64
8 persons,	25	161	6.44	1.24	5 persons,	33	206	6.24	0.80
9 persons,	18	118	6.56	1.37	6 persons,	26	179	6.88	0.87
10 persons,	12	84	7.00	1.43	7 persons,	13	87	6.69	1.05
11 persons,	3	24	8.00	1.38	8 persons,	11	74	6.73	1.19
12 persons,	1	5	5.00	2.40	9 persons,	6	43	7.17	1.26
34 persons,	1	54	54.00	0.63	10 persons,	6	44	7.33	1.36
Woburn. Ward 4,	574	3,822	6.66	0.69	11 persons,	2	13	6.50	1.69
1 person,	24	100	4.17	0.24	13 persons,	1	9	9.00	1.44
2 persons,	92	532	5.78	0.35	17 persons,	1	11	11.00	1.55
3 persons,	105	702	6.69	0.45	20 persons,	1	20	20.00	1.00
4 persons,	106	680	6.51	0.61	**NANTUCKET.**				
5 persons,	83	579	6.98	0.72	Nantucket,	981	7,287	7.43	0.41
6 persons,	66	457	6.92	0.87	1 person,	149	910	6.11	0.16
7 persons,	27	205	7.52	1.03	2 persons,	295	2,107	7.14	0.28
8 persons,	29	191	6.59	1.21	3 persons,	218	1,655	7.58	0.40
9 persons,	18	131	7.28	1.24	4 persons,	159	1,202	7.56	0.53
10 persons,	12	103	8.58	1.17	5 persons,	80	625	7.81	0.64
11 persons,	7	55	7.86	1.40	6 persons,	38	307	8.08	0.74
12 persons,	3	25	8.33	1.44	7 persons,	22	181	8.23	0.85
13 persons,	1	18	18.00	0.72	8 persons,	9	84	9.33	0.86
35 persons,	1	36	36.00	0.97	9 persons,	5	38	7.60	1.18
Woburn. Ward 5,	242	1,425	5.89	0.81	10 persons,	1	10	10.00	1.00
1 person,	4	11	2.75	0.36	11 persons,	2	19	9.50	1.16
2 persons,	42	264	6.29	0.32	12 persons,	1	11	11.00	1.09
3 persons,	36	214	5.94	0.50	16 persons,	1	100	100.00	0.16
4 persons,	38	207	5.45	0.73	28 persons,	1	40	40.00	0.70
5 persons,	35	200	5.71	0.88					

ROOMS: OCCUPIED DWELLING HOUSES — Continued.

COUNTIES, CITIES, TOWNS, AND NUMBER OF PERSONS TO A FAMILY.	Number of Families of Specified Size	Total Number of Rooms Occupied	Average Number of Rooms Occupied	Average Number of Persons to a Room	COUNTIES, CITIES, TOWNS, AND NUMBER OF PERSONS TO A FAMILY.	Number of Families of Specified Size	Total Number of Rooms Occupied	Average Number of Rooms Occupied	Average Number of Persons to a Room
NORFOLK.					**NORFOLK — Con.**				
Avon, ...	385	2,534	6.58	0.64	Brookline — Con.				
1 person,	13	46	3.54	0.28	10 persons,	57	584	10.25	0.98
2 persons,	74	431	5.82	0.34	11 persons,	40	460	11.50	0.96
3 persons,	86	573	6.66	0.45	12 persons,	16	222	13.88	0.86
4 persons,	68	466	6.85	0.58	13 persons,	13	190	14.62	0.89
5 persons,	56	379	6.77	0.74	14 persons,	7	74	10.57	1.32
6 persons,	34	222	6.53	0.92	15 persons,	5	98	19.60	0.77
7 persons,	24	167	6.96	1.01	16 persons,	3	59	19.67	0.81
8 persons,	16	121	7.56	1.06	17 persons,	1	7	7.00	2.43
9 persons,	7	50	7.14	1.26	18 persons,	2	36	18.00	1.00
10 persons,	3	18	6.00	1.67	19 persons,	1	50	50.00	0.38
11 persons,	2	15	7.50	1.47	20 persons,	1	17	17.00	1.18
14 persons,	1	9	9.00	1.56	22 persons,	1	12	12.00	1.83
26 persons,	1	37	37.00	0.70	25 persons,	1	15	15.00	1.67
Bellingham,	358	2,514	7.02	0.59	26 persons,	1	29	29.00	0.90
1 person,	23	141	6.13	0.16	27 persons,	1	20	20.00	1.35
2 persons,	80	536	6.70	0.30	29 persons,	1	17	17.00	1.71
3 persons,	71	481	6.77	0.44	31 persons,	1	55	55.00	0.56
4 persons,	54	383	7.09	0.56	72 persons,	1	115	115.00	0.63
5 persons,	34	244	7.18	0.70	Canton, . . .	908	7,023	7.26	0.66
6 persons,	46	338	7.35	0.82	1 person,	35	181	5.17	0.19
7 persons,	16	115	7.19	0.97	2 persons,	151	962	6.37	0.31
8 persons,	14	106	7.57	1.06	3 persons,	158	1,121	7.09	0.42
9 persons,	9	66	7.33	1.23	4 persons,	155	1,073	6.92	0.58
10 persons,	6	55	9.17	1.09	5 persons,	138	1,031	7.47	0.67
11 persons,	4	33	8.25	1.33	6 persons,	110	826	7.51	0.80
14 persons,	1	16	16.00	0.88	7 persons,	86	685	7.97	0.88
Braintree, .	1,254	8,721	6.95	0.61	8 persons,	51	385	7.55	1.06
1 person,	51	245	4.80	0.21	9 persons,	48	412	8.58	1.05
2 persons,	245	1,573	6.42	0.31	10 persons,	12	104	8.67	1.15
3 persons,	277	1,854	6.69	0.45	11 persons,	15	125	8.33	1.32
4 persons,	243	1,749	7.20	0.56	12 persons,	5	45	9.00	1.33
5 persons,	179	1,284	7.17	0.70	13 persons,	1	15	15.00	0.87
6 persons,	103	754	7.32	0.82	17 persons,	1	7	7.00	2.43
7 persons,	58	489	8.43	0.83	19 persons,	2	51	25.50	0.75
8 persons,	49	374	7.63	1.05	Cohasset, . .	586	4,644	7.92	0.53
9 persons,	25	191	7.64	1.18	1 person,	43	246	5.72	0.17
10 persons,	10	90	9.00	1.44	2 persons,	123	806	6.55	0.31
11 persons,	6	46	7.67	1.43	3 persons,	110	869	7.90	0.38
12 persons,	3	19	6.33	1.89	4 persons,	96	730	7.60	0.53
13 persons,	1	9	9.00	1.44	5 persons,	68	528	7.76	0.64
15 persons,	1	13	13.00	1.15	6 persons,	54	464	9.10	0.66
19 persons,	1	1	1.00	19.00	7 persons,	37	335	9.05	0.77
20 persons,	1	27	27.00	0.74	8 persons,	21	182	8.67	0.92
102 persons,	1	3	3.00	54.00	9 persons,	14	133	10.23	0.82
Brookline,	3,148	24,822	7.89	0.65	10 persons,	7	95	13.57	0.74
1 person,	113	307	2.72	0.37	11 persons,	6	81	13.50	0.81
2 persons,	319	1,634	5.12	0.39	12 persons,	3	41	13.67	0.88
3 persons,	459	2,980	6.51	0.46	13 persons,	4	58	14.50	0.90
4 persons,	510	3,755	7.36	0.54	14 persons,	1	23	23.00	0.61
5 persons,	527	4,115	7.81	0.64	15 persons,	1	15	15.00	1.00
6 persons,	450	4,122	9.16	0.66	19 persons,	1	18	18.00	1.06
7 persons,	311	2,880	9.26	0.76	Dedham, . .	1,613	11,697	7.25	0.62
8 persons,	186	1,797	9.66	0.83	1 person,	82	394	4.80	0.21
9 persons,	120	1,162	9.68	0.93	2 persons,	260	1,575	6.06	0.33

ROOMS: OCCUPIED DWELLING HOUSES — Continued.

COUNTIES, CITIES, TOWNS, AND NUMBER OF PERSONS TO A FAMILY.	Number of Families of Specified Size	Total Number of Rooms Occupied	Average Number of Rooms Occupied	Average Number of Persons to a Room
NORFOLK — Con.				
Dedham — Con.				
3 persons,	311	2,146	6.90	0.43
4 persons,	294	2,089	7.11	0.56
5 persons,	216	1,706	7.90	0.63
6 persons,	183	1,339	7.32	0.82
7 persons,	126	968	7.92	0.88
8 persons,	59	502	8.51	0.94
9 persons,	35	302	8.63	1.04
10 persons,	23	243	10.57	0.95
11 persons,	7	79	11.29	0.97
12 persons,	4	36	9.00	1.33
13 persons,	5	81	16.20	0.80
14 persons,	4	37	9.25	1.51
19 persons,	1	12	12.00	1.58
38 persons,	1	18	18.00	2.11
40 persons,	1	60	60.00	0.67
80 persons,	1	80	80.00	1.00
Dover,	148	1,139	7.70	0.59
1 person,	9	42	4.67	0.21
2 persons,	22	147	6.68	0.30
3 persons,	31	262	8.45	0.35
4 persons,	23	187	8.13	0.49
5 persons,	20	145	7.25	0.69
6 persons,	14	114	8.14	0.74
7 persons,	12	93	7.75	0.90
8 persons,	6	42	7.00	1.14
9 persons,	6	60	10.00	0.90
10 persons,	1	10	10.00	1.00
11 persons,	1	9	9.00	1.22
12 persons,	1	5	5.00	2.40
13 persons,	1	10	10.00	1.30
14 persons,	1	13	13.00	1.08
Foxborough,	828	5,784	6.99	0.56
1 person,	69	331	4.80	0.21
2 persons,	195	1,185	6.08	0.33
3 persons,	175	1,213	6.93	0.43
4 persons,	154	1,145	7.44	0.54
5 persons,	82	587	7.16	0.70
6 persons,	74	579	7.82	0.77
7 persons,	34	259	7.62	0.92
8 persons,	25	186	7.44	1.08
9 persons,	8	58	7.25	1.24
10 persons,	5	44	8.80	1.14
11 persons,	2	28	14.00	0.79
12 persons,	1	13	13.00	0.92
13 persons,	1	12	12.00	1.08
18 persons,	1	14	14.00	1.29
22 persons,	1	38	38.00	0.58
118 persons,	1	92	92.00	1.28
Franklin,	1,176	8,059	6.85	0.64
1 person,	58	232	4.00	0.25
2 persons,	217	1,285	5.92	0.34
3 persons,	242	1,610	6.65	0.45
4 persons,	229	1,511	6.60	0.61
5 persons,	164	1,146	6.99	0.72

COUNTIES, CITIES, TOWNS, AND NUMBER OF PERSONS TO A FAMILY.	Number of Families of Specified Size	Total Number of Rooms Occupied	Average Number of Rooms Occupied	Average Number of Persons to a Room
NORFOLK — Con.				
Franklin — Con.				
6 persons,	108	817	7.56	0.79
7 persons,	51	390	7.65	0.92
8 persons,	37	262	7.08	1.13
9 persons,	33	279	8.45	1.06
10 persons,	15	116	7.73	1.29
11 persons,	4	29	7.25	1.52
12 persons,	8	56	7.00	1.71
13 persons,	1	9	9.00	1.44
14 persons,	2	31	15.50	0.90
18 persons,	2	36	18.00	1.00
19 persons,	1	18	18.00	1.06
33 persons,	1	33	33.00	1.00
34 persons,	1	41	41.00	0.83
35 persons,	1	22	22.00	1.59
96 persons,	1	136	136.00	0.71
Holbrook,	571	3,792	6.64	0.61
1 person,	34	137	4.05	0.25
2 persons,	113	684	6.05	0.33
3 persons,	125	807	6.46	0.46
4 persons,	100	695	6.95	0.58
5 persons,	77	552	7.17	0.70
6 persons,	49	350	7.14	0.84
7 persons,	36	270	7.50	0.83
8 persons,	19	148	7.79	1.06
9 persons,	8	71	8.88	1.01
10 persons,	3	22	7.33	1.96
11 persons,	6	47	7.83	1.40
12 persons,	1	9	9.00	1.33
Hyde Park,	2,561	17,873	6.98	0.66
1 person,	82	313	3.82	0.26
2 persons,	365	2,022	5.54	0.35
3 persons,	461	3,062	6.64	0.45
4 persons,	498	3,550	7.13	0.56
5 persons,	366	2,892	7.36	0.68
6 persons,	297	2,303	7.75	0.77
7 persons,	197	1,526	7.75	0.80
8 persons,	121	938	7.75	1.03
9 persons,	54	457	8.46	1.06
10 persons,	45	379	8.42	1.19
11 persons,	17	132	7.76	1.42
12 persons,	13	123	9.46	1.27
13 persons,	6	44	7.33	1.77
14 persons,	5	56	11.20	1.25
15 persons,	1	16	16.00	0.94
16 persons,	3	26	8.67	1.85
17 persons,	1	8	8.00	2.13
18 persons,	1	13	13.00	1.38
20 persons,	1	13	13.00	1.54
Medfield,	415	3,048	7.34	0.61
1 person,	25	101	4.04	0.25
2 persons,	81	498	6.15	0.33
3 persons,	83	594	7.16	0.42
4 persons,	66	487	7.38	0.54
5 persons,	55	423	7.69	0.65

ROOMS: OCCUPIED DWELLING HOUSES — Continued.

Counties, Cities, Towns, and Number of Persons to a Family.	Number of Families of Specified Size	Total Number of Rooms Occupied	Average Number of Rooms Occupied	Average Number of Persons to a Room	Counties, Cities, Towns, and Number of Persons to a Family.	Number of Families of Specified Size	Total Number of Rooms Occupied	Average Number of Rooms Occupied	Average Number of Persons to a Room
NORFOLK — Con.					NORFOLK — Con.				
Medfield — Con.					Milton — Con.				
6 persons, . .	41	307	7.49	0.80	11 persons, . .	12	177	14.75	0.75
7 persons, . .	20	133	7.65	0.92	12 persons, . .	13	141	10.85	1.11
8 persons, . .	13	100	7.69	1.04	13 persons, . .	4	57	14.25	0.91
9 persons, . .	14	127	9.07	0.99	14 persons, . .	3	78	26.00	0.54
10 persons, . .	5	52	10.40	0.96	15 persons, . .	4	77	19.25	0.78
11 persons, . .	3	35	11.67	0.94	18 persons, . .	1	10	10.00	1.80
13 persons, . .	1	7	7.00	1.86	26 persons, . .	1	31	31.00	0.84
14 persons, . .	1	19	19.00	0.74	50 persons, . .	1	107	107.00	0.47
15 persons, . .	1	11	11.00	1.36	57 persons, . .	1	30	30.00	1.90
16 persons, . .	1	5	5.00	3.20	Needham, . .	802	5,458	6.78	0.65
18 persons, . .	1	7	7.00	2.57	1 person, . .	39	175	4.49	0.22
19 persons, . .	1	25	25.00	0.76	2 persons, . .	134	827	6.17	0.32
24 persons, . .	1	15	15.00	1.60	3 persons, . .	162	1,031	6.36	0.47
34 persons, . .	1	34	34.00	1.00	4 persons, . .	147	1,019	6.93	0.58
45 persons, . .	1	48	48.00	0.94	5 persons, . .	101	701	6.94	0.72
Medway, . .	732	5,296	7.23	0.55	6 persons, . .	82	604	7.37	0.81
1 person, . .	55	291	5.29	0.19	7 persons, . .	58	458	7.90	0.90
2 persons, . .	163	1,073	6.58	0.30	8 persons, . .	41	304	7.41	1.08
3 persons, . .	142	1,058	7.45	0.40	9 persons, . .	17	115	6.76	1.33
4 persons, . .	133	982	7.38	0.54	10 persons, . .	10	96	9.30	1.08
5 persons, . .	84	675	8.04	0.62	11 persons, . .	3	31	10.33	1.06
6 persons, . .	66	482	7.30	0.82	12 persons, . .	3	28	9.33	1.29
7 persons, . .	40	281	7.03	1.00	13 persons, . .	3	18	6.00	2.17
8 persons, . .	18	137	7.61	1.05	14 persons, . .	1	12	12.00	1.17
9 persons, . .	13	107	8.23	1.09	24 persons, . .	1	22	22.00	1.09
10 persons, . .	10	81	8.10	1.23	Norfolk, . .	210	1,584	7.53	0.59
11 persons, . .	4	43	10.75	1.02	1 person, . .	11	43	3.91	0.26
12 persons, . .	1	6	6.00	2.00	2 persons, . .	36	235	6.53	0.31
13 persons, . .	1	31	31.00	0.42	3 persons, . .	44	325	7.39	0.41
21 persons, . .	1	20	20.00	1.05	4 persons, . .	36	287	7.97	0.50
27 persons, . .	1	26	26.00	1.03	5 persons, . .	30	237	7.90	0.63
Millis, . . .	226	1,714	7.58	0.59	6 persons, . .	25	217	8.68	0.69
1 person, . .	11	46	4.18	0.24	7 persons, . .	13	114	8.77	0.80
2 persons, . .	33	239	7.24	0.28	8 persons, . .	5	41	8.20	0.98
3 persons, . .	51	377	7.39	0.41	9 persons, . .	9	76	8.44	1.07
4 persons, . .	36	267	7.42	0.54	11 persons, . .	1	6	6.00	1.83
5 persons, . .	34	262	7.71	0.65	Norwood, . .	363	2,286	6.29	0.73
6 persons, . .	22	160	7.27	0.83	1 person, . .	23	88	3.83	0.26
7 persons, . .	14	111	7.93	0.88	2 persons, . .	134	689	5.22	0.38
8 persons, . .	8	68	8.50	0.94	3 persons, . .	171	1,047	6.12	0.49
9 persons, . .	9	104	11.56	0.78	4 persons, . .	179	1,099	6.14	0.65
10 persons, . .	5	40	8.00	1.25	5 persons, . .	148	986	6.66	0.75
11 persons, . .	2	27	13.50	0.81	6 persons, . .	121	784	6.48	0.93
15 persons, . .	1	13	13.00	1.15	7 persons, . .	74	517	6.99	1.00
Milton, . . .	1,106	8,717	7.88	0.93	8 persons, . .	42	287	6.83	1.17
1 person, . .	38	192	5.05	0.20	9 persons, . .	33	222	6.73	1.34
2 persons, . .	157	913	5.82	0.34	10 persons, . .	15	92	6.13	1.63
3 persons, . .	191	1,255	6.57	0.46	11 persons, . .	12	106	8.83	1.25
4 persons, . .	170	1,253	7.37	0.54	12 persons, . .	7	70	10.90	1.20
5 persons, . .	156	1,144	7.33	0.68	13 persons, . .	2	27	13.50	0.96
6 persons, . .	141	1,202	8.52	0.70	20 persons, . .	1	14	14.00	1.43
7 persons, . .	87	805	9.25	0.76	25 persons, . .	1	22	22.00	1.14
8 persons, . .	68	615	9.04	0.88	QUINCY, . . .	4,373	27,592	6.31	0.75
9 persons, . .	39	417	10.69	0.84	1 person, . .	134	495	3.69	0.27
10 persons, . .	19	213	11.21	0.89	2 persons, . .	615	3,414	5.55	0.36

ROOMS: OCCUPIED DWELLING HOUSES — Continued.

Counties, Cities, Towns, and Number of Persons to a Family.	Number of Families of Specified Size	Total Number of Rooms Occupied	Average Number of Rooms Occupied	Average Number of Persons to a Room	Counties, Cities, Towns, and Number of Persons to a Family.	Number of Families of Specified Size	Total Number of Rooms Occupied	Average Number of Rooms Occupied	Average Number of Persons to a Room
NORFOLK — Con.					NORFOLK — Con.				
QUINCY — Con.					Quincy. Ward 2 — Con.				
3 persons, . .	756	4,416	5.84	0.51	13 persons, . .	2	16	8.00	1.63
4 persons, . .	785	4,882	6.22	0.64	14 persons, . .	2	20	10.00	1.40
5 persons, . .	717	4,561	6.36	0.79	Quincy. Ward 3, . .	983	5,559	5.66	0.84
6 persons, . .	509	3,414	6.71	0.89	1 person, . .	21	67	3.19	0.31
7 persons, . .	343	2,349	6.85	1.02	2 persons, . .	130	669	5.15	0.39
8 persons, . .	212	1,512	7.13	1.12	3 persons, . .	184	968	5.24	0.58
9 persons, . .	135	1,001	7.41	1.21	4 persons, . .	170	964	5.67	0.71
10 persons, . .	80	567	7.09	1.41	5 persons, . .	162	917	5.66	0.88
11 persons, . .	37	283	7.65	1.44	6 persons, . .	110	646	5.87	1.02
12 persons, . .	21	189	9.00	1.33	7 persons, . .	80	497	6.21	1.13
13 persons, . .	8	68	8.50	1.53	8 persons, . .	57	357	6.26	1.28
14 persons, . .	7	60	8.57	1.63	9 persons, . .	36	242	6.72	1.34
15 persons, . .	4	57	14.25	1.05	10 persons, . .	13	81	6.23	1.60
16 persons, . .	1	45	45.00	0.36	11 persons, . .	10	69	6.90	1.59
17 persons, . .	2	47	23.50	0.72	12 persons, . .	4	36	9.00	1.33
19 persons, . .	1	13	13.00	1.46	13 persons, . .	2	21	10.50	1.24
23 persons, . .	1	46	46.00	0.50	14 persons, . .	3	23	7.67	1.83
25 persons, . .	2	25	12.50	2.00	17 persons, . .	1	12	12.00	1.42
32 persons, . .	1	42	42.00	0.76	Quincy. Ward 4, . .	990	5,361	5.42	0.93
45 persons, . .	1	44	44.00	1.02	1 person, . .	25	84	3.36	0.30
49 persons, . .	1	62	62.00	0.79	2 persons, . .	114	516	4.53	0.44
Quincy. Ward 1, . .	790	5,470	6.92	0.65	3 persons, . .	151	739	4.89	0.61
1 person, . .	54	190	3.52	0.28	4 persons, . .	157	773	4.92	0.81
2 persons, . .	113	661	5.85	0.34	5 persons, . .	186	1,029	5.53	0.90
3 persons, . .	142	898	6.32	0.47	6 persons, . .	125	728	5.82	1.03
4 persons, . .	149	1,024	6.87	0.58	7 persons, . .	85	501	5.89	1.19
5 persons, . .	109	761	6.98	0.72	8 persons, . .	56	360	6.43	1.24
6 persons, . .	98	723	7.38	0.81	9 persons, . .	44	280	6.36	1.41
7 persons, . .	54	423	7.83	0.89	10 persons, . .	26	175	6.73	1.49
8 persons, . .	27	240	8.89	0.90	11 persons, . .	9	60	6.67	1.65
9 persons, . .	22	209	9.50	0.95	12 persons, . .	7	59	8.43	1.42
10 persons, . .	7	56	8.00	1.25	13 persons, . .	3	25	8.33	1.56
11 persons, . .	4	35	8.75	1.26	14 persons, . .	1	10	10.00	1.40
12 persons, . .	3	34	11.33	1.06	15 persons, . .	1	22	22.00	0.68
15 persons, . .	1	8	8.00	1.88	Quincy. Ward 5, . .	568	4,314	7.90	0.82
16 persons, . .	1	45	45.00	0.36	1 person, . .	4	16	4.00	0.25
17 persons, . .	1	35	35.00	0.49	2 persons, . .	88	571	6.49	0.31
19 persons, . .	1	13	13.00	1.46	3 persons, . .	117	813	6.95	0.43
23 persons, . .	1	46	46.00	0.50	4 persons, . .	104	751	7.22	0.55
25 persons, . .	2	25	12.50	2.00	5 persons, . .	90	698	7.76	0.64
45 persons, . .	1	44	44.00	1.02	6 persons, . .	71	556	7.83	0.77
Quincy. Ward 2, . .	584	3,962	6.68	0.70	7 persons, . .	43	357	8.30	0.84
1 person, . .	19	90	4.74	0.21	8 persons, . .	21	178	8.48	0.94
2 persons, . .	91	518	5.69	0.35	9 persons, . .	9	84	9.33	0.96
3 persons, . .	86	560	6.51	0.46	10 persons, . .	8	73	9.13	1.10
4 persons, . .	119	818	6.87	0.58	11 persons, . .	6	63	10.50	1.05
5 persons, . .	84	565	6.73	0.74	12 persons, . .	1	10	10.00	1.20
6 persons, . .	71	525	7.39	0.81	13 persons, . .	1	6	6.00	2.17
7 persons, . .	50	351	7.02	1.00	14 persons, . .	1	7	7.00	2.00
8 persons, . .	24	177	7.38	1.08	15 persons, . .	2	27	13.50	1.11
9 persons, . .	11	83	7.55	1.19	32 persons, . .	1	42	42.00	0.76
10 persons, . .	14	100	7.14	1.40	49 persons, . .	1	62	62.00	0.79
11 persons, . .	7	47	6.71	1.64	Quincy. Ward 6, . .	458	2,986	6.52	0.70
12 persons, . .	4	32	8.00	1.50	1 person, . .	11	48	4.36	0.23

ROOMS: OCCUPIED DWELLING HOUSES — Continued.

COUNTIES, CITIES, TOWNS, AND NUMBER OF PERSONS TO A FAMILY.	Number of Families of Specified Size	Total Number of Rooms Occupied	Average Number of Rooms Occupied	Average Number of Persons to a Room	COUNTIES, CITIES, TOWNS, AND NUMBER OF PERSONS TO A FAMILY.	Number of Families of Specified Size	Total Number of Rooms Occupied	Average Number of Rooms Occupied	Average Number of Persons to a Room
NORFOLK — Con.					**NORFOLK — Con.**				
Quincy, Ward 6 — Con.					Stoughton — Con.				
2 persons, . .	79	479	6.06	0.33	12 persons, . .	11	100	9.09	1.32
3 persons, . .	76	448	5.89	0.51	14 persons, . .	1	9	9.00	1.56
4 persons, . .	86	552	6.42	0.62	16 persons, . .	2	21	10.50	1.52
5 persons, . .	86	591	6.87	0.73	19 persons, . .	1	20	20.00	0.95
6 persons, . .	34	256	6.34	0.86	22 persons, . .	1	29	29.00	0.76
7 persons, . .	31	220	7.10	0.99	Walpole, . . .	688	4,891	7.11	0.61
8 persons, . .	27	200	7.41	1.08	1 person, . .	33	163	4.94	0.20
9 persons, . .	13	103	7.92	1.14	2 persons, . .	125	802	6.42	0.31
10 persons, . .	12	82	6.83	1.46	3 persons, . .	143	1,031	7.21	0.42
11 persons, . .	1	9	9.00	1.22	4 persons, . .	124	869	7.01	0.57
12 persons, . .	2	18	9.00	1.33	5 persons, . .	82	644	7.85	0.64
Randolph, . .	995	6,342	6.37	0.59	6 persons, . .	73	511	7.00	0.86
1 person, . .	61	293	4.80	0.21	7 persons, . .	45	330	7.33	0.95
2 persons, . .	170	1,037	6.10	0.33	8 persons, . .	26	215	8.27	0.97
3 persons, . .	178	1,239	6.96	0.43	9 persons, . .	20	157	7.85	1.15
4 persons, . .	181	1,296	7.13	0.56	10 persons, . .	7	49	7.00	1.43
5 persons, . .	112	811	7.24	0.69	11 persons, . .	3	27	9.00	1.22
6 persons, . .	82	639	7.79	0.77	12 persons, . .	4	43	10.75	1.12
7 persons, . .	50	379	7.58	0.92	18 persons, . .	1	7	7.00	2.57
8 persons, . .	38	303	7.97	1.00	23 persons, . .	1	18	18.00	1.28
9 persons, . .	19	183	9.63	0.93	43 persons, . .	1	25	25.00	1.72
10 persons, . .	9	79	8.78	1.14	Wellesley, . .	738	6,677	9.05	0.63
11 persons, . .	2	20	10.00	1.10	1 person, . .	28	107	3.82	0.26
12 persons, . .	1	10	10.00	1.20	2 persons, . .	116	775	6.68	0.30
17 persons, . .	2	29	14.50	1.17	3 persons, . .	130	939	7.22	0.42
Sharon, . . .	336	3,130	7.96	0.55	4 persons, . .	142	1,163	8.19	0.49
1 person, . .	35	216	6.17	0.16	5 persons, . .	96	796	8.29	0.60
2 persons, . .	53	359	6.77	0.30	6 persons, . .	72	592	8.22	0.73
3 persons, . .	65	509	7.83	0.38	7 persons, . .	55	501	9.11	0.77
4 persons, . .	78	630	8.08	0.50	8 persons, . .	24	206	8.58	0.93
5 persons, . .	62	487	7.85	0.64	9 persons, . .	22	188	8.55	1.05
6 persons, . .	41	363	8.85	0.68	10 persons, . .	13	133	10.23	0.98
7 persons, . .	28	241	8.61	0.81	11 persons, . .	12	137	11.42	0.96
8 persons, . .	13	117	9.00	0.89	12 persons, . .	4	70	17.50	0.69
9 persons, . .	5	50	10.00	0.90	13 persons, . .	4	52	13.00	1.00
10 persons, . .	4	47	11.75	0.85	14 persons, . .	3	49	16.33	0.86
11 persons, . .	2	20	10.00	1.10	15 persons, . .	2	32	16.00	0.94
12 persons, . .	2	19	9.50	1.26	16 persons, . .	1	20	20.00	0.80
13 persons, . .	2	28	14.00	0.93	17 persons, . .	1	17	17.00	1.00
14 persons, . .	1	13	13.00	1.08	20 persons, . .	1	18	18.00	1.11
18 persons, . .	1	21	21.00	0.86	21 persons, . .	1	38	38.00	0.55
24 persons, . .	1	10	10.00	2.40	24 persons, . .	1	29	29.00	0.83
Stoughton, . .	1,241	8,373	6.75	0.63	25 persons, . .	1	23	23.00	1.09
1 person, . .	77	349	4.53	0.22	29 persons, . .	1	25	25.00	1.16
2 persons, . .	233	1,425	6.12	0.33	32 persons, . .	1	26	26.00	1.23
3 persons, . .	235	1,582	6.73	0.45	33 persons, . .	1	28	28.00	1.18
4 persons, . .	213	1,429	6.71	0.60	40 persons, . .	1	43	43.00	0.93
5 persons, . .	175	1,200	6.86	0.73	55 persons, . .	1	47	47.00	1.17
6 persons, . .	129	1,014	7.86	0.76	59 persons, . .	1	60	60.00	0.98
7 persons, . .	68	490	7.21	0.97	71 persons, . .	1	39	39.00	1.82
8 persons, . .	45	332	7.38	1.08	124 persons, . .	1	142	142.00	0.87
9 persons, . .	35	262	7.49	1.20	324 persons, . .	1	382	382.00	0.85
10 persons, . .	12	87	7.25	1.38	Weymouth, . .	2,666	18,479	6.93	0.61
11 persons, . .	3	24	8.00	1.38	1 person, . .	102	464	4.55	0.22

ROOMS: OCCUPIED DWELLING HOUSES — Continued.

COUNTIES, CITIES, TOWNS, AND NUMBER OF PERSONS TO A FAMILY.	Number of Families of Specified Size	Total Number of Rooms Occupied	Average Number of Rooms Occupied	Average Number of Persons to a Room	COUNTIES, CITIES, TOWNS, AND NUMBER OF PERSONS TO A FAMILY.	Number of Families of Specified Size	Total Number of Rooms Occupied	Average Number of Rooms Occupied	Average Number of Persons to a Room
NORFOLK — Con.					**PLYMOUTH — Con.**				
Weymouth — Con.					Bridgewater — Con.				
2 persons,	563	3,213	6.30	0.31	9 persons,	16	136	8.50	1.06
3 persons,	599	4,057	6.77	0.44	10 persons,	2	22	11.00	0.91
4 persons,	501	3,460	6.91	0.58	11 persons,	4	31	7.75	1.42
5 persons,	367	2,743	7.47	0.67	12 persons,	2	20	10.00	1.20
6 persons,	230	1,687	7.33	0.82	13 persons,	3	49	16.33	0.80
7 persons,	156	1,137	7.29	0.96	14 persons,	3	42	14.00	1.00
8 persons,	111	814	7.33	1.09	15 persons,	1	15	15.00	1.00
9 persons,	42	316	7.52	1.20	18 persons,	1	8	8.00	2.25
10 persons,	27	257	9.51	1.05	169 persons,	1	130	130.00	1.30
11 persons,	15	134	8.93	1.23	1,015 persons,	1	588	588.00	1.73
12 persons,	5	45	9.00	1.33	**BROCKTON,**	7,700	47,423	6.16	0.70
13 persons,	4	41	10.25	1.27	1 person,	217	808	3.72	0.27
15 persons,	1	6	6.00	2.50	2 persons,	1,320	7,146	5.41	0.37
26 persons,	1	30	30.00	0.87	3 persons,	1,692	9,841	5.82	0.52
38 persons,	1	42	42.00	0.90	4 persons,	1,517	9,260	6.11	0.65
183 persons,	1	33	33.00	5.55	5 persons,	1,168	7,394	6.33	0.79
Wrentham,	634	4,849	7.72	0.53	6 persons,	760	4,963	6.53	0.92
1 person,	41	222	5.41	0.18	7 persons,	440	2,974	6.76	1.04
2 persons,	125	838	6.70	0.30	8 persons,	263	1,835	6.98	1.15
3 persons,	120	926	7.72	0.39	9 persons,	154	1,144	7.43	1.21
4 persons,	125	1,008	8.06	0.50	10 persons,	60	464	7.73	1.29
5 persons,	83	659	7.94	0.63	11 persons,	38	353	9.29	1.18
6 persons,	57	487	8.54	0.70	12 persons,	18	206	11.44	1.05
7 persons,	27	223	8.26	0.85	13 persons,	16	176	11.00	1.18
8 persons,	24	221	9.21	0.87	14 persons,	5	56	11.20	1.25
9 persons,	15	119	7.93	1.13	15 persons,	5	60	12.00	1.25
10 persons,	6	62	10.33	0.97	16 persons,	9	189	21.00	0.76
11 persons,	4	57	14.25	0.77	17 persons,	4	113	28.25	0.60
13 persons,	2	22	11.00	1.18	19 persons,	2	40	20.00	0.95
15 persons,	2	25	12.50	1.20	21 persons,	2	36	18.00	1.17
PLYMOUTH.					22 persons,	2	69	34.50	0.64
					25 persons,	1	3	3.00	8.33
Abington,	1,076	7,462	6.93	0.56	29 persons,	1	8	8.00	3.62
1 person,	53	230	4.34	0.23	30 persons,	1	17	17.00	1.76
2 persons,	221	1,361	6.16	0.32	31 persons,	1	80	80.00	0.39
3 persons,	243	1,625	6.69	0.45	33 persons,	1	45	45.00	0.73
4 persons,	205	1,495	7.29	0.55	37 persons,	1	50	50.00	0.74
5 persons,	154	1,189	7.72	0.65	42 persons,	1	42	42.00	1.00
6 persons,	101	763	7.55	0.79	44 persons,	1	42	42.00	1.05
7 persons,	51	380	7.82	0.89	*Brockton, Ward 1,*	935	6,558	7.01	0.64
8 persons,	25	192	7.68	1.04	1 person,	33	113	3.42	0.29
9 persons,	11	88	8.00	1.13	2 persons,	153	838	5.48	0.37
10 persons,	7	72	10.29	0.97	3 persons,	219	1,354	6.18	0.49
11 persons,	3	23	7.67	1.43	4 persons,	175	1,248	7.13	0.56
14 persons,	2	25	12.50	1.12	5 persons,	141	1,019	7.23	0.69
Bridgewater,	854	7,355	8.61	0.64	6 persons,	77	539	7.00	0.86
1 person,	39	245	6.03	0.47	7 persons,	45	361	8.02	0.87
2 persons,	188	1,354	7.20	0.28	8 persons,	29	263	9.07	0.88
3 persons,	167	1,264	7.57	0.40	9 persons,	25	220	8.80	1.02
4 persons,	154	1,207	7.84	0.51	10 persons,	11	99	9.00	1.11
5 persons,	114	906	7.95	0.63	11 persons,	5	49	9.80	1.12
6 persons,	84	725	8.63	0.70	12 persons,	5	80	16.00	0.75
7 persons,	42	351	8.36	0.84	13 persons,	4	55	13.75	0.95
8 persons,	32	272	8.50	0.94	14 persons,	2	19	9.50	1.47

ROOMS: OCCUPIED DWELLING HOUSES — Continued.

Counties, Cities, Towns, and Number of Persons to a Family	Number of Families of Specified Size	Total Number of Rooms Occupied	Average Number of Rooms Occupied	Average Number of Persons to a Room	Counties, Cities, Towns, and Number of Persons to a Family	Number of Families of Specified Size	Total Number of Rooms Occupied	Average Number of Rooms Occupied	Average Number of Persons to a Room
PLYMOUTH - Con.					**PLYMOUTH - Con.**				
Brockton, Ward 1 — Con.					*Brockton, Ward 4 — Con.*				
16 persons, . .	4	54	13.50	1.19	14 persons, . .	2	23	11.50	1.22
17 persons, . .	1	14	14.00	1.21	16 persons, . .	1	2	2.00	8.00
19 persons, . .	1	15	15.00	1.27	25 persons, . .	1	3	3.00	8.33
21 persons, . .	1	24	24.00	0.88	*Brockton. Ward 5,.*	1,126	6,374	5.66	0.79
22 persons, . .	2	69	34.50	0.64	1 person, . .	42	136	3.24	0.31
31 persons, . .	1	80	80.00	0.39	2 persons, . .	174	854	4.91	0.41
33 persons, . .	1	45	45.00	0.73	3 persons, . .	223	1,213	5.44	0.55
Brockton. Ward 2,.	1,050	7,178	6.71	0.66	4 persons, . .	196	1,105	5.64	0.71
1 person, . .	24	107	4.46	0.22	5 persons, . .	179	1,044	5.83	0.86
2 persons, . .	233	1,340	5.75	0.35	6 persons, . .	139	802	5.77	1.04
3 persons, . .	256	1,588	6.20	0.48	7 persons, . .	66	409	6.20	1.13
4 persons, . .	211	1,392	6.60	0.61	8 persons, . .	56	355	6.34	1.26
5 persons, . .	152	1,054	6.93	0.72	9 persons, . .	23	169	7.35	1.22
6 persons, . .	94	725	7.71	0.78	10 persons, . .	13	86	6.62	1.51
7 persons, . .	45	373	8.29	0.84	11 persons, . .	7	79	11.29	0.97
8 persons, . .	21	144	6.86	1.17	13 persons, . .	3	27	9.00	1.44
9 persons, . .	15	138	9.20	0.98	15 persons, . .	2	26	13.00	1.15
10 persons, . .	5	40	8.00	1.25	16 persons, . .	1	15	15.00	1.07
11 persons, . .	1	6	6.00	1.83	21 persons, . .	1	12	12.00	1.75
12 persons, . .	4	50	12.50	0.96	44 persons, . .	1	42	42.00	1.05
13 persons, . .	2	23	11.50	1.13	*Brockton. Ward 6,*	1,086	6,597	6.07	0.75
14 persons, . .	1	14	14.00	1.00	1 person, . .	40	150	3.75	0.27
16 persons, . .	1	18	18.00	0.89	2 persons, . .	152	837	5.51	0.36
17 persons, . .	3	99	33.00	0.52	3 persons, . .	228	1,298	5.69	0.53
30 persons, . .	1	17	17.00	1.76	4 persons, . .	204	1,186	5.81	0.69
37 persons, . .	1	50	50.00	0.74	5 persons, . .	156	961	6.16	0.81
Brockton. Ward 3,	1,198	7,295	6.09	0.69	6 persons, . .	126	804	6.38	0.94
1 person, . .	16	78	4.88	0.21	7 persons, . .	84	549	6.54	1.07
2 persons, . .	215	1,187	5.52	0.36	8 persons, . .	38	254	6.68	1.20
3 persons, . .	254	1,490	5.87	0.51	9 persons, . .	24	150	6.25	1.44
4 persons, . .	265	1,594	6.02	0.66	10 persons, . .	9	64	7.11	1.41
5 persons, . .	186	1,162	6.25	0.80	11 persons, . .	10	70	7.00	1.57
6 persons, . .	117	785	6.71	0.89	12 persons, . .	4	38	9.50	1.26
7 persons, . .	72	438	6.08	1.15	13 persons, . .	4	51	12.75	1.02
8 persons, . .	40	277	6.93	1.16	15 persons, . .	2	10	5.00	3.00
9 persons, . .	19	140	7.37	1.22	16 persons, . .	2	100	50.00	0.32
10 persons, . .	9	78	8.67	1.15	19 persons, . .	1	25	25.00	0.76
11 persons, . .	3	30	10.00	1.10	20 persons, . .	1	8	8.00	3.63
12 persons, . .	1	12	12.00	1.00	42 persons, . .	1	42	42.00	1.00
15 persons, . .	1	24	24.00	0.63	*Brockton. Ward 7,.*	1,196	7,349	6.14	0.66
Brockton. Ward 4,	1,059	6,072	5.58	0.79	1 person, . .	29	121	4.17	0.24
1 person, . .	33	103	3.12	0.32	2 persons, . .	219	1,234	5.63	0.35
2 persons, . .	174	856	4.92	0.41	3 persons, . .	294	1,758	5.98	0.50
3 persons, . .	218	1,140	5.23	0.57	4 persons, . .	245	1,516	6.19	0.65
4 persons, . .	221	1,228	5.56	0.72	5 persons, . .	184	1,186	6.45	0.78
5 persons, . .	170	968	5.69	0.87	6 persons, . .	96	624	6.50	0.92
6 persons, . .	111	684	6.16	0.97	7 persons, . .	64	443	6.92	1.01
7 persons, . .	64	401	6.27	1.12	8 persons, . .	32	226	7.06	1.13
8 persons, . .	47	316	6.72	1.19	9 persons, . .	22	156	7.09	1.27
9 persons, . .	26	171	6.58	1.37	10 persons, . .	6	51	8.50	1.18
10 persons, . .	7	46	6.57	1.52	11 persons, . .	3	22	7.33	1.50
11 persons, . .	9	97	10.78	1.02	13 persons, . .	2	12	6.00	2.17
12 persons, . .	4	26	6.50	1.85	Carver, . . .	262	1,714	6.54	0.50
13 persons, . .	1	8	8.00	1.63	1 person, . .	30	96	3.20	0.31

ROOMS: OCCUPIED DWELLING HOUSES — Continued.

COUNTIES, CITIES, TOWNS, AND NUMBER OF PERSONS TO A FAMILY.	Number of Families of Specified Size	Total Number of Rooms Occupied	Average Number of Rooms Occupied	Average Number of Persons to a Room	COUNTIES, CITIES, TOWNS, AND NUMBER OF PERSONS TO A FAMILY.	Number of Families of Specified Size	Total Number of Rooms Occupied	Average Number of Rooms Occupied	Average Number of Persons to a Room
PLYMOUTH - Con.					**PLYMOUTH — Con.**				
Carver — Con.					Hanover — Con.				
2 persons,	50	293	5.86	0.34	3 persons,	135	865	6.36	0.44
3 persons,	55	359	6.53	0.46	4 persons,	101	694	6.87	0.58
4 persons,	41	280	6.83	0.59	5 persons,	52	363	6.98	0.72
5 persons,	34	261	7.68	0.65	6 persons,	42	330	7.86	0.76
6 persons,	24	191	7.96	0.75	7 persons,	29	206	7.10	0.99
7 persons,	11	89	8.09	0.87	8 persons,	11	91	8.27	0.97
8 persons,	7	65	9.29	0.86	9 persons,	5	54	10.80	0.83
9 persons,	2	13	6.50	1.38	10 persons,	3	26	8.67	1.15
10 persons,	3	23	7.67	1.30	12 persons,	1	6	6.00	2.00
11 persons,	2	11	5.50	2.00	13 persons,	2	29	14.50	0.90
12 persons,	2	25	12.50	0.96	14 persons,	1	6	6.00	2.33
16 persons,	1	8	8.00	2.00	15 persons,	1	8	8.00	1.88
Duxbury,	532	4,840	9.10	0.41	17 persons,	1	10	10.00	1.70
1 person,	48	356	7.42	0.13	Hanson,	380	2,876	7.57	0.48
2 persons,	140	1,214	8.67	0.23	1 person,	24	127	5.29	0.19
3 persons,	115	1,016	8.83	0.34	2 persons,	84	647	7.70	0.26
4 persons,	94	786	8.36	0.48	3 persons,	104	792	7.62	0.39
5 persons,	51	454	8.90	0.56	4 persons,	66	508	7.70	0.52
6 persons,	33	311	9.42	0.64	5 persons,	49	386	7.88	0.63
7 persons,	22	227	10.32	0.68	6 persons,	28	229	8.18	0.73
8 persons,	10	104	10.40	0.77	7 persons,	12	90	7.50	0.93
9 persons,	11	116	10.55	0.85	8 persons,	6	48	8.00	1.00
10 persons,	5	76	15.20	0.66	9 persons,	3	21	7.00	1.29
12 persons,	1	22	22.00	0.55	10 persons,	4	28	7.00	1.43
19 persons,	1	68	68.00	0.28	Hingham,	1,164	8,741	7.51	0.55
50 persons,	1	90	90.00	0.56	1 person,	82	408	4.98	0.20
East Bridgewater,	726	5,371	7.40	0.54	2 persons,	227	1,562	6.88	0.29
1 person,	43	232	5.40	0.19	3 persons,	239	1,818	7.61	0.39
2 persons,	140	974	6.96	0.29	4 persons,	209	1,553	7.43	0.54
3 persons,	155	1,121	7.23	0.41	5 persons,	147	1,112	7.56	0.66
4 persons,	158	1,248	7.90	0.51	6 persons,	109	912	8.37	0.72
5 persons,	90	665	7.39	0.68	7 persons,	58	451	7.78	0.90
6 persons,	65	521	8.02	0.75	8 persons,	38	337	8.87	0.90
7 persons,	33	250	7.58	0.92	9 persons,	21	175	8.33	1.08
8 persons,	18	141	7.83	1.02	10 persons,	17	170	10.00	1.00
9 persons,	10	87	8.70	1.03	11 persons,	4	35	8.75	1.26
10 persons,	5	48	9.60	1.04	12 persons,	4	38	9.50	1.26
11 persons,	4	27	6.75	1.63	13 persons,	2	13	6.50	2.00
12 persons,	3	46	15.33	0.78	15 persons,	1	15	15.00	1.00
15 persons,	1	7	7.00	2.14	17 persons,	2	35	17.50	0.97
24 persons,	1	4	4.00	6.00	20 persons,	1	56	56.00	0.36
Halifax,	118	1,113	7.72	0.43	22 persons,	1	12	12.00	1.83
1 person,	24	130	5.42	0.18	26 persons,	1	2	2.00	13.00
2 persons,	35	267	7.63	0.26	37 persons,	1	37	37.00	1.00
3 persons,	29	254	8.76	0.34	Hull,	229	2,486	10.86	0.42
4 persons,	26	196	7.54	0.53	1 person,	10	43	4.30	0.23
5 persons,	11	95	8.64	0.58	2 persons,	35	257	7.34	0.27
6 persons,	12	120	10.00	0.60	3 persons,	43	391	9.09	0.33
7 persons,	7	51	7.29	0.96	4 persons,	44	355	8.07	0.50
8 persons,	2	16	8.00	1.00	5 persons,	30	356	11.87	0.42
10 persons,	2	14	7.00	1.43	6 persons,	27	488	18.07	0.33
Hanover,	544	3,705	6.81	0.55	7 persons,	19	166	8.74	0.80
1 person,	40	204	5.10	0.20	8 persons,	9	112	12.44	0.64
2 persons,	120	743	6.19	0.32	9 persons,	4	135	33.75	0.27

ROOMS: OCCUPIED DWELLING HOUSES — Continued.

PLYMOUTH — Con.

Hull — Con.

Counties, Cities, Towns, and Number of Persons to a Family	Number of Families of Specified Size	Total Number of Rooms Occupied	Average Number of Rooms Occupied	Average Number of Persons to a Room
10 persons,	4	63	15.75	0.63
11 persons,	1	30	30.00	0.37
13 persons,	1	8	8.00	1.63
14 persons,	1	55	55.00	0.25
28 persons,	1	27	27.00	1.04
Kingston,	477	3,496	7.33	0.50
1 person,	29	174	6.00	0.17
2 persons,	117	836	7.15	0.28
3 persons,	105	769	7.32	0.41
4 persons,	106	783	7.39	0.54
5 persons,	44	307	6.98	0.72
6 persons,	39	321	8.23	0.73
7 persons,	20	155	7.75	0.90
8 persons,	9	70	7.78	1.03
9 persons,	5	56	11.20	0.80
11 persons,	3	25	8.33	1.32
Lakeville,	233	1,743	7.48	0.50
1 person,	24	141	5.88	0.17
2 persons,	48	329	6.85	0.29
3 persons,	49	378	7.71	0.39
4 persons,	43	341	7.93	0.50
5 persons,	28	210	7.50	0.67
6 persons,	16	134	8.38	0.72
7 persons,	15	122	8.13	0.86
8 persons,	5	38	7.60	1.05
9 persons,	1	14	14.00	0.64
10 persons,	3	29	9.67	1.03
11 persons,	1	7	7.00	1.57
Marion,	213	2,167	10.17	0.35
1 person,	12	113	9.42	0.11
2 persons,	49	473	9.65	0.21
3 persons,	58	585	10.09	0.30
4 persons,	42	413	9.83	0.41
5 persons,	26	303	11.65	0.43
6 persons,	15	159	10.60	0.57
7 persons,	3	27	9.00	0.78
8 persons,	6	72	12.00	0.67
9 persons,	2	22	11.00	0.82
Marshfield,	511	3,946	7.72	0.45
1 person,	47	225	4.79	0.21
2 persons,	136	954	7.01	0.29
3 persons,	127	951	7.49	0.40
4 persons,	85	673	7.92	0.51
5 persons,	48	413	8.60	0.58
6 persons,	33	377	11.42	0.53
7 persons,	19	180	9.47	0.74
8 persons,	5	58	11.60	0.69
9 persons,	4	40	10.00	0.90
10 persons,	5	61	12.20	0.82
11 persons,	1	8	8.00	1.38
12 persons,	1	6	6.00	2.00
Mattapoisett,	301	2,332	7.75	0.44
1 person,	32	174	5.44	1.84
2 persons,	82	622	7.59	0.26

PLYMOUTH — Con.

Mattapoisett — Con.

Counties, Cities, Towns, and Number of Persons to a Family	Number of Families of Specified Size	Total Number of Rooms Occupied	Average Number of Rooms Occupied	Average Number of Persons to a Room
3 persons,	69	526	7.62	0.39
4 persons,	42	321	7.64	0.52
5 persons,	42	380	9.05	0.55
6 persons,	11	98	8.91	0.67
7 persons,	11	92	8.36	0.84
8 persons,	3	43	14.33	0.56
9 persons,	6	55	9.17	0.98
10 persons,	3	21	7.00	1.43
Middleborough,	1,673	12,168	7.27	0.55
1 person,	85	382	4.49	0.22
2 persons,	333	2,199	6.60	0.30
3 persons,	394	2,740	6.95	0.43
4 persons,	310	2,308	7.45	0.54
5 persons,	221	1,705	7.71	0.65
6 persons,	144	1,166	8.10	0.74
7 persons,	92	768	8.35	0.84
8 persons,	40	324	8.10	0.99
9 persons,	22	205	9.32	0.97
10 persons,	15	180	12.00	0.83
11 persons,	8	94	11.38	0.97
12 persons,	4	27	6.75	1.78
13 persons,	2	18	9.00	1.44
18 persons,	1	20	20.00	0.90
20 persons,	1	25	25.00	0.80
35 persons,	1	10	10.00	3.50
Norwell,	422	3,122	7.40	0.49
1 person,	38	241	6.34	0.16
2 persons,	96	669	6.97	0.29
3 persons,	105	723	6.89	0.44
4 persons,	72	567	7.88	0.51
5 persons,	49	397	8.10	0.62
6 persons,	22	190	8.64	0.69
7 persons,	16	125	7.81	0.90
8 persons,	10	88	8.80	0.91
9 persons,	9	79	8.78	1.03
11 persons,	4	33	8.25	1.33
13 persons,	1	10	10.00	1.30
Pembroke,	367	2,826	7.70	0.45
1 person,	50	273	5.46	0.18
2 persons,	93	682	7.33	0.27
3 persons,	80	653	8.16	0.37
4 persons,	68	582	8.56	0.47
5 persons,	30	233	7.77	0.64
6 persons,	22	176	8.00	0.75
7 persons,	10	83	8.30	0.84
8 persons,	7	69	9.86	0.81
9 persons,	4	33	8.25	1.09
10 persons,	2	30	15.00	0.67
11 persons,	1	12	12.00	0.92
Plymouth,	1,969	12,510	6.35	0.64
1 person,	119	548	4.61	0.22
2 persons,	372	2,120	5.70	0.35
3 persons,	454	2,698	5.94	0.50
4 persons,	358	2,293	6.41	0.62

ROOMS: OCCUPIED DWELLING HOUSES — Continued.

Counties, Cities, Towns, and Number of Persons to a Family.	Number of Families of Specified Size	Total Number of Rooms Occupied	Average Number of Rooms Occupied	Average Number of Persons to a Room
PLYMOUTH - Con.				
Plymouth — Con.				
5 persons,	263	1,784	6.78	0.74
6 persons,	169	1,197	7.08	0.85
7 persons,	111	764	6.88	1.02
8 persons,	55	373	6.78	1.18
9 persons,	31	235	7.58	1.49
10 persons,	17	112	6.59	1.52
11 persons,	6	53	8.83	1.25
12 persons,	4	37	9.25	1.30
13 persons,	2	40	20.00	0.65
14 persons,	2	32	16.00	0.88
15 persons,	1	6	6.00	2.50
16 persons,	1	60	60.00	0.27
17 persons,	1	20	20.00	0.85
18 persons,	1	50	50.00	0.36
21 persons,	1	38	38.00	0.55
50 persons,	1	50	50.00	1.00
Plympton,	162	1,122	6.93	0.49
1 person,	18	105	5.83	0.17
2 persons,	42	262	6.24	0.32
3 persons,	38	273	7.18	0.42
4 persons,	27	213	7.89	0.51
5 persons,	16	120	7.50	0.67
6 persons,	10	71	7.10	0.85
7 persons,	7	51	7.29	0.96
8 persons,	1	5	5.00	1.60
9 persons,	2	14	7.00	1.29
10 persons,	1	8	8.00	1.25
Rochester,	260	1,688	6.49	0.60
1 person,	13	68	5.23	0.19
2 persons,	56	349	6.23	0.32
3 persons,	56	354	6.32	0.47
4 persons,	44	293	6.66	0.60
5 persons,	36	228	6.33	0.79
6 persons,	32	228	7.13	0.84
7 persons,	14	102	7.29	0.96
8 persons,	5	30	6.00	1.33
9 persons,	2	13	6.50	1.38
12 persons,	2	23	11.50	1.04
Rockland,	1,331	8,802	6.61	0.65
1 person,	64	284	4.44	0.23
2 persons,	254	1,536	6.05	0.33
3 persons,	276	1,808	6.55	0.46
4 persons,	259	1,629	6.56	0.61
5 persons,	189	1,308	6.92	0.72
6 persons,	119	850	7.14	0.84
7 persons,	62	455	7.34	0.95
8 persons,	51	375	7.35	1.09
9 persons,	25	182	7.28	1.24
10 persons,	16	128	8.00	1.25
11 persons,	7	56	8.00	1.38
12 persons,	4	40	10.00	1.20
13 persons,	2	20	10.00	1.30
14 persons,	1	18	18.00	0.78
17 persons,	1	21	21.00	0.81
19 persons,	1	22	22.00	0.86

Counties, Cities, Towns, and Number of Persons to a Family.	Number of Families of Specified Size	Total Number of Rooms Occupied	Average Number of Rooms Occupied	Average Number of Persons to a Room
PLYMOUTH - Con.				
Scituate,	607	4,158	6.85	0.54
1 person,	65	329	5.06	0.20
2 persons,	129	808	6.26	0.32
3 persons,	133	931	7.00	0.43
4 persons,	114	803	7.04	0.57
5 persons,	60	433	7.22	0.69
6 persons,	47	392	7.70	0.78
7 persons,	26	298	7.81	0.90
8 persons,	16	136	8.50	0.94
9 persons,	4	33	8.25	1.09
10 persons,	7	52	7.43	1.35
11 persons,	3	26	8.67	1.27
12 persons,	2	31	15.50	0.77
13 persons,	1	11	11.00	1.18
Wareham,	801	5,708	6.41	0.56
1 person,	30	448	4.98	0.20
2 persons,	197	1,292	6.10	0.33
3 persons,	194	1,250	6.44	0.47
4 persons,	139	951	6.84	0.58
5 persons,	103	684	6.64	0.73
6 persons,	68	438	6.44	0.86
7 persons,	47	316	6.72	1.04
8 persons,	20	131	6.55	1.22
9 persons,	15	121	8.07	1.12
10 persons,	10	84	8.40	1.19
11 persons,	2	12	6.00	1.83
12 persons,	3	24	8.00	1.50
13 persons,	2	34	17.00	0.76
14 persons,	1	13	13.00	1.08
West Bridgewater,	469	3,633	7.42	0.53
1 person,	25	117	4.68	0.21
2 persons,	85	571	6.72	0.30
3 persons,	84	613	7.30	0.41
4 persons,	71	546	7.69	0.52
5 persons,	47	338	7.19	0.70
6 persons,	45	375	8.33	0.72
7 persons,	19	143	7.53	0.93
8 persons,	10	77	7.70	1.04
9 persons,	9	72	8.00	1.13
10 persons,	5	44	8.80	1.14
11 persons,	4	40	10.00	1.10
12 persons,	2	18	9.00	1.33
15 persons,	2	22	11.00	1.36
60 persons,	1	57	57.00	1.21
Whitman,	1,389	9,246	6.63	0.62
1 person,	49	222	4.53	0.22
2 persons,	269	1,652	6.14	0.53
3 persons,	302	1,896	6.28	0.48
4 persons,	287	1,906	6.64	0.49
5 persons,	194	1,357	6.99	0.71
6 persons,	125	896	7.17	0.84
7 persons,	62	426	6.87	1.02
8 persons,	51	373	7.31	1.09
9 persons,	21	153	7.29	1.24
10 persons,	16	119	7.44	1.34
11 persons,	4	35	8.75	1.26

ROOMS: OCCUPIED DWELLING HOUSES — Continued.

COUNTIES, CITIES, TOWNS, AND NUMBER OF PERSONS TO A FAMILY.	Number of Families of Specified Size	Total Number of Rooms Occupied	Average Number of Rooms Occupied	Average Number of Persons to a Room	COUNTIES, CITIES, TOWNS, AND NUMBER OF PERSONS TO A FAMILY.	Number of Families of Specified Size	Total Number of Rooms Occupied	Average Number of Rooms Occupied	Average Number of Persons to a Room
PLYMOUTH — Con.					SUFFOLK — Con.				
Whitman — Con.					Boston — Con.				
12 persons,	3	30	10.00	1.20	46 persons,	3	108	36.00	1.28
13 persons,	1	14	14.00	0.93	47 persons,	2	54	27.00	1.74
16 persons,	2	35	17.50	0.91	48 persons,	5	206	41.20	1.17
21 persons,	1	28	28.00	0.75	50 persons,	1	45	45.00	1.11
22 persons,	1	38	38.00	0.58	51 persons,	1	95	95.00	0.54
23 persons,	1	36	36.00	0.67	52 persons,	2	156	78.00	0.67
					53 persons,	1	53	53.00	1.00
SUFFOLK.					59 persons,	2	355	177.50	0.33
Boston,	103,306	618,598	5.99	0.80	62 persons,	2	84	42.00	1.48
1 person,	3,421	10,699	3.13	0.32	66 persons,	1	48	48.00	1.38
2 persons,	16,389	73,414	4.48	0.45	68 persons,	1	120	120.00	0.57
3 persons,	18,952	96,689	5.10	0.59	69 persons,	1	69	69.00	1.00
4 persons,	18,530	102,485	5.53	0.72	70 persons,	1	30	30.00	2.33
5 persons,	15,077	89,481	5.93	0.84	71 persons,	1	64	64.00	1.11
6 persons,	11,063	69,789	6.31	0.95	72 persons,	2	533	266.50	0.27
7 persons,	7,646	51,030	6.70	1.04	75 persons,	1	50	50.00	1.50
8 persons,	4,734	34,658	7.32	1.09	76 persons,	1	300	300.00	0.25
9 persons,	2,769	22,235	8.03	1.12	77 persons,	2	87	43.50	1.77
10 persons,	1,694	14,398	9.04	1.11	78 persons,	2	67	33.50	2.33
11 persons,	945	9,433	9.98	1.10	79 persons,	1	78	78.00	1.01
12 persons,	571	6,378	11.17	1.07	81 persons,	1	50	50.00	1.62
13 persons,	366	4,641	12.68	1.03	82 persons,	1	100	100.00	0.82
14 persons,	295	4,001	13.56	1.03	86 persons,	1	250	250.00	0.34
15 persons,	188	2,707	14.40	1.04	87 persons,	2	266	133.00	0.65
16 persons,	151	2,240	14.83	1.08	88 persons,	1	54	54.00	1.63
17 persons,	109	1,648	15.12	1.12	89 persons,	1	300	300.00	0.30
18 persons,	81	1,386	17.11	1.05	91 persons,	2	106	53.00	1.72
19 persons,	55	851	15.47	1.23	93 persons,	1	115	115.00	0.81
20 persons,	45	761	16.91	1.18	94 persons,	1	99	99.00	0.95
21 persons,	42	729	17.36	1.21	96 persons,	1	200	200.00	0.48
22 persons,	28	618	22.07	1.00	97 persons,	1	120	120.00	0.81
23 persons,	12	312	26.00	0.88	101 persons,	1	60	60.00	1.68
24 persons,	11	388	35.27	0.68	107 persons,	1	26	26.00	4.12
25 persons,	9	177	19.67	1.27	109 persons,	2	133	66.50	1.64
26 persons,	8	181	22.63	1.15	112 persons,	1	319	319.00	0.35
27 persons,	11	323	29.36	0.92	114 persons,	1	280	280.00	0.41
28 persons,	5	275	55.00	0.51	116 persons,	1	183	183.00	0.60
29 persons,	9	446	49.56	0.59	118 persons,	2	460	230.00	0.51
30 persons,	9	232	25.78	1.16	119 persons,	1	119	119.00	1.00
31 persons,	5	306	61.20	0.51	121 persons,	1	410	410.00	0.30
32 persons,	4	134	33.50	0.96	124 persons,	2	420	210.00	0.59
33 persons,	3	130	43.33	0.76	129 persons,	1	135	135.00	0.96
34 persons,	4	144	36.00	0.94	132 persons,	1	156	156.00	0.85
35 persons,	6	241	40.17	0.87	134 persons,	1	64	64.00	2.09
36 persons,	2	85	42.50	0.85	135 persons,	1	131	131.00	1.03
37 persons,	5	145	29.00	1.28	137 persons,	1	137	137.00	1.00
38 persons,	1	3	3.00	12.67	145 persons,	1	15	15.00	9.67
39 persons,	3	371	123.67	0.32	156 persons,	1	156	156.00	1.00
40 persons,	4	96	24.00	1.67	158 persons,	1	50	50.00	3.16
41 persons,	1	40	40.00	1.03	183 persons,	1	249	249.00	0.73
42 persons,	1	14	14.00	3.00	194 persons,	1	130	130.00	1.49
43 persons,	4	165	41.25	1.04	200 persons,	1	271	271.00	0.74
44 persons,	1	5	5.00	8.80	212 persons,	1	14	14.00	15.14
45 persons,	3	256	85.33	0.53	214 persons,	1	30	30.00	7.13

ROOMS: OCCUPIED DWELLING HOUSES — Continued.

COUNTIES, CITIES, TOWNS, AND NUMBER OF PERSONS TO A FAMILY.	Number of Families of Specified Size	Total Number of Rooms Occupied	Average Number of Rooms Occupied	Average Number of Persons to a Room	COUNTIES, CITIES, TOWNS, AND NUMBER OF PERSONS TO A FAMILY.	Number of Families of Specified Size	Total Number of Rooms Occupied	Average Number of Rooms Occupied	Average Number of Persons to a Room
SUFFOLK — Con.					**SUFFOLK — Con.**				
BOSTON — Con.					*Boston. Ward 2 — Con.*				
220 persons,	1	150	150.00	1.47	149 persons,	1	149	149.00	1.00
268 persons,	1	234	234.00	1.15	156 persons,	1	156	156.00	1.00
276 persons,	1	23	23.00	12.00	599 persons,	1	599	599.00	1.00
352 persons,	1	400	400.00	0.88	1,596 persons,	1	1,596	1,596.00	1.00
397 persons,	1	100	100.00	3.97	*Boston. Ward 3.*	3,164	17,045	5.39	0.82
399 persons,	1	153	153.00	2.61	1 person,	103	379	3.68	0.27
412 persons,	1	75	75.00	5.49	2 persons,	578	2,634	4.56	0.44
509 persons,	1	509	509.00	1.00	3 persons,	616	3,044	4.94	0.61
680 persons,	1	550	550.00	1.24	4 persons,	578	3,067	5.31	0.75
691 persons,	1	276	276.00	2.50	5 persons,	457	2,592	5.67	0.88
741 persons,	1	882	882.00	0.84	6 persons,	340	2,000	5.88	1.02
1,596 persons,	1	1,596	1,596.00	1.00	7 persons,	215	1,323	6.15	1.14
Boston. Ward 1,	4,671	26,861	5.75	0.78	8 persons,	130	895	6.88	1.16
1 person,	110	381	3.46	0.29	9 persons,	69	426	6.17	1.46
2 persons,	754	3,777	5.03	0.40	10 persons,	40	303	7.58	1.32
3 persons,	905	4,906	5.42	0.55	11 persons,	21	165	7.86	1.40
4 persons,	886	5,025	5.63	0.71	12 persons,	9	72	8.00	1.50
5 persons,	688	4,157	5.96	0.84	13 persons,	4	40	10.00	1.30
6 persons,	517	3,167	6.13	0.98	14 persons,	2	21	10.50	1.33
7 persons,	334	2,162	6.47	1.08	69 persons,	1	69	69.00	1.00
8 persons,	226	1,461	6.46	1.24	145 persons,	1	15	15.00	3.67
9 persons,	117	828	7.08	1.27	*Boston. Ward 4,*	3,010	17,061	5.67	0.78
10 persons,	66	506	7.67	1.30	1 person,	100	357	3.57	0.28
11 persons,	32	241	7.53	1.46	2 persons,	535	2,634	4.92	0.41
12 persons,	9	71	7.89	1.52	3 persons,	612	3,215	5.25	0.57
13 persons,	5	45	9.00	1.44	4 persons,	552	2,984	5.40	0.74
14 persons,	2	24	12.00	1.17	5 persons,	426	2,497	5.86	0.85
15 persons,	1	18	18.00	0.83	6 persons,	317	1,881	5.93	1.01
16 persons,	3	37	12.33	1.30	7 persons,	192	1,162	6.05	1.46
19 persons,	1	17	17.00	1.12	8 persons,	137	978	7.14	1.12
22 persons,	1	38	38.00	0.58	9 persons,	53	381	7.19	1.25
Boston. Ward 2,	4,144	23,889	5.76	0.90	10 persons,	37	276	7.46	1.34
1 person,	111	341	3.07	0.33	11 persons,	15	123	8.20	1.34
2 persons,	646	2,732	4.23	0.47	12 persons,	11	99	9.00	1.33
3 persons,	777	3,565	4.59	0.65	13 persons,	7	77	11.00	1.18
4 persons,	739	3,636	4.92	0.81	14 persons,	4	45	11.25	1.24
5 persons,	635	3,193	5.03	0.99	15 persons,	1	12	12.00	1.25
6 persons,	477	2,607	5.47	1.10	16 persons,	2	25	12.50	1.28
7 persons,	352	1,908	5.93	1.18	17 persons,	2	23	11.50	1.48
8 persons,	136	1,241	6.43	1.24	18 persons,	2	24	12.00	1.50
9 persons,	97	712	7.34	1.28	25 persons,	1	17	17.00	1.47
10 persons,	61	463	7.59	1.32	35 persons,	1	40	40.00	0.88
11 persons,	29	273	9.41	1.17	36 persons,	1	52	52.00	0.69
12 persons,	20	182	9.10	1.32	48 persons,	1	25	25.00	1.92
13 persons,	4	37	9.25	1.41	137 persons,	1	137	137.00	1.00
14 persons,	4	47	11.75	1.19	*Boston. Ward 5,*	2,588	15,858	6.12	0.82
15 persons,	3	36	12.00	1.25	1 person,	88	284	3.23	0.31
16 persons,	2	19	9.50	1.68	2 persons,	443	1,973	4.45	0.45
17 persons,	2	26	13.00	1.31	3 persons,	462	2,374	5.14	0.58
18 persons,	4	59	14.75	1.22	4 persons,	428	2,326	5.43	0.74
19 persons,	1	7	7.00	2.71	5 persons,	392	2,267	5.78	0.86
45 persons,	1	200	200.00	0.23	6 persons,	268	1,630	6.08	0.99
48 persons,	1	32	32.00	1.50	7 persons,	196	1,239	6.32	1.11
78 persons,	1	43	43.00	1.81	8 persons,	111	773	6.96	1.15

ROOMS: OCCUPIED DWELLING HOUSES — Continued.

Counties, Cities, Towns, and Number of Persons to a Family	Number of Families of Specified size	Total Number of Rooms Occupied	Average Number of Rooms Occupied	Average Number of Persons to a Room	Counties, Cities, Towns, and Number of Persons to a Family	Number of Families of Specified size	Total Number of Rooms Occupied	Average Number of Rooms Occupied	Average Number of Persons to a Room
SUFFOLK — Con.					**SUFFOLK — Con.**				
Boston. Ward 5 — Con.					*Boston. Ward 6 — Con.*				
9 persons,	80	636	7.95	1.13	44 persons,	1	5	5.00	8.80
10 persons,	35	243	6.94	1.44	45 persons,	1	41	41.00	1.10
11 persons,	22	176	8.00	1.38	48 persons,	1	49	49.00	0.98
12 persons,	18	150	8.33	1.44	52 persons,	1	127	127.00	0.41
13 persons,	12	126	10.50	1.24	72 persons,	1	500	500.00	0.14
14 persons,	6	74	12.33	1.14	76 persons,	1	300	300.00	0.25
15 persons,	7	90	12.86	1.17	87 persons,	1	200	200.00	0.44
16 persons,	4	58	14.50	1.10	96 persons,	1	200	200.00	0.48
17 persons,	3	38	12.67	1.34	124 persons,	1	120	120.00	1.03
18 persons,	2	25	12.50	1.44	*Boston. Ward 7,*	3,187	19,784	6.21	0.86
19 persons,	3	49	16.33	1.16	1 person,	289	647	2.24	0.43
20 persons,	1	14	14.00	1.43	2 persons,	534	1,778	3.33	0.60
21 persons,	1	15	15.00	1.40	3 persons,	461	1,863	4.11	0.73
23 persons,	1	15	15.00	1.53	4 persons,	442	1,992	4.51	0.89
26 persons,	2	65	32.50	0.80	5 persons,	328	1,821	5.55	0.90
34 persons,	1	36	36.00	0.94	6 persons,	254	1,561	6.15	0.98
114 persons,	1	280	280.00	0.41	7 persons,	208	1,395	6.71	1.04
741 persons,	1	882	882.00	0.84	8 persons,	162	1,363	8.41	0.95
Boston. Ward 6,	5,559	22,825	4.08	1.23	9 persons,	93	958	10.30	0.87
1 person,	266	475	1.79	0.56	10 persons,	77	849	11.03	0.91
2 persons,	799	2,159	2.70	0.74	11 persons,	57	634	11.12	0.99
3 persons,	878	2,534	2.89	1.04	12 persons,	41	473	11.54	1.04
4 persons,	901	2,841	3.15	1.27	13 persons,	35	509	14.54	0.89
5 persons,	833	3,036	3.64	1.37	14 persons,	31	402	12.97	1.08
6 persons,	626	2,348	3.75	1.60	15 persons,	26	447	17.19	0.87
7 persons,	503	2,000	3.98	1.76	16 persons,	23	385	16.74	0.96
8 persons,	366	1,768	5.03	1.59	17 persons,	13	184	14.15	1.20
9 persons,	172	915	5.32	1.69	18 persons,	12	173	14.42	1.25
10 persons,	105	673	6.41	1.56	19 persons,	8	121	15.13	1.26
11 persons,	48	350	7.29	1.51	20 persons,	8	131	16.38	1.22
12 persons,	23	237	10.30	1.16	21 persons,	11	158	14.36	1.46
13 persons,	19	177	9.32	1.46	22 persons,	4	107	26.75	0.82
14 persons,	9	147	16.33	0.86	23 persons,	1	14	14.00	1.64
15 persons,	5	72	14.40	1.04	24 persons,	2	32	16.00	1.50
16 persons,	5	82	16.40	0.98	25 persons,	2	23	11.50	2.17
17 persons,	3	60	20.00	0.85	26 persons,	1	18	18.00	1.44
18 persons,	6	105	17.50	1.03	27 persons,	2	37	18.50	1.46
19 persons,	5	104	20.80	0.91	29 persons,	2	112	56.00	0.52
20 persons,	8	159	19.88	1.01	30 persons,	1	20	20.00	1.50
21 persons,	3	48	16.00	1.31	31 persons,	1	14	14.00	2.21
22 persons,	4	100	25.00	0.88	37 persons,	1	22	22.00	1.68
23 persons,	1	20	20.00	1.15	39 persons,	1	225	225.00	0.17
24 persons,	2	142	71.00	0.34	46 persons,	1	60	60.00	0.77
25 persons,	1	12	12.00	2.08	100 persons,	1	33	33.00	3.30
27 persons,	3	113	37.67	0.63	118 persons,	1	350	350.00	0.34
28 persons,	1	100	100.00	0.28	121 persons,	1	410	410.00	0.30
29 persons,	2	46	23.00	1.26	124 persons,	1	300	300.00	0.41
30 persons,	3	73	24.33	1.23	194 persons,	1	136	136.00	1.43
31 persons,	1	200	200.00	0.16	*Boston. Ward 8,*	4,370	23,508	5.38	0.98
35 persons,	3	112	37.33	0.94	1 person,	185	492	2.66	0.38
38 persons,	1	3	3.00	12.67	2 persons,	682	2,371	3.48	0.58
39 persons,	1	120	120.00	0.33	3 persons,	713	2,763	3.88	0.77
40 persons,	3	36	12.00	3.33	4 persons,	680	2,874	4.23	0.95
43 persons,	1	16	16.00	2.69	5 persons,	586	2,560	4.37	1.14

ROOMS: OCCUPIED DWELLING HOUSES — Continued.

Counties, Cities, Towns, and Number of Persons to a Family.	Number of Families of Specified Size.	Total Number of Rooms Occupied.	Average Number of Rooms Occupied.	Average Number of Persons to a Room.	Counties, Cities, Towns, and Number of Persons to a Family.	Number of Families of Specified Size.	Total Number of Rooms Occupied.	Average Number of Rooms Occupied.	Average Number of Persons to a Room.
SUFFOLK — Con.					**SUFFOLK — Con.**				
Boston, Ward 8 — Con.					*Boston, Ward 9 — Con.*				
6 persons,	510	2,497	4.90	1.23	24 persons,	1	19	19.00	1.26
7 persons,	290	1,683	5.80	1.21	28 persons,	1	30	30.00	0.93
8 persons,	198	1,289	6.51	1.23	30 persons,	2	66	33.00	0.91
9 persons,	145	1,121	7.73	1.16	32 persons,	2	71	35.50	0.90
10 persons,	97	824	8.49	1.18	37 persons,	1	5	5.00	7.40
11 persons,	73	782	10.71	1.03	46 persons,	1	20	20.00	2.30
12 persons,	48	594	12.38	0.97	48 persons,	1	34	34.00	1.41
13 persons,	26	407	15.65	0.83	62 persons,	1	24	24.00	2.58
14 persons,	39	554	14.21	0.99	77 persons,	1	36	36.00	2.14
15 persons,	17	260	15.29	0.98	109 persons,	1	109	109.00	1.09
16 persons,	13	209	16.08	1.00	*Boston, Ward 10,*	4,471	31,465	7.04	0.72
17 persons,	10	159	15.90	1.07	1 person,	190	727	3.83	0.26
18 persons,	8	179	22.38	0.80	2 persons,	688	3,323	4.83	0.41
19 persons,	8	151	18.88	1.01	3 persons,	857	4,813	5.62	0.55
20 persons,	7	111	15.86	1.26	4 persons,	808	5,009	6.20	0.65
21 persons,	3	56	18.67	1.13	5 persons,	594	3,980	6.70	0.75
22 persons,	8	186	23.25	0.95	6 persons,	374	2,857	7.64	0.79
23 persons,	4	178	44.50	0.52	7 persons,	266	2,195	8.25	0.85
24 persons,	2	96	48.00	0.50	8 persons,	177	1,662	9.39	0.85
26 persons,	3	65	21.67	1.20	9 persons,	124	1,184	9.55	0.94
27 persons,	3	83	27.67	0.98	10 persons,	101	1,054	10.44	0.96
34 persons,	3	108	36.00	0.94	11 persons,	74	770	10.41	1.06
36 persons,	1	33	33.00	1.09	12 persons,	43	489	11.37	1.03
37 persons,	1	30	30.00	1.23	13 persons,	45	598	13.29	0.98
41 persons,	1	40	40.00	1.03	14 persons,	23	278	12.09	1.16
50 persons,	1	53	53.00	1.06	15 persons,	26	315	12.12	1.24
78 persons,	1	24	24.00	3.25	16 persons,	22	321	14.59	1.10
79 persons,	1	78	78.00	1.01	17 persons,	21	324	15.43	1.10
96 persons,	1	115	115.00	0.84	18 persons,	3	81	27.00	0.67
185 persons,	1	249	249.00	0.75	19 persons,	10	151	15.10	1.26
208 persons,	1	234	234.00	1.15	20 persons,	4	78	19.50	1.03
Boston, Ward 9,	4,682	24,765	5.29	0.94	21 persons,	2	30	15.00	1.40
1 person,	319	825	2.59	0.39	22 persons,	2	44	22.00	1.00
2 persons,	870	2,984	3.43	0.58	23 persons,	1	9	9.00	2.56
3 persons,	778	3,161	4.06	0.74	24 persons,	2	34	17.00	1.41
4 persons,	727	3,474	4.78	0.84	25 persons,	1	30	30.00	0.83
5 persons,	529	2,500	4.73	1.06	27 persons,	2	54	27.00	1.00
6 persons,	418	2,221	5.31	1.13	28 persons,	1	50	50.00	0.56
7 persons,	295	1,717	5.82	1.20	29 persons,	2	211	105.50	0.27
8 persons,	214	1,425	6.66	1.20	30 persons,	1	25	25.00	1.20
9 persons,	124	892	8.00	1.13	43 persons,	1	75	75.00	0.57
10 persons,	80	809	10.11	0.99	46 persons,	1	28	28.00	1.64
11 persons,	68	775	11.40	0.97	59 persons,	1	250	250.00	0.24
12 persons,	51	579	11.35	1.06	75 persons,	1	50	50.00	1.50
13 persons,	41	585	14.27	0.91	82 persons,	1	100	100.00	0.82
14 persons,	41	543	13.24	1.06	118 persons,	1	110	110.00	1.07
15 persons,	31	496	15.03	1.00	132 persons,	1	156	156.00	0.85
16 persons,	25	340	13.60	1.18	*Boston, Ward 11,*	3,770	35,008	9.29	0.57
17 persons,	9	130	14.44	1.18	1 person,	223	734	3.29	0.30
18 persons,	16	322	20.13	0.89	2 persons,	521	2,373	4.55	0.44
19 persons,	7	99	14.14	1.34	3 persons,	598	3,859	6.45	0.46
20 persons,	9	131	14.56	1.37	4 persons,	525	4,551	8.67	0.46
21 persons,	10	156	15.60	1.35	5 persons,	502	4,902	9.76	0.51
22 persons,	8	126	15.75	1.40	6 persons,	409	4,387	10.73	0.56

ROOMS: OCCUPIED DWELLING HOUSES — Continued.

COUNTIES, CITIES, TOWNS, AND NUMBER OF PERSONS TO A FAMILY.	Number of Families of Specified Size	Total Number of Rooms Occupied	Average Number of Rooms Occupied	Average Number of Persons to a Room	COUNTIES, CITIES, TOWNS, AND NUMBER OF PERSONS TO A FAMILY.	Number of Families of Specified Size	Total Number of Rooms Occupied	Average Number of Rooms Occupied	Average Number of Persons to a Room
SUFFOLK — Con.					**SUFFOLK — Con.**				
Boston. Ward 11 — Con.					*Boston. Ward 12 —* Con.				
5 persons,	349	3,678	11.55	0.64	30 persons,	1	28	28.00	1.07
6 persons,	206	2,549	12.23	0.65	37 persons,	1	33	33.00	1.12
9 persons,	145	1,884	12.99	0.69	39 persons,	1	26	26.00	1.50
10 persons,	110	1,556	14.15	0.71	62 persons,	1	60	60.00	1.03
11 persons,	61	819	13.43	0.82	70 persons,	1	30	30.00	2.33
12 persons,	39	622	15.95	0.75	86 persons,	1	250	250.00	0.34
13 persons,	33	487	14.76	0.88	91 persons,	1	31	31.00	2.94
14 persons,	20	290	14.50	0.97	94 persons,	1	99	99.00	0.95
15 persons,	11	192	17.45	0.86	134 persons,	1	64	64.00	2.09
16 persons,	7	133	19.00	0.84	214 persons,	1	30	30.00	7.13
17 persons,	12	210	17.50	0.97	352 persons,	1	400	400.00	0.88
18 persons,	5	75	15.00	1.20	694 persons,	1	276	276.00	2.50
19 persons,	2	26	13.00	1.46	*Boston. Ward 13,*	5,453	23,450	4.30	1.06
20 persons,	3	61	20.33	0.98	1 person,	210	622	2.96	0.34
21 persons,	4	96	24.00	0.88	2 persons,	835	2,986	3.58	0.56
24 persons,	1	45	45.00	0.53	3 persons,	976	3,840	3.93	0.76
29 persons,	1	20	20.00	1.50	4 persons,	974	3,978	4.08	0.98
25 persons,	1	37	37.00	0.76	5 persons,	815	3,547	4.35	1.15
32 persons,	2	63	31.50	1.02	6 persons,	635	2,893	4.56	1.32
33 persons,	1	79	79.00	0.42	7 persons,	445	2,161	4.86	1.44
35 persons,	1	71	71.00	0.49	8 persons,	266	1,421	5.34	1.50
40 persons,	1	48	48.00	1.38	9 persons,	147	821	5.59	1.61
48 persons,	1	120	120.00	0.57	10 persons,	66	417	6.32	1.58
71 persons,	1	64	64.00	1.11	11 persons,	35	253	7.23	1.52
89 persons,	1	300	300.00	0.57	12 persons,	19	139	7.32	1.64
91 persons,	1	75	75.00	1.21	13 persons,	11	94	8.55	1.52
97 persons,	1	120	120.00	0.81	14 persons,	4	37	9.25	1.51
112 persons,	1	319	319.00	0.35	15 persons,	5	76	15.20	0.99
116 persons,	1	193	193.00	0.60	16 persons,	2	24	12.00	1.33
Boston. Ward 12,	3,518	29,724	8.45	0.73	17 persons,	1	22	22.00	0.77
1 person,	119	446	3.75	0.27	18 persons,	2	31	15.50	1.16
2 persons,	548	2,642	4.82	0.41	19 persons,	3	37	12.33	1.54
3 persons,	578	3,516	6.08	0.49	25 persons,	1	31	31.00	0.81
4 persons,	496	3,457	6.97	0.57	31 persons,	1	20	20.00	1.55
5 persons,	400	3,034	7.59	0.66	*Boston. Ward 14,*	4,074	22,945	5.63	0.84
6 persons,	289	2,513	8.70	0.69	1 person,	111	373	3.36	0.30
7 persons,	211	2,090	9.91	0.71	2 persons,	656	2,989	4.56	0.44
8 persons,	199	2,062	10.38	0.77	3 persons,	786	4,022	5.12	0.59
9 persons,	145	1,672	11.53	0.78	4 persons,	735	3,918	5.33	0.75
10 persons,	125	1,487	11.90	0.84	5 persons,	611	3,449	5.64	0.89
11 persons,	84	1,058	12.60	0.87	6 persons,	461	2,735	5.93	1.01
12 persons,	91	1,187	13.04	0.92	7 persons,	299	1,830	6.12	1.14
13 persons,	48	645	13.44	0.97	8 persons,	189	1,238	6.55	1.22
14 persons,	59	862	14.61	0.96	9 persons,	111	805	7.25	1.24
15 persons,	31	433	13.97	1.07	10 persons,	57	475	8.33	1.20
16 persons,	27	389	14.41	1.11	11 persons,	27	251	9.30	1.18
17 persons,	23	339	14.74	1.15	12 persons,	10	74	7.40	1.62
18 persons,	17	253	14.88	1.21	13 persons,	9	85	9.44	1.38
19 persons,	4	47	11.75	1.62	14 persons,	6	66	11.00	1.27
20 persons,	3	53	17.67	1.13	15 persons,	2	31	15.50	0.97
21 persons,	5	90	18.00	1.17	17 persons,	1	15	15.00	1.13
23 persons,	2	46	23.00	1.00	18 persons,	1	13	13.00	1.38
25 persons,	1	14	14.00	1.79	107 persons,	1	26	26.00	4.12
28 persons,	1	58	58.00	0.48	680 persons,	1	550	550.00	1.24

ROOMS: OCCUPIED DWELLING HOUSES — Continued.

COUNTIES, CITIES, TOWNS, AND NUMBER OF PERSONS TO A FAMILY.	Number of Families of Specified Size	Total Number of Rooms Occupied	Average Number of Rooms Occupied	Average Number of Persons to a Room	COUNTIES, CITIES, TOWNS, AND NUMBER OF PERSONS TO A FAMILY.	Number of Families of Specified Size	Total Number of Rooms Occupied	Average Number of Rooms Occupied	Average Number of Persons to a Room
SUFFOLK — Con.					**SUFFOLK** — Con.				
Boston. Ward 15, .	3,992	22,546	5.65	0.83	*Boston. Ward 17* — Con.				
1 person, . .	90	318	3.53	0.28	18 persons, . .	1	12	12.00	1.50
2 persons, . .	598	2,763	4.62	0.43	212 persons, . .	1	14	14.00	15.14
3 persons, . .	763	3,871	5.07	0.59	*Boston. Ward 18,* . .	4,960	23,686	4.78	0.92
4 persons, . .	770	4,121	5.35	0.75	1 person, . .	180	531	2.95	0.34
5 persons, . .	627	3,670	5.85	0.85	2 persons, . .	955	3,791	3.98	0.50
6 persons, . .	431	2,499	5.80	1.03	3 persons, . .	1,007	4,320	4.29	0.70
7 persons, . .	318	1,965	6.18	1.13	4 persons, . .	908	4,154	4.57	0.87
8 persons, . .	171	1,162	6.80	1.18	5 persons, . .	695	3,401	4.89	1.02
9 persons, . .	115	838	7.29	1.24	6 persons, . .	471	2,500	5.31	1.13
10 persons, . .	56	395	7.05	1.42	7 persons, . .	329	1,917	5.83	1.20
11 persons, . .	29	233	8.03	1.37	8 persons, . .	183	1,114	6.09	1.31
12 persons, . .	6	61	10.17	1.18	9 persons, . .	100	712	7.12	1.26
13 persons, . .	10	112	11.20	1.16	10 persons, . .	62	476	7.68	1.30
14 persons, . .	4	47	11.75	1.19	11 persons, . .	27	225	8.33	1.32
18 persons, . .	1	16	16.00	1.13	12 persons, . .	17	141	8.29	1.45
43 persons, . .	1	54	54.00	0.80	13 persons, . .	6	67	11.17	1.16
200 persons, . .	1	271	271.00	0.74	14 persons, . .	8	101	12.63	1.11
220 persons, . .	1	150	150.00	1.47	15 persons, . .	5	53	10.60	1.42
Boston. Ward 16, . .	3,735	22,334	5.98	0.73	16 persons, . .	1	10	10.00	1.60
1 person, . .	68	253	3.72	0.27	17 persons, . .	1	11	11.00	1.55
2 persons, . .	642	3,271	5.10	0.39	19 persons, . .	1	13	13.00	1.46
3 persons, . .	798	4,388	5.50	0.55	22 persons, . .	1	17	17.00	1.29
4 persons, . .	727	4,222	5.81	0.69	23 persons, . .	1	16	16.00	1.44
5 persons, . .	536	3,294	6.15	0.81	26 persons, . .	1	13	13.00	2.00
6 persons, . .	401	2,642	6.59	0.91	29 persons, . .	1	30	30.00	0.97
7 persons, . .	250	1,770	7.08	0.99	158 persons, . .	1	50	50.00	3.16
8 persons, . .	155	1,129	7.28	1.10	276 persons, . .	1	23	23.00	12.00
9 persons, . .	81	649	8.01	1.12	*Boston. Ward 19,* . .	4,620	23,940	5.18	0.93
10 persons, . .	48	417	8.69	1.15	1 person, . .	122	413	3.39	0.30
11 persons, . .	17	151	8.88	1.24	2 persons, . .	627	2,641	4.21	0.47
12 persons, . .	6	60	10.00	1.20	3 persons, . .	789	3,696	4.68	0.64
13 persons, . .	1	9	9.00	1.44	4 persons, . .	884	4,370	4.94	0.81
14 persons, . .	2	39	19.50	0.72	5 persons, . .	713	3,657	5.13	0.97
16 persons, . .	1	10	10.00	1.60	6 persons, . .	542	2,967	5.47	1.10
20 persons, . .	1	15	15.00	1.33	7 persons, . .	408	2,242	5.50	1.27
45 persons, . .	1	15	15.00	3.00	8 persons, . .	242	1,441	5.95	1.34
Boston. Ward 17, . .	4,656	23,740	5.10	0.89	9 persons, . .	148	979	6.61	1.38
1 person, . .	119	345	2.90	0.34	10 persons, . .	69	523	7.58	1.32
2 persons, . .	734	3,082	4.20	0.48	11 persons, . .	30	256	8.53	1.29
3 persons, . .	884	4,113	4.65	0.64	12 persons, . .	22	182	8.27	1.45
4 persons, . .	921	4,472	4.86	0.82	13 persons, . .	7	69	9.86	1.32
5 persons, . .	695	3,756	5.40	0.93	14 persons, . .	3	29	9.67	1.45
6 persons, . .	549	2,902	5.29	1.07	15 persons, . .	4	52	13.00	1.15
7 persons, . .	360	2,092	5.81	1.20	16 persons, . .	1	7	7.00	2.29
8 persons, . .	186	1,193	6.41	1.25	19 persons, . .	1	15	15.00	1.27
9 persons, . .	119	821	6.90	1.30	21 persons, . .	1	30	30.00	0.70
10 persons, . .	66	461	6.98	1.43	23 persons, . .	1	14	14.00	1.64
11 persons, . .	23	193	8.39	1.31	25 persons, . .	1	20	20.00	1.25
12 persons, . .	11	92	8.36	1.43	27 persons, . .	1	36	36.00	0.75
13 persons, . .	8	79	9.88	1.32	31 persons, . .	1	42	42.00	0.74
15 persons, . .	2	20	10.00	1.50	37 persons, . .	1	55	55.00	0.67
16 persons, . .	5	67	13.40	1.19	77 persons, . .	1	51	51.00	1.51
17 persons, . .	2	26	13.00	1.31	389 persons, . .	1	153	153.00	2.61

ROOMS: OCCUPIED DWELLING HOUSES — Continued.

Counties, Cities, Towns, and Number of Persons to a Family.	Number of Families of Specified Size	Total Number of Rooms Occupied	Average Number of Rooms Occupied	Average Number of Persons to a Room
SUFFOLK — Con.				
Boston. Ward 20,	4,674	33,562	7.18	0.64
1 person,	86	393	4.22	0.24
2 persons,	732	4,239	5.79	0.35
3 persons,	818	5,325	6.51	0.46
4 persons,	918	6,375	6.94	0.58
5 persons,	772	5,723	7.41	0.67
6 persons,	542	4,262	7.86	0.76
7 persons,	363	3,067	8.45	0.83
8 persons,	293	1,820	8.71	0.92
9 persons,	116	982	8.53	1.01
10 persons,	58	570	9.83	1.02
11 persons,	29	285	9.83	1.12
12 persons,	17	184	10.82	1.11
13 persons,	7	107	15.29	0.85
14 persons,	4	57	14.25	0.98
15 persons,	1	8	8.00	1.88
16 persons,	1	11	11.00	1.45
18 persons,	1	18	18.00	1.00
19 persons,	1	14	14.00	1.36
29 persons,	2	47	23.50	1.23
33 persons,	1	15	15.00	2.20
47 persons,	1	42	42.00	1.12
81 persons,	1	50	50.00	1.62
Boston. Ward 21,	4,508	31,385	7.29	0.61
1 person,	53	279	5.26	0.19
2 persons,	721	3,968	5.46	0.37
3 persons,	862	5,429	6.30	0.48
4 persons,	884	6,306	7.13	0.56
5 persons,	683	5,218	7.64	0.65
6 persons,	446	3,752	8.41	0.71
7 persons,	302	2,707	8.96	0.78
8 persons,	168	1,528	9.10	0.88
9 persons,	81	797	9.84	0.91
10 persons,	41	459	11.20	0.89
11 persons,	31	356	11.48	0.96
12 persons,	12	147	12.25	0.98
13 persons,	5	64	12.80	1.02
14 persons,	5	76	15.20	0.92
15 persons,	5	63	12.60	1.19
16 persons,	1	12	12.00	1.33
17 persons,	1	15	15.00	1.13
21 persons,	2	50	25.00	0.84
31 persons,	1	30	30.00	1.03
33 persons,	1	36	36.00	0.92
135 persons,	1	131	131.00	1.03
Boston. Ward 22,	4,770	29,194	6.12	0.76
1 person,	68	270	3.97	0.25
2 persons,	746	3,649	4.89	0.41
3 persons,	921	5,068	5.47	0.55
4 persons,	915	5,412	5.91	0.68
5 persons,	802	4,954	6.18	0.81
6 persons,	528	3,538	6.70	0.90
7 persons,	340	2,355	6.93	1.01
8 persons,	217	1,603	7.39	1.08
9 persons,	110	850	7.73	1.16

Counties, Cities, Towns, and Number of Persons to a Family.	Number of Families of Specified Size	Total Number of Rooms Occupied	Average Number of Rooms Occupied	Average Number of Persons to a Room
SUFFOLK — Con.				
Boston. Ward 22 — Con.				
10 persons,	60	471	7.85	1.27
11 persons,	27	283	10.48	1.05
12 persons,	15	181	12.07	0.99
13 persons,	4	38	9.50	1.37
14 persons,	7	84	12.00	1.17
15 persons,	1	18	18.00	0.83
16 persons,	1	17	17.00	0.94
17 persons,	1	20	20.00	0.85
24 persons,	1	20	20.00	1.20
40 persons,	1	60	60.00	0.67
47 persons,	1	12	12.00	3.92
51 persons,	1	95	95.00	0.54
87 persons,	1	66	66.00	1.32
101 persons,	1	60	60.00	1.68
397 persons,	1	100	100.00	3.97
Boston. Ward 23,	3,896	25,308	6.55	0.72
1 person,	76	313	4.12	0.24
2 persons,	583	3,201	5.49	0.36
3 persons,	742	4,433	5.97	0.50
4 persons,	755	4,878	6.46	0.62
5 persons,	599	4,036	6.74	0.74
6 persons,	455	3,138	6.90	0.87
7 persons,	279	1,956	7.01	1.00
8 persons,	155	1,150	7.42	1.08
9 persons,	109	852	7.82	1.15
10 persons,	51	433	8.49	1.18
11 persons,	34	331	9.74	1.13
12 persons,	10	102	10.20	1.18
13 persons,	6	64	10.67	1.22
14 persons,	3	43	14.33	0.98
15 persons,	2	25	12.50	1.20
16 persons,	1	14	14.00	1.14
42 persons,	1	14	14.00	3.00
43 persons,	1	20	20.00	2.15
48 persons,	1	66	66.00	0.73
52 persons,	1	29	29.00	1.79
129 persons,	1	135	135.00	0.96
412 persons,	1	75	75.00	5.49
Boston. Ward 24,	3,944	27,611	7.00	0.66
1 person,	66	313	4.74	0.21
2 persons,	555	3,263	5.88	0.34
3 persons,	773	4,923	6.37	0.47
4 persons,	774	5,254	6.79	0.59
5 persons,	637	4,633	7.27	0.69
6 persons,	438	3,337	7.62	0.79
7 persons,	331	2,643	7.98	0.88
8 persons,	172	1,415	8.23	0.97
9 persons,	87	680	8.03	1.12
10 persons,	54	505	9.35	1.07
11 persons,	29	232	8.00	1.38
12 persons,	10	108	10.80	1.11
13 persons,	6	57	9.50	1.37
14 persons,	4	47	11.75	1.19
16 persons,	3	49	16.33	0.98

ROOMS: OCCUPIED DWELLING HOUSES — Continued.

COUNTIES, CITIES, TOWNS, AND NUMBER OF PERSONS TO A FAMILY.	Number of Families of Specified Size	Total Number of Rooms Occupied	Average Number of Rooms Occupied	Average Number of Persons to a Room.	COUNTIES, CITIES, TOWNS, AND NUMBER OF PERSONS TO A FAMILY.	Number of Families of Specified Size	Total Number of Rooms Occupied	Average Number of Rooms Occupied	Average Number of Persons to a Room.
SUFFOLK — Con.					SUFFOLK — Con.				
Boston. Ward 24 — Con.					*Chelsea. Ward 1,*	1,655	9,227	5.58	.81
17 persons,	1	7	7.00	2.43	1 person,	46	157	3.41	0.29
25 persons,	1	30	30.00	0.83	2 persons,	289	1,353	4.68	0.43
35 persons,	1	18	18.00	1.94	3 persons,	311	1,618	5.20	0.58
50 persons,	1	45	45.00	1.11	4 persons,	327	1,767	5.40	0.74
72 persons,	1	33	33.00	2.18	5 persons,	231	1,264	5.47	0.91
Boston. Ward 25,	3,172	21,249	6.70	0.71	6 persons,	178	1,065	5.98	1.00
1 person,	69	218	3.16	0.32	7 persons,	104	679	6.53	1.07
2 persons,	422	2,221	5.26	0.38	8 persons,	63	401	6.37	1.26
3 persons,	598	3,648	6.10	0.49	9 persons,	37	257	6.95	1.30
4 persons,	596	3,794	6.37	0.63	10 persons,	33	235	7.12	1.40
5 persons,	512	3,604	7.04	0.71	11 persons,	17	149	8.76	1.26
6 persons,	366	2,955	7.48	0.80	12 persons,	9	85	9.44	1.27
7 persons,	231	1,713	7.42	0.94	13 persons,	3	32	10.67	1.22
8 persons,	162	1,234	7.62	1.05	14 persons,	1	14	14.00	1.00
9 persons,	87	721	8.29	1.09	16 persons,	2	22	11.00	1.45
10 persons,	42	353	8.40	1.19	17 persons,	1	18	18.00	0.94
11 persons,	23	218	9.48	1.16	22 persons,	1	16	16.00	1.38
12 persons,	13	152	11.69	1.03	30 persons,	1	25	25.00	1.20
13 persons,	7	63	9.00	1.44	47 persons,	1	70	70.00	0.67
14 persons,	5	88	17.60	0.80	*Chelsea. Ward 2,*	1,712	9,461	5.53	0.80
15 persons,	2	20	10.00	1.50	1 person,	48	173	3.60	0.28
16 persons,	1	21	21.00	0.76	2 persons,	313	1,464	4.68	0.43
17 persons,	3	39	13.00	1.31	3 persons,	345	1,726	5.00	0.60
20 persons,	1	8	8.00	2.50	4 persons,	295	1,588	5.38	0.74
30 persons,	1	20	20.00	1.50	5 persons,	245	1,443	5.89	0.85
59 persons,	1	105	105.00	0.56	6 persons,	170	1,026	6.04	0.99
88 persons,	1	54	54.00	1.63	7 persons,	124	764	6.16	1.14
CHELSEA,	6,934	41,357	5.96	0.76	8 persons,	74	475	6.42	1.25
1 person,	165	588	3.56	0.28	9 persons,	52	322	6.19	1.45
2 persons	1,194	5,896	4.94	0.40	10 persons,	25	183	7.32	1.37
3 persons,	1,413	7,777	5.50	0.55	11 persons,	13	106	8.15	1.35
4 persons,	1,296	7,387	5.83	0.69	12 persons,	2	18	9.00	1.33
5 persons,	1,011	6,295	6.23	0.80	13 persons,	4	39	9.75	1.33
6 persons,	728	4,827	6.63	0.90	20 persons,	1	78	78.00	0.26
7 persons,	483	3,245	6.72	1.04	34 persons,	1	56	56.00	0.61
8 persons,	292	2,010	6.88	1.16	*Chelsea. Ward 3,*	1,561	9,339	5.98	0.76
9 persons,	169	1,188	7.03	1.28	1 person,	33	136	4.12	0.24
10 persons,	99	759	7.67	1.30	2 persons,	245	1,249	5.10	0.39
11 persons,	56	479	8.55	1.29	3 persons,	334	1,823	5.46	0.55
12 persons,	22	223	10.14	1.18	4 persons,	268	1,578	5.89	0.68
13 persons,	14	133	9.50	1.37	5 persons,	225	1,433	6.37	0.79
14 persons,	5	50	10.00	1.40	6 persons,	164	1,054	6.43	0.93
15 persons,	2	18	9.00	1.67	7 persons,	133	864	6.50	1.08
16 persons,	3	36	12.00	1.33	8 persons,	80	534	6.68	1.20
17 persons,	2	32	16.00	1.06	9 persons,	32	246	7.69	1.17
20 persons,	1	78	78.00	0.26	10 persons,	21	158	7.52	1.33
22 persons,	2	20	10.00	2.20	11 persons,	10	84	8.40	1.31
23 persons,	1	26	26.00	0.88	12 persons,	7	66	9.43	1.27
29 persons,	1	13	13.00	2.23	13 persons,	2	11	5.50	2.36
30 persons,	1	25	25.00	1.20	14 persons,	3	27	9.00	1.56
31 persons,	1	20	20.00	1.55	15 persons,	1	7	7.00	2.14
34 persons,	1	56	56.00	0.61	16 persons,	1	14	14.00	1.14
47 persons,	1	70	70.00	0.67	23 persons,	1	26	26.00	0.88
255 persons,	1	103	103.00	2.48	31 persons,	1	20	20.00	1.55

ROOMS: OCCUPIED DWELLING HOUSES — Continued.

COUNTIES, CITIES, TOWNS, AND NUMBER OF PERSONS TO A FAMILY.	Number of Families of Specified Size	Total Number of Rooms Occupied	Average Number of Rooms Occupied	Average Number of Persons to a Room
SUFFOLK — Con.				
Chelsea. Ward 4,	1,241	7,405	5.97	0.73
1 person,	29	94	3.24	0.31
2 persons,	222	1,038	4.68	0.43
3 persons,	263	1,537	5.84	0.51
4 persons,	223	1,342	6.02	0.66
5 persons,	194	1,206	6.22	0.80
6 persons,	132	914	6.92	0.87
7 persons,	72	480	6.93	1.01
8 persons,	49	339	6.92	1.16
9 persons,	33	236	7.15	1.26
10 persons,	7	57	8.14	1.23
11 persons,	12	89	7.42	1.48
12 persons,	1	22	22.00	0.55
13 persons,	1	8	8.00	1.63
14 persons,	1	9	9.00	1.56
15 persons,	1	11	11.00	1.36
22 persons,	1	4	4.00	5.50
Chelsea. Ward 5,	765	5,934	7.76	0.62
1 person,	9	28	3.11	0.32
2 persons,	125	795	6.36	0.31
3 persons,	169	1,073	6.71	0.45
4 persons,	153	1,112	7.27	0.55
5 persons,	116	949	8.18	0.61
6 persons,	84	768	9.14	0.66
7 persons,	50	439	8.78	0.80
8 persons,	26	261	10.04	0.80
9 persons,	15	127	8.47	1.06
10 persons,	13	126	9.69	1.03
11 persons,	4	51	12.75	0.86
12 persons,	3	32	10.67	1.13
13 persons,	4	43	10.75	1.21
17 persons,	1	14	14.00	1.21
29 persons,	1	13	13.00	2.23
255 persons,	1	103	103.00	2.48
Revere,	1,652	11,017	6.67	0.67
1 person,	31	142	4.58	0.22
2 persons,	275	1,038	5.36	0.34
3 persons,	342	2,140	6.26	0.48
4 persons,	289	1,829	6.33	0.63
5 persons,	206	1,824	6.85	0.73
6 persons,	133	1,388	7.19	0.83
7 persons,	93	724	7.78	0.90
8 persons,	69	545	7.90	1.01
9 persons,	46	381	8.28	1.09
10 persons,	16	112	7.60	1.43
11 persons,	17	142	8.35	1.32
12 persons,	7	61	8.71	1.38
13 persons,	3	24	8.00	1.63
14 persons,	3	35	11.67	1.20
17 persons,	1	15	15.00	1.13
26 persons,	1	20	20.00	1.30
Winthrop,	910	7,478	8.22	0.56
1 person,	17	140	8.24	0.12
2 persons,	122	821	6.73	0.30
3 persons,	188	1,462	7.78	0.39

COUNTIES, CITIES, TOWNS, AND NUMBER OF PERSONS TO A FAMILY.	Number of Families of Specified Size	Total Number of Rooms Occupied	Average Number of Rooms Occupied	Average Number of Persons to a Room
SUFFOLK — Con.				
Winthrop — Con.				
4 persons,	187	1,446	7.73	0.52
5 persons,	143	1,151	8.05	0.62
6 persons,	105	847	8.07	0.74
7 persons,	62	673	10.85	0.64
8 persons,	40	351	8.78	0.91
9 persons,	16	129	8.06	1.12
10 persons,	11	95	8.64	1.19
11 persons,	10	220	22.00	0.50
12 persons,	1	9	9.00	1.33
13 persons,	3	49	20.00	0.65
14 persons,	1	8	8.00	1.75
15 persons,	1	9	9.00	1.67
16 persons,	1	11	11.00	1.45
18 person,	1	4	4.00	4.50
42 persons,	1	12	42.00	1.00
WORCESTER.				
Ashburnham,	530	3,528	6.66	0.64
1 person,	29	156	5.38	0.19
2 persons,	118	713	6.04	0.33
3 persons,	119	736	6.18	0.40
4 persons,	99	688	6.95	0.58
5 persons,	54	376	6.96	0.72
6 persons,	45	303	6.73	0.89
7 persons,	31	229	7.39	0.95
8 persons,	11	91	8.27	0.97
9 persons,	12	86	7.17	1.26
10 persons,	4	25	6.25	1.60
11 persons,	2	16	8.00	1.38
12 persons,	1	6	6.00	2.00
13 persons,	1	16	16.00	0.81
14 persons,	1	19	19.00	0.74
19 persons,	1	17	17.00	1.12
26 persons,	1	22	22.00	1.18
31 persons,	1	29	29.00	1.07
Athol,	1,750	11,681	6.67	0.63
1 person,	108	458	4.24	0.24
2 persons,	340	1,802	5.59	0.36
3 persons,	391	2,462	6.30	0.48
4 persons,	337	2,263	6.72	0.60
5 persons,	218	1,528	7.01	0.71
6 persons,	143	1,018	7.12	0.84
7 persons,	77	615	7.99	0.88
8 persons,	55	390	7.09	1.13
9 persons,	31	215	6.94	1.30
10 persons,	20	173	8.65	1.16
11 persons,	7	59	8.43	1.31
12 persons,	8	73	9.13	1.32
13 persons,	5	46	9.20	1.41
15 persons,	1	8	8.00	1.88
17 persons,	2	28	14.00	1.21
21 persons,	1	57	57.00	0.37
22 persons,	1	26	26.00	0.85
29 persons,	1	35	35.00	0.83

ROOMS: OCCUPIED DWELLING HOUSES — Continued.

Counties, Cities, Towns, and Number of Persons to a Family.	Number of Families of Specified Size	Total Number of Rooms Occupied	Average Number of Rooms Occupied	Average Number of Persons to a Room	Counties, Cities, Towns, and Number of Persons to a Family.	Number of Families of Specified Size	Total Number of Rooms Occupied	Average Number of Rooms Occupied	Average Number of Persons to a Room
WORCESTER–Con.					WORCESTER–Con.				
Athol — Con.					Blackstone — Con.				
31 persons,	1	22	22.00	1.41	3 persons,	228	1,377	6.04	0.50
41 persons,	1	37	37.00	1.11	4 persons,	233	1,469	6.30	0.63
58 persons,	1	106	106.00	0.55	5 persons,	152	1,004	6.61	0.76
100 persons,	1	160	160.00	1.00	6 persons,	135	894	6.62	0.91
Auburn,	345	2,124	6.16	0.75	7 persons,	109	785	7.20	0.97
1 person,	15	56	3.73	0.27	8 persons,	72	520	7.22	1.11
2 persons,	49	268	5.47	0.37	9 persons,	32	327	10.22	0.88
3 persons,	65	385	5.92	0.51	10 persons,	29	202	6.97	1.44
4 persons,	60	398	6.63	0.60	11 persons,	14	105	7.50	1.47
5 persons,	51	347	6.80	0.73	12 persons,	5	36	7.20	1.67
6 persons,	34	209	6.15	0.98	13 persons,	6	59	9.83	1.32
7 persons,	32	208	6.50	1.08	14 persons,	2	24	12.00	1.17
8 persons,	16	94	5.88	1.36	15 persons,	2	39	19.50	0.77
9 persons,	9	62	6.89	1.31	20 persons,	1	14	14.00	1.43
10 persons,	6	43	7.17	1.40	25 persons,	1	25	25.00	1.00
11 persons,	4	26	6.50	1.69	26 persons,	1	33	33.00	0.79
12 persons,	1	5	5.00	2.40	33 persons,	1	28	28.00	1.18
13 persons,	2	12	6.00	2.17	41 person,	1	41	41.00	1.00
16 persons,	1	11	11.00	1.45	Bolton,	206	1,567	7.61	0.51
Barre,	558	4,686	8.40	0.49	1 person,	13	64	4.92	0.20
1 person,	55	339	6.16	0.16	2 persons,	46	284	6.11	0.33
2 persons,	136	908	6.90	0.29	3 persons,	42	306	7.29	0.41
3 persons,	117	949	8.11	0.37	4 persons,	46	369	8.02	0.50
4 persons,	88	702	7.98	0.50	5 persons,	22	196	8.91	0.56
5 persons,	66	585	8.86	0.56	6 persons,	14	116	8.29	0.72
6 persons,	39	348	8.92	0.67	7 persons,	11	94	8.55	0.82
7 persons,	22	241	1.10	0.64	8 persons,	4	38	9.50	0.84
8 persons,	12	117	9.75	0.82	9 persons,	4	59	14.75	0.61
9 persons,	6	51	8.50	1.06	10 persons,	2	25	12.50	0.80
10 persons,	6	41	6.83	1.46	11 persons,	1	9	9.00	1.22
11 persons,	2	13	6.50	1.69	12 persons,	1	10	10.00	1.20
12 persons,	3	70	2.33	0.51	Boylston,	177	1,263	7.14	0.58
15 persons,	2	53	26.50	0.57	1 person,	17	85	5.00	0.20
18 persons,	1	24	24.00	0.75	2 persons,	34	210	6.18	0.32
20 persons,	1	46	46.00	0.43	3 persons,	28	204	7.29	0.41
60 persons,	1	60	60.00	1.00	4 persons,	27	197	7.30	0.55
134 persons,	1	109	109.00	1.23	5 persons,	26	208	8.00	0.63
Berlin,	225	1,756	7.80	0.51	6 persons,	20	167	8.35	0.72
1 person,	18	112	6.22	0.16	7 persons,	11	84	7.64	0.92
2 persons,	57	420	7.37	0.27	8 persons,	7	37	5.29	1.51
3 persons,	35	291	8.31	0.36	9 persons,	2	15	7.50	1.20
4 persons,	38	297	7.82	0.51	10 persons,	4	49	12.25	0.82
5 persons,	29	229	7.90	0.63	11 persons,	1	7	7.00	1.57
6 persons,	18	143	7.94	0.76	Brookfield,	756	5,065	6.70	0.65
7 persons,	10	93	9.30	0.75	1 person,	40	174	4.35	0.23
8 persons,	9	72	8.00	1.00	2 persons,	138	857	6.21	0.32
9 persons,	5	37	7.40	1.22	3 persons,	153	980	6.41	0.47
10 persons,	3	37	12.33	0.81	4 persons,	143	974	6.81	0.59
11 persons,	1	10	10.00	1.10	5 persons,	85	605	7.12	0.70
13 persons,	1	10	10.00	1.30	6 persons,	78	564	7.23	0.83
14 persons,	1	5	5.00	2.80	7 persons,	42	282	6.71	1.04
Blackstone,	1,266	8,343	6.59	0.72	8 persons,	34	253	7.44	1.08
1 person,	43	218	5.07	0.20	9 persons,	18	145	8.06	1.12
2 persons,	199	1,143	5.74	0.35	10 persons,	7	45	6.43	1.56

ROOMS: OCCUPIED DWELLING HOUSES — Continued.

COUNTIES, CITIES, TOWNS, AND NUMBER OF PERSONS TO A FAMILY.	Number of Families of Specified Size	Total Number of Rooms Occupied	Average Number of Rooms Occupied	Average Number of Persons to a Room
WORCESTER—Con.				
Brookfield—Con.				
11 persons,	8	93	11.63	0.95
12 persons,	2	22	11.00	1.09
13 persons,	1	5	5.00	2.60
14 persons,	3	15	5.00	2.80
15 persons,	1	7	7.00	2.14
18 persons,	1	4	4.00	4.50
20 persons,	1	36	36.00	0.56
21 persons,	1	4	4.00	5.25
Charlton,	470	3,390	7.23	0.55
1 person,	25	145	5.80	0.17
2 persons,	105	672	6.40	0.31
3 persons,	105	726	6.91	0.43
4 persons,	86	675	7.85	0.51
5 persons,	56	473	8.45	0.59
6 persons,	38	269	7.08	0.85
7 persons,	22	153	6.95	1.01
8 persons,	9	73	8.11	0.99
9 persons,	12	95	7.92	1.14
10 persons,	4	20	5.00	2.00
11 persons,	2	21	10.50	1.05
12 persons,	3	22	7.33	1.64
13 persons,	2	33	16.50	0.79
17 persons,	1	22	22.00	0.77
Clinton,	2,278	13,735	6.03	0.84
1 person,	55	190	3.45	0.29
2 persons,	321	1,614	5.03	0.40
3 persons,	372	1,987	5.34	0.56
4 persons,	423	2,471	5.84	0.68
5 persons,	331	2,004	6.05	0.83
6 persons,	260	1,644	6.32	0.95
7 persons,	173	1,145	6.62	1.06
8 persons,	127	772	6.08	1.32
9 persons,	82	567	6.91	1.30
10 persons,	66	421	6.38	1.37
11 persons,	28	184	6.57	1.67
12 persons,	11	96	8.73	1.38
13 persons,	8	138	17.25	0.75
14 persons,	8	87	10.88	1.29
16 persons,	1	7	7.00	2.29
19 persons,	1	25	25.00	0.76
22 persons,	1	30	30.00	0.73
24 persons,	1	24	24.00	1.00
26 persons,	1	18	18.00	1.44
28 persons,	1	20	20.00	1.40
36 persons,	1	25	25.00	1.44
38 persons,	2	48	24.00	1.58
42 persons,	1	28	28.00	1.50
53 persons,	1	70	70.00	0.76
66 persons,	1	50	50.00	1.32
88 persons,	1	70	70.00	1.26
Dana,	196	1,298	6.62	0.55
1 person,	24	101	4.21	0.24
2 persons,	48	298	6.21	0.32
3 persons,	40	289	7.23	0.42

COUNTIES, CITIES, TOWNS, AND NUMBER OF PERSONS TO A FAMILY.	Number of Families of Specified Size	Total Number of Rooms Occupied	Average Number of Rooms Occupied	Average Number of Persons to a Room
WORCESTER—Con.				
Dana—Con.				
4 persons,	26	166	6.38	0.63
5 persons,	28	203	7.25	0.69
6 persons,	7	61	8.71	0.69
7 persons,	9	67	7.44	0.94
8 persons,	4	26	6.50	1.23
9 persons,	6	46	7.67	1.17
10 persons,	2	18	9.00	1.11
11 persons,	2	23	11.50	0.96
Douglas,	483	3,447	7.14	0.59
1 person,	38	200	5.26	0.19
2 persons,	90	640	7.11	0.28
3 persons,	98	697	7.11	0.42
4 persons,	76	549	7.22	0.55
5 persons,	70	502	7.17	0.70
6 persons,	33	233	7.06	0.85
7 persons,	29	224	7.72	0.91
8 persons,	28	201	7.18	1.11
9 persons,	6	64	10.67	0.84
10 persons,	6	52	8.67	1.15
11 persons,	6	48	8.00	1.38
13 persons,	1	11	11.00	1.18
15 persons,	1	10	10.00	1.50
27 persons,	1	16	16.00	1.69
Dudley,	628	3,976	6.33	0.81
1 person,	19	100	5.26	0.19
2 persons,	75	419	5.59	0.36
3 persons,	100	620	6.20	0.48
4 persons,	107	682	6.37	0.63
5 persons,	88	579	6.58	0.76
6 persons,	71	458	6.45	0.93
7 persons,	50	326	6.52	1.07
8 persons,	43	276	6.42	1.25
9 persons,	40	252	6.30	1.43
10 persons,	19	125	6.58	1.52
11 persons,	9	61	6.78	1.62
12 persons,	1	7	7.00	1.71
13 persons,	2	17	8.50	1.53
14 persons,	3	45	15.00	0.93
17 persons,	1	9	9.00	1.89
FITCHBURG,	5,686	34,560	6.08	0.76
1 person,	149	610	4.09	0.24
2 persons,	919	4,941	5.38	0.37
3 persons,	1,136	6,474	5.70	0.53
4 persons,	1,035	6,211	6.00	0.67
5 persons,	781	4,739	6.07	0.82
6 persons,	579	3,648	6.25	0.96
7 persons,	421	2,755	6.54	1.07
8 persons,	264	1,767	6.69	1.20
9 persons,	173	1,214	7.02	1.28
10 persons,	83	551	6.64	1.51
11 persons,	68	499	7.34	1.50
12 persons,	35	244	6.97	1.72
13 persons,	16	134	8.38	1.55
14 persons,	4	47	11.75	1.19

ROOMS : OCCUPIED DWELLING HOUSES — Continued.

WORCESTER—Con.
FITCHBURG — Con.

COUNTIES, CITIES, TOWNS, AND NUMBER OF PERSONS TO A FAMILY.	Number of Families of Specified Size	Total Number of Rooms Occupied	Average Number of Rooms Occupied	Average Number of Persons to a Room
15 persons,	7	72	10.29	1.46
17 persons,	4	28	7.00	2.43
18 persons,	1	26	26.00	0.69
22 persons,	1	12	12.00	1.83
23 persons,	3	112	37.33	0.62
24 persons,	2	55	27.50	0.87
27 persons,	1	80	80.00	0.34
32 persons,	1	15	15.00	2.13
37 persons,	1	95	95.00	0.39
80 persons,	1	75	75.00	1.07
111 persons,	1	217	217.00	0.51
Fitchburg. Ward 1,	897	5,334	5.95	0.82
1 person,	30	104	3.47	0.29
2 persons,	131	698	5.33	0.38
3 persons,	161	856	5.32	0.56
4 persons,	161	930	5.78	0.69
5 persons,	123	705	5.73	0.87
6 persons,	94	518	5.51	1.09
7 persons,	87	535	6.15	1.14
8 persons,	49	309	6.31	1.27
9 persons,	32	212	6.63	1.36
10 persons,	10	62	6.20	1.61
11 persons,	11	75	6.82	1.61
12 persons,	5	34	6.80	1.76
17 persons,	1	4	4.00	4.25
80 persons,	1	75	75.00	1.07
111 persons,	1	217	217.00	0.51
Fitchburg. Ward 2,	1,241	6,695	5.39	0.97
1 person,	18	73	4.06	0.25
2 persons,	155	760	4.90	0.41
3 persons,	210	1,027	4.89	0.61
4 persons,	198	1,023	5.17	0.77
5 persons,	174	949	5.28	0.95
6 persons,	147	801	5.45	1.10
7 persons,	116	627	5.41	1.30
8 persons,	66	386	5.85	1.37
9 persons,	58	367	6.33	1.42
10 persons,	41	234	5.71	1.75
11 persons,	27	159	5.89	1.87
12 persons,	16	106	6.63	1.81
13 persons,	2	13	6.50	2.00
14 persons,	2	11	5.50	2.55
15 persons,	5	47	9.40	1.60
17 persons,	3	24	8.00	1.13
18 persons,	1	26	26.00	0.69
22 persons,	1	12	12.00	1.83
27 persons,	1	80	80.00	0.34
Fitchburg. Ward 3,	941	5,749	6.28	0.75
1 person,	25	132	5.28	0.19
2 persons,	138	761	5.51	0.36
3 persons,	166	1,027	6.19	0.48
4 persons,	170	1,067	6.28	0.64
5 persons,	133	820	6.17	0.81
6 persons,	93	555	5.97	1.01

WORCESTER—Con.
Fitchburg. Ward 3 — Con.

COUNTIES, CITIES, TOWNS, AND NUMBER OF PERSONS TO A FAMILY.	Number of Families of Specified Size	Total Number of Rooms Occupied	Average Number of Rooms Occupied	Average Number of Persons to a Room
7 persons,	74	520	7.03	1.01
8 persons,	51	383	7.51	1.07
9 persons,	28	211	7.54	1.19
10 persons,	8	52	6.50	1.54
11 persons,	10	69	6.90	1.59
12 persons,	6	38	6.33	1.89
13 persons,	6	42	7.00	1.86
23 persons,	1	12	12.00	1.92
24 persons,	1	15	15.00	1.60
32 persons,	1	15	15.00	2.13
Fitchburg. Ward 4,	783	5,629	7.19	0.57
1 person,	36	124	3.44	0.29
2 persons,	159	920	5.79	0.35
3 persons,	197	1,271	6.45	0.48
4 persons,	154	1,078	7.00	0.57
5 persons,	86	627	7.29	0.80
6 persons,	69	578	8.38	0.72
7 persons,	39	365	9.36	0.75
8 persons,	19	166	8.74	0.92
9 persons,	15	131	8.73	1.03
10 persons,	6	94	15.67	0.64
11 persons,	4	81	20.25	0.54
12 persons,	1	12	12.00	1.00
13 persons,	4	47	11.75	1.11
14 persons,	1	15	15.00	0.26
15 persons,	2	25	12.50	1.20
37 persons,	1	95	95.00	0.39
Fitchburg. Ward 5,	845	5,254	6.23	0.64
1 person,	22	113	5.14	0.19
2 persons,	175	949	5.42	0.37
3 persons,	206	1,204	5.84	0.51
4 persons,	170	1,051	6.18	0.65
5 persons,	122	781	6.40	0.78
6 persons,	68	470	6.91	0.87
7 persons,	35	259	7.40	0.95
8 persons,	22	171	7.77	1.03
9 persons,	13	124	9.54	0.94
10 persons,	2	15	7.50	1.33
11 persons,	4	31	7.75	1.42
12 persons,	2	25	12.50	0.96
13 persons,	1	11	11.00	1.18
23 persons,	1	50	50.00	0.46
Fitchburg. Ward 6,	1,001	5,900	5.95	0.78
1 person,	18	64	3.56	0.28
2 persons,	164	853	5.30	0.38
3 persons,	196	1,089	5.56	0.54
4 persons,	182	1,062	5.84	0.69
5 persons,	143	887	6.20	0.81
6 persons,	108	696	6.44	0.93
7 persons,	70	449	6.41	1.09
8 persons,	57	352	6.18	1.59
9 persons,	27	169	6.26	1.44
10 persons,	16	94	5.88	1.70
11 persons,	12	84	7.00	1.57

ROOMS: OCCUPIED DWELLING HOUSES — Continued.

COUNTIES, CITIES, TOWNS, AND NUMBER OF PERSONS TO A FAMILY.	Number of Families Specified Size	Total Number of Rooms Occupied	Average Number of Rooms Occupied	Average Number of Persons to a Room	COUNTIES, CITIES, TOWNS, AND NUMBER OF PERSONS TO A FAMILY.	Number of Families Specified Size	Total Number of Rooms Occupied	Average Number of Rooms Occupied	Average Number of Persons to a Room
WORCESTER—Con.					**WORCESTER**—Con.				
Fitchburg, Ward 6—Con.					Hardwick—Con.				
12 persons,	5	29	5.80	2.07	12 persons,	2	13	6.50	1.85
13 persons,	3	21	7.00	1.86	13 persons,	2	22	11.00	1.18
14 persons,	1	21	21.00	0.67	14 persons,	2	23	11.50	1.22
23 persons,	1	50	50.00	0.46	15 persons,	1	6	6.00	2.50
24 persons,	1	40	40.00	0.60	17 persons,	1	21	21.00	0.81
Gardner,	2,062	11,818	5.73	0.78	26 persons,	1	21	21.00	1.24
1 person,	61	221	3.62	0.28	Harvard,	279	2,237	8.02	0.52
2 persons,	338	1,724	5.10	0.39	1 person,	16	98	6.13	0.16
3 persons,	427	2,366	5.54	0.54	2 persons,	56	391	6.98	0.29
4 persons,	388	2,143	5.52	0.72	3 persons,	62	462	7.45	0.40
5 persons,	321	1,881	5.86	0.85	4 persons,	53	450	8.49	0.47
6 persons,	182	1,089	5.98	1.00	5 persons,	34	259	7.62	0.66
7 persons,	141	884	6.27	1.12	6 persons,	17	169	9.94	0.60
8 persons,	86	553	6.43	1.24	7 persons,	18	187	10.39	0.67
9 persons,	52	327	6.29	1.43	8 persons,	12	116	9.67	0.83
10 persons,	32	211	6.59	1.52	9 persons,	4	29	7.25	1.24
11 persons,	15	94	6.27	1.76	10 persons,	1	9	9.00	1.11
12 persons,	6	34	5.67	2.12	11 persons,	2	18	9.00	1.22
13 persons,	5	32	6.40	2.03	12 persons,	1	10	10.00	1.20
15 persons,	3	31	10.33	1.45	14 persons,	1	18	18.00	0.78
16 persons,	1	36	36.00	0.44	24 persons,	2	21	10.50	2.29
21 persons,	1	27	27.00	0.78	Holden,	555	3,731	6.72	0.70
22 persons,	2	125	62.50	0.35	1 person,	36	193	5.36	0.19
24 persons,	1	40	40.00	0.60	2 persons,	90	554	6.16	0.32
Grafton,	1,106	7,696	6.96	0.66	3 persons,	88	567	6.44	0.47
1 person,	56	277	4.95	0.20	4 persons,	90	590	6.56	0.61
2 persons,	190	1,200	6.32	0.32	5 persons,	74	515	6.96	0.72
3 persons,	188	1,294	6.88	0.44	6 persons,	46	289	6.28	0.90
4 persons,	176	1,209	6.87	0.58	7 persons,	48	379	7.90	0.89
5 persons,	156	1,118	7.17	0.70	8 persons,	36	251	6.97	1.15
6 persons,	109	845	7.75	0.77	9 persons,	21	166	7.90	1.14
7 persons,	101	674	6.67	1.05	10 persons,	11	80	7.27	1.38
8 persons,	45	355	7.89	1.01	11 persons,	7	54	7.71	1.43
9 persons,	38	298	7.84	1.15	12 persons,	3	22	7.33	1.64
10 persons,	20	143	7.15	1.40	13 persons,	1	7	7.00	1.86
11 persons,	10	68	6.80	1.62	14 persons,	3	38	12.67	1.11
12 persons,	6	65	10.83	1.11	25 persons,	1	26	26.00	0.96
13 persons,	2	15	7.50	1.73	Hopedale,	307	2,261	7.36	0.61
14 persons,	2	12	6.00	2.33	1 person,	12	56	4.67	0.21
15 persons,	4	26	6.50	2.31	2 persons,	59	384	6.51	0.31
18 persons,	2	66	33.00	0.55	3 persons,	50	344	6.88	0.44
22 persons,	1	31	31.00	0.71	4 persons,	63	433	6.87	0.58
Hardwick,	533	3,791	7.11	0.70	5 persons,	38	316	8.32	0.60
1 person,	18	76	4.22	0.24	6 persons,	36	280	7.78	0.77
2 persons,	69	428	6.20	0.32	7 persons,	23	178	7.74	0.90
3 persons,	93	595	6.40	0.47	8 persons,	14	106	7.57	1.06
4 persons,	87	601	6.91	0.58	9 persons,	3	25	8.33	1.08
5 persons,	74	564	7.62	0.66	10 persons,	5	42	8.40	1.19
6 persons,	59	469	7.95	0.75	11 persons,	2	24	12.00	0.92
7 persons,	55	423	7.69	0.91	24 persons,	1	23	23.00	1.04
8 persons,	24	190	7.92	1.01	43 persons,	1	50	50.00	0.86
9 persons,	22	165	7.50	1.20	Hubbardston,	348	2,306	6.63	0.55
10 persons,	16	115	7.19	1.39	1 person,	35	168	4.80	0.21
11 persons,	7	59	8.43	1.31	2 persons,	78	476	6.10	0.33

ROOMS: OCCUPIED DWELLING HOUSES — Continued.

Counties, Cities, Towns, and Number of Persons to a Family.	Number of Families of Specified Size	Total Number of Rooms Occupied	Average Number of Rooms Occupied	Average Number of Persons to a Room
WORCESTER-Con.				
Hubbardston — Con.				
3 persons,	80	532	6.65	0.45
4 persons,	55	351	6.38	0.63
5 persons,	46	333	7.24	0.69
6 persons,	22	174	7.91	0.76
7 persons,	18	122	6.78	1.03
8 persons,	5	34	6.80	1.18
9 persons,	4	34	8.50	1.06
10 persons,	2	24	12.00	0.83
12 persons,	1	12	12.00	1.00
13 persons,	1	8	8.00	1.63
14 persons,	1	38	38.00	0.37
Lancaster,	452	3,644	8.06	0.60
1 person,	22	122	5.55	0.18
2 persons,	87	583	6.70	0.30
3 persons,	83	539	6.49	0.46
4 persons,	83	679	8.18	0.49
5 persons,	59	417	7.07	0.71
6 persons,	48	429	8.94	0.67
7 persons,	29	241	8.31	0.84
8 persons,	18	156	8.67	0.92
9 persons,	9	89	9.89	0.91
10 persons,	5	45	9.00	1.11
11 persons,	3	21	7.00	1.57
15 persons,	1	20	20.00	0.75
16 persons,	1	24	24.00	0.67
18 persons,	4	29	29.00	0.66
48 persons,	1	11	11.00	4.36
71 persons,	1	66	66.00	1.08
140 persons,	1	173	173.00	0.81
Leicester,	731	5,257	7.19	0.62
1 person,	34	185	5.44	0.18
2 persons,	115	725	6.30	0.32
3 persons,	140	947	6.76	0.44
4 persons,	141	1,002	7.11	0.56
5 persons,	110	802	7.29	0.69
6 persons,	75	584	7.79	0.77
7 persons,	38	303	7.97	0.88
8 persons,	34	229	7.39	1.08
9 persons,	18	149	8.28	1.09
10 persons,	17	166	9.76	1.02
11 persons,	6	49	8.17	1.35
12 persons,	3	36	12.00	1.00
13 persons,	1	11	11.00	1.18
15 persons,	2	69	34.50	0.43
Leominster,	2,181	13,789	6.32	0.67
1 person,	92	374	4.03	0.25
2 persons,	417	2,308	5.53	0.36
3 persons,	477	2,886	6.05	0.50
4 persons,	396	2,492	6.29	0.64
5 persons,	288	1,910	6.63	0.75
6 persons,	207	1,443	6.97	0.86
7 persons,	121	862	7.42	0.98
8 persons,	89	668	7.51	1.07
9 persons,	36	258	7.17	1.26

Counties, Cities, Towns, and Number of Persons to a Family.	Number of Families of Specified Size	Total Number of Rooms Occupied	Average Number of Rooms Occupied	Average Number of Persons to a Room
WORCESTER-Con.				
Leominster — Con.				
10 persons,	20	140	7.00	1.43
11 persons,	16	120	7.50	1.47
12 persons,	7	65	9.29	1.29
13 persons,	4	33	8.25	1.58
14 persons,	2	20	10.00	1.40
15 persons,	1	5	5.00	3.00
16 persons,	1	18	18.00	0.89
17 persons,	2	45	22.50	0.76
19 persons,	2	32	16.00	1.19
20 persons,	2	80	40.00	0.50
22 persons,	1	33	33.00	0.67
Lunenburg,	302	2,168	7.18	0.57
1 person,	17	95	5.59	0.18
2 persons,	65	423	6.51	0.40
3 persons,	65	447	6.88	0.44
4 persons,	51	381	7.47	0.54
5 persons,	37	277	7.49	0.67
6 persons,	26	186	7.15	0.84
7 persons,	14	109	7.79	0.90
8 persons,	13	106	8.15	0.98
9 persons,	5	55	11.00	0.82
10 persons,	3	33	11.00	0.91
11 persons,	3	32	10.67	1.03
12 persons,	2	18	9.00	1.33
16 persons,	1	6	6.00	2.67
Mendon,	234	1,885	8.06	0.47
1 person,	21	88	4.19	0.24
2 persons,	51	382	7.49	0.27
3 persons,	50	391	7.82	0.38
4 persons,	35	306	8.74	0.46
5 persons,	35	340	9.71	0.51
6 persons,	15	135	9.00	0.67
7 persons,	15	141	9.40	0.74
8 persons,	6	56	9.33	0.86
9 persons,	5	35	7.00	1.29
13 persons,	1	11	11.00	1.18
Milford,	2,116	14,021	6.63	0.84
1 person,	114	460	4.03	0.25
2 persons,	395	2,310	5.85	0.34
3 persons,	453	2,927	6.46	0.46
4 persons,	390	2,587	6.63	0.60
5 persons,	265	1,798	6.78	0.74
6 persons,	202	1,453	7.19	0.83
7 persons,	119	866	7.28	0.96
8 persons,	84	637	7.58	1.05
9 persons,	37	293	7.92	1.14
10 persons,	22	206	9.36	1.07
11 persons,	14	118	8.43	1.31
12 persons,	4	32	8.00	1.50
13 persons,	1	6	6.00	2.17
14 persons,	3	28	9.33	1.86
15 persons,	3	40	13.33	1.13
16 persons,	2	40	20.00	0.80
17 persons,	3	32	10.67	1.59

ROOMS: OCCUPIED DWELLING HOUSES — Continued.

COUNTIES, CITIES, TOWNS, AND NUMBER OF PERSONS TO A FAMILY.	Number of Families of Specified Size	Total Number of Rooms Occupied	Average Number of Rooms Occupied	Average Number of Persons to a Room	COUNTIES, CITIES, TOWNS, AND NUMBER OF PERSONS TO A FAMILY.	Number of Families of Specified Size	Total Number of Rooms Occupied	Average Number of Rooms Occupied	Average Number of Persons to a Room
WORCESTER-Con.					**WORCESTER**-Con.				
Milford — Con.					Northbridge — Con.				
19 persons, . .	2	67	33.50	0.57	3 persons, . .	198	1,206	6.09	0.49
26 persons, . .	1	35	35.00	0.74	4 persons, . .	159	1,063	6.31	0.63
41 persons, . .	1	60	60.00	0.68	5 persons, . .	152	998	6.57	0.76
51 persons, . .	1	26	26.00	1.96	6 persons, . .	125	775	6.20	0.97
Millbury, . . .	1,100	7,243	6.56	0.72	7 persons, . .	91	576	6.33	1.11
1 person, . .	40	211	5.28	0.19	8 persons, . .	68	443	6.51	1.23
2 persons, . .	178	1,027	5.77	0.35	9 persons, . .	41	272	6.63	1.36
3 persons, . .	200	1,269	6.35	0.47	10 persons, . .	15	110	7.33	1.36
4 persons, . .	211	1,377	6.53	0.61	11 persons, . .	20	124	6.20	1.77
5 persons, . .	153	1,063	6.56	0.76	12 persons, . .	5	56	11.20	1.07
6 persons, . .	100	674	6.74	0.89	13 persons, . .	3	18	6.00	2.17
7 persons, . .	71	497	7.00	1.00	14 persons, . .	1	8	8.00	1.75
8 persons, . .	45	318	7.07	1.13	16 persons, . .	3	21	7.00	2.29
9 persons, . .	45	336	7.47	1.24	17 persons, . .	1	11	11.00	1.55
10 persons, . .	32	211	6.59	1.52	20 persons, . .	1	16	16.00	1.25
11 persons, . .	12	76	6.33	1.74	22 persons, . .	1	21	21.00	1.05
12 persons, . .	5	41	8.20	1.46	33 persons, . .	1	37	37.00	0.89
13 persons, . .	3	33	11.00	1.18	44 persons, . .	1	50	50.00	0.88
14 persons, . .	2	18	9.00	1.56	North Brookfield, .	1,030	6,672	6.48	0.69
18 persons, . .	1	24	24.00	0.75	1 person, . .	44	198	4.50	0.22
62 persons, . .	1	2	2.00	31.00	2 persons, . .	197	1,104	5.60	0.36
96 persons, . .	1	96	96.00	1.00	3 persons, . .	184	1,191	6.47	0.46
New Braintree, .	114	167	8.22	0.58	4 persons, . .	154	970	6.30	0.64
1 person, . .	4	19	4.75	0.21	5 persons, . .	147	941	6.40	0.78
2 persons, . .	16	117	7.31	0.27	6 persons, . .	100	692	6.92	0.87
3 persons, . .	14	105	7.50	0.40	7 persons, . .	98	721	7.36	0.95
4 persons, . .	27	217	8.04	0.50	8 persons, . .	46	324	7.04	1.14
5 persons, . .	19	155	8.16	0.64	9 persons, . .	26	203	7.81	1.15
6 persons, . .	13	116	8.92	0.67	10 persons, . .	15	109	7.27	1.38
7 persons, . .	6	60	10.00	0.70	11 persons, . .	8	65	8.13	1.35
8 persons, . .	4	38	9.50	0.84	12 persons, . .	3	25	8.33	1.44
9 persons, . .	8	82	10.25	0.88	13 persons, . .	3	22	7.33	1.77
10 persons, . .	1	8	8.00	1.25	14 persons, . .	1	18	18.00	0.78
11 persons, . .	1	8	8.00	1.38	15 persons, . .	1	15	15.00	1.00
16 persons, . .	1	12	12.00	1.33	16 persons, . .	1	14	14.00	1.14
Northborough, . .	451	3,114	6.90	0.62	23 persons, . .	1	52	52.00	0.44
1 person, . .	26	114	4.38	0.23	25 persons, . .	1	8	8.00	3.13
2 persons, . .	72	465	6.46	0.31	Oakham, . .	161	1,342	8.34	0.45
3 persons, . .	96	652	6.59	0.46	1 person, . .	18	137	7.61	0.13
4 persons, . .	78	581	7.45	0.54	2 persons, . .	28	214	7.64	0.26
5 persons, . .	63	444	7.05	0.71	3 persons, . .	35	280	8.00	0.38
6 persons, . .	39	272	6.97	0.86	4 persons, . .	25	204	8.16	0.49
7 persons, . .	32	240	7.50	0.93	5 persons, . .	27	224	8.30	0.60
8 persons, . .	19	137	7.21	1.11	6 persons, . .	17	176	10.35	0.58
9 persons, . .	13	111	8.54	1.05	7 persons, . .	4	28	7.00	1.00
10 persons, . .	3	23	7.67	1.30	8 persons, . .	6	51	8.50	0.94
11 persons, . .	2	35	17.50	0.63	13 persons, . .	1	28	28.00	0.46
12 persons, . .	1	10	10.00	1.20	Oxford, . .	618	4,250	6.88	0.56
13 persons, . .	2	14	7.00	1.86	1 person, . .	53	289	5.45	0.18
14 persons, . .	1	9	9.00	1.56	2 persons, . .	157	1,042	6.64	0.30
15 persons, . .	1	7	7.00	2.14	3 persons, . .	117	854	7.30	0.41
Northbridge, . .	1,070	6,762	6.32	0.78	4 persons, . .	103	719	6.98	0.57
1 person, . .	39	193	4.95	0.20	5 persons, . .	67	471	7.03	0.71
2 persons, . .	145	824	5.68	0.35	6 persons, . .	44	303	6.89	0.87

550 CENSUS OF MASSACHUSETTS — 1895.

ROOMS: OCCUPIED DWELLING HOUSES — Continued.

COUNTIES, CITIES, TOWNS, AND NUMBER OF PERSONS TO A FAMILY.	Number of Families of Specified Size	Total Number of Rooms Occupied	Average Number of Rooms Occupied	Average Number of Persons to a Room
WORCESTER-Con.				
Oxford - Con.				
7 persons,	28	188	6.71	1.04
8 persons,	16	101	6.31	1.27
9 persons,	14	102	7.29	1.24
10 persons,	8	57	7.13	1.40
11 persons,	6	59	9.83	1.12
12 persons,	3	27	9.00	1.33
14 persons,	1	10	10.00	1.40
15 persons,	1	28	28.00	0.54
Paxton,	114	894	7.84	0.48
1 person,	5	28	5.60	0.18
2 persons,	25	218	8.72	0.23
3 persons,	28	211	7.54	0.40
4 persons,	29	238	8.21	0.49
5 persons,	10	64	6.40	0.78
6 persons,	7	42	6.00	1.00
7 persons,	5	47	9.40	0.74
8 persons,	3	21	7.00	1.14
9 persons,	1	15	15.00	0.60
11 persons,	1	10	10.00	1.10
Petersham,	254	1,981	7.80	0.48
1 person,	25	147	5.88	0.17
2 persons,	56	395	7.05	0.28
3 persons,	64	481	7.52	0.40
4 persons,	36	291	8.08	0.49
5 persons,	30	247	8.23	0.61
6 persons,	16	115	7.19	0.83
7 persons,	12	137	11.42	0.61
8 persons,	6	70	11.67	0.69
9 persons,	5	47	9.40	0.96
12 persons,	3	31	10.33	1.16
20 persons,	1	20	20.00	1.00
Phillipston,	114	896	7.83	0.52
1 person,	2	8	4.00	0.25
2 persons,	35	261	7.46	0.27
3 persons,	25	196	7.84	0.38
4 persons,	17	131	7.71	0.52
5 persons,	7	54	7.71	0.65
6 persons,	9	79	8.78	0.68
7 persons,	8	74	9.25	0.76
8 persons,	5	41	8.20	0.98
9 persons,	2	14	7.00	1.29
10 persons,	2	15	7.50	1.33
11 persons,	2	20	10.00	1.10
Princeton,	236	2,186	9.26	0.44
1 person,	16	123	7.69	0.13
2 persons,	50	365	7.30	0.27
3 persons,	54	447	8.28	0.36
4 persons,	39	420	10.77	0.37
5 persons,	20	174	8.70	0.57
6 persons,	23	198	8.61	0.70
7 persons,	16	192	12.00	0.58
8 persons,	6	47	7.83	1.02
9 persons,	3	21	7.00	1.29
10 persons,	6	119	19.83	0.50
11 persons,	3	80	26.67	0.41

COUNTIES, CITIES, TOWNS, AND NUMBER OF PERSONS TO A FAMILY.	Number of Families of Specified Size	Total Number of Rooms Occupied	Average Number of Rooms Occupied	Average Number of Persons to a Room
WORCESTER-Con.				
Royalston,	254	1,948	7.67	0.46
1 person,	19	93	4.89	0.20
2 persons,	62	467	7.53	0.27
3 persons,	66	471	7.14	0.42
4 persons,	45	356	7.91	0.51
5 persons,	26	268	10.31	0.49
6 persons,	21	162	7.71	0.78
7 persons,	10	96	9.60	0.73
8 persons,	2	16	8.00	1.00
9 persons,	3	19	6.33	1.42
Rutland,	225	1,502	6.68	0.65
1 person,	15	58	3.87	0.26
2 persons,	44	237	5.39	0.37
3 persons,	30	182	6.07	0.49
4 persons,	40	313	7.83	0.51
5 persons,	38	299	7.87	0.64
6 persons,	19	128	6.74	0.89
7 persons,	18	139	7.72	0.91
8 persons,	10	63	6.30	1.27
9 persons,	4	26	6.50	1.38
10 persons,	3	29	9.67	1.03
11 persons,	1	9	9.00	1.22
12 persons,	2	11	5.50	2.18
14 persons,	1	8	8.00	1.75
Shrewsbury,	381	2,917	7.66	0.52
1 person,	29	169	5.83	0.17
2 persons,	81	566	6.99	0.29
3 persons,	73	519	7.11	0.42
4 persons,	67	513	7.66	0.52
5 persons,	49	399	8.14	0.61
6 persons,	30	260	8.67	0.69
7 persons,	26	236	9.08	0.77
8 persons,	10	102	10.20	0.78
9 persons,	10	87	8.70	1.03
10 persons,	2	19	9.50	1.05
11 persons,	2	20	10.00	1.10
13 persons,	1	7	7.00	1.86
14 persons,	1	20	20.00	0.70
Southborough,	442	3,363	7.47	0.67
1 person,	22	120	5.45	0.18
2 persons,	85	576	6.78	0.30
3 persons,	89	613	6.89	0.44
4 persons,	74	495	6.69	0.60
5 persons,	47	325	6.91	0.72
6 persons,	52	371	7.13	0.84
7 persons,	27	211	7.81	0.90
8 persons,	11	74	6.73	1.19
9 persons,	12	93	7.75	1.16
10 persons,	5	54	10.80	0.93
11 persons,	1	9	9.00	1.22
12 persons,	1	7	7.00	1.71
13 persons,	3	28	9.33	1.39
14 persons,	1	10	10.00	1.40
15 persons,	1	12	12.00	1.25
17 persons,	2	20	10.00	1.70

ROOMS: OCCUPIED DWELLING HOUSES — Continued.

Counties, Cities, Towns, and Number of Persons to a Family	Number of Families of Specified Size	Total Number of Rooms Occupied	Average Number of Rooms Occupied	Average Number of Persons to a Room
WORCESTER—Con.				
Southborough—Con.				
18 persons,	3	33	11.00	1.64
20 persons,	1	16	16.00	1.25
21 persons,	2	17	8.50	2.47
55 persons,	1	67	67.00	0.82
62 persons,	1	2	2.00	31.00
128 persons,	1	150	150.00	0.85
Southbridge,	1,688	10,975	6.32	0.77
1 person,	63	259	4.11	0.24
2 persons,	240	1,378	5.74	0.35
3 persons,	308	1,883	6.11	0.49
4 persons,	267	1,684	6.31	0.63
5 persons,	202	1,304	6.46	0.77
6 persons,	196	1,313	6.70	0.90
7 persons,	155	1,001	6.46	1.08
8 persons,	93	609	6.55	1.22
9 persons,	61	388	6.36	1.41
10 persons,	51	336	6.59	1.52
11 persons,	28	251	8.96	1.23
12 persons,	13	85	6.54	1.84
13 persons,	3	26	8.67	1.50
14 persons,	4	38	9.50	1.47
16 persons,	1	18	18.00	0.89
21 persons,	2	52	26.00	0.81
24 persons,	1	50	50.00	0.48
Spencer,	1,625	10,270	6.32	0.74
1 person,	55	249	4.53	0.22
2 persons,	246	1,395	5.67	0.35
3 persons,	328	2,011	6.13	0.49
4 persons,	271	1,791	6.62	0.60
5 persons,	217	1,371	6.32	0.79
6 persons,	164	1,067	6.51	0.92
7 persons,	126	772	6.13	1.14
8 persons,	86	559	6.50	1.23
9 persons,	61	402	6.59	1.37
10 persons,	37	263	7.11	1.41
11 persons,	11	69	6.27	1.75
12 persons,	13	101	7.77	1.54
13 persons,	3	19	6.33	2.05
14 persons,	3	45	15.00	0.93
15 persons,	1	4	4.00	3.75
19 persons,	1	19	19.00	1.00
20 persons,	1	30	30.00	0.67
29 persons,	1	100	100.00	0.29
Sterling,	342	2,647	7.74	0.46
1 person,	39	216	5.54	0.18
2 persons,	80	548	6.85	0.29
3 persons,	80	665	8.31	0.36
4 persons,	62	501	8.08	0.50
5 persons,	26	204	7.85	0.64
6 persons,	22	177	8.05	0.75
7 persons,	13	119	9.15	0.76
8 persons,	9	77	8.56	0.94
9 persons,	7	62	8.86	1.02
10 persons,	3	56	18.67	0.54
13 persons,	1	22	22.00	0.59
WORCESTER—Con.				
Sturbridge,	434	3,194	7.35	0.60
1 person,	26	176	6.77	0.15
2 persons,	86	608	7.07	0.28
3 persons,	81	589	7.27	0.41
4 persons,	69	538	7.80	0.51
5 persons,	56	422	7.54	0.66
6 persons,	27	194	7.19	0.84
7 persons,	30	223	7.43	0.94
8 persons,	21	167	7.95	1.01
9 persons,	21	156	7.43	1.21
10 persons,	8	53	6.63	1.51
11 persons,	6	46	7.67	1.43
12 persons,	2	8	4.00	3.00
14 persons,	1	11	11.00	1.27
Sutton,	714	5,149	7.21	0.66
1 person,	33	190	5.76	0.17
2 persons,	130	936	7.20	0.28
3 persons,	118	833	7.06	0.42
4 persons,	107	784	7.30	0.55
5 persons,	92	684	7.43	0.67
6 persons,	80	584	7.30	0.82
7 persons,	57	393	6.89	1.02
8 persons,	27	188	6.96	1.15
9 persons,	22	165	7.50	1.20
10 persons,	17	105	6.18	1.62
11 persons,	13	94	7.23	1.52
12 persons,	8	46	5.75	2.09
13 persons,	6	50	8.33	1.56
14 persons,	2	40	20.00	0.70
31 persons,	1	30	30.00	1.03
46 persons,	1	30	30.00	1.53
Templeton,	718	4,831	6.73	0.60
1 person,	39	190	4.87	0.21
2 persons,	172	1,081	6.28	0.32
3 persons,	169	1,079	6.38	0.47
4 persons,	126	848	6.73	0.59
5 persons,	87	596	6.85	0.73
6 persons,	48	350	7.29	0.82
7 persons,	26	185	7.12	0.98
8 persons,	20	135	6.75	1.19
9 persons,	13	106	8.15	1.10
10 persons,	7	46	6.57	1.52
11 persons,	3	34	11.33	0.97
12 persons,	1	11	11.00	1.09
13 persons,	1	7	7.00	1.86
14 persons,	1	16	16.00	0.88
15 persons,	2	30	15.00	1.00
18 persons,	1	23	23.00	0.78
20 persons,	1	40	40.00	0.50
129 persons,	1	54	54.00	2.39
Upton,	524	3,886	7.42	0.55
1 person,	46	208	4.52	0.22
2 persons,	120	775	6.46	0.31
3 persons,	124	899	7.25	0.41
4 persons,	90	688	7.64	0.52

ROOMS: OCCUPIED DWELLING HOUSES — Continued.

Counties, Cities, Towns, and Number of Persons to a Family.	Number of Families of Specified Size	Total Number of Rooms Occupied	Average Number of Rooms Occupied	Average Number of Persons to a Room
WORCESTER—Con.				
Upton—Con.				
5 persons,	62	482	7.77	0.64
6 persons,	37	280	7.57	0.79
7 persons,	18	147	8.17	0.86
8 persons,	9	96	10.67	0.75
9 persons,	9	99	11.00	0.82
10 persons,	1	9	9.00	1.11
11 persons,	1	9	9.00	1.22
14 persons,	1	11	11.00	1.27
18 persons,	1	12	12.00	1.50
20 persons,	1	21	21.00	0.95
25 persons,	1	31	31.00	0.81
28 persons,	1	16	16.00	1.75
31 persons,	1	28	28.00	1.11
164 persons,	1	75	75.00	2.19
Uxbridge,	*12	5,678	6.39	0.62
1 person,	37	216	5.84	0.17
2 persons,	162	1,016	6.27	0.32
3 persons,	138	908	6.58	0.46
4 persons,	154	1,110	7.21	0.55
5 persons,	108	777	7.19	0.69
6 persons,	79	548	6.94	0.86
7 persons,	44	311	7.07	0.99
8 persons,	46	361	7.85	1.02
9 persons,	20	178	8.90	1.01
10 persons,	11	109	9.91	1.01
11 persons,	4	38	9.50	1.16
12 persons,	4	36	9.00	1.33
13 persons,	1	7	7.00	1.86
14 persons,	2	26	13.00	1.08
21 persons,	2	37	18.50	1.14
Warren,	980	6,682	6.82	0.66
1 person,	30	140	4.67	0.21
2 persons,	152	951	6.26	0.32
3 persons,	213	1,394	6.54	0.46
4 persons,	180	1,260	7.00	0.57
5 persons,	132	880	6.67	0.75
6 persons,	102	724	7.10	0.85
7 persons,	66	466	7.06	0.99
8 persons,	41	287	7.00	1.14
9 persons,	37	259	7.00	1.29
10 persons,	10	81	8.10	1.23
11 persons,	5	40	8.00	1.38
12 persons,	6	39	6.50	1.85
13 persons,	1	12	12.00	1.08
14 persons,	1	26	26.00	0.54
16 persons,	1	29	29.00	0.55
21 persons,	1	16	16.00	1.31
22 persons,	1	50	50.00	0.44
29 persons,	1	28	28.00	1.04
Webster,	1,716	10,082	5.88	0.77
1 person,	90	429	4.77	0.21
2 persons,	256	1,431	5.59	0.36
3 persons,	345	1,996	5.79	0.52
4 persons,	307	1,872	6.10	0.66

Counties, Cities, Towns, and Number of Persons to a Family.	Number of Families of Specified Size	Total Number of Rooms Occupied	Average Number of Rooms Occupied	Average Number of Persons to a Room
WORCESTER—Con.				
Webster—Con.				
5 persons,	210	1,189	5.66	0.88
6 persons,	194	1,002	5.63	1.07
7 persons,	116	676	5.83	1.20
8 persons,	83	500	6.02	1.33
9 persons,	62	407	6.56	1.37
10 persons,	24	175	7.29	1.37
11 persons,	15	101	6.73	1.63
12 persons,	7	45	6.43	1.87
17 persons,	1	5	5.00	3.40
19 persons,	1	19	19.00	1.00
22 persons,	1	33	33.00	0.67
23 persons,	1	38	38.00	0.61
32 persons,	1	15	15.00	2.13
34 persons,	1	32	32.00	1.06
50 persons,	1	27	27.00	1.85
Westborough,	1,031	7,589	7.36	0.69
1 person,	63	302	4.79	0.21
2 persons,	198	1,190	6.06	0.33
3 persons,	230	1,531	6.66	0.45
4 persons,	185	1,335	7.22	0.55
5 persons,	145	1,057	7.29	0.69
6 persons,	78	584	7.49	0.80
7 persons,	65	482	7.42	0.94
8 persons,	25	194	7.76	1.03
9 persons,	20	186	9.30	0.97
10 persons,	10	87	8.70	1.15
11 persons,	2	13	6.50	1.69
12 persons,	1	7	7.00	1.71
13 persons,	1	39	39.00	0.33
14 persons,	2	23	11.50	1.22
15 persons,	2	40	20.00	0.95
25 persons,	1	50	50.00	0.50
27 persons,	1	24	24.00	1.13
301 persons,	1	136	136.00	2.21
752 persons,	1	300	300.00	2.51
West Boylston,	648	4,365	6.73	0.68
1 person,	37	179	4.84	0.21
2 persons,	107	678	6.34	0.32
3 persons,	119	814	6.84	0.44
4 persons,	106	753	7.10	0.56
5 persons,	84	570	6.79	0.74
6 persons,	74	442	6.23	0.96
7 persons,	51	389	7.63	0.92
8 persons,	31	194	6.26	1.28
9 persons,	17	104	6.12	1.47
10 persons,	7	74	10.57	0.95
11 persons,	7	49	7.00	1.57
12 persons,	6	45	7.50	1.60
13 persons,	2	10	5.00	2.60
14 persons,	1	13	13.00	1.08
18 persons,	1	9	9.00	2.00
55 persons,	1	40	40.00	1.38
West Brookfield,	409	2,369	7.19	0.69
1 person,	41	218	5.32	0.19

ROOMS: OCCUPIED DWELLING HOUSES — Continued.

COUNTIES, CITIES, TOWNS, AND NUMBER OF PERSONS TO A FAMILY.	Number of Families of Specified Size	Total Number of Rooms Occupied	Average Number of Rooms Occupied	Average Number of Persons to a Room
WORCESTER—Con.				
West Brookfield — Con.				
2 persons,	108	710	6.57	0.30
3 persons,	76	555	7.30	0.41
4 persons,	64	466	7.28	0.55
5 persons,	55	450	8.18	0.64
6 persons,	31	245	7.90	0.76
7 persons,	18	155	8.61	0.81
8 persons,	8	58	7.25	1.10
9 persons,	6	43	7.17	1.26
10 persons,	1	12	12.00	0.83
11 persons,	1	27	27.00	0.41
Westminster,	370	2,483	6.71	0.53
1 person,	30	137	4.57	0.22
2 persons,	107	658	6.15	0.33
3 persons,	73	470	6.44	0.47
4 persons,	69	492	7.13	0.56
5 persons,	38	296	7.79	0.64
6 persons,	21	190	9.05	0.66
7 persons,	15	115	7.67	0.91
8 persons,	8	57	7.13	1.12
9 persons,	4	31	7.75	1.16
10 persons,	2	15	7.50	1.33
11 persons,	2	16	8.00	1.38
13 persons,	1	6	6.00	2.17
Winchendon,	1,078	7,004	6.50	0.64
1 person,	60	261	4.35	0.23
2 persons,	215	1,353	6.29	0.32
3 persons,	242	1,560	6.45	0.47
4 persons,	185	1,159	6.26	0.64
5 persons,	129	845	6.55	0.76
6 persons,	99	683	6.90	0.87
7 persons,	57	407	7.14	0.98
8 persons,	45	340	7.56	1.06
9 persons,	15	105	7.00	1.29
10 persons,	12	70	5.83	1.71
11 persons,	5	32	6.40	1.72
12 persons,	2	14	7.00	1.71
13 persons,	5	25	5.00	2.60
14 persons,	2	11	5.50	2.55
17 persons,	1	28	28.00	0.61
19 persons,	1	20	20.00	0.95
23 persons,	2	41	20.50	1.12
27 persons,	1	50	50.00	0.54
WORCESTER,	20,861	128,451	6.16	0.77
1 person,	585	2,237	3.82	0.26
2 persons,	3,255	17,019	5.23	0.38
3 persons,	3,945	22,463	5.69	0.53
4 persons,	3,966	23,601	5.95	0.67
5 persons,	3,164	19,321	6.11	0.82
6 persons,	2,170	13,784	6.35	0.94
7 persons,	1,570	10,178	6.48	1.08
8 persons,	955	6,352	6.65	1.20
9 persons,	573	3,981	6.95	1.30
10 persons,	259	1,908	7.37	1.36
11 persons,	160	1,234	7.71	1.43
WORCESTER—Con.				
WORCESTER—Con.				
12 persons,	92	839	9.12	1.32
13 persons,	34	357	10.50	1.24
14 persons,	24	338	14.08	0.99
15 persons,	22	359	16.32	0.92
16 persons,	16	180	18.00	0.83
17 persons,	9	141	15.67	1.09
18 persons,	7	158	22.57	0.80
19 persons,	5	75	15.00	1.27
20 persons,	3	61	20.33	0.98
21 persons,	2	25	12.50	1.68
22 persons,	3	81	27.00	0.81
23 persons,	4	180	45.00	0.51
24 persons,	8	302	37.75	0.64
25 persons,	4	151	37.75	0.66
27 persons,	1	40	40.00	0.68
28 persons,	2	72	36.00	0.78
29 persons,	1	18	18.00	1.61
31 persons,	2	111	55.50	0.56
32 persons,	2	68	34.00	0.94
35 persons,	1	33	33.00	1.06
37 persons,	2	141	70.50	0.52
38 persons,	1	60	60.00	0.63
40 persons,	2	91	45.50	0.88
41 persons,	1	42	42.00	0.98
44 persons,	1	13	13.00	3.38
46 persons,	1	60	60.00	0.77
49 persons,	1	14	14.00	3.50
53 persons,	1	54	54.00	0.98
62 persons,	1	46	46.00	1.37
64 persons,	1	43	43.00	1.49
66 persons,	1	134	134.00	0.49
69 persons,	1	66	66.00	1.05
99 persons,	1	47	47.00	2.11
113 persons,	1	108	108.00	1.05
150 persons,	1	173	173.00	0.87
172 persons,	1	51	51.00	3.37
188 persons,	1	380	380.00	0.49
205 persons,	1	100	100.00	2.05
227 persons,	1	149	149.00	1.52
529 persons,	1	324	324.00	1.63
1,055 persons,	1	688	688.00	1.53
Worcester, Ward 1,	2,417	15,528	6.42	0.71
1 person,	87	285	3.28	0.31
2 persons,	400	2,081	5.20	0.38
3 persons,	483	2,808	5.81	0.52
4 persons,	424	2,662	6.28	0.64
5 persons,	396	2,425	6.63	0.75
6 persons,	232	1,580	6.85	0.88
7 persons,	174	1,235	7.10	0.99
8 persons,	89	607	6.82	1.17
9 persons,	67	521	7.78	1.16
10 persons,	32	271	8.47	1.18
11 persons,	21	188	8.95	1.26
12 persons,	9	84	9.33	1.29

ROOMS: OCCUPIED DWELLING HOUSES — Continued.

COUNTIES, CITIES, TOWNS, AND NUMBER OF PERSONS TO A FAMILY.	Number of Families of Specified Size	Total Number of Rooms Occupied	Average Number of Rooms Occupied	Average Number of Persons to a Room	COUNTIES, CITIES, TOWNS, AND NUMBER OF PERSONS TO A FAMILY.	Number of Families of Specified Size	Total Number of Rooms Occupied	Average Number of Rooms Occupied	Average Number of Persons to a Room
WORCESTER—Con.					WORCESTER—Con.				
Worcester, Ward 1 —Con.					*Worcester, Ward 3 —Con.*				
13 persons, . .	6	81	13.50	0.96	18 persons, . .	3	80	26.67	0.08
14 persons, . .	5	103	20.60	0.68	19 persons, . .	2	26	13.00	1.46
15 persons, . .	5	73	14.60	1.03	20 persons, . .	1	15	15.00	1.33
16 persons, . .	1	21	21.00	0.76	21 persons, . .	1	16	16.00	1.31
17 persons, . .	3	53	17.67	0.96	23 persons, . .	1	100	100.00	0.23
18 persons, . .	3	60	20.00	0.90	24 persons, . .	3	110	36.67	0.65
19 persons, . .	2	34	17.00	1.12	27 persons, . .	1	40	40.00	0.68
20 persons, . .	1	32	32.00	0.63	32 persons, . .	1	50	50.00	0.64
21 persons, . .	1	9	9.00	2.33	35 persons, . .	1	33	33.00	1.06
22 persons, . .	1	23	23.00	0.96	37 persons, . .	1	100	100.00	0.37
25 persons, . .	2	50	25.00	0.92	41 persons, . .	1	42	42.00	0.98
28 persons, . .	1	32	32.00	0.88	49 persons, . .	1	14	14.00	3.50
26 persons, . .	1	134	134.00	0.49	188 persons, . .	1	380	380.00	0.49
32 persons, . .	1	65	65.00	1.05	520 persons, . .	1	324	324.00	1.65
Worcester, Ward 2,	2,653	17,208	6.49	0.76	*Worcester, Ward 4,*	2,712	14,814	5.40	0.91
1 person, . .	58	291	5.02	0.20	1 person, . .	47	183	3.89	0.26
2 persons, . .	414	2,286	5.52	0.36	2 persons, . .	340	1,665	4.90	0.41
3 persons, . .	546	3,160	5.79	0.52	3 persons, . .	476	2,442	5.13	0.58
4 persons, . .	537	3,218	5.99	0.67	4 persons, . .	517	2,682	5.19	0.77
5 persons, . .	402	2,537	6.31	0.79	5 persons, . .	449	2,392	5.33	0.94
6 persons, . .	293	1,891	6.45	0.93	6 persons, . .	328	1,787	5.45	1.10
7 persons, . .	180	1,204	6.69	1.05	7 persons, . .	202	1,429	5.45	1.28
8 persons, . .	106	806	7.60	1.05	8 persons, . .	164	967	5.90	1.36
9 persons, . .	61	440	7.21	1.25	9 persons, . .	81	488	6.02	1.49
10 persons, . .	23	160	6.96	1.44	10 persons, . .	38	235	6.18	1.62
11 persons, . .	16	147	9.19	1.20	11 persons, . .	18	118	6.56	1.68
12 persons, . .	6	66	11.00	1.09	12 persons, . .	12	87	7.25	1.66
13 persons, . .	2	12	6.00	2.17	13 persons, . .	4	28	7.00	1.86
14 persons, . .	2	18	9.00	1.56	14 persons, . .	1	20	20.00	0.70
15 persons, . .	1	9	9.00	1.67	19 persons, . .	1	15	15.00	1.27
17 persons, . .	1	11	11.00	1.55	20 persons, . .	1	14	14.00	1.43
29 persons, . .	1	18	18.00	1.61	31 persons, . .	1	38	38.00	0.82
53 persons, . .	1	54	54.00	0.98	150 persons, . .	1	173	173.00	0.87
64 persons, . .	1	43	43.00	1.49	172 persons, . .	1	51	51.00	3.37
227 persons, . .	1	149	149.00	1.52	*Worcester, Ward 5,*	3,028	15,901	5.25	0.96
1,055 persons, . .	1	688	688.00	1.53	1 person, . .	67	243	3.63	0.28
Worcester, Ward 3,	2,825	16,427	5.81	0.89	2 persons, . .	372	1,680	4.51	0.44
1 person, . .	103	356	3.46	0.29	3 persons, . .	458	2,180	4.76	0.63
2 persons, . .	405	1,869	4.61	0.43	4 persons, . .	561	2,846	5.07	0.79
3 persons, . .	440	2,279	5.18	0.58	5 persons, . .	511	2,585	5.06	0.99
4 persons, . .	489	2,611	5.34	0.75	6 persons, . .	349	1,886	5.40	1.11
5 persons, . .	426	2,256	5.30	0.94	7 persons, . .	277	1,487	5.37	1.30
6 persons, . .	326	1,779	5.46	1.10	8 persons, . .	190	1,117	5.88	1.36
7 persons, . .	247	1,426	5.77	1.21	9 persons, . .	127	772	6.08	1.48
8 persons, . .	149	834	5.60	1.43	10 persons, . .	44	323	7.34	1.36
9 persons, . .	100	633	6.33	1.42	11 persons, . .	28	170	6.07	1.81
10 persons, . .	45	288	6.40	1.56	12 persons, . .	18	126	7.00	1.71
11 persons, . .	38	279	7.34	1.50	13 persons, . .	7	53	7.57	1.72
12 persons, . .	20	191	9.55	1.26	14 persons, . .	4	40	10.00	1.40
13 persons, . .	3	18	6.00	2.17	15 persons, . .	5	83	16.60	0.90
14 persons, . .	1	58	14.50	0.97	16 persons, . .	2	23	11.50	1.39
15 persons, . .	6	130	21.67	0.69	18 persons, . .	1	18	18.00	1.00
16 persons, . .	3	67	22.33	0.72	22 persons, . .	1	18	18.00	1.22
17 persons, . .	2	23	11.50	1.48	24 persons, . .	2	54	27.00	0.89

ROOMS: OCCUPIED DWELLING HOUSES — Continued.

COUNTIES, CITIES, TOWNS, AND NUMBER OF PERSONS TO A FAMILY.	Number of Families of Specified Size	Total Number of Rooms Occupied	Average Number of Rooms Occupied	Average Number of Persons to a Room
WORCESTER-Con.				
Worcester. Ward 5 — Con.				
25 persons, . .	2	74	37.00	0.68
44 persons, . .	1	13	13.00	3.38
205 persons, . .	1	100	100.00	2.05
Worcester. Ward 6,	2,591	16,919	6.53	0.70
1 person, . .	59	265	4.49	0.22
2 persons, . .	415	2,397	5.78	0.35
3 persons, . .	502	3,111	6.20	0.48
4 persons, . .	507	3,309	6.53	0.61
5 persons, . .	363	2,452	6.75	0.74
6 persons, . .	277	1,926	6.95	0.86
7 persons, . .	199	1,403	7.05	0.99
8 persons, . .	122	848	6.95	1.15
9 persons, . .	59	411	6.97	1.29
10 persons, . .	39	275	7.05	1.42
11 persons, . .	21	171	8.14	1.35
12 persons, . .	15	121	8.07	1.49
13 persons, . .	4	40	10.00	1.30
14 persons, . .	3	28	9.33	1.50
15 persons, . .	1	12	12.00	1.25
16 persons, . .	1	16	16.00	1.00
17 persons, . .	1	16	16.00	1.06
22 persons, . .	1	40	40.00	0.55
32 persons, . .	1	18	18.00	1.78
58 persons, . .	1	60	60.00	0.43
Worcester. Ward 7,	2,452	15,770	6.43	0.96
1 person, . .	80	274	3.43	0.29
2 persons, . .	485	2,607	5.38	0.37
3 persons, . .	520	3,124	6.01	0.50
4 persons, . .	501	3,172	6.33	0.63
5 persons, . .	359	2,439	6.79	0.74
6 persons, . .	202	1,446	7.16	0.84
7 persons, . .	137	1,100	8.03	0.87
8 persons, . .	75	605	8.07	0.99
9 persons, . .	47	387	8.23	1.09
10 persons, . .	20	160	8.00	1.25
11 persons, . .	10	72	7.20	1.53

COUNTIES, CITIES, TOWNS, AND NUMBER OF PERSONS TO A FAMILY.	Number of Families of Specified Size	Total Number of Rooms Occupied	Average Number of Rooms Occupied	Average Number of Persons to a Room
WORCESTER-Con.				
Worcester. Ward 7 — Con.				
12 persons, . .	3	31	10.33	1.16
13 persons, . .	4	54	13.50	0.96
15 persons, . .	3	36	12.00	1.25
16 persons, . .	1	16	16.00	1.00
17 persons, . .	1	22	22.00	0.77
24 persons, . .	1	29	29.00	0.83
37 persons, . .	1	41	41.00	0.90
39 persons, . .	1	47	47.00	2.31
113 persons, . .	1	108	108.00	1.05
Worcester. Ward 8,	2,133	15,884	7.38	0.57
1 person, . .	84	340	4.05	0.25
2 persons, . .	424	2,424	5.72	0.35
3 persons, . .	520	3,359	6.46	0.46
4 persons, . .	430	3,101	7.21	0.55
5 persons, . .	288	2,235	7.76	0.64
6 persons, . .	163	1,479	9.07	0.96
7 persons, . .	94	894	9.51	0.74
8 persons, . .	60	568	9.47	0.85
9 persons, . .	31	329	10.61	0.85
10 persons, . .	18	196	10.89	0.92
11 persons, . .	8	89	11.13	0.96
12 persons, . .	9	133	14.78	0.81
13 persons, . .	4	71	17.75	0.73
14 persons, . .	5	71	14.20	0.99
15 persons, . .	1	16	16.00	0.94
16 persons, . .	2	37	18.50	0.96
17 persons, . .	1	16	16.00	1.06
23 persons, . .	1	30	30.00	0.77
24 persons, . .	2	109	54.50	0.44
25 persons, . .	2	77	38.50	0.65
28 persons, . .	1	40	40.00	0.70
31 persons, . .	1	73	73.00	0.42
40 persons, . .	2	91	45.50	0.88
46 persons, . .	1	60	60.00	0.77
63 persons, . .	1	46	46.00	1.37

ROOMS: OCCUPIED DWELLING HOUSES — Continued.

RECAPITULATION.

The State, and Number of Persons to a Family.	Number of Families of Specified Size	Total Number of Rooms Occupied	Average Number of Rooms Occupied	Average Number of Persons to a Room	The State, and Number of Persons to a Family.	Number of Families of Specified Size	Total Number of Rooms Occupied	Average Number of Rooms Occupied	Average Number of Persons to a Room
THE STATE, .	547,385	3,568,385	6.52	0.70	THE STATE—Con.				
1 person, .	21,836	95,391	4.37	0.23	55 persons, .	4	186	46.50	1.18
2 persons, .	91,786	514,059	5.60	0.36	56 persons, .	3	118	39.33	1.42
3 persons, .	106,436	647,758	6.09	0.49	57 persons, .	10	407	40.70	1.40
4 persons, .	99,152	632,775	6.38	0.63	58 persons, .	2	127	63.50	0.91
5 persons, .	78,156	519,147	6.64	0.75	59 persons, .	7	628	89.71	0.66
6 persons, .	56,460	385,414	6.86	0.87	60 persons, .	3	158	52.67	1.14
7 persons, .	37,173	261,602	7.04	0.99	61 persons, .	1	61	61.00	1.00
8 persons, .	23,202	169,286	7.30	1.10	62 persons, .	4	88	22.00	2.82
9 persons, .	13,771	104,682	7.60	1.18	63 persons, .	3	156	52.00	1.21
10 persons, .	7,896	63,473	8.10	1.23	64 persons, .	4	235	58.75	1.09
11 persons, .	4,352	37,769	8.68	1.27	65 persons, .	1	15	15.00	4.33
12 persons, .	2,281	21,927	9.61	1.25	66 persons, .	6	359	59.83	1.10
13 persons, .	1,399	15,421	11.02	1.18	67 persons, .	1	85	85.00	0.79
14 persons, .	877	10,871	12.40	1.13	68 persons, .	3	235	78.33	0.87
15 persons, .	547	7,280	13.31	1.13	69 persons, .	5	247	49.40	1.40
16 persons, .	384	5,754	15.10	1.06	70 persons, .	4	163	40.75	1.72
17 persons, .	285	4,392	15.41	1.10	71 persons, .	4	179	44.75	1.59
18 persons, .	224	3,811	17.01	1.06	72 persons, .	6	870	145.00	0.50
19 persons, .	163	3,088	18.94	1.00	74 persons, .	2	309	154.50	0.48
20 persons, .	156	3,143	20.15	0.99	75 persons, .	5	384	76.80	0.98
21 persons, .	115	2,192	19.06	1.10	76 persons, .	1	300	300.00	0.25
22 persons, .	101	2,471	24.47	0.90	77 persons, .	3	101	33.67	2.29
23 persons, .	63	1,618	25.68	0.90	78 persons, .	6	269	44.83	1.74
24 persons, .	76	2,161	28.43	0.84	79 persons, .	2	134	67.00	1.18
25 persons, .	65	1,463	22.51	1.11	80 persons, .	6	308	51.33	1.56
26 persons, .	39	930	23.85	1.09	81 persons, .	1	50	50.00	1.62
27 persons, .	44	1,397	31.75	0.85	82 persons, .	5	322	64.40	1.27
28 persons, .	38	1,273	33.50	0.84	84 persons, .	2	120	60.00	1.40
29 persons, .	44	1,477	33.57	0.86	85 persons, .	3	200	66.67	1.28
30 persons, .	28	948	33.86	0.89	86 persons, .	2	280	140.00	0.61
31 persons, .	27	1,284	47.56	0.65	87 persons, .	2	266	133.00	0.65
32 persons, .	23	744	32.35	0.99	88 persons, .	2	124	62.00	1.42
33 persons, .	23	837	36.39	0.91	89 persons, .	2	350	175.00	0.51
34 persons, .	26	980	37.69	0.90	91 persons, .	3	126	42.00	2.17
35 persons, .	28	937	33.46	1.05	93 persons, .	2	127	63.50	1.46
36 persons, .	19	692	36.42	0.99	94 persons, .	1	99	99.00	0.95
37 persons, .	25	1,084	43.36	0.85	96 persons, .	4	500	125.00	0.77
38 persons, .	19	649	34.16	1.11	97 persons, .	1	120	120.00	0.81
39 persons, .	16	1,012	63.25	0.62	98 persons, .	1	90	90.00	1.03
40 persons, .	16	577	36.06	1.11	99 persons, .	6	343	57.17	1.73
41 persons, .	13	424	32.62	1.26	100 persons, .	1	15	15.00	6.67
42 persons, .	11	334	30.36	1.38	101 persons, .	1	60	60.00	1.68
43 persons, .	17	700	41.18	1.04	103 persons, .	1	10	10.00	10.30
44 persons, .	12	390	32.50	1.35	105 persons, .	1	21	21.00	5.00
45 persons, .	10	536	53.60	0.84	107 persons, .	2	116	58.00	1.84
46 persons, .	10	289	28.90	1.59	109 persons, .	3	151	50.33	2.17
47 persons, .	13	594	45.69	1.03	111 persons, .	2	328	164.00	0.68
48 persons, .	8	291	36.38	1.32	112 persons, .	2	364	182.00	0.62
49 persons, .	9	292	32.44	1.51	113 persons, .	3	321	107.00	1.06
50 persons, .	13	545	41.92	1.19	114 persons, .	2	351	175.50	0.65
51 persons, .	6	292	48.67	1.05	116 persons, .	2	518	259.00	0.45
52 persons, .	4	247	61.75	0.84	118 persons, .	3	552	184.00	0.64
53 persons, .	9	353	39.22	1.35	119 persons, .	2	181	90.50	1.31
54 persons, .	4	173	43.25	1.25	120 persons, .	1	88	88.00	1.36

ROOMS: OCCUPIED DWELLING HOUSES — Concluded.

RECAPITULATION — Concluded.

THE STATE, AND NUMBER OF PERSONS TO A FAMILY.	Number of Families of Specified Size	Total Number of Rooms Occupied	Average Number of Rooms Occupied	Average Number of Persons to a Room	THE STATE, AND NUMBER OF PERSONS TO A FAMILY.	Number of Families of Specified Size	Total Number of Rooms Occupied	Average Number of Rooms Occupied	Average Number of Persons to a Room
THE STATE-Con.					THE STATE-Con.				
121 persons, . .	1	410	410.00	0.30	220 persons, . .	1	150	150.00	1.47
122 persons, . .	1	42	42.00	2.90	221 persons, . .	1	235	235.00	0.94
124 persons, . .	3	562	187.33	0.66	227 persons, . .	1	149	149.00	1.52
128 persons, . .	1	150	150.00	0.85	255 persons, . .	1	103	103.00	2.48
129 persons, . .	2	189	94.50	1.37	259 persons, . .	1	287	287.00	0.90
132 persons, . .	1	156	156.00	0.85	261 persons, . .	1	135	135.00	1.93
134 persons, . .	3	186	62.00	2.16	268 persons, . .	1	234	234.00	1.15
135 persons, . .	1	131	131.00	1.03	274 persons, . .	1	57	57.00	4.81
139 persons, . .	1	65	65.00	2.69	276 persons, . .	1	23	23.00	12.00
157 persons, . .	1	137	137.00	1.00	299 persons, . .	1	135	135.00	2.21
140 persons, . .	2	253	126.50	1.11	301 persons, . .	1	136	136.00	2.21
141 persons, . .	1	65	65.00	2.17	308 persons, . .	1	182	182.00	1.69
144 persons, . .	1	66	66.00	2.18	323 persons, . .	1	284	284.00	1.14
145 persons, . .	2	45	22.50	6.44	324 persons, . .	1	382	382.00	0.85
147 persons, . .	1	121	121.00	1.21	326 persons, . .	1	43	43.00	7.58
150 persons, . .	1	173	173.00	0.87	342 persons, . .	1	221	221.00	1.55
156 persons, . .	1	156	156.00	1.00	352 persons, . .	1	400	400.00	0.88
158 persons, . .	1	50	50.00	3.16	397 persons, . .	1	100	100.00	3.97
160 persons, . .	1	160	160.00	1.00	399 persons, . .	1	153	153.00	2.61
162 persons, . .	1	3	3.00	54.00	412 persons, . .	1	75	75.00	5.49
164 persons, . .	1	75	75.00	2.19	529 persons, . .	1	324	324.00	1.63
168 persons, . .	1	96	96.00	1.75	564 persons, . .	1	468	468.00	1.21
169 persons, . .	1	130	130.00	1.30	599 persons, . .	1	599	599.00	1.00
170 persons, . .	1	23	23.00	7.39	608 persons, . .	1	295	295.00	2.06
171 persons, . .	1	86	86.00	1.99	680 persons, . .	1	550	550.00	1.24
172 persons, . .	1	51	51.00	3.37	691 persons, . .	1	276	276.00	2.50
183 persons, . .	2	282	141.00	1.30	741 persons, . .	1	882	882.00	0.84
188 persons, . .	1	380	380.00	0.49	752 persons, . .	1	300	300.00	2.51
196 persons, . .	1	162	162.00	1.19	957 persons, . .	1	684	684.00	1.40
194 persons, . .	1	130	130.00	1.49	1,015 persons, . .	1	588	588.00	1.73
198 persons, . .	1	25	25.00	7.92	1,032 persons, . .	1	1,035	1,035.00	1.00
200 persons, . .	1	271	271.00	0.74	1,055 persons, . .	1	688	688.00	1.53
205 persons, . .	1	100	100.00	2.05	1,087 persons, . .	1	558	558.00	1.95
212 persons, . .	1	14	14.00	15.14	1,166 persons, . .	1	1,166	1,166.00	1.00
214 persons, . .	1	30	30.00	7.13	1,596 persons, . .	1	1,596	1,596.00	1.00
216 persons, . .	1	393	393.00	0.55					

ROOMS: OCCUPIED AND UNOCCUPIED DWELLING HOUSES.

OCCUPIED AND UNOCCUPIED ROOMS IN OCCUPIED AND UNOCCUPIED DWELLING HOUSES.

COUNTIES, CITIES, AND TOWNS.	OCCUPIED DWELLING HOUSES			Rooms in Unoccupied Dwelling Houses	TOTAL NUMBER OF ROOMS		
	Occupied Rooms	Unoccupied Rooms	Total		Occupied	Unoccupied	Occupied and Unoccupied
BARNSTABLE.	55,856	829	56,685	12,254	55,856	13,083	68,939
Barnstable, ...	8,557	74	8,631	1,479	8,557	1,553	10,110
Bourne, ...	3,094	32	3,126	1,493	3,094	1,525	4,619
Brewster, ...	1,827	9	1,855	434	1,827	443	2,270
Chatham, ...	4,553	103	4,656	1,143	4,553	1,246	5,799
Dennis, ...	4,222	39	4,261	656	4,222	695	4,917
Eastham, ...	988	13	1,001	184	988	197	1,185
Falmouth, ...	5,576	42	5,618	2,473	5,576	2,515	8,091
Harwich, ...	4,829	7	4,836	629	4,829	636	5,465
Mashpee, ...	388	-	388	42	388	42	430
Orleans, ...	2,820	100	2,920	626	2,820	726	3,546
Provincetown, ...	7,650	261	7,911	295	7,650	556	8,206
Sandwich, ...	3,235	112	3,347	581	3,235	693	3,928
Truro, ...	1,714	-	1,714	416	1,714	416	2,130
Wellfleet, ...	2,341	23	2,364	952	2,341	975	3,316
Yarmouth, ...	4,062	14	4,076	851	4,062	865	4,927
BERKSHIRE.	134,864	2,051	136,915	10,728	134,864	12,779	147,643
Adams, ...	10,177	408	10,585	570	10,177	978	11,155
Alford, ...	639	45	684	95	639	140	779
Becket, ...	1,616	16	1,632	238	1,616	254	1,870
Cheshire, ...	2,705	51	2,756	370	2,705	421	3,126
Clarksburg, ...	1,500	20	1,520	24	1,500	44	1,544
Dalton, ...	4,818	137	4,955	189	4,818	326	5,144
Egremont, ...	1,631	3	1,634	130	1,631	133	1,764
Florida, ...	650	4	654	106	650	110	760
Great Barrington, . . .	8,332	70	8,402	636	8,332	706	9,038
Hancock, ...	1,013	-	1,013	96	1,013	96	1,109
Hinsdale, ...	2,434	-	2,434	100	2,434	100	2,534
Lanesborough, ...	1,630	8	1,638	201	1,630	209	1,839
Lee, ...	6,732	80	6,812	352	6,732	432	7,164
Lenox, ...	4,442	44	4,486	1,096	4,442	1,140	5,582
Monterey, ...	1,021	6	1,027	167	1,021	173	1,194
Mount Washington, . . .	355	11	366	57	355	68	423
New Ashford, ...	263	-	263	49	263	49	312
New Marlborough, . . .	2,858	33	2,891	221	2,858	254	3,112
NORTH ADAMS, ...	25,393	443	25,836	951	25,393	1,394	26,787
Otis, ...	1,053	10	1,063	187	1,053	197	1,250
Peru, ...	569	-	569	88	569	88	657
PITTSFIELD, ...	30,994	423	31,417	1,627	30,994	2,050	35,044
Ward 1, ...	3,574	37	3,611	176	3,574	213	3,787
Ward 2, ...	5,215	111	5,326	180	5,215	291	5,506
Ward 3, ...	4,072	22	4,094	243	4,072	265	4,337
Ward 4, ...	5,027	58	5,085	334	5,027	392	5,419
Ward 5, ...	3,969	79	4,048	345	3,969	424	4,393
Ward 6, ...	5,057	76	5,133	171	5,057	247	5,304
Ward 7, ...	4,080	40	4,120	178	4,080	218	4,298

OCCUPIED AND UNOCCUPIED ROOMS IN OCCUPIED AND UNOCCUPIED DWELLING HOUSES — Continued.

COUNTIES, CITIES, AND TOWNS.	OCCUPIED DWELLING HOUSES			Rooms in Unoccupied Dwelling Houses	TOTAL NUMBER OF ROOMS		
	Occupied Rooms	Un-occupied Rooms	Total		Occupied	Unoccupied	Occupied and Unoccupied
BERKSHIRE — Con.							
Richmond,	1,377	19	1,396	163	1,377	182	1,559
Sandisfield,	1,794	20	1,814	422	1,794	442	2,236
Savoy,	977	-	977	63	977	63	1,040
Sheffield,	3,725	33	3,758	245	3,725	278	4,003
Stockbridge,	3,779	48	3,827	1,152	3,779	1,200	4,979
Tyringham,	802	26	828	172	802	198	1,000
Washington,	712	-	712	168	712	168	880
West Stockbridge,	2,319	39	2,358	210	2,319	249	2,568
Williamstown,	7,535	54	7,589	456	7,535	510	8,045
Windsor,	1,019	-	1,019	127	1,019	127	1,146
BRISTOL.	301,831	12,583	314,414	12,927	301,831	25,510	327,341
Acushnet,	2,282	28	2,310	161	2,282	189	2,471
Attleborough,	12,623	287	12,910	350	12,623	637	13,260
Berkley,	1,913	11	1,924	103	1,913	114	2,027
Dartmouth,	6,187	141	6,328	1,780	6,187	1,921	8,108
Dighton,	3,254	181	3,435	245	3,254	426	3,680
Easton,	7,145	86	7,231	557	7,145	643	7,788
Fairhaven,	6,468	67	6,535	503	6,468	570	7,038
FALL RIVER,	100,713	5,405	106,118	2,700	100,713	8,105	108,818
Ward 1,	13,322	982	14,304	239	13,322	1,221	14,543
Ward 2,	9,462	488	9,950	519	9,462	1,007	10,469
Ward 3,	10,249	283	10,532	184	10,249	467	10,716
Ward 4,	13,396	686	14,082	160	13,396	846	14,242
Ward 5,	9,771	599	10,370	292	9,771	891	10,662
Ward 6,	11,432	930	12,362	455	11,432	1,385	12,817
Ward 7,	9,733	326	10,059	193	9,733	519	10,252
Ward 8,	11,369	298	11,667	372	11,369	670	12,039
Ward 9,	11,979	813	12,792	296	11,979	1,099	13,078
Freetown,	2,123	43	2,166	357	2,123	380	2,503
Mansfield,	6,790	172	6,962	241	6,790	413	7,203
NEW BEDFORD,	75,827	2,890	78,717	2,069	75,827	4,959	80,786
Ward 1,	14,064	685	14,749	489	14,064	1,174	15,238
Ward 2,	11,209	334	11,543	300	11,209	634	11,843
Ward 3,	10,431	343	10,774	250	10,431	593	11,024
Ward 4,	11,745	383	12,128	263	11,745	646	12,391
Ward 5,	14,170	434	14,604	357	14,170	791	14,961
Ward 6,	14,208	711	14,919	410	14,208	1,121	15,329
North Attleborough,	10,357	476	10,833	614	10,357	1,090	11,447
Norton,	3,080	76	3,156	367	3,080	443	3,523
Raynham,	3,557	76	3,633	129	3,557	205	3,762
Rehoboth,	3,352	73	3,425	86	3,352	159	3,511
Seekonk,	2,428	72	2,500	90	2,428	162	2,590
Somerset,	3,865	254	4,119	250	3,865	504	4,369
Swansea,	3,214	31	3,245	48	3,214	79	3,293
TAUNTON,	41,645	2,044	43,689	1,497	41,645	3,541	45,186
Ward 1,	4,963	132	5,095	145	4,963	277	5,240
Ward 2,	5,453	321	5,774	172	5,453	493	5,946
Ward 3,	4,730	388	5,118	97	4,730	485	5,215
Ward 4,	5,782	256	6,038	450	5,782	706	6,488
Ward 5,	5,217	326	5,543	176	5,217	502	5,719
Ward 6,	4,858	143	5,001	84	4,858	227	5,085
Ward 7,	4,478	320	4,798	162	4,478	482	4,960
Ward 8,	6,164	158	6,322	211	6,164	369	6,533
Westport,	5,008	170	5,178	800	5,008	970	5,978

OCCUPIED AND UNOCCUPIED ROOMS IN OCCUPIED AND UNOCCUPIED DWELLING HOUSES — Continued.

COUNTIES, CITIES, AND TOWNS.	OCCUPIED DWELLING HOUSES			Rooms in Unoccupied Dwelling Houses	TOTAL NUMBER OF ROOMS		
	Occupied Rooms	Unoccupied Rooms	Total		Occupied	Unoccupied	Occupied and Unoccupied
DUKES.	9,875	393	10,268	7,784	9,875	8,177	18,052
Chilmark, ...	751	–	751	460	751	460	1,211
Cottage City, ...	2,279	105	2,384	5,521	2,279	5,626	7,905
Edgartown, ...	2,932	109	3,041	558	2,932	667	3,599
Gay Head, ...	215	–	215	12	215	12	227
Gosnold, ...	279	69	348	163	279	232	511
Tisbury, ...	2,236	92	2,328	782	2,236	874	3,110
West Tisbury, ...	1,183	18	1,201	288	1,183	306	1,489
ESSEX.	478,804	14,511	493,315	34,312	478,804	48,823	527,627
Amesbury, ...	15,365	502	15,867	610	15,365	1,112	16,477
Andover, ...	10,039	170	10,209	469	10,039	639	10,678
BEVERLY, ...	18,811	738	19,549	2,288	18,811	3,026	21,837
Ward 1, ...	4,014	40	4,054	99	4,014	139	4,153
Ward 2, ...	4,170	182	4,352	312	4,170	494	4,664
Ward 3, ...	3,805	138	3,943	122	3,805	260	4,065
Ward 4, ...	3,224	117	3,341	900	3,224	1,017	4,241
Ward 5, ...	2,055	36	2,091	855	2,055	891	2,946
Ward 6, ...	1,543	225	1,768	–	1,543	225	1,768
Boxford, ...	1,543	20	1,563	196	1,543	216	1,759
Bradford, ...	8,067	334	8,401	426	8,067	760	8,827
Danvers, ...	12,275	262	12,537	533	12,275	795	13,070
Essex, ...	2,858	88	2,946	445	2,858	533	3,391
Georgetown, ...	3,973	79	4,052	117	3,973	196	4,169
GLOUCESTER, ...	32,156	540	32,696	4,430	32,156	4,970	37,126
Ward 1, ...	4,140	60	4,200	1,008	4,140	1,068	5,208
Ward 2, ...	4,900	110	5,010	218	4,900	328	5,228
Ward 3, ...	4,738	111	4,849	69	4,738	180	4,918
Ward 4, ...	3,541	70	3,611	54	3,541	124	3,665
Ward 5, ...	5,844	75	5,919	231	5,844	306	6,150
Ward 6, ...	4,048	54	4,102	912	4,048	966	5,014
Ward 7, ...	3,023	26	3,049	39	3,023	65	3,088
Ward 8, ...	1,922	34	1,956	1,899	1,922	1,933	3,855
Groveland, ...	3,631	18	3,649	72	3,631	90	3,721
Hamilton, ...	2,411	–	2,411	1,722	2,411	1,722	4,133
HAVERHILL, ...	46,515	1,850	48,365	2,041	46,515	3,891	50,406
Ward 1, ...	4,581	210	4,791	282	4,581	492	5,073
Ward 2, ...	4,888	198	5,086	244	4,888	442	5,330
Ward 3, ...	5,151	168	5,319	121	5,151	289	5,440
Ward 4, ...	6,686	269	6,955	369	6,686	638	7,324
Ward 5, ...	15,035	687	15,722	564	15,035	1,251	16,286
Ward 6, ...	10,174	318	10,492	461	10,174	779	10,953
Ipswich, ...	7,945	54	7,999	509	7,945	563	8,508
LAWRENCE, ...	62,591	1,132	63,723	1,140	62,591	2,272	64,863
Ward 1, ...	10,060	248	10,308	129	10,060	377	10,437
Ward 2, ...	8,651	165	8,816	274	8,651	439	9,090
Ward 3, ...	10,069	121	10,190	24	10,069	145	10,214
Ward 4, ...	11,264	187	11,451	166	11,264	353	11,617
Ward 5, ...	12,667	215	12,882	179	12,667	394	13,061
Ward 6, ...	9,880	196	10,076	368	9,880	564	10,444
LYNN, ...	89,835	3,842	93,677	3,774	89,835	7,616	97,451
Ward 1, ...	2,312	70	2,382	170	2,312	240	2,552
Ward 2, ...	5,919	238	6,157	364	5,919	602	6,521
Ward 3, ...	21,898	956	22,854	1,052	21,898	2,008	23,906
Ward 4, ...	16,743	978	17,721	482	16,743	1,460	18,203
Ward 5, ...	19,197	692	19,889	708	19,197	1,400	20,597

OCCUPIED AND UNOCCUPIED ROOMS IN OCCUPIED AND UNOCCUPIED DWELLING HOUSES — Continued.

COUNTIES, CITIES, AND TOWNS.	OCCUPIED DWELLING HOUSES			Rooms in Unoccupied Dwelling Houses	TOTAL NUMBER OF ROOMS		
	Occupied Rooms	Unoccupied Rooms	Total		Occupied	Unoccupied	Occupied and Unoccupied
ESSEX — Con.							
LYNN — Con.							
Ward 6, ...	20,162	717	20,879	701	20,162	1,418	21,580
Ward 7, ...	3,604	191	3,795	297	3,604	488	4,092
Lynnfield, ...	1,515	19	1,534	107	1,515	126	1,641
Manchester, ...	3,430	118	3,548	1,747	3,430	1,865	5,295
Marblehead, ...	12,015	370	12,385	2,368	12,015	2,738	14,753
Merrimac, ...	4,282	194	4,476	312	4,282	506	4,788
Methuen, ...	8,933	171	9,104	284	8,933	455	9,388
Middleton, ...	1,471	81	1,552	160	1,471	241	1,712
Nahant, ...	1,426	238	1,664	2,600	1,426	2,838	4,264
Newbury, ...	2,671	106	2,777	383	2,671	489	3,160
NEWBURYPORT, ...	24,227	425	24,652	1,355	24,227	1,780	26,007
Ward 1, ...	3,893	27	3,920	220	3,893	247	4,140
Ward 2, ...	3,386	73	3,459	208	3,386	281	3,667
Ward 3, ...	4,908	26	4,934	240	4,908	266	5,174
Ward 4, ...	3,962	89	4,051	145	3,962	234	4,196
Ward 5, ...	3,576	121	3,697	208	3,576	329	3,905
Ward 6, ...	4,502	89	4,591	334	4,502	423	4,925
North Andover, . . .	5,509	47	5,556	399	5,509	446	5,955
Peabody, ...	15,466	596	16,062	363	15,466	959	16,425
Rockport, ...	6,997	254	7,251	782	6,997	1,036	8,033
Rowley, ...	2,373	22	2,395	113	2,373	135	2,508
SALEM, ...	48,572	1,368	49,940	2,195	48,572	3,563	52,135
Ward 1, ...	6,197	399	6,596	1,015	6,197	1,414	7,611
Ward 2, ...	9,356	306	9,662	321	9,356	627	9,983
Ward 3, ...	6,964	195	7,159	246	6,964	441	7,405
Ward 4, ...	7,598	194	7,792	130	7,598	324	7,922
Ward 5, ...	11,399	305	11,704	230	11,399	535	11,934
Ward 6, ...	6,858	169	7,027	253	6,858	422	7,280
Salisbury, ...	2,380	28	2,408	125	2,380	153	2,533
Saugus, ...	7,060	204	7,264	809	7,060	1,073	8,133
Swampscott, ...	5,702	236	5,938	864	5,702	1,100	6,802
Topsfield, ...	1,940	44	1,984	143	1,940	187	2,127
Wenham, ...	1,738	42	1,780	176	1,738	218	1,956
West Newbury, . . .	3,282	119	3,401	195	3,282	314	3,596
FRANKLIN.	68,207	1,673	69,880	4,654	68,207	6,327	74,534
Ashfield, ...	2,210	21	2,231	243	2,210	264	2,474
Bernardston, . . .	1,895	26	1,921	138	1,895	164	2,059
Buckland, . . .	2,585	86	2,671	129	2,585	215	2,800
Charlemont, . . .	2,034	33	2,067	93	2,034	126	2,160
Colrain, ...	2,514	70	2,584	92	2,514	162	2,676
Conway, ...	2,357	51	2,408	131	2,357	182	2,539
Deerfield, ...	5,097	8	5,105	274	5,097	282	5,379
Erving, ...	1,614	31	1,645	37	1,614	68	1,682
Gill, ...	1,633	52	1,685	45	1,633	97	1,730
Greenfield, . . .	10,509	166	10,675	378	10,509	544	11,053
Hawley, ...	869	15	884	72	869	87	956
Heath, ...	879	11	890	34	879	45	924
Leverett, ...	1,349	9	1,358	48	1,349	57	1,406
Leyden, ...	705	17	722	93	705	110	815
Monroe, ...	392	-	392	8	392	8	400
Montague, . . .	8,231	422	8,653	1,408	8,231	1,830	10,061
New Salem, . . .	1,569	37	1,606	74	1,569	111	1,680
Northfield, . . .	3,341	21	3,362	281	3,341	302	3,643

OCCUPIED AND UNOCCUPIED ROOMS IN OCCUPIED AND UNOCCUPIED
DWELLING HOUSES -- Continued.

COUNTIES, CITIES, AND TOWNS.	Occupied Rooms	Un-occupied Rooms	Total	Rooms in Unoccupied Dwelling Houses	Occupied	Unoccupied	Occupied and Unoccupied
FRANKLIN — Con.							
Orange,	8,775	367	9,142	315	8,775	682	9,457
Rowe,	785	18	803	188	785	206	991
Shelburne,	3,032	43	3,075	49	3,032	92	3,124
Shutesbury,	830	–	830	105	830	105	935
Sunderland,	1,299	5	1,304	44	1,299	49	1,348
Warwick,	1,297	–	1,297	153	1,297	153	1,450
Wendell,	802	17	819	155	802	172	974
Whately,	1,604	147	1,751	67	1,604	214	1,818
HAMPDEN.	209,488	6,802	216,350	10,423	209,488	17,285	226,773
Agawam,	3,711	19	3,730	201	3,711	220	3,931
Blandford,	1,859	24	1,883	329	1,859	353	2,212
Brimfield,	1,882	12	1,894	126	1,882	138	2,020
Chester,	2,525	77	2,602	226	2,525	303	2,828
CHICOPEE,	18,973	336	19,409	427	18,973	763	19,736
Ward 1,	3,085	57	3,142	6	3,085	63	3,148
Ward 2,	2,757	41	2,798	109	2,757	150	2,907
Ward 3,	2,541	59	2,600	5	2,541	64	2,605
Ward 4,	3,008	72	3,080	69	3,008	141	3,149
Ward 5,	3,373	26	3,399	43	3,373	69	3,442
Ward 6,	1,918	34	1,952	46	1,918	80	1,998
Ward 7,	2,291	47	2,338	149	2,291	196	2,487
East Longmeadow,	2,082	62	2,144	107	2,082	169	2,251
Granville,	2,032	–	2,032	169	2,032	169	2,201
Hampden,	1,438	93	1,531	82	1,438	175	1,613
Holland,	451	–	451	56	451	56	507
HOLYOKE,	43,167	2,295	45,462	1,557	43,167	3,852	47,019
Ward 1,	5,764	178	5,942	10	5,764	188	5,952
Ward 2,	7,831	582	8,413	122	7,831	704	8,535
Ward 3,	5,562	191	5,753	454	5,562	645	6,207
Ward 4,	5,938	868	6,806	137	5,938	1,005	6,943
Ward 5,	4,772	202	4,974	167	4,772	369	5,141
Ward 6,	6,126	186	6,312	95	6,126	281	6,407
Ward 7,	7,174	88	7,262	572	7,174	660	7,834
Longmeadow,	1,108	13	1,121	85	1,108	98	1,206
Ludlow,	2,941	27	2,968	123	2,941	150	3,091
Monson,	6,220	86	6,306	215	6,220	301	6,521
Montgomery,	355	–	355	17	355	17	372
Palmer,	9,367	180	9,547	473	9,367	653	10,020
Russell,	1,209	40	1,249	117	1,209	157	1,366
Southwick,	1,754	49	1,803	140	1,754	189	1,943
SPRINGFIELD,	77,438	2,708	80,146	4,669	77,438	7,377	84,815
Ward 1,	10,835	472	11,307	707	10,835	1,179	12,014
Ward 2,	9,876	514	10,390	336	9,876	850	10,726
Ward 3,	8,678	543	9,221	264	8,678	807	9,485
Ward 4,	10,636	364	11,000	417	10,636	781	11,417
Ward 5,	11,391	177	11,568	554	11,391	731	12,122
Ward 6,	8,480	421	8,901	542	8,480	963	9,443
Ward 7,	7,638	101	7,739	614	7,638	715	8,353
Ward 8,	9,904	116	10,020	1,235	9,904	1,351	11,255
Tolland,	651	5	656	164	651	169	820
Wales,	1,436	9	1,445	105	1,436	114	1,550
Westfield,	17,232	356	17,588	543	17,232	899	18,131
West Springfield,	8,486	426	8,912	281	8,486	707	9,193
Wilbraham,	3,021	45	3,066	211	3,021	256	3,277

OCCUPIED AND UNOCCUPIED ROOMS IN OCCUPIED AND UNOCCUPIED DWELLING HOUSES — Continued.

COUNTIES, CITIES, AND TOWNS.	OCCUPIED DWELLING HOUSES			Rooms in Unoccupied Dwelling Houses	TOTAL NUMBER OF ROOMS		
	Occupied Rooms	Un-occupied Rooms	Total		Occupied	Unoccupied	Occupied and Unoccupied
HAMPSHIRE.	85,062	1,569	86,631	3,719	85,062	5,288	90,350
Amherst,	8,622	109	8,731	144	8,622	253	8,875
Belchertown,	3,952	31	3,983	169	3,952	200	4,152
Chesterfield,	1,123	14	1,137	106	1,123	120	1,243
Cummington,	1,731	11	1,742	108	1,731	119	1,850
Easthampton,	6,809	87	6,896	283	6,809	370	7,179
Enfield,	1,921	9	1,930	36	1,921	45	1,966
Goshen,	516	33	549	102	516	135	651
Granby,	1,332	-	1,332	35	1,332	35	1,367
Greenwich,	1,061	-	1,061	65	1,061	65	1,126
Hadley,	3,129	28	3,157	88	3,129	116	3,245
Hatfield,	2,215	64	2,279	65	2,215	129	2,344
Huntington,	2,326	87	2,413	111	2,326	198	2,524
Middlefield,	808	26	834	243	808	269	1,077
NORTHAMPTON,	23,272	355	23,627	911	23,272	1,266	24,538
Ward 1,	3,151	60	3,211	53	3,151	113	3,264
Ward 2,	4,690	54	4,744	125	4,690	179	4,869
Ward 3,	4,160	70	4,230	159	4,160	229	4,389
Ward 4,	3,116	54	3,170	171	3,116	225	3,341
Ward 5,	2,806	-	2,806	92	2,806	92	2,898
Ward 6,	2,780	49	2,829	123	2,780	172	2,952
Ward 7,	2,569	68	2,637	188	2,569	256	2,825
Pelham,	858	46	904	127	858	173	1,031
Plainfield,	1,113	35	1,148	110	1,113	145	1,258
Prescott,	812	3	815	99	812	102	914
Southampton,	1,809	16	1,825	35	1,809	51	1,860
South Hadley,	6,071	192	6,263	186	6,071	378	6,449
Ware,	10,223	304	10,527	337	10,223	641	10,864
Westhampton,	861	10	871	44	861	54	915
Williamsburg,	3,259	85	3,344	133	3,259	218	3,477
Worthington,	1,239	24	1,263	182	1,239	206	1,445
MIDDLESEX.	719,835	19,606	739,441	50,374	719,835	69,980	789,815
Acton,	3,824	38	3,862	217	3,824	255	4,079
Arlington,	10,228	67	10,295	682	10,228	749	10,977
Ashby,	1,723	41	1,764	207	1,723	248	1,971
Ashland,	3,560	140	3,700	348	3,560	488	4,048
Ayer,	3,516	254	3,770	156	3,516	410	3,926
Bedford,	1,956	29	1,985	244	1,956	273	2,229
Belmont,	4,020	12	4,032	899	4,020	911	4,931
Billerica,	4,114	32	4,146	221	4,114	253	4,367
Boxborough,	556	16	572	22	556	38	594
Burlington,	938	51	989	110	938	161	1,099
CAMBRIDGE,	104,028	4,241	108,269	5,644	104,028	9,885	113,913
Ward 1,	22,615	533	23,148	1,032	22,615	1,565	24,180
Ward 2,	27,924	1,398	29,322	1,340	27,924	2,738	30,662
Ward 3,	14,173	684	14,857	284	14,173	968	15,141
Ward 4,	24,398	1,188	25,586	1,179	24,398	2,367	26,765
Ward 5,	14,918	438	15,356	1,809	14,918	2,247	17,165
Carlisle,	889	21	910	56	889	77	966
Chelmsford,	5,413	77	5,490	326	5,413	403	5,816
Concord,	7,575	102	7,677	494	7,575	596	8,171
Dracut,	3,389	59	3,448	261	3,389	320	3,709
Dunstable,	729	23	752	94	729	117	846
EVERETT,	26,948	1,137	28,085	3,198	26,948	4,335	31,283
Ward 1,	3,904	161	4,065	346	3,904	507	4,411

OCCUPIED AND UNOCCUPIED ROOMS IN OCCUPIED AND UNOCCUPIED DWELLING HOUSES — Continued.

COUNTIES, CITIES, AND TOWNS.	OCCUPIED DWELLING HOUSES			Rooms in Unoccupied Dwelling Houses	TOTAL NUMBER OF ROOMS		
	Occupied Rooms	Unoccupied Rooms	Total		Occupied	Unoccupied	Occupied and Unoccupied
MIDDLESEX — Con.							
EVERETT — Con.							
Ward 2,	3,674	130	3,804	599	3,674	729	4,403
Ward 3,	4,506	280	4,786	1,007	4,506	1,287	5,793
Ward 4,	4,525	164	4,689	429	4,525	593	5,118
Ward 5,	4,514	207	4,721	309	4,514	516	5,030
Ward 6,	5,825	195	6,020	508	5,825	703	6,528
Framingham,	15,468	234	15,702	2,014	15,468	2,248	17,716
Groton,	3,963	59	4,022	218	3,963	277	4,240
Holliston,	5,149	113	5,262	280	5,149	393	5,542
Hopkinton,	5,504	258	5,762	505	5,504	763	6,267
Hudson,	7,801	171	7,972	180	7,801	351	8,152
Lexington,	6,016	17	6,033	350	6,016	367	6,383
Lincoln,	1,631	42	1,673	155	1,631	197	1,828
Littleton,	2,001	26	2,027	88	2,001	114	2,115
LOWELL,	106,121	3,512	109,633	3,234	106,121	7,746	113,867
Ward 1,	11,382	318	11,700	182	11,382	500	11,882
Ward 2,	9,893	571	10,464	171	9,893	742	10,635
Ward 3,	12,809	529	13,438	323	12,809	892	13,761
Ward 4,	10,691	499	11,190	414	10,691	913	11,604
Ward 5,	9,836	562	10,398	246	9,836	808	10,644
Ward 6,	12,797	390	13,187	532	12,797	922	13,719
Ward 7,	14,755	478	15,233	501	14,755	979	15,734
Ward 8,	12,904	166	13,070	957	12,904	1,123	14,027
Ward 9,	10,994	259	11,253	608	10,994	867	11,861
MALDEN,	45,049	904	45,953	3,565	45,049	4,469	49,518
Ward 1,	6,542	68	6,610	383	6,542	451	6,993
Ward 2,	5,714	289	6,003	172	5,714	461	6,175
Ward 3,	6,669	118	6,787	570	6,669	688	7,357
Ward 4,	7,251	57	7,308	293	7,251	350	7,601
Ward 5,	6,723	149	6,872	692	6,723	841	7,564
Ward 6,	6,548	54	6,602	827	6,548	881	7,429
Ward 7,	5,602	169	5,771	628	5,602	797	6,399
MARLBOROUGH,	19,451	538	19,989	477	19,451	1,015	20,466
Ward 1,	2,196	82	2,278	123	2,196	205	2,401
Ward 2,	3,002	115	3,117	-	3,002	115	3,117
Ward 3,	3,363	87	3,450	74	3,363	161	3,524
Ward 4,	3,655	39	3,694	121	3,655	160	3,815
Ward 5,	2,774	71	2,845	52	2,774	123	2,897
Ward 6,	2,338	82	2,420	107	2,338	189	2,527
Ward 7,	2,123	62	2,185	-	2,123	62	2,185
Maynard,	4,287	20	4,307	145	4,287	165	4,452
MEDFORD,	22,854	381	23,235	2,451	22,854	2,832	25,686
Ward 1,	4,514	63	4,577	625	4,514	688	5,202
Ward 2,	3,693	85	3,778	206	3,693	291	3,984
Ward 3,	3,487	21	3,508	213	3,487	234	3,721
Ward 4,	2,861	20	2,881	152	2,861	172	3,033
Ward 5,	4,311	122	4,433	974	4,311	1,096	5,407
Ward 6,	3,988	70	4,058	281	3,988	351	4,339
Melrose,	20,071	136	20,207	2,969	20,071	3,105	23,176
Natick,	13,551	424	13,975	509	13,551	933	14,484
NEWTON,	44,911	372	45,283	4,776	44,911	5,148	50,059
Ward 1,	5,663	62	5,725	771	5,663	833	6,496
Ward 2,	8,538	63	8,601	886	8,538	949	9,487
Ward 3,	6,480	36	6,516	632	6,480	668	7,148
Ward 4,	5,530	101	5,631	822	5,530	923	6,453

OCCUPIED AND UNOCCUPIED ROOMS IN OCCUPIED AND UNOCCUPIED
DWELLING HOUSES — Continued.

COUNTIES, CITIES, AND TOWNS.	OCCUPIED DWELLING HOUSES			Rooms in Unoccupied Dwelling Houses	TOTAL NUMBER OF ROOMS		
	Occupied Rooms	Un-occupied Rooms	Total		Occupied	Unoccupied	Occupied and Unoccupied
MIDDLESEX — Con.							
NEWTON — Con.							
Ward 5, ...	6,709	34	6,743	685	6,709	719	7,428
Ward 6, ...	6,961	52	7,013	607	6,961	659	7,620
Ward 7, ...	5,030	24	5,054	373	5,030	397	5,427
North Reading, ...	1,589	13	1,602	98	1,589	111	1,700
Pepperell, ...	5,306	149	5,455	397	5,306	546	5,852
Reading, ...	8,198	112	8,310	494	8,198	606	8,804
Sherborn, ...	2,210	85	2,295	203	2,210	288	2,498
Shirley, ...	2,251	49	2,300	149	2,251	198	2,449
SOMERVILLE, ...	74,418	3,079	77,497	5,245	74,418	8,324	82,742
Ward 1, ...	14,018	767	14,785	600	14,018	1,367	15,385
Ward 2, ...	22,470	1,081	23,551	976	22,470	2,057	24,527
Ward 3, ...	20,079	461	20,540	1,744	20,079	2,205	22,284
Ward 4, ...	17,851	770	18,621	1,925	17,851	2,695	20,546
Stoneham, ...	10,507	105	10,612	451	10,507	556	11,063
Stow, ...	1,787	29	1,816	139	1,787	168	1,955
Sudbury, ...	1,979	45	2,024	102	1,979	147	2,126
Tewksbury, ...	4,511	17	4,528	288	4,511	305	4,816
Townsend, ...	3,614	60	3,674	239	3,614	299	3,913
Tyngsborough, ...	1,106	18	1,124	10	1,106	28	1,134
Wakefield, ...	12,944	430	13,374	841	12,944	1,271	14,215
WALTHAM, ...	28,995	495	29,490	1,799	28,995	2,294	31,289
Ward 1, ...	4,162	62	4,224	288	4,162	350	4,512
Ward 2, ...	3,959	86	4,045	266	3,959	352	4,311
Ward 3, ...	4,200	150	4,350	145	4,200	295	4,495
Ward 4, ...	4,277	51	4,328	349	4,277	400	4,677
Ward 5, ...	4,569	33	4,602	223	4,569	256	4,825
Ward 6, ...	4,440	113	4,553	303	4,440	416	4,856
Ward 7, ...	3,388	-	3,388	225	3,388	225	3,613
Watertown, ...	11,789	134	11,923	1,070	11,789	1,204	12,993
Wayland, ...	3,074	94	3,168	243	3,074	337	3,411
Westford, ...	3,635	59	3,694	187	3,635	246	3,881
Weston, ...	3,019	63	3,082	323	3,019	386	3,405
Wilmington, ...	2,202	23	2,225	329	2,202	352	2,554
Winchester, ...	9,838	72	9,910	1,147	9,838	1,219	11,057
WOBURN, ...	19,629	628	20,257	825	19,629	1,453	21,082
Ward 1, ...	3,519	5	3,524	305	3,519	310	3,829
Ward 2, ...	3,713	92	3,805	229	3,713	321	4,034
Ward 3, ...	3,634	31	3,665	82	3,634	113	3,747
Ward 4, ...	3,822	71	3,893	209	3,822	280	4,102
Ward 5, ...	1,425	46	1,471	-	1,425	46	1,471
Ward 6, ...	2,269	343	2,612	-	2,269	343	2,612
Ward 7, ...	1,247	40	1,287	-	1,247	40	1,287
NANTUCKET.	7,287	188	7,475	1,685	7,287	1,873	9,160
Nantucket, ...	7,287	188	7,475	1,685	7,287	1,873	9,160
NORFOLK.	210,776	4,080	214,856	15,197	210,776	19,277	230,053
Avon, ...	2,534	121	2,655	117	2,534	238	2,772
Bellingham, ...	2,514	31	2,545	188	2,514	219	2,733
Braintree, ...	8,721	194	8,915	521	8,721	715	9,436
Brookline, ...	24,822	518	25,340	2,755	24,822	3,273	28,095
Canton, ...	7,023	123	7,146	348	7,023	471	7,494
Cohasset, ...	4,644	4	4,648	12	4,644	16	4,660

OCCUPIED AND UNOCCUPIED ROOMS IN OCCUPIED AND UNOCCUPIED DWELLING HOUSES — Continued.

COUNTIES, CITIES, AND TOWNS.	OCCUPIED DWELLING HOUSES			Rooms in Unoccupied Dwelling Houses	TOTAL NUMBER OF ROOMS		
	Occupied Rooms	Un-occupied Rooms	Total		Occupied	Unoccupied	Occupied and Unoccupied
NORFOLK — Con.							
Dedham, ...	11,697	95	11,792	741	11,697	836	12,533
Dover, ...	1,139	11	1,150	63	1,139	74	1,213
Foxborough, ...	5,784	38	5,822	185	5,784	223	6,007
Franklin, ...	8,059	170	8,229	338	8,059	508	8,567
Holbrook, ...	3,792	107	3,899	225	3,792	332	4,124
Hyde Park, ...	17,873	466	18,339	1,080	17,873	1,546	19,419
Medfield, ...	3,048	67	3,115	122	3,048	189	3,237
Medway, ...	5,293	189	5,482	198	5,293	387	5,680
Millis, ...	1,714	89	1,803	231	1,714	320	2,034
Milton, ...	8,717	97	8,814	743	8,717	840	9,557
Needham, ...	5,438	48	5,486	495	5,438	543	5,981
Norfolk, ...	1,581	31	1,612	146	1,581	177	1,758
Norwood, ...	6,060	7	6,067	125	6,060	132	6,192
QUINCY, ...	27,592	765	28,357	3,199	27,592	3,964	31,556
Ward 1, ...	5,470	178	5,648	1,929	5,470	2,107	7,577
Ward 2, ...	3,902	87	3,989	191	3,902	278	4,180
Ward 3, ...	5,559	121	5,680	218	5,559	339	5,898
Ward 4, ...	5,361	186	5,547	229	5,361	415	5,776
Ward 5, ...	4,314	47	4,361	632	4,314	679	4,993
Ward 6, ...	2,986	146	3,132	-	2,986	146	3,132
Randolph, ...	6,312	65	6,377	376	6,312	441	6,753
Sharon, ...	3,130	112	3,242	637	3,130	749	3,879
Stoughton, ...	8,373	133	8,506	631	8,373	824	9,197
Walpole, ...	4,891	61	4,952	177	4,891	238	5,129
Wellesley, ...	6,677	56	6,733	458	6,677	514	7,191
Weymouth, ...	18,479	322	18,801	855	18,479	1,177	19,656
Wrentham, ...	4,869	100	4,969	231	4,869	331	5,200
PLYMOUTH.	171,153	4,330	175,483	23,509	171,153	27,839	198,992
Abington, ...	7,462	183	7,645	218	7,462	401	7,863
Bridgewater, ...	7,355	137	7,492	470	7,355	607	7,962
BROCKTON, ...	47,423	1,786	49,209	2,060	47,423	3,846	51,269
Ward 1, ...	6,558	266	6,824	229	6,558	495	7,053
Ward 2, ...	7,178	235	7,413	293	7,178	528	7,706
Ward 3, ...	7,295	127	7,422	320	7,295	447	7,742
Ward 4, ...	6,072	215	6,287	231	6,072	446	6,518
Ward 5, ...	6,374	358	6,732	432	6,374	790	7,164
Ward 6, ...	6,597	250	6,847	454	6,597	704	7,301
Ward 7, ...	7,349	335	7,684	71	7,349	406	7,755
Carver, ...	1,714	60	1,774	50	1,714	110	1,824
Duxbury, ...	4,840	63	4,903	1,536	4,840	1,599	6,439
East Bridgewater, . .	5,371	147	5,518	325	5,371	472	5,843
Halifax, ...	1,143	23	1,166	178	1,143	201	1,344
Hanover, ...	3,705	50	3,755	228	3,705	278	3,983
Hanson, ...	2,876	34	2,910	164	2,876	198	3,074
Hingham, ...	8,741	145	8,886	1,531	8,741	1,676	10,417
Hull, ...	2,486	23	2,509	4,194	2,486	4,217	6,703
Kingston, ...	3,496	50	3,546	334	3,496	384	3,880
Lakeville, ...	1,743	7	1,750	451	1,743	458	2,201
Marion, ...	2,167	127	2,294	823	2,167	950	3,117
Marshfield, ...	3,946	123	4,069	1,752	3,946	1,875	5,821
Mattapoisett, . . .	2,332	55	2,387	718	2,332	773	3,105
Middleborough, . . .	12,168	236	12,404	327	12,168	563	12,731
Norwell, ...	3,122	49	3,171	309	3,122	358	3,480

OCCUPIED AND UNOCCUPIED ROOMS IN OCCUPIED AND UNOCCUPIED
DWELLING HOUSES — Continued.

COUNTIES, CITIES, AND TOWNS.	OCCUPIED DWELLING HOUSES			Rooms in Unoccupied Dwelling Houses	TOTAL NUMBER OF ROOMS		
	Occupied Rooms	Unoccupied Rooms	Total		Occupied	Unoccupied	Occupied and Unoccupied
PLYMOUTH — Con.							
Pembroke, ...	2,826	26	2,852	343	2,826	369	3,195
Plymouth, ...	12,510	195	12,705	549	12,510	744	13,254
Plympton, ...	1,122	36	1,158	225	1,122	261	1,383
Rochester, ...	1,688	36	1,724	163	1,688	199	1,887
Rockland, ...	8,802	217	9,019	376	8,802	593	9,395
Scituate, ...	4,158	198	4,356	2,100	4,158	2,298	6,456
Wareham, ...	5,708	127	5,835	3,549	5,708	3,676	9,384
West Bridgewater, . . .	3,033	-	3,033	210	3,033	210	3,243
Whitman, ...	9,216	197	9,413	356	9,216	553	9,769
SUFFOLK.	678,450	37,510	715,960	43,181	678,450	80,691	759,141
Boston, ...	618,598	34,908	653,506	35,396	618,598	70,304	688,902
Ward 1, ...	26,861	1,470	28,331	1,125	26,861	2,595	29,456
Ward 2, ...	23,889	1,223	25,112	734	23,889	1,957	25,846
Ward 3, ...	17,045	894	17,939	316	17,045	1,210	18,255
Ward 4, ...	17,061	852	17,913	680	17,061	1,532	18,593
Ward 5, ...	15,838	761	16,599	485	15,838	1,246	17,084
Ward 6, ...	22,695	1,261	23,956	1,414	22,695	2,675	25,370
Ward 7, ...	19,781	1,235	21,016	1,468	19,781	2,703	22,484
Ward 8, ...	23,508	1,734	25,242	989	23,508	2,723	26,231
Ward 9, ...	24,765	2,069	26,834	1,047	24,765	3,116	27,881
Ward 10, ...	31,465	2,539	34,004	1,671	31,465	4,210	35,675
Ward 11, ...	35,008	1,375	36,383	2,465	35,008	3,840	38,848
Ward 12, ...	29,724	1,578	31,302	1,011	29,724	2,589	32,313
Ward 13, ...	23,450	1,978	25,428	449	23,450	2,427	25,877
Ward 14, ...	22,945	1,230	24,175	1,203	22,945	2,433	25,378
Ward 15, ...	22,546	1,308	23,854	594	22,546	1,902	24,448
Ward 16, ...	22,334	1,528	23,862	1,505	22,334	2,833	25,167
Ward 17, ...	23,740	1,770	25,510	1,216	23,740	2,986	26,726
Ward 18, ...	23,686	2,305	25,991	1,080	23,686	3,385	27,071
Ward 19, ...	23,940	1,111	25,051	1,665	23,940	2,776	26,716
Ward 20, ...	33,562	1,395	34,957	4,638	33,562	6,033	39,595
Ward 21, ...	31,393	1,001	32,394	1,867	31,393	3,468	34,861
Ward 22, ...	29,194	1,569	30,763	1,918	29,194	3,487	32,681
Ward 23, ...	25,308	903	26,211	2,223	25,308	3,126	28,434
Ward 24, ...	27,611	735	28,346	2,101	27,611	2,836	30,447
Ward 25, ...	21,249	484	21,733	1,732	21,249	2,216	23,465
Chelsea, ...	41,357	2,202	43,559	2,939	41,357	5,141	46,498
Ward 1, ...	9,227	563	9,790	536	9,227	1,099	10,326
Ward 2, ...	9,461	545	10,006	741	9,461	1,286	10,747
Ward 3, ...	9,330	398	9,728	730	9,330	1,128	10,458
Ward 4, ...	7,405	442	7,847	425	7,405	867	8,272
Ward 5, ...	5,934	254	6,188	507	5,934	761	6,695
Revere, ...	11,017	352	11,369	2,685	11,017	3,037	14,054
Winthrop, ...	7,478	48	7,526	2,161	7,478	2,209	9,687
WORCESTER.	436,897	19,415	456,312	22,266	436,897	41,681	478,578
Ashburnham, ...	3,528	171	3,699	423	3,528	594	4,122
Athol, ...	11,681	368	12,049	453	11,681	821	12,502
Auburn, ...	2,124	76	2,200	143	2,124	219	2,343
Barre, ...	4,686	96	4,782	509	4,686	605	5,291
Berlin, ...	1,756	14	1,770	151	1,756	165	1,921
Blackstone, ...	8,343	772	9,115	449	8,343	1,221	9,564
Bolton, ...	1,567	21	1,588	86	1,567	107	1,674

OCCUPIED AND UNOCCUPIED ROOMS IN OCCUPIED AND UNOCCUPIED DWELLING HOUSES — Continued.

COUNTIES, CITIES, AND TOWNS.	Occupied Dwelling Houses Occupied Rooms	Un-occupied Rooms	Total	Rooms in Unoccupied Dwelling Houses	Total Number of Rooms Occupied	Unoccupied	Occupied and Unoccupied
WORCESTER — Con.							
Boylston,	1,263	28	1,291	79	1,263	107	1,370
Brookfield,	5,065	167	5,232	459	5,065	626	5,691
Charlton,	3,399	35	3,434	128	3,399	163	3,562
Clinton,	13,735	501	14,236	377	13,735	878	14,613
Dana,	1,298	13	1,311	79	1,298	92	1,390
Douglas,	3,447	374	3,821	242	3,447	616	4,063
Dudley,	3,976	144	4,120	200	3,976	344	4,320
FITCHBURG,	34,591	1,153	35,744	1,469	34,591	2,622	37,213
Ward 1,	5,334	196	5,530	88	5,334	284	5,618
Ward 2,	6,695	132	6,827	186	6,695	318	7,013
Ward 3,	5,719	168	5,887	284	5,719	452	6,171
Ward 4,	5,629	220	5,849	346	5,629	566	6,195
Ward 5,	5,254	245	5,499	178	5,254	423	5,677
Ward 6,	5,960	192	6,152	387	5,960	579	6,539
Gardner,	11,818	566	12,384	274	11,818	840	12,658
Grafton,	7,696	169	7,865	355	7,696	524	8,220
Hardwick,	3,791	76	3,867	153	3,791	229	4,020
Harvard,	2,237	5	2,242	233	2,237	238	2,475
Holden,	3,731	73	3,804	207	3,731	280	4,011
Hopedale,	2,261	26	2,287	126	2,261	152	2,413
Hubbardston,	2,306	53	2,359	257	2,306	310	2,616
Lancaster,	3,644	179	3,823	391	3,644	570	4,214
Leicester,	5,257	84	5,341	133	5,257	217	5,474
Leominster,	13,789	193	13,982	351	13,789	544	14,533
Lunenburg,	2,168	38	2,206	115	2,168	153	2,321
Mendon,	1,885	27	1,912	116	1,885	143	2,028
Milford,	14,021	751	14,772	538	14,021	1,289	15,310
Millbury,	7,213	267	7,480	266	7,213	533	7,746
New Braintree,	937	31	968	–	937	31	968
Northborough,	3,114	123	3,237	195	3,114	318	3,432
Northbridge,	6,762	51	6,813	199	6,762	250	7,012
North Brookfield,	6,672	125	6,797	47	6,672	172	6,844
Oakham,	1,342	19	1,361	113	1,342	132	1,474
Oxford,	4,250	85	4,335	569	4,250	654	4,904
Paxton,	894	17	911	131	894	148	1,042
Petersham,	1,981	29	2,010	400	1,981	429	2,410
Phillipston,	893	11	904	148	893	159	1,052
Princeton,	2,186	41	2,227	439	2,186	480	2,666
Royalston,	1,948	59	2,007	290	1,948	349	2,297
Rutland,	1,502	28	1,530	52	1,502	80	1,582
Shrewsbury,	2,917	21	2,938	203	2,917	224	3,141
Southborough,	3,303	101	3,404	377	3,303	478	3,781
Southbridge,	10,675	253	10,928	505	10,675	758	11,433
Spencer,	10,270	758	11,028	474	10,270	1,232	11,502
Sterling,	2,647	122	2,769	1,306	2,647	1,428	4,075
Sturbridge,	3,191	175	3,366	119	3,191	294	3,485
Sutton,	5,149	147	5,296	81	5,149	228	5,377
Templeton,	4,831	123	4,954	398	4,831	521	5,352
Upton,	3,886	50	3,936	106	3,886	156	4,042
Uxbridge,	5,678	191	5,869	206	5,678	397	6,075
Warren,	6,682	359	7,041	290	6,682	649	7,331
Webster,	10,082	606	10,688	431	10,082	1,037	11,119
Westborough,	7,589	455	8,044	471	7,589	926	8,515
West Boylston,	4,363	59	4,422	386	4,363	445	4,808
West Brookfield,	2,939	76	3,015	89	2,939	165	3,104

OCCUPIED AND UNOCCUPIED ROOMS IN OCCUPIED AND UNOCCUPIED
DWELLING HOUSES — Concluded.

COUNTIES, CITIES, AND TOWNS.	OCCUPIED DWELLING HOUSES			Rooms in Unoccupied Dwelling Houses	TOTAL NUMBER OF ROOMS		
	Occupied Rooms	Un-occupied Rooms	Total		Occupied	Unoccupied	Occupied and Unoccupied
WORCESTER — Con.							
Westminster,	2,483	91	2,574	292	2,483	383	2,866
Winchendon,	7,004	207	7,211	288	7,004	495	7,499
WORCESTER,	128,451	8,562	137,013	4,899	128,451	13,461	141,912
Ward 1,	15,528	968	16,496	656	15,528	1,624	17,152
Ward 2,	17,208	928	18,136	700	17,208	1,628	18,836
Ward 3,	16,427	1,370	17,797	522	16,427	1,892	18,319
Ward 4,	14,814	1,005	15,819	179	14,814	1,184	15,998
Ward 5,	15,901	1,421	17,322	722	15,901	2,143	18,044
Ward 6,	16,919	938	17,857	736	16,919	1,674	18,593
Ward 7,	15,770	1,143	16,913	890	15,770	2,033	17,803
Ward 8,	15,884	789	16,673	494	15,884	1,283	17,167

RECAPITULATION.

THE STATE, AND COUNTIES.	OCCUPIED DWELLING HOUSES			Rooms in Unoccupied Dwelling Houses	TOTAL NUMBER OF ROOMS		
	Occupied Rooms	Un-occupied Rooms	Total		Occupied	Unoccupied	Occupied and Unoccupied
THE STATE.	3,568,385	125,600	3,693,985	253,013	3,568,385	378,613	3,946,998
Barnstable,	55,856	829	56,685	12,254	55,856	13,083	68,939
Berkshire,	134,864	2,051	136,915	10,728	134,864	12,779	147,643
Bristol,	301,831	12,583	314,414	12,927	301,831	25,510	327,341
Dukes,	9,875	393	10,268	7,784	9,875	8,177	18,052
Essex,	478,804	14,511	493,315	34,312	478,804	48,823	527,627
Franklin,	68,207	1,673	69,880	4,654	68,207	6,327	74,534
Hampden,	209,488	6,862	216,350	10,423	209,488	17,285	226,773
Hampshire,	85,062	1,569	86,631	3,719	85,062	5,288	90,350
Middlesex,	719,835	19,606	739,441	50,374	719,835	69,980	789,815
Nantucket,	7,287	188	7,475	1,685	7,287	1,873	9,160
Norfolk,	210,776	4,080	214,856	15,197	210,776	19,277	230,053
Plymouth,	171,153	4,330	175,483	23,509	171,153	27,839	198,992
Suffolk,	678,450	37,310	715,760	43,181	678,450	80,691	759,141
Worcester,	436,897	19,415	456,312	22,266	436,897	41,681	478,578

TENEMENTS:

OCCUPIED DWELLING HOUSES.

OCCUPIED AND UNOCCUPIED TENEMENTS IN OCCUPIED DWELLING HOUSES.

Counties, Cities, Towns, and Number of Tenements and Families.	Number of Occupied Dwelling Houses	Number of Occupied Tenements in Occupied Dwelling Houses	Number of Unoccupied Tenements in Occupied Dwelling Houses	Total Number of Tenements in Occupied Dwelling Houses
BARNSTABLE.				
Barnstable, ...	1,133	1,173	5	1,178
1 tenement (1 family), ...	1,094	1,094	-	-
2 tenements (2 families), ...	38	76	-	-
3 tenements (3 families), ...	1	3	-	-
Bourne, ...	402	429	7	436
1 tenement (1 family), ...	375	375	-	-
2 tenements (2 families), ...	27	54	-	-
Brewster, ...	242	255	2	257
1 tenement (1 family), ...	229	229	-	-
2 tenements (2 families), ...	13	26	-	-
Chatham, ...	489	543	23	566
1 tenement (1 family), ...	435	435	-	-
2 tenements (2 families), ...	54	108	-	-
Dennis, ...	784	817	10	827
1 tenement (1 family), ...	752	752	-	-
2 tenements (2 families), ...	31	62	-	-
3 tenements (3 families), ...	1	3	-	-
Eastham, ...	130	137	2	139
1 tenement (1 family), ...	123	123	-	-
2 tenements (2 families), ...	7	14	-	-
Falmouth, ...	656	722	8	730
1 tenement (1 family), ...	591	591	-	-
2 tenements (2 families), ...	64	128	-	-
3 tenements (3 families), ...	1	3	-	-
Harwich, ...	752	783	2	785
1 tenement (1 family), ...	721	721	-	-
2 tenements (2 families), ...	31	62	-	-
Mashpee, ...	74	81	-	81
1 tenement (1 family), ...	67	67	-	-
2 tenements (2 families), ...	7	14	-	-
Orleans, ...	356	375	14	389
1 tenement (1 family), ...	337	337	-	-
2 tenements (2 families), ...	19	38	-	-
Provincetown, ...	987	1,216	58	1,274
1 tenement (1 family), ...	784	784	-	-
2 tenements (2 families), ...	181	362	-	-
3 tenements (3 families), ...	19	57	-	-
4 tenements (4 families), ...	2	8	-	-
5 tenements (5 families), ...	1	5	-	-
Sandwich, ...	422	442	24	466
1 tenement (1 family), ...	403	403	-	-
2 tenements (2 families), ...	18	36	-	-
3 tenements (3 families), ...	1	3	-	-
Truro, ...	215	229	-	229
1 tenement (1 family), ...	201	201	-	-
2 tenements (2 families), ...	14	28	-	-

OCCUPIED AND UNOCCUPIED TENEMENTS IN OCCUPIED DWELLING HOUSES — Continued.

COUNTIES, CITIES, TOWNS, AND NUMBER OF TENEMENTS AND FAMILIES.	Number of Occupied Dwelling Houses	Number of Occupied Tenements in Occupied Dwelling Houses	Number of Unoccupied Tenements in Occupied Dwelling Houses	Total Number of Tenements in Occupied Dwelling Houses
BARNSTABLE — Con.				
Wellfleet,	314	332	4	336
1 tenement (1 family),	296	296	–	–
2 tenements (2 families),	18	36	–	–
Yarmouth,	520	535	3	538
1 tenement (1 family),	505	505	–	–
2 tenements (2 families),	15	30	–	–
BERKSHIRE.				
Adams,	1,345	1,604	88	1,692
1 tenement (1 family),	1,161	1,161	–	–
2 tenements (2 families),	129	258	–	–
3 tenements (3 families),	31	93	–	–
4 tenements (4 families),	19	76	–	–
5 tenements (5 families),	2	10	–	–
6 tenements (6 families),	1	6	–	–
Alford,	74	76	4	80
1 tenement (1 family),	72	72	–	–
2 tenements (2 families),	2	4	–	–
Becket,	201	219	3	222
1 tenement (1 family),	184	184	–	–
2 tenements (2 families),	16	32	–	–
3 tenements (3 families),	1	3	–	–
Cheshire,	278	297	8	305
1 tenement (1 family),	260	260	–	–
2 tenements (2 families),	17	34	–	–
3 tenements (3 families),	1	3	–	–
Clarksburg,	186	214	4	218
1 tenement (1 family),	163	163	–	–
2 tenements (2 families),	19	38	–	–
3 tenements (3 families),	3	9	–	–
4 tenements (4 families),	1	4	–	–
Dalton,	601	688	24	712
1 tenement (1 family),	527	527	–	–
2 tenements (2 families),	63	126	–	–
3 tenements (3 families),	9	27	–	–
4 tenements (4 families),	2	8	–	–
Egremont,	199	211	1	212
1 tenement (1 family),	187	187	–	–
2 tenements (2 families),	12	24	–	–
Florida,	91	93	1	94
1 tenement (1 family),	90	90	–	–
3 tenements (3 families),	1	3	–	–
Great Barrington,	1,006	1,136	12	1,148
1 tenement (1 family),	898	898	–	–
2 tenements (2 families),	93	186	–	–
3 tenements (3 families),	9	27	–	–
4 tenements (4 families),	5	20	–	–
5 tenements (5 families),	1	5	–	–
Hancock,	105	117	–	117
1 tenement (1 family),	94	94	–	–
2 tenements (2 families),	10	20	–	–
3 tenements (3 families),	1	3	–	–
Hinsdale,	314	346	–	346
1 tenement (1 family),	285	285	–	–
2 tenements (2 families),	26	52	–	–
3 tenements (3 families),	3	9	–	–

OCCUPIED AND UNOCCUPIED TENEMENTS IN OCCUPIED DWELLING HOUSES — Continued.

Counties, Cities, Towns, and Number of Tenements and Families.	Number of Occupied Dwelling Houses	Number of Occupied Tenements in Occupied Dwelling Houses	Number of Unoccupied Tenements in Occupied Dwelling Houses	Total Number of Tenements in Occupied Dwelling Houses
BERKSHIRE — Con.				
Lanesborough,	201	210	1	211
1 tenement (1 family),	192	192	-	-
2 tenements (2 families),	9	18	-	-
Lee,	797	922	13	935
1 tenement (1 family),	687	687	-	-
2 tenements (2 families),	98	196	-	-
3 tenements (3 families),	11	33	-	-
6 tenements (6 families),	1	6	-	-
Lenox,	519	581	11	592
1 tenement (1 family),	464	464	-	-
2 tenements (2 families),	50	100	-	-
3 tenements (3 families),	3	9	-	-
4 tenements (4 families),	2	8	-	-
Monterey,	110	115	1	116
1 tenement (1 family),	105	105	-	-
2 tenements (2 families),	5	10	-	-
Mount Washington,	31	31	1	32
1 tenement (1 family),	31	31	-	-
New Ashford,	29	30	-	30
1 tenement (1 family),	28	28	-	-
2 tenements (2 families),	1	2	-	-
New Marlborough,	316	325	4	329
1 tenement (1 family),	307	307	-	-
2 tenements (2 families),	9	18	-	-
NORTH ADAMS,	2,986	3,931	92	4,023
1 tenement (1 family),	2,280	2,280	-	-
2 tenements (2 families),	572	1,144	-	-
3 tenements (3 families),	83	249	-	-
4 tenements (4 families),	31	124	-	-
5 tenements (5 families),	7	35	-	-
6 tenements (6 families),	5	30	-	-
7 tenements (7 families),	3	21	-	-
8 tenements (8 families),	2	16	-	-
9 tenements (9 families),	1	9	-	-
10 tenements (10 families),	1	10	-	-
13 tenements (13 families),	1	13	-	-
Otis,	131	136	1	137
1 tenement (1 family),	126	126	-	-
2 tenements (2 families),	5	10	-	-
Peru,	69	71	-	71
1 tenement (1 family),	67	67	-	-
2 tenements (2 families),	2	4	-	-
PITTSFIELD,	3,806	4,342	75	4,417
1 tenement (1 family),	3,330	3,330	-	-
2 tenements (2 families),	433	866	-	-
3 tenements (3 families),	32	96	-	-
4 tenements (4 families),	9	36	-	-
5 tenements (5 families),	1	5	-	-
9 tenements (9 families),	1	9	-	-
Pittsfield, Ward 1,	506	552	8	560
1 tenement (1 family),	467	467	-	-
2 tenements (2 families),	33	66	-	-
3 tenements (3 families),	5	15	-	-
4 tenements (4 families),	1	4	-	-
Pittsfield, Ward 2,	621	722	19	741
1 tenement (1 family),	530	530	-	-

OCCUPIED AND UNOCCUPIED TENEMENTS IN OCCUPIED DWELLING
HOUSES — Continued.

COUNTIES, CITIES, TOWNS, AND NUMBER OF TENEMENTS AND FAMILIES.	Number of Occupied Dwelling Houses	Number of Occupied Tenements in Occupied Dwelling Houses	Number of Unoccupied Tenements in Occupied Dwelling Houses	Total Number of Tenements in Occupied Dwelling Houses
BERKSHIRE — Con.				
Pittsfield. Ward 2 — Con.				
2 tenements (2 families), ...	83	166	–	–
3 tenements (3 families), ...	6	18	–	–
4 tenements (4 families), ...	2	8	–	–
Pittsfield. Ward 3, ...	500	599	5	604
1 tenement (1 family), ...	411	411	–	–
2 tenements (2 families), ...	80	160	–	–
3 tenements (3 families), ...	8	24	–	–
4 tenements (4 families), ...	1	4	–	–
Pittsfield. Ward 4, ...	544	604	6 .	610
1 tenement (1 family), ...	497	497	–	–
2 tenements (2 families), ...	41	82	–	–
3 tenements (3 families), ...	4	12	–	–
4 tenements (4 families), ...	1	4	–	–
9 tenements (9 families), ...	1	9	–	–
Pittsfield. Ward 5, ...	444	546	15	561
1 tenement (1 family), ...	354	354	–	–
2 tenements (2 families), ...	82	164	–	–
3 tenements (3 families), ...	5	15	–	–
4 tenements (4 families), ...	2	8	–	–
5 tenements (5 families), ...	1	5	–	–
Pittsfield. Ward 6, ...	623	742	15	757
1 tenement (1 family), ...	512	512	–	–
2 tenements (2 families), ...	105	210	–	–
3 tenements (3 families), ...	4	12	–	–
4 tenements (4 families), ...	2	8	–	–
Pittsfield. Ward 7, ...	568	577	7	584
1 tenement (1 family), ...	559	559	–	–
2 tenements (2 families), ...	9	18	–	–
Richmond, ...	158	164	3	167
1 tenement (1 family), ...	152	152	–	–
2 tenements (2 families), ...	6	12	–	–
Sandisfield, ...	200	213	4	217
1 tenement (1 family), ...	187	187	–	–
2 tenements (2 families), ...	13	26	–	–
Savoy, ...	130	133	–	133
1 tenement (1 family), ...	127	127	–	–
2 tenements (2 families , ...	3	6	–	–
Sheffield, ...	450	481	5	486
1 tenement (1 family , ...	422	422	–	–
2 tenements (2 families , ...	25	50	–	–
3 tenements (3 families , ...	3	9	–	–
Stockbridge, ...	436	471	9	480
1 tenement (1 family), ...	403	403	–	–
2 tenements (2 families), ...	31	62	–	–
3 tenements (3 families , ...	2	6	–	–
Tyringham, ...	87	90	4	94
1 tenement (1 family), ...	84	84	–	–
2 tenements (2 families), ...	3	6	–	–
Washington, ...	87	87	–	87
1 tenement (1 family), ...	87	87	–	–
West Stockbridge, ...	312	324	7	331
1 tenement (1 family), ...	300	300	–	–
2 tenements (2 families), ...	12	24	–	–
Williamstown, ...	914	1,017	12	1,029
1 tenement (1 family), ...	822	822	–	–

OCCUPIED AND UNOCCUPIED TENEMENTS IN OCCUPIED DWELLING HOUSES — Continued.

COUNTIES, CITIES, TOWNS, AND NUMBER OF TENEMENTS AND FAMILIES.	Number of Occupied Dwelling Houses	Number of Occupied Tenements in Occupied Dwelling Houses	Number of Unoccupied Tenements in Occupied Dwelling Houses	Total Number of Tenements in Occupied Dwelling Houses
BERKSHIRE — Con.				
Williamstown — Con.				
2 tenements (2 families), ...	86	172	–	–
3 tenements (3 families), ...	2	6	–	–
4 tenements (4 families), ...	3	12	–	–
5 tenements (5 families), ...	1	5	–	–
Windsor, ...	127	135	–	135
1 tenement (1 family), ...	119	119	–	–
2 tenements (2 families), ...	8	16	–	–
BRISTOL.				
Acushnet, ...	263	294	5	299
1 tenement (1 family), ...	232	232	–	–
2 tenements (2 families), ...	31	62	–	–
Attleborough, ...	1,513	1,890	67	1,957
1 tenement (1 family), ...	1,187	1,187	–	–
2 tenements (2 families), ...	288	576	–	–
3 tenements (3 families), ...	27	81	–	–
4 tenements (4 families), ...	9	36	–	–
5 tenements (5 families), ...	2	10	–	–
Berkley, ...	238	256	3	259
1 tenement (1 family), ...	221	221	–	–
2 tenements (2 families), ...	16	32	–	–
3 tenements (3 families), ...	1	3	–	–
Dartmouth, ...	745	814	21	835
1 tenement (1 family), ...	678	678	–	–
2 tenements (2 families), ...	65	130	–	–
3 tenements (3 families), ...	2	6	–	–
Dighton, ...	428	461	33	494
1 tenement (1 family), ...	396	396	–	–
2 tenements (2 families), ...	31	62	–	–
3 tenements (3 families), ...	1	3	–	–
Easton, ...	979	1,061	19	1,080
1 tenement (1 family), ...	901	901	–	–
2 tenements (2 families), ...	75	150	–	–
3 tenements (3 families), ...	2	6	–	–
4 tenements (4 families), ...	1	4	–	–
Fairhaven, ...	755	898	12	910
1 tenement (1 family), ...	616	616	–	–
2 tenements (2 families), ...	135	270	–	–
3 tenements (3 families), ...	4	12	–	–
FALL RIVER, ...	8,069	17,948	1,146	19,094
1 tenement (1 family), ...	2,883	2,883	–	–
2 tenements (2 families), ...	2,737	5,474	–	–
3 tenements (3 families), ...	1,066	3,198	–	–
4 tenements (4 families), ...	881	3,524	–	–
5 tenements (5 families), ...	263	1,315	–	–
6 tenements (6 families), ...	186	1,116	–	–
7 tenements (7 families), ...	16	112	–	–
8 tenements (8 families), ...	20	160	–	–
9 tenements (9 families), ...	10	90	–	–
10 tenements (10 families), ...	2	20	–	–
11 tenements (11 families), ...	4	44	–	–
12 tenements (12 families), ...	1	12	–	–
Fall River. Ward 1, ...	1,156	2,342	217	2,559
1 tenement (1 family), ...	421	421	–	–
2 tenements (2 families), ...	465	930	–	–

OCCUPIED AND UNOCCUPIED TENEMENTS IN OCCUPIED DWELLING HOUSES — Continued.

COUNTIES, CITIES, TOWNS, AND NUMBER OF TENEMENTS AND FAMILIES.	Number of Occupied Dwelling Houses	Number of Occupied Tenements in Occupied Dwelling Houses	Number of Unoccupied Tenements in Occupied Dwelling Houses	Total Number of Tenements in Occupied Dwelling Houses
BRISTOL — Con.				
Fall River. Ward 1 — Con.				
3 tenements (3 families), ...	150	450	-	-
4 tenements (4 families), ...	81	324	-	-
5 tenements (5 families), ...	24	120	-	-
6 tenements (6 families), ...	13	78	-	-
7 tenements (7 families), ...	1	7	-	-
12 tenements (12 families), ...	1	12	-	-
Fall River. Ward 2, ...	823	1,677	92	1,769
1 tenement (1 family), ...	300	300	-	-
2 tenements (2 families), ...	319	638	-	-
3 tenements (3 families), ...	104	312	-	-
4 tenements (4 families), ...	82	328	-	-
5 tenements (5 families), ...	9	45	-	-
6 tenements (6 families), ...	9	54	-	-
Fall River. Ward 3, ...	832	2,247	73	2,320
1 tenement (1 family), ...	192	192	-	-
2 tenements (2 families), ...	293	586	-	-
3 tenements (3 families), ...	104	312	-	-
4 tenements (4 families), ...	146	584	-	-
5 tenements (5 families), ...	52	260	-	-
6 tenements (6 families), ...	26	156	-	-
7 tenements (7 families), ...	5	35	-	-
8 tenements (8 families), ...	6	48	-	-
9 tenements (9 families), ...	7	63	-	-
11 tenements (11 families), ...	1	11	-	-
Fall River. Ward 4, ...	872	2,241	131	2,372
1 tenement (1 family), ...	188	188	-	-
2 tenements (2 families), ...	320	640	-	-
3 tenements (3 families), ...	147	441	-	-
4 tenements (4 families), ...	148	592	-	-
5 tenements (5 families), ...	43	215	-	-
6 tenements (6 families), ...	22	132	-	-
7 tenements (7 families), ...	2	14	-	-
8 tenements (8 families), ...	1	8	-	-
11 tenements (11 families), ...	1	11	-	-
Fall River. Ward 5, ...	789	2,129	144	2,273
1 tenement (1 family), ...	215	215	-	-
2 tenements (2 families), ...	204	408	-	-
3 tenements (3 families), ...	133	399	-	-
4 tenements (4 families), ...	149	596	-	-
5 tenements (5 families), ...	45	225	-	-
6 tenements (6 families), ...	35	210	-	-
8 tenements (8 families), ...	2	16	-	-
9 tenements (9 families), ...	2	18	-	-
10 tenements (10 families), ...	2	20	-	-
11 tenements (11 families), ...	2	22	-	-
Fall River. Ward 6, ...	933	2,179	194	2,373
1 tenement (1 family), ...	317	317	-	-
2 tenements (2 families), ...	267	534	-	-
3 tenements (3 families), ...	207	621	-	-
4 tenements (4 families), ...	62	248	-	-
5 tenements (5 families), ...	36	180	-	-
6 tenements (6 families), ...	35	210	-	-
7 tenements (7 families), ...	4	28	-	-
8 tenements (8 families), ...	4	32	-	-
9 tenements (9 families), ...	1	9	-	-

OCCUPIED AND UNOCCUPIED TENEMENTS IN OCCUPIED DWELLING
HOUSES — Continued.

COUNTIES, CITIES, TOWNS, AND NUMBER OF TENEMENTS AND FAMILIES.	Number of Occupied Dwelling Houses	Number of Occupied Tenements in Occupied Dwelling Houses	Number of Unoccupied Tenements in Occupied Dwelling Houses	Total Number of Tenements in Occupied Dwelling Houses
BRISTOL. — Con.				
Fall River. Ward 7,	731	1,396	64	1,460
1 tenement (1 family),	312	312	-	-
2 tenements (2 families),	285	570	-	-
3 tenements (3 families),	52	156	-	-
4 tenements (4 families),	67	268	-	-
5 tenements (5 families),	4	20	-	-
6 tenements (6 families),	8	48	-	-
7 tenements (7 families),	2	14	-	-
8 tenements (8 families),	1	8	-	-
Fall River. Ward 8,	935	1,607	61	1,668
1 tenement (1 family),	526	526	-	-
2 tenements (2 families),	283	566	-	-
3 tenements (3 families),	49	147	-	-
4 tenements (4 families),	40	160	-	-
5 tenements (5 families),	18	90	-	-
6 tenements (6 families),	16	96	-	-
7 tenements (7 families),	2	14	-	-
8 tenements (8 families),	1	8	-	-
Fall River. Ward 9,	998	2,130	170	2,300
1 tenement (1 family),	412	412	-	-
2 tenements (2 families),	301	602	-	-
3 tenements (3 families),	120	360	-	-
4 tenements (4 families),	106	424	-	-
5 tenements (5 families),	32	160	-	-
6 tenements (6 families),	22	132	-	-
8 tenements (8 families),	5	40	-	-
Freetown,	313	342	9	351
1 tenement (1 family),	287	287	-	-
2 tenements (2 families),	24	48	-	-
3 tenements (3 families),	1	3	-	-
4 tenements (4 families),	1	4	-	-
Mansfield,	823	946	37	983
1 tenement (1 family),	705	705	-	-
2 tenements (2 families),	115	230	-	-
3 tenements (3 families),	1	3	-	-
4 tenements (4 families),	2	8	-	-
NEW BEDFORD,	7,480	12,221	569	12,790
1 tenement (1 family),	3,968	3,968	-	-
2 tenements (2 families),	2,676	5,352	-	-
3 tenements (3 families),	631	1,893	-	-
4 tenements (4 families),	109	436	-	-
5 tenements (5 families),	30	150	-	-
6 tenements (6 families),	52	312	-	-
7 tenements (7 families),	8	56	-	-
8 tenements (8 families),	2	16	-	-
9 tenements (9 families),	2	18	-	-
10 tenements (10 families),	2	20	-	-
New Bedford. Ward 1,	1,296	2,500	137	2,637
1 tenement (1 family),	572	572	-	-
2 tenements (2 families),	437	874	-	-
3 tenements (3 families),	208	624	-	-
4 tenements (4 families),	25	100	-	-
5 tenements (5 families),	8	40	-	-
6 tenements (6 families),	37	222	-	-
7 tenements (7 families),	6	42	-	-
8 tenements (8 families),	2	16	-	-
10 tenements (10 families),	1	10	-	-

OCCUPIED AND UNOCCUPIED TENEMENTS IN OCCUPIED DWELLING
HOUSES — Continued.

COUNTIES, CITIES, TOWNS, AND NUMBER OF TENEMENTS AND FAMILIES.	Number of Occupied Dwelling Houses	Number of Occupied Tenements in Occupied Dwelling Houses	Number of Unoccupied Tenements in Occupied Dwelling Houses	Total Number of Tenements in Occupied Dwelling Houses
BRISTOL — Con.				
New Bedford. Ward 2, ...	1,147	1,792	65	1,857
1 tenement (1 family), ...	609	609	-	-
2 tenements (2 families), ...	468	936	-	-
3 tenements (3 families), ...	49	147	-	-
4 tenements (4 families), ...	13	52	-	-
5 tenements (5 families), ...	4	20	-	-
6 tenements (6 families), ...	3	18	-	-
10 tenements (10 families), ...	1	10	-	-
New Bedford. Ward 3, ...	1,056	1,553	62	1,615
1 tenement (1 family), ...	594	594	-	-
2 tenements (2 families), ...	437	874	-	-
3 tenements (3 families), ...	17	51	-	-
4 tenements (4 families), ...	7	28	-	-
6 tenements (6 families), ...	1	6	-	-
New Bedford. Ward 4, ...	1,154	1,615	69	1,684
1 tenement (1 family), ...	775	775	-	-
2 tenements (2 families), ...	330	660	-	-
3 tenements (3 families), ...	26	78	-	-
4 tenements (4 families), ...	16	64	-	-
5 tenements (5 families), ...	5	25	-	-
6 tenements (6 families), ...	1	6	-	-
7 tenements (7 families), ...	1	7	-	-
New Bedford. Ward 5, ...	1,416	2,172	88	2,260
1 tenement (1 family), ...	835	835	-	-
2 tenements (2 families), ...	463	926	-	-
3 tenements (3 families), ...	82	246	-	-
4 tenements (4 families), ...	23	92	-	-
5 tenements (5 families), ...	8	40	-	-
6 tenements (6 families), ...	4	24	-	-
9 tenements (9 families), ...	1	9	-	-
New Bedford. Ward 6, ...	1,411	2,589	148	2,737
1 tenement (1 family), ...	583	583	-	-
2 tenements (2 families), ...	541	1,082	-	-
3 tenements (3 families), ...	249	747	-	-
4 tenements (4 families), ...	25	100	-	-
5 tenements (5 families), ...	5	25	-	-
6 tenements (6 families), ...	6	36	-	-
7 tenements (7 families), ...	1	7	-	-
9 tenements (9 families), ...	1	9	-	-
North Attleborough, ...	1,235	1,499	90	1,589
1 tenement (1 family), ...	988	988	-	-
2 tenements (2 families), ...	231	462	-	-
3 tenements (3 families), ...	15	45	-	-
4 tenements (4 families), ...	1	4	-	-
Norton, ...	372	401	16	417
1 tenement (1 family), ...	344	344	-	-
2 tenements (2 families), ...	27	54	-	-
3 tenements (3 families), ...	1	3	-	-
Raynham, ...	363	397	12	409
1 tenement (1 family), ...	331	331	-	-
2 tenements (2 families), ...	30	60	-	-
3 tenements (3 families), ...	2	6	-	-
Rehoboth, ...	403	451	13	464
1 tenement (1 family), ...	358	358	-	-
2 tenements (2 families), ...	42	84	-	-
3 tenements (3 families), ...	3	9	-	-

OCCUPIED AND UNOCCUPIED TENEMENTS IN OCCUPIED DWELLING
HOUSES — Continued.

COUNTIES, CITIES, TOWNS, AND NUMBER OF TENEMENTS AND FAMILIES.	Number of Occupied Dwelling Houses	Number of Occupied Tenements in Occupied Dwelling Houses	Number of Unoccupied Tenements in Occupied Dwelling Houses	Total Number of Tenements in Occupied Dwelling Houses
BRISTOL. — Con.				
Seekonk, ...	310	334	12	346
1 tenement (1 family), . . .	287	287	-	-
2 tenements (2 families), ...	22	44	-	-
3 tenements (3 families), ...	1	3	-	-
Somerset, ...	413	497	49	546
1 tenement (1 family), . . .	336	336	-	-
2 tenements (2 families), ...	73	146	-	-
3 tenements (3 families), ...	2	6	-	-
4 tenements (4 families), ...	1	4	-	-
5 tenements (5 families), ...	1	5	-	-
Swansea, ...	365	411	5	416
1 tenement (1 family), ...	322	322	-	-
2 tenements (2 families), ...	41	82	-	-
3 tenements (3 families), ...	1	3	-	-
4 tenements (4 families), ...	1	4	-	-
TAUNTON, ...	4,379	5,885	379	6,264
1 tenement (1 family), ...	3,062	3,062	-	-
2 tenements (2 families), ...	1,191	2,382	-	-
3 tenements (3 families), . . .	82	246	-	-
4 tenements (4 families), . . .	37	148	-	-
5 tenements (5 families), ...	4	20	-	-
8 tenements (8 families), ...	2	16	-	-
11 tenements (11 families), ...	1	11	-	-
Taunton. Ward 1, ...	518	669	22	691
1 tenement (1 family), . . .	372	372	-	-
2 tenements (2 families), ...	142	284	-	-
3 tenements (3 families), ...	3	9	-	-
4 tenements (4 families), ...	1	4	-	-
Taunton. Ward 2, ...	467	687	61	748
1 tenement (1 family), . . .	287	287	-	-
2 tenements (2 families), ...	158	316	-	-
3 tenements (3 families), ...	10	30	-	-
4 tenements (4 families), ...	9	36	-	-
5 tenements (5 families), ...	2	10	-	-
8 tenements (8 families), ...	1	8	-	-
Taunton. Ward 3, ...	424	691	69	760
1 tenement (1 family), . . .	222	222	-	-
2 tenements (2 families), ...	167	334	-	-
3 tenements (3 families), ...	18	54	-	-
4 tenements (4 families), ...	13	52	-	-
5 tenements (5 families), ...	2	10	-	-
8 tenements (8 families), ...	1	8	-	-
11 tenements (11 families), ...	1	11	-	-
Taunton. Ward 4, ...	607	737	45	782
1 tenement (1 family), . . .	485	485	-	-
2 tenements (2 families), ...	115	230	-	-
3 tenements (3 families), ...	6	18	-	-
4 tenements (4 families), ...	1	4	-	-
Taunton. Ward 5, ...	642	815	55	870
1 tenement (1 family), . . .	478	478	-	-
2 tenements (2 families), ...	157	314	-	-
3 tenements (3 families), ...	5	15	-	-
4 tenements (4 families), ...	2	8	-	-
Taunton. Ward 6, ...	503	715	28	743
1 tenement (1 family), ...	322	322	-	-
2 tenements (2 families), ...	155	310	-	-

OCCUPIED AND UNOCCUPIED TENEMENTS IN OCCUPIED DWELLING
HOUSES — Continued.

COUNTIES, CITIES, TOWNS, AND NUMBER OF TENEMENTS AND FAMILIES.	Number of Occupied Dwelling Houses	Number of Occupied Tenements in Occupied Dwelling Houses	Number of Unoccupied Tenements in Occupied Dwelling Houses	Total Number of Tenements in Occupied Dwelling Houses
BRISTOL — Con.				
Taunton. Ward 6 — Con.				
3 tenements (3 families), ...	21	63	-	-
4 tenements (4 families), ...	5	20	-	-
Taunton. Ward 7, ...	513	673	66	739
1 tenement (1 family), ...	367	367	-	-
2 tenements (2 families), ...	135	270	-	-
3 tenements (3 families), ...	8	24	-	-
4 tenements (4 families), ...	3	12	-	-
Taunton. Ward 8, ...	705	898	33	931
1 tenement (1 family), ...	529	529	-	-
2 tenements (2 families), ...	162	324	-	-
3 tenements (3 families), ...	11	33	-	-
4 tenements (4 families), ...	3	12	-	-
Westport, ...	647	702	29	731
1 tenement (1 family), ...	592	592	-	-
2 tenements (2 families), ...	55	110	-	-
DUKES.				
Chilmark, ...	93	95	-	95
1 tenement (1 family , ...	91	91	-	-
2 tenements (2 families , ...	2	4	-	-
Cottage City, ...	312	313	8	321
1 tenement (1 family , ...	311	311	-	-
2 tenements (2 families), ...	1	2	-	-
Edgartown, ...	351	377	24	401
1 tenement (1 family), ...	290	290	-	-
2 tenements (2 families), ...	38	76	-	-
3 tenements (3 families , ...	1	3	-	-
4 tenements (4 families , ...	2	8	-	-
Gay Head, ...	35	40	-	40
1 tenement (1 family), ...	30	30	-	-
2 tenements (2 families), ...	5	10	-	-
Gosnold, ...	35	38	3	41
1 tenement (1 family), ...	32	32	-	-
2 tenements (2 families), ...	3	6	-	-
Tisbury, ...	265	289	17	306
1 tenement (1 family , ...	240	240	-	-
2 tenements (2 families), ...	21	42	-	-
3 tenements (3 families , ...	1	3	-	-
4 tenements (4 families), ...	1	4	-	-
West Tisbury, ...	148	154	3	157
1 tenement (1 family , ...	142	142	-	-
2 tenements (2 families , ...	6	12	-	-
ESSEX.				
Amesbury, ...	1,956	2,281	101	2,382
1 tenement (1 family), ...	1,647	1,647	-	-
2 tenements (2 families), ...	296	592	-	-
3 tenements (3 families), ...	10	30	-	-
4 tenements (4 families), ...	3	12	-	-
Andover, ...	1,156	1,296	30	1,326
1 tenement (1 family), ...	1,040	1,040	-	-
2 tenements (2 families), ...	97	194	-	-
3 tenements (3 families), ...	15	45	-	-
4 tenements (4 families), ...	3	12	-	-
5 tenements (5 families), ...	1	5	-	-
BEVERLY, ...	2,049	2,914	121	3,035
1 tenement (1 family), ...	1,295	1,295	-	-
2 tenements (2 families , ...	679	1,358	-	-

OCCUPIED AND UNOCCUPIED TENEMENTS IN OCCUPIED DWELLING HOUSES — Continued.

COUNTIES, CITIES, TOWNS, AND NUMBER OF TENEMENTS AND FAMILIES.	Number of Occupied Dwelling Houses	Number of Occupied Tenements in Occupied Dwelling Houses	Number of Unoccupied Tenements in Occupied Dwelling Houses	Total Number of Tenements in Occupied Dwelling Houses
ESSEX — Con.				
BEVERLY — Con.				
3 tenements (3 families), ...	51	153	–	–
4 tenements (4 families), ...	17	68	–	–
5 tenements (5 families), ...	4	20	–	–
6 tenements (6 families), ...	2	12	–	–
8 tenements (8 families), ...	1	8	–	–
Beverly. Ward 1, ...	415	598	6	604
1 tenement (1 family), ...	260	260	–	–
2 tenements (2 families), ...	138	276	–	–
3 tenements (3 families), ...	10	30	–	–
4 tenements (4 families), ...	4	16	–	–
5 tenements (5 families), ...	2	10	–	–
6 tenements (6 families), ...	1	6	–	–
Beverly. Ward 2, ...	393	618	36	654
1 tenement (1 family), ...	209	209	–	–
2 tenements (2 families), ...	160	320	–	–
3 tenements (3 families), ...	15	45	–	–
4 tenements (4 families), ...	5	20	–	–
5 tenements (5 families), ...	2	10	–	–
6 tenements (6 families), ...	1	6	–	–
8 tenements (8 families), ...	1	8	–	–
Beverly. Ward 3, ...	399	610	27	637
1 tenement (1 family), ...	210	210	–	–
2 tenements (2 families), ...	171	342	–	–
3 tenements (3 families), ...	14	42	–	–
4 tenements (4 families), ...	4	16	–	–
Beverly. Ward 4, ...	392	528	22	550
1 tenement (1 family), ...	266	266	–	–
2 tenements (2 families), ...	118	236	–	–
3 tenements (3 families), ...	6	18	–	–
4 tenements (4 families), ...	2	8	–	–
Beverly. Ward 5, ...	247	306	7	313
1 tenement (1 family), ...	192	192	–	–
2 tenements (2 families), ...	51	102	–	–
3 tenements (3 families), ...	4	12	–	–
Beverly. Ward 6, ...	203	254	23	277
1 tenement (1 family), ...	158	158	–	–
2 tenements (2 families), ...	41	82	–	–
3 tenements (3 families), ...	2	6	–	–
4 tenements (4 families), ...	2	8	–	–
Boxford, ...	177	186	3	189
1 tenement (1 family), ...	168	168	–	–
2 tenements (2 families), ...	9	18	–	–
Bradford, ...	905	1,121	58	1,179
1 tenement (1 family), ...	708	708	–	–
2 tenements (2 families), ...	183	366	–	–
3 tenements (3 families), ...	10	30	–	–
4 tenements (4 families), ...	3	12	–	–
5 tenements (5 families), ...	1	5	–	–
Danvers, ...	1,333	1,653	52	1,705
1 tenement (1 family), ...	1,031	1,031	–	–
2 tenements (2 families), ...	285	570	–	–
3 tenements (3 families), ...	16	48	–	–
4 tenements (4 families), ...	1	4	–	–
Essex, ...	414	445	20	465
1 tenement (1 family), ...	383	383	–	–
2 tenements (2 families), ...	31	62	–	–

OCCUPIED AND UNOCCUPIED TENEMENTS IN OCCUPIED DWELLING
HOUSES — Continued.

COUNTIES, CITIES, TOWNS, AND NUMBER OF TENEMENTS AND FAMILIES.	Number of Occupied Dwelling Houses	Number of Occupied Tenements in Occupied Dwelling Houses	Number of Unoccupied Tenements in Occupied Dwelling Houses	Total Number of Tenements in Occupied Dwelling Houses
ESSEX — Con.				
Georgetown,	476	541	13	554
1 tenement (1 family),	415	415	-	-
2 tenements 2 families,	58	116	-	-
3 tenements (3 families),	2	6	-	-
4 tenements (4 families),	1	4	-	-
GLOUCESTER,	3,758	5,416	125	5,541
1 tenement (1 family),	2,577	2,577	-	-
2 tenements 2 families,	894	1,788	-	-
3 tenements (3 families),	164	492	-	-
4 tenements (4 families),	84	336	-	-
5 tenements (5 families),	20	100	-	-
6 tenements (6 families),	15	90	-	-
7 tenements (7 families),	2	14	-	-
8 tenements (8 families),	1	8	-	-
11 tenements (11 families),	1	11	-	-
Gloucester. Ward 1,	492	696	15	711
1 tenement (1 family),	328	328	-	-
2 tenements (2 families),	135	270	-	-
3 tenements (3 families),	22	66	-	-
4 tenements (4 families),	5	20	-	-
6 tenements (6 families),	2	12	-	-
Gloucester. Ward 2,	553	982	32	1,014
1 tenement (1 family),	268	268	-	-
2 tenements (2 families),	164	328	-	-
3 tenements (3 families),	47	141	-	-
4 tenements (4 families),	36	144	-	-
5 tenements (5 families),	8	40	-	-
6 tenements (6 families),	9	54	-	-
7 tenements (7 families),	1	7	-	-
Gloucester. Ward 3,	490	743	17	760
1 tenement (1 family),	300	300	-	-
2 tenements (2 families),	147	294	-	-
3 tenements (3 families),	28	84	-	-
4 tenements (4 families),	10	40	-	-
5 tenements (5 families),	5	25	-	-
Gloucester. Ward 4,	335	520	15	535
1 tenement (1 family),	216	216	-	-
2 tenements (2 families),	78	156	-	-
3 tenements (3 families),	23	69	-	-
4 tenements (4 families),	12	48	-	-
5 tenements (5 families),	5	25	-	-
6 tenements (6 families),	1	6	-	-
Gloucester. Ward 5,	691	893	16	909
1 tenement 1 family,	528	528	-	-
2 tenements (2 families),	138	276	-	-
3 tenements 3 families),	15	45	-	-
4 tenements (4 families),	9	36	-	-
8 tenements (8 families),	1	8	-	-
Gloucester. Ward 6,	534	704	13	717
1 tenement (1 family),	393	393	-	-
2 tenements (2 families),	125	250	-	-
3 tenements (3 families),	10	30	-	-
4 tenements (4 families),	5	20	-	-
11 tenements (11 families),	1	11	-	-
Gloucester. Ward 7,	415	587	10	597
1 tenement (1 family),	298	298	-	-

OCCUPIED AND UNOCCUPIED TENEMENTS IN OCCUPIED DWELLING
HOUSES — Continued.

COUNTIES, CITIES, TOWNS, AND NUMBER OF TENEMENTS AND FAMILIES.	Number of Occupied Dwelling Houses	Number of Occupied Tenements in Occupied Dwelling Houses	Number of Unoccupied Tenements in Occupied Dwelling Houses	Total Number of Tenements in Occupied Dwelling Houses
ESSEX — Con.				
Gloucester. Ward 7 — Con.				
2 tenements (2 families), ...	86	172	-	-
3 tenements (3 families), ...	18	54	-	-
4 tenements (4 families), ...	7	28	-	-
5 tenements (5 families), ...	2	10	-	-
6 tenements (6 families), ...	3	18	-	-
7 tenements (7 families), ...	1	7	-	-
Gloucester. Ward 8, ...	268	291	7	298
1 tenement (1 family), ...	246	246	-	-
2 tenements (2 families), ...	21	42	-	-
3 tenements (3 families), ...	1	3	-	-
Groveland, ...	505	560	3	563
1 tenement (1 family), ...	452	452	-	-
2 tenements (2 families), ...	51	102	-	-
3 tenements (3 families), ...	2	6	-	-
Hamilton, ...	295	315		315
1 tenement (1 family), ...	275	275	-	-
2 tenements (2 families), ...	20	40	-	-
HAVERHILL, ...	4,814	6,902	349	7,251
1 tenement (1 family), ...	3,030	3,030	-	-
2 tenements (2 families), ...	1,583	3,166	-	-
3 tenements (3 families), ...	141	423	-	-
4 tenements (4 families), ...	42	168	-	-
5 tenements (5 families), ...	6	30	-	-
6 tenements (6 families), ...	5	30	-	-
7 tenements (7 families), ...	1	7	-	-
8 tenements (8 families), ...	6	48	-	-
Haverhill. Ward 1, ...	389	573	36	609
1 tenement (1 family), ...	242	242	-	-
2 tenements (2 families), ...	121	242	-	-
3 tenements (3 families), ...	21	63	-	-
4 tenements (4 families), ...	2	8	-	-
5 tenements (5 families), ...	1	5	-	-
6 tenements (6 families), ...	1	6	-	-
7 tenements (7 families), ...	1	7	-	-
Haverhill. Ward 2, ...	476	631	40	671
1 tenement (1 family), ...	347	347	-	-
2 tenements (2 families), ...	115	230	-	-
3 tenements (3 families), ...	6	18	-	-
4 tenements (4 families), ...	7	28	-	-
8 tenements (8 families), ...	1	8	-	-
Haverhill. Ward 3, ...	508	781	32	813
1 tenement (1 family), ...	288	288	-	-
2 tenements (2 families), ...	189	378	-	-
3 tenements (3 families), ...	17	51	-	-
4 tenements (4 families), ...	10	40	-	-
5 tenements (5 families), ...	2	10	-	-
6 tenements (6 families), ...	1	6	-	-
8 tenements (8 families), ...	1	8	-	-
Haverhill. Ward 4, ...	812	957	54	1,011
1 tenement (1 family), ...	680	680	-	-
2 tenements (2 families), ...	120	240	-	-
3 tenements (3 families), ...	11	33	-	-
4 tenements (4 families), ...	1	4	-	-
Haverhill. Ward 5, ...	1,519	2,452	125	2,577
1 tenement (1 family), ...	747	747	-	-

OCCUPIED AND UNOCCUPIED TENEMENTS IN OCCUPIED DWELLING
HOUSES — Continued.

COUNTIES, CITIES, TOWNS, AND NUMBER OF TENEMENTS AND FAMILIES.	Number of Occupied Dwelling Houses	Number of Occupied Tenements in Occupied Dwelling Houses	Number of Unoccupied Tenements in Occupied Dwelling Houses	Total Number of Tenements in Occupied Dwelling Houses
ESSEX — Con.				
Haverhill. Ward 5 — Con.				
2 tenements (2 families), ...	666	1,332	-	-
3 tenements (3 families), ...	76	228	-	-
4 tenements (4 families), ...	20	80	-	-
5 tenements (5 families), ...	3	15	-	-
6 tenements (6 families), ...	3	18	-	-
8 tenements (8 families), ...	4	32	-	-
Haverhill. Ward 6, ...	1,110	1,508	62	1,570
1 tenement (1 family), ...	726	726	-	-
2 tenements (2 families), ...	372	744	-	-
3 tenements (3 families), ...	10	30	-	-
4 tenements (4 families), ...	2	8	-	-
Ipswich, ...	926	1,104	9	1,113
1 tenement (1 family), ...	779	779	-	-
2 tenements (2 families), ...	127	254	-	-
3 tenements (3 families), ...	13	39	-	-
4 tenements (4 families), ...	4	16	-	-
5 tenements (5 families), ...	2	10	-	-
6 tenements (6 families), ...	1	6	-	-
LAWRENCE, ...	6,735	10,783	227	11,010
1 family), ...	3,892	3,892	-	-
2 tenements (2 families), ...	2,120	4,240	-	-
3 tenements (3 families), ...	455	1,365	-	-
4 tenements (4 families), ...	175	700	-	-
5 tenements (5 families), ...	39	195	-	-
6 tenements (6 families), ...	37	222	-	-
7 tenements (7 families), ...	6	42	-	-
8 tenements (8 families), ...	4	32	-	-
9 tenements (9 families), ...	3	27	-	-
10 tenements (10 families), ...	1	10	-	-
12 tenements (12 families), ...	1	12	-	-
14 tenements (14 families), ...	1	14	-	-
32 tenements (32 families), ...	1	32	-	-
Lawrence. Ward 1, ...	1,170	1,805	50	1,855
1 tenement (1 family), ...	667	667	-	-
2 tenements (2 families), ...	404	808	-	-
3 tenements (3 families), ...	77	231	-	-
4 tenements (4 families), ...	15	60	-	-
5 tenements (5 families), ...	5	25	-	-
6 tenements (6 families), ...	1	6	-	-
8 tenements (8 families), ...	1	8	-	-
Lawrence. Ward 2, ...	841	1,331	33	1,364
1 tenement (1 family), ...	527	527	-	-
2 tenements (2 families), ...	208	416	-	-
3 tenements (3 families), ...	58	174	-	-
4 tenements (4 families), ...	36	144	-	-
5 tenements (5 families), ...	7	35	-	-
6 tenements (6 families), ...	1	6	-	-
7 tenements (7 families), ...	3	21	-	-
8 tenements (8 families . . .	1	8	-	-
Lawrence. Ward 3, ...	993	1,879	27	1,906
1 tenement (1 family), ...	437	437	-	-
2 tenements (2 families), ...	368	736	-	-
3 tenements (3 families), ...	114	342	-	-
4 tenements (4 families), ...	50	200	-	-
5 tenements (5 families), ...	11	55	-	-

OCCUPIED AND UNOCCUPIED TENEMENTS IN OCCUPIED DWELLING HOUSES — Continued.

Counties, Cities, Towns, and Number of Tenements and Families.	Number of Occupied Dwelling Houses	Number of Occupied Tenements in Occupied Dwelling Houses	Number of Unoccupied Tenements in Occupied Dwelling Houses	Total Number Tenements in Occupied Dwelling Houses
ESSEX — Con.				
Lawrence, Ward 3 — Con.				
6 tenements (6 families), ...	9	54	–	–
7 tenements (7 families), ...	2	14	–	–
9 tenements (9 families), ...	1	9	–	–
32 tenements (32 families)	1	32	–	–
Lawrence, Ward 4, ...	1,071	1,888	35	1,923
1 tenement (1 family), ...	537	537	–	–
2 tenements (2 families), ...	376	752	–	–
3 tenements (3 families), ...	99	297	–	–
4 tenements (4 families), ...	28	112	–	–
5 tenements (5 families), ...	12	60	–	–
6 tenements (6 families), ...	14	84	–	–
7 tenements (7 families), ...	1	7	–	–
8 tenements (8 families), ...	2	16	–	–
9 tenements (9 families), ...	1	9	–	–
14 tenements (14 families), .	1	14	–	–
Lawrence, Ward 5, ...	1,471	2,215	45	2,260
1 tenement (1 family), . . .	896	896	–	–
2 tenements (2 families), . . .	477	954	–	–
3 tenements (3 families), . . .	61	183	–	–
4 tenements (4 families), . . .	26	104	–	–
5 tenements (5 families), . . .	1	5	–	–
6 tenements (6 families), . . .	7	42	–	–
9 tenements (9 families), . . .	1	9	–	–
10 tenements (10 families), .	1	10	–	–
12 tenements (12 families), .	1	12	–	–
Lawrence, Ward 6, ...	1,189	1,665	37	1,702
1 tenement (1 family), . . .	828	828	–	–
2 tenements (2 families), . . .	287	574	–	–
3 tenements (3 families), . . .	46	138	–	–
4 tenements (4 families), . . .	20	80	–	–
5 tenements (5 families), . . .	3	15	–	–
6 tenements (6 families), . . .	5	30	–	–
LYNN, ...	10,045	14,144	773	14,917
1 tenement (1 family), . . .	6,588	6,588	–	–
2 tenements (2 families), . . .	2,864	5,928	–	–
3 tenements (3 families), . . .	396	1,188	–	–
4 tenements (4 families), . . .	70	280	–	–
5 tenements (5 families), . . .	13	65	–	–
6 tenements (6 families), . . .	10	60	–	–
7 tenements (7 families), . . .	3	21	–	–
14 tenements (14 families), .	1	14	–	–
Lynn, Ward 1, ...	332	387	14	401
1 tenement (1 family), . . .	278	278	–	–
2 tenements (2 families), . . .	53	106	–	–
3 tenements (3 families), . . .	1	3	–	–
Lynn, Ward 2, ...	804	968	51	1,019
1 tenement (1 family), . . .	653	653	–	–
2 tenements (2 families), . . .	140	280	–	–
3 tenements (3 families), . . .	9	27	–	–
4 tenements (4 families), . . .	2	8	–	–
Lynn, Ward 3, ...	2,564	3,602	178	3,780
1 tenement (1 family), . . .	1,653	1,653	–	–
2 tenements (2 families), . . .	809	1,618	–	–
3 tenements (3 families), . . .	81	243	–	–
4 tenements (4 families), . . .	17	68	–	–
5 tenements (5 families), . . .	4	20	–	–

OCCUPIED AND UNOCCUPIED TENEMENTS IN OCCUPIED DWELLING
HOUSES — Continued.

COUNTIES, CITIES, TOWNS, AND NUMBER OF TENEMENTS AND FAMILIES.	Number of Occupied Dwelling Houses	Number of Occupied Tenements in Occupied Dwelling Houses	Number of Unoccupied Tenements in Occupied Dwelling Houses	Total Number of Tenements in Occupied Dwelling Houses
ESSEX — Con.				
Lynn. Ward 4, ...	1,574	2,384	204	2,588
1 tenement (1 family), ...	964	964	-	-
2 tenements (2 families), ...	466	932	-	-
3 tenements (3 families), ...	109	327	-	-
4 tenements (4 families), ...	23	92	-	-
5 tenements (5 families), ...	5	25	-	-
6 tenements (6 families), ...	5	30	-	-
7 tenements (7 families), ...	2	14	-	-
Lynn. Ward 5, ...	1,914	2,875	140	3,015
1 tenement (1 family), ...	1,098	1,098	-	-
2 tenements (2 families), ...	706	1,412	-	-
3 tenements (3 families), ...	87	261	-	-
4 tenements (4 families), ...	16	64	-	-
5 tenements (5 families), ...	3	15	-	-
6 tenements (6 families), ...	3	18	-	-
7 tenements (7 families), ...	1	7	-	-
Lynn. Ward 6, ...	2,358	3,324	148	3,472
1 tenement (1 family), ...	1,537	1,537	-	-
2 tenements (2 families), ...	704	1,408	-	-
3 tenements (3 families), ...	102	306	-	-
4 tenements (4 families), ...	12	48	-	-
5 tenements (5 families), ...	1	5	-	-
6 tenements (6 families), ...	1	6	-	-
14 tenements (14 families), ...	1	14	-	-
Lynn. Ward 7, ...	499	604	38	642
1 tenement (1 family), ...	405	405	-	-
2 tenements (2 families), ...	86	172	-	-
3 tenements (3 families), ...	7	21	-	-
6 tenements (6 families), ...	1	6	-	-
Lynnfield, ...	183	211	4	215
1 tenement (1 family), ...	156	156	-	-
2 tenements (2 families), ...	26	52	-	-
3 tenements (3 families), ...	1	3	-	-
Manchester, ...	410	488	23	511
1 tenement (1 family), ...	335	335	-	-
2 tenements (2 families), ...	73	146	-	-
3 tenements (3 families), ...	1	3	-	-
4 tenements (4 families), ...	1	4	-	-
Marblehead, ...	1,433	2,003	80	2,083
1 tenement (1 family), ...	939	939	-	-
2 tenements (2 families), ...	438	876	-	-
3 tenements (3 families), ...	37	111	-	-
4 tenements (4 families), ...	18	72	-	-
5 tenements (5 families), ...	1	5	-	-
Merrimac, ...	495	605	35	640
1 tenement (1 family), ...	386	386	-	-
2 tenements (2 families), ...	108	216	-	-
3 tenements (3 families), ...	1	3	-	-
Methuen, ...	1,139	1,317	36	1,353
1 tenement (1 family), ...	970	970	-	-
2 tenements (2 families), ...	160	320	-	-
3 tenements (3 families), ...	9	27	-	-
Middleton, ...	199	219	18	237
1 tenement (1 family), ...	180	180	-	-
2 tenements (2 families), ...	18	36	-	-
3 tenements (3 families), ...	1	3	-	-

OCCUPIED AND UNOCCUPIED TENEMENTS IN OCCUPIED DWELLING HOUSES — Continued.

COUNTIES, CITIES, TOWNS, AND NUMBER OF TENEMENTS AND FAMILIES.	Number of Occupied Dwelling Houses	Number of Occupied Tenements in Occupied Dwelling Houses	Number of Unoccupied Tenements in Occupied Dwelling Houses	Total Number of Tenements in Occupied Dwelling Houses
ESSEX — Con.				
Nahant,	182	204	11	215
1 tenement (1 family),	163	163	-	-
2 tenements (2 families),	16	32	-	-
3 tenements (3 families),	3	9	-	-
Newbury,	346	360	20	380
1 tenement (1 family),	274	274	-	-
2 tenements (2 families),	40	80	-	-
3 tenements (3 families),	2	6	-	-
NEWBURYPORT,	2,977	3,479	86	3,565
1 tenement (1 family),	2,535	2,535	-	-
2 tenements (2 families),	396	792	-	-
3 tenements (3 families),	33	99	-	-
4 tenements (4 families),	12	48	-	-
5 tenements (5 families),	1	5	-	-
Newburyport. Ward 1,	515	601	6	607
1 tenement (1 family),	433	433	-	-
2 tenements (2 families),	74	148	-	-
3 tenements (3 families),	4	12	-	-
4 tenements (4 families),	2	8	-	-
Newburyport. Ward 2,	406	510	16	526
1 tenement (1 family),	324	324	-	-
2 tenements (2 families),	68	136	-	-
3 tenements (3 families),	7	21	-	-
4 tenements (4 families),	6	24	-	-
5 tenements (5 families),	1	5	-	-
Newburyport. Ward 3,	561	615	4	619
1 tenement (1 family),	510	510	-	-
2 tenements (2 families),	48	96	-	-
3 tenements (3 families),	3	9	-	-
Newburyport. Ward 4,	479	559	20	579
1 tenement (1 family),	468	468	-	-
2 tenements (2 families),	63	126	-	-
3 tenements (3 families),	7	21	-	-
4 tenements (4 families),	1	4	-	-
Newburyport. Ward 5,	446	528	23	551
1 tenement (1 family),	364	364	-	-
2 tenements (2 families),	73	146	-	-
3 tenements (3 families),	8	24	-	-
4 tenements (4 families),	1	4	-	-
Newburyport. Ward 6,	572	656	18	674
1 tenement (1 family),	496	496	-	-
2 tenements (2 families),	70	140	-	-
3 tenements (3 families),	4	12	-	-
4 tenements (4 families),	2	8	-	-
North Andover,	742	796	9	805
1 tenement (1 family),	691	691	-	-
2 tenements (2 families),	49	98	-	-
3 tenements (3 families),	1	3	-	-
4 tenements (4 families),	1	4	-	-
Peabody,	1,763	2,373	127	2,494
1 tenement (1 family),	1,243	1,243	-	-
2 tenements (2 families),	461	922	-	-
3 tenements (3 families),	30	90	-	-
4 tenements (4 families),	28	112	-	-
6 tenements (6 families),	1	6	-	-
Rockport,	896	1,236	38	1,274
1 tenement (1 family),	631	631	-	-

OCCUPIED AND UNOCCUPIED TENEMENTS IN OCCUPIED DWELLING
HOUSES — Continued.

COUNTIES, CITIES, TOWNS, AND NUMBER OF TENEMENTS AND FAMILIES.	Number of Occupied Dwelling Houses	Number of Occupied Tenements in Occupied Dwelling Houses	Number of Unoccupied Tenements in Occupied Dwelling Houses	Total Number of Tenements in Occupied Dwelling Houses
ESSEX — Con.				
Rockport — Con.				
2 tenements (2 families), ...	216	432	–	–
3 tenements (3 families), ...	31	93	–	–
4 tenements (4 families), ...	13	52	–	–
5 tenements (5 families), ...	2	10	–	–
6 tenements (6 families), ...	3	18	–	–
Rowley, ...	292	340	4	344
1 tenement (1 family), ...	246	246	–	–
2 tenements (2 families), ...	45	90	–	–
4 tenements (4 families), ...	1	4	–	–
SALEM, ...	4,865	7,623	302	7,925
1 tenement (1 family), ...	2,779	2,779	–	–
2 tenements (2 families), ...	1,682	3,364	–	–
3 tenements (3 families), ...	224	672	–	–
4 tenements (4 families), ...	132	528	–	–
5 tenements (5 families), ...	18	90	–	–
6 tenements (6 families), ...	18	108	–	–
7 tenements (7 families), ...	4	28	–	–
8 tenements (8 families), ...	4	32	–	–
10 tenements (10 families), ...	1	10	–	–
12 tenements (12 families), ...	1	12	–	–
Salem. Ward 1, ...	622	1,109	68	1,177
1 tenement (1 family), ...	279	279	–	–
2 tenements (2 families), ...	254	508	–	–
3 tenements (3 families), ...	48	144	–	–
4 tenements (4 families), ...	31	124	–	–
5 tenements (5 families), ...	6	30	–	–
6 tenements (6 families), ...	4	24	–	–
Salem. Ward 2, ...	963	1,369	54	1,423
1 tenement (1 family), ...	584	584	–	–
2 tenements (2 families), ...	356	712	–	–
3 tenements (3 families), ...	20	60	–	–
4 tenements (4 families), ...	2	8	–	–
5 tenements (5 families), ...	1	5	–	–
Salem. Ward 3, ...	701	1,028	41	1,069
1 tenement (1 family), ...	427	427	–	–
2 tenements (2 families), ...	231	462	–	–
3 tenements (3 families), ...	34	102	–	–
4 tenements (4 families), ...	8	32	–	–
5 tenements (5 families), ...	1	5	–	–
Salem. Ward 4, ...	795	1,181	42	1,223
1 tenement (1 family), ...	472	472	–	–
2 tenements (2 families), ...	279	558	–	–
3 tenements (3 families), ...	28	84	–	–
4 tenements (4 families), ...	13	52	–	–
5 tenements (5 families), ...	3	15	–	–
Salem. Ward 5, ...	1,048	1,881	62	1,943
1 tenement (1 family), ...	561	561	–	–
2 tenements (2 families), ...	313	626	–	–
3 tenements (3 families), ...	79	237	–	–
4 tenements (4 families), ...	64	256	–	–
5 tenements (5 families), ...	7	35	–	–
6 tenements (6 families), ...	14	84	–	–
7 tenements (7 families), ...	4	28	–	–
8 tenements (8 families), ...	4	32	–	–
10 tenements (10 families), ...	1	10	–	–
12 tenements (12 families), ...	1	12	–	–

OCCUPIED AND UNOCCUPIED TENEMENTS IN OCCUPIED DWELLING
HOUSES — Continued.

COUNTIES, CITIES, TOWNS, AND NUMBER OF TENEMENTS AND FAMILIES.	Number of Occupied Dwelling Houses	Number of Occupied Tenements in Occupied Dwelling Houses	Number of Unoccupied Tenements in Occupied Dwelling Houses	Total Number of Tenements in Occupied Dwelling Houses
ESSEX — Con.				
Salem. Ward 6, ...	734	1,055	35	1,090
1 tenement (1 family), ...	456	456	–	–
2 tenements (2 families), ...	249	498	–	–
3 tenements (3 families), ...	15	45	–	–
4 tenements (4 families), ...	14	56	–	–
Salisbury, ...	317	351	5	356
1 tenement (1 family), ...	284	284	–	–
2 tenements (2 families), ...	32	64	–	–
3 tenements (3 families), ...	1	3	–	–
Saugus, ...	965	1,065	44	1,109
1 tenement (1 family), ...	867	867	–	–
2 tenements (2 families), ...	96	192	–	–
3 tenements (3 families), ...	2	6	–	–
Swampscott, ...	703	823	46	869
1 tenement (1 family), ...	588	588	–	–
2 tenements (2 families), ...	110	220	–	–
3 tenements (3 families), ...	5	15	–	–
Topsfield, ...	215	264	9	273
1 tenement (1 family), ...	174	174	–	–
2 tenements (2 families), ...	35	70	–	–
3 tenements (3 families), ...	4	12	–	–
4 tenements (4 families), ...	2	8	–	–
Wenham, ...	206	234	8	242
1 tenement (1 family), ...	179	179	–	–
2 tenements (2 families), ...	26	52	–	–
3 tenements (3 families), ...	* 1	3	–	–
West Newbury, ...	394	440	20	460
1 tenement (1 family), ...	349	349	–	–
2 tenements (2 families), ...	44	88	–	–
3 tenements (3 families), ...	1	3	–	–
FRANKLIN.				
Ashfield, ...	225	252	3	255
1 tenement (1 family), ...	204	204	–	–
2 tenements (2 families), ...	19	38	–	–
3 tenements (3 families), ...	1	3	–	–
7 tenements (7 families), ...	1	7	–	–
Bernardston, ...	196	209	5	214
1 tenement (1 family), ...	184	184	–	–
2 tenements (2 families), ...	11	22	–	–
3 tenements (3 families), ...	1	3	–	–
Buckland, ...	332	387	19	406
1 tenement (1 family), ...	284	284	–	–
2 tenements (2 families), ...	42	84	–	–
3 tenements (3 families), ...	5	15	–	–
4 tenements (4 families), ...	1	4	–	–
Charlemont, ...	247	275	6	281
1 tenement (1 family), ...	220	220	–	–
2 tenements (2 families), ...	26	52	–	–
3 tenements (3 families), ...	1	3	–	–
Colrain, ...	324	366	17	383
1 tenement (1 family), ...	287	287	–	–
2 tenements (2 families), ...	32	64	–	–
3 tenements (3 families), ...	5	15	–	–
Conway, ...	286	309	11	320
1 tenement (1 family), ...	263	263	–	–
2 tenements (2 families), ...	23	46	–	–

OCCUPIED AND UNOCCUPIED TENEMENTS IN OCCUPIED DWELLING
HOUSES — Continued.

COUNTIES, CITIES, TOWNS, AND NUMBER OF TENEMENTS AND FAMILIES.	Number of Occupied Dwelling Houses	Number of Occupied Tenements in Occupied Dwelling Houses	Number of Unoccupied Tenements in Occupied Dwelling Houses	Total Number of Tenements in Occupied Dwelling Houses
FRANKLIN — Con.				
Deerfield, ...	635	674	2	676
1 tenement (1 family), ...	599	599	-	-
2 tenements (2 families), ...	33	66	-	-
3 tenements (3 families), ...	3	9	-	-
Erving, ...	217	256	6	262
1 tenement (1 family), ...	182	182	-	-
2 tenements (2 families), ...	32	64	-	-
3 tenements (3 families), ...	2	6	-	-
4 tenements (4 families), ...	1	4	-	-
Gill, ...	178	197	7	204
1 tenement (1 family), ...	161	161	-	-
2 tenements (2 families), ...	15	30	-	-
3 tenements (3 families), ...	2	6	-	-
Greenfield, ...	1,223	1,450	21	1,471
1 tenement (1 family), ...	1,022	1,022	-	-
2 tenements (2 families), ...	183	366	-	-
3 tenements (3 families), ...	11	33	-	-
4 tenements (4 families), ...	6	24	-	-
5 tenements (5 families), ...	1	5	-	-
Hawley, ...	103	110	3	113
1 tenement (1 family), ...	96	96	-	-
2 tenements (2 families), ...	7	14	-	-
Heath, ...	115	120	2	122
1 tenement (1 family), ...	110	110	-	-
2 tenements (2 families), ...	5	10	-	-
Leverett, ...	186	200	2	202
1 tenement (1 family), ...	172	172	-	-
2 tenements (2 families), ...	14	28	-	-
Leyden, ...	83	88	1	89
1 tenement (1 family), ...	78	78	-	-
2 tenements (2 families), ...	5	10	-	-
Monroe, ...	55	65	-	65
1 tenement (1 family), ...	45	45	-	-
2 tenements (2 families), ...	10	20	-	-
Montague, ...	954	1,349	93	1,442
1 tenement (1 family), ...	671	671	-	-
2 tenements (2 families), ...	210	420	-	-
3 tenements (3 families), ...	44	132	-	-
4 tenements (4 families), ...	21	84	-	-
5 tenements (5 families), ...	6	30	-	-
6 tenements (6 families), ...	2	12	-	-
New Salem, ...	219	233	4	237
1 tenement (1 family), ...	206	206	-	-
2 tenements (2 families), ...	12	24	-	-
3 tenements (3 families), ...	1	3	-	-
Northfield, ...	389	419	4	423
1 tenement (1 family), ...	363	363	-	-
2 tenements (2 families), ...	24	48	-	-
3 tenements (3 families), ...	1	3	-	-
5 tenements (5 families), ...	1	5	-	-
Orange, ...	1,055	1,380	73	1,463
1 tenement (1 family), ...	770	770	-	-
2 tenements (2 families), ...	257	514	-	-
3 tenements (3 families), ...	14	42	-	-
4 tenements (4 families), ...	8	32	-	-
6 tenements (6 families), ...	1	6	-	-

OCCUPIED AND UNOCCUPIED TENEMENTS IN OCCUPIED DWELLING HOUSES — Continued.

COUNTIES, CITIES, TOWNS, AND NUMBER OF TENEMENTS AND FAMILIES.	Number of Occupied Dwelling Houses	Number of Occupied Tenements in Occupied Dwelling Houses	Number of Unoccupied Tenements in Occupied Dwelling Houses	Total Number of Tenements in Occupied Dwelling Houses
FRANKLIN — Con.				
Orange — Con.				
8 tenements (8 families), ...	2	16	–	–
10 tenements (10 families), ...	1	10	–	–
Rowe, ...	108	123	6	129
1 tenement (1 family), ...	94	94	–	–
2 tenements (2 families), ...	13	26	–	–
3 tenements (3 families), ...	1	3	–	–
Shelburne, ...	322	392	11	403
1 tenement (1 family), ...	263	263	–	–
2 tenements (2 families), ...	52	104	–	–
3 tenements (3 families), ...	3	9	–	–
4 tenements (4 families), ...	4	16	–	–
Shutesbury, ...	121	125	–	125
1 tenement (1 family), ...	117	117	–	–
2 tenements (2 families), ...	4	8	–	–
Sunderland, ...	152	166	1	167
1 tenement (1 family), ...	138	138	–	–
2 tenements (2 families), ...	14	28	–	–
Warwick, ...	150	158	–	158
1 tenement (1 family), ...	142	142	–	–
2 tenements (2 families), ...	8	16	–	–
Wendell, ...	122	129	3	132
1 tenement (1 family), ...	116	116	–	–
2 tenements (2 families), ...	5	10	–	–
3 tenements (3 families), ...	1	3	–	–
Whately, ...	182	195	37	232
1 tenement (1 family), ...	170	170	–	–
2 tenements (2 families), ...	11	22	–	–
3 tenements (3 families), ...	1	3	–	–
HAMPDEN.				
Agawam, ...	489	553	4	557
1 tenement (1 family), ...	440	440	–	–
2 tenements (2 families), ...	43	86	–	–
3 tenements (3 families), ...	4	12	–	–
4 tenements (4 families), ...	1	4	–	–
11 tenements (11 families), ...	1	11	–	–
Blandford, ...	197	206	5	211
1 tenement (1 family), ...	189	189	–	–
2 tenements (2 families), ...	7	14	–	–
3 tenements (3 families), ...	1	3	–	–
Brimfield, ...	217	238	3	241
1 tenement (1 family), ...	199	199	–	–
2 tenements (2 families), ...	16	32	–	–
3 tenements (3 families), ...	1	3	–	–
4 tenements (4 families), ...	1	4	–	–
Chester, ...	314	354	16	370
1 tenement (1 family), ...	278	278	–	–
2 tenements (2 families), ...	32	64	–	–
3 tenements (3 families), ...	4	12	–	–
Chicopee, ...	2,280	3,042	70	3,112
1 tenement (1 family), ...	1,749	1,749	–	–
2 tenements (2 families), ...	418	836	–	–
3 tenements (3 families), ...	60	180	–	–
4 tenements (4 families), ...	44	176	–	–
5 tenements (5 families), ...	14	70	–	–

OCCUPIED AND UNOCCUPIED TENEMENTS IN OCCUPIED DWELLING HOUSES — Continued.

COUNTIES, CITIES, TOWNS, AND NUMBER OF TENEMENTS AND FAMILIES.	Number of Occupied Dwelling Houses	Number of Occupied Tenements in Occupied Dwelling Houses	Number of Unoccupied Tenements in Occupied Dwelling Houses	Total Number of Tenements in Occupied Dwelling Houses
HAMPDEN — Con.				
CHICOPEE — Con.				
6 tenements (6 families), ...	4	24	–	–
7 tenements (7 families), ...	1	7	–	–
Chicopee. Ward 1, ...	326	570	12	582
1 tenement (1 family), ...	195	195	–	–
2 tenements (2 families), ...	69	138	–	–
3 tenements (3 families), ...	25	75	–	–
4 tenements (4 families), ...	25	100	–	–
5 tenements (5 families), ...	10	50	–	–
6 tenements (6 families), ...	2	12	–	–
Chicopee. Ward 2, ...	325	394	8	402
1 tenement (1 family), ...	270	270	–	–
2 tenements (2 families), ...	45	90	–	–
3 tenements (3 families), ...	7	21	–	–
4 tenements (4 families), ...	2	8	–	–
5 tenements (5 families), ...	1	5	–	–
Chicopee. Ward 3, ...	294	417	14	431
1 tenement (1 family), ...	206	206	–	–
2 tenements (2 families), ...	72	144	–	–
3 tenements (3 families), ...	6	18	–	–
4 tenements (4 families), ...	5	20	–	–
5 tenements (5 families), ...	2	10	–	–
6 tenements (6 families), ...	2	12	–	–
7 tenements (7 families), ...	1	7	–	–
Chicopee. Ward 4, ...	339	421	13	434
1 tenement (1 family), ...	269	269	–	–
2 tenements (2 families), ...	61	122	–	–
3 tenements (3 families), ...	6	18	–	–
4 tenements (4 families), ...	3	12	–	–
Chicopee. Ward 5, ...	396	505	5	510
1 tenement (1 family), ...	299	299	–	–
2 tenements (2 families), ...	90	180	–	–
3 tenements (3 families), ...	3	9	–	–
4 tenements (4 families), ...	3	12	–	–
5 tenements (5 families), ...	1	5	–	–
Chicopee. Ward 6, ...	272	333	7	340
1 tenement (1 family), ...	226	226	–	–
2 tenements (2 families), ...	36	72	–	–
3 tenements (3 families), ...	5	15	–	–
4 tenements (4 families), ...	5	20	–	–
Chicopee. Ward 7, ...	338	402	11	413
1 tenement (1 family), ...	284	284	–	–
2 tenements (2 families), ...	45	90	–	–
3 tenements (3 families), ...	8	24	–	–
4 tenements (4 families), ...	1	4	–	–
East Longmeadow, ...	283	330	17	347
1 tenement (1 family), ...	239	239	–	–
2 tenements (2 families), ...	41	82	–	–
3 tenements (3 families), ...	3	9	–	–
Granville, ...	250	252	–	252
1 tenement (1 family), ...	248	248	–	–
2 tenements (2 families), ...	2	4	–	–
Hampden, ...	178	194	20	214
1 tenement (1 family), ...	163	163	–	–
2 tenements (2 families), ...	14	28	–	–
3 tenements (3 families), ...	1	3	–	–

OCCUPIED AND UNOCCUPIED TENEMENTS IN OCCUPIED DWELLING HOUSES — Continued.

COUNTIES, CITIES, TOWNS, AND NUMBER OF TENEMENTS AND FAMILIES.	Number of Occupied Dwelling Houses	Number of Occupied Tenements in Occupied Dwelling Houses	Number of Unoccupied Tenements in Occupied Dwelling Houses	Total Number of Tenements in Occupied Dwelling Houses
HAMPDEN — Con.				
Holland, ...	51	55	–	55
1 tenement (1 family), ...	47	47	–	–
2 tenements (2 families), . . .	4	8	–	–
HOLYOKE, ...	3,703	7,894	534	8,428
1 tenement (1 family), ...	2,276	2,276	–	–
2 tenements (2 families), . . .	586	1,172	–	–
3 tenements (3 families), . . .	246	738	–	–
4 tenements (4 families), . . .	163	652	–	–
5 tenements (5 families), . . .	73	365	–	–
6 tenements (6 families), . . .	139	834	–	–
7 tenements (7 families), . . .	55	385	–	–
8 tenements (8 families), . . .	115	920	–	–
9 tenements (9 families), . . .	16	144	–	–
10 tenements (10 families), . .	6	60	–	–
11 tenements (11 families), . .	8	88	–	–
12 tenements (12 families), . .	13	156	–	–
13 tenements (13 families), . .	2	26	–	–
14 tenements (14 families), . .	1	14	–	–
15 tenements (15 families), . .	3	45	–	–
19 tenements (19 families), . .	1	19	–	–
Holyoke, Ward 1, ...	433	1,145	40	1,185
1 tenement (1 family), ...	177	177	–	–
2 tenements (2 families), . . .	111	222	–	–
3 tenements (3 families), . . .	27	81	–	–
4 tenements (4 families), . . .	52	208	–	–
5 tenements (5 families), . . .	12	60	–	–
6 tenements (6 families), . . .	18	108	–	–
7 tenements (7 families), . . .	5	35	–	–
8 tenements (8 families), . . .	28	224	–	–
9 tenements (9 families), . . .	2	18	–	–
12 tenements (12 families), . .	1	12	–	–
Holyoke, Ward 2, ...	483	1,690	141	1,831
1 tenement (1 family), ...	148	148	–	–
2 tenements (2 families), . . .	80	160	–	–
3 tenements (3 families), . . .	49	147	–	–
4 tenements (4 families), . . .	25	100	–	–
5 tenements (5 families), . . .	14	70	–	–
6 tenements (6 families), . . .	44	264	–	–
7 tenements (7 families), . . .	22	154	–	–
8 tenements (8 families), . . .	44	352	–	–
9 tenements (9 families), . . .	4	36	–	–
10 tenements (10 families), . .	6	60	–	–
11 tenements (11 families), . .	8	88	–	–
12 tenements (12 families), . .	8	96	–	–
15 tenements (15 families), . .	1	15	–	–
Holyoke, Ward 3, ...	633	958	41	999
1 tenement (1 family), ...	472	472	–	–
2 tenements (2 families), . . .	91	182	–	–
3 tenements (3 families), . . .	38	114	–	–
4 tenements (4 families), . . .	9	36	–	–
5 tenements (5 families), . . .	3	15	–	–
6 tenements (6 families), . . .	9	54	–	–
7 tenements (7 families), . . .	4	28	–	–
8 tenements (8 families), . . .	6	48	–	–
9 tenements (9 families), . . .	1	9	–	–
Holyoke, Ward 4, ...	455	1,256	214	1,470
1 tenement (1 family, ...	181	181	–	–

OCCUPIED AND UNOCCUPIED TENEMENTS IN OCCUPIED DWELLING HOUSES — Continued.

COUNTIES, CITIES, TOWNS, AND NUMBER OF TENEMENTS AND FAMILIES.	Number of Occupied Dwelling Houses	Number of Occupied Tenements in Occupied Dwelling Houses	Number of Unoccupied Tenements in Occupied Dwelling Houses	Total Number of Tenements in Occupied Dwelling Houses
HAMPDEN — Con.				
Holyoke, Ward 4 — Con.				
2 tenements (2 families), ...	84	168	-	-
3 tenements (3 families), ...	65	195	-	-
4 tenements (4 families), ...	45	180	-	-
5 tenements (5 families , ...	19	95	-	-
6 tenements (6 families), ...	29	174	-	-
7 tenements (7 families), ...	14	98	-	-
8 tenements (8 families , ...	10	80	-	-
9 tenements (9 families), ...	6	54	-	-
12 tenements (12 families),. . . .	1	12	-	-
19 tenements (19 families), ...	1	19	-	-
Holyoke, Ward 5, ...	462	768	42	810
1 tenement (1 family), ...	292	292	-	-
2 tenements (2 families), ...	120	240	-	-
3 tenements (3 families), ...	18	54	-	-
4 tenements (4 families), ...	8	32	-	-
5 tenements (5 families), ...	9	45	-	-
6 tenements (6 families), ...	9	54	-	-
7 tenements (7 families), ...	2	14	-	-
8 tenements (8 families), ...	3	24	-	-
13 tenements (13 families), ...	1	13	-	-
Holyoke, Ward 6, ...	440	1,152	39	1,191
1 tenement (1 family), ...	258	258	-	-
2 tenements (2 families), ...	31	62	-	-
3 tenements (3 families), ...	46	138	-	-
4 tenements (4 families), ...	18	72	-	-
5 tenements (5 families), ...	16	80	-	-
6 tenements (6 families), ...	29	174	-	-
7 tenements (7 families), ...	8	56	-	-
8 tenements (8 families), ...	24	192	-	-
9 tenements (9 families), ...	3	27	-	-
12 tenements (12 families),. . . .	3	36	-	-
13 tenements (13 families),. . . .	1	13	-	-
14 tenements (14 families),. . . .	1	14	-	-
15 tenements (15 families), ...	2	30	-	-
Holyoke, Ward 7, ...	827	925	17	942
1 tenement (1 family), ...	748	748	-	-
2 tenements (2 families), ...	69	138	-	-
3 tenements (3 families), ...	3	9	-	-
4 tenements (4 families), ...	6	24	-	-
6 tenements (6 families), ...	1	6	-	-
Longmeadow, ...	134	146	2	148
1 tenement (1 family), ...	122	122	-	-
2 tenements (2 families), ...	12	24	-	-
Ludlow, ...	382	473	7	480
1 tenement (1 family), ...	315	315	-	-
2 tenements (2 families), ...	57	114	-	-
3 tenements (3 families), ...	2	6	-	-
4 tenements (4 families), ...	5	20	-	-
5 tenements (5 families), ...	2	10	-	-
8 tenements (8 families), ...	1	8	-	-
Monson, ...	735	872	15	887
1 tenement (1 family), ...	616	616	-	-
2 tenements (2 families), ...	104	208	-	-
3 tenements (3 families), ...	12	36	-	-
4 tenements (4 families), ...	3	12	-	-

OCCUPIED AND UNOCCUPIED TENEMENTS IN OCCUPIED DWELLING
HOUSES — Continued.

COUNTIES, CITIES, TOWNS, AND NUMBER OF TENEMENTS AND FAMILIES.	Number of Occupied Dwelling Houses	Number of Occupied Tenements in Occupied Dwelling Houses	Number of Unoccupied Tenements in Occupied Dwelling Houses	Total Number of Tenements in Occupied Dwelling Houses
HAMPDEN — Con.				
Montgomery, ...	62	63	-	63
1 tenement (1 family), ...	61	61	-	-
2 tenements (2 families), ...	1	2	-	-
Palmer, ...	1,276	1,382	37	1,419
1 tenement (1 family), ...	1,178	1,178	-	-
2 tenements (2 families), ...	91	182	-	-
3 tenements (3 families), ...	6	18	-	-
4 tenements (4 families), ...	1	4	-	-
Russell, ...	170	185	8	193
1 tenement (1 family), ...	159	159	-	-
2 tenements (2 families), ...	9	18	-	-
3 tenements (3 families), ...	1	3	-	-
5 tenements (5 families), ...	1	5	-	-
Southwick, ...	224	239	6	245
1 tenement (1 family), ...	209	209	-	-
2 tenements (2 families), ...	15	30	-	-
SPRINGFIELD, ...	8,457	11,741	524	12,265
1 tenement (1 family), ...	5,875	5,875	-	-
2 tenements (2 families), ...	2,232	4,464	-	-
3 tenements (3 families), ...	185	555	-	-
4 tenements (4 families), ...	96	384	-	-
5 tenements (5 families), ...	26	130	-	-
6 tenements (6 families), ...	20	120	-	-
7 tenements (7 families), ...	4	28	-	-
8 tenements (8 families), ...	9	72	-	-
9 tenements (9 families), ...	2	18	-	-
10 tenements (10 families), ...	4	40	-	-
13 tenements (13 families), ...	2	26	-	-
14 tenements (14 families), ...	1	14	-	-
15 tenements (15 families), ...	1	15	-	-
Springfield. Ward 1, ...	1,089	1,604	85	1,689
1 tenement (1 family), ...	605	605	-	-
2 tenements (2 families), ...	461	922	-	-
3 tenements (3 families), ...	17	51	-	-
4 tenements (4 families), ...	5	20	-	-
6 tenements (6 families), ...	1	6	-	-
Springfield. Ward 2, ...	1,054	1,758	108	1,866
1 tenement (1 family), ...	597	597	-	-
2 tenements (2 families), ...	344	688	-	-
3 tenements (3 families), ...	39	117	-	-
4 tenements (4 families), ...	44	176	-	-
5 tenements (5 families), ...	16	80	-	-
6 tenements (6 families), ...	7	42	-	-
7 tenements (7 families), ...	2	14	-	-
8 tenements (8 families), ...	2	16	-	-
9 tenements (9 families), ...	2	18	-	-
10 tenements (10 families), ...	1	10	-	-
Springfield. Ward 3, ...	771	1,360	107	1,467
1 tenement (1 family), ...	441	441	-	-
2 tenements (2 families), ...	229	458	-	-
3 tenements (3 families), ...	49	147	-	-
4 tenements (4 families), ...	22	88	-	-
5 tenements (5 families), ...	5	25	-	-
6 tenements (6 families), ...	12	72	-	-
7 tenements (7 families), ...	2	14	-	-
8 tenements (8 families), ...	5	40	-	-

OCCUPIED AND UNOCCUPIED TENEMENTS IN OCCUPIED DWELLING HOUSES — Continued.

COUNTIES, CITIES, TOWNS, AND NUMBER OF TENEMENTS AND FAMILIES.	Number of Occupied Dwelling Houses	Number of Occupied Tenements in Occupied Dwelling Houses	Number of Unoccupied Tenements in Occupied Dwelling Houses	Total Number of Tenements in Occupied Dwelling Houses
HAMPDEN — Con.				
Springfield. Ward 3 — Con.				
10 tenements (10 families), .	2	20	–	–
13 tenements (13 families), .	2	26	–	–
14 tenements (14 families), .	1	14	–	–
15 tenements (15 families), .	1	15	–	–
Springfield. Ward 4, .	1,058	1,435	67	1,502
1 tenement (1 family), .	759	759	–	–
2 tenements (2 families), .	258	516	–	–
3 tenements (3 families), .	23	69	–	–
4 tenements (4 families), .	10	40	–	–
5 tenements (5 families), .	5	25	–	–
8 tenements (8 families), .	2	16	–	–
10 tenements (10 families), .	1	10	–	–
Springfield. Ward 5, .	1,289	1,534	30	1,564
1 tenement (1 family), .	1,055	1,055	–	–
2 tenements (2 families), .	223	446	–	–
3 tenements (3 families), .	11	33	–	–
Springfield. Ward 6, .	1,004	1,390	86	1,476
1 tenement (1 family), .	651	651	–	–
2 tenements (2 families), .	327	654	–	–
3 tenements (3 families), .	19	57	–	–
4 tenements (4 families), .	7	28	–	–
Springfield. Ward 7, .	962	1,136	18	1,154
1 tenement (1 family), .	799	799	–	–
2 tenements (2 families), .	153	306	–	–
3 tenements (3 families), .	9	27	–	–
4 tenements (4 families), .	1	4	–	–
Springfield. Ward 8, .	1,230	1,524	23	1,547
1 tenement (1 family), .	968	968	–	–
2 tenements (2 families), .	237	474	–	–
3 tenements (3 families), .	18	54	–	–
4 tenements (4 families), .	7	28	–	–
Tolland, .	66	67	1	68
1 tenement (1 family), .	65	65	–	–
2 tenements (2 families), .	1	2	–	–
Wales, .	178	191	2	193
1 tenement (1 family), .	165	165	–	–
2 tenements (2 families), .	13	26	–	–
Westfield, .	2,057	2,593	74	2,667
1 tenement (1 family), .	1,580	1,580	–	–
2 tenements (2 families), .	436	872	–	–
3 tenements (3 families), .	26	78	–	–
4 tenements (4 families), .	13	52	–	–
5 tenements (5 families), .	1	5	–	–
6 tenements (6 families), .	1	6	–	–
West Springfield, .	1,069	1,360	87	1,447
1 tenement (1 family), .	809	809	–	–
2 tenements (2 families), .	236	472	–	–
3 tenements (3 families), .	17	51	–	–
4 tenements (4 families), .	7	28	–	–
Wilbraham, .	290	363	9	372
1 tenement (1 family), .	235	235	–	–
2 tenements (2 families), .	40	80	–	–
3 tenements (3 families), .	12	36	–	–
4 tenements (4 families), .	3	12	–	–

OCCUPIED AND UNOCCUPIED TENEMENTS IN OCCUPIED DWELLING HOUSES — Continued.

COUNTIES, CITIES, TOWNS, AND NUMBER OF TENEMENTS AND FAMILIES.	Number of Occupied Dwelling Houses	Number of Occupied Tenements in Occupied Dwelling Houses	Number of Unoccupied Tenements in Occupied Dwelling Houses	Total Number of Tenements in Occupied Dwelling Houses
HAMPSHIRE.				
Amherst,	921	1,064	25	1,089
1 tenement (1 family),	795	795	-	-
2 tenements (2 families),	115	230	-	-
3 tenements (3 families),	5	15	-	-
4 tenements (4 families),	6	24	-	-
Belchertown,	507	524	5	529
1 tenement (1 family),	494	494	-	-
2 tenements (2 families),	11	22	-	-
3 tenements (3 families),	1	3	-	-
5 tenements (5 families),	1	5	-	-
Chesterfield,	149	162	2	164
1 tenement (1 family),	136	136	-	-
2 tenements (2 families),	13	26	-	-
Cummington,	188	201	2	203
1 tenement (1 family),	176	176	-	-
2 tenements (2 families),	11	22	-	-
3 tenements (3 families),	1	3	-	-
Easthampton,	835	1,019	17	1,036
1 tenement (1 family),	683	683	-	-
2 tenements (2 families),	133	266	-	-
3 tenements (3 families),	11	33	-	-
4 tenements (4 families),	6	24	-	-
6 tenements (6 families),	1	6	-	-
7 tenements (7 families),	1	7	-	-
Enfield,	250	261	2	263
1 tenement (1 family),	239	239	-	-
2 tenements (2 families),	11	22	-	-
Goshen,	62	66	4	70
1 tenement (1 family),	58	58	-	-
2 tenements (2 families),	4	8	-	-
Granby,	165	171	-	171
1 tenement (1 family),	159	159	-	-
2 tenements (2 families),	6	12	-	-
Greenwich,	138	142	-	142
1 tenement (1 family),	135	135	-	-
2 tenements (2 families),	2	4	-	-
3 tenements (3 families),	1	3	-	-
Hadley,	374	390	5	395
1 tenement (1 family),	358	358	-	-
2 tenements (2 families),	16	32	-	-
Hatfield,	271	291	12	303
1 tenement (1 family),	251	251	-	-
2 tenements (2 families),	20	40	-	-
Huntington,	290	329	17	346
1 tenement (1 family),	260	260	-	-
2 tenements (2 families),	23	46	-	-
3 tenements (3 families),	5	15	-	-
4 tenements (4 families),	2	8	-	-
Middlefield,	85	92	7	99
1 tenement (1 family),	78	78	-	-
2 tenements (2 families),	7	14	-	-
NORTHAMPTON,	2,824	3,270	74	3,344
1 tenement (1 family),	2,441	2,441	-	-
2 tenements (2 families),	358	676	-	-
3 tenements (3 families),	31	93	-	-

OCCUPIED AND UNOCCUPIED TENEMENTS IN OCCUPIED DWELLING HOUSES — Continued.

COUNTIES, CITIES, TOWNS, AND NUMBER OF TENEMENTS AND FAMILIES.	Number of Occupied Dwelling Houses	Number of Occupied Tenements in Occupied Dwelling Houses	Number of Unoccupied Tenements in Occupied Dwelling Houses	Total Number of Tenements in Occupied Dwelling Houses
HAMPSHIRE — Con.				
NORTHAMPTON — Con.				
4 tenements (4 families), ...	11	44	-	-
5 tenements (5 families), ...	2	10	-	-
6 tenements (6 families), ...	1	6	-	-
Northampton. Ward 1, ...	377	480	10	490
1 tenement (1 family), ...	305	305	-	-
2 tenements (2 families), ...	53	106	-	-
3 tenements (3 families), ...	10	30	-	-
4 tenements (4 families), ...	7	28	-	-
5 tenements (5 families), ...	1	5	-	-
6 tenements (6 families), ...	1	6	-	-
Northampton. Ward 2, ...	453	507	10	517
1 tenement (1 family), ...	403	403	-	-
2 tenements (2 families), ...	47	94	-	-
3 tenements (3 families), ...	2	6	-	-
4 tenements (4 families), ...	1	4	-	-
Northampton. Ward 3, ...	500	607	16	623
1 tenement (1 family), ...	409	409	-	-
2 tenements (2 families), ...	79	158	-	-
3 tenements (3 families), ...	9	27	-	-
4 tenements (4 families), ...	2	8	-	-
5 tenements (5 families), ...	1	5	-	-
Northampton. Ward 4, ...	358	423	11	434
1 tenement (1 family), ...	294	294	-	-
2 tenements (2 families), ...	63	126	-	-
3 tenements (3 families), ...	1	3	-	-
Northampton. Ward 5, ...	416	445	-	445
1 tenement (1 family), ...	387	387	-	-
2 tenements (2 families), ...	29	58	-	-
Northampton. Ward 6, ...	357	412	10	422
1 tenement (1 family), ...	310	310	-	-
2 tenements (2 families), ...	40	80	-	-
3 tenements (3 families), ...	6	18	-	-
4 tenements (4 families), ...	1	4	-	-
Northampton. Ward 7, ...	363	396	17	413
1 tenement (1 family), ...	333	333	-	-
2 tenements (2 families), ...	27	54	-	-
3 tenements (3 families), ...	3	9	-	-
Pelham, ...	122	126	11	137
1 tenement (1 family), ...	118	118	-	-
2 tenements (2 families), ...	4	8	-	-
Plainfield, ...	102	109	7	116
1 tenement (1 family), ...	95	95	-	-
2 tenements (2 families), ...	7	14	-	-
Prescott, ...	96	106	1	107
1 tenement (1 family), ...	88	88	-	-
2 tenements (2 families), ...	7	14	-	-
4 tenements (4 families), ...	1	4	-	-
Southampton, ...	225	252	4	256
1 tenement (1 family), ...	199	199	-	-
2 tenements (2 families), ...	25	50	-	-
3 tenements (3 families), ...	1	3	-	-
South Hadley, ...	735	894	36	930
1 tenement (1 family), ...	608	608	-	-
2 tenements (2 families), ...	106	212	-	-
3 tenements (3 families), ...	13	39	-	-

OCCUPIED AND UNOCCUPIED TENEMENTS IN OCCUPIED DWELLING
HOUSES — Continued.

COUNTIES, CITIES, TOWNS, AND NUMBER OF TENEMENTS AND FAMILIES.	Number of Occupied Dwelling Houses	Number of Occupied Tenements in Occupied Dwelling Houses	Number of Unoccupied Tenements in Occupied Dwelling Houses	Total Number of Tenements in Occupied Dwelling Houses
HAMPSHIRE — Con.				
South Hadley — Con.				
4 tenements (4 families), ...	6	24	–	–
5 tenements (5 families), ...	1	5	–	–
6 tenements (6 families), ...	1	6	–	–
Ware, ...	1,208	1,523	67	1,590
1 tenement (1 family), ...	974	974	–	–
2 tenements (2 families), ...	189	378	–	–
3 tenements (3 families), ...	22	66	–	–
4 tenements (4 families), ...	15	60	–	–
5 tenements (5 families), ...	3	15	–	–
6 tenements (6 families), ...	5	30	–	–
Westhampton, ...	111	124	2	126
1 tenement (1 family), ...	98	98	–	–
2 tenements (2 families), ...	13	26	–	–
Williamsburg, ...	421	473	15	488
1 tenement (1 family), ...	370	370	–	–
2 tenements (2 families), ...	50	100	–	–
3 tenements (3 families), ...	1	3	–	–
Worthington, ...	152	155	4	159
1 tenement (1 family), ...	149	149	–	–
2 tenements (2 families), ...	3	6	–	–
MIDDLESEX.				
Acton, ...	469	529	6	535
1 tenement (1 family), ...	412	412	–	–
2 tenements (2 families), ...	54	108	–	–
3 tenements (3 families), ...	3	9	–	–
Arlington, ...	1,264	1,362	16	1,378
1 tenement (1 family), ...	1,171	1,171	–	–
2 tenements (2 families), ...	88	176	–	–
3 tenements (3 families), ...	5	15	–	–
Ashby, ...	218	233	8	241
1 tenement (1 family), ...	205	205	–	–
2 tenements (2 families), ...	11	22	–	–
3 tenements (3 families), ...	2	6	–	–
Ashland, ...	419	486	26	512
1 tenement (1 family), ...	354	354	–	–
2 tenements (2 families), ...	63	126	–	–
3 tenements (3 families), ...	2	6	–	–
Ayer, ...	442	528	47	575
1 tenement (1 family), ...	364	364	–	–
2 tenements (2 families), ...	74	148	–	–
3 tenements (3 families), ...	2	6	–	–
5 tenements (5 families), ...	2	10	–	–
Bedford, ...	235	251	6	257
1 tenement (1 family), ...	221	221	–	–
2 tenements (2 families), ...	12	24	–	–
3 tenements (3 families), ...	2	6	–	–
Belmont, ...	491	505	2	507
1 tenement (1 family), ...	477	477	–	–
2 tenements (2 families), ...	14	28	–	–
Billerica, ...	532	582	7	589
1 tenement (1 family), ...	490	490	–	–
2 tenements (2 families), ...	36	72	–	–
3 tenements (3 families), ...	5	15	–	–
5 tenements (5 families), ...	1	5	–	–

OCCUPIED AND UNOCCUPIED TENEMENTS IN OCCUPIED DWELLING HOUSES — Continued.

COUNTIES, CITIES, TOWNS, AND NUMBER OF TENEMENTS AND FAMILIES.	Number of Occupied Dwelling Houses	Number of Occupied Tenements in Occupied Dwelling Houses	Number of Unoccupied Tenements in Occupied Dwelling Houses	Total Number of Tenements in Occupied Dwelling Houses
MIDDLESEX — Con.				
Boxborough, ...	71	78	3	81
1 tenement (1 family), ...	64	64	–	–
2 tenements (2 families), ...	7	14	–	–
Burlington, ...	122	129	8	137
1 tenement (1 family), ...	115	115	–	–
2 tenements (2 families), ...	7	14	–	–
CAMBRIDGE, ...	11,837	17,193	978	18,171
1 tenement (1 family), . . .	8,319	8,319	–	–
2 tenements (2 families), ...	2,519	5,038	–	–
3 tenements (3 families), ...	638	1,914	–	–
4 tenements (4 families), ...	148	592	–	–
5 tenements (5 families), ...	73	365	–	–
6 tenements (6 families), ...	77	462	–	–
7 tenements (7 families), ...	24	168	–	–
8 tenements (8 families), ...	30	240	–	–
9 tenements (9 families), . . . , .	3	27	–	–
10 tenements (10 families), ...	3	30	–	–
11 tenements (11 families), ...	1	11	–	–
12 tenements (12 families), ...	1	12	–	–
15 tenements (15 families), ...	1	15	–	–
Cambridge, Ward 1, ...	2,306	2,943	114	3,057
1 tenement (1 family), ...	1,836	1,836	–	–
2 tenements (2 families), ...	353	706	–	–
3 tenements (3 families), ...	85	255	–	–
4 tenements (4 families), ...	12	48	–	–
5 tenements (5 families), ...	9	45	–	–
6 tenements (6 families), ...	6	36	–	–
8 tenements (8 families), ...	1	8	–	–
9 tenements (9 families), ...	1	9	–	–
Cambridge, Ward 2, ...	3,118	4,999	307	5,306
1 tenement (1 family), ...	1,941	1,941	–	–
2 tenements (2 families), ...	802	1,604	–	–
3 tenements (3 families), ...	232	696	–	–
4 tenements (4 families), ...	54	216	–	–
5 tenements (5 families), ...	34	170	–	–
6 tenements (6 families), ...	34	204	–	–
7 tenements (7 families), ...	7	49	–	–
8 tenements (8 families), ...	13	104	–	–
15 tenements (15 families), ...	1	15	–	–
Cambridge, Ward 3, ...	1,688	2,812	185	2,997
1 tenement (1 family), ...	952	952	–	–
2 tenements (2 families), ...	487	974	–	–
3 tenements (3 families), ...	172	516	–	–
4 tenements (4 families), ...	44	176	–	–
5 tenements (5 families), ...	13	65	–	–
6 tenements (6 families), ...	16	96	–	–
7 tenements (7 families), ...	2	14	–	–
8 tenements (8 families), ...	1	8	–	–
11 tenements (11 families), ...	1	11	–	–
Cambridge, Ward 4, ...	2,899	4,255	269	4,504
1 tenement (1 family), ...	2,074	2,074	–	–
2 tenements (2 families), ...	611	1,222	–	–
3 tenements (3 families), ...	113	339	–	–
4 tenements (4 families), ...	30	120	–	–
5 tenements (5 families), ...	15	75	–	–
6 tenements (6 families), ...	20	120	–	–

OCCUPIED AND UNOCCUPIED TENEMENTS IN OCCUPIED DWELLING HOUSES — Continued.

COUNTIES, CITIES, TOWNS, AND NUMBER OF TENEMENTS AND FAMILIES.	Number of Occupied Dwelling Houses	Number of Occupied Tenements in Occupied Dwelling Houses	Number of Unoccupied Tenements in Occupied Dwelling Houses	Total Number of Tenements in Occupied Dwelling Houses
MIDDLESEX — Con.				
Cambridge. Ward 4 — Con.				
7 tenements (7 families), ...	15	105	-	-
8 tenements (8 families), ...	15	120	-	-
9 tenements (9 families), ...	2	18	-	-
10 tenements (10 families), ...	3	30	-	-
12 tenements (12 families), ...	1	12	-	-
Cambridge. Ward 5, ...	1,829	2,204	103	2,307
1 tenement (1 family), ...	1,516	1,516	-	-
2 tenements (2 families), ...	266	532	-	-
3 tenements (3 families), ...	36	108	-	-
4 tenements (4 families), ...	8	32	-	-
5 tenements (5 families), ...	2	10	-	-
6 tenements (6 families), ...	1	6	-	-
Carlisle, ...	125	126	3	129
1 tenement (1 family), ...	124	124	-	-
2 tenements (2 families), ...	1	2	-	-
Chelmsford, ...	695	747	14	761
1 tenement (1 family), ...	645	645	-	-
2 tenements (2 families), ...	48	96	-	-
3 tenements (3 families), ...	2	6	-	-
Concord, ...	837	874	20	894
1 tenement (1 family), ...	802	802	-	-
2 tenements (2 families), ...	33	66	-	-
3 tenements (3 families), ...	2	6	-	-
Dracut, ...	440	475	12	487
1 tenement (1 family), ...	407	407	-	-
2 tenements (2 families), ...	32	64	-	-
4 tenements (4 families), ...	1	4	-	-
Dunstable, ...	96	106	4	110
1 tenement (1 family), ...	86	86	-	-
2 tenements (2 families), ...	10	20	-	-
EVERETT, ...	3,610	4,304	231	4,535
1 tenement (1 family), ...	2,981	2,981	-	-
2 tenements (2 families), ...	575	1,150	-	-
3 tenements (3 families), ...	47	141	-	-
4 tenements (4 families), ...	5	20	-	-
6 tenements (6 families), ...	2	12	-	-
Everett. Ward 1, ...	518	673	35	708
1 tenement (1 family), ...	377	377	-	-
2 tenements (2 families), ...	128	256	-	-
3 tenements (3 families), ...	12	36	-	-
4 tenements (4 families), ...	1	4	-	-
Everett. Ward 2, ...	479	583	29	612
1 tenement (1 family), ...	380	380	-	-
2 tenements (2 families), ...	94	188	-	-
3 tenements (3 families), ...	5	15	-	-
Everett. Ward 3, ...	615	729	55	784
1 tenement (1 family), ...	515	515	-	-
2 tenements (2 families), ...	88	176	-	-
3 tenements (3 families), ...	10	30	-	-
4 tenements (4 families), ...	2	8	-	-
Everett. Ward 4, ...	700	703	35	738
1 tenement (1 family), ...	697	697	-	-
2 tenements (2 families), ...	3	6	-	-
Everett. Ward 5, ...	699	779	42	821
1 tenement (1 family), ...	449	449	-	-

OCCUPIED AND UNOCCUPIED TENEMENTS IN OCCUPIED DWELLING
HOUSES — Continued.

COUNTIES, CITIES, TOWNS, AND NUMBER OF TENEMENTS AND FAMILIES.	Number of Occupied Dwelling Houses	Number of Occupied Tenements in Occupied Dwelling Houses	Number of Unoccupied Tenements in Occupied Dwelling Houses	Total Number of Tenements in Occupied Dwelling Houses
MIDDLESEX — Con.				
Everett. Ward 5 — Con.				
2 tenements (2 families), ...	131	262	-	-
3 tenements (3 families), ...	16	48	-	-
4 tenements (4 families), ...	2	8	-	-
6 tenements (6 families), ...	2	12	-	-
Everett. Ward 6, ...	698	837	35	872
1 tenement (1 family), ...	563	563	-	-
2 tenements (2 families), ...	131	262	-	-
3 tenements (3 families), ...	4	12	-	-
Framingham, ...	1,920	2,115	44	2,159
1 tenement (1 family), ...	1,730	1,730	-	-
2 tenements (2 families), ...	186	372	-	-
3 tenements (3 families), ...	3	9	-	-
4 tenements (4 families), ...	1	4	-	-
Groton, ...	476	508	11	519
1 tenement (1 family), ...	445	445	-	-
2 tenements (2 families , ...	30	60	-	-
3 tenements (3 families , ...	1	3	-	-
Holliston, ...	612	701	21	722
1 tenement (1 family), ...	525	525	-	-
2 tenements (2 families , ...	85	170	-	-
3 tenements (3 families , ...	2	6	-	-
Hopkinton, ...	714	752	49	801
1 tenement (1 family), ...	678	678	-	-
2 tenements (2 families), ...	34	68	-	-
3 tenements (3 families , ...	2	6	..	-
Hudson, ...	980	1,245	32	1,277
1 tenement (1 family), ...	748	748	-	-
2 tenements (2 families), ...	209	418	-	-
3 tenements (3 families), ...	13	39	-	-
4 tenements (4 families), ...	10	40	-	-
Lexington, ...	727	775	3	778
1 tenement (1 family), ...	682	682	-	-
2 tenements (2 families , ...	42	84	-	-
3 tenements (3 families , ...	3	9	-	-
Lincoln, ...	189	209	6	215
1 tenement (1 family), ...	171	171	-	-
2 tenements (2 families), ...	16	32	-	-
3 tenements (3 families), ...	2	6	-	-
Littleton, ...	227	256	4	260
1 tenement (1 family), ...	199	199	-	-
2 tenements (2 families), ...	27	54	-	-
3 tenements (3 families , ...	1	3	-	-
LOWELL, ...	11,963	16,885	848	17,733
1 tenement (1 family), ...	8,786	8,786	-	-
2 tenements (2 families , ...	2,312	4,624	-	-
3 tenements (3 families , ...	438	1,314	-	-
4 tenements (4 families), ...	170	680	-	-
5 tenements (5 families , ...	81	405	-	-
6 tenements (6 families , ...	87	522	-	-
7 tenements (7 families , ...	21	147	-	-
8 tenements (8 families), ...	21	168	-	-
9 tenements (9 families , ...	7	63	-	-
10 tenements (10 families), ...	1	10	-	-
12 tenements (12 families), ...	3	36	-	-
13 tenements (13 families), ...	1	13	-	-

OCCUPIED AND UNOCCUPIED TENEMENTS IN OCCUPIED DWELLING HOUSES — Continued.

COUNTIES, CITIES, TOWNS, AND NUMBER OF TENEMENTS AND FAMILIES.	Number of Occupied Dwelling Houses	Number of Occupied Tenements in Occupied Dwelling Houses	Number of Unoccupied Tenements in Occupied Dwelling Houses	Total Number of Tenements in Occupied Dwelling Houses
MIDDLESEX — Con.				
LOWELL — Con.				
14 tenements (14 families),	1	14	–	–
20 tenements (20 families),	1	20	–	–
23 tenements (23 families),	1	23	–	–
24 tenements (24 families),	1	24	–	–
36 tenements (36 families),	1	36	–	–
Lowell. Ward 1,	1,147	1,633	83	1,716
1 tenement (1 family),	882	882	–	–
2 tenements (2 families),	205	410	–	–
3 tenements (3 families),	23	69	–	–
4 tenements (4 families),	11	44	–	–
5 tenements (5 families),	7	35	–	–
6 tenements (6 families),	5	30	–	–
7 tenements (7 families),	3	21	–	–
8 tenements (8 families),	4	32	–	–
9 tenements (9 families),	3	27	–	–
12 tenements (12 families),	2	24	–	–
23 tenements (23 families),	1	23	–	–
36 tenements (36 families),	1	36	–	–
Lowell. Ward 2,	1,080	1,879	136	2,015
1 tenement (1 family),	564	564	–	–
2 tenements (2 families),	358	716	–	–
3 tenements (3 families),	92	276	–	–
4 tenements (4 families),	43	172	–	–
5 tenements (5 families),	7	35	–	–
6 tenements (6 families),	11	66	–	–
7 tenements (7 families),	2	14	–	–
8 tenements (8 families),	2	16	–	–
20 tenements (20 families),	1	20	–	–
Lowell. Ward 3,	1,407	2,038	123	2,161
1 tenement (1 family),	1,008	1,008	–	–
2 tenements (2 families),	280	560	–	–
3 tenements (3 families),	67	201	–	–
4 tenements (4 families),	20	80	–	–
5 tenements (5 families),	11	55	–	–
6 tenements (6 families),	16	96	–	–
7 tenements (7 families),	3	21	–	–
8 tenements (8 families),	1	8	–	–
9 tenements (9 families),	1	9	–	–
Lowell. Ward 4,	1,234	1,881	103	1,984
1 tenement (1 family),	761	761	–	–
2 tenements (2 families),	384	768	–	–
3 tenements (3 families),	51	153	–	–
4 tenements (4 families),	14	56	–	–
5 tenements (5 families),	10	50	–	–
6 tenements (6 families),	12	72	–	–
7 tenements (7 families),	1	7	–	–
14 tenements (14 families),	1	14	–	–
Lowell. Ward 5,	1,101	1,765	133	1,898
1 tenement (1 family),	667	667	–	–
2 tenements (2 families),	312	624	–	–
3 tenements (3 families),	74	222	–	–
4 tenements (4 families),	21	84	–	–
5 tenements (5 families),	10	50	–	–
6 tenements (6 families),	12	72	–	–
7 tenements (7 families),	1	7	–	–

OCCUPIED AND UNOCCUPIED TENEMENTS IN OCCUPIED DWELLING HOUSES — Continued.

COUNTIES, CITIES, TOWNS, AND NUMBER OF TENEMENTS AND FAMILIES.	Number of Occupied Dwelling Houses	Number of Occupied Tenements in Occupied Dwelling Houses	Number of Unoccupied Tenements in Occupied Dwelling Houses	Total Number of Tenements in Occupied Dwelling Houses
MIDDLESEX — Con.				
Lowell. Ward 5 — Con.				
8 tenements (8 families), ...	1	8	–	–
9 tenements (9 families), ...	2	18	–	–
13 tenements (13 families), ...	1	13	–	–
Lowell. Ward 6, ...	1,596	1,999	79	2,078
1 tenement (1 family), ...	1,340	1,340	–	–
2 tenements (2 families), ...	196	392	–	–
3 tenements (3 families), ...	28	84	–	–
4 tenements (4 families), ...	8	32	–	–
5 tenements (5 families), ...	14	70	–	–
6 tenements (6 families), ...	7	42	–	–
7 tenements (7 families), ...	1	7	–	–
8 tenements (8 families), ...	1	5	–	–
24 tenements (24 families , ...	1	24	–	–
Lowell. Ward 7, ...	1,514	2,383	105	2,488
1 tenement (1 family), ...	1,053	1,053	–	–
2 tenements (2 families), ...	300	600	–	–
3 tenements (3 families), ...	65	195	–	–
4 tenements (4 families), ...	35	140	–	–
5 tenements (5 families), ...	14	70	–	–
6 tenements (6 families , ...	23	138	–	–
7 tenements (7 families), ...	10	70	–	–
8 tenements (8 families), ...	12	96	–	–
9 tenements (9 families , ...	1	9	–	–
12 tenements (12 families)..	1	12	–	–
Lowell. Ward 8, ...	1,613	1,785	33	1,818
1 tenement (1 family), ...	1,471	1,471	–	–
2 tenements (2 families , ...	121	242	–	–
3 tenements (3 families), ...	14	42	–	–
4 tenements (4 families , ...	6	24	–	–
6 tenements (6 families , ...	1	6	–	–
Lowell. Ward 9, ...	1,241	1,522	53	1,575
1 tenement (1 family), ...	1,040	1,040	–	–
2 tenements (2 families , ...	156	312	–	–
3 tenements (3 families , ...	24	72	–	–
4 tenements (4 families), ...	12	48	–	–
5 tenements (5 families , ...	8	40	–	–
10 tenements (10 families , ...	1	10	–	–
MALDEN, ...	5,388	6,638	183	6,821
1 tenement (1 family), ...	4,236	4,236	–	–
2 tenements (2 families , ...	1,088	2,176	–	–
3 tenements (3 families), ...	39	117	–	–
4 tenements (4 families , ...	20	80	–	–
5 tenements (5 families), ...	2	10	–	–
6 tenements (6 families , ...	2	12	–	–
7 tenements (7 families , ...	1	7	–	–
Malden. Ward 1, ...	764	953	13	966
1 tenement (1 family), ...	588	588	–	–
2 tenements (2 families), ...	168	336	–	–
3 tenements (3 families , ...	3	9	–	–
4 tenements (4 families , ...	5	20	–	–
Malden. Ward 2, ...	713	1,091	64	1,155
1 tenement (1 family), ...	376	376	–	–
2 tenements (2 families), ...	311	622	–	–
3 tenements (3 families , ...	17	51	–	–
4 tenements (4 families , ...	6	24	–	–

OCCUPIED AND UNOCCUPIED TENEMENTS IN OCCUPIED DWELLING HOUSES — Continued.

COUNTIES, CITIES, TOWNS, AND NUMBER OF TENEMENTS AND FAMILIES.	Number of Occupied Dwelling Houses	Number of Occupied Tenements in Occupied Dwelling Houses	Number of Unoccupied Tenements in Occupied Dwelling Houses	Total Number of Tenements in Occupied Dwelling Houses
MIDDLESEX — Con.				
Malden. Ward 2 — Con.				
5 tenements (5 families), ...	1	5	–	–
6 tenements (6 families), ...	1	6	–	–
7 tenements (7 families), ...	1	7	–	–
Malden. Ward 3, ...	682	763	25	785
1 tenement (1 family), ...	605	605	–	–
2 tenements (2 families), ...	75	150	–	–
3 tenements (3 families), ...	1	3	–	–
5 tenements (5 families), ...	1	5	–	–
Malden. Ward 4, ...	853	1,024	11	1,035
1 tenement (1 family), ...	658	658	–	–
2 tenements (2 families), ...	164	328	–	–
3 tenements (3 families), ...	6	18	–	–
4 tenements (4 families), ...	5	20	–	–
Malden. Ward 5, ...	803	943	28	971
1 tenement (1 family), ...	672	672	–	–
2 tenements (2 families), ...	127	254	–	–
3 tenements (3 families), ...	1	3	–	–
4 tenements (4 families), ...	2	8	–	–
6 tenements (6 families), ...	1	6	–	–
Malden. Ward 6, ...	881	977	11	988
1 tenement (1 family), ...	790	790	–	–
2 tenements (2 families), ...	87	174	–	–
3 tenements (3 families), ...	3	9	–	–
4 tenements (4 families), ...	1	4	–	–
Malden. Ward 7, ...	712	887	33	920
1 tenement (1 family), ...	547	547	–	–
2 tenements (2 families), ...	156	312	–	–
3 tenements (3 families), ...	8	24	–	–
4 tenements (4 families), ...	1	4	–	–
MARLBOROUGH, ...	2,341	3,159	115	3,274
1 tenement (1 family), ...	1,616	1,616	–	–
2 tenements (2 families), ...	659	1,318	–	–
3 tenements (3 families), ...	44	132	–	–
4 tenements (4 families), ...	19	76	–	–
5 tenements (5 families), ...	2	10	–	–
7 tenements (7 families), ...	1	7	–	–
Marlborough. Ward 1, ...	255	317	16	333
1 tenement (1 family), ...	194	194	–	–
2 tenements (2 families), ...	55	110	–	–
3 tenements (3 families), ...	3	9	–	–
4 tenements (4 families), ...	1	4	–	–
Marlborough. Ward 2, ...	355	455	22	477
1 tenement (1 family), ...	280	280	–	–
2 tenements (2 families), ...	83	166	–	–
3 tenements (3 families), ...	3	9	–	–
Marlborough. Ward 3, ...	308	564	24	588
1 tenement (1 family), ...	297	297	–	–
2 tenements (2 families), ...	107	214	–	–
3 tenements (3 families), ...	14	42	–	–
4 tenements (4 families), ...	9	36	–	–
5 tenements (5 families), ...	1	5	–	–
Marlborough. Ward 4, ...	479	636	10	646
1 tenement (1 family), ...	346	346	–	–
2 tenements (2 families), ...	116	232	–	–
3 tenements (3 families), ...	11	33	–	–

OCCUPIED AND UNOCCUPIED TENEMENTS IN OCCUPIED DWELLING
HOUSES — Continued.

COUNTIES, CITIES, TOWNS, AND NUMBER OF TENEMENTS AND FAMILIES.	Number of Occupied Dwelling Houses	Number of Occupied Tenements in Occupied Dwelling Houses	Number of Unoccupied Tenements in Occupied Dwelling Houses	Total Number of Tenements in Occupied Dwelling Houses
MIDDLESEX — Con.				
Marlborough. Ward 4 — Con.				
4 tenements (4 families), ...	5	20	-	-
5 tenements (5 families), ...	1	5	-	-
Marlborough. Ward 5, ...	310	460	15	475
1 tenement (1 family), ...	177	177	-	-
2 tenements (2 families), ...	123	246	-	-
3 tenements (3 families), ...	6	18	-	-
4 tenements (4 families), ...	3	12	-	-
7 tenements (7 families), ...	1	7	-	-
Marlborough. Ward 6, ...	281	395	15	410
1 tenement (1 family), ...	170	170	-	-
2 tenements (2 families), ...	108	216	-	-
3 tenements (3 families), ...	3	9	-	-
Marlborough. Ward 7, ...	254	332	13	345
1 tenement (1 family), ...	182	182	-	-
2 tenements (2 families), ...	67	134	-	-
3 tenements (3 families), ...	4	12	-	-
4 tenements (4 families), ...	1	4	-	-
Maynard, ...	605	642	4	646
1 tenement (1 family), ...	570	570	-	-
2 tenements (2 families), ...	33	66	-	-
3 tenements (3 families), ...	2	6	-	-
MEDFORD, ...	2,811	3,172	80	3,252
1 tenement (1 family), ...	2,490	2,490	-	-
2 tenements (2 families), ...	295	590	-	-
3 tenements (3 families), ...	17	51	-	-
4 tenements (4 families), ...	7	28	-	-
5 tenements (5 families), ...	1	5	-	-
8 tenements (8 families), ...	1	8	-	-
Medford. Ward 1, ...	502	642	14	656
1 tenement (1 family), ...	488	488	-	-
2 tenements (2 families), ...	70	140	-	-
3 tenements (3 families), ...	3	9	-	-
5 tenements (5 families), ...	1	5	-	-
Medford. Ward 2, ...	468	544	18	562
1 tenement (1 family), ...	405	405	-	-
2 tenements (2 families), ...	54	108	-	-
3 tenements (3 families), ...	5	15	-	-
4 tenements (4 families), ...	4	16	-	-
Medford. Ward 3, ...	373	411	5	416
1 tenement (1 family), ...	343	343	-	-
2 tenements (2 families), ...	27	54	-	-
3 tenements (3 families), ...	2	6	-	-
8 tenements (8 families), ...	1	8	-	-
Medford. Ward 4, ...	384	426	4	430
1 tenement (1 family), ...	345	345	-	-
2 tenements (2 families), ...	37	74	-	-
3 tenements (3 families), ...	1	3	-	-
4 tenements (4 families), ...	1	4	-	-
Medford, Ward 5, ...	547	627	23	650
1 tenement (1 family), ...	472	472	-	-
2 tenements (2 families), ...	70	140	-	-
3 tenements (3 families), ...	5	15	-	-
Medford. Ward 6, ...	477	522	16	538
1 tenement (1 family), ...	437	437	-	-
2 tenements (2 families), ...	37	74	-	-

OCCUPIED AND UNOCCUPIED TENEMENTS IN OCCUPIED DWELLING HOUSES — Continued.

COUNTIES, CITIES, TOWNS, AND NUMBER OF TENEMENTS AND FAMILIES.	Number of Occupied Dwelling Houses	Number of Occupied Tenements in Occupied Dwelling Houses	Number of Unoccupied Tenements in Occupied Dwelling Houses	Total Number of Tenements in Occupied Dwelling Houses
MIDDLESEX — Con.				
Medford. Ward 6 — Con.				
3 tenements (3 families), ...	1	3	–	–
4 tenements (4 families), ...	2	8	–	–
Melrose, ...	2,474	2,685	26	2,711
1 tenement (1 family), ...	2,277	2,277	–	–
2 tenements (2 families), ...	184	368	–	–
3 tenements (3 families), ...	12	36	–	–
4 tenements (4 families), ...	1	4	–	–
Natick, ...	1,741	2,089	85	2,174
1 tenement (1 family), ...	1,420	1,420	–	–
2 tenements (2 families), ...	296	592	–	–
3 tenements (3 families), ...	23	69	–	–
4 tenements (4 families), ...	2	8	–	–
Newton, ...	5,102	5,528	80	5,608
1 tenement (1 family), ...	4,754	4,754	–	–
2 tenements (2 families), ...	292	584	–	–
3 tenements (3 families), ...	44	132	–	–
4 tenements (4 families), ...	6	24	–	–
5 tenements (5 families), ...	3	15	–	–
6 tenements (6 families), ...	2	12	–	–
7 tenements (7 families), ...	1	7	–	–
Newton. Ward 1, ...	743	830	17	847
1 tenement (1 family), ...	673	673	–	–
2 tenements (2 families), ...	57	114	–	–
3 tenements (3 families), ...	10	30	–	–
4 tenements (4 families), ...	2	8	–	–
5 tenements (5 families), ...	1	5	–	–
Newton. Ward 2, ...	1,084	1,107	14	1,121
1 tenement (1 family), ...	917	917	–	–
2 tenements (2 families), ...	75	150	–	–
3 tenements (3 families), ...	9	27	–	–
4 tenements (4 families), ...	2	8	–	–
5 tenements (5 families), ...	1	5	–	–
Newton. Ward 3, ...	671	719	8	727
1 tenement (1 family), ...	630	630	–	–
2 tenements (2 families), ...	34	68	–	–
3 tenements (3 families), ...	7	21	–	–
Newton. Ward 4, ...	643	685	19	704
1 tenement (1 family), ...	602	602	–	–
2 tenements (2 families), ...	40	80	–	–
3 tenements (3 families), ...	1	3	–	–
Newton. Ward 5, ...	804	856	8	864
1 tenement (1 family), ...	765	765	–	–
2 tenements (2 families), ...	29	58	–	–
3 tenements (3 families), ...	8	24	–	–
4 tenements (4 families), ...	1	4	–	–
5 tenements (5 families), ...	1	5	–	–
Newton. Ward 6, ...	768	826	9	845
1 tenement (1 family), ...	714	714	–	–
2 tenements (2 families), ...	46	92	–	–
3 tenements (3 families), ...	6	18	–	–
6 tenements (6 families), ...	2	12	–	–
Newton. Ward 7, ...	469	495	5	500
1 tenement (1 family), ...	453	453	–	–
2 tenements (2 families), ...	11	22	–	–
3 tenements (3 families), ...	3	9	–	–

OCCUPIED AND UNOCCUPIED TENEMENTS IN OCCUPIED DWELLING
HOUSES — Continued.

COUNTIES, CITIES, TOWNS, AND NUMBER OF TENEMENTS AND FAMILIES.	Number of Occupied Dwelling Houses	Number of Occupied Tenements in Occupied Dwelling Houses	Number of Unoccupied Tenements in Occupied Dwelling Houses	Total Number of Tenements in Occupied Dwelling Houses
MIDDLESEX — Con.				
Newton. Ward 7 — Con.				
4 tenements (4 families), ...	1	4	-	-
7 tenements (7 families), ...	1	7	-	-
North Reading, ...	204	228	3	231
1 tenement (1 family), ...	180	180	-	-
2 tenements (2 families), ...	24	48	-	-
Pepperell, ...	690	787	29	816
1 tenement (1 family), ...	595	595	-	-
2 tenements (2 families), ...	93	186	-	-
3 tenements (3 families), ...	2	6	-	-
Reading, ...	1,034	1,150	26	1,176
1 tenement (1 family), ...	923	923	-	-
2 tenements (2 families), ...	106	212	-	-
3 tenements (3 families), ...	5	15	-	-
Sherborn, ...	268	296	15	301
1 tenement (1 family), ...	250	250	-	-
2 tenements (2 families), ...	18	36	-	-
Shirley, ...	302	324	10	334
1 tenement (1 family), ...	283	283	-	-
2 tenements (2 families), ...	17	34	-	-
3 tenements (3 families), ...	1	3	-	-
4 tenements (4 families), ...	1	4	-	-
SOMERVILLE, ...	8,787	11,903	632	12,535
1 tenement (1 family), ...	6,126	6,126	-	-
2 tenements (2 families), ...	2,345	4,690	-	-
3 tenements (3 families), ...	236	708	-	-
4 tenements (4 families), ...	48	192	-	-
5 tenements (5 families), ...	12	60	-	-
6 tenements (6 families), ...	17	102	-	-
7 tenements (7 families), ...	1	7	-	-
8 tenements (8 families), ...	1	8	-	-
10 tenements (10 families), ...	1	10	-	-
Somerville. Ward 1, ...	1,578	2,302	158	2,460
1 tenement (1 family), ...	972	972	-	-
2 tenements (2 families), ...	520	1,040	-	-
3 tenements (3 families), ...	65	195	-	-
4 tenements (4 families), ...	13	52	-	-
5 tenements (5 families), ...	5	25	-	-
6 tenements (6 families), ...	3	18	-	-
Somerville. Ward 2, ...	2,647	3,875	228	4,103
1 tenement (1 family), ...	1,642	1,642	-	-
2 tenements (2 families), ...	858	1,716	-	-
3 tenements (3 families), ...	109	327	-	-
4 tenements (4 families), ...	20	80	-	-
5 tenements (5 families), ...	5	25	-	-
6 tenements (6 families), ...	10	60	-	-
7 tenements (7 families), ...	1	7	-	-
8 tenements (8 families), ...	1	8	-	-
10 tenements (10 families), ...	1	10	-	-
Somerville. Ward 3, ...	2,446	3,056	92	3,148
1 tenement (1 family), ...	1,885	1,885	-	-
2 tenements (2 families), ...	523	1,046	-	-
3 tenements (3 families), ...	31	93	-	-
4 tenements (4 families), ...	5	20	-	-
6 tenements (6 families), ...	2	12	-	-
Somerville. Ward 4, ...	2,116	2,670	154	2,824
1 tenement (1 family), ...	1,627	1,627	-	-

OCCUPIED AND UNOCCUPIED TENEMENTS IN OCCUPIED DWELLING HOUSES — Continued.

COUNTIES, CITIES, TOWNS, AND NUMBER OF TENEMENTS AND FAMILIES.	Number of Occupied Dwelling Houses	Number of Occupied Tenements in Occupied Dwelling Houses	Number of Unoccupied Tenements in Occupied Dwelling Houses	Total Number of Tenements in Occupied Dwelling Houses
MIDDLESEX — Con.				
Somerville. Ward 4 — Con.				
2 tenements (2 families), ...	444	888	-	-
3 tenements (3 families), ...	31	93	-	-
4 tenements (4 families), ...	10	40	-	-
5 tenements (5 families), ...	2	10	-	-
6 tenements (6 families), ...	2	12	-	-
Stoneham, ...	1,230	1,681	23	1,604
1 tenement (1 family), ...	1,161	1,161	-	-
2 tenements (2 families), ...	213	426	-	-
3 tenements (3 families), ...	11	33	-	-
4 tenements (4 families), ...	4	16	-	-
5 tenements (5 families), ...	1	5	-	-
Stow, ...	223	234	3	237
1 tenement (1 family), ...	212	212	-	-
2 tenements (2 families), ...	11	22	-	-
Sudbury, ...	244	272	10	282
1 tenement (1 family), ...	218	218	-	-
2 tenements (2 families), ...	24	48	-	-
3 tenements (3 families), ...	2	6	-	-
Tewksbury, ...	439	473	4	477
1 tenement (1 family), ...	406	406	-	-
2 tenements (2 families), ...	32	64	-	-
3 tenements (3 families), ...	1	3	-	-
Townsend, ...	465	512	13	525
1 tenement (1 family), ...	422	422	-	-
2 tenements (2 families), ...	40	80	-	-
3 tenements (3 families), ...	2	6	-	-
4 tenements (4 families), ...	1	4	-	-
Tyngsborough, ...	159	163	4	167
1 tenement (1 family), ...	156	156	-	-
2 tenements (2 families), ...	2	4	-	-
3 tenements (3 families), ...	1	3	-	-
Wakefield, ...	1,556	1,958	90	2,048
1 tenement (1 family), ...	1,201	1,201	-	-
2 tenements (2 families), ...	320	640	-	-
3 tenements (3 families), ...	25	75	-	-
4 tenements (4 families), ...	8	32	-	-
5 tenements (5 families), ...	2	10	-	-
WALTHAM, ...	3,856	4,276	110	4,386
1 tenement (1 family), ...	3,490	3,490	-	-
2 tenements (2 families), ...	328	656	-	-
3 tenements (3 families), ...	26	78	-	-
4 tenements (4 families), ...	10	40	-	-
6 tenements (6 families), ...	2	12	-	-
Waltham. Ward 1, ...	579	615	15	630
1 tenement (1 family), ...	546	546	-	-
2 tenements (2 families), ...	31	62	-	-
3 tenements (3 families), ...	1	3	-	-
4 tenements (4 families), ...	1	4	-	-
Waltham. Ward 2, ...	428	500	18	518
1 tenement (1 family), ...	368	368	-	-
2 tenements (2 families), ...	53	106	-	-
3 tenements (3 families), ...	4	12	-	-
4 tenements (4 families), ...	2	8	-	-
6 tenements (6 families), ...	1	6	-	-
Waltham. Ward 3, ...	554	651	32	683
1 tenement (1 family), ...	473	473	-	-

OCCUPIED AND UNOCCUPIED TENEMENTS IN OCCUPIED DWELLING HOUSES — Continued.

COUNTIES, CITIES, TOWNS, AND NUMBER OF TENEMENTS AND FAMILIES.	Number of Occupied Dwelling Houses	Number of Occupied Tenements in Occupied Dwelling Houses	Number of Unoccupied Tenements in Occupied Dwelling Houses	Total Number of Tenements in Occupied Dwelling Houses
MIDDLESEX — Con.				
Waltham, Ward 3 — Con.				
2 tenements (2 families), ...	69	138	-	-
3 tenements (3 families), ...	8	24	-	-
4 tenements (4 families), ...	4	16	-	-
Waltham, Ward 4, ...	602	646	14	660
1 tenement (1 family), ...	562	562	-	-
2 tenements (2 families), ...	37	74	-	-
3 tenements (3 families), ...	2	6	-	-
4 tenements (4 families), ...	1	4	-	-
Waltham, Ward 5, ...	580	639	7	646
1 tenement (1 family), ...	530	530	-	-
2 tenements (2 families), ...	45	90	-	-
3 tenements (3 families), ...	3	9	-	-
4 tenements (4 families), ...	1	4	-	-
6 tenements (6 families), ...	1	6	-	-
Waltham, Ward 6, ...	608	647	24	671
1 tenement (1 family), ...	571	571	-	-
2 tenements (2 families), ...	35	70	-	-
3 tenements (3 families), ...	2	6	-	-
Waltham, Ward 7, ...	505	578	-	578
1 tenement (1 family), ...	440	440	-	-
2 tenements (2 families), ...	58	116	-	-
3 tenements (3 families), ...	6	18	-	-
4 tenements (4 families), ...	1	4	-	-
Watertown, ...	1,533	1,650	28	1,678
1 tenement (1 family), ...	1,424	1,424	-	-
2 tenements (2 families), ...	105	210	-	-
3 tenements (3 families), ...	1	3	-	-
4 tenements (4 families), ...	2	8	-	-
5 tenements (5 families), ...	1	5	-	-
Wayland, ...	381	446	20	466
1 tenement (1 family), ...	323	323	-	-
2 tenements (2 families), ...	52	104	-	-
3 tenements (3 families), ...	5	15	-	-
4 tenements (4 families), ...	1	4	-	-
Westford, ...	475	526	10	536
1 tenement (1 family), ...	431	431	-	-
2 tenements (2 families), ...	39	78	-	-
3 tenements (3 families), ...	3	9	-	-
4 tenements (4 families), ...	2	8	-	-
Weston, ...	338	367	9	376
1 tenement (1 family), ...	309	309	-	-
2 tenements (2 families), ...	29	58	-	-
Wilmington, ...	301	338	6	344
1 tenement (1 family), ...	271	271	-	-
2 tenements (2 families), ...	25	50	-	-
3 tenements (3 families), ...	3	9	-	-
4 tenements (4 families), ...	2	8	-	-
Winchester, ...	1,207	1,301	17	1,318
1 tenement (1 family), ...	1,119	1,119	-	-
2 tenements (2 families), ...	82	164	-	-
3 tenements (3 families), ...	6	18	-	-
Woburn, ...	2,661	3,012	78	3,090
1 tenement (1 family), ...	2,347	2,347	-	-
2 tenements (2 families), ...	280	560	-	-
3 tenements (3 families), ...	31	93	-	-
4 tenements (4 families), ...	3	12	-	-

OCCUPIED AND UNOCCUPIED TENEMENTS IN OCCUPIED DWELLING HOUSES — Continued.

COUNTIES, CITIES, TOWNS, AND NUMBER OF TENEMENTS AND FAMILIES.	Number of Occupied Dwelling Houses	Number of Occupied Tenements in Occupied Dwelling Houses	Number of Unoccupied Tenements in Occupied Dwelling Houses	Total Number of Tenements in Occupied Dwelling Houses
MIDDLESEX — Con.				
Woburn. Ward 1, ...	453	509	1	510
1 tenement (1 family), ...	402	402	–	–
2 tenements (2 families), ...	46	92	–	–
3 tenements (3 families), ...	5	15	–	–
Woburn. Ward 2, ...	524	590	23	613
1 tenement (1 family), ...	463	463	–	–
2 tenements (2 families), ...	57	114	–	–
3 tenements (3 families), ...	3	9	–	–
4 tenements (4 families), ...	1	4	–	–
Woburn. Ward 3, ...	490	561	9	570
1 tenement (1 family), ...	425	425	–	–
2 tenements (2 families), ...	59	118	–	–
3 tenements (3 families), ...	6	18	–	–
Woburn. Ward 4, ...	501	574	15	589
1 tenement (1 family), ...	443	443	–	–
2 tenements (2 families), ...	45	90	–	–
3 tenements (3 families), ...	11	33	–	–
4 tenements (4 families), ...	2	8	–	–
Woburn. Ward 5, ...	209	242	12	254
1 tenement (1 family), ...	176	176	–	–
2 tenements (2 families), ...	33	66	–	–
Woburn. Ward 6, ...	306	343	9	352
1 tenement (1 family), ...	274	274	–	–
2 tenements (2 families), ...	27	54	–	–
3 tenements (3 families), ...	5	15	–	–
Woburn. Ward 7, ...	178	193	9	202
1 tenement (1 family), ...	164	164	–	–
2 tenements (2 families), ...	13	26	–	–
3 tenements (3 families), ...	1	3	–	–
NANTUCKET.				
Nantucket, ...	880	981	39	1,020
1 tenement (1 family), ...	779	779	–	–
2 tenements (2 families), ...	101	202	–	–
NORFOLK.				
Avon, ...	342	385	27	412
1 tenement (1 family), ...	299	299	–	–
2 tenements (2 families), ...	43	86	–	–
Bellingham, ...	314	358	5	363
1 tenement (1 family), ...	272	272	–	–
2 tenements (2 families), ...	40	80	–	–
3 tenements (3 families), ...	2	6	–	–
Braintree, ...	1,117	1,254	38	1,292
1 tenement (1 family), ...	989	989	–	–
2 tenements (2 families), ...	120	240	–	–
3 tenements (3 families), ...	7	21	–	–
4 tenements (4 families), ...	1	4	–	–
Brookline, ...	2,277	3,148	114	3,262
1 tenement (1 family), ...	1,824	1,824	–	–
2 tenements (2 families), ...	188	376	–	–
3 tenements (3 families), ...	173	519	–	–
4 tenements (4 families), ...	57	228	–	–
5 tenements (5 families), ...	16	80	–	–
6 tenements (6 families), ...	17	102	–	–

OCCUPIED AND UNOCCUPIED TENEMENTS IN OCCUPIED DWELLING HOUSES — Continued.

COUNTIES, CITIES, TOWNS, AND NUMBER OF TENEMENTS AND FAMILIES.	Number of Occupied Dwelling Houses	Number of Occupied Tenements in Occupied Dwelling Houses	Number of Unoccupied Tenements in Occupied Dwelling Houses	Total Number of Tenements in Occupied Dwelling Houses
NORFOLK — Con.				
Brookline — Con.				
8 tenements (8 families),	1	8	-	-
11 tenements (11 families),	1	11	-	-
Canton,	876	968	24	992
1 tenement (1 family),	793	793	-	-
2 tenements (2 families),	76	152	-	-
3 tenements (3 families),	5	15	-	-
4 tenements (4 families),	2	8	-	-
Cohasset,	577	586	1	587
1 tenement (1 family),	569	569	-	-
2 tenements (2 families),	7	14	-	-
3 tenements (3 families),	1	3	-	-
Dedham,	1,481	1,613	22	1,635
1 tenement (1 family),	1,365	1,365	-	-
2 tenements (2 families),	106	212	-	-
3 tenements (3 families),	8	24	-	-
4 tenements (4 families),	1	4	-	-
8 tenements (8 families),	1	8	-	-
Dover,	141	148	1	149
1 tenement (1 family),	134	134	-	-
2 tenements (2 families),	7	14	-	-
Foxborough,	723	828	7	835
1 tenement (1 family),	628	628	-	-
2 tenements (2 families),	87	174	-	-
3 tenements (3 families),	6	18	-	-
4 tenements (4 families),	2	8	-	-
Franklin,	984	1,176	32	1,208
1 tenement (1 family),	807	807	-	-
2 tenements (2 families),	164	328	-	-
3 tenements (3 families),	11	33	-	-
4 tenements (4 families),	2	8	-	-
Holbrook,	511	571	21	592
1 tenement (1 family),	451	451	-	-
2 tenements (2 families),	60	120	-	-
Hyde Park,	2,064	2,561	96	2,657
1 tenement (1 family),	1,644	1,644	-	-
2 tenements (2 families),	370	740	-	-
3 tenements (3 families),	37	111	-	-
4 tenements (4 families),	7	28	-	-
5 tenements (5 families),	4	20	-	-
8 tenements (8 families),	1	8	-	-
10 tenements (10 families),	1	10	-	-
Medfield,	348	415	16	431
1 tenement (1 family),	297	297	-	-
2 tenements (2 families),	43	86	-	-
3 tenements (3 families),	3	9	-	-
4 tenements (4 families),	3	12	-	-
5 tenements (5 families),	1	5	-	-
6 tenements (6 families),	1	6	-	-
Medway,	626	732	33	765
1 tenement (1 family),	536	536	-	-
2 tenements (2 families),	79	158	-	-
3 tenements (3 families),	7	21	-	-
4 tenements (4 families),	3	12	-	-
5 tenements (5 families),	1	5	-	-
Millis,	210	226	23	249
1 tenement (1 family),	199	199	-	-

OCCUPIED AND UNOCCUPIED TENEMENTS IN OCCUPIED DWELLING HOUSES — Continued.

COUNTIES, CITIES, TOWNS, AND NUMBER OF TENEMENTS AND FAMILIES.	Number of Occupied Dwelling Houses	Number of Occupied Tenements in Occupied Dwelling Houses	Number of Unoccupied Tenements in Occupied Dwelling Houses	Total Number of Tenements in Occupied Dwelling Houses
NORFOLK — Con.				
Millis — Con.				
2 tenements (2 families), .	8	16	-	-
3 tenements (3 families), .	2	6	-	-
5 tenements (5 families), .	1	5	-	-
Milton, .	1,903	1,106	19	1,125
1 tenement (1 family),	905	905	-	-
2 tenements (2 families), .	94	188	-	-
3 tenements (3 families), .	3	9	-	-
4 tenements 4 families, .	1	4	-	-
Needham, .	735	802	10	812
1 tenement 1 family,	675	675	-	-
2 tenements (2 families), .	53	106	-	-
3 tenements (3 families), .	7	21	-	-
Norfolk, .	179	210	6	216
1 tenement (1 family),	157	157	-	-
2 tenements (2 families), .	18	36	-	-
3 tenements (3 families), .	1	3	-	-
4 tenements (4 families), .	1	4	-	-
5 tenements (5 families), .	2	10	-	-
Norwood, .	866	963	2	965
1 tenement (1 family),	774	774	-	-
2 tenements (2 families), .	89	178	-	-
3 tenements (3 families), .	1	3	-	-
4 tenements (4 families), .	2	8	-	-
QUINCY, .	3,801	4,373	155	4,528
1 tenement 1 family,	3,294	3,294	-	-
2 tenements 2 families, .	453	906	-	-
3 tenements 3 families, .	44	132	-	-
4 tenements (4 families), .	9	36	-	-
5 tenements (5 families), .	1	5	-	-
Quincy. Ward 1, .	711	790	27	817
1 tenement (1 family),	641	641	-	-
2 tenements (2 families), .	63	126	-	-
3 tenements (3 families), .	5	15	-	-
4 tenements (4 families), .	2	8	-	-
Quincy. Ward 2, .	529	584	19	603
1 tenement 1 family,	478	478	-	-
2 tenements (2 families), .	47	94	-	-
3 tenements (3 families), .	4	12	-	-
Quincy. Ward 3, .	822	983	30	1,013
1 tenement (1 family),	673	673	-	-
2 tenements (2 families), .	138	276	-	-
3 tenements (3 families), .	10	30	-	-
4 tenements (4 families), .	1	4	-	-
Quincy. Ward 4, .	813	990	46	1,036
1 tenement (1 family),	665	665	-	-
2 tenements (2 families), .	123	246	-	-
3 tenements (3 families), .	21	63	-	-
4 tenements (4 families), .	4	16	-	-
Quincy. Ward 5, .	526	568	9	577
1 tenement (1 family),	488	488	-	-
2 tenements (2 families), .	36	72	-	-
4 tenements (4 families), .	2	8	-	-
Quincy. Ward 6, .	400	458	24	482
1 tenement (1 family),	349	349	-	-
2 tenements (2 families), .	46	92	-	-

OCCUPIED AND UNOCCUPIED TENEMENTS IN OCCUPIED DWELLING HOUSES — Continued.

COUNTIES, CITIES, TOWNS, AND NUMBER OF TENEMENTS AND FAMILIES.	Number of Occupied Dwelling Houses	Number of Occupied Tenements in Occupied Dwelling Houses	Number of Unoccupied Tenements in Occupied Dwelling Houses	Total Number of Tenements in Occupied Dwelling Houses
NORFOLK — Con.				
Quincy. Ward 6 — Con.				
3 tenements (3 families),	4	12	–	–
5 tenements (5 families),	1	5	–	–
Randolph,	824	905	12	917
1 tenement (1 family),	746	746	–	–
2 tenements (2 families),	75	150	–	–
3 tenements (3 families),	3	9	–	–
Sharon,	378	393	3	396
1 tenement (1 family),	365	365	–	–
2 tenements (2 families),	11	22	–	–
3 tenements (3 families),	2	6	–	–
Stoughton,	1,111	1,241	41	1,282
1 tenement (1 family),	991	991	–	–
2 tenements (2 families),	113	226	–	–
3 tenements (3 families),	5	15	–	–
4 tenements (4 families),	1	4	–	–
5 tenements (5 families),	1	5	–	–
Walpole,	620	688	13	701
1 tenement (1 family),	560	560	–	–
2 tenements (2 families),	54	108	–	–
3 tenements (3 families),	4	12	–	–
4 tenements (4 families),	2	8	–	–
Wellesley,	679	738	11	749
1 tenement (1 family),	624	624	–	–
2 tenements (2 families),	51	102	–	–
3 tenements (3 families),	4	12	–	–
Weymouth,	2,421	2,666	64	2,730
1 tenement (1 family),	2,193	2,193	–	–
2 tenements (2 families),	215	430	–	–
3 tenements (3 families),	10	30	–	–
4 tenements (4 families),	2	8	–	–
5 tenements (5 families),	1	5	–	–
Wrentham,	581	631	18	649
1 tenement (1 family),	534	534	–	–
2 tenements (2 families),	44	88	–	–
3 tenements (3 families),	3	9	–	–
PLYMOUTH.				
Abington,	912	1,076	38	1,114
1 tenement (1 family),	758	758	–	–
2 tenements (2 families),	144	288	–	–
3 tenements (3 families),	10	30	–	–
Bridgewater,	762	854	24	878
1 tenement (1 family),	675	675	–	–
2 tenements (2 families),	82	164	–	–
3 tenements (3 families),	5	15	–	–
BROCKTON,	5,255	7,700	360	8,060
1 tenement (1 family),	3,215	3,215	–	–
2 tenements (2 families),	1,957	3,914	–	–
3 tenements (3 families),	170	510	–	–
4 tenements (4 families),	10	40	–	–
5 tenements (5 families),	1	5	–	–
6 tenements (6 families),	1	6	–	–
10 tenements (10 families),	1	10	–	–
Brockton. Ward 1,	664	935	52	987
1 tenement (1 family),	414	414	–	–

OCCUPIED AND UNOCCUPIED TENEMENTS IN OCCUPIED DWELLING HOUSES — Continued.

COUNTIES, CITIES, TOWNS, AND NUMBER OF TENEMENTS AND FAMILIES.	Number of Occupied Dwelling Houses	Number of Occupied Tenements in Occupied Dwelling Houses	Number of Unoccupied Tenements in Occupied Dwelling Houses	Total Number of Tenements in Occupied Dwelling Houses
PLYMOUTH — Con.				
Brockton. Ward 1 — Con.				
2 tenements (2 families), ...	236	472	-	-
3 tenements (3 families), ...	13	39	-	-
10 tenements (10 families), ...	1	10	-	-
Brockton. Ward 2, ...	730	1,070	41	1,111
1 tenement (1 family), ...	419	419	-	-
2 tenements (2 families), ...	286	572	-	-
3 tenements (3 families), ...	21	63	-	-
4 tenements (4 families), ...	4	16	-	-
Brockton. Ward 3, ...	815	1,198	28	1,226
1 tenement (1 family), ...	466	466	-	-
2 tenements (2 families), ...	317	634	-	-
3 tenements (3 families), ...	30	90	-	-
4 tenements (4 families), ...	2	8	-	-
Brockton. Ward 4, ...	757	1,089	43	1,132
1 tenement (1 family), ...	459	459	-	-
2 tenements (2 families), ...	265	530	-	-
3 tenements (3 families), ...	32	96	-	-
4 tenements (4 families), ...	1	4	-	-
Brockton. Ward 5, ...	791	1,126	75	1,201
1 tenement (1 family), ...	485	485	-	-
2 tenements (2 families), ...	278	556	-	-
3 tenements (3 families), ...	27	81	-	-
4 tenements (4 families), ...	1	4	-	-
Brockton. Ward 6, ...	789	1,086	54	1,140
1 tenement (1 family), ...	516	516	-	-
2 tenements (2 families), ...	251	502	-	-
3 tenements (3 families), ...	21	63	-	-
5 tenements (5 families), ...	1	5	-	-
Brockton. Ward 7, ...	809	1,196	67	1,263
1 tenement (1 family), ...	456	456	-	-
2 tenements (2 families), ...	324	648	-	-
3 tenements (3 families), ...	26	78	-	-
4 tenements (4 families), ...	2	8	-	-
6 tenements (6 families), ...	1	6	-	-
Carver, ...	246	262	15	277
1 tenement (1 family), ...	230	230	-	-
2 tenements (2 families), ...	16	32	-	-
Duxbury, ...	503	532	8	540
1 tenement (1 family), ...	475	475	-	-
2 tenements (2 families), ...	27	54	-	-
3 tenements (3 families), ...	1	3	-	-
East Bridgewater, ...	642	726	28	754
1 tenement (1 family), ...	563	563	-	-
2 tenements (2 families), ...	74	148	-	-
3 tenements (3 families), ...	5	15	-	-
Halifax, ...	132	148	5	153
1 tenement (1 family), ...	116	116	-	-
2 tenements (2 families), ...	16	32	-	-
Hanover, ...	506	544	11	555
1 tenement (1 family), ...	468	468	-	-
2 tenements (2 families), ...	38	76	-	-
Hanson, ...	353	380	7	387
1 tenement (1 family), ...	326	326	-	-
2 tenements (2 families), ...	27	54	-	-
Hingham, ...	1,057	1,164	25	1,189
1 tenement (1 family), ...	957	957	-	-

OCCUPIED AND UNOCCUPIED TENEMENTS IN OCCUPIED DWELLING HOUSES — Continued.

COUNTIES, CITIES, TOWNS, AND NUMBER OF TENEMENTS AND FAMILIES.	Number of Occupied Dwelling Houses	Number of Occupied Tenements in Occupied Dwelling Houses	Number of Unoccupied Tenements in Occupied Dwelling Houses	Total Number of Tenements in Occupied Dwelling Houses
PLYMOUTH — Con.				
Hingham — Con.				
2 tenements (2 families),	95	190	–	–
3 tenements (3 families),	3	9	–	–
4 tenements (4 families),	2	8	–	–
Hull,	229	229	5	234
1 tenement (1 family),	229	229	–	–
Kingston,	425	477	10	487
1 tenement (1 family),	375	375	–	–
2 tenements (2 families),	48	96	–	–
3 tenements (3 families),	2	6	–	–
Lakeville,	220	233	1	234
1 tenement (1 family),	208	208	–	–
2 tenements (2 families),	11	22	–	–
3 tenements (3 families),	1	3	–	–
Marion,	205	213	7	220
1 tenement (1 family),	197	197	–	–
2 tenements (2 families),	8	16	–	–
Marshfield,	484	511	21	532
1 tenement (1 family),	457	457	–	–
2 tenements (2 families),	27	54	–	–
Mattapoisett,	281	301	10	311
1 tenement (1 family),	262	262	–	–
2 tenements (2 families),	18	36	–	–
3 tenements (3 families),	1	3	–	–
Middleborough,	1,396	1,673	39	1,712
1 tenement (1 family),	1,140	1,140	–	–
2 tenements (2 families),	240	480	–	–
3 tenements (3 families),	14	42	–	–
5 tenements (5 families),	1	5	–	–
6 tenements (6 families),	1	6	–	–
Norwell,	407	422	9	431
1 tenement (1 family),	392	392	–	–
2 tenements (2 families),	15	30	–	–
Pembroke,	345	367	3	370
1 tenement (1 family),	324	324	–	–
2 tenements (2 families),	20	40	–	–
3 tenements (3 families),	1	3	–	–
Plymouth,	1,615	1,969	35	2,004
1 tenement (1 family),	1,304	1,304	–	–
2 tenements (2 families),	280	560	–	–
3 tenements (3 families),	20	60	–	–
4 tenements (4 families),	10	40	–	–
5 tenements (5 families),	1	5	–	–
Plympton,	152	162	6	168
1 tenement (1 family),	142	142	–	–
2 tenements (2 families),	10	20	–	–
Rochester,	246	260	7	267
1 tenement (1 family),	233	233	–	–
2 tenements (2 families),	12	24	–	–
3 tenements (3 families),	1	3	–	–
Rockland,	1,186	1,331	46	1,377
1 tenement (1 family),	1,051	1,051	–	–
2 tenements (2 families),	127	254	–	–
3 tenements (3 families),	6	18	–	–
4 tenements (4 families),	2	8	–	–
Scituate,	569	607	20	627
1 tenement (1 family),	532	532	–	–

OCCUPIED AND UNOCCUPIED TENEMENTS IN OCCUPIED DWELLING HOUSES — Continued.

Counties, Cities, Towns, and Number of Tenements and Families.	Number of Occupied Dwelling Houses	Number of Occupied Tenements in Occupied Dwelling Houses	Number of Unoccupied Tenements in Occupied Dwelling Houses	Total Number of Tenements in Occupied Dwelling Houses
PLYMOUTH — Con.				
Scituate — Con.				
2 tenements (2 families), ...	36	72	–	–
3 tenements (3 families), ...	1	3	–	–
Wareham, ...	815	891	22	913
1 tenement (1 family), ...	748	748	–	–
2 tenements (2 families), ...	59	118	–	–
3 tenements (3 families), ...	7	21	–	–
4 tenements (4 families), ...	1	4	–	–
West Bridgewater, ...	578	409	–	409
1 tenement (1 family), ...	347	347	–	–
2 tenements (2 families), ...	31	62	–	–
Whitman, ...	1,210	1,389	37	1,426
1 tenement (1 family), ...	1,037	1,037	–	–
2 tenements (2 families), ...	168	336	–	–
3 tenements (3 families), ...	4	12	–	–
4 tenements (4 families), ...	1	4	–	–
SUFFOLK.				
Boston, ...	58,599	103,306	8,243	111,549
1 tenement (1 family), ...	33,470	33,470	–	–
2 tenements (2 families), ...	13,369	26,738	–	–
3 tenements (3 families), ...	8,454	25,362	–	–
4 tenements (4 families), ...	1,706	6,824	–	–
5 tenements (5 families), ...	637	3,185	–	–
6 tenements (6 families), ...	396	2,376	–	–
7 tenements (7 families), ...	205	1,435	–	–
8 tenements (8 families), ...	147	1,176	–	–
9 tenements (9 families), ...	56	504	–	–
10 tenements (10 families), ...	33	330	–	–
11 tenements (11 families), ...	30	330	–	–
12 tenements (12 families), ...	19	228	–	–
13 tenements (13 families), ...	15	195	–	–
14 tenements (14 families), ...	14	196	–	–
15 tenements (15 families), ...	12	180	–	–
16 tenements (16 families), ...	6	96	–	–
17 tenements (17 families), ...	10	170	–	–
18 tenements (18 families), ...	2	36	–	–
19 tenements (19 families), ...	3	57	–	–
20 tenements (20 families), ...	2	40	–	–
21 tenements (21 families), ...	1	21	–	–
22 tenements (22 families), ...	2	44	–	–
24 tenements (24 families), ...	1	24	–	–
25 tenements (25 families), ...	1	25	–	–
28 tenements (28 families), ...	3	84	–	–
30 tenements (30 families), ...	1	30	–	–
31 tenements (31 families), ...	1	31	–	–
38 tenements (38 families), ...	1	38	–	–
39 tenements (39 families), ...	1	39	–	–
42 tenements (42 families), ...	1	42	–	–
Boston, Ward 1, ...	2,843	4,671	301	4,972
1 tenement (1 family), ...	1,429	1,429	–	–
2 tenements (2 families), ...	1,034	2,068	–	–
3 tenements (3 families), ...	352	1,056	–	–
4 tenements (4 families), ...	25	100	–	–
5 tenements (5 families), ...	2	10	–	–
8 tenements (8 families), ...	1	8	–	–

OCCUPIED AND UNOCCUPIED TENEMENTS IN OCCUPIED DWELLING HOUSES — Continued.

COUNTIES, CITIES, TOWNS, AND NUMBER OF TENEMENTS AND FAMILIES.	Number of Occupied Dwelling Houses	Number of Occupied Tenements in Occupied Dwelling Houses	Number of Unoccupied Tenements in Occupied Dwelling Houses	Total Number of Tenements in Occupied Dwelling Houses
SUFFOLK — Con.				
Boston. Ward 2, ...	2,163	4,144	292	4,436
1 tenement (1 family), ...	822	822	-	-
2 tenements (2 families), ...	802	1,604	-	-
3 tenements (3 families), ...	467	1,401	-	-
4 tenements (4 families), ...	56	224	-	-
5 tenements (5 families), ...	7	35	-	-
6 tenements (6 families), ...	5	30	-	-
7 tenements (7 families), ...	4	28	-	-
Boston. Ward 3, ...	1,681	3,164	214	3,378
1 tenement (1 family), ...	666	666	-	-
2 tenements (2 families), ...	608	1,216	-	-
3 tenements (3 families), ...	372	1,116	-	-
4 tenements (4 families), ...	23	92	-	-
5 tenements (5 families), ...	5	25	-	-
6 tenements (6 families), ...	2	12	-	-
7 tenements (7 families), ...	3	21	-	-
8 tenements (8 families), ...	2	16	-	-
Boston. Ward 4, ...	1,851	3,010	183	3,193
1 tenement (1 family), ...	983	983	-	-
2 tenements (2 families), ...	640	1,280	-	-
3 tenements (3 families), ...	197	591	-	-
4 tenements (4 families), ...	17	68	-	-
5 tenements (5 families), ...	7	35	-	-
6 tenements (6 families), ...	3	18	-	-
7 tenements (7 families), ...	1	7	-	-
8 tenements (8 families), ...	1	8	-	-
9 tenements (9 families), ...	1	9	-	-
11 tenements (11 families), ...	1	11	-	-
Boston. Ward 5, ...	1,507	2,588	181	2,769
1 tenement (1 family), ...	769	769	-	-
2 tenements (2 families), ...	473	946	-	-
3 tenements (3 families), ...	219	657	-	-
4 tenements (4 families), ...	28	112	-	-
5 tenements (5 families), ...	8	40	-	-
6 tenements (6 families), ...	7	42	-	-
7 tenements (7 families), ...	2	14	-	-
8 tenements (8 families), ...	1	8	-	-
Boston. Ward 6, ...	1,854	5,559	417	5,976
1 tenement (1 family), ...	631	631	-	-
2 tenements (2 families), ...	296	592	-	-
3 tenements (3 families), ...	357	1,071	-	-
4 tenements (4 families), ...	223	892	-	-
5 tenements (5 families), ...	126	630	-	-
6 tenements (6 families), ...	71	426	-	-
7 tenements (7 families), ...	57	399	-	-
8 tenements (8 families), ...	42	336	-	-
9 tenements (9 families), ...	19	171	-	-
10 tenements (10 families), ...	5	50	-	-
11 tenements (11 families), ...	7	77	-	-
12 tenements (12 families), ...	6	72	-	-
13 tenements (13 families), ...	2	26	-	-
14 tenements (14 families), ...	5	70	-	-
15 tenements (15 families), ...	2	30	-	-
16 tenements (16 families), ...	1	16	-	-
17 tenements (17 families), ...	3	51	-	-
19 tenements (19 families), ...	1	19	-	-

OCCUPIED AND UNOCCUPIED TENEMENTS IN OCCUPIED DWELLING HOUSES — Continued.

COUNTIES, CITIES, TOWNS, AND NUMBER OF TENEMENTS AND FAMILIES.	Number of Occupied Dwelling Houses	Number of Occupied Tenements in Occupied Dwelling Houses	Number of Unoccupied Tenements in Occupied Dwelling Houses	Total Number of Tenements in Occupied Dwelling Houses
SUFFOLK — Con.				
Boston, Ward 7, ...	1,554	3,137	344	3,481
1 tenement (1 family), ...	959	959	-	-
2 tenements (2 families), ...	215	430	-	-
3 tenements (3 families), ...	139	417	-	-
4 tenements (4 families), ...	109	436	-	-
5 tenements (5 families), ...	52	260	-	-
6 tenements (6 families), ...	38	228	-	-
7 tenements (7 families), ...	8	56	-	-
8 tenements (8 families), ...	10	80	-	-
9 tenements (9 families), ...	7	63	-	-
10 tenements (10 families), . . .	5	50	-	-
11 tenements (11 families), . . .	4	44	-	-
12 tenements (12 families), . . .	2	24	-	-
13 tenements (13 families), . . .	2	26	-	-
14 tenements (14 families), . . .	1	14	-	-
15 tenements (15 families), . . .	1	15	-	-
17 tenements (17 families), . . .	1	17	-	-
18 tenements (18 families), . . .	1	18	-	-
Boston, Ward 8, ...	1,891	4,370	479	4,849
1 tenement (1 family), ...	874	874	-	-
2 tenements (2 families), ...	319	638	-	-
3 tenements (3 families), ...	349	1,047	-	-
4 tenements (4 families), ...	181	724	-	-
5 tenements (5 families), ...	69	345	-	-
6 tenements (6 families), ...	46	276	-	-
7 tenements (7 families), ...	18	126	-	-
8 tenements (8 families), ...	17	136	-	-
9 tenements (9 families), ...	6	54	-	-
10 tenements (10 families), . . .	4	40	-	-
11 tenements (11 families), . . .	1	11	-	-
12 tenements (12 families), . . .	2	24	-	-
13 tenements (13 families), . . .	1	13	-	-
14 tenements (14 families), . . .	1	14	-	-
15 tenements (15 families), . . .	1	15	-	-
16 tenements (16 families), . . .	1	16	-	-
17 tenements (17 families), . . .	1	17	-	-
Boston, Ward 9, ...	1,970	4,682	551	5,233
1 tenement (1 family), ...	963	963	-	-
2 tenements (2 families), ...	324	648	-	-
3 tenements (3 families), ...	322	966	-	-
4 tenements (4 families), ...	223	892	-	-
5 tenements (5 families), ...	87	435	-	-
6 tenements (6 families), ...	51	306	-	-
7 tenements (7 families), ...	27	189	-	-
8 tenements (8 families), ...	17	136	-	-
9 tenements (9 families), ...	6	54	-	-
10 tenements (10 families), . . .	2	20	-	-
11 tenements (11 families), . . .	2	22	-	-
12 tenements (12 families), . . .	2	24	-	-
13 tenements (13 families), . . .	1	13	-	-
16 tenements (16 families), . . .	2	32	-	-
42 tenements (42 families), . . .	1	42	-	-
Boston, Ward 10, ...	2,292	4,471	498	4,969
1 tenement (1 family), ...	1,453	1,453	-	-
2 tenements (2 families), ...	263	526	-	-
3 tenements (3 families), ...	274	822	-	-

OCCUPIED AND UNOCCUPIED TENEMENTS IN OCCUPIED DWELLING HOUSES — Continued.

COUNTIES, CITIES, TOWNS, AND NUMBER OF TENEMENTS AND FAMILIES.	Number of Occupied Dwelling Houses	Number of Occupied Tenements in Occupied Dwelling Houses	Number of Unoccupied Tenements in Occupied Dwelling Houses	Total Number of Tenements in Occupied Dwelling Houses
SUFFOLK — Con.				
Boston. Ward 10 — Con.				
4 tenements (4 families),	204	816	-	-
5 tenements (5 families),	24	120	-	-
6 tenements (6 families),	19	114	-	-
7 tenements (7 families),	13	91	-	-
8 tenements (8 families),	13	104	-	-
9 tenements (9 families),	5	45	-	-
10 tenements (10 families),	5	50	-	-
11 tenements (11 families),	2	22	-	-
12 tenements (12 families),	2	24	-	-
13 tenements (13 families),	2	26	-	-
14 tenements (14 families),	5	70	-	-
15 tenements (15 families),	1	15	-	-
17 tenements (17 families),	2	34	-	-
20 tenements (20 families),	1	20	-	-
21 tenements (21 families),	1	21	-	-
28 tenements (28 families),	1	28	-	-
31 tenements (31 families),	1	31	-	-
39 tenements (39 families),	1	39	-	-
Boston. Ward 11,	2,515	3,770	291	4,061
1 tenement (1 family),	2,036	2,036	-	-
2 tenements (2 families),	179	358	-	-
3 tenements (3 families),	149	447	-	-
4 tenements (4 families),	72	288	-	-
5 tenements (5 families),	27	135	-	-
6 tenements (6 families),	19	114	-	-
7 tenements (7 families),	7	49	-	-
8 tenements (8 families),	5	40	-	-
9 tenements (9 families),	2	18	-	-
10 tenements (10 families),	4	40	-	-
11 tenements (11 families),	4	44	-	-
12 tenements (12 families),	2	24	-	-
13 tenements (13 families),	1	13	-	-
15 tenements (15 families),	2	30	-	-
17 tenements (17 families),	2	34	-	-
18 tenements (18 families),	1	18	-	-
20 tenements (20 families),	1	20	-	-
24 tenements (24 families),	1	24	-	-
38 tenements (38 families),	1	38	-	-
Boston. Ward 12,	2,249	3,518	429	3,947
1 tenement (1 family),	1,688	1,688	-	-
2 tenements (2 families),	233	466	-	-
3 tenements (3 families),	199	597	-	-
4 tenements (4 families),	68	272	-	-
5 tenements (5 families),	17	85	-	-
6 tenements (6 families),	13	78	-	-
7 tenements (7 families),	6	42	-	-
8 tenements (8 families),	5	40	-	-
9 tenements (9 families),	5	45	-	-
10 tenements (10 families),	4	40	-	-
11 tenements (11 families),	5	55	-	-
13 tenements (13 families),	1	13	-	-
15 tenements (15 families),	3	45	-	-
22 tenements (22 families),	1	22	-	-
30 tenements (30 families),	1	30	-	-
Boston. Ward 13,	2,341	5,453	545	5,998
1 tenement (1 family),	657	657	-	-

OCCUPIED AND UNOCCUPIED TENEMENTS IN OCCUPIED DWELLING HOUSES — Continued.

COUNTIES, CITIES, TOWNS, AND NUMBER OF TENEMENTS AND FAMILIES.	Number of Occupied Dwelling Houses	Number of Occupied Tenements in Occupied Dwelling Houses	Number of Unoccupied Tenements in Occupied Dwelling Houses	Total Number of Tenements in Occupied Dwelling Houses
SUFFOLK — Con.				
Boston. Ward 13 — Con.				
2 tenements (2 families), ...	750	1,500	–	–
3 tenements (3 families), ...	743	2,229	–	–
4 tenements (4 families), ...	99	396	–	–
5 tenements (5 families), ...	53	265	–	–
6 tenements (6 families), ...	28	168	–	–
7 tenements (7 families), ...	20	140	–	–
8 tenements (8 families), ...	5	40	–	–
9 tenements (9 families), ...	2	18	–	–
10 tenements (10 families), ...	1	10	–	–
11 tenements (11 families), ...	1	11	–	–
17 tenements (17 families), ...	1	17	–	–
22 tenements (22 families), ...	1	22	–	–
Boston. Ward 14, ...	2,485	4,974	293	4,967
1 tenement (1 family), ...	1,418	1,418	–	–
2 tenements (2 families), ...	649	1,298	–	–
3 tenements (3 families), ...	370	1,110	–	–
4 tenements (4 families), ...	19	76	–	–
5 tenements (5 families), ...	14	70	–	–
6 tenements (6 families), ...	8	48	–	–
7 tenements (7 families), ...	3	21	–	–
8 tenements (8 families), ...	3	24	–	–
9 tenements (9 families), ...	1	9	–	–
Boston. Ward 15, ...	2,294	3,992	300	4,292
1 tenement (1 family), ...	1,074	1,074	–	–
2 tenements (2 families), ...	787	1,574	–	–
3 tenements (3 families), ...	407	1,221	–	–
4 tenements (4 families), ...	14	56	–	–
5 tenements (5 families), ...	7	35	–	–
6 tenements (6 families), ...	3	18	–	–
7 tenements (7 families), ...	2	14	–	–
Boston. Ward 16, ...	2,103	3,735	307	4,042
1 tenement (1 family), ...	1,067	1,067	–	–
2 tenements (2 families), ...	556	1,112	–	–
3 tenements (3 families), ...	449	1,347	–	–
4 tenements (4 families), ...	16	64	–	–
5 tenements (5 families), ...	4	20	–	–
6 tenements (6 families), ...	4	24	–	–
7 tenements (7 families), ...	3	21	–	–
8 tenements (8 families), ...	1	8	–	–
19 tenements (19 families), ...	1	19	–	–
25 tenements (25 families), ...	1	25	–	–
28 tenements (28 families), ...	1	28	–	–
Boston. Ward 17, ...	2,441	4,656	444	5,100
1 tenement (1 family), ...	1,109	1,109	–	–
2 tenements (2 families), ...	695	1,390	–	–
3 tenements (3 families), ...	513	1,539	–	–
4 tenements (4 families), ...	63	252	–	–
5 tenements (5 families), ...	27	135	–	–
6 tenements (6 families), ...	16	96	–	–
7 tenements (7 families), ...	9	63	–	–
8 tenements (8 families), ...	9	72	–	–
Boston. Ward 18, ...	2,303	4,960	556	5,516
1 tenement (1 family), ...	890	890	–	–
2 tenements (2 families), ...	676	1,352	–	–
3 tenements (3 families), ...	505	1,515	–	–

OCCUPIED AND UNOCCUPIED TENEMENTS IN OCCUPIED DWELLING HOUSES — Continued.

COUNTIES, CITIES, TOWNS, AND NUMBER OF TENEMENTS AND FAMILIES.	Number of Occupied Dwelling Houses	Number of Occupied Tenements in Occupied Dwelling Houses	Number of Unoccupied Tenements in Occupied Dwelling Houses	Total Number of Tenements in Occupied Dwelling Houses
SUFFOLK — Con.				
Boston. Ward 18 — Con.				
4 tenements (4 families), ...	136	544	–	–
5 tenements (5 families), ...	39	195	–	–
6 tenements (6 families), ...	22	132	–	–
7 tenements (7 families), ...	14	98	–	–
8 tenements (8 families), ...	8	64	–	–
9 tenements (9 families), ...	1	9	–	–
10 tenements (10 families), ...	1	10	–	–
11 tenements (11 families), ...	2	22	–	–
12 tenements (12 families), ...	1	12	–	–
13 tenements (13 families), ...	3	39	–	–
14 tenements (14 families), ...	2	28	–	–
15 tenements (15 families), ...	1	15	–	–
16 tenements (16 families), ...	1	16	–	–
19 tenements (19 families), ...	1	19	–	–
Boston. Ward 19, ...	2,344	4,620	260	4,880
1 tenement (1 family), ...	779	779	–	–
2 tenements (2 families), ...	519	1,038	–	–
3 tenements (3 families), ...	708	2,124	–	–
4 tenements (4 families), ...	68	272	–	–
5 tenements (5 families), ...	36	180	–	–
6 tenements (6 families), ...	25	150	–	–
7 tenements (7 families), ...	5	35	–	–
9 tenements (9 families), ...	1	9	–	–
10 tenements (10 families), ...	2	20	–	–
13 tenements (13 families), ...	1	13	–	–
Boston. Ward 20, ...	3,580	4,674	273	4,947
1 tenement (1 family), ...	2,750	2,750	–	–
2 tenements (2 families), ...	629	1,258	–	–
3 tenements (3 families), ...	188	564	–	–
4 tenements (4 families), ...	12	48	–	–
5 tenements (5 families), ...	7	35	–	–
6 tenements (6 families), ...	2	12	–	–
7 tenements (7 families), ...	1	7	–	–
Boston. Ward 21, ...	2,896	4,306	299	4,605
1 tenement (1 family), ...	2,005	2,005	–	–
2 tenements (2 families), ...	512	1,024	–	–
3 tenements (3 families), ...	340	1,020	–	–
4 tenements (4 families), ...	15	60	–	–
5 tenements (5 families), ...	7	35	–	–
6 tenements (6 families), ...	6	36	–	–
7 tenements (7 families), ...	1	7	–	–
8 tenements (8 families), ...	5	40	–	–
11 tenements (11 families), ...	1	11	–	–
12 tenements (12 families), ...	2	24	–	–
16 tenements (16 families), ...	1	16	–	–
28 tenements (28 families), ...	1	28	–	–
Boston. Ward 22, ...	2,850	4,770	332	5,102
1 tenement (1 family), ...	1,577	1,577	–	–
2 tenements (2 families), ...	690	1,380	–	–
3 tenements (3 families), ...	555	1,665	–	–
4 tenements (4 families), ...	12	48	–	–
5 tenements (5 families), ...	7	35	–	–
6 tenements (6 families), ...	6	36	–	–
8 tenements (8 families), ...	2	16	–	–
13 tenements (13 families), ...	1	13	–	–

OCCUPIED AND UNOCCUPIED TENEMENTS IN OCCUPIED DWELLING HOUSES — Continued.

COUNTIES, CITIES, TOWNS, AND NUMBER OF TENEMENTS AND FAMILIES.	Number of Occupied Dwelling Houses	Number of Occupied Tenements in Occupied Dwelling Houses	Number of Unoccupied Tenements in Occupied Dwelling Houses	Total Number of Tenements in Occupied Dwelling Houses
SUFFOLK — Con.				
Boston. Ward 23, ...	2,947	3,866	192	4,058
1 tenement (1 family), ...	2,199	2,199	–	–
2 tenements (2 families), ...	605	1,210	–	–
3 tenements (3 families), ...	130	390	–	–
4 tenements (4 families), ...	9	36	–	–
5 tenements (5 families), ...	2	10	–	–
6 tenements (6 families), ...	1	6	–	–
15 tenements (15 families), ...	1	15	–	–
Boston. Ward 24, ...	3,234	3,944	151	4,095
1 tenement (1 family), ...	2,620	2,620	–	–
2 tenements (2 families), ...	520	1,040	–	–
3 tenements (3 families), ...	92	276	–	–
4 tenements (4 families), ...	2	8	–	–
Boston. Ward 25, ...	2,602	3,172	111	3,283
1 tenement (1 family), ...	2,132	2,132	–	–
2 tenements (2 families), ...	395	790	–	–
3 tenements (3 families), ...	58	174	–	–
4 tenements (4 families), ...	12	48	–	–
5 tenements (5 families), ...	3	15	–	–
6 tenements (6 families), ...	1	6	–	–
7 tenements (7 families), ...	1	7	–	–
CHELSEA, ...	4,743	6,934	482	7,416
1 tenement (1 family), ...	2,953	2,953	–	–
2 tenements (2 families), ...	1,476	2,952	–	–
3 tenements (3 families), ...	258	774	–	–
4 tenements (4 families), ...	39	156	–	–
5 tenements (5 families), ...	10	50	–	–
6 tenements (6 families), ...	2	12	–	–
7 tenements (7 families), ...	3	21	–	–
8 tenements (8 families), ...	2	16	–	–
Chelsea. Ward 1, ...	1,089	1,655	130	1,785
1 tenement (1 family), ...	632	632	–	–
2 tenements (2 families), ...	367	734	–	–
3 tenements (3 families), ...	74	222	–	–
4 tenements (4 families), ...	13	52	–	–
5 tenements (5 families), ...	3	15	–	–
Chelsea. Ward 2, ...	1,138	1,712	123	1,835
1 tenement (1 family), ...	698	698	–	–
2 tenements (2 families), ...	341	682	–	–
3 tenements (3 families), ...	80	240	–	–
4 tenements (4 families), ...	12	48	–	–
5 tenements (5 families), ...	2	10	–	–
6 tenements (6 families), ...	2	12	–	–
7 tenements (7 families), ...	2	14	–	–
8 tenements (8 families), ...	1	8	–	–
Chelsea. Ward 3, ...	1,039	1,561	86	1,647
1 tenement (1 family), ...	600	600	–	–
2 tenements (2 families), ...	371	742	–	–
3 tenements (3 families), ...	58	174	–	–
4 tenements (4 families), ...	7	28	–	–
5 tenements (5 families), ...	2	10	–	–
7 tenements (7 families), ...	1	7	–	–
Chelsea. Ward 4, ...	846	1,241	94	1,335
1 tenement (1 family), ...	516	516	–	–
2 tenements (2 families), ...	283	566	–	–
3 tenements (3 families), ...	36	108	–	–

OCCUPIED AND UNOCCUPIED TENEMENTS IN OCCUPIED DWELLING HOUSES — Continued.

COUNTIES, CITIES, TOWNS, AND NUMBER OF TENEMENTS AND FAMILIES.	Number of Occupied Dwelling Houses	Number of Occupied Tenements in Occupied Dwelling Houses	Number of Unoccupied Tenements in Occupied Dwelling Houses	Total Number of Tenements in Occupied Dwelling Houses
SUFFOLK — Con.				
Chelsea. Ward 4 — Con.				
4 tenements (4 families), ...	7	28	–	–
5 tenements (5 families), ...	3	15	–	–
8 tenements (8 families), ...	1	8	–	–
Chelsea. Ward 5, ...	631	765	49	814
1 tenement (1 family), ...	507	507	–	–
2 tenements (2 families), ...	114	228	–	–
3 tenements (3 families), ...	10	30	–	–
Revere, ...	1,407	1,652	66	1,718
1 tenement (1 family), ...	1,183	1,183	–	–
2 tenements (2 families), ...	206	412	–	–
3 tenements (3 families), ...	16	48	–	–
4 tenements (4 families), ...	1	4	–	–
5 tenements (5 families), ...	1	5	–	–
Winthrop, ...	855	910	9	919
1 tenement (1 family), ...	805	805	–	–
2 tenements (2 families), ...	46	92	–	–
3 tenements (3 families), ...	3	9	–	–
4 tenements (4 families), ...	1	4	–	–
WORCESTER.				
Ashburnham, ...	446	530	36	566
1 tenement (1 family), ...	372	372	–	–
2 tenements (2 families), ...	67	134	–	–
3 tenements (3 families), ...	4	12	–	–
4 tenements (4 families), ...	3	12	–	–
Athol, ...	1,450	1,750	75	1,825
1 tenement (1 family), ...	1,206	1,206	–	–
2 tenements (2 families), ...	207	414	–	–
3 tenements (3 families), ...	28	84	–	–
4 tenements (4 families), ...	5	20	–	–
5 tenements (5 families), ...	1	5	–	–
6 tenements (6 families), ...	2	12	–	–
9 tenements (9 families), ...	1	9	–	–
Auburn, ...	277	345	17	362
1 tenement (1 family), ...	227	227	–	–
2 tenements (2 families), ...	42	84	–	–
3 tenements (3 families), ...	3	9	–	–
4 tenements (4 families), ...	3	12	–	–
6 tenements (6 families), ...	1	6	–	–
7 tenements (7 families), ...	1	7	–	–
Barre, ...	501	558	19	577
1 tenement (1 family), ...	449	449	–	–
2 tenements (2 families), ...	48	96	–	–
3 tenements (3 families), ...	3	9	–	–
4 tenements (4 families), ...	1	4	–	–
Berlin, ...	211	225	2	227
1 tenement (1 family), ...	198	198	–	–
2 tenements (2 families), ...	12	24	–	–
3 tenements (3 families), ...	1	3	–	–
Blackstone, ...	901	1,266	145	1,411
1 tenement (1 family), ...	635	635	–	–
2 tenements (2 families), ...	214	428	–	–
3 tenements (3 families), ...	24	72	–	–
4 tenements (4 families), ...	21	84	–	–
6 tenements (6 families), ...	4	24	–	–

OCCUPIED AND UNOCCUPIED TENEMENTS IN OCCUPIED DWELLING
HOUSES — Continued.

COUNTIES, CITIES, TOWNS, AND NUMBER OF TENEMENTS AND FAMILIES.	Number of Occupied Dwelling Houses	Number of Occupied Tenements in Occupied Dwelling Houses	Number of Unoccupied Tenements in Occupied Dwelling Houses	Total Number of Tenements in Occupied Dwelling Houses
WORCESTER — Con.				
Blackstone — Con.				
7 tenements (7 families), ...	1	7	-	-
8 tenements (8 families), ...	2	16	-	-
Bolton, ...	191	206	3	209
1 tenement (1 family), ...	177	177	-	-
2 tenements (2 families), ...	13	26	-	-
3 tenements (3 families), ...	1	3	-	-
Boylston, ...	147	177	5	182
1 tenement (1 family), ...	125	125	-	-
2 tenements (2 families), ...	19	38	-	-
3 tenements (3 families), ...	2	6	-	-
8 tenements (8 families), ...	1	8	-	-
Brookfield, ...	599	756	37	793
1 tenement (1 family), ...	466	466	-	-
2 tenements (2 families), ...	116	232	-	-
3 tenements (3 families), ...	11	33	-	-
4 tenements (4 families), ...	5	20	-	-
5 tenements (5 families), ...	1	5	-	-
Charlton, ...	420	470	7	477
1 tenement (1 family), ...	375	375	-	-
2 tenements (2 families), ...	41	82	-	-
3 tenements (3 families), ...	3	9	-	-
4 tenements (4 families), ...	1	4	-	-
Clinton, ...	1,694	2,278	114	2,392
1 tenement (1 family), ...	1,239	1,239	-	-
2 tenements (2 families), ...	376	752	-	-
3 tenements (3 families), ...	51	153	-	-
4 tenements (4 families), ...	13	52	-	-
5 tenements (5 families), ...	10	50	-	-
6 tenements (6 families), ...	3	18	-	-
7 tenements (7 families), ...	2	14	-	-
Dana, ...	175	196	4	200
1 tenement (1 family), ...	155	155	-	-
2 tenements (2 families), ...	19	38	-	-
3 tenements (3 families), ...	1	3	-	-
Douglas, ...	390	483	80	563
1 tenement (1 family), ...	319	319	-	-
2 tenements (2 families), ...	55	110	-	-
3 tenements (3 families), ...	10	30	-	-
4 tenements (4 families), ...	6	24	-	-
Dudley, ...	420	628	27	655
1 tenement (1 family), ...	301	301	-	-
2 tenements (2 families), ...	75	150	-	-
3 tenements (3 families), ...	18	54	-	-
4 tenements (4 families), ...	15	60	-	-
5 tenements (5 families), ...	6	30	-	-
6 tenements (6 families), ...	2	12	-	-
7 tenements (7 families), ...	3	21	-	-
FITCHBURG, ...	3,886	5,686	260	5,946
1 tenement (1 family), ...	2,569	2,569	-	-
2 tenements (2 families), ...	1,007	2,014	-	-
3 tenements (3 families), ...	217	651	-	-
4 tenements (4 families), ...	49	196	-	-
5 tenements (5 families), ...	23	115	-	-
6 tenements (6 families), ...	13	78	-	-
7 tenements (7 families), ...	3	21	-	-

OCCUPIED AND UNOCCUPIED TENEMENTS IN OCCUPIED DWELLING
HOUSES — Continued.

COUNTIES, CITIES, TOWNS, AND NUMBER OF TENEMENTS AND FAMILIES.	Number of Occupied Dwelling Houses	Number of Occupied Tenements in Occupied Dwelling Houses	Number of Unoccupied Tenements in Occupied Dwelling Houses	Total Number of Tenements in Occupied Dwelling Houses
WORCESTER — Con.				
FITCHBURG — Con.				
8 tenements (8 families), ...	3	24	–	–
9 tenements (9 families), ...	2	18	–	–
Fitchburg. Ward 1, ...	624	897	48	945
1 tenement (1 family), ...	405	405	–	–
2 tenements (2 families), ...	174	348	–	–
3 tenements (3 families), ...	39	117	–	–
4 tenements (4 families), ...	4	16	–	–
5 tenements (5 families), ...	1	5	–	–
6 tenements (6 families), ...	1	6	–	–
Fitchburg. Ward 2, ...	740	1,241	36	1,277
1 tenement (1 family), ...	443	443	–	–
2 tenements (2 families), ...	186	372	–	–
3 tenements (3 families), ...	63	189	–	–
4 tenements (4 families), ...	26	104	–	–
5 tenements (5 families), ...	10	50	–	–
6 tenements (6 families), ...	7	42	–	–
7 tenements (7 families), ...	1	7	–	–
8 tenements (8 families), ...	2	16	–	–
9 tenements (9 families), ...	2	18	–	–
Fitchburg. Ward 3, ...	649	911	33	944
1 tenement (1 family), ...	451	451	–	–
2 tenements (2 families), ...	153	306	–	–
3 tenements (3 families), ...	35	105	–	–
4 tenements (4 families), ...	4	16	–	–
5 tenements (5 families), ...	4	20	–	–
6 tenements (6 families), ...	1	6	–	–
7 tenements (7 families), ...	1	7	–	–
Fitchburg. Ward 4, ...	549	793	51	844
1 tenement (1 family), ...	370	370	–	–
2 tenements (2 families), ...	141	282	–	–
3 tenements (3 families), ...	27	81	–	–
4 tenements (4 families), ...	2	8	–	–
5 tenements (5 families), ...	5	25	–	–
6 tenements (6 families), ...	2	12	–	–
7 tenements (7 families), ...	1	7	–	–
8 tenements (8 families), ...	1	8	–	–
Fitchburg. Ward 5, ...	593	843	49	892
1 tenement (1 family), ...	385	385	–	–
2 tenements (2 families), ...	172	344	–	–
3 tenements (3 families), ...	31	93	–	–
4 tenements (4 families), ...	4	16	–	–
5 tenements (5 families), ...	1	5	–	–
Fitchburg. Ward 6, ...	731	1,001	43	1,044
1 tenement (1 family), ...	515	515	–	–
2 tenements (2 families), ...	181	362	–	–
3 tenements (3 families), ...	22	66	–	–
4 tenements (4 families), ...	9	36	–	–
5 tenements (5 families), ...	2	10	–	–
6 tenements (6 families), ...	2	12	–	–
Gardner, ...	1,573	2,062	133	2,195
1 tenement (1 family), ...	1,155	1,155	–	–
2 tenements (2 families), ...	357	714	–	–
3 tenements (3 families), ...	53	159	–	–
4 tenements (4 families), ...	6	24	–	–
5 tenements (5 families), ...	2	10	–	–

OCCUPIED AND UNOCCUPIED TENEMENTS IN OCCUPIED DWELLING
HOUSES — Continued.

COUNTIES, CITIES, TOWNS, AND NUMBER OF TENEMENTS AND FAMILIES.	Number of Occupied Dwelling Houses	Number of Occupied Tenements in Occupied Dwelling Houses	Number of Unoccupied Tenements in Occupied Dwelling Houses	Total Number of Tenements in Occupied Dwelling Houses
WORCESTER — Con.				
Grafton, ...	926	1,106	31	1,137
1 tenement (1 family), ...	771	771	–	–
2 tenements (2 families), ...	137	274	–	–
3 tenements (3 families), ...	11	33	–	–
4 tenements (4 families), ...	7	28	–	–
Hardwick, ...	460	533	11	544
1 tenement (1 family), ...	397	397	–	–
2 tenements (2 families), ...	55	110	–	–
3 tenements (3 families), ...	6	18	–	–
4 tenements (4 families), ...	2	8	–	–
Harvard, ...	262	279	1	280
1 tenement (1 family), ...	246	246	–	–
2 tenements (2 families), ...	15	30	–	–
3 tenements (3 families), ...	1	3	–	–
Holden, ...	415	555	19	574
1 tenement (1 family), ...	313	313	–	–
2 tenements (2 families), ...	76	152	–	–
3 tenements (3 families), ...	14	42	–	–
4 tenements (4 families), ...	8	32	–	–
6 tenements (6 families), ...	1	6	–	–
8 tenements (8 families), ...	1	8	–	–
Hopedale, ...	285	307	4	311
1 tenement (1 family), ...	265	265	–	–
2 tenements (2 families), ...	18	36	–	–
3 tenements (3 families), ...	2	6	–	–
Hubbardston, ...	311	348	6	354
1 tenement (1 family), ...	275	275	–	–
2 tenements (2 families), ...	35	70	–	–
3 tenements (3 families), ...	1	3	–	–
Lancaster, ...	395	452	30	482
1 tenement (1 family), ...	346	346	–	–
2 tenements (2 families), ...	44	88	–	–
3 tenements (3 families), ...	4	12	–	–
6 tenements (6 families), ...	1	6	–	–
Leicester, ...	594	731	14	745
1 tenement (1 family), ...	478	478	–	–
2 tenements (2 families), ...	99	198	–	–
3 tenements (3 families), ...	15	39	–	–
4 tenements (4 families), ...	4	16	–	–
Leominster, ...	1,046	2,181	34	2,215
1 tenement (1 family), ...	1,178	1,178	–	–
2 tenements (2 families), ...	426	852	–	–
3 tenements (3 families), ...	26	78	–	–
4 tenements (4 families), ...	8	32	–	–
5 tenements (5 families), ...	1	5	–	–
6 tenements (6 families), ...	1	6	–	–
7 tenements (7 families), ...	1	7	–	–
9 tenements (9 families), ...	1	9	–	–
14 tenements (14 families), ...	1	14	–	–
Lunenburg, ...	277	302	8	310
1 tenement (1 family), ...	256	256	–	–
2 tenements (2 families), ...	18	36	–	–
3 tenements (3 families), ...	2	6	–	–
4 tenements (4 families), ...	1	4	–	–
Mendon, ...	221	234	4	238
1 tenement (1 family), ...	209	209	–	–

OCCUPIED AND UNOCCUPIED TENEMENTS IN OCCUPIED DWELLING
HOUSES — Continued.

COUNTIES, CITIES, TOWNS, AND NUMBER OF TENEMENTS AND FAMILIES.	Number of Occupied Dwelling Houses	Number of Occupied Tenements in Occupied Dwelling Houses	Number of Unoccupied Tenements in Occupied Dwelling Houses	Total Number of Tenements in Occupied Dwelling Houses
WORCESTER — Con.				
Mendon — Con.				
2 tenements (2 families), ...	11	22	-	-
3 tenements (3 families), ...	1	3	-	-
Milford, ...	1,671	2,116	183	2,299
1 tenement (1 family), ...	1,310	1,310	-	-
2 tenements (2 families), ...	310	620	-	-
3 tenements (3 families), ...	26	78	-	-
4 tenements (4 families), ...	19	76	-	-
5 tenements (5 families), ...	4	20	-	-
6 tenements (6 families), ...	2	12	-	-
Millbury, ...	793	1,100	54	1,154
1 tenement (1 family), ...	560	560	-	-
2 tenements (2 families), ...	183	366	-	-
3 tenements (3 families), ...	31	93	-	-
4 tenements (4 families), ...	15	60	-	-
5 tenements (5 families), ...	3	15	-	-
6 tenements (6 families), ...	1	6	-	-
New Braintree, ...	114	114	5	119
1 tenement (1 family), ...	114	114	-	-
Northborough, ...	347	451	24	475
1 tenement (1 family), ...	260	260	-	-
2 tenements (2 families), ...	78	156	-	-
3 tenements (3 families), ...	4	12	-	-
4 tenements (4 families), ...	3	12	-	-
5 tenements (5 families), ...	1	5	-	-
6 tenements (6 families), ...	1	6	-	-
Northbridge, ...	836	1,070	12	1,082
1 tenement (1 family), ...	661	661	-	-
2 tenements (2 families), ...	139	278	-	-
3 tenements (3 families), ...	16	48	-	-
4 tenements (4 families), ...	17	68	-	-
5 tenements (5 families), ...	3	15	-	-
North Brookfield, ...	679	1,030	24	1,054
1 tenement (1 family), ...	411	411	-	-
2 tenements (2 families), ...	206	412	-	-
3 tenements (3 families), ...	45	135	-	-
4 tenements (4 families), ...	14	56	-	-
5 tenements (5 families), ...	2	10	-	-
6 tenements (6 families), ...	1	6	-	-
Oakham, ...	149	161	4	165
1 tenement (1 family), ...	138	138	-	-
2 tenements (2 families), ...	10	20	-	-
3 tenements (3 families), ...	1	3	-	-
Oxford, ...	562	618	18	636
1 tenement (1 family), ...	516	516	-	-
2 tenements (2 families), ...	38	76	-	-
3 tenements (3 families), ...	6	18	-	-
4 tenements (4 families), ...	2	8	-	-
Paxton, ...	109	114	3	117
1 tenement (1 family), ...	104	104	-	-
2 tenements (2 families), ...	5	10	-	-
Petersham, ...	232	254	5	259
1 tenement (1 family), ...	213	213	-	-
2 tenements (2 families), ...	16	32	-	-
3 tenements (3 families), ...	3	9	-	-

OCCUPIED AND UNOCCUPIED TENEMENTS IN OCCUPIED DWELLING HOUSES — Continued.

COUNTIES, CITIES, TOWNS, AND NUMBER OF TENEMENTS AND FAMILIES.	Number of Occupied Dwelling Houses	Number of Occupied Tenements in Occupied Dwelling Houses	Number of Unoccupied Tenements in Occupied Dwelling Houses	Total Number of Tenements in Occupied Dwelling Houses
WORCESTER — Con.				
Phillipston, ...	112	114	2	116
1 tenement (1 family), ...	110	110	-	-
2 tenements (2 families), ...	2	4	-	-
Princeton, ...	228	236	10	246
1 tenement (1 family), ...	221	221	-	-
2 tenements (2 families), ...	6	12	-	-
3 tenements (3 families), ...	1	3	-	-
Royalston, ...	233	254	6	260
1 tenement 1 family , ...	212	212	-	-
2 tenements (2 families), ...	21	42	-	-
Rutland, ...	213	225	5	230
1 tenement (1 family), ...	204	204	-	-
2 tenements 2 families, ...	7	14	-	-
3 tenements (3 families), ...	1	3	-	-
4 tenements 4 families, ...	1	4	-	-
Shrewsbury, ...	354	381	4	385
1 tenement 1 family, ...	327	327	-	-
2 tenements 2 families, ...	27	54	-	-
Southborough, ...	390	442	11	453
1 tenement (1 family), ...	344	344	-	-
2 tenements 2 families, ...	42	84	-	-
3 tenements (3 families), ...	3	9	-	-
5 tenements (5 families), ...	1	5	-	-
Southbridge, ...	1,379	1,688	47	1,735
1 tenement 1 family, ...	1,158	1,158	-	-
2 tenements (2 families), ...	172	344	-	-
3 tenements 3 families, ...	25	75	-	-
4 tenements (4 families), ...	16	64	-	-
5 tenements (5 families), ...	1	5	-	-
6 tenements (6 families), ...	7	42	-	-
Spencer, ...	1,157	1,625	170	1,795
1 tenement 1 family, ...	768	768	-	-
2 tenements (2 families), ...	322	644	-	-
3 tenements (3 families), ...	58	174	-	-
4 tenements 4 families, ...	6	24	-	-
5 tenements 5 families, ...	3	15	-	-
Sterling, ...	319	342	21	363
1 tenement 1 family, ...	296	296	-	-
2 tenements (2 families), ...	23	46	-	-
Sturbridge, ...	337	434	40	474
1 tenement (1 family), ...	262	262	-	-
2 tenements (2 families), ...	60	120	-	-
3 tenements (3 families), ...	10	30	-	-
4 tenements (4 families), ...	4	16	-	-
6 tenements (6 families), ...	1	6	-	-
Sutton, ...	529	714	25	739
1 tenement 1 family, ...	382	382	-	-
2 tenements (2 families), ...	124	248	-	-
3 tenements (3 families), ...	10	30	-	-
4 tenements (4 families), ...	11	44	-	-
5 tenements (5 families), ...	2	10	-	-
Templeton, ...	628	718	27	745
1 tenement (1 family), ...	542	542	-	-
2 tenements (2 families), ...	82	164	-	-
3 tenements (3 families), ...	4	12	-	-

OCCUPIED AND UNOCCUPIED TENEMENTS IN OCCUPIED DWELLING HOUSES — Continued.

COUNTIES, CITIES, TOWNS, AND NUMBER OF TENEMENTS AND FAMILIES.	Number of Occupied Dwelling Houses	Number of Occupied Tenements in Occupied Dwelling Houses	Number of Unoccupied Tenements in Occupied Dwelling Houses	Total Number of Tenements in Occupied Dwelling Houses
WORCESTER — Con.				
Upton, ...	418	524	9	533
1 tenement (1 family),	330	330	-	-
2 tenements (2 families), ...	73	146	-	-
3 tenements (3 families), ...	12	36	-	-
4 tenements (4 families), ...	3	12	-	-
Uxbridge, ...	641	812	38	850
1 tenement (1 family), ...	510	510	-	-
2 tenements (2 families), ...	103	206	-	-
3 tenements (3 families), ...	16	48	-	-
4 tenements (4 families), ...	12	48	-	-
Warren, ...	783	980	73	1,053
1 tenement (1 family), ...	630	630	-	-
2 tenements (2 families), ...	122	244	-	-
3 tenements (3 families), ...	23	69	-	-
4 tenements (4 families), ...	5	20	-	-
5 tenements (5 families), ...	2	10	-	-
7 tenements (7 families), ...	1	7	-	-
Webster, ...	935	1,716	121	1,837
1 tenement (1 family), ...	452	452	-	-
2 tenements (2 families), ...	303	606	-	-
3 tenements (3 families), ...	107	321	-	-
4 tenements (4 families), ...	39	156	-	-
5 tenements (5 families), ...	24	120	-	-
6 tenements (6 families), ...	9	54	-	-
7 tenements (7 families), ...	1	7	-	-
Westborough, ...	829	1,031	86	1,117
1 tenement (1 family), ...	640	640	-	-
2 tenements (2 families), ...	179	358	-	-
3 tenements (3 families), ...	7	21	-	-
4 tenements (4 families), ...	3	12	-	-
West Boylston, ...	562	648	12	660
1 tenement (1 family), ...	499	499	-	-
2 tenements (2 families), ...	49	98	-	-
3 tenements (3 families), ...	9	27	-	-
4 tenements (4 families), ...	2	8	-	-
5 tenements (5 families), ...	2	10	-	-
6 tenements (6 families), ...	1	6	-	-
West Brookfield, ...	353	409	15	424
1 tenement (1 family), ...	298	298	-	-
2 tenements (2 families), ...	54	108	-	-
3 tenements (3 families), ...	1	3	-	-
Westminster, ...	334	370	18	388
1 tenement (1 family), ...	302	302	-	-
2 tenements (2 families), ...	29	58	-	-
3 tenements (3 families), ...	2	6	-	-
4 tenements (4 families), ...	1	4	-	-
Winchendon, ...	890	1,078	40	1,118
1 tenement (1 family), ...	719	719	-	-
2 tenements (2 families), ...	162	324	-	-
3 tenements (3 families), ...	6	18	-	-
4 tenements (4 families), ...	1	4	-	-
6 tenements (6 families), ...	1	6	-	-
7 tenements (7 families), ...	1	7	-	-
WORCESTER, ...	11,153	20,961	1,730	22,591
1 tenement (1 family), ...	5,207	5,207	-	-
2 tenements (2 families), ...	3,344	6,688	-	-

OCCUPIED AND UNOCCUPIED TENEMENTS IN OCCUPIED DWELLING HOUSES — Continued.

Counties, Cities, Towns, and Number of Tenements and Families.	Number of Occupied Dwelling Houses	Number of Occupied Tenements in Occupied Dwelling Houses	Number of Unoccupied Tenements in Occupied Dwelling Houses	Total Number of Tenements in Occupied Dwelling Houses
WORCESTER — Con.				
WORCESTER — Con.				
3 tenements (3 families), ...	1,986	5,958	–	–
4 tenements (4 families), ...	359	1,436	–	–
5 tenements (5 families), ...	102	510	–	–
6 tenements (6 families), ...	86	516	–	–
7 tenements (7 families), ...	37	259	–	–
8 tenements (8 families), ...	20	160	–	–
9 tenements (9 families), ...	4	36	–	–
10 tenements (10 families), . . .	5	50	–	–
11 tenements (11 families), . . .	2	22	–	–
19 tenements (19 families), . . .	1	19	–	–
Worcester. Ward 1, ...	1,358	2,417	205	2,622
1 tenement (1 family), . . .	700	700	–	–
2 tenements (2 families), . . .	403	806	–	–
3 tenements (3 families), . . .	186	558	–	–
4 tenements (4 families), . . .	35	140	–	–
5 tenements (5 families), . . .	11	55	–	–
6 tenements (6 families), . . .	12	72	–	–
7 tenements (7 families), . . .	6	42	–	–
8 tenements (8 families), . . .	2	16	–	–
9 tenements (9 families), . . .	2	18	–	–
10 tenements (10 families), . . .	1	10	–	–
Worcester. Ward 2, ...	1,464	2,653	176	2,829
1 tenement (1 family), . . .	722	722	–	–
2 tenements (2 families), . . .	416	832	–	–
3 tenements (3 families), . . .	259	777	–	–
4 tenements (4 families), . . .	44	176	–	–
5 tenements (5 families), . . .	7	35	–	–
6 tenements (6 families), . . .	7	42	–	–
7 tenements (7 families), . . .	5	35	–	–
8 tenements (8 families), . . .	3	24	–	–
10 tenements (10 families), . . .	1	10	–	–
Worcester. Ward 3, ...	1,464	2,825	312	3,137
1 tenement (1 family), . . .	684	684	–	–
2 tenements (2 families), . . .	431	862	–	–
3 tenements (3 families), . . .	228	684	–	–
4 tenements (4 families), . . .	66	264	–	–
5 tenements (5 families), . . .	25	125	–	–
6 tenements (6 families), . . .	16	96	–	–
7 tenements (7 families), . . .	7	49	–	–
8 tenements (8 families), . . .	5	40	–	–
10 tenements (10 families), . . .	1	10	–	–
11 tenements (11 families), . . .	1	11	–	–
Worcester. Ward 4, ...	1,244	2,742	213	2,955
1 tenement (1 family), . . .	346	346	–	–
2 tenements (2 families), . . .	420	840	–	–
3 tenements (3 families), . . .	395	1,185	–	–
4 tenements (4 families), . . .	55	220	–	–
5 tenements (5 families), . . .	17	85	–	–
6 tenements (6 families), . . .	11	66	–	–
Worcester. Ward 5, ...	1,532	3,028	300	3,328
1 tenement (1 family), . . .	629	629	–	–
2 tenements (2 families), . . .	465	930	–	–
3 tenements (3 families), . . .	342	1,026	–	–
4 tenements (4 families), . . .	58	232	–	–
5 tenements (5 families), . . .	20	100	–	–

OCCUPIED AND UNOCCUPIED TENEMENTS IN OCCUPIED DWELLING HOUSES — Continued.

COUNTIES, CITIES, TOWNS, AND NUMBER OF TENEMENTS AND FAMILIES.	Number of Occupied Dwelling Houses	Number of Occupied Tenements in Occupied Dwelling Houses	Number of Unoccupied Tenements in Occupied Dwelling Houses	Total Number of Tenements in Occupied Dwelling Houses
WORCESTER — Con.				
Worcester. Ward 5 — Con.				
6 tenements (6 families), ...	15	90	–	–
7 tenements (7 families), .	3	21	–	–
Worcester. Ward 6, ...	1,514	2,591	171	2,762
1 tenement (1 family), ...	806	806	–	–
2 tenements (2 families), ...	456	912	–	–
3 tenements (3 families), ...	199	597	–	–
4 tenements (4 families , ...	29	116	–	–
5 tenements (5 families), ...	4	20	–	–
6 tenements (6 families), ...	9	54	–	–
7 tenements (7 families), ...	5	35	–	–
8 tenements (8 families), ...	4	32	–	–
9 tenements (9 families), ...	1	9	–	–
10 tenements (10 families), ...	1	10	–	–
Worcester. Ward 7, ...	1,325	2,452	212	2,664
1 tenement (1 family), ...	664	664	–	–
2 tenements (2 families), ...	386	772	–	–
3 tenements (3 families), ...	196	588	–	–
4 tenements (4 families), ...	38	152	–	–
5 tenements (5 families), ...	14	70	–	–
6 tenements (6 families), ...	9	54	–	–
7 tenements (7 families), ...	9	63	–	–
8 tenements (8 families), ...	5	40	–	–
9 tenements (9 families), ...	1	9	–	–
10 tenements (10 families , ...	1	10	–	–
11 tenements (11 families), ...	1	11	–	–
19 tenements (19 families), ...	1	19	–	–
Worcester. Ward 8, ...	1,252	2,153	141	2,294
1 tenement (1 family), ...	656	656	–	–
2 tenements (2 families), ...	367	734	–	–
3 tenements (3 families), ...	181	543	–	–
4 tenements (4 families), ...	34	136	–	–
5 tenements (5 families), ...	4	20	–	–
6 tenements (6 families), ...	7	42	–	–
7 tenements (7 families), ...	2	14	–	–
8 tenements (8 families), ...	1	8	–	–

OCCUPIED AND UNOCCUPIED TENEMENTS IN OCCUPIED DWELLING HOUSES — Concluded.

RECAPITULATION.

THE STATE, AND NUMBER OF TENEMENTS AND FAMILIES.	Number of Occupied Dwelling Houses	Number of Occupied Tenements in Occupied Dwelling Houses	Number of Unoccupied Tenements in Occupied Dwelling Houses	Total Number of Tenements in Occupied Dwelling Houses
THE STATE.	397,635	547,385	26,573	573,958
1 tenement (1 family),	294,700	294,700	-	-
2 tenements (2 families),	75,237	150,474	-	-
3 tenements (3 families),	18,469	55,407	-	-
4 tenements (4 families),	5,188	20,752	-	-
5 tenements (5 families),	1,607	8,035	-	-
6 tenements (6 families),	1,257	7,542	-	-
7 tenements (7 families),	413	2,891	-	-
8 tenements (8 families),	401	3,208	-	-
9 tenements (9 families),	109	981	-	-
10 tenements (10 families),	66	660	-	-
11 tenements (11 families),	49	539	-	-
12 tenements (12 families),	39	468	-	-
13 tenements (13 families),	21	273	-	-
14 tenements (14 families),	20	280	-	-
15 tenements (15 families),	17	255	-	-
16 tenements (16 families),	6	96	-	-
17 tenements (17 families),	10	170	-	-
18 tenements (18 families),	2	36	-	-
19 tenements (19 families),	5	95	-	-
20 tenements (20 families),	3	60	-	-
21 tenements (21 families),	1	21	-	-
22 tenements (22 families),	2	44	-	-
23 tenements (23 families),	1	23	-	-
24 tenements (24 families),	2	48	-	-
25 tenements (25 families),	1	25	-	-
28 tenements (28 families),	3	84	-	-
30 tenements (30 families),	1	30	-	-
31 tenements (31 families),	1	31	-	-
32 tenements (32 families),	1	32	-	-
36 tenements (36 families),	1	36	-	-
38 tenements (38 families),	1	38	-	-
39 tenements (39 families),	1	39	-	-
42 tenements (42 families),	1	42	-	-

DWELLING HOUSES:

NUMBER OF STORIES AND MATERIALS.

DWELLING HOUSES: NUMBER OF STORIES AND MATERIALS.

COUNTIES, CITIES, TOWNS, NUMBER OF STORIES TO DWELLING HOUSES, AND MATERIALS OF WHICH CONSTRUCTED.	Number of Occupied Dwelling Houses	Number of Unoccupied Dwelling Houses	Total Number of Dwelling Houses	COUNTIES, CITIES, TOWNS, NUMBER OF STORIES TO DWELLING HOUSES, AND MATERIALS OF WHICH CONSTRUCTED.	Number of Occupied Dwelling Houses	Number of Unoccupied Dwelling Houses	Total Number of Dwelling Houses
BARNSTABLE.				**BARNSTABLE —Con.**			
Barnstable,	1,133	178	1,311	**Chatham,**	489	141	630
Number of Stories.	1,133	178	1,311	*Number of Stories.*	489	141	630
1 story,	244	28	272	1 story,	6	17	23
1 story and attic,	567	67	634	1 story and attic,	398	92	490
Basement, 1 story, and attic,	2	–	2	Basement, 1 story, and attic,	10	2	12
2 stories,	247	52	299	2 stories,	20	10	30
2 stories and attic,	62	27	89	2 stories and attic,	50	18	68
Basement and 2 stories,	4	–	4	Basement and 2 stories,	2	–	2
Basement, 2 stories, and attic,	2	–	2	Basement, 2 stories, and attic,	3	2	5
3 stories,	3	1	4	*Materials.*	489	141	630
3 stories and attic,	2	3	5	Wood,	482	141	623
Materials.	1,133	178	1,311	Wood and brick,	7	–	7
Wood,	1,132	178	1,310	**Dennis,**	784	105	889
Brick and stone,	1	–	1	*Number of Stories.*	784	105	889
Bourne.	402	205	607	1 story and attic,	676	84	760
Number of Stories.	402	205	607	Basement, 1 story, and attic,	3	–	3
1 story,	7	–	7	2 stories,	1	–	1
1 story and attic,	318	130	448	2 stories and attic,	102	20	122
Basement, 1 story, and attic,	1	2	3	Basement, 2 stories, and attic,	1	–	1
2 stories,	9	14	23	3 stories,	1	–	1
2 stories and attic,	64	55	119	3 stories and attic,	–	1	1
Basement, 2 stories, and attic,	2	–	2	*Materials.*	784	105	889
3 stories,	–	3	3	Wood,	783	105	888
4 stories,	–	1	1	Wood and stone,	1	–	1
Not given,	1	–	1	**Eastham,**	130	27	157
Materials.	402	205	607	*Number of Stories.*	130	27	157
Wood,	401	203	604	1 story,	3	–	3
Wood and stone,	–	2	2	1 story and attic,	103	21	124
Not given,	1	–	1	Basement, 1 story, and attic,	1	–	1
Brewster.	242	54	296	2 stories,	10	1	11
Number of Stories.	242	54	296	2 stories and attic,	13	5	18
1 story,	42	11	53	*Materials.*	130	27	157
1 story and attic,	146	27	173	Wood,	130	27	157
Basement, 1 story, and attic,	1	–	1	**Falmouth.**	656	279	935
2 stories,	49	13	62	*Number of Stories.*	656	279	935
2 stories and attic,	3	1	4	1 story,	7	3	10
Basement and 2 stories,	–	1	1	1 story and attic,	385	123	508
3 stories,	1	1	2	Basement, 1 story, and attic,	2	1	3
Materials.	242	54	296	2 stories,	103	88	191
Wood,	241	52	293	2 stories and attic,	145	55	200
Wood and brick,	–	1	1	Basement and 2 stories,	4	2	6
Wood and stone,	1	1	2	Basement, 2 stories, and attic,	3	1	4
				3 stories,	7	5	12
				Basement and 3 stories,	–	1	1

DWELLING HOUSES: NUMBER OF STORIES AND MATERIALS — Continued.

Counties, Cities, Towns, Number of Stories to Dwelling Houses, and Materials of which Constructed.	Number of Occupied Dwelling Houses	Number of Unoccupied Dwelling Houses	Total Number of Dwelling Houses
BARNSTABLE — Con.			
Falmouth — Con.			
Materials.	656	279	935
Wood,	652	275	927
Brick,	1	–	1
Stone,	1	–	1
Wood and stone,	2	4	6
Harwich,	752	101	853
Number of Stories.	752	101	853
1 story,	2	–	2
1 story and attic,	657	90	747
Basement, 1 story, and attic,	6	1	7
2 stories,	7	1	8
2 stories and attic,	77	9	86
Basement, 2 stories, and attic,	3	–	3
Materials.	752	101	853
Wood,	752	101	853
Mashpee,	74	10	84
Number of Stories.	74	10	84
1 story and attic,	68	10	78
2 stories and attic,	6	–	6
Materials.	74	10	84
Wood,	74	10	84
Orleans,	356	89	445
Number of Stories.	356	89	445
1 story,	1	1	2
1 story and attic,	272	76	348
Basement, 1 story, and attic,	2	–	2
2 stories,	32	4	36
2 stories and attic,	44	8	52
Basement, 2 stories, and attic,	3	–	3
3 stories,	1	–	1
Basement and 3 stories,	1	–	1
Materials.	356	89	445
Wood,	355	89	444
Stone and cement,	1	–	1
Provincetown.	987	48	1,035
Number of Stories.	987	48	1,035
1 story,	130	15	145
1 story and attic,	490	20	510
Basement and 1 story,	6	–	6
Basement, 1 story, and attic,	24	2	26
2 stories,	218	7	225
2 stories and attic,	85	4	89
Basement and 2 stories,	14	–	14
Basement, 2 stories, and attic,	15	–	15
3 stories,	3	–	3
3 stories and attic,	1	–	1
Basement and 3 stories,	1	–	1
Materials.	987	48	1,035
Wood,	980	48	1,028
Wood and brick,	7	–	7
BARNSTABLE — Con.			
Sandwich,	422	69	491
Number of Stories.	422	69	491
1 story,	97	14	111
1 story and attic,	192	29	221
2 stories,	119	24	143
2 stories and attic,	14	2	16
Materials.	422	69	491
Wood,	421	69	490
Brick,	1	–	1
Truro.	215	58	273
Number of Stories.	215	58	273
1 story,	3	4	7
1 story and attic,	194	48	242
Basement, 1 story, and attic,	3	–	3
2 stories,	6	4	10
2 stories and attic,	6	2	8
Basement and 2 stories,	2	–	2
Basement, 2 stories, and attic,	1	–	1
Materials.	215	58	273
Wood,	215	58	273
Wellfleet.	314	149	463
Number of Stories.	314	149	463
1 story and attic,	227	122	349
Basement, 1 story, and attic,	4	8	12
2 stories,	20	5	25
2 stories and attic,	61	12	73
Basement and 2 stories,	–	1	1
Basement, 2 stories, and attic,	1	–	1
Basement and 3 stories,	–	1	1
Not given,	1	–	1
Materials.	314	149	463
Wood,	314	146	460
Wood and brick,	–	3	3
Yarmouth.	520	107	627
Number of Stories.	520	107	627
1 story,	41	6	47
1 story and attic,	391	75	466
Basement, 1 story, and attic,	1	–	1
2 stories,	30	13	43
2 stories and attic,	56	13	69
3 stories,	1	–	1
Materials.	520	107	627
Wood,	520	107	627
BERKSHIRE.			
Adams.	1,343	80	1,423
Number of Stories.	1,343	80	1,423
1 story,	15	1	16
1 story and attic,	249	35	284
Basement and 1 story,	10	–	10

DWELLING HOUSES: NUMBER OF STORIES AND MATERIALS — Continued.

COUNTIES, CITIES, TOWNS, NUMBER OF STORIES TO DWELLING HOUSES, AND MATERIALS OF WHICH CONSTRUCTED.	Number of Occupied Dwelling Houses	Number of Unoccupied Dwelling Houses	Total Number of Dwelling Houses
BERKSHIRE — Con.			
Adams — Con.			
Number of Stories — Con.			
Basement, 1 story, and attic, .	8	–	8
2 stories, ...	713	33	746
2 stories and attic, . . .	274	8	282
Basement and 2 stories, .	23	2	25
Basement, 2 stories, and attic,	17	1	18
3 stories, ...	20	–	20
3 stories and attic, . . .	11	–	11
Basement and 3 stories, .	3	–	3
Materials.	1,343	80	1,423
Wood, ...	1,206	79	1,285
Brick, ...	124	1	125
Stone, ...	1	–	1
Wood and brick, . .	12	–	12
Alford.	74	10	84
Number of Stories.	74	10	84
1 story, ...	3	–	3
1 story and attic, . .	51	6	57
Basement and 1 story, .	1	–	1
Basement, 1 story, and attic,.	2	–	2
2 stories, ...	16	4	20
Basement and 2 stories, .	1	–	1
Materials.	74	10	84
Wood, ...	74	10	84
Becket.	201	27	228
Number of Stories.	201	27	228
1 story, ...	5	–	5
1 story and attic, .	116	14	130
Basement, 1 story, and attic,.	6	3	9
2 stories, ...	67	8	75
2 stories and attic, . .	4	–	4
Basement and 2 stories,	3	2	5
Materials.	201	27	228
Wood, ...	200	27	227
Wood and stone, . .	1	–	1
Cheshire.	278	47	325
Number of Stories.	278	47	325
1 story, ...	11	1	12
1 story and attic, . .	153	39	192
Basement, 1 story, and attic,	4	–	4
2 stories, ...	79	6	85
2 stories and attic, . .	25	–	25
Basement and 2 stories, .	3	–	3
Basement, 2 stories, and attic,	1	1	2
3 stories, ...	1	–	1
Basement and 3 stories, .	1	–	1
Materials.	278	47	325
Wood, ...	278	47	325
BERKSHIRE — Con.			
Clarksburg.	186	5	191
Number of Stories.	186	5	191
1 story, ...	18	1	19
1 story and attic, . .	111	2	113
Basement and 1 story, .	1	–	1
Basement, 1 story, and attic,	11	–	11
2 stories, ...	35	2	37
2 stories and attic, . .	8	–	8
Basement and 2 stories, .	1	–	1
Basement and 3 stories, .	1	–	1
Materials.	186	5	191
Wood, ...	186	5	191
Dalton.	601	22	623
Number of Stories.	601	22	623
1 story, ...	9	–	9
1 story and attic, . .	148	8	156
Basement and 1 story, .	2	–	2
Basement, 1 story, and attic,.	1	–	1
2 stories, ...	400	14	414
2 stories and attic, . .	27	–	27
Basement and 2 stories, .	11	–	11
3 stories, ...	1	–	1
3 stories and attic, . .	1	–	1
Not given, ...	1	–	1
Materials.	601	22	623
Wood, ...	590	22	612
Brick, ...	7	–	7
Wood and brick, . .	2	–	2
Wood, brick, and stone, .	1	–	1
Not given, ...	1	–	1
Egremont.	199	12	211
Number of Stories.	199	12	211
1 story, ...	1	–	1
1 story and attic, . .	16	2	18
Basement, 1 story, and attic,	3	–	3
2 stories, ...	112	5	117
2 stories and attic, . .	56	2	58
Basement and 2 stories, .	9	–	9
Basement, 2 stories, and attic,	1	–	1
3 stories, ...	–	3	3
4 stories, ...	1	–	1
Materials.	199	12	211
Wood, ...	197	12	209
Brick, ...	1	–	1
Wood and brick, . .	1	–	1
Florida.	91	17	108
Number of Stories.	91	17	108
1 story, ...	6	2	8
1 story and attic, . .	64	11	75
Basement and 1 story, .	–	1	1

DWELLING HOUSES: NUMBER OF STORIES AND MATERIALS — Continued.

COUNTIES, CITIES, TOWNS, NUMBER OF STORIES TO DWELLING HOUSES, AND MATERIALS OF WHICH CONSTRUCTED.	Number of Occupied Dwelling Houses	Number of Unoccupied Dwelling Houses	Total Number of Dwelling Houses
BERKSHIRE — Con.			
Florida — Con.			
Number of Stories — Con.			
2 stories and attic, . . .	20	3	23
3 stories, ...	1	–	1
Materials.	21	17	108
Wood, ...	21	17	108
Great Barrington. . .	1,006	69	1,075
Number of Stories.	1,006	69	1,075
1 story, ...	29	2	31
1 story and attic, . . .	46	5	51
Basement and 1 story, . .	8	–	8
Basement, 1 story, and attic,	3	–	3
2 stories, ...	543	38	581
2 stories and attic, . . .	301	17	318
Basement and 2 stories, .	49	3	52
Basement, 2 stories, and attic,	12	1	13
3 stories, ...	10	2	12
3 stories and attic, . . .	2	–	2
Basement and 3 stories, .	2	–	2
Basement, 3 stories, and attic,	1	1	2
Materials.	1,006	69	1,075
Wood, ...	977	63	1,040
Brick, ...	17	1	18
Stone, ...	4	3	7
Wood and brick, . . .	6	1	7
Wood and stone, . . .	2	1	3
Hancock.	105	12	117
Number of Stories.	105	12	117
1 story, ...	1	–	1
1 story and attic, . . .	22	5	27
2 stories, ...	26	2	28
2 stories and attic, . . .	54	5	59
3 stories, ...	1	–	1
Basement, 3 stories, and attic,	1	–	1
Materials.	105	12	117
Wood, ...	104	11	115
Brick, . .	1	1	2
Hinsdale, ...	314	26	340
Number of Stories.	314	26	340
1 story, ...	28	–	28
1 story and attic, . . .	143	26	169
Basement and 1 story, . .	3	–	3
Basement, 1 story, and attic,	5	–	5
2 stories, ...	24	–	24
2 stories and attic, . . .	101	–	101
Basement and 2 stories, .	1	–	1
Basement, 2 stories, and attic,	3	–	3
3 stories, ...	1	–	1
3 stories and attic, . . .	1	–	1
Basement and 3 stories, .	1	–	1
Basement, 3 stories, and attic,	3	–	3

COUNTIES, CITIES, TOWNS, NUMBER OF STORIES TO DWELLING HOUSES, AND MATERIALS OF WHICH CONSTRUCTED.	Number of Occupied Dwelling Houses	Number of Unoccupied Dwelling Houses	Total Number of Dwelling Houses
BERKSHIRE — Con.			
Hinsdale — Con.			
Materials.	314	26	340
Wood, . .	306	26	332
Brick, ...	5	–	5
Stone, ...	3	–	3
Lanesborough, . . .	201	25	226
Number of Stories.	201	25	226
1 story, . .	60	8	68
1 story and attic, . . .	3	13	16
Basement and 1 story, . .	2	–	2
2 stories, ...	94	–	94
2 stories and attic, . . .	38	4	42
Basement and 2 stories, .	2	–	2
3 stories, ...	1	–	1
Basement and 3 stories, .	1	–	1
Materials.	201	25	226
Wood, . .	197	25	222
Wood and brick, . . .	3	–	3
Wood and stone, . . .	1	–	1
Lee.	797	42	839
Number of Stories.	797	42	839
1 story, . .	6	1	7
1 story and attic, . . .	199	13	212
Basement, 1 story, and attic, .	5	–	5
2 stories, ...	298	10	308
2 stories and attic, . . .	236	15	251
Basement and 2 stories, .	26	–	26
Basement, 2 stories, and attic,	12	3	15
3 stories, ...	10	–	10
3 stories and attic, . . .	3	–	3
Basement and 3 stories, .	1	–	1
Basement, 3 stories, and attic,	1	–	1
Materials.	797	42	839
Wood, . .	776	40	816
Brick, . .	14	–	14
Stone, . .	1	–	1
Wood and brick, . . .	6	1	7
Wood and stone, . . .	–	1	1
Lenox, ...	519	81	600
Number of Stories.	519	81	600
1 story, . .	18	4	22
1 story and attic, . . .	152	12	164
Basement and 1 story, . .	1	1	2
Basement, 1 story, and attic,	4	–	4
2 stories, ...	12	2	14
2 stories and attic, . . .	320	52	372
Basement and 2 stories, .	1	1	2
Basement, 2 stories, and attic,	5	6	11
3 stories, ...	4	1	5
3 stories and attic, . . .	1	2	3
4 stories, ...	1	–	1

DWELLING HOUSES: NUMBER OF STORIES AND MATERIALS — Continued.

COUNTIES, CITIES, TOWNS, NUMBER OF STORIES TO DWELLING HOUSES, AND MATERIALS OF WHICH CONSTRUCTED.	Number of Occupied Dwelling Houses	Number of Unoccupied Dwelling Houses	Total Number of Dwelling Houses
BERKSHIRE — Con.			
Lenox — Con.			
Materials.	519	81	600
Wood,	500	72	572
Brick,	9	4	13
Stone,	1	3	4
Wood and brick,	7	2	9
Wood and stone,	2	–	2
Monterey.	110	19	129
Number of Stories.	110	19	129
1 story,	15	1	16
1 story and attic,	36	9	45
2 stories,	7	2	9
2 stories and attic,	52	7	59
Materials.	110	19	129
Wood,	109	17	126
Stone,	–	1	1
Wood and brick,	1	–	1
Wood and stone,	–	1	1
Mount Washington.	31	9	40
Number of Stories.	31	9	40
1 story,	5	1	6
1 story and attic,	14	7	21
2 stories,	4	1	5
2 stories and attic,	3	–	3
Basement and 2 stories,	1	–	1
3 stories,	3	–	3
4 stories,	1	–	1
Materials.	31	9	40
Wood,	31	9	40
New Ashford.	29	7	36
Number of Stories.	29	7	36
1 story and attic,	17	7	24
2 stories and attic,	12	–	12
Materials.	29	7	36
Wood,	29	7	36
New Marlborough.	316	24	340
Number of Stories.	316	24	340
1 story,	3	–	3
1 story and attic,	48	5	53
Basement and 1 story,	1	–	1
Basement, 1 story, and attic,	1	–	1
2 stories,	257	19	276
2 stories and attic,	1	–	1
Basement and 2 stories,	4	–	4
Basement and 3 stories,	1	–	1
Materials.	316	24	340
Wood,	309	23	332
Brick,	5	1	6
Wood and brick,	2	–	2
BERKSHIRE — Con.			
NORTH ADAMS.	2,986	114	3,100
Number of Stories.	2,986	114	3,100
1 story,	47	2	49
1 story and attic,	431	12	443
Basement and 1 story,	6	–	6
Basement, 1 story, and attic,	37	–	37
2 stories,	1,863	71	1,934
2 stories and attic,	256	14	270
Basement and 2 stories,	166	9	175
Basement, 2 stories, and attic,	44	1	45
3 stories,	101	3	104
Basement and 3 stories,	12	1	13
Basement, 3 stories, and attic,	2	–	2
4 stories,	15	1	16
Not given,	6	–	6
Materials.	2,986	114	3,100
Wood,	2,855	113	2,968
Brick,	100	1	101
Stone,	2	–	2
Wood and brick,	20	–	20
Wood and stone,	2	–	2
Brick and stone,	1	–	1
Not given,	6	–	6
Otis.	131	25	156
Number of Stories.	131	25	156
1 story,	5	–	5
1 story and attic,	73	19	92
Basement, 1 story, and attic,	3	–	3
2 stories,	39	5	44
2 stories and attic,	9	1	10
Basement and 2 stories,	1	–	1
3 stories,	1	–	1
Materials.	131	25	156
Wood,	130	25	155
Brick,	1	–	1
Peru.	69	15	84
Number of Stories.	69	15	84
1 story,	35	14	49
1 story and attic,	1	–	1
2 stories,	33	1	34
Materials.	69	15	84
Wood,	67	15	82
Brick,	2	–	2
PITTSFIELD.	3,806	180	3,986
Number of Stories.	3,806	180	3,986
1 story,	31	1	32
1 story and attic,	315	12	327
Basement and 1 story,	3	–	3
Basement, 1 story, and attic,	1	–	1
2 stories,	2,597	122	2,719
2 stories and attic,	613	35	648

DWELLING HOUSES: NUMBER OF STORIES AND MATERIALS — Continued.

COUNTIES, CITIES, TOWNS, NUMBER OF STORIES TO DWELLING HOUSES, AND MATERIALS OF WHICH CONSTRUCTED.	Number of Occupied Dwelling Houses	Number of Unoccupied Dwelling Houses	Total Number of Dwelling Houses
BERKSHIRE — Con.			
PITTSFIELD — Con.			
Number of Stories — Con.			
Basement and 2 stories, . .	69	3	72
Basement, 2 stories, and attic,	20	2	22
3 stories,	88	3	91
3 stories and attic, . .	9	–	9
Basement and 3 stories, .	29	2	31
Basement, 3 stories, and attic,	1	–	1
4 stories,	18	–	18
4 stories and attic, . .	7	–	7
Basement and 4 stories, .	2	–	2
Basement, 4 stories, and attic,	2	–	2
Basement and 5 stories, .	1	–	1
Materials.	3,806	180	3,986
Wood,	3,612	172	3,784
Brick, .	154	5	159
Stone, .	7	2	9
Cement,	1	–	1
Wood and brick,	25	1	26
Wood and stone,	5	–	5
Brick and stone,	2	–	2
PITTSFIELD. WARD 1, .	506	22	528
Number of Stories.	506	22	528
1 story,	2	–	2
1 story and attic,	229	4	233
2 stories,	266	17	283
2 stories and attic, .	9	–	9
3 stories,	–	1	1
Materials.	506	22	528
Wood, .	478	22	500
Brick, .	13	–	13
Stone, .	1	–	1
Wood and brick,	14	–	14
PITTSFIELD. WARD 2, .	621	20	641
Number of Stories.	621	20	641
1 story,	3	–	3
1 story and attic,	3	1	4
2 stories,	556	15	571
2 stories and attic, .	50	3	53
Basement and 2 stories, .	4	–	4
Basement, 2 stories, and attic,	–	1	1
3 stories,	4	–	4
Basement and 3 stories, .	1	–	1
Materials.	621	20	641
Wood, .	618	20	638
Brick, .	2	–	2
Wood and brick,	1	–	1
PITTSFIELD. WARD 3, .	500	31	531
Number of Stories.	500	31	531
1 story,	4	–	4
Basement and 1 story, .	1	–	1
2 stories,	459	29	488

COUNTIES, CITIES, TOWNS, NUMBER OF STORIES TO DWELLING HOUSES, AND MATERIALS OF WHICH CONSTRUCTED.	Number of Occupied Dwelling Houses	Number of Unoccupied Dwelling Houses	Total Number of Dwelling Houses
BERKSHIRE — Con.			
PITTSFIELD. WARD 3 — Con.			
Number of Stories — Con.			
2 stories and attic, . .	27	2	29
Basement and 2 stories, .	4	–	4
3 stories,	5	–	5
Materials.	500	31	531
Wood, .	490	30	520
Brick, .	7	–	7
Stone, .	2	1	3
Wood and stone,	1	–	1
PITTSFIELD. WARD 4, .	544	30	574
Number of Stories.	544	30	574
1 story,	9	–	9
1 story and attic,	59	5	64
2 stories,	405	17	422
2 stories and attic, .	36	4	40
Basement and 2 stories, .	9	–	9
Basement, 2 stories, and attic,	3	1	4
3 stories,	12	1	13
Basement and 3 stories, .	10	2	12
4 stories,	1	–	1
Materials.	544	30	574
Wood, .	502	26	528
Brick, .	34	2	36
Stone, .	2	1	3
Cement,	1	–	1
Wood and brick,	1	1	2
Wood and stone,	4	–	4
PITTSFIELD. WARD 5, .	444	41	485
Number of Stories.	444	41	485
1 story,	4	–	4
1 story and attic,	17	2	19
Basement and 1 story, .	1	–	1
Basement, 1 story, and attic, .	1	–	1
2 stories,	264	23	287
2 stories and attic,	124	12	136
Basement and 2 stories, .	14	3	17
Basement, 2 stories, and attic,	2	–	2
3 stories,	11	1	12
3 stories and attic, .	3	–	3
Basement and 3 stories, .	1	–	1
Basement, 3 stories, and attic,	1	–	1
Basement and 5 stories, .	1	–	1
Materials.	444	41	485
Wood, .	433	40	473
Brick, .	10	1	11
Stone, .	1	–	1
PITTSFIELD. WARD 6, .	623	22	645
Number of Stories.	623	22	645
1 story,	8	–	8
1 story and attic, .	1	–	1
Basement and 1 story, .	1	–	1

DWELLING HOUSES: NUMBER OF STORIES AND MATERIALS — Continued.

COUNTIES, CITIES, TOWNS, NUMBER OF STORIES TO DWELLING HOUSES, AND MATERIALS OF WHICH CONSTRUCTED.	Number of Occupied Dwelling Houses	Number of Unoccupied Dwelling Houses	Total Number of Dwelling Houses	COUNTIES, CITIES, TOWNS, NUMBER OF STORIES TO DWELLING HOUSES, AND MATERIALS OF WHICH CONSTRUCTED.	Number of Occupied Dwelling Houses	Number of Unoccupied Dwelling Houses	Total Number of Dwelling Houses
BERKSHIRE—Con.				**BERKSHIRE—Con.**			
PITTSFIELD. WARD 6—Con.				**Sandisfield—Con.**			
Number of Stories—Con.				*Materials.*	200	54	254
2 stories,	255	9	264	Wood,	195	53	248
2 stories and attic,	333	13	346	Brick,	1	–	1
Basement and 2 stories,	7	–	7	Stone,	2	–	2
Basement, 2 stories, and attic,	11	–	11	Wood and brick,	2	–	2
3 stories,	7	–	7	Wood and stone,	–	1	1
Materials.	623	22	645	**Savoy.**	130	10	140
Wood,	620	22	642	*Number of Stories.*	130	10	140
Stone,	1	–	1	1 story,	24	3	27
Wood and brick,	2	–	2	1 story and attic,	92	6	98
				2 stories,	5	1	6
PITTSFIELD. WARD 7,	568	14	582	2 stories and attic,	9	–	9
Number of Stories.	568	14	582				
1 story,	1	1	2	*Materials.*	130	10	140
1 story and attic,	6	–	6	Wood,	130	10	140
2 stories,	392	12	404				
2 stories and attic,	34	1	35	**Sheffield.**	450	33	483
Basement and 2 stories,	31	–	31	*Number of Stories.*	450	33	483
Basement, 2 stories, and attic,	4	–	4	1 story and attic,	177	18	195
3 stories,	49	–	49	Basement, 1 story, and attic,	2	–	2
3 stories and attic,	6	–	6	2 stories,	6	–	6
Basement and 3 stories,	17	–	17	2 stories and attic,	260	14	274
4 stories,	17	–	17	Basement, 2 stories, and attic,	4	1	5
4 stories and attic,	7	–	7	3 stories and attic,	1	–	1
Basement and 4 stories,	2	–	2				
Basement, 4 stories, and attic,	2	–	2	*Materials.*	450	33	483
				Wood,	438	32	470
Materials.	568	14	582	Wood and brick,	11	–	11
Wood,	471	12	483	Wood and stone,	1	1	2
Brick,	88	2	90				
Wood and brick,	7	–	7	**Stockbridge.**	436	70	506
Brick and stone,	2	–	2	*Number of Stories.*	436	70	506
				1 story,	16	2	18
Richmond.	158	19	177	1 story and attic,	7	–	7
Number of Stories.	158	19	177	2 stories,	303	34	337
1 story,	11	1	12	2 stories and attic,	86	17	103
1 story and attic,	15	3	18	Basement and 2 stories,	15	5	20
2 stories,	78	11	89	Basement, 2 stories, and attic,	4	1	5
2 stories and attic,	52	4	56	3 stories,	3	3	6
Basement and 2 stories,	1	–	1	3 stories and attic,	–	2	2
3 stories and attic,	1	–	1	Basement and 3 stories,	–	3	3
				Basement, 3 stories, and attic,	1	3	4
Materials.	158	19	177	4 stories and attic,	1	–	1
Wood,	157	18	175				
Brick,	1	1	2	*Materials.*	436	70	506
				Wood,	420	58	478
Sandisfield.	200	54	254	Brick,	3	3	6
Number of Stories.	200	54	254	Stone,	1	2	3
1 story,	6	–	6	Wood and brick,	7	1	8
1 story and attic,	96	27	123	Wood and stone,	5	5	10
Basement, 1 story, and attic,	4	2	6	Wood, brick, and stone,	–	1	1
2 stories,	3	2	5				
2 stories and attic,	90	23	113	**Tyringham.**	87	17	104
Basement, 2 stories, and attic,	1	–	1	*Number of Stories.*	87	17	104
				1 story,	8	2	10

DWELLING HOUSES: NUMBER OF STORIES AND MATERIALS — Continued.

COUNTIES, CITIES, TOWNS, NUMBER OF STORIES TO DWELLING HOUSES, AND MATERIALS OF WHICH CONSTRUCTED.	Number of Occupied Dwelling Houses	Number of Unoccupied Dwelling Houses	Total Number of Dwelling Houses
BERKSHIRE — Con.			
Tyringham — Con.			
Number of Stories — Con.			
1 story and attic, . . .	30	5	35
Basement and 1 story, . .	1	2	3
2 stories, ...	46	1	47
2 stories and attic, . . .	–	2	2
Basement and 2 stories, . .	2	2	4
Basement, 2 stories, and attic,	–	2	2
Basement, 3 stories, and attic,	–	1	1
Materials.	87	17	104
Wood, ...	86	13	99
Brick, ...	1	1	2
Wood and stone, . . .	–	2	2
Brick and stone, . . .	–	1	1
Washington. . . .	87	20	107
Number of Stories.	87	20	107
1 story, ...	12	2	14
1 story and attic, . . .	48	11	59
Basement, 1 story, and attic,	2	–	2
2 stories, ...	23	7	30
2 stories and attic, . . .	2	–	2
Materials.	87	20	107
Wood, ...	86	20	106
Wood and stone, . . .	1	–	1
West Stockbridge. . .	312	35	347
Number of Stories.	312	35	347
1 story, ...	2	–	2
1 story and attic, . . .	135	26	161
Basement, 1 story, and attic,	1	–	1
2 stories, ...	120	9	129
2 stories and attic, . . .	50	–	50
Basement, 2 stories, and attic,	1	–	1
3 stories, ...	2	–	2
3 stories and attic, . . .	1	–	1
Materials.	312	35	347
Wood, ...	307	35	342
Brick, ...	2	–	2
Brick and stone, . . .	3	–	3
Williamstown. . . .	914	40	954
Number of Stories.	914	40	954
1 story, ...	17	1	18
1 story and attic, . . .	110	7	117
Basement, 1 story, and attic,	3	–	3
2 stories, ...	444	9	453
2 stories and attic, . . .	286	21	307
Basement and 2 stories, . .	17	–	17
Basement, 2 stories, and attic,	8	1	9
3 stories, ...	26	1	27
3 stories and attic, . . .	1	–	1
Basement and 3 stories, . .	1	–	1
4 stories, ...	1	–	1

COUNTIES, CITIES, TOWNS, NUMBER OF STORIES TO DWELLING HOUSES, AND MATERIALS OF WHICH CONSTRUCTED.	Number of Occupied Dwelling Houses	Number of Unoccupied Dwelling Houses	Total Number of Dwelling Houses
BERKSHIRE — Con.			
Williamstown — Con.			
Materials.	914	40	954
Wood, ...	886	39	925
Brick, ...	22	1	23
Stone, ...	2	–	2
Wood and brick, . . .	4	–	4
Windsor, ...	127	18	145
Number of Stories.	127	18	145
1 story, ...	11	2	13
1 story and attic, . . .	85	13	98
2 stories, ...	31	3	34
Materials.	127	18	145
Wood, ...	124	18	142
Brick, ...	2	–	2
Stone, ...	1	–	1
BRISTOL.			
Acushnet, ...	263	21	284
Number of Stories.	263	21	284
1 story, ...	11	3	14
1 story and attic, . . .	127	12	139
Basement and 1 story, . .	1	–	1
Basement, 1 story, and attic,	2	–	2
2 stories, ...	72	4	76
2 stories and attic, . . .	44	2	46
Basement and 2 stories, . .	2	–	2
Basement, 2 stories, and attic,	2	–	2
3 stories, ...	2	–	2
Materials.	263	21	284
Wood, ...	263	21	284
Attleborough. . . .	1,513	81	1,594
Number of Stories.	1,513	81	1,594
1 story, ...	52	31	83
1 story and attic, . . .	883	32	915
Basement and 1 story, . .	1	–	1
Basement, 1 story, and attic,	9	1	10
2 stories, ...	59	2	61
2 stories and attic, . . .	501	15	516
Basement, 2 stories, and attic,	4	–	4
3 stories, ...	1	–	1
3 stories and attic, . . .	3	–	3
Materials.	1,513	81	1,594
Wood, ...	1,509	81	1,590
Brick, ...	1	–	1
Stone, ...	2	–	2
Wood and brick, . . .	1	–	1
Berkley.	238	14	252
Number of Stories.	238	14	252
1 story, ...	189	13	202
Basement and 1 story, . .	5	–	5
2 stories, ...	44	1	45

DWELLING HOUSES: NUMBER OF STORIES AND MATERIALS — Continued.

COUNTIES, CITIES, TOWNS, NUMBER OF STORIES TO DWELLING HOUSES, AND MATERIALS OF WHICH CONSTRUCTED.	Number of Occupied Dwelling Houses	Number of Unoccupied Dwelling Houses	Total Number of Dwelling Houses
BRISTOL — Con			
Berkley — Con.			
Materials.	238	14	252
Wood,	237	14	251
Brick,	1	–	1
Dartmouth.	745	211	956
Number of Stories.	745	211	956
1 story,	14	7	21
1 story and attic,	329	74	403
Basement and 1 story,	1	–	1
Basement, 1 story, and attic,	31	2	33
2 stories,	10	5	15
2 stories and attic,	291	113	404
Basement, 2 stories, and attic,	27	4	31
3 stories,	–	3	3
3 stories and attic,	2	3	5
Materials.	745	211	956
Wood,	744	211	955
Wood and stone,	1	–	1
Dighton.	428	33	461
Number of Stories.	428	33	461
1 story,	9	1	10
1 story and attic,	304	24	328
Basement and 1 story,	–	1	1
Basement, 1 story, and attic,	10	–	10
2 stories,	1	–	1
2 stories and attic,	102	6	108
Basement, 2 stories, and attic,	2	1	3
Materials.	428	33	461
Wood,	420	31	451
Brick,	1	1	2
Wood and brick,	6	1	7
Wood and stone,	1	–	1
Easton.	979	87	1,066
Number of Stories.	979	87	1,066
1 story,	344	52	396
1 story and attic,	391	17	408
Basement and 1 story,	8	–	8
Basement, 1 story, and attic,	6	1	7
2 stories,	185	14	199
2 stories and attic,	33	–	33
Basement and 2 stories,	2	–	2
Basement, 2 stories, and attic,	1	–	1
3 stories,	8	2	10
4 stories,	1	1	2
Materials.	979	87	1,066
Wood,	971	82	1,053
Brick,	2	–	2
Stone,	5	4	9
Wood and brick,	1	–	1
Brick and cement,	–	1	1

COUNTIES, CITIES, TOWNS, NUMBER OF STORIES TO DWELLING HOUSES, AND MATERIALS OF WHICH CONSTRUCTED.	Number of Occupied Dwelling Houses	Number of Unoccupied Dwelling Houses	Total Number of Dwelling Houses
BRISTOL — Con.			
Fairhaven.	755	60	815
Number of Stories.	755	60	815
1 story,	38	5	43
1 story and attic,	146	18	164
Basement and 1 story,	1	–	1
Basement, 1 story, and attic,	1	2	3
2 stories,	226	12	238
2 stories and attic,	320	21	341
Basement and 2 stories,	1	–	1
Basement, 2 stories, and attic,	15	–	15
3 stories,	3	2	5
3 stories and attic,	1	–	1
Basement and 3 stories,	1	–	1
Basement, 3 stories, and attic,	1	–	1
Basement and 4 stories,	1	–	1
Materials.	755	60	815
Wood,	746	60	806
Brick,	3	–	3
Stone,	2	–	2
Wood and stone,	2	–	2
Brick and stone,	1	–	1
FALL RIVER.	8,082	293	8,375
Number of Stories.	8,082	293	8,375
1 story,	249	12	261
1 story and attic,	1,508	53	1,561
Basement and 1 story,	12	2	14
Basement, 1 story, and attic,	81	–	81
2 stories,	1,024	25	1,049
2 stories and attic,	3,531	55	3,586
Basement and 2 stories,	37	2	39
Basement, 2 stories, and attic,	139	1	140
3 stories,	1,220	54	1,274
3 stories and attic,	173	3	176
Basement and 3 stories,	29	2	31
Basement, 3 stories, and attic,	7	–	7
4 stories,	52	2	54
4 stories and attic,	4	–	4
Basement and 4 stories,	2	–	2
Basement, 4 stories, and attic,	1	–	1
5 stories,			
6 stories,			
Materials.	8,082	293	8,375
Wood,	7,584	291	7,875
Brick,	74	2	76
Stone,	30	1	–
Cement,	2	–	–
Wood and brick,	62	1	63
Wood and stone,	109	1	110
Wood and cement,	4	–	4
Brick and stone,	7	–	7
Wood, brick, and stone,	1	–	1
FALL RIVER. WARD 1.	1,156	24	1,180
Number of Stories.	1,156	24	1,180
1 story,	26	–	26

DWELLING HOUSES: NUMBER OF STORIES AND MATERIALS — Continued.

COUNTIES, CITIES, TOWNS, NUMBER OF STORIES TO DWELLING HOUSES, AND MATERIALS OF WHICH CONSTRUCTED.	Number of Occupied Dwelling Houses	Number of Unoccupied Dwelling Houses	Total Number of Dwelling Houses	COUNTIES, CITIES, TOWNS, NUMBER OF STORIES TO DWELLING HOUSES, AND MATERIALS OF WHICH CONSTRUCTED.	Number of Occupied Dwelling Houses	Number of Unoccupied Dwelling Houses	Total Number of Dwelling Houses
BRISTOL — Con.				**BRISTOL — Con.**			
FALL RIVER. WARD 1 — Con.				**FALL RIVER. WARD 3 — Con.**			
Number of Stories — Con.				*Number of Stories — Con.*			
1 story and attic, . . .	281	9	290	5 stories, ...	1	–	1
Basement and 1 story, . .	3	1	4	6 stories, ...	1	–	1
Basement, 1 story, and attic, .	13	–	13	*Materials.*	832	17	849
2 stories, ...	132	2	134	Wood, ...	784	17	801
2 stories and attic, . . .	512	6	518	Brick, ...	25	–	25
Basement and 2 stories, . .	4	–	4	Stone, ...	13	–	13
Basement, 2 stories, and attic,	14	1	15	Cement, ...	1	–	1
3 stories, ...	164	5	169	Wood and brick, . . .	6	–	6
3 stories and attic, . . .	2	–	2	Wood and stone, . . .	2	–	2
Basement and 3 stories, . .	2	–	2	Brick and stone, . . .	1	–	1
4 stories, ...	3	–	3				
Materials.	1,156	24	1,180	**FALL RIVER. WARD 4,**	872	13	885
Wood, ...	1,142	22	1,164	*Number of Stories.*	872	13	885
Stone, ...	–	1	1	1 story, ...	15	–	15
Wood and brick, . . .	1	1	2	1 story and attic, . . .	107	5	112
Wood and stone, . . .	11	–	11	Basement and 1 story, . .	1	–	1
Wood and cement, . . .	2	–	2	Basement, 1 story, and attic,	3	–	3
				2 stories, ...	41	1	42
FALL RIVER. WARD 2,	823	33	856	2 stories and attic, . . .	492	1	493
Number of Stories.	823	33	856	Basement and 2 stories, . .	2	–	2
1 story, ...	20	–	20	Basement, 2 stories, and attic,	12	–	12
1 story and attic, . . .	162	5	167	3 stories, ...	143	5	148
Basement and 1 story, . .	5	–	5	3 stories and attic, . . .	37	–	37
Basement, 1 story, and attic, .	18	–	18	Basement and 3 stories, . .	7	1	8
2 stories, ...	143	3	146	Basement, 3 stories, and attic,	1	–	1
2 stories and attic, . . .	359	5	364	4 stories, ...	8	–	8
Basement and 2 stories, . .	8	–	8	4 stories and attic, . . .	1	–	1
Basement, 2 stories, and attic,	6	–	6	Basement and 4 stories, . .	1	–	1
3 stories, ...	98	20	118	Basement, 4 stories, and attic,	1	–	1
3 stories and attic, . . .	3	–	3	*Materials.*	872	13	885
Basement and 3 stories, . .	1	–	1	Wood, ...	836	13	849
Materials.	823	33	856	Brick, ...	5	–	5
Wood, ...	812	33	845	Stone, ...	3	–	3
Brick, ...	9	–	9	Cement, ...	1	–	1
Wood and brick, . . .	1	–	1	Wood and brick, . . .	13	–	13
Wood and stone, . . .	1	–	1	Wood and stone, . . .	11	–	11
				Wood and cement, . . .	1	–	1
FALL RIVER. WARD 3,	832	17	849	Brick and stone, . . .	1	–	1
Number of Stories.	832	17	849	Wood, brick, and stone, . .	1	–	1
1 story, ...	32	3	35				
1 story and attic, . . .	78	–	78	**FALL RIVER. WARD 5,**	789	24	813
Basement, 1 story, and attic, .	8	–	8	*Number of Stories.*	789	24	813
2 stories, ...	90	4	94	1 story, ...	53	5	58
2 stories and attic, . . .	430	6	436	1 story and attic, . . .	94	10	104
Basement and 2 stories, . .	4	–	4	2 stories, ...	171	3	174
Basement, 2 stories, and attic,	47	–	47	2 stories and attic, . . .	243	2	245
3 stories, ...	84	4	88	Basement and 2 stories, . .	4	–	4
3 stories and attic, . . .	35	–	35	Basement, 2 stories, and attic,	1	–	1
Basement and 3 stories, . .	6	–	6	3 stories, ...	194	3	197
Basement, 3 stories, and attic,	2	–	2	3 stories and attic, . . .	24	–	24
4 stories, ...	13	–	13	4 stories, ...	5	1	6
Basement and 4 stories, . .	1	–	1	*Materials.*	789	24	813
				Wood, ...	713	23	736

DWELLING HOUSES: NUMBER OF STORIES AND MATERIALS — Continued.

COUNTIES, CITIES, TOWNS, NUMBER OF STORIES TO DWELLING HOUSES, AND MATERIALS OF WHICH CONSTRUCTED.	Number of Occupied Dwelling Houses	Number of Unoccupied Dwelling Houses	Total Number of Dwelling Houses
BRISTOL — Con.			
FALL RIVER. WARD 5 — Con.			
Materials — Con.			
Brick, .	3	1	4
Stone, .	1	-	1
Wood and brick, .	7	-	7
Wood and stone, .	64	-	64
Brick and stone, .	1	-	1
FALL RIVER. WARD 6, .	933	36	969
Number of Stories.	933	36	969
1 story, .	49	4	53
1 story and attic, .	185	7	192
Basement, 1 story, and attic,	3	-	3
2 stories, .	207	6	213
2 stories and attic, .	167	8	175
Basement and 2 stories, .	3	-	3
3 stories, .	289	11	300
3 stories and attic, .	9	-	9
4 stories, .	19	-	19
4 stories and attic, .	1	-	1
5 stories, .	1	-	1
Materials.	933	36	969
Wood, .	911	34	945
Brick, .	10	-	10
Stone, .	3	-	3
Wood and brick, .	1	1	2
Wood and stone, .	7	1	8
Brick and stone, .	1	-	1
FALL RIVER. WARD 7,	731	14	745
Number of Stories.	731	14	745
1 story, .	14	-	14
1 story and attic, .	87	1	88
Basement and 1 story, .	2	1	3
Basement, 1 story, and attic,	12	-	12
2 stories, .	52	1	53
2 stories and attic, .	432	9	441
Basement and 2 stories, .	4	-	4
Basement, 2 stories, and attic,	30	-	30
3 stories, .	60	2	62
3 stories and attic, .	22	-	22
Basement and 3 stories, .	5	-	5
Basement, 3 stories, and attic,	4	-	4
4 stories, .	4	-	4
4 stories and attic, .	2	-	2
5 stories, .	1	-	1
Materials.	731	14	745
Wood, .	687	14	701
Brick, .	17	-	17
Stone, .	6	-	6
Wood and brick, .	15	-	15
Wood and stone, .	3	-	3
Brick and stone, .	3	-	3
BRISTOL — Con.			
FALL RIVER. WARD 8, .	935	27	962
Number of Stories.	935	27	962
1 story, .	12	-	12
1 story and attic, .	273	7	280
Basement, 1 story, and attic,	9	-	9
2 stories, .	42	1	43
2 stories and attic, .	495	15	510
Basement and 2 stories, .	4	2	6
Basement, 2 stories, and attic,	18	-	18
3 stories, .	66	1	67
3 stories and attic, .	10	-	10
Basement and 3 stories, .	6	1	7
Materials.	935	27	962
Wood, .	924	27	951
Brick, .	4	-	4
Stone, .	4	-	4
Wood and stone, .	3	-	3
FALL RIVER. WARD 9,	998	21	1,019
Number of Stories.	998	21	1,019
1 story, .	28	-	28
1 story and attic, .	241	9	250
Basement and 1 story, .	1	-	1
Basement, 1 story, and attic,	15	-	15
2 stories, .	146	4	150
2 stories and attic, .	401	3	404
Basement and 2 stories, .	4	-	4
Basement, 2 stories, and attic,	11	-	11
3 stories, .	122	3	125
3 stories and attic, .	27	1	28
Basement and 3 stories, .	2	-	2
4 stories, .	-	1	1
Materials.	998	21	1,019
Wood, .	972	18	990
Brick, .	1	1	2
Wood and brick, .	17	2	19
Wood and stone, .	7	-	7
Wood and cement, .	1	-	1
Freetown.	313	48	361
Number of Stories.	313	48	361
1 story, .	26	25	51
1 story and attic, .	216	15	231
Basement and 1 story, .	1	-	1
Basement, 1 story, and attic,	9	-	9
2 stories, .	5	1	6
2 stories and attic, .	55	6	61
Basement, 2 stories, and attic,	1	1	2
Materials.	313	48	361
Wood, .	312	48	360
Wood and stone, .	1	-	1
Mansfield.	823	34	857
Number of Stories.	823	34	857
1 story, .	15	1	16

DWELLING HOUSES: NUMBER OF STORIES AND MATERIALS — Continued.

COUNTIES, CITIES, TOWNS, NUMBER OF STORIES TO DWELLING HOUSES, AND MATERIALS OF WHICH CONSTRUCTED.	Number of Occupied Dwelling Houses	Number of Unoccupied Dwelling Houses	Total Number of Dwelling Houses
BRISTOL — Con.			
Mansfield — Con.			
Number of Stories — Con.			
1 story and attic,	536	25	561
Basement, 1 story, and attic,	18	-	18
2 stories,	40	3	43
2 stories and attic,	202	4	206
3 stories,	11	1	12
4 stories,	1	-	1
Materials.			
Wood,	823	34	857
Wood,	821	34	855
Brick,	1	-	1
Wood and brick,	1	-	1
NEW BEDFORD,	7,480	210	7,690
Number of Stories.	7,480	210	7,680
1 story,	450	14	464
1 story and attic,	2,309	72	2,381
Basement and 1 story,	14	1	15
Basement, 1 story, and attic,	67	-	67
2 stories,	856	31	887
2 stories and attic,	2,901	72	2,973
Basement and 2 stories,	37	1	38
Basement, 2 stories, and attic,	196	2	198
3 stories,	509	13	522
3 stories and attic,	81	3	84
Basement and 3 stories,	17	1	18
Basement, 3 stories, and attic,	20	-	20
4 stories,	17	-	17
4 stories and attic,	1	-	1
5 stories,	1	-	1
Not given,	4	-	4
Materials.			
Wood,	7,480	210	7,680
Wood,	7,395	206	7,571
Brick,	70	-	70
Stone,	14	3	17
Wood and brick,	20	-	20
Wood and stone,	6	1	7
Brick and stone,	1	-	1
Not given,	4	-	4
NEW BEDFORD. WARD 1,	1,296	42	1,338
Number of Stories.	1,296	42	1,338
1 story,	326	11	337
1 story and attic,	110	4	114
Basement and 1 story,	2	-	2
Basement, 1 story, and attic,	3	-	3
2 stories,	374	13	387
2 stories and attic,	214	4	218
Basement and 2 stories,	6	-	6
Basement, 2 stories, and attic,	3	-	3
3 stories,	230	6	236
3 stories and attic,	1	3	7
Basement and 3 stories,	5	1	6
Basement, 3 stories, and attic,	5	-	5

COUNTIES, CITIES, TOWNS, NUMBER OF STORIES TO DWELLING HOUSES, AND MATERIALS OF WHICH CONSTRUCTED.	Number of Occupied Dwelling Houses	Number of Unoccupied Dwelling Houses	Total Number of Dwelling Houses
BRISTOL — Con.			
NEW BEDFORD. WARD 1-Con.			
Number of Stories — Con.			
4 stories,	13	-	13
Not given,	1	-	1
Materials.			
	1,296	42	1,338
Wood,	1,268	42	1,310
Brick,	19	-	19
Wood and brick,	8	-	8
Not given,	1	-	1
NEW BEDFORD. WARD 2,	1,147	31	1,178
Number of Stories.	1,147	31	1,178
1 story,	8	-	8
1 story and attic,	507	15	522
Basement and 1 story,	2	-	2
Basement, 1 story, and attic,	19	-	19
2 stories,	73	2	75
2 stories and attic,	446	12	458
Basement and 2 stories,	5	-	5
Basement, 2 stories, and attic,	24	-	24
3 stories,	46	2	48
3 stories and attic,	12	-	12
Basement and 3 stories,	4	-	4
Basement, 3 stories, and attic,	1	-	1
Materials.			
	1,147	31	1,178
Wood,	1,133	30	1,163
Brick,	8	-	8
Stone,	3	1	4
Wood and stone,	3	-	3
NEW BEDFORD. WARD 3,	1,056	28	1,084
Number of Stories.	1,056	28	1,084
1 story,	10	-	10
1 story and attic,	345	12	357
Basement and 1 story,	2	-	2
Basement, 1 story, and attic,	6	-	6
2 stories,	91	2	93
2 stories and attic,	540	12	552
Basement and 2 stories,	7	-	7
Basement, 2 stories, and attic,	18	2	20
3 stories,	27	-	27
3 stories and attic,	4	-	4
Basement, 3 stories, and attic,	4	-	4
4 stories,	2	-	2
Materials.			
	1,056	28	1,084
Wood,	1,044	27	1,071
Brick,	9	-	9
Stone,	3	1	4
NEW BEDFORD. WARD 4,	1,154	27	1,181
Number of Stories.	1,154	27	1,181
1 story,	53	-	53
1 story and attic,	321	10	331
Basement and 1 story,	4	1	5

DWELLING HOUSES: NUMBER OF STORIES AND MATERIALS — Continued.

COUNTIES, CITIES, TOWNS, NUMBER OF STORIES TO DWELLING HOUSES, AND MATERIALS OF WHICH CONSTRUCTED.	Number of Occupied Dwelling Houses	Number of Unoccupied Dwelling Houses	Total Number of Dwelling Houses
BRISTOL — Con.			
NEW BEDFORD. WARD 4-Con.			
Number of Stories — Con.			
Basement, 1-story, and attic,	29	–	29
2 stories,	113	3	116
2 stories and attic,	433	10	443
Basement and 2 stories,	10	1	11
Basement, 2 stories, and attic,	139	–	139
3 stories,	19	2	21
3 stories and attic,	16	–	16
Basement and 3 stories,	5	–	5
Basement, 3 stories, and attic,	9	–	9
Not given,	3	–	3
Materials.	1,154	27	1,181
Wood,	1,114	25	1,139
Brick,	24	–	24
Stone,	5	1	6
Wood and brick,	8	–	8
Wood and stone,	–	1	1
Not given,	3	–	3
NEW BEDFORD. WARD 5,	1,416	39	1,455
Number of Stories.	1,416	39	1,455
1 story,	33	3	36
1 story and attic,	497	15	512
Basement and 1 story,	3	–	3
Basement, 1 story, and attic,	5	–	5
2 stories,	82	3	85
2 stories and attic,	731	16	747
Basement and 2 stories,	4	–	4
Basement, 2 stories, and attic,	11	–	11
3 stories,	14	2	16
3 stories and attic,	35	–	35
Basement, 3 stories, and attic,	1	–	1
Materials.	1,416	39	1,455
Wood,	1,398	39	1,437
Brick,	9	–	9
Stone,	3	–	3
Wood and brick,	4	–	4
Wood and stone,	2	–	2
NEW BEDFORD. WARD 6,	1,411	43	1,454
Number of Stories.	1,411	43	1,454
1 story,	20	–	20
1 story and attic,	529	16	545
Basement and 1 story,	1	–	1
Basement, 1 story, and attic,	5	–	5
2 stories,	123	8	131
2 stories and attic,	537	18	555
Basement and 2 stories,	5	–	5
Basement, 2 stories, and attic,	1	–	1
3 stories,	173	1	174
3 stories and attic,	10	–	10
Basement and 3 stories,	3	–	3
4 stories,	2	–	2

COUNTIES, CITIES, TOWNS, NUMBER OF STORIES TO DWELLING HOUSES, AND MATERIALS OF WHICH CONSTRUCTED.	Number of Occupied Dwelling Houses	Number of Unoccupied Dwelling Houses	Total Number of Dwelling Houses
BRISTOL — Con.			
NEW BEDFORD. WARD 6-Con.			
Number of Stories — Con.			
4 stories and attic,	1	–	1
5 stories,	1	–	1
Materials.	1,411	43	1,454
Wood,	1,408	43	1,451
Brick,	1	–	1
Wood and stone,	1	–	1
Brick and stone,	1	–	1
North Attleborough.	1,235	82	1,317
Number of Stories.	1,235	82	1,317
1 story,	7	2	9
1 story and attic,	701	44	745
Basement and 1 story,	1	–	1
Basement, 1 story, and attic,	62	7	69
2 stories,	26	1	27
2 stories and attic,	402	28	430
Basement and 2 stories,	3	–	3
Basement, 2 stories, and attic,	26	–	26
3 stories,	2	–	2
3 stories and attic,	1	–	1
Basement and 3 stories,	2	–	2
Not given,	2	–	2
Materials.	1,235	82	1,317
Wood,	1,227	81	1,308
Brick,	3	1	4
Wood and brick,	3	–	3
Not given,	2	–	2
Norton.	372	46	418
Number of Stories.	372	46	418
1 story,	18	4	22
1 story and attic,	249	29	278
Basement, 1 story, and attic,	10	–	10
2 stories,	44	6	50
2 stories and attic,	44	7	51
Basement and 2 stories,	2	–	2
Basement, 2 stories, and attic,	3	–	3
3 stories,	2	–	2
Materials.	372	46	418
Wood,	361	45	406
Stone,	1	–	1
Wood and brick,	10	1	11
Raynham.	363	15	378
Number of Stories.	363	15	378
1 story,	3	–	3
1 story and attic,	264	10	274
Basement, 1 story, and attic,	13	2	15
2 stories,	1	–	1
2 stories and attic,	80	2	82
Basement, 2 stories, and attic,	2	1	3
Materials.	363	15	378
Wood,	361	15	376

DWELLING HOUSES: NUMBER OF STORIES AND MATERIALS — Continued.

COUNTIES, CITIES, TOWNS, NUMBER OF STORIES TO DWELLING HOUSES, AND MATERIALS OF WHICH CONSTRUCTED.	Number of Occupied Dwelling Houses	Number of Unoccupied Dwelling Houses	Total Number of Dwelling Houses
BRISTOL — Con.			
Raynham — Con.			
Materials — Con.			
Wood and brick, . . .	1	–	1
Brick and stone, . .	1	–	1
Rehoboth, ...	403	10	413
Number of Stories.	403	10	413
1 story, ...	62	2	64
1 story and attic, . .	260	3	263
Basement and 1 story, . .	3	–	3
Basement, 1 story, and attic,	11	–	11
2 stories, . . .	28	3	31
2 stories and attic, . .	37	2	39
Basement and 2 stories, . .	1	–	1
Basement, 2 stories, and attic,	1	–	1
Materials.	403	10	413
Wood, ...	399	10	409
Brick, ...	2	–	2
Wood and brick, . .	2	–	2
Seekonk, ...	310	12	322
Number of Stories.	310	12	322
1 story, . . .	49	2	51
1 story and attic, . .	179	8	187
Basement and 1 story, .	1	–	1
Basement, 1 story, and attic,	2	1	3
2 stories, ...	55	1	56
2 stories and attic, . .	22	–	22
3 stories, ...	2	–	2
Materials.	310	12	322
Wood, ...	308	12	320
Brick, ...	1	–	1
Wood and brick, . .	1	–	1
Somerset, ...	413	32	445
Number of Stories.	413	32	445
1 story, . . .	69	11	80
1 story and attic, . .	191	8	199
Basement, 1 story, and attic,	6	–	6
2 stories, . . .	26	5	31
2 stories and attic, . .	118	6	124
Basement and 2 stories, .	–	1	1
Basement, 2 stories, and attic,	3	1	4
Materials.	413	32	445
Wood, ...	409	31	440
Wood and brick, . .	4	–	4
Stone and cement, . .	–	1	1
Swansea, ...	365	6	371
Number of Stories.	365	6	371
1 story, . . .	5	–	5
1 story and attic, . .	178	3	181
Basement, 1 story, and attic,	4	–	4
2 stories, ...	80	1	81

COUNTIES, CITIES, TOWNS, NUMBER OF STORIES TO DWELLING HOUSES, AND MATERIALS OF WHICH CONSTRUCTED.	Number of Occupied Dwelling Houses	Number of Unoccupied Dwelling Houses	Total Number of Dwelling Houses
BRISTOL — Con.			
Swansea — Con.			
Number of Stories — Con.			
2 stories and attic, . .	89	2	91
Basement and 2 stories, . .	1	–	1
Basement, 2 stories, and attic,	3	–	3
3 stories, . . .	3	–	3
3 stories and attic, . .	1	–	1
Basement and 3 stories, .	1	–	1
Materials.	365	6	371
Wood, ...	363	6	369
Brick, ...	1	–	1
Wood and brick, . .	1	–	1
TAUNTON, ...	4,379	171	4,550
Number of Stories.	4,379	171	4,550
1 story, . . .	202	9	211
1 story and attic, . .	2,294	88	2,382
Basement and 1 story, . .	14	–	14
Basement, 1 story, and attic,	68	1	69
2 stories, ...	350	16	366
2 stories and attic, . .	1,350	53	1,403
Basement and 2 stories, . .	18	1	19
Basement, 2 stories, and attic,	27	1	28
3 stories, . . .	45	1	46
3 stories and attic, . .	6	1	7
Basement and 3 stories, . .	1	–	1
Basement, 3 stories, and attic,	1	–	1
4 stories, . . .	2	–	2
Not given, . . .	1	–	1
Materials.	4,379	171	4,550
Wood, ...	4,244	156	4,400
Brick, ...	101	13	114
Stone, ...	4	–	4
Cement, ...	1	–	1
Wood and brick, . .	24	1	25
Wood and stone, . .	1	1	2
Brick and stone, . .	3	–	3
Not given, . . .	1	–	1
TAUNTON. WARD 1, . .	518	18	536
Number of Stories.	518	18	536
1 story, . . .	7	1	8
1 story and attic, . .	297	12	309
Basement, 1 story, and attic,	12	–	12
2 stories, . . .	17	1	18
2 stories and attic, . .	171	4	175
Basement and 2 stories, . .	4	–	4
Basement, 2 stories, and attic,	1	–	1
3 stories, . . .	9	–	9
Materials.	518	18	536
Wood, ...	515	18	533
Brick, ...	1	–	1
Wood and brick, . .	2	–	2

COUNTIES, CITIES, TOWNS, NUMBER OF STORIES TO DWELLING HOUSES, AND MATERIALS OF WHICH CONSTRUCTED.	Number of Occupied Dwelling Houses	Number of Unoccupied Dwelling Houses	Total Number of Dwelling Houses
BRISTOL — Con.			
TAUNTON. WARD 2,	467	16	483
Number of Stories.	467	16	483
1 story,	116	4	120
1 story and attic,	40	2	42
Basement and 1 story,	3	–	3
2 stories,	70	4	74
2 stories and attic,	221	6	227
Basement and 2 stories,	2	–	2
Basement, 2 stories, and attic,	4	–	4
3 stories,	10	–	10
4 stories,	1	–	1
Materials.	467	16	483
Wood,	434	16	450
Brick,	21	–	21
Stone,	2	–	2
Cement,	1	–	1
Wood and brick,	7	–	7
Brick and stone,	2	–	2
TAUNTON. WARD 3,	424	9	433
Number of Stories.	424	9	433
1 story,	12	–	12
1 story and attic,	140	4	144
2 stories,	75	2	77
2 stories and attic,	182	3	185
Basement and 2 stories,	5	–	5
3 stories,	6	–	6
3 stories and attic,	2	–	2
Basement and 3 stories,	1	–	1
4 stories,	1	–	1
Materials.	424	9	433
Wood,	402	8	410
Brick,	21	1	22
Wood and brick,	1	–	1
TAUNTON. WARD 4,	607	49	656
Number of Stories.	607	49	656
1 story,	9	–	9
1 story and attic,	313	25	338
Basement, 1 story, and attic,	9	–	9
2 stories,	38	5	43
2 stories and attic,	222	16	238
Basement and 2 stories,	1	–	1
Basement, 2 stories, and attic,	8	1	9
3 stories,	7	1	8
3 stories and attic,	–	1	1
Materials.	607	49	656
Wood,	589	48	637
Brick,	10	–	10
Wood and brick,	8	–	8
Wood and stone,	–	1	1
TAUNTON. WARD 5,	642	21	663
Number of Stories.	642	21	663
1 story,	11	2	13

COUNTIES, CITIES, TOWNS, NUMBER OF STORIES TO DWELLING HOUSES, AND MATERIALS OF WHICH CONSTRUCTED.	Number of Occupied Dwelling Houses	Number of Unoccupied Dwelling Houses	Total Number of Dwelling Houses
BRISTOL — Con.			
TAUNTON. WARD 5 — Con.			
Number of Stories — Con.			
1 story and attic,	429	8	437
Basement, 1 story, and attic,	9	1	10
2 stories,	43	1	44
2 stories and attic,	141	9	150
Basement, 2 stories, and attic,	5	–	5
3 stories and attic,	4	–	4
Materials.	642	21	663
Wood,	640	20	660
Brick,	2	1	3
TAUNTON. WARD 6,	503	11	514
Number of Stories.	503	11	514
1 story,	27	–	27
1 story and attic,	238	9	247
Basement and 1 story,	3	–	3
Basement, 1 story, and attic,	26	–	26
2 stories,	29	–	29
2 stories and attic,	167	2	169
Basement, 2 stories, and attic,	6	–	6
3 stories,	7	–	7
Materials.	503	11	514
Wood,	474	10	484
Brick,	21	1	22
Stone,	2	–	2
Wood and brick,	5	–	5
Wood and stone,	1	–	1
TAUNTON. WARD 7,	513	19	532
Number of Stories.	513	19	532
1 story,	16	2	18
1 story and attic,	317	8	325
Basement and 1 story,	7	–	7
Basement, 1 story, and attic,	1	–	1
2 stories,	15	1	16
2 stories and attic,	153	8	161
Basement and 2 stories,	2	–	2
3 stories,	1	–	1
Not given,	1	–	1
Materials.	513	19	532
Wood,	511	19	530
Brick,	1	–	1
Not given,	1	–	1
TAUNTON. WARD 8,	705	28	733
Number of Stories.	705	28	733
1 story,	4	–	4
1 story and attic,	520	20	540
Basement and 1 story,	1	–	1
Basement, 1 story, and attic,	11	–	11
2 stories,	63	2	65
2 stories and attic,	93	5	98
Basement and 2 stories,	4	1	5

DWELLING HOUSES: NUMBER OF STORIES AND MATERIALS — Continued.

COUNTIES, CITIES, TOWNS. NUMBER OF STORIES TO DWELLING HOUSES, AND MATERIALS OF WHICH CONSTRUCTED.	Number of Occupied Dwelling Houses	Number of Unoccupied Dwelling Houses	Total Number of Dwelling Houses	COUNTIES, CITIES, TOWNS. NUMBER OF STORIES TO DWELLING HOUSES, AND MATERIALS OF WHICH CONSTRUCTED.	Number of Occupied Dwelling Houses	Number of Unoccupied Dwelling Houses	Total Number of Dwelling Houses
BRISTOL — Con.				**DUKES — Con.**			
TAUNTON. WARD 8 — Con.				**Edgartown — Con.**			
Number of Stories — Con.				*Number of Stories — Con.*			
Basement, 2 stories, and attic,	3	–	3	2 stories, ...	7	1	8
3 stories, ...	5	–	5	2 stories and attic, . . .	106	14	120
Basement, 3 stories, and attic,	1	–	1	Basement, 2 stories, and attic,	8	1	9
				3 stories, ...	–	1	1
Materials.	705	28	733	3 stories and attic, . . .	1	1	2
Wood, ...	679	17	696	Not given, ...	1	–	1
Brick, ...	24	10	34	*Materials.*	331	69	400
Wood and brick, . . .	1	1	2	Wood, ...	329	69	398
Brick and stone, . . .	1	–	1	Wood, brick, and stone, .	1	–	1
Westport.	647	105	752	Not given, ...	1	–	1
Number of Stories.	647	105	752				
1 story, ...	332	52	384	**Gay Head.**	35	2	37
1 story and attic, . . .	184	30	214	*Number of Stories.*	35	2	37
Basement and 1 story, . .	7	1	8	1 story, ...	1	–	1
Basement, 1 story, and attic,	3	–	3	1 story and attic, . . .	26	1	27
2 stories, ...	109	17	126	Basement, 1 story, and attic,	7	1	8
2 stories and attic, . . .	11	3	14	2 stories and attic, . . .	1	–	1
3 stories, ...	1	2	3	*Materials.*	35	2	37
Materials.	647	105	752	Wood, ...	23	1	24
Wood, ...	646	103	749	Brick, ...	1	–	1
Stone, ...	1	1	2	Stone, ...	4	1	5
Wood and stone, . . .	–	1	1	Wood and stone, . . .	7	–	7
DUKES.				**Gosnold.**	35	11	46
				Number of Stories.	35	11	46
Chilmark.	93	71	164	1 story, ...	3	–	3
Number of Stories.	93	71	164	1 story and attic, . . .	23	6	29
1 story, ...	5	15	20	Basement, 1 story, and attic,	2	–	2
2 stories, ...	75	49	124	2 stories, ...	3	–	3
2 stories and attic, . . .	13	7	20	2 stories and attic, . . .	3	5	8
				Basement, 3 stories, and attic,	1	–	1
Materials.	93	71	164	*Materials.*	35	11	46
Wood, ...	91	69	160	Wood, ...	34	11	45
Brick, ...	–	1	1	Wood, brick, and stone, .	1	–	1
Wood and brick, . . .	1	1	2	**Tisbury.**	263	99	362
Wood and stone, . . .	1	.	1	*Number of Stories.*	263	99	362
Cottage City. . . .	312	803	1,115	1 story, ...	8	8	16
Number of Stories.	312	803	1,115	1 story and attic, . . .	7	43	50
1 story, ...	28	64	92	Basement, 1 story, and attic,	166	–	166
1 story and attic, . . .	4	2	6	2 stories, ...	18	14	32
2 stories, ...	268	723	991	2 stories and attic, . . .	58	30	88
2 stories and attic, . . .	4	1	5	Basement, 2 stories, and attic,	3	–	3
3 stories, ...	6	10	16	3 stories, ...	1	4	5
4 stories, ...	2	3	5	Basement and 3 stories, .	2	–	2
Materials.	312	803	1,115	*Materials.*	263	99	362
Wood, ...	312	803	1,115	Wood, ...	261	99	360
				Wood and brick, . . .	1	–	1
Edgartown.	331	69	400	Wood and stone, . . .	1	–	1
Number of Stories.	331	69	400	**West Tisbury.** . . .	148	38	186
1 story, ...	5	–	5	*Number of Stories.*	148	38	186
1 story and attic, . . .	199	48	247	1 story, ...	5	1	6
Basement, 1 story, and attic,	4	3	7				

DWELLING HOUSES: NUMBER OF STORIES AND MATERIALS — Continued.

COUNTIES, CITIES, TOWNS, NUMBER OF STORIES TO DWELLING HOUSES, AND MATERIALS OF WHICH CONSTRUCTED.	Number of Occupied Dwelling Houses	Number of Unoccupied Dwelling Houses	Total Number of Dwelling Houses
DUKES — Con.			
West Tisbury — Con.			
Number of Stories — Con.			
1 story and attic, . . .	124	33	157
Basement, 1 story, and attic, .	5	–	5
2 stories, ...	4	1	5
2 stories and attic, . . .	10	2	12
3 stories, . . .	–	1	1
Materials.	148	38	186
Wood, ...	148	38	186
ESSEX.			
Amesbury.	1,996	86	2,042
Number of Stories.	1,996	86	2,042
1 story, ...	11	1	12
1 story and attic, . .	429	21	450
Basement and 1 story, . .	3	–	3
Basement, 1 story, and attic,	21	1	22
2 stories, ...	35	4	39
2 stories and attic, . .	1,334	24	1,358
Basement and 2 stories, .	2	–	2
Basement, 2 stories, and attic,	51	–	51
3 stories, ...	38	1	39
3 stories and attic, . .	25	4	29
Basement and 3 stories, .	3	–	3
4 stories, ...	3	–	3
Basement and 4 stories, .	1	–	1
Materials.	1,996	86	2,042
Wood, ...	1,923	85	2,008
Brick, ...	28	–	28
Wood and brick, . .	3	1	4
Wood and stone, . .	1	–	1
Brick and stone, . .	1	–	1
Andover. . . .	1,156	62	1,218
Number of Stories.	1,156	62	1,218
1 story, ...	22	2	24
1 story and attic, . .	356	29	385
2 stories, ...	210	6	216
2 stories and attic, . .	513	24	537
Basement, 2 stories, and attic,	10	1	11
3 stories, ...	41	–	41
3 stories and attic, . .	2	–	2
4 stories, ...	2	–	2
Materials.	1,156	62	1,218
Wood, ...	1,106	60	1,166
Brick, ...	24	–	24
Stone, ...	2	1	3
Wood and brick, . .	22	1	23
Wood and stone, . .	2	–	2
BEVERLY. . . .	2,049	216	2,265
Number of Stories.	2,049	216	2,265
1 story, ...	28	1	29
1 story and attic, . .	413	26	439

COUNTIES, CITIES, TOWNS, NUMBER OF STORIES TO DWELLING HOUSES, AND MATERIALS OF WHICH CONSTRUCTED.	Number of Occupied Dwelling Houses	Number of Unoccupied Dwelling Houses	Total Number of Dwelling Houses
ESSEX — Con.			
BEVERLY — Con.			
Number of Stories — Con.			
Basement and 1 story, . .	1	–	1
Basement, 1 story, and attic,	27	3	30
2 stories, ...	415	46	461
2 stories and attic, . .	1,026	123	1,149
Basement and 2 stories, .	9	1	10
Basement, 2 stories, and attic,	27	6	33
3 stories, ...	83	2	85
3 stories and attic, . .	10	5	15
Basement and 3 stories, .	2	–	2
Basement, 3 stories, and attic,	3	3	6
4 stories, ...	1	–	1
Not given, ...	4	–	4
Materials.	2,049	216	2,265
Wood, ...	2,030	212	2,242
Brick, ...	5	–	5
Stone, ...	–	2	2
Wood and brick, . .	8	1	9
Wood and stone, . .	2	1	3
Not given, ...	4	–	4
BEVERLY. WARD 1, . .	415	14	429
Number of Stories.	415	14	429
1 story, ...	5	–	5
1 story and attic, . .	39	2	41
Basement, 1 story, and attic, .	4	–	4
2 stories, ...	51	2	53
2 stories and attic, . .	304	10	314
Basement and 2 stories, .	1	–	1
Basement, 2 stories, and attic,	8	–	8
3 stories, ...	2	–	2
3 stories and attic, . .	1	–	1
Materials.	415	14	429
Wood, ...	413	14	427
Wood and brick, . .	1	–	1
Wood and stone, . .	1	–	1
BEVERLY. WARD 2, . .	393	32	425
Number of Stories.	393	32	425
1 story, ...	1	–	1
1 story and attic, . .	52	2	54
Basement, 1 story, and attic,	11	1	12
2 stories, ...	24	4	28
2 stories and attic, . .	236	20	256
Basement and 2 stories, .	3	–	3
Basement, 2 stories, and attic,	6	4	10
3 stories, ...	50	1	51
3 stories and attic, . .	6	–	6
Basement and 3 stories, .	1	–	1
Not given, ...	3	–	3
Materials.	393	32	425
Wood, ...	383	32	415
Brick, ...	2	–	2

DWELLING HOUSES: NUMBER OF STORIES AND MATERIALS — Continued.

COUNTIES, CITIES, TOWNS, NUMBER OF STORIES TO DWELLING HOUSES, AND MATERIALS OF WHICH CONSTRUCTED.	Number of Occupied Dwelling Houses	Number of Unoccupied Dwelling Houses	Total Number of Dwelling Houses
ESSEX — Con.			
BEVERLY. WARD 2 — Con.			
Materials — Con.			
Wood and brick, . . .	5	–	5
Not given, ...	3	–	3
BEVERLY. WARD 3, . .	389	18	417
Number of Stories.	389	18	417
1 story, ...	1	–	1
1 story and attic, . . .	123	4	127
Basement, 1 story, and attic, .	12	2	14
2 stories, ...	51	9	60
2 stories and attic, . . .	179	3	182
Basement and 2 stories, . .	1	–	1
Basement, 2 stories, and attic,	9	–	9
3 stories, ...	22	–	22
Basement, 3 stories, and attic,	1	–	1
Materials.	389	18	417
Wood, ...	388	18	416
Brick, ...	1	–	1
BEVERLY. WARD 4, . .	392	79	471
Number of Stories.	392	79	471
1 story, ...	8	1	9
1 story and attic, . . .	173	15	188
Basement and 1 story, . .	1	–	1
2 stories, ...	88	16	104
2 stories and attic, . . .	116	47	163
3 stories, ...	5	–	5
4 stories, ...	1	–	1
Materials.	392	79	471
Wood, ...	391	77	468
Stone, ...	–	2	2
Wood and brick, . . .	1	–	1
BEVERLY. WARD 5, . .	247	73	320
Number of Stories.	247	73	320
1 story, ...	5	–	5
1 story and attic, . . .	5	3	8
2 stories, ...	110	15	125
2 stories and attic, . . .	122	43	165
Basement and 2 stories, . .	2	1	3
Basement, 2 stories, and attic,	–	2	2
3 stories, ...	1	1	2
3 stories and attic, . . .	2	5	7
Basement, 3 stories, and attic,	–	3	3
Materials.	247	73	320
Wood, ...	245	71	316
Brick, ...	1	–	1
Wood and brick, . . .	1	1	2
Wood and stone, . . .	–	1	1
BEVERLY. WARD 6, . .	203	–	203
Number of Stories.	203	–	203
1 story, ...	8	–	8
1 story and attic, . . .	21	–	21
ESSEX — Con.			
BEVERLY. WARD 6 — Con.			
Number of Stories — Con.			
2 stories, ...	91	–	91
2 stories and attic, . . .	69	–	69
Basement and 2 stories, . .	2	–	2
Basement, 2 stories, and attic,	4	–	4
3 stories, ...	3	–	3
3 stories and attic, . . .	1	–	1
Basement and 3 stories, . .	1	–	1
Basement, 3 stories, and attic,	2	–	2
Not given, ...	1	–	1
Materials.	203	–	203
Wood, ...	200	–	200
Brick, ...	1	–	1
Wood and stone, . . .	1	–	1
Not given, ...	1	–	1
Boxford, ...	177	33	210
Number of Stories.	177	33	210
1 story, ...	5	5	10
1 story and attic, . . .	31	8	39
2 stories, ...	25	7	32
2 stories and attic, . . .	114	12	126
3 stories, ...	1	–	1
3 stories and attic, . . .	1	1	2
Materials.	177	33	210
Wood, ...	176	32	208
Stone, ...	1	–	1
Wood and stone, . . .	–	1	1
Bradford.	905	38	943
Number of Stories.	905	38	943
1 story, ...	8	1	9
1 story and attic, . . .	286	11	297
Basement, 1 story, and attic,	1	–	1
2 stories, ...	234	12	246
2 stories and attic, . . .	342	13	355
Basement and 2 stories, . .	2	–	2
Basement, 2 stories, and attic,	4	–	4
3 stories, ...	23	–	23
3 stories and attic, . . .	3	–	3
4 stories, ...	2	1	3
Materials.	905	38	943
Wood, ...	889	37	926
Brick, ...	16	1	17
Danvers, ...	1,333	61	1,394
Number of Stories.	1,333	61	1,394
1 story, ...	5	1	6
1 story and attic, . . .	596	24	620
Basement, 1 story, and attic,	32	2	34
2 stories, ...	61	3	64
2 stories and attic, . . .	608	28	636
Basement and 2 stories, . .	4	–	4

DWELLING HOUSES: NUMBER OF STORIES AND MATERIALS — Continued.

COUNTIES, CITIES, TOWNS, NUMBER OF STORIES TO DWELLING HOUSES, AND MATERIALS OF WHICH CONSTRUCTED.	Number of Occupied Dwelling Houses	Number of Unoccupied Dwelling Houses	Total Number of Dwelling Houses
ESSEX — Con.			
Danvers — Con.			
Number of Stories — Con.			
Basement, 2 stories, and attic,	3	–	3
3 stories,	21	2	23
3 stories and attic,	3	–	3
Basement, 3 stories, and attic,	–	1	1
Materials.	1,333	61	1,394
Wood,	1,308	90	1,398
Brick,	14	–	14
Stone,	2	–	2
Cement,	2	–	2
Wood and brick,	7	1	8
Essex,	414	63	477
Number of Stories.	414	63	477
1 story,	9	5	14
1 story and attic,	125	34	159
Basement and 1 story,	1	–	1
Basement, 1 story, and attic,	10	1	11
2 stories,	32	7	39
2 stories and attic,	212	13	225
Basement and 2 stories,	2	–	2
Basement, 2 stories, and attic,	14	3	17
3 stories,	9	–	9
Materials.	414	63	477
Wood,	412	63	475
Brick,	2	–	2
Georgetown,	476	18	494
Number of Stories.	476	18	494
1 story,	3	2	5
1 story and attic,	143	5	148
Basement, 1 story, and attic,	7	–	7
2 stories,	34	3	37
2 stories and attic,	276	8	284
Basement and 2 stories,	1	–	1
Basement, 2 stories, and attic,	5	–	5
3 stories,	5	–	5
3 stories and attic,	2	–	2
Materials.	476	18	494
Wood,	473	18	491
Brick,	2	–	2
Wood and brick,	1	–	1
GLOUCESTER,	3,758	447	4,205
Number of Stories.	3,758	447	4,205
1 story,	58	13	71
1 story and attic,	1,350	138	1,488
Basement and 1 story,	6	1	7
Basement, 1 story, and attic,	205	61	266
2 stories,	586	79	665
2 stories and attic,	1,243	103	1,346
Basement and 2 stories,	51	13	64
Basement, 2 stories, and attic,	112	15	127
ESSEX — Con.			
GLOUCESTER — Con.			
Number of Stories — Con.			
3 stories,	84	13	97
3 stories and attic,	39	5	44
Basement and 3 stories,	7	2	9
Basement, 3 stories, and attic,	5	1	6
4 stories,	–	1	1
Basement and 4 stories,	–	1	1
6 stories,	–	1	1
Not given,	12	–	12
Materials.	3,758	447	4,205
Wood,	3,712	442	4,154
Brick,	29	–	29
Stone,	2	1	3
Wood and stone,	2	4	6
Brick and stone,	1	–	1
Not given,	12	–	12
GLOUCESTER, WARD 1,	492	95	587
Number of Stories.	492	95	587
1 story,	4	1	5
1 story and attic,	246	37	283
Basement, 1 story, and attic,	32	–	32
2 stories,	10	12	22
2 stories and attic,	170	36	206
Basement and 2 stories,	2	1	3
Basement, 2 stories, and attic,	9	–	9
3 stories,	2	4	6
3 stories and attic,	10	2	12
Basement and 3 stories,	2	–	2
Basement, 3 stories, and attic,	–	1	1
4 stories,	–	1	1
Not given,	5	–	5
Materials.	492	95	587
Wood,	485	92	577
Brick,	1	–	1
Wood and stone,	1	3	4
Not given,	5	–	5
GLOUCESTER, WARD 2,	533	33	566
Number of Stories.	533	33	566
1 story,	2	2	4
1 story and attic,	164	6	170
Basement and 1 story,	5	1	6
Basement, 1 story, and attic,	40	1	41
2 stories,	96	4	100
2 stories and attic,	149	4	153
Basement and 2 stories,	23	10	33
Basement, 2 stories, and attic,	21	2	23
3 stories,	19	1	20
3 stories and attic,	10	2	12
Basement and 3 stories,	2	–	2
Basement, 3 stories, and attic,	1	–	1
Not given,	1	–	1

DWELLING HOUSES: NUMBER OF STORIES AND MATERIALS — Continued.

Counties, Cities, Towns, Number of Stories to Dwelling Houses, and Materials of which Constructed.	Number of Occupied Dwelling Houses	Number of Unoccupied Dwelling Houses	Total Number of Dwelling Houses
ESSEX — Con.			
GLOUCESTER. WARD 2 - Con.			
Materials.	533	33	566
Wood,	532	33	565
Not given,	1	–	1
GLOUCESTER. WARD 3,	490	9	499
Number of Stories.	490	9	499
1 story,	7	–	7
1 story and attic,	109	5	114
Basement, 1 story, and attic,	36	–	36
2 stories,	59	–	59
2 stories and attic,	218	4	222
Basement and 2 stories,	6	–	6
Basement, 2 stories, and attic,	22	–	22
3 stories,	24	–	24
3 stories and attic,	6	–	6
Basement and 3 stories,	1	–	1
Basement, 3 stories, and attic,	1	–	1
Not given,	1	–	1
Materials.	490	9	499
Wood,	484	9	493
Brick,	4	–	4
Stone,	1	–	1
Not given,	1	–	1
GLOUCESTER. WARD 4,	335	5	340
Number of Stories.	335	5	340
1 story,	8	–	8
1 story and attic,	44	1	45
Basement, 1 story, and attic,	7	–	7
2 stories,	63	3	66
2 stories and attic,	158	1	159
Basement and 2 stories,	4	–	4
Basement, 2 stories, and attic,	15	–	15
3 stories,	27	–	27
3 stories and attic,	6	–	6
Basement and 3 stories,	1	–	1
Not given,	2	–	2
Materials.	335	5	340
Wood,	310	5	315
Brick,	22	–	22
Brick and stone,	1	–	1
Not given,	2	–	2
GLOUCESTER. WARD 5,	691	19	710
Number of Stories.	691	19	710
1 story,	–	1	1
1 story and attic,	198	5	203
Basement, 1 story, and attic,	52	2	54
2 stories,	26	1	27
2 stories and attic,	361	8	369
Basement and 2 stories,	1	–	1
Basement, 2 stories, and attic,	38	–	38
3 stories,	3	1	4
3 stories and attic,	5	1	6
ESSEX — Con.			
GLOUCESTER. WARD 5 - Con.			
Number of Stories — Con.			
Basement and 3 stories,	1	–	1
Basement, 3 stories, and attic,	3	–	3
Not given,	3	–	3
Materials.	691	19	710
Wood,	687	19	706
Brick,	1	–	1
Not given,	3	–	3
GLOUCESTER. WARD 6,	534	120	654
Number of Stories.	534	120	654
1 story,	20	7	27
1 story and attic,	272	2	274
Basement, 1 story, and attic,	9	57	66
2 stories,	198	49	247
2 stories and attic,	30	3	33
Basement and 2 stories,	3	–	3
3 stories,	2	2	4
Materials.	534	120	654
Wood,	533	120	653
Wood and stone,	1	–	1
GLOUCESTER. WARD 7,	415	6	421
Number of Stories.	415	6	421
1 story,	12	–	12
1 story and attic,	174	2	176
Basement and 1 story,	1	–	1
Basement, 1 story, and attic,	16	–	16
2 stories,	126	2	128
2 stories and attic,	64	2	66
Basement and 2 stories,	12	–	12
Basement, 2 stories, and attic,	4	–	4
3 stories,	4	–	4
3 stories and attic,	2	–	2
Materials.	415	6	421
Wood,	415	6	421
GLOUCESTER. WARD 8,	268	160	428
Number of Stories.	268	160	428
1 story,	5	2	7
1 story and attic,	143	80	223
Basement, 1 story, and attic,	13	1	14
2 stories,	8	8	16
2 stories and attic,	93	45	138
Basement and 2 stories,	–	2	2
Basement, 2 stories, and attic,	3	13	16
3 stories,	3	5	8
Basement and 3 stories,	–	2	2
Basement and 4 stories,	–	1	1
6 stories,	–	1	1
Materials.	268	160	428
Wood,	266	158	424
Brick,	1	–	1

DWELLING HOUSES: NUMBER OF STORIES AND MATERIALS — Continued.

COUNTIES, CITIES, TOWNS, NUMBER OF STORIES TO DWELLING HOUSES, AND MATERIALS OF WHICH CONSTRUCTED.	Number of Occupied Dwelling Houses	Number of Unoccupied Dwelling Houses	Total Number of Dwelling Houses
ESSEX — Con.			
GLOUCESTER. WARDS—Con.			
Materials — Con.			
Stone,	1	1	2
Wood and stone,		1	1
Groveland.	505	9	514
Number of Stories.	505	9	514
1 story,	-	-	-
1 story and attic,	159	4	163
Basement, 1 story, and attic,	5	-	5
2 stories,	64	-	64
2 stories and attic,	267	5	272
3 stories,	2	-	2
Materials.	505	9	514
Wood,	505	9	514
Hamilton.	295	307	602
Number of Stories.	295	307	602
1 story,	19	38	57
1 story and attic,	134	232	366
Basement and 1 story,	-	1	1
Basement, 1 story, and attic,	1	1	2
2 stories,	20	20	40
2 stories and attic,	115	14	129
Basement, 2 stories, and attic,	1	1	2
3 stories,	4	-	4
3 stories and attic,	1	-	1
Materials.	295	307	602
Wood,	293	307	600
Wood and brick,	1	-	1
Wood and stone,	1	-	1
HAVERHILL.	4,814	235	5,049
Number of Stories.	4,814	235	5,049
1 story,	61	4	65
1 story and attic,	805	49	854
Basement and 1 story,	8	1	9
Basement, 1 story, and attic,	40	-	40
2 stories,	801	44	845
2 stories and attic,	2,302	97	2,399
Basement and 2 stories,	41	1	42
Basement, 2 stories, and attic,	34	4	38
3 stories,	550	15	565
3 stories and attic,	26	-	26
Basement and 3 stories,	41	3	44
Basement, 3 stories, and attic,	5	-	5
4 stories,	35	-	35
4 stories and attic,	1	-	1
Basement and 4 stories,	1	-	1
Basement and 5 stories,	1	-	1
Not given,	2	17	19
Materials.	4,814	235	5,049
Wood,	4,640	212	4,822
Brick,	150	3	153
Stone,	-	1	1

COUNTIES, CITIES, TOWNS, NUMBER OF STORIES TO DWELLING HOUSES, AND MATERIALS OF WHICH CONSTRUCTED.	Number of Occupied Dwelling Houses	Number of Unoccupied Dwelling Houses	Total Number of Dwelling Houses
ESSEX — Con.			
HAVERHILL. — Con.			
Materials — Con.			
Wood and brick,	43	2	45
Brick and stone,	9	-	9
Not given,	2	17	19
HAVERHILL. WARD 1,	389	32	421
Number of Stories.	389	32	421
1 story,	24	1	25
1 story and attic,	26	6	32
Basement and 1 story,	3	-	3
2 stories,	191	4	195
2 stories and attic,	54	3	57
Basement and 2 stories,	12	-	12
3 stories,	74	1	75
4 stories,	4	-	4
Not given,	1	17	18
Materials.	389	32	421
Wood,	349	14	363
Brick,	18	-	18
Wood and brick,	20	1	21
Brick and stone,	1	-	1
Not given,	1	17	18
HAVERHILL. WARD 2,	476	25	501
Number of Stories.	476	25	501
1 story and attic,	27	1	28
Basement, 1 story, and attic,	1	-	1
2 stories,	28	2	30
2 stories and attic,	286	16	302
Basement and 2 stories,	3	-	3
Basement, 2 stories, and attic,	16	-	16
3 stories,	84	3	87
Basement and 3 stories,	23	3	26
Basement, 3 stories, and attic,	2	-	2
4 stories,	4	-	4
Basement and 4 stories,	1	-	1
Basement and 5 stories,	1	-	1
Materials.	476	25	501
Wood,	416	24	440
Brick,	56	1	57
Wood and brick,	4	-	4
HAVERHILL. WARD 3,	508	14	522
Number of Stories.	508	14	522
1 story,	5	-	5
1 story and attic,	67	4	71
Basement, 1 story, and attic,	3	-	3
2 stories,	44	2	46
2 stories and attic,	294	8	302
Basement, 2 stories, and attic,	20	-	20
3 stories,	38	-	38
3 stories and attic,	6	-	6
4 stories,	15	-	15
4 stories and attic,	1	-	1

DWELLING HOUSES: NUMBER OF STORIES AND MATERIALS — Continued.

COUNTIES, CITIES, TOWNS, NUMBER OF STORIES TO DWELLING HOUSES, AND MATERIALS OF WHICH CONSTRUCTED.	Number of Occupied Dwelling Houses	Number of Unoccupied Dwelling Houses	Total Number of Dwelling Houses
ESSEX — Con.			
HAVERHILL. WARD 3 — Con.			
Materials.	508	14	522
Wood, ...	491	13	504
Brick, ...	17	1	18
HAVERHILL. WARD 4, .	812	46	858
Number of Stories.	812	46	858
1 story, ...	1	1	2
1 story and attic, . .	215	7	222
Basement, 1 story, and attic,	5	–	5
2 stories, ...	145	9	154
2 stories and attic, . .	392	26	418
Basement and 2 stories, . .	1	–	1
Basement, 2 stories, and attic,	21	3	24
3 stories, ...	27	–	27
Basement and 3 stories, . .	2	–	2
Basement, 3 stories, and attic,	3	–	3
Materials.	812	46	858
Wood, ...	797	44	841
Brick, ...	12	1	13
Stone, ...	–	1	1
Wood and brick, . . .	3	–	3
HAVERHILL. WARD 5, .	1,519	67	1,586
Number of Stories.	1,519	67	1,586
1 story, ...	26	2	28
1 story and attic, . .	302	23	325
Basement and 1 story, . .	4	–	4
Basement, 1 story, and attic,	15	–	15
2 stories, ...	271	12	283
2 stories and attic, . .	619	23	642
Basement and 2 stories, . .	23	1	24
Basement, 2 stories, and attic,	23	1	24
3 stories, ...	193	5	198
3 stories and attic, . .	18	–	18
Basement and 3 stories, . .	16	–	16
4 stories, ...	8	–	8
Not given, ...	1	–	1
Materials.	1,519	67	1,586
Wood, ...	1,467	67	1,534
Brick, ...	40	–	40
Wood and brick, . . .	11	–	11
Not given, ...	1	–	1
HAVERHILL. WARD 6, .	1,110	51	1,161
Number of Stories.	1,110	51	1,161
1 story, ...	5	–	5
1 story and attic, . .	168	8	176
Basement and 1 story, . .	1	1	2
Basement, 1 story, and attic,	10	–	10
2 stories, ...	122	15	137
2 stories and attic, . .	657	21	678
Basement and 2 stories, . .	2	–	2
Basement, 2 stories, and attic,	5	–	5
3 stories, ...	134	6	140
ESSEX — Con.			
HAVERHILL. WARD 6 — Con.			
Number of Stories — Con.			
3 stories and attic, . . .	2	–	2
4 stories, ...	4	–	4
Materials.	1,110	51	1,161
Wood, ...	1,090	50	1,140
Brick, ...	7	–	7
Wood and brick, . . .	5	1	6
Brick and stone, . . .	8	–	8
Ipswich.	926	82	1,008
Number of Stories.	926	82	1,008
1 story, ...	17	7	24
1 story and attic, . . .	217	30	247
Basement, 1 story, and attic,	10	–	10
2 stories, ...	41	2	43
2 stories and attic, . . .	572	41	613
Basement and 2 stories, . .	2	–	2
Basement, 2 stories, and attic,	19	–	19
3 stories, ...	38	2	40
3 stories and attic, . . .	3	–	3
Basement and 3 stories, . .	6	–	6
Basement, 3 stories, and attic,	1	–	1
Materials.	926	82	1,008
Wood, ...	916	82	998
Brick, ...	9	–	9
Wood and brick, . . .	1	–	1
LAWRENCE. . . .	6,735	120	6,855
Number of Stories.	6,735	120	6,855
1 story, ...	131	4	135
1 story and attic, . . .	2,014	39	2,053
Basement and 1 story, . .	1	–	1
Basement, 1 story, and attic,	27	–	27
2 stories, ...	1,316	21	1,337
2 stories and attic, . . .	2,255	49	2,304
Basement and 2 stories, . .	22	–	22
Basement, 2 stories, and attic,	18	–	18
3 stories, ...	819	4	823
3 stories and attic, . . .	40	2	42
Basement and 3 stories, . .	12	–	12
Basement, 3 stories, and attic,	1	–	1
4 stories, ...	74	1	75
4 stories and attic, . . .	1	–	1
5 stories, ...	3	–	3
Not given, ...	1	–	1
Materials.	6,735	120	6,855
Wood, ...	6,294	111	6,402
Brick, ...	395	4	399
Stone, ...	4	–	4
Wood and brick, . . .	15	1	16
Wood and stone, . . .	45	2	47
Brick and stone, . . .	3	1	4

DWELLING HOUSES: NUMBER OF STORIES AND MATERIALS — Continued.

COUNTIES, CITIES, TOWNS, NUMBER OF STORIES TO DWELLING HOUSES, AND MATERIALS OF WHICH CONSTRUCTED.	Number of Occupied Dwelling Houses	Number of Unoccupied Dwelling Houses	Total Number of Dwelling Houses	COUNTIES, CITIES, TOWNS, NUMBER OF STORIES TO DWELLING HOUSES, AND MATERIALS OF WHICH CONSTRUCTED.	Number of Occupied Dwelling Houses	Number of Unoccupied Dwelling Houses	Total Number of Dwelling Houses
ESSEX — Con.				ESSEX — Con.			
LAWRENCE — Con.				LAWRENCE. WARD 3 — Con.			
Materials — Con.				*Number of Stories* — Con.			
Brick and cement, . . .	8	1	9	Basement and 3 stories, . .	2	–	2
Wood, brick, and stone, .	3	–	3	4 stories, ...	10	–	10
Not given, ...	1	–	1	4 stories and attic, . . .	1	–	1
LAWRENCE. WARD 1, .	1,170	16	1,186	*Materials.*	383	6	389
Number of Stories.	1,170	16	1,186	Wood, ...	326	6	332
1 story, ...	30	–	30	Brick, ...	63	–	63
1 story and attic, . . .	537	4	541	Stone, ...	1	–	1
Basement, 1 story, and attic, .	10	–	10	Wood and stone, . . .	1	–	1
2 stories, ...	168	6	174	Brick and stone, . . .	1	–	1
2 stories and attic, . . .	338	6	344	Brick and cement, . . .	1	–	1
Basement, 2 stories, and attic,	5	–	5				
3 stories, ...	73	–	73	LAWRENCE. WARD 4, .	1,071	18	1,089
3 stories and attic, . . .	2	–	2	*Number of Stories.*	1,071	18	1,089
Basement and 3 stories, .	5	–	5	1 story, ...	24	1	25
4 stories, ...	2	–	2	1 story and attic, . . .	227	13	240
				Basement, 1 story, and attic,	3	–	3
Materials.	1,170	16	1,186	2 stories, ...	166	1	167
Wood, ...	1,022	12	1,034	2 stories and attic, . . .	385	2	387
Brick, ...	100	1	101	Basement, 2 stories, and attic,	2	–	2
Wood and brick, . . .	5	1	6	3 stories, ...	212	–	212
Wood and stone, . . .	39	2	41	3 stories and attic, . . .	15	–	15
Brick and stone, . . .	1	–	1	Basement and 3 stories, . .	2	–	2
Wood, brick, and stone, .	3	–	3	4 stories, ...	35	1	36
LAWRENCE. WARD 2, .	841	21	862	*Materials.*	1,071	18	1,089
Number of Stories.	841	21	862	Wood, ...	968	17	985
1 story, ...	15	–	15	Brick, ...	89	–	89
1 story and attic, . . .	245	5	250	Stone, ...	1	–	1
2 stories, ...	99	3	102	Wood and brick, . . .	6	–	6
2 stories and attic, . . .	300	10	310	Brick and cement, . . .	7	1	8
Basement, 2 stories, and attic,	1	–	1				
3 stories, ...	149	1	150	LAWRENCE. WARD 5, .	1,471	22	1,493
3 stories and attic, . . .	8	2	10	*Number of Stories.*	1,471	22	1,493
Basement and 3 stories, . .	2	–	2	1 story, ...	15	1	16
4 stories, ...	19	–	19	1 story and attic, . . .	376	6	382
5 stories, ...	3	–	3	Basement and 1 story, . .	1	–	1
				Basement, 1 story, and attic,	5	–	5
Materials.	841	21	862	2 stories, ...	470	8	478
Wood, ...	745	18	763	2 stories and attic, . . .	442	6	448
Brick, ...	93	3	96	Basement and 2 stories, .	18	–	18
Wood and brick, . . .	2	–	2	Basement, 2 stories, and attic,	2	–	2
Brick and stone, . . .	1	–	1	3 stories, ...	129	1	130
				3 stories and attic, . . .	4	–	4
LAWRENCE. WARD 3, .	383	6	389	Basement and 3 stories, . .	1	–	1
Number of Stories.	383	6	389	Basement, 3 stories, and attic,	1	–	1
1 story, ...	29	–	29	4 stories, ...	7	–	7
1 story and attic, . . .	203	4	207				
Basement, 1 story, and attic,	9	–	9	*Materials.*	1,471	22	1,493
2 stories, ...	197	2	199	Wood, ...	1,457	21	1,478
2 stories and attic, . . .	363	–	363	Brick, ...	9	–	9
Basement and 2 stories, . .	3	–	3	Stone, ...	2	–	2
Basement, 2 stories, and attic,	8	–	8	Wood and brick, . . .	1	–	1
3 stories, ...	161	–	161	Wood and stone, . . .	2	–	2
3 stories and attic, . . .	7	–	7	Brick and stone, . . .	1	1	1

DWELLING HOUSES: NUMBER OF STORIES AND MATERIALS — Continued.

COUNTIES, CITIES, TOWNS, NUMBER OF STORIES TO DWELLING HOUSES, AND MATERIALS OF WHICH CONSTRUCTED.	Number of Occupied Dwelling Houses	Number of Unoccupied Dwelling Houses	Total Number of Dwelling Houses	COUNTIES, CITIES, TOWNS, NUMBER OF STORIES TO DWELLING HOUSES, AND MATERIALS OF WHICH CONSTRUCTED.	Number of Occupied Dwelling Houses	Number of Unoccupied Dwelling Houses	Total Number of Dwelling Houses
ESSEX — Con.				ESSEX — Con.			
LAWRENCE. WARD 6, . .	1,189	37	1,226	LYNN. WARD 2, . . .	804	56	860
Number of Stories.	1,189	37	1,226	*Number of Stories.*	804	56	860
1 story, ...	18	2	20	1 story, ...	8	2	10
1 story and attic, . . .	426	7	433	1 story and attic, . . .	478	24	502
2 stories, ...	216	1	217	Basement, 1 story, and attic,	55	7	62
2 stories and attic, . . .	427	25	452	2 stories, ...	51	12	63
Basement and 2 stories, .	1	–	1	2 stories and attic, . . .	169	10	179
3 stories, ...	95	2	97	Basement and 2 stories, .	16	–	16
3 stories and attic, . . .	4	–	4	Basement, 2 stories, and attic,	7	–	7
4 stories, ...	1	–	1	3 stories, ...	18	1	19
Not given, ...	1	–	1	3 stories and attic, . .	2	–	2
Materials.	1,189	37	1,226	*Materials.*	804	56	860
Wood, ...	1,173	37	1,210	Wood, ...	799	56	855
Brick, ...	11	–	11	Brick, ...	3	–	3
Wood and brick, . . .	1	–	1	Wood and stone, . . .	2	–	2
Wood and stone, . . .	3	–	3				
Not given, ...	1	–	1	LYNN. WARD 3, . . .	2,564	111	2,675
				Number of Stories.	2,564	111	2,675
LYNN.	10,045	470	10,515	1 story, ...	7	2	9
Number of Stories.	10,045	470	10,515	1 story and attic, . . .	1,146	55	1,201
1 story, ...	133	16	149	Basement and 1 story, . .	1	–	1
1 story and attic, . . .	3,883	204	4,087	Basement, 1 story, and attic,	141	8	149
Basement and 1 story, . .	29	5	31	2 stories, ...	91	5	96
Basement, 1 story, and attic,	402	26	428	2 stories and attic, . . .	985	31	1,016
2 stories, ...	858	46	904	Basement and 2 stories, .	29	1	30
2 stories and attic, . . .	3,508	100	3,608	Basement, 2 stories, and attic,	61	6	67
Basement and 2 stories, .	151	7	158	3 stories, ...	73	3	76
Basement, 2 stories, and attic,	223	12	235	3 stories and attic, . . .	10	–	10
3 stories, ...	702	48	750	Basement and 3 stories, .	15	–	15
3 stories and attic, . . .	43	2	45	Basement, 3 stories, and attic,	2	–	2
Basement and 3 stories, .	77	2	79	4 stories, ...	2	–	2
Basement, 3 stories, and attic,	5	–	5	Not given, ...	1	–	1
4 stories, ...	26	2	28	*Materials.*	2,564	111	2,675
5 stories, ...	1	–	1	Wood, ...	2,532	106	2,638
Basement and 5 stories, .	2	–	2	Brick, ...	10	–	10
Not given, ...	5	–	5	Stone, ...	1	–	1
Materials.	10,045	470	10,515	Wood and brick, . . .	19	3	22
Wood, ...	9,892	459	10,351	Brick and stone, . . .	1	2	3
Brick, ...	84	4	88	Not given, ...	1	–	1
Stone, ...	2	–	2				
Wood and brick, . . .	50	4	54	LYNN. WARD 4, . . .	1,574	52	1,626
Wood and stone, . . .	7	–	7	*Number of Stories.*	1,574	52	1,626
Brick and stone, . . .	5	3	8	1 story, ...	15	4	19
Not given, ...	5	–	5	1 story and attic, . . .	237	12	249
				Basement and 1 story, . .	16	4	20
LYNN. WARD 1, . . .	332	32	364	Basement, 1 story, and attic,	16	1	17
Number of Stories.	332	32	364	2 stories, ...	207	6	213
1 story, ...	7	–	7	2 stories and attic, . . .	457	3	460
1 story and attic, . . .	239	29	268	Basement and 2 stories, .	65	4	69
Basement, 1 story, and attic,	9	–	9	Basement, 2 stories, and attic,	61	3	64
2 stories, ...	27	1	28	3 stories, ...	354	11	365
2 stories and attic, . . .	49	2	51	3 stories and attic, . . .	4	–	4
Basement and 2 stories, .	1	–	1	Basement and 3 stories, .	41	2	43
Materials.	332	32	364	4 stories, ...	16	2	18
Wood, ...	332	32	364				

DWELLING HOUSES: NUMBER OF STORIES AND MATERIALS — Continued.

COUNTIES, CITIES, TOWNS, NUMBER OF STORIES TO DWELLING HOUSES, AND MATERIALS OF WHICH CONSTRUCTED.	Number of Occupied Dwelling Houses	Number of Unoccupied Dwelling Houses	Total Number of Dwelling Houses
ESSEX — Con.			
LYNN. WARD 4 — Con.			
Number of Stories — Con.			
5 stories,	1	–	1
Basement and 5 stories,	2	–	2
Not given,	2	–	2
Materials.	1,574	52	1,626
Wood,	1,524	48	1,572
Brick,	26	2	28
Stone,	1	–	1
Wood and brick,	15	1	16
Wood and stone,	2	–	2
Brick and stone,	4	1	5
Not given,	2	–	2
LYNN. WARD 5,	1,914	82	1,996
Number of Stories.	1,914	82	1,996
1 story,	43	1	44
1 story and attic,	471	16	487
Basement and 1 story,	7	–	7
Basement, 1 story, and attic,	44	5	49
2 stories,	235	6	241
2 stories and attic,	855	25	880
Basement and 2 stories,	25	–	25
Basement, 2 stories, and attic,	63	3	66
3 stories,	146	26	172
3 stories and attic,	8	–	8
Basement and 3 stories,	8	–	8
Basement, 3 stories, and attic,	1	–	1
4 stories,	7	–	7
Not given,	1	–	1
Materials.	1,914	82	1,996
Wood,	1,876	81	1,957
Brick,	23	1	24
Wood and brick,	14	–	14
Not given,	1	–	1
LYNN. WARD 6,	2,358	91	2,449
Number of Stories.	2,358	91	2,449
1 story,	49	5	54
1 story and attic,	1,021	41	1,062
Basement and 1 story,	1	1	2
Basement, 1 story, and attic,	55	1	56
2 stories,	242	14	256
2 stories and attic,	821	21	842
Basement and 2 stories,	9	1	10
Basement, 2 stories, and attic,	19	–	19
3 stories,	108	7	115
3 stories and attic,	17	–	17
Basement, 3 stories,	12	–	12
Basement, 3 stories, and attic,	2	–	2
4 stories,	1	–	1
Not given,	1	–	1
Materials.	2,358	91	2,449
Wood,	2,332	90	2,422
ESSEX — Con.			
LYNN. WARD 6 — Con.			
Materials — Con.			
Brick,	21	1	22
Wood and brick,	1	–	1
Wood and stone,	3	–	3
Not given,	1	–	1
LYNN. WARD 7,	529	16	545
Number of Stories.	529	16	545
1 story,	4	2	6
1 story and attic,	271	27	298
Basement and 1 story,	1	–	1
Basement, 1 story, and attic,	52	4	56
2 stories,	5	2	7
2 stories and attic,	142	8	150
Basement and 2 stories,	6	1	7
Basement, 2 stories, and attic,	12	–	12
3 stories,	3	–	3
3 stories and attic,	2	2	4
Basement and 3 stories,	1	–	1
Materials.	489	46	545
Wood,	487	46	543
Brick,	1	–	1
Wood and brick,	1	–	1
Lynnfield.	143	12	155
Number of Stories.	143	12	155
1 story,	3	1	4
1 story and attic,	52	5	57
Basement and 1 story,	1	–	1
Basement, 1 story, and attic,	6	1	7
2 stories,	29	–	29
2 stories and attic,	92	5	97
Materials.	143	12	155
Wood,	141	12	153
Brick,	1	–	1
Stone,	1	–	1
Manchester.	410	121	531
Number of Stories.	410	121	531
1 story,	14	5	19
1 story and attic,	107	17	124
Basement, 1 story, and attic,	5	2	11
2 stories,	30	19	49
2 stories and attic,	202	53	255
Basement and 2 stories,	6	3	9
Basement, 2 stories, and attic,	31	15	46
3 stories,	7	5	12
Basement and 3 stories,	2	1	3
Basement and 4 stories,	–	1	1
Not given,	2	–	2
Materials.	410	121	531
Wood,	393	112	505
Brick,	6	–	6

DWELLING HOUSES: NUMBER OF STORIES AND MATERIALS — Continued.

COUNTIES, CITIES, TOWNS, NUMBER OF STORIES TO DWELLING HOUSES, AND MATERIALS OF WHICH CONSTRUCTED.	Number of Occupied Dwelling Houses	Number of Unoccupied Dwelling Houses	Total Number of Dwelling Houses
ESSEX — Con.			
Manchester — Con.			
Materials — Con.			
Stone, ...	3	2	5
Wood and brick, . . .	1	–	1
Wood and stone, . . .	5	5	10
Brick and stone, . . .	–	2	2
Not given, ...	2	–	2
Marblehead. . . .	1,433	238	1,671
Number of Stories.	1,433	238	1,671
1 story, ...	50	43	93
1 story and attic, . .	443	38	481
Basement and 1 story, . .	3	–	3
Basement, 1 story, and attic,	27	4	31
2 stories, ...	156	80	236
2 stories and attic, . .	641	57	698
Basement and 2 stories, . .	4	–	4
Basement, 2 stories, and attic,	38	5	43
3 stories, ...	57	10	67
3 stories and attic, . .	5	1	6
Basement and 3 stories, . .	6	–	6
Basement, 3 stories, and attic,	2	–	2
4 stories, ...	1	–	1
Materials.	1,433	238	1,671
Wood, ...	1,426	237	1,663
Brick, ...	6	1	7
Brick and stone, . . .	1	–	1
Merrimac. . . .	495	40	535
Number of Stories.	495	40	535
1 story, ...	9	2	11
1 story and attic, . .	33	6	39
Basement and 1 story, . .	3	–	3
Basement, 1 story, and attic,	3	–	3
2 stories, ...	214	14	228
2 stories and attic, . .	211	15	226
Basement and 2 stories, . .	7	1	8
Basement, 2 stories, and attic,	10	2	12
3 stories, ...	3	–	3
Basement, 3 stories, and attic,	1	–	1
Not given, ...	1	–	1
Materials.	495	40	535
Wood, ...	489	40	529
Brick, ...	5	–	5
Not given, ...	1	–	1
Methuen. . . .	1,139	38	1,177
Number of Stories.	1,139	38	1,177
1 story, ...	21	2	23
1 story and attic, . .	430	15	445
Basement and 1 story, . .	3	–	3
Basement, 1 story, and attic,	13	1	14
2 stories, ...	152	4	156
2 stories and attic, . .	463	13	566
Basement and 2 stories, . .	3	–	3
ESSEX — Con.			
Methuen — Con.			
Number of Stories — Con.			
Basement, 2 stories, and attic,	2	2	4
3 stories, ...	19	1	20
3 stories and attic, . .	2	–	2
Not given, ...	1	–	1
Materials.	1,139	38	1,177
Wood, ...	1,133	35	1,168
Brick, ...	1	1	2
Stone, ...	–	1	1
Wood and brick, . . .	2	–	2
Wood and cement, . . .	–	1	1
Brick and stone, . . .	1	–	1
Stone and cement, . . .	1	–	1
Not given, ...	1	–	1
Middleton. . . .	199	22	221
Number of Stories.	199	22	221
1 story, ...	3	1	4
1 story and attic, . .	92	12	104
Basement, 1 story, and attic,	2	–	2
2 stories, ...	2	1	3
2 stories and attic, . .	98	8	106
Basement, 2 stories, and attic,	1	–	1
3 stories, ...	1	–	1
Materials.	199	22	221
Wood, ...	196	22	218
Wood and brick, . . .	3	–	3
Nahant. . . .	182	215	397
Number of Stories.	182	215	397
1 story, ...	8	6	14
1 story and attic, . .	77	86	163
Basement and 1 story, . .	1	–	1
Basement, 1 story, and attic, .	25	7	32
2 stories, ...	13	12	25
2 stories and attic, . .	18	24	42
Basement and 2 stories, . .	15	12	27
Basement, 2 stories, and attic,	9	21	30
3 stories, ...	10	11	21
Basement and 3 stories, . .	3	32	35
Basement, 3 stories, and attic,	–	3	3
4 stories, ...	1	1	2
Not given, ...	2	–	2
Materials.	182	215	397
Wood, ...	178	206	384
Wood and brick, . . .	1	–	1
Wood and stone, . . .	–	9	9
Wood, brick, and stone, . .	1	–	1
Not given, ...	2	–	2
Newbury. . . .	316	73	389
Number of Stories.	316	73	389
1 story, ...	3	6	9
1 story and attic, . .	100	48	148

DWELLING HOUSES: NUMBER OF STORIES AND MATERIALS — Continued.

COUNTIES, CITIES, TOWNS, NUMBER OF STORIES TO DWELLING HOUSES, AND MATERIALS OF WHICH CONSTRUCTED.	Number of Occupied Dwelling Houses	Number of Unoccupied Dwelling Houses	Total Number of Dwelling Houses
ESSEX — Con.			
Newbury — Con.			
Number of Stories — Con.			
Basement and 1-story, . .	1	–	1
Basement, 1-story, and attic,	1	–	1
2-stories, ...	18	10	28
2-stories and attic, . .	185	9	194
3-stories, ...	7	–	7
4-stories, ...	1	–	1
Materials			
Wood, ...	316	73	389
Brick, ...	312	73	385
Wood and brick, . . .	2	–	2
Wood and stone, . . .	1	–	1
NEWBURYPORT. . .	1	–	1
Number of Stories.	2,977	188	3,165
1 story, ...	2,977	188	3,165
1 story and attic, . . .	24	16	40
Basement, 1-story, and attic,	182	15	197
2-stories, ...	5	–	5
2-stories and attic, . . .	330	29	359
Basement and 2-stories, .	2,015	103	2,118
Basement, 2-stories, and attic,	6	–	6
3-stories, ...	53	7	60
3-stories and attic, . . .	207	9	216
Basement and 3-stories, .	134	8	142
Basement, 3-stories, and attic,	1	–	1
4-stories, ...	15	–	15
5-stories, ...	4	–	4
	1	1	2
Materials.	2,977	188	3,165
Wood, ...	2,837	175	3,012
Brick, ...	123	12	135
Stone, ...	1	–	1
Wood and brick, . . .	12	1	13
Brick and stone, . . .	1	–	1
Brick and cement, . . .	3	–	3
NEWBURYPORT. WARD 1. . .	513	49	562
Number of Stories.	513	49	562
1 story, ...	11	16	27
1 story and attic, . . .	42	4	46
Basement, 1-story, and attic,	1	–	1
2-stories, ...	74	11	85
2-stories and attic, . . .	346	18	364
Basement and 2-stories, .	1	–	1
Basement, 2-stories, and attic,	10	–	10
3-stories, ...	17	–	17
3-stories and attic, . .	11	–	11
Materials.	513	49	562
Wood, ...	513	49	562
NEWBURYPORT. WARD 2, . .	406	26	432
Number of Stories.	406	26	432
1 story, ...	1	–	1
ESSEX — Con.			
NEWBURYPORT. WARD 2 — Con.			
Number of Stories — Con.			
1 story and attic, . . .	20	1	21
2-stories, ...	27	2	29
2-stories and attic, . . .	298	19	317
Basement, 2-stories, and attic,	6	1	7
3-stories, ...	54	3	57
Materials.	406	26	432
Wood, ...	398	24	422
Brick, ...	8	2	10
NEWBURYPORT. WARD 3, . .	561	29	590
Number of Stories.	561	29	590
1 story and attic, . . .	22	1	23
2-stories, ...	5	–	5
2-stories and attic, . . .	421	21	442
Basement, 2-stories, and attic,	16	2	18
3-stories, ...	14	–	14
3-stories and attic, . . .	73	5	78
Basement, 3-stories, and attic,	10	–	10
Materials.	561	29	590
Wood, ...	494	27	521
Brick, ...	64	2	66
Wood and brick, . . .	1	–	1
Brick and cement, . . .	2	–	2
NEWBURYPORT. WARD 4, . .	479	14	493
Number of Stories.	479	14	493
1 story, ...	11	–	11
1 story and attic, . . .	9	–	9
2-stories, ...	101	9	110
2-stories and attic, . . .	239	2	241
Basement and 2-stories, . .	5	–	5
3-stories, ...	82	2	84
3-stories and attic, . . .	27	–	27
4-stories, ...	4	–	4
5-stories, ...	1	1	2
Materials.	479	14	493
Wood, ...	441	12	453
Brick, ...	27	1	28
Wood and brick, . . .	9	1	10
Brick and stone, . . .	1	–	1
Brick and cement, . . .	1	–	1
NEWBURYPORT. WARD 5, . .	446	28	474
Number of Stories.	446	28	474
1 story and attic, . . .	29	1	30
2-stories, ...	122	7	129
2-stories and attic, . . .	246	14	260
Basement, 2-stories, and attic,	9	3	12
3-stories, ...	33	3	36
3-stories and attic, . . .	3	–	3
Basement, 3-stories, and attic,	4	–	4

DWELLING HOUSES: NUMBER OF STORIES AND MATERIALS — Continued.

COUNTIES, CITIES, TOWNS, NUMBER OF STORIES TO DWELLING HOUSES, AND MATERIALS OF WHICH CONSTRUCTED.	Number of Occupied Dwelling Houses	Number of Unoccupied Dwelling Houses	Total Number of Dwelling Houses
ESSEX — Con.			
NEWBURYPORT. WARD 5 — Con.			
Materials.	446	28	474
Wood,	428	24	452
Brick,	17	4	21
Wood and brick,	1	–	1
NEWBURYPORT. WARD 6,	572	42	614
Number of Stories.	572	42	614
1 story,	1	–	1
1 story and attic,	60	8	68
Basement, 1 story, and attic,	4	–	4
2 stories,	1	–	1
2 stories and attic,	465	29	494
Basement, 2 stories, and attic,	12	1	13
3 stories,	7	1	8
3 stories and attic,	20	3	23
Basement and 3 stories,	1	–	1
Basement, 3 stories, and attic,	1	–	1
Materials.	572	42	614
Wood,	563	39	602
Brick,	7	3	10
Stone,	1	–	1
Wood and brick,	1	–	1
North Andover.	742	53	795
Number of Stories.	742	53	795
1 story,	5	2	7
1 story and attic,	248	19	267
Basement and 1 story,	1	–	1
Basement, 1 story, and attic,	36	1	37
2 stories,	9	2	11
2 stories and attic,	424	24	448
Basement and 2 stories,	5	–	5
Basement, 2 stories, and attic,	1	–	1
3 stories,	10	5	15
3 stories and attic,	3	–	3
Materials.	742	53	795
Wood,	727	53	780
Brick,	12	–	12
Stone,	1	–	1
Wood and brick,	2	–	2
Peabody.	1,763	49	1,812
Number of Stories.	1,763	49	1,812
1 story,	6	1	7
1 story and attic,	581	16	597
Basement and 1 story,	1	–	1
Basement, 1 story, and attic,	22	–	22
2 stories,	227	8	235
2 stories and attic,	833	21	857
Basement and 2 stories,	11	–	11
Basement, 2 stories, and attic,	34	–	34
3 stories,	32	–	32
3 stories and attic,	10	–	10
ESSEX — Con.			
Peabody — Con.			
Number of Stories — Con.			
Basement and 3 stories,	1	–	1
Basement, 3 stories, and attic,	1	–	1
Not given,	4	–	4
Materials.	1,763	49	1,812
Wood,	1,734	48	1,782
Brick,	23	1	24
Wood and brick,	2	–	2
Not given,	4	–	4
Rockport.	896	114	1,010
Number of Stories.	896	114	1,010
1 story,	12	2	14
1 story and attic,	427	52	479
Basement and 1 story,	4	–	4
Basement, 1 story, and attic,	73	2	75
2 stories,	83	34	117
2 stories and attic,	245	16	261
Basement and 2 stories,	3	2	5
Basement, 2 stories, and attic,	33	3	36
3 stories,	9	2	11
3 stories and attic,	5	–	5
Basement and 3 stories,	1	–	1
Basement, 3 stories, and attic,	–	1	1
4 stories,	1	–	1
Materials.	896	114	1,010
Wood,	887	109	996
Brick,	1	–	1
Stone,	7	1	8
Wood and stone,	–	3	3
Brick and stone,	1	–	1
Wood, brick, and stone,	–	1	1
Rowley.	292	19	311
Number of Stories.	292	19	311
1 story,	8	2	10
1 story and attic,	106	10	116
Basement, 1 story, and attic,	4	–	4
2 stories,	10	1	11
2 stories and attic,	158	6	164
Basement, 2 stories, and attic,	4	–	4
3 stories,	2	–	2
Materials.	292	19	311
Wood,	292	19	311
SALEM.	4,863	265	5,128
Number of Stories.	4,863	265	5,128
1 story,	17	1	18
1 story and attic,	620	104	724
Basement and 1 story,	2	–	2
Basement, 1 story, and attic,	66	1	67
2 stories,	519	23	542
2 stories and attic,	2,729	91	2,820
Basement and 2 stories,	24	1	25

DWELLING HOUSES: NUMBER OF STORIES AND MATERIALS — Continued.

COUNTIES, CITIES, TOWNS, NUMBER OF STORIES TO DWELLING HOUSES, AND MATERIALS OF WHICH CONSTRUCTED.	Number of Oc- cupied Dwell- ing Houses	Number of Unoc- cupied Dwell- ing Houses	Total Num- ber of Dwell- ing Houses
ESSEX — Con.			
SALEM — Con.			
Number of Stories — Con.			
Basement, 2 stories, and attic,	155	2	157
3 stories, ...	636	34	670
3 stories and attic, . . .	52	3	55
Basement and 3 stories, . .	38	3	41
Basement, 3 stories, and attic,	10	–	10
4 stories, ...	19	2	21
4 stories and attic, . . .	1	–	1
Basement and 4 stories, . .	4	–	4
5 stories, ...	1	–	1
Materials.	4,863	265	5,128
Wood, ...	4,660	259	4,919
Brick, ...	151	5	156
Stone, ...	1	–	1
Wood and brick, . . .	40	1	41
Wood and stone, . . .	6	–	6
Brick and stone, . . .	3	–	3
Brick and cement, . . .	1	–	1
Stone and cement, . . .	1	–	1
SALEM. WARD 1, . . .	622	130	752
Number of Stories.	622	130	752
1 story, ...	5	–	5
1 story and attic, . . .	51	79	130
Basement, 1 story, and attic,	1	–	1
2 stories, ...	53	2	55
2 stories and attic, . . .	376	31	407
Basement, 2 stories, and attic,	5	–	5
3 stories, ...	117	17	134
3 stories and attic, . . .	10	1	11
Basement and 3 stories, .	2	–	2
4 stories, ...	1	–	1
5 stories, ...	1	–	1
Materials.	622	130	752
Wood, ...	577	130	707
Brick, ...	37	–	37
Wood and brick, . . .	8	–	8
SALEM. WARD 2, . . .	963	35	998
Number of Stories.	963	35	998
1 story, ...	1	1	2
1 story and attic, . . .	28	1	29
Basement and 1 story, . .	1	–	1
Basement, 1 story, and attic,	5	–	5
2 stories, ...	180	3	183
2 stories and attic, . . .	539	14	553
Basement and 2 stories, . .	12	1	13
Basement, 2 stories, and attic,	33	1	34
3 stories, ...	148	5	153
3 stories and attic, . . .	9	2	11
Basement and 3 stories, . .	7	1	8
Materials.	963	35	998
Wood, ...	909	32	941

COUNTIES, CITIES, TOWNS, NUMBER OF STORIES TO DWELLING HOUSES, AND MATERIALS OF WHICH CONSTRUCTED.	Number of Oc- cupied Dwell- ing Houses	Number of Unoc- cupied Dwell- ing Houses	Total Num- ber of Dwell- ing Houses
ESSEX — Con.			
SALEM. WARD 2 — Con.			
Materials — Con.			
Brick, ...	38	3	41
Wood and brick, . . .	12	–	12
Brick and stone, . . .	2	–	2
Brick and cement, . . .	1	–	1
Stone and cement, . . .	1	–	1
SALEM. WARD 3, . . .	701	27	728
Number of Stories.	701	27	728
1 story and attic, . . .	63	4	67
Basement, 1 story, and attic,	16	1	17
2 stories, ...	99	6	105
2 stories and attic, . . .	336	7	343
Basement and 2 stories, . .	6	–	6
Basement, 2 stories, and attic,	44	1	45
3 stories, ...	110	7	117
3 stories and attic, . . .	15	–	15
Basement and 3 stories, . .	6	–	6
Basement, 3 stories, and attic,	4	–	4
4 stories, ...	1	1	2
4 stories and attic, . . .	1	–	1
Materials.	701	27	728
Wood, ...	656	25	681
Brick, ...	40	1	41
Wood and brick, . . .	5	1	6
SALEM. WARD 4, . . .	795	18	813
Number of Stories.	795	18	813
1 story, ...	4	–	4
1 story and attic, . . .	132	3	135
Basement and 1 story, . .	1	–	1
Basement, 1 story, and attic,	28	–	28
2 stories, ...	39	3	42
2 stories and attic, . . .	436	8	444
Basement and 2 stories, . .	3	–	3
Basement, 2 stories, and attic,	28	–	28
3 stories, ...	98	3	101
3 stories and attic, . . .	12	–	12
Basement and 3 stories, . .	3	–	3
Basement, 3 stories, and attic,	4	–	4
4 stories, ...	4	1	5
Basement and 4 stories, . .	3	–	3
Materials.	795	18	813
Wood, ...	756	17	773
Brick, ...	25	1	26
Wood and brick, . . .	11	–	11
Wood and stone, . . .	3	–	3
SALEM. WARD 5, . . .	1,048	26	1,074
Number of Stories.	1,048	26	1,074
1 story and attic, . . .	100	5	105
Basement, 1 story, and attic,	11	–	11
2 stories, ...	80	2	82
2 stories and attic, . . .	626	17	643

DWELLING HOUSES: NUMBER OF STORIES AND MATERIALS — Continued.

COUNTIES, CITIES, TOWNS, NUMBER OF STORIES TO DWELLING HOUSES, AND MATERIALS OF WHICH CONSTRUCTED.	Number of Occupied Dwelling Houses	Number of Unoccupied Dwelling Houses	Total Number of Dwelling Houses
ESSEX — Con.			
SALEM. WARD 5 — Con.			
Number of Stories — Con.			
Basement and 2 stories, . .	2	–	2
Basement, 2 stories, and attic,	37	–	37
3 stories, ...	150	–	150
3 stories and attic, . . .	6	–	6
Basement and 3 stories, . .	20	2	22
Basement, 3 stories, and attic,	2	–	2
4 stories, ...	13	–	13
Basement and 4 stories, . .	1	–	1
Materials.	1,048	26	1,074
Wood, ...	1,035	26	1,061
Brick, ...	11	–	11
Wood and brick, . . .	2	–	2
SALEM. WARD 6, . . .	734	29	763
Number of Stories.	734	29	763
1 story, ...	7	–	7
1 story and attic, . . .	246	12	258
Basement, 1 story, and attic,	5	–	5
2 stories, ...	38	1	39
2 stories and attic, . . .	416	14	430
Basement and 2 stories, . .	1	–	1
Basement, 2 stories, and attic,	8	–	8
3 stories, ...	13	2	15
Materials.	734	29	763
Wood, ...	727	29	756
Stone, ...	1	–	1
Wood and brick, . . .	2	–	2
Wood and stone, . . .	3	–	3
Brick and stone, . . .	1	–	1
Salisbury.	317	18	335
Number of Stories.	317	18	335
1 story, ...	9	–	9
1 story and attic, . . .	117	10	127
2 stories, ...	22	2	24
2 stories and attic, . . .	167	6	173
3 stories, ...	2	–	2
Materials.	317	18	335
Wood, ...	317	16	333
Brick, ...	–	2	2
Saugus.	965	114	1,079
Number of Stories.	965	114	1,079
1 story, ...	12	1	13
1 story and attic, . . .	411	52	463
Basement and 1 story, . .	1	–	1
Basement, 1 story, and attic,	24	–	24
2 stories, ...	44	7	51
2 stories and attic, . . .	453	51	504
Basement and 2 stories, . .	1	1	2
Basement, 2 stories, and attic,	7	1	8
3 stories, ...	10	1	11
Not given, ...	2	–	2

COUNTIES, CITIES, TOWNS, NUMBER OF STORIES TO DWELLING HOUSES, AND MATERIALS OF WHICH CONSTRUCTED.	Number of Occupied Dwelling Houses	Number of Unoccupied Dwelling Houses	Total Number of Dwelling Houses
ESSEX — Con.			
Saugus — Con.			
Materials.	965	114	1,079
Wood, ...	955	114	1,069
Brick, ...	3	–	3
Stone, ...	1	–	1
Wood and brick, . . .	2	–	2
Wood and stone, . . .	2	–	2
Not given, ...	2	–	2
Swampscott, ...	703	65	768
Number of Stories.	703	65	768
1 story, ...	38	3	41
1 story and attic, . . .	348	22	370
2 stories, ...	305	33	338
2 stories and attic, . . .	4	2	6
3 stories, ...	8	5	13
Materials.	703	65	768
Wood, ...	700	63	763
Brick, ...	3	–	3
Stone, ...	–	1	1
Wood and stone, . . .	–	1	1
Topsfield.	215	15	230
Number of Stories.	215	15	230
1 story, ...	5	–	5
1 story and attic, . . .	75	3	78
Basement and 1 story, . .	1	–	1
Basement, 1 story, and attic,	1	1	2
2 stories, ...	8	2	10
2 stories and attic, . . .	119	8	127
Basement and 2 stories, . .	1	–	1
Basement, 2 stories, and attic,	1	–	1
3 stories, ...	1	–	1
3 stories and attic, . . .	2	–	2
Basement, 3 stories, and attic,	–	1	1
Not given, ...	1	–	1
Materials.	215	15	230
Wood, ...	213	15	228
Wood and brick, . . .	1	–	1
Not given, ...	1	–	1
Wenham.	206	20	226
Number of Stories.	206	20	226
1 story, ...	1	–	1
1 story and attic, . . .	104	8	112
Basement, 1 story, and attic,	1	–	1
2 stories and attic, . . .	99	12	111
3 stories and attic, . . .	1	–	1
Materials.	206	20	226
Wood, ...	202	20	222
Wood and brick, . . .	3	–	3
Wood and stone, . . .	1	–	1

DWELLING HOUSES: NUMBER OF STORIES AND MATERIALS — Continued.

Counties, Cities, Towns, Number of Stories to Dwelling Houses, and Materials of which Constructed.	Number of Occupied Dwelling Houses	Number of Unoccupied Dwelling Houses	Total Number of Dwelling Houses	Counties, Cities, Towns, Number of Stories to Dwelling Houses, and Materials of which Constructed.	Number of Occupied Dwelling Houses	Number of Unoccupied Dwelling Houses	Total Number of Dwelling Houses
ESSEX — Con.				**FRANKLIN — Con.**			
West Newbury,	394	25	419	**Buckland** — Con.			
Number of Stories.	394	25	419	*Number of Stories — Con.*			
1 story,	10	1	11	2 stories,	122	5	127
1 story and attic,	116	10	126	2 stories and attic,	4	–	4
Basement, 1 story, and attic,	2	1	3	Basement and 2 stories,	2	–	2
2 stories,	27	–	27	Basement, 2 stories, and attic,	1	–	1
2 stories and attic,	229	13	242				
Basement and 2 stories,	1	–	1	*Materials.*	352	23	355
Basement, 2 stories, and attic,	4	–	4	Wood,	329	23	352
3 stories,	2	–	2	Brick,	3	–	3
3 stories and attic,	1	–	1				
Basement and 3 stories,	1	–	1	**Charlemont.**	247	16	263
5 stories and attic,	1	–	1	*Number of Stories.*	247	16	263
				1 story,	9	1	10
Materials.	394	25	419	1 story and attic,	137	12	149
Wood,	387	24	411	Basement and 1 story,	1	–	1
Brick,	4	1	5	Basement, 1 story, and attic,	1	–	1
Stone,	2	–	2	2 stories,	3	2	5
Wood, brick, and stone,	1	–	1	2 stories and attic,	93	1	94
				Basement and 2 stories,	1	–	1
FRANKLIN.				Basement, 2 stories, and attic,	1	–	1
Ashfield.	225	30	255	3 stories and attic,	1	–	1
Number of Stories.	225	30	255				
1 story,	10	–	10	*Materials.*	247	16	263
1 story and attic,	–	2	2	Wood,	239	16	255
2 stories,	139	13	152	Brick,	8	–	8
2 stories and attic,	72	14	86				
Basement and 2 stories,	2	–	2	**Colrain.**	324	15	339
Basement, 2 stories, and attic,	1	–	1	*Number of Stories.*	324	15	339
3 stories,	–	1	1	1 story,	15	4	19
3 stories and attic,	1	–	1	1 story and attic,	172	6	178
				Basement, 1 story, and attic,	5	–	5
Materials.	225	30	255	2 stories,	69	5	74
Wood,	222	29	251	2 stories and attic,	36	–	36
Wood and brick,	3	–	3	Basement and 2 stories,	5	–	5
Wood and stone,	–	1	1	Basement, 2 stories, and attic,	1	–	1
				3 stories,	1	–	1
Bernardston.	196	19	215	3 stories and attic,	19	–	19
Number of Stories.	196	19	215	5 stories and attic,	1	–	1
1 story,	23	4	27				
1 story and attic,	110	11	121	*Materials.*	324	15	339
Basement, 1 story, and attic,	3	1	4	Wood,	287	15	302
2 stories,	17	2	19	Brick,	33	–	33
2 stories and attic,	40	1	41	Wood and brick,	3	–	3
Basement, 2 stories, and attic,	1	–	1	Wood and cement,	1	–	1
3 stories,	2	–	2				
				Conway.	286	22	308
Materials.	196	19	215	*Number of Stories.*	286	22	308
Wood,	195	19	214	1 story,	22	4	26
Brick,	1	–	1	1 story and attic,	137	13	150
				Basement and 1 story,	1	–	1
Buckland.	352	23	355	Basement, 1 story, and attic,	1	–	1
Number of Stories.	352	23	355	2 stories,	32	2	34
1 story,	13	5	18	2 stories and attic,	91	3	94
1 story and attic,	189	13	202	Basement and 2 stories,	1	–	1
Basement and 1 story,	1	–	1	3 stories,	1	–	1

DWELLING HOUSES: NUMBER OF STORIES AND MATERIALS — Continued.

COUNTIES, CITIES, TOWNS, NUMBER OF STORIES TO DWELLING HOUSES, AND MATERIALS OF WHICH CONSTRUCTED.	Number of Occupied Dwelling Houses	Number of Unoccupied Dwelling Houses	Total Number of Dwelling Houses
FRANKLIN — Con.			
Conway — Con.			
Materials.	286	22	308
Wood, .	282	21	303
Brick. .	4	1	5
Deerfield.	635	36	671
Number of Stories.	635	36	671
1-story,	21	–	21
1 story and attic,	31	3	34
2-stories,	358	20	378
2 stories and attic,	205	11	216
Basement and 2 stories, .	3	–	3
Basement, 2-stories, and attic,	7	2	9
3 stories,	10	–	10
Materials.	635	36	671
Wood, .	621	36	657
Brick, .	4	–	4
Stone, .	1	–	1
Wood and brick,	9	–	9
Erving.	217	5	222
Number of Stories.	217	5	222
1 story,	14	1	15
1 story and attic,	118	1	119
Basement, 1 story, and attic,	2	–	2
2-stories,	72	3	75
2 stories and attic,	8	–	8
Basement and 2 stories, .	2	–	2
Basement, 2 stories, and attic,	1	–	1
Materials.	217	5	222
Wood, .	216	5	221
Wood and brick,	1	–	1
Gill.	178	6	184
Number of Stories.	178	6	184
1 story,	11	1	12
1 story and attic,	107	3	110
2-stories,	27	1	28
2 stories and attic,	27	1	28
Basement, 2-stories, and attic,	1	–	1
3 stories,	4	–	4
3 stories and attic,	1	–	1
Materials.	178	6	184
Wood, .	168	6	174
Wood and brick,	1	–	1
Wood and stone,	1	–	1
Brick and stone,	8	–	8
Greenfield.	1,223	54	1,277
Number of Stories.	1,223	54	1,277
1 story,	29	3	32
1 story and attic,	434	19	453
Basement, 1 story, and attic, .	1	–	1
2 stories,	257	15	272
2 stories and attic, .	454	16	470
FRANKLIN — Con.			
Greenfield — Con.			
Number of Stories — Con.			
Basement and 2 stories, .	10	1	11
3-stories,	33	–	33
4-stories,	3	–	3
Not given,	2	–	2
Materials.	1,223	54	1,277
Wood, .	1,182	53	1,235
Brick, .	33	1	34
Stone, .	1	–	1
Wood and brick,	3	–	3
Wood and stone,	1	–	1
Brick and stone,	1	–	1
Not given, .	2	–	2
Hawley.	103	10	113
Number of Stories.	103	10	113
1 story,	3	1	4
1 story and attic,	85	7	92
2 stories,	8	2	10
2-stories and attic,	7	–	7
Materials.	103	10	113
Wood, .	101	10	111
Brick, .	1	–	1
Wood and brick,	1	–	1
Heath,	115	6	121
Number of Stories.	115	6	121
1 story,	1	–	1
1 story and attic,	79	5	84
Basement, 1 story, and attic,	1	–	1
2 stories,	3	–	3
2 stories and attic, .	31	1	32
Materials.	115	6	121
Wood, .	112	6	118
Wood and brick,	3	–	3
Leverett.	186	8	194
Number of Stories.	186	8	194
1 story,	30	3	33
1 story and attic,	96	4	100
Basement, 1 story, and attic,	1	–	1
2 stories,	29	1	30
2 stories and attic,	30	–	30
Materials.	186	8	194
Wood, .	186	8	194
Leyden.	83	13	96
Number of Stories.	83	13	96
1 story,	2	2	4
1 story and attic,	4	1	5
2 stories,	58	10	68
2 stories and attic, .	18	–	18
Basement and 2 stories, .	1	–	1

DWELLING HOUSES: NUMBER OF STORIES AND MATERIALS — Continued.

COUNTIES, CITIES, TOWNS, NUMBER OF STORIES TO DWELLING HOUSES, AND MATERIALS OF WHICH CONSTRUCTED.	Number of Occupied Dwelling Houses	Number of Unoccupied Dwelling Houses	Total Number of Dwelling Houses
FRANKLIN — Con.			
Leyden — Con.			
Materials.			
Wood,	83	13	96
Monroe,	55	1	56
Number of Stories.	55	1	56
1 story,	6	–	6
1 story and attic,	39	1	40
2 stories,	4	–	4
2 stories and attic,	5	–	5
Basement, 2 stories, and attic,	1	–	1
Materials.			
Wood,	55	1	56
Montague,	954	234	1,188
Number of Stories.	954	234	1,188
1 story,	12	48	60
1 story and attic,	280	71	351
Basement and 1 story,	3	15	18
Basement, 1 story, and attic,	12	11	23
2 stories,	150	54	204
2 stories and attic,	361	20	381
Basement and 2 stories,	3	11	14
Basement, 2 stories, and attic,	6	–	6
3 stories,	119	3	122
3 stories and attic,	6	1	7
Basement and 3 stories,	1	–	1
4 stories,	1	–	1
Materials.	954	234	1,188
Wood,	762	230	992
Brick,	186	4	190
Wood and brick,	6	–	6
New Salem,	219	11	230
Number of Stories.	219	11	230
1 story,	32	–	32
1 story and attic,	107	8	115
2 stories,	78	3	81
2 stories and attic,	1	–	1
3 stories,	1	–	1
Materials.	219	11	230
Wood,	211	11	222
Brick,	7	–	7
Wood and brick,	1	–	1
Northfield,	389	30	419
Number of Stories.	389	30	419
1 story,	36	5	41
1 story and attic,	189	14	203
Basement and 1 story,	1	–	1
2 stories,	130	–	138
2 stories and attic,	22	–	22
Basement and 2 stories,	2	–	2
3 stories,	4	2	6

COUNTIES, CITIES, TOWNS, NUMBER OF STORIES TO DWELLING HOUSES, AND MATERIALS OF WHICH CONSTRUCTED.	Number of Occupied Dwelling Houses	Number of Unoccupied Dwelling Houses	Total Number of Dwelling Houses
FRANKLIN — Con.			
Northfield — Con.			
Number of Stories — Con.			
3 stories and attic,	2	–	2
4 stories,	1	1	2
Basement and 4 stories,	2	–	2
Materials.	389	30	419
Wood,	372	29	401
Brick,	15	–	15
Wood and brick,	2	1	3
Orange,	1,053	41	1,094
Number of Stories.	1,053	41	1,094
1 story,	33	1	34
1 story and attic,	342	9	30
Basement and 1 story,	1	–	1
Basement, 1 story, and attic,	13	–	13
2 stories,	127	12	139
2 stories and attic,	427	16	443
Basement and 2 stories,	19	–	19
Basement, 2 stories, and attic,	28	2	30
3 stories,	17	1	18
3 stories and attic,	3	–	3
Basement and 3 stories,	1	–	1
4 stories,	1	–	1
Basement and 4 stories,	1	–	1
Materials.	1,053	41	1,094
Wood,	1,037	40	1,077
Brick,	9	1	10
Wood and brick,	6	–	6
Brick and stone,	1	–	1
Rowe,	108	27	135
Number of Stories.	108	27	135
1 story,	18	2	20
1 story and attic,	56	14	70
Basement, 1 story, and attic,	1	–	1
2 stories,	10	4	14
2 stories and attic,	23	6	29
Basement and 3 stories,	–	1	1
Materials.	108	27	135
Wood,	108	27	135
Shelburne,	322	6	328
Number of Stories.	322	6	328
1 story,	1	–	1
1 story and attic,	107	1	108
Basement, 1 story, and attic,	7	–	7
2 stories,	25	1	26
2 stories and attic,	171	4	175
Basement, 2 stories, and attic,	5	–	5
3 stories,	5	–	5
3 stories and attic,	1	–	1
Materials.	322	6	328
Wood,	307	6	313
Brick,	12	–	12

DWELLING HOUSES: NUMBER OF STORIES AND MATERIALS — Continued.

COUNTIES, CITIES, TOWNS, NUMBER OF STORIES TO DWELLING HOUSES, AND MATERIALS OF WHICH CONSTRUCTED.	Number of Occupied Dwelling Houses	Number of Unoccupied Dwelling Houses	Total Number of Dwelling Houses	COUNTIES, CITIES, TOWNS, NUMBER OF STORIES TO DWELLING HOUSES, AND MATERIALS OF WHICH CONSTRUCTED.	Number of Occupied Dwelling Houses	Number of Unoccupied Dwelling Houses	Total Number of Dwelling Houses
FRANKLIN — Con.				**HAMPDEN.**			
Shelburne — Con.				**Agawam,**	489	41	530
Materials — Con.				*Number of Stories.*	489	41	530
Stone, ...	2	–	2	1 story, ...	14	11	25
Wood and brick, . .	1	–	1	1 story and attic, . . .	268	22	290
				Basement and 1 story, . .	1	–	1
Shutesbury.	121	9	130	Basement, 1 story, and attic,	2	–	2
Number of Stories.	121	9	130	2 stories, ...	48	4	52
1 story, ...	102	7	109	2 stories and attic, . . .	149	4	153
1 story and attic, . . .	2	–	2	Basement and 2 stories, . .	2	–	2
2 stories, ...	17	1	18	Basement, 2 stories, and attic,	4	–	4
3 stories, ...	–	1	1	Basement and 3 stories, . .	1	–	1
Materials.	121	9	130	*Materials.*	489	41	530
Wood, ...	121	9	130	Wood, ...	486	41	527
				Brick, ...	2	–	2
Sunderland.	152	6	158	Wood and brick, . . .	1	–	1
Number of Stories.	152	6	158				
1 story, ...	19	2	21	**Blandford.**	197	36	233
1 story and attic, . . .	49	1	50	*Number of Stories.*	197	36	233
Basement and 1 story, . .	1	–	1	1 story and attic, . . .	85	17	102
2 stories, ...	81	3	84	Basement, 1 story, and attic, .	4	–	4
2 stories and attic, . . .	2	–	2	2 stories and attic, . . .	105	18	123
				Basement, 2 stories, and attic,	2	–	2
Materials.	152	6	158	3 stories, ...	1	–	1
Wood, ...	147	6	153	3 stories and attic, . . .	–	1	1
Brick, ...	5	–	5	*Materials.*	197	36	233
				Wood, ...	197	36	233
Warwick.	150	21	171				
Number of Stories.	150	21	171	**Brimfield,**	217	14	231
1 story, ...	13	4	17	*Number of Stories.*	217	14	231
1 story and attic, . . .	83	12	95	1 story, ...	3	1	4
Basement, 1 story, and attic, .	3	1	4	1 story and attic, . . .	89	2	91
2 stories, ...	41	1	42	Basement and 1 story, . .	1	–	1
2 stories and attic, . . .	10	3	13	2 stories, ...	4	–	4
				2 stories and attic, . . .	119	10	129
Materials.	150	21	171	Basement and 2 stories, . .	1	–	1
Wood, ...	150	21	171	3 stories, ...	–	1	1
Wendell.	122	25	147	*Materials.*	217	14	231
Number of Stories.	122	25	147	Wood, ...	209	13	222
1 story, ...	4	–	4	Brick, ...	7	1	8
1 story and attic, . . .	98	24	122	Wood and brick, . . .	1	–	1
2 stories, ...	1	–	1	**Chester.**	314	30	344
2 stories and attic, . . .	19	1	20	*Number of Stories.*	314	30	344
Materials.	122	25	147	1 story, ...	3	–	3
Wood, ...	122	25	147	1 story and attic, . . .	122	15	137
				Basement, 1 story, and attic,	4	1	5
Whately.	182	10	192	2 stories, ...	29	1	30
Number of Stories.	182	10	192	2 stories and attic, . . .	129	11	140
1 story, ...	2	1	3	Basement and 2 stories, . .	3	–	3
1 story and attic, . . .	89	7	96	Basement, 2 stories, and attic,	22	2	24
Basement, 1 story, and attic,	5	–	5	3 stories, ...	1	–	1
2 stories, ...	53	2	55	Basement and 3 stories, . .	1	–	1
2 stories and attic, . . .	33	–	33	*Materials.*	314	30	344
Materials.	182	10	192	Wood, ...	313	29	342
Wood, ...	181	10	191	Stone, ...	1	1	2
Brick, ...	1	–	1				

DWELLING HOUSES: NUMBER OF STORIES AND MATERIALS — Continued.

COUNTIES, CITIES, TOWNS, NUMBER OF STORIES TO DWELLING HOUSES, AND MATERIALS OF WHICH CONSTRUCTED.	Number of Occupied Dwelling Houses	Number of Unoccupied Dwelling Houses	Total Number of Dwelling Houses	COUNTIES, CITIES, TOWNS, NUMBER OF STORIES TO DWELLING HOUSES, AND MATERIALS OF WHICH CONSTRUCTED.	Number of Occupied Dwelling Houses	Number of Unoccupied Dwelling Houses	Total Number of Dwelling Houses
HAMPDEN — Con.				**HAMPDEN** — Con.			
CHICOPEE,	2,290	62	2,352	CHICOPEE. WARD 2 — Con.			
Number of Stories.	2,290	62	2,352	*Materials* — Con.			
1 story,	36	–	36	Stone,	1	–	1
1 story and attic,	388	12	400	Wood and brick,	4	–	4
Basement and 1 story,	2	–	2				
Basement, 1 story, and attic,	10	–	10	CHICOPEE. WARD 3,	294	1	295
2 stories,	849	16	865	*Number of Stories.*	294	1	295
2 stories and attic,	818	33	851	1 story,	5	–	5
Basement and 2 stories,	16	1	17	1 story and attic,	33	–	33
Basement, 2 stories, and attic,	21	–	21	2 stories,	15	–	15
3 stories,	70	–	70	2 stories and attic,	158	1	159
3 stories and attic,	65	–	65	3 stories,	22	–	22
Basement and 3 stories,	7	–	7	3 stories and attic,	53	–	53
4 stories,	7	–	7	4 stories,	7	–	7
Basement and 4 stories,	1	–	1	Basement and 4 stories,	1	–	1
Materials.	2,290	62	2,352	*Materials.*	294	1	295
Wood,	1,743	59	1,802	Wood,	139	–	139
Brick,	489	2	491	Brick,	126	–	126
Stone,	2	–	2	Wood and brick,	28	1	29
Wood and brick,	55	1	56	Brick and cement,	1	–	1
Brick and cement,	1	–	1				
				CHICOPEE. WARD 4,	339	7	346
CHICOPEE. WARD 1,	326	1	327	*Number of Stories.*	339	7	346
Number of Stories.	326	1	327	1 story,	1	–	1
1 story,	2	–	2	1 story and attic,	63	2	65
1 story and attic,	11	1	12	Basement, 1 story, and attic,	1	–	1
2 stories,	162	–	162	2 stories,	164	3	167
2 stories and attic,	112	–	112	2 stories and attic,	103	2	105
Basement and 2 stories,	3	–	3	3 stories,	6	–	6
Basement, 2 stories, and attic,	8	–	8	Basement and 3 stories,	1	–	1
3 stories,	18	–	18	*Materials.*	339	7	346
3 stories and attic,	9	–	9	Wood,	249	7	256
Basement and 3 stories,	1	–	1	Brick,	86	–	86
Materials.	326	1	327	Wood and brick,	4	–	4
Wood,	227	1	228				
Brick,	85	–	85	CHICOPEE. WARD 5,	396	5	401
Wood and brick,	14	–	14	*Number of Stories.*	396	5	401
				1 story,	1	–	1
CHICOPEE. WARD 2,	325	15	340	1 story and attic,	95	–	95
Number of Stories.	325	15	340	Basement, 1 story, and attic,	1	–	1
1 story,	7	–	7	2 stories,	212	4	216
1 story and attic,	53	1	54	2 stories and attic,	71	1	72
Basement and 1 story,	2	–	2	Basement and 2 stories,	2	–	2
Basement, 1 story, and attic,	8	–	8	3 stories,	11	–	11
2 stories,	79	5	84	3 stories and attic,	3	–	3
2 stories and attic,	150	8	158	*Materials.*	396	5	401
Basement and 2 stories,	9	1	10	Wood,	285	4	289
Basement, 2 stories, and attic,	8	–	8	Brick,	107	1	108
3 stories,	7	–	7	Wood and brick,	4	–	4
Basement and 3 stories,	2	–	2	CHICOPEE. WARD 6,	272	5	277
Materials.	325	15	340	*Number of Stories.*	272	5	277
Wood,	264	14	278	1 story,	4	–	4
Brick,	56	1	57	1 story and attic,	21	1	22

DWELLING HOUSES: NUMBER OF STORIES AND MATERIALS — Continued.

COUNTIES, CITIES, TOWNS, NUMBER OF STORIES TO DWELLING HOUSES, AND MATERIALS OF WHICH CONSTRUCTED.	Number of Occupied Dwelling Houses	Number of Unoccupied Dwelling Houses	Total Number of Dwelling Houses
HAMPDEN — Con.			
CHICOPEE. WARD 6 — Con.			
Number of Stories — Con.			
2 stories, ...	138	2	140
2 stories and attic, . . .	94	2	96
Basement and 2 stories, . .	2	–	2
Basement, 2 stories, and attic,	5	–	5
3 stories, ...	5	–	5
Basement and 3 Stories, . .	3	–	3
Materials.	272	5	277
Wood, ...	244	5	249
Brick, ...	27	–	27
Wood and brick, . . .	1	–	1
CHICOPEE. WARD 7, . .	338	28	366
Number of Stories.	338	28	366
1 story, ...	16	–	16
1 story and attic, . . .	112	7	119
2 stories, ...	79	2	81
2 stories and attic, . . .	130	19	149
3 stories, ...	1	–	1
Materials.	338	28	366
Wood, ...	335	28	363
Brick, ...	2	–	2
Stone, ...	1	–	1
East Longmeadow, . .	283	18	301
Number of Stories.	283	18	301
1 story and attic, . . .	55	3	58
Basement, 1 story, and attic,	2	–	2
2 stories, ...	123	13	136
2 stories and attic, . . .	100	2	102
Basement and 2 stories, . .	1	–	1
Basement, 2 stories, and attic,	2	–	2
Materials.	283	18	301
Wood, ...	278	18	296
Brick, ...	2	–	2
Wood and brick, . . .	2	–	2
Wood and stone, . . .	1	–	1
Granville, ...	250	23	273
Number of Stories.	250	23	273
1 story, ...	3	–	3
1 story and attic, . . .	110	9	119
Basement, 1 story, and attic, .	3	–	3
2 stories, ...	4	–	4
2 stories and attic, . . .	123	14	137
Basement, 2 stories, and attic,	7	–	7
Materials.	250	23	273
Wood, ...	249	21	270
Brick, ...	1	2	3
Hampden, ...	178	15	193
Number of Stories.	178	15	193
1 story, ...	1	–	1

COUNTIES, CITIES, TOWNS, NUMBER OF STORIES TO DWELLING HOUSES, AND MATERIALS OF WHICH CONSTRUCTED.	Number of Occupied Dwelling Houses	Number of Unoccupied Dwelling Houses	Total Number of Dwelling Houses
HAMPDEN — Con.			
Hampden — Con.			
Number of Stories — Con.			
1 story and attic, . . .	20	7	27
2 stories, ...	88	6	94
2 stories and attic, . . .	59	2	61
Basement and 2 stories, . .	7	–	–
Basement, 2 stories, and attic,	3	–	3
Materials.	178	15	193
Wood, ...	175	15	190
Stone, ...	1	–	1
Wood and brick, . . .	2	–	2
Holland, ...	51	8	59
Number of Stories.	51	8	59
1 story and attic, . . .	37	7	44
2 stories and attic, . . .	14	1	15
Materials.	51	8	59
Wood, ...	51	8	59
HOLYOKE, ...	3,703	187	3,890
Number of Stories.	3,703	187	3,890
1 story, ...	58	3	61
1 story and attic, . . .	294	12	306
Basement, 1 story, and attic,	10	1	11
2 stories, ...	735	45	780
2 stories and attic, . . .	1,259	84	1,343
Basement and 2 stories, . .	71	7	78
Basement, 2 stories, and attic,	77	7	84
3 stories, ...	548	17	565
3 stories and attic, . . .	157	9	166
Basement and 3 stories, . .	16	–	16
Basement, 3 stories, and attic,	4	–	4
4 stories, ...	423	2	425
4 stories and attic, . . .	22	–	22
Basement and 4 stories, . .	10	–	10
5 stories, ...	13	–	13
Basement and 5 stories, . .	1	–	1
Basement, 5 stories, and attic,	3	–	3
Not given, ...	2	–	2
Materials.	3,703	187	3,890
Wood, ...	2,156	151	2,307
Brick, ...	1,497	35	1,532
Stone, ...	6	–	6
Wood and brick, . . .	34	1	35
Wood and stone, . . .	3	–	3
Brick and stone, . . .	5	–	5
Not given, ...	2	–	2
HOLYOKE WARD 1, . .	433	2	435
Number of Stories.	433	2	435
1 story, ...	20	–	20
1 story and attic, . . .	52	–	52
Basement, 1 story, and attic,	1	–	1
2 stories, ...	103	1	104

DWELLING HOUSES: NUMBER OF STORIES AND MATERIALS — Continued.

COUNTIES, CITIES, TOWNS, NUMBER OF STORIES TO DWELLING HOUSES, AND MATERIALS OF WHICH CONSTRUCTED.	Number of Occupied Dwelling Houses	Number of Unoccupied Dwelling Houses	Total Number of Dwelling Houses
HAMPDEN — Con.			
HOLYOKE. WARD 1 — Con.			
Number of Stories — Con.			
2 stories and attic,	92	–	92
Basement and 2 stories,	3	–	3
3 stories,	64	1	65
3 stories and attic,	3	–	3
Basement and 3 stories,	1	–	1
4 stories,	91	–	91
4 stories and attic,	2	–	2
Basement and 4 stories,	1	–	1
Materials.	433	2	435
Wood,	180	–	180
Brick,	250	2	252
Stone,	1	–	1
Wood and brick,	2	–	2
HOLYOKE. WARD 2,	453	17	470
Number of Stories.	453	17	470
1 story,	5	1	6
1 story and attic,	2	–	2
2 stories,	46	1	47
2 stories and attic,	53	5	58
3 stories,	67	1	68
3 stories and attic,	104	9	113
Basement and 3 stories,	1	–	1
Basement, 3 stories, and attic,	3	–	3
4 stories,	144	–	144
4 stories and attic,	20	–	20
Basement and 4 stories,	1	–	1
5 stories,	3	–	3
Basement and 5 stories,	1	–	1
Basement, 5 stories, and attic,	3	–	3
Materials.	453	17	470
Wood,	202	15	217
Brick,	248	2	250
Brick and stone,	3	–	3
HOLYOKE. WARD 3,	633	51	684
Number of Stories.	633	51	684
1 story,	8	1	9
1 story and attic,	122	7	129
Basement, 1 story, and attic,	4	1	5
2 stories,	34	–	34
2 stories and attic,	377	33	410
Basement and 2 stories,	1	2	3
3 stories,	53	7	60
3 stories and attic,	9	–	9
Basement and 3 stories,	2	–	2
4 stories,	21	–	21
Basement and 4 stories,	2	–	2
Materials.	633	51	684
Wood,	539	51	590
Brick,	93	–	93
Wood and brick,	1	–	1

COUNTIES, CITIES, TOWNS, NUMBER OF STORIES TO DWELLING HOUSES, AND MATERIALS OF WHICH CONSTRUCTED.	Number of Occupied Dwelling Houses	Number of Unoccupied Dwelling Houses	Total Number of Dwelling Houses
HAMPDEN — Con.			
HOLYOKE. WARD 4,	455	12	467
Number of Stories.	455	12	467
1 story,	6	–	6
1 story and attic,	37	4	41
2 stories,	72	3	75
2 stories and attic,	148	4	152
Basement, 2 stories, and attic,	9	–	9
3 stories,	84	–	84
3 stories and attic,	39	–	39
Basement and 3 stories,	3	–	3
4 stories,	47	1	48
Basement and 4 stories,	4	–	4
5 stories,	6	–	6
Materials.	455	12	467
Wood,	234	11	245
Brick,	221	1	222
HOLYOKE. WARD 5,	462	24	486
Number of Stories.	462	24	486
1 story,	11	–	11
1 story and attic,	12	–	12
2 stories,	166	17	183
2 stories and attic,	154	5	159
Basement and 2 stories,	15	1	16
Basement, 2 stories, and attic,	5	1	6
3 stories,	70	–	70
3 stories and attic,	1	–	1
Basement and 3 stories,	4	–	4
Basement, 3 stories, and attic,	1	–	1
4 stories,	22	–	22
Not given,	1	–	1
Materials.	462	24	486
Wood,	266	8	274
Brick,	190	16	206
Stone,	1	–	1
Wood and brick,	2	–	2
Wood and stone,	2	–	2
Not given,	1	–	1
HOLYOKE. WARD 6,	440	9	449
Number of Stories.	440	9	449
1 story,	3	–	3
1 story and attic,	10	–	10
Basement, 1 story, and attic,	2	–	2
2 stories,	66	–	66
2 stories and attic,	31	–	31
Basement and 2 stories,	38	2	40
3 stories,	184	6	190
3 stories and attic,	1	–	1
Basement and 3 stories,	1	–	1
4 stories,	98	1	99
Basement and 4 stories,	2	–	2
5 stories,	4	–	4
Materials.	440	9	449
Wood,	47	–	47

DWELLING HOUSES: NUMBER OF STORIES AND MATERIALS — Continued.

COUNTIES, CITIES, TOWNS, NUMBER OF STORIES TO DWELLING HOUSES, AND MATERIALS OF WHICH CONSTRUCTED.	Number of Occupied Dwelling Houses	Number of Unoccupied Dwelling Houses	Total Number of Dwelling Houses
HAMPDEN — Con.			
HOLYOKE. WARD 6 — Con.			
Materials — Con.			
Brick,	388	9	397
Stone,	2	–	2
Wood and brick,	1	–	1
Brick and stone,	2	–	2
HOLYOKE. WARD 7,	827	72	899
Number of Stories.	827	72	899
1-story,	5	1	6
1 story and attic,	59	1	60
Basement, 1 story, and attic,	3	–	3
2-stories,	248	23	271
2-stories and attic,	404	37	441
Basement and 2 stories,	14	2	16
Basement, 2-stories, and attic,	63	6	69
3-stories,	26	2	28
Basement and 3 stories,	4	–	4
Not given,	1	–	1
Materials.	827	72	899
Wood,	688	66	754
Brick,	107	5	112
Stone,	2	–	2
Wood and brick,	28	1	29
Wood and stone,	1	–	1
Not given,	1	–	1
Longmeadow,	134	12	146
Number of Stories.	134	12	146
1 story,	11	1	12
1 story and attic,	35	2	37
Basement, 1 story, and attic,	2	–	2
2-stories,	75	7	82
2-stories and attic,	4	1	5
Basement and 2 stories,	2	1	3
Basement, 2-stories, and attic,	1	–	1
3-stories,	4	–	4
Materials.	134	12	146
Wood,	116	10	126
Brick,	12	1	13
Wood and brick,	5	1	6
Wood and stone,	1	–	1
Ludlow,	382	21	403
Number of Stories.	382	21	403
1-story,	63	6	69
1 story and attic,	16	1	17
Basement and 1 story,	1	–	1
2-stories,	189	12	201
2-stories and attic,	91	2	93
Basement and 2 stories,	3	–	3
Basement, 2 stories, and attic,	2	–	2
3-stories,	5	–	5
Basement and 3 stories,	2	–	2
HAMPDEN — Con.			
Ludlow — Con.			
Materials.	382	21	403
Wood,	377	21	398
Wood and brick,	5	–	5
Monson,	735	35	770
Number of Stories.	735	35	770
1-story,	52	–	52
1 story and attic,	339	26	365
Basement and 1 story,	4	–	4
Basement, 1 story, and attic,	16	1	17
2 stories,	212	8	220
2 stories and attic,	87	–	87
Basement and 2 stories,	8	–	8
Basement, 2 stories, and attic,	9	–	9
3 stories,	4	–	4
3 stories and attic,	2	–	2
Basement and 3 stories,	1	–	1
Basement and 4 stories,	1	–	1
Materials.	735	35	770
Wood,	729	35	764
Brick,	4	–	4
Stone,	1	–	1
Wood and brick,	1	–	1
Montgomery,	62	2	64
Number of Stories.	62	2	64
1 story,	25	–	25
1-story and attic,	9	–	9
Basement and 1-story,	1	–	1
2-stories,	26	2	28
2 stories and attic,	1	–	1
Materials.	62	2	64
Wood,	62	2	64
Palmer,	1,276	71	1,347
Number of Stories.	1,276	71	1,347
1-story,	10	1	11
1-story and attic,	304	25	329
Basement and 1 story,	5	1	6
Basement, 1 story, and attic,	48	2	50
2-stories,	183	13	196
2 stories and attic,	594	23	617
Basement and 2 stories,	16	–	16
Basement, 2 stories, and attic,	61	5	66
3 stories,	11	–	11
3 stories and attic,	43	1	44
Basement and 3 stories,	1	–	1
Materials.	1,276	71	1,347
Wood,	1,213	69	1,282
Brick,	29	–	29
Wood and brick,	26	2	28
Wood and stone,	8	–	8

DWELLING HOUSES: NUMBER OF STORIES AND MATERIALS — Continued.

COUNTIES, CITIES, TOWNS, NUMBER OF STORIES TO DWELLING HOUSES, AND MATERIALS OF WHICH CONSTRUCTED.	Number of Occupied Dwelling Houses	Number of Unoccupied Dwelling Houses	Total Number of Dwelling Houses
HAMPDEN—Con.			
Russell, ...	170	18	188
Number of Stories.	170	18	188
1 story, ...	10	1	11
1 story and attic, . . .	69	9	78
Basement, 1 story, and attic,	2	–	2
2 stories, ...	73	7	80
2 stories and attic, . .	1	1	2
Basement and 2 stories, . .	11	–	11
Basement, 2 stories, and attic,	1	–	1
3 stories, ...	2	–	2
Basement and 3 stories, .	1	–	1
Materials.	170	18	188
Wood, ...	168	18	186
Wood and brick, . . .	2	–	2
Southwick.	224	22	246
Number of Stories.	224	22	246
1 story and attic, .	118	17	135
Basement, 1 story, and attic,	7	–	7
2 stories and attic, . .	96	5	101
Basement, 2 stories, and attic,	3	–	3
Materials.	224	22	246
Wood, ...	222	22	244
Brick, ...	1	–	1
Wood and brick, . . .	1	–	1
SPRINGFIELD. .	8,457	610	9,067
Number of Stories.	8,457	610	9,067
1 story, ...	142	101	243
1 story and attic, . . .	1,174	98	1,272
Basement and 1 story, .	7	–	7
Basement, 1 story, and attic, .	30	–	30
2 stories, ...	2,648	142	2,790
2 stories and attic, . .	3,345	206	3,551
Basement and 2 stories, .	109	2	111
Basement, 2 stories, and attic,	118	7	125
3 stories, ...	614	41	655
3 stories and attic, . .	28	–	28
Basement and 3 stories, .	122	5	127
Basement, 3 stories, and attic,	9	1	10
4 stories, ...	92	5	97
Basement and 4 stories, .	9	–	9
5 stories, ...	6	2	8
Basement and 5 stories, .	1	–	1
6 stories, ...	1	–	1
Not given, ...	2	–	2
Materials.	8,457	610	9,067
Wood, ...	7,327	545	7,872
Brick, ...	991	55	1,046
Stone, ...	10	1	11
Cement, ...	2	1	3
Wood and brick, . .	111	1	112
Wood and stone, . .	2	2	4
Wood and cement, . .	–	3	3
Brick and stone, . .	8	1	9

COUNTIES, CITIES, TOWNS, NUMBER OF STORIES TO DWELLING HOUSES, AND MATERIALS OF WHICH CONSTRUCTED.	Number of Occupied Dwelling Houses	Number of Unoccupied Dwelling Houses	Total Number of Dwelling Houses
HAMPDEN—Con.			
SPRINGFIELD—Con.			
Materials—Con.			
Brick and cement, . .	3	–	3
Wood, brick, and stone, . .	1	1	2
Not given, ...	2	–	2
SPRINGFIELD. WARD 1,	1,089	67	1,156
Number of Stories.	1,089	67	1,156
1 story, ...	1	–	1
1 story and attic, . . .	86	3	89
Basement, 1 story, and attic,	3	–	3
2 stories, ...	103	6	109
2 stories and attic, . .	794	54	848
Basement and 2 stories, .	3	–	3
Basement, 2 stories, and attic,	12	1	13
3 stories, ...	76	3	79
Basement and 3 stories, .	8	–	8
4 stories, ...	3	–	3
Materials.	1,089	67	1,156
Wood, ...	1,003	64	1,067
Brick, ...	77	3	80
Wood and brick, . .	7	–	7
Brick and cement, . .	2	–	2
SPRINGFIELD. WARD 2,	1,054	49	1,103
Number of Stories.	1,054	49	1,103
1 story, ...	8	–	8
1 story and attic, . .	109	5	114
Basement and 1 story, . .	4	–	4
Basement, 1 story, and attic,	9	–	9
2 stories, ...	446	28	474
2 stories and attic, . .	278	13	291
Basement and 2 stories, .	30	–	30
Basement, 2 stories, and attic,	30	–	30
3 stories, ...	105	3	108
3 stories and attic, . .	6	–	6
Basement and 3 stories, .	7	–	7
4 stories, ...	20	–	20
5 stories, ...	1	–	1
6 stories, ...	1	–	1
Materials.	1,054	49	1,103
Wood, ...	829	44	873
Brick, ...	172	4	176
Wood and brick, . . .	53	1	54
SPRINGFIELD. WARD 3,	771	32	803
Number of Stories.	771	32	803
1 story, ...	10	1	11
1 story and attic, . .	49	5	54
Basement and 1 story, .	1	–	1
Basement, 1 story, and attic, .	2	–	2
2 stories, ...	157	9	166
2 stories and attic, . .	229	5	234
Basement and 2 stories, .	42	1	43
Basement, 2 stories, and attic,	30	3	33

DWELLING HOUSES: NUMBER OF STORIES AND MATERIALS — Continued.

Counties, Cities, Towns, Number of Stories to Dwelling Houses, and Materials of which Constructed.	Number of Occupied Dwelling Houses	Number of Unoccupied Dwelling Houses	Total Number of Dwelling Houses
HAMPDEN — Con.			
SPRINGFIELD. WARD 3 — Con.			
Number of Stories — Con.			
3 stories,	111	1	112
3 stories and attic,	15	–	15
Basement and 3 stories,	45	3	48
Basement, 3 stories, and attic,	2	1	3
4 stories,	67	3	70
Basement and 4 stories,	5	–	5
5 stories,	5	–	5
Basement and 5 stories,	1	–	1
Materials.	771	32	863
Wood,	395	15	410
Brick,	341	16	357
Stone,	2	1	3
Wood and brick,	31	–	31
Brick and stone,	2	–	2
SPRINGFIELD. WARD 4,	1,058	43	1,101
Number of Stories.	1,058	43	1,101
1 story,	6	–	6
1 story and attic,	57	3	60
Basement and 1 story,	1	–	1
Basement, 1 story, and attic,	6	–	6
2 stories,	196	3	199
2 stories and attic,	585	30	615
Basement and 2 stories,	17	–	17
Basement, 2 stories, and attic.	29	2	31
3 stories,	103	3	106
3 stories and attic,	3	–	3
Basement and 3 stories,	48	2	50
Basement, 3 stories, and attic,	1	–	1
4 stories,	1	–	1
Basement and 4 stories,	4	–	4
Not given,	1	–	1
Materials.	1,058	43	1,101
Wood,	858	28	886
Brick,	195	14	209
Stone,	4	–	4
Wood and brick,	15	–	15
Wood and stone,	2	–	2
Brick and stone,	2	1	3
Brick and cement,	1	–	1
Not given,	1	–	1
SPRINGFIELD. WARD 5,	1,289	64	1,353
Number of Stories.	1,289	64	1,353
1 story,	33	2	35
1 story and attic,	136	6	142
2 stories,	406	24	430
2 stories and attic,	599	31	630
Basement and 2 stories,	3	–	3
Basement, 2 stories, and attic,	2	–	2
3 stories,	47	1	48
3 stories and attic,	2	–	2
Basement and 3 stories,	1	–	1
HAMPDEN — Con.			
SPRINGFIELD. WARD 5 — Con.			
Materials.	1,289	64	1,353
Wood,	1,261	60	1,321
Brick,	24	1	25
Wood and brick,	1	–	1
Wood and stone,	–	2	2
Brick and stone,	3	–	3
Wood, brick, and stone,	–	1	1
SPRINGFIELD. WARD 6,	1,004	67	1,071
Number of Stories.	1,004	67	1,071
1 story,	40	6	46
1 story and attic,	161	12	173
Basement and 1 story,	1	–	1
Basement, 1 story, and attic,	2	–	2
2 stories,	416	19	435
2 stories and attic,	254	20	274
Basement and 2 stories,	8	1	9
Basement, 2 stories, and attic,	12	1	13
3 stories,	91	6	97
Basement and 3 stories,	13	–	13
Basement, 3 stories, and attic,	6	–	6
5 stories,	–	2	2
Materials.	1,004	67	1,071
Wood,	887	60	947
Brick,	111	6	117
Stone,	2	–	2
Cement,	2	1	3
Wood and brick,	1	–	1
Wood, brick, and stone,	1	–	1
SPRINGFIELD. WARD 7,	962	79	1,041
Number of Stories.	962	79	1,041
1 story,	16	6	22
1 story and attic,	209	9	218
Basement, 1 story, and attic,	5	–	5
2 stories,	316	20	336
2 stories and attic,	371	30	401
Basement and 2 stories,	2	–	2
Basement, 2 stories, and attic,	2	–	2
3 stories,	40	14	54
3 stories and attic,	1	–	1
Materials.	962	79	1,041
Wood,	932	74	1,006
Brick,	28	5	33
Wood and brick,	1	–	1
Brick and stone,	1	–	1
SPRINGFIELD. WARD 8,	1,230	209	1,439
Number of Stories.	1,230	209	1,439
1 story,	28	86	114
1 story and attic,	367	55	422
Basement, 1 story, and attic,	3	–	3
2 stories,	548	33	581
2 stories and attic,	235	23	258

DWELLING HOUSES: NUMBER OF STORIES AND MATERIALS — Continued.

COUNTIES, CITIES, TOWNS, NUMBER OF STORIES TO DWELLING HOUSES, AND MATERIALS OF WHICH CONSTRUCTED.	Number of Occupied Dwelling Houses	Number of Unoccupied Dwelling Houses	Total Number of Dwelling Houses
HAMPDEN — Con.			
SPRINGFIELD. WARD 8 - Con.			
Number of Stories — Con.			
Basement and 2 stories, . .	4	–	4
Basement, 2 stories, and attic.	1	–	1
3 stories, ...	41	10	51
3 stories and attic, . .	1	–	1
4 stories, ...	1	2	3
Not given, . . .	1	–	1
Materials.	1,230	209	1,439
Wood, ...	1,182	200	1,382
Brick, ...	43	6	49
Stone, . . .	2	–	2
Wood and brick, . .	2	–	2
Wood and cement, .	–	3	3
Not given, . . .	1	–	1
Tolland. . . .	66	22	88
Number of Stories.	66	22	88
1 story and attic, .	21	15	36
Basement, 1 story, and attic,	2	–	2
2 stories, . .	6	2	8
2 stories and attic, .	36	5	41
Basement, 2 stories, and attic,	1	–	1
Materials.	66	22	88
Wood, . . .	64	22	86
Stone, . . .	1	–	1
Wood and brick,	1	–	1
Wales. . . .	178	12	190
Number of Stories.	178	12	190
1 story, . . .	4	1	5
1 story and attic, .	89	7	96
2 stories, . .	9	–	9
2 stories and attic. .	76	4	80
Materials.	178	12	190
Wood, . . .	171	12	183
Brick, . . .	6	–	6
Stone, . . .	1	–	1
Westfield. . . .	2,057	72	2,129
Number of Stories.	2,057	72	2,129
1 story, . . .	33	1	34
1 story and attic, . .	346	15	361
Basement, 1 story, and attic,	2	–	2
2 stories, . . .	852	23	875
2 stories and attic, . .	705	31	736
Basement and 2 stories, .	31	1	32
Basement, 2 stories, and attic,	5	–	5
3 stories, . . .	70	1	71
3 stories and attic, . .	3	–	3
Basement and 3 stories, .	5	–	5
4 stories. . . .	1	–	1
Basement and 4 stories, .	1	–	1
5 stories, . . .	1	–	1
Not given, . . .	2	–	2
HAMPDEN — Con.			
Westfield — Con.			
Materials.	2,057	72	2,129
Wood, ...	1,921	66	1,987
Brick, ...	126	5	131
Wood and brick, . .	7	1	8
Wood and stone, . .	1	–	1
Not given, . . .	2	–	2
West Springfield. .	1,069	37	1,106
Number of Stories.	1,069	37	1,106
1 story, . . .	7	–	7
1 story and attic, . .	196	8	204
Basement and 1 story, .	1	–	1
Basement, 1 story, and attic,	1	–	1
2 stories, . .	512	17	529
2 stories and attic, . .	324	11	335
Basement and 2 stories, .	2	–	2
Basement, 2 stories, and attic,	1	–	1
3 stories, . . .	15	–	15
3 stories and attic, . .	9	1	10
Basement and 3 stories, .	1	–	1
Materials.	1,069	37	1,106
Wood, . . .	1,019	36	1,055
Brick, . . .	38	1	39
Wood and brick, . .	11	–	11
Brick and stone, . .	1	–	1
Wilbraham. . .	290	27	317
Number of Stories.	290	27	317
1 story, . . .	33	7	40
1 story and attic, . .	90	8	98
Basement, 1 story, and attic,	2	–	2
2 stories, . .	72	6	78
2 stories and attic, . .	76	5	81
Basement and 2 stories, .	–	1	1
3 stories, . . .	13	–	13
3 stories and attic, . .	2	–	2
Basement, 3 stories, and attic,	1	–	1
Basement, 4 stories, and attic,	1	–	1
Materials.	290	27	317
Wood, . . .	280	27	307
Brick, . . .	9	–	9
Wood and stone, . .	1	–	1
HAMPSHIRE.			
Amherst. . .	921	19	940
Number of Stories.	921	19	940
1 story, . . .	143	5	148
1 story and attic, . .	218	5	223
Basement, 1 story, and attic,	4	–	4
2 stories, . . .	214	6	220
2 stories and attic, . .	292	2	294
Basement and 2 stories, .	12	–	12
Basement, 2 stories, and attic,	3	–	3

DWELLING HOUSES: NUMBER OF STORIES AND MATERIALS — Continued.

COUNTIES, CITIES, TOWNS, NUMBER OF STORIES TO DWELLING HOUSES, AND MATERIALS OF WHICH CONSTRUCTED.	Number of Occupied Dwelling Houses	Number of Unoccupied Dwelling Houses	Total Number of Dwelling Houses
HAMPSHIRE — Con.			
Amherst — Con.			
Number of Stories — Con.			
3 stories, ...	25	1	26
3 stories and attic, . . .	6	–	6
Basement and 3 stories, .	2	–	2
Basement and 4 stories, .	2	–	2
Materials.	921	19	940
Wood, ...	868	19	887
Brick, ...	35	–	35
Stone, ...	1	–	1
Wood and brick, . . .	17	–	17
Belchertown, . . .	507	20	527
Number of Stories.	507	20	527
1 story and attic, . . .	200	11	211
Basement, 1 story, and attic, .	1	–	1
2 stories, ...	2	–	2
2 stories and attic, . . .	301	9	310
Basement, 2 stories, and attic,	1	–	1
3 stories and attic, . . .	2	–	2
Materials.	507	20	527
Wood, ...	497	20	517
Brick, ...	9	–	9
Stone, ...	1	–	1
Chesterfield, . . .	149	15	164
Number of Stories.	149	15	164
1 story, ...	2	–	2
1 story and attic, . . .	101	11	112
2 stories, ...	13	1	14
2 stories and attic, . . .	33	3	36
Materials.	149	15	164
Wood, ...	148	15	163
Brick, ...	1	–	1
Cummington, . . .	188	15	203
Number of Stories.	188	15	203
1 story, ...	29	3	32
1 story and attic, . . .	82	11	93
Basement and 1 story, . .	3	–	3
2 stories, ...	65	1	66
2 stories and attic, . . .	8	–	8
Basement and 2 stories, . .	1	–	1
Materials.	188	15	203
Wood, ...	185	14	199
Brick, ...	2	1	3
Wood and brick, . . .	1	–	1
Easthampton, . . .	835	43	878
Number of Stories.	835	43	878
1 story, ...	19	–	19
1 story and attic, . . .	286	31	317
2 stories, ...	415	11	426
2 stories and attic, . . .	100	1	101

COUNTIES, CITIES, TOWNS, NUMBER OF STORIES TO DWELLING HOUSES, AND MATERIALS OF WHICH CONSTRUCTED.	Number of Occupied Dwelling Houses	Number of Unoccupied Dwelling Houses	Total Number of Dwelling Houses
HAMPSHIRE — Con.			
Easthampton — Con.			
Number of Stories — Con.			
Basement, 2 stories, and attic,	1	–	1
3 stories, ...	9	–	9
3 stories and attic, . . .	1	–	1
Basement and 3 stories, .	1	–	1
4 stories, ...	2	–	2
Not given, ...	1	–	1
Materials.	835	43	878
Wood, ...	769	43	812
Brick, ...	61	–	61
Stone, ...	1	–	1
Cement, ...	1	–	1
Wood and brick, . . .	1	–	1
Brick and cement, . . .	1	–	1
Not given, ...	1	–	1
Enfield, ...	250	5	255
Number of Stories.	250	5	255
1 story, ...	17	–	17
1 story and attic, . . .	142	4	146
Basement, 1 story, and attic,	2	–	2
2 stories, ...	78	1	79
2 stories and attic, . . .	7	–	7
Basement and 2 stories, . .	3	–	3
3 stories, ...	1	–	1
Materials.	250	5	255
Wood, ...	249	5	254
Brick, ...	1	–	1
Goshen, ...	62	13	75
Number of Stories.	62	13	75
1 story, ...	1	–	1
1 story and attic, . . .	29	10	39
2 stories, ...	1	–	1
2 stories and attic, . . .	31	3	34
Materials.	62	13	75
Wood, ...	62	13	75
Granby, ...	165	5	170
Number of Stories.	165	5	170
1 story, ...	6	–	6
1 story and attic, . . .	65	2	67
2 stories, ...	15	2	17
2 stories and attic, . . .	79	1	80
Materials.	165	5	170
Wood, ...	164	5	169
Wood and brick, . . .	1	–	1
Greenwich, . . .	138	8	146
Number of Stories.	138	8	146
1 story, ...	3	–	3
1 story and attic, . . .	86	4	90
2 stories, ...	13	1	14
2 stories and attic, . . .	36	3	39

DWELLING HOUSES: NUMBER OF STORIES AND MATERIALS — Continued.

COUNTIES, CITIES, TOWNS, NUMBER OF STORIES TO DWELLING HOUSES, AND MATERIALS OF WHICH CONSTRUCTED.	Number of Occupied Dwelling Houses	Number of Unoccupied Dwelling Houses	Total Number of Dwelling Houses
HAMPSHIRE — Con.			
Greenwich — Con.			
Materials.			
Wood, ...	138	8	146
Hadley, ...	374	11	385
Number of Stories.	374	11	385
1 story, ...	14	2	16
1 story and attic, . . .	147	4	151
Basement, 1 story, and attic,	1	–	1
2 stories, ...	184	3	187
2 stories and attic, . .	24	–	24
Basement and 2 stories, . .	1	1	2
3 stories, ...	3	1	4
Materials.			
Wood, ...	362	11	373
Brick, ...	12	–	12
Hatfield.	271	11	282
Number of Stories.	271	11	282
1 story, ...	6	–	6
1 story and attic, . . .	18	4	22
2 stories, ...	144	6	150
2 stories and attic, . .	91	1	92
Basement and 2 stories, . .	1	–	1
Basement, 2 stories, and attic,	1	–	1
3 stories, ...	10	–	10
Materials.			
Wood, ...	262	11	273
Brick, ...	9	–	9
Huntington.	290	16	306
Number of Stories.	290	16	306
1 story, ...	8	–	8
1 story and attic, . . .	122	9	131
2 stories, ...	47	1	48
2 stories and attic, . .	107	6	113
Basement and 2 stories, . .	1	–	1
Basement, 2 stories, and attic,	2	–	2
3 stories, ...	3	–	3
Materials.			
Wood, ...	288	16	304
Brick, ...	2	–	2
Middlefield. . . .	85	25	110
Number of Stories.	85	25	110
1 story, ...	–	1	1
1 story and attic, . . .	31	13	44
2 stories, ...	4	2	6
2 stories and attic, . .	48	9	57
Basement, 2 stories, and attic,	1	–	1
3 stories and attic, . . .	1	–	1
Materials.			
Wood, ...	85	25	110

COUNTIES, CITIES, TOWNS, NUMBER OF STORIES TO DWELLING HOUSES, AND MATERIALS OF WHICH CONSTRUCTED.	Number of Occupied Dwelling Houses	Number of Unoccupied Dwelling Houses	Total Number of Dwelling Houses
HAMPSHIRE — Con.			
NORTHAMPTON. . .	2,824	119	2,943
Number of Stories.	2,824	119	2,943
1 story, ...	53	6	59
1 story and attic, . . .	808	34	842
Basement, 1 story, and attic,	26	–	26
2 stories, ...	1,400	53	1,453
2 stories and attic, . .	374	19	393
Basement and 2 stories, .	49	–	49
Basement, 2 stories, and attic,	13	2	15
3 stories, ...	74	1	75
3 stories and attic, . .	4	–	4
Basement and 3 stories, . .	4	–	4
Basement, 3 stories, and attic,	6	–	6
4 stories, ...	7	–	7
4 stories and attic, . .	1	–	1
Basement and 4 stories, . .	2	–	2
Basement, 4 stories, and attic,	2	–	2
7 stories, ...	–	4	4
Not given, ...	1	–	1
Materials.	2,824	119	2,943
Wood, ...	2,637	113	2,750
Brick, ...	159	6	165
Stone, ...	1	–	1
Cement, ...	2	–	2
Wood and brick, . . .	17	–	17
Wood and stone, . . .	2	–	2
Brick and stone, . . .	1	–	1
Brick and cement, . . .	1	–	1
Stone and cement, . . .	3	–	3
Not given, ...	1	–	1
NORTHAMPTON. WARD 1, . .	377	8	385
Number of Stories.	377	8	385
1 story, ...	16	–	16
1 story and attic, . . .	78	3	81
Basement, 1 story, and attic,	1	–	1
2 stories, ...	238	4	242
2 stories and attic, . .	13	1	14
Basement and 2 stories, .	6	–	6
Basement, 2 stories, and attic,	1	–	1
3 stories, ...	20	–	20
3 stories and attic, . .	1	–	1
4 stories, ...	1	–	1
Basement and 4 stories, . .	1	–	1
Not given, ...	1	–	1
Materials.	377	8	385
Wood, ...	327	8	335
Brick, ...	46	–	46
Cement, ...	1	–	1
Wood and brick, . . .	1	–	1
Brick and cement, . . .	1	–	1
Not given, ...	1	–	1
NORTHAMPTON. WARD 2, .	453	16	469
Number of Stories.	453	16	469
1 story, ...	3	–	3

DWELLING HOUSES: NUMBER OF STORIES AND MATERIALS — Continued.

Counties, Cities, Towns, Number of Stories to Dwelling Houses, and Materials of which Constructed.	Number of Occupied Dwelling Houses	Number of Unoccupied Dwelling Houses	Total Number of Dwelling Houses
HAMPSHIRE — Con.			
NORTHAMPTON. WARD 2 — Con.			
Number of Stories — Con.			
1 story and attic, . . .	47	2	49
2 stories, ...	199	4	203
2 stories and attic, . . .	144	8	152
Basement and 2 stories, . .	7	–	7
Basement, 2 stories, and attic,	4	2	6
3 stories, ...	35	–	35
3 stories and attic, . . .	2	–	2
Basement and 3 stories, . .	2	–	2
Basement, 3 stories, and attic,	2	–	2
4 stories, ...	6	–	6
Basement, 4 stories, and attic,	2	–	2
Materials.	453	16	469
Wood, ...	400	16	416
Brick, ...	50	–	50
Wood and brick, . . .	2	–	2
Wood and stone, . . .	1	–	1
NORTHAMPTON. WARD 3, .	500	18	518
Number of Stories.	500	18	518
1 story, ...	6	1	7
1 story and attic, . . .	83	1	84
Basement, 1 story, and attic, .	1	–	1
2 stories, ...	327	12	339
2 stories and attic, . . .	47	–	47
Basement and 2 stories, . .	20	–	20
Basement, 2 stories, and attic,	6	–	6
3 stories, ...	5	–	5
3 stories and attic, . . .	1	–	1
Basement, 3 stories, and attic,	3	–	3
4 stories and attic, . . .	1	–	1
7 stories, ...	–	4	4
Materials.	500	18	518
Wood, ...	480	18	498
Brick, ...	19	–	19
Cement, ...	1	–	1
NORTHAMPTON. WARD 4, .	358	21	379
Number of Stories.	358	21	379
1 story, ...	1	–	1
1 story and attic, . . .	77	5	82
Basement, 1 story, and attic,	1	–	1
2 stories, ...	166	8	174
2 stories and attic, . . .	108	8	116
Basement and 2 stories, . .	1	–	1
Basement, 2 stories, and attic,	1	–	1
3 stories, ...	2	–	2
Basement and 4 stories, . .	1	–	1
Materials.	358	21	379
Wood, ...	333	18	351
Brick, ...	23	3	26
Wood and brick, . . .	2	–	2

Counties, Cities, Towns, Number of Stories to Dwelling Houses, and Materials of which Constructed.	Number of Occupied Dwelling Houses	Number of Unoccupied Dwelling Houses	Total Number of Dwelling Houses
HAMPSHIRE — Con.			
NORTHAMPTON. WARD 5, .	416	13	429
Number of Stories.	416	13	429
1 story, ...	10	2	12
1 story and attic, . . .	274	5	279
Basement, 1 story, and attic,	7	–	7
2 stories, ...	92	5	97
2 stories and attic, . . .	28	1	29
Basement and 2 stories, .	1	–	1
3 stories, ...	4	–	4
Materials.	416	13	429
Wood, ...	402	12	414
Brick, ...	14	1	15
NORTHAMPTON. WARD 6, .	357	13	370
Number of Stories.	357	13	370
1 story, ...	6	–	6
1 story and attic, . . .	70	5	75
Basement, 1 story, and attic,	2	–	2
2 stories, ...	238	8	246
2 stories and attic, . . .	19	–	19
Basement and 2 stories, .	14	–	14
Basement, 2 stories, and attic,	1	–	1
3 stories, ...	4	–	4
Basement and 3 stories, .	2	–	2
Basement, 3 stories, and attic,	1	–	1
Materials.	357	13	370
Wood, ...	345	12	357
Brick, ...	5	1	6
Stone, ...	1	–	1
Wood and brick, . . .	1	–	1
Wood and stone, . . .	1	–	1
Brick and stone, . . .	1	–	1
Stone and cement. . . .	3	–	3
NORTHAMPTON. WARD 7, .	363	30	393
Number of Stories.	363	30	393
1 story, ...	11	3	14
1 story and attic, . . .	179	13	192
Basement, 1 story, and attic,	14	–	14
2 stories, ...	140	12	152
2 stories and attic, . . .	15	1	16
3 stories, ...	4	1	5
Materials.	363	30	393
Wood, ...	350	29	379
Brick, ...	2	1	3
Wood and brick, . . .	11	–	11
Pelham, ...	122	21	143
Number of Stories.	122	21	143
1 story, ...	5	–	5
1 story and attic, . . .	83	15	98
Basement, 1 story, and attic,	2	–	2
2 stories, ...	10	2	12
2 stories and attic, . . .	22	3	25
Basement, 2 stories, and attic,	–	1	1

DWELLING HOUSES: NUMBER OF STORIES AND MATERIALS — Continued.

COUNTIES, CITIES, TOWNS, NUMBER OF STORIES TO DWELLING HOUSES, AND MATERIALS OF WHICH CONSTRUCTED.	Number of Occupied Dwelling Houses	Number of Unoccupied Dwelling Houses	Total Number of Dwelling Houses
HAMPSHIRE — Con.			
Pelham — Con.			
Materials.	122	21	143
Wood, ...	122	21	143
Plainfield, ...	102	13	115
Number of Stories.	102	13	115
1 story, ...	1	–	1
1 story and attic, . . .	80	9	89
Basement, 1 story, and attic, .	1	–	1
2 stories, ...	2	1	3
2 stories and attic, . . .	18	3	21
Materials.	102	13	115
Wood, ...	99	13	112
Brick, ...	2	–	2
Wood and brick, . . .	1	–	1
Prescott, ...	96	13	109
Number of Stories.	96	13	109
1 story, ...	20	4	24
1 story and attic, . . .	44	7	51
2 stories, ...	2	1	3
2 stories and attic, . . .	29	1	30
Basement and 2 stories, . .	1	–	1
Materials.	96	13	109
Wood, ...	94	12	106
Brick, ...	–	1	1
Wood and brick, . . .	2	–	2
Southampton, . . .	225	6	231
Number of Stories.	225	6	231
1 story, ...	4	–	4
1 story and attic, . . .	90	2	92
2 stories, ...	3	–	3
2 stories and attic, . . .	127	4	131
3 stories, ...	1	–	1
Materials.	225	6	231
Wood, ...	216	6	222
Brick, ...	8	–	8
Wood and stone, . . .	1	–	1
South Hadley, . . .	735	27	762
Number of Stories.	735	27	762
1 story, ...	10	1	11
1 story and attic, . . .	184	6	190
Basement, 1 story, and attic, .	5	–	5
2 stories, ...	186	11	197
2 stories and attic, . . .	310	6	316
Basement and 2 stories, . .	10	–	10
Basement, 2 stories, and attic,	14	–	14
3 stories, ...	14	2	16
Basement, 3 stories, and attic,	1	1	2
Basement, 4 stories, and attic,	1	–	1
Materials.	735	27	762
Wood, ...	695	21	716

COUNTIES, CITIES, TOWNS, NUMBER OF STORIES TO DWELLING HOUSES, AND MATERIALS OF WHICH CONSTRUCTED.	Number of Occupied Dwelling Houses	Number of Unoccupied Dwelling Houses	Total Number of Dwelling Houses
HAMPSHIRE — Con.			
South Hadley — Con.			
Materials — Con.			
Brick, ...	35	6	41
Wood and brick, . . .	5	–	5
Ware, ...	1,208	45	1,253
Number of Stories.	1,208	45	1,253
1 story, ...	5	1	6
1 story and attic, . . .	142	6	148
Basement, 1 story, and attic, .	5	–	5
2 stories, ...	372	11	383
2 stories and attic, . . .	554	27	581
Basement and 2 stories, . .	24	–	24
Basement, 2 stories, and attic,	18	–	18
3 stories, ...	16	–	16
3 stories and attic, . . .	1	–	1
Basement and 3 stories, . .	10	–	10
4 stories, ...	1	–	1
Materials.	1,208	45	1,253
Wood, ...	1,144	45	1,189
Brick, ...	45	–	45
Stone, ...	1	–	1
Wood and brick, . . .	17	–	17
Wood and stone, . . .	1	–	1
Westhampton, . . .	111	6	117
Number of Stories.	111	6	117
1 story, ...	8	–	8
1 story and attic, . . .	21	1	22
2 stories, ...	21	1	22
2 stories and attic, . . .	61	4	65
Materials.	111	6	117
Wood, ...	111	6	117
Williamsburg, . . .	421	20	441
Number of Stories.	421	20	441
1 story, ...	63	7	70
1 story and attic, . . .	166	5	171
Basement and 1 story, . .	3	1	4
Basement, 1 story, and attic, .	1	3	4
2 stories, ...	177	2	179
2 stories and attic, . . .	5	1	6
Basement and 2 stories, . .	4	1	5
3 stories, ...	2	–	2
Materials.	421	20	441
Wood, ...	417	19	436
Wood and brick, . . .	4	–	4
Wood and stone, . . .	–	1	1
Worthington, . . .	152	22	174
Number of Stories.	152	22	174
1 story, ...	27	9	36
1 story and attic, . . .	48	5	53

DWELLING HOUSES: NUMBER OF STORIES AND MATERIALS — Continued.

Counties, Cities, Towns, Number of Stories to Dwelling Houses, and Materials of which Constructed.	Number of Occupied Dwelling Houses	Number of Unoccupied Dwelling Houses	Total Number of Dwelling Houses
HAMPSHIRE —Con.			
Worthington — Con.			
Number of Stories — Con.			
Basement and 1 story, . .	1	–	1
Basement, 1 story, and attic,	2	–	2
2 stories, ...	71	7	78
2 stories and attic, . . .	1	–	1
Basement and 2 stories, . .	1	–	1
3 stories, ...	1	1	2
Materials.	152	22	174
Wood, ...	152	22	174
MIDDLESEX.			
Acton.	469	27	496
Number of Stories.	469	27	496
1 story, ...	25	2	27
1 story and attic, . . .	164	13	177
Basement and 1 story, . .	3	–	3
Basement, 1 story, and attic,	5	–	5
2 stories, ...	218	10	228
2 stories and attic, . . .	33	2	35
Basement and 2 stories, .	9	–	9
3 stories, ...	6	–	6
Not given, ...	8	–	8
Materials.	469	27	496
Wood, ...	456	27	483
Wood and brick, . . .	5	–	5
Not given, ...	8	–	8
Arlington. . . .	1,264	84	1,348
Number of Stories.	1,264	84	1,348
1 story, ...	18	4	22
1 story and attic, . . .	118	3	121
Basement and 1 story, . .	1	–	1
Basement, 1 story, and attic,	1	3	4
2 stories, ...	460	25	485
2 stories and attic, . . .	576	42	618
Basement and 2 stories, .	6	1	7
Basement, 2 stories, and attic,	10	1	11
3 stories, ...	51	3	54
3 stories and attic, . . .	19	1	20
Basement and 3 stories, . .	3	1	4
Basement, 3 stories, and attic,	1	–	1
Materials.	1,264	84	1,348
Wood, ...	1,244	80	1,324
Brick, ...	4	–	4
Cement, ...	1	–	1
Wood and brick, . . .	8	–	8
Wood and stone, . . .	6	3	9
Wood and cement, . . .	1	–	1
Wood, brick, and stone, .	–	1	1
Ashby.	218	28	246
Number of Stories.	218	28	246
1 story, ...	37	6	43
MIDDLESEX — Con.			
Ashby — Con.			
Number of Stories — Con.			
1 story and attic, . . .	66	8	74
Basement and 1 story, . .	1	1	2
Basement, 1 story, and attic,	2	–	2
2 stories, ...	24	2	26
2 stories and attic, . . .	83	11	94
Basement and 2 stories, . .	1	–	1
Basement, 2 stories, and attic,	1	–	1
3 stories, ...	1	–	1
3 stories and attic, . . .	1	–	1
Basement and 3 stories, . .	1	–	1
Materials.	218	28	246
Wood, ...	207	26	233
Brick, ...	4	2	6
Wood and brick, . . .	7	–	7
Ashland.	419	45	464
Number of Stories.	419	45	464
1 story, ...	7	–	7
1 story and attic, . . .	131	15	146
2 stories, ...	52	10	62
2 stories and attic, . . .	212	19	231
3 stories, ...	16	1	17
4 stories, ...	1	–	1
Materials.	419	45	464
Wood, ...	412	43	455
Brick, ...	7	2	9
Ayer.	442	17	459
Number of Stories.	442	17	459
1 story, ...	9	1	10
1 story and attic, . . .	223	6	229
Basement and 1 story, . .	6	–	6
Basement, 1 story, and attic,	11	–	11
2 stories, ...	31	4	35
2 stories and attic, . . .	136	5	141
Basement and 2 stories, . .	2	–	2
Basement, 2 stories, and attic,	4	–	4
3 stories, ...	15	–	15
3 stories and attic, . . .	1	–	1
Basement and 3 stories, . .	1	1	2
Basement, 3 stories, and attic,	1	–	1
4 stories, ...	2	–	2
Materials.	442	17	459
Wood, ...	436	17	453
Brick, ...	5	–	5
Stone, ...	1	–	1
Bedford.	235	26	261
Number of Stories.	235	26	261
1 story, ...	2	1	3
1 story and attic, . . .	47	8	55
Basement, 1 story, and attic,	2	1	3

DWELLING HOUSES: NUMBER OF STORIES AND MATERIALS — Continued.

COUNTIES, CITIES, TOWNS, NUMBER OF STORIES TO DWELLING HOUSES, AND MATERIALS OF WHICH CONSTRUCTED.	Number of Occupied Dwelling Houses	Number of Unoccupied Dwelling Houses	Total Number of Dwelling Houses	COUNTIES, CITIES, TOWNS, NUMBER OF STORIES TO DWELLING HOUSES, AND MATERIALS OF WHICH CONSTRUCTED.	Number of Occupied Dwelling Houses	Number of Unoccupied Dwelling Houses	Total Number of Dwelling Houses
MIDDLESEX — Con.				**MIDDLESEX — Con.**			
Bedford — Con.				**Burlington.**	122	16	138
Number of Stories — Con.				*Number of Stories.*	122	16	138
2 stories, ...	28	3	31	1 story, ...	4	–	4
2 stories and attic, . .	148	11	159	1 story and attic, . . .	34	5	39
Basement, 2 stories, and attic,	2	1	3	Basement, 1 story, and attic,	1	–	1
3 stories, ...	1		1	2 stories, ...	14	2	16
3 stories and attic, . . .	3		3	2 stories and attic, . . .	68	9	77
Basement and 3 stories, .	1		1	3 stories, ...	1	–	1
Basement, 3 stories, and attic,	1	1	2				
Materials.	235	26	261	*Materials.*	122	16	138
Wood, ...	232	26	258	Wood, ...	121	16	137
Wood and brick, . . .	3	–	3	Stone, ...	1	–	1
Belmont, ...	491	83	574	**CAMBRIDGE,** . . .	11,857	662	12,489
Number of Stories.	491	83	574	*Number of Stories.*	11,857	662	12,489
1 story, ...	5	–	5	1 story, ...	146	14	160
1 story and attic, . . .	43	5	48	1 story and attic, . . .	694	69	763
Basement, 1 story, and attic,	3	–	3	Basement and 1 story, . .	7	1	8
2 stories, ...	170	15	185	Basement, 1 story, and attic,	166	8	174
2 stories and attic, . . .	245	59	304	2 stories, ...	2,684	123	2,807
Basement, 2 stories, and attic,	1	–	1	2 stories and attic, . . .	4,648	252	4,900
3 stories, ...	23	4	27	Basement and 2 stories, . .	268	9	277
3 stories and attic, . . .	1		1	Basement, 2 stories, and attic,	425	25	450
Materials.	491	83	574	3 stories, ...	2,277	135	2,412
Wood, ...	480	71	551	3 stories and attic, . . .	107	4	111
Brick, ...	8	3	11	Basement and 3 stories, . .	189	12	201
Wood and brick, . . .	2	–	2	Basement, 3 stories, and attic,	8	–	8
Wood and stone, . . .	–	1	1	4 stories, ...	189	6	195
Brick and stone, . . .	–	7	7	4 stories and attic, . . .	2	–	2
Brick and cement, . . .	1	1	2	Basement and 4 stories, . .	1	–	1
				5 stories, ...	24	–	24
Billerica, ...	532	25	557	Basement and 5 stories, . .	–	1	1
Number of Stories.	532	25	557	6 stories, ...	1	–	1
1 story, ...	6	–	6	Not given, ...	1	3	4
1 story and attic, . . .	123	6	129	*Materials.*	11,857	662	12,489
Basement, 1 story, and attic,	2	1	3	Wood, ...	10,875	603	11,478
2 stories, ...	5	–	5	Brick, ...	486	31	517
2 stories and attic, . . .	389	17	406	Stone, ...	8	–	8
3 stories, ...	5	1	6	Cement, ...	6	–	6
3 stories and attic, . . .	2	–	2	Wood and brick, . . .	403	18	421
Materials.	532	25	557	Wood and stone, . . .	26	1	27
Wood, ...	528	25	553	Brick and stone, . . .	26	6	32
Wood and brick, . . .	3	–	3	Brick and cement, . . .	4	–	4
Wood and stone, . . .	1	–	1	Wood, brick, and stone, .	2	–	2
Boxborough. . . .	71	3	74	Not given, ...	1	3	4
Number of Stories.	71	3	74				
1 story, ...	3	–	3	**CAMBRIDGE. WARD 1,** . .	2,303	125	2,428
1 story and attic, . . .	24	1	25	*Number of Stories.*	2,303	125	2,428
2 stories, ...	5	–	5	1 story, ...	13	–	13
2 stories and attic, . . .	38	2	40	1 story and attic, . . .	96	10	106
Basement, 2 stories, and attic,	1	–	1	Basement, 1 story, and attic,	27	1	28
Materials.	71	3	74	2 stories, ...	376	16	392
Wood, ...	66	3	69	2 stories and attic, . . .	1,157	60	1,217
Wood and brick, . . .	5	–	5	Basement and 2 stories, . .	53	1	54
				Basement, 2 stories, and attic,	73	7	80

DWELLING HOUSES: NUMBER OF STORIES AND MATERIALS — Continued.

COUNTIES, CITIES, TOWNS, NUMBER OF STORIES TO DWELLING HOUSES, AND MATERIALS OF WHICH CONSTRUCTED.	Number of Occupied Dwelling Houses	Number of Unoccupied Dwelling Houses	Total Number of Dwelling Houses
MIDDLESEX — Con.			
CAMBRIDGE. WARD 1 — Con.			
Number of Stories — Con.			
3 stories,	403	25	428
3 stories and attic,	48	2	50
Basement and 3 stories,	24	1	25
Basement, 3 stories, and attic,	5	–	5
4 stories,	24	–	24
4 stories and attic,	1	–	1
5 stories,	2	–	2
6 stories,	1	–	1
Not given,	–	2	2
Materials.	2,303	125	2,428
Wood,	2,184	112	2,296
Brick,	97	10	107
Stone,	2	–	2
Wood and brick,	19	–	19
Wood and stone,	–	1	1
Brick and stone,	1	–	1
Not given,	–	2	2
CAMBRIDGE. WARD 2,	3,118	129	3,247
Number of Stories.	3,118	129	3,247
1 story,	78	7	85
1 story and attic,	140	10	150
Basement and 1 story,	2	–	2
Basement, 1 story, and attic,	33	2	35
2 stories,	631	18	649
2 stories and attic,	1,084	45	1,129
Basement and 2 stories,	97	2	99
Basement, 2 stories, and attic,	140	7	147
3 stories,	756	27	783
3 stories and attic,	18	1	19
Basement and 3 stories,	62	7	69
Basement, 3 stories, and attic,	1	–	1
4 stories,	74	3	77
4 stories and attic,	1	–	1
5 stories,	1	–	1
Materials.	3,118	129	3,247
Wood,	2,902	118	3,020
Brick,	118	6	124
Stone,	1	–	1
Cement,	6	–	6
Wood and brick,	90	5	95
Brick and stone,	1	–	1
CAMBRIDGE. WARD 3,	1,688	49	1,737
Number of Stories.	1,688	49	1,737
1 story,	10	2	12
1 story and attic,	95	5	100
Basement and 1 story,	–	1	1
Basement, 1 story, and attic,	28	1	29
2 stories,	528	20	548
2 stories and attic,	473	9	482
Basement and 2 stories,	51	3	57
Basement, 2 stories, and attic,	69	1	70
MIDDLESEX — Con.			
CAMBRIDGE. WARD 3 — Con.			
Number of Stories — Con.			
3 stories,	367	6	373
3 stories and attic,	24	–	24
Basement and 3 stories,	19	–	19
4 stories,	19	–	19
5 stories,	2	–	2
Not given,	–	1	1
Materials.	1,688	49	1,737
Wood,	1,268	37	1,305
Brick,	104	–	104
Wood and brick,	272	10	282
Wood and stone,	24	–	24
Brick and stone,	18	1	19
Wood, brick, and stone,	2	–	2
Not given,	–	1	1
CAMBRIDGE. WARD 4,	2,899	142	3,041
Number of Stories.	2,899	142	3,041
1 story,	27	–	27
1 story and attic,	160	17	177
Basement and 1 story,	1	–	1
Basement, 1 story, and attic,	46	4	50
2 stories,	680	22	702
2 stories and attic,	1,191	48	1,239
Basement and 2 stories,	46	–	46
Basement, 2 stories, and attic,	132	7	139
3 stories,	431	38	469
3 stories and attic,	10	1	11
Basement and 3 stories,	80	3	83
Basement, 3 stories, and attic,	2	–	2
4 stories,	72	2	74
Basement and 4 stories,	1	–	1
5 stories,	19	–	19
Not given,	1	–	1
Materials.	2,899	142	3,041
Wood,	2,741	131	2,872
Brick,	136	8	144
Stone,	3	–	3
Wood and brick,	13	2	15
Brick and stone,	1	1	2
Brick and cement,	4	–	4
Not given,	1	–	1
CAMBRIDGE. WARD 5,	1,829	217	2,046
Number of Stories.	1,829	217	2,046
1 story,	18	5	23
1 story and attic,	203	27	230
Basement and 1 story,	4	–	4
Basement, 1 story, and attic,	32	–	32
2 stories,	469	47	516
2 stories and attic,	743	90	833
Basement and 2 stories,	18	3	21
Basement, 2 stories, and attic,	11	3	14
3 stories,	320	39	359

DWELLING HOUSES: NUMBER OF STORIES AND MATERIALS — Continued.

COUNTIES, CITIES, TOWNS, NUMBER OF STORIES TO DWELLING HOUSES, AND MATERIALS OF WHICH CONSTRUCTED.	Number of Occupied Dwelling Houses	Number of Unoccupied Dwelling Houses	Total Number of Dwelling Houses
MIDDLESEX — Con.			
CAMBRIDGE. WARD 5 — Con.			
Number of Stories — Con.			
3 stories and attic, . . .	7	–	7
Basement and 3 stories, .	4	1	5
4 stories, ...		1	1
Basement and 5 stories, .		1	1
Materials.	1,829	217	2,046
Wood, ...	1,780	205	1,985
Brick, ...	31	7	38
Stone, ...	2	–	2
Wood and brick, . . .	9	1	10
Wood and stone, . . .	2	–	2
Brick and stone, . . .	5	4	9
Carlisle.	125	8	133
Number of Stories.	125	8	133
1 story, ...	3	1	4
1 story and attic, . . .	11	1	12
2 stories, ...	36	3	39
2 stories and attic, . .	75	3	78
Materials.	125	8	133
Wood, ...	122	8	130
Wood and brick, . . .	3	–	3
Chelmsford. . . .	695	47	742
Number of Stories.	695	47	742
1 story, ...	73	6	79
1 story and attic, . . .	253	13	266
2 stories, ...	69	9	78
2 stories and attic, . .	296	19	312
Basement and 2 stories, .	1	–	1
Basement, 2 stories, and attic,	1	–	1
3 stories, ...	3	–	3
3 stories and attic, . .	1	–	1
Not given, ...	1	–	1
Materials.	695	47	742
Wood, ...	672	47	719
Brick, ...	12	–	12
Stone, ...	1	–	1
Wood and brick, . . .	8	–	8
Wood and stone, . . .	1	–	1
Not given, ...	1	–	1
Concord.	837	73	910
Number of Stories.	837	73	910
1 story, ...	9	2	11
1 story and attic, . . .	184	21	205
Basement and 1 story, . .	1	1	2
Basement, 1 story, and attic,	4	–	4
2 stories, ...	92	4	96
2 stories and attic, . .	511	40	551
Basement and 2 stories, .	4	1	5
Basement, 2 stories, and attic,	11	3	14
3 stories, ...	17	–	17

COUNTIES, CITIES, TOWNS, NUMBER OF STORIES TO DWELLING HOUSES, AND MATERIALS OF WHICH CONSTRUCTED.	Number of Occupied Dwelling Houses	Number of Unoccupied Dwelling Houses	Total Number of Dwelling Houses
MIDDLESEX — Con.			
Concord — Con.			
Number of Stories — Con.			
3 stories and attic, . . .	3	1	4
Basement and 3 stories, .	1	–	1
Materials.	837	73	910
Wood, ...	813	73	886
Brick, ...	8	–	8
Wood and brick, . . .	14	–	14
Wood and stone, . . .	1	–	1
Brick and stone, . . .	1	–	1
Dracut.	440	39	479
Number of Stories.	440	39	479
1 story, ...	4	–	4
1 story and attic, . . .	56	5	61
Basement and 1 story, . .	1	–	1
2 stories, ...	190	23	213
2 stories and attic, . .	187	11	198
Basement, 2 stories, and attic,	1	–	1
3 stories, ...	1	–	1
Materials.	440	39	479
Wood, ...	438	39	477
Brick, ...	1	–	1
Stone, ...	1	–	1
Dunstable.	96	15	111
Number of Stories.	96	15	111
1 story, ...	14	5	19
1 story and attic, . . .	34	3	37
Basement and 1 story, . .	1	–	1
2 stories, ...	47	7	54
Materials.	96	15	111
Wood, ...	94	14	108
Brick, ...	2	–	2
Wood and brick, . . .	–	1	1
EVERETT.	3,610	373	3,983
Number of Stories.	3,610	373	3,983
1 story, ...	90	23	113
1 story and attic, . . .	500	46	546
Basement and one story, .	8	2	10
Basement, 1 story, and attic,	20	1	21
2 stories, ...	654	87	741
2 stories and attic, . .	2,084	187	2,271
Basement and 2 stories, .	9	2	11
Basement, 2 stories, and attic,	46	6	52
3 stories, ...	171	18	189
3 stories and attic, . .	21	1	22
Basement and 3 stories, .	7	–	7
Materials.	3,610	373	3,983
Wood, ...	3,588	371	3,959
Brick, ...	19	2	21
Stone, ...	1	–	1
Wood and brick, . . .	2	–	2

DWELLING HOUSES: NUMBER OF STORIES AND MATERIALS — Continued.

Counties, Cities, Towns, Number of Stories to Dwelling Houses, and Materials of which Constructed	Number of Occupied Dwelling Houses	Number of Unoccupied Dwelling Houses	Total Number of Dwelling Houses
MIDDLESEX — Con.			
EVERETT. WARD 1,	518	45	563
Number of Stories.	518	45	563
1 story,	1	–	1
1 story and attic,	127	6	133
2 stories,	46	9	55
2 stories and attic,	281	20	301
Basement, 2 stories, and attic,	4	–	4
3 stories,	58	10	68
Basement and 3 stories,	1	–	1
Materials.	518	45	563
Wood,	518	45	563
EVERETT. WARD 2,	479	88	567
Number of Stories.	479	88	567
1 story,	38	17	55
1 story and attic,	95	18	113
Basement and 1 story,	6	2	8
Basement, 1 story, and attic,	19	1	20
2 stories,	39	7	46
2 stories and attic,	240	38	278
Basement and 2 stories,	3	1	4
Basement, 2 stories, and attic,	30	4	34
3 stories,	7	–	7
Basement and 3 stories,	2	–	2
Materials.	479	88	567
Wood,	477	88	565
Brick,	1	–	1
Stone,	1	–	1
EVERETT. WARD 3,	615	98	713
Number of Stories.	615	98	713
1 story,	43	6	49
1 story and attic,	26	1	27
2 stories,	318	52	370
2 stories and attic,	203	37	240
Basement and 2 stories,	2	–	2
Basement, 2 stories, and attic,	3	1	4
3 stories,	4	–	4
3 stories and attic,	16	1	17
Materials.	615	98	713
Wood,	614	98	712
Wood and brick,	1	–	1
EVERETT. WARD 4,	700	47	747
Number of Stories.	700	47	747
1 story and attic,	52	2	54
Basement and 1 story,	2	–	2
2 stories,	32	1	33
2 stories and attic,	584	42	626
Basement, 2 stories, and attic,	3	–	3
3 stories,	27	2	29
Materials.	700	47	747
Wood,	692	47	739
Brick,	8	–	8

Counties, Cities, Towns, Number of Stories to Dwelling Houses, and Materials of which Constructed	Number of Occupied Dwelling Houses	Number of Unoccupied Dwelling Houses	Total Number of Dwelling Houses
MIDDLESEX — Con.			
EVERETT. WARD 5,	600	37	637
Number of Stories.	600	37	637
1 story,	2	–	2
1 story and attic,	58	6	64
2 stories,	154	14	168
2 stories and attic,	328	14	342
Basement and 2 stories,	2	1	3
Basement, 2 stories, and attic,	4	1	5
3 stories,	50	1	51
Basement and 3 stories,	2	–	2
Materials.	600	37	637
Wood,	590	36	626
Brick,	9	1	10
Wood and brick,	1	–	1
EVERETT. WARD 6,	698	58	756
Number of Stories.	698	58	756
1 story,	6	–	6
1 story and attic,	142	13	155
Basement, 1 story, and attic,	1	–	1
2 stories,	65	4	69
2 stories and attic,	448	36	484
Basement and 2 stories,	2	–	2
Basement, 2 stories, and attic,	2	–	2
3 stories,	25	5	30
3 stories and attic,	5	–	5
Basement and 3 stories,	2	–	2
Materials.	698	58	756
Wood,	697	57	754
Brick,	1	1	2
Framingham.	1,920	267	2,187
Number of Stories.	1,920	267	2,187
1 story,	95	41	136
1 story and attic,	263	25	288
Basement and 1 story,	7	–	7
Basement, 1 story, and attic,	21	3	24
2 stories,	419	78	497
2 stories and attic,	1,048	106	1,154
Basement and 2 stories,	10	–	10
Basement, 2 stories, and attic,	12	4	16
3 stories,	39	8	47
3 stories and attic,	4	2	6
Basement, 3 stories, and attic,	2	–	2
Materials.	1,920	267	2,187
Wood,	1,905	263	2,168
Brick,	8	1	9
Stone,	2	–	2
Wood and brick,	4	2	6
Wood and cement,	1	1	2
Groton.	476	31	507
Number of Stories.	476	31	507
1 story,	11	1	12
1 story and attic,	172	15	187

DWELLING HOUSES: NUMBER OF STORIES AND MATERIALS — Continued.

Counties, Cities, Towns, Number of Stories to Dwelling Houses, and Materials of which Constructed.	Number of Occupied Dwelling Houses	Number of Unoccupied Dwelling Houses	Total Number of Dwelling Houses
MIDDLESEX — Con.			
Groton — Con.			
Number of Stories — Con.			
Basement, 1 story, and attic,	-	-	8
2 stories,	31	2	33
2 stories and attic,	239	12	251
Basement and 2 stories,	1	-	1
Basement, 2 stories, and attic,	-	-	8
3 stories,	3	1	4
Basement and 3 stories,	3	-	3
Materials.	476	31	507
Wood,	459	31	490
Brick,	7	-	7
Wood and brick,	10	-	10
Holliston.	612	39	651
Number of Stories.	612	39	651
1 story,	5	-	5
1 story and attic,	277	20	297
Basement and 1 story,	1	-	1
Basement, 1 story, and attic,	10	1	11
2 stories,	81	4	85
2 stories and attic,	217	13	230
Basement and 2 stories,	4	-	4
Basement, 2 stories, and attic,	3	-	3
3 stories,	12	1	13
4 stories,	1	-	1
Not given,	1	-	1
Materials.	612	39	651
Wood,	605	39	644
Brick,	2	-	2
Stone,	2	-	2
Wood and brick,	1	-	1
Wood and stone,	1	-	1
Not given,	1	-	1
Hopkinton.	714	73	787
Number of Stories.	714	73	787
1 story,	13	1	14
1 story and attic,	448	59	507
Basement, 1 story, and attic,	1	-	1
2 stories,	15	3	18
2 stories and attic,	226	10	236
Basement and 2 stories,	1	-	1
Basement, 2 stories, and attic,	1	-	1
3 stories,	7	-	7
3 stories and attic,	1	-	1
Basement, 3 stories, and attic,	1	-	1
Materials.	714	73	787
Wood,	705	72	777
Brick,	3	-	3
Wood and brick,	5	1	6
Wood and stone,	1	-	1
Hudson,	980	27	1,007
Number of Stories.	980	27	1,007
1 story,	11	2	13

Counties, Cities, Towns, Number of Stories to Dwelling Houses, and Materials of which Constructed.	Number of Occupied Dwelling Houses	Number of Unoccupied Dwelling Houses	Total Number of Dwelling Houses
MIDDLESEX — Con.			
Hudson — Con.			
Number of Stories — Con.			
1 story and attic,	388	10	398
Basement and 1 story,	2	-	2
Basement, 1 story, and attic,	20	1	21
2 stories,	101	1	102
2 stories and attic,	380	10	390
Basement and 2 stories,	11	1	12
Basement, 2 stories, and attic,	20	1	21
3 stories,	32	1	33
Basement and 3 stories,	5	-	5
4 stories,	1	-	1
Materials.	980	27	1,007
Wood,	969	27	996
Brick,	10	-	10
Wood and brick,	1	-	1
Lexington.	727	34	761
Number of Stories.	727	34	761
1 story,	62	1	63
1 story and attic,	62	4	66
2 stories,	526	21	547
2 stories and attic,	58	5	63
Basement and 2 stories,	4	1	5
3 stories,	14	2	16
Basement and 4 stories,	1	-	1
Materials.	727	34	761
Wood,	720	33	753
Brick,	5	-	5
Wood and brick,	1	-	1
Wood and stone,	1	1	2
Lincoln,	189	17	206
Number of Stories.	189	17	206
1 story,	8	1	9
1 story and attic,	28	2	30
Basement, 1 story, and attic,	1	-	1
2 stories,	32	3	35
2 stories and attic,	106	7	113
Basement and 2 stories,	1	-	1
Basement, 2 stories, and attic,	1	-	1
3 stories,	8	3	11
3 stories and attic,	4	-	4
Basement and 3 stories,	-	1	1
Materials.	189	17	206
Wood,	184	16	206
Brick,	2	1	3
Stone,	1	-	1
Wood and brick,	2	-	2
Littleton.	227	14	241
Number of Stories.	227	14	241
1 story,	-	3	3
1 story and attic,	76	4	80

DWELLING HOUSES: NUMBER OF STORIES AND MATERIALS — Continued.

COUNTIES, CITIES, TOWNS, NUMBER OF STORIES TO DWELLING HOUSES, AND MATERIALS OF WHICH CONSTRUCTED.	Number of Occupied Dwelling Houses	Number of Unoccupied Dwelling Houses	Total Number of Dwelling Houses	COUNTIES, CITIES, TOWNS, NUMBER OF STORIES TO DWELLING HOUSES, AND MATERIALS OF WHICH CONSTRUCTED.	Number of Occupied Dwelling Houses	Number of Unoccupied Dwelling Houses	Total Number of Dwelling Houses
MIDDLESEX — Con.				**MIDDLESEX — Con.**			
Littleton — Con.				LOWELL. WARD 1 — Con.			
Number of Stories — Con.				*Materials* — Con.			
2 stories, ...	1	–	1	Brick, ...	380	8	388
2 stories and attic, . . .	150	7	157	Stone, ...	2	–	2
Materials.	227	14	241	Wood and brick, . . .	24	1	25
Wood, ...	223	14	237	Brick and stone, . . .	5	–	5
Brick, ...	3	–	3	Brick and cement, . . .	1	–	1
Wood and brick, . . .	1	–	1	Wood, brick, and stone, .	1	–	1
LOWELL.	11,933	495	12,428	Not given, ...	1	–	1
Number of Stories.	11,933	495	12,428	LOWELL. WARD 2, . .	1,080	26	1,106
1 story, ...	174	11	185	*Number of Stories.*	1,080	26	1,106
1 story and attic, . . .	2,791	150	2,941	1 story, ...	25	1	26
Basement and 1 story, . .	3	–	3	1 story and attic, . . .	151	9	160
Basement, 1 story, and attic,	85	4	89	Basement, 1 story, and attic,	8	–	8
2 stories, ...	1,737	69	1,806	2 stories, ...	204	3	207
2 stories and attic, . . .	5,299	219	5,488	2 stories and attic, . . .	340	9	349
Basement and 2 stories, . .	36	1	37	Basement and 2 stories, . .	3	–	3
Basement, 2 stories, and attic,	152	3	155	Basement, 2 stories, and attic,	28	–	28
3 stories, ...	1,160	28	1,188	3 stories, ...	199	1	200
3 stories and attic, . . .	369	8	377	3 stories and attic, . . .	102	3	105
Basement and 3 stories, . .	21	–	21	Basement and 3 stories, . .	3	–	3
Basement, 3 stories, and attic,	8	1	9	4 stories, ...	16	–	16
4 stories, ...	108	–	108	4 stories and attic, . . .	1	–	1
4 stories and attic, . . .	6	–	6	*Materials.*	1,080	26	1,106
5 stories, ...	11	1	12	Wood, ...	843	22	865
6 stories, ...	1	–	1	Brick, ...	207	3	210
Not given, ...	2	–	2	Stone, ...	3	–	3
Materials.	11,933	495	12,428	Wood and brick, . . .	16	–	16
Wood, ...	11,034	478	11,512	Wood and stone, . . .	5	–	5
Brick, ...	727	14	741	Brick and stone, . . .	6	1	7
Stone, ...	28	–	28	LOWELL. WARD 3, . .	1,407	36	1,443
Wood and brick, . . .	109	1	110	*Number of Stories.*	1,407	36	1,443
Wood and stone, . . .	17	1	18	1 story, ...	10	–	10
Brick and stone, . . .	14	1	15	1 story and attic, . . .	357	10	367
Brick and cement, . . .	1	–	1	Basement, 1 story, and attic,	17	2	19
Wood, brick, and stone, .	1	–	1	2 stories, ...	125	–	125
Not given, ...	2	–	2	2 stories and attic, . . .	630	21	651
LOWELL. WARD 1, . .	1,147	21	1,168	Basement and 2 stories, . .	12	–	12
Number of Stories.	1,147	21	1,168	Basement, 2 stories, and attic,	17	–	17
1 story, ...	15	–	15	3 stories, ...	215	3	218
1 story and attic, . . .	107	4	111	3 stories and attic, . . .	14	–	14
2 stories, ...	119	3	122	Basement and 3 stories, . .	7	–	7
2 stories and attic, . . .	577	9	586	4 stories, ...	4	–	4
Basement and 2 stories, . .	2	–	2	*Materials.*	1,407	36	1,443
Basement, 2 stories, and attic,	10	–	10	Wood, ...	1,358	34	1,392
3 stories, ...	118	1	119	Brick, ...	22	1	23
3 stories and attic, . . .	157	4	161	Stone, ...	5	–	5
4 stories, ...	29	–	29	Wood and brick, . . .	13	–	13
4 stories and attic, . . .	1	–	1	Wood and stone, . . .	7	1	8
5 stories, ...	10	–	10	Brick and stone, . . .	2	–	2
6 stories, ...	1	–	1	LOWELL. WARD 4, . .	1,234	53	1,287
Not given, ...	1	–	1	*Number of Stories.*	1,234	53	1,287
Materials.	1,147	21	1,168	1 story, ...	1	–	1
Wood, ...	733	12	745				

DWELLING HOUSES: NUMBER OF STORIES AND MATERIALS — Continued.

COUNTIES, CITIES, TOWNS, NUMBER OF STORIES TO DWELLING HOUSES, AND MATERIALS OF WHICH CONSTRUCTED.	Number of Occupied Dwelling Houses	Number of Unoccupied Dwelling Houses	Total Number of Dwelling Houses
MIDDLESEX — Con.			
LOWELL. WARD 4 — Con.			
Number of Stories — Con.			
1 story and attic, . . .	255	9	262
Basement, 1 story, and attic,	3		3
2 stories, ...	173	1	174
2 stories and attic, . . .	652	33	685
Basement, 2 stories, and attic,	3	1	4
3 stories, ...	130	9	139
3 stories and attic, . . .	15	-	15
Basement, 3 stories, and attic,	2	-	2
4 stories, ...	2	-	2
Materials.	1,234	53	1,287
Wood, ...	1,198	53	1,251
Brick, ...	18		18
Stone, ...	1		1
Wood and brick, . . .	17		17
LOWELL. WARD 5, . .	1,101	35	1,136
Number of Stories.	1,101	35	1,136
1 story, ...	7	2	9
1 story and attic, . . .	151	12	163
Basement and 1 story, . .	1	-	1
Basement, 1 story, and attic,	19		19
2 stories, ...	113	5	118
2 stories and attic, . . .	613	11	624
Basement and 2 stories, . .	1		1
Basement, 2 stories, and attic,	24		24
3 stories, ...	141	5	146
3 stories and attic, . . .	12	-	12
Basement and 3 stories, . .	3		3
Basement, 3 stories, and attic,	2		2
4 stories, ...	13		13
Not given, ...	1		1
Materials.	1,101	35	1,136
Wood, ...	1,013	34	1,047
Brick, ...	61	1	62
Stone, ...	2		2
Wood and brick, . . .	23		23
Brick and stone, . . .	1		1
Not given, ...	1		1
LOWELL. WARD 6, . .	1,596	70	1,666
Number of Stories.	1,596	70	1,666
1 story, ...	43	3	46
1 story and attic, . . .	350	7	357
Basement, 1 story, and attic,	11	-	11
2 stories, ...	542	28	570
2 stories and attic, . . .	568	27	595
Basement, 2 stories, and attic,	10	1	11
3 stories, ...	79	3	82
3 stories and attic, . . .	3	-	3
4 stories, ...	9		9
5 stories, ...	1	1	2
Materials.	1,596	70	1,666
Wood, ...	1,592	70	1,662

COUNTIES, CITIES, TOWNS, NUMBER OF STORIES TO DWELLING HOUSES, AND MATERIALS OF WHICH CONSTRUCTED.	Number of Occupied Dwelling Houses	Number of Unoccupied Dwelling Houses	Total Number of Dwelling Houses
MIDDLESEX — Con.			
LOWELL. WARD 6 — Con.			
Materials — Con.			
Brick, ...	2	-	2
Stone, ...	2	-	2
LOWELL. WARD 7, . .	1,514	67	1,581
Number of Stories.	1,514	67	1,581
1 story, ...	2	-	2
1 story and attic, . . .	466	38	504
Basement, 1 story, and attic,	5	2	7
2 stories, ...	175	11	186
2 stories and attic, . . .	582	15	597
Basement, 2 stories, and attic,	5	-	5
3 stories, ...	186	1	187
3 stories and attic, . . .	52	-	52
Basement and 3 stories, . .	2	-	2
Basement, 3 stories, and attic,	1	-	1
4 stories, ...	34	-	34
4 stories and attic, . . .	4	-	4
Materials.	1,514	67	1,581
Wood, ...	1,475	66	1,541
Brick, ...	29	1	30
Stone, ...	7	-	7
Wood and brick, . . .	1	-	1
Wood and stone, . . .	2	-	2
LOWELL. WARD 8, . .	1,613	118	1,731
Number of Stories.	1,613	118	1,731
1 story, ...	60	4	64
1 story and attic, . . .	642	37	679
Basement and 1 story, . .	2	-	2
Basement, 1 story, and attic, .	14	-	14
2 stories, ...	196	17	213
2 stories and attic, . . .	652	55	707
Basement and 2 stories, . .	6	-	6
Basement, 2 stories, and attic,	11	-	11
3 stories, ...	25	4	29
3 stories and attic, . . .	5	-	5
Basement, 3 stories, and attic,	-	1	1
Materials.	1,613	118	1,731
Wood, ...	1,600	118	1,718
Brick, ...	4	-	4
Wood and brick, . . .	8	-	8
Wood and stone, . . .	1	-	1
LOWELL. WARD 9, . .	1,241	69	1,310
Number of Stories.	1,241	69	1,310
1 story, ...	11	1	12
1 story and attic, . . .	334	24	358
Basement, 1 story, and attic,	8	-	8
2 stories, ...	90	1	91
2 stories and attic, . . .	655	39	694
Basement and 2 stories, . .	12	1	13
Basement, 2 stories, and attic,	44	1	45
3 stories, ...	67	1	68
3 stories and attic, . . .	10	1	11

DWELLING HOUSES: NUMBER OF STORIES AND MATERIALS — Continued.

Counties, Cities, Towns, Number of Stories to Dwelling Houses, and Materials of which Constructed.	Number of Occupied Dwelling Houses	Number of Unoccupied Dwelling Houses	Total Number of Dwelling Houses
MIDDLESEX — Con.			
LOWELL. WARD 9 — Con.			
Number of Stories — Con.			
Basement and 3 stories, .	6	–	6
Basement, 3 stories, and attic,	3	–	3
4 stories,	1	–	1
Materials.	1,241	69	1,310
Wood, .	1,222	69	1,291
Brick, .	4	–	4
Stone, .	6	–	6
Wood and brick,	7	–	7
Wood and stone,	2	–	2
MALDEN.	5,388	450	5,838
Number of Stories.	5,388	450	5,838
1 story,	59	6	65
1 story and attic,	795	70	865
Basement and 1 story,	1	1	2
Basement, 1 story, and attic,	23	2	25
2 stories,	852	57	909
2 stories and attic,	3,345	290	3,635
Basement and 2 stories, .	38	4	42
Basement, 2 stories, and attic,	55	5	60
3 stories,	201	14	215
3 stories and attic,	12	–	12
Basement and 3 stories, .	3	1	4
Basement, 3 stories, and attic,	2	–	2
4 stories,	1	–	1
Not given,	1	–	1
Materials.	5,388	450	5,838
Wood, .	5,355	444	5,799
Brick, .	23	1	24
Stone, .	1	–	1
Cement,	–	1	1
Wood and brick,	7	4	11
Wood and stone,	1	–	1
Not given,	1	–	1
MALDEN. WARD 1,	764	58	822
Number of Stories.	764	58	822
1 story,	6	2	8
1 story and attic,	106	10	116
Basement, 1 story, and attic,	5	–	5
2 stories,	67	5	72
2 stories and attic,	544	39	583
Basement and 2 stories, .	5	–	5
Basement, 2 stories, and attic,	17	–	17
3 stories,	13	2	15
3 stories and attic,	1	–	1
Basement and 3 stories, .	1	–	1
Basement, 3 stories, and attic,	2	–	2
Materials.	764	58	822
Wood, .	759	58	817
Brick, .	1	–	1
Stone, .	1	–	1
Wood and brick,	3	–	3
MIDDLESEX — Con.			
MALDEN. WARD 2,	713	20	733
Number of Stories.	713	20	733
1 story,	24	1	25
1 story and attic,	119	6	125
Basement, 1 story, and attic,	3	–	3
2 stories,	63	1	64
2 stories and attic,	480	11	491
Basement and 2 stories, .	1	–	1
Basement, 2 stories, and attic,	2	–	2
3 stories,	16	1	17
3 stories and attic,	4	–	4
4 stories,	1	–	1
Materials.	713	20	733
Wood, .	712	19	731
Brick, .	1	–	1
Cement,	–	1	1
MALDEN. WARD 3,	682	52	734
Number of Stories.	682	52	734
1 story,	1	–	1
1 story and attic,	29	2	31
Basement, 1 story, and attic,	4	2	6
2 stories,	49	4	53
2 stories and attic,	554	40	594
Basement and 2 stories, .	3	–	3
Basement, 2 stories, and attic,	4	1	5
3 stories,	33	3	36
3 stories and attic,	4	–	4
Basement and 3 stories, .	1	–	1
Materials.	682	52	734
Wood, .	677	52	729
Brick, .	5	–	5
MALDEN. WARD 4,	833	41	874
Number of Stories.	833	41	874
1 story,	6	2	8
1 story and attic,	30	1	31
Basement and 1 story, .	1	–	1
Basement, 1 story, and attic,	3	–	3
2 stories,	227	9	236
2 stories and attic,	448	20	468
Basement and 2 stories, .	12	3	15
Basement, 2 stories, and attic,	16	2	18
3 stories,	86	4	90
3 stories and attic,	2	–	2
Basement and 3 stories, .	1	–	1
Not given,	1	–	1
Materials.	833	41	874
Wood, .	818	40	858
Brick, .	12	1	13
Wood and brick,	1	–	1
Wood and stone,	1	–	1
Not given,	1	–	1

DWELLING HOUSES: NUMBER OF STORIES AND MATERIALS — Continued.

COUNTIES, CITIES, TOWNS, NUMBER OF STORIES TO DWELLING HOUSES, AND MATERIALS OF WHICH CONSTRUCTED.	Number of Occupied Dwelling Houses	Number of Unoccupied Dwelling Houses	Total Number of Dwelling Houses
MIDDLESEX — Con.			
MALDEN. WARD 5,	806	86	889
Number of Stories.	806	86	889
1 story,	3	–	3
1 story and attic,	80	12	92
Basement, 1 story, and attic,	3	–	3
2 stories,	129	9	138
2 stories and attic,	555	61	616
Basement and 2 stories,	9	1	10
Basement, 2 stories, and attic,	2	1	3
3 stories,	22	2	24
Materials.	806	86	889
Wood,	799	85	884
Brick,	3	–	3
Wood and brick,	1	1	2
MALDEN. WARD 6,	881	113	994
Number of Stories.	881	113	994
1 story,	16	1	17
1 story and attic,	339	29	368
Basement and 1 story,	–	1	1
Basement, 1 story, and attic,	3	–	3
2 stories,	146	16	162
2 stories and attic,	349	64	413
Basement and 2 stories,	2	–	2
Basement, 2 stories, and attic,	6	1	7
3 stories,	20	–	20
Basement and 3 stories,	–	1	1
Materials.	881	113	994
Wood,	880	113	993
Brick,	1	–	1
MALDEN. WARD 7,	712	80	792
Number of Stories.	712	80	792
1 story,	3	–	3
1 story and attic,	95	10	105
Basement, 1 story, and attic,	2	–	2
2 stories,	171	13	184
2 stories and attic,	415	55	470
Basement and 2 stories,	6	–	6
Basement, 2 stories, and attic,	8	–	8
3 stories,	11	2	13
3 stories and attic,	1	–	1
Materials.	712	80	792
Wood,	710	77	787
Wood and brick,	2	3	5
MARLBOROUGH.	2,341	63	2,404
Number of Stories.	2,341	63	2,404
1 story,	22	–	22
1 story and attic,	657	27	684
Basement and 1 story,	5	1	6
Basement, 1 story, and attic,	54	2	56
2 stories,	514	13	527
2 stories and attic,	911	13	924
MIDDLESEX — Con.			
MARLBOROUGH — Con.			
Number of Stories — Con.			
Basement and 2 stories,	44	–	44
Basement, 2 stories, and attic,	97	4	101
3 stories,	27	3	30
3 stories and attic,	4	–	4
Basement and 3 stories,	2	–	2
Basement, 3 stories, and attic,	1	–	1
4 stories,	2	–	2
Not given,	1	–	1
Materials.	2,341	63	2,404
Wood,	2,300	63	2,363
Brick,	17	–	17
Wood and brick,	16	–	16
Wood and stone,	6	–	6
Wood, brick, and stone,	1	–	1
Not given,	1	–	1
MARLBOROUGH. WARD 1,	253	16	269
Number of Stories.	253	16	269
1 story,	2	–	2
1 story and attic,	91	7	98
Basement, 1 story, and attic,	1	–	1
2 stories,	45	8	53
2 stories and attic,	108	1	109
Basement and 2 stories,	1	–	1
Basement, 2 stories, and attic,	1	–	1
3 stories,	4	–	4
Materials.	253	16	269
Wood,	250	16	266
Brick,	2	–	2
Wood and brick,	1	–	1
MARLBOROUGH. WARD 2,	366	–	366
Number of Stories.	366	–	366
1 story,	1	–	1
1 story and attic,	124	–	124
2 stories,	111	–	111
2 stories and attic,	114	–	114
Basement and 2 stories,	5	–	5
Basement, 2 stories, and attic,	2	–	2
3 stories,	9	–	9
Materials.	366	–	366
Wood,	349	–	349
Brick,	3	–	3
Wood and brick,	7	–	7
Wood and stone,	6	–	6
Wood, brick, and stone,	1	–	1
MARLBOROUGH. WARD 3,	398	9	407
Number of Stories.	398	9	407
1 story,	5	–	5
1 story and attic,	97	2	99
Basement and 1 story,	5	–	5

DWELLING HOUSES: NUMBER OF STORIES AND MATERIALS — Continued.

Counties, Cities, Towns, Number of Stories to Dwelling Houses, and Materials of which Constructed	Number of Occupied Dwelling Houses	Number of Unoccupied Dwelling Houses	Total Number of Dwelling Houses
MIDDLESEX — Con.			
MARLBOROUGH. WARD 3 — Con.			
Number of Stories — Con.			
Basement, 1 story, and attic,	41	1	42
2 stories,	53	1	54
2 stories and attic,	135	3	138
Basement and 2 stories,	10	–	10
Basement, 2 stories, and attic,	45	2	47
3 stories,	1	–	1
3 stories and attic,	2	–	2
Basement and 3 stories,	1	–	1
Basement, 3 stories, and attic,	1	–	1
4 stories,	1	–	1
Not given,	1	–	1
Materials.	398	9	407
Wood,	392	9	401
Brick,	3	–	3
Wood and brick,	2	–	2
Not given,	1	–	1
MARLBOROUGH. WARD 4,	479	18	497
Number of Stories	479	18	497
1 story,	4	–	4
1 story and attic,	192	14	206
Basement, 1 story, and attic,	10	1	11
2 stories,	71	1	72
2 stories and attic,	185	1	186
Basement and 2 stories,	4	–	4
Basement, 2 stories, and attic,	9	1	10
3 stories,	3	–	3
3 stories and attic,	1	–	1
Materials.	479	18	497
Wood,	475	18	493
Wood and brick,	4	–	4
MARLBOROUGH. WARD 5,	310	6	316
Number of Stories	310	6	316
1 story,	4	–	4
1 story and attic,	6	–	6
Basement and 1 story,	–	1	1
2 stories,	189	1	190
2 stories and attic,	88	1	89
Basement and 2 stories,	15	–	15
Basement, 2 stories, and attic,	6	–	6
3 stories,	1	3	4
4 stories,	1	–	1
Materials.	310	6	316
Wood,	306	6	312
Brick,	4	–	4
MARLBOROUGH. WARD 6,	284	11	295
Number of Stories	284	11	295
1 story,	4	–	4
1 story and attic,	64	4	65
Basement, 1 story, and attic,	2	–	2
MIDDLESEX — Con.			
MARLBOROUGH. WARD 6 — Con.			
Number of Stories — Con.			
2 stories,	33	2	35
2 stories and attic,	148	7	155
Basement and 2 stories,	7	–	7
Basement, 2 stories, and attic,	20	1	21
3 stories,	5	–	5
Basement and 3 stories,	1	–	1
Materials.	284	14	295
Wood,	281	14	295
MARLBOROUGH. WARD 7,	254	–	254
Number of Stories	254	–	254
1 story,	2	–	2
1 story and attic,	86	–	86
2 stories,	12	–	12
2 stories and attic,	133	–	133
Basement and 2 stories,	2	–	2
Basement, 2 stories, and attic,	14	–	14
3 stories,	4	–	4
3 stories and attic,	1	–	1
Materials.	254	–	254
Wood,	247	–	247
Brick,	5	–	5
Wood and brick,	2	–	2
Maynard,	605	24	629
Number of Stories	605	24	629
1 story,	21	2	23
1 story and attic,	321	10	331
Basement and 1 story,	1	–	1
Basement, 1 story, and attic,	5	1	6
2 stories,	110	7	117
2 stories and attic,	114	3	117
Basement and 2 stories,	18	–	18
Basement, 2 stories, and attic,	5	–	5
3 stories,	9	1	10
Not given,	1	–	1
Materials.	605	24	629
Wood,	603	24	627
Wood and brick,	1	–	1
Not given,	1	–	1
MEDFORD,	2,811	286	3,097
Number of Stories	2,811	286	3,097
1 story,	60	9	69
1 story and attic,	379	18	397
Basement and 1 story,	1	–	1
Basement, 1 story, and attic,	20	1	21
2 stories,	844	126	970
2 stories and attic,	1,343	116	1,459
Basement and 2 stories,	24	2	26
Basement, 2 stories, and attic,	29	3	32
3 stories,	94	11	105

DWELLING HOUSES: NUMBER OF STORIES AND MATERIALS — Continued.

COUNTIES, CITIES, TOWNS, NUMBER OF STORIES TO DWELLING HOUSES, AND MATERIALS OF WHICH CONSTRUCTED.	Number of Occupied Dwelling Houses	Number of Unoccupied Dwelling Houses	Total Number of Dwelling Houses	COUNTIES, CITIES, TOWNS, NUMBER OF STORIES TO DWELLING HOUSES, AND MATERIALS OF WHICH CONSTRUCTED.	Number of Occupied Dwelling Houses	Number of Unoccupied Dwelling Houses	Total Number of Dwelling Houses
MIDDLESEX — Con.				**MIDDLESEX — Con.**			
MEDFORD — Con.				MEDFORD. WARD 3 — Con.			
Number of Stories — Con.				*Number of Stories — Con.*			
3 stories and attic, . . .	7	–	7	Basement and 2 stories, . .	3	2	5
Basement and 3 stories, . .	5	–	5	Basement, 2 stories, and attic,	8	3	11
Basement, 3 stories, and attic,	2	–	2	3 stories, ...	42	3	45
4 stories, ...	2	–	2	3 stories and attic, . . .	1	–	1
Not given, ...	1	–	1	Basement and 3 stories, . .	1	–	1
				4 stories, ...	2	–	2
Materials.	2,841	286	3,097				
Wood, ...	2,755	279	3,034	*Materials.*	375	20	383
Brick, ...	37	3	40	Wood, ...	351	17	368
Stone, ...	4	1	5	Brick, ...	11	–	11
Cement, ...	1	–	1	Stone, ...	2	1	3
Wood and brick, . . .	8	3	11	Cement, ...	1	–	1
Wood and stone, . . .	3	–	3	Wood and brick, . . .	5	2	7
Brick and stone, . . .	2	–	2	Wood and stone, . . .	3	–	3
Not given, ...	1	–	1				
				MEDFORD. WARD 4, . .	384	14	398
MEDFORD. WARD 1, . .	562	78	640	*Number of Stories.*	384	14	398
Number of Stories.	562	78	640	1 story, ...	3	–	3
1 story, ...	4	–	4	1 story and attic, . . .	43	2	45
1 story and attic, . . .	105	7	112	Basement, 1 story, and attic,	5	–	5
Basement, 1 story, and attic,	4	–	4	2 stories, ...	55	2	57
2 stories, ...	68	7	75	2 stories and attic, . . .	262	9	271
2 stories and attic, . . .	357	64	421	Basement and 2 stories, . .	3	–	3
Basement and 2 stories, . .	8	–	8	Basement, 2 stories, and attic,	6	–	6
Basement, 2 stories, and attic,	6	–	6	3 stories, ...	2	1	3
3 stories, ...	10	–	10	3 stories and attic, . . .	4	–	4
				Not given, ...	1	–	1
Materials.	562	78	640				
Wood, ...	559	77	636	*Materials.*	384	14	398
Brick, ...	1	1	2	Wood, ...	379	13	392
Wood and brick, . . .	2	–	2	Brick, ...	4	–	4
				Wood and brick, . . .	–	1	1
MEDFORD. WARD 2, . .	468	26	494	Not given, ...	1	–	1
Number of Stories.	468	26	494				
1 story, ...	3	1	4	MEDFORD. WARD 5, . .	547	113	660
1 story and attic, . . .	117	5	122	*Number of Stories.*	547	113	660
Basement, 1 story, and attic,	6	–	6	1 story, ...	39	6	45
2 stories, ...	83	6	89	1 story and attic, . . .	1	1	2
2 stories and attic, . . .	242	14	256	2 stories, ...	492	62	554
Basement and 2 stories, . .	3	–	3	3 stories, ...	12	4	16
Basement, 2 stories, and attic,	6	–	6	Basement and 3 stories, . .	3	–	3
3 stories, ...	8	–	8				
				Materials.	547	113	660
Materials.	468	26	494	Wood, ...	531	111	642
Wood, ...	466	26	492	Brick, ...	16	2	18
Brick and stone, . . .	2	–	2				
				MEDFORD. WARD 6, . .	477	35	512
MEDFORD. WARD 3, . .	373	20	393	*Number of Stories.*	477	35	512
Number of Stories.	373	20	393	1 story, ...	2	–	2
1 story, ...	9	2	11	1 story and attic, . . .	52	3	55
1 story and attic, . . .	61	–	61	Basement, 1 story, and attic,	2	–	2
Basement and 1 story, . .	1	–	1	2 stories, ...	75	7	82
Basement, 1 story, and attic,	3	1	4	2 stories and attic, . . .	311	22	333
2 stories, ...	71	2	73	Basement and 2 stories, . .	7	–	7
2 stories and attic, . . .	171	7	178	Basement, 2 stories, and attic,	3	–	3

DWELLING HOUSES: NUMBER OF STORIES AND MATERIALS — Continued.

COUNTIES, CITIES, TOWNS, NUMBER OF STORIES TO DWELLING HOUSES, AND MATERIALS OF WHICH CONSTRUCTED.	Number of Occupied Dwelling Houses	Number of Unoccupied Dwelling Houses	Total Number of Dwelling Houses	COUNTIES, CITIES, TOWNS, NUMBER OF STORIES TO DWELLING HOUSES, AND MATERIALS OF WHICH CONSTRUCTED.	Number of Occupied Dwelling Houses	Number of Unoccupied Dwelling Houses	Total Number of Dwelling Houses
MIDDLESEX — Con.				**MIDDLESEX — Con.**			
MEDFORD. WARD 6 — Con.				**Natick — Con.**			
Number of Stories — Con.				*Materials — Con.*			
3 stories,	20	3	23	Wood and brick,	2	–	2
3 stories and attic,	2	–	2	Wood and stone,	3	–	3
Basement and 3 stories,	1	–	1	**NEWTON.**	5,102	513	5,615
Basement, 3 stories, and attic,	2	–	2	*Number of Stories.*	5,102	513	5,615
Materials.	477	35	512	1 story,	103	4	107
Wood,	469	35	504	1 story and attic,	351	31	382
Brick,	5	–	5	Basement and 1 story,	18	1	19
Stone,	2	–	2	Basement, 1 story, and attic,	16	3	19
Wood and brick,	1	–	1	2 stories,	951	80	1,031
				2 stories and attic,	2,979	324	3,303
Melrose.	2,474	354	2,828	Basement and 2 stories,	46	2	48
Number of Stories.	2,474	354	2,828	Basement, 2 stories, and attic,	105	15	120
1 story,	14	–	14	3 stories,	499	49	548
1 story and attic,	350	28	378	3 stories and attic,	18	4	22
Basement and 1 story,	–	1	1	Basement and 3 stories,	7	–	7
Basement, 1 story, and attic,	21	1	22	Basement, 3 stories, and attic,	5	–	5
2 stories,	511	68	579	4 stories,	1	–	1
2 stories and attic,	1,462	246	1,708	Not given,	3	–	3
Basement and 2 stories,	11	–	11	*Materials.*	5,102	513	5,615
Basement, 2 stories, and attic,	35	–	35	Wood,	5,019	504	5,523
3 stories,	65	8	73	Brick,	43	3	46
3 stories and attic,	1	–	1	Stone,	11	–	11
Basement and 3 stories,	1	1	2	Wood and brick,	11	–	11
Basement, 3 stories, and attic,	1	1	2	Wood and stone,	14	3	17
4 stories,	1	–	1	Brick and stone,	1	3	4
Not given,	1	–	1	Not given,	3	–	3
Materials.	2,474	354	2,828	**NEWTON. WARD 1.**	743	72	815
Wood,	2,463	354	2,817	*Number of Stories.*	743	72	815
Brick,	2	–	2	1 story,	37	1	38
Stone,	3	–	3	1 story and attic,	101	11	112
Wood and brick,	1	–	1	Basement and 1 story,	6	1	7
Wood and stone,	2	–	2	Basement, 1 story, and attic,	7	3	10
Wood and cement,	1	–	1	2 stories,	231	9	240
Brick and stone,	1	–	1	2 stories and attic,	262	35	297
Not given,	1	–	1	Basement and 2 stories,	6	1	7
Natick.	1,741	69	1,810	Basement, 2 stories, and attic,	36	5	41
Number of Stories.	1,741	69	1,810	3 stories,	51	6	57
1 story,	64	4	68	3 stories and attic,	2	–	2
1 story and attic,	734	24	758	Basement and 3 stories,	3	–	3
Basement and 1 story,	1	–	1	Basement, 3 stories, and attic,	1	–	1
Basement, 1 story, and attic,	52	3	55	*Materials.*	743	72	815
2 stories,	153	11	164	Wood,	737	72	809
2 stories and attic,	655	22	677	Brick,	1	–	1
Basement and 2 stories,	5	–	5	Wood and brick,	4	–	4
Basement, 2 stories, and attic,	17	1	18	Wood and stone,	1	–	1
3 stories,	52	3	55	**NEWTON. WARD 2.**	1,004	100	1,104
3 stories and attic,	7	1	8	*Number of Stories.*	1,004	100	1,104
Basement and 3 stories,	1	–	1	1 story,	12	1	13
Materials.	1,741	69	1,810	1 story and attic,	15	4	19
Wood,	1,724	68	1,792	Basement and 1 story,	3	–	3
Brick,	12	1	13				

DWELLING HOUSES: NUMBER OF STORIES AND MATERIALS — Continued.

COUNTIES, CITIES, TOWNS, NUMBER OF STORIES TO DWELLING HOUSES, AND MATERIALS OF WHICH CONSTRUCTED.	Number of Occupied Dwelling Houses	Number of Unoccupied Dwelling Houses	Total Number of Dwelling Houses
MIDDLESEX — Con.			
NEWTON. WARD 2—Con.			
Number of Stories — Con.			
Basement, 1 story, and attic,	2	–	2
2 stories,	195	14	209
2 stories and attic,	729	75	804
Basement and 2 stories,	12	–	12
Basement, 2 stories, and attic,	7	3	10
3 stories,	25	3	28
3 stories and attic,	2	–	2
Basement and 3 stories,	1	–	1
Not given,	1	–	1
Materials.	1,004	100	1,104
Wood,	995	98	1,093
Brick,	5	1	6
Wood and brick,	2	–	2
Wood and stone,	–	1	1
Brick and stone,	1	–	1
Not given,	1	–	1
NEWTON. WARD 3,	671	68	739
Number of Stories.	671	68	739
1 story,	11	2	13
1 story and attic,	12	–	12
Basement and 1 story,	1	–	1
2 stories,	173	20	193
2 stories and attic,	409	39	448
Basement and 2 stories,	2	–	2
Basement, 2 stories, and attic,	1	–	1
3 stories,	58	6	64
3 stories and attic,	3	1	4
Basement, 3 stories, and attic,	1	–	1
Materials.	671	68	739
Wood,	661	68	729
Brick,	6	–	6
Stone,	1	–	1
Wood and stone,	3	–	3
NEWTON. WARD 4,	643	97	740
Number of Stories.	643	97	740
1 story,	16	–	16
1 story and attic,	78	6	84
Basement and 1 story,	2	–	2
Basement, 1 story, and attic,	2	–	2
2 stories,	142	21	163
2 stories and attic,	339	67	406
Basement and 2 stories,	14	–	14
Basement, 2 stories, and attic,	13	1	14
3 stories,	31	2	33
3 stories and attic,	2	–	2
Basement and 3 stories,	2	–	2
Basement, 3 stories, and attic,	2	–	2
Materials.	643	97	740
Wood,	637	94	731
Brick,	3	–	3
MIDDLESEX — Con.			
NEWTON. WARD 4—Con.			
Materials — Con.			
Stone,	3	–	3
Brick and stone,	–	3	3
NEWTON. WARD 5.	804	72	876
Number of Stories.	804	72	876
1 story,	13	–	13
1 story and attic,	60	3	63
2 stories,	82	6	88
2 stories and attic,	452	38	490
Basement and 2 stories,	1	–	1
Basement, 2 stories, and attic,	3	–	3
3 stories,	186	24	210
3 stories and attic,	5	1	6
4 stories,	1	–	1
Not given,	1	–	1
Materials.	804	72	876
Wood,	796	71	867
Brick,	3	1	4
Stone,	2	–	2
Wood and brick,	1	–	1
Wood and stone,	1	–	1
Not given,	1	–	1
NEWTON. WARD 6,	768	64	832
Number of Stories.	768	64	832
1 story,	14	–	14
1 story and attic,	77	4	81
Basement and 1 story,	6	–	6
Basement, 1 story, and attic,	5	–	5
2 stories,	91	4	95
2 stories and attic,	473	43	516
Basement and 2 stories,	8	1	9
Basement, 2 stories, and attic,	37	3	40
3 stories,	54	7	61
3 stories and attic,	2	2	4
Not given,	1	–	1
Materials.	768	64	832
Wood,	741	63	804
Brick,	13	–	13
Stone,	4	–	4
Wood and brick,	2	–	2
Wood and stone,	7	1	8
Not given,	1	–	1
NEWTON. WARD 7,	469	40	509
Number of Stories.	469	40	509
1 story and attic,	8	3	11
2 stories,	37	6	43
2 stories and attic,	315	27	342
Basement and 2 stories,	3	–	3
Basement, 2 stories, and attic,	8	3	11
3 stories,	94	1	95
3 stories and attic,	2	–	2

DWELLING HOUSES: NUMBER OF STORIES AND MATERIALS — Continued.

COUNTIES, CITIES, TOWNS. NUMBER OF STORIES TO DWELLING HOUSES, AND MATERIALS OF WHICH CONSTRUCTED.	Number of Occupied Dwelling Houses	Number of Unoccupied Dwelling Houses	Total Number of Dwelling Houses	COUNTIES, CITIES, TOWNS. NUMBER OF STORIES TO DWELLING HOUSES, AND MATERIALS OF WHICH CONSTRUCTED.	Number of Occupied Dwelling Houses	Number of Unoccupied Dwelling Houses	Total Number of Dwelling Houses
MIDDLESEX — Con.				**MIDDLESEX — Con.**			
NEWTON. WARD 7 — Con.				**Reading — Con.**			
Number of Stories — Con.				*Number of Stories — Con.*			
Basement and 3 stories, . .	1	–	1	Basement, 2 stories, and attic,	7	1	8
Basement, 3 stories, and attic,	1	–	1	3 stories, ...	7	–	7
				3 stories and attic, . . .	2	–	2
Materials.	469	40	509	Basement and 3 stories, .	1	–	1
Wood, ...	452	38	490	Not given, ...	2	–	2
Brick, ...	12	1	13				
Stone, ...	1	–	1	*Materials.*	1,034	55	1,089
Wood and brick, . . .	2	–	2	Wood, ...	1,031	55	1,086
Wood and stone, . . .	2	1	3	Brick, ...	1	–	1
				Not given, ...	2	–	2
North Reading, . .	204	14	218				
Number of Stories.	204	14	218	**Sherborn,**	268	25	293
1 story, ...	8	–	8	*Number of Stories.*	268	25	293
1 story and attic, . . .	57	7	64	1 story, ...	4	1	5
Basement, 1 story, and attic,	–	1	1	1 story and attic, . . .	55	7	62
2 stories, ...	51	3	54	2 stories, ...	57	5	62
2 stories and attic, . . .	84	3	87	2 stories and attic, . . .	151	11	162
Basement, 2 stories, and attic,	2	–	2	3 stories, ...	1	1	2
3 stories, ...	2	–	2				
				Materials.	268	25	293
Materials.	204	14	218	Wood, ...	267	25	292
Wood, ...	202	14	216	Brick, ...	1	–	1
Stone, ...	1	–	1				
Wood and brick, . . .	1	–	1	**Shirley.**	302	25	327
				Number of Stories.	302	25	327
Pepperell.	690	57	747	1 story, ...	12	3	15
Number of Stories.	690	57	747	1 story and attic, . . .	135	11	146
1 story, ...	9	1	10	Basement and 1 story, . .	2	–	2
1 story and attic, . . .	314	25	339	Basement, 1 story, and attic,	9	1	10
Basement and 1 story, . .	3	1	4	2 stories, ...	31	4	35
Basement, 1 story, and attic,	12	2	14	2 stories and attic, . . .	104	6	110
2 stories, ...	23	4	27	Basement and 2 stories, . .	1	–	1
2 stories and attic, . . .	311	24	335	Basement, 2 stories, and attic,	4	–	4
Basement and 2 stories, . .	3	–	3	3 stories, ...	1	–	1
Basement, 2 stories, and attic,	4	–	4	3 stories and attic, . . .	3	–	3
3 stories, ...	7	–	7				
3 stories and attic, . . .	1	–	1	*Materials.*	302	25	327
Basement and 3 stories, . .	2	–	2	Wood, ...	285	23	308
Not given, ...	1	–	1	Brick, ...	16	2	18
				Wood and brick, . . .	1	–	1
Materials.	690	57	747				
Wood, ...	674	53	727	**SOMERVILLE.** . . .	8,787	629	9,416
Brick, ...	8	2	10	*Number of Stories.*	8,787	629	9,416
Wood and brick, . . .	7	1	8	1 story, ...	122	8	130
Wood and cement, . . .	–	1	1	1 story and attic, . . .	460	48	508
Not given, ...	1	–	1	Basement and 1 story, . .	5	–	5
				Basement, 1 story, and attic, .	30	3	33
Reading.	1,034	55	1,089	2 stories, ...	1,407	91	1,498
Number of Stories.	1,034	55	1,089	2 stories and attic, . . .	5,015	334	5,349
1 story, ...	10	–	10	Basement and 2 stories, . .	269	12	281
1 story and attic, . . .	439	12	451	Basement, 2 stories, and attic,	342	29	371
Basement, 1 story, and attic,	5	–	5	3 stories, ...	1,037	95	1,132
2 stories, ...	48	6	54	3 stories and attic, . . .	34	3	37
2 stories and attic, . . .	512	36	548	Basement and 3 stories, . .	50	2	52
Basement and 2 stories, . .	1	–	1	Basement, 3 stories, and attic,	9	2	11
				4 stories, ...	6	–	6

DWELLING HOUSES: NUMBER OF STORIES AND MATERIALS — Continued.

COUNTIES, CITIES, TOWNS, NUMBER OF STORIES TO DWELLING HOUSES, AND MATERIALS OF WHICH CONSTRUCTED.	Number of Occupied Dwelling Houses	Number of Unoccupied Dwelling Houses	Total Number of Dwelling Houses
MIDDLESEX — Con.			
SOMERVILLE — Con.			
Number of Stories — Con.			
4 stories and attic, . . .	1	–	1
5 stories, ...	1	–	1
5 stories and attic, . . .	1	–	1
Materials.	8,787	629	9,416
Wood, ...	8,642	619	9,261
Brick, ...	131	10	141
Stone, ...	1	–	1
Wood and brick, . . .	12	–	12
Wood, brick, and stone, .	1	–	1
SOMERVILLE. WARD 1,	1,578	70	1,648
Number of Stories.	1,578	70	1,648
1 story, ...	7	–	7
1 story and attic, . . .	123	13	136
Basement and 1 story, . .	1	–	1
Basement, 1 story, and attic, .	6	–	6
2 stories, ...	360	10	370
2 stories and attic, . .	725	29	754
Basement and 2 stories, . .	36	4	40
Basement, 2 stories, and attic,	25	–	25
3 stories, ...	264	14	278
3 stories and attic, . .	19	–	19
Basement and 3 stories, . .	10	–	10
4 stories, ...	2	–	2
Materials.	1,578	70	1,648
Wood, ...	1,539	70	1,609
Brick, ...	37	–	37
Wood and brick, . . .	1	–	1
Wood, brick, and stone, .	1	–	1
SOMERVILLE. WARD 2,	2,647	115	2,762
Number of Stories.	2,647	115	2,762
1 story, ...	91	4	95
1 story and attic, . . .	123	9	132
Basement and 1 story, . .	2	–	2
Basement, 1 story, and attic,	14	3	17
2 stories, ...	569	25	594
2 stories and attic, . .	1,124	29	1,153
Basement and 2 stories, . .	139	4	143
Basement, 2 stories, and attic,	65	3	68
3 stories, ...	481	36	517
3 stories and attic, . .	5	1	6
Basement and 3 stories, .	28	1	29
4 stories, ...	4	–	4
4 stories and attic, . . .	1	–	1
5 stories, ...	1	–	1
Materials.	2,647	115	2,762
Wood, ...	2,593	107	2,700
Brick, ...	48	8	56
Wood and brick, . . .	6	–	6
SOMERVILLE. WARD 3,	2,446	219	2,665
Number of Stories.	2,446	219	2,665
1 story, ...	17	1	18
MIDDLESEX — Con.			
SOMERVILLE. WARD 3 — Con.			
Number of Stories — Con.			
1 story and attic, . . .	158	25	183
Basement, 1 story, and attic,	4	–	4
2 stories, ...	230	28	258
2 stories and attic, . . .	1,865	142	2,007
Basement and 2 stories, .	5	–	5
Basement, 2 stories, and attic,	5	–	5
3 stories, ...	155	21	176
3 stories and attic, . . .	6	1	7
Basement and 3 stories, .	1	1	2
Materials.	2,446	219	2,665
Wood, ...	2,408	218	2,626
Brick, ...	34	1	35
Stone, ...	1	–	1
Wood and brick, . . .	3	–	3
SOMERVILLE. WARD 4,	2,116	225	2,341
Number of Stories.	2,116	225	2,341
1 story, ...	7	3	10
1 story and attic, . . .	56	1	57
Basement and 1 story, . .	2	–	2
Basement, 1 story, and attic,	6	–	6
2 stories, ...	248	28	276
2 stories and attic, . . .	1,299	136	1,435
Basement and 2 stories, . .	89	4	93
Basement, 2 stories, and attic,	247	26	273
3 stories, ...	137	24	161
3 stories and attic, . . .	4	1	5
Basement and 3 stories, .	11	–	11
Basement, 3 stories, and attic,	9	2	11
5 stories and attic, . . .	1	–	1
Materials.	2,116	225	2,341
Wood, ...	2,102	224	2,326
Brick, ...	12	1	13
Wood and brick, . . .	2	–	2
Stoneham.	1,330	56	1,386
Number of Stories.	1,330	56	1,386
1 story, ...	17	–	17
1 story and attic, . . .	609	23	632
Basement and 1 story, . .	1	–	1
Basement, 1 story, and attic,	39	1	40
2 stories, ...	218	6	224
2 stories and attic, . . .	402	22	424
Basement and 2 stories, . .	8	2	10
Basement, 2 stories, and attic,	11	1	12
3 stories, ...	21	1	22
3 stories and attic, . . .	1	–	1
Basement and 3 stories, . .	2	–	2
4 stories, ...	1	–	1
Materials.	1,330	56	1,386
Wood, ...	1,329	54	1,383
Stone, ...	1	1	2
Wood and brick, . . .	–	1	1

DWELLING HOUSES: NUMBER OF STORIES AND MATERIALS — Continued.

COUNTIES, CITIES, TOWNS, NUMBER OF STORIES TO DWELLING HOUSES, AND MATERIALS OF WHICH CONSTRUCTED.	Number of Occupied Dwelling Houses	Number of Unoccupied Dwelling Houses	Total Number of Dwelling Houses
MIDDLESEX — Con.			
Stow.	223	20	243
Number of Stories.	223	20	243
1 story, ...	2	1	3
1 story and attic, . . .	32	5	37
Basement, 1 story, and attic,	4	–	4
2 stories, ...	45	2	47
2 stories and attic, . . .	133	11	144
Basement, 2 stories, and attic,	5	–	5
3 stories, ...	1	–	1
3 stories and attic, . . .	1	1	2
Materials.	223	20	243
Wood, ...	221	20	241
Brick, ...	1	–	1
Wood and brick, . . .	1	–	1
Sudbury.	244	17	261
Number of Stories.	244	17	261
1 story, ...	32	5	37
1 story and attic, . . .	14	5	19
2 stories, ...	50	–	50
2 stories and attic, . . .	143	6	149
Basement, 2 stories, and attic,	1	–	1
3 stories, ...	3	–	3
Basement and 3 stories, . .	1	1	2
Materials.	244	17	261
Wood, ...	241	17	258
Brick, ...	1	–	1
Wood and brick, . . .	2	–	2
Tewksbury.	439	46	485
Number of Stories.	439	46	485
1 story, ...	5	3	8
1 story and attic, . . .	195	14	209
Basement and 1 story, . .	1	–	1
Basement, 1 story, and attic,	5	–	5
2 stories, ...	55	17	72
2 stories and attic, . . .	171	11	182
Basement, 2 stories, and attic,	1	–	1
3 stories, ...	5	–	5
3 stories and attic, . . .	1	1	2
Materials.	439	46	485
Wood, ...	433	45	478
Brick, ...	1	–	1
Wood and brick, . . .	1	–	1
Wood and stone, . . .	3	1	4
Brick and stone, . . .	1	–	1
Townsend.	465	35	500
Number of Stories.	465	35	500
1 story, ...	48	10	58
1 story and attic, . . .	226	13	239
Basement and 1 story, . .	4	1	5
Basement, 1 story, and attic,	3	–	3
2 stories, ...	144	9	153
MIDDLESEX — Con.			
Townsend — Con.			
Number of Stories — Con.			
2 stories and attic, . . .	36	–	36
Basement, 2 stories, and attic,	1	2	3
3 stories, ...	2	–	2
Not given, ...	1	–	1
Materials.	465	35	500
Wood, ...	447	35	482
Brick, ...	4	–	4
Wood and brick, . . .	15	–	15
Not given, ...	1	–	1
Tyngsborough. . . .	159	2	161
Number of Stories.	159	2	161
1 story, ...	56	–	56
1 story and attic, . . .	18	–	18
Basement and 1 story, . .	1	–	1
2 stories, ...	79	2	81
2 stories and attic, . . .	2	–	2
Basement and 2 stories, . .	1	–	1
3 stories, ...	2	–	2
Materials.	159	2	161
Wood, ...	153	2	155
Brick, ...	2	–	2
Stone, ...	2	–	2
Wood and brick, . . .	1	–	1
Wood and stone, . . .	1	–	1
Wakefield.	1,556	103	1,659
Number of Stories.	1,556	103	1,659
1 story, ...	8	–	8
1 story and attic, . . .	445	26	471
Basement and 1 story, . .	1	–	1
Basement, 1 story, and attic,	60	1	61
2 stories, ...	73	6	79
2 stories and attic, . . .	865	64	929
Basement and 2 stories, . .	6	–	6
Basement, 2 stories, and attic,	36	1	37
3 stories, ...	49	5	54
3 stories and attic, . . .	10	–	10
Basement and 3 stories, . .	1	–	1
5 stories, ...	1	–	1
Not given, ...	1	–	1
Materials.	1,556	103	1,659
Wood, ...	1,540	103	1,643
Brick, ...	7	–	7
Wood and brick, . . .	7	–	7
Wood and stone, . . .	1	–	1
Not given, ...	1	–	1
WALTHAM.	3,856	268	4,124
Number of Stories.	3,856	268	4,124
1 story, ...	43	5	48
1 story and attic, . . .	192	11	203

DWELLING HOUSES: NUMBER OF STORIES AND MATERIALS — Continued.

COUNTIES, CITIES, TOWNS, NUMBER OF STORIES TO DWELLING HOUSES, AND MATERIALS OF WHICH CONSTRUCTED.	Number of Occupied Dwelling Houses	Number of Unoccupied Dwelling Houses	Total Number of Dwelling Houses	COUNTIES, CITIES, TOWNS, NUMBER OF STORIES TO DWELLING HOUSES, AND MATERIALS OF WHICH CONSTRUCTED.	Number of Occupied Dwelling Houses	Number of Unoccupied Dwelling Houses	Total Number of Dwelling Houses
MIDDLESEX — Con.				MIDDLESEX — Con.			
WALTHAM — Con.				WALTHAM. WARD 2 — Con.			
Number of Stories — Con.				*Materials* — Con.			
Basement, 1 story, and attic,	2	–	2	Brick and stone,	1	–	1
2 stories,	1,150	99	1,249	Not given,	1	–	1
2 stories and attic,	2,248	127	2,375				
Basement and 2 stories,	14	1	15	WALTHAM. WARD 3,	554	22	576
Basement, 2 stories, and attic,	71	12	83	*Number of Stories.*	554	22	576
3 stories,	108	11	119	1 story,	2	–	2
3 stories and attic,	16	2	18	1 story and attic,	79	1	80
Basement and 3 stories,	4	–	4	Basement, 1 story, and attic,	1	–	1
4 stories,	5	–	5	2 stories,	208	10	218
Basement, 4 stories, and attic,	1	–	1	2 stories and attic,	238	11	249
Not given,	2	–	2	Basement and 2 stories,	1	–	1
Materials.	3,856	268	4,124	Basement, 2 stories, and attic,	6	–	6
Wood,	3,802	262	4,064	3 stories,	13	–	13
Brick,	40	3	43	3 stories and attic,	4	–	4
Stone,	2	–	2	4 stories,	2	–	2
Wood and brick,	7	3	10	*Materials.*	554	22	576
Wood and stone,	2	–	2	Wood,	547	22	569
Brick and stone,	1	–	1	Brick,	7	–	7
Not given,	2	–	2				
				WALTHAM. WARD 4,	602	58	660
WALTHAM. WARD 1,	579	42	621	*Number of Stories.*	602	58	660
Number of Stories.	579	42	621	1 story,	2	–	2
1 story,	10	–	10	1 story and attic,	4	1	5
1 story and attic,	52	4	56	2 stories,	215	29	244
2 stories,	149	13	162	2 stories and attic,	345	21	366
2 stories and attic,	359	24	383	Basement and 2 stories,	4	–	4
Basement and 2 stories,	–	1	1	Basement, 2 stories, and attic,	10	4	14
3 stories,	7	–	7	3 stories,	21	1	22
3 stories and attic,	1	–	1	3 stories and attic,	1	2	3
Not given,	1	–	1	*Materials.*	602	58	660
Materials.	579	42	621	Wood,	594	58	652
Wood,	576	41	617	Brick,	8	–	8
Brick,	–	1	1	WALTHAM. WARD 5,	580	29	609
Stone,	2	–	2	*Number of Stories.*	580	29	609
Not given,	1	–	1	1 story,	10	–	10
				1 story and attic,	3	–	3
WALTHAM. WARD 2,	428	36	464	2 stories,	186	7	193
Number of Stories.	428	36	464	2 stories and attic,	304	10	314
1 story,	15	3	18	Basement and 2 stories,	6	–	6
1 story and attic,	32	5	37	Basement, 2 stories, and attic,	15	4	19
Basement, 1 story, and attic,	1	–	1	3 stories,	46	8	54
2 stories,	71	6	77	3 stories and attic,	4	–	4
2 stories and attic,	287	20	307	Basement and 3 stories,	4	–	4
Basement, 2 stories, and attic,	5	2	7	4 stories,	1	–	1
3 stories,	9	–	9	Basement, 4 stories, and attic,	1	–	1
3 stories and attic,	6	–	6	*Materials.*	580	29	609
4 stories,	1	–	1	Wood,	566	25	591
Not given,	1	–	1	Brick,	13	2	15
Materials.	428	36	464	Wood and brick,	1	2	3
Wood,	408	36	444	WALTHAM. WARD 6,	608	45	653
Brick,	12	–	12	*Number of Stories.*	608	45	653
Wood and brick,	4	–	4	2 stories,	130	15	145
Wood and stone,	2	–	2				

DWELLING HOUSES: NUMBER OF STORIES AND MATERIALS — Continued.

COUNTIES, CITIES, TOWNS. NUMBER OF STORIES TO DWELLING HOUSES, AND MATERIALS OF WHICH CONSTRUCTED.	Number of Occupied Dwelling Houses	Number of Unoccupied Dwelling Houses	Total Number of Dwelling Houses	COUNTIES, CITIES, TOWNS. NUMBER OF STORIES TO DWELLING HOUSES, AND MATERIALS OF WHICH CONSTRUCTED.	Number of Occupied Dwelling Houses	Number of Unoccupied Dwelling Houses	Total Number of Dwelling Houses
MIDDLESEX — Con.				**MIDDLESEX — Con.**			
WALTHAM. WARD 6 — Con.				**Wayland** — Con.			
Number of Stories — Con.				*Number of Stories* — Con.			
2 stories and attic, . . .	432	26	458	Basement and 2 stories, .	2	–	2
Basement and 2 stories, .	3	–	3	Basement, 2 stories, and attic,	7	–	7
Basement, 2 stories, and attic,	35	2	37	3 stories, ...	11	1	12
3 stories, ...	7	2	9	3 stories and attic, . .	1	–	1
4 stories, ...	1	–	1				
				Materials.	381	32	413
Materials.	608	45	653	Wood, ...	378	32	410
Wood, ...	607	44	651	Brick, ...	1	–	1
Wood and brick, . . .	1	1	2	Wood and brick, . . .	2	–	2
WALTHAM. WARD 7, . .	505	36	541	**Westford.**	475	28	503
Number of Stories.	505	36	541	*Number of Stories.*	475	28	503
1 story, ...	4	2	6	1 story, ...	2	–	2
1 story and attic, . . .	22	–	22	1 story and attic, . . .	240	15	255
2 stories, ...	191	19	210	Basement, 1 story, and attic, .	3	–	3
2 stories and attic, . . .	283	15	298	2 stories, ...	12	–	12
3 stories, ...	5	–	5	2 stories and attic, . . .	212	13	225
				Basement, 2 stories, and attic,	2	–	2
Materials.	505	36	541	3 stories, ...	3	–	3
Wood, ...	504	36	540	Basement and 3 stories, . .	1	–	1
Wood and brick, . . .	1	–	1				
				Materials.	475	28	503
Watertown. . .	1,533	140	1,673	Wood, ...	461	28	489
Number of Stories.	1,533	140	1,673	Brick, ...	5	–	5
1 story, ...	17	1	18	Stone, ...	1	–	1
1 story and attic, . . .	167	8	175	Wood and brick, . . .	7	–	7
Basement and 1 story, . .	3	1	4	Brick and stone, . . .	1	–	1
Basement, 1 story, and attic,	27	–	27				
2 stories, ...	136	7	143	**Weston.**	338	35	373
2 stories and attic, . . .	1,061	100	1,161	*Number of Stories.*	338	35	373
Basement and 2 stories, . .	5	–	5	1 story, ...	4	1	5
Basement, 2 stories, and attic,	43	15	58	1 story and attic, . . .	45	4	49
3 stories, ...	66	8	74	2 stories, ...	60	4	64
3 stories and attic, . . .	4	–	4	2 stories and attic, . . .	221	26	247
Basement and 3 stories, . .	2	–	2	3 stories, ...	8	–	8
Basement and 4 stories, . .	1	–	1				
Not given, ...	1	–	1	*Materials.*	338	35	373
				Wood, ...	330	34	364
Materials.	1,533	140	1,673	Brick, ...	–	1	1
Wood, ...	1,504	133	1,637	Stone, ...	3	–	3
Brick, ...	15	5	20	Wood and brick, . . .	4	–	4
Wood and brick, . . .	9	–	9	Wood and stone, . . .	1	–	1
Wood and stone, . . .	1	–	1				
Brick and stone, . . .	1	2	3	**Wilmington.** . . .	301	50	351
Wood, brick, and stone, .	2	–	2	*Number of Stories.*	301	50	351
Not given, ...	1	–	1	1 story, ...	8	1	9
				1 story and attic, . . .	41	13	54
Wayland.	381	32	413	Basement, 1 story, and attic,	2	–	2
Number of Stories.	381	32	413	2 stories, ...	97	19	116
1 story, ...	1	3	4	2 stories and attic, . . .	149	16	165
1 story and attic, . . .	123	8	131	Basement and 2 stories, . .	2	1	3
Basement and 1 story, . .	1	–	1	Basement, 2 stories, and attic,	1	–	1
Basement, 1 story, and attic, .	9	–	9	3 stories, ...	1	–	1
2 stories, ...	54	10	64				
2 stories and attic, . . .	172	10	182	*Materials.*	301	50	351
				Wood, ...	301	50	351

DWELLING HOUSES: NUMBER OF STORIES AND MATERIALS — Continued.

COUNTIES, CITIES, TOWNS, NUMBER OF STORIES TO DWELLING HOUSES, AND MATERIALS OF WHICH CONSTRUCTED.	Number of Occupied Dwelling Houses	Number of Unoccupied Dwelling Houses	Total Number of Dwelling Houses
MIDDLESEX — Con.			
Winchester, ...	1,207	133	1,340
Number of Stories.	1,207	133	1,340
1 story, ...	13	2	15
1 story and attic, . . .	106	4	110
Basement and 1 story, . .	3	–	3
Basement, 1 story, and attic,	3	–	3
2 stories, ...	184	13	197
2 stories and attic, . . .	836	103	939
Basement and 2 stories, . .	5	1	6
Basement, 2 stories, and attic,	7	–	7
3 stories, ...	44	10	54
3 stories and attic, . . .	4	–	4
Basement and 3 stories, . .	1	–	1
4 stories, ...	1	–	1
Materials.	1,207	133	1,340
Wood, ...	1,189	127	1,316
Brick, ...	15	5	20
Stone, ...	–	1	1
Wood and brick, . . .	3	–	3
WOBURN, ...	2,661	126	2,787
Number of Stories.	2,661	126	2,787
1 story, ...	36	1	37
1 story and attic, . . .	646	28	674
Basement and 1 story, . .	5	2	7
Basement, 1 story, and attic, .	31	2	33
2 stories, ...	259	16	275
2 stories and attic, . . .	1,586	72	1,858
Basement and 2 stories, . .	12	–	12
Basement, 2 stories, and attic,	47	4	51
3 stories, ...	30	1	31
3 stories and attic, . . .	6	–	6
Basement and 3 stories, . .	3	–	3
Materials.	2,661	126	2,787
Wood, ...	2,653	126	2,779
Brick, ...	4	–	4
Wood and brick, . . .	3	–	3
Wood and stone, . . .	1	–	1
WOBURN. WARD 1, . .	453	48	501
Number of Stories.	453	48	501
1 story, ...	1	1	2
1 story and attic, . . .	94	15	109
Basement, 1 story, and attic, .	4	2	6
2 stories, ...	25	1	26
2 stories and attic, . . .	308	29	337
Basement and 2 stories, . .	4	–	4
Basement, 2 stories, and attic,	6	–	6
3 stories, ...	8	–	8
3 stories and attic, . . .	3	–	3
Materials.	453	48	501
Wood, ...	452	48	500
Wood and brick, . . .	1	–	1
MIDDLESEX — Con.			
WOBURN. WARD 2, . .	524	35	559
Number of Stories.	524	35	559
1 story and attic, . . .	108	7	115
Basement and 1 story, . .	1	–	1
Basement, 1 story, and attic,	5	–	5
2 stories, ...	39	10	49
2 stories and attic, . . .	333	16	349
Basement and 2 stories, . .	2	–	2
Basement, 2 stories, and attic,	28	2	30
3 stories, ...	5	–	5
3 stories and attic, . . .	1	–	1
Basement and 3 stories, . .	2	–	2
Materials.	524	35	559
Wood, ...	523	35	558
Wood and stone, . . .	1	–	1
WOBURN. WARD 3, . .	490	14	504
Number of Stories.	490	14	504
1 story, ...	9	–	9
1 story and attic, . . .	115	–	115
Basement and 1 story, . .	3	2	5
Basement, 1 story, and attic,	1	–	1
2 stories, ...	60	5	65
2 stories and attic, . . .	288	6	294
Basement and 2 stories, . .	2	–	2
Basement, 2 stories, and attic,	3	–	3
3 stories, ...	8	1	9
Basement and 3 stories, . .	1	–	1
Materials.	490	14	504
Wood, ...	489	14	503
Brick, ...	1	–	1
WOBURN. WARD 4, . .	501	29	530
Number of Stories.	501	29	530
1 story, ...	8	–	8
1 story and attic, . . .	125	6	131
Basement, 1 story, and attic,	13	–	13
2 stories, ...	25	–	25
2 stories and attic, . . .	317	21	338
Basement and 2 stories, . .	1	–	1
Basement, 2 stories, and attic,	5	2	7
3 stories, ...	5	–	5
3 stories and attic, . . .	2	–	2
Materials.	501	29	530
Wood, ...	501	29	530
WOBURN. WARD 5, . .	209	–	209
Number of Stories.	209	–	209
1 story, ...	5	–	5
1 story and attic, . . .	60	–	60
Basement, 1 story, and attic,	3	–	3
2 stories, ...	53	–	53
2 stories and attic, . . .	85	–	85
Basement and 2 stories, . .	2	–	2
Basement, 2 stories, and attic,	1	–	1

DWELLING HOUSES: NUMBER OF STORIES AND MATERIALS — Continued.

COUNTIES, CITIES, TOWNS, NUMBER OF STORIES TO DWELLING HOUSES, AND MATERIALS OF WHICH CONSTRUCTED.	Number of Occupied Dwelling Houses	Number of Unoccupied Dwelling Houses	Total Number of Dwelling Houses
MIDDLESEX — Con.			
WOBURN. WARD 5 — Con.			
Materials.	209	–	209
Wood,	208	–	208
Wood and brick,	1	–	1
WOBURN. WARD 6,	306	–	306
Number of Stories.	306	–	306
1 story and attic,	96	–	96
Basement, 1 story, and attic,	5	–	5
2 stories,	16	–	16
2 stories and attic,	185	–	185
Basement and 2 stories,	1	–	1
Basement, 2 stories, and attic,	3	–	3
3 stories,	3	–	3
Materials.	306	–	306
Wood,	304	–	304
Brick,	1	–	1
Wood and brick,	1	–	1
WOBURN. WARD 7,	178	–	178
Number of Stories.	178	–	178
1 story,	13	–	13
1 story and attic,	51	–	51
Basement and 1 story,	1	–	1
2 stories,	41	–	41
2 stories and attic,	70	–	70
Basement, 2 stories, and attic,	1	–	1
3 stories,	1	–	1
Materials.	178	–	178
Wood,	176	–	176
Brick,	2	–	2
NANTUCKET.			
Nantucket.	880	420	1,300
Number of Stories.	880	420	1,300
1 story,	25	38	63
1 story and attic,	274	158	432
2 stories,	184	67	251
2 stories and attic,	375	127	502
Basement and 2 stories,	–	1	1
Basement, 2 stories, and attic,	17	5	22
3 stories,	2	14	16
3 stories and attic,	2	2	4
Basement and 3 stories,	–	2	2
4 stories,	–	3	3
4 stories and attic,	–	1	1
5 stories,	–	2	2
6 stories,	1	–	1
Materials.	880	420	1,300
Wood,	871	415	1,286
Brick,	9	5	14
NORFOLK.			
Avon,	342	14	356
Number of Stories.	342	14	356
1 story,	8	–	8
1 story and attic,	228	8	236
Basement and 1 story,	3	–	3
Basement, 1 story, and attic,	15	–	15
2 stories,	48	2	50
2 stories and attic,	33	2	35
Basement and 2 stories,	–	1	1
Basement, 2 stories, and attic,	4	–	4
3 stories,	1	1	2
Basement and 3 stories,	2	–	2
Materials.	342	14	356
Wood,	341	14	355
Stone,	1	–	1
Bellingham..	314	26	340
Number of Stories.	314	26	340
1 story,	5	–	5
1 story and attic,	210	18	228
Basement, 1 story, and attic,	6	1	7
2 stories,	2	2	4
2 stories and attic,	88	5	93
Basement and 2 stories,	1	–	1
Basement, 2 stories, and attic,	1	–	1
Not given,	1	–	1
Materials.	314	26	340
Wood,	309	26	335
Brick,	3	–	3
Wood and brick,	1	–	1
Not given,	1	–	1
Braintree.	1,117	64	1,181
Number of Stories.	1,117	64	1,181
1 story,	27	–	27
1 story and attic,	77	4	81
Basement and 1 story,	5	–	5
Basement, 1 story, and attic,	4	–	4
2 stories,	610	35	645
2 stories and attic,	283	19	302
Basement and 2 stories,	41	–	41
Basement, 2 stories, and attic,	10	–	10
3 stories,	54	6	60
3 stories and attic,	3	–	3
Basement and 3 stories,	1	–	1
Basement, 3 stories, and attic,	1	–	1
Not given,	1	–	1
Materials.	1,117	64	1,181
Wood,	1,108	64	1,172
Stone,	1	–	1
Wood and brick,	5	–	5
Wood and stone,	1	–	1
Wood, brick, and stone,	1	–	1
Not given,	1	–	1

DWELLING HOUSES: NUMBER OF STORIES AND MATERIALS — Continued.

COUNTIES, CITIES, TOWNS, NUMBER OF STORIES TO DWELLING HOUSES, AND MATERIALS OF WHICH CONSTRUCTED.	Number of Occupied Dwelling Houses	Number of Unoccupied Dwelling Houses	Total Number of Dwelling Houses
NORFOLK — Con.			
Brookline.	2,277	221	2,498
Number of Stories.	2,277	221	2,498
1 story,	3	–	3
1 story and attic,	48	1	49
Basement, 1 story, and attic,	1	–	1
2 stories,	353	17	370
2 stories and attic,	1,042	97	1,139
Basement and 2 stories,	39	–	39
Basement, 2 stories, and attic,	65	7	72
3 stories,	507	46	553
3 stories and attic,	60	10	70
Basement and 3 stories,	51	13	64
Basement, 3 stories, and attic,	38	16	54
4 stories,	41	5	46
Basement and 4 stories,	26	6	32
5 stories,	1	–	1
Basement and 5 stories,	1	–	1
6 stories,	–	3	3
Not given,	1	–	1
Materials.	2,277	221	2,498
Wood,	1,892	139	2,031
Brick,	262	64	326
Stone,	40	4	44
Wood and brick,	34	3	37
Wood and stone,	12	2	14
Wood and cement,	1	–	1
Brick and stone,	34	8	42
Brick and cement,	1	1	2
Stone and cement,	1	–	1
Canton.	876	43	919
Number of Stories.	876	43	919
1 story,	11	–	11
1 story and attic,	444	19	463
Basement, 1 story, and attic,	11	–	11
2 stories,	155	8	163
2 stories and attic,	241	14	255
Basement and 2 stories,	1	–	1
Basement, 2 stories, and attic,	5	2	7
3 stories,	4	–	4
3 stories and attic,	3	–	3
Basement, 3 stories, and attic,	1	–	1
Materials.	876	43	919
Wood,	870	43	913
Brick,	3	–	3
Stone,	2	–	2
Wood and brick,	1	–	1
Cohasset.	577	1	578
Number of Stories.	577	1	578
1 story,	20	–	20
1 story and attic,	340	1	341
Basement, 1 story, and attic,	16	–	16
2 stories,	10	–	10
2 stories and attic,	180	–	180

COUNTIES, CITIES, TOWNS, NUMBER OF STORIES TO DWELLING HOUSES, AND MATERIALS OF WHICH CONSTRUCTED.	Number of Occupied Dwelling Houses	Number of Unoccupied Dwelling Houses	Total Number of Dwelling Houses
NORFOLK — Con.			
Cohasset — Con.			
Number of Stories — Con.			
Basement, 2 stories, and attic,	6	–	6
3 stories and attic,	5	–	5
Materials.	577	1	578
Wood,	572	1	573
Stone,	2	–	2
Wood and brick,	2	–	2
Wood and stone,	1	–	1
Dedham.	1,481	93	1,574
Number of Stories.	1,481	93	1,574
1 story,	33	3	36
1 story and attic,	419	17	436
Basement and 1 story,	2	1	3
Basement, 1 story, and attic,	24	–	24
2 stories,	312	16	328
2 stories and attic,	635	47	682
Basement and 2 stories,	12	1	13
Basement, 2 stories, and attic,	7	–	7
3 stories,	30	7	37
3 stories and attic,	3	1	4
Basement and 3 stories,	1	–	1
4 stories,	1	–	1
Not given,	2	–	2
Materials.	1,481	93	1,574
Wood,	1,455	89	1,544
Brick,	4	–	4
Stone,	4	–	4
Wood and brick,	14	2	16
Wood and stone,	3	2	5
Not given,	1	–	1
Dover.	141	7	148
Number of Stories.	141	7	148
1 story,	3	–	3
1 story and attic,	51	3	54
2 stories,	14	–	14
2 stories and attic,	73	4	77
Materials.	141	7	148
Wood,	139	7	146
Wood and brick,	2	–	2
Foxborough.	723	28	751
Number of Stories.	723	28	751
1 story,	15	2	17
1 story and attic,	441	18	459
Basement, 1 story, and attic,	12	–	12
2 stories,	37	–	37
2 stories and attic,	190	8	198
Basement and 2 stories,	6	–	6
Basement, 2 stories, and attic,	13	–	13
3 stories,	7	–	7
3 stories and attic,	1	–	1
Basement, 3 stories, and attic,	1	–	1

DWELLING HOUSES: NUMBER OF STORIES AND MATERIALS — Continued.

COUNTIES, CITIES, TOWNS, NUMBER OF STORIES TO DWELLING HOUSES, AND MATERIALS OF WHICH CONSTRUCTED.	Number of Occupied Dwelling Houses	Number of Unoccupied Dwelling Houses	Total Number of Dwelling Houses
NORFOLK — Con.			
Foxborough — Con.			
Materials.	723	28	751
Wood,	718	28	746
Brick,	3	–	3
Stone,	2	–	2
Franklin.	984	44	1,028
Number of Stories.	984	44	1,028
1 story,	30	1	31
1 story and attic,	351	13	364
Basement and 1 story,	6	–	6
Basement, 1 story, and attic,	23	1	24
2 stories,	246	10	256
2 stories and attic,	270	16	286
Basement and 2 stories,	17	2	19
Basement, 2 stories, and attic,	23	–	23
3 stories,	14	–	14
3 stories and attic,	1	1	2
Basement, 3 stories, and attic,	2	–	2
Basement, 4 stories, and attic,	1	–	1
Materials.	984	44	1,028
Wood,	975	44	1,019
Brick,	7	–	7
Stone,	1	–	1
Wood and stone,	1	–	1
Holbrook.	511	35	546
Number of Stories.	511	35	546
1 story,	100	12	112
1 story and attic,	–	1	1
Basement and 1 story,	10	–	10
2 stories,	389	18	407
2 stories and attic,	1	–	1
Basement and 2 stories,	11	–	11
3 stories,	–	4	4
Materials.	511	35	546
Wood,	509	35	544
Brick,	2	–	2
Hyde Park.	2,064	137	2,201
Number of Stories.	2,064	137	2,201
1 story,	11	–	11
1 story and attic,	479	29	508
Basement, 1 story, and attic,	25	–	25
2 stories,	204	18	222
2 stories and attic,	1,095	72	1,167
Basement and 2 stories,	18	2	20
Basement, 2 stories, and attic,	31	4	35
3 stories,	195	3	198
Basement and 3 stories,	4	9	13
4 stories,	2	–	2
Materials.	2,064	137	2,201
Wood,	2,057	127	2,184
Brick,	6	9	15
Stone,	1	1	2
NORFOLK — Con.			
Medfield.	348	14	362
Number of Stories.	348	14	362
1 story,	6	–	6
1 story and attic,	82	2	84
Basement and 1 story,	1	–	1
Basement, 1 story, and attic,	4	–	4
2 stories,	13	4	17
2 stories and attic,	228	7	235
Basement, 2 stories, and attic,	3	–	3
3 stories,	8	1	9
3 stories and attic,	1	–	1
Basement and 3 stories,	1	–	1
Not given,	1	–	1
Materials.	348	14	362
Wood,	347	14	361
Wood and stone,	1	–	1
Medway.	626	26	652
Number of Stories.	626	26	652
1 story,	3	1	4
1 story and attic,	280	12	292
Basement and 1 story,	1	–	1
Basement, 1 story, and attic,	13	1	14
2 stories,	7	2	9
2 stories and attic,	300	10	310
Basement, 2 stories, and attic,	12	–	12
3 stories,	7	–	7
3 stories and attic,	2	–	2
4 stories,	1	–	1
Materials.	626	26	652
Wood,	623	25	648
Brick,	1	1	2
Stone,	1	–	1
Wood and brick,	1	–	1
Millis.	210	34	244
Number of Stories.	210	34	244
1 story,	21	7	28
1 story and attic,	1	–	1
2 stories,	122	25	147
2 stories and attic,	52	1	53
Basement and 2 stories,	7	1	8
Basement, 2 stories, and attic,	5	–	5
3 stories,	1	–	1
Basement and 3 stories,	1	–	1
Materials.	210	34	244
Wood,	204	34	238
Brick,	6	–	6
Milton.	1,003	79	1,082
Number of Stories.	1,003	79	1,082
1 story,	108	8	116
1 story and attic,	204	9	213
Basement and 1 story,	1	–	1
Basement, 1 story, and attic,	5	–	5

DWELLING HOUSES: NUMBER OF STORIES AND MATERIALS — Continued.

COUNTIES, CITIES, TOWNS, NUMBER OF STORIES TO DWELLING HOUSES, AND MATERIALS OF WHICH CONSTRUCTED.	Number of Occupied Dwelling Houses	Number of Unoccupied Dwelling Houses	Total Number of Dwelling Houses	COUNTIES, CITIES, TOWNS, NUMBER OF STORIES TO DWELLING HOUSES, AND MATERIALS OF WHICH CONSTRUCTED.	Number of Occupied Dwelling Houses	Number of Unoccupied Dwelling Houses	Total Number of Dwelling Houses
NORFOLK — Con.				NORFOLK — Con.			
Milton — Con.				**Norwood** — Con.			
Number of Stories — Con.				*Number of Stories* — Con.			
2 stories, ...	470	35	505	3 stories, ...	2	–	2
2 stories and attic, . . .	191	19	210	3 stories and attic, . . .	2	–	2
Basement and 2 stories, . .	4	–	4				
Basement, 2 stories, and attic,	4	1	5	*Materials.*	866	15	881
3 stories, ...	13	5	18	Wood, ...	861	15	876
3 stories and attic, . . .	3	2	5	Brick, ...	1	–	1
				Stone, ...	2	–	2
Materials.	1,003	79	1,082	Wood and stone, . . .	1	–	1
Wood, ...	986	79	1,065	Not given, ...	1	–	1
Brick, ...	5	–	5				
Stone, ...	7	–	7	**QUINCY.**	3,801	482	4,283
Wood and brick, . . .	4	–	4	*Number of Stories.*	3,801	482	4,283
Wood and stone, . . .	1	–	1	1 story, ...	46	22	68
				1 story and attic, . . .	1,584	194	1,778
Needham.	735	71	806	Basement and 1 story, . .	4	1	5
Number of Stories.	735	71	806	Basement, 1 story, and attic,	91	10	101
1 story, ...	12	1	13	2 stories, ...	296	80	376
1 story and attic, . . .	159	14	173	2 stories and attic, . . .	1,627	161	1,788
Basement and 1 story, . .	2	–	2	Basement and 2 stories, . .	12	4	16
Basement, 1 story, and attic,	16	4	20	Basement, 2 stories, and attic,	74	7	81
2 stories, ...	135	15	150	3 stories, ...	29	1	30
2 stories and attic, . . .	381	34	415	3 stories and attic, . . .	28	2	30
Basement and 2 stories, . .	6	1	7	Basement and 3 stories, . .	2	–	2
Basement, 2 stories, and attic,	6	–	6	Basement, 3 stories, and attic,	7	–	7
3 stories, ...	16	2	18	Basement and 4 stories, . .	1	–	1
4 stories, ...	2	–	2	*Materials.*	3,801	482	4,283
Materials.	735	71	806	Wood, ...	3,764	479	4,243
Wood, ...	728	71	799	Brick, ...	17	–	17
Wood and brick, . . .	4	–	4	Stone, ...	9	1	10
Wood and stone, . . .	3	–	3	Wood and brick, . . .	3	1	4
				Wood and stone, . . .	6	1	7
Norfolk.	179	20	199	Brick and stone, . . .	1	–	1
Number of Stories.	179	20	199	Not given, ...	1	–	1
1 story, ...	6	–	6				
1 story and attic, . . .	101	9	110	QUINCY. WARD 1, . . .	711	299	1,010
Basement, 1 story, and attic,	6	3	9	*Number of Stories.*	711	299	1,010
2 stories, ...	5	–	5	1 story, ...	18	18	36
2 stories and attic, . . .	58	8	66	1 story and attic, . . .	273	125	398
Basement and 2 stories, . .	1	–	1	Basement and 1 story, . .	–	1	1
Basement, 2 stories, and attic,	2	–	2	Basement, 1 story, and attic,	18	4	22
Materials.	179	20	199	2 stories, ...	50	62	112
Wood, ...	177	20	197	2 stories and attic, . . .	319	79	398
Brick, ...	1	–	1	Basement and 2 stories, . .	–	3	3
Not given, ...	1	–	1	Basement, 2 stories, and attic,	9	5	14
Norwood.	866	15	881	3 stories, ...	11	1	12
Number of Stories.	866	15	881	3 stories and attic, . . .	12	1	13
1 story, ...	8	–	8	Basement and 3 stories, . .	1	–	1
1 story and attic, . . .	439	5	444	*Materials.*	711	299	1,010
Basement, 1 story, and attic,	15	–	15	Wood, ...	696	297	993
2 stories, ...	15	1	16	Brick, ...	9	–	9
2 stories and attic, . . .	382	9	391	Stone, ...	2	1	3
Basement, 2 stories, and attic,	3	–	3	Wood and brick, . . .	1	–	1
				Wood and stone, . . .	4	1	5

DWELLING HOUSES: NUMBER OF STORIES AND MATERIALS — Continued.

COUNTIES, CITIES, TOWNS, NUMBER OF STORIES TO DWELLING HOUSES, AND MATERIALS OF WHICH CONSTRUCTED.	Number of Occupied Dwelling Houses	Number of Unoccupied Dwelling Houses	Total Number of Dwelling Houses
NORFOLK — Con.			
QUINCY. WARD 1 — Con.			
Materials — Con.			
Brick and stone, . . .	1	–	1
Not given, ...	1	–	1
QUINCY. WARD 2, . . .	529	23	552
Number of Stories.	529	23	552
1 story, ...	3	2	5
1 story and attic, . . .	341	9	350
Basement, 1 story, and attic, .	5	1	6
2 stories, ...	68	3	71
2 stories and attic. . . .	97	8	105
Basement and 2 stories, . .	5	–	5
Basement, 2 stories, and attic,	4	–	4
3 stories, ...	3	–	3
3 stories and attic, . . .	3	–	3
Materials.	529	23	552
Wood, ...	528	22	550
Brick, ...	1	–	1
Wood and brick, . . .	–	1	1
QUINCY. WARD 3, . .	822	35	857
Number of Stories.	822	35	857
1 story, ...	7	–	7
1 story and attic, . . .	430	16	446
Basement, 1 story, and attic, .	23	3	26
2 stories, ...	67	8	75
2 stories and attic, . . .	269	7	276
Basement, 2 stories, and attic,	17	1	18
3 stories and attic, . . .	3	–	3
Basement, 3 stories, and attic,	6	–	6
Materials.	822	35	857
Wood, ...	817	35	852
Brick, ...	1	–	1
Stone, ...	1	–	1
Wood and brick, . . .	2	–	2
Wood and stone, . . .	1	–	1
QUINCY. WARD 4, . .	813	43	856
Number of Stories.	813	43	856
1 story, ...	7	–	7
1 story and attic, . . .	391	21	412
Basement, 1 story, and attic, .	33	2	35
2 stories, ...	40	1	41
2 stories and attic, . . .	302	17	319
Basement and 2 stories, . .	5	1	6
Basement, 2 stories, and attic,	23	1	24
3 stories, ...	5	–	5
3 stories and attic, . . .	6	–	6
Basement, 3 stories, and attic,	1	–	1
Materials.	813	43	856
Wood, ...	804	43	847
Brick, ...	4	–	4
Stone, ...	5	–	5
NORFOLK — Con.			
QUINCY. WARD 5, . . .	526	82	608
Number of Stories.	526	82	608
1 story, ...	3	2	5
1 story and attic, . . .	41	23	64
Basement and 1 story, . .	3	–	3
Basement, 1 story, and attic,	1	–	1
2 stories, ...	28	6	34
2 stories and attic, . . .	425	50	475
Basement, 2 stories, and attic,	13	–	13
3 stories, ...	8	–	8
3 stories and attic, . . .	2	1	3
Basement and 3 stories, . .	1	–	1
Basement and 4 stories, . .	1	–	1
Materials.	526	82	608
Wood, ...	525	82	607
Brick, ...	1	–	1
QUINCY. WARD 6, . . .	400	–	400
Number of Stories.	400	–	400
1 story, ...	8	–	8
1 story and attic, . . .	108	–	108
Basement and 1 story, . .	1	–	1
Basement, 1 story, and attic,	11	–	11
2 stories, ...	43	–	43
2 stories and attic, . . .	215	–	215
Basement and 2 stories, . .	2	–	2
Basement, 2 stories, and attic,	8	–	8
3 stories, ...	2	–	2
3 stories and attic, . . .	2	–	2
Materials.	400	–	400
Wood, ...	397	–	397
Brick, ...	1	–	1
Stone, ...	1	–	1
Wood and stone, . . .	1	–	1
Randolph, ...	824	55	879
Number of Stories.	824	55	879
1 story, ...	2	2	4
1 story and attic, . . .	27	–	27
Basement, 1 story, and attic,	3	1	4
2 stories, ...	613	42	655
2 stories and attic, . . .	109	5	114
Basement and 2 stories, . .	23	1	24
Basement, 2 stories, and attic,	2	–	2
3 stories, ...	45	4	49
Materials.	824	55	879
Wood, ...	822	55	877
Stone, ...	2	–	2
Sharon, ...	378	81	459
Number of Stories.	378	81	459
1 story, ...	18	4	22
1 story and attic, . . .	34	5	39
2 stories, ...	172	44	216
2 stories and attic, . . .	143	19	162

DWELLING HOUSES: NUMBER OF STORIES AND MATERIALS -- Continued.

COUNTIES, CITIES, TOWNS, NUMBER OF STORIES TO DWELLING HOUSES, AND MATERIALS OF WHICH CONSTRUCTED.	Number of these occupied Dwelling Houses	Number of those occupied Dwelling Houses	Total Number of Dwelling Houses
NORFOLK — Con.			
Sharon — Con.			
Number of Stories — Con.			
3 stories,	11	7	18
3 stories and attic,	-	1	1
4 stories,	-	1	1
Materials.	378	81	459
Wood,	375	79	454
Stone,	2	1	3
Wood and brick,	1	-	1
Wood and stone,	-	1	1
Stoughton.	1,111	86	1,197
Number of Stories.	1,111	86	1,197
1 story,	41	5	46
1 story and attic,	377	25	402
Basement and 1 story,	5	4	9
Basement, 1 story, and attic,	4	-	4
2 stories,	8	-	8
2 stories and attic,	672	49	721
Basement, 2 stories, and attic,	1	-	1
3 stories,	1	-	1
3 stories and attic,	2	-	2
Not given,	-	3	3
Materials.	1,111	86	1,197
Wood,	1,110	83	1,193
Wood and stone,	1	-	1
Not given,	-	3	3
Walpole.	620	27	647
Number of Stories.	620	27	647
1 story,	3	1	4
1 story and attic,	274	13	287
Basement, 1 story, and attic,	31	-	31
2 stories,	27	1	28
2 stories and attic,	256	11	267
Basement, 2 stories, and attic,	21	1	22
3 stories,	7	-	7
Basement and 3 stories,	1	-	1
Materials.			
Wood,	620	27	647
Wellesley.	679	56	735
Number of Stories.	679	56	735
1 story,	9	-	9
1 story and attic,	23	3	26
Basement and 1 story,	1	-	1
Basement, 1 story, and attic,	2	-	2
2 stories,	222	18	240
2 stories and attic,	311	29	340
Basement and 2 stories,	21	2	23
Basement, 2 stories, and attic,	21	3	24
3 stories,	51	1	52
3 stories and attic,	6	-	6
Basement and 3 stories,	8	-	8

COUNTIES, CITIES, TOWNS, NUMBER OF STORIES TO DWELLING HOUSES, AND MATERIALS OF WHICH CONSTRUCTED.	Number of these occupied Dwelling Houses	Number of those occupied Dwelling Houses	Total Number of Dwelling Houses
NORFOLK — Con.			
Wellesley — Con.			
Number of Stories — Con.			
4 stories,	2	-	2
Basement, 4 stories, and attic,	1	-	1
Basement and 5 stories,	1	-	1
Materials.	679	56	735
Wood,	659	54	713
Brick,	7	-	7
Stone,	4	-	4
Wood and brick,	8	1	9
Wood and stone,	-	1	1
Not given,	1	-	1
Weymouth.	2,421	129	2,550
Number of Stories.	2,421	129	2,550
1 story,	19	5	24
1 story and attic,	1,544	71	1,615
Basement and 1 story,	3	-	3
Basement, 1 story, and attic,	143	5	148
2 stories,	178	15	193
2 stories and attic,	422	29	451
Basement and 2 stories,	11	-	11
Basement, 2 stories, and attic,	67	4	71
3 stories,	19	-	19
3 stories and attic,	12	-	12
Basement, 3 stories, and attic,	2	-	2
4 stories,	1	-	1
Materials.	2,421	129	2,550
Wood,	2,416	129	2,545
Brick,	1	-	1
Wood and brick,	4	-	4
Wrentham.	581	28	609
Number of Stories.	581	28	609
1 story,	23	1	24
1 story and attic,	354	15	369
Basement and 1 story,	1	-	1
Basement, 1 story, and attic,	4	-	4
2 stories,	29	2	31
2 stories and attic,	166	8	174
Basement, 2 stories, and attic,	2	1	3
3 stories,	2	1	3
Materials.	581	28	609
Wood,	578	28	606
Brick,	2	-	2
Stone,	1	-	1
PLYMOUTH.			
Abington.	912	29	941
Number of Stories.	912	29	941
1 story,	21	1	22
1 story and attic,	624	22	646
Basement and 1 story,	-	1	1
Basement, 1 story, and attic,	5	-	5

DWELLING HOUSES: NUMBER OF STORIES AND MATERIALS — Continued.

COUNTIES, CITIES, TOWNS, NUMBER OF STORIES TO DWELLING HOUSES, AND MATERIALS OF WHICH CONSTRUCTED.	Number of Occupied Dwelling Houses	Number of Unoccupied Dwelling Houses	Total Number of Dwelling Houses
PLYMOUTH — Con.			
Abington — Con.			
Number of Stories — Con.			
2 stories,	50	–	50
2 stories and attic,	203	5	208
Basement and 2 stories,	1	–	1
Basement, 2 stories, and attic,	5	–	5
3 stories,	2	–	2
3 stories and attic,	1	–	1
Materials.	912	29	941
Wood,	910	29	939
Brick,	2	–	2
Bridgewater,	762	60	822
Number of Stories.	762	60	822
1 story,	55	8	63
1 story and attic,	444	36	480
Basement, 1 story, and attic,	6	–	6
2 stories,	67	7	74
2 stories and attic,	179	9	188
Basement and 2 stories,	2	–	2
Basement, 2 stories, and attic,	2	–	2
3 stories,	5	–	5
3 stories and attic,	1	–	1
Basement, 3 stories, and attic,	1	–	1
Materials.	762	60	822
Wood,	756	60	816
Brick,	4	–	4
Wood and brick,	2	–	2
BROCKTON,	5,355	259	5,614
Number of Stories.	5,355	259	5,614
1 story,	239	15	254
1 story and attic,	2,274	133	2,407
Basement and 1 story,	7	2	9
Basement, 1 story, and attic,	46	–	46
2 stories,	571	24	595
2 stories and attic,	2,070	70	2,140
Basement and 2 stories,	16	6	22
Basement, 2 stories, and attic,	36	1	37
3 stories,	78	5	83
3 stories and attic,	5	1	6
Basement and 3 stories,	2	–	2
Basement, 3 stories, and attic,	2	–	2
4 stories,	3	–	3
Basement and 4 stories,	1	–	1
5 stories,	1	–	1
Not given,	4	2	6
Materials.	5,355	259	5,614
Wood,	5,322	255	5,577
Brick,	18	2	20
Stone,	4	–	4
Cement,	3	–	3
Wood and brick,	2	–	2
Wood and stone,	2	–	2
Not given,	4	2	6
PLYMOUTH — Con.			
BROCKTON. WARD 1,	664	30	694
Number of Stories.	664	30	694
1 story,	2	–	2
1 story and attic,	202	16	218
Basement, 1 story, and attic,	6	–	6
2 stories,	155	5	160
2 stories and attic,	254	8	262
Basement and 2 stories,	3	–	3
Basement, 2 stories, and attic,	9	–	9
3 stories,	20	1	21
3 stories and attic,	4	–	4
Basement and 3 stories,	1	–	1
4 stories,	3	–	3
5 stories,	1	–	1
Not given,	4	–	4
Materials.	664	30	694
Wood,	650	29	679
Brick,	7	1	8
Stone,	3	–	3
Not given,	4	–	4
BROCKTON. WARD 2,	730	36	766
Number of Stories.	730	36	766
1 story,	175	9	184
1 story and attic,	48	3	51
Basement and 1 story,	3	1	4
Basement, 1 story, and attic,	2	–	2
2 stories,	159	7	166
2 stories and attic,	321	14	335
Basement and 2 stories,	1	–	1
Basement, 2 stories, and attic,	1	–	1
3 stories,	19	2	21
3 stories and attic,	1	–	1
Materials.	730	36	766
Wood,	724	36	760
Brick,	6	–	6
BROCKTON. WARD 3,	815	35	850
Number of Stories.	815	35	850
1 story,	3	–	3
1 story and attic,	428	15	443
Basement, 1 story, and attic,	1	–	1
2 stories,	28	–	28
2 stories and attic,	344	14	358
Basement and 2 stories,	5	5	10
Basement, 2 stories, and attic,	4	–	4
3 stories,	1	1	2
Basement and 4 stories,	1	–	1
Materials.	815	35	850
Wood,	813	35	848
Brick,	2	–	2
BROCKTON. WARD 4,	757	39	796
Number of Stories.	757	39	796
1 story,	10	2	12

DWELLING HOUSES: NUMBER OF STORIES AND MATERIALS — Continued.

Counties, Cities, Towns, Number of Stories to Dwelling Houses, and Materials of which Constructed.	Number of Occupied Dwelling Houses	Number of Unoccupied Dwelling Houses	Total Number of Dwelling Houses
PLYMOUTH — Con.			
BROCKTON. WARD 4 — Con.			
Number of Stories — Con.			
1 story and attic,	390	26	416
Basement and 1 story,	1	–	1
Basement, 1 story, and attic,	11	–	11
2 stories,	57	2	59
2 stories and attic,	273	9	282
Basement and 2 stories,	2	–	2
Basement, 2 stories, and attic,	2	–	2
3 stories,	10	–	10
Basement, 3 stories, and attic,	1	–	1
Materials.	757	39	796
Wood,	754	39	790
Brick,	2	–	2
Stone,	1	–	1
Cement,	3	–	3
BROCKTON. WARD 5,	791	49	840
Number of Stories.	791	49	840
1 story,	21	4	25
1 story and attic,	428	24	452
Basement and 1 story,	2	–	2
Basement, 1 story, and attic,	12	–	12
2 stories,	44	2	46
2 stories and attic,	263	14	277
Basement and 2 stories,	3	1	4
Basement, 2 stories, and attic,	6	1	7
3 stories,	11	1	12
3 stories and attic,	–	1	1
Basement, 3 stories, and attic,	1	–	1
Not given,	–	1	1
Materials.	791	49	840
Wood,	791	48	839
Not given,	–	1	1
BROCKTON. WARD 6,	789	61	850
Number of Stories.	789	61	850
1 story,	19	–	19
1 story and attic,	410	42	452
Basement and 1 story,	1	1	2
Basement, 1 story, and attic,	11	–	11
2 stories,	47	7	54
2 stories and attic,	283	10	293
Basement and 2 stories,	2	–	2
Basement, 2 stories, and attic,	13	–	13
3 stories,	2	–	2
Basement and 3 stories,	1	–	1
Not given,	–	1	1
Materials.	789	61	850
Wood,	786	59	845
Brick,	1	1	2
Wood and brick,	1	–	1
Wood and stone,	1	–	1
Not given,	–	1	1
PLYMOUTH — Con.			
BROCKTON. WARD 7,	809	9	818
Number of Stories.	809	9	818
1 story,	9	–	9
1 story and attic,	368	7	375
Basement, 1 story, and attic,	3	–	3
2 stories,	81	1	82
2 stories and attic,	332	1	333
Basement, 2 stories, and attic,	1	–	1
3 stories,	15	–	15
Materials.	809	9	818
Wood,	807	9	816
Wood and brick,	1	–	1
Wood and stone,	1	–	1
Carver,	246	8	254
Number of Stories.	246	8	254
1 story,	23	–	23
1 story and attic,	164	6	170
2 stories,	41	2	43
2 stories and attic,	18	–	18
Materials.	246	8	254
Wood,	245	8	253
Wood and brick,	1	–	1
Duxbury,	503	162	665
Number of Stories.	503	162	665
1 story,	18	7	25
1 story and attic,	302	86	388
Basement and 1 story,	1	–	1
Basement, 1 story, and attic,	9	2	11
2 stories,	122	44	166
2 stories and attic,	49	20	69
Basement and 2 stories,	–	1	1
Basement, 2 stories, and attic,	–	1	1
3 stories,	2	1	3
Materials.	503	162	665
Wood,	492	158	650
Brick,	4	–	4
Wood and brick,	7	4	11
East Bridgewater,	642	41	683
Number of Stories.	642	41	683
1 story,	9	1	10
1 story and attic,	479	31	510
Basement and 1 story,	1	–	1
Basement, 1 story, and attic,	7	–	7
2 stories,	9	3	12
2 stories and attic,	128	6	134
Basement and 2 stories,	1	–	1
Basement, 2 stories, and attic,	7	–	7
Not given,	1	–	1
Materials.	642	41	683
Wood,	639	39	678
Brick,	–	2	2

DWELLING HOUSES: NUMBER OF STORIES AND MATERIALS — Continued.

COUNTIES, CITIES, TOWNS, NUMBER OF STORIES TO DWELLING HOUSES, AND MATERIALS OF WHICH CONSTRUCTED.	Number of Occupied Dwelling Houses	Number of Unoccupied Dwelling Houses	Total Number of Dwelling Houses
PLYMOUTH — Con.			
East Bridgewater — Con.			
Materials — Con.			
Wood and brick, . . .	2	–	2
Not given, ...	1	–	1
Halifax.	132	19	151
Number of Stories.	132	19	151
1 story, ...	7	1	8
1 story and attic, . .	95	14	109
Basement and 1 story, . .	1	–	1
2 stories, ...	14	1	15
2 stories and attic, . .	14	3	17
4 stories, ...	1	–	1
Materials.	132	19	151
Wood,. .	131	18	149
Wood and brick, . .	1	1	2
Hanover.	506	35	541
Number of Stories.	506	35	541
1 story, . .	12	2	14
1 story and attic, . .	364	29	393
Basement, 1 story, and attic,	5	–	5
2 stories, ...	31	1	32
2 stories and attic, . .	94	3	97
Materials.	506	35	541
Wood,. .	500	34	534
Wood and brick, . .	6	1	7
Hanson.	353	24	377
Number of Stories.	353	24	377
1 story, . .	6	2	8
1 story and attic, . .	295	19	314
2 stories, ...	12	1	13
2 stories and attic, . .	39	2	41
3 stories, ...	1	–	1
Materials.	353	24	377
Wood,. .	352	24	376
Wood and stone, . .	1	–	1
Hingham.	1,057	158	1,215
Number of Stories.	1,057	158	1,215
1 story, . .	66	7	73
1 story and attic, . .	466	56	522
Basement and 1 story, .	4	3	7
Basement, 1 story, and attic,	54	6	60
2 stories, ...	370	44	414
2 stories and attic, . .	70	26	96
Basement and 2 stories, .	6	1	7
Basement, 2 stories, and attic,	10	7	17
3 stories, ...	10	8	18
3 stories and attic, . .	1	–	1
Materials.	1,057	158	1,215
Wood,. .	1,041	153	1,194
Brick, .	1	–	1
PLYMOUTH — Con.			
Hingham — Con.			
Materials — Con.			
Stone, ...	–	1	1
Wood and brick, . .	14	4	18
Wood and stone, . .	1	–	1
Hull.	229	510	739
Number of Stories.	229	510	739
1 story, . .	9	6	15
1 story and attic, . .	–	2	2
Basement, 1 story, and attic,	1	–	1
2 stories, ...	91	259	350
2 stories and attic, . .	64	149	213
Basement and 2 stories, .	20	31	51
Basement, 2 stories, and attic,	15	17	32
3 stories, ...	17	34	51
3 stories and attic, . .	–	2	2
Basement and 3 stories, .	8	8	16
Basement, 3 stories, and attic,	2	1	3
Basement and 4 stories, .	1	–	1
5 stories, ...	1	1	2
Materials.	229	510	739
Wood,. .	227	510	737
Wood and stone, . .	2	–	2
Kingston.	425	43	468
Number of Stories.	425	43	468
1 story, . .	10	1	11
1 story and attic, . .	233	25	258
Basement, 1 story, and attic,	22	–	22
2 stories, ...	3	–	3
2 stories and attic, . .	153	17	170
Basement, 2 stories, and attic,	1	–	1
3 stories, ...	3	–	3
Materials.	425	43	468
Wood,. .	414	42	456
Brick,. .	1	–	1
Wood and brick, . .	10	1	11
Lakeville.	220	65	285
Number of Stories.	220	65	285
1 story, . .	7	8	15
1 story and attic, . .	176	44	220
2 stories, ...	15	8	23
2 stories and attic, . .	22	5	27
Materials.	220	65	285
Wood,. .	219	65	284
Wood and stone, . .	1	–	1
Marion.	205	75	280
Number of Stories.	205	75	280
1 story, . .	3	1	4
1 story and attic, . .	132	47	179
Basement, 1 story, and attic,	3	–	3
2 stories and attic, . .	65	25	90

DWELLING HOUSES: NUMBER OF STORIES AND MATERIALS—Continued.

COUNTIES, CITIES, TOWNS, NUMBER OF STORIES TO DWELLING HOUSES, AND MATERIALS OF WHICH CONSTRUCTED.	Number of Occupied Dwelling Houses	Number of Unoccupied Dwelling Houses	Total Number of Dwelling Houses	COUNTIES, CITIES, TOWNS, NUMBER OF STORIES TO DWELLING HOUSES, AND MATERIALS OF WHICH CONSTRUCTED.	Number of Occupied Dwelling Houses	Number of Unoccupied Dwelling Houses	Total Number of Dwelling Houses
PLYMOUTH – Con.				**PLYMOUTH – Con.**			
Marion – Con.				**Middleborough – Con.**			
Number of Stories – Con.				*Materials – Con.*			
Basement, 2 stories, and attic,	1	1	2	Stone,	1	–	1
3 stories,	1	–	1	Not given,	1	–	1
4 stories,	–	1	1				
				Norwell,	407	43	450
Materials.	205	75	280	*Number of Stories.*	407	43	450
Wood,	205	75	280	1 story,	19	1	20
				1 story and attic,	245	30	275
Marshfield,	484	329	813	Basement and 1 story,	2	–	2
Number of Stories.	484	329	813	Basement, 1 story, and attic,	2	3	5
1 story,	22	27	49	2 stories,	106	5	111
1 story and attic,	327	205	532	2 stories and attic,	31	3	34
Basement and 1 story,	–	1	1	Basement, 2 stories, and attic,	1	1	2
Basement, 1 story, and attic,	6	–	6	3 stories,	1	–	1
2 stories,	32	56	88				
2 stories and attic,	89	34	123	*Materials.*	407	43	450
Basement and 2 stories,	2	4	6	Wood,	405	42	447
Basement, 2 stories, and attic,	1	–	1	Wood and brick,	2	1	3
3 stories,	5	2	7				
				Pembroke,	345	54	399
Materials.	484	329	813	*Number of Stories.*	345	54	399
Wood,	480	329	809	1 story,	16	5	21
Brick,	2	–	2	1 story and attic,	267	39	306
Wood and brick,	2	–	2	Basement and 1 story,	2	–	2
				Basement, 1 story, and attic,	–	1	1
Mattapoisett,	281	72	353	2 stories,	7	1	8
Number of Stories.	281	72	353	2 stories and attic,	52	8	60
1 story,	5	2	7	Basement and 2 stories,	1	–	1
1 story and attic,	175	36	211				
Basement, 1 story, and attic,	3	–	3	*Materials.*	345	54	399
2 stories,	20	6	26	Wood,	344	54	395
2 stories and attic,	76	25	101	Wood and brick,	1	–	4
3 stories,	1	3	4				
3 stories and attic,	1	–	1	**Plymouth,**	1,615	67	1,682
				Number of Stories.	1,615	67	1,682
Materials.	281	72	353	1 story,	103	8	111
Wood,	280	72	352	1 story and attic,	361	19	380
Stone and cement,	1	–	1	Basement, 1 story, and attic,	10	–	10
				2 stories,	477	13	490
Middleborough,	1,396	43	1,439	2 stories and attic,	543	20	563
Number of Stories.	1,396	43	1,439	Basement and 2 stories,	41	1	42
1 story,	199	8	207	Basement, 2 stories, and attic,	52	–	52
1 story and attic,	788	22	810	3 stories,	20	4	24
Basement and 1 story,	4	1	5	3 stories and attic,	2	–	2
Basement, 1 story, and attic,	14	–	14	Basement and 3 stories,	6	2	8
2 stories,	152	11	163				
2 stories and attic,	218	–	218	*Materials.*	1,615	67	1,682
Basement and 2 stories,	1	–	1	Wood,	1,594	65	1,659
Basement, 2 stories, and attic,	10	–	10	Brick,	8	2	10
3 stories,	7	1	8	Wood and brick,	11	–	11
3 stories and attic,	1	–	1	Wood and stone,	1	–	1
Basement and 3 stories,	1	–	1	Brick and stone,	1	–	1
Not given,	1	–	1				
				Plympton,	152	29	181
Materials.	1,396	43	1,439	*Number of Stories.*	152	29	181
Wood,	1,388	43	1,431	1 story,	126	16	142
Brick,	6	–	6	1 story and attic,	1	–	1

DWELLING HOUSES: NUMBER OF STORIES AND MATERIALS — Continued.

COUNTIES, CITIES, TOWNS, NUMBER OF STORIES TO DWELLING HOUSES, AND MATERIALS OF WHICH CONSTRUCTED.	Number of Occupied Dwelling Houses	Number of Unoccupied Dwelling Houses	Total Number of Dwelling Houses
PLYMOUTH — Con.			
Plympton — Con.			
Number of Stories — Con.			
Basement and 1 story, . .	1	–	1
2 stories, ...	16	9	25
2 stories and attic, . . .	8	4	12
Materials.	152	29	181
Wood, ...	152	29	181
Rochester.	246	18	264
Number of Stories.	246	18	264
1 story, ...	180	9	189
1 story and attic, . . .	28	3	31
Basement and 1 story, . .	3	–	3
Basement, 1 story, and attic,	2	–	2
2 stories, ...	28	6	34
2 stories and attic, . . .	4	–	4
Basement and 2 stories, . .	1	–	1
Materials.	246	18	264
Wood, ...	246	17	263
Wood and brick, . . .	–	1	1
Rockland.	1,186	58	1,244
Number of Stories.	1,186	58	1,244
1 story, ...	9	2	11
1 story and attic, . . .	942	48	990
Basement, 1 story, and attic,	10	–	10
2 stories, ...	41	4	45
2 stories and attic, . . .	173	4	177
Basement, 2 stories, and attic,	6	–	6
3 stories, ...	4	–	4
3 stories and attic, . . .	1	–	1
Materials.	1,186	58	1,244
Wood, ...	1,172	58	1,230
Brick, ...	1	–	1
Wood and brick, . . .	13	–	13
Scituate.	569	253	822
Number of Stories.	569	253	822
1 story, ...	47	21	68
1 story and attic, . . .	376	127	503
2 stories, ...	114	81	195
2 stories and attic, . . .	28	23	51
Basement and 2 stories, . .	1	–	1
3 stories, ...	2	–	2
Basement and 3 stories, . .	1	–	1
4 stories and attic, . . .	–	1	1
Materials.	569	253	822
Wood, ...	569	253	822
Wareham.	815	508	1,323
Number of Stories.	815	508	1,323
1 story, ...	651	391	1,042
1 story and attic, . . .	1	–	1
Basement and 1 story, . .	8	2	10
PLYMOUTH — Con.			
Wareham — Con.			
Number of Stories — Con.			
2 stories, ...	60	85	145
2 stories and attic, . . .	88	24	112
Basement, 2 stories, and attic,	1	–	1
3 stories, ...	3	2	5
3 stories and attic, . . .	1	–	1
Basement and 3 stories, . .	1	1	2
4 stories, ...	1	2	3
Basement, 4 stories, and attic,	–	1	1
Materials.	815	508	1,323
Wood, ...	813	508	1,321
Stone, ...	1	–	1
Stone and cement, . . .	1	–	1
West Bridgewater. . .	378	27	405
Number of Stories.	378	27	405
1 story, ...	2	–	2
1 story and attic, . . .	269	16	285
Basement, 1 story, and attic,	2	–	2
2 stories, ...	25	1	26
2 stories and attic, . . .	80	10	90
Materials.	378	27	405
Wood, ...	377	27	404
Wood and brick, . . .	1	–	1
Whitman.	1,210	51	1,261
Number of Stories.	1,210	51	1,261
1 story, ...	45	2	47
1 story and attic, . . .	871	40	911
Basement and 1 story, . .	1	–	1
Basement, 1 story, and attic,	5	–	5
2 stories, ...	75	2	77
2 stories and attic, . . .	200	6	206
Basement and 2 stories, . .	1	–	1
3 stories, ...	12	1	13
Materials.	1,210	51	1,261
Wood, ...	1,203	51	1,254
Brick, ...	2	–	2
Wood and brick, . . .	5	–	5
SUFFOLK.			
BOSTON.	58,599	3,525	62,124
Number of Stories.	58,599	3,525	62,124
1 story, ...	526	43	569
1 story and attic, . . .	1,887	108	1,995
Basement and 1 story, . .	47	6	53
Basement, 1 story, and attic,	346	13	359
2 stories, ...	8,310	500	8,810
2 stories and attic, . . .	15,642	1,197	16,839
Basement and 2 stories, . .	905	34	939
Basement, 2 stories, and attic,	1,678	83	1,761
3 stories, ...	15,440	762	16,202
3 stories and attic, . . .	1,752	84	1,836

DWELLING HOUSES: NUMBER OF STORIES AND MATERIALS — Continued.

COUNTIES, CITIES, TOWNS, NUMBER OF STORIES TO DWELLING HOUSES, AND MATERIALS OF WHICH CONSTRUCTED.	Number of Occupied Dwelling Houses	Number of Unoccupied Dwelling Houses	Total Number of Dwelling Houses	COUNTIES, CITIES, TOWNS, NUMBER OF STORIES TO DWELLING HOUSES, AND MATERIALS OF WHICH CONSTRUCTED.	Number of Occupied Dwelling Houses	Number of Unoccupied Dwelling Houses	Total Number of Dwelling Houses
SUFFOLK — Con.				**SUFFOLK — Con.**			
BOSTON — Con.				BOSTON. WARD 1 — Con.			
Number of Stories — Con.				*Materials — Con.*			
Basement and 3 stories, . .	3,859	227	4,086	Brick, ...	149	15	164
Basement, 3 stories, and attic,	1,852	74	1,926	Stone, ...	1	–	1
4 stories, ...	2,764	133	2,897	Wood and brick, . . .	19	–	19
4 stories and attic, . . .	217	18	235				
Basement and 4 stories, . .	2,362	143	2,505	BOSTON. WARD 2, . .	2,163	85	2,248
Basement, 4 stories, and attic,	144	14	158	*Number of Stories.*	2,163	85	2,248
5 stories, ...	439	29	468	1 story, ...	35	4	39
5 stories and attic, . . .	3	–	3	1 story and attic, . . .	88	3	91
Basement and 5 stories, . .	287	23	310	Basement and 1 story, . .	3	–	3
Basement, 5 stories, and attic,	2	–	2	Basement, 1 story, and attic,	101	7	108
6 stories, ...	43	6	49	2 stories, ...	244	14	258
6 stories and attic, . . .	1	–	1	2 stories and attic, . . .	547	29	576
Basement and 6 stories, . .	49	16	65	Basement and 2 stories, . .	54	2	56
Basement, 6 stories, and attic,	1	–	1	Basement, 2 stories, and attic,	151	2	153
7 stories, ...	5	–	5	3 stories, ...	681	20	701
7 stories and attic, . . .	1	–	1	3 stories and attic, . . .	76	2	78
Basement and 7 stories, . .	7	–	7	Basement and 3 stories, . .	119	1	120
8 stories, ...	6	–	6	Basement, 3 stories, and attic,	30	–	30
Basement and 8 stories, . .	1	–	1	4 stories, ...	17	1	18
Not given, ...	23	12	35	4 stories and attic, . . .	1	–	1
				Basement and 4 stories, . .	12	–	12
Materials.	58,599	3,525	62,124	Basement, 4 stories, and attic,	1	–	1
Wood, ...	40,870	2,396	43,266	Not given, ...	3	–	3
Brick, ...	15,564	876	16,440	*Materials.*	2,163	85	2,248
Stone, ...	401	44	445	Wood, ...	1,694	66	1,760
Cement, ...	17	–	17	Brick, ...	425	18	443
Wood and brick, . . .	468	20	488	Wood and brick, . . .	31	1	32
Wood and stone, . . .	54	7	61	Brick and stone, . . .	3	–	3
Wood and cement, . . .	5	1	6	Brick and cement, . . .	1	–	1
Brick and stone, . . .	1,164	163	1,327	Not given, ...	3	–	3
Brick and cement, . . .	29	6	35				
Stone and cement, . . .	4	–	4	BOSTON. WARD 3, . .	1,681	32	1,713
Wood, brick, and stone, . .	1	–	1	*Number of Stories.*	1,681	32	1,713
Not given, ...	22	12	34	1 story, ...	5	–	5
				1 story and attic, . . .	22	3	25
BOSTON. WARD 1, . .	2,843	130	2,973	Basement, 1 story, and attic,	9	–	9
Number of Stories.	2,843	130	2,973	2 stories, ...	141	3	144
1 story, ...	48	3	51	2 stories and attic, . . .	399	6	405
1 story and attic, . . .	229	14	243	Basement and 2 stories, . .	21	–	21
Basement and 1 story, . .	1	–	1	Basement, 2 stories, and attic,	38	1	39
Basement, 1 story, and attic,	101	1	102	3 stories, ...	925	16	941
2 stories, ...	510	33	543	3 stories and attic, . . .	30	1	31
2 stories and attic, . . .	629	27	656	Basement and 3 stories, . .	36	–	36
Basement and 2 stories, . .	69	5	74	Basement, 3 stories, and attic,	6	–	6
Basement, 2 stories, and attic,	110	2	112	4 stories, ...	34	–	34
3 stories, ...	973	42	1,015	Basement and 4 stories, . .	8	–	8
3 stories and attic, . . .	21	–	21	5 stories, ...	–	1	1
Basement and 3 stories, . .	137	3	140	Basement and 5 stories, . .	2	1	3
Basement, 3 stories, and attic,	5	–	5	*Materials.*	1,681	32	1,713
4 stories, ...	9	–	9	Wood, ...	1,440	26	1,466
4 stories and attic, . . .	1	–	1	Brick, ...	202	5	207
Materials.	2,843	130	2,973	Wood and brick, . . .	33	–	33
Wood, ...	2,674	115	2,789	Brick and cement, . . .	6	1	7

DWELLING HOUSES: NUMBER OF STORIES AND MATERIALS — Continued.

COUNTIES, CITIES, TOWNS, NUMBER OF STORIES TO DWELLING HOUSES, AND MATERIALS OF WHICH CONSTRUCTED.	Number of Occupied Dwelling Houses	Number of Unoccupied Dwelling Houses	Total Number of Dwelling Houses	COUNTIES, CITIES, TOWNS, NUMBER OF STORIES TO DWELLING HOUSES, AND MATERIALS OF WHICH CONSTRUCTED.	Number of Occupied Dwelling Houses	Number of Unoccupied Dwelling Houses	Total Number of Dwelling Houses
SUFFOLK — Con.				**SUFFOLK — Con.**			
BOSTON. WARD 4,	1,851	74	1,925	BOSTON. WARD 6 — Con.			
Number of Stories.	1,851	74	1,925	*Number of Stories — Con.*			
1 story,	8	1	9	Basement, 1 story, and attic,	9	–	9
1 story and attic,	115	3	118	2 stories,	145	10	155
Basement and 1 story,	1	–	1	2 stories and attic,	140	5	145
Basement, 1 story, and attic,	9	1	10	Basement and 2 stories,	10	–	10
2 stories,	259	15	274	Basement, 2 stories, and attic,	37	2	39
2 stories and attic,	429	13	442	3 stories,	483	29	512
Basement and 2 stories,	38	1	39	3 stories and attic,	243	10	253
Basement, 2 stories, and attic,	50	1	51	Basement and 3 stories,	68	7	75
3 stories,	793	35	828	Basement, 3 stories, and attic,	65	1	66
3 stories and attic,	66	2	68	4 stories,	418	25	443
Basement and 3 stories,	32	1	33	4 stories and attic,	30	1	31
Basement, 3 stories, and attic,	3	1	4	Basement and 4 stories,	36	–	36
4 stories,	43	–	43	Basement, 4 stories, and attic,	4	–	4
Basement and 4 stories,	2	–	2	5 stories,	79	8	87
Not given,	3	–	3	5 stories and attic,	1	–	1
				Basement and 5 stories,	9	–	9
Materials.	1,851	74	1,925	6 stories,	6	1	7
Wood,	1,595	70	1,665	7 stories,	2	–	2
Brick,	237	4	241	8 stories,	1	–	1
Stone,	1	–	1	Not given,	–	1	1
Wood and brick,	7	–	7				
Brick and stone,	1	–	1	*Materials.*	1,854	102	1,956
Brick and cement,	7	–	7	Wood,	579	26	605
Not given,	3	–	3	Brick,	1,215	75	1,290
				Cement,	1	–	1
BOSTON. WARD 5,	1,507	47	1,554	Wood and brick,	53	–	53
Number of Stories.	1,507	47	1,554	Brick and stone,	6	1	7
1 story,	7	–	7				
1 story and attic,	24	–	24	BOSTON. WARD 7,	1,554	128	1,682
Basement, 1 story, and attic,	8	–	8	*Number of Stories.*	1,554	128	1,682
2 stories,	134	6	140	1 story,	9	–	9
2 stories and attic,	332	10	342	Basement and 1 story,	2	–	2
Basement and 2 stories,	3	–	3	2 stories,	75	10	85
Basement, 2 stories, and attic,	49	4	53	2 stories and attic,	96	14	110
3 stories,	769	20	789	Basement and 2 stories,	18	3	21
3 stories and attic,	64	5	69	Basement, 2 stories, and attic,	150	29	179
Basement and 3 stories,	33	–	33	3 stories,	233	15	248
Basement, 3 stories, and attic,	17	–	17	3 stories and attic,	197	14	211
4 stories,	65	2	67	Basement and 3 stories,	57	8	65
Basement and 5 stories,	1	–	1	Basement, 3 stories, and attic,	278	13	291
Not given,	1	–	1	4 stories,	297	12	309
				4 stories and attic,	9	1	10
Materials.	1,507	47	1,554	Basement and 4 stories,	49	2	51
Wood,	1,062	19	1,081	Basement, 4 stories, and attic,	3	–	3
Brick,	390	22	412	5 stories,	62	4	66
Stone,	2	2	4	Basement and 5 stories,	4	–	4
Wood and brick,	42	1	43	6 stories,	9	2	11
Brick and stone,	2	–	2	Basement and 6 stories,	1	–	1
Brick and cement,	8	3	11	7 stories,	2	–	2
Not given,	1	–	1	8 stories,	3	–	3
				Not given,	–	1	1
BOSTON. WARD 6,	1,854	102	1,956				
Number of Stories.	1,854	102	1,956	*Materials.*	1,554	128	1,682
1 story,	30	1	31	Wood,	203	18	221
1 story and attic,	38	1	39				

DWELLING HOUSES: NUMBER OF STORIES AND MATERIALS — Continued.

COUNTIES, CITIES, TOWNS, NUMBER OF STORIES TO DWELLING HOUSES, AND MATERIALS OF WHICH CONSTRUCTED.	Number of Occupied Dwelling Houses	Number of Unoccupied Dwelling Houses	Total Number of Dwelling Houses
SUFFOLK — Con.			
BOSTON, WARD 7 — Con.			
Materials — Con.			
Brick, ...	1,314	103	1,417
Stone, ...	9	4	13
Wood and brick, . . .	8	–	8
Brick and stone, . . .	20	2	22
Not given, ...	–	1	1
BOSTON, WARD 8, . .	1,891	83	1,974
Number of Stories.	1,891	83	1,974
1 story, ...	22	1	23
1 story and attic, . . .	6	2	8
Basement and 1 story, . .	8	1	9
Basement, 1 story, and attic,	2	–	2
2 stories, ...	130	12	142
2 stories and attic, . .	116	5	121
Basement and 2 stories, . .	18	–	18
Basement, 2 stories, and attic,	87	3	90
3 stories, ...	368	14	382
3 stories and attic, . .	318	12	330
Basement and 3 stories, . .	143	1	144
Basement, 3 stories, and attic,	180	4	184
4 stories, ...	243	12	255
4 stories and attic, . .	64	5	69
Basement and 4 stories, .	86	5	91
Basement, 4 stories, and attic,	20	1	21
5 stories, ...	58	2	60
5 stories and attic, . .	1	–	1
Basement and 5 stories, . .	10	1	11
Basement, 5 stories, and attic,	1	–	1
6 stories, ...	4	2	6
Basement and 6 stories, . .	1	–	1
7 stories and attic, . .	1	–	1
Basement and 7 stories, . .	1	–	1
Not given, ...	3	–	3
Materials.	1,891	83	1,974
Wood, ...	359	22	381
Brick, ...	1,474	58	1,532
Stone, ...	14	–	14
Wood and brick, . . .	19	–	19
Wood and stone, . . .	10	1	11
Wood and cement, . . .	2	–	2
Brick and stone, . . .	10	1	11
Brick and cement, . . .	1	1	2
Not given, ...	2	–	2
BOSTON, WARD 9, . .	1,970	91	2,061
Number of Stories.	1,970	91	2,061
1 story, ...	34	–	34
1 story and attic, . . .	16	1	17
Basement and 1 story, . .	5	–	5
Basement, 1 story, and attic,	1	–	1
2 stories, ...	76	11	87
2 stories and attic, . . .	91	3	94

COUNTIES, CITIES, TOWNS, NUMBER OF STORIES TO DWELLING HOUSES, AND MATERIALS OF WHICH CONSTRUCTED.	Number of Occupied Dwelling Houses	Number of Unoccupied Dwelling Houses	Total Number of Dwelling Houses
SUFFOLK — Con.			
BOSTON, WARD 9 — Con.			
Number of Stories — Con.			
Basement and 2 stories, . .	32	1	33
Basement, 2 stories, and attic,	268	8	276
3 stories, ...	250	13	263
3 stories and attic, . . .	77	2	79
Basement and 3 stories, . .	177	11	188
Basement, 3 stories, and attic,	428	24	452
4 stories, ...	235	1	236
4 stories and attic, . .	13	1	14
Basement and 4 stories, . .	203	10	213
Basement, 4 stories, and attic,	11	1	12
5 stories, ...	34	1	35
Basement and 5 stories, . .	15	2	17
6 stories, ...	2	–	2
Basement and 7 stories, . .	1	–	1
Not given, ...	1	1	2
Materials.	1,970	91	2,061
Wood, ...	292	21	313
Brick, ...	1,455	66	1,521
Stone, ...	1	–	1
Wood and brick, . . .	29	2	31
Wood and stone, . . .	4	1	5
Brick and stone, . . .	189	–	189
Not given, ...	1	1	2
BOSTON, WARD 10, . .	2,292	121	2,413
Number of Stories.	2,292	121	2,413
1 story, ...	9	1	10
1 story and attic, . . .	17	3	20
Basement and 1 story, . .	3	3	6
Basement, 1 story, and attic,	3	–	3
2 stories, ...	62	2	64
2 stories and attic, . . .	100	6	106
Basement and 2 stories, . .	57	–	57
Basement, 2 stories, and attic,	52	–	52
3 stories, ...	136	16	152
3 stories and attic, . .	26	–	26
Basement and 3 stories, . .	831	51	882
Basement, 3 stories, and attic,	58	1	59
4 stories, ...	340	17	357
4 stories and attic, . . .	1	–	1
Basement and 4 stories, . .	519	21	540
Basement, 4 stories, and attic,	1	–	1
5 stories, ...	24	–	24
Basement and 5 stories, . .	33	–	33
6 stories, ...	4	–	4
Basement and 6 stories, . .	9	–	9
Not given, ...	7	–	7
Materials.	2,292	121	2,413
Wood, ...	222	9	231
Brick, ...	1,697	73	1,770
Stone, ...	45	11	56
Wood and brick, . . .	2	–	2

DWELLING HOUSES: NUMBER OF STORIES AND MATERIALS — Continued.

COUNTIES, CITIES, TOWNS, NUMBER OF STORIES TO DWELLING HOUSES, AND MATERIALS OF WHICH CONSTRUCTED.	Number of Occupied Dwelling Houses	Number of Unoccupied Dwelling Houses	Total Number of Dwelling Houses
SUFFOLK — Con.			
BOSTON. WARD 10 — Con.			
Materials — Con.			
Brick and stone, . . .	318	28	346
Not given, ...	8	-	8
BOSTON. WARD 11, .	2,515	260	2,775
Number of Stories.	2,515	260	2,775
1 story,	-	1	1
1 story and attic, . . .	4	1	5
Basement and 1 story, . .	1	-	1
2 stories, ...	81	6	87
2 stories and attic, . . .	70	3	73
Basement and 2 stories, . .	6	1	7
Basement, 2 stories, and attic,	18	1	19
3 stories, ...	180	8	188
3 stories and attic, . . .	204	10	214
Basement and 3 stories, . .	300	55	355
Basement, 3 stories, and attic,	275	16	291
4 stories, ...	84	6	90
4 stories and attic, . . .	70	8	78
Basement and 4 stories, . .	876	92	968
Basement, 4 stories, and attic,	75	12	87
5 stories, ...	18	5	23
5 stories and attic, . . .	1	-	1
Basement and 5 stories, . .	204	19	223
Basement, 5 stories, and attic,	1	-	1
6 stories, ...	3	-	3
Basement and 6 stories, . .	35	16	51
Basement, 6 stories, and attic,	1	-	1
7 stories, ...	1	-	1
Basement and 7 stories, . .	5	-	5
Basement and 8 stories, . .	1	-	1
Not given, ...	1	-	1
Materials.	2,515	260	2,775
Wood, ...	185	7	192
Brick, ...	1,672	110	1,782
Stone, ...	209	22	231
Wood and brick, . . .	3	-	3
Wood and stone, . . .	-	1	1
Brick and stone, . . .	444	119	563
Not given, ...	2	1	3
BOSTON. WARD 12, .	2,249	85	2,334
Number of Stories.	2,249	85	2,334
1 story, ...	3	-	3
1 story and attic, . . .	12	1	13
Basement and 1 story, . .	1	-	1
Basement, 1 story, and attic,	5	-	5
2 stories, ...	40	-	40
2 stories and attic, . . .	115	11	126
Basement and 2 stories, . .	6	-	6
Basement, 2 stories, and attic,	39	3	42
3 stories, ...	200	17	217
3 stories and attic, . . .	67	3	70
Basement and 3 stories, . .	294	10	304
SUFFOLK — Con.			
BOSTON. WARD 12 — Con.			
Number of Stories — Con.			
Basement, 3 stories, and attic,	412	6	418
4 stories, ...	434	17	451
4 stories and attic, . . .	22	2	24
Basement and 4 stories, . .	427	11	438
Basement, 4 stories, and attic,	24	-	24
5 stories, ...	131	4	135
Basement and 5 stories, . .	6	-	6
6 stories, ...	10	-	10
Basement and 6 stories, . .	1	-	1
Materials.	2,249	85	2,334
Wood, .	258	10	268
Brick, .	1,882	69	1,951
Stone, .	34	2	36
Cement, .	3	-	3
Wood and brick, .	37	3	40
Brick and stone, .	34	-	34
Brick and cement, .	1	1	2
BOSTON. WARD 13, .	2,341	48	2,389
Number of Stories.	2,341	48	2,389
1 story, ...	20	-	20
1 story and attic, . . .	78	2	80
Basement and 1 story, . .	3	1	4
Basement, 1 story, and attic,	21	-	21
2 stories, ...	227	7	234
2 stories and attic, . . .	376	12	388
Basement and 2 stories, . .	83	1	84
Basement, 2 stories, and attic,	55	-	55
3 stories, ...	1,032	20	1,052
3 stories and attic, . . .	78	-	78
Basement and 3 stories, . .	236	4	240
Basement, 3 stories, and attic,	17	-	17
4 stories, ...	102	1	103
Basement and 4 stories, . .	8	-	8
5 stories, ...	5	-	5
Materials.	2,341	48	2,389
Wood, ...	2,033	41	2,074
Brick, ...	264	6	270
Cement, ...	1	-	1
Wood and brick, . . .	38	1	39
Brick and stone, . . .	1	-	1
Brick and cement, . . .	4	-	4
BOSTON. WARD 14, .	2,485	142	2,627
Number of Stories.	2,485	142	2,627
1 story, ...	16	6	22
1 story and attic, . . .	33	1	34
Basement and 1 story, . .	5	1	6
Basement, 1 story, and attic,	8	1	9
2 stories, ...	720	56	776
2 stories and attic, . . .	242	10	252
Basement and 2 stories, . .	66	-	66

DWELLING HOUSES: NUMBER OF STORIES AND MATERIALS — Continued.

Counties, Cities, Towns. Number of Stories to Dwelling Houses, and Materials of which Constructed.	Number of Occupied Dwelling Houses	Number of Unoccupied Dwelling Houses	Total Number of Dwelling Houses
SUFFOLK — Con.			
BOSTON. WARD 14 — Con.			
Number of Stories — Con.			
Basement, 2 stories, and attic,	40	1	41
3 stories,	1,075	57	1,132
3 stories and attic,	18	2	20
Basement and 3 stories,	200	4	204
Basement, 3 stories, and attic,	6	–	6
4 stories,	50	2	52
Basement and 4 stories,	3	–	3
5 stories,	2	–	2
Basement and 5 stories,	1	–	1
Not given,	–	1	1
Materials.	2,485	142	2,627
Wood,	2,080	121	2,211
Brick,	355	18	373
Stone,	4	–	4
Wood and brick,	28	2	30
Brick and stone,	8	–	8
Not given,	–	1	1
BOSTON. WARD 15,	2,294	68	2,362
Number of Stories.	2,294	68	2,362
1 story,	10	1	11
1 story and attic,	59	5	64
Basement, 1 story, and attic,	19	2	21
2 stories,	498	22	520
2 stories and attic,	351	12	363
Basement and 2 stories,	96	–	96
Basement, 2 stories, and attic,	146	2	148
3 stories,	726	14	740
3 stories and attic,	21	1	22
Basement and 3 stories,	353	8	361
Basement, 3 stories, and attic,	4	–	4
4 stories,	6	–	6
4 stories and attic,	2	–	2
5 stories,	1	–	1
Basement and 5 stories,	1	–	1
6 stories,	1	–	1
Not given,	–	1	1
Materials.	2,294	68	2,362
Wood,	2,094	59	2,153
Brick,	169	7	176
Cement,	10	–	10
Wood and brick,	17	1	18
Wood and stone,	2	–	2
Wood and cement,	2	–	2
Not given,	–	1	1
BOSTON. WARD 16,	2,103	126	2,229
Number of Stories.	2,103	126	2,229
1 story,	32	5	37
1 story and attic,	26	1	27
Basement, 1 story, and attic,	1	–	1
2 stories,	396	23	419
2 stories and attic,	658	55	713
SUFFOLK — Con.			
BOSTON. WARD 16 — Con.			
Number of Stories — Con.			
Basement and 2 stories,	27	1	28
Basement, 2 stories, and attic,	9	–	9
3 stories,	848	38	886
3 stories and attic,	13	1	14
Basement and 3 stories,	63	1	64
Basement, 3 stories, and attic,	2	–	2
4 stories,	21	–	21
Basement and 4 stories,	3	–	3
5 stories,	–	1	1
6 stories,	1	–	1
Basement and 6 stories,	2	–	2
Not given,	1	–	1
Materials.	2,103	126	2,229
Wood,	1,905	104	2,009
Brick,	159	14	173
Stone,	2	–	2
Wood and brick,	4	–	4
Wood and stone,	1	–	1
Brick and stone,	31	8	39
Not given,	1	–	1
BOSTON. WARD 17,	2,441	129	2,570
Number of Stories.	2,441	129	2,570
1 story,	19	1	20
1 story and attic,	81	11	92
Basement, 1 story, and attic,	1	1	2
2 stories,	527	24	551
2 stories and attic,	631	20	651
Basement and 2 stories,	50	3	53
Basement, 2 stories, and attic,	51	4	55
3 stories,	961	53	1,014
3 stories and attic,	26	1	27
Basement and 3 stories,	45	3	48
4 stories,	48	4	52
Not given,	1	4	5
Materials.	2,441	129	2,570
Wood,	1,919	92	2,011
Brick,	504	31	535
Stone,	2	–	2
Wood and brick,	14	2	16
Wood and stone,	1	–	1
Not given,	1	4	5
BOSTON. WARD 18,	2,303	132	2,435
Number of Stories.	2,303	132	2,435
1 story,	18	2	20
1 story and attic,	34	4	38
Basement, 1 story, and attic,	3	–	3
2 stories,	316	10	326
2 stories and attic,	322	34	356
Basement and 2 stories,	68	4	72
Basement, 2 stories, and attic,	27	3	30
3 stories,	755	32	787

DWELLING HOUSES: NUMBER OF STORIES AND MATERIALS — Continued.

COUNTIES, CITIES, TOWNS, NUMBER OF STORIES TO DWELLING HOUSES, AND MATERIALS OF WHICH CONSTRUCTED.	Number of Occupied Dwelling Houses	Number of Unoccupied Dwelling Houses	Total Number of Dwelling Houses
SUFFOLK — Con.			
BOSTON. WARD 18 — Con.			
Number of Stories — Con.			
3 stories and attic, . . .	22	3	25
Basement and 3 stories, . .	461	29	490
Basement, 3 stories, and attic,	6	2	8
4 stories, ...	137	6	143
4 stories and attic, . . .	2	–	2
Basement and 4 stories, . .	108	1	109
Basement, 4 stories, and attic,	3	–	3
5 stories, ...	20	2	22
6 stories, ...	1	–	1
Materials.	2,303	132	2,435
Wood, ...	1,254	81	1,335
Brick, ...	1,013	49	1,062
Stone, ...	10	–	10
Wood and brick, . . .	8	–	8
Wood and stone, . . .	–	1	1
Brick and stone, . . .	18	1	19
BOSTON. WARD 19, . .	2,144	136	2,280
Number of Stories.	2,144	136	2,280
1 story, ...	12	1	13
1 story and attic, . . .	75	1	76
Basement, 1 story, and attic,	3	–	3
2 stories, ...	217	26	243
2 stories and attic, . . .	402	13	415
Basement and 2 stories, . .	26	2	28
Basement, 2 stories, and attic,	24	–	24
3 stories, ...	1,111	68	1,179
3 stories and attic, . . .	43	1	44
Basement and 3 stories, . .	118	9	127
Basement, 3 stories, and attic,	48	5	53
4 stories, ...	44	10	54
Basement and 4 stories, . .	20	–	20
6 stories, ...	1	–	1
Materials.	2,144	136	2,280
Wood, ...	1,730	87	1,817
Brick, ...	319	43	362
Stone, ...	23	2	25
Wood and brick, . . .	9	1	10
Wood and stone, . . .	1	–	1
Brick and stone, . . .	61	3	64
Brick and cement, . . .	1	–	1
BOSTON. WARD 20, . .	3,589	472	4,061
Number of Stories.	3,589	472	4,061
1 story, ...	63	5	68
1 story and attic, . . .	191	17	208
Basement and 1 story, . .	2	–	2
Basement, 1 story, and attic,	8	–	8
2 stories, ...	608	40	648
2 stories and attic, . . .	2,131	347	2,478
Basement and 2 stories, . .	19	–	19
Basement, 2 stories, and attic,	36	3	39
3 stories, ...	490	45	535

COUNTIES, CITIES, TOWNS, NUMBER OF STORIES TO DWELLING HOUSES, AND MATERIALS OF WHICH CONSTRUCTED.	Number of Occupied Dwelling Houses	Number of Unoccupied Dwelling Houses	Total Number of Dwelling Houses
SUFFOLK — Con.			
BOSTON. WARD 20 — Con.			
Number of Stories — Con.			
3 stories and attic, . . .	11	4	15
Basement and 3 stories, . .	23	10	33
Basement, 3 stories, and attic,	1	–	1
4 stories, ...	6	–	6
5 stories, ...	–	1	1
Materials.	3,589	472	4,061
Wood, ...	3,506	464	3,970
Brick, ...	72	8	80
Stone, ...	1	–	1
Wood and brick, . . .	4	–	4
Wood and stone, . . .	4	–	4
Brick and stone, . . .	1	–	1
Wood, brick, and stone, .	1	–	1
BOSTON. WARD 21, . .	2,896	151	3,047
Number of Stories.	2,896	151	3,047
1 story, ...	12	1	13
1 story and attic, . . .	39	–	39
Basement, 1 story, and attic,	7	–	7
2 stories, ...	333	7	340
2 stories and attic, . . .	1,303	61	1,364
Basement and 2 stories, . .	64	4	68
Basement, 2 stories, and attic,	118	5	123
3 stories, ...	840	55	895
3 stories and attic, . . .	58	3	61
Basement and 3 stories, . .	31	2	33
Basement, 3 stories, and attic,	6	1	7
4 stories, ...	75	11	86
4 stories and attic, . . .	2	–	2
Basement and 4 stories, . .	1	1	2
Basement, 4 stories, and attic,	1	–	1
5 stories, ...	3	–	3
Basement and 5 stories, . .	1	–	1
6 stories, ...	1	–	1
8 stories, ...	1	–	1
Materials.	2,896	151	3,047
Wood, ...	2,560	108	2,668
Brick, ...	268	39	307
Stone, ...	24	–	24
Wood and brick, . . .	32	4	36
Wood and stone, . . .	3	–	3
Brick and stone, . . .	9	–	9
BOSTON. WARD 22, . .	2,850	179	3,029
Number of Stories.	2,850	179	3,029
1 story, ...	8	2	10
1 story and attic, . . .	89	5	94
Basement and 1 story, . .	1	–	1
Basement, 1 story, and attic,	3	–	3
2 stories, ...	571	26	597
2 stories and attic, . . .	1,045	75	1,120
Basement and 2 stories, . .	21	–	21
Basement, 2 stories, and attic,	20	1	21

DWELLING HOUSES: NUMBER OF STORIES AND MATERIALS — Continued.

COUNTIES, CITIES, TOWNS, NUMBER OF STORIES TO DWELLING HOUSES, AND MATERIALS OF WHICH CONSTRUCTED.	Number of Occupied Dwelling Houses	Number of Unoccupied Dwelling Houses	Total Number of Dwelling Houses
SUFFOLK — Con.			
BOSTON. WARD 22 — Con.			
Number of Stories — Con.			
3 stories, ...	924	53	977
3 stories and attic, . . .	39	4	43
Basement and 3 stories, . .	85	6	91
Basement, 3 stories, and attic,	2	–	2
4 stories, ...	37	6	43
Basement and 4 stories, . .	1	–	1
Basement, 4 stories, and attic,	1	–	1
5 stories, ...	2	–	2
6 stories, ...	–	1	1
8 stories, ...	1	–	1
Materials.	2,850	179	3,029
Wood, ...	2,607	143	2,750
Brick, ...	226	34	260
Stone, ...	3	–	3
Wood and brick, . . .	7	–	7
Wood and stone, . . .	7	1	8
Wood and cement, . . .	–	1	1
BOSTON. WARD 23, . .	2,947	248	3,195
Number of Stories.	2,947	248	3,195
1 story, ...	42	1	43
1 story and attic, . . .	213	7	220
Basement and 1 story, . .	4	–	4
Basement, 1 story, and attic,	10	–	10
2 stories, ...	506	35	541
2 stories and attic, . . .	1,872	174	2,046
Basement and 2 stories, . .	9	–	9
Basement, 2 stories, and attic,	32	4	36
3 stories, ...	243	23	266
3 stories and attic, . . .	11	1	12
Basement and 3 stories, . .	3	3	6
Basement, 3 stories, and attic,	1	–	1
4 stories, ...	1	–	1
Materials.	2,947	248	3,195
Wood, ...	2,922	242	3,164
Brick, ...	12	3	15
Stone, ...	4	–	4
Wood and brick, . . .	4	1	5
Wood and stone, . . .	1	2	3
Stone and cement, . . .	4	–	4
BOSTON. WARD 24, . .	3,234	238	3,472
Number of Stories.	3,234	238	3,472
1 story, ...	16	3	19
1 story and attic, . . .	274	10	284
Basement and 1 story, . .	2	–	2
Basement, 1 story, and attic,	5	–	5
2 stories, ...	826	60	886
2 stories and attic, . . .	1,795	134	1,929
Basement and 2 stories, . .	27	5	32
Basement, 2 stories, and attic,	26	2	28
3 stories, ...	233	22	255

COUNTIES, CITIES, TOWNS, NUMBER OF STORIES TO DWELLING HOUSES, AND MATERIALS OF WHICH CONSTRUCTED.	Number of Occupied Dwelling Houses	Number of Unoccupied Dwelling Houses	Total Number of Dwelling Houses
SUFFOLK — Con.			
BOSTON. WARD 24 — Con.			
Number of Stories — Con.			
3 stories and attic, . . .	13	2	15
Basement and 3 stories, . .	1	–	1
4 stories, ...	4	–	4
6 stories and attic, . . .	1	–	1
Not given, ...	1	–	1
Materials.	3,234	238	3,472
Wood, ...	3,222	236	3,458
Brick, ...	2	2	4
Stone, ...	1	–	1
Wood and brick. . . .	6	–	6
Wood and stone, . . .	1	–	1
Brick and stone, . . .	1	–	1
Not given, ...	1	–	1
BOSTON. WARD 25, . .	2,602	218	2,820
Number of Stories.	2,602	218	2,820
1 story, ...	48	3	51
1 story and attic, . . .	124	12	136
Basement and 1 story, . .	5	–	5
Basement, 1 story, and attic,	9	–	9
2 stories, ...	668	42	710
2 stories and attic, . . .	1,450	118	1,568
Basement and 2 stories, . .	17	1	18
Basement, 2 stories, and attic,	35	2	37
3 stories, ...	211	37	248
3 stories and attic, . . .	10	–	10
Basement and 3 stories, . .	13	–	13
Basement, 3 stories, and attic,	2	–	2
4 stories, ...	9	–	9
Not given, ...	1	3	4
Materials.	2,602	218	2,820
Wood, ...	2,465	209	2,674
Brick, ...	89	4	93
Stone, ...	11	1	12
Cement, ...	2	–	2
Wood and brick, . . .	14	1	15
Wood and stone, . . .	19	–	19
Wood and cement, . . .	1	–	1
Brick and stone, . . .	1	–	1
Not given, ...	–	3	3
CHELSEA.	4,743	333	5,076
Number of Stories.	4,743	333	5,076
1 story, ...	43	–	43
1 story and attic, . . .	207	14	221
Basement and 1 story, . .	1	1	2
Basement, 1 story, and attic,	61	7	68
2 stories, ...	1,016	93	1,109
2 stories and attic, . . .	1,576	85	1,661
Basement and 2 stories, . .	170	15	185
Basement, 2 stories, and attic,	216	8	224
3 stories, ...	1,021	78	1,099
3 stories and attic, . . .	73	6	79

DWELLING HOUSES: NUMBER OF STORIES AND MATERIALS — Continued.

COUNTIES, CITIES, TOWNS, NUMBER OF STORIES TO DWELLING HOUSES, AND MATERIALS OF WHICH CONSTRUCTED.	Number of Occupied Dwelling Houses	Number of Unoccupied Dwelling Houses	Total Number of Dwelling Houses
SUFFOLK — Con.			
CHELSEA — Con.			
Number of Stories — Con.			
Basement and 3 stories, . .	291	18	309
Basement, 3 stories, and attic,	13	-	13
4 stories, ...	39	3	42
Basement and 4 stories, . .	14	-	14
5 stories and attic, . . .	1	-	1
Basement and 5 stories, . .	1	-	1
Not given, ...	-	5	5
Materials.	4,743	333	5,076
Wood, ...	3,771	254	4,025
Brick, ...	927	70	997
Stone, ...	5	1	6
Wood and brick, . . .	28	3	31
Wood and stone, . . .	1	-	1
Brick and stone, . . .	7	-	7
Brick and cement, . . .	4	-	4
Not given, ...	-	5	5
CHELSEA. WARD 1, . .	1,089	67	1,156
Number of Stories.	1,089	67	1,156
1 story, ...	11	-	11
1 story and attic, . . .	51	2	53
Basement, 1 story, and attic,	25	2	27
2 stories, ...	196	12	208
2 stories and attic, . . .	327	20	347
Basement and 2 stories, . .	55	6	61
Basement, 2 stories, and attic,	37	-	37
3 stories, ...	265	21	286
3 stories and attic, . . .	26	-	26
Basement and 3 stories, . .	59	3	62
Basement, 3 stories, and attic,	2	-	2
4 stories, ...	27	1	28
Basement and 4 stories, . .	7	-	7
5 stories and attic, . . .	1	-	1
Materials.	1,089	67	1,156
Wood, ...	788	52	840
Brick, ...	285	15	300
Stone, ...	1	-	1
Wood and brick, . . .	9	-	9
Brick and stone, . . .	6	-	6
CHELSEA. WARD 2, . .	1,138	87	1,225
Number of Stories.	1,138	87	1,225
1 story, ...	16	-	16
1 story and attic, . . .	61	8	69
Basement and 1 story, . .	1	-	1
Basement, 1 story, and attic,	15	1	16
2 stories, ...	313	31	344
2 stories and attic, . . .	280	16	296
Basement and 2 stories, . .	26	1	27
Basement, 2 stories, and attic,	103	8	111
3 stories, ...	225	13	238
3 stories and attic, . . .	35	6	41
Basement and 3 stories, . .	37	2	39
SUFFOLK — Con.			
CHELSEA. WARD 2 — Con.			
Number of Stories — Con.			
Basement, 3 stories, and attic,	10	-	10
4 stories, ...	11	-	11
Basement and 4 stories, . .	5	-	5
Not given, ...	-	1	1
Materials.	1,138	87	1,225
Wood, ...	902	65	967
Brick, ...	226	20	246
Stone, ...	1	-	1
Wood and brick, . . .	4	1	5
Brick and stone, . . .	1	-	1
Brick and cement, . . .	4	-	4
Not given, ...	-	1	1
CHELSEA. WARD 3, . .	1,039	79	1,118
Number of Stories.	1,039	79	1,118
1 story, ...	7	-	7
1 story and attic, . . .	69	4	73
Basement and 1 story, . .	-	1	1
Basement, 1 story, and attic,	18	4	22
2 stories, ...	151	21	172
2 stories and attic, . . .	391	9	400
Basement and 2 stories, . .	47	5	52
Basement, 2 stories, and attic,	44	-	44
3 stories, ...	236	24	260
3 stories and attic, . . .	6	-	6
Basement and 3 stories, . .	68	5	73
4 stories, ...	1	2	3
Basement and 4 stories, . .	1	-	1
Not given, ...	-	4	4
Materials.	1,039	79	1,118
Wood, ...	852	49	901
Brick, ...	178	25	203
Wood and brick, . . .	9	1	10
Not given, ...	-	4	4
CHELSEA. WARD 4, . .	846	45	891
Number of Stories.	846	45	891
1 story, ...	5	-	5
1 story and attic, . . .	16	-	16
Basement, 1 story, and attic,	3	-	3
2 stories, ...	76	8	84
2 stories and attic, . . .	336	16	352
Basement and 2 stories, . .	39	1	40
Basement, 2 stories, and attic,	25	-	25
3 stories, ...	213	12	225
3 stories and attic, . . .	4	-	4
Basement and 3 stories, . .	126	8	134
Basement, 3 stories, and attic,	1	-	1
Basement and 4 stories, . .	1	-	1
Basement and 5 stories, . .	1	-	1
Materials.	846	45	891
Wood, ...	629	37	666

DWELLING HOUSES: NUMBER OF STORIES AND MATERIALS — Continued.

Counties, Cities, Towns, Number of Stories in Dwelling Houses, and Materials of which Constructed.	Number of Occupied Dwelling Houses	Number of Unoccupied Dwelling Houses	Total Number of Dwelling Houses
SUFFOLK — Con.			
CHELSEA. WARD 4—Con.			
Materials—Con.			
Brick,	243	7	220
Wood and brick,	3	1	4
Wood and stone,	1	–	1
CHELSEA. WARD 5,	631	55	686
Number of Stories.	631	55	686
1 story,	4	–	4
1 story and attic,	10	–	10
2 stories,	280	21	301
2 stories and attic,	242	24	266
Basement and 2 stories,	3	2	5
Basement, 2 stories, and attic,	7	–	7
3 stories,	2	8	10
3 stories and attic,	2	–	2
Basement and 3 stories,	1	–	1
Materials.	631	55	686
Wood,	600	51	651
Brick,	25	3	28
Stone,	3	1	4
Wood and brick,	3	–	3
Revere,	1,407	336	1,743
Number of Stories.	1,407	336	1,743
1 story,	21	14	35
1 story and attic,	247	88	335
Basement and 1 story,	2	–	2
Basement, 1 story, and attic,	10	4	14
2 stories,	305	99	404
2 stories and attic,	666	98	764
Basement and 2 stories,	63	5	68
Basement, 2 stories, and attic,	35	10	45
3 stories,	51	12	63
3 stories and attic,	1	–	1
Basement and 3 stories,	5	–	5
Basement, 3 stories, and attic,	1	–	1
4 stories,	–	1	1
Not given,	–	5	5
Materials.	1,407	336	1,743
Wood,	1,392	327	1,719
Brick,	15	8	23
Wood and brick,	–	1	1
Winthrop,	855	291	1,146
Number of Stories.	855	291	1,146
1 story,	36	22	58
1 story and attic,	224	96	320
Basement and 1 story,	1	–	1
Basement, 1 story, and attic,	13	1	14
2 stories,	189	77	266
2 stories and attic,	342	83	425
Basement and 2 stories,	9	4	13
Basement, 2 stories, and attic,	18	3	21
3 stories,	19	5	24

Counties, Cities, Towns, Number of Stories in Dwelling Houses, and Materials of which Constructed.	Number of Occupied Dwelling Houses	Number of Unoccupied Dwelling Houses	Total Number of Dwelling Houses
SUFFOLK — Con.			
Winthrop — Con.			
Number of Stories — Con.			
3 stories and attic,	3	–	3
4 stories,	1	–	1
Materials.	855	291	1,146
Wood,	852	290	1,142
Brick,	–	1	1
Wood and brick,	2	–	2
Wood and stone,	1	–	1
WORCESTER.			
Ashburnham.	446	60	506
Number of Stories.	446	60	506
1 story and attic,	287	41	328
Basement, 1 story, and attic,	5	1	6
2 stories,	10	2	12
2 stories and attic,	136	16	152
3 stories,	7	–	7
Basement and 3 stories,	1	–	1
Materials.	446	60	506
Wood,	432	55	487
Brick,	12	3	15
Wood and brick,	2	2	4
Athol,	1,450	67	1,517
Number of Stories.	1,450	67	1,517
1 story,	21	1	22
1 story and attic,	564	34	598
Basement and 1 story,	2	–	2
Basement, 1 story, and attic,	55	4	59
2 stories,	80	3	83
2 stories and attic,	639	24	663
Basement and 2 stories,	2	–	2
Basement, 2 stories, and attic,	35	–	35
3 stories,	41	–	41
3 stories and attic,	2	1	3
Basement and 3 stories,	5	–	5
4 stories,	3	–	3
Not given,	1	–	1
Materials.	1,450	67	1,517
Wood,	1,436	66	1,502
Brick,	12	1	13
Wood and brick,	2	–	2
Auburn,	277	21	298
Number of Stories.	277	21	298
1 story,	37	5	42
1 story and attic,	151	12	163
Basement, 1 story, and attic,	2	–	2
2 stories,	51	3	54
2 stories and attic,	29	1	30
Basement and 2 stories,	4	–	4
Basement, 2 stories, and attic,	2	–	2
3 stories,	1	–	1

DWELLING HOUSES: NUMBER OF STORIES AND MATERIALS — Continued.

Counties, Cities, Towns, Number of Stories to Dwelling Houses, and Materials of which Constructed	Number of Occupied Dwelling Houses	Number of Unoccupied Dwelling Houses	Total Number of Dwelling Houses
WORCESTER — Con.			
Auburn — Con.			
Materials.	277	21	298
Wood, ...	276	21	297
Brick, ...	1	–	1
Barre, ...	501	71	572
Number of Stories.	501	71	572
1 story, ...	172	31	203
1 story and attic, . .	64	6	70
2 stories, ...	241	27	268
2 stories and attic, . .	18	4	22
3 stories, ...	3	2	5
3 stories and attic, . .	2	1	3
Basement and 3 stories, .	1	–	1
Materials.	501	71	572
Wood, ...	488	66	554
Brick, ...	11	5	16
Wood and brick, . .	2	–	2
Berlin, ...	211	26	237
Number of Stories.	211	26	237
1 story, ...	1	–	1
1 story and attic, . .	96	20	116
Basement, 1 story, and attic,	5	1	6
2 stories, ...	4	1	5
2 stories and attic, . .	102	4	106
Basement, 2 stories, and attic,	1	–	1
3 stories, ...	2	–	2
Materials.	211	26	237
Wood, ...	201	26	227
Brick, ...	5	–	5
Wood and brick, . .	2	–	2
Wood and stone, . .	1	–	1
Wood and cement, . .	2	–	2
Blackstone, . . .	901	50	951
Number of Stories.	901	50	951
1 story, ...	9	3	12
1 story and attic, . .	412	29	441
Basement and 1 story, .	–	1	1
Basement, 1 story, and attic,	65	3	68
2 stories, ...	186	5	191
2 stories and attic, . .	195	7	202
Basement and 2 stories, .	7	1	8
Basement, 2 stories, and attic,	16	–	16
3 stories, ...	4	–	4
3 stories and attic, . .	4	–	4
Basement and 3 stories, .	2	–	2
4 stories, ...	1	1	2
Materials.	901	50	951
Wood, ...	823	47	870
Brick, ...	23	–	23
Stone, ...	4	–	4
Wood and brick, . .	13	–	13

Counties, Cities, Towns, Number of Stories to Dwelling Houses, and Materials of which Constructed	Number of Occupied Dwelling Houses	Number of Unoccupied Dwelling Houses	Total Number of Dwelling Houses
WORCESTER — Con.			
Blackstone — Con.			
Materials — Con.			
Wood and stone, . .	35	3	38
Wood, brick, and stone, .	3	–	3
Bolton, ...	191	11	202
Number of Stories.	191	11	202
1 story, ...	25	1	26
1 story and attic, . .	45	2	47
Basement, 1 story, and attic,	1	–	1
2 stories, ...	17	–	17
2 stories and attic, . .	100	8	108
Basement and 2 stories, .	1	–	1
Basement, 2 stories, and attic,	2	–	2
Materials.	191	11	202
Wood, ...	182	11	193
Brick, ...	9	–	9
Boylston, ...	147	10	157
Number of Stories.	147	10	157
1 story, ...	12	–	12
1 story and attic, . .	49	7	56
2 stories, ...	71	3	74
2 stories and attic, . .	14	–	14
3 stories, ...	1	–	1
Materials.	147	10	157
Wood, ...	141	10	151
Brick, ...	4	–	4
Wood and brick, . .	2	–	2
Brookfield, ...	599	59	658
Number of Stories.	599	59	658
1 story, ...	37	10	47
1 story and attic, . .	183	25	208
Basement and 1 story, .	7	1	8
Basement, 1 story, and attic,	8	2	10
2 stories, ...	251	12	263
2 stories and attic, . .	80	6	86
Basement and 2 stories, .	18	–	18
Basement, 2 stories, and attic,	3	–	3
3 stories, ...	9	2	11
Basement and 3 stories, .	1	–	1
4 stories, ...	–	1	1
Not given, ...	2	–	2
Materials.	599	59	658
Wood, ...	568	54	622
Brick, ...	22	3	25
Stone, ...	3	–	3
Wood and brick, . .	4	2	6
Not given, ...	2	–	2
Charlton, ...	420	21	441
Number of Stories.	420	21	441
1 story, ...	29	5	34
1 story and attic, . .	211	8	219

DWELLING HOUSES: NUMBER OF STORIES AND MATERIALS -- Continued.

COUNTIES, CITIES, TOWNS, NUMBER OF STORIES TO DWELLING HOUSES, AND MATERIALS OF WHICH CONSTRUCTED.	Number of Occupied Dwelling Houses	Number of Unoccupied Dwelling Houses	Total Number of Dwelling Houses
WORCESTER — Con.			
Charlton — Con.			
Number of Stories — Con.			
Basement and 1 story, . .	1	–	1
Basement, 1 story, and attic,	2	–	2
2 stories, ...	134	6	140
2 stories and attic, . . .	39	2	41
Basement and 2 stories, . .	4	–	4
Materials.	420	21	441
Wood, .	401	21	422
Brick, .	6	–	6
Stone, .	3	–	3
Wood and brick,	9	–	9
Wood and stone,	1	–	1
Clinton, . . .	1,694	59	1,753
Number of Stories.	1,694	59	1,753
1 story, . . .	46	4	50
1 story and attic, . .	540	30	570
Basement and 1 story, . .	3	1	4
Basement, 1 story, and attic,	50	2	52
2 stories, . . .	382	11	393
2 stories and attic, . .	451	9	460
Basement and 2 stories, . .	52	–	52
Basement, 2 stories, and attic,	64	–	64
3 stories, . .	70	2	72
3 stories and attic, . .	5	–	5
Basement and 3 stories, . .	16	–	16
Basement, 3 stories, and attic,	5	–	5
4 stories, . . .	9	–	9
Basement and 4 stories, . .	1	–	1
Materials.	1,694	59	1,753
Wood, .	1,605	56	1,661
Brick, .	85	3	88
Cement, .	1	–	1
Wood and stone,	1	–	1
Wood and cement, . .	2	–	2
Dana.	175	12	187
Number of Stories.	175	12	187
1 story and attic, . .	121	10	131
2 stories, . .	4	1	5
2 stories and attic, . .	47	–	47
3 stories, . .	3	1	4
Materials.	175	12	187
Wood, .	173	12	185
Brick, .	1	–	1
Wood and brick,	1	–	1
Douglas. . . .	390	29	419
Number of Stories.	390	29	419
1 story, . . .	25	3	28
1 story and attic, . .	202	17	219
Basement and 1 story, . .	6	–	6
Basement, 1 story, and attic,	15	1	16
WORCESTER — Con.			
Douglas — Con.			
Number of Stories — Con.			
2 stories, ...	54	5	59
2 stories and attic, . .	68	1	69
Basement and 2 stories, .	1	1	2
Basement, 2 stories, and attic,	15	1	16
3 stories, . . .	3	–	3
Basement and 3 stories, .	1	–	1
Materials.	390	29	419
Wood, .	373	29	402
Brick, .	10	–	10
Wood and brick,	7	–	7
Dudley.	420	22	442
Number of Stories.	420	22	442
1 story, .	1	–	1
1 story and attic, . .	211	13	224
Basement and 1 story, .	1	–	1
Basement, 1 story, and attic,	12	–	12
2 stories, . . .	24	1	25
2 stories and attic, . .	137	6	143
Basement and 2 stories, .	7	–	7
Basement, 2 stories, and attic,	17	–	17
3 stories, . .	3	2	5
3 stories and attic, . .	4	–	4
Basement and 3 stories, .	1	–	1
Basement, 3 stories, and attic,	2	–	2
Materials.	420	22	442
Wood, .	399	20	419
Brick, .	8	–	8
Stone, .	7	–	7
Wood and brick, .	4	1	5
Stone and cement, .	2	–	2
Wood, brick, and stone, .	–	1	1
FITCHBURG, . .	3,886	182	4,068
Number of Stories.	3,886	182	4,068
1 story, . . .	17	5	22
1 story and attic, . .	1,473	85	1,558
Basement and 1 story, . .	3	–	3
Basement, 1 story, and attic,	104	12	116
2 stories, . . .	403	20	423
2 stories and attic, . .	1,310	43	1,353
Basement and 2 stories, . .	91	4	95
Basement, 2 stories, and attic,	96	5	101
3 stories, . .	295	5	300
3 stories and attic, . .	44	1	45
Basement and 3 stories, . .	27	–	27
Basement, 3 stories, and attic,	4	1	5
4 stories, . . .	12	–	12
4 stories and attic, . .	1	–	1
Basement and 4 stories, .	1	–	1
5 stories, . . .	2	–	2
Not given, . . .	3	1	4

DWELLING HOUSES: NUMBER OF STORIES AND MATERIALS — Continued.

Counties, Cities, Towns, Number of Stories to Dwelling Houses, and Materials of Which Constructed.	Number of Occupied Dwelling Houses	Number of Unoccupied Dwelling Houses	Total Number of Dwelling Houses	Counties, Cities, Towns, Number of Stories to Dwelling Houses, and Materials of Which Constructed.	Number of Occupied Dwelling Houses	Number of Unoccupied Dwelling Houses	Total Number of Dwelling Houses
WORCESTER — Con.				**WORCESTER — Con.**			
FITCHBURG — Con.				FITCHBURG. WARD 3 — Con.			
Materials.	3,886	182	4,068	*Number of Stories — Con.*			
Wood, .	3,640	172	3,812	Basement, 1 story, and attic,	25	2	27
Brick, .	180	6	186	2 stories,	68	2	70
Stone, .	3	-	3	2 stories and attic,	228	7	235
Wood and brick,	32	1	33	Basement and 2 stories,	27	-	27
Wood and stone,	1	2	3	Basement, 2 stories, and attic,	21	-	21
Brick and stone,	27	-	27	3 stories,	41	3	44
Stone and cement,	1	-	1	3 stories and attic,	4	-	4
Not given,	2	1	3	Basement and 3 stories,	4	-	4
FITCHBURG. WARD 1, .	624	16	640	Basement, 3 stories, and attic,	1	1	2
Number of Stories.	624	16	640	*Materials.*	649	26	675
1 story,	2	4	6	Wood, .	594	20	614
1 story and attic,	325	8	333	Brick, .	47	4	51
Basement, 1 story, and attic,	27	1	28	Stone, .	2	-	2
2 stories,	40	-	40	Wood and brick,	6	1	7
2 stories and attic,	161	2	163	Wood and stone,	-	1	1
Basement and 2 stories,	8	-	8	FITCHBURG. WARD 4, .	549	32	581
Basement, 2 stories, and attic,	19	1	20	*Number of Stories.*	549	32	581
3 stories,	31	-	31	1 story,	7	-	7
3 stories and attic,	9	-	9	1 story and attic,	108	12	120
Basement and 3 stories,	1	-	1	Basement, 1 story, and attic,	3	3	6
5 stories,	1	-	1	2 stories,	62	4	66
Materials.	624	16	640	2 stories and attic,	273	9	282
Wood, .	612	16	628	Basement and 2 stories,	9	1	10
Brick, .	7	-	7	Basement, 2 stories, and attic,	15	-	15
Wood and brick,	4	-	4	3 stories,	63	2	65
Wood and stone,	1	-	1	3 stories and attic,	15	1	16
FITCHBURG. WARD 2, .	740	28	768	Basement and 3 stories,	3	-	3
Number of Stories.	740	28	768	Basement, 3 stories, and attic,	1	-	1
1 story,	3	-	3	4 stories,	6	-	6
1 story and attic,	273	14	287	4 stories and attic,	1	-	1
Basement and 1 story,	1	-	1	5 stories,	1	-	1
Basement, 1 story, and attic,	25	1	26	Not given,	2	-	2
2 stories,	118	4	122	*Materials.*	549	32	581
2 stories and attic,	203	5	208	Wood, .	483	32	515
Basement and 2 stories,	35	2	37	Brick, .	31	-	31
Basement, 2 stories, and attic,	19	1	20	Wood and brick,	5	-	5
3 stories,	42	-	42	Brick and stone,	27	-	27
3 stories and attic,	6	-	6	Stone and cement,	1	-	1
Basement and 3 stories,	12	-	12	Not given,	2	-	2
Basement, 3 stories, and attic,	2	-	2	FITCHBURG. WARD 5, .	593	24	617
Not given,	1	1	2	*Number of Stories.*	593	24	617
Materials.	740	28	768	1 story and attic,	145	8	153
Wood, .	678	27	705	2 stories,	65	9	74
Brick, .	49	-	49	2 stories and attic,	257	7	264
Wood and brick,	13	-	13	Basement and 2 stories,	7	-	7
Not given,	-	1	1	Basement, 2 stories, and attic,	17	-	17
FITCHBURG. WARD 3, .	649	26	675	3 stories,	57	-	57
Number of Stories.	649	26	675	3 stories and attic,	3	-	3
1 story,	2	-	2	Basement and 3 stories,	5	-	5
1 story and attic,	228	11	239	4 stories,	6	-	6
				Basement and 4 stories,	1	-	1

DWELLING HOUSES: NUMBER OF STORIES AND MATERIALS — Continued.

COUNTIES, CITIES, TOWNS, NUMBER OF STORIES TO DWELLING HOUSES, AND MATERIALS OF WHICH CONSTRUCTED.	Number of Occupied Dwelling Houses	Number of Unoccupied Dwelling Houses	Total Number of Dwelling Houses
WORCESTER — Con.			
FITCHBURG. WARD 5 — Con.			
Materials.	593	24	617
Wood,	574	23	597
Brick,	18	1	19
Stone,	1	–	1
FITCHBURG. WARD 6,	731	56	787
Number of Stories.	731	56	787
1 story,	3	1	4
1 story and attic,	394	32	426
Basement and 1 story,	2	–	2
Basement, 1 story, and attic,	24	5	29
2 stories,	50	1	51
2 stories and attic,	208	13	221
Basement and 2 stories,	5	1	6
Basement, 2 stories, and attic,	5	3	8
3 stories,	31	–	31
3 stories and attic,	7	–	7
Basement and 3 stories,	2	–	2
Materials.	731	56	787
Wood,	699	54	753
Brick,	28	1	29
Wood and brick,	4	–	4
Wood and stone,	–	1	1
Gardner.	1,573	43	1,616
Number of Stories.	1,573	43	1,616
1 story,	27	1	28
1 story and attic,	905	33	938
Basement, 1 story, and attic,	29	–	29
2 stories,	88	3	91
2 stories and attic,	449	6	455
Basement and 2 stories,	3	–	3
Basement, 2 stories, and attic,	21	–	21
3 stories,	45	–	45
3 stories and attic,	2	–	2
Basement and 3 stories,	2	–	2
4 stories,	2	–	2
Materials.	1,573	43	1,616
Wood,	1,553	42	1,595
Brick,	16	–	16
Wood and brick,	4	–	4
Wood and stone,	–	1	1
Grafton.	926	51	977
Number of Stories.	926	51	977
1 story,	24	2	26
1 story and attic,	343	22	365
Basement and 1 story,	5	1	6
Basement, 1 story, and attic,	30	–	30
2 stories,	209	14	223
2 stories and attic,	302	9	311
Basement and 2 stories,	6	1	7
Basement, 2 stories, and attic,	3	1	4
3 stories,	4	–	4
Not given,	–	1	1

COUNTIES, CITIES, TOWNS, NUMBER OF STORIES TO DWELLING HOUSES, AND MATERIALS OF WHICH CONSTRUCTED.	Number of Occupied Dwelling Houses	Number of Unoccupied Dwelling Houses	Total Number of Dwelling Houses
WORCESTER — Con.			
Grafton — Con.			
Materials.	926	51	977
Wood,	915	48	963
Brick,	7	1	8
Wood and brick,	4	1	5
Not given,	–	1	1
Hardwick.	460	21	481
Number of Stories.	460	21	481
1 story,	5	–	5
1 story and attic,	163	6	169
Basement, 1 story, and attic,	9	1	10
2 stories,	27	5	32
2 stories and attic,	221	8	229
Basement, 2 stories, and attic,	4	–	4
3 stories,	4	–	4
3 stories and attic,	27	1	28
Materials.	460	21	481
Wood,	455	20	475
Brick,	4	1	5
Cement,	1	–	1
Harvard.	262	34	296
Number of Stories.	262	34	296
1 story,	15	12	27
1 story and attic,	73	5	78
Basement and 1 story,	1	–	1
Basement, 1 story, and attic,	1	–	1
2 stories,	36	3	39
2 stories and attic,	129	13	142
Basement, 2 stories, and attic,	6	1	7
3 stories,	1	–	1
Materials.	262	34	296
Wood,	251	33	284
Brick,	1	1	2
Wood and brick,	10	–	10
Holden.	415	31	446
Number of Stories.	415	31	446
1 story,	9	–	9
1 story and attic,	215	23	238
Basement and 1 story,	1	–	1
Basement, 1 story, and attic,	3	1	4
2 stories,	4	–	4
2 stories and attic,	174	6	180
Basement and 2 stories,	1	–	1
Basement, 2 stories, and attic,	5	1	6
3 stories and attic,	3	–	3
Materials.	415	31	446
Wood,	406	31	434
Brick,	8	–	8
Wood and brick,	4	–	4
Hopedale.	285	18	303
Number of Stories.	285	18	303
1 story and attic,	152	11	163

DWELLING HOUSES: NUMBER OF STORIES AND MATERIALS — Continued.

COUNTIES, CITIES, TOWNS, NUMBER OF STORIES TO DWELLING HOUSES, AND MATERIALS OF WHICH CONSTRUCTED.	Number of Occupied Dwelling Houses	Number of Unoccupied Dwelling Houses	Total Number of Dwelling Houses
WORCESTER — Con.			
Hopedale — Con.			
Number of Stories — Con.			
Basement, 1 story, and attic,	18	–	18
2 stories,	14	–	14
2 stories and attic,	86	7	93
Basement, 2 stories, and attic,	2	–	2
3 stories,	8	–	8
3 stories and attic,	4	–	4
Basement and 3 stories,	1	–	1
Materials.	285	18	303
Wood,	281	18	299
Stone,	1	–	1
Cement,	1	–	1
Wood and stone,	2	–	2
Hubbardston,	311	36	347
Number of Stories.	311	36	347
1 story,	25	1	26
1 story and attic,	160	22	182
2 stories,	120	13	133
2 stories and attic,	3	–	3
3 stories,	2	–	2
Not given,	1	–	1
Materials.	311	36	347
Wood,	307	36	343
Brick,	3	–	3
Stone,	1	–	1
Lancaster,	395	38	433
Number of Stories.	395	38	433
1 story,	2	–	2
1 story and attic,	160	15	175
Basement, 1 story, and attic,	5	1	6
2 stories,	47	4	51
2 stories and attic,	168	14	182
Basement and 2 stories,	2	–	2
Basement, 2 stories, and attic,	4	2	6
3 stories,	4	1	5
3 stories and attic,	2	–	2
Basement and 3 stories,	1	–	1
4 stories,	–	1	1
Materials.	395	38	433
Wood,	367	34	401
Brick,	7	2	9
Stone,	1	–	1
Wood and brick,	17	2	19
Wood and stone,	2	–	2
Wood, brick, and stone,	1	–	1
Leicester,	594	16	610
Number of Stories.	594	16	610
1 story,	7	–	7
1 story and attic,	300	11	311
Basement and 1 story,	2	–	2

COUNTIES, CITIES, TOWNS, NUMBER OF STORIES TO DWELLING HOUSES, AND MATERIALS OF WHICH CONSTRUCTED.	Number of Occupied Dwelling Houses	Number of Unoccupied Dwelling Houses	Total Number of Dwelling Houses
WORCESTER — Con.			
Leicester — Con.			
Number of Stories — Con.			
Basement, 1 story, and attic,	17	–	17
2 stories,	36	1	37
2 stories and attic,	217	4	221
Basement and 2 stories,	2	–	2
Basement, 2 stories, and attic,	8	–	8
3 stories,	1	–	1
3 stories and attic,	2	–	2
6 stories,	1	–	1
Not given,	1	–	1
Materials.	594	16	610
Wood,	584	15	599
Brick,	7	1	8
Wood and brick,	3	–	3
Leominster,	1,643	49	1,692
Number of Stories.	1,643	49	1,692
1 story,	25	–	25
1 story and attic,	408	20	428
Basement, 1 story, and attic,	12	1	13
2 stories,	472	13	485
2 stories and attic,	634	10	644
Basement and 2 stories,	20	–	20
Basement, 2 stories, and attic,	9	1	10
3 stories,	56	3	59
3 stories and attic,	3	–	3
Basement and 3 stories,	3	–	3
4 stories,	1	–	1
Not given,	–	1	1
Materials.	1,643	49	1,692
Wood,	1,620	48	1,668
Brick,	17	–	17
Wood and brick,	6	–	6
Not given,	–	1	1
Lunenburg,	277	18	295
Number of Stories.	277	18	295
1 story,	29	4	33
1 story and attic,	97	6	103
Basement and 1 story,	1	1	2
2 stories,	87	5	92
2 stories and attic,	60	2	62
Basement and 2 stories,	2	–	2
3 stories and attic,	1	–	1
Materials.	277	18	295
Wood,	272	18	290
Brick,	2	–	2
Wood and brick,	3	–	3
Mendon,	221	16	237
Number of Stories.	221	16	237
1 story,	4	1	5
1 story and attic,	134	8	142

DWELLING HOUSES: NUMBER OF STORIES AND MATERIALS — Continued.

COUNTIES, CITIES, TOWNS. NUMBER OF STORIES TO DWELLING HOUSES, AND MATERIALS OF WHICH CONSTRUCTED.	Number of Occupied Dwelling Houses	Number of Unoccupied Dwelling Houses	Total Number of Dwelling Houses	COUNTIES, CITIES, TOWNS. NUMBER OF STORIES TO DWELLING HOUSES, AND MATERIALS OF WHICH CONSTRUCTED.	Number of Occupied Dwelling Houses	Number of Unoccupied Dwelling Houses	Total Number of Dwelling Houses
WORCESTER — Con.				**WORCESTER — Con.**			
Mendon — Con.				**New Braintree.**	114	–	114
Number of Stories — Con.				*Number of Stories.*	114	–	114
Basement and 1 story, . .	1	–	1	1 story, ...	5	–	5
Basement, 1 story, and attic,	11	3	14	1 story and attic, . . .	29	–	29
2 stories, ...	7	–	7	2 stories, ...	79	–	79
2 stories and attic, . . .	55	3	58	2 stories and attic, . . .	1	–	1
Basement and 2 stories, . .	2	–	2				
Basement, 2 stories, and attic,	7	1	8	*Materials.*	114	–	114
				Wood, ...	113	–	113
Materials.	221	16	237	Brick, ...	1	–	1
Wood, ...	217	14	231				
Stone, ...	–	1	1	**Northborough.** . . .	347	23	370
Wood and brick, . . .	4	–	4	*Number of Stories.*	347	23	370
Wood and stone, . . .	–	1	1	1 story, ...	24	4	28
				1 story and attic, . . .	131	6	137
Milford.	1,671	73	1,744	Basement and 1 story, . .	8	1	9
Number of Stories.	1,671	73	1,744	Basement, 1 story, and attic,	3	–	3
1 story, ...	31	2	33	2 stories, ...	83	5	88
1 story and attic, . . .	754	39	793	2 stories and attic, . . .	93	4	97
Basement and 1 story, . .	2	–	2	3 stories, ...	4	3	7
Basement, 1 story, and attic,	136	2	138	3 stories and attic, . . .	1	–	1
2 stories, ...	120	10	130				
2 stories and attic, . . .	484	15	499	*Materials.*	347	23	370
Basement and 2 stories, . .	30	–	30	Wood, ...	319	21	340
Basement, 2 stories, and attic,	71	4	75	Brick, ...	24	1	25
3 stories, ...	29	1	30	Stone, ...	1	–	1
3 stories and attic, . . .	8	–	8	Wood and brick, . . .	2	–	2
Basement and 3 stories, . .	1	–	1	Wood and stone, . . .	1	–	1
Basement, 3 stories, and attic,	2	–	2	Brick and stone, . . .	–	1	1
4 stories, ...	3	–	3				
				Northbridge. . . .	836	34	870
Materials.	1,671	73	1,744	*Number of Stories.*	836	34	870
Wood, ...	1,644	73	1,717	1 story, ...	21	6	27
Brick, ...	22	–	22	1 story and attic, . . .	364	11	375
Stone, ...	5	–	5	Basement and 1 story, . .	–	2	2
Wood and brick, . . .	3	–	3	Basement, 1 story, and attic,	51	–	51
				2 stories, ...	29	5	34
Millbury.	793	32	825	2 stories and attic, . . .	309	9	318
Number of Stories.	793	32	825	Basement and 2 stories, . .	13	–	13
1 story, ...	26	1	27	Basement, 2 stories, and attic,	40	1	41
1 story and attic, . . .	302	11	313	3 stories, ...	7	–	7
Basement and 1 story, . .	3	1	4	3 stories and attic, . . .	1	–	1
Basement, 1 story, and attic,	42	1	43	Basement, 3 stories, and attic,	1	–	1
2 stories, ...	61	7	68				
2 stories and attic, . . .	316	11	327	*Materials.*	836	34	870
Basement and 2 stories, . .	10	–	10	Wood, ...	788	32	820
Basement, 2 stories, and attic,	16	–	16	Brick, ...	14	2	16
3 stories, ...	15	–	15	Stone, ...	2	–	2
3 stories and attic, . . .	1	–	1	Wood and brick, . . .	31	–	31
Basement and 3 stories, . .	1	–	1	Wood and stone, . . .	1	–	1
Materials.	793	32	825	**North Brookfield.** . .	679	5	684
Wood, ...	739	30	769	*Number of Stories.*	679	5	684
Brick, ...	34	2	36	1 story, ...	7	–	7
Wood and brick, . . .	17	–	17	1 story and attic, . . .	239	3	242
Wood and stone, . . .	2	–	2	Basement and 1 story, . .	3	–	3
Not given, ...	1	–	1	Basement, 1 story, and attic,	98	–	98

DWELLING HOUSES: NUMBER OF STORIES AND MATERIALS — Continued.

COUNTIES, CITIES, TOWNS, NUMBER OF STORIES TO DWELLING HOUSES, AND MATERIALS OF WHICH CONSTRUCTED.	Number of Occupied Dwelling Houses	Number of Unoccupied Dwelling Houses	Total Number of Dwelling Houses
WORCESTER — Con.			
North Brookfield — Con.			
Number of Stories — Con.			
2 stories,	14	–	14
2 stories and attic,	232	2	234
Basement and 2 stories,	3	–	3
Basement, 2 stories, and attic,	64	–	64
3 stories,	8	–	8
3 stories and attic,	3	–	3
Basement and 3 stories,	6	–	6
Basement, 3 stories, and attic,	2	–	2
Materials.	679	5	684
Wood,	665	4	669
Brick,	10	1	11
Stone,	2	–	2
Wood and brick,	2	–	2
Oakham,	149	17	166
Number of Stories.	149	17	166
1 story,	5	2	7
1 story and attic,	65	10	75
Basement, 1 story, and attic,	1	–	1
2 stories,	7	–	7
2 stories and attic,	68	5	73
3 stories,	1	–	1
Basement, 3 stories, and attic,	1	–	1
Not given,	1	–	1
Materials.	149	17	166
Wood,	146	17	163
Brick,	1	–	1
Stone,	1	–	1
Wood and brick,	1	–	1
Oxford,	562	85	647
Number of Stories.	562	85	647
1 story and attic,	318	27	345
Basement and 1 story,	1	–	1
Basement, 1 story, and attic,	10	2	12
2 stories,	9	12	21
2 stories and attic,	212	41	253
Basement, 2 stories, and attic,	8	2	10
3 stories,	4	1	5
Materials.	562	85	647
Wood,	548	77	625
Brick,	6	2	8
Stone,	1	–	1
Wood and brick,	3	–	3
Wood and stone,	4	6	10
Paxton,	109	20	129
Number of Stories.	109	20	129
1 story,	3	3	6
1 story and attic,	6	8	14
2 stories,	56	2	58
2 stories and attic,	41	7	48

COUNTIES, CITIES, TOWNS, NUMBER OF STORIES TO DWELLING HOUSES, AND MATERIALS OF WHICH CONSTRUCTED.	Number of Occupied Dwelling Houses	Number of Unoccupied Dwelling Houses	Total Number of Dwelling Houses
WORCESTER — Con.			
Paxton — Con.			
Number of Stories — Con.			
Basement, 2 stories, and attic,	2	–	2
3 stories,	1	–	1
Materials.	109	20	129
Wood,	108	20	128
Wood and stone,	1	–	1
Petersham,	232	57	289
Number of Stories.	232	57	289
1 story,	7	2	9
1 story and attic,	114	33	147
2 stories,	4	3	7
2 stories and attic,	101	18	119
Basement, 2 stories, and attic,	3	1	4
3 stories,	1	–	1
3 stories and attic,	1	–	1
Basement and 3 stories,	1	–	1
Materials.	232	57	289
Wood,	231	56	287
Wood and brick,	1	–	1
Wood and stone,	–	1	1
Phillipston,	112	18	130
Number of Stories.	112	18	130
1 story,	14	3	17
1 story and attic,	56	7	63
2 stories,	41	6	47
2 stories and attic,	1	2	3
Materials.	112	18	130
Wood,	112	18	130
Princeton,	228	39	267
Number of Stories.	228	39	267
1 story,	3	–	3
1 story and attic,	109	19	128
Basement, 1 story, and attic,	3	–	3
2 stories,	25	5	30
2 stories and attic,	72	9	81
Basement and 2 stories,	1	1	2
Basement, 2 stories, and attic,	3	2	5
3 stories,	6	–	6
Basement and 3 stories,	3	1	4
Basement, 3 stories, and attic,	–	1	1
4 stories,	1	–	1
Basement and 4 stories,	1	–	1
5 stories,	1	–	1
Basement and 5 stories,	–	1	1
Materials.	228	39	267
Wood,	220	35	255
Brick,	5	2	7
Stone,	1	–	1
Wood and brick,	2	1	3
Wood and stone,	–	1	1

DWELLING HOUSES: NUMBER OF STORIES AND MATERIALS—Continued.

COUNTIES, CITIES, TOWNS, NUMBER OF STORIES TO DWELLING HOUSES, AND MATERIALS OF WHICH CONSTRUCTED.	Number of Occupied Dwelling Houses	Number of Unoccupied Dwelling Houses	Total Number of Dwelling Houses
WORCESTER—Con.			
Royalston.	233	40	273
Number of Stories.	233	40	273
1 story,	4	5	9
1 story and attic,	144	26	170
Basement, 1 story, and attic,	—	1	1
2 stories,	74	7	81
2 stories and attic,	7	1	8
Basement and 2 stories,	3	—	3
3 stories and attic,	1	—	1
Materials.	233	40	273
Wood,	232	40	272
Wood and stone,	1	—	1
Rutland.	213	7	220
Number of Stories.	213	7	220
1 story,	5	—	5
1 story and attic,	110	3	113
2 stories,	5	—	5
2 stories and attic,	91	4	95
3 stories,	1	—	1
4 stories,	1	—	1
Materials.	213	7	220
Wood,	212	7	219
Brick,	1	—	1
Shrewsbury.	354	29	383
Number of Stories.	354	29	383
1 story,	12	3	15
1 story and attic,	108	9	117
Basement, 1 story, and attic,	1	—	1
2 stories,	20	8	28
2 stories and attic,	206	8	214
Basement, 2 stories, and attic,	3	1	4
3 stories,	2	—	2
3 stories and attic,	1	—	1
Basement, 3 stories, and attic,	1	—	1
Materials.	354	29	383
Wood,	347	29	376
Brick,	6	—	6
Wood and stone,	1	—	1
Southborough.	390	50	440
Number of Stories.	390	50	440
1 story,	3	—	3
1 story and attic,	153	24	177
Basement, 1 story, and attic,	2	—	2
2 stories,	17	3	20
2 stories and attic,	205	23	228
Basement, 2 stories, and attic,	3	—	3
3 stories,	4	—	4
3 stories and attic,	3	—	3
Materials.	390	50	440
Wood,	380	48	428
Brick,	2	1	3

COUNTIES, CITIES, TOWNS, NUMBER OF STORIES TO DWELLING HOUSES, AND MATERIALS OF WHICH CONSTRUCTED.	Number of Occupied Dwelling Houses	Number of Unoccupied Dwelling Houses	Total Number of Dwelling Houses
WORCESTER—Con.			
Southborough—Con.			
Materials—Con.			
Stone,	1	—	1
Wood and brick,	6	1	7
Wood, brick, and stone,	1	—	1
Southbridge.	1,379	72	1,451
Number of Stories.	1,379	72	1,451
1 story,	59	3	62
1 story and attic,	469	15	484
Basement and 1 story,	8	2	10
Basement, 1 story, and attic,	44	2	46
2 stories,	334	27	361
2 stories and attic,	340	12	352
Basement and 2 stories,	34	4	38
Basement, 2 stories, and attic,	55	3	58
3 stories,	24	1	25
3 stories and attic,	1	1	2
Basement and 3 stories,	5	—	5
Basement, 3 stories, and attic,	2	1	3
4 stories,	3	—	3
Basement and 6 stories,	1	—	1
Not given,	—	1	1
Materials.	1,379	72	1,451
Wood,	1,310	68	1,378
Brick,	67	4	71
Stone,	1	—	1
Wood and brick,	1	—	1
Spencer.	1,157	60	1,217
Number of Stories.	1,157	60	1,217
1 story,	56	1	57
1 story and attic,	204	14	218
Basement and 1 story,	8	—	8
Basement, 1 story, and attic,	54	1	55
2 stories,	257	19	276
2 stories and attic,	384	17	401
Basement and 2 stories,	48	4	52
Basement, 2 stories, and attic,	111	3	114
3 stories,	18	—	18
3 stories and attic,	3	—	3
Basement and 3 stories,	10	1	11
Basement, 3 stories, and attic,	1	—	1
4 stories,	2	—	2
Basement and 4 stories,	1	—	1
Materials.	1,157	60	1,217
Wood,	1,143	60	1,203
Brick,	12	—	12
Wood and brick,	2	—	2
Sterling.	319	228	547
Number of Stories.	319	228	547
1 story,	1	55	56
1 story and attic,	118	129	247
Basement and 1 story,	3	1	4

DWELLING HOUSES: NUMBER OF STORIES AND MATERIALS — Continued.

COUNTIES, CITIES, TOWNS, NUMBER OF STORIES TO DWELLING HOUSES, AND MATERIALS OF WHICH CONSTRUCTED.	Number of Occupied Dwelling Houses	Number of Unoccupied Dwelling Houses	Total Number of Dwelling Houses
WORCESTER — Con.			
Sterling — Con.			
Number of Stories — Con.			
Basement, 1 story, and attic,	11	–	11
2 stories,	32	31	63
2 stories and attic,	143	12	155
Basement, 2 stories, and attic,	4	–	4
3 stories,	5	–	5
3 stories and attic,	1	–	1
Basement and 3 stories,	1	–	1
Materials.	319	228	547
Wood,	310	226	536
Brick,	6	2	8
Cement,	1	–	1
Wood and brick,	2	–	2
Sturbridge.	337	33	370
Number of Stories.	337	33	370
1 story,	19	4	23
1 story and attic,	101	10	111
Basement and 1 story,	1	1	2
Basement, 1 story, and attic,	11	1	12
2 stories,	56	11	67
2 stories and attic,	139	6	145
Basement and 2 stories,	6	–	6
Basement, 2 stories, and attic,	1	–	1
3 stories and attic,	1	–	1
Basement and 3 stories,	1	–	1
4 stories,	1	–	1
Materials.	337	33	370
Wood,	317	28	345
Brick,	7	–	7
Stone,	10	4	14
Wood and brick,	1	1	2
Brick and stone,	2	–	2
Sutton,	529	11	540
Number of Stories.	529	11	540
1 story,	38	–	38
1 story and attic,	278	11	289
Basement and 1 story,	5	–	5
Basement, 1 story, and attic,	7	–	7
2 stories,	41	–	41
2 stories and attic,	154	–	154
Basement, 2 stories, and attic,	2	–	2
3 stories,	2	–	2
3 stories and attic,	1	–	1
4 stories,	1	–	1
Materials.	529	11	540
Wood,	514	11	525
Brick,	12	–	12
Wood and brick,	3	–	3
Templeton,	628	51	679
Number of Stories.	628	51	679
1 story,	9	2	11

COUNTIES, CITIES, TOWNS, NUMBER OF STORIES TO DWELLING HOUSES, AND MATERIALS OF WHICH CONSTRUCTED.	Number of Occupied Dwelling Houses	Number of Unoccupied Dwelling Houses	Total Number of Dwelling Houses
WORCESTER — Con.			
Templeton — Con.			
Number of Stories — Con.			
1 story and attic,	394	28	422
Basement, 1 story, and attic,	5	–	5
2 stories,	57	2	59
2 stories and attic,	152	17	169
Basement and 2 stories,	–	1	1
Basement, 2 stories, and attic,	3	–	3
3 stories,	5	1	6
Basement and 3 stories,	2	–	2
4 stories,	1	–	1
Materials.	628	51	679
Wood,	617	48	665
Brick,	6	3	9
Wood and brick,	5	–	5
Upton.	418	14	432
Number of Stories.	418	14	432
1 story,	18	1	19
1 story and attic,	183	10	193
Basement, 1 story, and attic,	36	–	36
2 stories,	16	–	16
2 stories and attic,	136	3	139
Basement and 2 stories,	2	–	2
Basement, 2 stories, and attic,	19	–	19
3 stories,	5	–	5
3 stories and attic,	1	–	1
Basement and 4 stories,	1	–	1
Not given,	1	–	1
Materials.	418	14	432
Wood,	410	14	424
Brick,	2	–	2
Wood and brick,	4	–	4
Wood and stone,	1	–	1
Not given,	1	–	1
Uxbridge.	641	30	671
Number of Stories.	641	30	671
1 story,	30	2	32
1 story and attic,	325	16	341
Basement and 1 story,	1	1	2
Basement, 1 story, and attic,	23	2	25
2 stories,	21	–	21
2 stories and attic,	208	6	214
Basement and 2 stories,	7	2	9
Basement, 2 stories, and attic,	14	–	14
3 stories,	5	–	5
3 stories and attic,	2	1	3
Basement and 3 stories,	4	–	4
6 stories and attic,	1	–	1
Materials.	641	30	671
Wood,	593	23	616
Brick,	36	4	40
Stone,	3	–	3
Wood and brick,	6	1	7

DWELLING HOUSES: NUMBER OF STORIES AND MATERIALS — Continued.

COUNTIES, CITIES, TOWNS, NUMBER OF STORIES TO DWELLING HOUSES, AND MATERIALS OF WHICH CONSTRUCTED.	Number of Occupied Dwelling Houses	Number of Unoccupied Dwelling Houses	Total Number of Dwelling Houses
WORCESTER — Con.			
Uxbridge — Con.			
Materials — Con.			
Wood and stone,	3	–	3
Brick and stone,	–	2	2
Warren.	783	39	822
Number of Stories.	783	39	822
1 story,	19	4	23
1 story and attic,	185	8	193
Basement, 1 story, and attic,	3	–	3
2 stories,	304	16	320
2 stories and attic,	219	10	229
Basement and 2 stories,	26	–	26
Basement, 2 stories, and attic,	10	–	10
3 stories,	10	1	11
3 stories and attic,	4	–	4
Basement and 3 stories,	3	–	3
Materials.	783	39	822
Wood,	741	36	777
Brick,	37	3	40
Wood and brick,	5	–	5
Webster,	935	68	1,003
Number of Stories.	935	68	1,003
1 story,	12	–	12
1 story and attic,	353	55	408
Basement and 1 story,	3	–	3
Basement, 1 story, and attic,	71	1	72
2 stories,	36	–	36
2 stories and attic,	331	7	338
Basement and 2 stories,	11	–	11
Basement, 2 stories, and attic,	87	3	90
3 stories,	15	2	17
3 stories and attic,	3	–	3
Basement and 3 stories,	5	–	5
Basement, 3 stories, and attic,	1	–	1
4 stories,	5	–	5
4 stories and attic,	2	–	2
Materials.	935	68	1,003
Wood,	886	67	953
Brick,	27	1	28
Stone,	16	–	16
Wood and brick,	6	–	6
Westborough.	829	57	886
Number of Stories.	829	57	886
1 story,	8	1	9
1 story and attic,	342	24	366
Basement and 1 story,	2	–	2
Basement, 1 story, and attic,	16	2	18
2 stories,	34	3	37
2 stories and attic,	349	20	369
Basement and 2 stories,	3	–	3
Basement, 2 stories, and attic,	28	4	32
3 stories,	36	3	39

COUNTIES, CITIES, TOWNS, NUMBER OF STORIES TO DWELLING HOUSES, AND MATERIALS OF WHICH CONSTRUCTED.	Number of Occupied Dwelling Houses	Number of Unoccupied Dwelling Houses	Total Number of Dwelling Houses
WORCESTER — Con.			
Westborough — Con.			
Number of Stories — Con.			
3 stories and attic,	4	–	4
Basement and 3 stories,	3	–	3
4 stories,	4	–	4
Materials.	829	57	886
Wood,	791	54	845
Brick,	15	1	16
Wood and brick,	22	2	24
Wood and stone,	1	–	1
West Boylston.	562	45	607
Number of Stories.	562	45	607
1 story,	–	–	–
1 story and attic,	271	16	287
Basement and 1 story,	2	–	2
Basement, 1 story, and attic,	27	1	28
2 stories,	40	2	42
2 stories and attic,	175	8	183
Basement and 2 stories,	5	–	5
Basement, 2 stories, and attic,	10	2	12
3 stories,	17	1	18
3 stories and attic,	2	–	2
Basement and 3 stories,	2	–	2
Basement, 3 stories, and attic,	2	–	2
4 stories,	1	–	1
Not given,	–	12	12
Materials.	562	45	607
Wood,	538	30	568
Brick,	17	1	18
Wood and brick,	7	2	9
Not given,	–	12	12
West Brookfield.	353	13	366
Number of Stories.	353	13	366
1 story,	3	–	3
1 story and attic,	98	6	104
2 stories,	13	3	16
2 stories and attic,	228	4	232
3 stories,	7	–	7
3 stories and attic,	4	–	4
Materials.	353	13	366
Wood,	346	13	359
Brick,	1	–	1
Wood and brick,	5	–	5
Wood and stone,	1	–	1
Westminster.	334	40	374
Number of Stories.	334	40	374
1 story,	2	–	2
1 story and attic,	200	25	225
Basement, 1 story, and attic,	1	–	1
2 stories,	10	2	12
2 stories and attic,	118	13	131

DWELLING HOUSES: NUMBER OF STORIES AND MATERIALS — Continued.

COUNTIES, CITIES, TOWNS, NUMBER OF STORIES TO DWELLING HOUSES, AND MATERIALS OF WHICH CONSTRUCTED.	Number of Occupied Dwelling Houses	Number of Unoccupied Dwelling Houses	Total Number of Dwelling Houses
WORCESTER — Con.			
Westminster — Con.			
Number of Stories — Con.			
Basement, 2 stories, and attic,	2	–	2
3 stories and attic,	1	–	1
Materials.	334	40	374
Wood,	324	37	361
Brick,	5	2	7
Wood and brick,	5	1	6
Winchendon.	890	43	933
Number of Stories.	890	43	933
1 story,	4	2	6
1 story and attic,	554	23	577
Basement, 1 story, and attic,	8	–	8
2 stories,	36	5	41
2 stories and attic,	272	13	285
3 stories,	15	–	15
4 stories,	1	–	1
Materials.	890	43	933
Wood,	886	42	928
Brick,	3	1	4
Stone,	1	–	1
WORCESTER.	11,153	461	11,614
Number of Stories.	11,153	461	11,614
1 story,	211	20	231
1 story and attic,	2,134	131	2,265
Basement and 1 story,	17	1	18
Basement, 1 story, and attic,	96	7	103
2 stories,	1,529	57	1,586
2 stories and attic,	3,743	151	3,894
Basement and 2 stories,	135	6	141
Basement, 2 stories, and attic,	233	9	242
3 stories,	2,326	52	2,378
3 stories and attic,	118	3	121
Basement and 3 stories,	272	12	284
Basement, 3 stories, and attic,	20	–	20
4 stories,	213	7	220
4 stories and attic,	6	–	6
Basement and 4 stories,	22	1	23
Basement, 4 stories, and attic,	4	–	4
5 stories,	48	4	52
5 stories and attic,	1	–	1
Basement and 5 stories,	8	–	8
6 stories,	2	–	2
Basement and 6 stories,	1	–	1
7 stories,	2	–	2
Not given,	12	–	12
Materials.	11,153	461	11,614
Wood,	10,078	406	10,484
Brick,	873	43	916
Stone,	26	6	32
Cement,	1	–	1
Wood and brick,	148	6	154

COUNTIES, CITIES, TOWNS, NUMBER OF STORIES TO DWELLING HOUSES, AND MATERIALS OF WHICH CONSTRUCTED.	Number of Occupied Dwelling Houses	Number of Unoccupied Dwelling Houses	Total Number of Dwelling Houses
WORCESTER — Con.			
WORCESTER — Con.			
Materials — Con.			
Wood and stone,	2	–	2
Wood and cement,	1	–	1
Brick and stone,	15	–	15
Brick and cement,	2	–	2
Wood, brick, and stone,	1	–	1
Not given,	6	–	6
WORCESTER. WARD 1,	1,358	50	1,408
Number of Stories.	1,358	50	1,408
1 story,	3	–	3
1 story and attic,	140	4	144
Basement, 1 story, and attic,	11	1	12
2 stories,	195	3	198
2 stories and attic,	584	29	613
Basement and 2 stories,	6	–	6
Basement, 2 stories, and attic,	31	3	34
3 stories,	283	6	289
3 stories and attic,	29	–	29
Basement and 3 stories,	23	1	24
Basement, 3 stories, and attic,	7	–	7
4 stories,	28	1	29
4 stories and attic,	1	–	1
Basement and 4 stories,	5	–	5
5 stories,	7	2	9
5 stories and attic,	1	–	1
Basement and 5 stories,	2	–	2
Not given,	2	–	2
Materials.	1,358	50	1,408
Wood,	1,150	36	1,186
Brick,	189	14	203
Stone,	4	–	4
Wood and brick,	12	–	12
Brick and stone,	1	–	1
Not given,	2	–	2
WORCESTER. WARD 2,	1,464	75	1,539
Number of Stories.	1,464	75	1,539
1 story,	8	1	9
1 story and attic,	346	25	371
Basement and 1 story,	4	–	4
Basement, 1 story, and attic,	18	3	21
2 stories,	183	10	193
2 stories and attic,	416	29	445
Basement and 2 stories,	33	1	34
Basement, 2 stories, and attic,	38	2	40
3 stories,	321	2	323
3 stories and attic,	5	–	5
Basement and 3 stories,	56	2	58
Basement, 3 stories, and attic,	2	–	2
4 stories,	15	–	15
Basement and 4 stories,	2	–	2
5 stories,	4	–	4
Basement and 5 stories,	3	–	3

DWELLING HOUSES: NUMBER OF STORIES AND MATERIALS — Continued.

COUNTIES, CITIES, TOWNS, NUMBER OF STORIES TO DWELLING HOUSES, AND MATERIALS OF WHICH CONSTRUCTED.	Number of Occupied Dwelling Houses	Number of Unoccupied Dwelling Houses	Total Number of Dwelling Houses
WORCESTER—Con.			
WORCESTER, WARD 2-Con.			
Materials.	1,464	75	1,539
Wood, .	1,344	70	1,414
Brick, .	78	4	82
Stone, .	4	-	4
Wood and brick,	29	1	30
Wood and stone,	1	-	1
Brick and stone,	6	-	6
Brick and cement,	1	-	1
Wood, brick, and stone,	1	-	1
WORCESTER. WARD 3,	1,464	45	1,509
Number of Stories.	1,464	45	1,509
1 story,	89	1	90
1 story and attic,	256	12	268
Basement and 1 story,	5	1	6
Basement, 1 story, and attic,	8	-	8
2 stories,	274	5	279
2 stories and attic,	416	18	434
Basement and 2 stories,	41	-	41
Basement, 2 stories, and attic,	26	-	26
3 stories,	243	4	247
3 stories and attic,	19	1	20
Basement and 3 stories,	18	1	19
Basement, 3 stories, and attic,	1	-	1
4 stories,	42	2	44
4 stories and attic,	2	-	2
Basement and 4 stories,	1	-	1
5 stories,	16	-	16
7 stories,	1	-	1
Not given,	6	-	6
Materials.	1,464	45	1,509
Wood, .	1,281	42	1,323
Brick, .	145	1	146
Stone, .	2	-	2
Wood and brick,	30	2	32
Wood and stone,	1	-	1
Wood and cement,	1	-	1
Brick and stone,	2	-	2
Not given,	2	-	2
WORCESTER. WARD 4,	1,244	16	1,260
Number of Stories.	1,244	16	1,260
1 story,	17	-	17
1 story and attic,	138	5	143
Basement, 1 story, and attic,	2	-	2
2 stories,	268	6	274
2 stories and attic,	351	1	352
Basement and 2 stories,	4	1	5
Basement, 2 stories, and attic,	19	-	19
3 stories,	387	2	389
3 stories and attic,	19	1	20
Basement and 3 stories,	14	-	14
Basement, 3 stories, and attic,	3	-	3
4 stories,	21	-	21
Basement and 4 stories,	1	-	1
WORCESTER—Con.			
WORCESTER. WARD 4-Con.			
Materials.	1,244	16	1,260
Wood, .	1,210	16	1,226
Brick, .	21	-	21
Wood and brick,	13	-	13
WORCESTER. WARD 5,	1,532	82	1,614
Number of Stories.	1,532	82	1,614
1 story,	41	6	47
1 story and attic,	422	32	454
Basement and 1 story,	1	-	1
Basement, 1 story, and attic,	9	-	9
2 stories,	128	9	137
2 stories and attic,	498	25	523
Basement and 2 stories,	13	1	14
Basement, 2 stories, and attic,	31	2	33
3 stories,	327	7	334
3 stories and attic,	20	-	20
Basement and 3 stories,	18	-	18
4 stories,	17	-	17
5 stories,	5	-	5
Not given,	2	-	2
Materials.	1,532	82	1,614
Wood, .	1,418	73	1,491
Brick, .	81	1	82
Stone, .	4	5	9
Wood and brick,	29	3	32
WORCESTER. WARD 6,	1,514	82	1,596
Number of Stories.	1,514	82	1,596
1 story,	13	12	25
1 story and attic,	485	33	518
Basement, 1 story, and attic,	19	1	20
2 stories,	163	11	174
2 stories and attic,	491	10	501
Basement and 2 stories,	7	-	7
Basement, 2 stories, and attic,	15	-	15
3 stories,	264	10	274
3 stories and attic,	7	-	7
Basement and 3 stories,	22	2	24
Basement, 3 stories, and attic,	2	-	2
4 stories,	20	3	23
Basement and 4 stories,	2	-	2
Basement, 4 stories, and attic,	1	-	1
5 stories,	3	-	3
Materials.	1,514	82	1,596
Wood, .	1,444	73	1,517
Brick, .	64	9	73
Wood and brick,	5	-	5
Brick and stone,	1	-	1
WORCESTER. WARD 7,	1,325	71	1,396
Number of Stories.	1,325	71	1,396
1 story,	22	-	22
1 story and attic,	152	14	166

DWELLING HOUSES: NUMBER OF STORIES AND MATERIALS — Continued.

Counties, Cities, Towns, Number of Stories to Dwelling Houses, and Materials of which Constructed.	Number of Occupied Dwelling Houses	Number of Unoccupied Dwelling Houses	Total Number of Dwelling Houses	Counties, Cities, Towns, Number of Stories to Dwelling Houses, and Materials of which Constructed.	Number of Occupied Dwelling Houses	Number of Unoccupied Dwelling Houses	Total Number of Dwelling Houses
WORCESTER — Con.				**WORCESTER — Con.**			
WORCESTER. WARD 7 - Con.				**WORCESTER. WARD 8 - Con.**			
Number of Stories — Con.				*Number of Stories — Con.*			
Basement and 1 story, . .	7	–	7	2 stories, ...	65	1	66
Basement, 1 story, and attic,	24	2	26	2 stories and attic, . . .	570	23	593
2 stories, ...	243	12	255	Basement and 2 stories, . .	9	–	9
2 stories and attic, . . .	417	16	433	Basement, 2 stories, and attic,	52	1	53
Basement and 2 stories, . .	22	3	25	3 stories, ...	208	5	213
Basement, 2 stories, and attic,	21	1	22	3 stories and attic, . . .	9	–	9
3 stories, ...	293	16	309	Basement and 3 stories, . .	69	4	73
3 stories and attic, . . .	10	1	11	Basement, 3 stories, and attic,	3	–	3
Basement and 3 stories, .	52	2	54	4 stories, ...	23	–	23
Basement, 3 stories, and attic,	2	–	2	4 stories and attic, . . .	3	–	3
4 stories, ...	47	1	48	Basement and 4 stories, . .	5	–	5
Basement and 4 stories, . .	6	1	7	Basement, 4 stories, and attic,	3	–	3
5 stories, ...	5	2	7	5 stories, ...	8	–	8
Basement and 5 stories, . .	2	–	2	Basement and 5 stories, . .	1	–	1
Materials.	1,325	71	1,396	6 stories, ...	2	–	2
Wood, ...	1,148	61	1,209	Basement and 6 stories, . .	1	–	1
Brick, ...	144	9	153	7 stories, ...	1	–	1
Stone, ...	8	1	9	Not given, ...	2	–	2
Wood and brick, . . .	20	–	20	*Materials.*	1,252	40	1,292
Brick and stone, . . .	4	–	4	Wood, ...	1,083	35	1,118
Brick and cement, . . .	1	–	1	Brick, ...	151	5	156
WORCESTER. WARD 8,	1,252	40	1,292	Stone, ...	4	–	4
Number of Stories.	1,252	40	1,292	Cement, ...	1	–	1
1 story, ...	18	–	18	Wood and brick, . . .	10	–	10
1 story and attic, . . .	195	6	201	Brick and stone, . . .	1	–	1
Basement, 1 story, and attic,	5	–	5	Not given, ...	2	–	2

RECAPITULATION.

The State, Number of Stories to Dwelling Houses, and Materials of which Constructed.	Number of Occupied Dwelling Houses	Number of Unoccupied Dwelling Houses	Total Number of Dwelling Houses	The State, Number of Stories to Dwelling Houses, and Materials of which Constructed.	Number of Occupied Dwelling Houses	Number of Unoccupied Dwelling Houses	Total Number of Dwelling Houses
THE STATE.	397,633	30,861	428,494	**THE STATE — Con.**			
1 story,	11,505	2,108	13,613	*1 story and attic — Con.*			
Wood, ...	11,251	2,074	13,325	Stone, ...	58	6	64
Brick, ...	197	23	220	Cement, ...	4	–	4
Stone, ...	23	5	28	Wood and brick, . .	101	5	106
Cement, ...	1	–	1	Wood and stone, . .	52	7	59
Wood and brick, . .	18	1	19	Wood and cement, . .	5	2	7
Wood and stone, . .	7	–	7	Brick and stone, . .	2	–	2
Wood and cement, . .	1	3	4	Brick and cement, . .	1	–	1
Brick and stone, . .	2	2	4	Stone and cement, . .	3	–	3
Stone and cement, . .	1	–	1	Wood, brick, and stone, .	1	–	1
Not given, . . .	4	–	4	Not given, . . .	1	–	1
1 story and attic,	100,611	8,688	109,300	*Basement and 1 story,* .	553	86	639
Wood, ...	99,979	8,639	108,618	Wood, ...	523	81	604
Brick, ...	404	39	443	Brick, ...	16	3	19

DWELLING HOUSES: NUMBER OF STORIES AND MATERIALS — Continued.
RECAPITULATION — Continued.

THE STATE, NUMBER OF STORIES TO DWELLING HOUSES, AND MATERIALS OF WHICH CONSTRUCTED.	Number of Occupied Dwelling Houses	Number of Unoccupied Dwelling Houses	Total Number of Dwelling Houses
THE STATE — Con.			
Basement and 1 story — Con.			
Stone, ...	3	–	3
Wood and brick, . .	10	1	11
Wood and stone, . .	1	1	2
Basement, 1 story, and attic,	5,255	345	5,600
Wood, ...	4,861	327	5,258
Brick, ...	60	3	63
Stone, ...	16	2	18
Cement, . . .	2	–	2
Wood and brick, . .	185	9	194
Wood and stone, . .	58	3	61
Wood and cement, . .	1	–	1
Brick and stone, . .	–	1	1
Wood, brick, and stone, .	2	–	2
2 stories, ...	71,416	6,318	77,734
Wood, ...	68,597	6,118	74,715
Brick, ...	2,220	141	2,361
Stone, ...	98	10	108
Cement, ...	14	–	14
Wood and brick, . .	408	26	434
Wood and stone, . .	56	15	71
Wood and cement, . .	2	1	3
Brick and stone, . .	11	4	15
Brick and cement, . .	2	1	3
Stone and cement, . .	7	1	8
Wood, brick, and stone, .	1	1	2
2 stories and attic, . .	142,452	9,396	151,848
Wood, ...	138,612	9,102	147,714
Brick, ...	2,742	156	2,898
Stone, ...	131	16	147
Cement, ...	6	1	7
Wood and brick, . .	730	40	770
Wood and stone, . .	153	36	189
Wood and cement, . .	5	–	5
Brick and stone, . .	55	14	69
Brick and cement, . .	9	–	9
Wood, brick, and stone, .	8	1	9
Not given, . . .	1	–	1
Basement and 2 stories, .	4,269	289	4,558
Wood, ...	3,556	244	3,800
Brick, ...	491	35	526
Stone, ...	17	1	18
Cement, ...	2	1	3
Wood and brick, . .	177	4	181
Wood and stone, . .	16	4	20
Brick and stone, . .	4	–	4
Brick and cement, . .	4	–	4
Wood, brick, and stone, .	2	–	2
Basement, 2 stories, and attic,	7,319	516	7,835
Wood, ...	6,053	418	6,471
Brick, ...	868	60	928
Stone, ...	20	4	24
Cement, ...	2	–	2

THE STATE, NUMBER OF STORIES TO DWELLING HOUSES, AND MATERIALS OF WHICH CONSTRUCTED.	Number of Occupied Dwelling Houses	Number of Unoccupied Dwelling Houses	Total Number of Dwelling Houses
THE STATE — Con.			
Basement, 2 stories, and attic — Con.			
Wood and brick, . .	262	18	280
Wood and stone, . .	57	12	69
Wood and cement, . .	1	1	2
Brick and stone, . .	53	2	55
Wood, brick, and stone, .	3	1	4
2 stories, ...	34,384	1,897	36,281
Wood, ...	27,461	1,482	28,943
Brick, ...	6,236	351	6,587
Stone, ...	71	6	77
Cement, ...	7	–	7
Wood and brick, . .	426	28	454
Wood and stone, . .	71	7	78
Wood and cement, . .	2	–	2
Brick and stone, . .	88	18	106
Brick and cement, . .	17	4	21
Stone and cement, . .	2	–	2
Wood, brick, and stone, .	3	1	4
3 stories and attic, . .	3,989	211	4,200
Wood, ...	2,020	125	2,145
Brick, ...	1,773	79	1,852
Stone, ...	21	–	21
Wood and brick, . .	123	4	127
Wood and stone, . .	21	1	22
Brick and stone, . .	26	2	28
Brick and cement, . .	1	–	1
Stone and cement, . .	3	–	3
Wood, brick, and stone, .	1	–	1
Basement and 3 stories, .	5,433	374	5,807
Wood, ...	1,927	125	2,052
Brick, ...	3,035	161	3,196
Stone, ...	31	17	48
Cement, ...	2	–	2
Wood and brick, . .	126	5	131
Wood and stone, . .	1	5	6
Wood and cement, . .	1	–	1
Brick and stone, . .	297	60	357
Brick and cement, . .	10	–	10
Wood, brick, and stone, .	3	1	4
Basement, 3 stories, and attic,	2,119	119	2,238
Wood, ...	262	25	287
Brick, ...	1,698	82	1,780
Stone, ...	18	4	22
Wood and brick, . .	21	–	21
Wood and stone, . .	6	2	8
Wood and cement, . .	1	–	1
Brick and stone, . .	111	5	116
Brick and cement, . .	1	1	2
Wood, brick, and stone, .	1	–	1
4 stories, ...	4,267	189	4,456
Wood, ...	672	27	699
Brick, ...	3,389	149	3,538
Stone, ...	53	3	56

DWELLING HOUSES: NUMBER OF STORIES AND MATERIALS — Continued.
RECAPITULATION — Continued.

THE STATE, NUMBER OF STORIES TO DWELLING HOUSES, AND MATERIALS OF WHICH CONSTRUCTED.	Number of Occupied Dwelling Houses	Number of Unoccupied Dwelling Houses	Total Number of Dwelling Houses	THE STATE, NUMBER OF STORIES TO DWELLING HOUSES, AND MATERIALS OF WHICH CONSTRUCTED.	Number of Occupied Dwelling Houses	Number of Unoccupied Dwelling Houses	Total Number of Dwelling Houses
THE STATE — Con.				THE STATE — Con.			
4 stories — Con.				*6 stories — Con.*			
Cement,	1	–	1	Stone,	3	1	4
Wood and brick,	58	1	59	Brick and stone,	6	–	6
Wood and stone,	2	–	2	*6 stories and attic,*	2	–	2
Brick and stone,	80	6	86	Wood,	2	–	2
Brick and cement,	11	2	13	*Basement and 6 stories,*	51	16	67
Not given,	1	1	2	Brick,	26	6	32
4 stories and attic,	274	20	294	Stone,	5	6	11
Wood,	26	3	29	Brick and stone,	20	4	24
Brick,	234	16	250	*Basement, 6 stories, and attic,*	1	–	1
Wood and brick,	5	–	5	Brick,	1	–	1
Wood and stone,	1	–	1	*7 stories,*	7	4	11
Brick and stone,	7	1	8	Wood,	–	4	4
Brick and cement,	1	–	1	Brick,	5	–	5
Basement and 4 stories,	2,475	152	2,627	Wood and brick,	1	–	1
Wood,	30	2	32	Brick and stone,	1	–	1
Brick,	1,805	71	1,876	*7 stories and attic,*	1	–	1
Stone,	148	10	158	Brick,	1	–	1
Cement,	2	–	2	*Basement and 7 stories,*	7	–	7
Wood and brick,	7	–	7	Brick,	3	–	3
Brick and stone,	482	68	550	Stone,	1	–	1
Brick and cement,	1	1	2	Brick and stone,	3	–	3
Basement, 4 stories, and attic,	158	15	173	*8 stories,*	6	–	6
Wood,	2	1	3	Brick,	2	–	2
Brick,	132	9	141	Brick and stone,	4	–	4
Stone,	4	–	4	*Basement and 8 stories,*	1	–	1
Wood and brick,	4	–	4	Brick,	1	–	1
Brick and stone,	16	5	21	*Not given,*	150	63	213
5 stories,	560	40	600	Wood,	9	6	15
Wood,	8	7	15	Brick,	9	1	10
Brick,	503	28	531	Not given,	132	56	188
Stone,	15	4	19				
Cement,	1	–	1	**AGGREGATES.**	397,633	30,861	428,494
Wood and brick,	4	–	4				
Wood and stone,	1	–	1	*Number of Stories.*	397,633	30,861	428,494
Brick and stone,	28	1	29	1 story,	11,505	2,108	13,613
5 stories and attic,	8	–	8	1 story and attic,	100,611	8,698	109,309
Wood,	2	–	2	Basement and 1 story,	553	86	639
Brick,	6	–	6	Basement, 1 story, and attic,	5,255	345	5,600
Basement and 5 stories,	304	25	329	2 stories,	71,416	6,318	77,734
Wood,	5	1	6	2 stories and attic,	142,452	9,366	151,818
Brick,	143	10	153	Basement and 2 stories,	4,269	289	4,558
Stone,	79	5	84	Basement, 2 stories, and attic,	7,319	516	7,835
Wood and brick,	1	–	1	3 stories,	34,384	1,897	36,281
Brick and stone,	74	8	82	3 stories and attic,	3,989	211	4,200
Brick and cement,	2	1	3	Basement and 3 stories,	5,433	374	5,807
Basement, 5 stories, and attic,	5	–	5	Basement, 3 stories, and attic,	2,119	119	2,238
Wood,	3	–	3	4 stories,	4,267	189	4,456
Brick,	1	–	1	4 stories and attic,	274	20	294
Brick and stone,	1	–	1	Basement and 4 stories,	2,475	152	2,627
6 stories,	51	10	61	Basement, 4 stories, and attic,	158	15	173
Wood,	2	1	3	5 stories,	560	40	600
Brick,	40	8	48	5 stories and attic,	8	–	8

DWELLING HOUSES: NUMBER OF STORIES AND MATERIALS — Concluded.

RECAPITULATION — Concluded.

THE STATE, NUMBER OF STORIES TO DWELLING HOUSES, AND MATERIALS OF WHICH CONSTRUCTED.	Number of Occupied Dwelling Houses	Number of Unoccupied Dwelling Houses	Total Number of Dwelling Houses	THE STATE, NUMBER OF STORIES TO DWELLING HOUSES, AND MATERIALS OF WHICH CONSTRUCTED.	Number of Occupied Dwelling Houses	Number of Unoccupied Dwelling Houses	Total Number of Dwelling Houses
AGGREGATES — Con.				AGGREGATES — Con.			
Number of Stories — Con.				*Materials.*	397,633	30,861	428,494
Basement and 5 stories, . .	304	25	329	Wood, ...	365,933	28,812	394,745
Basement, 5 stories, and attic.	5	–	5	Brick, ...	26,041	1,431	27,472
6 stories, ...	51	10	61	Stone, ...	815	100	915
6 stories and attic, . . .	2	–	2	Cement, ...	44	2	46
Basement and 6 stories, . .	51	16	67	Wood and brick, . . .	2,667	142	2,809
Basement, 6 stories, and attic,	1	–	1	Wood and stone, . . .	583	13	596
7 stories, ...	7	4	11	Wood and cement, . . .	19	7	26
7 stories and attic, . . .	1	–	1	Brick and stone, . . .	1,371	201	1,572
Basement and 7 stories, . .	7	–	7	Brick and cement, . . .	60	10	70
8 stories, ...	6	–	6	Stone and cement, . . .	16	1	17
Basement and 8 stories, . .	1	–	1	Wood, brick, and stone, .	25	5	30
Not given, ...	150	63	213	Not given, ...	139	57	196

TABULAR ANALYSES

FOR THE FOLLOWING PRESENTATIONS:

The tables respecting rooms, tenements, and dwelling houses relate directly to the housing of the people, and to the distribution of the population by rooms. This, of course, forms a basis for deductions as to the concentration of the population within certain territorial limits, and shows whether or not undue crowding exists in any quarter. Heretofore comparisons of density of population have generally rested upon the number of persons per acre. For the first time in any State Census, and indeed in any Census in this country, the population is distributed by rooms. That is to say, from the tables presented we may see the exact number of rooms occupied in the aggregate by families of each specified size, and the average number of persons to each room; and this information is obtainable for each town and city, and for each ward in a city, with aggregates for the State. Whether or not undue concentration of the population exists may be determined with much greater approach to accuracy from such data, than from any comparison based merely on the ground area occupied.

In analyzing this, the first table of the series relating to rooms, tenements, and dwelling houses, we shall, as usual, confine ourselves to the recapitulation. This may be found on pages 556, 557. The total number of families in the State is 547,385, and these families occupy 3,568,385 rooms; the average number of rooms per family being 6.52, and the average number of persons to a room, 0.70. Families of one person each occupy on the average 4.37 rooms; families of two persons each, 5.60 rooms; and families of three persons each, 6.09 rooms. There are in the State more families of three persons each than are found of any other size, the total number of such families being 106,436; and the average number of persons to a room in such families is 0.49. Taking the State as a whole, there are no evidences of undue crowding, notwithstanding the density of our population; that is to say, whatever crowding may exist in certain quarters of our large cities does not appear in the general average. Certain peculiarities shown in the table need explanation. For example, several instances occur of large families in which each person occupies a single room. The first example of this kind in the table is found in the families of 19 persons each, there being 163 such families in the State; the average number of rooms to each family being 18.94, and the average number of persons to a room, one. Another instance will be found in a single family of 61 persons, each person occupying one room. In general, it may be said that these large families having a single room assigned to each person are reported from penal institutions, comprise persons occupying dormitories in connection with colleges, or include other cases wherein certain aggregations of the population are classed as families for Census purposes, and the number of rooms assigned to each such family, and therefore the average number to each person, is more or less arbitrary. Other instances appear of families showing an abnormally large number of persons to a room. For example, the table shows a single family of 162 persons occupying three rooms, or an average of 54 persons to each room. This is an Italian colony, living in barracks, and classed as a single family; and, in general, it may be said that wherever an abnormally large number of persons to a room appears in the table, it is because these persons, although considered independent families for Census purposes, are really aggregations of persons living in camps, or in barracks, or in hospital wards, or other similar places, the number of rooms occupied being thus reduced below the normal, and the average number of persons to a room correspondingly increased.

The average number of persons to a family in the State has been shown by a preceding table to be 4.57. The families containing five persons or less, include in the aggregate 1,312,104 persons, or 52.48 per cent of the entire population of the State. So far as the State as a whole is concerned, the average number of persons to a room in the tenements occupied by these families is less than one; the highest average being found in connection with the families of five persons each, namely, 0.75, and the lowest in connection with the families composed of but a single person each, this average being 0.23.

The average number of rooms occupied by the families of five persons each is 6.64. If such a family includes father, mother, and three children, it can be readily accommodated in a five-room tenement without serious crowding. Such a tenement would enable the family to have a kitchen, sitting room, and three sleeping rooms; or, a kitchen, dining room, sitting room (or parlor), and two sleeping rooms.

In order to enable a closer comparison of the concentration of the population in the different counties and in the cities, two analysis tables are inserted, the first summarizing the aggregates for the counties.

THE STATE, AND COUNTIES.	Population	Total Number of Rooms Occupied	Average Number of Rooms Occupied per Family	Average Number of Persons to a Room
THE STATE.	2,500,183	3,568,385	6.52	0.70
Barnstable,	27,654	55,856	6.92	0.50
Berkshire,	86,292	134,864	7.17	0.64
Bristol,	219,019	301,831	6.33	0.73
Dukes,	4,238	9,875	7.56	0.43
Essex,	330,393	478,804	6.46	0.69
Franklin,	40,145	68,207	7.08	0.59
Hampden,	152,938	209,488	6.39	0.73
Hampshire,	54,710	85,062	7.24	0.64
Middlesex,	499,217	719,835	6.69	0.69
Nantucket,	3,016	7,287	7.43	0.41
Norfolk,	134,819	210,776	7.10	0.64
Plymouth,	101,498	171,153	6.89	0.59
Suffolk,	539,799	678,450	6.01	0.80
Worcester,	306,445	436,897	6.49	0.70

The first line of this table reproduces the facts for the State, which we have already brought forward from the recapitulation of the main table; the other lines show the total population of each county, the total number of rooms occupied, the average number of rooms occupied per family, and the average number of persons to a room. It is at once apparent that, speaking only of the average conditions in the different counties, the number of persons to a room does not rise above one; the highest average being found in the county of Suffolk, which contains the city of Boston, wherein the average number of persons to a room is 0.80, and the lowest in the county of Nantucket, which is composed of the single town of Nantucket, the average number of persons to a room in this county being 0.41.

The next table presents the facts for the cities.

Cities.	Population	Total Number of Rooms Occupied	Average Number of Rooms Occupied per Family	Average Number of Persons to a Room
Beverly,	11,806	18,811	6.46	0.63
Boston,	496,920	618,598	5.99	0.80
Brockton,	33,165	47,423	6.16	0.70
Cambridge,	81,643	104,028	6.05	0.78
Chelsea,	31,264	41,357	5.96	0.76
Chicopee,	16,420	18,973	6.24	0.87
Everett,	18,573	26,948	6.26	0.69
Fall River,	89,203	100,713	5.61	0.89
Fitchburg,	26,409	34,591	6.08	0.76
Gloucester,	28,211	32,156	5.94	0.88
Haverhill,	30,209	46,515	6.74	0.65
Holyoke,	40,322	43,167	5.47	0.93
Lawrence,	52,164	62,591	5.80	0.83
Lowell,	84,367	106,121	6.28	0.80
Lynn,	62,354	89,835	6.35	0.69
Malden,	29,708	45,049	6.79	0.66
Marlborough,	14,977	19,451	6.16	0.77
Medford,	14,474	22,854	7.20	0.63
New Bedford,	55,251	75,827	6.20	0.73
Newburyport,	14,552	21,227	6.96	0.60
Newton,	27,590	44,911	8.12	0.61
North Adams,	19,135	25,393	6.46	0.75
Northampton,	16,746	23,272	7.12	0.72
Pittsfield,	20,461	30,994	7.14	0.66
Quincy,	20,712	27,592	6.31	0.75
Salem,	34,473	48,372	6.35	0.71
Somerville,	52,200	74,418	6.25	0.70
Springfield,	51,522	77,438	6.60	0.67
Taunton,	27,115	41,645	7.08	0.65
Waltham,	20,876	28,995	6.78	0.72
Woburn,	14,178	19,629	6.52	0.72
Worcester,	98,767	128,451	6.16	0.77

The largest city, Boston, contains a population of 496,920 persons, occupying in the aggregate 618,598 rooms, the average number of rooms to each family being 5.99, and the average number of persons to a room, 0.80. So far as our largest city is concerned, it is, therefore, shown that, on the average, the number of persons to a room does not exceed one. In a Tenement House Census of Boston, taken by this Bureau in 1891, it was shown that, considering rented tenements only, the average number of persons to a room for the city was 0.91. It was found, however, that in certain sections of the city a higher average existed, the highest being found at the North End, so-called, where the average number of persons to a room in rented tenements was 1.47. In the present Census, which includes all classes of tenements, it will be found by reference to the main table, pages 535 to 542, that the highest average number of persons to a room in Boston is in the present Ward 6, which also includes the North End district, this average being 1.23. The average number of persons to a room is higher in the city of Holyoke than in any other city, this average being 0.93. In Holyoke, the aggregate population, 40,322, occupies 43,167 rooms, the average number of rooms occupied being 5.47 per family, this being the smallest average number of rooms occupied per family in any city. The largest average number of rooms occupied per family in the cities, namely, 8.12, is found in the city of Newton. The smallest average number of persons to a room, is, however, found in the city of Newburyport, this average being 0.60.

We present an analysis table showing the city and town population compared, with respect to occupancy of rooms.

CLASSIFICATION.	Population	Total Number of Rooms Occupied	Average Number of Rooms Occupied per Family	Average Number of Persons to a Room
THE STATE.	2,500,183	3,568,385	6.52	0.70
Cities, ...	1,635,767	2,150,345	6.21	0.76
Towns, ...	864,416	1,418,040	7.06	0.61

The total population in the cities, 1,635,767, occupies in the aggregate 2,150,345 rooms; the average number of rooms to each family being 6.21, and the average number of persons to a room, 0.76. In the towns the population is 864,416, the total number of rooms occupied being 1,418,040, and the average number of rooms occupied by each family, 7.06, while the average number of persons to a room is 0.61.

Rooms: Occupied and Unoccupied Dwelling Houses.

The recapitulation of the presentation relating to rooms in occupied and unoccupied dwelling houses is presented on page 572. The information contained in it is so plainly presented that no special analysis in text is required to bring out the main facts. The occupied dwelling houses in the State contained 3,693,985 rooms. Of these, at the date of the enumeration, 3,568,385 were occupied and 125,600 unoccupied. The rooms in the unoccupied dwelling houses numbered 253,013, the total number of rooms in occupied and unoccupied houses aggregating 3,946,998. Of these, including occupied and unoccupied dwellings, there were 378,613 rooms entirely unoccupied at the date of the enumeration.

The facts as to the cities are brought forward in the following analysis table :

CITIES.	OCCUPIED DWELLING HOUSES			Rooms in Unoccupied Dwelling Houses	Total Number of Occupied and Unoccupied Rooms	Total Number of Unoccupied Rooms
	Occupied Rooms	Unoccupied Rooms	Total			
Beverly, ...	18,811	738	19,549	2,288	21,837	3,026
Boston, ...	618,598	34,908	653,506	35,396	688,902	70,304
Brockton, ...	47,423	1,786	49,209	2,030	51,239	3,816
Cambridge, ...	104,028	4,241	108,269	5,644	113,913	9,885
Chelsea, ...	41,357	2,202	43,559	2,939	46,498	5,141
Chicopee, ...	18,973	336	19,309	427	19,736	763
Everett, ...	26,948	1,137	28,085	3,198	31,283	4,335
Fall River, ...	100,713	5,405	106,118	2,700	108,818	8,105
Fitchburg, ...	34,591	1,153	35,744	1,469	37,213	2,622
Gloucester, ...	32,156	540	32,696	4,430	37,126	4,970
Haverhill, ...	46,515	1,850	48,365	2,041	50,406	3,891
Holyoke, ...	43,167	2,295	45,462	1,557	47,019	3,852
Lawrence, ...	62,591	1,132	63,723	1,140	64,863	2,272
Lowell, ...	106,121	3,812	109,933	3,934	113,867	7,746
Lynn, ...	89,835	3,842	93,677	3,774	97,451	7,616
Malden, ...	45,049	904	45,953	3,565	49,518	4,469
Marlborough, ...	19,451	538	19,989	477	20,466	1,015
Medford, ...	22,854	381	23,235	2,451	25,686	2,832
New Bedford, ...	75,827	2,890	78,717	2,069	80,786	4,959
Newburyport, ...	24,227	425	24,652	1,355	26,007	1,780
Newton, ...	44,911	372	45,283	4,776	50,059	5,148
North Adams, ...	25,393	443	25,836	951	26,787	1,394
Northampton, ...	23,272	355	23,627	911	24,538	1,266
Pittsfield, ...	30,994	423	31,417	1,627	33,044	2,030
Quincy, ...	27,592	765	28,357	3,199	31,556	3,964

| CITIES. | OCCUPIED DWELLING HOUSES | | | Rooms in Unoccupied Dwelling Houses | Total Number of Occupied and Unoccupied Rooms | Total Number of Unoccupied Rooms |
	Occupied Rooms	Unoccupied Rooms	Total			
Salem, ...	48,372	1,568	49,940	2,195	52,135	3,763
Somerville, ...	74,418	3,079	77,497	5,245	82,742	8,324
Springfield, ...	77,438	2,708	80,146	4,669	84,815	7,377
Taunton, ...	41,645	2,044	43,689	1,497	45,186	3,541
Waltham, ...	28,995	495	29,490	1,799	31,289	2,294
Woburn, ...	19,629	628	20,257	825	21,082	1,453
Worcester, ...	128,451	8,562	137,013	4,899	141,912	13,461

In the city of Boston, the occupied dwelling houses contained 653,506 rooms. There were, however, 34,908 rooms in these houses which were unoccupied at the date of the enumeration. The additional unoccupied rooms, in dwelling houses entirely unoccupied, brings the aggregate number of unoccupied rooms to 70,304. These figures, as we shall hereafter point out in connection with other tables, throw light upon the possibility of increase of population within the limits of the rooms at present available for occupancy. In Fall River, to take for illustration a leading textile factory city, the total number of rooms unoccupied at the date of the enumeration was 8,105; of these, 2,700 were in houses entirely unoccupied. In Worcester, to cite a manufacturing city in which the industries are varied, but chiefly metals and metallic goods and machinery, there were 13,461 unoccupied rooms, of which 4,899 were in entirely unoccupied dwellings. In Lynn, a leading city devoted to the manufacture of boots and shoes, there were 7,616 unoccupied rooms, of which 3,774 were in entirely unoccupied houses. In Holyoke, the seat of the paper industry, there were only 3,852 unoccupied rooms, of which 1,557 were in unoccupied houses. It is not necessary to multiply examples, as similar comparisons can be made to any extent at the pleasure of the reader.

The final analysis table contrasts the facts for the cities and towns, in comparison with aggregates for the State.

| CLASSIFICATION. | OCCUPIED DWELLING HOUSES | | | Rooms in Unoccupied Dwelling Houses | Total Number of Occupied and Unoccupied Rooms | Total Number of Unoccupied Rooms |
	Occupied Rooms	Unoccupied Rooms	Total			
THE STATE.	3,568,385	125,600	3,693,985	253,013	3,946,998	378,613
Cities, ...	2,150,345	91,957	2,242,302	115,477	2,357,779	207,434
Towns, ...	1,418,040	33,643	1,451,683	137,536	1,589,219	171,179

From this table it will be seen that the total number of unoccupied rooms in the cities of the Commonwealth at the date of the enumeration was 207,434, while in the towns the number of such rooms was 171,179. In the cities, 115,477 unoccupied rooms were in dwelling houses entirely unoccupied, while in the towns the number of such rooms was 137,536.

Tenements: Occupied Dwelling Houses.

The presentation relating to tenements shows for each city and town, and for each ward in a city, the total number of occupied dwelling houses, the number of occupied or unoccupied tenements in such houses, and also the total number of tenements whether occupied or not. The recapitulation appears on page 637, and, so far as the State at large is concerned, it shows that the 397,633 occupied dwelling houses contained 547,385 occupied tenements; the number of unoccupied tenements being 26,573, and the total number of tenements available for occupancy in occupied dwelling houses, 573,958. The occupied houses are presented so as to show the number of tenements in each. There were, for instance, 294,700 single tenements in the occupied houses, each, of course, being occupied by a single family; at the other end of the scale we find one occupied dwelling containing 42 tenements. The two-tenement occupied houses numbered 75,237; the three-tenement occupied houses, 18,469; the four-tenement occupied houses, 5,188; the five-tenement occupied houses, 1,607; the six-tenement occupied houses, 1,257; the seven-tenement occupied houses, 413; the eight-tenement occupied houses, 401; and the nine-tenement occupied houses, 109. From this point onward, as the number of tenements per house increases, the number of such houses rapidly decreases. The word "tenement" in this presentation is used in its broadest sense as indicating any place of abode, without regard to its character.

The facts as to the number of occupied and unoccupied tenements for the counties are summarized in the following analysis table:

THE STATE, AND COUNTIES.	Number of Occupied Dwelling Houses	Number of Occupied Tenements in Occupied Dwelling Houses	Number of Unoccupied Tenements in Occupied Dwelling Houses	Total Number of Tenements in Occupied Dwelling Houses
THE STATE.	397,633	547,385	26,573	573,958
Barnstable, ...	7,476	8,069	162	8,231
Berkshire, ...	16,294	18,810	388	19,198
Bristol, ...	30,093	47,708	2,526	50,234
Dukes, ...	1,217	1,306	55	1,361
Essex, ...	54,234	74,092	2,803	76,895
Franklin, ...	8,177	9,637	337	9,974
Hampden, ...	23,072	32,793	1,441	34,234
Hampshire, ...	10,231	11,744	319	12,063
Middlesex, ...	86,596	107,654	4,122	111,776
Nantucket, ...	880	981	39	1,020
Norfolk, ...	25,789	29,685	814	30,499
Plymouth, ...	20,631	24,830	799	25,629
Suffolk, ...	65,604	112,802	8,800	121,602
Worcester, ...	47,339	67,274	3,968	71,242

The total number of tenements in occupied dwelling houses in Suffolk County was 121,602. These tenements were found in 65,604 occupied houses, the number of unoccupied tenements being 8,800. To contrast the facts shown in this county with those which appear in the county of Franklin, which is an agricultural county, we note that the total number of tenements in occupied houses in Franklin County was 9,974, found in 8,177 houses, the number of unoccupied tenements in such houses being 337. That is to say, in Suffolk County, which contains the city of Boston, the number of tenements in occupied houses approximated twice the number of houses, or, on the average, nearly two tenements to a house; while in Franklin County the number of tenements exceeded the number of houses by less than 22 per cent. In Middlesex County, to cite one of the most populous counties, in which, however, the figures are not affected by the conditions existing within the municipal limits of Boston, we find there were 111,776 tenements in 86,596 occupied dwellings, 4,122 of these being vacant at the date of the enumeration.

The facts as to the cities can be easily compared by means of the following table:

CITIES.	Number of Occupied Dwelling Houses	Number of Occupied Tenements in Occupied Dwelling Houses	Number of Unoccupied Tenements in Occupied Dwelling Houses	Total Number of Tenements in Occupied Dwelling Houses
Beverly, ...	2,049	2,914	121	3,035
Boston, ...	58,599	103,306	8,243	111,549
Brockton, ...	5,355	7,700	360	8,060
Cambridge, ...	11,837	17,193	978	18,171
Chelsea, ...	4,743	6,934	482	7,416
Chicopee, ...	2,290	3,042	70	3,112
Everett, ...	3,610	4,304	231	4,535
Fall River, ...	8,069	17,948	1,146	19,094
Fitchburg, ...	3,886	5,686	260	5,946
Gloucester, ...	3,758	5,416	125	5,541
Haverhill, ...	4,814	6,902	349	7,251
Holyoke, ...	3,703	7,894	534	8,428
Lawrence, ...	6,735	10,783	227	11,010
Lowell, ...	11,933	16,885	848	17,733
Lynn, ...	10,045	14,144	773	14,917
Malden, ...	5,388	6,638	183	6,821
Marlborough, ...	2,341	3,159	115	3,274
Medford, ...	2,811	3,172	80	3,252
New Bedford, ...	7,480	12,221	569	12,790
Newburyport, ...	2,977	3,479	86	3,565
Newton, ...	5,102	5,528	80	5,608
North Adams, ...	2,986	3,931	92	4,023
Northampton, ...	2,824	3,270	74	3,344
Pittsfield, ...	3,806	4,342	75	4,417
Quincy, ...	3,801	4,373	155	4,528
Salem, ...	4,863	7,623	302	7,925
Somerville, ...	8,787	11,903	632	12,535
Springfield, ...	8,457	11,741	524	12,265
Taunton, ...	4,379	5,885	379	6,264
Waltham, ...	3,856	4,276	110	4,386
Woburn, ...	2,661	3,012	78	3,090
Worcester, ...	11,153	20,861	1,730	22,591

The city of Boston contained 111,549 tenements in occupied dwelling houses at the date of the enumeration, the number of such houses being 58,599. Of these tenements, 8,243 were unoccupied. These figures show that there were available for occupancy, on the average, nearly two tenements to each occupied house. Comparing these figures with those previously presented for the counties, we note that the city of Boston alone contained about the same number of tenements in its occupied dwelling houses as were found in the entire county of Middlesex: but the tenements in the occupied dwelling houses in Middlesex County, which numbered 111,776, were found in 86,596 houses, while, as we have said, the 111,549 tenements in Boston were found in 58,599 houses. It is exceedingly interesting to compare the different cities with respect to the tenements available for occupancy in the dwelling houses which were occupied at the date of the enumeration. While, as we have remarked, the tenements in the city of Boston average nearly two to each occupied house, we find in the city of Newton only 5,608 tenements in 5,102 houses, or slightly more than one tenement to a house on the average. In Newton, also, the number of unoccupied tenements in the occupied houses was but 80, or slightly less than one and one-half per cent of the total number of tenements; while, in the city of Boston, there were 8,243 unoccupied tenements, or about seven per cent of the total number of tenements. In the city of Fall River, devoted to the cotton industry, there were found 19,094 tenements in 8,069 occupied houses, an average of 2.37 per house; in Holyoke, 8,428 tenements in 3.703 houses, an average of 2.28 per house; in Lynn, 14,917 tenements in 10,045 houses, an average of 1.49 per house; in Lowell, 17,733 tenements in 11,933 houses, an average of 1.49 per house; and in Lawrence, 11,010 tenements in 6,735 houses, an average of 1.63 per house. These cities are all devoted to manufacturing. In Malden, there were only 6,821 tenements in 5,388 houses, an average of 1.27 per house; in Medford, 3,252 tenements in 2,811 houses, an average of 1.16 per house; and in Waltham, 4,386 tenements in 3,856 houses, an average of 1.14 per house. These cities, like Newton, are largely residential. As the cities increase in size, the tendency to increase the number of tenements per house is clearly shown in the table, and the larger number of tenements per house found in the manufacturing cities as compared with the residential cities is also plainly apparent.

The final table contrasts the cities and towns with respect to tenements.

CLASSIFICATION.	Number of Occupied Dwelling Houses	Number of Occupied Tenements in Occupied Dwelling Houses	Number of Unoccupied Tenements in Occupied Dwelling Houses	Total Number of Tenements in Occupied Dwelling Houses
THE STATE.	397,633	547,385	26,573	573,958
Cities, ...	225,098	346,465	20,011	366,476
Towns, ...	172,535	200,920	6,562	207,482

The cities as a whole contained 366,476 tenements, found in 225,098 occupied dwelling houses, an average of 1.63 per house, while the towns contained 207,482 tenements, found in 172,535 houses, an average of 1.20 per house. In the State, as a whole, there were 573,958 tenements, found in 397,633 occupied houses, an average of 1.44 per house. In the cities, 20,011 tenements in occupied houses were entirely unoccupied, or 5.46 per cent of the total number of tenements in such houses. In the towns, 6,562 unoccupied tenements were found in occupied houses, or 3.16 per cent of the total number of tenements in such houses.

Dwelling Houses: Number of Stories and Materials.

The presentation relating to dwelling houses correlates the information as to occupied and unoccupied dwellings with other data showing the number of stories and materials of construction. This information is presented fully in the table for each town and city. The recapitulation for the State, pages 738 to 741, shows that the total number of one-story houses was 13,613; those having one story and an attic numbering 109,309; while the basement and one-story houses numbered 639. There were 5,600 houses having a basement, a single story, and an attic. The two-story houses numbered 77,734; those having two stories and an attic, 151,818; while the basement and two-story houses numbered 4,558. There were 7,835 houses having a basement, two stories, and an attic. The three-story houses numbered 36 281, while the houses having three stories and an attic numbered 4,200, and those having a basement and three stories 5,807. There were also 2,238 houses having a basement, three stories, and an attic. The four-story houses numbered 4,456, and there were 2,627 having a basement and four stories, while 294 had four stories and an attic, and 173, a basement, four stories, and an attic. The houses of five stories numbered 600, and those having a basement and five stories, 329. There were also 61 six-story houses, 67 having a basement and six stories, 11 seven-story houses, seven having a basement and seven stories, six eight-story houses, one having a basement and eight stories, and a few others of different combinations which are fully shown in the table. Under the classification employed, the most numerous classes are the houses having one story and an attic, which numbered 109,309, those having two stories, which numbered 77,734, and those having two stories and an attic, which numbered 151,818.

The data as to the material of which the 428,494 dwelling houses were constructed are brought forward in the following series of analysis tables. The first gives the figures for the occupied dwelling houses in the cities and towns and also in the State for 1895, placed in comparison with the figures for the Census of 1885 for the same cities and towns.

OCCUPIED DWELLING HOUSES: MATERIALS OF WHICH CONSTRUCTED.	THE STATE		CITIES		TOWNS	
	1885	1895	1885	1895	1885	1895
Wood, ...	284,606	365,933	139,820	197,220	144,786	168,713
Brick, ...	24,038	26,041	22,208	23,648	1,830	2,393
Stone, ...	567	815	427	590	140	225
Cement, ...	127	44	114	36	13	8
Wood and brick, ...	608	2,667	317	1,794	291	873
Wood and stone, ...	44	503	17	328	27	175
Wood and cement, . . .	6	19	3	10	3	9
Brick and stone, ...	237	1,371	223	1,308	14	63
Brick and cement, . . .	7	60	7	57	–	3
Stone and cement, . . .	3	16	2	9	1	7
Wood, brick, and stone, . .	5	25	3	12	2	13
Not given, ...	–	139	–	86	–	53
TOTALS, ...	310,248	397,633	163,141	225,098	147,107	172,535

From this table we learn that in 1895 there were, in the State, 365,933 occupied dwelling houses constructed of wood, 197,220 of these being in the cities and 168,713 in the towns. Of the 26,041 occupied dwelling houses built of brick, 23,648 were found in the cities and but 2,393 in the towns.

The second analysis table shows the number of unoccupied dwelling houses in the cities and towns and in the State and the materials of which constructed.

UNOCCUPIED DWELLING HOUSES: MATERIALS OF WHICH CONSTRUCTED.	THE STATE		CITIES		TOWNS	
	1885	1895	1885	1895	1885	1895
Wood, ...	13,352	28,812	3,393	11,297	9,959	17,515
Brick, ...	1,090	1,431	958	1,211	132	220
Stone, ...	81	100	58	64	23	36
Cement, ...	11	2	8	2	3	–
Wood and brick, ...	19	142	3	79	16	63
Wood and stone, ...	3	93	–	27	3	66
Wood and cement, . . .	–	7	–	4	–	3
Brick and stone, ...	24	201	23	178	1	23
Brick and cement, . . .	–	10	–	7	–	3
Stone and cement, . . .	–	1	–	–	–	1
Wood, brick, and stone, . .	–	5	–	1	–	4
Not given, ...	–	57	–	40	–	17
TOTALS, ...	14,580	30,861	4,443	12,910	10,137	17,951

There were 28,812 unoccupied dwelling houses built of wood in the State in 1895, of which 11,297 were in the cities and 17,515 in the towns.

The third table shows equivalent facts for both occupied and unoccupied dwelling houses for the cities and towns and for the State.

TOTAL DWELLING HOUSES: MATERIALS OF WHICH CONSTRUCTED.	THE STATE		CITIES		TOWNS	
	1885	1895	1885	1895	1885	1895
Wood, ...	297,958	394,745	143,213	208,517	154,745	186,228
Brick, ...	25,128	27,472	23,166	24,859	1,962	2,613
Stone, ...	648	915	485	654	163	261
Cement, ...	138	46	122	38	16	8
Wood and brick, ...	627	2,809	320	1,873	307	936
Wood and stone, ...	47	596	17	355	30	241
Wood and cement, . . .	6	26	3	14	3	12
Brick and stone, ...	261	1,572	246	1,486	15	86
Brick and cement, . . .	7	70	7	64	–	6
Stone and cement, . . .	3	17	2	9	1	8
Wood, brick, and stone, . .	5	30	3	13	2	17
Not given, ...	–	196	–	126	–	70
TOTALS, ...	324,828	428,494	167,584	238,008	157,244	190,486

From the above table it is seen that of the total number of dwelling houses in the State, namely, 428,494, there were 394,745 which were constructed of wood. Of these, 208,517 were located in cities, and 186,228 in towns. These figures show how largely wood is used in Massachusetts as a material of construction for dwellings, and they also show that in this respect the cities form no exception to the towns; indeed, the number of wooden houses within city limits exceeds, as will be seen, the number in the towns. The number of brick houses in the State is 27,472, and of these the cities contain by far the larger part, the aggregate number of such houses in the cities being 24,859, while brick houses in the towns number only 2,613. There were found only 915 houses constructed entirely of stone. Of these, 654 were in the cities and 261 in the towns. The other combinations of materials presented in the table need not be particularly referred to, as they are plainly apparent.

The arrangement of the table enables comparisons to be made between the facts for 1885 and those of the present Census. For example, the total number of houses has risen in the decade from 324,828 to 428,494, an increase of 31.91 per cent. The houses within city limits have increased from 167,584 to 238,008, an increase of 42.02 per cent; while those in towns have increased from 157,244 to 190,486, an increase of 21.14 per cent. In the State at large the wooden houses have increased from 297,958 to 394,745, an increase of 32.48 per cent; the brick houses from 25,128 to 27,472, an increase of 9.33 per cent; and the stone houses from 648 to 915, an increase of 41.20 per cent. While the use of brick in the construction of dwelling houses, so far as shown by the number of houses constructed of that material in the cities, does not show so great a gain as is shown by the increase in houses of all kinds, nevertheless, in the towns, the gain in brick houses is greater than the gain in houses of all kinds. For example, the number of brick houses in cities has increased in the decade from 23,166 to 24,859, an increase of 7.31 per cent, while in the towns, they have increased from 1,962 to 2,613, a gain of 33.18 per cent.

The next table presents a comparison of occupied, unoccupied, and total dwelling houses in the counties for the years 1885 and 1895.

THE STATE, AND COUNTIES.	OCCUPIED DWELLING HOUSES		UNOCCUPIED DWELLING HOUSES		TOTAL DWELLING HOUSES	
	1885	1895	1885	1895	1885	1895
THE STATE.	310,248	397,633	14,580	30,861	324,828	428,494
Barnstable, ...	7,585	7,476	803	1,620	8,388	9,096
Berkshire, ...	13,730	16,294	672	1,184	14,402	17,478
Bristol, ...	23,203	30,093	769	1,487	23,972	31,580
Dukes, ...	1,103	1,217	909	1,093	2,012	2,310
Essex, ...	43,095	54,234	1,819	3,951	44,914	58,185
Franklin, ...	7,290	8,177	467	684	7,757	8,861
Hampden, ...	17,853	23,072	469	1,395	18,322	24,467
Hampshire, ...	8,847	10,231	348	498	9,195	10,729
Middlesex, ...	60,600	86,596	2,139	6,223	62,739	92,819
Nantucket, ...	999	880	202	420	1,201	1,300
Norfolk, ...	19,321	25,789	806	1,916	20,127	27,705
Plymouth, ...	16,463	20,631	1,676	3,040	18,139	23,671
Suffolk, ...	51,108	65,604	2,021	4,485	53,129	70,089
Worcester, ...	39,051	47,339	1,480	2,865	40,531	50,204

The occupied dwelling houses in 1895 in the State as a whole numbered 397,633, or 92.80 per cent of the total number of houses shown in the table; in 1885, they numbered 310,248, or 95.51 per cent of the total number of houses. On the other hand, there were, of course, 7.20 per cent of the total houses unoccupied in 1895, and 4.49 per cent unoccupied in 1885. Similar comparisons for each of the counties may be made from the table.

In the following table, similar data are presented for the cities:

CITIES.	OCCUPIED DWELLING HOUSES		UNOCCUPIED DWELLING HOUSES		TOTAL DWELLING HOUSES	
	1885	1895	1885	1895	1885	1895
Beverly, ...	1,509	2,049	122	216	1,631	2,265
Boston, ...	45,998	58,599	1,531	3,525	47,529	62,124
Brockton, ...	3,188	5,355	17	259	3,205	5,614
Cambridge, ...	8,977	11,837	232	662	9,209	12,499
Chelsea, ...	4,114	4,743	94	333	4,208	5,076
Chicopee, ...	1,624	2,290	27	62	1,651	2,352
Everett, ...	1,107	3,610	21	373	1,128	3,983
Fall River, ...	5,266	8,069	54	209	5,320	8,278
Fitchburg, ...	2,540	3,886	42	182	2,582	4,068
Gloucester, ...	3,077	3,758	146	447	3,223	4,205
Haverhill, ...	3,681	4,814	61	235	3,742	5,049
Holyoke, ...	2,565	3,703	47	187	2,612	3,890
Lawrence, ...	5,369	6,735	163	120	5,532	6,855
Lowell, ...	9,390	11,933	450	495	9,840	12,428
Lynn, ...	7,243	10,045	140	470	7,383	10,515
Malden, ...	2,909	5,388	75	450	2,984	5,838
Marlborough, ...	1,591	2,341	20	63	1,611	2,404
Medford, ...	1,613	2,811	51	286	1,664	3,097
New Bedford, ...	5,130	7,480	90	210	5,220	7,690
Newburyport, ...	2,713	2,977	81	188	2,794	3,165
Newton, ...	3,467	5,102	98	513	3,565	5,615
North Adams, ...	1,979	2,986	7	114	1,986	3,100

CITIES.	OCCUPIED DWELLING HOUSES		UNOCCUPIED DWELLING HOUSES		TOTAL DWELLING HOUSES	
	1885	1895	1885	1895	1885	1895
Northampton, ...	2,157	2,824	51	119	2,208	2,943
Pittsfield, ...	2,599	3,806	69	180	2,668	3,986
Quincy, ...	2,166	3,801	28	482	2,194	4,283
Salem, ...	4,040	4,863	153	265	4,193	5,128
Somerville, ...	4,849	8,787	126	629	4,975	9,416
Springfield, ...	5,976	8,457	158	610	6,134	9,067
Taunton, ...	3,530	4,379	103	171	3,633	4,550
Waltham, ...	2,612	3,856	100	268	2,712	4,124
Woburn, ...	2,109	2,661	16	126	2,125	2,787
Worcester, ...	8,053	11,153	70	461	8,123	11,614

Without reproducing the figures, we merely point out that 94.33 per cent of the total dwelling houses in the city of Boston were occupied in 1895, and 96.78 per cent in 1885. Selecting a few of the leading manufacturing cities, the following percentages result from the data contained in the table : In Fall River, 97.48 per cent of the dwelling houses were occupied in 1895 and 98.98 per cent in 1885 : in Worcester, 96.03 per cent were occupied in 1895, and 99.14 per cent in 1885 : in Holyoke, 95.19 per cent were occupied in 1895, and 98.20 per cent in 1885 : in Lowell, the occupied dwelling houses constituted 96.02 per cent of the total number in 1895, and 95.43 per cent in 1885. These and similar comparisons may be carried to any extent by means of the figures contained in the table, but it is not necessary to enlarge upon them here.

The final table presents the data for the cities and towns in the aggregate so as to be compared with each other and with the aggregates for the State.

CLASSIFICATION.	OCCUPIED DWELLING HOUSES		UNOCCUPIED DWELLING HOUSES		TOTAL DWELLING HOUSES	
	1885	1895	1885	1895	1885	1895
THE STATE.	310,248	397,633	14,580	30,861	324,828	428,494
Cities, ...	163,141	225,098	4,443	12,910	167,584	238,008
Towns, ...	147,107	172,535	10,137	17,951	157,244	190,486

In the cities as a whole, 94.58 per cent of the total number of dwelling houses were occupied in 1895, as against 97.35 per cent occupied in 1885 : in the towns, on the other hand, 90.58 per cent were occupied in 1895, as against 93.55 per cent in 1885.

Averages and Comparative Totals:
Rooms, Tenements, and Dwelling Houses.

ROOMS, TENEMENTS, AND DWELLING HOUSES.

	COUNTIES, CITIES, AND TOWNS.	POPULATION			Number of Families	DWELLING HOUSES			OCCUPIED DWELLING HOUSES		
		Males	Females	Both Sexes		Occupied	Unoccupied	Total	Occupied Tenements	Unoccupied Tenements	Total Tenements
1	BARNSTABLE.	13,294	14,360	27,654	8,069	7,476	1,620	9,096	8,069	162	8,231
2	Barnstable,.	1,944	2,111	4,055	1,173	1,133	178	1,311	1,173	5	1,178
3	Bourne,	772	808	1,580	429	402	205	607	429	7	436
4	Brewster,	437	464	901	255	242	54	296	255	2	257
5	Chatham,	808	911	1,809	543	489	141	630	543	23	566
6	Dennis,	1,164	1,381	2,545	817	784	105	889	817	10	827
7	Eastham,	234	242	476	137	130	27	157	137	2	139
8	Falmouth,	1,283	1,372	2,655	722	656	279	935	722	8	730
9	Harwich,	1,253	1,279	2,532	783	752	101	853	783	2	785
10	Mashpee,	178	152	330	81	74	10	84	81	–	81
11	Orleans,	559	639	1,198	375	356	89	445	375	14	389
12	Provincetown,	2,215	2,340	4,555	1,216	987	48	1,035	1,216	58	1,274
13	Sandwich,	734	846	1,580	442	422	69	491	442	24	466
14	Truro,.	402	413	815	220	215	58	273	220	–	220
15	Wellfleet,	449	519	968	332	314	149	463	332	4	336
16	Yarmouth,	772	883	1,655	535	520	107	627	535	3	538
17	BERKSHIRE.	42,525	43,767	86,292	18,810	16,294	1,184	17,478	18,810	388	19,198
18	Adams,	3,712	4,125	7,837	1,604	1,343	80	1,423	1,604	88	1,692
19	Alford,.	152	128	280	76	74	10	84	76	4	80
20	Becket,	483	405	888	219	201	27	228	219	3	222
21	Cheshire,	599	577	1,176	297	278	47	325	297	8	305
22	Clarksburg,	502	507	1,009	214	186	5	191	214	4	218
23	Dalton,	1,506	1,704	3,210	688	601	22	623	688	24	712
24	Egremont,	406	430	836	211	199	12	211	211	1	212
25	Florida,	223	202	425	93	91	17	108	93	1	94
26	Great Barrington,	2,332	2,462	4,794	1,136	1,006	69	1,075	1,136	12	1,148
27	Hancock,	266	245	511	117	105	12	117	117	–	117
28	Hinsdale,	821	829	1,650	346	314	26	340	346	–	346
29	Lanesborough,	434	414	848	210	201	25	226	210	1	211
30	Lee,	1,973	2,093	4,066	922	797	42	839	922	13	935
31	Lenox,	1,529	1,343	2,872	581	519	81	600	581	11	592
32	Monterey,	241	223	464	115	110	19	129	115	1	116
33	Mount Washington,	76	60	136	31	31	9	40	31	1	32
34	New Ashford,	68	48	116	30	29	7	36	30	–	30
35	New Marlborough,	682	606	1,288	325	316	24	340	325	4	329
36	NORTH ADAMS,.	9,350	9,785	19,135	3,931	2,986	114	3,100	3,931	92	4,023
37	Otis,	289	229	518	136	131	25	156	136	1	137
38	Peru,	146	159	305	71	69	15	84	71	–	71
39	PITTSFIELD,	9,838	10,623	20,461	4,342	3,806	180	3,986	4,342	75	4,417
40	Ward 1,.	1,428	1,408	2,836	552	506	22	528	552	8	560
41	Ward 2,.	1,658	1,868	3,526	722	621	20	641	722	19	741
42	Ward 3,.	1,285	1,340	2,625	599	500	31	531	599	5	604
43	Ward 4,.	1,198	1,582	2,780	604	544	30	574	604	6	610
44	Ward 5,.	1,328	1,359	2,687	546	444	41	485	546	15	561
45	Ward 6,.	1,684	1,790	3,474	742	623	22	645	742	15	757
46	Ward 7,.	1,257	1,276	2,533	577	568	14	582	577	7	584

Occupied Rooms	Unoccupied Rooms	Total Rooms	Males to a Family	Females to a Family	Persons to a Family	Persons to an Occupied Dwelling House	Estimated Population of Unoccupied Dwelling Houses	Estimated Population of Unoccupied Tenements in Occupied Dwelling Houses	Estimated Population if all Dwelling Houses were fully Occupied	Families to each Occupied Dwelling House	Persons to each Occupied Dwelling House	Rooms to each Occupied Tenement	Persons to each Room in Occupied Tenements	
55,856	13,083	68,939	1.65	1.78	3.43	3.70	5,994	556	34,204	1.08	3.43	6.92	0.50	1
8,557	1,553	10,110	1.66	1.80	3.46	3.58	637	17	4,709	1.04	3.46	7.29	0.47	2
3,094	1,525	4,619	1.80	1.88	3.68	3.93	806	26	2,412	1.07	3.68	7.21	0.51	3
1,827	443	2,270	1.71	1.82	3.53	3.72	291	7	1,109	1.05	3.53	7.16	0.49	4
4,553	1,246	5,799	1.65	1.68	3.33	3.70	522	77	2,408	1.11	3.33	8.38	0.40	5
4,222	695	4,917	1.43	1.69	3.12	3.25	341	31	2,917	1.04	3.12	5.17	0.60	6
988	197	1,185	1.71	1.76	3.47	3.66	99	7	582	1.05	3.47	7.21	0.48	7
5,576	2,515	8,091	1.78	1.90	3.68	4.05	1,130	29	3,814	1.10	3.68	7.72	0.48	8
4,829	636	5,465	1.60	1.63	3.23	3.37	340	6	2,878	1.04	3.23	6.17	0.52	9
388	42	430	2.20	1.87	4.07	4.46	45	-	375	1.09	4.07	4.79	0.85	10
2,820	726	3,546	1.49	1.70	3.19	3.37	300	45	1,543	1.05	3.19	7.52	0.42	11
7,650	556	8,206	1.82	1.93	3.75	4.61	221	218	4,984	1.23	3.75	6.29	0.60	12
3,235	693	3,928	1.66	1.91	3.57	3.74	258	86	1,924	1.05	3.57	7.32	0.49	13
1,714	416	2,130	1.76	1.80	3.56	3.79	220	-	1,035	1.07	3.56	7.48	0.48	14
2,341	975	3,316	1.35	1.57	2.92	3.08	459	12	1,439	1.06	2.92	7.05	0.41	15
4,062	865	4,927	1.44	1.65	3.09	3.18	340	9	2,004	1.03	3.09	7.59	0.41	16
134,864	12,779	147,643	2.26	2.33	4.59	5.30	5,941	1,781	94,014	1.15	4.59	7.17	0.64	17
10,177	978	11,155	2.32	2.57	4.89	5.84	467	430	8,734	1.19	4.89	6.34	0.77	18
639	140	779	2.00	1.68	3.68	3.78	38	15	333	1.03	3.68	8.41	0.44	19
1,616	254	1,870	2.20	1.85	4.05	4.42	119	12	1,019	1.09	4.05	7.58	0.55	20
2,705	421	3,126	2.02	1.94	3.96	4.23	199	32	1,407	1.07	3.96	9.11	0.43	21
1,500	44	1,544	2.34	2.37	4.71	5.42	27	19	1,055	1.15	4.71	7.01	0.67	22
4,818	326	5,144	2.19	2.48	4.67	5.34	147	112	3,439	1.14	4.67	7.00	0.67	23
1,631	133	1,764	1.92	2.04	3.96	4.20	50	4	890	1.06	3.96	7.73	0.51	24
650	110	760	2.40	2.17	4.57	4.67	79	5	509	1.02	4.57	6.99	0.65	25
8,332	706	9,038	2.05	2.17	4.22	4.77	329	51	5,174	1.13	4.22	7.35	0.58	26
1,013	96	1,109	2.27	2.10	4.37	4.87	58	-	569	1.11	4.37	8.66	0.50	27
2,434	100	2,534	2.37	2.40	4.77	5.25	137	-	1,787	1.10	4.77	7.03	0.68	28
1,630	209	1,839	2.07	1.97	4.04	4.22	106	4	958	1.04	4.04	7.76	0.52	29
6,732	432	7,164	2.14	2.27	4.41	5.10	214	57	4,337	1.16	4.41	7.30	0.60	30
4,442	1,140	5,582	2.63	2.31	4.94	5.53	448	54	3,374	1.12	4.94	7.65	0.65	31
1,021	173	1,194	2.09	1.94	4.03	4.22	80	4	548	1.05	4.03	8.88	0.45	32
355	68	423	2.45	1.94	4.39	4.39	40	4	180	1.00	4.39	11.45	0.38	33
263	49	312	2.27	1.60	3.87	4.00	28	-	144	1.03	3.87	8.77	0.44	34
2,858	254	3,112	2.10	1.86	3.96	4.08	98	16	1,402	1.03	3.96	8.70	0.45	35
25,393	1,394	26,787	2.38	2.49	4.87	6.41	731	448	20,314	1.32	4.87	6.46	0.75	36
1,053	197	1,250	2.13	1.68	3.81	3.95	99	4	621	1.04	3.81	7.74	0.49	37
569	88	657	2.06	2.24	4.30	4.42	66	-	371	1.03	4.30	8.01	0.54	38
30,994	2,050	33,044	2.26	2.45	4.71	5.58	969	353	21,782	1.14	4.71	7.14	0.66	39
3,574	213	3,787	2.59	2.55	5.14	5.60	123	41	3,090	1.09	5.14	6.47	0.79	40
5,215	291	5,506	2.29	2.59	4.88	5.68	114	93	3,735	1.16	4.88	7.22	0.68	41
4,072	265	4,337	2.14	2.24	4.38	5.25	165	22	2,810	1.20	4.38	6.80	0.64	42
5,027	392	5,419	1.98	2.62	4.60	5.11	153	28	2,961	1.11	4.60	8.32	0.55	43
3,969	424	4,393	2.43	2.49	4.92	6.05	248	74	3,009	1.23	4.92	7.27	0.68	44
5,057	247	5,304	2.27	2.41	4.68	5.58	123	70	3,667	1.19	4.68	6.82	0.69	45
4,080	218	4,298	2.18	2.21	4.39	4.46	62	31	2,626	1.02	4.39	7.07	0.62	46

ROOMS, TENEMENTS, AND DWELLING HOUSES — Continued.

	COUNTIES, CITIES, AND TOWNS.	Population Males	Females	Both Sexes	Number of Families	Dwelling Houses Occupied	Unoccupied	Total	Occupied Dwelling Houses Occupied Tenements	Unoccupied Tenements	Total Tenements
	BERKSHIRE - Con.										
1	Richmond, . . .	354	347	701	164	158	19	177	164	3	167
2	Sandisfield,. . .	401	401	802	213	200	54	254	213	4	217
3	Savoy, ...	256	248	504	133	130	10	140	133	-	133
4	Sheffield, . . .	944	953	1,897	481	450	33	483	481	5	486
5	Stockbridge, . .	996	1,081	2,077	471	436	70	506	471	9	480
6	Tyringham, . .	186	177	363	90	87	17	104	90	4	94
7	Washington, . .	256	187	423	87	87	20	107	87	-	87
8	West Stockbridge, .	608	649	1,257	324	312	35	347	324	7	331
9	Williamstown, . .	2,615	2,272	4,887	1,017	914	40	954	1,017	12	1,029
10	Windsor, . . .	301	255	556	135	127	18	145	135	-	135
11	BRISTOL.	105,582	113,437	219,019	47,708	30,093	1,487	31,580	47,708	2,526	50,234
12	Acushnet, . . .	568	547	1,115	294	263	21	284	294	5	299
13	Attleborough, . .	4,029	4,259	8,288	1,800	1,513	81	1,594	1,800	67	1,867
14	Berkley, . . .	482	473	955	256	238	14	252	256	3	259
15	Dartmouth, . .	1,599	1,508	3,107	814	745	211	956	814	21	835
16	Dighton, . . .	916	881	1,797	461	428	33	461	461	33	494
17	Easton, . . .	2,286	2,166	4,452	1,061	979	87	1,066	1,061	19	1,080
18	Fairhaven, . . .	1,554	1,784	3,338	808	755	60	815	898	12	910
19	FALL RIVER, . .	42,794	46,499	89,293	17,948	8,069	209	8,278	17,948	1,146	19,094
20	Ward 1, . . .	5,410	5,736	11,146	2,342	1,156	24	1,180	2,342	217	2,559
21	Ward 2, . . .	4,192	4,532	8,724	1,677	823	33	856	1,677	92	1,769
22	Ward 3, . . .	5,624	5,827	11,451	2,247	832	17	849	2,247	73	2,320
23	Ward 4, . . .	4,824	5,644	10,468	2,241	872	13	885	2,241	131	2,372
24	Ward 5, . . .	5,135	5,474	10,609	2,129	789	24	813	2,129	144	2,373
25	Ward 6, . . .	6,004	6,290	12,264	2,179	933	36	969	2,179	194	2,373
26	Ward 7, . . .	2,970	3,427	6,397	1,396	731	14	745	1,396	64	1,460
27	Ward 8, . . .	3,278	4,054	7,332	1,607	935	27	962	1,607	61	1,668
28	Ward 9, . . .	5,267	5,545	10,812	2,130	998	21	1,019	2,130	170	2,300
29	Freetown, . . .	725	680	1,405	342	313	48	361	342	9	351
30	Mansfield, . . .	1,793	1,929	3,722	946	823	34	857	946	37	983
31	NEW BEDFORD, .	26,158	29,093	55,251	12,221	7,480	210	7,690	12,221	569	12,790
32	Ward 1, . . .	6,456	6,736	13,192	2,500	1,206	42	1,238	2,500	137	2,637
33	Ward 2, . . .	3,730	4,061	7,791	1,792	1,147	31	1,178	1,792	65	1,857
34	Ward 3, . . .	2,451	3,185	5,636	1,553	1,056	28	1,084	1,553	62	1,615
35	Ward 4, . . .	2,943	3,345	6,288	1,615	1,154	27	1,181	1,615	69	1,684
36	Ward 5, . . .	4,144	4,960	9,104	2,172	1,416	39	1,455	2,172	88	2,260
37	Ward 6, . . .	6,434	6,706	13,140	2,589	1,411	43	1,454	2,589	148	2,737
38	North Attleborough, .	3,145	3,431	6,576	1,499	1,235	82	1,317	1,489	90	1,589
39	Norton, . . .	760	854	1,614	401	372	46	418	401	16	417
40	Raynham, . . .	751	767	1,518	397	363	15	378	397	12	409
41	Rehoboth, . . .	958	852	1,810	451	403	10	413	451	13	464
42	Seekonk, . . .	793	672	1,465	334	310	12	322	334	12	346
43	Somerset, . . .	1,040	943	1,983	497	413	32	445	497	49	546
44	Swansea, . . .	830	797	1,627	411	365	6	371	411	5	416
45	TAUNTON, . .	13,147	13,968	27,115	5,885	4,379	171	4,550	5,885	379	6,264
46	Ward 1, . . .	1,389	1,413	2,802	669	518	18	536	669	22	691
47	Ward 2, . . .	1,365	1,507	2,872	687	467	16	483	687	61	748
48	Ward 3, . . .	1,460	1,579	3,039	691	424	9	433	691	69	760
49	Ward 4, . . .	1,394	1,595	2,989	737	607	49	656	737	45	782
50	Ward 5, . . .	1,850	1,991	3,841	815	642	21	663	815	55	870
51	Ward 6, . . .	1,539	1,563	3,102	715	503	11	514	715	28	743

ROOMS, TENEMENTS, AND DWELLING HOUSES — Continued.

Occupied Rooms	Unoccupied Rooms	Total Rooms	Males to a Family	Females to a Family	Persons to a Family	Persons to an Occupied Dwelling House	Estimated Population of Unoccupied Dwelling Houses	Estimated Population of Unoccupied Tenements in Occupied Dwelling Houses	Estimated Population if all Houses were fully Occupied	Families to each Occupied Dwelling House	Persons to each Occupied Tenement	Rooms to each Occupied Tenement	Persons to each Room in Occupied Tenements	
1,377	182	1,559	2.16	2.11	4.27	4.44	84	13	798	1.04	4.27	8.40	0.51	1
1,794	442	2,236	1.88	1.88	3.76	4.01	217	15	1,034	1.07	3.77	8.42	0.45	2
977	63	1,040	1.93	1.86	3.79	3.88	39	-	543	1.02	3.79	7.35	0.52	3
3,725	278	4,003	1.96	1.98	3.94	4.22	159	20	2,056	1.07	3.94	7.74	0.51	4
3,779	1,200	4,979	2.11	2.30	4.41	4.76	333	40	2,450	1.08	4.41	8.02	0.55	5
802	198	1,000	2.07	1.96	4.03	4.17	71	16	450	1.03	4.03	8.91	0.45	6
712	168	880	2.71	2.15	4.86	4.86	97	-	520	1.00	4.86	8.18	0.50	7
2,319	249	2,568	1.88	2.00	3.88	4.65	141	27	1,425	1.04	3.88	7.16	0.54	8
7,535	510	8,045	2.57	2.24	4.81	5.35	214	58	5,159	1.11	4.81	7.41	0.65	9
1,019	127	1,146	2.23	1.89	4.12	4.38	79	-	635	1.06	4.12	7.55	0.55	10
301,833	25,510	327,343	2.21	2.38	4.59	7.28	19,825	11,594	241,438	1.59	4.59	6.35	0.73	11
2,282	189	2,471	1.93	1.86	3.79	4.24	89	19	1,223	1.12	3.79	7.76	0.49	12
12,623	637	13,260	2.73	2.26	4.59	5.48	444	294	9,026	1.25	4.59	6.63	0.66	13
1,913	114	2,027	1.88	1.85	3.73	4.01	56	11	1,022	1.08	3.73	7.47	0.50	14
6,187	1,921	8,108	1.97	1.85	3.82	4.17	880	80	4,067	1.09	3.82	7.00	0.50	15
3,254	426	3,680	1.99	1.91	3.90	4.20	139	129	2,065	1.08	3.90	7.06	0.55	16
7,145	643	7,788	2.16	2.04	4.20	4.55	396	80	4,325	1.08	4.20	6.73	0.62	17
6,468	570	7,038	1.73	1.99	3.72	4.42	265	45	3,648	1.19	3.72	7.20	0.52	18
100,713	8,105	108,818	2.38	2.59	4.97	11.06	2,312	5,096	97,211	2.22	4.97	5.61	0.89	19
13,522	1,221	14,743	2.31	2.45	4.76	9.64	231	1,033	12,410	2.03	4.76	5.69	0.84	20
9,462	1,007	10,469	2.50	2.70	5.20	10.60	350	478	9,552	2.04	5.20	5.64	0.92	21
10,249	467	10,716	2.50	2.60	5.10	13.76	234	372	12,057	2.70	5.10	4.56	1.12	22
13,396	846	14,242	2.15	2.52	4.67	12.00	156	612	11,236	2.57	4.67	5.98	0.78	23
9,771	891	10,662	2.41	2.57	4.98	13.45	323	717	11,649	2.70	4.98	4.59	1.09	24
11,432	1,385	12,817	2.76	2.87	5.63	13.14	473	1,092	13,820	2.34	5.63	5.25	1.07	25
9,733	519	10,252	2.13	2.45	4.58	8.75	123	293	6,813	1.91	4.58	6.97	0.66	26
11,369	670	12,039	2.04	2.52	4.56	7.84	212	278	7,822	1.72	4.56	7.07	0.64	27
11,979	1,099	13,078	2.47	2.61	5.08	10.83	227	864	11,903	2.13	5.08	5.62	0.90	28
2,123	380	2,503	2.12	1.99	4.11	4.49	216	37	1,658	1.09	4.11	6.21	0.66	29
6,790	413	7,203	1.89	2.04	3.93	4.52	154	145	4,021	1.15	3.93	7.18	0.55	30
75,827	4,959	80,786	2.14	2.38	4.52	7.39	1,552	2,572	59,375	1.63	4.52	6.20	0.73	31
14,064	1,174	15,238	2.58	2.70	5.28	10.18	428	723	14,343	1.93	5.28	5.63	0.94	32
11,209	634	11,843	2.08	2.27	4.35	6.79	210	283	8,284	1.56	4.35	6.26	0.70	33
10,431	593	11,024	1.58	2.05	3.63	5.34	150	225	6,011	1.47	3.63	6.72	0.54	34
11,745	646	12,391	1.82	2.14	3.96	5.54	150	273	6,811	1.40	3.96	7.27	0.54	35
14,170	791	14,961	1.91	2.28	4.19	6.43	251	369	9,724	1.53	4.19	6.52	0.64	36
14,208	1,121	15,329	2.49	2.59	5.08	9.31	400	752	14,292	1.85	5.08	5.49	0.92	37
10,357	1,090	11,447	2.10	2.29	4.39	5.32	436	395	7,407	1.21	4.39	6.91	0.63	38
3,080	443	3,523	1.89	2.13	4.02	4.34	200	64	1,878	1.08	4.02	7.68	0.52	39
3,557	205	3,762	1.89	1.93	3.82	4.18	63	46	1,627	1.09	3.82	8.96	0.43	40
3,352	159	3,511	2.12	1.89	4.01	4.49	45	52	1,907	1.12	4.01	7.43	0.54	41
2,428	162	2,590	2.38	2.01	4.39	4.73	57	53	1,575	1.08	4.39	7.27	0.60	42
3,865	504	4,369	2.09	1.90	3.99	4.80	154	196	2,333	1.20	3.99	7.78	0.51	43
3,214	79	3,293	2.02	1.94	3.96	4.46	27	20	1,674	1.13	3.96	7.82	0.51	44
41,645	3,541	45,186	2.24	2.37	4.61	6.19	1,058	1,747	29,920	1.34	4.61	7.08	0.65	45
4,963	277	5,240	2.08	2.11	4.19	5.41	97	92	2,991	1.29	4.19	7.42	0.56	46
5,453	493	5,946	1.99	2.19	4.18	6.15	98	255	3,225	1.47	4.18	7.94	0.53	47
4,730	485	5,215	2.11	2.29	4.40	7.17	65	204	3,408	1.63	4.40	6.85	0.64	48
5,782	706	6,488	1.89	2.17	4.06	4.92	241	183	3,413	1.21	4.06	7.85	0.52	49
5,217	502	5,719	2.27	2.44	4.71	5.98	126	259	4,226	1.27	4.71	6.40	0.74	50
4,858	227	5,085	2.15	2.19	4.34	6.17	68	122	3,292	1.42	4.34	6.79	0.64	51

ROOMS, TENEMENTS, AND DWELLING HOUSES — Continued.

	COUNTIES, CITIES, AND TOWNS.	POPULATION			Number of Families	DWELLING HOUSES			OCCUPIED DWELLING HOUSES		
		Males	Females	Both Sexes		Occupied	Unoccupied	Total	Occupied Tenements	Unoccupied Tenements	Total Tenements
	BRISTOL — Con.										
	TAUNTON — Con.										
1	Ward 7, . . .	1,509	1,524	3,033	673	513	19	532	673	66	739
2	Ward 8, . . .	2,641	2,796	5,437	898	705	28	733	898	33	931
3	Westport, . . .	1,344	1,334	2,678	702	647	105	752	702	29	731
4	DUKES.	2,057	2,181	4,238	1,306	1,217	1,093	2,310	1,306	55	1,361
5	Chilmark, . .	151	153	304	95	93	71	164	95	–	95
6	Cottage City, .	508	530	1,038	313	312	803	1,115	313	8	321
7	Edgartown, . .	527	598	1,125	377	331	69	400	377	24	401
8	Gay Head, . . .	90	79	169	40	35	2	37	40	–	40
9	Gosnold, . . .	88	52	140	38	35	11	46	38	3	41
10	Tisbury, . . .	477	525	1,002	289	263	99	362	289	17	306
11	West Tisbury, .	216	244	460	154	148	38	186	154	3	157
12	ESSEX.	161,913	168,480	330,393	74,092	54,234	3,951	58,185	74,092	2,803	76,895
13	Amesbury, . .	4,780	5,206	9,986	2,281	1,956	86	2,042	2,281	101	2,382
14	Andover, . . .	2,913	3,232	6,145	1,296	1,156	62	1,218	1,296	30	1,326
15	BEVERLY, . . .	5,728	6,078	11,806	2,914	2,049	216	2,265	2,914	121	3,035
16	Ward 1, . . .	1,328	1,348	2,676	598	415	14	429	598	6	604
17	Ward 2, . . .	1,124	1,319	2,443	618	383	32	427	618	36	654
18	Ward 3, . . .	1,176	1,266	2,442	610	399	18	417	610	27	637
19	Ward 4, . . .	952	1,059	2,011	528	392	79	471	528	22	550
20	Ward 5, . . .	601	692	1,293	306	247	73	320	306	7	313
21	Ward 6, . . .	547	484	1,031	254	203	–	203	254	23	277
22	Boxford, . .	359	368	727	186	177	33	210	186	3	189
23	Bradford, . .	2,222	2,514	4,736	1,121	905	38	943	1,121	58	1,179
24	Danvers, . .	3,958	4,223	8,181	1,653	1,333	61	1,394	1,653	52	1,705
25	Essex, . . .	809	778	1,587	445	414	63	477	445	20	465
26	Georgetown, . .	999	1,051	2,050	541	476	18	494	541	13	554
27	GLOUCESTER, . .	16,257	11,954	28,211	5,416	3,758	447	4,205	5,416	125	5,541
28	Ward 1, . . .	1,682	1,516	3,198	696	492	95	587	696	15	711
29	Ward 2, . . .	2,763	2,265	5,028	982	533	33	566	982	32	1,014
30	Ward 3, . . .	3,467	1,723	5,190	743	490	9	499	743	17	760
31	Ward 4, . . .	2,276	1,185	3,461	520	335	5	340	520	15	535
32	Ward 5, . . .	2,296	2,048	4,344	893	691	19	710	893	16	909
33	Ward 6, . . .	1,464	1,479	2,943	704	534	120	654	704	13	717
34	Ward 7, . . .	1,697	1,141	2,838	587	415	6	421	587	10	597
35	Ward 8, . . .	612	597	1,209	291	268	160	428	291	7	298
36	Groveland, . .	1,118	1,215	2,333	560	505	9	514	560	3	563
37	Hamilton, . .	685	671	1,356	315	295	307	602	315	–	315
38	HAVERHILL, . .	14,535	15,674	30,209	6,902	4,814	235	5,049	6,902	349	7,251
39	Ward 1, . . .	1,271	1,377	2,648	573	389	32	421	573	36	609
40	Ward 2, . . .	1,105	1,408	2,513	631	476	25	501	631	40	671
41	Ward 3, . . .	1,696	1,847	3,543	781	508	14	522	781	32	813
42	Ward 4, . . .	1,890	2,095	3,985	957	812	46	858	957	54	1,011
43	Ward 5, . . .	5,632	5,636	11,268	2,452	1,519	67	1,586	2,452	125	2,577
44	Ward 6, . . .	2,941	3,311	6,252	1,508	1,110	51	1,161	1,508	62	1,570
45	Ipswich, . .	2,178	2,542	4,720	1,104	926	82	1,008	1,104	9	1,113
46	LAWRENCE, .	25,107	27,057	52,164	10,783	6,735	120	6,855	10,783	227	11,010
47	Ward 1, . . .	4,199	4,369	8,568	1,805	1,170	16	1,186	1,805	50	1,855
48	Ward 2, . . .	3,374	3,610	6,984	1,331	841	21	862	1,331	33	1,364
49	Ward 3, . . .	4,161	4,817	8,978	1,879	993	6	999	1,879	27	1,906

ROOMS, TENEMENTS, AND DWELLING HOUSES — Continued.

Occupied Rooms	Unoccupied Rooms	Total Rooms	Males to a Family	Females to a Family	Persons to a Family	Persons to an Occupied Dwelling House	Estimated Population of Unoccupied Dwelling Houses	Estimated Population of Unoccupied Tenements in Occupied Dwelling Houses	Estimated Population if all Dwelling Houses were fully Occupied	Families to each Occupied Dwelling House	Persons to each Occupied Dwelling House	Rooms to each Occupied Tenement	Persons to each Room in Occupied Tenements	
4,478	482	4,960	2.24	2.27	4.51	5.91	112	208	3,445	1.31	4.51	6.65	0.68	1
6,164	369	6,533	2.04	3.11	6.05	7.71	216	200	5,833	1.27	6.05	6.86	0.88	2
5,008	970	5,978	1.91	1.90	3.81	4.14	435	110	5,223	1.69	3.81	7.13	0.56	3
9,875	8,177	18,052	1.58	1.67	3.25	3.48	3,804	179	8,221	1.07	3.25	7.56	0.42	4
751	460	1,211	1.59	1.61	3.20	3.27	232	-	536	1.62	3.20	7.91	0.40	5
2,279	5,626	7,905	1.62	1.70	3.32	3.33	2,674	27	3,759	1.00	3.32	7.28	0.46	6
2,932	667	3,599	1.40	1.58	2.98	3.40	285	72	1,432	1.14	2.98	7.78	0.38	7
215	12	227	2.25	1.98	4.23	4.83	10	-	179	1.14	4.23	5.58	0.79	8
279	232	511	2.31	1.37	3.68	4.00	44	11	195	1.09	3.68	7.34	0.50	9
2,236	874	3,110	1.65	1.82	3.47	3.81	377	59	1,458	1.10	3.47	7.74	0.45	10
1,183	306	1,489	1.40	1.59	2.99	3.11	118	9	587	1.04	2.99	7.68	0.39	11
478,804	48,823	527,627	2.19	2.27	4.46	6.09	24,062	12,501	366,956	1.37	4.46	6.43	0.69	12
15,365	1,112	16,477	2.10	2.28	4.38	5.11	439	442	10,807	1.17	4.38	6.74	0.65	13
10,039	639	10,678	2.25	2.49	4.74	5.32	330	142	6,617	1.12	4.74	7.75	0.61	14
18,811	3,026	21,837	1.96	2.09	4.05	5.76	1,244	490	13,940	1.42	4.05	6.46	0.65	15
4,014	139	4,153	2.22	2.25	4.47	6.45	90	27	2,793	1.44	4.47	6.71	0.67	16
4,170	494	4,664	1.82	2.13	3.95	6.22	199	142	2,784	1.57	3.95	6.75	0.59	17
3,805	260	4,065	1.93	2.07	4.00	6.32	110	108	2,960	1.53	4.00	6.23	0.64	18
3,224	1,017	4,241	1.80	2.01	3.81	5.13	405	84	2,500	1.55	3.81	6.11	0.62	19
2,055	891	2,946	1.96	1.97	3.93	4.87	356	28	1,587	1.24	3.93	6.72	0.59	20
1,543	225	1,768	2.15	1.91	4.06	5.08	-	93	1,324	1.25	4.06	6.07	0.67	21
1,543	216	1,759	1.93	1.98	3.91	4.11	136	12	875	1.05	3.91	8.59	0.47	22
8,067	760	8,827	1.98	2.24	4.22	5.23	199	245	5,189	1.24	4.22	7.20	0.59	23
12,275	795	13,070	2.39	2.56	4.95	6.14	375	257	8,813	1.24	4.95	7.43	0.67	24
2,858	533	3,391	1.82	1.75	3.57	3.83	241	71	1,899	1.07	3.57	6.42	0.56	25
3,975	195	4,160	1.85	1.94	3.79	4.31	78	49	2,177	1.14	3.79	7.34	0.72	26
32,156	4,970	37,126	3.00	2.21	5.21	7.51	3,357	651	32,219	1.44	5.21	5.94	0.88	27
4,140	1,068	5,208	2.41	2.18	4.59	6.50	618	69	3,885	1.41	4.59	5.95	0.77	28
4,900	328	5,228	2.81	2.31	5.12	9.43	311	164	5,503	1.84	5.12	4.90	1.03	29
4,738	180	4,918	4.67	2.32	6.99	10.59	95	119	5,404	1.52	6.99	6.58	1.10	30
3,541	124	3,665	4.58	2.28	6.66	10.33	52	100	3,613	1.55	6.66	6.54	0.98	31
5,844	306	6,150	2.57	2.29	4.86	6.29	120	78	4,542	1.29	4.86	6.54	0.74	32
4,048	966	5,014	2.08	2.10	4.18	5.51	661	54	3,658	1.32	4.18	5.75	0.73	33
3,023	65	3,088	2.89	1.94	4.83	6.84	41	48	2,927	1.41	4.83	5.15	0.94	34
1,922	1,933	3,855	2.10	2.05	4.15	4.51	722	29	1,969	1.09	4.15	6.60	0.65	35
3,631	90	3,721	2.00	2.17	4.17	4.62	42	13	2,388	1.11	4.17	6.48	0.64	36
2,411	1,722	4,133	2.17	2.13	4.30	4.60	1,412	-	2,768	1.07	4.30	7.65	0.56	37
46,515	3,891	50,406	2.11	2.27	4.38	6.28	1,476	1,529	33,214	1.43	4.38	6.74	0.65	38
4,581	492	5,073	2.22	2.40	4.62	6.81	218	166	3,062	1.47	4.62	7.99	0.58	39
4,888	442	5,330	1.75	2.23	3.98	5.28	132	159	2,804	1.33	3.98	7.75	0.51	40
5,151	289	5,440	2.17	2.37	4.54	6.97	98	145	3,786	1.54	4.54	6.90	0.60	41
6,686	638	7,324	1.97	2.19	4.16	4.91	226	225	4,436	1.18	4.16	6.99	0.60	42
15,035	1,251	16,286	2.30	2.30	4.60	7.42	497	575	12,940	1.61	4.60	6.15	0.75	43
10,174	779	10,953	1.95	2.20	4.15	5.63	287	257	6,796	1.36	4.15	6.75	0.61	44
7,945	563	8,508	1.98	2.30	4.28	5.10	418	39	5,177	1.19	4.28	7.20	0.59	45
62,501	2,272	64,863	2.33	2.51	4.84	7.75	950	1,099	54,193	1.60	4.84	5.80	0.83	46
10,060	377	10,437	2.33	2.42	4.75	7.32	117	238	8,923	1.54	4.75	5.57	0.85	47
8,651	439	9,090	2.54	2.71	5.25	8.30	174	173	7,231	1.58	5.25	6.50	0.81	48
10,069	145	10,214	2.22	2.56	4.78	9.04	54	129	9,161	1.89	4.78	5.36	0.89	49

ROOMS, TENEMENTS, AND DWELLING HOUSES — Continued.

	COUNTIES, CITIES, AND TOWNS.	Males	Females	Both Sexes	Number of Families	Occupied	Unoccupied	Total	Occupied Tenements	Unoccupied Tenements	Total Tenements
	ESSEX — Con.										
	LAWRENCE — Con.										
1	Ward 4, .	4,802	5,167	9,969	1,888	1,071	18	1,089	1,888	35	1,923
2	Ward 5, .	4,764	5,169	9,933	2,215	1,471	22	1,493	2,215	45	2,260
3	Ward 6, .	3,807	3,925	7,732	1,665	1,189	37	1,226	1,665	37	1,702
4	LYNN, .	30,173	32,181	62,354	14,144	10,045	470	10,515	14,144	773	14,917
5	Ward 1, .	765	814	1,579	387	332	32	364	387	14	401
6	Ward 2, .	1,933	2,003	3,936	968	804	56	860	968	51	1,019
7	Ward 3, .	7,046	7,813	14,859	3,602	2,364	111	2,675	3,602	178	3,780
8	Ward 4, .	5,669	5,843	11,512	2,384	1,574	52	1,626	2,384	204	2,588
9	Ward 5, .	6,076	6,784	12,860	2,875	1,914	82	1,996	2,875	140	3,015
10	Ward 6, .	7,316	7,616	14,932	3,324	2,358	91	2,449	3,324	148	3,472
11	Ward 7, .	1,368	1,308	2,676	604	499	46	545	604	38	642
12	Lynnfield, .	408	410	818	211	183	12	195	211	4	215
13	Manchester, .	893	983	1,876	488	410	121	531	488	23	511
14	Marblehead, .	3,649	4,022	7,671	2,003	1,433	238	1,671	2,003	80	2,083
15	Merrimac, .	1,111	1,190	2,301	605	495	40	535	605	35	640
16	Methuen, .	2,760	2,930	5,690	1,317	1,139	38	1,177	1,317	36	1,353
17	Middleton, .	428	410	838	219	199	22	221	219	18	237
18	Nahant, .	425	440	865	204	182	215	397	204	11	215
19	Newbury, .	760	729	1,489	360	316	73	389	360	20	380
20	NEWBURYPORT, .	6,616	7,936	14,552	3,479	2,977	188	3,165	3,479	86	3,565
21	Ward 1, .	1,097	1,275	2,372	601	513	49	562	601	5	606
22	Ward 2, .	1,046	1,285	2,331	510	406	26	432	510	16	526
23	Ward 3, .	1,196	1,470	2,666	615	561	29	590	615	4	619
24	Ward 4, .	1,029	1,292	2,321	559	479	14	493	559	20	579
25	Ward 5, .	1,016	1,220	2,236	538	446	28	474	538	23	561
26	Ward 6, .	1,232	1,394	2,626	656	572	42	614	656	18	674
27	North Andover, .	1,765	1,804	3,569	796	742	53	795	796	9	805
28	Peabody, .	5,262	5,245	10,507	2,373	1,763	49	1,812	2,373	121	2,494
29	Rockport, .	2,966	2,323	5,289	1,236	806	114	1,010	1,236	38	1,274
30	Rowley, .	656	616	1,272	340	292	19	311	340	4	344
31	SALEM, .	16,270	18,203	34,473	7,623	4,863	265	5,128	7,623	302	7,925
32	Ward 1, .	2,369	2,637	5,006	1,109	622	130	752	1,109	68	1,177
33	Ward 2, .	2,692	2,955	5,647	1,369	963	35	998	1,369	54	1,423
34	Ward 3, .	1,925	2,460	4,385	1,028	701	27	728	1,028	41	1,069
35	Ward 4, .	2,429	2,806	5,235	1,181	795	18	813	1,181	42	1,223
36	Ward 5, .	4,816	5,095	9,911	1,881	1,048	26	1,074	1,881	62	1,943
37	Ward 6, .	2,039	2,250	4,289	1,055	734	29	763	1,055	35	1,090
38	Salisbury, .	642	658	1,300	351	317	18	335	351	5	356
39	Saugus, .	2,189	2,308	4,497	1,065	965	114	1,079	1,065	44	1,109
40	Swampscott, .	1,534	1,725	3,259	823	703	65	768	823	46	869
41	Topsfield, .	516	517	1,033	264	215	15	230	264	9	273
42	Wenham, .	431	455	886	234	206	20	226	234	8	242
43	West Newbury, .	811	832	1,643	440	394	25	419	440	20	460
44	FRANKLIN.	20,263	19,882	40,145	9,637	8,177	684	8,861	9,637	337	9,974
45	Ashfield, .	523	490	1,013	252	225	30	255	252	3	255
46	Bernardston, .	389	389	778	209	196	19	215	209	5	214
47	Buckland, .	785	763	1,548	387	332	23	355	387	19	406
48	Charlemont, .	526	515	1,041	275	247	16	263	275	6	281
49	Colrain, .	851	759	1,610	366	324	15	339	366	17	383
50	Conway, .	657	647	1,304	309	286	22	308	309	11	320

ROOMS, TENEMENTS, AND DWELLING HOUSES — Continued.

Occupied Rooms	Unoccupied Rooms	Total Rooms	Males to a Family	Females to a Family	Persons to a Family	Persons to an Occupied Dwelling House	Estimated Population of Unoccupied Dwelling Houses	Estimated Population of Unoccupied Tenements in Occupied Dwelling Houses	Estimated Population if all Dwelling Houses were fully Occupied	Families to each Occupied Dwelling House	Persons to each Occupied Dwelling House	Persons to each Occupied Tenement	Rooms to each Occupied Tenement	Persons to each Room in Occupied Tenements	
11,264	353	11,617	2.54	2.74	5.28	9.31	168	185	10,322	1.76	5.28	5.97	0.89		1
12,667	394	13,061	2.15	2.33	4.48	6.75	149	202	10,284	1.51	4.48	5.72	0.78		2
9,880	564	10,444	2.28	2.31	4.64	6.50	241	172	8,315	1.40	4.64	5.93	0.78		3
89,835	7,616	97,451	2.13	2.28	4.41	6.21	2,019	2,400	68,682	1.41	4.41	6.35	0.69		4
2,312	240	2,552	1.98	2.10	4.08	4.76	172	57	1,788	1.17	4.08	5.97	0.68		5
5,919	602	6,521	2.00	2.07	4.07	4.90	274	208	4,418	1.20	4.07	6.11	0.66		6
21,898	2,008	23,906	1.96	2.17	4.13	5.80	644	765	16,228	1.40	4.13	6.08	0.68		7
16,743	1,460	18,203	2.58	2.45	4.83	7.31	380	985	12,877	1.51	4.83	7.02	0.69		8
19,197	1,400	20,597	2.11	2.36	4.47	6.72	551	626	14,037	1.50	4.47	6.68	0.67		9
20,162	1,418	21,580	2.20	2.29	4.49	6.33	576	665	16,175	1.41	4.49	6.07	0.74		10
3,604	488	4,092	2.26	2.17	4.43	5.36	247	168	3,091	1.21	4.43	5.97	0.74		11
1,515	126	1,641	1.94	1.94	3.88	4.47	54	16	888	1.15	3.88	7.18	0.54		12
5,430	1,865	5,295	1.88	2.01	3.84	4.58	554	88	2,518	1.19	3.84	7.03	0.55		13
12,015	2,738	14,753	1.82	2.01	3.83	5.25	1,273	506	9,230	1.40	3.83	6.00	0.64		14
4,282	506	4,788	1.83	1.97	3.80	4.05	186	133	2,620	1.22	3.80	7.08	0.54		15
8,933	455	9,388	2.16	2.22	4.32	5.00	190	156	6,056	1.16	4.32	6.78	0.64		16
1,471	241	1,712	1.96	1.87	3.83	4.21	93	69	1,000	1.10	3.83	6.72	0.57		17
1,426	2,868	4,294	2.08	2.16	4.24	4.75	1,021	47	1,963	1.12	4.24	6.90	0.61		18
2,971	489	3,460	2.11	2.03	4.14	4.71	344	83	1,946	1.14	4.14	7.42	0.56		19
24,227	1,780	26,007	2.00	2.28	4.18	4.80	919	350	15,830	1.17	4.18	6.96	0.60		20
3,893	247	4,140	1.83	2.12	3.95	4.62	226	20	2,618	1.17	3.95	6.48	0.61		21
3,386	281	3,667	2.05	2.52	4.57	5.74	149	73	2,553	1.26	4.57	6.64	0.60		22
4,908	266	5,174	1.94	2.39	4.33	4.75	138	17	2,821	1.10	4.33	7.08	0.54		23
3,962	234	4,196	1.84	2.31	4.15	4.85	68	83	2,472	1.17	4.15	7.09	0.50		24
3,576	329	3,905	1.89	2.27	4.16	5.01	140	96	2,472	1.21	4.16	6.65	0.63		25
4,502	423	4,925	1.88	2.12	4.00	4.59	193	72	2,891	1.15	4.00	6.86	0.58		26
5,509	446	5,955	2.22	2.26	4.48	4.81	255	40	3,864	1.07	4.48	6.92	0.65		27
15,466	959	16,425	2.22	2.23	4.43	5.96	292	556	11,355	1.25	4.43	6.72	0.68		28
6,997	1,036	8,033	2.40	1.88	4.28	5.90	673	163	6,125	1.38	4.28	5.66	0.76		29
2,375	133	2,508	1.93	1.81	3.74	4.38	83	15	1,570	1.16	3.74	6.98	0.54		30
48,372	3,763	52,135	2.13	2.59	4.72	7.00	1,879	1,365	37,717	1.57	4.72	6.35	0.71		31
6,197	1,414	7,611	2.13	2.38	4.51	8.05	1,047	397	6,290	1.78	4.51	5.50	0.81		32
9,356	627	9,983	1.96	2.16	4.12	5.86	295	222	6,074	1.42	4.12	6.83	0.60		33
6,964	441	7,405	1.87	2.40	4.27	6.26	169	175	4,729	1.47	4.27	6.77	0.63		34
7,598	524	7,922	2.06	2.37	4.43	6.58	118	186	5,539	1.49	4.43	6.45	0.69		35
11,399	535	11,934	2.56	2.71	5.27	9.46	246	327	10,484	1.79	5.27	6.06	0.87		36
6,858	422	7,280	1.93	2.14	4.07	5.84	169	142	4,990	1.44	4.07	6.50	0.63		37
2,580	155	2,735	1.83	1.87	3.70	4.10	74	19	1,385	1.11	3.70	6.78	0.55		38
7,060	1,073	8,133	2.05	2.37	4.22	4.66	551	186	5,214	1.10	4.22	6.63	0.64		39
5,702	1,100	6,802	1.86	2.10	3.96	4.64	502	182	3,713	1.17	3.96	6.95	0.57		40
1,940	187	2,127	1.95	1.96	3.91	4.80	72	35	1,140	1.23	3.91	7.35	0.53		41
1,738	218	1,956	1.84	1.95	3.79	4.30	86	30	1,002	1.14	3.79	7.43	0.51		42
3,282	314	3,596	1.84	1.89	3.73	4.17	104	75	1,822	1.12	3.73	7.46	0.50		43
68,207	6,327	74,534	2.11	2.06	4.17	4.91	3,358	1,465	44,508	1.18	4.17	7.08	0.59		44
2,210	264	2,474	2.08	1.94	4.02	4.50	135	12	1,160	1.12	4.02	8.77	0.46		45
1,895	164	2,059	1.86	1.86	3.72	3.97	75	19	872	1.07	3.72	9.07	0.41		46
2,585	215	2,800	2.03	1.97	4.00	4.66	107	76	1,737	1.17	4.00	6.68	0.60		47
2,034	126	2,160	1.92	1.87	3.79	4.21	67	23	1,131	1.11	3.79	7.40	0.51		48
2,514	162	2,676	2.03	2.07	4.40	4.97	75	75	1,709	1.13	4.40	6.87	0.64		49
2,357	182	2,539	2.13	2.09	4.22	4.56	100	46	1,450	1.08	4.22	7.63	0.55		50

ROOMS, TENEMENTS, AND DWELLING HOUSES — Continued.

	COUNTIES, CITIES, AND TOWNS.	POPULATION				DWELLING HOUSES			OCCUPIED DWELLING HOUSES		
		Males	Females	Both Sexes	Number of Families	Occupied	Unoccupied	Total	Occupied Tenements	Unoccupied Tenements	Total Tenements
	FRANKLIN — Con.										
1	Deerfield, . . .	1,550	1,457	3,007	674	635	36	671	674	2	676
2	Erving, . . .	490	474	964	256	217	5	222	256	6	262
3	Gill, ...	699	383	1,082	197	178	6	184	197	7	204
4	Greenfield, . .	2,987	3,242	6,229	1,450	1,223	54	1,277	1,450	21	1,471
5	Hawley, . . .	250	218	468	110	103	10	113	110	3	113
6	Heath, . . .	250	226	476	120	115	6	121	120	2	122
7	Leverett, . . .	379	365	744	200	186	8	194	200	2	202
8	Leyden, . . .	185	178	363	88	83	13	96	88	1	89
9	Monroe, . . .	176	122	298	65	55	1	56	65	–	65
10	Montague, . .	3,076	2,982	6,058	1,349	954	234	1,188	1,349	93	1,442
11	New Salem, . .	438	431	869	233	219	11	230	233	4	237
12	Northfield, . .	754	1,097	1,851	419	389	30	419	419	4	423
13	Orange, . . .	2,690	2,671	5,361	1,390	1,053	41	1,094	1,390	75	1,465
14	Rowe, ...	283	215	498	123	108	27	135	123	6	129
15	Shelburne, . .	750	810	1,560	392	322	6	328	392	11	403
16	Shutesbury, . .	218	226	444	125	121	9	130	125	–	125
17	Sunderland, . .	381	315	696	166	152	6	158	166	1	167
18	Warwick, . . .	321	278	599	158	150	21	171	158	–	158
19	Wendell, . . .	293	236	529	129	122	25	147	129	3	132
20	Whately, . . .	392	363	755	195	182	10	192	195	37	232
21	HAMPDEN.	74,133	78,805	152,938	32,793	23,072	1,395	24,467	32,793	1,441	34,234
22	Agawam, . . .	1,237	1,171	2,408	533	489	41	530	533	4	537
23	Blandford, . .	437	412	849	206	197	36	233	206	5	211
24	Brimfield, . .	498	464	962	238	217	14	231	238	3	241
25	Chester, . . .	700	729	1,429	354	314	30	344	354	16	370
26	CHICOPEE, . .	8,095	8,325	16,420	3,042	2,290	62	2,352	3,042	70	3,112
27	Ward 1, . .	1,608	1,661	3,269	570	326	1	327	570	12	582
28	Ward 2, . .	802	950	1,752	394	325	15	340	394	8	402
29	Ward 3, . .	1,440	1,377	2,817	417	294	1	295	417	14	431
30	Ward 4, . .	1,050	1,208	2,258	421	339	7	346	421	13	434
31	Ward 5, . .	1,360	1,290	2,650	505	396	5	401	505	5	510
32	Ward 6, . .	822	876	1,698	333	272	5	277	333	7	340
33	Ward 7, . .	1,013	963	1,976	402	338	28	366	402	11	413
34	East Longmeadow, . .	863	728	1,591	330	283	18	301	330	17	347
35	Granville, . .	522	483	1,005	252	250	23	273	252	–	252
36	Hampden, . .	374	369	743	194	178	15	193	194	20	214
37	Holland, . .	107	92	199	55	51	8	59	55	–	55
38	HOLYOKE, . .	19,198	21,124	40,322	7,894	3,703	187	3,890	7,894	534	8,428
39	Ward 1, . .	2,849	3,165	6,014	1,145	433	2	435	1,145	40	1,185
40	Ward 2, . .	4,373	4,485	8,858	1,690	453	17	470	1,690	141	1,831
41	Ward 3, . .	2,461	2,562	5,023	958	633	51	684	958	41	999
42	Ward 4, . .	3,233	3,548	6,781	1,256	455	12	467	1,256	214	1,470
43	Ward 5, . .	1,574	2,005	3,579	768	462	24	486	768	42	810
44	Ward 6, . .	2,717	2,981	5,698	1,152	440	9	449	1,152	39	1,191
45	Ward 7, . .	1,991	2,378	4,369	925	827	72	899	925	17	942
46	Longmeadow, . .	290	330	620	146	134	12	146	146	2	148
47	Ludlow, . . .	1,314	1,248	2,562	473	382	21	403	473	7	480
48	Monson, . . .	1,802	1,884	3,736	872	735	35	770	872	15	887
49	Montgomery, . .	151	124	275	63	62	2	64	63	–	63
50	Palmer, . . .	3,345	3,513	6,858	1,382	1,276	71	1,347	1,382	37	1,419
51	Russell, . . .	440	406	846	185	170	18	188	185	8	193

ROOMS, TENEMENTS, AND DWELLING HOUSES — Continued.

Occupied and Unoccupied Dwelling Houses			Averages, Etc.											
Occupied Rooms	Unoccupied Rooms	Total Rooms	Males to a Family	Females to a Family	Persons to a Family	Persons to an Occupied Dwelling House	Estimated Population of Unoccupied Dwelling Houses	Estimated Population of Unoccupied Tenements in Occupied Dwelling Houses	Estimated Population if all Dwelling Houses were fully Occupied	Families to each Occupied Dwelling House	Persons to each Occupied Dwelling House	Rooms to each Occupied Tenement	Persons to each Room in Occupied Tenements	
5,097	282	5,379	2.30	2.46	4.46	4.74	171	9	3,187	1.06	4.46	7.50	0.59	1
1,614	68	1,682	1.92	1.85	3.77	4.44	22	23	1,099	1.18	3.77	6.30	0.60	2
1,623	97	1,730	3.55	1.94	5.49	6.08	36	38	1,156	1.11	5.49	8.29	0.66	3
10,509	544	11,053	2.06	2.24	4.30	5.09	275	90	6,504	1.10	4.30	7.25	0.59	4
869	87	956	2.27	1.98	4.25	4.54	45	13	526	1.07	4.25	7.90	0.54	5
879	45	924	2.09	1.88	3.97	4.14	25	8	509	1.04	3.97	7.33	0.54	6
1,349	57	1,406	1.90	1.82	3.72	4.00	32	7	786	1.08	3.72	6.75	0.55	7
705	110	815	2.10	2.03	4.13	4.37	57	4	424	1.06	4.13	8.01	0.51	8
392	8	400	2.71	1.87	4.58	5.42	5	-	303	1.18	4.58	6.03	0.76	9
8,231	1,830	10,061	2.28	2.21	4.49	6.35	1,486	418	7,392	1.41	4.49	6.10	0.74	10
1,569	111	1,680	1.88	1.85	3.73	3.97	44	15	928	1.06	3.73	6.73	0.55	11
3,541	102	3,643	1.80	2.62	4.42	4.76	143	18	2,012	1.08	4.42	7.97	0.55	12
8,775	682	9,457	1.94	1.92	3.86	5.09	240	282	5,852	1.32	3.86	6.31	0.61	13
785	206	991	2.30	1.75	4.05	4.61	124	24	646	1.14	4.05	6.58	0.63	14
3,032	92	3,124	1.91	2.07	3.98	4.84	20	44	1,633	1.22	3.98	7.73	0.51	15
830	105	935	1.74	1.81	3.55	3.67	33	-	477	1.03	3.55	6.64	0.55	16
1,299	49	1,348	2.29	1.90	4.19	4.58	27	4	727	1.00	4.19	7.83	0.54	17
1,297	153	1,450	2.03	1.76	3.79	3.99	84	-	683	1.05	3.79	8.21	0.46	18
802	172	974	2.27	1.83	4.10	4.34	109	12	650	1.06	4.10	6.22	0.66	19
1,604	214	1,818	2.01	1.86	3.87	4.15	42	143	940	1.07	3.87	8.23	0.47	20
209,488	17,285	226,773	2.26	2.40	4.66	6.65	9,249	6,715	168,802	1.42	4.66	6.39	0.73	21
2,711	220	3,031	2.23	2.12	4.35	4.92	202	17	2,627	1.13	4.35	6.71	0.65	22
1,859	353	2,212	2.12	2.00	4.12	4.31	155	21	1,025	1.05	4.12	9.02	0.46	23
1,882	138	2,020	2.09	1.95	4.04	4.43	62	12	1,056	1.10	4.04	7.91	0.51	24
2,525	303	2,828	1.98	2.06	4.04	4.55	137	65	1,651	1.13	4.04	7.13	0.57	25
18,973	763	19,736	2.66	2.74	5.40	7.17	445	378	17,243	1.35	5.40	6.24	0.87	26
3,085	63	3,148	2.82	2.92	5.74	10.03	10	69	3,348	1.75	5.74	5.41	1.06	27
2,757	150	2,907	2.04	2.41	4.45	5.39	81	36	1,869	1.21	4.45	7.00	0.64	28
2,541	64	2,605	3.46	3.50	6.75	9.58	10	95	2,922	1.42	6.76	6.09	1.11	29
3,008	141	3,149	2.49	2.87	5.36	6.06	47	70	2,375	1.24	5.36	7.14	0.75	30
3,373	69	3,442	2.69	2.56	5.25	6.69	33	26	2,703	1.28	5.25	6.68	0.79	31
1,918	80	1,998	2.47	2.63	5.10	6.24	31	36	1,765	1.22	5.10	5.76	0.89	32
2,291	196	2,487	2.52	2.40	4.92	5.85	164	54	2,394	1.19	4.92	5.70	0.86	33
2,082	169	2,251	2.61	2.21	4.82	5.62	101	82	1,774	1.17	4.82	6.31	0.76	34
2,032	169	2,201	2.07	1.92	3.99	4.02	92	-	1,097	1.01	3.99	8.06	0.49	35
1,438	175	1,613	1.93	1.90	3.83	4.17	63	77	883	1.09	3.83	7.41	0.52	36
451	56	507	1.95	1.67	3.62	3.90	31	-	230	1.08	3.62	8.20	0.44	37
43,167	3,852	47,019	2.43	2.68	5.11	10.89	2,036	2,720	45,087	2.13	5.11	5.47	0.93	38
5,764	188	5,952	2.49	2.76	5.25	13.89	28	210	6,232	2.64	5.25	5.03	1.04	39
7,831	704	8,535	2.59	2.65	5.24	19.55	352	730	9,929	3.73	5.24	4.63	1.13	40
5,562	645	6,207	2.57	2.67	5.24	7.94	405	215	5,643	1.51	5.24	5.81	0.90	41
5,938	1,005	6,943	2.57	2.83	5.40	14.90	179	1,156	8,116	2.76	5.40	4.73	1.14	42
4,772	369	5,141	2.05	2.61	4.66	7.75	186	196	3,961	1.66	4.66	6.21	0.75	43
6,126	281	6,407	2.56	2.59	4.95	12.95	117	195	6,008	2.62	4.95	5.32	0.93	44
7,174	660	7,834	2.15	2.57	4.72	5.28	380	80	4,829	1.12	4.72	7.76	0.61	45
1,108	98	1,206	1.99	2.26	4.25	4.63	56	9	685	1.09	4.25	7.59	0.56	46
2,911	150	3,061	2.78	2.64	5.42	6.71	141	38	2,741	1.24	5.42	6.15	0.88	47
6,220	301	6,521	2.14	2.16	4.30	5.10	179	65	3,990	1.19	4.30	7.13	0.56	48
535	17	552	2.40	1.97	4.37	4.44	9	-	284	1.02	4.37	8.49	0.51	49
9,367	653	10,020	2.42	2.54	4.96	5.37	381	184	7,423	1.08	4.96	6.78	0.73	50
1,209	157	1,366	2.38	2.19	4.57	4.98	90	37	973	1.09	4.57	6.54	0.70	51

ROOMS, TENEMENTS, AND DWELLING HOUSES — Continued.

	COUNTIES, CITIES, AND TOWNS.	POPULATION			Number of Families	DWELLING HOUSES			OCCUPIED DWELLING HOUSES		
		Males	Females	Both Sexes		Occupied	Unoccupied	Total	Occupied Tenements	Unoccupied Tenements	Total Tenements
	HAMPDEN — Con.										
1	Southwick, . . .	510	451	961	229	224	22	246	239	6	245
2	SPRINGFIELD, . .	24,651	26,871	51,522	11,741	8,457	610	9,067	11,741	524	12,265
3	Ward 1, . . .	3,405	3,494	6,899	1,604	1,089	67	1,156	1,604	85	1,689
4	Ward 2, . . .	3,886	4,012	7,898	1,758	1,054	49	1,103	1,758	108	1,866
5	Ward 3, . . .	3,152	3,045	6,197	1,300	771	32	803	1,300	167	1,467
6	Ward 4, . . .	2,652	3,557	6,209	1,435	1,058	43	1,101	1,435	67	1,502
7	Ward 5, . . .	2,886	3,540	6,426	1,534	1,289	64	1,353	1,534	30	1,564
8	Ward 6, . . .	2,983	3,170	6,153	1,390	1,004	67	1,071	1,390	86	1,476
9	Ward 7, . . .	2,202	2,448	4,650	1,136	962	79	1,041	1,136	18	1,154
10	Ward 8, . . .	3,485	3,605	7,090	1,524	1,230	209	1,439	1,524	23	1,547
11	Tolland, . . .	171	138	309	67	66	22	88	67	1	68
12	Wales, . . .	405	378	783	191	178	12	190	191	2	193
13	Westfield, . .	5,175	5,488	10,663	2,593	2,057	72	2,129	2,593	74	2,667
14	West Springfield,	2,951	3,174	6,125	1,390	1,069	37	1,106	1,390	87	1,447
15	Wilbraham, . .	837	903	1,740	363	290	27	317	363	9	372
16	HAMPSHIRE.	26,061	28,649	54,710	11,744	10,231	498	10,729	11,744	319	12,063
17	Amherst, . . .	2,427	2,358	4,785	1,064	921	19	940	1,064	25	1,089
18	Belchertown, . .	1,115	1,046	2,161	524	507	20	527	524	5	529
19	Chesterfield, .	301	288	589	162	149	15	164	162	2	164
20	Cummington, . .	367	383	750	201	188	15	203	201	2	203
21	Easthampton, . .	2,242	2,548	4,790	1,019	835	43	878	1,019	17	1,036
22	Enfield, . . .	512	478	990	261	250	5	255	261	2	263
23	Goshen, . . .	160	144	304	66	62	13	75	66	4	70
24	Granby, . . .	394	354	748	171	165	5	170	171	-	171
25	Greenwich, . .	243	238	481	142	138	8	146	142	-	142
26	Hadley, . . .	894	810	1,704	390	374	11	385	390	5	395
27	Hatfield, . . .	669	593	1,262	291	271	11	282	291	12	303
28	Huntington, . .	722	728	1,450	329	290	16	306	329	17	346
29	Middlefield, . .	197	189	386	92	85	25	110	92	7	99
30	NORTHAMPTON, . .	7,434	9,312	16,746	3,270	2,824	119	2,943	3,270	74	3,344
31	Ward 1, . . .	1,013	1,157	2,170	480	377	8	385	480	10	490
32	Ward 2, . . .	967	2,277	3,244	507	453	16	469	507	10	517
33	Ward 3, . . .	1,370	1,502	2,872	607	500	18	518	607	16	623
34	Ward 4, . . .	1,239	1,249	2,488	423	358	21	379	423	11	434
35	Ward 5, . . .	1,046	1,090	2,136	445	416	13	429	445	-	445
36	Ward 6, . . .	871	1,032	1,903	412	357	13	370	412	10	422
37	Ward 7, . . .	928	1,005	1,933	396	363	30	393	396	17	413
38	Pelham, . . .	246	240	486	126	122	21	143	126	11	137
39	Plainfield, . .	231	219	450	109	102	13	115	109	7	116
40	Prescott, . .	208	193	401	106	96	13	109	106	1	107
41	Southampton, . .	537	517	1,054	252	225	6	231	252	4	236
42	South Hadley, . .	2,064	2,380	4,443	894	735	27	762	894	36	930
43	Ware, . . .	3,576	4,075	7,651	1,523	1,208	45	1,253	1,523	67	1,590
44	Westhampton, . .	241	235	476	124	111	6	117	124	2	126
45	Williamsburg, . .	950	1,005	1,955	473	421	20	441	473	15	488
46	Worthington, . .	341	307	648	155	152	22	174	155	4	159
47	MIDDLESEX.	239,323	259,894	499,217	107,654	86,596	6,223	92,819	107,654	4,122	111,776
48	Acton, ...	980	998	1,978	529	469	27	496	529	6	535
49	Arlington, . . .	3,067	3,448	6,515	1,362	1,264	84	1,348	1,362	16	1,378
50	Ashby, . . .	413	391	804	233	218	28	246	233	8	241

ROOMS, TENEMENTS, AND DWELLING HOUSES — Continued.

Occupied Rooms	Unoccupied Rooms	Total Rooms	Males to a Family	Females to a Family	Persons to a Family	Persons to an Occupied Dwelling House	Estimated Population of Unoccupied Dwelling Houses	Estimated Population of Unoccupied Tenements in Occupied Dwelling Houses	Estimated Population if all Dwelling Houses were fully Occupied	Rooms to each Occupied Dwelling House	Persons to each Occupied Dwelling House	Rooms to each Occupied Tenement	Persons to each Room in Occupied Tenements	
1,754	189	1,943	2.13	1.89	4.02	4.29	94	24	1,079	1.07	4.02	7.34	0.55	1
77,438	7,377	84,815	2.10	2.29	4.39	6.09	3,715	2,590	57,587	1.59	4.39	6.60	0.67	2
10,835	1,179	12,014	2.12	2.18	4.30	6.54	425	566	7,600	1.47	4.30	6.75	0.64	3
9,876	850	10,726	2.21	2.28	4.49	7.49	367	485	8,750	1.67	4.49	5.92	0.80	4
8,678	807	9,485	2.32	2.24	4.56	8.04	257	488	6,942	1.76	4.56	6.38	0.71	5
10,636	781	11,417	1.85	2.48	4.33	5.87	252	290	6,754	1.56	4.33	7.41	0.58	6
11,391	731	12,122	1.88	2.31	4.19	4.99	349	126	6,871	1.10	4.19	7.43	0.56	7
8,480	963	9,443	2.15	2.28	4.43	6.13	411	581	6,945	1.38	4.43	6.10	0.73	8
7,638	715	8,353	1.94	2.15	4.09	4.83	382	74	5,106	1.18	4.09	6.72	0.61	9
9,904	1,351	11,255	2.29	2.36	4.65	5.76	1,204	107	8,401	1.24	4.65	6.50	0.72	10
651	169	820	2.55	2.06	4.61	4.68	103	5	417	1.02	4.61	9.72	0.47	11
1,436	114	1,550	2.12	1.98	4.10	4.40	53	8	844	1.07	4.10	7.52	0.55	12
17,232	899	18,131	1.99	2.12	4.11	5.18	577	304	11,544	1.26	4.11	6.65	0.62	13
8,486	707	9,193	2.17	2.33	4.50	5.73	212	392	6,729	1.27	4.50	6.24	0.72	14
3,021	256	3,277	2.30	2.40	4.70	6.00	102	43	1,945	1.25	4.70	8.32	0.58	15
85,062	5,288	90,350	2.22	2.44	4.66	5.35	2,664	1,487	58,861	1.15	4.66	7.24	0.64	16
8,622	253	8,875	2.28	2.22	4.50	5.20	99	113	4,997	1.16	4.50	8.10	0.55	17
3,952	200	4,152	2.13	1.99	4.12	4.26	85	21	2,267	1.03	4.12	7.54	0.55	18
1,123	120	1,243	1.86	1.78	3.64	3.95	59	7	655	1.09	3.64	6.93	0.52	19
1,731	119	1,850	1.83	1.90	3.73	3.99	60	7	817	1.07	3.73	8.61	0.43	20
6,809	370	7,179	2.20	2.50	4.70	5.74	247	80	5,117	1.22	4.70	6.68	0.70	21
1,921	45	1,966	1.96	1.83	3.79	3.96	29	8	1,018	1.04	3.79	7.56	0.52	22
516	135	651	2.43	2.18	4.61	4.90	64	18	386	1.06	4.61	7.82	0.59	23
1,332	35	1,367	2.30	2.07	4.37	4.53	23	–	771	1.04	4.37	7.79	0.56	24
1,061	65	1,126	1.71	1.68	3.39	3.49	28	–	509	1.03	3.39	7.47	0.45	25
3,129	116	3,245	2.29	2.08	4.37	4.56	50	22	1,776	1.04	4.37	8.02	0.54	26
2,215	129	2,344	2.30	2.04	4.34	4.66	51	52	1,365	1.07	4.34	7.61	0.57	27
2,326	198	2,524	2.20	2.21	4.41	5.00	80	75	1,905	1.13	4.41	7.07	0.62	28
808	230	1,077	2.14	2.06	4.20	4.54	114	29	529	1.08	4.20	8.78	0.48	29
23,272	1,296	24,568	2.27	2.85	5.12	5.93	700	579	17,851	1.16	5.12	7.12	0.72	30
3,151	113	3,264	2.11	2.41	4.52	5.76	46	45	2,261	1.27	4.52	6.56	0.69	31
4,690	170	4,860	1.91	4.49	6.40	7.16	115	64	3,423	1.12	6.40	9.23	0.69	32
4,160	229	4,389	2.26	2.47	4.73	5.74	103	76	3,051	1.21	4.73	6.85	0.69	33
3,116	225	3,341	2.93	2.95	5.88	6.95	146	65	2,699	1.18	5.88	7.37	0.80	34
2,806	92	2,898	2.35	2.45	4.80	5.13	67	–	2,203	1.07	4.80	6.31	0.76	35
2,780	172	2,952	2.11	2.51	4.62	5.33	69	46	2,018	1.15	4.62	6.75	0.68	36
2,569	256	2,825	2.31	2.54	4.88	5.33	160	83	2,176	1.09	4.88	6.49	0.75	37
858	173	1,031	1.95	1.91	3.86	3.98	84	42	612	1.03	3.86	6.81	0.57	38
1,113	145	1,258	2.12	2.01	4.13	4.41	57	29	536	1.07	4.13	10.23	0.40	39
812	102	914	1.96	1.82	3.78	4.18	54	4	459	1.10	3.78	7.96	0.49	40
1,809	51	1,860	2.13	2.05	4.18	4.68	28	17	1,099	1.12	4.18	7.18	0.58	41
6,071	378	6,449	2.50	2.67	4.97	6.04	163	179	4,785	1.22	4.97	6.79	0.73	42
10,223	641	10,864	2.35	2.67	5.02	6.33	285	396	8,272	1.26	5.02	6.71	0.75	43
861	54	915	1.94	1.90	3.84	4.29	26	8	510	1.12	3.84	6.94	0.55	44
3,259	218	3,477	2.01	2.12	4.13	4.64	93	62	2,110	1.12	4.13	6.89	0.60	45
1,239	206	1,445	2.20	1.98	4.18	4.26	94	17	759	1.02	4.18	7.99	0.52	46
719,835	69,980	789,815	2.22	2.42	4.64	5.76	35,844	19,126	554,187	1.24	4.64	6.69	0.69	47
3,824	255	4,079	1.85	1.89	3.74	4.22	114	22	2,114	1.13	3.74	7.28	0.52	48
10,228	749	10,977	2.25	2.53	4.78	5.15	433	76	7,024	1.08	4.78	7.51	0.64	49
1,723	248	1,971	1.77	1.68	3.45	3.69	103	28	935	1.07	3.45	7.39	0.47	50

ROOMS, TENEMENTS, AND DWELLING HOUSES — Continued.

	COUNTIES, CITIES, AND TOWNS.	POPULATION			DWELLING HOUSES				OCCUPIED DWELLING HOUSES		
		Males	Females	Both Sexes	Number of Families	Occupied	Unoccupied	Total	Occupied Tenements	Unoccupied Tenements	Total Tenements
	MIDDLESEX — Con.										
1	Ashland, . . .	1,015	1,075	2,090	486	419	45	464	486	26	512
2	Ayer, ...	1,018	1,083	2,101	528	442	17	459	528	47	575
3	Bedford, . . .	623	546	1,169	251	235	26	261	251	6	257
4	Belmont, . . .	1,519	1,324	2,843	505	491	83	574	505	2	507
5	Billerica, . . .	1,301	1,276	2,577	582	532	25	557	582	7	589
6	Boxborough, . .	172	135	307	78	71	3	74	78	3	81
7	Burlington, . .	316	258	574	129	122	16	138	129	8	137
8	CAMBRIDGE, . .	39,831	41,812	81,643	17,193	11,837	662	12,499	17,193	978	18,171
9	Ward 1, . .	7,814	8,067	15,881	2,943	2,303	125	2,428	2,943	114	3,057
10	Ward 2, . .	10,894	11,738	22,632	4,999	3,118	129	3,247	4,999	307	5,306
11	Ward 3, . .	7,303	6,693	13,996	2,812	1,688	49	1,737	2,812	185	2,997
12	Ward 4, . .	8,914	9,767	18,681	4,235	2,899	142	3,041	4,235	269	4,504
13	Ward 5, . .	4,906	5,547	10,453	2,204	1,829	217	2,046	2,204	103	2,307
14	Carlisle, . . .	268	224	492	126	125	8	133	126	3	129
15	Chelmsford, . .	1,611	1,551	3,162	747	695	47	742	747	14	761
16	Concord, . . .	3,157	2,018	5,175	874	837	73	910	874	20	894
17	Dracut, . . .	1,325	1,118	2,443	475	440	39	479	475	12	487
18	Dunstable, . . .	207	193	400	106	96	15	111	106	4	110
19	EVERETT, . . .	9,057	9,516	18,573	4,304	3,610	373	3,983	4,304	231	4,535
20	Ward 1, . .	1,590	1,548	3,138	673	518	45	563	673	35	708
21	Ward 2, . .	1,289	1,338	2,627	583	479	88	567	583	29	612
22	Ward 3, . .	1,515	1,575	3,090	729	615	98	713	729	55	784
23	Ward 4, . .	1,380	1,496	2,876	703	700	47	747	703	35	738
24	Ward 5, . .	1,539	1,614	3,153	779	600	27	627	779	42	821
25	Ward 6, . .	1,744	1,945	3,689	837	698	58	756	837	35	872
26	Framingham, . .	4,570	4,942	9,512	2,115	1,929	267	2,187	2,115	44	2,159
27	Groton, . . .	1,078	1,114	2,192	508	476	31	507	508	11	519
28	Holliston, . . .	1,309	1,409	2,718	701	612	39	651	701	21	722
29	Hopkinton, . .	1,469	1,515	2,984	752	714	73	787	752	49	801
30	Hudson, . . .	2,733	2,775	5,508	1,245	980	27	1,007	1,245	32	1,277
31	Lexington, . . .	1,692	1,806	3,498	775	727	34	761	775	3	778
32	Lincoln, . . .	626	485	1,111	209	189	17	206	209	6	215
33	Littleton, . . .	569	567	1,136	256	227	14	241	256	4	260
34	LOWELL, . . .	38,961	45,436	84,267	16,885	11,933	495	12,428	16,885	848	17,733
35	Ward 1, . .	4,085	5,423	9,508	1,633	1,147	21	1,168	1,633	85	1,716
36	Ward 2, . .	5,034	5,459	10,493	1,879	1,080	26	1,105	1,879	136	2,015
37	Ward 3, . .	4,301	4,944	9,245	2,038	1,407	36	1,443	2,038	123	2,161
38	Ward 4, . .	4,385	4,856	9,241	1,881	1,234	53	1,287	1,881	103	1,984
39	Ward 5, . .	4,003	4,449	8,452	1,765	1,101	35	1,136	1,765	133	1,898
40	Ward 6, . .	4,236	4,996	9,232	1,999	1,526	70	1,966	1,999	79	2,078
41	Ward 7, . .	6,018	7,100	13,118	2,383	1,514	67	1,581	2,383	105	2,488
42	Ward 8, . .	3,653	4,287	7,940	1,785	1,613	118	1,731	1,785	33	1,818
43	Ward 9, . .	5,116	3,922	7,068	1,522	1,241	69	1,310	1,522	53	1,575
44	MALDEN, . . .	13,923	15,785	29,708	6,638	5,388	450	5,838	6,638	183	6,821
45	Ward 1, . .	1,795	2,310	4,105	953	764	58	822	953	13	966
46	Ward 2, . .	2,633	2,697	5,330	1,091	713	20	733	1,091	64	1,155
47	Ward 3, . .	1,524	2,055	3,579	763	682	52	734	763	23	786
48	Ward 4, . .	2,325	2,475	4,800	1,024	833	41	874	1,024	11	1,035
49	Ward 5, . .	1,822	2,109	3,931	943	803	86	889	943	28	971
50	Ward 6, . .	2,017	2,195	4,212	977	881	113	994	977	11	988
51	Ward 7, . .	1,807	1,944	3,751	887	712	80	792	887	33	920
52	MARLBOROUGH, .	7,469	7,508	14,977	3,159	2,341	63	2,404	3,159	115	3,274
53	Ward 1, . .	679	656	1,335	317	253	16	269	317	16	333

ROOMS, TENEMENTS, AND DWELLING HOUSES — Continued.

Occupied and Unoccupied Dwelling Houses			Averages, Etc.												
Occupied Rooms	Unoccupied Rooms	Total Rooms	Males to a Family	Females to a Family	Persons to a Family	Persons to an Occupied Dwelling House	Estimated Population of Unoccupied Dwelling Houses	Estimated Population of Unoccupied Tenements in Occupied Dwelling Houses	Estimated Population if all Dwelling Houses were fully Occupied	Families to each Occupied Dwelling House	Persons to each Occupied Tenement	Rooms to each Occupied Tenement	Persons to each Room in Occupied Tenements	
3,560	488	4,048	2.09	2.21	4.30	4.99	225	112	2,427	1.16	4.30	7.83	0.59	1
3,516	410	3,926	1.93	2.05	3.98	4.75	81	187	2,369	1.19	3.98	6.66	0.60	2
1,956	273	2,229	2.48	2.18	4.66	4.97	129	28	1,326	1.07	4.66	7.79	0.60	3
4,020	911	4,931	3.01	2.62	5.63	5.79	481	11	3,735	1.03	5.63	7.96	0.71	4
4,114	253	4,367	2.24	2.19	4.43	4.84	121	31	2,729	1.09	4.43	7.07	0.63	5
556	38	594	2.21	1.73	3.94	4.32	15	12	332	1.10	3.94	7.13	0.55	6
938	161	1,099	2.45	2.00	4.45	4.70	75	36	685	1.06	4.45	7.27	0.61	7
104,028	9,885	113,913	2.32	2.43	4.75	6.80	4,568	4,646	90,857	1.45	4.75	6.05	0.78	8
22,615	1,565	24,180	2.66	2.74	5.40	6.90	863	616	17,300	1.28	5.40	7.68	0.70	9
27,924	2,738	30,662	2.18	2.35	4.53	7.26	937	1,291	24,960	1.60	4.53	5.79	0.81	10
14,173	968	15,141	2.00	2.38	4.98	8.29	406	921	15,326	1.67	4.98	5.04	0.99	11
24,398	2,367	26,765	2.10	2.31	4.41	6.44	914	1,186	20,781	1.46	4.41	5.76	0.77	12
14,918	2,247	17,165	2.22	2.52	4.74	5.72	1,241	488	12,182	1.23	4.74	6.77	0.70	13
889	77	966	2.12	1.78	3.90	3.94	32	12	556	1.01	3.90	7.06	0.55	14
5,413	403	5,816	2.16	2.07	4.23	4.55	214	59	3,435	1.07	4.23	7.25	0.58	15
7,575	596	8,171	3.61	2.31	5.92	6.18	451	118	5,744	1.04	5.92	8.67	0.68	16
3,389	320	3,709	2.79	2.35	5.14	5.55	216	62	2,721	1.08	5.14	7.13	0.72	17
729	117	846	1.95	1.82	3.77	4.07	63	15	478	1.10	3.77	6.88	0.55	18
26,948	4,335	31,283	2.11	2.21	4.32	5.14	1,917	908	21,488	1.19	4.32	6.23	0.69	19
3,904	507	4,411	2.36	2.30	4.66	6.06	273	165	3,574	1.50	4.66	5.80	0.80	20
3,674	729	4,403	2.21	2.30	4.51	5.48	482	131	3,240	1.22	4.51	6.30	0.72	21
4,506	1,287	5,793	2.08	2.16	4.24	5.02	402	233	3,815	1.19	4.24	6.18	0.69	22
4,525	593	5,118	1.96	2.13	4.09	4.11	193	143	3,212	1.00	4.09	6.44	0.64	23
4,514	516	5,030	1.98	2.07	4.05	5.26	195	170	3,518	1.30	4.05	5.79	0.70	24
5,825	703	6,528	2.08	2.33	4.41	5.29	307	154	4,150	1.20	4.41	6.96	0.63	25
15,468	2,248	17,716	2.16	2.34	4.50	4.95	1,322	198	11,632	1.10	4.50	7.31	0.61	26
3,963	277	4,240	2.12	2.19	4.31	4.61	143	47	2,382	1.07	4.31	7.80	0.55	27
5,149	393	5,542	1.87	2.01	3.88	4.44	173	81	2,972	1.15	3.88	7.85	0.53	28
5,504	763	6,267	1.95	2.02	3.97	4.18	395	195	3,484	1.05	3.97	7.32	0.54	29
7,801	351	8,152	2.03	2.23	4.26	5.42	146	136	5,590	1.27	4.26	6.27	0.68	30
6,016	367	6,383	2.18	2.33	4.51	4.81	164	14	3,676	1.07	4.51	7.76	0.58	31
1,631	197	1,828	3.00	2.52	5.52	5.88	100	32	1,245	1.11	5.52	7.80	0.68	32
2,001	114	2,115	2.22	2.22	4.44	5.00	70	18	1,224	1.13	4.44	7.82	0.57	33
106,121	7,746	113,867	2.31	2.69	5.00	7.07	3,500	4,240	92,107	1.41	5.00	6.28	0.80	34
11,382	500	11,882	2.50	3.32	5.82	8.29	174	485	10,105	1.42	5.82	6.95	0.84	35
9,883	742	10,625	2.68	2.90	5.58	9.72	253	759	11,505	1.74	5.58	5.27	1.06	36
12,869	892	13,761	2.11	2.43	4.54	6.57	297	558	10,040	1.45	4.54	6.31	0.72	37
10,691	913	11,604	2.33	2.58	4.91	7.49	397	506	10,144	1.52	4.91	5.68	0.86	38
9,836	808	10,644	2.27	2.52	4.79	7.68	269	637	9,358	1.60	4.79	5.57	0.86	39
12,797	922	13,719	2.17	2.50	4.67	5.85	410	369	10,111	1.25	4.67	6.40	0.73	40
14,755	979	15,734	2.52	2.98	5.50	8.66	580	578	14,276	1.57	5.50	6.19	0.89	41
12,904	1,123	14,027	2.05	2.40	4.45	4.92	581	147	8,908	1.11	4.45	7.23	0.62	42
10,994	867	11,861	2.05	2.57	4.62	5.67	391	245	7,674	1.23	4.62	7.22	0.64	43
45,049	4,469	49,518	2.10	2.38	4.48	5.51	2,489	820	33,008	1.23	4.48	6.79	0.66	44
6,542	451	6,993	1.88	2.43	4.31	5.37	311	56	4,472	1.25	4.31	6.86	0.63	45
5,714	461	6,175	2.42	2.47	4.89	7.48	150	313	5,793	1.53	4.89	5.24	0.93	46
6,669	688	7,357	2.00	2.69	4.69	5.25	273	108	3,969	1.12	4.69	8.74	0.54	47
7,251	350	7,601	2.27	2.42	4.69	5.76	236	52	5,088	1.23	4.69	7.08	0.66	48
6,723	841	7,564	1.93	2.24	4.17	4.90	421	117	4,460	1.17	4.17	7.13	0.58	49
6,548	881	7,429	2.06	2.25	4.31	4.78	540	47	4,799	1.11	4.31	6.70	0.64	50
5,602	797	6,399	2.04	2.19	4.23	5.27	422	140	4,313	1.23	4.23	6.32	0.67	51
19,451	1,015	20,466	2.36	2.38	4.74	6.40	403	545	15,925	1.35	4.74	6.16	0.77	52
2,196	205	2,401	2.14	2.07	4.21	5.28	84	67	1,486	1.25	4.21	6.93	0.61	53

ROOMS, TENEMENTS, AND DWELLING HOUSES — Continued.

	COUNTIES, CITIES, AND TOWNS.	POPULATION			Number of Families	DWELLING HOUSES			OCCUPIED DWELLING HOUSES		
		Males	Females	Both Sexes		Occupied	Unoccupied	Total	Occupied Tenements	Unoccupied Tenements	Total Tenements
	MIDDLESEX — Con.										
	MARLBOROUGH — Con.										
1	Ward 2,	1,072	1,133	2,205	455	366	-	366	455	22	477
2	Ward 3,	1,522	1,447	2,969	564	398	9	407	564	24	588
3	Ward 4,	1,613	1,689	3,302	636	479	18	497	636	10	646
4	Ward 5,	969	965	1,934	460	310	6	316	460	15	475
5	Ward 6,	841	848	1,689	395	281	14	295	395	15	410
6	Ward 7,	773	770	1,543	332	254	-	254	332	13	345
7	Maynard,	1,520	1,570	3,090	642	605	24	629	642	4	646
8	**MEDFORD,**	7,043	7,431	14,474	3,172	2,811	286	3,097	3,172	80	3,252
9	Ward 1,	1,521	1,491	3,012	642	562	78	640	642	14	656
10	Ward 2,	1,054	1,251	2,305	544	468	26	494	544	18	562
11	Ward 3,	829	1,095	1,924	411	373	20	393	411	5	416
12	Ward 4,	1,010	946	1,956	426	384	14	398	426	4	430
13	Ward 5,	1,518	1,437	2,955	627	547	113	660	627	23	650
14	Ward 6,	1,111	1,211	2,322	522	477	35	512	522	16	538
15	Melrose,	5,548	6,417	11,965	2,685	2,474	354	2,828	2,685	26	2,711
16	Natick,	4,234	4,580	8,814	2,080	1,741	69	1,810	2,089	85	2,174
17	**NEWTON,**	12,355	15,235	27,590	5,528	5,102	513	5,615	5,528	80	5,608
18	Ward 1,	1,993	2,294	4,287	830	743	72	815	830	17	847
19	Ward 2,	2,488	2,924	5,412	1,107	1,004	100	1,104	1,107	14	1,121
20	Ward 3,	1,484	1,949	3,433	719	671	68	739	719	8	727
21	Ward 4,	1,509	2,065	3,574	685	643	97	740	685	19	704
22	Ward 5,	1,939	2,175	4,114	856	804	72	876	856	8	864
23	Ward 6,	1,931	2,309	4,240	836	768	64	832	836	9	845
24	Ward 7,	1,011	1,519	2,530	495	469	40	509	495	5	500
25	North Reading,	422	413	835	228	204	14	218	228	3	231
26	Pepperell,	1,650	1,671	3,321	787	690	57	747	787	29	816
27	Reading,	2,235	2,482	4,717	1,150	1,034	55	1,089	1,150	26	1,176
28	Sherborn,	584	862	1,446	286	268	25	293	286	15	301
29	Shirley,	654	745	1,399	324	302	25	327	324	10	334
30	**SOMERVILLE,**	24,917	27,283	52,200	11,903	8,787	629	9,416	11,903	632	12,535
31	Ward 1,	4,834	5,293	10,127	2,302	1,578	70	1,648	2,302	158	2,460
32	Ward 2,	8,338	8,858	17,196	3,875	2,647	115	2,762	3,875	228	4,103
33	Ward 3,	6,158	6,808	13,056	3,056	2,446	219	2,665	3,056	92	3,148
34	Ward 4,	5,587	6,234	11,821	2,670	2,116	225	2,341	2,670	154	2,824
35	Stoneham,	3,070	3,214	6,284	1,581	1,330	56	1,386	1,581	23	1,604
36	Stow,	473	447	920	234	223	20	243	234	3	237
37	Sudbury,	603	538	1,141	272	244	17	261	272	10	282
38	Tewksbury,	1,653	1,726	3,379	473	439	46	485	473	4	477
39	Townsend,	880	900	1,780	512	465	35	500	512	13	525
40	Tyngsborough,	324	311	635	165	159	2	161	165	4	167
41	Wakefield,	3,962	4,342	8,304	1,958	1,556	103	1,659	1,958	90	2,048
42	**WALTHAM,**	9,638	11,238	20,876	4,276	3,856	268	4,124	4,276	110	4,386
43	Ward 1,	1,426	1,494	2,920	615	579	42	621	615	15	630
44	Ward 2,	1,390	1,546	2,936	500	428	36	464	500	18	518
45	Ward 3,	1,590	1,786	3,376	651	554	22	576	651	32	683
46	Ward 4,	1,414	1,657	3,071	646	602	58	660	646	14	660
47	Ward 5,	1,222	1,665	2,887	639	580	29	609	639	7	646
48	Ward 6,	1,274	1,644	2,918	647	608	45	653	647	24	671
49	Ward 7,	1,322	1,446	2,768	578	505	36	541	578	-	578
50	Watertown,	3,740	4,048	7,788	1,650	1,533	140	1,673	1,650	28	1,678
51	Wayland,	1,026	1,000	2,026	446	381	32	413	446	20	466

ROOMS, TENEMENTS, AND DWELLING HOUSES — Continued.

Occupied Rooms	Unoccupied Rooms	Total Rooms	Males to a Family	Females to a Family	Persons to a Family	Persons to an Occupied Dwelling House	Estimated Population of Unoccupied Dwelling Houses	Estimated Population of Unoccupied Tenements in Occupied Dwelling Houses	Estimated Population if all Dwelling Houses were fully Occupied	Families to each Occupied Dwelling House	Persons to each Occupied Dwelling House	Rooms to each Occupied Tenement	Persons to each Occupied Tenement	Persons to each Occupied Room	
3,002	115	3,117	2.36	2.49	4.85	6.02	–	107	2,312	1.24	4.85	6.00	0.73		1
3,363	161	3,524	2.70	2.56	5.26	7.46	67	126	3,162	1.42	5.26	5.96	0.88		2
3,655	160	3,815	2.54	2.65	5.19	6.89	124	52	3,478	1.33	5.19	5.75	0.90		3
2,774	123	2,897	2.10	2.10	4.20	6.24	37	63	2,634	1.48	4.20	6.03	0.70		4
2,338	189	2,527	2.13	2.15	4.28	6.01	84	64	1,857	1.41	4.28	5.92	0.72		5
2,123	62	2,185	2.33	2.32	4.65	6.07	–	60	1,903	1.31	4.65	6.39	0.73		6
4,287	165	4,452	2.37	2.44	4.81	5.11	123	19	3,292	1.06	4.81	6.08	0.72		7
22,854	2,832	25,686	2.22	2.84	5.15	5.15	1,473	365	16,312	1.13	4.56	7.20	0.63		8
4,514	688	5,202	2.37	2.32	4.69	5.36	418	66	3,496	1.14	4.69	7.03	0.67		9
3,693	291	3,984	1.94	2.30	4.24	4.93	128	76	2,569	1.16	4.24	6.79	0.62		10
3,487	234	3,721	2.02	2.66	4.68	5.16	103	23	2,050	1.10	4.68	8.48	0.55		11
2,861	172	3,033	2.37	2.22	4.59	5.09	71	18	2,045	1.11	4.59	6.72	0.68		12
4,511	1,096	5,407	2.42	2.29	4.71	5.40	616	108	3,673	1.15	4.71	6.88	0.69		13
3,988	351	4,339	2.13	2.32	4.45	4.87	170	71	2,563	1.09	4.45	7.64	0.58		14
20,071	3,105	23,176	2.07	2.39	4.46	4.84	1,713	116	13,794	1.09	4.46	7.48	0.60		15
13,551	933	14,484	2.03	2.19	4.22	5.06	349	359	9,522	1.20	4.22	6.49	0.65		16
44,911	5,148	50,059	2.23	2.76	4.99	5.41	2,775	389	30,764	1.08	4.99	8.12	0.61		17
5,663	833	6,496	2.40	2.77	5.17	5.77	415	88	4,790	1.12	5.17	6.82	0.76		18
8,538	949	9,487	2.25	2.64	4.89	5.39	539	68	6,019	1.10	4.89	7.71	0.63		19
6,480	668	7,148	2.06	2.71	4.77	5.12	348	58	3,819	1.07	4.77	9.01	0.53		20
5,530	923	6,453	2.20	3.02	5.22	5.56	559	99	4,212	1.07	5.22	8.07	0.65		21
6,709	719	7,428	2.27	2.54	4.81	5.12	569	58	4,521	1.06	4.81	7.84	0.61		22
6,961	659	7,620	2.31	2.76	5.07	5.52	353	46	4,639	1.09	5.07	8.33	0.61		23
5,030	397	5,427	2.04	3.07	5.11	5.39	216	26	2,772	1.06	5.11	10.16	0.50		24
1,589	111	1,700	1.85	1.81	3.66	4.09	57	11	903	1.12	3.66	6.97	0.53		25
5,306	546	5,852	2.10	2.12	4.22	4.81	274	122	3,717	1.14	4.22	6.74	0.63		26
8,198	606	8,804	1.94	2.16	4.10	4.56	251	107	5,075	1.11	4.10	7.13	0.58		27
2,210	288	2,498	2.04	3.02	5.06	5.40	135	76	1,657	1.07	5.06	7.73	0.65		28
2,251	198	2,449	2.02	2.30	4.32	4.63	116	43	1,558	1.07	4.32	6.95	0.62		29
74,418	8,324	82,742	2.10	2.29	4.39	5.94	3,736	2,774	58,710	1.35	4.39	6.25	0.70		30
14,018	1,367	15,385	2.10	2.50	4.40	6.42	449	695	11,271	1.46	4.40	6.09	0.72		31
22,470	2,057	24,527	2.15	2.29	4.44	6.50	748	1,042	18,956	1.46	4.44	5.80	0.77		32
20,079	2,205	22,284	2.01	2.26	4.27	5.34	1,169	383	14,618	1.25	4.27	6.57	0.65		33
17,851	2,695	20,546	2.09	2.34	4.43	5.59	1,258	682	13,761	1.26	4.43	6.09	0.66		34
10,507	556	11,063	1.94	2.03	3.97	4.72	264	91	6,639	1.19	3.97	6.65	0.60		35
1,787	168	1,955	2.02	1.91	3.93	4.13	83	12	1,015	1.05	3.93	7.64	0.51		36
1,979	147	2,126	2.21	1.98	4.19	4.68	80	42	1,263	1.11	4.19	7.28	0.58		37
4,511	305	4,816	3.49	3.65	7.14	7.70	354	29	3,792	1.08	7.14	9.54	0.75		38
3,614	299	3,913	1.72	1.76	3.48	3.83	134	45	1,959	1.10	3.48	7.06	0.49		39
1,106	28	1,134	1.99	1.91	3.90	3.99	8	16	659	1.03	3.90	6.79	0.57		40
12,944	1,271	14,215	2.02	2.22	4.24	5.34	550	382	9,256	1.26	4.24	6.61	0.64		41
28,995	2,294	31,289	2.25	2.63	4.88	5.41	1,450	537	22,863	1.31	4.88	6.78	0.72		42
4,162	350	4,512	2.32	2.43	4.75	5.04	212	71	3,203	1.06	4.75	6.77	0.70		43
3,959	352	4,311	2.78	3.09	5.87	6.86	247	106	3,289	1.17	5.87	7.92	0.74		44
4,200	295	4,495	2.44	2.75	5.19	6.09	134	166	3,676	1.18	5.19	6.45	0.80		45
4,277	400	4,677	2.19	2.56	4.75	5.10	296	67	3,434	1.07	4.75	6.62	0.72		46
4,569	256	4,825	1.91	2.61	4.52	4.98	144	32	3,063	1.10	4.52	7.15	0.63		47
4,440	416	4,856	1.97	2.54	4.51	4.80	216	108	3,242	1.06	4.51	6.86	0.66		48
3,388	225	3,613	2.29	2.50	4.79	5.48	197	–	2,905	1.14	4.79	5.86	0.82		49
11,789	1,204	12,993	2.27	2.45	4.72	5.08	711	132	8,631	1.08	4.72	7.14	0.66		50
3,074	337	3,411	2.30	2.24	4.54	5.32	170	91	2,287	1.17	4.54	6.89	0.66		51

ROOMS, TENEMENTS, AND DWELLING HOUSES — Continued.

COUNTIES, CITIES, AND TOWNS.	POPULATION			Number of Families	DWELLING HOUSES			OCCUPIED DWELLING HOUSES		
	Males	Females	Both Sexes		Occupied	Unoccupied	Total	Occupied Tenements	Unoccupied Tenements	Total Tenements
MIDDLESEX — Con.										
1 Westford, .	1,223	1,195	2,418	526	475	28	503	526	10	536
2 Weston, .	877	833	1,710	367	338	35	373	367	9	376
3 Wilmington, .	715	705	1,420	338	301	50	351	338	6	344
4 Winchester, .	2,928	3,222	6,150	1,301	1,207	133	1,340	1,301	17	1,318
5 WOBURN, .	7,000	7,178	14,178	3,012	2,661	126	2,787	3,012	78	3,090
6 Ward 1, .	1,314	1,311	2,625	509	453	48	501	509	1	510
7 Ward 2, .	1,478	1,403	2,881	590	524	35	559	590	23	613
8 Ward 3, .	1,165	1,344	2,509	561	490	14	504	561	9	570
9 Ward 4, .	1,248	1,374	2,622	574	501	29	530	574	15	589
10 Ward 5, .	602	559	1,161	242	209	–	209	242	12	254
11 Ward 6, .	689	724	1,413	343	306	–	306	343	9	352
12 Ward 7, .	504	463	967	193	178	–	178	193	9	202
13 **NANTUCKET.**	1,315	1,701	3,016	981	880	420	1,300	981	39	1,020
14 Nantucket, .	1,315	1,701	3,016	981	880	420	1,300	981	39	1,020
15 **NORFOLK.**	64,780	70,039	134,819	29,685	25,789	1,916	27,705	29,685	814	30,499
16 Avon, .	818	808	1,626	385	342	14	356	385	27	412
17 Bellingham, .	721	760	1,481	358	314	26	340	358	5	363
18 Braintree, .	2,660	2,651	5,311	1,254	1,117	64	1,181	1,254	38	1,292
19 Brookline, .	6,826	9,338	16,164	3,148	2,277	221	2,498	3,148	114	3,262
20 Canton, .	2,207	2,429	4,636	968	876	43	919	968	24	992
21 Cohasset, .	1,148	1,326	2,474	586	577	1	578	586	1	587
22 Dedham, .	3,476	3,735	7,211	1,613	1,481	93	1,574	1,613	22	1,635
23 Dover, .	345	323	668	148	141	7	148	148	1	149
24 Foxborough, .	1,542	1,677	3,219	828	723	28	751	828	7	835
25 Franklin, .	2,459	2,677	5,136	1,176	984	44	1,028	1,176	32	1,208
26 Holbrook, .	1,127	1,171	2,298	571	511	35	546	571	21	592
27 Hyde Park, .	5,760	6,066	11,826	2,561	2,064	137	2,201	2,561	96	2,657
28 Medfield, .	883	989	1,872	415	348	14	362	415	16	431
29 Medway, .	1,438	1,475	2,913	732	626	26	652	732	33	765
30 Millis, .	484	522	1,006	226	210	34	244	226	23	249
31 Milton, .	2,562	2,956	5,518	1,106	1,003	79	1,082	1,106	19	1,125
32 Needham, .	1,749	1,762	3,511	802	735	71	806	802	10	812
33 Norfolk, .	471	411	882	210	179	20	199	210	6	216
34 Norwood, .	2,437	2,137	4,574	963	866	15	881	963	2	965
35 QUINCY, .	10,608	10,104	20,712	4,373	3,801	482	4,283	4,373	155	4,528
36 Ward 1, .	1,712	1,850	3,562	790	711	299	1,010	790	27	817
37 Ward 2, .	1,408	1,333	2,741	584	529	23	552	584	19	603
38 Ward 3, .	2,502	2,194	4,696	983	822	35	857	983	30	1,013
39 Ward 4, .	2,658	2,306	4,964	990	813	43	856	990	46	1,036
40 Ward 5, .	1,297	1,372	2,669	568	526	82	608	568	9	577
41 Ward 6, .	1,031	1,049	2,080	458	400	–	400	458	24	482
42 Randolph, .	1,825	1,869	3,694	905	824	55	879	905	12	917
43 Sharon, .	839	878	1,717	393	378	81	459	393	3	396
44 Stoughton, .	2,570	2,702	5,272	1,241	1,111	86	1,197	1,241	41	1,282
45 Walpole, .	1,500	1,494	2,994	688	620	27	647	688	13	701
46 Wellesley, .	1,470	2,759	4,229	738	679	56	735	738	11	749
47 Weymouth, .	5,592	5,699	11,291	2,666	2,421	129	2,550	2,666	64	2,730
48 Wrentham, .	1,263	1,321	2,584	631	581	28	609	631	18	649

ROOMS, TENEMENTS, AND DWELLING HOUSES — Continued.

Occupied Rooms	Unoccupied Rooms	Total Rooms	Males to a Family	Females to a Family	Persons to a Family	Persons to an Occupied Dwelling House	Estimated Population of Unoccupied Dwelling Houses	Estimated Population of Unoccupied Tenements in Occupied Dwelling Houses	Estimated Population were fully Occupied	Families to each Occupied Dwelling House	Persons to each Occupied Dwelling House	Rooms to each Occupied Tenement	Persons to each Occupied Tenement	
3,635	246	3,881	2.33	2.27	4.60	5.09	143	46	2,097	1.19	4.60	6.91	0.67	1
3,019	386	3,405	2.39	2.37	4.96	5.06	177	42	1,929	1.09	4.96	8.23	0.57	2
2,202	352	2,554	2.11	2.09	4.20	4.72	238	25	1,081	1.12	4.20	6.51	0.64	3
9,838	1,219	11,057	2.25	2.48	4.73	5.10	678	80	6,968	1.08	4.73	7.50	0.63	4
19,629	1,453	21,082	2.33	2.38	4.71	5.23	672	207	15,217	1.18	4.71	6.52	0.72	5
3,519	310	3,829	2.58	2.58	5.16	5.79	278	5	2,908	1.12	5.16	6.91	0.75	6
3,710	321	4,031	2.50	2.58	4.88	5.59	193	112	3,196	1.13	4.88	6.29	0.78	7
3,634	113	3,747	2.08	2.39	4.47	5.12	72	40	2,854	1.11	4.47	6.48	0.69	8
3,822	280	4,102	2.18	2.39	4.57	5.23	152	49	2,843	1.15	4.57	6.05	0.80	9
1,425	46	1,471	2.40	2.31	4.80	5.56	-	58	1,229	1.15	4.80	5.83	0.81	10
2,269	343	2,612	2.01	2.11	4.12	4.62	-	57	1,460	1.12	4.12	6.02	0.62	11
1,247	40	1,287	2.61	2.40	5.01	5.45	-	43	1,202	1.08	5.01	6.46	0.78	12
7,287	1,873	9,160	1.34	1.73	3.07	3.43	1,441	129	4,577	1.11	3.07	7.43	0.41	13
7,287	1,873	9,160	1.34	1.73	3.07	3.43	1,441	129	4,577	1.11	3.07	7.43	0.41	14
210,776	19,277	230,053	2.18	2.36	4.54	5.23	10,021	3,895	188,536	1.15	4.54	7.10	0.64	15
2,534	238	2,772	2.12	2.10	4.22	4.75	67	114	1,807	1.13	4.22	6.58	0.64	16
2,514	219	2,733	2.02	2.12	4.14	4.72	123	21	1,625	1.14	4.14	7.02	0.59	17
8,721	715	9,436	2.12	2.12	4.24	4.75	304	161	5,776	1.12	4.24	6.95	0.61	18
24,822	3,273	28,095	2.17	2.96	5.13	7.10	1,569	585	18,315	1.38	5.13	7.89	0.65	19
7,023	471	7,494	2.28	2.51	4.79	5.29	227	115	4,978	1.11	4.79	7.28	0.66	20
4,044	16	4,060	1.96	2.26	4.22	4.29	4	4	2,482	1.02	4.22	7.92	0.53	21
11,997	836	12,833	2.15	2.32	4.47	4.87	453	98	7,762	1.09	4.47	7.25	0.62	22
1,139	74	1,213	2.23	2.18	4.51	4.74	33	5	703	1.05	4.51	7.70	0.59	23
5,784	223	6,007	1.86	2.03	3.89	4.45	125	27	3,671	1.15	3.89	6.90	0.56	24
8,059	508	8,567	2.00	2.28	4.37	5.22	230	149	5,306	1.20	4.37	6.85	0.64	25
3,792	332	4,124	1.97	2.95	3.02	4.50	158	84	2,540	1.12	4.02	6.64	0.61	26
17,873	1,546	19,419	2.25	2.37	4.62	5.73	785	444	13,055	1.24	4.62	6.28	0.66	27
3,048	189	3,237	2.13	2.38	4.51	5.38	75	72	2,019	1.19	4.51	7.54	0.61	28
5,293	387	5,680	1.94	2.02	3.98	4.65	121	151	3,365	1.17	3.98	7.23	0.55	29
1,714	320	2,034	2.11	2.31	4.45	4.79	163	192	1,271	1.08	4.45	7.58	0.59	30
8,717	840	9,557	2.32	2.67	4.99	5.50	435	95	6,048	1.10	4.99	7.88	0.63	31
5,438	543	5,981	2.18	2.20	4.38	4.78	339	44	3,891	1.09	4.38	6.78	0.65	32
1,581	177	1,758	2.24	1.96	4.20	4.96	99	25	1,006	1.17	4.20	7.55	0.56	33
6,060	132	6,192	2.53	2.22	4.75	5.28	70	10	4,993	1.11	4.75	6.29	0.75	34
27,592	3,964	31,556	2.43	2.31	4.74	5.45	2,627	735	24,074	1.15	4.74	6.91	0.75	35
5,470	2,107	7,577	2.17	2.34	4.51	5.01	1,498	122	5,182	1.11	4.51	6.92	0.65	36
3,902	278	4,180	2.41	2.28	4.69	5.18	119	89	2,949	1.10	4.69	6.68	0.70	37
5,559	339	5,898	2.55	2.23	4.78	5.71	290	143	5,039	1.20	4.78	5.96	0.84	38
5,361	415	5,776	2.68	2.33	5.01	6.11	265	230	5,457	1.22	5.01	5.42	0.93	39
4,314	679	4,993	2.28	2.42	4.70	5.07	416	42	3,127	1.08	4.70	7.60	0.62	40
2,986	146	3,132	2.25	2.29	4.54	5.20	-	109	2,189	1.15	4.54	6.52	0.70	41
6,312	441	6,753	2.02	2.06	4.08	4.48	246	49	3,989	1.10	4.08	6.97	0.59	42
3,130	749	3,879	2.14	2.23	4.37	4.54	368	13	2,698	1.04	4.37	7.96	0.55	43
8,373	824	9,197	2.07	2.18	4.25	4.75	409	174	5,855	1.12	4.25	6.75	0.65	44
4,891	238	5,129	2.18	2.17	4.35	4.83	130	57	3,181	1.11	4.35	7.11	0.61	45
6,677	514	7,191	1.99	3.74	5.73	6.23	349	65	4,641	1.60	5.73	9.05	0.63	46
18,479	1,177	19,656	2.10	2.14	4.24	4.66	601	271	12,163	1.10	4.24	6.93	0.61	47
4,869	331	5,200	2.00	2.10	4.10	4.45	125	74	2,783	1.09	4.10	7.72	0.53	48

ROOMS, TENEMENTS, AND DWELLING HOUSES — Continued.

	COUNTIES, CITIES, AND TOWNS.	POPULATION			Number of Families	DWELLING HOUSES			OCCUPIED DWELLING HOUSES		
		Males	Females	Both Sexes		Occupied	Unoccupied	Total	Occupied Tenements	Unoccupied Tenements	Total Tenements
1	PLYMOUTH.	50,694	50,804	101,498	24,830	20,651	3,040	23,671	24,830	799	25,629
2	Abington, . . .	2,040	2,167	4,207	1,076	912	29	941	1,076	38	1,114
3	Bridgewater, . . .	2,722	1,964	4,686	854	762	60	822	854	24	878
4	BROCKTON, .	16,559	16,606	33,165	7,700	5,355	259	5,614	7,700	360	8,060
5	Ward 1, .	2,059	2,110	4,169	935	664	30	694	935	52	987
6	Ward 2, .	2,067	2,260	4,327	1,070	750	36	766	1,070	41	1,111
7	Ward 3, .	2,567	2,478	5,045	1,198	815	35	850	1,198	28	1,226
8	Ward 4, .	2,369	2,423	4,792	1,089	757	39	796	1,089	43	1,132
9	Ward 5, .	2,566	2,480	5,046	1,126	791	49	840	1,126	75	1,201
10	Ward 6, .	2,596	2,344	4,940	1,086	789	61	850	1,086	54	1,140
11	Ward 7, .	2,335	2,511	4,846	1,196	809	9	818	1,196	67	1,263
12	Carver, . . .	546	470	1,016	262	246	8	254	262	15	277
13	Duxbury, . . .	945	1,021	1,966	532	503	102	605	532	8	540
14	East Bridgewater, .	1,441	1,453	2,894	726	642	41	683	726	28	754
15	Halifax, . . .	266	231	497	148	132	19	151	148	5	153
16	Hanover, . . .	1,009	1,042	2,051	544	506	35	541	544	11	555
17	Hanson, . . .	708	672	1,380	380	353	24	377	380	7	387
18	Hingham, . . .	2,299	2,520	4,819	1,164	1,057	158	1,215	1,164	25	1,189
19	Hull, ...	536	508	1,044	229	229	510	739	229	5	234
20	Kingston, . . .	847	899	1,746	477	425	43	468	477	10	487
21	Lakeville, . . .	439	431	870	233	220	65	285	233	1	234
22	Marion, . . .	328	431	759	213	205	75	280	213	7	220
23	Marshfield, . .	830	930	1,760	511	484	329	813	511	21	532
24	Mattapoisett, . .	490	542	1,032	301	281	72	353	301	10	311
25	Middleborough, .	3,205	3,484	6,689	1,673	1,396	43	1,439	1,673	39	1,712
26	Norwell, . . .	771	769	1,540	422	407	43	450	422	9	431
27	Pembroke, . . .	634	589	1,223	367	345	54	399	367	3	370
28	Plymouth, . . .	3,863	4,094	7,957	1,969	1,615	67	1,682	1,969	35	2,004
29	Plympton, . . .	268	281	549	162	152	29	181	162	6	168
30	Rochester, . . .	535	486	1,021	260	236	18	254	260	7	267
31	Rockland, . . .	2,757	2,766	5,523	1,331	1,186	58	1,244	1,331	46	1,377
32	Scituate, . . .	1,115	1,131	2,246	607	569	243	822	607	20	627
33	Wareham, . . .	1,765	1,902	3,667	891	815	508	1,323	891	22	913
34	West Bridgewater, .	877	870	1,747	409	378	27	405	409	-	409
35	Whitman, . . .	2,879	2,865	5,744	1,389	1,210	51	1,261	1,389	37	1,426
36	SUFFOLK.	260,675	279,124	539,799	112,802	65,604	4,485	70,089	112,802	8,800	121,602
37	BOSTON, . . .	259,666	257,254	496,920	103,306	58,599	3,525	62,124	103,306	8,243	111,549
38	Ward 1, . .	10,363	10,644	21,007	4,671	2,843	130	2,973	4,671	301	4,972
39	Ward 2, . .	11,505	10,083	21,588	4,144	2,163	85	2,248	4,144	292	4,436
40	Ward 3, . .	6,841	7,102	13,943	3,164	1,681	32	1,713	3,164	214	3,378
41	Ward 4, . .	6,654	6,721	13,375	3,010	1,851	74	1,925	3,010	183	3,193
42	Ward 5, . .	6,994	5,992	12,986	2,588	1,507	47	1,554	2,588	181	2,769
43	Ward 6, . .	14,805	13,055	27,860	5,559	1,854	102	1,956	5,559	417	5,976
44	Ward 7, . .	9,049	7,924	16,973	3,157	1,554	128	1,682	3,157	344	3,481
45	Ward 8, . .	12,143	10,987	23,130	4,370	1,891	83	1,974	4,370	479	4,849
46	Ward 9, . .	11,398	11,776	23,174	4,682	1,970	91	2,061	4,682	551	5,233
47	Ward 10, . .	10,070	12,484	22,554	4,471	2,292	121	2,413	4,471	498	4,969
48	Ward 11, . .	7,975	12,555	19,930	3,770	2,515	260	2,775	3,770	291	4,061
49	Ward 12, . .	9,188	12,403	21,591	3,518	2,249	85	2,334	3,518	429	3,947
50	Ward 13, . .	12,695	12,205	24,900	5,453	2,341	48	2,389	5,453	545	5,998
51	Ward 14, . .	9,635	9,551	19,186	4,074	2,485	142	2,627	4,074	293	4,367
52	Ward 15, . .	8,975	9,648	18,623	3,992	2,294	68	2,362	3,992	300	4,292

ROOMS, TENEMENTS, AND DWELLING HOUSES — Continued.

Occupied Rooms	Unoccupied Rooms	Total Rooms	Males to a Family	Females to a Family	Persons to a Family	Persons to an Occupied Dwelling House	Estimated Population of Unoccupied and Occupied Dwelling Houses	Estimated Population of Unoccupied Tenements in Occupied Dwelling Houses	Estimated Population if all Dwelling Houses were fully Occupied	Families to each Occupied Dwelling House	Persons to each Occupied Tenement	Rooms to each Occupied Tenement	Persons to each Room in Occupied Tenements	
171,153	27,839	198,992	2.04	2.05	4.09	4.92	14,957	3,268	119,723	1.20	4.09	6.89	0.59	1
7,462	401	7,863	1.90	2.01	3.91	4.61	134	149	4,490	1.18	3.91	6.93	0.56	2
7,355	607	7,962	3.19	2.30	5.49	6.45	369	152	5,187	1.12	5.49	8.61	0.64	3
47,423	3,816	51,239	2.15	2.16	4.31	6.19	1,683	1,552	36,820	1.44	4.31	6.16	0.70	4
6,558	495	7,053	2.20	2.26	4.46	6.28	188	252	4,580	1.41	4.46	7.01	0.64	5
7,178	528	7,706	1.93	2.11	4.04	5.95	213	165	4,706	1.47	4.04	6.71	0.60	6
7,295	447	7,742	2.14	2.07	4.21	6.19	217	118	5,280	1.47	4.21	6.09	0.69	7
6,072	446	6,518	2.18	2.22	4.40	6.83	247	189	5,228	1.44	4.40	5.58	0.79	8
6,374	790	7,164	2.28	2.20	4.48	6.38	318	95	5,605	1.42	4.48	5.66	0.79	9
6,597	704	7,301	2.39	2.16	4.55	6.25	382	246	5,508	1.38	4.55	6.07	0.75	10
7,349	406	7,755	1.95	2.10	4.05	5.99	54	271	5,171	1.48	4.05	6.11	0.66	11
1,714	110	1,824	2.09	1.79	3.88	4.15	56	58	1,107	1.07	3.88	6.54	0.59	12
4,840	1,599	6,439	1.78	1.92	3.70	3.91	635	50	2,629	1.06	3.70	9.10	0.41	13
5,371	472	5,843	1.99	2.00	3.99	4.51	185	112	3,391	1.15	3.99	7.40	0.54	14
1,143	201	1,344	1.80	1.76	3.56	3.77	72	17	586	1.12	3.56	7.72	0.48	15
3,705	278	3,983	1.85	1.92	3.77	4.05	142	41	2,231	1.08	3.77	6.81	0.55	16
2,876	198	3,074	1.86	1.77	3.63	3.91	94	25	1,499	1.08	3.63	7.57	0.48	17
8,741	1,676	10,417	1.98	2.16	4.14	4.56	729	194	5,645	1.30	4.14	7.63	0.55	18
2,486	4,217	6,703	2.34	2.22	4.56	4.56	2,326	23	3,393	1.00	4.56	10.80	0.42	19
3,496	384	3,880	1.78	1.88	3.66	4.11	177	37	1,960	1.12	3.66	7.33	0.50	20
1,743	458	2,201	1.88	1.85	3.73	3.95	237	4	1,131	1.06	3.73	7.48	0.50	21
2,167	950	3,117	1.54	2.02	3.56	3.70	278	25	1,992	1.04	3.56	10.17	0.35	22
3,946	1,875	5,821	1.61	1.78	3.44	3.64	1,398	72	3,090	1.06	3.44	7.72	0.45	23
2,382	773	3,105	1.63	1.80	3.43	3.67	294	31	1,930	1.07	3.43	7.75	0.44	24
12,168	563	12,731	1.92	2.08	4.00	4.70	206	196	7,061	1.20	4.00	7.27	0.55	25
3,122	358	3,480	1.81	1.82	3.63	3.75	161	35	1,756	1.04	3.63	7.30	0.49	26
2,826	369	3,195	1.73	1.60	3.33	3.54	191	19	1,424	1.06	3.33	7.70	0.43	27
12,510	744	13,254	1.96	2.08	4.04	4.95	359	141	8,428	1.22	4.04	6.35	0.64	28
1,122	261	1,383	1.65	1.74	3.39	3.61	105	20	674	1.07	3.39	6.93	0.49	29
1,688	199	1,887	2.06	1.87	3.93	4.15	75	28	1,121	1.06	3.93	6.49	0.60	30
8,802	593	9,395	2.07	2.08	4.15	4.66	276	161	5,984	1.12	4.15	6.61	0.61	31
4,158	2,298	6,456	1.84	1.86	3.70	3.95	999	71	5,349	1.07	3.70	6.85	0.54	32
5,708	3,576	9,284	1.98	1.80	3.78	4.16	2,008	83	5,548	1.09	3.78	6.41	0.59	33
3,053	210	3,263	2.14	2.13	4.27	4.62	125	—	1,872	1.08	4.27	7.42	0.58	34
9,216	553	9,769	2.08	2.06	4.14	4.75	242	156	6,120	1.15	4.14	6.63	0.62	35
678,450	80,691	759,141	2.31	2.48	4.79	8.23	50,312	42,152	618,863	1.72	4.79	6.01	0.80	36
618,598	70,304	688,902	2.32	2.49	4.81	8.48	29,592	39,649	566,464	1.76	4.81	5.89	0.80	37
20,861	2,595	23,456	2.22	2.28	4.50	7.79	961	1,355	23,223	1.64	4.50	5.75	0.78	38
23,889	1,957	25,846	2.75	2.46	5.21	9.08	848	1,521	25,967	1.92	5.21	5.75	0.90	39
17,045	1,210	18,255	2.16	2.25	4.41	8.20	265	944	15,152	1.88	4.41	5.39	0.82	40
17,061	1,532	18,593	2.21	2.23	4.44	7.23	535	813	14,723	1.63	4.44	5.67	0.78	41
15,838	1,246	17,084	2.70	2.32	5.02	8.62	405	999	14,300	1.72	5.02	6.12	0.82	42
22,635	2,675	25,270	2.66	2.35	5.01	15.06	1,563	2,088	31,482	3.00	5.01	4.08	1.23	43
19,781	2,703	22,484	2.88	2.55	5.41	10.92	1,798	1,801	20,252	2.02	5.41	6.51	0.86	44
23,598	2,723	23,231	2.78	2.51	5.29	12.23	1,945	2,531	26,079	2.31	5.29	5.58	0.98	45
24,765	3,116	27,881	2.43	2.52	4.95	11.76	1,070	2,727	26,971	2.58	4.95	5.29	0.94	46
31,465	4,210	35,675	2.25	2.79	5.04	9.84	1,191	2,510	28,255	1.95	5.04	7.04	0.72	47
35,008	3,840	38,848	1.96	3.33	5.29	7.92	2,059	1,539	23,528	1.50	5.29	9.29	0.57	48
29,724	2,589	32,313	2.61	3.53	6.14	9.00	86	2,634	25,041	1.36	6.14	8.45	0.73	49
23,450	2,427	25,877	2.33	2.24	4.57	10.64	511	2,491	27,302	2.33	4.57	4.30	1.06	50
22,945	2,433	25,378	2.37	2.34	4.71	7.72	1,096	1,380	21,602	1.64	4.71	5.63	0.84	51
22,546	1,902	24,448	2.25	2.42	4.67	8.12	552	1,401	20,576	1.74	4.67	5.65	0.83	52

ROOMS, TENEMENTS, AND DWELLING HOUSES — Continued.

	COUNTIES, CITIES, AND TOWNS.	Males	Females	Both Sexes	Number of Families	Occupied	Unoccupied	Total	Occupied Tenements	Unoccupied Tenements	Total Tenements
	SUFFOLK — Con.										
	BOSTON — Con.										
1	Ward 16,	7,664	8,656	16,320	3,735	2,103	126	2,229	3,735	307	4,042
2	Ward 17,	10,128	10,986	21,114	4,656	2,441	129	2,570	4,656	444	5,100
3	Ward 18,	10,641	11,038	21,679	4,960	2,303	132	2,435	4,960	556	5,516
4	Ward 19,	10,508	11,864	22,372	4,620	2,144	136	2,280	4,620	260	4,880
5	Ward 20,	9,893	11,635	21,528	4,674	3,589	472	4,061	4,674	273	4,947
6	Ward 21,	8,079	11,195	19,274	4,396	2,896	151	3,047	4,396	299	4,605
7	Ward 22,	10,445	11,844	22,289	4,770	2,850	179	3,029	4,770	332	5,102
8	Ward 23,	8,736	9,547	18,283	3,866	2,947	248	3,195	3,866	192	4,058
9	Ward 24,	8,589	9,651	18,240	3,944	3,234	238	3,472	3,944	151	4,095
10	Ward 25,	7,283	7,708	15,001	3,172	2,602	218	2,820	3,172	111	3,283
11	CHELSEA,	15,273	15,991	31,264	6,934	4,743	333	5,076	6,934	482	7,416
12	Ward 1,	3,666	3,813	7,479	1,655	1,089	67	1,156	1,655	130	1,785
13	Ward 2,	3,723	3,862	7,585	1,712	1,138	87	1,225	1,712	123	1,835
14	Ward 3,	3,521	3,601	7,122	1,561	1,039	79	1,118	1,561	86	1,647
15	Ward 4,	2,530	2,857	5,387	1,241	846	45	891	1,241	94	1,335
16	Ward 5,	1,853	1,858	3,691	765	631	55	686	765	49	814
17	Revere,	3,721	3,702	7,423	1,652	1,407	336	1,743	1,652	66	1,718
18	Winthrop,	2,015	2,177	4,192	910	855	291	1,146	910	9	919
19	WORCESTER,	152,056	154,389	306,445	67,274	47,339	2,865	50,204	67,274	3,968	71,242
20	Ashburnham,	1,070	1,078	2,148	530	446	60	506	530	36	566
21	Athol,	3,735	3,629	7,364	1,750	1,450	67	1,517	1,750	75	1,825
22	Auburn,	821	777	1,598	345	277	21	298	345	17	362
23	Barre,	1,150	1,128	2,278	558	501	71	572	558	19	577
24	Berlin,	451	446	897	225	211	26	237	225	2	227
25	Blackstone,	3,116	2,923	6,039	1,266	901	50	951	1,266	145	1,411
26	Bolton,	398	399	797	206	191	11	202	206	3	209
27	Boylston,	389	340	729	177	147	10	157	177	5	182
28	Brookfield,	1,689	1,590	3,279	756	599	59	658	756	37	793
29	Charlton,	975	902	1,877	470	420	21	441	470	7	477
30	Clinton,	5,291	6,206	11,497	2,278	1,694	59	1,753	2,278	114	2,392
31	Dana,	353	364	717	196	175	12	187	196	4	200
32	Douglas,	1,032	993	2,025	483	390	29	419	483	80	563
33	Dudley,	1,611	1,592	3,203	628	420	22	442	628	27	655
34	FITCHBURG,	13,037	13,372	26,409	5,686	3,886	182	4,068	5,686	260	5,946
35	Ward 1,	2,197	2,179	4,376	807	624	16	640	807	48	945
36	Ward 2,	3,289	3,221	6,510	1,241	740	28	768	1,241	36	1,277
37	Ward 3,	2,108	2,191	4,299	911	649	26	675	911	33	944
38	Ward 4,	1,497	1,717	3,214	793	549	32	581	793	51	844
39	Ward 5,	1,646	1,704	3,350	843	593	24	617	843	49	892
40	Ward 6,	2,300	2,360	4,660	1,001	731	56	787	1,001	43	1,044
41	Gardner,	4,735	4,447	9,182	2,062	1,573	43	1,616	2,062	133	2,195
42	Grafton,	2,455	2,646	5,101	1,106	926	51	977	1,106	31	1,137
43	Hardwick,	1,376	1,279	2,655	533	460	21	481	533	11	544
44	Harvard,	574	588	1,162	279	202	34	206	279	1	280
45	Holden,	1,302	1,300	2,602	555	415	31	446	555	19	574
46	Hopedale,	698	679	1,377	307	285	18	303	307	4	311
47	Hubbardston,	659	615	1,274	348	311	36	347	348	6	354
48	Lancaster,	978	1,202	2,180	452	395	38	433	452	30	482
49	Leicester,	1,541	1,698	3,239	731	594	16	610	731	14	745
50	Leominster,	4,504	4,707	9,211	2,181	1,643	49	1,692	2,181	34	2,215

ROOMS, TENEMENTS, AND DWELLING HOUSES — Continued.

Occupied Rooms	Unoccupied Rooms	Total Rooms	Males to a Family	Females to a Family	Persons to a Family	Persons to an Occupied Dwelling House	Estimated Population of Unoccupied Dwelling Houses	Estimated Population of Unoccupied Tenements in Occupied Dwelling Houses	Estimated Population if all Dwelling Houses were fully Occupied	Families to each Occupied Dwelling House	Persons to each Occupied Tenement	Rooms to each Occupied Tenement	Persons to each Room in Occupied Tenements	
22,334	2,833	25,167	2.05	2.32	4.37	7.76	978	1,342	18,640	1.78	4.37	5.98	0.73	1
23,740	2,986	26,726	2.17	2.36	4.53	8.65	1,116	2,011	24,241	1.91	4.53	5.10	0.89	2
23,686	3,385	27,071	2.14	2.23	4.37	9.41	1,242	2,430	25,361	2.15	4.37	4.78	0.92	3
23,940	2,776	26,716	2.27	2.57	4.84	10.43	1,418	1,258	25,048	2.15	4.84	5.18	0.93	4
33,562	6,033	39,595	2.12	2.49	4.61	6.00	2,882	1,239	25,019	1.30	4.61	7.18	0.64	5
31,393	3,468	34,861	1.88	2.60	4.48	6.60	1,006	1,440	21,720	1.49	4.48	7.29	0.61	6
29,194	3,487	32,681	2.19	2.48	4.67	7.82	1,490	1,550	25,239	1.67	4.67	6.12	0.73	7
25,308	3,126	28,434	2.26	2.47	4.73	6.20	1,538	908	20,729	1.31	4.73	6.55	0.72	8
27,611	2,836	30,447	2.18	2.44	4.62	5.64	1,342	608	20,289	1.22	4.62	7.00	0.66	9
21,249	2,216	23,465	2.30	2.43	4.73	5.77	1,258	525	16,784	1.22	4.73	6.70	0.71	10
41,257	5,141	46,498	2.20	2.31	4.51	6.59	2,194	2,174	35,932	1.46	4.51	5.96	0.76	11
9,227	1,099	10,326	2.22	2.30	4.52	6.87	460	588	8,527	1.52	4.52	5.58	0.81	12
9,461	1,286	10,747	2.17	2.26	4.43	6.67	580	545	8,710	1.50	4.43	5.53	0.80	13
9,330	1,128	10,458	2.25	2.31	4.56	6.85	541	392	8,305	1.50	4.56	5.98	0.73	14
7,405	867	8,272	2.04	2.30	4.34	6.27	287	408	6,992	1.47	4.34	5.97	0.73	15
5,934	761	6,695	2.39	2.43	4.82	5.85	322	236	4,249	1.21	4.82	7.76	0.62	16
11,017	3,037	14,054	2.25	2.24	4.49	5.28	1,774	296	9,395	1.17	4.49	6.67	0.67	17
7,478	2,209	9,687	2.22	2.39	4.61	4.90	1,426	41	5,690	1.06	4.61	8.22	0.56	18
436,807	41,681	478,578	2.26	2.30	4.56	6.47	18,837	18,094	345,073	1.42	4.56	6.49	0.70	19
3,528	594	4,122	2.02	2.03	4.05	4.82	289	146	2,783	1.19	4.05	6.06	0.61	20
11,681	821	12,502	2.14	2.07	4.21	5.08	340	316	8,820	1.21	4.21	6.67	0.63	21
2,124	219	2,343	2.38	2.25	4.63	5.77	121	79	1,798	1.25	4.63	6.16	0.75	22
4,686	605	5,291	2.06	2.02	4.08	4.55	323	78	2,670	1.11	4.08	8.39	0.49	23
1,756	165	1,921	2.01	1.98	3.99	4.25	111	8	1,016	1.07	3.99	7.80	0.51	24
8,343	1,221	9,564	2.46	2.31	4.77	6.70	335	692	7,006	1.41	4.77	6.59	0.72	25
1,567	107	1,674	1.93	1.94	3.87	4.17	46	12	855	1.08	3.87	7.61	0.51	26
1,263	107	1,370	2.20	1.92	4.12	4.96	50	21	800	1.20	4.12	7.14	0.58	27
5,065	626	5,691	2.24	2.10	4.34	5.47	328	161	3,763	1.26	4.34	6.70	0.65	28
3,399	163	3,562	2.07	1.92	3.99	4.47	94	28	1,999	1.12	3.99	7.23	0.55	29
13,735	878	14,613	2.32	2.73	5.05	6.70	401	576	12,474	1.34	5.05	6.03	0.84	30
1,298	92	1,390	1.80	1.86	3.66	4.10	49	15	781	1.12	3.66	6.62	0.55	31
3,447	616	4,063	2.14	2.05	4.19	5.89	151	335	2,512	1.24	4.19	7.14	0.59	32
3,976	344	4,320	2.56	2.54	5.10	7.65	168	118	3,509	1.50	5.10	6.65	0.81	33
34,591	2,622	37,213	2.29	2.35	4.64	6.80	1,238	1,206	28,853	1.46	4.64	6.08	0.76	34
5,334	284	5,618	2.45	2.46	4.88	7.01	112	234	4,722	1.44	4.88	5.95	0.82	35
6,695	318	7,013	2.65	2.60	5.25	8.80	246	189	6,945	1.68	5.25	5.39	0.97	36
5,719	452	6,171	2.31	2.41	4.72	6.02	172	156	4,627	1.40	4.72	6.28	0.75	37
5,629	566	6,195	1.89	2.16	4.05	5.85	187	207	3,908	1.44	4.05	7.10	0.57	38
5,254	423	5,677	1.95	2.02	3.97	5.65	136	195	3,681	1.42	3.97	6.23	0.64	39
5,960	579	6,539	2.30	2.36	4.66	6.37	357	290	5,217	1.37	4.66	5.95	0.78	40
11,818	840	12,658	2.29	2.16	4.45	5.84	251	592	10,025	1.31	4.45	5.73	0.78	41
7,696	524	8,220	2.22	2.39	4.61	5.51	281	145	5,525	1.19	4.61	6.86	0.66	42
3,791	229	4,020	2.58	2.40	4.98	5.77	121	55	2,851	1.16	4.98	7.11	0.70	43
2,237	238	2,475	2.05	2.11	4.16	4.44	151	4	1,717	1.06	4.16	8.02	0.52	44
3,731	280	4,011	2.35	2.34	4.69	6.27	194	89	2,885	1.34	4.69	6.72	0.70	45
2,261	152	2,413	2.28	2.21	4.49	4.83	87	18	1,482	1.08	4.49	7.36	0.61	46
2,306	310	2,616	1.89	1.77	3.66	4.10	148	22	1,444	1.12	3.66	6.63	0.55	47
3,644	570	4,214	2.16	2.66	4.82	5.52	210	145	2,335	1.14	4.82	8.06	0.60	48
5,257	217	5,474	2.11	2.32	4.43	5.45	87	62	3,888	1.23	4.43	7.19	0.62	49
13,789	544	14,333	2.06	2.16	4.22	5.61	275	143	9,029	1.33	4.22	6.32	0.67	50

ROOMS, TENEMENTS, AND DWELLING HOUSES — Continued.

	COUNTIES, CITIES, AND TOWNS.	POPULATION			Number of Families	DWELLING HOUSES			OCCUPIED DWELLING HOUSES		
		Males	Females	Both Sexes		Occupied	Unoccupied	Total	Occupied Tenements	Unoccupied Tenements	Total Tenements
	WORCESTER — Con.										
1	Lunenburg, . . .	626	611	1,237	302	277	18	295	302	8	310
2	Mendon, . . .	462	427	889	234	221	16	237	234	4	238
3	Milford, . . .	4,354	4,605	8,959	2,116	1,671	73	1,744	2,116	183	2,299
4	Millbury, . . .	2,619	2,603	5,222	1,100	793	32	825	1,100	54	1,154
5	New Braintree, . .	292	250	542	114	114	–	114	114	5	119
6	Northborough, . .	975	965	1,940	451	347	23	370	451	24	475
7	Northbridge, . .	2,732	2,554	5,286	1,070	836	34	870	1,070	12	1,082
8	North Brookfield, .	2,248	2,387	4,635	1,030	679	5	684	1,030	24	1,054
9	Oakham, . . .	308	297	605	161	149	17	166	161	4	165
10	Oxford, . . .	1,147	1,243	2,390	618	562	85	647	618	18	636
11	Paxton, . . .	234	192	426	114	109	20	129	114	3	117
12	Petersham, . . .	493	459	952	254	232	57	289	254	5	259
13	Phillipston, . . .	248	212	460	114	112	18	130	114	2	116
14	Princeton, . . .	491	461	952	236	228	39	267	236	10	246
15	Royalston, . . .	454	436	890	254	233	40	273	254	6	260
16	Rutland, . . .	526	452	978	225	213	7	220	225	5	230
17	Shrewsbury, . .	784	740	1,524	381	354	29	383	381	4	385
18	Southborough, . .	1,274	949	2,223	442	390	50	440	442	11	453
19	Southbridge, . .	4,043	4,207	8,250	1,688	1,379	72	1,451	1,688	47	1,735
20	Spencer, . . .	3,784	3,830	7,614	1,625	1,157	60	1,217	1,625	170	1,795
21	Sterling, . . .	604	614	1,218	342	319	228	547	342	21	363
22	Sturbridge, . . .	948	962	1,910	434	337	33	370	434	40	474
23	Sutton, . . .	1,770	1,650	3,420	714	529	11	540	714	25	739
24	Templeton, . . .	1,488	1,427	2,915	718	628	51	679	718	27	745
25	Upton, ...	908	1,242	2,150	524	418	14	432	524	9	533
26	Uxbridge, . . .	1,780	1,766	3,546	812	641	30	671	812	38	850
27	Warren, . . .	2,197	2,233	4,430	980	783	39	822	980	73	1,053
28	Webster, . . .	3,799	4,000	7,799	1,716	935	68	1,003	1,716	121	1,837
29	Westborough, . .	2,611	2,624	5,235	1,031	829	57	886	1,031	86	1,117
30	West Boylston, . .	1,447	1,521	2,968	648	562	45	607	648	12	660
31	West Brookfield, .	717	750	1,467	409	353	13	366	409	15	424
32	Westminster, . .	632	683	1,315	370	334	40	374	370	18	388
33	Winchendon, . .	2,257	2,233	4,490	1,078	890	43	933	1,078	40	1,118
34	WORCESTER, . .	48,803	49,904	98,707	20,861	11,153	461	11,614	20,861	1,730	22,591
35	Ward 1, . .	5,611	5,489	11,100	2,417	1,358	50	1,408	2,417	205	2,622
36	Ward 2, . .	6,424	6,665	13,089	2,653	1,464	75	1,539	2,653	176	2,829
37	Ward 3, . .	7,636	7,001	14,637	2,825	1,464	45	1,509	2,825	312	3,137
38	Ward 4, . .	6,729	6,762	13,491	2,742	1,244	16	1,260	2,742	213	2,955
39	Ward 5, . .	8,053	7,232	15,285	3,028	1,532	82	1,614	3,028	300	3,328
40	Ward 6, . .	5,677	6,158	11,835	2,591	1,514	82	1,596	2,591	171	2,762
41	Ward 7, . .	4,756	5,596	10,352	2,452	1,325	71	1,396	2,452	212	2,664
42	Ward 8, . .	3,977	5,001	8,978	2,154	1,252	40	1,292	2,153	141	2,294

ROOMS, TENEMENTS, AND DWELLING HOUSES--Continued.

Occupied Rooms	Unoccupied Rooms	Total Rooms	Males to a Family	Females to a Family	Persons to a Family	Persons to an Occupied Dwelling House	Estimated Population of Unoccupied Dwelling Houses	Estimated Population of Unoccupied Tenements in Occupied Dwelling Houses	Estimated Population if all Dwelling Houses were fully Occupied	Families to each Dwelling House	Persons to each Occupied Dwelling House	Rooms to each Occupied Tenement	Persons to each Room in Occupied Tenements	
2,168	152	2,321	2.07	2.03	4.10	4.47	80	32	1,350	1.09	4.10	7.18	0.57	1
1,885	143	2,028	1.97	1.83	3.80	4.02	64	15	968	1.96	3.80	8.03	0.47	2
14,021	1,289	15,310	2.06	2.17	4.23	5.36	391	774	10,124	1.27	4.23	6.03	0.64	3
7,213	533	7,746	2.38	2.37	4.75	6.59	211	257	5,990	1.39	4.75	6.56	0.72	4
937	31	968	2.56	2.19	4.75	4.75	-	24	566	1.00	4.75	8.22	0.58	5
3,114	318	3,432	2.16	2.14	4.30	5.59	129	103	2,172	1.30	4.30	6.90	0.62	6
6,762	250	7,012	2.55	2.39	4.94	6.32	215	59	5,601	1.28	4.94	6.72	0.78	7
6,672	172	6,844	2.18	2.32	4.50	6.83	34	108	4,777	1.52	4.50	6.18	0.69	8
1,342	132	1,474	1.91	1.85	3.76	4.06	69	17	989	1.08	3.76	8.34	0.45	9
4,250	654	4,904	1.86	2.01	3.87	4.25	361	79	2,821	1.10	3.87	6.88	0.59	10
894	148	1,042	2.05	1.69	3.74	3.91	78	11	615	1.05	3.74	7.84	0.48	11
1,981	429	2,410	1.94	1.81	3.75	4.10	234	19	1,205	1.09	3.75	7.80	0.48	12
893	159	1,052	2.18	1.86	4.04	4.11	74	8	542	1.02	4.04	7.83	0.52	13
2,186	480	2,666	2.08	1.95	4.03	4.18	163	40	1,155	1.04	4.03	9.26	0.44	14
1,948	349	2,297	1.79	1.71	3.50	3.82	153	21	1,064	1.09	3.50	7.67	0.46	15
1,502	80	1,582	2.34	2.01	4.35	4.59	82	22	1,032	1.06	4.35	6.68	0.65	16
2,917	224	3,141	2.06	1.94	4.00	4.31	125	18	1,605	1.08	4.00	7.66	0.52	17
3,303	478	3,781	2.88	2.15	5.03	5.79	285	55	2,563	1.13	5.03	7.47	0.67	18
10,675	758	11,433	2.40	2.49	4.89	5.98	481	299	8,011	1.22	4.89	6.92	0.77	19
10,270	1,232	11,502	2.33	2.36	4.69	6.58	395	797	8,806	1.40	4.69	6.32	0.74	20
2,647	1,428	4,075	1.77	1.79	3.56	3.82	871	75	2,164	1.07	3.56	7.74	0.46	21
3,191	294	3,485	2.18	2.22	4.40	5.07	187	176	2,273	1.29	4.40	7.35	0.60	22
5,149	228	5,377	2.48	2.31	4.79	6.47	71	129	3,611	1.35	4.79	7.21	0.66	23
4,831	521	5,352	2.07	1.99	4.06	4.64	287	110	3,262	1.14	4.06	6.73	0.69	24
3,886	156	4,042	1.73	2.37	4.10	5.14	72	37	2,250	1.25	4.10	7.42	0.55	25
5,678	397	6,075	2.19	2.18	4.37	5.53	103	166	3,878	1.27	4.37	6.99	0.62	26
6,682	649	7,331	2.24	2.28	4.52	5.66	221	339	4,681	1.25	4.52	6.82	0.66	27
10,082	1,037	11,119	2.21	2.33	4.54	5.84	567	549	8,915	1.84	4.54	5.88	0.77	28
7,589	926	8,515	2.53	2.55	5.08	6.51	599	467	6,092	1.24	5.08	7.36	0.69	29
4,363	445	4,808	2.23	2.35	4.58	5.28	238	55	3,261	1.15	4.58	6.73	0.68	30
2,930	165	3,104	1.75	1.84	3.59	4.16	54	34	1,775	1.16	3.59	7.19	0.50	31
2,483	383	2,866	1.71	1.84	3.55	3.94	155	64	1,567	1.11	3.55	6.71	0.53	32
7,004	495	7,499	2.10	2.07	4.17	5.04	217	167	4,874	1.23	4.17	6.50	0.64	33
128,451	13,461	141,912	2.34	2.39	4.73	8.86	4,084	8,183	111,034	1.87	4.73	6.36	0.77	34
15,528	1,624	17,152	2.32	2.27	4.59	8.37	409	941	12,450	1.78	4.59	6.32	0.71	35
17,208	1,628	18,836	2.42	2.51	4.93	8.94	671	868	14,028	1.81	4.93	6.49	0.76	36
16,427	1,892	18,319	2.70	2.48	5.18	10.00	459	1,616	16,765	1.93	5.18	5.81	0.89	37
14,814	1,184	15,998	2.45	2.47	4.92	10.84	173	1,948	14,712	2.20	4.92	5.40	0.91	38
15,901	2,143	18,044	2.66	2.39	5.05	9.98	818	1,515	17,618	1.98	5.05	5.25	0.96	39
16,919	1,674	18,593	2.19	2.38	4.57	7.82	641	781	13,257	1.71	4.57	6.53	0.79	40
15,770	2,033	17,803	1.94	2.28	4.22	7.81	555	805	11,802	1.85	4.22	6.43	0.66	41
15,884	1,283	17,167	1.85	2.32	4.17	7.17	287	588	9,883	1.72	4.17	7.38	0.57	42

ROOMS, TENEMENTS, AND DWELLING HOUSES — Concluded.

RECAPITULATION.

	THE STATE, AND COUNTIES	POPULATION			Number of Families	DWELLING HOUSES			OCCUPIED DWELLING HOUSES		
		Males	Females	Both Sexes		Occu-pied	Unoc-cupied	Total	Occu-pied Tene-ments	Unoc-cupied Tene-ments	Total Tene-ments
1	THE STATE.	1,214,701	1,285,482	2,500,183	547,385	397,633	30,861	428,494	547,385	26,573	573,958
2	Barnstable, . . .	13,294	14,360	27,654	8,069	7,476	1,620	9,096	8,069	162	8,231
3	Berkshire, . . .	42,525	43,767	86,292	18,810	16,294	1,184	17,478	18,810	388	19,198
4	Bristol, . . .	105,582	113,457	219,019	47,708	30,093	1,487	31,580	47,708	2,526	50,234
5	Dukes, . . .	2,057	2,181	4,238	1,306	1,217	1,093	2,310	1,306	55	1,361
6	Essex, ...	161,943	168,480	330,586	74,092	54,234	3,951	58,185	74,092	2,803	76,895
7	Franklin, . . .	20,293	19,852	40,145	9,637	8,177	684	8,861	9,637	337	9,974
8	Hampden, . . .	74,134	78,805	152,368	32,793	23,072	1,395	24,467	32,793	1,441	34,234
9	Hampshire, . .	26,061	28,649	54,710	11,744	10,231	498	10,729	11,744	319	12,063
10	Middlesex, . .	239,323	250,894	499,217	107,654	86,596	6,223	92,819	107,654	4,122	111,776
11	Nantucket, . .	1,315	1,701	3,016	981	880	420	1,300	981	39	1,020
12	Norfolk, . . .	64,780	70,039	134,819	29,685	25,789	1,916	27,705	29,685	814	30,499
13	Plymouth, . . .	50,694	50,804	101,498	24,830	20,634	3,040	23,674	24,830	799	25,620
14	Suffolk, . . .	260,675	279,124	539,799	112,802	65,604	4,485	70,089	112,802	8,800	121,602
15	Worcester, . .	152,056	154,389	306,445	67,274	47,339	2,865	50,204	67,274	3,968	71,242

RECAPITULATION. AVERAGES PER AREAS.

	THE STATE, AND COUNTIES.	Areas * (Square Miles)	Persons to a Square Mile	Families to a Square Mile
1	THE STATE.	8,040	310.97	68.08
2	Barnstable, ...	290	95.36	27.82
3	Berkshire, ...	1,000	86.29	18.81
4	Bristol, ...	530	413.24	90.02
5	Dukes, ...	120	35.32	10.88
6	Essex, ...	500	660.79	148.18
7	Franklin, ...	680	59.04	14.17
8	Hampden, ...	670	228.27	48.94
9	Hampshire, ...	540	101.31	21.75
10	Middlesex, ...	805	620.15	133.73
11	Nantucket, ...	60	50.27	16.35
12	Norfolk, ...	526	256.31	56.44
13	Plymouth, ...	727	140.00	34.25
14	Suffolk, ...	44	12,268.16	2,563.68
15	Worcester, ...	1,550	197.71	43.40

* Land surface only.

ROOMS, TENEMENTS, AND DWELLING HOUSES — Concluded.

RECAPITULATION.

Occu-pied Rooms	Unoc-cupied Rooms	Total Rooms	Males to a Family	Fe-males to a Family	Per-sons to a Family	Per-sons to an Occu-pied Dwell-ing House	Esti-mated Popu-lation of Occu-pied Dwell-ing Houses	Estimated Population of Unoc-cupied Tenements in Occu-pied Dwelling Houses	Estima-ted Popu-lation if all Dwelling Houses were fully Occupied	Fami-lies to each Occu-pied Dwel-ling House	Per-sons to each Occu-pied Tene-ment	Rooms to each Occu-pied Tene-ment	Per-sons to each Room in Occu-pied Tene-ments	
3,568,385	378,613	3,946,998	2.22	2.35	4.57	6.29	194,116	121,459	2,815,738	1.38	4.57	6.52	0.70	1
55,856	13,083	68,939	1.65	1.78	3.43	3.70	5,994	556	24,204	1.08	3.43	6.92	0.50	2
134,864	12,779	147,643	2.26	2.33	4.59	5.30	5,941	1,781	94,014	1.15	4.59	7.17	0.64	3
301,831	25,510	327,341	2.21	2.38	4.59	7.28	10,825	11,594	241,458	1.59	4.59	6.33	0.73	4
9,875	8,177	18,052	1.58	1.67	3.25	3.48	3,894	179	8,221	1.07	3.25	7.56	0.43	5
478,804	48,823	527,627	2.19	2.27	4.46	6.09	24,062	12,501	366,956	1.37	4.46	6.46	0.69	6
68,207	6,327	74,534	2.11	2.06	4.17	4.91	3,558	1,405	44,008	1.18	4.17	7.08	0.59	7
209,488	17,285	226,773	2.26	2.40	4.66	6.63	9,249	6,715	168,992	1.42	4.66	6.39	0.73	8
85,062	5,288	90,350	2.22	2.44	4.66	5.35	2,664	1,487	58,861	1.15	4.66	7.24	0.64	9
719,835	69,980	789,815	2.22	2.42	4.64	5.76	35,844	19,126	554,187	1.24	4.64	6.69	0.69	10
7,287	1,873	9,160	1.34	1.73	3.07	3.43	1,441	129	4,577	1.11	3.07	7.43	0.41	11
210,776	19,277	230,053	2.18	2.36	4.54	5.23	10,021	3,696	148,536	1.15	4.54	7.10	0.64	12
171,153	27,839	198,992	2.04	2.05	4.09	4.92	14,957	3,268	119,723	1.20	4.09	6.89	0.59	13
678,450	80,691	759,141	2.31	2.48	4.79	8.23	30,912	42,152	618,863	1.72	4.79	6.01	0.80	14
436,897	41,681	478,578	2.26	2.30	4.56	6.47	18,557	18,094	346,076	1.42	4.56	6.49	0.70	15

RECAPITULATION. AVERAGES PER AREAS.

Dwellings† to a Square Mile	Acres to a Person	Acres to a Family	Acres to a Dwelling†	Square feet to a Person	Square feet to a Family	Square feet to a Dwelling†	
53.30	2.06	9.40	12.01	89,650	409,478	523,096	1
31.37	6.71	23.00	29.40	292,356	1,001,950	888,823	2
17.48	7.42	34.02	36.62	323,071	1,482,105	1,595,057	3
59.58	1.55	7.11	10.74	67,462	309,708	467,877	4
19.25	18.12	58.81	33.25	789,384	2,561,568	1,448,229	5
116.37	0.97	4.32	5.50	42,190	188,134	239,567	6
13.03	10.84	45.16	49.11	472,221	1,967,138	2,139,410	7
36.52	2.80	13.08	17.53	122,131	569,589	763,417	8
19.87	6.32	29.43	32.21	275,166	1,281,875	1,403,144	9
115.30	1.03	4.79	5.55	44,955	208,465	241,784	10
21.67	12.73	39.14	29.54	554,610	1,705,101	1,286,695	11
52.67	2.50	11.34	12.15	108,768	493,988	529,292	12
32.65	4.57	18.69	19.60	199,135	814,009	853,865	13
1,592.93	0.05	0.25	0.40	2,272	10,874	17,501	14
32.39	3.24	14.75	19.76	141,009	642,321	869,710	15

† Includes both occupied and unoccupied dwelling houses.

TABULAR ANALYSIS.

The presentation entitled " Averages and Comparative Totals: Rooms, Tenements, and Dwelling Houses," brings together the leading facts as to the number of families, occupied and unoccupied dwelling houses, occupied and unoccupied tenements, and occupied and unoccupied rooms, with averages showing males to a family, females to a family, persons to a family, persons to each occupied dwelling house, estimated population of unoccupied dwelling houses, estimated population of unoccupied tenements in occupied dwelling houses, estimated population if all dwelling houses were fully occupied, families to each occupied dwelling house, persons to each occupied tenement, rooms to each occupied tenement, and persons to each room in the occupied tenements. The recapitulation for the State, by counties, appears on pages 780,781. The estimates referred to above have, of course, been based upon the ascertained facts: that is, the estimated population of the unoccupied dwelling houses has been based upon the average number of persons found in the occupied dwelling houses, and the other estimates have been made up in a similar manner.

Taking the first line of the recapitulation, which presents the facts for the State, and disregarding the figures showing population, families, and dwelling houses, which are comprised in the first 13 columns of the table and which have been alluded to in the analysis of previous tables, we note that the average number of males to a family for the State is 2.22, and the average number of females 2.35, the average number of persons of both sexes being 4.57. The average number of persons to an occupied dwelling is 6.29. The estimated population of the unoccupied dwelling houses, based upon this last figure, is 194,116, and the estimated population of the unoccupied tenements in the occupied dwelling houses is 121,439. These two estimates aggregate 315,555, which is the estimated population that could be housed in the dwelling houses found entirely unoccupied and in the unoccupied tenements of occupied dwelling houses. This number of persons, added to the total population of the State, namely, 2,500,183, gives an estimated population of 2,815,738, if the dwelling houses and tenements which were unoccupied at the time of the enumeration were as fully occupied as the occupied dwelling houses and tenements. That is to say, this figure represents the population that could be housed in the houses and tenements at present existing, without more crowding than is found in the tenements that are at present occupied. This indicates the limit of expansion within the present tenements available for housing the people, without diminishing the average space occupied by each family. A similar estimate appears for each county, and the estimates may be compared with the actual population shown in the third column of the table. In such a comparison some remarkable differences are disclosed. In Suffolk County, for example, the actual population was 539,799. The estimated population, if all dwelling houses were fully occupied, is 618,863, an increase of 14.65 per cent. In Dukes County, on the other hand, the actual population was 4,238, while, if all the dwelling houses were fully occupied, the population would become 8,221, an increase of 93.98 per cent. This

[783]

possible increase in Dukes County is larger than in any other, and is partly due to the existence of numerous vacant houses at the time of the enumeration, intended for summer occupancy only, and which later in the season would have been filled with temporary residents.

The percentages of possible increase in population within the limits of the dwelling houses and tenements already existing, without increasing the families and persons to each occupied dwelling house and tenement, beyond the averages shown in the table, may be seen from the following statement for each of the counties and for the State :

THE STATE, AND COUNTIES.	Actual Population	Estimated Population if all Dwelling Houses were fully Occupied	Percentages of Possible Increase
THE STATE.	2,500,183	2,815,738	12.62
Barnstable,	27,654	34,204	23.69
Berkshire,	86,292	94,014	8.95
Bristol,	219,019	241,438	10.24
Dukes,	4,238	8,221	93.98
Essex,	330,393	366,956	11.07
Franklin,	40,145	44,908	11.86
Hampden,	152,938	168,902	10.44
Hampshire,	54,710	58,861	7.59
Middlesex,	499,217	554,187	11.01
Nantucket,	3,016	4,577	51.76
Norfolk,	134,819	148,536	10.17
Plymouth,	101,498	119,723	17.96
Suffolk,	539,799	618,863	14.65
Worcester,	306,445	343,076	11.95

The average number of males and females to each family, the average number of persons to a family, the average number of persons and families to each occupied dwelling house, the average number of persons to each occupied tenement, the average number of rooms to each occupied tenement, and the average number of persons to each room in the occupied tenements, for each of the cities, are brought forward in the following analysis table :

CITIES.	Males to a Family	Females to a Family	Persons to a Family	Persons to an Occupied Dwelling House	Families to each Occupied Dwelling House	Persons to each Occupied Tenement	Rooms to each Occupied Tenement	Persons to each Room in the Occupied Ten- ements
Beverly,	1.96	2.09	4.05	5.76	1.42	4.05	6.46	0.63
Boston,	2.32	2.49	4.81	8.48	1.76	4.81	5.99	0.80
Brockton,	2.15	2.16	4.31	6.19	1.44	4.31	6.16	0.70
Cambridge,	2.32	2.43	4.75	6.90	1.45	4.75	6.05	0.78
Chelsea,	2.20	2.31	4.51	6.59	1.46	4.51	5.96	0.76
Chicopee,	2.66	2.74	5.40	7.17	1.33	5.40	6.24	0.87
Everett,	2.11	2.21	4.32	5.14	1.19	4.32	6.26	0.69
Fall River,	2.38	2.59	4.97	11.06	2.22	4.97	5.61	0.89
Fitchburg,	2.29	2.35	4.64	6.80	1.46	4.64	6.08	0.76
Gloucester,	3.00	2.21	5.21	7.51	1.44	5.21	5.94	0.88
Haverhill,	2.11	2.27	4.38	6.28	1.43	4.38	6.74	0.65
Holyoke,	2.43	2.68	5.11	10.89	2.13	5.11	5.47	0.93
Lawrence,	2.33	2.51	4.84	7.75	1.60	4.84	5.80	0.83

CITIES.	Males to a Family	Females to a Family	Persons to a Family	Persons to an Occupied Dwelling House	Families to each Occupied Dwelling House	Persons to each Occupied Tenement	Rooms to each Occupied Tenement	Persons to each Room in Occupied Tenements
Lowell,	2.31	2.69	5.00	7.07	1.41	5.00	6.28	0.80
Lynn,	2.13	2.28	4.41	6.21	1.41	4.41	6.35	0.69
Maiden,	2.10	2.38	4.48	5.51	1.23	4.48	6.79	0.66
Marlborough,	2.36	2.38	4.74	6.40	1.35	4.74	6.16	0.77
Medford,	2.22	2.34	4.56	5.15	1.13	4.56	7.20	0.63
New Bedford,	2.14	2.38	4.52	7.39	1.63	4.52	6.20	0.73
Newburyport,	1.90	2.28	4.18	4.89	1.17	4.18	6.96	0.60
Newton,	2.23	2.76	4.99	5.41	1.08	4.99	8.12	0.61
North Adams,	2.38	2.49	4.87	6.41	1.32	4.87	6.46	0.75
Northampton,	2.27	2.85	5.12	5.93	1.16	5.12	7.12	0.72
Pittsfield,	2.26	2.45	4.71	5.38	1.14	4.71	7.14	0.66
Quincy,	2.43	2.31	4.74	5.45	1.15	4.74	6.31	0.75
Salem,	2.13	2.39	4.52	7.09	1.57	4.52	6.35	0.71
Somerville,	2.10	2.29	4.39	5.94	1.35	4.39	6.25	0.70
Springfield,	2.10	2.29	4.39	6.09	1.39	4.39	6.60	0.67
Taunton,	2.24	2.37	4.61	6.19	1.34	4.61	7.08	0.65
Waltham,	2.25	2.63	4.88	5.41	1.11	4.88	6 78	0.72
Woburn,	2.33	2.38	4.71	5.33	1.13	4.71	6.52	0.72
Worcester,	2.34	2.39	4.73	8.86	1.87	4.73	6.16	0.77

The United States Census for 1890 presented for each leading city in the country a statement showing the number of occupied dwellings, number of families, and the average number of persons to a dwelling and to a family. This information is given in the following table, in order that the figures may be compared with the facts obtained for the cities in Massachusetts in the present Census:

CITIES.	UNITED STATES CENSUS — 1890			
	Number of Occupied Dwellings	Number of Families	Persons to an Occupied Dwelling	Persons to a Family
Albany, N. Y.,	13,153	20,433	7.22	4.65
Allegheny, Pa.,	16,543	20,805	6.36	5.06
Atlanta, Ga.,	11,447	13,353	5.72	4.91
Baltimore, Md.,	72,112	86,654	6.02	5.01
Brooklyn, N. Y.,	82,282	170,970	9.80	4.72
Buffalo, N. Y.,	37,290	51,461	6.86	4.97
Camden, N. J.,	12,362	12,667	4.72	4.60
Charleston, S. C.,	8,164	11,196	6.73	4.91
Chicago, Ill.,	127,871	220,320	8.60	4.99
Cincinnati, O.,	33,487	63,530	8.87	4.67
Cleveland, O.,	43,835	53,052	5.96	4.93
Columbus, O.,	16,179	18,050	5.45	4.88
Dayton, O.,	12,366	13,217	4.95	4.63
Denver, Colo.,	18,010	19,730	5.93	5.41
Des Moines, Iowa,	9,923	10,488	5.05	4.78
Detroit, Mich.,	36,992	42,209	5.57	4.88
Evansville, Ind.,	9,091	9,743	5.58	5.21
Grand Rapids, Mich.,	11,411	13,393	5.28	4.50
Hartford, Conn.,	6,553	11,596	8.12	4.59
Indianapolis, Ind.,	21,138	23,063	4.99	4 57

CITIES.	UNITED STATES CENSUS — 1890			
	Number of Occupied Dwellings	Number of Families	Persons to an Occupied Dwelling	Persons to a Family
Jersey City, N. J., ...	18,562	34,434	8.78	4.73
Kansas City, Mo., ...	23,140	26,734	5.74	4.96
Lincoln, Neb., ...	8,848	9,256	6.23	5.96
Los Angeles, Cal., ...	10,368	11,056	4.86	4.56
Louisville, Ky., ...	24,999	32,970	6.45	4.89
Memphis, Tenn., ...	11,567	13,354	5.58	4.83
Milwaukee, Wis., ...	32,888	41,519	6.22	4.92
Minneapolis, Minn., ...	25,281	32,901	6.52	5.01
Nashville, Tenn., ...	13,746	15,487	5.54	4.92
Newark, N. J., ...	23,296	38,906	7.81	4.67
New Haven, Conn., ...	11,194	17,381	7.26	4.68
New Orleans, La., ...	43,000	48,582	5.63	4.98
New York, N. Y., ...	81,828	312,766	18.52	4.84
Omaha, Neb., ...	20,194	22,485	6.96	6.25
Paterson, N. J., ...	9,870	16,815	7.94	4.66
Philadelphia, Pa., ...	187,052	205,135	5.60	5.10
Pittsburg, Pa., ...	37,725	45,584	6.33	5.23
Providence, R. I., ...	17,639	29,242	7.49	4.52
Reading, Pa., ...	11,693	12,326	5.02	4.76
Richmond, Va., ...	12,538	15,678	6.49	5.19
Rochester, N. Y., ...	23,954	27,312	5.59	4.90
San Francisco, Cal., ...	47,183	52,535	6.34	5.69
Scranton, Pa., ...	12,263	14,839	6.13	5.07
St. Joseph, Mo., ...	9,460	9,902	5.53	5.28
St. Louis, Mo., ...	60,937	91,756	7.41	4.92
St. Paul, Minn., ...	20,976	25,832	6.35	5.15
Syracuse, N. Y., ...	15,641	19,277	5.64	4.57
Toledo, O., ...	15,842	17,113	5.14	4.76
Trenton, N. J., ...	11,428	11,901	5.03	4.83
Troy, N. Y., ...	7,805	12,895	7.81	4.73
Washington, D. C., ...	38,798	43,967	5.94	5.24
Wilmington, Del., ...	11,878	12,473	5.17	4.93

The average number of persons to a family in the city of Boston is 4.81. This average was exceeded in 1890 in the following cities: Allegheny, Atlanta, Baltimore, Buffalo, Charleston, Chicago, Cleveland, Columbus, Denver, Detroit, Evansville, Kansas City, Lincoln, Louisville, Memphis, Milwaukee, Minneapolis, Nashville, New Orleans, New York, Omaha, Philadelphia, Pittsburg, Richmond, Rochester, San Francisco, Scranton, St. Joseph, St. Louis, St. Paul, Trenton, Washington, and Wilmington. The average number of persons to each occupied dwelling house in Boston is 8.48. The average number of persons to an occupied dwelling was larger than this in 1890 in the following cities: Brooklyn, Chicago, Cincinnati, Jersey City, and New York. The marked difference between the conditions existing in the city of New York and the other cities mentioned in the table is perhaps the most striking feature of the comparison. In New York the average number of persons to an occupied dwelling was 18.52; the largest average number of persons found to an occupied dwelling in any other city is shown in Brooklyn, where the average was 9.80. The cities of Fall River and Holyoke, however, contained a larger average number of persons to an occupied dwelling house than was found in the city of Brooklyn, or than was found in any of the cities shown except New York, these averages, respectively, being 11.06 and 10.89. Excluding Brooklyn

and New York from the table derived from the United States Census, we find that the
city which had the next largest average number of persons to an occupied dwelling is
Cincinnati, the average being 8.87. This is larger than the average number of persons
to an occupied dwelling house in the city of Boston, and approximately the same as the
average number of persons to an occupied dwelling found in Worcester, namely, 8.86.
Jersey City had an average of 8.78 persons to an occupied dwelling, and Chicago an
average of 8.60, while an average of 8.12 was found in the city of Hartford. Below
these cities, the city having the largest average number of persons to an occupied dwelling was Paterson, the average being 7.94. The average in the city of Albany was
7.22; in Newark, 7.81; in New Haven, 7.26; in Providence, 7.49; in St. Louis, 7.41;
and in Troy, 7.81. The cities in Massachusetts in which these figures are approximated
are: Chicopee, 7.17; Gloucester, 7.51; Lawrence, 7.75; Lowell, 7.07; New Bedford,
7.39; and Salem, 7.09. Other comparisons may be made from the tables.

The number of occupied dwellings, number of families, average number of persons to an occupied dwelling, and the average number of persons to a family, in each
of the States and Territories, according to the United States Census of 1890, are shown
in the following table:

STATES AND TERRITORIES.	UNITED STATES CENSUS — 1890			
	Number of Occupied Dwellings	Number of Families	Persons to an Occupied Dwelling	Persons to a Family
Alabama,	281,602	287,292	5.37	5.27
Arizona,	13,338	13,495	4.47	4.42
Arkansas,	209,190	213,620	5.39	5.28
California,	235,925	245,710	5.12	4.92
Colorado,	81,127	84,276	5.08	4.89
Connecticut,	130,779	165,890	5.71	4.50
Delaware,	33,882	34,578	4.97	4.87
District of Columbia,	138,798	43,967	5.94	5.24
Florida,	78,816	80,059	4.97	4.89
Georgia,	342,874	352,059	5.36	5.22
Idaho,	17,852	18,113	4.73	4.66
Illinois,	669,812	778,015	5.71	4.92
Indiana,	452,043	467,146	4.85	4.69
Iowa,	379,318	388,517	5.04	4.92
Kansas,	292,086	297,358	4.89	4.80
Kentucky,	335,990	354,463	5.53	5.24
Louisiana,	204,341	214,123	5.47	5.22
Maine,	135,255	150,355	4.89	4.40
Maryland,	84,204	202,179	5.66	5.16
Massachusetts,	355,280	479,790	6.30	4.67
Michigan,	434,370	455,004	4.82	4.60
Minnesota,	229,678	247,975	5.67	5.25
Mississippi,	235,656	241,148	5.47	5.35
Missouri,	485,320	528,295	5.52	5.07
Montana,	26,934	27,501	4.91	4.81
Nebraska,	201,470	206,820	5.26	5.12
Nevada,	10,066	10,170	4.55	4.50
New Hampshire,	76,665	87,348	4.91	4.31
New Jersey,	247,342	308,339	5.84	4.69
New Mexico,	34,671	35,504	4.43	4.33
New York,	895,593	1,308,015	6.70	4.59
North Carolina,	301,571	306,952	5.37	5.27

STATES AND TERRITORIES.	UNITED STATES CENSUS — 1890			
	Number of Occupied Dwellings	Number of Families	Persons to an Occupied Dwelling	Persons to a Family
North Dakota, ...	37,918	38,478	4.82	4.75
Ohio, ...	720,414	785,291	5.10	4.68
Oklahoma, ...	14,942	15,029	4.14	4.11
Oregon, ...	61,925	63,791	5.07	4.92
Pennsylvania, ...	999,364	1,061,626	5.26	4.95
Rhode Island, ...	52,250	75,010	6.61	4.61
South Carolina, ...	217,195	222,941	5.30	5.16
South Dakota, ...	68,894	70,250	4.77	4.68
Tennessee, ...	323,136	334,194	5.47	5.29
Texas, ...	402,422	411,251	5.56	5.44
Utah, ...	37,285	38,816	5.58	5.36
Vermont, ...	69,817	75,869	4.76	4.38
Virginia, ...	292,654	304,673	5.66	5.44
Washington, ...	68,833	70,977	5.08	4.92
West Virginia, ...	136,378	140,359	5.59	5.43
Wisconsin, ...	316,163	335,456	5.34	5.03
Wyoming, ...	11,880	12,065	5 11	5.03
THE UNITED STATES, ...	11,483,318	12,690,152	5.45	4.93

In Massachusetts in 1890, according to this table, there were 355,280 occupied dwellings containing 479,790 families. The average number of persons to a dwelling was 6.30, and the average number of persons to a family, 4.67. We have seen that in the present Census the number of occupied dwellings becomes 397,633, and the number of families 547,385, while the average number of persons to each occupied dwelling house is 6.29, approximately the same as was shown to each occupied dwelling in the Census of 1890; the average number of persons to a family now being 4.57, as against 4.67, the figure shown in 1890. The average number of persons shown in the present Census to each occupied dwelling house exceeds the average number per dwelling found in any State in the Census of 1890 except in the States of New York and Rhode Island, where the averages were, respectively, 6.70 and 6.61. The average number of persons to a family in Massachusetts, as shown by the present Census, is exceeded by the average number of persons to a family shown by the Census of 1890 in the following States, the average in each case being annexed: Alabama, 5.27; Arkansas, 5.28; California, 4.92; Colorado, 4.89; Delaware, 4.87; District of Columbia, 5.24; Florida, 4.89; Georgia, 5.22; Idaho, 4.66; Illinois, 4.92; Indiana, 4.69; Iowa, 4.92; Kansas, 4.80; Kentucky, 5.24; Louisiana, 5.22; Maryland, 5.16; Michigan, 4.60; Minnesota, 5.25; Mississippi, 5.35; Missouri, 5.07; Montana, 4.81; Nebraska, 5.12; New Jersey, 4.69; New York, 4.59; North Carolina, 5.27; North Dakota, 4.75; Ohio, 4.68; Oregon, 4.92; Pennsylvania, 4.95; Rhode Island, 4.61; South Carolina, 5.16; South Dakota, 4.68; Tennessee, 5.29; Texas, 5.44; Utah, 5.36; Virginia, 5.44; Washington, 4.92; West Virginia, 5.43; Wisconsin, 5.03; and Wyoming, 5.03. That is to say, in 40 States, nearly the whole number, the average number of persons to a family, as shown by the Census of 1890, exceeds the average number of persons to a family shown in Massachusetts by the present Census. The average number of persons to a family in the United States as a whole was 4.93, which is also in excess of the average shown in Massachusetts.

The recapitulation on pages 780, 781 gives an interesting table of averages per areas, or, in other words, distributes the population according to the area of land surface, and also shows the number of acres and square feet to each person, and to each family and dwelling, for the State and for each county.

Referring to the first line of this recapitulation, we find that the State has an area of 8,040 square miles, this being the land surface only. The average number of persons to a square mile is 310.97, and the average number of families to a square mile 68.08. The average number of dwellings to each square mile, including both occupied and unoccupied dwelling houses, is 53.30. This apportionment of land area, allows, on the average, 2.06 acres to each person, 9.40 acres to each family, and 12.01 acres to each dwelling; or 89,650 square feet of land area to each person, 409,478 square feet to each family, and 523,093 square feet to each dwelling. In the county of Suffolk each person has, on the average, an allotment of 2,272 square feet, each family has 10,874 square feet, and each dwelling 17,501 square feet. These, of course, are the most limited areas found in the State. At the other extremity of the scale stands the county of Dukes, comprising the island of Martha's Vineyard and the islands within the town of Gosnold. Here each person has, on the average, 789,384 square feet, each family 2,561,-568 square feet, and each dwelling 1,448,229 square feet; or, on the average, 18.12 acres to each person, 58.81 acres to each family, and 33.25 acres to each dwelling. These figures are approximated in the counties of Franklin and Nantucket, while the most limited areas, except in the county of Suffolk, are found in the counties of Essex, Middlesex, and Bristol. If the comparison is based on the average number of square feet to each person, these three counties rank in the order named.

A comparison of areas for the State as shown by the Censuses of 1885 and 1895 is presented in the following table:

CLASSIFICATION.									1885	1895
Area* (square miles),	.	.	.	.	.	.	.	.	8,040	8,040
Persons to a square mile,	.	.	.	.	.	.	.	.	241.56	310.97
Families to a square mile,	.	.	.	.	.	.	.	.	52.79	68.08
Dwellings† to a square mile,	.	.	.	.	.	.	.	40.40	53.30
Acres to a person,	.	.	.	.	.	.	.	.	2.65	2.06
Acres to a family,	.	.	.	.	.	.	.	.	12.12	9.40
Acres to a dwelling,†	.	.	.	.	.	.	.	.	15.84	12.01
Square feet to a person,	.	.	.	.	.	.	.	.	115,410	89,650
Square feet to a family,	.	.	.	.	.	.	.	.	528,121	409,478
Square feet to a dwelling,†	.	.	.	.	.	.	.	690,034	523,093

* Land surface only.   † Includes both occupied and unoccupied dwelling houses.

The area of the State in square miles, including land surface only, is, of course, the same in 1895 as in 1885. The number of persons to a square mile in 1895 is 310.97, as against 241.56 in 1885. The average number of families to a square mile, which in 1885 was 52.79, has risen to 68.08. The number of dwellings to a square mile, including both occupied and unoccupied dwellings, has risen from 40.40 to 53.30. On the average, each person in the Commonwealth had an allotment of 2.65 acres in 1885, but in 1895 this has fallen to 2.06. The average number of acres to a family, which in 1885 was 12.12, has fallen to 9.40. The average number of acres to a dwelling has fallen from 15.84 to 12.01. On the average, each person in 1885 occupied 115,410 square feet, but under the increase in population, each person now has, on the average, only 89,650 square feet. The number of square feet to a family has fallen from 528,121 to 409,478, and the average number of square feet to each dwelling, from 690,034 to 523,093. This comparison shows quite clearly the effect of the increase of population upon a territory which is incapable of expansion, and while the comparisons which have been made in connection with previous tables indicate that undue concentration of the population is still confined to limited areas and to a few sections in certain cities and towns, it is, nevertheless, true that the area available to each person is, as a matter of averages, constantly growing smaller, and that the decrease, when measured at intervals of 10 years, is quite material.

NATIVE AND FOREIGN BORN.

NATIVE AND FOREIGN BORN.

COUNTIES, CITIES, TOWNS, AND SEX.	Native Born	Foreign Born	PERCENTAGES Native Born	PERCENTAGES Foreign Born	COUNTIES, CITIES, TOWNS, AND SEX.	Native Born	Foreign Born	PERCENTAGES Native Born	PERCENTAGES Foreign Born
BARNSTABLE.					**BERKSHIRE — Con.**				
Barnstable,	3,822	233	94.25	5.75	Alford,	259	21	92.50	7.50
Males,	1,841	103	45.40	2.54	Males,	139	13	49.65	4.64
Females,	1,981	130	48.85	3.21	Females,	120	8	42.85	2.86
Bourne,	1,486	94	94.05	5.95	Becket,	723	165	81.42	18.58
Males,	727	45	46.01	2.85	Males,	388	95	43.69	10.70
Females,	759	49	48.04	3.10	Females,	335	70	37.73	7.88
Brewster,	831	70	92.23	7.77	Cheshire,	975	201	82.91	17.09
Males,	406	31	45.06	3.44	Males,	487	112	41.41	9.53
Females,	425	39	47.17	4.33	Females,	488	89	41.50	7.56
Chatham,	1,764	45	97.51	2.49	Clarksburg,	801	298	79.39	20.61
Males,	878	20	48.53	1.11	Males,	397	105	39.35	10.40
Females,	886	25	48.98	1.38	Females,	404	193	40.04	10.21
Dennis,	2,436	109	95.72	4.28	Dalton,	2,659	551	82.83	17.17
Males,	1,115	49	43.81	1.93	Males,	1,284	222	40.00	6.92
Females,	1,321	60	51.91	2.35	Females,	1,375	329	42.83	10.25
Eastham,	462	14	97.06	2.94	Egremont,	787	49	94.14	5.86
Males,	230	4	48.32	0.84	Males,	382	24	45.69	2.87
Females,	232	10	48.74	2.10	Females,	405	25	48.45	2.99
Falmouth,	2,284	371	86.03	13.97	Florida,	347	78	81.65	18.35
Males,	1,111	172	41.85	6.47	Males,	172	51	40.47	12.00
Females,	1,173	199	44.18	7.50	Females,	175	27	41.18	6.35
Harwich,	2,370	162	93.60	6.40	Great Barrington,	3,910	884	81.56	18.44
Males,	1,181	72	46.64	2.85	Males,	1,902	430	39.67	8.97
Females,	1,189	90	46.96	3.55	Females,	2,008	454	41.89	9.47
Mashpee,	319	11	96.67	3.33	Hancock,	483	28	94.52	5.48
Males,	173	5	52.43	1.51	Males,	252	14	49.31	2.74
Females,	146	6	44.24	1.82	Females,	231	14	45.21	2.74
Orleans,	1,132	66	94.49	5.51	Hinsdale,	1,274	376	77.21	22.79
Males,	527	32	43.99	2.67	Males,	628	193	38.06	11.70
Females,	605	34	50.50	2.84	Females,	646	183	39.15	11.09
Provincetown,	3,228	1,327	70.87	29.13	Lanesborough,	738	110	87.03	12.97
Males,	1,529	686	33.57	15.06	Males,	374	60	44.10	7.08
Females,	1,699	641	37.30	14.07	Females,	364	50	42.93	5.89
Sandwich,	1,344	236	85.06	14.94	Lee,	3,224	842	79.29	20.71
Males,	632	102	40.00	6.46	Males,	1,528	445	37.58	10.94
Females,	712	134	45.06	8.48	Females,	1,696	397	41.71	9.77
Truro,	690	125	84.66	15.34	Lenox,	2,119	753	73.78	26.22
Males,	338	64	41.47	7.86	Males,	1,099	430	38.27	14.97
Females,	352	61	43.19	7.48	Females,	1,020	323	35.51	11.25
Wellfleet,	900	68	92.98	7.02	Monterey,	423	41	91.16	8.84
Males,	419	30	43.29	3.09	Males,	216	25	46.55	5.39
Females,	481	38	49.69	3.93	Females,	207	16	44.61	3.45
Yarmouth,	1,583	72	95.65	4.35	Mount Washington,	120	16	88.23	11.77
Males,	746	26	45.08	1.57	Males,	65	11	47.79	8.09
Females,	837	46	50.57	2.78	Females,	55	5	40.44	3.68
					New Ashford,	107	9	92.24	7.76
BERKSHIRE.					Males,	63	5	54.31	4.31
					Females,	44	4	37.93	3.45
Adams,	5,020	2,817	64.05	35.95	New Marlborough,	1,127	161	87.50	12.50
Males,	2,392	1,320	30.52	16.85	Males,	592	90	45.96	6.99
Females,	2,628	1,497	33.53	19.10	Females,	535	71	41.54	5.51

NATIVE AND FOREIGN BORN — Continued.

COUNTIES, CITIES, TOWNS, AND SEX	Native Born	Foreign Born	Native Born %	Foreign Born %
BERKSHIRE—Con.				
NORTH ADAMS, .	13,666	5,469	71.42	28.58
Males, . . .	6,565	2,785	34.31	14.55
Females, .	7,101	2,684	37.11	14.03
Otis, ...	500	18	96.52	3.48
Males, . .	283	6	54.63	1.16
Females, .	217	12	41.89	2.32
Peru, ...	269	36	88.20	11.80
Males, . .	127	19	41.64	6.23
Females, . .	142	17	46.56	5.57
PITTSFIELD, .	15,913	4,548	77.77	22.23
Males, . .	7,629	2,209	37.28	10.80
Females, .	8,284	2,339	40.49	11.43
Richmond, .	547	154	78.03	21.97
Males, . .	273	81	38.94	11.56
Females, .	274	73	39.09	10.41
Sandisfield, . .	741	61	92.39	7.61
Males, . . .	372	29	46.38	3.62
Females, .	369	32	46.01	3.99
Savoy, . . .	471	33	93.45	6.55
Males, . . .	235	21	46.62	4.17
Females, . .	236	12	46.83	2.38
Sheffield, . . .	1,703	194	89.77	10.23
Males, . .	844	100	44.49	5.27
Females, .	859	94	45.28	4.96
Stockbridge, . .	1,708	369	82.23	17.77
Males, . .	820	176	39.48	8.47
Females, .	888	193	42.75	9.30
Tyringham, . .	344	19	94.77	5.23
Males, . .	176	10	48.49	2.75
Females, .	168	9	46.28	2.48
Washington, . .	342	81	80.85	19.15
Males, . .	193	43	45.62	10.17
Females, .	149	38	35.23	8.98
West Stockbridge, .	1,030	227	81.94	18.06
Males, . .	495	113	39.38	8.99
Females, .	535	114	42.56	9.07
Williamstown, .	3,874	1,013	79.27	20.73
Males, . .	2,123	492	43.44	10.07
Females, .	1,751	521	35.83	10.66
Windsor, . .	504	52	90.65	9.35
Males, . .	274	27	49.28	4.86
Females, .	230	25	41.37	4.49
BRISTOL.				
Acushnet, . .	995	120	89.24	10.76
Males, . .	493	75	44.22	6.72
Females, .	502	45	45.02	4.04
Attleborough, .	6,213	2,075	74.96	25.04
Males, . .	3,054	975	36.84	11.77
Females, .	3,159	1,100	38.12	13.27
Berkley, . .	847	108	88.69	11.31
Males, . .	418	64	43.77	6.70
Females, .	429	44	44.92	4.61
Dartmouth, .	2,623	484	84.42	15.58
Males, . .	1,321	278	42.51	8.95
Females, .	1,302	206	41.91	6.63

COUNTIES, CITIES, TOWNS, AND SEX	Native Born	Foreign Born	Native Born %	Foreign Born %
BRISTOL—Con.				
Dighton, . . .	1,495	302	83.20	16.80
Males, . . .	749	167	41.68	9.29
Females, . .	746	135	41.52	7.51
Easton, . . .	3,338	1,114	74.98	25.02
Males, . .	1,702	584	38.23	13.12
Females, .	1,636	530	36.75	11.90
Fairhaven, .	2,859	479	85.65	14.35
Males, . .	1,323	231	39.63	6.92
Females, .	1,536	248	46.02	7.43
FALL RIVER, .	44,683	44,520	50.09	49.91
Males, . . .	21,803	20,901	24.44	23.43
Females, .	22,880	23,619	25.65	26.48
Freetown, . .	1,222	183	86.98	13.02
Males, . . .	608	117	43.28	8.32
Females, .	614	66	43.70	4.70
Mansfield, . .	3,157	565	84.82	15.18
Males, . .	1,528	265	41.05	7.12
Females, .	1,629	300	43.77	8.06
NEW BEDFORD, .	32,597	22,714	58.89	41.11
Males, . .	15,364	10,794	27.81	19.53
Females, .	17,173	11,920	31.08	21.58
North Attleborough,	5,024	1,552	76.40	23.60
Males, . . .	2,436	709	37.05	10.78
Females, .	2,588	843	39.35	12.82
Norton, . .	1,396	218	86.49	13.51
Males, . . .	655	105	40.58	6.51
Females, .	741	113	45.91	7.00
Raynham, . .	1,312	206	86.43	13.57
Males, . .	639	112	42.09	7.38
Females, .	673	94	44.34	6.19
Rehoboth, . .	1,586	224	87.62	12.38
Males, . . .	818	140	45.19	7.74
Females, .	768	84	42.43	4.64
Seekonk, . .	1,181	284	80.61	19.39
Males, . .	607	186	41.43	12.70
Females, .	574	98	39.18	6.69
Somerset, . .	1,574	409	79.37	20.63
Males, . .	798	242	40.24	12.21
Females, .	776	167	39.13	8.42
Swansea, . .	1,349	278	82.91	17.09
Males, . .	672	158	41.30	9.71
Females, .	677	120	41.61	7.38
TAUNTON, . .	19,340	7,775	71.33	28.67
Males, . .	9,532	3,615	35.16	13.33
Females, .	9,808	4,160	36.17	15.34
Westport, . .	2,189	489	81.74	18.26
Males, . .	1,086	258	40.55	9.64
Females, .	1,103	231	41.19	8.62
DUKES.				
Chilmark, . .	302	2	99.34	0.66
Males, . .	150	1	49.34	0.33
Females, .	152	1	50.00	0.33
Cottage City, .	808	230	77.84	22.16
Males, . .	389	119	37.47	11.47
Females, .	419	111	40.37	10.69

NATIVE AND FOREIGN BORN — Continued.

COUNTIES, CITIES, TOWNS, AND SEX.	Native Born	Foreign Born	PERCENTAGES Native Born	Foreign Born	COUNTIES, CITIES, TOWNS, AND SEX.	Native Born	Foreign Born	PERCENTAGES Native Born	Foreign Born
DUKES — Con.					ESSEX — Con.				
Edgartown,	1,008	117	89.60	10.40	LAWRENCE,	27,862	24,302	53.41	46.59
Males,	470	57	41.78	5.06	Males,	13,614	11,493	26.10	22.03
Females,	538	60	47.82	5.34	Females,	14,248	12,809	27.31	24.56
Gay Head,	164	5	97.04	2.96	LYNN,	46,060	16,294	73.87	26.13
Males,	87	3	51.48	1.77	Males,	22,595	7,578	36.24	12.15
Females,	77	2	45.56	1.19	Females,	23,465	8,716	37.63	13.98
Gosnold,	120	20	85.71	14.29	Lynnfield,	716	102	87.53	12.47
Males,	71	17	50.71	12.15	Males,	355	53	43.40	6.48
Females,	49	3	35.00	2.14	Females,	361	49	44.13	5.99
Tisbury,	916	86	91.42	8.58	Manchester,	1,406	470	74.94	25.06
Males,	433	44	43.21	4.39	Males,	673	220	35.87	11.73
Females,	483	42	48.21	4.19	Females,	733	250	39.07	13.33
West Tisbury,	421	39	91.52	8.48	Marblehead,	6,767	904	88.22	11.78
Males,	196	20	42.61	4.35	Males,	3,289	360	42.88	4.69
Females,	225	19	48.91	4.13	Females,	3,478	544	45.34	7.09
					Merrimac,	1,977	324	85.92	14.08
ESSEX.					Males,	940	171	40.85	7.43
					Females,	1,037	153	45.07	6.65
Amesbury,	7,452	2,534	74.62	25.38	Methuen,	3,733	1,957	65.61	34.39
Males,	3,542	1,258	35.47	12.40	Males,	1,832	928	32.20	16.31
Females,	3,910	1,286	39.15	12.98	Females,	1,901	1,029	33.41	18.08
Andover,	4,454	1,691	72.48	27.52	Middleton,	706	132	84.25	15.75
Males,	2,179	734	35.46	11.94	Males,	360	68	42.96	8.11
Females,	2,275	957	37.02	15.58	Females,	346	64	41.29	7.64
BEVERLY,	9,636	2,170	81.62	18.38	Nahant,	597	268	69.02	30.98
Males,	4,737	991	40.12	8.40	Males,	308	117	35.61	13.52
Females,	4,899	1,179	41.50	9.98	Females,	289	151	33.41	17.46
Boxford,	647	80	89.00	11.00	Newbury,	1,307	182	87.78	12.22
Males,	318	41	43.74	5.64	Males,	647	113	43.45	7.59
Females,	329	39	45.26	5.36	Females,	660	69	44.33	4.63
Bradford,	3,995	741	84.35	15.65	NEWBURYPORT,	11,593	2,959	79.66	20.34
Males,	1,882	340	39.74	7.18	Males,	5,379	1,237	36.96	8.50
Females,	2,113	401	44.61	8.47	Females,	6,214	1,722	42.70	11.84
Danvers,	6,315	1,896	77.19	22.81	North Andover,	2,526	1,043	70.78	29.22
Males,	3,074	884	37.57	10.81	Males,	1,254	511	35.14	14.31
Females,	3,241	982	39.62	12.00	Females,	1,272	532	35.64	14.91
Essex,	1,384	193	87.84	12.16	Peabody,	7,876	2,661	74.96	25.04
Males,	705	104	44.43	6.55	Males,	3,929	1,333	37.39	12.69
Females,	689	89	43.41	5.61	Females,	3,947	1,328	37.57	12.35
Georgetown,	1,864	186	90.93	9.07	Rockport,	3,261	2,028	61.66	38.34
Males,	898	101	43.81	4.92	Males,	1,680	1,286	31.77	24.31
Females,	966	85	47.32	4.15	Females,	1,581	742	29.89	14.03
GLOUCESTER,	16,880	11,354	59.83	40.17	Rowley,	1,154	118	90.72	9.28
Males,	8,657	7,680	30.69	26.94	Males,	599	57	47.09	4.48
Females,	8,223	3,731	29.14	13.23	Females,	555	61	43.63	4.80
Groveland,	1,912	421	81.95	18.05	SALEM,	23,708	10,765	68.77	31.23
Males,	926	192	39.69	8.23	Males,	11,329	4,941	32.87	14.33
Females,	986	229	42.26	9.82	Females,	12,379	5,824	35.90	16.90
Hamilton,	1,068	288	78.76	21.24	Salisbury,	1,202	98	92.46	7.54
Males,	521	164	38.42	12.10	Males,	594	48	45.60	3.69
Females,	547	124	40.34	9.14	Females,	608	50	46.77	3.85
HAVERHILL,	22,831	7,378	75.58	24.42	Saugus,	3,657	840	81.32	18.68
Males,	11,038	3,497	36.54	11.57	Males,	1,791	398	39.83	8.85
Females,	11,793	3,881	39.04	12.85	Females,	1,866	442	41.49	9.83
Ipswich,	3,432	1,288	72.71	27.29	Swampscott,	2,606	653	79.96	20.04
Males,	1,647	531	34.89	11.25	Males,	1,270	264	38.97	8.10
Females,	1,785	757	37.82	16.04	Females,	1,336	389	40.99	11.94

NATIVE AND FOREIGN BORN — Continued.

COUNTIES, CITIES, TOWNS, AND SEX.	Native Born	Foreign Born	Percentages Native Born	Percentages Foreign Born
ESSEX — Con.				
Topsfield,	929	104	89.94	10.06
Males,	464	52	44.92	5.03
Females,	465	52	45.02	5.03
Wenham,	797	89	89.95	10.05
Males,	391	40	44.13	4.52
Females,	406	49	45.82	5.53
West Newbury,	1,375	268	83.69	16.31
Males,	680	131	41.39	7.97
Females,	695	137	42.30	8.34
FRANKLIN.				
Ashfield,	953	60	94.08	5.92
Males,	484	39	47.78	3.85
Females,	469	21	46.30	2.07
Bernardston,	725	53	93.19	6.81
Males,	363	26	46.66	3.34
Females,	362	27	46.53	3.47
Buckland,	1,396	352	77.26	22.74
Males,	610	175	39.41	11.30
Females,	586	177	37.85	11.44
Charlemont,	986	55	94.72	5.28
Males,	493	33	47.36	3.17
Females,	493	22	47.36	2.11
Colrain,	1,367	243	84.91	15.09
Males,	702	149	43.60	9.26
Females,	665	94	41.31	5.83
Conway,	1,132	172	86.81	13.19
Males,	567	90	43.48	6.90
Females,	565	82	43.33	6.29
Deerfield,	2,396	611	79.68	20.32
Males,	1,209	341	40.21	11.34
Females,	1,187	270	39.47	8.98
Erving,	815	149	84.54	15.46
Males,	409	81	42.43	8.40
Females,	406	68	42.11	7.06
Gill,	934	148	86.32	13.68
Males,	584	115	53.97	10.63
Females,	350	33	32.35	3.05
Greenfield,	5,152	1,077	82.71	17.29
Males,	2,480	507	39.81	8.14
Females,	2,672	570	42.90	9.15
Hawley,	451	17	96.37	3.63
Males,	241	9	51.50	1.92
Females,	210	8	44.87	1.71
Heath,	454	22	95.38	4.62
Males,	233	17	48.95	3.57
Females,	221	5	46.43	1.05
Leverett,	723	21	97.18	2.82
Males,	364	15	48.95	2.01
Females,	359	6	48.25	0.81
Leyden,	336	27	92.56	7.44
Males,	171	14	47.10	3.86
Females,	165	13	45.46	3.58
Monroe,	229	69	76.85	23.15
Males,	117	59	39.26	19.80
Females,	112	10	37.59	3.35

COUNTIES, CITIES, TOWNS, AND SEX.	Native Born	Foreign Born	Percentages Native Born	Percentages Foreign Born
FRANKLIN — Con.				
Montague,	4,125	1,933	68.09	31.91
Males,	2,057	1,019	33.96	16.82
Females,	2,068	914	34.13	15.09
New Salem,	783	86	90.11	9.89
Males,	390	48	44.88	5.52
Females,	393	38	45.23	4.37
Northfield,	1,651	200	89.20	10.80
Males,	672	82	36.30	4.43
Females,	979	118	52.90	6.37
Orange,	4,597	764	85.75	14.25
Males,	2,271	419	42.36	7.82
Females,	2,326	345	43.39	6.43
Rowe,	383	115	76.91	23.09
Males,	206	77	41.37	15.46
Females,	177	38	35.54	7.63
Shelburne,	1,408	152	90.26	9.74
Males,	669	81	42.89	5.19
Females,	739	71	47.37	4.55
Shutesbury,	413	31	93.02	6.98
Males,	204	14	45.95	3.15
Females,	209	17	47.07	3.83
Sunderland,	578	118	83.05	16.95
Males,	305	76	43.82	10.92
Females,	273	42	39.23	6.03
Warwick,	513	86	85.64	14.36
Males,	263	58	43.91	9.68
Females,	250	28	41.73	4.68
Wendell,	451	78	85.26	14.74
Males,	245	48	46.32	9.07
Females,	206	30	38.94	5.67
Whately,	647	108	85.70	14.30
Males,	326	66	43.18	8.74
Females,	321	42	42.52	5.56
HAMPDEN.				
Agawam,	1,908	500	79.24	20.76
Males,	984	253	40.87	10.50
Females,	924	247	38.37	10.26
Blandford,	828	21	97.53	2.47
Males,	426*	11	50.18	1.29
Females,	402	10	47.35	1.18
Brimfield,	857	105	89.08	10.92
Males,	436	62	45.32	6.45
Females,	421	43	43.76	4.47
Chester,	1,272	157	89.01	10.99
Males,	616	84	45.11	5.88
Females,	656	73	45.90	5.11
CHICOPEE,	9,359	7,061	57.00	43.00
Males,	4,565	3,530	27.80	21.50
Females,	4,794	3,531	29.20	21.50
East Longmeadow,	976	615	61.35	38.65
Males,	479	384	30.11	24.13
Females,	497	231	31.24	14.52
Granville,	902	103	89.75	10.25
Males,	465	57	46.27	5.67
Females,	437	46	43.48	4.58

NATIVE AND FOREIGN BORN — Continued.

COUNTIES, CITIES, TOWNS, AND SEX.	Native Born	Foreign Born	PERCENTAGES Native Born	PERCENTAGES Foreign Born
HAMPDEN — Con.				
Hampden, . . .	595	148	80.08	19.92
Males, . . .	298	76	40.11	10.23
Females, . . .	297	72	39.97	9.69
Holland, . . .	180	19	90.45	9.55
Males, . . .	95	12	47.74	6.03
Females, . . .	85	7	42.71	3.52
HOLYOKE, . . .	22,247	18,075	55.17	44.83
Males, . . .	10,780	8,418	26.73	20.88
Females, . . .	11,467	9,657	28.44	23.95
Longmeadow, . .	511	109	82.42	17.58
Males, . . .	238	52	38.39	8.38
Females, . . .	273	57	44.03	9.20
Ludlow, . . .	1,544	1,018	60.27	39.73
Males, . . .	782	532	30.53	20.76
Females, . . .	762	486	29.74	18.97
Monson, . . .	2,998	748	80.03	19.97
Males, . . .	1,463	399	39.06	10.65
Females, . . .	1,535	349	40.97	9.32
Montgomery, . .	260	15	94.55	5.45
Males, . . .	141	10	51.28	3.63
Females, . . .	119	5	43.27	1.82
Palmer, . . .	4,533	2,325	66.10	33.90
Males, . . .	2,171	1,174	31.66	17.12
Females, . . .	2,362	1,151	34.44	16.78
Russell, . . .	683	163	80.73	19.27
Males, . . .	347	93	41.02	10.99
Females, . . .	336	70	39.71	8.28
Southwick, . . .	859	102	89.39	10.61
Males, . . .	449	61	46.72	6.35
Females, . . .	410	41	42.67	4.26
SPRINGFIELD, . .	38,828	12,694	75.36	24.64
Males, . . .	18,644	6,007	36.19	11.66
Females, . . .	20,184	6,687	39.17	12.98
Tolland, . . .	262	47	84.79	15.21
Males, . . .	145	26	46.93	8.41
Females, . . .	117	21	37.86	6.80
Wales, . . .	652	131	83.27	16.73
Males, . . .	333	72	42.53	9.19
Females, . . .	319	59	40.74	7.54
Westfield, . . .	8,692	1,971	81.52	18.48
Males, . . .	4,246	929	39.82	8.71
Females, . . .	4,446	1,042	41.70	9.77
West Springfield, .	4,740	1,385	77.39	22.61
Males, . . .	2,324	627	37.94	10.24
Females, . . .	2,416	758	39.45	12.37
Wilbraham, . .	1,345	395	77.30	22.70
Males, . . .	661	176	37.99	10.11
Females, . . .	684	219	39.31	12.59
HAMPSHIRE.				
Amherst, . . .	4,275	510	89.34	10.66
Males, . . .	2,191	236	45.79	4.93
Females, . . .	2,084	274	43.55	5.73
Belchertown, . .	1,860	301	86.07	13.93
Males, . . .	961	154	44.47	7.13
Females, . . .	899	147	41.60	6.80

COUNTIES, CITIES, TOWNS, AND SEX.	Native Born	Foreign Born	PERCENTAGES Native Born	PERCENTAGES Foreign Born
HAMPSHIRE — Con.				
Chesterfield, . .	568	21	96.43	3.57
Males, . . .	289	12	49.06	2.04
Females, . . .	279	9	47.37	1.53
Cummington, . .	717	33	95.60	4.40
Males, . . .	346	21	46.13	2.80
Females, . . .	371	12	49.47	1.60
Easthampton, . .	3,363	1,427	70.21	29.79
Males, . . .	1,579	663	32.97	13.84
Females, . . .	1,784	764	37.24	15.95
Enfield, . . .	776	214	78.38	21.62
Males, . . .	405	107	40.91	10.81
Females, . . .	371	107	37.47	10.81
Goshen, . . .	283	21	93.09	6.91
Males, . . .	148	12	48.68	3.95
Females, . . .	135	9	44.41	2.96
Granby, . . .	607	141	81.15	18.85
Males, . . .	304	90	40.64	12.03
Females, . . .	303	51	40.51	6.82
Greenwich, . .	460	21	95.63	4.37
Males, . . .	232	11	48.23	2.29
Females, . . .	228	10	47.40	2.08
Hadley, . . .	1,354	350	79.46	20.54
Males, . . .	686	208	40.26	12.20
Females, . . .	668	142	39.20	8.34
Hatfield, . . .	992	270	78.61	21.39
Males, . . .	513	156	40.65	12.36
Females, . . .	479	114	37.96	9.03
Huntington, . .	1,221	229	84.21	15.79
Males, . . .	603	119	41.59	8.20
Females, . . .	618	110	42.62	7.59
Middlefield, . .	337	49	87.31	12.69
Males, . . .	170	27	44.04	7.00
Females, . . .	167	22	43.27	5.69
NORTHAMPTON, .	12,564	4,182	75.02	24.98
Males, . . .	5,465	1,969	32.63	11.76
Females, . . .	7,099	2,213	42.39	13.22
Pelham, . . .	458	28	94.24	5.76
Males, . . .	235	11	48.36	2.26
Females, . . .	223	17	45.88	3.50
Plainfield, . . .	440	10	97.78	2.22
Males, . . .	225	6	50.00	1.33
Females, . . .	215	4	47.78	0.89
Prescott, . . .	386	15	96.26	3.74
Males, . . .	201	7	50.12	1.75
Females, . . .	185	8	46.14	1.99
Southampton, . .	915	139	86.81	13.19
Males, . . .	453	84	42.98	7.97
Females, . . .	462	55	43.83	5.22
South Hadley, . .	3,122	1,321	79.27	29.73
Males, . . .	1,385	669	31.17	15.06
Females, . . .	1,737	652	39.10	14.67
Ware, . . .	4,460	3,191	58.29	41.71
Males, . . .	2,107	1,469	27.54	19.20
Females, . . .	2,353	1,722	30.75	22.51
Westhampton, . .	418	58	87.82	12.18
Males, . . .	206	35	43.28	7.35
Females, . . .	212	23	44.54	4.83

NATIVE AND FOREIGN BORN — Continued.

COUNTIES, CITIES, TOWNS, AND SEX.	Native Born	Foreign Born	PERCENTAGES Native Born	PERCENTAGES Foreign Born
HAMPSHIRE—Con.				
Williamsburg, . .	1,594	361	81.53	18.47
Males, . . .	783	167	40.05	8.54
Females, . .	811	194	41.48	9.93
Worthington, . .	626	22	96.60	3.40
Males, . . .	327	14	50.46	2.16
Females, . .	299	8	46.14	1.24
MIDDLESEX.				
Acton, . . .	1,620	358	81.90	18.10
Males, . . .	787	193	39.78	9.76
Females, . .	833	165	42.12	8.34
Arlington, . .	4,611	1,904	70.77	29.23
Males, . . .	2,163	904	33.20	15.88
Females, . .	2,448	1,000	37.57	15.35
Ashby, . . .	745	59	92.66	7.34
Males, . . .	386	27	48.01	3.36
Females, . .	359	32	44.65	3.98
Ashland, . .	1,663	427	79.57	20.43
Males, . . .	802	213	38.37	10.19
Females, . .	861	214	41.20	10.24
Ayer, . . .	1,719	382	81.82	18.18
Males, . . .	834	184	39.70	8.75
Females, . .	885	198	42.12	9.43
Bedford, . .	856	313	73.22	26.78
Males, . . .	451	172	38.57	14.72
Females, . .	405	141	34.65	12.06
Belmont, . .	1,796	1,047	63.17	36.83
Males, . . .	884	635	31.09	22.34
Females, . .	912	412	32.08	14.49
Billerica, . .	1,819	758	70.59	29.41
Males, . . .	933	368	36.21	14.28
Females, . .	886	390	34.38	15.13
Boxborough, . .	260	47	84.69	15.31
Males, . . .	142	30	46.26	9.77
Females, . .	118	17	38.43	5.54
Burlington, . .	456	118	79.44	20.56
Males, . . .	246	70	42.85	12.20
Females, . .	210	48	36.59	8.36
CAMBRIDGE, . .	53,388	28,255	65.39	34.61
Males, . . .	26,525	13,306	32.49	16.30
Females, . .	26,863	14,949	32.90	18.31
Carlisle, . .	406	86	82.52	17.48
Males, . . .	219	49	44.51	9.96
Females, . .	187	37	38.01	7.52
Chelmsford, . .	2,374	788	75.08	24.92
Males, . . .	1,206	405	38.14	12.87
Females, . .	1,168	383	36.94	12.11
Concord, . .	3,839	1,336	74.18	25.82
Males, . . .	2,371	786	45.81	15.19
Females, . .	1,468	550	28.37	10.63
Dracut, . .	1,607	836	65.78	34.22
Males, . . .	860	465	35.20	19.04
Females, . .	747	371	30.58	15.18
Dunstable, . .	359	41	89.75	10.25
Males, . . .	183	24	45.75	6.00
Females, . .	176	17	44.00	4.25

COUNTIES, CITIES, TOWNS, AND SEX.	Native Born	Foreign Born	PERCENTAGES Native Born	PERCENTAGES Foreign Born
MIDDLESEX - Con.				
EVERETT, . . .	13,258	5,235	71.27	28.73
Males, . . .	6,466	2,591	34.81	13.95
Females, . .	6,772	2,744	36.46	14.78
Framingham, . .	7,383	2,129	77.62	22.38
Males, . . .	3,581	980	37.65	10.39
Females, . .	3,802	1,140	39.97	11.99
Groton, . . .	1,847	345	84.26	15.74
Males, . . .	929	149	42.38	6.80
Females, . .	918	196	41.88	8.94
Holliston, . .	2,234	484	82.19	17.81
Males, . . .	1,073	236	39.48	8.68
Females, . .	1,161	248	42.71	9.13
Hopkinton, . .	2,418	566	81.03	18.97
Males, . . .	1,195	274	40.05	9.18
Females, . .	1,223	292	40.98	9.79
Hudson, . . .	4,127	1,181	77.75	22.25
Males, . . .	1,963	570	36.98	10.74
Females, . .	2,164	611	40.77	11.51
Lexington, . .	2,561	937	73.22	26.78
Males, . . .	1,220	472	34.88	13.49
Females, . .	1,341	465	38.34	13.29
Lincoln, . . .	705	406	63.46	36.54
Males, . . .	368	258	33.13	23.22
Females, . .	337	148	30.33	13.32
Littleton, . .	891	245	78.43	21.57
Males, . . .	437	132	38.47	11.62
Females, . .	454	113	39.96	9.95
LOWELL, . . .	47,023	37,344	55.74	44.26
Males, . . .	22,152	16,779	26.26	19.88
Females, . .	24,871	20,565	29.48	24.38
MALDEN, . . .	20,719	8,989	69.74	30.26
Males, . . .	9,864	4,059	33.21	13.66
Females, . .	10,855	4,930	36.53	16.60
MARLBOROUGH, . .	11,151	3,826	74.45	25.55
Males, . . .	5,524	1,945	36.88	12.99
Females, . .	5,627	1,881	37.57	12.56
Maynard, . . .	1,903	1,187	61.59	38.41
Males, . . .	921	599	29.81	19.38
Females, . .	982	588	31.78	19.03
MEDFORD, . . .	10,852	3,622	74.98	25.02
Males, . . .	5,259	1,784	36.34	12.32
Females, . .	5,593	1,838	38.64	12.70
Melrose, . . .	8,955	3,010	74.84	25.16
Males, . . .	4,214	1,334	35.22	11.15
Females, . .	4,741	1,676	39.62	14.01
Natick, . . .	7,086	1,728	80.39	19.61
Males, . . .	3,395	839	38.52	9.52
Females, . .	3,691	889	41.87	10.09
NEWTON, . . .	18,871	8,719	68.40	31.60
Males, . . .	8,715	3,640	31.59	13.19
Females, . .	10,156	5,079	36.81	18.41
North Reading, . .	737	98	88.26	11.74
Males, . . .	363	59	43.47	7.07
Females, . .	374	39	44.79	4.67
Pepperell, . .	2,691	630	81.03	18.97
Males, . . .	1,337	313	40.26	9.42
Females, . .	1,354	317	40.77	9.55

NATIVE AND FOREIGN BORN — Continued.

COUNTIES, CITIES, TOWNS, AND SEX.	Native Born	Foreign Born	Percentages Native Born	Percentages Foreign Born
MIDDLESEX – Con.				
Reading,	3,799	918	80.54	19.46
Males,	1,811	424	38.39	8.99
Females,	1,988	494	42.15	10.47
Sherborn,	1,045	401	72.27	27.73
Males,	440	144	30.43	9.96
Females,	605	257	41.84	17.77
Shirley,	1,042	357	74.48	25.52
Males,	488	166	34.88	11.87
Females,	554	191	39.60	13.65
SOMERVILLE,	36,989	15,211	70.86	29.14
Males,	17,944	6,973	34.37	13.56
Females,	19,045	8,238	36.49	15.78
Stoneham,	5,010	1,274	79.73	20.27
Males,	2,428	642	38.64	10.21
Females,	2,582	632	41.09	10.06
Stow,	719	204	78.15	21.85
Males,	370	103	40.21	11.20
Females,	349	98	37.94	10.65
Sudbury,	925	216	81.07	18.93
Males,	470	133	41.19	11.66
Females,	455	83	39.88	7.27
Tewksbury,	1,866	1,513	55.22	44.78
Males,	905	748	26.78	22.14
Females,	961	765	28.44	22.64
Townsend,	1,600	180	89.89	10.11
Males,	781	99	43.88	5.56
Females,	819	81	46.01	4.55
Tyngsborough,	516	119	81.26	18.74
Males,	257	67	40.47	10.55
Females,	259	52	40.79	8.19
Wakefield,	5,999	2,305	72.24	27.76
Males,	2,874	1,088	54.61	13.10
Females,	3,125	1,217	37.63	14.66
WALTHAM,	14,565	6,071	70.92	29.08
Males,	6,869	2,769	32.90	13.27
Females,	7,836	3,302	38.02	15.81
Watertown,	5,436	2,352	69.80	30.21
Males,	2,628	1,112	33.74	14.28
Females,	2,808	1,240	36.06	15.92
Wayland,	1,633	393	80.60	19.40
Males,	832	194	41.06	9.58
Females,	801	199	39.54	9.82
Westford,	1,598	820	66.09	33.91
Males,	821	402	33.95	16.63
Females,	777	418	32.14	17.28
Weston,	1,274	436	74.50	25.50
Males,	662	215	38.72	12.57
Females,	612	221	35.78	12.93
Wilmington,	1,110	310	78.17	21.83
Males,	553	162	38.94	11.41
Females,	557	148	39.23	10.42
Winchester,	4,321	1,829	70.26	29.74
Males,	2,090	838	33.98	13.63
Females,	2,231	991	36.28	16.11
WOBURN,	9,963	4,215	70.27	29.73
Males,	4,853	2,147	34.23	15.14
Females,	5,110	2,068	36.04	14.59

COUNTIES, CITIES, TOWNS, AND SEX.	Native Born	Foreign Born	Percentages Native Born	Percentages Foreign Born
NANTUCKET.				
Nantucket,	2,766	250	91.71	8.29
Males,	1,220	95	40.45	3.15
Females,	1,546	155	51.26	5.14
NORFOLK.				
Avon,	1,392	234	85.61	14.39
Males,	708	110	43.54	6.77
Females,	684	124	42.07	7.62
Bellingham,	1,179	302	79.61	20.39
Males,	567	154	38.28	10.40
Females,	612	148	41.33	9.99
Braintree,	4,111	1,200	77.41	22.59
Males,	2,006	654	37.77	12.31
Females,	2,105	546	39.64	10.28
Brookline,	10,120	5,744	64.46	35.54
Males,	4,780	2,046	29.57	12.66
Females,	5,640	3,698	34.89	22.88
Canton,	3,442	1,194	74.24	25.76
Males,	1,650	557	35.59	12.02
Females,	1,792	637	38.65	13.74
Cohasset,	1,970	504	79.65	20.57
Males,	947	204	38.28	8.12
Females,	1,023	300	41.35	12.25
Dedham,	5,273	1,968	73.12	26.88
Males,	2,600	876	36.05	12.15
Females,	2,673	1,062	37.07	14.73
Dover,	567	161	75.90	24.10
Males,	264	81	39.52	12.13
Females,	243	80	36.38	11.97
Foxborough,	2,707	512	84.09	15.91
Males,	1,299	243	40.35	7.55
Females,	1,408	269	43.74	8.36
Franklin,	3,952	1,184	76.95	23.05
Males,	1,870	589	36.41	11.47
Females,	2,082	595	40.54	11.58
Holbrook,	2,007	291	87.34	12.66
Males,	989	138	43.04	6.00
Females,	1,018	153	44.30	6.66
Hyde Park,	8,476	3,350	71.67	28.33
Males,	4,186	1,574	35.40	13.31
Females,	4,290	1,776	36.27	15.02
Medfield,	1,506	366	80.45	19.55
Males,	677	206	36.17	11.00
Females,	829	160	44.28	8.55
Medway,	2,415	498	82.91	17.09
Males,	1,206	232	41.40	7.96
Females,	1,209	266	41.51	9.13
Millis,	786	220	78.13	21.87
Males,	376	108	37.37	10.74
Females,	410	112	40.76	11.13
Milton,	3,720	1,798	67.42	32.58
Males,	1,815	747	32.89	13.54
Females,	1,905	1,051	34.53	19.04
Needham,	2,372	1,139	67.56	32.44
Males,	1,187	562	33.81	16.00
Females,	1,185	577	33.75	16.44

NATIVE AND FOREIGN BORN — Continued.

COUNTIES, CITIES, TOWNS, AND SEX.	Native Born	Foreign Born	PERCENTAGES Native Born	PERCENTAGES Foreign Born	COUNTIES, CITIES, TOWNS, AND SEX.	Native Born	Foreign Born	PERCENTAGES Native Born	PERCENTAGES Foreign Born
NORFOLK — Con.					**PLYMOUTH — Con.**				
Norfolk, . . .	655	227	74.26	25.74	Hanson, . .	1,244	136	90.14	9.86
Males, .	349	122	59.57	13.83	Males, . .	629	79	45.57	5.73
Females, . .	306	105	34.69	11.91	Females, . .	615	57	44.57	4.13
Norwood, . .	3,221	1,353	70.42	29.58	Hingham, . .	3,893	926	80.78	19.22
Males, . .	1,664	773	36.38	16.90	Males, . .	1,861	438	38.62	9.09
Females, . .	1,557	580	34.04	12.68	Females, . .	2,032	488	42.16	10.13
QUINCY, . .	13,582	7,130	65.58	34.42	Hull, . . .	786	258	75.29	24.71
Males, . .	6,828	3,780	32.97	18.25	Males, . .	418	118	40.04	11.30
Females, . .	6,754	3,350	32.61	16.17	Females, . .	368	140	35.25	13.41
Randolph, . .	3,054	640	82.67	17.33	Kingston, . .	1,467	279	84.02	15.98
Males, . .	1,510	315	40.87	8.53	Males, . .	717	130	41.06	7.45
Females, . .	1,544	325	41.80	8.80	Females, . .	750	149	42.96	8.53
Sharon, . .	1,349	368	78.57	21.43	Lakeville, . .	799	71	91.84	8.16
Males, . .	649	190	37.80	11.06	Males, . .	393	46	45.17	5.29
Females, . .	700	178	40.77	10.37	Females, . .	406	25	46.67	2.87
Stoughton, . .	4,197	1,075	79.61	20.39	Marion, . .	728	31	95.92	4.08
Males, . .	2,042	528	38.73	10.02	Males, . .	314	14	41.37	1.84
Females, . .	2,155	547	40.88	10.37	Females, . .	414	17	54.55	2.24
Walpole, . .	2,305	689	76.99	23.01	Marshfield, . .	1,587	173	90.17	9.83
Males, . .	1,129	371	37.71	12.39	Males, . .	764	86	43.41	4.89
Females, . .	1,176	318	39.28	10.62	Females, . .	823	87	46.76	4.94
Wellesley, . .	3,178	1,051	75.15	24.85	Mattapoisett, . .	958	74	92.83	7.17
Males, . .	1,048	422	24.78	9.98	Males, . .	449	41	43.51	3.97
Females, . .	2,130	629	50.37	14.87	Females, . .	509	33	49.32	3.20
Weymouth, . .	9,392	1,899	83.18	16.82	Middleborough, . .	5,841	848	87.32	12.68
Males, . .	4,597	995	40.72	8.81	Males, . .	2,781	424	41.57	6.34
Females, . .	4,795	904	42.46	8.01	Females, . .	3,060	424	45.75	6.34
Wrentham, . .	2,218	366	85.84	14.16	Norwell, . .	1,412	128	91.69	8.31
Males, . .	1,080	183	41.80	7.08	Males, . .	717	54	46.56	3.50
Females, . .	1,138	183	44.04	7.08	Females, . .	695	74	45.13	4.81
					Pembroke, . .	1,095	128	89.53	10.47
PLYMOUTH.					Males, . .	565	69	46.20	5.64
					Females, . .	530	59	43.33	4.83
Abington, . .	3,661	546	87.02	12.98	Plymouth, . .	6,409	1,548	80.54	19.46
Males, . .	1,787	253	42.48	6.01	Males, . .	3,113	750	39.12	9.43
Females, . .	1,874	293	44.54	6.97	Females, . .	3,296	798	41.42	10.03
Bridgewater, . .	3,523	1,163	75.18	24.82	Plympton, . .	483	66	87.98	12.02
Males, . .	1,895	827	40.44	17.65	Males, . .	237	31	43.17	5.65
Females, . .	1,628	336	34.74	7.17	Females, . .	246	35	44.81	6.37
BROCKTON, . .	25,138	8,027	75.80	24.20	Rochester, . .	928	93	90.89	9.11
Males, . .	12,577	3,982	37.92	12.01	Males, . .	478	57	46.82	5.58
Females, . .	12,561	4,045	37.88	12.19	Females, . .	450	36	44.07	3.53
Carver, . .	878	138	86.42	13.58	Rockland, . .	4,529	994	82.00	18.00
Males, . .	451	95	44.39	9.35	Males, . .	2,254	503	40.81	9.11
Females, . .	427	43	42.03	4.23	Females, . .	2,275	491	41.19	8.89
Duxbury, . .	1,751	215	89.06	10.94	Scituate, . .	1,958	288	87.18	12.82
Males, . .	844	101	42.93	5.14	Males, . .	972	143	43.28	6.36
Females, . .	907	114	46.13	5.80	Females, . .	986	145	43.90	6.46
East Bridgewater, .	2,445	449	84.49	15.51	Wareham, . .	2,800	567	83.16	16.84
Males, . .	1,210	231	41.81	7.98	Males, . .	1,427	338	42.38	10.04
Females, . .	1,235	218	42.68	7.53	Females, . .	1,373	229	40.78	6.80
Halifax, . .	433	64	87.12	12.88	West Bridgewater, .	1,393	354	79.74	20.26
Males, . .	227	39	45.67	7.85	Males, . .	684	193	39.15	11.05
Females, . .	206	25	41.45	5.03	Females, . .	709	161	40.59	9.21
Hanover, . .	1,815	236	88.49	11.51	Whitman, . .	4,906	838	85.42	14.58
Males, . .	890	119	43.40	5.80	Males, . .	2,453	426	42.71	7.41
Females, . .	925	117	45.09	5.71	Females, . .	2,453	412	42.71	7.17

NATIVE AND FOREIGN BORN — Continued.

COUNTIES, CITIES, TOWNS, AND SEX.	Native Born	Foreign Born	PERCENTAGES Native Born	PERCENTAGES Foreign Born
SUFFOLK.				
Boston, . . .	316,522	180,398	63.70	36.30
Males, . . .	156,241	83,425	51.44	16.70
Females, . . .	160,281	96,973	32.26	19.51
CHELSEA, . .	21,208	10,056	67.84	32.16
Males, . . .	10,436	4,847	33.38	15.47
Females, . . .	10,772	5,219	34.46	16.69
Revere, . . .	5,298	2,125	71.37	28.63
Males, . . .	2,659	1,062	35.82	14.31
Females, . . .	2,639	1,063	35.55	14.32
Winthrop, . . .	3,080	1,112	73.47	26.53
Males, . . .	1,486	529	35.45	12.62
Females, . . .	1,594	585	38.02	13.91
WORCESTER.				
Ashburnham, . .	1,847	301	85.99	14.01
Males, . . .	913	157	42.51	7.30
Females, . . .	934	144	43.48	6.71
Athol, . . .	6,088	1,276	82.67	17.33
Males, . . .	3,009	726	40.86	9.86
Females, . . .	3,079	550	41.81	7.47
Auburn, . . .	1,082	516	67.71	32.29
Males, . . .	548	273	34.29	17.09
Females, . . .	534	243	33.42	15.20
Barre, . . .	1,867	411	81.96	18.04
Males, . . .	928	222	40.74	9.74
Females, . . .	939	189	41.22	8.30
Berlin, . . .	786	111	87.63	12.37
Males, . . .	390	61	43.48	6.80
Females, . . .	396	50	44.15	5.57
Blackstone, . .	3,745	2,224	62.01	37.99
Males, . . .	1,883	1,233	31.18	20.42
Females, . . .	1,862	1,061	30.83	17.57
Bolton, . . .	665	132	83.44	16.56
Males, . . .	324	74	40.65	9.29
Females, . . .	341	58	42.79	7.27
Boylston, . . .	572	157	78.46	21.54
Males, . . .	314	75	43.07	10.29
Females, . . .	258	82	35.39	11.25
Brookfield, . .	2,370	709	78.38	21.62
Males, . . .	1,292	397	39.40	12.11
Females, . . .	1,278	312	38.98	9.51
Charlton, . . .	1,590	287	84.71	15.29
Males, . . .	841	134	44.80	7.14
Females, . . .	749	153	39.91	8.15
Clinton, . . .	6,893	4,604	59.95	40.05
Males, . . .	3,296	1,995	28.67	17.35
Females, . . .	3,597	2,609	31.28	22.70
Dana, . . .	628	89	87.59	12.41
Males, . . .	302	51	42.12	7.11
Females, . . .	326	38	45.47	5.30
Douglas, . . .	1,593	433	78.63	21.37
Males, . . .	799	234	39.44	11.55
Females, . . .	794	199	39.19	9.82
Dudley, . . .	1,945	1,258	60.72	39.28
Males, . . .	981	630	30.63	19.67
Females, . . .	964	628	30.09	19.61

COUNTIES, CITIES, TOWNS, AND SEX.	Native Born	Foreign Born	PERCENTAGES Native Born	PERCENTAGES Foreign Born
WORCESTER—Con.				
Fitchburg, . .	17,349	9,090	65.69	34.31
Males, . . .	8,489	4,548	32.15	17.22
Females, . . .	8,860	4,512	33.54	17.09
Gardner, . . .	6,390	2,792	69.59	30.41
Males, . . .	3,194	1,541	34.79	16.78
Females, . . .	3,196	1,251	34.80	13.63
Grafton, . . .	3,410	1,691	66.85	33.15
Males, . . .	1,701	754	33.35	14.78
Females, . . .	1,709	937	33.50	18.37
Hardwick, . . .	1,693	962	63.77	36.23
Males, . . .	871	505	32.81	19.02
Females, . . .	822	457	30.96	17.21
Harvard, . . .	959	203	82.53	17.47
Males, . . .	456	118	39.24	10.16
Females, . . .	503	85	43.29	7.31
Holden, . . .	1,876	726	72.10	27.90
Males, . . .	917	385	35.24	14.80
Females, . . .	959	341	36.86	13.10
Hopedale, . .	1,123	254	81.55	18.45
Males, . . .	568	130	41.25	9.44
Females, . . .	555	124	40.30	9.01
Hubbardston, . .	1,105	169	86.73	13.27
Males, . . .	566	93	44.43	7.30
Females, . . .	539	76	42.30	5.97
Lancaster, . .	1,648	532	75.60	24.40
Males, . . .	730	248	33.49	11.37
Females, . . .	918	284	42.11	13.03
Leicester, . .	2,421	818	74.75	25.25
Males, . . .	1,180	361	36.43	11.15
Females, . . .	1,241	457	38.32	14.10
Leominster, . .	7,327	1,884	79.55	20.45
Males, . . .	3,569	935	38.75	10.15
Females, . . .	3,758	949	40.80	10.30
Lunenburg, . .	1,085	152	87.71	12.29
Males, . . .	555	71	44.87	5.74
Females, . . .	530	81	42.84	6.55
Mendon, . . .	805	84	90.55	9.45
Males, . . .	419	43	47.13	4.84
Females, . . .	386	41	43.42	4.61
Milford, . . .	6,766	2,193	75.52	24.48
Males, . . .	3,256	1,098	36.34	12.26
Females, . . .	3,510	1,095	39.18	12.22
Millbury, . . .	3,541	1,684	67.81	32.19
Males, . . .	1,721	808	32.96	17.19
Females, . . .	1,820	783	34.85	15.00
New Braintree, . .	426	116	78.60	21.40
Males, . . .	223	69	41.14	12.73
Females, . . .	203	47	37.46	8.67
Northborough, . .	1,454	486	74.95	25.05
Males, . . .	726	240	37.42	12.84
Females, . . .	728	237	37.53	12.21
Northbridge, . .	3,077	2,209	58.21	41.79
Males, . . .	1,569	1,163	29.68	22.00
Females, . . .	1,508	1,046	28.53	19.79
North Brookfield, . .	3,674	961	79.27	20.73
Males, . . .	1,760	488	37.97	10.53
Females, . . .	1,914	473	41.30	10.20

NATIVE AND FOREIGN BORN — Continued.

COUNTIES, CITIES, TOWNS, AND SEX.	Native Born	Foreign Born	Percentages Native Born	Percentages Foreign Born	COUNTIES, CITIES, TOWNS, AND SEX.	Native Born	Foreign Born	Percentages Native Born	Percentages Foreign Born
WORCESTER - Con.					WORCESTER - Con.				
Oakham, . . .	541	64	89.42	10.58	Sturbridge, . .	1,521	389	79.64	20.36
Males, . . .	275	33	45.45	5.46	Males, . . .	747	201	39.11	10.52
Females, . .	266	31	43.97	5.12	Females, . .	774	188	40.53	9.84
Oxford, . . .	1,922	468	80.42	19.58	Sutton, . . .	2,309	1,111	67.51	32.49
Males, . . .	925	222	38.70	9.29	Males, . . .	1,186	584	34.67	17.08
Females, . .	997	246	41.72	10.29	Females, . .	1,123	527	32.84	15.41
Paxton, . . .	357	69	83.80	16.20	Templeton, . .	2,473	442	84.84	15.16
Males, . . .	191	43	44.83	10.10	Males, . . .	1,262	226	43.30	7.75
Females, . .	166	26	38.97	6.10	Females, . .	1,211	216	41.54	7.41
Petersham, . .	819	133	86.03	13.97	Upton, . . .	1,874	276	87.16	12.84
Males, . . .	416	77	43.70	8.09	Males, . . .	801	107	37.25	4.98
Females, . .	403	56	42.33	5.88	Females, . .	1,073	169	49.91	7.86
Phillipston, . .	417	43	90.65	9.35	Uxbridge, . .	2,600	946	73.32	26.68
Males, . . .	226	22	49.13	4.78	Males, . . .	1,296	484	36.55	13.65
Females, . .	191	21	41.52	4.57	Females, . .	1,304	462	36.77	13.03
Princeton, . .	788	164	82.77	17.23	Warren, . . .	3,248	1,182	73.32	26.68
Males, . . .	401	90	42.12	9.46	Males, . . .	1,601	596	36.14	13.45
Females, . .	387	74	40.65	7.77	Females, . .	1,647	586	37.18	13.23
Royalston, . .	795	95	89.33	10.67	Webster, . . .	4,606	3,193	59.06	40.94
Males, . . .	405	49	45.51	5.50	Males, . . .	2,212	1,587	28.36	20.35
Females, . .	390	46	43.82	5.17	Females, . .	2,384	1,606	30.70	20.59
Rutland, . . .	806	172	82.42	17.58	Westborough, .	4,113	1,122	78.57	21.43
Males, . . .	422	104	43.15	10.63	Males, . . .	2,089	522	39.91	9.97
Females, . .	384	68	39.27	6.95	Females, . .	2,024	600	38.66	11.46
Shrewsbury, . .	1,347	177	88.39	11.61	West Boylston, .	2,016	952	67.92	32.08
Males, . . .	691	93	45.34	6.10	Males, . . .	994	453	33.49	15.26
Females, . .	656	84	43.05	5.51	Females, . .	1,022	499	34.43	16.82
Southborough, .	1,522	791	68.47	31.53	West Brookfield,	1,283	184	87.46	12.54
Males, . . .	811	405	36.48	20.83	Males, . . .	616	101	41.99	6.89
Females, . .	711	238	31.99	10.70	Females, . .	667	83	45.47	5.65
Southbridge, .	5,442	2,808	65.96	34.04	Westminster, .	1,167	148	88.75	11.25
Males, . . .	2,673	1,370	32.40	16.61	Males, . . .	563	69	42.82	5.24
Females, . .	2,769	1,438	33.56	17.43	Females, . .	604	79	45.93	6.01
Spencer, . . .	5,958	1,656	78.25	21.75	Winchendon, .	3,535	955	78.73	21.27
Males, . . .	2,935	849	38.55	11.15	Males, . . .	1,757	500	39.15	11.14
Females, . .	3,023	807	39.70	10.60	Females, . .	1,778	455	39.60	10.13
Sterling, . . .	1,062	156	87.19	12.81	WORCESTER, .	67,114	31,653	67.95	32.05
Males, . . .	533	71	43.76	5.83	Males, . . .	33,120	15,743	33.53	15.94
Females, . .	529	85	43.43	6.98	Females, . .	33,994	15,910	34.42	16.11

NATIVE AND FOREIGN BORN — Concluded.

RECAPITULATION: BY COUNTIES.

COUNTIES, AND SEX.	Native Born	Foreign Born	PERCENTAGES Native Born	PERCENTAGES Foreign Born	COUNTIES, AND SEX.	Native Born	Foreign Born	PERCENTAGES Native Born	PERCENTAGES Foreign Born
BARNSTABLE, . .	24,651	3,003	89.14	10.86	HAMPSHIRE, . .	41,796	12,914	76.40	23.60
Males, .	11,853	1,441	42.86	5.21	Males, .	19,814	6,247	36.22	11.41
Females, .	12,798	1,562	46.28	5.65	Females, .	21,982	6,667	40.18	12.19
BERKSHIRE, . .	66,708	19,584	77.30	22.70	MIDDLESEX, .	342,560	156,657	68.62	31.38
Males, .	32,769	9,756	37.97	11.31	Males, .	166,044	73,279	33.26	14.68
Females, .	33,939	9,828	39.33	11.39	Females, .	176,516	83,378	35.36	16.70
BRISTOL, . .	134,920	84,999	61.60	38.40	NANTUCKET, .	2,766	250	91.71	8.29
Males, .	65,606	39,076	29.96	18.25	Males, .	1,220	95	40.45	3.15
Females, .	69,314	44,123	31.64	20.15	Females, .	1,546	155	51.26	5.14
DUKES, .	3,739	499	88.23	11.77	NORFOLK, . .	99,386	35,483	73.72	26.28
Males, .	1,796	261	42.58	6.16	Males, .	48,023	16,757	35.62	12.43
Females, .	1,943	238	45.85	5.61	Females, .	51,363	18,676	38.10	13.85
ESSEX, .	283,695	96,698	70.73	29.27	PLYMOUTH, .	82,860	18,638	81.64	18.36
Males, .	114,097	47,816	34.54	14.47	Males, .	41,107	9,587	40.50	9.45
Females, .	119,598	48,882	56.19	14.80	Females, .	41,753	9,051	41.14	8.91
FRANKLIN, .	53,398	6,747	86.19	16.81	SUFFOLK, . .	346,108	193,091	64.12	35.88
Males, .	16,635	3,058	41.44	9.11	Males, .	170,822	89,833	31.65	16.64
Females, .	16,763	3,989	41.75	7.70	Females, .	175,286	103,838	32.47	19.24
HAMPDEN, .	105,031	47,907	68.67	31.33	WORCESTER, . .	217,635	88,810	71.02	28.98
Males, .	51,088	23,045	33.40	15.07	Males, .	107,438	44,618	35.06	14.56
Females, .	53,943	24,862	35.27	16.26	Females, .	110,197	44,192	35.96	14.42

RECAPITULATION. FOR THE STATE.

THE STATE, AND SEX.	Native Born	Foreign Born	* PERCENTAGES OF TOTAL POPULATION Native Born	* PERCENTAGES OF TOTAL POPULATION Foreign Born
THE STATE, .	1,735,253	764,930	69.41	30.59
Males, .	848,312	366,389	33.93	14.65
Females, .	886,941	398,541	35.48	15.94

* See note, page 851.

RECAPITULATION. PERCENTAGES.

THE STATE, AND COUNTIES.	PERCENTAGES MALES Native Born	PERCENTAGES MALES Foreign Born	PERCENTAGES FEMALES Native Born	PERCENTAGES FEMALES Foreign Born	THE STATE, AND COUNTIES.	PERCENTAGES MALES Native Born	PERCENTAGES MALES Foreign Born	PERCENTAGES FEMALES Native Born	PERCENTAGES FEMALES Foreign Born
THE STATE,	69.84	30.16	69.00	31.00	THE STATE—Con.				
Barnstable, . .	89.16	10.84	89.12	10.88	Hampshire, . .	76.03	23.97	76.73	23.27
Berkshire, . .	77.06	22.94	77.54	22.46	Middlesex, . .	69.38	30.62	67.92	32.08
Bristol, . .	62.14	37.86	61.10	38.90	Nantucket, . .	92.78	7.22	90.89	9.11
Dukes, . .	87.31	12.69	89.09	10.91	Norfolk, . .	74.13	25.87	73.33	26.67
Essex, . .	70.47	29.53	70.99	29.01	Plymouth, . .	81.09	18.91	82.18	17.82
Franklin, . .	81.97	18.03	84.44	15.56	Suffolk, . .	65.53	34.47	62.80	37.20
Hampden, . .	68.91	31.09	68.45	31.55	Worcester, . .	70.66	29.34	71.38	28.62

COLOR AND RACE.

[815]

COLOR AND RACE.

COUNTIES, CITIES, TOWNS, AND SEX.	White	Colored	Indian	Japanese	Chinese	PERCENTAGES				
						White	Colored	Indian	Japanese	Chinese
BARNSTABLE.										
Barnstable, . . .	3,961	94	–	–	–	97.68	2.32	–	–	–
Males, . . .	1,906	38	–	–	–	47.00	0.94	–	–	–
Females, . . .	2,055	56	–	–	–	50.68	1.38	–	–	–
Bourne, . . .	1,561	19	–	–	–	98.80	1.20	–	–	–
Males, . . .	760	12	–	–	–	48.10	0.76	–	–	–
Females, . . .	801	7	–	–	–	50.70	0.44	–	–	–
Brewster, . . .	882	19	–	–	–	97.89	2.11	–	–	–
Males, . . .	430	7	–	–	–	47.72	0.78	–	–	–
Females, . . .	452	12	–	–	–	50.17	1.33	–	–	–
Chatham, . . .	1,807	1	1	–	–	99.88	0.06	0.06	–	–
Males, . . .	808	–	–	–	–	49.64	–	–	–	–
Females, . . .	999	1	1	–	–	50.24	0.06	0.06	–	–
Dennis, . . .	2,542	3	–	–	–	99.88	0.12	–	–	–
Males, . . .	1,162	2	–	–	–	45.66	0.08	–	–	–
Females, . . .	1,380	1	–	–	–	54.22	0.04	–	–	–
Eastham, . . .	476	–	–	–	–	100.00	–	–	–	–
Males, . . .	234	–	–	–	–	49.16	–	–	–	–
Females, . . .	242	–	–	–	–	50.84	–	–	–	–
Falmouth, . . .	2,630	24	–	–	1	99.06	0.90	–	–	0.04
Males, . . .	1,271	11	–	–	1	47.87	0.41	–	–	0.04
Females, . . .	1,359	13	–	–	–	51.19	0.49	–	–	–
Harwich, . . .	2,520	12	–	–	–	99.52	0.48	–	–	–
Males, . . .	1,247	6	–	–	–	49.25	0.24	–	–	–
Females, . . .	1,273	6	–	–	–	50.27	0.24	–	–	–
Mashpee, . . .	40	88	202	–	–	12.12	26.67	61.21	–	–
Males, . . .	23	51	104	–	–	6.97	15.46	31.51	–	–
Females, . . .	17	37	98	–	–	5.15	11.21	29.70	–	–
Orleans, . . .	1,198	–	–	–	–	100.00	–	–	–	–
Males, . . .	559	–	–	–	–	46.66	–	–	–	–
Females, . . .	639	–	–	–	–	53.34	–	–	–	–
Provincetown, . .	4,500	53	–	–	2	98.79	1.16	–	–	0.05
Males, . . .	2,183	30	–	–	2	47.92	0.66	–	–	0.05
Females, . . .	2,317	23	–	–	–	50.87	0.50	–	–	–
Sandwich, . . .	1,560	20	–	–	–	98.73	1.27	–	–	–
Males, . . .	725	9	–	–	–	45.89	0.57	–	–	–
Females, . . .	835	11	–	–	–	52.84	0.70	–	–	–
Truro, . . .	807	8	–	–	–	99.02	0.98	–	–	–
Males, . . .	398	4	–	–	–	48.84	0.49	–	–	–
Females, . . .	409	4	–	–	–	50.18	0.49	–	–	–
Wellfleet, . . .	967	1	–	–	–	99.90	0.10	–	–	–
Males, . . .	448	1	–	–	–	46.28	0.10	–	–	–
Females, . . .	519	–	–	–	–	53.62	–	–	–	–
Yarmouth, . . .	1,649	6	–	–	–	99.64	0.36	–	–	–
Males, . . .	771	1	–	–	–	46.59	0.06	–	–	–
Females, . . .	878	5	–	–	–	53.05	0.30	–	–	–
BERKSHIRE.										
Adams, . . .	7,825	10	–	–	2	99.85	0.12	–	–	0.03
Males, . . .	3,705	5	–	–	2	47.28	0.06	–	–	0.03
Females, . . .	4,120	5	–	–	–	52.57	0.06	–	–	–

COLOR AND RACE — Continued.

COUNTIES, CITIES, TOWNS, AND SEX.	White	Colored	Indian	Japanese	Chinese	PERCENTAGES				
						White	Colored	Indian	Japanese	Chinese
BERKSHIRE — Con.										
Alford, ...	275	5	-	-	-	98.21	1.79	-	-	-
Males, ...	150	2	-	-	-	53.57	0.72	-	-	-
Females, . . .	125	3	-	-	-	44.64	1.07	-	-	-
Becket, ...	885	3	-	-	-	99.66	0.34	-	-	-
Males, ...	481	2	-	-	-	54.16	0.23	-	-	-
Females, . . .	404	1	-	-	-	45.50	0.11	-	-	-
Cheshire, ...	1,175	1	-	-	-	99.91	0.09	-	-	-
Males, ...	598	1	-	-	-	50.85	0.09	-	-	-
Females, . . .	577	-	-	-	-	49.06	-	-	-	-
Clarksburg, . . .	1,007	2	-	-	-	99.80	0.20	-	-	-
Males, ...	501	1	-	-	-	49.65	0.10	-	-	-
Females, . . .	506	1	-	-	-	50.15	0.10	-	-	-
Dalton, ...	3,159	50	-	-	1	98.41	1.56	-	-	0.03
Males, ...	1,481	24	-	-	1	46.14	0.75	-	-	0.03
Females, . . .	1,678	26	-	-	-	52.27	0.81	-	-	-
Egremont, . . .	833	3	-	-	-	99.64	0.36	-	-	-
Males, . . .	405	1	-	-	-	48.44	0.12	-	-	-
Females, . . .	428	2	-	-	-	51.20	0.24	-	-	-
Florida, ...	425	-	-	-	-	100.00	-	-	-	-
Males, . . .	223	-	-	-	-	52.47	-	-	-	-
Females, . . .	202	-	-	-	-	47.53	-	-	-	-
Great Barrington, .	4,642	146	-	-	6	96.83	3.05	-	-	0.12
Males, ...	2,260	66	-	-	6	47.14	1.38	-	-	0.12
Females, . . .	2,382	80	-	-	-	49.69	1.67	-	-	-
Hancock, ...	501	10	-	-	-	98.04	1.96	-	-	-
Males, ...	259	7	-	-	-	50.68	1.37	-	-	-
Females, . . .	242	3	-	-	-	47.36	0.59	-	-	-
Hinsdale, ...	1,598	52	-	-	-	96.85	3.15	-	-	-
Males, . . .	797	24	-	-	-	48.30	1.46	-	-	-
Females, . . .	801	28	-	-	-	48.55	1.69	-	-	-
Lanesborough, . .	812	36	-	-	-	95.75	4.25	-	-	-
Males, ...	413	21	-	-	-	48.70	2.48	-	-	-
Females, . . .	399	15	-	-	-	47.05	1.77	-	-	-
Lee, ...	3,963	101	-	-	2	97.47	2.48	-	-	0.05
Males, ...	1,915	56	-	-	2	47.10	1.37	-	-	0.05
Females, . . .	2,048	45	-	-	-	50.37	1.11	-	-	-
Lenox, ...	2,794	78	-	-	-	97.28	2.72	-	-	-
Males, ...	1,496	33	-	-	-	52.09	1.15	-	-	-
Females, . . .	1,298	45	-	-	-	45.19	1.57	-	-	-
Monterey, . . .	457	6	1	-	-	98.49	1.29	0.22	-	-
Males, ...	239	1	1	-	-	51.50	0.22	0.22	-	-
Females, . . .	218	5	-	-	-	46.99	1.07	-	-	-
Mount Washington, .	136	-	-	-	-	100.00	-	-	-	-
Males, ...	76	-	-	-	-	55.88	-	-	-	-
Females, . . .	60	-	-	-	-	44.12	-	-	-	-
New Ashford, . .	116	-	-	-	-	100.00	-	-	-	-
Males, ...	68	-	-	-	-	58.62	-	-	-	-
Females, . . .	48	-	-	-	-	41.38	-	-	-	-
New Marlborough, .	1,288	-	-	-	-	100.00	-	-	-	-
Males, ...	682	-	-	-	-	52.95	-	-	-	-
Females, . . .	606	-	-	-	-	47.05	-	-	-	-
NORTH ADAMS, .	19,072	48	1	-	14	99.67	0.25	0.01	-	0.07
Males, ...	9,317	18	1	-	14	48.69	0.09	0.01	-	0.07
Females, . . .	9,755	30	-	-	-	50.98	0.16	-	-	-
Otis, ...	501	16	1	-	-	96.72	3.09	0.19	-	-
Males, ...	280	9	-	-	-	54.05	1.74	-	-	-
Females, . . .	221	7	1	-	-	42.67	1.35	0.19	-	-

COLOR AND RACE — Continued.

COUNTIES, CITIES, TOWNS, AND SEX.	White	Colored	Indian	Japanese	Chinese	PERCENTAGES				
						White	Colored	Indian	Japanese	Chinese
BERKSHIRE — Con.										
Peru, ...	294	11	–	–	–	96.39	3.61	–	–	–
Males, ...	140	6	–	–	–	45.90	1.97	–	–	–
Females, . . .	154	5	–	–	–	50.49	1.64	–	–	–
PITTSFIELD, . . .	20,160	291	1	–	9	98.53	1.42	0.01	–	0.04
Males, ...	9,686	143	–	–	9	47.34	0.70	–	–	0.04
Females, . . .	10,474	148	1	–	–	51.19	0.72	0.01	–	–
Richmond, . . .	690	7	4	–	–	98.43	1.00	0.57	–	–
Males, ...	353	1	–	–	–	50.36	0.14	–	–	–
Females, . . .	337	6	4	–	–	48.07	0.86	0.57	–	–
Sandisfield, . . .	801	1	–	–	–	99.88	0.12	–	–	–
Males, ...	400	1	–	–	–	49.88	0.12	–	–	–
Females, . . .	401	–	–	–	–	50.00	–	–	–	–
Savoy, ...	504	–	–	–	–	100.00	–	–	–	–
Males, ...	256	–	–	–	–	50.79	–	–	–	–
Females, . . .	248	–	–	–	–	49.21	–	–	–	–
Sheffield, . . .	1,733	141	3	–	–	92.41	7.43	0.16	–	–
Males, ...	869	72	3	–	–	45.81	3.79	0.16	–	–
Females, . . .	884	69	–	–	–	46.60	3.64	–	–	–
Stockbridge, . . .	1,995	82	–	–	–	96.05	3.95	–	–	–
Males, ...	954	42	–	–	–	45.93	2.02	–	–	–
Females, . . .	1,041	40	–	–	–	50.12	1.93	–	–	–
Tyringham, . . .	390	3	–	–	–	99.17	0.83	–	–	–
Males, ...	184	2	–	–	–	50.69	0.55	–	–	–
Females, . . .	176	1	–	–	–	48.48	0.28	–	–	–
Washington, . . .	423	–	–	–	–	100.00	–	–	–	–
Males, ...	236	–	–	–	–	55.79	–	–	–	–
Females, . . .	187	–	–	–	–	44.21	–	–	–	–
West Stockbridge, . .	1,230	27	–	–	–	97.85	2.15	–	–	–
Males, ...	594	14	–	–	–	47.26	1.11	–	–	–
Females, . . .	636	13	–	–	–	50.59	1.04	–	–	–
Williamstown, . . .	4,757	147	–	–	3	96.93	3.01	–	–	0.06
Males, ...	2,548	64	–	–	3	52.14	1.31	–	–	0.06
Females, . . .	2,189	83	–	–	–	44.79	1.70	–	–	–
Windsor, ...	556	–	–	–	–	100.00	–	–	–	–
Males, ...	301	–	–	–	–	54.14	–	–	–	–
Females, . . .	255	–	–	–	–	45.86	–	–	–	–
BRISTOL.										
Acushnet, . . .	1,107	7	1	–	–	99.28	0.63	0.09	–	–
Males, ...	564	3	1	–	–	50.58	0.27	0.09	–	–
Females, . . .	543	4	–	–	–	48.70	0.36	–	–	–
Attleborough, . . .	8,182	102	–	–	4	98.72	1.23	–	–	0.05
Males, ...	3,975	50	–	–	4	47.96	0.60	–	–	0.05
Females, . . .	4,207	52	–	–	–	50.76	0.63	–	–	–
Berkley, ...	951	4	–	–	–	99.58	0.42	–	–	–
Males, ...	478	4	–	–	–	50.05	0.42	–	–	–
Females, . . .	473	–	–	–	–	49.53	–	–	–	–
Dartmouth, . . .	3,067	40	–	–	–	98.71	1.29	–	–	–
Males, ...	1,576	23	–	–	–	50.72	0.74	–	–	–
Females, . . .	1,491	17	–	–	–	47.99	0.55	–	–	–
Dighton, ...	1,772	25	–	–	–	98.61	1.39	–	–	–
Males, ...	904	12	–	–	–	50.31	0.66	–	–	–
Females, . . .	868	13	–	–	–	48.30	0.73	–	–	–
Easton, ...	4,438	13	–	–	1	99.69	0.29	–	–	0.02
Males, ...	2,274	11	–	–	1	51.08	0.25	–	–	0.02
Females, . . .	2,164	2	–	–	–	48.61	0.04	–	–	–

COLOR AND RACE — Continued.

COUNTIES, CITIES, TOWNS, AND SEX	White	Colored	Indian	Japanese	Chinese	PERCENTAGES White	Colored	Indian	Japanese	Chinese
BRISTOL — Con.										
Fairhaven,	3,297	40	1	-	-	98.77	1.20	0.03	-	-
Males, .	1,536	17	1	-	-	46.01	0.51	0.03	-	-
Females,	1,761	23	-	-	-	52.76	0.69	-	-	-
Fall River, .	88,885	272	1	-	45	99.64	0.31	*-	-	0.05
Males, .	42,542	117	-	-	45	47.69	0.13	-	-	0.05
Females,	46,343	155	1	-	-	51.95	0.18	*-	-	-
Freetown,	1,398	7	-	-	-	99.50	0.50	-	-	-
Males, .	724	1	-	-	-	51.53	0.07	-	-	-
Females,	674	6	-	-	-	47.97	0.43	-	-	-
Mansfield,	3,708	12	-	-	2	99.63	0.32	-	-	0.05
Males, .	1,784	7	-	-	2	47.93	0.19	-	-	0.05
Females,	1,924	5	-	-	-	51.70	0.13	-	-	-
New Bedford, .	53,650	1,565	18	-	18	97.10	2.82	0.04	-	0.04
Males, .	25,437	694	9	-	18	46.03	1.25	0.02	-	0.04
Females,	28,213	871	9	-	-	51.07	1.57	0.02	-	-
North Attleborough,	6,544	28	-	-	4	99.51	0.43	-	-	0.06
Males, .	3,128	13	-	-	4	47.57	0.20	-	-	0.06
Females,	3,416	15	-	-	-	51.94	0.23	-	-	-
Norton, .	1,597	17	-	-	-	98.95	1.05	-	-	-
Males, .	747	13	-	-	-	46.28	0.81	-	-	-
Females,	850	4	-	-	-	52.67	0.24	-	-	-
Raynham,	1,483	35	-	-	-	97.69	2.31	-	-	-
Males, .	731	20	-	-	-	48.15	1.32	-	-	-
Females,	752	15	-	-	-	49.54	0.99	-	-	-
Rehoboth,	1,792	18	-	-	-	99.01	0.99	-	-	-
Males, .	946	12	-	-	-	52.27	0.66	-	-.	-
Females,	846	6	-	-	-	46.74	0.33	-	-	-
Seekonk, .	1,430	34	1	-	-	97.61	2.32	0.07	-	-
Males, .	773	19	1	-	-	52.76	1.30	0.07	-	-
Females,	657	15	-	-	-	44.85	1.02	-	-	-
Somerset, .	1,981	2	-	-	-	99.90	0.10	-	-	-
Males, .	1,039	1	-	-	-	52.40	0.05	-	-	-
Females,	942	1	-	-	-	47.50	0.05	-	-	-
Swansea, .	1,596	31	-	-	-	98.09	1.91	-	-	-
Males, .	815	15	-	-	-	50.09	0.92	-	-	-
Females,	781	16	-	-	-	48.00	0.99	-	-	-
Taunton,	26,974	131	-	-	10	99.48	0.48	-	-	0.04
Males, .	13,070	67	-	-	10	48.20	0.25	-	-	0.04
Females,	13,904	64	-	-	-	51.28	0.23	-	-	-
Westport,	2,657	19	2	-	-	99.21	0.71	0.08	-	-
Males, .	1,331	12	1	-	-	49.70	0.45	0.04	-	-
Females,	1,326	7	1	-	-	49.51	0.26	0.04	-	-
DUKES.										
Chilmark,	303	1	-	-	-	99.67	0.33	-	-	-
Males, .	151	-	-	-	-	49.67	-	-	-	-
Females,	152	1	-	-	-	50.00	0.33	-	-	-
Cottage City, .	970	65	-	-	3	93.45	6.26	-	-	0.29
Males, .	473	32	-	-	3	45.57	3.08	-	-	0.29
Females,	497	33	-	-	-	47.88	3.18	-	-	-
Edgartown,	1,057	28	-	-	-	97.51	2.49	-	-	-
Males, .	511	16	-	-	-	45.42	1.42	-	-	-
Females,	586	12	-	-	-	52.09	1.07	-	-	-
Gay Head, .	16	6	147	-	-	9.46	3.56	86.98	-	-
Males, .	8	3	79	-	-	4.73	1.78	46.74	-	-
Females,	8	3	68	-	-	4.73	1.78	40.24	-	-

* Less than one one-hundredth of one per cent.

COLOR AND RACE — Continued.

COUNTIES, CITIES, TOWNS, AND SEX.	White	Colored	Indian	Japanese	Chinese	PERCENTAGES White	Colored	Indian	Japanese	Chinese
DUKES — Con.										
Gosnold, ...	133	7	-	-	-	95.00	5.00	-	-	-
Males, ...	82	6	-	-	-	58.57	4.29	-	-	-
Females, . . .	51	1	-	-	-	36.43	0.71	-	-	-
Tisbury, ...	977	24	-	-	1	97.50	2.40	-	-	0.10
Males, ...	467	9	-	-	1	46.60	0.90	-	-	0.10
Females, . . .	510	15	-	-	-	50.90	1.50	-	-	-
West Tisbury, . .	450	10	-	-	-	97.83	2.17	-	-	-
Males, ...	212	4	-	-	-	46.09	0.87	-	-	-
Females, . . .	238	6	-	-	-	51.74	1.30	-	-	-
ESSEX.										
Amesbury, . . .	9,936	46	-	-	4	99.50	0.46	-	-	0.04
Males, ...	4,760	16	-	-	4	47.67	0.16	-	-	0.04
Females, . . .	5,176	30	-	-	-	51.83	0.30	-	-	-
Andover, ...	6,089	54	-	-	2	99.09	0.88	-	-	0.03
Males, ...	2,892	19	-	-	2	47.06	0.31	-	-	0.03
Females, . . .	3,197	35	-	-	-	52.03	0.57	-	-	-
BEVERLY, . . .	11,758	38	-	-	10	99.59	0.32	-	-	0.09
Males, ...	5,796	12	-	-	10	48.33	0.10	-	-	0.09
Females, . . .	6,052	26	-	-	-	51.26	0.22	-	-	-
Boxford, ...	727	-	-	-	-	100.00	-	-	-	-
Males, ...	359	-	-	-	-	49.38	-	-	-	-
Females, . . .	368	-	-	-	-	50.62	-	-	-	-
Bradford, ...	4,717	17	-	-	2	99.60	0.36	-	-	0.04
Males, ...	2,215	5	-	-	2	46.77	0.11	-	-	0.04
Females, . . .	2,502	12	-	-	-	52.83	0.25	-	-	-
Danvers, ...	8,161	18	-	-	2	99.76	0.22	-	-	0.02
Males, ...	3,949	7	-	-	2	48.27	0.09	-	-	0.02
Females, . . .	4,212	11	-	-	-	51.49	0.13	-	-	-
Essex, ...	1,584	3	-	-	-	99.81	0.19	-	-	-
Males, ...	809	-	-	-	-	50.98	-	-	-	-
Females, . . .	775	3	-	-	-	48.83	0.19	-	-	-
Georgetown, . . .	2,047	3	-	-	-	99.85	0.15	-	-	-
Males, ...	998	1	-	-	-	48.68	0.05	-	-	-
Females, . . .	1,049	2	-	-	-	51.17	0.10	-	-	-
GLOUCESTER, . .	28,173	9	-	-	29	99.87	0.03	-	-	0.10
Males, ...	16,223	5	-	-	29	57.51	0.02	-	-	0.10
Females, . . .	11,950	4	-	-	-	42.36	0.01	-	-	-
Groveland, . . .	2,328	5	-	-	-	99.79	0.21	-	-	-
Males, ...	1,116	2	-	-	-	47.84	0.08	-	-	-
Females, . . .	1,212	3	-	-	-	51.95	0.13	-	-	-
Hamilton, . . .	1,347	9	-	-	-	99.34	0.66	-	-	-
Males, ...	681	4	-	-	-	50.22	0.30	-	-	-
Females, . . .	666	5	-	-	-	49.12	0.36	-	-	-
HAVERHILL, . . .	29,907	284	-	1	17	99.00	0.94	-	*-	0.06
Males, ...	14,381	137	-	1	16	47.60	0.45	-	*-	0.06
Females, . . .	15,526	147	-	-	1	51.40	0.49	-	-	*-
Ipswich, ...	4,697	19	-	-	4	99.51	0.40	-	-	0.09
Males, ...	2,168	6	-	-	4	45.93	0.12	-	-	0.09
Females, . . .	2,529	13	-	-	-	53.58	0.28	-	-	-
LAWRENCE, . . .	52,033	98	-	-	33	99.75	0.19	-	-	0.06
Males, ...	25,027	47	-	-	33	47.98	0.09	-	-	0.06
Females, . . .	27,006	51	-	-	-	51.77	0.10	-	-	-
LYNN, ...	61,555	767	1	-	31	98.72	1.23	*-	-	0.05
Males, ...	29,762	380	-	-	31	47.73	0.61	-	-	0.05
Females, . . .	31,793	387	1	-	-	50.99	0.62	*-	-	-

* Less than one one-hundredth of one per cent.

COLOR AND RACE — Continued.

COUNTIES, CITIES, TOWNS, AND SEX.	White	Colored	Indian	Japanese	Chinese	White	Colored	Indian	Japanese	Chinese
ESSEX — Con.										
Lynnfield,	804	14	-	-	-	98.29	1.71	-	-	-
Males,	404	4	-	-	-	49.39	0.49	-	-	-
Females,	400	10	-	-	-	48.90	1.22	-	-	-
Manchester,	1,868	5	-	2	1	99.57	0.27	-	0.11	0.05
Males,	887	3	-	2	1	47.28	0.16	-	0.11	0.05
Females,	981	2	-	-	-	52.29	0.11	-	-	-
Marblehead,	7,636	33	-	-	2	99.54	0.43	-	-	0.03
Males,	3,636	11	-	-	2	47.40	0.14	-	-	0.03
Females,	4,000	22	-	-	-	52.14	0.29	-	-	-
Merrimac,	2,300	-	-	-	1	99.96	-	-	-	0.04
Males,	1,110	-	-	-	1	48.24	-	-	-	0.04
Females,	1,190	-	-	-	-	51.72	-	-	-	-
Methuen,	5,683	5	1	-	1	99.87	0.09	0.02	-	0.02
Males,	2,755	4	-	-	1	48.42	0.07	-	-	0.02
Females,	2,928	1	1	-	-	51.45	0.02	0.02	-	-
Middleton,	835	3	-	-	-	99.64	0.36	-	-	-
Males,	425	3	-	-	-	50.71	0.36	-	-	-
Females,	410	-	-	-	-	48.93	-	-	-	-
Nahant,	863	2	-	-	-	99.77	0.23	-	-	-
Males,	423	2	-	-	-	48.90	0.23	-	-	-
Females,	440	-	-	-	-	50.87	-	-	-	-
Newbury,	1,487	2	-	-	-	99.87	0.13	-	-	-
Males,	760	-	-	-	-	51.04	-	-	-	-
Females,	727	2	-	-	-	48.83	0.13	-	-	-
NEWBURYPORT,	14,461	87	-	-	4	99.37	0.60	-	-	0.03
Males,	6,583	29	-	-	4	45.23	0.20	-	-	0.03
Females,	7,878	58	-	-	-	54.14	0.40	-	-	-
North Andover,	3,562	4	3	-	-	99.80	0.11	0.09	-	-
Males,	1,763	-	2	-	-	49.39	-	0.06	-	-
Females,	1,799	4	1	-	-	50.41	0.11	0.03	-	-
Peabody,	10,494	12	-	-	1	99.87	0.12	-	-	0.01
Males,	5,256	5	-	-	1	50.02	0.05	-	-	0.01
Females,	5,238	7	-	-	-	49.85	0.07	-	-	-
Rockport,	5,286	1	-	-	2	99.94	0.02	-	-	0.04
Males,	2,963	1	-	-	2	56.02	0.02	-	-	0.04
Females,	2,323	-	-	-	-	43.92	-	-	-	-
Rowley,	1,265	7	-	-	-	99.45	0.55	-	-	-
Males,	653	3	-	-	-	51.34	0.23	-	-	-
Females,	612	4	-	-	-	48.11	0.32	-	-	-
SALEM,	34,266	181	-	2	24	99.40	0.52	-	0.01	0.07
Males,	16,170	74	-	2	24	46.91	0.21	-	0.01	0.07
Females,	18,096	107	-	-	-	52.49	0.31	-	-	-
Salisbury,	1,297	3	-	-	-	99.77	0.23	-	-	-
Males,	641	1	-	-	-	49.31	0.07	-	-	-
Females,	656	2	-	-	-	50.46	0.16	-	-	-
Saugus,	4,462	35	-	-	-	99.22	0.78	-	-	-
Males,	2,165	24	-	-	-	48.14	0.54	-	-	-
Females,	2,297	11	-	-	-	51.08	0.24	-	-	-
Swampscott,	3,240	16	-	-	3	99.42	0.49	-	-	0.09
Males,	1,525	6	-	-	3	46.79	0.19	-	-	0.09
Females,	1,715	10	-	-	-	52.63	0.30	-	-	-
Topsfield,	1,033	-	-	-	-	100.00	-	-	-	-
Males,	516	-	-	-	-	49.95	-	-	-	-
Females,	517	-	-	-	-	50.05	-	-	-	-
Wenham,	883	3	-	-	-	99.66	0.34	-	-	-
Males,	429	2	-	-	-	48.42	0.23	-	-	-
Females,	454	1	-	-	-	51.24	0.11	-	-	-

COLOR AND RACE — Continued.

COUNTIES, CITIES, TOWNS, AND SEX.	White	Colored	Indian	Japanese	Chinese	PERCENTAGES				
						White	Colored	Indian	Japanese	Chinese
ESSEX — Con.										
West Newbury, .	1,642	1	-	-	-	99.94	0.06	-	-	-
Males, ...	811	-	-	-	-	49.36	-	-	-	-
Females, . .	831	1	-	-	-	50.58	0.06	-	-	-
FRANKLIN.										
Ashfield, ...	1,009	4	-	-	-	99.60	0.40	-	-	-
Males, ...	521	2	-	-	-	51.43	0.20	-	-	-
Females, . .	488	2	-	-	-	48.17	0.20	-	-	-
Bernardston, . . .	778	-	-	-	-	100.00	-	-	-	-
Males, ...	389	-	-	-	-	50.00	-	-	-	-
Females, . . .	389	-	-	-	-	50.00	-	-	-	-
Buckland, . . .	1,548	-	-	-	-	100.00	-	-	-	-
Males, ...	785	-	-	-	-	50.71	-	-	-	-
Females, . . .	763	-	-	-	-	49.29	-	-	-	-
Charlemont, . . .	1,027	14	-	-	-	98.66	1.34	-	-	-
Males, ...	519	7	-	-	-	49.86	0.67	-	-	-
Females, . . .	508	7	-	-	-	48.80	0.67	-	-	-
Colrain, ...	1,609	-	1	-	-	99.94	-	0.06	-	-
Males, ...	850	-	1	-	-	52.80	-	0.06	-	-
Females, . . .	759	-	-	-	-	47.14	-	-	-	-
Conway, ...	1,297	7	-	-	-	99.46	0.54	-	-	-
Males, ...	657	-	-	-	-	50.38	-	-	-	-
Females, . . .	640	7	-	-	-	49.08	0.54	-	-	-
Deerfield, . . .	2,980	26	-	-	1	99.10	0.87	-	-	0.03
Males, ...	1,531	18	-	-	1	50.92	0.60	-	-	0.03
Females, . . .	1,449	8	-	-	-	48.18	0.27	-	-	-
Erving, ...	964	-	-	-	-	100.00	-	-	-	-
Males, ...	490	-	-	-	-	50.83	-	-	-	-
Females, . . .	474	-	-	-	-	49.17	-	-	-	-
Gill, ...	1,075	3	-	3	1	99.35	0.28	-	0.28	0.09
Males, . .	693	2	-	3	1	64.04	0.19	-	0.28	0.09
Females, . . .	382	1	-	-	-	35.31	0.09	-	-	-
Greenfield, . .	6,213	14	-	-	2	99.74	0.23	-	-	0.03
Males, ...	2,980	5	-	-	2	47.84	0.08	-	-	0.03
Females, . . .	3,233	9	-	-	-	51.90	0.15	-	-	-
Hawley, ...	468	-	-	-	-	100.00	-	-	-	-
Males, . .	250	-	-	-	-	53.42	-	-	-	-
Females, . . .	218	-	-	-	-	46.58	-	-	-	-
Heath, ...	475	1	-	-	-	99.79	0.21	-	-	-
Males, ...	249	1	-	-	-	52.31	0.21	-	-	-
Females, . . .	226	-	-	-	-	47.48	-	-	-	-
Leverett, . . .	725	19	-	-	-	97.45	2.55	-	-	-
Males, ...	369	10	-	-	-	49.60	1.34	-	-	-
Females, . . .	356	9	-	-	-	47.85	1.21	-	-	-
Leyden, ...	363	-	-	-	-	100.00	-	-	-	-
Males, ...	185	-	-	-	-	50.96	-	-	-	-
Females, . . .	178	-	-	-	-	49.04	-	-	-	-
Monroe, ...	295	1	2	-	-	98.99	0.34	0.67	-	-
Males, ...	174	-	2	-	-	58.39	-	0.67	-	-
Females, . . .	121	1	-	-	-	40.60	0.34	-	-	-
Montague, . . .	6,054	2	-	-	2	99.94	0.03	-	-	0.03
Males, ...	3,074	-	-	-	2	50.75	-	-	-	0.03
Females, . . .	2,980	2	-	-	-	49.19	0.03	-	-	-
New Salem, . . .	867	2	-	-	-	99.76	0.24	-	-	-
Males, ...	437	1	-	-	-	50.28	0.12	-	-	-
Females, . . .	430	1	-	-	-	49.48	0.12	-	-	-

COLOR AND RACE — Continued.

COUNTIES, CITIES, TOWNS, AND SEX	White	Colored	Indian	Japanese	Chinese	PERCENTAGES				
						White	Colored	Indian	Japanese	Chinese
FRANKLIN — Con.										
Northfield,	1,846	3	1	1	-	99.73	0.17	0.05	0.05	-
Males,	754	-	-	-	-	40.73	-	-	-	-
Females,	1,092	3	1	1	-	59.00	0.17	0.05	0.05	-
Orange,	5,354	3	-	-	4	99.86	0.06	-	-	0.08
Males,	2,686	-	-	-	4	50.10	-	-	-	0.08
Females,	2,668	3	-	-	-	49.76	0.06	-	-	-
Rowe,	498	-	-	-	-	100.00	-	-	-	-
Males,	283	-	-	-	-	56.83	-	-	-	-
Females,	215	-	-	-	-	43.17	-	-	-	-
Shelburne,	1,559	-	-	-	1	99.93	-	-	-	0.07
Males,	749	-	-	-	1	48.01	-	-	-	0.07
Females,	810	-	-	-	-	51.92	-	-	-	-
Shutesbury,	444	-	-	-	-	100.00	-	-	-	-
Males,	218	-	-	-	-	49.10	-	-	-	-
Females,	226	-	-	-	-	50.90	-	-	-	-
Sunderland,	686	10	-	-	-	98.56	1.44	-	-	-
Males,	378	3	-	-	-	54.31	0.43	-	-	-
Females,	308	7	-	-	-	44.25	1.01	-	-	-
Warwick,	599	-	-	-	-	100.00	-	-	-	-
Males,	321	-	-	-	-	53.59	-	-	-	-
Females,	278	-	-	-	-	46.41	-	-	-	-
Wendell,	529	-	-	-	-	100.00	-	-	-	-
Males,	293	-	-	-	-	55.39	-	-	-	-
Females,	236	-	-	-	-	44.61	-	-	-	-
Whately,	754	1	-	-	-	99.87	0.13	-	-	-
Males,	391	1	-	-	-	51.79	0.13	-	-	-
Females,	363	-	-	-	-	48.08	-	-	-	-
HAMPDEN.										
Agawam,	2,401	7	-	-	-	99.71	0.29	-	-	-
Males,	1,232	5	-	-	-	51.16	0.21	-	-	-
Females,	1,169	2	-	-	-	48.55	0.08	-	-	-
Blandford,	842	7	-	-	-	99.18	0.82	-	-	-
Males,	433	4	-	-	-	51.00	0.47	-	-	-
Females,	409	3	-	-	-	48.18	0.35	-	-	-
Brimfield,	952	9	1	-	-	98.96	0.94	0.10	-	-
Males,	493	5	-	-	-	51.25	0.52	-	-	-
Females,	459	4	1	-	-	47.71	0.42	0.10	-	-
Chester,	1,425	4	-	-	-	99.72	0.28	-	-	-
Males,	698	2	-	-	-	48.85	0.14	-	-	-
Females,	727	2	-	-	-	50.87	0.14	-	-	-
CHICOPEE,	16,410	6	-	-	4	99.94	0.04	-	-	0.02
Males,	8,088	3	-	-	4	49.26	0.02	-	-	0.02
Females,	8,322	3	-	-	-	50.68	0.02	-	-	-
East Longmeadow,	1,589	2	-	-	-	99.87	0.13	-	-	-
Males,	863	-	-	-	-	54.24	-	-	-	-
Females,	726	2	-	-	-	45.63	0.13	-	-	-
Granville,	1,003	2	-	-	-	99.80	0.20	-	-	-
Males,	520	2	-	-	-	51.74	0.20	-	-	-
Females,	483	-	-	-	-	48.06	-	-	-	-
Hampden,	721	22	-	-	-	97.04	2.96	-	-	-
Males,	361	13	-	-	-	48.59	1.75	-	-	-
Females,	360	9	-	-	-	48.45	1.21	-	-	-
Holland,	199	-	-	-	-	100.00	-	-	-	-
Males,	107	-	-	-	-	53.77	-	-	-	-
Females,	92	-	-	-	-	46.23	-	-	-	-

COLOR AND RACE — Continued.

COUNTIES, CITIES, TOWNS, AND SEX.	White	Colored	Indian	Japanese	Chinese	PERCENTAGES				
						White	Colored	Indian	Japanese	Chinese
HAMPDEN — Con.										
HOLYOKE, . . .	40,262	49	-	-	20	99.85	0.10	-	-	0.05
Males, . . .	19,169	9	-	-	20	47.54	0.02	-	-	0.05
Females, . . .	21,093	51	-	-	-	52.31	0.08	-	-	-
Longmeadow, . . .	618	2	-	-	-	99.68	0.32	-	-	-
Males, . . .	288	2	-	-	-	46.45	0.32	-	-	-
Females, . . .	330	-	-	-	-	53.23	-	-	-	-
Ludlow, ...	2,561	1	-	-	-	99.96	0.04	-	-	-
Males, . . .	1,313	1	-	-	-	51.25	0.04	-	-	-
Females, . . .	1,248	-	-	-	-	48.71	-	-	-	-
Monson, . . .	3,680	56	-	-	-	98.50	1.50	-	-	-
Males, . . .	1,824	38	-	-	-	48.69	1.02	-	-	-
Females, . . .	1,866	18	-	-	-	49.81	0.48	-	-	-
Montgomery, . . .	275	-	-	-	-	100.00	-	-	-	-
Males, . . .	151	-	-	-	-	54.91	-	-	-	-
Females, . . .	124	-	-	-	-	45.09	-	-	-	-
Palmer, ...	6,833	24	-	-	1	99.64	0.35	-	-	0.01
Males, . . .	3,336	8	-	-	1	48.65	0.12	-	-	0.01
Females, . . .	3,497	16	-	-	-	50.99	0.23	-	-	-
Russell, ...	846	-	-	-	-	100.00	-	-	-	-
Males, . . .	440	-	-	-	-	52.01	-	-	-	-
Females, . . .	406	-	-	-	-	47.99	-	-	-	-
Southwick, . . .	952	9	-	-	-	99.06	0.94	-	-	-
Males, . . .	505	5	-	-	-	52.55	0.52	-	-	-
Females, . . .	447	4	-	-	-	46.51	0.42	-	-	-
SPRINGFIELD, . .	50,596	901	2	1	22	98.20	1.75	*-	*-	0.05
Males, . . .	24,240	388	1	-	22	47.05	0.75	*-	-	0.05
Females, . . .	26,356	513	1	1	-	51.15	1.00	*-	*-	-
Tolland, . . .	292	17	-	-	-	94.50	5.50	-	-	-
Males, . . .	161	10	-	-	-	52.10	3.24	-	-	-
Females, . . .	131	7	-	-	-	42.40	2.26	-	-	-
Wales, . . .	774	9	-	-	-	98.85	1.15	-	-	-
Males, . . .	400	5	-	-	-	51.08	0.64	-	-	-
Females, . . .	374	4	-	-	-	47.77	0.51	-	-	-
Westfield, . . .	10,557	101	-	-	5	99.00	0.95	-	-	0.05
Males, . . .	5,119	51	-	-	5	48.00	0.48	-	-	0.05
Females, . . .	5,438	50	-	-	-	51.00	0.47	-	-	-
West Springfield, . .	6,109	14	-	-	2	99.74	0.23	-	-	0.03
Males, . . .	2,945	4	-	-	2	48.08	0.07	-	-	0.03
Females, . . .	3,164	10	-	-	-	51.66	0.16	-	-	-
Wilbraham, . . .	1,733	7	-	-	-	99.60	0.40	-	-	-
Males, . . .	833	4	-	-	-	47.87	0.23	-	-	-
Females, . . .	900	3	-	-	-	51.73	0.17	-	-	-
HAMPSHIRE.										
Amherst, . . .	4,611	166	4	2	2	96.37	3.47	0.08	0.04	0.04
Males, . . .	2,354	65	4	2	2	49.20	1.36	0.08	0.04	0.04
Females, . . .	2,257	101	-	-	-	47.17	2.11	-	-	-
Belchertown, . . .	2,148	13	-	-	-	99.40	0.60	-	-	-
Males, . . .	1,111	4	-	-	-	51.41	0.19	-	-	-
Females, . . .	1,037	9	-	-	-	47.99	0.41	-	-	-
Chesterfield, . . .	589	-	-	-	-	100.00	-	-	-	-
Males, . . .	301	-	-	-	-	51.10	-	-	-	-
Females, . . .	288	-	-	-	-	48.90	-	-	-	-
Cummington, . . .	749	1	-	-	-	99.87	0.13	-	-	-
Males, . . .	366	1	-	-	-	48.80	0.13	-	-	-
Females, . . .	383	-	-	-	-	51.07	-	-	-	-

* Less than one one-hundredth of one per cent.

COLOR AND RACE — Continued.

COUNTIES, CITIES, TOWNS, AND SEX.	White	Colored	Indian	Japanese	Chinese	PERCENTAGES				
						White	Colored	Indian	Japanese	Chinese
HAMPSHIRE — Con.										
Easthampton, . . .	4,778	10	-	-	2	99.75	0.21	-	-	0.04
Males, ...	2,238	2	-	-	2	46.73	0.04	-	-	0.04
Females, . . .	2,540	8	-	-	-	53.02	0.17	-	-	-
Enfield, ...	988	2	-	-	-	99.80	0.20	-	-	-
Males, ...	510	2	-	-	-	51.52	0.20	-	-	-
Females, . . .	478	-	-	-	-	48.28	-	-	-	-
Goshen, ...	303	1	-	-	-	99.67	0.33	-	-	-
Males, ...	160	-	-	-	-	52.63	-	-	-	-
Females, . . .	143	1	-	-	-	47.04	0.33	-	-	-
Granby, ...	747	1	-	-	-	99.86	0.14	-	-	-
Males, ...	394	-	-	-	-	52.67	-	-	-	-
Females, . . .	353	1	-	-	-	47.19	0.14	-	-	-
Greenwich, . . .	481	-	-	-	-	100.00	-	-	-	-
Males, ...	243	-	-	-	-	50.52	-	-	-	-
Females, . . .	238	-	-	-	-	49.48	-	-	-	-
Hadley, ...	1,703	1	-	-	-	99.94	0.06	-	-	-
Males, ...	893	1	-	-	-	52.40	0.06	-	-	-
Females, . . .	810	-	-	-	-	47.54	-	-	-	-
Hatfield, ...	1,255	7	-	-	-	99.45	0.55	-	-	-
Males, ...	663	6	-	-	-	52.54	0.47	-	-	-
Females, . . .	592	1	-	-	-	46.91	0.08	-	-	-
Huntington, . . .	1,444	6	-	-	-	99.58	0.42	-	-	-
Males, ...	719	3	-	-	-	49.58	0.21	-	-	-
Females, . . .	725	3	-	-	-	50.00	0.21	-	-	-
Middlefield, . . .	382	4	-	-	-	98.96	1.04	-	-	-
Males, ...	194	3	-	-	-	50.26	0.78	-	-	-
Females, . . .	188	1	-	-	-	48.70	0.26	-	-	-
NORTHAMPTON, . .	16,647	94	-	-	5	99.41	0.56	-	-	0.03
Males, ...	7,377	52	-	-	5	44.05	0.31	-	-	0.03
Females, . . .	9,270	42	-	-	-	55.36	0.25	-	-	-
Pelham, ...	483	3	-	-	-	99.38	0.62	-	-	-
Males, ...	245	1	-	-	-	50.41	0.21	-	-	-
Females, . . .	238	2	-	-	-	48.97	0.41	-	-	-
Plainfield, . . .	449	1	-	-	-	99.78	0.22	-	-	-
Males, ...	230	1	-	-	-	51.11	0.22	-	-	-
Females, . . .	219	-	-	-	-	48.67	-	-	-	-
Prescott, ...	401	-	-	-	-	100.00	-	-	-	-
Males, ...	208	-	-	-	-	51.87	-	-	-	-
Females, . . .	193	-	-	-	-	48.13	-	-	-	-
Southampton, . .	1,051	2	-	1	-	99.72	0.19	-	0.09	-
Males, ...	537	-	-	-	-	50.95	-	-	-	-
Females, . . .	514	2	-	1	-	48.77	0.19	-	0.09	-
South Hadley, . .	4,435	6	-	2	-	99.82	0.14	-	0.04	-
Males, ...	2,051	3	-	-	-	46.16	0.07	-	-	-
Females, . . .	2,384	3	-	2	-	53.66	0.07	-	0.04	-
Ware, ...	7,649	-	-	-	2	99.97	-	-	-	0.03
Males, ...	3,574	-	-	-	2	46.71	-	-	-	0.03
Females, . . .	4,075	-	-	-	-	53.26	-	-	-	-
Westhampton, . .	476	-	-	-	-	100.00	-	-	-	-
Males, ...	241	-	-	-	-	50.63	-	-	-	-
Females, . . .	235	-	-	-	-	49.37	-	-	-	-
Williamsburg, . .	1,954	1	-	-	-	99.95	0.05	-	-	-
Males, ...	950	-	-	-	-	48.59	-	-	-	-
Females, . . .	1,004	1	-	-	-	51.36	0.05	-	-	-
Worthington, . .	648	-	-	-	-	100.00	-	-	-	-
Males, ...	341	-	-	-	-	52.62	-	-	-	-
Females, . . .	307	-	-	-	-	47.38	-	-	-	-

COLOR AND RACE — Continued.

COUNTIES, CITIES, TOWNS, AND SEX.	White	Colored	Indian	Japanese	Chinese	PERCENTAGES				
						White	Colored	Indian	Japanese	Chinese
MIDDLESEX.										
Acton, ...	1,976	2	-	-	-	99.90	0.10	-	-	-
Males, . . .	979	1	-	-	-	49.49	0.05	-	-	-
Females, . .	997	1	-	-	-	50.41	0.05	-	-	-
Arlington, . .	6,449	61	-	-	5	98.99	0.93	-	-	0.08
Males, . . .	3,034	28	-	-	5	46.57	0.43	-	-	0.08
Females, . .	3,415	33	-	-	-	52.42	0.50	-	-	-
Ashby, ...	804	-	-	-	-	100.00	-	-	-	-
Males, . . .	413	-	-	-	-	51.37	-	-	-	-
Females, . .	391	-	-	-	-	48.63	-	-	-	-
Ashland, . . .	2,082	6	-	-	2	99.61	0.29	-	-	0.10
Males, . . .	1,009	4	-	-	2	48.27	0.19	-	-	0.10
Females, . .	1,073	2	-	-	-	51.34	0.10	-	-	-
Ayer, ...	2,080	21	-	-	-	99.00	1.00	-	-	-
Males, . . .	1,006	12	-	-	-	47.88	0.57	-	-	-
Females, . .	1,074	9	-	-	-	51.12	0.43	-	-	-
Bedford, . . .	1,168	1	-	-	-	99.91	0.09	-	-	-
Males, . . .	622	1	-	-	-	53.20	0.09	-	-	-
Females, . .	546	-	-	-	-	46.71	-	-	-	-
Belmont, . . .	2,833	8	-	-	2	99.65	0.28	-	-	0.07
Males, . . .	1,513	4	-	-	2	53.22	0.14	-	-	0.07
Females, . .	1,320	4	-	-	-	46.43	0.14	-	-	-
Billerica, . . .	2,554	23	-	-	-	99.11	0.89	-	-	-
Males, . . .	1,287	14	-	-	-	49.94	0.55	-	-	-
Females, . .	1,267	9	-	-	-	49.17	0.34	-	-	-
Boxborough, . .	302	5	-	-	-	98.37	1.63	-	-	-
Males, . . .	168	4	-	-	-	54.73	1.30	-	-	-
Females, . .	134	1	-	-	-	43.64	0.33	-	-	-
Burlington, . .	571	3	-	-	-	99.48	0.52	-	-	-
Males, . . .	315	1	-	-	-	54.88	0.17	-	-	-
Females, . .	256	2	-	-	-	44.60	0.35	-	-	-
CAMBRIDGE, . .	78,733	2,849	1	4	56	96.44	3.49	*-	*-	0.07
Males, . . .	38,428	1,342	1	4	56	47.07	1.65	*-	*-	0.07
Females, . .	40,305	1,507	-	-	-	49.37	1.84	-	-	-
Carlisle, . . .	492	-	-	-	-	100.00	-	-	-	-
Males, . . .	268	-	-	-	-	54.47	-	-	-	-
Females, . .	224	-	-	-	-	45.53	-	-	-	-
Chelmsford, . .	3,160	2	-	-	-	99.94	0.06	-	-	-
Males, . . .	1,610	1	-	-	-	50.92	0.03	-	-	-
Females, . .	1,550	1	-	-	-	49.02	0.03	-	-	-
Concord, . . .	5,108	60	7	-	-	98.70	1.16	0.14	-	-
Males, . . .	3,099	55	3	-	-	59.88	1.06	0.06	-	-
Females, . .	2,009	5	4	-	-	38.82	0.10	0.08	-	-
Dracut, . . .	2,441	2	-	-	-	99.92	0.08	-	-	-
Males, . . .	1,323	2	-	-	-	54.16	0.08	-	-	-
Females, . .	1,118	-	-	-	-	45.76	-	-	-	-
Dunstable, . .	399	1	-	-	-	99.75	0.25	-	-	-
Males, . . .	206	1	-	-	-	51.50	0.25	-	-	-
Females, . .	193	-	-	-	-	48.25	-	-	-	-
EVERETT, . .	18,106	455	-	-	12	97.49	2.45	-	-	0.06
Males, . . .	8,822	223	-	-	12	47.50	1.20	-	-	0.06
Females, . .	9,284	232	-	-	-	49.99	1.25	-	-	-
Framingham, . .	9,470	37	-	-	5	99.56	0.39	-	-	0.05
Males, . . .	4,548	17	-	-	5	47.81	0.18	-	-	0.05
Females, . .	4,922	20	-	-	-	51.75	0.21	-	-	-
Groton, . . .	2,143	49	-	-	-	97.76	2.24	-	-	-
Males, . . .	1,050	28	-	-	-	47.90	1.28	-	-	-
Females, . .	1,093	21	-	-	-	49.86	0.96	-	-	-

* Less than one one-hundredth of one per cent.

COLOR AND RACE — Continued.

COUNTIES, CITIES, TOWNS, AND SEX.	White	Colored	Indian	Japanese	Chinese	PERCENTAGES White	Colored	Indian	Japanese	Chinese
MIDDLESEX — Con.										
Holliston,	2,712	4	-	-	2	99.79	0.14	-	-	0.07
Males,	1,305	2	-	-	2	48.02	0.07	-	-	0.07
Females,	1,407	2	-	-	-	51.77	0.07	-	-	-
Hopkinton,	2,983	-	-	-	1	99.97	-	-	-	0.03
Males,	1,468	-	-	-	1	49.20	-	-	-	0.03
Females,	1,515	-	-	-	-	50.77	-	-	-	-
Hudson,	5,290	16	-	-	2	99.66	0.30	-	-	0.04
Males,	2,523	8	-	-	2	47.53	0.15	-	-	0.04
Females,	2,767	8	-	-	-	52.13	0.15	-	-	-
Lexington,	3,479	17	-	-	2	99.46	0.48	-	-	0.06
Males,	1,683	7	-	-	2	48.11	0.20	-	-	0.06
Females,	1,796	10	-	-	-	51.35	0.28	-	-	-
Lincoln,	1,075	35	1	-	-	96.76	3.15	0.09	-	-
Males,	611	14	1	-	-	55.00	1.26	0.09	-	-
Females,	464	21	-	-	-	41.76	1.89	-	-	-
Littleton,	1,127	9	-	-	-	99.21	0.79	-	-	-
Males,	568	1	-	-	-	50.00	0.09	-	-	-
Females,	559	8	-	-	-	49.21	0.70	-	-	-
LOWELL,	84,206	136	-	1	24	99.81	0.16	-	*-	0.03
Males,	38,840	66	-	1	24	46.04	0.07	-	*-	0.03
Females,	45,366	70	-	-	-	53.77	0.09	-	-	-
MALDEN,	29,369	326	-	1	12	98.86	1.10	-	*-	0.04
Males,	13,755	156	-	-	12	46.30	0.53	-	-	0.04
Females,	15,614	170	-	1	-	52.56	0.57	-	*-	-
MARLBOROUGH,	14,939	33	-	1	4	99.74	0.22	-	0.01	0.03
Males,	7,449	16	-	-	4	49.73	0.11	-	-	0.03
Females,	7,490	17	-	1	-	50.01	0.11	-	0.01	-
Maynard,	3,089	-	-	-	1	99.97	-	-	-	0.03
Males,	1,519	-	-	-	1	49.16	-	-	-	0.03
Females,	1,570	-	-	-	-	50.81	-	-	-	-
MEDFORD,	14,297	169	1	-	7	98.77	1.17	0.01	-	0.05
Males,	6,956	79	1	-	7	48.05	0.55	0.01	-	0.05
Females,	7,341	90	-	-	-	50.72	0.62	-	-	-
Melrose,	11,852	105	-	-	8	99.05	0.88	-	-	0.07
Males,	5,493	47	-	-	8	45.91	0.39	-	-	0.07
Females,	6,359	58	-	-	-	53.14	0.49	-	-	-
Natick,	8,772	42	-	-	-	99.52	0.48	-	-	-
Males,	4,212	22	-	-	-	47.79	0.25	-	-	-
Females,	4,560	20	-	-	-	51.73	0.23	-	-	-
NEWTON,	27,220	354	-	-	16	98.66	1.28	-	-	0.06
Males,	12,190	149	-	-	16	44.18	0.54	-	-	0.06
Females,	15,030	205	-	-	-	54.48	0.74	-	-	-
North Reading,	834	1	-	-	-	99.88	0.12	-	-	-
Males,	421	1	-	-	-	50.42	0.12	-	-	-
Females,	413	-	-	-	-	49.46	-	-	-	-
Pepperell,	3,305	16	-	-	-	99.52	0.48	-	-	-
Males,	1,641	9	-	-	-	49.41	0.27	-	-	-
Females,	1,664	7	-	-	-	50.11	0.21	-	-	-
Reading,	4,706	8	-	-	3	99.77	0.17	-	-	0.06
Males,	2,230	2	-	-	3	47.28	0.04	-	-	0.06
Females,	2,476	6	-	-	-	52.49	0.13	-	-	-
Sherborn,	1,434	12	-	-	-	99.17	0.83	-	-	-
Males,	582	2	-	-	-	40.25	0.14	-	-	-
Females,	852	10	-	-	-	58.92	0.69	-	-	-
Shirley,	1,392	7	-	-	-	99.50	0.50	-	-	-
Males,	651	3	-	-	-	46.53	0.22	-	-	-
Females,	741	4	-	-	-	52.97	0.28	-	-	-

* Less than one one-hundredth of one per cent.

COLOR AND RACE — Continued.

COUNTIES, CITIES, TOWNS, AND SEX.	White	Colored	Indian	Japanese	Chinese	PERCENTAGES				
						White	Colored	Indian	Japanese	Chinese
MIDDLESEX — Con.										
Somerville, . . .	32,101	72	-	-	27	99.81	0.14	-	-	0.05
Males, . . .	24,857	33	-	-	27	47.62	0.06	-	-	0.05
Females, . . .	27,244	39	-	-	-	52.19	0.08	-	-	-
Stoneham, . . .	6,253	27	-	-	4	99.51	0.43	-	-	0.06
Males, . . .	3,054	12	-	-	4	48.60	0.19	-	-	0.06
Females, . . .	3,199	15	-	-	-	50.91	0.24	-	-	-
Stow, . . .	920	-	-	-	-	100.00	-	-	-	-
Males, . . .	473	-	-	-	-	51.41	-	-	-	-
Females, . . .	447	-	-	-	-	48.59	-	-	-	-
Sudbury, . . .	1,154	7	-	-	-	99.39	0.61	-	-	-
Males, . . .	599	4	-	-	-	52.50	0.35	-	-	-
Females, . . .	555	3	-	-	-	46.89	0.26	-	-	-
Tewksbury, . . .	3,331	47	1	-	-	98.58	1.39	0.03	-	-
Males, . . .	1,629	23	1	-	-	48.21	0.68	0.03	-	-
Females, . . .	1,702	24	-	-	-	50.37	0.71	-	-	-
Townsend, . . .	1,768	12	-	-	-	99.33	0.67	-	-	-
Males, . . .	876	4	-	-	-	49.22	0.22	-	-	-
Females, . . .	892	8	-	-	-	50.11	0.45	-	-	-
Tyngsborough, . .	635	-	-	-	-	100.00	-	-	-	-
Males, . . .	324	-	-	-	-	51.02	-	-	-	-
Females, . . .	311	-	-	-	-	48.98	-	-	-	-
Wakefield, . . .	8,283	17	-	-	4	99.75	0.20	-	-	0.05
Males, . . .	3,952	6	-	-	4	47.59	0.07	-	-	0.05
Females, . . .	4,331	11	-	-	-	52.16	0.13	-	-	-
Waltham, . . .	20,824	36	-	-	16	99.75	0.17	-	-	0.08
Males, . . .	9,602	20	-	-	16	46.00	0.09	-	-	0.08
Females, . . .	11,222	16	-	-	-	53.75	0.08	-	-	-
Watertown, . . .	7,725	56	-	-	7	99.19	0.72	-	-	0.09
Males, . . .	3,713	20	-	-	7	47.67	0.26	-	-	0.09
Females, . . .	4,012	36	-	-	-	51.52	0.46	-	-	-
Wayland, . . .	2,023	2	-	-	1	99.85	0.10	-	-	0.05
Males, . . .	1,023	2	-	-	1	50.49	0.10	-	-	0.05
Females, . . .	1,000	-	-	-	-	49.36	-	-	-	-
Westford, . . .	2,414	4	-	-	-	99.83	0.17	-	-	-
Males, . . .	1,223	-	-	-	-	50.58	-	-	-	-
Females, . . .	1,191	4	-	-	-	49.25	0.17	-	-	-
Weston, . . .	1,709	1	-	-	-	99.94	0.06	-	-	-
Males, . . .	877	-	-	-	-	51.29	-	-	-	-
Females, . . .	832	1	-	-	-	48.65	0.06	-	-	-
Wilmington, . . .	1,412	8	-	-	-	99.44	0.56	-	-	-
Males, . . .	711	4	-	-	-	50.07	0.28	-	-	-
Females, . . .	701	4	-	-	-	49.37	0.28	-	-	-
Winchester, . . .	6,043	107	-	-	-	98.26	1.74	-	-	-
Males, . . .	2,893	35	-	-	-	47.04	0.57	-	-	-
Females, . . .	3,150	72	-	-	-	51.22	1.17	-	-	-
Woburn, . . .	13,958	218	1	-	1	98.45	1.53	0.01	-	0.01
Males, . . .	6,889	110	-	-	1	48.59	0.77	-	-	0.01
Females, . . .	7,069	108	1	-	-	49.86	0.76	0.01	-	-
NANTUCKET.										
Nantucket, . . .	2,956	60	-	-	-	98.07	1.99	-	-	-
Males, . . .	1,303	12	-	-	-	43.20	0.40	-	-	-
Females, . . .	1,653	48	-	-	-	54.81	1.59	-	-	-
NORFOLK.										
Avon, . . .	1,620	5	-	-	1	99.63	0.31	-	-	0.06
Males, . . .	815	2	-	-	1	50.13	0.12	-	-	0.06
Females, . . .	805	3	-	-	-	49.50	0.19	-	-	-

COLOR AND RACE — Continued.

COUNTIES, CITIES, TOWNS, AND SEX.	White	Colored	Indian	Japanese	Chinese	PERCENTAGES				
						White	Colored	Indian	Japanese	Chinese
NORFOLK — Con.										
Bellingham, . . .	1,475	3	3	-	-	99.60	0.20	0.20	-	-
Males, . . .	719	-	2	-	-	48.55	-	0.13	-	-
Females, . . .	756	3	1	-	-	51.05	0.20	0.07	-	-
Braintree, . . .	5,302	6	-	-	3	99.82	0.12	-	-	0.06
Males, . . .	2,654	3	-	-	3	49.96	0.06	-	-	0.06
Females, . . .	2,648	3	-	-	-	49.86	0.06	-	-	-
Brookline, . . .	16,048	104	1	1	10	99.28	0.64	0.01	0.01	0.06
Males, . . .	6,782	32	1	1	10	41.95	0.20	0.01	0.01	0.06
Females, . . .	9,266	72	-	-	-	57.33	0.44	-	-	-
Canton, . . .	4,612	23	-	-	1	99.48	0.50	-	-	0.02
Males, . . .	2,193	13	-	-	1	47.31	0.28	-	-	0.02
Females, . . .	2,419	10	-	-	-	52.17	0.22	-	-	-
Cohasset, . . .	2,466	8	-	-	-	99.68	0.32	-	-	-
Males, . . .	1,144	4	-	-	-	46.24	0.16	-	-	-
Females, . . .	1,322	4	-	-	-	53.44	0.16	-	-	-
Dedham, . . .	7,131	72	3	-	5	98.89	1.00	0.04	-	0.07
Males, . . .	3,434	37	-	-	5	47.62	0.51	-	-	0.07
Females, . . .	3,697	35	3	-	-	51.27	0.49	0.04	-	-
Dover, . . .	646	2	-	-	-	99.70	0.30	-	-	-
Males, . . .	343	2	-	-	-	51.35	0.30	-	-	-
Females, . . .	323	-	-	-	-	48.35	-	-	-	-
Foxborough, . . .	3,201	18	-	-	-	99.44	0.56	-	-	-
Males, . . .	1,528	14	-	-	-	47.47	0.43	-	-	-
Females, . . .	1,673	4	-	-	-	51.97	0.13	-	-	-
Franklin, . . .	5,131	3	-	-	2	99.90	0.06	-	-	0.04
Males, . . .	2,454	3	-	-	2	47.78	0.06	-	-	0.04
Females, . . .	2,677	-	-	-	-	52.12	-	-	-	-
Holbrook, . . .	2,293	5	-	-	-	99.78	0.22	-	-	-
Males, . . .	1,124	3	-	-	-	48.91	0.13	-	-	-
Females, . . .	1,169	2	-	-	-	50.87	0.09	-	-	-
Hyde Park, . . .	11,713	108	-	-	5	99.05	0.91	-	-	0.04
Males, . . .	5,707	48	-	-	5	48.26	0.41	-	-	0.04
Females, . . .	6,006	60	-	-	-	50.79	0.50	-	-	-
Medfield, . . .	1,867	4	-	-	1	99.73	0.22	-	-	0.05
Males, . . .	880	2	-	-	1	47.01	0.11	-	-	0.05
Females, . . .	987	2	-	-	-	52.72	0.11	-	-	-
Medway, . . .	2,911	2	-	-	-	99.94	0.06	-	-	-
Males, . . .	1,437	1	-	-	-	49.33	0.03	-	-	-
Females, . . .	1,474	1	-	-	-	50.61	0.03	-	-	-
Millis, . . .	1,000	6	-	-	-	99.40	0.60	-	-	-
Males, . . .	481	3	-	-	-	47.81	0.30	-	-	-
Females, . . .	519	3	-	-	-	51.59	0.30	-	-	-
Milton, . . .	5,459	53	5	-	1	98.93	0.96	0.09	-	0.02
Males, . . .	2,533	25	3	-	1	45.90	0.45	0.06	-	0.02
Females, . . .	2,926	28	2	-	-	53.03	0.51	0.03	-	-
Needham, . . .	3,492	17	-	1	1	99.46	0.48	-	0.03	0.03
Males, . . .	1,736	12	-	-	1	49.44	0.34	-	-	0.03
Females, . . .	1,756	5	-	1	-	50.02	0.14	-	0.03	-
Norfolk, . . .	882	-	-	-	-	100.00	-	-	-	-
Males, . . .	471	-	-	-	-	53.40	-	-	-	-
Females, . . .	411	-	-	-	-	46.60	-	-	-	-
Norwood, . . .	4,557	12	5	-	-	99.63	0.26	0.11	-	-
Males, . . .	2,426	8	3	-	-	53.04	0.17	0.07	-	-
Females, . . .	2,131	4	2	-	-	46.59	0.09	0.04	-	-
QUINCY, . . .	20,694	6	-	-	12	99.91	0.03	-	-	0.06
Males, . . .	10,591	5	-	-	12	51.13	0.03	-	-	0.06
Females, . . .	10,103	1	-	-	-	48.78	*	-	-	-

* Less than one one-hundredth of one per cent.

COLOR AND RACE — Continued.

COUNTIES. CITIES TOWNS, AND SEX.	White	Colored	Indian	Japanese	Chinese	White	Colored	Indian	Japanese	Chinese
						PERCENTAGES				
NORFOLK — Con.										
Randolph, . . .	5,991	-	-	-	5	99.92	-	-	-	0.08
Males, . . .	3,822	-	-	-	3	49.92	-	-	-	0.08
Females, . . .	3,809	-	-	-	-	50.00	-	-	-	-
Sharon, . . .	1,706	11	-	-	-	99.36	0.64	-	-	-
Males, . . .	833	4	-	-	-	48.63	0.23	-	-	-
Females, . . .	873	7	-	-	-	50.73	0.41	-	-	-
Stoughton, . . .	5,256	27	6	-	3	99.32	0.51	0.11	-	0.06
Males, . . .	2,561	9	5	-	3	48.43	0.17	0.09	-	0.06
Females, . . .	2,688	18	1	-	-	50.89	0.34	0.02	-	-
Walpole, . . .	2,987	7	-	-	-	99.77	0.23	-	-	-
Males, . . .	1,495	5	-	-	-	49.94	0.16	-	-	-
Females, . . .	1,492	2	-	-	-	49.83	0.07	-	-	-
Wellesley, . . .	4,273	15	-	-	1	99.62	0.36	-	-	0.02
Males, . . .	1,461	8	-	-	1	34.55	0.19	-	-	0.02
Females, . . .	2,772	7	-	-	-	65.07	0.17	-	-	-
Weymouth, . . .	11,251	11	-	-	5	99.65	0.31	-	-	0.04
Males, . . .	5,567	20	-	-	5	49.31	0.18	-	-	0.04
Females, . . .	5,684	15	-	-	-	50.34	0.13	-	-	-
Wrentham, . . .	2,565	20	-	-	-	99.22	0.78	-	-	-
Males, . . .	1,259	10	-	-	-	48.49	0.39	-	-	-
Females, . . .	1,311	10	-	-	-	50.73	0.39	-	-	-
PLYMOUTH.										
Abington, . . .	4,394	8	2	-	3	99.69	0.19	0.04	-	0.08
Males, . . .	2,063	4	1	-	3	48.31	0.08	0.02	-	0.08
Females, . . .	2,161	4	1	-	-	51.38	0.11	0.02	-	-
Bridgewater, . . .	4,398	5	1	-	2	98.12	1.82	0.02	-	0.04
Males, . . .	2,571	46	-	-	2	57.00	1.05	-	-	0.04
Females, . . .	1,827	29	1	-	-	41.12	0.77	0.02	-	-
Brockton, . . .	42,928	208	3	-	26	99.28	0.63	0.01	-	0.08
Males, . . .	16,416	117	2	-	26	49.49	0.55	0.01	-	0.08
Females, . . .	16,512	90	1	-	-	49.79	0.28	*-	-	-
Carver, . . .	886	22	1	-	-	97.74	2.16	0.10	-	-
Males, . . .	504	14	1	-	-	52.27	1.37	0.10	-	-
Females, . . .	402	8	-	-	-	45.47	0.79	-	-	-
Duxbury, . . .	1,904	10	-	-	-	99.49	0.51	-	-	-
Males, . . .	942	3	-	-	-	47.92	0.15	-	-	-
Females, . . .	1,014	7	-	-	-	51.57	0.36	-	-	-
East Bridgewater, . .	2,880	8	-	-	1	99.69	0.28	-	-	0.03
Males, . . .	1,433	2	-	-	1	49.69	0.07	-	-	0.03
Females, . . .	1,447	6	-	-	-	50.00	0.21	-	-	-
Halifax, . . .	497	-	-	-	-	100.00	-	-	-	-
Males, . . .	296	-	-	-	-	55.52	-	-	-	-
Females, . . .	241	-	-	-	-	46.48	-	-	-	-
Hanover, . . .	2,602	10	-	-	-	99.07	0.93	-	-	-
Males, . . .	1,080	9	-	-	-	48.76	0.44	-	-	-
Females, . . .	1,052	10	-	-	-	50.31	0.49	-	-	-
Hanson, . . .	1,308	12	-	-	-	99.13	0.87	-	-	-
Males, . . .	703	5	-	-	-	50.94	0.36	-	-	-
Females, . . .	605	7	-	-	-	48.19	0.51	-	-	-
Hingham, . . .	4,711	99	4	-	2	97.82	2.06	0.08	-	0.04
Males, . . .	2,248	47	2	-	2	46.65	0.98	0.04	-	0.04
Females, . . .	2,463	52	2	-	-	51.17	1.08	0.04	-	-
Hull, . . .	1,059	5	-	-	-	99.52	0.48	-	-	-
Males, . . .	552	4	-	-	-	50.96	0.38	-	-	-
Females, . . .	507	1	-	-	-	48.56	0.10	-	-	-

* Less than one one-hundredth of one per cent.

COLOR AND RACE — Continued.

COUNTIES, CITIES, TOWNS, AND SEX.	White	Colored	Indian	Japanese	Chinese	PERCENTAGES				
						White	Colored	Indian	Japanese	Chinese
PLYMOUTH — Con.										
Kingston,	1,745	-	-	-	1	99.94	-	-	-	0.06
Males,	846	-	-	-	1	48.45	-	-	-	0.06
Females,	899	-	-	-	-	51.49	-	-	-	-
Lakeville,	856	11	3	-	-	98.39	1.26	0.35	-	-
Males,	434	5	-	-	-	49.89	0.57	-	-	-
Females,	422	6	3	-	-	48.50	0.69	0.35	-	-
Marion,	750	9	-	-	-	98.81	1.19	-	-	-
Males,	323	5	-	-	-	42.55	0.66	-	-	-
Females,	427	4	-	-	-	56.26	0.53	-	-	-
Marshfield,	1,758	2	-	-	-	99.88	0.12	-	-	-
Males,	849	1	-	-	-	48.24	0.06	-	-	-
Females,	909	1	-	-	-	51.64	0.06	-	-	-
Mattapoisett,	1,030	2	-	-	-	99.80	0.20	-	-	-
Males,	489	1	-	-	-	47.38	0.10	-	-	-
Females,	541	1	-	-	-	52.42	0.10	-	-	-
Middleborough,	6,626	57	3	-	3	99.06	0.86	0.04	-	0.04
Males,	3,177	22	3	-	3	47.50	0.33	0.04	-	0.04
Females,	3,449	35	-	-	-	51.56	0.53	-	-	-
Norwell,	1,462	78	-	-	-	94.94	5.06	-	-	-
Males,	733	38	-	-	-	47.60	2.46	-	-	-
Females,	729	40	-	-	-	47.34	2.60	-	-	-
Pembroke,	1,220	3	-	-	-	99.75	0.25	-	-	-
Males,	633	1	-	-	-	51.76	0.08	-	-	-
Females,	587	2	-	-	-	47.99	0.17	-	-	-
Plymouth,	7,847	102	8	-	-	98.62	1.28	0.10	-	-
Males,	3,813	44	6	-	-	47.92	0.55	0.08	-	-
Females,	4,034	58	2	-	-	50.70	0.73	0.02	-	-
Plympton,	549	-	-	-	-	100.00	-	-	-	-
Males,	268	-	-	-	-	48.82	-	-	-	-
Females,	281	-	-	-	-	51.18	-	-	-	-
Rochester,	1,016	4	1	-	-	99.51	0.39	0.10	-	-
Males,	533	1	1	-	-	52.20	0.10	0.10	-	-
Females,	483	3	-	-	-	47.31	0.29	-	-	-
Rockland,	5,511	5	-	-	7	99.78	0.09	-	-	0.13
Males,	2,747	3	-	-	7	49.74	0.05	-	-	0.13
Females,	2,764	2	-	-	-	50.04	0.04	-	-	-
Scituate,	2,246	-	-	-	-	100.00	-	-	-	-
Males,	1,115	-	-	-	-	49.64	-	-	-	-
Females,	1,131	-	-	-	-	50.36	-	-	-	-
Wareham,	3,347	18	1	-	1	99.41	0.53	0.03	-	0.03
Males,	1,757	7	-	-	1	52.18	0.21	-	-	0.03
Females,	1,590	11	1	-	-	47.23	0.32	0.03	-	-
West Bridgewater,	1,746	1	-	-	-	99.94	0.06	-	-	-
Males,	876	1	-	-	-	50.14	0.06	-	-	-
Females,	870	-	-	-	-	49.80	-	-	-	-
Whitman,	5,687	37	13	1	6	99.01	0.64	0.23	0.02	0.10
Males,	2,845	18	9	1	6	49.55	0.31	0 16	0.02	0.10
Females,	2,842	19	4	-	-	49.48	0.33	0.07	-	-
SUFFOLK.										
Boston,	486,625	9,472	10	7	805	97.93	1.91	*-	*-	0.16
Males,	234,081	4,775	4	7	799	47.11	0.96	*-	*-	0.16
Females,	252,545	4,697	6	-	6	50.82	0.95	*-	-	*-
Chelsea,	30,527	693	5	-	39	97.64	2.22	0.02	-	0.12
Males,	14,901	330	4	-	38	47.66	1.05	0.02	-	0.12
Females,	15,626	363	1	-	1	49.98	1.17	*-	-	*-

* Less than one one-hundredth of one per cent.

COLOR AND RACE — Continued.

COUNTIES, CITIES, TOWNS, AND SEX.	White	Colored	Indian	Japanese	Chinese	PERCENTAGES White	Colored	Indian	Japanese	Chinese
SUFFOLK — Con.										
Revere,	7,347	67	4	-	5	98.98	0.90	0.05	-	0.07
Males,	3,682	30	4	-	5	49.60	0.41	0.05	-	0.07
Females,	3,665	37	-	-	-	49.38	0.49	-	-	-
Winthrop,	4,156	34	-	-	2	99.14	0.81	-	-	0.05
Males,	2,000	13	-	-	2	47.71	0.31	-	-	0.05
Females,	2,156	21	-	-	-	51.43	0.50	-	-	-
WORCESTER.										
Ashburnham,	2,145	2	-	1	-	99.86	0.09	-	0.05	-
Males,	1,067	2	-	1	-	49.67	0.09	-	0.05	-
Females,	1,078	-	-	-	-	50.19	-	-	-	-
Athol,	7,347	13	-	-	4	99.76	0.18	-	-	0.06
Males,	3,722	9	-	-	4	50.54	0.12	-	-	0.06
Females,	3,625	4	-	-	-	49.22	0.06	-	-	-
Auburn,	1,597	1	-	-	-	99.94	0.06	-	-	-
Males,	821	-	-	-	-	51.58	-	-	-	-
Females,	776	1	-	-	-	48.56	0.06	-	-	-
Barre,	2,275	3	-	-	-	99.87	0.13	-	-	-
Males,	1,148	2	-	-	-	50.40	0.08	-	-	-
Females,	1,127	1	-	-	-	49.47	0.05	-	-	-
Berlin,	897	-	-	-	-	100.00	-	-	-	-
Males,	451	-	-	-	-	50.28	-	-	-	-
Females,	446	-	-	-	-	49.72	-	-	-	-
Blackstone,	6,658	1	-	-	-	99.98	0.02	-	-	-
Males,	3,116	-	-	-	-	51.60	-	-	-	-
Females,	2,922	1	-	-	-	48.38	0.02	-	-	-
Bolton,	793	4	-	-	-	99.50	0.50	-	-	-
Males,	395	3	-	-	-	49.56	0.38	-	-	-
Females,	398	1	-	-	-	49.94	0.12	-	-	-
Boylston,	722	7	-	-	-	99.04	0.96	-	-	-
Males,	386	3	-	-	-	52.95	0.41	-	-	-
Females,	336	4	-	-	-	46.09	0.55	-	-	-
Brookfield,	3,268	9	-	-	2	99.67	0.27	-	-	0.06
Males,	1,682	5	-	-	2	51.30	0.15	-	-	0.06
Females,	1,586	4	-	-	-	48.37	0.12	-	-	-
Charlton,	1,876	1	-	-	-	99.94	0.05	-	-	-
Males,	975	-	-	-	-	51.94	-	-	-	-
Females,	901	1	-	-	-	48.00	0.06	-	-	-
Clinton,	11,492	2	-	-	3	99.96	0.02	-	-	0.02
Males,	5,286	2	-	-	3	45.98	0.02	-	-	0.02
Females,	6,206	-	-	-	-	53.98	-	-	-	-
Dana,	716	1	-	-	-	99.86	0.14	-	-	-
Males,	352	1	-	-	-	49.09	0.14	-	-	-
Females,	364	-	-	-	-	50.77	-	-	-	-
Douglas,	2,017	9	-	-	-	99.56	0.44	-	-	-
Males,	1,030	3	-	-	-	50.84	0.15	-	-	-
Females,	987	6	-	-	-	48.72	0.29	-	-	-
Dudley,	3,179	24	-	-	-	99.26	0.74	-	-	-
Males,	1,599	12	-	-	-	49.93	0.37	-	-	-
Females,	1,580	12	-	-	-	49.33	0.37	-	-	-
Fitchburg,	26,344	51	-	-	14	99.76	0.19	-	-	0.05
Males,	12,995	28	-	-	14	49.21	0.11	-	-	0.05
Females,	13,349	23	-	-	-	50.55	0.08	-	-	-
Gardner,	9,114	66	-	-	2	99.26	0.72	-	-	0.02
Males,	4,698	35	-	-	2	51.17	0.38	-	-	0.02
Females,	4,416	31	-	-	-	48.09	0.34	-	-	-

COLOR AND RACE — Continued.

COUNTIES, CITIES, TOWNS, AND SEX.	White	Colored	Indian	Japanese	Chinese	PERCENTAGES				
						White	Colored	Indian	Japanese	Chinese
WORCESTER — Con.										
Grafton, ...	5,090	10	–	–	1	99.78	0.20	–	–	0.02
Males, ...	2,448	6	–	–	1	47.99	0.12	–	–	0.02
Females, . . .	2,642	4	–	–	–	51.79	0.08	–	–	–
Hardwick, . . .	2,654	1	–	–	–	99.96	0.04	–	–	–
Males, ...	1,375	1	–	–	–	51.79	0.04	–	–	–
Females, . . .	1,279	–	–	–	–	48.17	–	–	–	–
Harvard, . . .	1,146	16	–	–	–	98.62	1.38	–	–	–
Males, ...	565	9	–	–	–	48.62	0.78	–	–	–
Females, . . .	581	7	–	–	–	50.00	0.60	–	–	–
Holden, . . .	2,369	3	–	–	–	99.88	0.12	–	–	–
Males, ...	1,300	2	–	–	–	49.96	0.08	–	–	–
Females, . . .	1,299	1	–	–	–	49.92	0.04	–	–	–
Hopedale, . . .	1,370	7	–	–	–	99.49	0.51	–	–	–
Males, ...	694	4	–	–	–	50.40	0.29	–	–	–
Females, . . .	676	3	–	–	–	49.09	0.22	–	–	–
Hubbardston, . .	1,268	6	–	–	–	99.52	0.48	–	–	–
Males, ...	656	3	–	–	–	51.49	0.24	–	–	–
Females, . . .	612	3	–	–	–	48.03	0.24	–	–	–
Lancaster, . . .	2,152	28	–	–	–	98.72	1.28	–	–	–
Males, ...	969	9	–	–	–	44.45	0.41	–	–	–
Females, . . .	1,183	19	–	–	–	54.27	0.87	–	–	–
Leicester, . . .	3,236	3	–	–	–	99.91	0.09	–	–	–
Males, ...	1,539	2	–	–	–	47.52	0.06	–	–	–
Females, . . .	1,697	1	–	–	–	52.39	0.03	–	–	–
Leominster, . . .	9,166	38	–	–	7	99.51	0.41	–	–	0.08
Males, ...	4,477	20	–	–	7	48.60	0.22	–	–	0.08
Females, . . .	4,689	18	–	–	–	50.91	0.19	–	–	–
Lunenburg, . . .	1,236	1	–	–	–	99.92	0.08	–	–	–
Males, ...	626	–	–	–	–	50.61	–	–	–	–
Females, . . .	610	1	–	–	–	49.31	0.08	–	–	–
Mendon, ...	847	32	10	–	–	95.28	3.60	1.12	–	–
Males, ...	441	16	5	–	–	49.61	1.80	0.56	–	–
Females, . . .	406	16	5	–	–	45.67	1.80	0.56	–	–
Milford, ...	8,262	16	–	–	4	99.78	0.18	–	–	0.04
Males, ...	4,343	7	–	–	4	48.48	0.08	–	–	0.04
Females, . . .	4,506	9	–	–	–	51.31	0.10	–	–	–
Millbury, ...	5,220	–	–	–	2	99.96	–	–	–	0.04
Males, ...	2,617	–	–	–	2	50.11	–	–	–	0.04
Females, . . .	2,603	–	–	–	–	49.85	–	–	–	–
New Braintree, . .	542	–	–	–	–	100.00	–	–	–	–
Males, ...	292	–	–	–	–	53.87	–	–	–	–
Females, . . .	250	–	–	–	–	46.13	–	–	–	–
Northborough, . .	1,937	3	–	–	–	99.85	0.15	–	–	–
Males, ...	973	2	–	–	–	50.16	0.10	–	–	–
Females, . . .	964	1	–	–	–	49.69	0.05	–	–	–
Northbridge, . .	5,280	5	–	–	1	99.89	0.09	–	–	0.02
Males, ...	2,729	2	–	–	1	51.63	0.03	–	–	0.02
Females, . . .	2,551	3	–	–	–	48.26	0.06	–	–	–
North Brookfield, .	4,625	8	–	–	2	99.79	0.17	–	–	0.04
Males, ...	2,241	5	–	–	2	48.35	0.11	–	–	0.04
Females, . . .	2,384	3	–	–	–	51.44	0.06	–	–	–
Oakham, . . .	906	2	–	–	–	99.67	0.33	–	–	–
Males, ...	396	2	–	–	–	50.58	0.33	–	–	–
Females, . . .	297	–	–	–	–	49.09	–	–	–	–
Oxford, ...	2,350	40	–	–	–	98.33	1.67	–	–	–
Males, ...	1,129	18	–	–	–	47.24	0.75	–	–	–
Females, . . .	1,221	22	–	–	–	51.09	0.92	–	–	–

COLOR AND RACE. 825

COLOR AND RACE—Continued.

COUNTIES, CITIES. TOWNS, AND SEX	White	Colored	Indian	Japanese	Chinese	PERCENTAGES White	Colored	Indian	Japanese	Chinese
WORCESTER — Con.										
Paxton,	426	-	-	-	-	100.00	-	-	-	-
Males,	234	-	-	-	-	54.93	-	-	-	-
Females,	192	-	-	-	-	45.07	-	-	-	-
Peter-ham,	947	5	-	-	-	99.47	0.53	-	-	-
Males,	490	3	-	-	-	51.47	0.32	-	-	-
Females,	457	2	-	-	-	48.00	0.21	-	-	-
Phillipston,	460	-	-	-	-	100.00	-	-	-	-
Males,	248	-	-	-	-	53.91	-	-	-	-
Females,	212	-	-	-	-	46.09	-	-	-	-
Princeton,	952	-	-	-	-	100.00	-	-	-	-
Males,	491	-	-	-	-	51.58	-	-	-	-
Females,	461	-	-	-	-	48.42	-	-	-	-
Royalston,	890	-	-	-	-	100.00	-	-	-	-
Males,	454	-	-	-	-	51.01	-	-	-	-
Females,	436	-	-	-	-	48.99	-	-	-	-
Rutland,	978	-	-	-	-	100.00	-	-	-	-
Males,	526	-	-	-	-	53.78	-	-	-	-
Females,	452	-	-	-	-	46.22	-	-	-	-
Shrewsbury,	1,521	2	1	-	-	99.80	0.13	0.07	-	-
Males,	781	2	1	-	-	51.24	0.13	0.07	-	-
Females,	740	-	-	-	-	48.56	-	-	-	-
Southborough,	2,201	22	-	-	-	99.01	0.99	-	-	-
Males,	1,265	9	-	-	-	56.90	0.41	-	-	-
Females,	936	13	-	-	-	42.11	0.58	-	-	-
Southbridge,	8,215	30	-	-	5	99.58	0.36	-	-	0.06
Males,	4,028	10	-	-	5	48.83	0.12	-	-	0.06
Females,	4,187	20	-	-	-	50.75	0.24	-	-	-
Spencer,	7,605	7	-	-	2	99.88	0.09	-	-	0.03
Males,	3,779	3	-	-	2	49.63	0.04	-	-	0.03
Females,	3,826	4	-	-	-	50.25	0.05	-	-	-
Sterling,	1,207	11	-	-	-	99.10	0.90	-	-	-
Males,	600	4	-	-	-	49.26	0.33	-	-	-
Females,	607	7	-	-	-	49.84	0.57	-	-	-
Sturbridge,	1,872	38	-	-	-	98.01	1.99	-	-	-
Males,	928	20	-	-	-	48.58	1.05	-	-	-
Females,	944	18	-	-	-	49.43	0.94	-	-	-
Sutton,	3,411	9	-	-	-	99.74	0.26	-	-	-
Males,	1,768	2	-	-	-	51.70	0.05	-	-	-
Females,	1,643	7	-	-	-	48.04	0.21	-	-	-
Templeton,	2,910	5	-	-	-	99.83	0.17	-	-	-
Males,	1,485	3	-	-	-	50.95	0.10	-	-	-
Females,	1,425	2	-	-	-	48.88	0.07	-	-	-
Upton,	2,149	1	-	-	-	99.95	0.05	-	-	-
Males,	907	1	-	-	-	42.18	0.05	-	-	-
Females,	1,242	-	-	-	-	57.77	-	-	-	-
Uxbridge,	3,529	16	-	-	1	99.52	0.46	-	-	0.02
Males,	1,771	8	-	-	1	49.95	0.23	-	-	0.02
Females,	1,758	8	-	-	-	49.57	0.23	-	-	-
Warren,	4,405	22	-	-	3	99.43	0.50	-	-	0.07
Males,	2,182	12	-	-	3	49.25	0.27	-	-	0.07
Females,	2,223	10	-	-	-	50.18	0.23	-	-	-
Webster,	7,777	9	9	-	4	99.71	0.12	0.12	-	0.05
Males,	3,789	4	2	-	4	48.58	0.05	0.03	-	0.05
Females,	3,988	5	7	-	-	51.13	0.07	0.09	-	-
Westborough,	5,213	19	-	-	3	99.58	0.36	-	-	0.06
Males,	2,594	15	-	-	2	49.55	0.29	-	-	0.04
Females,	2,619	4	-	-	1	50.03	0.07	-	-	0.02

COLOR AND RACE — Continued.

Counties, Cities, Towns, and Sex	White	Colored	Indian	Japanese	Chinese	Percentages				
						White	Colored	Indian	Japanese	Chinese
WORCESTER — Con.										
West Boylston, . .	2,962	6	-	-	-	99.80	0.20	-	-	-
Males, ...	1,443	4	-	-	-	48.62	0.13	-	-	-
Females, . . .	1,519	2	-	-	-	51.18	0.07	-	-	-
West Brookfield, . .	1,466	-	-	-	1	99.93	-	-	-	0.07
Males, ...	716	-	-	-	1	48.81	-	-	-	0.07
Females, . . .	750	-	-	-	-	51.12	-	-	-	-
Westminster, . . .	1,313	2	-	-	-	99.84	0.16	-	-	-
Males, ...	631	1	-	-	-	47.98	0.08	-	-	-
Females, . . .	682	1	-	-	-	51.86	0.08	-	-	-
Winchendon, . . .	4,482	6	-	-	2	99.82	0.13	-	-	0.05
Males, ...	2,251	4	-	-	2	50.14	0.08	-	-	0.05
Females, . . .	2,231	2	-	-	-	49.68	0.05	-	-	-
WORCESTER, . . .	97,607	1,104	4	1	51	98.83	1.12	*-	*-	0.05
Males, ...	48,275	534	2	1	51	48.88	0.54	*-	*-	0.05
Females, . . .	49,332	570	2	-	-	49.95	0.58	*-	-	-

RECAPITULATION: BY COUNTIES.

Counties, and Sex	White	Colored	Indian	Japanese	Chinese	Percentages				
						White	Colored	Indian	Japanese	Chinese
BARNSTABLE, . . .	27,100	348	203	-	3	98.00	1.26	0.73	-	0.01
Males, . . .	13,015	172	104	-	3	47.07	0.62	0.37	-	0.01
Females, . . .	14,085	176	99	-	-	50.93	0.64	0.36	-	-
BERKSHIRE, . . .	84,967	1,277	11	-	37	98.47	1.48	0.01	-	0.04
Males, . . .	41,867	616	5	-	37	48.52	0.72	*-	-	0.04
Females, . . .	43,100	661	6	-	-	49.95	0.76	0.01	-	*-
BRISTOL, ...	216,509	2,402	24	-	84	98.85	1.10	0.01	-	0.04
Males, . . .	104,374	1,111	13	-	84	47.65	0.51	0.01	-	0.04
Females, . . .	112,135	1,291	11	-	-	51.20	0.59	*-	-	-
DUKES, ...	3,946	141	147	-	4	93.11	3.33	3.47	-	0.09
Males, . . .	1,904	70	79	-	4	44.93	1.65	1.87	-	0.09
Females, . . .	2,042	71	68	-	-	48.18	1.68	1.60	-	-
ESSEX, ...	328,426	1,784	5	5	173	99.41	0.54	*-	*-	0.05
Males, . . .	160,921	813	2	5	172	48.71	0.25	*-	*-	0.05
Females, . . .	167,505	971	3	-	1	50.70	0.29	*-	-	*-
FRANKLIN, . . .	40,016	110	4	4	11	99.68	0.27	0.01	0.01	0.03
Males, . . .	20,226	50	3	3	11	50.38	0.12	0.01	0.01	0.03
Females, . . .	19,790	60	1	1	-	49.30	0.15	*-	*-	-
HAMPDEN, . . .	151,640	1,240	3	1	54	99.15	0.81	*-	*-	0.04
Males, . . .	73,519	559	1	-	54	48.07	0.36	*-	-	0.04
Females, . . .	78,121	681	2	1	-	51.86	0.45	*-	*-	-
HAMPSHIRE, . . .	54,371	319	4	5	11	99.38	0.58	0.01	0.01	0.02
Males, . . .	25,900	144	4	2	11	47.34	0.26	0.01	*-	0.02
Females, . . .	28,471	175	-	3	-	52.04	0.32	-	0.01	-
MIDDLESEX, . . .	493,485	5,489	12	7	224	98.81	1.10	*-	*-	0.05
Males, . . .	236,492	2,595	7	5	224	47.37	0.52	*-	*-	0.05
Females, . . .	256,993	2,894	5	2	-	51.48	0.58	*-	*-	-
NANTUCKET, . . .	2,956	60	-	-	-	98.01	1.99	-	-	-
Males, . . .	1,303	12	-	-	-	43.20	0.40	-	-	-
Females, . . .	1,653	48	-	-	-	54.81	1.59	-	-	-

* Less than one one-hundredth of one per cent.

COLOR AND RACE — Concluded.

RECAPITULATION: BY COUNTIES — Concluded.

COUNTIES AND SEX.	White	Colored	Indian	Japanese	Chinese	White	Colored	Indian	Japanese	Chinese
						\multicolumn{5}{c}{PERCENTAGES}
NORFOLK,	134,168	572	23	2	54	99.52	0.42	0.02	*-	0.04
Males,	64,438	273	14	1	54	47.80	0.20	0.01	*-	0.04
Females,	69,730	299	9	1	-	51.72	0.22	0.01	*-	-
PLYMOUTH,	100,600	805	40	1	52	99.12	0.79	0.04	*-	0.05
Males,	50,218	398	25	1	52	49.48	0.39	0.03	*-	0.05
Females,	50,382	407	15	-	-	49.64	0.40	0.01	-	-
SUFFOLK,	528,656	10,266	19	7	851	97.94	1.90	*-	*-	0.16
Males,	254,664	5,148	12	7	844	47.18	0.95	*-	*-	0.16
Females,	273,992	5,118	7	-	7	50.76	0.95	*-	-	*-
WORCESTER,	304,578	1,727	24	2	114	99.59	0.57	*-	*-	0.04
Males,	151,079	852	10	2	113	49.30	0.28	*-	*-	0.04
Females,	153,499	875	14	-	1	50.09	0.29	*-	-	*-

RECAPITULATION. FOR THE STATE.

THE STATE AND SEX.	White	Colored	Indian	Japanese	Chinese	White	Colored	Indian	Japanese	Chinese
						\multicolumn{5}{c}{† PERCENTAGES OF TOTAL POPULATION}
THE STATE,	2,471,418	26,540	519	34	1,672	98.85	1.06	0.02	*-	0.07
Males,	1,199,920	12,813	279	26	1,663	47.99	0.51	0.01	*-	0.07
Females,	1,271,498	13,727	240	8	9	50.86	0.55	0.01	*-	*-

† See note, page 851.

RECAPITULATION. PERCENTAGES.

THE STATE AND COUNTIES.	\multicolumn{5}{c}{MALES}					\multicolumn{5}{c}{FEMALES}
	White	Colored	Indian	Japanese	Chinese	White	Colored	Indian	Japanese	Chinese
THE STATE,	98.78	1.06	0.02	*-	0.14	98.91	1.07	0.02	*-	*-
Barnstable,	97.90	1.30	0.78	-	0.02	98.08	1.23	0.69	-	-
Berkshire,	98.45	1.45	0.01	-	0.09	98.48	1.51	0.01	-	-
Bristol,	98.86	1.05	0.01	-	0.08	98.85	1 14	0.01	-	-
Dukes,	92.56	3.40	3.84	-	0.20	93.63	3.25	3.12	-	-
Essex,	99.39	0.50	*-	*-	0.11	99.42	0.58	*-	-	*-
Franklin,	99.67	0.25	0.01	0.01	0.06	99.68	0.30	0.01	0.01	-
Hampden,	99.17	0.76	*-	-	0.07	99.13	0.87	*-	*-	-
Hampshire,	99.38	0.55	0.02	0.01	0.04	99.38	0.63	-	0.01	-
Middlesex,	98.82	1.09	*-	*-	0.09	98.89	1.11	*-	*-	-
Nantucket,	99.09	0.91	-	-	-	97.18	2.82	-	-	-
Norfolk,	99.47	0.42	0.02	*-	0.09	99.56	0.43	0.01	*-	-
Plymouth,	99.06	0.79	0.05	*-	0.10	99.17	0.80	0.03	-	-
Suffolk,	97.69	1.98	0.01	*-	0.32	98.16	1.84	*-	-	*-
Worcester,	99.36	0.56	0.01	*-	0.07	99.42	0.57	0.01	-	*-

* Less than one one-hundredth of one per cent.

CONJUGAL CONDITION.

[839]

CONJUGAL CONDITION.

COUNTIES, CITIES, TOWNS, AND SEX.	Single	Married	Widowed	Divorced	Unknown	PERCENTAGES				
						Single	Married	Widowed	Divorced	Unknown
BARNSTABLE.										
Barnstable, . . .	1,799	1,830	413	11	2	44.37	45.13	10.18	0.27	0.05
Males, . . .	919	918	101	6	-	22.67	22.64	2.49	0.14	-
Females, . . .	880	912	312	5	2	21.70	22.49	7.69	0.13	0.05
Bourne, . . .	765	673	129	2	11	48.42	42.60	8.17	0.12	0.69
Males, . . .	395	333	34	1	9	25.00	21.08	2.15	0.06	0.57
Females, . . .	370	340	95	1	2	23.42	21.52	6.02	0.06	0.12
Brewster, . . .	408	400	87	6	-	45.29	44.40	9.65	0.66	-
Males, . . .	210	202	22	3	-	23.31	22.42	2.44	0.33	-
Females, . . .	198	198	65	3	-	21.98	21.98	7.21	0.33	-
Chatham, . . .	759	883	164	3	-	41.95	48.81	9.06	0.17	-
Males, . . .	410	447	40	1	-	22.66	24.71	2.21	0.06	-
Females, . . .	349	436	124	2	-	19.30	24.10	6.85	0.11	-
Dennis, . . .	1,064	1,186	283	12	-	41.81	46.60	11.12	0.47	-
Males, . . .	488	583	89	4	-	19.18	22.91	3.50	0.15	-
Females, . . .	576	603	194	8	-	22.63	23.69	7.62	0.32	-
Eastham, . . .	210	215	51	-	-	44.12	45.17	10.71	-	-
Males, . . .	109	107	18	-	-	22.90	22.48	3.78	-	-
Females, . . .	101	108	33	-	-	21.22	22.69	6.93	-	-
Falmouth, . . .	1,281	1,129	242	3	-	48.25	42.52	9.12	0.11	-
Males, . . .	640	569	72	2	-	24.11	21.43	2.71	0.07	-
Females, . . .	641	560	170	1	-	24.14	21.09	6.41	0.04	-
Harwich, . . .	1,100	1,274	145	11	2	43.44	50.32	5.73	0.43	0.08
Males, . . .	603	640	5	3	2	23.81	25.28	0.20	0.12	0.08
Females, . . .	497	634	140	8	-	19.63	25.04	5.53	0.31	-
Mashpee, . . .	186	118	26	-	-	56.36	35.76	7.88	-	-
Males, . . .	113	59	6	-	-	34.24	17.88	1.82	-	-
Females, . . .	73	59	20	-	-	22.12	17.88	6.06	-	-
Orleans, . . .	496	577	122	3	-	41.40	48.17	10.18	0.25	-
Males, . . .	236	285	36	2	-	19.70	23.79	3.00	0.17	-
Females, . . .	260	292	86	1	-	21.70	24.38	7.18	0.08	-
Provincetown, . .	2,220	1,984	340	9	2	48.73	43.56	7.46	0.20	0.05
Males, . . .	1,132	992	82	7	2	24.85	21.78	1.80	0.15	0.05
Females, . . .	1,088	992	258	2	-	23.88	21.78	5.66	0.05	-
Sandwich, . . .	799	614	166	1	-	50.57	38.86	10.51	0.06	-
Males, . . .	373	310	50	1	-	23.61	19.62	3.17	0.06	-
Females, . . .	426	304	116	-	-	26.96	19.24	7.34	-	-
Truro, ...	401	341	73	-	-	49.29	41.84	8.96	-	-
Males, . . .	217	172	13	-	-	26.63	21.10	1.60	-	-
Females, . . .	184	169	60	-	-	22.57	20.74	7.36	-	-
Wellfleet, . . .	385	451	131	1	-	39.77	46.59	13.53	0.11	-
Males, . . .	187	229	33	-	-	19.31	23.66	3.41	-	-
Females, . . .	198	222	98	1	-	20.46	22.93	10.12	0.11	-
Yarmouth, . . .	684	809	154	7	1	41.53	48.88	9.31	0.42	0.06
Males, . . .	329	401	37	4	1	19.88	24.23	2.24	0.24	0.06
Females, . . .	355	408	117	3	-	21.45	24.65	7.07	0.18	-
BERKSHIRE.										
Adams, . . .	4,552	2,890	384	11	-	58.08	36.88	4.90	0.14	-
Males, . . .	2,189	1,425	96	2	-	27.93	18.18	1.23	0.03	-
Females, . . .	2,363	1,465	288	9	-	30.15	18.70	3.67	0.11	-

CONJUGAL CONDITION — Continued.

COUNTIES, CITIES, TOWNS, AND SEX.	Single	Married	Widowed	Divorced	Un-known	Single	Married	Widowed	Divorced	Un-known
						— PERCENTAGES				

COUNTIES, CITIES, TOWNS, AND SEX.	Single	Married	Widowed	Divorced	Un-known	Single	Married	Widowed	Divorced	Un-known
BERKSHIRE — Con.										
Alford, . . .	128	132	18	2	–	45.72	47.14	6.43	0.71	–
Males, . . .	78	67	5	2	–	27.86	23.93	1.79	0.71	–
Females, . .	50	65	13	–	–	17.86	23.21	4.64	–	–
Becket. . . .	438	376	72	2	–	49.33	42.54	8.11	0.22	–
Males, . . .	264	192	26	1	–	29.78	21.62	2.93	0.11	–
Females, . .	174	184	46	1	–	19.60	20.72	5.18	0.11	–
Cheshire, . . .	566	520	90	–	–	48.13	44.22	7.65	–	–
Males, . . .	307	265	27	–	–	26.11	22.54	2.29	–	–
Females, . .	259	255	63	–	–	22.02	21.68	5.36	–	–
Clarksburg, . .	536	427	44	2	–	53.12	42.32	4.36	0.20	–
Males, . . .	267	215	19	1	–	26.46	21.31	1.88	0.10	–
Females, . .	269	212	25	1	–	26.66	21.01	2.48	0.10	–
Dalton, . . .	1,843	1,135	228	3	1	57.42	35.36	7.10	0.09	0.03
Males, . . .	884	566	53	2	1	27.54	17.64	1.65	0.06	0.03
Females, . .	959	569	175	1	–	29.88	17.72	5.45	0.03	–
Egremont, . . .	400	377	57	2	–	47.84	45.10	6.82	0.24	–
Males, . . .	201	186	19	–	–	24.04	22.25	2.27	–	–
Females, . .	199	191	38	2	–	23.80	22.85	4.55	0.24	–
Florida, . . .	225	164	36	–	–	52.94	38.59	8.47	–	–
Males, . . .	122	85	16	–	–	28.71	20.00	3.76	–	–
Females, . .	103	79	20	–	–	24.23	18.59	4.71	–	–
Great Barrington, .	2,488	1,883	418	5	–	51.90	39.28	8.71	0.11	–
Males, . . .	1,254	946	130	2	–	26.16	19.73	2.71	0.04	–
Females, . .	1,234	937	288	3	–	25.74	19.55	6.00	0.07	–
Hancock, . . .	267	210	33	1	–	52.25	41.10	6.46	0.19	–
Males, . . .	148	107	10	1	–	28.96	20.94	1.96	0.19	–
Females, . .	119	103	23	–	–	23.29	20.16	4.50	–	–
Hinsdale, . . .	977	556	116	1	–	59.21	33.70	7.03	0.06	–
Males, . . .	508	277	36	–	–	30.79	16.79	2.18	–	–
Females, . .	469	279	80	1	–	28.42	16.91	4.85	0.06	–
Lanesborough, . .	417	367	60	4	–	49.17	43.28	7.08	0.47	–
Males, . . .	231	183	17	3	–	27.24	21.58	2.01	0.35	–
Females, . .	186	184	43	1	–	21.93	21.70	5.07	0.12	–
Lee, ...	2,203	1,551	300	12	–	54.18	38.15	7.38	0.29	–
Males, . . .	1,088	791	89	5	–	26.75	19.46	2.19	0.12	–
Females, . .	1,115	760	211	7	–	27.43	18.69	5.19	0.17	–
Lenox, ...	1,730	970	167	5	–	60.24	33.78	5.81	0.17	–
Males, . . .	976	491	59	3	–	33.98	17.10	2.05	0.11	–
Females, . .	754	479	108	2	–	26.26	16.68	3.76	0.06	–
Monterey, . . .	224	194	42	4	–	48.28	41.81	9.05	0.86	–
Males, . . .	128	96	16	1	–	27.59	20.69	3.45	0.21	–
Females, . .	96	98	26	3	–	20.69	21.12	5.60	0.65	–
Mount Washington, .	63	60	11	2	–	46.32	44.12	8.09	1.47	–
Males, . . .	40	31	3	2	–	29.41	22.79	2.21	1.47	–
Females, . .	23	29	8	–	–	16.91	21.33	5.88	–	–
New Ashford, . .	62	48	6	–	–	53.45	41.38	5.17	–	–
Males, . . .	39	24	5	–	–	33.62	20.69	4.31	–	–
Females, . .	23	24	1	–	–	19.83	20.69	0.86	–	–
New Marlborough, .	619	562	106	1	–	48.06	43.63	8.23	0.08	–
Males, . . .	361	280	41	–	–	28.03	21.74	3.18	–	–
Females, . .	258	282	65	1	–	20.03	21.89	5.05	0.08	–
NORTH ADAMS, .	10,781	7,284	1,938	32	–	56.31	38.07	5.42	0.17	–
Males, . . .	5,407	3,644	289	10	–	28.25	19.05	1.51	0.05	–
Females, . .	5,374	3,640	749	22	–	28.09	19.02	3.91	0.12	–
Otis, ...	250	222	41	5	–	48.26	42.85	7.92	0.97	–
Males, . . .	161	109	16	3	–	31.08	21.04	3.09	0.58	–
Females, . .	89	113	25	2	–	17.18	21.81	4.83	0.39	–

CONJUGAL CONDITION — Continued.

COUNTIES, CITIES, TOWNS, AND SEX.	Single	Married	Widowed	Divorced	Un-known	PERCENTAGES Single	Married	Widowed	Divorced	Un-known
BERKSHIRE — Con.										
Peru, ...	167	117	20	1	–	54.75	38.36	6.56	0.33	–
Males, ...	80	59	6	1	–	26.23	19.34	1.97	0.33	–
Females, . . .	87	58	14	–	–	28.52	19.02	4.59	–	–
PITTSFIELD, . . .	11,730	7,531	1,160	36	4	57.83	36.81	5.67	0.17	0.02
Males, ...	5,753	3,785	283	13	4	28.12	18.50	1.38	0.06	0.02
Females, . . .	5,977	3,746	877	23	–	29.21	18.31	4.29	0.11	–
Richmond, . . .	382	282	35	2	–	54.49	40.23	5.00	0.28	–
Males, ...	197	142	14	1	–	28.10	20.26	2.00	0.14	–
Females, . . .	185	140	21	1	–	26.39	19.97	3.00	0.14	–
Sandisfield, . .	385	352	60	5	–	48.00	43.89	7.48	0.63	–
Males, ...	203	175	22	1	–	25.31	21.82	2.74	0.13	–
Females, . . .	182	177	38	4	–	22.69	22.07	4.74	0.50	–
Savoy, ...	239	221	43	1	–	47.42	43.85	8.53	0.20	–
Males, ...	123	111	21	1	–	24.40	22.02	4.17	0.20	–
Females, . . .	116	110	22	–	–	23.02	21.83	4.36	–	–
Sheffield, . . .	963	760	168	6	–	50.77	40.06	8.85	0.32	–
Males, ...	510	377	53	4	–	26.89	19.87	2.79	0.21	–
Females, . . .	453	383	115	2	–	23.88	20.19	6.06	0.11	–
Stockbridge, . .	1,134	793	143	7	–	54.60	38.18	6.89	0.33	–
Males, ...	558	390	45	3	–	26.87	18.77	2.17	0.14	–
Females, . . .	576	403	98	4	–	27.73	19.41	4.72	0.19	–
Tyringham, . . .	178	157	26	1	1	49.03	43.25	7.16	0.28	0.28
Males, ...	100	80	5	1	–	27.54	22.04	1.38	0.28	–
Females, . . .	78	77	21	–	1	21.49	21.21	5.78	–	0.28
Washington, . .	231	150	34	–	8	54.61	35.46	8.04	–	1.89
Males, ...	141	80	12	–	3	33.33	18.91	2.84	–	0.71
Females, . . .	90	70	22	–	5	21.28	16.55	5.20	–	1.18
West Stockbridge, .	658	472	126	1	–	52.35	37.55	10.02	0.08	–
Males, ...	340	225	43	–	–	27.05	17.90	3.42	–	–
Females, . . .	318	247	83	1	–	25.30	19.65	6.60	0.08	–
Williamstown, . .	2,779	1,839	262	7	–	56.87	37.63	5.36	0.14	–
Males, ...	1,616	923	74	2	–	33.07	18.89	1.51	0.04	–
Females, . . .	1,163	916	188	5	–	23.80	18.74	3.85	0.10	–
Windsor, . . .	302	220	34	–	–	54.32	39.56	6.12	–	–
Males, ...	178	110	13	–	–	32.02	19.78	2.34	–	–
Females, . . .	124	110	21	–	–	22.30	19.78	3.78	–	–
BRISTOL.										
Acushnet, . . .	531	475	107	2	–	47.62	42.60	9.60	0.18	–
Males, ...	296	235	35	2	–	26.55	21.07	3.14	0.18	–
Females, . . .	235	240	72	–	–	21.07	21.53	6.46	–	–
Attleborough, . .	4,415	3,367	460	21	25	53.27	40.63	5.55	0.25	0.30
Males, ...	2,243	1,674	92	3	17	27.06	20.20	1.11	0.04	0.20
Females, . . .	2,172	1,693	368	18	8	26.21	20.43	4.44	0.21	0.10
Berkley, . . .	430	433	88	4	–	45.06	45.34	9.21	0.42	–
Males, ...	241	217	21	3	–	25.24	22.72	2.20	0.31	–
Females, . . .	189	216	67	1	–	19.79	22.62	7.01	0.11	–
Dartmouth, . . .	1,489	1,369	238	9	2	47.93	44.06	7.66	0.29	0.06
Males, ...	832	685	76	6	–	26.78	22.04	2.45	0.19	–
Females, . . .	657	684	162	3	2	21.15	22.02	5.21	0.10	0.06
Dighton, . . .	878	765	147	7	–	48.86	42.57	8.18	0.39	–
Males, ...	494	384	35	3	–	27.49	21.37	1.94	0.17	–
Females, . . .	384	381	112	4	–	21.37	21.20	6.24	0.22	–
Easton, . . .	2,371	1,765	305	11	–	53.26	39.64	6.85	0.25	–
Males, ...	1,292	882	103	9	–	29.02	19.81	2.32	0.20	–
Females, . . .	1,079	883	202	2	–	24.24	19.83	4.53	0.05	–

CONJUGAL CONDITION — Continued.

COUNTIES, CITIES, TOWNS, AND SEX.	Single	Married	Widowed	Divorced	Unknown	PERCENTAGES Single	Married	Widowed	Divorced	Unknown
BRISTOL — Con.										
Fairhaven, . . .	1,577	1,473	276	12	-	47.24	44.13	8.27	0.36	-
Males, . . .	749	731	67	7	-	22.43	21.90	2.01	0.21	-
Females, . .	828	742	209	5	-	24.81	22.23	6.26	0.15	-
FALL RIVER, . .	55,032	31,267	4,788	106	10	59.45	35.65	5.37	0.12	0.01
Males, . . .	25,904	15,452	1,292	46	10	29.04	17.32	1.45	0.05	0.01
Females, . .	27,128	15,815	3,496	60	-	30.41	17.73	3.92	0.07	-
Freetown, . . .	739	543	112	6	5	52.59	38.65	7.97	0.43	0.36
Males, . . .	414	274	29	4	4	29.46	19.50	2.06	0.29	0.29
Females, . .	325	269	83	2	1	23.13	19.15	5.91	0.14	0.07
Mansfield, . . .	1,875	1,583	257	7	-	50.38	42.53	6.90	0.19	-
Males, . . .	942	791	57	3	-	25.31	21.25	1.53	0.08	-
Females, . .	933	792	200	4	-	25.07	21.28	5.37	0.11	-
NEW BEDFORD, .	30,280	21,361	3,503	93	14	54.80	38.66	6.34	0.17	0.03
Males, . . .	14,733	10,550	840	29	6	26.66	19.10	1.52	0.05	0.01
Females, . .	15,547	10,811	2,663	64	8	28.14	19.56	4.82	0.12	0.02
North Attleborough,.	3,593	2,537	429	17	-	54.64	38.58	6.52	0.26	-
Males, . . .	1,757	1,267	115	6	-	26.72	19.27	1.75	0.09	-
Females, . .	1,836	1,270	314	11	-	27.92	19.31	4.77	0.17	-
Norton, . . .	836	630	137	11	-	51.80	39.03	8.49	0.68	-
Males, . . .	391	320	43	6	-	24.23	19.82	2.67	0.37	-
Females, . .	445	310	94	5	-	27.57	19.21	5.82	0.31	-
Raynham, . . .	708	685	119	6	-	46.64	45.13	7.84	0.39	-
Males, . . .	370	344	35	2	-	24.37	22.66	2.51	0.13	-
Females, . .	338	341	84	4	-	22.27	22.47	5.53	0.26	-
Rehoboth, . . .	907	766	131	4	2	50.11	42.32	7.24	0.22	0.11
Males, . . .	511	384	59	2	2	28.23	21.22	3.26	0.11	0.11
Females, . .	396	382	72	2	-	21.88	21.10	3.98	0.11	-
Seekonk, . . .	771	594	94	5	1	52.63	40.55	6.41	0.34	0.07
Males, . . .	447	311	30	4	1	30.51	21.23	2.05	0.27	0.07
Females, . .	324	283	64	1	-	22.12	19.32	4.36	0.07	-
Somerset, . . .	1,012	839	126	6	-	51.03	42.31	6.36	0.30	-
Males, . . .	568	432	37	3	-	28.64	21.79	1.87	0.15	-
Females, . .	444	407	89	3	-	22.39	20.52	4.49	0.15	-
Swansea, . . .	809	684	127	7	-	49.72	42.04	7.81	0.43	-
Males, . . .	438	350	39	3	-	26.92	21.51	2.40	0.18	-
Females, . .	371	334	88	4	-	22.80	20.53	5.41	0.25	-
TAUNTON, . . .	15,078	10,086	1,921	27	3	55.61	37.19	7.09	0.10	0.01
Males, . . .	7,614	4,982	536	12	3	28.08	18.37	1.98	0.05	0.01
Females, . .	7,464	5,104	1,385	15	-	27.53	18.82	5.11	0.05	-
Westport, . . .	1,324	1,129	216	9	-	49.44	42.16	8.06	0.34	-
Males, . . .	697	562	80	5	-	26.03	20.99	2.98	0.19	-
Females, . .	627	567	136	4	-	23.41	21.17	5.08	0.15	-
DUKES.										
Chilmark, . . .	117	155	34	-	-	38.49	50.33	11.18	-	-
Males, . . .	61	78	14	-	-	20.07	25.00	4.60	-	-
Females, . .	56	77	20	-	-	18.42	25.33	6.58	-	-
Cottage City, . .	467	478	88	5	-	44.99	46.05	8.48	0.48	-
Males, . . .	254	236	15	3	-	24.47	22.73	1.45	0.29	-
Females, . .	213	242	73	2	-	20.52	23.32	7.03	0.19	-
Edgartown, . .	488	481	148	8	-	43.38	42.75	13.16	0.71	-
Males, . . .	247	241	36	3	-	21.96	21.42	3.20	0.26	-
Females, . .	241	240	112	5	-	21.42	21.33	9.96	0.45	-
Gay Head, . .	97	60	11	1	-	57.40	35.50	6.51	0.59	-
Males, . . .	57	29	3	1	-	33.73	17.16	1.77	0.59	-
Females, . .	40	31	8	-	-	23.67	18.34	4.74	-	-

CONJUGAL CONDITION — Continued.

COUNTIES, CITIES, TOWNS, AND SEX.	Single	Married	Widowed	Divorced	Un-known	PERCENTAGES				
						Single	Married	Widowed	Divorced	Un-known
DUKES — Con.										
Gosnold, . . .	53	77	9	1	-	37.86	55.00	6.43	0.71	-
Males, . . .	35	48	4	1	-	25.00	34.29	2.86	0.71	-
Females, . . .	18	29	5	-	-	12.86	20.71	3.57	-	-
Tisbury, . . .	459	436	100	7	-	45.81	43.51	9.98	0.70	-
Males, . . .	242	211	22	2	-	24.15	21.05	2.20	0.20	-
Females, . . .	217	225	78	5	-	21.66	22.46	7.78	0.50	-
West Tisbury, . .	193	222	41	3	1	41.96	48.26	8.91	0.65	0.22
Males, . . .	104	111	-	1	-	22.61	24.13	-	0.22	-
Females, . .	89	111	41	2	1	19.35	24.13	8.91	0.43	0.22
ESSEX.										
Amesbury, . . .	5,357	5,885	683	32	29	53.65	58.90	6.84	0.32	0.29
Males, . . .	2,615	1,917	206	14	28	26.19	19.20	2.06	0.14	0.28
Females, . . .	2,742	1,968	477	18	1	27.46	19.70	4.78	0.18	0.01
Andover, . . .	3,702	1,984	453	6	-	60.24	32.29	7.37	0.10	-
Males, . . .	1,846	973	92	2	-	30.04	15.84	1.49	0.03	-
Females, . . .	1,856	1,011	361	4	-	30.20	16.45	5.88	0.07	-
BEVERLY, . . .	6,003	4,869	848	29	27	51.61	40.73	7.18	0.25	0.23
Males, . . .	3,072	2,423	202	4	27	26.02	20.52	1.71	0.04	0.23
Females, . . .	3,021	2,386	646	25	-	25.59	20.21	5.47	0.21	-
Boxford, . . .	369	298	60	-	-	50.75	41.00	8.25	-	-
Males, . . .	189	149	21	-	-	25.99	20.50	2.89	-	-
Females, . . .	180	149	39	-	-	24.76	20.50	5.36	-	-
Bradford, . . .	2,410	2,028	279	19	-	50.89	42.82	5.89	0.40	-
Males, . . .	1,132	1,005	79	6	-	23.90	21.22	1.67	0.13	-
Females, . . .	1,278	1,023	200	13	-	26.99	21.60	4.22	0.27	-
Danvers, . . .	4,440	3,101	624	10	6	54.27	37.90	7.63	0.12	0.08
Males, . . .	2,239	1,538	175	3	3	27.37	18.79	2.14	0.04	0.04
Females, . . .	2,201	1,563	449	7	3	26.90	19.11	5.49	0.08	0.04
Essex, . . .	797	708	137	5	-	46.44	44.61	8.63	0.32	-
Males, . . .	406	352	47	4	-	25.59	22.18	2.96	0.25	-
Females, . . .	354	356	90	1	-	20.85	22.43	5.67	0.07	-
Georgetown, . .	989	855	201	5	-	48.24	41.71	9.80	0.25	-
Males, . . .	505	421	72	1	-	24.63	20.54	3.51	0.05	-
Females, . . .	484	434	129	4	-	23.61	21.17	6.29	0.20	-
GLOUCESTER, . .	16,623	9,874	1,625	56	33	58.92	35.09	5.76	0.20	0.12
Males, . . .	10,429	5,250	520	29	29	36.97	18.61	1.85	0.10	0.10
Females, . . .	6,194	4,624	1,105	27	4	21.95	16.39	3.91	0.10	0.02
Groveland, . . .	1,221	912	200	-	-	52.34	39.09	8.57	-	-
Males, . . .	595	464	59	-	-	25.51	19.89	2.52	-	-
Females, . . .	626	448	141	-	-	26.83	19.20	6.05	-	-
Hamilton, . . .	689	565	101	1	-	50.81	41.67	7.45	0.07	-
Males, . . .	354	298	33	-	-	26.11	21.98	2.43	-	-
Females, . . .	335	267	68	1	-	24.70	19.69	5.02	0.07	-
HAVERHILL, . .	15,667	12,422	2,021	86	13	51.86	41.12	6.69	0.29	0.04
Males, . . .	7,794	6,171	527	34	9	25.80	20.42	1.74	0.12	0.03
Females, . . .	7,873	6,251	1,494	52	4	26.06	20.70	4.95	0.17	0.01
Ipswich, . . .	2,606	1,746	359	9	-	55.21	36.99	7.61	0.19	-
Males, . . .	1,199	866	108	5	-	25.40	18.35	2.29	0.10	-
Females, . . .	1,407	880	251	4	-	29.81	18.64	5.32	0.09	-
LAWRENCE, . .	29,912	18,576	3,304	63	9	57.34	36.19	6.33	0.12	0.02
Males, . . .	14,749	9,498	842	17	1	28.28	18.21	1.61	0.03	*-
Females, . . .	15,163	9,078	2,462	46	8	29.06	17.98	4.72	0.09	0.02
LYNN, ...	32,369	25,590	4,161	204	30	51.91	41.04	6.67	0.33	0.05
Males, . . .	16,311	12,748	1,008	79	27	26.16	20.44	1.61	0.13	0.05
Females, . . .	16,058	12,842	3,153	125	3	25.75	20.60	5.06	0.20	*-

* Less than one one-hundredth of one per cent.

CONJUGAL CONDITION — Continued.

COUNTIES, CITIES, TOWNS, AND SEX.	Single	Married	Widowed	Divorced	Un-known	PERCENTAGES				
						Single	Married	Widowed	Divorced	Un-known
ESSEX — Con.										
Lynnfield, . . .	399	346	72	1	–	48.78	42.30	8.80	0.12	–
Males, . . .	209	174	25	–	–	25.55	21.27	3.06	–	–
Females, . .	190	172	47	1	–	23.23	21.03	5.74	0.12	–
Manchester, . .	973	769	133	1	–	51.87	40.99	7.09	0.05	–
Males, . . .	463	389	41	–	–	24.68	20.73	2.19	–	–
Females, . .	510	380	92	1	–	27.19	20.26	4.90	0.05	–
Marblehead, . .	3,915	3,150	699	17	–	51.04	40.80	7.94	0.22	–
Males, . . .	1,923	1,552	169	5	–	25.07	20.23	2.20	0.07	–
Females, . .	1,992	1,578	440	12	–	25.97	20.57	5.74	0.15	–
Merrimac, . . .	1,064	1,038	162	7	–	47.55	45.11	7.04	0.30	–
Males, . . .	552	518	37	4	–	23.99	22.51	1.61	0.17	–
Females, . .	542	520	125	3	–	23.56	22.60	5.43	0.13	–
Methuen, . . .	3,053	2,218	403	14	2	53.66	38.98	7.08	0.24	0.04
Males, . . .	1,542	1,101	113	3	1	27.10	19.35	1.99	0.05	0.02
Females, . .	1,511	1,117	290	11	1	26.56	19.63	5.09	0.19	0.02
Middleton, . .	401	363	74	–	–	47.85	43.32	8.83	–	–
Males, . . .	214	183	31	–	–	25.53	21.84	3.70	–	–
Females, . .	187	180	43	–	–	22.32	21.48	5.13	–	–
Nahant, . . .	464	348	50	3	–	53.64	40.23	5.78	0.35	–
Males, . . .	216	189	19	1	–	24.97	21.85	2.19	0.12	–
Females, . .	248	159	31	2	–	28.67	18.38	3.59	0.23	–
Newbury, . . .	766	615	103	5	–	51.44	41.30	6.92	0.34	–
Males, . . .	428	305	24	3	–	28.75	20.48	1.61	0.20	–
Females, . .	358	310	79	2	–	22.69	20.82	5.31	0.14	–
NEWBURYPORT, .	7,658	5,559	1,313	42	–	52.40	38.20	9.02	0.29	–
Males, . . .	3,556	2,771	290	19	–	24.30	19.04	1.99	0.13	–
Females, . .	4,102	2,788	1,023	23	–	28.19	19.16	7.03	0.16	–
North Andover, .	2,025	1,337	206	1	–	56.74	37.46	5.77	0.03	–
Males, . . .	1,031	675	59	–	–	28.89	18.91	1.65	–	–
Females, . .	994	662	147	1	–	27.85	18.55	4.12	0.03	–
Peabody, . . .	5,874	3,963	650	8	12	55.94	37.72	6.18	0.08	0.11
Males, . . .	3,067	1,978	201	4	12	29.19	18.83	1.94	0.04	0.11
Females, . .	2,807	1,985	449	4	–	26.72	18.89	4.27	0.04	–
Rockport, . . .	2,645	2,326	320	–	–	49.97	43.98	6.05	–	–
Males, . . .	1,560	1,390	106	–	–	29.50	24.58	2.00	–	–
Females, . .	1,085	1,026	214	–	–	20.47	19.40	4.05	–	–
Rowley, . . .	605	576	85	6	–	47.56	45.29	6.68	0.47	–
Males, . . .	335	287	32	2	–	26.33	22.57	2.51	0.16	–
Females, . .	270	289	53	4	–	21.23	22.72	4.17	0.31	–
SALEM, . . .	19,576	12,410	2,386	54	47	56.79	36.00	6.92	0.15	0.14
Males, . . .	9,403	6,211	600	23	33	27.28	18.01	1.74	0.07	0.10
Females, . .	10,173	6,199	1,786	31	14	29.51	17.99	5.18	0.08	0.04
Salisbury, . .	608	583	102	7	–	46.77	44.85	7.84	0.54	–
Males, . . .	311	290	38	3	–	23.92	22.31	2.92	0.23	–
Females, . .	297	293	64	4	–	22.85	22.54	4.92	0.31	–
Saugus, . . .	2,295	1,908	285	8	1	51.03	42.43	6.34	0.18	0.02
Males, . . .	1,152	944	91	1	1	25.62	20.99	2.05	0.02	0.02
Females, . .	1,143	964	194	7	–	25.41	21.44	4.31	0.16	–
Swampscott, . .	1,600	1,433	224	2	–	49.10	43.97	6.87	0.06	–
Males, . . .	765	709	60	–	–	23.48	21.75	1.84	–	–
Females, . .	835	724	164	2	–	25.62	22.22	5.03	0.06	–
Topsfield, . .	536	383	113	1	–	51.89	37.08	10.94	0.09	–
Males, . . .	291	191	34	–	–	28.17	18.49	3.29	–	–
Females, . .	245	192	79	1	–	23.72	18.59	7.65	0.09	–
Wenham, . . .	428	398	60	–	–	48.31	44.92	6.77	–	–
Males, . . .	208	198	25	–	–	23.48	22.35	2.82	–	–
Females, . .	220	200	35	–	–	24.83	22.57	3.95	–	–

CONJUGAL CONDITION — Continued.

COUNTIES, CITIES, TOWNS, AND SEX.	Single	Married	Widowed	Divorced	Un-known	PERCENTAGES Single	Married	Widowed	Divorced	Un-known
ESSEX — Con.										
West Newbury, . .	794	712	132	5	–	48.33	43.34	8.03	0.30	–
Males, . . .	412	357	40	2	–	25.08	21.73	2.43	0.12	–
Females, . .	382	355	92	3	–	23.25	21.61	5.60	0.18	–
FRANKLIN.										
Ashfield, . . .	476	444	93	–	–	46.99	43.83	9.18	–	–
Males, . . .	270	225	28	–	–	26.65	22.21	2.77	–	–
Females, . .	206	219	65	–	–	20.34	21.62	6.41	–	–
Bernardston, . .	369	333	71	3	2	47.43	42.80	9.12	0.39	0.26
Males, . . .	190	169	26	2	2	24.42	21.72	3.34	0.26	0.26
Females, . .	179	164	45	1	–	23.01	21.08	5.78	0.13	–
Buckland, . . .	792	653	100	3	–	51.16	42.18	6.46	0.20	–
Males, . . .	437	324	22	2	–	28.23	20.93	1.42	0.13	–
Females, . .	355	329	78	1	–	22.93	21.25	5.04	0.07	–
Charlemont, . .	466	503	73	1	–	44.76	48.32	6.82	0.10	–
Males, . . .	248	254	25	1	–	23.82	24.40	2.21	0.10	–
Females, . .	218	249	48	–	–	20.94	23.92	4.61	–	–
Colrain, . . .	835	667	101	1	6	51.86	41.43	6.27	0.06	0.38
Males, . . .	479	331	37	1	3	29.75	20.56	2.30	0.06	0.19
Females, . .	356	336	64	–	3	22.11	20.87	3.97	–	0.19
Conway, . . .	668	541	93	2	–	51.22	41.49	7.13	0.16	–
Males, . . .	356	272	28	1	–	27.30	20.86	2.14	0.08	–
Females, . .	312	269	65	1	–	23.92	20.63	4.99	0.08	–
Deerfield, . . .	1,598	1,155	249	4	1	53.15	38.41	8.28	0.13	0.03
Males, . . .	892	582	74	1	1	29.67	19.36	2.46	0.03	0.03
Females, . .	706	573	175	3	–	23.48	19.05	5.82	0.10	–
Erving, . . .	447	458	58	1	–	46.37	47.51	6.02	0.10	–
Males, . . .	242	228	20	–	–	25.10	23.65	2.08	–	–
Females, . .	205	230	38	1	–	21.27	23.86	3.94	0.10	–
Gill, ...	696	335	48	3	–	64.32	30.96	4.44	0.28	–
Males, . . .	514	165	17	3	–	47.50	15.25	1.57	0.28	–
Females, . .	182	170	31	–	–	16.82	15.71	2.87	–	–
Greenfield, . .	3,301	2,458	443	23	4	53.90	39.46	7.11	0.37	0.06
Males, . . .	1,648	1,232	99	5	3	26.46	19.78	1.59	0.08	0.04
Females, . .	1,653	1,226	344	18	1	26.54	19.68	5.52	0.29	0.02
Hawley, . . .	221	212	35	–	–	47.22	45.30	7.48	–	–
Males, . . .	129	107	14	–	–	27.57	22.86	2.99	–	–
Females, . .	92	105	21	–	–	19.65	22.44	4.49	–	–
Heath, . . .	233	202	36	5	–	48.95	42.44	7.56	1.05	–
Males, . . .	134	101	12	3	–	28.15	21.22	2.52	0.63	–
Females, . .	99	101	24	2	–	20.80	21.22	5.04	0.42	–
Leverett, . . .	354	333	54	3	–	47.58	44.76	7.26	0.40	–
Males, . . .	193	166	20	–	–	25.94	22.31	2.69	–	–
Females, . .	161	167	34	3	–	21.64	22.45	4.57	0.40	–
Leyden, . . .	174	154	35	–	–	47.93	42.43	9.64	–	–
Males, . . .	94	78	13	–	–	25.89	21.49	3.58	–	–
Females, . .	80	76	22	–	–	22.04	20.94	6.06	–	–
Monroe, . . .	172	107	18	–	1	57.72	35.91	6.04	–	0.33
Males, . . .	110	62	4	–	–	36.91	20.81	1.34	–	–
Females, . .	62	45	14	–	1	20.81	15.10	4.70	–	0.33
Montague, . .	3,340	2,345	363	6	4	55.13	38.71	5.99	0.10	0.07
Males, . . .	1,785	1,177	108	2	4	29.47	19.43	1.78	0.03	0.07
Females, . .	1,555	1,168	255	4	–	25.66	19.28	4.21	0.07	–
New Salem, . .	412	380	75	–	2	47.41	43.73	8.63	–	0.23
Males, . . .	216	189	31	–	2	24.85	21.75	3.57	–	0.23
Females, . .	196	191	44	–	–	22.56	21.98	5.06	–	–

CONJUGAL CONDITION — Continued.

COUNTIES, CITIES, TOWNS, AND SEX.	Single	Married	Widowed	Divorced	Un-known	PERCENTAGES				
						Single	Married	Widowed	Divorced	Un-known
FRANKLIN — Con.										
Northfield, . . .	1,034	679	128	10	-	55.86	36.68	6.92	0.54	-
Males, . . .	372	339	37	6	-	49.10	18.31	2.00	0.32	-
Females, . .	662	340	91	4	-	35.76	18.37	4.92	0.22	-
Orange, . . .	2,521	2,507	317	16	-	47.02	46.76	5.92	0.30	-
Males, . . .	1,336	1,255	92	7	-	24.92	23.41	1.72	0.13	-
Females, . .	1,185	1,252	225	9	-	22.10	23.35	4.20	0.17	-
Rowe, ...	264	201	33	-	-	53.01	40.56	6.63	-	-
Males, . . .	172	102	9	-	-	34.54	20.48	1.81	-	-
Females, . .	92	99	24	-	-	18.47	19.88	4.82	-	-
Shelburne, . . .	745	678	134	3	-	47.76	43.46	8.59	0.19	-
Males, . . .	378	339	33	-	-	24.23	21.73	2.12	-	-
Females, . .	367	339	101	3	-	23.53	21.73	6.47	0.19	-
Shutesbury, . .	181	210	48	5	-	40.76	47.30	10.81	1.13	-
Males, . . .	90	108	17	3	-	20.27	24.32	3.83	0.68	-
Females, . .	91	102	31	2	-	20.49	22.98	6.98	0.45	-
Sunderland, . .	344	295	57	-	-	49.43	42.38	8.19	-	-
Males, . . .	211	149	21	-	-	30.32	21.40	3.02	-	-
Females, . .	133	146	36	-	-	19.11	20.98	5.17	-	-
Warwick, . . .	286	275	36	2	-	47.74	45.91	6.01	0.34	-
Males, . . .	166	142	12	1	-	27.71	23.71	2.00	0.17	-
Females, . .	120	133	24	1	-	20.03	22.20	4.01	0.17	-
Wendell, . . .	255	240	33	1	-	48.20	45.37	6.24	0.19	-
Males, . . .	153	123	16	1	-	28.92	23.25	3.03	0.19	-
Females, . .	102	117	17	-	-	19.28	22.12	3.21	-	-
Whately, . . .	357	334	50	4	-	48.61	44.24	6.63	0.52	-
Males, . . .	296	168	16	2	-	27.29	22.25	2.12	0.26	-
Females, . .	161	166	34	2	-	21.32	21.99	4.51	0.26	-
HAMPDEN.										
Agawam, . . .	1,296	951	157	4	-	53.82	39.50	6.52	0.16	-
Males, . . .	704	479	52	2	-	29.23	19.90	2.16	0.08	-
Females, . .	592	472	105	2	-	24.59	19.60	4.36	0.08	-
Blandford, . . .	449	344	53	3	-	52.89	40.52	6.24	0.35	-
Males, . . .	243	172	19	3	-	28.62	20.26	2.24	0.35	-
Females, . .	206	172	34	-	-	24.27	20.26	4.00	-	-
Brimfield, . . .	503	367	91	1	-	52.29	38.15	9.46	0.10	-
Males, . . .	280	184	34	-	-	29.11	19.13	3.53	-	-
Females, . .	223	183	57	1	-	23.18	19.02	5.93	0.10	-
Chester, . . .	686	643	94	6	-	48.00	45.00	6.58	0.42	-
Males, . . .	343	321	33	3	-	24.00	22.47	2.31	0.21	-
Females, . .	343	322	61	3	-	24.00	22.53	4.27	0.21	-
CHICOPEE, . . .	9,464	6,060	924	25	7	57.64	36.54	5.63	0.15	0.04
Males, . . .	4,784	3,044	246	14	7	29.14	18.54	1.50	0.08	0.04
Females, . .	4,680	2,956	678	11	-	28.50	18.00	4.13	0.07	-
East Longmeadow, .	912	606	71	-	2	57.32	38.09	4.46	-	0.13
Males, . . .	524	312	25	-	2	32.93	19.61	1.57	-	0.13
Females, . .	388	294	46	-	-	24.39	18.48	2.89	-	-
Granville, . . .	502	406	93	4	-	49.95	40.40	9.25	0.40	-
Males, . . .	281	198	40	3	-	27.96	19.70	3.98	0.30	-
Females, . .	221	208	53	1	-	21.99	20.70	5.27	0.10	-
Hampden, . . .	341	322	77	3	-	45.90	43.34	10.36	0.40	-
Males, . . .	185	161	25	3	-	24.90	21.67	3.37	0.40	-
Females, . .	156	161	52	-	-	21.00	21.67	6.99	-	-
Holland, . . .	93	87	19	-	-	46.73	43.72	9.55	-	-
Males, . . .	54	46	7	-	-	27.13	23.12	3.52	-	-
Females, . .	39	41	12	-	-	19.60	20.60	6.03	-	-

CONJUGAL CONDITION — Continued.

COUNTIES, CITIES, TOWNS, AND SEX.	Single	Married	Widowed	Divorced	Unknown	PERCENTAGES Single	Married	Widowed	Divorced	Unknown
HAMPDEN — Con.										
HOLYOKE, . . .	24,460	13,810	2,005	50	17	60.66	34.25	4.97	0.08	0.04
Males, . . .	11,824	6,849	502	10	13	60.52	16.99	1.24	0.03	0.03
Females, . . .	12,636	6,961	1,503	20	4	31.34	17.26	3.73	0.05	0.01
Longmeadow, . .	334	240	44	2	–	55.87	38.71	7.10	0.32	–
Males, . . .	159	119	10	2	–	25.65	19.19	1.61	0.32	–
Females, . . .	175	121	34	–	–	28.22	19.52	5.49	–	–
Ludlow, . . .	1,479	953	127	3	–	57.73	37.19	4.96	0.12	–
Males, . . .	778	503	31	2	–	30.37	19.63	1.21	0.08	–
Females, . . .	701	450	96	1	–	27.36	17.56	3.75	0.04	–
Monson, . . .	2,018	1,478	246	3	1	53.87	39.45	6.57	0.08	0.03
Males, . . .	1,038	753	68	2	1	27.71	20.10	1.82	0.05	0.03
Females, . . .	980	725	178	1	–	26.16	19.35	4.75	0.03	–
Montgomery, . .	143	119	12	1	–	52.00	43.27	4.37	0.36	–
Males, . . .	83	62	5	1	–	30.18	22.55	1.82	0.36	–
Females, . . .	60	57	7	–	–	21.82	20.72	2.55	–	–
Palmer, . . .	3,874	2,763	400	19	2	55.39	37.37	5.83	0.28	0.03
Males, . . .	1,909	1,383	122	9	2	27.84	19.00	1.78	0.13	0.03
Females, . . .	1,965	1,260	278	10	–	28.65	18.37	4.05	0.15	–
Russell, . . .	459	315	70	2	–	54.25	37.23	8.27	0.23	–
Males, . . .	246	166	27	1	–	29.08	19.62	3.19	0.12	–
Females, . . .	213	149	43	1	–	25.18	17.61	5.08	0.12	–
Southwick, . .	471	422	59	9	–	49.01	43.91	6.14	0.94	–
Males, . . .	266	215	23	6	–	27.68	22.37	2.39	0.63	–
Females, . . .	205	207	36	3	–	21.33	21.54	3.75	0.31	–
SPRINGFIELD, . .	27,445	20,345	3,500	95	46	53.27	39.49	6.96	0.19	0.09
Males, . . .	13,558	10,130	803	34	36	26.32	19.66	1.73	0.07	0.07
Females, . . .	13,887	10,215	2,697	62	10	26.95	19.83	5.23	0.12	0.02
Tolland, . . .	162	121	25	1	–	52.43	39.16	8.09	0.32	–
Males, . . .	101	63	6	1	–	32.69	20.39	1.94	0.32	–
Females, . . .	61	58	19	–	–	19.74	18.77	6.15	–	–
Wales, . . .	404	321	49	9	–	51.59	41.00	6.26	1.15	–
Males, . . .	217	167	17	4	–	27.71	21.33	2.17	0.51	–
Females, . . .	187	154	32	5	–	23.88	19.67	4.09	0.64	–
Westfield, . . .	5,415	4,402	795	51	–	50.78	41.28	7.46	0.48	–
Males, . . .	2,760	2,191	201	23	–	25.88	20.54	1.89	0.22	–
Females, . . .	2,655	2,211	594	28	–	24.90	20.74	5.57	0.26	–
West Springfield, .	3,339	2,401	369	12	4	54.51	39.20	6.02	0.20	0.07
Males, . . .	1,659	1,196	90	2	4	27.08	19.53	1.47	0.03	0.07
Females, . . .	1,680	1,205	279	10	–	27.43	19.67	4.55	0.17	–
Wilbraham, . .	1,033	575	126	6	–	59.37	33.05	7.24	0.34	–
Males, . . .	513	285	37	2	–	29.48	16.38	2.13	0.11	–
Females, . . .	520	290	89	4	–	29.89	16.67	5.11	0.23	–
HAMPSHIRE.										
Amherst, . . .	2,684	1,707	389	5	–	56.09	35.67	8.13	0.11	–
Males, . . .	1,502	843	81	1	–	31.39	17.62	1.69	0.02	–
Females, . . .	1,182	864	308	4	–	24.70	18.05	6.44	0.09	–
Belchertown, . .	1,123	878	146	9	5	51.97	40.63	6.76	0.41	0.23
Males, . . .	620	437	49	7	2	28.69	20.23	2.27	0.32	0.09
Females, . . .	503	441	97	2	3	23.28	20.40	4.49	0.09	0.14
Chesterfield, . .	254	283	52	–	–	43.12	48.05	8.83	–	–
Males, . . .	134	142	25	–	–	22.75	24.11	4.24	–	–
Females, . . .	120	141	27	–	–	20.37	23.94	4.59	–	–
Cummington, . .	324	355	69	2	–	43.20	47.34	9.20	0.26	–
Males, . . .	158	180	28	1	–	21.07	24.00	3.73	0.13	–
Females, . . .	166	175	41	1	–	22.13	23.34	5.47	0.13	–

CONJUGAL CONDITION — Continued.

COUNTIES, CITIES, TOWNS, AND SEX.	Single	Married	Widowed	Divorced	Unknown	PERCENTAGES Single	Married	Widowed	Divorced	Unknown
HAMPSHIRE - Con.										
Easthampton,	2,750	1,696	337	7	-	57.41	35.41	7.03	0.15	-
Males,	1,301	857	83	1	-	27.16	17.90	1.73	0.02	-
Females,	1,449	839	254	6	-	30.25	17.51	5.30	0.13	-
Enfield,	479	442	68	1	-	48.39	44.64	6.87	0.10	-
Males,	265	221	25	1	-	26.77	22.32	2.53	0.10	-
Females,	214	221	43	-	-	21.62	22.32	4.34	-	-
Goshen,	163	118	21	-	2	53.62	38.81	6.91	-	0.66
Males,	93	57	8	-	2	30.59	18.75	2.63	-	0.66
Females,	70	61	13	-	-	23.03	20.06	4.28	-	-
Granby,	394	295	56	3	-	52.67	39.44	7.49	0.40	-
Males,	224	148	21	1	-	29.94	19.79	2.81	0.13	-
Females,	170	147	35	2	-	22.73	19.65	4.68	0.27	-
Greenwich,.	218	203	58	2	-	45.32	42.20	12.06	0.42	-
Males,	117	101	23	2	-	24.32	21.00	4.78	0.42	-
Females,	101	102	35	-	-	21.00	21.20	7.28	-	-
Hadley,	942	610	150	2	-	55.28	35.80	8.80	0.12	-
Males,	530	306	57	1	-	31.10	17.96	3.34	0.06	-
Females,	412	304	93	1	-	24.18	17.84	5.46	0.06	-
Hatfield,	692	494	76	-	-	54.83	39.15	6.02	-	-
Males,	393	248	28	-	-	31.14	19.65	2.22	-	-
Females,	299	246	48	-	-	23.69	19.50	3.80	-	-
Huntington,	760	585	104	3	-	52.41	40.21	7.17	0.21	-
Males,	392	292	37	1	-	27.03	20.14	2.55	0.07	-
Females,	368	293	67	2	-	25.38	20.07	4.62	0.14	-
Middlefield,	203	155	28	-	-	52.59	40.16	7.25	-	-
Males,	112	77	8	-	-	29.02	19.95	2.07	-	-
Females,	91	78	20	-	-	23.57	20.21	5.18	-	-
NORTHAMPTON,.	9,987	5,714	1,026	18	1	59.63	34.12	6.13	0.11	0.01
Males,	4,363	2,824	241	5	1	26.05	16.86	1.44	0.03	0.01
Females,	5,624	2,890	785	13	-	33.58	17.26	4.69	0.08	-
Pelham,	242	210	34	-	-	49.80	43.21	6.99	-	-
Males,	126	107	13	-	-	25.93	22.02	2.67	-	-
Females,	116	103	21	-	-	23.87	21.19	4.32	-	-
Plainfield, .	194	212	44	-	-	43.11	47.11	9.78	-	-
Males,	109	107	15	-	-	24.22	23.78	3.33	-	-
Females,	85	105	29	-	-	18.89	23.33	6.45	-	-
Prescott,	184	187	27	3	-	45.89	46.63	6.73	0.75	-
Males,	102	93	11	2	-	25.44	23.19	2.74	0.50	-
Females,	82	94	16	1	-	20.45	23.44	3.99	0.25	-
Southampton,	547	407	99	1	-	51.90	38.62	9.39	0.09	-
Males,	298	205	33	1	-	28.28	19.45	3.13	0.09	-
Females,	249	202	66	-	-	23.62	19.17	6.26	-	-
South Hadley,	2,613	1,595	229	6	-	58.81	35.90	5.15	0.14	-
Males,	1,196	795	60	3	-	26.92	17.89	1.35	0.07	-
Females,	1,417	800	169	3	-	31.89	18.01	3.80	0.07	-
Ware, .	4,525	2,683	440	3	-	59.14	35.07	5.75	0.04	-
Males,	2,116	1,333	124	3	-	27.66	17.42	1.62	0.04	-
Females,	2,409	1,350	316	-	-	31.48	17.65	4.13	-	-
Westhampton,	246	204	26	-	-	51.68	42.86	5.46	-	-
Males,	129	104	8	-	-	27.10	21.85	1.68	-	-
Females,	117	100	18	-	-	24.58	21.01	3.78	-	-
Williamsburg,	1,008	783	159	5	-	51.56	40.05	8.13	0.26	-
Males,	519	387	41	3	-	26.55	19.79	2.09	0.16	-
Females,	489	396	118	2	-	25.01	20.26	6.04	0.10	-
Worthington,	330	279	39	-	-	50.93	43.05	6.02	-	-
Males,	186	140	15	-	-	28.71	21.60	2.31	-	-
Females,	144	139	24	-	-	22.22	21.45	3.71	-	-

CONJUGAL CONDITION — Continued.

COUNTIES, CITIES, TOWNS, AND SEX.	Single	Married	Widowed	Divorced	Un-known	PERCENTAGES Single	Married	Widowed	Divorced	Un-known
MIDDLESEX.										
Acton,	937	870	166	2	3	47.37	43.99	8.39	0.10	0.15
Males,	498	441	39	–	2	51.17	52.30	1.97	–	0.10
Females,	439	429	127	2	1	22.20	21.69	6.42	0.10	0.05
Arlington,	3,605	2,409	408	2	1	56.71	36.97	6.26	0.04	0.02
Males,	1,764	1,191	110	1	1	27.07	18.28	1.69	0.02	0.02
Females,	1,961	1,218	298	1	–	29.64	18.69	4.57	0.02	–
Ashby,	573	344	78	7	2	46.40	42.78	9.70	0.87	0.25
Males,	213	172	25	1	2	26.50	21.39	3.11	0.12	0.25
Females,	160	172	53	6	–	19.90	21.39	6.59	0.75	–
Ashland,	1,160	761	165	4	–	55.50	36.41	7.90	0.19	–
Males,	583	378	51	3	–	27.89	18.09	2.44	0.14	–
Females,	577	383	114	1	–	27.61	18.32	5.46	0.05	–
Ayer,	1,078	855	167	1	–	51.31	40.69	7.95	0.05	–
Males,	541	423	53	1	–	25.75	20.16	2.52	0.05	–
Females,	537	432	114	–	–	25.56	20.56	5.43	–	–
Bedford,	652	436	80	1	–	55.77	37.30	6.81	0.09	–
Males,	379	221	23	–	–	32.42	18.91	1.96	–	–
Females,	273	215	57	1	–	23.35	18.39	4.88	0.09	–
Belmont,	1,715	975	153	–	–	60.32	34.30	5.38	–	–
Males,	923	543	53	–	–	32.47	19.10	1.86	–	–
Females,	792	432	100	–	–	27.85	15.20	3.52	–	–
Billerica,	1,443	949	178	7	–	56.00	36.82	6.91	0.27	–
Males,	782	481	34	4	–	30.35	18.66	1.32	0.16	–
Females,	661	468	144	3	–	25.65	18.16	5.59	0.11	–
Boxborough,	143	146	16	2	–	46.58	47.55	5.22	0.65	–
Males,	89	75	8	–	–	28.99	24.43	2.61	–	–
Females,	54	71	8	2	–	17.59	23.12	2.61	0.65	–
Burlington,	323	201	50	–	–	56.27	35.02	8.71	–	–
Males,	192	103	21	–	–	33.46	17.94	3.66	–	–
Females,	131	98	29	–	–	22.82	17.08	5.05	–	–
CAMBRIDGE,	47,552	28,631	5,562	87	21	58.24	35.07	6.56	0.11	0.02
Males,	24,270	14,262	1,256	24	19	29.73	17.47	1.54	0.05	0.02
Females,	23,282	14,369	4,306	63	2	28.51	17.60	5.02	0.08	*
Carlisle,	248	200	42	2	–	50.41	40.65	8.53	0.41	–
Males,	147	103	16	2	–	29.88	20.96	3.25	0.41	–
Females,	101	97	26	–	–	20.53	19.72	5.28	–	–
Chelmsford,	1,645	1,305	207	5	–	52.02	41.27	6.55	0.16	–
Males,	879	654	77	1	–	27.80	20.68	2.44	0.03	–
Females,	766	651	130	4	–	24.22	20.59	4.11	0.13	–
Concord,	3,350	1,554	263	7	1	64.75	30.03	5.08	0.14	0.02
Males,	2,244	815	93	5	–	43.36	15.75	1.79	0.10	–
Females,	1,106	739	170	2	1	21.37	14.28	3.29	0.04	0.02
Dracut,	1,412	851	138	1	41	57.80	34.83	5.65	0.04	1.68
Males,	808	418	57	1	41	33.08	17.11	2.33	0.04	1.68
Females,	604	433	81	–	–	24.72	17.72	3.32	–	–
Dunstable,	188	172	37	3	–	47.00	43.09	9.25	0.75	–
Males,	96	87	22	2	–	24.00	21.75	5.50	0.50	–
Females,	92	85	15	1	–	23.00	21.25	3.75	0.25	–
EVERETT,	9,565	7,960	1,021	20	7	51.50	42.85	5.50	0.11	0.04
Males,	4,804	3,955	286	9	3	25.86	21.29	1.54	0.05	0.02
Females,	4,761	4,005	735	11	4	25.64	21.56	3.96	0.06	0.02
Framingham,	5,343	3,518	610	14	27	56.17	36.99	6.41	0.15	0.28
Males,	2,651	1,745	142	5	27	27.87	18.35	1.49	0.05	0.28
Females,	2,692	1,773	468	9	–	28.30	18.64	4.92	0.10	–
Groton,	1,182	803	199	8	–	53.92	36.63	9.08	0.37	–
Males,	613	400	60	5	–	27.96	18.25	2.74	0.23	–
Females,	569	403	139	3	–	25.96	18.38	6.34	0.14	–

* Less than one one-hundredth of one per cent.

CONJUGAL CONDITION — Continued.

COUNTIES, CITIES, TOWNS, AND SEX.	Single	Married	Widowed	Divorced	Un-known	PERCENTAGES				
						Single	Married	Widowed	Divorced	Un-known
MIDDLESEX — Con.										
Holliston, . . .	1,365	1,095	253	7	-	50.15	40.29	9.31	0.25	-
Males, . . .	686	547	74	2	-	25.24	20.15	2.72	0.07	-
Females, . .	677	548	179	5	-	24.91	20.16	6.59	0.18	-
Hopkinton, . . .	1,624	1,104	256	-	-	54.42	37.00	8.58	-	-
Males, . . .	826	544	99	-	-	27.68	18.25	3.32	-	-
Females, . .	798	560	157	-	-	26.74	18.77	5.26	-	-
Hudson, . . .	2,743	2,260	326	27	3	51.68	41.62	6.14	0.51	0.05
Males, . . .	1,355	1,086	80	10	2	25.53	20.46	1.51	0.19	0.03
Females, . .	1,388	1,125	246	17	1	26.15	21.16	4.63	0.32	0.02
Lexington, . .	1,906	1,259	322	11	-	54.49	35.99	9.21	0.31	-
Males, . . .	933	638	116	5	-	26.67	18.24	3.32	0.14	-
Females, . .	973	621	206	6	-	27.82	17.75	5.89	0.17	-
Lincoln, . . .	702	347	60	2	-	63.19	31.23	5.40	0.18	-
Males, . . .	419	188	19	-	-	37.72	16.92	1.71	-	-
Females, . .	283	159	41	2	-	25.47	14.31	3.69	0.18	-
Littleton, . . .	644	420	71	-	1	56.69	36.97	6.25	-	0.09
Males, . . .	321	226	22	-	-	28.26	19.89	1.94	-	-
Females, . .	323	194	49	-	1	28.43	17.08	4.31	-	0.09
LOWELL, . . .	48,793	29,769	5,655	127	23	57.83	35.29	6.70	0.15	0.03
Males, . . .	22,855	14,661	1,347	49	19	27.08	17.38	1.59	0.05	0.03
Females, . .	25,968	15,108	4,308	78	4	30.75	17.91	5.11	0.09	*-
MALDEN, . . .	16,125	11,625	1,916	37	5	54.28	39.13	6.45	0.12	0.02
Males, . . .	7,668	5,814	430	6	5	25.81	19.57	1.45	0.02	0.02
Females, . .	8,457	5,811	1,486	31	-	28.47	19.56	5.00	0.10	-
MARLBOROUGH, . .	8,573	5,620	754	21	9	57.24	37.52	5.04	0.14	0.06
Males, . . .	4,429	2,825	204	4	7	29.57	18.86	1.36	0.03	0.05
Females, . .	4,144	2,795	550	17	2	27.67	18.66	3.68	0.11	0.01
Maynard, . . .	1,715	1,185	188	1	1	55.50	38.35	6.09	0.03	0.03
Males, . . .	856	594	68	1	1	27.70	19.23	2.20	0.03	0.03
Females, . .	859	591	120	-	-	27.80	19.12	3.89	-	-
MEDFORD, . . .	7,883	5,660	923	8	-	54.46	39.10	6.38	0.06	-
Males, . . .	3,982	2,828	228	5	-	27.51	19.53	1.58	0.04	-
Females, . .	3,901	2,832	695	3	-	26.95	19.57	4.80	0.02	-
Melrose, . . .	6,300	4,871	784	7	3	52.65	40.71	6.55	0.06	0.03
Males, . . .	2,940	2,423	181	3	1	24.57	20.25	1.51	0.03	0.01
Females, . .	3,360	2,448	603	4	2	28.08	20.46	5.04	0.03	0.02
Natick, . . .	4,783	3,352	657	22	-	54.27	38.03	7.45	0.25	-
Males, . . .	2,378	1,660	191	5	-	26.98	18.83	2.17	0.06	-
Females, . .	2,405	1,692	466	17	-	27.29	19.20	5.28	0.19	-
NEWTON, . . .	16,108	9,835	1,608	29	10	58.38	35.65	5.83	0.10	0.04
Males, . . .	7,050	4,904	382	11	8	25.55	17.78	1.39	0.03	0.03
Females, . .	9,058	4,931	1,226	18	2	32.83	17.87	4.44	0.07	0.01
North Reading, . .	421	350	64	-	-	50.42	41.92	7.66	-	-
Males, . . .	224	182	16	-	-	26.83	21.80	1.91	-	-
Females, . .	197	168	48	-	-	23.59	20.12	5.75	-	-
Pepperell, . . .	1,743	1,328	230	20	-	52.48	39.99	6.93	0.60	-
Males, . . .	909	663	70	8	-	27.37	19.96	2.11	0.24	-
Females, . .	834	665	160	12	-	25.11	20.03	4.82	0.36	-
Reading, . . .	2,373	1,965	371	8	-	50.31	41.66	7.87	0.16	-
Males, . . .	1,165	982	84	4	-	24.70	20.82	1.78	0.08	-
Females, . .	1,208	983	287	4	-	25.61	20.84	6.09	0.08	-
Sherborn, . . .	762	557	123	4	-	52.70	38.52	8.50	0.28	-
Males, . . .	330	219	35	-	-	22.82	15.15	2.42	-	-
Females, . .	432	338	88	4	-	29.88	23.37	6.08	0.28	-
Shirley, . . .	743	558	101	7	-	52.39	39.89	7.22	0.50	-
Males, . . .	360	272	28	4	-	25.02	19.44	2.00	0.29	-
Females, . .	383	286	73	3	-	27.37	20.45	5.22	0.21	-

* Less than one one-hundredth of one per cent.

CONJUGAL CONDITION. 843

CONJUGAL CONDITION — Continued.

COUNTIES, CITIES, TOWNS, AND SEX.	Single	Married	Widowed	Divorced	Unknown	PERCENTAGES Single	Married	Widowed	Divorced	Unknown
MIDDLESEX — Con.										
SOMERVILLE,	27,501	21,264	3,252	77	6	52.68	40.92	6.23	0.15	0.02
Males,	13,457	10,624	813	20	3	25.77	20.35	1.56	0.04	0.01
Females,	14,044	10,740	2,439	57	3	26.91	20.57	4.67	0.11	0.01
Stoneham,	3,064	2,694	497	29	–	48.79	42.87	7.91	0.46	–
Males,	1,577	1,345	134	14	–	25.10	21.40	2.13	0.22	–
Females,	1,487	1,349	363	15	–	23.66	21.47	5.78	0.24	–
Stow,	451	401	68	–	–	49.02	43.59	7.39	–	–
Males,	251	203	19	–	–	27.28	22.07	2.06	–	–
Females,	200	198	49	–	–	21.74	21.52	5.33	–	–
Sudbury,	618	406	115	2	–	54.16	35.58	10.08	0.18	–
Males,	357	207	39	–	–	31.29	18.14	3.42	–	–
Females,	261	199	76	2	–	22.87	17.44	6.66	0.18	–
Tewksbury,	1,865	1,087	358	–	59	55.19	32.17	10.89	–	1.75
Males,	952	517	168	–	16	28.17	15.30	4.97	–	0.48
Females,	913	570	200	–	43	27.02	16.87	5.92	–	1.27
Townsend,	784	802	189	3	2	44.04	45.06	10.62	0.17	0.11
Males,	418	404	53	3	2	23.48	22.70	2.98	0.17	0.11
Females,	366	398	136	–	–	20.56	22.36	7.64	–	–
Tyngsborough,	328	247	56	1	3	51.65	38.90	8.82	0.16	0.47
Males,	183	123	15	–	3	28.82	19.37	2.36	–	0.47
Females,	145	124	41	1	–	22.83	19.53	6.46	0.16	–
Wakefield,	4,594	3,551	502	16	1	52.92	40.11	6.77	0.19	0.01
Males,	2,167	1,923	152	9	1	26.10	19.66	1.83	0.11	0.01
Females,	2,227	1,608	410	7	–	26.82	20.45	4.94	0.08	–
WALTHAM,	12,022	7,459	1,352	39	4	57.59	35.73	6.48	0.18	0.02
Males,	5,652	3,685	288	9	4	27.08	17.65	1.38	0.04	0.02
Females,	6,370	3,774	1,064	30	–	30.51	18.08	5.10	0.14	–
Watertown,	4,498	2,804	476	8	2	57.76	36.00	6.11	0.10	0.03
Males,	2,211	1,411	115	1	2	28.39	18.11	1.48	0.01	0.03
Females,	2,287	1,393	361	7	–	29.37	17.89	4.63	0.09	–
Wayland,	1,112	761	149	4	–	54.89	37.56	7.35	0.20	–
Males,	599	378	48	1	–	29.57	18.66	2.36	0.05	–
Females,	513	383	101	3	–	25.32	18.90	4.99	0.15	–
Westford,	1,334	893	180	10	1	55.17	36.93	7.44	0.42	0.04
Males,	700	445	74	4	–	28.95	18.40	3.06	0.17	–
Females,	634	448	106	6	1	26.22	18.53	4.38	0.25	0.04
Weston,	985	621	104	–	–	57.60	36.32	6.08	–	–
Males,	529	309	39	–	–	30.94	18.07	2.28	–	–
Females,	456	312	65	–	–	26.66	18.25	3.80	–	–
Wilmington,	728	602	87	3	–	51.27	42.39	6.13	0.21	–
Males,	393	290	30	2	–	27.68	20.42	2.11	0.14	–
Females,	335	312	57	1	–	23.59	21.97	4.02	0.07	–
Winchester,	3,513	2,263	366	8	–	57.12	36.80	5.95	0.13	–
Males,	1,703	1,131	89	5	–	27.69	18.39	1.45	0.08	–
Females,	1,810	1,132	277	3	–	29.43	18.41	4.50	0.05	–
WOBURN,	8,224	5,036	907	10	1	58.00	35.52	6.39	0.08	0.01
Males,	4,212	2,516	267	5	–	29.70	17.75	1.88	0.04	–
Females,	4,012	2,520	640	5	1	28.30	17.77	4.51	0.04	0.01
NANTUCKET.										
Nantucket,	1,283	1,294	415	24	–	42.54	42.90	13.76	0.80	–
Males,	571	642	88	14	–	18.93	21.28	2.92	0.47	–
Females,	712	652	327	10	–	23.61	21.62	10.84	0.33	–
NORFOLK.										
Avon,	848	650	123	5	–	52.15	39.98	7.56	0.31	–
Males,	442	329	42	5	–	27.18	20.24	2.58	0.31	–
Females,	406	321	81	–	–	24.97	19.74	4.98	–	–

CONJUGAL CONDITION — Continued.

Counties, Cities, Towns, and Sex.	Single	Married	Widowed	Divorced	Un-known	Percentages: Single	Married	Widowed	Divorced	Un-known
NORFOLK — Con.										
Bellingham,	750	613	103	6	-	51.25	41.39	6.95	0.41	-
Males,	375	302	39	5	-	25.32	20.39	2.63	0.34	-
Females,	384	311	64	1	-	25.93	21.00	4.32	0.07	-
Braintree,	2,731	2,241	351	6	2	51.42	42.19	6.23	0.12	0.04
Males,	1,405	1,158	92	3	2	26.45	21.80	1.73	0.06	0.04
Females,	1,326	1,083	259	3	-	24.97	20.39	4.50	0.06	-
Brookline,	9,969	5,265	916	9	5	61.67	52.57	5.67	0.06	0.03
Males,	4,002	2,622	195	3	4	24.76	16.22	1.21	0.02	0.02
Females,	5,967	2,643	721	6	1	36.91	16.35	4.46	0.04	0.01
Canton,	2,828	1,461	343	4	-	61.00	31.51	7.40	0.09	-
Males,	1,369	728	109	1	-	29.53	15.70	2.35	0.03	-
Females,	1,459	733	234	3	-	31.47	15.81	5.05	0.06	-
Cohasset,	1,405	905	153	11	-	56.79	36.58	6.19	0.44	-
Males,	648	452	43	5	-	26.19	18.27	1.74	0.20	-
Females,	757	453	110	6	-	30.60	18.31	4.45	0.24	-
Dedham,	4,097	2,531	570	7	6	56.82	35.10	7.90	0.10	0.08
Males,	2,036	1,235	197	3	5	28.24	17.13	2.73	0.04	0.06
Females,	2,061	1,296	373	4	1	28.58	17.97	5.17	0.06	0.02
Dover,	391	225	51	-	1	58.53	33.68	7.64	-	0.15
Males,	210	113	21	-	1	31.44	16.91	3.15	-	0.15
Females,	181	112	30	-	-	27.09	16.77	4.49	-	-
Foxborough,	1,567	1,361	280	11	-	48.68	42.28	8.70	0.34	-
Males,	759	690	87	6	-	23.58	21.44	2.70	0.18	-
Females,	808	671	193	5	-	25.10	20.84	6.00	0.16	-
Franklin,	2,772	2,008	330	16	10	53.97	39.10	6.42	0.31	0.20
Males,	1,351	1,008	90	5	5	26.30	19.63	1.75	0.10	0.10
Females,	1,421	1,000	240	11	5	27.67	19.47	4.67	0.21	0.10
Holbrook,	1,165	984	146	3	-	50.70	42.82	6.35	0.13	-
Males,	592	493	42	-	-	25.76	21.45	1.83	-	-
Females,	573	491	104	3	-	24.94	21.37	4.52	0.13	-
Hyde Park,	6,592	4,498	710	23	3	55.74	38.04	6.00	0.19	0.03
Males,	3,323	2,245	186	4	2	28.10	18.99	1.57	0.06	0.02
Females,	3,269	2,253	524	19	1	27.64	19.05	4.43	0.16	0.01
Medfield,	1,029	691	145	7	-	54.97	36.91	7.75	0.37	-
Males,	489	347	46	1	-	26.12	18.54	2.46	0.05	-
Females,	540	344	99	6	-	28.85	18.37	5.29	0.32	-
Medway,	1,494	1,181	285	3	-	51.29	40.54	8.07	0.10	-
Males,	787	593	57	1	-	27.02	20.35	1.96	0.03	-
Females,	707	588	178	2	-	24.27	20.19	6.11	0.07	-
Millis,	510	424	67	5	-	50.69	42.15	6.66	0.50	-
Males,	253	208	21	2	-	25.14	20.68	2.09	0.20	-
Females,	257	216	46	3	-	25.55	21.47	4.57	0.30	-
Milton,	3,375	1,812	325	3	3	61.17	32.84	5.89	0.05	0.05
Males,	1,588	888	83	-	3	28.78	16.09	1.51	-	0.05
Females,	1,787	924	242	3	-	32.39	16.75	4.38	0.05	-
Needham,	1,977	1,318	213	3	-	56.31	37.54	6.07	0.08	-
Males,	1,006	669	74	-	-	28.65	19.05	2.11	-	-
Females,	971	649	139	3	-	27.66	18.49	3.96	0.08	-
Norfolk,	452	368	59	3	-	51.25	41.72	6.69	0.34	-
Males,	270	183	18	-	-	30.61	20.75	2.04	-	-
Females,	182	185	41	3	-	20.64	20.97	4.65	0.34	-
Norwood,	2,588	1,743	234	8	1	56.58	38.11	5.12	0.17	0.02
Males,	1,471	884	78	3	1	32.16	19.33	1.71	0.06	0.02
Females,	1,117	859	156	5	-	24.42	18.78	3.41	0.11	-
QUINCY,	11,974	7,617	1,097	22	2	57.81	36.78	5.30	0.11	*-
Males,	6,436	3,820	335	16	1	31.07	18.45	1.62	0.08	*-
Females,	5,538	3,797	762	6	1	26.74	18.33	3.68	0.03	*-

* Less than one one-hundredth of one per cent.

CONJUGAL CONDITION — Continued.

COUNTIES, CITIES, TOWNS, AND SEX.	Single	Married	Widowed	Divorced	Unknown	PERCENTAGES Single	Married	Widowed	Divorced	Unknown
NORFOLK — Con.										
Randolph, . . .	1,914	1,419	345	16	-	51.81	58.41	9.34	0.44	-
Males, . .	965	735	117	8	-	26.12	19.89	3.17	0.22	-
Females, . .	949	684	228	8	-	25.69	18.52	6.17	0.22	-
Sharon, . .	912	645	151	8	1	53.11	37.57	8.79	0.47	0.06
Males, . .	459	326	52	2	-	26.73	18.99	3.02	0.12	-
Females, . .	453	319	99	6	1	26.38	18.58	5.77	0.35	0.06
Stoughton, . .	2,839	2,004	415	12	2	53.85	58.02	7.87	0.22	0.04
Males, . .	1,434	996	132	6	2	27.20	18.90	2.50	0.11	0.04
Females, . .	1,405	1,008	283	6	-	26.65	19.12	5.37	0.11	-
Walpole, . .	1,623	1,161	200	6	4	54.21	38.77	6.68	0.20	0.14
Males, . .	852	591	54	1	2	28.46	19.74	1.80	0.03	0.07
Females, . .	771	570	146	5	2	25.75	19.03	4.88	0.17	0.07
Wellesley, . .	2,815	1,139	268	3	4	66.56	26.94	6.34	0.07	0.09
Males, . .	840	572	55	-	3	19.86	13.53	1.30	-	0.07
Females, . .	1,975	567	213	3	1	46.70	13.41	5.04	0.07	0.02
Weymouth, . .	5,864	4,633	774	20	-	51.93	41.03	6.86	0.18	-
Males, . .	3,042	2,330	211	9	-	26.94	20.64	1.87	0.08	-
Females, . .	2,822	2,303	563	11	-	24.99	20.39	4.99	0.10	-
Wrentham, . .	1,358	980	231	15	-	52.55	37.93	8.94	0.58	-
Males, . .	696	488	75	4	-	26.94	18.89	2.90	0.15	-
Females, . .	662	492	156	11	-	25.61	19.04	6.04	0.43	-
PLYMOUTH.										
Abington, . . .	2,057	1,816	320	13	1	48.89	43.17	7.61	0.31	0.02
Males, . .	1,022	901	109	7	1	24.29	21.42	2.59	0.17	0.02
Females, . .	1,035	915	211	6	-	24.60	21.75	5.02	0.14	-
Bridgewater, . .	2,571	1,649	408	8	50	54.86	35.19	8.71	0.17	1.07
Males, . .	1,523	926	218	5	50	32.50	19.76	4.65	0.11	1.07
Females, . .	1,048	723	190	3	-	22.36	15.43	4.06	0.06	-
BROCKTON, . .	17,188	13,920	1,896	107	54	51.83	41.97	5.72	0.32	0.16
Males, . .	8,998	6,981	493	35	52	27.13	21.05	1.49	0.11	0.15
Females, . .	8,190	6,939	1,403	72	2	24.70	20.92	4.23	0.21	0.01
Carver, . .	521	395	92	8	-	51.28	38.88	9.05	0.79	-
Males, . .	301	201	37	7	-	29.63	19.78	3.64	0.69	-
Females, . .	220	194	55	1	-	21.65	19.10	5.41	0.10	-
Duxbury, . .	912	836	213	5	-	46.39	42.52	10.83	0.26	-
Males, . .	452	418	73	2	-	22.99	21.26	3.71	0.11	-
Females, . .	460	418	140	3	-	23.40	21.26	7.12	0.15	-
East Bridgewater, .	1,399	1,232	251	12	-	48.84	42.57	8.67	0.42	-
Males, . .	746	608	79	8	-	25.77	21.01	2.73	0.28	-
Females, . .	653	624	172	4	-	22.57	21.56	5.94	0.14	-
Halifax, . .	222	218	57	-	-	44.67	43.86	11.47	-	-
Males, . .	136	111	19	-	-	27.37	22.33	3.82	-	-
Females, . .	86	107	38	-	-	17.30	21.53	7.65	-	-
Hanover, . .	974	901	167	9	-	47.49	43.93	8.14	0.44	-
Males, . .	496	451	59	3	-	24.18	21.99	2.88	0.15	-
Females, . .	478	450	108	6	-	23.31	21.94	5.26	0.29	-
Hanson, . .	619	636	118	7	-	44.85	46.09	8.55	0.51	-
Males, . .	347	322	37	2	-	25.14	23.33	2.68	0.15	-
Females, . .	272	314	81	5	-	19.71	22.76	5.87	0.36	-
Hingham, . .	2,542	1,864	405	7	1	52.75	38.68	8.40	0.15	0.02
Males, . .	1,227	949	118	4	1	25.46	19.69	2.45	0.09	0.02
Females, . .	1,315	915	287	3	-	27.29	18.99	5.95	0.06	-
Hull, . . .	544	434	48	1	17	52.11	41.57	4.60	0.09	1.63
Males, . .	287	223	20	-	6	27.49	21.36	1.92	-	0.57
Females, . .	257	211	28	1	11	24.62	20.21	2.68	0.09	1.06

CONJUGAL CONDITION — Continued.

COUNTIES, CITIES, TOWNS, AND SEX.	Single	Married	Widowed	Divorced	Un-known	PERCENTAGES				
						Single	Married	Widowed	Divorced	Un-known
PLYMOUTH — Con.										
Kingston, . . .	848	744	146	8	-	48.57	42.61	8.36	0.46	-
Males, . . .	435	367	43	2	-	24.91	21.02	2.46	0.12	-
Females, . .	413	377	103	6	-	23.66	21.59	5.90	0.34	-
Lakeville, . . .	432	359	74	5	-	49.66	41.26	8.51	0.57	-
Males, . . .	231	180	26	2	-	26.55	20.69	2.99	0.23	-
Females, . .	201	179	48	3	-	23.11	20.57	5.52	0.34	-
Marion, . . .	346	328	82	3	-	45.59	43.21	10.80	0.40	-
Males, . . .	152	163	11	2	-	20.03	21.47	1.44	0.27	-
Females, . .	194	165	71	1	-	25.56	21.74	9.36	0.13	-
Marshfield, . .	801	799	159	1	-	45.51	45.40	9.03	0.06	-
Males, . . .	410	393	47	-	-	23.30	22.33	2.67	-	-
Females, . .	391	406	112	1	-	22.21	23.07	6.36	0.06	-
Mattapoisett, .	457	449	120	6	-	44.28	43.51	11.63	0.58	-
Males, . . .	234	223	28	5	-	22.67	21.61	2.71	0.49	-
Females, . .	223	226	92	1	-	21.61	21.90	8.92	0.09	-
Middleborough, .	3,203	2,908	559	18	1	47.89	43.47	8.36	0.27	0.01
Males, . . .	1,561	1,468	168	7	1	23.34	21.94	2.51	0.11	0.01
Females, . .	1,642	1,440	391	11	-	24.55	21.53	5.85	0.16	-
Norwell, . . .	722	662	150	6	-	46.88	42.99	9.74	0.39	-
Males, . . .	387	328	52	4	-	25.13	21.30	3.37	0.26	-
Females, . .	335	334	98	2	-	21.75	21.69	6.37	0.13	-
Pembroke, . .	542	571	107	3	-	44.32	46.69	8.75	0.24	-
Males, . . .	313	279	41	1	-	25.60	22.81	3.35	0.08	-
Females, . .	229	292	66	2	-	18.72	23.88	5.40	0.16	-
Plymouth, . . .	4,037	3,343	561	16	-	50.74	42.01	7.05	0.20	-
Males, . . .	2,045	1,665	147	6	-	25.70	20.92	1.85	0.08	-
Females, . .	1,992	1,678	414	10	-	25.04	21.09	5.20	0.12	-
Plympton, . . .	250	235	60	4	-	45.54	42.80	10.93	0.73	-
Males, . . .	130	116	21	1	-	23.68	21.13	3.83	0.18	-
Females, . .	120	119	39	3	-	21.86	21.67	7.10	0.55	-
Rochester, . .	508	445	63	4	1	49.76	43.58	6.17	0.39	0.10
Males, . . .	289	221	21	3	1	28.31	21.64	2.06	0.29	0.10
Females, . .	219	224	42	1	-	21.45	21.94	4.11	0.10	-
Rockland, . . .	2,913	2,205	394	11	-	52.74	39.93	7.13	0.20	-
Males, . . .	1,524	1,109	118	6	-	27.59	20.08	2.14	0.11	-
Females, . .	1,389	1,096	276	5	-	25.15	19.85	4.99	0.09	-
Scituate, . . .	1,101	950	188	7	-	49.02	42.30	8.37	0.31	-
Males, . . .	581	475	57	2	-	25.87	21.15	2.54	0.08	-
Females, . .	520	475	131	5	-	23.15	21.15	5.83	0.23	-
Wareham, . . .	1,656	1,435	265	10	1	49.18	42.62	7.87	0.30	0.03
Males, . . .	944	736	79	5	1	28.03	21.86	2.35	0.15	0.03
Females, . .	712	699	186	5	-	21.15	20.76	5.52	0.15	-
West Bridgewater, .	973	687	83	3	1	55.70	39.32	4.75	0.17	0.06
Males, . . .	533	338	6	-	-	30.51	19.35	0.34	-	-
Females, . .	440	349	77	3	1	25.19	19.97	4.41	0.17	0.06
Whitman, . . .	2,838	2,525	367	14	-	49.41	43.96	6.39	0.24	-
Males, . . .	1,503	1,248	125	3	-	26.17	21.73	2.17	0.05	-
Females, . .	1,335	1,277	242	11	-	23.24	22.23	4.22	0.19	-
SUFFOLK.										
Boston, . . .	284,740	176,745	34,023	688	714	57.30	35.57	6.85	0.14	0.14
Males, . . .	142,404	88,407	8,220	175	450	28.65	17.79	1.66	0.04	0.09
Females, . .	142,336	88,338	25,803	513	264	28.65	17.78	5.19	0.10	0.05
Chelsea, . . .	17,129	11,973	2,104	31	27	54.79	38.30	6.73	0.10	0.08
Males, . . .	8,741	5,946	553	14	19	27.96	19.02	1.77	0 04	0.06
Females, . .	8,388	6,027	1,551	17	8	26.83	19.28	4.96	0.06	0.02

CONJUGAL CONDITION — Continued.

COUNTIES, CITIES, TOWNS, AND SEX.	Single	Married	Widowed	Divorced	Un-known	PERCENTAGES				
						Single	Married	Widowed	Divorced	Un-known
SUFFOLK — Con.										
Revere, . . .	3,991	3,696	376	20	–	53.76	49.90	5.07	0.27	–
Males, . . .	2,108	1,543	91	9	–	28.40	20.58	1.23	0.12	–
Females, . .	1,883	1,523	285	11	–	25.36	20.32	3.84	0.15	–
Winthrop, . . .	2,149	1,768	266	8	1	51.26	42.18	6.35	0.19	0.02
Males, . . .	1,060	887	64	3	1	25.29	21.16	1.53	0.07	0.02
Females, . .	1,089	881	202	5	–	25.97	21.02	4.82	0.12	–
WORCESTER.										
Ashburnham, . .	1,044	899	204	1	–	48.80	41.85	9.50	0.05	–
Males, . . .	572	451	46	1	–	26.63	20.99	2.14	0.05	–
Females, . .	472	448	158	–	–	21.97	20.86	7.36	–	–
Athol, ...	3,961	3,128	607	27	1	48.90	42.48	8.24	0.37	0.01
Males, . . .	1,950	1,576	196	12	1	26.48	21.40	2.66	0.17	0.01
Females, . .	1,951	1,552	411	15	–	22.42	21.08	5.58	0.20	–
Auburn, . . .	968	614	74	2	–	56.82	38.43	4.63	0.12	–
Males, . . .	474	315	31	1	–	29.66	19.72	1.94	0.06	–
Females, . .	434	299	43	1	–	27.16	18.71	2.69	0.06	–
Barre, ...	1,199	871	194	9	5	52.63	38.24	8.52	0.39	0.22
Males, . . .	645	443	53	5	4	28.31	19.45	2.33	0.22	0.17
Females, . .	554	428	141	4	1	24.32	18.79	6.19	0.17	0.05
Berlin, . . .	442	366	85	4	–	49.28	40.80	9.48	0.44	–
Males, . . .	235	184	32	–	–	26.29	20.51	3.57	–	–
Females, . .	207	182	53	4	–	23.08	20.29	5.91	0.44	–
Blackstone, . .	3,584	2,010	419	26	–	59.35	35.28	6.94	0.43	–
Males, . . .	1,967	1,008	132	9	–	32.57	16.69	2.19	0.15	–
Females, . .	1,617	1,002	287	17	–	26.78	16.59	4.75	0.28	–
Bolton, . . .	369	332	91	5	–	46.30	41.65	11.42	0.63	–
Males, . . .	198	159	38	3	–	24.84	19.95	4.77	0.38	–
Females, . .	171	173	53	2	–	21.46	21.70	6.65	0.25	–
Boylston, . . .	370	292	66	1	–	50.75	40.05	9.06	0.14	–
Males, . . .	211	148	30	–	–	28.94	20.30	4.12	–	–
Females, . .	159	144	36	1	–	21.81	19.75	4.94	0.14	–
Brookfield, . .	1,704	1,359	207	9	–	51.97	41.45	6.31	0.27	–
Males, . . .	934	680	70	5	–	28.49	20.74	2.13	0.15	–
Females, . .	770	679	137	4	–	23.48	20.71	4.18	0.12	–
Charlton, . . .	924	827	117	9	–	49.23	44.06	6.23	0.48	–
Males, . . .	520	411	38	6	–	27.70	21.90	2.02	0.32	–
Females, . .	404	416	79	3	–	21.53	22.16	4.21	0.16	–
Clinton, . . .	6,876	3,928	676	17	–	59.81	34.17	5.88	0.14	–
Males, . . .	3,178	1,954	155	4	–	27.64	17.00	1.35	0.05	–
Females, . .	3,698	1,974	521	13	–	32.17	17.17	4.53	0.11	–
Dana, ...	323	325	60	8	1	45.05	45.32	8.37	1.12	0.14
Males, . . .	158	163	26	5	1	22.03	22.73	3.63	0.70	0.14
Females, . .	165	162	34	3	–	23.02	22.59	4.74	0.42	–
Douglas, . . .	1,014	807	192	13	–	50.05	39.83	9.48	0.64	–
Males, . . .	549	414	60	10	–	27.10	20.44	2.96	0.49	–
Females, . .	465	393	132	3	–	22.95	19.39	6.52	0.15	–
Dudley, . . .	1,909	1,077	179	8	–	60.54	33.63	5.59	0.24	–
Males, . . .	997	530	80	4	–	31.13	16.55	2.50	0.12	–
Females, . .	912	547	99	4	–	29.41	17.08	3.09	0.12	–
FITCHBURG, . .	14,700	10,175	1,464	47	23	55.66	38.53	5.54	0.18	0.08
Males, . . .	7,478	5,113	411	17	18	28.31	19.36	1.56	0.07	0.07
Females, . .	7,222	5,062	1,053	30	5	27.35	19.17	3.98	0.11	0.02
Gardner, . . .	4,882	3,908	423	19	–	52.62	42.56	4.61	0.21	–
Males, . . .	2,636	1,991	98	10	–	28.71	21.68	1.07	0.11	–
Females, . .	2,196	1,917	325	9	–	23.91	20.88	3.54	0.10	–

CONJUGAL CONDITION — Continued.

COUNTIES, CITIES, TOWNS, AND SEX.	Single	Married	Widowed	Divorced	Un-known	PERCENTAGES				
						Single	Married	Widowed	Divorced	Un-known
WORCESTER - Con.										
Grafton, . . .	2,855	1,931	305	9	1	55.97	37.85	5.98	0.18	0.02
Males, . . .	1,387	962	101	4	1	27.19	18.86	1.98	0.08	0.02
Females, . .	1,468	969	204	5	-	28.78	18.99	4.00	0.10	-
Hardwick, . . .	1,554	940	159	2	-	58.55	35.40	5.99	0.08	-
Males, . . .	832	476	67	1	-	31.34	17.93	2.52	0.04	-
Females, . .	722	464	92	1	-	27.19	17.47	3.47	0.04	-
Harvard, . . .	593	464	104	1	-	51.03	39.93	8.95	0.09	-
Males, . . .	299	239	36	-	-	25.73	20.57	3.10	-	-
Females, . .	294	225	68	1	-	25.30	19.36	5.85	0.09	-
Holden, . . .	1,490	936	174	1	1	57.26	35.97	6.69	0.04	0.04
Males, . . .	774	471	56	-	1	29.75	18.10	2.15	-	0.04
Females, . .	716	465	118	1	-	27.51	17.87	4.54	0.04	-
Hopedale, . .	727	592	55	1	2	52.80	42.99	3.99	0.07	0.15
Males, . . .	386	295	15	-	2	28.03	21.42	1.09	-	0.15
Females, . .	341	297	40	1	-	24.77	21.57	2.90	0.07	-
Hubbardston, . .	614	531	123	2	4	48.19	41.68	9.66	0.16	0.31
Males, . .	342	270	42	2	3	26.84	21.20	3.30	0.16	0.23
Females, . .	272	261	81	-	1	21.35	20.48	6.36	-	0.08
Lancaster, . .	1,289	730	178	3	-	58.21	33.49	8.16	0.14	-
Males, . . .	568	367	41	2	-	26.05	16.84	1.88	0.09	-
Females, . .	701	363	137	1	-	32.16	16.65	6.28	0.05	-
Leicester, . . .	1,828	1,193	217	1	-	56.44	36.83	6.70	0.03	-
Males, . . .	888	589	63	1	-	27.42	18.18	1.95	0.03	-
Females, . .	940	604	154	-	-	29.02	18.65	4.75	-	-
Leominster, . .	4,644	3,923	614	20	10	50.42	42.60	6.66	0.22	0.10
Males, . . .	2,357	1,967	168	7	5	25.59	21.36	1.82	0.08	0.05
Females, . .	2,287	1,956	446	13	5	24.83	21.24	4.84	0.14	0.05
Lunenburg, . .	617	547	71	2	-	49.88	44.22	5.74	0.16	-
Males, . . .	330	278	17	1	-	26.68	22.47	1.38	0.08	-
Females, . .	287	269	54	1	-	23.20	21.75	4.36	0.08	-
Mendon, . . .	455	346	81	6	1	51.18	38.92	9.11	0.68	0.11
Males, . . .	250	182	27	3	-	28.12	20.47	3.04	0.34	-
Females, . .	205	164	54	3	1	23.06	18.45	6.07	0.34	0.11
Milford, . . .	4,845	3,392	704	16	2	54.08	37.86	7.86	0.18	0.02
Males, . . .	2,451	1,706	189	7	1	27.36	19.04	2.11	0.08	0.01
Females, . .	2,394	1,686	515	9	1	26.72	18.82	5.75	0.10	0.01
Millbury, . . .	2,934	1,868	345	4	101	56.19	35.77	6.63	0.08	1.93
Males, . . .	1,470	944	163	1	101	28.15	18.08	1.97	0.02	1.93
Females, . .	1,464	924	212	3	-	28.04	17.69	4.06	0.06	-
New Braintree, . .	390	194	45	2	1	55.35	35.80	8.31	0.36	0.18
Males, . . .	170	97	23	1	1	31.36	17.90	4.25	0.18	0.18
Females, . .	130	97	22	1	-	23.99	17.90	4.06	0.18	-
Northborough, . .	991	708	145	6	-	51.08	41.13	7.48	0.31	-
Males, . . .	522	406	45	2	-	26.91	20.93	2.32	0.10	-
Females, . .	469	392	100	4	-	24.17	20.20	5.16	0.21	-
Northbridge, . .	3,063	1,950	268	4	1	57.94	36.89	5.07	0.08	0.02
Males, . . .	1,664	981	85	1	1	31.47	18.56	1.61	0.02	0.02
Females, . .	1,399	969	183	3	-	26.47	18.33	3.46	0.06	-
North Brookfield,	2,549	1,770	308	8	-	54.99	38.19	6.64	0.18	-
Males, . . .	1,279	880	85	4	-	27.59	18.99	1.83	0.09	-
Females, . .	1,270	890	223	4	-	27.40	19.20	4.81	0.09	-
Oakham, . . .	300	246	55	4	-	49.50	40.66	9.09	0.66	-
Males, . . .	166	123	17	2	-	27.44	20.33	2.81	0.33	-
Females, . .	134	123	38	2	-	22.15	20.33	6.28	0.33	-
Oxford, . . .	1,217	970	190	9	4	50.92	40.58	7.95	0.38	0.17
Males, . . .	603	476	63	4	1	25.23	19.91	2.64	0.17	0.04
Females, . .	614	494	127	5	3	25.69	20.67	5.31	0.21	0.13

CONJUGAL CONDITION — Continued.

COUNTIES. CITIES. TOWNS. AND SEX.	Single	Married	Widowed	Divorced	Unknown	PERCENTAGES Single	Married	Widowed	Divorced	Unknown
WORCESTER - Con.										
Paxton, . . .	186	208	31	1	-	43.66	48.83	7.28	0.23	-
Males, . . .	113	105	16	-	-	48.52	24.65	3.76	-	-
Females, . .	73	103	15	1	-	17.14	24.18	3.52	0.23	-
Petersham, . .	475	377	92	7	1	49.80	39.60	9.66	0.74	0.11
Males, . . .	270	190	27	6	-	28.36	19.96	2.84	0.63	-
Females, . .	205	187	65	1	1	21.53	19.64	6.82	0.11	0.11
Phillipston, . .	218	201	40	1	-	47.39	43.69	8.70	0.22	-
Males, . . .	129	99	19	1	-	28.04	21.52	4.13	0.22	-
Females, . .	89	102	21	-	-	19.35	22.17	4.57	-	-
Princeton, . .	484	391	77	-	-	50.84	41.07	8.09	-	-
Males, . . .	261	200	30	-	-	27.42	21.01	3.15	-	-
Females, . .	223	191	47	-	-	23.42	20.06	4.94	-	-
Royalston, . .	383	416	81	-	-	44.16	46.74	9.10	-	-
Males, . . .	219	209	26	-	-	24.61	23.48	2.92	-	-
Females, . .	174	207	55	-	-	19.55	23.26	6.18	-	-
Rutland, . . .	525	391	59	2	1	53.68	39.98	6.04	0.20	0.10
Males, . . .	305	199	21	1	-	31.18	20.35	2.15	0.10	-
Females, . .	220	192	38	1	1	22.50	19.63	3.89	0.10	0.10
Shrewsbury, . .	769	615	134	6	-	50.46	40.36	8.79	0.39	-
Males, . . .	423	311	46	4	-	27.76	20.41	3.01	0.26	-
Females, . .	346	304	88	2	-	22.70	19.95	5.78	0.13	-
Southborough, . .	1,286	793	144	-	-	57.85	35.67	6.48	-	-
Males, . . .	804	417	53	-	-	36.17	18.75	2.39	-	-
Females, . .	482	376	91	-	-	21.68	16.92	4.09	-	-
Southbridge, . .	4,904	2,907	431	4	4	59.44	35.24	5.22	0.05	0.05
Males, . . .	2,484	1,431	123	1	4	30.11	17.35	1.49	0.01	0.05
Females, . .	2,420	1,476	308	3	-	29.33	17.89	3.73	0.04	-
Spencer, . . .	4,358	2,843	394	17	2	57.24	37.34	5.17	0.22	0.03
Males, . . .	2,211	1,409	153	9	2	29.04	18.51	2.00	0.12	0.03
Females, . .	2,147	1,434	241	8	-	28.20	18.83	3.17	0.10	-
Sterling, . . .	544	565	107	2	-	44.66	46.39	8.79	0.16	-
Males, . . .	293	283	26	2	-	24.05	23.24	2.14	0.16	-
Females, . .	251	282	81	-	-	20.61	23.15	6.65	-	-
Sturbridge, . .	1,030	735	145	-	-	55.93	38.48	7.59	-	-
Males, . . .	536	362	50	-	-	28.06	18.95	2.62	-	-
Females, . .	494	373	95	-	-	25.87	19.53	4.97	-	-
Sutton, . . .	1,957	1,247	201	4	11	57.22	36.46	5.88	0.12	0.32
Males, . . .	1,075	612	70	2	11	31.43	17.80	2.05	0.06	0.32
Females, . .	882	635	131	2	-	25.79	18.57	3.83	0.06	-
Templeton, . .	1,445	1,238	222	10	-	49.57	42.47	7.62	0.34	-
Males, . . .	803	613	70	2	-	27.55	21.03	2.40	0.07	-
Females, . .	642	625	152	8	-	22.02	21.44	5.22	0.27	-
Upton, . . .	1,110	848	175	12	5	51.03	39.44	8.14	0.56	0.23
Males, . . .	441	412	46	5	4	20.51	19.17	2.14	0.23	0.18
Females, . .	669	436	129	7	1	31.12	20.27	6.00	0.33	0.05
Uxbridge, . .	1,922	1,353	254	14	3	54.29	38.16	7.16	0.40	0.08
Males, . . .	1,016	687	72	2	3	28.65	19.68	2.03	0.06	0.08
Females, . .	906	666	182	12	-	25.55	18.78	5.13	0.34	-
Warren, . . .	2,408	1,783	234	5	-	54.36	40.25	5.28	0.11	-
Males, . . .	1,249	802	56	-	-	28.20	20.13	1.26	-	-
Females, . .	1,159	801	178	5	-	26.16	20.12	4.02	0.11	-
Webster, . . .	4,385	2,947	449	18	-	56.22	37.79	5.76	0.23	-
Males, . . .	2,204	1,471	114	10	-	28.26	18.86	1.46	0.13	-
Females, . .	2,181	1,476	335	8	-	27.96	18.93	4.30	0.10	-
Westborough, . .	2,830	1,944	419	10	2	59.38	36.56	8.00	0.19	0.04
Males, . . .	1,558	944	123	4	2	29.98	18.03	2.35	0.08	0.04
Females, . .	1,552	970	296	6	-	25.83	18.53	5.65	0.11	-

CONJUGAL CONDITION — Continued.

COUNTIES, CITIES, TOWNS, AND SEX.	Single	Married	Widowed	Divorced	Un-known	PERCENTAGES				
						Single	Married	Widowed	Divorced	Un-known
WORCESTER - Con.										
West Boylston, . .	1,651	1,117	185	13	2	55.63	37.63	6.23	0.44	0.07
Males, . . .	823	563	55	4	2	27.73	18.96	1.85	0.14	0.07
Females, . .	828	554	130	9	-	27.90	18.67	4.38	0.30	-
West Brookfield, .	681	655	122	9	-	46.42	44.65	8.32	0.61	-
Males, . .	349	325	36	7	-	23.79	22.15	2.46	0.48	-
Females, .	332	330	86	2	-	22.63	22.50	5.86	0.13	-
Westminster, . .	597	588	127	3	-	45.40	44.71	9.66	0.23	-
Males, . . .	293	293	44	2	-	22.28	22.28	3.35	0.15	-
Females, .	304	295	83	1	-	23.12	22.43	6.31	0.08	-
Winchendon, . .	2,344	1,827	303	16	-	52.21	40.69	6.75	0.35	-
Males, . .	1,236	909	106	6	-	27.53	20.25	2.36	0.13	-
Females, .	1,108	918	197	10	-	24.68	20.44	4.39	0.22	-
WORCESTER, . .	56,190	36,773	5,567	179	58	56.89	37.23	5.64	0.18	0.06
Males, . . .	28,917	18,340	1,518	48	40	29.27	18.57	1.54	0.05	0.04
Females, .	27,273	18,433	4,049	131	18	27.62	18.66	4.10	0.13	0.02

RECAPITULATION: BY COUNTIES.

COUNTIES, AND SEX.	Single	Married	Widowed	Divorced	Un-known	PERCENTAGES				
						Single	Married	Widowed	Divorced	Un-known
BARNSTABLE, . .	12,557	12,484	2,526	69	18	45.41	45.14	9.13	0.25	0.07
Males, . . .	6,361	6,247	638	34	14	23.00	22.59	2.31	0.12	0.05
Females. . .	6,196	6,237	1,888	35	4	22.41	22.55	6.82	0.13	0.02
BERKSHIRE, . .	47,917	32,822	5,378	161	14	55.53	38.03	6.23	0.19	0.02
Males, . . .	24,452	16,437	1,563	65	8	28.34	19.04	1.81	0.08	0.01
Females, .	23,465	16,385	3,815	96	6	27.19	18.99	4.42	0.11	0.01
BRISTOL, . .	122,655	82,351	13,581	370	62	56.00	37.60	6.20	0.17	0.03
Males, . .	60,933	40,827	3,621	158	43	27.82	18.64	1.66	0.07	0.02
Females, .	61,722	41,524	9,960	212	19	28.18	18.96	4.54	0.10	0.01
DUKES, . .	1,874	1,907	431	25	1	44.22	45.00	10.17	0.59	0.02
Males, . . .	1,000	952	94	11	-	23.60	22.46	2.22	0.26	-
Females, .	874	955	337	14	1	20.62	22.54	7.95	0.33	0.02
ESSEX, . .	178,871	128,068	22,538	707	206	54.14	38.76	6.82	0.22	0.06
Males, . .	91,053	64,395	6,026	268	171	27.56	19.49	1.83	0.08	0.05
Females, .	87,818	63,673	16,512	439	38	26.58	19.27	4.99	0.14	0.01
FRANKLIN, . .	20,551	16,699	2,779	96	20	51.19	41.60	6.92	0.24	0.05
Males, . . .	11,021	8,387	829	41	15	27.45	20.89	2.07	0.10	0.04
Females, .	9,530	8,312	1,950	55	5	23.74	20.71	4.85	0.14	0.01
HAMPDEN, . .	85,282	57,791	9,496	290	79	55.76	37.79	6.21	0.19	0.05
Males, . .	42,509	28,919	2,513	127	65	27.80	18.91	1.64	0.08	0.04
Females, .	42,773	28,872	6,983	163	14	27.96	18.88	4.57	0.11	0.01
HAMPSHIRE, .	30,862	20,093	3,677	70	8	56.41	36.72	6.72	0.13	0.02
Males, . .	14,985	10,004	1,034	33	5	27.39	18.28	1.89	0.06	0.01
Females, .	15,877	10,089	2,643	37	3	29.02	18.44	4.83	0.07	0.01
MIDDLESEX, .	278,719	186,820	32,720	721	237	55.83	37.42	6.55	0.15	0.05
Males, . .	137,513	92,944	8,443	254	169	27.54	18.62	1.69	0.05	0.04
Females, .	141,206	93,876	24,277	467	68	28.29	18.80	4.86	0.10	0.01
NANTUCKET, .	1,283	1,294	415	24	-	42.54	42.90	13.76	0.80	-
Males, . .	571	642	88	14	-	18.93	21.28	2.92	0.47	-
Females, .	712	652	327	10	-	23.61	21.62	10.84	0.33	-
NORFOLK, . .	75,848	49,877	8,815	255	44	56.26	37.00	6.54	0.17	0.03
Males, . .	37,100	25,005	2,551	93	31	27.52	18.55	1.89	0.07	0.02
Females, .	38,748	24,872	6,264	142	13	28.74	18.45	4.65	0.10	0.01

CONJUGAL CONDITION — Concluded.

RECAPITULATION: BY COUNTIES — Concluded.

COUNTIES, AND SEX.	Single	Married	Widowed	Divorced	Un-known	PERCENTAGES				
						Single	Married	Widowed	Divorced	Un-known
PLYMOUTH,	51,176	42,546	7,353	296	127	50.42	41.92	7.24	0.29	0.13
Males,	26,807	21,400	2,252	122	113	26.41	21.09	2.22	0.12	0.11
Females,	24,369	21,146	5,101	174	14	24.01	20.83	5.02	0.17	0.02
SUFFOLK,	308,009	193,522	36,779	747	742	57.06	35.85	6.81	0.14	0.14
Males,	154,313	96,753	8,938	201	470	28.59	17.92	1.65	0.04	0.09
Females,	153,696	96,769	27,841	546	272	28.47	17.93	5.16	0.10	0.05
WORCESTER,	169,426	116,971	19,162	639	247	55.29	38.17	6.25	0.21	0.08
Males,	87,432	58,525	5,639	251	209	28.53	19.10	1.84	0.08	0.07
Females,	81,994	58,446	13,523	388	38	26.76	19.07	4.41	0.13	0.01

RECAPITULATION. FOR THE STATE.

THE STATE, AND SEX.	Single	Married	Widowed	Divorced	Un-known	* PERCENTAGES OF TOTAL POPULATION				
						Single	Married	Widowed	Divorced	Un-known
THE STATE,	1,385,030	943,245	165,650	4,450	1,808	55.40	37.73	6.62	0.18	0.07
Males,	696,050	471,437	44,229	1,672	1,313	27.84	18.86	1.76	0.07	0.05
Females,	688,980	471,808	121,421	2,778	495	27.56	18.87	4.86	0.11	0.02

*See note at bottom of page.

RECAPITULATION. PERCENTAGES.

THE STATE AND COUNTIES.	PERCENTAGES									
	MALES					FEMALES				
	Single	Married	Widowed	Divorced	Un-known	Single	Married	Widowed	Divorced	Un-known
THE STATE.	57.50	38.81	3.64	0.14	0.11	53.60	36.70	9.44	0.22	0.04
Barnstable,	47.85	46.99	4.80	0.26	0.10	43.15	43.43	13.15	0.24	0.03
Berkshire,	57.50	38.65	3.68	0.15	0.02	53.61	37.44	8.72	0.22	0.01
Bristol,	57.71	38.67	3.43	0.15	0.04	54.41	36.60	8.78	0.19	0.02
Dukes,	48.61	46.28	4.57	0.54	–	49.07	43.79	15.45	0.64	0.05
Essex,	56.24	39.77	3.72	0.16	0.11	52.13	37.79	9.80	0.26	0.02
Franklin,	54.31	41.33	4.09	0.20	0.07	48.02	41.87	9.82	0.28	0.02
Hampden,	57.54	39.01	3.39	0.17	0.09	54.28	36.64	8.86	0.20	0.02
Hampshire,	57.50	38.39	3.57	0.12	0.02	55.42	35.22	9.22	0.13	0.01
Middlesex,	57.46	38.84	3.55	0.10	0.07	54.33	36.12	9.34	0.18	0.03
Nantucket,	43.42	48.82	6.69	1.07	–	41.86	38.33	19.22	0.59	–
Norfolk,	57.27	38.60	3.94	0.14	0.05	55.32	35.51	8.95	0.20	0.02
Plymouth,	52.88	42.22	4.44	0.24	0.22	47.97	41.62	10.04	0.34	0.03
Suffolk,	59.20	37.11	3.43	0.08	0.18	55.06	34.67	9.97	0.20	0.10
Worcester,	57.50	38.49	3.71	0.16	0.14	53.11	37.86	8.76	0.25	0.02

NOTE. — On page 806, at the close of the presentation for native and foreign born, two recapitulations are given, one for the State, and the other for the State and Counties, by sex. In the first recapitulation, the total population is taken as the basis for figuring percentages for native born and foreign born, and the number of native born and foreign born males and native born and foreign born females. In the second recapitulation, the whole number of males is taken as 100 per cent in figuring the percentages of native born and foreign born males, and the whole number of females is taken as 100 per cent in figuring the percentages of native born and foreign born females. The use of these different bases causes a slight variation in the percentages for the State in the two recapitulations, and this explanation is supplied in order that these variations may not be considered errors in computation.

The same variations occur in the percentages on page 827, at the close of the presentation for color and race, and in the tables above on this page, the explanation of these variations previously given being equally applicable thereto.

SOLDIERS, SAILORS, AND MARINES.

SOLDIERS, SAILORS, AND MARINES.

COUNTIES, CITIES, AND TOWNS.	Soldiers	Sailors	Marines	Total	COUNTIES, CITIES, AND TOWNS.	Soldiers	Sailors	Marines	Total
BARNSTABLE.	316	134	33	483	BRISTOL.	2,394	299	77	2,770
Barnstable,	79	13	6	98	Acushnet,	17	6	1	24
Bourne,	28	3	3	34	Attleborough,	157	12	2	171
Brewster,	12	-	3	15	Berkley,	28	7	-	35
Chatham,	20	3	2	25	Dartmouth,	46	5	1	52
Dennis,	16	5	-	21	Dighton,	46	-	2	48
Eastham,	7	1	-	8	Easton,	64	10	-	74
Falmouth,	23	3	2	28	Fairhaven,	63	19	2	84
Harwich,	31	1	2	34	FALL RIVER,	583	61	22	676
Mashpee,	3	4	-	7	Freetown,	59	2	-	61
Orleans,	15	1	-	16	Mansfield,	101	-	2	103
Provincetown,	31	-	8	39	NEW BEDFORD,	504	122	17	643
Sandwich,	30	1	3	34	North Attleborough,	99	6	6	111
Truro,	4	-	-	4	Norton,	37	1	-	38
Wellfleet,	4	95	-	99	Raynham,	38	1	2	41
Yarmouth,	13	4	4	21	Rehoboth,	36	8	3	47
					Seekonk,	27	1	-	28
BERKSHIRE.	1,275	15	10	1,300	Somerset,	45	8	1	54
Adams,	67	-	1	68	Swansea,	23	1	1	25
Alford,	7	-	-	7	TAUNTON,	389	22	15	426
Becket,	22	-	-	22	Westport,	22	7	-	29
Cheshire,	33	-	-	33					
Clarksburg,	26	1	-	27	DUKES.	55	29	-	84
Dalton,	47	-	1	48	Chilmark,	-	-	-	-
Egremont,	16	-	-	16	Cottage City,	23	3	-	26
Florida,	10	-	-	10	Edgartown,	8	17	-	25
Great Barrington,	89	-	-	89	Gay Head,	1	2	-	3
Hancock,	7	-	-	7	Gosnold,	-	3	-	3
Hinsdale,	20	-	-	20	Tisbury,	15	3	-	18
Lanesborough,	15	-	-	15	West Tisbury,	8	1	-	9
Lee,	82	1	-	83					
Lenox,	24	-	-	24	ESSEX.	6,059	533	86	6,678
Monterey,	12	-	-	12	Amesbury,	147	2	5	154
Mount Washington,	2	-	-	2	Andover,	86	2	5	93
New Ashford,	4	1	-	5	BEVERLY,	320	35	1	356
New Marlborough,	32	-	-	32	Boxford,	18	-	-	18
NORTH ADAMS,	231	3	3	237	Bradford,	117	6	1	124
Otis,	16	-	-	16	Danvers,	218	10	5	233
Peru,	7	-	-	7	Essex,	55	1	-	56
PITTSFIELD,	262	5	3	270	Georgetown,	112	2	-	114
Richmond,	6	1	-	7	GLOUCESTER,	292	53	5	350
Sandisfield,	27	-	1	28	Groveland,	75	1	-	76
Savoy,	14	-	-	14	Hamilton,	30	3	-	33
Sheffield,	56	1	-	57	HAVERHILL,	586	28	13	627
Stockbridge,	30	-	-	30	Ipswich,	115	6	-	121
Tyringham,	11	-	-	11	LAWRENCE,	409	40	6	455
Washington,	8	-	-	8	LYNN,	1,290	107	14	1,411
West Stockbridge,	21	-	-	21	Lynnfield,	28	2	-	30
Williamstown,	62	2	1	65	Manchester,	52	6	1	59
Windsor,	9	-	-	9	Marblehead,	300	38	4	342

SOLDIERS, SAILORS, AND MARINES — Continued.

COUNTIES, CITIES, AND TOWNS.	Soldiers	Sailors	Marines	Total	COUNTIES, CITIES, AND TOWNS.	Soldiers	Sailors	Marines	Total
ESSEX - Con.					HAMPDEN — Con.				
Merrimac,	44	1	-	45	Longmeadow,	15	-	-	15
Methuen,	76	2	4	82	Ludlow,	32	-	-	32
Middleton,	26	-	-	26	Monson,	80	-	-	80
Nahant,	21	6	-	27	Montgomery,	3	-	-	3
Newbury,	53	1	2	56	Palmer,	81	9	-	90
NEWBURYPORT,	312	29	12	353	Russell,	16	1	-	17
North Andover,	18	-	-	18	Southwick,	27	-	-	27
Peabody,	192	12	1	205	SPRINGFIELD,	718	25	15	758
Rockport,	62	21	-	83	Tolland,	7	-	-	7
Rowley,	48	1	-	49	Wales,	25	-	-	25
SALEM,	637	103	5	745	Westfield,	216	1	6	223
Salisbury,	42	3	-	45	West Springfield,	78	2	3	83
Saugus,	94	7	-	101	Wilbraham,	28	1	1	30
Swampscott,	59	2	1	62					
Topsfield,	44	3	-	47	HAMPSHIRE.	852	14	6	872
Wenham,	37	-	1	38	Amherst,	89	-	1	90
West Newbury,	44	-	-	44	Belchertown,	61	-	-	61
					Chesterfield,	18	-	-	18
FRANKLIN.	800	11	4	815	Cummington,	21	-	-	21
Ashfield,	28	-	-	28	Easthampton,	63	2	1	66
Bernardston,	21	-	-	21	Enfield,	29	-	1	30
Buckland,	29	1	1	31	Goshen,	15	-	-	15
Charlemont,	18	-	-	18	Granby,	19	-	-	19
Colrain,	38	2	-	40	Greenwich,	22	-	-	22
Conway,	27	-	-	27	Hadley,	20	1	-	21
Deerfield,	49	-	-	49	Hatfield,	17	-	-	17
Erving,	30	-	1	31	Huntington,	19	-	-	19
Gill,	13	1	-	14	Middlefield,	2	-	-	2
Greenfield,	97	2	-	99	NORTHAMPTON,	209	4	2	215
Hawley,	15	-	-	15	Pelham,	18	-	-	18
Heath,	10	-	-	10	Plainfield,	12	-	-	12
Leverett,	24	-	-	24	Prescott,	11	-	-	11
Leyden,	13	-	-	13	Southampton,	21	-	-	21
Monroe,	4	-	-	4	South Hadley,	64	3	-	67
Montague,	85	-	-	85	Ware,	60	4	1	65
New Salem,	23	-	-	23	Westhampton,	14	-	-	14
Northfield,	30	2	1	33	Williamsburg,	34	-	-	34
Orange,	120	1	1	122	Worthington,	14	-	-	14
Rowe,	9	-	-	9					
Shelburne,	40	-	-	40	MIDDLESEX.	6,997	366	123	7,486
Shutesbury,	21	-	-	21	Acton,	65	2	-	67
Sunderland,	11	-	-	11	Arlington,	79	3	1	83
Warwick,	13	2	-	15	Ashby,	25	1	-	26
Wendell,	12	-	-	12	Ashland,	61	2	-	63
Whately,	20	-	-	20	Ayer,	50	-	-	50
					Bedford,	17	3	-	20
HAMPDEN.	1,908	55	31	1,994	Belmont,	27	-	-	27
Agawam,	48	1	1	50	Billerica,	47	2	-	49
Blandford,	27	-	-	27	Boxborough,	6	-	-	6
Brimfield,	38	-	-	38	Burlington,	11	-	-	11
Chester,	27	-	-	27	CAMBRIDGE,	856	81	18	955
CHICOPEE,	125	4	1	130	Carlisle,	13	-	-	13
East Longmeadow,	9	3	-	12	Chelmsford,	79	3	1	83
Granville,	22	-	-	22	Concord,	81	5	-	86
Hampden,	27	-	1	28	Dracut,	24	2	1	27
Holland,	8	-	-	8	Dunstable,	9	-	-	9
HOLYOKE,	251	8	3	262	EVERETT,	276	21	11	308

SOLDIERS, SAILORS, AND MARINES — Continued.

COUNTIES, CITIES, AND TOWNS.	Soldiers	Sailors	Marines	Total	COUNTIES, CITIES, AND TOWNS.	Soldiers	Sailors	Marines	Total
MIDDLESEX—Con.					NORFOLK—Con.				
Framingham	142	7	1	150	Milton	58	4	-	62
Groton	44	2	-	46	Needham	43	3	-	46
Holliston	79	1	-	80	Norfolk	25	-	-	25
Hopkinton	47	2	-	49	Norwood	54	-	-	54
Hudson	131	2	-	133	QUINCY	257	50	5	312
Lexington	59	2	-	61	Randolph	125	5	2	132
Lincoln	15	-	-	15	Sharon	54	2	-	56
Littleton	19	-	-	19	Stoughton	110	18	-	128
LOWELL	908	35	13	956	Walpole	61	3	2	66
MALDEN	393	21	15	429	Wellesley	49	5	2	56
MARLBOROUGH	255	8	2	265	Weymouth	311	9	2	322
Maynard	34	4	-	38	Wrentham	53	2	2	57
MEDFORD	233	18	5	256					
Melrose	190	12	3	205	PLYMOUTH	2,512	164	40	2,716
Natick	228	7	2	237	Abington	134	2	-	136
NEWTON	241	11	11	263	Bridgewater	78	4	1	83
North Reading	33	1	-	34	BROCKTON	542	42	3	587
Pepperell	58	-	-	58	Carver	28	-	-	28
Reading	121	3	-	124	Duxbury	84	2	7	93
Sherborn	21	-	-	21	East Bridgewater	75	4	-	79
Shirley	24	2	-	26	Halifax	20	1	-	21
SOMERVILLE	680	48	18	746	Hanover	72	3	-	75
Stoneham	199	3	-	202	Hanson	54	-	1	55
Stow	26	3	-	29	Hingham	120	10	1	131
Sudbury	23	-	-	23	Hull	30	-	-	30
Tewksbury	29	1	-	30	Kingston	44	4	-	48
Townsend	75	-	-	75	Lakeville	18	4	-	22
Tyngsborough	16	-	-	16	Marion	18	3	6	27
Wakefield	203	9	-	212	Marshfield	94	5	-	99
WALTHAM	241	9	11	261	Mattapoisett	23	19	1	43
Watertown	98	9	-	107	Middleborough	196	16	2	214
Wayland	40	1	-	41	Norwell	59	2	1	62
Westford	56	3	1	60	Pembroke	69	3	-	72
Weston	22	1	2	25	Plymouth	144	11	4	159
Wilmington	32	1	-	33	Plympton	29	4	-	33
Winchester	61	5	3	69	Rochester	25	9	1	35
WOBURN	197	10	4	211	Rockland	171	4	2	177
					Scituate	82	4	-	86
NANTUCKET	67	10	-	77	Wareham	89	3	5	97
Nantucket	67	10	-	77	West Bridgewater	52	1	-	52
					Whitman	163	4	5	172
NORFOLK	2,223	163	41	2,427					
Avon	38	4	-	42	SUFFOLK	5,675	867	205	6,747
Bellingham	27	1	-	28	BOSTON	4,755	779	194	5,728
Braintree	113	6	1	120	CHELSEA	755	67	10	832
Brookline	141	9	6	156	Revere	105	15	1	121
Canton	54	3	1	58	Winthrop	60	6	-	66
Cohasset	41	-	7	48					
Dedham	103	15	-	118	WORCESTER	4,948	90	44	5,082
Dover	19	-	-	19	Ashburnham	58	-	-	58
Foxborough	74	5	-	79	Athol	173	2	1	176
Franklin	76	1	1	78	Auburn	19	4	-	23
Holbrook	38	1	-	39	Barre	60	2	-	62
Hyde Park	162	15	5	182	Berlin	24	1	-	25
Medfield	42	-	-	42	Blackstone	49	4	-	53
Medway	79	2	4	85	Bolton	29	-	-	29
Millis	16	-	1	17					

SOLDIERS, SAILORS, AND MARINES — Concluded.

COUNTIES, CITIES, AND TOWNS.	Soldiers	Sailors	Marines	Total	COUNTIES, CITIES, AND TOWNS.	Soldiers	Sailors	Marines	Total
WORCESTER-Con.					WORCESTER-Con.				
Boylston, . . .	28	1	-	29	Oakham, . . .	14	-	1	15
Brookfield, . .	78	-	2	80	Oxford, . . .	54	-	-	54
Charlton, . . .	52	-	1	53	Paxton, . . .	16	-	-	16
Clinton, . . .	115	1	1	117	Petersham, . .	28	-	-	28
Dana, . . .	30	-	-	30	Phillipston, . .	16	-	-	16
Douglas, . . .	52	-	-	52	Princeton, . .	25	-	-	25
Dudley, . . .	26	1	-	27	Royalston, . .	29	-	-	29
FITCHBURG, . .	346	5	2	353	Rutland, . . .	30	-	-	30
Gardner, . . .	152	1	2	155	Shrewsbury, . .	54	2	-	56
Grafton, . . .	93	3	-	96	Southborough, .	37	-	-	37
Hardwick, . .	39	-	1	40	Southbridge, . .	68	-	-	68
Harvard, . . .	17	-	-	17	Spencer, . . .	156	-	2	158
Holden, . . .	47	2	-	49	Sterling, . . .	37	-	-	37
Hopedale, . .	27	-	-	27	Sturbridge, . .	48	-	-	48
Hubbardston, . .	36	-	-	36	Sutton, . . .	44	1	-	45
Lancaster, . .	34	3	-	37	Templeton, . .	77	-	-	77
Leicester, . .	50	-	1	51	Upton, . . .	52	-	-	52
Leominster, . .	202	1	2	205	Uxbridge, . .	53	-	-	53
Lunenburg, . .	34	-	-	34	Warren, . . .	51	-	-	51
Mendon, . . .	36	-	-	36	Webster, . . .	87	2	1	90
Milford, . . .	173	4	-	177	Westborough, .	149	3	2	154
Millbury, . . .	96	4	-	100	West Boylston, .	54	-	-	54
New Braintree, .	5	-	-	5	West Brookfield, .	47	-	1	48
Northborough, .	43	1	-	44	Westminster, . .	40	-	-	40
Northbridge, . .	57	-	-	57	Winchendon, . .	94	-	-	94
North Brookfield, .	86	1	-	87	WORCESTER, . .	1,222	41	24	1,287

RECAPITULATION.

THE STATE, AND COUNTIES.	Soldiers	Sailors	Marines	Total
THE STATE.	36,081	2,750	700	39,531
Barnstable, ...	316	134	33	483
Berkshire, ...	1,275	15	10	1,300
Bristol, ...	2,394	299	77	2,770
Dukes, ...	55	29	-	84
Essex, ...	6,059	533	86	6,678
Franklin, ...	800	11	4	815
Hampden, ...	1,908	55	31	1,994
Hampshire, ...	852	14	6	872
Middlesex, ...	6,997	366	123	7,486
Nantucket, ...	67	10	-	77
Norfolk, ...	2,223	163	41	2,427
Plymouth, ...	2,512	164	40	2,716
Suffolk, ...	5,675	867	205	6,747
Worcester, ...	4,948	90	44	5,082

TABULAR ANALYSES

FOR THE FOLLOWING PRESENTATIONS:

Native and Foreign Born.

The presentation showing the population classified as native and foreign born, for each town and city, is contained on pages 791 to 802. The recapitulation, to which we shall allude in this analysis, appears on page 803. So far as the State at large is concerned, this recapitulation shows that the native born persons number 1,735,253, of whom 848,312 are males and 886,941 females. The foreign born number 764,930, of whom 366,389 are males and 398,541 are females. Expressed in percentages, the native born constitute 69.41 per cent, or about 69 persons in every 100, of the total population, while the foreign born constitute 30.59, or about 31 persons in every 100, of the total population. The native born males constitute 33.93 per cent, and the native born females 35.48 per cent of the total population, while the foreign born males constitute 14.65 per cent, and the foreign born females 15.94 per cent of the total population. The percentage of foreign born persons varies considerably in the different counties, being largest in the county of Bristol, where it reaches 38.40, and smallest in the county of Nantucket, where it is but 8.29. The percentages in the different counties are shown in the recapitulation. From them we may note that about 62 persons in every 100 (61.60 per cent), in the county of Bristol, are native born; and taking the other counties in order, beginning with the lowest and closing with the highest, we obtain the following statement as to the number of native born persons in every 100 of the population: Suffolk County, about 64 (64.12 per cent); Middlesex County, about 69 (68.62 per cent); Hampden County, about 69 (68.67 per cent); Essex County, about 71 (70.73 per cent); Worcester County, about 71 (71.02 per cent); Norfolk County, about 74 (73.72 per cent); Hampshire County, about 76 (76.40 per cent); Berkshire County, about 77 (77.30 per cent); Plymouth County, about 82 (81.64 per cent); Franklin County, about 83 (83.19 per cent); Dukes County, about 88 (88.23 per cent); Barnstable County, about 89 (89.14 per cent); while in the county of Nantucket, consisting of the insular town of Nantucket, the native born number about 92 in every 100 (91.71 per cent).

The following table shows the number of native and foreign born persons in the State and in each of the counties in 1895, and also, for purposes of comparison, in 1885, with percentages:

THE STATE, AND COUNTIES.	NUMBER				PERCENTAGES			
	1885		1895		1885		1895	
	Native Born	Foreign Born	Native Born	Foreign Born	Native Born	Foreign Born	Native Born	Foreign Born
THE STATE.	1,415,274	526,867	1,735,253	764,930	72.87	27.13	69.41	30.59
Barnstable,	27,208	2,637	24,651	3,003	91.16	8.84	89.14	10.86
Berkshire,	57,435	16,393	66,708	19,584	77.80	22.20	77.30	22.70
Bristol,	106,626	51,872	134,920	84,099	67.27	32.73	61.60	38.40
Dukes,	3,869	266	3,739	499	93.57	6.43	88.23	11.77
Essex,	198,237	65,490	233,695	96,698	75.17	24.83	70.73	29.27
Franklin,	31,939	5,510	33,398	6,747	85.29	14.71	83.19	16.81
Hampden,	81,550	35,214	105,031	47,907	69.84	30.16	68.67	31.33
Hampshire,	37,919	10,553	41,796	12,914	78.23	21.77	76.40	23.60
Middlesex,	255,887	101,424	342,560	156,657	71.61	28.39	68.62	31.38
Nantucket,	2,973	169	2,766	250	94.62	5.38	91.71	8.29
Norfolk,	78,830	23,312	99,386	35,433	77.18	22.82	73.72	26.28
Plymouth,	70,638	11,042	82,860	18,638	86.48	13.52	81.64	18.36
Suffolk,	279,988	141,121	346,108	193,691	66.49	33.51	64.12	35.88
Worcester,	182,175	61,864	217,635	88,810	74.65	25.35	71.02	28.98

From this table the increase in the number of foreign born during the decade is clearly seen. Confining our comparison to percentages, we find that in the State, as a whole, the percentage of foreign born has risen from 27.13 to 30.59. In each of the counties an increase is noted, although in the county of Berkshire the change is very slight, the percentage in 1885 being 22.20 and in 1895, 22.70. In the other counties the increases in percentages are as follows: Barnstable, 8.84 to 10.86; Bristol, 32.73 to 38.40; Dukes, 6.43 to 11.77; Essex, 24.83 to 29.27; Franklin, 14.71 to 16.81; Hampden, 30.16 to 31.33; Hampshire, 21.77 to 23.60; Middlesex, 28.39 to 31.38; Nantucket, 5.38 to 8.29; Norfolk, 22.82 to 26.28; Plymouth, 13.52 to 18.36; Suffolk, 33.51 to 35.88; and Worcester, 25.35 to 28.98. With respect to the native born, we may base the following statement on the percentages shown in the table: the number of native born in the State is now about 69 in every 100, as against about 73 in every 100 in 1885; in Barnstable County the number of native born persons in every 100 shows a decline in 1895 as compared with 1885 from about 91 to about 89; in Berkshire, from about 78 to about 77; in Bristol, from about 67 to about 62; in Dukes, from about 94 to about 88; in Essex, from about 75 to about 71; in Franklin, from about 85 to about 83; in Hampden, from about 70 to about 69; in Hampshire, from about 78 to about 76; in Middlesex, from about 72 to about 69; in Nantucket, from about 95 to about 92; in Norfolk, from about 77 to about 74; in Plymouth, from about 86 to about 82; in Suffolk, from about 66 to about 64; and in Worcester, from about 75 to about 71.

A comparison for the cities may be made from the following table:

CITIES	NUMBER				PERCENTAGES			
	1885		1895		1885		1895	
	Native Born	Foreign Born	Native Born	Foreign Born	Native Born	Foreign Born	Native Born	Foreign Born
Beverly,	7,833	1,353	9,636	2,170	85.27	14.73	81.62	18.38
Boston,	257,098	133,295	316,522	180,398	65.86	34.14	63.70	36.30
Brockton,	16,751	4,032	25,138	8,027	80.60	19.40	75.80	24.20
Cambridge,	40,473	19,185	53,388	28,255	67.84	32.16	65.39	34.61
Chelsea,	19,128	6,581	21,208	10,056	74.40	25.60	67.84	32.16
Chicopee,	6,934	4,582	9,359	7,061	60.21	39.79	57.00	43.00

CITIES.	NUMBER				PERCENTAGES			
	1885		1895		1885		1895	
	Native Born	Foreign Born	Native Born	Foreign Born	Native Born	Foreign Born	Native Born	Foreign Born
Everett, ...	4,610	1,215	13,238	5,335	79.14	20.86	71.27	28.73
Fall River, . . .	28,912	27,958	44,683	44,520	50.84	49.16	50.09	49.91
Fitchburg, . . .	11,688	3,687	17,349	9,060	76.02	23.98	65.69	34.31
Gloucester, . . .	14,689	7,014	16,880	11,331	67.68	32.32	59.83	40.17
Haverhill, . . .	17,634	4,161	22,831	7,378	80.91	19.09	75.58	24.42
Holyoke, . . .	14,007	13,888	22,247	18,075	50.21	49.79	55.17	44.83
Lawrence, . . .	21,765	17,097	27,862	24,302	56.01	43.99	53.41	46.59
Lowell, ...	38,224	25,883	47,023	37,344	59.63	40.37	55.74	44.26
Lynn, ...	35,099	9,768	46,060	16,294	78.70	21.30	73.87	26.13
Malden, ...	12,074	4,333	20,719	8,989	73.59	26.41	69.74	30.26
Marlborough, . .	8,078	2,863	11,151	3,826	73.83	26.17	74.45	25.55
Medford, . . .	6,928	2,114	10,852	3,622	76.62	23.38	74.98	25.02
New Bedford, . .	23,137	10,256	32,537	22,711	69.29	30.71	58.89	41.11
Newburyport, . .	11,110	2,606	11,593	2,959	81.00	19.00	79.66	20.34
Newton, ...	14,265	5,494	18,871	8,719	72.19	27.81	68.40	31.60
North Adams, . .	9,149	3,391	13,666	5,469	72.96	27.04	71.42	28.58
Northampton, . .	9,542	3,354	12,564	4,182	73.99	26.01	75.02	24.98
Pittsfield, . . .	11,092	3,374	15,913	4,548	76.68	23.32	77.77	22.23
Quincy, ...	8,460	3,685	13,582	7,130	69.66	30.34	65.58	34.42
Salem, ...	20,489	7,601	23,708	10,765	72.94	27.06	68.77	31.23
Somerville, . . .	22,471	7,500	36,989	15,211	74.98	25.02	70.86	29.14
Springfield, . . .	28,635	8,940	38,828	12,694	76.21	23.79	75.36	24.64
Taunton, . . .	17,105	6,569	19,340	7,775	72.25	27.75	71.33	28.67
Waltham, . . .	10,596	4,013	14,805	6,071	72.53	27.47	70.92	29.08
Woburn, . . .	8,225	3,525	9,963	4,215	70.00	30.00	70.27	29.73
Worcester, . . .	48,207	20,182	67,114	31,653	70.49	29.51	67.95	32.05
Cities, ...	805,408	379,499	1,065,619	570,448	67.97	32.03	65.14	34.86
Towns, ...	609,866	147,368	669,634	194,782	80.54	19.46	77.47	22.53
THE STATE, . .	1,415,274	526,867	1,735,253	764,930	72.87	27.13	69.41	30.59

Each of the cities shows an increase in the percentage of foreign born in 1895 as compared with 1885, except Holyoke, Marlborough, Northampton, Pittsfield, and Woburn. In the following cities, however, this increase is very slight, the percentages for each period being annexed: Fall River, from 49.16 to 49.91; Medford, from 23.38 to 25.02; Newburyport, 19 to 20.34; North Adams, 27.04 to 28.58; Springfield, 23.79 to 24.64; Taunton, 27.75 to 28.67; and Waltham, from 27.47 to 29.08. The city which shows the greatest increase in the percentage of foreign born is the city of New Bedford, in which city the percentage has increased from 30.71 to 41.11. A considerable increase is also shown in the cities of Fitchburg, Everett, and Gloucester. In Fitchburg, the percentage has increased from 23.98 to 34.31; in Everett, from 20.86 to 28.73; and in Gloucester, from 32.32 to 40.17. The decreases in the percentages of foreign born in the cities which show a decline are as follows: Holyoke, from 49.79 to 44.83; Marlborough, 26.17 to 25.55; Northampton, 26.01 to 24.98; Pittsfield, 23.32 to 22.23; and Woburn, 30 to 29.73. In the cities in the aggregate, 34.86 per cent of the total population is foreign born in 1895 as compared with 32.03 per cent in 1885. In the towns of the Commonwealth, 22.53 per cent of the total population is foreign born as against 19.46 per cent in 1885.

The following analysis table presents the population of the city of Boston by wards, classified as native born and foreign born:

CITY OF BOSTON.	Total Population	Native Born	Foreign Born	PERCENTAGES OF TOTAL POPULATION	
				Native Born	Foreign Born
BOSTON, ...	496,920	316,522	180,398	63.70	36.30
Males, ...	239,666	156,241	83,425	31.44	16.79
Females, ...	257,254	160,281	96,973	32.26	19.51
Ward 1, ...	21,007	13,656	7,351	65.01	34.99
Males, ...	10,363	6,875	3,488	32.73	16.60
Females, ...	10,644	6,781	3,863	32.28	18.39
Ward 2, ...	21,588	12,375	9,213	57.32	42.68
Males, ...	11,505	6,771	4,734	31.36	21.93
Females, ...	10,083	5,604	4,479	25.96	20.75
Ward 3, ...	13,943	9,765	4,178	70.04	29.96
Males, ...	6,841	4,826	2,015	34.61	14.45
Females, ...	7,102	4,939	2,163	35.43	15.51
Ward 4, ...	13,375	9,285	4,090	69.42	30.58
Males, ...	6,654	4,721	1,933	35.30	14.45
Females, ...	6,721	4,564	2,157	34.12	16.13
Ward 5, ...	12,986	8,574	4,412	66.02	33.98
Males, ...	6,994	4,668	2,326	35.94	17.91
Females, ...	5,992	3,906	2,086	30.08	16.07
Ward 6, ...	27,860	12,030	15,830	43.18	56.82
Males, ...	14,805	6,463	8,342	23.20	29.94
Females, ...	13,055	5,567	7,488	19.98	26.88
Ward 7, ...	16,973	9,290	7,683	54.73	45.27
Males, ...	9,049	5,114	3,935	30.13	23.19
Females, ...	7,924	4,176	3,748	24.60	22.08
Ward 8, ...	23,130	12,025	11,105	51.99	48.01
Males, ...	12,143	6,520	5,623	28.19	24.31
Females, ...	10,987	5,505	5,482	23.80	23.70
Ward 9, ...	23,174	13,693	9,481	59.09	40.91
Males, ...	11,398	6,933	4,465	29.92	19.27
Females, ...	11,776	6,760	5,016	29.17	21.64
Ward 10, ...	22,554	15,767	6,787	69.91	30.09
Males, ...	10,070	7,348	2,722	32.58	12.07
Females, ...	12,484	8,419	4,065	37.33	18.02
Ward 11, ...	19,930	12,995	6,935	65.20	34.80
Males, ...	7,375	5,691	1,684	28.55	8.45
Females, ...	12,555	7,304	5,251	36.65	26.35
Ward 12, ...	21,591	15,470	6,121	71.65	28.35
Males, ...	9,188	6,915	2,273	32.03	10.53
Females, ...	12,403	8,555	3,848	39.62	17.82
Ward 13, ...	24,900	13,939	10,961	55.98	44.02
Males, ...	12,695	7,249	5,446	29.11	21.87
Females, ...	12,205	6,690	5,515	26.87	22.15
Ward 14, ...	19,186	13,063	6,123	68.09	31.91
Males, ...	9,635	6,653	2,982	34.68	15.54
Females, ...	9,551	6,410	3,141	33.41	16.37
Ward 15, ...	18,623	12,524	6,099	67.25	32.75
Males, ...	8,975	6,195	2,780	33.27	14.93
Females, ...	9,648	6,329	3,319	33.98	17.82
Ward 16, ...	16,320	11,504	4,816	70.49	29.51
Males, ...	7,664	5,509	2,155	33.76	13.20
Females, ...	8,656	5,995	2,661	36.73	16.31

CITY OF BOSTON.	Total Population	Native Born	Foreign Born	PERCENTAGES OF TOTAL POPULATION	
				Native Born	Foreign Born
BOSTON — Con.					
Ward 17, ...	21,114	13,703	7,411	64.90	35.10
Males, ...	10,128	6,761	3,367	32.02	15.95
Females, ...	10,986	6,942	4,044	32.88	19.15
Ward 18, ...	21,679	13,174	8,505	60.77	39.23
Males, ...	10,641	6,542	4,099	30.18	18.91
Females, ...	11,038	6,632	4,406	39.59	20.32
Ward 19, ...	22,372	13,471	8,901	60.21	39.79
Males, ...	10,508	6,320	4,188	28.25	18.72
Females, ...	11,864	7,151	4,713	31.96	21.07
Ward 20, ...	21,528	15,535	5,993	72.16	27.84
Males, ...	9,893	7,320	2,573	34.00	11.95
Females, ...	11,635	8,215	3,420	38.16	15.89
Ward 21, ...	19,274	14,248	5,026	73.92	26.08
Males, ...	8,079	6,305	1,774	32.71	9.21
Females, ...	11,195	7,943	3,252	41.21	16.87
Ward 22, ...	22,289	14,687	7,602	65.89	34.11
Males, ...	10,445	7,054	3,391	31.65	15.22
Females, ...	11,844	7,633	4,211	34.24	18.89
Ward 23, ...	18,283	12,267	6,016	67.10	32.90
Males, ...	8,736	5,999	2,737	32.81	14.97
Females, ...	9,547	6,268	3,279	34.29	17.93
Ward 24, ...	18,240	13,244	4,996	72.61	27.39
Males, ...	8,589	6,418	2,171	35.19	11.90
Females, ...	9,651	6,826	2,825	37.42	15.49
Ward 25, ...	15,001	10,238	4,763	68.25	31.75
Males, ...	7,293	5,071	2,222	33.81	14.81
Females, ...	7,708	5,167	2,541	34.44	16.94

Bearing in mind that the foreign born population of the city as a whole constitutes 36.30 per cent of the total population, or, in other words, that about 36 persons in every 100 of the total population are foreign born, we note that this percentage is exceeded in the following wards, the percentages being in each case annexed: ward 2, 42.68; ward 6, 56.82; ward 7, 45.27; ward 8, 48.01; ward 9, 40.91; ward 13, 44.02; ward 18, 39.23; and ward 19, 39.79. The ward which has the largest percentage of foreign born is ward 6, which includes what is popularly known as the North-End District. Here the foreign born constitute nearly 57 in every 100 of the total population. On the other hand, ward 21 has the smallest percentage of foreign born, namely, 26.08, or about 26 persons in every 100 of the total population. This is nearly paralleled in ward 24, where the foreign born number about 27 in every 100 of the total population, or 27.39 per cent.

It may be interesting to compare the percentages of foreign born in different districts of the city. Wards 1 and 2 constitute East Boston, including also the islands in the harbor. The total population of these wards and islands is 42,595, the number of foreign born being 16,564, or about 39 persons in every 100 (38.89 per cent). Wards 3, 4, and 5 constitute the Charlestown District, the total population being 40,304, of which 12,680 are foreign born, or about 31 persons in every 100 (31.46 per cent). South Boston includes wards 13, 14, and 15, with a small part of ward 16. The total population of the district is 67,913, of which it is estimated that 24,692 are foreign born, or about 36 persons in every 100 (36.36 per cent). The Back Bay territory, so called, is rather indefinitely bounded, but portions of wards 10 and 11 fall within this section, the estimated population of the district being 21,244, of which it is estimated that 6,862 are foreign born, or about 32 persons in every 100 (32.30 per cent). Ward 25 comprises the

Brighton District. Here the total population is 15,001, the foreign born numbering 4,763, or about 32 persons in every 100 (31.75 per cent). West Roxbury comprises the whole of ward 23 and part of ward 22. In these wards, respectively, the foreign born population constitutes 32.90 per cent and 34.11 per cent of the total population, or from 33 to 34 persons in the 100. Wards 20 and 24, with a part of ward 16, make up the Dorchester District. In these wards, respectively, the foreign born population constitutes 27.84, 27.39, and 29.51 per cent of the total population, or from about 27 to 30 persons in every 100. Wards 17, 18, 19, 21, and a part of ward 22 comprise Roxbury. In ward 17, the foreign born constitute 35.10 per cent of the total population, or about 35 persons in every 100; in wards 18 and 19, respectively, the percentages are 39.23 and 39.79, or from about 39 to 40 persons in every 100; in ward 21 the percentage is 26.08, or about 26 persons in the 100; while in ward 22 the percentage is 34.11, or about 34 persons in the 100. In nearly every ward the foreign born males and the foreign born females form percentages of the total population which do not differ very widely, but an exception is found in ward 11, a large part of which falls within the Back Bay territory. Here the males who are foreign born constitute 8.45 per cent of the total population, while the females constitute 26.35 per cent of the total population, this excess of females being undoubtedly due to the fact of the presence in that ward of a considerable number of foreign born females engaged in domestic service. The subject of the foreign influence upon the growth of the city, as well as its influence upon the growth of the entire population of the State, will be further treated in discussing the tables relating to place of birth and parent nativity, to be hereafter presented.

Color and Race.

The presentation, pages 805 to 828, shows the distribution of the population by color and race. The recapitulation is contained upon page 827. The entire white population of the State is 2,471,418; colored, 26,540; Indian, 519; Japanese, 34; and Chinese, 1,672. Expressed in percentages, 98.85 per cent is white, 1.06 colored, 0.02 Indian, 0.07 Chinese, while the Japanese comprise less than one one-hundredth of one per cent. The white males number 1,199,920, or 47.99 per cent of the total population, and the white females 1,271,498, or 50.86 per cent of the total population. The colored males number 12,813 and the colored females 13,727, or 0.51 per cent and 0.55 per cent, respectively, of the total population. The Indian males number 279 and the Indian females 240, each constituting one one-hundredth of one per cent of the total population. Eight Japanese females and nine Chinese females appear in the enumeration. The percentages of white persons of the total population do not greatly vary in the different counties, rising from 93.11 in the county of Dukes to 99.68 in the county of Franklin. The percentage of colored persons of the total population is largest in the county of Dukes, this percentage being 3.33, and next largest in Nantucket and Suffolk, in which counties the percentages of colored persons are 1.99 and 1.90, respectively. In the following counties, besides those named, the percentage of colored persons of total population rises above one per cent: Barnstable, 1.26; Berkshire, 1.48; Bristol, 1.10; and Middlesex, 1.10. No Indians were enumerated in the county of Nantucket, while the Indian population was less than one one-hundredth of one per cent of the total population in the counties of Essex, Hampden, Middlesex, Suffolk, and Worcester. The largest percentage of Indians was found in the county of Dukes, namely, 3.47. No Japanese were found in Barnstable, Berkshire, Bristol, Dukes, or Nantucket counties, while the Japanese population did not exceed one one-hundredth of one per cent in any county, and was less than one one-hundredth of one per cent in the counties of Essex, Hampden, Middlesex, Norfolk, Plymouth, Suffolk, and Worcester. The largest number of Chinese was found in the county of Suffolk, where persons of this race constituted 0.16 per cent of the total population. No Chinese were enumerated in the county of Nantucket.

Conjugal Condition.

The distribution of the population according to conjugal condition appears in the table on pages 829 to 852, the recapitulation being found upon page 851. The number of single persons enumerated was 1,385,030, or 55.49 per cent of the total population; the number of married persons being 943,245, or 37.73 per cent of the total population. The widowed* number 165,650, or 6.62 per cent of the total population; the divorced, 4,450, or 0.18 per cent of the total population; while there were 4,808 persons for whom the facts as to conjugal condition could not be ascertained, constituting, however, but seven one-hundredths of one per cent of the total population. The single males number 696,050, or 27.84 per cent of the total population, and the single females 688,980, or 27.56 per cent of the total population. It will be seen, therefore, that upon the basis of percentages of the total population, no great difference appears between the sexes among the single persons. This is also true with respect to the married persons, who include 471,437 males and 471,808 females, constituting, respectively, 18.86 and 18.87 per cent of the total population. The widowed females number 121,421, or 4.86 per cent of the total population, a number greatly in excess of the males included under this head who aggregate 44,229, or 1.76 per cent of the total population. The divorced persons include 1,672 males and 2,778 females; while the persons whose conjugal condition was unknown were very largely males, who number in the aggregate 1,313 as against 495 females of this class. The percentage which the single persons constitute of the total population is largest in the county of Suffolk, this percentage being 57.06, and smallest in the county of Nantucket, namely, 42.54. The percentage which the widowed persons constitute of the total population is largest in the county of Nantucket, namely, 13.76. In Dukes County the percentage of widowed persons of the total population is 10.17, the next largest percentage, namely, 9.43, being found in the county of Barnstable. The percentage of widowed persons of the total population is smallest in the county of Bristol, namely, 6.20, although this varies but slightly from the percentages found in several other counties, and in the State as a whole. In no county does the proportion of divorced persons rise so high as one per cent.

Soldiers, Sailors, and Marines.

The table, pages 853 to 858, shows the total number of persons living in the Commonwealth on May 1, 1895, who served as either soldiers, sailors, or marines, in the War of the Rebellion, with aggregates. The recapitulation for the State appears on page 858, from which it will be seen that at the time of the enumeration there were living in Massachusetts, 36,081 soldiers of the late war, 2,750 sailors, and 700 marines, or, in the aggregate, 39,531 veterans of the different branches of the service. The distribution of these persons, by counties, is also shown in the recapitulation, but need not be especially pointed out here.

The returns included a certain number of persons under more than one designation; for example, "soldier and marine," "soldier and sailor," etc. To avoid duplications in presentation, however, all such persons appear in the table under the single head "soldier." The number designated as soldiers, therefore, includes some who were enrolled in other branches of the service, besides having served in the army. It is possible, also, that wives on account of a failure to understand clearly the nature of the inquiry, which was applicable only to survivors of the War of the Rebellion, may, in some instances, have returned their husbands as soldiers when they were merely at present enrolled in the militia. Every effort was made to guard against this misconception, however, and if such instances occurred it was impossible to detect the error, as it was also impossible to prevent omissions which may have occurred on account of lack of knowledge as to the fact in question on the part of those upon whom the enumerator was obliged to depend for information, no means of verification being available to the Bureau. The figures, while undoubtedly in the main correct, should be regarded as approximate rather than absolute.

---

* Including under this head, for convenience of tabulation, persons of either sex deprived by death of husband or wife, and not re-married.

Lightning Source UK Ltd.
Milton Keynes UK
UKHW041048260520
363901UK00003B/635